W9-AWY-141

TO THE STUDENT: A Study Guide for this textbook is available through your college bookstore under the title STUDY GUIDE FOR BUSINESS LAW and COMPREHENSIVE BUSINESS LAW by Elizabeth M. Crocker and Ann R. Henry. The Study Guide can help you with course material by acting as a tutorial, review, and study aid. If the Study Guide is not in stock, ask the bookstore manager to order a copy for you.

BUSINESS LAW

THE SERIES IN BUSINESS LAW

BUSINESS LAW
Principles and Cases
Fourth Edition

Daniel V. Davidson
Radford University

Brenda E. Knowles
Indiana University at South Bend

Lynn M. Forsythe
California State University, Fresno

Robert R. Jespersen
University of Arkansas at Little Rock

Wadsworth Publishing Company
Belmont, California

Copyright © 1993 by Wadsworth Publishing Company. Copyright © 1990 by PWS-Kent Publishing Company. Copyright © 1984 and 1987 by Kent Publishing Company.

All rights reserved. No part of this book may be reproduced, stored in a retrieval system, or transcribed, in any form or by any means—electronic, mechanical, photocopying, recording, or otherwise—without the prior written permission of the publisher, Wadsworth Publishing Company, Belmont, California 94002.

Library of Congress Cataloging-in-Publication Data
Business law : principles and cases / Daniel V. Davidson . . . [et al.].—4th ed.
   p.   cm.
    Includes bibliographical references and index.
    ISBN 0-534-93280-0
    1. Commercial law—United States—Cases.   I. Davidson, Daniel V.
  KF888.B817 1992
  346.73'07—dc20   92-26530
  [347.3067]   CIP

 This book is printed on recycled, acid-free paper.

Printed in the United States of America
93 94 95 96 97—10 9 8 7 6 5 4 3 2

Editor-in-Chief: John-Paul Lenney
Assistant Editor: Susan Gay
Production Editor/Designer: Kirby Lozyniak
Manufacturing Coordinator: Lisa Flanagan
Compositor: Modern Graphics, Inc.
Cover Printer: John P. Pow Company, Inc.
Printer and Binder: Arcata Graphics/Halliday Lithograph

To Dee, Jaime and Tara

To my parents, Madge L. and Ernest E. Knowles, and all my other teachers

To James and Michael Poptanich for their love and patience, and to Aileen and Robert Zollweg for their inspiration

To Shirley

CONTENTS

CHAPTER 20   Title, Risk of Loss, and Bulk Sales   400

CHAPTER 21   Warranties and Product Liability   415

CHAPTER 22   Remedies for Breach of the Sales Contract   432

PART 5
Debtor-Creditor Relations

534

PREFACE

STATEMENT OF PURPOSE

Law cannot be made simple, nor can it be made easy. However, it is our strong conviction that law does not have to be made any more difficult, and on this premise we have written this text for undergraduate students. The purpose of *Business Law: Principles and Cases, Fourth Edition,* is to make the myriad of topics of business law comprehensible to the beginning student by using plain language, relevant and realistic examples, pertinent cases, and a clear writing style. While we do not intend to familiarize students with all the technical intricacies of the law, we do hope to stimulate their interest in those intricacies and to make them aware of how law affects their lives.

No matter what discipline business students select as a major field of study, they will encounter many legal issues during their professional lives. This text covers a substantial number of those issues. Among them are contracts, sales, commercial paper, debtor-creditor relations, agency, partnerships, corporations, government regulations, property protection, and international business. This text cannot supply the solution to all the potential legal problems involved in these areas; however, it can help students to recognize the legal issues that such problems present and to decide when to seek the appropriate help. The study of this book will not make anyone a lawyer, but it will help to make students aware of when a lawyer is needed.

The book is divided into ten parts, with the divisions based on the traditional topical areas of business law. Such an approach allows the instructor to select those topics germane to any course in which the text is used. It is suitable for use in a single-semester, comprehensive-coverage course or as the text for a multiple-semester, sequential series of courses. While the text is not specifically geared to the CPA examination, it does cover each of the business law topics included in the examination, and thus should be of considerable value to the accounting major.

Part I, "Foundations of American Law," introduces the American legal system by examining the logic behind the law and the reasons for studying business law. Chapter 2 explains the structure of the court system and the role of the United States Constitution in our legal system. Tort law and the concept of private duty are introduced in Chapter 3, and Chapter 4 focuses on the area of criminal law and the concept of public duty. Chapter 5 is an unusual and distinctive feature of the book. It leads the student, step-by-step, through the stages of a civil law suit, with explanations of *what* is being done at each stage of the proceedings and *why* it is being done. Chapter 6 is also distinctive, exposing the student to two professional relationships: the attorney-client relationship and the legal liability of the accountant. Chapter 7 introduces the crucial topic of business ethics.

Part II deals with the topic that forms the foundation of business law: the law of contracts. Although the modern complexities of business have led to a number of specialized areas of law, contract law forms the base upon which these specialized areas are built. A clear understanding of contract law is therefore essential to an understanding of the various other areas of business law. Chapter 8 explores the development of contract law and the different classifications of contracts. Chapter 9 looks at the formation of the agreement between parties—the area of offer and acceptance. Chapter 10 discusses the concept of consideration—the exchange of value between parties that makes the contract enforceable. Chapter 11 illustrates the limitations on who can enter a contract—the concept of capacity. Chapter 12 focuses on illegal agreements, underscoring the requirement that a contract must have a legal purpose to be valid. Chapter 13 examines the voluntary nature of the contract—the concept of reality of consent. Chapter 14 looks into the occasional need for formality in contract law and the need for a written agreement. Contracts between two parties often affect the rights of a third person not a party of the contract; Chapter 15 explores some of the rights and duties of the third persons so affected. Chapters 16 and 17 deal with the release of some contract obligations, or discharges, and the remedies available for nonperformance of other contractual obligations.

Part III, "The Law of Sales," introduces the Uniform Commercial Code (UCC), the modern, comprehensive law that governs many domestic commercial transactions. Although any contract for the sale of goods falls within Article 2 of the UCC, very few people are aware of their rights and duties in this area. Merchants need to be especially cognizant of the different legal aspects of sales law. Of special interest, and growing importance, are warranties and product liability, which are the subject of Chapter 21. The recent consumer movement has made both these areas particularly important to any business that deals in goods.

Part IV focuses on commercial paper, another area governed by the UCC. Millions of checks are issued every week to pay bills, to purchase goods and services, or to receive cash. Every loan made involves the use of some type of promissory note. Both checks and promissory notes are types of commercial paper and both are governed by Article 3 of the UCC. Knowing how and when to use a negotiable instrument can be extremely important to a business, especially in terms of profit generation and liability.

Part V, "Debtor-Creditor Relations," offers a truly comprehensive coverage of this subject. Three detailed chapters are devoted to secured transactions; two chapters focus on bankruptcy and alternatives to bankruptcy. Extensive coverage has been given to these topics because they are two of the most difficult areas in business law to master, and the extra coverage allows greater detail in explanation, resulting in better treatment of the fundamental concepts. The breakdown of secured transactions into three chapters emphasizes the major stages of a security interest from creation through enforcement. The analysis of bankruptcy in two chapters emphasizes the alternative nature of the options available to the debtor. Chapter 31 deals with the Bankruptcy Reform Act, the Bankruptcy Amendments and Federal Judgeship Act of 1984, and the general concepts of a "straight" bankruptcy under Chapter 7. This chapter also explains why the Bankruptcy Reform Act was declared unconstitutional and how the 1984 Amendments have clarified this area of law. Chapter 32 examines the alternatives to a "straight" bankruptcy, both within bankruptcy law and under traditional state laws.

Part VI devotes three chapters to the important area of the law of agency. Agency is a specialized type of employment in which one person is authorized to represent another in business transactions. Without the law of agency, modern business as we know it would be impossible. Thus, a thorough knowledge and understanding of this area are of special importance to a business student. Agency is not combined with the general topic of employment because agency is an important enough topic to stand alone. Also, nonagency employment is primarily an aspect of contract law, a subject covered earlier in the text, and as such is controlled by government regulation, which is the focus of Part VIII.

Part VII, "Business Organizations," consists of nine chapters. The first three examine the partnership as a business form: its formation, operation, and termination. Chapter 38 provides a detailed discussion of the problems involved in winding up this particular type of business. The next six chapters deal with aspects of the corporation as a business form. Included are chapters on the formation of a corporation, the operation of the business, and the management of the firm. Also included is a timely chapter on the effects of mergers, consolidations, and other acquisitions of the corporation. The last two chapters in Part VII treat the topics of franchising and securities regulations. Because so many corporations use securities as a source of funds, familiarity with securities regulations is an important consideration in avoiding liability for securities fraud. The Foreign Corrupt Practices Act, partially enforced by the Securities and Exchange Commission, is included in the coverage of this topic.

Part VIII, "Government Regulation," is another feature of the text. It not only covers the major antitrust statutes but also explains the theories that justify government regulation of business. Also included are chapters on environmental protection, one of the most controversial areas of business law, consumer protection, and labor and fair employment practice. Part VIII deals comprehensively with the environment within which all American businesses must operate, and an awareness of these issues is essential to a successful business career.

Part IX, "Property Protection," examines a number of diverse yet related topics: real and personal property, bailments, insurance, wills, estates, and trusts. These chapters provide some of the basic information needed to protect personal assets. Chapters 49 and 50 deal with acquisition, transfer, and protection of personal and real property. Chapter 51 covers the topic of insurance, the protection of that property from hazards. Wills, estates, and trusts—the planning of an estate to provide for one's heirs and family—are the subjects of Chapters 52 and 53.

Part X, "The Emerging Business Environment," is unique in that it discusses the two topics of computers and the law and international business. The intent is to provide an overview of these increasingly important areas, which promise to have a substantial impact on the future of business and business law. Although coverage of any single issue is limited, the overall treatment effectively introduces each of the topics.

Multinational corporations present special problems and unique opportunities for the future. Awareness of the legal issues to be faced in this area will be extremely important for the successful businessperson of the future. As society increases the demands it makes upon corporations, business leaders will need to respond to these demands or face ever-increasing government regulation. The pervasive nature of computers and the law must interrelate.

CHANGES IN THE FOURTH EDITION

Business Law: Principles and Cases continues its tradition of success with a variety of features which benefit both student and instructor.

- Excellent, updated figures and tables that show students examples of documents and help them visualize concepts.

- One of the leading researchers in international business, Carolyn Hotchkiss (Babson College), has completely revised Chapter 55, *International Business*. Professor Hotchkiss has updated the chapter with the goal of clarifying the complicated and ever-changing global environment.

- An updated coverage of bankruptcy law which includes a pro-creditor approach that has emerged since 1984.

- Up-to-date coverage of topics includes the latest important changes in the UCC and additional new landmark cases that better illustrate concepts covered in the text.

- Chapters on business ethics and computers and the law have been thoroughly revised and updated.

- Labor and employment regulations coverage has been substantially re-worked to reflect new statutory enactments, especially those concerning the physically challenged.
- Corporate law coverage includes several new cases that set the current standard for measuring anti-takeover devices.

Written and designed with the student in mind, *Business Law: Principles and Cases* provides a variety of pedagogical features to assist in the learning process.

PEDAGOGICAL FEATURES

Chapter Outlines

The topical outlines that open each chapter alert the student to the chapter coverage and help to provide a structured study approach.

Marginal Notes and Glossary

Brief definitions of key terms appear in the margins throughout the text. These marginal notes provide a working understanding of the phrases without disrupting the student's efforts to read the material. More complete definitions are provided in the Glossary, and the student may also choose to consult a law dictionary for even more detail.

Cases and Case Index

Numerous condensed cases are used to illustrate legal points throughout the text. These include both classic, landmark cases and many of the most recent decisions pertaining to business law. The actual court opinions have been "briefed" into a four-part format: a statement of facts, the issues upon which the decision hinges, the holding of the court, and the reasoning behind the holding. The Case Index at the end of the book allows the reader easy access to this material. A number of hypothetical cases intended to illustrate particular points of law also appear in several places throughout the text.

Illustrations

The text includes helpful illustrations—flowcharts, diagrams, legal forms and documents, summary and comparative tables. A list of these follow this preface.

"You Be The Judge"

New to the fourth edition, these boxed inserts summarize current events that relate to a major chapter topic and ask the reader to resolve the facts and consider the situation as if he or she were deciding the outcome. While there is often no correct answer, citations to the actual event, articles about the event, as well as avenues for class discussion are provided in the Instructor's Manual. This feature, found in half of the chapters, encourages critical thinking, motivates class discussion, and provides possible writing assignments for students.

Summaries

The text of each chapter closes with a narrative summary of the material presented in the chapter. The summaries are not meant to completely cover the material, but to aid the student in a general review.

Discussion Questions and Case Problems

Each chapter includes questions and problems, some dealing with the principles and terms covered in the chapter and some designed to test general comprehension of the material.

Most chapters include case problems that are based on actual court opinions. Since these problems give the case name and citation, students can look up the actual case to compare their answers and reasoning with those of the court. These chapter-ending questions and problems can be used as a study tool in reviewing the material, as classroom discussion material, or for out-of-class writing assignments.

Appendices

Four appendices provide easy access to actual source material referred to in the text and footnotes throughout the book. Appendix A includes Articles 1–9 of the Uniform Commercial Code; Appendix B presents the United States Constitution; Appendix C contains the Uniform Limited Partnership Act with the 1985 amendments. Appendix D contains the Revised Uniform Limited Partnership Act with the 1985 amendments.

SUPPLEMENTAL ITEMS

Student Study Guide

Elizabeth Crocker and Ann Henry, both of the University of Arkansas, have prepared a comprehensive Study Guide to accompany the text. This Study Guide includes study hints, review of key terms and general principles, application questions, and essay questions to help the student master the subject and its vocabulary.

Instructor's Manual

The Instructor's Manual outlines each chapter's material in the form of teaching hints. A segment called "Trouble Spots" highlights those areas that traditionally confuse students because of the complexity of the material or the language of the law. This section suggests methods of avoiding these traditional problems by calling the student's attention to them in advance. The Instructor's Manual also includes teaching hints, answers to the text's chapter-ending questions and problems, suggestions and background information for the "You Be The Judge" boxes, and a list of excerpts from the "Business and the Law" videos which can be used in regular lecture classes.

Transparencies

A set of eighty acetate transparencies is available to help instructors graphically illustrate some of the more difficult concepts presented in the text. These consist of illustrations, both from the text and from other sources; they include summary charts, legal documents, and various other facsimile items.

**Test Bank and
Trilogy Computerized
Test Bank**

For each chapter, the Test Bank provides 3800 test items including the following types of questions:

- twenty-five true/false, directed at both application and vocabulary;
- twenty-five multiple choice, aimed primarily at application, with some vocabulary and recognition included;
- ten short answer and application questions, measuring the student's ability to list key concepts and define legal terms;
- five hypothetical essay questions that involve analysis and application of legal reasoning and critical thinking skills for resolution of hypothetical situations;
- four critical thinking and analysis questions derived from court opinions dealing with the topical material. The citation to the opinion is included.

This mix provides sufficient flexibility and enough possible questions to satisfy a wide variety of instructional needs. The computerized version of the same test items is IBM-PC compatible and is available in both 5¼″ and 3½″ formats.

Telecourse Guide

Includes learning objectives, a topic overview, assignments, a list of key terms, a self-test, and "Your Opinion, Please" section which asks the student to apply concepts.

A STATEMENT OF GRATITUDE

Putting a textbook together "from whole cloth" is difficult under the most ideal of conditions. To do so when geographically separated is even more difficult, and we could not have done it without the help, support, encouragement, and belief of the following people:

Al Bruckner, our editor. His help, guidance, and encouragement have been invaluable. In addition, his enthusiasm provided a necessary adrenaline boost whenever we began to tire. Susan Gay, our assistant editor. Susan was always there to act as a liaison for the author team, both among us and between us and the company. She also provided the coordination of details, communications, and correspondence so essential to making our multiregional writing effort possible. Kirby Lozyniak, our production editor, who took the individual quirks and foibles of our writing styles and turned them into a well-written textbook, and did so with never a complaint voiced to us. Carolyn Hotchkiss (Babson College) for her expertise and efforts in revising Chapter 55, *International Business*. And a special thanks to two very special people—Dick Crews and Rolf Janke. Dick was our first editor, and he guided us through two editions. When Dick retired, Rolf stepped in and led us through the third edition. The support and confidence each gave us made the work bearable, and we will be eternally grateful to both of them.

We also wish to express our gratitude to The American Law Institute, which granted us permission to reprint excerpts from the *Restatement (Second) of Contracts* (copyright 1982 by The American Law Institute; reprinted with the permission of The American Law Institute), *Restatement (Second) of Torts* (copyright 1977 by The American Law Institute; reprinted with the permission of The American Law Institute), and *Restatement (Second) of Agency* (copyright 1958 by The American Law Institute; reprinted with the permission of The American Law Institute).

Finally, our thanks to the many reviewers who read over our manuscripts and offered constructive criticism to strengthen the finished product. Throughout, they were critical, supportive, and encouraging. Their efforts and suggestions were essential to the final product.

William Dennis Ames
Indiana University of Pennsylvania

Walter A. Authur
Manchester Community College

Gilbert T. Cave
Lakeland Community College

Randy T. Davis
Richland College

Patricia L. DeFrain
Glendale College

Lizbeth G. Ellis
New Mexico State University

Frank S. Forbes
University of Nebraska, Omaha

Marsha E. Haas
College of Charleston

Susan S. Jarvis
University of Texas, Pan American

Wayne Lewis
Union College

Violet Eva Molnar
Riverside Community College

Joan S. Ryan
Lane Community College

Edward F. Shafer
Rochester Community College

Karen J. Vehlow
Northwest Nazarene College

Dennis A. Wallace
Strayer College

Amy Oakes Young
Louisiana State University, Shreveport

A NOTE TO THE STUDENTS

As you read this text, you may find yourself occasionally frustrated by the use of such terms as *generally, usually, ordinarily, in most cases, as a rule,* and the like. When this happens, remember this: Most business law is based on state law, and there are many variations among several states. These variations make it impossible—and unwise—to make definite statements about some legal subjects. In addition, although there *are* general rules of law, there are also exceptions to the general rules. Since space and time limitations would make it impossible to list all these exceptions in any one introductory text, we have gone with the majority rule unless otherwise noted.

Also remember that if these generalities are frustrating for you, they are equally frustrating for your instructor, for attorneys who are arguing these principles in the various courts of the land, and for the judges who have to decide the cases being argued!

It is our sincere hope that we have put together a text that is not only a valid educational tool but also a book that is enjoyable to read. Business law is a serious and important topic, but it is also potentially entertaining and interesting one. This book is designed to emphasize the importance and seriousness of the topic while underscoring the interest it contains. We feel we have been successful in our efforts, and we hope that you agree.

Daniel V. Davidson
Brenda E. Knowles
Lynn M. Forsythe
Robert R. Jespersen

LIST OF FIGURES

ABOUT THE AUTHORS

DANIEL V. DAVIDSON received both his B.S. in Business Administration and his J.D. in Law from Indiana University, Bloomington. He has previously taught at Central Connecticut State College, St. Cloud State University in Minnesota, the University of Arkansas, and California State University at Fresno. He is currently serving as the Associate Dean of the College of Business and Economics at Radford University in Virginia.

Professor Davidson has been the recipient of four awards for teaching. In 1975 he was named Outstanding Teacher of the Year at Central Connecticut State College. In 1979 he received the Outstanding Faculty Award from Beta Alpha Psi, and in 1980 he was named the *Razorback Award* winner as the Outstanding Business Professor, both at the University of Arkansas. In 1984 Professor Davidson was awarded the Meritorious Performance Award at California State University at Fresno.

Professor Davidson is an active member of the Academy of Legal Studies in Business (formerly the American Business Law Association) and its Southern Regional. He has held several offices in the Southern Regional, including president, and is currently serving as the Senior Advisory Editor of the *Southern Law Journal* and of the *Proceedings* of the region's annual meeting.

BRENDA E. KNOWLES received a B.A. *magna cum laude* from the University of Evansville, an M.A. from Miami University, and a J.D. from the Indiana University School of Law (Bloomington). She is an Associate Professor of Business Law at Indiana University at South Bend, where she has been the recipient of the Amoco Foundation Excellence in Teaching Award, a system-wide, all-university teaching award. She has also been active in FACET, the faculty colloquium on excellence in teaching, which is a system-wide, all-university effort to encourage effective teaching and learning in the academic community. She is also a member of Beta Gamma Sigma.

Professor Knowles specializes in research on employment discrimination, antitrust, and intellectual property law. She publishes her work in professional journals and has won an award for her research. In addition, she has been recognized both nationally and locally for her professional and civic accomplishments, most recently through the W. George Pinnell Award for outstanding **service** to Indiana University.

Professor Knowles is an active member of the Academy of Legal Studies in Business (formerly the American Business Law Association) and of several regionals. More specifically, she is a past President of the ALSB and a past President of the Tri-State Regional. She is licensed to practice law in Indiana, and is a member of the American, Indiana State, and St. Joseph County Bar Associations.

LYNN M. FORSYTHE is Professor of Business Law and the former Director of Graduate Business Programs at California State University, Fresno. She received her B.A. from the Pennsylvania State University and her J.D. from the University of Pittsburgh School of Law and has passed the bar examination in both California and Pennsylvania.

Professor Forsythe has been an estate and gift tax attorney for the Internal Revenue Service and has taught business law, administrative law, government regulation of business, real estate law, business ethics, estate planning and business and society. She is the author of numerous articles on business law and the teaching of business law. She has held the positions of staff editor, coeditor and reviewer for the *Journal of Legal Studies Education* and served as the Editor-in-Chief for the 1987–1989 term. She is currently an advisory editor.

Professor Forsythe is a member of Beta Gamma Sigma. She has been active in the American Bar Association, for which she chaired subcommittees and panels, including an American Law Institute–American Bar Association program; and the American Business Law Association, for which she served as program coordinator for the 1983 annual meeting and as liaison to the National Conference of Commissioners on Uniform State Laws and as a member of the Executive Committee of the American Business Law Association. Having previously held each of the other offices of the Western Business Law Association, she served as president in 1986–1987.

ROBERT R. JESPERSEN is Professor of Business Law and Adjunct Professor of Law at the University of Arkansas at Little Rock. He has also served as associate dean, director of the M.B.A. program, and director of the executive development program at U.A.L.R. He holds the A.B. and A.M. degrees from Columbia University, the J.D. from the University of Houston, and the LL.M. from the University of Texas at Austin.

Professor Jespersen has practiced law in Texas and Arkansas, and is a retired Judge Advocate of the U.S. Marine Corps, having reached the rank of Colonel. He has served as a faculty member and administrative officer at the University of Houston, Princeton University, and Columbia University. His public service includes appointment as Assistant Attorney General of Texas.

Professor Jespersen served three years in Africa, first as Headmaster of the Kurisini International Education Centre in Dar es Salaam, Tanzania, and then as Senior Advisor to the Association of African Universities in Accra, Ghana. He is a former president of the Southern Regional Business Law Association (now the SALSB) and the American Business Law Association (now the ALSB). He is currently President of the Arkansas Chapter of the Federalist Society for Law and Public Policy Studies.

BUSINESS LAW

PART 1

Foundations of American Law

Ignorance of the law is no excuse. The basic truth of this old adage seems simple and obvious. However, the simplicity of the truth hides the complexity of the law. Each citizen—and resident—of this country has "constructive notice" of the law. Each person is expected to be aware of, and to abide by, all the laws of the land. Yet the enormity of "the law" makes such an expectation futile. No one person can really *know* "the law," but every person is expected to obey it. Thus, a built-in contradiction exists in the system.

This opening part of the book will introduce the reader to the law as it exists in the United States. Broad legal philosophies will be presented briefly. The American legal system will be outlined. The concept of private duty and torts and the concept of public duty and crimes will be introduced. A civil lawsuit will be explained. Finally, the section will examine a special legal-professional area and will discuss business ethics.

Each part of this book will shed some light on and offer some insights into areas that the reader may not have previously explored. A thorough knowledge of law takes years of specialized study, and this text alone will not provide it. But it will begin to open the doors of understanding for the student and to remove that "ignorance of the law [that] is no excuse."

CHAPTER 1

Introduction

OUTLINE

WHAT IS THE RELATIONSHIP BETWEEN LAW, ORDER, AND JUSTICE?

Law

This book is about understanding the law of business. Before we begin our study, however, we must answer a basic question: What is *law*? There are many definitions, ranging from the philosophical to the practical. Plato said law was social control. Blackstone said it was rules specifying what was right and what was wrong. For our purposes, however, we shall define law as *rules that must be obeyed*. People who disobey these rules are subject to **sanctions** that could result in their having to do something they would not voluntarily do, such as paying money to someone or going to jail. Our society has many kinds of rules, but not all rules can be considered "law." For example, a rule in baseball says that after three strikes you are out. That is not law. All laws are rules, but not all rules are laws. What differentiates a law from a rule is its *enforceability*. People who do not follow the rules in baseball are not arrested or taken to court. They are simply ejected from the game. In contrast, people who break laws can be made accountable for their actions.

Sanctions Coercive means.

There are many different kinds of legal rules. One kind defines a definite way of making a contract or a will. A second forbids certain kinds of conduct; **criminal law** is an excellent example of this kind of legal rule. A third category has been established to compensate persons who have been injured because someone else breached a duty. For example, when an automobile manufacturer builds a car negligently, and its **negligence** is the direct cause of an injury, the manufacturer may have to pay the injured person money damages. Finally, there are rules that our legislative bodies and courts establish to take care of their everyday business. For example, all states have a rule concerning the maximum number of days defendants have before they must answer a lawsuit. This is an example of **procedural law.**

Criminal law That body of law dealing with public wrongs called crimes.

Negligence Failure to do something that a reasonable person would do, or doing something that a reasonable and prudent person would not do.

Procedural law Methods of enforcing rights or obtaining redress for their invasion; machinery for carrying on a lawsuit.

We will view the law as a body of rules that establish a certain level of social conduct, breaches of which are grounds for enforcement in courts of law. Enforcement consists of one of three legal remedies: (1) paying money damages, (2) being subject to a court order that directs a person to do or not do something (an injunction), or (3) going to jail or prison. The law is not unlike the controlling function in management, in which a standard is established (a law), performance is measured against that standard (the facts), and actual performance is corrected so the standard can be achieved (through the use of a legal remedy).

Order

The manner in which the law usually looks at *order* is in the form of a legal command issued by a judge. But we are not concerned with order in that sense. Another way of looking at order is as *the absence of chaos*. Chaos, as you know, is confusion and total disorganization. If the laws of a society were always followed and never broken, perfect order would result. There would be no crime, and everyone would be safe. For example, no one would run red lights and cause injuries to others; all orders would be legal and no one would break them; and neighbors would get along with neighbors without arguing. History tells us that no society in which there was perfect order has ever existed. Our society would come very close to perfect order if we allowed ourselves to be treated as though we were in the military. All police states have a great deal of order but very little justice. Nazi Germany was an example of this condition.

The words *law* and *order* are often linked together. It is natural to link them because if the law is followed, there will be order. It is precisely because the law is not followed all the time by all the people that there is not perfect order. Society is always somewhat chaotic and disorganized. One of the reasons people do not always obey the law is that often they are not aware of what the law is. For example, every contract, whether oral or written, could be organized in such a way that it would always be legally enforceable. But since not everyone knows the law of contracts, it is quite impossible for all contracts to be legally enforceable. For this reason, the law presumes that all citizens know the law, whether, in fact, they do or do not. This position, theoretically at least, creates an incentive for all citizens to study the law. If the law did not presume that everyone knows the law, the result would be more chaos than exists already. In that case, individuals accused of breaking the law would have an excellent defense: They did not know they were breaking it. Our educational system plays an important role in allowing us to learn the law. A perfect society, of course, would not need any laws. Until that day arrives, every society will have to establish certain laws designed to create order.

Justice

Just as all life is a search for reality, all law should be a search for justice. Although justice *is* fairness, the concept of fairness is less abstract than that of justice and thus is easier to deal with on a practical level. For example, when a millionaire accused of murder obtains the best criminal trial lawyer in the country to defend him and is either acquitted or receives a small sentence, many people ask: Is that fair? When you were a child and saw bullies pick on someone smaller than themselves, you probably asked yourself the same question: Is that fair? In these situations, the results are clearly unfair and therefore unjust. As Lenny Bruce once said, "They call it the Halls of Justice because the only place you get justice is in the halls."

Commutative justice The attempt to give all persons their due on the assumption that all persons are equal.

There are two kinds of justice: commutative and distributive. **Commutative justice** attempts to give all persons what is due them. It places everyone on an equal footing. An example of commutative justice is a contract that requires a person who sold some property for $60,000 to carry out his part of the bargain even though he subsequently discovers he could have sold the property for $80,000; the law usually will not take into account the fact that he was a high school dropout and that the person he dealt with was a college graduate. **Distributive justice**, on the other hand, does not place everyone on an equal level. It holds that some people should get more and others less

Distributive justice The attempt to "distribute" justice in a way that considers inequalities among individuals.

because people are unequal, and it is up to "justice" to establish equality through a disproportionate allocation of benefits. Distributive justice could be used as a philosophical basis for affirmative action programs, which attempt to make up for past unconstitutional discrimination. In a free society such as ours, the best we can do is *seek* to achieve justice. It is improbable that we could ever achieve perfect justice in every case.

The Nexus: Practicability

"The law," then, is really a system consisting of law, order, and justice. Combined, they make up the American legal system. All the elements should be balanced in perfect equilibrium so that one element does not adversely affect any other. If we had total order, we would have very little justice; if we had total justice, we might have very little order. The *nexus* (link between elements) of the two concepts is the point of *practicability*. For example, to achieve perfect justice with respect to traffic violations, we would have to have jury trials with counsel to ascertain precisely whether a citizen did in fact violate the speed limit. However, the costs of such a venture would be so prohibitive that no municipality or other local jurisdiction could afford to pay for it. Accordingly, most traffic courts tend to achieve "assembly line" justice rather than perfect justice. Such is the practicability inherent in the relationship among law, order, and justice.

THE LAW AS AN ARTIFICIAL LANGUAGE SYSTEM

Many terms used in the law are also used in everyday speech, but they have totally different meanings in the law. This text will define the terms for you, either in the chapter or in the Glossary at the back of the book. The list of terms is seemingly endless: *offer, acceptance, consideration, guaranty,* and so on. Since the terms may have different connotations within the law, be on guard for subtle shifts in meaning. If you are in doubt, reread the passage again or check for other definitions in the Glossary. In addition, it is impossible to discuss the law intelligently without reference to some words that are limited to the law for their definition. For lack of a better term, these words are called **jargon**. Examples include *estoppel, appellee, assignee, bailee, causa mortis, caveat vendor, quid pro quo,* and *codicil*.

Jargon   The technical terminology of a particular profession.

You make no assumptions when you study a foreign language; therefore, make none about the law. Remember these three rules about our artificial language system, and you will encounter minimal difficulty in mastering this material:

1. Legal terms may appear to be synonyms for everyday words, but they are not.
2. Legal terms may have more than one legal meaning.
3. Some legal terms have no relation to everyday language.

THE LAW OF BUSINESS

Law merchant Those rules of trade and commerce used by merchants in England after 1066.

Common law The unwritten law that is based on custom, usage, and court decisions; different from statute law, which consists of laws passed by legislatures.

The law of business began as a private system administered outside the regular law courts in England. It was called the **law merchant** because it was administered in courts established in the various merchant guilds. It eventually was integrated into the English **common law** court system. Today the law of business includes contracts, sales, commercial paper, secured transactions, agency, partnerships, corporations, and insurance.

WHY STUDY THE LAW OF BUSINESS?

Preventive law Law designed to prevent harm or wrongdoing before it occurs.

This textbook could be called a primer in **preventive law.** As a businessperson, you should understand the legal implications of what you are doing; as a consumer, you will find such understanding valuable. If you understand the issues raised here and can apply your knowledge to particular business situations, you may save yourself great expense later. For example, when you study the Statute of Frauds, you will learn that if two persons enter into a contract that is reduced to writing and only one of the two parties signs the contract, only the party who signed the contract can be sued on it. That means the party who did not sign the contract has two options: (1) to comply with the contract if acceptable or (2) to breach the contract knowing that the other, in general, cannot sue successfully. The party who signed it has no options; he or she must comply or stand ready to be sued. This is because the Statute of Frauds states that certain contracts must be in writing in order to be enforceable. Therefore, a party cannot be sued on such a contract unless that person signed it. If a tenant signed a lease but the landlord did not, the tenant could be sued on the lease, but the landlord, in general, could not. Business is a very practical subject. The law of business is just as practical.

Another reason for studying the law of business is that it will help you develop valuable decision-making skills. It will also sensitize you to particular situations in which you may need the assistance of a lawyer. In real estate transactions, for example, you will discover that the buyer or seller needs the assistance of a lawyer *before* an earnest money contract is signed rather than after. Skillful legal draftsmanship in drawing up the contract is where a lawyer can be most useful.

WHAT ARE THE NEEDS OF A LEGAL SYSTEM?

The Need to Be Reasonable

A legal system must be reasonable. The laws under which people live must be based on assumptions that are provable. These various assumptions can be proved through reliance upon facts. The law stating that persons driving motor vehicles must stop at red lights and may proceed on green lights is based on the fact that chaos would result if busy intersections did not have lights or stop signs. Speeding laws are reasonable since it can be demonstrated that higher speeds on busy streets are related to higher numbers of accidents.

In addition to being reasonable, laws must be applied reasonably. A law stating that persons will have property taken away from them if they do not pay for the property is certainly reasonable; but it would not be reasonably applied if a person stopped paying for the property and, without notice, the property were removed by the person to whom the money was owed. The person owing the money would first have to be told that the money was due and payable and then be given a chance to say why the money could not be paid. Then, if the money still were not paid, the person to whom the amount was due could repossess the property through legal process.

The Need to Be Definite

The law must be definite, not vague. For example, a law stating that all contracts "in excess of approximately $500" must be in writing would not clearly specify when a contract must be in writing. The Statute of Frauds, however, states that all contracts in excess of $500 must be in writing, which makes it very clear. If one has a contract for $499.99, it need not be in writing; a contract for $500.01 must be in writing. Sometimes the law is unable to state precisely what one must do in all circumstances. In such cases, the law uses the word _reasonable_ instead of setting precise parameters. If an automobile hits a pedestrian and causes injury, the pedestrian may sue the driver of the vehicle. In this situation, the law does not state that speed in excess of a particular amount is sufficient to find the driver at fault. If all you had to go on was that the speed limit was fifty-five miles per hour and the car was going fifty miles per hour, would you find the driver at fault? You simply do not have enough information. You would need to know more about the driver. Did the driver have a current operator's license? If the driver had to wear glasses when driving, were they worn? Was the driver intoxicated or otherwise under the influence of drugs? Did the driver get enough sleep the night before? One could continue seeking facts about the driver, the automobile, the road conditions, the time of day, and so on. Under these conditions, the law would ask the question: Was the driver's conduct reasonable under the circumstances? If so, it will be written off as an accident; if not, the driver will be liable for any injury to the pedestrian. In the final analysis, the law provides an answer. Thus, the law is definite.

The Need to Be Flexible

To say that the law must be both definite and flexible is not a contradiction in terms. The law needs to be definite in order to establish a standard. The law must be flexible so that it can be applied in many different _individual_ situations. For example, in many **community property** states, the divorce court judge has flexibility in dividing the community property of the two parties. If a couple, both aged twenty-five, have a community estate of $500,000 and there are no children to consider, how much should each get? You simply do not have enough facts to answer the question. What if the man is a brain

Community property Property owned in common by a husband and wife as a kind of marital property in a form of marital partnership.

surgeon with a yearly income of $300,000 and his wife is a high school dropout with no employment skills? Their joint community property amounts to $500,000. A division of $400,000 to the wife and $100,000 to the husband might be appropriate under those circumstances. In the future, the husband can always go out and earn much more than his wife because he has a marketable skill. In such a situation, a judge would be persuaded by the skill of the advocates as well. If lawyers are not persuasive, their clients will get less. Yielding to persuasion makes our system flexible. If trees did not bend in the wind, they would break. Our legal system is like those trees: It must bend without breaking.

The Need to Be Practical

Because people depend on it to guide their actions, the law needs to be practical and oriented to action rather than to thought. This is not to say that there are not some very thoughtful ideas behind the law, but it is *not* a philosophical system; it is a *real* system. One can prove or not prove just about anything in a philosophical system, because it is not real. The law, however, must deal with real issues created by real people. These issues take the form of a legal conflict. For example, suppose a world-famous concert pianist earns over $200,000 per year. While driving home one night her car stalls at a railroad intersection. The pianist attempts without success to start the car. A train is rapidly approaching. She decides to abandon the car and flee, but the doors and windows are all electronically controlled and are jammed. The train hits the car, and the driver's hands are crushed by the collapsing metal. The pianist sues, and the court decides that the automobile manufacturer was negligent in constructing the vehicle. Although the law cannot wave a magic wand and replace the pianist's hands, it can assess money damages and give the pianist the present value of what she would have earned from playing the piano for the rest of her life. That is not an ideal solution, but it is a practical one. If the law were not practical, it would be useless.

The Need to Be Published

If we had the best set of laws imaginable but no one knew of them, they would be useless. Therefore, all laws must be published. It is for this reason that the law properly presumes that all persons know the law.

The Need to Be Final

If a controversy exists and it is possible to use the legal system to resolve it, one thing is certain: At some point in the future, the matter will be resolved. It may not be resolved to the full satisfaction of the person who "won" the case, but it will be resolved. In this sense, the law is like a political election. On election day, someone wins and someone loses. The outcome is final. In criminal law, if the defendant wins the case in trial court, that is the end of the matter. The prosecutor cannot appeal in most situations. A defendant who is convicted in trial court can appeal to the highest court in the state system. If the defendant does not gain a reversal, that is the end of the matter, unless the United States Supreme Court chooses to review the case. The process is much like a ping-pong ball that keeps bouncing back and forth until someone finally wins and the ball comes to rest. Many cases end in a **settlement**, which

Settlement A form of legally binding agreement that "settles" a lawsuit.

Plea Bargaining   *Process of settlement used in criminal cases.*

means that the matter is not carried to trial, but the parties agree to end the matter on their own. The settlement agreed on is incorporated into the court's final judgment. In criminal cases, the same sort of process is called **plea bargaining**. More than 75 percent of all cases, criminal and civil, are disposed of in this manner. However the process is accomplished, it results in a final judgment. Table 1.1 outlines the needs of a legal system.

WHAT ARE THE PURPOSES OF A LEGAL SYSTEM?

Achieving Justice

As previously discussed, justice is basically fairness. Sometimes we achieve it and sometimes we don't. In the law of business, we deal more with commutative justice—giving each person his due—than with distributive justice. In a contract, for example, commutative justice gives each person that to which the person is entitled under the contract—no more, no less. The rule of *caveat emptor* (let the buyer beware) is an example of how the law allocates risk in a business transaction. If the buyer does not thoroughly examine the goods before they are bought, the buyer will be prevented from seeking redress in the courts if what is bought does not conform to the buyer's expectations. If the buyer had examined the goods before the purchase, flaws could have been discovered and the sale might not have been made.

There is a trend, however, to introduce elements of distributive justice into the law of business. The courts, legislatures, and administrative agencies are attempting to reallocate the risks of business transactions by taking into account the status of the parties. For example, in 1976 the Federal Trade

TABLE 1.1   The Needs of a Legal System

LEGAL SYSTEM	ANARCHY/CHAOS
Reasonable → Rules	Arbitrary and/or unreasonable rules
→ Application	Uneven/biased application
Definite rules and limits	Vague or unclear rules, no defined limits
Flexible standards (to keep up with changes in society and technology)	Rigid and unbending standards (Stone-Age rules in a modern world)
Practical rules based on reality	Hypothetical or impractical rules based on wishful thinking
Published (communicated)	Unpublished—"surprise rules"
Final—to put an end to a case at a particular time	Ongoing, continuous—never seeming to end!

Unconscionability Condition of being so unreasonably favorable to one party, or so one-sided, as to shock the conscience.

Commission established a new rule concerning consumer transactions that resulted in more protection for the consumer. You will learn more about this matter in the discussion of the holder in due course doctrine in Chapter 25.

Another limit placed upon the doctrine of commutative justice is that of **unconscionability.** An eighteenth-century English case provides an excellent working definition of unconscionable contracts as contracts that are so unfair "no man in his senses and not under delusion would make [them] on the one hand, and no honest and fair man would accept [them] on the other."[1] Our legal system must always consider that some contracts ought not to be enforced even if they fully comply with all the rules concerning contract formation. You will learn more about this subject in the discussion of reality of consent in Chapter 13.

Providing Police Power

Since justice is the ultimate purpose of a legal system, providing police power may be viewed as an intermediate purpose of a legal system. When most students see the term *police power,* they usually envision a person in a blue uniform with a badge and gun. That is just one part of the power we call police power. Police power is inherent in all governments. This power allows for the creation and enforcement of laws designed to protect the public's health, safety, and general welfare.[2] Laws and ordinances concerning police, fire, sanitation, and social welfare departments in state and local governments stem from this power.

Maintaining Peace and the Status Quo

Injunction A court order prohibiting a person or persons from doing a certain thing or, on the other hand, ordering that something be done.

Ever since the days of ancient England, one of the clearest purposes of the law has been to "keep the King's peace." All modern torts and crimes can trace their origin to a simple breaching of the King's peace. Today, laws that govern the relationships between private individuals, such as the laws governing assault, battery, trespass, and false imprisonment, are private forms of keeping the peace. Allied with keeping the peace is the concept of maintaining the status quo—that is, keeping things the way they are. It is natural for the law to maintain the status quo unless changing things will benefit society. In cases where irreparable injury is alleged, it is possible, upon a proper showing, to obtain an **injunction** from a court that will maintain the status quo until the matter is finally resolved.

Providing Answers

Appellate court A court that has the power to review the decisions of lower courts.

On a philosophical plane, the law should be just; but on a practical plane, it should provide answers. Sometimes the answers the law provides are not satisfactory answers. If a person sues a neighbor concerning a nuisance the neighbor is allegedly creating, and the neighbor wins the case in trial court, the person who sued can appeal the decision to the next higher court. In most states this higher court is called an **appellate court.** If an appellate court rules

[1]Earl of Chesterfield v. Janssen, 28 Eng. Rep. 82, 100 (Ch. 1750).
[2]Drysdale v. Prudden, 195 N.C. 722, 143 S.E. 530, 536 (1928).

in favor of the person who allegedly created the nuisance, a further appeal may be taken to the state's highest court. In that court, however, the person who originally sued may win and thereby receive a satisfactory answer. Your business law professor may be more interested in raising questions for you to consider than in providing answers, which is as it should be in a college classroom. That same person, however, as a practicing lawyer, would be more interested in obtaining answers for clients than in raising legal questions. A legal system in which there were no answers would be ridiculous.

Providing Protection

Civil rights   The rights in the first ten amendments to the Constitution (the Bill of Rights) and due process and equal protection under the Fourteenth Amendment.

The law protects all kinds of interests. You have already seen that the law concerns itself with protecting individuals. The tort law of assault and battery is a classic example of protection of the individual. The law also protects persons less obviously when it protects their **civil rights**. Civil rights laws are extremely important in modern litigation and have their historical antecedent in the first ten amendments to our federal Constitution. The Constitution appears as an appendix to this book; it would be worthwhile for you to refresh your memory about its features at this time. Persons are protected in the free exercise of their speech, are free to choose or not to choose a religion, can peacefully assemble, and may petition their government for a redress of grievances (a rarely used freedom). The right to keep and bear arms, the right to be free of unreasonable searches and seizures, the right against compulsory self-incrimination, the right to a grand jury, the right against double jeopardy, the right to a jury trial, and the right to bail are some of the more important civil rights.

The government is also in the business of protecting *itself*. A government's self-protection is an ancient right that goes back to Roman law. It is based on the concept that if the sovereign is **sovereign**, it cannot be attacked legally. This rule still stands, although the federal government and many states have passed special statutes allowing suit for torts to be brought against them.

Sovereign   Above or superior to all others; that from which all authority flows.

Finally, the law is concerned with the protection of property. All property is either personal or real. *Personal property* is all property with the exception of real property. In general, if property is movable, it is personal property. *Real property,* on the other hand, is land and whatever is affixed to land, like a house. Our legal system has a variety of laws that protect property.

Enforcing Intent

The law of contracts is based on *freedom of contract*. It is this rule that allows each of us to be our own legislator. We make our own laws as long as the contracts into which we enter do not violate the general principles of contract law. For example, you may wish to enter into a contract with a supplier of goods. You may want to make the contract today so that it will immediately bind the other party. Perhaps you have found a good price and do not think you will find a better one. Your problem is that you do not presently have the money to pay for the goods, but you know that you could easily resell them for an immediate cash profit within ten days after delivery. You should, therefore, seek a provision in the contract stating that the buyer will pay the seller for the goods eleven days after receipt of the goods. Of course, if you cannot resell the goods within ten days, you will have a problem, but that is a question of business judgment and not of law.

Providing Rehabilitation

Both criminal law and civil law are directed toward rehabilitation. Criminal law should, among other things, rehabilitate the criminal. If people who enter jails or prisons are not rehabilitated by the time they leave, all we are doing is maintaining free hotels for criminals. Civil law is directed toward the rehabilitation of debtors. The Constitution gives Congress the power to make laws concerning bankruptcy. Bankruptcy laws have developed to the point that anyone can use the protection of the law to escape financial difficulty and to create a new financial life. For example, take a twenty-five-year-old university honors graduate. The graduate decides to enter the computer software business because of her knowledge of computer programming. At first, business booms. She decides to expand, and banks help in financing a major expansion. Suddenly the market shifts and the business has much more in debts than in assets. Is it not fair to allow this person to seek protection under the bankruptcy law and begin again? What is the alternative? To allow this person to spend the rest of her working life trying to pay off the debt would be counterproductive. Let her start afresh and profit from her mistakes.

Facilitating Commercial Transactions

One of the major characteristics of the American legal system is that it facilitates commercial transactions. For example, if everyone had to have cash to purchase an automobile, the number of automobiles sold in the United States would be reduced by millions. To a great degree, our society is built upon the automobile. The steel, energy, and transportation industries are directly related to the automobile. Accordingly, the extension of credit for the purchase of automobiles greatly facilitates trade. The use of checks and credit cards also accelerates commercial transactions. The taking of a security interest (see Chapter 28) in goods expedites trade to persons who might otherwise not be in a financial position to make the purchase. The United States legal system fosters free and open competition and facilitates trade. This characteristic of the legal system has done much to make the United States the business and financial giant it is today. Table 1.2 outlines the purposes of a legal system.

WHAT ARE THE SOURCES OF THE AMERICAN LEGAL SYSTEM?

Our legal system is based on the Constitution, treaties, statutes, ordinances, administrative regulations, common law, case law, and equity. These elements of the American legal system are interconnected. Each of the elements is separate, but when the elements are interconnected, they make up the system. These elements must be thought of as a system, since a change in one element cannot be considered in isolation. Such a change will affect one or more parts

TABLE 1.2   The Purposes of a Legal System

PURPOSE	REASON
Achieving justice.	To provide "justice" so that the needs of the members of the society are addressed.
Providing police power.	To provide a social structure so that "wronged" individuals do not have to resort to self-help; to give society control of the system.
Maintaining peace and the status quo.	To provide each member of the society with a feeling of personal security and a structure upon which each individual can rely.
Providing answers.	The practical counterpoint to achieving justice; lets the members of society know what is expected of them and what they may expect of others.
Providing protection.	To define and establish social guidelines and protect the entire society if any of these guidelines are not followed and obeyed.
Enforcing intent.	A free society must allow people to agree to act, and it must provide some methods for ensuring that these agreements are honored.
Providing rehabilitation.	To allow a person who violates the guidelines of the society to have a second chance; recognizes that anyone can make a mistake.
Facilitating commercial transactions.	Our society supports freedom of contract and private ownership of property; each of these concepts requires the ability to trade one's assets, and the easier it is to do so, the better for business.

of the system. In a civil rights suit, a person may allege a violation of constitutional rights (Fourteenth Amendment), a statutory right (Civil Rights Act of 1964), an administrative regulation (Equal Employment Opportunity Commission guideline), past decisions of the court (**stare decisis**), and equity (if all else fails, the person should win because it is fair). The important thing to remember is that all the parts are interrelated and that the whole is more than the sum of the parts.

Stare decisis   To abide by, or adhere to, decided cases; policy of courts to stand by decided cases and not to disturb a settled point.

Constitutions   A *constitution* is the *fundamental law of a nation*. It may be written or unwritten. The British constitution is said to be unwritten. Clearly, the United States Constitution *is* written. It allocates the powers of government and also sets limits on those powers. Our founding fathers knew that all tyrants had two powers: the power of the purse and the power of the sword. The Constitution places the power of the purse exclusively with the Congress and the power of the sword with the executive branch. Our third branch of government, the judiciary, has neither the power of the purse nor the power of the

Judicial review The power of the courts to say what the law is.

sword, and yet it has the power to decide the constitutionality of the laws passed by Congress. In the case of *Marbury* v. *Madison*,[3] the United States Supreme Court for the first time applied the doctrine of **judicial review**. That case held that the Supreme Court has the power to decide whether laws passed by Congress comply with the Constitution. If they do not, they are unconstitutional and thus of no force or effect. We will discuss the unique nature of the Constitution, and the *Marbury* v. *Madison* case, further in the next chapter.

Our states also have constitutions, and they are the fundamental laws of those jurisdictions. The U.S. Constitution is the supreme legal document in the United States; any conflict between it and state constitutions will result in the latter yielding to the federal document.

Treaties

Treaties, which are *formal agreements between two or more nations,* are the only element of our legal system that does not stem from the Constitution. Treaties are made, not with the authority of the Constitution, but under the authority of the United States. This difference is important, since the power to make a treaty is a function of sovereignty and not one of a constitution. In most cases, treaties require enabling legislation passed by Congress. The case of *Missouri* v. *Holland*[4] established that statutes passed in accordance with a valid treaty cannot be declared unconstitutional. Once made, treaties also become the supreme law of the land.

Statutes

Statutes are the *acts of legislative bodies.* They command or prohibit the doing of something. The word *statute* is preferred when one is referring to legislative acts in order to distinguish it from such other "laws" as ordinances, regulations, common law, and case law. The best example of state statutory law is found in the Uniform Commercial Code (UCC) (see Appendix A). All fifty states, the District of Columbia, and the United States Virgin Islands have adopted this law. It is the subject of many of the chapters contained in this book. The UCC covers the following subjects: sales, commercial paper, bank deposits and collections, letters of credit, bulk transfers, documents of title, investment securities, and secured transactions.

Ordinances

Ordinances are *laws passed by municipal bodies.* Cities, towns, and villages, if incorporated, have the power to establish laws for the protection of the public's health, safety, and welfare. These entities are to be distinguished from counties, which generally do not have legislative power. Counties usually have the power to enforce state laws within their boundaries.

Administrative Regulations

Administrative regulations are *rules promulgated by governmental bodies created by the legislative branch of government,* such as the Federal Trade

[3]1 Cranch 137, 2 L.Ed. 60 (1803).
[4]252 U.S. 416, 40 S.Ct. 382, 64 L.Ed. 641 (1920).

Commission on the federal level and an insurance commission on the state level. These bodies have unusual powers, which will be discussed in Chapter 45. The rules and regulations of these entities have the full force and effect of law.

Common Law and Law Merchant

Common law consists of "those principles and rules of action, relating to the government and security of persons and property, which derive their authority solely from usages and customs of immemorial antiquity, or from the judgments and decrees of the courts recognizing, affirming, and enforcing such usages and customs."[5] *Law merchant* is the body of rules used by merchants that was based on usage and custom. This is the predecessor of the modern law of business.

Case Law

Case law exists in the many reported cases emanating from federal and state courts. It is quite often up to judges to interpret statutes in order to apply them to actual cases and controversies. These interpretations place what lawyers call a "judicial gloss" on the statute. You will not know what a particular statute really stands for until you have read not only the statute but also the cases that have interpreted that statute. *Case law,* then, is *the law as pronounced by judges.*

Stare decisis is an ancient doctrine that means *the question has been decided.* For example, if a particular legal point is well settled in a certain jurisdiction, a future case with substantially the same facts will be decided in accordance with the principle that has already been decided. It is for this reason, as well as others, that lawyers do a great deal of legal research. An opportunity to "make law," as it is called, occurs when a legal point is in conflict. For example, many states are divided into various judicial districts, and each of these districts may issue written legal opinions. If two or more districts have published conflicting opinions on a particular point, and the state's supreme court has *not* issued an opinion on the point, the time is ripe for the creation of a new rule, statewide, that will resolve the matter once and for all.

Equity

Equity has been defined as *a body of rules applied to legal controversies when there is no adequate remedy at law.* These rules are based not on technicalities but rather on the principles outlined by Justinian during his reign as the Byzantine emperor of Rome (A.D. 527–565): "to live honestly, to harm nobody, [and] to render to every man his due." These rules were developed outside the common law courts in England by an officer of the king called the chancellor. Today the rules of law and equity are joined into one system. The injunction is an equitable remedy, but before our courts will issue an injunction, the person requesting it must show proof of an inadequate remedy at law. For example, if your neighbors are burning rubber tires on their property

---

[5]Western Union Tel. Co. v. Call Pub. Co., 181 U.S. 92, 21 S.Ct. 561, 45 L.Ed. 765 (1901).

and the prevailing wind carries the obnoxious odor directly across your property, their action will destroy the peaceful use and enjoyment of your land. In general, no amount of money damages would be sufficient to allow them to continue to burn rubber tires. In that case, you would have an inadequate remedy at law, and you could request that the court issue an injunction to stop your neighbors from burning those tires. In a larger sense, however, equity may be viewed as a doctrine that results in the legal system's adhering to the principle of fairness. Figure 1.1 outlines the sources of the American legal system.

HOW IS THE LAW CLASSIFIED?

Federal Versus State Law

Our legal system is divided into two branches: federal and state. American lawyers must learn not only the law of their states but the law of the federal courts as well. In addition, lawyers must know the *majority rule*. The majority rule is simply the rule that most states have adopted. Quite often, there is also a *minority* rule that a smaller number of states follow. Rarely, if at all, do the states agree on everything.

Common Versus Statutory Law

As discussed earlier, our system consists of both common and statutory law. The European legal system does not have a common law; European law is

FIGURE 1.1   The Sources of the American Legal System

F = federal	S = state	
F, S	Constitution	Supreme law of the land; fundamental basis of domestic law.
F	Treaties	Not based on the Constitution; formal agreements between nations; fundamental basis of international law/relations.
F, S	Statutes	Acts of the legislature; control of domestic conduct; subject to limits imposed by the Constitution.
S	Ordinances	Laws passed by municipal bodies and designed to control purely local problems, subject to any limits imposed by statutes or by the Constitution.
F, S	Administrative Regulations	Acts of administrative agencies; control of specific areas of conduct; subject to any limits imposed by statutes or by the Constitution.
S	Common Law and Law Merchant	Principles and rules that have developed over time and are based on custom and usage; provide coverage when statutes and the Constitution do not.
F, S	Case Law	Precedent, established interpretations of areas of law in which the courts define what the law is.
F, S	Equity	Special rules and relief when "the law" does not provide a proper and/or adequate remedy.

totally statutory. The statutes are grouped into codes, and the codes are administered by judges. Judges do not make law in the European system. Judges in England and the United States have the power to "make law" by interpreting statutes, and those interpretations become law.

Civil Versus Criminal Law

Another dichotomy in our legal system is its division into civil and criminal law. *Civil law* is *private law wherein one person sues another person. Criminal law* is *public law in which a government entity sues a person;* for example, if a person becomes violently abusive and attacks another individual, and thus inflicts bodily harm upon the innocent individual, the district attorney as the representative of a government entity may prosecute the attacker for assault. If convicted, the attacker may go to jail or prison. In addition, the person who was injured may sue the attacker in court for money damages. The additional suit would not constitute **double jeopardy** or its civil law equivalent, **res judicata,** since there are two different theories of action: civil and criminal.

Double jeopardy   A rule of criminal law that states that a person will not be twice exposed to conviction for the same offense.

Res judicata   A rule of civil law that states that a person will not be twice exposed to liability for the same wrong.

Substantive Versus Procedural Law

Substantive law deals with *rights and duties given or imposed by the legal system. Procedural law* is devoted to *how those rights and duties are enforced.* For example, the law of contracts is substantive law. The law of pleadings describes how one goes about enforcing those rights or duties. A controversy over the matter of contractual consideration or the lack of it is a substantive matter, but how one goes about getting that matter into a court is a matter of procedure. Where one files the lawsuit, what must be alleged, how one serves the lawsuit on the defendant, and how long the defendant has to answer the allegations are all examples of procedural law. This book is devoted primarily to *substantive* law.

YOU BE THE JUDGE

The U.S. Supreme Court acts on approximately 5,000 cases a year. Of these, only about 4% are granted an oral review. Because this percentage is so small, the litigant's initial goal is to devise a strategy to convince the justices that a case has significance. Four of the nine justices must agree that a case has merit in order to schedule an oral argument before the complete court. The justices follow different procedures in reaching a decision as to which cases should be granted review.

Chief Justice William Rehnquist and Justices Byron White, Harry Blackmun, Sandra O'Connor, Antonin Scalia, and Anthony Kennedy currently pool the efforts. On a rotating basis, one law clerk from their combined pool of approximately twenty-three clerks prepares a summary of each case. This summary is then distributed to all six justices. Some justices rely solely on the summary in deciding whether the case is granted review. Other justices review some of the petitions based on what they read in the summary.

Justices Thurgood Marshall and John Stevens do not participate in the pooling arrangement. They rely on their own individual clerks to review the petitions and to make recommendations.

Justice William Brennan, who retired in 1990, generally scanned the petitions himself. Brennan felt that to transfer the review function to someone else would be " . . . an indefensible abdication of his responsibilities. . . ."[1] He may be the last justice to personally read the petitions. These are the various practices that influence a person's ability to obtain Supreme Court review.

Justice David Souter took Brennan's place on the bench. Which approach should he follow? If you were appointed to the U.S. Supreme Court, what would you do and why?

Source: "Only Clerks May Be Screening Petitions To Supreme Court in Post-Brennan Era," Stephen Wermiel, *The Wall Street Journal,* Thursday, October 11, 1990, page B8.

SUMMARY

Law consists of rules that must be obeyed. These rules must be obeyed because they can be enforced in courts of law. Order is the absence of chaos. Our legal system strives to create and to maintain order. Justice is fairness. Commutative justice seeks to give each person what is due him or her. Distributive justice seeks to give each person more, or less, than what is due. The goal of distributive justice is to balance the unequal distributions that exist in society. Our legal system seeks constantly to balance law, order, and justice. Its ultimate goal is to achieve equilibrium.

The law is an artificial language system. It uses words from everyday conversation, but it adds different meanings. It also uses words that are unique to the law. The law of business includes contracts, sales, commercial paper, secured transactions, agency, partnerships, corporations, and insurance. By studying the law of business, you will learn how to avoid legal problems. If legal problems should develop, however, this knowledge will sensitize you to their ramifications. As a result, you will know when an attorney should be consulted.

A legal system needs to be <u>reasonable</u>, <u>definite</u>, <u>practical</u>, published, and final. A legal system should be directed toward achieving justice. It does so by properly utilizing police power; by keeping the peace or maintaining the status quo when irreparable injury is threatened; by providing answers; by protecting people, property, and government; by enforcing intent; by rehabilitating people; and by facilitating commercial transactions.

Our legal system is like a three-dimensional chess game in which a move in one subsystem can affect other subsystems. The sources of the American legal system are constitutions, treaties, statutes, ordinances, administrative regulations, common law, the law merchant, case law, and equity. The law is a multifaceted, bifurcated system of federal and state law, common and statutory law, civil and criminal law, and substantive and procedural law.

DISCUSSION QUESTIONS

1. Why do you think St. Augustine said that states without justice are robber bands enlarged?

2. Are law, order, and justice equally weighted parts of our legal system, or do one or two outweigh the other? Explain.

3. Why is the law an artificial language system? Turn to the Glossary and look up five legal terms whose meanings in the law differ from their meanings in everyday usage. Look up five legal terms that have meanings unique to the law. What are the definitions?

4. What rational arguments can you make for *not* having a knowledge of the law? What arguments can you make for having a knowledge of the law?

5. Philosopher John Rawls said, "Justice is the first virtue of social institutions, as truth is of systems of thought." Discuss.

6. The Federal Tort Claims Act allows the United States government to be sued under certain circumstances. Why do you think this statute was enacted? Why are intentional torts exceptions to the law?

7. What is stare decisis? Once a question has been decided, is there no way for the rule to be changed?

8. The UCC was developed by the National Conference of Commissioners on Uniform State Laws and the American Law Institute. What advantage is there to such an organization?

9. Jeremy Bentham (1748–1832), an English lawyer, is best known for his utilitarian philosophy that the object of law should be to achieve the "greatest happiness of the greatest number." Discuss the implications of the following statement based upon your knowledge of common versus statutory law.

> Do you know how they make [common law]? Just as a man makes laws for his dog. When your dog does anything you want to break him of, you wait until he does it and then beat him. This is the way you make law for your dog, and this is the way judges make laws for you and me. They won't tell a man beforehand. . . . The French have had enough of this dog-law; they are turning it as fast as they can into statute law, that everybody may have a rule to go by. . . . (Bentham, 5 *Works* 231.)

10. On numerous occasions, Mochan telephoned a person and used language that was obscene, lewd, and filthy. After the person complained to the police, Mochan was indicted and convicted of a common law misdemeanor since there was no criminal statute covering obscene telephone calls. Discuss the outcome of this case with respect to the rule that our laws need to be published. (*Commonwealth* v. *Mochan*, 177 Pa. Super. 454, 110 A.2d 788 [1955].)

CHAPTER 2

The American Legal System

OUTLINE

THE FEDERAL CONSTITUTION

The Constitution of the United States is unique for two reasons: it is the oldest written national constitution, and it was the first to design a government based on the concept of a separation of powers. It was created in reaction to the tyranny of English rule. England has an unwritten constitution and a system of government that tends to merge the legislative, executive, and judicial functions. In contrast, our written constitution created a governmental structure with three separate "compartments" and a series of checks and balances whereby the power of one "compartment" is offset by that of the others.

Because their study of history taught them that all tyrants had at least two powers—the power of the purse and the power of the sword—our founding fathers placed the power of the purse (fiscal and monetary) in the legislative branch of government and the power of the sword (armed forces) in the executive branch. They gave the third branch of government the power that ultimately was to be called the power of *judicial review*. This power allows the third branch of government to make the ultimate decision as to where and how the other two powers may be properly exercised. We shall discuss this power in greater detail later.

Allocation of Power

Legislative Power   Article 1 of the Constitution creates a Congress consisting of two houses: the Senate and the House of Representatives. Congress has the power to levy and collect taxes, pay debts, and pass all laws with respect to certain enumerated powers, such as providing for the common defense and general welfare, regulating commerce, borrowing and coining money, establishing post offices and highways, promoting science and the arts, and creating courts inferior to that of the Supreme Court.

Executive Power   Article 2 creates the executive branch of government by creating the offices of president and vice-president. The president is the commander-in-chief of the armed forces of the United States. In addition, the president has the power to make treaties and to nominate ambassadors, judges, and other officers of the United States. The Senate must confirm all presidential appointments. Without Senate confirmation, the appointee cannot take office. The vice-president serves for the president when the president is unable to serve and is the president of the Senate.

Judicial Power   Article 3 vests the judicial power of the United States in one Supreme Court and in such other inferior courts as Congress may create. All federal judges in the United States are nominated by the president; if they are confirmed by the Senate, they serve in office for the rest of their lives, during good behavior.

The actual wording of Article 3 limits rather than expands the judicial power. Limitations placed on the power flow from the words **"cases . . .**

Cases and controversies
Claims brought before the court by regular proceedings to protect or enforce rights or to prevent or punish wrongs.

[and] controversies" that appear in Section 2. In general, the federal courts are limited to hearing and deciding cases and controversies only. Constitutional law has evolved to the point where, today, the following areas are not within the realm of cases and controversies:

1. advisory opinion
2. moot point
3. lack of standing
4. political question

limits that constrain judicial power.

Advisory opinion A formal opinion by a judge, court, or law officer on a question of law submitted by a legislative body or a government official but not presented in an actual case.

The doctrine of the separation of powers requires that our courts deal only with judicial matters. An **advisory opinion** is one wherein the executive branch refers a question to the judicial branch for a nonbinding opinion. That is not the purpose of our judicial system. Accordingly, whenever a member of the executive branch requires an advisory opinion, the question is referred to the justice department within the executive branch for an opinion of the attorney general. In our system of government, the attorney general is the appropriate person to issue an advisory opinion. The following case illustrates that the judicial power is limited to real controversies and does not encompass advisory opinions.

G.T.E. Sylvania, Inc. v. Consumers Union
445 U.S. 375 (1980)

FACTS   Consumers Union brought an action under the Freedom of Information Act to obtain from the Consumer Product Safety Commission reports on television-related accidents. The U.S. District Court dismissed the case. The U.S. Court of Appeals reversed and remanded. The U.S. Supreme Court granted certiorari and also remanded. On remand, the Court of Appeals further remanded for a trial on the merits, and certiorari was again granted by the Supreme Court.

ISSUE   Does this action present a sufficient case or controversy to establish proper jurisdiction, even though the Commission agreed with the requester that the documents should be released?

HOLDING   Yes. There was sufficient case or controversy.

REASONING   "The purpose of the case-or-controversy requirement is to limit the business of federal courts to questions presented in the adversary context and in a form historically viewed as capable of resolution through the judicial process. . . . The clash of adverse parties sharpens the presentation of issues upon which the court so largely depends for illumination of difficult questions." However, here the CPSC and the requester do not want precisely the same result because television manufacturers obtained an injunction to prevent the release of the information in question. Thus, the parties actually do not want precisely the same outcome. To allow the CPSC to release the information would subject it to attack for violating the injunction, which would have no effect on the requester.

Moot point A subject for argument that is unsettled or undecided; a point not settled by judicial decision.

The federal courts will hear only cases that are appropriate for a judicial solution. In the case of *Defunis* v. *Odergard,*[1] the Supreme Court stated that the question of whether a student should be admitted to a law school was a **moot point** because by the time the Court could have issued its opinion, the student would have been on the brink of graduation. Accordingly, as an example of judicial efficiency, it chose not to write an opinion on the merits of the suit.

Standing Legal involvement; the right to sue.

Only persons who can assert that they have actually been harmed or injured have **standing** to sue. For example, if you saw a person punch someone in the nose, you would not have standing to sue the aggressor for assault and battery. The person who was hit would have standing to sue since he was the one who was injured. The following case discusses one aspect of standing.

Flast v. *Cohen*
392 U.S. 83 (1968)

FACTS A federal taxpayer brought suit to prohibit the spending of federal monies to finance instructional materials in parochial schools. The spending was authorized under the Elementary and Secondary Education Act of 1965. The suit was based on the grounds that such expenditures were in violation of the First Amendment guaranteeing freedom of religion.

ISSUE Does a taxpayer have standing to sue?

HOLDING Yes. In such a case a taxpayer does have standing.

REASONING "The fundamental aspect of standing is that it focuses on the party seeking to get his complaint before a federal court and not on the issues he wishes to have adjudicated." The party seeking relief must have a personal stake in the outcome of the controversy so as to assure a *concrete* awareness. Under certain circumstances, a taxpayer may have a personal stake in the outcome. Therefore, there is no absolute bar to a federal taxpayer suit. This case raised the sole question of the standing of individuals who assert only their status as taxpayers. Since the taxpayer in this case successfully asserted that this legislation exceeds specific constitutional limits, he had standing to sue.

Political questions Questions concerning government, the state, or politics, which are thus more properly settled at the ballot box than in the courtroom.

Judicial restraint A holding or pressing back from action by a court.

Even though many **political questions** in our society involve real controversies, the doctrine of our courts is that they will not hear them. This rule is based on the concept of **judicial restraint**. For example, if a citizen should assert that a state is not based on a republican form of government, that claim would not be heard in our federal courts because it is a political question. If a citizen thinks that our nation's foreign policy is incorrect, our courts could not be used to debate the point because it is a political question. But is *leg-*

[1]416 U.S. 312 (1974).

islative apportionment—the ratio of legislative representation to constituents—a political question? The following case resolved that question.

Baker v. Carr
369 U.S. 186 (1962)

FACTS   The plaintiffs alleged that the apportionment of the state legislature under Tennessee state law was unequal since rural voters had greater representation than urban voters.

ISSUE   Is state legislative apportionment a political question and therefore **nonjusticiable?**

HOLDING   No. It is a constitutional question and is therefore justiciable.

REASONING   The claim of the **appellants** that "they are being denied equal protection is justifiable, provided discrimination is sufficiently shown . . . the right to relief under the equal protection clause is not diminished by the fact that the discrimination relates to political rights . . . the nonjusticiability of a political question is primarily a function of the separation of powers . . . the question here is the consistency of state action with the federal Constitution. We have no question decided, or to be decided, by a political branch of government coequal with this court . . . when challenges to state action respecting matters of the administration of the affairs of the state and the officers through whom they are conducted have rested on claims of Constitutional deprivation which are amenable to judicial correction, this court has acted upon its view of the merit of the claim."

Nonjusticiable Not subject to the jurisdiction of a court.

Appellants Persons who appeal the decision of a lower court to a higher court.

Now that you know the four limits that constrain judicial power, we will consider the one concept that has expanded judicial power. When you read the Constitution, you will not find the specific power of judicial review mentioned. That is because it is a court-created power. The chief justice of the United States in 1803, John Marshall, created this doctrine of the law in the landmark case of *Marbury* v. *Madison*.[2] This power is based on an interpretation of the Constitution that our courts may examine the actions of the legislative and executive branches of government to ascertain whether those actions conform to the Constitution. If they do not, the courts have the power to declare those actions unconstitutional and therefore unenforceable. Thus, the Supreme Court can declare an act of Congress invalid. This concept of judicial power does not exist in England, where the Parliament is supreme. Therefore, the branch of government that has neither the power of the purse nor the power of the sword has all the power, in a sense, because it has the power to say what is right. Since 1803, the power of our courts to judicially review all actions of the legislative and executive branches of government has gone unchallenged. It is the keystone of our doctrine of the separation of powers. Furthermore, this power of the Supreme Court to invalidate legisla-

[2]1 Cranch 137, 2 L.Ed. 60 (1803).

tion also extends to all state legislation because of the supremacy clause of the federal Constitution.

The Watergate crisis, remembered by many as a low point in American history, may be viewed as a high point with respect to the doctrine of judicial review. In 1974 President Nixon was ordered to produce the now-famous Watergate tapes for use in a federal prosecution. President Nixon claimed executive privilege and rejected the order to turn over the tapes to the federal prosecutor. The Supreme Court, in a unanimous opinion, denied his claim and ordered him to release the tapes. President Nixon complied with the order of the Supreme Court, thus ending a constitutional crisis and becoming the first president to resign from office.

The following case contains the most famous Supreme Court opinion. It created the doctrine of judicial review.

Marbury v. *Madison*
1 Cranch 137, 2 L.Ed. 60 (1803)

FACTS

Mandamus A type of writ that issues from a court of superior jurisdiction commanding the performance of a particular act specified therein.

Congress enacted a statute that revised the federal judicial system. In accordance with that law, President John Adams signed the commission for a Washington, D.C., justice of the peace, William Marbury, but the commission never reached him. The new president's secretary of state, James Madison, withheld Marbury's commission. Marbury sought relief by filing an action in the Supreme Court asking that Madison show cause why a **mandamus** should not be issued directing Madison to deliver his commission.

ISSUE

If Marbury is entitled to a remedy, is mandamus the appropriate remedy?

HOLDING

No. Congress cannot expand the jurisdiction of the Supreme Court. The jurisdiction of the Supreme Court is contained in the Constitution, and Congress can neither expand nor contract it.

REASONING

Writ A mandatory precept issuing from a court of justice and couched in the form of a letter ordering some designated activity.

"The peculiar delicacy of this case, the novelty of some of its circumstances, and the real difficulty attending the points which occur in it require a complete exposition of the principles on which the opinion to be given by the court is founded. . . . It only remains to be inquired whether [the remedy] can issue from this court. . . . If this court is not authorized to issue a **writ** of Mandamus . . . it must be because the law is unconstitutional, and therefore absolutely incapable of conferring the authority, and assigning the duties which its words purport to confer and assign. . . . The act to establish the judicial courts of the United States authorizes the Supreme Court to issue Writs of Mandamus in cases warranted by the principles and usages of law, to any courts appointed or persons holding office, under the authority of the United States. . . . However, the Constitution says that the Supreme Court shall have original jurisdiction in all cases affecting ambassadors, other public ministers and consuls, and those in which a state shall be a party. In all other cases, the Supreme Court shall have appellate jurisdiction. . . . The authority given to the Supreme Court, by the act establishing the judicial courts of the United States, to issue Writs of Mandamus to public officers, appears not to be warranted by the Constitution, and it becomes necessary to inquire whether a jurisdiction so conferred can be exercised. . . . The powers of the legislature are defined and limited. . . . It is a proposition too plain to be contested, that the Constitution controls only legislative acts repugnant to it; or, that the legislature may alter the Constitution by an ordinary act. . . . Certainly all those who have formed written constitutions contemplate them as forming the fundamental and paramount law of the nation, and consequently, the theory of every such government must be, that an act of the legislature, repugnant to the Constitution, is void. . . . It is emphatically the province and duty of the judicial department to say what the law is. . . . If two laws conflict with each other, the courts must decide on the operation of each. . . . If, then, the courts are to regard the Constitution, and the Constitution is superior to any ordinary act of the legislature, the Constitution, and no such ordinary act, must govern the case to which they both apply. . . . Thus, the particular phraseology of the Constitution of the United States conforms and strengthens the principle, supposed to be essential to all written constitutions, that a law repugnant to the Constitution is void, and that courts, as well as other departments, are bound by that instrument."

Figure 2.1 outlines the allocation of constitutional power.

Limitation of Power

Habeus corpus The name given to a variety of writs issued to bring a party before a court or judge.

The original Constitution that was signed on 17 September 1787 contained a number of rights pertaining to individuals. The ancient and most celebrated prerogative writ in English law was the right to **habeus corpus.** This right may be used by all persons who have been deprived of their liberty. The writ is addressed to the person who detains an individual; it commands that person

FIGURE 2.1 Allocation of Constitutional Powers

ARTICLE 1 LEGISLATIVE POWERS	1. Legislative powers are vested in Congress. 2. House of Representatives members shall serve two-year terms, based on the population of the states. 3. Senate members shall serve six-year terms, with each state allocated two senators. 4. All revenue bills must arise in the House of Representatives. 5. Congress has the power to collect and levy taxes, to provide for a common defense, to provide for general welfare, and to coin money (among other powers). 6. Congress has the power to raise an army and a navy and to declare wars. 7. The Senate is empowered to try all impeachments.
ARTICLE 2 EXECUTIVE POWERS	1. The executive power is vested in a president who is elected for a term in office of four years. 2. The president and the vice-president are selected by the vote of the Electoral College. 3. The president is the commander-in-chief of the army, the navy, and the militia of the states. 4. The president has the power, with the advice and consent of the Senate, to make treaties and to make federal appointments, including ambassadors, consuls, and federal judges.
ARTICLE 3 JUDICIAL POWERS	1. The judicial power is vested in one Supreme Court and in such subordinate courts as Congress establishes. 2. Federal judges hold their offices for life during good behavior, and their salaries may not be diminished. 3. The federal courts have exclusive jurisdiction over federal questions and concurrent jurisdiction over certain diversity of citizenship cases.

to produce the individual in a court and requires that court to determine whether the person has been rightfully detained. The following case, which was decided 5:4, demonstrates how the modern Court is narrowing this right.

Woodard v. Hutchins
464 U.S. 377 (1984)

FACTS
: The State of North Carolina filed an application to vacate the order of a circuit court judge that granted a stay of execution. The application for the stay of execution included repetitious and novel claims as to why it should be granted. At no time did Hutchins deny that he deliberately murdered three police officers.

ISSUE
: Will the Supreme Court hear successive petitions for habeus corpus petitions?

HOLDING
: No.

REASONING
: "This case is a clear example of the abuse of the writ. . . . All three of Hutchins' claims could and should have been raised in his first petition for federal *habeus corpus*. . . . A pattern seems to be developing in capital cases of multiple review in which claims are brought forward—often in piecemeal fashion—only after the execution date is set or becomes imminent. Federal courts should not continue to tolerate—even in capital cases—this type of abuse of the writ of *habeus corpus*."

Another right established in the Constitution was that no bills of attainder were to be passed by Congress. A *bill of attainder* is a "legislative trial" whereby a person is judged a felon or worse by act of the legislature and not by a court of law.

Ex post facto   After the fact; pertaining to an act or fact occurring after some previous act or fact.

Congress was also denied the right to enact **ex post facto** laws. For example, if a citizen entered into a transaction that was perfectly legal in January, Congress would be prevented from declaring that transaction illegal in a statute passed after January.

Other individual rights, such as trial by jury in most criminal cases, were contained in the original Constitution, but those just mentioned are particularly notable.

Amendments to the Constitution

Four years after the Constitution was signed, the first ten amendments to the Constitution were passed. These first ten amendments, known as the Bill of Rights, were designed to assure that certain individual rights were protected. Over the years an additional twenty-six amendments to the Constitution have been passed and other amendments proposed. The amendments to the Constitution reflect the concerns of the citizens with certain topics and reflect changes in the society over which the Constitution itself serves as the supreme law. Figure 2.2 deals with several of the amendments to the Constitution.

FIGURE 2.2 Selected Constitutional Amendments

THE BILL OF RIGHTS (1791)

Amendment	Protections
1	Guarantees freedom of religion, freedom of speech and of the press, and the rights to peaceably assemble and to petition the government for redress of grievances.
2	Guarantees the right to keep and bear arms.
3	Guarantees that no soldiers shall be quartered in private homes during times of peace without the consent of the homeowner.
4	Prohibits unreasonable searches and seizures; requires that warrants be issued only upon probable cause.
5	Guarantees the right to a grand jury; prohibits double jeopardy; protects against self-incrimination; assures due process of law; protects against deprivations of property without just compensation.
6	Guarantees the right to a fair, speedy, and public trial; the right to an impartial jury; the right to an attorney; and the right to confront witnesses and accusers.
7	Guarantees the right to a trial by jury in civil cases.
8	Prohibits cruel and unusual punishment; prohibits the setting of excessive bail.
9	Specifies that rights not specifically named are retained by the people.
10	Those powers not delegated to the federal government nor prohibited to it by the states are reserved to the states or to the people.

The Civil War Amendments

13 (1865)	Prohibits slavery or involuntary servitude, except as a criminal punishment following conviction of the crime.
14 (1868)	Grants U.S. citizenship to all persons born or naturalized in the United States; prohibits any attempts to abridge the privileges of citizenship; prohibits any state from depriving any person of life, liberty, or property without due process of law; mandates that states provide equal protection under the law to any persons within the jurisdiction of the state.
15 (1870)	Prohibits denial or interference with the right to vote on account of race, color, or previous condition of servitude.

Selected Other Amendments

16 (1913)	Permits Congress to levy and collect income taxes without apportionment among the states and without regard to the census.
19 (1920)	Extends the right to vote to women.
26 (1971)	Extends the right to vote to 18-year-olds; prohibits age discrimination in the right to vote.

THE COURTS AND JURISDICTION

The basic concept with respect to our courts is one of *jurisdiction, the legal power of a court to decide a particular matter.*

In this section, we will examine four aspects of jurisdiction:

1. subject matter jurisdiction
2. jurisdiction over the person
3. concurrent versus exclusive jurisdiction
4. venue

Subject Matter Jurisdiction

Subject matter jurisdiction
The power of a court to hear only certain kinds of questions.

In our discussion of the Constitution, we said that the Supreme Court was limited to deciding cases and controversies. In addition, Article 3 of the Constitution defines the **subject matter jurisdiction** of the Supreme Court as all cases in law and equity arising under the Constitution, the statutes of the United States, and all treaties. The subject matter jurisdiction granted to the Supreme Court is extensive. A state juvenile court, on the other hand, is limited solely to hearing matters concerning children. If an adult were brought before a juvenile court, the court would lack jurisdiction, since it may decide only matters concerning youngsters. Likewise, a federal bankruptcy court may not decide a criminal matter, since its jurisdiction is limited to bankruptcy matters.

Jurisdiction Over the Person

Plaintiff   A person who files a lawsuit; the person who complains.

Defendant   A person who answers a lawsuit; the person complained about.

Once a court has the appropriate subject matter jurisdiction, it must also have jurisdiction over the *persons* whose rights, duties, or obligations will be decided by the court. For example, if both the **plaintiff** and the **defendant** are residents of state X, state X has jurisdiction over them. On the other hand, if the plaintiff is a resident of state X but the defendant is a resident of state Y, state X may not have proper jurisdiction over the defendant. In such a case, it is probable that the more appropriate forum would be a federal court, for reasons that will be stated later. If the plaintiff wanted to sue the defendant in a state court, the plaintiff might have to go to state Y and sue the defendant there, since a *defendant's* state of residence is almost always appropriate.

All states have laws called *long-arm statutes.* Suppose a resident of state Y drives a car on the roads of state X and injures a resident of state X. In that situation, the courts of state X would have jurisdiction over the person of the resident of state Y, since it would be unfair for the resident of state X to have to go to state Y to sue. Under these laws, a state can also exercise jurisdiction over corporations that are incorporated in one state, have offices in a second state, and do business in a third state. In that situation, the courts of all three states would have **in personam** jurisdiction over the corporation.

In personam   Directed against or with reference to a specific person.

If a state cannot obtain in personam jurisdiction on either of these grounds (residency or long-arm statutes), another approach can be used. If an individual or a corporation has property in one state but resides in another, the state in which the property is located can exercise jurisdiction over the property on the basis of what the law calls **in rem** jurisdiction.

In cases of either in personam or in rem jurisdiction, notice to the defendant must be properly served by process. Proper **service of process** includes *actual notice,* in which one is personally served by an officer of the court, or notice served publicly in a newspaper. Notice in a newspaper would be used in those cases where actual notice could not be obtained after a reasonable attempt to do so. In that case, it is called *constructive service.* With regard to long-arm statutes, proper notice is usually service at the office of the state's secretary of state.

In rem   Directed against a thing with reference to no specific person and consequently against or with reference to all whom it might concern.

Service of process   Delivery, in person or otherwise, of a writ or notice to the person named so as to inform that person of the nature and terms of the writ or notice.

Concurrent Versus Exclusive Jurisdiction

In certain cases, both state and federal courts may exercise jurisdiction. If so, it is called *concurrent jurisdiction.* On the other hand, certain matters can be heard only by federal courts; this is called *exclusive jurisdiction.* Examples of exclusive jurisdiction are suits in which the United States is a party, some areas of admiralty law, bankruptcy, copyright, federal crimes, and patent cases.

ONLY ONE PARTY HAS JURISDICTION

Venue

Once a court establishes that it has proper jurisdiction over the subject matter and the person, it must then ascertain whether proper venue exists. *Venue* literally means "neighborhood." In a legal sense, however, it means *the proper geographical area or district where a suit may be brought.* For example, if both the plaintiff and the defendant are residents of the same state, in personam jurisdiction exists in that state's court. But which state court? The question is usually answered with respect to the area in which a particular court is located and in which the defendant's residence is also located. Venue could be proper in the area in which an incident, such as an automobile accident, occurred. The venue laws of each state spell out in great detail the appropriate court in which the filing of the suit would be proper.

Conflict of Laws

Conflict of laws is *the legal doctrine that resolves any variance between the laws of two or more conflicting jurisdictions.* It deals primarily with the subject matter jurisdiction of any particular court. For example, assume that a citizen of state A entered into a contract with a citizen of state B while both of them were residing in state C. The contract concerned goods that were located in state D, and the goods were to be shipped to state E. While the goods were in transit, they were stopped and taken by a citizen of state F who was a creditor of the citizen of state A. What should the citizen of state B do to get the goods? In which state should suit be filed? What law should that state apply—the law of state A, B, C, D, E, or F? It could be that the citizen of state B would win if the laws of states A, C, or E were applied but would lose if the laws of states B, D, or F were applied. We will not attempt to resolve this question in this text, since it is clearly too complex for a first course in the law of business. You need only be aware of the complexity of this matter and the often quite simple solution to the problem—that is, the contracting parties agree ahead of time that if there should be any dispute concerning the contract, the laws of a particular state would apply. That is called *preventive law.*

Federal Courts

In addition to the general grounds discussed previously with respect to jurisdiction, there are two specific grounds for federal jurisdiction: (1) federal question and (2) diversity of citizenship *plus* amount in controversy.

Federal question jurisdiction derives directly from Article 3 of the Constitution. *Federal questions* are *questions that pertain to the federal Constitution, statutes of the United States, and treaties of the United States.* Also included today are all regulations of federal administrative agencies. For example, if a person were denied a job because of race, that would raise a federal question, since such discrimination would raise questions of violations of the Constitution, federal statutes, and federal regulations as well. If a publishing company brought an action asserting that its copyright had been infringed by another publishing company, it would raise a federal question, since copyright is both a constitutional and a statutory question. States do not have the right to issue copyrights.

Federal question jurisdiction preempts the need for diversity of citizenship and vice versa. *Diversity of citizenship* exists *when the plaintiff is a citizen of one state and the defendant is a citizen of another.* It also exists *when one party is a foreign country and the other is a citizen of a state.* The primary reason for this basis for jurisdiction is that if a citizen of state X had to file suit in state Y in order to obtain jurisdiction over that person, it is possible that the court of state Y might favor its citizen over the citizen of state X. In that case, the plaintiff could file suit in federal court.

When federal jurisdiction is based on diversity of citizenship, there is a further requirement for the majority of the approximately 75,000 cases that are filed in federal courts annually: a *minimum amount* in question. Title 28, Section 1332(a), of the United States Code now requires that the amount in question must exceed $50,000 in diversity cases. Cases in which the federal courts have exclusive jurisdiction do not have a minimum amount requirement. The purpose behind the amount is to prevent federal courts from dealing with trifles. This rule complies with an ancient Latin legal maxim: *de minimus non curat lex* ("the law takes no account of trifles").

Most federal cases are highly complex, and the precise amount is a matter that sometimes is not known until after the lawsuit is filed. Accordingly, the courts look to the amount that the plaintiff, in good faith, has determined to be the amount in dispute. This is called the *plaintiff viewpoint rule.*

Figure 2.3 depicts the two grounds for federal jurisdiction.

Specialized Courts

Congress has, from time to time, created courts of limited jurisdiction. At present, these courts include the claims court, court of military appeals, court of international trade, and the tax court.

FIGURE 2.3 The Two Grounds for Federal Jurisdiction

**FOR FEDERAL JURISDICTION
THE CASE MUST INVOLVE**

EITHER
Federal Question

The controlling law involves a federal statute, rule, or regulation; an issue of U.S. Constitutional law; or a treaty.

The case involves a consul or ambassador as a party.

The case involves maritime or admiralty law.

The United States is a party to the action.

The case is between two or more states.

OR
Diversity of Citizenship

At least one party on each side of the controversy is a citizen of a different state than the other parties.

+

**A Minimum Amount in Controversy
(Excluding Costs and Interest)**

The minimum amount for which the plaintiff must sue is currently $50,000.

Congress has created *federal district courts* in every state. Each state has at least one; some states have many. Rhode Island, for example, has one district, and Texas has four. The courts contained in each district constitute the general trial courts of the federal system.

All of the district courts are grouped into circuits. Currently there are thirteen circuits. Each circuit has a court of appeals in which appeals from the trial courts are heard. For the most part, the decisions of these *circuit courts of appeals* are final. In a very few cases, further appeal may be made to the Supreme Court.

The thirteen federal judicial circuits and their seats are First: Boston, MA; Second: New York, NY; Third: Philadelphia, PA; Fourth: Richmond, VA; Fifth: New Orleans, LA; Sixth: Cincinnati, OH; Eighth: St. Louis, MO; Ninth: San Francisco, CA; Tenth: Denver, CO; Eleventh: Atlanta, GA; Twelfth: District of Columbia, Washington, D.C.; Thirteenth: Federal Circuit, Washington, D.C.

The *Supreme Court* sits at the apex of the American judicial system. *It is the only court created by the Constitution*. It has nine judges, called justices. They are nominated by the president and confirmed by the Senate, and they serve for life, as do all federal judges except those appointed to serve in the specialized courts.

As mentioned previously, the Supreme Court must hear certain cases. These cases arise under the following conditions:

1. whenever the highest state court declares a federal law invalid

2. whenever the highest state court declares a state law valid in situations in which it was challenged by application of a federal law

3. whenever a federal court declares a federal statute unconstitutional and the government was a party to the suit

4. whenever a federal appellate court declares a state statute invalid on the grounds that it violates federal law

5. whenever a federal three-judge court has ruled in a civil case involving an equitable remedy

Certiorari A writ used by the court in order to review a case.

Certiorari, which means *"to be more fully informed,"* is used whenever the Supreme Court desires to hear a particular case even though there is no right of appeal. It is through this device that most cases are heard in the Court. No hard and fast rules exist in connection with this route other than that a minimum of four justices must agree to hear the case. Nevertheless, there are certain situations in which this route is followed:

1. whenever two or more circuit courts of appeals have conflicting rules with respect to the same question

2. whenever the highest state court has decided a question in such a manner that it is in conflict with prior decisions of the United States Supreme Court

3. whenever the highest state court has decided a question that has not yet been determined by the Supreme Court

4. whenever a circuit court of appeals has decided a state law question that is in conflict with established state law

5. whenever a circuit court of appeals has decided a federal question that has not yet been decided by the Supreme Court

State Courts

All states have *inferior trial courts*. These include justice courts (courts presided over by justices of the peace, most of whom are not lawyers), municipal courts, juvenile courts, domestic relations courts, traffic courts, small claims courts, and probate courts. For the most part, they are not *courts of record*— that is, there is no record of the trial. In cases of appeals from their decisions, there is a *trial de novo,* "a new trial," in a court of general jurisdiction.

The more significant cases involving matters of state law originate in *courts of general jurisdiction* (courts having the judicial power to hear all matters with respect to state law). In some jurisdictions, there are two courts on the same level. One court is charged with resolving all **questions of law** and the other with resolving all matters of **equity.** An example of a question of law is a suit seeking money damages. Most business law cases fall into that category. Equity questions involve the issuing of an injunction. Rarely, if ever, do business law cases involve the issuing of an injunction.

Questions of law A term used in contrast to fact; questions to be decided by the court.

Equity The spirit and habit of fairness, justness, and right dealing that should regulate human intercourse.

Each state has at least one *court of appeals*. It is usually called the supreme court, but not always. In New York State, for example, the "supreme court" is a court of general jurisdiction, whereas the Court of Appeals is the highest court in the state. Sometimes there are also intermediate courts of appeals, as in the federal system.

Figure 2.4 describes how a typical state system and the federal system make up the American judicial system.

FIGURE 2.4 The American Judicial System

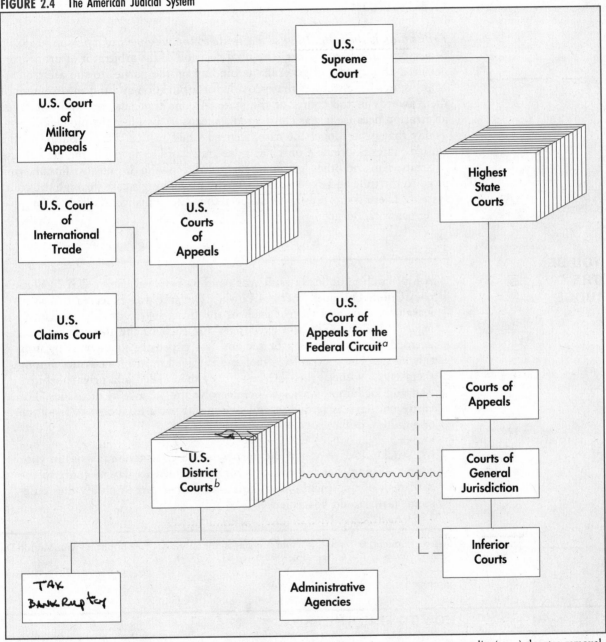

Note: Solid line (———) denotes direct appeal; dotted line (----) denotes appeal in some cases; wavy line( ) denotes removal jurisdiction.
[a] Takes appeals from some specialized courts.
[b] Bankruptcy courts exist as units of the district courts.
[c] In some cases, there is direct Supreme Court review.

Note: See pg. 70, Fig. 4.4 for the stages of a criminal procedure and pg. 90, Fig. 15.10, for the stages of a civil procedure.

ARBITRATION

Arbitration is *the submitting of a dispute to the judgment of a person or group of persons called arbitrators.* The final decision of the arbitrator or arbitrators is called an *award* and generally is binding on the parties to the arbitration. Many states have statutes that provide for arbitration and the enforcement of their awards in the courts of the state. At one time, the law did not favor arbitration because it was considered a means of avoiding the judicial system. Today that is no longer the case. Retired Chief Justice Warren Burger of the United States Supreme Court has gone on record as favoring the greater use of arbitration and other legitimate means of resolving disputes without having to go to the time and expense connected with moving a case through the court system. There is no reason to suspect that Chief Justice William Rehnquist disagrees with Burger.

YOU BE THE JUDGE

A multimillion dollar lawsuit was pending between Pacific Gas & Electric, Union Oil, and Thermal Power. The suit was expected to last at least one year, and to cost each of the firms several million dollars in legal fees alone. The top executives for each of the three companies decided that there was a better and less expensive manner of fighting this battle. These executives met and resolved most of the issues among themselves, without their lawyers. They then called in a private arbitration and mediation service to help resolve the balance of the issues. The entire matter was settled within one month, at a total cost of less than one million dollars.

If a stockholder of one of the parties filed a class action lawsuit in your court, alleging that the corporation was denied its day in court to the detriment of the stockholders, and asking the court to nullify the settlement, how would you rule?

Source: "Coming to Terms—Without Bringing in the Lawyers," Jane Birnbaum with Morton D. Sosland, *Business Week*, April 13, 1992, page 63.

HOW TO FIND THE LAW

We have already referred to some legal cases in this and the previous chapter. Other cases will be cited in succeeding chapters. If you should want to go to the library and read any one of these cases in its entirety, you will have to know how to find the law.

Federal Court Cases   If you were looking for the case *Mitsubishi Motors Corporation* v. *Soler Chrysler-Plymouth, Inc.*, 473 U.S. 614, 87 L.Ed.2d 444, 105 S.Ct. 3346 (1985), for example, you would find it in any one of three sources. First, the United States Government Printing Office publishes the official *United States Reports*. The case would be found on page 614 of volume 473. Alternatively, you could find the case on page 444 of the 87th volume of *Lawyers Edition, Second* published by the Lawyers Cooperative Publishing Company. Finally, you could find the case in the 105th volume of the *Supreme Court Reporter*, published by West Publishing Company, at page 3346.

All cases decided by the circuit courts of appeals are found in the *Federal Reporter*. If you were looking for the case of *United States* v. *Douglas Aircraft Company*, you would find it at 169 F.2d 755 (9th Cir. 1948). You would go to volume 169 of the *Federal Reporter, Second Series*, and turn to page 755. The (9th Cir. 1948) means that the case was decided by the Ninth Circuit Court of Appeals, which sits in San Francisco and hears cases from district courts in Washington, Montana, Oregon, Idaho, Nevada, Arizona, Alaska, Hawaii, and California. The case was decided in 1948.

U.S. district court cases are found in the *Federal Supplement Series*. If you were looking for the case of *Hoeflich* v. *William S. Merrell Co.*, you would find it at 288 F. Supp. 659 (E.D. Pa. 1968). Following our established procedure, look for volume 288 of the *Federal Supplement*. The case would be found on page 659. The (E.D. Pa. 1968) means that the case was decided in the United States District Court for the Eastern District of Pennsylvania in 1968.

State Court Cases   The *National Reporter System* contains seven regional reporters for state cases plus two separate state reporters. They are as follows:

1. *Atlantic Reporter*—Connecticut, Delaware, Maine, Maryland, New Hampshire, New Jersey, Pennsylvania, Rhode Island, Vermont, and the District of Columbia Municipal Court of Appeals

2. *Northeastern Reporter*—Illinois, Indiana, Massachusetts, New York, and Ohio

3. *Northwestern Reporter*—Iowa, Michigan, Minnesota, Nebraska, North Dakota, South Dakota, and Wisconsin

4. *Pacific Reporter*—Alaska, Arizona, California, Colorado, Hawaii, Idaho, Kansas, Montana, Nevada, New Mexico, Oklahoma, Oregon, Utah, Washington, and Wyoming

5. *Southeastern Reporter*—Georgia, North Carolina, South Carolina, Virginia, and West Virginia

6. *Southwestern Reporter*—Arkansas, Kentucky, Missouri, Tennessee, and Texas

7. *Southern Reporter*—Alabama, Florida, Louisiana, and Mississippi

8. *New York Supplement*
9. *California Reporter*

SUMMARY

The federal Constitution is unique because it created the doctrine of separation of powers. As a result, our government is divided into three distinct branches: legislative, executive, and judicial.

The judicial power is not unlimited. For example, courts may not issue advisory opinions or decide moot cases or political questions. In all cases, the plaintiff must have standing to sue.

The doctrine of judicial review was created by Chief Justice John Marshall in the landmark case of *Marbury* v. *Madison*. The doctrine represents an expansion of judicial power, since it allows the Supreme Court to determine whether a statute passed by Congress is in compliance with the Constitution or whether the executive branch has acted in accordance with the Constitution.

Our court system is based on the concept of jurisdiction. Jurisdiction means the power to speak the law. It is divided into subject matter jurisdiction or in personam jurisdiction and can be either concurrent or exclusive. A federal court's jurisdiction is based on either federal question or diversity of citizenship jurisdiction. In all diversity cases, the jurisdictional amount of $50,000 must be met. Federal courts are specialized, district, appellate, or supreme. Venue, on the other hand, is a question of whether the case is filed in the proper court.

All cases reported in the state court systems may be found by referring to the *National Reporter System.* All cases reported in the federal court system may be found by referring to the *Federal, Federal Supplement,* or *United States Reports.*

DISCUSSION QUESTIONS

1. Why is our federal Constitution considered unique?
2. What is the significance of the case of *Marbury* v. *Madison?*
3. Where is the constitutional protection of habeus corpus found? What does the term mean?
4. What is meant by the term *jurisdiction?*
5. What is a federal question?
6. Why do some state courts have only one court of general jurisdiction, whereas others have two?
7. What is meant by this citation: 234 S.W. 358 (1946)?
8. In *Baker* v. *Carr* the issue of state legislative apportionment was determined to be a judicial question and not a political question. What arguments can you make that it really was a political question and therefore nonjusticiable? Why do you think the Supreme Court acted as it did?
9. The highest court in a state determines that a state law violates the federal Constitution. Can that decision be reviewed by the United States Supreme Court, or is the decision of the state court final?
10. Go to the nearest law library and determine who was counsel for the plaintiff in *Flast* v. *Cohen.*

CASE PROBLEMS

1. The text indicates that a moot point is one that is undecided. If that is so, would a case be barred in which the parties carefully stipulated all the facts: a so-called test case? (*Chicago & Grand Trunk Ry.* v. *Wellman*, 143 U.S. 339 [1892].)

2. Does a taxpayer have standing to sue the federal government challenging the creation of a Christmas postage stamp for the reason that it violates the establishment of religion clause of the First Amendment? (*P.O.A.U.* v. *Watson*, 407 F.2d 1264 [D.C. Cir. 1968].)

3. Was the conducting of the Vietnam war by presidential authority, without a congressional declaration of war in accordance with Art. I, Sec. 8. Cl. 11 of the Constitution, a "political question"? (*Mora* v. *McNamara*, 389 U.S. 934 [1967].)

4. Does segregation of children in public schools on the basis of race, even though the physical facilities and other "tangible" factors may be equal, deprive the children of the minority group of equal educational opportunities? Discuss with respect to the Fourteenth Amendment. (*Brown* v. *Board of Education*, 347 U.S. 483 [1954].)

5. The plaintiff sued the defendant in a New York court. The defendant was served in person at his residence in the state of Connecticut. Does the New York court have jurisdiction to grant the plaintiff appropriate relief? (*Garfein* v. *McInnis*, 248 N.Y. 261, 162 N.E. 73 [1928].)

6. Producers of chemicals used for pesticides sued the U.S. Administrator of the Environmental Protection Agency challenging Section 3(c)(1)(D) of the Federal Insecticide, Fungicide, and Rodenticide Act (FIFRA). That section allowed parties to submit disputes to binding arbitration. The producers alleged that the law violated Article III of the U.S. Constitution by allocating to arbitrators the function of the courts. The District Court held that the Congress acted unconstitutionally by assigning judicial powers to arbitrators. On appeal, did the Supreme Court affirm or reverse? Why? (*Thomas* v. *Union Carbide*, 473 U.S. 568, 87 L.Ed.2d 409, 105 S.Ct. 3325 [1985].)

7. Federal courts apply the so-called American Rule that a party who prevails in litigation ordinarily is not entitled to collect attorneys' fees from the losing party. This court-adopted rule has an exception contained in the Civil Rights Attorneys' Fees Awards Act, 42 U.S.C. 1988. Do you think that, under the statute, defendants who prevail should also be awarded attorneys' fees? (*Christiansburg Garment Co.* v. *EEOC*, 434 U.S. 412 [1978].)

8. X agrees to arbitrate any disputes he might have with Y. However, X makes the same type of agreement with A, B, and C as well. If A, B, C, and Y all have disputes with X that raise common issues of fact and law, may a federal court consolidate all four arbitration proceedings so that they will be heard at one time and place? (*Seguro de Servidio* v. *McAuto*, 878 F.2d 5 [1st Cir. Puerto Rico 1989].)

CHAPTER 3

Torts

OUTLINE

OBJECTIVES OF TORT LAW

Tort law is concerned with a body of "private" wrongs, whereas *criminal law,* which we shall study in the next chapter, is concerned with "public" wrongs. The laws have evolved over hundreds of years to support the protection of an individual's rights with respect to property and person. Tort law, therefore, reflects civilized society. Torts provide a mechanism for persons who have been wronged to seek remedies in our court system. In general, the remedy sought is money damages. The way that people avoid committing these wrongs is to adhere to various "duties." For example, society recognizes a duty to refrain from physically injuring other persons or their property. Society also recognizes a duty to refrain from humiliating others.

Because tort law recognizes certain duties, it raises the question of exactly which rights society should protect through the imposition of duties. For example, should society recognize as a wrong only behavior that was intended to be a wrong? Or should society recognize as a wrong not only intended wrong but also an unintended wrong that was due to someone's negligence? Should society also recognize as a wrong unintended behavior in which the person was not negligent? These are the questions that we shall discuss in this chapter.

Society has developed the body of tort law to resolve social and economic policy questions. The law has to take into consideration the social usefulness of the conduct of persons, the interests asserted by the plaintiff, the justification (if any) for the defendant's conduct, the economic burden that would be placed upon the defendant if liability were imposed, the question of spreading the cost of liability from one to many persons, and the unique problem of respecting past decisions and yet maintaining flexibility within the legal system by providing solutions to modern problems.

THEORIES OF TORT LIABILITY

This chapter discusses intentional torts, negligence, and strict liability. Table 3.1 depicts the three theories of tort liability. *Intentional torts* are those wrongs in which the persons charged must have acted in such a manner that they either wanted to harm someone or knew that what they did would result in harm. Suppose that someone said something offensive to you, and you said, "If you don't stop that, I'll punch you in the nose." If that person did not stop it, and you punched him in the nose, the law states that you were wrong. You committed the tort of *battery* on the other person. (Provocation is not an issue here, since the law does not recognize the privilege of striking someone unless you are struck first.)

The law of *negligence* is based on a concept of fault in which the areas of morals and law have been intermingled. The question raised here is how

TABLE 3.1   The Three Theories of Tort Liability

TORT LIABILITY		
INTENTIONAL TORTS	**NEGLIGENCE**	**STRICT LIABILITY IN TORT**
The accused knows or should know the conduct would be likely to cause injury.	The conduct of the accused is compared to the "reasonable and prudent person."	The accused is involved in conduct that is deemed extremely hazardous.
Involves a simple duty to avoid the act or conduct.	Involves a reasonable duty to avoid the act or conduct.	Involves a strict duty to avoid the act or conduct.
There must be a showing of fault.	There must be a showing of fault.	There is no need to show "fault."
The harm must be foreseeable.	The harm must be foreseeable.	The harm must be foreseeable.

society apportions the costs of accidents. Society must often make a moral statement when an injury occurs. Suppose a child darts out from behind a parked car an instant before the driver's car reaches that point; the driver immediately brakes in an effort to avoid hitting the child but is unable to stop in time to avoid the accident. In all likelihood, this accident would be considered unavoidable—it occurred without any negligence on the part of the driver. The child, even though injured, would be denied any compensation from the driver for the accident.

On the other hand, if a child walking across the street in a designated crosswalk was hit by an automobile because the driver was drunk or the car's brakes were faulty, society says that the driver breached a duty to drive the car in a reasonable manner. Accordingly, the driver will have to pay for damages suffered by the child. Although the child is just as injured in the first example as in the second example, society denies compensation in the first case but not in the second.

Strict liability finds persons liable even if their conduct was unintentional or nonnegligent; that is, even if it wasn't their fault, they're liable. Some activities are classified as either ultrahazardous or abnormally dangerous, and if injury results from either of those situations, the actor will be held liable. For example, suppose you have a pet rattlesnake in a sealed glass cage and you place the cage in your back yard with signs on the fence that say: Danger—Poisonous Snake, Beware. If the snake somehow gets out and bites someone, you will be held liable. The law would prevent you from trying to prove how careful you were. It would say that your rattlesnake caused injury, and you will simply have to pay.

INTENTIONAL TORTS

Assault

Assault is the threat or reasonable apprehension that one person will strike another. For example, verbal threats, no matter how belligerent, are not an assault. The verbal threat must be accompanied by some overt act. The threats can be used to show intent, but there must be some act short of actually striking the other person. Pointing an unloaded pistol at a person is an assault if the other person has no way of knowing whether the pistol is loaded or not.

Battery

Privilege A particular or peculiar benefit or advantage beyond the common advantages of other citizens; a right, power, franchise, or immunity held by a person beyond the course of the law.

Some legal authorities have defined *battery* as a consummated assault. It is the touching or striking of another without that person's permission. The law places a high value on the dignity of the human body and will not tolerate a contact that is without *consent* or **privilege.** For example, removing a chair from a person who briefly stood up and began to sit down again is a battery when the person hits the floor. The key element in that case is that the actor intended the natural consequence of removing the chair: falling to the ground. As far as the law is concerned, it is the same as pushing the person to the ground. On the other hand, if the removal of the chair had been unintended, there could not have been a battery. The following case is an example of the extent to which the law will go to protect its citizens from being charged with intentional acts.

People v. Tate
68 Ill. App.3d 881, 386 N.E.2d 584 (1979)

FACTS Tate was carrying two one-foot-long sticks connected by a link chain, a device commonly called "karate sticks." Under the authority of Ill. Criminal Code Section 24-1(a)(1), the police determined that the "karate sticks" were bludgeons and arrested Tate. Tate contended that he was enrolled in the Golden Dome Karate School and that the sticks were athletic equipment rather than weapons.

ISSUE Are karate sticks bludgeons?

HOLDING No.

REASONING A bludgeon is a "short stout stick or club, with one end loaded or thicker and heavier than the other, used as a weapon." There is nothing in the record to indicate that one end of the karate sticks was loaded or thicker and heavier than the other end. The court, therefore, concluded that karate sticks do not fall within the definition of a bludgeon.

Note: Although this is a criminal case rather than a tort case, it points out that our courts are very careful when evaluating any law that includes "intent" as an element. "Intent" means that a reasonable person would conclude from the objective facts that the actor did that with which he is charged.

Defamation

Slander Any oral statement that tends to expose a person to public ridicule or to injure a person's reputation.

Libel Any *written* or printed statement that tends to expose a person to public ridicule or to injure a person's reputation.

There are two forms of defamation: *slander* and *libel*. The reason for the two forms, each of which has different elements, is that each was developed in a different English court. Slander, which is spoken defamation, was developed in the English church courts (the ecclesiastical courts that had jurisdiction over spiritual matters). Libel (written defamation) was developed in the Star Chamber (an English common law court that had jurisdiction over cases in which the ordinary course of justice was so obstructed by one party that no inferior court could have its process obeyed). The tort of defamation is an exception to the First Amendment's guarantee of free speech. Accordingly, United States courts have changed some of the common law rules.

Slander is spoken communication that causes a person to suffer a loss of reputation. The common law rule distinguished between *slander per se* and *slander per quod*. Slander per se occurs when a person says that another person is seriously immoral, seriously criminal, has a social disease, or is unfit as a business or professional person. In those cases, there is no need to prove actual damages. Slander per quod is any other type of oral defamatory statement.

Libel is written communication that causes a person to suffer a loss of reputation. There are also two kinds of libel. *Libel per se* is libelous without having to resort to the context in which the remark appeared. For example, if a newspaper printed a story that referred to a person as a "known assassin for hire," there is no need to show the context of the statement. On the other hand, *libel per quod* requires proof of the context. For example, suppose a television talk show host says that a particular woman just gave birth to a child. In order to prove that it was libel, the woman would have to prove that she was not married and that she had not made public knowledge of her cohabiting, but unmarried, private life. The following case describes how American courts have tailored the English doctrine to our own situation with respect to public officials.

New York Times Company v. Sullivan
376 U.S. 255 (1964)

FACTS Sullivan was a city commissioner in Montgomery, Alabama. He alleged that he had been libeled by the *New York Times* when it carried a full-page advertisement in which certain charges were made against the city with respect to the treatment of Dr. Martin Luther King, Jr.

ISSUE "To determine the extent to which the constitutional protections for speech and press limit a state's power to award damages in a libel action brought by a public official against critics of his official conduct."

HOLDING This was not libel because there was no showing of *malice*.

REASONING " . . . Debate on public issues should be uninhibited, robust, and wide-open, and . . . it may well include vehement, caustic, and sometimes unpleasantly sharp attacks on government and public officials. . . . The constitutional guarantees require, we think, a federal rule that prohibits a public official from recovering damages for a defamatory falsehood relating to his official conduct unless he proves that the statement was made with 'actual malice'—that is, with knowledge that it was false or with reckless disregard of whether it was false or not. . . . We hold that the Constitution delimits a state's power to award damages for libel in actions brought by public officials against critics of their official conduct."

The *New York Times* case is a landmark in American jurisprudence. Since 1964, the Supreme Court, in a number of cases, has extended the holding to "public figures" as well as public officials. A public figure is a person who has a degree of prominence in society. Thus, a person who chooses to become active in society and who not only receives but actually solicits attention in the media would be classified a public figure. Furthermore, the court has extended the definition of a public official to include candidates for public office as well as incumbents.

False Imprisonment

False imprisonment is the detention of one person by another against the former's will and without just cause. This tort protects a person from the loss of liberty and freedom of movement. For example, if after the end of a college class your professor locked the door and said that no one could leave the room, that action would be false imprisonment. Sometimes standing in a doorway and refusing to let a person pass is also false imprisonment. On the other hand, being stopped by a store detective when there is just cause to consider the person a shoplifter is not false imprisonment.

Mental Distress

A growing body of law concerns situations that fall far short of assault but, for public policy reasons, have been recognized as a tort by the courts. The law will protect an individual from suffering *serious indignity* that *causes emotional distress*. This right, however, is balanced against the interest of the state in not opening the courts to frivolous and trivial claims. In this context, liability has been found where an airline unreasonably insulted a passenger on an aircraft. Also, liability was found where a bill collector unreasonably humiliated a debtor. In that regard, you should know that federal law now specifically controls the activities of bill collectors, and the court-made rules concerning liability have been modified by the federal statute. Liability has also been found where a mortician displayed a dead body without its having been embalmed. In that case, damages were recovered by near relatives.

Invasion of Privacy

Actionable Furnishing legal grounds for an action.

Under common law, there was no tort of invasion of privacy. Recently, however, our courts have begun to recognize that unwarranted invasions of privacy are **actionable**. *Privacy* refers to an individual's right to be left alone. A person's privacy is invaded if that person is subjected to unwarranted intrusions into his or her right to be left alone. These unwarranted intrusions have led to lawsuits and to the awarding of damages for the person whose privacy was invaded. Liability has been found for the public disclosure of private matters, such as wiretapping a private citizen's telephone without permission. The use of a famous person's name or photograph without permission is an invasion of privacy when the name or the photograph is used to promote a commercial product.

Trespass

In common law, trespass was the most common tort. Today, the general tort of "trespass" has evolved into some of the specific torts we have already discussed, but trespass remains as the tort used to define *actions that protect both real and personal property interests, normally against infringements.* A person who ventures onto the land of another without permission is a trespasser. The only question is one of damages. Even if the person trespassed through mistake and did no harm, there will be "nominal" damages of, say, one dollar. If, on the other hand, the person had trespassed before and had been warned, more than nominal damages would be assessed in order to compensate the owner for the unwarranted invasion of land. Of course, the trespasser will be liable for any damages done.

Conversion

Conversion occurs when a person intentionally exercises exclusive control over the personal property of another without permission. In such a case, the converter is liable for damages. If a person actually obtains possession of the property lawfully but is then told by the owner to return it and does not do so, that person is still a converter. Once damages are paid, there is no need for the converter to return the property. If return is sought, the proper action is one for **replevin.**

Replevin   A personal action brought to recover possession of goods unlawfully taken.

Fraud

Fraud is an extremely complex tort. It concerns the misrepresentation of a material fact made with the intention to deceive. If an innocent person reasonably relies on the misrepresentation and is damaged as a result, the injured person may successfully sue for fraud. Accordingly, there are five elements of fraud:

1. A material fact (not an opinion) was involved.
2. The fact was misrepresented (a falsehood).
3. The falsehood was made with the intent to deceive *(scienter)*.
4. The falsehood was one on which another person justifiably relied (reliance).
5. That person was injured as a result (damage).

For example, whenever a jeweler sells a rhinestone as a diamond with the knowledge that it is a rhinestone, the action is fraud. Whenever a bank customer obtains a loan on the basis of a false financial statement, it is fraud. Whenever a landowner sells "one hundred" acres of land with the knowledge that it is only fifty acres, it is fraud. Whenever a corporation solicits persons to buy stock for the purpose of building a new plant when in reality the corporation wanted the money to pay off existing liabilities, it is fraud. The list is endless. Figure 3.1 outlines the intentional torts discussed in this chapter.

Defenses to Intentional Torts

Implied consent A concurrence of wills manifested by signs, actions, or facts, or by inaction or silence, which raises a presumption that agreement has been given.

Consent   Even though a tort has been committed, the law may not compensate the injured party if, in fact, that person consented to the tort. Most cases involve issues of **implied consent**. The law will not infer consent unless it is reasonable under the circumstances. For example, football players obviously batter each other throughout the course of a game. Therefore, even though the tort of battery may have been committed, it is not actionable, because the law views each player as having consented to the touching. However, if a player intentionally exceeds the implied consent, he may be liable for the tort.

Privilege   Permission is given voluntarily, whether it is expressed or implied. The law also recognizes a nonvoluntary defense beyond permission. Because the law seeks to protect certain social interests more than others, it developed the concept of privilege. Privilege is recognized in the following situations:

1. If someone moves to strike you, you have the ancient privilege of self-defense.

 FIGURE 3.1   Intentional Torts

Specific Tort	Definition
Assault	The *threat* or reasonable apprehension that one person will strike another
Battery	A consummated assault
Defamation	Slander (spoken) Libel (written)
False Imprisonment	The detention of one person by another against his or her will and without just cause
Mental Distress	The suffering of a serious indignity
Invasion of Privacy	Unwarranted intrusions on the privacy of another
Trespass	Actions to protect real and personal property from harm or infringement
Conversion	Occurs when a person intentionally exercises exclusive control over the personal property of another without permission
Fraud	The misrepresentation of a material fact made with the intention to deceive

2. Retail businesspersons have a privilege to detain persons who they reasonably believe have committed theft.

3. Persons whose property is stolen have the privilege of going onto another person's property in order to retrieve it.

4. Judges and legislators have the privilege of saying things that might be slander under other circumstances in order to stimulate debate and encourage independence of thought and action.

Necessity   Whenever a person commits what would otherwise be a land trespass for self-protection, the law recognizes that necessity would disallow the landowner nominal damages. For example, if you were in a boat on a lake and a storm suddenly developed, you could enter a private cove, tie up to a private dock, and find shelter on the land in order to protect yourself. There would be no trespass.

Truth   Truth is the best defense with respect to the tort of defamation. If an individual accuses a businessperson of being a crook and is sued for defamation, the individual will win if it can be proved that the businessperson is a "fence" for stolen property. Figure 3.2 depicts the defenses to intentional torts.

FIGURE 3.2   Defenses to Intentional Torts

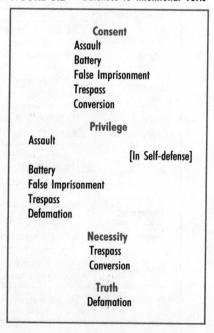

Consent
Assault
Battery
False Imprisonment
Trespass
Conversion

Privilege
Assault
[In Self-defense]
Battery
False Imprisonment
Trespass
Defamation

Necessity
Trespass
Conversion

Truth
Defamation

NEGLIGENCE

Negligence exists when four conditions are met. First, the defendant must have owed the plaintiff a duty. Second, the defendant must have breached the duty. Third, the breach of that duty must be the actual as well as the "legal" cause of the plaintiff's injury. Fourth, that injury must be one that the law recognizes and for which money damages may be recovered.

Duty

We live in a legal system in which we all have a duty to protect other persons from harm. The question the courts must examine is what degree of duty exists under what specific circumstances.

The *reasonable-and-prudent-person* rule has been established in negligence law in order to determine the "degree" of duty.

In the discussion on intentional torts, we emphasized that the key element in finding liability is determining that the defendant intended harm. For example, if a defendant points a gun at the plaintiff and pulls the trigger, we can determine that the defendant intended some sort of harm to the plaintiff. We infer intent from overt behavior. Negligence stands in sharp contrast to intentional torts. With respect to intentional torts, we all have a simple duty to avoid liability-causing behavior. However, with respect to negligence, we all have a "reasonable" duty to avoid this type of behavior. This standard is more difficult to define, explain, and apply than is the standard of simple duty. Generally, however, the law states that *reasonable duty is a standard of ordinary skill and care, based on the facts of each individual case.*

If, while you were quietly fishing on the shore of a lake, you saw another fisherman one hundred feet away fall out of his boat and begin to drown, does the common law place on you a duty to help him? The answer is no, because you did not create the hazard in the first place. On the other hand, suppose you owned a boat yard on the lake and the fisherman rented his boat from you. If the boat sprung a leak because it was defective when rented, thereby causing the fisherman to drown, you would have breached your duty to rent safe boats. You created the harm in the second situation but not in the first.

Both intentional torts and negligence are based on the concept of *fault.* Strict liability has nothing to do with fault. All theories of liability, however, have to do with **foreseeability.**

Foreseeability The knowledge or notice that a result is likely to occur if a certain act occurs.

Foreseeability deals with the likelihood that something will happen in the future. It is not very difficult to see that if you point a loaded gun at someone and pull the trigger, you will cause that person harm. But suppose you get in your car and drive down a dark street, within the speed limit and with your lights on. A child darts out from behind a parked car, and you hit the child. Were you negligent, or was it merely an unavoidable accident? This is a more difficult question. Foreseeability is determined by what a "reasonable and prudent person" would expect. Thus, the foreseeability of a child darting into the street in front of your car would depend on such factors as the degree of darkness, the lateness of the hour, how densely populated the area was (i.e., rural or urban, residential or business), other children observed in the area, signs regarding children at play, and so forth. Until these factors are considered, no determination of the foreseeability of the child's action, and thus of your negligence—or lack thereof—can be made.

In order to test for a duty in any particular situation, the law has constructed a person against whom the conduct of the defendant will be compared. This purely hypothetical person is known as the *reasonable and prudent person*—not perfect, merely reasonable. Three areas help to define the reasonable and prudent person: knowledge, investigation, and judgment.

Knowledge As the amount of knowledge existing in the world increases, so does the amount of knowledge that the reasonable and prudent person is expected to possess. In this sense, therefore, the law presumes that we have complete knowledge of the law. If we did not have this rule, it would be silly for us to have any legal rules at all, for if we had no knowledge of the law how could we be expected to obey it?

Investigation Before you drive a car, for example, the law presumes that you will have ascertained that the brakes are working properly. If you are a drug manufacturer, the law presumes that you will have discovered that your drug does not cause any harmful side effects; if it does, you will have violated the standard of care of a reasonable and prudent person.

Judgment You have heard some people say that one person has "good" judgment or another has "bad" judgment. The law measures both persons against the same standard. In a tort case, the defendant had better have acted reasonably or else he will be found to have breached the duty of reasonable care. We have no hard and fast rules here. The outcome always depends on the facts of each case. A missing fact, once supplied, can change the outcome. Therefore, before we begin any activity, the law expects us to ask ourselves such questions as What is the likelihood that this particular activity will harm someone else? If harm might come, what is the likelihood of the extent of the harm? What must I give up in order to avoid the risk to others?

Let's say that you just got a new rifle and want to test it, and adjust the sights (or scope) for maximum accuracy for the deer season. You find an isolated field in the country and set up a target at the base of a bald hill 300 yards away. No one else is present. After firing the first shot, however, you begin to attract a crowd. Assume that with each shot the crowd gets larger. At what point do you decide to stop shooting in order to avoid injury to an innocent person? The decision to stop involves the exercise of reason. The exercise of reason is judgment.

Statutory Standard In some cases, the law solves the problem of limits, such as we have just raised, by providing a standard contained in a statute. For example, most laws state that when it begins to get dark, all drivers are required to turn on their car lights. If, while traveling down a road at night without your lights on, you hit and injure a pedestrian, the law will conclude that you breached a standard of reasonableness, no matter what your excuse. Most of these statutes provide a criminal penalty, but that penalty is truly irrelevant in a civil proceeding such as a tort case. The majority rule is that breaching the statutory standard is **negligence per se.** In a minority of states, breaching the statutory standard is only "some evidence of negligence" and is not conclusive.

Negligence per se Inherent negligence; negligence without a need for further proof.

Breach of Duty

In general, the plaintiff has to prove that the defendant caused injury by not adhering to the standard of the *reasonable and prudent person*. In some cases, however, that strict requirement of proof is relaxed. In these cases the law has developed the doctrine of *res ipsa loquitur*, which means "the thing speaks for itself." It applies in situations where circumstantial proof is sufficient. In order to apply solely circumstantial evidence, the injury must be such that it meets the following three tests: (1) it ordinarily does not occur in the absence of someone's negligence, (2) it must be caused by a device within the control of the defendant, and (3) the plaintiff in no way has contributed to his or her own injury. For example, if a patient submits to an operation to remove infected tonsils and leaves the operating room with a surgical instrument imbedded in her throat, there is no need to require direct testimony on the point. It speaks for itself. The physician was negligent.

Causation

The heart of the law of negligence is causation. Causation has two components: actual cause and proximate cause.

Actual Cause The law determines whether X is the actual cause of Y by raising the question of whether but for X, Y would not have happened. This is called the *but-for test*. For example, a defendant in an automobile accident case may have failed to signal a turn properly. But if the accident would have happened even if he had signaled properly, the failure to signal is not the actual cause of the accident. It fails the but-for test.

Proximate Cause After actual cause has been established, the scene shifts to what the law calls *policy questions*. Such questions have nothing to do with whether the defendant actually did the act. What is decided here is whether the law should hold the defendant liable or not. At some point the law will say, "Enough." Beyond this point the defendant will not be held liable. In order to solve these policy questions, the law has developed a three-pronged test:

1. What is the likelihood that this particular conduct will injure other persons?
2. If injury should occur, what is the degree of seriousness of the injury?
3. What is the interest that the defendant must sacrifice to avoid the risk of causing the injury?

For example, if it is determined that the defendant was negligent with respect to Tommy, but Bob tried to rescue Tommy and suffered some injury as a result, the defendant will be held liable for Bob's injuries as well as Tommy's because it is foreseeable that people will try to rescue someone in peril. The following case is considered by experts to be the landmark case with respect to proximate cause.

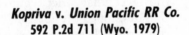

Kopriva v. Union Pacific RR Co.
592 P.2d 711 (Wyo. 1979)

FACTS On 19 December 1974 a bridge was damaged by the defendant, causing the rerouting of all vehicular traffic to a highway that normally took only westbound traffic, thus forcing that highway to take both eastbound and westbound traffic. Kopriva was seriously injured in an automobile accident on that stretch of highway on 21 May 1975. She brought an action against the railroad for negligence. The district court dismissed the action and the plaintiff appealed.

ISSUE Was the railroad's negligence a remote or a proximate cause of Kopriva's injuries?

HOLDING The railroad's negligence was a remote cause.

REASONING Even though the accident would not have occurred but for the railroad's negligence in 1974, that does not mean that it will be held liable in this case. "The proximate cause of an injury is that cause which in natural and continuous sequence, unbroken by an efficient intervening cause, produces the injury, and without which the result would not have occurred." The negligence of a driver of the automobile that directly caused Kopriva's injuries was such an intervening cause.

Harm If the plaintiff is not injured, the defendant will not be held liable in damages. For example, a driver speeding down a road at 180 miles per hour is clearly breaching the duty to drive in a safe and reasonable manner; but if a person is not injured thereby, no one can successfully sue for negligence.

YOU BE THE JUDGE

On 30 October 1985, Sylvia Seegrist shot ten people, fatally wounding three of them, at the Springfield Mall located near Philadelphia. In February, 1990, a jury found the Springfield Mall liable for the damages

Ms. Seegrist had inflicted. The jury apparently accepted the plaintiffs' argument that the presence of a larger and better-trained security staff would have prevented the incident. Moreover, the jury apparently believed the plaintiffs' psychiatrist's testimony that the mall was under a duty to have Ms. Seegrist committed to a mental institution owing to several occurrences of her bizarre behavior (including threats of violence) at the mall during the previous year. The defendant's psychiatrist, in disagreeing with the plaintiffs' expert, determined that the odds of the plaintiffs' dying in a mass murder, such as the one executed by Ms. Seegrist, would be about one in thirty million. He also noted that, before this violence, no mass murder had ever occurred at a shopping center. Thus, according to the defendant's expert, the mall had no duty to attempt to institutionalize Ms. Seegrist and that such an attempt, given the legal constraints involved, would have failed anyway.

If you were the appellate judge, would you uphold the jury's verdict? On what elements of negligence law would you focus in arriving at your decision?

Source: "Was a Mall to Blame for Mass Murder?," Lawrence W. Sherman, *The Wall Street Journal*, April 4, 1990, page A22.

Defenses to Negligence

Assumption of the Risk   The common law developed a doctrine in which the defendant will win if it can be proved that the plaintiff assumed the risk. The law calls this *volenti non fit injuria*. For example, have you ever examined cigarette packages? They bear various warnings, some of which are "Surgeon General's Warning: Smoking by pregnant women may result in fetal injury, premature birth, and low birth weight," or "Quitting smoking now greatly reduces serious risks to your health," or "Cigarette smoke contains carbon monoxide." A longtime cigarette smoker who contracts lung cancer and sues the cigarette manufacturer will most likely lose, because the manufacturer will defend on the basis of the plaintiff's voluntarily assuming the risk.

Contributory Negligence   If a plaintiff had been wearing a black raincoat at night and, while jaywalking across a street, had been hit by a car that was exceeding the speed limit, the defendant could assert that the plaintiff actually contributed to the injury. If the state in which the case was being heard followed the rule of *contributory negligence,* and if contributory negligence were successfully asserted, the plaintiff would lose because contributory negligence would **bar** recovery.

Bar   In the legal sense, to prevent or to stop.

Comparative Negligence   In a growing number of jurisdictions, the doctrine of contributory negligence has been replaced by the doctrine of *comparative negligence*. Here, the fact finder (usually the jury) determines to what degree the plaintiff contributed to his injury. Provided that the plaintiff did not contribute more than 50 percent to his injury, the percentage will be used in making the ultimate award of damages. For example, if he is injured to the extent of $100,000 in damages but contributed 35 percent to his injury, he will be awarded $65,000 instead of losing completely, as he would under the doctrine of contributory negligence. The following case is an application of the rule of comparative negligence in federal court.

Lewis v. Timco, Inc.
716 F.2d 1425 (5th Cir. 1983) 74 ALR Fed. 293

FACTS Lewis was injured while working as a crew member on a drilling barge. He was employed by Timco. His injury occurred when a design defect in a piece of equipment he was using caused it to malfunction resulting in a cable wrapping itself around him.

ISSUE "Whether the doctrine of comparative fault applies in a product liability suit . . . under the maritime jurisdiction of the federal courts."

HOLDING The doctrine of comparative fault applies in a product liability suit under the maritime jurisdiction of the federal courts.

REASONING If the injury did not occur solely through the malfunction of the equipment but occurred as a result of *both* the equipment and the operator (Lewis), the recovery of money damages must be reduced by the degree to which the plaintiff contributed to his injury. "Admiralty courts have long engaged in the exercise of comparing plaintiff's negligence to both fault and nonfault based upon the liability of plaintiffs . . . comparative fault has long been an accepted risk-allocating principle under the maritime law. . . . We are persuaded that general considerations of fairness and efficiency support a comparative fault defense in (this) action."

STRICT LIABILITY AND PRODUCT LIABILITY

Recall that with respect to intentional torts, we all have a duty to avoid such behavior. With respect to negligence, we have a duty to use reasonable care. We now examine two situations in which the law states that our duty is absolute to avoid such behavior, regardless of whether we are at fault or not.

Whenever a person undertakes an extremely hazardous activity and it is foreseeable that injury could result from it, that person will be held "strictly liable" if injury does result, whether or not the person was at fault. *Strict liability* means *without regard to fault*. For example, if you use explosives on your property and by so doing cause windows to be blown out of an adjoining neighbor's house, you will be held liable no matter how careful you were in handling those explosives. The following case created this doctrine of the law.

Rylands v. Fletcher
L.R. 3 H.L. 330 (1868)

FACTS The defendants were mill owners in Lancashire, England. They constructed a reservoir on their land. The water in the reservoir broke through and flowed into an abandoned coal mine shaft. The flooding of the well overflowed into the adjoining property owner's coal mine and caused injury.

ISSUE What should a landowner's liability be for the nonnatural use of the land if it causes damage to another?

HOLDING The landowner should be liable for the abnormal use of land.

REASONING The lower court said, "We think that the true rule of law is that the person who for his own purposes brings on his land and collects and keeps there anything likely to do mischief if it escapes, must keep it at his peril, and if he does not do so is **prima facie** answerable for all the damage which is the natural consequence of its escape." The House of Lords (the highest "court" in England), however, said that the rule applies only to nonnatural use of land versus " . . . any purpose for which it might in the ordinary course of the enjoyment of land be used." Therefore, the rule applies only to abnormal activity.

Prima facie At first sight; on the first appearance; on the face of it.

Through the development of the doctrine of strict liability, our courts have shifted emphasis from ultrahazardous activity to dangerous activity. The *Restatement (Second) of Torts*,[1] Section 402A, has established the rule with respect to products: a vendor will be held liable for a product containing a defect sufficient to make the product unreasonably dangerous to a person who uses the product, provided that the product has not been substantially changed. The following case illustrates this point.

Greenman v. Yuba Products, Inc.
59 Cal.2d 67, 377 P.2d 897 (1963)

FACTS Greenman's wife bought him a Shopsmith power tool for Christmas. While he was using the tool, it struck him and inflicted serious injuries. He sued the manufacturer for negligence.

ISSUE Is proof of negligence required if the facts reflect that a product was defectively manufactured?

HOLDING No. Liability will attach without any showing of negligence.

REASONING "A manufacturer is strictly liable in tort when an article he places on the market, knowing that it is to be used without inspection for defects, proves to have a defect that causes injury to a human being. The purpose of such

[1]*Restatement (Second) of Torts* is a publication of the American Law Institute that states the current version of the common law of torts. An authoritative source, it is used by courts but is not binding on them.

liability is to insure that the costs of injuries resulting from defective products are borne by the manufacturers that put such products on the market rather than by the injured persons who are powerless to protect themselves. . . . To establish the manufacturer's liability it was sufficient that plaintiff proved that he was injured while using the Shopsmith in a way it was intended to be used as a result of a defect in the design and manufacture of which plaintiff was not aware that made the Shopsmith unsafe for its intended use."

SUMMARY

Tort law is designed to protect an individual's rights with respect to person and property. To do this, the law uses the device of "duty." Tort law deals with "private" wrongs, whereas criminal law deals with "public" wrongs.

There are three theories of tort liability: intentional torts, negligence, and strict liability. Intentional torts are those in which a person either intended to harm someone or knew that harm would result from the action. Intentional torts to persons are assault, battery, defamation, false imprisonment, mental distress, and invasion of privacy. Intentional torts to property are trespass and conversion. The defenses of consent, privilege, necessity, and truth apply to both categories.

Negligence is the unintentional causing of harm that could have been prevented if the defendant had acted as a reasonable and prudent person. Strict liability is a separate basis of tort liability because it has nothing to do with either intent or negligence. Our legal system has declared that certain activities are so dangerous that if harm results, the actor will be found liable.

Central to a discussion of all three theories of liability are the concepts of duty and foreseeability. Duty means a certain kind of conduct and therefore is action oriented. Intentional torts establish that one has a duty to avoid them. Negligence establishes that one has a "reasonable" duty to avoid it. Strict liability, on the other hand, establishes a strict duty so that no matter how reasonable the conduct, there is automatic liability if harm occurs. Foreseeability concerns thought rather than action. If the hypothetical reasonable and prudent person would have foreseen harm, there is liability.

DISCUSSION QUESTIONS

1. What are the objectives of tort law?
2. A person decides to go shopping at the XYZ Department Store. While in the Sportswear Department, the store detective suspects the person of stealing a swimsuit. The detective approaches the person and says, "Excuse me, but would you mind if I asked you a few questions?" The person responds with, "Well, I'm really in quite a rush. I'm on my lunch hour and I have to get back to work." Nevertheless, the person submits to the questioning. The questioning lasts for twenty minutes. Has there been a false imprisonment? Would your answer be any different if the detective had said, "Excuse me, I suspect you of stealing swimsuits. Would you mind if I asked you a few questions?"

3. A hotel waiter asks a male guest, "Is this woman your wife or your mistress?" Is the hotel liable for the waiter's insult? Would your answer be any different if the waiter had asked, "Is this woman your wife or your daughter?"

4. Someone knocks on your front door; after you have admitted him, he accuses you of having a "loathsome" disease and of being a rapist. Has he committed a tort against you? Would your answer be any different if he said the same things in the presence of another person?

5. Why is it that intentional torts, negligence, and strict liability all involve the issue of foreseeability?

6. We all have a duty to protect other persons from harm. How does tort law resolve the question of the extent of that duty?

7. A manufacturer of chemical products markets suntan oil without sufficiently investigating the fact that under certain circumstances the vapors of the product become inflammable. Suppose a person uses the product, and as he rubs the oil on his chest, it ignites and burns him. Can he successfully sue the manufacturer for its negligence? Why?

8. It can be scientifically proved that pollution in the smokestacks of a steel plant in Beaumont, Texas, is carried in the clouds over the Gulf of Mexico and deposited on the city of Orlando, Florida. It is also known that the pollutants carry cancer-causing chemicals. On what theory can a person who contracted cancer while living in Orlando successfully sue the steel plant? Discuss your answer with respect to proximate cause.

9. Because you love skydiving, you decide to open a parachute-jumping school. Before students can take the training and make a jump, you require that they sign a voluntary statement that frees you of all liability if they should be harmed. A student makes a jump, but the parachute fails to open. On the basis of those facts, could you be successfully sued for wrongful death? Would it make any difference if it develops that the student simply did not pull the ripcord?

10. A gorilla escapes from a traveling circus, enters a shopping center, and destroys $347,500 worth of property. Will all suits be successful against the circus, or can the circus win if it proves it was not at fault?

CASE PROBLEMS

1. The defendant entered a hotel dining room carrying a walking stick under his arm. He approached the plaintiff and threatened to "whip the hell out of" him if he didn't sign an apology prepared by the defendant. Has an assault occurred? (*Trogden* v. *Terry,* 172 N.C. 540, 90 S.E. 583 [1916].)

2. The defendant threw a punch at Larry, intending to hit Larry when he did so. Unfortunately, he missed Larry with the punch. Instead he struck Daryl. The defendant had no intention of striking Daryl at any time. Has the defendant committed a battery on Daryl? (*Carnes* v. *Thompson,* 48 S.W.2d 903 [Mo. 1932].)

3. The defendant published the following: "These progressive dealers listed here sell Armour's Star Bacon in the new window-top carton." If one of the dealers listed specialized in kosher meat exclusively, has a defamation taken place (kosher meat dealers do not deal in bacon)? (*Braun* v. *Armour & Co.,* 254 N.Y. 514, 173 N.E. 845 [1930].)

4. Taylor sustained personal injuries in an automobile accident because Carter had left her car in a parking lot and had failed to set the parking brake. Taylor had seen the runaway car at a distance of 125 feet, but because she was talking to a passenger had failed to avoid the car and was hit. If Taylor sues Carter for negligence, who should prevail, and why? (*Taylor* v. *Carter,* 2 NC App. 78, 162 S.E.2d 607 [1968].)

5. Kelley was injured when an assailant shot him in the course of an armed robbery. Kelley sued the manufacturer of the handgun the robber had used, seeking monetary damages. Who should win? Explain. (*Kelley* v. *R. G. Industries, Inc.,* 497 A.2d 1143 [Md. 1985].)

6. The defendant falsely asserted that his warehouse was fireproof. Based on the assertion, the plaintiff deposited his goods in the warehouse and was issued a warehouse receipt stating that the defendant would not be liable for loss owing to fire. A fire occurred and the goods were destroyed. What would be the result and why? (*Rosenblatt* v. *John F. Ivory Storage Co.,* 262 Mich. 513, 247 N.W. 733 [1933].)

7. The defendant shot the plaintiff's dog while it was in the process of attacking the defendant's sheep. Will

the defendant win the lawsuit on the basis of privilege? Why, or why not? (*Granier* v. *Chagnon,* 122 Mont. 327, 203 P.2d 982 [1949].)

8. The plaintiff fell down an unlighted stairway in the defendant's public building. The plaintiff's injury occurred at night. A city ordinance required that stairways in buildings open to the public be constantly lighted. Discuss with respect to the tort of negligence. (*Monsour* v. *Excelsior Tobacco Co.,* 115 S.W.2d 219 [Mo. App. 1938].)

9. The defendant operated an amusement park ride in which it could be observed that some patrons fell down because they could not maintain their balance on a moving belt. The plaintiff observed the ride, paid for a turn, and fell down, fracturing his kneecap. Discuss with respect to assumption of the risk. (*Murphy* v. *Steeple-*

chase Amusement Co., 250 N.Y. 479, 166 N.E. 173 [1929].)

10. Palsgraf was standing on a railroad platform waiting for her train. Another passenger attempted to board a train that was pulling out of the station. A railroad employee standing nearby attempted to give the passenger a "boost" to help him board the moving train. In the process, a package the passenger was carrying was dropped onto the tracks and exploded. The concussion from the explosion caused some scales standing at the opposite end of the railroad platform to fall on Palsgraf, causing severe injury. Palsgraf has sued the railroad for her injuries, alleging negligence by the employee. Is the railroad liable for the injury to Palsgraf? Explain fully. (*Palsgraf* v. *Long Island Railroad,* 284 N.Y. 339, 162 N.E. 99 [1928].)

CHAPTER 4

Crimes and Business

OUTLINE

WHY STUDY CRIMINAL LAW?

You may wonder why a business law textbook contains a chapter on criminal law. Our reason for including this brief overview of crimes is that businesses are constantly confronted with the *effects* of such crimes as embezzlement, forgery, and fraud, to cite only a few of the kinds of crimes that will be discussed later in the chapter. To prevent a crime from happening, or to deal effectively with a crime once it has occurred, you have to know what the crime is and what the legal ramifications are.

OBJECTIVES OF CRIMINAL LAW

The objectives of criminal law are the protection of persons and property, the deterrence of criminal behavior, the punishment of criminal activity, and the rehabilitation of the criminal.

Protection of Persons and Property

Someone once said that a lock was designed to keep an honest person honest. It is for the same reason that the state declares certain conduct to be illegal. The state believes that all persons and their property should be protected from harm. In Chapter 3, you learned that tort law also protects persons and property. The difference between tort law and criminal law is that tort law results in money damages, whereas criminal law results in loss of freedom by sending a person to jail or prison. Private interests are served through the awarding of damages. The public interest is served by punishing criminal activity. If all persons respected everyone else's person or property, there would be very little reason for criminal law.

Deterrence of Criminal Behavior

Deterrent   A danger, difficulty, or other consideration that stops or prevents a person from acting.

A key to the hoped-for reduction in criminal behavior is that our criminal laws present a sufficient **deterrent** to antisocial behavior. The presumption inherent in criminal law is that if we make the punishment sufficiently harsh, persons who might do something criminal are prevented from doing so because they fear punishment. If enough people fear the punishment, they will not commit a criminal act.

In our society, however, the Constitution states that there shall be no cruel and unusual punishment. Certainly, if our laws allowed the death penalty for even minor offenses, there would probably be fewer minor offenses. But is that just? To lose one's life for stealing a loaf of bread seems too high a price to pay for fewer loaves of bread being stolen. The problem is to decide how much punishment will deter criminal behavior without going too far.

Punishment of Criminal Activity

Since we most likely will be unable to deter all criminal activity, our laws accept that a certain level of criminal activity will exist in society. Accordingly, we punish criminal activity for punishment's sake. There is no such thing as a free lunch: If a criminal takes something without paying for it, the criminal law makes that individual pay for it through deprivation of freedom for a period of time.

Rehabilitation of the Criminal

Once convicted, a criminal will begin to serve a sentence in a jail or prison. But that is not where our criminal justice system ends. Our government has designed various programs to educate and train criminals in legitimate occupations during the period of incarceration. Upon release, therefore, there should be no reason to return to a life of crime. Sometimes a sentence is suspended; that is, it is not put into effect. In such cases, the court supervises the individuals' activities to ensure that they have learned from their mistakes. Figure 4.1 depicts the four objectives of criminal law.

BASES OF CRIMINAL RESPONSIBILITY

All crimes consist of two elements: a criminal *act* and an appropriate *mental state*. If only one element is present, there can be no crime. For example, if you decide that you are going to rob a bank and then do nothing about it, you have not committed a crime. Similarly, if a cigarette you are smoking in a motel ignites the draperies in your room and causes the motel to burn down,

FIGURE 4.1 Objectives of Criminal Law

Protection of Persons and Property	Sanctions imposed by society against wrongdoers Preservation of the "social fabric" Ensures that society will protect the people within so that "self-help" is not needed or encouraged
Deterrence of Criminal Behavior	Threat of sanctions discourage criminal conduct Sanctions must be sufficiently harsh to deter, without violating the provisions of the Constitution
Punishment of Criminal Activity	Persons who violate the criminal law are punished by fine and/or imprisonment Deprivation of property and/or freedom is the "fee" that a person pays for violation of the criminal law Society punishes the criminal so that the victim/victim's family do not feel obligated to do so
Rehabilitation of the Criminal	Provide educational opportunities and medical treatment to make the person convicted of the crime "marketable" so that the perceived need to commit crime is removed Supervision of parolees and supervision of people who receive suspended sentences to ensure that they are not falling into prior patterns

you have not committed a crime. In the latter case, you may be liable in tort for negligence, but you have not committed the crime of arson.

The Act

The law will impose criminal liability for an illegal act that is voluntarily committed. For example, if you were kidnapped and your abductor forced you to rob a bank under threat of death, obviously the act of robbing the bank was not voluntary. On the other hand, what about a failure to act? In that respect, the following case is informative.

Jones v. Unites States
308 F.2d 307 (D.C. Cir. 1962)

FACTS   The defendant failed to provide for an infant, thus causing the infant's death by malnutrition. The defendant was not the child's mother.

ISSUE   Was the defendant's failure to act a violation of a legal or a moral duty?

HOLDING   It was a violation of a moral duty; thus it is not actionable.

REASONING   A failure to act that amounts to a failure of a moral duty will never result in criminal liability. Only a failure to act that violated a statute or breached a contractual duty, a failure to perform as volunteered, or status as the parent or guardian of the infant would have resulted in the failure of a legal duty on the part of this defendant.

Mental State

Jurisprudence   The philosophy and science of law.

To be held criminally responsible for an illegal act, the actor must intend to do that which is done. Various terms have been used to describe this mental state: *consciously, intentionally, maliciously, unlawfully,* and *willfully,* to name just a few. These terms once had a place in our **jurisprudence** as the concept of mental state was being developed, but today our approach to the problem is more systematic. This current approach involves the use of one of five terms, depending on the specific requirements of the statute, and shows more specifically the *degree* of intent than the older terms. The terms used are as follows:

1. *Purpose*—An actor acts with purpose if it is his conscious objective to do that which is done.
2. *Knowledge*—An actor acts with knowledge if she is aware of what she is doing.
3. *Recklessness*—An actor acts with recklessness if he disregards a substantial and unjustifiable risk that criminal harm or injury may result from his action.

4. *Negligence*—An actor acts in a criminally negligent way if she should have known that a substantial and unreasonable risk of harm would result from her action.

5. *Strict liability*—An actor will be held strictly liable if he acts in a manner that our criminal law declares criminal even if none of the above four elements is present. The justification for this theory is that it is used primarily for crimes that have a light punishment—for example, violating public health laws with respect to the sale of food. This theory is also used in statutory rape cases simply because our society has a vested interest in protecting our youth.

The following case shows that the application of the proper term is critical in determining the outcome of a trial.

State v. Crocker
435 A.2d 58 (Me. 1981)

FACTS — Five-year-old Timothy Crocker died of severe malnourishment, dehydration, and a head wound. Timothy's father was charged with murder by "depraved indifference," a mental state between recklessness and negligence and normally used as the test for negligent manslaughter.

ISSUE — Is Timothy's father guilty of murder?

HOLDING — Yes. The court felt that the requisite mental state was proved at trial.

REASONING — A person is guilty of murder by "depraved indifference" if he engages in conduct that manifests that degree of indifference to the value of a human life so that the death of another human being results. The defendant argued that the term "depraved indifference" is unconstitutionally vague because it is the same standard as that of criminally negligent manslaughter. The court, however, found that murder is properly charged if the conduct is "so heinous in the eyes of the law as to constitute murder." Here, Timothy's entire head was covered with bruises, both eyes were blackened, and black and blue marks covered his entire body. He weighed only thirty-one pounds whereas a child of his age should have weighed approximately forty-five pounds. Therefore, this was not a matter of negligence, but rather one of "depraved indifference."

Figure 4.2 depicts the two bases of criminal responsibility.

SERIOUSNESS OF THE OFFENSE

Criminal law classifies all offenses into three categories according to their level of seriousness. These categories are, from least to most serious, misdemeanors, felonies, and treason.

FIGURE 4.2   The Bases of Criminal Responsibility

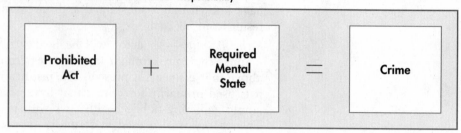

Misdemeanors

Misdemeanors are *minor offenses that are punishable by confinement of up to one year in a city or county jail, a small fine, or both.*

Felonies

Felonies are *major offenses punishable by confinement from one year to life in a state or federal prison, a large fine, or both.* In some states special capital felony statutes provide for the sentence of death.

Treason

Treason is the most serious offense against the state. It consists of *waging war against the state* or of *giving aid and comfort to our enemies in time of war.* Figure 4.3 depicts the seriousness of the offense.

SELECTED CRIMES

This text does not allow space to list all of the common crimes. We will mention selected crimes that have applications for either detection or prevention in the marketplace.

Arson

Arson is *the intentional burning of any property by fire or explosion.* Originally this crime was restricted to the burning of a house. Today the crime has been expanded to include the burning of all real property and just about all personal property.

Burglary

Burglary is *the breaking and entering of a structure with the intent to commit a felony.* Originally this crime was restricted to the breaking and entering of a house at night, but it too has been expanded to include more activity.

Embezzlement

Embezzlement is *the taking of money or other property by an employee who has been entrusted with the money or property by his or her employer.*

Forgery

Forgery is *the making or altering of a negotiable instrument or credit card invoice in order to create or to shift legal liability for the instrument.* It gen-

FIGURE 4.3   Seriousness of the Offense

SEVERITY	CLASSIFICATION	PUNISHMENT
Most Serious	Treason (waging war against the state; giving comfort to the enemy in time of war)	Death sentence Exile Life imprisonment
	Felonies (major offenses against society, including murder, arson, rape, and burglary)	One year or more (minimum) Life imprisonment or the death sentence Sentenced to a state or federal prison
Least	Misdemeanors (minor offenses against society, including traffic offenses, petty theft, and DUI)	Fine and/or incarceration for up to one year Sentenced to the city or county jail

Defraud   To deprive a person of property or of any interest, estate, or right by fraud, deceit, or artifice.

erally consists of signing another person's name to a check, promissory note, or credit card invoice or altering an amount on any of those documents. To win any such case, the state must prove that the accused acted with the intent to **defraud,** as illustrated in the following case.

State v. LaRue
5 Wash. App. 299, 487 P.2d 255 (1971)

FACTS   LaRue was convicted of the crime of forgery for attempting to purchase an electric razor by offering a stolen money order in payment. After signing the name "Goldsmith" in the blank designated "purchaser's name," LaRue endorsed the money order with the name "Goldsmith." Subsequently it was discovered that the money order had been stolen. LaRue attempted to flee but was apprehended.

ISSUE   Is LaRue guilty of forgery?

HOLDING   Yes.

REASONING   LaRue argued that he is not guilty of forgery because his signature had no effect on the validity of the money order. However, forgery is the "fraudulent making or alteration of a writing to the prejudice of another man's rights or as the false making or material alteration, with intent to defraud, of any writing which, if genuine, might apparently be of legal efficacy or the foundation of legal liability." Under that test, LaRue is guilty of forgery: The falseness of the writing is the critical element of the offense.

Fraud

Fraud is a broad term that covers many specific situations. The English courts were very slow to criminalize fraudulent behavior, preferring to let tort law handle most situations. Over the years, however, legislation was passed in both England and the United States to overcome the rather insensitive view of "[we] are not to indict one for making a fool of another."[1] Today most states have statutes that cover variations of what is generally called *theft by deception*. For example, if a seller of goods created the impression that certain goods were worth $1,000 when, in fact, they were worth only $10, the action would be theft by deception if the purchase were made.

Larceny

Larceny is *the wrongful taking and carrying away of the personal property of another without the owner's consent and with the intent to deprive the owner of the property permanently*. The most common forms of larceny are shoplifting and pickpocketing. The use of force is not needed.

Robbery

Robbery is a form of aggravated theft. It is basically *larceny plus the threat to use violence or force*. The following case distinguishes a good-faith belief from the bad faith required for criminal intent.

People v. *Butler*
55 Cal. Rptr. 511, 421 P.2d 703 (1967)

FACTS Butler got into an argument with his employer over the question of wages due him. Guns were drawn, shots were fired . . . and Butler took his employer's wallet.

ISSUE Will the mistaken belief that one had a right to property negate the felonious intent necessary for a robbery conviction?

HOLDING Yes. A good-faith belief will negate intent to commit robbery.

REASONING "It has long been the rule in this state and generally throughout the country that a bona fide belief, even though mistakenly held, that one has a right or claim to the property negates felonious intent."

A Comment on Corporations

There is a growing tendency in many states to hold corporations criminally responsible when their officers and agents commit criminal actions in the execution of their office. Punishment is usually in the form of a fine. If a fine is assessed against the corporation for the criminal activity of its officers and agents, who really suffers? The officers and agents? No, because they will have been separately tried and convicted for their behavior. The stockholders do. The question, then, is: Should innocent stockholders suffer the loss in the form of lower earnings?

[1]Regina v. Jones, 91 Eng. Rep. 330 (1703).

A Comment on the Racketeer Influenced and Corrupt Organizations (RICO) Statute 18 U.S.C. § 1961 et seq.

The RICO statute was made law in 1970. Since that time, Congress has amended the law, and many courts have interpreted many of its sections. The definitions of terms used in the statute are found in section 1961. Section 1962 lists the activities that are prohibited. Criminal and civil penalties are found in section 1963, and sections 1965 to 1968 cover procedural rules.

According to the law's legislative history, it was the intent of Congress to remedy a serious problem: the infiltration of criminals into legitimate businesses as both a "cover" for their criminal activity and as a means of "laundering" profits derived from their crimes.

Since this law focuses on legitimate business activities, it continues to present a concern for all business organizations. The following case extends the definition of a business "enterprise" to include public as well as private entities.

United States v. *Grzywacz*
603 F.2d 682 (7th Cir. 1979)

FACTS   The District Court convicted three former police officers of violating the RICO statute by using their former status to solicit and accept bribes from various businesses.

ISSUE   Does the term "enterprise" as defined by 18 U.S.C. 1961 (4) include public entities as well as private entities?

HOLDING   Yes.

REASONING   "Consideration of past precedent, legislative history, and the plain words of the statute convince us that the RICO statute admits of a broader, less constricted interpretation. We believe that public entities and individuals may constitute section 1961 (4) enterprises through which racketeering is conducted."

SELECTED DEFENSES

The four classic defenses to criminal liability are duress, insanity, intoxication, and justification.

Duress

Duress exists when *the accused was coerced into criminal conduct by threat or use of force that any person of reasonable firmness could not resist.* Not all states have this defense, and those that do have differences with respect to the crimes to which it is applicable. The following case cites the three essential elements of the defense.

United States v. Contento-Pachon
723 F.2d 691 (9th Cir. 1984)

FACTS   The defendant was convicted of unlawful possession with intent to distribute a narcotic substance. During the trial, the defendant attempted to introduce evidence of duress. The trial court excluded it.

ISSUE   Should the court have allowed the evidence to be introduced?

HOLDING   Yes.

REASONING   There are three elements to the defense of duress:

1. an immediate threat of death or serious bodily harm

2. a well-grounded fear that the threat will be carried out

3. no reasonable opportunity to escape the threatened harm

The defendant offered evidence on each of the three elements. Therefore, his evidence should have been allowed.

Insanity

Insanity exists when, *as a result of a mental disease or defect, the accused either did not know that what he was doing was wrong or could not prevent himself from doing what he knew to be wrong.* This defense has been under increasing attack for a variety of reasons, but chiefly because after almost 200 years the definition is still ambiguous. It has been applied to less than 1 percent of all criminal cases and has been successful in only a very small number of those cases.

Lipscomb v. State
609 S.W.2d 15 (Ark. 1980)

FACTS   Lipscomb was convicted of robbery and sentenced to fifteen years' imprisonment. He argued that the trial court erred in not making a pretrial determination of his insanity plea.

ISSUE   What is the proper test to determine if the defendant is not guilty by reason of insanity?

HOLDING   The proper test is whether the defendant could conform his conduct to the law or appreciate the criminality of his conduct.

REASONING   Prior law used the test that "the existence of an insane delusion is a defense to a crime only when the imaginary state of facts, if real, would justify or excuse the crime." Today, the proper test is that "a person is not criminally responsible for his conduct if at the time of that conduct, as a result of mental disease or mental defect, he lacked the capacity either to appreciate the criminality of his conduct or to conform his conduct to the requirements of the law."

Intoxication

Intoxication may be either *voluntary* or *involuntary*. Voluntary intoxication is not a defense unless it negates the specific intent required by a statute. For example, the crime of rape is said to require a general intent. Intoxication, therefore, would not be a valid defense. On the other hand, assault with the intent to commit rape is said to require specific intent. In that case, intoxication could be a valid defense. Generally, involuntary intoxication is a good defense. Involuntary intoxication could occur if one were forced to drink an alcoholic beverage against one's will or without one's knowledge.

Justification

Justification exists when *a person believes an act is necessary in order to avoid harm to himself or to another person.* The key to this defense is that whatever the person does in order to avoid harm must be lesser than the harm to be avoided. For example, sometimes property has to be destroyed in order to prevent the spread of fire. Also, a druggist may dispense a drug without a prescription if to do so would save a person's life.

YOU BE THE JUDGE

Holden Charles Hollom, age 51, was a cab driver for Luxor Cab Co. He had approximately twenty-five years' experience driving cabs. Late one night while driving his cab near San Francisco's Civic Center, Hollom and another cab driver watched Ocie James McClure snatch a purse from a tourist. McClure punched the victim and knocked her to the ground. (The tourist was subsequently taken to the hospital for treatment of minor injuries.) The cabbies chased McClure several blocks, yelling at him to stop. Hollom made a sharp turn onto the sidewalk to block McClure's path. Thinking McClure was about to get away, Hollom drove forward and pinned McClure against a building wall. According to McClure's attorney, he suffered two severe leg fractures, a severed artery, and a torn calf muscle.

McClure had previous theft convictions. In this instance, he pleaded guilty to robbery and was sentenced to ten years in prison. McClure initiated a civil law suit against Hollom and Luxor Cab Co. for his hospital bills. If you were the judge deciding this case in a nonjury trial, what would you do and why? Did Hollom commit any crimes or use unreasonable force to make the arrest?

Sources: "Verdict Brings Donations to 'Hero' Cabbie," *The Los Angeles Times*, Monday, February 17, 1992, page A3, and "SF cabbie looks forward to second day in court, and the reality of justice," *The Fresno Bee*, Sunday, March 29, 1992, page A3.

THE LAW OF CRIMINAL PROCEDURE

Criminal procedure is the *area of law that deals with the judicial process in a criminal case*. It is concerned with assuring criminal justice without infringing on individual rights. The drafters of the U.S. Constitution were determined to avoid the excesses and abuses that had been faced under English rule. As a result, the area of criminal procedure was very important. There was a desire to protect the rights of the individual to the greatest extent possible without making law enforcement impossible.

The Constitution contains numerous criminal procedure provisions and protections, among them the guarantees of **due process** and **equal protection.** The defendant must be informed of the charges against him, must be tried before an impartial tribunal, must be permitted to confront witnesses against him, and cannot be compelled to testify against himself. The defendant is entitled to a speedy trial, may not be held subject to excessive **bail,** and may not be subjected to cruel and unusual punishment if convicted. No citizen may be subjected to unreasonable searches and seizures, and the only evidence that may be admitted at trial is evidence properly and lawfully obtained. Figure 4.4 depicts the stages of criminal procedure.

The law carries a *presumption* of innocence until the defendant is proved guilty, and the burden of proof that must be satisfied in a criminal trial is the heaviest such burden in American jurisprudence. The state must convince the jury of the defendant's guilt **beyond a reasonable doubt,** or the defendant must be acquitted.

A police officer acting with probable cause may arrest and accuse an individual of committing a crime, or the arrest may occur under a warrant issued by a judge. A police officer who has probable cause to believe that a crime has been committed, or is being committed, may take the suspect into custody without obtaining a warrant. If an arrest warrant is used, it must be issued by a judge based on probable cause. The judge may find probable cause

Due process The proper exercise of judicial authority as established by general concepts of law and morality.

Equal protection Treatment of all persons before the courts as any other person would be treated before the courts.

Bail The procurement of release of a person charged with a crime by assuring his future attendance in the court.

Beyond a reasonable doubt The degree of proof required in a criminal trial, which is proof to a moral certainty not subject to any other *reasonable* interpretation.

FIGURE 4.4   The Stages of Criminal Procedure

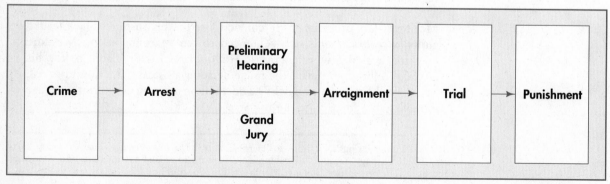

Crime → Arrest → Preliminary Hearing / Grand Jury → Arraignment → Trial → Punishment

to believe that a crime has been committed only on the basis of a sworn, written complaint that names the person to be arrested or adequately describes him.

Once arrested and charged with criminal conduct, the accused must be given a preliminary hearing. At the preliminary hearing, a magistrate determines whether there is probable cause to proceed to a trial. Should the magistrate decide that there is no probable cause, or that there is not enough evidence to proceed to trail, or that there is virtually no chance to obtain a conviction, the charges against the accused will be dropped, and the accused will be released from custody.

Grand jury A jury whose duty it is to receive complaints of criminal conduct and to return a bill of indictment if convinced a trial should be held.

Indictment A written accusation of criminal conduct issued to a court by a grand jury.

A **grand jury** may also be involved in the pretrial stages of criminal proceedings. A grand jury is a panel charged with determining whether there is reason to believe that a person has committed a crime. After hearing the evidence presented by the prosecutor, the grand jury will issue an **indictment** if it believes that the accused has committed a crime. The state will then proceed to trial on the basis of this indictment.

The following case raises the question of whether an indictment must be dismissed if, at times, unauthorized persons are present during a session of a grand jury.

United States v. Computer Sciences Corporation
689 F.2d 1181 (4th Cir. 1982)

FACTS The District Court dismissed all fifty-seven counts in an indictment because on five occasions during an eighteen-month period some unauthorized persons were present during a session of the grand jury.

ISSUE Does Rule 6 (d) of the Federal Rules of Criminal Procedure require dismissal of the indictment?

HOLDING No.

REASONING Under the general rule, the counts must be dismissed if unauthorized persons are present during the deliberations of a grand jury. However, "[a] review of the record satisfies us that the invasions of the grand jury proceedings were rare, inadvertent and nonprejudicial to any defendant. . . . [E]ach situation should be addressed on a *sui generis* basis. . . . In the course of a grand jury investigation lasting eighteen months, intrusions by unauthorized persons occurred on [only] five occasions. . . . Each intrusion was brief, lasting no more than a minute or two. . . . Each intrusion brought the proceedings to an abrupt halt, and no testimony was taken in the presence of the unauthorized persons. . . . Attainable reality, not perfection, here suffices. . . . [But] [p]rosecutors should not consider what we have written as in any way amounting to an encouragement to depart from scrupulous compliance with Fed.R.Crim.P. 6 (d). . . ."

Arraigned Called before a court to enter a plea on an indictment.

Once the grand jury has issued an indictment or the magistrate at a preliminary hearing has determined that probable cause exists, the accused is **arraigned.** At the arraignment, the accused is informed of the charges against

Nolo contendere A plea in a criminal proceeding that has the same effect as a plea of guilty but that may not be used as evidence of guilt.

him, and, if necessary, the court appoints an attorney to represent the defendant. The defendant then enters a plea to the charges pending against him. If the plea so entered is guilty or **nolo contendere,** the court moves to the sentencing stage. If the plea is not guilty, a trial date is set and bail is determined, if appropriate.

At the trial, the state has the burden of proving its case beyond a reasonable doubt, and it must satisfy this burden within the established rules of evidence. Any violation of the rules of evidence will result in the exclusion of the improper evidence, and often the exclusion of the evidence will destroy the state's case. When this happens, the defendant will be acquitted.

If the defendant is found guilty, the court moves to the sentencing stage. Sentencing is governed by legislative guidelines to some extent, but the guidelines are normally very broad and somewhat vague, and a great deal of judicial discretion is usually involved in sentencing. Under current federal law, judges have much less discretion in sentencing than most state court judges.

SUMMARY

Criminal law is designed to protect persons and property from harm. In addition, it should deter criminal behavior. The best protection, of course, is the absence of criminal activity. However, since there is always bound to be some criminal activity, the law should punish criminals for their wrongful acts and try to rehabilitate them while they are incarcerated.

Criminal responsibility is based on two essential elements, one physical and the other mental. The physical element is an overt act. The mental element is actually one of the following: intent, negligence, or strict liability. There is a similarity to tort law, but the interests that are protected are different. Tort law protects private interests, whereas criminal law protects public interests. Accordingly, one can be held liable twice for the same act, once in tort law and once in criminal law. This is not double jeopardy (a second prosecution after the first trial for the same offense) because there are two distinct bases of liability.

All crimes are either misdemeanors or felonies. Misdemeanors are the less serious crimes; felonies, the more serious. Treason involves acts to overthrow the government on the part of a person who owes allegiance to that government.

The selected crimes discussed in the chapter are arson, burglary, embezzlement, forgery, fraud, larceny, and robbery. The defenses mentioned are duress, insanity, intoxication, and justification.

The law of criminal procedure is very technical. An individual suspected of committing a crime may be arrested only upon probable cause, either by the arresting officer or by a judge issuing an arrest warrant. Once arrested, the accused is entitled to a preliminary hearing that requires another finding of probable cause in order to proceed to a trial. A grand jury may also be used, issuing an indictment if it believes that the accused has committed a crime.

If there should be a trial, the state must prove its case beyond a reasonable doubt, and it must do so under numerous constitutional guarantees, such as due process, equal protection, and the rules of evidence. Only upon conviction may an accused person be sentenced to a fine or imprisonment.

DISCUSSION QUESTIONS

1. With respect to the individual citizen, what is the meaning of the following quote from *Lanzetta* v. *New Jersey:* "No one may be required at peril of life, liberty, or property to speculate as to the meaning of penal statutes"?

2. Of the four objectives of criminal law, which should have precedence over the others? Why? Which should have the least precedence? Why?

3. If merely thinking about a crime is not punishable under criminal law, why are both the act and the mental state required in order to decide criminal responsibility?

4. If a restaurant cashier takes money that rightfully should have been placed in the restaurant's checking account, what crime, if any, has been committed? Why?

5. If a house were on fire during a drought, would a volunteer firefighter who dynamited the surrounding houses in order to save the rest of the community have any criminal responsibility? Explain.

6. In 1951, twenty-one corporations were convicted on criminal price-fixing charges in violation of federal antitrust laws and were fined a total of $822,500. The judge who sentenced them said, "The real blame is to be laid at the doorstep of corporate defendants and those who guide and direct their policy." What is to be gained by society when fines are inflicted on corporations rather than imposing prison sentences on those officers and agents who actually committed the criminal activity?

7. An individual's business is losing money. She decides to burn down her place of business, collect the proceeds of her insurance, and start over again. The building burns down, but a drifter sleeping in the building at the time is burned to death. What is the liability for the actor: arson, homicide, both, or neither? Why?

8. If an individual were observed entering a store yard at night and carrying a ladder and a bag of tools, could that person be convicted of attempted burglary?

9. The Model Penal Code is a proposed criminal code that many states have used to revise and modernize their criminal laws. It consolidates larceny, embezzlement, false pretense, extortion, blackmail, fraudulent conversion, receiving stolen property, and all other similar offenses into the one general offense of theft. What advantages can you find to this approach?

10. Crimes are either *mala in se* (morally wrong) or *mala prohibita* (wrong because the law says they are wrong). To which category does the crime of arson belong? To which does income tax evasion belong? Why?

CASE PROBLEMS

1. A New York statute made it a crime for a person to have no visible means of support and to live without employment. Such a law is commonly called a vagrancy statute. Discuss the legality of the statute with respect to the two bases of criminal responsibility. (*Fenster* v. *Leary*, 20 N.Y.2d 309, 229 N.E.2d 426 [1967].)

2. A defendant was accused of having been involved in a heroin distribution scheme. He attempted to introduce evidence of duress. The evidence was that he was in a "depressed" state, that he was tense and nervous, and that if he hadn't involved himself in the scheme, there would have been "consequences." Should the trial court have allowed the evidence? Why? (*United States* v. *Hernandez*, 608 F.2d 741 [9th Cir. 1979].)

3. RICO was designed to apply to legitimate businesses that had been infiltrated by criminals. Can RICO be used against criminals who operate illegitimate businesses such as a gambling business? Why? (*United States* v. *Cappetto,* 502 F.2d 1351 [7th Cir. 1974].)

4. Federal law requires that government attorneys appearing before grand juries be "specifically directed" by the Attorney General. (See 28 U.S.C. 515 [a].) A government attorney appeared before a grand jury pursuant to a letter from an assistant attorney general. Is that proper grounds for a dismissal of the indictment? Give reasons for your answer. (*United States* v. *Agrusa,* 520 F.2d 370 [8th Cir. 1975].)

5. A fifteen-year-old was tried as a juvenile for being in the company of another boy who stole a woman's wallet. He was confined for up to six years (until he was twenty-one). If he had been convicted of the same crime as an adult he would have been fined $5 to $50 or jailed for not more than two months. Discuss with respect to the reason, or lack thereof, for the length of his confinement. (*In re Gault,* 387 U.S. 1 [1967].)

6. In a criminal case, the prosecution sought discovery of the name of a defense-related psychiatrist. Defense counsel objected on the grounds that he had not decided to call the psychiatrist as a witness and, therefore, his name was not discoverable. What outcome, and why? (*State* v. *Pawlyk,* 115 Wash.2d 457, 800 P.2d 338 [1980].)

7. The defendant was convicted of embezzlement. In his appeal, he argued that he was not guilty of the crime since the money came into his possession as the operator of a collection agency, and, as an independent businessman, he could not have been the employee or agent for the business that lost the money. Discuss. (*State* v. *Riggins,* 8 Ill.2d 78, 132 N.E.2d 519 [1956].)

8. A lawyer was retained to represent an individual accused of disorderly conduct. In a meeting with his client, the lawyer said that his fee would be $200 and that he would need an additional $2000 to buy the silence of the arresting officer. In fact, the arresting officer subsequently told the lawyer that the client was not in any trouble and that the matter would be dropped. Nevertheless, the attorney kept the $2200. Discuss. (*Graham* v. *United States,* 187 F.2d 87 [1950].)

9. The defendant was convicted of assault with intent to murder. He argued that he could not have had the mental intent to murder since, prior to the assault, he became voluntarily intoxicated. Discuss. (*Roberts* v. *People,* 19 Mich. 401 [1870].)

10. The defendant was convicted of murdering a peace officer, a capital offense. The defendant argued that he was not aware that the victim was a peace officer. The facts were that the victim appeared at the scene after the defendant's estranged wife called the police for assistance. In an attempt to get the defendant to put down his weapon, the officer said: "Freeze! Stop! Police! Drop your weapon." What outcome, and why? (*Havard* v. *State,* 800 S.W.2d 195 [Tex. Crim. App. 1989].)

CHAPTER 5

Anatomy of a
Civil Lawsuit

OUTLINE

THE PROBLEM

Nic Grant, a college sophomore, had saved some of his earnings from a part-time job to take his girlfriend, Nancy Griffin, to dinner at the most expensive restaurant in town, Chez Joey. This was an important date for him, and he wanted to impress Nancy with his interest in her.

That night he called for Nancy at seven o'clock and took her to the restaurant, which was on the top floor of the town's tallest building. As soon as the elevator door opened, he knew he had made the right decision. It was beautiful. The interior was exotic. Soft music could be heard in the background. The head waiter ushered them to their table, and the waiter quickly appeared to take their order. They ordered a delicately dry white wine to go with their fresh swordfish, the specialty of the house. Nic could see that Nancy was having a wonderful time. When the swordfish was served, it was partially covered with a sauce that had an unusual taste. Since neither of them had had swordfish before, they took no further notice of it and ate the fish.

Using his newly obtained credit card, Nic paid the bill. He said goodnight to Nancy at eleven o'clock and was home by eleven-thirty. Before he went to bed, he felt some rumbling in his stomach, but he discounted it as merely the aftereffects of new food. He couldn't sleep, however, and things got worse. He called out to his roommate, Tom. At one-thirty in the morning, Tom carried Nic to his car and drove him to the nearest hospital with an emergency room.

Nic spent the next five days in the hospital. He lost his job because he didn't show up for work Monday night and failed to take his mid-term examinations, which caused him to drop out of college for the semester. Nancy, who didn't have a job, suffered the same physical problem Saturday night and also dropped out of school. Nic's roommate, Tom, who was taking a course in business law, advised Nic to consult a lawyer.

CLIENT'S INTERVIEW WITH A LAWYER

Contingency fee   A fee that is possible but not assured; a fee stipulated to be paid to an attorney for services rendered in conducting a suit or other proceeding only if the case is won.

The local bar association referred Nic to an attorney. At the interview Nic recounted for the attorney, Lyn Carroll, all the facts of that fateful evening. The attorney asked whether Nic had notified the restaurant, and he said no. Ms. Carroll said that something could be done about the matter and that she might be able to help Nancy as well. The three agreed to meet on Monday to discuss, read, and sign the client-attorney contract. A copy of this document is shown in Figure 5.1. As indicated in the contract, payment was to be based on a **contingency fee**.

FIGURE 5.1   Client-Attorney Contract

AGREEMENT

THIS CONTRACT entered into, by, and between NIC GRANT and NANCY GRIFFIN, herein referred to as CLIENTS, and LYN CARROLL, hereinafter referred to as ATTORNEY, WITNESSETH:

1. Clients hereby retain and employ attorney to represent them in the prosecution of their claim and cause of action for damages sustained by them as a result of eating food at Chez Joey on 17 June 1991 at 9876 Appian Way, Smithville, Texas, resulting in injuries and damages to clients.

2. Clients agree to pay attorney for her services rendered pursuant to this employment contract at the rate of one-third (33⅓ percent) of the net amount recovered, if any.

3. All necessary and reasonable costs, expenses, investigation, preparation for trial, and litigation expenses shall be initially paid for by attorney and then deducted from the amount of any settlement or recovery, and the division between the parties shall be made after deduction of said expenses. Furthermore, clients shall reimburse attorney for all such costs and expenses even if no recovery is made or, in the alternative, if the costs and expenses should exceed the amount of the recovery.

4. Attorney agrees to undertake the representation of clients in the prosecution of the above claims and causes of action, using her highest professional skill to further the interest of said clients in all matters in connection with their claims and causes of action, and to diligently pursue said claims and causes of action.

5. No settlement or other disposition of the matter shall be made by attorney without the written approval of clients.

IN WITNESS WHEREOF, the parties hereto have executed this instrument in triplicate originals this 26th day of June 1991.

CLIENT _____
                                    NIC GRANT

CLIENT _____
                                    NANCY GRIFFIN

ATTORNEY _____
                                    LYN CARROLL

INVESTIGATION OF THE FACTS

In the interviews with her clients and in subsequent telephone conversations, the information displayed in Figure 5.2 was obtained by Ms. Carroll. On the basis of this preliminary information, Attorney Carroll obtained medical releases from both clients in order to obtain the hospital and medical records.

FIGURE 5.2   Preliminary Information

ACTIONS	INFORMATION	
	Nic Grant	
	4321 South Medford, Apt. 32	
	Smithville, Texas 88903	
	(123) 521-2394 (Home)	
	NONE (Work)	
	DOB 21 May 1968	
	Nancy Griffin	
	1234 North Mitford, Apt. 9B	
	Smithville, Texas 88909	
	(123) 522-4932 (Home)	
	NONE (Work)	
	DOB 24 Dec 1969	
Get Credit Card Copy	Date of Injury	17 June 1991
	Place of Injury	Chez Joey
		9876 Appian Way
		Smithville, Texas 88906
	Nature of Injury	WARRANTY: Breach of Implied Warranty of Merchantability—Contract—Sale of Goods (UCC)
Get Hospital and Doctor's Records	Treatment	Grant—Doctor's Hospital 18–22 June 1991
	Physician	Billy Lee, M.D. Professional Building Smithville, Texas 88901
	Treatment	Griffin—none
	Physician	Alfred Lowens, M.D. 8323 Farkleberry Lane Smithville, Texas 88901

Nic turned over his copy of the credit card invoice reflecting payment for the meals. The medical release appears in Figure 5.3.

After reviewing the file, Ms. Carroll wrote to the university that Grant and Griffin had been attending for proof that they had been withdrawn from classes after 17 June 1991. She also wrote to Grant's former employer for proof that he had been fired on 20 June 1991. Once all the material requested was in the file, the preliminary investigation came to a close. It evidenced that Nic and Nancy had both eaten contaminated swordfish, based on a chemical analysis of the contents of their stomachs, and had contracted food poisoning.

FIGURE 5.3   Medical Release

MEDICAL AUTHORIZATION

TO: _____

I hereby authorize and request you to allow my attorney, LYN CARROLL, free access to any and all hospital and/or medical records or reports in your possession or custody and, upon request of LYN CARROLL, to furnish to her, at my expense, a full and complete report concerning your medical examination and treatment of

_____

_____

Date

_____

     Name

_____

     Address

(The term *ptomaine poisoning* was used beginning in 1870 to include various nitrogen compounds formed during the decomposition of proteins. Today, however, investigators have determined that most food poisoning is due to other factors, including bacteria, especially salmonella organisms, as well as chemicals.) At this point, Ms. Carroll sat down and wrote a letter to an officer of Chez Joey. The letter is displayed in Figure 5.4 on page 80.

NEGOTIATION OF SETTLEMENT

Suit Abbreviation of "lawsuit," the formal legal proceeding used to solve a legal problem.

Upon receipt of the letter of notice, Mr. Durand called his insurance company and informed them of its contents. The insurance carrier immediately assigned an adjuster to the case. The adjuster contacted Ms. Carroll to ascertain the nature of the injuries and discovered the information shown in Figure 5.5 on page 81. On the basis of this information, the adjuster attempted to negotiate a settlement by offering $1454.15 to Mr. Grant and $175.00 to Ms. Griffin. Since the offer covered only out-of-pocket medical expenses, it was rejected, and Ms. Carroll filed **suit** on 24 July 1991.

FIGURE 5.4   Letter of Notice

LYN CARROLL, J.D.
Attorney at Law
Suite 654
Smithville Savings Building
Smithville, Texas 88905

6 July 1991

Mr. Joseph E. Durand
President
Chez Joey, Inc.
9876 Appian Way   RE: *Nic Grant and Nancy Griffin* v. *Chez Joey, Inc.*
Smithville, Texas 88906   **d/b/a** Chez Joey

Dear Mr. Durand:

I have been retained by Mr. Nic Grant and Ms. Nancy Griffin to represent them in a cause of action arising from their having dinner at your restaurant on 17 June 1991 and, as a direct result, having contracted food poisoning. My investigation indicates that their injuries were caused by having eaten contaminated swordfish, which is a breach of the implied warranty of merchantability and is thus actionable under the Texas Uniform Commercial Code, Section 2-314.

Should you or your liability carrier wish to discuss this matter with me in order to achieve a just and equitable settlement, please get in touch with me within twelve days from the date of this letter. If I do not hear from you or your representative within that period, I shall file suit against you without further notice.

Sincerely,

Lyn Carroll

LC:rj
cc: Mr. Grant
cc: Ms. Griffin

D/b/a Abbreviation for "doing business as" that is used whenever one person operates a business under another name.

Complaint In civil practice, the plaintiff's first pleading.

Summons A writ requiring the sheriff to notify the person named that the person must appear in court to answer a complaint.

FILING OF THE SUIT

Figure 5.6 shows the Plaintiff's Original Petition. After this **complaint** was filed, the clerk of the court issued a **summons** and delivered it to the sheriff so that he could serve the summons along with the complaint on the defendant. Both the summons and the complaint were in this case personally delivered to the defendant. Since the defendant is a corporation, they were delivered

FIGURE 5.5 Summary of the Insurance Adjustor's Findings

DAMAGES

Mr. Grant
1.	Cost of meal	$67.00
2.	Trans. to hosp.	5.00
3.	Hospital bill	1250.15
4.	Doctor bill	137.00
5.	Lost wages	unknown
6.	Tuition for 1 sem.	550.00
7.	Books	75.00
	TOTAL	**$2084.15**

Ms. Griffin
1.	Doctor bill	$175.00
2.	Tuition for 1 sem.	550.00
3.	Books	60.00
	TOTAL	**$785.00**

	GRAND TOTAL	**$2869.15**

FIGURE 5.6 Plaintiff's Original Petition

Plaintiff's Original Petition
No. 23465

NIC GRANT and NANCY GRIFFIN	) **IN THE DISTRICT COURT**)) **MALFUSIA COUNTY**
V.	) **STATE OF TEXAS**
Chez Joey, Inc. d/b/a/ Chez Joey	) **156th JUDICIAL DISTRICT**)

TO THE HONORABLE JUDGE OF SAID COURT:

NOW COME NIC GRANT and NANCY GRIFFIN, hereinafter called PLAINTIFFS, complaining of CHEZ JOEY, Inc., a domestic corporation doing business in the State of Texas as Chez Joey, hereinafter called DEFENDANT, who may be served with citation by service upon their statutory agent, JOSEPH E. DURAND, 9876 Appian Way, Smithville, Malfusia County, Texas, and for cause of action would respectfully show unto the court that:

FIGURE 5.6   continued

I

On or about 17 June 1991, plaintiffs had dinner at Chez Joey restaurant. They ordered, were served, and consumed the specialty of the house, broiled swordfish with house sauce. Mr. Grant paid $67.00 for the two meals. Later that evening plaintiffs became violently ill, had high temperatures, vomited, lost control of their bowels, and required medical and hospital attention. A subsequent examination of the contents of their respective stomachs revealed that the swordfish was contaminated, thus causing the plaintiffs to contract food poisoning.

II

Defendant's breach of the implied warranty of merchantability is a violation of the Texas Uniform Commercial Code, Section 2-314, the pertinent portion of which is quoted verbatim:

(1) Unless excluded or modified . . . a warranty that the goods shall be merchantable is implied in a contract for their sale if the seller is a merchant with respect to goods of that kind. Under this section the serving for value of food or drink to be consumed either on the premises or elsewhere is a sale.

III

As a result of defendant's breach of the implied warranty of merchantability, plaintiffs have incurred, and will continue to incur, various medical expenses; they have suffered, and will continue to suffer, pain; Mr. Grant has been unable to work and has lost wages in the sum of $600.00, and his ability to earn in the immediate future has been temporarily impaired; plaintiffs have suffered a loss of tuition incurred in the course of furthering their education by having to drop out of school.

WHEREFORE, plaintiffs pray judgment against defendant in the sum of $10,000.00, their costs, and all other proper relief.

LYN CARROLL
Attorney at Law
Suite 654
Smithville Savings Building
Smithville, Texas 88905
(123) 525-1234

to Mr. Durand, the registered agent for the corporation. Figure 5.7 displays a copy of the defendant's answer.

At this point in the proceedings, the issue is *joined*, meaning the plaintiffs have sued the defendant in a court of law and the defendant has filed an answer. Before trial, it is the duty of both attorneys to simplify the legal issues, amend their complaint and answer, and limit the number of expert witnesses, if any.

FIGURE 5.7 Defendant's Answer

Defendant's Original Answer
No. 23465

NIC GRANT	) **IN THE DISTRICT COURT**
and	
NANCY GRIFFIN	) **MALFUSIA COUNTY**
V.	) **STATE OF TEXAS**
CHEZ JOEY, INC.	) **156th JUDICIAL DISTRICT**
d/b/a/ CHEZ JOEY	)

TO THE HONORABLE JUDGE OF SAID COURT:

COMES NOW CHEZ JOEY, INC., d/b/a/ CHEZ JOEY, defendant in the above styled and numbered cause, and for answer to Plaintiff's Original Petition would respectfully show unto the court:

I

Defendant denies each and every material allegation contained in Plaintiff's Original Petition.

WHEREFORE, having fully answered, defendant prays that the complaint be dismissed, for his costs, and for all other proper relief.

JONES, MURPHY, SABBATINO, and SCHWARTZ
Suite 1010
First National Bank Building
Smithville, Texas 88905
(123) 525-9876

By _____
ATTORNEYS FOR DEFENDANT

On 14 August 1991 a copy of this answer was mailed to Ms. Lyn Carroll, attorney for plaintiffs, Suite 654, Smithville Savings Building, Smithville, Texas 88905.

By _____
JEFFERSON JONES

YOU BE THE JUDGE

> The city of Chicago has approximately 60 miles of underground freight tunnels running beneath a section of the city known as the Loop. The Chicago River runs very close to these tunnels in a number of places. A leak developed in one of the tunnels, a fact known to a top city official. He discovered that it would cost $50,000 to repair the leak. He decided to wait until the city was better able to afford the repair bill, or until he could find a less expensive method for repairing the leak.
>
> Before any repairs were made, the leak erupted from a minor nuisance to a major flood. Over 250 million gallons of water poured into the old tunnels, causing the power company to shut off electricity to the Loop region which forced hundreds of businesses to close. It is estimated that damages will exceed $1 billion.
>
> Assume that a taxpayer's group wanted to file suit in this case. Who would they sue and on what basis would the suit be filed?

Source: "The cost of not putting a finger in the dike," *U.S. News & World Report,* April 27, 1992, page 13.

PRETRIAL PROCEEDINGS

Now begins what is called the discovery process. *Discovery* is a general term that applies to *a group of specific methods of narrowing the issue.* The reason lawyers use the process is that it results in either shortening the actual trial, if there is one, or eliminating the need for a trial if the case is settled before trial. If one side can see that there is no way they could win the suit, it is in their best interests to settle the case. The "scope" of discovery is very broad. Accordingly, one can discover all that is relevant even if the evidence could not be introduced at trial. The test is that it must be reasonably calculated to lead to admissible evidence.

Depositions

Impeach To call into question the veracity of a witness by means of evidence brought forth for that purpose.

A *deposition* is *the reducing to writing of a witness's* sworn *testimony outside of court.* This is done routinely today either to preserve testimony for someone who, for good cause, may not be able to be present at the trial or to subsequently **impeach** the witness when the party does appear at trial and gives evidence that conflicts with what he or she gave at the time the deposition was taken. For example, if a witness in this case said that she saw both Nic and Nancy at Chez Joey's on June 17 but later at the trial contradicted her own testimony, the deposition would be used to show the jury that the witness is unreliable. A deposition may be obtained from any party or witness.

Interrogatories

Interrogatories are *written questions from one side to the other*. Like depositions, interrogatories produce a written record of answers to questions. Because both the questions and the answers are written, however, the answers are not as spontaneous as in a deposition. The answer is made under oath, but the respondent has the time to think out and carefully phrase the written answers to the questions posed. Interrogatories may be obtained from all parties to the lawsuit but not from all witnesses. That is, if a witness is neither a plaintiff nor a defendant (the two groups that comprise the parties), an interrogatory may not be obtained.

Production of Documents and Things

In many lawsuits, testimony alone is insufficient to win the case. In our case, since the testimony of Nic and Nancy would be insufficient, Ms. Carroll will introduce the records of the two doctors, the hospital, and the credit card invoice. Because of the circumstances of this case, Ms. Carroll may also request the production of records in the possession of Chez Joey reflecting when and where the fish was bought and any internal communications used in its kitchen explaining the procedure used in preparing swordfish. The legal form used to obtain those documents is called a **subpoena duces tecum.** The following case raises the questions of the scope of a subpoena duces tecum and the extent of an attorney's Fifth Amendment privilege against self-incrimination.

Subpoena duces tecum   A court order to produce evidence at the trial.

Re Zisook
430 N.E.2d 1037 (Ill. 1981)

FACTS Zisook was an attorney, practicing law in a professional corporation. He was sued by one of his clients, who sought the production of certain documents in Zisook's possession to prove his (the client's) case. When Zisook refused to provide the documents, the client asked the court to issue a *subpoena duces tecum* for these documents. Zisook failed to comply with the *subpoena duces tecum,* and the bar association instituted disciplinary proceedings against Zisook to decide whether his right to practice law should be suspended.

ISSUE Should Zisook be suspended from the practice of law for failing to comply?

HOLDING Yes.

REASONING Every natural person possesses the civil right against compulsory self-incrimination. However, in this case Zisook chose an inappropriate way to assert this right. An attorney who is a sole practitioner may assert the right but an attorney who is in practice as a professional corporation cannot claim the right because the documents are the property of the corporation and not the property of any natural person.

Physical or Mental Examination

Whenever the physical or mental condition of a party to the suit is in question, the court may order that party to submit to an examination by a physician. In this case, it is not so much the present condition of the plaintiffs as their physical condition on June 17–18 that is in question. Therefore, an examination at this point will probably not be pursued.

Request for Admission

One party can serve upon the other party a written request for an *admission,* which takes the form of *a question asked by one party to which the answer is either yes or no.* If the party who is to respond fails to answer in a stated period of time (usually thirty days), the matter is deemed admitted. Figure 5.8 depicts the five discovery devices.

The Result of Discovery

As a result of the discovery process, the attorneys for Chez Joey inform their client that the law of implied warranties with respect to merchantability imposes an absolute liability upon the merchant (Chez Joey) for the fitness of the food. It makes no difference that the restaurant did everything it could reasonably do to prevent such injury from occurring. Mr. Jones recommends settlement for $5,000. Mr. Durand accepts the advice of counsel. Ms. Carroll informs her clients of the offer and recommends rejection. Nic and Nancy agree, and the case goes to trial.

Motion for a Summary Judgment

Summary judgment A judgment issued by the court based on the pleadings due to the absence of any issues of material facts.

At this point, it is most likely that Lyn Carroll would introduce a motion for a summary judgment because no substantial fact questions appear to be in dispute; it is merely a matter of applying the law. In such a case, a motion for summary judgment is appropriate. The motion will be granted if, after a review of the pleadings, depositions, affidavits, and other filings it appears that there is no genuine issue of any material fact. Nevertheless, let us assume that there is an issue of fact and continue with the process.

THE TRIAL

Jury Selection

Voir dire An oath given to jurors stating that they swear to answer truthfully all questions asked them in order to determine their competence to serve on the jury.

Most states require prospective jurors to complete a juror information form. The form elicits information on which the respective attorneys base their questions to the jury in what is called the **voir dire** examination. This is an important part of the trial. The information offered by the jurors in response to the questions from counsel are used by counsel as the basis of their challenging jurors as biased and thus ineligible for service. In this case, for example, if a potential juror worked for Chez Joey, Ms. Carroll would challenge that person and request that the judge excuse the person. On the other hand, if one of the prospective jurors was a student at Nic and Nancy's university, Mr. Jones would examine the student very carefully to see whether he or she would favor a fellow student.

FIGURE 5.8 Pretrial Proceedings

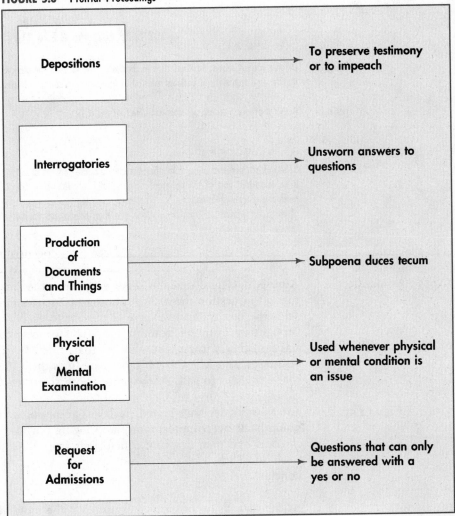

Depositions	To preserve testimony or to impeach
Interrogatories	Unsworn answers to questions
Production of Documents and Things	Subpoena duces tecum
Physical or Mental Examination	Used whenever physical or mental condition is an issue
Request for Admissions	Questions that can only be answered with a yes or no

Opening Statements   After the jury is chosen, each side has an opportunity to tell the jury what it intends to prove.

Direct Examination   Ms. Carroll questions her witnesses.

Expert Witnesses   An expert witness is a professional person who appears in a trial to offer an opinion from facts that have been produced at trial. The following case discusses the propriety of cross-examining an expert witness regarding his or her status as a "professional witness."

Sears v. Rutishauser
102 Ill.2d 402, 466 N.E.2d 210 (1984)

FACTS   Defense counsel wished to impeach a medical expert witness for the plaintiff by questioning him with respect to the number and frequency of patients referred to him by the plaintiff's attorney.

ISSUE   Is this a proper question on cross-examination?

HOLDING   Yes.

REASONING   "The modern personal injury trial often becomes a battle between expert witnesses. . . . An expert medical witness is an important part of the technique of personal injury litigation. The principal safeguard against errant expert testimony is cross examination. . . . Therefore, opposing counsel may probe bias, partisanship, or financial interest of an expert witness on cross-examination and that includes the number and frequency of referrals which he has received from an attorney."

Cross-Examination

After Ms. Carroll questions each of her witnesses, Mr. Jones has an opportunity to question them. Skillful use of cross-examination by competent counsel is the best means we have at present to ascertain the truth of the matters brought up in direct examination. (This process continues until Ms. Carroll has no other witnesses to call. At that time Mr. Jones directly examines his witnesses, and Ms. Carroll cross-examines them until the defense has no further witnesses to call. At that time, both sides "rest" their cases.)

Closing Arguments

After both sides have rested, each has an opportunity to persuade the jury by going back over the testimony and laying out all the facts that were proved in court and then drawing conclusions from those facts that best support its position. Thus, the attorneys take the same set of facts and draw opposite conclusions.

Judgment

Adduced   Given as proof.

Petit jurors   Ordinary jurors comprising the panel of twelve for the trial of a civil or criminal action.

At the conclusion of closing arguments, the judge discusses the law with the jury and charges them to answer certain questions with respect to the evidence **adduced** at trial. After the jury withdraws from the courtroom, they deliberate and reach their decision, called the *verdict*. At that time the verdict is announced in open court. In this case, the jury, whose members are referred to as **petit jurors**, hold for the plaintiffs for $7500. The judgment is the court's official decision and appears in Figure 5.9.

Appeal

At this point, attorneys for Chez Joey could file a notice of appeal and thus have an opportunity to be heard in a higher court; but since the decision is in accordance with the law, no appeal is filed and the case finally comes to an end. Chez Joey now owes the plaintiffs $7500. Figure 5.10 depicts the stages of a trial.

FIGURE 5.9 Court's Judgment

IN THE 156th DISTRICT COURT OF MALFUSIA COUNTY, STATE OF TEXAS

NIC GRANT)	
and	**PLAINTIFFS**
NANCY GRIFFIN)	
V.	
CHEZ JOEY, INC.	
d/b/a/ CHEZ JOEY)	**DEFENDANT**

No. 23465

JUDGMENT

On the 12th day of November 1991 this cause came to be heard, plaintiffs appearing in person and by their attorney, LYN CARROLL, and defendant appearing in person and by his attorneys, JONES, MURPHY, SABBATINO, and SCHWARTZ. All parties announcing ready for trial, a jury composed of Mae Brown and eleven others of the regular panel of the petit jurors of this court was selected and impaneled and sworn according to law to try the issues of fact arising in this cause. After the introduction of all the evidence, the instructions of the court, and the arguments of counsel, said jury retired to consider its verdict, and after deliberating thereon returned unto court the following verdict:

We, the jury, find in favor of the plaintiffs, Nic Grant and Nancy Griffin, and assess their damages as $5000.00 and $2500.00, respectively.

_____

MAE BROWN, FOREMAN

IT IS, THEREFORE, BY THE COURT, CONSIDERED, ORDERED, AND ADJUDGED that the plaintiffs, NIC GRANT and NANCY GRIFFIN, have and recover of and from the defendant, Chez Joey, Inc. d/b/a/ Chez Joey the sums of $5000.00 and $2500.00, respectively, plus their court costs herein expended. Said judgment shall bear interest from this date until paid at the rate of TEN PERCENT PER ANNUM.

ENTERED this 13th day of November 1991.

_____

DISTRICT JUDGE

APPROVED AS TO FORM:

_____

Attorney for Plaintiffs

_____

Attorneys for Defendant

FIGURE 5.10 The Stages of a Trial

| Jury Selection | → | Opening Statements | → | Direct Examination | → | Cross Examination | → | Closing Arguments | → | Judgment | → | Appeal (if any) |

NOTE: FINALITY

In this chapter, you have witnessed one of the great virtues of the law: finality. Whenever a cause of action has been litigated and reduced to a judgment and all appeals have been exhausted, the matter finally comes to an end. In that case the doctrine of res judicata applies. *Res judicata* means that whenever a court issues a final judgment, the subject matter of that lawsuit is finally decided between the parties to the suit. This doctrine prevents further suits from being brought. The matter finally comes to rest.

The following case discusses the question of the appropriateness of applying the doctrine of res judicata.

Cotton States Mutual Ins. Co. v. Anderson
749 F.2d 663 (11th Cir. 1984)

FACTS   An insurance company challenged the constitutionality of Georgia's no-fault insurance statute. On appeal from the trial court's decision, the State of Georgia (Anderson) raised the question for the first time that the insurance company was estopped from raising the question of the unconstitutionality of the statute because it had raised an almost identical argument in prior litigation.

ISSUE   Will the doctrine of res judicata prevent a litigant from relitigating the same issue if it is raised for the first time on appeal and not in the trial court?

HOLDING   Yes and no.

REASONING   The reason the issue was not raised in the trial court was because the other case had not been finally decided prior to the time when this trial court announced its decision. Therefore, it is understandable that it would be raised for the first time on appeal. Res judicata is proper "if the issue in the subsequent proceeding is identical to the one involved in the prior action, the issue was actually litigated, and the determination of the issue was necessary in the prior action." However, the court chose to exercise its discretion and not apply the doctrine because "[f]ederal courts must be slow to declare state statutes unconstitutional" on the basis of the important principle of federalism. The court then went on to analyze the statute and found that it was constitutional.

SUMMARY

Lawsuits are based on factual circumstances. The facts create the legal issues. Therefore, it is up to the client to reveal all the facts to his or her attorney. If all the facts are not known, the attorney might draw the wrong legal conclusion. If the facts warrant a lawsuit, the first thing the attorney should do is to apprise the potential defendant of liability and seek to settle the case without filing suit.

Attorneys' fees are an important consideration in deciding whether the client should sue. The case that we discussed involved a contingency fee arrangement, whereby if the plaintiffs had lost the case, their attorney would have received no fees. There are two other bases for attorneys' fees, which are not mentioned in the chapter: flat rate and hourly rate. In those cases, the attorney would have received compensation whether or not she had won the case. Whatever fee arrangement exists, it is mentioned in the contract, either oral or written, that creates the attorney-client relationship.

Before a lawsuit is filed, the attorney has a duty to investigate the facts to determine whether sufficient evidence exists to justify litigation. Before filing suit, however, an opportunity is usually provided for the defendant to settle the matter.

After suit is filed, the discovery process takes place. Discovery is designed to "narrow" the legal issues, thus enhancing pretrial settlement or reducing the duration of the actual trial. Trial is the last stage of the preappellate process.

The doctrine of res judicata means that when a court issues a final judgment, the subject matter of the case cannot be relitigated between the same parties.

DISCUSSION QUESTIONS

1. Refer to the attorney-client contract and answer this question: if Lyn Carroll spent forty-five hours on this case but lost the lawsuit, would she be due the reasonable value of her services instead of the 33⅓ percent she would have received if she had won? Explain your answer.

2. Would Attorney Carroll have had a more difficult time proving her case if Nic had paid for the meals in cash? Why?

3. Give one reason for the rejection of the first offer to settle the case for $1454.15 and $175.00. Explain your answer.

4. What is a deposition?

5. What is an interrogatory? How does it differ from a deposition?

6. What is a subpoena duces tecum?

7. What is the reason for using a request for admission?

8. What are the stages of a trial? Explain each one.

9. Why didn't the defendant appeal the decision of the trial court?

10. What is res judicata?

CASE PROBLEMS

1. A deposition was used in a trial instead of the person appearing as a witness. If the rules of civil procedure allow this only if the party offering the deposition has been, after due diligence, unable to procure the attendance of the witness, what do you think would constitute "due diligence"? (*Hertz v. Graham*, 292 F.2d 443 [2d Cir. 1961].)

2. The defendant objected to interrogatories that asked him to define a dishonest act in general and to state if certain acts were dishonest. If interrogatories are to be "liberally construed," should the questions be allowed? (*Leumi Financial Corp. v. Hartford Accident & Indemnity Co.*, 295 F.Supp. 539 [S.D.N.Y. 1969].)

3. The rules of discovery are quite broad, but are they broad enough to include the opposing party's expert witness report? (*Franks v. National Dairy Products Corp.*, 41 F.R.D. 234 [W.D. Tex. 1966].)

4. The rules of civil procedure allow for the physical and mental examination of all "parties." The defendant objected to his being examined, asserting that the rule is intended for plaintiffs. Discuss. (*Schlagenhauf v. Holder*, 379 U.S. 194 [1964].)

5. Is the purpose of the rule that allows for a request for admission the discovery of information or the elimination at trial of having to prove points that cannot be fairly contested? (*McSparran v. Hanigan*, 225 F.Supp. 628 [1963].)

6. Should an appellate court consider an argument that was raised for the first time on appeal if the argument was based on a case that was decided after the trial in this case? (*Davis v. United States*, 413 F.2d 1226 [5th Cir. 1969].)

7. The Federal Rules of Civil Procedure provide, *inter alia*, that a motion for a summary judgment "shall be served at least ten days before the time fixed for the hearing" on the motion. Can a trial court grant a movant's *oral* motion for a summary judgment? Why? (*Hanson v. Polk County Land, Inc.*, 608 F.2d 129 [5th Cir. 1979].)

8. In a personal injury case the trial court rejected the plaintiff attorney's questions about whether the prospective jurors had read any literature or heard any discussion on the amounts of verdicts in personal injury cases, and, if so, whether they formed any opinions concerning the topic. Did the trial court rule properly? (*Kujawa v. Baltimore Transit Co.*, 224 Md. 195, 167 A.2d 196 [1961].)

9. The judge participated in examining the witnesses by asking various questions. By so doing, the judge helped or hurt one side or the other. If a trial judge has a duty to make clear to the jury the facts and circumstances pertinent to the case, do you think that either attorney has a valid ground to object? Discuss. (*United States v. Ostendorff*, 371 F.2d 729 [4th Cir. 1966].)

10. Does a spouse in a divorce proceeding have a right to discovery of the records of a closely held corporation in which the other spouse serves as president but not as a stockholder? (*Fox v. Fox*, 96 App. Div. 2d 571, 465 N.Y.S.2d 260 [1983].)

CHAPTER 6

The Attorney-Client Relationship and the Accountant's Legal Liability

OUTLINE

THE ROLE OF THE ATTORNEY

As we discussed in Chapter 5, the attorney-client relationship is largely governed by contract law. The client normally will hire an attorney to represent the client in a particular matter. The attorney then will perform the agreed services for a fee. The amount of the fee should be agreed on in advance, along with any other factors the parties need to negotiate or settle. The more aspects the parties agree to in the contract, the fewer areas will be subject to disagreement later.

The client should be aware that the attorney may occupy different types of legal roles while representing the client. The attorney may, in some instances, be acting as an **agent** for the client. In such a role, the attorney is subject to the control of the **principal,** the client. (See Chapter 33 for a discussion of the duties of an agent.) In other instances, the attorney will be acting as an **independent contractor** who is representing the client. While acting in this capacity, the attorney is not subject to the control of the client. The client will have determined the *ends* to be accomplished, but the attorney/independent contractor is responsible for the *means* chosen to accomplish those ends. The attorney must choose means that comply with the Code of Professional Responsibility and state statutes, regardless of the client's desires. An understanding of the role played by the attorney will often prevent misunderstanding by the client.

Agent   A person authorized by another individual to act for that other individual, normally in the conduct of business.

Principal   The employer of an agent; the person who gives authority to the agent to represent his or her interests.

Independent contractor   One who contracts to do a job or perform a task, but according to his or her own methods and not subject to the control of the employer.

The Adversarial Process

The Anglo-American legal system is based on a unique premise. Early in the development of English common law, it was determined that the *adversarial process* should be followed in trials. Under the adversarial process, *each side to a lawsuit is to present its case in its most favorable light.* Neither side to the lawsuit is required to present "the truth." Rather, the finder of fact (the jury, or the judge if there is no jury) is expected to *find* the truth by examining the conflicting evidence presented by each adversary.

The plaintiff in a civil case, or the state in a criminal case, will present evidence and testimony in a manner that best supports the plaintiff's own viewpoint. All the evidence is expected to show why the plaintiff or the state should win the case. Once the plaintiff has completed this presentation, the defendant takes his or her turn. The defendant will present evidence and testimony to best support the defendant's viewpoint. This evidence may be intended to refute the evidence of the plaintiff (or of the state) or to support the position of the defendant. Once the defendant has completed the presentation, the finder of fact will deliberate over the evidence and testimony presented by both sides. The general idea is that an impartial third party—the finder of fact—will find the truth by hearing what each side feels are its strongest arguments.

To help the finder of fact resolve the legal conflict, certain burdens of proof are imposed by the law. As noted in Chapter 4, in order to obtain a

Clear and convincing proof
A degree of proof that tends to establish the truth in a case beyond a well-founded doubt.

Preponderance of proof The greater weight of evidence; a degree of proof that makes the conclusion sought more likely than not.

criminal conviction, the state must provide proof *beyond a reasonable doubt* for its case. In other words, a *reasonable* person could not doubt the truth of the state's evidence. In civil cases the plaintiff has the burden of proof, but not to the same degree as in a criminal proceeding. The plaintiff will have to prove the case by **clear and convincing proof** or by a **preponderance of proof.** Both these tests require the plaintiff to establish sufficient evidence that the plaintiff's position is most likely the truth. A failure to satisfy the necessary burden of proof will result in a verdict for the other party.

An Officer of the Court

To practice law in the United States, a person must be admitted to the bar. Admission to the bar is governed by state bar associations, state statutes, and state courts. Each state has its own bar association; admission to the bar in one state does not mean admission to any other state's bar. The normal requirements for admission to a bar include graduation from a law school, passing a state bar examination, and presenting satisfactory proof of high moral standards.

Bar membership is a jealously guarded privilege. Once attained, it carries with it certain duties and responsibilities. Attorneys who are admitted to the bar are expected to conduct their professional—and even personal—lives in an appropriate manner, to act in a way that reflects favorably on the profession, and to adhere to the Code of Professional Responsibility. In addition, each attorney is deemed an officer of the court, and as such must act appropriately.

As an *officer of the court,* an attorney "is responsible for the purity and fairness of all his dealings in court."[1] The attorney must avoid obvious misconduct, such as fraud, deceit, or dishonesty; refrain from serving as counsel in any cases in which the attorney expects to appear as a witness; refrain from asserting unwarranted or improper legal claims; report to the court any frauds perpetrated against the court; and avoid any appearance of impropriety.

Privilege

In order for the adversarial process to work, each attorney must adequately represent his or her client. To do so, the attorney must have access to any relevant information the client possesses. The concept of attorney-client *privilege* was developed to facilitate attorney-client communication by *protecting the attorney from being forced to divulge to third parties any communications with the client.*

The purpose of privilege is to preserve the secrets and confidences of the client. The general feeling is that only by ensuring confidentiality can the client feel free to discuss any matter with the attorney. In addition, the protection afforded by privilege allows the attorney to obtain information beyond that which the client might otherwise volunteer.

Before privilege will be recognized, the communication must be secret and confidential. The type of communication that is protected by privilege is either

[1]In re Application of Griffiths, 162 Conn. 249, 254 (1972).

legal advice of any kind sought by the client from a legal advisor or any communications made in confidence by a legal advisor to the client. Such communications are permanently privileged and protected against disclosure by either the attorney or the client unless the client waives the protection.

The existence of privilege is denied when the attorney is aware of any intent by the client to commit a criminal act. Under such circumstances, the attorney may reveal the plan and any other information needed to prevent the commission of the criminal act.

The following case illustrates how far the courts are willing to go to protect attorney-client privilege.

Kevlik v. Goldstein
724 F.2d 844 (1st Cir. 1984)

FACTS

Kevlik was driving an automobile in Derry, New Hampshire. In the automobile with him were his brother and another person, Southmayd. The three were allegedly stopped by the Derry police, unlawfully arrested, beaten, and denied medical attention. All three were charged with disorderly conduct and resisting arrest and with simple assault. At trial, all three were acquitted of all charges.

As a result, all three men filed suit against the city of Derry. Southmayd, on the advice of his father, retained an attorney named McNamara, of the law firm of Wiggin and Nourie, to represent him in the case, paying a $200 retainer at the time. Southmayd met with McNamara after McNamara filed an appearance, and the full story was told to him. When McNamara learned the extent of the case, he withdrew as Southmayd's attorney, citing a conflict of interests since his firm represented the Derry police department's insurer. When the Kevliks got to trial, they sought to have the firm of Wiggin and Nourie disqualified as counsel to the defendant owing to a conflict of interest and to the access the firm might have to privileged information between McNamara and Southmayd, which might harm their case.

ISSUE

Does an attorney-client privilege exist in this setting? Is there a conflict with the Code of Professional Responsibility and the firm of Wiggin and Nourie?

HOLDING

Yes, to both issues. Southmayd had made confidential communications with McNamara, and the information that had been communicated to him could be harmful to the case being presented by the Kevliks.

REASONING

The withdrawal of McNamara from the case prior to any trial was irrelevant. At the time of the communication between McNamara and Southmayd the attorney-client privilege became applicable. A subsequent withdrawal did not change the nature of the communications made earlier.

The Kevliks intended to call Southmayd (who had previously settled out of court with the city of Derry) as a witness. The possession of the information communicated to McNamara by Southmayd gives the appearance of impropriety. Such an appearance of impropriety is a violation of the Code of Professional Responsibility. An attorney who possesses information relevant to the controversy at hand of such a delicate nature must disqualify himself. Accordingly, the firm of Wiggin and Nourie must be disqualified in this case.

THE ROLE OF THE ACCOUNTANT

In many respects, accountants occupy a position similar to that occupied by attorneys. Attorneys are governed in their professional conduct by the Code of Professional Conduct and by state statutes. Accountants are governed by generally accepted accounting principles (GAAP) and generally accepted auditing standards (GAAS). Accountants also must comply with codes of professional ethics and with state statutes. Both attorneys and accountants are highly trained and strictly regulated professionals.

Accountants are governed to a great extent by the *contracts* they make with their clients. The terms of the contract go a long way toward defining the duties of the accountant to the client. An accountant who is independent is hired to provide services as an *independent contractor*. The client establishes the ends to be attained in the contract, but the accountant selects the means for attaining those ends on the basis of professional judgment, GAAP, and GAAS.

Accountants perform much of their work for the use and benefit of *third persons*—persons who are not a party to the contract. These third persons may have rights against the accountant as third-party beneficiaries under the contract, even though they are not a party to the contract. (See Chapter 15, The Rights of Third Parties.) In addition, accountants may face liability to third persons under various statutes. These statutory provisions are designed to protect the investing public from securities manipulations or the general public from tax evasions and frauds.

Common Law

Under the common law, accountants face three types of potential liability. They can be found liable to their clients for any breaches of contract. They can be found liable to their clients under tort law for negligence or for fraud. And in certain circumstances, they can be found liable to third parties under tort law for negligence or fraud.

When an accountant enters a contract with a client, the accountant owes the client a duty to honor the terms of the contract. Any failure to honor the terms of the contract or to perform the contract within the stated time period constitutes a breach of contract. Once a breach is established, the client can sue for—and collect—any reasonable and foreseeable damages that arise as a result of the breach. (For a detailed discussion of remedies for breach of contract, see Chapter 17.) The potential liability is normally substantially higher than the fees the accountant is to collect. For example, a simple tax return preparation may carry a fee of $40. But if the accountant makes an error, he or she faces fines of at least $100, plus any interest and penalties imposed on the client.

The accountants are governed in their dealings with clients not only by the terms of their contracts but also by standards imposed by law. Accountants are expected to exercise reasonable care in their dealings with clients. But the degree of care deemed reasonable is measured against a hypothetical person, a prudent accountant. In other words, accountants must exercise the degree of care and skill normally possessed by members of the accounting profession. A failure to satisfy this degree of care and skill will make an accountant liable *in tort* to the client.

An accountant will be deemed guilty of *negligence* if he or she fails to exercise the care and skill that a reasonable, prudent accountant would exercise under similar circumstances. Although this test requires accountants to meet the demanding standards of the accounting profession, it does *not* make them absolutely responsible for the accuracy of their work. So long as accountants satisfy generally accepted accounting principles and auditing standards and act in good faith with integrity, they will not be liable for simple errors in judgment. By the same token, accountants are not *required* to discover every impropriety or **defalcation** in their clients' books and records. However, if these defalcations or improprieties have gone undiscovered because of negligence, the accountants will be liable for any losses suffered by their clients due to the negligent failure to discover the problem.

An accountant may be liable for *fraud* under two different circumstances: findings of actual fraud or findings of constructive fraud. An accountant's intentional misstatement of a **material fact** to mislead the client will result in a finding of **actual fraud,** provided the client relies on the misstated fact to his or her detriment. Actual fraud against the client is very unusual for an independent accountant. **Constructive fraud** will be found if the accountant is grossly negligent in the performance of duty. The accountant who is so negligent as to "disregard the truth" will be deemed guilty of constructive fraud.

The duty an accountant owes to third persons is frequently misunderstood. Again, the major tort theories are negligence and fraud. But the third person is not in **privity of contract** with the accountant, so the right to sue for damages is less obvious. The third person must prove not only that the tort occurred but also that the accountant owed a duty to the third person to perform the work properly.

In order for a third person who is injured by the negligence of an accountant to seek remedies for the negligence, the third person must show that the accountant knew the work was being done for the benefit of the third person. In some jurisdictions, the accountant must know the work was intended for a particular third person. In other jurisdictions, it is sufficient to show that the third person was part of a group that would normally rely on the work of the accountant. For example, a negligently prepared financial statement used by the client in a loan application could subject the accountant to liability to the bank if the accountant knew the statement was to be used as part of the loan application. But the same statement would not subject the accountant to liability to the bank if the accountant could not have known the statement would be used in the loan application.

Defalcation   The acts of a defrauder in the commission of the fraud.

Material fact   A fact a reasonable person would rely on in deciding whether to act.

Actual fraud   Intentional misstatement of a material fact for the purpose of inducing action by the other party.

Constructive fraud   Fraud in effect, although not necessarily in intent.

Privity of contract   The connection or relationship that exists between two or more contracting parties.

Third persons may also seek recovery for fraud committed by the accountant, whether actual or constructive fraud. Any third person who can show that he or she relied on the accountant's work and that the work was fraudulently prepared can collect damages for the fraud from the accountant. Notice that there is no need to show any expectation of reliance or usage by the third person to recover for fraud.

The following cases involve third-party proceedings against accountants based on allegations of negligence and fraud. Both were heard and decided simultaneously by the New York Court of Appeals. Although the facts in the cases were similar, the court's opinions were different.

Credit Alliance Corporation v. Arthur Andersen & Co.
483 N.E.2d 110 (N.Y. 1985)

FACTS Credit Alliance Corporation (Credit) regularly provided financing to L. B. Smith, a Virginia corporation. During 1978 Credit advised Smith that, as a condition to extending any additional financing, Credit would insist upon examining audited financial statements of Smith's business. Smith provided consolidated financial statements prepared by Arthur Andersen & Co. for the years 1976 and 1977. These statements contained an auditor's report that the statements had been prepared in compliance with GAAS and GAAP and accurately reflected the financial condition of Smith. When Smith returned for additional financing in 1979, additional consolidated financial statements prepared by Arthur Andersen & Co. were presented to Credit. By 1980, Smith had filed for relief in bankruptcy, having defaulted on loans from credit totaling several million dollars. Credit sued Arthur Andersen & Co., alleging negligence and fraud by the accountants in the preparation of the consolidated financial statements of Smith that had been relied on by Credit.

ISSUE Did Arthur Andersen & Co. have sufficient contracts with Credit to be held liable in this case?

HOLDING No. Andersen was not in privity of contract with Credit, nor was there sufficient showing of notice of Andersen as to the use to be made of the statements as to be equated with privity.

REASONING While allegations were made that Andersen knew, or should have known, that Smith was showing the financial statements to Credit, there was no allegation that the reports were for a particular purpose or that Andersen was employed to prepare reports in order for Smith to obtain financing. Andersen neither dealt with Credit nor prepared the statements for the use of Credit. Absent a showing of some conduct by Andersen designed to encourage Credit to provide financing to Smith, Andersen is not guilty of any wrongdoing, nor should Andersen be held liable to Credit.

European American Bank and Trust Company v. Strauhs & Kays
483 N.E.2d 110 (N.Y. 1985)

FACTS European American Bank and Trust (EAB) made substantial loans to Majestic Electro Industries and its subsidiaries in 1979. Soon thereafter EAB advanced additional funds to Majestic to allow it to acquire Brite Lite lamps. Throughout this entire period Majestic employed the accounting firm of Strauhs & Kays (S&K) to audit its financial records. EAB relied on the financial statements prepared by S&K in determining the maximum amounts it was willing to lend Majestic, frequently communicating with S&K in writing or orally to clarify certain aspects of the financial statements prepared by S&K. Majestic subsequently filed for bankruptcy, leaving numerous loans from EAB unpaid. EAB sued S&K, alleging negligence and fraud in the preparation of the financial statements on which EAB had relied to its detriment.

ISSUE   Did S&K have sufficient contracts with EAB to be held liable in this case? If so, was the conduct of S&K sufficient to amount to negligence or fraud in this situation?

HOLDING   Yes, there were sufficient contracts to allow S&K to be held liable, and yes, the conduct was sufficient to amount to negligence and fraud.

REASONING   S&K was well aware that the primary aim and end of its preparation of the financial statements was to allow its client, Majestic, to procure financing from EAB. It was alleged, and not denied, that S&K frequently discussed the financial statements it had prepared for Majestic with EAB, both orally and in writing. It was also established that S&K regularly overstated the value of the assets of Majestic and understated the company's liabilities. While there was no privity between S&K and EAB, the communications between them were the practical equivalent of privity and provided the nexus for holding S&K liable in this case.

Federal Securities Statutes

Registration statement   A statement that must be filed with the Securities and Exchange Commission before a security can be offered for sale.

Security   Any note, stock, bond, certificate of interest, or investment contract, or any interest or instrument commonly known as a security.

The Securities Act of 1933 and the Securities Exchange Act of 1934 impose potential civil and criminal liabilities against accountants. These two acts are covered in detail in Chapter 44. In this section, we examine only the liabilities and responsibilities of the accountant under the acts.

Under the Securities Act of 1933, the accountant is quite vulnerable to civil liability. The accountant may be found liable to anyone who purchases a security covered by a **registration statement**. If the accountant prepared any financial statements included in the registration statement and if the statement *contains* a false statement or *omits* a material fact, the accountant is potentially liable. To establish a case, any purchaser of the **security** need only show that he suffered a loss on the security. The accountant must then disprove liability. The only defense that will disprove liability is a showing that the accountant made a reasonable investigation of the information; that the accountant reasonably believed his work was correct, complete, and truthful; *and* that he did *in fact* believe that the work was correct, complete, and truthful. Unless the accountant can prove a lack of liability, he is held liable for any loss suffered by the purchaser.

The Securities Exchange Act of 1934 is less biased against the accountant. The accountant still faces potential civil liability, but the purchaser has a substantially heavier burden of proof. In order to hold the accountant liable for any false or misleading statements made in the financial statements, the purchaser must prove three things:

1. The price of the security was affected by the false or misleading statement.

[handwritten: INFO USED FOR DECISION]

2. The purchaser relied on the false or misleading statement in making the purchase.

3. The purchaser was not aware of the inaccuracy of the statement.

[handwritten: didn't know it was inaccurate]

Even if the purchaser can prove all three necessary elements, the accountant may not be liable. The defense to civil liability under the 1934 Act is a showing of **due diligence** and good faith in preparing the statement.

An accountant may also face criminal liability under both the 1933 and the 1934 Acts. If it is shown that the accountant *willfully* made false statements or *willfully* omitted material facts, the accountant faces a potential fine of up to $10,000, up to five years of imprisonment, or both. The following case deals with the issue of the criminal liability of accountants.

Due diligence A fair, proper, and common degree of care that persons of ordinary prudence would exercise in the same circumstances.

United States v. Natelli
527 F.2d 311 (1975)

FACTS   Anthony Natelli was the partner in charge of the Washington, D.C., office of Peat, Marwick, Mitchell & Co. (Peat) and the engagement partner in Peat's audit of the National Student Marketing Corporation (Marketing). Joseph Scansaroli was also an employee of Peat and was assigned as the audit supervisor on the Marketing audit. Marketing prepared and issued a proxy statement in connection with a special meeting of the stockholders to consider an amendment to the corporate charter that would increase the capital stock of Marketing and to seek approval of a merger of six companies into Marketing. The proxy statement contained financial statements prepared by Peat, and these statements contained false and misleading information. It was alleged that this information was willfully and knowingly made by the auditors. Net sales and profits were substantially overstated, and about $1 million in reported net sales for 1968 proved to be nonexistent by the date of the proxy statement. Criminal charges were brought against both Natelli and Scansaroli for intentionally misstating the financial condition of the company in the statements included in the proxy statement, and both were convicted. Each appealed the conviction.

ISSUE   Did the auditors have knowledge of the errors contained in the proxy statement, or act with reckless disregard for the truth or falsity of the statements, so that a criminal conviction could be upheld?

HOLDING   With regard to Natelli, yes. With regard to Scansaroli, the issue was unclear. His conviction was reversed and his case remanded for a new trial. (His conviction was subsequently upheld upon petition by the government.)

REASONING   Natelli discovered several "suspicious" matters during the preparation of the financial statements and the certification of these statements in the proxy statement. He testified that he checked some of these matters with the account executive in charge for Marketing, but did not check further. He also carefully worded his footnotes to the financial statement in a manner that concealed the suspicious issues and his questions about these issues. Natelli also chose not to disclose the $1 million in net sales which proved to be nonexistent by the date of the proxy statement. In addition, he had Scansaroli "verify" commitments from firms that they were going to use Marketing's services by telephoning these firms. No written verifications were sought, and a mere statement that the companies Scansaroli called were *considering* using Marketing's services was deemed sufficient to include the gross charges that would be paid if the services were used as actual earnings for the period the firms were considering using the services.

Internal Revenue Provisions

Many accountants derive a substantial portion of their incomes from preparing tax returns for clients. Professional preparation of tax returns can carry substantial potential liability for the preparer.

If the preparer *negligently* understates the tax liability of the taxpayer, the preparer can be fined $250 per return.[2] If the preparer *willfully* understates the tax liability of the taxpayer, the penalty increases to $1000 per return.[3] Making a false return or aiding in the preparation of a false return is a crime punishable by a fine of up to $5000, imprisonment of up to three years, or both.[4]

In addition, the Tax Reform Act of 1986 has added or amended the penalties imposed on the taxpayer for various violations of the Internal Revenue Code. For example, a failure to pay taxes carries a penalty of 1 percent per month, as compared to the penalty prior to the Reform Act of ½ percent per month.[5] The penalty for negligence under the new law is 5 percent of the taxes due, and the scope of negligence is expanded to include any failure to make a reasonable effort to comply with the Code and any careless disregard of the rules of Internal Revenue.[6] This is in addition to any conduct that would have been negligent under the prior laws. The fraud penalties have also been increased, from 50 percent to 75 percent. However, the higher penalty rate is only applicable to the portion of the tax underpayment that is fraudulent, and the taxpayer is allowed to prove that the underpayment is not fraudulent.[7] In any of these cases, the tax preparer may be liable to the taxpayer for these penalties if the preparer is the party who is responsible for the penalty assessment.

Privilege

Unlike the attorney-client relationship, the accountant-client relationship does not carry automatic privilege for confidential communications. Any accountant-client privilege that exists does so only by express state statute. The vast majority of states do not recognize any privileged communications between accountant and client. Even if state law recognizes the privilege, no federal court will recognize it or honor it in a federal court proceeding.

At the present time, there are seventeen different states that recognize the existence of an accountant-client privilege.[8] The statutes are not identical and broad, general statements about the nature of accountant-client privilege cannot be made. Some of the states grant the privilege only to CPAs, and others

---

[2]Internal Revenue Code, Section 6694(a).

[3]Ibid., Section 6694(b).

[4]Internal Revenue Code, Section 7206.

[5]Ibid., Section 6651 as amended by Section 1502 of the Tax Reform Act of 1986.

[6]Ibid., Section 6653 as amended by Section 1503 of the Tax Reform Act of 1986.

[7]Ibid.

[8]The states that have adopted some form of accountant-client privilege are Arizona, Colorado, Florida, Georgia, Illinois, Indiana, Iowa, Kentucky, Louisiana, Maryland, Michigan, Missouri, Montana, Nevada, New Mexico, Pennsylvania, and Tennessee. In addition, Puerto Rico recognizes the privilege.

extend the privilege to all public accountants. Some of the states deny the existence of the privilege in any criminal or bankruptcy proceedings, but allow it otherwise. And some of the states are unclear as to whether the privilege belongs to the accountant or to the client. In at least two of the states (Illinois and New Mexico) court opinions have interpreted the privilege as belonging to the accountant and *not* to the client.

In the following case, the issue of the extent of the privilege was involved. Notice how narrowly the court defined the privilege, and to whom it belongs.

People v. *Zimbelman*
572 P.2d 830 (Colo. 1977)

FACTS   Knox and Zimbelman each owned one-half of the stock in Balto Industries, Inc. Knox was in poor health and desired to sell his share of the business so he could retire. Zimbelman prepared financial statements and a general report on the company, which he presented to Knox in conjunction with an offer to buy Knox's shares. Zimbelman misstated the position of the company and otherwise committed fraud in these reports.

After the sale was completed, Knox died. His family discovered the fraudulent representations that Zimbelman had made and filed civil and criminal charges against Zimbelman for the fraud. In the criminal proceedings, the state of Colorado called Hook as a witness. Hook had prepared financial statements and had audited the books of Balto shortly before the reports were prepared by Zimbelman. Colorado statutes provide for accountant-client privilege, and Zimbelman asserted this privilege in an effort to prevent Hook from testifying.

ISSUE   Can Zimbelman assert the accountant-client privilege in this case in order to prevent Hook from testifying?

HOLDING   No. Balto Industries, Inc., and not Zimbelman, was the client, so only Balto can assert the privilege provided by the statute.

REASONING   The Colorado statute is very specific. Only the client possesses privilege, and since the corporation is a legal person, only Balto in this case had the privilege. Zimbelman was not the client, despite his 50-percent ownership of the stock of the corporation. If the corporation had asserted the privilege, the testimony of Hook would have been disallowed. But since Balto did not assert the privilege, the testimony was allowable. (Based on the testimony of Hook and others, Zimbelman was convicted of the criminal charges brought against him.)

Working Papers   An accountant's *working papers* are those papers and documents prepared by the accountant during the course of the employment; they are used in preparing the final financial statements. These working papers are the *accountant's* property, and not the property of the client. The client is entitled only to the finished work product. The accountant needs the working papers as proof of the care and quality of the work performed. They are to be treated confidentially and protected zealously. But they are never to be turned over to the client. (Nor may they be given to any third parties without the express permission of the client.) To do so is to stand defenseless in the face of lawsuits for negligence, fraud, and statutory liability.

SUMMARY

The Anglo-American legal system follows the adversarial process. Each side to a case or controversy presents its evidence in its most favorable light. The finder of fact decides the facts of the case on the basis of these conflicting presentations. In order for the process to work, skilled advocates are needed. Attorneys fulfill the roles of skilled advocates in the United States. An attorney is admitted to the bar and acts as an officer of the court in representing the client. One aspect of the role of legal counselor for the client is the concept of privilege. Communications made between an attorney and a client are legally protected from disclosure for as long as the client desires confidentiality.

Accountants face multiple types of potential liability for the work they perform. Under common law principles, an accountant may be liable to a client for breach of contract or to a client or third persons for negligence or fraud. In addition, there are potential civil and criminal liabilities under federal securities laws for errors of commission or omission in preparing financial statements for use in registration statements. The Internal Revenue Code also provides for both civil and criminal liabilities for errors made by tax preparers.

The concept of privilege, so important to the attorney-client relationship, normally does not apply to accountants. There is no common law privilege for accountants, nor any federal court privilege. The working papers prepared by an accountant belong to the accountant, not to the client. An accountant's working papers are extremely important as proof of the quality of the work performed.

DISCUSSION QUESTIONS

1. What is the theory behind the adversarial process as a method of finding facts in a trial?

2. What is the purpose of attorney-client privilege, and when does this privilege exist?

3. What standards are used to determine whether an accountant is guilty of negligence? Are these standards appropriate, or should some other standards be used?

4. What must a third person prove in order to hold an accountant liable for constructive fraud? For actual fraud? Why are these two types of fraud treated differently?

5. What are the standards for holding an accountant civilly liable under the Securities Act of 1933? Under the Securities Exchange Act of 1934? Why do these acts have different standards?

6. Roberts is subpoenaed to appear in a federal court to testify against his former client, Smith. One of the questions asked of Roberts concerns a confidential communication between Smith and Roberts. Before Roberts can answer the question, Smith objects, asserting that the communication is privileged. What result should occur if Roberts is a former accountant of Smith? If Roberts is a former attorney of Smith? If there is a different answer, why?

7. Betty, a CPA, negligently prepared financial statements for use in a registration statement covered by the Securities Act of 1933. Phillip purchased some of these securities and has lost a large amount of money on his purchase. Phillip has decided to sue Betty to collect damages. What must Phillip do in order to be able to collect damages from Betty in this case?

8. Suppose that the American legal system were changed so that the role of the attorney was to find and to present the truth to the court, rather than to act as an

advocate for his or her client. Suppose further that the responsibility of "finding and presenting the truth" was declared the most important aspect of an attorney's role. How would such a change affect the attorney-client privilege? Do you feel that the change would increase or decrease justice?

9. Mike, an accountant, prepared the tax returns for Diane in 1987. In his preparation of these returns, Mike disregarded several of the new provisions of the Tax Reform Act of 1986. As a result, Diane's tax liability has been understated by $1000. The Internal Revenue Service audited Diane's return and discovered the understatement of her liability. Diane has settled her tax audit with the IRS and then sought remedies against Mike. What results should occur, and why?

10. Gary, a CPA, has prepared financial statements for Apex, Inc., for the past several years. Gary was recently fired by Apex, and the president of Apex has demanded that Gary surrender all his documents and data concerning Apex to the president, including any working papers in Gary's possession. What should Gary do in this situation? Why?

CASE PROBLEMS

1. Lang was general counsel for First National Bank. Several shareholders of the bank sued the bank's board of directors for alleged mismanagement of bank funds. The plaintiffs attempted to get Lang to aid them in this suit. The board of directors sought a court order to prevent Lang from associating with the plaintiffs or to disclose any secret information he obtained from the board. What was the result? (*Housler* v. *First National Bank of East Islip*, 484 F. Supp. 1321 [E.D. N.Y. 1980].)

2. Sam, an attorney, sued Rose, his former client, for legal fees allegedly earned but not paid. Rose and her attorney sought the right to inspect Sam's work records from the earlier case. Sam refused to produce the records, citing privilege rules. What was the result? (*Brandt* v. *Smith*, 634 F.2d 796 [5th Cir. 1981].)

3. Stern hired Touche to prepare certified financial statements, which were to be used in seeking credit for its operations. Stern had falsified its financial statements. Touche did not discover these falsifications, but should have done so. Touche prepared and certified the financial statements, and Ultramares extended credit to Stern, based on the certified statements. Stern defaulted on the loan, and Ultramares sued Touche for negligence and fraud in preparing the statements. Was the failure by Touche to discover the falsifications sufficient to establish constructive fraud? Explain fully. (*Ultramares Corporation* v. *Touche*, 255 N.Y. 170, 174 N.E. 441 [1931].)

4. Drake purchased stock in Thor Power Company based on fictitious financial statements. The statements were certified by Peat, Marwick. Drake sued Peat, Marwick for applying inappropriate accounting procedures. Peat, Marwick defended by arguing that it did not profit from the allegedly inflated security prices. If the suit is filed under the Securities Exchange Act of 1934, what will be the result? (*Drake* v. *Thor Power Tool Co.*, 282 F. Supp. 94 [N.D. Ill. 1967].)

5. Roth was the president of Continental Corporation. He also owned 25 percent of the company's stock. Roth also managed Valley Commercial, an affiliate of Continental. Roth regularly borrowed money from Valley, after having Valley borrow the money from Continental. Roth was unable to repay a loan from Valley, which meant that Valley could not repay Continental. Roth put up collateral of approximately 80 percent of the loan to secure the loan. The auditors certified that the collateral was in excess of the loan amount, even though they knew it was for less than the amount owed. Were the auditors guilty of criminal conduct in this case, based on their knowing certification of false financial statements? Does it make any difference that the auditors did not profit in any manner from their certification of the statements? (*United States* v. *Simon*, 425 F.2d 796 [2nd Cir. 1969].)

6. Nay was the president and principal stockholder of First Securities, a brokerage firm. Ernst and Ernst, a CPA firm, performed the audits for First Securities for twenty years. During that twenty-year period, Nay induced Hochfelder and others to invest funds in allegedly high-yielding escrow accounts. In fact, the accounts were fictitious, and Nay was converting the funds to his own personal use. Upon the suicide of Nay, the fictitious nature of the accounts was discovered. Hochfelder sued Ernst and Ernst for his losses, alleging a violation of the Securities Exchange Act of 1934 in the auditing of the records of First Securities. There were no allegations of

fraud or intentional misconduct by the CPA firm, but rather a charge of negligent nonfeasance for failing to discover the fraud. If the CPA firm had done nothing improper in its auditing practices, should it be held liable for not having discovered this fraudulent program implemented by Nay? (*Ernst & Ernst* v. *Hochfelder*, 425 U.S. 185 [1976].)

7. A businessman hired a CPA firm to prepare financial statements for his businesses. The firm was aware that the statements so prepared were to be used for the procurement of additional financing and also for the purpose of obtaining investors so that the businesses could be incorporated. The CPA firm accepted the job and guaranteed that its report of the business would be accurate for any category within $5,000. The final statements submitted by the firm misstated the Accounts Payable total of the business by $33,689. The businessman used the statements prepared by the firm to obtain additional financing and also incorporated a portion of the business, again using the statements prepared by the firm. The corporation has filed suit against the CPA firm, alleging negligent preparation of the financial statements. The firm is defending on a lack of privity of contract and on allegations of contributory negligence. What should the court rule? (*Ryan* v. *Kanne*, 170 N.W.2d 395 [Iowa 1969].)

8. Emle sued Patentex for alleged patent infringements. One of the attorneys representing Patentex in the case had formerly served as an attorney for Emle. Emle objected to the presence of this attorney as a representative of Patentex and sought his removal from the trial. The grounds asserted by Emle for the removal of the attorney was a possible violation of the attorney-client privilege. What should the judge rule? (*Emle Industries, Inc.* v. *Patentex, Inc.*, 487 F.2d 562 [2nd cir. 1973].)

9. McLean was induced to purchase stock in Technodyne by representations concerning past sales and future sales potential. These representations were false. McLean claims to have relied, in part, on financial statements prepared and certified by C&S in deciding to invest in Technodyne. C&S had prepared financial statements that were accurate in every respect except one, and that one (Accounts Receivable) was misstated despite the best efforts of C&S to determine the truth of the figures. McLean sued C&S for the $200,000 he lost on his investment in Technodyne, basing his suit on erroneous financial statements and common law fraud. Should C&S be liable to McLean in this situation? Explain fully. (*McLean* v. *Alexander*, 599 F.2d 1190 [1979].)

10. A number of stockholders in First American filed a class action lawsuit against First American, its board of directors, its officers, and its controlling stockholders. The current president of First American, Schweitzer, had previously been the attorney for the company. He was questioned by the stockholders concerning matters that had arisen during his time as counsel for the firm and before he became the president. Schweitzer and the attorney in the case both objected, basing the objections on attorney-client privilege. Should attorney-client privilege prevent stockholders of a corporation from gaining testimony or evidence in a lawsuit involving the corporation? Explain your answer fully. (*Garner* v. *Wolfinbarger*, 430 F.2d 1093 [1970].)

C H A P T E R   7

Business Ethics

CAPITALISM

- SUPPLY
- DEMAND

- PRICE
- QUALITY
- SELECTION

O U T L I N E

ETHICAL THEORIES

The study of ethics and ethical principles is well known in philosophy, but it is relatively new to business. Business students have long been used to "hard and fast" answers and theories in their courses. "Debits equal credits" is a given in accounting classes, and accounting students can tell at a glance if the debits and credits are equal. If they are not equal, the student knows that a problem exists and can then attempt to find the problem and resolve it. However, the fact that the debits and credits are equal does not guarantee that there is no problem. An error could still exist, but it is not as obvious. Business ethics is somewhat similar to this latter situation. Studying ethical theories and principles is not nearly as "hard and fast" as most business courses, and problems are not nearly as obvious in an ethical setting as they are in the example above. Yet, questions of ethics—particularly questions of *business* ethics—are among the most important questions the businessperson of this era will face.

Ethics can be defined as *the system or code of morals of a particular person, religion, group, or profession.*[1] Such a definition does not provide much help in the area of business ethics, however, because the "group" is too diverse to have a single system or code of morals. Similarly, "business" is not a single profession like law or medicine. And while it is probably true that some people "worship the almighty dollar," business cannot properly be viewed as a religion. Thus, for most people, the study of business ethics comes down to an analysis of the system or code of morals of a particular person—the particular businessperson whose conduct is being evaluated. Unfortunately, the ethical standard too often applied is the ethical standard of the observer and not that of the observed person. In order to properly treat the ethical issues of a businessperson, some framework must be established for analysis, and some basic understanding of the ethical parameters of business needs to be developed.

Consequential and Nonconsequential Principles

Before a framework for the analysis of business ethics can be developed, some decisions must be made as to what values and standards are being measured, and on what basis the measurement is being made. There are two broad categories of ethical theories. Ethical theories may be based on *consequential* (teleological) principles or on *nonconsequential* (deontological) principles. Consequential principles judge the ethics of a particular action by the consequences of that action. Consequential ethics determine the "rightness" or "wrongness" of any action by determining the ratio of good to evil that the action will produce. The "right" action is that action that produces the greatest ratio of good to evil of any of the available alternatives. The two major

[1]*Moral Issues in Business,* 3rd ed., Barry (Belmont, Cal.: Wadsworth, 1986), p. 5.

theories of ethical behavior under the consequential principles are egoism and utilitarianism.

Nonconsequential principles tend to focus on the concept of duty. Under the nonconsequential approach, a person acts ethically if that person is faithful to his duty regardless of the consequences that follow from being faithful to that duty. If a person carries out his or her duties, the greatest good occurs *because* the duty of the individual is carried out. If each individual carries out his or her duty, society knows what to expect from each individual in any given situation. This situation provides for greater long-term continuity than would arise if every individual based every choice on the consequences of each particular action. Society imposes duties to maximize the values that society wants. The categorical imperative advanced by Immanuel Kant in the late eighteenth century is the best-known theory in support of the nonconsequential principles of ethics.

Egoism

The doctrine that self-interest is the proper goal of all human action is known as *egoism*.[2] In this doctrine, each person is expected to act in a manner that maximizes his or her long-term interests. In so doing, society benefits because each individual acts in a manner that produces the greatest ratio of good to evil, and the sum of these "good-producing" actions is the greatest good for the society.

One common misconception of egoism is that all egoists are hedonistic seekers of pleasure. This concept focuses on pleasure as being equal to one's best interests. In fact, an egoist may well choose to act in a "selfless" manner because doing so will further the long-term self-interests of that person to a greater degree than will any short-term pleasures he or she may enjoy. An egoist may be willing to make a personal sacrifice today in order to receive some benefit in the future, and doing so is consistent with the doctrine of egoism. Similarly, an egoist may simply obtain self-gratification from performing acts that benefit others, so that such actions further one's long-term interests by increasing one's satisfaction.

In the same manner that an individual may follow egoism, so may an organization. From an organizational perspective, egoism involves those actions that best promote the long-term interests of the organization. Thus a corporation may establish a minority hiring program or a college scholarship program and in so doing may well be acting in a totally egoistic manner. Such programs may advance the long-term interests of the corporation by improving its public image, reducing social tensions, or avoiding legal problems that might otherwise have arisen. The short-term expenses incurred in such programs are more than offset by the benefits to be derived in the future, so that the programs may appear to be generous and public-spirited when in reality they are undertaken for "selfish" reasons.

[2]Ibid., p. 36.

Utilitarianism

The other major consequential approach is utilitarianism. To a utilitarian, the proper course of conduct is that which produces the greatest good for the greatest number. Rather than focusing on the interests of the individual, utilitarianism focuses on the interests of the society. The appropriate act is the one that best serves the interests of the social group as a whole, regardless of the impact on any given individual or subgroup of the social group. In theory, a utilitarian does not care if the "good" is immediate or long-term. The only concern is whether the "good" to be derived—whenever it is derived—is the greatest possible "good" available among the alternatives.

There are two primary types of utilitarianism, act utilitarianism and rule utilitarianism. Act utilitarianism is concerned with individual acts and the effect on the social group that such acts will cause. To an act utilitarian, each individual must act in the manner that will produce the greatest net benefit to the group, even if such acts involve the breaking of a rule. To an act utilitarian, telling a "little white lie" may be the ethical thing to do if telling the truth would cause more harm that telling the lie, or if telling the lie would produce more good than would result from telling the truth.

A rule utilitarian believes that a strict adherence to the rules of the social group will, by definition, produce the greatest good for the greatest number. A rule utilitarian follows all the rules of the society without exception unless the society decides that some specific exceptions are needed to make the rule more ethical. Since the ends justify the means, and since the rules strictly define the means, the proper course of conduct is simple. Follow the rules, and the proper ends will be attained automatically. This principle applies across the board, whether the acts are those of an individual or of an organization within the society. The rules reflect social values, and obedience to those rules maximizes social values and social good.

The Categorical Imperative

The nonconsequential principles of ethical theory are best exemplified by the categorical imperative developed by Immanuel Kant, a German philosopher of the eighteenth century. Kant felt that there were universal moral principles that existed without regard to the circumstances of the moment. When people follow these universal moral principles they are acting ethically. When they do not follow these universal principles, they are acting unethically. Individual variations and consequences are irrelevant. The universal moral principles impose a duty on each person, and the performance of that duty is what determines the "rightness" or "wrongness" of any action.

To Kant, there were perfect duties and imperfect duties. Perfect duties were things that a person must always refrain from doing; imperfect duties were things that a person must do, but only on certain occasions. For example, a perfect duty might be that a merchant must never cheat a customer. An imperfect duty might be that a merchant may need to contribute to charity, but only occasionally, and based in part on the merchant's ability to make a contribution at a particular time.

Based on his theories, Kant developed his "categorical imperative." The categorical imperative, simply stated, says that each person should act in such a way that his or her action could become the universal law. <u>*Each* person is expected to act as *every* person ought to act in a perfectly ethical and moral world.</u> The rules to be followed are unconditional, and adherence to those rules is imperative. If each person carries out his or her *duty* by following the "universal law," society will be properly served by each individual.

This approach to ethics is also applicable to organizations. An organization is judged in the same manner as an individual; the organization is expected to obey the categorical imperative, just as an individual is expected to obey it. The organization is to act according to its duty, with its actions being judged against the universal law standard—would such conduct be proper if all organizations were to act in the same manner? The organization would be expected to act in a manner that discharged its duty to every aspect of society, which would include a recognition of the rights of others and the duty owed to others.

Whether consequential or nonconsequential, these theories provide a possible framework for evaluating the ethics of business and the people who operate business. Unfortunately, there is no universally accepted theory or approach to ethics in general, let alone to business ethics. Each firm in the business environment can select a theory of ethics to follow in developing its own ethical approach to conducting its business. To do so, however, the businessperson must also take into account some other factors, which we will now discuss.

YOU BE THE JUDGE

At 3:45 p.m. on Monday, March 30, 1992, the tiny human being Theresa Ann Campo Pearson stopped breathing. She was just ten days old. On her 25th day in the womb, for reasons not entirely understood, the tube around her embryonic central nervous system failed to close at one end, and she never developed a brain. Theresa's parents did not know this until her mother was eight months pregnant.

When they learned their baby would die within days of birth, the parents made a decision: they would petition the courts to declare Theresa brain dead so that they could offer her kidneys, lungs, liver, and heart to infants awaiting transplants.

With that, a public debate began. Doctors, lawyers, and ethicists weighed in on both sides. Without a brain, most agreed, Theresa was hardly a complete person. On the other hand, taking organs while her brainstem kept her heart and lungs "alive" was a line many did not want to cross. Opponents warned against starting down the "slippery slope" toward further devaluation of human life and toward a view of ailing people as merely collections of spare parts.

> The parents filed their petition to have Theresa declared brain dead by the courts. Weigh the alternatives, consider the case carefully, and render your opinion.

Source: "The amazing grace of ordinary people," Merrill McLoughlin, *U.S. News & World Report,* April 13, 1992, page 11.

THE CHANGING SOCIAL ENVIRONMENT

Over the years, business has changed, and as business has changed the attitudes of society toward business have changed. The early days of commerce featured primarily local trade, with mainly hand-crafted goods produced and sold by local merchants and craftsmen. Under these circumstances, the rule of **caveat emptor** was followed, and the success of any business was, to a great extent, dependent upon the reputation of its operator.

Caveat emptor   Let the buyer beware.

Eventually, business began to industrialize and gained an increased capacity for productivity. As business began to produce more, it was able to expand its geographic market from local to regional. This expansion caused a minor change, although the buyer still had to beware. No longer could the buyer expect to be personally acquainted with the seller. Although the reputation of the seller remained important, much of the spread of that reputation was now by hearsay. The buyer and seller were becoming separated by distance.

As industrialization continued to expand, transportation and communication began to grow and develop. The advent of the railroads allowed truly national business operations for the first time. With the opportunity to deal on a national scale, manufacturers became aware of "economies of scale." The age of "bigger is better" had arrived. Now caveat emptor took on more meaning. The buyer could no longer rely on a seller's reputation, since sellers began to combine into trusts, and the available substitutes for any seller's products began to decline.

For the first time, the public expectation of business made a drastic change. The public began to request government intervention to protect the consumer and the workers from "big business." And the government responded with what business must have felt was a vengeance. The Interstate Commerce Commission, the various antitrust statutes, the Securities and Exchange Commission, and a myriad of other agencies and acts were passed in relatively rapid succession. The list of alphabet agencies and acts seemed endless to business.

Why did this happen? Fundamentally because business did not meet the expectations and the demands of the public. Was business acting illegally? In most cases, no! Was business acting unethically? From our contemporary perspective, it probably was; from a historical point of view, probably not.

The key element to remember is that in most cases business was being conducted in a manner that had been socially and legally acceptable up to that time. However, the societal perspective was changing and the demands of the society were moving in a new direction, and business refused to recognize these changes. When businesses did not respond to what society demanded, the legislatures intervened to force businesses to respond. The changing social environment forced changes in the business environment.

In the following case, the stockholders of a corporation challenged a decision by the board of directors that would have resulted in a reduced profit picture for the firm. Notice how the court defined the *duty* of the corporation. After reading the case, think about how a similar case might be resolved today.

Dodge v. *Ford Motor Co.*
170 N.W. 668 (1919)

FACTS   The Dodge brothers as shareholders of Ford Motor Company brought suit to compel the payment of dividends by the company and for other relief under the laws of the state of Michigan. At the time of the suit, Ford Motors had assets in excess of $132 million, total liabilities of just over $18 million, and a capital surplus of nearly $112 million. Ford was at that time paying a dividend of 5 percent *per month* and had also paid "special dividends" of $41 million in the five prior years, or $20 per dollar of stock. Henry Ford declared that henceforth there would be no special dividends and that certain socially beneficial programs would be started with the financial support of the Ford Motor Company.

ISSUE   May the board of directors of a corporation place the interests of the public ahead of the interests of the stockholders of the corporation by discontinuing these special dividends and by rerouting funds for nonbusiness purposes?

HOLDING   No. The directors have a duty to the business and to the stockholders and must honor that duty. Directors may not change the goals of the business in order to devote themselves to other purposes.

REASONING   The directors of a corporation have a duty to be exercised in good faith, the duty to operate a business. The first duty is to the shareholders and to the business. Any acts that are detrimental to the business are not to be taken, even for humanitarian purposes. Humanitarian acts should be conducted by individuals with their personal funds and not with corporate funds. (Note: Ford Motor Company was ordered to pay a special dividend of $19 million in addition to the regular 5 percent per month dividend it had been paying.)

Compare the reasoning of the court in the following case with the reasoning the court applied to the *Dodge* v. *Ford Motors Co.* case. Notice the difference in the public attitude toward charitable contributions, as evidenced by the New Jersey statute of 1930.

A. P. Smith Mfg. Co. v. Barlow
13 N.J. 145, 98 A.2d 581 (1953)

FACTS A. P. Smith Mfg. Co., incorporated in 1896, was engaged in the manufacture and sale of valves, fire hydrants, and special equipment. Over the years the business had regularly contributed to the local community chest and occasionally to Upsala College and Newark University. In 1951 the board of directors adopted a resolution stating that it would be in the best interests of the firm to contribute $1500 to Princeton University. Several of the stockholders questioned the appropriateness of this contribution, and the corporate officers sought a declaratory judgment upholding the decision of the board.

ISSUE Was the action of the board of directors **ultra vires** and thus beyond the scope of permissible conduct for the corporation?

HOLDING No. This contribution was within the scope of authority of the board of directors and the corporation.

REASONING A 1930 New Jersey statute expressly provided for corporate contributions to "charitable, philanthropic or benevolent instrumentalities conducive to public welfare" and authorized boards of directors to make such contributions as the board might "deem expedient and as in their judgment will contribute to the protection of the corporate interest." While limitations were imposed, the contribution in question in this case was nowhere near the maximum permissible charitable contribution. The president of the company testified that he felt the contribution was a sound investment and that the firm would gain good will in the community from such a donation. It was also pointed out that if private contributions were to disappear, funding for private schools or other charities would have to come from the government. The court then ruled that the contribution was **intra vires**.

Ultra vires Acts beyond the scope of the power of a corporation; unauthorized corporate conduct.

Intra vires Action within the power of a corporation; authorized corporate conduct.

THE SOCIAL CONTRACT THEORY

Many business executives today argue that American business is too regulated. These people see domestic business drowning in a sea of bureaucratic red tape while less-regulated foreign firms are assuming control of the economy. They want to be unfettered, set free from the "excessive" regulations and allowed to freely compete with foreign producers.

Although this attitude can be justified from a purely economic position, it fails to take into account the "social contract" between business and society. This social contract defines the permissible scope of business conduct and goes beyond the purely economic issues. Society wants more from business than profits, and business *must* accept this mandate if business is to survive. To do otherwise is to breach the social contract.

The social contract theory basically posits that business can exist only because society *allows* it to exist and that business must satisfy the demands of the society if it is to be allowed to continue. If business does not satisfy the demands of society, society will change the rules of the game, and in so changing the rules, the permission that business now has may well be revoked.

Society today expects (and demands) more from business than mere profits. Environmental concerns, consumer safety and protection, and quality of life must also be provided for in the production process. If these added demands cause costs to rise, so be it. If business as we know it will not meet these demands voluntarily, the demands will be met by regulation—or by society's changing the form of business.

THE PROBLEM OF BUSINESS ETHICS

A basic problem faces any business in its efforts to be "ethical": There are no fixed guidelines to follow, no formal codes of ethics to set the standards. The legal profession has a Code of Professional Responsibility; the medical profession has its Hippocratic oath; the accounting profession has a code of ethics; the real estate industry has a code of conduct; other professions have codes to guide them. But business has no code, no "road map" of ethical conduct. The closest thing business has to an ethical guideline is the law. If a business obeys the law, it is acting legally and is seemingly meeting its minimum social requirements. However, this forces business into the sea of red tape, and it makes business *reactive*—responding to legislative demands—rather than *proactive*—establishing its own path.

Given this problem, what can be done to provide a solution? At the present time, probably nothing in the large sense. But each industry can attempt to develop a code of ethics for that particular industry, in much the same manner that the real estate industry has developed a code for its members. If an industry-wide approach will not work, each firm can develop a code of ethics for its employees.

The Human Element

Amoral Neither moral nor immoral, not judged by moral standards.

Too often in the past business has acted as an **amoral** institution. Workers were expected to leave their personal values at the front gate when they reported to work. The workers were expected to be loyal agents of the employer. If a course of conduct was good for the employer, it was to be followed by the employee. If a course of conduct was not good for the employer, the employee was not to follow it. The attitudes and opinions of the employees were ignored.

This attitude was described—and then rebutted—by Alex C. Micholos in his article "The Loyal Agent's Argument."[3] This argument runs as follows:

1. As a loyal agent of some principal, I ought to serve his interests as he would serve them himself if he had my expertise.

2. He would serve his own interests in a thoroughly egoistic way.

[3]*Ethical Theory and Business,* 2d ed., Beauchamp and Bowie (Englewood Cliffs, N.J.: Prentice-Hall, 1983), p. 247.

3. Therefore, as a loyal agent of this principal, I ought to operate in a thoroughly egoistic way in his behalf.

In order to operate in a thoroughly egoistic manner, a person acts in the way that best advances his or her interests, presuming that everyone else is doing the same thing. If each person maximizes personal interests, the society as a whole will be better off.

The gist of the loyal agent's argument is that the loyal agent will put the principal first in any conflicts of interests. The agent is more concerned with being *first* than with being *nice*. However, there is a weakness to the argument, and Micholos spends the balance of his article rebutting the basic premise of the loyal agent's argument. Too many people feel that a loyal agent, if acting in a truly egoistic manner, has a license—if not a duty—to act immorally and unethically if doing so will advance the interests of the principal. Micholos argued that the truly loyal agent must exercise due care and skill in performing his or her duties and must act in a socially acceptable manner while furthering the interests of the principal. To do otherwise is to be disloyal.

In the following case, the court had to deal with the issue of an employer allegedly terminating an "employment at will" situation, when the employee alleged that the termination was due to her refusal to continue an experimental formula that was potentially harmful to the persons who might use it. Notice how the court treats each of these conflicting issues in its opinion.

Pierce v. Ortho Pharmaceutical Corporation
417 A.2d 505 (N.J. 1980)

FACTS   Dr. Pierce was employed by Ortho as the director of a medical research team. One of the projects the team was involved with was a liquid medication to be used in the treatment of chronic diarrhea. The medication was designed to be used by infants, children, and the elderly. The original formula contained a high concentration of saccharin, the use of which was objected to by Dr. Pierce. Ortho pressured the research team to begin clinical testing of the liquid medication, but Dr. Pierce refused to begin testing. Dr. Pierce insisted that Ortho wait approximately three months until a revised formula that did not contain saccharin could be developed and ready for use. Ortho relieved Dr. Pierce of her duties as director of the research team. Dr. Pierce then resigned her position, alleging that Ortho pressured her into resigning her position with the firm.

ISSUE   May an employment at will be freely terminated by the employer at any time and for any reason? If that reason involves a violation of public policy, may the employee seek damages for wrongful discharge?

HOLDING   Generally speaking, an employer in an employment at will is free to terminate the employment relationship at any time, with or without cause. However, firing an employee for a reason that violates public policy is not "in good faith" and may result in liability for wrongful discharge.

REASONING   In wrongful discharge cases, the court must balance the interests of the employee, the employer, and the public. Employees have an interest in knowing they will not be fired for exercising legal rights; employers have an interest in running their businesses as they see fit, so long as they do not violate public policy; and the public has an interest in employment stability. Employees who are members of a profession have a special duty to abide not only by federal and state law, but also by the codes of ethics of their professions. These duties may force employees to refuse to perform certain acts that violate any of the duties. The employee should not be subject to discharge for adhering to these duties. However, an employee does not have the right to interfere with an employer's business because a required act is in conflict with the employee's personal morals, as opposed to a recognized professional code of conduct or ethics. In this case, Dr. Pierce objected to the use of saccharin in the liquid medication. She was not asked to violate her professional code of ethics nor the Hippocratic oath. She was not asked to violate FDA regulations regarding the testing of new medications. She had a difference of opinion with her employer. She was reassigned to other projects. Since she viewed this reassignment as a demotion, she resigned. These facts do not lead to a finding of wrongful discharge.

Loyal Agent

If you refer to the chapters on agency (Chapters 33, 34, and 35), you will discover that the agent has a duty to obey the *lawful* orders of the principal. The agent is not empowered, or allowed, to follow unlawful orders. The loyal agent's argument is an excellent model for agents to obey, provided that the agent remembers that there are limits to loyalty. A corporation or any other principal should remember that the agent is a person, and as a person the agent has certain attitudes, values, and principles to which he or she must be true if he or she is to be happy in life or in work.

The Legal Aspect

The American legal system contains numerous "ethical" components. For example, a person is presumed innocent until proven guilty. Each person is entitled to due process of the law and to equal protection under the law. There is a protection against self-incrimination and a right to legal counsel in criminal proceedings. Freedoms of speech and religion, among others, are guaranteed by the Constitution.

Business law also attempts to reflect the morality of the society and to promote ethical conduct in the realm of business. The law of sales imposes a duty on the parties to a sales contract to act in good faith. Bankruptcy is designed to give an *honest* debtor a fresh start. As already discussed, agency law imposes the duties of good faith and loyalty on the agent. And there are other examples of the ethical and/or moral aspects of business law.

The laws regulating business have developed to a great extent under the social contract theory. Governmental regulations of business were enacted initially, in many cases, in response to a public demand for protection from the abuses and excesses of "big business." The antitrust laws discussed in Chapter 46 were intended to control business and to protect the ideal of a free and competitive economic society. The abusive practices of the railroads, the oil companies, the meat packers, and others during the nineteenth century led to a public outcry for reform and to governmental intervention in response to these outcries. Eventually these same laws were used to combat other perceived wrongs committed by the business community. For example, the Federal Trade Commission has begun to require corrective advertising from firms found guilty of misleading or deceptive advertisements in an effort to increase the sale of their products. In the following case, note how the FTC alleges that the marketing campaign of the firm is deceptive and attempts to force the advertiser to use honesty in its ads.

Ger-Ro-Mar, Inc. v. Federal Trade Commission
518 F.2d 33 (1975)

FACTS   Ger-Ro-Mar, Inc. was a California corporation, doing business as Symbra'Ette, Inc. The business involved the manufacturing and sale of brassieres, girdles, swimwear, and lingerie through a company-controlled system of distributors. Symbra'Ette "sold" distributorships at five levels, ranging from Key Distributor (the lowest level) to Regional Manager (the highest level). Distributors were encouraged to recruit Key Distributors and set up a network, with sponsors of the Key Distributors receiving a percentage of the sales from their network. People in the four highest levels purchased their inventory from Symbra'Ette at discounts, with the size of the discount based on the level and the dollar volume. Key Distributors purchased from their sponsors.
The FTC challenged the networking scheme of Symbra'Ette as a lottery and as inherently misleading. The agency also alleged that the literature provided by Symbra'Ette falsely stated the profits that District Managers and Regional Managers could reasonably expect by participating in this program.

ISSUE   Is this sort of multilevel marketing program inherently misleading and thus a violation of Section 5 of the Federal Trade Commission Act? Was the profit potential stated in the literature exaggerated and thus misleading?

HOLDING   No (multilevel marketing plan) and yes (profit potential as described in the literature).

REASONING   The FTC argued that the recruiting plan would lead to literally hundreds of millions of people within one year. The court rejected this argument, looking instead at the actual number of distributors. The court felt that there was no showing that even the most credulous prospective investor was likely to be misled by the marketing plan. The per se condemnation of the plan by the FTC was unsupported by even a trace of evidence and was therefore rejected by the court. The sales manuals and literature prepared by Symbra'Ette, on the other hand, were overly optimistic and thus misleading. The claims were misleading, and the literature must be amended to remedy this problem. A more realistic statement of profit potential and advancement potential must be included in the literature distributed by the company.

The apparent success of the antitrust laws encouraged both the public and the government in the use of statutes to force business to meet the demands of the public. The consumer movement of the 1960s led to a number of protective statutes by both the federal and the state governments. The federal government was most concerned about protecting consumer credit, based on the importance of credit in our modern society. However, there were also federal statutes that dealt with consumer product safety. Similarly, the state governments enacted safety statutes and also dealt with home solicitation. In each of these areas, the government became involved only after a perceived problem was identified, public demands for protection were raised, and the business community failed or refused to adequately meet the demands of the public.

The decades of the 1960s and the 1970s also saw an increased public awareness of and concern over pollution of the environment. Again, a number of protests and a great deal of public action were ignored by the business community in general, and once again governmental intervention was the tool used to correct the problem. These governmental environmental protection statutes were intended to clean up the environment in order to protect the quality of life for our population and wildlife and for future generations. Again, the government only became involved after the business community failed to present any viable solutions to the problems concerning the public.

The areas of consumer protection and environmental regulation are each covered in Chapter 47. The statutory treatment of these problems provides relatively rigid and potentially expensive protections to the public. Similar protections could have been developed by the business community with a great deal less rigidity and a great deal less expense if business had been willing to meet the challenge directly on its own. Instead, by waiting until the government told it what to do, business faces a much stricter regulatory environment in which to operate.

The labor movement is another example of the unwillingness of business to face a developing situation, which led to a multitude of regulations. Business refused to recognize the union movement, and it refused to bargain collectively in good faith with the workers. As a result, the workers obtained statutory rights to unionize and to bargain collectively. These rights are, again, rigid and technical and more stringent that they would have been if business had voluntarily recognized the same principles. In a similar vein, we find such matters as occupational safety, civil rights of the employees, and a number of other areas rigidly regulated owing to the unwillingness of business to self-regulate. These topics are dealt with in some detail in Chapter 48.

In each of these areas and in a number of others the social contract theory is obvious. Society perceived problems and demanded that certain corrective steps be taken to alleviate these problems. Business had an opportunity to take the corrective steps in a fashion devised by business, but failed—or refused—to do so. The government stepped in to resolve the problems in a rigid, statutory manner when no satisfactory solutions were advanced by business.

THE PROBLEM CONTINUES

Despite a continuing attempt by many businesses to avoid the problem of business ethics in the hope that it will "go away," contemporary ethical problems illustrate the seriousness of the issue. In addition, recent court opinions show an increased judicial awareness of the social responsibilities of corporations. Several years ago, Ford Motor Company engineers discovered a potentially hazardous defect in the construction design of the newly developed (at the time) Ford Pinto. The defect presented the possibility of a gas tank rupture, with a resulting fire hazard, if the Pinto were subjected to a rear-end collision. However, Ford's management applied a cost-benefit analysis and determined that it was cheaper for the corporation to pay damages in the lawsuits that were likely to arise due to the design defect than it was to recall the cars and correct the defect. With hindsight, it is obvious that the management made an improper decision from a cost perspective. But what about the ethical issues raised by this decision? How many consumers lost confidence in Ford over this act? How does the public feel about the case and its implications?

More recently, the courts awarded Pennzoil a multibillion dollar settlement in a lawsuit against Texaco for Texaco's conduct in attempting to prevent a merger between Pennzoil and Getty Oil. The court based its decision on the *unethical* interference and conduct of Texaco.

Other cases will undoubtedly arise in the future, and the likelihood of liability for unethical conduct may be the spur needed to force business to recognize and to honor its ethical obligations.

A SUGGESTION FOR BUSINESS

American businesses need to develop a model or a framework of ethical behavior. Most likely, no single model can be developed that will apply equally well to every industry within the American economy, but it is possible to suggest a general outline for business that can be tailored by each industry to the particular needs and demands of that industry. For example, business should probably lean toward the consequential ethical theories rather than toward the nonconsequential theories. Consequential ethical theories are more easily understood and more readily accepted by the general public than the more esoteric concepts that go with a nonconsequential approach. In addition, consequential theories are more flexible and thus allow changes as society and technology advance.

Business also should consider its public relations image in deciding how to proceed within the consequential area. A utilitarian approach, one concerned with the greater good of the society, would be more acceptable to society than an egoistic approach. Society already tends to view business as *egotistic*, and many people seem to have trouble distinguishing between egoistic and egotistic. To avoid this problem of comprehension and understanding, business should probably select the utilitarian approach. Such an approach also fits into the social contract theory, which business must already satisfy if it is to be "allowed" to continue.

Business should avoid "hard and fast" rules because of the changing social environment, especially with the rapid changes of the modern technological age. This does not mean that business should not have rules and standards but, rather, that the rules and standards should be flexible enough to change as society and the business environment change. Business also should advocate the loyal agent argument, with the loyal agent of the business acting as an agent should—with the best long-term interests of the principal in mind. This means that an agent should act in a proper and legal manner to further the best interests of the principal and should not be encouraged to take short cuts in the short run for immediate profit without regard to the rules or the interests of society.

Whenever possible, businesses should learn to work with the government in establishing statutory regulations of the business environment. By taking a proactive rather than a reactive role, business can not only protect its own best interests but also use its active stance to show that business cares about society and the interests of the public. This would not only improve the public relations posture of business but would also show a serious effort to conform to the social contract.

The development of a comprehensive business ethic will not be easy, nor will it be greeted with open arms by many business leaders. However, the alternative is excessive regulation, public distrust, and a general malaise in the business community. Steps can be taken that will benefit both business and society. To do so can only be good for business.

SUMMARY

Over the history of this country, the social environment in which business operates has changed drastically. As the social environment has changed, the demands of society on business have also changed. Business has been slow to recognize or to accept these changes, however.

The social contract theory says that business must respond to the demands of the society, or the society is permitted to change the "rules of the game" to ensure that business will comply. If business does not act as society demands, society will have the legislature enact rules to force compliance.

Even if business wants to act ethically, it is difficult for business to do so. There are no clear-cut guidelines for business to follow in adopting a code of ethics, and interfirm agreements as to what should be done could be challenged as a conspiracy in violation of the antitrust laws. Still, some effort must be made. Business can make this effort by recognizing the human element, the fact that its employees are humans with human wants, desires, and values. Business needs to recognize that unless it responds voluntarily, the legislature will often intervene. Finally, business needs to recognize that the courts are beginning to recognize an ethical aspect of conduct. Cases like the Pinto case and the Pennzoil-Texaco case will help to establish a new line of precedent concerning business ethics and the liability of the firms that fail to toe the ethical line.

DISCUSSION QUESTIONS

1. What is the social contract theory, and how does it affect the role of a corporation within the society in which it operates?

2. Do you feel that a state supreme court today would resolve the fact situation presented in *Dodge* v. *Ford Motor Co.* in the same manner as the Michigan Supreme Court did in 1919? Why?

3. Should the federal government develop a model code of ethics for all businesses in the United States to follow? If so, why? If not, who should develop such a code? Why?

4. What should be considered in the establishment of a code of ethics for any particular business?

5. Explain the "loyal agent's argument" as described by Micholos. What, if anything, is wrong with the argument?

6. Should a legal system be concerned with ethical is-sues and moral values, or should it be concerned only with the allocation of justice?

7. What could/should business do to prevent further federal regulations requiring "ethical" conduct in the business environment?

8. Do you agree with the "ethical" opinion of the court in the Pennzoil-Texaco case? Why?

9. The FTC has become active in the area of advertising, requiring corrective advertising in some cases. Do you feel that corrective advertising is an appropriate remedy when a firm is found guilty of false or misleading advertising? Why?

10. Is business ruled by a "game theory" in which bluffing is a proper part of the game, or is business obligated to act in an honest and forthright manner without regard to any "game theory"?

CASE PROBLEMS

1. Bayard was a truck driver for McLean Trucking. He had been employed by McLean for over twenty-two years and was also the union shop steward at the company's plant. Bayard was sent by McLean to pick up a load of goods. The load exceeded the state maximum weight limit, and Bayard refused to drive the truck with the excessive load on board. As a result of this refusal, McLean discharged Bayard. Can McLean legally fire Bayard under these circumstances? (*Bayard* v. *National Labor Relations Board*, 505 F.2d 342 [1974].)

2. Capiello was an employee at will of Ragen Industries, employed as a commission salesman. Cappiello had earned substantial commissions that had not yet been paid and had a contract pending that would result in a very large commission. His supervisor discharged Cappiello without cause, allegedly to appropriate these accrued and pending commissions for himself. Cap-piello sued for wrongful discharge, seeking as damages both his accrued and pending commissions and punitive damages. Assuming that each of Cappiello's allegations was true, should punitive damages be awarded in this situation? Do ethical considerations allow for a jury award in excess of actual damages? Discuss fully. (*Cappiello* v. *Ragen Precision Industries, Inc.*, 471 A.2d 432 [N.J. Super. A.D. 1984].)

3. Duke Power Company employed ninety-five employees, fourteen of whom were black. The company revised its hiring and promotion policies so that a high school diploma and a minimum score on an intelligence test were both required in order to be hired or promoted. Thirteen of the black employees challenged this new standard as discriminatory and violative of their rights. From an ethical perspective, should a company be able to impose such employment and promotion

standards? (*Griggs et al.* v. *Duke Power Company*, 401 U.S. 424 [1970].)

4. The secretary of labor, acting under the provisions of OSHA, passed a standard limiting occupational exposure to cotton dust. Representatives of the cotton industry challenged the standard as unreasonable since there was no cost-benefit analysis to support the standard. Should such a standard be upheld only on the basis of a cost-benefit analysis, or are there more important ethical considerations involved? (*American Textile Manufacturers Institute, Inc.* v. *Donovan*, 452 U.S. 490 [1981].)

5. Seaton was a registered representative of a member firm of the National Association of Securities Dealers (NASD). The NASD promulgated rules designed to protect investors, including a rule that members shall observe high standards of commercial honor and just and equitable principles of trade. Seaton was accused of conducting private security transactions without prior written notification and of filing false and misleading applications. As a result, Seaton was suspended from any association with any NASD member for one year. Is such a suspension ethically valid, presuming that all charges against Seaton were proven? What ethical issues are involved in such a decision? (*Seaton* v. *Securities and Exchange Commission*, 670 F.2d 309 [D.C. 1982].)

6. Colgate-Palmolive and its advertising agency developed a "mock-up" of sandpaper to demonstrate the moistening abilities of Rapid Shave, a product developed by Colgate. The FTC discovered that a "mock-up" was being used in the commercials and issued a cease and desist order against the commercials. Colgate argued that Rapid Shave would actually perform as indicated in the commercial and that the "mock-up" looked better on television than real sandpaper. Is the use of an undisclosed "mock-up" and the creation of a particular belief in the mind of the viewing public misleading? What ethical grounds are involved in such a situation? (*Federal Trade Commission* v. *Colgate-Palmolive Co.*, 380 U.S. 374 [1964].)

7. The Federation of Homemakers, a consumer protection group, challenged the labeling of frankfurters as misleading and asked the secretary of agriculture to enforce the Wholesome Meats Act more strictly. The central issue in the challenge was the use of the term "all meat" on frankfurter labels when, in fact, the frank-furters could contain up to 15 percent nonmeat ingredients. The secretary of agriculture resisted the group's challenge, asserting that in the meat industry the term "all meat" was generally understood to mean that some nonmeat additives could be used. Should the manufacturers of frankfurters be allowed to label their product as "all meat" when it is really only 85 percent meat? Why? Is this an ethical issue, a legal issue, or both? (*Federation of Homemakers* v. *Hardin*, 328 F. Supp. 181 [D.C. D.C. 1971].)

8. Park is the chief executive officer of Acme Markets, a retail food chain. Acme Markets was charged with storing its food in a building contaminated by rodents, a violation of the Federal Food, Drug, and Cosmetic Act. The government charged both Acme Markets and Park for violations of the act. Park asserts that he is not guilty of the charge because he told another officer of the firm to correct the problem and should not be held responsible for the other officer's failure to act properly. Evaluate Park's argument from a general ethical perspective. (*U.S.* v. *Park*, 721 U.S. 658 [1975].)

9. A registered investment adviser was in the habit of secretly purchasing securities for himself, advising his clients that the securities he had purchased were good long-term investments, and then selling his own holdings in the securities when the market price rose, in part due to the investments of his clients. Evaluate this conduct from an ethical perspective. (*SEC* v. *Capital Gains Research Bureau*, 375 U.S. 180 [1963].)

10. The employees of Gissel Packing Company were considering the formation of a union under NLRB guidelines. The president of the company learned of the union drive and decided to persuade the employees that joining a union was not in their best interests or the best interests of the company. In a talk to the employees, the president pointed out that the company was not very solid financially and that a strike would probably result in the closing of the plant and the loss of a great many jobs. In a subsequent letter to the employees, the president asserted that the organizing union was a "strike-happy outfit" that would destroy the profitability of the firm and force a plant shutdown. The union lost the NLRB election and filed an unfair labor practice charge against the company and the president for the preelection communications. Evaluate the conduct of the president from an ethical perspective. (*NLRB* v. *Gissel Packing Co., Inc.*, 395 U.S. 575 [1969].)

PART 2

The Law of Contracts

The law of contracts forms the foundation of business law. Virtually every aspect of business involves contracts, as does much of a person's normal life. When you rent an apartment, you sign—or orally agree to—a contract known as a lease; when you take a job, you enter a contract of employment; any purchase of goods, services, or real estate involves some form of contract. Loans are evidenced by a type of contract known as a promissory note. Even the marital relationship is a type of contract.

This part of the book will examine the traditional elements of contract law—the so-called common law of contracts. Later parts will consider various special types of contracts, among them sales, commercial paper, secured transactions, and insurance. These specialized forms are probably more familiar to you than the basic form and may seem more timely and relevant. Keep in mind the fact that all of these specialized forms are merely variations of the basic form. The common law elements are present in each special contract; thus, you must understand those common law elements before you can properly utilize these specialized forms.

CHAPTER 8

An Introduction to the Law of Contracts

OUTLINE

THE IMPORTANCE OF CONTRACT LAW

Of all the aspects of law examined in this text, probably none is as significant overall or as pervasive in our lives as the law of contracts. Virtually every personal or business activity involves contract law: Charging a birthday gift on a credit card, buying and insuring a car, leasing an apartment, writing a check, paying for college, and working at an establishment covered by an employment agreement, for example. Even filling up our gasoline tanks involves international contract law, since we receive much of our oil as a result of international contracts.

The law of contracts affects our most mundane activities, as well as some rather sensational ones, such as _surrogacy_ contracts (whereby women agree contractually to have babies for infertile couples) or lawsuits between famous "live-in" couples involving _palimony_ (requests by one member of an unmarried couple that the other pay alimony or a similar form of financial support after the couple's breakup). In this chapter, we deal with broad categories of contracts and contractual situations. In later chapters we will consider many of these topics in more detail as we attempt to understand an area of the law that is as old as Moses yet as new as today's developments.

Commercial Law Contracts

Mercantile Having to do with business, commerce, or trade.

Free enterprise Freedom to conduct a legitimate business for profit.

When most of us think of the word _contracts_, we envision the **mercantile** world. Indeed, our system of **free enterprise** has historically stressed the importance of freedom of contract and a corresponding protection of contractual rights. It was not always so. Blackstone's _Commentaries on the Laws of England_, first published in 1756, devoted 380 pages to real property law but only 28 pages to contracts. Thus, to Blackstone the law of contracts apparently was a subdivision of the law of property rather than the independent branch of law as we know it today.[1]

Part of the reason for this perception lies in the historical development of contract law. Although always broadly a part of the common law, mercantile traditions grew out of the law merchant, which represented the accumulation of commercial customs from as early as Phoenician times. The mercantile courts were separate from courts of law, and the merchants (or guilds) administered their own rules and customs. Hence, the evolution of commercial law remained outside the mainstream of legal development until fairly late in English history, the end of the seventeenth century.[2] In the late 1800s, after the assimilation of the law merchant into the common law, several acts of Parliament dealt with commercial law subjects.

Not surprisingly, then, various legal bodies in the United States, influenced by these English precedents, penned a wide variety of statutes covering

---

[1]A. G. Guest, ed., _Anson's Law of Contracts_, 25th ed. (Oxford: Clarendon Press, 1979), p. 1.
[2]Paul Conway, _Outline of the Law of Contracts_, 3rd ed. (Irvington-on-Hudson, N.Y.: American Legal Publications, 1968), p. 10.

American commercial law (for example, the Uniform Negotiable Instruments Law and the Uniform Sales Act). By the 1930s several such acts existed. Because each state had not completely adopted these acts, however, commercial remedies differed from state to state. Moreover, these acts were already somewhat outmoded and thus not reflective of modern commercial practices. For these reasons, and especially to effect an integration of these contradictory statutes, in the 1940s the American Law Institute and the National Conference of Commissioners on Uniform State Laws began to prepare what we today call the Uniform Commercial Code.[3]

The UCC, as the Uniform Commercial Code is commonly known, revolutionized prior approaches to commercial transactions by viewing commercial transactions as a single subject of the law.[4] The drafters saw, for example, that a sale of goods may constitute one facet of such a transaction. They also realized that a check may be used for payment of the purchase price of the goods or that, alternatively, the seller may retain a **security interest** in the goods to ensure payment of the balance of the debt. An examination of the Uniform Commercial Code reveals articles on sales, **commercial paper,** bank deposits and collections, and **secured transactions,** which correspond roughly to the scenarios described above. The UCC has fulfilled its original goals of simplifying, clarifying, and modernizing the law governing commercial transactions; permitting the continued expansion of commercial practices through custom, usage, and agreement of the parties; and making uniform the law among the various jurisdictions (Section 1-102[2] and Comment 1). Louisiana, while it has incorporated some of the articles of the UCC into its commercial laws, is unique in that it has not wholly adopted the UCC. Most states' commercial statutes, with minor variations, have reproduced the UCC articles in their entirety. Excerpts from the Code are included in Appendix A.

In addition to the Uniform Commercial Code, the National Conference of Commissioners on Uniform State Laws has drafted other statutes for possible adoption by the states. Examples include the Uniform Partnership Act and the Uniform Consumer Credit Code, among others. These laws have regularized commercial transactions so that transactions from state to state will be more consistent with each other. Such uniformity fosters predictability of result without necessarily sacrificing the law's capacity to change when commercial practices dictate change. You will need to check your particular jurisdiction to see whether your state has adopted these uniform acts and codes or whether it instead relies on its own statutes to cover these legal areas.

Common Law Contracts

The existence of statutes concerned with commercial contract law should not overshadow the importance of common law contracts. Many doctrines regarding modern-day contracts stem from "judge-made" law, or decisions

---

Security interest An interest in personal property or fixtures that secures payment or performance of an obligation.

Commercial paper Negotiable instruments; checks, drafts, notes, and certificates of deposit; instruments that are used as credit instruments and/or as substitutes for money and that are governed by Article 3 of the UCC.

Secured transactions Credit arrangements, covered by Article 9 of the UCC, in which the creditor has a security interest in certain assets of the debtor.

---

[3]Bradford Stone, *Uniform Commercial Code in a Nutshell* (St. Paul, Minn.: West, 1975), pp. 1–2.

[4]Ibid., p. 3.

growing out of contractual disputes from earlier times. Contract disputes being decided on a daily basis in jurisdictions around the country significantly add to this body of precedents. In addition, even the UCC states that common law contract law supplements the UCC in those areas where the statute is silent. It is appropriate, then, that most of our discussion in the succeeding chapters will center around *common law* contract principles—that is, principles derived from the judgments and decrees of courts.

Definition of a Contract

As you would expect, there are many definitions for the word *contract*. In general, a *contract* is *a legally binding and legally enforceable promise, or set of promises, between two or more competent parties.* Put another way, a contract is "a promise or set of promises for the breach of which the law gives a remedy, or the performance of which the law in some way recognizes as a duty."[5] Most of us intuitively understand what a contract is. Still, situations exist that may at first glance appear to be contracts but are not.

For example, let's assume that you are a Rolling Stones fan. The Stones are in the United States for a concert tour. You are extremely anxious to attend a concert because, given Mick Jagger's age, you fear that this may be your last chance to see them. A friend promises you tickets to the show, and you are of course elated. Two days later, your friend calls to tell you he is taking an "old flame" instead of you. As you hang up, your anger and disappointment cause you to think about suing your friend. After all, you had an agreement, and he has broken a promise to you. You *deserve* to collect for the harm you have suffered.

Did your agreement give rise to a legally enforceable contract? Would a court protect your expectations and award you damages? The short answer is probably no. Most courts would see this situation as a breached social obligation, not a breached contractual obligation. Nevertheless, you may occasionally read of people suing in small claims courts for the expenses incurred in making plans for dates and finding that they have been stood up. If the plaintiffs win these "contract" actions (and sometimes they do), the results are generally overturned if appealed, because the more settled rule would call such situations broken social obligations, not breached contracts. Put another way, you should be aware that a court will not call all agreements "contracts."

Contrast this situation with one in which you call a Stones' ticket outlet, give the staff member your credit card number, and order two concert tickets. When you arrive at the box office days before the concert, you are informed that the tickets have been sold to someone else. Can you successfully sue this time? Perhaps you can, because this situation is not exactly a social obligation and seems instead to have created binding *economic* obligations on both sides. Thus, to protect your economic expectations, a court may call this a contract and award you damages. Hence, the part of the definition that alludes to a "legally enforceable" or "legally binding" agreement is quite significant be-

[5]*Restatement (Second) of Contracts,* Section 1 (1981).

cause it means that not every promise, agreement, or expectation is a contract. In essence, a contract is any agreement between two or more parties that a court will recognize as one that creates legally binding duties and obligations between the parties.

YOU BE THE JUDGE

> Kevin Ross attended Creighton University on an athletic scholarship from 1978-1982. Achieving only a "D" average, he used up his athletic eligibility without graduating from the university. After leaving Creighton, Ross attended remedial classes with grade school children. As a consequence, Ross subsequently sued Creighton for negligence (specifically, educational malpractice), negligent admission, and negligent infliction of emotional distress. In addition, Ross argued breach of contract based on his alleged promise to play basketball in exchange for Creighton's alleged promise to allow him meaningful participation in its academic program. Creighton also allegedly promised to provide tutors and other special assistance. He argued that, owing to Creighton's failure to live up to its promises, he had suffered damages in the form of educational deficiencies.
>
> The appeals court ruled against Ross on his three negligence theories. If you were the judge, how would you rule on the breach of contract claim? What are your views concerning the *ethics* of the parties?

Source: "Court: Some Education Claims OK," Randall Samborn, *The National Law Journal,* March 23, 1992, page 3.

Elements of a Contract

Given the law's emphasis on promises or mutual assent, it is not surprising that the first requirement for a valid contract is an *agreement*. Basically, an agreement consists of an offer and an acceptance of that offer. The law necessarily looks at the agreement from the viewpoint of a reasonably prudent person and asks whether such a person would believe that an offer and an acceptance had actually occurred.

Second, the agreement must be supported by *consideration*, something bargained for and given in exchange for a promise.

Third, the parties must have *capacity*, or the legal ability to contract.

Fourth, the contract must be based on the *genuine assent* of each party. If one party has procured the assent of the other person by fraud or duress, for example, courts may set the contract aside owing to the lack of genuine assent to the agreement by the disadvantaged party.

Public policy The general attitude of the public toward certain conduct; the public sense of morality, good conduct, and acceptable behavior to which citizens must conform.

Fifth, the subject matter of the contract must be *legal.* The legality of the bargain would be questionable, for instance, if the parties agreed to do something that would violate a statute or **public policy**.

Aqveement
Lonsideration
Capacity
Assent
Legal
Proper Form

Sixth, in some cases a contract must be in *proper form.* Despite the fact that courts ordinarily will enforce oral contracts (even though it is risky to contract orally because of the difficulties of trying to prove exactly what was said), some categories of contracts must be in writing to be legally effective.

In summary, to be valid, a contract must be (1) based on an agreement, (2) supported by consideration, (3) made by parties having the capacity to contract, (4) based on these parties' genuine assent, (5) grounded in a legal undertaking, and (6) expressed in proper form, if applicable. We will discuss each of these requirements in detail in succeeding chapters. Figure 8.1 shows the elements of a contract.

In the following case, the court considered many of these same concepts in reaching its decision.

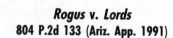

Rogus v. Lords
804 P.2d 133 (Ariz. App. 1991)

FACTS   David Lords, Marge Rogus, and Sylvia Waters were licensed real estate salespersons or brokers. All were members of the Mesa-Chandler-Tempe Board of Realtors (the Board). In 1985, Lords, representing landowners, solicited offers to purchase a certain parcel of real property from Sylvia Waters. Although Lords did not have a written listing agreement, he did have a verbal listing agreement from the owners. Waters later obtained a written offer from Walter Bush to purchase the property. The offer contained Bush's name, address, and phone number and provided for payment of a real estate commission of 6 percent. Rogus and Waters would receive one-half of the commission and Lords the other one-half. Waters gave the written offer to Lords, who submitted it to the owners. The owners then contacted Bush directly and negotiated a sale of the property to Bush on terms virtually identical to those contained in the original offer, except that the commission provision had been deleted. No real estate commission was ever paid in connection with Bush's purchase of the property. Rogus and Waters subsequently brought this breach of contract action against Lords to recover $66,000, the commission they would have received from Bush's original offer to purchase the property. Rogus and Waters based their lawsuit on the Board's Code of Ethics, which, in their interpretation, created a contractual relationship between real estate agents and would therefore allow them to sue Lords, the "listing" agent, for the real estate commission they had allegedly earned.

ISSUE   Did the obligations set forth in the Board's Code of Ethics give rise to a contractual relationship that would entitle Rogus and Waters to recover for breach of contract from a fellow member of the Board?

HOLDING   No. The realtor members intended the Board's Code of Ethics to constitute a noncontractual pledge of moral conduct rather than a contract that would give rise to enforceable rights between members.

REASONING   For an enforceable contract to exist, there must be an offer, an acceptance, consideration, and sufficient specification of terms so that a court can ascertain the obligations involved in the transaction. The requirement of certainty is relevant to the ultimate element of contract formation; that is, whether the parties have manifested assent or an intent to be bound. The language of the Code of Ethics—for example, "The term REALTOR has come to connote competency, fairness, and high integrity resulting from adherence to a lofty ideal of moral conduct in business relations. . . ."—constitutes evidence that the Board members intended to impose upon themselves a moral, not a contractual, obligation with respect to their relations with the public and one another. Moreover, in order to be binding, an agreement must be definite and certain so that a court can exactly fix the liability of the parties. Not only were the obligations set forth in the Code of Ethics generally aspirational in nature, but the Code also failed to include any terms providing for specific enforcement of ethical violations by an individual member against another member. Furthermore, the Code made no reference to the obligations assumed by the members. Therefore, this lack of specificity in the terms of the Code indicated that the parties never intended it to bind them contractually. Hence, in the absence of other evidence, the Code of Ethics did not constitute a contract between the parties that would enable Rogus and Waters to bring an action for damages against Lords.

FIGURE 8.1   Elements of a Contract

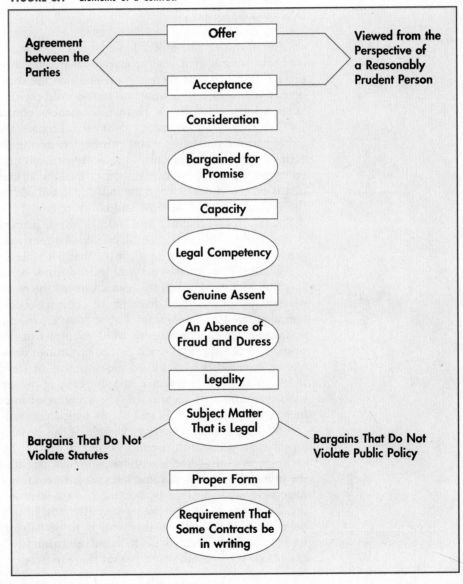

FROM STATUS TO CONTRACT AND BACK AGAIN

As mentioned earlier, the development of contract law occurred relatively late in English legal history. One reason for this stems from the social hierarchies set by the feudal society that prevailed throughout Europe between the eleventh and thirteenth centuries. In such a rigid, stratified society, each person occupied a special status or social position. Consequently, one's social circumstances determined the rights owed to one and the conduct expected of one. For example, feudal lords owed few duties to lowly serfs; but serfs owed their lives to their lords.

Imagine the disruptive effect contract law, which calls for the performance of mutual duties and obligations, would have had on such a social order. It is not surprising, then, that property law assumed foremost importance during these times. If a serf were the property of the lord, courts did not have to bother with protecting what the state would consider the serf's rather trivial expectations. Accordingly, the development of contract law was unnecessary.

Yet, as England became a commercial center, the law merchant and contracts became more important. Moreover, during the social and political reforms of the late eighteenth and nineteenth centuries, the rise of capitalistic ethics brought with it demands for freedom of contract. This political emphasis on the importance of the individual and of private property accelerated the growth of what we now call contract law. To a largely agrarian society dedicated to self-reliance and individualism, protection of expectations and enforcement of obligations took on added importance. The demise of a status-oriented society ushered in a contractually oriented social order.

Ironically, as an aftermath of the industrial revolution, the twentieth century has witnessed numerous restrictions on the nineteenth century's adoption of virtually unrestricted freedom of contract. Legislatures and courts have curtailed freedom of contract. Labor laws, environmental protection statutes, and consumer enactments are a few examples of how lawmakers have lately restricted freedom of contract. Similarly, through common law decisions, courts have hampered the continued development of freedom of contract by protecting individuals who have little bargaining power even *after* these persons have consummated a contract. The doctrine of *unconscionability,* which we mentioned in Chapter 1, and about which you will learn more in Chapters 10 and 13, provides a perfect example of this protection. Suppose two parties have bargained. If, in the court's opinion, one of them (usually a corporation or business entity) had grossly superior bargaining power, or leverage, over the other, the court will sometimes set such contracts aside on the grounds of unconscionability—that is, because *the contract is shockingly oppressive or grossly unfair to one of the parties*. (Do not, however, make the mistake of believing *you* can rely on this remedy to get out of each and every contract for which you belatedly wish to avoid responsibility!) Such developments have convinced some commentators that this progression shows an interesting circularity; that is, a movement from "status" to "contract" and back to "status" again.

CLASSIFICATIONS OF CONTRACTS

Contracts can be categorized or distinguished in various ways. These categories are not always mutually exclusive, and several different terms may apply to the same contract. For example, suppose a restaurant orders produce and meat from its supplier at set prices, and the supplier promises to deliver on a predetermined schedule. The understanding between these parties invokes several categories of contracts simultaneously: In short, this agreement is an informal, bilateral, valid, express contract.

Formal Versus Informal Contracts

The distinction between formal and informal contracts comes from the method used in creating the contract. As you may recall, in early common law times, the contracting parties generally engaged in certain formalities (hence the term *formal*). To be valid, for example, a contract had to be under seal; that is, the document had to be closed with wax and imprinted with one's insignia, or distinctive mark. Nowadays, very few contracts have to be under seal because most jurisdictions have abolished the need for certain classes of private contracts or instruments to be under seal. A seal, if used, does not affect the legal validity of most contracts. This trend toward eliminating sealed, or formal, contracts demonstrates that the need for ceremonies and formalities to ensure validity has largely passed. The more common category of contracts today consists of *informal* (or simple) contracts. In these, the emphasis is not on the form or mode of expression but instead on giving effect to the promises of the parties. Informal contracts do not require a seal. Such contracts may be either oral or written and in fact may even be implied from the conduct of the parties.

Unilateral Versus Bilateral Contracts

As you have learned, every contract has at least two contracting parties. The person who makes an offer (called the *offeror*) generally promises to do something or to pay a certain amount if the person to whom the offer has been made (called the *offeree*) will comply with the offeror's request. Usually, then, in return for this promise, the offeror demands a certain act or a certain promise of the offeree as acceptance. The form of the acceptance demanded determines whether the contract is a *unilateral contract (promise on one side only)* or a *bilateral contract (promises on both sides)*.

If the offeror promises to pay the offeree $50 for plowing the offeror's garden, this contract is unilateral. Only one person (the offeror) has promised to do anything. The offeree accepts the offer by doing the requested act (that is, plowing). By *performing* the act, the offeree *accepts* the offer.

In contrast, if one party (the promisor) makes a promise and the other party (the promisee) accepts the offer by promising to do the requested act, a bilateral contract exists because there are promises on both sides of the agreement. To use the same example, assume the offeror promises to pay the offeree $50 if the offeree will promise to plow the offeror's garden. When the offeree accepts by so promising, an exchange of promises has occurred, and a bilateral contract has resulted. Try to apply these concepts to the following case.

Kuhnhoffer v. Naperville
Community School District 203
758 F. Supp. 468 (N.D. Ill. 1991)

FACTS   From 1979 to 1988, the Naperville Community School District 203 (the School District) employed Larry Kuhnhoffer as a school bus driver. At the end of each school year, Kuhnhoffer received a letter from the School District thanking him for his work during the year and inviting him to return as a bus driver for the following year. On 27 May 1988, Kuhnhoffer received the following letter from the School District:

> Dear Mr. Kuhnhoffer:
>
> Thank you for your work for Naperville students during the 1987–88 school year. We appreciate your efforts and recognize the important role which you play in the District's educational program.
>
> Based on your performance this year and the staff needs which we anticipate at this time, we are looking forward to your return to your position for the 1988–89 school year.
>
> I hope that you will find your summer to be enjoyable and rewarding. If I can be of any assistance, please do not hesitate to call me.
>
> Sincerely,
>
> (signed) Dr. Michael L. Kiser
>
> Assistant Superintendent for Personnel

On 26 July 1988, just two months after Kuhnhoffer had received that letter, the Naperville Police Department arrested him for driving under the influence of alcohol. Kuhnhoffer refused to submit to a Breathalyzer test upon his arrest. Shortly after Kuhnhoffer's arrest, the Office of the Illinois Secretary of State (the Secretary of State) notified the Illinois State Board of Education (the Board of Education) that Kuhnhoffer would begin serving a six-month summary suspension of his driving privileges on 10 September 1988. The Board of Education, in turn, notified the DuPage County Educational Service Region that Kuhnhoffer's bus driver's permit would be suspended as of September 10 and that he would not be eligible to reapply for his permit until 11 March 1992. Dr. Kiser, the assistant superintendent of the School District, received the same notification from the Board of Education. Since the 1988–1989 school year began on 25 August 1988, all school bus drivers were to report to work on or before 24 August 1988. Approximately two weeks before this date, Kiser informed Kuhnhoffer that, owing to Kuhnhoffer's DUI arrest, the School District could not hire him as a school bus driver. Kuhnhoffer sued the School District for breach of contract.

ISSUE   Did the 27 May letter sent by Kiser to Kuhnhoffer, coupled with the parties' course of dealing over the previous nine years, create an implied contract of employment?

HOLDING   No. The School District's offer contemplated the formation of a unilateral contract. Because an offer for a unilateral contract is accepted by performance, no contract could result between Kuhnhoffer and the School District until he commenced performance. Without a valid license, Kuhnhoffer could not fully perform his end of the bargain; hence, no contract ever came into existence.

REASONING According to Kuhnhoffer, the 27 May letter, coupled with the parties' course of dealing over the previous nine years, was sufficient to create an implied contract of employment. While Kuhnhoffer was correct in asserting that express or implied contracts may create property interests, Kuhnhoffer's argument presupposed that the parties had an existing employment agreement. However, the School District denied that a contract had ever been formed. It contended that the 27 May letter had constituted not an offer but an "invitation" for possible future employment. This distinction, though merely a semantic one, in these circumstances became irrelevant because whether or not the letter constituted an offer of employment, the School District had properly revoked its "offer" prior to acceptance. Moreover, this case involves the principles associated with unilateral contracts. A unilateral contract arises from a promise made by one party in exchange for the other party's act or performance. Here, the School District offered to employ Kuhnhoffer in exchange for Kuhnhoffer's performance; the offer did not solicit a return promise from Kuhnhoffer (and none was given). Because Kuhnhoffer could accept the offer for a unilateral contract only by performance, the School District was not contractually bound until Kuhnhoffer commenced performance. Accordingly, the School District remained free to revoke the offer any time prior to acceptance. After learning of the six-month suspension of Kuhnhoffer's license, the School District promptly notified Kuhnhoffer that he would not be hired as a bus driver for the 1988–1989 school year. This action, which constituted a revocation of the offer, was certainly justified. After all, school bus drivers must have a valid driver's license. Kuhnhoffer could not maintain a bus driver's permit if his driver's license had been suspended. Without a valid driver's license, Kuhnhoffer could not fully perform his end of the bargain and thus could not accept the School District's offer of a unilateral contract.

Valid, Voidable, Void, and Unenforceable Contracts

A *valid contract* is one that *is legally binding and enforceable*.

In contrast, a *voidable contract* is one that *may be either affirmed or rejected at the option of one or more of the contracting parties*. The agreement is nonetheless valid until it is rejected or disaffirmed. For example, if a person buys a car in the belief that it has been driven only 50,000 miles when in actuality it has 250,000 miles on it, that contract may be voidable on the basis of fraud or misrepresentation. However, the contract is valid and fully enforceable *until* the buyer disaffirms it.

Void agreements, though they may outwardly appear to be contracts, can never have any legal effect. They *are unenforceable and never become contracts because they lack one of the essential elements of a contract*. An agreement to murder someone is void and cannot be enforced by a court because it lacks the element of legality.

On the other hand, it is possible to have a seemingly binding contract that *will not be given effect in a court of law*. Suppose, for example, that the contract involved is one that must be in writing (such as a contract for a sale of goods priced at $500 or more); if the contract is oral, it will be *unenforceable*. Note that otherwise the contract appears to meet all the criteria of a valid contract.

Express Versus Implied Contracts

An *express contract* is one in which *the parties set forth their intentions specifically and definitely*, either in writing or orally. Most contracts are of this type.

An *implied contract* is one that *must be discerned or inferred from the actions or conduct of the parties*. Even though the parties should have expressed their intentions more clearly, it is still possible to conclude that a true contract exists. We often call these agreements *contracts implied in fact* because, based on the facts, it is possible to say that despite the absence of explicit language to this effect, the parties intended to create a contract.

Assume, for example, that two parties have had a well-known, years' long understanding that grain will be accepted when delivered. If one party takes grain to the elevator and the elevator refuses to accept it, the facts of the parties' prior, long-standing relationship and their previous conduct may allow a court to enforce this agreement as a contract implied in fact. Practically speaking, many agreements have express provisions and also include terms that must be discerned from the actions of the parties. In short, a given contract may not fall neatly into one or the other of these categories. In the case that follows, the judge refused to find either an express contract or a contract implied in fact.

Fletcher, Barnhardt & White, Inc. v. Matthews
397 S.E.2d 81 (N.C. App. 1990)

FACTS   Fletcher, Barnhardt & White, Inc. (the firm) sells individualized promotional materials to businesses throughout the Southeast. In October 1984, the firm hired Jeffrey Matthews as a sales representative. The firm paid Matthews a base salary during his first year of employment plus commissions that he earned. After his first year of employment, the firm compensated Matthews solely on the basis of the commissions earned. After being on straight commission salary for approximately six months, Matthews approached the firm and requested permission to draw against his commissions. A "draw" is an arrangement in which a sales representative receives a predetermined amount of money each pay period. Thus, in a month when Matthews earned few commissions, he would receive the set amount of pay; and in a month when commissions exceeded the draw, the firm would retain the excess to repay any deficits incurred during months in which the draw exceeded the commissions earned. The firm initially set Matthews's draw at $1,750 per two-week pay period and increased this amount in May 1986 to $1,950 per pay period. Along with his paycheck, Matthews received a monthly statement that advised him of his commissions for that month versus the draw he was receiving. In months when his commissions exceeded his draw, the firm applied the excess to any deficits that had accrued. In October 1987, Matthews began the initial steps to form a business to compete with the firm. On 7 February 1988, Matthews went to the home of Mr. Fletcher, the president of the firm, and informed Fletcher of his intention to leave the firm's employ and begin operating his own company. Matthews, after that exchange, indicated that he would pay back the money Fletcher, in behalf of the firm, had demanded. After receiving no payments from Matthews, on 18 May 1989 the firm sued him to recover the deficit in his draw account.

ISSUE   Had the firm and Matthews entered into a contract that made Matthews personally liable for the deficit in his draw account?

HOLDING   No. The parties had not entered into any agreement concerning the consequences of a salesperson's terminating his or her employment with a deficit owed to the firm.

REASONING   When a material term of a contract is absent, the agreement is not legally binding on the parties. The failure of the parties to consider whether Matthews might be personally liable for the excess advances over commissions indicated the absence of an express contract. Furthermore, Matthews's statements that he would repay the money to the firm occurred *after* he had terminated his employment; thus, the statements were unenforceable because they were not supported by consideration. Finally, the parties' failure to agree at any point that Matthews would be personally liable for the deficits in the draw account, besides indicating the lack of an express contract, also showed that no implied contract in fact had ever come into existence. Hence, in the absence of either an express contract or an implied contract in fact concerning Matthews's personal liability, the firm could not recover the deficits in the draw account. Rather, the firm should have protected its interests by executing a contract covering these matters, limiting the amount of the draw, requiring a promissory note from Matthews, or firing him.

Executory Versus Executed Contracts

An *executory contract* is one in which *some condition or promise has not yet been completed by one or more of the parties*. For instance, if one person agrees to buy a television set from Honest John's, the contract is executory; the television still has to be delivered and the buyer must pay for it. If the buyer pays for the television prior to delivery, the contract is likewise executory, although technically the buyer has executed his or her part of the contract.

As you may have surmised, an *executed contract* is one in which *all conditions or promises have been fully completed or performed*. In the last example, when Honest John's delivers the television set, the contract will be executed. Neither party has anything further to do.

Quasi Contracts Versus Contracts Implied in Fact

Unjust enrichment   Benefits unfairly received or retained by a person and to which the person is not entitled unless the person pays the reasonable value of them.

One type of implied contract deserves special attention. This is a contract implied in law, or a *quasi contract*. Lawsuits alleging quasi contract as the basis for recovery may also be called suits for **unjust enrichment**. Under certain circumstances, the law will "create" a contract for the parties, despite their wishes and intentions, in order to prevent the unjust enrichment of one party. In these circumstances, even though it may be clear that the parties did not actually contract with each other, the parties will be treated as if they had contracted. A *contract implied in fact,* which was discussed earlier, is also an implied contract. It differs from a contract implied in law in that sufficient facts or evidence of conduct exists for a court to find that the parties actually meant to contract with each other. Their transaction was perhaps a bit sloppy; that is, we might wish for more explicit language. But we can with some certainty conclude that the parties intended a binding agreement between themselves. A contract implied in fact is thus a "true" contract. In contrast, a *contract implied in law* is *a fiction engineered by a court so as to effect justice between two parties*. Unlike a contract implied in fact, this is not a "true" contract, hence the name quasi contract.

An illustration should help to clarify further the difference between a contract implied in fact and a contract implied in law. Assume that Mattie is sitting on her front porch when a painting crew appears. Actually, the painting crew has the wrong address (111 Riverside instead of 1111 Riverside). Mattie nevertheless allows the crew to paint her house and later tries to argue that since she had not asked for the services, she should not have to pay for them. To prevent the unjust enrichment of Mattie at the painters' expense, most

Detriment Any loss or harm suffered by a person or property.

courts would force Mattie to pay the painters for the benefit she has received (a newly painted house) or, put another way, for the **detriment** suffered by the painters (the cost of their supplies, services, and so on). Mattie would be liable in quasi contract or a contract implied in law only for the reasonable value of the services rendered; the painters cannot "gouge" her by charging, after the fact, an exorbitant price. A contract implied in fact does not exist here because nothing in the facts suggests that Mattie and the painting company had dealt with each other before the crew arrived at Mattie's house. Evidence of an intention to contract, however sloppy the execution of the contract, would have made this a true contract, or a contract implied in fact. Instead, the court *creates* a contract—a quasi contract or contract implied in law—to prevent the unjust enrichment of Mattie.

Do not be misled into believing that every time one person receives a benefit, a quasi-contractual recovery will be possible. Remember that the policy underlying such recoveries is the avoidance of injustice. Mattie has to pay because she knowingly allowed the painters to proceed. Had she not been present, however, the painters would probably be unable to hold Mattie liable because the services were conferred on her as a result of the painters' negligence or mistake. (They had come to the wrong house.) In these circumstances, it would not be inequitable to allow Mattie to retain the benefits bestowed on her. By the same token, a person who confers a gift (for example, let us assume Mattie's brother contracts with a painting company to redo Mattie's dilapidated house as a surprise for her) or one who volunteers a service (a neighbor who decides to paint Mattie's house while Mattie is away for the weekend) will not be able to recover later from Mattie in quasi contract either. The same will be true of a person who buys supplies in a mistaken belief there is a contract, or who incurs foreseeable difficulties and later tries to make the recipients of the services pay for these extra costs or services on a quasi-contractual theory. Still, it is wise to remember that courts can, in a given circumstance, create a contract in order to avoid injustice.

Analyze the following case in light of these principles.

Perkins v. Daugherty
722 S.W.2d 907 (Ky. App. 1987)

FACTS   Perkins, in partnership with Kindred Homes, Inc. (Kindred), began developing Crosswoods Subdivision. Daugherty, a licensed engineer, was retained to do the engineering and contracting work for the subdivision. There was no written contract between Daugherty and the developers; rather, he worked by verbal agreement. Perkins and Kindred later dissolved their partnership, each taking a portion of the property. Daugherty, however, continued to work on Kindred's portion of the property and planned to complete his work on Perkins's property, as well, after finishing Kindred's. Daugherty still had no written contract with either Perkins or Kindred. Daugherty subsequently worked on Perkins's property until it became apparent that Perkins had obtained the help of another engineer for the

Lien A legal charge or encumbrance against property.

Counterclaimed Presented a cause of action in opposition to the plaintiff's.

project. At that time, Daugherty sent Perkins a bill for $18,256.52. When Perkins did not pay the amount due, Daugherty filed an engineer's **lien** against Perkins's property. This action, in turn, led Perkins to sue Daugherty for damages allegedly incurred by the wrongful filing of the lien. Daugherty **counterclaimed** for the amount of the bill, plus interest on the lien.

ISSUE Should Daugherty receive compensation for the work done for Perkins on the basis of either a contract implied in fact or a contract implied in law?

HOLDING Yes. Daugherty should receive compensation based on a contract implied in law.

REASONING The evidence was insufficient to show a contract implied in fact. However, Daugherty could recover on a contract implied in law owing to Perkins's unjust enrichment. A contract implied in law is not based on a contract but is a legal fiction invented to permit a recovery where the law of natural justice says there should be a recovery as if promises were made. Courts may allow such a recovery regardless of the intentions of the parties and may even, in some cases, violate such intentions. Perkins's requests that Daugherty begin working for him as soon as possible, Perkins's knowledge that Daugherty had begun the work, and the substantially lower fee charged Perkins by the second engineer as a result of Daugherty's previous efforts entitled Daugherty to an award based on a contract implied in law.

Table 8.1 shows the different types of contracts.

TABLE 8.1 Classifications of Contracts

TYPE OF CONTRACT	DEFINITION	EXAMPLE
Formal	One created by certain rituals, ceremonies, or formalities.	A contract that requires notarization, such as a transfer of an automobile title to another person. *seal*
Informal	One created through oral or written statements or through the parties' conduct; needs no special rituals.	An oral contract to buy a used compact disk player costing $400.
Unilateral	One created by a promise given in exchange for an act.	A contract in which the borrower agrees to pay back the $400 consumer loan obtained from a bank.
Bilateral	One created by a promise given in exchange for another promise.	A contract in which one person promises to sell her dental equipment and another promises to buy the equipment.
Valid	One that manifests all the essential elements of a contract.	A contract to buy a car from a dealership.
Voidable	One that manifests all the essential elements of a contract and is legally binding unless disaffirmed by one or more of the contracting parties.	A contract to sell a termite-ridden house when the seller has knowledge of the extensive termite damage.
Void	One that lacks the essential elements of a contract.	A contract in which a lender charges the borrower a 40-percent rate of interest on a loan.

TABLE 8.1   continued

TYPE OF CONTRACT	DEFINITION	EXAMPLE
Unenforceable	One that manifests the essential elements of a contract but will not be given effect by a court of law.	An oral contract to guarantee the payment of another person's debts if that person fails to pay.
Express	One created by the parties' setting out their intentions specifically and definitely.	A contract that lists the price, the terms of the sale, the delivery date, and other details regarding the purchase of a car.
Implied	One discerned or inferred from the actions or conduct of the parties.	
• Implied in fact	Despite the absence of explicit language, the parties intended to contract with each other; a true contract.	A contract consisting of an offer to give someone an heirloom upon her marriage. On her wedding day, the bride asks for the heirloom.
• Implied in law	Contract created by a court for the parties, despite their wishes and intentions, in order to avoid injustice and/or the unjust enrichment of one party.	A contract to provide landscaping around a home in a development. When the homeowner fails to pay, a court orders the owner of the development to pay the landscaper because of the enhanced value of the development.
Executory	One in which some promise or obligation remains unfulfilled.	A contract to sell a horse, saddle, and bridle. The seller forgets to bring the saddle on the date of delivery.
Executed	One in which all parties have completed their promises or obligations under the terms of the agreement.	A contract to buy a computer for $2,000 with delivery effected by the seller in exchange for the buyer's giving a certified check for $2,000 at the time of delivery.

SUMMARY

Probably no area of the law affects us as often as the law of contracts. Commercial law, especially the Uniform Commercial Code's integration of older statutes and common law rules, has become increasingly important in the United States. For the first time many statutes exist that attempt to harmonize areas of the law that previously varied from state to state. Besides statutes, the common law has also spawned numerous contract principles that affect the legal environment of business. Although the word *contract* has many definitions, a common one states that a contract is a legally binding and legally enforceable promise or set of promises between two or more competent parties.

To have a valid contract, six requirements are necessary: (1) an agreement, (2) supported by consideration, (3) made by parties having the capacity to contract, (4) based on these parties' genuine assent, (5) grounded in a legal undertaking, and (6) expressed in proper form, if applicable. Historically, contracts were of minor importance because a feudal social order was uninterested in protecting parties' expectations. With the advent of freedom of contract and rising industrialism, contract law had outstripped property law in significance by the nineteenth century. Ironically, today the law appears to be swinging back to a concern with status, as evidenced by protective statutes and common law decisions. Contracts may be classified as formal or informal; unilateral or bilateral; valid, voidable, void, or unenforceable; express or implied; and executed or executory. These categories are not necessarily mutually exclusive. A contract implied in fact consists of evidence of sufficient facts or conduct from which a court can conclude that the parties intended a binding agreement between themselves. A contract implied in fact is thus a true contract. A quasi contract, or contract implied in law, is not a true contract. It is a different type of implied contract in which a court will create a contract for the parties, despite their wishes and intentions, in order that justice may be served. However, not every situation in which a benefit has been conferred gives rise to a quasi contract.

DISCUSSION QUESTIONS

1. Define the term *contract*.
2. Distinguish between a contractual obligation and a social obligation.
3. Name and define the six requirements for a valid contract.
4. Why do some commentators state that the history of contract law has swung from status to contract and back again?
5. Explain the following categories of contracts: (1) formal, (2) informal, (3) unilateral, (4) bilateral, (5) valid, (6) voidable, (7) void, (8) unenforceable, (9) express, (10) implied, (11) executory, and (12) executed.
6. What are the legal requirements for showing a quasi contract?

7. What is the Uniform Commercial Code, and why is it important?
8. Suppose Joan asks the bank for a loan. What kind of a contract would result from the bank's granting her this loan?
9. A contract involving an interest in land (such as a contract for the sale of a house) must be in writing. What is the legal effect of an oral contract in this situation?
10. What is the difference between a contract implied in fact and a contract implied in law?

CASE PROBLEMS

1. Michael and Mary Dursteler entered into a written contract to sell their mink ranch to Michael's brother, Dennis, and his wife, Gloria. The contract provided for a down payment of $10,000 and periodic payments thereafter. The parties also agreed to establish an interim partnership to operate the business while the buyers became acquainted with mink ranching. Within a few months, the parties found themselves at odds over various issues that the contract had not addressed, including how the partnership would initially raise the money to run the ranch, how the buyers would secure food for the mink, and how the partnership would re-

port its income and expenses. Was there an enforceable contract between the parties? If there was none, could the buyers nonetheless sue the sellers for the value of the benefits the buyers had conferred on the sellers (e.g., the $10,000 down payment and $850 in feed)? (*Dursteler v. Dursteler,* 697 P.2d 1244 [Idaho App. 1985].)

2. Lorena G. Rouse sued Peoples Natural Gas Company (Peoples) for breach of an implied employment contract. Although there was no written employment contract between Rouse and Peoples, Rouse argued that a contract implied in fact arose from certain provisions in Peoples's employment manual and from Peoples's prior conduct, including Peoples's promoting her, giving her positive performance evaluations, and increasing her salary. Rouse contended that Peoples's termination of her employment with the company was not in accordance with the procedures set out in the employment manual and thus represented a breach of Peoples's employment contract with Rouse. Could the terms of an employment manual form the basis for a contract implied in fact? (*Rouse* v. *Peoples Natural Gas Company,* 605 F. Supp. 230 [D. Kan. 1985].)

3. During a heat wave, Celeste Ahern found that her air conditioner, though still running, was failing to cool her home. She picked a service person, James M. Knecht, out of the Yellow Pages based on his advertisement, which stressed honesty. After arriving with his helper, Knecht gave Mrs. Ahern the following quotation for the work he needed to do: making the service call of $69 combined with the $85 charge for diagnosing problems in the system ($154); raising and leveling the condenser and slab ($210); wet washing the condenser and coils ($138); checking, cleaning, and tightening all electrical connections ($69); leak checking eight service connections with a leak detection instrument and stopping the obvious leak at the condenser with a suction nut and seal cap ($72); and installing instruments for monitoring the coolant and adding all required freon to bring the unit back up to service ($119). The total amount quoted to Mrs. Ahern (to her amazement) equaled $762. When Mrs. Ahern told Knecht that she needed to leave the house to attend to other business, he told her that he required payment at the time the work was done. Therefore, Mrs. Ahern agreed to prepare a check in the amount of $762, which she left with Knecht. After she departed, Knecht and his helper raised and leveled the condenser and slab merely by shoveling several inches of landscaping gravel (taken from Mrs. Ahern's patio) under the slab. Moreover, during the process of adding

the freon, Knecht apparently further disabled the unit by mistakenly switching the compressor's wires. Consequently, Mrs. Ahern hired another service person, who fixed the unit properly for $72. Mrs. Ahern and her husband subsequently sued to recover the $762 paid to Knecht. What grounds could a court use to set aside the agreement with Knecht? (*Ahern* v. *Knecht,* 563 N.E.2d 787 [Ill. App. 1990].)

4. Dr. Chanda took twenty-eight rolls of already developed Super-8 movie film to a Fotomat outlet in Melbourne, Florida, in April, 1980, in order to have the film images transferred to videotape as a way of saving the images, which were deteriorating. This film contained depictions of his honeymoon, his graduation from medical school, his son's birth, and other events of great sentimental value to Chanda. The Fotomat clerk prepared an order form that contained a conspicuous, bold-type statement that limited Fotomat's liability for loss, damage, or delay during film processing to the replacement cost of a nonexposed roll of film and/or a blank cassette of similar size. Fotomat expressly disclaimed liability for all other loss or damage. Dr. Chanda read this clause, asked the clerk about it, and signed it. The film was later lost and never found. Dr. Chanda sued for damages, arguing that the limitation of liability provision was unconscionable. Should the court set this contract aside on the grounds of unconscionability? (*Fotomat Corporation of Florida* v. *Chanda,* 464 So.2d 626 [Fla. App. 1985].)

5. Arduini was a tenured teacher who had begun his duties for the 1979–1980 school year on 27 August 1979. On 13 September 1979, Arduini received a "contractual continued service notification" that stated his salary for the 1979–1980 school year and included a copy of a liquidated damages policy adopted by the school board on 6 August 1979. This policy allowed the school district to deduct 4 percent of the contract salary as liquidated damages from the pay of any teacher who resigned on his or her own initiative during the school year. When Arduini resigned from his position on 19 October 1979, the school board, in accordance with this policy, withheld 4 percent of Arduini's salary. Arduini sued, arguing that he was not bound by this liquidated damages policy because it was not part of the contract between him and the school board. The school board contended that the liquidated damages clause was part of a unilateral contract formed between Arduini and the board when he began performance of the act contemplated by the contract (commencing his

teaching duties). According to the board, Arduini thus had accepted the contract and the liquidated damages clause some time after 13 September 1979, when he had received official notice of the policy. Who was correct? (*Arduini* v. *Board of Education of Pontiac Township High School*, 441 N.E.2d 73 [Ill. 1985].)

6   Mary Dobos was admitted to Boca Raton Community Hospital with a condition serious enough to cause her doctor to order around-the-clock nursing care. The hospital, on Dobos's doctor's orders, asked Nursing Care Services, Inc., to perform nursing services for two weeks while Dobos was in the hospital and for a second two-weeks' period while Dobos was at home. Mrs. Dobos, who was mentally alert during the at-home period, later argued that she should not be liable for Nursing Care Services, Inc.'s fees because she had neither signed a written contract nor orally agreed to be liable for these services. Should Dobos be liable for the $3,723.90 in fees, and, if so, under what theory? (*Nursing Care Services, Inc.* v. *Dobos*, 380 So.2d 516 [Fla. App. 1980].)

7   Michelle Marvin alleged that in 1964 she and Lee Marvin had entered into an oral agreement that while they lived together, they would share their earnings and property and hold themselves out to the public as husband and wife. She took Marvin's name and allegedly agreed to give up her career as an entertainer and singer in order to devote her time to Lee as a companion and homemaker. She asserted that in return Lee had agreed to provide her with financial support for the rest of her life. Michelle and Lee lived together until 1970, when he asked her to leave his household. Upon Lee's subsequent refusal to provide further support for her, Michelle sued him for one-half of the property acquired during their relationship. Could one party to a non-marital relationship sue the other for a distribution of property in the absence of an express contract if the parties' conduct demonstrated an implied contract or some other tacit understanding between them? (*Marvin* v. *Marvin*, 557 P.2d 106 [Cal. 1976].)

8   Jan Victor Hirschmann, the assistant chief of medicine at the Veterans Administration (VA) Medical Center in Seattle, Washington, submitted a request for a twelve-month extended leave for educational purposes on 8 December 1983. The request included six months' leave with full pay for training in London, England. Questions arose within the VA as to whether it should pay for leaves involving training outside the United States. Dr. Hirschmann eventually took the leave without pay from September, 1984, through September, 1985, and then sued the VA for the six months' pay he claimed the VA had arbitrarily and capriciously withheld from him. Did the United States Claims Court have jurisdiction to hear Hirschmann's complaint under the Tucker Act, which states that the Claims Court has jurisdiction to "render judgment upon any claim against the United States founded either upon the Constitution, or any act of Congress or any regulation of an executive department, or upon any express or implied contract with the United States"? (*Hirschmann* v. *U.S.*, 11 Cl. Ct. 338 (1986].)

9   The Strupps had borrowed $68,500 from People's Bank & Trust Company (People's) for use in their farming operations. The Strupps had promised to repay the loan out of their 1980 crop harvest. But owing to a drought in 1980, the Strupps had defaulted on part of this loan. However, as a result of this drought, they became eligible for a Farmers Home Administration (FmHA) disaster emergency loan. The Strupps hoped such a loan would give them sufficient funds to operate their farm for the 1981 growing season and also allow them to pay off the loan on which they had defaulted. An FmHA official assured the Strupps that they were eligible for such an emergency loan and furthermore that they would be able to get an "interim loan" from a commercial lender that would permit them to begin their 1981 plantings while the FmHA processed their loan. People's agreed to become this "interim lender" based on several phone conversations with FmHA officials in April and June. In reliance on these agreements, People's advanced $72,851.88 to the Strupps. During the summer, the Strupps began divorce proceedings. As a result of these marital problems, Mr. Strupp deeded back to the original owner a farm he had been buying on a land contract because he decided to give up farming. The FmHA then refused to close the emergency loan because the FmHA had intended to use this farm to secure the Strupps' repayment of the loan. The FmHA soon afterward called People's to advise it that the FmHA loan would not be closed owing to the unavailability of the land as security. After the FmHA's cancellation of the Strupps' loan, People's sued the government for the amount extended to the Strupps in the interim loan. Had People's dealings with the FmHA provided the basis for the Claims Court's jurisdiction over claims brought against the government for either an express or implied in fact contract? (*People's Bank & Trust Co.* v. *U.S.*, 11 Cl. Ct. 554 [1987].)

10   On 12 May 1978, Siders purchased a home from

the Odaks. She also executed an option agreement permitting her to purchase an additional 1.3 acres of adjoining land at any time within three years from the date of purchase on giving thirty days' written notice. Hence, the option was valid until 12 May 1981. In February, 1981, Siders orally notified the Odaks of her intent to exercise this option. The parties later disagreed about whether the Odaks had waived the requirement of a written notice. Nonetheless, the Odaks ultimately fused to sell Siders the additional acreage. When Siders sued to have the optioned land conveyed to her, the Odaks contended that the option agreement was a unilateral contract that could be accepted only by full performance (i.e., the actual purchase of the land) prior to the expiration date of 12 May 1981. Were the Odaks correct? (*Siders* v. *Odaks,* 513 N.Y.S.2d 549 [N.Y. App. Div. 1987].)

CHAPTER 9

Contractual Agreement: Mutual Assent

OUTLINE

THE FIRST STEP IN CONTRACT FORMATION

Agreement is the essence of a contract. Once there has been a *valid offer* by the offeror (the person making the offer) and a *valid acceptance* by the offeree (the person to whom the offer is made), we are well on our way to having a legally binding contract, because there are generally few problems with consideration, capacity, genuine assent, legality, and proper form, the remaining requirements for a contract. On the other hand, precisely because these two aspects of contract formation are so important, courts will closely examine the words and conduct of the parties to determine whether a **bona fide** offer and acceptance are indeed present. From common law times, numerous rules have developed for checking the authenticity of the offer and the acceptance. Broadly speaking, under these rules it is fairly difficult to contract, because courts require rather clear-cut statements that the parties are freely and voluntarily entering into a particular agreement. Conversely, under the Uniform Commercial Code, a court can more easily infer a bona fide offer and acceptance from the conduct of the parties, even if the parties have omitted terms like price, mode of payment, or mode of delivery. In this chapter, we discuss the reasons for these developments.

Bona fide In good faith; honest; without deceit; innocent.

MUTUAL ASSENT

The assent of both parties to the agreement is a requirement of the initial phase of contract formation. This assent must be mutual, and the parties must agree to exactly the same terms. In short, both parties must actually intend to be bound to the terms embodied in the offer and acceptance. Without mutual assent, there can be no agreement.

THE OBJECTIVE THEORY OF CONTRACTS

Given the necessity for mutual assent, the question of how to judge whether the parties have mutually consented to the transaction naturally arises. If you are in a particularly mischievous mood, you may say to a friend, "Tom, I'll let you buy my stereo outfit for $100; that's the offer." Since Tom knows the components are worth at least $1,000, Tom quickly says, "I'll take it." Does this exchange constitute a valid offer and acceptance? Will you have to sell the stereo, or will you be allowed to say that you were kidding and did not intend to make an offer?

Common law rules tell us that the offeror must exhibit a clear and present intent to offer. You fairly straightforwardly enumerated the terms of the offer,

Objective Capable of being observed and verified without being distorted by personal feelings and prejudices.

Subjective Capable of being observed and verified through individual feelings and emotions.

it seems. Would it nevertheless be apparent from your statement that you were only kidding?

The law determines whether or not a valid offer exists by an **objective** standard. To decide whether an offer has been made, common law requires a court or a jury to put itself in the offeree's place (that is, in Tom's shoes) to ascertain if a reasonable offeree would believe that you were serious in offering the stereo at this price. Since your words and conduct will be judged by an objective (instead of **subjective**) test, your secret intent (for instance, that you were joking and did not really want to sell the stereo) cannot be shown. Hence, in this example a court may find that you have made a valid offer to Tom.

Obviously, this result depends heavily on the facts. If you are clearly jesting, are excited, or are even visibly angry, details supporting the existence of these facts might lead to a different result. Hence, a word to the wise would be to beware of making "offers" you do not mean, since under both the common law and the Uniform Commercial Code you may be stuck with them.

The following case illustrates these important concepts.

City of Everett v. *Estate of Sumstad*
631 P.2d 366 (Wash. 1981)

FACTS Mr. and Mrs. Mitchell are the proprietors of a small secondhand store. On 12 August 1978 the Mitchells attended Alexander's Auction, where they frequently had shopped to obtain merchandise for their own use and for use as inventory in their business. At the auction the Mitchells purchased a used safe with an inside compartment for $50. As they were told by the auctioneer when they purchased the safe, the Mitchells found that the inside compartment of the safe was locked. The safe was one of two safes that were part of the Sumstad estate. Several days after the auction, the Mitchells took the safe to a locksmith to have the locked compartment opened. The locksmith found $32,207 inside. The Everett Police Department, notified by the locksmith, impounded the money.

ISSUE Was there in fact a sale of the safe and its unknown contents to the Mitchells at the auction?

HOLDING Yes. There was a sale of the safe and its contents, as revealed by the terms of the agreement in light of the surrounding circumstances.

REASONING The objective manifestation theory of contracts stresses the outward manifestation of assent made by each party to the other. The subjective intention of the parties is irrelevant. A contract has, strictly speaking, nothing to do with the personal, or individual, intent of the parties. A contract is an obligation attached by the mere force of law to certain acts of the parties, usually words, that ordinarily accompany and represent a known intent. The inquiry, then, focuses on the outward manifestations of intent by a party to enter into a contract as judged by the reasonable meaning of a person's words and acts. If the offeror, judged by a reasonable standard, manifests an intention to agree in regard to the matter in question, agreement is established. Here the facts showed that the auctioneer had told the bidders that both this safe and the other one had come from an estate, that both were still locked, that neither had been opened, that the required combinations and keys were unavailable for either, and that all sales were final. Furthermore, there was no statement in which the auctioneer reserved the rights to any contents of the safe to the estate. Under these circumstances, reasonable persons would conclude that the auctioneer had manifested an objective intent to sell the safe and its contents and that the parties had mutually assented to enter into that sale of the safe and the contents of the locked compartment.

OFFER

Let us look more closely at this first phase of reaching agreement, the offer. An *offer* generally involves *an indication (by a promise or another commitment) of one's willingness to do or refrain from doing something in the future.* An offer implicitly invites another person to assent to the promise or commitment in order to seal the bargain.

Clear Intention to Contract and Definiteness of the Offer

Given this definition, an offer must show a *clear intention to contract* and be *definite* in all respects if it is to constitute a genuine common law offer. An agreement to agree at some future time, for example, lacks these prerequisites of a common law offer. Similarly, statements of opinion, statements of intention, and preliminary negotiations do not result in bona fide offers because they lack definiteness. But reasonable people will differ as to what is a clear, definite offer and what is instead only preliminary negotiations or dickering. Since these are questions of fact that a judge or jury may later decide, caution is of course desirable. If you want to make an offer, be specific in all particulars. On the other hand, haggling or dickering lacks this definiteness regarding the details of the transaction and your intentions. Such preliminary negotiations are ordinarily too vague to constitute a valid offer. Winning or losing a lawsuit may turn on such minute distinctions as how a court will interpret the words expressed by the parties. For example, are the words, "I can send you two carloads at $5000 per carload" identical in intent to "I offer to send you two carloads at $5000 per carload"? Many people would view these statements as virtually identical, but a strict common law interpretation will treat only the second statement as a bona fide offer. The other statement will be treated as an indication of a willingness to negotiate, but it will not rise to the level of a bona fide offer.

Despite the common law's requirement that an offer be definite in all its material (or essential) terms, you should be aware that the Uniform Commercial Code relaxes this common law prerequisite in several significant ways. For instance, the UCC in Section 2-204 states that a contract for sale under the Code will not fail for indefiniteness as long as the parties have intended to form a contract and a reasonably certain basis for giving an appropriate remedy exists, even though one or more of the terms of the agreement have been left open. In addition, the UCC contains several so-called gap-filling provisions whereby the court can supply the terms omitted by the parties,

Output contract A contract that calls for the buyer to purchase all of the production of the seller during the term of the contract.

Requirements contract A contract in which the seller agrees to provide as much of a product or service as the buyer needs during the contract term.

including price, place of delivery, mode of payment, and so on.[1] Moreover, the Code validates **output** and **requirements** contracts, both of which would be too indefinite for common law courts to enforce.[2] Because the Code is predicated on the idea that commercial people (merchants) want to deal with each other, it has eliminated some of the ticklish technicalities that impeded contract formation under the common law. You will learn more about this and other revolutionary changes in the common law brought about by the Uniform Commercial Code in Chapters 18–22.

Advertisements and Auctions

The law in general does not treat *advertisements* as valid offers, but rather as *invitations to deal, or statements of intention to sell certain merchandise*. Advertisements are characterized in this fashion because they usually lack sufficient specificity to become offers. Instead, the law views advertisements as invitations for persons to come in and make offers for the types of goods and at the prices indicated in the advertisements. A contrary rule that advertisements are equal to offers would presuppose that a merchant has an unlimited supply of merchandise. Thus, the principle that advertisements ordinarily are not offers protects merchants from the hardships that a contrary rule might produce. On occasion, however, an advertisement, catalogue, circular, price list, or price quotation will show sufficient detail for a court to say that a valid offer exists. Such a result, however exceptional, sometimes occurs, as the following case demonstrates.

Harris v. Time, Inc.
237 Cal. Rptr. 584 (Cal. App. 1987)

FACTS Joshua Gnaizda, the three-year-old son of a prominent Bay Area attorney, received an offer from Time, Inc. (Time) in an envelope that contained two see-through windows that only partially revealed the envelope's contents. One window showed Joshua's name and address. The other revealed the following statement: "JOSHUA A. GNAIZDA, I'LL GIVE YOU THIS VERSATILE NEW CALCULATOR WATCH FREE Just for Opening this Envelope Before Feb. 15, 1985." Beneath the offer was a picture of the calculator watch itself. However, upon opening the envelope, Joshua's mother realized that the see-through window had not revealed the full text of Time's offer. Specifically, printed below the picture of the calculator watch were the following additional words: "AND MAILING THIS CERTIFICATE TODAY!" Thus, the see-through window did not allow these words to be visible before opening the envelope. The certificate itself clearly required that Joshua purchase a subscription to *Fortune* magazine in order to receive the free calculator watch. Joshua's father, suing on his son and Mark Harris's behalf for $15,000 in punitive damages, contended that Time's failure to supply Joshua with a calculator watch represented a breach of contract.

ISSUE Was the text of the unopened mailer an offer rather than an advertisement?

[1]See Uniform Commercial Code, Sections 2-305, 2-309, and 2-310.
[2]Ibid., Section 2-306.

HOLDING	Yes. The text technically constituted a bona fide offer. However, the frivolous nature of the lawsuit mandated its dismissal.
REASONING	The law usually treats advertisements as mere invitations to bargain, not offers. However, an advertisement can constitute an offer and can form the basis of a unilateral contract if it calls for performance of a specific act without further communication and leaves nothing for future negotiation. The text of Time's unopened mailer technically represented an offer to enter into a unilateral contract: The promisor had made a promise (i.e., to give the recipient a calculator watch) in exchange for the performance of an act by the promisee (i.e., the opening of the envelope). Hence, this communication represented an exception to the general rule. Once Time had made an offer proposing the formation of a unilateral contract and the Gnaizdas had supplied the required consideration by opening the envelope and exposing themselves to the sales pitch within, there was an enforceable contract, assuming the Gnaizdas had given Time notice of their performance. But the legal maxim *de minimus non curat*—"the law disregards trifles"—necessitated the dismissal of the case, owing to the inappropriateness of a court's being used as a vehicle by those whose only real damage is feeling foolish for having opened junk mail.

Normally, courts will require a showing that the merchant has placed some limitation on the advertised goods before courts will find that the advertisement constitutes an offer. For example, the merchant may have specified a time limit, such as "for one day only," on the advertisement. Or the merchant may have designated a quantity limit, such as "while they last" or "to the first ten customers," on the advertisement. In such a situation, the courts are somewhat more likely to find that the advertisement is an offer and not an invitation to deal or to negotiate. Again, courts will utilize the objective standard of what a reasonable person would have thought as the deciding factor.

Auctions are similar to advertisements in that the seller is not actually the offeror, although he or she may appear to be offering the goods for sale through the auctioneer. In reality, the bidder is the offeror. For a sale to occur, the seller must accept the bid. The seller can even refuse to sell to the highest bidder unless the auction is publicized as "without reserve." In this type of auction, the seller must let the goods go to the highest bidder; he or she cannot withdraw the goods if the price bid is too low. Once the auctioneer lets the hammer fall, the seller has accepted the bid. But until this point, the bidder can withdraw the offer and thus avoid the formation of a contract of sale. Section 2-328 of the Uniform Commercial Code covers these points, which will be discussed again in Chapter 20.

Communication of the Offer to the Offeree

Another requirement for a bona fide offer is that the offeror (or his or her agent) must communicate the offer to the offeree. At first glance this rule may seem nonsensical. How, you may ask, can a person accept an offer if he or she is ignorant about the existence of the offer? Believe it or not, that sometimes happens. For example, assume that two parties have been haggling over the terms of a real estate transaction. After much correspondence, the would-be buyer (offeree) writes, "Okay, you win. I will pay $80,000 for the land,"

and mails the letter to the offeror. A day later, before the arrival of the mail, the would-be seller (offeror) coincidentally arrives at the same figure, and writes, "This is my final offer. I will sell you the land for $80,000. Take it or leave it," and mails this letter to the offeree. Later, the offeror wants to sell this land to a third person who is interested in purchasing it, but the original offeree is alleging that he and the offeror now have a contract for $80,000. Despite the claims of the original offeree, the offeror probably can sell the land to the third party because most courts will hold that the first party (the original offeree) has not validly accepted the offer. This is true because *at the time* of the would-be buyer's purported acceptance, no offer to sell the land at a price of $80,000 had been communicated to the original offeree. And, as mentioned previously, an offer has no legal effect until the offeror (or his or her agent) communicates it to the offeree. Courts would liken the correspondences in this example to identical offers crossing in the mail, each asking for and necessitating an acceptance before any valid contract would ensue, and neither receiving the required acceptance.

This requirement of communicating the offer to the offeree sometimes arises in the context of *general offers*. Although most offers are made by one person to another, offers made to the general public or a similar class of large numbers of persons are perfectly legal. A reward (such as for the arrest and conviction of the persons who have been vandalizing an office complex) represents the best example of a general offer. Even though some case results to the contrary exist, most courts will require that the party who performs the act contemplated by the reward (here, the identification of the vandals so as to lead to their prosecution and conviction) must have known of the reward and have intended the act as acceptance of that offer. Under this view, a general offer must be communicated to the offeree in order for a valid acceptance to occur. A person who coincidentally had identified the vandals without knowledge of the reward would be ineligible to receive the reward under the rule followed in a majority of jurisdictions.

Note that in the next case, the court used such common law principles to determine the identity of the person to whom the offeror had *intended* to communicate the offer.

Lucas v. *Godfrey*
467 N.W.2d 180 (Wis. App. 1991)

FACTS Robyn Warren Godfrey had been George Lucas's secretary for several years. She performed various office duties, including picking up the mail. From time to time, Godfrey received personal mail at the office address, a post office box. This controversy centers around a contest entry form sent to that address. The *Reader's Digest* sweepstakes is a promotional effort on the part of the magazine designed, among other things, to increase subscription sales. The magazine sends contest "eligibility cards" to people around the country, who then enter the sweepstakes by returning the card to the magazine. The magazine obtains lists of subscribers to various other publications and mails promotional materials and contest eligibility cards to persons whose names appear on these lists. The cards contain number codes, indicating the particular magazine subscriber list from which the *Reader's Digest* had taken the recipient's name and address. *Reader's Digest* sent one such eligibility card, addressed by computer, to "Robyn W. Lucas" at the office post office box address. Godfrey crossed out the initial and the name "Lucas," inserted her surname in its place, and returned the card. The magazine eventually selected this card as the winner of a $150,000 prize. The code number on the card indicated that the name and mailing address had been taken from a list of subscribers to *Ellery Queen's Mystery Magazine (Ellery Queen)*. Godfrey was an *Ellery Queen* subscriber, but Lucas was not. The circulation director of *Ellery Queen* testified that, for a period of time, Godfrey's subscription was listed in the name Robyn W. Lucas. The magazine had corrected this error and at some point Godfrey began receiving the magazine in her own name. When Godfrey's receipt of the sweepstakes prize became known, Lucas sued Godfrey and *Reader's Digest,* claiming that he was entitled to the money. Godfrey answered and cross-claimed, seeking a judgment that the money was hers. In light of these competing claims, *Reader's Digest* deposited the $150,000 with the court, asking it to decide whether Lucas or Godfrey was entitled to claim the prize.

ISSUE Was there a contract between *Reader's Digest* and either Godfrey or Lucas?

HOLDING Yes. The contract was between the magazine and Godfrey, who, as the intended offeree, had accepted the offer by returning the sweepstakes card.

REASONING Lucas submitted that because *Reader's Digest* had addressed the card to "Robyn W. Lucas," and because Robyn Warren Godfrey is not "Robyn W. Lucas," she could not recover. (Under that reasoning, of course, neither could Lucas.) Contract law, however, holds that the manifested intention of the offeror determines the person or persons in whom is created a power of acceptance. According to *Reader's Digest's* general counsel, the magazine sent the contest eligibility card to the Lucas post office box to get the contest materials and the magazine's promotional messages to prospective customers—in this particular case, active subscribers to *Ellery Queen.* Hence, these facts admit of a single reasonable inference: that *Reader's Digest* intended to offer entry in its sweepstakes to a person whose name appeared on the list of active subscribers to *Ellery Queen* and who would receive mail at the address taken from that magazine's subscriber list—Post Office Box 579, Wisconsin Rapids, Wisconsin. The fact that the card was addressed to Robyn W. Lucas, rather than Robyn Godfrey, is explained by the manner in which Godfrey's name was originally—and mistakenly—listed in the *Ellery Queen* subscriber files. The evidence indicated that any error in listing Godfrey's name that appeared in the *Ellery Queen* files, and thus on the *Reader's Digest* sweepstakes computer-generated contest mailing label, was indeed inadvertent and thus would not detract from the validity of the *Reader's Digest's* sweepstakes offer. An entrant or contestant who performed the act requested—returning the card—would accept the offer to enter the contest and thus form a valid and binding contract with the promoter. Consequently, by accepting the offer *Reader's Digest* had made to her, Godfrey became eligible for the prize. When the *Reader's Digest* selected her number as the winner, she, not Lucas, was entitled to receive the $150,000 prize.

YOU BE THE JUDGE

The FBI had placed Leo Joseph Koury, an accused contract killer, on its 10 Most-Wanted List in 1979. In 1988, the FBI offered a $25,000 reward for information leading to his capture. Koury died in San Diego, California, of a brain hemorrhage on June 17, 1991. He had been admitted to the hospital under the alias of William Franklin Biddle, a fact the county later discovered and brought to the attention of the FBI. The county argued that because it had helped the FBI determine that Koury was dead, it deserved the reward. The FBI nonetheless refused to turn over the money to the county on the rationale that the agency had offered the reward for information that would lead to Koury's arrest, which was impossible because of Koury's death.

If you were deciding this lawsuit, would you force the FBI to turn over the reward money to the county? Would your decision differ if it were based on *ethical* grounds?

Sources: "Most-Wanted Man Dies of Hemorrhage," *The Fresno Bee*, June 23, 1991, page A-11, and "FBI Says It Won't Fork Over $25,000 as Reward for Finding Fugitive Dead," *The Fresno Bee*, June 27, 1991, page D8.

Figure 9.1 summarizes the steps of reaching an agreement.

Duration of the Offer

Usually, offers will comply with the rules and will be legally effective. The next question that often arises concerns the *duration* of the offer; that is, how long will it remain open? Basically, there are four methods for terminating an offer: (1) lapse, (2) revocation, (3) rejection, and (4) acceptance.

It is quite possible that the offeror will set the life span for the offer by stating in the offer when it will terminate. This sets up the potential **lapse** of the offer. For instance, an offer may state, among other things, "This offer will remain open for thirty days." If after thirty days the offeree has not responded, the offer automatically lapses. The offeror is under no legal duty to communicate the fact that the offer has lapsed to the offeree. After thirty days, the offeror can make the same offer to anyone else without worrying about facing a lawsuit from the first offeree.

In many cases, the offeror neglects to state any time period in the offer. How long does the offeree have before he or she must respond in these situ-

Lapse The expiration or the loss of an opportunity because of the passage of a time limit within which the opportunity had to be exercised.

FIGURE 9.1 Offer: The First Phase of Reaching an Agreement

A bona fide offer by the offeror must:	• Show a clear *intention* to contract.
	• Be *definite* in all respects.
	• Be *communicated to the offeree* or his or her agent.
Communications by the offeror unreflective of a bona fide offer include:	• Any undisclosed secret intent.
	• Statements made in jest or strong excitement.
	• Preliminary negotiations.
	• Price quotations.
	• Dickering.
	• Advertisements.
	• Invitations to deal.

ations? To avoid lapse, the offeree must accept within a reasonable time. Determination of what constitutes a reasonable time becomes a question of fact that a judge or jury decides. The trier of fact will consider such things as industry conditions, customs, and usages of trade. In volatile commodities markets, an offer may lapse in a matter of moments. On the other hand, given a downturn in the real estate market, a period of days or weeks may be a reasonable time if the offer involves a sale of real property. To avoid such uncertainties, the offeror should state specifically when the offer lapses.

Lapse also may occur by operation of law. That is, regardless of the wishes of the parties, an offer automatically lapses upon the following occurrences: (1) the death or insanity of the offeror or offeree, (2) the **supervening** illegality of the subject matter of the offer, or (3) the destruction of the subject matter involved in the offer. In other words, if Joe Olivetti offers to sell his car to Joan Hays but dies before she accepts, the offer automatically lapses. Joe's estate does not have to inform Joan of his death. Similarly, if two days after Joe makes the offer, his city passes an ordinance stating that sales of private cars without safety stickers are illegal, Joe's offer will lapse if the car does not have a sticker. If lightning strikes the car and destroys it, the offer lapses. No communication to Joan is necessary in these last instances either.

Another method of terminating an offer, besides lapse, is **revocation.** Under common law, the offeror possesses virtually unlimited rights to revoke at any time before acceptance. This is true whether or not the offeror uses the word *revoke*, as long as an intention to terminate the offer is clear.

In general, revocation does not become effective until it is communicated to (or received by) the offeree. Interestingly, such communication may be effective whether communicated directly or indirectly. Using our earlier example, Joe may state bluntly, "Joan, I revoke my offer to you." Alternatively, Joan may hear that Joe has sold the car to Len Hill. There has been an effective revocation in either case.

Usually, Joe will be dealing only with Joan or, at most, with a few parties. This is not the case with a general offer to the public. If Joe has lost his prize Dalmatian, Jake, and has offered a reward for the return of or information about the dog, he need only revoke his offer in the same manner (or medium) in which he has made the original offer. Because it would be too burdensome to require Joe to communicate with every possible "taker" of his offer, public revocation suffices. It is even effective against a person who has not seen the advertisement and who later comes forward with information about Jake.

Methods do exist for taming this seemingly unlimited power of revocation by the Joes of the world. Joan may prohibit Joe's power of revocation by forcing Joe to promise to keep the offer open for a stated time. The promise itself will not protect Joan from revocation. But if she takes an **option** on the car, Joe is legally bound to hold the offer open for a period of time agreed

Supervening Coming or happening as something additional or unexpected.

Revocation The cancellation, rescission, or annulment of something previously done or offered.

Option A privilege given to the offeree, for consideration, to accept an offer at any time during a preset period, with the understanding that the offer cannot be revoked during the stated period; a contract to keep an offer open for some agreed-upon time period.

on. Joan will have to pay Joe for the option; but once she does so, he cannot sell the car to anyone else during the option period without breaching this option contract. Usually, Joan is under no obligation to exercise the option. If she does not, Joe can keep the money or other consideration paid to him for the option. If Joan does exercise the option, normally the money paid for the option will be subtracted from the purchase price. Depending on the bargaining position of the parties, however, this is not always the case.

Another exception to the rule that an offeror can revoke an offer at any time before acceptance comes from the Uniform Commercial Code, Section 2-205.

> An offer *by a merchant* [emphasis added] to buy or sell goods which by its terms gives assurance that it will be held open is not revocable, for lack of consideration, during the time stated, or if no time is stated, for a reasonable time, but in no event may such period of irrevocability exceed three months.

The Code demands that merchants, as professionals, keep their word even if they have been given no consideration for their assurances. Simply put, the Code dramatically changes the common law doctrine regarding the offeror's right to revoke when the offeror is a **merchant** and the other provisions of Section 2-205 have been met.

Finally, the doctrine of **promissory estoppel** may prohibit offerors from revoking their offers. Under this theory, offerors will be prevented (estopped) from asserting a defense otherwise available to them (generally that they as common law offerors have the right to revoke the offer). In order for Joan, the offeree in our earlier example, to assert this doctrine successfully, she must show that (1) Joe, the offeror, promised or represented to her that he would hold the offer open; (2) she relied on these promises or representations; (3) she suffered a detriment thereby (maybe she passed up another car because she thought she would get Joe's); and (4) injustice can be avoided only by forcing the offeror to leave the offer open. In several cases, plaintiffs have used this doctrine to cut off the offeror's power of revocation.

Thus far, we have dwelt on the offeror's power to terminate the offer. The offeree, of course, may refuse the offer and thereby terminate it. The law calls the offeree's power of termination **rejection**. Like revocations, rejections are not effective until communicated by the offeree to the offeror. Thus, Joan may reject Joe's offer by telling Joe she is no longer interested in the car.

The usual rule holds that an offer cannot later be accepted after lapse, revocation, or rejection because after these events the offer has expired. However, if the parties are nonetheless still willing to deal, there may be a valid agreement subsequent to one of these events. The parties generally are not obligated to continue the transaction unless they find it advantageous to do so.

Merchant   A person who regularly deals in goods of the kind or has the knowledge or skill peculiar to the practices or goods involved in the transaction.

Promissory estoppel   A doctrine that prohibits a promisor from denying the making of a promise or from escaping the liability for that promise because of the justifiable reliance of the promisee that the promise would be kept.

Rejection   A refusal to accept what is offered.

For a good example of some of these concepts, including the application of promissory estoppel in a real-life context, read the next case.

Zeman v. Lufthansa German Airlines
699 P.2d 1274 (Alaska 1985)

FACTS   Zeman was a contractor who in October, 1978, had offered to build a thirty-six-unit building for Lufthansa German Airlines' (Lufthansa's) accommodations for its personnel in Anchorage. Lufthansa in January, 1979, had sent Zeman a letter saying "as soon as we are able to convince ourselves that the completion of the building will be within a fortnight, the agreement we have in mind can be signed." Zeman responded that he was confident he could meet the occupancy date required and that he looked forward to entering into an agreement with Lufthansa. Zeman proceeded with the construction of the building intended for Lufthansa. He also consented to a judgment against himself for delinquent payments on the property acquired for the building owing to his belief that Lufthansa's signing of the lease would provide funds for paying off these delinquencies. However, Lufthansa informed him in late July, 1979, that the airlines would not be housed in Zeman's building. Zeman could not find other renters and therefore, in late 1979, lost the building to the bank that had financed the construction. Zeman thereafter sued Lufthansa for breach of contract and promissory estoppel. The lower court granted Lufthansa's motion for summary judgment.

ISSUE   Did Zeman have a binding contract with Lufthansa? If not, could promissory estoppel be applied against Lufthansa to force the airline to live up to the alleged agreement with Zeman?

HOLDING   Summary judgment was inappropriate because substantial issues of fact existed as to the interpretation of certain ambiguous letters between the parties. Thus, the case was **remanded** to the trial court for a determination of whether there was mutual assent between the parties and of certain facts to ascertain whether Zeman alternatively would be able to pursue his promissory estoppel theory.

Remanded   Sent back to an inferior court for further action.

REASONING   The trial court had found that there was no mutual assent between the parties, that there was instead only a nonbinding agreement to agree. Yet because the record in this case contained evidence that could reasonably be interpreted to indicate definiteness as to mutual assent and material terms, a reversal of the summary judgment as to these issues and a remand of the case for trial was necessary. Moreover, it was not clear whether Zeman had substantially changed his position in reliance on any of Lufthansa's statements. Zeman, in order to make out a case of promissory estoppel, must be able to show that (1) the action induced amounted to a substantial change of position, (2) the action was either actually foreseen or reasonably foreseeable by the promisor, (3) an actual promise was made and itself induced the action or **forbearance** in reliance thereon, and (4) enforcement would be necessary in the interest of justice. Zeman argued that he had undergone substantial changes of position in reliance on Lufthansa's statements even though he had always intended to build the apartment complex. Thus, a remand of the case to the lower court was necessary to determine the substantiality of the costs associated with accelerated financing for the project and with furnishing the apartments for Lufthansa's special requests. If either of these costs proved substantial, Zeman could pursue the promissory estoppel theory. Otherwise, he could not.

Forbearance   A refraining from action.

The following recent Supreme Court case illustrates that our legal system places such importance on the doctrine of promissory estoppel that it will uphold the concept even in the face of a constitutional challenge. As you read the case, consider the ethical implications of the newspapers' actions.

Cohen v. Cowles Media Company
59 U.S.L.W. 4773 (June 24, 1991)

FACTS

During the closing days of the 1982 Minnesota gubernatorial race, Dan Cohen, an active Republican associated with Wheelock Whitney's Independent-Republican gubernatorial campaign, approached reporters from the *St. Paul Pioneer Press Dispatch* (the *Pioneer Press*) and the *Minneapolis Star and Tribune* (the *Star Tribune*) and offered to provide documents relating to a candidate in the upcoming election. Cohen made clear to the reporters that he would provide the information only if they gave him a promise of confidentiality. Reporters from both papers promised to keep Cohen's identity anonymous; and Cohen turned over copies of two public court records concerning Marlene Johnson, the Democratic-Farmer-Labor candidate for lieutenant governor. The first record indicated that Johnson had been charged in 1969 with three counts of unlawful assembly and the second that she had been convicted in 1970 of petit theft. The first charges were eventually dismissed, and the one for petit theft was later **vacated.** After consultation and debate, the editorial staffs of the two newspapers independently decided to publish Cohen's name as part of their stories concerning Johnson. In their stories, both papers identified Cohen as the source of the court records, indicated his connection to the Whitney campaign, and included denials by Whitney campaign officials of any role in the matter. The same day the stories appeared, Cohen's employer fired him. Cohen then sued the publishers of the *Pioneer Press* and the *Star Tribune,* alleging breach of contract owing to the application of promissory estoppel. The newspapers argued that enforcement of their promise of confidentiality under a theory of promissory estoppel would violate their First Amendment rights.

Vacated Set aside; nullified; rendered void.

ISSUE

Did the First Amendment prohibit Cohen from recovering damages, under state promissory estoppel law, for a newspaper's breach of a promise of confidentiality given to him in exchange for information?

HOLDING

No. The First Amendment did not confer on the press a constitutional right to disregard promises that state law would otherwise enforce.

REASONING

A well established line of cases holds that generally applicable laws do not offend the First Amendment simply because their enforcement against the press has incidental effects on its ability to gather and report the news. It is therefore beyond dispute that "[t]he publisher of a newspaper has no special immunity from the application of general laws. He has no special privilege to invade the rights and liberties of others" [*Associated Press* v. *NLRB*]. Accordingly, enforcement of such general laws against the press is not subject to stricter scrutiny than would be applied to enforcement against other persons or organizations. There can be little doubt that the Minnesota doctrine of promissory estoppel is a law of general applicability; it does not target or single out the press. Rather, the doctrine is generally applicable to the daily transactions of all citizens of Minnesota. Moreover, the First Amendment does not forbid its application to the press, particularly since application of Minnesota's promissory estoppel doctrine in this case will not "punish" the newspaper for publishing truthful information that was lawfully obtained. Here, Minnesota law simply requires those making promises to keep them. The parties themselves, as in this case, determine the scope of their legal obligations. Hence, any restrictions that may be placed on the publication of truthful information are self-imposed. Furthermore, whether the newspapers actually obtained Cohen's name "lawfully"— at least for purposes of publishing it—remains unclear, for they acquired it only by making a promise that they failed to honor. According to Cohen, the breach of this promise caused him to lose his job, lowered his earning capacity, and caused him damages in excess of $50,000. Still, the newspapers argue that permitting Cohen to maintain a cause of action for promissory estoppel will inhibit truthful reporting because news organizations will have legal incentives not to disclose a confidential source's identity even when that person's identity is itself newsworthy. But if this is the case, it involves no more than the incidental, and constitutionally insignificant, consequence of applying to the press a generally applicable law that requires individuals who make certain kinds of promises to keep them. The case is remanded to the Minnesota Supreme Court where that court should consider whether it will uphold, on promissory estoppel grounds, the jury verdict awarding $200,000 in compensatory damages to Cohen.

ACCEPTANCE

Acceptance is the usual mode of terminating an offer. As noted earlier, this represents a significant moment for the offeror and offeree because they now have an agreement. Barring problems with consideration, capacity, genuineness of assent, legality, or proper form, a binding contract now exists.

Acceptance involves the *offeree's assent to all the terms of the offer*. Because this is so, the offeree's intention to be bound to the total offer must be clear. Hence, the offeree's uncommunicated mental reservations will not be binding on the offeror. As with offers, courts apply the objective test to see whether the acceptance is valid. That the acceptance is oral, written, or implied (e.g., through an act such as cashing a check) generally does not affect its validity, as long as the offer has been communicated to the offeree (or the offeree's agent), and it is the offeree (or the offeree's agent) who accepts. The case that follows illustrates these points.

Moore v. *Kuehn*
602 S.W.2d 713 (Mo. App. 1980)

FACTS
After fire had damaged Kuehn's building, an insurance adjuster employed by the company with which Kuehn had coverage contacted Moore about a written estimate for the necessary repair work. The adjuster approved Moore's estimate of $7600 and instructed Moore to submit a written proposal to Kuehn in that amount. When Moore did so, Kuehn told him that he, Kuehn, wanted to look over the proposal more closely before signing it. However, he told Moore, ''The roof ought to be fixed, so get on it.'' Moore proceeded to do all the repairs suggested in the proposal. Kuehn retained his copy of the proposal but never signed it. After the completion of the work, the insurer settled with Kuehn for $12,069.48, based on Moore's $7600.00 estimate and the separate estimates of two other companies that had aided in the restoration of the building. Kuehn received a check in the amount of $12,069.48 and wrote out checks to the three companies involved in the rebuilding. Moore's check from Kuehn, however, was in the amount of only $5500. Kuehn assured him that the balance of $2100 would be paid when Moore finished a small number of specified items that needed completion or correction. Moore did so, apparently to Kuehn's satisfaction, but was thereafter told by Kuehn that he could not pay Moore owing to insufficient funds. Moore's subsequent extrajudicial attempts to recover the claimed balance due and the payment for extras were unsuccessful. Kuehn claimed there was no contract between him and Moore for the completed repairs and the extras.

ISSUE   Was there a valid contract between Kuehn and Moore based on Kuehn's acceptance of Moore's proposal regarding repairs?

HOLDING   Yes. There was such a contract, so Moore should receive $2,531 in damages.

REASONING It is a well-settled rule of law that an offeree may orally accept a written offer. The result is an oral contract embodying the terms of the writing. In light of this rule, there could be little doubt that Moore and Kuehn had entered into an express oral contract for the repair of the roof. Upon receiving the written proposal, Kuehn had told Moore, "The roof ought to be fixed, so get on it." The only offer made to Kuehn at that point, and the only offer to which his acceptance could conceivably have had reference, involved Kuehn's property. The terms of that writing necessarily controlled the oral contract established at that point. Moreover, Kuehn's silent acquiescence in and acceptance of Moore's performance of the other repair work listed in the proposal constituted an implied acceptance of the contract as it related to those items. The manifestation of acceptance of an offer need not occur only through spoken or written word; it may also come through the offeree's conduct or failure to act. The evidence indicated that the writing was the sole offer made by Moore to Kuehn; that Kuehn was aware of the terms of that offer; that he instructed Moore to complete one of the items proposed; that he subsequently permitted Moore, without objection, to complete all the work proposed in the writing and in fact cooperated with him in one facet of the job; and that he accepted the benefits of Moore's performance. There was no evidence that Kuehn had either questioned the necessity of any of the proposed repairs or contested the proposed contract price. In view of this evidence, Kuehn's contemporaneous refusals to sign the proposal were such that they indicated that he had in fact impliedly assented to Moore's full performance in accordance with the proposal. Consequently, a contract existed between the litigants for the repairs listed in the proposal.

Mirror Image Rule

Under common law rules, an acceptance must be not only clear but also unconditional. This concept, called the *mirror image* or *matching-ribbons rule* of common law, means that the acceptance must match, term by term, the provisions in the offer. Any deviation from these terms, whether by alteration, addition, or omission, makes the acceptance invalid and tantamount to a rejection of the offer originally made.

Any deviation from the terms of the offer brings about a qualified acceptance, known as a *counteroffer*. Counteroffers terminate offers unless the original offeror remains willing to accept the terms of the counteroffer. As you have seen in other contexts, such offerors are not obligated to do so unless they still want to deal. Therefore, if you desire to enter into a contract with the offeror, you should pay close attention to the language of the acceptance. Mere inquiries, requests, and terms implied by law, if part of the acceptance, do not invalidate it. Thus, if Joan says, "I'll take the car at $2000 as you offered, but I'd like you to throw in the snow tires," a valid acceptance probably exists (Joan's added statement is a request). Contrast this with Joan's saying, "I accept *if* you throw in the snow tires." The latter statement sounds more like a provision or a condition and may make the purported acceptance legally ineffective unless Joe is prepared to let Joan have the snow tires as part of the deal.

In the following case, the court applied the mirror image rule in concluding that the writings reflected a counteroffer and thus the lack of any mutual assent to the terms of the purported agreement.

D'Agostino v. Bank of Ravenswood
563 N.E.2d 886 (Ill. App. 1990)

FACTS Steve Spanos, owner of the building located at 3928–32 N. Broadway in Chicago, was three years behind in property tax payments. Spanos listed the property for sale with a real estate broker, William Vranas. On 8 May 1986, Vranas presented Spanos with a written offer from Vincenzo D'Agostino to purchase the property for $230,000. An earnest money check in the amount of $1000 was submitted with the offer. Spanos testified that when he received the offer on 13 May 1986, he drew a line through the $230,000 figure, raised the price to $235,000, initialed the price change, and signed the offer at the bottom. Later that day, Vranas informed Spanos that D'Agostino would not accept the offer at $235,000. Spanos then orally agreed with Vranas during a subsequent telephone conversation that he would reduce the price to the original $230,000. D'Agostino later drew a line through the $235,000 figure that Spanos had inserted in the offer, reduced the price to $230,000, and initialed the change. But Spanos never initialed the document after D'Agostino had changed the written price back to $230,000. The parties continued, without success, to draft a contract that manifested a price acceptable to both. D'Agostino made another offer on 29 May that included mortgage and inspection contingencies as well as certain seller's warranties. Shortly thereafter, Spanos rejected this offer; and on 10 June, Spanos sold the property to another buyer. Upon learning of this sale, D'Agostino sued the Bank of Ravenswood, the trustee for Spanos, for **specific performance** of the contract.

Specific performance An equitable remedy provided by the courts when monetary damages would be insufficient and the object of the contract is unique and in which the court orders performance of the contract exactly as agreed.

ISSUE Did the agreement dated 8 May 1986 represent an enforceable contract between Spanos and D'Agostino?

HOLDING No. Spanos's response was a counteroffer that rejected the original offer. Since no valid contract had been formed, D'Agostino was not entitled to specific performance.

REASONING An acceptance requiring any modification or change of terms constitutes a rejection of the original offer and becomes a counteroffer that the original offeror must accept before a valid contract is formed. In the present case, Spanos had rejected D'Agostino's original offer of 8 May when he drew a line through the $230,000 figure, increased the price to $235,000, initialed the price change, and signed the offer at the bottom. Spanos's actions created a counteroffer rather than an acceptance. Spanos's oral acquiescence to the previously offered price constituted merely an acceptance of a rejected offer. Because later acceptance ordinarily cannot revive a rejected offer, the evidence showed that a valid contract never came into existence. Accordingly, D'Agostino was not entitled to specific performance.[3]

The Uniform Commercial Code continues its relaxation of common law rules in Section 2-207 by permitting a contract to arise between the parties even if the offeree adds terms or includes different terms in the purported acceptance. This provision of the UCC reflects the drafters' knowledge of commercial realities, specifically the fact that buyers and sellers in commercial

---

[3]The court also held that Spanos's failure to sign the document after the alleged oral agreement to reduce the price to the original $230,000 made the contract unenforceable because of noncompliance with the Statute of Frauds. You will learn in Chapter 14 that the Statute of Frauds requires that the defendant sign any contract involving a sale of land. Otherwise, a court generally will refuse to give effect to the contractual terms.

settings generally exchange their respective forms (for example, purchase order forms or order acknowledgment forms), which may contain contradictory terms. Rather than hamper commercial dealings by judging the inconsistent terms under the common law rule that any variances in the material terms of the offer and acceptance constitute a counteroffer and hence a rejection of the original offer, the UCC drafters permit a contract to arise between the parties unless the offeree has expressly indicated that his or her acceptance of the offer is conditioned on the offeror's assent to these additional or different terms. Section 2-207 furthermore sets out a scheme for determining the operative terms of the contract in these circumstances. For instance, between merchants the additional terms automatically become part of the contract without the offeror's consent unless the original offer expressly requires the offeree to accept the terms of the offer, the additional terms materially alter the contract (that is, they would unfairly surprise or be unduly oppressive of the offeror), or the offeror has notified the offeree that he or she will not accept the new terms. This same section of the Code also states that conduct by both parties that recognizes the existence of a contract is sufficient to establish a contract for sale even though the writings of the parties do not otherwise establish a contract. You will learn more about these concepts in succeeding chapters, but you should at this point at least have some appreciation of the alterations of common law rules embodied in the Code and the underlying rationales for these changes.

Manner and Time of Acceptance

Besides accepting unconditionally, the offeree must avoid one other pitfall in order to effect a valid acceptance: The offeree must accept in exactly the mode specified by the offeror in the offer. Thus, should the offeror say that acceptance must occur by a telegram, a letter would not constitute an effective acceptance. Similarly, if the offer says, "Acceptance required by return mail," an acceptance placed in the mail two days later would be invalid. Finally, when the offer says, "Acceptance effective only when received," a contract will not arise until the offeror receives the acceptance.

Nevertheless, the offeror may not care to stipulate the mode necessary for a valid acceptance. In such cases, the offeree can use any *reasonable* medium of communication, as long as he or she acts within a reasonable time. Usually, the offeree will choose the same medium as was used by the offeror. By implication, this medium is a reasonable and authorized mode of communication. Hence, in the absence of a stipulated method of acceptance, if the offeror makes the offer via the mail, the offeree's mailing of an acceptance represents a reasonable mode of acceptance and thus a valid response. Another medium, such as the telephone, may be reasonable, and therefore authorized as well, if this medium has been used in the prior dealings between the parties or if it is sanctioned by local or industry custom.

Use of an authorized mode of communication in such circumstances takes on particular significance because, in most states, these acceptances become legally effective at the time of dispatch (mailing, wiring, and so on). This is called the *mailbox rule* or *implied agency rule* because the post office or telegraph office is deemed to be the agent of the offeror. To illustrate, assume that the offeror has not stipulated the mode of acceptance in an offer that was mailed to the offeree on 28 September. The offeror subsequently attempts to revoke the offer on 1 October and then learns that the offeree had mailed an acceptance to the offeror on 30 September. A contract exists as of 30 September, and thus there is no "mere offer" that can be revoked by the offeror. The fact that the acceptance was not received by the offeror until after he or she attempted to revoke the offer is irrelevant. The law treats the post office as the offeror's agent and thus concludes that the offeror "received" the acceptance on 30 September, the date the letter was received by the post office. Because some letters never arrive, it would be advisable for the offeree to secure postal or telegraphic receipts in order to prove after the fact the date on which the acceptance had actually been dispatched.

In contrast, where the offeree has used an unauthorized mode of communication, the strict rule states that the acceptance is not effective until it is actually received by the offeror, and the mailbox rule is not applicable. Even so, some courts will enforce the agreement if the acceptance, though communicated via an unauthorized mode, is timely, especially if the courts can construe the offeror's language about the proper mode as a suggestion rather than a stipulation or condition. The Uniform Commercial Code lends credence to such decisions by sanctioning acceptances "in any manner and by any medium reasonable in the circumstances" (Section 2-206[1][a]).

As you can see, the time of contract formation is crucial. The mailbox rule allows acceptance, and hence a contract, to occur even before the offeror knows of the acceptance. Such acceptances cut off the offeror's otherwise almost unlimited right to revoke, because revocation must occur before acceptance in order for an attempted revocation to be effective. Offerors can curtail the effect of the mailbox rule by stipulating that acceptances will not be effective until received by them. Note, too, that in any event, the mailbox rule applies only to acceptances: Revocations and rejections do not take effect until they are communicated to (that is, are received by) the offeree and offeror, respectively. Moreover, revocations and rejections do not become legally binding upon dispatch, as acceptances sometimes do.

Using these principles, evaluate the actions—and the ethics—of the offeror in the following case.

Martin v. Government Employees Insurance Company
565 N.E.2d 197 (Ill. App. 1990)

FACTS   Royce L. Martin works for the United States Postal Service. Government Employees Insurance Company (GEICO) conducts a mail-order automobile insurance business nationally. In March 1986, Martin's existing insurance coverage for his 1985 Pontiac Firebird was due to expire, so he obtained a GEICO form in the post office before that date.

This form gave him the opportunity to obtain a free quotation from GEICO of the rates available for auto insurance, based on the information solicited in the form. The form requested, among other things, the potential insured's occupation; social security number; name of current insurance company and date current insurance expired; driver's license suspension or revocation information, including any convictions for driving under the influence of drugs or alcohol; and history of accidents or traffic violations. GEICO's form encouraged interested persons "to take a few minutes right now to complete and return the postage-paid FREE QUOTATION REQUEST. If you qualify, you'll know in just a few days how much GEICO might save you." The form further noted that if a potential insured did not meet GEICO's underwriting requirements, he or she might "still obtain the same quality auto coverage and service from one of [GEICO's] affiliates, at somewhat higher rates and for a 6-month policy term." Martin completed the form and returned it to GEICO. The company sent him a "personal quote sheet," an application for insurance, a cover letter, and step-by-step instructions for completing the "application process." According to Martin, when he received the quote sheet and application from GEICO (instead of an affiliate), he assumed that he had met GEICO's underwriting requirements and did not seek replacement insurance elsewhere. The application required some additional information from Martin, but many of the questions were ones that he had answered previously in the quotation request. At least one additional question was new, however: Whether the applicant had any physical impairments. Martin answered that he is deaf. He sent in his application and check on 14 March 1986. On 27 March 1986, Martin's automobile was stolen. He reported the loss to GEICO the same day, by telephone. By a "GEICO Claim-Gram" dated 3 April 1986, Martin received GEICO's request for his policy number in order to process the claim. At about the same time, GEICO returned Martin's application and check. The check had been stamped for deposit only but had not been deposited. A policy control number sticker had been torn off the face of the check. An accompanying memorandum, dated 2 April 1986, stated that GEICO could not consider Martin's memorandum until he had completed answers to certain questions. The requested information, however, already had been furnished or did not apply. Martin returned the application and check to GEICO. Shortly thereafter, GEICO again returned his check and application with no explanation. Upon the recovery of his vandalized automobile, Martin once more demanded adjustment of his claim and tendered his premium payment. By letter dated 19 June 1986, however, GEICO denied liability and refused to pay on the grounds that Martin had not completed the application and that GEICO had not approved it. Martin then filed suit for breach of contract against GEICO.

ISSUE

Had GEICO and Martin entered into a contract of insurance at the time Martin reported the loss of his automobile?

HOLDING

No. The express language in GEICO's materials had not created an offer that Martin could have accepted merely by submitting the application and check. Consequently, Martin's loss was not insured by GEICO.

REASONING

The GEICO representations unequivocally put Martin, the applicant, on notice that he was not to consider the application form an offer from GEICO, but rather a "request" for coverage, which GEICO would grant only when GEICO had approved the application. Exhortations to "act today" and "join the GEICO family of 'good drivers' " should not lead a reasonable applicant to believe his or her coverage began upon mailing in the application when the same materials expressly conditioned coverage on approval of the application. Because GEICO most likely would have accepted Martin's application and would have provided coverage had the theft of the car not occurred when it did, from a business or public relations standpoint, GEICO's position appears questionable, particularly in light of its attempt to attract government employees. Yet ignoring GEICO's reservation of the right to approve the application would do serious damage to the common law of contracts, since GEICO's right to approve the application equates with the acceptance of the prospective insured's offer. Unfortunately for Martin, GEICO's stamping his check for deposit and offering a policy control number on the face of it did not constitute a **constructive** acceptance of his mailed-in application. While these facts suggest that GEICO was processing Martin's application, these internal practices did not represent an objective manifestation to Martin that GEICO had actually accepted his offer. GEICO's explicit, unambiguous statement that it would not extend coverage before approval of the application showed that GEICO had taken care to draft its materials in such a way as to prevent an applicant from assuming that, by mailing in the form and check, he or she would create a binding contract for immediate coverage. Had the GEICO materials

Constructive Inferred; amounting to or involving the act assumed.

remained silent on the issue of reserving approval, or had the timing of coverage been left completely open, it would have been reasonable to assume that a contract had been created when Martin had completed the application process. In such a situation, Martin's reasonable expectations of immediate coverage would have been fulfilled because there would have been nothing in the materials to indicate that any further consideration of the application would have been necessary. Hence, the effective date of coverage under the contract would also have coincided with the date on which the application had been mailed. Contract theory would support such a result because of the common law mailbox rule, which recognizes that the mailed acceptance of an offer is effective when mailed, not when received or acknowledged.

Silence

As the foregoing discussion implies, some overt act necessarily accompanies acceptance. For this reason, acceptance requires a clear intent to accept. Thus, the settled weight of authority holds that mere silence by the offeree cannot constitute acceptance. However, in some isolated cases the prior dealings of the parties may permit acceptance based on silence. The following case illustrates the necessity of an overt act to constitute an acceptance.

Karsch v. Carr
807 S.W.2d 96 (Mo. App. 1990)

FACTS   In the spring of 1987, John M. Karsch informed Robert C. Carr that he was interested in buying property consisting of approximately 1,364 acres in Washington County. At the time, Karsch viewed the land and told Carr that he wanted to construct a large lake on the property. Thereafter, Carr and Karsch continued negotiations toward the purchase of the property. In December 1987, Carr mailed a draft form of an agreement for the sale of the real estate to Karsch. The proposed contract recited a purchase price of $340,000 and named the grantees as John Karsch and his wife or any corporate name to be used. Neither party signed this draft form of the contract. On 8 January 1988, Karsch told Carr that he was willing to pay $240,000 for the property, but Carr rejected that offer. The next day, Karsch offered to pay $265,200 for the property and showed Carr a handwritten memorandum of the terms he (Karsch) had prepared, including an amount representing the down payment, the interest rate, the length of the payment period, the monthly payment amount, etc. After further negotiations, on 14 January 1988, Carr informed Karsch that he and the other sellers would sell the property to Karsch for $265,200. On that same date, Carr received from Karsch the original memorandum prepared by Karsch as well as a $5000 check. On 3 February 1988, Carr personally delivered the following items to Karsch in an envelope: a general warranty deed for the property signed by all the sellers, the promissory note, the deed of trust, the title insurance commitment, and Karsch's original memorandum of terms. Karsch kept the documents and expressed no dissatisfaction with them. On 10 February, Karsch learned from an engineer who had inspected the property that it would not be "economically practical" to build a one-hundred-acre lake on the property. On 17 February 1988, Karsch informed Carr that he did not intend to purchase the property and cited as his reason the fact that he would not be able to construct on the property a lake as large as he wanted. Carr, however, refused to release Karsch from the alleged contract. Karsch then returned the documents to Carr and filed a **declaratory judgment** action against Carr to determine if there were an enforceable contract between them.

Declaratory judgment   A decision by a court that merely sets out the rights of the parties without ordering either party to perform any actions.

ISSUE   Had Carr and Karsch entered into a contract for the sale of the property?

HOLDING No. Karsch's actions in taking the documents without objection and retaining them from 3 February until 17 February did not evince an acceptance of Carr's proposed terms.

REASONING As a general rule, silence or inaction cannot constitute acceptance of an offer. If the offeree has no duty to speak, the offeror may not translate the offeree's silence into an acceptance merely because the offeror attaches that effect to it. Karsch did not at any time communicate his acceptance of Carr's terms to Carr. In fact, within two weeks of receiving the documents, Karsch clearly rejected Carr's offer. Hence, because Karsch's acts did not manifest an acceptance, no enforceable contract ever came into existence.

Bilateral Versus Unilateral Contracts

The last major issue that relates to acceptance turns on whether the contract, if formed, would be bilateral or unilateral. The weight of authority holds that an offer that contemplates the making of a *bilateral* contract may be accepted by either a direct communication of a promise to the offeror or a counter-promise inferred from the offeree's conduct or other circumstances. When the offer instead contemplates the formation of a *unilateral* contract, it is usually unnecessary for the offeree to communicate acceptance. The offeree accepts the offer by merely completing the act called for in the offer. Subsequent notice to the offeror is not required. Besides, such notice would be redundant because the offeror will eventually learn of the acceptance when the offeree requests payment for the services rendered. Nevertheless, disputes may arise between the parties as to how much time an offeree has for completing the performance mentioned in the unilateral contract. If the offeror says, "I'll pay you $50 to chop firewood for me," and the offeree says, "Okay," the offeree may think chopping wood at any time within the next two months will constitute a binding acceptance. On the other hand, the offeror may get nervous when the firewood is not in the wood rack within two weeks and therefore may make the same offer to someone else, who completes the job sooner. In such circumstances, the offeror may not want to pay the first offeree for the wood delivered two months later; enough wood has already been supplied. Because of such timing problems, courts remain somewhat hostile to unilateral contracts, and construe alleged contracts as bilateral if they can. More importantly, contracting parties can avoid such timing problems by setting down all the pertinent details (delivery date, price, and so on) in advance in writing, whether the offeror proposes a unilateral or a bilateral contract. Good business planning, even in everyday affairs, helps avoid potential legal difficulties.

The Uniform Commercial Code eliminates many of the distinctions made in the common law between bilateral and unilateral contracts by specifying that unless the parties unambiguously indicate otherwise, "an order or other offer to buy goods for prompt or current shipment shall be construed as inviting acceptance either by a prompt promise to ship or by the prompt or current shipment of conforming or nonconforming goods. . . ." (Section 2-206[1][b]). In the first instance, a bilateral contract would be formed; in the second, a unilateral contract. Acceptance would be effective in either case.

SUMMARY

Agreement represents perhaps the most important aspect of contract formation. To have agreement, there must be an offer and an acceptance. Assent to a contract must be mutual. Courts employ an objective test to assess whether the parties have mutually assented to the terms of the agreement. Such a test asks whether a reasonable offeree would believe that the offeror has made an offer. No secret intent can be shown. An offer is an indication (by a promise or another commitment) of one's willingness to do or to refrain from doing something in the future. The offer must exhibit a clear and present intent to contract and be definite in all respects in order to be a genuine offer under common law. Statements of opinion, statements of intention, and preliminary negotiations are too indefinite to be offers. The same is true of most advertisements: The law usually construes them as invitations for persons to come in and make offers for the types of goods and at the prices indicated in the advertisements. An offer has no legal effect until the offeror communicates it to the offeree. General offers are perfectly legal; but many jurisdictions require that they, too, be communicated to the offeree in order for a valid acceptance to occur.

The four methods of terminating an offer are (1) lapse, (2) revocation, (3) rejection, and (4) acceptance. Generally, neither a revocation nor a rejection takes legal effect until communicated to or received by the other party. However, if an offeree uses an authorized mode of communication, an acceptance may be effective on dispatch. The offeror's power of revocation may be limited by options, by the "firm offer" provision of the Uniform Commercial Code, or by promissory estoppel. All three doctrines have certain elements that must be met before the offeree can cut off the offeror's right to revoke. Acceptance is the usual mode of terminating an offer. A bona fide offer and acceptance bring about an agreement, which in most cases will be tantamount to a contract. Acceptance involves the offeree's assent to all the terms of the offer. The acceptance must be clear and must be communicated to the offeror. Under the mirror image rule of the common law, an acceptance has to match, term by term, the provisions in the offer. A qualified acceptance—one that deviates from the original terms—is called a counteroffer. A counteroffer terminates the original offer and in effect is a rejection of the offer.

If the offeror has not stipulated the mode necessary for a valid acceptance, use of any reasonable (or authorized) mode of communication will make the acceptance effective on dispatch. This is called the mailbox rule. If, in contrast, the offeree has used an unauthorized mode, acceptance must be received to be effective; the mailbox rule will be inapplicable. The mailbox rule does not apply to revocations or rejections. Silence by the offeree ordinarily does not constitute acceptance. In bilateral contracts, communication of the acceptance usually is necessary, but this is not true for unilateral contracts. In unilateral contracts, the offeree accepts the offer merely by completing the act called for in the offer. Because of the problems that can arise from disputes concerning how much time the offeree has to accept in unilateral contracts, courts are hostile to this category of contracts. The Uniform Commercial Code eliminates many of the common law distinctions between bilateral and unilateral contracts.

DISCUSSION QUESTIONS

1 What does a court mean by *mutual assent*?
2 Explain the phrase *objective theory of contracts*.
3 Briefly state the common law rules surrounding a valid offer.
4 Name and define the ways in which an offer can terminate.
5 Is an advertisement a bona fide offer? Why or why not?

6 In what situations will lapse occur by operation of law?
7 Discuss the common law rules of revocation.
8 Name and list the elements for each of the methods available for terminating the offeror's power of revocation.
9 What are counteroffers, and how do they arise?
10 Explain the term *mailbox rule* and its significance.

CASE PROBLEMS

1 Sandra Speckel was injured when a car driven by Laurri Perkins collided with a truck in which Sandra was a passenger. In December, 1983, Speckel's attorney, Stephen Eckman, demanded the insurance policy limits of $50,000 to settle the case. In January, 1984, Perkins's attorney, Donald Wheat, informed Eckman that he had sent Eckman's demand to Perkins's insurance company for consideration even though he himself thought Wheat's settlement demand was too high. No more correspondence occurred between the parties until about a week before the scheduled trial, when Wheat sent the following letter, dated 14 April 1984, to Eckman:

> Dear Mr. Eckman:
>
> In reviewing my file concerning this claim and the upcoming trial, I note that we have a demand in our file for policy limits of $50,000.00. While I agree that the case has some value, I cannot agree that this is a limits case.
>
> At this point in time I have authority to offer you $50,000.00 in settlement of your claim against my client and her mother. I would appreciate hearing from you at your earliest

> convenience and would be pleased to carry any offer you may wish to make back to my client's insurance company for their consideration.
> Very truly yours,
> /s/Donald A. Wheat/cjh

Wheat never saw this letter, which his secretary had signed, and was unaware that his secretary had erroneously typed $50,000 rather than $15,000 as he had dictated. Eckman accepted the offer of $50,000 on behalf of his client on 17 April 1984. Eckman argued that the letter was a valid offer, enforceable as a contract upon Eckman's acceptance of it, because Wheat's subjective intention was irrelevant. Wheat contended that the internal inconsistency in the wording of his letter imposed a duty of inquiry on the offeree when factors raising a presumption of error existed. Who should win? (*Speckel by Speckel* v. *Perkins*, 364 N.W.2d 890 [Minn. App. 1985].)
2 Kern's Bakery decided to change the wrapping material used to package its products and discussed the proposed changes with R-P Packaging's (R-P's) representatives. On 28 December 1977, Kern's plant manager gave R-P's representative a verbal "order" for cellophane wrap. R-P's 4 January 1978 order acknowl-

edgment form contained specifications, delivery instructions, an order date, and quantity. "Later" was typed in the space for the contract price; "W/A" was written in the space entitled "acknowledgment date." At the bottom of the acknowledgment form was typed: "Produce printing plates per artwork sent to Frank Tarpley, but first send photostats with color stripe to customers for approval before etching." R-P's representative testified that "W/A" stood for "will advise," which meant R-P did not have the customer's approval to proceed. R-P did not proceed with the artwork because Kern had never approved it. In the meantime, on 3 January 1978, Kern's was purchased by Flowers Baking Company. As part of the contract for sale, Kern's represented that all pending contracts of more than $5000 to which it was a party had been listed in the agreement. Kern's further agreed to indemnify Flowers (i.e., make up any losses suffered by Flowers) against all liability arising from any misrepresentation by Kern's. The order for cellophane from R-P was not listed. R-P's order acknowledgment arrived after Flowers had assumed control and was never received by Kern's. Flowers ultimately agreed to buy some wrapping material from R-P, accepted it, but then rejected it when the material was too short for the bakery trays. R-P sued Kern's and Flowers for $13,357.11, the purchase price of the packaging material. The court ruled there was no contract between R-P and Kern's under the UCC. Flowers argued there was sufficient evidence under UCC Section 2-204 to prove a contract had existed between R-P and Kern's. Who was correct? (*Flowers Baking Co. of Lynchburg, Incorporated* v. *R-P Packaging Incorporated*, 329 S.E.2d 462 [Va. 1985].)

3. Globe Life and Accident Insurance Company (Globe) issued a life insurance policy insuring the life of Alexis D. Reddick to his mother, Mrs. Reddick, on 1 December 1987 through 1 December 1988. Mrs. Reddick did not pay the premium due on 1 December 1988. Accordingly, after the expiration of the thirty-one-day grace period, the coverage, pursuant to the terms of the policy, automatically lapsed as of the due date. On 5 January 1989, Globe sent the following letter to Mrs. Reddick:

Dear Policyholder:
We're sorry, but at this time your Globe Life Insurance Policy is in danger of lapsing. Our records show that we have not received the premium that was due on 1 December

1988. . . . PLEASE ACT NOW! Send in your payment, along with the attached notice, and the benefits of your policy will remain in full force. We must receive your payment by 20 January 1989.

The final notice that accompanied this letter stated, "PAYMENT IS NEEDED SO YOUR INSURANCE WILL NOT LAPSE." Alexis D. Reddick died on 17 January 1989. On 20 January 1989, Mrs. Reddick notified Globe of the death and mailed in the requested premium. Globe did not receive the premium until after the 20th. When Globe did not pay under the life insurance policy for Alexis's death, Mrs. Reddick sued for breach of contract. She argued that the 5 January 1989 letter had extended the grace period and that, pursuant to the mailbox rule, she had accepted Globe's offer to extend the insurance coverage to 20 January in a timely fashion. How should a court rule in this case? (*Reddick* v. *Globe Life and Accident Insurance Company*, 575 So.2d 207 [Fla. App. 1990].)

4. Mid-State Federal Savings Bank (Mid-State) owned a residential subdivision known as Ethan's Glen, which it had acquired through a foreclosure sale. Marketing and Management Associates, Inc. (MMA), consisting of corporations owned by Lloyd Boggio, Bob Bidwell (deceased), and Jeff Andrews, became interested in the property. During July and August, 1986, MMA and Mid-State negotiated for the sale and purchase of Ethan's Glen. During this period, several drafts of a "Contract for Sale and Purchase" were exchanged between the two parties. In the various versions, one of the parties typically would delete one or more items, and the other party would in turn reinstate the items. On 8 September, Mid-State prepared and signed the last version of the agreement, which was sent to MMA for its execution. The document was signed and witnessed without change by MMA and returned to Mid-State with a letter dated 10 September from Lloyd Boggio. The letter included the following information:

As you suggested, we are ignoring in this document the following issues:
1. Interest reserve [a lender's loan to the buyer to pay the interest on the loan] for the development loan;
2. Interest reserve for the construction loan; and

3. Permanent financing for our buyers at 90% of the selling price and without a requirement to deliver some number of contracts before we are allowed to close an individual buyer (no pre-sale requirement).

We are relying on your assurances that everyone at Mid-State is aware that all of these are essential to our development and marketing plans, and are a prerequisite for ultimately concluding this purchase.

On 8 October, MMA sent Mid-State its proposed Development Business Plan, which set forth details regarding the deferred matters that Boggio's letter had mentioned. Two weeks later, Mid-State advised MMA that "the deal was not going to work." MMA nevertheless insisted that the sale should close on its financing terms as of 10 November 1986. Mid-State responded that it was "terminating the contract" because Mid-State had never agreed to the terms of the financing demanded by MMA. Did an enforceable contract exist between Mid-State, the seller, and MMA, the buyer? (*Mid-State Federal Savings Bank* v. *Marketing and Management Associates, Inc.*, 570 So.2d 1016 [Fla. App. 1990].)

5. Klein, a construction equipment wholesaler, sued Pitman Manufacturing for breach of contract on its alleged failure to sell Klein certain fully assembled truck bodies. Pitman responded that Klein's second purchase order to purchase unassembled bodies had been rejected by a Pitman counteroffer to sell the unassembled truck bodies at a reduced rate if Klein would first satisfy the balance owed from the first purchase order. Pitman argued that since Klein had not accepted this counteroffer, Pitman had the right to cancel the original contract. Who was right? (*Edward Klein Truck and Heavy Equipment Company, Inc.* v. *Pitman Manufacturing Company*, 512 F. Supp. 101 [W.D. Pa. 1981].)

6. In 1984, Koch had enrolled in a group insurance policy that provided $100,000 in accidental death benefits. In 1985, American Heritage Life Insurance Company (American Heritage) sent Koch a premium notice that included an application for increasing the death benefits under the policy to $150,000. The application provided that this increased coverage would "become effective upon the first day of the month following the receipt of [Koch's] premium payment." Koch signed the application on 26 March 1985, and on 29 March 1985, mailed the application and the check for the additional premium to American Heritage's agent, Orsdel. Orsdel received the application and additional premium on 3 April 1985. Koch subsequently died in an automobile accident on 16 April 1985. When American Heritage paid Mrs. Koch only $100,000, she argued that the mailbox rule made the post office the agent of American Heritage and that her husband's mailing of the letter on 29 March 1985 constituted the company's "receipt" of the premium payment and thus validated the additional coverage as of 1 April 1985, prior to Mr. Koch's death. Should a court find this argument persuasive? (*American Heritage Life Insurance Company* v. *Koch*, 721 S.W.2d 611 [Tex. App. 1986].)

7. The Simses sought the assistance of a Baton Rouge store owner, Betty Lou Stokes, in opening a retail women's lingerie shop in Metairie, Louisiana. The agreement between the parties set out Stokes's responsibilities which included, among other things, that Stokes be present for a minimum number of days at the Metairie store "unless both parties agree otherwise." The Simses ultimately sued for a $7500 payment they had made to Stokes on the ground that she had worked in the Metairie store for one day only and thus had breached their agreement. Stokes argued that the Simses knew that the language "unless both parties agree otherwise" was an escape clause insisted upon by Stokes because she knew her daughter's complications from a pregnancy might make travel to Metairie difficult. The Simses contended that Stokes had asked for the clause "in case things came up," and they denied that they knew specifically what Stokes had meant by this phrase. The Simses further stated that it was their understanding that if something did come up, the parties would mutually agree that Stokes could be absent. Was there a contract between the Simses and Stokes? (*Sims-Smith Ltd.* v. *Stokes*, 466 So.2d 480 [La. App. 1985].)

8. Wheeler made an offer on property owned by Ronald D. Woods and Debra Woods Lane. The offer required the sellers to accept the offer in writing on or before midnight on 11 March 1984, in order for the offer to become binding. Woods and Lane ultimately attempted to accept Wheeler's offer by calling Western Union and sending two mailgrams indicating their acceptance on 12 March. Wheeler received these mailgrams on 13 March. When Wheeler found out that Woods and Lane had sold the property to another purchaser, he sued the sellers owing to his belief that he had an enforceable contract with them. Was his reasoning correct? (*Wheeler* v. *Woods*, 723 P.2d 1224 [Wyo. 1986].)

9. W. E. Gilbert & Associates (Gilbert) sued South Carolina National Bank for breach of an alleged contract for construction management services. In early 1981 the bank had developed a construction plan that it tentatively planned to implement over the ensuing year and a half. The bank had solicited applications from firms that desired to be the construction manager for the bank's projects and had selected Gilbert. However, three months later, the bank terminated its relationship with Gilbert. Gilbert then sued the bank, arguing that a contract had been established by a Gilbert brochure, a letter from the bank that lacked information about either the number of projects for which the bank would need management services or the compensation to be paid, and a letter from Gilbert that proposed a fee schedule but left for future reference the compensation to be paid for smaller projects. Would you agree with Gilbert? (*W. E. Gilbert & Associates* v. *South Carolina National Bank*, 330 S.E.2d 307 [S.C. App. 1985].)

10. In early 1984, Ashton Springer, the principal of plaintiff Elvin Associates, began efforts to mount a Broadway musical production about the life and music of Mahalia Jackson. He wrote to defendant Aretha Franklin seeking her agreement to appear in the title role. Franklin called Springer, expressed her strong interest in the production, and told Springer to contact her agents at the William Morris Agency. Springer spoke with Phil Citron and Katy Rothacker of that agency, and in several conversations with the latter discussed the basic financial terms that would govern Franklin's agreement to appear. After an exchange of several proposals and counterproposals, near the end of February 1984, Rothacker called Springer and informed him that Franklin had accepted his final proposal. In the interim, Springer had already set about making the necessary arrangements to get the production going. During a conversation about rehearsal and performance dates, Franklin indicated to Springer that there were no other conflicting engagements on her schedule. In the second week of March, Springer and director-choreographer Faison flew to Detroit to meet with Franklin to discuss various aspects of the production, including rehearsal and performance dates. Franklin agreed to a tentative schedule that called for rehearsals to begin in April and performances to begin in May. After he returned to New York, Springer began negotiating limited partnership agreements with various investors to finance the "Mahalia" production. He also began calling promoters and

theaters in various cities in an effort to reserve dates for performances. During these discussions, he learned for the first time that Franklin had recently cancelled several performances, purportedly owing to a newly acquired fear of flying. Springer spoke with Citron at William Morris regarding these incidents, and Citron reassured Springer that no such problem existed here. Springer also spoke with Franklin, who reassured him that she wanted to do the show and that she would fly as often as necessary. Springer offered to make alternative arrangements for transportation to the various performance sites and to alter the performance schedule to accommodate slower forms of transportation. But Franklin told Springer that she was uncomfortable traveling more than 200 miles per day by ground transportation. Moreover, she strongly assured him that she would overcome her fear of flying. On 23 March 1984, several of Franklin's representatives met with Springer to finalize the agreement. The only major issue left unresolved at the close of this meeting was the location for rehearsals. Franklin's representatives had requested that they occur in Detroit, but Faison subsequently vetoed this proposal, stressing that the lighting and costume designers to be engaged all were in New York. Springer did not convey this information directly to Franklin, but she ultimately learned through her agents that the rehearsals would take place in New York. In the ensuing weeks, the parties exchanged several drafts of the agreement. A final draft of the contract was ready for signature as of 7 June, the date scheduled for Franklin to come to New York to begin rehearsals for the show. Springer had, in the intervening weeks, made all the arrangements necessary for rehearsals to begin. He had hired set, lighting, and costume designers, plus stage and technical crews, and he had reserved dance studios. Springer was in frequent communication with Franklin during this period, as were Faison and other members of the production staff, concerning such varied matters as the compositions to be performed, the costumes she would wear, and the hiring of her own regular backup singers to perform in the chorus. At one point, Franklin even sang one of the production songs to Springer over the telephone. During this period, Faison therefore made final determinations as to the compositions to be performed and as to the cast and chorus. As planned, rehearsals began on 4 June without Franklin and continued for several days. Franklin did not arrive in New York on 7 June and, indeed, never came to New York for the rehearsals. Springer immediately sought an explanation from Franklin's representatives, who informed him that she would not fly. Springer paid the cast through the end of the week and then suspended the production. He attempted to secure another well-known performer to fill the title role, but none of the performers whom he contacted would agree to step into the role at that point. Hence, Springer ultimately abandoned this second at-tempt to mount a production of "Mahalia." Springer, suing in the name of Elvin Associates, later brought a lawsuit against Franklin for breach of contract and promissory estoppel. Should he win this case? (*Elvin Associates* v. *Franklin,* 735 F. Supp. 1177 [S.D. N.Y. 1990].)

C H A P T E R   10

Consideration: The Basis of the Bargain

O U T L I N E

THE BARGAIN AS A CONTRACT THEORY

Despite the rather checkered history that surrounds its principles, no doctrine of common law is as firmly entrenched today as the concept of *consideration*. Though it is shrouded in historical traditions, we nevertheless must come to grips with its tenets if we are to understand modern contract law.

Remember that early in the history of contracts the parties underwent elaborate rituals, such as sealing their contracts with wax and placing their insignia in the wax, in order to demonstrate their willingness to be bound to the terms embodied in the agreement. Although few contracts are under seal today, owing largely to the inconvenience of formalizing every contract, the idea that the parties ought to be actually bargaining and exchanging something of value rather than merely making empty promises has lingered. Filling this ideological gap was the evolution of the notion that the presence of consideration indicates an exchange of something of value by the parties, resulting in an agreement between the parties. Thus, consideration shows that some obligation or duty worthy of a court's protection actually exists. It also establishes that the parties are acting deliberately and intend to bind themselves to the terms of the agreement. Because it rids contracts of excessive formality while encouraging exchanges between people, the doctrine of consideration initially appears well suited to commercial and economic activity and hence to the study of business law. Nevertheless, some of the legal results under this doctrine seem quite harsh. For this reason, theories have emerged that permit an agreement to be binding in some cases despite the lack of consideration. Your overall comprehension will increase if you try to remember the historical context surrounding this quaint doctrine.

DEFINITION

Waiver The voluntary surrender of a legal right; the intentional surrender of a right.

Among the many definitions of the term *consideration,* one of the most common states that consideration is *a waiver, or promised waiver, of rights bargained for in exchange for a promise.* It always consists of either a benefit to the promisor or a detriment to the promisee, bargained for and given in exchange for a promise. In view of previous discussion, you should not be surprised to see the words *bargain, promise,* and *exchange* playing such a prominent role in this definition. Consideration usually takes the form of money, but it may consist of an intangible, noneconomic benefit or detriment or anything of "value" to the parties.

Consideration as an Act or a Forbearance

Implicit in this doctrine is the necessity of the parties' bargaining over some present event or object and exchanging something of value in order to bind themselves to do (or to refrain from doing) something. It is important, then, to check the parties' language closely. Words that sound like promises may

Illusory   Fallacious; nominal as opposed to substantial; of false appearance.

actually be **illusory** ones because the parties have not really committed themselves in any manner to the bargain. If one party never really agrees to do anything (for example, if Sharon Hall says, "I will sell you my car for $8000 *if I feel like it*"), the promise is illusory and unenforceable because no consideration is present.

In unilateral contracts, consideration manifests itself in an act or a forbearance to act (the consideration comes from refraining from engaging in a legal act). For example, suppose your parents promise you a new car if you will earn straight As in school. If you do, the agreement is supported by consideration and will be enforceable in a court of law, assuming you live in a state where family members can sue each other if they breach (that is, fail to perform) this agreement.

Now apply our definition of consideration to see why the agreement is enforceable. You waived your right to unlimited leisure time in exchange for your parents' promise. You and your parents bargained about the straight As, so the car is not a gift to you. You must do something (study more than you would like) or refrain from doing something (watching television and engaging in other leisure activities) to earn it. Furthermore, your parents, the **promisors,** received a benefit (the satisfaction of knowing you are an honor student) while you, the **promisee,** suffered a detriment (studying hard all year) as a result of this bargain. Your act of making perfect grades has therefore been given in exchange for your parents' promise to buy you a car. Note that the benefit they have received has no dollars-and-cents economic value, yet the benefit is sufficient consideration to support their side of the bargain. They will receive what they asked of you.

Promisors   Those who make a promise or commitment.

Promisee   One to whom a promise or commitment has been made.

Check your understanding of these principles as you consider the next case.

Taylor v. Bonilla
801 S.W.2d 553 (Tex. App. 1990)

FACTS   In December, 1985, Scott Taylor met with Tony Bonilla to discuss surrendering Taylor's whole life insurance policy and obtaining its accumulated cash surrender value. Although the parties disagreed about whether Taylor intended to replace the policy when he first contacted Bonilla, they did not dispute the fact that during the meeting the two men discussed Taylor's obtaining a $100,000 term life policy as a "replacement" of the surrendered whole life policy. During the same meeting, Bonilla completed and Taylor signed a number of forms drafted by New York Life Insurance Company (New York Life). These forms included an application for the term policy and a form requesting the surrender of the whole life policy and the return of its accumulated cash value. On the term policy application, Bonilla, New York Life's agent, noted that the whole life policy would terminate upon the issuance of the new term policy. In addition, Taylor signed a sheet entitled "Important Notice Regarding Replacement," which included the following warning:

> If after studying the information made available to you, you do decide to replace the existing life insurance with our company with a new life insurance policy issued by our company, you are urged not to take action to terminate or alter your existing life insurance coverage until after you have been issued

the new policy, examined it, and have found it acceptable to you. If you should terminate or otherwise materially alter your existing coverage and fail to qualify for the life insurance for which you have applied, you may find yourself unable to purchase other life insurance or able to purchase it only at substantially higher rates.

Taylor never gave Bonilla a check for the first premium on the term policy. In addition, he failed to complete a policy loan form or a dividend withdrawal form, either of which would have allowed him to use the accumulated cash value of the whole life policy to pay the first premium on the term policy. Approximately two weeks before his death, Taylor received a New York Life check in "full settlement of all claims" under the whole life policy. Taylor negotiated the check. During the same two-week period, Bonilla received the newly issued term policy. Before Bonilla could deliver the policy to Taylor, however, Taylor was killed in a car wreck. When Mrs. Taylor called Bonilla to inform him of her husband's death and to ask about his coverage with New York Life, Bonilla told her that the new term policy was not yet in force because no premium had been paid on it. Mrs. Taylor revealed that her husband had, before his death, received a check from New York Life and had cashed it. Bonilla then told her he would determine the status of the whole life policy and let her know what he had learned. Later, Bonilla called to tell her that, because Taylor had accepted payment of the cash value of the policy by negotiating New York Life's check, the surrender of the whole life policy had been completed before the accident. Consequently, Bonilla concluded that Taylor had died without any coverage by New York Life. Mrs. Taylor subsequently sued Bonilla and New York Life for breach of contract.

ISSUE   Did Taylor's surrender of the whole life policy serve as consideration for the issuance of the new (i.e., the term life) policy?

HOLDING   Yes. The surrender of valid contract rights, which one is not bound to surrender, constitutes valuable consideration for a return promise.

REASONING   Fundamental contract principles support the proposition that, when no other consideration is shown, mutual obligations by parties to an agreement will furnish sufficient consideration to constitute a binding agreement. In addition, the general rule is that a promisee's surrender of valid contractual rights, which one is not bound to surrender, constitutes valuable consideration for a return promise. New York Life's contention that Taylor had paid no consideration is correct only in the sense that he had neither remitted a check or cash with the application nor completed a dividend withdrawal or policy loan form to pay the premium out of the cash value of the whole life policy. Taylor had, however, surrendered his right for the whole life policy to continue in force under the policy's automatic premium protection clause (i.e., the accumulated cash value of the policy would cover any premium payments Taylor had failed to make). In addition, under other terms of the policy, Taylor had a right to keep the policy in force and to expect the company to pay its face amount to the designated beneficiary on his death. Neither party argues that Taylor would have had that right if the policy had been effectively surrendered. Therefore, upon the surrender of the policy, Taylor gave up his valuable contractual right to have the insurance company pay the face amount of the policy to the beneficiary of his choice. Taylor relinquished this right in return for a promise from the company to provide him with term insurance, conditioned only on his meeting underwriting guidelines. And sufficient evidence existed to show that the parties intended that, upon Taylor's surrender of the whole life policy, the company would in fact issue him a new term policy. Thus, Taylor's surrender of the first policy constituted legally valuable consideration for the issuance of the new policy.

Consideration as a Promise to Act or to Forbear

Both the *Taylor* case and your hypothetical bargain with your parents concerning the new car evince the formation of a unilateral contract. The analysis would be the same, however, if you had *promised* to earn straight As in exchange for your parents' promise to buy the car. In that situation, a bilateral contract would have been created, with the respective promises constituting the consideration to support the agreement, as long as the promises were genuine and not illusory.

Take this example one step further. If, for instance, your parents breach this contract and you want to sue them, they may bargain with you about dropping the lawsuit. If they promise to pay you $1,000 if you do not sue, in exchange for your promise to forego legal action, you will have made another enforceable contract. You know the reasons: A promise to act or to forbear from a certain action, bargained for and given in exchange for another promise, is consideration. Therefore, you should be able to convince a court to force your parents to pay, should they refuse to do so.

However, as the following case indicates, forbearance alone may be insufficient to constitute consideration if the party bases his or her forbearance on a worthless claim.

State ex rel Ludwick v. Bryant
697 P.2d 858 (Kan. 1985)

FACTS   Virginia Bryant owned and operated a day-care service called Tender Loving Care, Inc. (TLC). On 31 July 1981, the check written on TLC's account by Bryant as part of the corporation's second-quarter wage report to the Kansas Department of Human Resources (Human Resources) was returned for insufficient funds. TLC stopped all operations in August, 1981. In October, 1981, Bryant individually filed a petition in bankruptcy and listed Human Resources as a creditor. On 29 April 1982, Bryant received a discharge in bankruptcy, but the debt owed by TLC to Human Resources was not allowed in the bankruptcy action because the bankruptcy court held Bryant was not personally liable for the taxes owed by TLC to the state. On 12 July 1982, a representative of Human Resources asked Bryant to come to its office. While there, she was told she needed to pay the $231.79 debt of TLC. When she mentioned she had received a discharge in bankruptcy, department officials told her that she needed to pay the debt, since state unemployment taxes could not be discharged in bankruptcy. She eventually signed a personal guarantee to pay off TLC's debt on an installment basis. Bryant later contacted her attorney, who informed the department that the debt covered by the personal guarantee had been discharged in bankruptcy and that, further, the guarantee lacked consideration. Human Resources argued that consideration had been present, since both Bryant and TLC had benefited from the guarantee's provisions relating to mode of payment and from the department's resultant forbearance from suit on the debt.

ISSUE   Was Bryant's guarantee to pay TLC's debt supported by consideration so as to create a valid contract between Bryant and Human Resources?

HOLDING   No. There was no consideration present in Bryant's guarantee because Human Resources' forbearance to sue Bryant and TLC was based on a worthless claim and as such provided no consideration to support the contract.

REASONING   Kansas follows the traditional rule that any forbearance to prosecute or defend a claim or action, or to do an act that one is not legally bound to perform, usually represents sufficient consideration for a contract based thereon, unless the claim or defense is obviously invalid, worthless, or frivolous. Here, the debt owed by TLC was incapable of either enforcement or collection, making Human Resources's agreement to forbear without value. Hence, no consideration to support Bryant's execution of the guarantee ever came into existence.

Adequacy of Consideration

Going back to our earlier example, can your parents win if they try to argue that $8000 for a new car is too much, or that you are really doing nothing (that is, becoming an honor student hardly constitutes a detriment to you) to secure your side of the bargain? They can try, but courts generally will not be receptive to such arguments. The classic rule states that courts will not inquire into the adequacy of the consideration. Courts instead will assume that the parties themselves remain the best judges of how much their bargain is worth and whether their performances are substantially equivalent. Courts ordinarily will not "second guess" the parties after the fact. The following case illustrates this important principle.

Buckingham v. *Wray*
366 N.W.2d 753 (Neb. 1985)

FACTS In November, 1979, John C. Wray II, an Omaha, Nebraska, auto parts dealer, and C. Norris Buckingham entered into a written agreement whereby Wray agreed to stock and maintain an inventory for an auto parts store, K-B Auto, owned by Buckingham in Carson, Iowa. The contract also required Wray to purchase the K-B inventory at 90 percent of the inventory's original cost. The contract provided that in addition Wray would be reimbursed for his travel to and from Buckingham's Iowa store but would not receive any compensation for his services to K-B Auto. Wray, moreover, could receive discounts from wholesale suppliers on purchases of inventory for K-B Auto under the terms of the contract. Unfortunately, K-B Auto eventually went out of business; and Buckingham sought performance of the contract provision relating to Wray's purchase of the K-B Auto inventory. Unable to locate Wray, Buckingham brought suit against Wray concerning the inventory that Buckingham had been unable to liquidate when K-B Auto had closed. Wray argued that there was no valid contract between him and Buckingham because the consideration to support their agreement had been inadequate.

ISSUE Was the parties' agreement supported by consideration, even though by its terms Wray was to receive no compensation for any services he rendered to K-B Auto?

HOLDING Yes. There was sufficient value in the promises made by the parties to constitute adequate consideration to support the agreement between Wray and Buckingham.

REASONING The general rule is that consideration will be deemed sufficient to support a contract if there is any detriment to the promisee or benefit to the promisor. Moreover, courts generally will not inquire into the adequacy of the consideration for a contract, which fact is left instead to the personal judgment of the parties, unless the inadequacy is so great as to suggest fraud. The lack of compensation for Wray's services did not in itself negate the existence of consideration, since compensation and consideration are neither identical nor synonymous. Valuable consideration to support a contract need not be translatable into dollars and cents. If consideration consists of performance or a promise of performance, which the promisor treats and considers as having value to the promisor, there is sufficient consideration for a contract. The promises of the parties and Wray's ability to receive discounts on purchases for his own stores as a result of the increased wholesale purchases made possible by Buckingham's purchases constituted adequate consideration to support the Buckingham-Wray contract.

There are, however, exceptions to the general rule that courts will not inquire into the adequacy of the consideration. If there is evidence that fraud, duress, undue influence, mistake, or other similar situations may have been present in the formation of the contract, adequacy of consideration becomes a much more significant issue. Courts in these situations may permit one or more of the litigants to back out of the deal. The doctrine of unconscionability under either the common law or the Uniform Commercial Code (see Section 2-302 of the UCC, which holds that a court may refuse to enforce a contract if it is shockingly unfair or oppressive) can in some circumstances also form a further basis for overturning bargains when the consideration appears to be grossly inadequate. But remember that courts do not routinely use this rationale to overturn bargaining between parties.

CONSIDERATION IN SPECIAL CONTEXTS

Let us now look at the doctrine of consideration in the special contexts of contracts for the sale of goods, suretyship contracts, liquidated and unliquidated debt situations, and composition agreements.

Contracts for the Sale of Goods

As we learned in Chapter 9, the "firm offer" provision of the Uniform Commercial Code (Section 2-205) states that an offer to buy or sell goods by a merchant who gives assurance in writing that the offer will be held open may be irrevocable for a period of up to three months even if no consideration has been paid to the offeror. Intended to encourage commercial activity that is free from hagglings about "options," this provision dramatically changes the common law rules concerning consideration. Thus, even in the absence of consideration, courts will enforce a UCC "firm offer." The same is true of modifications under the UCC: They, too, are enforceable without consideration (Section 2-209[1]). The common law would require consideration in both situations. In this context, we should refer again to output and requirements contracts, two types of sales contracts mentioned earlier in Chapter 9. Unless the language of these contracts indicates otherwise, courts ordinarily enforce output and requirements contracts as contracts supported by consideration. These courts reason that consideration is present in the form of the respective detriments suffered by the buyer and seller in obligating themselves to deal exclusively with the other party in these circumstances. The promises undergirding such contracts, then, are nonillusory, making the bargains enforceable.

Suretyship Contracts

Default A failure to do what should be done, especially in the performance of a contractual obligation, without legal excuse or justification for the nonperformance.

In contrast to some situations covered by the UCC in which the requirement of consideration is relaxed, the common law definitely requires consideration in suretyship contracts. Such contracts always involve three parties: a principal debtor, a creditor, and a surety. The surety agrees to be liable to the creditor in the event of the principal debtor's **default**. This is a typical commercial transaction. To illustrate, let us assume that Chan Wai (the principal debtor) wishes to buy a new car. She may seek financing from a credit union (the creditor), which in turn may require that she bolster her credit (and decrease its risk) by having another person (such as her father or mother) sign the note as a surety.

If the principal debtor and surety simultaneously promise to pay the promissory note, these promises will be supported by a single consideration (the loan of money to Chan Wai by the credit union). Both promises will be supported by consideration and hence will be enforceable. If, in contrast, the credit union lends the money for the car to Chan Wai and *later* asks a surety to promise to pay in the event of her default, this second promise must be supported by new consideration before the surety's promise is legally binding. As we shall learn, Chan Wai's preexisting obligation to the credit union (because the loan has already been made) does not constitute consideration for enforcing the surety's subsequent promise to pay the credit union.

Liquidated Debts

On the same rationale, if one owes a debt to another person, part payment of that debt is not consideration for full discharge of the debt. For instance, assume Jim Hays has his dentist perform a root canal treatment on him. At the outset, the dentist tells Jim the treatment will cost $190; and Jim agrees that this is a fair price. If Jim pays $150, he cannot successfully argue that this part payment is consideration for full discharge of the debt. Put in legal terms, the dentist will be able to argue that Jim is under a preexisting duty to pay the entire $190. Since neither party has waived any rights and since no bargaining has been done in exchange for this promise to pay $150, there is, by definition, an absence of consideration here. Hence, by the settled rule, Jim is liable for the entire bill, or $190. Central to this discussion is the fact that the debt is *liquidated;* that is, *the amount owed is not disputed.* Jim has agreed to pay $190, and he should not, after the fact, be allowed to escape this obligation. If he could, commercial dealings would be thrown into shambles!

Unliquidated Debts

Suppose that Jim has initially agreed to pay $190 for the root canal treatment. However, after the dentist treats him, Jim continues to have soreness around the gums and the treated tooth is still sensitive to thermal changes. Although he wants to live up to his obligation to pay his debt, he does not believe he should pay the dentist the entire amount because he is not entirely satisfied with the results of the treatment. At the point when Jim expresses these objections to the dentist, the debt is *unliquidated;* that is, the *precise amount owed is in dispute.* If Jim sends the dentist a check for $150 in these circumstances—particularly if he in some fashion indicates that this amount represents full payment for his entire indebtedness—the dentist should understand that cashing Jim's check would permit him to argue that he owes her nothing more. Her act of cashing the check shows that she has impliedly agreed to accept $150 as full payment of the debt. Hence, she would be subject to the common law rule that payment toward an unliquidated debt that is intended as and accepted as full payment is consideration for full discharge of the debt. Therefore, if the dentist wishes to collect the entire $190 she alleges Jim owes, and in order to protect her rights fully, she should not cash Jim's check for $150. Instead she should return it to Jim with a note stating that she is not agreeing to accept the tendered amount as full payment of the debt. If she is strapped for cash, she may be able to cash the check and try to preserve her rights against Jim by endorsing it "with full reservation of all rights." Ideally, she should refrain from cashing the check to avoid the application of the rule that partial payment of an unliquidated debt that is accepted (expressly or impliedly) as full payment of the debt *is* consideration for a full discharge of that debt.

Alternatively, Jim and the dentist may negotiate and ultimately agree that $150 is the amount owed. In this case, each receives a benefit (Jim, by paying $40 less than he thought he would have to pay; the dentist, by getting most of the $190), and each suffers a detriment (Jim, by believing $150 is still too much; the dentist, by thinking she has lost $40) as a result of the bargained-for promise to pay. This notion of an exchange of rights is a hallmark of consideration.

One last note is appropriate. When Jim and the dentist agree on the $150 sum, technically there is a compromise (of the unliquidated debt) that subsequently has led to a satisfaction and an accord. A *compromise* is the *settlement of a disputed claim by the mutual agreement of the parties*. The agreement as to the amount is an *accord,* and the fulfillment of the agreement (the payment of the agreed-upon amount) is a *satisfaction*.

Composition Agreements

Bankruptcy An area of law designed to give an "honest debtor" a fresh start; the proceedings undertaken against a person or a firm under the bankruptcy laws.

Unliquidated debt situations form the basis for a court's enforcement of a *composition agreement,* or *an agreement between a debtor and a group of creditors to accept a smaller percentage of the debt owed in full satisfaction of the claim,* as consideration for full discharge of the debt. Even though you will not study **bankruptcy** until Chapter 31, you probably are aware that the bankruptcy of the debtor poses grave financial risks for the creditor, because in bankruptcy proceedings a creditor ordinarily realizes only a few cents on every dollar owed. Consequently, it is often in the creditor's best interest to give the debtor more time to pay (before the creditor forces the debtor into bankruptcy) or to agree with other creditors to accept smaller sums in full cancellation of larger claims through a composition agreement. As an example, suppose the debtor owes creditors A, B, and C $6000, $4000, and $2000, respectively. The creditors may each agree to accept 50 percent of the respective debts as full satisfaction of their claims against the debtor. Thus, if the debtor pays creditor A $3000, creditor B $2000, and creditor C $1000, none

[handwritten marginal note: Composition - remedy for all "Chapter" of Bankruptcy law.]

of the three will be able to sue for the remaining amount. Courts analogize the result here to a settlement of an unliquidated debt situation, in which the resultant compromise between the debtor and a creditor represents a satisfaction and accord for the debts. Similarly, in composition agreements, those agreed to by the debtor and a group of creditors, payments accepted by the creditors are supported by consideration and thus constitute full discharge of the debts.

Some courts would instead characterize the sums owed to the three creditors as liquidated debts and would find insufficient consideration in the subsequent agreement to justify full discharge of the debts. Ironically, these same courts in the next breath might sanction such agreements on public policy grounds (the debtor's avoidance of bankruptcy and the creditors' realization of partial payment). Whatever the rationale, courts clearly favor composition agreements and therefore enforce them.

ABSENCE OF CONSIDERATION

Under certain circumstances courts will find a total absence of consideration and will not enforce the agreement that the parties have shaped.

Illusory Promises

As mentioned earlier, promises that do not bind the promisor to a commitment are *illusory promises*. Such promises can be performed without any benefit to the promisor or without any detriment to the promisee and hence are not supported by consideration. A promise "to order such goods as we may wish" or "as we may want from time to time" is not a genuine promise at all; it only appears to set up a binding commitment. Instead, it actually allows the promisor to order nothing. Such "will, wish, or want contracts," as they are often called, are void because they lack consideration. Contracts that purport to reserve an immediate right of arbitrary **cancellation** fall into this category of contracts as well. Because of the potential unfairness of allowing one side to free itself from an agreement to which the other side considers itself bound by merely giving notice of cancellation, courts are hostile to attempted exercises of a right of arbitrary cancellation. Courts therefore try to find some actual or implied limitations on the purported immediate right of arbitrary cancellation so as to make it a nonillusory, or binding, promise. Since consideration would exist for such promises, the agreement would be enforceable.

Cancellation Any action shown on the face of a contract that indicates an intent to destroy the obligation of the contract.

Preexisting Duty

As already mentioned briefly, if one performs an act (or refrains from doing something) that one has a preexisting obligation to do (or refrain from doing), settled law holds that such a person has suffered no detriment. Consequently, no consideration is present to support the underlying promise or performance.

Classic examples of these results come from cases involving law enforcement officers. Assume you live next door to a policewoman. Now imagine your neighbor coming to you with this proposition: For $50 she will patrol around your house while you are gone on a trip. Since this sounds like a good deal to you, you agree. But you have second thoughts later and do not pay her. When she sues you in small claims court, she will probably lose because she has a preexisting duty (imposed by law) to try to keep your home free from burglaries. She has suffered no detriment in patrolling around your house, so there is no consideration to support her promise to you.

The following case illustrates the concept that there is no consideration to support a bargain in which one party is only promising to do what he or she already has an obligation to do.

Gross v. Diehl Specialties International, Inc.
776 S.W.2d 879 (Mo. App. 1989)

FACTS Diehl Specialties International, Inc. (Diehl) had employed George Gross under a fifteen-year employment contract originally executed in 1977. The owner of the company, Harry Schenberg, had produced a nondairy product for customers allergic to cows' milk, but the formulation could not withstand pasteurization. Schenberg requested Gross's technical assistance in reformulating the product, Vitamite, for commercial usage. After Gross had successfully reformulated the product, on 24 August 1977, Gross and Diehl entered into an employment contract. The agreement established Gross as Diehl's general manager for fifteen years and set Gross's compensation at $14,400 annually, plus cost of living increases. Furthermore, when 10 percent of Diehl's gross profits exceeded the annual salary, Gross would receive an additional amount of compensation equal to the difference between his compensation and 10 percent of the gross profits for that year. In addition, during the term of the agreement, Gross would receive a royalty of 1 percent of the selling price of all the products produced by Diehl that utilized one or more of Gross's inventions or formulae. Following the term of the agreement, that amount would increase to 2 percent of the selling price. The contract further provided that during the term of the agreement, Gross and Diehl would own the inventions and formulae equally and that following the term of the agreement the ownership would revert to Gross. During the term of the agreement Diehl had exclusive rights to the use of the inventions and formulae and after the term of agreement a nonexclusive right of use. At the time of the execution of this contract, sales had risen from virtually nothing in 1976 to $750,000 annually, due to the development of Vitamite and a chocolate-flavored product formulated by Gross called Chocolite. Eventually Schenberg, who was in declining health, desired to sell his company. In 1982, with yearly sales amounting to $7,500,000, he sold the company to the Diehl family enterprises for $3,000,000. Prior to the sale, the Diehl family insisted on the execution of a new contract between Gross and the firm. Otherwise, the Diehls would substantially reduce the amount the family would pay for Schenberg's business. The new contract executed on 24 August 1982 reduced the expressed term of the contract to ten years, making the expiration date the same as in the original contract; maintained Gross's base salary of $14,400 effective September 1982, thereby eliminating any cost of living increases incurred since the original contract; retained the 10 percent of gross profit provision, provided that the firm would exclusively own Gross's inventions and formulae during the term of the contract and after its termination; and retained the 1 percent royalty during the term of the agreement. The Diehls made no other changes in the agreement except that under this new contract, Gross would receive no royalties after the term of the agreement. Gross received no compensation for executing the new contract, he was not a party to Schenberg's sale of the company, and he received nothing tangible from that sale. After the sale, Gross assumed the title and responsibilities of president of Diehl with additional duties but no additional compensation. In 1983 and 1984, the business of the firm declined severely; and in October, 1984, the firm terminated Gross's employment. When a dispute subsequently arose between Gross and Diehl as to the ownership of the inventions and formulae, Gross sought a declaratory judgment as to whether he or the firm rightfully owned this intellectual property. The trial court held that the 1982 agreement, not the 1977 one, constituted the operative agreement between the parties. Gross then argued on appeal that since Diehl had given no consideration for the 1982 agreement, the 1977 contract therefore remained in effect.

ISSUE   Had Diehl given consideration for the 1982 agreement?

HOLDING   No. Diehl had merely promised to carry out a preexisting contractual duty; hence, Diehl had given no consideration to support this new agreement.

REASONING   A modification of a contract constitutes the making of a new contract, and such new contract must be supported by consideration. When a contract has not been fully performed at the time of the new agreement, the substitution of a new provision, resulting in a modification of the obligations on *both* sides, for a provision in the old contract still unperformed will constitute sufficient consideration for the new contract. Although consideration may consist of either a detriment to the promisee or a benefit to the promisor, a promise to carry out an already existing contractual duty does not amount to consideration. Under the 1982 contract, Diehl assumed no detriment it did not already have. The term of the contract expired on the same date under both contracts, and Diehl undertook no greater obligations than those previously set out in the 1977 contract. Gross, on the other hand, received less than he had enjoyed under the original contract, since the firm in the 1982 agreement reduced his base pay to the 1977 amount despite the provision in the 1977 contract for cost of living adjustments. The new agreement also took away Gross's equal ownership in the formulae during the term of the contract and after its termination. Similarly, Gross lost all royalties after termination of the agreement and the right to use and license the formulae subject to the firm's right to nonexclusive use upon the payment of royalties. Simply put, in exchange for nothing, Diehl acquired exclusive ownership of the formulae during and after the agreement had terminated, turned its nonexclusive use after termination into exclusive use and control, and achieved a reduction in Gross's base salary. Because Diehl did no more than promise to carry out an already existing contractual duty, Diehl had provided no consideration for the 1982 agreement. Diehl nevertheless maintained that consideration had passed to Gross because the purchase of the firm by the Diehl family might not have occurred without the later agreement. Diehl also maintained that the purchase had provided Gross with continued employment and a financially viable employer. Yet the evidence showed that Gross had enjoyed continued employment with the same employer under the 1977 agreement and that nothing in the 1982 agreement had provided for any additional financial protection for Gross. The essence of Diehl's position was that Schenberg had received more from his sale of the company because of the new agreement than he would have obtained without it. Traditional contract principles, however, make it difficult to convert Schenberg's windfall into a benefit to Gross. Consequently, the 1977 agreement, not the one executed in 1982, constituted the operative agreement between the parties.

Besides obligations or duties imposed by law, preexisting duties may stem from contractual agreements. There are numerous cases dealing with these situations. To use a simple example, suppose G & H Painting Service has contracted with you to paint your basement for $900. Halfway through the job, the crew boss tells you he will dismiss the crew unless you agree to pay him $200 more (he has just seen the latest consumer price index and knows inflation is winning against him). Because you are planning a party two days hence, you grudgingly say yes. The question, of course, is do you have to pay $900 or $1100? Based on the doctrine of preexisting obligations, you will generally have to pay only $900, since the firm already owes you the duty of finishing the basement. But if you subsequently want G & H to lay a concrete patio for you, your promise to pay $500 in return for G & H's work on the patio is supported by new consideration—G & H has not obligated itself to construct the patio as part of the original agreement—and you must pay $500 more for this additional work.

To return to the earlier example, assume now that in the middle of winter there is a freakish humid spell that causes a paint-resistant fungus to grow in your basement. As a result, G & H has to paint the walls three times to cover them. If this condition arose after the firm began the work, most courts would characterize this blight as an unforeseen or unforeseeable difficulty and would order you to pay the higher price. The same would hold true if you and the firm had canceled the original contract and had started anew with different promises and obligations. In both situations, consideration would support the new promises. Strikes, inflation in the prices of raw materials, and lack of access to raw materials do not meet the test of "unforeseen or unforeseeable difficulties"; and new promises extracted on these bases would ordinarily lack consideration and thus be unenforceable.

Moral Consideration

We have noted that harsh outcomes sometimes result from the application of the doctrine of consideration. Promises made from a so-called *moral obligation* embody one such subcategory of consideration and are generally not enforced. In general, courts adhere strictly to the requirement of consideration in these contexts.

For example, suppose your child has been saved without injury from the jaws of a snarling Doberman pinscher because of the efforts of a passerby. The person who saved your child unfortunately suffers deep cuts that eventually require cosmetic surgery. Faced with such generosity, who among us would not promise this person the world? You are only human, so you offer to pay this Good Samaritan's lost wages while she is in the hospital. As time passes, however, you grow less willing to pay; and finally you cease paying her altogether. If she sues you, you will usually win because a court will conclude that she has bestowed a gift on you—that is, saving the child. Consequently, no consideration is present (note, too, that there was no bargaining *before* the humanitarian gesture in exchange for your promise to pay). Because of your self-interest, *you* may not think this particular result under this doctrine is harsh; but almost anyone else reading about this situation would. Therefore, in a few jurisdictions, courts would reject the settled rule by holding that the Good Samaritan could win. Note, though, that this would be the position taken by a minority of courts. The next case follows the majority rule.

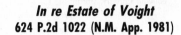

In re Estate of Voight
624 P.2d 1022 (N.M. App. 1981)

FACTS Four months before he died, while in Illinois, Mr. Voight gave two promissory notes for $13,500 each to his stepsons, John and Thomas Kapsa, for debts owed to the stepsons by their mother, Voight's deceased wife. When Mr. Voight died, the Kapsas sued Voight's estate to collect on the promissory notes.

ISSUE Were the promissory notes supported by consideration so as to be valid contracts?

HOLDING No. Moral consideration does not constitute legal consideration.

REASONING Under Illinois law (which governs the issues here), a person has no legal obligation to assume the debt of his or her deceased spouse. Furthermore, a moral obligation alone is not valid consideration for a promise to pay. Since Mr. Voight never had a legal duty to pay the Kapsas the money his wife owed them, the only consideration for the promissory notes was the moral duty he had felt. This was not sufficient to make the notes valid and enforceable in Illinois.

Past Consideration

Stipend A fixed sum of money paid periodically for services or to defray expenses.

Related to this doctrine of moral consideration is the doctrine of *past consideration*. This issue typically arises when a person retires and the former boss agrees to pay the employee a small **stipend** "in consideration of twenty-five years of faithful service." Since the old services are executed (completed or finished), they cannot form the basis for a new promise. The same is true of a promise to pay a relative based on the promisor's "love and affection" for the promisee. Notice that in both cases there is no bargaining and no *exchange* of anything of value. Accordingly, neither of the promises is supported by consideration and neither would be enforceable. As traditional legal authority holds, "Past consideration is *no* consideration." The following case illustrates this point.

Tindall v. Konitz Contracting, Inc.
783 P.2d 1376 (Mont. 1989)

FACTS Francis M. Tindall operated a general contracting business centered in Lewistown, Montana, that primarily dealt with crushing gravel for secondary roadways and runways. In 1979, Tindall met Thomas Konitz, who at that time was employed by another general contracting firm. Tindall wanted to retire, and the two men had several discussions regarding the sale of Tindall's business to Konitz. On 1 August 1979, Konitz and Tindall consummated the sale of the business through the signing of three documents. Both parties realized that the only way Konitz could successfully take over the business was through Tindall's initial support and active assistance, including Tindall's bonding capacity. During the next few months, Konitz bid on three jobs. Tindall, however, signed the bid forms and furnished the bonds. Although Tindall was granted these jobs, Konitz did the actual work and paid the bond premiums. The payments received on the jobs went first to Tindall, who did not withhold any service charges for the use of his bonding capacity. During the spring of 1981, Tindall began pressuring Konitz to sign a personal service contract in Tindall's behalf. The contract provided that Konitz would pay Tindall for his services at a rate of 4 percent of the gross contract price for Tindall's assistance in the bidding, preparation, and other administrative services necessary to complete the contract and another 3.5 percent whenever Tindall acted as a guarantor or surety on the contract. Although Konitz initially refused to sign the personal service contract, he ultimately relented when Tindall threatened to put Konitz out of business by going to Konitz's suppliers, bankers, and bonding companies and by repossessing Konitz's equipment. The personal service contract that Tindall prepared and that Konitz signed stated that Tindall had helped bid and bond five jobs and that Tindall therefore was entitled to $138,629.80, in payments of $1000 a month beginning 1 August 1984. Owing to Konitz's improved financial condition, Konitz decided not to make the 1 August payment. When Tindall sued him for breach of contract, Konitz asserted that no consideration existed for the personal service contract.

ISSUE   Had Tindall given consideration in exchange for Konitz's signing of the personal service contract?

HOLDING   No. Tindall's assistance constituted past consideration, which is insufficient to support a promise.

REASONING   Consideration is an essential element of a contract. Neither party disputes the fact that Konitz initially required Tindall's bonding capacity and that Tindall had therefore assisted Konitz with bonding for the first few jobs, but all these jobs were bonded and executed prior to the signing of the personal service contract in November, 1981. By the time Konitz signed the personal service contract in 1981, he had already developed a bonding capacity for himself and no longer needed Tindall's assistance. The general rule is that past consideration is not sufficient to support a promise. This rule of common law contract principles applies because the detriment had already been incurred and therefore could not have been bargained for in exchange for the promise. Similarly, in these circumstances, Tindall had tendered his "consideration"—the signing of the personal service contract—prior to the bonding assistance. Konitz's promise to pay Tindall $138,629.80 thus was unenforceable because it was supported by past consideration.

EXCEPTIONS TO THE BARGAINING THEORY OF CONSIDERATION

As should now be apparent, whether or not the parties have bargained with a resulting exchange of value appears to be of crucial importance under the common law rules surrounding consideration. Still, courts will enforce agreements despite a lack of consideration in the following four situations: (1) promissory estoppel, (2) charitable subscriptions, (3) promises made after the statute of limitations has expired, and (4) promises to repay debts after a discharge in bankruptcy.

Promissory Estoppel   In Chapter 9, we discussed promissory estoppel in the context of preventing an offeror's revocation of the offer. To recapitulate, we said that courts apply this equitable doctrine in order to avoid injustice. Essentially, the elements are the same whether we are dealing with offers or with consideration. In both, the promisor makes a definite promise that he or she expects, or should reasonably expect, will induce the plaintiff/promisee to act (or refrain from acting) in a manner that may be detrimental to the latter person; accordingly, the promisor will be held to his or her promise to avoid injustice. Simply put, the promisor will be prevented from asserting a defense (here, that there is no consideration) normally available to the promisor.

In the case of the employer who offered to pay his employee "in consideration of twenty-five years of faithful service," promissory estoppel might be used as a substitute for consideration to enable the employee to win. In other words, if the employer has in fact paid the former employee $100 a month for ten years, and the employee has given up opportunities for part-time employment owing to an expectation of continued stipends, some courts will conclude that the employer must continue the payments despite the absence of bargaining or of an exchange of anything of value.

Charitable Subscriptions

Likewise, promissory estoppel may help promisees win in the category of *charitable subscriptions,* which is another exception to the requirement of consideration. You can probably guess how this legal issue—*the promise to pay a certain sum to a nonprofit charity*—arises.

Typically, a generous person wishes to donate a sizable amount to a worthy charity and promises to do so. Later this humanitarian zeal wanes; the person no longer wishes to live up to the agreement. If you were the donor, what would you argue? In all likelihood, you would try to argue that you intended to bestow a gift. Since consideration is by definition lacking in a gift (there is no bargaining and no exchange of value), you could not be held liable for this promise.

Ordinarily, though, a would-be donor will have to live up to the agreement because charitable institutions rely on the belief that the amount pledged in subscriptions will be forthcoming and because people make pledges based on the knowledge that other people will be making similar pledges. Courts, of course, believe that charitable institutions (like universities, hospitals, or churches) serve noble purposes. Thus, in addition to resorting to promissory estoppel as a substitute for consideration as shown above, courts may alternatively enforce the promise on public policy grounds.

Promises Made After Expiration of the Statute of Limitations

State statutes of limitations set time limits on when creditors can bring suit against debtors for sums owed to them. Ordinarily this period is from two to six years, after which the creditor cannot maintain suit against the debtor. Sometimes the debtor wants to repay the debt even if this time limit has passed. As we have already learned, there seems to be no consideration present in such a circumstance; there is no bargaining, and it may be argued that the debtor's promise represents moral consideration at best.

But our analysis would be wrong under most state statutes and decisions, because the debtor's new promise to pay will be enforced if it is in writing.

The public policy of encouraging people to pay their debts probably forms the basis for this exception to the bargaining theory of consideration.

As the next case shows, the written promise must be specific.

Curry v. Winnfield
398 So.2d 97 (La. App. 1981)

FACTS   Curry was the holder of a promissory note executed by Winnfield on 26 June 1973. The note was secured by a real estate mortgage and was payable in thirty-six monthly installments commencing on 26 July 1972. Winnfield made no payments on the note. The statute of limitations for suing on such notes in Louisiana is five years. However, Curry did not file suit until 24 March 1980, more than five years after the default. On 9 April 1980, Winnfield wrote to Curry's attorney, "Please write me if I could work out some kind of agreement with the note."

ISSUE   Was the letter of April 9 a sufficient promise to pay to eliminate the running of the statute of limitations?

HOLDING   No. This acknowledgment of debt was not a sufficient promise to allow Curry to sue despite the running of the statute of limitations.

REASONING   At the time the letter was written, the statute of limitations had already been exceeded. Yet, a natural obligation to pay the note still existed, even though the time period for filing suit had passed. Nevertheless, for a natural obligation to be sufficient consideration for a new contract, there must be a new promise to pay the debt in order to eliminate Curry's bar to recovery posed by the running of the statute of limitations. The language contained in the letter did not amount to a new promise to pay the debt and therefore did not constitute a renunciation by Winnfield of the running of the statute of limitations.

Promises to Pay Debts After Bankruptcy Discharges

The same policy applies and the result is similar when a debtor subsequently promises to pay a debt after he or she has received a discharge in bankruptcy. Again, no consideration underlies this new promise, but most states will allow the enforcement of the promise, provided that the debtor make the promise to pay in open court and with a full understanding of its significance, as required by the Bankruptcy Reform Act of 1978. (Bankruptcy is covered in detail in Chapters 31 and 32.)

YOU BE THE JUDGE

Before their marriage in 1984, a Colorado couple entered into a prenuptial agreement in which each promised to put the other through college. At the time of their divorce, the husband had completed his college degree but the wife had not. The wife subsequently sued the husband for breach of contract based on the prenuptial agreement. The husband countered by saying that the prenuptial agreement constituted a contract

FIGURE 10.1 Consideration: A Summary

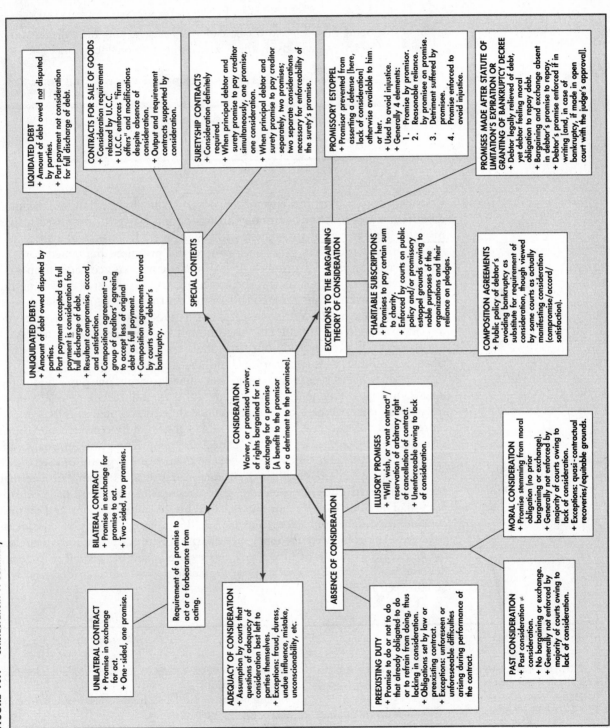

LIQUIDATED DEBT
+ Amount of debt owed not disputed by parties.
+ Part payment not consideration for full discharge of debt.

CONTRACTS FOR SALE OF GOODS
+ Consideration requirement relaxed by U.C.C.
+ U.C.C. enforces "firm offers" and modifications despite absence of consideration.
+ Output and requirement contracts supported by consideration.

SURETYSHIP CONTRACTS
+ Consideration definitely required.
+ When principal debtor and surety promise to pay creditor simultaneously, one promise, one consideration.
+ When principal debtor and surety promise to pay creditor separately, two promises; two separate considerations necessary for enforceability of the surety's promise.

PROMISSORY ESTOPPEL
+ Promisor prevented from asserting a defense (here, lack of consideration) otherwise available to him or her.
+ Used to avoid injustice.
+ Generally 4 elements:
 1. Promise by promisor.
 2. Reasonable reliance by promisee on promise.
 3. Detriment suffered by promisee.
 4. Promise enforced to avoid injustice.

PROMISES MADE AFTER STATUTE OF LIMITATION'S EXPIRATION OR GRANTING OF BANKRUPTCY DECREE
+ Debtor legally relieved of debt, yet debtor feeling moral obligation to repay debt.
+ Bargaining and exchange absent in debtor's promise to repay.
+ Debtor's promise enforced if in writing (and, in case of bankruptcy, if made in open court with the judge's approval).

UNLIQUIDATED DEBTS
+ Amount of debt owed disputed by parties.
+ Part payment accepted as full payment is consideration for full discharge of debt.
+ Resultant compromise, accord, and satisfaction.
+ Composition agreement—a group of creditors' agreeing to accept less of original debt as full payment.
+ Composition agreements favored by courts over debtor's bankruptcy.

SPECIAL CONTEXTS

EXCEPTIONS TO THE BARGAINING THEORY OF CONSIDERATION

CHARITABLE SUBSCRIPTIONS
+ Promises to pay certain sum to charity.
+ Enforced by courts on public policy and/or promissory estoppel grounds owing to noble purposes of the organizations and their reliance on pledges.

COMPOSITION AGREEMENTS
+ Public policy of debtor's avoiding bankruptcy as substitute for requirement of consideration, though viewed by some courts as actually manifesting consideration (compromise/accord/ satisfaction).

CONSIDERATION
Waiver, or promised waiver, of rights bargained for in exchange for a promise [A benefit to the promisor or a detriment to the promisee].

BILATERAL CONTRACT
+ Promise in exchange for promise to act.
+ Two-sided, two promises.

UNILATERAL CONTRACT
+ Promise in exchange for act.
+ One-sided, one promise.

Requirement of a promise to act or a forbearance from acting.

ADEQUACY OF CONSIDERATION
+ Assumption by courts that questions of adequacy of consideration best left to parties themselves.
+ Exceptions: fraud, duress, undue influence, mistake, unconscionability, etc.

ABSENCE OF CONSIDERATION

ILLUSORY PROMISES
+ "Will, wish, or want contract" / reservation of arbitrary right of cancellation of contract.
+ Unenforceable owing to lack of consideration.

MORAL CONSIDERATION
+ Promise stemming from moral obligation (no prior bargaining or exchange).
+ Generally not enforced by majority of courts owing to lack of consideration.
+ Exceptions: quasi-contractual recoveries/equitable grounds.

PREEXISTING DUTY
+ Promise to do or not to do that already obligated to do or to refrain from doing, thus lacking in consideration.
+ Obligations set by law or preexisting contract.
+ Exceptions: unforeseen or unforeseeable difficulties arising during performance of the contract.

PAST CONSIDERATION
+ Past consideration ≠ consideration.
+ No bargaining or exchange.
+ Generally not enforced by majority of courts owing to lack of consideration.

in which being married was the consideration for paying for college, and since the marriage was over, there was failure of consideration.

If you were the decisionmaker, for whom would you rule and why?

Source: "Law," Ellen Joan Pollock, *The Wall Street Journal*, April 17, 1992, page B1.

SUMMARY

Consideration is a firmly entrenched doctrine in modern law. A common definition states that consideration consists of any waiver or promised waiver of rights bargained for in exchange for a promise. It exists when there is a benefit to the promisor or a detriment to the promisee bargained for and given in exchange for a promise. In unilateral contracts, consideration may take the form of an act or a forbearance to act. In bilateral contracts, the respective promises constitute consideration. In the absence of fraud, duress, undue influence, or unconscionability, courts will generally not inquire into the adequacy of the consideration. Although no consideration is necessary under the UCC provisions about firm offers and modifications of sales contracts, consideration is necessary to hold a surety liable.

The doctrine of preexisting obligations mandates that one pay a liquidated debt in full; part payment is not consideration for full discharge of the debt. In contrast, part payment of an unliquidated debt, if accepted as full payment, represents a compromise of the debt and is supported by consideration. Such satisfaction and accord completely cancel the debt. The same rationale validates composition agreements between the debtor and a group of creditors.

Agreements based on illusory promises or promises grounded in either preexisting legal duties or preexisting contractual relationships lack consideration. The same is true of promises based on moral obligations and on past consideration. The four exceptions to the "bargaining" theory of consideration are (1) promissory estoppel, (2) charitable subscriptions, (3) promises made after the statute of limitations has expired, and (4) promises to repay debts after discharges in bankruptcy. Agreements without consideration will be enforced in these situations.

[handwritten margin notes: "Benefit to promisor or Detriment to promisee"; "Enforced"]

DISCUSSION QUESTIONS

1. How did the concept of consideration develop historically?
2. Define *consideration*.
3. Can "doing nothing" ever be consideration to support a promise?

4. Why do courts refuse to inquire into the adequacy of consideration?
5. Discuss how the UCC treats consideration in contracts for the sale of goods.
6. Explain why part payment of a liquidated debt is

not consideration for full discharge of the debt, but part payment accepted as full payment for an unliquidated debt is.

7. What are composition agreements, and how are they related to the doctrine of consideration?

8. When will courts enforce new promises made about the subject matter of an earlier contract?

9. Why do the doctrines of moral or past consideration permit harsh results?

10. Explain the four situations in which courts will enforce agreements despite a lack of bargaining (and hence consideration).

CASE PROBLEMS

1. Jackie Mohr worked as a secretary for Arachnid, Inc. (Arachnid). On 13 February 1989, Mohr and Arachnid entered into a written agreement for the payment of six months' severance pay if Mohr's employment should cease as a result of a significant change in the ownership of the firm's stock. The agreement was to be effective only if such termination occurred within one year of the date of the agreement. On 24 February 1989, owing to a shareholder buyout, the ownership of the company changed significantly. Mohr was notified on 12 April 1989 that her employment would terminate. At that time, Arachnid paid Mohr two weeks' severance pay. When Mohr sued for breach of contract, Arachnid argued that the agreement was void and unenforceable because Mohr had provided no consideration. Did Mohr's continuing to work for Arachnid constitute consideration sufficient to support an express agreement to pay severance wages? (*Mohr v. Arachnid, Inc.*, 559 N.E.2d 1098 [Ill. App. 1990].)

2. James "Buster" Douglas and his manager, John P. Johnson, had signed a boxing promotional agreement with Don King Productions, Inc. (DKP) for $25,000 on 31 December 1988. The agreement provided DKP with the "sole and exclusive right to secure and arrange all professional boxing bouts" for Douglas for the term of the agreement. DKP in turn obligated itself to promote not less than four bouts requiring Douglas's services during the annual period ending 25 February 1990 and, for two years thereafter, no fewer than three bouts per year, on the dates and at sites designed by DKP, and against opponents designated by DKP after consultation with Douglas and Johnson. The parties promised to negotiate and agree on the purses payable by DKP to Douglas for bouts undertaken pursuant to the agreement, with all purses remaining subject to a floor of $25,000 plus $10,000 in training expenses per bout. The promotional agreement also set forth DKP's intention to promote a heavyweight championship bout involving Douglas and provided that the three-year term of the agreement would be automatically extended in the event that Douglas were recognized as world champion, "to cover the entire period [Douglas was] world champion and a period of two years following" Douglas's loss of the title. Under the agreement, Douglas promised not to "participate in any bouts other than bouts promoted or co-promoted by DKP" nor "render . . . services as a professional boxer" to any entity other than DKP. Douglas also represented that he would not enter into any oral or written contract that "conflict[ed] in any material respect with the provisions" of the agreement or that either "purport[ed] to grant similar or conflicting rights" to any person other than DKP or that "might interfere with [Douglas's] full and complete performance" of the agreement. Pursuant to this promotional agreement, Douglas participated in three bouts arranged by DKP during the first year ending 26 February 1990. The last of these involved the heavyweight championship bout held on 10 February 1990 in Tokyo, Japan, between Douglas and then-heavyweight champion Michael Tyson. In accordance with the promotional agreement, which called for the monetary terms of each bout to be negotiated and set forth in a separate agreement, Douglas and Johnson entered into a bout agreement for that fight, pursuant to which Douglas would be paid $1.3 million, inclusive of training expenses. Douglas won the bout and became the undisputed heavyweight champion of the world. Relations between Don King and the Douglas camp soured, however, when King, who was also Tyson's promoter, objected to the alleged "long count" that had occurred during the eighth round of the fight. Tyson had knocked Douglas down during that round, but Douglas was on his feet before the referee concluded the count. Douglas subsequently knocked out Tyson in the tenth round.

King's objection temporarily placed in doubt the official recognition of Douglas's victory over Tyson. Shortly after this championship bout, Douglas and Johnson executed a contract with the Mirage Hotel for Douglas, now the heavyweight champion, to fight two bouts at the hotel for a minimum of $50 million. But the Mirage Hotel contracts would not be binding until Douglas and Johnson obtained a release from DKP of its allegedly exclusive promotional rights or, alternatively, a judicial declaration that the promotion and bout agreements were void and unenforceable. In filing suit for a declaratory judgment, Douglas and Johnson argued that the contractually specified million-dollar purse represented inadequate consideration because this figure amounted to a "mere token" of Douglas's value as the world heavyweight champion. Should a court accept Douglas and Johnson's arguments in these circumstances? (*Don King Productions, Inc.* v. *Douglas,* 742 F. Supp. 741 [S.D.N.Y. 1990].)

3. Price worked as a salesperson for Mercury Supply Company (Mercury), a cleaning materials and janitorial supplies company, near Nashville. Weil, the owner of the company, gave Price several promotions over the years, and in March, 1975, changed Price's title to vice-president for sales. There was no change in Price's compensation at that time, and his duties remained the same as they had been in his earlier positions of sales manager and sales coordinator. According to Price, Weil at this time orally promised him that he would never have to worry about employment because of the service he had rendered to the company in the past. Price also stated that Weil told him he had been hired as the vice-president for sales of Mercury for the rest of his life or until he retired. Unfortunately, over the years, the relationship between Price and Weil cooled; and Weil discharged Price on 2 March 1981. Price later argued that in March, 1975, the parties had entered into a valid oral employment contract in which he had been hired as the vice-president for sales of Mercury for the rest of his life or until his retirement. Was there consideration present to support this alleged agreement? (*Price* v. *Mercury Supply Company, Inc.,* 682 S.W.2d 924 [Tenn. App. 1984].)

4. Leiter was an associate in a law firm with Parkhurst, Fraser, and Newlin. Because of Leiter's alleged conflict of interest in a sale of property that had resulted in damages to the law firm, on 24 July 1974, Leiter agreed to pay his three associates $4500 each within five years. Leiter died after making this agreement, and his estate later refused to pay the lawyers by arguing that there was no consideration to support Leiter's agreement with them. Was the agreement a valid compromise of Parkhurst, Fraser, and Newlin's claims? (*In re Estate of Leiter,* 409 N.E.2d 91 [Ill. App. 1980].)

5. In July, 1975, Pennsylvania Blue Shield (Blue Shield), the trade name of Medical Services Association of Pennsylvania, solicited bids for the lease of a computer. These bids were to be received by Blue Shield no later than 12:00 noon on 18 August 1975. Universal Computer Systems, Inc. (Universal), through its president, Warren Wilson, contacted Joel Gebert, the sole Blue Shield contact for the request for bids, and obtained Gebert's assurance that he (Gebert) would have the bid proposal picked up at the Allegheny Airlines ticket counter in Harrisburg on the morning of 18 August 1975, in time for the 12:00 noon deadline. Pursuant to Gebert's promise, Wilson dispatched his bid proposal by Allegheny Airlines' PDQ Service on 18 August 1975, at approximately 8:30 A.M. When Wilson called Gebert to give him the waybill number so that the proposal could be picked up, Gebert informed Wilson that he had changed his mind regarding his promise to pick up the bid proposal and would not do so. After many difficulties, Wilson finally persuaded Allegheny Airlines to release the package to a courier other than the addressee, Blue Shield; but the package arrived at Blue Shield after 12:00 noon and was rejected as untimely. Wilson argued that if the proposal had arrived in a timely fashion, Universal's bid would have been the lowest and that the firm should therefore receive damages in the amount of the expected profit on the contract. Was either Gebert or Wilson's promise illusory? If either was illusory, could Universal use promissory estoppel as a substitute for consideration? (*Universal Computer Systems, Inc.* v. *Medical Services Association of Pennsylvania,* 474 F. Supp. 472 [M.D. Pa. 1979], *modified* 628 F.2d 820 [3d Cir. 1980].)

6. Lenaxa State Bank (the bank) had loaned Thurston approximately $34,000 for use in his lawn care business. Since Thurston had not paid the notes as they had become due, Lenaxa notified Thurston that it would foreclose on the security agreements and repossess the collateral on the notes if Thurston did not take some action on the notes. Thurston and the bank subsequently agreed to execute a $20,000 second mortgage on Thurston's home. The bank further promised not to file this mortgage for two weeks so that Thurston could collect $23,000 in accounts receivable. If Thurston

brought in the monies, Lenaxa promised it would destroy the mortgage. Thurston did not pay, so the bank filed the mortgage. Thurston argued there was no consideration to support the second mortgage because the bank had foreclosed; hence, there had been no forbearance. But the bank asserted there had been forbearance to sue for a time sufficient to constitute consideration. What should a court decide? (*Safety Federal Savings and Loan Association* v. *Thurston*, 648 P.2d 267 [Kan. App. 1982].)

7. Thomas was injured in March, 1981, while working for Rooks Transit Lines, Inc. On 9 November 1981, Thomas filed to collect insurance benefits from Michigan Mutual Insurance Company, Rooks's insurer. On 3 December 1981, the insurance company's adjuster contacted Thomas's attorney and offered to settle the claim for $664. On 29 December 1981, Thomas's attorney called the adjuster and informed him that Thomas had agreed to accept this settlement. The adjuster told the attorney that he would issue a check for $664 when Thomas had signed a voluntary dismissal and had mailed it to his attention. On 27 January 1981, Thomas's attorney informed the insurance company that Thomas had had a "change of heart" and that Thomas no longer wished to accept the $664. The insurance company argued that a valid settlement or compromise of the claim had occurred and that Thomas was obligated to accept the $664. Was the company correct? (*Thomas* v. *Michigan Mutual Insurance Company*, 358 N.W.2d 902 [Mich. App. 1984].)

8. Hamilton Bancshares, Inc. (Hamilton) entered into a "stock purchase option" with the Leroys whereby Hamilton could buy bank stock from the Leroys within an eighty-day period if it chose to do so. Each option was purportedly granted "in consideration of the sum of one dollar . . . it had paid. . . ." Hamilton also gave the Leroys $5000 in earnest money, "to be applied to the purchase price of the shares subject to the option in the event that the option is exercised and to be refunded to [Hamilton] in the event that this option is not exercised." Five weeks later, the Leroys attempted to withdraw the option, at which point Hamilton rejected this attempted withdrawal and exercised the option. The Leroys contended that since the $1 had not in fact been paid to them as recited in the option agreement, there was no consideration and hence no contract. The Leroys thus characterized the option agreement as an offer that could be withdrawn any time prior to acceptance. The Leroys further argued that since the $5000 was to

be refunded to Hamilton if the option were not exercised, the $5000 was of no benefit to them and therefore did not constitute consideration either. Hamilton admitted that the $1 had not in fact been paid but asserted that the Leroys' use of the earnest money for the period of the option constituted consideration sufficient to support the option. Who had the better argument, the Leroys or Hamilton? (*Hamilton Bancshares, Inc.* v. *Leroy*, 476 N.E.2d 788 [Ill. App. 1985].)

9. William B. Marty, Jr. became an employee of Cubic Corporation (Cubic) in December, 1976. At that time, he signed an invention and secrecy agreement in which he agreed to disclose to the company any ideas or inventions he conceived on company time, to assign to the company all rights in any such discoveries, to cooperate in obtaining patents on these inventions, and to refrain from disclosing any of Cubic's secret inventions or processes. Under the agreement, Cubic promised to pay the expenses of obtaining a patent, $75 on the employee's execution of the patent application, and $75 if the patent were obtained. In mid-May, 1977, Marty thought of an idea for an electronic warfare simulator (EWS), a device for training pilots in electronic warfare. Cubic personnel viewed the idea favorably, funded an internal project to study Marty's concept, and submitted the EWS proposal to the Navy. In June, 1978, Marty, without Cubic's knowledge, applied for a patent on his invention and received the patent in 1979. When Marty offered to license the EWS to Cubic, Cubic insisted that the patent belonged to it and that Marty should assign the patent to the company. Cubic ultimately made Marty's continued employment contingent on this assignment. Marty steadfastly refused to make the requested assignment, and Cubic terminated his employment in 1980. When Cubic sued Marty for breach of contract, he argued that the agreement was unenforceable because the "token" bonus of $150 constituted consideration too inadequate to support a promise to convey the invention to Cubic. He also contended that his employment could not serve as the consideration for the agreement because Cubic had hired him before he had signed it. Should a court accept Marty's reasoning? (*Cubic Corporation* v. *Marty*, 229 Cal. Rptr. 828 [Cal. App. 1986].)

10. In 1982, First Interstate Bank financed a tractor and trailer for C. H. Betterton. From the outset, Betterton had difficulty making the loan payments. On 15 February 1984, Betterton met with a bank official, Stiles, who allegedly warned him that unless he paid off all

the arrearages on his loans, the bank would immediately take measures to collect the debt. Betterton first told her the truck was in a Tucson repair shop. He then allegedly suggested to Stiles that he could bring the loan up to date and keep his payments current by having the broker for whom he worked (i.e., a person who secures contracts for transportation services and sees that they are paid for) take the payments out of his paycheck and transfer them directly to the bank. The broker agreed to make such payments in Betterton's behalf. Betterton, the broker, and the garage owner who was repairing Betterton's truck all believed Stiles had promised to forgo repossession of the truck if the repairs were completed and the payments were made by the broker directly to the bank. However, Stiles had not told Betterton and the others that she had ordered Auto Recovery Bureau (ARB) to repossess the tractor-trailer rig. More importantly, she had not canceled this order after reaching the new agreement with Betterton. The very next day, ARB repossessed the truck while Betterton was making a delivery in Phoenix. When Betterton sued Stiles for breach of contract, the trial court held that no consideration underlay Betterton's agreement with Stiles because he was already under a preexisting duty to keep the truck in good repair pursuant to the terms of the security agreement he had signed with the bank. The lower court did not discuss at all the effect of Betterton's promise to have his broker make the payments directly to the bank. Should the appellate court uphold the lower court's decision? (*Betterton* v. *First Interstate Bank,* 800 F.2d 732 [8th Cir. 1986].)

C H A P T E R 11

Contractual Capacity: The Ability to Agree

O U T L I N E

LEGAL CAPACITY

age - Contract
mental capacity
Id 18 yrs old
Voidable
but not void

Our examination of contract law has stressed the importance of *the parties' mutual assent* to an agreement and some *evidence of their commitment* to be bound to the duties and obligations set out in that agreement. In learning about the legal requisites for agreement and consideration, objective factors like the words uttered or the value exchanged have merited most of our attention. We now place these matters aside and begin instead to concentrate on who the parties to the contract are and their *capacity,* or legal ability, to form a valid contract. Capacity, the third requirement for a valid contract, mandates that the parties to the contract have *the legal ability to bind themselves to the contract and to enforce any promises made to them.* However, incapacity, or lack of such capacity, is the exception, not the rule. Hence, the burden of proof regarding incapacity falls on the party raising it as a defense to enforcement of the contract or as a basis for **rescission** of the contract.

Rescission An annulment or cancellation; a termination of the contract through restoration of the parties to the status quo.

To determine *contractual capacity,* the law looks at the relative bargaining power of the parties involved. Historically, older persons have taken care of the younger members of society. The law attempts to protect children, who remain less adept at bargaining, from overreaching by those who represent more experienced bargainers by allowing children under a certain age to disaffirm (or withdraw from) the contract. The same is true of persons who lack mental capacity, such as insane persons: Contracts made by these persons may be absolutely void, voidable (the insane person can disaffirm the contract), or even valid (if, for example, contract formation occurs during a lucid period). Thus, the existence or absence of legal capacity and the consequences of proving incapacity depend heavily on the facts and on a given person's status. Indeed, the law often uses the status of a person as a basis for making legal distinctions and may in fact **circumscribe** the legal rights of any persons falling within these classifications. For this reason many jurisdictions limit the contractual rights of minors, insane persons, intoxicated persons, aliens, and convicts. In earlier times, the common law also curtailed the rights of married women to contract through laws called Married Women's Property Acts. Most states have eliminated these statutory restrictions, but some vestiges of these acts may remain in a few states. The extent of the legal disability placed on such classes of individuals comprises the central thrust of this chapter.

Circumscribe Limit the range of activity associated with something.

MINORS

Most jurisdictions no longer follow the earlier common law rule that any person of either sex under twenty-one years of age is a *minor* (or an *infant*). Most states have changed this rule by statute to allow for achievement of *majority status* (that is, adult status) as early as age eighteen for almost all

Emancipation Freedom from the control or power of another; release from parental care and the attainment of legal independence.

Disaffirmance/ Rescission

purposes. (A common exception involves the purchasing of alcoholic beverages.) Other states allow for termination of infancy status upon marriage or emancipation.

To protect minors in their dealings with adults, the law allows minors to disaffirm (or avoid) their contracts with adults except in certain specialized cases, such as contracts involving necessaries (things that directly foster the minor's well-being). When the minor decides not to perform the legal obligations contemplated in the agreement by *disaffirming* the contract, this action results in a voidable contract. The minor has the option of performing the contract, but it is usually voidable on his or her part. The converse is not true: The adult who has contracted with a minor will ordinarily be unable to use the infancy of the minor to avoid the contract unless the minor allows the adult to disaffirm the contract. Simply put, do not contract with minors! Or, if you do, realize that the minor's powers may, in a given instance, be quite pervasive. Practically speaking, besides refusing to deal with minors, you can curtail their powers of avoidance by insisting that a parent or other adult co-sign the contract with them. In this fashion you will have effectively limited the minor's power of *rescission, the ability to have the contract set aside*. This is true because even if the minor disaffirms the contract, the adult co-signer will still remain liable on it.

Analyze the following case in light of these principles.

Smoky, Inc. v. McCray
396 S.E.2d 794 (Ga. App. 1990)

FACTS   Julie Ann McCray was taking a riding lesson conducted by Deirdre Dunn in a riding ring at the Rocky Pine Ranch. McCray was circling Dunn on a horse controlled by a longe line held by Dunn. Because the longe line regulated the direction of the horse's movement, McCray could ride the horse and work on leg strength and balance without touching the reins, although her feet were in the stirrups. Terry Meier, the son of the president of the ranch, and two other boys entered the ring with three ponies, which were on halters, and moved to the far end of the ring. The parties at trial disputed whether one of the ponies thereupon escaped from Terry's control as he was adjusting the saddle stirrups or whether Terry, at the behest of his sister, Karen Meier, released the pony in order to play a trick on another equestrienne also working in the far end of the ring. At any rate, the pony ran to the other end of the ring, startling McCray's mount. McCray fell and broke her arm. LeMan McCray and Mary Catherine McCray, as the parents of Julie Ann McCray, later brought suit against Smoky, Inc. d/b/a Rocky Pine Ranch, to recover damages for the injuries incurred by their daughter when she fell off the horse. At trial, the judge refused to admit an agreement waiving all claims against Smoky, Inc. that Julie had signed when she was fourteen years old.

ISSUE   Was this agreement voidable under Georgia law owing to infancy?

HOLDING   Yes. Julie could disaffirm this agreement, signed when she was an infant, because it did not involve a necessary and thus represented a voidable contract.

REASONING   The trial court properly refused to admit at trial the agreement signed by Julie Ann McCray, which Smoky, Inc. had tendered for the sole purpose of enabling the jury to determine whether McCray had waived all claims against it.

The trial court found that at the time of the execution of the agreement, McCray had been fourteen years old and unaccompanied by any parent or guardian. Moreover, as a contract by a minor for an item not a necessary under Georgia law, the agreement was voidable as a matter of law. Furthermore, according to Georgia precedents, "A contract by which an infant [waives] a claim which he [or she] may have for damages against another for personal injuries received by the infant is voidable, and may be disaffirmed by the infant. The institution or maintenance by the infant of a suit against the other contracting party [here, Smoky, Inc.] to recover damages for the injuries sustained by the infant amounts to a disaffirmance by the infant of the contract."

Misrepresentation of Age

What if the minor intentionally misrepresents his or her age? For example, suppose seventeen-year-old Marcie tells the salesperson at Ace Used Cars that she is twenty-one and pulls out a falsified driver's license to "prove it." If Marcie later tries to avoid the contract with Ace, can Ace argue that this intentional misrepresentation prevents rescission? Under the law of most jurisdictions, the minor can still disaffirm the contract. (But in these circumstances, many times the adult will be able to disaffirm as well, despite the usual rule to the contrary.) Some states hold that such a misrepresentation cuts off the minor's power of disaffirmance. Alternatively, some states allow rescission but force the minor to put the adult back in the position he or she would have been in but for the contract. In other words, assuming the same facts as above, some states will allow Marcie to disaffirm the contract but will either force her to return the car or will hold her liable in quasi contract for the reasonable value of the benefit Ace has conferred on her by furnishing her with the car. Also, Marcie will probably have to pay for any damage done to the car while it has been in her custody.

This result follows the usual rule that upon disaffirmance, the minor must return to the adult the property or other consideration that was the object of the contract, if possible. Strong policy reasons exist for this rule, called the *duty of restoration*. It clearly seems unfair to let the minor "have it both ways"—that is, get out of the contract and yet retain the consideration. The law therefore says that if the minor wants to avoid a contract, he or she must *totally* avoid it.

Sometimes, however, the minor cannot return the property or other consideration because it has been damaged or destroyed. Ace will be very upset if Marcie asks for the money that she has already paid on the car as well as total release from the contract and in exchange presents Ace with a demolished car. In most states the minor will get exactly what he or she wishes because merely giving the car back fulfills the minor's duty of restoration. But in some states, Ace will be able to set off any payments received from the seventeen-year-old due to the damaged condition of the car. These states add to the duty of restoration the *duty of restitution*. In short, these jurisdictions require the minor to give the adult consideration sufficient to put the adult back in the economic position the adult enjoyed at the beginning of the transaction between the parties.

The case that follows illustrates many of these points.

Scott Eden Management v. Kavovit
563 N.Y.S.2d 1001 (Sup. 1990)

FACTS In 1984, when defendant Andrew M. Kavovit was twelve years of age, he and his parents entered into a contract with Scott Eden Management (Scott Eden) in which Scott Eden became the exclusive personal manager to supervise and promote Andrew's career in the entertainment industry. This agreement ran initially from 8 February 1984 to 8 February 1986, with an extension for another three years to 8 February 1989. It entitled Scott Eden to a 15-percent commission on Andrew's gross compensation, notwithstanding any earlier termination of the agreement. In 1986, Andrew signed an agency contract with the Andreadis Agency (Andreadis), a licensed agent selected by Scott Eden pursuant to industry requirements. This contract involved an additional 10-percent commission. Thereafter, Andrew signed several contracts for his services. The most important contract, from a financial and career point of view, secured a role for Andrew on "As the World Turns," a long-running television soap opera. Income from this employment contract appears to have commenced on 28 December 1987 and continued through 28 December 1990, with a strong possibility for renewal. One week before the expiration of the contract with Scott Eden, Andrew's attorney notified Scott Eden of Andrew's disaffirmance on the basis of infancy. Until then, Andreadis had been forwarding Scott Eden its commissions; but by letter of 4 February 1989, Andrew's father, David Kavovit, advised Andreadis that Andrew's salary should go directly to Andrew and that he would send Andreadis its 10 percent. Thereafter, Scott Eden received no additional commissions. Scott Eden then instituted suit, seeking money damages for the commissions owed to it.

ISSUE Did a fifteen-year-old child actor have the right to disaffirm his contract with his exclusive personal manager, Scott Eden?

HOLDING Yes. However, to avoid the unjust enrichment of the infant, the infant must pay Scott Eden the fees and commissions due to it under its managerial contract.

REASONING An infant's contract is voidable, and the infant has an absolute right to disaffirm. This aspect of the law of contracts became well entrenched in the common law by the early fifteenth century. In bringing this action and defending against the summary judgment motion, Scott Eden fully recognizes the principle of law involved here and in no way challenges the infant's right to disaffirm. Rather, Scott Eden relies upon a corollary to the main rule, which also evolved early in the common law: "After disaffirmance, the infant is not entitled to be put in a position superior to such a one as he would have occupied if he had never entered into his voidable agreement. He is not entitled to retain an advantage from a transaction which he repudiates. The privilege of infancy is to be used as a shield and not as a sword." The restoration of consideration requirement also finds voice in statutes, one of which states that the infant need not tender restoration of benefits received prior to disaffirmance, "but the court may make a tender of restoration a condition of its judgment, and may otherwise in its judgment so adjust the equities between the parties that unjust enrichment is avoided." The restoration of consideration principle, as interpreted by the courts, has, for example, resulted in the infant's being responsible for the wear and tear on the goods returned by him or her. In other such cases, the minor's inability to return the benefits obtained effectively precludes the minor from disaffirming the contract in order to get back the consideration given. Once a performance contract has been signed, the personal manager is entitled to its percentage fee, subject only to the condition subsequent that the client perform and earn the fee. When the client signs a performance contract, it is with the understanding that the gross amount to be paid is not solely for him. It is the expectation of all parties—the agent, the performer and, in this case, the soap opera production company—that 15 percent of that gross amount belongs to the personal manager. To the extent that the performer obtains that 15 percent for himself, he is unjustly enriched. If a court adopts the argument asserted by the Kavovits, the infant would be put in a position superior to that which he would have occupied had he never entered into the contract with Scott Eden. He would be retaining an advantage from the repudiated transaction; that is, using the privilege of infancy as a sword rather than a shield. Not only is this manifestly unfair, but it would undermine the policy underlying the rule allowing disaffirmance. If the infant may rescind the contract with the manager immediately after signing a lucrative performance contract, yet still retain the benefits of the performance contract, no reputable manager will expend any efforts on behalf of an infant. In this case, adjustment of the equities so as to prevent unjust enrichment, as suggested by New York statutory provisions, leads to the conclusion that Andrew and his parents must continue to pay to Scott Eden all commissions owed to Scott Eden under its contract, as they become due. Thus, on the first two causes of action, summary judgment is denied to the Kavovits and is granted to Scott Eden to the extent that it shall be restored to its original condition. Moreover, inasmuch as Scott Eden will no longer be involved in the day-to-day personal management of the infant, it is entitled to periodic statements regarding Andrew's income and the sources thereof, as well as to annual inspections of the books and records kept with regard to Andrew's income.

Bona fide purchaser A person who purchases in good faith, for value, and without notice of any defects or defenses affecting the sale or transaction.

Changing the circumstances of our previous example a bit, let us assume that Marcie had traded in another car when she had purchased the now-demolished one from Ace. When she avoids the contract, Ace has to return this trade-in to the minor as well in order to fulfill the adult's corresponding duty of restitution. If Ace has already sold this car to a **bona fide purchaser,** the minor cannot get the car back but can recover the price paid by the third party to Ace.

When minors like Marcie attempt to disaffirm transactions with adults, no special words or acts are required to effect an avoidance. Disaffirmances may be made orally or in writing, formally (by a lawsuit) or informally, directly or indirectly. (The minor's conveying the car to someone else when the minor reaches majoritarian age is an avoidance of the contract with Ace Used Cars.)

The minor's power of disaffirmance, whether the contract is executory or executed, ordinarily extends through his or her minority and for a reasonable time after achieving majority. As we have seen before, and as shown in the following case, how long a reasonable time is becomes a question of fact for a judge or jury to decide in light of all the circumstances.

Bobby Floars Toyota, Inc. v. Smith
269 S.E.2d 320 (N.C. App. 1980)

FACTS   Charles Edward Smith, Jr., purchased an automobile from Bobby Floars Toyota, Inc. (Floars) on 15 August 1973. On that date the defendant was seventeen years old; he would have his eighteenth birthday on 25 September 1973. Smith executed a purchase money security agreement to finance $2362.00, the balance due on the purchase price of the automobile, payable in thirty installments of $99.05 each. After having made eleven monthly payments, ten of which were made after his eighteenth birthday, Smith voluntarily returned the automobile to Floars and defaulted on his payment obligations. The automobile was sold for $700.00, leaving a deficiency of $821.52. Floars brought this action to recover damages in the amount of the deficiency.

ISSUE   Was Smith's voluntary relinquishment of the automobile ten months after attaining the age of majority a timely disaffirmance of his contract with Floars?

HOLDING   No. Ten months constituted an unreasonable time within which to elect between disaffirmance and ratification, and Smith was therefore liable to Floars.

REASONING   The settled rule is that the conventional contracts of an infant (that is, a minor), except those for necessaries and those authorized by statute, are voidable at the election of the infant and may be disaffirmed by the infant during minority or within a reasonable time after reaching majority. The definition of a reasonable time depends on the circumstances of each case; defining a hard-and-fast rule regarding precise time limits is impossible. Nevertheless, Smith's attempted disaffirmance in this case was untimely.

Ratification

Ratification means that the minor has in some fashion indicated (1) *approval of the contract made while he or she is an infant* and (2) *an intention to be bound to the provisions of that contract*. Ratification, then, represents the opposite of disaffirmance and cuts off any right to disaffirm. Ratification takes two separate forms: express and implied. Even with express ratifications, or those situations in which the minor explicitly and definitely agrees to accept the obligations of the contract, the policy of protecting minors is so strong that many states require express ratifications to be in writing. The more common type of ratification occurs through indirect means, such as conduct that shows approval of the contract, even though the minor has said nothing specifically about agreeing to be bound to it. To illustrate, failure to make a timely disaffirmance constitutes an implied ratification of an executed contract. Thus, a minor who is not diligent in disaffirming within a reasonable time after attaining majority will have impliedly ratified the contract. Such lack of action does not ordinarily bring about ratification of an executory contract, however. Some courts, moreover, will hold that, by itself, partial payment of a debt is usually not tantamount to ratification, unless payment is coupled to the minor's express intention to be bound to the contract. In any event, ratification cannot occur until the minor achieves majoritarian status. If ratification *were* possible beforehand, the law's protection of minors would be meaningless. The *Floars* case cited previously provides a good illustration of these principles.

Bobby Floars Toyota, Inc. v. Smith
269 S.E.2d 320 (N.C. App. 1980)

FACTS   Same as in the earlier citation.

ISSUE   Had Smith impliedly ratified the contract?

HOLDING   Yes. Smith's acceptance of the benefits and continuation of payments under the contract constituted a ratification of it and prevented a later disaffirmance.

REASONING   Affirmation, or conduct showing ratification, would be sufficient to bind the infant, regardless of whether a reasonable time for disaffirmance had passed. The facts here demonstrated that Smith's continued possession and operation of the car after his eighteenth birthday and the ten monthly payments made after he turned eighteen were tantamount to ratification and precluded Smith's subsequent attempt at disaffirmance.

Necessaries

Even in the absence of ratification, minors will be liable for transactions whereby they have been furnished "necessaries." *Necessaries* formerly encompassed only food, clothing, and shelter; but the law has broadened the rule to cover other *things that directly foster the minor's well-being*. The basis for the minor's liability is *quasi* contract, which you learned about in Chapter 8. (There can be no liability in *contract* law owing to the lack of capacity, remember?) If an adult has supplied necessaries to the minor, the law will imply liability for the reasonable value of those necessaries. Often, though, the law will not impose liability on the minor for the cost of necessaries unless the minor's parents are unable to discharge their obligation to support their child and pay for such essentials.

The definition of necessaries depends on the minor's circumstances, or social and economic station in life. In this sense, the rule is applied somewhat subjectively. Although food, clothing, and shelter are covered, is a fur coat a necessary for which the minor is liable? It may be, depending on the minor's social station. Similarly, loans for medical or dental services or education may also be necessaries in some situations. Numerous cases involve cars, and many courts hold that a car, especially if it is used for coming and going to work, is a necessary for which the minor remains liable. Clearly, the definition of what constitutes a necessary changes as community values and mores change.

The following case illustrates several points about the potential liability for necessaries that can arise on the part of both the infant and the parents of that infant.

University of Cincinnati Hospital v. Cohen
566 N.E.2d 187 (Ohio App. 1989)

FACTS   Jennifer Cohen, who was seventeen at the time and supported by her parents, sustained serious injuries in an automobile collision. A helicopter transported her from the scene of the accident to the University of Cincinnati Hospital for emergency treatment and care. Between 14 September 1985 and 3 December 1985, she accumulated charges of $221,274.17. Subsequently, Jennifer's mother assigned (i.e., voluntarily transferred) to the hospital all the rights and benefits under her (i.e., the mother's) employer's hospital insurance plan. After Jennifer reached the age of majority, the hospital brought action against Jennifer and her parents, jointly, and moved for a summary judgment. At the hearing on the motion, the hospital's counsel informed the trial judge that the parents and the hospital had entered into a settlement agreement, but that the hospital would proceed against Jennifer, who had denied liability. Jennifer's counsel argued that she had not contracted with the hospital for the services furnished her, and, as a minor, she was not liable for them.

ISSUE Did Jennifer's minority absolve her from liability for medical services furnished to her by the hospital?

HOLDING No. A minor who had sustained injuries and incurred substantial medical bills remained liable for and could not avoid the debt, since emergency medical services constituted necessaries; the custodial parents likewise remained liable for the debt under an implied contract because of the parents' duty to support children as required by Ohio law.

REASONING Ohio follows the common law rule providing that a minor's contracts, except for necessaries, are voidable at his or her option. This liability-for-necessaries exception is not based on contract principles; rather, it stems from quasi contract and unjust enrichment imposed at the time an implied contract for the reasonable value of necessaries furnished to the minor arises. Since medical services constitute necessaries, a parent having custody of a child is likewise liable for the debt under an implied contract for the minor child's medical care because of the duty to support required by Ohio statutes. If the parents fail or refuse to pay for emergency medical care furnished to save the minor's life, the provider hospital or physician may then look to the child for payment. Jennifer also contends that if she is liable for the hospital's charges for medical services despite her minority, her parents' settlement agreement with the hospital constitutes an accord and satisfaction as to the debt. A presumption that the hospital relied on the parents' credit for payment exists, since Jennifer lives with her parents. Therefore, the relationship between Jennifer and her parents creates primary and secondary liability, and the hospital must first look to the parents for payment. A compromise and settlement by parents, who are primarily liable, resulting from payment of a lesser amount in full satisfaction of an unliquidated claim constitutes an accord and satisfaction and discharges the debt of the minor who is secondarily liable. However, the terms of the parents' settlement agreement with the hospital negate such an accord and satisfaction. Obviously, Jennifer does not intend to join in the settlement agreement with her parents, since she has consistently maintained that she is not liable to the hospital. More significant, however, is the rule that a liquidated debt or claim cannot be compromised by payment of a lesser sum unless there is consideration separate from the terms of the compromise and settlement. In this case, Jennifer does not challenge the accuracy or reasonableness of the hospital's charges. Therefore, it represents a liquidated debt. Furthermore, her parents' agreement with the hospital is not for payment of a lesser amount in satisfaction of its $221,274.17 claim. The agreement merely gives her parents a one-year grace period to pay on the balance, while also forgiving the interest during that period if they make two $50,000 payments within ninety days of the execution of the agreement. In short, the agreement does nothing but buy the parents more time to pay. Finally, Jennifer has not satisfied her burden of proof for an accord and satisfaction, since there is no evidence that her parents have actually performed the terms of the agreement. Moreover, she has not offered any proof that the hospital intended to discharge Jennifer's debt in return for her parents' promise. Therefore, the trial judge correctly granted the hospital's motion for summary judgment.

Special Statutes

Legislatures in many states have passed special statutes making minors liable in a variety of circumstances. Under such laws, minors may be responsible for educational loans, medical or dental expenses, insurance policies, banking account contracts, transportation by common carrier (for example, airline tickets), and other expenses. These statutes protect the interests of those persons who have dealt with minors who, despite their age, are exhibiting the skills and maturity of adults.

Torts and Crimes

The law similarly protects the interests of adults when an adult has suffered losses owing to a minor's torts and crimes. Thus, minors generally cannot disaffirm liability for torts and crimes, areas of the law we discussed in Chapters 3 and 4, unless the minor is of "tender years," or too young to understand the consequences of his or her acts. Minors may also escape liability in these areas if the imposition of tort liability will bring about the enforcement of a contract the minor has previously disaffirmed. Note how, in this latter context, the law has chosen once again to protect minors at the expense of adults.

INSANE PERSONS

Like minors, insane persons may lack the capacity to make a binding contract. However, the law in this area is somewhat more complicated.

To be *insane,* a person must be *so mentally infirm or deranged as to be unable to understand what he or she is agreeing to or the consequences attendant upon that agreement.* The causes of such disability—lunacy, mental retardation, senility, or alcohol or drug abuse—are irrelevant.

Effects of Transactions by Insane Persons

Guardians Persons legally responsible for taking care of the affairs of another who lacks the legal capacity to do so.

The contracts of persons who have been adjudged insane through court proceedings are absolutely void. Only their **guardians** have the legal capacity to contract on their behalf. However, the contracts of other insane persons are voidable. To disaffirm a contract, the person using insanity as a defense must prove that he or she was actually insane at the time of contracting. If the person were instead lucid and understood the nature and consequences of the contract, that person would remain bound to the contract.

This power of an insane person to avoid contracts also extends to the heirs or personal representative of a deceased insane person. A living insane person's guardian possesses similar powers. Upon regaining sanity, a formerly insane person may nonetheless ratify a contract made during the period of insanity.

Determining whether a transaction by an insane person is void, voidable, or enforceable depends heavily on the facts, as the following case illustrates.

Lloyd v. *Jordan*
544 So.2d 957 (Ala. 1989)

FACTS George Lloyd purchased an annuity from the Executive Life Insurance Company of Beverly Hills, California, in September, 1983, and named his daughters by a previous marriage, Jordan and Pitts, as co-beneficiaries. George Lloyd also executed a will in June, 1985, that devised all of his property to Jordan and Pitts and made no provision for Olivia Lloyd, George Lloyd's second wife. It appears that although they had divorced after the execution of the will, George Lloyd and Olivia Lloyd remarried in August, 1987. At that time, Olivia Lloyd obtained a change of beneficiary form from Executive Life, and George Lloyd allegedly executed the form to change the beneficiary of the annuity to Olivia Lloyd. After George Lloyd's death, Jordan and Pitts petitioned the probate court to enter an order designating them as the proper beneficiaries of the annuity on the ground that Lloyd had been mentally incompetent and had lacked capacity to execute the change of beneficiary form. Testimony from George Lloyd's

Non compos mentis Not of sound mind; insane.

physician indicated that Lloyd had been showing signs of mental instability and chronic dementia in April, 1987; and, in fact, he was declared **non compos mentis** in September, 1987.

ISSUE

Did George Lloyd, owing to his deteriorating mental condition, lack legal capacity in August, 1987, when he changed the beneficiaries of the annuity from his daughters to his wife, Olivia?

HOLDING

Yes. Because George Lloyd was mentally incapable of understanding the effect of the change of beneficiary form, he had lacked the capacity to execute this form.

REASONING

Contracts of insane persons are absolutely void, and a contract executed before the maker's adjudication of insanity or the appointment of a guardian becomes suspect when it appears that apparent consent to the contract may have been unreal because of mental incapacity. As Alabama precedents note, the validity of a contract hinges on whether the parties possess not only the legal status affording capacity to contract, but also the mental competence affording capacity to consent. No contract exists in circumstances in which one of the parties was, by reason of physical debility, age, mental aberration, or otherwise, incapable of understanding and appreciating the nature, force, and effect of the agreement allegedly made or in which he was unable to do so because insane, or mentally infirm, or because of incapacity resulting from lunacy, idiocy, senile dementia, imbecility, or any other defect or disease of the mind, whatever the cause. However, mere mental weakness falling short of incapacity to appreciate the business in hand will not invalidate a contract, nor will mere mental weakness or unsoundness to some degree, in the absence of fraud or undue influence. A person's physical condition not adversely affecting mental competence is immaterial; and neither age, sickness, extreme distress, nor debility of body will affect the capacity to make a contract if sufficient intelligence remains to enable the party to understand the transaction. Courts, of course, will not necessarily invalidate a person's contracts because of age, feebleness of mind, loss of memory, fatigue, or ill health. When other inequitable grounds (such as duress, undue influence, or overreaching) accompany the mental incapacity or weakness, however, grounds for invalidation of the contract may exist; mental weakness may render a person more susceptible to these factors. Consequently, courts will not avoid a contract on the ground of mental incapacity or weakness unless the incapacity is of such a character that, at the time of execution, the person has no reasonable perception or understanding of the nature and terms of the contract or unless undue influence (or the like) accompanies the incapacity. Testimony at the trial from George Lloyd's physician indicated that in April, 1987, before executing the change of beneficiary form, Lloyd had suffered mental instability and the onset of chronic dementia (mental deterioration or senility). Olivia Lloyd and George Lloyd had remarried in August, 1987; shortly thereafter, Olivia Lloyd had obtained the change of beneficiary form for George Lloyd to sign. Moreover, Olivia Lloyd had testified that she "couldn't say" that George Lloyd had known what he was doing on the day he had signed the form. George Lloyd's mental condition was apparently deteriorating to the extent that a court had declared him non compos mentis and had appointed a guardian for him one month after the execution of the form. Therefore, sufficient evidence existed to support the trial court's finding that George Lloyd had been incapable of understanding and appreciating the nature and effect of the change of beneficiary form that he had signed.

Necessaries

By analogy to the rules covering minors, the law makes insane persons liable for necessaries in quasi contract. The categories of goods and services deemed necessaries for minors generally extend to insane persons. In the context of insanity, fewer controversies should arise regarding whether medical or legal services are necessaries, as they probably constitute necessaries for which the insane person is liable.

YOU BE THE JUDGE

Pauline L. Harrison is the 73-year-old daughter of Henry Francis Du Pont and a descendant of the founders of Du Pont Co. One month after suffering a stroke in the spring of 1990, Mrs. Harrison set up a trust to manage her 360,000 shares of Du Pont stock, worth about $25 million, for her chief beneficiaries, her children and grandchildren. However, Mrs. Harrison later sued to have this trust agreement nullified. She argued that she was incompetent when she signed the agreement; that she did not understand the trust agreement was irrevocable; and that her children had forced her to sign the agreement owing to their disenchantment with her June 1990 marriage to Boyd de Brossard, a retired investment broker, to whom the descendants allegedly feared Mrs. Harrison would leave all her assets. To rebut Mrs. Harrison's claim of incompetency, the descendants presented evidence in court that on May 23, 1990, three weeks after her stroke and about a week before signing the trust documents, Mrs. Harrison and Mr. de Brossard had won a game of duplicate bridge, during which Mrs. Harrison had showed her customary high level of expertise. According to the descendants' lawyers, Mrs. Harrison's ability to follow the bidding rules and strategies of duplicate bridge demonstrated that she possessed the requisite mental faculties to understand the trust agreement. Mrs. Harrison's lawyers countered that the ability to utilize her skills as a "life master" of bridge was irrelevant to Mrs. Harrison's understanding of an unfamiliar subject such as the terms of a trust agreement.

Did Mrs. Harrison's duplicate bridge victory, achieved shortly before she signed the trust agreement, show that she had sufficient mental capacity to understand the effect of her actions in signing the trust documents? If you were the judge in this nonjury trial, how would you rule?

Sources: "Bridge Is Indeed a Game of Suits, But Not Often This Kind of Suit," Jonathan M. Moses, *The Wall Street Journal,* February 4, 1992, page B1, and "Law," Scott McMurray and Christi Harlan, *The Wall Street Journal,* May 1, 1992, page B8.

INTOXICATED PERSONS

If a person is so thoroughly intoxicated that he or she does not understand the nature or consequences of the agreement being made, this mental disability approaches that of an insane person. Hence, under certain circumstances, such a person can disaffirm any such agreement. However, this power of possible disaffirmance depends on the degree of intoxication involved, which in turn involves a question of fact. As you would expect, slight degrees of intoxication do not constitute cause for disaffirmance of a contract.

Whether the intoxication was involuntary or voluntary may bear on the result, too. If a plaintiff has plied the defendant with liquor, any resulting intoxication may be a factor in a finding of incapacity, fraud, or overreaching that will release the defendant from the agreement. Even voluntary intoxication can sometimes result in a voidable contract if the facts support this conclusion.

Upon regaining sobriety, the formerly intoxicated person may either avoid or ratify the contract. The rules about acting within a reasonable time apply here as well; if the person does not quickly disaffirm the contract, an implied ratification will be found. Courts are generally hostile to avoiding contracts on the basis of intoxication except in unusual circumstances. Still, in the next case a judge invalidated part of an agreement owing to one party's chronic intoxication.

Galloway v. *Galloway*
281 N.W.2d 804 (N.D. 1979)

FACTS   Henry Galloway had sued his wife Betty for divorce. Betty was an alcoholic; but her husband testified that at the time she agreed to the divorce, she was lucid, sober, and fully capable of entering into the agreement, which had been presented to the court in September. Five days after the judge had accepted the agreement and granted the divorce, Betty asked that this judgment be set aside.

ISSUE   Did Betty's alcoholism render her incapable of contracting?

HOLDING   The evidence raised many doubts about Betty's capacity to contract at the time she had entered the agreement and for an extended period afterward. Therefore, the court properly set aside the part of the agreement that dealt with the property settlement but upheld the divorce.

REASONING   Parties capable of contracting remain essential to the existence of any contract. Although a court had not declared Betty judicially incompetent until four months after her signing of the agreement, some evidence indicated that her judgment had been impaired and that she had been drinking just days prior to signing the agreement. Since some evidence showed that Betty may have been incompetent to judge her rights and interests in relation to the agreement, the provisions of the agreement relating to the property settlement were set aside.

ALIENS

An *alien* is *a citizen of a foreign country*. Most of the disabilities to which an alien was formerly subject have been removed, usually through treaties. Thus, a *legal* alien can ordinarily enter contracts and pursue gainful employment without legal disabilities, just as any United States citizen can. Some states make distinctions based on the alien's right to hold or convey personal property (generally authorized under such statutes) and the right to hold, convey, or inherit real property (some restrictions may apply here). *Enemy* aliens, or those who are residents of countries with whom we are officially at war, cannot enforce contracts during the period of hostility but sometimes can after the war is over.

Given the large numbers of illegal aliens in the United States, this area of the law (and related ethical questions) promises to be ripe for future developments.

CONVICTS

In many states, conviction of a felony or treason carries with it certain contractual disabilities. For instance, laws may prohibit convicts from conveying property during their periods of incarceration. Such disabilities, if applicable, exist only during imprisonment. Upon release from prison, these persons have full rights to contract.

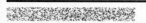

MARRIED WOMEN

Under early common law, married women's contracts were void. Women were viewed as their husband's property and as otherwise lacking in capacity to make contracts. This common law disability, reflected in Married Women's Property Acts, has been eliminated by statute or by judicial decision in almost all states.

Table 11.1 summarizes the contractual capacities of minors, insane persons, intoxicated persons, aliens, convicts, and married women.

TABLE 11.1 Contractual Capacity

	CLASSIFICATION OF CONTRACT			
CLASS OF PERSON	**VALID**	**VOIDABLE**	**VOID**	**EXCEPTIONS**
1. Minors		X (upon return of consideration to seller)		1. Misrepresentation of age, which eliminates power of rescission in some jurisdictions. 2. Failure to rescind within a reasonable time after achieving majority (implied ratification). 3. Express ratification after achieving majority (necessity of a writing in some jurisdictions). 4. Necessaries (liability in quasi contract in some cases if parents unable to pay). 5. Special statutes making minors liable.

TABLE 11.1 continued

CLASS OF PERSON	CLASSIFICATION OF CONTRACT			EXCEPTIONS
	VALID	VOIDABLE	VOID	
2. Insane persons				
a. Those adjudged insane			X	1. Capacity by guardians to contract on these persons' behalf.
b. Sane persons	X			
c. Those insane but not adjudged by a court to be so		X		1. Ratification possible during periods of lucidity. 2. Necessaries (liability in quasi contract in some circumstances).
3. Intoxicated persons				
a. Sober persons	X			
b. Slightly intoxicated persons	X			
c. Seriously intoxicated persons		X		1. Subsequent express ratification upon regaining sobriety possible. 2. Failure to rescind within a reasonable time after achieving sobriety in involuntary intoxication circumstances (implied ratification).
4. Aliens				
a. Legal aliens	X			1. Some restrictions sometimes regarding ownership of real property.
b. Enemy aliens				
1. during hostilities			X	
2. after hostilities are ended	X			
5. Convicts				
a. During incarceration			X	
b. Upon release	X			
6. Married women	X			1. Some anachronistic restrictions perhaps remaining in a few states.

SUMMARY

Minors, insane persons, intoxicated persons, aliens, and convicts may lack contractual capacity. Previously these restrictions applied to married women, too. In other words, these classes of people may lack the legal ability to bind themselves to an agreement and to enforce any promises made to them.

The contracts of a minor, usually defined as a person under age eighteen, are often voidable, even when the minor has misrepresented his or her age, at the option of the minor. This power of disaffirmance ordinarily extends through the person's minority and for a reasonable time after attaining majority. However, after reaching majority, a minor may ratify, or approve, the contract. Ratification may be express or implied. Even in the absence of ratification, a minor will be liable for necessaries in quasi contract. The definition of necessaries depends on the minor's station in life and the parent's ability to provide for the minor. Sometimes special statutes broaden a minor's areas of liability. A minor will almost always be liable for any tort and crime unless the minor is very young or the imposition of tort liability will bring about the enforcement of a contract previously disaffirmed by the minor.

The contracts of insane persons may be void, voidable, or valid. To be insane, a person must demonstrate sufficient mental derangement to be unable to understand what he or she is agreeing to or the consequences attendant upon that agreement. Such agreements are void, but contracts entered into during periods of lucidity are enforceable. Upon regaining sanity, a person may either ratify the contract or avoid it. Insane persons are liable for necessaries, just as minors are.

Total intoxication may render a person incapable of entering into a binding contract, but slight intoxication will not. Upon regaining sobriety, the person may either disaffirm or ratify the contract. However, courts are generally hostile to avoiding contracts on the basis of intoxication except in unusual circumstances.

Aliens, or persons who are citizens of foreign countries, may face legal disabilities with regard to contractual capacity. This is especially true of enemy aliens or residents of countries with whom our country is officially at war. Convicts and even married women may have limited rights to contract as well. State statutes should be consulted to determine the degree of disability, if any, that exists for these persons.

DISCUSSION QUESTIONS

1. Why is the law concerned with the concept of capacity to contract?

2. Why do smart businesspeople say, "Don't deal with minors"?

3. Can minors disaffirm contracts if they have misrepresented their ages at the time of contracting?

4. How long does an infant's power to rescind a contract last?

5. What is ratification, and how can it occur?

6. Define *necessaries*.

7. Can an insane person's contracts ever be enforceable? Why or why not?

8. Explain the law as it relates to intoxication as a basis for contractual capacity.

9. How can alienage become a basis for contractual disability?

10. Discuss the current state of the law regarding the legal disabilities of convicts and married women.

CASE PROBLEMS

1. The Bundys had contracted with Dalton to put vinyl siding on the house in which they resided. Dalton had assumed the house belonged to them. However, when Dalton attempted to collect for the work he had performed after the Bundys had not paid him, Dalton discovered that the house belonged to the Bundys' daughter, Janet, who was twelve years old. Was the vinyl a "necessary" for which Janet could have been held liable despite her minority? (*Dalton* v. *Bundy*, 666 S.W.2d 443 [Mo. App. 1984].)

2. Rogers, a nineteen-year-old, secured the services of a professional employment agency and did not pay the agency's service charge. In North Carolina at this time, twenty-one constituted the age of majority. Were such services a "necessary", and was Rogers therefore liable to the agency despite his infancy? (*Gastonia Personnel Corporation* v. *Rogers*, 172 S.E.2d 19 [N.C. 1970].)

3. George Ferling, on 6 April 1981, drove his friend, Vivian Abernathy, and her daughter to the Mercantile Bank, where he added Abernathy's name to his bank account as a joint tenant. The bank employee testified that she had explained to Ferling the effect of this change and that Ferling appeared to understand what she was telling him. Some months before, on 16 December 1980, Ferling had been hospitalized with lung cancer. The doctors at that time believed that Ferling's cancer had spread to his brain because he was disoriented as to time and place. However, by January, 1981, he became oriented as to time and place and seemed to be improving. Ferling had stayed at Abernathy's home during his illness. She had taken care of him, and he had said he wanted to marry her. Upon Ferling's death, $20,401.89, the amount in Ferling's checking account, had passed to Abernathy as the joint tenant. Ferling's estate sued Abernathy for this money on the ground that Ferling had been mentally incompetent on 6 April 1981 when he had added Abernathy's name to his account. Should the estate prevail in this lawsuit? (*Estate of Ferling* v. *Abernathy*, 670 S.W.2d 109 [Mo. App. 1984].)

4. Debra Hughes, an unwed mother, had her baby at age sixteen. Two months later, Debra and the father of the child, Bruce Haack, were married. When Debra's parents did not pay for her hospital bills, the hospital sued both Debra and her husband. Was Debra liable? Could Bruce be held liable even though the marriage had taken place after the birth of the baby? (*Madison General Hospital* v. *Haack*, 369 N.W.2d 663 [Wis. 1985].)

5. Webster Street Partnership, Ltd. (Webster Street), had entered into a lease agreement with Sheridan and Wilwerding, who were both minors. Webster Street was aware of this fact. Both boys had left home voluntarily, with the understanding that they could return to their parents' residence whenever they desired. The boys disaffirmed the contract with Webster Street on 12 November 1982 when they were behind on the rent. Sheridan achieved majoritarian status on 5 November 1982, but Wilwerding never achieved his majority during the time period in question. Webster Street argued that the rental property was a "necessary" for which the boys were liable. Was Webster Street correct? Was Sheridan's disaffirmance valid, since he had become an adult legally on 5 November 1982? (*Webster Street Partnership, Ltd.* v. *Sheridan*, 368 N.W.2d 439 [Neb. 1985].)

6. The junior class of Springfield High School on 19 November 1980 signed a contract with the "Music Machine," a sound system operated by Michael Hebert, to provide music for their junior prom in May, 1981. The contract was signed by Wayne Howes, one of the class sponsors, and was approved by the principal of the school. In February, 1981, the school learned that the "Music Machine" was not a live band but a disc jockey sound system using tapes and records. Since the prin-

cipal deemed such a nonlive sound system inappropriate for the prom, both he and Howes wrote to Hebert and informed Hebert the services of the "Music Machine" would not be required. When Hebert sued the school board, the principal, and Howes for breach of contract, the trial court held that only the members of the junior class were parties to the contract. Was the trial court correct in its conclusion that the junior class could be sued? (*Hebert v. Livingston Parish School Board,* 438 So.2d 1141 [La. App. 1983].)

7. Scherer and his wife got an uncontested divorce in the Dominican Republic. Scherer later argued that he had been drinking and taking Valium when he had signed the divorce agreement. Was such intoxication sufficient to render Scherer legally incapable of contracting? (*Scherer v. Scherer,* 405 N.E.2d 40 [Ind. App. 1980].)

8. Farrar was seventeen when she entered into a contract with the Oak Park Swedish Health Spa. She used her father's MasterCharge to pay for this membership, and her father paid the amount due to MasterCharge. Farrar later attempted to disaffirm the contract on the grounds of infancy. Did Farrar's father ratify her contract with the spa by paying MasterCharge? (*Farrar v. Swedish Health Spa,* 337 So.2d 911 [La. App. 1976].)

9. Halbman, a minor, contracted with Lemke for a 1968 Oldsmobile. A connecting rod broke, resulting in a garage repair bill of $637.40. Halbman never paid this bill and later attempted to disaffirm his contract with Lemke. Lemke sought to recoup the damages (i.e., those represented by the garage repair bill) to the car up to the time of disaffirmance. Did Halbman, upon successfully disaffirming the contract, owe Lemke a duty of restitution for the damages to the car? (*Halbman* v. *Lemke,* 298 N.W.2d 562 [Wis. 1980].)

10. In May, 1987, at the age of 83, Henderson Smith conveyed to Lorene Smith, his son's widow, a 23.5-acre parcel of land. In November, 1987, after Smith's death, his other son, Robert, filed suit to have the deed set aside owing to incapacity on his father's part and fraud, deceit, and undue influence on Lorene Smith's part. Several witnesses at trial spoke of Smith's confusion, the weakness of his intellect, and the fact that various people had taken care of Smith's business affairs, his housekeeping, and his errands. Moreover, a court had set aside a land conveyance made in the early 1980s; and the grantee of a 1985 land conveyance had voluntarily rescinded it because of the grantee's belief that Smith had not understood what he was doing when he had deeded the property away to the grantee. The trial court directed a verdict in favor of Lorene Smith. Should the appellate court uphold this decision? (*Smith* v. *Smith,* 574 So.2d 644 [Miss. 1990].)

CHAPTER 12

Legal Agreements

O U T L I N E

REQUIREMENT OF LEGALITY

By this time, you are undoubtedly aware of the emphasis of American contract law on bargaining and contract formation through the agreement of the parties. Yet, as with most human activities, the permissible boundaries for such conduct remain limited. Society at large may have a stake in the agreement the parties have forged. An agreement to bribe public officials or to murder someone, for instance, has definite repercussions for society that extend beyond the parties who initiated the bargain. The law, then, imposes a requirement that the subject matter and purpose of the bargain be legal in order for the bargain to be recognized as a valid contract. In this sense, the term *illegal contract* probably constitutes a misnomer; a bargain in general cannot attain the status of "contract" if it is tainted with illegality. Hence, such "contracts" are void. Most business transactions are perfectly legal, but the prudent businessperson and citizen will be sensitive to the possibility that a bargain, however innocent it outwardly seems, may nevertheless involve a violation of a statute, common law, or public policy. In such cases, the law characterizes such a bargain as illegal. An understanding of the types of bargains that are typically illegal and of the effects of these transactions therefore seems desirable. Accordingly, an examination of these and similar concepts forms the focus of this chapter.

COMPONENTS OF ILLEGALITY

The most widely accepted definition of *illegality*, taken from the *Restatement (Second) of Contracts*, Section 512, states that *a bargain is illegal if its performance is criminal, tortious, or otherwise opposed to public policy.*

Both the subject matter of the bargain and the realization of its objectives must be permissible under state and federal statutes. Sometimes these statutes impose criminal penalties for their violation (for example, a person may face imprisonment for *arson*, or malicious burning, if that person bargains with someone to set fire to his or her home or business in order to collect fire insurance proceeds). Other statutes may prohibit certain kinds of bargains without imposing criminal penalties on those who violate these statutes. For instance, to protect the public from unqualified tradespeople, a city ordinance may require all plumbers to hold licenses before they will be allowed to practice the plumbing trade. Suppose Sue Weiss hires Logan Plumbing to fix her kitchen sink and later refuses to pay because Logan did not have the necessary license at the time the services were rendered. In many jurisdictions Sue will win this case in court if Logan sues to collect. These courts will view the bargain between Sue and Logan as illegal and therefore refuse to permit the plumbing company to collect from the customer for the value of the services rendered.

Tortious Relating to private or civil wrongs or injuries.

The desire to protect the public also underlies the prohibition of bargains involving **tortious** conduct (for instance, an agreement between two parties for the purpose of defrauding a third).

Similarly, even in the absence of an agreement that violates a statute or one that requires the commission of a tort, courts may declare any bargain that will be detrimental to the public at large illegal on public policy grounds. Although the concept of *public policy* may fluctuate as different courts apply different standards, courts have increasingly used this rationale in a variety of contexts in which there appears to be no other basis for protecting the peace, health, or morals of the community. For example, a bank may offer a rather one-sided night depository agreement in which it refuses to accept liability for a deposit placed in its after-hours slot, even if the loss stems from the negligence of its own employee and the depositor can prove that he or she actually deposited the amount in question with the bank. It is difficult to characterize the bank's conduct as either criminal or tortious, yet its treatment of consumers seems exceedingly unfair or shocking. The concept of public policy—here, the protection of depositors' expectations that the bank will take proper care of their deposits and the protection of consumers against one-sided agreements—will permit a court to invalidate such agreements on the grounds of illegality. A court may characterize such agreements as **exculpatory clauses** or **contracts of adhesion** (depositors may have had no choice but to accept the bank's terms).

Exculpatory clause A part of an agreement in which a prospective plaintiff agrees in advance not to seek to hold the prospective defendant liable for certain things for which the prospective defendant would otherwise be liable.

Contracts of adhesion Contracts whose terms are not open to negotiation—the offeree must "take it or leave it."

In general, an illegal bargain is void and hence unenforceable. This is ordinarily true whether the agreement is executory or fully executed. Usually a court merely leaves the parties where it finds them. Neither party, then, can sue the other. Exceptions to the general rule that courts will not give relief to parties who have created an illegal bargain do exist, however. But, as the following case shows, when there are no public policy bases for suspending the usual rule, a court will refuse to give effect to a bargain tainted with illegality.

Wagner v. State
364 N.W.2d 246 (Iowa 1985)

FACTS

Petition for post-conviction relief A legal challenge to the constitutionality of a sentence handed down by a federal or state judge in which a prisoner asks for the sentence imposed to be set aside.

Wagner was an inmate at the Iowa State Penitentiary on 2 September 1981 when a riot occurred at the prison. During the riot, fires and other property damage ensued, and inmates held staff members hostage. As part of the negotiations to end the riot, the warden promised in writing that officials would take no reprisals against certain inmates, including Wagner. However, on 9 September, Wagner was charged with disciplinary violations for his actions during the disturbance. He was the only individual on the list of those to whom the warden had promised no reprisals who, nonetheless, received sanctions. As a result, his "good time" was forfeited, which in turn led to the revocation of his scheduled parole on 18 September 1981. In his **petition for post-conviction relief,** Wagner argued that the state had breached the no-reprisals agreement when it disciplined him for his conduct during the riot.

ISSUE   Was the no-reprisals agreement, made by the warden under duress and in a violent situation, enforceable?

HOLDING   No. Such an agreement was illegal and void.

REASONING   Any agreement for immunity or amnesty that is produced by unlawful threats, such as the hostage situation in this case, is contrary to public policy and void. Promises extorted through violence and coercion are not promises at all; instead, they are void from the beginning and unenforceable as a matter of public policy. The state could have lived up to such an agreement if it had decided that valid reasons for doing so existed. But a court will refuse to uphold such an agreement in circumstances such as these when the state has decided not to abide by its earlier agreement.

MALA IN SE AND *MALA PROHIBITA* BARGAINS

Early on, many courts became dissatisfied with the rule that illegal contracts are absolutely void. Some of these courts therefore distinguished between *bargains that violate statutes because they are evil in themselves (mala in se)* and *bargains that have been merely forbidden by statute (mala prohibita)*. The first type (for instance, an agreement to murder someone) fell within the general rule and was void. However, some courts were prepared to view bargains included within the second type as voidable rather than void, depending on the nature and effect of the act prohibited by the statute. To illustrate, one case involved the sale of cattle in violation of a law stating that all cattle sold must be tested for brucellosis (a serious disease in cattle) sometime within the thirty-day period preceding the sale. The court clearly could have used this statutory violation as a basis for holding the agreement void. Yet the court concluded that this bargain was *mala prohibita,* not *mala in se,* because the contract was neither in bad faith nor contrary to public policy, and therefore enforced the contract.[1]

You may disagree with the court's interpretation of this infraction of the law. But you should know that in deciding the legality of an agreement, some courts have continued to distinguish between *mala in se* and *mala prohibita* bargains. More recent commentators have criticized these distinctions as invalid by arguing that any bargain that violates a statute is absolutely void no matter what the rationale behind the prohibition involves. This represents the position most widely accepted today. Nevertheless, the continued use of these terms demonstrates the tendency of courts to weigh differences in the degree of evil and to determine the availability of judicial relief accordingly. We will see further examples of this tendency later in the chapter. However, courts almost universally recognize two categories of bargains as *mala in se:* agreements to commit a crime and agreements to commit a tort.

[1] *First National Bank of Shreveport* v. *Williams,* 346 So.2d 257, 264 (La. App. 1977).

AGREEMENTS VIOLATIVE OF STATUTES

The agreement we mentioned earlier involving arson could be called a *mala in se* bargain because the subject matter of the agreement itself, the commission of a crime, is morally unacceptable. The same would be true of an agreement to kill someone, a so-called murder contract. Neither party could enforce such agreements; they would be absolutely void.

AGREEMENTS TO COMMIT A TORT

Chattels Articles of personal (as opposed to real) property; any interests in property that are less than a freehold or a fee interest in land.

Likewise, an agreement that involves the commission of a tort is illegal and void. Besides fraud, which was mentioned earlier, such bargains may involve agreements to damage the good name of a competitor, to inflict mental distress on a third party, or to trespass against another's **chattels** or property in order to cause injury to the property.

AGREEMENTS VIOLATIVE OF STATUTES

As you know, statutes prohibit many activities. Determining whether a particular activity violates a statute (assuming the activity is not *mala in se*) requires that courts resort first to the words of the underlying statute. Then courts must assess the legislative intent and, finally, examine the social effects of giving or refusing a remedy in the particular situation. The next case is instructive.

Stampco Construction Co., Inc. v. *Guffey*
572 N.E.2d 510 (Ind. App. 1991)

FACTS Stampco Construction Co., Inc. (Stampco) performed work under contracts for the construction of public works. W. Keith Guffey (Keith) and Wendell Guffey (Wendell) were both employees of Stampco between July, 1984, and October, 1985. At that time, Indiana statutes and the federal Davis Bacon Act mandated payment of prevailing wages for workers employed on public works projects. Keith worked on the Muncie Sanitary District and Community Development projects for $13 per hour. He also worked on the Blair's Green Acres project (the Blair's project) for $350 per week from June to October, 1985. Stampco employed Wendell on the Blair's project and paid him $8 per hour for regular hours and $12 per hour for overtime. On 30 October 1985, Keith signed an affidavit of release in exchange for $500 cash and a $1500 I.O.U. That affidavit released Stampco from the payment of minimum wages and prevailing wages for work performed on public works projects. After Stampco had terminated Keith and Wendell's employment, both filed suit seeking compensation for the difference between the wages paid and those to which they had been entitled under the prevailing scale of wages. The trial court awarded Keith $8,146.74 and Wendell $2,502.11 and then trebled these awards pursuant to Indiana statutory provisions. Stampco argued that Keith and Wendell had waived such statutory benefits by agreeing to accept lower wages and that Keith's release similarly had waived any claim he might have had for unpaid wages against Stampco.

ISSUE   Were Keith and Wendell precluded from bringing lawsuits under the prevailing wage statutes owing to their agreements with Stampco?

HOLDING   No. They could sue under these statutes because the agreements with Stampco violated public policy and hence were illegal.

REASONING   In determining the question of law of whether an agreement violates public policy, a court must look at all the circumstances of a particular case. A court should keep in mind that refraining from unnecessarily restricting freedom of contract furthers the public's best interests. Moreover, a court should not hold agreements void as against public policy unless such contracts clearly contravene what the legislature has declared to be public policy or unless they clearly tend to injure the public in some fashion. A 1983 case held that Indiana's prevailing wage statute does not infringe upon the liberty to contract and thus is constitutional. Prevailing wage statutes on both the state and federal levels protect public works employees from substandard wages. Here, Stampco's employment agreements with Keith and Wendell violated both Indiana's statute and the federal Davis Bacon Act that require paying wages at the prevailing rate. As a general rule, courts characterize as void any contracts made in violation of a statute. Hence, condoning Stampco's failure to follow the law would violate public policy. Moreover, allowing agreements, settlements, or releases of claims in such circumstances would permit unscrupulous contractors to force employees to submit to economic pressures and accept lower wages. Such employment agreements are void as against public policy, illegal, and unenforceable because these agreements would subvert the federal and state legislatures' intentions to protect public works employees.

It is worthwhile to explore some categories of activities that courts ordinarily find violative of statutes. Among them are price-fixing agreements, performance of services without a license, Sunday laws, and wagering and usury statutes.

Price-Fixing Agreements

Monopolies   The power of firms to carry on a business or a trade to the exclusion of all competitors.

Oligopolies   Economic conditions in which a small number of firms dominates the market but no one firm controls it.

The purpose of price-fixing agreements generally is to restrain competition so as to create **monopolies** or **oligopolies** in order to control price fluctuations. The Sherman Antitrust Act, the Clayton Act, and the Federal Trade Commission Act, discussed in Chapter 46, comprise the major federal legislative enactments that make such bargains illegal. Price-fixing agreements may also violate state statutes; or alternatively, courts may invalidate them on public policy grounds.

Performance of Services Without a License

Agreements relating to the performance of services without a license may constitute another type of statutory violation. Recall our earlier example involving Sue Weiss and Logan Plumbing Company. To protect the public from unqualified persons, state statutes often require the licensing of such professions as law, medicine, and public accountancy and such trades as electrical work, contracting, and plumbing. Before the state grants a license, the would-be practitioner usually must demonstrate minimal competency, after achieving the required educational qualifications, by successfully passing an examination. In such cases, the absence of a license prevents the professional or tradesperson from enforcing the bargain. Thus, if Sue's state requires Logan Plumbing to use professionally licensed plumbers, and the plumbers are not professionally licensed, Logan cannot force Sue to pay, because this bargain is illegal and void. However, assuming that Logan botches Sue's work and causes flooding in her kitchen, in most jurisdictions Sue will be able to recover her damages from Logan despite the absence of a license.

In contrast to a regulatory licensing scheme such as the one just mentioned, some states require licensing primarily as a revenue-producing mechanism rather than as a device for protecting the health and welfare of its citizens. If the primary intent of the licensing requirement is to produce revenue, the lack of a license will not affect the contract between the parties. If that were the case, Sue would have to compensate Logan.

It pays to remember that courts have fairly wide discretion in these matters and may take into account such factors as the absence of harm resulting from failure to obtain the license, the extent of the knowledge of the persons involved, and the relative "guilt" of the respective parties. If, for example, a court deems the amount forfeited by the unlicensed professional large enough to constitute a penalty, the professional ordinarily will be able to sue for the fee despite the lack of a license. As mentioned before, even in statutes assigning criminal sanctions, courts will look closely at the legislative intent of the statute in deciding whether to give or to withhold remedies.

Sunday Laws

Sunday laws, so named because they *prohibit the formation or performance of contracts on Sundays,* are troublesome because the terms of such statutes vary widely from state to state. The most common type of statute prohibits the conducting of secular business, or one's "ordinary calling" (such as selling merchandise), on Sunday. (You may be familiar with Sunday laws that forbid the sale of certain alcoholic beverages.) Exceptions usually involve works of charity or necessity, which can be accomplished on Sunday without fear of sanctions.

A violation of a Sunday statute in some jurisdictions voids the contract, unless the party asking for recovery can show, for instance, that he or she had no knowledge that the contract was executed on Sunday or that the agreement, though initiated on Sunday, was not accepted (and thus did not ripen into a contract) until later in the week.

Litigants in some jurisdictions have challenged the constitutionality of such statutes. These laws, by singling out Sunday as a "day of rest" from mercantile activity, may violate the First Amendment's prohibition against a governmentally established religion. In other words, Sunday is not the "Sabbath" for all Americans; yet state governments' enactments of such laws arguably put the interests of one religious group ahead of the interests of others and thus raise constitutional questions.

Wagering Statutes

Wagering contracts and lotteries are illegal in most states because of statutes prohibiting gambling, betting, and other games of chance. The underlying rationale for these laws focuses on the protection of the public from the crime and familial discord often associated with gambling. To constitute illegal wagering, the activity must involve a person's paying consideration or value in the hope of receiving a prize or other property by chance. Wagering in the legal sense always involves a scheme in which risk has been *artificially* created; hence, insurance contracts or stock transactions in which risk is an inherent feature do not comprise situations that implicate illegal wagering. On the other hand, raffles may be viewed by the courts as unlawful wagering. For instance, because of relatively soft demand in the housing market, some enterprising couples in various parts of the country have recently attempted to raffle off their homes. The conduct of these people has violated the wagering statutes of some of these jurisdictions. It should be noted, however, that public lotteries are perfectly legal in many states. Additionally, if the participant is not required to give something of value in order to take part in the activity, it is probably not a lottery and consequently is probably legal.

YOU BE THE JUDGE

The music channels, MTV and VH-1, sponsor numerous contests every year. In 1989, VH-1 gave away 36 Corvettes all to the same person in its "VH-1 Corvette Collection." In another contest, MTV, through its "Hellbent Roadhops Contest," gave away six Harley Davidson motorcycles, six leather jackets, six helmets, and six trips to Boston to six different viewers. Barry Glick sued MTV and VH-1 arguing that these sweepstakes constitute illegal gambling because the contests obligate viewers to pay in order to play. Most contestants enter by dialing 900 telephone numbers at two dollars per call. The music channels' attorneys countered with evidence that while most of the 1.1 million viewers had used the 900 numbers, 136,506 contestants had mailed in their entries; and 30,094 had utilized a toll-free number that they had requested by mail. Glick characterized himself as a Don Quixote figure bent on defending the poor from the toll charges and other abuses. Glick's attorney also noted another potential motive for filing the suit: a 19th century New Jersey law that permits citizen lawsuits against operators of illegal lotteries and bettors; this law allows the plaintiff to receive one-half of the total amount wagered if the bettors fail to ask for their money back within six months.

> Was Mr. Glick correct in characterizing the VH-1 and MTV sweep-stakes as illegal gambling? If you were presiding over this lawsuit, how would you decide it?

Source: "This Man Wants His MTV (to Stop All Those Contests)," Mark Robichaux, *The Wall Street Journal,* May 12, 1992, page A5.

Usury Statutes

Usurious contracts occur when *a loan of money is made at a greater profit (or rate of interest) than state law permits.* For usury to exist, there must be a loan of money (or an agreement to extend the maturity of a monetary debt) for which the debtor agrees to repay the principal at a rate that exceeds the legal rate of interest. In addition, the lender must intend to violate the usury laws. If these elements are present, the resultant contract is illegal. In most states, a usurious lender will be unable to collect any interest and may also be subject to criminal or other statutory penalties. In some states, only the amount of excess interest is denied; the lender can recover the remaining interest and principal. In a few states, the agreement is void; the lender receives no interest, no principal.

Because such wide variations exist among state usury laws, it is difficult to generalize. Loans to corporations may be exempt from a jurisdiction's usury statutes, as may short-term loans, especially if the lender will be incurring large risks in making the loans. **Acceleration clauses** and **prepayment clauses** are generally not usurious. The same is true of service fees that reflect the incidental costs of making a loan—filing and recording fees, for example. Sales under revolving charge accounts (open-ended credit accounts) or **conditional sales contracts** ordinarily are not usurious even if a higher-than-lawful rate is charged. Two reasons have been forwarded in justification of this position: (1) A bona fide conditional sale on a deferred-payment basis is not a loan of money, and (2) the finance charge is merely a part of an increased purchase price reflective of the seller's risk in giving up possession of personal property (clothes, refrigerators, blenders, and the like) that depreciates quickly in value. **Time-price differential sales contracts** may or may not be usurious, depending on applicable state law and/or special consumer protection statutes. Time-price differential sales contracts involve an offer to sell at a designated price for cash (say $6000 for an automobile) or at a higher price on credit (say $7500). Even though the maximum legal rate of interest in this state may be 18 percent, the 25 percent actual rate represented by the credit price will not be usurious as long as the final price reflects the credit nature of the sale rather than an intent to evade the usury laws.

The trend today is to raise the maximum interest rate and to increase the exceptions to the usury laws. Moreover, federally guaranteed loans allow interest rates that would otherwise violate state law. These factors have seriously eroded the original purpose of usury laws—the protection of debtors from excessive rates of interest. But, as mentioned earlier, little uniformity

Acceleration clauses Clauses in contracts that advance the date for payment based on the occurrence of a condition or the breach of a duty.

Prepayment clauses Contract clauses that allow the debtor to pay the debt before it is due without penalty.

Conditional sales contracts Sales contracts in which the transfer of title to the buyer is subject to a condition, most commonly the payment of the full purchase price by the buyer.

Time-price differential sales contracts Contracts with a difference in price based on the date of payment, with one price for an immediate payment and another price if the payment is at a later date.

exists in the various states' usury statutes; so it is wise to consult these statutes if you are in doubt about the legality of a particular transaction. The case that follows illustrates a typical situation implicating the possible application of usury laws.

Title & Trust Company of Florida v. Parker
468 So.2d 520 (Fla. App. 1985)

FACTS The Parkers, California residents, were approached in May, 1980, by representatives of a California corporation known as EAC, Inc. (EAC), who proposed that the Parkers lend EAC $200,000. EAC promised to repay the Parkers $305,000 ninety days later in exchange for this loan. As security for the loan, the Parkers received a mortgage on a parcel of real estate in Jacksonville, Florida, that EAC allegedly owned. Although the loan was evidenced by a note with a stated principal of $305,000 and a per annum interest rate of 18 percent, the true principal involved was $200,000, of which amount only $175,000 was eventually distributed to EAC. Thus, the actual interest rate involved in the transaction amounted to 52 percent per annum and exceeded 200 percent for the ninety days. Prior to the distribution of the loan proceeds, the Parkers received a title insurance commitment covering the mortgaged Jacksonville property from Title & Trust Company of Florida (Title & Trust). Subsequently, Title & Trust discovered that the deed under which EAC allegedly held title to the property was a forgery. Thus, Title & Trust refused to issue a title insurance policy covering the Jacksonville parcel. In the meantime, before Title & Trust had given notice to Mr. Parker of EAC's defective title, the Parkers had already given the loan principal to the EAC officers. The Parkers sued Title & Trust for breach of its commitment to provide title insurance when Title & Trust refused to reimburse the Parkers for their "loss." The Parkers asked for $305,000, the face value of the insurance commitment. Title & Trust argued that the Parkers had sustained no "loss" under the policy when their interest in the Florida property had been declared null and void in the true owners' quiet title suit against the Parkers and EAC because under the Florida usury statute the Parkers' note and mortgage were unenforceable.

ISSUE Could the Parkers recover from Title & Trust the face value of the title insurance commitment issued by Title & Trust even though the agreement in which the Florida property had been given as security for the loan was usurious?

HOLDING No. Although the Parkers had sustained a loss, to award the Parkers the face value of the policy would give effect to the usurious part of the agreement and thus violate the public policy of the state.

REASONING Courts, in general, have an affirmative duty to avoid allowing a party who violates public policy to receive any substantial benefits from his or her wrongdoing. Florida's statutes evidenced a clear legislative declaration of a public policy against usury, including both the forfeiture of usurious interest and the nonenforcement of a criminally usurious debt. Accordingly, the trial judge properly disallowed that portion of the damages predicated on the usurious interest rate by awarding the Parkers $175,000 in damages rather than $305,000, the face amount of the policy, or the total coverage afforded by the commitment issued by Title & Trust.

AGREEMENTS VIOLATIVE OF PUBLIC POLICY

As we saw in the *Wagner* case, judges more and more frequently resort to public policy as a basis for invalidating agreements. In holding that a contract is void on public policy grounds, the court is deciding the legality of the agreement before it in light of the public interests involved. Hence, public policy frequently becomes an alternative ground for finding illegality. A court may strike down a contract to fix prices because the agreement violates statutes (e.g., the Sherman Act), or it may choose to invalidate the same agreement on public policy grounds, citing the damage to the public that such a covenant poses. The *Stampco* decision indicates the law's use of this double-edged sword, since one basis for the statute at issue in that case was a public policy basis: prevention of injury to the public interest that otherwise may result by a public works employee's succumbing to the employer's unscrupulous offers to pay wages lower than those mandated by prevailing wage statutes. However, because *public policy* is such a wide-ranging term, courts often have to juggle competing interests in judging the legality of certain types of bargains.

In what is unquestionably one of the most controversial cases of the last few decades, the New Jersey Supreme Court had to balance such statutory directives and public policies in disposing of the widely publicized "Baby M" case, which follows.

In re Baby M
537 A.2d 1227 (N.J. 1988)

FACTS   In February, 1985, William Stern and Mrs. Mary Beth Whitehead entered into a surrogacy contract in which Mrs. Whitehead agreed to bear a child for Stern and his infertile wife. The contract provided that through artificial insemination using Mr. Stern's sperm, Mrs. Whitehead would become pregnant, bear the child, deliver it to Mr. Stern, and terminate her maternal rights so that Mr. and Mrs. Stern could adopt the baby. Mr. Stern, for his part, agreed to attempt the artificial insemination and to pay $10,000 to Mrs. Whitehead upon the delivery of the child to him after its birth. In a separate contract, Mr. Stern agreed to pay $7500 to the Infertility Center of New York, which had brought the parties together. Mrs. Whitehead gave birth to a healthy baby girl on 27 March 1986. The Sterns named her Melissa; Mrs. Whitehead named her Sara. When the Sterns visited the hospital, Mrs. Whitehead told them she was not sure if she could give up the baby. But on 30 March 1986, she did so. Later that evening, however, she went to the Sterns' house and pleaded with them to let her have a week with the baby because she was suffering greatly about giving up the child. Concerned about the possibility of Mrs. Whitehead's committing suicide, the Sterns agreed, believing Mrs. Whitehead would keep her word. When it became apparent that Mrs. Whitehead would not return the child to the Sterns, Mr. Stern filed suit, seeking enforcement of the surrogacy contract and permanent custody of the child. Mrs. Whitehead, in the meantime, had fled the state; and the Sterns were unable to reacquire possession of Melissa for over four months.

ISSUE   Was such a surrogacy contract legal and enforceable in New Jersey?

HOLDING   No. Such a contract violated both New Jersey statutory law and the public policies of the state.

REASONING   The trial court was wrong in enforcing the contract, terminating Mrs. Whitehead's parental rights, and allowing Mrs. Stern to adopt the child. Specifically, the surrogacy contract conflicted with laws prohibiting the use of money in connection with adoptions, laws requiring proof of parental unfitness or abandonment before courts could order termination of parental rights or grant adoptions, and laws making surrender of custody and consent to adoption revocable in private placement adoptions. Besides violating statutory law, the surrogacy contract also contravened several public policies of the state: that children should remain with and be brought up by both the natural parents;

that the rights of natural parents are equal concerning their child, with a father's right being no greater than a mother's; that consent to surrender of a child must be voluntary; and that the best interests of the child be taken into account in determining the fitness of the custodial father, the effect on the child of not living with her natural mother, and so forth. Hence, this surrogacy contract created and was based on principles directly contrary to New Jersey laws. Simply put, it guaranteed the separation of a child from its mother; it permitted adoption regardless of the adoptive parent's suitability; it totally ignored the child; it took the child from the mother regardless of her wishes and her maternal fitness; and it did all this and accomplished all its goals through the use of money. Moreover, the potential degradation of some women that might result from this arrangement had not been considered. In sum, the harmful consequences of this surrogacy arrangement, particularly the arrangement's irrevocability and the money that purported to form the consideration for it, infected the entire contract. Therefore, in New Jersey, a surrogate mother's agreement to sell her child was void.

Covenants Not to Compete

Covenants not to compete, also called *restrictive covenants,* are *express promises that a seller of a business or an employee who leaves a company will not engage in the same or a similar business or occupation for a period of time in a certain geographic area.* Such bargains may or may not be legal. If the purpose of these "noncompete clauses" is to protect the buyer of a business from the possibility that the seller will set up shop two blocks from the original business establishment, or the former employer from the possibility that the ex-employee will sign on with a competitor, the restrictions on the seller or former employee, if reasonable in *time* and in *geographic scope,* will ordinarily be upheld as legal. But, as mentioned earlier, these situations are complicated by competing policies. It is clearly unfair to shackle unduly the employment opportunities of the seller (or former employee), who has to make a living. Similarly, if we curtail this person's business activities or occupational activities, we are in effect insulating the buyer (or former employer) from competition and may thereby unwittingly bring about higher prices. For this reason, many courts use public policy considerations in scrutinizing these restrictive covenants and in arriving at their decisions.

Usually such covenants are incidental to the sale of a business or to an employment contract. (Agreements not to compete that have no other purpose than the curtailing of competition are illegal as restraints on trade and are violations of antitrust law.) If, however, under the facts and circumstances, a particular covenant not to compete is unreasonably restrictive in time or geographic scope, it is within a court's power to rewrite the covenant so that it is less restrictive (a process called *blue-penciling*) and hence reasonable. But, as you have been cautioned in the past, do not expect courts to save you from bad (or illegal) bargains. Blue-penciling is comparatively rare. In fact, most courts would reject this approach, void the restrictive covenant, and construe the agreement without any reference to the covenant not to compete.

The next case shows how the question of the legality of a restrictive covenant can become the basis for a lawsuit.

Technical Aid Corporation v. *Allen*
591 A.2d 262 (N.H. 1991)

FACTS   Technical Aid Corporation (Technical Aid) is in the business of providing temporary and contract professionals to industry. Technical Aid hired Allen on or about 20 April 1981. When he first reported for work on 27 April 1981, a company employee told Allen that the company expected him to sign an employment contract containing a number of restrictive covenants. Because Allen had not known of this contract, he wanted to take it home to have a lawyer look at it. However, because he could not work for Technical Aid without signing the contract immediately and because he had already given notice to his previous employer, Allen felt he had no choice but to sign it. The contract contained the following restrictions: 1) that he would not, while in Technical Aid's employ, engage in any activity whatsoever that would compete with Technical Aid; 2) that he would not, in the event of the termination of this agreement, engage in a competitive business with Technical Aid, for a period of eighteen months, within a radius of one hundred miles of any office to which Technical Aid had assigned him while in its employ; 3) that he would not, for the same period, attempt to divert from Technical Aid any personnel, goodwill, or business; and 4) that he would not divulge any confidential information acquired while in Technical Aid's employ. After working in Technical Aid's national office for a number of years, Allen transferred to the Nashua, New Hampshire, office. In 1985, Allen decided to leave Technical Aid. Together with Redmond, a former employee of the company, Allen formed E & S, a temporary personnel business. In April, 1986, they leased office space for E & S; and on 10 May 1986, Allen resigned from Technical Aid. Thereafter, he worked for E & S, participating only in management; he neither solicited nor serviced customers. Technical Aid subsequently sued Allen for violations of various restrictive covenants contained in his employment contract with the company.

ISSUE   Were these restrictive covenants enforceable?

HOLDING   Yes. The restrictive covenants overall were enforceable, despite the unenforceability of one provision, because this unenforceable term was not essential to the agreed-on exchange and because Technical Aid had not engaged in serious misconduct.

REASONING   The law does not look with favor on contracts in restraint of trade or competition; hence, courts narrowly construe such contracts. Nonetheless, restrictive covenants are valid and enforceable if the restraint is reasonable given the particular circumstances of the case. To determine the reasonableness of a restrictive covenant ancillary to an employment contract, New Hampshire courts will employ a three-pronged test: First, is the restriction greater than necessary to protect the legitimate interests of the employer? Second, does the restriction impose an undue hardship on the employee? And third, is the restriction injurious to the public interest? If the courts answer any of these questions in the affirmative, the restriction in question is unreasonable and unenforceable. The contract contains a number of restrictive covenants. Judging the validity of the first of these (the covenant against competition) at the outset involves identifying the legitimate interests of the employer and determining whether the restraint is narrowly tailored to protect those interests. Here, Technical Aid's interest derives from Allen's contact with its customers. When an employee is put in a position involving client contact, it is natural that some of the goodwill emanating from the client is directed to the employee rather than to the employer. Thus, the employer has a legitimate interest in preventing its employees from appropriating this goodwill to its detriment. For a restrictive covenant based on an employee's client contact to protect narrowly the legitimate interests of the employer, the geographic scope of the restriction generally must be limited to that area in which the employee had client contact, as that usually constitutes the extent of the area in which the employer's goodwill is subject to appropriation by the employee. For salespersons, this area often corresponds to the territory to which they are assigned to make sales. As a salesperson in Technical Aid's Nashua sales office, Allen's territory included the entire state of New Hampshire and possibly Vermont and part of Massachusetts. However, the covenant against competition prohibits Allen from engaging in competition anywhere within a one-hundred mile radius of the Nashua office. This area includes large portions of Maine, Massachusetts, Rhode Island, and Connecticut. Because Allen could not, as an employee of Technical Aid, solicit business in these regions, it remains highly unlikely that he would be able to appropriate any of Technical Aid's goodwill there. Hence, the geographic limitation is greater than necessary to protect the legitimate interests of Technical Aid; and the covenant against competition fails to meet the first prong of the reasonableness test. For similar reasons, this covenant also fails to meet the second prong of the reasonableness test, since the covenant imposes an undue hardship on Allen. When the restriction is greater than necessary to protect the legitimate interests of the employer, any adverse effect caused by that part of the restriction deemed unnecessary constitutes an undue hardship on the employee. Here, the covenant against competition, to the extent that it prohibits Allen from engaging in competition with Technical Aid beyond his assigned sales territory, seriously limits Allen's employment opportunities without providing any legitimate benefit to Technical Aid. Thus, this covenant imposes an undue hardship on Allen. Finally, the evidence fails to show that the covenant against competition has injured the public interest. Although the restriction does limit the public's ability to choose, the mere fact of some limitation does not suffice as injury to the public interest. If it did, courts could find no restrictive covenant reasonable, as any restriction would curtail to some degree the public's ability to choose. A restrictive covenant must unreasonably limit the public's right to choose before courts will find it injurious to the public interest. Although the covenant against competition does not seem injurious to the public interest, because it violates two prongs of the reasonableness test, the covenant against competition is unreasonable and unenforceable as written. The second restrictive covenant of the contract (the covenant against servicing customers) encompasses far less activity than that covered by the covenant against competition. Like the covenant against competition, however, the geographic scope of the covenant against servicing customers is greater than necessary to protect the legitimate interests of Technical Aid. Technical Aid has clients far outside Allen's allotted territory; indeed, it purports to be not only a national but an international organization. Accordingly, Technical Aid has no legitimate interest in protecting its entire client base from Allen. Therefore, for the majority of Technical Aid's customers, Allen has no advantage over any other complete stranger; he has no special hold on their goodwill. As with the previous covenant, the lack of a legitimate interest behind this covenant means that its restriction imposes an undue hardship on Allen; particularly since he, in addition, could violate the covenant without so realizing, owing to his lack of awareness of the identities of all Technical Aid's customers worldwide. Although there is no evidence that the covenant against servicing customers is injurious to the public interest, it fails to meet the first two prongs of the reasonableness test and is, therefore, unenforceable as written. The last restriction—in which Allen agreed to refrain from diverting personnel, goodwill, or business from Technical Aid—is no greater than necessary to protect the firm's business. As to these restrictions regarding its own staff, Technical Aid certainly has a legitimate interest in retaining the services of its current employees about whom an ex-employee has become knowledgeable. To hold otherwise would be to encourage employers to limit the contacts between its employees, thereby reducing the employers' vulnerability to former employees' recruiting away current employees. Moreover, the eighteen-month duration for the restrictions appears reasonable as well. Technical Aid, in effect, seeks a time period for the goodwill owed it—but directed to Allen—to dissipate. As such, this period does not seem excessive. As a final matter, the restrictions of paragraph 6 bear examination. Paragraph 6 prohibits Allen from engaging in activity competitive to Technical Aid while in its employ. The legitimate interests of an employer in enforcing a restrictive covenant remain considerably stronger during the employee's term of employment than subsequent to it. Employers are entitled to undivided loyalty from their present employees. Such a restriction is not a hardship to the employee, who by definition is not being prevented from plying his or her trade, nor is it injurious to the public interest. Therefore, this restriction is reasonable and enforceable. According to the *Restatement (Second) of Contracts,* Section 184, courts may give the enforceable terms of a contract effect if the unenforceable terms are not essential to the agreed exchange and if the party seeking enforcement has not engaged in serious misconduct.

Exculpatory Clauses   Agreements to commit torts are illegal. Indeed, there seems to be little justi-fication for a court's validating an agreement that has as its purpose an in-tentional breach of the duty of reasonable care to others. On the other hand, is there anything illegal about a bargain in which one party tries in advance to limit its liability in a particular set of circumstances? There unfortunately is no clear-cut answer to this question. Courts judge the legality of such *exculpatory clauses*, or bargains in which one person agrees *in advance* to exonerate another person's activities from liability, on a case-by-case basis. You are probably familiar with many such attempts at exculpation. For example, a certain dry cleaner always writes on his customers' tickets, "Not responsible for elastic and buttons." When customers sign the tickets, the dry cleaner can argue that the customers have agreed to hold him harmless for any damages to those parts of their clothing. Restaurants that have signs saying "Not responsible for belongings left in booths" are attempting to achieve the same end. In general, these and other agreements in which one party promises not to hold the other liable for tortious or wrongful conduct are legal. In many jurisdictions, statutes covering workers' compensation, innkeepers, and landlord-tenant relationships make the issue of liability for these particular areas moot. However, in the absence of statutes or clear precedents, courts look closely to see whether the party who agrees to assume the risk of tortious conduct without any recovery has done so voluntarily. In other words, the courts consider whether the party who has initiated the exculpatory clause has superior bargaining power (or superior knowledge) over the other person. (Recall the bank deposit example earlier in this chapter.) If so, courts may strike down the exculpatory clause as being contrary to public policy. Courts often use words like *oppressive, unconscionable,* and *unfair* when invalidating such clauses.

If the court believes an *adhesion contract* exists—that is, a contract drafted by the stronger party in order to force unfavorable terms on the weaker party—the court will probably find the clause contrary to public policy and thus illegal. This finding is by no means an easy task, however. Courts will necessarily weigh a variety of factors such as the age of the parties, their respective degrees of expertise, their mental condition at the time they signed the clause (was the injured party drunk when he signed the exculpatory clause just before climbing onto the "mechanical bull" in Joe's Pub?), and whether the language of the clause was in fine print. After analyzing these and other facts and policies, the court decides the legality of such clauses.

The *Porubiansky* and *Topp* cases illustrate the disposition of exculpatory clause issues by two different courts.

Porubiansky v. Emory University
275 S.E.2d 163 (Ga. App. 1980)
Affirmed, 282 S.E.2d 903 (Ga. 1981)

FACTS   Porubiansky was accepted as a patient at Emory University's School of Dentistry Clinic. Before becoming a patient, she was told that all treatment would be administered by dental students and employees under the direction of a licensed dentist or by a licensed dentist. Porubiansky signed a consent form in which she agreed to hold the clinic and its personnel harmless for any injuries arising out of any dental treatment rendered. After about five months of care, she had a clinic dentist remove an impacted tooth. During this procedure, the dentist noticed that her jaw was broken and told her so. She sued Emory, alleging that her jaw was broken during the negligent removal of her tooth. The clinic denied this and pleaded the exculpatory clause in the consent form as a defense.

ISSUE

Was the exculpatory clause legal and hence a valid defense?

HOLDING

No. The clause was illegal.

REASONING

The exculpatory clause was void as against public policy, since the law requires that dentists possess and exercise a reasonable amount of care and skill. Thus, the public interest of the state of Georgia would not be served if dentists, or dental clinics vested with the responsibility of training future dentists, were permitted to relieve themselves from liability for their own negligence.

Topp Copy Products, Inc. v. Singletary
591 A.2d 298 (Pa. Super. 1991)

FACTS

Topp Copy Products, Inc. (Topp Copy) entered into a commercial lease for the first floor of a multistoried building. Singletary was the owner of the building and the landlord on the commercial lease. In an apartment located above the premises leased by Topp Copy, a toilet developed a leak, resulting in substantial water damage to Topp Copy's inventory stored in the leased unit. The plumbing fixture that broke and caused the subsequent water damage to this inventory was not located in Topp Copy's leased unit. Topp Copy (the lessee) sued Singletary (the lessor) alleging negligence. Singletary, in turn, contended that an exculpatory clause in the parties' lease agreement barred Topp Copy's suit for the water damage caused by the broken plumbing fixture. This clause, in paragraph 19, released Singletary "from any and all liability for damages that may result from the bursting, stoppage and leakage of any water pipe, . . . watercloset, . . . and drain, and from all liability for any and all damage caused by the water . . . and contents of said water pipes, . . . waterclosets and drains." Topp Copy argued that this exculpatory clause did not apply to its damage because the clause explicitly failed to relieve the landlord of liability for his own negligence and because the clause was ambiguous when read in context with another clause in the agreement. Specifically, Topp Copy asserted that the language of paragraph 15 of the lease—"[a]ll damages or injuries done to the said premises other than those caused by fire and by ordinary wear and tear or by the acts or *omission of the landlord* shall be repaired by the lessee herein. . . ."—made the exculpation by paragraph 19 ambiguous.

ISSUES

Was the exculpatory clause in paragraph 19 of the lease enforceable? Did that clause relieve Singletary of liability for his own negligent conduct?

HOLDING

Yes. The exculpatory clause was enforceable. However, the ambiguity of the clause's language would preclude Singletary's successfully arguing that the clause immunized him from liability for his own negligent acts.

REASONING

In Pennsylvania, an exculpatory clause generally is valid whenever it satisfies three conditions: 1) The clause does not contravene any policy of law (that is, it is not a matter of interest to the public or state); 2) the contract is between persons relating entirely to their own private affairs; and 3) each party is a free bargaining agent, in that the agreement is not in effect a mere contract of adhesion. Once the clause fulfills these conditions and thus becomes a valid contract, the contract must meet four additional standards in order to be interpreted and construed to relieve a person of liability for his or her own acts of negligence. These four standards hold that 1) a court must construe the contract immunizing a party from liability for negligence strictly, since the law does not favor such a party; 2) the contract must state the intention of the parties with the greatest particularity, beyond doubt by express stipulation, and no inference from words of general import can establish it; 3) a court must construe the contract against the party seeking immunity from liability; and 4) the burden of establishing this immunity rests on the party seeking the protection of the clause. These seven considerations demonstrate that Pennsylvania law does not view contracts providing for the immunity of parties from their own negligent acts positively. Rather, under Pennsylvania law, courts will subject exculpatory clauses included in lease agreements to a detailed and thorough review to determine their validity and enforceability. The reason the law looks with disfavor on exculpatory clauses stems from the fact that they excuse defendants from maintaining reasonable standards of care. Under such clauses, defendants may be negligent with impunity. Because generally the law seeks to discourage negligence and to require that wrongdoers remain liable for their wrongful acts, courts interpret the validity and enforceability of exculpatory clauses in a limiting fashion and strictly construe the language against the clause's author. In this case, the exculpatory clause does satisfy the initial three conditions required for validity. This clause, included in a commercial lease entered into between a business tenant and an individual landlord, does not implicate any matters of public or state interest; rather, the clause is included in an agreement relating completely to the parties' private affairs. Moreover, Topp Copy does not contend that the commercial lease at issue represents a contract of adhesion. Although the instant exculpatory clause meets the initial three conditions for validity, Topp Copy specifically argues that the clause, although initially valid, does not immunize Singletary from his own negligent acts. Relying on the additional four standards of construction, Topp Copy maintains that the exculpatory clause uses words of general import and is ambiguous when read in conjunction with paragraph 15 of the lease. According to Topp Copy, because the exculpatory clause does not meet the four standards of construction, Pennsylvania courts cannot give it effect to immunize Singletary from liability for his own negligent conduct. The exculpatory clause in paragraph 19 releases and discharges Singletary *"from any and all liability for damages that may result from the bursting, stoppage and leakage of any water"* (emphasis added). These are plainly words of general import and demonstrate that the parties had not, via the exculpatory clause, intended to exculpate Singletary for acts of Singletary's own negligence.

EXCEPTIONS: UPHOLDING ILLEGAL AGREEMENTS

As mentioned earlier, the general rule is that an illegal bargain is void; the court leaves the parties where they are as a result of the bargain. Despite this general rule, there are some situations in which a party may bring a successful suit based on an illegal agreement. Usually one cannot sue for enforcement of an illegal executory agreement, but in certain circumstances one may sue if the performance called for in the bargain has been rendered.

Parties Not *in Pari Delicto*

When one of the parties is less guilty than the other, the law states that the parties are not *in pari delicto (they are not equally at fault or equally wrong)*. This allows the less-guilty person to recover if recovery would serve the public interest in some way. For instance, the less-guilty party may be a member of a class of persons a regulatory statute was designed to protect. If, in our earlier example, the statute requiring the licensing of plumbers were a regulatory as opposed to a revenue-raising statute, Sue would not be *in pari delicto* ("in equal wrong") with the plumber who had failed to comply with the statute. If she had given him $100 as a down payment on a garbage disposal, she could recover this money. A policy of protecting the public from unlicensed tradespeople would be advanced by allowing her recovery. Such results, then, focus on the conduct of the less-guilty party rather than on the illegality of the subject matter of the contract. Similarly, if Joanne works for a photographer who does not have a license as required by a local ordinance, she can still recover the wages due her if she does not know about her boss's noncompliance. The illegality here may be termed *incidental,* or **collateral.**

Notice how the court applied many of these concepts in deciding the next case.

Collateral   Secondary.

National Petrochemical Company of Iran v. M/T Stolt Sheaf
930 F.2d 240 (2d Cir. 1991)

FACTS

On 7 April 1980, in response to the seizure of the United States Embassy in Tehran and the taking of fifty-two American diplomatic personnel as hostages by Iranian militants, President Carter severed diplomatic relations with Iran and issued Executive Order 12205. The order proscribed, among other things, "[t]he sale, supply or other transfer, by any person subject to the jurisdiction of the United States, of any items, commodities or products . . . from the United States . . . either to or destined for Iran." In June, 1980, National Petrochemical Company of Iran (NPC) sought to purchase supplies of certain urgently needed chemicals for delivery to Iran. The mutual trade embargoes existing between the United States and Iran, however, rendered NPC's prior sources unavailable. NPC therefore approached various traders and brokers in order to secure new sources of supply. Consequently, Monnris Enterprises (Monnris) of Dubai, United Arab Emirates, contracted with NPC to act as a middleman for NPC's purchase of the needed chemicals from Rotex Chemie Brunst & Co. of Hamburg, West Germany (Rotex). Rotex acted in this transaction, however, through a Swiss affiliate, Formula S.A., because West Germany, like the United States, had placed restraints on shipments to Iran. Although the pertinent documents called for shipment of the chemicals from "any West European and UAE Ports," these chemicals were in fact purchased from suppliers in the United States and shipped from Houston, Texas, aboard the *Stolt Sheaf.* Although the original **charter party** called for delivery of the cargo from Texas to Barcelona, Spain, a subsequent addendum to that charter party specified Iran as the ultimate destination of the cargo. When war broke out between Iran and Iraq in September, 1980, the tanker, the *Stolt Sheaf,* notified NPC that it was invoking the war risk clause of the charter party. The tanker also requested that the charterer, Rotex, name an alternate destination for the cargo aboard the *Stolt Sheaf,* which by then was in the vicinity of Iran. Thereafter, by a second addendum to the charter party, Rotex ordered the *Stolt Sheaf* to Taiwan, where Rotex successfully resold the cargo. Although Rotex purportedly made the sale in Taiwan for the account of NPC, none of the proceeds from Rotex and Formula ever reached NPC. In the resulting legal proceedings in Germany, Kuhn Mohamed, the proprietor of Monnris at the time of this transaction, stated in an affidavit that Monnris's relationship with NPC in this transaction evolved from NPC's need for a middleman who could secure the necessary contracts for circumventing the effect of the trade sanctions applying to Iran. Mohamed also acknowledged that he knew by 21 August 1980, approximately a month before their intended delivery to Iran, that the *Stolt Sheaf* was bringing the chemicals from the United States through Barcelona, where new bills of lading would be issued either for that vessel or for another one. Ashgar Bakhtiari, head of NPC's procurement department in 1980, also submitted a statement in the German proceedings that indicated Bakhtiari's knowledge that the bills of lading would not necessarily reflect the true destination of the cargo in order to avoid the effects of the regulations concerning economic sanctions. When NPC sued the *Stolt Sheaf* for negligently and conspiratorially allowing Rotex's sale of the cargo in Taiwan, the *Stolt Sheaf* argued that NPC could not recover owing to the underlying illegality of the contracts.

Charter party   A document setting forth the arrangements whereby one person takes over a ship for the conveyance of goods to one or more ports; also called a charter.

ISSUES
Were the contracts that NPC was seeking to enforce illegal? If so, was NPC nevertheless entitled to recover because it was not *in pari delicto* with those who had intentionally violated the trade embargoes?

HOLDING
Yes and no. NPC could not enforce these agreements because they were admittedly part of a larger plan to violate the United States's trade embargoes against Iran. Moreover, NPC's knowledge of the illegal origin of the cargo precluded its asserting that it was not *in pari delicto* with the other parties who had violated the trade embargoes.

REASONING
NPC claimed that the contracts at issue in this suit were legal because the individual agreements, viewed separately, fell outside the embargoes against shipments from the United States to Iran. Executive Order 12205, by its terms, applied to "any person subject to the jurisdiction of the United States." Thus, NPC contended that because Formula and Monnris were not subject to the jurisdiction of the United States, their contracts to supply goods to Iran similarly lay outside the scope of the embargoes. Likewise, NPC claimed, the defendants, as foreign entities, could properly contract to make the shipments. However, the proposition that foreign entities that undertake to deliver goods from a United States port in violation of American law were not, in doing so, "subject to the jurisdiction of the United States" would merit little support. Moreover, this reasoning would ignore the undisputed fact that each contract was a component, in the words of NPC's complaint, of a "scheme to transport the cargoes for payment of monies between the U.S. and Iran, without detection in contravention of the then existing laws and trade embargoes between the two countries." Under New York contract law, a perfectly legitimate contract may become unenforceable owing to its "direct connection" with an illegal transaction. Thus, even assuming that, viewed in isolation, the contracts underlying its claims were legal, U.S. courts would prohibit NPC from enforcing those agreements because the contracts were part of a larger plan to violate the United States's trade embargoes. However, NPC argued further that its ignorance of the illegal origin of the cargo would permit it to enforce the contract, notwithstanding any illegality, because NPC was not *in pari delicto* with those who had intentionally violated the trade embargoes. True, NPC might be entitled to enforce the contracts if it had been truly unaware of the illegality. Yet NPC admitted in its complaint that Monnris Enterprises had acted as NPC's agent in securing the chemicals from Rotex. Further, Bakhtiari's statement in the German proceedings acknowledged that the embargoes had forced NPC to "work through agents and middlemen" in order to avoid the regulations giving effect to the economic sanctions. Mohamed's affidavit in the German litigation made clear that Monnris's role in the transaction at issue had resulted from its seeking precisely such a middleman role in the circumstances posed by the trade embargoes against Iran. Moreover, Mohamed had unequivocally stated that he had been told on 21 August 1980 that the chemicals at issue in this case had been shipped from the United States. Thus, Monnris, NPC's agent, knew of the illegal nature of the transaction—that goods were being shipped from the United States to Iran. This knowledge was, in turn, attributable to NPC, because it is a basic tenet of the law of agency that the knowledge of an agent is imputed to the principal. In sum, the evidence showed that NPC was *in pari delicto* as to the *Stolt Sheaf* shipment and hence could not recover the proceeds of the sale in Taiwan.

Repentance

Even if the parties are *in pari delicto*, the law will allow recovery by the person who shows repentance of the illegal bargain by rescinding the bargain before it is consummated. For example, let us assume that a partnership attempts to bribe a state senator for favorable legislation. This agreement would be illegal because it is harmful to the public. If one of the partners attempts to rescind the transaction before the money is delivered to the senator, he or she can do so. The law calls this *repentance*. Courts justify the partner's recovery of the money because such a result furthers the public interest of deterring illegal schemes.

Partial Illegality

Agreements may consist of several different promises supported by different considerations. Courts will enforce the parts of the bargain that involve legal promises and legal considerations while refusing to enforce those parts of the bargain that are illegal, if courts can sever these promises. If, instead, either the illegal promise or the illegal consideration (or both) wholly taints the agreement, the entire agreement is declared void by such courts. Cases, such as the *Technical Aid* decision, that involve a restrictive covenant can provide good examples of *partial illegality*. If a court finds the restrictive covenant to be unreasonable in scope, the judge may sever it from the rest of the agreement because it is illegal. The court will, however, ordinarily enforce the remainder of the contract—the sale of a business, for example—because the balance of the contract is perfectly legal; it is divisible from the illegal portion. In short, courts will give effect to those provisions capable of standing as a contract following the severing or divisibility of the illegal portion.

Figure 12.1 shows the components of legality and illegality in contracts.

FIGURE 12.1   The Requirement of Legality as an Element of Contract Formation and Enforcement

ILLEGALITY ⟵————   ————⟶ LEGALITY

Mala in Se Bargains (inherently and completely illegal)

a. "Agreements" to commit crimes

b. "Agreements" to commit torts

Mala Prohibita Bargains (illegal because forbidden by statute)

a. Price fixing agreements

b. Performances of services without licenses under regulatory licensing schemes

c. Sunday laws

d. Wagering statutes

e. Usury statutes

Bargains Comprised of Subject Matters That Are Not Tortious, Criminal, or Otherwise Violative of Public Policy

Bargains Involving Public Policy Considerations

a. Covenants not to compete

If unreasonable in time and geographical scope / If reasonable in time and geographical scope

b. Exculpatory clauses

If clauses are in fine print and drafter has vastly superior bargaining power / If clauses are conspicuous and parties have equal bargaining power

c. Agreements in which one party is not in pari delicto

d. Agreements in which one party repents before the illegal bargains are consummated

e. Agreements in which the legal portions can be severed from the illegal portions

SUMMARY

The law imposes a requirement that the subject matter and purpose of a bargain be legal in order for the bargain to be recognized as a valid contract. A bargain is illegal if its performance is criminal, tortious, or otherwise opposed to public policy. Some courts distinguish between bargains that violate statutes because they are evil in themselves (*mala in se*) and bargains that are merely forbidden by statute (*mala prohibita*). Many types of bargains violate statutes, such as price-fixing agreements, bargains in contravention of Sunday laws, wagering agreements, and usurious transactions. Performance of services without a license may make the agreement void if the statute is regulatory. In contrast, if the statute requires licensing as a revenue-enhancing measure, lack of a license will not void the bargain. Judges today look increasingly to public policy factors when deciding cases. Covenants not to compete (promises to refrain from engaging in the same or a similar business for a period of time in a certain geographic area) and exculpatory clauses (attempts to disclaim liability for negligence or other torts), if too restrictive or one-sided, may be struck down on public policy grounds.

There are some exceptions to the rule that illegal bargains are void. These exceptions include agreements in which the parties are not *in pari delicto,* or of equal guilt; agreements in which one party repents of the illegal bargain before its consummation; and agreements in which courts can sever the legal portions from the illegal segments.

DISCUSSION QUESTIONS

1. What is the difference between a *mala in se* and a *mala prohibita* bargain?
2. What is an exculpatory clause? Is it always legal? Why or why not?
3. What are covenants not to compete? What standards do courts use to judge their legality?
4. Describe the difference between a regulatory statute and a revenue-producing statute. What relief will courts give for the violation of these statutes?

5. What is a Sunday law?
6. Why are wagering and lotteries illegal in most jurisdictions?
7. What is a usurious contract?
8. What kinds of common financing devices would not violate usury laws?
9. Describe the three most important exceptions to the general rule that an illegal bargain is void.
10. What is an adhesion contract?

CASE PROBLEMS

1. In 1988, Ogelean Riddick sold the Suncoast Beauty School of Florida, Inc., to Suncoast Beauty College, Inc., a Florida corporation, and JoAnn Phillips. Riddick, in exchange for a payment of $20,000 from Suncoast Beauty College, Inc. and Phillips, executed a covenant not to compete, which stated:

For a period of five (5) years from date of closing and transfer of the business interest and assets, SUNCOAST BEAUTY SCHOOL OF FLORIDA, INC. and OGELEAN RIDDICK, as an individual, will not directly or indirectly for themselves or on behalf of any person, persons, partnership or corporation engage or attempt to engage in the ownership or operation of a beauty school in Pinellas County, Florida; nor aid or assist anyone else, except the Buyer, to do so within these limits; nor solicit in any manner any past accounts of the business; nor have any interest, directly or indirectly, in such a business; except that Ogelean Riddick, individually, may perform inspections for National Accrediting Commission of Cosmetology Arts and Sciences (NACCAS), and may be a free-lance conductor of seminars and a teacher of instructors and students in the beauty school environment.

However, Riddick subsequently opened a hair salon within one mile of the location of the beauty school. Suncoast Beauty College, Inc. and Phillips filed suit against Riddick for breach of the covenant not to compete. Would their lawsuit succeed? (*Riddick* v. *Suncoast Beauty College, Inc.*, 579 So.2d 855 [Fla. App. 1991].)

2. Portable Embryonics, Inc. (Portable) was in the business of performing nonsurgical bovine embryo transfers for clients in Montana and other states. Dr. Albert C. Mills, III (Mills) and his wife are the sole shareholders of Portable. Portable employed Gary Porter and Alton James from 1977 until 1988. Technicians such as Mills, Porter, and James remove fertilized eggs from donor cows and then implant the embryos into recipient cows, which serve as surrogate mothers; alternatively, they freeze the embryos for later use. In the spring of 1980, Portable prepared an employment contract that contained provisions for the protection of trade secrets and restrictions concerning employees who departed the company. James signed the contract on 17 April 1980, and Porter signed on 6 May 1980. Porter and James terminated their employment with Portable in February, 1988, and, within a few days, formed J. P. Genetics, Inc., a Montana corporation. J. P. Genetics, Inc. also performs nonsurgical bovine embryo transfers. When Mills learned that J. P. Genetics, Inc. had successfully lured away many of Portable's clients, Mills, citing the employment agreement, sued Porter and James for breach of contract, breach of loyalty, fraud, and bad faith. Porter and James, in turn, cited Montana statutes that characterized ova or embryo transfers on animals as the practice of veterinary medicine and that made the practice of veterinary medicine without a license a misdemeanor. Using these statutes, Porter and James argued that the purported employment contracts were illegal and unenforceable. Given these facts, should a court find in favor of Portable or Porter and James? (*Portable Embryonics, Inc.* v. *J. P. Genetics,* 810 P.2d 1197 [Mont. 1991].)

3. William "Rick" Malecha sued the St. Croix Valley Skydiving Club, Inc. for damages arising from injuries he had suffered from a skydiving accident. On 27 August 1983, Malecha and two friends had taken a skydiving course of five hours' duration. He had paid for the training that morning and at some point during the day had signed a waiver of liability form. Among other things, the agreement specified that the club could not be "held responsible or liable for any negligence implied or otherwise." Malecha sustained serious injuries when his parachute failed to open as he made his first jump in the afternoon of the 27th. When Malecha sued the club for negligence, it contended that his signing the agreement had released it from liability. What arguments should Malecha make in his own behalf? (*Malecha* v. *St. Croix Valley Skydiving Club,* 392 N.W.2d 727 [Minn. App. 1986].)

4. Vitality Centers, Inc. (Vitality) had leased an automatic telephone system from Potomac Leasing Company (Potomac). Potomac had bought the equipment from Leads Unlimited, Inc., the manufacturer, and had then entered into a lease agreement with Vitality. In essence, Potomac served an intermediary function after the manufacturer had located a would-be customer; but Potomac itself had no knowledge of the equipment. Indeed, the lease that Vitality had signed recited that fact. After it had made a few payments on the noncancellable, forty-eight-month lease, Vitality sent the equipment back to Potomac. When Potomac sued to enforce the lease, Vitality asserted that the subject matter of the lease was illegal and that the contract was therefore void. Unknown to Potomac, Vitality had used the equipment to dial phone numbers randomly to leave advertising messages and to record the responses of the persons answering the calls. Arkansas statutes prohibited all such activities. Should a court allow Vitality to raise the alleged illegality of the lease as a defense to Potomac's enforcement of the lease? (*Potomac Leasing Company* v. *Vitality Centers, Inc.,* 718 S.W.2d 928 [Ark. 1986].)

5. Richard Zientara had asked his friend and co-worker, Chester Kaszuba, to have his wife, Bernice, purchase an Illinois lottery ticket for Zientara at her place of work in Illinois. Zientara and the Kaszubas were all Indiana residents. Kaszuba agreed, and Zientara therefore gave him an envelope containing the purchase price and the numbers selected for the ticket. Zientara's number won a lottery worth $1,696,800, but Kaszuba refused to give Zientara the ticket and even made an effort to claim the ticket for himself. As a result, Zientara filed suit against the Kaszubas on several theories, including breach of contract. The Kaszubas argued that the transaction with Zientara was an illegal and therefore an unenforceable transaction because the Indiana Constitution prohibits lotteries. Would a court find this assertion persuasive? (*Kaszuba* v. *Zientara*, 506 N.E.2d 1 [Ind. 1987].)

6. In January and February, 1987, Doye Baker lent Daymon Howard $55,000, with four advances of funds that ended on 18 February. Baker agreed to finance the loan over a period of seven years, at 15 percent interest per annum, with monthly payments of $1,061.32 beginning 1 March 1987. The loan agreement between the parties was oral, and it was completed on 18 February. Baker testified that on that day, "When we were discussing it, [Howard] asked me what his payments would be on the $55,000 at the 15 percent interest, and I did have an amortization book, and that is where we came up with a figure of $1,061.00, whatever it is." Howard did not execute a promissory note or any other instrument evidencing the loan. However, between 18 February and 1 March, after the parties had agreed on the terms of the loan, Baker gave Howard a printed amortization schedule setting forth the amount of the loan, the rate of interest, and the 84 payments of $1,061.32 each required under the original agreement. After Howard had made eight payments and a part of the ninth, he quit paying on the loan. Texas statutes stated that the maximum legal rate of interest for oral agreements is 10 percent; for a written contract, Texas law allowed interest rates higher than 10 percent before requiring the lender to forfeit, as a penalty, three times the amount of usurious interest charged. Was this a usurious contract under Texas law because it was an oral agreement, or did the unsigned amortization schedule make it a written contract? (*Baker* v. *Howard*, 799 S.W.2d 450 [Tex. App. 1990].)

7. Anabas Export, Ltd. (Anabas) sold and delivered stickers featuring Michael Jackson's portrait to Alper Industries, Inc. (Alper) for resale and distribution by Alper. Anabas had not obtained Jackson's written permission to use his picture, as required by New York law. When Anabas sued Alper for the contract price, Alper argued that the sale of the stickers was void and unenforceable. Was Alper right? Why or why not? (*Anabas Export, Ltd.* v. *Alper Industries, Inc.*, 603 F. Supp. 1275 [S.D.N.Y. 1985].)

8. Kimbrough and Fox had been partners in a business known as ARA Rental and were also the equal owners of a corporation called C & G Inc., which consisted primarily of pieces of real property and equipment. When they decided to end their business relationship with each other, they divided these assets into two parcels. On 21 December 1979, Kimbrough and Fox tossed a coin to determine who would get each parcel. As a result of this coin toss, Kimbrough received what he deemed to be the less desirable parcel of property. Kimbrough later sued to have this agreement set aside on the ground that the coin toss violated the state's wagering statute and thus was void. How would you rule in this case if you were the judge? (*Kimbrough* v. *Fox*, 631 S.W.2d 606 [Tex. App. 1982].)

9. Wheeler was an industrial engineer who had performed industrial engineering services for Bucksteel Co. (Bucksteel). Oregon law provided that no one could practice engineering in the state unless he or she were registered and had obtained the required certificate to practice engineering. When Wheeler sued Bucksteel for services rendered, Bucksteel argued that the company owed Wheeler nothing because his failure to register as an engineer had made the contract for his services illegal. Was Bucksteel correct? (*Wheeler* v. *Bucksteel Co.*, 698 P.2d 995 [Or. App. 1985].)

10. San Benito Bank sued Rio Grande Music Company (RG Music) on a promissory note signed by Paco Betancourt, the founder of RG Music. Part of the company's "business" involved the smuggling of electronic equipment into Mexico. The bank had agreed to treat incoming checks drawn against Mexican banks in payment for the smuggled goods as "cash collections." When several of these checks were dishonored, Betancourt signed the promissory note that was at issue in the case to make up the deficiencies owed to the bank. When the bank sued to collect on this promissory note, RG Music contended that the bank's knowledge that the company was using the funds in illegal transactions made the note unenforceable. Was RG Music absolved from liability owing to this underlying illegality? (*San Benito Bank & Trust Company* v. *Rio Grande Music Company*, 686 S.W.2d 635 [Tex. App. 1985].)

C H A P T E R 13

Genuineness of the Contractual Assent

O U T L I N E

REALITY OF CONSENT

We have already briefly discussed the proposition that a valid offer and acceptance form the heart of all contracts. We have also seen that an agreement supported by consideration, made by parties having the ability to contract, and based on a subject that is legal should issue into a valid contract. But appearances can be deceptive. Before we check to see whether the agreement necessitates proper form (that is, whether the contract must be in writing), a topic we will take up in the next chapter, we first have to ascertain whether the parties have *genuinely* assented to the contract. Put another way, is the consent given by the parties real; or are the facts actually different from those to which they have outwardly agreed? The existence of fraud, misrepresentation, mistake, duress, undue influence, or unconscionability precludes the mutual assent that is the foundation of modern contract law. Since these matters are of some consequence in our private and business dealings, we will now turn our attention to a discussion of them and their legal effect.

FRAUD

Fraud is a word we all use fairly loosely, mainly because it lends itself to many definitions. At base, it consists of deception or hoodwinking; and it seems to involve a communication of some sort. But as one ancient case notes, "[a] nod or a wink, or a shake of the head or a smile" will do.[1] Sometimes even silence will suffice.

The essence of fraud is hard to pin down. One common definition states that fraud is *a deliberate misrepresentation of a material fact with the intent to induce another person to enter into a contract that will be injurious to that person.* The essence of fraud becomes clearer as we break down this definition into smaller components.

Elements of Fraud To constitute fraud, the misrepresentation or misstatement must concern a *fact.* A fact is something reasonably subject to exact knowledge. Thus, a statement about the size of a car engine or the dimensions of a lot are probably factual.

To show this first element of fraud, then, the plaintiff will have to prove that the defendant misstated a fact. Predictions, statements of value, and expressions of opinions do not generally equate with misrepresentations of fact; nor do misstatements of law.

Actually, in any given situation, it may be difficult to distinguish a fact from an opinion. Suppose a car salesperson says to you, "This little dandy will get you down the road at a pretty good clip. It has a great engine. It's a

[1]Walters v. Morgan, 3 DeF., F. & J. 718, 724 (1861).

V-6, and those engines have been very serviceable." The first two remarks are probably opinions, also known as "puffs" or "dealer's talk." The statement about the type of engine probably constitutes a fact. You may be unhappy, for instance, if you find a V-8 engine in the car after you purchase it; or if you find out V-6s have many problems and the salesperson knows this. In such a case, you may want to argue that you have been a victim of misrepresentation. However, courts tend to discount statements of value because of genuine differences in the way people assess things. When Joe says, "That ring is worth a thousand dollars," unless Joe is a jewelry dealer or an expert and the other person is not, most courts will refuse to call Joe's statement a fact. Joe may believe that his wedding ring is that dear, based, at least in part, on sentimentality. Such statements of value, because they are not factual, ordinarily do not constitute this first element of a showing of fraud.

2. The second element that a plaintiff must prove to recover in fraud involves the *materiality* of the fact that was allegedly misstated. A fact is not material unless the plaintiff considers it of some importance when making the decision to enter the contract. To use our earlier example, you may not care one whit if the engine is a V-6. If you do not, the lack of a V-6 in the car you buy will not be a material fact. A court will enforce the bargain despite your protestations. The mileage of the car, the number of previous owners, the extent of the **warranties** given—all these facts will ordinarily be material to you. Misstatements about these facts may therefore lead to liability if you prove the other elements of fraud.

The element of fraud that is most unpleasant, as well as most difficult to prove, is the defendant's *knowledge of the falsity of his or her statement.* Sometimes called **scienter**, this means an evil intent. In other words, the defendant knew, or should have known, that he or she was misstating an important fact at the time of making the statement. Outright lies would, of course, meet this third requirement. Interestingly, the defendant may also be liable for reckless use of the truth or for a statement made without verifying its accuracy when verification is possible. To illustrate, assume that a prospective buyer says to the homeowner, "I guess the property line extends to that fence, doesn't it?" The homeowner nods yes, even though the line actually does not extend that far. What the homeowner may later call laziness may nevertheless be circumstantial evidence of the existence of *scienter* because that person presumably can ascertain fairly easily the boundaries of the property by checking the title. If the buyer purchases in reliance on this statement, a cause of action in fraud may be possible.

Closely related to the requirement of knowledge of the falsity of the statement is an *intent to deceive.* As noted earlier, deception is the hallmark of fraud. This element is difficult to disprove if the first three elements have been established, because courts can usually find no satisfactory reason for a defendant's misstatements except an intent to induce the plaintiff into accepting a sharp bargain.

4. The plaintiff must also prove that he or she *relied on the deception.* This

Warranties Representations that become part of the contract and that are made by a seller of goods at the time of the sale as to the character, quality, or nature of the goods.

Scienter Guilty knowledge; specifically, one party's prior knowledge of the cause of a subsequent injury to another person.

showing will not be particularly burdensome, assuming the plaintiff's reliance is reasonable. For example, if Tom inspects a lakefront cottage with a front porch that is on the verge of caving into the lake, a court will not allow him to cry "foul" (or "fraud") if the porch crumbles into the water one month after Tom buys the cottage. The same will be true even if the owner has said the cottage is structurally sound. Clearly, Tom should have been aware of such a *patent* (obvious) defect. Since his reliance is unreasonable, he will not win if he sues for fraud. Changing the facts to involve carpenter ant infestation rather than a sagging porch, if we assume the insect damage is a *latent* defect (hidden/unobservable by the human eye), Tom may win unless the court thinks Tom's refraining from ordering a pest inspection is in itself unreasonable.

The final element of a plaintiff's proof, *detriment*, or injury, normally is not difficult to show. In our last example, Tom can argue that his damages amount to the sum needed to rid the cottage of carpenter ants and to repair the substructure of the dwelling. Alternatively, Tom may ask for rescission of the contract. If granted by a court, he will turn the cottage over to the original owner, and the owner will make restitution of the price Tom has paid for the property.

The following case illustrates what happens when a plaintiff is unsuccessful in proving all the elements of fraud.

Scott v. *Bodor, Inc.*
571 N.E.2d 313 (Ind. App. 1991)

FACTS   Bodor, Inc. (Bodor) is a closely held Indiana corporation wholly owned by Robert and Stephen Kesler. In 1983, John Scott contacted Bodor to offer his services as a financial planner. Scott told Robert Kesler that he could offer Bodor a variety of plans that would provide income tax advantages to Bodor. Bodor eventually retained Scott; and, over several years, he set up various insurance and investment plans for Bodor. He also provided tax planning advice to the company and to Robert Kesler. Eventually, Scott became Bodor's general financial advisor, with unfettered access to Bodor's offices and financial information. Bodor's officers trusted Scott and never consulted third parties for advice concerning any financial arrangements that Scott had made on behalf of Bodor. In 1985, Bodor's officers met with Scott to discuss the company's tax situation for the year. Suggesting that a supplemental income plan would be extremely beneficial, Scott recommended that Bodor's officers meet with Thomas J. Brown, the owner of Thomas J. Brown & Associates, Inc. and a person Scott proclaimed to be an expert in "supplemental income" plans. In November, 1985, Brown flew to Indiana from Tampa, Florida, to pitch the plan to Robert and Stephen Kesler, accountant Raymond Plummer, controller John Bishopp, and Scott at Bodor's corporate offices. Scott introduced Brown to the Bodor officers as his associate, and Brown explained the "supplemental income" plan to the Bodor officers. According to Brown, the "supplemental income" plan had two features that were extremely important to Bodor: The corporation could take an immediate tax deduction for any funds it contributed to the program and could retrieve any funds it had paid in if it needed to do so. When Steve Kesler asked if the plan were a life insurance vehicle, Brown replied that it was primarily an investment vehicle with a small life insurance component. Robert Kesler then told Scott that he did not want the program if it were only a life insurance policy, but Scott assured him that it was an investment procedure. Neither Brown nor Scott mentioned that the program in actuality consisted exclusively of a whole life insurance policy, and the plan brochure prepared by Brown did not mention that the funding of the plan would occur exclusively through life insurance. Within a month after the meeting, Robert Kesler decided to implement the plan. He also decided, however, that Bodor should not make the $260,000 principal payment that Scott and Brown had suggested but should instead contribute only $130,000 in the first year. He notified Scott of this decision; and Scott began to prepare the documents, including the insurance applications for Bodor's principal officers, necessary to implement the plan. Each of the insured officers underwent a physical examination as part of the application process. Each of the insured officers also signed a policy application, and Robert signed each application in his capacity as president of Bodor, the policy owner. When presented to the Bodor officers to be signed, the policy applications specified neither the cost nor the amount of insurance to be procured; Scott filled in that information after he had obtained the signatures on the applications. Scott also prepared for Robert's signature a letter to the insurer to accompany the first principal payment. This letter did not specify that all the funds Bodor would supply actually represented insurance premiums. In late December, 1985, after the completion of the paperwork, Bodor issued its check for $130,000 to fund the first year of the plan and took a $130,000 deduction for the 1985 tax year. In March, 1986, three months after the implementation of the plan, Scott presented amended insurance applications to Robert for his signature. These applications, the first documents to state the face value of the insurance policy that any Bodor officer had seen, did not set out the nature or the cost of the insurance to be procured. Robert, as was his custom with regard to documents prepared for Bodor by Scott, signed the applications without reading them. Moreover, despite Robert Kesler's requests for such documentation, Scott never presented Bodor's officers with copies of the insurance policies or any other documents concerning the "supplemental income" plan. In the second year of the plan, 1986, Bodor earned greater profits and increased its contribution to the plan to $240,000 in order to earn a larger deduction. In order to make the second-year payment, Bodor borrowed $240,000 from the Ameritrust National Bank. Bodor deducted the $240,000 principal payment from its 1986 taxes. In April, 1987, Bodor's officers discovered that the $370,000 that Bodor had put into the plan was not tax deductible. When Robert Kesler met with Scott, Scott confirmed that the contributions to the plan were not deductible. Robert demanded the immediate withdrawal of Bodor's funds from the plan and asked for the return of these funds. Scott ultimately informed Robert that most of Bodor's funds in the plan would not be returned. In fact, Bodor managed to recover only $117,000 of its $370,000 investment before terminating all its business dealings with Brown and Scott. When Bodor sued Scott for fraud, Scott moved for a **summary judgment** on this issue.

Summary judgment A judgment rendered in favor of one party before trial and on the basis of the pleadings, owing to an absence of any genuine issue of facts.

ISSUE Had Scott and Brown's statements concerning the alleged "supplemental income" plan amounted to fraud?

HOLDING Yes. The lack of evidence establishing that Bodor knew that the funding of the plan would derive exclusively from the purchase of life insurance, coupled with Scott's (and Brown's) express assurances that it would not, constituted sufficient evidence of fraud to withstand a motion for summary judgment.

REASONING Actionable fraud consists of five elements: (1) the one accused of fraud (the defendant) must have made at least one representation of a past or existing fact, (2) which was false, (3) which the defendant knew to be false or made with reckless disregard as to its truth or falsity, (4) upon which the plaintiff reasonably relied, and (5) which harmed the plaintiff. Scott and Brown argued that Bodor had failed to produce evidence tending to show that they had made any misrepresentations of material fact. They denied that their statements concerning the tax deductibility of the funds involved misrepresentations of past or existing fact. According to Scott and Brown, even assuming they had made misstatements, the misstatements were, at most, misstatements of law. They further argued that, in Indiana, misstatements of law can never form the basis of fraud since everyone is presumed to know the law; and, consequently, the allegedly defrauded party cannot justifiably have relied on the misstatements. While this assertion correctly states the law in Indiana, exceptions to this general rule exist. Here, for example, Bodor introduced evidence tending to show that the defendants made misrepresentations of law and fact. The factual misrepresentations dealt with the form and structure of the proposed plan, and the legal misrepresentations concerned the tax deductible status of the plan. To the extent that the legal misrepresentations were premised on the factual misrepresentations, thereby impairing the plaintiffs' ability to discover the law applicable to the true facts, the legal misrepresentations constituted a sufficient basis for an action in fraud. These facts, if proven at trial, would invoke the exception to the general rule that legal misrepresentations cannot form the basis for fraud. Defendants next submitted that their misrepresentations concerning Bodor's ability to retrieve funds from the plan at will represented predictions of future events and, hence, were not actionable fraud under Indiana law. Granted, Indiana adheres to the common law rule that mere statements of opinion or promises of future action cannot constitute material misrepresentations capable of supporting an action in fraud. However, Scott and Brown's representations concerning Bodor's ability to retrieve funds from the plan consisted of representations concerning past or existing facts—the present features or terms of the proposed plan—and not mere statements of opinion or promises of future action. Robert Kesler stated that he had not read the policy application amendments when he signed on behalf of Bodor because he had a confidential relationship with Scott and was accustomed to signing documents prepared by Scott for Bodor without reviewing them. Scott and Brown maintained that Bodor had no right to rely on their misrepresentations. They first pointed out that, under Indiana law, a party has no right to rely on a statement if he or she failed to exercise ordinary care in guarding against fraud. However, there was evidence supporting the inference that Bodor had relied on Scott and Brown, self-proclaimed experts in the field, for tax planning advice. In addition, the evidence demonstrated that neither Bodor nor its agents possessed tax planning expertise. In sum, genuine issues of material fact as to the making of the misrepresentations and reliance upon them and as to whether the misrepresentations, if made, would support recovery for actual fraud existed in this case. Accordingly, the trial court's denial of defendants' motion for partial summary judgment merited affirmance.

Successful proof of a cause of action in fraud usually justifies *rescission,* or the setting aside of the contract. Hence, such contracts are voidable at the option of the injured party (Tom, in the example we used earlier). As mentioned, an alternative to rescission is recovery of damages sufficient to restore Tom to the *status quo,* or the position he would have been in had the facts of the transaction mirrored his conception of them at the time of his acceptance. The facts of each case normally will dictate which remedy a plaintiff will elect to pursue. Tom, as plaintiff, faces one final pitfall: He must act as quickly as possible, or he may waive his cause of action, as will be explained later.

Silence

No discussion of fraud is complete without a reference to *silence* and its effect on whether a court will grant relief. The common law steadfastly held that "mere silence is not fraud." This conclusion was predicated on the belief that fraud necessitates some sort of overt communication. Since by definition silence denotes the total absence of any statement, the rule arose that one could not be liable for fraud unless one had said or done something (remember our first element requiring a misstatement or misrepresentation of a fact). Many jurisdictions now reject this rule and hold, for instance, that the seller should voluntarily tell Tom of any drainage, ventilation, or other problems in order to encourage nonconcealment and honesty in business transactions. Similarly, if the buyer asks a question, the seller must answer truthfully and correct any wrong assumptions under which the buyer may be operating. A seller's silence in such instances today may not save the seller from possible legal liability. Still, the strict rule is that there is generally no duty to speak.

Even the common law, however, deemed some situations so fraught with the possibility of injury or detriment that it placed a duty to speak on the party possessing the information. We have already examined one of these situations, that of latent defects. There is also a duty to speak in situations in which the parties owe each other **fiduciary** duties, or duties that arise from a relationship of trust. For example, an investment advisor should inform her client of her part ownership in ABC Corporation if the client asks her whether ABC stock is a "good deal." Similarly, if you are applying for insurance coverage, you cannot be silent if you are asked questions about your medical history. To avoid fraud, you must, for example, disclose the existence of a heart condition. Finally, a statement made in preliminary negotiations (such as, "This car has never been in a wreck") that is no longer true at the time of the execution of the contract (the car was hit from behind in the meantime) must be disclosed in order to escape a possible lawsuit based on fraud.

These are a few examples of situations in which there is an absolute duty to speak. Failure to speak is tantamount to fraud. In other situations, there may or may not be a duty to speak, as the next case shows. As you read and analyze this case, go beyond the legal principles to consider the ethics of the seller's actions as well.

Fiduciary One who holds a special position of trust or confidence and who is thereby expected to act with the utmost good faith and loyalty.

Hauben v. Harmon
605 F.2d 920 (5th Cir. 1979)

FACTS

Condemnation The process by which privately held land is taken for a public use despite the owner's objection and lack of consent.

Hauben sued Harmon for fraud and misrepresentation and sought rescission of a land sale contract he had entered into with Harmon. The land Hauben had purchased lies in a district where land is subject to **condemnation** by the state of Florida for flood control purposes. Harmon had not disclosed the state's possible condemnation to Hauben prior to the sale. Some months after the execution of the contract, the state filed a condemnation suit, and Hauben sued for rescission of the contract based on fraud.

ISSUE

Did Harmon's nondisclosure to Hauben of the fact of possible condemnation constitute fraud?

HOLDING

No. Harmon's failure to disclose this fact was not tantamount to fraud.

REASONING

Before signing the contract, Hauben had inspected the property on two occasions, and Harmon's broker had also encouraged Hauben to call the local zoning board if he had any questions about the property. Even though Harmon had been in contact with the supervisors of the flood control project regarding the possible condemnation of this land, whether the piece of land sold to Hauben would be condemned remained purely speculative. Although nondisclosure of a material fact may justify a finding of fraud, a failure to disclose mere possibilities could not amount to a failure to disclose material facts. Moreover, here the buyer and seller apparently had equivalent access to information concerning the property; so it was not fraud that the seller knew facts unknown to the buyer yet refrained from telling the buyer of those facts.

MISREPRESENTATION

We have spoken at length about fraud. We can handle the subject of *misrepresentation* much more summarily. Basically, everything we have previously noted about fraud is true of a cause of action involving misrepresentation, with one notable exception: Misrepresentation lacks the elements of *scienter* and intent to deceive. Nevertheless, misrepresentation (often called *innocent misrepresentation* to differentiate it from fraud) can lead to the imposition of legal remedies. The property owner's statement about the property boundaries may amount to innocent misrepresentation if *scienter* cannot be proved. Misrepresentation, or *the innocent misstatement of a material fact that is relied on with resultant injury,* makes the contract voidable at the option of the injured party. Rescission thus remains a possible (and in many jurisdictions the exclusive) remedy. Again, the plaintiff must act in a timely manner so as not to waive the cause of action.

Practically speaking, most plaintiffs allege both fraud and misrepresentation in the same suit. Fraud is harder to prove but is a more desirable theory from the plaintiff's point of view because successful proof of fraud brings with it the possibility of recovery of damages under the tort of deceit. The elements of deceit are identical to those of fraud. Upon a showing of deceit, a court may award *punitive* damages (damages beyond the actual losses suffered) in addition to the actual damages normally recoverable for fraud. But even if the plaintiff fails to prove fraud (and its twin, deceit), recovery on grounds of misrepresentation is possible. At the very least, a showing of fraud or misrepresentation will be grounds for rescission.

In the next case, the judge wrestled with the doctrinal differences between fraud and misrepresentation.

Alabi v. *DHL Airways, Inc.*
583 A.2d 1358 (Del. Super. 1990)

FACTS   DHL Airways, Inc. (DHL) operates a worldwide air express service for small packages and envelopes. On 25 April 1986, Mabayomije Alabi called DHL's Philadelphia office requesting an envelope pickup for delivery to his cousin in London, England. Alabi claimed, and DHL did not deny, that he then inquired whether DHL could insure the envelope for $15,000. The DHL representative indicated that the maximum insurance Alabi could purchase was $10,000. Alabi had used DHL's services numerous times before April, 1986, and had been supplied with a stack of envelopes and airway bills by a representative of DHL. Prior to the arrival of the courier, Alabi filled out the airway bill and sealed the contents of the envelope. On the arrival of the courier, Alabi inquired once more about the possibility of insuring the envelope for $15,000; the courier again mentioned the limit of $10,000. Alabi paid the courier $76 for the contract of carriage and for the purchase of $10,000 worth of insurance. The airway bill utilized by DHL was a six-by-eight-inch, six-copy, NCR paper containing terms on both sides. On the front of the bill were spaces for a description of the contents, requests for insurance, and the insured amount, if the shipper elected to insure the shipment. A statement disclaiming liability for all damages and warranties and limiting liability to $100 appeared below the insurance information blocks. In addition, there was a place for the shipper's signature; and in that block appeared the declaration, "I WARRANT THAT ALL DETAILS GIVEN HEREIN ARE TRUE AND CORRECT." The reverse side of the airway bill contained eleven paragraphs that constituted DHL's terms and conditions applicable to the shipments accepted by DHL referenced on the front of the bill. Paragraph 11 listed the materials not deemed acceptable for shipment by DHL. Listed first among those was "currency." Paragraph 2, entitled "SHIPPER'S OBLIGATIONS AND ACKNOWLEDGEMENTS [sic]" provided:

> The Shipper warrants that each article in the shipment is properly described on this AIRBILL and has not been declared by DHL to be unacceptable for transport, and that the shipment is properly marked and addressed and packed to ensure safe transportation with ordinary care in handling. The Shipper hereby acknowledges that DHL may abandon and/or release any item consigned by the Shipper to DHL, which DHL has declared to be unacceptable or which the Shipper has undervalued for Customs' purposes or misdescribed hereon, whether intentionally or otherwise, without incurring any liability whatsoever to the Shipper and the Shipper will save and defend, **indemnify** and hold DHL harmless for all claims, fines and expenses arising therefrom.

Indemnify To reimburse a party for a loss suffered by that party for the benefit of another.

On the airway bill in a block marked "description of contents," Alabi wrote "documents regarding school bills." The courier examined the airway bill, did not question Alabi about the contents, and accepted the envelope for delivery. In actuality, according to Alabi, the envelope contained $15,000 in cash. Alabi's envelope arrived in London, but DHL was unable to deliver the envelope the day it arrived. DHL stored the envelope overnight at its London facility; and the next day, when DHL prepared to attempt delivery again, it discovered that the envelope was missing. DHL notified Alabi of the loss and conducted a search for the envelope. The search, which included the help of the police, was unsuccessful, and the envelope's whereabouts remained unknown. Alabi sued DHL for compensatory damages for DHL's failure to deliver an express document envelope, which allegedly contained $15,000 in cash. DHL moved for summary judgment, arguing that Alabi's misrepresentation concerning the contents of the envelope rendered both the contract of carriage and the contract of insurance unenforceable.

ISSUE Did Alabi's statement regarding the contents of the envelope amount to either innocent misrepresentation or fraud?

HOLDING Because it was not clear whether Alabi's statement constituted either innocent misrepresentation or fraud, the granting of DHL's motion for summary judgment would be improper. Rather, a full airing of the facts in the context of a trial would be appropriate.

REASONING DHL had sought summary judgment, claiming that Alabi's contracts with it were voidable owing to his alleged misrepresentation of the contents of the envelope. Under settled law, a contract may be voidable on the basis of misrepresentation, be it a fraudulent or an innocent misrepresentation. As such, a defendant can assert misrepresentation as an affirmative defense to an action on the contract. In the instant case, two contracts, one for carriage and one for insurance, remained in dispute. However, both contracts arose from essentially the same transaction and the alleged misrepresentation was the same as to both. The *Restatement (Second) of Contracts* provides probably the clearest discussion of the elements that a defendant would need to show in order to prevail when asserting misrepresentation as a defense. Simply put, for a contract to be voidable, a party must show all four of the following elements: 1) that there was a misrepresentation, 2) that the misrepresentation was either fraudulent or material, 3) that the misrepresentation induced the recipient to enter into the contract, and 4) that the recipient's reliance on the misrepresentation was reasonable. The first issue centered on whether the labeling of the envelope, allegedly containing $15,000 in cash, as "documents regarding school bills" constituted a misrepresentation. A misrepresentation is "an assertion that is not in accordance with the facts." Although Alabi asserted that "documents" suffices as a general description of currency, this was an untenable position. Such terms as negotiable instruments and certificates might suffice as a description of cash only because they would indicate to the reader that the contents of the envelope have an inherent value. However, the term "documents regarding school bills" would not indicate that the contents are inherently valuable to third-party **interlopers** or others in DHL's position. Because Alabi's description did not

Interlopers Those who intrude or interfere wrongfully.

accord with the now-alleged fact that there was cash in the envelope, it constituted a misrepresentation of the contents. The second element—whether the misrepresentation was fraudulent or material—would merit scrutiny. If the misrepresentation were nonfraudulent or innocent, it must be material for the contract to be voidable. On the other hand, if the misrepresentation were fraudulent, it need not be material for the contract to be voidable. Alabi claimed that the description was as accurate as he could make it without inviting theft. To some extent Alabi's assertion purposely misled DHL about the contents of the shipment. However, Alabi also claimed that he was unaware that DHL would reject shipments of cash. Thus, it was not clear at this stage of the proceedings whether the misrepresentation was fraudulent as a matter of law. Alternatively, under the second element, if the misrepresentation is not fraudulent, one must still decide if it is nevertheless material. According to the *Restatement,* a misrepresentation is material if it would be likely to induce a reasonable person to manifest assent, or if the maker knows that it would be likely to induce the recipient to do so. In the instant case, Alabi had in his possession airbills (or bills of lading). Furthermore, Alabi had frequently utilized DHL's services for two years prior to the shipment at issue in this case. Nothing contained in the record indicated that DHL's airway bill form had changed in those two years. Based on this long-time use of DHL's services, Alabi could not complain now that he was unaware of the terms and conditions contained on the airway bill. Therefore, Alabi's signing of the airway bill bound him to those terms and conditions. Given that Alabi must be charged with the knowledge that DHL would not accept cash for delivery, the misrepresentation became material. Since Alabi had reason to know DHL would not accept cash and since he had described the shipment as otherwise, he had induced DHL to enter into a contract to which it would not otherwise assent. The third element—whether the misrepresentation induced DHL to enter into the contract—would require a misrepresentation that substantially contributed to DHL's decision to manifest its assent. The party's reliance on the misrepresentation, however, need not be the sole or even the predominant factor in influencing his conduct. In the instant case, nothing in the record indicated that DHL had failed to attach importance to the misrepresentation. The fourth element, whether DHL's reliance on the misrepresentation was reasonable, would examine whether the recipient's reliance was justified. Prior to shipping and giving the envelope to DHL, Alabi twice inquired about the availability of $15,000 worth of insurance. This would indicate that the document's value belied the description on the airway bill. DHL argued that following this line of reasoning would impose on DHL a duty to inspect every envelope. On the other hand, DHL did reserve the right to inspect the envelopes it accepted for delivery. DHL would not reserve such a right if it did not believe that at some point or on some occasion it would want to check the contents because it had reason to believe that a description was inaccurate. Although DHL apparently realizes that it is not always reasonable to rely on the description supplied by a shipper, where that point or occasion falls would remain a question of fact that the trier of fact must determine. Further, because the misrepresentation at issue underlay both the contract of carriage and the contract of insurance, the analysis would be the same as to both. Therefore, a material issue of fact existed as to the reasonableness of DHL's reliance on the description supplied by Alabi. SInce DHL had not established all four elements of its affirmative defense as a matter of law, granting summary judgment would be improper in this case.

Figure 13.1 describes the elements of misrepresentation and fraud and shows the analysis the court may follow in determining the presence of either as a defense to a contract. Use this figure to supplement your understanding of these two topics.

MISTAKE

Human nature is such that people often try to unravel transactions because they have made an error about some facet of the deal. Imagine the havoc that

FIGURE 13.1   The Elements of Fraud and Misrepresentation

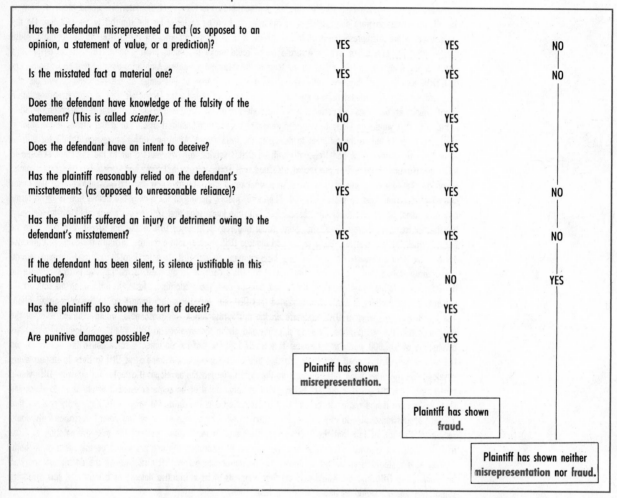

Has the defendant misrepresented a fact (as opposed to an opinion, a statement of value, or a prediction)?	YES	YES	NO
Is the misstated fact a material one?	YES	YES	NO
Does the defendant have knowledge of the falsity of the statement? (This is called *scienter*.)	NO	YES	
Does the defendant have an intent to deceive?	NO	YES	
Has the plaintiff reasonably relied on the defendant's misstatements (as opposed to unreasonable reliance)?	YES	YES	NO
Has the plaintiff suffered an injury or detriment owing to the defendant's misstatement?	YES	YES	NO
If the defendant has been silent, is silence justifiable in this situation?		NO	YES
Has the plaintiff also shown the tort of deceit?		YES	
Are punitive damages possible?		YES	

Plaintiff has shown misrepresentation.

Plaintiff has shown fraud.

Plaintiff has shown neither misrepresentation nor fraud.

would arise if courts readily accepted these hindsight arguments. The result would be a decrease in contracts, since people would be wary of dealing with each other. As you no doubt realize, such unpredictability would unduly hamper commercial pacts. On the other hand, we have repeatedly stressed the importance of mutual assent in contract law. Thus, the law, on policy grounds, wishes to set the contract aside if the error is so great that it has tainted the parties' consent to the agreement.

The legal doctrine of *mistake* tries to balance these competing interests. Mistake occurs when *the parties are wrong about the existence or absence of a past or present fact that is material to their transaction.* Note that the parties must be wrong about material *facts.* Thus, legal mistake is not synonymous with ignorance, inability, or inaccurate judgments relating to value or quality. Courts will rescind contracts on the ground of mistake *only* if the error is so fundamental that it cannot be said that the parties' states of mind were in agreement about the essential facts of the transaction. Mistakes as to law, in contrast, will oftentimes not form grounds for rescission of the contract. There are two kinds of mistake: unilateral and bilateral (or mutual) mistake.

Unilateral Mistake

As the term implies, in a *unilateral mistake, only one party is mistaken about a material fact*. The general rule, with some exceptions, is that the courts will not rescind such contracts. The parties are held to their bargains as forged.

Unilateral mistakes often occur because of misplaced expectations of value. Let us suppose that Jacques goes to an antique store to look for a Duncan Phyfe table. He finds a table that he believes to be a Duncan Phyfe, and without mentioning his belief to the store owner, pays a hefty price for it. Later that evening, a friend informs him the table is not a Duncan Phyfe. If Jacques tries to avoid the contract, he will not be successful because only he was mistaken about a material fact—that is, that the table was a Duncan Phyfe. He was also mistaken as to value. In such unilateral mistake situations, courts take a "hands off" approach and leave the parties with the bargains they have made. Rescission of the contract is not granted.

The result here could be different if the store owner knew (or should have known) of Jacques's error or in some other fashion acted fraudulently or unconscionably. But the facts do not support such a conclusion; if they did, courts might allow rescission of the contract, despite the unilateral mistake.

Likewise, courts will suspend the general rule of refusing to grant relief for unilateral mistakes in situations in which the mistake is a result of business computations. As the next decision illustrates, certain requirements must be met; but, in general, courts will grant rescission in such circumstances if the rescission will not injure any third parties. Note that rescission was the remedy given in the following case even though only Dick was in error (that is, the mistake was unilateral).

Dick Corporation v. Associated Electric Cooperative, Inc.
475 F.Supp. 15 (W.D. Mo. 1979)

FACTS Dick Corporation (Dick) was a construction firm. In submitting a bid for the construction of a power plant, Dick made a mistake of $1,000,000. Dick bid $13,600,000 when it meant to bid $14,600,000. This occurred because the number $100,000 was placed on the summary sheet instead of the correct figure of $1,100,000. Dick was the lowest bidder on the project; but because of the discrepancy between its bid and the next lowest bid ($15,674,000), the engineering firm to which Dick had sent the bid had asked Dick to recheck its figures. The next morning, Dick called to say it had discovered its error. Dick wanted to perform the contract at the corrected price; and the Cooperative wanted it to do so, since even at the corrected price Dick was the lowest bidder.

ISSUE

Did Dick's unilateral mistake merit a court's giving the remedy of **reformation?**

HOLDING

Yes. The court reformed the contract to the correct sum of $14,600,000.

REASONING

When a bidder for a public contract makes a unilateral mistake in preparing the bid owing to incorrect business computations, and the mistake is otherwise remediable, the bidder may obtain equitable relief by rescission or cancellation of the contract. Such relief will not be granted unless the error were made in good faith, prompt notice of the error were given, and the offeree had not altered its position because of the bid so as to suffer a hardship if relief were given. Put another way, the prerequisites for obtaining appropriate equitable relief are 1) the mistake must be of such consequence that enforcement would be unconscionable; 2) the mistake must relate to the substance of the matter under consideration; 3) the mistake must have occurred in good faith and regardless of the exercise of ordinary care; 4) it must be possible to return the other party to the status quo; and 5) no other circumstances exist that would make granting relief inequitable. Since both parties wanted the contract to continue, the court therefore ordered reformation and corrected the bid to $14,600,000.

Reformation Equitable remedy whereby a court corrects a written instrument in order to remove a mistake and to make the agreement conform to the terms to which the parties originally had agreed.

Bilateral Mistake

If both parties are in error about the essence of the agreement, bilateral (or mutual) *mistake* exists. Courts will rescind such agreements on the rationale that, owing to a mistake about the existence, identity, or nature of the subject matter of the contract, a valid agreement has not occurred. If a mutual mistake of fact is present, either party may disaffirm this voidable contract unless rescission will cause injuries to innocent third parties. This is so because the parties' minds have not met on the salient facts of the transaction. For example, assume an American company contracts with a foreign company (headquartered in New York) for hand-loomed rugs. The firms contract in April, but, unknown to both parties, a warehouse fire had destroyed the rugs in March. The destruction of the subject matter makes the contract voidable on the grounds of bilateral mistake: The parties have made an error regarding a significant fact—that is, that the rugs existed at the time of contract formation. **Ambiguities** are another cause of mutual mistake. If the American buyer believes that the term *rugs* means room-sized carpets, but, because of language difficulties, the foreign seller envisions rugs as identical in size to wall hangings, this ambiguity may constitute mutual mistake. If so, rescission will be justifiable. The following case involves a much simpler case of bilateral (or mutual) mistake.

Ambiguities Uncertainties regarding the meanings of expressions used in contractual agreements.

Harding v. *Willie*
458 N.W.2d 612 (Iowa App. 1990)

FACTS

Dale Harding is the owner of a home in Eagle Grove. Prior to 10 January 1987, Harding listed the real estate for sale. On 3 January 1987, B. V. Willie and his wife inspected the home for possible purchase or rental. Willie, an attorney, and Harding, a doctor, had been friends for many years. When Willie noticed a crack in the ceiling and inquired about it, Harding informed Willie that a water leakage problem had existed in that area but had been fixed in 1985 and had not leaked since. On 12 January 1987, Willie made an offer on the house; Harding accepted it the next day. Willie paid earnest money in the amount of $5,000, with the contract balance of $85,000 due on 1 March 1987. On 1 March 1987, when Willie went to the residence to make a final inspection before the closing on 2 March 1987, Willie observed water leaking through a crack in the ceiling and in the garage. On 2 March, the scheduled closing date, Willie informed the real estate agent that he was rescinding the contract because of the leaks. Although Harding subsequently rented the property to another party, in August, 1987, Harding filed a petition at law seeking specific performance of the contract or money damages for breach of contract. Willie argued that the contract was void owing either to a mutual mistake of fact or to fraud. Following trial, the district court entered judgment against Willie for $29,155.79, plus interest and court costs.

ISSUE   Was the contract void owing to a mutual mistake of fact or to fraud?

HOLDING   Yes. Owing to Harding and Willie's mutual mistake of a material fact as to whether the roof leaked, there was no meeting of the parties' minds; hence, no contract ever existed between the parties.

REASONING   Willie contended the contract is void owing to a mutual mistake of fact or to fraud on the part of Harding. A mistake of fact is one of the fundamental grounds of equitable relief, and an agreement based on a mutual mistake between two parties as to their relative and respective rights entitles either party to have the agreement set aside. When a material mutual mistake made by the parties in respect to the subject matter of a contract exists, in contemplation of law there is no contract, because the minds of the parties do not meet. Yet under the doctrine of mutual mistake, the mistake must be both "mutual" and "material." Here, unquestionably either a mutual mistake occurred or Harding committed fraud. On his examination of the home, Willie noticed the crack in the ceiling and inquired about it. Harding, at the very least, stated that while there had been a leak in the past, there was "absolutely no problem" with the roof. Regardless of how he said it, Harding either knew the roof still leaked, which would constitute fraud, or thought the roof was repaired and did not leak, which would lead to a mutual mistake of fact. No evidence of fraud on Harding's part was apparent here: The roof had been fixed, the parties were friends, and Harding had the roof fixed again as quickly as possible. However, both parties acted under the assumption that the roof would not leak. Harding was mistaken because he had had the roof repaired and expected those repairs to last. Willie was mistaken because of the representations made by the seller, Harding. Willie also reasonably relied on Harding's representations. They were friends; and although there was no evidence that a fiduciary relationship existed (as claimed by Willie), enough of a relationship existed to make trusting the other's statements a reasonable action. Willie—who might, as an attorney, consequently be aware that an investigation is ordinarily a good idea—could still rely on the statements of a friend, at least concerning personal business transactions. As a matter of fact, once Willie saw the crack, he did investigate: He asked the seller the condition of the crack. Willie might have undertaken a further investigation, but it would have led to the contractor who fixed the roof, who probably would have said, "The roof is still good; I fixed it." Because Willie could not have obtained any further knowledge than the seller possessed, Willie had not failed to exercise ordinary care and prudence in this business transaction. Finally, Harding claimed that the mutual mistake was not material, owing to the relatively low cost of repairing the leak. But the contract in this instance involved the purchase of a home. Parties often consider a home a necessity because shelter is a necessity, and parties enter into contracts based on the assumption that the home will provide shelter. Given this, a leak in the roof certainly would constitute a material consideration. Therefore, a mutual mistake of a material fact existed; and, as a result, the minds of the parties had not met. Accordingly, no contract was ever made. Hence, the trial court should have granted judgment in favor of Willie for the amount of the earnest money paid, plus interest.

Reformation

If a court can easily remedy the mistake, a court may *reform* the contract, or *rewrite it to reflect the parties' actual intentions* (as the *Dick Corporation* court did). In our last example, involving the hand-loomed rugs, assuming these rugs were obtainable, once the ambiguity comes to light, reformation would permit a court to make the subject matter of the contract room-sized rugs. After resort to a court's equitable powers of reformation, the contract would be fully enforceable. Be aware, though, that large backlogs of court cases form a substantial impediment to the availability of reformation as a practical remedy. As we have discussed throughout this unit on contracts, take pains to ascertain exactly what your agreement means beforehand. You will thereby avoid a great many frustrations (and expenses).

**YOU BE
THE
JUDGE**

Thirteen-year-old Bryan Wrzesinski of Addison, Illinois, who has approximately 40,000 baseball cards in his collection, bought a 1968 Nolan Ryan/Jerry Koosman rookie baseball card for $12.00 (plus tax). On the day of the sale, the Ball-Mart part-time clerk who sold him the card (which was marked $1200) was particularly frazzled and harried. As a consequence, the clerk—who had little knowledge of cards—thought there was a decimal point in the price and hence sold the card for $12.00. However, Bryan, according to most accounts, knew exactly what a "bargain" he was getting. Joe Irmen, the owner of Ball-Mart, subsequently sued Bryan for either the recovery of the card or for damages, even though a sign in the shop said, "All sales final." On 5 March, during the trial in the Du Page County small claims court, Bryan testified that on the previous night he had traded the disputed card for a 1967 Tom Seaver and a 1965 Joe Namath rookie card worth an estimated $2200, even though Judge Ann Jorgensen had instructed Bryan to retain the card, pending the trial. On hearing this bombshell, Judge Jorgensen stopped the proceedings and ordered Bryan's lawyer to produce the card. Back in court two days later, the lawyer produced the card. The unidentified new owner had agreed to relinquish it temporarily, provided that the court would place it in a protective holder with the court's exhibit number affixed thereon (thus assuring that the card would be even more valuable owing to the notoriety of the case).

If you were in Judge Jorgensen's place, how would you characterize the legal issues involved here? How would you decide the case? Do you have any sentiments concerning Bryan, his lawyer, and the new owner's ethics?

Sources: "Scorecard," Steve Wulf, appearing in *Sports Illustrated,* March 18, 1991, pages 9 and 10.
"Ridiculous Values Are Missing Point of Baseball Cards," Bill Moor, appearing in *South Bend Tribune,* March 12, 1991, page C-10.

DURESS

There can be no genuine assent to the terms of an agreement in which one person has assented while under duress. The person who has so assented can ask for rescission on the contract on the ground of duress.

Asserting the defense of *duress* means alleging that *one has been forced into the contract against one's will.* To constitute duress, the coercion must be so extreme that the victim has lost all ability to assent freely and voluntarily to the transaction. Given this definition, courts look for evidence of physical threats or threats that, if carried out, would cause intense mental anguish. Forcing a person to sign a contract at gunpoint would, of course, represent duress. To most courts, so would a spouse's threat to tell the parties' children that the other spouse has committed adultery. If, as a result of this intimidation, the spouse signs over a disproportionate share of the marital property, courts could rescind this agreement on the basis of duress. Similarly, courts generally view threats to institute criminal actions (even if there is a basis for these) in order to extract a contractual agreement as duress. Courts, however, ordinarily do not see threats of civil suits as equaling duress. Note how the court construed the threat involved in the case that follows.

Germantown Manufacturing Co. v. Rawlinson
491 A.2d 138 (Pa. Super. 1985)

FACTS

Confession of judgment notes Promissory notes in which the defendant has given the plaintiff written permission to enter a judgment in favor of the plaintiff against the defendant in the event of a lawsuit.

Robert Rawlinson was the assistant controller at the Germantown Manufacturing Company. As such, he had embezzled over $327,000 from the company. On the discovery of this misappropriation of funds, a representative of the company's insurer came to the Rawlinsons' house to have Mr. and Mrs. Rawlinson sign two **confession of judgment notes** to cover the embezzled funds. The first note was for $160,000—the amount Mr. Rawlinson admitted having taken. The second was for all amounts in excess of $160,000 that Rawlinson subsequently was determined to have embezzled. The insurance company representative allegedly indicated to Mrs. Rawlinson that since the Rawlinsons had $160,000 readily available, the judgment was, in effect, already satisfied. He also stated that there would be no criminal prosecution of Mr. Rawlinson if the Rawlinsons cooperated. Mrs. Rawlinson understood this to mean that if she signed the confession of judgment notes, her husband would not go to jail. During this meeting, she was crying and was visibly upset about what her husband had done. She also had recently suffered a miscarriage. The first note ultimately was satisfied, but the total amount owed on the second note turned out to be over $212,000. Mrs. Rawlinson therefore asked the court to open judgment on the second note so that she could assert the defenses of fraud, misrepresentation, and duress to avoid her obligation on the second note.

ISSUE

Was Mrs. Rawlinson's signature on the second note procured by fraud, misrepresentation, and/or duress so as to permit the court to open judgment on that note?

HOLDING

Yes. Mrs. Rawlinson's signature had been obtained by fraudulent misrepresentations, and she had agreed to be liable on the note while under duress.

REASONING   The representative of the insurance company had made a fraudulent misrepresentation while asking her to sign *both* notes when he stated that the judgment was, in effect, satisfied. The misrepresentations were also material because they had induced her to sign the second note. Had she known the true terms of the second note, she would not have signed it. Hence, Mrs. Rawlinson had presented sufficient evidence of duress to constitute a meritorious defense and thus render the contract voidable. Moreover, the representative's statements included a threat to instigate a criminal prosecution against Mrs. Rawlinson's spouse. Thus, the "choice" available to Mrs. Rawlinson appeared to involve impermissible coercion. Her only alternative was to refuse to sign the note and thus place an unbearable stress on her marriage. This lack of meaningful choice represented the epitome of duress and unconscionability as well. Given the presence of fraud, misrepresentation, duress, and unconscionability, Mrs. Rawlinson should be allowed to open judgment on the note and to avoid its application to her.

The discussion to this point has focused on personal duress. Recently, the doctrine of economic duress has become prevalent. *Economic duress* occurs when *one party is forced to agree to a further, wrongful, and coercive demand (usually a price increase) as a consequence of receiving the commodities or services to which he or she is entitled under the original contract.* In most instances, the injured party cannot obtain the goods or services elsewhere. We can use our earlier example of the hand-loomed rugs to illustrate this concept. Assume that the New York–based rug company has the only hand-loomed rugs around, and the American buyer has agreed to pay $2500 per rug. Economic duress exists if the seller tells the American buyer (who has orders for the rugs waiting to be filled) that he can have the rugs only if he is willing to pay $4000 apiece for them. The buyer needs the rugs in order to fill his contracts and is faced with a lack of alternative sources for the goods (owing to the unique nature of the rugs). Basing its decision on the concept of economic duress, a court may force the seller to sell the rugs at the original price of $2500 or allow the American buyer to recover any difference in price after the fact.

Whether a court will grant a recovery to a plaintiff who alleges economic duress (or business compulsion) depends heavily on the particular facts of a given situation. For a good example of this proposition, read the next case.

Brock v. Entre Computer Centers
933 F.2d 1253 (4th Cir. 1991)

FACTS   Entre Computer Centers, Inc. (Entre), a Delaware corporation with its headquarters and principal place of business in McLean, Virginia, is a franchisor of approximately 150 retail computer stores located across the United States. Jerry Brock became interested in starting an Entre franchise after reading an ad in the *Wall Street Journal*. Brock subsequently traveled to Vienna, Virginia, for a franchise "visitation day" during which Entre made prepared presentations regarding its formula for success. Brock later alleged that Entre made untrue representations at that time. In particular, Brock maintained that Entre had made false promises regarding the availability of IBM products to Entre franchisees. On 20 March 1984, Brock entered into a franchise agreement with Entre for the establishment of an Entre Computer Center store in Beaumont, Texas, and ten days later entered into a second franchise agreement for a store in Baton Rouge, Louisiana. These franchise agreements, among other things, stated that Entre would not consent to a transfer of ownership by the franchisee to a third party unless the franchisee signed a general release of all claims against Entre. After signing the franchise agreements, Brock began operation of the stores, which, unfortunately, were unsuccessful from the very beginning. In early 1986, Brock decided to sell the Beaumont and Baton Rouge centers. Entre would not consent to Brock's transfers of the centers to third parties unless Brock first signed the releases called for in the franchise agreements. Brock thereupon entered into two general releases with Entre. Each release was virtually identical to the first release that Brock had signed when he became an Entre franchisee. After the execution of these releases, Brock sold the Beaumont and Baton Rouge stores to third parties. Brock later sued Entre for fraud, asserting in addition that Entre's procurement of the releases through economic duress had made the releases legally invalid.

ISSUE Were the releases invalid owing to economic duress?

HOLDING No. Entre's promise to enforce its rights under the original agreement unless Brock executed the requested releases did not constitute a wrongful threat that had destroyed his freedom to act. Hence, Entre's conduct had not amounted to economic duress.

REASONING Brock asserted that he had entered into the releases owing to economic duress; and, as a result, the releases were invalid. There are three elements to a claim of economic duress: 1) wrongful acts or threats, 2) financial distress caused by the wrongful acts or threats, and 3) the absence of any reasonable alternative to the terms presented by the wrongdoer. Furthermore, to prove economic duress, a plaintiff such as Brock must establish that Entre had made a wrongful threat that was of such character as to destroy the free agency of the party to whom the threat was directed (here, Brock). The evidence in this case failed to show these elements. Even assuming that Brock's portrayal of the dire financial condition of the centers was correct, Brock, the franchisee, had expressly agreed in the franchise agreements, at a time when he was under no financial distress whatsoever, that he would not transfer the businesses without Entre's consent, and that Entre had the right to condition its consent on the execution of a general release in Entre's favor. Thus, Entre had made no wrongful threat that destroyed Brock's free agency; rather, Entre had only required the franchisee to do what he already had agreed to do. The only possible threat involved in this case was that Entre had promised to enforce its rights under the original agreement by withholding its consent to the transfer of the franchises unless Brock executed the requested releases. At the time he had entered into the original agreement, Brock was experiencing no economic difficulty. He was under no obligation to enter into that agreement and was free to negotiate if he did not want to be bound by the release provision. However, Brock did enter into that agreement at a time when he was perfectly free to walk away from the deal. As a result, the releases Entre had provided Brock pursuant to the original agreement had not been procured through economic duress. Furthermore, Brock's additional assertion that the releases were based on a mutual mistake and were not valid contracts because he had believed that he had no choice but to sign the releases was equally meritless. First of all, Brock had not shown that Entre also held this "mistaken" view. Thus, the essential element of mutual mistake—a requirement that both parties hold the mistaken view—was missing here. Moreover, Brock could not even establish his own "mistaken" view. Objective evidence in the form of the franchise agreements showed that Brock knew that he had to sign a release in order to sell his franchise. He had expressly agreed to this provision when he initially signed the franchise agreements. Thus, Brock had not shown that he held a mistaken belief shared by Entre at the time of the signing of the original agreement.

As has been true of most reality-of-consent situations discussed in this chapter, contracts made under duress are ordinarily voidable. Hence, rescission may be effected at the option of the injured party *unless* the injured party ratifies the contract by acquiescing in the coercive conduct for an unreasonably long time. However, sometimes in such cases the conduct exemplifying duress is so extreme that a court will find the contract void. Threats directed at third parties (such as a relative) may give rise to duress of this sort if one party enters into the contract to protect the innocent third party from these threats by the wrongdoer.

UNDUE INFLUENCE

Closely related to duress is the concept of undue influence. Indeed, many courts view it as a subcategory of duress. Like duress, its existence depends heavily on the facts.

Undue influence is the *use of a relationship of trust and confidence to extract contractual advantages.* Newspapers are full of examples of such situations. Recall the allegations of undue influence involving nurses who have been named beneficiaries of their patients' sizable estates or lawyers who have enormously benefited from their clients' **testamentary** dispositions. Since the favored nurse or lawyer has the ability to dominate or overreach the other party, the law often allows the rescission of such contracts. Because of the domination by another, the contracting party has actually not exerted his or her free will in entering into the contract but instead has given effect to the will or wishes of the other party.

Testamentary Pertaining to a will.

The law will presume undue influence in certain circumstances, notably in fiduciary relationships. In the example of the lawyer that we just cited, the mere existence of the relationship will require the lawyer to prove that the client made the disposition free from the lawyer's coercion. The law will demand that the lawyer, as a fiduciary, act with utmost good faith in dealing with persons who will be predisposed to follow whatever the lawyer advises. Like lawyers, parents may enjoy fiduciary relationships with their children, doctors with their patients, accountants with their clients, and so on. It is sometimes difficult for courts to determine when the persuasiveness of the fiduciary has become so intense that the other party has lost all vestiges of free will. But when they are convinced that this has occurred, they permit rescission of the challenged contract.

UNCONSCIONABILITY

You may have noted some similarities between the concept of unconscionability, which we discussed in Chapter 10, and the ideas we have been considering in this chapter. Especially in the context of consumer law, some courts have set contracts aside when they have found the bargaining power of the parties so unequal as to be commercially shocking or unreasonably oppressive.

In Chapter 12, we learned that some courts call such agreements contracts of adhesion, meaning that one party to the contract is able to impose its will on the other party through overreaching. The Uniform Commercial Code validates this approach in Section 2-302, but not all states have adopted this section of the UCC. Nevertheless, unconscionability may signal a lack of meaningful assent to a contract and may justify a court's subsequent intervention in behalf of the injured party.

SUMMARY

To have a valid contract, the assent of the parties must be genuine. The existence of fraud, misrepresentation, mistake, duress, undue influence, or unconscionability precludes the reality of consent that serves as the foundation of modern contract law. Fraud is a deliberate misrepresentation of a material fact with the intent to induce another person to enter a contract that will be injurious to that person. Predictions, statements of value, opinions, and misstatements of law do not constitute fraud. Probably the most difficult element to prove is the defendant's knowledge of the falsity of the statement, or *scienter*. The plaintiff's reliance on the deception must be reasonable, or the plaintiff will be precluded from recovering. Successful proof of fraud makes the contract voidable and justifies rescission. Although the common law held that mere silence is not fraud, there were exceptions to this doctrine even in early common law times. Today, the judicial trend is to force disclosure of material facts if their concealment may injure the other party. Innocent misrepresentation may also result in legal liability.

Mistake occurs when the parties are wrong about the existence or absence of a past or present fact that is material to their transactions. There are two types of mistake: unilateral (one person is in error) and bilateral/mutual (both parties are in error). Courts will generally not rescind unilateral mistakes unless the other party knows, or should have known, of the mistaken party's error or uses it to take unconscionable advantage of the injured party. In these cases, as in situations involving errors in business computations, courts will allow rescission. If a mutual or bilateral mistake of fact is present, either party can disaffirm the contract. Ambiguity, for example, may lead to rescission. The equitable remedy of reformation allows a court to rewrite a contract to reflect the parties' actual intentions, but courts will not always permit reformation.

Duress exists when a person's will has been overridden as a result of another person's threats. Duress may be either personal or economic, the latter occurring when a seller wrongfully or coercively withholds scarce commodities or services in order to extract a higher contract price. Undue influence is the use of a relationship of trust and confidence to gain contractual advantages. In certain relationships, the law will presume undue influence. The existence of unconscionability may signal a lack of meaningful assent to a contract and thus constitute grounds for a court's setting aside the contract.

DISCUSSION QUESTIONS

1. Can an opinion be equivalent to fraud?
2. When is a fact material?
3. What sorts of conduct may indicate the defendant's knowledge of a statement's falsity?
4. Discuss the requirement of a plaintiff's reliance when alleging fraud. What are the implications of this requirement?
5. How does silence relate to the legal theory of fraud?

6. In what situations is there a legal duty to speak?
7. Name, define, and explain the remedies for the two types of mistakes.
8. Define *duress*.
9. Discuss the recently emerging doctrine of economic duress.
10. In what circumstances will the law presume undue influence? Why?

CASE PROBLEMS

1. The Jacobses sued the Gallery of Homes and its agent, Howard Wolfley, for damages resulting from Wolfley's alleged misrepresentations. During negotiations between the Jacobses, who were represented by Wolfley, and the Phillippis, the sellers of the real estate in question, the Phillippis offered to sell the house at an interest rate of 12 percent with a balloon payment (the entire balance of the unpaid mortgage) due and payable within one year. Wolfley conveyed this offer to the Jacobses, who instructed Wolfley to make a further counteroffer of 10 percent for the first six months and 12 percent for the second six months. However, Wolfley did not inform the Phillippis of the further counteroffer by the Jacobses. Thus, the Phillippis believed that their offer of 12 percent interest had been accepted. The parties subsequently signed a real estate contract that provided for an interest rate of 12 percent and for a balloon payment of the balance plus interest within twelve months. The terms of this contract were complete and visible for review by the Jacobses. The Jacobses ultimately defaulted on this contract when they failed to make the scheduled balloon payment. The Jacobses then sued to have the real estate contract rescinded on the ground of mutual mistake owing to their belief that the interest rate for the first six months should have been 10 percent, not 12 percent. Should a court grant rescission in these circumstances? (*Jacobs* v. *Phillippi*, 697 P.2d 132 [N.M. 1985].)

2. On 25 August 1987, Helen Turner was involved in an automobile accident with Sheila A. Lucas, who was operating an automobile owned by Donnie M. Lucas. Both Mrs. Turner and the Lucases were insured by State Farm Mutual Automobile Insurance Company (State

Farm). Following the accident, Mrs. Turner was directed by her State Farm agent to the State Farm claims office. She met with Debra Pendergrass on 26 August 1987, the day following the accident. At the meeting, Mrs. Turner assumed Ms. Pendergrass was acting as her adjuster and not that of Mrs. Lucas; and, in fact, Ms. Pendergrass was not initially aware that Mrs. Turner was insured by State Farm because only the Lucas file was present. After some discussion, Ms. Pendergrass presented to Mrs. Turner an agreement and release providing $500 for "pain and suffering and inconvenience" and for payment of medical expenses up to $5000. Although Mrs. Turner told Ms. Pendergrass she had injured her foot, neck, and back and had an appointment with a doctor that afternoon, Mrs. Turner signed the release. However, Mrs. Turner did not cash the $500 draft and returned it to State Farm after consulting with her attorney. At trial, Mrs. Turner testified that she thought the agreement was for inconvenience and payment of medical bills. When asked if she had considered the agreement to be a complete release of the Lucases, she replied: "No, I did not consider this a release at all." She testified that she had attempted to read the agreement but could not because she did not have her glasses with her. The cross-examination of Ms. Pendergrass at trial showed that Ms. Pendergrass had not checked Mrs. Turner's policy and file on the computer and thus had never advised Mrs. Turner of her rights under the policy in any fashion until after Mrs. Turner had signed the release. Moreover, Ms. Pendergrass admitted that she had never revealed during her conversation with Mrs. Turner that she was serving in a dual capacity (i.e., representing both the Lucases and Mrs.

Turner) on this claim. When State Farm sued for a declaratory judgment (a judgment by a court that merely sets out the rights of the parties in a given situation without ordering any performance by either party) sustaining the validity of the release, Mrs. Turner sought rescission of the release. Assuming Mrs. Turner's signing of the release had constituted a unilateral mistake, could a court nonetheless grant this request for rescission? (*State Farm Mutual Automobile Insurance Company v. Turner*, 399 S.E.2d 22 [S.C. App. 1990].)

3. The City of Dana Point, California, had adopted the Dana Point Specific Plan (the DPSP), which recognized the area's scenic views of the harbor, coast, and mountains as one of the area's primary natural resources. The city also had adopted land use regulations that conformed with the DPSP and that restricted the nature and type of development permitted in Dana Point. Seeking to build a residential development on its Dana Point property, Southwest Diversified, Inc. (Southwest) filed a tentative tract map with the county Environmental Management Agency and applied for use, zoning, and coastal permits. By applying for these permits, Southwest subjected its project to a public hearing review process before the DPSP Board of Review and the Orange County Planning Commission, among others. Southwest's development proposal requested certain concessions it was not otherwise entitled to receive and to which there was substantial opposition in the neighboring community. To achieve the necessary approval, Southwest actively solicited the support of nearby residents, including Clyde Lacher and others. The neighbors' primary concerns lay in protecting their views. During the latter part of 1987 and through the summer of 1988, Southwest, through its agents, Richard Garlinghouse and Mark Buell, conducted and attended several meetings with interested neighbors. During such meetings, Southwest's agents allegedly asserted that the homes built in the development would be erected on the natural, existing grade, without using fill dirt; would be set back from the street twenty-five feet; and would be situated to maximize Lacher and the neighbors' views. Garlinghouse claimed that no structure built on Southwest's property would exceed one story in height above the street level of Calle La Primavera. During the permit approval process, Southwest represented to the county's planning commission that it would 1) provide split-level building pads and step-down units to preserve the natural form of the property's terrain and 2) limit homes along Calle La Primavera to single-story plans using

structural designs that preserved the views of nearby residents. In reliance on Southwest's representations, Lacher and the other residents acquiesced in the development plans and, at hearings before the DPSP review board and the county's planning commission, recommended approval of the project. Only after the project had been approved and construction had begun did the following facts come to light: that Southwest had no intention of building on the existing grade, but had planned to bring in fill dirt to raise certain sites and had done so; that the promised one-story homes were in fact significantly higher; and that Southwest had exploited the property's terrain to increase its view potential without consideration of the harm to the views of Lacher and the others. Lacher and the neighbors argued that if they, the other residents, and the administrative review agencies had known the true facts about the development, approval of the project would not have been obtained by Southwest without conditions being imposed that would have protected the views of the nearby residents. As a result, Lacher and the others argued, Southwest's actions had deprived them of substantial ocean, coastline, and mountain views that the DPSP otherwise protected, causing a diminution in their property's value as well as severe emotional distress. They subsequently sued Southwest for fraud in inducing them to support Southwest's request for governmental approval of the project. How should a court rule in this case? (*Lacher v. Superior Court*, 281 Cal. Rptr. 640 [Cal. App. 1991].)

4. Clearwater Construction & Engineering, Inc. (Clearwater) and Wickes Forest Industries (Wickes) entered into a contract for the construction of several forest service roads called the Van Buren project. This contract extended through 31 December 1976. Clearwater did not complete the contract by this date because logging operations had hampered its excavation work. On 1 February 1977, the parties executed a second agreement that extended the completion date on the Van Buren project until 31 December 1977. Clearwater experienced similar difficulties in completing the project by the 1977 date, owing, in Clearwater's view, to Wickes's failure to remove the right-of-way logs. Clearwater later filed suit for damages for the failure of Wickes to pay Clearwater the contract price. At trial Clearwater argued that the 1977 agreement was either a binding, valid contract that Wickes had breached or that, alternatively, the agreement was invalid as the product of unlawful economic duress. Clearwater asserted that the economic duress derived from Wickes's

alleged breaches of the original contract, which breaches had placed Clearwater in so precarious a financial condition that Clearwater had been forced to sign the 1977 agreement against its will in order to save itself from financial ruin. Wickes contended that Clearwater had an adequate remedy at law for the alleged breach of the original contract and thus that no economic duress was present. Wickes also maintained that whether economic duress had existed was irrelevant anyway, since Clearwater had, by its conduct, ratified the 1977 agreement. Did the evidence show that Clearwater had entered the 1977 agreement as the result of economic duress? Alternatively, had Clearwater ratified the 1977 agreement by its subsequent conduct? (*Clearwater Construction & Engineering, Inc.* v. *Wickes Forest Industries,* 697 P.2d 1146 [Idaho 1985].)

5. Michael La Fleur suffered a work-related injury in January, 1975, when a forklift blade fell on his right foot. The company doctor thought the injury was superficial, even though La Fleur had continued to experience pain. A physician from the employer's insurance company diagnosed the injury as a sprain. In August, 1976, after the termination of his employment, La Fleur accepted a lump-sum settlement of $4000 from the insurer in which he agreed as part of the release that the settlement represented the total amount of workers' compensation due him. However, after entering into this agreement, La Fleur experienced increasing discomfort in his right foot and was diagnosed as having arterial occlusive disease. As a result, he underwent several operations and eventually had both legs amputated above the knees. Hence, La Fleur was permanently confined to a wheelchair. An expert witness testified that the disease had existed at the time of the accident but had escaped diagnosis because it was difficult to detect. This expert also concluded that the forklift accident had aggravated this preexisting arterial disease and had led to the amputation of the right leg. The added stress to the left leg that had resulted from the amputation of the right leg in turn caused the amputation of the left leg. La Fleur sued the employer and its insurer for rescission of the lump-sum agreement on the ground of mutual mistake. Should a court grant this requested remedy? (*La Fleur* v. *C.C. Pierce Co., Inc.,* 496 N.E.2d 827 [Mass. 1986].)

6. Life Investors Insurance Company (Life Investors) sued Citizens National Bank of Wisner (Citizens) and the personal representative of Merle Gralheer's estate for the alleged overpayment of insurance proceeds to Citizens. Gralheer had borrowed money from Citizens, which had required him to purchase life insurance each time he had signed a note with the bank. When Gralheer died of cancer, Life Investors had paid the entire claim—$38,000—because Citizens's other insurance carrier, United Life Insurance Company (United Life), had denied liability. Under United Life's policies, debtors who have cancer or heart disease were not eligible for coverage. Life Investors therefore sued Citizens for $19,000, the amount of overpayment, claiming fraudulent misrepresentation and mutual mistake. On appeal, Citizens argued that the trial court had committed reversible error in failing to require Life Investors to elect between these two theories before presenting its case. Were these theories so inconsistent that the insurer should have chosen one or the other? (*Life Investors Insurance Company of America* v. *Citizens National Bank of Wisner,* 392 N.W.2d 771 [Neb. 1986].)

7. Four children of Delphine Wagner attempted to have the court appoint a conservator to manage Mrs. Wagner's estate because of her advanced age and the undue influence of two of her daughters, Clarinda and Clara Mae. Specifically, Mrs. Wagner had leased land—previously farmed by some of the petitioners—to another concern, resulting in a 160 percent greater income to Mrs. Wagner. At the time of the conservatorship hearing, Mrs. Wagner was seventy-nine years old and recently widowed. The doctors who had examined Mrs. Wagner testified that she was oriented as to time and place, in good health, and neat and clean. The doctors also had characterized Mrs. Wagner as strong-willed, feisty, and opinionated. The children asking for the conservator also had described their mother as bull-headed and stubborn. The evidence regarding one of the siblings' alleged undue influence was a statement by another sibling that Clarinda was with her mother all the time, that Clarinda was opinionated, and that Clarinda was probably telling her mother how to do everything. Should a court in these circumstances find that Mrs. Wagner had been subject to undue influence? (*In re Estate of Wagner,* 367 N.W.2d 736 [Neb. 1985].)

8. Orlandi leased approximately 3000 acres of West Virginia land to Goodell under a minimum royalty lease. Under the lease, Goodell was obligated to pay certain specified sums in advance for each of the first four years. No relationship existed between the payment schedule and any given quantity of coal that might be mined. After signing the lease, Goodell hired a contract miner who, based on May, 1979, drillings, concluded that the

site contained too much rock to be profitably mined. Goodell made no further attempts to exploit his rights under the lease. When Goodell failed to make the first scheduled royalty payment, Orlandi sued. Goodell countered that the contract had been signed under a mutual mistake of fact as to the presence of merchantable and mineable coal on the property. Since no such coal was available, Goodell argued, the contract should be rescinded. How should the judge decide this case? (*Orlandi* v. *Goodell,* 760 F.2d 78 [4th Cir. 1985].)

9. Linda Chapman agreed to buy real estate from the Hoseks. About a month after she had signed the purchase agreement, the institution through which she had planned to finance the purchase informed her that the land was located in a flood-hazard area and that she would have to buy flood insurance as a prerequisite to obtaining the mortgage. Chapman, in addition, allegedly learned that during heavy rains the Hoseks' property had been damaged from flooding and had been made inaccessible. Therefore, seven weeks after signing the purchase agreement, Chapman sued the Hoseks and the listing and selling brokers for rescission of the contract on the ground of fraud. Chapman contended that the defendants had concealed facts material to the transaction—the requirement of flood insurance and the propensity of the area to flood during heavy rains—and that these misrepresentations constituted fraud. Was Chapman correct? Could the defendants argue in defense that the information cited by Chapman was a matter of public record and that she had been negligent in failing to discover the truth? (*Chapman* v. *Hosek,* 475 N.E.2d 593 [Ill. App. 1985].)

10. Lester Barrer's home had been sold at a tax sale to satisfy tax liabilities owed to the Internal Revenue Service (IRS). Because the Internal Revenue Code provides for the redemption of real property within 120 days of the sale of the property, the IRS informed Barrer that he could redeem his home by paying $17,400 to the IRS or to Curtis, the purchaser of the property, by 22 October 1981. On 20 October 1981, Barrer spoke with Emily Womack, the president of Women's National Bank (WNB), with whom Barrer was professionally acquainted, about a loan. Barrer and Womack later disputed several key points of information Barrer had provided in his loan application, including, among other things, the fact that Columbia First Federal Savings and Loan Association (Columbia), the holder of the principal mortgage on the home, had begun foreclosure proceedings on his home because he was six months behind in his mortgage payments. Barrer testified that he had said he "thought" he was two months behind; Womack, in contrast, testified that Barrer had said he was current on his payments. Barrer had disclosed the $30,000 tax liability that had forced the tax sale but had not indicated a contingent liability for an additional $11,000 owed by his corporation but which, at that time, had not been asserted against him personally. Although Barrer had not shown on the loan application that he had approximately $1500 in unsatisfied debts pending against him, he had answered yes to a question asking whether he were the subject of any pending lawsuits. Without securing a credit report on Barrer, the bank had loaned him the $17,400 needed to redeem his home. Barrer had given the check to the IRS on 22 October 1981, believing that his home had been saved. That afternoon, Curtis, the tax sale purchaser, phoned WNB and spoke to an official there. Curtis provided the official with information about Barrer's arrearages with Columbia and the fact that the IRS was planning to hold another tax sale as soon as the $17,400 was paid. Based on this information and a credit report that was belatedly run on Barrer, the bank stopped payment on the $17,400 check it had given to Barrer. Barrer therefore was unable to redeem his home, and Curtis became the owner of it. When Barrer sued the bank for damages to compensate him for the loss of equity in his home, the bank alleged that Barrer's innocent misrepresentations provided it with grounds for rescinding the contract with him. Would you agree with the bank's asserted defense? (*Barrer* v. *Women's National Bank,* 761 F.2d 752 [D.C. Cir. 1985].)

CHAPTER 14

Interpretation and Proper Form of Contracts

OUTLINE

THE IMPORTANCE OF FORM

In the preceding chapters, we discussed in detail the six requirements for a contract: offer, acceptance, consideration, capacity, legality, and reality of consent. Since we now understand the essentials of contract formation, we are ready to tackle some of the issues that may arise out of the contract itself. For instance, although the parties may have tried to be as precise as possible, questions about what the contract "really says" and whether certain conditions have been met may crop up as the parties begin their performance. One classic case involved a dispute over the word *chicken*. A Swiss buyer thought *chicken* meant broilers and fryers, or tender, juicy chicken. The New York seller, however, shipped stewing chicken to fulfill part of the contract; the Swiss buyer was not amused. As these parties found out, much to the disappointment of the buyer, contract **interpretation** often becomes an extremely important matter.

Interpretation The process of discovering the meaning of a contract; the defining, discovering, and explaining of unclear language.

If the parties cannot resolve their differences, they will call on a court to decide what the disputed terms mean. As aids for this task, courts have certain standards they can apply to unravel even the most ambiguous terms and phrases. However, other rules of law may limit these interpretive capacities. Judges are necessarily wary of tampering with a writing that the parties seemingly mean to represent the final expression of their intentions. For this reason, the **parol evidence** rule states that oral testimony ordinarily is not admissible to add to, alter, or vary the terms of a written agreement. In certain situations, parol evidence will be admissible to clear up ambiguities (such as the meaning of the word *chicken* mentioned earlier). Reference to the trade usages and customs of a particular industry may dispose of these types of ambiguity. Simply put, writing a contract does not guarantee that the subsequent performance of the contract will remain free of semantic wranglings. But the alternative of contracting orally makes little sense because oral transactions multiply the potential interpretive problems.

Parol evidence Oral statements.

In addition, according to the **Statute of Frauds,** certain categories of contracts must be in writing to be enforceable. The contract involving chickens, a type of goods, constitutes one example, assuming the contract price equals or exceeds $500. Others include contracts not to be completed within one year from the date of their making, contracts involving interests in land, contracts to answer for the debt of another, promises of **executors** and **administrators** to pay a claim against the estate of the deceased out of their own funds, and contracts made in consideration of marriage. The writing in these situations provides evidence that the parties really did contract about the matters in dispute, and it avoids the **perjuries** traditionally and historically associated with these categories of contracts. In most other situations, the parties are free to contract orally, even though it is unwise to do so. This interplay among contract interpretation, the parol evidence rule, and the Statute of Frauds forms the subject of this chapter.

Statute of Frauds A statute requiring that specified types of contracts must be in writing in order to be enforceable.

Executors The persons named and appointed in a will by the testator to carry out the administration of the estate as established by the will.

Administrators The persons who have been empowered by an appropriate court to handle the estate of a deceased person.

Perjuries False statements made under oath during court proceedings.

JUDICIAL INTERPRETATION

In previous chapters, we dwelled on the importance of a *meeting of the minds* of the parties to the contract. Imprecise though this phrase is, it highlights one of the essential elements of a contract: The parties of necessity must have indicated, by their words or conduct, an intention to agree about some matter. Yet because language is an imprecise vehicle of expression, it may subsequently become apparent that the parties were not binding themselves to identical terms and courses of action (witness our "chicken" controversy). When this variance in expectations surfaces, disputes arise. If the parties cannot resolve these disputes, courts inherit the task of interpreting what the contract "really says."

Interpretation is *the process of determining the meaning of the words and other manifestations of intent that the parties have used in forging their agreement when the language of the agreement is not clear.* Ascertaining the parties' intent in order to enforce the contract as the parties wished is not easy. Problems arise primarily because words are symbols of expression and can take on an almost infinite number of meanings. Moreover, words do not exist in a vacuum. Determining how a certain party intended to use words or actions therefore becomes a factual issue. A court must examine one party's understanding and conduct in the situation, but it must also be conscious of how other reasonable persons would have understood these same words and actions under similar circumstances. In deciding between two competing views, courts often must consider the intentions of the parties through a frame of reference usually called the "reasonable person," or objective, approach. This perspective allows the court to choose the interpretation that would be most consonant with the expectations of a prudent person in the same circumstances. Though not a perfect method, it at least ensures that the interpretation the court chooses is not so divergent from normality that it becomes nonsensical.

Standards

Because interpretation involves comparing the parties' words and conduct from some other perspective, certain standards of interpretation have evolved over the years. Probably the most common one is the standard of *general usage,* or the meaning that a reasonably prudent person who was aware of all operative uses and who was acquainted with the circumstances involved prior to and during the making of the agreement would attach to the agreement. For example, assume a relative of yours signs an agreement in which he gives $10,000 as a life membership fee for admission to a nursing home. Assume further that the agreement states that for a trial period of two months, either your relative or the nursing home can suspend the agreement. On the occurrence of that event, the $10,000 (minus $200 per month) will be returned. What if your relative unfortunately dies after one month in the home?

Can your relative's estate recover the $9800, or has the life membership fee been paid irrevocably?

By resorting to the standard of general usage, a court in a similar case decided that a reasonable person in your relative's place at the time of the execution of the contract would have understood the provision to mean that unless and until life membership status were obtained, the nursing home should return the money (less the amounts specified) to him. The court also asserted that if the nursing home had intended to retain the money in the event of a probationary member's death, it should have expressly stated this fact in the contract. Had the facts been different, the court might have applied the standard of *limited usage* (the meaning given to language in a particular locale) instead of the standard of general usage. Other standards that courts may apply in interpreting ambiguous contractual or statutory language are discussed in the following sections.

Total Integration

The standards employed in contract interpretation may turn on whether the contract is totally integrated. A *totally integrated contract* is one that *represents the parties' final and complete statement of their agreement*. Such a contract may be neither contradicted nor supplemented by evidence of prior agreements or expressions. The law assumes that the writing supersedes terms set out earlier in preliminary negotiations.

Partial Integration

If a *writing is intended to be the final statement* of the parties' agreement *but is incomplete,* it is a *partially integrated contract*. Such a writing may not be contradicted by evidence of earlier agreements or expressions, but it may be supplemented by evidence of additional, consistent terms. Perhaps your relative and the nursing home orally agreed that his personal physician (rather than the nursing home's) will provide needed medical care. If the parties leave this provision out, the contract represents a partially integrated writing. Since this provision does not appear to contradict the original agreement, some courts may allow the parties to add it to the agreement later.

Rules of Integration

In general, the more formal and complete the instrument, the more likely a court will find it to be a totally integrated agreement. According to the rules of integration, exchanges of letters, telegrams, and memoranda may indicate the formation of a contract; but they may not represent the final intentions of the parties. Rather, these communications may show only tentative and preliminary agreement. Some judges employ different standards of interpretation, depending on whether there has been integration. When no integration has occurred, some would use the standard of reasonable expectation—that is, the meaning one party would reasonably expect the other to attribute to a term, given what the first party has said or done. If John is trying to buy a "fully equipped" car and a dispute later arises as to whether an air conditioner is included, a court will need to scrutinize the car salesperson's representations. If the agreement is integrated, a judge may instead apply the standard of limited usage—the meaning of the term as understood locally and in the trade—to see whether "fully equipped" cars ordinarily include air conditioners.

Rules of Interpretation   To supplement the appropriate standard of interpretation, courts also use rules of interpretation. Although authorities disagree as to the relative importance of these rules, you should be aware of the following common ones:

1. Courts should attempt to give effect to the manifested intentions of the parties.
2. Courts should examine the contract as a whole in order to ascertain the intentions of the parties.
3. Courts should give ordinary words their ordinary meanings and technical words their technical meanings, unless the circumstances indicate otherwise.
4. Subject to the requirements of the parol evidence rule (discussed later in this chapter), courts should take into account all the circumstances surrounding the transaction.

Other rules state that reasonable constructions are favored when unreasonable alternative constructions are possible, that the main purpose of the agreement and all parts of the instrument will be given effect if possible, that special and specific words or provisions control general ones, that written words control printed ones, that words will be construed most strictly against the party who drafts the agreement, and that contracts affecting the public interest will be construed in favor of the public.

The case that follows demonstrates how vital interpretation is in determining what the wording of a contract means when disagreements subsequently develop. Note that the court used some of the concepts we have discussed in disposing of this case.

Rodriguez v. General Accident Insurance Company of America
808 S.W.2d 379 (Mo. 1991)

FACTS   On 11 September 1987, Gail Rodriguez received injuries when the vehicle she was driving collided with a vehicle operated by John Fruehwirth. Fruehwirth's insurance company paid Rodriguez $50,000, the limits of liability under Fruehwirth's insurance policy. Rodriguez sought the balance of her damages from her insurance carrier, General Accident Insurance Company of America (General Accident) pursuant to the policy's "underinsured motorist coverage." The face sheet of the policy in question showed various coverages for two automobiles, including underinsured motorist coverage, with a limit of $50,000 on each vehicle. The salient portions of the Underinsured Motorist Coverage Endorsement provided the following:

Underinsured Motorist Coverage

INSURING AGREEMENT

A. We will pay damages which an "insured" is legally entitled to recover from the owner or operator of an "underinsured motor vehicle" because of "bodily injury,"

   1. Sustained by an "insured". . . .

C. "Underinsured motor vehicle" means a land motor vehicle or trailer of any type to which a bodily injury liability bond or policy applies at the time of the accident but its limit for bodily injury liability is less than the limit of liability for this coverage.

LIMIT OF LIABILITY

A. The limit of liability shown in the schedule for this coverage is our maximum limit of liability for all damages resulting from any one accident. *This is the most we will pay regardless of the number of:*

   1. "Insureds";
   2. Claims made;
   3. *Vehicles or premiums shown in the Declarations;* or
   4. Vehicles involved in the accident. *However, the limit of liability shall be reduced by all sums paid because of the "bodily injury" by or on behalf of persons or organizations who may be legally responsible.* This includes all sums paid under part A of this policy [emphases added].

General Accident declined to pay, citing this contractual language. Owing to the alleged ambiguity of the wording of the contract, the Rodriguezes then brought this action, seeking both to recover under the uninsured motorist coverage and to have their underinsured motorist coverage "stacked," thereby realizing a total of $100,000 in underinsured motorist coverage. The trial court sustained General American's motion for summary judgment, holding that under the insurance contract, Fruehwirth was not an "underinsured motorist." The Rodriguezes appealed this decision.

ISSUE   Was the Rodriguezes' insurance contract sufficiently ambiguous to warrant the application of the objective reasonable expectations test to resolve this alleged ambiguity?

HOLDING   No. In the absence of statutes or public policies requiring the construction advocated by the Rodriguezes, the law would mandate the enforcement of insurance policies as written when such policies are unambiguous.

REASONING   The Rodriguezes argue that the ambiguity of their insurance contract with General Accident entitles them to a resolution of this ambiguity consistent with their objective reasonable expectations. They further submit that application of the objective reasonable expectations doctrine renders their underinsured motorist coverage as excess coverage entitling them to $50,000 in coverage beyond that previously paid by Fruehwirth's insurer. The law holds that an ambiguity arises when there is duplicity, indistinctness, or uncertainty in the meaning of the words used in the contract. If there is a conflict between a technical definition within a contract and the meaning that the average lay person would reasonably understand, a court will apply the lay person's definition unless it plainly appears that the parties intended the technical meaning. The law will not permit a court to create an ambiguity in order to distort the language of an unambiguous policy or in order to enforce a particular construction it believes more appropriate. Thus, where insurance policies are unambiguous, in the absence of a statute or public policy requiring coverage, courts will enforce such agreements as written. The contract between General Accident and the Rodriguezes clearly states that an underinsured motor vehicle is a vehicle whose limits for bodily injury liability are "less than the limit of liability for this coverage." By their own admission, the Rodriguezes acknowledge that Fruehwirth's liability insurance coverage was $50,000. Since Fruehwirth's coverage equals the limit of liability under the Rodriguezes' policy, Fruehwirth would not qualify as an underinsured motorist as defined by the Rodriguezes' policy. Moreover, a set-off provision of the Rodriguezes' policy, which provides that "the limit of liability shall be reduced by all sums paid because of the 'bodily injury' by or on behalf of persons or organizations who may be legally responsible. . . ."

reinforces this definition of underinsured motorist. Indeed, this provision sets off the $50,000 paid by Fruehwirth's insurer against the $50,000 coverage provided by General Accident. The underinsured motorist coverage, therefore, does not, as the Rodriguezes argue, equate with excess coverage. Instead, that coverage provides a total amount of protection General Accident will pay to the Rodriguezes if the other persons legally responsible for Mrs. Rodriguez's injuries have lesser liability limits than those provided under the Rodriguezes' underinsured motorist coverage. The Rodriguezes also contend that the court should permit them to "stack" the underinsured motorist coverage of each of their two vehicles insured by the General Accident policy, thereby yielding a combined limit of $100,000. The contract language applicable to this issue—"The limit of liability shown in the schedule for this coverage is the maximum limit of liability for all damages resulting from any one accident. This is the most we will pay regardless of the number of . . . vehicles or premiums shown in the Declarations"—clearly and unambiguously constitutes an antistacking provision. In the absence of ambiguity and any public policy violations, courts will enforce the clear language of the contract. Hence, the trial court in these circumstances properly granted summary judgment in favor of General Accident.

YOU BE THE JUDGE

> The Philadelphia Orchestra sued Walt Disney Co. for one-half the estimated $120 million in profits resulting from the 1991 home video and laser disk re-release of the film classic, "Fantasia." (In 1938, the orchestra, under famed conductor Leopold Stokowski, recorded the music for the film.) The orchestra argued that, as a "joint author" of the film, it should share in the proceeds from these new versions. The orchestra further submitted that Disney had never secured the orchestra's permission before releasing the 1991 versions of the film. Disney had, in 1957, asked for, and received, the orchestra's permission to release a sound recording of the music from "Fantasia," in exchange for Disney's payment of a royalty.
>
> Obviously, home videos and laser disk technologies did not exist in 1938 at the time of the signing of the original contract. How would you decide this case, given this contractual ambiguity?

Source: "Disney Is Sued by Orchestra over " 'Fantasia,' " Richard Turner, *The Wall Street Journal*, May 7, 1992, pages B-1 and B-5.

Conduct and Usages of Trade

The conduct of the parties often aids in contract interpretation. If the court is in doubt, it will follow the interpretation placed on the agreement by the parties themselves. For example, when one party has accepted for years a grade of wool inferior to the contract specifications, evidence of this conduct will be admissible in determining how to interpret the specifications. As you will learn in Chapter 18, Uniform Commercial Code Section 2-208, on course of performance, course of dealing, usage of trade, and contract construction, incorporates this rule of interpretation. You should therefore note its importance to the concept of contract interpretation and the courts' increasing reliance on it in Code transactions.

PAROL EVIDENCE RULE

So far, we have explored some of the concepts and rules dealing with contract interpretation. In so doing, we have stressed the importance of ascertaining the parties' intentions. We now turn to another important facet of contract law that is closely related to interpretation, the *parol evidence rule*. This rule is predicated on the belief that *oral evidence should not be admissible to alter, add to, or vary the terms of an integrated, written contract*. If the parties appear to have intended the writing as the final expression of their agreement, to allow later oral or written evidence that contradicts that writing will call into question the whole process of reducing one's agreement to writing. For instance, assume that Larry and Lynn sign a contract for the sale of a used car. They both agree, in a completed writing, that the price of the car is $6000. If one of the parties later tries to argue that the price is higher or lower, the parol evidence rule will preclude oral testimony to this effect, should litigation ensue as a result of this dispute. Imagine the havoc a contrary rule would cause. Courts therefore uphold the sanctity of totally integrated contracts by applying the parol evidence rule.

Because the parol evidence rule is designed to uphold a policy of protecting writings—those instruments representing the final intentions and terms of the parties—it is actually a rule of **substantive law** rather than a rule of evidence.

For a good example of how the parol evidence rule can become an issue, read the following case.

Substantive law The portion of the law that regulates rights, in contrast to law that grants remedies or enforces rights.

Magnetic Copy Services, Inc. v. Seismic Specialists, Inc.
805 P.2d 1161 (Colo. App. 1990)

FACTS   Magnetic Copy Services, Inc. (MCS) is a Colorado corporation that engages in the business of copying magnetic tapes. Seismic Specialists, Inc. (SSI) is a Colorado corporation that conducts seismic surveys in areas of potential oil and gas exploration by generating sound waves through a dynamite blast or other vibration equipment. SSI then records sound waves on magnetic tapes, which companies such as MCS duplicate for sale to SSI customers. On 22 October 1986, MCS and SSI signed a contract, prepared by MCS, involving MCS's copying of SSI's field tapes. The contract stated: "SSI agrees to provide MCS 3,000 field tapes to be copied for its clients within one year of this agreement. . . . MCS will pay SSI a commission of $10.00 per tape. . . ." A year after the execution of the contract, SSI had provided only 1399 tapes to MCS for copying. Nevertheless, SSI continued to provide tapes to MCS for copying during the fall of 1987. During this one-year period, several events pertinent to the parties' agreement occurred. For instance, SSI lost one or two of its primary customers, which loss reduced the number of tapes SSI could produce to provide for copying to MCS. In addition, SSI had several hundred tapes copied by companies other than MCS because its customers either wanted a shorter turnaround time on the copying than MCS could provide or wanted a different copying method used. Moreover, during this one-year contract period, MCS had cash-flow difficulties; and at times it delayed making payments to SSI after it (MCS) had received payment from these customers. At those times, SSI allowed MCS significant flexibility in making its payments. MCS claimed that SSI's failure to produce 3000 tapes within one year of the contract constituted a breach of the contract and that SSI was, therefore, not entitled to its commission on certain tapes, including the last 43 tapes provided before 22 October 1987, the anniversary date of the signing of the contract. Furthermore, MCS argued that it need not pay a commission to SSI for the 538 tapes copied during the months of November and December, 1987. At trial, the court had allowed SSI and MCS's employees to testify about the provision specifying that SSI would provide 3000 tapes to MCS. SSI's employees testified that the reference in the contract to 3000 tapes constituted a goal, not a guarantee. These employees, however, also testified that SSI had always intended to provide 3000 tapes but was not able to do so within the year. MCS's employees testified that they had construed SSI's statement as a promise or commitment to provide 3000 tapes within one year. MCS, moreover, viewed the terms of the contract as clear and unambiguous and thus asserted that the trial court had improperly varied the terms of the contract by the use of parol evidence.

ISSUE   Did the trial court commit reversible error in admitting parol evidence concerning this contract provision?

HOLDING   Yes. Because the contract provision in dispute here was unambiguous, the trial court erred in admitting parol evidence regarding its terms.

REASONING   In the absence of an ambiguity, extrinsic evidence cannot vary the terms of a written agreement. Moreover, courts must enforce an unambiguous agreement according to its express terms. The determination of whether a contract is ambiguous remains a question of law for the court, and thus the trial court's conclusion will not necessarily bind an appellate court. Settled law holds that the mere disagreement between the parties regarding the proper interpretation of a contract does not, in itself, create an ambiguity. Here, SSI argued that the contract is ambiguous because of the omission of the term "guarantee" and that the testimony that SSI's promise to provide 3000 tapes merely connoted a goal is therefore admissible to confirm the ambiguity and to explain the intent of the parties. However, the phrase "agrees to provide" constituted an unambiguous promise by SSI to provide MCS with 3000 tapes within a year of the contract. Furthermore, the contract did not condition SSI's performance on any set of circumstances and did not state or imply that providing 3000 tapes within a year represented merely a goal or objective. However, the trial court had used testimony from SSI regarding the 3000 tape "goal," admitted without objection, as a basis for modifying the contract; and SSI had implicitly argued that MCS's failure to object to this parol evidence would mandate the affirmance of the trial court's determination. The parol evidence rule is one of substantive law, not merely one of evidence. Therefore, if, as here, a contract is unambiguous, the trial court, even if it has received parol evidence without objection, must ignore it. As S. Williston, *Contracts,* Section 631 states: "[since] parol testimony with respect to prior or contemporaneous agreements is not admissible to vary, contradict, or add to the terms of a written instrument [because the parol evidence rule] is one of substantive law, and not a mere rule of evidence, testimony introduced in violation of the rule, even in the absence of objection thereto, can be given no legal effect." Although the trial court could consider parol evidence to determine if a contract is ambiguous, if, as here, after hearing the evidence the court concludes that the contract is unambiguous, the court should strike the parol evidence. Therefore, the trial court erred in using parol evidence to vary the terms of an unambiguous contract; and its interpretation of the contract premised thereon accordingly could not stand.

EXCEPTIONS TO THE PAROL EVIDENCE RULE

Courts will disregard the parol evidence rule and will admit parol evidence in certain circumstances. The following circumstances are among the more common in which the parol evidence rule is not applied.

Partially Integrated Contracts

The policy base that underlies the parol evidence rule is not as compelling in situations in which the contract is partially integrated (that is, incomplete). In such cases, although the writing may not be contradicted by evidence of earlier terms, it may be supplemented by evidence of additional, consistent terms. (Recall our earlier example of your relative's medical care in the nursing home.)

Mistake, Fraud, and Other "Reality-of-Consent" Situations

Parol evidence is admissible to show mistake, fraud, duress, and failure of consideration, the kinds of situations we covered in Chapter 13. Since the existence of these situations casts doubt on the validity of the integrated writing, there is no overwhelmingly persuasive policy reason to justify exclusion of contradictory oral statements.

Ambiguities and Conditions Precedent

Courts will also allow parol evidence in order to clear up ambiguities (remember our "chicken" example) and to show that the agreement was not to become binding on the parties until a condition precedent (that is, a certain act or event must occur before the other party has a duty to perform or before a contract exists) was met, such as reduction of the agreement to writing or approval of the contract by a party's attorney. However, courts may allow evidence about a condition precedent only if this evidence does not contradict the written terms of the contract at issue.

Uniform Commercial Code

Sections 2-202 and 2-208 of the Uniform Commercial Code deal with the parol evidence rule. Basically, the Code recognizes the rule but then reduces its impact by stating that evidence of course of dealing (conduct), usage of trade, and course of performance is admissible. Courts can also admit evidence of consistent, additional terms unless they find that the parties intended the writing as a complete and exclusive statement of the terms of the agreement. Moreover, the Code sets up priorities among these types of evidence: The express terms of the agreement control course of performance, course of dealing, and usage of trade. Evidence relating to course of performance in turn controls admissions about course of dealing and usage of trade.

STATUTE OF FRAUDS

The historical ancestor for the parol evidence rule's policy of upholding the terms expressed in the parties' integrated writings is the original Statute of Frauds. Called An Act for the Prevention of Frauds and Perjuries, the English

Parliament passed this law in 1677. Because perjury was so widespread in lawsuits involving oral contracts, Parliament decreed that certain classes of contracts must be *in writing* to be enforceable. Thus, the term *Statute of Frauds* is somewhat misleading, since such statutes deal with the requirement of a writing rather than with reality-of-consent situations like fraud. (The term *frauds* refers to the wholesale misrepresentations or perjured statements made to early English courts.) Every state has a statute of frauds modeled on the original one.

The Statute of Frauds requires that certain types of contracts be in writing before courts will enforce them. If the subject matter of the contract involves a type of contract thus enumerated in the Statute of Frauds, the agreement generally cannot be oral but instead must be in writing before a court will give it effect. The Statute of Frauds never arises as a legal issue unless a valid contract exists.

Affirmative defense   A defense to a cause of action that must be raised by the defendant.

The Statute of Frauds is also an **affirmative defense,** one used by a person who does not want a contract to be enforced against himself or herself. A defendant who wishes to utilize this defense must expressly plead it, or it will be waived; if a waiver is found, an oral contract that would otherwise have been unenforceable because of a violation of the Statute of Frauds will be enforced against the defendant. Courts have been somewhat hostile to Statute of Frauds claims because of the injustice such statutes can cause. Consequently, some courts construe these statutes broadly and find various rationales for removing the contract at issue from the coverage of the statute, which allows the court to enforce oral contracts that would otherwise not be enforceable.

Types of Contracts Covered

We will examine six categories of contract covered by the Statute of Frauds: contracts to answer for the debt of another, contracts for interests in land, contracts not to be performed within one year of the date of their making, promises of executors and administrators of estates, contracts made in consideration of marriage, and contracts for sales of goods priced at $500 or more.

Contracts to Answer for the Debt of Another   Ordinarily, oral promises between two persons may be perfectly valid and enforceable in courts. When Linda orally promises to pay George $200 for a used cash register and he orally promises to sell it to her, a contract exists between the two parties. We call such promises *original* promises because both parties have promised to be *primarily* liable in all events if something should go awry in the transaction.

Guarantor   One who promises to answer for the payment of a debt or the performance of an obligation if the person liable in the first instance fails to make payment or to perform.

Surety   A person who promises to pay or to perform in the event that the principal debtor fails to do so.

Sometimes people agree to be liable secondarily—that is, only in the event someone else defaults. Such agreements, called *collateral contracts,* are promises to answer for the debt or default of another. Collateral contracts typically involve three persons: the debtor (original promisor), the creditor (the promisee), and the third party, who is generally called a **guarantor** or **surety.** Notice that a collateral contract exhibits definite characteristics:

1. There are three parties (but not all three-party transactions are collateral contracts; **novations,** for example, are not collateral contracts).

2. There are two promises, one original (debtor to creditor) and the other collateral (third party to creditor).

3. The second promise is a promise to accept only collateral, or secondary, liability resulting from the default of another.

Novations Substitutions by mutual agreement of new contracts in place of preexisting ones, whether between the same parties or with new parties replacing one or more of the original ones.

Since such collateral promises are somewhat unusual (we generally assume people will be responsible for their own debts but not for another person's), the purpose of this provision of the Statute of Frauds is to require evidence—through a writing—of this undertaking of possible secondary liability.

The *intent of the parties* determines whether a three-party transaction involves a collateral contract, which must be in writing to be enforceable, or an original contract, which may be enforceable even if oral. For example, if Stein wants his grandson to have a car, he may cosign a note at a bank for the child. This is a three-party situation (Stein, his grandson, and the bank), but it is *not* a collateral contract. Stein and his grandson are joint, original promisors to the bank. As such, Stein is accepting liability in all events. The bank can sue *either* him or his grandson if the grandson defaults on the car payments.

If, however, Stein wishes to be only secondarily liable and the note is phrased so that he is, the contract is a collateral one. In the event of default, the bank must sue the grandson *without success before* Stein can be held liable. Note that the intent of the parties is crucial in determining the type of contract—original or collateral—that is involved. If it is deemed a collateral contract, the bank is protecting itself from a defense based on the Statute of Frauds by requiring the transaction to be in writing.

Because courts are generally hostile to the Statute of Frauds, there is an exception to the rule that a collateral contract must be in writing to be enforceable. This is called the *leading-object* or *main-purpose exception:* When the third party agrees to be liable chiefly for the purpose of obtaining an economic benefit for himself or herself personally, the second promise, even if oral, will be enforceable. Change our earlier example to one in which Stein *orally* tells the bank he will pay *if* his grandson defaults. When the grandson does not pay and the bank sues Stein, Stein will use the Statute of Frauds as his defense: There is no writing, and the contract appears to be a collateral one. If, however, the bank can prove that before Stein agreed to be liable, Stein knew that the institution was about to force the grandson into bankruptcy, which in turn would mean that Stein might lose sizable loans he had made to his grandson, the bank may be able to show that Stein's leading object in making the promise involved preventing economic loss to himself. Proving this, the bank can argue that Stein's conduct makes him the equivalent of an original promisor—he was willing to pay and to assume liability in all events, not just secondarily—in order to protect his economic position vis-à-vis his grandson's impending bankruptcy. The wise businessperson avoids such potential legal problems by requiring all promises to be in writing rather than relying on oral ones.

The next case illustrates many of these concepts.

Al Booth's, Inc. v. Boyd-Scarp Enterprises, Inc.
518 So.2d 422 (Fla. App. 1988)

FACTS   Al Booth's, Inc. (Booth's), a supplier, sued Boyd-Scarp Enterprises, Inc. (Boyd-Scarp) and James Rathmann for nonpayment following delivery of various appliances to Rathmann's new home being built by Boyd-Scarp. Booth's, aware of Boyd-Scarp's financial problems, allegedly contacted Rathmann prior to delivery, asking him to guarantee payment. The evidence indicated that Rathmann had orally promised to pay in the event the builder, Boyd-Scarp, did not and that Booth's had then delivered the goods. Booth's appealed from a summary judgment holding that Booth's could not recover from Rathmann owing to the Statute of Frauds. Booth's maintained that the trial court had erred in ruling that the Statute of Frauds barred its recovery on Rathmann's oral collateral promise to pay the debt of the builder, Boyd-Scarp.

ISSUE   Was Rathmann's oral promise to pay Booth's in the event Boyd-Scarp failed to pay Booth's, unenforceable under the Statute of Frauds because it represented a collateral promise to answer for the debt or default of another?

HOLDING   No. Although Rathmann's promise constituted such a collateral promise, because Rathmann's leading object in making the promise involved an immediate pecuniary benefit to him (i.e., delivery of the appliances to his new home), his promise remained enforceable, even though it was oral, because it fell outside the coverage of the Statute of Frauds.

REASONING   The Florida Statute of Frauds provides in relevant part that "no action shall be brought . . . to charge the defendant upon any special promise to answer for the debt . . . of another person . . . unless the agreement or promise upon which such action shall be brought, or some note or memorandum thereof shall be in writing and signed by the party to be charged. . . ." This statutory language creates a distinction between direct promises and collateral promises to pay debts. Where the alleged oral promise is a direct promise that obligates a person in the first instance, it falls outside the Statute of Frauds and is enforceable. In the present case, the evidence, including that proffered by Booth's in its bookkeeper's affidavit, reflects that if in fact Rathmann had made a promise, it was a promise to pay in the event Boyd-Scarp did not. Such a promise would be a promise to answer for the debt of another. However, despite the cases relied on by Rathmann and the language above, this does not necessarily mean that the Statute of Frauds would bar Booth's recovery. Indeed, Rathmann's oral promise in this case would not fall within the purview of the Statute of Frauds. The pivotal question on the applicability of that statute centers on whether the promise is, in fact, an actual assumption of the liability of another with consideration flowing only to such other or, to the contrary, is an original undertaking of the promisor himself supported by independent consideration flowing to him. Florida case law on this point accords with the weight of authority in following the "leading object" rule, wherein if the promise to pay the debt of another is independent and unconditional, and is made for a valuable consideration of direct pecuniary value to the promisor (that is to say, the "leading object" being to benefit the promisor), the transaction falls outside the statute's coverage. In short, when the leading object of the promise or agreement is to become guarantor or surety to the promisee for a debt for which a third party is and continues to be primarily liable, the agreement, whether made before or after or at the time of the promise with the principal, is within the statute and not binding unless evidenced by writing. On the other hand, when the leading object of the promisor is to subserve some interest or purpose of his or her own, despite the fact that the effect is to pay or discharge the debt of another, this promise is not within the statute. Hence, the "leading object" rule recognizes that an important difference exists between cases in which the promisor makes the promise for the benefit of another and in which the promisor makes it for his or her own pecuniary benefit. If the promisor's main purpose was to advance his or her own interests and he or she has received a substantial, immediate, and pecuniary benefit, the promise falls outside the Statute of Frauds. Numerous decisions from other states have applied this rule to factual situations analogous to that presented here. Since evidence existed indicating that Rathmann had agreed to guarantee payment and that the promise had been for his own economic benefit, the "leading object" rule would apply to take the promise out of the Statute of Frauds. This being so, the trial court had improperly entered summary judgment for Rathmann.[1]

Mortgages Conditional transfers of property as security for a debt.

Leases Contracts that grant the right to use and occupy realty.

Easements Limited rights to use and enjoy the land of another.

Contracts for Interests in Land Any agreement that involves buying, selling, or transferring interests in land must be in writing to be enforceable. **Mortgages, leases, easements,** and sales agreements about standing timber and buildings attached to the land should also be in writing to satisfy the Statute of Frauds. Thus, if you orally offer to buy someone's house and the seller accepts your offer, this contract will be unenforceable because it does not comply with the Statute of Frauds.

Courts will nevertheless enforce oral contracts for the sale of land if the purchaser has paid part of the purchase price and, with the seller's consent, takes possession of the land and makes valuable improvements on it. This equitable remedy is called the *doctrine of part performance*. For example, assume Green moves onto Berry's land and, with Berry's oral permission, tears down an old garage, repaints the entire house, and rebuilds a barn, all at Green's expense. Green also has paid $5000 to Berry before undertaking these actions. When Berry later tries to claim there was no enforceable contract of sale between the two, a court can nonetheless order specific performance of the contract despite noncompliance with the Statute of Frauds. Courts justify such an exception to the requirement of a writing on the ground that the conduct of the parties prior to litigation shows the existence of a contract. Courts in such cases conclude that the parties' conduct can be explained only by the actual presence of such a contract. Equity will also give remedies in such situations to avoid the unjust enrichment of the seller.

Contracts Not to Be Performed Within One Year of the Date of Their Making According to the Statute of Frauds, a promise in a contract that cannot be performed within one year from the date of the making of the agreement must be in writing to be enforceable. To illustrate, an oral promise to haul milk for a dairy producer during a one-year period cannot be valid under the Statute of Frauds in situations in which it would be objectively impossible to haul the

---

[1]The court noted that Rathmann could not assert as a defense the UCC provision of the Statute of Frauds, which states that contracts involving sales of goods priced at $500 or more must be in writing, because Rathmann's receiving and accepting the goods fell within one of the exceptions to the UCC provision and thus made the contract, though oral, enforceable.

gallonage of milk contracted for in less than one year. This would be the case if the parties had entered into the contract on 15 December, with the term of the contract stated as running from 1 January to 31 December of the next year. Such a contract is one *not to be performed within one year of the date of its making* (15 December); therefore, under the Statute of Frauds, to be enforceable, it must be in writing. Courts have reacted hostilely to this section of the statute because of its harsh effects on the person who may suffer losses as a result of the rule's application. Thus, courts often have limited the coverage of this proviso to situations in which performance cannot *possibly* occur within one year's time (as in our example above). This limitation has led to rather strained results. For example, a bilateral contract in which an employee promises to work for an employer "for the employer's lifetime" sounds as if it invariably cannot be performed within one year. Some courts, however, interpret such language to mean that since it is *possible*—though not *probable*—that the employer might die within a year, an oral contract would be enforceable despite the Statute of Frauds. Under this approach, if the contract in our earlier example had obligated the hauler to transport the milk for "as long as the dairy farmer produces milk," such courts would reason that the dairy farmer could possibly cease operations within one year, thereby making the contract capable of being performed within one year from the date of the making of the contract. However remote this possibility, the fact that such a contingency *could* happen makes the oral contract enforceable and this section of the Statute of Frauds inapplicable. Other courts, though, would adopt the stricter approach and hold that the contracts at issue in both cases must be in writing to be enforceable. For two different courts' views of this matter, see the following cases.

D & N Boening, Inc. v. *Kirsch Beverages, Inc.*
472 N.E.2d 992 (N.Y. 1984)

FACTS   D & N Boening, Inc. (Boening) was the exclusive subdistributor of "Yoo Hoo" Chocolate beverages in Nassau and Suffolk Counties, New York. Although there was no written contract between Boening and American Beverage Corp. (American), the prime distributor of "Yoo Hoo," American had agreed verbally to continue the franchise arrangement as long as Boening performed satisfactorily, exerted its best efforts, and acted in good faith. In 1982, Kirsch Beverage purchased American and shortly thereafter terminated Boening's subdistributorship. Boening then sued Kirsch for breach of contract. Kirsch, in turn, asserted that, under New York law, the agreement was void because it was barred by the Statute of Frauds.

ISSUE   Did this agreement have to be in writing under the Statute of Frauds because it was one that could not be performed within one year from the date of its making?

HOLDING   Yes. The oral agreement between the parties called for performance of an indefinite duration and could only be terminated within one year by a breach of the agreement during that year. As such, the agreement fell within the coverage of the Statute of Frauds and was void under New York law.

REASONING The underlying rationale for the Statute of Frauds' requirement of a signed writing for a contract not to be performed within one year from the date of its making was the mistrust of witnesses' memories regarding matters involving time periods longer than one year. In addition, courts have historically shrunk from giving too broad an interpretation to this provision of the statute. Their tendency instead has been to limit its application to those contracts that by their very terms have absolutely no possibility in fact and law of full performance within one year. Under New York case precedents, the mere possibility of a breach within the first year of an agreement does not take the agreement out of the statute. These cases' reasoning applies to this particular agreement, since according to its terms, the agreement required American to continue the Boening subdistributorship indefinitely: There was no expiration date, and no options to terminate the agreement were reserved to either party. Indeed, the agreement could have continued in perpetuity unless Boening had failed to perform its subdistributorship satisfactorily, to exert its best efforts, and to act in good faith. Such a failure would not have constituted a permitted manner of performance; rather, it would have been a breach of the agreement. Being terminable only by Boening's breach, the agreement was not one that by its terms could be performed within one year. As such, it came within the coverage of the Statute of Frauds and was unenforceable under New York law because it was unwritten.

Argonaut Insurance Companies v. *Medical Liability Mutual Insurance Company*
760 F. Supp. 1078 (S.D.N.Y. 1991)

FACTS Since the mid-1960s, physicians who are members of the Medical Society of the State of New York (MSSNY) have received medical malpractice liability insurance coverage from three insurance companies. The initial coverage, furnished by Wausau Insurance Company (Wausau), ran from the inception of the coverage to 30 June 1974. When Wausau stopped writing that coverage, Argonaut Insurance Companies (Argonaut) succeeded it and wrote medical liability insurance for MSSNY members from 1 July 1974 to 30 June 1975. Argonaut then ceased its coverage and was succeeded by Medical Liability Mutual Insurance Company (MLMIC). MLMIC commenced its coverage on 1 July 1975, which coverage continues to the present day. The insurance industry calls this type of nonoverlapping coverage "end-to-end" coverage. The policies MLMIC issues to covered physicians consist of annual policies so that MLMIC maintains the coverage for a particular physician by writing a new policy for that physician at the end of each policy year. Apparently this constitutes the industry practice in such insurance policies. A claim for medical malpractice may arise from a single diagnosis or treatment or from a physician's allegedly negligent treatment of a patient over a number of years (for example, negligent failure to diagnose cancer). This latter situation represents a "continuous treatment" medical malpractice claim. Within the parlance of medical malpractice insurance, a "continuous treatment case" involves allegations of malpractice spanning more than one policy period when there is a single insurer involved. An "end-to-end case" involves allegations of malpractice spanning more than one policy period when there are two or more insurers involved. Because of Argonaut's relatively brief appearance as malpractice insurer for MSSNY physicians, it found itself involved in continuous treatment cases in which the plaintiff alleged malpractice beginning during the period of Wausau's coverage, extending through Argonaut's period of coverage, and continuing into MLMIC's coverage. This put Argonaut into a relationship with the other two insurance companies regarding, among other things, the costs of defending against the action (e.g., attorneys' fees, investigation expenses, and so on). A continuous treatment case alleging malpractice beginning during the policy year 1 July 1974 through 30 June 1975 and extending thereafter concerned only Argonaut and MLMIC, since Wausau had dropped out of the picture. A question of obvious mutual concern, then, involved the allocation of defense costs among insurers in end-to-end cases. Until February, 1987, Argonaut shared end-to-end defense costs equally with Wausau and MLMIC (or with MLMIC only, if the malpractice claim did not arise until after Wausau's coverage had ceased). However, during that month Argonaut put both Wausau and MLMIC on notice that it would no longer allocate end-to-end defense costs equally when the policy periods of the respective insurers were unequal. Both MLMIC and Wausau maintained that the prior agreement to allocate defense costs equally had bound Argonaut; and the two companies therefore instructed defense attorneys handling such cases to bill the fees and expenses on an equal basis among the insurance companies concerned. Since February, 1987, Argonaut had continued to pay on that basis, under protest and with all rights reserved, to avoid the resultant prejudice to itself and its insureds if Argonaut had placed defense counsel in the center of this conflict among the insurance companies. Argonaut subsequently commenced this action for declaratory and injunctive relief and for restitution of the defense costs paid by Argonaut under protest in excess of its pro rata share in end-to-end coverage cases. Subsequently, the court dismissed Wausau from the action. Argonaut and MLMIC continued to litigate the issue, culminating in their cross-motions for summary judgment. Argonaut argued that the alleged agreement that bound it to share end-to-end defense costs equally was unenforceable under the Statute of Frauds.

ISSUE   Did an exchange of memoranda that had given rise to an alleged agreement between Argonaut and MLMIC to share equally the expenses of defending overlapping coverage claims fall within the Statute of Frauds because it involved an agreement that could not be performed within one year from the making thereof?

HOLDING   No. Because the companies could have disposed of each malpractice claim falling within their coverage by motion, settlement, or trial within one year, the Statute of Frauds did not cover the alleged agreement. Hence, the agreement was enforceable against Argonaut.

REASONING   Argonaut contends that its purported agreement to share defense costs equally with MLMIC falls within the Statute of Frauds of New York, which provides in part that "a. Every agreement, promise or undertaking is void, unless it or some note or memorandum thereof be in writing, and subscribed by the party to be charged therewith, or by his lawful agent, if such agreement, promise or undertaking: 1. By its terms is not to be performed within one year from the making thereof. . . ." Argonaut further maintains that the exchange of correspondence quoted earlier is not sufficient to satisfy the statute. In this case, however, the alleged agreement does not fall within the Statute of Frauds. The provision on which Argonaut relies applies to an agreement that "by its terms" could not be performed within one year. Unless the wording of the agreement requires that construction, the agreement does not fall within the statute. In the case at bar, the parties could have disposed of each malpractice claim falling within Argonaut's coverage by motion, settlement, or trial within one year. Such a result remains unlikely, but likelihood is not the issue. Application of the Statute of Frauds depends on the explicit terms of the agreement. To fall outside the Statute of Frauds in New York, the contract must be one that by its terms can be performed within a year—even if, as a practical matter, it were well nigh impossible of performance within a year. Therefore, the agreement to share expenses, which Argonaut allegedly entered into with MLMIC, does not fall within the Statute of Frauds. But that does not end the inquiry: It must still appear that the exchange of correspondence has given rise to a binding contract. In considering Argonaut's theory as pleaded in the complaint, the malpractice cases forming the basis for this action involve only those cases in which the malpractice plaintiff alleges negligence during Argonaut's one-year policy and also alleges continued treatment and negligence during the period of two or more of the successive annual policies issued by MLMIC. Malpractice during the year of Argonaut's coverage and only during the first succeeding year of MLMIC's coverage would, even on Argonaut's theory, result in an even allocation of the costs of defense. Although Argonaut bases its claim primarily on its perception of fairness, MLMIC resists anything other than the equal division of the costs of defense. Consequently, MLMIC contends that in an exchange of correspondence beginning in 1977, Argonaut agreed to the equal division of defense costs among the insurance companies concerned. The evidence shows that a series of letters between Argonaut's claims supervisor, Marvin Kipnes, and his counterpart at MLMIC, John Andreotta, culminated in a 10 July 1979 letter from Kipnes stating, among other things, that the companies had "both reaffirmed [their] willingness to participate jointly in the investigation and defense of cases involving end-to-end coverage, whenever possible, and share equally in the expenses associated with same." To implement these procedures, Argonaut's Malpractice Claim Department prepared a draft letter to be sent to MLMIC with respect to malpractice claims falling within the joint concerns of the two companies. One line in this letter stated, "Obviously, we have an end-to-end coverage situation. As such, we have agreed to share equally in the expenses associated with the instigation and defense of this matter. . . ." Courts must determine whether an exchange of memoranda between the parties will give rise to a binding and enforceable contract by examining (1) the language of the agreement; (2) the context of the negotiations; (3) the existence of open terms; (4) partial performance; and (5) the necessity of putting the agreement in final form, as indicated by the customary form of such transactions. Of those factors, the first, "the language of the agreement," remains the most important. In the case at bar, Kipnes's exchange of correspondence with Andreotta clearly expressed an intent by Argonaut to be bound by the procedures Kipnes himself suggested. In the 24 October 1977 letter, Kipnes characterized his suggestions, including the equal division of defense costs, as "proposals" and recommended them to Andreotta as "a means of standardizing these procedures" between the insurance companies involved. In his 4 November 1977 reply on behalf of MLMIC, Andreotta noted his "full agreement with the approach" proposed by Kipnes and stated that he had even circulated copies of Argonaut's 24 October 1977 letter and copies of his response to his staff so that they could have "this correspondence to serve as a guideline for future activity." Argonaut's subsequent correspondence, including the drafting of the form letter to be used in processing claims, implemented Kipnes's proposal, to which Andreotta had agreed. Thus, "partial performance" of the agreement by Argonaut is evident; and the "context of the negotiations" consists of the insurance companies' attempts to work out guidelines and procedures for the prompt and efficient handling of claims. Hence, a number of factors favor the conclusion that Argonaut and MLMIC entered into a binding agreement for the division of defense costs. And because this agreement can be performed within one year from the date of its making, the contract falls outside the Statute of Frauds.

Some jurisdictions allow recovery for oral contracts that would otherwise be unenforceable because they extend for periods longer than one year when one party to the contract will be able to complete its performance within one year, even though the other party will be unable to do so. Courts may also apply promissory estoppel, which we learned about in earlier chapters, to allow recovery for otherwise unenforceable contracts.

Promises by Executors and Administrators of Estates   Promises by executors and administrators of estates to pay estate claims out of their own personal funds must be in writing to be enforceable. Since such agreements would be relatively unusual, the courts require a writing as evidence that the parties actually reached such an agreement.

Promises Made in Consideration of Marriage   Like the previous category, unilateral promises to pay money or to transfer property in consideration of a promise to marry are so uncommon that the law requires that such promises also be in writing in order to be enforceable. If the Benson family promises to pay $20,000 and to transfer the ownership of their condominium in Florida to Jim Lloyd if Jim promises to marry their daughter, Celie, the Bensons' promise must be in writing, according to the Statute of Frauds. By analogy, antenuptial (or prenuptial) agreements, which couples enter into before marriage and which typically spell out the disposition of the marital property should the marriage end in divorce, must ordinarily also be in writing if they are to be enforceable.

Contracts for Sales of Goods Priced at $500 or More   In addition to the five common law categories of contracts that have to be in writing to be enforceable under the Statute of Frauds that we have just discussed, the Uniform Commercial Code also has several provisions that implicate the Statute of Frauds. The most important of these is UCC Section 2-201, which states that contracts for sales of goods priced at $500 or more are not enforceable unless there is a writing sufficient to indicate that a contract for sale has been made between the parties and the writing is signed by the person against whom enforcement of the contract is sought. Therefore, according to the Statute of Frauds, a contract for a sale of produce—since the Code would classify produce as *goods* (i.e., identifiable, movable, personal property)—priced at $500 or more must be in writing. The Code further states that a writing is *not* insufficient if it omits or incorrectly states a term agreed on, but courts will refuse to enforce the agreement beyond the quantity of goods mentioned in such writing.

Under Section 2-201, however, courts will enforce oral contracts if (1) the goods are to be specially manufactured for the buyer and are not suitable for sale to others in the ordinary course of the seller's business, (2) the buyer makes a partial payment or a partial acceptance (although the contract will be enforced only for the portion of goods paid for or accepted), or (3) the party being sued admits in court (or in court documents) that a contract was made for a certain quantity of goods.

The Statute of Frauds section in the Code also contains a novel provision that may trap the unaware merchant. A **merchant** who receives a signed written confirmation (for example, "This is to confirm our sale to you of 2000 bushels of apples, #6 grade, at $1.25/bushel, delivery Tuesday, /s/ Seller") and does not object to it in writing within ten days is bound to the contract. The policy underlying this result is a familiar one: valid oral contract on the terms stated must exist if the other party (who, as a merchant, is considered a "pro") does not object to the confirmation. The moral of this section of the Code is: Answer your mail, merchants!

Merchant   A person who deals in goods of the kind, or otherwise, through his or her occupation, holds himself or herself out as having knowledge or skill peculiar to the practice or goods involved in the transaction.

Writing

As we have seen in other contexts, the writing required to satisfy the Statute of Frauds may be rather minimal. It may take the form of letters, telegrams, receipts, or memoranda. The writing must, at a minimum, identify the parties to the agreement, the subject matter of the agreement, and all material terms and conditions. Several writings may be pieced together as long as they all refer to the same transaction.

Signature

Similarly, anything intended by the parties as a signature will suffice to satisfy the Statute of Frauds. This would, of course, include written signatures; but courts have even held stamped signatures or stationery letterheads to be sufficient. The memorandum need not be signed by both parties as long as the party against whom enforcement is sought (or the party's authorized agent) has signed.

Notice how the court utilized these principles in deciding the following case.

Barber & Ross Co. v. Lifetime Doors, Inc.
810 F.2d 1276 (4th Cir. 1987), *cert. denied* 108 S.Ct. 86 (1987)

FACTS   Barber & Ross (B & R) purchases millwork products, including doors, from manufacturers, prepares them for installation in new homes, and sells them to new home builders. Lifetime Doors, Inc. (Lifetime) is a large manufacturer of doors. In 1982, B & R began to buy various types of doors from Lifetime. In early 1983, Lifetime supplied B & R with sales literature that promised new purchasers "continuous production availability . . . in full proportion to monthly needs" that would ensure that purchasers could "order flexible quantities" in shipments of a "desired number" if they joined Lifetime's VIP Club. B & R's president entered into an oral agreement with Lifetime whereby Lifetime promised to supply B & R's requirements of four truckloads of six-panel doors each month, in return for which B & R would purchase doors exclusively from Lifetime. From the middle of March to the middle of May that year, B & R purchased both flush and six-panel doors exclusively from Lifetime under this agreement. However, in May, Lifetime suggested that B & R should purchase the six-panel doors from other manufacturers owing to Lifetime's shortages of these types of doors. In July, Lifetime instituted an "allocation system" that tied purchases of the more popular six-panel doors to sales of the less desirable flush doors. This system caused B & R to buy more flush doors than it needed and simultaneously resulted in B & R's receiving fewer six-panel doors. In September, B & R terminated its contractual relationship with Lifetime, citing the negative effects on B & R's business caused by Lifetime's policy. B & R then sued Lifetime, claiming that Lifetime's allocation system had violated the antitrust laws and that Lifetime had breached the requirements contract between the parties. The trial court awarded B & R $2.1 million on these claims. On appeal, Lifetime argued that there could be no breach of contract because the alleged requirements contract was unenforceable under the Statute of Frauds.

ISSUE   Was the alleged contract unenforceable under the Statute of Frauds?

HOLDING   No. There was sufficient writing to indicate that the parties had formed a contract for the sale of goods; and this writing had been signed by the party against whom enforcement was sought.

REASONING   The written sales brochures Lifetime had given to B & R met the requirements of the Statute of Frauds's signature requirement because the Lifetime Doors trademark that appeared on the documents was sufficient to authenticate the brochures. The writings also stated a sufficiently definite quantity for purposes of the statute because they referred to meeting the purchaser's needs. To be enforceable under this category of the Statute of Frauds, a writing must provide a basis for believing that the offered oral evidence rests on a real transaction. The writing need not, however, conclusively establish the existence of a contract to fulfill the requirements of the Statute of Frauds. Because the writings in this case had promised that Lifetime would meet the monthly needs of B & R, they were sufficient to support B & R's claim that an oral agreement had been reached to form a requirements contract.

Table 14.1 explains the scope of the Statute of Frauds, the elements required to find coverage, and exceptions to the general rules.

TABLE 14.1   The Statute of Frauds

TYPES OF CONTRACTS COVERED (AND WHICH MUST BE IN WRITING)	ELEMENTS	EXCEPTIONS
1. Contracts to answer for the debt of another.	1. There are three parties. 2. There are two promises, one original (debtor to creditor) and the other collateral (third party guarantor to creditor). 3. The second promise is a promise to accept only secondary liability resulting from the default of another. 4. The intent of the parties determines whether a three-party transaction involves a collateral contract (which must be in writing) or an original contract (which can be oral yet still enforceable).	1. Novations and other three-party transactions are not guaranty contracts but joint, original contracts. 1. The "leading object" or "main purpose" doctrine.
2. Contracts for interests in land.	1. The agreement involves buying, selling, or transferring interests in land. 2. Leases, easements, and sales agreements about standing timber and buildings attached to the land are also covered.	1. Doctrine of part performance.
3. Contracts not to be performed within one year of the date of their making.	1. Contracts in which it is impossible to perform the contract completely within one year of the *date* of the creation of the contract are involved.	1. Courts may circumvent the application of the statute by resort to the fiction that it is *possible* (albeit not probable) for the contracts to be performed within one year from the date of their making. 2. Part performance by one party. 3. Circumstances that justify the application of promissory estoppel.
4. Contracts for a sale of goods priced at $500 or more (UCC §2-201).	1. The contract involves a sale of goods.	1. Between merchants, a written confirmation sent by one party to another must be objected to by the other within 10 days or the Statute of Frauds will be satisfied.

TABLE 14.1   continued

TYPES OF CONTRACTS COVERED (AND WHICH MUST BE IN WRITING)	ELEMENTS	EXCEPTIONS
		2. Oral contracts involving (a) specially manufactured goods not readily resalable in the ordinary course of the seller's business, (b) goods for which payment has been received, (c) goods for which acceptance has been made, or (d) an admission in a court proceeding by the person against whom enforcement is sought that a contract for sale was made, are enforceable.
	2. The price of the goods must be at least $500. 3. The writing is not insufficient if it omits or incorrectly states an agreed-on term, but the contract will be unenforceable beyond the quantity of goods shown in the writing. 4. The writing must be signed by the person against whom enforcement is sought or the authorized agent or broker of that person.	
5. Promises by executors and administrators of estates.	1. The executors or administrators have promised to pay estate claims out of their own personal funds.	
6. Promises made in consideration of marriage.	1. One person has promised another person to pay a given amount or otherwise to perform a contractual duty to induce that person to enter a marriage.	

SUMMARY

Interpretation is the process of determining the meaning of words and other manifestations of intent that the parties have used in forging their agreement. Over the years, certain standards and rules of interpretation, based on whether the contract is totally integrated or partially integrated, have evolved. A totally integrated contract represents the parties' final and complete statement of their agreement and cannot be contradicted. Similarly, a partially integrated contract is intended to be the parties' final statement, but it is incomplete. It may be supplemented with consistent, additional terms. The conduct of the parties and usages of trade may aid in contract interpretation.

The parol evidence rule states that oral evidence is not admissible to alter, add to, or vary the terms of an integrated, written contract. However, the parol evidence rule will not be applied in some circumstances: partially integrated contracts; agreements suggesting mistake, duress, or fraud; ambiguity; conditions precedent; or in some commercial contexts.

In accordance with the Statute of Frauds, certain types of contracts must be in writing to be enforceable. These include collateral contracts, contracts for sales or transfers of interests in land, contracts not to be performed within one year from the date of their making, contracts for sales of goods priced at $500 or more, promises of executors and administrators of estates, and promises made in consideration of marriage. However, very little in the way of a memorandum or signature is necessary to satisfy the Statute of Frauds.

DISCUSSION QUESTIONS

1. What is the process of contract interpretation?
2. What is the legal difference between a totally integrated contract and a partially integrated contract?
3. Name any three rules of interpretation.
4. How are conduct and usages of trade important in contract interpretation?
5. Give an original example of a contract interpretation problem.
6. What is the parol evidence rule?
7. Name and discuss the exceptions to the parol evidence rule.

8. Explain the basis for the Statute of Frauds, historically and currently.
9. What are the most important characteristics of a collateral contract, or a contract to guarantee the debt of another? Also, explain the exception to the rule that collateral contracts must be in writing.
10. Describe the exceptions to the rule that a contract for a sale of goods priced at $500 or more must be in writing.

CASE PROBLEMS

1. Marvin Mann had an insurance contract with State Farm Mutual Automobile Insurance Company (State Farm) whereby the company insured Mann against "losses" to his car, including "theft." The insurance policy specifically excluded coverage for losses to the auto occurring while the auto was in the possession of

another person under a conditional sale or purchase agreement. Mann had transferred possession of the auto to another individual in exchange for a personal check for the purchase price in the course of what Mann believed was a sale of the auto. However, the check was returned to Mann owing to insufficient funds. The "buyer" later admitted that he knew the check would be dishonored and had intended to defraud Mann into parting with possession of the auto. The auto was never recovered. State Farm denied liability under the two provisions noted. Would you agree with State Farm's interpretation of the contract? (*Mann v. State Farm Mutual Automobile Insurance Company,* 698 P.2d 925 [Okla. 1985].)

2. John Parkos and Sheila Searcy had signed a lease-purchase agreement in which Searcy had agreed to operate a restaurant on commercial premises owned by Parkos. When Parkos subsequently tried to evict Searcy, she argued that the written lease-purchase agreement entitled her to remain in possession. Parkos, in turn, asserted that the agreement was invalid under the Statute of Frauds because the agreement had incorrectly identified the lessor and lessee, had omitted the exhibit that would have described the real property in detail, and had omitted the price and terms of payment. Who had the better argument here, Parkos or Searcy? (*Parkos v. Searcy,* 589 A.2d 1197 [R.I. 1991].)

3. Pine Tree Electric Company, Inc. (Pine Tree), an electrical contractor, had for years bought electrical equipment and supplies from Graybar Electric Co., Inc. (Graybar), an electrical equipment and parts supplier. In 1978, however, Graybar cut off credit sales to Pine Tree because of Pine Tree's failure to pay its bills on time. In order to help its cash flow problems, Pine Tree solicited investors. Hollis Sawyer, a relative of one of Pine Tree's employees, advanced about $300,000 to Pine Tree. Sawyer effected a reorganization of the company in which he ended up with all the voting power as the sole preferred stockholder and as vice-president of the firm. Pine Tree shortly thereafter resumed its relationship with Graybar but soon missed two monthly payments owed to Graybar. At a meeting of Pine Tree and Graybar executives devoted to straightening out these credit problems, Sawyer allegedly told the Graybar representatives that if Pine Tree did not pay its account, he would. Graybar allegedly wrote a letter five days later memorializing the outcome of these discussions. Following this meeting, Graybar reopened Pine Tree's line of credit. When Pine Tree was later forced into invol-

untary bankruptcy, Graybar sued Sawyer on the basis of this alleged guarantee. Sawyer argued that no contract of guarantee had been formed and that if one had been formed, the Statute of Frauds barred Graybar's suit. Who was correct? (*Graybar Electric Co., Inc. v. Sawyer,* 485 A.2d 1384 [Me. 1985].)

4. The City of Yonkers sued Otis Elevator Company (Otis) for breaking an alleged promise to remain in the city. The city argued that in 1976 it had obtained approximately $12 million of urban renewal funding to allow Otis to expand and modernize its plant. The city asserted that Otis's receipt of these funds imposed on Otis an obligation to remain in Yonkers for a "reasonable period of time, i.e., not less than 60 years." Thus, when Otis attempted to leave Yonkers for New Jersey in 1981, the city brought suit against the company. The city at trial ultimately conceded that no written contract imposed that obligation on Otis, nor had Otis made any express oral promise to that effect. Could a court nonetheless impose such an obligation on Otis, or would such a result violate the Statute of Frauds? (*City of Yonkers v. Otis Elevator Company,* 649 F. Supp. 716 [S.D. N.Y. 1986].)

5. Since 1940, Jacob Heller had occupied two suites of law offices at 51 Chambers Street, New York City. In 1965, New York City acquired title to the building in a condemnation proceeding. From 1965 to 1980, Heller was a month-to-month tenant. In 1980, Heller and George Croucher, then director of the Bureau of Property Management for New York City, entered into an oral agreement whereby Heller agreed to relinquish Suite 1409 on the condition that the monthly rent for Suite 1425 remain at $201 and that the term of tenancy last until Heller died. The city nevertheless attempted to terminate the lease in 1984, when Heller was eighty years old. Heller argued that his tenancy was protected by the oral lease, but the city contended that the Statute of Frauds barred any oral contract that by its terms could not be performed within one year from the date of its making. Who would win? Why? (*City of New York v. Heller,* 487 N.Y.S.2d 288 [N.Y. Civ. Ct. 1985].)

6. Mr. and Mrs. George Christou had resided at Rose Hill with George's brother, James, for years and had been paying half of the mortgage and real estate taxes during that time. When James moved out, the Christous began paying the entire mortgage and the full amount of the taxes, even though James's name appeared as owner on the deed to Rose Hill. Mrs. Christou contended that these payments had resulted from a 1981

oral agreement whereby George had given up his interest in the family bakery in exchange for James's giving up his interest in Rose Hill. James subsequently refused to convey Rose Hill to Mrs. Christou and George and instead allegedly put Rose Hill in the name of Lena Christou, George and James's mother. At that point, when George refused to join Mrs. Christou in her efforts to enforce the 1981 agreement, Mrs. Christou alone sued George, James, and Lena. Mrs. Christou argued that these mortgage and real estate tax payments constituted part performance of such magnitude as to take the alleged oral contract to convey Rose Hill to her and George out of the Statute of Frauds. Was she correct? (*Christou* v. *Christou*, 487 N.Y.S. 2d 192 [N.Y. App. Div. 1985].)

7. In the fall of 1984, the Corinth Gas and Water Department was seeking a building suitable for housing its maintenance department and for storing its equipment and spare parts. In December, 1984, John Putt approached Wayne McGee, department manager, and Dennis Coleman, a department employee, and told them his building was for sale for $100,000. On 14 January 1985, McGee appeared at the regular monthly meeting of the Utilities Commission and reported his conversation with Putt. After negotiations and several inspections, on 11 March 1985, the Commission formally approved the purchase, as evidenced by the following minutes entry: "Commissioner Martin reported that they had obtained the agreement of John Putt to sell the building on Old Highway 45 (Tate Street) to the City for $95,000.00 with him to retain the shed immediately north of the building." The minutes were signed by commission officers and approved at the 8 April 1985 meeting. However, the minutes failed to reflect any agreement between the commission and Putt regarding any possible outstanding encumbrances or judgments or the possible proration of taxes. In time, the commission turned the matter over to its lawyer in order to conclude the transaction. On examining the title to the property and checking the courthouse records, the commission's lawyer found judgment liens of approximately $16,000 against the property. After Putt had objected to the city's deducting this amount and a prorated tax for 1985 from the $95,000, the city refused to conclude the transaction. When Putt sued the city for breach of contract, the city asserted the Statute of Frauds as its defense, arguing that no written memorandum memorializing the alleged agreement existed. Could a court recognize the minutes of the commission's meeting as a

sufficient memorandum to satisfy the Statute of Frauds? (*Putt* v. *City of Corinth*, 579 So.2d 534 [Miss. 1991].)

8. National Microsales Corporation (NMC) is a Connecticut corporation engaged in the business of buying and selling computer output microfilming (COM) equipment. Chase Manhattan Bank, N.A. (Chase) a national bank, entered into negotiations in 1988 with NMC to sell some of its used COM equipment to NMC for resale. When Chase subsequently sold the equipment to a third party, NMC filed a breach of contract action against Chase. In June, 1989, Chase moved for summary judgment on the basis of the Statute of Frauds. NMC cross-moved for summary judgment, striking Chase's affirmative defense of the Statute of Frauds on the ground that the "merchant's exception" (i.e., Section 2-201[2]) to the statute covered these contracts. Although a factual dispute as to whether Chase was a "merchant" for UCC purposes existed, the evidence showed that Chase had disposed of $6.5 million dollars' worth of COM equipment. NMC also pointed out Chase's adoption of uniform procedures for purchasing new equipment and disposing of used equipment and other "surplus fixed assets," including procedures for soliciting bids from prospective purchasers of surplus property. However, George J. Stehle, Chase's vice-president in charge of office purchasing and contracts administration, testified that Chase never purchases goods for resale and that Chase has no specialized knowledge concerning the goods that it buys for its own use. He also stated that Chase is unfamiliar with the market for the equipment that it purchases and that when it disposes of surplus goods, it generally sells them to resellers, rather than end users, and usually sells the equipment for less than fair market value. Did Chase's status as a merchant preclude it from relying on the Statute of Frauds as an affirmative defense to the buyer's action for breach of contract? (*National Microsales Corporation* v. *Chase Manhattan Bank, N.A.,* 761 F. Supp. 304 [S.D.N.Y. 1991].)

9. Attorney Thomas Drake entered into an oral contract with Perry Skundor according to which Drake had agreed to represent Skundor's adult son, David, in a felony case. Although Skundor had paid Drake a $350 retainer, had secured Drake as his son's counsel, had paid for his son's polygraph examination, and had investigated drug rehabilitation centers for his son, he refused at the time of the trial seven months later to sign a promissory note guaranteeing the payment of his son's legal fees. Rather, Skundor insisted that his son was

responsible for paying them. Drake, however, never received any payment from David. Could Perry Skundor, the father, successfully assert the Statute of Frauds as his defense when Drake sued him for the unpaid attorneys' fees? (*Drake, Phillips, Kuenzli & Clark* v. *Skundor*, 501 N.E.2d 88 [Ohio App. 1986].)

10. Earl Maddox brought an action against his former employer, Corbett Plywood Company, and its parent company, Baxley Veneer and Clete Company (Baxley), alleging breach of an employment contract. Maddox asserted that when the lumber mill's owner, Horace Corbett, had recruited him to work as general manager of the mill, Corbett had promised him that he could stay on the job until age 65. Maddox had left other lucrative employment to accept the job at the mill and had worked at the mill for two years without taking a vacation. Sometimes he had worked long hours. However, no written employment contract existed between the parties. When Corbett died in 1981, the mill fired Maddox one month later. Maddox sued for breach of contract. At trial, the employer moved for a directed verdict, arguing that Georgia's Statute of Frauds makes oral contracts for employment longer than one year unenforceable. Maddox responded that the contract was enforceable because he had partially performed the contract within the meaning of a Georgia statute stating that oral contracts of employment for longer than one year are unenforceable unless "there has been part performance of the contract as would render it a fraud on the party refusing to comply if the court did not compel a performance." The trial court denied Baxley's motion for a directed verdict and refused to grant Baxley's requested instruction regarding what conduct would constitute part performance too insufficient to remove the contract from the operation of the Statute of Frauds. The jury returned a verdict in favor of Maddox for $87,000. Baxley subsequently appealed this verdict. Should the appellate court reverse the jury's verdict? (*Baxley Veneer and Clete Company* v. *Maddox*, 404 S.E.2d 554 [Ga. 1991].)

CHAPTER 15

The Rights of Third Parties

OUTLINE

ADDITION OF THIRD PARTIES TO THE RELATIONSHIP

A contract influences the legal rights of the two parties who enter it. It may also influence the financial position of other people. In some situations, these other people are so significant in the contract that they have legal rights under the contract and can file a lawsuit to enforce these contractual rights. The two kinds of situations are those in which the third party is significant when the contract is initially formed and those in which the third party is added later. This chapter deals with whether these other people have enforceable legal rights.

THIRD-PARTY BENEFICIARY CONTRACTS

Persons and corporations that receive rights in a contract to which they have not agreed are called *beneficiaries*. It is really more appropriate to call this kind of beneficiary a third *person* because the additional person is not a *party* to the contract. However, we shall use the common terminology and refer to this person as a third party.

The two people who enter into the contract are commonly called the promisor and the promisee. The *promisor* is the party who promises to perform; the *promisee* is the party to whom that promise is made. Often in third-party beneficiary contracts, the promise is to deliver goods to or perform a service directly for a third party. For example, Jane was very busy; to save time in shopping for a Father's Day present and mailing it to her father in St. Cloud, Minnesota, she ordered an expensive shirt from the Neiman-Marcus catalog to be gift wrapped and delivered to her father. This arrangement is a third-party beneficiary contract. Her father is the third-party beneficiary. A beneficiary does not need to know about the contract in order for it to be valid.

Because these third parties are called beneficiaries, it is generally assumed that they receive something beneficial and good, but this is not always the case. The legal requirement for an intended beneficiary is that at least one of the contracting parties, usually the promisee, intended to have goods delivered to or services performed for that third party. The third party may not necessarily desire them. The beneficiary may, in fact, be very displeased on receipt of the goods or services, as when a company offers to throw a cream pie in the face of any third-party beneficiary that the promisee designates.

An Incidental Beneficiary

Probably the most important factor in determining the rights of a third party is whether or not the third party is an intended or an incidental beneficiary. When the original parties to the contract, or at least one of them, *meant* to affect a noncontracting person by establishing the contract, the noncontracting person is an *intended beneficiary*. Intended beneficiaries have legal rights.

If the benefit or action to the noncontracting party was *accidental,* or *not intended,* this party is an *incidental beneficiary.*

As an example of an incidental beneficiary, suppose an owner of a vacant city lot decides to build a high-rise garage on it. The owner enters into a contract with a builder to construct the garage. The neighboring lot has a high-rise office building on it, so the owner of the office building will benefit financially by the construction of the garage. This person is an incidental beneficiary, because neither the builder nor the original owner intended to benefit that person.

An Intended Beneficiary

An intended beneficiary does not have to be mentioned by name in the contract. It is sufficient for the parties to *clearly intend* to give the beneficiary rights under the agreement. In the absence of a clear expression of such an intent, the contracting parties are presumed to act for themselves. Sometimes the intended beneficiary may be one person from a group of people for whose benefit the contract was established. Automobile insurance, for example, is a contract between an insurance company and a driver, but it is also partially for the benefit of other drivers and pedestrians who share the road.

The distinction between intended and incidental beneficiaries is discussed in the case that follows; the legal relationships in the case are diagrammed in Figure 15.1.

Allan v. *Bekins Archival Service, Inc.*
154 Cal. Rptr. 458 (Cal. App. 1979)

FACTS Allan was the announcer and master of ceremonies in the television series called "Celebrity Bowling." He also had a partnership interest in the show, which was produced from 1970 to 1976. The producer of the show entered into a contract with Bekins Archival Service to store, inventory, and ship the videotapes of the series to distributors and tape-duplicating firms when authorized by the producer. Bekins was to receive a monthly fee for this service. The producer deposited 114 tapes with Bekins.

Bekins shipped tapes 1 through 26, as authorized. The tapes were never returned but Bekins's monthly inventory

FIGURE 15.1 Legal Relationships in *Allan* v. *Bekins Archival Services, Inc.*

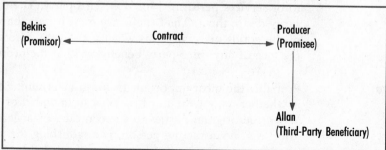

reported that the tapes had been returned to Bekins. Consequently, the producer destroyed the duplicates of these tapes. Due to the loss of these tapes, the producer was unable to perform an agreement to have the series rebroadcast. If the series had been rebroadcast, Allan would have been entitled to royalty payments. Bekins had solicited business by representing that it had a specialized facility and that it recognized the high monetary value of the tapes.

ISSUE   Was Allan an intended third-party beneficiary of the contract between the producer and Bekins?

HOLDING   Yes. It can be inferred that the contract was made for Allan's benefit.

REASONING   To be an intended (express) beneficiary a person need not be named in the contract. If Allan can show that he is a person or member of a class for whose benefit the contract was made, he should recover. The intent to benefit the third party need not be manifested by the promisor (Bekins). It is sufficient if the promisor realizes that the promisee (the producer) has this intent. The decision may not extend to bit actors in a series, who have a smaller financial interest in the tapes.

A Donee Beneficiary

The rights of an intended third-party beneficiary in a contract *may* be affected by the relationship between the promisee and the third party. If the promisee *means to make a gift to the third party*, the third party is a *donee beneficiary*. Life insurance policies are excellent examples of third-party beneficiary contracts. If a husband purchases a $100,000 life insurance policy from Prudential Insurance Company of America and names his wife as the beneficiary, she is a donee beneficiary. The husband has no legal obligation to purchase this insurance. (He might be under a legal obligation to purchase life insurance under some marital contracts or divorce decrees, but this is uncommon.) He is, in effect, planning a gift to his wife that will take effect at his death. She is a donee beneficiary. This example is shown in Figure 15.2.

Prudential Insurance Company, the promisor, promises to deliver $100,000 to the promisee's wife if the promisee dies under situations covered by the policy. If Prudential refuses to pay, the wife could sue the company directly

FIGURE 15.2   Donee Beneficiary

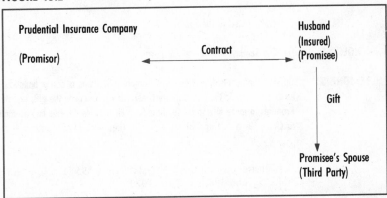

as an intended third party. Prudential (the promisor) could use the same legal defenses against the wife (third party) as it could against the husband (promisee). These defenses might include lack of capacity to enter into a contract; lack of mutual assent; illegality in the contract; mistake in contract formation; fraudulent statements about the promisee's health; an improperly formed contract; or cancellation of the policy. The promisor would not have to make a payment if the cause of death was excluded by the terms of the contract. In addition, the courts usually disallow recovery by the beneficiary if the promisee has failed to perform his or her duty under the contract.[1]

According to the law in some states, the donee beneficiary's rights cannot be terminated after the contract is made. However, the promisee can still defeat the rights of the donee by not performing his or her contractual obligations.[2] In other states, the beneficiary's right is limited to situations in which the beneficiary knows about the contract and has accepted it verbally or by reliance on its terms. If the beneficiary has accepted the contract, the beneficiary has a *vested* interest in it. In these states, a beneficiary with a vested interest must consent before there can be a rescission of the contract. This rule applies to both donee and **creditor beneficiaries**. Even so, a donee beneficiary cannot prevent the promisee from taking some action that will defeat the rights of the donee beneficiary; for example, breaching the contract by refusing to pay for the goods or services.

In the following case, the court considered the legal rights of a donee beneficiary who was promised a gift of a house.

Creditor beneficiary   A person who is entitled to performance by the promisee.

Oman v. Yates
422 P.2d 489 (Wash. 1967)

FACTS   The Sundays agreed to sell a house to Oman. Oman signed the contract, but under the agreement she was not going to pay for the property; Rheims was going to pay the *complete* purchase price to the Sundays, in cash. Rheims wrote a check for the down payment, but his bank account lacked sufficient funds to cover the check. The Sundays did not receive any payment on the contract. Rheims died, and Yates was named the executor of Rheims's estate.

ISSUE   Is Oman entitled to the house?

HOLDING   No. The Sundays did not receive payment.

REASONING   Oman is not entitled to specific performance. She was a donee beneficiary and could not require Rheims or his estate to complete the gift. Delivery is necessary to complete the gift, and the property was never delivered to Oman. Promises to make gifts in the future are not enforceable. Rheims had no contractual obligation to deliver the property to Oman. In a suit against the promisor, third-party beneficiaries have the same rights as the promisee. Oman

---

[1] 2 Williston on Contracts, 3rd ed., Section 395 (1959), p. 1066.
[2] Ibid., Section 396, pp. 1067, 1070.

could not require the Sundays to transfer the property to her, as they were not paid. Defenses that are valid against the promisee are valid against the third-party beneficiary.

The Sundays could have requested specific performance, but they requested monetary damages instead. A settlement was worked out and they received monetary damages from Rheims's estate.

A Creditor Beneficiary

Mortgage insurance Insurance that will pay off a mortgage on a home if a contingency occurs.

If the promisee owed a legal duty to the third party, the third party is a *creditor beneficiary.* Again, a life insurance policy is an excellent example. A working couple wishes to purchase a house with a $100,000 mortgage. The bank is willing to lend them $100,000 based on the value of the home and both of their salaries. Since the bank feels that the husband could not afford the monthly payments without his wife's salary, the bank makes the loan contingent on the purchase of **mortgage insurance** on her life. She agrees to purchase $100,000 of mortgage insurance from Metropolitan Life Insurance Company. The bank is a creditor beneficiary. This arrangement is diagrammed in Figure 15.3.

If the wife dies during the term of the mortgage, the bank can sue Metropolitan directly on the insurance contract. Metropolitan can use any defenses that it had against the wife as defenses against the bank.

If the wife tries to cancel the policy, the bank could successfully sue the wife, because canceling the insurance policy and not replacing it would be a breach of the contract between the bank and the wife. The bank, however, would probably allow her to substitute another insurance policy from a different company if the coverage was essentially the same. In reality, if the bank does not trust the wife to make the premium payments, it will require her to make the payments through the bank; then the bank would know that the payments are being made.

The differences between donee and creditor beneficiaries are not great. They both have basically the same rights against the promisor. Although many

FIGURE 15.3 Creditor Beneficiary

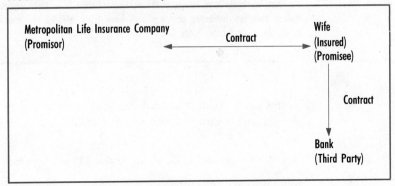

states say that the rights of a creditor beneficiary are directly derived from the promisee, courts usually provide the same type of protection for the donee beneficiary as they do for the creditor beneficiary. The only real differences are their rights against the promisee, and even these differences are becoming less pronounced. The distinction between creditor and donee beneficiaries is completely dropped by the *Restatement (Second) of Contracts*,[3] which relies solely on the distinction between intended and incidental beneficiaries. The donee-creditor distinction is also beginning to disappear in some states, such as California.[4]

A third party cannot successfully claim any better rights than those provided in the contract. The next case examines the importance of the underlying legal rights.

Harris v. Superior Court (Mirsaidi)
233 Cal. Rptr. 186 (Cal. App. 1986)

FACTS

Arbitration Submission of claim to people (arbitrators) who will determine rights.

The Harrises claimed that Dr. Mirsaidi was negligent in the birth of their daughter. They wished to have the dispute settled by **arbitration.** However, Dr. Mirsaidi wished to have the dispute settled by a court. The Harrises received medical care from Dr. Mirsaidi and Hawthorne Community Medical Group, Inc., under a prepaid health services program provided through Mr. Harris's employer. The enrollment form signed by Mr. Harris stated, "I agree that any claim asserted by a Member . . . against Maxicare, Hawthorne Community Medical Group, Inc., [three other entities], their employees or other contracting health professionals, pharmacies, or their employees for bodily injury to or death of a member, is subject to binding arbitration."

ISSUE

Did Dr. Mirsaidi have the right to choose either arbitration or litigation?

HOLDING

No. He was a third-party beneficiary of the contract entered into by Mr. Harris and Hawthorne Community Medical Group.

REASONING

The contract clause clearly provided that Hawthorne Community Medical Group was a party to the agreement. Hawthorne Community Medical Group could only provide medical care through its employees, like Dr. Mirsaidi. Dr. Mirsaidi could not accept patients and payments under the terms of the contract *and* deny the arbitration clause. He knew or should have known of the existence of the clause. Third parties cannot gain greater rights under the contract than the contracting parties already have. If Dr. Mirsaidi had been allowed to choose litigation, he would have been given greater rights.

In this case, the mother and daughter were also third-party beneficiaries under the insurance contract the father signed.

[3]*Restatement (Second) of Contracts*, Section 302 and Introductory Note to Chapter 14, at 438 and 439.
[4]*Allan* v. *Bekins Archival Service*, Inc., 154 Cal. Rptr. 458, at 463, footnote 8.

Analysis of Third-Party Beneficiary Contracts	In analyzing a situation involving a potential third party, the following questions should be addressed:

1. Was the additional person involved from the beginning, or was that person added later?
2. Did the promisee intend to benefit the third party, or was it an accident?
3. Was the promisee making a gift to the third party, or was the promisee fulfilling a contract obligation to the third party? |

DEFINING ASSIGNMENTS AND DELEGATIONS

If the third person becomes involved after the initial contract formation, that person is not a third-party beneficiary. Instead, the relationship may be either an assignment or a delegation. To understand the distinction between assignments and delegations, it is essential to remember the distinction between rights and duties. Contractual *rights* are the parts of the contract that a person is entitled to *receive*. Examples would be delivery of goods, payment for work completed, and discounts for early payment. Contractual *duties* are the parts of the contract that a person is obligated to *give*. These could include working an eight-hour day, paying 20 percent interest on credit card charges, and providing repair services. Rights can be assigned, and duties can be delegated. Although even judges and lawyers may be careless in their terminology, duties cannot be assigned. The rules of law dealing with delegation will always be applied to duties.

ASSIGNMENTS

An *assignment* occurs *when a person transfers a contractual right to someone else*. The transferor is called the *assignor,* and the recipient is called the *assignee*. After the assignment occurs, the assignor has completely lost all contractual rights. The assignor's right has been extinguished, and now it belongs exclusively to the assignee. The other party to the original contract, the promisor, now has to deliver the promised goods or services to the assignee. The assignee is the only party entitled to them.

For example, a tenant is renting a house from a landlord. Under the lease, the tenant must pay $400 per month for rent. The landlord is in default on a personal loan obtained from the bank and assigns the $400 per month rent payment to the bank. The landlord (the assignor) has given up the legal right to the money. That right now belongs exclusively to the assignee, the bank. This situation is diagrammed in Figure 15.4.

FIGURE 15.4   Assignment

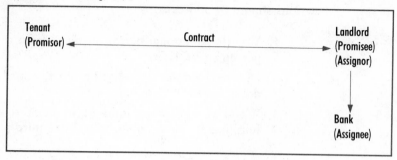

<table>
<tr><td>Tenant
(Promisor)</td><td>◄ —————— Contract —————— ►</td><td>Landlord
(Promisee)
(Assignor)</td></tr>
<tr><td></td><td></td><td>▼</td></tr>
<tr><td></td><td></td><td>Bank
(Assignee)</td></tr>
</table>

Formalities Required for Assignments

Generally, an assignment does not have to follow any particular format. Assignors must use words that indicate an intent to vest a present right in the contract to the assignee. This means that the assignor intends to transfer the right immediately, not at some time in the future. A writing is not required unless the state Statute of Frauds applies. This includes the Statute of Frauds provisions in the Uniform Commercial Code as adopted by the state. As with other contractual provisions, it is preferable to reduce the assignment to writing. The assignment must contain an adequate description of the rights that are being assigned. In the following case, the judge analyzed the requirements for an assignment.

Mission Valley East, Inc. v. County of Kern
174 Cal. Rptr. 300 (Cal. App. 1981)

FACTS   The county tax collector arranged for seven parcels of land to be sold at a public tax sale. Under applicable California law, the owners could file a claim to receive any excess proceeds received by the tax collector for one year after the sale. (Excess proceeds are the amounts the tax collector receives minus the taxes owed and the tax collector's costs.) Neal, the attorney for Mission Valley East, Inc., wrote the owners and offered them $100 each for their remaining interests in the parcels. He led them to believe that their interests were almost worthless and that his client had purchased the property at the tax sale and needed a quitclaim deed and an assignment to obtain title insurance. Mission Valley East, Inc., had not purchased the parcels. After buying the quitclaim deeds and assignments, Mission Valley East filed a claim for the excess proceeds. The assignors were not aware that they had the right to excess proceeds.

ISSUE   Did the assignments transfer to Mission Valley East, Inc., the right to the excess proceeds?

HOLDING   No. There was no showing of intent to make such an assignment.

REASONING   Personal rights to claim money are freely assignable, but proof of the intention to assign any rights must be clear and positive. The assignment must describe the subject matter with sufficient particularity to identify the rights assigned. In this case, the deeds limited the assignment to the assignor's rights in real property and did not include personal rights, such as the right to excess proceeds. The rights to the excess proceeds were not specifically mentioned in the assignment.

Consideration is not required in order to have a valid assignment. Although the assignee need not give up consideration in exchange for the contract right, consideration is generally present. This factor affects the legal relationship between the assignor and the assignee. That relationship can be either a contract or a gift. It is generally a contract, especially in business settings. In our earlier example, the landlord assigned the payments to the bank so the bank would not sue the landlord or take other action to collect. People in business are not in the habit of making gifts to other businesspeople. A gift assignment would occur, for example, if a sales representative for a concrete company assigned the 10 percent Christmas bonus he earned to his eldest daughter for her college education fund.

Notice of the Assignment

Since the assignment extinguishes the assignor's rights and creates rights for the assignee, one would assume that the promisor must be told about the assignment. Surprisingly, this is not a legal requirement; An assignment is perfectly valid even though the promisor is never informed. An assignee would want to give notice to the promisor for a number of reasons, particularly if the assignor is potentially unethical or dishonest.

If the promisor *has* received notice of the assignment and then pays the promisee or delivers performance to the promisee, the promisor will still be obligated to pay or deliver performance to the assignee. In many instances, the promisor is not told about the assignment, and the promisee receives the performance and transfers it to the assignee. If the promisor has not been given notice and the assignor receives performance and does not transfer it to the assignee, the assignee would have to take action against the assignor, who may have absconded with the funds.

In some cases, dishonest assignors have "benefited" by selling the *same* contract right to more than one assignee. Of course, if the second assignee has notice or knowledge of the prior assignment, that person will receive the assignment subject to the rights of the first assignee. In most cases the second assignee lacks notice. Dishonest assignors generally disappear with the funds and leave the innocent assignees to resolve their conflicting claims. Two theories are widely used by the courts to resolve these problems. One theory is that the first assignee to receive the assignment received all the rights; the assignor had nothing to assign to later assignees. This theory, commonly referred to as the *first-in-time approach* or the *American Rule,* is applied in some states. For example, if Anita, the promisee, assigned her right to Joel on January 1 and then assigned her right to Larry on January 15, Joel would receive the right according to this rule.

Other states apply the rule that the first assignee to actually give notice to the promisor receives the better right. This is called the *first-to-give-notice approach* or the *English Rule*. It is followed in California, Florida, and a few other states. In the prior example, if Larry had given notice to the promisor first, he would have prevailed under the English Rule. One of the policies underlying this rule is that a prudent assignee who is about to pay value for the assignment would check with the promisor. A promisor who had notice of earlier assignments would tell the prospective purchaser, and this step would prevent additional assignments. The advantage of giving notice should be obvious.

Under either rule of law, the assignor would be liable for fraud if he or she can be located with the money. However, there is nothing wrong with a promisee (assignor) dividing up the contract rights and assigning *different* contract rights to different assignees.

Nonassignable Rights

Assignments have become an important aspect of our business and financial structure. They are important techniques for selling goods and obtaining cash. A common business practice among retail outlets is to sell expensive items on time. The retailer assigns the monthly payments to a credit corporation in exchange for cash. The retailer then uses the cash to buy more merchandise. A common example of this practice occurs when a buyer purchases an automobile financed through a car dealership. Because of the importance of assignments in commercial transactions, courts are now predisposed to allow assignments. This favorable perspective is obvious in the courts' treatment of contract assignments. Assignments do not require the approval of the promisor. Even when the promisor vehemently opposes the assignment, the courts generally will allow it.

To prevent the assignment, the promisor must prove to the court that one of the following conditions exists:

1. The assignment would *materially* change the duty of the promisor.
2. The assignment would *materially* impair the chance of return performance.
3. The assignment would *materially* increase the burden or risk imposed by the contract.

The promisor must convince the court that he or she would be in a substantially worse position if the assignment were allowed. These requirements are included in Section 2-210(2) of the Uniform Commercial Code and are applicable unless the language of the contract contains other provisions.

When the assignment materially changes the promisor's duty, the promisor must perform a substantially different type or degree of work. Many assignments involve assigning monthly payments. As this simply requires that the promisor change the address on the monthly envelopes, the promisor's duty is not substantially different. As an example of a substantially different duty, suppose a promisor promised to paint the exterior of any one house and that this promise was made to Lynda, who owns a 1000-square-foot single-level house. Lynda assigns the right to Joanne, who owns a 2500-square-foot two-story house. The promisor could convince the court that this assignment materially affects the promisor's duty.

If the assignment impairs the chance of return performance, it increases the chance that the promisor will not receive consideration from the promisee. For example, Chris wanted to have her portrait painted. She located a talented but struggling artist, John, who would paint the portrait for $200. John explained that he needed the money to buy canvas and quality oil paint before he started. Chris agreed to pay him the money on the first of the month. John was to start the portrait on the fifteenth. Now John wants to assign that payment to his landlord for unpaid rent. Chris could convince the court that this assignment would impair her chance of receiving the portrait.

An assignment will not be allowed if it increases the risk or burden of the contract. If John, the artist, tries to assign only $150 of the payment to his landlord, Chris may be able to convince the court that this assignment increases the burden or risk imposed by their contract, as John might purchase very cheap materials.

The proassignment attitude of the courts is also evidenced by their interpretation of the language in the promisor-promisee contract. Even if the contract states that "no assignment shall be made" or that "there shall be no assignment without the prior consent of the promisor," most courts will still allow the assignment. Courts interpret these clauses as promises or covenants not to assign the rights. The assignor is then held legally responsible for making the assignment and must pay the promisor for any loss caused by the assignment. Often the promisor cannot prove any loss in court, so this is a rather hollow right. These clauses can also be interpreted by courts as preventing the transfer of the contract duties. This latter approach is followed by Section 2-210(3) of the Uniform Commercial Code. If the contracting parties really want to prevent assignments, they must use clauses like "all assignments shall be void" or "any attempt at assignment shall be null and void." Most courts will interpret this language as actually removing the power to make assignments.

The law has not always favored assignments. Some states still limit certain types of assignments. Common examples are prohibitions or limitations on the assignment of wages. Statutes in Alabama, California, Connecticut, District of Columbia, Missouri, and Ohio generally prohibit the assignment of future wages. In addition, California and Connecticut and many other states have special rules that apply to assignments of wages as security for small loans.[5]

---

[5]*Restatement (Second) of Contracts,* Statutory Note to Chapter 15 at pages 7–9.

Rights Created by the Assignment

An assignee obtains the same legal rights in the contract that the assignor had. If the assignee sues the promisor, the promisor generally may use the same defenses against the assignee that were available against the assignor. Examples of these defenses would include fraud, duress, undue influence, and breach of contract by the assignor. The promisor will not, however, be able to use *every* conceivable defense against an assignee. The assignee's rights against the promisor were at issue in the following case; the order of events is diagrammed in Figure 15.5.

Hefley v. Jones
687 F.2d 1383 (10th Cir. 1982)

FACTS   Jones contracted to sell a number of heifers and steers to Bonnett in two different contracts entered into on 2 March 1978 and 16 March 1978. On March 6 Bonnett agreed to sell to Hefley and Martin the heifers he had just bought from Jones; on March 24 he agreed to sell to Hefley and Martin steers he had bought from Jones. Bonnett and Jones contracted with each other again on 9 March and 10 April in which Jones was the purchaser. Bonnett appeared to breach these latter contracts and disappeared with the $81,500 down payment he had received from Jones. Jones refused to deliver the steers and heifers to Hefley and Martin. (The parties were trading cattle futures. The actual delivery dates were months in the future.)

FIGURE 15.5   Legal Relationships in *Hefley* v. *Jones*

Jones refused to deliver the cattle to Hefley and Martin on Contracts I and III. Jones was the seller in Contracts I and III. He was the purchaser in Contracts II and IV.

ISSUE	Had Bonnett made a valid, enforceable assignment of his contract rights to Hefley and Martin?
HOLDING	Yes. A valid assignment had been made.
REASONING	The Oklahoma Commercial Code applies because cattle are goods. The Code does not require any particular language to create an assignment. Contractual language may be interpreted in light of the course of dealing between the parties and the usage in the trade or business. Cattle are often sold many times between the original sale by the rancher and the ultimate purchase by a feedlot. The rancher delivers the cattle to the final purchaser and collects the remaining amount due on the purchase price. Commissions are settled through the chain of purchases. Bonnett had sold Jones's cattle contracts in the past. Jones's counterclaim against Bonnett on the other contracts had not matured at the time of the assignment, so it could not be used as a setoff against the assignee.

Warranties Implied by the Assignor

An assignor who makes an assignment implies that certain things are true about the assigned rights, namely, that (1) the right is a valid legal right, and (2) there are no valid defenses to the assigned right. These warranties need not be expressly stated but can instead be implied. If the assignor breaches the warranties, the assignee can successfully sue.

Waiver of Defenses Clause

A *waiver of defenses clause* in a contract attempts to give the assignee better legal rights than the assignor had. Often it is part of a standard printed contract prepared by the assignee or assignor and signed by the promisor. The consumer (promisor) is generally not aware that the contract contains a waiver of defenses clause or does not understand what it means. In the clause, *the promisor promises to give up legal defenses in any later lawsuit by the assignee.* In other words, the promisor agrees not to exert defenses like fraud in the inducement or breach of warranty against any subsequent assignees. Figure 15.6 shows the effect on the promisor-assignee relationship of a valid waiver of defenses clause. Part A indicates what would happen if the assignor sued the promisor. Part B indicates what would happen if the assignee sued the promisor. If the clause is effective it reduces the promisor's bargaining power. For example, if a purchaser buys a product on time and the product is defective, a common reaction is to stop making payments. A waiver of defenses clause means that the buyer must continue to make the payments. Consumer groups and government agencies have often opposed waiver of defenses clauses because they reduce a consumer's bargaining power. Such a clause *is* generally enforceable under Section 9-206(1) of the Uniform Commercial Code, unless there is a different rule under statute or court decision for buyers or lessees of consumer goods.[6] Some states with statutes forbidding or limiting these clauses include Alaska, District of Columbia, Missouri, Ohio, and Washington.[7] The Federal Trade Commission enacted a regulation barring these agreements in contracts by consumers.[8]

[6]Under the Uniform Commercial Code, the assignee would be subject to the same defenses as a holder in due course of a negotiable instrument.
[7]*Restatement (Second) of Contracts,* Statutory Note to Chapter 15 at page 10.
[8]16 C.F.R. Section 433.1–.3 (1975).

FIGURE 15.6   Comparison of the Contract Rights of the Assignor and Assignee*

CONTRACT WITHOUT A WAIVER OF DEFENSES CLAUSE	CONTRACT WITH A VALID WAIVER OF DEFENSES CLAUSE
A. Lawsuit by Assignor Defenses Promisor ◄──✗── Assignor	A. Lawsuit by Assignor Defenses Promisor ◄──✗── Assignor
B. Lawsuit by Assignee Defenses Promisor ◄──✗── Assignee	B. Lawsuit by Assignee Defenses Promisor ◄──✗── Assignee

Legend
Plaintiff ─────► Defendant
Defenses   Defenses will not be successful.
◄──✗── Lawsuit will not be successful.

*This figure assumes that the Promisor has valid defenses that can be proven in court.

DELEGATIONS

Assignments and delegations may occur simultaneously. Initially, however, it will be easier to understand delegations if they are analyzed as a completely separate concept. In a *delegation, the promisor locates a new promisor to perform the duties under the contract.* The original promisor is called the *delegator,* and the new promisor is called the *delegatee.* For example, suppose a purchaser buys a new automobile from a car dealer. One of the terms of that contract is that the dealer promises to provide certain warranty work on the car for three years. The mechanic employed by the car dealer quits, so the dealer contracts with a garage to do the warranty work. This particular delegation is illustrated in Figure 15.7. As with assignments, there may be consideration for the delegation, but that is not necessary. If there is no consideration, the delegation is really a gift from the new promisor to the old promisor.

The purchaser of the car, the promisee, can sue the car dealer who made the promise if the warranty work is not performed. The purchaser can also generally sue the delegatee for failure to perform. In many states the purchaser can sue both the delegator and the delegatee at the same time, but the courts will not permit the purchaser to collect twice.

The relationship between the delegator and the delegatee may be that of a contract or of a gift. If a contract relationship is present, the delegator has the right to sue the delegatee for nonperformance. If a gift relationship is present, the court would hold that the delegatee promised to make a gift in

FIGURE 15.7   Delegation

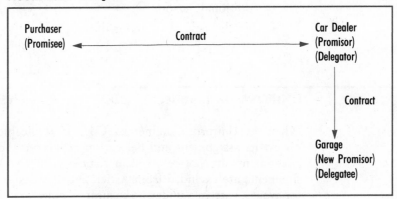

the future but failed to deliver it. Generally, promises to make gifts in the future are not enforceable without promissory estoppel.

Delegations do not occur unless the delegatee assumes the contract duties. This assumption can be either expressly stated or implied. The trend in court decisions is to imply the assumption of the duties, especially when there is an assignment and a delegation. An example would occur when the parties state that there is an "assignment of the contract" or an "assignment of all my rights under the contract." Such statements are *generally* interpreted as indicating an assignment, a delegation of the duties by the delegator, and an acceptance of the duties by the delegatee unless there is a clear indication of a contrary intention. This position is followed by the Uniform Commercial Code, Section 2-210(4), and the *Restatement (Second) of Contracts,* Section 328.

Delegations do not have the preferred status in the eyes of the law that assignments do. Courts are more inclined to deny a delegation. If the contract between the promisor and the promisee states that "there shall be no delegations," the courts will prevent delegations. The same is true if the contract calls for personal performance. Courts are also more likely to decide that a delegation is unfair to the promisee. Under the Uniform Commercial Code, Section 2-210(1), duties cannot be delegated if the agreement states that there will be no delegation or the promisor has a substantial interest in having the delegator perform the contract. Section 2-210(3) indicates that a contract clause that prohibits the assignment of "the contract" is to be construed as preventing only a delegation of the contract duties to the assignee.

To characterize an assignment or a delegation situation, one should answer the following questions:

1. Was the additional person involved from the beginning or added later?
2. Did the additional person undertake to perform a contract duty or become entitled to a contract right? Or both?

3. Did the language of the original contract prevent this transfer to an additional person?

4. Did the type of rights or duties prevent this transfer to an additional person?

UNIFORM COMMERCIAL CODE PROVISIONS

When the Uniform Commercial Code is applicable, businesspeople need to review its assignment and delegation provisions. Some questions concerning assignments are not resolved in Article 9 of the Code. Certain types of assignments are excluded from Article 9 by Section 9-104; for example, claims for wages, interests under an insurance policy, claims arising from the commission of a tort, and deposits in banks. Under Sections 9-201 and 9-203, provisions of Article 9 may be subordinated to state statutes regulating installment sales to consumers. Section 2-210 of the Code covers assignments and delegations under contracts for the sale of goods. (This is only a brief overview of the Code provisions.)

YOU BE THE JUDGE

The owners of Clark's Restaurant in Boston tried to negotiate a sale of the business. The lease stated that the landlord was granted the right to approve all future subtenants of the property. The restaurant argued that the lease really requires good faith and fair dealing in the approval of subtenants. The landlord argued that the lease should be interpreted literally, i.e., a lease that requires the landlord's consent means the landlord's actual consent.

If you were the judge deciding this case, how would you interpret the contract clause?

Source: "Law," Jonathan M. Moses and Junda Woo, *The Wall Street Journal,* Tuesday, March 17, 1992, page B12.

SUMMARY

An additional person who is involved in a contract from the beginning may be a third-party beneficiary. If the promisor or promisee meant to affect the third person under the contract, that person will be an intended beneficiary and will have enforceable rights. Intended beneficiaries can file lawsuits to protect their own legal rights. If they sue the promisor, the promisor can use against them the same defenses that are valid against the promisee. Creditor beneficiaries can sue a promisee who tries to cancel the contract. Donee beneficiaries will generally not be successful in a suit against the promisee because the donee beneficiary did not receive the gift.

An additional party who becomes involved after the contract is formed may be an assignee or a delegatee. An assignee receives a contract right from the transferor. An assignment extinguishes the contract right of the assignor and sets up this contract right exclusively in the assignee. A delegatee assumes the transferor's obligation to perform under the contract. The delegator will still be obligated to perform if the delegatee does not.

DISCUSSION QUESTIONS

1. Julia promised to buy her son, Jonathan, a car from Ted McNare's Volkswagen if Jonathan graduated from college. Does Ted McNare have any rights in the contract? Why or why not?
2. Monkey Business employs costumed personnel who dress like apes, belly dancers, and clowns to deliver singing telegrams. If you hired Monkey Business to deliver a birthday greeting to your boss, what are the legal rights of Monkey Business, you, and your boss?
3. Some states have statutes prohibiting or limiting assignment of wages. What public policies might the state legislatures have been trying to promote with these statutes?
4. Should waiver of defenses clauses be enforced? What are the advantages and disadvantages of these clauses?

5. Is there any reason why an assignment of the Jones-Bonnett contract should not be allowed in *Hefley* v. *Jones*, 687 F.2d 1383 (10th Cir. 1982)?
6. What are the differences between assignees and third-party beneficiaries? In what ways are they similar?
7. Why do American courts favor assignments?
8. When will an assignment be allowed if the contract does not mention assignments?
9. What happens if the assignor assigns the identical contract right to three assignees? Who should recover from whom?
10. How do assignments and delegations differ from each other?

CASE PROBLEMS

1. Stevens Air Systems contracted with Health Care Services Corporation (HCS) to provide health care to employees. HCS contracted with Omaha Indemnity to cover the catastrophic illnesses of these employees. The insurer signed the contract with the knowledge that HCS intended to benefit the Stevens employees who participated in the health plan. Were these employees intended third-party beneficiaries who could sue Omaha? Should contrary language in the HCS-Omaha contract influence this decision? (*Gilmore* v. *Omaha Indemnity*, 158 Cal. Rptr. 229 [Cal. App. 1979].)
2. Mrs. Murphy's nineteen-year-old son was killed in an accident caused by Pollard, who was insured by All-

state. Allstate already paid her the amount of money specified by the policy limits. Mrs. Murphy seeks to enforce a state law that requires insurance companies to use good faith and fair dealing in settling claims. Is Mrs. Murphy entitled to sue Allstate as a third-party beneficiary for failing to settle the claim fairly? (*Murphy* v. *Allstate Insurance Company*, 132 Cal. Rptr. 424 [Cal. 1976], 553 P.2d 584.)
3. Raymond Robson, Sr. and Raymond Robson, Jr. had a contract in which the father was to receive all of his son's shares in their company when the son died. In addition, the father was to pay $500 per month from the company proceeds to his son's wife for five years

following the son's death or until she remarried, whichever occurred first. Two days before Robson, Jr.'s death, the two men modified the contract. This modification removed the father's obligation to make payments to the widow from the company proceeds. Birthe Robson and Robson, Jr. were separated at the time of his death and a divorce action was pending. Is Birthe Robson a third-party beneficiary of the contract between her husband and her father-in-law? Does she have enforceable rights? (*Robson* v. *Robson*, 514 F. Supp. 99 [N.D. Ill. 1981].)

4.   A general release was negotiated and signed between the general contractor, Robbins, Inc., and the subcontractor, Hirsch. (The release was given for $36,000 and indicated that Hirsch would not be responsible for any difficulties arising from the project.) The owner of the premises sued to recover the amount that the owner had to pay to Sears, a tenant, who suffered damages allegedly due to the defective work performed by the subcontractor. A substantial part of the building had collapsed. Is the owner an intended third party of the general release and consequently bound by the release? (*Sears, Roebuck and Co.* v. *Jardel Co.*, 421 F.2d 1048 [3rd Cir. 1970].)

5.   Beaty, a professional basketball player, signed a contract to play for Kirst. General Insurance Company posted a security bond for his salary. Beaty's "contract" was sold to Daniels, then to the Stars, and then to the Spirits of St. Louis. Under the last contract, the Spirits were supposed to pay Beaty, but they have not been doing so. Can Beaty enforce the Stars-Spirits contract? Can Kirst or General Insurance Company enforce the Stars-Spirits contract? Why or why not? (*Kirst* v. *Silna*, 163 Cal. Rptr. 230 [Cal. App. 1980].)

6.   Williams was injured while working on a drilling rig at Amchitka Island, Alaska. He was working for Parco, Inc. Parco had contracted with the Atomic Energy Commission (AEC) to drill certain test holes at Amchitka. Fenix & Scisson had a contract with the AEC to furnish engineering services in conjunction with drilling and mining operations there. Under this contract, Fenix & Scisson was required to inspect drilling operations and to recommend any improvements to the AEC. The firm also was required to take reasonable safety precautions in the performance of its work. This contract was supplemented by provisions that Fenix & Scisson had responsibility for overall industrial safety at the site. At the time of the accident, there were seven Parco employees on the job and one Fenix & Scisson

employee on the job. Does Fenix & Scisson have a contractual duty to Williams? Is he an intended third-party beneficiary of their contract with AEC? (*Williams* v. *Fenix & Scisson, Inc.*, 608 F.2d 1205 [9th Cir. 1979].)

7.   Patrick Puccia sold his restaurant to two buyers. He took back a note and second mortgage and transferred the note to the Bank of Palatine for collateral on other loans. The purported assignment dated 10 March 1981 provided as follows:

> For value received, I hereby assign all my rights, title, and interest in and to: That certain note and trust dated 3-9-81 from the Bank & Trust Company of Arlington Heights, Trustee under trust no. 2635 dated 11-15-80 in the amount of $225,000 payable to Patrick Puccia [illegible] [to] the Bank of Palatine.

Did the purported assignment adequately describe the item to be assigned, even though the word "deed" was omitted from the term "trust deed"? (*Klehm* v. *Grecian Chalet, Ltd.*, 518 N.E.2d 187 [Ill. App. 1987].)

8.   Mrs. Lara entered Kern County General Hospital to give birth. After the child was born, Mrs. Lara died. The hospital was not paid for medical services provided to the child. Under the state law, Mr. Lara, a seasonal farmworker, was billed for the services. The hospital assigned their claim to Kern County Collection Service, a private organization. Should this assignment be allowed? What defenses may be available against the assignee? (*Lara* v. *Kern County Board of Supervisors*, 130 Cal. Rptr. 668 [Cal. App. 1976].)

9.   The Owens signed a contract to purchase a Motorola stereo record player and 140 albums from Universal. The contract said that the record player would be "free." The Owens could pay $698.00 cash or $849.72 if they paid over time. They agreed to pay over time. They signed the contract and a note. The printed terms on the back of the note indicated that the note would be assigned to Unico, and it was. Unico controlled numerous aspects of Universal's business. The contract stated, "Buyer agrees not to set up any claim against such seller as a defense, counterclaim, or offset to any action by an assignee for any unpaid balance of the purchase price or for possession of the property." The Owens were to make payments for 3 years; Universal was to make periodic deliveries of the albums for 5⅓ years. Universal became insolvent, and the Owens did not receive most of their albums. Do the Owens have

to pay Unico on the note? Should they have to make payment? Why or why not? (*Unico* v. *Owen,* 232 A.2d 405 [N.J. 1967].)

10. Milford owned a stud horse that he sold to Stewart. Under the terms of the written contract, Stewart was to allow Milford two breedings a year from the horse as long as the horse lived. This agreement stated that it was valid "regardless [of] to whom the horse may be sold," and the agreement was filed with the county clerk. Stewart sold the horse to McKinnie, who had read and understood the Milford-Stewart contract. McKinnie refused to honor the terms of the Milford-Stewart contract. Is McKinnie bound by the contract? Why or why not? (*McKinnie* v. *Milford,* 597 S.W.2d 953 [Tex. App. 1980].)

C H A P T E R   16

Methods of Discharging the Contract

O U T L I N E

TERMINATION OF THE CONTRACT

When parties contract with one another, each party naturally assumes that the other party will faithfully and satisfactorily perform according to the terms of the agreement. Consequently, whenever the parties do what the contract calls for, we say that they have discharged their duties under the contract. *Discharge of a contract* involves *the legally valid termination of a contractual duty.* Upon discharge, the agreement between the parties has been fulfilled; the parties' duties and obligations to one another end at this time. The law groups the many methods for discharging contracts into four main categories: discharge by performance; discharge by agreement of the parties; discharge by operation of law; and discharge by nonperformance.

Complete performance represents one method of discharging a contract; but the law will, in certain circumstances, allow degrees of performance—*substantial performance,* for instance. Discharge may also result from the *agreement of the parties,* that is, through a release, a rescission, an accord and satisfaction, a novation, or other method. Similarly, a contract discharge will occur by *operation of law* in cases involving bankruptcy decrees, the expiration of the statute of limitations period, and material alterations of contracts. Discharge by nonperformance comes about if the parties can invoke the doctrine of impossibility or the doctrine of commercial frustration. Breach of the contract, whether actual or anticipatory, also discharges the contract, as does noncompliance with the contract's conditions. We will study these various methods of discharging contracts in this chapter.

DISCHARGE BY PERFORMANCE

Complete Performance

The simplest, most common, and most satisfactory method of discharge consists of *complete performance.* (Yet, as we will see later, rendering complete performance may be easier said than done.) If Johnson has agreed to deliver five carloads of grain, and Kreczewski has promised to pay $2000 per carload, complete performance will occur when Johnson makes the deliveries to Kreczewski and Kreczewski pays Johnson. The *parties' exact fulfillment of the terms of the contract* satisfies the intent of their agreement and their reason for contracting. Complete performance also extinguishes all the legal duties and rights that the contract originally set up. (Note, too, that performance will be complete if one of the parties *tenders* either the grain or the payment—that is, unconditionally offers to perform his contractual obligation and can so perform. That person will have completely performed the contract even if the other person does not accept the grain or the payment.)

As long as Johnson is fulfilling Kreczewski's reasonable expectations under the contract, discharge by complete performance will ensue once the parties have met their respective obligations under the agreement. However, if

Johnson during the course of the deliveries does not live up to the letter of the agreement as to the quality of the grain sent to Kreczewski, Kreczewski should give Johnson prompt notice of these defects and should state formally that he expects complete performance. Kreczewski's failure to take such actions may allow Johnson to argue after the fact that Kreczewski has waived his right to expect complete performance.

In some circumstances, one party's performance does not mirror precisely the rights and obligations enumerated in the agreement. In such cases, the other party may question whether this degree of performance adequately fulfills the requisites of the contract.

Substantial Performance

The issue raised by such a question involves the legal sufficiency of less-than-complete performance. The law does not always require exact performance of a contract; hence, *minor deviations* from the performance contemplated in the contract may not preclude the discharge of the contract. This type of performance is called *substantial performance*. A party who has substantially performed may receive the payment agreed to by the parties. However, because substantial performance nevertheless represents a type of contract breach, because the performance is not perfect and is instead a notch below the parties' reasonable expectations under the contract, the other party may sue for the damages occasioned by substantial, as opposed to complete, performance.

Before the doctrine of substantial performance is available to discharge the responsibilities of a performing party, two criteria must be met. First, the breach must not have been material; in other words, the defective performance must not destroy the value or purpose of the contract.[1] Second, the breach cannot be willful; that is, the deviations must not result from bad-faith conduct.

It should be noted that contracts that require one party to perform "to the satisfaction" of the other party may be held to a higher standard of "substantiality." In fact, in certain cases, such as those involving custom tailoring, some courts hold that the personal, subjective expectations of the dissatisfied party must be met in order to discharge the contract. Other courts hold that performance is substantial if the performance rendered will satisfy our old friend, "the reasonably prudent person under the same or similar circumstances." Courts generally will apply this latter test when performance is not based on personal tastes or aesthetic preferences (as may be involved in our custom tailoring example) but rather on satisfaction as to merchantability or mechanical utility (as in the purchase of a car).

Usually, however, the courts are more willing to apply the concept of substantial performance to construction contracts than to sales contracts. This is so because a disgruntled buyer has a duty to return or to reject a defective suit, whereas a dissatisfied occupier of land necessarily must keep the defective

---

[1]A material breach, as we will see in later sections of this chapter, occurs when the performance rendered falls appreciably below the level of performance the parties reasonably expected under the terms of the contract. Such a breach discharges the other party from the contract.

house or garage. The possibility of the unjust enrichment of the landowner makes the doctrine of substantial performance more attractive to courts in construction situations than in most other commercial contexts.

The next case illustrates some of these principles.

F. A. Gray, Inc. v. Weiss
519 A.2d 716 (Me. 1986)

FACTS   At Weiss's invitation, F. A. Gray, Inc. (Gray) submitted a written and signed $3895 proposal to Weiss for the preparation and painting of Weiss's house and barn. After discussions with Gray, Weiss asked Gray to do the job using stain instead of paint. After changing the word "paint" to "stain," Weiss signed and returned Gray's written proposal. Gray then began work on Weiss's house and barn. Before Gray had completed the work, however, Weiss became dissatisfied with the appearance of the buildings and insisted that Gray stop. When Weiss refused to pay Gray for the work completed, Gray sought to recover the full contract price. Weiss argued that Gray had breached the contract by proceeding to do the job with an inappropriate covering material that Gray, by virtue of its expertise, should have refused to use.

ISSUE   Could Gray recover for its work pursuant to the contract?

HOLDING   Yes. Gray's use of the oil stain did not preclude a court's finding that it had substantially performed the contract.

REASONING   There is no ready formula for determining what, in any particular case, amounts to "substantial performance" sufficient to justify a judgment for the contract price, lessened by deductions for asserted claims of defects or omissions. Such a determination is always a question of fact or a matter of degree. The factors courts take into account include the work called for by the contract, the extent to which there has been compliance, the ratio of the cost of curing the defects and omissions to the total contract price, and the importance of any defects or omissions to the purpose of the contract. When a contractor has in good faith completed substantial performance of the terms of the contract, with only slight omissions and defects that the contractor can readily remedy, the contractor may recover the contract price, less the damages resulting from these omissions. Deficient workmanship may constitute the difference between substantial and full performance, but such faulty workmanship will not necessarily bar recovery on the contract. The contract at issue required that Gray "thoroughly scrape, prime all bare wood, caulk loose joints, putty loose sash[es], and apply one coat [of] oil-base house stain." The contract further provided that "all work [should] be completed in a workmanlike manner according to standard practice." The records revealed that Weiss had selected stain as the material to be used after a discussion with Gray and that Gray had advised Weiss against the use of stain. In fact, Gray had finally agreed to use the stain only on the condition that Weiss approve a test patch before Gray would proceed. Weiss then approved the test patch Gray had stained. Because the contract specifically required stain rather than paint, Gray's use of an oil-based stain could not completely preclude his recovery under the contract.

DISCHARGE BY AGREEMENT OF THE PARTIES

The parties themselves can specifically agree to discharge the contract. Provisions to that effect may be part of the original contract between the parties or part of a new contract drafted expressly to discharge the initial contract.

Release

Release represents a common method for discharging the legal rights one party has against another. To be valid, a *release* should be in *writing*, should be supported by *consideration*, and should effect an *immediate relinquishment* of rights or claims owed to another. For example, a landowner may sign a release in which he or she agrees to discharge the builder from the original contractual obligations, usually in exchange for money. Insurance companies commonly execute similar releases to be signed by the insured parties when the insurers pay for the insured parties' injuries.

Rescission

Sometimes the parties may find it advantageous to call off their deal. The law calls this process *rescission*. A contract of *rescission* is a *voluntary, mutual surrender and discharge of contractual rights and duties whereby the parties are returned to the original status quo*. A valid rescission is legally binding. In general, rescission may be either in writing or oral (subject, you will recall, to the Statute of Frauds' requirements under Section 2-209 of the UCC— moreover, rescissions of realty contracts often must be written); formal or informal; express or implied.

The simplest method of rescission involves the termination of executory bilateral contracts. If Johnson and Kreczewski in our earlier example *mutually agree to cancel* their transaction, *express rescission* has occurred. On the other hand, they may subsequently agree that Johnson will deliver seven boxcars of grain instead of five. *Substituting this later agreement* for the old one brings about an *implied rescission* of the earlier agreement. However, problems often ensue if the parties attempt rescission of a unilateral contract (or a bilateral contract where one party has fully executed his or her duties). In these situations, some courts will infer a promise to pay for the performance rendered or require that consideration be paid to the party who has performed before they will grant rescission. Courts ordinarily resolve these issues by trying to ascertain the intent of the parties; but as we have learned, this task is often a difficult one.

Note how the court applied these concepts in the case that follows.

Mor-Wood Contractors, Inc. v. Ottinger
562 N.E.2d 1247 (Ill. App. 1990)

FACTS

In June, 1987, the Ottingers purchased an undeveloped parcel of property in the Village of Hawthorn Woods (the Village). On 30 June 1987, J. & W. Trenching Service, Inc. filed with the Lake County Health Department an application for a permit to build a septic system for the property on the Ottingers' behalf. The site plan accompanying the application showed a proposed septic field to the west of the planned home with a proposed drainage swale to be cut on the southwest portion of the lot. The Health Department issued the Ottingers a septic permit on approximately 21 July 1987, based on J. & W.'s application. In July, 1987, the Ottingers retained an architect to draw up plans for the construction of a single-family home on the property. The architect's site plan showed that the house was to be set slightly counterclockwise on the lot instead of being perfectly square within it. The site plan also indicated that the lot was to be graded to create a valley or swale sloping away from the southwest corner of the home. The Ottingers and Mor-Wood contractors, Inc. (Mor-Wood) began negotiations for a contract for construction of a house on the property. On 30 August 1987, the parties entered into a contract under which Mor-Wood was to grade the property and construct the home pursuant to the architect's plans and specifications by 1 February 1988. Two of the contract's provisions, relevant here, stated:

> 1) If the Contractor fails to correct defective Work or persistently fails to carry out the Work in accordance with the contract Documents, the Owner, by a written order, may order the Contractor to stop the Work, or any portion thereof, until the cause for such order has been eliminated. 2) If the Contractor defaults or persistently fails or neglects to carry out the Work in accordance with the Contract Documents or fails to perform any provision of the Contract, the Owner, after seven days' written notice to the Contractor . . . may make good such deficiencies and may deduct the cost thereof . . . from the payment then or thereafter due the Contractor or, at his option . . . may terminate the contract and take possession of the site and of all materials, equipment, tools, and construction equipment and machinery thereon owned by the Contractor and may finish the work by whatever method he may deem expedient. . . .

Mor-Wood retained Lake-Cook Trenching as a subcontractor for the project, and Lake-Cook applied to the Health Department for a new septic permit on 21 September 1987. Accompanying the application was a site plan showing the septic field to the south of the home instead of to its west and without the swale indicated on the architect's plans. This site plan also depicted the planned home as sitting square within the lot rather than being turned slightly counterclockwise. After the issuance of the permit on 21 October 1987, Tim Morvay of Mor-Wood testified that, while the lot was being graded, Craig Ottinger insisted that the swale be cut even though Morvay indicated that it would traverse the septic area. The excavator who cut the swale testified that he had cut it at Ottinger's insistence and over Morvay's objection. Morvay testified that he then called the Health Department to examine the site to determine if the swale cut necessitated reevaluation of the septic field. A Health Department inspector visited the job site and, as a result of his inspection, sent a letter to the Ottingers on 6 November 1987 revoking the septic permits as of that day, owing to the swale's interference with septic lines and its reduction of the available septic absorption area. Morvay testified that, after he learned of the letter, he discussed the septic problems with Ottinger and ordered a new soil test. On 17 November, Morvay met with Ottinger to pick up a check for partial payment under the contract; Ottinger issued the check to Mor-Wood. That day the Village posted a "stop work" order on the Ottingers' property because of the revoked septic permits. After discovering the stop-work order on the property, Ottinger stopped payment on the check the same day. Morvay denied that he had known that the stop-work order had been posted when he had collected the check from Ottinger. On 17 November, Ottinger met with attorney Lawrence Rochell to discuss the situation. Rochell sent a letter to Mor-Wood's attorney, restating his client's concern that the Morvays had attempted to secure a check from Ottinger despite their alleged knowledge that a stop-work order had been posted. The letter indicated that Mor-Wood had failed to give the Ottingers copies of subcontractor affidavits as requested and that Mor-Wood's negligence had led to the stop-work order's being issued after the revocation of the septic permit. The letter stated that the Ottingers were exercising their rights under the contract by demanding that Mor-Wood "stop any further work at the project site." Mor-Wood's workers left the job site on or about 19 November and removed all of Mor-Wood's equipment at this time. The parties and their attorneys did not meet again until 8 December 1987. At that meeting, each party contended that the problem with the septic field had been caused by the other party. The meeting concluded with each side submitting a list of damages to the other. The Ottingers subsequently completed construction of the home without Mor-Wood's involvement. They retained PAF & Associates to redesign the septic field, which, when modified slightly, received the Health Department's approval. Carpenter George G. Carlberg testified that the Ottingers had retained him to finish the framing work on the house. Carlberg estimated that Mor-Wood had completed 75 percent of the rough work and one-third of the full carpentry work before he had begun working on the house. Carlberg stated that the prior work on the house constituted "a well constructed job." In the litigation that followed, Mor-Wood sued the Ottingers for the reasonable value of the services rendered in partially constructing the Ottingers' home, which had resulted from the Ottingers' alleged rescission of the construction contract. The Ottingers, in turn, argued that Mor-Wood had breached the contract by abandoning it.

ISSUE   Had the letter from the Ottingers' attorney effected a rescission of the contract?

HOLDING   Yes. The phrasing of the letter, in conjunction with Mor-Wood's later evacuation of the job site, had constituted a rescission of the contract.

REASONING   The Ottingers claimed that the 18 November 1987 letter sent by their attorney, Rochell, to Mor-Wood's attorney had not constituted either a termination of Mor-Wood or a rescission of the contract. The trial court apparently had focused on Rochell's demand that Mor-Wood "stop any further work at the project site" and the statement that "recission [sic] of the contract would be in [Mor-Wood's] best interests." The Ottingers, on the other hand, stressed the closing line of the letter, which had stated that Rochell would be "happy to discuss this further." The Ottingers contended that the plain language of the letter indicated that they had not intended to terminate Mor-Wood or to rescind the contract. The letter made it clear that the Ottingers' demand that Mor-Wood cease work on the project grew out of the second contractual provision. The Ottingers argued, however, that although this section does deal with termination, it also separately empowered the Ottingers to "make good" deficiencies in Mor-Wood's work. Thus, the Ottingers contended, Rochell's letter had merely notified Mor-Wood that the Ottingers would exercise this right under the contract. However, this interpretation of Rochell's letter was untenable for two reasons. First, some of the defects noted in Rochell's letter pertained to Mor-Wood's failure to provide the Ottingers with the subcontractor affidavits, a deficiency the Ottingers could not "make good" themselves. Second, the letter never expressed the Ottingers' intention to "make good" any deficiencies in Mor-Wood's performance. Instead, the letter demanded that Mor-Wood stop work completely, a demand more consistent with outright termination. If the Ottingers had merely wished to order Mor-Wood to cease work while it remedied the deficiencies in its performance, they could have done so without terminating the contract. The Ottingers' attorney's reference to the section dealing with termination of the contract of necessity highlights the Ottingers' authority to terminate the contract. Hence, the trial court correctly determined that Rochell's letter had constituted an attempt to terminate the contract (or rescind it) on behalf of the Ottingers. Generally, rescission means the cancelling of a contract so as to restore the parties to their initial status. Rescission can arise in two settings: First, rescission of a contract can occur by the mutual agreement of the parties, and second, rescission also comprises an equitable remedy which a court can afford to one party under a contract because of the one party's fraud or substantial nonperformance or breach. A party seeking rescission must restore the other party to the status quo existing at the time of the making of the contract. Although the law sometimes uses the terms "abandonment" and "rescission" interchangeably, authorities urge the drawing of a distinction: "Where, upon a material breach by one party, the other party treats the breach as total by refusing to perform further and by maintaining an action for damages for such total breach, he is said to abandon further performance, but such abandonment is not technically a rescission of the contract, but a mere acceptance of a situation created by the wrongdoing of the adverse party" (17 Am. Jur. 2d, *Contracts,* Sect. 484 (1964)). In the instant case, the Ottingers' use of the word "abandonment" appeared to mean *unilateral* abandonment or, in other words, a breach of Mor-Wood's obligation to perform under the contract. The Ottingers argued that Mor-Wood's removal of equipment from the job site and the failure to return would constitute "abandonment," or a breach of the contract. The trial court, on the other hand, had found that the Ottingers' termination of Mor-Wood by the 18 November letter, combined with Mor-Wood's evacuation of the job site, effected a rescission of the contract. The record supported the trial court's determination, since the Ottingers had terminated Mor-Wood and had demanded that Mor-Wood stop working on the project. Thus, based on the trial court's finding that Mor-Wood did not breach the contract, if any party here abandoned the contract, it was the Ottingers. In any event, the trial court correctly determined that the contract had been rescinded. A proposal to rescind may become binding if it is accepted before it is withdrawn, and rescission of the contract can be implied from the course of the parties' conduct. Here, the trial court found that Mor-Wood's decision to leave the job site after receiving the termination letter from the Ottingers' attorney would constitute an effective rescission of the contract. The evidence presented at trial amply supported this conclusion. Mor-Wood elected to treat the contract as rescinded and to seek recovery under **quantum meruit** for the reasonable value of the services it had performed for the Ottingers before the rescission of the contract. Where one party repudiates a contract and refuses to be bound by it, the injured party may treat the contract as rescinded and recover under quantum meruit so far as he has performed. Here, the rescission at issue was mutual; so there is no injured

Quantum meruit An equitable remedy allowing one to recover the reasonable value of the services rendered.

party *per se* as there might be in the case of a breached contract. However, as settled law holds, "Where one of the parties to a contract, while the contract is still executory, directs the other not to proceed further with the performance thereof, the latter may bring an action for damages for the breach of the contract or an action upon quantum meruit for the value of the services rendered and any materials furnished" (17 Am. Jur. 2d., *Contracts,* Section 519 (1964)). Thus, the trial court correctly determined that Mor-Wood could recover under quantum meruit.

**Accord and
Satisfaction**

As we learned in Chapter 10 when we discussed consideration in unliquidated debt situations, the parties may agree to *accept performance different from that required by their original bargain.* An agreement of this sort is called an *accord. When the parties comply with the accord, satisfaction* occurs, and discharge of the original claim by accord and satisfaction (that is, substituted performance) has resulted. The process of accord and satisfaction requires evidence of assent. Moreover, an accord will not be legally binding unless and until the performance required in the accord (that is, the "satisfaction") is rendered.

Novation

Just as the parties may agree to substituted performances, so they may agree to substituted parties. A *novation* is a contract that effects an *immediate discharge of a previously existing contractual obligation, creates a new contractual obligation or duty, and includes as a party to this new agreement one who was neither owed a duty nor obligated to perform in the original contract.* A novation, then, is a contract in which a new party is substituted for one of the parties in the previous contract. The novation immediately discharges an obligation, whereas an accord, by contrast, is not executed until performance occurs. As you would expect, both the assent of the person to whom the obligation is owed (usually the creditor) and the assent of the new obligor (third party) are required for a valid novation. The assent of the previous debtor is usually not required, although that party can disclaim the benefit of the discharge if desired. The novation, in addition, must be supported by valid consideration.

To illustrate a novation, assume that Mary has leased an apartment for twelve months. After six months, Mary faces a reassignment to a job in another state. If Mary can find a new tenant who is willing to take over the balance of her lease and if Mary's landlord will agree to substitute this new tenant in place of Mary, thereby releasing Mary from her lease obligations, a novation will exist. The old contract has been changed by a substitution of a new party for one of the old parties, with the consent of the remaining "old" party.

DISCHARGE BY OPERATION OF LAW

We have seen in other contexts that the law itself can mandate the discharge of certain contracts. As you will learn in Chapter 31, bankruptcy decrees may grant to honest debtors a discharge of contractual obligations by operation of law. Most of the time a creditor will not receive the total owed, and yet the discharge in bankruptcy prevents the creditor from later suing the debtor for nonperformance (usually nonpayment). Most states, however, allow the debtor to revive the obligation by a later promise to pay the creditor, subject to the Bankruptcy Act's provisions.

Statutes of limitations in all jurisdictions establish time periods within which lawsuits for different claims must be brought. Noncompliance with these statutory time limits may discharge contractual claims by operation of law. For example, if according to the relevant state statute claims for breach of contract must be brought within six years of the date of the alleged breach, any claims asserted in a lawsuit brought after this time limit are unenforceable. When the transaction involves a sale of goods, Section 2-725 of the UCC states that the injured party must ordinarily file suit within four years of the occurrence of the breach. The underlying claim is discharged by operation of law if a suit is not filed within this period. Periods of limitations differ from jurisdiction to jurisdiction, so each state's statutes should be checked.

The law also may grant a discharge of any contract that has been materially altered by one of the parties to the agreement. Before this rule will be applied it must be shown that the alteration was done intentionally and without the consent of the other party. Thus, if Johnson changes the carload price of the grain on the written contract from $2000 to $5000, Kreczewski can obtain a discharge of the contract through operation of law, basing the request for discharge on Johnson's material alteration of the written agreement without permission.

DISCHARGE BY NONPERFORMANCE

Under certain circumstances, nonperformance may discharge a contract. Still, as mentioned before, do not expect courts to apply these doctrines in order to save you from a bad bargain.

Impossibility

Until the middle of the last century, courts rejected outright the doctrine of impossibility as a method of discharging contracts. *Impossibility* as a legal concept refers to *an unforeseen event or condition that precludes the party's performing as promised.* For instance, such events as the destruction of the subject matter of the contract without the fault of either party (Johnson's wheat burns before being loaded), supervening illegality (after the contract's formation, a law is passed that makes it illegal for trains to carry agricultural products into certain states), or conduct by one party that makes performance by the other party impossible (Kreczewski contracts for every possible car in carrying out other deals so that Johnson cannot procure the necessary cars for their transaction) generally discharge contracts. These examples denote *objective impossibility* (nonperformance of the contract is unavoidable; *no one* can perform the contract in these circumstances).

Another instance of objective impossibility that may constitute grounds for discharging the contract involves the death or disability of either party to a personal services contract (Johnson hires Pollock to paint his portrait, and Pollock has a debilitating heart attack). This contingency forms an exception to the general rule that a contract will be binding and thus not dischargeable except through performance despite the death or disability of either party, unless the parties have agreed otherwise. The contract would not be discharged, however, if another painter is acceptable to Johnson.

On the other hand, courts have held that circumstances involving subjective impossibility (as opposed to objective impossibility such as destruction of the subject matter) will not discharge contractual obligations. *Subjective impossibility* consists of nonperformance owing to personal, as contrasted to external, impossibility. In such cases, the contract *can* be performed, but *this particular person* is unable to fulfill the obligations contemplated in the contract. For this reason, nonperformance owing to insolvency, shortages of materials, strikes, riots, droughts, and price increases will ordinarily not discharge contracts. However, some courts will temporarily suspend the duty to perform until the conditions causing the inability to perform have passed. More liberal courts may even discharge the contract if later performance will place an appreciably greater burden on the one obligated to perform. Given this division of opinion, the parties often will try to protect their rights by including express provisions covering the types of contingencies just described. Still, it is up to the courts to decide the validity of any such clauses.

The court in the next case applied the general rule about subjective impossibility in refusing to allow it as a method of discharging this particular contract.

Board of Education of the City of Chicago v. Chicago Teachers Union, Local 1
412 N.E.2d 587 (Ill. App. 1980)

FACTS   In June, 1977, the Chicago Board of Education closed all schools and laid off all employees one day early for economic reasons. The union alleged that the one-day, end-of-school layoff was a breach of its collective bargaining agreement with the board. The board argued that its actions were justified because of deficits in the board's budget. The trial court ordered that all teachers be paid for this one-day layoff.

ISSUE   Were the deficits an unforeseen event that rendered the contract incapable of being performed?

HOLDING   No. The doctrine of impossibility was inapplicable to the facts of this case.

REASONING   The board, once it makes an appropriation for teachers' salaries in its budget, thereby implementing the salary provisions of the collective bargaining agreement, is contractually obligated to pay teachers for the period specified. Since the Education Fund showed an operating surplus, there was insufficient evidence of a lack of funds to justify personnel layoffs. Moreover, impossibility of performance will not discharge a contract where the event causing the impossibility can be foreseen and guarded against in the contract. The contingency of lack of funds was foreseeable in light of the board's accumulated deficit and could have been expressly provided for in the agreement. Furthermore, even the insolvency of a promisor will not discharge one from one's duty to perform. For these reasons, the board's obligation to its teachers could not be excused on the ground of impossibility of performance.[2]

Commercial Frustration

Because of the harshness of the general rule that impossibility will ordinarily not discharge the performance called for in a contract, the doctrine of *commercial frustration* (or frustration of purpose) has recently emerged as a basis for excused nonperformance. Courts will not invoke this doctrine to excuse performance, however, unless the *essential purpose and value of the contract have been frustrated*. If the parties could (or should) have reasonably foreseen the resultant frustration, courts will hold the nonperforming party to the terms of the bargain. Hence, courts will not utilize this doctrine to release parties from bad bargains. It is important to understand that in these cases performance is possible; but the value of the contract has been frustrated or destroyed by a supervening event that was not reasonably anticipated at the contract's formation. The Uniform Commercial Code uses the term *commercially impracticable* (Section 2-615) in a similar manner to excuse nonperformance in cases of severe shortages of raw materials owing to war, embargo, local crop failure, and other similar reasons. These factors must have caused a marked increase in price or must have totally precluded the seller from obtaining the supplies necessary for performance before courts will allow discharge.

The next case, in which the court accepted the doctrine of commercial frustration as a defense, is instructive on many levels.

Chase Precast Corporation v. *John J. Paonessa Company, Inc.*
56 N.E.2d 603 (Mass. 1991)

FACTS   In 1982, the Commonwealth of Massachusetts, through the Department of Public Works (the Department), entered into two contracts with the John J. Paonessa Company, Inc. (Paonessa) for resurfacing and improvements to two stretches of Route 128. Part of each contract called for replacing a grass median strip between the north- and southbound lanes with concrete surfacing and precast concrete median barriers. Paonessa entered into two contracts with Chase Precast Corporation (Chase) under which Chase was to supply, in the aggregate, 25,800 linear feet of concrete median barriers according to the specifications of the Department for highway construction. Chase had specified the quantity and type of barriers to be supplied in two purchase orders it had prepared. The highway reconstruction began in the spring of 1983. In May, the Department began receiving protests from angry residents who objected to the use of the concrete median barriers and the removal of the grass median strip. Paonessa and Chase became aware of the protest around 1 June. On 6 June, a group of about one hundred citizens filed an

[2]On appeal, the Supreme Court of Illinois held that the board had discretionary power to impose a layoff for economic reasons, that it had exercised this power reasonably, and that this power could not be restricted by contract. (*Board of Education of the City of Chicago* v. *Chicago Teachers Union, Local 1*, 430 N.E.2d 1111 [Ill. 1981].)

action in the Superior Court to stop the installation of the concrete median barriers and other aspects of the work. On 7 June, anticipating modification by the department, Paonessa notified Chase by letter to stop producing concrete barriers for the projects. Chase did so on receipt of the letter the following day. On 17 June, the Department and the citizens' group entered into a settlement providing, in part, that no additional concrete median barriers would be installed. On 23 June, the Department deleted the permanent concrete median barriers item from its contracts with Paonessa. Before stopping production on 8 June, Chase had produced approximately one-half of the concrete median barriers called for by its contracts with Paonessa and had delivered most of them to the construction sites. Paonessa paid Chase at the contract price for all that Chase had produced. Although Chase had suffered no out-of-pocket expense as a result of the cancellation of the remaining portion of the barriers, it sued Paonessa to recover the profits it allegedly had lost owing to the cancellation of the contracts to supply the median barriers. Paonessa defended on the grounds of impossibility and frustration of purpose.

ISSUE Would either the doctrine of impossibility or the doctrine of frustration of purpose serve as a defense to immunize Paonessa from liability?

HOLDING The doctrine of frustration of purpose would immunize Paonessa from liability because the parties had not, at the time of contract formation, contemplated the cancellation of the items and thus had not allocated in the contract the risk of such cancellation to either party.

REASONING Massachusetts courts have long recognized and applied the doctrine of impossibility as a defense to an action for breach of contract. Under Massachusetts courts' construction of that doctrine,

> where from the nature of the contract it appears that the parties must from the beginning have contemplated the continued existence of some particular specified thing as the foundation of what was to be done, then, in the absence of any warranty that the thing shall exist . . . the parties shall be excused . . . [when] performance becomes impossible from the accidental perishing of the thing without the fault of either party.

On the other hand, although Massachusetts courts have referred to the doctrine of frustration of purpose in a few decisions, such courts have never clearly defined it. However, other jurisdictions have explained the doctrine as follows: When an event neither anticipated nor caused by either party, the risk of which was not allocated by the contract, destroys the object or purpose of the contract, thus destroying the value of performance, the parties are excused from further performance. At least one Massachusetts precedent has called frustration of purpose a "companion rule" to the doctrine of impossibility. Both doctrines concern the effect of supervening circumstances on the rights and duties of the parties. The difference lies in the effect of the supervening event. Under frustration, performance remains possible; but the expected value of performance to the party seeking to be excused has been destroyed by the fortuitous event. Clearly, frustration of purpose represents a more accurate label for the defense argued in this case than impossibility of performance, since performance was not literally impossible. Nothing prevented Paonessa from honoring its contract to purchase the remaining sections of median barrier, whether or not the Department would approve their use in the road construction. The principal question in both kinds of cases remains whether an unanticipated circumstance, the risk of which should not fairly be thrown on the promisor, has made performance vitally different from what was reasonably to be expected. Another definition of frustration of purpose is found in the *Restatement (Second) of Contracts,* Section 265: "Where, after a contract is made, a party's principal purpose is substantially frustrated without his fault [or her] by the occurrence of an event the non-occurrence of which was a basic assumption on which the contract was made, his [or her] remaining duties to render performance are discharged, unless the language or the circumstances indicate the contrary." This definition is nearly identical to the defense of "commercial impracticability" found in the Uniform Commercial Code, Section 2-615. That section states that performance is excused when it has been made "impracticable by the occurrence of a contingency the non-occurrence of which was a basic assumption on which the contract was made." In the present case, Paonessa bore no responsibility for the Department's elimination of the median barriers from the projects. Therefore, whether

Paonessa can rely on the defense of frustration turns on whether elimination of the barriers was a risk allocated by the contracts to Paonessa. Simply put, given the commercial circumstances in which the parties dealt, was the contingency that developed one that the parties could reasonably have foreseen as a real possibility that could affect performance? Or, alternatively, was it one of that variety of risks that the parties were tacitly assigning to the promisor by their failure to provide for it explicitly? If it was, performance will be required. If it could not be so considered, performance is excused. This becomes a question for the trier of fact. Paonessa's contracts with the Department contain a standard provision allowing the Department to eliminate items or portions of work found unnecessary. The purchase order agreements between Chase and Paonessa do not contain a similar provision. Yet this difference in the contracts does not mandate the conclusion that Paonessa assumed the risk of reduction in the quantity of the barriers. Chase knew the barriers were for Department projects and was aware of the Department's power to decrease quantities of contract items, since Chase had supplied median barriers to the Department in the past. The provision giving the Department the power to eliminate items or portions thereof was standard in its contracts. In this case, even if the parties were aware generally of the Department's power to eliminate contract items, the judge could reasonably have concluded that they had not contemplated the cancellation for a major portion of the project of such a widely used item as concrete median barriers and had not allocated the risk of such cancellation. Hence, the doctrine of frustration of purpose would discharge Paonessa's remaining duties to render performance and immunize it from liability to Chase for lost profits.

Actual Breach

Breach of contract occurs when one or more of the contracting parties *fails to perform* the obligations set up by the contract. That different *degrees* of breach exist somewhat complicates the issue. A *complete* or *actual* breach of contract involves the nonperformance of a duty that is so *material* and essential to the agreement that the other party is justified in treating the agreement as at an end. The Uniform Commercial Code in Sections 2-703 and 2-711 embraces this common law principle. Actual breach generally discharges the other party's obligation to perform under the terms of the contract. However, rather than canceling the contract upon breach, the injured (or nonbreaching) party may elect instead to hold the nonperforming party to the contract through various types of remedies, which we will discuss in Chapter 17.

The following case deals with a situation in which each party to the contract accused the other party of breach. Note how the court resolved the issues.

Marshall Construction, Ltd. v. Coastal Sheet Metal & Roofing, Inc.
569 So.2d 845 (Fla. App. 1990)

FACTS   On 20 February 1988, Marshall Construction, Ltd. (Marshall) entered into a general contract with the State of Florida for the repair and replacement of the roofs of buildings 51, 52, and 53 at Florida State Hospital in Chattahoochee, Florida, for the sum of $239,095. The contract called for substantial completion within 120 days after the date of the notice to proceed and final completion within 30 days after the date of substantial completion. The contract required Marshall to pay liquidated damages in the event that Marshall failed to complete the contract within the time specifications. In March, 1988, Marshall and Coastal Sheet Metal & Roofing, Inc. (Coastal) entered into an oral contract to replace the roofs of buildings 51, 52, and 53. Coastal was to perform the work; Marshall was to receive

$7,265 for its bond premium and for its fee; and Coastal was to receive the balance of Marshall's contract with the state. Coastal agreed to replace the roofs according to the specifications of the architect. Coastal received notice to proceed on 28 March 1988, and Coastal was given 120 days for substantial completion and an additional 30 days for final completion. A problem subsequently developed with the roofing system installed in building 51 because water had penetrated the roof insulation. Both parties agreed that the new roof on the east wing of building 51 needed replacing because of these defects. Coastal admitted that it could not afford to proceed with the work and could not repair the defective roof unless Marshall paid it for the work already completed. On 15 June 1988, Coastal stopped work on the project. Marshall requested several times that Coastal continue the work, and Coastal refused to work until it had received payment. On 24 June 1988, Marshall ordered Coastal off the job and hired someone else to complete the work. Coastal subsequently filed a complaint against Marshall seeking damages for breach of an oral contract, alleging that Marshall had wrongfully discharged Coastal from the contract prior to the completion of the construction. Coastal also claimed it was entitled to the performance bond issued to Marshall by the Continental Insurance Company on the roofing project. Marshall filed a counterclaim seeking damages for Coastal's breach of contract and negligent workmanship.

ISSUE   Had Coastal's actions in failing to replace the roofing system amounted to a material breach of its contract with Marshall?

HOLDING   Yes. Coastal's refusal to repair the roof without further payment represented a material breach of the contract that would discharge Marshall's duty to pay Coastal.

REASONING   A well-settled contract principle states that unexpected difficulty, expense, or hardship does not excuse a party from performance of its obligations under a contract. In addition, in order to maintain an action for breach of contract, a claimant must first establish performance on its part of the contractual obligations imposed in the contract. Here, Coastal failed to install the roofing system on the east wing as required under the contract. When Coastal refused to repair the work without further payment, it committed a material breach that entitled Marshall to treat the breach as a discharge of its duty to pay Coastal until Coastal repaired the defective roof and fulfilled its contractual duties. The terms of the contract had required substantial completion by 25 July 1988, and Coastal had refused to return to work without being paid; these facts completely justified Marshall's concluding that a material breach had occurred and then ordering Coastal off the job. No substantial, competent evidence surfaced to support a finding that Marshall had breached the contract. Rather, the undisputed evidence demonstrated that Coastal had committed a material breach of the contract. This breach, in turn, excused Marshall's obligation to pay Coastal until Coastal completed the repairs to the roof.

Anticipatory Breach   Sometimes one of the contracting parties will indicate in advance, through words or conduct, that he or she does not intend to abide by the terms of the contract. To illustrate, if Johnson unequivocally tells Kreczewski before the time performance is due that he will not send the grain as scheduled, Johnson will have wrongfully repudiated the contract. Johnson's action in legal terms is called *anticipatory breach* or *anticipatory repudiation*. In this situation, as in actual breaches, the injured party need not limit its potential responses to discharge of the contract.

The Uniform Commercial Code sanctions a kind of anticipatory repudiation in circumstances less definite than those allowable under the common law. Section 2-609 of the Code states that when reasonable grounds for insecurity arise with respect to one party's performance, the other party may demand adequate assurances of due performance and suspend performance until such assurances are forthcoming. If thirty days pass without reply, the party who has demanded the assurances may deem the contract repudiated. Kreczewski's actual or apparent **insolvency,** for example, may cause Johnson to invoke the provisions of Section 2-609. If Kreczewski does not respond within thirty days, Johnson may then treat the contract as repudiated. (See Section 2-610.)

Insolvency   Inability to pay one's debts as they become due.

Conditions

The presence of conditions may result in nonperformance that will justify discharge of a contract.

A promise is a vow or an agreement that places on the promisor a duty to do something or to refrain from doing something. A *condition,* in contrast, is *an act or event that limits or qualifies a promise.* The condition must occur before the promisor has a duty to perform or to refrain from performing.

Authorities classify conditions in two ways. The first category emphasizes the *timing* of the qualifying occurrence (the condition) in relation to the promised performance. Three subsets of this category include *conditions precedent, concurrent conditions,* and *conditions subsequent.* The second category stems from the *manner* in which the conditions arise. Conditions created by law are called *constructive* (or *implied*) *conditions.* By contrast, conditions created by the agreement of the parties themselves are called *express conditions.*

Under the first category, an agreement may explicitly state that a *certain act or event must occur before the other party has a duty to perform or before a contract exists.* If so, a *condition precedent* exists. For example, a person may promise (for consideration) to buy a car if the seller can deliver the car within ten days. A duty to buy the car does not arise unless and until the seller fulfills the condition. Thus the timing of the condition and any later duty to perform go together. To be a condition precedent rather than a mere promise, the parties must indicate that the condition is an essential, vital aspect of the transaction. The buyer in our example will have to prove that delivery within ten days is essential to the transaction if the buyer later wishes to sue for rescission of the contract or for damages on the ground that the seller has not delivered the car on time. A common condition precedent involves a buyer's signing a contract for the purchase of a new house subject to the sale of the buyer's current residence. The buyer views this provision as an important consideration regarding his or her willingness to enter into the contract.

Concurrent conditions, related to conditions precedent in regard to the timing of the condition and the promised performance, obligate the parties *to perform at the same time.* Concurrent conditions (for instance, the transfer of goods in exchange for payment) underlie most commercial sales.

A *condition subsequent* is *any occurrence that the parties have agreed will cut off an existing legal duty.* It may also be a contingency, the happening or performance of which will defeat a contract already in effect. When a sales contract involving grain storage states that the contract will be of no effect if fire destroys the grain, a condition subsequent exists. Genuine conditions subsequent are rare. What may sound like a condition subsequent—for example, "Acme Insurance will not pay for casualty losses if premises are not occupied"—will be construed by many courts as a condition precedent. Courts that would characterize such a provision as a condition subsequent would interpret the clause as stating that the occurrence of the condition (vacant premises) will cut off an existing legal duty (payment of the casualty loss). Other courts would say that it is a condition precedent (premises must be kept occupied) that merely sounds like a condition subsequent because of the phrasing. Procedurally this distinction can be significant. If it is a condition precedent, the insured has the burden of proof; if it is a condition subsequent, the insurer has the burden of proof. When the evidence is conflicting, the party who has the burden of proof often loses.

Express conditions—for example, "This sale can be consummated only by a payment of cash"—are those *spelled out by the parties* explicitly or implied in fact. A *constructive condition* is one not expressed by the parties, but rather *read into the contract in order to serve justice* (that is, the condition is implied in law). Differentiating between an express condition implied in fact and a constructive condition can be difficult. For example, a provision regarding place of delivery normally is a condition precedent in a contract involving grain, but if such a condition is lacking, and in the absence of clear intent, a court may imply that the place for delivery is the seller's place of business (see UCC Section 2-308).

Nonperformance of an express condition precedent (such as posting a performance bond) causes a failure of condition that nullifies the other party's duty to perform and discharges the contract. Similarly, the presence of an express condition *subsequent* (meaning that the occurrence of a particular event cuts off all ongoing contractual duties) discharges the obligations of both parties. For example, the buyer's returning goods before payment is due under the terms of a contract in which the buyer had reserved this right would constitute discharge of the contract. But to avoid a breach of an express condition, courts ordinarily require strict compliance. In contrast, substantial compliance generally avoids a breach of a constructive condition.

The following case deals with the issue of a condition precedent in an employment context.

Hapney v. Central Garage, Inc.
579 So.2d 127 (Fla. App. 1991)

FACTS   Central Garage, Inc., d/b/a Gulfcoast Auto and Automotive Accessories (Gulfcoast), is a Florida corporation engaged in the installation, repair, and maintenance of auto air conditioners and related auto accessories. It has facilities in Tampa, St. Petersburg, Sarasota, and Ft. Myers and draws customers from other surrounding areas. In 1988, David Hapney, an experienced installer and repairer of auto and truck air-conditioning systems, began to work for Gulfcoast.

As a condition of Hapney's employment, he entered into an "Employee Confidentiality Agreement and Covenant Not To Compete," which provided that for three years following the termination of his employment, Hapney would not offer, as an agent, employee, owner, or distributor, similar products or services on behalf of a competitor of Gulfcoast on the west coast of Florida from Crystal River to Naples or inland one hundred miles. On 14 July 1989, Hapney voluntarily terminated his employment and began working for a direct competitor of Gulfcoast. On 1 August 1989, Gulfcoast instituted an action to enforce the covenant not to compete against Hapney and his new employer, despite the following facts: While employed by Gulfcoast, Hapney had received no significant training in the installation and repair of automobile air-conditioning systems, beyond the knowledge and skill that he already possessed; he had received significant training in the installation of cruise controls and cellular telephones in automobiles; he had had no significant contacts with and had developed no significant relationships with Gulfcoast's customers; and he had acquired no trade secrets or confidential business information from Gulfcoast. Hapney argued that in determining the legality of a covenant not to compete in addition to evaluating the reasonableness of the covenant as to time and geographical scope, a court must also consider, as a condition precedent, whether the covenant reasonably relates to protecting a legitimate interest of the employer.

ISSUE   Was the existence of a legitimate, protectible interest on the employer's part a condition precedent for a court's finding a valid restrictive covenant?

HOLDING   Yes. For a covenant not to compete to be valid and enforceable in Florida, such a condition precedent must exist.

REASONING   A review of the laws and decisions of the states outside Florida that permit employee noncompetition agreements reveals an overwhelming majority requiring, at a minimum, that such contracts be reasonably related to the protection of a "legitimate business interest" or concern a "protectible interest" of the employer. The rule, generally stated, is that an employer may not enforce a post-employment restriction on a former employee simply to eliminate competition per se; rather, the employer must establish the legitimate business interest it is protecting. This rule represents an expression of common sense that both insulates the employer from unfair competition and recognizes the right of an individual, in a free and competitive society, to earn an honest living and better his or her status along the way. In a broader sense, all consumers benefit from the availability of goods and services, the quality and price of which are determined by fair competition, unfettered by artificial monopolistic practices. Moreover, a plain reading of the applicable law dispels any notion that the legislature intended to dispense with the bedrock requirement that covenants of this nature must relate to a legitimate business interest of the employer in order to restrict or impinge upon the right to pursue and earn a living guaranteed by Florida's constitution. Such employer legitimate interests may include (1) trade secrets and confidential business lists, records, and information; (2) customer goodwill; and (3) to a limited degree, extraordinary or specialized training provided by the employer. Although the third category remains difficult to define with any degree of precision, to merit recognition as a protectible interest, the employer must provide more in training than that acquired by simply performing the tasks associated with a job. The resolution of this question is pertinent here because Hapney, although thoroughly schooled in the installation and repair of auto air conditioners at the time of his employment by Gulfcoast, did acquire the knowledge and experience necessary to install and repair cruise control units and cellular telephones while in the employ of Gulfcoast. To constitute a protectible interest, however, the training or education provided must be extraordinary, or that which goes beyond what is usual, regular, common, or customary in the industry in which the employee is employed. The rationale is that if an employer has dedicated time and money to the extraordinary training and education of an employee, whereby the employee attains a unique skill or an enhanced degree of sophistication in an existing skill, permitting that employee to use those skills to the benefit of a competitor when the employee has contracted not to do so is unfair. The precise degree of training or education that rises to the level of a protectible interest varies from industry to industry and is a factual determination to be made by the trial court. Needless to say, skills acquired by following the directions on the box or learned by a person of ordinary education by reading a manual do not meet the test. Such is the case of Hapney, who extended his air-conditioning installation and repair skills to include cruise control units and cellular telephones. In sum, (1) a covenant not to compete that prohibits competition per se violates public policy and is void; (2) a condition precedent to the validity of a covenant not to compete entered into by an agent, independent contractor, or employee is the existence of a legitimate business interest of the employer to be protected; (3) it is the employer's burden to plead and prove the underlying protectible interest; (4) trade secrets, customer lists, and the right to prevent direct solicitation of existing customers are, per se, legitimate business interests subject to protection; and (5) other business interests, such as, but not limited to, extraordinary training or education, may constitute protectible interests depending on the proof **adduced.** As applied to this case, Gulfcoast had failed to plead or prove a legitimate business interest to be protected as the foundation of Hapney's covenant not to compete.

Adduced Given as a reason or proof; cited as an example.

Table 16.1 shows various methods for discharging a contract, detailing both the methods of discharge and the general rules applied to each method.

TABLE 16.1 Methods of Discharging Contracts

TYPE OF DISCHARGE	GENERAL RULES

1. Discharge by performance
  a. Complete performance: the parties' exact fulfillment of the terms of the contract.
  b. Substantial performance: less than perfect performance that complies with the essential portions of the contract.
	1. Tender of delivery or payment completes the contract.
	1. Applicable only to nonmaterial and nonwillful breaches.
	2. Injured party may sue for damages resulting from the minor deviations that have led to substantial (as opposed to complete) performance.

2. Discharge by agreement of the parties
  a. Release: the surrender of a legal claim.
 	
  b. Rescission: the voluntary mutual surrender and discharge of contractual rights and duties whereby the parties are returned to the original status quo.
  c. Accord and satisfaction: agreement whereby the parties decide to accept performance different from that required by their original bargain and then the parties' compliance with this new agreement.
  d. Novation: a contract that effects an immediate discharge of a previously existing contractual duty, creates a new contractual obligation or duty, and includes as a party to this new agreement one who was neither owed a duty nor obligated to perform in the original contract.
	1. Author of release should put it in writing, support it with consideration, and use it as an immediate relinquishment of rights or claims owed to another.
	1. May be either written or oral (subject to the Statute of Frauds), formal or informal, expressed or implied.
	1. Actual agreement and subsequent performance necessary.
	
	1. Assent of creditor and new obligor required.
	2. Different from an accord and satisfaction in that it effects an immediate discharge of an obligation rather than a discharge predicated on a subsequent performance.

TABLE 16.1   continued

TYPE OF DISCHARGE	GENERAL RULES
3. Discharge by operation of law	
a. Bankruptcy: discharge of the debtor's contractual obligations by court decree.	1. Revival of the obligation possible if done in compliance with applicable statutory provisions.
b. Statute of limitations: definite statutory time period during which a lawsuit must be commenced or be barred forever.	1. Applicable time periods differ from state to state.
c. Material alteration of the contract: serious change in the contract effected by a party to the contract.	1. Must be done intentionally and without the consent of the other party.
4. Discharge by nonperformance	
a. Impossibility: unforeseen event or condition that precludes the possibility of the party's performing as promised.	1. Only objective (as opposed to subjective) impossibility leads to discharge.
	2. Includes such events as destruction of the contract's subject matter without the fault of either party, supervening illegality, death or disability of either party whose performance is essential to the performance of the contract, and conduct by one party that makes performance by the other party impossible.
b. Commercial frustration: destruction of the essential purpose and value of the contract.	1. Destruction of the value of the contract brought about by a supervening event not reasonably anticipated at the contract's formation.
	2. Term "commercially impracticable."
c. Breach: nonperformance of the obligations set up by the contract.	
1. Complete (or actual) breach.	1. Nonperformance of a duty so material and essential to the agreement that the other party is justified in treating the agreement as at an end.
2. Anticipatory breach: indication in advance by one of the contracting parties that he or she does not intend to abide by the terms of the contract.	1. Covered by both the common law and the UCC.
d. Conditions: limitations or qualifications placed on a promise.	
1. Express conditions: those in which the parties explicitly or impliedly in fact set out the limitations to which their promises will be subject.	1. Strict compliance with express conditions necessary to avoid a breach.
2. Constructive conditions: those read into the contract or implied in law in order to serve justice.	2. Substantial compliance with constructive conditions necessary to avoid a breach.
3. Condition precedent: performance contingent on the happening of a future event; failure of the condition precedent nullifies the other party's duty to perform and discharges the parties.	
4. Condition subsequent: the occurrence of a particular event cuts off all ongoing contractual duties and discharges the obligations of both parties.	

SUMMARY

Discharge of a contract refers to the legally valid termination of a contractual duty. Performance may be either complete or substantial. Both degrees of performance ordinarily discharge the contract. The parties may themselves agree to discharge the contract. Release, rescission, accord and satisfaction, and novation are examples of this method of discharging contracts. Bankruptcy decrees, the running of statutes of limitations, and material alterations of the contract will justify discharge of a contract by operation of law. In some circumstances, the nonperformance of one of the parties will discharge a contract. Courts that find evidence of destruction of the subject matter, intervening illegality, or conduct by one party that makes performance by the other party objectively impossible will excuse the resultant nonperformance. This is the doctrine of impossibility. However, in many other situations, impossibility will not justify discharge of the contract. The doctrine of commercial frustration has consequently arisen to mitigate the harshness of the common law's rejection of impossibility as a defense to nonperformance. Breach, whether actual or anticipatory, may also bring about discharge of the contract. The nonoccurrence of express conditions precedent and the occurrence of express conditions subsequent, in addition to constructive conditions, may cause discharge of a contract as well.

DISCUSSION QUESTIONS

1. What are the four main methods of contract discharge?

2. What conditions must be met before substantial performance is legally possible? Does substantial performance always constitute a breach of the contract?

3. What characteristics must be present before a release is valid?

4. What is rescission?

5. Describe how accord and satisfaction occur.

6. How are accord and satisfaction different from a novation?

7. Explain fully the doctrine of impossibility and the doctrine of commercial frustration as they relate to discharge of contracts.

8. What sorts of situations will discharge a contract by operation of law?

9. Define and explain the legal consequences of anticipatory breach under the common law and the Uniform Commercial Code.

10. What is a complete, or material, breach of contract? What are the injured party's options when a complete breach occurs?

CASE PROBLEMS

1. Richard Au became a Gulf Oil dealer in 1971. His contract obligated him to sell Gulf products at carwash centers owned by Au in Ohio for ten years. Gulf agreed to loan Au money for structural improvements and construction of the carwash centers and to provide Au with special allowances and subsidies that permitted Au to sell Gulf products at competitive prices. The contract stated that Au had to pay the outstanding balance of any such loans if Au ever breached the contract. In case of a breach, Gulf had the option of terminating all con-

tracts with Au by giving him ten days' notice of its decision. The oil crisis of 1973 led to Gulf's discontinuing its special allowances and subsidies. As a result, Au's profit margins declined, and he purchased less gasoline each year. In 1980, Gulf terminated Au without notice for Au's failure to pay $7000 for a shipment of gasoline. Au filed suit against Gulf, contending that Gulf's failure to pay him the special allowances and thereby to keep him and other Gulf dealers competitive constituted a breach of contract. Gulf had failed to perform substantially under the contract and had prevented him from so performing, Au asserted. He also argued that Gulf could not recover the $7000 because Gulf had failed to satisfy the condition precedent requiring ten days' written notice prior to termination of the contract. Were Au's arguments valid? (*Au Rustproofing Center* v. *Gulf Oil Corporation*, 755 F.2d 1231 [6th Cir. 1985].)

2. C. B. Dodge Company (Dodge) owned some land in Seattle on the shore of Lake Washington. In 1908, the Dodge Company had executed a quitclaim deed concerning a narrow strip of the property that bordered the lake so that the city could construct what is now Lake Washington Boulevard. The deed contained three conditions, one of which reserved the right, for Dodge itself and for its successors and assigns, to build and maintain a boathouse along the shore of Lake Washington. The city was responsible for acquiring the land necessary for the boathouse and for allowing the building and use of it. Breach of this condition allowed the grantor, Dodge, or its successors to forfeit the grant. In 1983, Jack M. Martin, one of the successors to the Dodge land, and others asked the city for permission to build a boathouse. The Martins then attempted to exercise their right to forfeit the city's interest in the land along which Lake Washington is located. The city admitted that the language in the deed created a condition subsequent, but argued that the condition subsequent was no longer enforceable due to the passage of time. The city also maintained that the subsequent lowering of Lake Washington had made compliance with the condition subsequent legally impossible. The city claimed that because the state had given the newly uncovered shore land to the city on the condition that the land be used as a park, the city could not allow the construction of a private boathouse on this site. Would you accept these arguments if you were a judge? (*Martin* v. *City of Seattle*, 728 P.2d 1091 [Wash. App. 1986].)

3. Ben Lindsey was hired by the University of Arizona as head basketball coach in April, 1982. Lindsey's contract with Arizona, a National Collegiate Athletic Association (NCAA) member, made him attractive to shoe manufacturers and distributors. One such distributor, Classco, offered Lindsey a shoe endorsement contract worth $30,000 and seventy-five pairs of Adidas shoes if Lindsey would encourage his basketball players to wear Adidas brand basketball shoes during the season. Throughout the 1982–1983 basketball season, the players, with few exceptions, wore Adidas brand shoes. When the university fired Lindsey as head coach in March, 1983, Classco refused to fulfill its second-year agreement with him. Classco argued that Lindsey's termination as head coach operated as a condition subsequent that extinguished Classco's obligation to perform. Should a court accept Classco's assertion? (*Lindsey* v. *Classco*, 642 F. Supp. 250 [D. Ariz. 1986].)

4. In November, 1980, Paul L. Gould individually and as president of Paul L. Gould, Inc. entered into a contract with P. A. Argentinis for the construction of a custom-designed house. The agreement incorporated the house plans and specifications prepared for Argentinis by professional architects. The contract contained Gould's various express warranties, including a warranty against water leakage into the premises for one year after closing. The house was to be ready for occupation by 1 May 1981. The closing took place in April, 1981. Gould took from Argentinis a purchase money mortgage for the final $50,000 of the total sale price of $334,000. Although a certificate of occupancy had been issued, the Argentinis family was unable to occupy the house as scheduled because forty to fifty items of construction remained unfinished. After further negotiation, the parties reached a supplemental agreement modifying the terms of the mortgage. The parties agreed to a modified promissory note and mortgage for $43,000 and a cash payment of $3000, which was to be released on completion of those construction items deemed unsatisfactory. The Argentinis family moved into the house in early July, 1981, and the cash payment and documents were released to Gould from escrow. Some items due for completion later that month or "within a reasonable period of time" had not yet been performed. Of principal concern to Argentinis were the lack of water pressure in the house and the contaminated well water. He subsequently discovered that the well had been placed, without a permit, too near a septic system and sewer drain. In addition, the basement remained vulnerable to flooding during rains. Storm

flooding occurred within the warranty period, again in June, 1982, and twice more in April, 1983, causing substantial damage to personal and real property. Argentinis made repeated demands on Gould within the warranty period to rectify the problems of the improperly sited well, the flooding basement, and numerous other significant deficiencies. Gould refused to repair the defects unless given an unconditional release concerning all such defects and the right to determine those defects for which he had borne responsibility. Argentinis refused to give this release, refused to make payments on the outstanding debt, and brought suit against Gould for breach of contract and breach of express warranties. Gould sought to foreclose the $43,000 mortgage. The parties tried these consolidated actions before an attorney trial referee who found for Argentinis on the contract claims and on Gould's foreclosure action, ruling that Gould should not receive the final contract payment because he had not substantially completed construction. The trial court accepted the referee's report in September, 1989, and rendered judgments consistent with that report; this appeal followed. Among other things, Gould claimed that the referee's conclusion that the company had not substantially completed the construction had been against the weight of evidence. He stated that Argentinis's architects had performed inspections as the work progressed and had approved the materials and workmanship. Moreover, Gould submitted, the town building inspector had found that the project met all but one minor code requirement and had thus issued a valid certificate of occupancy. Had Gould substantially performed this contract? (*Argentinis* v. *Gould*, 579 A.2d. 1078 [Conn. App. 1990].)

5. Jake Adams was seriously injured while racing a motorcycle at the Cherokee Dragway. Adams had signed a document entitled "RELEASE AND WAIVER OF LIABILITY AND INDEMNITY AGREEMENT" in which Adams had agreed not to sue the dragway for injuries. Embossed in red and beneath the signature of Jake Adams was the statement, "I HAVE READ THIS RELEASE." Adams argued that the release was not binding on him because he had not read it prior to signing, had not known it was a release from liability, and instead had assumed it was merely the registration form for the race. Did Adams's failure to read the release invalidate its legal effect? (*Adams* v. *Roark*, 686 S.W.2d 73 [Tenn. 1985].)

6. E. B. Sherman, Inc. (Sherman) had sold its rights to serve as the Florida sales representative of certain lighting fixture manufacturers to Robert Mirizio and Ben Smith in exchange for $50,850. As part of this agreement, Sherman had furnished its Florida customers' list to Mirizio and Smith. As it turned out, the rights Mirizio and Smith had purchased were actually nontransferable; on learning this fact, Mirizio and Smith had notified Sherman of their intent to rescind the contract. What theory (or theories) would they use to support their claim for rescission? (*E. B. Sherman, Inc.* v. *Mirizio*, 556 So.2d. 1145 [Fla. App. 2 Dist. 1989].)

7. Riverbend Products, Inc. (Riverbend) processes and sells tomato paste and frozen citrus products. It has processing plants in Visalia, California, and Yuma, Arizona. On 14 July 1988, Cliffstar Corporation (Cliffstar) ordered 3.2 million pounds of tomato paste from Riverbend. In the same purchase order, Cliffstar attempted to purchase an option on an additional 500,000 pounds of paste. Delivery of the paste was to be spread over the following year, until 30 June 1989. Riverbend accepted the order in writing on 25 July 1988 but rejected Cliffstar's requested option "due to the uncertainty of the incoming tonnage." Between October and December 1987, Riverbend had forecast sales for the 1988 tomato crop of approximately 53 million pounds of tomato paste. By combining firm contracts with spot buys, Riverbend planned to acquire sufficient numbers of raw tomatoes to support its sales forecast. Thereafter, Riverbend received oral and written orders for approximately 78 million pounds of tomato paste. It remained disputed, however, whether Riverbend had accepted these orders and thus had entered into contracts to supply this amount. About the time of the formation of the Cliffstar-Riverbend contract and extending into the early fall, a shortage developed in the tomato crop in Arizona and California. The combined 1988 Arizona and California tomato harvest came in at about 8.45 percent less than early season estimates. Riverbend's contract growers delivered only 95,000–100,000 tons of the 170,000 tons of tomatoes for which Riverbend had contracted, or about 56–58 percent. Shortages developed in other parts of the country as well. Riverbend had become aware of the Arizona shortage by 1 August 1988 and of the California shortage by September, 1988, when its processing plants had completed canning the shortened supply. Owing to these shortages, Riverbend failed to deliver the 3.2 million pounds of paste to Cliffstar. Instead, Riverbend allocated its available supply among its customers. Riverbend first notified Cliffstar by letter on 27 September

1988 that all contracts would have to be reevaluated. Riverbend then notified Cliffstar by letter on 21 November 1988 that Cliffstar would be allocated 1 million pounds of paste. Riverbend did not allocate to each of its customers an equal percentage of their orders. Between 21 November 1988 and 23 January 1989, Riverbend and Cliffstar engaged in oral and written settlement-modification negotiations. The parties disputed whether Cliffstar had agreed to an allocation or had otherwise modified the initial contract with Riverbend. In any event, Riverbend delivered substantially less than 1 million pounds of paste to Cliffstar. When Cliffstar demanded its full contract amount, this lawsuit ensued. Riverbend defended its failure to deliver by citing the UCC doctrine of commercial impracticability. Would this defense be successful in these circumstances? (*Cliffstar Corporation* v. *Riverbend Products, Inc.*, 750 F. Supp. 81 [W.D. N.Y. 1990].)

8. When he retired in July, 1983, John R. Hunt, M.D., purchased a "claims-made" professional liability insurance policy from St. Paul Fire and Marine Insurance Company (St. Paul). The policy provided coverage for claims made from 1983 through 29 July 1986, regardless of when the acts or omissions giving rise to any such claim had occurred. The policy specifically and unambiguously stated that in order to be covered, a claim must "be made while this agreement is in effect." Additionally, the policy answered the question, "When is a claim made?" as follows: "A claim is made on the date you first report an incident or injury to us or our agent." A patient of Dr. Hunt had filed a medical malpractice claim against him on 29 August 1985. Dr. Hunt had failed to answer the complaint, and a default judgment had been entered against him on 17 April 1987 in the amount of $250,000. Because the patient's claim had not been reported to St. Paul until July 1987, the company denied coverage because notice of the claim had not been given until after the expiration of the policy. Dr. Hunt died on 28 February 1988. On 23 August 1988, St. Paul brought a declaratory judgment action, requesting that the court declare that no coverage had existed as to the medical malpractice claim here at issue. Lenore Hunt, as the personal representative of Dr. Hunt's estate, answered the complaint and in that answer alleged that Dr. Hunt's failure to provide notice had been "excused as a result of [his] infirmity and incapacity. . . ." During Dr. Hunt's life, he had not been adjudicated an incompetent or an incapacitated person, nor had a conservator or guardian ever been appointed to tend to his affairs. Nevertheless, at the trial of this declaratory judgment action, the jury had determined that Dr. Hunt was unable to give notice of the claim in question to St. Paul during the period of August, 1985, to 29 July 1986 because of a mental impairment. The jury also found that his inability to give notice of the claim had not been reasonably foreseeable to Dr. Hunt at the time he had purchased the policy. Based on these findings, together with the facts stipulated by the parties, the trial court had declared that coverage by St. Paul did exist for the patient's claim to the policy limits. The court had further found that St. Paul remained liable for post-judgment interest on that amount from the date of judgment and for the reasonable attorneys' fees incurred by the estate in defending the lawsuit. On appeal, St. Paul contended that Dr. Hunt's mental impairment would not excuse noncompliance with the notice provisions of the policy. Specifically, it alleged that, under a claims-made policy such as at issue here, the insured's duty to provide notice of a claim is a material condition precedent to coverage and that impossibility or impracticability of performance does not excuse the failure to comply with such a condition. Should a court accept St. Paul's reasoning in these circumstances? (*St. Paul Fire and Marine Insurance Company* v. *Estate of John R. Hunt, M.D.*, 811 P.2d. 432 [Colo. App. 1991].)

9. In February, 1985, Judy McDonald and Bedford Datsun (Bedford) entered into a sales contract for an automobile. Bedford agreed to deliver the automobile in the middle part of April, 1985, and the deal would be closed at that time in order to accommodate McDonald's financial arrangements. McDonald paid a deposit of $100 and agreed to trade in a 1982 Cadillac Cimarron for $6300, with the condition that the trade-in was subject to reappraisal at the time of the delivery of the new automobile. Bedford telephoned McDonald on 17 April to inform her that her automobile had been shipped from Chicago prior to that date. That same day, McDonald visited Bedford. She was concerned that the added mileage on her Cadillac might reduce the trade-in allowance. The salesperson, though not the used car appraiser, inspected the car and assured her that the added mileage would not affect the trade-in allowance. On 4 May Bedford advised McDonald that her automobile had not arrived, but requested her to bring her trade-in automobile to the dealership for a reappraisal. At this time, the appraiser devalued the trade-in by $500. McDonald protested this action, refused to accept her

deposit back, and then proposed that the parties split the $500 difference. Bedford refused, saying it would not compromise. McDonald left the dealership after asking the salesperson to telephone her as soon as the new automobile had arrived. On 8 May, McDonald telephoned Bedford to say that she would accept the devaluation of her trade-in. Bedford told her that her automobile had been delivered on 6 May and transferred in a lease transaction to another person that same day. Bedford stated that it had consequently canceled McDonald's sales contract and refunded her deposit, which she received on 8 May. Bedford sold the new automobile for the same price as contracted for by McDonald, but with no trade-in allowed. Following a trial without a jury, the court found that Bedford had been in possession of McDonald's automobile on 4 May and thus refused to accept Bedford's representations that the automobile had not arrived until 6 May. The court determined that Bedford had sold McDonald's automobile to another party because it had received a better bargain. According to the court, by lowering the trade-in value of the Cadillac, Bedford had attempted to evade its contract with McDonald. The court concluded that McDonald had not breached the contract. On appeal, Bedford claimed that the trial court had erred in finding that Bedford, not McDonald, had breached the sales contract. Bedford argued that McDonald's refusal to pay, and her subsequent offer to split, the additional $500 on the trade-in had constituted an anticipatory repudiation of the existing sales contract that had excused performance on Bedford's part. How should the appellate court rule on Bedford's contention? (*McDonald v. Bedford Datsun,* 570 N.E.2d. 299 [Ohio App. 1989].)

10. W. E. Erickson Construction Company (Erickson) sued Congress-Kenilworth Corporation (C-K) for sums due for the construction of a concrete water slide known as "Thunder Mountain Rapids." Erickson argued that a corporate resolution—apparently rendered in order to allow Erickson to secure financing on behalf of C-K—that authorized the transfer of the land on which the slide was built to Erickson as security for payment and a subsequent letter acknowledging C-K's indebtedness of $550,000 to Erickson represented an accord and satisfaction that made C-K liable to Erickson. Did the correspondence between the parties indicate that the terms of the original contract and the amount of fees due under this contract were sufficiently in dispute to constitute an accord and satisfaction? (*W. E. Erickson Construction, Inc.* v. *Congress-Kenilworth Corporation,* 477 N.E.2d 513 [Ill. App. 1985].)

C H A P T E R 17

Contractual Remedies

O U T L I N E

TYPES OF REMEDIES

Despite the parties' original intentions, the possibility exists that one party will fail to live up to the contractual obligations. As we have already learned, such nonperformance constitutes a breach of the contract and entitles the injured party to certain remedies, assuming the injured party does not wish to waive (or ignore) the breach. A *remedy* is *a cause of action resulting from breach of a contract.* After the occurrence of a breach, remedies attempt to satisfy the parties' expectations as of the time of the contract's formation. Remedies fall into two main categories: those resulting from a court's exercise of its powers "at law" (*legal* remedies) and those arising from a court's use of its powers of equity (**equitable** remedies). Although you as a layperson have probably always used the term *legal remedies* to encompass both types of relief, in this chapter you will learn to identify the sorts of situations in which it is appropriate for a court to order one kind of relief or the other. You also will become aware of the fact that these types of remedies usually are mutually exclusive.

The most common legal remedy sought consists of *damages,* or the amount of money that will put the injured party in the same position he or she would have been in had the other party performed. The injured party must *mitigate,* or minimize, these damages; but having fulfilled this legal duty, the injured party should be able at the very least to receive *compensatory damages,* those that will put the party in the same economic position that would have been enjoyed had the agreement been performed. If the facts permit, the injured party moreover may receive *consequential damages,* those indirect or special damages springing from the effects or aftermath of the breach itself; *punitive damages,* those damages over and above the actual damages that a court may award in order to deter the defendant from future malicious conduct; and *liquidated damages,* those agreed on by the parties in advance in the event of breach. A court may also give *nominal damages* (a small amount of compensation) for minor, technical contractual breaches that cause no actual losses.

In some situations, money damages will inadequately compensate the injured party for the loss of the bargain occasioned by the breach. Injured persons in these cases ordinarily resort to *equitable* remedies. These possible modes of relief include *rescission,* the cancellation or termination of the contract through the restoration of the parties to the status quo. Restoration is accomplished by *restitution*—the return of the goods, money, or property involved in the contract or the recovery of the reasonable value of the services rendered. *Specific performance,* or the court-ordered enforcement of the contract according to its exact terms, is an alternative type of equitable remedy, as is *quasi contract,* which we discussed in Chapter 8. *Quasi contract,* you may remember, refers to the situation in which a court creates a contract for the parties, despite their wishes and intentions, in order to prevent the unjust enrichment of one party. (The remedy available in quasi contract is restitution

Equitable Arising from the branch of the legal system designed to provide a remedy where no remedy existed at common law; a system designed to provide "fairness" when there was no suitable remedy "at law."

based, allowing the injured party to recover the reasonable value of the services rendered.) *Reformation* (the court's rewriting of a contract in order to remove a mistake and to make the agreement conform to the terms to which the parties originally agreed) and *injunctions* (court-ordered writs directing a person to do or to refrain from doing some specified act) are two other equitable remedies.

Discretionary   Having the freedom to make certain decisions.

Courts' powers to award equitable remedies are **discretionary;** hence, courts will not normally give equitable remedies if the injured party has "unclean hands" (that is, has shown bad faith or dishonesty); if the injured party has unduly delayed bringing the lawsuit; if a **forfeiture** of property will result from the conferring of an equitable decree; if the court itself will necessarily have to supervise the implementation of the remedy granted; or if the remedy at law (ordinarily money damages, as you will recall) is available, determinable, and adequate.

Forfeiture   The loss of a right or privilege as a penalty for certain conduct.

The parties may in advance attempt to limit the remedies available to the injured party. We previously discussed such efforts in the context of exculpatory clauses in Chapter 12. The UCC restricts this common law right to limit remedies in Section 2-719 by sanctioning contracts containing exclusive remedies provisions unless the exclusive remedy fails in its essential purpose (as in a contract that limits the exclusive remedy to repair and replacement of faulty parts of a computer printer that turns out to be a "lemon" and cannot be fixed satisfactorily). The Code, in Section 2-719, also forbids contractual limitations of consequential damages for personal injuries from the use of consumer goods. (The UCC dubs limitations on these sorts of damages **prima facie unconscionable** but notes that limitations of damages in purely commercial settings are not.)

Prima facie   At first sight; on its face; something presumed to be true because of its appearance unless disproved by evidence to the contrary.

Unconscionable   Blatantly unfair and one sided; so unfair as to shock the conscience.

It has been said that for every legal wrong there is a legal remedy. We will explore in this chapter some of the contractual remedies that are obtainable.

DAMAGES

When one party breaches a contract, the other party is entitled to payment for lost expectations. The injured party therefore can bring an action for *damages,* or *the sum of money that will place the party in the same economic position that would have been enjoyed had the contract been performed.*

It is not necessary that the injured party be able to compute exactly what the damages were, as long as the losses were the natural and proximate consequences of the breach. In computing damages, courts ask whether the breaching party, as a reasonable person, should have foreseen at the time of contracting that these injuries would result from breach. If the nonperforming party should have foreseen the losses, courts will award damages to the injured party. The amount of damages awarded will of course depend heavily on the facts of the case.

Compensatory Damages

The most common type of damages is *compensatory damages,* or those *sums of money that will place the injured party in the same economic position that would have been attained had the contract been performed.* Such damages are also called *actual* damages. Injured parties may recover only the damages that the parties can reasonably foresee. The 1854 English case, *Hadley* v. *Baxendale,* enunciated this doctrine, which is still widely accepted as a limitation on the damages recoverable for breach of contract. Under the *Hadley* v. *Baxendale* rule, then, courts will ordinarily confine compensatory damages awards to those losses naturally arising from the breach, or those the parties may have reasonably contemplated or foreseen, at the time of contract formation, as the probable result of a breach of the contract. Compensatory damages include all damages directly attributable to the loss of the bargain previously agreed on by the parties, including lost profits and any incidental expenses incurred as a result of the breach. In a sale of goods, courts usually compute the difference between the contract price and the market price in formulating the actual damages. The same is ordinarily true of land contracts. Thus, if Miranda Construction Company, a developer of real estate for its own particular purposes, orders three bulldozers from Welling Machinery Company and, unfortunately, none of the bulldozers functions properly under such circumstances, Miranda should be able to recover the general or *direct damages* or losses occasioned by the defective equipment. Miranda's costs of repairing the machines constitute one type of direct loss. Alternatively, if Miranda has to buy new bulldozers at higher prices, Miranda will be able to recover the costs associated with obtaining this substitute performance.

Assuming that Miranda's bad luck continues and a seller with whom Miranda has contracted to buy land for investment purposes fails to go through with this realty contract, Miranda can sue the reneging seller for the difference between the price of this piece of land and the one Miranda eventually purchases to take its place. Miranda also can sue for such expenses as the additional brokers' fees or commissions involved in obtaining the second parcel of real estate, since these losses flow directly and foreseeably from the seller's breach as well. However, Miranda in both cases must deduct any expenses saved as a result of the breaches.

The following case deals with some of the concepts we have just discussed and illustrates the complexity of the computation of damages.

Snyder v. *Bio-Lab, Inc.*
405 N.Y.S.2d 596 (N.Y. Sup.Ct. 1978)

FACTS   Snyder had used a teat dip manufactured by Bio-Lab on his dairy cows in order to prevent infectious mastitis, an inflammation of the udder that destroys milk-producing cells. The use of the dip severely burned the udders and teats of 59 of Snyder's 130 milking cows. Of these 59 cows, 39 were rendered useless as milk producers and were sent to slaughter; 9 were sold for beef; and the remaining 11, not as seriously injured as the others, were kept in the herd.

ISSUE   Could Snyder recover as compensatory damages lost profits, including the market value of the slaughtered animals and the loss in milk production occasioned by the incident?

HOLDING   Yes. Snyder should receive damages, subject to some offsets, for these losses.

REASONING   The usual measure of damages for injury to, or destruction of, personal property is the amount that will return the owner, monetarily, to the status he or she enjoyed before the loss. The market value at the time of the loss, or the difference in market value before and after the injury, will generally be the measure applied. Any special value, particular qualities, or capabilities—such as a high rate of milk production or registration—are generally considered as factors making up market value. Thus, Snyder could recover the fair market value of the 48 slaughtered and sold cows ($43,742), but must offset the salvage value of the animals ($10,441), for a loss of $33,301. Furthermore, Snyder could recover the loss of profits for a three-month period following the injury, during which time Snyder attempted to replace the slaughtered cows with cows of equal quality ($7512.44). He could also receive damages for the lost profits attributable to the introduction of the replacement animals into the herd, since experts had testified that the remaining cows produced significantly less milk when the replacement cows were added to the herd. To determine the time period for which these damages were recoverable, it was necessary to compare the earlier production rates of the cows with the production rates after the incident, taking into account the damaged and slaughtered cows, the unaffected cows, and the replacement cows. Hence, the loss attributable to the incident's impact on the remaining cows was $13,010.13 for the relevant five-month period. Given the $1306.00 in special damages that were undisputed, Snyder was awarded $55,129.57 in damages.

Consequential Damages

Besides compensatory damages, it is also possible for plaintiffs like Snyder and Miranda to receive *consequential damages*. Consequential damages are those indirect or special damages springing from the effects or aftermath (i.e., the consequences) of the breach itself. Assume that in addition to the contracts mentioned, Miranda loses a grading contract with the city because the bulldozers will not work and loses several rental contracts from retailers who wished to be part of a mall Miranda was planning to develop on the real estate he had tried to purchase. Can Miranda sue Welling and the seller for the losses accruing from these special circumstances and not just from the direct breach? To determine liability or the lack thereof, a court will apply the "reasonable person" test to see whether such lost contracts were a foreseeable result of Welling and the seller's breach. A judge will not award purely speculative or conjectural damages; but if a court finds Welling and the seller knew, or should have known, at the time of contract formation, of Miranda's circumstances and the potential effect of their breaches on Miranda, it may award incidental or consequential damages. The Uniform Commercial Code also recognizes this doctrine in Sections 2-715 and 2-710.

The following case indicates some of the factors a court will take into account before awarding consequential damages.

Redgrave v. Boston Symphony Orchestra, Inc.
855 F.2d 888 (1st Cir. 1988)

FACTS   Vanessa Redgrave, the noted actress, sued the Boston Symphony Orchestra, Inc. (BSO) for breach of contract. Redgrave alleged that the BSO had cancelled its Boston and New York performances of *Oedipus Rex,* in which Redgrave was to appear as a narrator, in retaliation for Redgrave's public expressions of support for the Palestinian Liberation Organization (PLO). The BSO contended that it had cancelled the performances owing to its concern for physical security and the risk of disruptions that would impair the artistic integrity of the performances. Redgrave argued she should receive as actual damages her performance fee of $31,000 and, in addition, consequential damages for the harm to her professional career caused by the BSO's cancellation of her contract.

ISSUE   Should the BSO be liable for consequential damages arising from the loss of professional opportunities?

HOLDING   Yes. The BSO was liable for the consequential damages represented by Redgrave's loss of one Broadway offer.

REASONING   The district court jury found that the BSO's cancellation of the *Oedipus Rex* concerts had caused consequential harm to Redgrave's professional career and that this harm had been a foreseeable consequence within the contemplation of the parties at the time they had entered into the contract. However, the district court judge overturned the jury's verdict of $100,000 because of the court's belief that Redgrave had not met the strict standards required by the First Amendment for the recovery of such damages involving communicative activity. According to the district court, any statements of opinion by the BSO as reflected in the BSO cancellation and subsequent press release would be protected absolutely under the First Amendment and would bar the recovery of consequential damages. However, the district court had erroneously confused communication *about* the BSO's contract cancellation with the notion of an implied communication of a particular message *by* the BSO regarding Redgrave. Furthermore, under the district court's ruling, the cancellation of almost any contract with a notable figure could effectively be transformed into a statement protected by the First Amendment, thereby unnecessarily diluting the protections intended by contract law. Thus, although Redgrave would have to meet the strict contract requirements for finding consequential damages, no additional requirements would have to be imposed in this case because of the strictures of the First Amendment. In order for Redgrave to prove that the BSO's cancellation had resulted in the loss of other professional opportunities, it would be necessary for her to present sufficient facts for a jury reasonably to infer that Redgrave had lost wages and professional opportunities subsequent to April, 1982; that such losses had been the natural and probable result of the BSO's cancellation rather than the result of other, independent factors; that this harm had been a foreseeable consequence within the contemplation of the parties to the contract when it had been made; and that damages for such losses were capable of being ascertained by reference to some definite standard. The BSO had introduced evidence that Redgrave's political activities and statements had generated widespread media attention prior to the incident with the BSO. Therefore, to the extent that Redgrave might have experienced a decline in the quality of film offers received subsequent to April, 1982, that decline could have resulted from Redgrave's political views and not the BSO's cancellation. Thus, it had been Redgrave's burden to introduce enough facts for a jury reasonably to infer that any decline in film and Broadway offers had been proximately caused by the BSO cancellation and not by the fact that producers independently had been concerned with the same factors that had motivated the BSO. The testimony of one Broadway producer who had considered hiring Redgrave had revealed that he had been affected by the BSO cancellation because the BSO was a premier arts organization dependent on the same type of support his theater was. From this testimony, a jury reasonably could have inferred that the BSO's cancellation had not just highlighted for this producer the potential problems that hiring Redgrave would cause but had actually been a cause of his decision. Hence, Redgrave had presented sufficient evidence to prove consequential damages of $12,000, the fee arrangement contemplated by him for Redgrave's appearance in his production, minus the expenses she personally would have incurred had she appeared in the play. Because she had been unable to prove the other allegations of lost professional opportunities, the appellate court overturned the jury's $100,000 consequential damages award to Redgrave as erroneous.

Duty of Mitigation

In determining whether to give damages and, if so, how to measure them, courts place on the injured party the duty to *mitigate* (or minimize) these damages if possible. In other words, the injured party must *take affirmative steps to prevent escalation of the losses brought about by the breaching party.* In our bulldozer example, courts will expect Miranda to attempt to procure substitute bulldozers, assuming this is possible without undue risk or expense. If Miranda does not undertake such reasonable steps, his failure to mitigate damages will preclude his receiving consequential damages. Rather, the court will limit his losses to those accruing directly from the breach. But if Miranda can prove it was impossible to obtain substitute bulldozers, most courts will excuse his failure to mitigate. The duty of mitigation does not require the injured party to go to superhuman lengths. If the risks or expenses in mitigation attempts are unreasonably great, there is no duty to mitigate.

Punitive Damages

In contrast to their willingness to make compensatory and consequential damages available to injured parties, courts generally will not allow the recovery of punitive damages in breach of contract situations. *Punitive,* or *exemplary, damages* are imposed *not to compensate the injured party but to punish the wrongdoer in order to deter future conduct of this sort.* The old common law rule was that punitive damages were never appropriate for breaches of contract. Though still rare, some statutes now permit the imposition of punitive damages in contractual situations (such as **treble damages** under the antitrust laws). Furthermore, some courts have been willing to grant punitive damages in situations in which one party has acted willfully. An insurance company that unduly delays paying off legitimate contractual claims against it may be subject to punitive damages in order to discourage this type of conduct. Consumer transactions also may form the basis for an award of punitive damages if the circumstances so warrant.

Treble damages A statutory remedy in antitrust actions that allows the successful plaintiff to recover three times the damages suffered as a result of the antitrust violation.

In the following case, the Supreme Court upheld a punitive damage award in a contract action involving an insurance company. On appeal, the insurance company challenged the jury's discretion to award such damages under the common law as unconstitutional. Note how the Court dealt with this challenge.

Pacific Mutual Life Insurance Company v. Haslip
111 S. Ct. 1032 (1991)

FACTS   Beginning in August, 1981, Cleopatra Haslip and other employees of Roosevelt City, Alabama, had paid premiums to Lemmie L. Ruffin, Jr., a Pacific Mutual Life Insurance Company (Pacific Mutual) agent, for health and life insurance.

After her hospitalization in January, 1982, Haslip discovered that she had no insurance coverage. Apparently, Ruffin had failed to remit the premiums he had collected to the appropriate insurers, with the result that Haslip's policies had lapsed without her knowledge. Haslip sued Pacific Mutual for damages in fraud owing to Ruffin's misappropriation of these premiums and sought to hold the company liable on a theory of **respondeat superior.** Following the court's charge instructing the jury that it could award punitive damages if it determined liability for fraud existed, the jury, among other things, returned a verdict for Haslip of over $1 million against Pacific Mutual and Ruffin. This sum included a punitive damages award representing more than four times the amount of compensatory damages Haslip had claimed. The Supreme Court of Alabama affirmed, specifically upholding the punitive damages award. On appeal to the United States Supreme Court, Pacific Mutual argued that the punitive damages award assessed against it violated the due process clause of the Fourteenth Amendment.

Respondeat superior Doctrine asserting that an employer is liable for the wrongful acts of an employee.

ISSUE

Would the due process clause of the Fourteenth Amendment, which requires fundamental fairness, act as a check on undue jury discretion to award punitive damages and, in the absence of any express statutory limits, thus place outer limits on the size of such civil damages awards?

HOLDING

No. The common law method for assessing punitive damages, consistently upheld by state and federal courts for many years, did not demonstrate such inherent unfairness as to deny defendants due process.

REASONING

Punitive damages have long been a part of traditional state tort law in the United States. And as early as the 1700s in England, Blackstone appeared to note their use. Moreover, the early American cases (in the 1780s and 1790s) that used the traditional common law approach allowed the jury, after a court's instructing it to consider the gravity of the wrong and the need to deter similar wrongful conduct, initially to determine the amount of the punitive damages award. Trial and appellate courts then reviewed the jury's determination to ensure its reasonableness. Furthermore, it would appear that every state and federal court that has considered the question has ruled that the common law method for assessing punitive damage does not in itself violate due process, since the method does not appear to be so inherently unfair as to be per se unconstitutional. In addition, the common law method for assessing punitive damages was well established before the enactment of the Fourteenth Amendment. On the other hand, it would be just as inappropriate to say that, because courts have recognized punitive damages for so long, their imposition is never unconstitutional. One must concede that unlimited jury discretion (or unlimited judicial discretion) in the fixing of punitive damages might invite extreme results that jar one's constitutional sensibilities. In fact, concerns about punitive damages that "run wild" abound. Yet one need not, and indeed one cannot, draw a mathematically bright line between the constitutionally acceptable and the constitutionally unacceptable that would fit every case. Nonetheless, general concerns of reasonableness and adequate guidance for the court when the case is tried to a jury properly enter into this constitutional calculus. In this case, the punitive damages assessed by the jury against Pacific Mutual did not violate the due process clause of the Fourteenth Amendment for the following reasons. First, the trial court's punitive damages instruction, stating that the purpose of punitive damages is to punish the defendant and to protect the public by deterring future wrongdoing and that the jury had to consider the character and degree of wrong shown and the necessity of preventing similar wrong, reasonably accommodated Pacific Mutual's interest in rational decision making and the state's interest in meaningful individual assessment of appropriate deterrence and retribution without giving the jury undue discretion. Hence, no violation of the due process clause resulted from this instruction. Second, Alabama's posttrial procedures for scrutinizing punitive damages awards, which required trial courts to reflect in the record their reasons for interfering with the verdict or their refusing to do so on grounds of the excessiveness of the damages, included such factors as a consideration of the culpability of the defendant's conduct, the desirability of discouraging others from similar conduct, and the impact on the parties or innocent third parties. Such posttrial procedures ensured meaningful and adequate review of punitive damages awards. Similarly, in this case, under Alabama law, the Alabama Supreme Court's review of this punitive damages award, by first undertaking a comparative analysis and then applying detailed substantive standards for evaluating the award to ensure that the award did not exceed the amount that would accomplish society's goals of punishment and deterrence, constituted an appropriate method to help assure the reasonableness of the amount of punitive damages and the rationality of the award in furthering the purposes of deterrence and punishment. In short, the Alabama Supreme Court's postverdict review ensured that punitive damages awards were not grossly out of proportion to the severity of the offense and had some understandable relationship to compensatory damages. Such procedural safeguards, including instructions to the jury on the nature and purpose of punitive damages awards, posttrial review of the punitive damages award by the trial court's consideration of certain enumerated factors, and the subsequent comparative analysis by the Alabama Supreme Court that applied detailed substantive standards developed for evaluating punitive damages awards, imposed a sufficiently definite and meaningful constraint on the discretion of Alabama fact finders in awarding punitive damages to ensure that such awards were not grossly disproportionate to the severity of the offense and were adequate to protect the due process rights of an insurer whose agent had defrauded the insureds. In sum, the standard of proof requiring the jury to be "reasonably satisfied from the evidence" before it could impose punitive damages under Alabama law, when buttressed by other existing procedural and substantive protections, was constitutionally sufficient, notwithstanding the desirability of requiring a higher standard of proof. Finally, then, a punitive damages award of over $800,000 against an insurer whose agent had defrauded an insured was not excessive and did not violate the insurer's due process rights, even though the award exceeded by more than four times the amount of compensatory damages, more than 200 times the out-of-pocket expenses incurred by the insured, and greatly exceeded the fine that Alabama law imposed for insurance fraud.

YOU BE THE JUDGE

A plaintiff brought a discrimination suit against a roller rink and a deputy sheriff who had arrested the plaintiff. A Virginia jury awarded the plaintiff compensatory damages of $25,000 and punitive damages of $175,500. Under Virginia law, punitive damages that either "shock the conscience of the court" or derive from a jury influenced by "passion or prejudice" are "excessive" and, hence, unenforceable.

In a second case, a West Virginia couple who lived near a landfill and who had filed a lawsuit against its owners received nothing in compensatory damages, but the jury awarded them $105,000 in punitive damages. West Virginia law obligates a judge to uphold a punitive damages award unless the award is "monstrous" or lacks any "foundation in the evidence."

Assume that the defendants have asked you, the appellate judge, to consider the fairness of these two awards under the constitutional guidelines established in *Pacific Mutual Life Insurance Co. v. Haslip.* How would you rule in each case?

Source: "Law," Christi Harlan and Milo Geyelin, *The Wall Street Journal,* December 16, 1991, page B2.

Notice how the Supreme Court emphasized the policy underpinnings for a jury's award of punitive damages and the existence of various procedural and substantive protections that would act as a curb on the jury's otherwise unfettered discretion to award *any* amount of damages, no matter how gargantuan the award might be. In addition, ponder the ethical conduct of Pacific Mutual's agent that subjected the company to legal liability.

Use the following case to test your understanding of the principles discussed to this point.

National Advertising Company v. Wilson Auto Parts, Inc.
569 N.E.2d 997 (Ind. App. 1991)

FACTS In April, 1985, Wilson Auto Parts, Inc. (Wilson) executed a written agreement with National Advertising Company (National) for advertising space on one of its outdoor billboards. The agreement set forth the size of the billboard (12 feet by 36 feet), the unit charge ($375 per month), and the length of the lease (three years). Eighteen months before the lease expired, National removed the billboard on which Wilson's advertisement had appeared and replaced the billboard with a larger one. National did not notify Wilson in advance of the removal of either the advertisement or the billboard. Shortly after removing Wilson's advertisement, but before contracting with Cellular One, National advised Wilson of the availability of the larger billboard but at a unit price higher than that for which Wilson had contracted. Wilson rejected the offer and insisted that National honor the terms of the original agreement. National offered Wilson another location for the placement of the advertisement, but Wilson rejected this offer by insisting that the location of its advertising was unique and that another location would be unsatisfactory. National also offered to place Wilson's advertisement on the larger billboard for the original contract price of $375 per month, but after the expiration of Cellular One's contract. Thereafter, National leased the larger billboard space to another advertiser (Cellular One) at a unit price of $1590 per month for one year. Wilson sued National for breach of contract and received compensatory damages of $21,870 (but no punitive damages) after a **bench trial.** National appealed, asserting that the judge should not have awarded Wilson compensatory damages because Wilson had suffered no losses. Wilson cross-appealed, contending that the trial court's failure to award it punitive damages amounted to reversible error.

Bench trial A trial without a jury in which the judge alone decides the case.

ISSUE Was Wilson entitled to compensatory and punitive damages?

HOLDING Yes and no. Wilson, because of the loss of the benefit of his bargain caused by National's breach of contract, had merited the trial court's award of compensatory damages. But the absence of fraud or malice in National's conduct made Wilson ineligible for punitive damages; hence, the trial court had reasoned correctly in failing to award Wilson punitive damages.

REASONING National argued that the judge should not have granted Wilson compensatory damages because the advertiser had suffered no actual losses. National maintained that in a breach of contract action, two methods of establishing damages exist: (1) lost profits and (2) the benefit of the bargain. As to lost profits, National correctly asserted that the record contains no evidence that Wilson had lost any revenue because of National's breach of contract. As to the benefit of the bargain rationale, National submitted that the proper computation consists of the amount by which the market value of the 12-by-36-foot sign for the unexpired term was exceeded by the amount Wilson had obligated itself to pay under the contract for the sign. National contended that the monthly fair market value of the sign was $375, precisely the monthly amount that the contract had required Wilson to pay; and hence under the "benefit of the bargain" standard, the court should not have allowed Wilson to recover damages. However, National's argument contained fatal flaws. The evidence at trial showed that the parties had agreed that the monthly

Stipulation   Agreement by both parties concerning facts placed before a court.

rental value of the 12-by-36-foot advertising billboard was $375 on *30 April 1985*. The monthly rental value of the 14-by-48-foot monopole billboard was $1590 in late 1986. The parties' **stipulation** had focused on the monthly rental value of the billboard at the time of the execution of the contract. There was no stipulation concerning the monthly rental value of the 12-by-36-foot sign in November, 1986, which was at or near the time of the contract's breach. On the other hand, evidence in the record existed from which the trial court could have determined its value. For example, Wilson had contracted for billboard advertising space at a specific location, namely, the east side of 45th and North Keystone, facing north. The location of the billboard itself had intrinsic value independent of the actual size of the billboard. Hence, although it was true that National had placed a newer and larger sign on the east side of 45th and North Keystone, facing north, the value of the advertising space on the smaller sign was not necessarily substantially different from the value of the advertising space on the larger sign. The trial court found that National had rented advertising space on the newer sign for $1590 per month. The record revealed that National had offered Wilson advertising space on the newer sign at the rate of $375 per month. The record further showed that other billboards in the immediate vicinity had been renting for $1750 per month. Thus, the trial court had sufficient evidence on which to conclude that the value of the advertising space at the location of the billboard had been $1590 per month at the time National had breached its contract with Wilson. A damage award does not require any specific degree of certainty, as long as the evidence supports the amount awarded and the award is not based on speculation or conjecture. A party who suffers from a breach of contract is entitled to recover the benefit of his or her bargain. Consequently, when a party breaches a contract to provide advertising space, the nonbreaching party's benefit of the bargain is measured by the difference between the fair market value of the advertising space before the loss and the fair market value at the time of the loss. In this case, the trial court awarded compensatory damages to Wilson in the amount of $21,870.00. The court calculated this award by measuring the difference between the fair market value of the advertising space before the loss and the fair market value at the time of loss. Because the evidence had supported this amount, which figure was not based upon speculation or conjecture, the trial court had not erred in its computation of damages. National next contended that the trial court erred in neglecting to include in its judgment any consideration of Wilson's failure to mitigate damages. National argued that since Wilson had made no effort to reduce or mitigate its losses, a court should bar it from recovering compensatory damages. As a general rule, a nonbreaching party must mitigate damages. However, this general rule is not without exception or limitation. The breaching party has the burden of proving that the nonbreaching party has failed to use reasonable diligence to mitigate damages. The record indicated that National had offered Wilson advertising space on other of its billboard signs at different locations throughout the city for the same monthly rental Wilson was paying on its original contract. National also had offered to place Wilson's advertisement on the larger billboard once the Cellular One contract had expired (nearly a year after the offer had been made). In explaining why Wilson had declined National's offers, John Wilson, the president of Wilson Auto Parts, Inc., testified that the location of the 12-by-36-foot sign was unique; the sign was in close proximity to his business; traffic could see it from at least two different directions; and the advertisement distinguished Wilson from his competitors located in the immediate area. The record also showed that John Wilson had sought alternative advertising from at least one other outdoor advertising sign company, which had a billboard approximately 150 yards from his original sign; however, the monthly rental at $1750 had been cost prohibitive. Given these facts, National had not carried its burden of proving Wilson failed to use reasonable diligence to mitigate damages. Moreover, because of the unique location of this particular sign, Wilson was not required to obtain advertising space at another location. Nor was Wilson obligated to wait for a year in order to use the sign at the location for which it had contracted. In short, the trial court had not erred in declining to make any finding concerning mitigation of damages. On cross-appeal, Wilson contended that the trial court had erred in failing to award punitive damages. Wilson argued that National had knowingly, willfully, and wrongfully removed Wilson's advertisement; and, in spite of Wilson's objections, National had rented the advertising space to another advertiser. Injured parties ordinarily cannot recover punitive damages in breach of contract actions in the absence of clear and convincing evidence that the breaching party's conduct showed malice, fraud, gross negligence, or oppressiveness and that the breaching party's acts were inconsistent with the hypothesis that the tortious conduct resulted from a mistake of law or fact, an honest error of judgment, overzealousness, mere negligence, or other noniniquitous human failings. Because there was no clear and convincing evidence that malice, fraud, gross negligence, or oppressive conduct had accompanied National's conduct, the trial court's failure to award Wilson punitive damages had not constituted reversible error.

Liquidated Damages

The parties may agree *in advance* that *on breach of contract a certain sum of money will be paid* to the injured party. This remedy is called *liquidated damages*. The amount agreed to in advance by the parties fully satisfies any liability attendant on the breach that has occurred. Courts will enforce such provisions if (1) the amount agreed on is reasonable and not out of proportion to the apparent injury resulting from the breach and (2) calculation of the resulting damages in advance and with any accuracy would be difficult, if not impossible. UCC Section 2-718 takes a similar approach in the context of sales contracts.

Our contractor from earlier in the chapter, Miranda, may well find himself subject to such a clause. Construction contracts typically have clauses assessing a per-day charge for delays in completing a building on time. As long as the per-day charge is reasonable, courts generally uphold these clauses because of the difficulty of ascertaining the amount of damages that breach of such a contract would cause.

Courts will not enforce *penalties*, however. Penalties consist of amounts unrelated to the possible damages that may occur and are usually excessively large. Such an arbitrary lump sum, even if the parties have agreed to it as satisfaction of a breach, will be void. The case that follows illustrates some of these points.

Kvassay v. Murray
808 P.2d 896 (Kan. App. 1991)

FACTS On 22 February 1984, Kvassay, who had been an independent insurance adjuster, contracted to sell 24,000 cases of baklava to Great American at $19 per case. Under the contract, the sales were to occur over a one-year period with Great American as Kvassay's only customer. The contract included a clause that provided: "If Buyer refuses to accept or repudiates delivery of the goods sold to him, under this Agreement, Seller shall be entitled to damages, at the rate of $5.00 per case, for each case remaining to be delivered under this Contract." Early in this contractual relationship, checks issued by Great American were dishonored for insufficient funds. Frequently one of the Murrays (the controlling shareholders of Great American) issued a personal check for the amount due. After producing approximately 3000 cases, Kvassay stopped manufacturing the baklava because the Murrays had refused to purchase any more of the product. In April, 1985, Kvassay filed suit for damages arising from the collapse of his baklava baking business. The trial court deemed the liquidated damages provision unreasonable (and hence unenforceable) because of the great disparity between Kvassay's previous yearly income (about $20,000) and the liquidated damages claim ($105,000). The court also refused to permit Kvassay to recover damages for lost profits. Kvassay appealed these findings by the trial court.

ISSUE Was the liquidated damages clause in the contract unreasonable?

HOLDING No. The court erred in using Kvassay's previous income as a yardstick for judging the reasonableness of the liquidated damages clause; hence, the appellate court remanded the case for further consideration of the criteria the trial court should have applied in determining the validity of the clause.

REASONING Kvassay's first line of attack focused on the trial court's ruling that the amount of liquidated damages sought by him was unreasonable, therefore making the liquidated damages clause unenforceable. Kvassay claimed $105,000 in losses under the liquidated damages clause of the contract, representing $5 per case for the approximately 21,000 cases of baklava that he was unable to deliver. The trial court determined that Kvassay's use of expected profits to formulate liquidated damages was improper because the business enterprise lacked duration, permanency, and recognition. The court then compared Kvassay's previous yearly income (about $20,000) with the claim for liquidated damages ($105,000) and found the disparity so great as to make the clause unenforceable. Since the contract involved the sale of goods between merchants, the Uniform Commercial Code (UCC) governed the transaction. This Kansas statute reads in part: "(1) Damages for breach by either party may be liquidated in the agreement but only at an amount which is reasonable in the light of the anticipated or actual harm caused by the breach, the difficulties of proof of loss, and the inconvenience or nonfeasibility of otherwise obtaining an adequate remedy. A term fixing unreasonably large liquidated damages is void as a penalty." Non-UCC cases in Kansas judge the validity of liquidated damages clauses under a two-step test: Damages must be reasonable and difficult to ascertain. Under the UCC, however, reasonableness is the only test; the Kansas UCC provides three criteria by which to measure the reasonableness of liquidated damages clauses: (1) the anticipated or actual harm caused by the breach, (2) the difficulty of proving loss, and (3) the difficulty of obtaining an adequate remedy. In its ruling, the trial court deemed the liquidated damages clause unreasonable in light of Kvassay's income before he had entered into the manufacturing contract with Great American. The Kansas UCC would provide no such basis for contrasting income under a previous, unrelated employment arrangement with the liquidated damages sought under a manufacturing contract. Indeed, the traditional goal of the law in cases where a buyer breaches a manufacturing contract is to place the seller in the same position he or she would have occupied if the vendee had preformed the contract. Thus, liquidated damages under the contract in this case must be measured against the anticipated or actual loss under the baklava contract. Consequently, the trial court erred in using Kvassay's previous income as a yardstick. A better measure of the validity of the liquidated damages clause in this case would stem from a comparison of the actual lost profits caused by the breach with the $5 per case amount set by the clause. However, Kvassay made no attempt during the bench trial to prove actual profits or actual costs of production. Thus, the trial court could not compare the $5 liquidated damages clause in the contract with the actual profits lost by the breach. It was not until the jury trial that Kvassay had attempted to prove the actual profits lost as part of his damages. Given the trial court's ruling that lost profits were not recoverable and could not be presented to the jury, it is questionable whether the court would have permitted evidence concerning lost profits at the bench trial. In short, the trial court utilized an impermissible factor to issue its ruling on the liquidated damages clause and did not directly address the correct statutory factors. Accordingly, the trial court's analysis represented reversible error that would necessitate a remand for further consideration of the reasonableness of the liquidated damages clauses in light of the three criteria set out in the Kansas UCC. Kvassay also contended that the trial court erred in ruling that damages for lost profits were not recoverable. As noted, the trial court made this ruling prior to hearing any evidence on the issue of lost profits. In ruling that Kvassay could not recover lost profits, the court held as a matter of law that this bakery business had not been in existence a sufficient length of time to calculate future profits and serve as a basis for the recovery of damages. However, the UCC would govern the damages in this case, and the trial court erred in finding the UCC inapplicable. The general rule governing damages is: "The remedies provided by this act shall be liberally administered to the end that the aggrieved party may be put in as good a position as if the other party had fully performed." In addition, the Kansas UCC specifically allows lost profits as damages. In this case, Kvassay attempted to present an ample basis on which to determine profits earned on the baklava produced under the contract, including the testimony of a certified public accountant, who had stated that, from an accounting standpoint, at least 5 percent of the baklava contract needed to be completed before profits could be determined with "reasonable certainty." In this case, 12.5 percent of the contract had been completed. Given the quantity of evidence offered to prove the profitability of Kvassay's business, the trial court was premature in ruling, as a matter of law, that Kvassay could not prove lost profits. Kvassay should have been permitted to offer his evidence and meet his burden of proof regarding such damages.

Nominal Damages

We have noted that for most breaches of contract, an action for damages may be possible. However, in certain cases, especially those involving a minor, or technical, breach, the injured party sustains no actual losses or damages. A court may nevertheless award *a small amount of compensation* (say $1) for the breach. This type of remedy is called *nominal damages*. Sometimes a court or jury awards nominal damages because the injured party has not been able to prove the substantial damages that he or she claims to have suffered. Upon proof of a breach, the injured party is therefore entitled only to nominal damages, the token sum that a court will require the defendant to pay as an acknowledgment of the wrongful conduct in which he or she has engaged.

EQUITABLE REMEDIES

When the "at law" remedy of damages is unavailable, indeterminable, or inadequate, courts in the exercise of their powers of equity may award certain remedies. The plaintiff's eligibility to receive such fairness-oriented relief will depend on the absence of bad faith on the plaintiff's part and similar factors. Simply put, a plaintiff will not necessarily receive equitable remedies just because he or she asks for them. When they are available, the most significant types of equitable relief include rescission and restitution, specific performance, quasi contract, reformation, and injunction.

Rescission and Restitution

As we learned in the last chapter, the parties may voluntarily agree to rescind, or to set aside, their contract before rendering performance. This type of rescission discharges the contract. But rescission may also occur as a result of a material breach of the agreement. *Rescission* in this context refers to the cancellation or termination of the contract through the restoration of the parties to the status quo. Upon such rescission, the injured party may ask for restitution. *Restitution,* or the return of the goods, money, or property involved in the contract or the recovery of the reasonable value of the services rendered, is the legal term that describes the process by which the parties are returned to their original positions at the time of contract formation. In essence, then, restitution relies on quasi-contractual principles rather than on the original agreement, because once rescission has occurred, the original contract no longer exists. To avoid the unjust enrichment of the breaching party, the law permits restitution by allowing the plaintiff to sue in quasi contract in order to recover. For this reason, in most jurisdictions, one cannot sue for both damages and restitution. Most jurisdictions treat damages and restitution as mutually exclusive remedies; the injured party must elect to pursue one remedy or the other. If Miranda has paid Welling for the bulldozers, on Welling's breach he can treat the contract as at an end (that is, rescind it) and then recover the money (consideration) already paid to Welling in order to avoid the unjust enrichment of Welling. Or, alternatively, Miranda can sue for damages. The "election of remedies" doctrine prevents Miranda from recovering twice at common law. The UCC explicitly rejects this principle in Sections 2-703 and 2-711, demonstrating yet another way in which the Code has changed the common law.

In the following case, the court utilized the principle of rescission in arriving at its decision.

Wall v. *Foster Petroleum Corporation*
791 P.2d 1148 (Colo. App. 1989)

FACTS

In July, 1979, John Wall purchased a newly constructed single-family residence from Foster Petroleum Corporation (Foster) for $149,500. Foster built the house for Wall in an area it was developing for sale. Immediately after the purchase, Wall added improvements costing approximately $11,000. In the spring of 1980, Wall discovered that water had seeped into the basement and that cracks had developed in the basement slab, in the dry-wall portions of the basement, and in the upper levels of the house. Wall contacted Foster and Don Ice, the general contractor. They retained an engineer who performed soil tests and found that the house was situated on a type of soil that, when mixed with water, expands and puts pressure on the foundation and other structural components. In June, 1981, Wall filed a complaint against Foster and Ice for damages based on negligence and breach of warranty. In 1984, he amended his complaint to request rescission as an alternative form of relief. The trial court determined that Foster had not conducted soil tests and that Foster had constructed the residence on expansive soil that had swelled on contact with water, causing damage to both the residence and Wall's personal property. The court did not determine that Foster was negligent in failing to test the soil, but it did conclude that the damage to the residence remained permanent and incurable, thus violating the **implied warranty of habitability** and entitling Wall to rescission. Foster argued that because Wall could repair the house, the court should have awarded Wall money damages, not rescission.

Implied warranty of habitability A promise or warranty made by a builder that a home is free of major defects.

ISSUE

Was rescission the appropriate remedy here?

HOLDING

Yes. Foster's breach was substantial and ongoing. As a consequence, a court would have difficulties assessing the amount of damages; hence, the court's decision to order rescission of the contract was proper.

REASONING

Foster argued that the evidence did not support the trial court's determination that the damage to the residence was significant enough to warrant rescinding the contract. According to Foster, the fact that the house could be repaired entitled Wall to contract damages rather than to rescission. Here, Foster was neither negligent in building the house nor fraudulent in its representations. However, the implied warranty of habitability would arise whenever the builder-vendor held itself out as having the expertise to construct a livable dwelling; and rescission remained an appropriate remedy for misrepresentation, even if the seller had not realized the falsity of the misrepresentation. Generally, a court may grant rescission if the facts show that there is a substantial breach, that the injury caused is irreparable, or that damages would be inadequate, difficult, or impossible to assess. Here, the evidence supported the trial court's determination that the breach was substantial and the damage incurable. In addition, given the ongoing nature of the problems, damages would be difficult, if not impossible, to assess. Accordingly, rescission of the contract was warranted. Foster next contended that Wall's delay in asserting his claim for rescission and in failing to tender title to the property precluded this claim. Although a party must rescind a contract within a reasonable time, what constitutes a reasonable time depends on the facts of a particular case, as determined by the trier of fact. In this case, the trial court concluded that the continuous and changing nature of the construction problems excused Wall's failure to demand rescission earlier (the complaint initially had requested only contract damages and not rescission). The evidence also indicated that the problems had continued and worsened after the filing of the complaint. It further showed that Wall had undertaken continuous evaluations concerning the damage to his house to ascertain the extent of the problem and the approach he should pursue. Hence, Wall's actions constituted a legitimate effort to resolve the matter without resorting to rescission. Therefore, the evidence supported the trial court's determination that Wall had acted within a reasonable time in rescinding the contract. Accordingly, because the injury was substantial and irreparable, thus making an award of damages inadequate, and because there was a substantial breach of the implied warranty of habitability, the court had properly awarded rescission to Wall. Consequently, Foster must pay Wall $149,500, the amount paid for the house, subject to the condition precedent that Wall convey the property free and clear of all encumbrances to Foster.

Specific Performance

Whenever the remedy represented by damages or restitution would be inadequate or unjust, the injured party may ask a court to order *specific performance*. In these cases, *a court compels the breaching party to perform according to the exact terms of the agreement.*

Courts rely on uniqueness as one factor in deciding whether to grant specific performance. Since land is by definition unique, courts ordinarily grant specific performance for breaches of land contracts. For example, should you try to buy a prairie-style home on the river, money damages for breach of that contract are unfulfilling: Money can buy a house similar to the one in the contract, but not *that* particular house. The inherent uniqueness of real estate may therefore convince a court to order the breaching party to convey the house to you—that is, give you specific performance—in order that justice may be done. The same may be said of contracts involving unique goods or chattels (articles of movable personal property). If Bogan breaches a contract to sell a Rembrandt painting, in the absence of fraud or illegality a court can compel Bogan to convey the painting to the buyer. But when the injured party can easily obtain the personal property or chattels, specific performance is an inappropriate remedy: Money damages will be adequate in these cases.

Money damages ordinarily will not satisfy the parties in situations involving personal services contracts. If these contracts are at issue, courts are reluctant to force the parties into a relationship in which at least one of the parties will be unhappy. For example, when Reggie Jackson wanted to break his contract with the Oakland A's and play for the Yankees, how could the A's be sure Jackson would give his best efforts if he really wanted to play for the Yankees? For this reason, and because courts are reluctant to force a party into what one party may characterize as "involuntary servitude," courts ordinarily do not grant specific performance in contracts that consist of personal services. The A's instead could sue Reggie and the Yankees for money damages.

The court wrangled with the issue of specific performance in the following case.

The Connecticut National Bank v. Trans World Airlines, Inc.
762 F. Supp. 76 (S.D.N.Y. 1991)

FACTS   In February, 1986, Trans World Airlines, Inc. (TWA) entered into an Equipment Trust Agreement (the Agreement) with the Connecticut National Bank (CNB). The Agreement, commonly known as a sale/leaseback, provided that CNB would purchase ten aircraft and approximately ninety-six jet engines from TWA and would then lease them back to TWA until 1 February 1996. In connection with the lease/purchase, CNB received Senior Secured Trust Notes (the Notes), some of which matured on 1 February 1991 and others of which were scheduled to mature on 1 February 1996. The aggregate original principal of these Notes amounted to approximately $312 million, with the principal on the 1991 Notes being worth $100 million and the balance being covered by the 1996 Notes. The Agreement provided that TWA would pay all the necessary interest and principal on the Notes directly to CNB, as trustee, which in turn would pay the noteholders, or the trust beneficiaries. TWA also guaranteed payment to the beneficiaries and agreed to **indemnify** CNB. Finally, the Agreement stated that once the lease had expired and TWA had paid off the Notes, the equipment would revert back to TWA. TWA met its obligations in a satisfactory fashion until 31 January 1991. At that time, TWA failed to make the required payments of approximately $57 million, $9 million of which represented interest on the 1991 and 1996 Notes and the other $48 million of which represented the remaining principal on the then-matured 1991 Notes. Consequently, CNB failed to pay the beneficiaries, since the Agreement specifically obligated CNB to pay the beneficiaries only to the extent that TWA had paid CNB. CNB then demanded return of its property and immediate payment of the approximately $81 million presently due as principal on the 1996 Notes. Although the Agreement specifically afforded CNB these remedies, TWA failed to make any payments and did not return any of CNB's property. Therefore, CNB, on 26 March 1991, filed a lawsuit seeking specific performance of the Agreement's default remedies, including the return of the equipment located inside and outside the United States, delivery of various records relating to the property, and a permanent injunction preventing TWA from removing any of the property from the United States. TWA argued that a court's requiring specific performance of the Agreement's default provisions would be inappropriate because CNB had a remedy at law. In addition, TWA asserted that requiring it to return the property in light of the tremendous ramifications such an order might have on both TWA and the public at large would be inequitable.

Indemnify To reimburse a party for a loss suffered by that party for the benefit of another.

ISSUE   Should a court grant CNB's motion for summary judgment and order specific performance of the agreement?

HOLDING   Yes. Specific performance represented the most appropriate and fairest remedy because granting CNB an "at law" remedy (i.e., money damages) would in essence leave CNB remediless; if TWA had possessed the cash to pay CNB, presumably TWA would not have defaulted in the first place.

REASONING   This case did not involve the ordinary situation in which a party demands specific performance of a contractual obligation, although CNB's complaint denominated its demands as such. The contractual obligation placed on TWA consisted of its paying money in exchange for the use of CNB's property. Technically, if CNB were demanding specific performance of TWA's obligations, CNB would be demanding that TWA pay the money it owes pursuant to the Agreement. Such a demand, of course, would be futile, since TWA has already failed to pay. Instead, CNB sought to have the property returned—the precise remedy to which the parties had previously agreed. Thus, CNB did not really seek specific performance of TWA's obligations; rather, CNB sought to enforce an agreed-on contractual remedy in the event of a default. Under this rationale, CNB clearly was entitled to the return of the property. Moreover, even if one considered CNB's demands traditional claims for specific performance of a contractual obligation, CNB would merit a summary judgment. Yet, according to TWA, CNB would be adequately protected if it secured a money judgment against TWA for the amount due on the Notes. In TWA's view, since the Agreement required CNB to make payments to the beneficiaries solely from the funds it actually had received from TWA, CNB allegedly would suffer no loss or risk because of TWA's failure to pay or return the property. TWA further argued that since it must maintain the planes and engines under strict guidelines from the Federal Aviation Administration, no risk of damage to the property could occur. However, TWA's suggestion that by obtaining a money judgment CNB would be adequately protected was nothing short of specious. Because TWA has been teetering on the brink of bankruptcy for years, its possession of cash in its coffers to satisfy such a judgment remained very unlikely. Indeed, if TWA had had the money, it presumably would not have defaulted in the first place. Therefore, the likely scenario under TWA's view would be that after obtaining such a judgment, CNB would attach TWA's property (the planes and engines) to satisfy the judgment. This result would return the parties precisely to the position they find themselves in today. Requiring such actions would be extremely unfair to CNB in light of the fact that the Agreement itself provided such a remedy in the event of a default. In addition, the fact that TWA might be adequately safeguarding the property would remain irrelevant. It was CNB's property, so CNB had the right to demand its return. Indeed, with respect to the balance of equities, it would be difficult to imagine a more grievous wrong than permitting TWA to continue to use CNB's property without bothering to pay for it. Of course, a judgment that would force TWA to turn over the property might well diminish TWA's ability to serve consumers and might also represent a threat to the jobs of TWA employees. However, one of the reasons TWA had enunciated for its failure to meet its obligations under the Agreement centered on a lack of customers. Moreover, recent newspaper articles indicated that TWA had received permission to sell certain of its international routes to another carrier. This fact suggested that TWA possessed more planes and engines than it would actually need. This aside, the actual threat to TWA remained unclear. TWA's fleet included 207 planes, and only 10 planes were completely involved in the repossession. As to the 62 engines involved in the Agreement, TWA had failed to explain how many planes would be affected by their return. Finally, if one were to compare this action to an eviction proceeding when a tenant has failed to pay rent, the tenant could always argue that he or she will experience greater hardships than the landlord who is simply losing money, especially if the tenant is taking care of the property. Once again, this would bring about an illogical result and would mean that a landlord could never evict a tenant who fails to pay rent. Just as the landlord could evict a tenant, the law could require the lessee of property who fails to pay to return the property to the owner. Finally, TWA argued that a court should excuse it from satisfying the contract because events beyond its control had prevented it from possessing sufficient funds to meet its obligations. Specifically, TWA asserted that the recent Persian Gulf War, which had resulted in decreased air travel, owing to fears of terrorism and increased oil prices, had curtailed its cash flow. Without a doubt, all airlines had experienced certain financial difficulties because of events in the Middle East. But none of these factors excused TWA from its obligations. Moreover, all of the alleged factors having an impact upon TWA's profits constituted clearly foreseeable risks of doing business in an international forum. In short, TWA could not demonstrate its entitlement to relief from meeting its obligations, since all of the factors it had mentioned fell well within the foreseeable at the time of its entering into the Agreement.

Just as damages and restitution generally are mutually exclusive remedies, so too are damages and specific performance. The following case illustrates the principle that damages and specific performance are mutually exclusive.

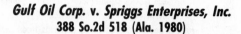

Gulf Oil Corp. v. *Spriggs Enterprises, Inc.*
388 So.2d 518 (Ala. 1980)

FACTS Spriggs had bought land from Diamondhead after Diamondhead had promised it would not sell any of its property located between this land and Interstate 10 if that property were to be used for a service station. Four years later, Diamondhead nevertheless sold property to Gulf Oil, which intended to construct a service station on this property in spite of a restriction on the property that said it could be used only for a convenience store with no more than two gasoline pumps. Spriggs sued for fraud and breach of contract based on Diamondhead's refusal to live up to the restrictive covenant. The jury awarded Spriggs $250,000 in actual damages and $1,000,000 in punitive damages. In addition, the court ordered specific performance of the original agreement.

ISSUE Could Spriggs receive both damages and specific performance in the same suit?

HOLDING No. These remedies were mutually exclusive, so Spriggs would have to elect one remedy or the other.

REASONING In assessing damages of $1,250,000 against Gulf while at the same time ordering specific performance, the lower court had committed reversible error. Because damages and specific performance are inconsistent remedies for suits arising out of the same contract, Spriggs, the injured party, must accordingly elect his remedy.

Quasi Contract/ Reformation/ Injunction

Two concepts that we have discussed on several occasions in the contracts section, *quasi contract* and *reformation,* bear mentioning again before we leave the topic of equitable remedies. The other, an *injunction,* or a writ issued by a court of equity ordering a person to do or refrain from doing some specified act, does not arise as often in the context of contracts. But you should nonetheless be aware that it is another type of equitable remedy. Quasi contract involves the situation in which a court creates a contract for the parties, despite their wishes and intentions, in order to prevent the unjust enrichment of one party. When the parties have not entered into a contract, but one party has knowingly received a benefit to which he or she is not entitled, an *unjust enrichment* has occurred. Since there is no contract, the injured party cannot seek remedies in contract. However, in the interests of equity and fairness, the injured party may receive a restitution-based remedy, the reasonable value of the services rendered. Reformation, on the other hand, concerns a court's rewriting a contract in order to remove a mistake and to make the agreement conform to the terms to which the parties originally agreed. (We discussed reformation in Chapter 13.)

WAIVER OF BREACH

Even though we have spent a great deal of this chapter studying the various remedies available to an injured party when the other party breaches the contract, we noted in the beginning of the chapter that the injured party may

Waiver The voluntary, intentional surrender of a legal right.

be willing to accept less than complete performance. The law terms the injured party's giving up the right to receive the performance set out in the contract a **waiver** of breach. Once a waiver of breach occurs, the waiver in effect eliminates the breach, and the performance required under the contract continues as if the breach had never happened. In essence, waiver of breach precludes the termination or rescission of the contract; it serves as a method of keeping the contract operative between the parties. As usual, though, the nonbreaching party can later recover damages for anything that constitutes less than complete performance. Thus, if only one of the bulldozers delivered to Miranda were slightly defective or if Welling had been only slightly late in making what was otherwise a satisfactory delivery, Miranda may choose to waive such breaches in order to receive Welling's performance under the rest of the contract.

A waiver of breach ordinarily applies only to the matter waived and not inevitably to the rest of the contract. The same is true of subsequent breaches of the contract: Normally the first waiver will not cover additional, later breaches, especially when the later breaches bear no relation to the first one. However, the waiving party may want to stand on his or her rights after the first waiver and indicate unambiguously that he or she will not tolerate future breaches. This action will eliminate the possibility of the breaching party's arguing that the waivers were so numerous and systematic that the breaching party believed less than complete performance was acceptable for the duration of the contract. Still, waiver remains a common business response in those circumstances in which the continuation of the contract would further the interests of the injured party.

Table 17.1 classifies various common types of contractual remedies.

TABLE 17.1   Types of Contractual Remedies

TYPE OF REMEDY	DEFINITION
Legal Remedies (money damages)	Those damages resulting from a court's exercise of its powers "at law."
Compensatory damages	Awarded to a nonbreaching party in order to compensate him or her for the actual, foreseeable harm or loss caused by the breach.
Consequential damages	Indirect or special damages springing from the effects or aftermath (i.e., the consequences) of the breach itself; not recoverable unless the breaching party knew, or should have known, at the time of contract formation, of the potential effect of a breach on the nonbreaching party.
Punitive damages	Unusual award by court to punish for willful, wanton, malicious harm caused to a nonbreaching party.

TABLE 17.1   continued

TYPE OF REMEDY	DEFINITION
Nominal damages	Inconsequential sum that establishes that plaintiff had a cause of action but suffered no measurable pecuniary loss.
Liquidated damages	A provision in a contract that a stated sum of money or property will be paid, or forfeited if previously deposited, if one of the parties fails to perform in accordance with the contract; enforceable unless unreasonable.
Mitigation of damages	Duty placed on the party who suffers any type of damages to reduce the actual losses, if he or she is able to do so.
Equitable Remedies	Those remedies arising from a court's use of its powers of equity.
Rescission and restitution	The cancellation or abrogation of a contract and the return of the previously rendered consideration or its value; may be mutually agreed to by the parties to a contract or awarded as a remedy by the court.
Specific performance	An order by a court to render a contractually promised performance.
Quasi contract	A court's requiring that one who has received a benefit pay for the benefit conferred in order to prevent the unjust enrichment of the other party.
Reformation	A court's correction of an agreement to conform to the intentions of the parties.
Injunction	An order enjoining a person to act or restraining a person from doing some act.
Waiver of Breach	A party's relinquishment, repudiation, or surrender of a right that he or she has to seek a remedy for breach of contract.

SUMMARY

Upon one party's breach of a contract, the other party is free to pursue several kinds of remedies unless the injured party waives the breach. Remedies fall into two main categories, legal ("at law") and equitable remedies. Usually a party sues for compensatory damages, or the amount of money that will place the party in the same economic position that he or she would have enjoyed had the contract been performed. Because the breaching party is liable for the foreseeable consequences of the breach, courts may award these actual losses and may even grant consequential losses or special damages if the facts so warrant. The injured party must mitigate the damages unless doing so will cause unreasonable expense or unreasonable risk. Failure to mitigate will limit the injured party to the recovery of direct losses.

Courts impose punitive damages to punish the wrongdoer in order to deter future malicious conduct. Some modern courts and statutes reject the old common law rule that punitive damages can never constitute appropriate remedies for breaches of contract. The parties may agree in advance on the sum of money to be paid for breaches of certain types. Such liquidated damages clauses are enforceable unless a court construes them as penalties. If the party sustains no actual damages, nominal damages may be awarded.

When the "at law" remedy of damages is unavailable, indeterminable, or inadequate, courts may order equitable remedies. Rescission and restitution constitute one such remedy and involve the termination of the contract through the restoration of the parties to the status quo. Damages and restitution are mutually exclusive remedies, so the injured party must elect (or choose) one remedy or the other.

If either damages or restitution will be inadequate, a court may order specific performance. This is an equitable remedy that compels the breaching party to perform according to the terms of the agreement. Courts usually grant specific performance when the subject matter of the contract is unique, but they are reluctant to grant specific performance in suits involving non-unique goods or personal services contracts.

Quasi contract, reformation, and injunctions, or writs ordering a person to do or refrain from doing some specified act, represent other types of equitable relief.

The injured party may choose to waive the breach in order to keep the contract going between the parties. Waiver of breach, or the injured party's giving up the right to receive the performance set out in the contract, does not preclude the injured party's seeking recovery for damages resulting from the breach, however.

DISCUSSION QUESTIONS

1. What is a remedy?
2. Name and define the two main types of remedies.
3. Explain how courts assess the existence of compensatory and consequential damages.
4. Define the duty of mitigation.
5. What is the relationship of punitive damages to contractual breaches?
6. Describe what liquidated damages are and under what conditions courts will enforce liquidated damages clauses.

7. Why does the remedy of restitution differ from an action in damages?
8. Under what circumstances is specific performance an appropriate remedy?
9. What is the legal consequence of waiving a breach of contract?
10. Define the term *injunction*.

CASE PROBLEMS

1. Dean Van Horn Consulting Associates, Inc. (Van Horn) employed Charles Wold, whom Van Horn trained in business consulting, including accounting, tax preparation, and advising clients, who were primarily doctors and dentists. When he became a full-time employee, Wold signed an employment contract that contained a restrictive covenant obligating him to pay Van Horn as damages a set percentage of any billings Wold made to clients for services rendered if Wold, within three years of leaving Van Horn's employ, set up a competing corporation in violation of the noncompete clause contained in the employment contract. Wold formed a corporation called Professional Consulting Group, Inc. (PCG) immediately after he left Van Horn's. When Van Horn sued Wold on the basis of the restrictive covenant, Wold argued that Van Horn must be able to prove specific amounts of actual damages suffered in order to receive liquidated damages under a contract. Was Wold correct? (*Dean Van Horn Consulting Associates* v. *Wold*, 367 N.W.2d 556 [Minn. Ct. App. 1985].)

2. George Halas, Sr. was the founder of the Chicago Bears and the club's president until his death on 31 October 1983. The Chicago Bears was originally incorporated as an Illinois corporation on 1 April 1922. George Halas, Sr.'s children, George Halas, Jr. and Virginia McCaskey, had acquired stock in the team through prior gifts and sales. Until his death in 1979, George Halas, Jr. also assisted his father in managing the team. At the time of his son's death, George Halas, Sr. owned 76.5 shares, or a 49.35-percent interest, in the Bears. The estate of George Halas, Jr. owned 30.5 shares representing a 19.68-percent interest in the Bears. Virginia McCaskey and others owned the remaining outstanding shares. In his will, George Halas, Jr. directed that his 30.5 shares be held in separate trusts for the benefit of his children, Stephen and Christine. In addition to naming his father executor of his estate, George Halas, Jr. also appointed his father trustee of his children's trusts. In July, 1980, Thomas Chuhak was appointed guardian ad litem (a guardian appointed by a court to prosecute or defend the rights of a child who is involved in a lawsuit) to represent Stephen and Christine Halas. In October, 1981, Mr. Chuhak obtained a court order requiring that the executor of the estate give Chuhak "30 days advance notice in writing in the event the Executor decides to sell, convey, mortgage, encumber, . . . or

effect a redemption of any of the shares of stock issued by the Chicago Bears Club, Inc., . . ." In July, 1981, at a special meeting of the shareholders, a proposal to reorganize the Bears was discussed. The proposal called for the execution of stock exchange agreements and a merger with a newly formed Delaware corporation structured to achieve various objectives for the shareholders. The purpose of the reorganization was to (1) "freeze" the value of stock owned by Halas, Sr. and shift future appreciation to the grandchildren in order to save estate taxes, (2) maintain control of the Bears within the family, and (3) reduce income taxes on rental income derived from the skyboxes that were to be built at the stadium. On 20 October 1981, the shareholders signed a pre-organization subscription agreement providing for the exchange of their shares in the Illinois corporation for shares in a soon-to-be-formed Delaware corporation. The Chicago Bears Football Club subsequently was incorporated in Delaware, and the directors of the Illinois corporation approved the subscription agreement and the stock exchange agreement. On 7 December 1981, George Halas, Sr. executed a stock exchange agreement on behalf of the testamentary trusts, which received 183 shares of Class C common stock in the Delaware corporation in exchange for their 30.5 shares of common stock in the Illinois corporation. On 16 December 1981, the Illinois Bears was merged into the Delaware Bears. George Halas, Sr. gave no notice of the reorganization to either the guardian ad litem or the beneficiaries. The successor executor filed suit, alleging injury to the estate of George Halas, Jr. by virtue of the restrictions that the reorganization had imposed on the transfer of stock under the Delaware corporation's certificate of incorporation that were not present in the articles of the Illinois corporation. These restrictions, among other things, restricted the transfer of stock and gave the corporation the right of first refusal for sixty days should a shareholder wish to transfer any shares. Following a bench trial, the trial court held that George Halas, Sr. had breached his fiduciary duties by failing to give notice of the reorganization to the guardian ad litem and by failing to protect the interests of Stephen and Christine in the reorganization. Because there were sufficient votes to bring about the reorganization without the votes of the shares held in trust for the benefit of Stephen and Christine, the trial court declined to rescind the reorganization or declare it void. Despite evidence that the restrictions on the transfer of the stock and the right of first approval with its sixty-day waiting period—two significant aspects of the reorganization—had reduced the value of the stock, the trial court awarded only nominal damages of $1. Should the appellate court uphold this result? (*In re Estate of Halas,* 568 N.E.2d 170 [Ill. App. 1991].)

3. Koenings was a staff attorney with the Joseph Schlitz Brewing Company (Schlitz). When Schlitz became the target of a friendly takeover attempt by G. Heileman Brewing Company (Heileman) in 1981, Schlitz's board of directors offered so-called golden parachute contracts, which allowed for a continuation of salary for a stated time period after termination of employment, to seventy key management employees as a method of making the takeover of the company less attractive to Heileman. In one provision of this contract, Schlitz promised to allow employees to treat any reduction in the employee's level of responsibilities as a termination. If the employee elected to take advantage of the termination procedure, the company promised to pay the balance of the employee's salary for the time period stated in the contract. Even though Heileman's attempt to take over Schlitz failed, Schlitz soon thereafter merged with Stroh's. This merger, Koenings argued, resulted in a substantial reduction of his responsibilities. Thus, he took a job with another company and sued Schlitz for the thirteen months' salary remaining under the "golden parachute" contract. Did the failure of Schlitz to include a clause, wherein Koenings agreed that any salary earned from another firm would be used to mitigate these liquidated damages, make the termination provision of the contract unreasonable and therefore void on public policy grounds as a penalty? (*Koenings* v. *Joseph Schlitz Brewing Co.,* 377 N.W.2d 593 [Wis. 1985].)

4. In August, 1980, Camel Investments, Inc. (Camel) purchased Webber Oil Company from Orval and Vivian Webber. Camel paid the Webbers $250,000 in cash as a down payment and gave the Webbers a note for the balance of $1,075,000. The purchase agreement provided that Camel could offset sums due by Camel to the Webbers under the note by amounts due by the Webbers to Camel under the agreement. As part of the agreement, the Webbers retained one retail station known as WOCO #3. They promised to purchase all their gasoline from Camel and agreed not to compete with Camel in Okaloosa County in any way for a three-year period except by operating WOCO #3. In March,

1981, the Webbers' son, Ronald, began a petroleum distribution business, SAV-A-TON Petroleum, Inc., that directly competed with Camel in the county. The Webbers had provided some of the initial capital for this corporation. Because the Webbers began purchasing a substantial amount of gasoline from SAV-A-TON, Camel began offsetting $3000 per month on the note payment, the amount Camel calculated to be its lost profits. From this point on, the Webbers purchased almost all their gasoline from SAV-A-TON. In the subsequent lawsuit involving the parties, could Camel recover damages in the form of lost profits for both the Webbers' breach of the gasoline purchase provision and the covenant not to compete? (*Camel Investments, Inc.* v. *Webber,* 468 So.2d 340 [Fla. Dist. Ct. App. 1985].)

5. Transamerica Productions, Inc. (Transamerica), a film distributor, sued Kelly for removing from distribution a film about the rich and powerful that starred Carl Betz and Dina Merrill. Transamerica argued that this removal represented a breach of its motion picture distribution contract with Kelly. Transamerica therefore demanded $50,000 in damages for its lost profits. Kelly submitted that the marketing of a new film was such a speculative venture that there would be insufficient evidence on which a court could compute the alleged damages. Should a court accept Kelly's argument? (*Southwestern Financial Corp.* v. *Kelly,* 233 Cal. Rptr. 639 [Cal. App. 1987].)

6. Bart Schuman, a real estate syndicator in Los Angeles, had asked Frank Short to act as a banker for the proposed syndication of Eastwind Village, an apartment complex in Indianapolis, Indiana. The property was to be purchased from Eden United, Inc. After extended discussions, Short left a May, 1981, meeting with Eden's representative confident that he and Eden had reached agreement on the deal. After an inspection of the property, the parties had amended the agreement to require Eden to obtain from Chatlee, the current owner, warranties that Chatlee would maintain the property in the condition found by Short during the inspection and would close with Short under the terms of the Short-Eden agreement should Eden default and not close on the property. During the months that followed, the transaction dragged; Eden delayed ordering the title work and postponed the closing. At a 17 August 1981 meeting, Eden proposed a mortgage containing provisions that were more stringent than the mortgages reviewed by Short in May and that in fact made the deal unworkable for Short. After negotiations, Eden ulti-

mately agreed to make the changes requested by Short. The closing documents, however, were presented exactly as they had been prior to the 17 August meeting. For example, the mortgage contained no grace period on monthly payments and no requirement of notice for late payments. Short assumed these matters would be resolved with additional drafting at the closing. He arrived at the closing financially ready to complete the deal. However, Eden refused to assign the warranties of condition obtained from Chatlee or to negotiate any of the other issues until the closing statement, which called for an additional $133,000 in taxes, had been signed and accepted. The closing ended abruptly with the Eden people walking out. When Eden failed to meet the terms of its escrow arrangement with Chatlee and defaulted on that deal, Chatlee began working with Short to close on Eastwind. Chatlee reached agreement with Short on the financial terms and made the changes in the Short-Chatlee mortgage that Short had requested in July. However, when Chatlee and Short tried to close under the terms of the Short-Eden agreement, Eden blocked the escrowed Eden-Chatlee closing documents without justification, demanded compensation if Chatlee sold directly to Short, offered to allow Chatlee to sell to any purchaser except Short without interference, and proposed alternative purchasers for brokerage fees far less than the sums demanded from the proposed Short-Chatlee closing. Ultimately, Eden's actions forced both Chatlee and Short to abandon the transaction. Short later sued Eden for tortious interference with contract. Would the evidence support an award of punitive damages against Eden? (*Eden United, Inc.* v. *Short,* 573 N.E.2d 920 [Ind. App. 1991].)

7. The Reuben H. Donnelley Corporation (Donnelley) had omitted the Midland Hotel (Midland) from its 1981 *Chicago Visitors Guide* listing for "Hotels" (although it had mentioned the hotel under "Banquet Rooms"). Midland was the only downtown business so omitted. Midland filed suit against Donnelley to recover the lost net profits allegedly caused by this breach of contract, and a jury awarded the hotel $500,000 on this theory. On appeal, Donnelley asserted that the award had been improper because the hotel had made few efforts to mitigate its damages and because the trial judge had failed to instruct the jury that lost profits would be allowed only if their loss was reasonably within the contemplation of the defaulting party at the time the contract was formed. How should the appellate court rule on this appeal? (*Midland Hotel Corporation* v. *Reuben H.*

Donnelley Corporation, 501 N.E.2d 1280 [Ill. App. 1986], mod. 515 N.E.2d 61 [Ill. 1987].)

8. Gowing contracted with Blue Lakes Apartments, Ltd. (Blue Lakes) to purchase two condominiums for $54,000 each. This purchase contract allowed Blue Lakes to recommend the institution from which Gowing would seek financing for the purchase. Blue Lakes interpreted this clause to mean that if Gowing could not get financing from this source, Blue Lakes could reject Gowing as a purchaser so long as Blue Lakes returned Gowing's $5400 deposit. The bank that Blue Lakes had recommended approved Gowing's application for one unit but denied his application for the other. Although the bank failed to notify Gowing of this denial, the bank did notify Blue Lakes, which returned Gowing's deposit. Because the condominiums had appreciated in value to $60,000 and because Gowing had purchased the condominiums for resale purposes, Gowing sued the bank for specific performance, even though Blue Lakes had sold the second unit to a third party prior to the trial. Assuming the court had found that Blue Lakes' interpretation of the financing clause was incorrect, that is, that Gowing did not have to rely on Blue Lakes' recommendation as to financing exclusively, could the court award Gowing compensatory damages rather than specific performance? Should the court award Gowing punitive damages? (*Blue Lakes Apartments, Ltd.* v. *Gowing,* 464 So.2d 705 [Fla. Dist. Ct. App. 1985].)

9. Morhlang agreed to purchase a lot from Draper, a developer, for $14,875. As part of the purchase agreement, Draper promised to bear the cost of relocating a gas company line and paving a street that abutted the lot. When Draper discovered that the cost of relocating the gas line would be $10,050, Draper offered to substitute another lot for the one Morhlang had chosen. Morhlang, who had obtained financing for the lot, sued Draper for specific performance of the agreement. Should a court award Morhlang his requested remedy? (*Morhlang* v. *Draper,* 365 N.W.2d 443 [Neb. 1985].)

10. In early 1984, Carter Hawley Hale Stores, Inc. (Carter Hawley) hired David Dworkin as president of its Neiman-Marcus division. His five-year employment contract included an "evergreen" provision: At the end of each year, another year was added to the back of the contract, thus giving Dworkin, in effect, a new five-year contract. The contract provided for a base salary and a number of other benefits, including stock options, annual bonus potential, and various executive perquisites. After Carter Hawley had spun off its Neiman-Marcus

division to a newly formed company, Neiman-Marcus Group, Inc. (NMG) Dworkin's relationship with Richard Marcus, the Neiman-Marcus chairman and chief executive officer, deteriorated; by late October, 1987, Dworkin was out as the Neiman-Marcus president. He contended that his firing had represented a breach of his employment contract; NMG asserted that he had resigned pursuant to a resignation agreement. For five months after Dworkin's departure, NMG continued to pay the amount of Dworkin's monthly base salary, $37,500. Dworkin then assumed the presidency of Bon-wit Teller, a smaller retailing firm. He wrote to NMG demanding payment of damages for breach of his employment contract. In the litigation that followed, a jury awarded Dworkin $790,000 in damages for the breach of contract occasioned by NMG's wrongful discharge. On appeal, NMG argued that Dworkin's salary from Bonwit-Teller, his new employer, was higher than he would have received from Neiman-Marcus and thus barred his recovering damages from NMG. How should the appellate court rule in this case? (*Neiman-Marcus Group, Inc.* v. *Dworkin*, 919 F.2d 368 [5th Cir. 1990].)

PART 3
The Law of Sales

*T*he early common law of contracts was adequate for the society in which it developed, but it was inappropriate—if not inadequate—for a commercial society. As commerce developed and became more widespread, changes in the law were needed. A more modern set of rules than the common law was necessary to govern the business environment. Out of this need the *law merchant* was developed.

The sociological and technological advances of the twentieth century made the law merchant as outmoded for this era as the common law had been for the industrial revolution. Once again, new rules were needed. And once again, new rules were developed. This time the new legal area was called the Uniform Commercial Code (UCC).

One of the areas governed by the UCC is the law of sales. This area involves transactions in *goods*—tangible personal property. When a person buys groceries at the supermarket, goods are being purchased. An automobile is considered goods. So are major appliances, furniture, and clothing, among other things. An average American consumer will buy thousands of goods over his or her lifetime. Each of these transactions is governed by the UCC, Article 2, Sales. However, few consumers know or understand the laws that govern such transactions.

CHAPTER 18

Formation of the Sales Contract

OUTLINE

THE SCOPE OF ARTICLE 2

The common law coverage of contracts provides a good framework for studying agreements between people. However, as society progressed and developed in England and in the United States, some elements of the common law became outdated. When this occurred, the law-making bodies often stepped in to try to resolve the problems presented by a changing society. One result of this intervention is the Statute of Frauds, which requires that certain types of contracts be in writing in order to be enforceable. (See Chapter 14.) Another example of legislative intervention to help the law keep pace with society is Article 2 of the Uniform Commercial Code. Article 2 governs the *sale* of *goods*.

Goods

Goods are defined in Section 2-105(1) of the Code. According to that section, *goods* mean *all things that are movable at the time they are identified to the contract*. The Code lists several things that are specifically included as goods, such as specially manufactured items; the unborn young of animals; growing crops; and things attached to land, if they are to be separated from the land for their sale. The Code also specifically excludes some things, declaring them not to be goods. Examples are **money** when used as a payment for sale; investment securities; and **things in action,** such as rights under a contract yet to be performed. (Things in action are also sometimes referred to as *choses in action.*)

Money   A legally recognized medium of exchange authorized or adopted by a government.

Things in action   A personal right; an intangible claim not yet reduced to possession.

Sales

Article 2 only covers the *sale* of goods. Goods have already been defined, but what is a sale? According to Section 2-106(1), a *sale* is *the passing of title from the seller to the buyer for a price*. This is the only definition of a sale in Article 2, but there are several related and similar terms. For example, the words *contract* and *agreement,* when used in Article 2, refer to either the present or the future sale of goods. *Contract for sale* covers both a present sale and a contract to sell goods in the future. A *present sale* is a sale made at the time the contract is made.

Transactions under Article 2 must involve two persons. One is the *buyer,* the person who purchases, or agrees to purchase, the goods. The other person is the *seller,* who provides, or agrees to provide, the goods covered by the contract.

The law of sales is very broad. It covers every sale of goods, whether made by a seller who is a merchant or by one who is a nonmerchant, and whether made to a buyer who is a merchant or to one who is a nonmerchant. Regardless of the status of the parties, Article 2 controls the sale. However, the status of the parties may affect how strictly the sale is regulated by the Code; the key factor here is the status of the parties as merchants or nonmerchants.

Expert A person with a high degree of skill or with a specialized knowledge.

Employee A person working for salary or wages and who is subject to control by the employer.

A *merchant* is defined as a person who deals in the type of goods involved, or who claims to be an **expert** in the type of goods involved, or who has an **employee** who is an expert in the type of goods involved.[1] Any other persons would be considered nonmerchants under the Code.

If neither party to the contract is a merchant, the Code requires that they act in *good faith*. This means that both parties must perform in an honest manner. If both parties to the contract are merchants, the Code requires that they act in good faith and in a *commercially reasonable manner*. This means they both must act honestly and that they must follow the normal fair dealings of their trades. If one party is a merchant and the other is a nonmerchant, each must meet the standards that go with the status occupied. The merchant must act in good faith and in a commercially reasonable manner. The nonmerchant must act in good faith.

YOU BE THE JUDGE

Article 2 of the Uniform Commercial Code requires merchants to act in a commercially reasonable manner. The Code also provides that merchants give an implied warranty of merchantability in the sale of goods. This warranty requires, among other things, that labeled products must conform to their labels.

Food producers include ingredients on the labels of the foods they sell in grocery stores, and also use "buzz words" in the naming of their products. The labels may say that the food is "low fat" or "fresh," and may make reference to the number of calories per serving or to the recommended daily allowance of various nutrients. This label information is frequently misleading and seldom useful.

Assume a consumer group has filed a suit, asking for damages based on breach of the warranty of merchantability. How would you rule in this case, and why?

Source: "The Fight over Food Labels," Christine Gorman, *Time,* July 15, 1991, page 52.

The following case shows how one court decided whether a party was a merchant. Similar reasoning is likely to be followed by other courts facing the question of whether a party in a transaction is a merchant.

[1]Uniform Commercial Code, Section 2-104(1).

Musil v. *Hendrich*
627 P.2d 367 (Kan. App. 1981)

FACTS   Musil and Hendrich were both hog farmers, raising hogs for sale and slaughter. Both raised pigs and both also purchased hogs and pigs. Hendrich had been in the business for over thirty years and Musil for thirteen years. In September, 1977, Hendrich approached Musil at a sale barn in Colorado and told him that he had some feeder pigs for sale. Musil subsequently visited Hendrich's farm, looked at the feeder pigs, and bought sixty of them. At the time of the sale the pigs appeared to be healthy, although a few had dysentery. After two weeks some of the feeder pigs appeared wobbly, and soon several of them died. Over the next month, Musil lost nearly sixty pigs, some of them the feeder pigs purchased from Hendrich and the rest from his general hog population. A postmortem examination revealed that the pigs were infected with swine dysentery, pneumonia, atrophic rhinitis, and whipworm parasitism, all fairly common ailments in swine. If properly treated, none of the infections would affect the merchantability of the hogs. Musil contacted Hendrich about the sick pigs and asked Hendrich to make reparation. When Hendrich refused, Musil filed suit. Among his grounds for seeking damages was a breach of the implied warranty of merchantability in the sale of the pigs.

ISSUE   Is Hendrich a merchant, so that the implied warranty of merchantability would be given to the buyer, Musil? Was the warranty of merchantability breached in this case?

HOLDING   Yes, Hendrich was a merchant. No, the warranty of merchantability was not breached.

REASONING   The court reviewed the UCC definition of "merchant" and applied the tests contained therein to Hendrich. The first test is: Does the person regularly deal in goods of the kind involved? Hendrich had been in the hog business for over thirty years, and he sold between fifty and one hundred pigs each month. The second test is: Does the person by his occupation hold himself out as having knowledge or skills peculiar to the practices or goods involved in the transaction? All the information presented at trial established that Hendrich did indeed hold himself out as an expert in the hog industry. Thus, Hendrich was a merchant in the sale of pigs and hogs, and as such he did give the buyer, Musil, the implied warranty of merchantability. However, there was no showing that the warranty was breached in this sale. The veterinarians who testified said that the infections were common to pigs and did not affect merchantability *if properly treated*. Musil himself testified that at the time of the sale he had noted that some of the pigs had dysentery, but he was not overly concerned about the matter. From the evidence, the court properly concluded that Hendrich was a merchant and that there was no breach of the implied warranty of merchantability.

FORMING THE CONTRACT

A contract for the sale of goods is normally formed in the same manner as a contract formed at common law. The Code recognizes that a contract exists whenever the parties act as if they have an agreement.[2] But the Code also goes beyond the common law. In an effort to reflect commercial reality, the Code will sometimes recognize a contract that would not be considered binding at common law.

[2]Ibid., Section 2-204(1).

Thus, in Section 2-204(2), the Code recognizes a contract when the time of the agreement is uncertain. And in Section 2-204(3), the Code permits a contract to stand even though some terms, such as price or quantity, are omitted from the agreement. At common law, the omission of any of these terms would negate the existence of a contract. The courts would rule that the attempted contract failed owing to "indefiniteness of the terms." Under the UCC, if the parties *intend* to have a contract, and if remedies can be found in case there is a breach, the mere lack of some terms is held to be unimportant. A contract will be found to exist, and the missing terms will be supplied under other provisions of the Code.

Offer and Acceptance

As in regular contract law, a contract for the sale of goods needs both an offer and an acceptance. These technical requirements are covered by UCC Section 2-206. This section states that unless an offer obviously requires otherwise, the offer can be accepted in any manner reasonable under the circumstances.

It should be remembered that at common law the acceptance had to comply exactly with all the terms of the offer. Any variation was treated as a *counteroffer* (an attempt to vary the terms of the original offer) rather than as an acceptance. The Code has attempted to change this requirement.

Suppose the seller received an offer that included the following clause: "Acceptance should be made by sending a white pigeon carrying your note of acceptance tied to its left leg." At common law, a seller could *only* accept by tying a note to the left leg of a white pigeon. If the message was tied to the right leg, or if the pigeon was gray, the seller was deemed to have made a counteroffer.

Under the Code, the seller can accept by complying, or by nearly complying, or by using any other method of accepting that is reasonable. Thus, under some circumstances, the Code even permits the acceptance of an offer by performing rather than by communicating.

Conforming goods Goods that fit the description contained in the contract; goods that people in the industry would recognize as the goods described.

Nonconforming goods Goods that do not fit the description contained in the contract.

Accommodation Something supplied for convenience or to satisfy a need.

Seasonably Timely Something occurring in a prompt or timely manner.

For example, an offer to buy goods may call for prompt shipment of the goods. In this case, the seller can accept by promptly shipping **conforming goods** to the buyer. Or the offer could be accepted if the seller notified the buyer that the goods would be shipped promptly. Or the seller could accept by promptly shipping **nonconforming goods** to the buyer. However, in the last case, the seller would not only have accepted the offer but would also (possibly) have breached the contract that was entered into by the shipment-as-acceptance. According to Section 2-206(1)(b), a seller who receives an order or other offer, with the offer calling for acceptance by prompt shipment, may ship nonconforming goods as an **accommodation** to the buyer, and the shipment will not be treated as an acceptance of the offer. In order to qualify as an accommodation shipment, the seller must **seasonably** notify the buyer that nonconforming goods have been shipped and that the buyer has the option of accepting these (counteroffered) goods or rejecting them and returning them to the seller at the seller's expense. If the seller fails to give the required seasonable notification, the buyer may treat the goods shipped as an acceptance of the offer—and as a breach of the contract, since the goods do not conform.

The seller who accepts by means of a prompt or current shipment must be careful. Assume the seller accepts by shipping but does not notify the buyer. If the buyer neither receives the goods nor hears from the seller within a reasonable time, the buyer may treat the offer as lapsed before acceptance.[3] When this happens, the buyer has no duty to pay for the goods when they finally arrive. This leaves the seller with unsold goods at some distant point and no contract remedies to fall back on.

Standard Form Contracts

Very often both parties to the contract are merchants. When this situation occurs, it is also common to have the offer made on a standard form from the offeror and the acceptance made on a standard form prepared by the offeree/acceptor. A *standard form* is a *preprinted contract form,* with blanks left in certain places for later completion as the final contract terms are agreed to by the parties. Use of a standard form contract would normally have negated the contract at common law, but the Code makes allowance for it.

Under Section 2-207(1), an acceptance that is made within a reasonable time is effective, even if it includes terms that add to or differ from the terms of the original offer. The only exception is when the acceptance is *expressly* made subject to an agreement to the new or different terms.

If the purported acceptance includes new or different terms, the Code provides a solution.[4] The new terms are treated as *proposed additions* to the contract. If the contract is between merchants, the new terms become a part of the contract unless one of the following conditions exists:

1. The offer explicitly limits acceptance to the terms of the offer.
2. The new terms materially alter the contract.
3. The offeror objects to the new terms within a reasonable time.

If the contract is not between merchants, the courts will not normally uphold the new terms unless it can be shown that both parties accepted them.

If the offeree proposes different terms, Section 2-207(3) controls. This section states that when the parties *act* as if they have a contract, they *have* a contract. And if they have writings, the writings will be construed so that an agreement exists. The written contract will consist of the terms on which the parties agree, as well as of the terms included by one party without any objection by the other party. But it will *not* include any terms that contradict other terms, that have been objected to by one of the parties, or that materially

---

[3]Ibid., Section 2-206(2).
[4]Ibid., Section 2-207(2).

alter the basic agreement. Table 18.1 shows how a "conflict of forms" problem would be resolved.

The following case shows one way in which the courts may resolve a "battle of the forms" between merchants. Compare the court's results with Table 18.1.

TABLE 18.1   A "Conflict of Forms" Resolution

IF THE OFFER SAYS	AND	IF THE ACCEPTANCE SAYS	THE CONTRACT WILL SAY
Include "A"		Nothing on "A"	Include "A"
Include "A"		Include "A"	Include "A"
Nothing on "A"		Include "A"	Include "A" (Maybe)[1]
Nothing on "A"		Exclude "A"	Exclude "A" (Maybe)[2]
Include "A"		Exclude "A"	Nothing on "A" (Maybe)[3]
Exclude "A"		Include "A"	Nothing on "A" (Maybe)[4]
Exclude "A"		Exclude "A"	Exclude "A"
Exclude "A"		Nothing on "A"	Exclude "A"

[1]The contract will include "A" unless including "A" will materially alter the duties of the parties, the offeror objects to the inclusion of "A," or the offer specifically limits acceptance to the offer's original terms.

[2]The contract will exclude "A" unless excluding "A" will materially alter the duties of the parties, the offeror objects to the exclusion of "A," or the offer specifically limits acceptance to the offer's original terms.

[3]The contract will not mention "A" unless the exclusion of "A" will materially alter the duties of the parties, the offeror objects to the exclusion of "A," or the offer specifically limits acceptance to the offer's original terms.

[4]The contract will not mention "A" unless the inclusion of "A" will materially alter the duties of the parties, the offeror objects to the inclusion of "A," or the offer specifically limits acceptance to the offer's original terms.

Application of Doughboy Industries, Inc.
17 A.D.2d 216, 233 N.Y.S.2d 488 (1962)

FACTS   The parties began doing business together in February 1960, performing two contracts. In each contract, each party used its own "standard form" to offer and/or to accept. On 6 May 1960, the buyer sent its purchase order to the seller in New York, ordering 20,000 pounds of film and asking for more film on a "hold basis," subject to change. The seller accepted and sent its written acknowledgment form, which included an arbitration clause, to the buyer in Wisconsin. The buyer subsequently wanted to reduce the goods placed on "hold basis," and the seller then refused to reduce the quantity.

ISSUE   Should the controversy be settled by arbitration in New York, in accordance with the seller's form, or by litigation in Wisconsin, the buyer's location?

HOLDING   The controversy is to be settled by litigation.

REASONING   The arbitration clause can be viewed as a material alteration or as a term nullified by a conflicting provision in the buyer's form. In either case, it will not be included as a part of the ultimate contract. Many prior New York cases had held that an agreement to arbitrate is material and not to be included by implication. In addition, the buyer's form (the first form issued) required the buyer to sign any later terms proposed by the other party. The buyer never signed such an agreement to arbitrate.

The presence of an arbitration clause as an added term will not automatically be treated as a material alteration. In the following case, the court upheld an arbitration clause in the seller's confirmation.

Schulze and Burch Biscuit Company v. *Tree Top, Inc.*
831 F.2d 709 (7th Cir. 1987)

FACTS   Schulze and Burch (Schulze) and Tree Top had done business together nine times in the past, with each transaction being more or less the same type of contract. Schulze would order dehydrated apple powder from Tree Top and use the powder in making strawberry and blueberry toastettes, which it would then sell to Nabisco. On 27 April 1984, Schulze telephoned Tree Top and ordered 40,000 pounds of the apple powder. Schulze informed Tree Top that, as usual, the sale was subject to a Schulze purchase order, and gave Tree Top the number of the relevant purchase order. No copy of the purchase order was ever sent to Tree Top. The purchase order limited the terms of the contract to the terms included in the purchase order. Soon thereafter Tree Top sent a written confirmation to Schulze. The confirmation form included an arbitration clause in bold print on its face. Schulze did not object to this confirmation, nor had it objected to any of the previous confirmation forms in prior contracts. Schulze subsequently filed this suit, alleging that the powder had been so full of apple stems and splinters that it clogged the machinery, did not meet the specifications of the contract, and constituted a breach of contract. Tree Top filed a motion to stay the proceedings pending arbitration.

ISSUE   Should this controversy be submitted to arbitration as per the confirmation, or was the arbitration clause a material alteration to the contract between the parties?

HOLDING   The case should properly have been submitted to arbitration. Under the circumstances of this case, the arbitration clause was not a material alteration.

REASONING   Courts have held that the addition of an arbitration clause is not a material alteration if the other party had reason to know that the clause would be included in the confirmation and was not unreasonably taken by surprise by the clause. In this case, Schulze had never sent its purchase order to Tree Top and had never notified Tree Top that the purchase order was to be the sole source of contract terms. Tree Top also presented evidence that the prior course of dealings between the parties gave notice to Schulze that an arbitration clause would be included. Since there was a prior course of dealings, and since only the Tree Top form was exchanged by the parties, Schulze cannot properly maintain that the inclusion of the clause was an unreasonable surprise or a material alteration. The submission of the case to arbitration is upheld.

Firm Offers

Another area that gets special treatment for merchants under the Code is the area of firm offers.[5] At common law, an offer could be freely revoked by the offeror at any time before its acceptance. This right to revoke existed even though the offeror might have "promised" to keep the offer open for some given time period. Such a situation makes it very difficult for the offeree to make detailed plans.

The Code recognizes that the offeree may have to make plans and explore options before accepting an offer. The offeree may not be able to use promissory estoppel (see Chapter 9), but he or she may still be harmed if an offer is revoked. To eliminate this potential problem, the Code guarantees that firm offers cannot be freely revoked before acceptance. If a merchant *promises in writing* to keep an offer open and unmodified for some specified time, and *signs* the writing, a *firm offer* exists. The offer cannot be revoked by the offeror during the time the offeror agreed to keep the offer open. And if no time was specified, it cannot be revoked for a "reasonable time." But the reasonable time cannot exceed three months.

Statute of Frauds

So far, the discussion has focused on the intent to have a contract. However, some technical rules will override intent. One of these involves the *Statute of Frauds,* which requires that a contract for the sale of goods for $500 or more must be in writing to be enforceable.[6] An oral agreement in this area is normally unenforceable.

Again, the Code attempts to recognize modern commercial reality in this area. If the parties have *any* writing signed by the party being sued, that writing is sufficient to satisfy the statute. Omitted terms or incorrectly stated terms will not defeat the proof of the contract.[7]

Confirmation A written memorandum of the agreement; a notation that provides written evidence that an agreement was made.

When both parties are merchants, a different rule applies. Suppose one merchant sends a written **confirmation** that would be binding on the sender. The other merchant will also be bound by the confirmation unless he or she objects to its contents *in writing* within ten days after receiving it.[8] This rule forces merchants to read their forms and to cooperate with other merchants.

Finally, Section 2-201(3) of the Code lists three exceptions to the general provisions of the Statute of Frauds:

1. No writing is needed when the goods are to be *specially* manufactured for the buyer and are of such a nature that they cannot be resold by the seller in the ordinary course of his business, and when the seller has made a substantial start in performing the contract.

2. No writing is needed if the party being sued admits in court or in the legal proceedings that the contract existed.

[5] Ibid., Section 2-205.
[6] Ibid., Section 2-201(1).
[7] Ibid.
[8] Ibid., Section 2-201(2).

3. No writing is needed for any portion of the goods already delivered and accepted *or* already paid for and accepted.

Parol evidence rule   A rule stating that when contracts are in writing, only the writing can be used to show the terms of the contract.

When the parties have a written agreement, the **parol evidence rule** applies; that is, this writing is meant to be the final agreement, and the writing cannot be contradicted by any oral agreement made at the same time as or before the writing.[9] But the writing can be explained or supplemented by additional evidence. Either party may show that course of dealings, usage of trade, or course of performance gives special meanings to certain terms of the writing. And either party may introduce evidence of additional, consistent terms to fill out any apparent gaps in the written agreement.

Course of dealings refers to any prior conduct or contracts between the parties. Prior conduct sets up a pattern that a party may reasonably expect will be followed in the present setting.[10] *Usage of trade* refers to a widely recognized and accepted industry practice. When usage of trade is proved, it is expected to be followed by the parties.[11] *Course of performance* involves repeated performance between the parties in their present contract. If neither party objects to the performance, it is considered appropriate to continue so performing.[12] In interpreting a contract, the court will first look to the express language used by the parties. Whenever possible, the court will read the express language of the agreement and then consider the course of performance, any course of dealings, and any usages of trade in a consistent manner. However, if a consistent interpretation is not possible, express terms control any other interpretation. Course of performance controls over either course of dealings or usage of trade, and course of dealings controls over usage of trade.

In the following case, the court had to decide whether a contract existed by virtue of course of performance and course of dealings.

Smith-Scharff Paper Company v. P. N. Hirsch & Co. Stores, Inc.
754 S.W.2d 928 (Mo. App. 1988)

FACTS   Smith-Scharff was a distributor of paper products. One of its customers was P. N. Hirsch, who purchased paper bags imprinted with the P. N. Hirsch logo from Smith-Scharff. The two companies had been doing business virtually continuously since 1947. Smith-Scharff kept a supply of Hirsch bags in stock so that purchase orders could be filled in a timely manner. Hirsch was aware of this practice and kept Smith-Scharff up to date on its business forecasts. When P. N. Hirsch was liquidated and its stores sold to Dollar General, the president of Smith-Scharff promptly called the president of P. N. Hirsch, seeking assurances that the bags Smith-Scharff had in stock would be purchased. He was told that Hirsch would honor all of its commitments. Subsequently, Smith-Scharff sent Hirsch a bill for $65,000, representing the amount of all Hirsch bags in stock. Over the next six months Hirsch ordered and paid

[9]Ibid., Section 2-202.
[10]Ibid., Section 1-205(1).
[11]Ibid., Section 1-205(2).
[12]Ibid., Section 2-208(1).

for $45,000 worth of the bags, leaving Smith-Scharff with an inventory of just over $20,000. Smith-Scharff sued for this amount.

ISSUE	Was there a contract between Smith-Scharff and P. N. Hirsch for the sale of all of these bags?
HOLDING	Yes. The parties did have a contract.
REASONING	P. N. Hirsch argued that the amount of this alleged contract fell within the Statute of Frauds. In the absence of a writing, there was no enforceable agreement. The court found, however, that these goods were specially manufactured and thus fell outside the coverage of the Statute of Frauds. The court also found that the course of dealings between the parties led to upholding the contract implied by the conduct of the parties. P. N. Hirsch was aware that Smith-Scharff kept a supply of bags on hand for its benefit and took no steps to curtail this practice. In addition, the president of Hirsch assured the president of Smith-Scharff that the remaining inventory of bags would be purchased by Hirsch. A contract existed between the parties, and P. N. Hirsch must perform the contract as agreed.

Course of dealings and course of performance are normally based on current or prior conduct of the parties with one another. As such, both are readily apparent and difficult to deny. Some trade usage patterns are less obvious, especially since the usage of trade may be applicable to situations in which one (or even both) of the parties are not merchants. For example, in California it is a standard usage of trade to use a formal bill of sale to transfer an automobile, truck, or boat by contract (see Figure 18.1).

It is generally the obligation of the parties to acquaint themselves with the usages of trade that apply and to comply with them if necessary.

GENERAL OBLIGATIONS

In general, the parties to a sales contract are to act in *good faith*. In addition, any merchant who is a party to a sales contract is obligated to act in a *commercially reasonable manner*. These two standards are broad enough that they adequately regulate the basic sales contract. The drafters of the Code decided, however, that more specific provisions were needed to supplement these rules and standards.

The most basic and obvious obligation is spelled out in Section 2-301. Under that section, the seller is to transfer and deliver conforming goods to the buyer. The buyer is then to accept and pay for the goods so delivered. Both parties are to perform in accordance with the terms of the contract. Conforming goods are goods that are within the description of the goods as set out in the contract.[13] (Delivery will be covered in Chapter 19, under "Seller's Duties.") Payment by the buyer will normally be in money. However, Section 2-304 permits payment in money, goods, realty, or "other." The

[13]Ibid., Section 2-106(2).

FIGURE 18.1 Bill of Sale

BILL OF SALE

VEHICLE LICENSE NO. OR VESSEL CF NO.

VEHICLE OR HULL IDENTIFICATION NO.   MAKE   BODY TYPE   MODEL   YEAR

FOR MOTOR-
CYCLES ONLY: ENGINE NO.

For the sum of _____ Dollars

($ _____) and/or other valuable consideration in the amount of

$ _____ , the receipt of which is hereby acknowledged, I/we did sell,

transfer and deliver to _____
(BUYER)

ADDRESS   CITY   STATE   ZIP CODE

on the _____ day of _____ 19 ___ , my/our right, title
and interest in and to the above described vehicle or vessel.

I/We certify under penalty of perjury that: (1) I/We are the lawful owner(s)
of the vehicle/vessel and (2) I/We have the right to sell it, and (3) I/We guarantee and will defend the title to the vehicle/vessel against the claims and
demands of any and all persons arising prior to this date and (4) the vehicle/
vessel is free of all liens and encumbrances.

Signature
of Seller X _____ Date _____

ADDRESS   CITY   STATE   ZIP CODE

Courtesy of Bingham Toyota, Clovis, California.

manner of payment, whatever the form, will normally be spelled out in the contract.

So now we have both parties acting in good faith, with the seller selling and the buyer buying. And, of course, all is being done according to the terms of the contract. If that was all that Article 2 said, the rules of contracts from common law would be more than adequate to cover sales. The true value of the Code's coverage of sales is what it provides, if, or when, the contract is defective, incomplete, or unclear in some area.

Unconscionability   For example, Section 2-302 makes provisions for *unconscionable* contracts or contract clauses. Unconscionability means so unfair or so one-sided as to shock the conscience. Unlike the common law, which presumed that equal bargaining power existed, the Code realized that some parties can "force a bargain" on the other party. If the court feels that a contract is unconscionable, it may refuse to enforce the contract. If the court feels that only a clause of the contract is unconscionable, it normally will enforce all of the contract except the challenged clause.

The following case illustrates one way in which the court has attacked unconscionability.

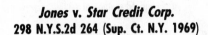

Jones v. *Star Credit Corp.*
298 N.Y.S.2d 264 (Sup. Ct. N.Y. 1969)

FACTS   Mr. and Mrs. Jones, who were on welfare, agreed to buy a freezer from a salesman representing Your Shop At Home Service. The freezer had a base price of $900. After the addition of finance charges, insurance, and sales tax, the total purchase price was $1234.80. (Various damages and costs added in the case brought the total to $1439.69.) The Joneses had paid $619.88 when this suit was filed. Star Credit Corp. claimed that the Joneses still owed $819.81. The court determined that the freezer had a maximum value *at retail* of $300 when it was purchased.

ISSUE   Is this contract unconscionable under the provision of the UCC?

HOLDINGS   Yes. Charging $1439.69 for a $300 freezer is unconscionable as a matter of law.

REASONING   The limited financial resources of the buyers were known to the seller, leading to the conclusion that advantage was taken of the buyers. The parties were grossly unequal in bargaining power. Since the buyers have already paid more than $600 for a $300 freezer, the creditor has been adequately compensated. No further payments are due.

Open Terms   The Code also recognizes that the parties may intend to have a contract even though the contract may omit some elements. In an effort to give the parties the "benefit of their bargain," the Code allows the omitted terms to be filled in by the court. (Remember, the court will *complete* a contract for the parties, but it will not *write* or make a contract for the parties.)

What happens when the parties intend to create a contract but fail to set a price? In such a case, Section 2-305 controls. Under this section, the price can be set by either of the parties or by some external factor. If nothing is said about price, the price is a *reasonable* price at the time of delivery of the goods. If the price is to be set by one of the parties, that party must set the price in good faith. A bad-faith price may be treated by the other party as a cancellation of the contract, or the other party may set a reasonable price and perform the contract.

In the following case, the court demonstrated the flexibility provided by the Code in interpreting a contract that would have failed at common law.

North Central Airlines, Inc. v. *Continental Oil Co.*
574 F.2d 582 (D.C. Cir. 1978)

FACTS   The parties had entered a contract for the sale of oil. The price of the oil was to be determined by averaging the posted prices of a particular type of oil. After the contract was entered, the federal government began to regulate the price of oil and introduced a new "two-tier" pricing system. Under the new federal price regulation, the contract method of pricing could not be followed.

ISSUE   If the agreed method of setting prices cannot be used, what price will be charged?

HOLDING   A reasonable price will be substituted for the contract price-setting mechanism.

REASONING   According to UCC Section 2-305(1), when the agreed price standard fails, a reasonable price will be substituted, leaving the rest of the contract according to its original terms.

Sometimes the parties set a price and otherwise agree to contract terms except for *delivery.* Again, the Code provides a method to save the contract and to resolve the problem. Three different delivery sections may be utilized.

First, under Section 2-307 the seller is to make a complete delivery in one shipment unless the contract allows for several shipments. However, if the seller tenders a partial delivery and the buyer does not object, the seller can continue to make partial shipments *until* the buyer objects.

Second, Section 2-308 covers the place for delivery. If the contract is silent as to the place of delivery, delivery is at the *seller's* place of business. (Law students often miss this point. At first glance, it seems illogical. In reality, it is very logical. When a person buys a toaster or a can of beans, that person takes delivery at the store—the seller's place of business.) If the seller has no place of business, delivery is at the seller's residence. If the goods are known by both parties to be at some other place, the other place is the proper place for the delivery.

Third, Section 2-309 covers the time for delivery. If the contract is silent about when delivery is to occur, delivery is to be within a reasonable time. Reasonable time here means reasonable in both clock time and in calendar time. The seller is to make delivery during normal business hours (clock time), and the seller is not allowed to delay unduly the number of days before delivery (calendar time).

In addition to these rules, the Code resolves several other potential problems. Under Section 2-306, the Code specifically allows requirement contracts and output contracts. In a *requirement contract,* the seller provides all of a certain good that the buyer *needs.* In an *output contract,* the buyer purchases all of a certain good that the seller *produces.* Both types of contract were often declared unenforceable at common law since they were too indefinite in terms. Table 18.2 summarizes the open terms of a sales contract.

TABLE 18.2   Open Terms in a Sales Contract

OPEN TERM	TREATMENT	CODE SECTION
Price	The buyer or the seller sets the price *in good faith* if the contract so provides.	2-305(2)
	The price is a reasonable price at the time and the place of delivery.	2-305(1)
Delivery	If no place for delivery is mentioned, delivery is presumed to be at the seller's place of business. If the seller has no place of business, delivery is presumed to be at the seller's residence.	2-308(a)
	If the goods to the contract are identified, and if both parties know the goods are at a place other than the seller's location, delivery is presumed to occur at the location of the goods.	2-308(b)
	If the time for delivery is not mentioned, delivery is to occur within a reasonable time, considering the nature of the goods (calendar time), and at a reasonable time, considering the nature of the buyer's business (clock time).	2-309
Payment	Payment is expected at the time and place of delivery unless some other payment terms are expressly included in the contract. Payment is expected to be in any commercially reasonable manner, unless the contract states otherwise. If the seller insists on cash payment at the time of delivery, but did not specify cash payment in the contract, the buyer must be given a reasonable opportunity to procure cash.	2-310

Options

The Code also deals with *options*. If a contract calls for an unspecified product mix, the assortment of goods is at the *buyer's* option.[14] If the contract is silent as to how the goods are to be shipped, the shipping arrangements are at the *seller's* option.[15] However, if a party having an option delays unduly, the other party may act. A party may elect to wait until hearing what is being done by the other party or may proceed on his own. Thus, if the buyer does not notify the seller as to the product mix desired, the seller may delay shipping any goods, and the delay is excused.[16] Or the seller may select his own assortment

[14]Ibid., Section 2-311(2).
[15]Ibid.
[16]Ibid., Section 2-311(3)(a).

and ship them, providing he acts in good faith.[17] Or the seller may treat the delay as a breach of contract by the buyer and seek remedies for the breach. (Remedies for breach of a sales contract are covered in Chapter 22.)[18]

Cooperation

As a final and overriding obligation, the parties are required to cooperate with one another in the performance of their duties. Any failure to cooperate or any interference with the performance of the other party can be treated as a breach of contract or as an excuse for a delayed performance.

ARTICLE 2A: LEASES

Leasing goods rather than purchasing them has become a fairly common business practice in recent years. The lessee acquires the right to use and possess the goods for the lease period, without any concern about depreciation or resale at the end of the term. In addition, the lessee often is given the option to purchase the goods at their book value at the termination of the lease. The lessor receives payment for the use of the goods and retains title to those goods. The lease arrangement contains some benefits for each party, but it also has presented some problems. Although the *sale* of goods is governed by Article 2 of the UCC, the *leasing* of goods was until recently governed by common law principles, which were somewhat archaic and out of date in a modern commercial setting. As a result, a new article was developed for inclusion in the UCC—Article 2A, Leases.

The concepts embodied in Article 2A are not new. For several years courts have been drawing analogies between the sale of goods and the leasing of goods and have applied sales principles to leases. Article 2A is merely confirming by statute what was already being done in practice. Generally speaking, Article 2A treats leases in the same manner as Article 2 treats sales. This treatment includes giving to the lessee warranties of merchantability if the lessor is a merchant in goods of the type covered by the lease and the warranty of fitness for a particular purpose if the lessor has reason to know of any particular purpose for which the goods are leased and knows that the lessee is relying on the expertise of the lessor in leasing the particular goods.

Leases also are categorized under the new provisions. One of these categories is a "consumer lease," in which the goods are leased for personal, household, or family use, and in which the total payments under the lease contract (excluding renewals or purchases at the end of the lease term) do not exceed $25,000. Leases that are not "consumer leases" are, by default, commercial leases. A second category is a "finance lease," one in which the lessor does not select, manufacture, or supply the goods; the lessor acquires the

[17]Ibid., Section 2-311(3)(b).
[18]Ibid.

goods in connection with the lease; and the lessee receives a copy of the contract evidencing the lessor's purchase or acquisition of the goods before the lessee signs the lease.

One major difference between Article 2 provisions governing sales and Article 2A provisions governing leases is in the area of warranty law. Warranty protections under Article 2A are substantially more generous than the corresponding protections available under Article 2. Both articles provide for a four-year statute of limitations in seeking remedies for a breach of warranty. However, under Article 2, the four-year period begins to run when the goods are delivered to the buyer (Section 2-725). This is true even if the defect that results in a breach of warranty is not discovered (or discoverable) for four or five years from the date of delivery. By contrast, in Section 2-506 of Article 2A, the four-year period does not begin to run until the cause of action accrues, and the cause of action does not accrue until the defect is discovered, or should be discovered, by the aggrieved party. Thus Article 2A is more proconsumer in the warranty area than Article 2, upon which it is modeled.

As Article 2A becomes more widely adopted, and as cases begin to accumulate to establish judicial interpretation of the provisions of the article, lease law promises to become an important element of commercial law.

SUMMARY

This chapter introduced the law of sales and Article 2 of the Uniform Commercial Code. It is important to distinguish sales contracts from other types of contracts. Article 2 attempts to deal with "commercial reality" in the sale of goods, whereas common law developed strict and rigid rules for the treatment of contracts. Article 2 also recognizes the difference between a merchant—a person who "specializes" in dealing with a particular type of goods—and a nonmerchant—a "casual dealer" in the goods.

The Code provides built-in flexibility in the formation of sales contracts. *Intent,* rather than form, is the key element in sales. Offers and acceptances are likely to be found if the parties act as if they have an agreement. The Code even provides methods to supply missing terms, if it seems appropriate to do so in order to carry out the wishes and intentions of the parties.

The Statute of Frauds remains operative under Article 2, but its provisions are less restrictive than they were under common law. Three exceptions to the Statute of Frauds are built into the Code, and the past dealings of the parties may also be taken into consideration in deciding what the parties have agreed to do.

Some general obligations are imposed on the parties to prevent or minimize abuses of the less rigid rules of Article 2. The parties are required to act in good faith, they may not act unconscionably, and they must cooperate with one another. Performance options are available to either party if the other party fails to cooperate fully or properly.

Article 2A, which deals with the leasing of goods, has been proposed as an addition to the UCC. This Article, which provides that leases of goods will be treated in virtually the same manner as the sale of goods, is likely to be adopted in the near future by all of the states which follow Article 2.

DISCUSSION QUESTIONS

1. How does the UCC define "goods"?
2. What is a "sale," according to Article 2?
3. What are the three separate conditions that will qualify a person as a merchant? Why are merchants treated differently from nonmerchants under Article 2?
4. How can an offer be accepted under the law of sales? What must an offeror do to restrict the manner of acceptance?
5. The seller sent the buyer a form offering to sell certain goods. The buyer returned a form accepting the offer. The forms did not agree on every point. Do the parties have a contract? If so, what are its terms? If not, why?
6. What are the exceptions to the Statute of Frauds under Article 2 of the law of sales?
7. What constitutes a sufficient writing between merchants to satisfy the Statute of Frauds?
8. What are the basic duties of a merchant seller in a sales contract? Of a merchant buyer?
9. If the contract is silent as to the place of delivery, where should delivery take place?
10. When should delivery be tendered? Explain fully.

CASE PROBLEMS

1. Bunge Corp. was a major purchaser of corn. Bunge signed three contracts with Toppert, each calling for the delivery of 10,000 bushels of corn to Bunge. Bunge offered Toppert a fourth contract, but Toppert did not accept. Bunge was to pay for each contract as it was performed. Toppert delivered the corn for the first contract and began delivery on the second. Bunge refused to pay for the first. Bunge's reason for refusing to pay was that he wanted to force Toppert and Toppert's family to sign additional contracts. Is this a valid reason? Explain fully. (*Toppert* v. *Bunge Corp.*, 377 N.E.2d 324 [Ill. 1978].)

2. Campbell owned and operated a grain elevator. He orally agreed with a number of farmers to buy 7000 bushels of soybeans at $5.30 per bushel. Campbell then signed and mailed to the farmers a written confirmation of the agreement. This written confirmation was the only writing involved, and the farmers/sellers did not sign it. The farmers denied that they were bound by the agreement because of the Statute of Frauds. Is their contention sound? (*Campbell* v. *Yokel,* 313 N.E.2d 628 [Ill. 1974].)

3. John, a candy manufacturer, purchased gelatin from Stein. John normally telephoned his orders to Stein and then sent a written purchase order later. Stein would send John a sales agreement with each shipment of gelatin. Stein's sales agreement included an arbitration clause. John felt one order of gelatin was unfit for his use, and he sued Stein. Stein asked the court to remove the case to arbitration. What should the court decide? Why? (*Just Born, Inc.* v. *Stein, Hall & Co.,* 13 UCC Rep. 431 [Pa. Ct. Com. Pleas 1971].)

4. Kemper, a retailer, had been doing business with Celebrity, a wholesaler, for five years. Whenever Kemper received any defective goods from Celebrity, Kemper would set those goods aside. Later, if the Celebrity salesman verified that the goods were defective, Kemper's account would be adjusted to reflect the defective merchandise. In the case in question, Kemper set aside allegedly defective goods for subsequent inspection by the Celebrity salesman. The salesman refused to verify or to adjust the account, claiming that the invoice required written objection regarding any nonconformity and a return of defective goods within five days of de-

livery. Did Kemper properly reject the goods in this case (based on course of dealings), or was the rejection improper (based on the specific language of the invoice)? Explain. (*Celebrity, Inc.* v. *Kemper*, 632 P.2d 743 [N.M. 1981].)

5. LTV was manufacturing all-terrain vehicles for use in Asia. The vehicles had to be crated in order to be shipped. LTV entered an oral agreement with Bateman, calling for Bateman to produce packing crates built to LTV's specifications. LTV later refused to accept the crates prepared by Bateman. When Bateman sued, LTV raised the Statute of Frauds as a defense to the enforceability of the contract. Does Bateman need a writing in order to enforce this contract? Explain. (*LTV Aerospace Corp.* v. *Bateman*, 492 S.W.2d 703 [Tex. 1973].)

6. Newman owned and operated a mobile home sales company. He advertised that his sales included a complete set-up of any mobile homes purchased from his lot. Moses agreed to purchase a mobile home from Newman, and arrangements were made to deliver the mobile home and set it up on Moses' lot. On February 9, Newman delivered the mobile home, blocked it up, removed the tires and axles, and hooked up the water and sewer lines. Moses' fiancee cleaned the interior, moved some kitchen items in, and inspected the mobile home. She discovered a broken window and a broken water pipe and informed Newman of these facts. It was also pointed out to Newman that no door keys had been given to Moses. On February 10, before Newman could correct any of these problems, the mobile home was destroyed by a wind storm. Moses claims that he had never accepted the mobile home and that Newman had never delivered conforming goods to the buyer. Did Newman tender delivery, and did Moses accept delivery of the mobile home? (*Moses* v. *Newman*, 658 S.W.2d 119 [Tenn. App. 1983].)

7. Casual Slacks entered into a written contract to sell clothing to Warren's, with delivery to be made during "June–August." Casual shipped the clothes in three roughly equal shipments, one a month. After the shipments, Casual received a check from Warren's for a substantially smaller amount than the contract called for. Casual refused to accept this check and sued Warren's for the full contract price. Warren's defended against the lawsuit by alleging that Casual had breached the contract by improper shipment. According to Warren's, the clothing industry had a particular meaning for

the term "June–August" that Casual had not followed. As a result, Warren's had suffered substantial losses, and the lesser amount of the check was to reflect those losses. How should the court treat this parol evidence of a usage of trade in conjunction with the written contract? Explain fully. (*Warren's Kiddie Shoppe, Inc.* v. *Casual Slacks, Inc.*, 171 S.E.2d 643 [Ga. App. 1969].)

8. Nicole owned and operated a "pony cart" amusement ride that had been purchased from Jones. Jones had originally purchased the ride from the manufacturer and had operated the ride for about two months before selling it to Nicole. Allen was injured while getting off the ride. Allen's guardian sued Nicole for negligence and sued both Nicole and Jones for breach of warranty and for strict liability. Is Jones a "merchant" and therefore liable for breach of warranty in this case? Why? (*Allen* v. *Nicole, Inc.*, 412 A.2d 824 [N.J. 1980].)

9. Fyke operated a wholesale nursery. For two years, Fyke purchased trees from Hoffman's, another nursery. Fyke complained to Hoffman on several occasions that the trees delivered were of poor quality and condition and not of the size ordered. However, no written notices were sent, and no other demands were made by Fyke. After two years, Fyke refused to pay his outstanding balance of $9000 and stopped doing business with Hoffman. Hoffman sued for the balance owed, and Fyke countersued for breach of contract and breach of warranty. How should the case be resolved? (*Hoffman's Double Bar Pine Nursery* v. *Fyke*, 633 P.2d 516 [Colo. App. 1981].)

10. Nations ordered nine pumps from Process for installation in a government facility. The pumps were ordered by means of a purchase order prepared by Nations and sent to Process. Process promptly shipped nine pumps to Nations, but the pumps so delivered did not conform to the specifications of the purchase order. Nations accepted the pumps and installed them, but informed Process that the pumps did not conform to the specifications of the order. Process negotiated with Nations and eventually shipped conforming pumps. Nations refused to accept these pumps or to pay for them. Did the parties have an enforceable contract, or had Process breached by initially shipping nonconforming pumps? (*Nations Enterprise, Inc.* v. *Process Equipment Co.*, 579 P.2d 655 [Colo. App. 1978].)

CHAPTER 19

Performance of the Sales Contract

OUTLINE

SELLER'S DUTIES

The seller in a contract for the sale of goods has a very simple basic duty. The seller is to *tender delivery* of *conforming goods* according to the terms of the contract. The parties can agree to make delivery in any manner they desire. If they do not agree, or if they simply fail to consider how delivery is to occur, the Uniform Commercial Code covers the topic for them. Section 2-503 explains tender of delivery.

The seller has properly tendered delivery by putting and holding conforming goods at the buyer's disposition and then notifying the buyer that the goods are available. Normally the contract will tell the seller when and where to make the goods "available." When it does not, the seller must make his or her tender at a reasonable time and place, and the buyer must provide facilities suitable for receiving the goods.

This all sounds technical and confusing, but in reality delivery is fairly simple. There are five possible ways delivery can occur:

Common carrier A company in the business of transporting people or goods for a fee and holding itself out as serving the general public.

Bailee One to whom goods are delivered with the understanding that they will be returned at a future time.

Document of title A written evidence of ownership or of rights to something.

1. The buyer personally takes the goods from the seller.
2. The seller personally takes the goods to the buyer.
3. The seller ships the goods to the buyer by means of a **common carrier.**
4. The goods are in the hands of a third person (**bailee**), and no documents of title are to be involved.
5. The goods are in the hands of a third person, and the seller is to deliver some **document of title** to the buyer.

If the seller properly tenders delivery under any of these situations and the goods are conforming, the seller has performed his or her duty under the contract. Tender entitles the seller to have the buyer accept the goods and to receive payment for the goods.[1]

If the buyer and the seller make the delivery personally and directly (possibilities 1 and 2), proper tender is obvious. The seller will provide properly packaged goods to the buyer. The buyer will accept the goods and pay for them. Very neat, and very simple.

If the goods are in the hands of a third person, referred to as a bailee, delivery becomes somewhat more complicated. The seller in these cases must either provide the buyer with a **negotiable** document of title covering the goods (possibility 5) or get some acknowledgment from the bailee that the goods now belong to the buyer (possibility 4). If the buyer objects to anything less than a negotiable document of title, the seller must provide a negotiable document in order to prove that a proper tender of delivery was made.[2]

Negotiable Transferable either by an endorsement and delivery or by delivery alone.

The UCC treats the topic of documents of title in Article 7. This article,

[1]Uniform Commercial Code, Section 2-507(1).
[2]Ibid., Section 2-503(4)(a), (b).

entitled "Warehouse Receipts, Bills of Lading, and Other Documents of Title," specifies the rights and the duties of all relevant parties in the handling of documents of title, whether those documents are negotiable or nonnegotiable. In addition to the coverage of a document of title by Parts 1 and 2 (for a warehouse receipt) or Parts 1 and 3 (for a bill of lading), both Parts 4 and 5 of this article deal with warehouse receipts and bills of lading if the document of title in question is negotiable. However, only Part 4 is also involved if the document of title is nonnegotiable. In order to reduce the amount of statutory coverage involved, and to avoid the problems of determining whether there has been a "due negotiation" of the document making the holder a "holder by due negotiation," most commercial warehousemen and common carriers simply issue nonnegotiable documents of title.

Most carriers prefer to use a nonnegotiable document of title to protect themselves. Figure 19.1 shows the first page of such a document. Figure 19.2 shows the provisions listed on the back of the same document. Note provision #8 and the nine boldfaced lines at the bottom of Figure 19.2. These two areas limit and control how a seller of stored goods may tender delivery to a buyer.

None of the methods of delivery that we have described is very troublesome. The problems in understanding delivery normally arise when a common carrier enters the picture (possibility 3). Now the seller must give the goods to the carrier, the carrier must transport the goods to the buyer, and the buyer must accept the transported goods and make payment for them. As one might expect, the more parties involved in a transaction, the more likely problems and confusion will enter the picture.

The seller must provide for reasonable carriage of the goods, taking into account the nature of the goods, the need for speed, and any other factors that will affect the delivery. The seller then must obtain and deliver to the buyer any necessary documents concerning the carriage, and the seller must promptly notify the buyer of the shipment.[3] Again, all these steps seem obvious, and none should cause any undue problems or hardships. The problems arise when the parties use technical and/or legal terms without understanding their meaning.

Figure 19.3 illustrates the type of contract a seller may have to enter in order to send the goods by means of a common carrier.

STANDARD SHIPPING TERMS

Every shipping contract must take one of two positions: it is either a *shipment* contract or a *destination* contract. In a shipment contract, once the seller makes a proper contract for the carriage of the goods and surrenders the goods to the care of the carrier, the goods belong to the buyer. The buyer has

[3]Ibid., Section 2-504.

FIGURE 19.1   A Nonnegotiable Warehouse Receipt (Front)

NON-NEGOTIABLE
WAREHOUSE RECEIPT AND CONTRACT

I. ACCEPTANCE OF WAREHOUSE RECEIPT CONTRACT AND SIGNATURE IDENTIFICATION

BEKINS MOVING & STORAGE CO.   Date _____ 19 _____

Gentlemen:

    I hereby acknowledge receiving your warehouse receipt and contract, Storage Lot Number _____ ,
and I have read the provisions, limitations, terms and conditions on the reverse side of this agreement. I hereby accept its
terms and conditions, and affix my official signature hereto for your files.

A. _____
                               (PRINT YOUR NAME IN FULL)

_____ _____ _____ _____
(STREET)   (CITY)   (STATE)   (ZIP)

Home Phone: _____   _____
Work Phone: _____   (SIGNATURE)

B. You are also authorized to accept orders for access, delivery or removal of my goods from:

_____
        (IN YOUR OWN HANDWRITING PRINT IN AUTHORIZED PERSON'S NAME)

_____ _____ _____ _____
(STREET)   (CITY)   (STATE)   (ZIP)

_____
        (SIGNATURE OF PERSON AUTHORIZED ABOVE)

C. As Depositor, I understand that value protection in the amount of $ _____ at an additional monthly charge of $ _____ per
month has been ordered for my account. I acknowledge that the amount of value protection represents the actual cash
value of the property placed into storage. If value protection is not desired or Depositor wants to declare a higher value,
please indicate below. Depositor agrees and understands that if value protection is not desired then the value of the
property placed into storage, and the Company's liability in case of loss or damage arising out of Company's negligence or
for any cause for which it may be liable for each or any article or the contents of any package or container stored hereunder
or later received does not exceed and is limited to sixty (60¢) cents per pound per article, upon which agreed value the rates are
based, the Depositor having been given the opportunity to declare a higher amount of value and to pay an additional
charge and having elected not to do so.

Value Protection is not Desired _____ Please Initial and Date

Value Protection in the amount of $ _____ *is Desired.* _____ Please Initial and Date

D. In the event that the actual cash value of the entire lot of property stored on which the Depositor has declared a lump
sum value is in excess of the lump sum amount so declared by the Depositor, it is agreed that the Depositor shall be
regarded as being his own insurer to the extent of the difference, and the Depositor shall bear that proportion of any loss
which the undeclared amount bears to the actual cash value of the property.

CUSTOMER'S COPY — RETAIN IN SAFE PLACE

II. NON-NEGOTIABLE WAREHOUSE RECEIPT AND CONTRACT

RECEIVED FOR THE ACCOUNT OF _____ _____ (hereinafter called the

Depositor) whose latest known address is _____

_____ the goods described on the inventory attached and
by this reference made a part hereof (contents and condition of contents unknown) to be handled on monthly storage in
warehouse situated at _____ at the monthly storage charge
of _____ dollars subject to the provisions, limitations, terms and conditions herein printed on the face and reverse side
hereof, all of which are agreed and assented to by the Depositor for himself and his heirs; and to be delivered to said Depositor
upon payment of all charges. Storage rate herein is based on declared value of sixty (60¢) cents per pound per article, unless the
Depositor has declared a higher value and agreed to the rate for higher value.

Storage Lot No. _____   Date _____ 19 _____

SEE PROVISIONS, LIMITATIONS, TERMS AND   **BEKINS MOVING & STORAGE CO.**
CONDITIONS OF CONTRACT ON REVERSE SIDE   By _____

W 15/1282   © THE BEKINS COMPANY 1977

Courtesy of Bekins Moving and Storage, Fresno, California.

FIGURE 19.2   A Nonnegotiable Warehouse Receipt (Back)

III. PROVISIONS, LIMITATIONS, TERMS AND CONDITIONS OF WAREHOUSE RECEIPT AND CONTRACT

1. OWNERSHIP OF GOODS: The Depositor has represented to the Company that the Depositor has the lawful possession of and legal right and authority to store all of the property herein described, and upon the provisions, limitations, terms and conditions herein set forth, and if there be any controversy or litigation concerning the property, the Depositor agrees to pay all storage and other charges which this Company may incur or become liable for or by judgment be compelled to pay in connection therewith, and this Company shall have a lien on said property for all storage and other charges.

2. TERMS OF PAYMENT: Payments for storage and other charges are due and payable upon the date of this receipt and on the same date of each succeeding month thereafter. Delinquent accounts shall incur interest at the maximum amount permitted by law commencing on the 61st day after payment is due.

3. ADDITIONS TO STORAGE LOT: Any additional goods hereafter delivered by the Depositor to the Company for storage as a part of this lot while this receipt is outstanding shall be subject to the terms and conditions hereof.

4. CORRECTION OF ERRORS: Unless notice is given in writing to the Company within thirty (30) days after either the mailing of this receipt to the Depositor or the delivery of this receipt personally to the Depositor, the attached inventory will be deemed to be correct, complete, and the terms and conditions accepted and shall likewise be binding on any future additions made to this lot.

5. LIABILITY OF COMPANY: A. Except as set forth in paragraphs B through D the Company agrees to indemnify the Depositor for all physical loss or damage to property while in the care, custody and control of the Company within a 50 mile radius of the warehouse. The total liability of the company for physical loss or damage shall in no event exceed: (1) the amount of the value declared by the Depositor or sixty (60¢) cents per pound per article; (2) the cost of repairing damaged property; (3) the cost of replacing lost or destroyed property with material of like kind and quality; (4) the actual cash value of such property at time and place of loss.

B. The Company shall not be liable for any loss, damage or delay caused by or resulting from:

(1) An act, omission or order of Depositor or owner, or the agent thereof;

(2) Depreciation, deteriorization, obsolescence and ordinary wear and tear;

(3) The nature of the article or any defect, characteristic or inherent vice thereof including susceptibility to damage because of atmospheric conditions such as temperature and humidity;

(4) Earthquake, flood, rising waters, acts of God or any other cause beyond the control of the Company;

(5) Strikes, lockouts, labor disturbances, riots, civil commotions, or the act of any person or persons taking part in such occurrence or disorder;

(6) Hostile or warlike action in time of peace or war by any authority maintaining or using military forces, nuclear reaction, nuclear radiation or radioactive contamination, insurrection, rebellion, revolution, civil war, usurped power, or any action taken by government authority against such occurrence;

(7) Breakage of glass, chinaware or similar articles of a brittle or fragile nature unless packed and unpacked by the Company;

(8) Insects, moth, vermin, unless the Depositor can establish that said insects, moth, vermin or rodent were not in his articles when delivered to the Company.

C. The Company shall not be liable for consequential damages from negligent delay or proximately caused by the physical loss or damage to any property unless they are specifically set forth in writing stating the nature and extent of the consequential damages that may be incurred in the event of either negligent delay or physical loss or damage to the property stored and the company acknowledges to the depositor in writing that it agrees to be liable for such consequential damages.

D. The Company shall not assume liability for loss or damage to articles of extraordinary value unless: (1) the depositor, in writing, specifically lists each such article specifically designating it as an article of extraordinary value; (2) the value of each such article is clearly indicated, and (3) the company is afforded the opportunity prior to acceptance of the property into storage to pack and otherwise provide adequate protection to such article (at company's pub-

lished charges) if in the estimation of the company, the depositor's packing or packaging is determined to be inadequate for the protection of such article.

As used herein, the term "articles of extraordinary value" refers to those articles which because of uniqueness or rarity have a value substantially in excess of the cost of newly manufactured items of substantially the same type and quality apart from such uniqueness or rarity, such as, but not limited to (1) musical instruments of rare quality, or (2) historical significance, (3) original manuscripts, (4) first editions, or (5) autographed copies of books, (6) antique furniture, (7) heirlooms, (8) paintings, (9) sculptures, (10) other works of art, (11) hobby collections, and (12) exhibits.

6. SERVICE TO STORED GOODS: Many instruments and articles by their nature, frequently require attention and adjustment both during storage and after removal. The Company will not furnish any such attention or adjustment as part of its service. The services of this Company are limited to storage, packing, moving and shipping, and it does not accept liability in respect to such attention or adjustment. Should the Company at its discretion, determine that moth-treating all or a portion of the goods stored hereunder is necessary for the protection of the goods of other persons stored in the warehouse, it may moth-treat same and add its charges therefor to the amount payable by the Depositor hereunder.

7. BUILDING — WATCHMAN: It is understood that the building is of fire-resistant contruction, but no guarantee is given that the contents of same cannot be destroyed by fire. No night watchman shall be required.

8. DELIVERY AND ACCESS TO GOODS: The goods deposited hereunder will be ready for delivery or access during regular working days, on 24 hours notice, from the Depositor or any other specified person on his or her behalf on presentation of written authority executed by said Depositor and providing that all storage and other charges owing to the Company are paid in full. No transfer of this receipt will be recognized unless all charges are paid and transfer is entered on the books of the Company and a charge paid therefor. A warehouse labor charge will be made for placing goods in storage and for removing to platform for delivery. An additional charge will be made for all access to or part delivery of goods.

9. CHANGE OF ADDRESS: Notice of any change of address of the Depositor must be given by the Depositor to the Company, in writing and acknowledged in writing by the Company on the following monthly statement, and no notice of any change of address shall be valid or binding against the Company, if given in any other manner, and it is hereby expressly understood and agreed that all notices of any nature to the Depositor shall be sent to the latest known address as shown on the face of this warehouse receipt until such written notice of change is received by said Company, and acknowledged by it in writing on the following monthly statement.

10. SATISFACTION OF WAREHOUSEMAN'S LIEN: This Company shall have a lien upon any and all property deposited with it by Depositor, or on the proceeds thereof in its hand, for all lawful charges for storage and preservation of same or any part thereof, also for all lawful claims for money advanced, interest, transportation, labor, wrapping, weighing, coopering, and all other charges and expenses in relation to such property, or any part thereof, and also for all reasonable charges and expenses for notice and advertisement of sale and for the sale of the property where default has been made in satisfying this Company's lien. This lien may be enforced by the Company at any time either by public or private sale of the goods with or without a judicial hearing.

11. TIME FOR FILING CLAIM: As a condition precedent to recovery, a claim for any loss, damage, injury, overcharge or delay must be filed in writing with the Company within 60 days after delivery to depositor, or in the case of failure to make delivery, then within 60 days after a reasonable time for delivery has elapsed, and suit must be instituted against company within two years and one day from the date when notice in writing is given by the company to the claimant that company has disallowed the claim or any part or parts thereof specified in the notice. Where a claim is not filed or suit is not instituted thereon in accordance with the foregoing provisions, company shall not be liable and such claim shall not be paid.

DO NOT LOSE OR MISPLACE THIS RECEIPT

PRESENT THIS WAREHOUSE RECEIPT AND A WRITTEN ORDER WHEN ANY GOODS ARE TO BE WITHDRAWN. GOODS WILL BE DELIVERED ONLY UPON RECEIPT OF A WRITTEN ORDER SIGNED BY THE PERSON IN WHOSE NAME THEY ARE STORED.

THIS WAREHOUSE RECEIPT MUST BE RETURNED WHEN ALL THE GOODS ENUMERATED IN THE INVENTORY ARE WITHDRAWN.

TITLE TO PACKING MATERIALS PASSES TO CUSTOMER IMMEDIATELY UPON DELIVERY AT POINT OF ORIGIN.

Courtesy of Bekins Moving and Storage, Fresno, California.

FIGURE 19.3 A Nonnegotiable Airbill (Bill of Lading)

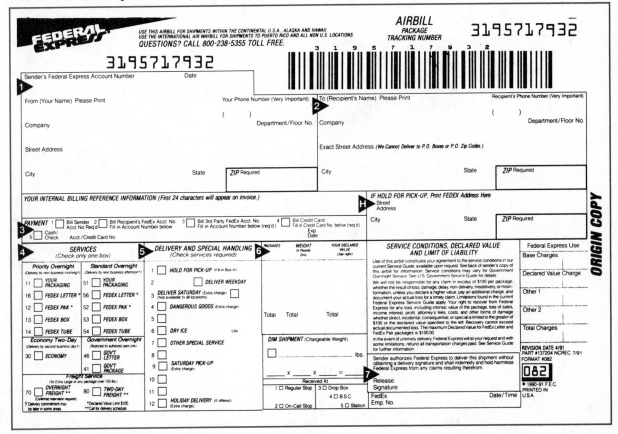

Courtesy of Federal Express Corporation, Memphis, Tennessee.

Risk of loss Financial responsibility in case of injury, harm, or destruction of the subject matter.

title and **risk of loss.** The seller has performed his or her part of the contract. In contrast, in a destination contract, the seller retains title and all risk of loss until the carrier gets the goods to the buyer or wherever the goods are supposed to go under the contract. The seller has not performed until the goods reach their destination. (Title and risk of loss are covered in detail in Chapter 20.)

Under UCC Section 2-303, the parties can agree to allocate or share the risk of loss during transit. However, this sort of arrangement seems to be the exception rather than the rule. Most parties seem to ignore the problem of loss during shipment until a loss occurs. And, at that point, it is too late to begin negotiating about what to do if a loss occurs. Because of this normal oversight, and because so many shipments use standard terms, the UCC has allocated risk of loss and a number of other things when the parties to a contract use any of these standard shipping terms. If the parties do not designate how loss is to be allocated, and if the contract does not specify whether it is a shipment contract or a destination contract, the law presumes that the contract is a shipment contract. Thus, once the seller properly transfers the goods to the carrier and makes arrangements for the transportation of the goods, the title and the risk of loss pass to the buyer.

F.O.B.

F.O.B. means "free on board." When this term is used, the seller quotes a price for the goods to the buyer "F.O.B." This quoted price is the total cost to the buyer for the goods, including any transportation or loading expenses incurred, at the named place. The buyer is responsible for any costs incurred beyond the F.O.B. point named in the contract. *Free on board* may be either a shipment contract term or a destination contract term, depending on the place named. If the contract terms are F.O.B. and the named place is the place of shipment (the *seller's* location), the contract is a *shipment contract*. *Once the seller has the goods loaded by the carrier, the seller has fully performed.* If the contract terms are F.O.B. and named place is the destination (the *buyer's* location), the contract is a *destination contract*. *The seller has not performed until the goods arrive at the final point,* and thus the seller has the risk of damages during transit.[4]

F.A.S.

F.A.S. means "free along side," and is a standard shipping term for seagoing transportation. This term is normally followed by the name of a vessel and the name of a port. When a seller quotes the price to the buyer "F.A.S.," the seller is telling the buyer that this is the total cost of the goods, including any expenses incurred, to get the goods to the named location. Again, the buyer is responsible for any costs incurred (loading, transportation, insurance, and so on) beyond the F.A.S. point named in the contract. *The seller is required only to get the goods to the named vessel and port.* Having done so, the seller has performed. The buyer then has all the risks of loading, transporting, and unloading the goods. The buyer is responsible from the dock of shipment to the buyer's location.[5]

There is a recent trend to treat F.A.S. as a seagoing F.O.B. term, with the term being either a shipment contract or a destination contract, depending on the named port. This current usage is gradually replacing the more traditional and more correct treatment of F.A.S. as a shipment contract term, with *ex-ship* being the more traditional and more correct term for a destination contract.

Ex-Ship

The term *ex-ship* always involves a destination contract. The seller quotes a price to the buyer "ex-ship," which means the price the buyer is to pay to receive tender of the goods *off* the named ship *at* the named dock. Like F.A.S., *ex-ship* indicates that the transportation is by sea. However, now *the seller is*

---

[4]Ibid., Section 2-319(1)(a), (b).
[5]Ibid., Section 2-319(2).

responsible for getting the goods both to the named vessel and port and un-loaded from the vessel. Here the seller has the risks of loading, transport, and unloading the goods. Until the goods reach the destination dock, they are the seller's responsibility.[6]

C.I.F. and C & F

C.I.F. means cost, insurance, freight. C & F means cost and freight. When either of these terms is used, *the seller quotes a lump-sum price to the buyer.* That single price will include the cost of the goods, the freight to get the goods to the buyer, and possibly the cost of the insurance to cover the goods during the carriage.[7] Both terms are deemed to be shipment contracts, with the buyer assuming all the risks associated with the transportation. Under both of these terms the seller pays the carrier for the transportation and then includes these freight charges as part of the price quoted to the buyer. The buyer repays the seller for the expenses of the carriage.

No Arrival, No Sale

Under a *no arrival, no sale contract, the seller is facing the risk of loss if the goods are damaged or destroyed during transit.* However, even if the goods are damaged or destroyed, the seller may not be responsible to the buyer to perform the contract. If it can be shown that the seller shipped conforming goods, and it is not shown that the seller caused the loss or damage, the seller is released from the duty to perform.[8] However, if the goods shipped were not conforming or if the seller caused the loss, the seller is still obligated to ship conforming goods.

C.O.D.

Collect on delivery is a destination contract with a special feature: *The buyer is required to pay for the goods on tender by the carrier, but is not permitted to inspect the goods until payment has been made.* If the buyer is unable or unwilling to pay on tender, the goods are returned to the seller, and the buyer is held for breach of contract.

INTERVENING RIGHTS

Once the seller's single duty has been performed, the focus of the sales contract shifts. The seller has performed, but it is not yet time for the buyer to perform. First, the buyer had an intervening right, the right to inspect the goods. If this inspection results in a discovery of some nonconformity, the seller *may* have a right to cure the defective performance to avoid a breach. Only after these intervening rights have been exercised or waived does the duty of the buyer to perform arise.

[6]Ibid., Section 2-322.
[7]Ibid., Section 2-320.
[8]Ibid., Section 2-324.

Inspection

The right of the buyer to inspect the goods is covered in UCC Section 2-513. This section empowers the buyer to inspect the goods in any reasonable manner and at any reasonable time and place. This includes inspection after the goods arrive at their destination, if the seller ships the goods.

The buyer bears the expense of inspection. This serves two functions: (1) it encourages the buyer to use a more reasonable method of inspection since the buyer must pay for it, and (2) it eliminates "phantom" inspections, with the expenses billed to the other person. If the inspection reveals that the goods do not conform to the contract, the buyer is entitled to recover the expenses of the inspection from the seller, along with any other damages the buyer may be entitled to recover. (This and other remedies will be discussed in Chapter 22.)

There are two circumstances in which the buyer is required to pay for the goods before being allowed to inspect them. If the contract calls for *payment against documents* or if it is *C.O.D.*, inspection before payment is not allowed. However, such a preinspection payment is not treated as an acceptance under the code.[9] In contrast, if the right to inspect the goods before payment exists, a preinspection payment is treated as an acceptance.

If the buyer fails to inspect, or refuses to inspect, or inspects poorly, the buyer may waive some rights. Any defects that should be noticed or discovered by a reasonable inspection may not be argued after an unreasonable inspection. The one exception is when the seller promises to correct, or *cure*, the problem and then fails to do so. In other words, unless the defect is hidden (so that a reasonable inspection would not reveal it), the buyer must "speak now, or forever hold his peace."

Cure

Often the buyer will discover, on inspection, that the goods do not conform exactly to the description in the contract. When this happens, the buyer must make a decision. Either (1) the nonconformity is minor, or of little or no consequence, in which case the buyer will normally accept the goods despite the nonconformity; or (2) the goods are too different from those described in the contract to be acceptable. When this happens, the buyer must promptly notify the seller, specifying in detail the problems with the goods that result in nonconformity.

If the time for performance has not yet expired, the Code gives the seller a chance to avoid being held in breach. The seller may *cure* the defect in the goods, *putting the goods into conformity with the contract.*[10] However, the cure must be completed within the time period in which the original contract was to be performed. No extension of time is permitted without the buyer's permission.

Occasionally, a seller ships nonconforming goods and reasonably expects the buyer to accept them despite the nonconformity. Such an expectation may

[9]Ibid., Sections 2-512, 2-513(3).
[10]Ibid., Section 2-508(1).

be realistically based on typical past dealings between the parties. In such a case, if the buyer decides to stand by the literal terms of the contract and refuses to accept the nonconforming goods, and so informs the seller, the UCC gives the seller a right to cure *even if* the time for performance is past.[11] If the seller informs the buyer of an intention to cure the defect, the seller is given a reasonable time to cure by substituting conforming goods so that the seller's performance is in compliance with the contract.

In the following case, the seller showed a willingness to cure defective performance, but the buyers refused to allow the seller a chance to cure. As a result, the buyers waived their right to rescind the contract under the provisions of the UCC.

Stephenson v. *Frazier*
399 N.E. 2d 794 (Ind. App. 1980)

FACTS   In July, 1974, the Stephensons purchased a modular home from Frazier. The total contract price of $22,500 included the installation of a septic system and the construction of a foundation for the home on property owned by the Stephensons. During the installation of the modular home, the Stephensons complained to Frazier about a number of alleged defects in the home and in the foundation that was being constructed. (The defects alleged included loose paneling, a water mark in the bathroom, broken storm window frames, a wrinkled roof, missing aluminum siding, crooked window frames, a missing mirror, and missing axles and wheels.) The Stephensons also argued that the foundation was improperly built. Frazier replied that he thought the foundation was "100 percent" and that if they did not like it, they could take him to court. At that point the Stephensons ordered Frazier and his crew to leave and told them that the property was "off limits" to them. The following day Frazier notified the Stephensons that he was ready to install the septic system and complete the installation of the modular home. The Stephensons responded that Frazier could not complete the job in a satisfactory manner and asserted that they wanted to rescind the contract.

ISSUE   Were the Stephensons entitled to a rescission of the contract and the return of the purchase price of the modular home?

HOLDING   No. The Stephensons were not allowed to rescind and must perform the contract with Frazier.

REASONING   The sale of the modular home was covered by the UCC, Article 2, which states that the seller has the right to cure nonconformance on notice to the buyer of an intent to do so. Frazier's letter the day after the disagreement showed a clear intent to cure the defects, and the refusal of the Stephensons to permit this right to cure prohibited rescission based on any alleged defects in the home. The court treated the alleged defects in the construction of the foundation under Indiana common law, asserting that the sale of the home was governed by the UCC, but the foundation was a "service" to be judged under common law contract principles. The court held that the alleged problems with the foundation amounted to a material breach of contract if true, and remanded the case for reconsideration on this matter.

---

[11]Ibid., Section 2-508(2).

BUYER'S DUTIES

The buyer's duties on the sales contract arise after the seller's duties have been completed and the intervening rights of the parties have been exercised, if these intervening rights in fact exist in the contract. Since the buyer is not required to inspect the goods, a failure to inspect operates as a waiver, and the buyer's duty to perform arises. If the buyer inspects and discovers a defect, the seller may have a right to cure. If the seller does in fact cure, the duty of the buyer arises. The buyer has a duty to *accept* the goods and to *pay* for the goods.

Acceptance

The UCC states that the buyer can accept the goods, and thus be obligated to pay for them, in a number of ways.[12] After having had a reasonable time to inspect the goods, the buyer is deemed to have accepted them in one of the following ways:

1. By signifying that the goods are conforming to the contract.
2. By signifying that the goods do not conform, but that they will be retained and accepted despite the nonconformity.
3. By failing to make a proper **rejection** of the goods if they are nonconforming.
4. By doing anything that is not consistent with the seller's ownership of the goods.

Rejection   A refusal to accept upon proper tender.

As mentioned earlier, acceptance obligates the buyer to pay for the goods at the contract price. It also prevents rejection of the accepted goods unless the defect was hidden or the seller promised to cure the defect and then failed to do so. Also, the acceptance of any part of a **commercial unit** is treated as an acceptance of the entire commercial unit.[13]

Commercial unit   The normal "package" size for the industry involved and the type of goods being sold; an unbroken "unit."

The following case dealt with the issue of a hidden defect.

Hummel v. Skyline Dodge, Inc.
589 P.2d 73 (Colo. App. 1978)

FACTS   Hummel was a used car dealer; Skyline Dodge was a new and used car dealer. A customer wanted Hummel to trade a used Dodge Dart for one of Hummel's cars. Hummel took the Dart to Skyline to see whether they would buy it from Hummel if Hummel took it in trade. Skyline's sales manager took the car for a test drive, looked it over, and agreed to buy it from Hummel. Hummel then traded with the owner, delivered the Dart to Skyline, and received payment for the car. Several days later, Skyline discovered that the Dart had a bent frame and was in

[12]Ibid., Section 2-606(1).
[13]Ibid., Sections 2-606(2), 2-607.

very bad condition. Skyline asked Hummel to take the car back. When Hummel refused, Skyline stopped payment on its check. Hummel sued on the check, and Skyline countersued for damages.

ISSUES	Had Skyline Dodge accepted the car when it took possession from Hummel? Were the defects in the car hidden, so that the acceptance, if it occurred, could be revoked on discovery of the defects?
HOLDINGS	Yes, Skyline had accepted the car; no, the defects were not hidden.
REASONING	An acceptance was found because Skyline had examined the car and issued a check "without reservation." Payment following a cursory inspection is a valid acceptance. The defect was not hidden because Skyline had both the equipment and the expert personnel to examine the car thoroughly. It failed to do so through its own fault, not due to any action by Hummel.

In the following case, the court found that the buyer had accepted the goods by failing to properly reject them despite an apparent nonconformity.

Plateq Corp. v. *Machlett Laboratories, Inc.*
456 A.2d 786 (Conn. 1983)

FACTS	Machlett Laboratories placed an order with Plateq for two lead-covered steel tanks. These tanks were to be used for the testing of x-ray tubes. According to the contract, delivery of the tanks was to occur at the Plateq plant, but the tanks were to be inspected for any possible radiation leaks after they were installed at the Machlett location. When the tanks were nearly completed, a Machlett engineer conducted a preliminary inspection. During this inspection he noticed some deviations from the specifications and pointed out these problems to Plateq. Plateq promised to have the problems corrected by the following day in time for the tanks to be delivered. The Machlett engineer agreed, and said that a truck would be sent to pick up the tanks shortly. Instead, Machlett sent a note of cancellation to Plateq and refused to accept the tanks.
ISSUE	Did Machlett properly reject the goods?
HOLDING	No. The conduct of Machlett and its engineer did not constitute a proper rejection.
REASONING	Plateq had substantially completed its performance under the contract when the Machlett engineer made his preliminary inspection. When the engineer pointed out some deviation, Plateq agreed to correct the problems. At this time the performance period had not yet expired, and Plateq had the right and the opportunity to cure the defect. Machlett's attempt to cancel the contract was an improper rejection that prevented Plateq from completing its performance as scheduled. An improper rejection is treated as an acceptance, and Plateq is entitled to the contract price.

Payment

Once the seller tenders delivery and the buyer accepts, or fails to reject properly, the buyer has a duty to tender payment. Likewise, in the case of a C.O.D. contract or a payment against documents, the buyer has a duty to tender payment. The buyer is allowed to tender payment in any manner that is nor-

Cash Money, an officially recognized medium of exchange.

mal in the ordinary course of business, typically by check or draft. A seller who is not satisfied with this can demand **cash**. But in so doing, the seller must allow the buyer a reasonable extension of time to obtain cash.[14] This would normally be viewed as one banking day.

Once the buyer tenders payment, the normal contract for the sale of goods is fully performed. Each of the parties received what it wanted, and nothing further is required. However, some contracts have special problems. Some of these problems will be discussed next; others will be discussed in Chapter 22, on remedies.

SPECIAL PROBLEMS

The commercial world is crowded with businesses trying to get "a foot in the door," or trying to keep "a foot in the door," or just looking for a new gimmick that will give them an edge. As a result, some new forms of business dealings have arisen. The UCC has attempted to deal with two of these new areas—sale on approval and sale or return—that resemble an old area—consignments. The Code deals with these new areas in Sections 2-326 and 2-327.

Sale on Approval

A *sale on approval* exists if *the buyer "purchases" goods primarily for personal use with the understanding that the goods can be returned, even if they conform to the contract.* The buyer is given a reasonable time to examine, inspect, and try the goods at the seller's risk. Neither title nor risk of loss passes to the buyer until and unless the buyer accepts the goods. The buyer is deemed to have accepted the goods if one of the following occurs:

1. The buyer signifies acceptance.
2. The buyer does not return the goods.
3. The buyer subjects the goods to unreasonable usage.

The following example involves a contract for sale on approval.

Sam "purchases" a new lawn mower with a thirty-day "free home trial." He uses the mover six times in three weeks, cutting his lawn and in no way abusing the product. After the third week Sam returns the mower and refuses to pay the purchase price. Since this was a sale on approval and Sam never approved, he is not responsible for the price.

---

[14]Ibid., Section 2-511(1), (2).

Sale or Return

A *sale or return* exists if *the buyer "purchases" goods primarily for resale with the understanding that the unsold goods may be returned to the seller even if they conform to the contract.* In this situation, both title and risk of loss lie with the goods. Goods stolen from the buyer cannot be returned, so they are "sold" to the buyer. The seller must be paid for them.

The following example indicates how the purpose of a sale or return differs from the purpose of a sale on approval.

Sam "purchases" some automobile stereo systems from Smooth Sounds, Inc. on a sale-or-return contract. Sam displays the stereo in his service station. If a customer wants an auto stereo system, Sam will sell it and install it. Sam can return any unsold units to Smooth Sounds for a refund or for credit on future goods. However, a thief breaks into Sam's station and steals the stereos. Sam must pay Smooth Sounds for the stereos since he cannot return them.

Consignment

In a *consignment, the owner of the goods allows a consignee to display and sell the goods for the owner/consignor.* The UCC treats such an arrangement as a sale or return unless one of the following occurs:

1. The consignor ensures that signs are posted specifying that the goods on display are consigned goods.
2. The consignor proves that the creditors of the consignee were generally aware of the consignments.
3. The consignor complies with the rules for secured transactions under Article 9 (see Chapters 28 and 29).

Obviously, the Code has limited, if not eliminated, consignment in the modern business world. Most such arrangements today are merely treated as sale-or-return contracts. The importance of such a distinction is shown in the following case.

Collier v. B & B Sales, Inc.
471 S.W.2d 151 (Tex. 1971)

FACTS   B & B Sales was a supplier of stereo equipment. B & B entered into a contract with Collier that called for B & B to deliver stereo equipment to Collier. The invoice called for the equipment to be picked up from Collier if it had not been sold within ninety days. After the goods were delivered, but before the ninety days had expired, Collier's store was burglarized and all the equipment purchased from B & B was stolen. B & B demanded payment for the goods from Collier. Collier argued that the transaction had been a consignment, and that B & B had risk of loss.

ISSUE

Was this a consignment, so that B & B had risk of loss, or was this a sale or return so that Collier had risk of loss?

HOLDING

This transaction was a sale or return, so that Collier had risk of loss.

REASONING

The agreement between Collier and B & B treated the transaction as a sale, and the invoice sent to Collier indicated that this was a sale but that any unsold goods would be taken back by B & B after ninety days. This meant that the goods belonged to Collier for the ninety-day period. According to UCC Section 2-326, this was a sale or return, in which title and risk of loss run with possession. Collier had possession and therefore risk of loss.

If a consignment is involved, the risk of loss is treated differently, as the following case shows. Compare the result in this case with the result in the *Collier* case preceding this one.

Employers Casualty Company v. Peterson
609 S.W.2d 579 (Tex. Civ. App. 1980)

FACTS

Nathan Shay operated a jewelry business in Texas. The Petersons had purchased jewelry from Shay, and Shay had sold jewelry for the Petersons in prior transactions. In October, 1976, the Petersons asked Shay to sell a diamond ring, a pair of diamond earrings, and several other items of jewelry for them. Shay picked up the jewelry from the Petersons, giving them a receipt that stated the "customer's estimate of value" and the notation, "To be sold at the agreed prices above." Two days later Peterson called Shay and stated that he had decided not to sell the jewelry at the stated price and instructed Shay to return the jewelry to the Petersons. Shay then informed the Petersons that the diamond ring (valued at $9800) had been stolen from Shay's business. The Petersons then filed a claim with their homeowner's insurance company, Employers Casualty, for the value of the ring. Employers denied liability, claiming that the transaction with Shay was a sale or return and therefore Shay owned the ring at the time of the theft. Thus, the ring was not insured under the Petersons' policy at that time.

ISSUE

Was this a sale or return, so that Shay had risk of loss, or was this a consignment, so that the Petersons retained title, and the jewelry was still covered by their homeowner's insurance?

HOLDING

This was a consignment, so that the Petersons still retained title, and the jewelry was still covered by their homeowner's insurance.

REASONING

The insurance company relied on *Collier* v. *B & B Sales, Inc.* to establish that a sale or return was involved and that risk of loss had therefore passed to Shay. The court disagreed. In *Collier* a bill of sale specified the right of the buyer to return any unsold goods for refund or credit. In the instant case, a receipt in which Shay agreed to sell the described items for "the agreed prices above," was, in the court's opinion, evidence that Shay was acting as an agent for the Petersons and that the goods were on consignment. There was no showing by the insurer that the Petersons ever intended to sell the jewelry to Shay or that Shay ever intended to buy it. Rather, all the evidence indicated an intention that Shay was to act as an agent for the Petersons, who still owned the jewelry. This evidence led to the determination that a consignment was involved and that the Petersons properly filed the claim with the insurer for the value of the stolen ring.

Auctions

Auctions receive special mention under UCC Section 2-328. In an *auction, the auctioneer, on behalf of the seller, sells the goods to the highest bidder.* The auctioneer does not give the same warranties to a buyer that other sellers of goods give.

A sale at auction is not complete until the auctioneer accepts a bid. Even then, if a bid is made while the auctioneer is in the process of **"knocking down,"** the auctioneer may elect to reopen bidding.

"Knocking down" The acceptance of a bid by an auctioneer, signified by the fall of the gavel after the announcement that the goods are "Going, going, gone!"

The goods at an auction are presumed to be put up "with reserve." An auction will be deemed "without reserve" only if by its terms it is specifically and expressly stated to be "without reserve." *With reserve* means that the auctioneer may declare all the bids to be too low and may refuse to accept any bids or to make any sale. In contrast, if the auction is *without reserve,* the highest bid made must be accepted and a sale made.

What if the *seller* enters a bid, directly or indirectly, in an effort to drive up the bidding? The winning bidder in such a case may choose to renounce his or her bidding and to avoid the sale or may elect to take the goods at the last good-faith bid before the seller entered the bidding.[15]

PRIMER ON ARTICLE 7

Article 7 of the Uniform Commercial Code deals with documents of title, especially warehouse receipts and bills of lading. Documents of title are involved in the sale of goods when the seller is to tender delivery through a third person bailee. Under Article 7, the person who issues a document of title covering the goods is a "bailee," whether the document of title is a warehouse receipt (signifying stored goods) or a bill of lading (signifying goods shipped by common carrier). The buyer under Article 2 is also known as the "consignee" under Article 7. The consignee is entitled to receive the goods or to negotiate the document of title, if negotiable. The person who deposits the goods with the third person/bailee is the seller under Article 2 and the "consignor" under Article 7.

Documents of title can be either "negotiable" or "nonnegotiable," depending upon the tenor of the document. If the document calls for delivery of the goods to "the order" of a named consignee or "to bearer," that document is negotiable. The consignee, if specifically named, negotiates the document by endorsing it and delivering it to another person. The consignee may also negotiate the document by delivery alone (no endorsement is needed) if the document calls for delivery of the goods "to bearer." A person to whom a negotiable document of title is negotiated, and who purchases the document in good faith and without any notice of defenses or claims against the document, receives the document by due negotiation. This means that the person

[15]Ibid., Section 2-328(4).

has good title to the goods covered by the document and has title to the document of title itself. It also entitles the holder to receive delivery of the goods from the bailee free from any defenses or claims not included in the document itself.

A warehouseman assumes liability for any damages to the goods stored with him or her if the damages are caused by a failure to exercise reasonable care. The warehouseman also has a warehouseman's lien on the goods for storage and transportation charges, insurance, and expenses reasonably necessary to preserve the goods.

A carrier of goods must exercise the degree of care reasonable for the goods and assumes liability for any damages to the goods carried by him or her, subject to common law restrictions. The carrier may limit liability to the value stated by the consignor, if rates are set in part by the value stated, provided that the consignor has the option to declare a higher value and to insure the goods accordingly.

The bailee *must* deliver the goods described in and covered by the document to the consignee or to the holder by due negotiation, unless one of the special exceptions provided in UCC 7-403 excuses the bailee from this duty.

The provisions of Article 7 operate in conjunction with Article 2 when there is a contract for the sale of goods and provision for delivery of those goods through a third person/bailee.

SUMMARY

In the performance of a sales contract, each party has some duty or duties to perform, and each has some right that may be asserted. The seller is to tender delivery of conforming goods as per the contract. The buyer is to accept and pay for the goods so tendered. The buyer normally has the right to inspect the goods before accepting or paying. If the inspection discloses any defects, the seller frequently has the right to cure, or correct the defect in the goods or in the performance.

The parties to a sale often use standard shipping terms. These terms have been defined by the UCC as forming either a shipment contract or a destination contract. In a shipment contract, the buyer bears the risks of loss or damage during transportation. In a destination contract, the seller bears the risks of loss or damage during transportation.

Some special problems have developed from modern business practices. Before the adoption of the UCC, consignments were frequently used to sell goods. Today, consignments have virtually been replaced by sale-on-approval and sale-or-return contracts. Each area is specially treated under Article 2, as are auctions.

DISCUSSION QUESTIONS

1. According to the UCC, what constitutes a proper tender of delivery?

2. What is the legal effect of a shipment contract as compared with that of a destination contract?

3. Explain the buyer's right of inspection. Include how, when, and where inspection may occur.

4. Assume that the seller in a sales contract did not mention the manner of payment in the agreement, although the contract did specify that payment was due upon delivery. What must the seller do in order to receive payment in money rather than in some other commercially reasonable manner? Explain.

5. What would an owner/consignor need to show in order to establish that goods in the hands of a merchant were consigned goods rather than goods that had been sold under a sale-or-return (or other sales) contract? Why might the owner/consignor want or need to establish that a consignment exists?

6. Acme Corp., a Boston business, entered a contract to sell goods to Zephyr, a Chicago retailer. The contract called for Zephyr to pay $10,000 for the goods "F.O.B. Chicago." Under this contract, which party is responsible for the risk of shipping the goods, and why?

7. Biltless Mfg. sent goods to Smart Set Co. under a "no arrival, no sale" contract. After the goods were sent but before they arrived, Biltless learned it could double its profit in another market. If Biltless recovers the goods from the carrier, what rights can Smart Set assert? Explain.

8. Scott, a merchant, sent Roy some goods under a contract. Roy was to receive the goods by December 18. On December 12, Roy received nonconforming goods from Scott, and Roy promptly called Scott to inform him of the nonconformity. What should Scott do to avoid being sued for breach?

9. Mary and Agnes are merchants. Mary sent goods to Agnes under a contract. Agnes glanced at the boxes and paid Mary for the goods. Agnes later discovered that the goods were of inferior quality and design. What rights does Agnes have against Mary, and why? What, if anything, should Agnes have done differently?

10. Farm Goods, Inc. sold Ralph a tractor under a sale-on-approval contract. After Ralph plowed twenty acres, he lent the tractor to his neighbor Ben. Once Ben had plowed another forty acres, Ralph informed Farm Goods that he was returning the tractor, since it did not meet with his approval. Farm Goods is suing Ralph. What will be the result, and why?

CASE PROBLEMS

1. The Giffees purchased a mobile home from Fegett in 1970. In 1971, Mrs. Giffee became ill, and the Giffees had the mobile home moved back to Fegett's lot so that it could be displayed and offered for resale. Fegett agreed to relay any offers he received on the mobile home to the Giffees. One of Fegett's creditors attached and removed a number of mobile homes from Fegett's lot, including the one owned by the Giffees. The Giffees are now suing Fegett for the value of the mobile home, alleging that the arrangement was a sale or return and that Fegett had risk of loss on the mobile home. What should the court rule in this case? (*Founders Investment Corp.* v. *Fegett* [Ky. App. 1978].)

2. Compton entered a contract with Baker that called for Compton to deliver heating and cooling equipment in a building owned by Baker. The contract called for Baker to pay Compton $12,000 on the delivery by Compton of the equipment for the first two floors of the building. Compton delivered the equipment three weeks later and demanded payment as per the contract. Baker refused to pay the $12,000, offering instead to pay $3000. Compton rejected this counteroffer. Baker then told Compton to remove the equipment delivered to date and return it for a refund. However, when Compton showed up to reclaim the equipment, Baker had locked the doors and would not allow Compton access to the equipment. Baker then sued, seeking a rescission of the contract. Baker also claimed that Compton had failed to mitigate damages by not returning the equipment for a refund. Compton countersued for

breach of contract. What result should occur? Explain fully. (*Baker* v. *Compton*, 455 N.E.2d 382 [Ind. App. 1983].)

3. The plaintiff, a wholesale jeweler, delivered two diamonds to the defendant, a retail jeweler, so that the defendant could display the diamonds and attempt to sell them for the plaintiff. Ten days after the defendant received the diamonds, they were stolen from his store. There was no showing of any fault on the part of the defendant for the theft of the diamonds. Is the defendant liable to the plaintiff for the value of the diamonds stolen from the store? On what legal theory would you decide the question? (*Harold Klein & Co., Inc.* v. *Lapardo*, 308 A.2d 538 [N.H. 1973].)

4. Scampoli purchased a new color television set from Wilson, paying cash for the purchase. Wilson guaranteed ninety days' free service and a one-year warranty on all parts. The set was delivered to Scampoli, but when it was turned on it did not perform properly. The delivery man promised to send a repairman to correct the problem. Two days later a service representative arrived and attempted to correct the problem. After working on the set for some time, the service representative told the buyer he would have to take the set back to the shop to adjust it properly. The buyer refused to allow the removal of the set for repair, insisting that she was entitled to a "new" set and not one that had been "repaired." The buyer retained the set but demanded a refund of the purchase price. Can the dealer properly perform this contract by making adjustments or minor repairs, or must he substitute a new television for the one delivered? Explain fully. (*Wilson* v. *Scampoli*, 228 A.2d 848 [D.C. App. 1967].)

5. In January, the Murrays bought a motor home from Holiday Rambler, paying $11,000 for it. From the very beginning, the Murrays had problems with the motor home, and by July it had been returned to Holiday Rambler for repairs and adjustments nine times. Holiday Rambler paid for all of these repairs and adjustments. In July, the Murrays took a trip in the motor home and encountered numerous difficulties. The motor home stalled while climbing a mountain, the brakes failed while descending a mountain, the electric system caught on fire, and gas fumes became so bad the Murrays were forced to evacuate the vehicle. Despite all these problems, the Murrays managed to get the motor home back to their home and then back to the dealer. Holiday Rambler offered to provide additional free repairs, but the Murrays declined and instead demanded

a rescission of the contract. Does Holiday Rambler have the right to cure the defects in this situation, or can the Murrays revoke their acceptance of the product? Explain your answer fully. (*Murray* v. *Holiday Rambler, Inc.*, 265 N.W.2d 513 [Wis. 1978].)

6. Lumber Sales contracted to deliver five boxcars of lumber to Brown. Brown admitted receiving four carloads but denied receiving the fifth and refused to pay for the fifth carload of lumber. The evidence established that the fifth boxcar was delivered to the railroad siding as called for in the contract but that the lumber was apparently stolen from the car before Brown inspected it or took possession of it. Under these circumstances, who should bear the risk of loss? What legal theory would you use to decide the question? (*Lumber Sales, Inc.* v. *Brown*, 469 S.W.2d 888 [Tenn. 1971].)

7. In January, Stridiron purchased a new Renault automobile from Island Cars. Less than two weeks later, Stridiron returned the car to Island Cars for repairs, due to an oil leak. Island kept the car for five days making repairs. Two months later Stridiron returned the car again, this time for replacement of the roller gears in the electric sun roof. Repairs took two days. In May, Stridiron returned the car to Island because it stalled every time it was shifted into third gear. The alternator, regulator, and battery had to be replaced. Stridiron received his car back on June 11, but three days later it had to be towed back to Island because it would not start. Finally, in September, all needed repairs were completed. Stridiron returned the keys to Island and refused to take possession of the car at that time. Stridiron then sued, seeking to revoke his acceptance of the sales contract, based on hidden defects that substantially impaired the value of the car. Island objected, claiming that they had to be given a reasonable opportunity to cure any defects in the car. Did the conduct of Island Car amount to a seasonable cure of defects, or should Stridiron be permitted to revoke? Explain fully. (*Stridiron* v. *I.C., Inc.*, 578 F. Supp. 997 [1984].)

8. Karinol entered into a contract with Pestana that called for Karinol to send a shipment of watches to Pestana. There were no provisions in this contract for allocating the risk of loss, and no standard shipping terms were used in the agreement. Karinol made appropriate arrangements for sending the goods to Pestana, delivered the goods to the carrier, and notified Pestana that the goods were en route. Unfortunately, the goods never arrived at the Pestana warehouse. Each party asserts that the other party had risk of loss in this con-

tract. Which party should bear the risk of loss and why? (*Pestana* v. *Karinol Corp.*, 367 So.2d 1096 [Fla. 1979].)

9. Northern Bank Note Company (Northern) of Chicago is in the business of printing bonds and securities for corporate clients. Halstead Hospital (Halstead), a Kansas corporation, hired Northern to print industrial revenue bonds and to deliver these bonds to Halstead's counsel in New York. The bond closing was scheduled for December 18, and Northern agreed to have the bonds at the signature company in New York on December 17 for inspection and signing. Northern hired a courier to deliver the bonds, but somehow one of the four boxes was not delivered, causing a delay in the bond closing and costing Halstead a substantial amount of money. Halstead sued Northern for the loss, alleging that the contract was a destination contract, so that Northern had risk of loss. Northern argued that the contract was a shipment contract, so that Halstead had risk of loss. How should this case be resolved? Explain fully. (*Halstead Hospital, Inc.* v. *Northern Bank Note Co.*, 33 UCC Rep. 1665 [10th Cir. 1982].)

10. A building contractor telephoned a concrete company in February, asking about prices and terms for concrete. The concrete company quoted a price and stated that the price as quoted would be adhered to for "the year." The building contractor agreed to the price, and the concrete company began to supply concrete for various jobs of the contractor. Concrete was supplied for the balance of the calendar year at the quoted price. The following January and February the concrete company supplied concrete as requested, but billed the contractor for a higher price. He refused to pay the higher price, alleging that the price quoted to him was effective for twelve full months, ending at the end of February of the second year. The concrete company argued that, by usage of trade, prices regularly changed as of January 1. How should this case be resolved? Explain your reasoning. (*Loizeaux Builders Supply Co.* v. *Donald B. Ludwig Co.*, 366 A.2d 721 [N.J. 1976].)

CHAPTER 20

Title, Risk of Loss, and Bulk Sales

OUTLINE

TITLE TO GOODS

When the term *title* is used, it refers to *legal ownership*. The legal owner of goods is said to have title. When goods are sold, title passes from the seller to the buyer. Title is a very important concept, but in some respects it is not as important today as it was in the past, at least under Article 2.

Historic Importance

Under common law, title was of paramount importance. Nearly all aspects of the contract hinged on title and its location. Risk of loss was placed on the party having title. The outcome of many lawsuits depended on who had title, so the courts spent a great deal of time and energy on this issue.

Modern Rule

The UCC specifically states that all the rights, duties, and remedies of any party apply without regard to title unless title is specifically required.[1] However, in recognition of the importance of title, some provisions have been made to help in locating title in the sale of goods.

Under the Code, title passes from the seller to the buyer when the seller completes performance of *delivery*. Thus, the type of delivery contract becomes important in determining which party has title. If the delivery contract is a shipment contract, title passes to the buyer at the time and place of shipment. If the contract is a destination contract, title passes to the buyer when delivery is tendered at the destination. These rules apply even though the seller may claim to have "reserved title." The Code states that a **reservation of title** is, in reality, only the reservation of a security interest.

In the following case, the seller claimed to retain title to the goods. When the buyer subsequently resold the goods, the seller brought criminal charges against the buyer. Notice how the court used the UCC to resolve the criminal case.

Reservation of title An attempt by the seller to retain title until the buyer has fully performed the contract; a denial by the seller that the buyer owns the goods.

Commonwealth v. Jett
326 A.2d 508 (Pa. 1974)

FACTS The Jetts purchased an organ from Menchey Music. The organ was delivered to the Jetts, but Menchey claimed that it "retained title" until the installment sales contract had been fully paid. The Jetts made several payments on the contract and then defaulted in their payments. Menchey tried on several occasions to collect the payments that had been missed and finally obtained a writ of **replevin** in order to recover the organ. Unfortunately, when the writ was served, it was discovered that the Jetts had sold the organ. Menchey then brought criminal charges against the Jetts for fraudulent conversion of its (Menchey's) property, the organ.

Replevin Recover goods unlawfully taken from the person who is rightfully entitled to possession of the goods.

ISSUE Did Menchey Music have title to the organ at the time the Jetts sold it, so that the sale represented a criminal conversion?

[1]Uniform Commercial Code, Section 2-401.

HOLDING	No. Under the provisions of the UCC, title had passed to the Jetts so that their sale of the organ was not criminal.
REASONING	Even though this was a criminal case, its resolution depended on the commercial law that controlled the transaction, the UCC. Article 2 permits the parties to choose the time and the manner in which title will vest in the buyer, but such a choice requires explicit agreement. If the parties do not explicitly agree, title will pass as provided in Section 2-401. A seller is not permitted to retain title in an installment sales contract because such a retention would negate the provisions of Article 9 on Secured Transactions. In order to carry out the policies of the UCC, an attempt to reserve or retain title by the seller must be treated as a reservation of a security interest. Thus, title had passed to the Jetts, and since the Jetts had title at the time they sold the organ, they could not have committed a fraudulent conversion of Menchey's property.

In some sales contracts, the goods are *not to be delivered*. Again, the Code specifies how title is to pass. If the goods are not to be moved and the seller is to deliver a document of title, title passes when and where the document is given to the buyer. If no documents are to be delivered, title passes at the time and place the contract is made.

Of course, under any set of circumstances, title cannot pass unless the goods are in *existence* and *identified* to the contract. The existence of the goods presents no problem: Either the goods exist or they do not exist. However, identification can present a problem. Goods are identified to a contract when they are shipped, marked, or *otherwise designated* by the seller as the goods that will satisfy the contract.[2] (Determining what qualifies as "otherwise designated" is a question of fact.)

Revests Is vested again; is acquired a second time.

Occasionally title will pass from the buyer back to the seller. If the buyer *rejects* the goods, or refuses to accept, receive, or retain them, title **revests** in the seller.[3] This is true even if the buyer is acting improperly by refusing the goods. Likewise, if the buyer properly revokes an acceptance, title revests in the seller.

Attach To tie, bind, fasten, or connect; to seize property under court order.

The location of title is still important in the area of *creditor rights*. A creditor of one of the parties may be able to **attach** any goods that belong to that party. Thus, creditors are very anxious to know where title lies. This also helps to explain the UCC's treatment of consignments, discussed in Chapter 19. The Code is very careful in spelling out the rights of each party when creditors are involved. Section 2-402 deals with the rights of creditors of the seller when goods are sold. The rights of an **unsecured creditor** of the seller are limited by the rights of the buyer to recover the goods once the goods are identified to the contract. In a legal tug-of-war between the buyer and a creditor of the seller, the buyer normally will win if the goods have been identified as the goods covered by the sales contract.

Unsecured creditor A general creditor; a creditor whose claim is not "covered" by collateral.

[2]Ibid., Section 2-501(1)(b).
[3]Ibid., Section 2-401(4).

**Fraudulent
Retention**

Another problem arises when, as sometimes happens, the seller "sells" goods but *retains possession*. In such a case, the seller's creditors can treat the sale as *void* if the retention by the seller is fraudulent under state law. The seller's only defense is that of being a merchant who retained the goods in good faith in the ordinary course of business for a commercially reasonable time. Thus, a seller who holds identified goods in "lay-away" would have a valid defense to the fraudulent retention charge. But a seller who holds the goods without a valid reason could be in trouble.

The following hypothetical case illustrates a fraudulent retention by the seller.

John, a blacksmith deeply in debt, feared his creditors would sue him and take his equipment to pay the debts. To prevent this, he "sold" his equipment to Lil, who let John retain possession of "her" equipment. When John's creditors tried to attach the equipment to satisfy the debts, John denied he owned it. He produced the bill of sale as proof. The sale would be fraudulent since John retained the goods after the sale in bad faith. The creditors thus could treat the sale as void and attach the equipment.

Conclusive presumption An inference of the truth or the falsity of a fact from which a result *must* follow as a matter of law.

Different states treat the issue of fraudulent retention differently. There are three possible rules for a state to follow. In some states a fraudulent retention by the seller is treated as a **conclusive presumption** of fraud; if a seller sells goods and then retains possession of those goods for any reason other than a commercial reason, the seller is deemed guilty of fraud. Other states view a retention of the goods by the seller after the sale as prima facie proof of fraud; the seller is presumed to be guilty of fraud unless the seller is able to show good cause for the retention. In yet other states, the retention of the goods by the seller is viewed as merely one bit of evidence, to be viewed together with all the other evidence, in determining whether a fraud has occurred.

**Voidable Title and
Entrustment**

As a general rule, any person who sells goods can transfer to the buyer only those rights that are equal to or less than the rights the seller possesses in those goods. Thus, a person who has valid title (i.e., the owner of the goods) can sell the goods and pass valid title to the buyer. A person who has void title (i.e., a thief) has no true title to the goods and passes void title to the buyer. The true owner of the goods may legally reclaim the goods from the person who bought the goods from the thief, if and when the true owner discovers the location of the goods. However, a person who has *voidable title* may legally transfer rights that are better than he or she possesses in the goods. A person with voidable title may legally pass full and valid title to a buyer *if* that buyer is a good-faith purchaser for value. For example, a person who acquires goods through fraud or misrepresentation has voidable title to those goods. The person who was defrauded or who was the victim of the misrepresentation may avoid the transaction and recover title to the goods if the avoidance occurs while the defrauding or misrepresenting party still has possession of the goods. However, if the defrauding or misrepresenting party sells the goods before any attempt to avoid the transaction occurs, the buyer may have full and valid title to the goods.

The issue of **entrustment** presents similar problems regarding voidable title and the passage of valid title.[4] An entrustment occurs when possession of the goods is given to a merchant who regularly deals in goods of that kind (often for repairs). The entruster, the person who delivers possession of the goods to the merchant, gives the merchant voidable title, which gives the merchant the legal power to transfer all of the entruster's rights to a good-faith purchaser who purchases the entrusted goods from the merchant in the ordinary course of business. Thus, an owner who takes his or her goods to a merchant for repairs entrusts those goods to the merchant. If the merchant happens to sell the entrusted goods to a customer in the ordinary course of business, and if the customer acted in good faith, the customer takes valid title to the goods. Of course, the entruster does have rights and remedies against the merchant to whom the goods were entrusted. The following two examples show the difference between an entrustment and a mere **bailment**.

Entrustment The delivery of goods to a merchant in goods of that type.

Bailment the transfer of the possession of goods with the understanding that the goods will be returned later.

Betty took her watch to Roger's Jewelry to have it repaired. Roger's sells new and used watches in its normal business dealings. If a customer comes into the store and "purchases" Betty's watch, that customer will own the watch. Betty's only recourse will be to sue Roger's for her loss. By entrusting the watch to Roger's, she gave Roger's the legal power to transfer good title.

Roger took his watch to Betty's Radio Shop to have it repaired. Although Betty's does not deal in watches, Betty sometimes repairs watches for her friends, and she agrees to do this for Roger. If a customer comes into Betty's and "purchases" Roger's watch, Roger can recover the watch from the customer. Since Betty does not deal in watches, the transaction with Roger was not an entrustment, and Betty's could not legally transfer title to the customer.

The following case deals with the issue of entrustment of goods to a merchant and also with the requirement that the buyer of the entrusted goods must act in good faith in the ordinary course of business in order to acquire good title.

[4]Ibid., Section 2-403.

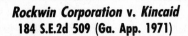

Rockwin Corporation v. Kincaid
184 S.E.2d 509 (Ga. App. 1971)

FACTS

Rockwin was an Alabama corporation involved in the manufacture and sale of mobile homes. In March, 1977, Rockwin delivered a 1970 model mobile home to Western Mobile-Homes, a Georgia retailer of mobile homes. Western also received an invoice with the mobile home, cautioning Western that the invoice should not be viewed as conveying title and that title could be transferred only by a manufacturer's certificate of origin. (Western never received a manufacturer's certificate of origin.) Soon thereafter, Western sold the mobile home and delivered it to Kincaid, who paid in full with a check. Western never paid Rockwin for the mobile home, and Rockwin filed a **trover** suit to recover the mobile home from Kincaid.

Trover An action to recover the value of personal property wrongfully converted by another person, to the detriment of the owner.

ISSUE

Did Kincaid acquire good title to the mobile home in the transaction with Western?

HOLDING

Yes. Kincaid was a good-faith purchaser in the ordinary course of business and acquired good title in the transaction with Western.

REASONING

The court found that Rockwin had entrusted the mobile home to Western, a merchant who regularly dealt in goods of that type, thereby empowering Western to transfer all of Rockwin's rights in the mobile home to a good-faith purchaser. The court also found that Kincaid was a good-faith purchaser in the ordinary course of business and had no notice or knowledge of any restrictions placed on Western by Rockwin or of the invoice sent to Western by Rockwin. Since both parties to the contract for the entrusted goods performed fully, title had passed to Kincaid on his payment for the mobile home and Western's delivery of the mobile home to Kincaid. Rockwin argued that under Georgia law Kincaid could not acquire title until he acquired a Georgia certificate of title for the mobile home, and since he never acquired such a certificate, he never acquired good title under Georgia law. The court rejected this argument, interpreting the relevant statute as one requiring a buyer to acquire a new Georgia certificate of title only if an old Georgia certificate of title had previously been issued and therefore needed to be replaced. In this case, since a Georgia certificate had never been issued on the mobile home, Kincaid did not need to get a replacement certificate in order to assert valid title.

Insurable Interest

The term *insurable interest* refers to *the right to purchase insurance on goods to protect one's property rights and interests in the goods.*[5] The buyer gains an insurable interest when existing goods are identified to the contract even if the goods are nonconforming. If the goods are not identified, the buyer gains an insurable interest once identification occurs. Likewise, if the goods are not yet in existence, the buyer gains an insurable interest as soon as the goods come into existence.

The seller has an insurable interest in the goods for as long as the seller retains title to or any security interest in the goods; and either party has an insurable interest if that party also has a risk of loss. Notice that title is not necessary for an insurable interest to exist.

Table 20.1 outlines the circumstances in which title and risk of loss are

[5]Ibid., Section 2-501.

TABLE 20.1   The Movement of Title and Risk of Loss

FORM OF DELIVERY	CIRCUMSTANCES IN WHICH TITLE PASSES TO BUYER (SECTION 2-401)	CIRCUMSTANCES IN WHICH RISK OF LOSS SHIFTS TO BUYER (SECTION 2-509)
1. Delivery by carrier		
a. With shipment contract	At the time and place of shipment	When carrier receives the goods
b. With destination contract	Upon tender of delivery	When delivery is tendered at destination
2. Delivery by warehouseman		
a. Via negotiable document of title	Upon delivery of document to buyer	When buyer receives the document
b. Via nonnegotiable document of title	Upon delivery of document to buyer	After the buyer has a reasonable time to notify the bailee
c. With no document of title	At the time and place of contract	Upon bailee's acknowledgment of buyer's right to goods
3. Personal delivery		
a. By merchant seller	At the time and place of contract	Upon delivery of goods to buyer
b. By nonmerchant seller	At the time and place of contract	Upon tender of goods to buyer

transferred from the seller to the buyer in the different types of sales contracts we have discussed. We will take up the subject of risk of loss in the next section.

RISK OF LOSS

The term *risk of loss* refers to *the financial responsibility between the parties if the goods are lost, damaged, or destroyed before the buyer has accepted them*. Notice that risk of loss refers to the relationship between the *buyer* and the *seller*. It does not refer to the possibility that an independent carrier of the goods may be liable. Nor does it refer to the possible liability of any insurer of the goods or of their delivery. The allocation of risk of loss often depends on the method of the performance.

A buyer who has risk of loss must pay the seller for the goods if the goods were properly shipped. This situation arises most commonly in a shipment contract: If the seller shipped conforming goods, but during the journey the goods were damaged, destroyed, or lost, the buyer is liable and must perform the contract as agreed. Of course, the buyer may have recourse against the carrier or against an insurer for the loss, but such recourse involves a separate contract or relationship and does not affect the buyer's liability to the seller.

If the contract involved is a destination contract, the seller bears the risk of loss. In this situation, any lost, damaged, or destroyed goods are the responsibility of the seller. The seller will be required to ship more goods or to make up the loss to the buyer in some other manner. And the seller will then have to proceed against the carrier or the insurer for any remedies that may be available.

In the next case, a shipment contract was presumed rather than specified. Any time a destination contract is not specified, the court treats the contract as a shipment contract.

Pestana v. Karinol Corporation
367 So.2d 1096 (Fla. App. 1979)

FACTS   On 4 March 1975, Nahim Amar B., a resident of Mexico, entered into a contract with Karinol, an exporting company from Miami. The terms of the contract, contained in a one-page invoice written in Spanish, called for Amar to purchase sixty-four electronic watches for $6006. A notation at the bottom of the contract read, "Please send the merchandise in cardboard boxes duly strapped with metal bands via air parcel post to Chetumal. Documents to Banco de Commercio De Quintano Roo S.A." There were no provisions in the contract specifically allocating the risk of loss while the goods were in the possession of the carrier, nor were any standard shipping terms used. The evidence established that on 11 April 1975 Karinol properly packaged and shipped the watches to Belize, Central America, to an agent of Amar. The cartons arrived in Belize 15 April and were stored in the air freight cargo room. On 2 May, Amar's agent opened the boxes and discovered that there were no watches in the boxes. Mr. Pestana, as the representative of Amar (who had died in the interim) sued Karinol and its insurer, alleging that the watches were lost or stolen while under the care and control of Karinol and while Karinol had risk of loss. Karinol filed a cross-complaint alleging that Amar had risk of loss and that Karinol thus was not liable.

ISSUE   Which party had risk of loss in this case?

HOLDING   Amar had risk of loss, based on the finding of the court that the contract in question was a shipment contract.

REASONING   A shipment contract is presumed under the UCC unless the contract specifies that a destination contract was intended by the parties. In a shipment contract risk of loss passes to the buyer when the goods are delivered to the carrier for shipment to the buyer. The contract in question contained no standard shipping terms and did not specify that the contract was a destination contract, so a shipment contract must be presumed. There was adequate evidence that Karinol had performed its duty under the contract by properly packaging and shipping the goods to Amar. The fact that the notation on the invoice called for the goods to be "sent to" Chetumal, Mexico, does not change the basic nature of the agreement. The contract was a shipment contract, Amar had risk of loss, and Karinol fulfilled its duty.

In the following case, the court found that a shipment contract was involved, so risk of loss had passed to the buyer when the carrier received the goods from the seller.

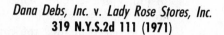

Dana Debs, Inc. v. *Lady Rose Stores, Inc.*
319 N.Y.S.2d 111 (1971)

FACTS
Lady Rose sent a written order to Dana Debs for the purchase of 288 garments. The purchase order called for Dana Debs to "ship via Stuart, 453 W. 57th St." Stuart picked up the goods and gave Dana Debs a receipt for the merchandise. Four days later, Stuart informed Dana Debs that it (Stuart) had lost the entire shipment. Dana Debs then informed Lady Rose of the loss and sent Lady Rose a bill for the goods.

ISSUE
Which party had the risk of loss when the goods were lost by Stuart?

HOLDING
Lady Rose had the risk of loss and must pay for the shipment.

REASONING
The carrier arrangements established a shipment contract. Dana Debs was instructed to "ship via Stuart." Once Stuart took possession of the goods, Dana Debs had done everything called for in the contract, and the title and risk of loss had passed to Lady Rose Stores.

In contracts that do not involve the use of an independent carrier, the risk of loss will frequently depend on how adequately the parties have performed. Several possibilities are explored next.

Breach of Contract

If the seller breaches the contract by sending nonconforming goods, risk of loss remains with the seller until either the seller cures the defect or the buyer accepts the goods despite the nonconformity.[6] In order for this provision to apply, the goods must be so nonconforming that the buyer may properly reject the tender of delivery.

Sometimes the buyer accepts the goods that the seller sent but later finds them to be nonconforming. When this occurs, the buyer often has the right to revoke acceptance (see Chapter 22). When accepting the goods, the buyer assumed risk of loss. When the nonconformity is discovered and the acceptance is revoked, what happens? The buyer retains risk of loss, *but only to the extent* of the buyer's insurance coverage. Any loss in excess of the insurance rests on the seller.

Repudiation   Rejection of an offered or available right or privilege,
or of a duty or relation.

Sometimes the buyer breaches a contract, usually by **repudiation**, after the goods are identified but before they are delivered. In such a case, risk of loss has not yet shifted from the seller to the buyer. As a result, the risk still rests on the seller. However, since the buyer is in breach, any loss in excess of the seller's insurance coverage rests on the buyer. Of course, the buyer will face this possible loss only for a commercially reasonable time.

No Breach of Contract

If the contract is *not* breached, risk of loss is much more technical. It is difficult to determine where risk of loss resides until the entire contract is

[6]Ibid., Section 2-510.

reviewed. The UCC recognizes four distinct contract possibilities to allocate risk of loss when the contract has not been breached.[7] In addition, the parties can by contract agree to allocate the risk.

The first situation arises in a contract whereby the seller sends the goods by means of a *carrier*. If the goods are sent by means of a *shipment* contract, risk of loss passes to the buyer when the goods are delivered to the carrier. This is true even if the seller reserves rights in the goods pending payment.

In contrast, the seller may enter into a *destination* contract with the carrier. Risk of loss then does not pass to the buyer until the goods are properly tendered at the point of destination. Once the goods are made available to the buyer, the buyer has risk of loss.

The second situation arises when the goods are in the hands of a *bailee* and they are not to be physically delivered. When the bailee is holding the goods, the contract must be very carefully analyzed. The contract may call for the seller to deliver a negotiable document of title to the buyer. If so, risk of loss passes when the buyer receives the document from the seller. If the seller is not to use a negotiable document of title but does use a nonnegotiable document, risk of loss passes only after the buyer has a reasonable opportunity to present the document to the bailee. And sometimes no document at all is used. In such cases, risk of loss passes to the buyer only after the bailee acknowledges the rights of the buyer in the goods.

The third situation arises when the goods are in the possession of the *seller* and a carrier is not to be used. Under these circumstances, the *status* of the seller is the key. If the seller is a merchant, risk of loss does not pass to the buyer until the buyer takes possession of the goods. If the seller is not a merchant, risk of loss passes on *tender* of delivery to the buyer. The following two examples show how risk of loss varies with the status of the seller.

Joan is a used car dealer. She enters a contract with Bob to sell him a car. She tells Bob that the keys are in the car and to go pick it up at any time. Before Bob gets there, the car is destroyed by a fire. Since Joan is a merchant, she still has risk of loss. She will have to provide Bob with another car or refund his money.

Jack is *not* a car dealer of any sort. He enters a contract to sell his car to Marie. He tells her the keys are in the car, and she can pick it up at any time. This is a tender of delivery. Before Marie gets the car, it is destroyed by a fire. She must bear the loss since Jack was a nonmerchant.

The fourth set of circumstances applies to a *sale on approval*. Here risk of loss remains with the seller until the buyer accepts the goods by approval

[7]Ibid., Section 2-509.

of the sale. Of course, the various ways the buyer can "accept" should be kept in mind.

Finally, the parties can *agree* to allocate risk of loss in any way they wish. Risk of loss can be divided in any manner the parties feel is proper. Such an agreement must be very explicit, or the Code provisions just discussed will be applied.

BULK SALES

Some years ago, several owners of troubled businesses began following a questionable business practice. Finding themselves in a bind, with business off, assets depleted, and their creditors demanding payment, these owners elected to take a less than ethical way out of their dilemma. They sold their business— lock, stock, and barrel—for cash and disappeared before their creditors knew what had happened. Faced with a new owner, an unsecured creditor could not assert a claim against the business assets. (*Secured* creditors, however, were protected under Article 9. See Chapters 28–30, on secured transactions.)

In an effort to prevent such occurrences, the drafters of the UCC included Article 6, "Bulk Transfers." Article 6 outlines the only proper and protected method for selling businesses that fall under its coverage. A failure to follow the rules may result in some very substantial losses for the buyer.

Article 6 begins its coverage by defining a *bulk transfer* as "any transfer in bulk and not in the ordinary course of the transferor's business of a major part of the materials, supplies, merchandise or other inventory."[8] In addition, if the seller transfers a *substantial* part of the equipment in connection with a bulk transfer of inventory, the equipment is also part of the bulk transfer and is thus covered by Article 6.[9] Finally, Article 6 is restricted in coverage to businesses that have the sale of merchandise from stock as their principal business function. Service enterprises such as a barber shop are not covered; however, a bakery would be covered.

Notice that no figures are used in the "definitions." A *major part* of the materials, supplies, or merchandise probably means *over half*, and a *substantial part* of the equipment probably means *less than half*. The final determination lies with the courts. The absence of an absolute figure allows a case-by-case analysis, but, more important, it does not leave the room for maneuvering that a definitely stated percentage would. Any businessperson in doubt about whether the sale is a bulk transfer would be well advised to comply with Article 6.

If the sale is a bulk transfer, the buyer and the seller need to show they have taken four separate steps. If these steps are properly taken, the buyer

[8]Ibid., Section 6-102(1).
[9]Ibid., Section 6-102(2).

obtains the goods free of any unsecured claims by the seller's creditors. If the parties fail to properly satisfy any step, the seller's secured and unsecured creditors may all assert their claims against the *buyer* as well as the seller.

The first step is taken by the seller. The seller must prepare a list of creditors, in writing and under oath. The list must include the name and address of every creditor and the amount of each creditor's claim. The *seller* is responsible for the accuracy of this list. Any errors or omissions cannot be held against the buyer unless the buyer knew of the error and ignored it.[10]

The second step is taken by both the buyer and the seller. The two parties must prepare a list of all items being transferred. The list must include sufficient identification to inform an interested party of what was sold. The buyer must retain the property list and the list of creditors for six months following the sale or must file them with a designated public office.[11]

The third step is taken by the buyer. The buyer must notify every creditor on the creditor list of the sale and when it will occur. This notice must be given at least ten days before the buyer pays for the goods *or* receives them, whichever happens first. Any creditor who is on the list and who is not notified may ignore the sale and proceed against the goods even after the sale. This rule does not apply if the bulk transfer is made by auction.[12]

The fourth step is also taken by the buyer. The buyer is responsible for seeing that the payments that he or she makes are applied to the seller's debts. It is the duty of the buyer to distribute the money to the listed creditors first, with any surplus going to the seller. And if the money will not cover all the debts, the buyer must pay the creditors **pro rata**.[13]

Pro rata Proportionately; according to percentages.

These steps seem to impose a heavy duty on the buyer, but the rationale underlying them is one of public policy: The buyer of a business or its assets should know that the seller has debts, and the buyer is thus in a position to prevent losses by the creditor; the creditor is seldom in the same position; and the seller cannot always be trusted to perform properly. However, the law does protect a buyer who follows the rules, as the next case illustrates.

Adrian Tabin Corp. v. *Climax Boutique, Inc.*
338 N.Y.S.2d (Sup. Ct. N.Y. 1972)

Affidavit A written statement made under oath.

L. D. J. Dresses made a bulk sale of its business to Climax Boutique through Paul Warman, a principal in Climax Boutique. L. D. J. Dresses provided an **affidavit** to the buyers that it had no debts and that there were no creditors. The buyers ran a lien search and discovered no liens outstanding against L. D. J. At the time of the bulk sale, Adrian Tabin Corp. was a creditor of L. D. J. Adrian Tabin claimed that since it was not notified of the sale, the sale was void as to its claim.

[10]Ibid., Section 6-104(2), (3).
[11]Ibid., Section 6-103.
[12]Ibid., Section 6-105.
[13]Ibid., Section 6-106.

ISSUE   Is the claim of the creditor valid against a buyer in bulk who was unaware of the creditor?

HOLDING   No. The good faith of the buyer in bulk cuts off the claim of the creditor.

REASONING   The UCC bulk sale provisions place the responsibility for the accuracy of a creditor list on the seller. The buyer is not liable for any errors or omissions on the creditor list unless the buyer *knows* of the error. Here the purchaser had no knowledge of the creditor, and the purchaser had conducted an inquiry. The creditor's claim in the sold assets is cut off.

SUMMARY

In this chapter, we examined the concept and importance of title to goods. Under the UCC, title passes at any time the parties agree. If the parties do not agree, title passes when the seller completes his or her performance. Title can revest in the seller if the buyer refuses to accept the goods, rejects them, or revokes the acceptance. The primary area in which title is important today is that of creditor rights.

The concept of risk of loss is much more important under the Code than it was under common law. Risk of loss refers to the party—buyer or seller—who must bear the burden of lost, damaged, or destroyed goods when the loss occurs during the performance stage of the contract.

A bulk sale is any sale of a major part of the seller's business that is not made in the ordinary course of business. The Code's provisions on bulk sales are designed to protect the seller's creditors.

DISCUSSION QUESTIONS

1. Under Article 2 of the Uniform Commercial Code, when does title pass from the seller to the buyer?
2. What does a seller mean when he or she attempts to "reserve title" to the goods being sold? What is the legal effect of such a reservation of title under Article 2?
3. What is an insurable interest? Can more than one party have an insurable interest in goods?
4. What does the term *risk of loss* mean in the law of sales?
5. In a bulk sale, what are the four steps required under Article 6? Who is responsible for each step?
6. George sells some goods to Harry. Harry leaves the goods in George's possession. Some of George's creditors attempt to attach the goods, alleging that the sale is void as far as their rights are concerned since George

retained possession. If George is not a merchant, what should the result be? Will the same result occur in every state? Why?
7. Harvey takes his watch to Ralph's Repair Shop and asks Ralph to fix it. Ralph repairs all sorts of things but does not sell anything regularly. One of Ralph's employees sells Harvey's watch to a customer. Who has title to the watch? What should Harvey do?
8. Scott shipped nonconforming goods to Ellen under a sales contract. The goods were shipped under a shipment contract. When the goods arrived, they had been damaged. Who bears the risk of loss between Scott and Ellen, and why?
9. Jim, a merchant, sold goods to Dennis. Dennis was to pick them up later that day. When Dennis arrived to

pick up the goods, he discovered they were damaged. Jim insisted that since Dennis had paid for them, Dennis was responsible for the damage. Was Jim correct or not? Explain.

10. Acme's owner has decided to go out of business.

He has offered to sell all of his inventory and equipment to Stan if Stan will pay cash. Stan suspects that Acme is in financial trouble, and he asks you what he should do to protect himself. What advice would you give? Be specific.

CASE PROBLEMS

1. Bowman purchased a Cessna airplane in 1969. He purchased an insurance policy on the plane from American Home Assurance, with the policy to run from 23 December 1969 through 23 December 1970. On 12 December 1970, Bowman agreed to sell the airplane to Hemmer. The plane was destroyed before Hemmer took possession. Bowman submitted a claim to his insurance company, but they denied liability, alleging that Bowman had no insurable interest in the plane as of 12 December 1970. Bowman sued American Home Assurance. What should the result be? (*Bowman* v. *American Home Assurance Co.*, 213 N.W.2d 446 [Neb. 1973].)

2. Harrison, a Connecticut merchant, ordered clothing from Ninth Street East, Ltd., a California manufacturer. The contract and all invoices stated that delivery was to be "FOB Los Angeles," and all documents specified "Goods Shipped at Purchaser's Risk." The carrier arrived at Harrison's business, and the driver attempted to deliver the goods, but the store manager insisted that the carrier must unload the truck. The carrier refused to do so. Harrison complained to Ninth Street East. During this controversy, the goods were lost by the carrier. Which party has risk of loss? Explain your reasoning. (*Ninth Street East, Ltd.* v. *Harrison*, 259 A.2d 772 [1968].)

3. Ramos purchased a new motorcycle from Wheel Sports, paying the full purchase price. Ramos received all the necessary papers to register and insure the motorcycle. However, Ramos left the motorcycle with Wheel Sports until he returned from his vacation. While Ramos was on vacation, the motorcycle was stolen from Wheel Sports. Who must bear the risk of loss? Explain fully. (*Ramos* v. *Wheel Sports Center*, 409 N.Y.S.2d 505 [1978].)

4. Martin agreed to purchase a truck and a haystack mover from Melland's, trading in his old truck and haystack mover as part of the deal. Martin transferred the title on the trade-in to Melland immediately but

retained possession and continued to use the old truck and mover until the new ones were ready. While Martin was still using his old truck and haystack mover, they were destroyed by a fire. Who must bear the risk of loss? (*Martin* v. *Melland's, Inc.*, 283 N.W.2d 76 [N.D. 1979].)

5. Halifax was a licensed loan company. It borrowed money from several sources and then loaned those funds to its customers. Halifax sold its business to Credithrift and used the proceeds of the sale to repay Commercial Bank, one of its creditors. No notice of the sale, nor any proceeds from the sale, was given to Guggenheim, another creditor of Halifax. Halifax is not available, and Guggenheim has sued Credithrift for the amount owed by Halifax, alleging that the sale was made in violation of the Bulk Sales Act so that the buyer is liable for the preexisting debts of the bulk seller. Is this a bulk sale? Explain your answer fully. (*Credithrift Financial Corporation* v. *Guggenheim*, 232 So.2d 400 [Fla. 1970].)

6. The Albermarle School Board hired Graves to build a new school. Graves hired Electrical as a subcontractor. Electrical agreed to furnish all labor and materials for the electrical work. As part of the subcontract, Electrical would sell the electrical supplies to Graves so that Graves could be reimbursed by the School Board, and Electrical would then install the supplies in the new school. Electrical was in debt to National Bank and granted the bank a security interest on all of its supplies and equipment. Electrical has defaulted on its loan with National and the bank is claiming that the "sale" of the electrical supplies to Graves was fraudulent, with Electrical retaining possession, and thus the bank can rightfully repossess these supplies. Graves asserts that it is a good-faith purchaser and therefore not subject to National's claims. Who should prevail in this case? (*Graves Construction Company, Inc.* v. *Rockingham National Bank*, 263 S.E.2d 408 [Va. 1980].)

7. Dunlop entered into a contract with Ada Oil to sell

Ada 436 tires. These tires were delivered to Ada Oil by Ryder Truck Lines. The truck containing the tires was driven to the loading dock of Ada Oil on a Friday, and Ryder was instructed to return to pick up its trailer on the following Monday. It was discovered the following Monday that the trailer containing the tires had been stolen from the Ada Oil premises. Ada Oil claims that since the tires had not yet been unloaded, delivery had not yet been tendered, and risk of loss had not yet passed to the buyer. Dunlop argues that Ada has risk of loss and must pay for the shipment. How should the case be resolved? (*Ada Oil Co.* v. *Dunlop Tire & Rubber Corp.*, 550 S.W.2d 129 [Tex. Civ. App. 1977].)

8. Sacks wanted to purchase a particular type of television. He called several stores until he located a store that carried the type of television he desired. Sacks then arranged for Smith, who had a history of purchasing items with bad checks, to go to the store and purchase the television for him. Sacks then purchased the television from Smith after Smith had purchased the television from the merchant, paying for it with a bad check. Sacks claims that Smith had voidable title, and that his (Sacks's) purchase gave Sacks good title, superior to the title of the merchant. Does Sacks have good title to the television? Explain fully. (*Sacks* v. *State*, 360 N.E.2d 21 [Ind. App. 1977].)

9. Hayward entered into a contract to purchase a boat from Postma. By the terms of the contract, Postma was to receive the boat from the manufacturer, install a number of options, and deliver the boat to Lake Macatawa. Hayward issued a promissory note to Postma to pay for the boat and granted Postma a security interest in the boat. One clause of the security agreement called for Hayward to maintain adequate insurance on the boat. After Postma received the boat from the manufacturer, but before the boat had been delivered to the lake, a fire at Postma's destroyed the boat. Hayward asked Postma to pay off the note covering the boat, and Postma refused. Hayward argues that Postma has risk of loss, and Postma argues that Hayward should have been carrying insurance to protect against any loss to the boat. Which party is correct? What legal theories should be used to resolve this case? (*Hayward* v. *Postma*, 188 N.W.2d 31 [Mich. 1971].)

10. On July 12, Ward agreed to purchase a car from Bryant, with Ward agreeing to make weekly payments until the full purchase price was paid and Bryant retaining title until payment in full was received. Ward accompanied Bryant to Bryant's home to take possession of the car. Several days later, on July 15, Bryant executed a bill of sale and signed the transfer portion of the tag receipt. On the day of the sale, Ward took several of his friends for a drive in his new car. During the drive, Ward struck and killed a pedestrian. The mother of the pedestrian sued Ward as the driver and Bryant as the owner of the automobile. Bryant's insurance company subsequently was brought into the case as well. If Bryant was still the owner of the automobile at the time of the accident, his insurance company is liable under the terms of the insurance contract with Bryant. If, however, Ward was the owner, neither Bryant nor his insurance company was liable. Who owned the car at the time of the accident? Explain fully. (*American Mutual Fire Insurance Company* v. *Cotton States Mutual Insurance Company*, 253 S.E.2d 825 [Ga. App. 1979].)

C H A P T E R 21

Warranties and Product Liability

O U T L I N E

THE CONCEPT OF WARRANTIES

A *warranty* is "a promise that a proposition of fact is true."[1] Since a warranty is a promise, it becomes *a part of the contract* in the sale of goods. Warranty protection is very often the best protection that a buyer can have in a sale. Warranties are of three types: **express, implied,** and **statutory.** The fact that one type of warranty is present does not mean that the other types are absent. In fact, all three types may be present in one contract.

At common law, the courts presumed that the parties to a contract had equal bargaining power. They also strongly believed in "freedom of contract." Thus, the courts were reluctant to interfere in the contractual relationship. The rule of caveat emptor—let the buyer beware—was regularly followed. As the commercial world matured, the positions of the parties to a sales contract began to change. It became less likely that the parties would truly have equal bargaining power—and less likely that the seller of the goods had also manufactured them. The courts and legislatures began to seek means of protecting the consumer. Implied and statutory warranties and product liability provided those means. The consumer has now become so protected that many people feel the rule is caveat venditor—let the seller beware!

Express Actually stated; communicated from one party to the other.

Implied Imposed by operation of law; presumed to be present under the circumstances.

Statutory Created by statute; imposed by law.

EXPRESS WARRANTIES

An *express warranty* can be given only by the *seller*. Such a warranty is said by the UCC to be a part of "the basis of the bargain." Section 2-313 mentions three different ways in which the seller creates an express warranty:

1. Any *affirmation* of a fact or a promise that relates to the goods creates an express warranty that the goods will match the fact or the promise.
2. Any *description* of the goods creates an express warranty that the goods will match the description.
3. Any *sample* or *model* of the goods creates an express warranty that the goods will conform to the sample or the model.

Any of these three methods creates an express warranty if it is a part of "the basis of the bargain." It is not necessary for the seller to use such words as *warrant* or *guarantee*. It is not even necessary for the seller to *intend* to create an express warranty. All that is necessary is that the seller employ one of these methods in a manner that causes the buyer reasonably to believe that a warranty is given.

The Uniform Sales Act, which preceded the UCC, required the buyer to

[1]*Black's Law Dictionary*, rev. 4th ed., 1968.

show *reliance* before an express warranty was found. The UCC seems to have removed the requirement of proving reliance. Instead, reliance appears to be presumed. The rule under the Code is that the seller must *disprove the existence of an express warranty*. In other words, if the buyer can prove the seller affirmed a fact, described the goods, or used a model or a sample, an express warranty is presumed. To disprove the existence of the warranty, the seller must show proof that the conduct described by the buyer was *not* the basis of the bargain. If such proof cannot be shown, the express warranty will be included in the contract.

Express warranties focus on *facts*. Mere opinions of the seller are not taken to be warranties. The seller is also allowed a certain amount of "puffing." However, there is often a fine line between opinion and fact, and the seller should be extremely careful. If a statement is **quantifiable,** it is likely to be treated as a fact. If the statement is **relative,** it normally will be treated as opinion. Thus, the statement "this car gets thirty miles per gallon" likely would be treated as a warranty. But "this is a good car" likely would not be a warranty.

Figure 21.1 illustrates the difficulty faced by the court in deciding whether something is a matter of fact or a matter of opinion. There is a great deal of "gray area" between those things that are obvious facts and those things that are obviously opinion, and the court has the task of deciding whether something within this "gray area" is a fact or is an opinion.

If the seller conveys an impression to the buyer and that impression is based on obvious facts, an express warranty exists. If the seller conveys information to the buyer that is obviously opinion, the seller is involved in "sales talk" or "puffing," and no express warranty is given. If the words, acts, or deeds of the seller fall within the "gray area," the court will consider the relative expertise of the parties, the ability of the buyer to ascertain the truth of the assertions of the seller, and the reliance the buyer places in the seller. These words, acts, or deeds may be treated by the courts as assertions of fact, and the courts therefore may find an express warranty exists despite the intent of the seller.

The seller also needs to be careful in advertising. Advertisements that claim certain characteristics for a product may be treated by the courts as affirmations of fact and thus as express warranties. The following example shows how an advertisement may be viewed by the court in an express warranty case.

Quantifiable Capable of exact statement; measurable, normally in numbers.

Relative Not capable of exact statement; as compared to some other standard or model or system; also known as comparative.

FIGURE 21.1 Finding an Express Warranty

| Obvious Fact | Gray Area | Obvious Opinion |

A television advertisement for the Pik Pen Company, manufacturers of disposable ball point pens, shows a couple on a picnic. The couple has several cans but no can opener. One of them reaches into a pocket, removes a Pik Pen, and punches a hole in the top of a can. As the camera pulls back, a voice says, "Pik Pens for 79 cents. Not just a great writing instrument."

If a customer decides to use his or her Pik Pen to open a can, and the pen shatters and causes injury to the customer during this attempted use, a good argument could be made that the commercial had created a belief in the mind of the customer that this use was expressly warranted by the commercial. (But if the Pik Pen company were to use a disclaimer in the commercial—normally by scrolling script across the bottom of the screen—the courts would be likely to find that the commercial did *not* create an express warranty.)

Finally, the Code views the timing of the statement or conduct from the buyer's perspective. Under Section 2-209(1), a modification of a sales contract is valid without consideration. This means that the seller can create an express warranty before the contract is formed, while forming the contract, or after the contract is formed.

Sellers should remember two things: If they *know* a fact, they should state it honestly; if they do *not* know, they should not speculate! It is too easy to give an express warranty without realizing it.

The following case is one of the landmark cases in express warranty law. Notice how the court viewed the relative knowledge of the parties and the special circumstances of the case in reaching its finding of fact.

Wat Henry Pontiac Co. v. Bradley
210 P.2d 348 (Sup. Ct. Okla. 1949)

FACTS   On 22 October 1944, Mrs. Bradley went to Wat Henry Pontiac to purchase a used car. She dealt with the used car sales manager. Mrs. Bradley testified that she asked many questions, and the seller assured her the car was in good condition. He allegedly said: "This is a car I can recommend" and "It is in A-1 shape." Mrs. Bradley stated that she had to travel to Camp Shelby, Mississippi, with her seven-month-old child to see her husband, and she asked for a test drive. The sales manager replied that the car was mechanically perfect, but that because of wartime gas rationing she could not give it a test drive. She bought the car and drove it home. Several days later, after she had set out for Camp Shelby, the car broke down and required extensive repairs. The sales manager, a former mechanic, testified that he gave no warranties and that he explained to Mrs. Bradley that there were no warranties on the car.

ISSUE   Did the seller give any express warranties on the car in this sale?

HOLDING   Yes. Under the circumstances of this case, the seller did give express warranties.

REASONING Mrs. Bradley was ignorant of the facts in this case. The defects in the car were hidden, and the buyer was not allowed a test drive. The seller was an expert in automobiles. He had served a long time as a mechanic and so stated to the buyer. His statements as to the condition of the car constituted a warranty and not mere opinion.

IMPLIED WARRANTIES

As pointed out in the preceding section, express warranties are a part of the contract. They are not present unless given by the seller. The court will not find an express warranty unless it is created by the seller as a basis of the bargain. In contrast, *implied warranties are imposed by law.* Implied warranties are present unless voluntarily surrendered by the buyer or excluded by the seller.

The UCC recognizes four possible types of implied warranties: title, infringement, merchantability, and fitness for a particular purpose. Some, all, or none of the warranties may be present in any given contract, depending on the circumstances surrounding the transaction.

Warranty of Title

Every contract for the sale of goods carries a warranty of title by the seller *unless* such a warranty is excluded by specific language warning the buyer that title is not guaranteed or *unless* the sale is made under circumstances that put the buyer on notice that title is not guaranteed.[2] If neither of these conditions is present, warranty of title exists. A warranty of title ensures the buyer of the following:

> The transfer of the goods is proper.
>
> The buyer is receiving good title.
>
> The goods are free of hidden security interests, encumbrances, or liens.

In other words, the buyer is assured that no one may assert a hidden claim to the goods that is superior to the claim of the buyer.

In the following case, an apparently innocent seller of goods was found to have breached the warranty of title in his sale.

Ricklefs v. *Clemens*
531 P.2d 94 (Kan. 1975)

FACTS In March, 1971, Clemens sold a Corvette Stingray to Ricklefs for $1500 plus Ricklef's 1969 Pontiac trade-in. At the time of the sale, Clemens delivered to Ricklefs a certificate of title for the car. According to the title certificate, the

[2]Uniform Commercial Code, Section 2-312.

car was a 1969 Corvette, and the title was free of all liens and encumbrances not specifically noted on the certificate. In December, 1971, Ricklefs was informed by an FBI agent that the car was stolen and that if he (Ricklefs) continued to operate the car he was likely to be arrested. Ricklefs subsequently contacted Clemens and demanded restitution.

ISSUE   Do the facts show a breach of the implied warranty of title in this case?

HOLDING   Yes. According to the Official Comments of the UCC, a disturbance of quiet possession is one method of establishing a breach of warranty of title.

REASONING   The warranty of title that a seller gives to a buyer should allow the buyer to rely on the fact that he will not be drawn into any later contests to establish ownership of the goods. Any facts that subsequently come to light that cast a substantial shadow over title are sufficient to constitute a breach of the warranty of title. In this case, the warning from the FBI agent that Ricklefs might be arrested for the continued operation of the automobile that had allegedly been stolen was sufficient to cast such a shadow over his title and thus to constitute a breach of the warranty of title. The fact that Clemens may have been innocent of any wrongdoing is irrelevant.

Section 2-312 of the UCC specifies that every seller of goods gives an implied warranty of title unless the contract contains specific language that the warranty is being excluded or the circumstances of the sale are such that the buyer should realize that the seller does not warrant title. Thus, a merchant who is entrusted with goods (see Chapter 20 for a discussion of entrustments) gives a warranty of title if the merchant sells the entrusted goods to a good-faith purchaser. If the merchant had voidable title to the entrusted goods, the buyer received good title, and there is no breach of the warranty. However, if the goods entrusted to the merchant had been stolen, the person who purchased the goods from the merchant would receive void title, and the merchant would be liable for breach of the implied warranty of title.

Warranty Against Infringement

A warranty against infringement can be given by either the buyer or the seller, although it is normally given by the seller.[3] None of the other implied warranties can be given by the buyer. The *infringement* protected against is the *rightful claim of any third person. Patent* infringement is probably the most common type of problem dealt with under this warranty. Another area that is becoming increasingly important is copyright. Videotapes, audio tapes, and computer software normally are copyrighted, and all are easy to copy without a great deal of equipment, expertise, or expense. Experts estimate that "pirated" copies of copyright-protected materials cost each of these industries millions of dollars per year, and more attention is being paid to the protection and enforcement of copyrights. As this trend continues, an increase in the number of cases involving the warranty against infringements should occur. This topic promises to be an area of growth in litigation over the next several years.

[3]Ibid., Section 2-312(3).

To give this warranty, the seller must be a merchant who regularly deals in the type of goods involved. The buyer who warrants against infringement need not be a merchant. Any buyer who furnishes specifications to the seller for a special manufacture of goods must warrant against infringement if the seller complies with the specifications.

Warranty of Merchantability

Probably the most commonly breached, and the most commonly asserted, implied warranty is the warranty of merchantability. A warranty of merchantability is given whenever a merchant of goods, including a merchant of food or drink, makes a sale. Failure to satisfy any of the following six criteria means that the goods are not merchantable and that the warranty has been breached:[4]

1. Goods must pass without objection in the trade, under the description in the contract.

Fungible Virtually identical and interchangeable; not different from other goods of the same description.

2. If goods are **fungible,** they must be of fair average quality within the description.
3. Goods must be suitable for their ordinary purpose and use.
4. Goods must be of even kind, quality, and quantity.
5. Goods must be adequately contained, packaged, and labeled as required under the agreement.
6. Goods must conform to the promises and facts contained on the label, if any.

Under this warranty, merchant sellers have been found liable because of bobby pins in soft drink containers, worms in canned peas, a decomposing mouse in a soda bottle, and a hair dye that caused the buyer's hair to fall out.

Because numerous merchantability cases have involved disputes over food and drink, the courts have developed special rules to determine merchantability in these cases. Some states follow the "foreign-natural" test; others follow the "reasonable expectations" test. Under the foreign-natural test, a chicken bone in a chicken salad sandwich would not involve a breach since chicken bones are "natural" to chicken. But a cherry pit in a chicken salad would be "foreign" and thus would establish a breach. Under the reasonable expectations test, the court attempts to establish what a reasonable person would expect to find in the food. Any foreign object would show a breach, but so would some natural objects. Thus, a chicken bone in a chicken salad sandwich might show a breach if it is unreasonable to expect to find a bone in such a sandwich. The reasonable expectations in any given case would be a question of fact.

The following case illustrates the approach a court might take in a merchantability-of-food case.

[4]Ibid., Section 2-314(2).

Webster v. Blue Ship Tea Room
347 Mass. 421, 198 N.E.2d 309 (1964)

FACTS

One Saturday in 1959, Webster, her sister, and her aunt entered the Blue Ship Tea Room. Webster, who was born and raised in New England, initially ordered clam chowder and crabmeat salad. When she was informed that there was no clam chowder, she ordered a cup of fish chowder. After she ate three or four spoonfuls of the chowder, she became aware that something was lodged in her throat. She could not swallow or clear her throat by gulping. At Massachusetts General Hospital, she had two esophagoscopies, in the second of which a fish bone was found in her throat and removed.

ISSUE

"Whether a fish bone lurking in a fish chowder, about the ingredients of which there is no other complaint, constitutes a breach of implied warranty under applicable provisions of the Uniform Commercial Code?"

HOLDING

No. The fish chowder, as served, was fit to be eaten and was merchantable. There was no breach of implied warranty.

REASONING

At trial, the judge charged the jury with the following: "Was the fish chowder fit to be eaten and wholesome? . . . [N]obody is claiming that the fish itself wasn't wholesome. . . . But the bone of contention here—I don't mean that for a pun—but was this fish bone a foreign substance that made the fish chowder unwholesome or not fit to be eaten?" Webster emphasized the high standard to which the sale of food is held by the courts. But the Blue Ship Tea room urged the court to remember that Webster was a native New Englander who had eaten fish chowder before, and that "fish chowder, as it is served and enjoyed by New Englanders, is a hearty dish, originally designed to satisfy the appetites of our seamen and fishermen." In reaching its conclusion, the court examined *The American Woman's Cookbook, A New English Dictionary, The House of Seven Gables,* Fannie Farmer, and *The Boston Cooking School Cook Book.* Based on its research, the court stated: "Thus we consider a dish which for many long years, if well made, has been made generally as outlined above [omitted]. It is not too much to say that a person sitting down in New England to consume a good New England fish chowder embarks on a gustatory adventure which may entail the removal of some fish bones from the bowl as he proceeds. We are not inclined to tamper with age-old recipes by any amendment reflecting the plaintiff's view of the effect of the Uniform Commercial Code upon them. . . . We should be prepared to cope with the hazards of fish bones, the occasional presence of which, in the light of a hallowed tradition, do not impair their fitness or merchantability."

Warranty of Fitness for a Particular Purpose

Any seller, whether a merchant or a nonmerchant, may give the implied warranty of fitness for a particular purpose. In order for this warranty to come into existence, the following conditions must be present:[5]

1. The seller must know that the buyer is contemplating a particular use for the goods.
2. The seller must know that the buyer is relying on the seller's skill, judgment, or knowledge in selecting the proper goods for the purpose.
3. The buyer must not restrict the seller's range of choices to a particular brand or price range or otherwise limit the scope of the seller's expert judgment.

[5]Ibid., Section 2-315.

Notice that the warranty here is for a *particular* purpose. Also note that merchantability covers *normal* purpose or use. Thus, even if the warranty of fitness for a particular purpose is not found, the warranty of merchantability will normally be available to protect the buyer. However, if the seller is not a merchant, the buyer may have to prove the warranty of fitness for a particular purpose in order to have any implied warranty protection.

Occasionally a case will involve allegations that the warranties of merchantability and fitness for a particular purpose have both been breached. With the courts' growing tendency to protect the buyer, the seller in such a case is quite likely to lose on at least one of the warranties and may lose on both counts, as the seller in the following case discovered.

Vlases v. *Montgomery Ward & Co.*
377 F.2d 846 (3d Cir. 1967)

FACTS Vlases purchased 2000 chickens from Montgomery Ward to start a chicken business. After receiving the birds, Vlases discovered that they were afflicted with avian leukosis, a bird cancer. Vlases sued Montgomery Ward for breach of its implied warranties of merchantability and fitness for a particular purpose. Montgomery Ward claimed that the disease is not detectable in baby chicks, and that the chickens could have become ill after the sale.

ISSUE Did this sale violate the implied warranties of merchantability and fitness for a particular purpose?

HOLDING Yes. The seller is responsible for breach of warranty when inferior goods are sold.

REASONING The purpose of implied warranties is to make the seller responsible for selling inferior goods. That the defect was difficult to discover is not an adequate defense. The law does not care what precautions the seller took. The issue is merely the quality of the goods provided to the buyer. The quality was inferior. No exclusions of the warranties were present. The warranties were therefore breached.

STATUTORY WARRANTIES

Before 1975, many consumers faced certain problems in the area of warranty law: Many manufacturers disclaimed warranty protection, leaving the consumer with little or no protection; and most manufacturers put the warranty terms inside a sealed package so the consumer did not know what warranty provisions were involved until after the sale. The warranty terms inside the package frequently were in the form of a "warranty card." The instructions to the buyer were for the buyer to complete the card and return it to the manufacturer in order to obtain his or her warranties. In fact, these cards often specified that the buyer was agreeing to accept the *express* warranties the manufacturer was offering as the exclusive warranties in the contract. By completing and returning the card, the buyer was surrendering any implied warranties he or she possessed in exchange for a very restricted sixty- or ninety-day express warranty coverage proposed by the merchant. As a result of these problems, the Magnuson-Moss Act–Consumer Product Warranty Act became law in 1975.[6] This law covers any consumer good manufactured after 3 January 1975. The manufacturer must provide the consumer with presale warranty information. The manufacturer also should set up informal settlement procedures to benefit the consumer.

The manufacturer does not have to give any express warranties under the statute. However, according to the law, a manufacturer who does give an express warranty must designate it as either *full* or *limited*. To qualify as a full warranty, the warranty must meet at least four requirements:

1. It must warrant that defects will be remedied within a reasonable time.
2. It must conspicuously display any exclusions or limitations of consequential damages.
3. An implied warranty must not be limited in time.
4. It must warrant that if attempts to remedy defects fail, the consumer will be allowed to select either a refund or a replacement.

Any warranty that is not full is limited. In a limited warranty, implied warranties may be limited to a reasonable time, frequently the same time as the express warranties.

WARRANTY EXCLUSIONS

The seller can modify or exclude warranties. The simplest way to exclude an *express* warranty is not to give one. If the seller is careful, no express warranties will exist. Sometimes a seller will create an express warranty orally but will attempt to exclude any express warranties in writing. In this case, the court will turn to UCC Section 2-316(1). The court will take the warranty and the exclusion as consistent with one another if possible; otherwise, the warranty will override the exclusion.

Excluding or modifying *implied* warranties is not so easy. To exclude or modify a warranty of merchantability, either orally or in writing, the word *merchantability* must be used. If the exclusion is written, the exclusion must be conspicuous. To exclude or modify a warranty of fitness for a particular purpose, the exclusion must be written, and it must be conspicuous; no oral exclusions of fitness are allowed.[7]

---

[6] 15 USCA, Sections 2301–2312.
[7] UCC, Section 2-316(2).

Under Section 2-316(3), it is possible to exclude all implied warranties of quality under three sets of circumstances (which normally do not exclude title or infringement protections):

1. Language such as "as is" or "with all faults" must be used properly so that the buyer is duly informed that no implied warranties are given.
2. If the buyer has thoroughly examined the goods or has refused to examine them before the sale, no implied warranty is given for defects that the examination should have revealed.
3. Under course of dealings, course of performance, or usage of trade, implied warranties are not given as a matter of common practice.

In the following case, the court was faced with the question of whether a written disclaimer of warranty was properly given so that the buyer was aware of the disclaimer.

Fairchild Industries v. *Maritime Air Services, Ltd.*
333 A.2d 313 (Md. 1975)

FACTS In 1969, the parties entered into a contract for the lease of a helicopter from Fairchild to Maritime. The lease contained an option to buy, which was exercised by Maritime in 1969. Accordingly, the parties entered into a purchase agreement. This agreement consisted of a printed form furnished by Fairchild, and with all relevant provisions being typed on the form. Among the provisions typed into the agreement was a paragraph that asserted that the sale was to be made "as is" and that the seller was giving no warranties, express or implied, except the warranty of title. When Maritime encountered problems with the helicopter, it asserted that the helicopter was not merchantable and that Fairchild was liable for breach of the implied warranties of the sale. Fairchild alleged that no implied warranties were present in the sale.

ISSUE Did the inclusion of the paragraph in the sales agreement operate as an effective disclaimer of the implied warranties in this sale?

HOLDING No. The attempt to disclaim the warranties was not conspicuous and was therefore ineffective as a disclaimer.

REASONING Section 2-316 of the UCC is designed to protect buyers from unexpected and unbargained disclaimers of warranty protections. The Code requires that such disclaimers be conspicuous if they are in writing so that a buyer will not be taken unaware after the sale is consummated. A seller may not claim, after the fact, that a writing was intended to be conspicuous. Fairchild could have typed the alleged disclaimer in uppercase letters rather than in the lowercase that were actually used. Unless a written disclaimer is properly communicated, it is of no effect. Since Fairchild did not properly disclaim the implied warranties, the implied warranties are present.

If warranties do exist, the next question is, *whom* do they protect? At common law, the answer was simple but unsatisfactory. Since the warranty was a part of the contract, it extended only to a party to the contract. Thus, the buyer was covered, but no one else. The UCC has changed this. Section 2-318 contains the following three alternative provisions, and each state has selected *one* of the alternatives:

1. Warranties extend to any member of the buyer's family or household or any guest in the buyer's home if it is reasonable to expect that person to use or consume the goods.
2. Warranties extend to *any natural person* (human being) who could reasonably be expected to use or consume the goods.
3. Warranties extend to *any person* (remember, a corporation is a *legal person*) who could reasonably be expected to use or consume the goods.

The seller may not exclude or modify the extension of the warranties to those third-party beneficiaries.

PRODUCT LIABILITY

Occasionally, a situation arises in which a person is injured by goods and no warranty provisions are available to protect the injured party. When such a situation occurs, the injured party is not without remedy. He or she may discover that although warranty protections are lacking, potential remedies are available under tort law. The injured party may be able to assert *negligence* or even *strict tort liability*.

At common law, negligence could be used in only two circumstances. The injured party could recover damages on the ground of negligence by showing that he or she was in privity of contract with the negligent party. Because in most instances the injured party was in contact only with an innocent intermediate party, and not with the negligent manufacturer, this requirement effectively removed the possibility of suing for negligence. The other circumstance ignored the privity requirement. If the goods were found to be *imminently* or *inherently dangerous*, privity was not required. A product is imminently dangerous if it is reasonably certain to threaten death or severe bodily harm. An item is inherently dangerous if it is dangerous by its nature. Imminent danger is commonly found in negligent production; inherent danger, in negligent use.

In 1916, the American courts effectively laid the privity defense to rest. In the landmark case of *MacPherson* v. *Buick Motor Co.*, the court allowed an injured plaintiff to sue a manufacturer and to recover damages despite a lack of privity. Other courts quickly adopted the *MacPherson* rule, and, as a result, privity of contract is seldom asserted as a negligence defense today.

In the following case, the plaintiff's lack of privity was raised as a defense to the lawsuit. The court rejected the lack of privity defense and allowed the case to proceed on its merits.

Embs v. *Pepsi-Cola Bottling Co. of Lexington, Kentucky, Inc.*
528 S.W.2d 703 (Ky. 1975)

FACTS   Embs was shopping at Stamper's Cash Market. She went to an upright soft drink cooler, removed several bottles from the cooler, and placed them in her basket. As she turned away from the cooler, she heard a sound like a shotgun. She looked and saw a gash in her leg, broken glass on the floor, and soda pop on her dress. Embs was taken to the hospital by Mrs. Stamper, who told her that a Seven-Up bottle had exploded and that several other Seven-Up bottles had similarly exploded that week.

Pepsi-Cola Bottling Company was the local bottler of the Seven-Up and loaded all the Seven-Up bottles delivered to the Stamper's Cash Market. Arnold Vice was the local distributor of Seven-Up, and he delivered and unloaded all the Seven-Up in stock at the store. Mrs. Embs sued all three for strict product liability owing to the explosion of the bottle. The defense asserted by all three was lack of privity of contract with Mrs. Embs.

ISSUE   Were the defendants liable to Mrs. Embs despite a lack of privity of contract between her and any of the three defendants?

HOLDING   Yes. The lack of privity of contract is irrelevant in a case such as this.

REASONING   The public policy of the state is furthered by minimizing the risk of personal injury and property damage, and this can best be done by charging the costs against the manufacturers and retailers who can procure liability insurance, spreading the cost of such insurance to their customers. Given this public policy objective, it makes no sense to protect one class of persons from injury but not another. The imposition of strict liability without regard to privity of contract effectively discourages the distribution of defective products and imposes no unreasonable burden on the businesses. The injured third party should be compensated, and the multiple defendants should trace the defect for allocation to one of them. The burden should not be placed on the innocent party.

The other basis for recovery for an injured party is *strict tort liability*. This theory is set out in *Restatement (Second) of Torts*, Section 402A. Section 402A is widely followed by the courts of the United States. The section states:

(1) One who sells any product in a defective condition unreasonably dangerous to the user or consumer or to his property is subject to liability for physical harm thereby caused to the ultimate user or consumer, or to his property, if
    (a) the seller is engaged in the business of selling such a product, and
    (b) it is expected to and does reach the user or consumer without substantial change in the condition in which it is sold.
(2) The rule stated in subsection (1) applies although
    (a) the seller has exercised all possible care in the preparation and sale of his product, and
    (b) the user or consumer has not bought the product from or entered into any contractual relation with the seller.

The following case shows how the theory of strict tort liability is currently being applied. Notice that the injured plaintiff is asserting a defect in design and also that he should recover for injuries that were *increased*, as opposed to *caused*, by the allegedly defective design. Such rulings apparently will continue to be the thrust of strict tort liability for some time to come.

Larsen v. General Motors Corp.
391 F.2d 495 (8th Cir. 1968)

FACTS   Larsen was driving a 1963 Chevrolet Corvair, with the permission of its owner. While operating the car, Larsen was involved in an accident. The impact occurred on the left front corner of the Corvair, causing a severe rear thrust of the steering column into Larsen's head. Larsen alleged that the Corvair was negligently designed and that a design defect increased his injuries. He alleged (1) negligence in design, (2) negligent failure to warn drivers, and (3) breach of the warranty of merchantability. General Motors based its defense on a lack of duty to make cars safe during a collision.

ISSUE   Is the manufacturer liable for negligent design of the product?

HOLDING   Yes. This defect led to a readily foreseeable zone of danger for the operator of the car.

REASONING   The manufacturer has a duty to use reasonable care in designing its product so that the article is safe for its intended use. The product must be reasonably fit and free of hidden defects. For an automobile, the probability of an accident is very high. Injuries from such accidents are readily foreseeable. It is irrational to limit the liability of the manufacturer to those situations in which the defect causes the accident. Where the injury to the occupant is enhanced by the manufacturer's lack of reasonable care, the manufacturer is liable.

YOU BE THE JUDGE

> The Consumer Federation of America and the Public Interest Research Group (PIRG) proposed that the Consumer Product Safety Commission (CPSC) enact a regulation requiring warning labels for certain dangerous toys. The proposal would require that marbles and small balls (less than 1.68 inches in diameter) as well as balloon packages have warning labels. Each of these products has been considered dangerous due to the fact that infants sometimes swallow them, leading to death or serious injury. The evidence presented showed that an average of 8 infants per year die from choking after ingesting either a marble or a balloon. Despite the evidence, the CPSC decided against enacting the labeling requirement regulation.
>
> Assume that the Consumer Federation of America and PIRG are seeking judicial relief. How would you rule, and why?

Source: "One small step for consumerism sanity," James J. Kilpatrick, *Roanoke Times & World News*, May 3, 1992, page F3.

SUMMARY

Warranty law and product liability are two major areas of consumer protection—a subject that has been receiving an increasing amount of attention for some years.

Warranty protection comes in three broad forms: express warranties, which are given by the seller; implied warranties, which are imposed by law; and statutory warranties, which are primarily concerned with disclosures to consumer-purchasers. Warranties are considered a part of the contract covering the sale of goods.

Warranties may be excluded by the seller or surrendered by the buyer. The method of exclusion depends on the type of warranty involved.

Under product liability, the manufacturer or the seller may be held liable because of negligence in making, designing, or packaging the product. The manufacturer may also be held strictly liable, despite any lack of due care. This is true if the product, in its normal use, in imminently or inherently dangerous.

DISCUSSION QUESTIONS

1. According to Article 2 of the UCC, when does a seller give a buyer express warranties in a sales contract?

2. What does a seller warrant to the buyer in the implied warranty of title?

3. When does a buyer of goods receive an implied warranty of merchantability? What assurances does the buyer receive with this warranty?

4. What is the difference between a "full warranty" and a "limited warranty" under the Magnuson-Moss Act–Consumer Warranty Protection Act?

5. What are the requirements that must be satisfied before a seller will be found liable for strict tort liability under Section 402A of the *Restatement (Second) of Torts*?

6. George is negotiating with Steve for the sale of a boat. George tells Steve the boat will easily pull three water-skiers. Steve buys the boat and discovers that if there are three skiers, the boat will not move fast enough to allow them to get up on their skis. If Steve attempts to sue George, what legal theories should be asserted? Explain.

7. Carl saw an advertisement on television in which a driver drove his new four-wheel-drive "Macho" up the side of a building to the garage on the roof. (Carl did not pay attention to the disclaimer scrolling across the bottom of the screen.) Carl had recently purchased a new "Macho," and he decided to drive it up the side of his apartment building. The "Macho" and Carl both were injured in Carl's efforts, and Carl has filed suit against Macho Motors, alleging breach of an express warranty. What result should occur? Explain.

8. Bob is buying a stereo from Earl. Bob asks Earl about the distortion figures for the stereo. Earl does not know the correct answer, but he does not want Bob to realize his lack of knowledge. What will happen if Earl answers, and his answer is incorrect? How should Earl answer?

9. A manufacturer negligently built a door so that the lock would not hold properly. Debbie bought the door for her home. The lock did not hold, and a burglar robbed Debbie because of the improperly functioning lock. May Debbie sue the manufacturer for negligence?

10. Rayex sold sunglasses advertised as safe for baseball. A high school athlete was using the baseball sunglasses when he misplayed a fly ball. The ball hit the glasses and they shattered, blinding the athlete in one eye. It was subsequently discovered that the lenses of the sunglasses were unreasonably thin and not impact-resistant. How should the athlete argue to establish strict tort liability?

CASE PROBLEMS

1. Kidde hired J. M. Thompson to construct a building according to plans and specifications supplied by Kidde. Thompson subsequently hired Gateway as a subcontractor for the sole purpose of installing the roof to the building. It was agreed that Gateway was to use a mechanically attached roof system (MARS) consisting of a rubber roofing membrane attached to the building by batten bars and then sealed and waterproofed. As part of its agreement, Gateway offered Kidde a five-year express warranty that the roof would remain waterproof and leakproof. Kidde rejected the express warranty offered by Gateway. The MARS roof installed by Gateway began leaking immediately after installation. Gateway made numerous attempts to remedy the problem, but was never successful. Kidde has decided to sue Gateway for breach of the implied warranty of merchantability. Gateway alleges that Kidde rejected any and all warranties when Kidde rejected the express warranty. Did the rejection of the express warranty by Kidde amount to a rejection of all warranties? Explain your answer. (*Westover Products, Inc.* v. *Gateway Roofing Co., Inc.,* 380 S.E.2d 369 [N.C. App 1989]).

2. Dunham was using a hammer to fit a pin into a tractor accessory. While he was "tapping" the pin into place, the hammer broke and a chip from the hammer struck him in the eye. As a result, he lost his vision in the injured eye. Dunham sued both the manufacturer, V & B, and the distributor, Belknap, alleging strict liability in tort. The manufacturer and the distributor based their defense on the fact that the hammer contained no defect in construction. What should be the result? (*Dunham* v. *Vaughan & Bushnell Mfg. Co.,* 42 Ill.2d 339, 247 N.E.2d 401 [1969].)

3. Flory purchased a mobile home from Alamo Mobile Homes. The mobile home was manufactured by Silvercrest. The mobile home, as delivered, was defective, and Flory spent a substantial sum in hiring people to remedy its numerous defects. Several months after the sale was completed, Silvercrest mailed a document to Flory that purported to disclaim any and all implied warranties of quality in the mobile home. Flory sued both the seller, Alamo Mobile Homes, and the manufacturer, Silvercrest, for compensatory and consequential damages, alleging product liability, breach of warranty, and fraud. Silvercrest denied that it was liable due to a lack of privity with Flory and alleged that it had disclaimed any

warranties if its lack of privity defense was denied. Did Silvercrest's lack of privity with Flory constitute a valid defense? Had Silvercrest properly disclaimed any implied warranties? Explain fully on both issues. (*Flory* v. *Silvercrest Industries, Inc.,* 633 P.2d 424 [Ariz. App. 1980].)

4. Garnes purchased a new color television set from Sears. The set was used in the Garnes home for six months. One evening Garnes turned the set on, and twenty minutes later the television burst into flames, causing damage to the set and the surrounding property of Garnes. Garnes sued Sears for damages, alleging breach of warranty and strict product liability. Sears denied that the television was defective or unreasonably dangerous, and thus denied that it was liable. How should this case be resolved? Explain fully. (*Liberty Mutual Insurance* Co. v. *Sears, Roebuck and Company,* 406 A.2d 1254 [1979].)

5. Sheeskin was carrying a six-pack of Coca-Cola to his shopping cart in a supermarket when one of the bottles exploded. As a result of the explosion, Sheeskin lost his balance, fell to the floor, and suffered multiple injuries. He sued both the supermarket and Coca-Cola Bottling, alleging breach of warranties of merchantability and negligence. What should be the result? (*Sheeskin* v. *Giant Foods, Inc.,* 318 A.2d 874 [Md. 1974].)

6. Tarulli purchased an exotic bird from Birds in Paradise. At the time of the sale, Birds in Paradise asked Tarulli to have the bird examined by a veterinarian. Tarulli declined to have the bird examined. Subsequently, the bird Tarulli had purchased died. It appeared that the bird was ill at the time of the sale. Tarulli sued Birds in Paradise for breach of the implied warranty of merchantability. Birds in Paradise denied that Tarulli received the warranty due to his failure to "inspect" the bird. How should the case be decided? (*Tarulli* v. *Birds in Paradise,* 26 UCC 872 [N.Y. 1979].)

7. Klages was employed as a night auditor at Conley's Motel. While working, Klages had been the victim of an armed robbery at the motel. In order to protect himself in the event of another robbery, Klages purchased a mace pen from General Ordinance. The pen was advertised as a device that would cause "instantaneous incapacitation" of an attacker. The pen also was advertised to be as effective as a gun without the perma-

nent injury from using a gun. Shortly after purchasing the pen, Klages was again held up by an armed robber. He squirted the robber with the mace, hitting him in the face with the mace discharge. The robber was not instantaneously incapacitated, however, and he shot Klages in the head. As a result of the gunshot wound, Klages lost all sight in his right eye. Klages has sued the manufacturer of the mace pen for misrepresentation. What should be the result in this case? (*Klages* v. *General Ordinance Equipment Corporation*, 367 A.2d 207 [Pa. 1976].)

8. Heckman was using a power press manufactured by Federal Press. While operating the press, Heckman's hand was caught in the mechanism and severely injured. The press as manufactured did not have a "guarding device" to prevent injuries such as the one suffered by Heckman. As a result, Heckman sued Federal for defective design and for producing an unreasonably dangerous product. What result should occur in this case? (*Heckman* v. *Federal Press Co.*, 587 F.2d 612 [3rd Cir. 1978].)

9. Geigy manufactured an herbicide designed for use in weed and grass control in agriculture. The bags Geigy used to package the herbicide contained a printed panel on the side that purported to disclaim any implied warranties. The herbicide was sold to and distributed by various agricultural supply companies. Willoughby, hoping to solve the grass and weed infestation problem in his corn crop, approached the manager of AgSupply, a local firm, for advice. The manager recommended the Geigy product and agreed to apply the herbicide personally to Willoughby's crop. Willoughby's crop was severely damaged by the chemicals, and he sued both AgSupply and Geigy for breach of warranty. Geigy al-

leged that the disclaimer on the bag precluded its liability even though Willoughby never saw the bag or had an opportunity to read the disclaimer. Was the disclaimer on the bag effective against Willoughby? Explain. (*Willoughby* v. *Ciba-Geigy Corporation*, 601 S.W.2d 385 [Tex. Civ. App. 1980].)

10. Tiner purchased a "general purpose" winch from Motor Truck in 1970. The winch was manufactured by Sperry and sold through Motor Truck, an authorized distributor. At the time of the sale, Tiner told Motor Truck that he needed a device suitable for hauling both material and personnel to great heights. Motor Truck recommended a Model 23, with modifications to increase its cable capacity. Tiner purchased a Model 23 winch and had it modified by a truck equipment company as per the recommendation of Motor Truck. In 1975, McKnelly, an employee of Tiner, was being raised to a radio tower on the winch when the cable was severed. McKnelly fell approximately one hundred feet and suffered serious injuries. He sued Sperry and Motor Truck for breach of express warranties and for product liability. Sperry alleged that there is a distinction between winches, which are to be used for moving heavy loads at slow speeds, and hoists, to be used for moving light loads and personnel at high speeds, and that this distinction is generally known in the industry. Thus Sperry argued that it should not be held liable due to the misuse of the winch. McKnelly argued that such a distinction is not generally known or recognized. He also argued that the term "general purpose" winch warranted the use to which the winch was put. How should this case be decided? Explain fully. Which factors were most persuasive to you in your decision? (*McKnelly* v.

CHAPTER 22

Remedies for Breach of the Sales Contract

OUTLINE

THE REASON FOR REMEDIES

The overwhelming majority of sales contracts are performed by the parties as expected. The seller will tender conforming goods to the buyer at the time and place of delivery. The buyer then will inspect the goods, accept them, and pay the seller the price agreed to in the contract. Of course, not every tender is letter perfect. But when the tender of delivery is flawed, the seller normally will cure the defect. Again, the parties are left with their bargain as agreed.

However, in some cases the tender is never made, or it is made in so insubstantial a manner that it is treated as a breach of contract. Furthermore, some sellers refuse to cure a defective performance or lack the time to do so, and some buyers refuse to pay the agreed price or are unable to do so. Under these circumstances, the other party must look to *remedies* to minimize the effect of the breach.

This chapter will examine remedies from the seller's viewpoint and then from the buyer's viewpoint. In either case, certain remedies will be available at some times and other remedies at other times. The last part of the chapter will explore some technical rules that affect how and when remedies may be sought or established.

SELLER'S REMEDIES

If the buyer wrongfully rejects goods, refuses to pay for the goods, or otherwise breaches the contract, the seller is entitled to remedies. The possible remedies available to the seller depend on *when* the buyer breaches. The seller has six possible remedies if the breach is *before* acceptance. If the breach is *after* acceptance, the seller has two possible remedies. Figure 22.1 summarizes the types of preacceptance and postacceptance remedies available to the seller. We will discuss each of these in turn.

Preacceptance

If the buyer breaches the contract *before* accepting the goods, the seller may seek up to six different remedies. The seller does not have to choose just one possible remedy: As many of the six can be used as are needed in the particular case.

The first possible remedy is to *withhold delivery of the goods*. The seller does not have to deliver or to continue delivering goods to a buyer who is not willing to perform the contract properly. In addition, if the seller discovers that the buyer is insolvent, the seller may withhold delivery unless the buyer pays in cash all prior charges *and* the cost of the current shipment.

The second possible seller's remedy is a little more complicated. It is known as *stoppage of delivery in transit*.[1] To use this remedy, the goods must be in

[1] Uniform Commercial Code, Section 2-705.

FIGURE 22.1   Seller's Remedies

1. **Preacceptance Remedies**

   If, before accepting the goods, the buyer repudiates or breaches the contract or becomes insolvent, the seller may do any, or all, of the following:

   a. Withhold delivery of goods still in the seller's possession.

   b. Stop delivery of goods in transit (subject to some size-of-shipment limitations).

   c. Identify goods to the contract in order to establish the amount of damages (which includes the right to decide to complete construction or to terminate work in process).

   d. Resell any goods, or any work in process, in the seller's possession.

   e. Sue for damages based on the resale or on lost profits, or sue for the performance of the contract.

   f. Cancel all future performance owed to the buyer under the contract.

2. **Postacceptance Remedies**

   If the buyer accepts delivery of the goods and then fails or refuses to pay for them, the seller may do one or both of the following:

   a. Sue for the amount due under the contract.

   b. Reclaim the goods, provided the buyer is insolvent *and* the seller can assert the claim within ten days of the delivery (a written misrepresentation of solvency waives the ten-day limit).

Carrier   A third party hired to deliver the goods from the seller to the buyer.

the possession of a third person—a **carrier** or a bailee. If the seller discovers that the buyer is *insolvent,* the seller may stop delivery of any goods in the possession of a third person. If the buyer *breaches* the contract, the seller may also be able to stop the delivery; however, before the seller can stop delivery because of a breach, the delivery must be of a *carload, truckload, planeload,* or larger shipment.

The seller also must make provisions to protect the carrier or the bailee before a stoppage is permitted. The seller must notify the carrier or bailee in enough time to reasonably allow a stoppage and must indemnify that carrier or bailee for any charges or damages suffered because of the stoppage.

The third remedy for the seller allows the seller to exercise some discretion in the treatment of unidentified goods.[2] If the buyer breaches the contract, the seller may *identify goods* to the contract that were unidentified before the breach, thus helping to establish damages. Also, the seller may decide either to *complete goods* that were incomplete or to *stop production* and *resell* the goods for scrap. Either of these options may be used provided that the seller is exercising reasonable business judgment.

The fourth seller's remedy gives the seller the right to *resell* those goods that are still in the seller's possession.[3] A seller who does resell the goods, and who does so in good faith in a commercially reasonable manner, may also be able to collect damages from the buyer. If so, the damages are figured by

[2]Ibid., Section 2-704.
[3]Ibid., Section 2-706.

taking the resale price from the contract price, adding consequential damages, and subtracting any expenses saved.

The seller may elect to resell in a public sale or in a private sale and may resell the entire lot of goods as a unit or by individual units. All the seller has to do is establish that the resale was totally commercially reasonable. This means that the method, time, place, and terms all must be shown to be reasonable. And the seller must give the breaching buyer notice of the sale, if possible.

Normally, the issue of reasonableness will be raised in a private sale, but if given notice, the buyer has little opportunity to defeat the resale. In a public resale, reasonableness is well defined. Except for recognized futures, the resale can be made only on *identified* goods. It must occur at a normal place for a public sale unless the goods are perishable. The breaching buyer must be given notice of the time and place of the resale. Notice must be given as to where the goods are located so prospective bidders can inspect them. If the seller fails to meet any of these criteria, the resale is not commercially reasonable, and therefore the seller cannot recover any damages.

If the seller resells the goods for more than the contract price, an interesting situation arises. If the buyer breached, the seller may keep the excess. If the buyer rightfully rejected the goods, the seller may still keep the excess, but now the excess is defined as anything above the buyer's security interest.

The fifth option available to the seller is to *sue the buyer*. The seller may elect to sue for damages, for lost profits, or for the contract price.[4] If the seller has not yet completed the goods or has not yet identified the goods, the seller normally will sue for damages. Damages are determined by taking the difference between the contract price and the market price at the time and place of breach, adding any incidental damages, and subtracting any expenses saved.

The seller may discover that the damages computed do not put him or her in as good a position as performance of the contract would have. If so, the seller may elect to sue for lost profits. The seller will show the profits that full performance would have netted and sue for this amount plus the recovery of any expenses reasonably incurred.

If the seller is unable to resell the goods, and the goods have been identified to the contract, the seller may elect to sue for the contract price. However, an election to sue for the contract price places a burden on the seller. The seller must hold the goods for the buyer and deliver them to the buyer when the buyer pays for them.

The final preacceptance seller's remedy is the right to *cancel*. On giving notice to the buyer, the seller can cancel all future performance due to the buyer under the contract. Cancellation does not discharge the buyer or hinder the seller in collecting or enforcing any other rights or remedies resulting from the breach.

[4]Ibid., Sections 2-708, 2-709.

Postacceptance

Once the goods have been *accepted* by the buyer, and the buyer has breached the contract, the seller may select either or both of two remedies.

The first of these remedies is by far the more common. The seller may *sue the buyer* for the price of the goods. Since the buyer has accepted, the buyer's duty to pay is established. Thus, winning the case is almost a certainty. However, many buyers who do not pay are *unable* to pay. They are insolvent. In such a situation, winning the case is a Pyrrhic victory—the winner suffers nearly as much as the loser.

If the buyer has accepted goods, and the buyer is insolvent, the seller probably will rely on the second available postacceptance remedy: The seller will attempt to *reclaim* the goods.[5] To do so, the seller must prove that the following two situations occurred:

1. The buyer received the goods on credit *while insolvent*.
2. The seller demanded the return of the goods within ten days of delivery to the buyer.

This remedy is obviously of limited value, since many credit terms are for thirty days or longer and the seller has only ten days in which to act. But there is one exception. If the buyer *misrepresented* his or her solvency *in writing* to the seller within three months before delivery, the ten-day limit does not apply.

It is possible, at least in theory, for a seller to use all eight remedies in a single contract upon a breach by the buyer. In order to use all eight possible remedies, the circumstances would have to be unusual (to say the least), and the conduct of the buyer would have to fit within certain guidelines. Although such a confluence of circumstances is highly unlikely, it could happen, as in the following example.

Tara entered into a contract with Jaime that called for Jaime to produce and deliver 1000 video games to Tara each month for the next twelve months. Tara was to make payments for each shipment within thirty days of receipt. Jaime did not ordinarily allow deferred or delayed payment, but Tara had provided a written financial statement that presented a picture of a very profitable business. (As it turned out, the financial statement was fraudulent; Tara was, in fact, insolvent at the time of the contract.)

Jaime purchased sufficient raw materials to produce eight months' worth of goods and began the manufacturing process. The first two monthly shipments had been sent to Tara, the third monthly shipment had been turned over to a common carrier for delivery, and monthly shipment number four was ready for pickup by the common carrier when Jaime learned that Tara was insolvent. The goods for monthly shipments five through eight were, at that time, in various stages of "work in process," and the balance of the raw materials to complete the contract had been ordered by Jaime. Jaime decided to seek any and all remedies that might be available under Article 2.

[5]Ibid., Section 2-702(2).

Jaime first looked at the preacceptance remedies. He decided to withhold delivery of the fourth shipment to the carrier and to notify the carrier to stop the goods that were already in transit (the third shipment). The goods in shipments three and four had been identified to the contract, as was the work in process. Jaime decided to stop the work in process and to sell the partially completed goods for scrap. He also decided to resell the completed goods that were stopped in transit and the goods withheld from delivery. Jaime also called Tara and canceled all future performance on the contract due to the insolvency of Tara. Since Tara was insolvent, Jaime sued for damages on shipments three through eight and for lost profits on shipments nine through twelve.

Jaime then decided to exercise the postacceptance remedies. He reclaimed all the unsold goods still in Tara's possession from shipments one and two and sued for the amount due under the contract for all goods that Tara had disposed of before Jaime was able to assert his right to reclaim the goods from Tara.

BUYER'S REMEDIES

The buyer also has a range of possible remedies. And like the seller, the buyer's remedy options depend on the timing of the breach. The buyer has six preacceptance and three postacceptance remedies available. These remedies are summarized in Figure 22.2.

FIGURE 22.2   Buyer's Remedies

1. **Preacceptance Remedies**
   If the seller fails to tender delivery of conforming goods, the buyer may do any, or all, of the following:
   a. Sue for damages for the breach of contract.
   b. Cover and sue for any damages resulting from the cost of cover.
   c. Seek specific performance if the goods are unique or replevin if the goods are not unique but cover could not be obtained.
   d. Claim any identified goods still in the possession of the seller, provided the seller has become insolvent within ten days of receiving a payment from the buyer.
   e. Resell any nonconforming goods shipped by the seller in order to minimize the overall losses involved.
   f. Cancel any future duties under the contract, without surrendering any present rights.
2. **Postacceptance Remedies**
   If the seller delivers nonconforming goods, with a nonconformity that is hidden or that was not cured despite the seller's assurance that cure would be effected, the buyer may do the following:
   a. Revoke the acceptance *if* the nonconformity substantially impairs the value of the contract, which then allows the buyer to seek any preacceptance remedies.
   b. Sue for damages *if* the nonconformity is not sufficient to allow for revocation.
   c. Seek recoupment by deducting the damages suffered from the amount owed the seller under the contract.

[6]Ibid., Section 2-713.

Preacceptance   Before the buyer accepts, the seller may breach by nondelivery or by delivery of nonconforming goods. Under either circumstance, the buyer may elect any or all of the following remedies.

The buyer's first remedy is to *sue for damages*.[6] The buyer is allowed to recover the excess of market price over contract price at the time of breach and at the place of delivery. To this amount are added any additional damages. This amount is then reduced by any expenses the buyer might have saved because of the breach.

In the following case, the court was asked to determine if damages were properly calculated.

Miller v. Titeca
628 P.2d 670 (Mont. 1981)

FACTS   Miller and Titeca entered into a contract on 20 July 1978. The contract called for the sale of eighty head of mixed calves, with Titeca to deliver the calves on or before 15 November 1978. The payment was calculated at the market price on the date of the contract. At the time of the agreement, Miller's agent gave Titeca a check for $2000 as a down payment on the calves. Three weeks later Titeca informed the agent that, due to personal problems, he would not be able to deliver on schedule, and the agent should get replacement calves. On 28 September 1978, Titeca phoned Miller and told Miller that he would not be able to deliver the calves until after 1 January 1979. Miller said that he had already resold the calves to a buyer in Minnesota and expected delivery. On 29 October, Miller sent a letter to Titeca, warning him of the need to deliver the calves and extending the delivery date to 15 December 1978. Following a heavy snowfall on November 8, Titeca returned the uncashed down-payment check to Miller's agent. It was attached to a letter stating that delivery by the deadline was impossible and requesting additional time to tender delivery. After Miller again demanded delivery by the deadline and was again informed that such a delivery would be impossible, Miller filed suit on 8 December, asking for specific performance or for damages if the seller did not deliver by the deadline. Titeca raised several defenses to the lawsuit, including impossibility on two grounds: that he did not own the cattle to be sold and that inclement weather prevented delivery. He also challenged the method used by Miller to compute the damages sought.

ISSUES   Was performance by the seller excused due to impossibility? Did the buyer fail to mitigate damages and/or improperly calculate the damages being sought?

HOLDINGS   No, the seller never established impossibility. No, the buyer's damages were calculated solely on the basis of changes in market prices.

REASONING   The fact that the seller did not own the cattle described in the contract at the time the contract was made is irrelevant. The object of the contract was lawful when made, and performance was possible by the time performance was due. Similarly, the heavy snowfall did not render performance impossible since the seller was able to drive to the location of the cattle daily to feed and care for them and since snow in Montana in December is not unforeseen or unforeseeable. As to the measure of damages, the buyer simply applied the relevant sections of the Uniform Commercial Code, calculating the difference between the market price at the time of the breach and the contract price as specified in the contract. Since the UCC specifically provides this as a method of measuring damages, the alleged failure of the buyer to mitigate damages by purchasing replacement cattle is not relevant. (The seller's wife was the owner of the cattle in the contract, and he never attempted to explain why it was impossible for him to acquire these cattle to fulfill the contract or why he could not obtain other cattle elsewhere to satisfy the contract.)

The second remedy available to the buyer is that of *cover*.[7] The buyer covers by buying *substitute* goods from another source within a reasonable time of the breach. If the goods obtained through cover cost more than the contract price, the buyer may collect the excess costs from the breaching seller, plus other expenses incurred in effecting cover.

The third remedy is available if the goods cannot be obtained by cover. The buyer may seek *specific performance* or *replevin*.[8] If the goods are unique, the court may order specific performance, and the seller will have to deliver the goods in accordance with the contract. If the goods are not unique but are unavailable from other sources at the time, replevin is available. Once the buyer shows an inability to cover, the court will order replevin.

The fourth remedy is probably rare in actual practice. *If* the seller has identified the goods to the contract, and *if* the buyer has paid some or all of the contract price, and *if* the seller becomes insolvent within ten days of receipt of the payment, the buyer can *claim the identified goods*.[9] The likelihood of this chain of events occurring is not very high. But if it does occur, the buyer is protected.

The fifth remedy available to the buyer frequently baffles and amazes students: Under appropriate circumstances, the *buyer* may *resell* the goods. This remedy becomes available when the seller ships nonconforming goods to the buyer. On receipt of the nonconforming goods, the buyer must notify the seller of the nonconformity. Furthermore, if the buyer is a merchant, the buyer must request instructions from the seller as to disposal of the goods. If no instructions are given, the buyer must attempt to resell the goods for the seller. The resale must be reasonable. A buyer who does resell may deduct an appropriate amount for expenses and commissions and then apply the balance to the damages resulting from the breach. Any excess must be returned to the seller.

The final preacceptance remedy available to the buyer is the right to *cancel*. On discovery of a breach by the seller, the buyer may notify the seller that all future obligations of the buyer are cancelled. Cancellation will not affect any other rights or remedies of the buyer under contract.

Postacceptance

Once the buyer has accepted the goods, the focus shifts. A buyer who accepts *cannot* reject the goods. However, the buyer *may* be able to *revoke* the ac-

[7]Ibid., Section 2-712.
[8]Ibid., Section 2-716.
[9]Ibid., Section 2-502.

ceptance. Revocation is permitted if the defect is hidden, or if the defect was to be *cured* by the seller and no cure occurred.[10] Revocation is available only if the defect **substantially impairs** the value of the goods to the buyer. If the buyer properly revokes acceptance, the buyer is said to have rejected the initial delivery and is permitted to assert preacceptance remedies.

Substantially impairs Makes worth a great deal less, seriously harms or injures, or reduces in value.

The buyer may accept the goods and later discover a defect or other breach that is not sufficient to permit a revocation. When this happens, the buyer will select the second possible remedy, *suit for damages*.[11]

Notice in each of the following cases how revocation can be used by an innocent buyer of defective goods. Also notice how the buyer who wishes to revoke must act in a reasonable and timely manner in order to exercise this remedy.

Schumaker v. *Ivers*
238 N.W.2d 284 (S.D. 1976)

FACTS   In November, the Schumakers visited a music store owned by Ivers to look at electric organs. Ivers recommended a particular model to the Schumakers and suggested that they allow him to deliver it to them on a trial basis. In December, the organ was delivered to the Schumakers. The Schumakers noticed nothing wrong with the organ and the next week they paid the full purchase price for it. At that time they also discussed warranty protections and service with Ivers. About two weeks later, the organ began to malfunction. The Schumakers called Ivers to complain, and he promised to have a serviceman come by to repair the organ. Nearly three months later the serviceman arrived. His efforts to repair the organ failed, and in May, the Schumakers demanded a refund for the purchase. Instead Ivers delivered a replacement organ. This organ also proved defective, and again the Schumakers demanded a refund. In June, Ivers attempted to redeliver the original organ, allegedly repaired and in good working order, but the Schumakers refused. Finally, in August, the Schumakers filed suit to revoke their acceptance and to recover the purchase price.

ISSUE   Can the Schumakers revoke their acceptance of the organ nine months after it was delivered?

HOLDING   Yes. The Schumakers acted properly throughout the transaction, and their revocation was timely in these circumstances.

REASONING   The Schumakers had informed Ivers that they wanted to revoke their acceptance and receive a refund of their payment in May, after numerous attempts to repair the original organ had failed. When they accepted the second organ, it was clearly with the understanding that this organ would work properly. When it failed to so operate, the Schumakers notified Ivers of their intent to revoke in a timely manner. The Schumakers had cooperated with Ivers throughout the transaction, and they had notified Ivers properly, so they were allowed to revoke.

[10]Ibid., Section 2-608.
[11]Ibid., Section 2-607.

In the following case, the court ruled that holding the goods was not retaining them, and so the right of the buyer to revoke still existed.

O'Shea v. *Hatch*
640 P.2d 515 (N.M. App. 1982)

FACTS   In January, 1976, the O'Sheas purchased a colt from Hatch. At the time of the sale the O'Sheas informed Hatch that they wanted a horse that could be used as a show horse, could be ridden by their teen-aged daughter, and would be suitable and safe around children. Hatch assured them that the horse was a registered gelding of gentle nature and was suitable for use by children. The O'Sheas purchased the horse, sent him to a trainer for "green breaking" for saddle riding, and then took the horse to their home in Lubbock, Texas. The O'Sheas soon noticed that the horse exhibited stallion-like characteristics; that is, he was aggressive and uncontrollable. They had the horse inspected by a veterinarian, who informed them that the horse had not been properly gelded and was a ridgeling. In April, 1976, the O'Sheas notified Hatch that the horse was not suitable and demanded the return of their purchase money plus expenses. Hatch refused. The O'Sheas then had the horse properly gelded. In January, 1980, the O'Sheas filed suit against Hatch.

ISSUE   Did the conduct of the O'Sheas in having the horse gelded, and in retaining him for four years, constitute an acceptance despite the nonconformity and thus preclude rescission or damages?

HOLDING   No. The O'Sheas gave Hatch timely notice of the defects in the horse and made an effective revocation of their acceptance in April, 1976.

REASONING   When the O'Sheas learned that the horse was a ridgeling, they informed Hatch. Hatch at that point told the O'Sheas to have the veterinarian operate on the horse and he (Hatch) would pay for it. Under such circumstances, Hatch cannot use the fact that the O'Sheas followed his instructions to show that they had accepted the horse despite the nonconformity. As to the retention of the horse by the O'Sheas for the remainder of the four years, the court pointed out that Hatch refused to rescind the sale or to return their purchase price and expenses. When a buyer properly revokes acceptance, and the buyer receives no instructions from the seller as to how to return or dispose of the goods, the buyer is entitled to retain possession until such instructions are received. Here, the O'Sheas were never given such instructions. Thus, their retention was valid under the provisions of the Code. Their revocation was timely and proper. They are entitled to their verdict.

The third remedy available to the buyer is *recoupment*. Normally this third remedy will be used together with the second. The buyer will notify the seller that the buyer is recouping by deducting damages from the contract price owed to the seller. If the seller does not object, recoupment is used. If the seller objects, the buyer may not recoup but can still sue for damages.

MODIFICATIONS

The parties to the contract are allowed to tailor their remedies to fit the particular contract. The parties may, by *expressly including* it in the contract, provide for remedies *in addition to* the remedies provided by the Uniform Commercial Code.[12] Or they may provide for remedies *instead of* those provided by the Code. Or they may place a *limit* on the remedies that may be used.

If the parties so desire, they can select one remedy that is to be used as the exclusive remedy for their particular contract. Such an exclusive remedy must be followed unless circumstances change so that the remedy no longer adequately covers the damages.

Consequential damages may be excluded or limited by the parties in the contract. Such an agreement will be enforced unless the court finds it to be unconscionable.

The parties may also provide for **liquidated damages** if the provision is reasonable, the difficulty of setting the loss is substantial, and establishing actual loss would be inconvenient, if not impossible.[13] Of course, if the amount designated as liquidated damages is found unreasonable, the clause is void.

Sometimes the seller justifiably withholds delivery from the buyer when the buyer has paid part of the contract price. In such a case, the *buyer,* even though in breach, can recover any payments made *in excess of* any liquidated damages called for in the contract or, if there is no liquidated-damages amount, the *lesser* of 20 percent of the total contract value or $500.

Consequential damages
Damages or losses that occur as a result of the initial wrong but that are not *direct* and *immediate.*

Liquidated damages An amount expressly stipulated by the parties to the contract as the measure of damages if a breach occurs.

SPECIAL PROBLEMS

In determining *when* remedies may be obtained and *what* remedies to seek, several special problems may arise. The courts need to know whether a breach has occurred. If there has been a breach, the courts need to know when it occurred and if any legal excuses are involved. Some of these problems will be analyzed next.

Anticipatory Repudiation

Repudiate   To reject or refuse an offered or available right or privilege or a duty or relation.

Occasionally one of the parties to a contract will **repudiate** his or her obligations *before* performance is due.[14] If such a repudiation will substantially reduce the value to be received by the other party, the other party may choose *one* of three courses of conduct:

1. He or she may await performance for a commercially reasonable time *despite* the repudiation.
2. Or this party may treat the repudiation as an *immediate* breach and seek any available remedies.
3. Or the party may suspend his or her own performance under the contract.

[12]Ibid., Section 2-719.
[13]Ibid., Section 2-718.
[14]Ibid., Section 2-610.

A repudiating party is allowed to *retract* the repudiation at any time up to and including the date performance is due, if the other party permits a retraction.[15] No retraction is allowed if the nonrepudiating party has canceled the contract or has *materially* changed position in reliance on the repudiation. A retraction reestablishes the contract rights and duties of each party.

Adequate Assurances

When the parties enter a contract for the sale of goods, each expects to receive the benefit of the bargain made. If, before performance is due, either party feels *insecure* in expecting performance, the insecure party may demand assurances of performance.[16] The insecure party must make a *written* demand for assurance that performance will be tendered when due. Until the assurances are given, the requesting party may **suspend** performance. If no assurance is given within thirty days of request, it is treated as repudiation of the contract.

Suspend To cause to cease for a time; to become inoperative for a time; to stop temporarily.

Excused Performance

Sometimes a seller may be *forced* into a delay in making delivery, may not be able to make delivery, or may have to make only a partial delivery. Normally this would be treated as a breach. However, some of these situations fall into the area of *excused performance* and hence are *not* treated as a breach.[17]

Performance is excused, in whole or in part, if performance has become *impracticable* because of the occurrence of some event whose *nonoccurrence* was a basic assumption of the contract. Also, performance is excused if the seller's delay or lack of performance is based on compliance with a *governmental order or regulation*.

In the following case, "impracticability" and the timeliness of the seller's notice to the buyer of a problem with performance were both at issue.

Glassner v. Northwest Lustre Craft Company, Inc.
591 P.2d 419 (Or. App. 1979)

FACTS

Glassner entered into a contract with Northwest Lustre Craft in which Glassner was to receive various items of china dishes and glassware. Northwest delivered the goods ordered, with the exception of eight dessert plates. Northwest had notified Glassner that the eight dessert plates were not available at the time of the original delivery due to a strike at the manufacturer's plant, had refunded the amount for the eight plates, and had promised to send them as soon as they were available, at which time Glassner could pay for them separately. Glassner notified Northwest that the contract was being rescinded, tendered back the goods she had received, and demanded her full payment be refunded to her. When Northwest refused, Glassner sued.

[15]Ibid., Section 2-611.
[16]Ibid., Section 2-609.
[17]Ibid., Section 2-615.

ISSUE   Was the failure of Northwest to tender a complete delivery of the goods sufficient to allow for a rescission of the contract by the buyer?

HOLDING   No. The strike at the manufacturer's plant made delivery of the eight dessert plates impracticable, but the seller gave timely notice of the delay in delivery. There was no breach, and thus rescission was not proper.

REASONING   Glassner relied on pre-Code cases from Oregon to argue that the missing plates were an integral part of the contract and that the failure to deliver them with the balance of the goods ordered amounted to a breach, so that rescission was available. However, the UCC controlled this case and superseded the cases relied on by Glassner. The relevant Code section specifies that "delay in delivery or nondelivery in whole or in part" is not a breach "if performance as agreed has been made impracticable by the occurrence of a contingency the non-occurrence of which was a basic assumption on which the contract was made," provided the seller has given the buyer seasonable notice. The strike in this case was such a contingency, and Northwest had given timely notice. Furthermore, Northwest was ready, willing, and able to deliver the eight plates a short time later. Thus the delay in performance was excused, rescission was not appropriate since there was no breach, and Northwest is entitled to the payment for the eight plates.

Seasonably Timely; being done in the right time; occurring within a reasonable, prompt time period.

If the seller has an excuse for less than full performance, the seller must notify the buyer **seasonably**. If performance will be reduced but not eliminated, the seller is allowed to *allocate* deliveries among customers in a reasonable manner. On receiving notice of a planned allocation due to some excuse, the buyer must elect whether to terminate the contract or to modify it.[18] Modifying it means accepting the partial delivery as a substitute performance. A failure to modify within thirty days will be treated as a termination.

Duty to Particularize

When the buyer rightfully rejects goods, the buyer must do so properly.[19] If the goods are rejected owing to a *curable* defect, the buyer may reject only by stating *exactly* what the defect is. A failure to do so will preclude the use of that defect in court to prove breach. And if the buyer cannot prove breach, the seller will be deemed to have performed properly. Thus, a *failure to particularize* will result in the buyer's being required to pay for the goods or in liability to the seller.

STATUTE OF LIMITATIONS

Any lawsuit for breach of a sales contract must be started within four years of the breach, unless the contract itself sets a shorter time period. (The time period cannot be less than one year.) The fact that a breach is not discovered when it occurred is not material. The time limitation begins at *breach,* not at *discovery.* This reemphasizes the need for a buyer to inspect goods carefully and completely in order to protect his or her interests.

[18]Ibid., Section 2-616.
[19]Ibid., Section 2-605.

SUMMARY

Although most sales contracts are fully performed and the performance is normally satisfactory, sometimes a nonperformance occurs. When nonperformance is found, the innocent party usually seeks remedies for breach of contract.

When the buyer fails to perform, the seller will seek remedies. The available remedies depend on when the buyer breached. If the buyer breached before acceptance, the seller will seek one or more of six preacceptance remedies. If the buyer accepts the goods and then breaches, the seller will seek one or both of two postacceptance remedies. By the same token, if the seller breaches, the buyer will seek remedies. Again, the buyer's available remedies will depend on when the seller breached. If the seller breached before the buyer accepted the goods, the buyer may seek one or more of six remedies. If the seller breaches after the buyer accepts, the buyer has three available remedies.

Occasionally a nonperformance turns out not to be a breach. It may involve a special problem that excuses performance or affects the rights of the innocent party. Great care must be exercised by both parties in these special problem areas.

DISCUSSION QUESTIONS

1. What remedies may a seller seek if the buyer breaches a sales contract before the buyer has accepted the goods?

2. What are the seller's two postacceptance remedies, and when may the seller utilize either of them?

3. What are the three postacceptance remedies available to the buyer, and when may the buyer utilize each of them?

4. What is an *anticipatory repudiation,* and how does it affect the law of sales?

5. What is meant by a "duty to particularize," and how does this duty affect the rights of the parties to a sales contract?

6. Ace Mfg. agreed to produce and sell some goods to Sampson. The contract called for ten shipments of twenty-five units each. After satisfactorily completing five shipments, Ace sent the sixth shipment. Order number 7 was then in process. Sampson wrongfully rejected shipment number 6. Ace decided to complete the work on number 7 and to sue Sampson for the price on shipments 6 and 7 and for lost profits on the others. Samp-

son argued that Ace could not complete number 7 at his (Sampson's) expense. Who is correct? Explain.

7. Tom shipped goods to Martin via Allied Parcel Service. After the goods were shipped, Tom discovered that Martin was insolvent. What may Tom do in this situation? What obligation does Tom have to Allied?

8. Roberto, the seller, was in possession of goods that Suzanne had wrongfully rejected. Roberto sold the goods to Brenda for one-half the contract price without telling anyone about the sale. May Roberto collect the unpaid balance of the contract price from Suzanne? Explain.

9. Bob and Sam entered into a contract that called for Sam to deliver goods to Bob and for Bob to pay $1500. Bob gave Sam a $500 deposit on the goods. During the contract period, Sam discovered that Bob was insolvent and decided to withhold delivery of the goods to Bob. While Bob admits that he is in breach, he also asserts that he is entitled to restitution for his deposit on the goods. Is Bob entitled to restitution, and if so, how much is he to recover from Sam?

10. Martha entered into a contract with Amy that called for Amy to manufacture and deliver goods to Martha, with delivery to occur in six months. Three months later, Martha phoned Amy and repudiated the contract. At the time, Martha thought she could obtain the goods from another source at a substantially lower price. When Martha realized that her repudiation would operate as a breach, she immediately called Amy, apologized for her conduct, and attempted to retract her repudiation. What are Amy's rights in this case?

CASE PROBLEMS

1. The Detroit Screwdriver Co. agreed to specially manufacture a stud-driving machine for Ladney. Before Detroit completed the machine, Ladney called and canceled. Detroit immediately stopped working on the machine and sued Ladney for breach of contract. Ladney argued that by halting production, Detroit had acted in bad faith and could therefore collect no damages. What should be the result? (*Detroit Power Screwdriver Co.* v. *Ladney,* 25 Mich. App. 478, 181 N.W.2d 828 [1979].)

2. Garfinkel purchased carpeting form Lehman and had it installed. On installation, Garfinkel noticed an unsightly condition in the carpet. The defect immediately was called to the attention of Lehman, who sent representatives to try to correct the condition. These efforts did not succeed, and Garfinkel notified Lehman that he (Garfinkel) was rejecting the carpet, demanded its removal, and insisted on a refund. Lehman argued that, by leaving the carpet on the floor, Garfinkel had accepted it as delivered. What result should occur? (*Garfinkel* v. *Lehman Floor Covering Co.,* 60 Misc.2d 72, 302 N.Y.S.2d 167 [1969].)

3. In connection with the centennial of the purchase of Alaska from Russia, the Centennial Development Co. hired Van Wormer to mint 50,000 anniversary coins. Centennial Development canceled the contract before Van Wormer had completed performance. Van Wormer sued for lost profits of three cents per coin. Centennial Development objected to this measure of damages. What result should occur? (*Anchorage Centennial Development Co.* v. *Van Wormer & Rodrigues,* 443 P.2d 596 [Alaska 1968].)

4. Eastern ordered 150 lawnmowers from Turf Man Sales and accepted delivery of the mowers on March 28. At the time of the order, Eastern was insolvent, was unable to pay for the mowers, and had no intention of paying for them. On 4 April, Turf Man learned of the financial condition of Eastern and made a demand by telephone for the return of the mowers. On April 8, Turf Man made demand on the court-appointed receivers of Eastern for return of the mowers. Is Turf Man within its rights under the UCC to recover the mowers, or does Turf Man have to exert physical control over the goods in order to recover them? Discuss fully. (*Metropolitan Distributors* v. *Eastern Supply Co.,* 21 D. & C.2d 128 [Pa. 1959].)

5. Aubrey purchased a computer system from Tandy to perform certain functions that were explained to Tandy prior to the sale. The Tandy salesperson determined that Tandy did not have any software that would perform the tasks desired, but that such software would work on a Tandy computer. The Tandy salesperson did not mention to Aubrey that Tandy would not stand behind the software purchased elsewhere. When the recommended software would not perform as expected on the Tandy computer and could not be modified to do so, Aubrey notified Tandy of a desire to rescind the contract, alleging that the failure of the software to perform the specified tasks substantially impaired the value of the entire contract. Tandy denied that it had breached the contract, that there was any problem with the Tandy computer, or that rescission was a proper remedy. What result should occur? Explain. (*Aubrey's R. V. Center, Inc.* v. *Tandy Corporation,* 731 P.2d 1124 [Wash. App. 1987].)

6. Purdon contracted with Birkner for the purchase of 3500 Christmas trees. The trees were to be "Number One" grade trees, being over 5½ feet tall and of good shape and form. When the trees were delivered, Purdon objected that the trees were inferior. Birkner, a wholesaler with thirty-two years of experience in the industry, assured Purdon that the trees were as described. Purdon believed Birkner, retained the trees, and attempted to sell them. At the close of the Christmas season, Purdon had sold only 600 trees, and he refused to pay for them as per the contract. Birkner sued for breach of contract, and Purdon counterclaimed that he had revoked his ac-

ceptance of the trees and was not liable. What result should occur? (*Birkner* v. *Purdon,* 183 N.W.2d 598 [Mich. 1970].)

7. Mott had a contract to purchase 4000 bushels of grain from Svihovec, with delivery to occur in March. Mott refused to accept a delivery in March due to an alleged shortage of boxcars. Mott similarly refused delivery in April or in May. Finally, in June, Svihovec sold the grain to another party. In September Mott demanded delivery from Svihovec, and when delivery was refused, Mott sued for breach of contract. What result should occur? (*Mott Equity Elevator* v. *Svihovec,* 236 N.W.2d 900 [N.D. 1975].)

8. Wegematic advertised that it had produced a revolutionary, new type of digital computer. On the basis of these advertisements, the United States agreed to purchase one of the new computers. Wegematic failed to deliver the computer as agreed, alleging that the delay was due to unforeseen technological difficulties. Is this a valid excuse for nondelivery? (*United States* v. *Wegematic,* 360 F.2d 674 [2d Cir. 1966].)

9. Dura-Wood and Century Forest both are in the business of treating cross-ties for industrial and commercial use. Dura-Wood signed a contract to deliver cross-ties to Smith. Dura-Wood did not have enough cross-ties on hand and contacted Century Forest by telephone to purchase the 20,000 cross-ties it needed, at $8.60 per tie. The following day, the Dura-Wood agent sent a letter to Century Forest restating the content of the conversation and the agreement reached therein. Century Forest never replied to the letter. When the agent for Dura-Wood subsequently contacted Century Forest as to delivery, Century Forest stated that it would not deliver the ties and was canceling the contract. Dura-Wood sued for breach of contract, and Century Forest relied on the defense of a lack of any writing, as required by the Statute of Frauds. What result should occur? What is the basis for your decision? (*Dura-Wood Treating Company* v. *Century Forest Industries, Inc.,* 675 F.2d 745 [5th Cir. 1982].)

10. Richter approached Tatum, a dealer in foreign cars, to purchase a used Ferrari Daytona coupe for a total price of $17,500. Tatum did not have the car in stock but was able to locate one in Connecticut. Tatum acquired all relevant information and prepared an invoice and a bill of sale for the car. When the car was delivered, it turned out to be a European version designed for racing and was not suitable for highway operation. Tatum refused to accept this car for Richter even though Richter was willing to accept the car. When Tatum was unable to locate another Ferrari Daytona, Richter brought an action in replevin to claim the originally delivered car from Richter. Under these circumstances, could Richter use replevin to obtain the car from Tatum? (*Tatum* v. *Richter,* 373 A.2d 923 [Md. App. 1977].)

PART 4

The Law of Commercial Paper

*C*ommercial paper takes many forms. In its most familiar form, we know it as the check that we look forward to on payday and that our creditors look forward to on their paydays. If you have ever taken a loan from a bank, you have signed some type of promissory note, which is another form of commercial paper.

Merriam-Webster defines commercial paper as "short-term negotiable instruments arising out of commercial transactions." Millions of such instruments are signed each day, not only because they are a safe and convenient means of doing business that eliminates the risk of dealing in cash, but also because they are acceptable in the commercial world as a credit instrument and/or as a substitute for money.

This part of the text explores commercial paper and how and why it is so widely used and so readily accepted in the modern commercial world. The text also will deal with the topics of *electronic fund transfers* and bank-customer relations.

C H A P T E R 23

An Introduction to Commercial Paper

O U T L I N E

HISTORIC OVERVIEW

Promissory note   A written promise to pay a sum of money at a future time unconditionally.

Drafts   Orders for the payment of money drawn by one person on another.

Commercial paper of some type has been present in nearly every society that has developed a substantial commercial system. Documents very similar to the contemporary **promissory note** have been dated back to about 2100 B.C. The merchants of Europe were using negotiable documents on a broad scale by the thirteenth century. In fact, the use of **drafts** was so widespread that a substantial portion of the law merchant was devoted to their proper treatment.

Commercial paper had become so pervasive by the late nineteenth century that the English Parliament began to enact special statutes to govern its use. Following the example of the English, the National Conference of Commissioners on Uniform State Laws drafted the *Uniform Negotiable Instruments Law* (NIL) for the United States in 1896. Each of these statutes merely attempted to cover the common law rules that had been developed over the years.

The NIL was designed to unify and codify the rules and laws of each jurisdiction regarding all negotiable commercial documents. However, the breadth of the topical coverage made the NIL unwieldy and difficult to apply to the commercial world of the twentieth century.

Thus, the *Uniform Commercial Code* (UCC) was written to comply more readily with the demands of the modern business world. It has been adopted by every state in the union except Louisiana, and Louisiana has adopted some portions, including Articles 3 and 4. The UCC, or "the Code" as it is frequently called, has standardized and clarified the rules of commercial paper while retaining most of the traditional rules and views of the topic. The codification of commercial paper is located in Article 3 of the Code.

THE SCOPE OF ARTICLE 3

The Uniform Commercial Code is divided into eleven articles. Each article has a different purpose and is designed to do a different thing. For example, Article 1 deals with general concepts and definitions, among other things. Articles 10 and 11 deal with the effective dates of coverage and some technical details. The remaining eight articles (Article 2 through Article 9) are each devoted to a particular topic of commercial law. The article dedicated to commercial paper is Article 3.

Negotiable instruments   Written promises or orders for the payment of a sum certain of money to order or to bearer.

Subject to   Liable, subordinate, subservient, inferior, obedient to; governed or affected by.

The Code's coverage of commercial paper is restricted to **negotiable instruments,** as defined in Section 3-103, and is limited to these instruments. Section 3-103(1) states that Article 3 governs neither money, nor documents of title, nor investment securities. Moreover, Section 3-103(2) cross-references to the coverages of Articles 4 (bank collections and deposits) and 9 (secured transactions), stating that Article 3 is **subject to** these referenced articles.

Documents Instruments on which are recorded matter that may be used as evidence; written instruments used to prove a fact.

Thus, one finds that Article 3 covers negotiable instruments but not other types of commercial or negotiable **documents** and that two other articles of the Code may supplement, complement, or override the provisions of Article 3.

FUNCTIONS AND FORMS

Commercial paper has two major *functions:* It is designed to serve as a substitute for money, and it is designed to serve as a credit instrument. In satisfying either use, it carries certain contract rights, certain property rights, and some special rights due exclusively to its nature as commercial paper.

Every negotiable instrument is presumed to be a contract, but not every contract is a negotiable instrument. The difference between a contract and a negotiable instrument is one of *form*. To be negotiable, an instrument must be (1) current in trade and (2) payable in money. These criteria are obviously too broad and too vague to be of much practical significance. Accordingly, Article 3 has more fully defined the requirements an instrument must meet in order to be negotiable. (These requirements are dealt with in detail in Chapter 24.)

UCC Section 3-104 lists the four forms a negotiable instrument may take. Every negotiable instrument must be in one of these forms:

1. drafts (may be demand instruments or time instruments; the drawee may be any legal person or party)
2. checks (must be a demand instrument; the drawee must be a bank)
3. promissory note (may be a demand instrument, but is normally a time instrument)
4. certificate of deposit (may be a demand instrument, but is normally a time instrument; the maker is normally a bank)

The first two forms of commercial paper, drafts and checks, are one class of negotiable instruments; this class is known as *order* paper. Promissory notes (often referred to as "notes") and certificates of deposit (usually referred to as "CDs") constitute the class of negotiable instruments known as *promise* paper.

ORDER PAPER ("THREE-PARTY" PAPER)

The distinctive features of order paper, or three-party paper, are that each instrument contains an *order* to pay money and that at least *three parties* are necessary to fill the legal roles involved. The order element will be pointed out in the following sections, and the rules governing this class of negotiable instrument will be explained in the final portion of the chapter. The three parties are the drawer, the drawee, and the payee. As noted, this class consists of drafts and checks.

Drafts

A *draft* is *an instrument in which one party, the drawer, issues an instrument to a second party, the payee.* The draft is accepted by the payee as a substitute for money. The payee expects to receive money at some time from the third party, the drawee. The reason the payee expects to receive money from the drawee is contained in the basic form of the instrument. As will be pointed out, the drawer issues an order to the drawee to pay a sum of money. This order, coupled with the three roles involved, distinguishes drafts from promise paper. The components of a draft are illustrated in Figure 23.1.

Checks

Demand instrument   An instrument that is due at once; a present debt or obligation.

Time instrument   An instrument that is due at a future, determinable time or date.

The most common type of order paper is a *check.* Checks are special types of drafts. Like a draft, a check necessitates the involvement of three parties, but there are two differences. A check is, by definition, a **demand instrument**; in contrast, a draft may be a demand instrument or a **time instrument**. And on a check, *the drawee must be a bank*; in contrast, anyone may be the drawee on a draft. Figure 23.2 illustrates the various elements of a check.

In both a check and a draft, the drawee is obligated to the drawer. This obligation is normally a debt owed to the drawer. When the drawer *orders* the drawee to pay, the drawer is directing the drawee as to how the debt should be discharged or partially discharged. The order to the drawee to pay,

FIGURE 23.1   A Bank Draft

Courtesy of Crestar Bank (formerly United Virginia Bank) of Radford, Virginia.
(1) The order. (2) Words of negotiability. (3) The payee. (4) The amount, in numbers. (5) The amount, in words. (6) The date of issue. (7) The drawer's signature. (8) The drawee.

FIGURE 23.2 A Check

JAMES C. MORRISON
1765 SHERIDAN DRIVE
YOUR CITY, STATE 09087

1226

Date _____ (6) _____ $\frac{68\text{-}2}{510}$

(1)   (2)
Pay to the order of _____ (3) _____ $ (4)

(5)

Dollars

CRESTAR (8)
Crestar Bank
Richmond, Virginia

NOT NEGOTIABLE
SAMPLE - VOID
<u>DO   NOT   CASH!</u>
(7)

⑈000067894⑈ 12345678⑈ 226

Courtesy of Crestar Bank, Radford, Virginia.
(1) The order. (2) Words of negotiability. (3) The payee. (4) The amount, in numbers. (5) The amount, in words. (6) The date of issue. (7) The drawer's signature. (8) The drawee.

coupled with the obligation to pay, assures the payee that payment will probably be made by the drawee at the appropriate time.

The Order Both a check and a draft contain an order. The drawer orders the drawee to pay the instrument. The language used is not a request. The drawer does not "ask," or "hope," or even "expect" the drawee to pay. The drawer *demands* that payment be made. If you look at Figure 23.1 or Figure 23.2, you will see that the drawer tells the drawee to *"Pay to the order of (Payee)."* It should also be noted that the *order* is the word *pay;* the phrase "to the order of" is *not* the order. This phrase is a term of negotiability. Its meaning will be explained in the next chapter, which deals with negotiability.

The Drawer The person who *draws* an order instrument, who *gives* the order to the drawee, and who **issues** the instrument to the payee is known as the *drawer*. This person originates the check or the draft. The drawer does not pay the payee directly. The drawee is expected to pay the payee or the **holder**, upon proper **presentment**. That is why the drawer gives the drawee the order. The drawer expects the order to be obeyed because of a prior agreement or relationship between the drawer and the drawee. If the order is obeyed, the drawee pays the payee or holder, and both the drawer and the drawee have performed.

The Drawee The party to whom the order on the check or draft is *directed* is the *drawee*. The drawee is told by the drawer to "pay to the order of" the

Issues Puts into circulation.

Holder One legally in possession of a negotiable instrument by means of a negotiation.

Presentment The act of giving a negotiable instrument to the drawee or maker for acceptance and/or payment.

Accept Make an engagement to pay the negotiable instrument in money when due.

payee. It is the drawee who is expected to make payment to the presenting party. However, the drawee has no duty to the payees or to the holder to pay, despite the order. The only duty the drawee has is a duty owed to the drawer. The duty of the drawee is to **accept** the instrument. Before acceptance, there is only the prospect that the drawee will pay when the time for payment arrives. Once the drawee accepts, the drawee has a contractual obligation to pay the presenter. This relationship is illustrated in Figure 23.3.

The Payee The *payee* is the person to whom the instrument is *originally issued*. The payee may be specifically designated, as in "Pay to the order of *Jane Doe*"; the payee may be an office or title, as in "Pay to order of *Treasurer of Truro County*"; or the particular payee may be unspecified, as in "Pay to the order of *bearer*." The payee may decide to seek payment personally, or the payee may decide to further negotiate the instrument. The words "to the order of" allow the payee to order the drawee to make payment to some other party. ("To the order of" means to whomever the payee orders, literally allowing the negotiation of the instrument.)

PROMISE PAPER ("TWO-PARTY" PAPER)

The class of negotiable instruments covering notes and CDs is promise paper or two-party paper. The distinctive features of this class are that each instrument contains a *promise* to pay (or to repay) money and that only *two parties* are necessary to fill the legal roles involved. These two parties are known as the **maker** and the payee.

Maker One who makes or executes a promise-paper negotiable instrument.

The term *two-party* is confusing to many people. Many stores have signs

FIGURE 23.3   The Parties on Order Paper

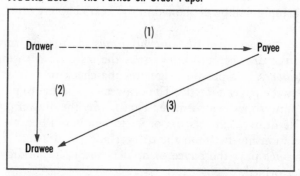

(1) The drawer is *presumed* to have a contract with the payee since the instrument was issued. (2) The drawer is *presumed* to have a contract or an understanding with the drawee that will cause the drawee to obey the *order*. (3) The payee and the drawee have *no* contract and *no* understanding on the instrument in question until both *presentment* and *acceptance* occur.

prominently posted stating that they do not accept "two-party checks." These so-called two-party checks are, in reality, checks that are being negotiated by the payee to a later holder. The store does not want to accept a check unless it receives it *directly* from the drawer. But there is no such legal creature as a *check* that is "two-party paper."

The promise element of promise paper will be pointed out in the following sections, and the rules governing this class of negotiable instrument will be explained in the final portion of the chapter.

Promissory Notes

The promissory note is the oldest known form of negotiable instrument. It is normally used as a credit instrument, executed either at the time credit is extended or as evidence of a preexisting debt not yet repaid.

In a note, one party (the maker) *promises* to pay the other party (the payee) a sum of money at some future time. The promise may call for a lump-sum payment, or it may call for installment payments over time. The note may specify the payment of interest in addition to the principal; it may have the interest included in the principal; or it may be interest free. The note may recite details about **collateral**. Despite any or all of these possibilities, the basic form is constant. Such an instrument is illustrated in Figure 23.4.

Collateral A security given in addition to the direct security, intended to guaranty its validity or ensure its performance.

Certificates of Deposit

A *certificate of deposit* (or a CD, as it is commonly called) is a special type of note issued by a *bank* as an acknowledgment of money *received*, with a *promise* to repay the money at some future date. Many people think of a CD as a time savings account, in contrast to a passbook savings account. In reality, though, a CD is not a savings account at all. It is most commonly a time deposit of money with a bank.

A CD normally pays higher interest than a savings account, with the interest varying according to the amount of time the certificate is to run. Most certificates run for some multiple of six months, and they are available in some multiple of $1000. However, a number of banks offer CDs for shorter time periods, such as ninety days. Some banks are beginning to offer CDs for multiples of $100. One type of CD is illustrated in Figure 23.5.

Many banks today offer some variation of a "saver's certificate," which is non-negotiable, rather than a negotiable certificate of deposit. It appears that the CD is becoming extinct, although some CDs still exist. However, the widespread replacement of CDs with other forms of certificates makes this an area of primarily historic interest.

The Promise Promise paper is so called because it contains a promise. The maker of the instrument *promises* to pay an amount of money to the payee or to a holder. The instrument does not say that the maker "might" pay, or will "probably" pay, or will "agree" to pay. The instrument says that the maker *promises* to pay an amount of money to the payee or to the order of the payee.

FIGURE 23.4   A Promissory Note

Great American Federal
Savings Bank

DIVISIONS:
SAN DIEGO FEDERAL
LAGUNA FEDERAL
SAN JOAQUIN FIRST FEDERAL
PEOPLES FEDERAL
FIRST FEDERAL OF SOUTH PASADENA
RIVERSIDE SAVINGS
KAWEAH SAVINGS
SONOMA COUNTY SAVINGS

PROMISSORY NOTE

Loan No.

Borrower(s)
Name(s) _____ and _____
               first   middle   last   first   middle   last

(1)   (2) Address   **(3)**   **(2)**
Borrower (jointly and severally if more than one) promises to pay to Great American Federal Savings Bank ("Lender"), or order, in U.S. money, at its office in San Diego, California, or elsewhere Lender designates, principal and interest on unpaid principal from the date advanced until paid, in amount, annual rate and consecutive monthly installments as follows:

Principal $ **(4)**   Annual Interest Rate   %

Installments $ on the same day of month beginning

Minimum Interest $ 100.00

Interest will be computed on the basis of a 12 month year and 30 day month. The date of payment, whether early or late, will be disregarded for purposes of allocating the payment between principal and interest; each payment will be treated for this purpose as though made on its due date.

PREPAYMENT: Full or partial prepayment may be made without penalty except Borrower will pay any minimum interest amount specified. Borrower will tell Lender in writing that Borrower is making a prepayment. Lender will use all prepayments to reduce the principal subject to its right to first apply payments received to any past due interest or other charges. Partial prepayments will not delay the due dates nor change the amount of monthly payments unless Lender agrees in writing to those delays or changes. Full prepayment may be made at any time. Lender may require that partial prepayment be made on the same day as monthly payments are due. Lender may also require that the amount of any partial prepayment be equal to the amount of principal that would have been part of the next one or more monthly payments.

LATE CHARGE: Borrower will pay a late charge of 5% of each installment not paid within 15 days of its due date, or $5.00, whichever is greater.

DEFAULT AND ACCELERATION: If Borrower fails to timely pay any installment when due or to perform any provision contained in any document securing this Note, Lender may, at Lender's option, declare all sums owed hereunder immediately due and payable. Borrower will pay all reasonable expenses and attorney's fees of Lender in any action relating to Borrower's obligations.

SELLER, IF ANY: Borrower intends to use some or all of the loan proceeds to pay _____,
as Seller, amounts due Seller under a contract between Seller and Borrower, dated _____
Borrower represents that a true and correct copy of the contract has been furnished to Lender and that it contains the entire agreement between Seller and Borrower. The following notice applies only to the named Seller, if any, and to the proceeds hereof paid to said Seller under the described contract.

NOTICE: ANY HOLDER OF THIS CONSUMER CREDIT CONTRACT IS SUBJECT TO ALL CLAIMS AND DEFENSES WHICH THE DEBTOR COULD ASSERT AGAINST THE SELLER OF GOODS OR SERVICES OBTAINED WITH THE PROCEEDS HEREOF. RECOVERY HEREUNDER BY THE DEBTOR SHALL NOT EXCEED AMOUNTS PAID BY THE DEBTOR HEREUNDER.

NON-WAIVER: By accepting payment after its due date or after notice of default, Lender will not waive its right to prompt payment when due of other sums, or to declare a default, or to proceed with any remedy it has. Without affecting the liability of anyone else, Lender may release anyone liable, may change payment terms, and add, alter, substitute, or release security.

☐ This Note is secured by a Security Agreement.
☐ This Note is unsecured.

BEFORE SIGNING ORIGINAL, WE RECEIVED AND READ A COMPLETED COPY HEREOF.

(5)
_____   _____   _____   _____
Borrower's Signature   Date   Borrower's Signature   Date

_____   _____   _____   _____
Borrower's Signature   Date   Borrower's Signature   Date

(Sign Original Only)

C-1-424 (Rev. 6/83)

Courtesy of Great American Federal Savings Bank of San Diego and Fresno, California.
(1) The *promise*. (2) Words of negotiability. (3) The *payee*. (4) The amount borrowed. (5) The signature of the *maker*.

FIGURE 23.5 A Negotiable Certificate of Deposit

NEGOTIABLE CERTIFICATE OF DEPOSIT

San Diego Federal
SAVINGS AND LOAN ASSOCIATION

600 B Street, San Diego, California 92183

NO. **5014**

DATE **(1)**

THIS CERTIFIES THAT THERE HAS BEEN DEPOSITED IN SAN DIEGO FEDERAL SAVINGS AND LOAN ASSOCIATION

THE SUM OF **(2)**

DOLLARS $ **(3)** VOIDED

PAYABLE TO THE ORDER OF **(4)** VOIDED

UPON PRESENTATION AND SURRENDER OF THIS CERTIFICATE PROPERLY ENDORSED AT

OFFICE

	INTEREST RATE % PER ANNUM	INTEREST AMOUNT	MATURITY DATE	TOTAL AMOUNT PAYABLE
			(5)	**(6)**

This deposit bears interest from the date hereof to the maturity date at the stated rate computed for the actual number of days elapsed on the basis of a 360-day year payable on the maturity date. This certificate is not payable before maturity and bears no interest after maturity.

(FIXED RATE/FIXED TERM)

SAN DIEGO FEDERAL SAVINGS AND LOAN ASSOCIATION

(7)

Authorized Signature

Courtesy of Great American Federal Savings Bank (formerly San Diego Federal) of San Diego and Fresno, California.

(1) The date of issue. (2) The amount of the "deposit," in words. (3) The amount of the "deposit," in numbers. (4) The *payee*. (5) The maturity date. (6) The amount to be paid. (7) The signature of the *maker*.

The Maker The duties performed by the drawer and the drawee on order paper are effectively combined in promise paper: Both duties fall to the *maker*. The maker *makes the promise* ("I promise to pay to the order of [the payee]"); the maker *issues the instrument to the payee;* and the maker *pays the instrument upon proper presentment*. However, there is one important difference from order paper. While the drawee is not obligated to any holder until acceptance, the maker *is* liable to a holder from the date of original issue. This obligation is illustrated in Figure 23.6.

The Payee As in order paper, the payee is the party to whom the instrument is originally issued. Again, the payee may be specifically designated by name, or designated by title or office, or unspecified. The payee on promise paper

FIGURE 23.6 The Parties on Promise Paper

Maker ———————— **(1)** ————————▶ Payee

(1) The maker is *presumed* to have a contract with the payee since an instrument has been issued, and the maker is obligated to accept and to pay the instrument upon proper presentment by the payee or by a holder.

is the person to whom the promise is made by the maker. By contrast, the payee on order paper is the person to whom the drawee is directed (ordered) to make payment.

USES OF NEGOTIABLE INSTRUMENTS

Negotiable instruments are widely used in our economy. They are used as a substitute for money. They are used for convenience. They are used as credit instruments. They are used to pay bills, to buy things, and to borrow. Some of the most important uses of each type are set out in the following sections.

Checks

The most commonly used type of negotiable instrument is a check. Many people use checks rather than cash for regular daily purchases. Checks are regularly written to the supermarket for groceries, to the utility companies to pay bills, to the landlord to pay the rent, and to the bank to make loan payments. In addition, many working people receive their salaries or wages in periodic paychecks from their employers.

Checks are widely used because they are easily written, easily carried, and widely accepted. Carrying and using checks is safer than carrying and using cash. If a person loses a blank, unsigned check, no harm is done. All that was lost was a piece of paper. If a person loses cash, the money is gone. The bank will not take an unsigned check, but it will take lost money. Great care should be taken with checks. A signed check, otherwise blank, is nearly as good as cash. Anyone finding such a check can complete the blanks and possibly receive cash for it as completed, to the detriment of the depositor/"drawer."

Drafts

Businesses often use drafts to pay for merchandise ordered, especially when the buyer and the seller are in different states. Drafts may be payable "at sight" (that is, on demand), or they may be "time drafts" (that is, they are payable at a future date). Often a seller of goods will send a draft to the buyer for acceptance. If the buyer accepts, he or she has agreed to pay any holder who makes proper presentment. Such a draft is called a *trade acceptance*.

With the recent liberalization of federal and state banking laws and regulations, a number of changes have occurred in the area of commercial paper. One of these changes has been in the area of drafts. Today many credit unions offer accounts similar to the checking accounts offered by banks and savings and loan institutions. These drafting accounts offer the same privileges for credit union depositors as are available to depositors of banks. Technically, however, these are *not* checking accounts; there are some minor differences (share drafts are discussed in more detail in Chapter 27). A sample "share draft" is illustrated in Figure 23.7.

Promissory Notes

Promissory notes most often are used as instruments of credit. They also are used as evidence to show a preexisting debt. Any time a customer borrows

FIGURE 23.7   A Share Draft

IMA C. U. DRAFT

GET MORE OF ME AT THE

CREDIT UNION OFFICE

(1) _____ 19 _____

75-148/919

PAY TO THE ORDER OF ____(2)____ $ (3)

(4)

DOLLARS

TO: **Educational Employees Credit Union**

455 E. BARSTOW AVE.—(209) 224-7788

FRESNO, CALIFORNIA 93710

Payable Through: First Bank (N.A.)-Northfield, MN

) (5)

(6)

PURPOSE _____

⑂ ⑆091901480⑈536

Courtesy of Educational Employees Credit Union of Fresno, California.
(1) The date of issue. (2) The payee. (3) The amount, in numbers. (4) The amount, in words.
(5) The drawee. (6) The signature of the drawer.

Mortgage note   A contract binding all of a property to secure payment of a promissory note.

Installment note   A promissory note calling for periodic payments at predetermined times.

money from a bank, the borrower must sign a promissory note. This signed note proves the existence of the debt, the amount owed, the manner of repayment, and any other terms important to the loan agreement. Notes are so widely used that special types of notes have developed. Real estate loans normally involve a **mortgage note**. Automobile loans usually involve an **installment note**. Many banks also use a device called a commercial loan note or a signature note for short-term unsecured loans (loans made without collateral).

Certificates of Deposit

A certificate of deposit is an instrument issued by a bank evidencing a debt owed to a depositor. These instruments commonly call for the bank to pay to a proper presenter the amount deposited plus interest at a stated future date. Although regularly thought of as a type of special savings account, CDs are really credit instruments. They recognize money "borrowed" by the bank from its depositor.

SUMMARY

Article 3 of the Uniform Commercial Code involves negotiable instruments, also known as commercial paper. These negotiable instruments serve two major functions: They operate as a substitute for money, and they are used as credit instruments. All negotiable instruments are "current in trade" and are payable in money.

There are two major classes of commercial paper, and two types of negotiable instrument are included in each class. The first class, order paper, is used primarily as a substitute for money. This class consists of checks and drafts. The necessary parties involved in this class of instrument are the drawer, the drawee, and the payee. The other class, promise paper, is primarily a credit instrument. It consists of promissory notes and certificates of deposit. The necessary parties involved are the maker and the payee.

DISCUSSION QUESTIONS

1. Who is expected to make payment on a negotiable instrument that is designated as "order paper," and why is that party expected to make payment?

2. Who is expected to make payment on a negotiable instrument that is designated as "promise paper," and why is that party expected to make payment?

3. What requirements distinguish a check from a draft?

4. A check or a draft must contain a communication from the drawer to the drawee. What form does this communication take? How is this different from promise paper?

5. Who may serve as the drawee on a check? Who may serve as the drawee on a draft? Is the difference as to who may serve as the drawee significant?

6. What are the two major functions of commercial paper, and which function is most likely to be involved with each type of commercial paper?

7. What duty or duties is/are performed by the "maker" on promise paper? What do we call the party or parties who perform comparable duties on order paper?

8. What is the duty of the drawee to the drawer on order paper at the time of issue? What is the duty of the drawee to the payee on order paper upon issue? Why?

9. When does the duty of the maker to pay the instrument arise on promise paper? When does the duty of the drawee to pay the instrument arise on order paper?

10. Technically, only four types of commercial paper exist. However, people enter into a number of different types of contracts involving commercial paper accounts. How many different types of checking accounts are offered by your bank? How many different types of promissory notes are used by your bank? Why are there so many types of accounts or notes?

CHAPTER 24

Negotiability

OUTLINE

FORMAL REQUIREMENTS

Defenses   Arguments offered by the defendant as reasons in law or fact why the plaintiff should not recover.

Commercial paper has a special place in business law. Under certain circumstances, the holder of a negotiable instrument is permitted to collect the money despite any **defenses** the maker or drawer can assert. The instrument, if correctly made or drawn, will move easily through the commercial world. However, the law is very jealous of these potential benefits. To carry the benefits of negotiability, an instrument must meet the formal requirements of negotiability. These requirements are set out in Section 3-104(1) of the UCC:

Unconditional   Not limited or affected by any condition.

> Any writing to be a negotiable instrument within this Article must
> (a)   be signed by the maker or drawer; and
> (b)   contain an **unconditional** promise or order to pay a sum certain in money and no other promise, order, obligation or power given by the maker or drawer except as authorized by this Article; and
> (c)   be payable on demand or at a definite time; and
> (d)   be payable to order or to bearer.

These elements are pictured in Figure 24.1. Notice that *every* element must be present. The absence of any element negates negotiability. The paper does not become worthless, but it is no longer negotiable under the law. And that means no holder would have the protections afforded by Article 3. The person holding the paper would still have potential contract rights, however.

Writing Requirement

Commercial paper represents an **intangible right,** the right to collect money at some future time. However, to satisfy the requirements of Article 3, the proof of this right must be tangible. The simplest way to prove that the right exists is to put it in writing. As defined in Section 1-201(46), a writing includes "printing, typewriting or any other intentional reduction to tangible form."

For many people, the type of negotiable instrument most frequently encountered is a check. Most checks are in a standard form, preprinted on paper. Similarly, many drafts are preprinted, in standard form, on paper; most certificates of deposit are preprinted on paper; and many notes are preprinted in a form readily adaptable to the needs of the lender/preparer. These preprinted, standardized forms are familiar, and they contain blanks at all the appropriate places to streamline their completion. However, such convenience is just that— a convenience. It is *not* a necessity.

Commercial paper is equally valid when prepared by handwriting on a scratch pad. Or on a matchbook cover. Or on virtually any other relatively permanent thing. For example, several years ago, on a television series entitled "Love American Style," a couple was marooned on a desert island. The only thing they had for entertainment was a deck of cards. According to the plot, they spent their time playing gin. When they were rescued, the young woman had won $1 million. As evidence, she had a check . . . written on her stom-

FIGURE 24.1   The Elements of Negotiability

Is it *written*?

No   Yes

Is it *signed* by the maker or drawer?

No   Yes

Does it contain an *unconditional* promise or order?

No   Yes

Does it call for payment of a *sum certain*?

No   Yes

IT IS A *CONTRACT,* GOVERNED BY COMMON LAW.

Is it payable in *money*?

No   Yes

Is it payable at a *determinable time*?

No   Yes

Is it payable *to order* or *to bearer*?

No   Yes

IT IS *NEGOTIABLE* UNDER ARTICLE 3.

ach! Despite the comedy implications so heavily emphasized, such a check would be valid.

On April 15, a disgruntled taxpayer completed his tax return. When he mailed in his return, he included a check for the taxes due and a note. The note said: "You've been trying to get it for years, and you've finally succeeded. Here's the shirt off my back." The note was pinned to his check, which was written on his undershirt.

However, the joke was on him. The IRS cashed it!

**Signature
Requirement**

On a check or a draft, an order is given by the drawer. On a note or a CD, a promise is given by the maker. Given the widespread use of preprinted forms as negotiable instruments, some protection is needed from fraud or trickery. The UCC tries to minimize the potential for fakery by requiring a *signature* by the maker or the drawer. Most people think of a signature as a manual subscription, an autograph. That is a signature, but it is not the only possible type of signature.

A corporation, being an inanimate creature, cannot sign its own name. Yet corporations need to "sign" checks. The checks can, of course, be signed by agents of the corporation. But even this is impractical. Some corporations issue thousands of checks each month. An authorized signer would spend nearly an entire career "autographing" checks for the corporation.

Fortunately, the UCC solved this problem. The solution is found in Section 1-201(39), which defines a signature as *any mark or symbol executed with the present intent to authenticate a writing.* Thus, a corporation can use a stamp to sign checks. Likewise, a negotiable instrument can be signed by affixing an *X,* or a thumbprint, or any other intentionally affixed symbol.

There are problems with unusual types of signatures. They may be so strange that people will be hesitant to accept them or the instrument containing them. And the unusual signature must be proved by the person trying to claim the instrument.[1]

It makes no difference where the instrument is signed. Although it is normal to sign in the lower right-hand corner of the face of the instrument, the signature can be anywhere. For example, in a note beginning "I, Mary Smith, promise to pay," Mary Smith's signature following the word *I* would be sufficient.

One of the ways in which a signature can be made on a negotiable instrument is shown in the following case.

First Security Bank of Brookfield v. Fastwich, Inc.
612 S.W.2d 799 (Mo. 1981)

FACTS   The Smiths were the officers and directors of Fastwich. As officers of the corporation, they were authorized to borrow money on behalf of the firm. Fastwich needed funds, and the Smiths approached First Security Bank for a loan. First Security loaned the firm $10,000 and prepared a promissory note as evidence of the debt. In the upper left hand corner of the note was typed "Fastwich, Inc." In the lower right hand corner of the note was the following:
[Typed]FASTWICH, INC.
[Signed]John J. Smith, Jr. [s]Carolyn Smith
[s] Gary D. Smith   [s]Cheryl J. Smith
Fastwich subsequently defaulted on the loan, and the bank attempted to collect the money owed. Fastwich denied that it was liable to the bank because the bank failed to establish the validity of its signature on the note since the name was merely typed.

[1]Uniform Commercial Code, Section 3-307(1)(a).

ISSUE   Was Fastwich's signature on the note? If so, was the signature valid?

HOLDING   Yes. Fastwich's signature was on the note, and the presence of the signature carries a presumption of validity.

REASONING   Section 3-307 of the Code presumes that all signatures are genuine or authorized unless the action involves an obligation of a person who has died or who has become incompetent. Absent one of those circumstances, the defendant must introduce evidence that the signature is a forgery or was not authorized. In this case, Fastwich failed to introduce any evidence that called the validity of the signature into question, so the signature must be presumed to be genuine. The Code permits a signature by typing, and it permits a signature by authorized representatives. Both appear to be present in this case. Fastwich's signature was, therefore, on the instrument, and the signature must be presumed to be valid until it is shown to be otherwise.

Unconditional Promise or Order Requirement

Negotiable instruments are designed to move easily through the commercial world. To serve effectively as a substitute for money, a negotiable instrument must be freely transferable. It also needs to be in a form that people can accept. These needs are met by the requirement that the promise made, or the order given, be *unconditional.* A person taking possession of a negotiable instrument wants to know that payment can be reasonably expected under *every* circumstance. A prospective holder would not be eager to accept an instrument that says payment *might* be made or will be made *only if* something happens. The holder wants an unconditional promise that the money will be paid.

The Code has gone to great lengths to define *unconditional.* Section 3-105 lists ten different things that do *not* make the promise or order conditional. However, a reading of this section by the uninitiated may be confusing. As a result, the courts frequently rely on the so-called four-corner rule. The four-corner rule requires that every necessary bit of information to determine rights on an instrument be contained within its four corners; that is, the information must be found *on the instrument itself.* If the holder must look to some source of information other than the instrument in order to determine rights, the instrument is not negotiable. (The four-corner rule also applies to *time of payment* and *sum certain* requirements.)

Several standard statements frequently found on a negotiable instrument are deemed to be *not* conditional. Some of the more important of these follow:[2]

1. A statement of consideration as *the basis* for the instrument is not a condition to payment. This is true whether the consideration has been performed or has merely been promised. And it is true if the instrument says it was issued "as per agreement," or uses words of similar meaning. Since the instrument is presumed to be issued because of an agreement, a statement that this is true does not make payment conditional.

[2]Ibid., Section 3-105(1).

2. A statement that the instrument arose from a separate agreement or that it refers to a separate agreement does not make payment conditional. This is true even if the separate agreement sets out the rights for acceleration of payment.

3. A statement concerning security interests or collateral connected to the instrument will not make payment conditional. This is true even if the holder may, at various times, demand that additional collateral be put forward to protect the interests of any holders involved.

4. A statement indicating that a particular *account* is to be debited or that a particular fund is expected to provide reimbursement is not conditional. Nor is it conditional if the entire assets of a partnership, unincorporated association, trust, or estate are listed as the sole source of payment.

However, it is deemed conditional, and therefore a denial of negotiability, if payment is restricted to a particular source of funds other than those just mentioned.[3]

Thus, a statement that a particular note is to be paid from the proceeds from selling a car is conditional. No holder would be able to rely on payment in such a note unless it was known that (1) the car had been sold, and (2) the selling price was at least as great as the note amount.

It is also deemed a condition if the instrument is *subject to* or *governed by* a separate agreement or document.[4] This means that an instrument drafted "as per our contract" is negotiable. But an instrument "subject to our contract" is *not* negotiable. Such subtle differences can be confusing at times.

In the following case, a note was treated as non-negotiable because of its reference to a separate contract that was to be treated as a part of the "note."

Salomonsky v. Kelly
349 S.E.2d 358 (Va. 1986)

FACTS   In March, 1976, Williamson agreed to sell his interest in Lake Manor Associates in equal shares to Salomonsky and Armstrong. In return, Salomonsky and Armstrong each agreed to give Williamson 400 shares of a stock with a value of $15 per share and a non-interest-bearing note in the amount of $4000. The notes were executed on 15 March 1976. On the same date, the parties executed an agreement that was incorporated in the notes by reference and referred to the notes. Both notes payable to the order of Williamson contained the following language: "FOR VALUE RECEIVED, the undersigned promises to pay to the order of J. MONTE WILLIAMSON, . . . the principal sum of Four Thousand Dollars ($4,000.00), payable as set forth in that certain agreement dated March 15, 1976, an executed copy of which is attached hereto and made a part hereof by this reference." The agreement set forth various conditions that had to be satisfied before the debt became due and payable. These conditions were met in

[3]Ibid., Section 3-105(2)(b).
[4]Ibid., Section 3-105(2)(a).

October, 1981. In early 1982, Williamson orally demanded payment. He made written demand for payment in May, 1982, and when he did not receive his money, he filed suit in June 1982. Salomonsky and Armstrong defended by relying on the Statute of Limitations, which they alleged bars the collection of the notes.

ISSUE Were these notes negotiable instruments, and thus barred by the Statute of Limitations, or mere contracts, in which case they are enforceable?

HOLDING These notes were mere contracts and thus were not yet barred by the Statute of Limitations.

REASONING The clause included in each of the notes that the notes were "payable as set forth in that agreement dated March 15, 1976" made the notes non-negotiable. The language of the clause requiring the holder of the note to look to another agreement for the terms of payment violates the UCC requirement that the instrument must be unconditional in order to be negotiable. Since the notes in question are not negotiable, they are simply contracts to pay money, subject to certain conditions. The Statute of Limitations would have begun to run on 15 March 1976 (the date of issue), if the notes were negotiable, but in this case it did not begin to run until October, 1981 (the date the conditions for payment were satisfied), because these were mere contracts. Since no other defenses were raised, the notes are valid and enforceable and must be paid. (Williamson died during the appeal, and Kelly, his executor, was substituted in both cases.)

Sum Certain Requirement

A holder of a negotiable instrument must know how much money is to be received when the instrument is paid. The amount is commonly specified exactly, which makes the determination simple, but this is not necessary to satisfy the *sum certain* requirement. To meet the requirement of a sum certain, *the amount must be calculable from the face of the instrument*. This requirement once again raises the four-corner rule. All the necessary information must be on the instrument for the calculation of the total amount due, even if the calculation has not been done.

Under Section 3-106(1), the sum is certain even if it is to be paid under any of the following conditions:

1. with stated interest or by stated installments
2. with stated different rates of interest before and after default or a specified date
3. with a stated discount or addition if paid before or after the date fixed for payment
4. "with **exchange**" or "less exchange," whether at a fixed rate or at the current rate
5. with costs of collection or an attorney's fee, or both, upon default

Exchange Interchange or conversion of the money of two countries or of current and uncurrent monies with an allowance for differences in value.

Judgment rate Rate of interest prescribed by the laws of the particular state or country, which must be paid in all cases where the law allows interest regardless of the debtor's consent.

As if these provisions are not enough, Section 3-118(d) provides that a statement that the instrument is payable "with interest" still carries a sum certain. The rationale is that "with interest" means interest at the **judgment rate,** and the holder has *constructive notice* of what the judgment rate is for

Current rate   Rate of interest currently being charged by financial institutions and recognized as the "going rate" or the "market rate."

the jurisdiction. However, payment of interest at the **current rate** is not a sum certain. The current rate varies, and the holder would need to look beyond the four corners to determine the amount due.

Money Requirement

Since commercial paper serves as a substitute for money, payment must ultimately be made in *money*. Money is defined as *a medium of exchange authorized or adopted by a domestic or foreign government as part of its currency.*[5] Thus, gold and silver are *not* money, but pounds sterling, lira, drachmas, and the like are.

There are really only two problems with payment "in money." The first problem arises when payment is stated in a foreign currency. The second problem involves alternatives for payment. The UCC resolves the first problem, and a number of cases decided under the NIL apparently resolved the second. (Although the NIL is no larger in effect, the precedents set by its cases are still valid, though this is open to argument.)

Under Section 3-107(2), when foreign currency is called for, the instrument must be read carefully. If the instrument *specifies* the foreign currency, payment must be made in that currency. But if the foreign currency is merely *stated,* payment may be made either in the foreign currency or in U.S. dollars at the exchange rate on the payable date.

To understand the second problem, suppose that an instrument calls for the payment of $2000 or ten ounces of gold; is this instrument negotiable? The answer depends on who has the option. If the *maker* or *drawer* can decide which medium to offer at the due date, the instrument is *not* negotiable. However, if the *holder* has the option of choosing the money or the alternative, the instrument *is* negotiable. The reasoning behind this rule is that if the holder has the option, the money *must* be available, thus satisfying the requirement of payment in money. The alternative payment form gives the holder a hedge against inflation, thus making the instrument more enticing and increasing its marketability.

Determinable Time Requirement

A holder wants to know not only how much money will be paid (sum certain), and in what medium (money), but also *when* payment can be expected. The question of when will depend on the instrument, but it must be payable either *on demand* (Section 3-108) or at a *definite time* (Section 3-109).

An instrument is payable on demand when payment is to be made *at sight,* or *at presentment,* or when no time for payment is stated. Any form of instrument may be payable on demand, but promise paper (notes and CDs) normally is not payable on demand. A check *must* be payable on demand, by definition. Thus, a **postdated check** is technically no longer a check; rather, it is a time draft.

Postdated check   Check delivered before its date, generally payable at sight or on presentment on or after the day of its date.

The payee or holder must be able to tell when the instrument is payable by looking at the face of the instrument. Unless the instrument *specifies* that

[5]Ibid., Section 1-201(24).

it is to be paid at some future date (payable at a definite time), it is payable on demand. On demand means whenever the holder presents it to the drawee or maker. A check has no time provisions (see Figure 23.2). It normally is dated *when* issued with the date of issue. It is payable from that date forward. If a drawer issues a check on June 1 but dates it June 15, the check is not payable on demand. The check has become a *time draft*.

An instrument is payable at a definite time if, by its terms, it is payable at a time that can be determined from its face. This definite time frequently will be some stated future date, as "24 September 19XX." Or it may be at some time after a stated date, such as "90 days after 3 March 19XX." Either of these dates would be definite even if some provision was made for accelerating the payment date. And they would be definite with a provision for extending the time, if the holder has the option of extension, or even if the maker or **acceptor** has the option of extending the time. However, in this last situation the extension must be a predetermined definite period, not to exceed the original term.

The UCC also stipulates that payment is at a definite time if payment is a stated period after sight (that is, after presentment). Thus, an instrument calling for payment "60 days after sight" is payable at a definite time. Although the holder must act (present the instrument to the drawee to establish the date of sight), once the act is done, the date for payment is definite.

However, one must be careful in this area. According to Section 3-109(2), payment is *not* at a definite time if it is to occur only upon an act or occurrence that is of uncertain date. This is true even if the event has already occurred. For example, an instrument payable "30 days after Uncle Charlie dies" is not negotiable, even if Uncle Charlie has already died. The holder would have to go outside the instrument to determine the time of occurrence before the time to pay the instrument could be set. The following case illustrates this point.

Acceptor The person who accepts a negotiable instrument (generally the drawee) or who engages to be primarily liable for its payment.

Matter of Estate of Balkus
381 N.W.2d 593 (Wis. App. 1985)

FACTS   James T. Balkus died intestate on December 4, 1983. Shortly after his death, his sister, Ann Vesely, examined his personal property and discovered six deposit slips from a savings account maintained by Balkus. On each of these six slips was the following notation: "Payable to Ann Balkus Vesely on P.O.D. The full amount and other deposits." Each slip was also dated and signed by Balkus. (The parties agreed that *P.O.D.* meant "payable on death.") Vesely also found two promissory notes, both of which were payable to her order. Each note was for $6000 plus interest at 5 percent. Vesely filed claims against the Balkus estate for the amounts represented by the six deposit slips and the two promissory notes. The circuit court denied her claims, and she appealed.

ISSUE   Were these negotiable instruments under Wisconsin law, and was Vesely a holder in due course of these instruments?

HOLDING   The deposit slips were not negotiable instruments, so that Vesely could not be a holder in due course (HDC). The promissory notes were negotiable instruments, but Vesely was not an HDC on them either.

REASONING   The court ruled that the deposit slips were not negotiable instruments since they were not payable on demand or at a definite time. Since they were payable only on the death of Balkus, they were payable only on an event uncertain as to the time of occurrence. The promissory notes were negotiable instruments, but Vesely was not a holder in due course because they had never been delivered by the maker. As a general rule, a promissory note that is not delivered is of no effect. Since these notes never were delivered, Vesely has no rights on either of them. The denial of her claims by the circuit court is affirmed.

Words of Negotiability Requirement

To be negotiable, even if every other element is present, an instrument must contain words of negotiability. The words of negotiability are "Pay to order" or "Pay to bearer." The reason these words are so important is that the law reads them as authorizing the free transfer of the instrument. Failing to use one of these terms is a denial of free transferability and therefore a denial of negotiability.

If an instrument that is otherwise negotiable calls for payment by stating "Pay to Pete Jones," (rather than "Pay to the order of Pete Jones"), it is not negotiable. By its terms, *only* Pete Jones is authorized to receive payment; he cannot transfer payment. However, an endorsement that says "Pay to Pete Jones" would not affect negotiability. Endorsements cannot negate negotiability once it exists.

To be payable *to order,* the terms of the instrument must state that it is payable *to the order or assigns of a specified individual* or to a *specified individual or to the individual's order.*[6] The designated individual may be a *person,* as in "Pay to Paula Lopez or order"; an *office,* as in "Pay to the order of the Treasurer of Washington County"; an *estate* or *trust,* as in "Pay to the order of the Johnson Estate"; or an unincorporated association, as in "Pay to the XYZ Partnership or order." An instrument payable to order requires an endorsement to be negotiated (see Chapter 25, on negotiation and endorsements).

If no particular individual is designated, the instrument must be payable *to bearer* to be negotiable. An instrument is payable to bearer when, by its terms, it is payable to bearer or to the order of bearer; or to "cash" or the order of "cash"; or to a named person or bearer, as in "Pay to Joe Jakes or bearer" or "Pay to the Order of Joe Jakes or bearer" (Section 3-111). No endorsement is legally needed to negotiate an instrument payable to bearer, although most holders will request (or demand) an endorsement for added protection.

CONSTRUCTION AND INTERPRETATION

In an effort to minimize problems and to reduce the number of lawsuits involving commercial paper, the drafters of the UCC added some special sec-

[6]Ibid., Section 3-110(1).

tions. These sections deal with recurring problem areas and define how they are to be treated.

The first of these sections is 3-112, which covers certain *terms* and *omissions* that do not affect negotiability. Most of the coverage is devoted to terms. Subsection (b) says that a statement that collateral has been given as security, or that such collateral may be sold in case of default, has no effect on negotiability. Similarly, subsection (c) says that a promise to maintain or to protect any collateral given will not affect negotiability. And subsections (d) and (e) allow provisions covering **confession of judgment** or the waiver of other legal rights without affecting negotiability. However, these subsections do require that no rights be waived before the due date of the instrument. A blanket waiver, especially by confession of judgment, without regard to the due date will effectively destroy negotiability.

The omission area is covered in subsection (1). Here the Code says that omitting any statement of consideration as a reason for issuing an instrument has no effect. Likewise, the omission of a stated place for payment or drawing does not deny negotiability.

More commonly, problems arise over meaning rather than negotiability. For this reason, Section 3-118 covers several standard ambiguities. The rules set forth in this section apply to *every* instrument.

If there is a reasonable doubt whether the instrument is a draft or a note, the *holder* may treat it as either. Further, a draft that names the drawer as the drawee is treated as a note.

If an instrument has internal contradictions, the Code says that *handwritten* terms control over typewritten or printed (that is, typeset) terms. If the conflict is between typewritten and printed terms, typewritten ones control. And if the ambiguity is between words and numbers, the words control *if they are clear*. However, if the words are ambiguous, the numbers control. If a check reads

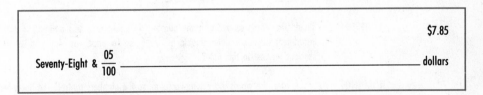

the check would be for seventy-eight and 05/100 dollars ($78.05). But if the check reads

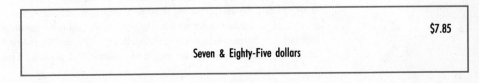

Confession of judgment A judgment in which the defendant, instead of entering a plea, confesses the action; a written commitment whereby the defendant consents to allowing the plaintiff to confess a judgment against the defendant.

the check would be for seven and 85/100 dollars ($7.85). The next case deals
with just such an issue of ambiguity.

Wall v. *East Texas Teachers Credit Union*
533 S.W.2d 918 (Tex. 1976)

FACTS   Wall signed a promissory note, payable to the order of the East Texas Teachers Credit Union, that was ambiguous
and allegedly usurious. The note read as follows:

$19,896.01

                                                    Note No. 22724 Account No. 3329-99
                                                          May 7, 1971

For Value Received, I/We jointly and severally, promise to pay to the **EAST TEXAS TEACHERS
CREDIT UNION,** or order, at LONGVIEW, TEXAS the sum of Nineteen hundred eight
hundred ninety-six————and 01/100 Dollars, **payable in 1 installment of** Seven thousand————and NO/100 Dollars, **and 1 installment of** Seven thousand————
and NO/Dollars 1 at $6803.48 due September 15, 1971 (x) **which includes principal and interest**
( ) **plus interest on the unpaid balances at the rate of** One percent **per month both before and after
maturity, the installments to be paid** (x) **monthly** ( ) **semi-monthly** ( ) **weekly** ( ) **bi-weekly
beginning** June 15, 1971
Collateral: Shares, 170 head mixed cattle

                                          SIGNATURE OF MAKER
SIGNATURE OF WITNESSES   **AND COMAKERS**   **ADDRESS**

_____   (X)_____   _____

At the time of the suit there had been no payments of principal or interest. Wall argued that the ambiguity in the
note had to be interpreted by the rule that words control over numbers, so that he owed $2796.01 ($1900 plus
$896.01). Wall also argued that there was no way to tell when the first two installment payments were due from
the note. Finally, Wall argued that the interest was usurious and that he was entitled to a penalty of twice the
interest, as provided for by Texas law.

ISSUES   Should the words control over the numbers in interpreting this ambiguous note? Were the dates for the first two
installment payments determinable in this note? To what was Wall entitled in the way of penalty/offset for the
usurious interest in this note?

HOLDINGS   In this case, the words did not make sense, so the numbers control. The dates for payment of the installments were
determinable from the note, read as a whole. Wall was entitled to the penalties for usury before interest was added
to his note.

REASONING   The wording in the note was grammatically incorrect and involved an unorthodox use of words. Combined with the
call for the payment of three installments, each of which was greater than the alleged full amount of the note (from
literally reading the words), this use of words is ambiguous, and the numbers must, therefore, control. Although
the dates of the installments are not stated immediately adjacent to the amount of the installments, the box checked
later that calls for payment monthly beginning 15 June 1971, and the statement that the final installment was to
be paid 15 September 1971, allowed for a proper determination of when the installments were due. The maximum

interest under Texas law was 10 percent per annum, and the penalty for usurious interest is twice the amount of usurious interest contracted for. To add the interest to the note and then to subtract twice the interest is, in effect, giving the borrower only penalty/offset of the interest. Thus, the penalty should be to subtract double the interest from the principal and to deny interest on the loan to the credit union.

Finally, unless the instrument specifies, a provision for interest is interpreted as meaning interest at the judgment rate for the jurisdiction where the instrument is to be paid. Also, interest is considered to run from the date of the instrument, unless a different period is specified. If the instrument bears interest but is not dated, interest runs from the date of issue.

SUMMARY

This chapter examined the technical requirements for negotiability of an instrument under Article 3. The first requirement is that the instrument be written, or reduced to tangible form. Next, the instrument must be signed by the maker or the drawer. The promise (for notes or CDs) or the order (for checks or drafts) must be unconditional. All of the terms necessary for payment must be included on the face of the instrument.

The instrument must be payable in money, a recognized governmental currency. The amount of the payment must be a sum certain, which means the amount can be computed from the face of the instrument. In addition, the time of payment must be determinable from the face of the instrument, or it must be payable on demand. Finally, the instrument must contain "words of negotiability." This means it must be payable "to order" or "to bearer."

In case the instrument contains ambiguities, the code provides a method of interpretation. Handwriting controls over typing and over printing. Typing controls over printing. Words control over numbers if the words make sense. If the words do not make sense, the numbers control.

DISCUSSION QUESTIONS

1. How can a negotiable instrument be "signed" by a nonhuman entity?

2. Normally any attempt to restrict payment to a certain source of funds makes the instrument conditional. Why is this considered a condition on payment? Give examples to support your answer.

3. What is meant by the phrase *sum certain in money?*

4. Why is an instrument payable "30 days after sight" payable at a definite time? How is the date of "sight" determined?

5. Would the following instrument be considered negotiable?

I promise to pay to the order of Chris Jamison four thousand dollars ($4000.00) plus 8% interest. Interest is to be figured from 9-1-90.

Donald McDonald

6. The courts haves consistently held that an I.O.U. is not negotiable. The following is a typical I.O.U.:

I.O.U. $300

(s) *Donald McDonald*

Why would such a document be deemed non-negotiable? Be specific.

7. Glenda issued a promissory note to Ralph. Ralph transferred the note to Phil. When Phil tried to collect from Glenda, she refused to pay. The note stated that interest was payable "at the prime rate." Assume the case hinges on the negotiability of the note, and that all other elements are satisfactory. Is this note a negotiable instrument? Explain your answer.

8. Don drew a draft payable to the order of Pam. The draft called for the payment of $750 for an oak dining room suite. How could this payment be worded so that it would be a negotiable instrument?

9. Marvella issued a time draft to Herman, with payment "6 months to the day after our marriage." He married her on January 4; she divorced him on May 11; and he demanded payment on July 4, all of the same year. Was the draft a negotiable instrument? Discuss fully. What rights may Herman assert?

10. Bob issued a note to Larry. The note had the following terms included in its body:

> Interest at 14% per annum. [This term was printed.]
> Interest at 14 ¼%. [This term was typewritten.]
> Plus interest. [This term was handwritten.]

How will interest be calculated on the note, and why?

CASE PROBLEMS

1. Schleider arranged with his dentist to have certain dental work performed. In order to pay for the dental work, Schleider issued an instrument to the dentist. The instrument contained a promise by Schleider to pay to the order of the dentist $480. The instrument also contained the following clause: "In case of death of maker, all payments not due at death are cancelled." The dentist transferred the instrument to Reserve Plan two days later. Schleider claims that the dental work was never performed and refuses to pay Reserve Plan. Reserve Plan asserts that it is a holder in due course and is entitled to payment despite the adequacy of the dental work. If the instrument is a negotiable instrument, Schleider has to pay Reserve Plan. Is the instrument negotiable? Explain fully. (*Reserve Plan, Inc. v. Schleider*, 145 N.Y.S. 2d 122 [1955].)

2. Holly Hills executed and delivered a promissory note and a mortgage to Rogers and Blythe. The note in question contained the following clause: "This note with interest is secured by a mortgage on real estate, of even date herewith, made by the maker [Holly Hills] hereof in favor of the said payee . . . the terms of said mortgage are by this reference made a part hereof." Rogers and Blythe subsequently transferred the note and the mortgage to Charter Bank as security on another note. Eventually Holly Hills dishonored the note. The bank sued both Holly Hills and Rogers and Blythe, asserting that it was entitled to collect since it qualified as a holder in due course. Was this note negotiable, so that Charter Bank could be a holder in due course? Explain your answer. (*Holly Hills Acres, Ltd.* v. *Charter Bank of Gainesville*, 314 So.2d 209 [Fla. 1975].)

3. Hellman hired Evenson to sell an apartment complex that Hellman owned. Evenson located a buyer, and the buyer and Hellman worked out the details for the sale of the complex. At the conclusion of the negotiations, Hellman issued a promissory note to Evenson for $12,500 as payment for Evenson's work in selling the apartment complex. The buyer later defaulted on the sales contract, and Hellman refused to honor the promissory note he had issued to Evenson. When Evenson sued to collect the note, Hellman argued that there was a condition attached to payment of the note, namely that the buyer complete the sale as agreed. Since the

buyer did not complete the sale, Hellman argues that he is not liable to Evenson for the note. Assuming that the note is in every other respect negotiable, should the court admit Hellman's parol evidence concerning conditions for payment? (*Evenson v. Hlebechuk*, 305 N.W.2d 13 [N.D. 1981].)

4. Yost executed and delivered to Appliances, Inc. an undated ninety-day promissory note payable to the order of Appliances, Inc. When ninety days had elapsed, Appliances, Inc. demanded payment, and Yost refused to honor the note. Yost asserts that the note was not a negotiable instrument and that he is therefore not liable to Appliances, Inc. for the money allegedly owed on the note. Is the note negotiable? What rights, if any, belong to Appliances, Inc. in this case? (*Appliances, Inc. v. Yost*, 29 UCC Rep. Serv. 560 [Conn. 1980].)

5. Briggs signed and issued the following note:

June 6, 1985

Ninety days after the above date, I promise to pay to the order of Three Thousand Four Hundred Dollars $ _____

_____ **Dollars**

_____

The party in possession of this note argues that the note is a bearer-negotiable instrument. Briggs argues that the note is not negotiable. Who is correct and why? (*Broadway Management Corp. v. Briggs*, 332 N.E.2d 131 [Ill. 1975].)

6. The Glendora Bank sued Davis to collect on a promissory note that Davis had issued. The only issue in the case was whether the note was negotiable. The note contained the following clause:

> This note is given in payment of merchandise and is to be liquidated by payments received on account of sale of such merchandise.

Is this a negotiable promissory note? Explain (*Glendora Bank v. Davis*, 267 P. 311 [Cal. 1928].)

7. Barton executed and issued an instrument to Hudgens that promised to pay $3000 to the order of Hudgens "upon evidence of an acceptable permanent loan of $290,000 for Barton, and Barton's acceptance of the

commitment." Hudgens obtained a loan commitment for Barton, but Barton did not accept the loan. Hudgens then sued Barton on the "promissory note." Is the instrument in question a promissory note? Why? (*Barton v. Scott Hudgens Realty & Mortgage, Inc.*, 222 S.E.2d 126 [Ga. App. 1975].)

8. The Campbells issued a note payable to the order of Strand in the amount of $11,250, plus interest. The note was issued to purchase shares in a limited partnership that Strand promised to establish but never came into existence. Strand subsequently endorsed and delivered the note to Centerre Bank for value. When the Campbells defaulted on the note, Centerre Bank sued for the balance due. The Campbells defended on two grounds: (1) there was a failure of consideration because the limited partnership was never established and (2) a clause in the note stating that interest may vary with bank rates charged to Strand made the note nonnegotiable, so that the bank could not be a holder in due course. How should this case be resolved? Be certain you treat both major issues raised by the Campbells. (*Centerre Bank of Branson v. Campbell*, 744 S.W.2d 490 [Mo. App. 1988].)

9. NRX Technologies issued notes that were unconditionally guaranteed by three members of its board of directors. The corporation accepted the proceeds of the notes, and at least one of the directors was given stock and stock options in exchange for his guarantee. The directors denied liability for their guarantees and alleged that the notes and the guarantees were incomplete when signed and therefore should not be binding on them. Should this defense be valid? Why? (*Kornfeld v. NRX Technologies, Inc.*, 465 N.E.2d 30 [N.Y. 1984].)

10. McDonald stole numerous money orders from the Unites States Post Office, along with an imprinting machine. McDonald used the machine to prepare a number of money orders for the maximum amount of $100, endorsed them, and cashed them at First Bank. First Bank then presented the money orders to the government and was paid for them. The government is now suing First Bank to recover the money paid to the bank on the money orders. The bank argues that the money orders are negotiable instruments, so the bank is protected by the UCC. The government argues that a money order is not a negotiable instrument. Which side is correct on this issue? Which party should prevail? (*United States v. The First National Bank of Boston*, 263 F. Supp. 298 [D.C. Mass. 1967].)

CHAPTER 25

Negotiation and Holders in Due Course

OUTLINE

TRANSFER

Negotiable instruments are intended to flow through the commercial world. In order to "flow," the instrument needs to be transferred from person to person. The form these transfers take determines the rights that can be asserted by each person gaining possession of the instrument.

The entire process begins with a transfer known as an *issue*. UCC Section 3-102(1)(a) defines an issue as the first delivery of an instrument to a holder or a **remitter**. Either the maker or the drawer causes the instrument to be prepared and initially placed into one of the streams of commerce.

A negotiable instrument, once issued, is presumed to support an underlying contract. It also contains all the necessary elements to be a contract, and as such it can be *assigned*. As we explained in Chapter 15, an assignment is the voluntary transfer of one's legal rights. In an assignment, one party, the assignor, transfers his or her rights under a contract to another party, the assignee. The assignee takes these rights *subject to* any and all claims, defenses, and **setoffs** available to the obligor (the party expected to perform the contract). This means the assignee may very well be unable to enforce the rights transferred because of some defense or defect the obligor can assert on the contract.

These same rights and defenses apply to the transfer of a negotiable instrument by means of an assignment,[1] which presents a problem. Since assignees can have no greater rights than those of their assignors, very few people would be willing to accept a negotiable instrument by such a transfer. The possibility of collecting the money due would be too speculative. The assignee could seldom be certain that the promise would be kept or that the order would be obeyed at the due date, since some defense might exist that would override the original obligation. Obviously, something more is needed to protect the possessor of the commercial paper and to facilitate the free flow of commercial paper through commercial channels. That something more is provided by the UCC, and it is known as *negotiation*.

A negotiation is the transfer of a negotiable instrument *in such a manner* that the transferee becomes a *holder*.[2] To determine the "manner" needed, one must examine the form of the instrument. If the instrument is payable *to order,* it must be properly **endorsed** and **delivered** to be negotiated. If the instrument is payable *to bearer,* delivery alone is sufficient to constitute negotiation.

For example, a check that says "Pay to the order of *Ollie Oliver*" must be endorsed by Ollie Oliver before it can be negotiated. If Ollie simply delivers the check to another person without endorsing it, the transfer would be an assignment. The terms imposed by the drawer—pay to the order of Ollie

Remitter A person who sends or transmits money to another, especially by purchasing a cashier's check or bank draft.

Setoffs Rights that exist between two parties, each of whom owes an ascertained amount to the other, to set off their respective debts by way of mutual reduction so that only the net amount will be paid.

Endorsed Signed with one's name so that the endorser's rights in the negotiable instrument are transferred to another.

Delivered Placed within the actual or constructive possession or control of another.

---

[1]Uniform Commercial Code, Section 3-201.
[2]Ibid., Section 3-201(1).

Oliver—require that Ollie *prove* he is transferring his rights. His endorsement provides that proof.

In contrast, a check that says "Pay to the order of *bearer*" does not need to be endorsed in order to be negotiated. Delivery alone is enough to show negotiation. The terms imposed by the drawer at the time of issue—pay to the order of bearer—tell the drawee that anyone in possession is entitled to payment.

If the instrument requires an endorsement, the endorsement must be written on the instrument itself or on an *allonge,* a paper so firmly affixed to the instrument as to become a part of the instrument. Also, to be a negotiation, the endorsement must transfer the entire instrument or the entire unpaid balance. Any attempt to transfer less than the entire balance of the instrument is treated as a partial assignment, not as a negotiation.[3]

The following case illustrates the concept of a transfer as an assignment and not as a negotiation.

Waters v. Waters
498 S.W.2d 236 (Tex. App. 1973)

FACTS   Jerry Waters and his ex-wife, Patsy Waters, entered a property settlement as part of their divorce. Part of the property settlement agreement was that a note Jerry had issued to Patsy's father should be paid to Patsy. The note, payable to Jim Still, was delivered to Patsy, but it was not endorsed by the payee. Some time later Jim Still died. Patsy sued Jerry on the note, and Jerry denied that Patsy was entitled to enforce the note.

ISSUE   Was Patsy entitled to enforce the promissory note?

HOLDING   Yes. The evidence established that Patsy was the owner of the note, and as such she was permitted to seek collection on it from the maker.

REASONING   The lack of any endorsement by Jim Still does not preclude Patsy's rights. The owner of a promissory note may transfer it without any endorsement or without any written assignment. The lack of any endorsements prevented Patsy from attaining the status of holder. But she can still seek to collect as an assignee or as a donee in a gift.

ENDORSEMENTS

An *endorsement* must be placed on a negotiable instrument that is payable to *order* before it can be effectively negotiated. In addition, each endorsement on an instrument *creates an additional contract* between the endorser and all subsequent holders. For this reason, many people will not accept the transfer

[3]Ibid., Section 3-202(2), (3).

FIGURE 25.1 The Endorsement Matrix

	Unqualified	Qualified
Special	1	2
Blank	3	4
Restrictive	5	6

of a *bearer* instrument unless the transferor endorses it. Even though bearer paper may legally be negotiated by delivery alone, the transferee usually demands the added security of the endorsement contract. To further emphasize the importance of endorsements, the UCC states in Section 3-402 that "unless the instrument clearly indicates that a signature is made in some other capacity it is an endorsement."

There are two reasons for endorsing an instrument. One reason is to affect *negotiation*. The other is to affect *liability*. The endorsements that affect negotiation tell the holder that another endorsement is needed to negotiate the instrument further (a *special* endorsement); that no further endorsements are needed in order to negotiate the instrument further (a *blank* endorsement); or that the instrument has been restricted to some special channel of commerce, such as banking (a *restrictive* endorsement). The endorsements that affect liability either (1) admit and/or agree to honor the contract of endorsement (an *unqualified* endorsement) or (2) expressly deny any liability on the contract the endorsement represents (a *qualified* endorsement). Every endorsement must affect negotiation as well as liability. Thus, each endorsement must fit one of the boxes in the matrix shown in Figure 25.1.

Notice that each box is numbered. We will use these numbers to refer back to the matrix as we discuss some examples of the various types of endorsements. Throughout the examples, we will be using the check shown in Figure 25.2.

Special Endorsement

A *special* endorsement *specifies the party to whom the instrument is to be paid or to whose order it is to be paid.*[4] This means that a special endorsement makes the instrument *order* paper. Even if the instrument was issued as bearer paper, a special endorsement will turn it into order paper. The party specified will have to endorse it before it can be negotiated further. Figure 25.3 shows an example of a special endorsement.

Blank Endorsement

A *blank* endorsement *does not specify the party to whom the instrument is to be paid.* The normal form of a blank endorsement is a mere signature. Such

[4]Ibid., Section 3-204(1).

FIGURE 25.2   The Check as Issued

FIGURE 25.3   A Special Endorsement

an endorsement makes the instrument *bearer* paper.[5] As such it is negotiable by delivery alone, without any need for further endorsements. In Figure 25.4, (3) would be a blank endorsement.

Notice that at this point the check has every endorsement that is necessary for negotiation. Should the check now be lost or stolen, the finder or the thief could effectively negotiate it. To protect against such an occurrence, Section 3-204(3) empowers any holder to **convert** a blank endorsement into a special endorsement. This is done by writing appropriate words above the blank endorsement, as is shown in Figure 25.5. Here a holder added the words "Pay to Mata Harry, or order" above Charlie Chenn's endorsement. This phrase could have been added by Charlie Chenn when he negotiated the check to Mata Harry. More likely, Mata Harry added the phrase after she received the check from Charlie Chenn. By adding the phrase, she has protected herself against losing the check or having it stolen.

Convert   To change from one form or function to another.

---

[5]Ibid., Section 3-204(2).

FIGURE 25.4   A Blank Endorsement

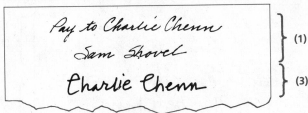

FIGURE 25.5   A Blank Endorsement Converted to a Special Endorsement

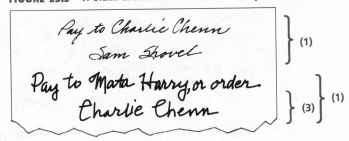

**Restrictive
Endorsement**

A *restrictive* endorsement purports to prohibit any further negotiation of the instrument. Or it is conditional. Or it contains words that indicate it is to be deposited or collected, such as "for deposit," "for collection," or "pay any bank." Or it has some other restriction specified as to its use.[6]

However, once an instrument as issued satisfies all the tests of negotiability, no endorsement can remove its negotiable status.[7] Even with a restrictive endorsement, further negotiation and transfer is permitted. In Figure 25.6, (5) shows a restrictive endorsement.

It should be noted that each of these sample endorsements refers to the *unqualified* endorsement column of the matrix set out in Figure 25.1. The reason for this is contained in UCC Section 3-414. Under this section, an endorsement is presumed to be unqualified. To be *qualified*, the endorsement must contain specific words of qualification.

Dishonored   Refused for acceptance or payment upon proper presentment.

Notice   Information; knowledge of a fact or a state of affairs.

**Unqualified
Endorsement**

An *unqualified* endorsement *carries with it a contract*. The endorser is committed to the *endorsee* (the person to whom the instrument is transferred by endorsement) or to any later endorser if the instrument is **dishonored**, and proper **notice** is given. The normal order of payment among the endorsers is

[6]Ibid., Section 3-205(1), (2), (3), (4).
[7]Ibid., Section 3-206(1).

FIGURE 25.6   A Restrictive Endorsement

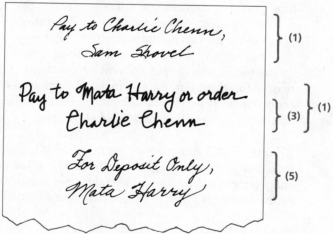

the reverse of the order in which they endorse.[8] Thus, endorser number 4 would collect from number 3; number 3 would collect from number 2; and number 2 would collect from number 1. This is known as the secondary chain of liability and will be covered in more detail in Chapter 26.

Qualified Endorsement

A *qualified endorsement is one that denies contract liability.* The endorser includes words such as "without recourse" in the endorsement. These words have the legal effect of telling later endorsers that the qualifying endorser will *not* repay them if the instrument is dishonored. By accepting a qualified endorsement in a negotiation, the later endorsers also agree to the contract terms of the qualified endorsement. In Figure 25.7, each of the earlier endorsements is shown as unqualified; in Figure 25.8, each is shown as qualified.

FIGURE 25.7   Unqualified Endorsements

Pay to Charlie Chenn,
Sam Shovel — (1)

Pay to Mata Harry or order
Charlie Chenn — (3) } (1)

For Deposit Only,
Mata Harry — (5)

[8]Ibid., Section 3-414(1), (2).

FIGURE 25.8 Qualified Endorsements

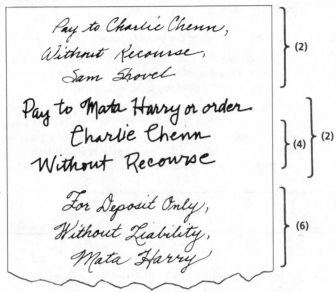

Note the specific language necessary to change an endorsement from the presumed unqualified endorsement to a qualified endorsement.

In the following case, the court had to deal with the issue of a special endorsement and its effect on subsequent negotiations. Notice the effect that the endorsement had on an attempt to further negotiate the notes in question.

In the following case, the court had to deal with the issue of a special endorsement and its effect on subsequent negotiations. Notice the effect that the endorsement had on an attempt to further negotiate the notes in question.

Klomann v. Sol K. Graff & Sons
317 N.E.2d 608 (Ill. 1974)

FACTS Sol K. Graff & Sons were real estate brokers. They were involved in the sale and exchange of a number of properties on behalf of Fred Klomann. As a result of these transactions, Sol K. Graff & Sons owed Klomann $13,000. The firm issued three promissory notes payable to the order of Klomann and totalling $13,000 as payment of the account.

Fred Klomann later negotiated these notes to his daughter by special endorsement. His daughter examined the notes and returned them to her father for collection without endorsing them. Some time later Fred Klomann scratched out the name of his daughter in the special endorsements, substituted the name of his wife, and transferred possession of the notes to his wife. The following month Fred's wife demanded payment on the notes from Sol K. Graff & Sons. Payment was refused, and she filed suit on the notes.

ISSUE Does Georgia Klomann (Fred's wife) have sufficient rights in the notes to collect them from the maker?

HOLDING   No. The rights in these notes belonged to the special endorsee, Candace Klomann (Fred's daughter), and were never transferred by her.

REASONING   Section 3-204 of the Uniform Commercial Code provides:

> (1) A special endorsement specifies the person to whom or to whose order it makes the instrument payable. Any instrument specially endorsed becomes payable to the order of the special endorsee and may be further negotiated only by his endorsement.

In this case, the notes were specially endorsed to Candace, and she never endorsed or negotiated the notes thereafter. Rather, she returned them to her father for collection. Instead of collecting the notes, he altered the special endorsements without permission or authority and attempted to negotiate the notes again. At that time, Fred Klomann had no rights in the notes, and this second transfer by Fred vested in the transferee only such rights as were held by the transferor. Since Fred had no rights, he transferred no rights to Georgia.

HOLDER

At the beginning of this chapter, we examined the transfer of negotiable instruments. It was pointed out that a transfer leaves the transferee in the role of assignee. And it was stated that a *negotiation* leaves the transferee in the role of a *holder*.

The role of holder is important in negotiable instruments. It normally carries contractual rights against several parties involved with the instrument. It also normally carries **warranty rights** against some parties involved with the instrument. And it is an essential element before a party can become a *holder in due course*, perhaps the most favored position in the law of commercial paper.

A holder is *a person in possession of a negotiable instrument drawn, issued, or endorsed to him, to his order, to bearer, or in blank.* Thus, the holder either receives the original issue from the maker or drawer or receives a negotiation through endorsement and/or delivery. A holder has the right to transfer, negotiate, discharge, or enforce the instrument in the holder's own name.[9] However, a holder is subject to any defenses on the instrument that a maker or drawer can assert.

Warranty rights   Rights to enforce implied promises that certain facts in relation to the negotiable instrument are, or shall be, as they were stated or promised to be.

HOLDER IN DUE COURSE

Burden of proof   The legal necessity of affirmatively proving a fact or facts on an issue raised between the parties in a cause of action.

To overcome even one of the defenses on the instrument that may be available to the maker or drawer, the holder needs to acquire holder in due course status. Great care needs to be exercised here. The **burden of proof** of having

[9]Ibid., Sections 1-201(20), 3-301.

holder in due course status lies with the person claiming the status.[10] A holder must prove he or she is a holder in due course; such status is not presumed. A holder or an assignee is subject to any defense the drawer or maker can assert. A holder in due course is subject only to some defenses of the maker or drawer. The holder in due course prevails over most available defenses.

The Code defines a *holder in due course* as a holder who takes an instrument *for value, in good faith,* and *without notice* of any defenses or defects affecting the instrument.[11] The issues of value and good faith are relatively simple to establish. However, the "without notice" issue can be difficult to prove at times.

For Value

Section 3-303 sets out three methods of *giving value* for an instrument. Notice that each method involves actual performance by the holder, not just a commitment to perform in the future. The first method is either to perform the agreed consideration or to acquire a security interest in the instrument. *Doing* something is a giving of value here, but *promising* to do something is not. The second method is to take the instrument as payment for, or as security on, a preexisting debt or obligation. This method is valid even if the claim is not yet due. The third method is to give a negotiable instrument in exchange for the one received or to make an irrevocable commitment to a third person (not the transferor) as the basis for the transfer. Once the holder can prove that value was given, the holder goes on to the next test.

In the following case, the question of whether a party was a holder in due course (HDC) hinged on the presence of value.

Schulingkamp v. Aicklen
534 So.2d 1327 (La. App. 4 Cir. 1988)

FACTS The Aicklens issued a note payable to the order of Schulingkamp in the amount of $10,500 and dated 15 November 1984. The note was given to the payee in conjunction with an offer to purchase real estate. The payee had not accepted the offer by 21 December 1984, at which time the Aicklens sent a telegram withdrawing their offer. On 28 December 1984, Schulingkamp purported to have accepted the original offer and so notified the Aicklens through her attorney.

ISSUE Did Schulingkamp give value for the note in this case?

HOLDING No. While value is presumed on the issuance of a note, if the maker questions value, the payee must prove that consideration/value was given.

REASONING While the payee claims that she had tacitly accepted the offer prior to the date the offer was withdrawn, she admits that she never signed an acceptance until after the date of withdrawal by the Aicklens. She took no steps to show

---

[10]Ibid., Section 3-307(3).
[11]Ibid., Section 3-302(1).

this alleged tacit acceptance and, in fact, did not reply to several attempts by the Aicklens to find out the status of their offer. As a matter of law in Louisiana, a payee is given the presumption that the instrument in question was given for value received, unless the maker of the note casts doubt on the issue of consideration. Once such doubt is cast, the burden of proof shifts to the payee to prove consideration by a preponderance of evidence. In this case, the makers raised the issue of lack of consideration, which forced the payee to show that consideration had been given. To show that, she would need to show that she had accepted the offer. She failed to do so; thus she had not given value. She may not enforce the note.

In Good Faith

The next requirement is that the holder take the instrument in *good faith*. Good faith is defined as honesty in fact in the transaction.[12] This requirement is actually measured by a negative test. The holder acted with good faith if bad faith is not present. To show lack of good faith, it must be proved that the holder either had *actual knowledge* of a defect in the instrument or *ignored* facts that would show the defect. Usually, all the holder needs to do is to allege good faith. The burden of proof then will shift to the maker or drawer. It will be up to the maker or drawer to prove bad faith, or actual knowledge of some defect, by the holder. Very few cases involve bad faith.

Without Notice of Defects or Defenses

The final requirement to establish holder in due course status is that the holder take the instrument *without notice* of any defenses or defects on the instrument. Section 3-304 of the Code lists certain areas that affect the notice provision. Each of these areas is examined in the following sections.

Facts That Are Notice   A purchaser of a negotiable instrument has notice of a defect if the instrument is incomplete in some material respect. Thus, a missing signature or a missing amount would be notice. So would a missing date on a *time* instrument. But a missing date on a *demand* instrument, such as a check, is not notice since it is not material. It is not material because a demand instrument is payable at issue, and even if it is not dated, it has been issued. The simple fact of its existence proves that it has been issued.

Notice of a defect also exists if the instrument is visibly altered or bears visible evidence of a forgery. Notice exists if the instrument is irregular on its face. This means that an erasure of an obligation of a party or of an amount is notice of a defect.

A holder who takes an instrument stamped "NSF" (not sufficient funds), or "Payment Stopped," or "Paid" would have notice of a defense or defect on the instrument. It has been presented, and it has been dishonored or paid. The holder knows this by looking at the face of the instrument. Taking an **overdue** instrument is also considered notice. An instrument is overdue if the holder has reason to know that any payment is overdue or is in default or that acceleration has occurred. A demand instrument is overdue after demand has been made *or* after an unreasonable time lapse following issue. While

Overdue Unpaid beyond its maturity date.

[12]Ibid., Section 1-301(19).

unreasonable time is ambiguous, some guidelines are available. A reasonable time for a draft would normally be longer than that for a check but shorter than that for a demand note. And a reasonable time on a non-interest-bearing note would be shorter than on an interest-bearing note. A reasonable time on a check is presumed to be thirty days. Reasonable times on other instruments would depend on the instrument itself, the community it is circulated in, and any other relevant factors. Each case must be handled differently.

In the following case, a drawer of a check argued that a holder had notice of a defense so that the holder could not be a holder in due course.

Jaeger & Branch, Inc. v. *Pappas*
433 P.2d 605 (Utah 1967)

FACTS   Pappas was building a hotel in Park City, Utah. He had been purchasing a number of materials from Allo Distributing Company of North Hollywood, California. Pappas had ordered a shipment of carpeting from Allo, and Allo had arranged to purchase and ship the carpeting to Pappas. The carpeting had been ordered from Jaeger & Branch. Jaeger & Branch had the shipment delayed pending payment from Allo. When Pappas called Allo to find out where the carpet was, Allo asked Pappas to call Jaeger to try to straighten things out. Pappas called Jaeger and gave Jaeger assurance that the carpeting would be paid for promptly. Pappas sent a check payable to the order of Allo, Allo promptly endorsed the check and delivered it to Jaeger, and Jaeger deposited the check with his bank. In the meantime, the carpeting shipment had been released and delivered to Pappas.

After the conversation with Jaeger, Pappas called Allo again and informed Allo that unless Allo sent "everything you say you're going to," Pappas would place a stop payment order on the check. Pappas did, in fact, place a stop payment order on the check so that the check was returned to Jaeger. Jaeger sued Pappas for the amount of the check, and Pappas denied that Jaeger was a holder in due course.

ISSUE   Did Jaeger have notice of any defenses on the check issued by Pappas?

HOLDING   No. Nothing in the facts would provide Jaeger with notice of any defenses on this check.

REASONING   From a review of the facts and the evidence of the case, the court could find nothing that would have placed Jaeger on notice of any defenses on the check. The mere fact that Pappas had called Jaeger before issuing the check to Allo is not sufficient to provide notice. While it is true that a holder must act in a reasonable manner and should make inquiry if the facts indicate the possibility of a defense on the instrument, the reverse is also true. If there is nothing to indicate a defense exists, the holder need not make inordinate inquiries. In this case, there was nothing to indicate that the check was subject to any defenses, and Jaeger acted properly. He qualified as a holder in due course and is entitled to collect the check.

Facts That Are Not Notice   The UCC, Section 3-304(4), states that the following facts, standing alone, are not notice even if the holder has knowledge of the fact:

Antedated Affixed with an earlier date; dated before the instrument was written.

Accommodation party One who has signed an instrument without receiving value and for the purpose of lending his or her name to some other person as a means of securing credit.

1. The instrument was **antedated** or postdated.
2. The instrument was issued or negotiated for an executory promise, *unless* the holder has notice of defenses to the promise.
3. Any party has signed as an **accommodation party.**
4. A formerly incomplete instrument was completed.
5. Any person negotiating the instrument is or was a fiduciary.
6. There was a default on an interest payment on the instrument.

In addition, it is not treated as notice if any party has filed or recorded a document, if the holder would otherwise qualify as a holder in due course. And before notice is effective, it must be received in a time and a manner that give a reasonable opportunity to act on the information.[13] Notice must be received before the holder receives the instrument. Once the holder has received the instrument, later notice is irrelevant.

EFFECT OF HOLDER IN DUE COURSE STATUS

The status of holder in due course is a preferred legal position. The holder in due course takes an instrument free of *personal defenses.* Although the holder in due course is subject to *real defenses,* he or she will be able to enforce the instrument against any other defense or defect. This position is far superior to that of a mere holder or an assignee. A holder or an assignee is subject to any and every defense or defect in the instrument, real or personal.

Personal Defenses

A mere holder, an assignee, or a transferee takes possession of a negotiable instrument subject to every available defense. In contrast, a holder in due course takes the instrument subject only to *real* defenses. The HDC is not subject to personal (sometimes referred to as limited) defenses. A *personal defense* is one that affects the *agreement* for which the instrument was issued. It does *not* affect the *validity* of the instrument. The validity of the instrument is not in question; it is acknowledged to be valid. The underlying agreement is the point of contention. A real defense, on the other hand, questions the legal validity of the instrument.

The most common types of personal defenses are those available on a simple contract. The most common of these contract defenses are failure of consideration, fraud, duress, and breach of warranty. In addition, the holder frequently may be faced with the personal defenses of nondelivery, theft, payment, or any other cancellation.

Most of the simple contract defenses were covered in Part 2 ("The Law of Contracts") and need no further review here. However, fraud does need

[13]Ibid., Section 3-304(5), (6).

some added coverage because negotiable instrument law recognizes two types of fraud. One type, fraud in the *inducement,* is a personal defense. The other type, fraud in the *execution,* is a real defense.

Fraud in the inducement is a personal defense because the fraud committed is a fraud related to the *agreement.* The maker or drawer *intentionally* and *knowingly* issues a negotiable instrument to the payee. However, this issue is made to support an underlying agreement, and the agreement is based on fraudulent representations. The underlying contract is voidable because of the fraud, but the instrument is valid, subject only to a personal defense.

Of the other personal defenses not based on simple contract defenses, only one will be covered here. Nondelivery of the instrument needs special treatment. (The rest are covered in Chapter 26, in the section on discharge.) To issue an instrument, the maker or drawer must *deliver* the instrument to the payee or to an authorized representative of the payee. If the payee gains possession of the instrument without the knowledge or consent of the maker or drawer, the defense of nondelivery is available against a mere holder. Another type of nondelivery occurs when the maker or drawer gives the payee possession, but with a condition attached before delivery is effective. The condition may be that the payee perform some act, which is then not performed. Technically, delivery never occurred because the condition was never satisfied, and the defense of nondelivery can be raised as a personal defense.

Real Defenses

A *real defense,* sometimes referred to as a universal defense, *challenges the validity of the instrument itself.* If a real defense can be established, the negotiable instrument is voided by operation of law, and no one can enforce the instrument. Thus, even a holder in due course will lose to a real defense. It should be kept in mind that if a maker or drawer alleges a real defense, the maker or drawer must establish the defense as real. A failure to do so will normally still leave a valid personal defense, but such a defense will not prevail against a holder in due course.

Section 3-305 of the UCC lists five potential types of real defenses. These defenses are covered in the following sections.

Infancy   The first real defense is infancy, but only "to the extent that it is a defense to a simple contract."[14] To determine whether infancy is a real defense, state law must be examined. If the statutes in the state where the instrument is issued allow infancy to be asserted as a defense to the underlying contract, the infancy may also be raised as a real defense on the instrument. Even if state law does not give such a broad defense, it is still useful as a personal defense; however, a holder in due course can override that defense.

Other Incapacity, Duress, or Illegality   The second real defense is "such other incapacity, or duress, or illegality of the transactions, as renders the obligation

[14]Ibid., Section 3-305(2)(a).

of the party a nullity."[15] Again, the relevant state law will be controlling. If the state statutes void the transaction, the instrument also is voided. If not, the defense is merely personal in nature. An example would be the issuance of a check to pay a gambling debt. If gambling agreements are illegal in the state, a defense exists on the instrument, but it is probably only a personal defense. However, if the check contains a notation that it is meant as payment for a gambling debt, the defense becomes real. The instrument itself now reflects the illegality.

Other types of illegality that might affect a negotiable instrument, and hence operate as a real defense on the instrument, include usury, agreements that violate public policy, and attempting to do business in a state when not licensed to do so. In the following case, a merchant was conducting business in a state where the merchant was not licensed. Notice how the court handles the defense in the case.

Pacific National Bank v. Hernreich
398 S.W.2d 221 (Ark. 1966)

FACTS Hernreich operated a jewelry store in Fort Smith, Arkansas. He would periodically purchase diamonds from salesmen of the Sebel Company, a foreign corporation that was not licensed to do business in the state of Arkansas. Sebel then would discount the notes Hernreich signed when he purchased the diamonds, selling them to Pacific National Bank.

Hernreich executed three notes in early 1963, payable to the order of Sebel. Sebel then sold the notes to the bank. Shortly thereafter Sebel died, and the company was dissolved. When the notes came due, Hernreich refused to pay them.

ISSUE Can a holder in due course of promissory notes collect the notes from the maker despite the illegality of the execution of the notes?

HOLDING No. The illegality affecting these notes was a real defense and as such will defeat the claims of a holder in due course.

REASONING An Arkansas statute states that any foreign corporation that fails to properly register to do business within the state of Arkansas cannot make any contracts in the state, and any alleged contracts so entered cannot be enforced in either law or equity. The promissory notes Hernreich signed were contracts entered into with an unregistered corporation—Sebel Company. As such these notes were void *ab initio*, and the status of the bank as a holder in due course is irrelevant.

Ab initio From the beginning.

Fraud The third real defense is fraud in the *execution*. In this defense, the maker or drawer must prove two things: (1) lack of knowledge of the instruments signed and (2) no reasonable opportunity to discover the nature or

---

[15]Ibid., Section 3-305(2)(b).

terms of the instrument.[16] To establish this defense, the maker or drawer must *prove* that discovering the nature of the signed instrument was not reasonable at the time of signing. Such proof will be virtually impossible unless the signing person is either illiterate or is involved in a strange set of circumstances. The following hypothetical case illustrates such a setting.

Freddy Hornet, a famous rock musician, was signing autographs outside a theater after a performance. Sonya Smith, among others, shoved a paper in front of Freddy for him to sign. However, the paper she shoved was a promissory note, payable to her order, for $50,000. Freddy signed it without reading it, and Sonya left the theater area. Sonya later sued Freddy to collect the money called for in the note.

If Freddy can prove these facts, he will have a real defense and will not have to pay the note.

Discharge in Insolvency   The fourth real defense is a "discharge in insolvency proceedings."[17] This area basically refers to a discharge in bankruptcy proceedings. Bankruptcy is a federally guaranteed *privilege,* and federal law prevails over conflicting state law. The federal bankruptcy law discharges the enforceability of the instrument, creating a statutory real defense on the instrument. (Bankruptcy is covered in Chapter 31.)

Other Discharges   The final real defense is "any other discharge of which the holder has notice when he takes the instrument."[18] This defense is misleading. Referring to it as a real defense is probably improper in theory, if not in fact. To be a holder in due course, a holder cannot have notice of any problems, defenses, or defects in the instrument. If the holder has notice, the holder cannot qualify as an HDC. Thus, the notice referred to in the Code defeats HDC status. Having this notice has the same effect as a real defense, but it is really a denial of holder in due course protection. This means that since the holder has notice, he cannot be an HDC; but *if* he were an HDC, he would lose since he faces a real defense.

In addition to the real defenses, a maker or drawer can avoid liability on an instrument against an HDC under two other circumstances. Once circumstance may afford total avoidance: Section 4-404 states that an *unauthorized* signature is wholly inoperative against the person whose name is signed unless that person ratifies the signing or is not allowed to deny its validity. Thus, a forgery is a possible defense against even a holder in due course.

The other circumstance may afford partial avoidance: Section 4-407 states that if an instrument is materially *altered* through no fault of the maker or

---

[16]Ibid., Section 3-305(2)(c).
[17]Ibid., Section 3-305(2)(d).
[18]Ibid., Section 3-305(2)(e).

drawer, an HDC may enforce it as originally issued (the alteration is a real defense to the extent altered). If the alteration is due to the fault of the maker or drawer, the defense is merely personal and cannot be asserted against a holder in due course.

In the following case, the court had to deal with a material alteration, in the form of an unauthorized completion of a note, and the rights of a holder in due course of the note in question.

Virginia Capital Bank v. *Aetna Casualty & Surety Company*
343 S.E.2d 81 (Va. 1986)

FACTS   Paul Tibbs, doing business as Paul's Auto Sales, had a long-standing course of dealings with Virginia Capital Bank and Mathews General Insurance Company. Tibbs purchased business insurance from Mathews, borrowing money from the bank to finance the premium. Tibbs normally signed, in blank, a promissory note on the bank's form and delivered the form to Mathews. Mathews then calculated the premiums and interest, completed the note, and delivered the note to the bank. The bank advanced the money called for in the note to Mathews, and Tibbs paid the note. Tibbs conducted business with Mathews and the bank in this manner from 1958 to 1980. In March, 1980, Tibbs signed a blank note form and delivered the note to Mathews, who told Tibbs the note would be for approximately $960. However, Mathews filled the note in for $9600 principal and $696 interest, endorsed the note in his business name, and presented the note to the bank. The bank paid Mathews $9600 and took possession of the note. Tibbs made a few payments on the note and then informed the bank that the note had been completed improperly and he (Tibbs) was not making any more payments.

ISSUE   Could the bank enforce the note against the maker and/or the payee as presented?

HOLDING   Yes. The bank was a holder in due course, and the alteration in this case provided a mere personal defense.

REASONING   Tibbs as the maker and Mathews as the endorser/presenter of the note both are liable to the bank for the note as presented. The bank is an HDC, and the alteration here provides a personal defense, so the bank must seek its remedies from the other parties to the negotiation. (The bank had sued its insurer for payment under its banker's blanket bond policy, but the insurer denied liability under the policy. The court agreed that the policy did not cover this situation, but that the bank was protected by the provisions of the UCC and the protections afforded an HDC in this situation.)

STATUTORY LIMITATIONS

The protected status given to holders in due course makes abuses possible. If a payee obtains an instrument by wrongful means and then negotiates it to an HDC, the maker or drawer will nearly always be obliged to pay the instrument. As will be seen in the next chapter, the maker or drawer can sue the payee to recover the money paid. However, the payee must be *found* to be sued. And the finding may not be easy. If the payee and the "HDC" are working together, the maker or drawer is easily taken, usually with no chance of recovering.

Because of this potential, the Federal Trade Commission (FTC) passed a regulation in 1976 designed to protect *consumers*. This regulation modifies the holder in due course rules in some circumstances. If a consumer credit transaction is involved, the instrument used must contain the following notice, printed prominently:

ANY HOLDER OF THIS CONSUMER CREDIT CONTRACT IS SUBJECT TO ALL CLAIMS AND DEFENSES WHICH THE DEBTOR COULD ASSERT AGAINST THE SELLER OF GOODS OR SERVICES OBTAINED PURSUANT HERETO OR WITH THE PROCEEDS HEREOF. RECOVERY HEREUNDER BY THE DEBTOR SHALL NOT EXCEED AMOUNTS PAID BY THE DEBTOR HEREUNDER.

The effect of the rule is to make even an HDC subject to any defenses available against the payee, which is a tremendous protection for the consumer. This rule may have a great impact on the use of consumer credit contracts in the future.

If the notice is present in a consumer credit transaction, any holder of the instrument has agreed *by the terms of the instrument* to remain subject to any defenses of the maker or drawer. This means that a consumer could avoid payment to any HDC in possession of the instrument if the consumer could avoid payment to the payee.

Unfair trade practice Conduct not previously considered improper under the law but now prohibited by the Federal Trade Commission in the interest of the general public.

If the notice is not included in a consumer credit transaction, an **unfair trade practice** is involved. The consumer can file suit against any holders who are deemed to have committed an unfair trade practice for all damages involved.

The following case is one the consumer probably would have lost before the passage of the FTC rule.

Jefferson Bank & Trust Co. v. Stamatiou
384 So.2d 388 (La. 1980)

FACTS   Stamatiou purchased a truck from Key Dodge, signing a chattel mortgage and sale agreement. The agreement included a promissory note and the FTC clause that preserves the consumer debtor's rights against subsequent holders in due course. The agreement also specified that the note was to be assigned to Jefferson Bank & Trust Co. Shortly after the sale, Stamatiou alleged that the truck had become inoperable. As a result, he notified Key Dodge and Jefferson Bank that he wanted to rescind the contract. Jefferson Bank later instituted this lawsuit against Stamatiou for the unpaid loan amount, alleging that Stamatiou used the truck as business equipment and not as a consumer good.

ISSUE   Is the FTC clause preserving defenses in consumer credit sales valid in a nonconsumer credit transaction?

HOLDING   Yes. If the clause is included in the agreement, it is a part of the contract despite the debtor's status.

REASONING   Freedom of contract is a right of the parties. They can include any contractual clauses they desire. The mere fact that Jefferson Bank later argued that the clause was not meant to apply except for consumer credit contracts is immaterial. They put it in; they must honor it. The defenses that could be asserted against Key Dodge can also be asserted against Jefferson Bank. The bank was put on notice by the terms of the contract that any defenses good against Key Dodge were also good against the Bank.

SUMMARY

A negotiable instrument can be transferred in a number of ways. The original transfer from the maker or the drawer is an issue. Once issued, it can be further transferred by assignment or by negotiation. An assignment gives the assignee no special rights or protections. In contrast, a negotiation may confer some individual rights on the recipient. When a negotiation occurs, the transferee becomes a holder.

Most negotiations involve the use of an endorsement. Endorsements may affect further negotiation, and they may affect liability of the parties. Special, blank, and restrictive endorsements affect negotiations. Qualified and unqualified endorsements affect liability.

Once a negotiation occurs, the holder has the opportunity to achieve the most favored status in commercial paper: He or she may become a holder in due course. A holder in due course is a holder who takes an instrument in good faith, for value, and without notice of any defenses or defects on the instrument. A holder in due course can defeat a personal defense. A real defense will defeat a holder in due course.

The Federal Trade Commission enacted a special rule in 1976 to protect consumers. The rule denies any protection against any defenses, even for an HDC, on a consumer credit instrument.

DISCUSSION QUESTIONS

1. Why is the distinction between assignments and negotiations so important?

2. How can a holder endorse an instrument to minimize his or her potential secondary liability?

3. Arnita issued Carol a check payable to the order of Carol. Carol sold the check to Lynn, but neglected to endorse it. At this point, what is Lynn's legal status? What duty, if any, does Carol owe to Lynn?

4. Terry issued a check to Phil. Phil endorsed the check and delivered it to Irene. The name of the payee on the check had originally been Ben, but Terry had crossed out Ben's name and replaced it with Phil's name. To show what he had done, Terry initialed the changed payee. Under these circumstances, can Irene be a holder in due course?

5. Ann is in possession of a check that Dan issued to her. She would like to mail the check to her bank, to be deposited to her checking account. How should she endorse the check to give herself maximum protection, and why does such an endorsement give maximum protection?

6. Lloyd has a promissory note originally issued by

Randy. However, Lloyd is afraid Randy might default on the note when it comes due. Jim is willing to buy the note from Lloyd. Is there a way for Lloyd to endorse the note to minimize his potential loss if Randy dishonors the note?

7. Denise issued the following check to Bill:

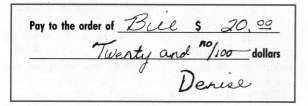

Pay to the order of *Bill* $ *20.00*

Twenty and no/100 dollars

Denise

Bill adds the number 2 before the "20.00" and adds the words *Two Hundred* before the "Twenty." He then negotiates the check to Sarah, an HDC. How much will Denise have to pay Sarah, and why?

8. Charles has a note issued by David. He discovers that David is about to go through a bankruptcy, so he negotiates the note to Richard. Richard qualifies as a holder in due course. What are Richard's rights against David?

9. Sam calls on Brenda, asking to demonstrate a new carpet cleaner. After the demonstration, he make his sales pitch, but Brenda refuses to buy. Sam then pulls out a pad of paper and asks Brenda to sign so that Sam "can get paid by the boss for the demonstration." Brenda signs a promissory note. What' defense, if any, can Brenda later assert on the note?

10. John's Television Sales and Service offered credit terms to its customers who desired them. The customer signed a promissory note for the amount of the credit, and after the customer took the television, John sold the signed note to his bank. The notes provided by John did not contain the FTC consumer credit language. If a customer has a personal defense on his or her purchase from John, may the customer raise that defense against the bank as well? Why?

CASE PROBLEMS

1. Higgins executed a promissory note payable to the order of Westerly Hospital. The hospital endorsed the note in blank and negotiated it to a bank, with the hospital guaranteeing payment if Higgins defaulted. Higgins defaulted, the hospital paid the note as guaranteed, and the bank delivered the note to the hospital. The hospital sued Higgins to collect. Higgins contended that the hospital is not a holder and therefore may not sue. Is Higgins correct? (*Westerly Hospital* v. *Higgins*, 256 A.2d 506 [R.I. 1969].)

2. Vanotti agreed to purchase some land in Arizona from a developer. He signed a promissory note for $4400 to cover the purchase. The note gave Vanotti the right to rescind the sale for six months. The developer negotiated the note to Salter. Three months after signing the note, Vanotti decided to rescind the contract. Salter sued Vanotti on the note, claiming that he (Salter) was entitled to payment as a holder in due course. Is Salter correct? Explain fully. (*Salter* v. *Vanotti*, 599 P.2d 962 [Colo. App. 1979].)

3. Affinity Pictures wanted to rent a theatre to exhibit one of its films. Affinity approached Mann Theatres and arranged to rent the Boulevard Theatre for two weeks at a rental of $5442 per week. Saka, one of the film's producers, delivered two checks to Mann as payment of the rental fee. Mann took both checks to its bank. The bank honored one check but dishonored the other. Mann called Saka about the dishonored check, and Saka said the check would be paid the following week. As a result, Mann permitted the second week of occupancy. When the check was again dishonored, Mann sued Saka. Was Mann a holder in due course on the dishonored check? Explain your reasoning. (*Saka* v. *Mann Theatres*, 575 P.2d 1335 [Nev. 1978].)

4. Seinfeld wrote three checks payable to the order of Wolfson. The checks totaled $160,000. Wolfson promised Seinfeld that the checks would not be negotiated, and Seinfeld delivered them to Wolfson. Wolfson immediately deposited the checks to the Wolfson account. At the time of the deposit, the Wolfson account was overdrawn by $57,000. Despite this, Wolfson asked for immediate access to the funds, and the bank honored this request. (Had the bank inquired of Seinfeld's bank about Seinfeld's balance, it would have learned that he had only $2000 on deposit.) Wolfson withdrew the funds deposited, and Seinfeld's bank dishonored the checks on presentment. Wolfson's bank has sued Seinfeld for the total of the checks, alleging that it is an HDC. Sein-

feld answered that he had been subjected to fraud in the inducement. Furthermore, since the bank had not acted in good faith it was not an HDC and thus was subject to Seinfeld's defense. Had the bank acted in good faith in this case? (*Seinfeld* v. *Commercial Bank & Trust Company*, 405 So.2d 1039 [Fla. App. 1981].)

5. Warnock purchased a cashier's check payable to herself and drawn on the Pueblo Bank. Warnock subsequently endorsed the cashier's check, and her attorney, Quick, wrote below her endorsement "for deposit only." Soon thereafter, Quick deposited the check in an account that he (Quick) maintained at the La Junta Bank. Warnock died two years later, and her estate made demand on the La Junta Bank for the amount of the cashier's check. When the bank refused, the estate sued, claiming that the bank had acted improperly by not honoring the restrictive endorsement on the check (the check was not deposited to Warnock's account). Did the bank ignore the restrictive endorsement and thus make itself liable to the estate? If Quick had not added the words "for deposit only," would a different result occur? (*Travis* v. *La Junta State Bank*, 694 P.2d 350 [Colo. App. 1984].)

6. Dental Supply had an employee who endorsed checks payable to the order of Dental Supply by means of a rubber stamp. The stamp did not restrictively endorse the checks, but endorsed them in blank. The employee cashed thirty-five of the checks that she had stamped rather than deposit them and retained the money for her personal use. When Dental Supply learned what had happened, it sued the bank for conversion of its funds. Is the bank liable to the firm for conversion of the funds? Is the bank liable on any other grounds? Discuss fully (*Palmer & Ray Dental Supply of Abilene, Inc.,* v. *First National Bank*, 477 S.W.2d 954 [Tex. Civ. App. 1972].)

7. Money Mart cashes payroll and government checks for a fee. Epicycle is a Colorado corporation that pays its employees by check. Cronin, an employee of Epicycle, had previously borrowed money from Epicycle, and Epicycle deducted payments from Cronin's pay. In February, Cronin was terminated by Epicycle, but an Epicycle employee who was not aware of the indebtedness issued Cronin his final paycheck for the full amount of his pay, $280, without deducting any amount for his debt. Cronin cashed his check at Money Mart, and Epicycle issued a stop payment order on the paycheck. When Epicycle's bank returned the check "payment stopped," Money Mart sued, claiming to be a holder in

due course. The Superior Court ruled that Money Mart was not a holder in due course because it was in the business of cashing checks and should have verified the validity of the check before cashing it. Was Money Mart an HDC, or did its status as a party that regularly cashed checks for a fee impose a higher standard on it than is imposed on other holders? Explain. (*Money Mart Check Cashing Center, Inc.* v. *Epicycle Corporation*, 677 P.2d 1372 [Colo. 1983].)

8. Murphy issued a check payable to the order of Brownsworth. Brownsworth took the check to Manufacturers Bank seeking a cashier's check to replace the check given to him by Murphy. Manufacturers Bank called the drawee bank to ascertain that the check issued by Murphy was good, received a positive reply, and took the check issued by Murphy as payment for the cashier's check requested by Brownsworth. Murphy subsequently issued a stop payment order on the check. When Manufacturers Bank sued to collect the amount of the check, Murphy asserted that Manufacturers could not be a holder in due course since it lacked good faith in the transaction. As evidence of this lack of good faith, Murphy asserted that Brownsworth was not a regular customer of the bank, so the bank should not have issued a cashier's check in this situation. Does the argument advanced by Murphy establish a lack of good faith? Explain. (*Manufacturers & Traders Trust Co.* v. *Murphy*, 369 F. Supp. 11 [Penn. 1974].)

9. Favor issued a promissory note to Cochise Park as payment for land that Favor was purchasing. As a part of the deal, Cochise Park gave Favor a "Money Back Guarantee and Exchange Agreement" as a separate document. This separate document granted Favor the right to withdraw from the transaction and to receive his promissory note back if he was not satisfied with the sale. Two weeks later Cochise Park sold the note to Yaffe, and then Cochise Park filed for bankruptcy. Favor inspected the land, was dissatisfied with it, and demanded the return of his promissory note according to the separate document's provisions. Yaffe, who knew nothing of the separate document, refused to return the note and sued Favor for the note. What result should occur? Explain. (*Favor* v. *Yaffe*, 605 S.W.2d 342 [Tex. 1980].)

10. Sardou executed and delivered a promissory note to Harvey. Harvey then endorsed the note with the following language: "For valuable consideration, we hereby assign all of our rights title and interest in the within installment note to W. O. Stewart. /s/ Harvey." The

note was defaulted on by Sardou, and Stewart sued Harvey as the endorser of the note. Harvey alleges that the endorsement he used was a qualified endorsement, so he is not liable to Stewart for the default on the note by Sardou. Is the endorsement a qualified endorsement? What are the rights of Stewart and of Harvey in this case? (*Coulter* v. *Stewart,* 379 P.2d 910 [Ariz. 1963].)

C H A P T E R 26

Liability and Discharge

O U T L I N E

BASIC CONCEPTS

Commercial paper is used as a substitute for money. However, at some point, the holder of the paper is going to want the money for which the paper was substituted. This desire normally will lead to a presentment to the maker or drawee. In most cases, the maker or drawee then will pay the money as provided; the instrument will be canceled; and its commercial life will terminate. Unfortunately, such a series of events does not happen every time. Some makers or drawees refuse to pay the presented instrument. When this occurs, the issue of *liability* arises. And some holders inadvertently fail to make a proper presentment. When this occurs, the concept of *discharge* arises.

THE CHAINS OF LIABILITY

The term *liability* refers to an obligation to pay the negotiable instrument involved. There are several possible types of liability in commercial paper. The obligation to pay may be based either on **primary liability** or on **secondary liability**. The liability also may be based on contract principles, warranty principles, or the admissions of one of the parties.

Primary liability Liability of the party to be looked to first for payment.

Primary Parties

Secondary liability Liability of parties on a negotiable instrument upon default by the primary party.

The *maker* of a note is the primary party on that note. It is the maker to whom the holder will look first for payment, and the maker is expected to pay. The *drawee* is the primary party on a check or a draft. It is the drawee to whom the holder will look first for payment, and the drawee is expected to pay.

A substantial difference exists between the position of the primary party on a note and that of a primary party on a check or a draft. On a note, the maker is primarily liable as soon as the note is issued. This is because the primary party, the maker, is also the person who gives the promise to pay. The maker is in a contractual relationship with the payee on issue of the instrument. By contrast, the drawee is not primarily liable on a check or a draft until a holder makes *presentment* and the drawee accepts the instrument as presented. This is because two contractual relationships are involved in order paper: the contract between the drawer and the payee and the contract between the drawer and the drawee. The contractual relationship between the drawee and the payee does not exist until the drawee accepts the instrument, thereby agreeing to honor the order of the drawer. Thus, a note has primary liability from issue, but a check or a draft has a mere *expectation* that primary liability will exist at a future time.

Secondary Parties

The *drawer* of a check or a draft and the *endorsers* of any negotiable instrument are secondary parties on that instrument. Secondary parties face potential secondary liability on an instrument. A secondary party agrees, by acting either as the drawer or as the endorser, to pay the instrument *if certain condition are met*. To hold a secondary party liable, a person holding the instrument must prove three things: (1) *presentment* was properly made, (2) the primary party *dishonored* the instrument, and (3) *notice* of the dishonor was properly given to the secondary party. In addition, each secondary party faces certain warranty liabilities by virtue of being a secondary party. These liabilities will be discussed later in this chapter.

Presentment

Clearinghouse Device or association for the adjustment and payment of daily balances between banks in a city.

Presentment is *a demand for acceptance or for payment* of a negotiable instrument. The demand is made to the maker, the drawee, or the acceptor of the instrument by the presenter. The presentment can be made through a **clearinghouse** or at a place specified in the instrument. If the presentment is made through the mail, presentment occurs when the mail is *received*. This puts the danger of postal delay on the presenting party. If the presentment is to be made at a specified place and if the person who is to receive it is not there at the proper time, presentment is excused. This removes the danger of drawee or maker absence from the presenter. If a note is payable at a bank in the United States or a draft is to be accepted at such a bank, the note or draft must be presented at that bank.[1]

The rules of presentment are very important, because presentment must be made before a dishonor can be shown. And dishonor must be shown before any secondary party (except the drawer) can be held on his or her liability. The only exception to this rule is if presentment is *excused*.

The rules that govern presentment are fairly straightforward. Section 3-503 of the UCC explains the *time* for presentment: The holder must make presentment within a reasonable time, or the presentment is improper. The reasonable time concept has two components: the time must be reasonable in both a *clock* sense (time of day) and a *calendar* sense (day of the week).

In every case, presentment must be made at a reasonable time of day— that is, during normal working hours. An alleged presentment made at a bank or business address at three o'clock in the morning would be improper and would not be effective to prove a dishonor.

The clock concept is obvious, but the calendar one is a little confusing. If the instrument is *not* a check, the proper time for presentment is determined by the language of the instrument. According to UCC Section 3-503(1):

1. If the instrument is payable at, or a specific time after, a stated date, presentment for acceptance must be made *on* or *before* the date set for payment.

2. If the instrument is payable after sight, it must be presented for accep-

---

[1]Uniform Commercial Code, Section 3-504(1), (2), (4).

tance (establishing "sight") within a reasonable time of its date or its issue, whichever is later.

3. If a date for payment is specified, presentment must be made on *that date*.

4. If the instrument is accelerated, presentment is due within a reasonable time after the acceleration.

Certified Assured in writing that the instrument has been accepted by the bank and that payment will be made on proper presentment.

In contrast, the holder of a check must abide by different rules, unless the check has been **certified**. The holder must present the check to the drawee bank within thirty days of its date or its issue, whichever is later, to hold the drawer liable *on that check*. A delay beyond this thirty-day period will not excuse the drawer from liability. Such a delay will merely excuse the liability on that particular check. The drawer may be forced to redeem the check by paying cash or by issuing a new negotiable instrument to replace the original check. A second time limit is also involved with an uncertified check: The check must be presented within seven days of an endorsement to retain the liability of the endorser. Thus, a check presented within thirty days of its issue but more than seven days after an endorsement could be enforced against the drawer, but not against the endorser.

Once presentment is made, the focus shifts to the maker, drawee, or acceptor. If the presentment is made for *acceptance,* the drawee has until the close of business the next business day to accept the instrument. And if the holder agrees in good faith, another business day may be granted to the drawee to decide whether to accept the instrument.[2] If the presentment is made for *payment,* the drawee, acceptor, or maker may delay paying the instrument until an investigation is made to decide that payment would be proper. However, payment must be made *before* the close of the business day on which the presentment was made.[3] Any delay beyond these time limits is treated as a dishonor of the instrument presented.

Persons receiving a presentment do have some protection. They can require some proof from the presenter of the presenter's right to have the check; and requesting these proofs is *not* treated as a dishonor. They can require the presenter to show them the instrument. They can demand reasonable identification of the presenter. They can require a showing of authority to make the presentment. They can demand the surrender of the instrument upon payment in full. If the presenter fails or refuses to comply with any of these requests, the presentment is considered improper. However, the presenter is allowed a reasonable time to comply with any of the requests.[4]

The importance of presentment is illustrated in the following case.

[2]Ibid., Section 3-506(1).
[3]Ibid., Section 3-506(2).
[4]Ibid., Section 3-505.

Estate of Kohlhepp v. *Mason*
478 P.2d 339 (Utah 1970)

FACTS Hannah Kohlhepp died testate on 3 January 1969. Her will was admitted to probate on 28 January 1969. Mervin Holt was the executor of the estate, as provided in the will. One of the provisions of the will gave Hal Mason the right to purchase a dry farm owned by Kohlhepp on Kohlhepp's death, if he so desired. The purchase price specified in the will was $10,000. On 7 April 1969, Mason filed a notice of his intent to purchase the dry farm. On 29 August 1969, Holt unilaterally determined that a reasonable time for the purchase had expired. Holt notified Mason that he had twenty-five days to deposit $10,000 with the court, or he would be presumed to have withdrawn his intent to purchase. Following further negotiations and hearings, Mason was given a deadline of 7 November 1969 at 5:00 P.M. to deposit the $10,000 with Holt. If the funds were so deposited, Holt was to execute and deliver a deed to Mason; if no such deposit was made, Mason's rights under the will would terminate. Mason was able to deposit an uncertified check with the court clerk by the deadline. The following Monday, Holt sent his secretary to pick up the check for his endorsement and presentment. The secretary (apparently of her own volition) asked the drawee bank if the check would be paid on that date if presented. The bank stated that, as of that date, the check would not be honored, and the bank put a notation on the check: "Drawn against uncollected funds." The secretary returned to Holt's office without the check, but with a photocopy of the check with the notation. At that point, Holt sent a letter to Mason and to his lender stating that since the check had been dishonored on presentment, Mason had breached his court-imposed duty, and his rights were terminated. Mason objected to this interpretation, and the cause of action began.

ISSUE Had the check been dishonored on proper presentment?

HOLDING No. The check was never properly presented, so there was no dishonor.

REASONING Presentment is a demand for acceptance or payment made on the maker, acceptor, or drawee by or on behalf of the holder. In this case Holt never took possession of the check, never endorsed it, and never presented it to the bank for payment or acceptance. There was no evidence that his secretary was empowered to act on his behalf, nor that the secretary actually demanded payment or acceptance. A check itself is not an assignment of funds, but it operates as a suspension of the underlying obligation until presentment. In this case Mason deposited the check by the deadline, as required, and therefore met his obligation. Since there was no showing of presentment, there is no evidence that he was not ready, willing, and able to perform on presentment. Mason must be given a reasonable time to pay the $10,000.

Acceptance

When the drawee decides to accept an instrument, the drawee must sign the instrument. *By signing the draft or check, the drawee agrees to honor the instrument as presented.* This act of *acceptance* fixes the primary liability of the drawee. (An order instrument has no primary liability until it has been accepted by the drawee.)

The acceptance can be made even if the instrument is incomplete, but it must be made for the instrument as presented. Suppose the drawee tries to change the terms of the draft in the acceptance. The presenter can treat this as a dishonor or can agree to the changed terms. However, if this **draft-varying**

Draft-varying acceptance A purported acceptance, valid only if the presenter will agree to terms not included in the instrument itself.

FIGURE 26.1 The Chains of Liability

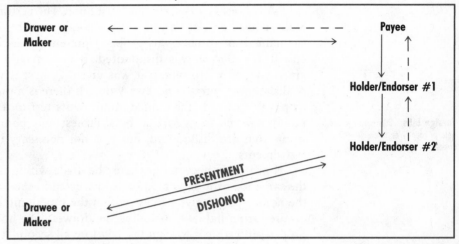

The (potential) primary liability moves in a *clockwise* manner, following the solid lines. Upon dishonor, the holder is thrown into the secondary chain of liability. Secondary liability moves in a *counterclockwise* manner, following the dotted lines. It should be remembered that this is only an illustration and that there could be more or fewer holders/endorsers than are shown here. It should also be noted that the *maker* occupies the positions of both the drawer and the drawee.

acceptance is agreed to by the presenter, the drawer and every endorser are discharged from secondary liability.

Dishonor

An instrument is *dishonored* when *proper presentment is made, and acceptance and/or payment is refused.* A dishonor also occurs when presentment is excused and the instrument is not accepted or paid.[5] (Under UCC Section 3-507(3), the return of an instrument for lack of a proper endorsement is *not* a dishonor.) The failure of the primary party to accept the instrument within the proper time is also a dishonor. A check returned because of insufficient funds or because of a stop payment order is dishonored. A refusal by the primary party is a dishonor. Dishonor is a *denial* of primary liability, and it activates the secondary liability of endorsers and of the drawer (see Figure 26.1). Remember that before dishonor, the secondary parties faced only *potential* secondary liability. The act of dishonor may, and usually will, move this liability from potential to actual.

Protest

Once an instrument is dishonored, the holder is thrown into the secondary chain of liability (see Figure 26.1). Following the secondary chain involves going back to prior holders to recover the amount of the instrument. However, in order to follow the secondary chain, the holder must follow certain steps.

[5]Ibid., Section 3-507.

One of these steps involves *protest,* although this particular step is fairly rare. A protest is a *certificate* of dishonor. The certificate is made by a United States consul or vice-consul or by a notary public.[6] The certificate states that the named instrument was properly presented (or that presentment was excused) and that it was dishonored. It also may state that notice has been given and, if so, to whom it was given. Protest is not needed in every case of dishonor. Protest is necessary only if there is a dishonor on a draft drawn or payable outside the United States or its territories. These drafts are commonly referred to as **foreign bills.** Protest may be used on any other instruments that are dishonored, but it is not necessary on any other dishonored instruments.

Foreign bills Bills drawn in one state or country on a foreign state or country.

If protest is necessary, it must be made within the proper time (which is the same for protest as for notice, discussed in the following section). Should the holder fail to give protest within the time limit, *all* secondary parties are excused from liability, including the drawer. The holder who fails to make a proper protest on a foreign bill will lose all secondary claims and will end up collecting nothing on the instrument.

Notice

When the dishonored instrument is drawn and payable in the United States or its territories and possessions, no protest is required. However, the holder still has an obligation. The holder must give *notice* to prior parties in order to establish their secondary liabilities. The notice may be given to any or all persons who may be liable on the instrument. And it may be given *by* any person who has received notice, in addition to the holder.[7]

The notice may be given in any reasonable manner. It may be written or oral. It may be given in any terms or in any form, as long as it adequately *identifies the instrument* and *states that it was dishonored.*[8] The UCC is concerned with the rights of the holder. Allowance is even made for an error in the description of the instrument in the notice. A **misdescription** will not affect the validity of the notice unless it misleads the person being notified.

Misdescription Error or falsity in the description of the subject matter that is misleading on a material point.

Midnight deadline Midnight of the next banking day following the banking day on which the relevant item or notice is received.

The notice must be given in a timely manner. A bank must give notice before its **midnight deadline.** The holder of a dishonored instrument must give notice by midnight of the third business day following dishonor. Finally, a prior party who has received notice has three business days after receiving notice to give notice to holders prior to his or her possession.[9]

The following case shows what can happen to a bank that fails to act within its time limits.

[6]Ibid., Section 3-509(1).
[7]Ibid., Section 3-508(1).
[8]Ibid., Section 3-508(3).
[9]Ibid., Section 3-508(2).

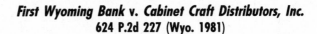

First Wyoming Bank v. Cabinet Craft Distributors, Inc.
624 P.2d 227 (Wyo. 1981)

FACTS Quality Kitchens delivered a $10,000 check to Cabinet Craft as payment on account. Cabinet Craft deposited the check with Security Bank in Billings, Montana. Security Bank then placed the check in the bank collection system. The check moved through the system to First Wyoming Bank, the drawee. First Wyoming then sent the check by courier to the computer center for processing. The courier arrived at the computer center with the check, but decided not to await the processing due to flooding of the main road back to First Wyoming's locale. The check was returned to First Wyoming three days later, and First Wyoming dishonored the check due to insufficient funds in the drawer's account. Cabinet Craft sued the bank for the value of the check due to its delay in deciding to dishonor the instrument.

ISSUE Did First Wyoming dishonor the check in a timely manner? If it did not, was its delay in dishonoring the check excused?

HOLDING No to both issues. The check's dishonor was unduly delayed, and the delay was not excused under the Code.

REASONING The UCC allows a bank to delay its dishonor under some circumstances, providing the bank acts with due diligence. However, the bank bears the burden of proving its due diligence in order to take advantage of the excuse. In this case, the bank failed to establish its due diligence for two reasons. First, when the checks were not promptly returned from the computer center, the bank did not make any inquiries as to the location of the checks that had been sent there for processing. Second, the courier could have taken a secondary route back from the computer center to the bank even if the main road was indeed flooded. By choosing to have the checks flown back by commercial airline rather than having the courier wait for them and then drive them back as was normally done, the bank acted in a less than diligent manner. The bank's delay was unexcused, and the bank therefore is liable for the check.

It is normal for each party to give notice to his or her immediate transferor. However, sometimes the transferor cannot be found or, when found, cannot pay. For that reason, a holder should give notice to every prior party who can be located. This increases the chances that the holder eventually will recover on the dishonored instrument.

A failure to give proper or timely notice will operate as a release from the conditional secondary liability for all the secondary parties *except* the drawer. It should be observed that this is different from the rule on protests. An improper protest releases the drawer along with the other parties, but improper notice does not release the drawer.

Frequently, the duty to make presentment or to give protest or notice is *waived* or *excused*. When these situations arise, Section 3-511 of the Code controls. A delay in giving notice or protest is excused when the party is unaware that action is needed or when the delay is due to circumstances beyond the control of the holder. However, in the second case, the holder must act with reasonable *diligence* once the cause of the delay passes. This section of the Code may also excuse presentment, protest, or notice completely. A complete excuse will arise under any of the following three circumstances.[10]

1. The party to be charged has expressly or impliedly waived the right.
2. The party to be charged has dishonored the instrument or has no right to expect or to require acceptance or payment.
3. The presentment, protest, or notice cannot be made with reasonable diligence.

LIABILITY

A negotiable instrument is a *contract* with special treatment under the law. One recognition of contract law principles is found in UCC Section 3-401. This section states that "no person is liable on an instrument unless his signature appears thereon." However, once the signature is found, the signing party faces potential liability. The type of liability depends on the capacity in which it was signed. Again, the Code helps. According to Section 3-402, every signature is *presumed* to be an endorsement unless the instrument clearly indicates some other capacity.

The maker of promise paper and the acceptor of order paper give a contract. Each agrees to pay the instrument according to the terms of the instrument at the time of his or her engagement or *as completed* if it was incomplete. The drawer of order paper promises to pay any holder or any endorser the amount of the instrument if it is dishonored.[11]

The endorsers of commercial paper also give a contract by the act of endorsing, unless the endorsement is qualified. By the act of endorsing, the endorser promises that upon dishonor and *proper* notice, he or she will pay the instrument *as endorsed* to any subsequent holder. The endorsers are presumed to be liable to one another on a dishonored instrument in the order endorsed, moving from bottom to top.[12]

Two other parties *may* be involved in contractual liability on commercial paper: the accommodation party and the guarantor. Each of these parties has special potential contract liability. An *accommodation party* is a person who signs an instrument to "lend his name," or his credit, to another party. He signs as a favor, usually without getting anything out of the transaction. The accommodation party is liable to subsequent parties in the capacity in which he signed.[13] If required to pay because of his secondary liability, he is entitled to recover from the accommodated party.

[10]Ibid., Section 3-511(2).
[11]Ibid., Section 3-413(1), (2).
[12]Ibid., Section 3-414.
[13]Ibid., Section 3-415.

A *guarantor* is a person who adds the words "payment guaranteed," or their equivalent, to a signature on an instrument. A guarantor waives the need for presentment, protest, or notice and waives any protection under the Statute of Frauds. A guarantor promises to pay the holder for a dishonored instrument without the need to go to any other party.[14]

In addition to the basic contract liabilities just discussed, persons who present or transfer negotiable instruments make certain *warranties*. These warranties carry with them the possibility of liabilities also, and warranty liabilities cannot be disclaimed as contract ones can. An endorser may deny contract liability by the use of a qualified endorsement. But warranty liability is still present even if the endorsement is qualified, unless the qualified endorsement specifically excludes warranties. An endorser could qualify the endorsement so that warranties are also excluded, even though endorsing with such a qualification to later holders makes the endorsement highly unusual. The endorser who would use such an endorsement would be well protected, but the instrument would be very difficult to transfer since few subsequent holders would be willing to accept such a negotiation.

The warranties involved in commercial paper are set out in Section 3-417 of the UCC. There are two major categories of warranties: *presentment* warranties and *transfer* warranties. Presentment warranties are fairly simple. Any person who obtains acceptance or payment, and any prior transferor, warrants the following facts to the acceptor or payor:[15]

1. The person has good title, or is authorized to act by a person with good title, to obtain acceptance or payment.
2. The person has no *knowledge* that the signature of the maker or of the drawer is unauthorized.
3. The instrument has not been materially altered.

In transfer warranties, any person who transfers an instrument *for consideration* warrants the following facts to the transferee:[16]

1. The person has good title, or is authorized by a person having good title, to make the transfer.
2. All signatures are genuine or authorized.
3. The instrument has not been materially altered.
4. No defenses of any party are good against the transferor.
5. The person has no *knowledge* of any insolvency proceedings that affect the instrument.

[14]Ibid., Section 3-416.
[15]Ibid., Section 3-417(1).
[16]Ibid., Section 3-417(2).

In addition, if the transfer is made by means of an endorsement, the endorser gives the transfer warranties to any and all subsequent good-faith holders. The only variation in the transfer warranties arises when the transfer is made by means of a qualified endorsement. In that case, the qualified endorser gives all the same warranties *except* for the one that concerns defenses (item 4). Qualified endorsers warrant only that they have no *knowledge* of any defenses that are good against them, not that there are no defenses.[17]

SPECIAL PROBLEMS

Imposters Persons who assume the identity or title of another for the purpose of deception.

Figure 26.2 summarizes the order of liability on a negotiable instrument. As was pointed out earlier, a person's signature must appear on an instrument before that person can be held liable on the instrument. Thus, a forgery or an unauthorized signature is normally of no legal effect. However, an unauthorized signature can be *ratified* by the named person, and it then becomes fully effective.[18] In some circumstances, **imposters** can sign, and the signature is fully effective. Under Section 3-405, an imposter may sign the name of the *payee* if he induced the maker or drawer to issue the instrument to him thinking he was the payee. This is known as the *imposter rule*. A similar set of facts leads to the *fictitious-payee rule*. Under this rule, the maker or drawer is induced to issue a check or a note to a named payee. However, the payee who is named has no right to the instrument and did not know of its issuance. The person who induced the issuance may sign for the "fictitious payee," and the signature is fully effective.[19] The following hypothetical cases illustrate these two special problem areas.

Fred stole a radio from Herb. Fred then approached Thelma, told her that he was Herb, and offered to sell the radio to her. Thelma wrote a check payable to the order of Herb to pay for the radio. Under the imposter rule, Fred may effectively endorse the check by writing Herb's name, UCC Section 3-404 on unauthorized signatures notwithstanding.

Steve worked for Acme. Part of his job was preparing checks to be used in paying bills and then taking those checks to Mr. Burton to be signed for the company. Steve slipped a check payable to Hall and Associates in among the other checks for Mr. Burton to

---

[17]Ibid., Section 3-417(3).
[18]Ibid., Section 3-404(2).
[19]Ibid., Section 3-405(1)(b).

FIGURE 26.2 Liability on a Negotiable Instrument

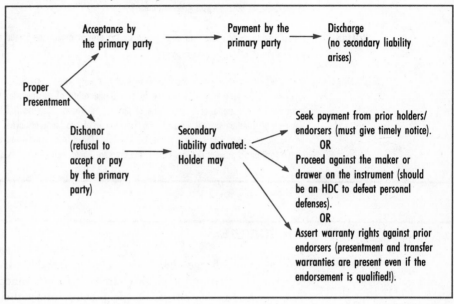

sign. In fact, no money was owed to Hall and Associates. If Steve later removes the phony check and endorses it "Hall and Associates," the endorsement is valid under the fictitious-payee rule, UCC Section 3-404 notwithstanding.

In the following case, the court was faced with an imposter-endorsed check and had to use the imposter rule to resolve the issues.

Philadelphia Title Insurance Co. v. Fidelity-Philadelphia Trust Co.
419 Pa. 78, 212 A.2d 222 (1965)

FACTS Edmund Jezemski and his wife, Paula, were separated and living apart. Edmund was the executor and sole heir of the estate of his mother. Included in the estate was a parcel of real estate in Philadelphia. Paula arranged for a mortgage on this property without the knowledge or the consent of Edmund. Paula arrived at the office of an attorney with a man she introduced as her husband, Edmund. She then executed a deed conveying the property from the estate of Edmund's mother to Paula and Edmund as tenants by the entireties, executed a mortgage from the Title Company, and took a check payable to the order of Paula and Edmund Jezemski from the Title Company. Paula and "Edmund" endorsed the check, and Paula cashed the check, which eventually was paid by Fidelity-Philadelphia Trust Company.

When Edmund learned what had happened, he brought an action to have the mortgage and the deed set aside. The Title Company then sued the bank to recover the amount of the check.

ISSUE	Is the bank liable for paying a check made payable to an imposter and then endorsed by that imposter and presented to the bank in an otherwise proper manner?
HOLDING	No. The issuance of a check to an imposter by the drawer makes the forged endorsement of the imposter effective against the drawer.
REASONING	Normally, a forgery is wholly inoperative against the party whose signature is forged unless ratified by that person. However, an exception exists when the forgery is the result of an imposter who induces the drawer to issue the instrument to the imposter in the name of the person whose signature is forged. The UCC specifically deals with this type of situation so that, in a situation where one of two innocent parties must bear the loss, the loss is placed on the party better able to have prevented the loss. The drawer who issues an instrument to an imposter is in a better position to prevent the loss than is the innocent bank, which merely honors the endorsement of the imposter.

DISCHARGE

The term *discharge* means *to remove liability or potential liability on a negotiable instrument.* A discharge can take place in a number of ways. Some methods discharge all the parties, and others discharge only a few. The most important and most common types of discharge are explained in the following sections.

Payment or Satisfaction

The most common type of discharge is the payment or other satisfaction of the instrument.[20] In the vast majority of cases, the primary party pays the instrument on presentment and cancels it (or otherwise marks it as paid). If this were not so, negotiable instruments would not be so readily accepted in the commercial world.

There are only two exceptions to payment operating as a discharge. A payment will not operate as a discharge when it is made in bad faith to a thief or to a person holding through or after a thief. And it will not operate as a discharge if the paying party makes a payment that violates a restrictive endorsement. (*Note:* An intermediary bank or a nondepository bank *may* be discharged even though it ignores the restrictive endorsement, provided it acts in good faith.) In these examples, the bad faith of the payor does not remove liability. The proper party, the person who should have received payment, is still entitled to payment, and the liability of the wrongfully paying party remains.

Tender of Payment

If a party *tenders payment* in full to a holder *when an instrument is due* or later, and the holder *refuses* the payment, a discharge occurs.[21] The party

---

[20]Ibid., Section 3-603.
[21]Ibid., Section 3-604.

tendering payment is discharged to a limited extent. No additional interest can be added to the instrument after the date of the tender, nor can any other costs or attorney's fees be added to the instrument. Any other parties on the instrument (endorsers, drawers, and the like) are *totally* discharged if, to collect on the instrument, they could theoretically have sued the party who made the tender of payment.

Cancellation and Renunciation

A holder may discharge a party by canceling that party's signature on the instrument or by canceling the instrument itself.[22] Cancellation may be shown either by striking out a portion, such as one signature, or by striking out the entire instrument. It can also be shown by destroying or mutilating a signature or the entire instrument. To be effective, the cancellation must be done intentionally.

Renunciation operates as a discharge whenever the holder *delivers a written* and *signed* statement to the discharged party that renounces (gives up) any rights against that person.[23] Such a discharge is good against the renouncing party but not against any later holders, unless they were aware of the renunciation.

Impairment

Under the UCC Section on impairment, a holder may elect to release some party from liability on the instrument.[24] Or a holder may decide to release some *collateral* that is being used to secure payment of the instrument. However, in so doing, the holder also will discharge some or even all of the secondary parties on the instrument. When the holder releases a particular prior party, the holder also releases any *other* prior party who might have had recourse against the originally released party. And when a holder releases collateral, the holder releases *every* prior party, since each prior party might have had recourse against the collateral. There are only two exceptions to these rules:

1. If a prior party agrees to the release of another party or to a release of the collateral, the agreeing party is not discharged by the release.
2. If the holder *expressly* reserves rights against a party, that party is not released or discharged. However, the releases by the holder are also *not* effective as far as the nondischarged party is concerned. In other words, the party who was expressly not discharged does not have any change in his or her position.

Table 26.1 summarizes the main types of discharge.

[22]Ibid., Section 3-605.
[23]Ibid.
[24]Ibid., Section 3-606.

TABLE 26.1   Discharges of a Negotiable Instrument

COMPLETE DISCHARGE	PARTIAL DISCHARGE
Payment or satisfaction of the instrument • by the primary party discharges all liability on the instrument. • by a secondary party discharges the liability of the secondary party. Cancellation of the instrument • discharges all liability on the instrument by cancelling the instrument itself.	Tender of payment • cancels secondary liability and establishes the maximum liability of the primary party who tendered payment. Renunciation • cancels rights against the person to whom the discharge is delivered. Cancellation of an Endorsement • cancels the liability of the person whose endorsement has been cancelled. Impairment • cancels the secondary liability of all parties whose rights are impaired unless those parties agree to the release or impairment.

Other Discharges

If a party is a former holder of an instrument and later *reacquires* the instrument, a partial discharge occurs.[25] Any person who held the note *between* the two holdings of the reacquiring party is discharged from liability to the reacquiring party. And if the reacquiring party *strikes out* the endorsements of the intervening persons, they are totally discharged on the instrument. For example, if George holds a note, endorses it to Betty, and then buys it back from Betty, Betty is discharged from liability to George.

A fraudulent material alteration also acts as a discharge.[26] If the alteration is fraudulent and material, any party who does not consent to the alteration is totally discharged from liability under most circumstances. A holder in due course may still enforce the instrument as it was *originally issued* even though it has been materially altered.

Finally, any undue delay in presentment operates as a discharge for all prior endorsers. An undue delay in giving notice of a dishonor will operate as a discharge of all prior endorsers and *may* discharge a drawer or maker. And an undue delay in a *necessary* protest will operate as a discharge of all the prior parties, both endorsers and drawer.[27]

When the delay involves notice, and payment was to be made at a named bank, the drawer or maker may be discharged. However, to be discharged, the following facts must be shown:

[25]Ibid., Section 3-208.
[26]Ibid., Section 3-407.
[27]Ibid., Section 3-502.

1. The bank became insolvent *during the undue delay*.
2. The maker or drawer lost funds held by the bank that were intended to cover the instrument.
3. The maker or drawer assigned in writing his or her rights against the bank for the lost funds to the holder.

SUMMARY

As formal contracts, negotiable instruments carry certain contract responsibilities and liabilities. The maker of promise paper has primary liability. The drawee of order paper faces potential primary liability. Once the drawee accepts an instrument, the drawee has primary liability. If the primary liability is denied or refused, every prior holder is secondarily liable. In addition, the drawer of order paper is secondarily liable on a dishonored instrument.

In order for the holder to enforce the primary liability of the instrument, proper presentment must be made on the maker or drawee. At that point, the primary party will either accept the instrument or dishonor it. If dishonor occurs, the holder will give notice to prior parties to establish their secondary liability. The holders may also be required to give protest, especially on foreign bills.

Negotiable instruments carry both contract liability and warranty liability. The warranty liability may be transfer warranty liability or presentment warranty liability.

The final stage for most instruments is discharge. Discharge can be, and normally is, based on payment or satisfaction. Some discharges are partial, discharging either a portion of the liability or a few of the parties. Tender of payment is a partial discharge. Cancellation, renunciation, and impairment are all discharges of some of the secondary parties.

DISCUSSION QUESTIONS

1. What is the legal consequence of failing to file a formal protest on the dishonor of a foreign bill? Is the result any different if the instrument involved is not a foreign bill?

2. In order to show proper presentment, what must the presenting party establish?

3. There are five transfer warranties. Do they differ when qualified and unqualified endorsements are used? If so, how?

4. Why does the UCC grant a discharge when collateral is impaired? Explain fully.

5. What three options are available to the holder of an instrument that has been dishonored after proper presentment? Under what circumstances should the holder pursue any or all of the options available?

6. Bernie was the holder of a time draft payable on 7 September 19XX. When Bernie looked at his calendar, he saw that September 7 fell on a Sunday. What should Bernie do to establish proper presentment?

7. Bill issued a check to Sarah on 1 June 19XX. Sarah endorsed it over to Mike on June 6, and Mike endorsed it over to Pete on June 10. Pete took the check to the

bank on 8 July 19XX, and the bank dishonored the check. What rights can Pete assert against *each* of the other parties? How should he proceed?

8. Amy transferred a note to Jim by delivery alone. At the time of the transfer, the maker of the note was involved in an insolvency proceeding. Jim was unable to collect the note from the maker. What are his rights against Amy?

9. Joe issued an interest-bearing demand note to Jane.

Jane negotiated the note to Larry. Larry in turn negotiated it to Tom. Joe offered to pay Tom, but Tom refused the payment. What effect does Tom's refusal have on *each* of the other parties?

10. Dan issued a check to Ron. Ron fraudulently raised the amount payable from $100 to $400. He then negotiated the check to Sam, a holder in due course. If the bank dishonors the check, what are Sam's rights against Ron? Against Dan? Explain.

CASE PROBLEMS

1. Kirby agreed to purchase land from Bergfeld and gave Bergfeld a check for $20,000 at the time of closing. Bergfeld took the check to his bank and asked that the cashier telephone Kirby's bank to verify that sufficient funds were on deposit to cover the check. The bookkeeper at Kirby's bank stated that sufficient funds were not on deposit at that time. Bergfeld refused to sell the land to Kirby, and Kirby sued for specific performance of the contract. Had Bergfeld made proper presentment of the check? Had the check been dishonored so that Kirby was in breach? (*Kirby* v. *Bergfeld,* 182 N.W.2d 205 [Neb. 1970].)

2. Cotton issued a negotiable promissory note to Jones in 1955. Over the next twelve years, until the death of Jones in 1967, Cotton made regular payments on the note. After Jones died, a paper was found among his personal effects. The paper called for the cancellation of any unpaid balance on the note Cotton had issued if Jones died before Cotton. Cotton alleged that this paper was a valid renunciation. Jones's estate argued that it was not valid. What should be the result? Explain. (*Greene* v. *Cotton,* 457 S.W.2d 493 [Ky. 1970].)

3. American Music and Disneyland Records entered into a series of contracts. After the contracts were performed, American Music owed Disneyland Records $93,000. To cover this debt, ten promissory notes were issued, payable to Disneyland. Each note was signed by Irv Schwartz individually, with no mention in the notes of American Music. When the notes were not paid, Disneyland sued Schwartz. Schwartz argued that Disneyland should have sued American Music and not Schwartz. What should be the result? Explain fully. (*Schwartz* v. *Disneyland Vista Records,* 383 So.2d 117 [Fla. 1980].)

4. Ridley issued a check payable to the order of Clem-

ents and drawn on his bank in Tennessee. Clements endorsed the check to Continental, and Continental deposited the check to its account at Central Bank. Central mailed the check to the drawee bank in Tennessee, asking the drawee to "Check for collection—Return if not paid in three days." Several days later, Central Bank called the bank in Tennessee and inquired about the check. On being informed that the check was not good, Central Bank asked the drawee to continue to try to collect on the check. One month later, when the amount of the check remained uncollected, the drawee returned it to Central Bank. Central Bank sued Clements for the amount of the check, based on his endorsement. Clements alleged that his liability was discharged by the bank's failure to give him timely notice of the dishonor. What result should occur in this case? Explain your answer. (*Clements* v. *Central Bank of Georgia,* 270 S.E.2d 194 [Ga. App. 1980].)

5. Shea applied to Franklin Bank for a loan so that he could purchase an automobile from his father-in-law, MacMurray. Franklin Bank approved the loan application and issued a check payable to the order of Shea and MacMurray. Shea later presented the check to the Chase Manhattan Bank, and Chase Manhattan paid Shea the face amount of the check in cash. The check as accepted by Chase Manhattan had a forged endorsement purportedly by MacMurray. Chase Manhattan alleges that MacMurray's "endorsement" falls within the imposter rule, but Franklin Bank argues that it is an inoperative forgery. Which bank is correct, and why? (*Franklin National Bank* v. *Chase Manhattan Bank, N.A.,* 328 N.Y.S.2d 25 [1972].)

6. Mobilla endorsed a promissory note "without recourse" and discounted the note to Union Bank. The signature of the maker on the note was a forgery, and

the bank was unable to collect from the maker named on the note. When the bank sued Mobilla, he raised the qualified endorsement as a defense to the bank's action. Should the qualified endorsement of the payee preclude the bank's claim against the payee? On what theory should the bank pursue its remedies? (*The Union Bank v. Mobilla*, 43 Erie Co. Leg. J. 45 [Pa. 1959].)

7. Brufach issued a promissory note payable to the order of Leffingwell. The note called for monthly payments for five years, with the entire unpaid balance and principal due in the sixty-first month. The note also contained an acceleration clause. Eighteen months later, Leffingwell endorsed the note over to Zimmerman. Eventually Brufach defaulted on the note, and Zimmerman sued both Brufach and Leffingwell for the unpaid balance. Leffingwell argued that he should not be held liable for the note since Zimmerman did not proceed first against Brufach. Should Zimmerman be able to collect from Leffingwell in this case? Explain your answer. (*Val Zimmerman Corp. v. Leffingwell*, 318 N.W.2d 781 [Wis. 1982].)

8. Finance Company opened a checking account with National Bank. Over the course of a year, an automobile dealer submitted completed loan applications and promissory notes from its customers to Finance Company. Finance Company issued checks payable to the order of the borrower so that the automobile purchases could be completed. Nine of these "borrowers" were fictitious, and the automobile dealer personally endorsed these nine checks with the names of the alleged "borrowers," presented them to the bank, and received cash for them. When Finance Company discovered this scheme, it demanded that National Bank return the money paid out for these checks. National Bank refused to do so. Ultimately, Finance Company's insurance company paid the losses and then sued the bank as sub-

rogee (person taking the place of) of Finance Company. Is the bank liable for these checks? Explain fully. (*Fidelity and Casualty Company of New York v. Constitution National Bank*, 356 A.2d 117 [Conn. 1975].)

9. Kaiser entered into a lease agreement with Northwest that called for Kaiser to make monthly payments to Northwest for rent, taxes, and maintenance. A controversy arose over the terms of the lease, but Kaiser continued to send Northwest his checks every month. Northwest held these checks without making presentment for some time. Finally, ten months later, Northwest presented all ten checks to the bank. A number of the checks were refused by the bank since they were considered "stale" and because insufficient funds were on deposit at the time. Northwest has demanded payment from Kaiser for these dishonored checks, and Kaiser has asserted that he was discharged from liability due to the undue delay in making presentment. Who should prevail and why? (*Kaiser v. Northwest Shopping Center, Inc.*, 544 S.W.2d 785 [Tex. 1976].)

10. Penn Mutual issued a check payable to the order of Morris. The check was drawn against Penn Mutual's account at Girard Bank. Eventually the check was deposited by Payung at the Mount Holly Bank. The check as deposited contained a forgery of the Morris endorsement and an endorsement by Payung. Mount Holly Bank transferred the check through normal banking channels to Central Penn (which paid Mount Holly the full amount of the check) and on to Girard Bank. Girard paid Central Penn for the check on presentment. Girard has sued Mount Holly for breach of presentment warranties on the check due to the forged endorsement. Mount Holly defended by arguing that the drawer was negligent, and thus Mount Holly is relieved of liability. How should this case be resolved? (*Girard Bank v. Mount Holly Bank*, 474 F. Supp 1225 [1979].)

CHAPTER 27

Bank-Customer Relations

OUTLINE

BASIC CONCEPTS

In the United States today, nearly every business organization has a checking account. In addition, many, if not most, of the adults in this country have checking accounts. Workers receive their pay by check. Checking account information is normally required on credit and loan applications. Millions of checks move through the economic system each day. Yet very few people actually understand this checking system they are using.

A new customer walking into a bank follows the signs that lead to the "New Accounts" desk. Upon sitting down at this desk, the novice depositor is inundated with trivial information and details. Several different types of accounts—interest plus checking, free checking, ready-reserve checking, and so on—are briefly mentioned in passing; multiple colors and styles of checks are displayed; a "signature card" is handed to the customer with instructions to "sign at the X"; a deposit ticket is prepared; and a deposit is made in the customer's name in this new account. Before *really* knowing what has happened, the new customer is back on the street, the proud possessor of a personal checking account. And more likely than not, the customer has no idea of what all this legally means.

By signing a signature card, the customer has entered a multirole legal relationship with the bank. The signature card represents a *contract* that the customer accepts on signing the signature card, even though he or she probably is unaware of any of its terms or conditions. In addition, the customer is now governed by Part 4 of Article 4 of the Uniform Commercial Code, which governs the bank-customer relationship. The customer has entered into an *agency* relationship and has agreed to a *debtor-creditor* relationship, as well.

Service charges Charges imposed by the bank on the customer for the rendering of certain specified services in handling the customer's account.

The contract that the customer entered is relatively simple. It covers such things as **service charges** that can be imposed, minimum balance requirements for the customer's account, and technical terms and conditions. Likewise, the coverage afforded by Article 4 of the Code is fairly simple. Basically, it spells out the *mandatory* rights and duties of each of the parties. These will be dealt with later in the chapter.

The agency portion of the agreement is a complete surprise to most depositors. (Agency is covered in Chapters 33 through 35.) To put it simply, the bank is the *agent* and the depositor is the *principal*. An agent is required to obey any *lawful order* of the principal that deals with the agency. This explains in part the language used on a check. The depositor/principal is *ordering* the agent/bank to "Pay to the order of" someone. The check does not say "Please pay" or "I would appreciate it if you would pay." It says "PAY!" This language is an *order*, and the order is usually lawful. Therefore, the bank must obey that order or face possible liability to the depositor for the disobedience.

The final relationship is variable. Normally, the customer will have a

Overdraft The act of checking out more money than one has on deposit in a bank, which is in the nature of a loan, implying a promise to pay.

positive balance in the checking account. As a result, the customer is a *creditor* of the bank, and the bank is a *debtor* of the customer. Occasionally the bank will pay an **overdraft** on the customer's account. When this happens, the customer has a negative balance in the account, and the roles reverse. Now the bank is a creditor of the customer, and the customer is a debtor to the bank.

THE CUSTOMER: RIGHTS AND DUTIES

Statement A summation of the customer's activities with the account for the period, accompanied by the items paid by the bank in good faith to support the debit entries on the statement.

Stop payment An order issued by the drawer to the drawee that a specified check or draft *not* be paid on proper presentment.

The first and main duty of a customer is to act with due care and diligence. Whether writing a check, inspecting a monthly **statement**, or endorsing a check; whether making a deposit or cashing a check—the customer is required to act in a careful and reasonable manner. If customers remember that it is their money being handled, and that carelessness could cause them to *lose* that money, they are more likely to be careful.

Customers have several rights that they may exercise. They may **stop payment** on a previously issued check, and they may collect damages from the bank if the bank errs in the handling of the account. But before they can exercise these rights, customers must show that they have acted properly and/or that the bank has acted improperly.

For example, suppose that Louis issues a check to pay for some merchandise. The merchant presents the check to the bank for payment, and the bank dishonors the check. Louis is now likely to have some problems with the merchant. He may have to pay the merchant a "handling fee" or a "service charge" for the returned check. He may face a lawsuit filed by the merchant to collect the amount of the check plus costs and interest. And in many states he *may* face a *criminal* charge for passing *hot* (bad) checks.

But what if the dishonor was due to an error by the bank, not to any carelessness or wrongdoing on Louis's part? Louis will still have to settle his own problems with the merchant, but the criminal action will be dropped. And Louis will be able to proceed against the bank for collection of any and all damages he might have suffered in this ordeal.

According to UCC Section 4-402, the bank is liable to its customer for any damages *proximately caused* by a *wrongful* dishonor of the customer's check. The damages expressly covered in the section include the following:

1. damages due to an arrest
2. damages due to a prosecution
3. any other consequential damages that can actually be proved

From this language, it sounds as if the customer will end up in a reasonably good position: The customer will recover the "handling fees," the interest, and any other costs paid to the merchant; the customer will recover any

Proximate cause That which, in a natural and continuous sequence, produces the injury, and without which the injury would not have occurred.

damages related to the arrest; and the bank will end up taking all the losses on this case. In seeking damages from the bank, however, the customer must prove that the bank's conduct was the **proximate cause** of the losses suffered by the customer. Such proof is often difficult. If the bank can show that the customer contributed to the loss, the bank probably will owe nothing, and the customer will collect nothing. The hypothetical case that follows represents the type of problem that might prevent the customer's victory.

Bob had a balance in his checking account of $120.15. He made a deposit on Friday of $900, using a blank deposit slip provided by the bank. In completing the deposit slip, Bob accidentally wrote his account number incorrectly. The following Tuesday, Bob wrote a $500 check to Sam's Stereo to purchase a turntable. Sam took the check to the bank on Wednesday, and the bank returned it unpaid due to insufficient funds. Sam assessed Bob with a $10 service charge and demanded that Bob repurchase the check, along with a 10 percent "interest fee." Sam also filed criminal charges for the "hot check."

Bob paid $100 bail to get out of jail after his arrest, and he paid Sam the $560 in cash to get the proceedings dropped. If Bob now sues the bank, he will learn a shocking lesson. Bob's negligence caused the loss, so the bank is not liable. If Bob had used his own *personalized, precoded* deposit slips, he probably would have won. Since he didn't, he will lose.

The customer also has a right to issue *stop payment* orders to the bank. If done properly, the bank must obey this order to stop payment, or it will face liability to the customer for any damages caused by disobeying the order. To be effective and to be properly made, the order must be given to the bank in a reasonable manner. That is, the bank must receive a *complete* description of the check (number, payee, amount, date, reason) with enough "lead time" to allow the bank to react to the order.[1] A minimum of a few hours will normally be required, and it may take as long as a full banking day to get the word out to the bank's various branch offices.

The customer can give either an *oral* or a *written* stop payment order. If made orally, the order is valid for fourteen calendar days. After fourteen days it expires unless it has been put into writing. A written order is good for six months, and it can be renewed for additional six-month periods.[2] Of course, every renewal will entail another service charge.

If the customer properly gives the bank a stop payment order, and the bank pays the check despite the order, the customer *may* be able to collect damages from the bank. To do so, the customer will have to *prove* that she

[1]Uniform Commercial Code, Section 4-403(1).
[2]Ibid., Section 4-403(2).

suffered damages because the check was paid.[3] To prove this, she will have to show that the presenter could not have collected from her (the customer) *if* payment had been stopped as ordered. If the customer would have lost a case to the presenter, she will not be able to collect any damages from the bank for paying the check despite the stop payment order.

In the following case the court was faced with a rather unusual stop payment order request from a bank's customer.

Thompson Poultry v. First National Bank of New York
255 N.W.2d 856 (Neb. 1977)

FACTS S&H Poultry, Inc. purchased a bank money order from First National Bank of New York on 7 February 1973 and delivered the money order to Thompson Poultry as payment for a load of poultry products. After S&H received the poultry, it decided to go out of business and returned the shipment to Thompson the same day. Thompson refused to return the money order to S&H, and S&H asked First National Bank to stop payment on the bank money order.

ISSUE Can a bank stop payment on a bank money order?

HOLDING No. A bank money order is essentially the same as a cashier's check, and payment cannot be stopped.

REASONING The court ruled that the bank money order was the equivalent of a cashier's check; that is, a bill of exchange drawn by a bank upon itself and accepted in advance by the act of issuance. As such, it is not subject to countermand by either the purchaser or the issuing bank. The court also stated that a bank money order, purchased for adequate consideration, stands by its own foundation as an independent, unconditional, and primary obligation of the bank. Under such circumstances, the bank may not stop payment. The bank money order must be honored by the bank.

Reconcile To make consistent or compatible; to bring into harmony or agreement.

The bank periodically must send statements to its customers. The customer has a duty to examine and to **reconcile** this statement. A failure to do so will result in a waiver of rights in favor of the bank. And the reconciliation must be made *promptly*, since undue delay also operates as a waiver of rights and claims against the bank.[4] The bank satisfies its duty to provide a statement to the customer by mailing it or by holding it available for the customer, if the customer so requests. The customer satisfies his duty by promptly and carefully examining and balancing the statement when it is received.

By failing to make a prompt examination, the customer cannot assert against the bank

1. an unauthorized customer signature,
2. a material alteration of the check, or

---

[3]Ibid., Section 4-403(3).
[4]Ibid., Section 4-406(1).

3. any other unauthorized signatures or alterations made *by the same person,*

provided that the customer had a reasonable time to examine the statement and to notify the bank of any problems or irregularities. The "reasonable time" available to the customer may not exceed fourteen calendar days.[5]

To complete the statement inspection duty, the customer must report any unauthorized signatures and/or any material alterations within one year of the statement date or lose the right to raise these issues. And any unauthorized endorsements must be reported to the bank within three years of the statement date, or the right to raise this issue is lost.[6]

If the customer notifies the bank *within* fourteen days of receiving the statement, he or she gets *all* the money back on the unauthorized signatures, and the alteration amount back on the alterations. If notice is given to the bank after fourteen days but within one year, the customer recovers the amount of the *first* signature or the *first* alteration by *each* signer or alterer. And the customer puts the bank on notice for any future signings or alterations. However, the customer cannot recover on any of the checks between the first one and the date of notice. If notice is over one year after the statement date, the customer cannot recover anything from the bank. If there is an unauthorized endorsement, it must be reported to the bank within three years, or the customer cannot recover anything from the bank.

The following case illustrates the duty of a customer to reconcile the statement.

K & K Manufacturing, Inc. v. Union Bank
628 P.2d 44 (Ariz. 1981)

FACTS   Knight was the president and majority stockholder of K & K Manufacturing. The only two employees of K & K were Knight and Garza, the bookkeeper. Garza's duties included preparing checks for Knight to sign and reconciling the bank statements for the K & K account and for Knight's personal account. From March, 1977, through January, 1978, Garza forged Knight's signature on nearly seventy checks. The forged checks were worth over $60,000, with nearly $50,000 from K & K's accounts and over $11,000 from Knight's personal account. The bank informed Knight numerous times during this period that his personal account was overdrawn, but Knight never investigated or questioned this fact. An audit of the company's books revealed Garza's actions, and Knight sued the bank for the losses, alleging that the bank had breached its contract by honoring the forgeries.

ISSUE   Is the bank liable for the losses suffered by Knight due to the forgeries by Garza?

HOLDING   No. The bank had done nothing improper in this case and had not breached its contract.

[5]Ibid., Section 4-406(2).
[6]Ibid., Section 4-406(4).

REASONING   A bank customer has a duty to reconcile his statements and to notify the bank of any alterations, forgeries, or irregularities. A customer is not excused from his duty to act in a careful and prudent manner because the customer has erroneously placed his trust in a dishonest employee. A bank's depositors are chargeable with the knowledge of any facts that an honest employee would have discovered by acting in a reasonable and prudent manner. In this case, a reasonable and prudent examination of the bank statements would have revealed the forgeries in the bank statement of May, 1977, and would have allowed Knight to give the bank notice at that time. By waiting until after January, 1978, Knight had acted improperly.

THE BANK: RIGHTS AND DUTIES

Since the bank is the agent of the customer, it must obey any lawful orders of the customer. This duty to obey gives the bank a very important right: It can charge to the customer's account *any* item that is properly payable from the customer's account. The bank can pay the check even if payment creates an overdraft.[7] The bank can also pay a check that was incomplete when issued and then completed by some later holder. The bank may even know that a holder completed the check and still pay it as completed. The only exception is when the bank has notice that the completion was improper or was done in bad faith.[8]

In accordance with the rules that govern timely presentment, the bank may refuse to honor any *stale checks*. A stale check is one that is more than six months old and has not been certified. If the bank dishonors a stale check, it is not liable to the customer for any damages. However, the bank may, at its option, honor a stale check. Again, the bank will not be liable for any damages suffered by the customer if it honors the check in good faith.[9] It should be remembered that a written stop payment is good for six months, the period after which a check becomes stale. Suppose a customer issues a written stop payment order. Six months elapse without the check ever being presented, and the customer does not renew the stop payment order. The payee now presents the check to the bank. The check is stale. A stop payment order had been in effect on that check. The bank honors the check. If the bank can prove that it acted in good faith, it will face no liability for its payment of the stale, once-stopped check.

Under normal agency rules, if the principal dies or becomes incompetent, the agency terminates by operation of law. After this termination, if the agent continues to perform its agency duties, the agent becomes personally liable, and the principal has no liability. This rule would be impractical in commercial paper, so the UCC expressly changes it. As applied to the bank-customer

[7]Ibid., Section 4-401(1).
[8]Ibid., Section 4-401(2).
[9]Ibid., Section 4-404.

relationship, agencies do not automatically end at the instant of the principal's death or incompetence.

Under Section 4-405(1), the bank is fully authorized to perform its banking functions on the account of a customer who has died or has become incompetent until the bank *knows* of the occurrence and has had adequate time to react to the news. Even if the bank knows of the customer's death, its power to act is not terminated. Section 4-405(2) permits the bank to continue to honor checks drawn on the account for ten days after the date of a death unless a stop payment is placed on the account by an interested party.

Sometimes banks make mistakes. A bank may honor an instrument that had a stop payment order covering it, or it may do something else that allows the customer to recover damages from the bank. When this happens, the bank has some protection: It is entitled to **subrogation**. Subrogation means that the bank is given the rights that some other parties could have raised if the bank had not made improper payment. UCC Section 4-407 gives the bank three different sets of rights to assert through subrogation:

Subrogation The substitution of one person in the place of another with reference to a lawful claim, demand, or right.

1. the rights of a holder in due course against the maker or drawer
2. the rights of the payee or any other holder against the maker or drawer
3. the rights of the drawer or maker against the payee or any other holders

Thus, the bank has the rights of both sides and of every interested party. From this buffet of rights, the bank can select the set of rights that give it the greatest likelihood of winning the case.

The bank has the right to enforce the terms of its contract with the customer. Among other things, this right allows the bank to impose certain service charges and fees against many of its customers each month. The bank may be able to collect a specific amount every month; it may be able to collect a specific amount in any month the customer's account balance falls below a certain amount; or it may be able to charge a specific amount for every check written by the customer. The bank will impose a service charge for handling a stop payment order. Likewise, it may charge a customer when it pays an overdraft or when it dishonors a check, if honoring it would have created an overdraft. These service charges are specified in the contract the customer agreed to when the signature card was signed.

The duties of the bank are simple. The bank is required to honor the terms and conditions of its contract. It is required to obey the rules of agency and to act in good faith in a commercially reasonable manner.

SPECIAL PROBLEMS

Two areas deserve further mention: Certified checks and unauthorized signatures.

Certified Checks

A *certified check is one that has already been accepted by the drawee bank.*[10] In other words, the bank has assumed primary liability and agreed to pay the check on a later presentment. Certification can be done at the request of the drawer or of any holder. A refusal by the bank to certify the check is *not* a dishonor.

How does certification occur? Either the drawer or a holder presents the check to the bank and requests certification. If the bank agrees to certify, it follows certain steps. First, it *charges* the account of the customer and *credits* its own "Certified Check Account." Thus, the money is held by the bank in the bank's own account, and the customer has already "paid" the amount of the check. Second, the bank punches a hole in the encoded account number of the check to ensure that the check will not be paid a second time on a later presentment. Third, a stamp is made on the face of the check, and the terms of the certification are written into the stamped form.

If the drawer seeks and receives the certification, the drawer remains secondarily liable until final payment. However, if a holder seeks and receives the certification, the drawer and all prior endorsers are discharged from liability.

Unauthorized Signatures

Under UCC Section 1-201(43), an *unauthorized signature is one made without any authority express or implied,* and it includes a forgery. An unauthorized signature is wholly inoperative against the person whose name was signed unless that person later ratifies the signing. It cannot be used to impose liability on the purported signer. However, in some circumstances, an unauthorized and unratified signature is still binding on the purported signer. According to Section 3-406, if a person contributes to the unauthorized signing through *negligence,* he or she will be held liable to any good-faith holder of the instrument.

Many businesses "sign" checks by means of a stamp. The business may leave the stamp and its checks in a place where they are easily reached by a nonauthorized person (most likely a thief). Such conduct on the part of the business is negligent, and the negligence leads to the unauthorized "signing." In such circumstances, the business may not later assert the defense that the signing was unauthorized if the holder is a holder in good faith. Notice that the holder does *not* have to be a holder in due course; the fact that the holder is in good faith is sufficient. The *negligence* of the wronged party is the key: The wronged party must be negligent, and the negligence must cause the loss. Otherwise, the unauthorized signature cannot be used against the person whose name was signed.

---

[10]Ibid., Section 3-411.

YOU BE
THE
JUDGE

Congressional debates over restructuring banking regulations to rejuvenate the banking system and fears about the liquidity of the FDIC both point to the existence of some serious problems in the United States banking industry. While the debate so far has been concerned with how to solve the problems, a better question might be whether solutions should be sought at all.

People who desire "traditional banking services" use alternatives to banks to find these services today. Drafting accounts, money market accounts, or cash management accounts can be opened through credit unions or brokerage firms, some of which provide insurance coverage equal to that offered by the FDIC. Car loans can be obtained through the dealer from whom you purchase your automobile. Home mortgages can be obtained through insurance companies and Wall Street securities firms. Even automatic teller machines are being offered by nonbanks. At the end of 1990 in the United States, banks only held 16% of the outstanding residential mortgages, and less than 50% of the outstanding automobile loans.

Given the current state of the banking industry, and the availability of alternative sources of "traditional banking services," do you feel that we should bother to restructure the rules and regulations governing banking, or should we let banks "sink or swim" in a competitive environment?

Source: "Do We Really Need Banks Anymore?", Bernard Baumohl, *Time,* July 15, 1991, page 49.

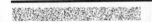

CREDIT UNION SHARE DRAFT ACCOUNTS

The use of share draft accounts through credit unions has increased in recent years. Many individuals are selecting an account with a credit union rather than with a bank due to more personalized treatment by the credit union, lower charges and fees, or a number of other reasons. These share draft accounts operate in most respects like a checking account opened at a bank, but there are a few differences. A credit union does not return the customer's canceled checks in a monthly bank statement. Rather, the credit union will send the customer a synopsis of the activities on the account for the period, normally a month. This synopsis will list the drafts that were presented and accepted, but it will not include the cancelled drafts. The customer must reconcile the statement on the basis of the summation and then go to the credit union office to straighten out any problems, examine drafts for alterations, or look for unauthorized signatures.

The drawer of a share draft has the same right to stop payment on the draft as the drawer on a check possesses. And the same time limits—fourteen days for an oral order, six months for a written order—operate on the stop payment order directed to the credit union/drawee.

These share draft accounts also have instruments that are payable on demand, the same as a check. Further, the drawer can postdate, or antedate, the share draft. The treatment in nearly every respect is the same as the treatment given to checks. The differences tend to be minor and technical and have little impact on the customer or the customer's use of the account.

ELECTRONIC FUND TRANSFERS

Recent technological advances have provided banking with a new method of doing business and with a new type of service. This new method of doing business is the *electronic fund transfer* (EFT), which allows for computerization of checking accounts and for faster (theoretically), more accurate banking transactions. The Electronic Fund Transfer Act, which became effective in 1980, provides the basic legal framework for this method of doing business. In addition, the UCC's Permanent Editorial Board is considering revisions to the Code to reflect the advent of electronic banking. This method of financial dealing eventually may make the current checking or drafting account obsolete, or nearly so, due to the delays and expenses of handling checks or drafts when compared to electronic banking.

Four methods of electronic fund transfers have become widely used. One method is the Point of Sale (POS) terminal and the "debit" card. In a POS transaction, the customer presents the merchant with a debit card, the merchant imprints the card and has the customer sign, and the funds are transferred from the customer's account to the merchant's account. The transaction is similar in format to the use of a credit card, but there should be no delay for the merchant in receiving the money from the sale. Unfortunately, often the use of a POS transaction is no faster or safer for the merchant than the use of a check. In most parts of the country the POS transaction must be processed through a clearinghouse in the same manner as a check, and the transfer of funds to the merchant is no faster than it would be with a check. In addition, the cost is slightly higher for a POS than for a check when a clearinghouse is involved.

A second, and more familiar, method is the use of Automated Teller Machine (ATM) transfers. The bank customer inserts his or her card in the machine, enters his or her personal identification number (PIN), and selects a transaction. The customer can make a deposit, a withdrawal, a transfer from one account to another, a payment, or a number of other banking transactions.

If the bank is a participant in a network, the customer may be able to authorize payments to predetermined accounts by phone. Here, the customer calls the bank and, using the buttons on a Touch-Tone® phone, can designate preselected "payees" who will be paid an amount determined by punching in the amount of the "electronic check" so that the funds are automatically transferred.

Finally, there are preauthorized automatic payments and preauthorized direct deposits. In both cases, regular amounts are deducted from, or added to, the customer's account balance on designated dates to ensure that payment (or credit) is received without any worries about forgetting to send in the check or drive to the bank to make the deposit.

In general, a consumer who uses EFTs has the same types of rights and duties as a consumer who has a checking or drafting account with a financial institution. For example, a customer can place a stop payment order on a preauthorized payment by notifying the bank orally or in writing at least three days prior to the date for preauthorized payment. A consumer can recover damages from a financial institution for failure to make EFT payments as instructed, provided the consumer has sufficient funds on deposit.

Numerous protections exist for the consumer who is using EFTs as well. For example, consumer liability is limited in case of unauthorized use of an account, provided the consumer gives proper and timely notice to the bank. The bank has the burden of proof to establish either that the use was in fact authorized or that the customer did not give proper and/or timely notice.

As the public becomes more familiar and more comfortable with electronic fund transfers, the use of this form will grow and develop. And as that happens, the use of checks will begin to decline. The decline will be gradual at first, but by the next century we may do virtually all of our banking electronically.

SUMMARY

The most frequently used negotiable instrument is the check. As a result, special attention must be paid to the bank-customer relationship. When a customer opens a checking account, a multirole relationship is created. The bank and the customer have a contract, they are involved in an agency, they have a debtor-creditor relationship, and they are controlled by Article 4 of the UCC.

Customers have a duty to exercise due care in their dealings with their accounts. They are required to inspect their statements carefully and promptly for any irregularities, alterations, or unauthorized signings. They may also issue stop payment orders to the bank. Since the bank is the agent of its customers, it is obligated to obey such orders.

The bank is required to abide by the terms of its contract with the customer. It must pay properly drawn checks if the customer has sufficient funds, and it must act in good faith.

Certified checks and unauthorized signatures can present special problems. A certified check is one that has been accepted by the bank and then circulated through the normal channels of commerce. Unauthorized signings are sometimes caused by the negligence of the customer; in such a case, the bank is not liable for honoring the unauthorized signing.

Credit unions have become actively involved in the business of providing accounts to customers. Credit union share draft accounts, similar to checking accounts in virtually every aspect, have become a common alternative to the traditional checking accounts offered by banks. The credit unions tend to have lower minimum balance requirements and lower fees and charges for their credit union members who elect to open share draft accounts.

Electronic fund transfers are the probable wave of the future. By using the capacity and speed of computers and by eliminating the paper required by traditional checking accounts, funds can be moved more quickly, more accurately, more efficiently, and more inexpensively than is possible with checking accounts. This is a developmental area that will grow rapidly over the next several years.

DISCUSSION QUESTIONS

1. Where do the terms and conditions of the contract between the bank and the customer originate?

2. What should a stop payment order include?

3. What is the bank customer's duty with respect to the bank statement sent to the customer each month? What should the customer do to maximize his or her protection in meeting this duty? Explain.

4. How does the duty and authority of a bank as an agent for the customer differ from the duty and authority of an agent in other circumstances when the principal dies or becomes incompetent? Why do you think this difference exists?

5. Denise made a deposit at her bank on a personalized deposit slip. She was not aware that the deposit was mistakenly credited to the account of another customer. She wrote a check that would have been good if the deposit had been properly credited to her account, but it was dishonored due to insufficient funds. What are her rights in this situation?

6. Vicki issued a stop payment order on a check she

had issued to a gas station. The bank paid the check over the stop payment order. What must Vicki prove to recover her money on this check from the bank?

7. James received his bank statement August 1. He examined it and discovered a forgery on August 14. He notified the bank on August 18. A second forgery by the same person was presented to the bank and honored by the bank on August 16. What are the rights of James and of the bank on the second forged check? Explain fully.

8. Bob issued a check to Carl. Carl negotiated it to Dave. Dave negotiated it to Edna. Edna went to the bank seeking certification of the check. The bank refused to certify the check. Has the bank dishonored the check? What are Edna's rights against each of the parties?

9. Freddy's Fenders pays all of its bills by check. The checks are signed by means of a rubber stamp. A thief breaks into the office of Freddy's Fenders, breaks open the locked desk, and steals some checks. He then opens

the safe and steals the rubber signature stamp. The bank unknowingly cashes several of these stolen checks when they are presented. What are the rights of Freddy's Fenders against the bank in this case?

10. What is an electronic fund transfer? What are the current methods for transferring funds electronically?

CASE PROBLEMS

1. C.I.T. issued two checks totaling $11,000 to McCarthy. McCarthy endorsed and deposited the checks in his account, to be collected. C.I.T. placed a stop payment order on the checks with its bank before the checks were presented. Upon presentment, the bank accidentally honored the checks despite the stop payment. The bank then charged C.I.T.'s account for the $11,000. C.I.T. sued to have its account credited for the $11,000. If the only defense C.I.T. has is personal in nature, what should be the result? (*Universal C.I.T. Credit Corp.* v. *Guaranty Bank & Trust Co.,* 161 F. Supp. 790 [Mass. 1958].)

2. A church opened a checking account with First National Bank. The checks had to be signed by Jordan and Jackson, two elders of the congregation. Bank statements were to be mailed to Jordan. Over the span of one year, fifty checks were issued by Jordan, with Jordan forging Jackson's signature on each of the checks. The church sued the bank to recover on the fifty forged checks. What should be the result? (*Jackson* v. *First National Bank of Memphis,* 403 S.W.2d 109 [Tenn. App. 1966].)

3. Kendall discovered that his business was in trouble and that he had too little money to continue operating the business until things improved. He then received an agreement from his bank whereby the bank agreed to cover any overdrafts on Kendall's checking account until the business became profitable. The bank then dishonored several checks drawn by Kendall due to insufficient funds. Kendall sued the bank for the damages caused by these dishonors. What should be the result? (*Kendall Yacht Corp.* v. *United California Bank,* 50 Cal.3d 949, 123 Cal. Rptr. 848 [Cal. App. 1975].)

4. Giardano borrowed $9500 from the bank in order to pay for two trucks he had agreed to buy. The bank issued a cashier's check payable to the order of Fiero, the seller of the trucks. Giardano delivered the cashier's check to Fiero and took possession of the trucks. He immediately discovered that both trucks were defective and asked the bank to stop payment on the cashier's check. The bank refused to issue a stop payment order and honored the check upon presentment. Giardano defaulted on the loan from the bank, and when the bank sued, he raised the defense that the bank should have stopped payment on the cashier's check so that no money would have been lost. Is Giardano's argument persuasive? Could the bank have stopped payment on the cashier's check? (*National Newark & Essex Bank* v. *Giardano,* 268 A.2d 327 [N.J. 1970].)

5. Harvey made reservations at a resort hotel that had advertised in a national magazine. The hotel required advance payment by cashier's check, which Harvey sent to the hotel just before his arrival. When Harvey arrived at the hotel, he found that the advertisements were misleading and that he had been cheated. He immediately checked out and called the bank to try to stop payment on the cashier's check. Must the bank honor the stop payment order that Harvey placed? (*Moon Over the Mountains, Ltd.* v. *Marine Midland Bank,* 87 Misc.2d 918, 386 N.Y.S.2d 974 [1976].)

6. Shaw and Nauman were joint tenants in a checking account, a savings account, and a safety deposit box, all with Union Bank. After Nauman died, Shaw took possession of the safety deposit box and the checking account funds. When Shaw attempted to acquire the savings account funds, the bank refused to surrender them without a release from the state tax commission. Shaw obtained the release and presented a savings withdrawal form to Union Bank. The bank then prepared a cashier's check for the account balance but refused to release it to Shaw without a probate of the Nauman estate. Shaw then hired an attorney to probate the estate, only to discover that, due to the small size of the estate, probate was not necessary. When the bank finally released the funds, Shaw filed suit against the bank, seeking to recover lost interest, the cost of the unnecessary probate, and mental pain and suffering. Is Shaw entitled to damages from the bank in this case? If so, on what basis should damages be awarded? (*Shaw* v.

Union Bank and Trust Company, 640 P.2d 953 [Okla. 1981].)

7. On 30 June 1972, Ragusa issued a check for $5000 drawn on State Bank and payable to the order of Southern Masonry. Ragusa was informed by Southern Masonry that the check had been lost or stolen, and a replacement check was issued to Southern Masonry. At the same time, Ragusa placed a verbal stop payment order on the first check. In July, 1975, the first check was deposited by Southern Masonry in its account with BNO, which then presented the check to State Bank. State Bank accepted the check and charged the Ragusa account. When Ragusa received his monthly statement, he returned the check to the bank and demanded that his account be recredited for the $5000 and the check returned to BNO because (1) a stop payment order had been placed on the check and (2) the check was stale, being three years old. The bank agreed to return the check and recredit the Ragusa account. However, the Federal Reserve refused State Bank's request for a refund due to the delay in returning the check, and State Bank again charged the Ragusa account for the check. Ragusa is now suing to recover his money from the bank. Is Ragusa entitled to recover the $5000, plus damages suffered? Explain your answer fully. (*Charles Ragusa & Son* v. *Community State Bank,* 360 So.2d 231 [La. App. 1978].)

8. Tenn was approached by Hawley with a proposed business opportunity. Tenn was interested but wanted additional time to think the deal over. However, he did give Hawley a check for $6000, which Hawley was "to hold" until Tenn made a decision. Hawley deposited the check in his bank, and the bank presented the check to the drawee. The drawee accepted the check even though Tenn did not have sufficient funds on deposit to cover the check. When Tenn learned what had occurred, he tried to recover from Hawley but was unable to do so. Tenn now denies the authority of the bank to pay the overdraft on his account and refuses to repay the bank. The bank has sued Tenn for the monies advanced in excess of Tenn's balance. Is Tenn correct, or is the bank entitled to recover the overdraft from Tenn? Explain fully. (*City Bank of Honolulu* v. *Tenn,* 469 P.2d 816 [Haw. 1970].)

9. Sims deposited a check with her bank. The drawee bank was located in another city, and the depository bank had a policy of "holding" the deposit credit for three days to allow the check to "clear." One of the tellers at the depository bank mistakenly placed a ten-day hold on the funds, so several small checks written by Sims after the three-day period but before the ten-day period had expired were dishonored by the bank. Sims is suing the bank for wrongful dishonor of these checks, seeking the following damages: $1.50 for a long-distance phone call to clarify the acceptance of the check; $130 for lost wages, since Sims took a week off owing to her embarrassment; and $500 for mental suffering and inconvenience. What should Sims collect from the bank? (*Bank of Louisville Royal* v. *Sims,* 435 S.W.2d 57 [Ky. 1968].)

10. On October 4, GMAC drew four checks payable to the order of Huber Chevrolet and totaling $21,700. Huber deposited the checks in its account with the bank, using the restrictive endorsement "for deposit only." Huber then drew a check for $26,000 against the account. On October 25, the bank and GMAC each learned that Huber had become insolvent. The bank "froze" Huber's checking account, and GMAC issued stop payment orders on the four checks. On October 28, the bank dishonored the $26,000 check drawn by Huber on its presentment. When GMAC sought a setoff against the bank for the four checks, the bank denied that GMAC could assert any rights because the bank was an HDC and not subject to personal defenses. Did the bank give value in this case, so that it qualified as an HDC? Why? (*General Motors Acceptance Corporation* v. *Bank of Carroll County,* 226 S.E.2d 815 [Ga. App. 1976].)

PART 5

Debtor-Creditor Relations

*A*t one time, lending money was considered a dishonorable occupation. Under canon law, moneylenders were not allowed to charge interest on loans. To do so was to commit a sin. Moreover, people did not often borrow in those days; when they wanted to buy something, they usually saved until they could pay cash for the purchase.

With the arrival of the industrial revolution, things began to change. Borrowing, and the use of credit, became an important aspect of good business management. If a business could borrow the money to buy equipment and then use that equipment to generate income over and above the cost of the loan, the business was ahead. Unfortunately, some businesses did not generate enough profits to repay the loan. When this happened, defaults occurred.

Eventually, legal methods were developed to protect the parties to credit transactions. Creditors were allowed to *secure* the debt by taking legal rights on certain assets of the debtor. And debtors were sometimes allowed to escape onerous debt burdens and start over with a clean slate. This part of the text deals with the rights—and the duties—of debtors and creditors, an especially important topic in our consumer-oriented American economy.

C H A P T E R   28

Secured Transactions: Security Interests and Perfection

O U T L I N E

CREDIT FINANCING AND ARTICLE 9

Credit is an extremely important aspect of current American business practices. Without it, many successful firms would never have gotten started. Yet the person who extends credit (the creditor) undertakes the risk that the person to whom he or she has given credit (the debtor) will not be able to repay the debt in full. Understandably, the creditor wishes to be protected against such losses before they occur. The Uniform Commercial Code's methods of creating protection for the creditor form the basis of this chapter's discussion.

We have already seen that a commercial transaction in one of its simplest forms may involve a sale of goods in which the buyer pays cash. Alternatively, the buyer may use a check or draft to pay for all (or a portion of) the goods. In this chapter, we shall examine a third method of closing a commercial transaction: The buyer may give the owner of the goods a *security interest*. The portion of the Uniform Commercial Code that deals with these matters is Article 9, "Secured Transactions; Sales of **Accounts** and **Chattel Paper**."

Despite the availability of several methods of structuring a commercial transaction, use of secured transactions is very common in business today; hence, an understanding of Article 9 is crucial. To illustrate, let us assume that Bart Brown wishes to buy a meat freezer and a cash register for his new restaurant business. He may pay for part of the sale in cash and receive possession of the items in exchange for giving the seller of the goods a security interest in this equipment. Such a security interest "secures" or ensures payment by the buyer so that if Bart does not pay the seller, the latter can repossess the goods. Thus, a secured transaction allows buyers to receive goods sooner than they would have if they had been forced to pay cash; and, at the same time, it permits sellers to protect themselves by retaining the right of repossession in the event of a buyer's nonpayment. As we shall see, sellers must comply with several additional rules under Article 9 relating to perfection and priorities to ensure that they will have first rights to the equipment in the event of Bart's **default**. We will discuss these concepts further in this chapter and in Chapter 29.

Using the terminology adopted by the Code, we can further characterize the seller as the *secured party* ("a lender, seller, or other person in whose favor there is a security interest, including a person to whom accounts or chattel paper have been sold").[1] Bart is of course the *debtor* ("the person who owes payment or other performance of the obligation secured, whether or not he owns or has rights in the collateral, and includes the seller of accounts or chattel paper").[2] Bart and the seller presumably have entered into a *security agreement* ("the agreement which creates or provides for a security interest").[3]

Accounts Rights to payments for goods sold or leased or for services rendered that are not evidenced by an instrument or chattel paper.

Chattel paper A writing that evidences both a monetary obligation and a security interest in specific goods.

Default A failure to do what should be done, especially in the performance of a contractual obligation, without legal excuse or justification for the nonperformance.

---

[1]Uniform Commercial Code, Section 9-105(m).
[2]Ibid., Section 9-105(d). This section further states that "[w]here the debtor and the owner of the collateral are not the same person, the term 'debtor' means the owner of the collateral in any provision of the Article dealing with the collateral, the obligor in any provision dealing with the obligation, and may include both where the context so requires. . . ."
[3]Ibid., Section 9-105(1).

The freezer and cash register constitute *collateral* ("the property subject to a security interest").[4] Article 9's applications are very broad, since it may cover relatively simple business transactions like the one we have described; or it may extend to highly complex forms of business financing, such as accounts receivable financing.[5]

The 1972 Official Text of Article 9 differs substantially from the 1962 Official Text. Most states have adopted the 1972 version; but since some states still follow the 1962 rules, you should check your jurisdiction to see which version applies. We will use the 1972 Official Text of Article 9 in Chapters 28–30.

Part of the richness of Article 9 stems from its unified approach to secured financing. Before the UCC came into being, there existed a wide variety of security devices that had arisen rather haphazardly in response to perceived security financing needs. These devices—known by such strange names as "pledges," "chattel mortgages," "conditional sales," "trust receipts," and "factor's liens"—were very technical. Hence, a seller who had mistakenly chosen the wrong device or who had not complied with the ticklish requirements of a particular device might later find that he or she had no valid security interest. Moreover, these devices remained limited in scope; they could not reach **general intangibles** such as television or motion picture rights or the goodwill of a business or service, which most of us today would recognize as important sources of commercial collateral. Finally, these devices placed great emphasis on who had held title during the course of the parties' dealings.

General intangibles Personal property other than goods, accounts, chattel paper, instruments, documents, or money; for example, goodwill, literary rights, patents, or copyrights.

The Code's creation of a single device, the Article 9 security interest, as a substitute for the numerous devices that had grown up as a result of a hundred years' worth of common law and statutory developments was welcome indeed. Article 9's rejection of the older devices' distinctions based on form (and concepts of "title")[6] has led to a simplified structure. This format more accurately reflects the wide variety of present-day secured financing transactions and allows for commercial recognition of new forms of financing without requiring the legislatures to pass new statutes or change old ones. This chapter will focus on some of the provisions of Article 9 that illustrate the Code's breadth and flexibility.

SCOPE OF ARTICLE 9

In general, according to Section 9-102, Article 9

> applies (a) to any transaction (regardless of its form) which is intended to create a security interest in personal property or fixtures including goods,

[4]Ibid., Section 9-105(c). Collateral also includes accounts and chattel paper that have been sold.
[5]Ibid., Section 9-106.
[6]Section 9-202 makes the concept of title—that is, whether the secured party or the debtor has title to the collateral—immaterial under the Code.

documents, instruments, general intangibles, chattel paper or accounts and also (b) to any sale of accounts or chattel paper.

By a "security interest," Article 9 means "an interest in personal property or fixtures which secures payment or performance of an obligation."[7] The personal property or collateral that will be subject to a security interest takes many forms. Moreover, the Code categorizes collateral according to either (1) the *nature* of the collateral or (2) its *use*. Thus, *documents* (warehouse receipts, bills of lading, and other documents of title); *instruments* (drafts, certificates of deposit, stocks, and bonds); *proceeds* (whatever is received upon the sale, exchange, collection, or other disposition of collateral or proceeds); and three kinds of collateral defined earlier—*accounts, chattel paper,* and *general intangibles*—represent the types of collateral the Code classifies primarily on the basis of their *nature.*

Goods are the most common type of collateral, and a more detailed discussion of this category illustrates how the Code classifies collateral on the basis of the debtor's *use*. According to the Code, "goods" include all things that are movable at the time the security interest attaches or that are fixtures.[8] The Code further distinguishes goods with regard to the debtor's use of them. *Consumer goods* consist of those used or bought for use primarily for personal, family, or household purposes. Thus, a debtor may give a security interest in his or her furniture or car to a secured party. *Equipment* includes goods used or bought for use primarily in business. Bart's freezer and cash register are equipment collateral, as a truck would be for the electric company. *Farm products* are also a type of goods. The Code defines farm products as crops, livestock, or supplies used or produced in farming operations. Interestingly, then, a farmer may give a security interest in wheat, corn, cows, or even milk, since the Code covers the products of crops or livestock in their unmanufactured states as well.[9] *Inventory,* defined as goods held by a person for sale or lease or raw materials used or consumed in a business, is another type of goods. Inventory differs from consumer goods and equipment because inventory is held for sale rather than use.[10] Such things as coal or packages for goods are inventory, as is a dealer's supply of cars or a merchant's supply of tires, paint, clothing, or toys. The last type of goods that the Code delineates is *fixtures*. Goods are fixtures when they become so related to particular real estate that an interest in them arises under real estate law.[11] Furnaces and central air-conditioning units are fixtures.

Given these differences in definition, it is not surprising that the Code

[7]Uniform Commercial Code, Section 1-201(37).
[8]Ibid., Section 9-105(h). Goods may also include such things as standing timber, growing crops, and the unborn young of animals.
[9]Ibid., Section 9-109(1), (2), (3).
[10]Ibid., Section 9-109(4), Official Comment 3.
[11]Ibid., Section 9-313(1)(a).

makes these classes of goods mutually exclusive. In other words, the same property cannot at the same time and to the same person be both equipment and inventory. In borderline cases—for example, a social worker's car or a farmer's pickup—the principal use to which the property has been put determines the type of collateral involved.[12] Because the Code's rules regarding perfection, priorities, and default often turn on the type of collateral involved (as we shall see further in Chapters 29 and 30), you should be aware of the importance of knowing which category of collateral is present in a given transaction.

Whatever the kind of collateral that is subject to the security interest, the Code drafters apparently meant Article 9 to apply to all *consensual* security interests in personal property and fixtures as well as to certain sales of accounts and chattel paper (often called "assignments").[13] In our earlier example, we can say that Bart Brown and the seller of the meat freezer and the cash register have freely agreed to enter into this commercial transaction. Since personal property is involved (the freezer and register are "goods"), Bart has agreed to let the seller retain an interest in the goods until Bart pays for them (a method of ensuring the performance of Bart's obligations) and the seller, in turn, has agreed to give the goods to Bart now (even though the seller has not received the total price for them) in exchange for the right to repossess the freezer and register if Bart does not pay. This transaction therefore fulfills all the requirements of an enforceable security interest.

Given the necessity for consent between the parties, Article 9 accordingly does not apply to a "security interest" that arises by **operation of law** rather than through the agreement of the parties. Examples of such situations include a **mechanic's lien** on Bart's restaurant that an unpaid contractor obtains as a result of renovating Bart's place of business. The lien represents the money Bart owes for the labor and materials involved in the construction of the restaurant. Since Bart and the contractor have not agreed in advance that the contractor will have an interest in Bart's restaurant, this is a nonconsensual arrangement that arises as a consequence of the parties' *status* (the contractor is a creditor who now is using the restaurant as security for the debt Bart owes) rather than as a result of *mutual consent*. It is therefore not an Article 9 security interest.

This result also stems from the fact that Article 9 in general does not apply to real property or real estate. Instead, as mentioned, it applies only to security interests in *personal* property. Hence, Article 9 has no bearing on land mortgages or on landlords' liens. And although it specifically includes within its scope the old methods of creating security interests (for example, pledges, chattel mortgages, and factor's liens),[14] it specifically exempts from its coverage security interests that are subject to any federal statute and certain

Operation of law Certain automatic results that must occur following certain actions or facts because of established legal principles and not as the result of any voluntary choice by the parties involved.

Mechanic's lien A statutory protection given to certain builders, artisans, and providers of material that grants a lien on the building and the land improved by such persons.

[12]Ibid., Section 9-109, Official Comment 2.
[13]Ibid., Section 9-104(c).
[14]Ibid., Section 9-102(2).

other categories of transactions, including wage and salary claims and claims resulting from court judgments.[15]

In some cases, a transaction, although covered by Article 9, may also be subject to any local statutes governing usury, retail installment sales, and the like (for example, the Uniform Consumer Credit Code). In those situations, in the event of a conflict, the provisions of any such statute, and not Article 9, are controlling.[16]

One test to use in deciding whether Article 9 applies is to ask whether the transaction *is intended* to have effect as security. If the answer is yes, Article 9 probably covers the transaction.

SECURITY INTEREST

As we have just noted, Article 9 broadly defines the term *security interest* as *an interest in personal property or fixtures that secures payment or performance of an obligation.* One of the assets of the Code, as previously discussed, derives from the flexibility of such sweeping definitions. And, in fact, courts have had few problems in recognizing a security interest. Despite this seeming simplicity of definition, one area—that of leases "intended as security" in contrast to "true" leases—has caused businesspeople and courts some difficulties.

The Code states definitively that Article 9 applies to "a lease intended as security."[17] It also notes that whether a lease is intended as security must be determined by the facts of each case and that the inclusion of an option to purchase does not in and of itself make the lease one intended for security. On the other hand, a provision that on the expiration of the lease the person who is leasing (called the "lessee") becomes the owner, or has the option of buying the property for very little money, makes the lease one intended as security.[18] In this latter situation, the transaction more closely resembles an installment sales contract, especially when, as is often the case, the "rental" payments equal the selling price of the property subject to the "lease." The "lessor" (the person leasing the personal property to another) is actually a secured party who is using the monthly leasing payments as monthly installments on a conditional sales agreement. This transaction *would* be subject to the Code's provisions because it would be a lease intended as security, not a true lease.

Why, one may ask, is this an important distinction anyway? The answer will become clear when we discuss the process of "perfection." If such a lease

[15]Ibid., Section 9-104.
[16]Ibid., Sections 9-201, 9-203(4).
[17]Ibid., Section 9-102(2).
[18]Ibid., Section 1-201(37).

is intended as security, it will be subject to Article 9's filing requirements. A true lease will not be because in general Article 9 does not apply to situations in which one pays merely for the right to use the goods for a specified period of time without ever becoming the owner of the leased property. Debtors in Article 9 transactions are trying to buy the property that is the object of the security interest. At the same time, secured parties are retaining an interest in the property until this transfer of ownership is accomplished by the debtor's paying all that is owed. In a true lease, the parties never contemplate such an eventual transfer of ownership.

Thus, if we change the facts of our earlier hypothetical case and have Bart lease the freezer and cash register, assuming this is a true lease, Article 9 does not govern. However, if in effect the owner of the freezer and register is retaining *title* to the goods to ensure that Bart will pay for the goods, we have a *lease intended as security;* and the parties must follow Article 9's rules. This means, as we will see later, that if Bart goes bankrupt, the **trustee in bankruptcy** will be able to get the equipment because Bart will be deemed the owner of the equipment. He has in effect been *paying* for the items on an installment sales basis, even though the parties have called the transaction a "lease." By not filing, the original owner of the equipment has not perfected his or her interest in the equipment and will not be able to repossess the equipment (or any other type of collateral). Since the law in these circumstances treats the bankruptcy trustee as a **lien creditor,** the trustee will have superior rights to those of our unperfected original owner.

The following case does not involve the trustee in bankruptcy, but it illustrates the necessity of following the Code's rules if a court later characterizes the transaction at issue as a lease intended as security.

Trustee in bankruptcy The person appointed by the bankruptcy court to act as trustee of the debtor's property for the benefit and protection of the creditors.

Lien creditor One whose debt is secured by a claim on specific property.

Walton v. *Howard*
403 S.E.2d 91 (Ga. App. 1991)

FACTS   Howard entered into a contract entitled a "Lease/Purchase Agreement" with Walton regarding a John Deere tractor. In exchange, Walton agreed to "sell" the equipment to Howard for Howard's promise to pay off the amount in arrears that Walton owed to John Deere Finance Plans, Inc. (John Deere) and to take over the future monthly installment payments owed on the equipment until all the debts owed under the financing agreement between Walton and John Deere had been paid. The agreement granted Howard the right to a bill of sale for the equipment on payment of $1 and other consideration once the lien in favor of John Deere had terminated. In the interim, the parties considered the monthly payments as "lease payments" between Walton and Howard. The agreement imposed on Howard the duty to pay taxes and to provide insurance on the equipment. Howard furthermore paid Walton $4000 for Walton's equity in the equipment and then made six monthly payments of over $1000 to John Deere before falling into arrears. When Howard was three months behind in payments, Walton repossessed the equipment and retained it in his possession without notice of intent either to retain the collateral in satisfaction of the debt or to dispose of it to satisfy the debt. Howard subsequently brought suit against Walton for breach of contract or, in the alternative, for a judgment ordering Walton to return the equipment. The trial judge found the written agreement a security agreement subject to Georgia's Commercial Code and granted Howard the right to redeem the collateral on payment of the remaining debt plus $400 for interest on the sum paid by Walton to John Deere to extinguish the lien. Walton appealed this decision.

ISSUE   Was the lease a true lease or a lease intended as security and hence covered under Georgia's Commercial Code?

HOLDING   The lease was subject to Georgia's Commercial Code because the lease agreement had created a security interest; as such, it did not constitute a true lease but rather a conditional sale.

REASONING   The trial court rightly concluded that Howard and Walton had entered into a secured transaction. The agreement granted Howard the right to purchase the equipment for a nominal sum after John Deere had received the final monthly installment payment. Pursuant to the definition of "security interest" in Georgia's Commercial Code, "an agreement that upon compliance with the terms of the lease, the lessee shall become or has the option to become the owner of the property for no additional consideration or for a nominal consideration does make the lease one intended for security." Additional factors that tend to establish that a transaction is a conditional sale instead of a true lease include an initial down payment and the placing of responsibility for payment of taxes and insurance on the lessee. In this case, the evidence showed that Howard, referred to in the agreement as "Lessee/Buyer," had made a down payment of $4000 to compensate Walton, the "Lessor/Seller," for Walton's equity interest in the equipment. The agreement also required Howard to pay taxes and insurance. Hence, ample evidence existed to support the finding that the agreement had created a security interest. Having determined that the agreement had created a security interest, the trial court had not erred in finding that the Commercial Code covered the agreement. Moreover, the court had not erred, pursuant to such statute, in awarding Howard the right to redeem the equipment on the payment of the amount due under the agreement ($6954) plus $400 for interest to Walton to reimburse Walton for paying off the prior lien on the equipment.

CREATION AND ENFORCEABILITY OF THE SECURITY INTEREST

A security interest is of negligible value unless it is valid and enforceable. It therefore behooves the owner of the freezer and the register in our earlier hypothetical case to attain the status of a *secured creditor* (or secured party). In this way, if Bart, the debtor, later cannot or will not pay for the equipment, the secured party will be able to repossess the goods and, if perfected, enjoy priority over the claims that other third parties, such as the bankruptcy trustee, may assert regarding the property. However, before the secured party has an enforceable security interest in the collateral, the security interest must "attach."[19] *Attachment* concerns the process by which the secured party and the debtor create the security interest and thereby confer on the secured party certain enforceable rights to the collateral vis-à-vis the debtor. Attachment does not give the secured party rights necessarily superior to those obtained by other creditors (an additional step called perfection is necessary to accomplish this). Nevertheless, as the first step in the creation and enforceability of a security interest, attachment remains extremely important.

[19]Ibid., Section 9-203.

According to the UCC, attachment occurs when a prospective secured party does all of the following:

1. enters into a *security agreement* whereby the prospective secured party and the debtor agree that a security interest will attach
2. possesses a security agreement signed by the debtor or, alternatively, retains possession of the collateral
3. ascertains that the debtor has rights in the collateral
4. gives value

The omission of any of the requirements just listed invalidates the security interest. Such an argument underlies the next case.

Wawak v. Affiliated Food Stores, Inc.
15 UCC Rep. Serv.2d 276 (Ark. 1991)

FACTS Billy J. Wawak and Earlene Wawak began operating the Oak Grove Supermarket in 1978. The Wawaks acquired their stock from Affiliated Food Stores, Inc. (Affiliated), which secured its account with them by a security agreement and a UCC financing statement covering the inventory of the supermarket. In 1986 the Wawaks made arrangements to sell the supermarket to Robert S. Davis, operating under the names Bob's Thriftway and Bob's Supermarket of Arkansas. Davis and the Wawaks signed an agreement under which Davis began operating the supermarket on 28 January 1986 while the documents of sale were being prepared. Davis made immediate arrangements with Affiliated Food Stores to purchase inventory for the Oak Grove Supermarket and executed a security agreement and financing statement with Affiliated covering the inventory of the supermarket. The financing statement and security agreement were properly recorded in February. In April, Davis and the Wawaks completed their transaction; Davis executed a security agreement and financing statement covering the inventory to secure the indebtedness due the Wawaks; and Davis properly recorded these instruments on 8 April 1986. After eighteen months, Davis declared bankruptcy; and on 15 January 1988, the Wawaks took possession of the supermarket and inventory from the trustee in bankruptcy. The Wawaks sought a declaratory judgment that their security interest was prior and superior to the security interest of Affiliated because no attachment had occurred owing to Davis's lack of any rights in the collateral. When the court ruled that the security interest of Affiliated Food Stores, Inc. was prior to that of the Wawaks, the Wawaks appealed.

ISSUE Did Davis have sufficient rights in the collateral for attachment to have occurred?

HOLDING Yes. Davis, as the buyer in possession of the supermarket, had had sufficient rights in the collateral to satisfy this requirement of attachment.

REASONING The Wawaks maintain that under Arkansas statute a security interest does not attach until the debtor has "rights in the collateral." They contend that Davis had no rights in the inventory of the supermarket (the collateral) until 7 April 1986, when the sale was completed. Prior to 7 April, they submit that Davis merely functioned as a "manager" or "bailee." However, Davis was effectively the buyer in possession of a going concern, fully empowered to convey title to the collateral to purchasers in the ordinary course of business. The profits, as well as the losses, were his from and after 28 January 1986, when he took possession and began operating the supermarket. Moreover, the final purchase documents reflect that the sale to Davis became effective on 27 January 1986. The fact that the sale was still in process on 7 February 1986 does not mean that, within the context of the law, he was without rights in the collateral. Although the Code does not define "rights in the collateral," and Arkansas courts have not had occasion to construe the term, other states have done so in precedents stating, for example, that "possession of the collateral, accompanied by a contingent right of ownership, has been held sufficient for a security interest to attach. . . . An interest greater than naked possession has been deemed a sufficient right in the collateral to satisfy the requirements of statutes similar [to the one in issue]. . . ." Under these authorities, Davis had rights in the collateral. Moreover, Arkansas law provides that when all the applicable steps to perfect a security interest are taken before the interest attaches, it is perfected at the time it attaches. As one commentator has noted, "Perfection [the completion of all security agreement steps, plus filing] under section 4-9-303 does not require a particular sequence of events. Thus, a security interest [can be] perfected even though the financing statement was filed prior to the time the security interest attached. . . ." Here, even if it were correct that Davis's rights in the collateral had not matured until 7 April on the conclusion of the sale, the Wawaks had failed to perfect their security interest by filing until 8 April, whereas the security interest of Affiliated became perfected on 7 April at the instant Davis's rights in the collateral attached.

Pledge A debtor's delivery of collateral to a creditor, the collateral to be possessed by the creditor until the debt is paid.

Notice that the *Wawak* case took into account the fact that Davis was in possession of the supermarket. However, attachment by possession more appropriately centers on the creditor's physically retaining the goods used as collateral. For example, a simple **pledge** of a coin collection in which the owner of the collection insists, in accordance with the agreement, on keeping it until the debtor pays for it ordinarily will be enforceable because attachment will have occurred. In most cases, however, as in our situation involving Bart, the debtor will not agree to the secured party's retaining possession of the collateral (without his meat freezer "on site," Bart will have few customers!). Thus, in lieu of possession, a signed security agreement will be necessary before the security interest is valid.

To comply with the Code, security agreements must

1. be in writing
2. create or provide for a security interest
3. reasonably identify the collateral
4. be signed by the debtor[20]

Although these requirements seem simple, a great deal of litigation has resulted from a creditor's failure to use forms that include this minimal information or from a failure to fill out these forms correctly. A security agreement may contain many other terms as well, such as the amount of the indebtedness and the terms of payment; liability in the event of risk of loss or damage to the collateral; a requirement of insurance on and the maintenance and repair of the collateral; a warranty by the debtor that he or she owns the collateral free from liens or security interests; a statement of the debtor's rights (if any)

[20]Ibid., Sections 9-203(1), 9-110.

regarding removal of the collateral to another location; and a description of events that constitute default by the debtor. The security agreement shown in Figure 28.1 includes some of these terms.

A security agreement also may extend the security interest of the secured party to all collateral of the kind that is the subject of the agreement, which the debtor may acquire *after* entering into this agreement. Thus, if Bart, after entering into a security agreement with the seller of the freezer, obtains an industrial grade bread-making machine, use of an *after-acquired property clause* in the original security agreement means that the seller may also get the bread-making machine if Bart ultimately fails to pay for the freezer and the cash register. Or, alternatively, assume Bart is a seller of radios and that he gives a security interest to a creditor who has provided him with an inventory of radios. Every time Bart sells one of the original radios and uses the money from this sale to purchase another radio to replenish his inventory, the cred-

FIGURE 28.1   Security Agreement Form

SECURITY AGREEMENT USED WITH
LOAN ON
GOODS, FIXTURES, OR EQUIPMENT

_____ , 19 _____

_____
(NAME)

_____
(NO. AND STREET)   (CITY)   (COUNTY)   (STATE)

(Hereinafter called "Debtor") hereby grants to St. Joseph Bank and Trust Company, South Bend, Indiana (Hereinafter called "Bank"), a security interest in the following property together with all tools, accessories, parts, equipment and accessions now attached to or which may hereafter at any time be placed in or added to the property; also any replacements of such property herein described (hereinafter called "Collateral"):

_____
_____
_____

The security interest granted hereby is to secure payment and performance of the liabilities and obligations of debtor to Bank of every kind and description, direct or indirect, absolute or contingent, due or to become due, now existing or hereafter arising (hereinafter called "Obligations").

Debtor hereby warrants and covenants:

   1. The collateral is being acquired for the following primary uses:____ personal, or family use,____business use, or ____farming operations

   2. The Collateral_____will____ will not be acquired with the proceeds of the loan provided for in this Agreement. (In the event the Collateral will be acquired with the proceeds of the loan, the Bank may disburse such proceeds to the seller of the Collateral.)

   3. In the event the Collateral will be attached to real estate, the description of such real estate and the known owner of record of such real estate are set forth hereafter. If the Collateral is attached to such real estate prior to the perfection of the security interest granted herein, the Debtor will, on demand, furnish the Bank with a disclaimer or disclaimers executed by persons having an interest in such real estate. Real estate described;_____

_____
_____

   4. The Collateral will be kept at the address of the Debtor set out below, which in the case of a business is the address of the principal office of such business within this state. Debtor will not remove the Collateral from the state without the prior written consent of the Bank. If the Collateral is being acquired for farming use and the Debtor is not a resident of Indiana, the Collateral will be kept at the address set forth in the description of the Collateral. Debtor will immediately give written notice to the Bank of any change of address and in the case of a business, any change in its principal place of business and if the Collateral consists of equipment normally used in more than one state, any use of the Collateral in any jurisdiction other than a state in which the Debtor shall have previously advised the Bank such Collateral will be used.

FIGURE 28.1   continued

5. Debtor has, or will acquire, full and clear title to the Collateral and except for the security interest granted herein, will at all times keep the Collateral free from any adverse lien, security interest or encumbrance.

6. No financing statement covering all or any portion of the Collateral is on file in any public office.

7. Debtor authorizes the Bank at the expense of the Debtor to execute and file on its behalf a financing statement or statements in those public offices deemed necessary by the Bank to protect its security interest in the Collateral. Debtor will deliver or cause to be delivered to the Bank any certificates of titles to the Collateral with the security interest of the Bank noted thereon.

8. Debtor will not sell or offer to sell or otherwise transfer the Collateral or any interest therein without the prior written consent of the Bank.

9. Debtor will at all times keep the Collateral insured against loss, damage, theft and other risks in such amounts, under such policies and with such companies as shall be satisfactory to the Bank, which policies shall provide that any loss thereunder shall be payable to the Bank as its interest may appear and the Bank may apply the proceeds of the insurance against the outstanding indebtedness of the Debtor, regardless of whether all or any portion of such indebtedness is due or owing. All policies of insurance so required shall be placed in the possession of the Bank.

Upon failure of the Debtor to procure such insurance or to remove any encumbrance upon the Collateral or if such insurance is concelled, the indebtedness secured hereby shall become immediately due and payable at the option of the Bank, without notice or demand, or the Bank may procure such insurance or remove any encumbrance on the Collateral and the amount so paid by the Bank shall be immediately repayable and shall be added to and become a part of the indebtedness secured hereby and shall bear interest at the same note rate as the indebtedness secured hereby until paid.

10. Debtor will keep the Collateral in good order and repair and will not waste or destroy the Collateral or any portion thereof. Debtor will not use the Collateral in violation of any statute or ordinance or any policy of insurance thereon and the Bank may examine and inspect such Collateral at any reasonable time or times wherever located.

11. Debtor will pay promptly when due all taxes and assessments upon the Collateral or for its use or operation.

12. The occurrence of any one of the following events shall constitute default under this Security Agreement: (a) nonpayment when due of any installment of the indebtedness hereby secured or failure to perform any agreement contained herein; (b) any statement, representation, or warranty at any time furnished the Bank is untrue in any material respect as of the date made; (c) Debtor becomes insolvent or unable to pay debts as they mature or makes an assignment for the benefit of creditors or any proceeding is instituted by or against the Debtor alleging that such Debtor is insolvent or unable to pay debts as they mature; (d) entry of judgment against the Debtor; (e) loss, theft, substantial damage, destruction, sale or encumbrance to or of all or any portion the Collateral, or the making of any levy, seizure or attachment, thereof or thereon; (f) death of the Debtor who is a natural person or of any partner of the Debtor which is a partnership; (g) dissolution, merger or consolidation or transfer of a substantial portion of the property of the Debtor which is a corporation or partnership; or (h) the Bank deems itself insecure for any other reason whatsoever.

When an event of default shall be existing, the note or notes and any other liabilities may at the option of the Bank and without notice or demand be declared and thereupon immediately shall become due and payable and the Bank may exercise from time to time any rights and remedies of a secured party under the Uniform Commercial Code or other applicable law. Debtor agrees in the event of default to make the Collateral available to the Bank at a place acceptable to the Bank which is convenient to the Debtor. If any notification or disposition of all or any portion of the Collateral is required by law, such notification shall be deemed reasonable and properly given if mailed at least ten (10) days prior to such disposition, postage prepaid to the Debtor at its latest address appearing on the records of the Bank. Expenses of retaking, holding, repairing, preparing for sale and selling, shall include the Bank's reasonable attorneys' fees and expenses. Any proceeds of the disposition of the Collateral will be applied by the Bank to the payment of expenses of retaking, holding, repairing, preparing for sale and selling the Collateral, including reasonable attorneys' fees and legal expenses and any balance of such proceeds will be applied by the Bank to the payment of the indebtedness then owing the Bank.

No delay on the part of the Bank in the exercise of any right or remedy shall operate as a waiver thereof, and no single or partial exercise by the Bank of any right or remedy shall preclude other or further exercise thereof or the exercise of any other right or remedy. If more than one party shall execute this Agreement, the term "Debtor" shall mean all parties signing this Agreement and each of them, and such parties shall be jointly and severally obligated hereunder. The neuter pronoun, when used herein, shall include the masculine and the feminine and also the plural. If this Agreement is not dated when executed by the Debtor, the Bank is authorized, without notice to the Debtor, to date this Agreement.

This Agreement has been delivered at South Bend, Indiana, and shall be construed in accordance with the laws of the State of Indiana. Wherever possible each provision of this Agreement shall be interpreted in such manner as to be effective and valid under applicable law, but if any provision of this Agreement shall be prohibited by or invalid under applicable law, such provision shall be ineffective to the extent of such prohibition or invalidity, without invalidating the remainder of such provision or the remaining provisions of this Agreement.

This Agreement shall be binding upon the heirs, administrators and executors of the Debtor and the rights and privileges of the Bank hereunder shall inure to the benefit of its successors and assigns.

_____

Address: _____

_____   _____

F1025

Courtesy of Trustcorp Bank, South Bend, Indiana (formerly St. Joseph Bank and Trust Company, South Bend, Indiana).

itor's security interest in the original inventory of radios leaves the first radio, affixes to the proceeds, follows the proceeds through Bart's bank account, and affixes to the radio purchased to restock the inventory. Such after-acquired property clauses are common in secured transactions.

In the following case, one party disputed whether the financing statement had adequately described the property in question. (Financing statements, which we shall discuss in some detail shortly, consist of forms placed in the public records that indicate a secured party's retention of a security interest in certain collateral.)

In re Shore Haven Motor Inn, Inc.
124 Bankr. 617 (Bkrtcy. S.D. Fla. 1991)

FACTS

In December of 1987, the creditor, James Lavin, extended a loan to the debtor, South Haven Motor Inn, Inc. (South Haven), in the amount of $1,500,000 and secured the debt by a wraparound mortgage on the debtor's real property. The mortgage contained a clause wherein the debtor pledged as collateral the profits and rents derived from the hotel operation. The parties also executed and recorded a chattel mortgage (i.e., a security agreement) covering the goods, chattels, furniture, and appliances (including any proceeds thereof) situated on the property of the debtor. The creditor filed a financing statement with the Florida secretary of state on 4 February 1988, that listed as collateral all the furniture, goods, and appliances on the property of the debtor. Neither the security agreement nor the financing statement indicated that the loan was secured by the accounts receivable of the debtor. This fact notwithstanding, the creditor argued that it has the right to the cash collateral generated from the hotel operation on two grounds. First, the creditor asserted that it has a valid, perfected security interest in the hotel revenues of the debtor by virtue of the duly recorded wraparound mortgage. The creditor claimed that the room rates collected by the debtor from the operation of the hotel are "rents"; hence, the creditor maintained, the assignment of rents clause in the mortgage vests the creditor with absolute ownership of the rents following the debtor's default on the loan. Moreover, the creditor claimed that the filed financing statement covers the revenues of the hotel (i.e., the accounts receivable).

ISSUES

Were the revenues derived from the debtor's operation of the hotel "rents" subject to the security interest created by the recorded mortgage? Did a financing statement listing as collateral the goods, furniture, and appliances in each of the debtor's hotel rooms preserve for the creditor an interest in the debtor's accounts receivable?

HOLDINGS

No to each issue. The "rents" represent personalty, or personal property, that would not be subject to the wraparound mortgage on the real property. And the omission of any description of accounts receivable in the financing statement would leave the creditor unperfected and unsecured as to the hotel revenues (i.e., the accounts receivable) generated by the debtor's hotel operations.

REASONING

Numerous courts have addressed the issue of whether revenues derived from the operation of a hotel are "rents" subject to the security interest created by a recorded mortgage deed. Most jurisdictions have characterized hotel revenues as personalty, not rents. Such courts typically have reasoned that guests in a hotel or motel do not pay rent under a lease. Rather, they enter into a contract that provides them with a limited right to use the premises as mere licensees. Because licensees do not acquire an interest in the realty to which the license obtains, the revenues from such licenses represent personalty, or personal property. Thus, because the revenues derived from the debtor's hotel operation are personalty, a creditor must perfect a security interest in such personalty pursuant to Article 9 of the Florida Uniform Commercial Code. The lien spelled out in the creditor's wraparound mortgage on the realty, therefore, would not cover the revenues generated from the debtor's hotel operation. Alternatively, the creditor asserts that it has a perfected security interest in the revenues by virtue of the recorded security agreement and financing statement. A financing statement must contain, among other things, a statement indicating the types, or describing the items, of collateral. The description of the collateral in a financing statement is sufficient if it reasonably informs third parties that items in possession of the debtor may be subject to a prior security interest, thus putting third parties on notice that further inquiry may be necessary. The financing statement filed by the creditor here, although somewhat illegible, contains an addendum describing the items pledged as collateral by the debtor. This addendum lists the goods, furniture, and appliances in each of the hotel rooms of the debtor but does not describe the accounts receivable of the debtor as an item of collateral. Consequently, this omission of any reference to accounts receivable represents an inadequate description of the collateral and leaves the creditor unsecured vis-à-vis the hotel revenues generated by the debtor.

The need for evidence of the parties' intentions forms the basis for requiring such information on the security agreement. If the parties have spelled out their respective rights and duties in advance, there should be fewer disputes over the terms of the agreement and over the property that represents the collateral for the obligation secured.

PERFECTION

So far, we have focused primarily on the relationship between the creditor and the debtor and how the creditor may protect his or her interest in the collateral by becoming a secured party. Yet in that earlier discussion we noted that the processes leading to the creation and enforceability of a secured interest only give the secured party rights greater than those of the debtor; they do not necessarily confer on the secured party superior rights to the collateral vis-à-vis other creditors and the bankruptcy trustee. Now we turn to a discussion of how secured parties can protect themselves against such third parties who also may be claiming rights in the collateral. In other words, how can the seller/secured party in our earlier example protect the freezer and register from Bart's other business creditors (for example, produce suppliers) if Bart's financial situation deteriorates to the point that either the produce suppliers or—if Bart is on the verge of insolvency—the trustee in bankruptcy is trying to get all of Bart's equipment to satisfy Bart's creditors' claims against him?

Perfection is the process by which secured parties protect their collateral from the clutches of later creditors who have also given value when the debtor has used the same pieces of equipment as collateral for loans from them. The date of perfection, in turn, represents the date from which the law measures priorities if there are competing claims among other perfected creditors. The topic of priorities among secured parties will be addressed in Chapter 29.

In general, perfection occurs in one of three ways: By the creditor's filing a financing statement, by the creditor's taking possession of the collateral, or by the creditor's doing nothing beyond attachment. The last type is called *automatic perfection* (or perfection by attachment); and, as we shall learn, it is the method sellers of high-volume, relatively inexpensive items like televisions or stereos ordinarily choose. Rather than filing a financing statement or taking possession of the collateral, such creditors instead rely solely on their security agreement with the debtor to perfect their interests in the collateral.

The policy underlying the first two methods involves giving public notice of the existence of the security interest. In other words, the drafters of the Code believed that to deserve the status of a perfected secured creditor, the would-be secured party ought to undertake some affirmative action. And by either filing or possessing, the secured party is doing something that will give anyone looking for a security interest in the collateral notice of the secured party's claim. In the third situation, the nature of the collateral makes the costs of providing public notice arguably higher than the benefits to be gained from filing; for this reason, the Code does not place any affirmative duties on the secured creditor in these situations beyond attachment. Table 28.1 summarizes the methods of perfecting a security interest in various types of collateral.

Filing

Letters of credit Agreements made at the request of a customer that the bank will honor drafts or other demands for payment on compliance with the conditions specified in the credit.

Whether filing is necessary in order to perfect a security interest depends on the type of collateral involved. If the collateral is accounts or general intangibles, filing is ordinarily the only method of perfection.[21] For goods (including fixtures), chattel paper, and negotiable documents, the secured party may file but is not obligated to do so. Because of their negotiability, interests in money, instruments, and **letters of credit** can never be perfected by filing (possession is the usual method).[22] If filing is necessary, Section 9-403 of the UCC states that the presentation of a financing statement and the required fees to the appropriate state or local filing officer and that officer's acceptance of the statement constitutes filing. Hence, the device that the Code uses to give notice of the security interest is a *financing statement*. (An alternative method of filing, which we will not discuss in detail, involves registering the security interest according to the requirements of statutes other than the UCC, such as state acts covering the certification of title for automobiles, trailers, mobile homes, and boats.) According to Section 9-402, to be legally effective, a financing statement must contain certain information: the names of the debtor and secured party; their addresses; a statement indicating the types, or describing the items, of collateral; and the signature of the debtor. Figure 28.2 represents a typical financing statement. The filing of such a document allows third parties to obtain information about the security interest from either the

[21]Ibid., Sections 9-302, 9-401.
[22]Ibid., Section 9-304(1).

TABLE 28.1   Methods of Perfecting a Security Interest

TYPE OF COLLATERAL	PERFECTION METHOD (GENERALLY)
Consumer goods (excluding motor vehicles and fixtures)	Automatic (if a purchase money security interest)
	Possession
	Filing
Equipment	Filing
	Possession
Farm products	Filing
	Possession
Inventory (including motor vehicles)	Filing
	Possession
Fixtures	Filing
	Automatic (if a purchase money security interest)
	Possession (in theory)
Proceeds	Filing
	Automatic (if security interest in original collateral perfected)
Documents (negotiable)	Filing
	Possession
	Automatic (for 21 days)
Instruments	Possession
	Automatic (for 21 days)
Chattel paper	Filing
	Possession
Accounts	Filing
	Automatic (in some instances)
General intangibles	Filing
Letters of credit	Possession
Motor vehicles	Filing
	Compliance with state certificate of title statutes
Aircraft, copyrights, and the like	Filing (under applicable federal statutes, not under the UCC)

secured party or the debtor. Thus, if Bart wants credit from a wholesaler, and the latter wants to take a security interest in Bart's equipment before extending credit, the wholesaler will check the public records for financing statements to see which of Bart's equipment is already subject to security interests held by other creditors. This information will help the wholesaler make its decision about whether to extend credit to Bart.

The question of whether a copy of the security agreement, if filed, con-

FIGURE 28.2 Financing Statement Form

Courtesy of Trustcorp Bank, South Bend, Indiana (formerly St. Joseph Bank and Trust Company, South Bend, Indiana).

stitutes the legal equivalent of a financing statement has arisen repeatedly. The Code notes that filing the security agreement will constitute an effective filing if it contains the information required for a financing statement and if it has been signed by the debtor.[23] But because the description of the collateral in the security agreement serves to create enforceable rights in the collateral for the secured party, it must necessarily be more detailed than the information set out in the financing statement, which only provides public notice of

[23]Ibid., Section 9-402(1).

a claimed interest in the collateral. Given these differing rationales, it is therefore probably wise not to treat security agreements and financing statements interchangeably for filing purposes, as the following case demonstrates.

Sommers v. *International Business Machines*
640 F.2d 686 (5th Cir. 1981)

FACTS Sommers, the trustee in bankruptcy, sued International Business Machines (IBM) and West Publishing Company (West) for certain personal property in the debtor's estate, even though IBM and West had claimed perfected interests in this property. West had sold $20,875 worth of law books to Legal Cooperatives, Inc. (LCI). Thereafter, West had filed a financing statement with the secretary of state of the state of Texas. The financing statement had contained the names and addresses of LCI as the debtor and West as the secured party. It had been signed by West, but not by the debtor, LCI. Also, it had not described the collateral; instead, it had contained the following notation: "LAW BOOKS SEE ATTACHED SECURITY AGREEMENT." A photostatic reproduction of the purchase order had been attached to the financing statement. The trustee in bankruptcy had tried to avoid LCI's obligation to West on the grounds that the purchase order did not qualify as a security agreement under the UCC since it did not contain language granting the vendor a security interest in the goods, or, alternatively, on the grounds that the financing statement had not met the requirements of Section 9-402 of the UCC since it was not signed by the debtor and did not contain an adequate description of the collateral.

ISSUES Was the purchase order signed by an LCI officer a security agreement? If so, was it properly perfected?

HOLDINGS Yes, it was a security agreement. No, it had not been properly perfected.

REASONING The language in the purchase order to the effect that West had retained title to the books until they had been paid for was sufficient to reserve a security interest in the books to West. But a copy of the security agreement was not effective as a financing statement even if it had fulfilled all but one of the requirements of a financing statement (that is, the debtor had not signed the financing statement). The statutory requirements for a financing statement had to be met if a security agreement were filed as a financing statement. In addition, to call the omission of a formal requisite—here, the signature of one of the secured parties—a "minor error which was not seriously misleading" was unpersuasive. Therefore, because West's security interest in the collateral was unperfected, the trustee in bankruptcy could claim the books.

As implied in the *Sommers* case, a financing statement that substantially complies with the Code's requirements will be effective even though it contains *minor* errors that are not seriously misleading.[24] This provision of the Code is indicative of one policy of Article 9, which is to simplify the filing requirements and "to discourage the fanatical and impossibly refined reading of such statutory requirements in which courts have occasionally indulged themselves."[25] Nevertheless, as the next case shows, failure to provide an address may preclude perfection of the security interest.

[24]Ibid., Section 9-402(8).
[25]Ibid., Section 9-402, Official Comment 9.

In re L & K Transportation Co., Inc.
8 Bankr. 921 (D. Mass. 1981)

FACTS The debtor had bought a trucking business and had given the seller a security interest in, among other things, a **common carrier** certificate. The debtor had become bankrupt, and the trustee in bankruptcy had challenged the security interest. The financing statement had not included the debtor's address.

ISSUE Did the omission of the debtor's address on the financing statement invalidate the legal effectiveness of the filed statement?

HOLDING Yes. This financing statement did not legally perfect the seller's security interest because of the omitted information.

REASONING The trustee was correct. Although the Code should be liberally construed and applied in order to promote its underlying purposes and policies of simplifying and clarifying commercial transactions, and despite the fact that a financing statement is to be upheld "even though it contains minor errors which are not seriously misleading," this was not such a minor error. Unless it could be shown that the debtor was so well known that there would be no question of its identity, this financing statement would not perfect the seller's interest. In fact, the evidence had shown that the debtor was clearly not so well known that mail could be delivered to it by utilizing its name alone as an address. Thus, the absence of the debtor's address on the financing statement had precluded the establishment of a valid security interest.

Common carrier A person or firm offering to the public, for compensation, the service of transporting people or goods.

The financing statement ordinarily will be effective if it contains enough information to cause the party searching the records to look further, which will enable that party to discover the perfected security interest. Note that in the following case, however, the court believed the defect in the financing statement was so seriously misleading that it invalidated the attempt to perfect the security interest.

In re Nowling
124 Bankr. 858 (N.D. Fla. 1991)

FACTS The debtors, Billy and Brenda Nowling, operated a lawnmower shop prior to filing for bankruptcy under Chapter 7 of the Bankruptcy Code in August, 1987. The Nowlings did business as "B&B Equipment." All their business stationery, invoices, and business cards used the name "B&B Equipment." On 26 June 1986, the Nowlings executed a security agreement in the name of "B&B Equipment" with Roberts Supply, Inc. (Roberts), along with a financing statement that Roberts filed centrally with the secretary of state. This financing statement listed "B&B Equipment" as the debtor. Roberts sold various merchandise to the Nowlings on credit, which merchandise the Nowlings ultimately returned to Roberts for credit, prior to the bankruptcy filing. Venn, as trustee, sought to avoid this transfer as a preference under Section 547 of the Bankruptcy Code, which allows the trustee to avoid transfers to "unsecured" creditors. (If Roberts were a "secured" creditor of the debtors, the return of items for credit would not represent a voidable preference under Section 547.)

ISSUE

Was the financing statement filed by Roberts solely in the trade name of the debtors (and not in their individual names) sufficient to perfect a security interest in the merchandise returned by the Nowlings?

HOLDING

No. The financing statement filed by Roberts solely in the trade name of the debtors inadequately identified the debtors and, as such, under Florida law was insufficient to perfect a security interest in the merchandise at issue.

REASONING

A determination of the adequacy of the notice provided by the financing statement necessitates consideration of Article 9 of Uniform Commercial Code, which provides: "A financing statement is sufficient if it gives the names of the debtor and the secured party, is signed by the debtor, gives an address of the secured party from which information concerning the security interest may be obtained, gives a mailing address of the debtor, and contains a statement indicating the types, or describing the items, of collateral." Regarding the identification of the debtor, the UCC provides in pertinent part: "A financing statement sufficiently shows the name of the debtor if it gives the individual, partnership, or corporate name of the debtor, whether or not it adds other trade names or names of partners." A third subsection also provides generally: "A financing statement substantially complying with the requirements of this section is effective even though it contains minor errors which are not seriously misleading." The bankruptcy judge correctly noted in his order that the purpose of the UCC filing system involves giving notice to interested parties that a security interest exists in the property of the debtor. A financing statement is effective as long as it puts any searcher on inquiry. The law also considers the trustee to be in the position of a hypothetical but prudent creditor. The judge concluded that any reasonably prudent creditor conducting a search with the secretary of state would have discovered Roberts's financing statement because the statement consisted of a technical defect that was "not seriously misleading." Yet the commentary underlying another Florida amendment notes that, since the secured party or other person searching the record may likely be unaware of trade names, filing a financing statement under trade names would not suffice to perfect a security interest in collateral, since such filings *would* seriously mislead the searcher. The other basis for the bankruptcy judge's decision stemmed from his conclusion that the debtors' filing their bankruptcy petition as "Billy and Brenda Nowling, d/b/a B&B Equipment" had put the trustee on notice to search for a financing statement under both the trade and individual names. However, as the trustee pointed out, Section 544 of the Bankruptcy Code permits a trustee to avoid a transfer of property to an unsecured creditor "without regard to any knowledge of the trustee or of any creditor." Thus, even actual knowledge on the part of the trustee will not suffice if the statement is defective. Further, the Florida legislature amended the law in 1979 so that creditors with knowledge would have priority over unperfected security interests. This section applies to Venn; moreover, the parties agree with the bankruptcy judge that the Bankruptcy Act puts the trustee in the place of a hypothetical lien creditor. Roberts acknowledges that the trustee's knowledge of the encumbrance is irrelevant to the question of the perfection of the security interest. But Roberts asserts that the trustee's knowledge of the fact that the Nowlings were doing business under a trade name different from their individual names had placed on the trustee the duty to inquire into recordings under both names. Roberts, however, cites no authority for this untenable proposition. If *actual knowledge* of the encumbrance itself is insufficient to defeat a lien creditor's priority over an unperfected security interest, *constructive notice* of the fact that a debtor goes by two different names should be **a fortiori** insufficient. Hence, neither of the grounds relied on by the trial court is persuasive. Moreover, a form filed in only a trade name (and not in the individual names of the debtors) remains insufficient to perfect a security interest in the subject property. Consequently, a remand of the case to the Bankruptcy Division for further proceedings was warranted.

A fortiori   All the more; said of a conclusion that follows with even greater logical necessity than another already accepted in the argument.

Numerous other courts have held that the creditor's filing of a financing statement that lists the debtor's trade or business name rather than its legal name constitutes an insufficient filing to perfect a security interest under Section 9-402. However, because the law differs among the various jurisdictions on this point, the creditor's precision in filing the appropriate information often determines whether the courts deem the security interest at issue perfected or unperfected.

You should also be aware that sometimes a creditor will file a financing statement even before the completion of the security agreement. But even though a financing statement may be filed before a security agreement is made or a security interest otherwise attaches,[26] filing before attachment does not constitute perfection.[27] Without attachment at some later time, no perfection ever occurs.

The Code's flexibility is nowhere more apparent than in its handling of the proper place for filing the financing statement. The Code does not take a stance on whether filings should be local or statewide, an issue that had caused a great many pre-Code problems. Instead, in Section 9-401(1), it provides three different options that depend on the type of collateral involved, thus allowing the respective states to choose the method they believe is most conducive to giving notice of claims.

A financing statement generally is effective for a period of five years from the date of filing, after which the security interest lapses (or becomes unperfected) unless the secured party files a continuation statement before this lapse.[28] The secured party may file such a statement within six months prior to the expiration of the financing statement. The secured party must sign the continuation statement, identify the original statement by file number, and state that the original statement still remains in effect.[29] The filing of a continuation statement prolongs the effectiveness of the original financing statement for five years, and the Code does not limit the number of such statements that a secured party can file.

Assuming that the secured party has neither released all or part of the collateral described in the financing statement[30] nor assigned its security interest to another,[31] the Code imposes certain additional duties on the secured party. For example, the secured party must comply within two weeks whenever the debtor requests a statement of account or a list of collateral from the secured party. (Presumably the debtor will request such information because of a lack of certainty about the total amount owed.) Failure to comply may make the secured party liable for losses to the debtor caused by the noncompliance and may, in rare cases, even cost the secured party its security interest. This will be true regarding any security interests reflected in the lists written up by the debtor should any persons be misled by the secured party's failure to comply (as, for instance, by failing to correct the list).[32] On the other hand,

[26]Ibid., Section 9-402(1).
[27]Ibid., Section 9-303(1).
[28]Ibid., Section 9-403(2), (3).
[29]Ibid.
[30]Ibid., Section 9-406.
[31]Ibid., Section 9-405(2).
[32]Ibid., Section 9-208(2).

the Code protects the secured party from burdensome requests by limiting the debtor to one such list or statement every six months. The secured party may charge ten dollars for each additional request within this time period.[33]

Once there are no outstanding obligations under the financing statement, the Code sets out a procedure that may require the secured party to file a termination statement noting discharge of the obligations and/or termination of the financing agreement. Where consumer goods are concerned, the Code places an affirmative duty on the secured party to file a termination statement within one month or within ten days following written demand by the debtor once the debtor has completely paid for the goods. In all other cases, however, the secured party need not file a termination statement unless the debtor requests such a filing.[34] But when compliance is necessary, the Code subjects noncomplying secured parties to certain penalties. Termination statements, which refer to the appropriate financing statement by file number, clear the public records so that the presence of old, irrelevant financing statements will not leave a would-be creditor with an unrealistic picture of a credit applicant's creditworthiness and reliability.

Possession

As mentioned earlier, the secured party's possession of the collateral is in some cases the method used for perfecting the security interest.[35] Historically, when financing arrangements were more primitive, possession of the personal property was the surest sign of ownership; hence, perfection by possession was the most popular method. Even today secured parties ordinarily must perfect security interests in letters of credit, money, and instruments in this manner and may perfect goods, negotiable documents, or chattel paper in this fashion as well. For instance, a bank may require a debtor to give it possession of the debtor's stocks and bonds as collateral for securing a loan. As noted earlier, this is called a pledge.

As we will discuss in more detail later, the type of collateral involved is relevant in determining whether perfection can occur by possession. If the creditor's possession of collateral (and the debtor's resultant *lack* of possession) is to serve as public notice of the security interest to other parties, the collateral must be tangible; that is, one must be able to see, touch, or move it. All the types of collateral mentioned in the preceding paragraph as perfectible by possession have this attribute. On the other hand, contract rights, accounts that constitute a significant portion of the debtor's business, and general intangibles merely represent rights and have no physical embodiment. Thus, they can never be perfected by possession; filing is necessary.

Automatic Perfection

Automatic perfection is the method ordinarily used for perfecting *purchase money security interests* in consumer goods.[36] As mentioned earlier, in these

---

[33]Ibid., Section 9-208(3).
[34]Ibid., Section 9-404(1).
[35]Ibid., Section 9-305.
[36]Ibid., Section 9-302(1)(d).

situations, *perfection occurs on attachment alone.* A look at the nature of these transactions shows why filing is unnecessary. The Code defines a purchase money security interest as one retained by the seller of the collateral to secure all or part of its price or taken by a person who by making advances or incurring an obligation gives value to enable the debtor to acquire rights in the collateral.[37]

Typically, a seller will retain a purchase money security interest in the collateral, whether it be a stove, refrigerator, washing machine, or stereo. This means that the seller will usually sell to the buyer, on an installment basis, goods that the buyer will use for personal purposes. The seller will in turn retain a security interest in the consumer goods—for instance, a stereo—to secure the unpaid purchase price. If the buyer misses any installment payments, the seller can repossess the collateral. The secured party's purchase money security interest is perfectible the moment the transaction has occurred because there is a written security agreement signed by the debtor, the secured party has given value, and the debtor has rights in the collateral (that is, attachment has occurred). All of this will have happened (thanks to the modern wonder of "form contracts") a short time before the debtor walks out with the stereo in hand.

Given the type of collateral involved (consumer goods) and the frequency with which such transactions occur, the UCC has commonsensibly followed pre-Code law in eliminating the filing requirement for these types of commercial deals. It would make little sense to require a merchant to pay the filing fees and other administrative costs associated with filing for every $100 item sold. Moreover, there would be few benefits from filing in such situations, since consumer goods—already low in price and prone to rapid deterioration—are not the types of property later secured parties would want as collateral anyway. Therefore, the public notice to such creditors afforded by filing would have little value and would only clutter the filing offices. The same rationale underlies the availability of automatic perfection as a method for perfecting certain transfers of accounts, documents, and instruments, as well.

Note that the court had occasion to resort to many of these concepts in deciding how to dispose of the interesting case that follows.

In re Lockovich
124 Bankr. 660 (W.D. Pa. 1991)

FACTS On about 20 August 1986, John J. and Clara Lockovich purchased a 22-foot 1986 Chapparel Villian III boat from the Greene County Yacht Club (the Club) for $32,500. The Lockoviches (Debtors) paid $6000 to the Club and executed

[37]Ibid., Section 9-107.

a "security agreement/lien contract" that set forth the purchase and finance terms. In the contract, the Lockoviches granted a security interest in the boat to the holder of the contract. When Gallatin National Bank (Gallatin) paid the Yacht Club $26,757.14 on the Lockoviches' behalf, the Club assigned the contract to Gallatin. Gallatin then filed the financing statements in the appropriate Greene County office and with the secretary of the Commonwealth of Pennsylvania. Greene County was the county in which Gallatin was located, but the Lockoviches were residents of Allegheny County. The filing of the financing statements therefore was ineffective to perfect the security interest in the boat. The Lockoviches subsequently defaulted under the terms of the security agreement to Gallatin by failing to remit payments as required. Before Gallatin could take action, the Lockoviches filed for relief under Chapter 11 of the Bankruptcy Code. Gallatin then sought to enforce its rights pursuant to the security agreement. On 2 October 1989, the Bankruptcy Court denied Gallatin's motion, holding that because Gallatin had failed to perfect its security interest in the boat by filing, it was an unsecured creditor. As a holder of an unperfected security interest, Gallatin's right to the boat remained inferior to that of the debtor-in-possession, a hypothetical leinholder pursuant to the bankruptcy laws.

ISSUE   Did Gallatin have to file a financing statement in order to perfect its purchase money security interest in the boat?

HOLDING   No. Gallatin held a purchase money security interest in a consumer good (the boat) and hence did not have to file a financing statement in order to achieve the status of secured party.

REASONING   To perfect a security interest in collateral under the Code, a secured party must file a financing statement in the office of the Secretary of the Commonwealth and in the appropriate office of the county in which the debtor resides. Yet the Pennsylvania UCC permits several exceptions to this general rule depending on the type of collateral: "(a) General Rule—A financing statement must be filed to perfect all security interests except the following . . . (4) a purchase money security interest in consumer goods; but filing is required for a motor vehicle required to be registered." Three significant problems exist in determining the automatic perfection of purchase money interests in consumer goods. First, what is a purchase money security interest? Second, what are "consumer goods"? Third, can massive and expensive items qualify as consumer goods? As to the first question, a purchase money security interest consists of one "(1) taken or retained by the seller of the collateral to secure all or part of its price; or (2) taken by a person who by making advances or incurring an obligation gives value to enable the debtor to acquire rights in or the use of collateral if such value is in fact so used." The parties do not dispute the fact that the security interest held by Gallatin amounts to a purchase money security interest. As to the remaining questions—which involve issues of first impression in this state—a court's analysis must focus on whether a $32,500 watercraft is a consumer good under Pennsylvania law. In Pennsylvania, "consumer goods" include those used or bought for use primarily for personal, family, or household purposes. Such goods are not classified according to design or intrinsic nature, but according to the use to which the owner puts them. The Lockoviches never maintained that they utilize the boat for anything other than for their personal use. Under the clear mandate of the Code, a consumer good subject to exception from the filing of financing statements is determined by the use or intended use of the good; design, size, weight, shape, and cost remain irrelevant. In fact, if a millionaire decides to purchase the Queen Mary for his or her personal or family luxury on the high seas, under the Code, the great Queen is nothing but a common consumer good. There need be no debate as to cost, size, or life expectancy. In short, creditors must be confident that when they enter into a commercial transaction, they will play by the rules as written in the Code. Those who do not believe Pennsylvania law should permit an expensive boat to fall within the classification of consumer goods have two legislative solutions available. One is to require explicitly the filing of security interests in motorboats. The other approach, adopted in some states, involves limiting the value to which the consumer goods exemption applies. Durable, valuable consumer goods on which a creditor is likely to rely for collateral encompass more than motorboats or mobile homes. If motorboats or other expensive items are to be excluded from the dictates of the Pennsylvania UCC provision in dispute, either via specific exemptions or a fixed ceiling price for consumer goods below which no financing statements are required, such determinations are necessarily for the Pennsylvania legislature. For present analysis, the boat is a consumer good and, pursuant to Pennsylvania law, Gallatin did not have to file a financing statement in order to perfect its security interest in the boat. Since Gallatin has a valid security interest in the boat, it can enforce its security interest under the bankruptcy laws.

RELATED TOPICS

Two other topics deserve consideration before we leave the issues covered in this chapter: Multistate transactions and proceeds.

Multistate Transactions

A related aspect of perfection involves the problem of collateral, such as equipment, that the debtor can move across state or county lines. The Code's rules for such situations, expressed in Section 9-103, are very complex. In general, the Code says that with respect to ordinary goods, the secured party should perfect its interest by filing or by some other method in the state where the collateral is located. Upon the debtor's removal of the collateral, the secured party should file in the new jurisdiction.

If a purchase money security interest is involved and both parties at the time of the creation of the security interest understand that the debtor will move the collateral to another jurisdiction, the law of the new jurisdiction controls perfection for thirty days after the debtor receives possession, assuming the collateral is moved in that time. To avoid losing priority of perfection, the secured party ought to file in both jurisdictions. If collateral has previously been perfected in one jurisdiction and then is moved to another, it remains perfected for its period of original perfection or for four months, whichever expires first. Thus, the secured party should file in the new jurisdiction before this four-month period expires.

The removal of motor vehicles from jurisdiction to jurisdiction is covered by state certificate of title laws and by the Code.[38] Because these laws are very complicated, a wise secured creditor will keep abreast of the debtor's removal of these vehicles in order to do everything possible to retain a perfected security interest in them. Generally speaking, a secured party will need to re-perfect (usually by filing) within four months of the collateral's removal to the new jurisdiction if the new jurisdiction is a non–title certificate state. If, in contrast, the jurisdiction to which the debtor has removed the motor vehicle requires perfection by notation of the security interest on the title, reperfection in this situation will not occur by filing in the new jurisdiction but rather by the secured party's noting its interest on the motor vehicle's certificate of title. In such circumstances, the secured party may have longer than four months in which to reperfect, since reperfection will be necessary only when the debtor requests the surrender of the vehicle's title in order to receive new registration

---

[38]Ibid., Section 9-103(1)(a), (2); 9-302(3)(b), (4).

papers in the new state. At that time, the prudent secured party will note its interest again on the new certificate of title and thus remain perfected.

For an interesting illustration of these concepts, examine the next case.

Trans Canada Credit Corporation, Ltd. v. *Kosack*
590 A.2d 1295 (Pa. Super. 1991)

FACTS
Trans Canada Credit Corporation, Ltd. (Trans Canada), a Canadian corporation, lent money to DiCicco and secured its interest in the loan proceeds with a chattel mortgage. By the terms of the chattel mortgage, Trans Canada could take immediate possession of the vehicle DiCicco purchased upon either DiCicco's removal of the vehicle from Canada or DiCicco's sale or transfer of the vehicle. DiCicco later removed the vehicle from Canada and obtained a Pennsylvania certificate of title on or about 14 April 1987. The certificate of title did not have an endorsement indicating Trans Canada's lien as en encumbrance on the vehicle, but it did bear a notation indicating that the vehicle was an "out of state" vehicle. On 16 May 1987, DiCicco sold the secured vehicle to Kosack, an automobile broker and dealer. Kosack subsequently resold the vehicle at an interstate auto auction. In January, 1988, Trans Canada made application in Pennsylvania to perfect its security interest. This statute allows the perfection of a security interest in the Commonwealth of Pennsylvania before or after the expiration of a four-month period within which an out-of-state lien might otherwise be perfected under the laws of the jurisdiction where the motor vehicle had been located when the secured interest had attached. Thus, Trans Canada subsequently characterized this filing in January, 1988, as a "reperfection" of the security interest. Trans Canada, after making several unsuccessful demands on Richard Kosack d/b/a Family Motors, filed this lawsuit for $4875, the uncontested fair market value of the automobile at the time Kosack resold it at an auto auction. A nonjury trial resulted in a verdict in favor of Kosack. On consideration of posttrial motions, the trial court granted **judgment non obstante veredicto** in favor of Trans Canada due to its belief that Trans Canada, as a validly perfected creditor, had priority regarding the sold automobile.

> **Judgment non obstante ver-
> edicto (or judgment n.o.v.)**
> Literally, judgment notwithstanding
> the verdict; a judgment entered by
> the court in favor of the plaintiff in
> circumstances in which the jury has
> rendered a verdict for the defen-
> dant (or vice versa).

ISSUE
Did the perfection of Trans Canada's security interest in Canada cover the removal of the automobile to Pennsylvania and thus give Trans Canada priority regarding the automobile?

HOLDING
Yes. A valid out-of-state lien continues perfected in Pennsylvania, even if the certificate of title does not reflect the lien, for four months. Moreover, the notation on the Pennsylvania title reflecting a prior out-of-state title should have put a dealer such as Kosack on inquiry notice as to a claimed prior security interest.

REASONING
Trans Canada argued that the relevant Pennsylvania statute provides:

> (ii) If the name of the lienholder is not shown on an existing certificate of title issued by that jurisdiction, the security interest continues perfected in this Commonwealth for four months after a first certificate of title of the vehicle is issued in this Commonwealth, and, thereafter if, within the four-month period, it is perfected in this Commonwealth. The security interest may also be perfected in this Commonwealth after the expiration of the four-month period, in which case perfection dates from the time of perfection in this Commonwealth.

Trans Canada therefore claimed that where an out-of-state lien is not shown on the existing certificate of title, a security interest continues perfected in the commonwealth for four months after a first certificate of title for the vehicle has been issued in the commonwealth regardless of whether the security interest holder applies for its perfection before or after the expiration of the four months. In contrast, Kosack maintained that Trans Canada, having failed to perfect within four months, could enjoy a perfected security interest only from the time of actual application. The Canadian title proffered to the commonwealth for retitling indisputably did not note the encumbrance of Trans Canada's interest from Canada. However, as Trans Canada pointed out, a notation on the Pennsylvania title (which Kosack had acknowledged would indicate that the Pennsylvania title had been derived from a prior out-of-state title) should have placed Kosack on inquiry notice. Kosack had been a dealer in automobiles for forty years and was sophisticated in the matter of automobile titles and security interests. The plain language of the statute gives an absolute and unconditional four-month period within which an out-of-state security interest, if the same were perfected under the law of the jurisdiction where the vehicle was located when the security interest attached, continues perfected in the Commonwealth of Pennsylvania for four months following a Pennsylvania issuance of title. Thus, Trans Canada's security interest had been perfected both when DiCicco had sold the vehicle to Kosack and when Kosack subsequently had sold the vehicle at the auto auction. The law of Ontario, the applicable out-of-state law, does not require notice of an encumbrance to be noted on the Ontario title. To the contrary, under Ontario law, the interest is perfected on the registration of a financing statement. Hence, as settled law holds, if the title to an automobile originates in a jurisdiction where there is no requirement that a perfected security interest appear on the face of the title and the automobile is brought into another jurisdiction and new certificate of title is issued showing no security interest, the holder of the security interest continues to have a perfected security interest for four months from the date of the issuance of a new title. That the security holder fails to perfect its interest until after the expiration of the four-month period does not matter. The purpose of the statute is to give the security interest holder a four-month period to recover the auto without such recovery being foreclosed by the defense of a bona fide purchaser for value. The purpose of a foreign title notation can only be to alert a purchaser that he or she should make further inquiry as to the foreign title. This is true particularly when the purchaser is not an unsophisticated consumer but rather one who deals in automobiles.

Proceeds

The final point to be made about security interests and perfection is that the Code allows a secured party's interest to reach the proceeds of the debtor's disposition of the collateral.[39] In other words, the secured party has a "lien" (similar to that which we just discussed in the context of multistate transactions) that "floats" over the collateral and includes as "proceeds" whatever is received on the sale, exchange, collection or other disposition of the collateral.[40] If Bart were to sell the freezer and cash register to another person, the secured party's interest in the collateral would extend even to the cash proceeds realized from this sale. Thus, the issue of proceeds, and the Code's treatment of it, implicates not only perfection rules but also priority rules (especially when, as is often the case, the trustee in bankruptcy is involved as well).

SUMMARY

A secured transaction assures payment by the buyer: If the buyer does not pay the seller, the seller's security interest will allow the seller to repossess the property. A secured transaction typically involves a secured party, a debtor, a security agreement, and collateral. The Code categorizes collateral according

[39]Ibid., Section 9-204.
[40]Ibid., Section 9-306.

to its nature or its use. One type of collateral is goods; the different classes of goods are mutually exclusive. Collateral may also consist of documents, instruments, letters of credit, proceeds, accounts, chattel paper, and general intangibles. Article 9 applies to consensual security interests in personal property or fixtures but not to those arising by operation of law. It covers leases meant as security but not "true" leases. Attachment is the process by which the secured party creates an enforceable security interest in the collateral. A signed security agreement is evidence that attachment has occurred.

Perfection refers to the method by which secured parties protect themselves against later creditors of the debtor. Perfection can take place in one of three ways: (1) by the creditor's filing a valid financing statement, (2) by the creditor's possession of the collateral, and (3) by automatic perfection. The method of perfection that the secured party should use often depends on the type of collateral involved. If filing is the applicable method, a legally effective financing statement must be used.

The Code's rules regarding multistate transactions are very complex, but the secured party should check them whenever the debtor moves the collateral from one jurisdiction to another in order to ensure continuation of perfection. The secured party generally can reach the proceeds of the debtor's later disposition of the collateral if he or she has met certain requirements under the Code.

DISCUSSION QUESTIONS

1. What is a secured transaction?
2. Define a security interest.
3. Name and define the various types of property recognized by the Code as collateral.
4. If I do not pay the mechanic who fixes my car and he or she obtains a judgment against me, does the mechanic have an Article 9 security interest in my car? Why or why not?
5. What is the difference between a "true lease" and a "lease intended as security"?
6. What is attachment, and what are the requirements for it?

7. Name the criteria necessary for a valid security agreement.
8. Define perfection and discuss in detail the three methods by which perfection occurs.
9. What kinds of defects will cause a financing statement to be ineffective?
10. What problems can arise if Debbie Dunn has given her bank a security interest in bulldozers, and she moves the bulldozers from Indiana to Michigan?

CASE PROBLEMS

1. A farmer had granted a security interest in his chickens to a bank and a government agency. Upon the farmer's bankruptcy, both creditors claimed the chickens. The bank had taken a security interest in all of the debtor's "inventory." The agency argued chickens are livestock and therefore farm products, not inventory,

under the Code. Did the bank's security interest cover the chickens? (*In re Northeast Chick Services* v. *Collins*, 43 Bankr. 326 [D. Mass. 1985].)

2. Owens made a loan of $25,000 to Howard. Two promissory notes signed by Howard, each containing the words "SECURITY: 1956 GMC bus," evidenced the loan. As security for payment of the notes, Howard endorsed the certificate of title for the bus and delivered the certificate to Owens. Five months later, Howard sold the bus to Simplot for $45,000, to be paid in installments. After Simplot had paid the last installment, he took possession of the bus and received from Howard a bill of sale stating that the bus was free of all liens and encumbrances. When Simplot asked for the certificate of title, Howard told him it was lost. Simplot requested that the Idaho Department of Transportation conduct a title search; at the same time, he also applied for a transfer of title. Meanwhile, after Owens had approached Howard and unsuccessfully demanded payment of the loan, Owens applied for a certificate of title showing Howard as the owner and Owens as the lienholder. Despite Simplot's pending application, the Department of Transportation issued Owens the requested title. The Department also issued a certificate of title to Simplot. The certificate designated him as the owner and showed no liens or encumbrances. Sometime later, Howard notified Simplot that Owens was claiming a security interest in the bus. At Simplot's request, the Idaho Department of Transportation held a hearing to determine the parties' respective interests. The Department concluded that Simplot owned the bus, but that the title remained encumbered by Owens's lien. Simplot then filed this action, claiming ownership free of all liens and seeking an award of damages against Howard. Simplot based his claim on the fact that the promissory notes bearing the notation "SECURITY: 1956 GMC bus," in conjunction with Howard's execution and delivery of the certificate of title to the bus to Owens, constituted actions legally inadequate to create a security interest and to effect attachment of such an interest. Would you agree with Simplot? (*Simplot* v. *William C. Owens, M.D., P.A.*, 805 P.2d. 449 [Idaho 1990].)

3. Silverline Building and Maintenance Company (Silverline) contracted with the District of Columbia (the District) in December, 1983, to perform janitorial services in two office buildings occupied by the District. At approximately the same time, Silverline entered into a factoring arrangement with Thomas Funding Corporation (Thomas) in which Silverline assigned its right to payment pursuant to its contracts with the District to Thomas in exchange for money Silverline received from Thomas to use as working capital. Silverline notified the District of the assignment by letter and directed the District to make payments to Thomas on receipt of Silverline's invoices. In addition, Thomas filed a financing statement with the Recorder of Deeds covering "all now owned and hereafter acquired accounts, contract rights . . . [and] general intangibles of the debtor." The financing statement, however, inadvertently identified the debtor as "Silvermine Building Maintenance Co.," mistakenly substituting the letter "m" for the second letter "l" in the word Silverline. Until October, 1984, the District paid Thomas the amount due Silverline under the janitorial service contracts. In April and May, 1984, the Internal Revenue Service (IRS) had made assessments against Silverline for unpaid federal income taxes totaling $22,370.19. On 5 October 1984, the IRS filed a notice of tax lien against Silverline with the Recorder of Deeds and served the District with a notice of tax levy against any property or rights to property belonging to Silverline. At the time, the District owed $18,747 on the janitorial service contracts for work performed during September, 1984. Instead of paying the amount owed under the contracts to Thomas, the District paid this amount to the IRS on 1 January 1985. Thomas then brought suit against the District for the amount due under the Silverline contracts, $18,747. Thomas, as a perfected secured party, would have full rights to the $18,747. However, if Thomas had failed to perfect its interest in the assignment of the accounts, Silverline would retain a property interest on which a third-party lien creditor, such as the IRS, could attach a lien. The IRS argued that the misspelling of Silverline's name on the financing statement had made the filing by Thomas invalid. Was the misspelling of Silverline's name as "Silvermine" an error so seriously misleading as to render the financing statement ineffective for the purposes of putting a third party on notice that Silverline had given Thomas a security interest in the accounts? (*District of Columbia* v. *Thomas Funding Corporation*, 15 UCC Reporting Service 2d 242 [D.C. Cir. 1991].)

4. Bellman offered to buy cattle from Rohweder at $625 per head. Because Bellman could not obtain financing to complete the purchase, Rohweder entered a "share agreement"—not uncommon in the cattle business—under which Bellman would breed the Rohweder cows and care for all the cows and calves. For these services, Bellman would receive 40 percent of the calf

crop. Rohweder would remain the owner and receive the rest of the calves. Pursuant to this arrangement, Rohweder delivered 710 cows to pastures Bellman had rented in Nebraska. Later, Bellman began to experience financial difficulties and filed for bankruptcy. Aberdeen Production Credit Association (PCA) had security agreements with Bellman, and upon his bankruptcy, argued that the after-acquired property clauses in these agreements covered Rohweder's livestock, as well. Rohweder contended that he at all times had remained the owner of the cattle and had only relinquished possession to Bellman. Rohweder asserted that PCA's alleged security interest was invalid because Bellman's mere possession of the livestock and Bellman's unexercised option to purchase had not given the debtor sufficient rights in the collateral for a security interest to attach. Who had the better argument? (*Rohweder* v. *Aberdeen Production Credit Association,* 765 F.2d 109 [8th Cir. 1985].)

5. The Renslows, the debtors, granted Prairie State Bank (the Bank) a security interest in twelve guns. The Bank perfected its interest as of 13 April 1981 by filing a financing statement in Illinois and by taking possession of the guns in November, 1981. The Renslows then moved to Arizona and in August, 1982, regained the guns from the Bank, which had been holding them. The Internal Revenue Service (IRS) obtained tax liens against the debtors in June and October, 1982. In September, 1982, the guns were stolen. Although the guns had been insured, the insurer did not know to whom to pay the insurance proceeds, since both the IRS and the Bank claimed them. The evidence showed that the Bank had failed to reperfect its interest within a four-month period after the guns had been sent to the debtors' new location in Arizona and that the IRS's lien had been obtained after that four months' time. Who had priority as to the insurance proceeds, the Bank or the IRS? (*Prairie State Bank* v. *Internal Revenue Service,* 745 P.2d 966 [Ariz. App. 1987].)

6. Heritage House Interiors, Inc. (Heritage House) is in the business of selling and installing furniture, accessories, and furnishings. In order to obtain inventory, Heritage House and Chicago Pacific Corporation, by and through its division known as Pennsylvania House (Pennsylvania House), entered into a security agreement in August, 1988. Pursuant to this agreement, Pennsylvania House agreed to sell furniture and accessories to Heritage House. In turn, Heritage House granted Pennsylvania House a security interest in (1) all furniture and accessories purchased by Heritage House from Penn-

sylvania House and (2) the proceeds of this collateral. The security agreement noted that the agreements were "for the benefit of [Pennsylvania House], its successors and assigns." In connection with the security agreement, Heritage House filed a financing statement with the Florida secretary of state. The financing statement identified the secured party as "Pennsylvania House, a division of Chicago Pacific Corporation, 137 North 10th Street, Lewisburg, PA 17837." The financing statement described Pennsylvania House's collateral as "all inventory of the debtor previously acquired from the secured party, or hereafter acquired from the secured party, specifically including Pennsylvania House furniture and including Pennsylvania House accessories, as well as accounts receivable, chattel paper, and proceeds from sale of such inventory." In January, 1989, Chicago Pacific Corporation merged with Maytag Corporation (Maytag). Maytag, as the surviving corporation, succeeded by operation of law to all rights and property of Chicago Pacific. Pennsylvania House, now a division of Maytag, remained in the same business location and continued to sell furniture and accessories to Heritage House. In June, 1989, LADD Furniture, Inc., (LADD) agreed to purchase the assets of Pennsylvania House–Maytag, excluding "any of [Maytag's] claims or causes of action against third parties relating to the assets, properties, business or operations . . . arising out of transactions occurring prior to the closing date." In July, 1989, LADD and its wholly owned subsidiary, Pennsylvania House, Inc., entered into an assignment and assumption agreement whereby LADD assigned the interests it would acquire in Pennsylvania House–Maytag to Pennsylvania House, Inc. The same day, Maytag assigned to Pennsylvania House, Inc. the assets of Pennsylvania House–Maytag. Pennsylvania House, Inc. continued to sell furniture and accessories to Heritage House under the prior agreements involving Heritage House and Pennsylvania House and Pennsylvania House–Maytag.

In June, 1990, Heritage House filed its voluntary petition for relief under Chapter 11 of the Bankruptcy Code. At the time, Heritage House owed Pennsylvania House, Inc. $426,505.78, and its inventory included furniture and accessories valued at approximately $195,000, which items had been purchased from Pennsylvania House, Pennsylvania House–Maytag, or Pennsylvania House, Inc. The final transaction in this complex chain of events occurred in September, 1990, when Maytag and LADD assigned "any and all security interests and causes of action" they had against Heritage House to Pennsylvania House, Inc. Despite the transfers of assets among Pennsylvania House, Pennsylvania House–Maytag, LADD, and Pennsylvania House, Inc., the physical location of the entity doing business with Heritage House had always remained the same. Thus, except for the name of the secured party, all of the information contained in the financing statement continued to be correct. Heritage House claimed that the financing statement filed by Pennsylvania House was insufficient to perfect any interest Pennsylvania House, Inc. might have had in the inventory. Despite the complicated facts surrounding this matter, the narrow question involved in the subsequent litigation between the parties focused on whether Pennsylvania House, Inc. enjoyed a perfected and enforceable security interest in the furniture that Heritage House had purchased from Pennsylvania House, Pennsylvania House–Maytag, and Pennsylvania House, Inc. and the proceeds therefrom, where the financing statement filed by Pennsylvania House had never been amended and where neither Pennsylvania House–Maytag nor Pennsylvania House, Inc. had ever entered into a new security agreement with Heritage House. If you were the judge, how would you decide this issue? (*In re Heritage House Interiors, Inc.*, 122 Bankr. 605 [M.D. Fla. 1990].)

7. In August, 1988, Laurel Explosives, Inc. (Laurel), filed an action against H & P Coal Company (H & P) seeking to recover on a debt secured by a Caterpillar D9H tractor. A default judgment granted against H & P upheld the validity of Laurel's security interest in the Caterpillar D9H tractor. Subsequently, Laurel filed a lawsuit against First National Bank & Trust Company of Corbin (First National), which had possession of the Caterpillar D9H tractor, because First National had claimed that it possessed a security interest in the tractor that was superior to Laurel's. First National maintained that its security interest, which was perfected more than two years after Laurel's, was nonetheless superior because the financing statement it had filed correctly listed the serial number of the tractor, whereas the security agreement Laurel had filed as a financing statement contained an error. The evidence showed that Laurel's security agreement described the tractor as a "CATERPILLAR D9H #90VO4695 (TRACTOR)" instead of #90V4695. First National subsequently filed two financing statements that listed the tractor as secured collateral. The first described the tractor as "One (1) Caterpillar Tractor D8H, Serial No. 90V4695." But

First National's second financing statement correctly described the tractor as "CAT D9H TRACTOR S/N 90V4695." Laurel argued that the serial number in its security agreement, which erroneously included a zero before the last four digits, would not be seriously misleading and that this description would give adequate notice of Laurel's claimed security interest in this particular tractor. Thus, Laurel asserted that its security interest should enjoy priority over First National's. Was Laurel correct? (*Laurel Explosives Inc.* v. *First National Bank & Trust Company of Corbin*, 801 S.W.2d 336 [Ky. App. 1990].)

8. Essex was in the business of selling yachts at retail. Hartford National Bank (HNB) had provided Essex's initial capital of $60,000 in exchange for which Essex had given HNB a security interest in all its present and after-acquired inventory. First Pennsylvania Bank (Pennsylvania) had earlier become a purchase money secured party and as such had also retained a security interest in Essex's after-acquired property. HNB had perfected by filing before Pennsylvania. Thus, when Essex defaulted on its obligations to HNB, HNB had repossessed nine boats (all of Essex's inventory) that had been in Essex's possession, at which time Pennsylvania had asserted its security interest in the boats, as well. At trial, the evidence showed that under Pennsylvania's arrangement with Essex and the manufacturer of seven of the nine boats in question, Pennsylvania had held title and would transfer the title to any boat sold directly to the purchaser. Essex at no time had held title to the boats, The court therefore concluded that, as to the seven boats, Essex had never acquired any rights in them and that HNB's security interest had not attached to them. Should the appellate court overturn this result? (*Hartford National Bank and Trust Company* v. *Essex Yacht Sales, Inc.*, 492 A.2d 230 [Conn. App. 1985].)

9. The Findleys raised catfish on a so-called catfish farm. Sunburst Bank (the Bank), the secured party, had filed a financing statement in the county where the Findleys resided but had not filed any such statement in the county in which the catfish ponds were located. In contesting the Bank's security interest, the Findleys argued that since "crops" are included within the definition of "farm products," their catfish were therefore crops. As such, according to the Findleys, in order to create a security interest and then to perfect a lien on catfish under Section 9-203, a reasonable description of the location of the catfish ponds should have been an integral part of the security agreement and financing

statement. Were the Findleys correct? (*In re Findley*, 76 Bankr. 547 [N.D. Miss. 1987].)

10. Valley Bank and Rockwell International Credit Corporation (Rockwell) were creditors of Curtis Press. Valley Bank held a security interest in "all of the equipment" of Curtis Press, while Rockwell held a purchase money security interest in a particular piece of Curtis's equipment. Both secured parties had duly perfected their interests in the state of Idaho. However, Curtis later moved the equipment to Wyoming and then defaulted on the obligations owed to both creditors. In this case, a Wyoming UCC statute required Rockwell and Valley Bank to reperfect their security interests within four months after the collateral had entered that state, but neither creditor did so. After this period expired, Valley Bank located the equipment and reperfected its security interest by taking possession of the collateral. Rockwell then belatedly reperfected its security interest by filing a continuation statement with the Wyoming secretary of state. When Rockwell asked Valley Bank to relinquish the equipment, the bank declined. Rockwell then sued the bank, arguing that its interest in the collateral was superior. Which party would prevail in the lawsuit for the collateral? (*Rockwell International Credit Corporation* v. *Valley Bank*, 707 P.2d 517 [Idaho App. 1985].)

CHAPTER 29

Secured Transactions: Priorities

OUTLINE

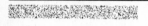

THE CODE AND COMPETING CLAIMS FOR THE SAME COLLATERAL

In Chapter 28, we examined the process of attachment and perfection, the methods by which secured parties protect their respective interests in the collateral against the debtor and against later creditors of the debtor, especially the trustee in bankruptcy, who, under the bankruptcy laws, occupies the status of a lien creditor. As mentioned, the date of perfection becomes particularly significant when, as is sometimes the case, upon the debtor's default, several secured parties claim a perfected security interest in the same collateral. The Uniform Commercial Code's system for deciding which competing claim is superior—that is, which claim has priority—is the focus of this chapter.

PRIORITIES

A secured party's priority over other creditors is of enormous practical importance. The one catastrophe every creditor fears most is the bankruptcy of the debtor. The reason for this is simple: In the event of bankruptcy, each creditor runs the risk of receiving only a few cents of every dollar loaned to the debtor. Yet, as we have previously discussed, a creditor can maximize the chances of recovering the money owed by attaining the status of a perfected secured party. This status will give the creditor first claims to the collateral and thus the best chance (generally by selling the collateral) of realizing most, if not all, of the debt. A perfected secured party, then, will have priority over general (or unsecured) creditors and lien creditors, including the trustee in bankruptcy. After the secured party has disposed of the collateral, any money in excess of that owed to the secured party may be applied to the claims of these other creditors. In many instances, however, no money will be available to satisfy these latter claims. Thus, we cannot overemphasize the importance of becoming a secured party.

CONFLICTING INTERESTS IN THE SAME COLLATERAL

Not surprisingly, given the advantages attendant on being a secured party, most creditors strive to achieve this status. This fact in turn leads to the possibility that several secured parties will claim a security interest in the same collateral. How, then, can we determine who among this class of favored parties has priority? Or, to use informal lingo, who has "first dibs" on the collateral?

The UCC's rules on priorities, contained in Section 9-312, are difficult to unravel and understand. In general, the Code validates a "first-in-time, first-in-right" approach whereby those who have perfected their claims first will have priority. For example, if two competing security interests have been perfected by filing, the first to be filed has priority, whether the security interest attached before or after filing.[1] For this reason, it makes sense for a creditor/lender to file a financing statement covering the transaction even *before* all the requirements for attachment have been met, because it is the date of filing that will control who has priority in the collateral. Thus, the time of attachment is often less important than the time of perfection (here, by filing), even though there can be no perfection without attachment.

For example, suppose that Third Bank files a financing statement covering the inventory in Penny Pope's Sporting Goods store on 10 December 1991 and Fourth Bank files such a statement on the same inventory on 1 February 1992. Third Bank will have priority over Fourth Bank, even though Fourth Bank may have given value first and thus have attached its interest before Third Bank did. However, note that neither Third Bank nor Fourth Bank can have a perfected interest until attachment occurs. Simply put, Third Bank's earlier filing gives it a superior interest in the inventory under the UCC's "first-to-file" rules. Because the Code determines priorities from the time of filing—if all secured parties have filed—it behooves a would-be secured party to file as soon as possible.

The Code's drafters have justified this "race to the recording office" as a necessary protection of the public filing system. In the drafters' view, Fourth Bank, though it has attached its interest first, cannot complain, because it could have checked the public records and thus have learned of Third Bank's claimed interest before taking its security interest. According to the drafters, lenders like Third Bank who plan to make a series of subsequent advances and who have filed first should be able to make those later advances without having, as a condition of protection, to check each time for filings *later* than theirs.[2] Hence, in our hypothetical case, Third Bank will have priority because it has filed first.

The following case illustrates these and other aspects of the Code's priorities rules.

Genoa National Bank v. *Sorensen*
304 N.W.2d 659 (Neb. 1981)

FACTS Sorensen, a farmer, had granted security interests in his growing crops to two different persons, Fichtl and Nelson. Both creditors had filed financing statements locally, but they had not filed until 3 November and 17 November 1978, respectively, with the Public Service Commission, as required by a Nebraska law that had become effective on 2 September 1977. In the meantime, on 11 October 1978, Genoa National Bank had obtained a judgment

---

[1]Uniform Commercial Code, Section 9-312(5)(a).
[2]Ibid., Section 9-312, Official Comment 5.

Levy execution To seize and sell property to satisfy a judgment.

against Sorensen based on promissory notes that Sorensen owed to the bank. On 19 October 1978, the bank had caused the sheriff to **levy execution** on the grain that had been harvested from the land covered by Fichtl and Nelson's security agreements. Fichtl and Nelson argued that their liens were prior and superior to the bank's.

ISSUE

Were Fichtl and Nelson perfected secured parties so that their interests would take priority over that of a **judgment creditor?**

HOLDING

Yes. Their liens were perfected before the bank had acquired its judgment lien and thus were superior to the bank's lien.

REASONING

Judgment creditor A creditor who has obtained a court verdict that allows the enforcement of an execution, or seizure and sale of property.

Constructive notice Information that a person is treated as knowing, whether actually known or not

Central filing was required for growing crops but not for harvested crops. Thus, when the crops were harvested, the locally filed financing statements became sufficient to perfect the security interests and therefore had priority over the judgment lien, which had not been obtained until after the crops had been harvested. The evidence was clear beyond contradiction that if the crops had remained "unharvested" until such time as the judgment creditor had obtained its judgment and levied execution, it would clearly have priority over the security creditors who had failed to file their financing statements in the offices of both the county clerk and the Public Service Commission. But in this case, long before the judgment creditor had acquired any interest on which levy could have been executed, the crops had been harvested and taken to an elevator. The bank's argument that if a filing is improperly made at the outset, it may never be corrected or made valid was incorrect because the purpose of filing is to give **constructive notice** to the world and actual notice to those who would take the trouble to look. Thus, if at any time after 21 October 1977, the date on which the crops had been harvested, and 11 October 1978, the date on which the bank had acquired its judgment lien, Fichtl or Nelson had wished to take further action to perfect their respective liens on harvested crops, they would have been required simply to refile their financing statement in the office of the county clerk where it was already on file. Acceptance of the bank's position would mean that even though there was a financing statement on file in the office of the county clerk before the bank had acquired its judgment and levied execution, and it was proper in all respects as to harvested crops, the court should nevertheless ignore that financing statement because the security holders had not had a second stamp placed on the document after the crops had been harvested. To make such a requirement would be to ignore the Code's clearly stated position that if a filing is properly perfected when made, a change in status will not deprive the holder of its lien interest. Further, a financing statement may be filed before the security interest attaches. Therefore, Fichtl and Nelson's filings had been made in advance of their acquiring their interest in the harvested crops and attaching at such time as the crops were harvested, thereby eliminating the requirement of a duplicate filing. Hence, the better rule, and the one supported both by the language of the UCC and logic, required that if an otherwise unperfected lien is not filed at all the proper places at the time of filing, but through the passage of time or change in character of the property becomes a proper filing under the provisions of the Uniform Commercial Code, the lien also becomes properly perfected and is superior to all other liens not otherwise perfected prior to the time that the previous security lien had been perfected.

Order of Perfection

As we learned in Chapter 28, filing represents one of three alternative methods of perfection. With purchase money security interests in consumer goods, for instance, one may rely on automatic perfection; or one may perfect by taking possession of the collateral. In all such cases (that is, where there has been no filing by any of the parties), the first to perfect takes priority.

Order of Attachment

If for some reason none of the parties has perfected its security interest, the first interest to attach enjoys priority. However, relying on attachment alone as a vehicle for attaining priority is not advisable because an *unperfected* secured creditor will not enjoy a preferred status in bankruptcy proceedings. Simply stated, to gain priority over other secured parties and over the trustee in bankruptcy, it is imperative to file as soon as possible if filing is an acceptable mode for perfecting a security interest in the type of collateral involved, or, if filing is not appropriate, to perfect one's interest as soon as possible in the appropriate manner.

The seller in the following case unfortunately learned this rule the hard way.

Crystal Bar, Inc. v. Cosmic, Inc.
758 F. Supp. 543 (D. S.D. 1991)

FACTS
In March, 1984, Crystal Bar, Inc. (Crystal Bar), Reese M. Williams individually, and the Reese Williams Trust sold 200 shares of capital stock (a minority interest); a liquor license; and the business assets, inventory, and stock in trade of Crystal Bar to Cosmic, Inc. (Cosmic) under a written "Purchase Agreement." The total purchase price was $225,000, with a down payment of $50,000 and the balance financed by the assumption of $40,468.58 of the sellers' debts and $164,531.42 amortized monthly at 12 percent per annum for ten years. The parties characterized the purchase agreement as an option to purchase and never perfected it as a security agreement under the South Dakota statutory provisions dealing with secured transactions. In December, 1984, Cosmic, as assignor, entered into an assignment with codefendant Virgil Hauff, assignee, covering the property subject to the prior purchase agreement. In this assignment, Hauff agreed to assume all the obligations of Cosmic under the original purchase agreement ($159,174.41). In a similar manner to the original purchase agreement, the assignment reserved title pending final payment. Again, Cosmic failed to perfect the assignment as a security agreement. Hauff subsequently defaulted by failing to make his monthly payments in August and September, 1989. Crystal Bar mailed a notice of default to Hauff in September. The total delinquency amounted to $110,545.15. The Internal Revenue Service also claimed a lien on the property described in the two agreements for income, withholding, and social security taxes due to the government by Hauff and his wife. Because the liquor license, estimated to be worth $75,000–$100,000, represented Hauff's major asset, the IRS sought to satisfy a portion or all of its lien through its levy on this property. The IRS argued that because the seller had failed to perfect its security interest in the property, the IRS's interest was superior to that of Crystal Bar.

ISSUE
Would the holder of a tax lien enjoy priority over the holder of an unperfected security interest in the liquor license?

HOLDING
Yes. Article 9 would cover the liquor license; and since the secured party, which had sold its business to the debtor, had failed to perfect its interest in the liquor license in accordance with Article 9, the IRS as a lien holder would have priority.

REASONING
The Federal Tax Lien Act provides that a federal tax lien attaches to all property, whether real or personal, belonging to a taxpayer, whenever such a person fails to pay taxes. The IRS had filed tax liens against Virgil D. Hauff and Karen M. Hauff on 27 June 1988, 26 December 1988, and 13 October 1989. Regarding the priority of a lien creditor over an unperfected security interest, the South Dakota UCC states, "(1) Except as provided in subsection (2), an unperfected security interest is subordinate to the rights of: (b) A person who becomes a lien creditor before the security interest is perfected; . . . (3) A 'lien creditor' means a creditor who has acquired a lien on the property involved by attachment, levy, or the like and includes an assignee for [the] benefit of creditors from the time of

[the] assignment, and a trustee in bankruptcy from the date of the filing of the petition or a receiver in equity from the time of appointment." In South Dakota, a liquor license is considered "property." Under the UCC, therefore, it represents a general intangible subject to a security interest in favor of a creditor. Under South Dakota UCC statutes, a security interest in a general intangible must be filed in order to protect it from the claims of third parties. Accordingly, since Crystal Bar had failed to file properly the security interest created by the purchase agreement, it enjoyed only an unperfected interest in the license. Since an unperfected security interest is subordinate to the rights of a third party (in this case, the IRS) that becomes a lien creditor before the security interest is perfected, the IRS liens deserved first priority. All Crystal Bar needed to do to protect itself was to perfect its security interest. In its final argument, Crystal Bar maintained that since the parties had labeled the purchase agreement an option, the agreement did not give rise to a "security interest." However, calling a security agreement an option does not make it an option; the location of the title is immaterial. Moreover, according to South Dakota statutes, "Each provision of this chapter with regard to rights, obligations and remedies applies whether title to collateral is in the secured party or in the debtor." Hence, the clear intent of the law of South Dakota is to bring contracts of the type being considered here under the umbrella of a "security interest."

EXCEPTIONS

We will now turn our attention to some very important exceptions to the general rules of priorities. The first of these deals with a purchase money security interest that is held by a purchase money secured party.

Purchase Money Security Interests

For reasons that soon will become clear, a purchase money secured party enjoys priority over interests that precede his or her interest in time, provided the party complies with certain provisions of the Code. In other words, a purchase money security interest contradicts our previously described "first-to-file-or-to-perfect" rules on priorities. An analysis of the types of commercial situations that involve purchase money security interests and purchase money secured parties will explain why the Code sanctions a special status for these interests.

As we learned in Chapter 28, a security interest is a purchase money security interest to the extent that it is "(a) taken or retained by the seller of the collateral to secure all or part of its price; or (b) taken by a person who by making advances or incurring an obligation gives value to enable the debtor to acquire rights in or the use of collateral if such value is in fact so used."[3] As should be apparent from this definition, purchase money secured parties typically are sellers or lenders who, by their extensions of credit, permit the debtor to acquire rights in the collateral. But not all sellers or lenders qualify for purchase money secured party status. We will be able to understand how purchase money secured parties differ from other secured parties if we reexamine our earlier example involving Third Bank and Penny Pope.

This time let us assume that Third Bank has agreed to finance Penny's

[3]Ibid., Section 9-107.

inventory. As her inventory financier, Third Bank agrees to give Penny letters of credit (or a line of credit) on which Penny can draw at irregular intervals and from which the bank can issue future advances of funds to her as she needs them. To protect itself, Third Bank creates and perfects a security interest in all present and after-acquired property of Penny's and all proceeds thereof. In such situations, Third Bank has a so-called floating lien over Penny's inventory, since the lien covers the items of inventory as they stand on the shelf and even "floats" over other inventory and property that Penny acquires through subsequent advances or loans from Third Bank. Third Bank's "lien" also covers the proceeds of any items that Penny sells. Generally speaking, Third Bank will compel Penny to maintain a certain ratio of inventory and will gauge her repayment of the loans and its later advances with reference to this ratio. Typically, Third Bank will ask Penny to promise to refrain from *double financing,* or using this same inventory as collateral for a subsequent loan from another creditor, say, Fourth Bank.

We can understand Third Bank's reasons for protecting its security interest in the inventory: The bank is well aware that, should Penny's business go bankrupt, it will need to have priority if it is going to realize any money from its extension of credit. Hence, on the one hand, the law wants to protect secured parties like Third Bank so that they will be willing to extend credit to businesspeople like Penny. One way to accomplish this is to give them priority if they are the first to file or to perfect.

But, on the other hand, it seems unfair for Third Bank to have the ability to restrict unduly Penny's access to credit. Potential subsequent creditors may see Third Bank's previously filed financing statement on the inventory and may refuse to extend Penny credit because of Third Bank's seeming priority based on its compliance with the first-to-file-or-to-perfect rules. Where will she get credit if, for some reason, Third Bank refuses to give her more loans or advances?

The UCC attempts to balance both Penny's and Third Bank's interests by giving priority to purchase money security interests. In other words, if Fourth Bank advances money (say, $10,000) to enable Penny to acquire additional inventory, Fourth Bank will have priority over Third Bank to the extent of the value given—here, $10,000—because the law characterizes Fourth Bank as a purchase money secured party in these circumstances. (Third Bank, as the inventory financier and the holder of an after-acquired property and future advances clauses, is a nonpurchase money secured party here.) However, to earn this priority, Fourth Bank will have to fulfill certain requirements, depending on the type of collateral involved.

If the collateral is inventory, Fourth Bank enjoys priority over Third Bank's conflicting security interest in the same inventory (and in identifiable cash proceeds) received on or before the delivery of the inventory to a buyer (here, Penny). This will be true provided that the purchase money security interest has been perfected by filing at the time the debtor receives possession of the inventory, and the purchase money secured party notifies *in writing* any persons who have previously filed financing statements covering inventory of the same types that he or she (the purchase money secured party) has or expects to acquire a purchase money security interest in the inventory of the debtor. The purchase money secured party must also describe the inventory by item or type. To acquire priority over Third Bank, Fourth Bank must meet these requirements.[4]

To those who feel this "superpriority" for purchase money secured parties is unfair to inventory financiers like Third Bank, the drafters of the Code offer the following policy justifications. The notification procedures required by the Code will tip off Third Bank that Penny is "double financing." At this point, if it believes itself vulnerable, Third Bank may curtail future advances to Penny and may, assuming that the security agreement so provides and that it gives notice, demand payment from Penny (by arguing that such double financing constitutes a condition of default). Third Bank thus has ways of protecting itself from Penny if it so desires, and in the meantime Penny has acquired new avenues of credit. Third Bank also has the added protection of knowing that it will still have priority with regard to the inventory if Fourth Bank does not comply with the Code's requirements.

If the security interest covers noninventory collateral (such as equipment or consumer goods), Fourth Bank, as a purchase money secured party, will have priority over Third Bank, as a holder of a conflicting security interest in the same collateral or its proceeds, if the purchase money security interest is perfected at the time the debtor receives possession of the collateral or within ten days thereafter.[5] Hence, it is clear that the type of collateral involved dictates what a creditor must do to achieve purchase money secured party status. Why is less required (a ten-day "grace period" for filing and no need to give notice to holders of previously filed security interests) of one who wishes to attain priority in noninventory collateral? Apparently, the drafters of the Code believed that arrangements for periodic advances against incoming property are unusual outside the inventory field; thus, they did not think there was a need to notify noninventory secured parties, because, in fact, only in rare instances would such a previous financier even exist. Simply put, equipment and consumer goods are not usually valuable enough for several creditors to have taken security interests in them. To illustrate, if Penny buys a new refrigerator to preserve the "bounce" of the tennis balls she is selling, the refrigerator will be equipment because she uses it in her business. Should Fourth Bank lend her the money to buy the refrigerator, it will become a purchase money secured party if it files a financing statement within ten days of Penny's receipt of the refrigerator. It will have priority over Third Bank, despite lack of notice to the latter, even if Third Bank has filed a financing statement indicating an interest in "all inventory, *equipment,* and after-

[4]Ibid., Section 9-312(3).
[5]Ibid., Section 9-312(4).

acquired property of Penny Pope's Sporting Goods Store." If Fourth Bank does not file within ten days, Third Bank will have a priority claim to the refrigerator under the usual first-to-file-or-to-perfect rules.

If there are two or more competing purchase money security interests in the same type of collateral, the Code applies to the usual first-to-file-or-to-perfect rule in determining priority in this situation. Thus, the purchase money secured party who files first will have superior rights.

The following case illustrates the types of legal issues that arise in the context of purchase money security interests.

Davis Bros., Inc. v. United Bank of Littleton
701 P.2d 642 (Colo. App. 1985)

FACTS   United Bank of Littleton (the Bank) and Davis Bros., Inc. (Davis Bros.) were creditors of Drug Fair, a retail drug store and pharmacy. On 14 November 1975, the Bank filed a financing statement covering all the debtor's inventory, furniture, fixtures, equipment, accounts receivable, and all after-acquired property. On 27 September 1976, Davis Bros. filed a financing statement to secure payment of a $62,822.28 note. The statement listed as collateral Drug Fair's inventory, prescription records, and all "drug and sundry inventory of debtor which debtor has purchased or may purchase from secured party and in which secured party has taken or will take a purchase money security interest." Davis Bros. subsequently supplied Drug Fair with merchandise for sale in its business on a weekly credit basis. The Bank learned of Davis Bros.' financing statement on 16 February 1977 as the result of a lien search. However, Davis Bros. did not give the Bank any other notice that it had or expected to acquire a purchase money security interest in debtor's inventory. During April, 1979, the Bank took possession of and sold Drug Fair's inventory and prescription records without giving Davis Bros. notice of the sale. At the time of the sale, Drug Fair owed Davis Bros. $7,951.84 on an open account for drugs and sundries purchased from Davis Bros. after the filing of Davis Bros.' financing statement. This amount was over and above the amount due on the note. Davis Bros. then brought suit for an accounting of the proceeds of the sale and for damages for conversion of the items in which it had priority. The trial court granted summary judgment as to Davis Bros.' claim for conversion of the debtor's prescription records and the drugs and sundries for which Davis Bros. had a purchase money security interest. Following trial on the issue of damages, the court entered judgment for $25,000 for conversion of the prescription records and $7,951.84 plus interest at the rate of 18 percent per annum for conversion of the drugs and sundries.

ISSUE   Did the judge err in granting damages to Davis Bros. for conversion of the drugs and sundries because the Bank had priority in these items?

HOLDING   Yes. Although the evidence showed that the Bank had converted the prescription records, the Bank nonetheless enjoyed priority in the inventory items allegedly converted, since Davis Bros. had not complied with the statutory requirements for gaining priority in these circumstances.

REASONING   Colorado's UCC statute requires a purchase money secured party in inventory to perfect its interest by the time the debtor receives possession of the collateral and to give notice to the holder of a conflicting security interest who has previously filed a financing statement covering the same types of inventory in order to enjoy priority vis-à-vis other creditors in inventory. This notice should state that the person giving the notice has or expects to acquire a purchase money security interest in the inventory of the debtor and should describe the inventory by item or type. Davis

Bros.' failure to send written notice to the Bank made it ineligible to attain priority as a purchase money secured party. Therefore, the Bank, as the result of its previously filed financing statement, enjoyed priority in the inventory in question and by definition could not be liable for conversion of the inventory.

Bona Fide Purchaser of Consumer Goods

Besides purchase money secured parties, another class of persons who may have priority over a previously perfected security interest is the bona fide purchaser of consumer goods.[6] Recall from Chapter 28 that "consumer goods" are goods that have been used or bought for use primarily for personal, family, or household purposes.[7] Thus, this section of the Code limits priority to the purchase of this type of collateral. Examination of this Code provision shows further limitations, since to enjoy priority over a previously perfected security interest, a buyer must be ignorant of the security interest, must pay value, and must use the goods for personal, family, or household purposes.

To illustrate, assume that Henry Smith wishes to sell his refrigerator to Margaret Hernandez. Margaret does not know it, but Handley, the owner of the appliance store where Henry bought the refrigerator, has a perfected security interest in this consumer good (Handley is relying on automatic perfection—that is, the mere attachment of the security interest). If Margaret pays value and uses the refrigerator in her home, she will have priority; in other words, she will retain the refrigerator even if Handley tries to repossess it from her, should Henry default in his payments. However, if Margaret plans to use the refrigerator in her dental office for the purpose of keeping anesthetics cold, Handley will win because Margaret does not fit Section 9-307(2)'s definition of a bona fide purchaser (because of her nonpersonal use of the collateral).

So far, we have been assuming that Handley will rely on automatic perfection, which, as discussed in Chapter 28, is the mode generally preferred by the Handleys of the world because they can thereby avoid the expense and inconvenience of filing. However, under Section 9-307(2), if Handley files a financing statement covering a consumer good before a buyer purchases it, Handley, not the bona fide purchaser, will have a priority claim to it. Handley, then, must decide whether the possibility that a refrigerator will be sold to a bona fide purchaser outweighs the inconvenience of filing. If he thinks it does, he should file in order to attain priority; if not, he can rely on automatic perfection to keep him secure from the claims of everyone except this specialized type of bona fide purchaser.

The secured party in the next case undoubtedly regretted its failure to file a financing statement on the fixture that was in dispute.

---

[6]Ibid., Section 9-307(2).
[7]Ibid., Section 9-109(1).

Kibbe v. *Rohde*
427 A.2d 1163 (Pa. Super. 1981)

FACTS   The Patz Company had retained a security interest in the barn cleaner that it had sold to the Bulls but had neglected to file a financing statement on this fixture. The Kibbes later bought the land on which the barn cleaner had been installed. Some time after the sale, Rohde, an employee of Patz, removed the barn cleaner because Patz had not been paid for it. The Kibbes sued Rohde and Patz for trespass and for the value of the barn cleaner, asserting that they were bona fide purchasers for value of the farm and its fixtures.

ISSUE   Did the Kibbes merit the status of bona fide purchasers for value because they had bought the farm and the barn cleaner without knowledge of Patz's security interest in the barn cleaner?

HOLDING   Yes. They were bona fide purchasers for value.

REASONING   A lawyer had searched the appropriate records for the Kibbes before the sale and had found no liens on the property. Since this had been the only knowledge available to the Kibbes at the time they had become purchasers, there was no evidence showing that the Kibbes had any knowledge or notice of Patz's security claim. Accordingly, the jury verdict against Patz for trespass and for conversion of the barn cleaner was correct.

Buyer in the Ordinary Course of Business

A buyer in the ordinary course of business may, according to Section 9-307(1), have priority over a perfected security interest. To use our earlier example, when Henry Smith buys the refrigerator from Handley's Appliance Store, he is a buyer in the ordinary course of business. *Anyone who buys goods from a merchant seller in a standard (as opposed to an extraordinary) transaction is a buyer in the ordinary course of business.* As such, Henry will take the refrigerator free of a security interest created by his seller (Handley may have given a security interest in his inventory of appliances to Third Bank), even though the security interest is perfected and even if Henry (as a savvy business law student) knows of Third Bank's security interest. The policy reasons for such a result are probably obvious: Will the Henrys across our country buy refrigerators (or stereos or garden tractors) out of a seller's stock of trade or inventory if the Third Banks of our nation can repossess these items? Hardly. Therefore, buyers in the ordinary course of business—by definition those who may know of the existence of a perfected security interest in the goods but who buy in good faith and without knowledge that the sale of them is in violation of the ownership rights or security interest of a third party—have priority in such competing claims situations. Although many people use the terms *bona fide purchaser* and *buyer in the ordinary course of business* interchangeably, they are distinct concepts. We more appropriately term one *consumer* who has bought goods from another consumer in an occasional sale a bona fide purchaser. Buyers in the ordinary course of business, in contrast, are purchasers who are buying from a seller who routinely sells from inventory or otherwise regularly engages in such transactions.

As the next case indicates, buyers who engage in nonroutine business transactions will not enjoy priority as buyers in the ordinary course of business would.

Bank of Illinois v. Dye
517 N.E.2d 38 (Ill. App. 1987)

FACTS   Bank of Illinois (the Bank) was a "floor-plan" financier of Gordon McGrath, who did business as McGrath Auto Sales (McGrath). The Bank, on 16 July 1984, filed a financing statement that covered "new and used motor vehicles" acquired by McGrath and that authorized McGrath to sell, lease, and consume its inventory in the ordinary course of business. In July, 1985, McGrath pledged a 1985 Buick Riviera to R. Edward Dye, delivered a duplicate Indiana certificate of title to the vehicle, and received in return a $15,300 advance. Although the parties later disputed the date that the vehicle had come into Dye's possession, they did agree that the Bank's security interest was created, under the floor-plan financing, prior to Dye's taking possession of the car. Dye also testified that he and Gordon McGrath had been close friends for over thirty years. He said that, from the early 1980s through 1985, he had bought and sold eight or ten cars through McGrath at a dealers' auction in Indianapolis. McGrath had suggested to Dye that he could cut costs by allowing McGrath to keep the "paperwork" including the certificates of title, while he, Dye, used a set of dealer's license plates on the cars. Dye admitted that, as a result, he had had no proof of ownership of any of the vehicles; but he had not found that unusual, because he and Gordon had been "very good friends." He indicated further that he was "sure" Gordon McGrath had handled the transactions concerning the vehicles he had bought and sold in a manner different from those involving other people who had purchased cars from the dealership. As to the "purchase" of the 1985 Buick Riviera, Dye testified that he had paid the same price for the car as McGrath had paid for it; he had paid no taxes on it until December, 1985; he had received no certificate of title until December, 1985; he had always used McGrath's dealer's plates; he had signed a document representing to the state that the sale had occurred in December rather than June; and he had returned the car to McGrath's lot whenever McGrath had needed to show the car to "prospective clients." Apparently, McGrath had never informed Dye of the Bank's security interest. Dye argued that he had been a buyer in the ordinary course of business who could take the car free of the Bank's security interest.

ISSUE   Was Dye a buyer in the ordinary course of business?

HOLDING   No. He was not a buyer in the ordinary course of business. Therefore, the Bank could recover the Buick from him.

REASONING   Although Dye argued that McGrath's sale to him was "in the ordinary course of business," owing to the fact that he and McGrath had engaged in other similar transactions, the crucial questions centered around whether the transaction between the buyer and seller was "customary in the business" and whether the buyer was "a typical buyer in an ordinary business transaction with the seller." Here, the incidents surrounding Dye's purchase of the vehicle from McGrath had indicated that the sale was not in the ordinary course of business. For example, McGrath had sold the vehicle at the same price at which he had purchased it. Furthermore, McGrath had added no sum to the sales price that represented the required Illinois tax payments. Indeed, McGrath had never paid such a tax, and, eventually, Dye himself had paid the tax in December, 1985. No certificate of title had been assigned to Dye or requested until December, 1985, when Dye purportedly had learned for the first time that McGrath was having difficulties. McGrath had also allowed Dye to use McGrath's dealer's license plates, and Dye had thus participated in a fraud against the state of Illinois, which had been entitled to a registration fee for the vehicle. Moreover, Dye had participated with McGrath in sending a false document to the secretary of state representing the date of the sale as December, 1985, rather than June, 1985. Finally, the vehicle had been made available to McGrath after the sale so that it had always been present on the seller's floor when a check of the "floor-planned" vehicles was made by the Bank, including one occasion when the Bank had made an unannounced check. Most of the foregoing unusual aspects of the transaction had given the impression to the outside world and to Dye that McGrath had not parted with his ownership of the automobile. In total, these factors were so atypical and uncustomary as to negate any argument that the sale had been in the ordinary course of business.

Common Law and Statutory Liens

Under Section 9-310 of the Code, certain liens that arise by operation of law have priority over a perfected security interest in the collateral. For instance, if Monty Moore takes his car to Avenue Auto Repair (AAR) and does not pay Harry, the owner of AAR, Harry will have a common law or statutory lien on the car to the extent of the money owed him for his services or materials. Harry can retain possession of the car; and, in the event of Monty's default, he can force Westside Savings and Loan, the secured party for Monty's car, to pay him for his repairs before Westside realizes any proceeds from the sale of Monty's car.

Fixtures

As discussed in Chapter 28, generally Article 9 does not cover security interests in real estate. However, as you may remember, in addition to covering personal property, Article 9 also encompasses fixtures (goods that have become so related to real estate that an interest in them arises under real estate law). In many parts of the country, factories, schools, and homes almost invariably have a fixture called a furnace. In most cases, a mortgagee (the party who loaned the money for the purchase of the land) has a security interest in the real property, while a secured party may have retained an interest in the furnace. Knock-down, drag-out fights over priority sometimes occur as a result of this dovetailing of real property and personal property interests if the seller of the furnace wishes to repossess the furnace but confronts the mortgagee of the land, who claims the furnace as part of his or her real estate security interest.

Section 9-313 of the Code sets out rules for settling these problems. According to the Code, a perfected security interest in fixtures has priority over the conflicting interest of an **encumbrancer** or owner of real estate when (1) the security interest is a purchase money security interest; (2) the security interest is perfected by a fixture filing—that is, filing in the office where a real estate mortgage would be filed or recorded—before the goods become fixtures (or within ten days thereafter); and (3) the debtor has an interest of record in the real estate or is in possession of it. Thus, if Fire Power Furnace Company sells Earl LePage, the lessee of Port-Hole Pub, a furnace on an installment basis and retains a security interest in the furnace until it is paid for, Fire Power will have priority over Earl's lessor (or the mortgagee of the

Encumbrancer The holder of a claim relating to real or personal property.

Pub) if (1) it is a purchase money secured party and (2) it perfects its security interest before the furnace is installed (or within ten days of that time).[8]

Similarly, a perfected security interest in fixtures will have priority if (1) the fixtures are readily removable factory or office machines or readily removable replacements of domestic appliances that are consumer goods and (2) before the goods become fixtures, the security interest is perfected by any method permitted under Article 9.[9] Therefore, if Don Dunn's garbage disposal disintegrates and he buys one from Hosinski's Appliance Store through a conditional sales contract, Hosinski's will have priority over Don's mortgagee (whose mortgage covers not only the real property but the plumbing and appliances) if it perfects its security interest before it installs the disposal in Don's home. Since you no doubt remember that perfection of such consumer goods may occur through attachment, Hosinski's will have priority as of the moment Don signs the security agreement.

It may, however, be in Hosinski's best interests to perfect by resorting to a fixture filing, because such a filing will ensure its priority over subsequent encumbrancers or purchasers whose interests arise after Hosinski's.

When the secured party has priority over all owners and encumbrancers of the real estate, that party may, on default, sever and remove the collateral (such as the furnace) from the real estate. A secured party who elects to do this has a duty to reimburse any encumbrancer or owner of the real estate who is not the debtor for any physical injury caused to the property by the removal. Correspondingly, a person entitled to reimbursement may refuse permission to remove until the secured party gives adequate security for the performance of this obligation.[10]

The following case involves the unraveling of priorities in a fixture. Notice how the court applied real estate law and UCC statutes to determine priority.

Matter of Cliff's Ridge Skiing Corporation
123 Bankr. 753 (Bkrtcy. W.D. Mich. 1991)

FACTS   On 28 October 1987, Cliff's Ridge Skiing Corporation (Debtor) filed for relief under Chapter 11 of the Bankruptcy Code. On 4 January 1988, the case was converted to a Chapter 7 case. The Debtor's assets were sold pursuant to a court order dated 28 July 1988. One of the assets sold was a chairlift. The sale proceeds received from the chairlift ($22,500) were placed in an interest-bearing escrow account pending a court determination of the creditors' entitlements to the proceeds. Three creditors, First National Bank and Trust Company of Marquette (First National), Cliff's Ridge Development Co. (Cliff's Ridge), and First of America Bank—Marquette, N.A. (FOA), each claimed legal entitlement to the escrowed proceeds and the interest earned therefrom. The facts showed the following: On 24 July 1980, FOA loaned Cliff's Ridge the sum of $300,000 pursuant to a note; Cliff's Ridge executed a mortgage and a security agreement to secure the repayment of this debt. The mortgage granted FOA an interest in certain real property

---

[8]Ibid., Section 9-313(4)(a).
[9]Ibid., Section 9-313(4)(c).
[10]Ibid., Section 9-313(8).

owned by Cliff's Ridge together with "all improvements now or hereafter created on the property . . . and all fixtures now or hereafter attached to the property. . . ." Although FOA properly filed and perfected the mortgage and security agreement, it never made a fixture filing. On 4 February 1982, the Debtor assumed the obligations owed to FOA by Cliff's Ridge. In April or May, 1982, the Debtor bought a chairlift. On 22 November 1982, Cliff's Ridge conveyed its real property (a ski hill) to the Debtor pursuant to a warranty deed and a mortgage, which was subject to the prior mortgage granted by Cliff's Ridge to FOA. The mortgage, properly perfected by filing on 23 November 1982, was specifically subordinated to the prior mortgage granted to FOA. Moreover, this mortgage did not expressly grant Cliff's Ridge an interest in the Debtor's fixtures, whether then owned or after acquired; the mortgage granted an interest only in the conveyed real property. On 13 December 1982, the Debtor, the Economic Development Commission (EDC), and First National executed a loan agreement, which provided that (1) First National would loan $175,000 to the EDC to be used to purchase the chairlift; and (2) First National would receive a perfected security interest in the chairlift, if FOA would subordinate any security interest it might claim with respect to the chairlift to First National. At the time of this loan agreement, the parties apparently had failed to recognize that Cliff's Ridge might claim an interest in the chairlift pursuant to its prior mortgage. Next, on 14 December 1982, a financing statement, intended as a fixture filing, was filed, listing the EDC as the secured party and First National as the assignee. The real property description was attached to the financing statement. (Through the years, the required continuation statements were filed as well.)

ISSUES

Was the chairlift a fixture? Which creditor had priority and thus should receive the proceeds of the sale of the chairlift?

HOLDINGS

Yes. The chairlift was a fixture. First National, owing to the subordination agreement, had first priority to the proceeds.

REASONING

Goods are "fixtures" when they become so related to particular real estate that an interest in them arises under real estate law. The parties have stipulated that the chairlift had been engineered to be erected on the realty and had been adapted to the ski hill real property. Under governing Michigan law, this personal property therefore had become a fixture. Under Michigan law, a creditor can utilize two methods to create and perfect an interest in fixtures. A creditor may (1) utilize procedures under Michigan real estate law or (2) take a security interest under the Uniform Commercial Code as adopted in Michigan. Under the first method, once a mortgage creates an interest in fixtures under Michigan real estate law, the interest must be perfected by recording the mortgage in the county where the real property is located. Under the second method, in which a security interest in fixtures may be created and perfected under the UCC without reference to state real estate law, a financing statement must be filed. To be sufficient, a financing statement covering fixtures must satisfy the five requirements of a financing statement and meet the following conditions: state that it covers this type of collateral; recite that it is to be recorded in the real estate records; contain a description of the real estate where the fixtures are located, which description is sufficient to provide constructive notice under state real estate mortgage law; and, if the debtor does not have an interest of record in the real estate, disclose the owner of record. The financing statement covering such fixtures must be filed where a mortgage on the real estate would be recorded; i.e., the register of deeds in the county in which the real estate is located. When a sufficient financing statement is filed in the proper place, a "fixture filing" occurs. After a proper fixture filing, a secured party has a perfected interest in the fixture and may enforce its security interest against other persons according to designated priorities. When a fixture becomes complemental to real property, it becomes a permanent **accession;** and the fixture becomes part of the security with regard to any existing mortgage.

Accession An article later attached to a principal article of personal property that becomes so closely incorporated with the principal article that it cannot be detached therefrom without injury to the principal article.

    The language in both FOA's prior recorded mortgage and the Cliff Ridge mortgage on the real property is sufficient to create and perfect their respective interests in the chairlift fixture under state real estate law. Moreover, First National holds a perfected personal property interest in the chairlift under the UCC. Consequently, all three creditors have validly perfected interests in the proceeds of the sale of the chairlift. First National asserts that it, as the holder of a purchase money security interest in the chairlift, should receive the sale proceeds because it holds an interest superior to FOA and Cliff Ridge's mortgage interests. The general rule of priority is that a security interest in fixtures is subordinate to a conflicting interest held by a mortgagee of the related real estate. Under the general rule, then, FOA and Cliff's Ridge's mortgage interests would be superior to First National's interest. One exception to the general rule governs where (1) the security interest in fixtures is a purchase money security interest, (2) the interest of the mortgagee arose before the goods became fixtures, (3) a valid fixture filing occurred before the goods became fixtures or within ten days thereafter, or (4) the debtor has an interest of record in the real estate. The first requirement raises the threshold issue: Does First National hold a purchase money security interest? The relevant UCC provision states: "A security interest is a 'purchase money security interest' to the extent that it is (a) taken or retained by the seller of the collateral to secure all or part of its price; or (b) taken by a person who by making advances or incurring an obligation gives value to enable the debtor to acquire rights in or the use of collateral if such value is in fact so used." The Debtor purchased the chairlift from the Breckenridge Ski Area sometime after April or May, 1982. Therefore, First National was not the "seller of the collateral" and thus no purchase money security interest arose under Michigan law. First National had advanced funds to the Debtor pursuant to the loan transaction on 17 December 1982 and 23 December 1982, yet the chairlift was delivered in August 1982. Because delivery of the chairlift occurred approximately four months before First National had made any loan advance, the value given by First National did not "enable" the Debtor to acquire the chairlift. Further, whether the value, i.e., the funds disbursed by First National, was "in fact so used" by the Debtor to purchase the chairlift remained unclear. Indeed, the delivery and construction dates would indicate that the Debtor had either paid or incurred the cost prior to the time First National had made the cash advances. Hence, First National had failed to meet its burden of proof that it held a purchase money security interest in the chairlift. Accordingly, the general fixture priority rule initially would govern. Therefore, in the absence of FOA's subordination, the priority of the parties' interests in the chairlift would be: First, FOA as a real estate encumbrancer; second, Cliff's Ridge as a real estate encumbrancer; and third, First National as the holder of a perfected security interest. However, the subordination agreement between FOA and First National had consensually altered these respective initial priorities. The effect of the subordination agreement should be construed as FOA and First National's having "traded places" to the extent of the money advanced by First National to the Debtor for the chairlift loan that remains unpaid or the remaining mortgage balance owed to FOA by the Debtor, whichever is less. (Such a construction would do no damage to Cliff's Ridge's interest and its original priority position, either.) Consequently, owing to the subordination agreement, First National had priority as to all the escrowed proceeds from the sale of the chairlift and the interest earned therefrom.

Figure 29.1 illustrates the attachment and the perfection of a security interest. It also examines the order of priorities in the event of a conflict among the creditors seeking to enforce their rights in the same collateral.

SUMMARY

The rules on priorities represent the Code's attempt to decide who, among validly perfected secured parties, has superior rights to the collateral. In general, the Code validates a "first-in-time, first-in-right" approach. Thus, if competing security interests have been perfected by filing, the first to be filed has priority, whether the security interest attached before or after filing. If neither party has filed, the first party to perfect has priority. And if no one has perfected, the first interest to attach has superior rights to the collateral. There are some exceptions to these priority rules. For instance, a purchase money secured party may prevail over earlier, perfected creditors if the party follows

FIGURE 29.1 Anatomy of a Security Interest, Attachment, Perfection, and Priority

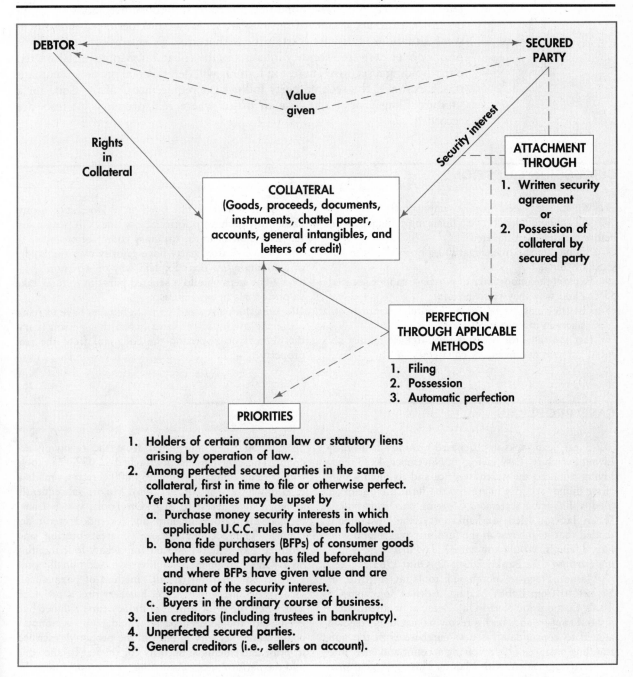

DEBTOR

SECURED PARTY

Value given

Security interest

Rights in Collateral

ATTACHMENT THROUGH

1. Written security agreement
   or
2. Possession of collateral by secured party

COLLATERAL
(Goods, proceeds, documents, instruments, chattel paper, accounts, general intangibles, and letters of credit)

PERFECTION THROUGH APPLICABLE METHODS

1. Filing
2. Possession
3. Automatic perfection

PRIORITIES

1. Holders of certain common law or statutory liens arising by operation of law.
2. Among perfected secured parties in the same collateral, first in time to file or otherwise perfect. Yet such priorities may be upset by
   a. Purchase money security interests in which applicable U.C.C. rules have been followed.
   b. Bona fide purchasers (BFPs) of consumer goods where secured party has filed beforehand and where BFPs have given value and are ignorant of the security interest.
   c. Buyers in the ordinary course of business.
3. Lien creditors (including trustees in bankruptcy).
4. Unperfected secured parties.
5. General creditors (i.e., sellers on account).

certain Code provisions that make distinctions according to the type of collateral involved. Similarly, bona fide purchasers of consumer goods and buyers in the ordinary course of business may defeat prior perfected interests in some situations. Likewise, certain liens that arise by operation of law have priority over perfected security interests in the collateral. Moreover, a secured party holding a security interest in fixtures will defeat a real property claimant if, for example, the secured party follows the requirements of the Code for a "fixture filing," or a filing in an office where real property interests are recorded.

DISCUSSION QUESTIONS

1. Why is the issue of priority important?
2. Why should a lender file a financing statement even before the deal is completed?
3. Enumerate the rules regarding priorities in the absence of filing.
4. Explain the importance of purchase money secured parties and why they merit priority.
5. List the rules for becoming a purchase money secured party in inventory collateral.
6. List the rules for becoming a purchase money secured party in noninventory collateral.

7. What is a bona fide purchaser? Does such a purchaser always have priority? How does this person differ from a buyer in the ordinary course of business?
8. Does a secured party have priority over the holder of a common law lien? Explain why or why not.
9. What steps should a secured party in fixtures take to protect his or her interest?
10. Why does a secured party in fixtures have to reimburse the owner of the land (when that person is not the debtor) on removing the collateral from the real property?

CASE PROBLEMS

1. Sarah Jean Jackson purchased furniture from Easy Living Furniture (Easy Living) in November, 1983. Easy Living financed the purchase price and retained a purchase money security interest in the furniture but never filed a financing statement covering this transaction. When Jackson filed for bankruptcy, the trustee contended that its interest in the furniture was superior to Easy Living's. Would you agree? (*Ledford* v. *Easy Living Furniture,* 52 Bankr. 706 [S.D. Ohio 1985].)
2. James Freeman purchased tools at a price of $1,261.40 from Bobby Majors, a dealer for Snap-On Tools Corporation (Snap-On). Because he already had a significant balance on his revolving account, Freeman agreed to consolidate his new purchase with the outstanding balance of his revolving account and enter into a security agreement with Majors. This agreement provided for a "purchase money security interest" and listed as "property" the $1,261.40 in new purchases and

$826.07 in tools transferred from the revolving account. Thus, the agreement attached $2,087.47 in tools to secure an obligation of $1,643.00 (Freeman made a cash down payment of $412.06). Majors subsequently assigned his interest to Snap-On Tools, which transformed the agreement into an "extended credit account." The account became interest bearing and required payments of $85.60 for twenty-four months. Snap-On's agreement with Freeman additionally provided for a "first-in-first-out" method of payment allocation to the time balance. Furthermore, it provided that when the prior purchase money time balance had been paid, the secured party would retain a nonpurchase money security interest in the property described in prior agreements as security for the net balance due and the performance of any other obligations under the agreement. This is the only language in the agreement that made reference to the release of the "purchase money" security status as Freeman forwarded payments on the account. Freeman continued to purchase tools on credit from Majors after the establishment of the extended credit account, and the charges were posted to the revolving account. When Freeman made another significant purchase, a consolidation followed. This time the outstanding balance of the extended credit account was consolidated with the balance of the new revolving account and the new purchase. This consolidated security agreement also provided for a "purchase money security interest." After this consolidation, Freeman continued to purchase tools on credit; and the entire process was repeated four months later. This third and final consolidation was perfected by the filing of a UCC financing statement. This perfection of the security agreement occurred before Freeman voluntarily petitioned for bankruptcy. However, the Bankruptcy Code allows a debtor such as Freeman to avoid a lien that consists of a nonpossessory, nonpurchase money security interest. Freeman, in attempting to avoid Snap-On's lien on the tools purchased, argued that a purchase money security interest used to secure the purchase price of goods sold in a particular transaction is transformed into a nonpurchase money security interest when antecedent or after-acquired debt is consolidated with the new purchase under one contract. Given the UCC's definition of a purchase money security interest, should a court find Freeman's argument persuasive? (*In re Freeman*, 124 Bankr. 840 [N.D. Ala. 1991].)

3. Computer Accounting Incorporated (CAI) had been providing accounting services to Pacific Mountain Corporation (PMC). PMC had been in the market for a computer to perform its accounting work. Eventually, the parties had agreed to purchase a Honeywell, Inc. (Honeywell) computer system. In May, 1978, CAI entered into an "Original Equipment Manufacturer" (OEM) contract with Honeywell to sell the latter's computers. This document provided that a security interest would be retained in any equipment Honeywell delivered to CAI until CAI's "obligations [had been] paid in full." CAI then confirmed existing orders with Honeywell for two computer systems, one for PMC and one for CAI. In June, 1978, CAI prepared and forwarded a written purchase agreement to PMC that provided that most of the equipment would remain in the possession of CAI and would be used by CAI when not in use by PMC. In late September or early October, 1978, CAI and PMC agreed that a subsidiary of PMC, Consolidated Commercial Investors Corporation (CCIC), would

be substituted as purchaser. The equipment then was leased to CAI, apparently for tax advantages. On 9 October 1978, to finance this transaction, CCIC executed a loan agreement with Puget Sound National Bank whereby CCIC granted the bank a security interest in the computer. On 20 October 1978, the bank filed its financing statement. The computer was delivered to CAI but did not function properly. Although CCIC paid CAI in full for the system, the computer was never delivered to CCIC. CAI then refused to pay Honeywell, CCIC defaulted on its loan, and the bank brought and won an action to acquire possession of the collateral. When Honeywell argued that its interest in the computer was superior to the bank's, the court held CCIC was a buyer in the ordinary course of business and thus took the computer free of Honeywell's security interest. Honeywell then countered with the argument that CCIC could not be a buyer in the ordinary course of business because the goods had never been delivered to CCIC. Was possession of the goods a prerequisite for becoming a buyer in the ordinary course of business? (*Puget Sound National Bank* v. *Honeywell, Inc.*, 698 P.2d 584 [Wash. App. 1985].)

4. Between February and May, 1982, Mark Products U.S., Inc. (Mark Products) sold seismic exploration equipment to a consortium called the Vibrosearch companies. The equipment was sold on an open account, unsecured basis, with payment due thirty days following delivery. Mark Products shipped the goods to the various states in which the Vibrosearch companies operated. By May, all deliveries had been made and received. In June, 1982, InterFirst Bank Houston, N.A. (InterFirst) loaned the parent company, Vibrosearch, Inc., $9 million and established a $2.5 million line of credit. These loans were evidenced by two promissory notes, both dated 30 June 1982, and secured by guaranty agreements and security agreements in favor of InterFirst. The security agreements covered all of the Vibrosearch companies' assets, including all the seismic exploration equipment sold by Mark Products. In early July, InterFirst filed the required financing statements in the appropriate states and in Texas, the principal place of business of Vibrosearch, Inc. As of 16 July 1982, the amount of indebtedness owed by the Vibrosearch companies to InterFirst was $8,314,003.60. By that time, Mark Products had become concerned over the Vibrosearch companies' outstanding indebtedness and had sought additional security. Hence, on 16 July 1982, Vibrosearch, Inc., executed a promissory note in

favor of Mark Products in the principal amount of $772,854.03, representing the balance of the unpaid purchase price of the equipment. Simultaneously, Vibrosearch, Inc., also signed a financing statement and a security agreement, the latter of which provided that Vibrosearch, Inc., would not sell, lease, rent, or otherwise dispose of the equipment without the written consent of Mark Products. In addition, it purported to grant Mark Products a first priority security interest in the seismic exploration equipment. On 1 September 1982, Mark Products filed a financing statement with the state of Texas, but did not file financing statements in any other states. Mark Products argued that it had held a purchase money security interest as of 3 September 1982 that took priority over InterFirst's secured claim. It further asserted that the Vibrosearch companies had not become a "debtor" and the goods had not become "collateral" for purposes of Section 9-107 until the security agreement had come into existence. Moreover, Mark Products asserted, the grace period for filing under the purchase money security interest provision would start to run only after there was a "debtor" in possession of "collateral." Should a court agree with Mark Products' claim and find that it had priority over InterFirst? (*Mark Products U.S., Inc.* v. *InterFirst Bank Houston, N.A.,* 737 S.W.2d. 389 [Tex. App. 1987].)

5. Northwestern Sales, Inc. (Northwestern) sold its inventory to Prairie Distributors (Prairie) in March, 1978, with Northwestern retaining a security interest in Prairie's inventory, after-acquired property, proceeds, and accounts receivable for the unpaid balance of the purchase price. Northwestern filed a financing statement with the Morton County Register of Deeds on 19 April 1978 and with the secretary of state on 21 June 1978. Mandan Security Bank (MSB), which had financed part of Prairie's purchase and had taken a security interest in Prairie's accounts receivable and inventory, filed a financing statement with the secretary of state on 10 May 1978. On 2 March 1979, Northwestern assigned to Ruben Elhard, its sole shareholder, all of its rights and interests, including the $125,000 promissory note and "all security interests and financing statements" executed by Prairie in favor of Northwestern. In May, 1979, Prairie began doing business with Tappan and entered into a security agreement on 11 May 1979 with Tappan. Tappan notified MSB in writing that it had or expected to acquire a purchase money security interest in Prairie's inventory but had not so notified Elhard or Northwestern. However, Tap-

pan had called Northwestern's president to inquire about details in Northwestern's filing that Tappan had found confusing. Tappan filed a financing statement with the secretary of state on 19 June 1979. When Elhard ultimately sued Prairie to recover on his unpaid promissory note, he claimed priority over Tappan, the purchase money secured party, on the ground that Tappan's telephone conversation with Northwestern's president had been insufficient to satisfy the notification procedures placed on purchase money secured parties under the Code. Was Elhard right? (*Elhard* v. *Prairie Distributors, Inc.,* 366 N.W.2d 465 [N.D. 1985].)

6. Hamilton Bank (the Bank) and ITT Corporation (ITT) were secured creditors of Diaconx Corporation (Diaconx). Upon Diaconx's bankruptcy, a dispute developed regarding the status of ITT's security interest vis-à-vis the Bank's. All the parties agreed that in April, 1984, the Bank had obtained a perfected security interest in the property of the debtor, including after-acquired inventory, and that ITT later had obtained a perfected purchase money security interest in certain inventory thereafter obtained by the debtor. They further agreed that ITT had given notice to the Bank of its security interest before Diaconx had received the property at issue here, but only after ITT had perfected the security interest by filing. Diaconx argued that ITT's failure to give notice of the lien claim to the Bank, prior to perfection, had subordinated ITT's security interest to that of the Bank. ITT responded that its providing notice prior to Diaconx's obtaining the relevant inventory had been sufficient to establish its priority over the Bank. Under Section 9-312, who had the better argument? (*In re Diaconx Corporation,* 79 Bankr. 602 [E.D. Pa. 1987].)

7. National Bank of Commerce of Mississippi (the Bank) perfected a purchase money security interest in a John Deere tractor purchased by Williams in March, 1979, with a loan from the Bank. The Farmers Home Administration (FmHA) subsequently obtained a second lien on the tractor as security for a 1982 loan to Williams. On 9 March 1984, the Bank's 1979 financing statement expired without the Bank's having filed a continuation statement within the six months before the statement had lapsed. When Williams defaulted on his loan with the Bank, the Bank repossessed the tractor and sold it. After retaining the amount due it on the loan, the Bank forwarded the remainder to the FmHA. The FmHA, however, contended that the Bank should have paid it the entire sales price because its lien had

priority over the Bank's owing to the lapsed financing statement. The Bank argued that it had reperfected its purchase money security interest (by possession) upon its repossessing of the tractor in 1986 and thus still enjoyed priority over the FmHA. Would this argument persuade a court to rule in the Bank's favor? (*In re Williams*, 82 Bankr. 430 [Bkrtcy. N.D. Miss. 1988].)

8. On 3 August 1978, Citizens and Southern Bank (C&S) filed a financing statement covering all equipment, inventory, accounts receivable, chattel paper, instruments, proceeds, and all after-acquired property of its debtor Randall Helton d/b/a United TV. On 27 November 1978, Helton entered into an "inventory financing agreement" with Appliance Buyers Credit Corporation (ABCC) to finance the occasional acquisition of inventory from King's Appliance. On 24 November 1978, ABCC filed a financing statement listing itself as the secured party and Helton as the debtor and covering all television sets, stereos, radio, organs, pianos, and other equipment. On 1 December 1978, ABCC sent notification to C&S that it had or expected to acquire a purchase money security interest in Helton's inventory and described the inventory by item or type. ABCC eventually assigned the security interest in the inventory so financed to King's Appliance, which had shipped merchandise to Helton. When Helton defaulted on his obligations both to C&S and to King's Appliance, C&S took possession of all Helton's inventory and gave notice of its intention to sell the inventory to satisfy Helton's indebtedness. King's Appliance argued that as ABCC's assignee it held a perfected security interest in part of the inventory that was prior to that of C&S. C&S asked for and got a summary judgment on the ground that the UCC absolutely requires the purchase money secured party to give notification in writing to the holder of the conflicting security interest *before* the date on which the purchase money secured party files its financing statement. Would you agree with the court's interpretation of Section 9-312(3)(b)? (*King's Appliance & Electronics, Inc.* v. *Citizens & Southern Bank of Dublin*, 278 S.E.2d 733 [Ga. App. 1981].)

9. First Community Bank (FCB) filed suit in bankruptcy court to request that the court allow it to liquidate its asserted security interest in a Three Buoys Sunseeker boat and to collect the remainder of the proceeds derived from the sale of a second boat. The trustee claimed that FCB had no right to the proceeds being held in escrow because FCB had failed to perfect a security interest in either the boat or the proceeds. The

debtor, Beacon Light Marina Yacht Club, Inc. (Beacon), had purchased a Sunseeker houseboat from Executive Yacht and Boat Sales (Executive). Beacon sold time-share interests in the boat for use by purchasers for specified periods during the year. In July, 1988, Dixie Financial Corporation of Virginia (Dixie) executed a loan to Beacon to refinance the marina where the boats were situated. After receiving a note and security agreement, Dixie filed financing statements to perfect its interest in the debtor's furniture, fixtures, machinery, equipment, inventory, and accounts receivable. Dixie later assigned all its rights and interests in the note and security agreement to FCB. FCB never obtained possession of the certificate of title to the Sunseeker and never noted its asserted security interest on the title. Rather, it relied totally on the collateral package received from Dixie in arguing that it was a validly perfected secured party in inventory because Beacon was a dealer in boats. However, the trustee later argued that Beacon had used the boat as equipment and that state law in Virginia required perfection of liens on such equipment in accordance with state watercraft statutes and regulations (i.e., notation of the secured party's interest on the certificate of title). The trustee asserted that the absence of such a notation and FCB's failure to have the title in its possession made it an unperfected party whose interest in the boat and proceeds was subordinate to the rights of the bankruptcy trustee, whom the law views as a hypothetical lien creditor. Would you agree with the trustee? (*In re Beacon Light Marina Yacht Club, Inc.*, 125 Bankr. 154 [Bkrtcy. W.D. Va. 1990].)

10. C Tek Software, Inc. (C Tek) is the owner of ClienTrak, computer software sold to companies in the financial services industry, principally banks and insurance companies. The software stores information and generates correspondence. On 26 October 1987, New York State Business Venture Partnership (NYSBVP) perfected a security interest in some pieces of hardware owned by C Tek as well as the source code and all ownership rights to the computer software ClienTrak including copyrights 1983, 1984, 1985, 1986, and 1987. On 17 June 1988, C Tek entered into a Master Distribution Agreement (MDA) with Intelligent Investment Systems (IIS). The MDA was a ten-year licensing agreement that gave IIS the exclusive worldwide right to sell and develop the ClienTrak software. Under the MDA, IIS promised to pay C Tek royalties, which would decrease in amount over time as IIS made changes to the software. Most important, the MDA granted IIS the

right "to produce, copy, distribute and market deriva-tive versions of the software and documentation with-out limitation." At the time of the execution of the MDA, the ClienTrak software was at version 3.7.2B. It would have taken a group of programmers about five years to produce independently comparable software. IIS made revisions to thousands of lines of source code after re-ceiving its licensing rights under the MDA and had em-ployed several programmers to make the changes, to assist users, and to raise the software to version 4.1.8. The differences between this source code and the prior version delivered to IIS at the time of the execution of the MDA consists of three types of modifications. First, the overwhelming majority of changes involved the elimination of "bugs," or minor defects in the source code that prevent the software's operating as intended. Second, some minor changes were made to make the display and controls more user friendly. Third, three major changes were made to the import function, the report customizer, and the communications message ex-change. This last group of changes are the only ones a programmer would call "enhancements"; no new "modules" were added to the five modules existing in version 3.7.2B. IIS, in addition, always retained the ca-pability to return version 3.7.2B to NYSBVP. On 6 April 1989, C Tek filed for bankruptcy. In an earlier pro-ceeding, the bankruptcy judge had recognized NYSBVP's validly perfected security interest in the ClienTrak soft-ware. Assuming that in the present proceeding a court would find that IIS's modifications of the software were copyrightable as a derivative work, could NYSBVP foreclose on the source code because the modifications to the source code represented an accession? Or, alter-natively, should the court refuse to follow the doctrine of accession and give to IIS the ownership rights to such changes free and clear of NYSBVP's lien because the changes IIS had made to the source code could be sev-ered from the underlying work? (*In re C-Tek Software, Inc.*, 127 Bankr. 501 [Bkrtcy. D. N.H. 1991].)

CHAPTER 30

Secured Transactions: Default

OUTLINE

THE CODE AND DEFAULT

The previous chapters dealing with secured transactions considered the methods by which secured parties can protect their interests in the collateral. Neither the debtor nor the secured party, however, wants to speak the unspeakable: the possibility that the debtor will *default,* or fail to meet the obligations set out in the security agreement. Still, this unspeakable moment sometimes occurs.

The default of the debtor represents a bittersweet moment for the secured party. On the one hand, default distresses the secured party because it reveals that the debtor may be unable or unwilling to pay the debt to the secured party. But on the other hand, the secured party has worked hard to preserve his or her status as one superior to an unsecured lender and as one who thus has rights to the collateral on default. In brief, Part 5 of Article 9 allows the secured party, on the debtor's default, to take possession of the collateral and to dispose of it in satisfaction of the secured party's claim. Yet, in so doing, the Code provides the debtor with certain protections and makes the secured party liable for any noncompliance with applicable Code provisions.

Interestingly, the Code does not define the term *default.* Basically, the parties decide what will constitute default, and the security agreement embodies these conclusions. Nonpayment by the debtor constitutes perhaps the easiest definition of default. But as Figure 28.1 showed, default clauses are often broad and lengthy. Security agreements also often include acceleration clauses by which the secured party demands that all payments be made immediately. In the absence of bad faith and unconscionability, courts routinely uphold these clauses.

On default, the secured party may resort to various alternative remedies. Using non-Code remedies, the secured party may become a judgment creditor, may **garnish** the debtor's wages, or may **replevy** the goods. Code remedies include strict foreclosure (retention of the collateral in satisfaction of the debt) and resale of the collateral. In Section 9-501(1), the UCC further provides that non-Code and Code rights and remedies on default are cumulative. Yet it is clear that secured parties must be unsuccessful in enforcing their rights by one method before they can utilize another method against the debtor. Neither the Code nor case law sanctions an approach whereby a secured creditor may employ non-Code and Code remedies simultaneously against the debtor.

Garnish   Receive assets of the debtor that are in the hands of a third party in order to satisfy a debt owed.

Replevy   Acquire possession of goods unlawfully held by another.

NON-CODE REMEDIES

Foreclose   Cut off an existing ownership right in property.

The Code says that on default, secured parties may seek a court judgment, may **foreclose,** or may otherwise enforce the security agreement by any avail-

Writ of execution A writing, issued by a court, enforcing a judgment or decree.

Garnishment A legal proceeding in which assets of a debtor that are in the hands of a third person are ordered held by the third person or turned over to the creditor in full or partial satisfaction of the debt.

able judicial procedure.[1] Accordingly, secured parties can use their Code remedies of repossession and resale with the possibility of a deficiency judgment for which the debtor is liable, or they can follow the non-Code remedy of becoming judgment creditors by filing suit, obtaining a judgment, and having the sheriff use a **writ of execution** to levy on the goods and then sell them at a public sale. The proceeds of this sale are paid to the secured party. Another non-Code alternative to levying on the goods involves **garnishment** of a set percentage of the debtor's wages. Although there are certain advantages to following these non-Code remedies (in cases where the value of the collateral has decreased so far that the possibility of reaching assets beyond the collateral would be desirable), in practice most creditors elect the tidier and speedier remedies of repossession and resale that the UCC allows.

RIGHT OF REPOSSESSION

Unless already in possession of the collateral, a secured party has the right to take possession of the collateral on the debtor's default. In so doing, that party may employ "self-help" measures; that is, secured parties can repossess the collateral themselves without judicial procedures *if* they can do so without breaching the peace.[2] Repossession carries with it inherent dangers, however. Besides risking possible tort liability if the repossession involves a breach of the peace, the secured party also risks UCC liability[3] and the loss of the right to a deficiency judgment. Needless to say, this aspect of the Code has spawned numerous lawsuits. In general, the courts assess such factors as whether the secured party entered the debtor's home or driveway without permission and whether the debtor agreed to the repossession. Although it is difficult to make generalizations in this area, if the creditor repossesses an automobile from a public street and the debtor fails to object to this procedure, most courts will hold that there has been no breach of the peace. Nevertheless, in recent years, some questions have arisen as to the constitutionality of this "self-help" provision of the Code on the ground that repossession without notice to the debtor may deprive the debtor of due process rights.[4] Statutes authorizing replevin may be subject to the same constitutional argument.

The next case illustrates one court's disposition of this constitutional question.

[1]Uniform Commercial Code, Section 9-501(1).
[2]Ibid., Section 9-503.
[3]Ibid., Section 9-507.
[4]Fuentes v. Shevin, 407 U.S. 67 (1972); Mitchell v. W.T. Grant Co., 416 U.S. 600 (1974).

Jefferds v. *Ellis*
522 N.Y.S.2d 398 (N.Y. App. Div. 1987)

FACTS   Jefferds had "leased" a tractor truck from Ellis under a "home-drafted" agreement that said nothing about default or Ellis's right of repossession. After Jefferds had paid nine monthly installments of $460 each without default, Ellis seized the vehicle in question without prior notice and without any judicial process. Ellis seized the truck when the vehicle was temporarily parked by Jefferds on the land of a third party with the keys left in the vehicle. Ellis's reasons for seizing the truck were based on his subjective view that Jefferds had not been taking satisfactory care of it and that, as a result, the vehicle was becoming unsafe. When Jefferds sought the return of the truck, Ellis argued that Section 9-503 of the Code permitted self-help repossessions and that his actions were legal since the "lease" was actually a secured transaction and thus subject to the UCC's provisions.

ISSUE   Was Ellis's unilateral act of repossessing the truck under an agreement that had made no mention of repossession and that had occurred in circumstances in which the "lessee"/buyer was current with regard to payments owed permissible under the UCC and constitutional under New York law?

HOLDING   Yes. The court held that Section 9-503 was constitutional in the circumstances of this case.

REASONING   The lower court was incorrect in holding that the rights afforded to a secured party on default under Section 9-503 unconstitutionally deprived Jefferds of his right to due process because he had not been given a judicial hearing prior to the repossession. No logical reason has been advanced as to why a repossession under a conditional sales contract, such as the one in this case, should be treated differently from repossession under a chattel mortgage pursuant to UCC Sections 9-503 and 9-504, the latter of which New York courts previously had determined to be constitutionally permissible. Hence, the holdings by New York courts to the effect that peaceable self-help remedies by secured creditors do not involve "state action" governed by the Fourteenth Amendment but rather constitute private action, were consonant with the holdings of the courts of many other states and clearly applied to the repossession of Jefferds's truck, as well.

Besides repossession by self-help, the Code also sanctions the secured party's requiring the debtor to assemble the collateral at a reasonably convenient place to be designated by the secured party if the security agreement provides for this.[5] Moreover, when the collateral consists of heavy equipment that makes physical removal burdensome or expensive, the Code permits the secured party to render the equipment unusable and to dispose of the collateral on the debtor's premises, thus eliminating the need for physically removing the collateral.

These rules do not cover accounts and general intangibles, because one cannot possess purely intangible collateral. When the debtor is in default with regard to these types of collateral, the secured party may notify the person who is obligated on the intangibles to make payments directly to him or her.

[5]Uniform Commercial Code, Section 9-503.

The secured party may also take control of any proceeds to which he or she is entitled under the UCC.[6]

STRICT FORECLOSURE

After default and repossession, the secured party may decide *to retain the collateral in complete satisfaction of the debt.*[7] This remedy is called the secured party's right of *strict foreclosure.* Strict foreclosure may be attractive to the secured party for several reasons: (1) The value of the collateral may be approximately equal to the debt, (2) the expenses of court actions are avoided, (3) there can be no subsequent controversies about whether the resale price was fair, and (4) the UCC sets out matter-of-factly the requirements for effecting strict foreclosure.

However, to effect strict foreclosure, the secured party must comply with certain requirements, which include the following:

1. The secured party must send written notice of his or her intention to retain the collateral to
   a. the debtor, unless the debtor has signed *after* default a statement renouncing his or her right to force a sale of the collateral (in the case of consumer goods, no other notice need be sent);
   b. many other secured parties who have in writing notified the secured party who is foreclosing that they claim an interest in the collateral.
2. The secured party must wait twenty-one days after sending notice in order to receive objections in writing to the secured party's proposed retention of the collateral.[8]

If the secured party receives no such objections, he or she can utilize the remedy of strict foreclosure; but the secured party will thereby give up any claims to a deficiency judgment.

In contrast, strict foreclosure is not permissible in certain situations:

1. Whenever the secured party actually receives written objections from those entitled to notification within twenty-one days, the secured party must sell the collateral.
2. If the collateral consists of consumer goods and the debtor has paid 60 percent of the cash price of a purchase money security interest or

[6]Ibid., Section 9-502.
[7]Ibid., Section 9-505(2).
[8]Ibid.

60 percent of the loan in all other cases, the secured party must sell the collateral unless the debtor has, *after* default, renounced in writing the right to require a sale of the collateral.[9]

The policy behind this UCC provision recognizes the debtor's substantial equity in the collateral and the fact that resale may result in a surplus that would by right belong to the debtor. Therefore, in the absence of the debtor's renunciation of the right to demand resale, the secured party cannot retain the collateral. This section also contains penalties for noncompliance: When the secured party is obligated to sell the collateral, failure to do so within ninety days makes the secured party liable in either **conversion** or damages (under a statutory formula enumerated in the Code).[10]

Conversion   The unauthorized and wrongful exercise of dominion and control over the personal property of another to the harm of that other person.

RESALE OF REPOSSESSED COLLATERAL

On the other hand, the secured party may choose initially to satisfy the debtor's obligation by reselling, leasing, or otherwise disposing of the collateral.[11] In fact, secured parties use this remedy of foreclosure by sale much more frequently than strict foreclosure. The liberality of the Code's provision for resale allows the secured party to realize the highest resale price possible and at the same time to reduce the possibility of a deficiency judgment. In this way, both the secured party and the debtor benefit.

The sale may be either public or private, subject always to the requirement that the method, manner, time, place, and terms of such sale be commercially reasonable.[12] A public sale, or auction, is the more ordinary occurrence; but the Code encourages private sales when, as is often the case, a private sale through commercial channels will increase the chances for a higher resale price.

Notice

Secured parties usually must notify debtors of the time and place of any public or private sale. When the collateral consists of nonconsumer goods, foreclosing secured parties must in addition notify any other secured party who has notified them in writing of a claimed interest in the collateral. A secured party who claims an interest must notify the foreclosing secured party before the latter sends notification to the debtor or before the debtor renounces his or her rights. Thus, the burden is on the claimant secured parties to notify the foreclosing secured party of their interest before a corresponding duty to notify them of sale ever arises. In certain circumstances, the secured party may

[9]Ibid., Section 9-505(1).
[10]Ibid.
[11]Ibid., Section 9-504.
[12]Ibid., Section 9-504(3).

nonetheless dispense with notification if the collateral is perishable, threatens to decline speedily in value, or is of a type customarily sold on a recognized market.[13] The policy reason for notification stems from a belief that those who have an interest in the collateral—the debtor and **junior secured parties**— may want to bid on the collateral or send their friends to do so.

Junior secured parties Any secured parties whose security interests are subordinate to that of the priority secured party (here, the foreclosing secured party).

A debtor may agree contractually to waive this required notice. The case that follows illustrates how a court may treat such a waiver.

Van Bibber v. *Norris*
419 N.E.2d 115 (Ind. 1981)

FACTS   Norris sued Van Bibber and American Fletcher National Bank (AFNB) for damages for the wrongful repossession of his mobile home and the loss of its contents. One of the provisions in the security agreement Norris had signed allowed AFNB to accelerate the amount due and to repossess without notice on Norris's default. Norris argued that since AFNB had routinely accepted late payments without declaring a default, a duty had arisen to notify him of AFNB's intention to repossess.

ISSUE   Did AFNB have a duty to notify Norris of repossession despite the waiver of notice stated in the acceleration clause?

HOLDING   No. There was no such duty.

REASONING   A security agreement in general is to be enforced according to its terms. Hence, an agreement containing a nonwaiver and a nonmodification clause would give the secured party the right to take possession of the collateral without notice on default.

Commercially Reasonable Sale

A great deal of litigation has arisen from the Code provision stating that the sale itself must be commercially reasonable. According to the UCC, the fact that a better price might have been obtained at a different time or by a different method does not in itself make the sale commercially unreasonable. Similarly, sales in conformity with the commercial practices of dealers in the type of collateral sold or sales made in the usual manner on recognized markets demonstrate commercial reasonableness as well. Likewise, a court's approval of a sale or the sanctioning of a sale by a creditors' committee makes the sale commercially reasonable.[14] In these cases, the debtor's argument that the resale price is insufficient will not constitute grounds for a court's denying the secured party a deficiency judgment. But, in some circumstances, a court may deny a secured party its right to a deficiency judgment. The following case illustrates how one court grappled with the concept of commercial reasonableness.

[13]Ibid.
[14]Ibid., Section 9-507(2).

Bank of Chapmanville v. Workman
406 S.E.2d. 58 (W.Va. 1991)

FACTS   On 26 July 1982, the Workmans bought a 1982 Duke mobile home and entered into an installment loan contract with the Bank of Chapmanville (the Bank) whereby the Workmans promised to pay $38,703.60 in 120 monthly payments over a period of ten years in exchange for the Bank's retaining a security interest in the mobile home. Five years later, the Workmans failed to make the June and July, 1987, payments; and on 19 August 1987, the Bank sent them a written "notice of right to cure default." On 24 August 1987, Ms. Workman met with the Bank's loan officer, Charles Dale. The Bank claimed that Ms. Workman told Dale that she and her husband could no longer afford the mobile home and that the Bank could repossess it. The Workmans, on the other hand, contended that they had attempted to negotiate a schedule for catching up on their payments, but that the Bank had insisted on repossession. On 2 September 1987, the Bank sent the Workmans a "final demand letter." At the Bank's request, the Workmans vacated the mobile home. Later they moved to North Carolina. Whether Ms. Workman provided the Bank with their address and telephone number in North Carolina remained unclear. On 26 September 1987, the Bank sent to the Workmans by certified mail a "notice of public sale" dated 25 September 1987. The Bank sent the notice to the same address to which it had sent the "notice of right to cure default" and the "final demand letter," both of which the Workmans had received. The "notice of public sale" was returned unclaimed around 15 October 1987. The Bank placed a single "notice of public sale" in the legal notices section of the 1 October 1987 issue of the *Logan Banner* newspaper and posted a copy of the notice in the courthouse. This notice, among other things, stated that the Bank of Chapmanville would, on Friday 23 October 1987, at the hour of 11:00 A.M., sell at public auction at the front step of the mobile home in Garretts Fork, Logan County, West Virginia, a certain mobile home described in the security agreement as a 1982 Duke 14-by-70-foot mobile home, serial number 10068. The public auction took place on 23 October 1987. No bidders attended, and the Bank sold the mobile home to itself for $10,614. The Bank did not have the home appraised before the public sale, but consulted the NADA guide; the sale price was lower than the NADA reference value. The Bank applied the sale price to the balance owed by the Workmans, leaving a deficiency of $7873.25 as of the date of sale. On 29 February 1988, four and one-half months after the repossession, the Bank sold the mobile home to a private person, Michael Mays, for $13,000. When the Bank sold the mobile home to Mays, it did not credit its net profit from that sale to the Workmans' deficiency debt. The Workmans therefore argued that because the Bank had engaged in a commercially unreasonable sale, it should be barred from seeking a deficiency judgment and should be made to pay the statutory damages the UCC sets out for these kinds of omissions.

ISSUE   Had the secured creditor conducted a commercially reasonable sale of the mobile home?

HOLDING   Maybe yes, maybe no. The notice of sale might have been so general as to make the sale of the mobile home commercially unreasonable. However, since the evidence was in conflict on this issue, only a jury could decide this question. A remand to the trial court for a determination of this issue therefore was proper.

REASONING   The Workmans' first point—that the Bank had improperly failed to credit its net profit from the sale—was not correct. If a secured creditor buys a repossessed good from itself at a public sale conducted in a commercially reasonable manner and then resells it for a higher price, the secured creditor has done nothing wrong, provided the creditor's purchase price is not unreasonably low. However, if a secured creditor buys low at its own commercially unreasonable "public sale" and only after this sale earnestly attempts to sell the good in a commercially reasonable manner, its behavior is at least as bad as that which the statutory damage provisions of the UCC are designed to discourage. The Workmans alleged that the Bank had engaged in this kind of misconduct and thus should be barred from seeking a deficiency judgment and be made to pay statutory damages. West Virginia law has adopted UCC provision 9-504 in mandating a sale that is commercially reasonable in every respect of the disposition of the collateral. Here, even if the Bank had adequately attempted to provide the Workmans with public notice of the public sale, evidence revealed three aspects of the published notice that a jury could find disturbing: (1) The notice lacks a specific address, (2) no telephone number is given for inquiries about the mobile home, and (3) no mention is made of an opportunity to inspect before sale. Although such deficiencies would not render every public sale commercially unreasonable, they do illustrate that the trial court had erred in directing a verdict for the Bank. Moreover, because there was no other advertisement of the "public sale," this legal notice had to serve as an effective advertisement to potential buyers as well as notice to the debtors. Thus, the sufficiency of the notice's description of the location of the public sale went to the issue of the commercial reasonableness of the sale. The Bank pointed out that Garretts Fork is a rural community without road names and numbers; thus, it might be awkward to give the address, or rather directions, in the notice. However, the Bank did not even place a "For Sale" sign on the mobile home; and the record suggested that there are many mobile homes in Garretts Fork. The only way a potential buyer would know where to look for the mobile home would be to call the Bank, and the notice, by lacking a telephone number, did not encourage such inquiries. After selling the mobile home to itself at the repossession sale, the Bank placed an advertisement in the *Logan Banner* that described the mobile home and listed the Bank's telephone number. The trial court would not allow the Workmans to present evidence concerning the later advertisement. The Workmans wanted to show that the Bank had utilized one standard of what was commercially reasonable when selling for the Workmans' account and another when selling for its own account. Hence, the court should have allowed the newspaper advertisement into evidence because its probative value far outweighed the possible unfair prejudice to the Bank. In addition, the judge could have cured any potential unfair prejudice with an instruction to the jury that a secured creditor is not required to use the same selling method when reselling goods for its own account as it uses at a repossession sale. Hence, whether the Bank's sale of the mobile home had been commercially reasonable remained unclear. Because of the conflicting evidence, the issue became a question only a jury could decide. If, on remand, the jury were to find that the Bank's sale of the mobile home was commercially unreasonable, the court would need to address the question of whether a secured creditor's commercially unreasonable disposition of collateral bars it from seeking a deficiency judgment, an issue of first impression in West Virginia.

Proceeds

The Code even sets out the order for applying the proceeds of the sale.[15] According to the Code, the secured party must apply the proceeds realized from the disposition of the collateral in this order:

1. payment of the reasonable expenses of retaking and disposing of the collateral, including reasonable attorneys' fees if provided by the security agreement

2. satisfaction of the debt owed to the secured party

3. payment of remaining proceeds to eligible junior secured parties in the same collateral

4. payment to the debtor of any surplus and corresponding liability on the debtor's part for any deficiency, unless the parties have otherwise agreed

[15]Ibid., Section 9-504(1), (2).

DEBTORS' RIGHTS

It is possible that no sale will ever occur because the debtor has the right to redeem the collateral at any time before the secured party has disposed of it. *Redemption* consists of the debtor's extinguishing the secured party's security interest by tendering payment of all obligations due, including expenses incurred by the secured party in retaking and preparing the collateral for disposition (usually resale) and in arranging for the resale. Such expenses also may include attorneys' fees and legal expenses. A debtor who can accomplish redemption before sale or strict foreclosure can retain the collateral. On the other hand, a debtor may, after default, agree to waive the right to redeem.[16] The debtor presumably could not waive such rights in the original security agreement; rather, default must precede such waivers.

In the following case, the secured party's disregard of the debtor's rights in the collateral left the secured party vulnerable to a punitive damages award in favor of the debtor.

Friendly Credit Union v. *Campbell*
579 So.2d. 1288 (Ala. 1991)

FACTS   Freddie B. Campbell, an employee of International Paper Company, borrowed approximately $12,000 from Friendly Credit Union in February, 1986, to purchase a truck. Campbell signed a security agreement with the credit union, giving it a security interest in the vehicle to secure the loan. Monthly payments of $337.50 were regularly deducted from Campbell's paychecks until 21 March 1987, when a lockout occurred at International Paper. As a result of the lockout, the credit union posted a notice in the union hall stating that monthly payments on all loans were waived after 31 March 1987. Apparently the credit union was proceeding under Paragraph 15 of its security agreement, which provided, "In the event that . . . there is a strike . . . failure to make any payments hereunder for a period not to exceed ninety days, during the continuation of such a strike shall not constitute a default hereunder. . . ." When the lockout continued after the ninety-day period had expired, the credit union issued another notice allowing the payment of interest only on all loans. In July, 1987, Campbell contacted the credit union about the payment of interest on his loan. In order to make the interest payments, Campbell turned over to the credit union $465.29 from his Christmas savings account and approximately $900 from a personal and holiday vacation fund. In December, 1987, in response to pressure from regulatory agencies, the credit union notified Campbell that his "interest only" payments no longer satisfied his obligation under the original purchase agreement. The National Credit Union Administration (NCUA) had directed the credit union to require that loan payments, including all amounts in arrears, would become due no later than 31 July 1987. As a result of the NCUA's advice, the credit union gave Campbell three options: (1) catch up the payments on his loan by paying the amount in arrears and making the $337.50 monthly payments called for by his original loan obligation, (2) pay off the total balance of the loan, or (3) refinance the loan. Campbell, still unemployed, could choose only the refinancing option. He tried to refinance by applying for a loan with another institution, but it denied Campbell's application because of the insufficiency of his income. Friendly Credit Union denied his request for refinancing for the same reason. Due to his inability to meet the credit union's demands, which had been increased from those originally agreed on, Campbell's vehicle was peaceably

---

[16]Ibid., Section 9-501(3), 9-506.

repossessed. On 14 March 1988, the credit union notified Campbell that he had fourteen days in which to pay the balance of his loan ($10,650.38 plus interest) in order to redeem his truck. Still unemployed, Campbell could not redeem his truck under the terms of this notice. The credit union sold his truck for $6417 on 24 March 1988—before the end of the period in which Campbell had been told he could redeem his truck. That sale resulted in a deficiency of $4277.04. Campbell's subsequent lawsuit alleged that he had not been in default according to the modified "interest only" agreement he had made with Friendly Credit Union. Owing to the existence of the agreement that had modified Campbell's duty to pay interest only, Campbell asserted that the credit union should be estopped from requiring the payment of the total amount or the amount in arrears plus the current monthly payments. Campbell's estoppel theory was supported by his alleged reliance on the contract modifications he had made with Friendly Credit Union. Campbell asserted that the repossession therefore was invalid and amounted to a conversion of his vehicle. Campbell's complaint also stated that: (1) the sale of the truck was commercially unreasonable; and (2) the credit union's notice concerning his period of redemption had indicated that he would have until 28 March 1988 to redeem his truck. It is undisputed that the credit union had cut short the period in which he had been told he could redeem his truck, since the truck was sold on 24 March 1988. Because the sale of the truck had left Campbell with a deficiency of $4277.04, he claimed he had suffered injury.

ISSUE Was Campbell in default when the credit union sold his truck?

HOLDING No. Campbell was not in default under the modified contract at the time of the sale of the truck.

REASONING Campbell was not in default under the terms of the modified July, 1987, contract. The credit union's written notice allowing "interest only" payments amounted to a written public offer satisfying Alabama statutory law. Campbell's payment of the interest with money taken from his vacation and Christmas funds signaled his acceptance of the credit union's modified offer. Evidence supporting Campbell's argument that he had relied on the modified "interest only" arrangement certainly existed. For example, Campbell had released his Christmas and vacation funds to the credit union in order to satisfy the modified agreement allowing interest payments only. Thus, the jury could have found that Friendly Credit Union was estopped from changing the terms of Campbell's payment, based on his reliance on the credit union's past actions. According to the modified agreement with the credit union, Campbell was not in default. Consequently, Friendly Credit Union's repossession of the truck, when he had not been in default, constituted conversion, for a creditor may validly repossess the property only of a defaulting party. Settled law holds that if a jury infers from the evidence presented that the plaintiff has suffered actual injury or loss, the plaintiff is entitled to at least nominal damages. Furthermore, under Alabama law, a plaintiff's right to recover nominal damages supports the jury's award of punitive damages when the defendant's actions are oppressive and malicious. Hence, the evidence supported an award of punitive damages, particularly since evidence existed to show that Campbell had suffered actual losses. Given this evidence, the jury could have awarded Campbell nominal or actual damages, and because it could have awarded such damages, it could also have awarded punitive damages, if the circumstances of the defendant's actions would otherwise support such an award.

SECURED PARTIES' DUTIES

Besides having to observe the previously mentioned duties regarding disposition of the collateral, secured parties also have the duty of taking reasonable care of the collateral while it is in their possession, either before or after default. They are liable for any losses caused by their failure to meet this obligation, but they do not lose their security interests if such a loss occurs.[17] Unless the parties have otherwise agreed, the secured party can charge to the debtor payment of reasonable expenses, such as insurance and taxes, incurred in the custody, preservation, or use of the collateral. Moreover, the Code places the risk of accidental loss or damage on the debtor to the extent of any deficiency in insurance coverage. The secured party also may hold as additional security any increase or profits (except money) received from the collateral, but the secured party should either turn over any money so received to the debtor or apply it to reduce the secured obligation. There is a duty to keep the collateral identifiable except for **fungible** collateral that may be commingled. The secured party may either repledge the collateral on terms that do not violate the debtor's right to redeem it or use the collateral if this will help to preserve it or its value (for example, in an ongoing business, the operation of equipment that has been given as security).[18]

Fungible Virtually identical; interchangeable; descriptive of things that belong to a class and that are not identifiable individually.

Once the expenses of holding the collateral have been defrayed, as mentioned, the secured party must turn over any remaining proceeds to the debtor. On the other hand, the debtor remains liable for any deficiency—the difference between the available proceeds and the amount of indebtedness and expenses that remain—unless the parties have agreed otherwise or state law eliminates this obligation.[19]

Debtors sometimes try to argue that the amount received from the sale of the collateral (the usual basis for computing deficiencies or surpluses), if lower than the collateral's market value, makes the sale commercially unreasonable. But courts ordinarily do not respond favorably to such arguments as long as fraud is not present and the secured party has attempted in good faith to attract buyers. Similarly, these arguments generally will not affect the rights of the purchaser at the sale: The purchaser takes the collateral free and clear of such claims if the purchase is made in good faith.[20]

However, a secured party's failure to comply with the duties regarding disposition of the collateral may subject the secured party to statutory liability under Section 9-507 for losses by debtors or junior secured parties and, if consumer goods are involved, to a damages formula that sets up a statutory penalty. As we learned earlier, some courts also will deny the secured party the right to a deficiency judgment as a consequence of noncompliance or misbehavior.

The following case involves allegations that the secured party had failed to live up to its duty to take reasonable care of the collateral. In reading the case, try to determine whether the secured party could have taken better care of the collateral and whether the care taken was reasonable and adequate.

[17]Ibid., Section 9-207(3).
[18]Ibid., Section 9-207(2).
[19]Ibid., Section 9-504(2).
[20]Ibid., Section 9-504(4).

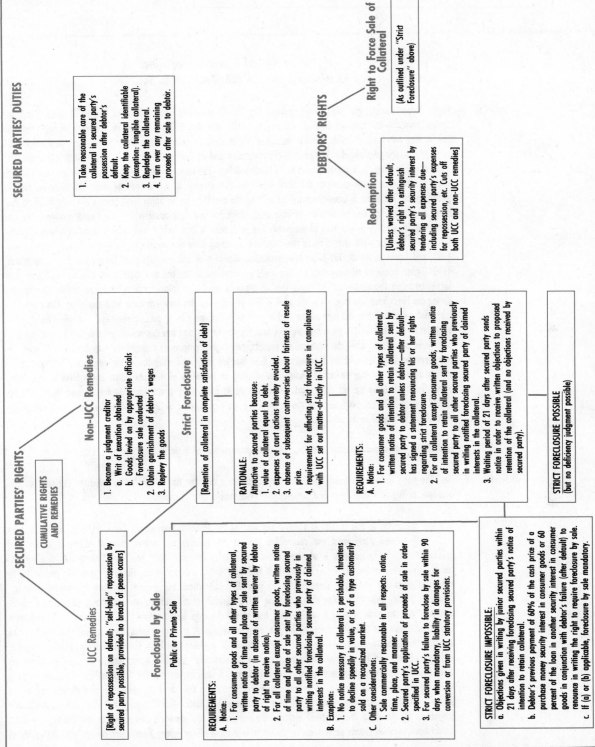

DIAGRAM 30.1 Concepts Regarding Default

In re Biglari Import Export, Inc.
15 UCC Rep. Serv.2d 280 (Bankr. W.D. Tex. 1991)

FACTS   Biglari Import Export, Inc. (the Debtor) operates The Ritz Oriental Rug Gallery. In 1986, Biglari borrowed operating capital from the International Bank of Commerce (IBOC), granting IBOC a lien on its inventory of rugs. Later in the lending relationship, IBOC became concerned about Biglari's business and loan performance and asked that some of the rugs be pledged to the bank. Biglari complied and ultimately delivered forty rugs into IBOC's possession. IBOC stored the rugs in a storage room in its bank building. The room, though not designed as a collateral storage vault, is the same room in which the bank stores its own records. It has a concrete floor, no windows, and no public access. The room is located toward the rear of the building, on an upper level, and is the only room on that level. A winding stairway leads to a vestibule area, which has one door opening out to a fenced courtyard and one door into the employee-only area of the bank. The back door is kept locked, and only bank officers have a key to this door. The rugs were, according to the witnesses, removed from this room only on two occasions, once in July, 1988, and again in March, 1990. On both occasions, Biglari took out the rugs and brought them back. In March, 1990, Biglari removed all forty rugs so they could be aired out in the sun and mothballed (the standard procedure for maintaining the quality of the rugs). One of Biglari's employees (along with an assistant) picked up the rugs during the lunch hour one day, while the bank officer in charge of this loan was away from the office. The employees told bank personnel that the loan officer had approved their coming by to pick up the rugs, and someone from the bank let them into the storage room. No one had the employees sign any paperwork relative to checking the rugs out. Three days later, after the mothballing process, two Biglari employees brought the rugs back to the bank. No one from the bank checked the bundles to be sure that all forty rugs were there. The rugs were returned to the storage room, where they remained undisturbed. During an inventory of the rugs taken at the bank in December, 1990, the bank came up ten rugs short. Later, during its bankruptcy proceedings, Biglari argued that the judge should reduce IBOC's secured claim by the value of the ten rugs because of IBOC's alleged failure to take reasonable care of the collateral in its possession.

ISSUE   Had IBOC used reasonable care in the custody and preservation of Biglari's rugs?

HOLDING   Yes. The basic manner in which IBOC had stored the rugs and the bank's conduct in releasing the rugs on two occasions to Biglari's employees had satisfied the "reasonable care" standard.

REASONING   The law applicable to this matter is Texas's adoption of the Uniform Commercial Code, which in applicable part says, "[A] secured party must use reasonable care in the custody and preservation of collateral in his [sic] possession. . . ." The question is whether, under the facts of this case, IBOC had used "reasonable care" in the custody and preservation of Biglari's rugs. If it had not, it " . . . [would be] liable for any loss caused by its failure to meet any obligation imposed by the preceding subsections but [would] not lose its security interest." However, Biglari had the burden of establishing IBOC's breach of the duty to use reasonable care. The evidence indicated that the basic manner in which IBOC had stored the rugs would satisfy the "reasonable care" standard. The room, while not expressly designed for the purpose of storing rugs, was adequately secure, confirmed by the fact that the same room housed the bank's own records. In addition, the bank limited access to bank employees; and only officers had keys to the back door. The "reasonable care" standard would impose no greater obligations than these for storing and preserving these rugs. However, Biglari highlighted the "mothballing" incident, pointing to the bank's release of the rugs to two employees of Biglari on their oral representation of authority and to the bank's failure to confirm the return of all forty rugs three days later. Biglari argued that this laxity in the bank's procedures for handling the collateral violated the reasonable care standard. According to the Debtor, the bank should have required proper express authorization from a bank officer before it permitted anyone into the collateral storage area or permitted the removal of any of the collateral. Furthermore, in Biglari's opinion, if the bank had counted the rugs when they were returned after the mothballing, it would have caught the shortfall immediately (assuming that this is when the shortfall occurred) and could have contacted Biglari immediately, presumably so Biglari could have taken prompt steps to intercept the dishonest employees. Nevertheless, Biglari's argument overlooked the fact that IBOC had released the rugs to Biglari's own employees; and it had been Biglari's own employees who had brought the rugs back to the bank three days later. The bank could not bear responsibility for the conduct of Biglari's employees to a greater degree than Biglari's own responsibility. Given that there was just as much evidence to suggest wrongdoing on the part of Biglari or its employees (e.g., refusals by Biglari's insurance companies to honor claims made by the firm), a court should not hold IBOC liable under the reasonable care standard simply because the rugs ended up missing.

SUMMARY

When a debtor defaults, the secured party may pursue either non-Code or Code remedies. Under the Code, the secured party may take possession of the collateral and either retain it in complete satisfaction of the debt (strict foreclosure) or dispose of it by public or private sale (foreclosure by sale). In either case, notification of the debtor and perhaps other parties must take place if the secured party is to escape Code liability. The secured party's right of strict foreclosure may be limited by such things as the debtor's paying 60 percent of the price of collateral consisting of consumer goods.

If a sale is undertaken, it must be conducted in a commercially reasonable manner. The Code also enumerates the order in which the proceeds of a sale should be applied, assuming a sale has occurred. However, the debtor may cut off the secured party's right to foreclosure by sale or strict foreclosure by redeeming the collateral before the secured party disposes of it by resale or retention. When the secured party is in possession of the collateral either before or after default, the party must take reasonable care of the collateral. Failure to live up to this and other duties subjects the secured party to liability for any losses caused thereby, to possible damages under a statutory formula, and to possible denial of the right to a deficiency judgment. Debtors ordinarily are liable for any deficiency that remains after the sale or other disposition of the collateral.

DISCUSSION QUESTIONS

1. What is default?
2. What kinds of non-Code remedies can the secured party pursue?
3. Describe fully the UCC's treatment of the right of repossession.

4. Explain the requirements necessary for effecting strict foreclosure.
5. Name the situations in which strict foreclosure is not permissible.

6. Discuss the rules relating to foreclosure by sale or resale of the repossessed collateral.

7. How can one tell whether a sale has been conducted in a "commercially reasonable" manner?

8. Enumerate the order in which proceeds are applied after a sale.

9. What is redemption?

10. List the secured party's duties of reasonable care of the collateral and the liabilities that may result from a secured party's failure to observe his or her applicable duties.

CASE PROBLEMS

1. Schmode's, Inc. (Schmode's) sold to Harco Leasing Company (Harco) a 1978 International tractor truck and a 1970 Hobbs trailer. Harco and the Wilkinsons entered into a conditional sales agreement with respect to the truck and the trailer. Schmode's guaranteed to Harco that if the Wilkinsons defaulted on their obligations, resulting in Harco's reclaiming the truck and trailer from the Wilkinsons, Schmode's would repurchase them from Harco. The Wilkinsons defaulted and on 19 December 1979 delivered the truck and trailer to Schmode's. Schmode's repaired the collateral and tried to sell it. When these efforts failed, Schmode's began leasing it to others through mid-April, 1983, during which time the collateral was operated a minimum of 204,000 miles. Schmode's honored its agreement with Harco and paid the sum due Harco from the Wilkinsons. The collateral was sold publicly on 28 April 1983. The Wilkinsons argued that Schmode's retention and use of the collateral for almost three years amounted to strict foreclosure and that the Wilkinsons therefore could not be held liable for any deficiency judgment. Were the Wilkinsons correct? (*Schmode's, Inc.* vs. *Wilkinson*, 361 N.W.2d 557 [Neb. 1985].)

2. First National Bank of Pulaski, Tennessee (First National), was the secured creditor of Gary and Katie Jones. When the Joneses became unable to make the payments on their loan, First National repossessed the farm equipment that the Joneses had used as security for their indebtedness and sold the property at a sale. The Joneses argued that First National's sale had violated Section 9-504 because First National's notification to the Joneses of the sale a few days prior to it had been oral. Must a secured party give written notice of the sale in order to comply with the Code's resale provision? (*Jones* v. *First National Bank of Pulaski*, 505 So.2d 352 [Ala. 1987].)

3. On 8 February 1985, Clyde Parrish, Jr. obtained a loan from the McChord Credit Union (McChord) in order to purchase a 1985 Honda Accord. The debt owed to McChord ($10,014) was guaranteed by Clyde, Sr. Clyde, Jr. made the required monthly payments of $225.75 until October, 1986, when he sold the car to Stephanie Irons. Irons made the monthly payments to McChord until April, 1988, when she ceased payments. On 5 January 1989, McChord filed an action for the entire balance due on the note. McChord named as defendants Clyde, Jr. and his wife; Clyde, Sr. and his wife; and Stephanie Irons and her husband. McChord took possession of the Honda automobile and advertised it for sale in the Pierce County Credit Union's newsletter and on signs posted in the Credit Union lobby. McChord sold the car on 20 March 1989 for $3500. None of the Parrishes received notice of the sale until May, 1989. Clyde, Sr. acknowledged, however, that he had been aware that McChord had had possession of the car in April, 1989. Clyde, Sr. contended that he and his son both were entitled to proper notification of McChord's sale of the car. He claimed that McChord's failure to provide such notice violates the UCC and precludes McChord from recovering a deficiency judgment. Was a guarantor such as Clyde, Sr. a "debtor" and thus entitled to statutory notice of the creditor's proposed sale of the collateral? (*McChord Credit Union* v. *Parrish*, 809 P.2d 759 [Wash. App. 1991].)

4. The Backeses sold a restaurant to the Carlisles and the Martins, who began business as Village Corner, Inc., in July, 1984. By December, 1984, the debtors had ceased making payments; and by 1 February 1985, they had defaulted on the promissory note they had signed with the Backeses. On 29 March the Backeses took possession of the premises; and on 1 April they sold the collateral to new tenants without notifying the Carlisles and Martins of the sale. The Backeses argued that the sale fell within one of the exceptions to the Code's no-

tice requirement, since on March 29 they had had only two options: to sell the collateral to the new tenant for whatever the new tenant offered or to remove the collateral and sell it for a possibly lesser amount. At that point, the Backeses asserted, they had been confronted with a take-it-or-leave-it proposition. Because the new tenant had planned to move in on April 1, they contended, there had been insufficient time for notice. Thus, because the property had threatened to decline speedily in value, the Backeses had justifiably dispensed with notice to the Carlisles and Martins. Should a court accept this argument? (*Backes* v. *Village Corner, Inc.*, 242 Cal. Rptr. 716 [Cal. App. 1987].)

5. Would a secured creditor be guilty of breaching the peace and therefore of illegally repossessing a vehicle if it had unauthorizedly entered the driveway of the debtor's residence to remove the vehicle? Would a repossession be illegal if the secured party had broken into the debtor's place of business and replaced the locks with new ones? (*Butler* v. *Ford Motor Credit Company*, 829 F.2d 568 [5th Cir. 1987] and *Riley State Bank of Riley* v. *Spillman*, 750 P.2d 1024 [Kan. 1988].)

6. The Wipperts operated a cattle ranch east of Browning, Montana, on the Blackfeet Indian Reservation. The Wipperts had borrowed $44,729.97 from the Blackfeet Tribal Credit Program and had used "all cattle now owned or hereafter owned by [them]" as collateral for the loan. When the Wipperts defaulted, the tribe informed them by letter that it planned to sell the collateral. However, the letter said nothing about the time and place of the proposed sale, even though the security agreement between the Wipperts and the tribe had required the tribe to give the Wipperts five days' prior written notice of the time and place of the sale. The cattle were sold at public auction, leaving a deficiency of $17,698. The Wipperts maintained that the tribe's failure to give them notice as required by the security agreement and Montana's UCC statute precluded the tribe's receiving a deficiency judgment. The tribe argued that since this collateral was of a type customarily sold on a recognized market, i.e., cattle sold at auction, notice of sale was not required. Who had the better argument? (*Wippert* v. *Blackfeet Tribe*, 695 P.2d 461 [Mont. 1985].)

7. Guaranty Bank & Trust Company (Guaranty Bank) and the Small Business Administration (SBA) originally litigated their lien priority dispute concerning the debtors' farm equipment before a bankruptcy court judge. That judge had held that the lien of Guaranty Bank

enjoyed priority over that of the SBA. The United States District Court for the Northern District of Mississippi had affirmed that decision, but the Fifth Circuit Court of Appeals had reversed the decision. In the meantime, Guaranty Bank, in its preparations for a foreclosure sale, had posted public notices and had sent copies of the notice to local equipment dealers, the debtors' attorney, and the attorney representing the SBA. Guaranty Bank's attorney had conducted the foreclosure sale during legal hours on 10 September 1987. Prior to the sale, Guaranty Bank had had the farm equipment appraised by Jerry Mitchell, an employee of the Yokley and Lundy Auction Company (Yokley and Lundy), who had valued the equipment at $40,000–$55,000. His appraisal worksheet, which reflected his evaluation of the individual items, had noted a total value of between $41,312.50 and $42,000. After receiving the appraisal, Guaranty Bank had calculated its foreclosure bid as $25,000. Mitchell had testified, without contradiction, that he had thought this bid was reasonable under the circumstances. At the foreclosure sale, Guaranty Bank had been the only bidder and had purchased the equipment for the $25,000 price. Pursuant to the provisions of the earlier court order, Guaranty Bank had deposited this amount in an interest-bearing account. The following day, Guaranty Bank had put the equipment in an auction sale being conducted by Yokley and Lundy. According to Mitchell, the equipment had been sold "without reservation"; i.e., the equipment would not be pulled from the sale and Guaranty Bank would take whatever price the equipment brought. At this auction, Guaranty Bank had received net proceeds of $39,748.29. Following the Fifth Circuit's reversal of the two earlier decisions, Guaranty Bank had paid the SBA the $25,000 price that it had bid at the foreclosure sale plus accrued interest of $2848.11, or a total payment of $27,848.11. The legal question on remand centered on whether the court should permit Guaranty Bank to retain the difference in the price that it had paid at the foreclosure sale and the amount that it had received at the auction sale, an alleged "profit" totaling $14,748.29 ($39,748.29 less $25,000). The three underlying issues that the court would face included (1) whether Guaranty Bank had owed a fiduciary duty to the SBA in disposing of the farm equipment, (2) whether Guaranty Bank's foreclosure sale of the equipment had met the UCC commercial reasonableness standard, and (3) whether equity would dictate that Guaranty Bank pay over the excess proceeds received at the auction sale to the SBA. How would you answer these questions if you were the judge? (*In re Whatley,* 126 Bankr. 231 [Bkrtcy. N.D. Miss. 1991].)

8. Between October, 1983, and August, 1985, Selvais operated a diesel repair business but was unable to make his payment obligations to Fritts. On 30 August 1985, Fritts declared Selvais to be in default and repossessed the collateral pursuant to Fritts's rights under the security agreement. At that time, the parties executed a repossession agreement. In this agreement, Selvais and the corporation under which Selvais conducted his business, Beltech Enterprises, Inc. (Beltech), admitted default, tendered the collateral for repossession, and waived any right to notice of a public or private sale of the collateral and of any proposal by Fritts to retain the collateral in satisfaction of the debt. The agreement further provided that Fritts would release Selvais from any liability for any deficiency in excess of $75,000. Upon repossession, Fritts reentered the premises and operated the business in his own name for a period of two to five weeks, after which time Fritts incorporated the business under the name of Tarheel Diesel Service, Inc. (Tarheel). Fritts was the only shareholder in the corporation, and Fritts and his wife were the officers of the corporation. Fritts then transferred the repossessed collateral to Tarheel in exchange for a promissory note made to Fritts by Tarheel in the amount of $26,415. Fritts signed this note in his capacity as president of Tarheel. In February, 1988, Fritts filed this action seeking a deficiency judgment in the amount of $75,000. At trial, Selvais argued that Fritts, after repossession, had retained the collateral and had thereby discharged any claim for a deficiency against him. Specifically, Selvais claimed that Tarheel was Fritts's "alter ego" and should not be considered as a separate entity. If a court disregards the corporate entity, Fritts would be deemed to have retained the collateral himself in satisfaction of Selvais's obligation and would thereby be precluded from seeking any deficiency under North Carolina law. Would a court find this argument persuasive? (*Fritts* v. *Selvais,* 404 S.E.2d 505 [N.C. App. 1991].)

9. Ford Motor Credit Company (FMCC) was the floor-plan inventory financier for Suburban Ford. The security agreement between the parties permitted FMCC to take immediate possession of the collateral without legal process upon Suburban's default. As a result of an audit on 11 March 1981, FMCC realized Suburban Ford was in default and demanded payment. The business closed on 13 March 1981. The owners of Suburban Ford argued that FMCC was liable to them in tort because FMCC's actions had caused the collapse of the agency. They also contended that the sale of the cars had not been commercially reasonable, since FMCC had sold the cars in bulk rather than leaving the vehicles with the dealership, which could have sold them at retail for higher prices. Were Suburban Ford's contentions persuasive? (*Ford Motor Credit Company* v. *Suburban Ford,* 699 P.2d 992, cert. denied, 474 U.S. 995 [1985].)

10. United Missouri Bank of Kirkwood (the Bank) loaned David Goodman $7306.03 for the purchase of a Ford van and retained a security interest in the van. The Bank repossessed the van on 5 December 1980 when Goodman had become two months behind in his payments. On 8 December, the Bank notified Mann that he would have ten days to redeem the collateral or it would be offered for sale. Goodman also was informed he could redeem the van any time prior to the actual disposition. The approximate amount in question was $2078.77. The Bank advertised the sale on 17 December 1980 and, on 22 December, received a written bid for $1200, which was later accepted. Other lower bids were received and rejected. The buyer took possession in late December, 1980, or early January, 1981, and after the first application was denied, owing to technical deficiencies, a repossession title was issued on 28 January. Goodman also advertised the van for sale at $3200, a price at which he received some inquiries but no offers. On 21 January 1981, Goodman's attorney attempted to redeem the collateral but, since the van already had been sold, was refused. Goodman argued that the Bank had converted the van in selling it and in refusing Goodman's offer to redeem the van. Would you agree? (*Mann* v. *United Missouri Bank of Kirkwood,* 689 S.W.2d 830 [Mo. App. 1985].)

CHAPTER 31

Straight Bankruptcy

OUTLINE

HISTORIC BACKGROUND

When the colonists broke away from England to set up the United States of America, they had a strong desire to avoid problems that they had encountered under the English system of government. The United States Constitution and the Bill of Rights were drafted specifically to prevent some of these problems. One problem area was the treatment of debtors.

In England, persons unable or unwilling to pay their debts were very commonly thrown into debtors' prison. Once in prison, a debtor might remain there for years waiting for friends or family to raise funds to repay the debt or until the creditors agreed to the debtor's release. Less commonly, the debtor would agree to some form of indentured servitude. Under such an agreement, the debtor had to work for a preset number of years at little or no salary to repay the debt.

To prevent such treatment of debtors in this country, the founding fathers made provisions in the Constitution for bankruptcy. Article I, Section 8, of the United States Constitution says: "The Congress shall have the Power . . . to establish . . . uniform Laws on the subject of Bankruptcies throughout the United States."

For much of the history of the United States, some form of federal bankruptcy regulation has existed. Although the Constitution seemingly calls for exclusive federal control of this area, the bankruptcy laws have tended to coexist with state law in many areas. In fact, state law often is used to define problems or to provide solutions to bankruptcy problems.

Until very recently, bankruptcy was governed by the federal Bankruptcy Act, enacted in 1898. This act was quite technical, and many people found it confusing. In 1978, Congress passed a new law, the Bankruptcy Reform Act, which took effect 1 October 1979. The Bankruptcy Reform Act had two major purposes. It was designed to provide for fair and equitable treatment of the creditors in the distribution of the debtor's property. But, more important, it was designed to give an "honest debtor" a "fresh start."

Unfortunately, the Bankruptcy Reform Act had some technical problems (discussed below) that resulted in its being declared unconstitutional. As a result, the Bankruptcy Amendments and Federal Judgeship Act of 1984[1] was enacted. This new act was intended to clarify the jurisdiction of the bankruptcy courts and to resolve the constitutional problems presented by the Bankruptcy Reform Act. At the same time, Congress made the new bankruptcy coverage more sensitive to the needs of the creditors and made some effort to reduce or eliminate the problem of debtor abuses that had occurred under the former bankruptcy laws.

[1]P.L. 98–353.

THE BANKRUPTCY REFORM ACT

Adjunct Added or joined to another.

The Bankruptcy Reform Act called for a whole new adjudicative system of bankruptcies. Under the act, each United States district court was to contain a separate, **adjunct** bankruptcy court. These bankruptcy courts were to be staffed by bankruptcy *judges,* each of whom was to serve a fourteen-year term. The bankruptcy judges were to be appointed by the president, subject to approval by the Senate. It was hoped that this new system, which replaced the "referees" acting through the district courts, would simplify and speed up bankruptcy proceedings.

The new bankruptcy court–bankruptcy judge system encountered a major roadblock when, on 28 June 1982, the United States Supreme Court declared the Bankruptcy Reform Act unconstitutional. As a result of this ruling, the entire area of bankruptcy jurisdiction was in doubt. The case that raised the challenge to the Bankruptcy Reform Act involved the Northern Pipeline Company. Northern Pipeline filed a petition in bankruptcy in January, 1980. As a part of its petition, Northern Pipeline sued Marathon Pipe Line Company in the bankruptcy court, alleging that Marathon Pipe Line had breached a contract. Marathon sought dismissal of the suit on the grounds that the bankruptcy courts established by the Bankruptcy Reform Act were unconstitutional. The United States Supreme Court handed down its opinion in *Northern Pipeline Construction Co.* v. *Marathon Pipe Line Co.*[2] on 28 June 1982. This opinion upheld the position of Marathon Pipe Line and totally confused the validity of bankruptcy coverage under the Bankruptcy Reform Act.

Article III of the United States Constitution requires that the judicial power of the United States must be exercised by judges who have life tenure during good behavior and who are not subject to salary diminution. Such protections insulate federal judges from possible coercion by the legislature. The bankruptcy judges established by Congress in the Bankruptcy Reform Act under the powers of Article I lacked either of these protections. These judges were to serve for a term of fourteen years, not for life; and their salaries were to be established by statute, subject to adjustment. In addition, the Court ruled that Congress had improperly delegated too much power to the new bankruptcy courts, allowing these courts to exercise jurisdiction over *all matters* arising under bankruptcy laws. The Court ruled that bankruptcy courts may not exercise Article III powers over any constitutional or state-created areas of law, but rather must restrict their authority to specific bankruptcy topics.

The Supreme Court granted Congress an extension to 4 October 1982 to reconstitute the bankruptcy courts or to limit their jurisdiction. Congress did not react to the Court's opinion by the deadline, but President Reagan requested an additional extension to 24 December 1982 so the matter could be

[2]458 U.S. 50 (1982).

studied further. This deadline also passed with no solution presented by Congress.

For nearly two years, Congress did nothing to resolve the problem. During this period the bankruptcy courts continued to operate under an "emergency rule" suggested by the Judicial Conference of the United States and accepted by the United States Courts of Appeals. This emergency rule, approved in some form by nearly all of the U.S. District Courts, allowed the bankruptcy courts to hear all bankruptcy cases in their entirety unless one of the parties to the action requested the District Court to remove the case due to improper jurisdiction. The orders of the bankruptcy court could be appealed to the District Courts, and the District Courts, at their discretion, could either accept the findings of the bankruptcy court or hold a new hearing on the matter.

Thus the Bankruptcy Reform Act was implemented under this emergency rule until Congress finally moved to resolve the problems presented by the opinion in *Northern Pipeline*. Since the substantive aspects of the Bankruptcy Reform Act had not been challenged in that opinion, they continued to be followed under the emergency rules.

The act has four major operative sections, called chapters. These chapters are Chapter 7, "Liquidation"; Chapter 9, "Adjustments of Debts of a Municipality"; Chapter 11, "Reorganization"; and Chapter 13, "Adjustments of Debts of an Individual with Regular Income." In a Chapter 7 proceeding, the debtor's **nonexempt** assets are sold, the proceeds are distributed to the creditors, and a discharge is normally granted. Under Chapters 9, 11, and 13, the debtor *restructures* and *rearranges* things so that the creditors will (normally) be paid in full. In this chapter, we will examine a straight bankruptcy proceeding—that is, a Chapter 7 liquidation. In the next chapter, we will look at other bankruptcy proceedings available under Chapters 11 and 13 and at alternatives to bankruptcy.

Nonexempt assets Those assets available under the law for the payment and satisfaction of the debtor's creditors.

BANKRUPTCY AMENDMENTS AND FEDERAL JUDGESHIP ACT OF 1984

President Reagan signed the Bankruptcy Amendments and Federal Judgeship Act of 1984 into law on 10 July 1984. This act addresses the problems presented by *Northern Pipeline* by restructuring and redefining the bankruptcy court system and its jurisdiction. In addition, it makes a number of substantive changes to the Bankruptcy Reform Act and its coverage.

Under the new law, bankruptcy judges are still to be appointed for a term of fourteen years at an initial salary of $66,100 per year.[3] (Since the tenure and the salary both are established by statute and are subject to changes by

[3]The salary was increased to $82,300 in 1989.

the legislature, the bankruptcy judges still are not Article III judges, the original problem addressed by the court in *Northern Pipeline*.) The appointments are to be made by the U.S. Court of Appeals in which the District Court is located. These appointments are to be made from a slate of nominees recommended to the Circuit Court by the judicial councils of each circuit. Only persons who apply to the judicial council for a judgeship may be considered for recommendation by the Court of Appeals. The judicial council is to submit a list of three nominees for each judgeship. The Court of Appeals will then either select one of the nominees or reject all of them and request a new submission.

Since these bankruptcy judges are not Article III judges, the bankruptcy courts have only limited jurisdiction under the law. The 1984 Amendments grant exclusive and original jurisdiction in all bankruptcy matters to the U.S. District Court. The District Court *may* then refer any or all such cases to the bankruptcy court for adjudication. However, after referral to the bankruptcy court, the case may be withdrawn by the District Court, either on its own motion or on the motion of any party to the proceedings, "for cause shown." The meaning of "for cause shown" will need to be defined by the courts in a number of cases before the limits imposed by that phrase are known.

STRAIGHT BANKRUPTCY

To many people, the term *bankruptcy* means just one thing—a *liquidation of the debtor's assets in order to obtain a discharge from debts*. This form of bankruptcy carries some very negative connotations to many people. These people view a *straight* bankruptcy, or a Chapter 7 proceeding, as an admission of failure. Rather than viewing this as a "fresh start" for an "honest debtor," they feel that it is a "cop-out" by a "deadbeat." However, times are changing. More and more people are beginning to realize that a liquidation is a financial and legal option designed to help a person who has been flooded by debt. The stigma of failure is being removed, and the number of Chapter 7 proceedings is increasing annually. There are two types of Chapter 7 bankruptcies: voluntary and involuntary.

Voluntary Bankruptcy

Any person, firm, or corporation may file a voluntary bankruptcy petition, with *five* exceptions:

1. railroads
2. government units
3. banks
4. savings and loan associations
5. insurance companies

Insolvent The condition of being unable to pay one's debts; lacking the means or property to pay one's debts.

The debtor who files a voluntary petition does not even need to be **insolvent**. If a debtor desires to eliminate the debts, the debtor can file the petition, consent to the court's jurisdiction, and receive a discharge. In theory, a debtor with $1 million in cash and *total* debts of $250 could file for bankruptcy. In practice, such an event is extremely unlikely.

The 1984 Bankruptcy Amendments have made one major substantive change in this area. Prior to the 1984 Act, bankruptcy was viewed as a *right* of the debtor, and the *need* of the debtor was not considered by the court. As a result, a number of debtors apparently were abusing the bankruptcy system, using Chapter 7 proceedings to eliminate unsecured debts they could have repaid in full.[4] The law now permits the bankruptcy judge to hold a hearing designed to determine the need of the debtor for the relief being sought. If the judge feels that granting the relief would be a "substantial abuse" of Chapter 7, the petition is dismissed.

In addition, the law requires that all debtors be made aware of the alternative provisions of Chapter 13 repayment plans before they are allowed to file a Chapter 7 petition. By so doing, it is hoped that more debtors will elect a repayment plan rather than a liquidation procedure. This will work to the benefit of the creditors and may also help a number of debtors by allowing them to retain more of their assets than they would under a Chapter 7 liquidation.

Involuntary Bankruptcy

Often a debtor will get deeply in debt and try to avoid bankruptcy. When this happens, the creditors frequently will decide to petition the debtor into bankruptcy against his or her will. They do so by initiating an involuntary bankruptcy proceeding.

An *involuntary* petition may be filed against any person, firm, or corporation that meets certain criteria, with *seven* exceptions:

the *five* debtors who may *not* file a voluntary petition

farmers

charitable corporations

A *farmer* is defined as an individual who received more than 80 percent of gross income in the prior year from the operation of a farm that he or she owns and operates.

If a debtor does not fall within one of these exceptions, the debtor is potentially subject to an involuntary petition. The vast majority of debtors in this country do not fit into one of these exceptions. However, the creditors who file the petition must show that three criteria—one related to conduct, one to numbers, and one to debt—are satisfied before they may file.

[4]*Monograph #23, Consumer Bankruptcy Study; Consumers' Right to Bankruptcy.* Credit Research Center, 1982.

Conduct Creditors must allege, and prove, that the debtor is "guilty" of one of two acts: Either the debtor is not paying debts as they become due, *or* the debtor appointed a receiver or made a general assignment for the benefit of the creditors within the 120 days that preceded the filing of the petition. Under the latter test, the receiver or assignee must have taken possession of the debtor's property.

Number The proper number of creditors for the particular debtor must join in the petition. If the debtor has a *total* of twelve creditors or more, *at least* three of them must sign the petition. If the debtor has fewer than twelve creditors, one or more creditors must file.

Contingent Possible, but not assured; doubtful or uncertain; dependent on the occurrence of some future event that is itself uncertain or questionable.

Debt The creditors who file the petition must have an aggregate claim against the debtor of *at least* $5000 that is neither secured nor **contingent**. A debtor with less than $5000 in general unsecured debts may not be involuntarily petitioned into bankruptcy.

The following example shows one problem that petitioning creditors may face.

Bob has seven creditors. He has made no payments for four months to any of them. He owes Ralph, one of the creditors, $6000. Ralph has $2000 in collateral. Unless another creditor with at least $1000 in unsecured debt will join Ralph on a petition, Ralph cannot institute an involuntary petition.

If a debtor is involuntarily petitioned into bankruptcy, the debtor may deny that he is bankrupt and request a trial. A debtor who wins a trial can collect damages from the creditors who signed the petition.

THE BANKRUPTCY PROCEEDING

Order for relief A transferral of jurisdiction over the debtor's estate to the bankruptcy court.

Once a petition is filed, the judge will issue an **order for relief** (unless the debtor files an answer denying bankruptcy and demands a trial). At this point, the proceeding is in motion, and it will continue until the final orders are entered. Upon entering the order for relief, the judge promptly appoints an *interim trustee*. The interim trustee takes possession of the debtor's property until a permanent trustee can be selected.

The filing of a petition in bankruptcy operates as an *automatic stay* against creditors who are involved in any legal actions against the debtor. The creditors must suspend any legal actions already commenced and must delay filing any new actions, pending the outcome of the bankruptcy proceedings. Similarly, the creditors may not initiate any repossession actions against the assets of the debtor. This automatic stay provision is designed to ensure that all the creditors are afforded equitable treatment under the bankruptcy proceedings by preventing any one creditor from gaining an advantage through his actions at the expense of the other creditors.

The court will call for a meeting of the creditors within a reasonable time of the order for relief. The debtor, the interim trustee, and the creditors—but not the judge—will all attend this meeting. The debtor is expected to submit to an examination by the creditors concerning the debtor's assets, liabilities, and anything else the creditors feel is important. Although the debtor may not like it, it is best to cooperate fully: A refusal to cooperate may result in a denial of **discharge.** The creditors may elect a permanent trustee at this meeting. If no trustee is elected, the interim trustee becomes the permanent trustee by court appointment.

Discharge The release of the debtor from the obligation of all debts that were proved in the proceedings so that they are no longer a charge against the debtor.

The permanent trustee is the key figure in the bankruptcy proceeding. The trustee is the representative of the *debtor's* estate, and the trustee will attempt to preserve this estate to protect the interests of the *unsecured creditors.* The estate that the trustee preserves is made up of all the property the debtor has when the case is begun and any property the debtor acquires within the 180 days following the petition-filing date. The trustee must gather all of these assets, liquidate the *nonexempt* assets, and generally handle the creditors' claims. The trustee also raises objections to the granting of a discharge if the debtor gives cause to do so. The trustee may be helped by a *creditors' committee,* a group of at least three and at most eleven unsecured creditors who consult with the trustee as needed.

The debtor has certain duties to perform, as well. The debtor must file a relatively detailed series of schedules that are intended to reveal his or her financial position so that the bankruptcy court can properly evaluate the need for relief and so that the interests of the various creditors can be protected. The debtor must provide a list of creditors, both secured and unsecured, the address of each creditor, and the amount of debt owed to each. The debtor also must provide a schedule of his financial affairs and a listing of all property owned, even if that property will be claimed as an exempt asset. Finally, the debtor must provide a list of current income and expenses. This list may show that the debtor should be in a Chapter 13 repayment plan rather than a Chapter 7 liquidation proceeding. If it does, the court may, on its own motion, dismiss the Chapter 7 proceeding following a hearing and encourage the debtor to refile under Chapter 13. However, the law also carries with it a presumption in favor of the debtor. The debtor is presumed to be entitled to receive the order of relief for whatever chapter was chosen by the debtor. The schedules are to be prepared by the debtor under oath and signed. Knowingly submitting false information in these schedules is a crime under the bankruptcy law.

The debtor also must cooperate fully with the trustee and surrender all property to the trustee. Finally, the debtor must attend any and all hearings and comply with all orders of the court. If this is done, a discharge normally will result.

The debtor can *exempt* some assets from the trustee's liquidation. This exemption is, surprisingly, governed by *state* statutes. If state law permits, the debtor may elect to take either the state exemptions or the federal exemptions. If no such choice is allowed by state law, the debtor must take the state exemptions. Under no circumstances may the debtor take both sets of exemptions.

Over thirty states have elected the override provision, requiring the debtor to take the state exemptions. And even if the debtor is in a state that allows the choice of either the federal or the state exemptions, another limitation has been imposed by the 1984 Amendments. In a joint filing, both the husband and the wife must select the same exemptions, either state or federal. They no longer will be allowed to select the exemptions individually, which allowed one to take the federal exemptions while the other took the state exemptions.

Certain types of property are exempt under most state statutes. Typically, a debtor who elects (or is required) to take the state exemptions will be able to retain the following types of assets for his or her "fresh start":

some cash

residence or homestead

clothing

tools of the trade

insurance

In some states, the debtor also may exempt one automobile. In addition, the debtor is allowed to exempt some "benefits" for public policy reasons:

veteran's benefits

social security benefits

unemployment compensation benefits

disability benefits

alimony

The Bankruptcy Reform Act exempts the following property from the proceeding:

1. equity in the debtor's home of up to $7500

2. if there is no equity in the home or if the equity is less than $7500, the unused portion of the $7500 in a joint petition or $3750 in an individual petition

3. equity in one automobile of up to $1200

4. household goods and clothing, up to $200 per item and up to $4000 aggregate

5. jewelry up to $500

6. tools of the debtor's trade, including books, up to $750

7. any unmatured life insurance policies owned by the debtor

The act also permits a debtor to convert goods from nonexempt classes to exempt classes before filing the bankruptcy petition. And if there is a lien on, or security interest attached to, otherwise exempt property, the debtor can redeem it—which automatically exempts it—by paying off the lien-holding creditor.

Allowable Claims

Once the permanent trustee has assumed control of the estate and the exempt property has been removed from the estate, the serious business of bankruptcy begins. Those claims of creditors that are *allowable* must be filed. Only allowable debts may participate in the distribution of the estate. Allowable claims may be filed by the debtor, by the creditor, or even by the trustee. But they *must* be filed within six months of the first creditors' meeting.

Nearly every debt that existed before the order for relief will be allowable. There are four major exceptions to this statement. The following four debts are not allowable, or at least are not *fully* allowable:

1. claims that would be unenforceable against the debtor, such as contracts based on fraud or duress

2. claims for interest that are figured beyond the petition date, since interest may no longer accrue once a petition is filed

3. damages based on a lease violation or termination, to some extent (the landlord can claim a debt only up to the greater of one year's rent *or* 15 percent of the balance of the lease [with a three-year maximum] plus any unpaid rent already due and payable)

4. damages based on breach of an employment contract, if those damages *exceed* one year's compensation, plus unpaid wages due and payable

The following example shows how allowable claims are used.

Nancy filed a voluntary bankruptcy petition on August 1. At that time, she was three months behind on her rent, and she still had ten years remaining on her lease. She was also two weeks behind on her payroll. Both of her employees had two years remaining on their employment contracts.

Nancy's landlord can assert a claim only for twenty-one months of rent (three months already due plus 15 percent of ten years remaining on the lease, or eighteen months). Each of Nancy's employees can claim only fifty-four weeks of wages (two weeks already earned plus one year) for breach of the employment contract.

The landlord's claim for the other eight and a half years and each employee's claim for the other year will not be allowed.

Recovery of Property   While administering a debtor's estate, a trustee may discover that the debtor committed certain improper actions. A trustee who discovers such conduct is obligated to recover the transferred property for the benefit of the unsecured creditor. These improper acts fall into two major categories: *voidable preferences* and *fraudulent conveyances*.

YOU BE THE JUDGE

> One of the owners of a savings and loan institution was under federal investigation for alleged wrongdoings that led to the failure of the S & L. Eventually, 38 federal criminal charges were filed against the owner for alleged misuses of thrift funds. The owner retained a criminal attorney to represent him in the case, paying a $300,000 retainer for the attorney's services. Following a six-week trial, the owner was convicted of 23 counts, and acquitted of the other 15, receiving a sentence of five years in federal prison.
>
> Several months later, the owner filed for bankruptcy court protection. He had debts of about $700 million dollars, including the claims of the federal thrift regulators, and assets of only about $2.5 million. The trustee has asserted that the payment of the $300,000 retainer to the criminal attorney is an improper payment. How would you rule on the trustee's assertion?

Source: "Lawyer's Fee Jeopardized by Bankruptcy," Christi Harlan and Jonathan M. Moses, *The Wall Street Journal,* May 4, 1992, page B13.

Voidable Preferences   A *voidable preference* is a *payment made by a debtor to one or a few creditors at the expense of the other creditors in that particular creditor class.* This is not as complicated as it may seem at first glance.

A transfer is deemed *preference,* and therefore voidable, if all the following five conditions are met:

1. The transfer benefits a creditor.
2. The transfer covers a preexisting debt.
3. The debtor is insolvent at the time of the transfer. (A debtor is *presumed* to be insolvent during the ninety days preceding the date of the petition; this presumption is rebuttable by the debtor.)
4. The transfer is made during the ninety days preceding the petition date.
5. The transfer gave the creditor who received it a greater percentage of the creditor's claim than fellow creditors will receive as a result of the transfer.

A transfer is not deemed a preference if it fits *any* one of the following tests:

1. The transfer is for a new obligation, as opposed to a preexisting debt.
2. The transfer is made in the ordinary course of business.
3. The transfer involves a purchase money security interest (see Chapter 28).
4. The transfer is a payment on a *fully* secured claim.
5. The transfer is for normal payments made to creditors within ninety days prior to the petition, if the payments *total* less than $600 per creditor.

The following case illustrates the importance of timing in a bankruptcy proceeding and shows how the court literally defines the conduct of the parties.

Matter of Duffy
3 B.R. 263 (1980)

FACTS   Duffy entered into a long-term lease agreement with Avis Rent-a-Car. He failed to make numerous payments due under the lease, and Avis threatened to repossess the leased car. On 30 July 1979, Duffy mailed Avis a check for $400. (The check was postdated 3 August 1979.) Avis presented the check, and Duffy's bank paid Avis the face amount of the check on 6 August 1979. Duffy eventually filed a petition for relief under the bankruptcy laws. This petition was filed ninety-four days after he mailed the check to Avis, but only eighty-eight days after the check was paid by the bank. The trustee in bankruptcy challenged the payment to Avis as a voidable preference, arguing that since Avis received the money within the ninety days preceding the petition, the debt was paid within the ninety days. Avis argued that, since the check was *received* outside the ninety-day period, the payment was not a preference. Avis also argued that, even if the payment were within the ninety-day period, Avis had given new value by agreeing not to repossess the leased automobile.

ISSUE   Was payment made to Avis within the ninety days preceding the petition, so that it is presumed to be a voidable preference? If payment was within ninety days, did Avis give new value, so as to rebut the presumption of a voidable preference?

HOLDING   Yes, payment was made within the ninety-day period. No, Avis did not give "new value" when it elected not to repossess the leased automobile.

REASONING   Under the law of commercial paper, a check is not paid "until accepted and honored by the bank." This acceptance and honoring occurred within the ninety-day period preceding the bankruptcy petition, so the voidable preference rules are applicable. The payment is presumed to be a preference, and Avis failed to rebut this presumption. Avis did not give new value by its forbearance from repossession of the automobile. The forbearance by Avis did not enhance the estate of the debtor, and the conduct of Avis in no way aided the other creditors. The payment is a voidable preference, and the trustee can recover the $400 payment for the benefit of the debtor's estate.

Fraudulent Conveyance A *fraudulent conveyance* is a *transfer by a debtor that involves actual or constructive fraud*. Actual fraud is involved if the debtor *intended* to hinder or delay a creditor in recovering a debt. An example of such a transfer would be a sale by the debtor to a relative so a creditor could not foreclose on the asset. Constructive fraud is involved when the debtor sells an asset for *inadequate* consideration and as a result of the sale becomes insolvent, or if the debtor is already insolvent at the time of the unreasonable sale. It is also deemed constructive fraud to engage in a business that is undercapitalized. Any fraudulent conveyance made during the one year preceding the petition may be set aside by the trustee under federal law. And some *state* statutes permit the avoidance of such conveyances during the preceding two to five years. The trustee uses the time period that most strongly favors the creditors.

Distribution of Proceeds

Once the trustee has gathered and liquidated all available assets and allowed all allowable claims, the estate is distributed to the creditors. The Bankruptcy Reform Act contains a mandatory priority list of debts. Each class of creditors takes its turn, and no class may receive any payments until all higher-priority classes are paid in full. All creditors *within* a given class will be paid on a pro rata basis until either the claims are paid in full or the estate is exhausted.

The highest priority of claims is the expense of handling the estate. All of the costs incurred by the trustee in preserving and administering the bankruptcy must be paid first.

The next class of claims involves debts that arise in the ordinary course of business *between* the date the petition is filed and the date the trustee is appointed.

The third and fourth priorities are interrelated. Priority 3 is wages earned by employees of the debtor during the ninety days preceding the petition, up to a maximum of $2000 per employee. Priority 4 is unpaid contributions by an employer to employee benefit plans, if they arise during the 180 days before the petition, up to $2000 per employee. However, these claims are reduced by any claims paid in priority 3. Thus, the maximum priority for each employee is a total of $2000. Any claims in excess of this amount go to the bottom of the list.

The fifth priority is given to grain farmers who have a claim against the owner or operator of a grain storage facility and to U.S. fishermen who have a claim against individuals who operate a fish storage or fish processing facility. In either case, the priority is limited to $2000 per individual creditor.

The sixth priority is claims by consumers for goods or services paid for but not received. The maximum here is $900 per person as a priority, with any surplus claim going to the bottom of the list.

The final priority claim is in favor of debts owed to government units. This class is basically made up of taxes due during the three years preceding the petition.

After all priority claims are paid, the balance of the estate is used to pay general unsecured creditors. When all unsecured creditors have been paid in full, any monies left are paid to the debtor. Normally the funds will not cover the general creditor claims, and a pro rata distribution is necessary. This leaves the creditors with less money than they were owed. The debtor must hope for a *discharge* to make the balance of the claims uncollectible. Figure 31.1 summarizes the distribution of proceeds.

Discharge

A discharge can be granted only to an *individual* and only if he or she is an honest debtor. A discharge will be denied if the debtor made a fraudulent conveyance or does not have adequate books and records. In addition, a debtor will be denied a discharge if he or she refuses to cooperate with the court during the proceedings. And no discharge will be granted if a discharge was received during the previous six years. A denial of discharge means that the unpaid portions of any debts continue and are fully enforceable after the proceedings end.

Even if a discharge is granted, some claims are not affected. Under the Bankruptcy Reform Act, certain debts continue to be fully enforceable against the debtor even though the debtor received a discharge. The following ten major classes of debts are not affected by a discharge:

1. taxes due to any government unit
2. debts that arose because of fraud by the debtor concerning his financial condition
3. claims not listed by the creditors or by the debtor in time for treatment in the proceedings
4. debts incurred through embezzlement or theft
5. alimony
6. child support
7. liabilities due to malicious torts of the debtor
8. fines imposed by a government unit
9. claims that were raised in a previous case in which the debtor did not receive a discharge
10. student loans, unless the loan is at least five years in arrears

In addition to these ten classes of debts, the 1984 Amendments addressed the problem of debtors who "load up" with debts just prior to filing a petition, knowing the proceedings will discharge these recently incurred debts. Under the law, any debtor purchases from one creditor of $500 or more in "luxury" goods or services that are incurred within forty days of the petition are presumed to be nondischargeable. Similarly, any cash advances of $1000 or more that are received from one creditor within the twenty days prior to the petition are presumed to be nondischargeable. The debtor will have the burden of

FIGURE 31.1   Distribution of Proceeds

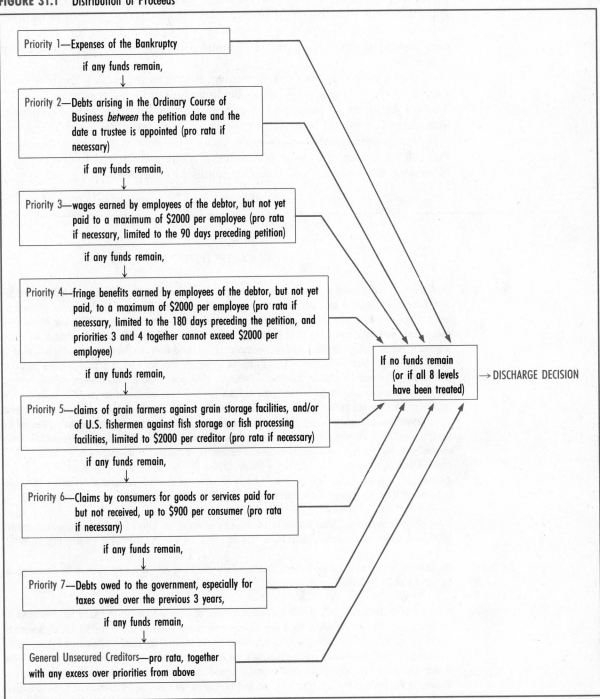

proof and will have to convince the court that these debts were not fraudulently incurred with the intent of receiving a discharge in order to have these debts discharged. Notice that a discharge is possible but that the debtor has the burden of proof! Figure 31.2 summarizes the steps in a bankruptcy proceeding.

Finally, even if a discharge is granted, it may be revoked. If the trustee or a creditor requests a revocation of the discharge, the request may be granted. The request must be made within one year of the discharge, and the debtor must have committed some wrongful act, such as fraud during the proceedings. The possibility of revocation encourages the debtor to remain honest. In the following case, the court was asked to deny a discharge to the debtors. Note how narrowly the court defines conduct by the debtors.

In re Knott
32 B.R. 252 (1983)

FACTS

W. B. Knott, Jr. was involved in farming and in land speculation. During the years 1974 through 1982, he and his wife, Virginia, had received approximately twenty-four loans from Citizens Bank and Trust Company (Citizens) as well as other loans from other lenders. At the time of the bankruptcy petition, in October, 1982, four of the loans from Citizens were outstanding. As part of the ongoing financial relationship between Knott and Citizens, Knott was required to submit updated financial statements annually. Citizens used these statements to determine how much it was willing to lend Knott during the year. The financial statements were not used to procure any one particular loan. Knott had submitted a financial statement in December, 1979, that showed that Knott owned eighteen building lots in the Bonneville subdivision. In fact, these eighteen lots had been transferred to Landville Realty, Inc., a corporation wholly owned by Knott and his wife. Three of the loans from Citizens that were still unpaid at the time of the petition had been made during 1980, so that the making of these loans was at least partially influenced by the December, 1979, financial statement. Knott encountered financial difficulties in 1981 that continued into 1982, eventually causing him to file a voluntary petition in bankruptcy. At the time of the petition, Knott failed to list a one-third interest in some land known as The Stable. Citizens objected to the granting of a discharge to Knott, alleging that Knott was not an "honest debtor" due to his erroneous financial statement of December, 1979, and to his failure to list his interest in The Stables in his list of assets accompanying his petition in October, 1982.

ISSUES

Did Knott intend to deceive Citizens Bank and Trust when he submitted the "false" financial statement in December, 1979? Did Knott conceal property to hinder, delay, and defraud his creditors in his listing of assets in October, 1982?

HOLDING

No, Knott did not intend to deceive Citizens Bank and Trust. No, Knott did not conceal assets to hinder, delay, or defraud any of his creditors.

REASONING

It is true that the December, 1979, financial statement included eighteen building lots that Knott had transferred to Landville Realty, but Landville Realty was a corporation wholly owned by the Knotts, so that his net worth was not affected by the erroneous listing of title to these building lots. In addition, the lending officer from Citizens stated that he did not read the financial statement carefully and did not know if the revelation as to the location of title to these lots would have affected the Bank's decision to lend money to Knott. In order for the court to deny a discharge in bankruptcy in this type of situation, the creditor must establish that the debtor made false representations knowing they were false and intending to deceive the creditor. The creditor also must show reliance and harm due

FIGURE 31.2 The Bankruptcy Proceeding

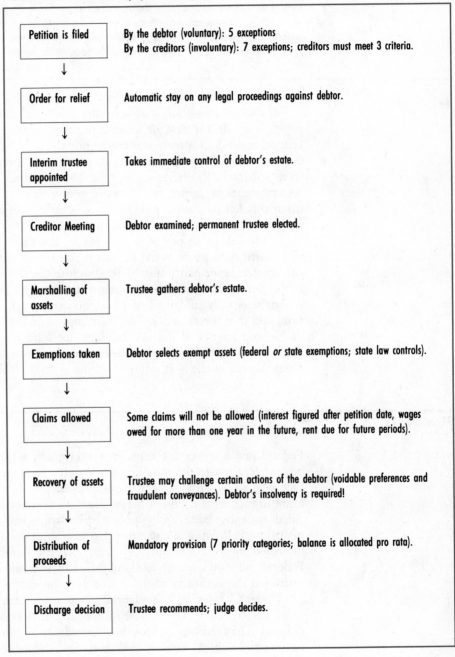

Petition is filed	By the debtor (voluntary): 5 exceptions By the creditors (involuntary): 7 exceptions; creditors must meet 3 criteria.
↓	
Order for relief	Automatic stay on any legal proceedings against debtor.
↓	
Interim trustee appointed	Takes immediate control of debtor's estate.
↓	
Creditor Meeting	Debtor examined; permanent trustee elected.
↓	
Marshalling of assets	Trustee gathers debtor's estate.
↓	
Exemptions taken	Debtor selects exempt assets (federal *or* state exemptions; state law controls).
↓	
Claims allowed	Some claims will not be allowed (interest figured after petition date, wages owed for more than one year in the future, rent due for future periods).
↓	
Recovery of assets	Trustee may challenge certain actions of the debtor (voidable preferences and fraudulent conveyances). Debtor's insolvency is required!
↓	
Distribution of proceeds	Mandatory provision (7 priority categories; balance is allocated pro rata).
↓	
Discharge decision	Trustee recommends; judge decides.

to the false statements and must show all of this with clear and convincing evidence. Citizens failed to satisfy the court of the elements required. As to the concealment of property in the petition, Knott testified that he and his wife hastily filed the petition, inadvertently omitting this property. On questioning by the creditors at the creditors meeting, Knott amended his schedule to include the property. There was no evidence of any attempt to hinder, delay, or defraud the creditors. The objections of the bank are not sufficient to deny the discharge.

On some occasions, a debtor who has been granted a discharge in bankruptcy may decide that he would like to repay the creditor despite the discharge. If the debtor truly wants to repay the debt, he may voluntarily *reaffirm* the debt and then repay it. However, the requirements for a reaffirmation were substantially increased by the 1984 Amendments. Prior to the 1984 Amendments, a debtor could reaffirm any debts at virtually any time. Too often this led to a debtor reaffirming debts out of a sense of guilt following the discharge and putting himself in the same sort of financial position as had originally led to the petition. As a result, the 1984 Amendments require that any reaffirmations be made in writing and filed with the court. In addition, the written agreement must be filed before the debtor is granted a discharge. If the debtor has an attorney, the attorney must file a declaration that the debtor was fully informed of his rights, voluntarily agreed to the reaffirmation, and that the agreement will not impose an undue hardship on the debtor or his dependents. If the debtor does not have an attorney, the court must approve the reaffirmation, and the court will not grant approval unless the repayment is in the best interests of the *debtor*.

SUMMARY

Federal law governs the topic of bankruptcy, which is designed to give an honest debtor a fresh start. The Bankruptcy Reform Act, which took effect in October, 1979, provided for the establishment of bankruptcy courts as a separate branch of the United States district court system. These courts are presided over by bankruptcy judges who specialize in handling bankruptcy petitions. Following a constitutional challenge to the bankruptcy courts established by the Bankruptcy Reform Act, the Bankruptcy Amendments and Federal Judgeship Act of 1984 modified these bankruptcy courts and severely restricted the authority of the courts and the judges.

Under Chapter 7 ("Liquidation"), bankruptcy can be initiated by the debtor or by the creditors. The debtor initiates the proceedings by filing a voluntary petition. The creditors initiate the proceedings by filing an involuntary petition against the debtor. Five "public interest" corporations are prohibited from filing a voluntary petition; any other debtor may file such a petition, even if solvent. Creditors may file an involuntary petition against most debtors, but only if the debtor has acted improperly, *and* the proper number of creditors join the petition, *and* the proper amount of unsecured debts is involved.

Once the petition is filed, a judge appoints a trustee to administer the bankrupt's estate. The trustee is to preserve the estate for the protection of the unsecured creditors. The debtor is allowed some exemptions so that a fresh start is possible. The rest of the estate is available for settling debts.

Once the exempt property is removed, the balance of the estate is liquidated and the proceeds are applied to the allowable claims of the creditors.

The proceeds are applied first to priority classes as set up by the Bankruptcy Reform Act. After all priority classes are paid in full, the remaining proceeds are applied to the claims of the unsecured creditors. The debtor will then seek a discharge. If the debtor has been honest and has cooperated, a discharge probably will be granted. If not, the debts will continue.

DISCUSSION QUESTIONS

1. What are the two major purposes of the Bankruptcy Reform Act?

2. Who are the five types of debtors who cannot file a voluntary petition for a Chapter 7 bankruptcy? Who are the seven types of debtors who cannot be involuntarily petitioned into Chapter 7 bankruptcy? Why do you think these debtors are excluded from Chapter 7 proceedings?

3. What three "tests" must the creditors meet in order to petition a debtor into bankruptcy involuntarily?

4. Ronald is involved in a bankruptcy. The state in which he lives allows the debtor to select either the federal or the state exemptions. The state exemptions completely exempt the debtor's homestead. Ronald does not own a home. What should he do? Why?

5. Martha has filed a bankruptcy petition, dated August 1. She has as one of her debts a $30,000 loan dated June 1 that had 18 percent interest and was due on December 1. How much of this total indebtedness is allowable in the bankruptcy proceeding?

6. How does bankruptcy law deal with the problem of a debtor "loading up" with debts just prior to filing the petition? Is this treatment an appropriate solution to the problem of a debtor who "loads up" with debts?

7. What does the most recent bankruptcy coverage provide for credit card companies and other unsecured creditors to improve their position over the position they enjoyed under the Bankruptcy Reform Act? Does this new treatment make a substantial difference? Should this have been done, or should the old treatment have been retained?

8. Herb was having financial problems. In a desperate attempt to save his business, he ordered a new product line from Ace Equipment. Herb paid for the new goods on delivery by Ace. Herb's creditors filed a bankruptcy petition five weeks later. If the trustee challenges the payment to Ace as a voidable preference, what will happen? Explain fully.

9. Sam knew he was about to go bankrupt. Just days before he filed his petition, he sold his new Lincoln to his secretary for $300. What must the secretary prove in order to keep the Lincoln? Explain.

10. Sharon ordered a new washing machine and drier from Honest Al's Appliances. She paid the full $1300 at the time. Before receiving the machines, Sharon was notified that Honest Al had gone bankrupt. What are Sharon's rights? Explain.

CASE PROBLEMS

1. While insolvent, and within the ninety days preceding the filing of a petition, the debtor transferred property to a creditor as payment of a preexisting debt. The creditor had a security interest, and the collateral was worth more than the debt. Was this a voidable preference? (*In re Conn*, 9 Bankr. 431 [1981].)

2. Mazzola was the sole stockholder of Dennis M. Construction Company, a business involved in building

private homes. Dennis M. built and sold a home to LaVangie, who claimed that the house was defective as built. When LaVangie was unable to reach a settlement with the firm, he attached some property owned by Mazzola. Mazzola managed to have the attachment released, and he immediately sold the property and applied the proceeds to several other debts of the corporation. Two months later Mazzola filed a petition in bankruptcy. Among the debts he listed for discharge was the claim by LaVangie. In his petition he included several statements that LaVangie claims were made fraudulently or with reckless disregard for the truth. LaVangie is challenging the granting of a discharge to Mazzola. How should the court rule in this case? Explain your reasoning. (*In re Mazzola,* 4 B.R. 179 [1980].)

3. On 24 August 1981, Ellison gave Harbin a check for $7700 to pay for goods Harbin had sold and delivered to Ellison more than forty-five days earlier. Harbin deposited the check in his account at American Bank, which presented the check to the drawee bank. The drawee bank dishonored the check and returned it to American. American resubmitted the check to the drawee on 15 September, and the check was honored at that time. Ellison filed a bankruptcy petition on 23 November 1981. The trustee has demanded that Harbin return the $7700 to the estate, alleging that this payment was a preferential transfer. Harbin denied that this was a preference. What result? (*Matter of Ellison,* 31 B.R. 545 [1983].)

4. The Karachi Cab Company borrowed money from Wapnick, using its taxi licenses as security for the loan. Wapnick attempted to perfect the security interest, but filed her financing statement in the wrong office so that the security interest was improperly perfected. Karachi Cab went bankrupt shortly thereafter, and the trustee in bankruptcy attempted to avoid the security interest of Wapnick. Can the trustee in bankruptcy defeat the security interest of Wapnick in this case? Explain fully. (*In re Karachi Cab Co.,* 21 Bankr. 822 [1982].)

5. Baker has filed for a discharge in bankruptcy under Chapter 7. She has monthly take-home pay of $650 and monthly expenses of $925. Among the debts listed by Baker in her petition are three student loans totalling $6600. She can establish that she has special circumstances and that the repayment of the three loans would cause her an undue hardship. In this situation can the court grant a discharge from the student loans? (*Baker v. University of Tennessee at Chattanooga,* 10 Bankr. 870 [1981].)

6. Thexton, a farmer, filed a voluntary bankruptcy petition. He elected to take the state exemptions, which provided for a debtor to exempt his or her homestead. Under Kansas law, the homestead exemption applies to up to 160 acres of land, if the land is occupied by the family as its principal residence. The debtor also had an oil and gas lease for the oil and gas beneath his land. The trustee agreed that the land itself was subject to exemption, but urged the court to rule that the unaccrued royalties were personal property and as such were not included in the homestead exemption. The debtor conceded that all royalties accrued to the date of the petition should be turned over to the trustee, but argued that the unaccrued royalties were exempt. How should the court resolve this issue? Explain your answer fully. (*In re Thexton,* 39 B.R. 367 [1984].)

7. Jenkins owed Friedman $225,000 in losses arising from trading in commodities futures. Friedman attempted to involuntarily petition Jenkins into bankruptcy and to have the trustee recover some properties and assets that Jenkins had transferred to other creditors. Friedman argued that these transfers were voidable preferences under bankruptcy law. Jenkins resisted the involuntary petition, arguing that he was a farmer and therefore immune from an involuntary petition. Jenkins, admittedly, was engaged in operating a farm and had received gross income of $60,000 from his farming operations. He also had received $3000 from the sale of insurance. But Friedman asserted that a $330,000 loan Jenkins received should also be counted as income so that Jenkins could not receive the necessary percentage of income from farming operations to be classified as a farmer. Is Jenkins a farmer under the standards of the bankruptcy laws? (*Jenkins v. Petitioning Creditor Ray E. Friedman,* 664 F.2d 184 [8th Cir. 1981].)

8. Turpin filed a petition in bankruptcy, and filed all the necessary schedules and information. However, he did not include his interests in a pension fund or a profit-sharing plan to which he was entitled under his employment. The trustee in bankruptcy argued that these assets had to be included and had to be transferred to the trustee. Turpin argued that these were more similar to future wages, to which he was not yet entitled, and thus should not be included or transferred to the trustee. Who should prevail? (*Matter of Turpin,* 644 F.2d 472 [5th Cir. 1981].)

9. The Blanton Smith Corporation (Smith) regularly purchased oil from Gulf Oil through Gulf's agent, Boyd.

Smith normally paid for the oil it purchased by check, with these checks dated fifty to sixty days after the invoice date. The checks were delivered to Boyd, who deposited them in his account and then wrote a check to Gulf drawn against his own account. Smith filed a petition in bankruptcy, and the trustee demanded that Gulf return $30,000 that it had received as payments on the Smith account in the ninety days preceding the petition, arguing that these payments amounted to preferential transfers. Gulf insisted that the payments it received were valid and not preferential for one of two reasons: (1) Smith had received new value for the payments, which exempts the payments from recovery for preferences; or (2) Gulf received its funds from Boyd, not Smith, and therefore Gulf was not the proper party from whom the trustee should be seeking recovery. How should the court resolve this case? (*In re Blanton Smith Corporation,* 37 B.R. 303 [1984].)

10. Kaiser purchased a home in Miami for $300,000. He had the house put in his wife's name rather than in his name or in their names. He paid all expenses and maintenances from his corporate funds rather than from personal funds. Two years later, Kaiser filed a Chapter 7 bankruptcy petition and did not list the Miami house as one of his assets. The trustee in bankruptcy argued that Kaiser had committed a fraudulent transfer of assets by placing the house in his wife's name and asked the court to include the house in the debtor's estate. What should the court do in this case? (*In re Kaiser,* 722 F.2d 1580 [2d Cir. 1983].)

C H A P T E R   32

Alternatives to Straight Bankruptcy

O U T L I N E

OTHER BANKRUPTCY PLANS

In the last chapter, we examined a Chapter 7 liquidation proceeding, commonly referred to as a straight bankruptcy. Many people have the mistaken idea that Chapter 7 proceedings are all the Bankruptcy Reform Act covers. In reality, several other types of proceedings are also available under the Bankruptcy Reform Act. The first sections of this chapter will discuss two of these proceedings: A corporate reorganization under Chapter 11 of the Bankruptcy Reform Act and a wage earner's repayment plan under Chapter 13 of the act. Neither of these plans calls for a liquidation of the debtor's assets in order to cover the debts; and under both plans, the creditors can reasonably expect to be paid in full by the debtor. In the last sections of the chapter, we will discuss alternatives to bankruptcy. These nonbankruptcy alternatives normally are available under state statutes, in contrast to the federal statutes that provide for bankruptcy.

Reorganizations

Chapter 11 bankruptcy proceedings, known as *reorganizations,* are designed to allow the debtor to adjust his or her financial situation. Chapter 11 is used by debtors to avoid liquidations. Although reorganizations are designed primarily for use by corporate debtors, individuals are also allowed to use the reorganization format.

The major advantages of a reorganization are that it allows a business to continue, and it forces creditors who object to go along with the plan despite their objections. In addition, the creditors normally will receive more than they would have in a liquidation under Chapter 7.

Any debtor who could use Chapter 7, *except* stockbrokers and commodity brokers, may also use Chapter 11. Moreover, railroads, which are prohibited from using Chapter 7, may use Chapter 11. Like a liquidation proceeding, a reorganization may be either voluntary or involuntary. And the same limitations apply here as apply to a liquidation petition (refer to pages 613–616 for a description of how petitions may be initiated).

The Proceedings   Once the petition has been filed, the court will do three things:

1. It will enter an order for relief.
2. It will appoint a trustee, if requested to do so by any interested party.
3. It will appoint creditor committees to represent the creditors. (Equity security holders will be represented by a separate committee.)

If no interested party asks for the appointment of a trustee, the *debtor* is permitted to retain possession and control of the assets and/or the business. The committees appointed by the court will meet with the trustee if one is

Debtor in possession A debtor who does not turn possession of his or her assets over to a trustee.

Examiner A person appointed by the court to investigate the financial position and condition of the debtor.

Classes of creditors Categories of creditors based on the nature of the obligation that gives rise to the debt.

Impaired Rendered less valuable or less enforceable.

appointed, or with the **debtor in possession** if no trustee is appointed, to discuss the treatment of the proceedings. The committees also will investigate the debtor's finances and financial potential, and they will help prepare a plan for reorganizing that will benefit all the interested parties.

In the event that no one asks for the appointment of a trustee, the court may appoint an **examiner**. The examiner or the trustee will investigate the debtor and the debtor's business activities and business potential. On the basis of this investigation, a recommendation will be made to the court. The recommendation may be a reorganization plan, or it may be a suggestion that the proceedings be transferred from Chapter 11 to Chapter 7 (liquidation) or to Chapter 13 (wage earner plan). The court normally will follow such a recommendation unless a good reason not to follow it is presented.

The Plan   The purpose of a reorganization is to develop a *plan* under which the debtor can avoid liquidation while somehow managing to satisfy the claims of the creditors. Obviously, the right to propose a plan can be very important. If the debtor remains in possession (that is, no trustee is appointed), *only* the debtor may propose a plan during the first 120 days after the order for relief. *Any* interested party (debtor, creditor, stockholder, or trustee) may propose a plan under any of three conditions:

1. if a trustee is appointed
2. if the debtor fails to propose a plan within the 120-day period
3. if the debtor proposes a plan within 120 days, but it is not accepted by all affected **classes of creditors** within 180 days of the order for relief

For a plan to be confirmed, it must designate all claims by class as well as specify which classes will be **impaired** and which will *not* be impaired. It must also show how the plan can be implemented successfully. Among factors that the court will examine are the following:

1. plans to sell any assets
2. plans to merge, consolidate, or divest
3. plans to satisfy, or modify, any liens or claims
4. plans to issue new stock to generate funds

If new stock is to be issued, it *must* have voting rights. No new nonvoting stock may be issued under a reorganization plan.

Each class of creditors that is impaired is allowed to vote on the plan. A class is deemed to have accepted the plan if creditors having at least two-thirds of the dollar amount involved *and* more than one-half of the total number of creditors approve it. If a creditor class is not impaired by the plan, it does not need to approve the plan.

Despite the vote, no plan can be accepted or rejected by the creditors. The final word is left to the court. The court will hold a hearing on the plan, and the court may confirm or reject it. The court may confirm a plan if it was accepted by at least one class of creditors. If all the creditor classes approve the plan, the court normally will confirm it. Similarly, if all the creditor classes reject the plan, the court normally will reject it. But final word is with the court alone. The vote of the creditor classes simply provides the court with guidance.

Once the court approves a plan, it becomes binding on everyone affected by it. The court will look at the plan's fairness to each interested group, especially those creditors impaired by the plan. And the court will look at the viability of the plan. Finally, if the court feels the plan will not work or is not fair, the court can order the proceedings converted to a Chapter 7 liquidation. This last-ditch power encourages everyone involved to act in good faith, since Chapter 11 usually is better than Chapter 7 for all concerned.

In the following case, the court rejected a proposed plan because it was neither feasible nor fair to the priority creditors.

In re Lakeside Global II, Ltd.
116 B.R. 499 (Bkrtcy. S.D. Tex. 1989)

FACTS   Lakeside Global II, Ltd. (Global) owned two garden-type apartment complexes, Bankside and Lakeside, both purchased from McNeil Real Estate Funds (McNeil). In 1986, Global defaulted on its debts for these two properties, and litigation ensued. Lincoln National Investment Management Co., Ltd. (Lincoln) posted the Bankside property for foreclosure, and McNeil arranged to become mortgagee in possession. Three weeks later Global filed for protection under Chapter 11 of the Bankruptcy Code. McNeil had both properties appraised in November, 1986. The fair market value of Bankside was set at $3,640,000 and of Lakeside at $4,281,000. For purposes of evaluating the reorganization plan, all parties have stipulated the values of the properties as $3,000,000 for Bankside and $3,620,000 for Lakeside. On 28 October 1987, McNeil proposed a fourth amended plan for reorganization. Under this plan, which would conclude 31 December 1991, $225,000 would be invested in the properties for capital improvements. All administrative expenses, priority claims, and unsecured claims would be paid in full in the short term, with minimal payments to lienholders until the conclusion of the plan. At that time, the projected appreciation of the property would result in balloon payments to pay all lienholders in full. Global supported the plan proposed by McNeil. American Savings Bank (ASB) and Lincoln objected to the plan. ASB also proposed its own plan calling for a change in the management of the properties.

ISSUE   Is the plan proposed by McNeil feasible, and, if so, is it fair to the creditors?

HOLDING   No. This plan is neither feasible nor fair to the creditors, especially the priority creditors.

REASONING   The court must evaluate a plan to determine if the plan can be realistically carried out and to ensure that the plan is not likely to be followed by the liquidation of the debtor or the need for additional financial reorganization. The court should not confirm "visionary schemes which promise creditors and equity security holders more under a proposed plan than the debtor can possibly attain after confirmation." This plan presents such a visionary scheme. The earning power of the business is questionable. The sum called for in the plan is to be generated from net operating cash flows and the proceeds of a sale from some source as yet unknown, based on estimates of increases in value that the court is not convinced will occur. The plan proposed by McNeil is rejected. The court also rejected the plan proposed by ASB and strongly urged the parties to reopen negotiations to take advantage of the temporary protections of bankruptcy to achieve a workable plan.

Repayment Plans

Chapter 13 of the Bankruptcy Reform Act is designed to allow a debtor with a regular source of income to adjust the debts and to repay all creditors. Chapter 13 plans are available only to individual debtors; they cannot be used by corporations. They are available only to debtors who have less than $100,000 in unsecured debts and less than $350,000 in secured debts. Debtors who exceed either maximum will have to use Chapter 7, Chapter 11, or some nonbankruptcy alternative.

The Proceedings   In many respects, a repayment plan is the simplest bankruptcy proceeding for an individual debtor. The court will issue an order for relief, and a trustee will be appointed. The trustee will perform the investigation duties that would be followed under a reorganization, but only if the debtor operates a business. And the trustee will carry out the plan proposed by the debtor, if the plan is approved by the court.

The Plan   The debtor must file a proposed repayment plan with the court. The plan must provide equal treatment to each creditor claim within any given class of creditors. This does *not* mean that each class must be treated equally— only that *within* each class, every creditor must be treated equally. The plan also must make some provisions for clearing up any defaulted debts or defaulted payments on debts. The plan must not call for payments beyond a three-year period, unless the court feels that a longer period is necessary. Even then, the plan must be carried out within five years.

The court will approve the plan if the following conditions are met:

1. The plan appears to be fair to all parties.
2. The plan is in the best interests of the creditors.
3. It appears that the debtor can conform to the plan.
4. The plan proposes to pay at least as much as would have been paid under Chapter 7.

Once approved, the plan is binding on all parties, with or without their consent. At that point, the debtor must turn over to the trustee enough of the debtor's income to make the payments called for under the plan.

If the debtor performs the plan as approved, the court will grant a discharge. The discharge terminates all debts provided for in the plan—if they are dischargeable in a liquidation—that received their full share under the plan. In addition, the court can intercede and grant a discharge *during* the plan, even though the plan has not been completely carried out. The court will do so *only* if the following three factors are present:

1. The debtor cannot complete the plan owing to circumstances beyond the debtor's control.
2. The general (lowest-priority) creditors have received at least as much as they would have received in a liquidation.
3. The court does not feel it would be practical to alter the plan.

The likelihood of such a court intervention during the plan is not very high, but the option is there. And, once again, the desire to provide a fresh start for an honest debtor is obvious.

In the next case, because the court did not feel the debtor was being honest, it denied him a "fresh start."

In re Yee
7 Bkrtcy. 747 (1980)

FACTS Yee was a financial analyst. His annual pay was $16,800. He had total debts of nearly $13,000, including debts of $2600 on a National Direct Student Loan and $380 in parking tickets. He proposed a repayment plan under Chapter 13 whereby he would pay $30 a month for thirty-six months and have all his debts discharged. He had no assets not subject to exemption, so that in a liquidation his creditors would receive nothing. The court denied his repayment plan on the grounds that it was not filed in good faith.

ISSUE Can the court deny a repayment plan that proposes token payments and that would result in the discharge of substantial debts after minimal payments?

HOLDING Yes. If the court finds a lack of good faith, it may deny a Chapter 13 repayment plan.

REASONING Unlike a Chapter 7 proceeding, in which the court has virtually no role, a Chapter 13 plan must meet with judicial approval. Here Mr. Yee had proposed a plan that would permit him to escape his debts rather than repay them. After expenses, his plan would pay only about 7 percent of his debt. Such minimal payments would constitute an abuse of Chapter 13. The plan is denied owing to an absence of good faith.

Notice how much more understanding the court becomes when the debtor is an "honest debtor" as envisioned in the Bankruptcy Code. Compare the result in this case with the result in *Yee*.

In re Jones
31 B.R. 485 (1983)

FACTS
Jones filed a petition for relief under Chapter 13 of the Bankruptcy Code on 14 August 1982. All of her scheduled debts were unsecured and totaled approximately $28,230. The principal portion of the debt is a judgment obtained by the Illinois Department of Public Aid for $18,288 for the recovery of overpayments of public aid benefits. Jones proposed a plan that called for her to pay 10 percent of all of her unsecured debts. Under the plan, Jones would pay $210 per month for thirty-six months. After deducting fixed expenses and the cost of the plan, Jones would be left with $80 per month to be applied to her necessary living expenses for herself and her four children. The Illinois Department of Public Aid objected to the plan, alleging that the plan should treat the department's judgment as a separate category of debt and also alleging that the plan was not proposed in good faith.

ISSUE
Did the plan as proposed meet the necessary standard of good faith?

HOLDING
Yes. The debtor proposed a plan that met the standards of fundamental fairness. Given her circumstances, this plan was proposed in good faith and should be confirmed.

REASONING
Chapter 13 proceedings allow a debtor to be discharged from debts that would not be discharged under Chapter 7. Thus, even though the claim of the Department of Public Aid would not be discharged under Chapter 7, it may be dischargeable under Chapter 13. The department's assertion that a discharge of 90 percent of its claim violates good faith is without merit. The payments proposed by Jones represent her best effort, and that satisfies the good faith requirement. A divorced mother with four children who has proposed a plan that provides only $80 per month beyond her fixed expenses and the payments called for under the plan cannot be said to be acting in bad faith. The purpose of Chapter 13 is to provide debtors with a meaningful opportunity to rehabilitate. This plan meets that purpose and is affirmed.

1984 *Amendments*   The Bankruptcy Amendments of 1984 have tightened the requirements for a Chapter 13 repayment plan. The new standards also reduce the burden on the courts, since the good faith of the debtor, as in *Yee,* is not an issue. Rather, a more tangible standard than the apparent good faith of the debtor has been substituted.

The more recent law allows any unsecured creditor to block the debtor's proposed repayment plan if the plan does not meet one of two criteria:

1. The plan calls for the payment of 100 percent of the creditor's claim; or

2. the plan calls for the debtor to pay 100 percent of all income not necessary to support the debtor's immediate family for at least three years.

Unless the debtor shows that the plan satisfies one of these two criteria, the Chapter 13 repayment plan will be rejected by the court. The debtor will then have to file a new plan, change over to a Chapter 7 proceeding, or withdraw the petition.

Under the 1978 Bankruptcy Reform Act, debtor payments under a repayment plan did not begin until the plan was confirmed by the court. This gave many debtors a four- to six-month "grace period" in which the debtor retained all of his or her assets but made no payments, to the detriment of the creditors. The 1984 Amendments call for payments to begin *within* thirty days of the filing of the plan, subject to confirmation of the plan by the court. The debtor makes these payments to the trustee, who hold the monies paid until confirmation of the plan by the court and then distributes them to the various creditors. If the debtor fails to make payments to the trustee in a timely manner, the plan can be dismissed by the court.

Finally, the 1984 Amendments provide for modification of the plan after it is confirmed. The trustee, the debtor, or any creditor may petition the court to increase or decrease the debtor's payments whenever the debtor's circumstances or income warrant such a modification. Prior to the 1984 Amendments decreases were possible, but increases were not permitted.

The three bankruptcy alternatives discussed in these two chapters are designed to give an honest debtor a fresh start. An individual may use any of the three alternatives. Most businesses can use two of the three alternatives. Figure 32.1 compares these three bankruptcy alternatives.

NONBANKRUPTCY ALTERNATIVES

In many cases, a debtor or creditor will object to undergoing a bankruptcy, perhaps because of a distaste for the stigma of bankruptcy or for a number of other reasons. But a wish to avoid bankruptcy does not remove the financial problems of the debtor. Often the debtor or creditor will select a nonbankruptcy alternative to "get out from under." Whether such a decision will work depends on a number of factors.

Prejudgment Remedies

The creditors of a troubled debtor frequently will use some *prejudgment procedure* in an effort either to get paid or to force the debtor into acting before a judicial verdict is issued. Three major prejudgment procedures are available to creditors.

The first remedy is **attachment.** A creditor may go to the clerk of the court and obtain a writ of attachment on the basis of the creditor's word that the debtor has not satisfied some claim. Usually, the creditor must post a bond to cover any potential liability in case the attachment is not made in good faith.

The creditor will then have the sheriff levy on as much of the debtor's estate as is needed to satisfy the claim of the attaching creditor. The sheriff will take control over these assets until the proceedings terminate.

Attachment The act or process of taking, apprehending, or seizing persons or property by virtue of a writ, summons, or other judicial order and bringing the same into the custody of the law.

FIGURE 32.1   Comparison of Bankruptcy Proceedings

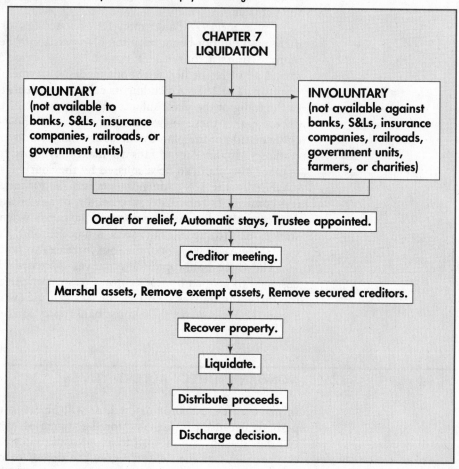

Once the attachment occurs, the creditor must proceed to get a judgment against the debtor. If a judgment is obtained, the assets may be sold to cover the judgment unless the debtor pays outright in order to have the assets released. If the creditor fails to get a judgment within some preset time period, the attachment and lien will expire.

Attachments frequently lead to bankruptcy petitions. The creditors who did not seek an attachment will file an involuntary petition, alleging that the attaching creditor has received a preference. If they petition within four months of the attachment, the courts normally will overturn the attachment.

The second major prejudgment remedy is a *garnishment*. (A garnishment can also be used as a postjudgment remedy under some circumstances.) In a garnishment, the targeted assets are in the hands of some third person and not in the hands of the debtor. The assets that the third person controls belong

FIGURE 32.1 continued

FIGURE 32.1   continued

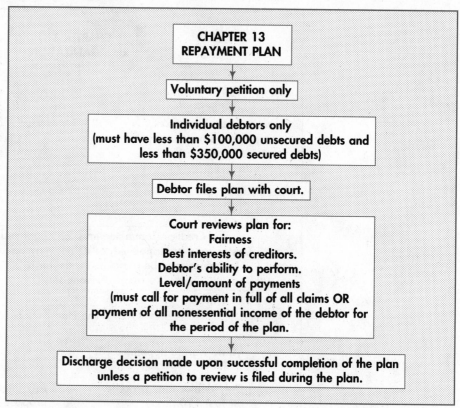

CHAPTER 13
REPAYMENT PLAN

Voluntary petition only

Individual debtors only
(must have less than $100,000 unsecured debts and
less than $350,000 secured debts)

Debtor files plan with court.

Court reviews plan for:
Fairness
Best interests of creditors.
Debtor's ability to perform.
Level/amount of payments
(must call for payment in full of all claims OR
payment of all nonessential income of the debtor for
the period of the plan.

Discharge decision made upon successful completion of the plan
unless a petition to review is filed during the plan.

to the debtor or are owed to the debtor. For example, a checking account balance *belongs* to the debtor but is "held" by the bank. The debtor's wages are *owed* to the debtor but are "held" by the employer.

The creditor will officially notify the third person to hold, or retain, the assets pending a judgment. A third person who ignores this notification will become *personally* liable to the creditor when a judgment is entered. Normally, the freezing of the debtor's checking account or paycheck will "encourage" the debtor to resolve the dispute rapidly.

The third major prejudgment remedy is *receivership*. This remedy is not a favored prejudgment choice today, unless it is initiated by the debtor, because of the ready availability of bankruptcy relief. In a receivership, the court appoints a disinterested third person to manage the affairs of the debtor. This receiver is responsible for preserving the debtor's estate until a judgment is reached. Liens on the property of the debtor continue under a receivership, but the property affected cannot be bothered without permission of the court.

Postjudgment Remedies

Unless the debtor pays the debt or the creditor cancels it, the parties eventually must resolve the case by some other means. This normally is done by the entry of a judgment by the court. A creditor who wins the case and receives a judgment probably will seek one of three major postjudgment remedies to satisfy his or her claim.

The first of these is an *execution*. In an execution, the creditor will attempt to seize and sell as many of the debtor's assets as are needed to cover the judgment. This is done by procuring a writ of execution from the court and then having the sheriff levy on the debtor's assets. After the sheriff levies, the assets seized are appraised, a notice of sale is made, and the goods are sold. (The sale is usually at a public auction, commonly referred to as a judicial sale.) The proceeds of the sale or a predetermined percentage of the appraised value, whichever is higher, will be applied to the debts owed to the creditor. (The percentage varies from state to state, since this is a state remedy.)

Redeem To buy back; to liberate an estate or article from mortgage or pledge by paying the debt for which it stood as security.

The debtor is usually allowed to **redeem** any real property and some personal property within a fixed period after the sale by paying the purchaser the necessary amount. A purchaser should also be aware that only the debtor's interest in the asset has been purchased. There may very well be other liens or claims or other problems to be confronted later. Thus, the selling price usually is fairly low.

The second major postjudgment remedy is a *supplementary proceeding*. A supplementary proceeding can be used only if the writ of execution is unsatisfied. In a supplementary proceeding, the creditors attempt to discover any assets of the debtor by examining and questioning any interested parties. If assets are discovered, the creditors can have a receiver appointed to preserve the assets or they can have the court order a sale of the assets.

The third major postjudgment remedy is a *garnishment*. Garnishments were already discussed as a prejudgment remedy, but there is a slight difference here. *Before* a judgment is entered, the third person is instructed to *hold the assets*. *After* a judgment is entered, the third person is told to *turn the assets over* to cover the debts owed. If wages are garnished, some amount must be left to allow the debtor to subsist until the debt is paid.

The next case shows one limitation of a garnishment.

Peterson v. Peterson
571 P.2d 1369 (Utah 1977)

FACTS The plaintiff and the defendant were divorced. As part of the divorce decree, the plaintiff was to receive child support payments. The defendant fell behind in these payments, and the plaintiff sought a writ of garnishment against the defendant's checking account to obtain the delinquent payments. The defendant objected to the writ, arguing that the money in the account belonged to his second wife and not to him.

ISSUE Are funds in a checking account subject to garnishment if the garnishee did not earn the funds?

HOLDING   No. A garnishment can be used only against monies of the garnishee.

REASONING   The defendant in this case had not worked in over a year. The funds in the checking account were almost entirely derived from the earnings of the defendant's current spouse. Both parties considered the funds on deposit to belong to the spouse. None of the money "belonged" to the defendant. Since the garnishment was improper, it was set aside.

Debtor-Initiated Remedies

Debtors often decide to get out from under on their own by initiating remedies under state law rather than seeking a discharge in bankruptcy. A debtor who so decides usually will choose one of two options.

The first option is an *assignment for the benefit of creditors.* Here the debtor freely and voluntarily transfers property to a third person, in trust, to pay the creditors. Creditor consent is not needed, and once the transfer is made, the property is beyond the reach of the creditors. Unfortunately for the debtor, such a transfer does not result in an automatic discharge. Not only that, it may result in the filing of a bankruptcy petition by the creditors.

To avoid these problems, many debtors prefer to reach a *contractual agreement* with the creditors. Such an agreement *does* require creditor consent, but it will also result in discharge. The debtor may seek a composition or an extension, or both.

In a *composition,* each creditor who is involved agrees to take *less* money than is owed, if the money is paid immediately, as full satisfaction of the debt. Such an arrangement is a contract between the debtor and the creditors as well as among the creditors. Thus, at least two creditors must join before the composition is valid. Otherwise, it would be invalid because of lack of consideration (see Chapter 10).

In an *extension,* the creditors agree to a longer repayment period in order to receive full payment. Again, the courts view it as a dual contract between debtor and creditors and among the creditors.

In either a composition or an extension, the contract among the creditors is based on their acceptance of a change in performance in exchange for an agreement by each not to file suit to collect the original contract. Thus, both a composition and an extension are supported by consideration. Each is a contract. And the court will enforce either as it would enforce any other contract.

SUMMARY

An embattled debtor need not always go through liquidation in order to make a fresh start. Other bankruptcy and nonbankruptcy remedies may work equally well.

Under bankruptcy, the debtor may seek a reorganization under Chapter

11 or a repayment plan under Chapter 13. Each of these requires court approval of the plan, and each requires the debtor to propose the plan in good faith. In a reorganization, the debtor adjusts his or her financial position to allow a business to continue. In a repayment plan, the debtor proposes a method of repaying debts over a three-to-five-year period. Good faith and fairness are essential in both plans.

Some creditors seek nonbankruptcy remedies under state law. The creditor may seek either prejudgment remedies to force the debtor to act or postjudgment remedies in order to collect. Either type of action may result in a bankruptcy proceeding. The debtor may also seek a nonbankruptcy remedy under state law. This normally will involve a contract with the creditors and frequently will result in a bankruptcy proceeding.

DISCUSSION QUESTIONS

1. What role does the examiner or the trustee play in a reorganization under Chapter 11?

2. What does the court look at in deciding whether to approve a repayment plan under Chapter 13?

3. What will happen to the debtor under a repayment plan if, owing to a change in circumstances, he or she cannot complete the plan as approved by the court?

4. What public policy considerations might lead a court to prefer a Chapter 11 reorganization over a Chapter 7 liquidation for a corporation? What considerations would lead the court to order a removal from Chapter 11 to Chapter 7 when a corporation files its petition for reorganization under Chapter 11?

5. Under the Bankruptcy Reform Act, a Chapter 13 proceeding was often judged by the good faith of the debtor in proposing the plan. The 1984 Amendments have replaced the debtor's good faith criterion with a new test. How can this test be used to successfully determine whether the debtor is allowed to use a repayment plan or will be subjected to a liquidation proceeding instead?

6. What is the difference between a prejudgment and a postjudgment garnishment proceeding?

7. Why does the law specify that a minimum percentage of appraised value must be applied to debts in an execution? Does this rule reflect more of a public policy concern for the debtor or for the creditor?

8. Why would a debtor make an assignment for the benefit of his or her creditors?

9. Why would a creditor be willing to agree to a composition agreement? Why would a composition agreement occasionally be better for the creditor than a bankruptcy proceeding?

10. How is an extension plan similar to a Chapter 13 repayment plan? How is it different from a Chapter 13 repayment plan? Which seems to be better for the debtor?

CASE PROBLEMS

1. Miller and Fox entered a contract for the sale of some horses. When Miller failed to produce papers on one of the horses as required by the contract, Fox refused to pay for the horse. Miller then obtained a writ of attachment against Fox for the unpaid balance. Fox objected to the attachment since Miller had breached the contract. Can Miller enforce the attachment when he (Miller) is in breach? (*Miller* v. *Fox*, 571 P.2d 804 [Mont. 1977].)

2. CISI was a data processing company handling Visa and MasterCard credit transactions for retail merchants. On 31 March 1983, CISI filed a voluntary petition for relief under Chapter 11 and ceased its credit card division's operations. Prior to stopping the oper-

ation of its credit card division, CISI transferred $278,000 from its account with FNBB to its account with Hamilton Bank. (FNBB paid the retail merchants for their credit card vouchers upon authorization from CISI.) Credit card vouchers still outstanding and awaiting payment from FNBB after the petition was filed amounted to $294,000, which FNBB had to pay. FNBB demanded the return of the funds CISI had transferred to Hamilton Bank, claiming that the funds were the property of FNBB in the form of a constructive trust. The other creditors of CISI object to this argument, claiming that FNBB is a mere creditor with no greater rights to these funds than any other creditor. These other creditors also assert that allowing FNBB to claim these funds would amount to a preferential transfer in violation of the Bankruptcy Code. How should the court treat the $278,000 transferred to the Hamilton Bank? Why? (*In re Computer Input Services, Inc.*, 33 B.R. 292 [1983].)

3. Telemart, a retail grocer, filed a Chapter 11 petition on September 13. Lewis, one of Telemart's suppliers, had delivered $60,000 worth of merchandise on credit to Telemart between August 27 and September 25. When Lewis learned of the Telemart petition, Lewis demanded a return of all the goods as provided by the UCC, Article 2. Is Lewis entitled to a return of the goods under the UCC, or do the goods remain with the bankrupt's estate for treatment and distribution under the bankruptcy laws? (*In the Matter of Telemart Enterprises, Inc.*, 524 F.2d 761 [1975].)

4. Whitman filed a petition for a repayment plan under Chapter 13 of the Bankruptcy Code. One of her debts was an automobile loan from Memphis Bank. The loan carried an interest rate of 21 percent. The bankruptcy court felt that this rate was too high, and ordered Whitman to repay the bank the loan at an interest rate of 10 percent. The bank has appealed this ruling of the bankruptcy court. Should the loan be repaid at the 21 percent called for by the loan agreement, at the 10 percent established by the bankruptcy court, or some other rate? Explain your reasoning. (*Memphis Bank & Trust Co. v. Whitman*, 692 F.2d 427 [6th Cir. 1982].)

5. Wilson Foods filed a petition for relief under Chapter 11 of the Bankruptcy Code while remaining in possession of the business. Immediately on filing its petition, Wilson filed a complaint against the United Food and Commercial Workers International Union, seeking a judgment permitting the rejection of collective bargaining agreements. Wilson also independently reduced the

wages of its employees after it filed for reorganization, and the union asked the National Labor Relations Board (NLRB) to intercede on behalf of the workers. The NLRB claims that Wilson's conduct is an unfair labor practice that is prohibited by federal law. Should the NLRB be allowed to hold administrative proceedings to determine whether Wilson has acted in an improper manner prior to the bankruptcy proceeding, or should the bankruptcy court preempt the NLRB in this case? (*In re Wilson Foods Corporation*, 31 B.R. 269 [1983].)

6. Johns-Manville was a major producer of asbestos products. Asbestos exposure to its customers had led to some 16,000 lawsuits being filed against Johns-Manville, with many more lawsuits expected in the future. As a result of the potential liabilities faced by the company from these lawsuits, Johns-Manville filed for a Chapter 11 reorganization. Several creditors of Johns-Manville asserted that the filing was not in good faith and should be dismissed by the court. Among the grounds asserted for this challenge was the fact that Johns-Manville was a very successful corporation and was not insolvent or close to insolvency. Should the court dismiss the petition? (*In re Johns-Manville Corporation*, 36 Bankr. 727 [1984].)

7. Landmark has as its only substantial asset an apartment complex. City Federal, the only creditor in its class, had a first mortgage on the property in the amount of $2,250,000 and carried an interest rate of 9½ percent. Landmark filed a petition for relief under Chapter 11 and proposed a reorganization plan that was approved by all creditors except City Federal. Under the Landmark plan, City Federal was to receive no payments for the first fifteen months of the plan and interest only on the mortgage, at a rate of 12½ percent, beginning in month 16 and running through month 36. The plan also called for Landmark to issue a new note, payable in full in three years, to City Federal to replace any and all liabilities owed to City Federal. Should the court approve this plan over the objection of City Federal? What factors will the court need to consider in determining whether to approve the plan? (*Matter of Landmark at Plaza Park, Ltd.*, 7 B.R. 653 [1980].)

8. Hebert filed a petition for relief under Chapter 13 of the Bankruptcy Code on 8 September 1983. The court approved the plan on 29 March 1984. The plan called for payment to the IRS of $163 a month for thirty-six months and then of $318 a month for twenty-four months. The plan specified, and the court agreed, that these payments did not include interest. The IRS did

not object to the plan prior to its confirmation but later informed Hebert that interest would be accrued on the unpaid balance owed. Hebert has asked the court to hold the IRS in contempt of court and to prohibit the accrual of interest on the unpaid balance. How should the court rule in this matter? Why? (*In re Hebert,* 61 B.R. 44 [1986].)

9. The Keffers filed for relief under Chapter 13 of the Bankruptcy Code. They proposed a repayment plan that called for the payment of approximately 10 percent of the amount they owed to their unsecured creditors. One of the unsecured creditors, Credithrift, objected to court approval of the plan. Credithrift argued that the conduct of Mr. Keffer in "pawning" certain items of personal property that had been pledged as collateral to secure the Credithrift loan constituted bad faith, and that the presence of bad faith by the debtors requires the court to deny the plan unless it calls for payment in full of all the unsecured debts. Should the court agree with Credithrift in this situation and deny the plan as proposed? What factors should the court consider in reaching its decision? (*In re Keffer,* 87 B.R. 509 [Bkrtcy. S.D. Ohio 1988].)

10. On 2 February 1990, Boullion filed for relief under Chapter 13. On 22 March 1990 Boullion filed a complaint against Sapp seeking to determine the validity of a lien on the Boullion residence. (Sapp was the holder of a second lien on the real estate containing the Boullion residence.) When Sapp did not respond to the complaint, Boullion moved for a default judgment against Sapp and for release of the lien on the real estate. Chapter 13 allows a plan to provide the modification of the rights of holders of secured claims other than a claim secured only by a security interest in real property that is the debtor's principal residence. Can Boullion circumvent the stated limitation of the Bankruptcy Code by means of a default judgment against Sapp? What should the court decide in this case? (*In re Boullion,* 123 B.R. 549 [Bkrtcy. W.D. Tex. 1990].)

PART 6
The Law of Agency

*O*ne of humanity's fondest dreams is to be able to be in more than one place at the same time. Obviously, this is a physical impossibility. Fortunately, though, the law has found a way to do *legally* what cannot be done *physically*. By using an agent, a person can legally be in more than one place at a time.

An *agent* is a person empowered to "be you," within the scope of the agency. Whatever the agent hears, you "heard." Whatever an agent says, you "said." Whatever an agent does, you "did." In other words, you are legally responsible for your agent's conduct—within the scope of the agency.

There are obvious benefits to be derived from "being" in many places at one time, but there are also many potential problems if your various representatives do not conduct themselves properly. Part 6 explores these benefits and potential problems.

33
THE CREATION AND TERMINATION OF AN AGENCY

34
AGENCY: LIABILITY FOR CONTRACTS

35
AGENCY: LIABILITY FOR TORTS

CHAPTER 33

The Creation and Termination of an Agency

OUTLINE

AGENCY LAW AND AGENCY RELATIONSHIPS

Agency law deals with the relationships between workers and the people who hire workers. It includes their duties and responsibilities both to each other and to the public at large. No one can really avoid agency law. Almost everyone at some time works as an employee or hires an employee. Moreover, agency relationships arise not only in business situations but also in non-business situations, as, for example, when a person returns books to the library for a friend.

Most agency relationships do not require litigation because they run smoothly. To resolve the legal problems that do arise, one must look to agency law, contract law, and tort law. In most of these subject areas, the court will rely heavily on state law. Much of the law of agency has been studied by the American Law Institute and is discussed in their publication, *Restatement (Second) of Agency*. Restatements are treatises that summarize detailed recommendations of what the law should be on a particular subject. Although Restatements are not legislature- or court-made law, they become part of the legal precedents when courts rely on them and incorporate them into court decisions. The *Restatement (Second) of Agency* states:

1. Agency is the fiduciary relation which results from the manifestation of consent by one person to another that the other shall act on his behalf and subject to his control, and consent by the other so to act.
2. The one for whom action is to be taken is the principal.
3. The one who is to act is the agent.[1]

An agency relationship is consensual in nature. It is based on the concept that the parties mutually agree that (1) the agent will act on behalf of the principal, and (2) the agent will be subject to the principal's direction and control. In addition, the parties must be competent to act as principal and agent.

RESTRICTIONS ON CREATING AN AGENCY RELATIONSHIP

A broad range of situations are affected by agency law, from a small partnership with two partners to a corporation with thousands of employees, and from a highly skilled petroleum engineer to a sixteen-year-old babysitter. In fact, everything a corporation does, it does through agents. There are very few restrictions on who can form agency relationships and what can be done through agency relationships.

[1]*Restatement (Second) of Agency* (Philadelphia: American Law Institute, 1958), Section 1.

Capacity to Be a Principal

With the exception of minors and incompetents, any person can appoint an agent. It is generally true that any person having capacity to *contract* has capacity to employ a servant agent or a nonservant agent. (The distinction between these two agents is that a principal has more control over the actions of the former than over those of the latter.) Since agency is a consensual relationship, the principal must have capacity to give a legally operative consent.[2]

Some states have determined that a minor lacks capacity to be a principal. In other states, a minor has the capacity to enter into an agency relationship, but the agency relationship is voidable. (The *Restatement [Second] of Agency*, Section 20, takes the second position.) In these states, the agreements entered into by the minor's agent would also be voidable to the same extent that the minor's own contracts would be voidable. The key to understanding this concept is remembering that the contract is really entered into by the principal.

Capacity to Be an Agent

Generally, anyone can be an agent. Even persons who do not have capacity to act for themselves—for example, minors or insane persons—can act as agents for someone else. It is the capacity of the *principal*, not that of the agent, that is controlling. Obviously, however, principals should exercise care to appoint agents who are able to make sound decisions.

Duties an Agent Can Perform

Generally, an agent can be assigned to do almost any task. There are, however, some nondelegable duties, such as the following:

1. an employer's duty to provide safe working conditions[3]
2. a person's duty under some contract terms
3. a landlord's duty to tenants
4. a **common carrier's** duty to passengers
5. a person's duty under a license issued to that person
6. the duty of a person engaged in inherently dangerous work to take adequate precautions to avoid harm

Common carrier A company in the business of transporting people or goods for a fee and holding itself out as serving the general public.

Other nondelegable duties are defined by various state statutes. These may consist of many different types. If the duty is nondelegable and the principal attempts to delegate the duty to someone else, the principal will be personally liable if the task is not properly completed. *Nondelegable duties* really mean that the *task* can be delegated, but the *responsibility for its proper completion* cannot.

A person who hires another to engage in ultrahazardous activities will be liable for any injury that results. This rule applies whether the person who is hired is a servant or an **independent contractor**.

Independent contractor Person hired to perform a task but not subject to the control of the employer.

[2]Ibid., Section 20, Comment b.
[3]Ibid., Section 492, Comment a.

FIGURE 33.1   Distinction Between Special Agents and General Agents

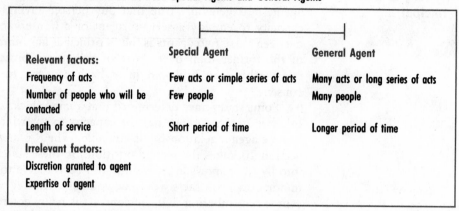

Relevant factors:	Special Agent	General Agent
Frequency of acts	Few acts or simple series of acts	Many acts or long series of acts
Number of people who will be contacted	Few people	Many people
Length of service	Short period of time	Longer period of time
Irrelevant factors:		
Discretion granted to agent		
Expertise of agent		

TYPES OF AGENCY RELATIONSHIPS

The distinction between general and special agents is a matter of degree. A *special agent* is *employed to complete one transaction or a simple series of transactions*. The relationship covers a relatively limited period and is not continuous. A *general agent* is *hired to conduct a series of transactions over time*. The amount of **discretion** the agent has is immaterial in making the distinction between general and special agents. The expertise of the agent is also immaterial.

Discretion   The right to use one's own judgment in making a decision between the alternatives.

General and Special Agents

In deciding whether an agent is a general agent or a special agent, courts should look at all of the following factors:

1. the number of acts that will be completed to achieve the authorized result

2. the number of people who will be dealt with before achieving the desired result

3. the length of time that will be necessary to achieve the desired result[4]

The manager of a card shop is a general agent. In contrast, a person who delivers a package to a customer of the store on a one-time basis is a special agent. Categorizing an agent who is between these two extremes can be difficult. As Figure 33.1 shows, a continuum of relationships exists between the role of special agents and that of general agents. Toward the center of the line

[4]Ibid., Section 3, Comment a.

it is difficult to determine if the worker is more like a special agent or more like a general agent.

Gratuitous Agents

Payment is not necessary in a principal-agent relationship. If a person volunteers services without an agreement or an expectation of payment, that person may still be an agent. The requirements for a *gratuitous agency* are that *one person volunteered to help another, and the person being helped accepted this assistance.* For instance, Susie was visiting Joel, who had some yard work to do. Susie offered to help. While she was pruning a tree, she carelessly sawed off a limb, which fell on a car belonging to Joel's neighbor. The courts could find that Susie was Joel's agent, in which case Joel would be liable for the damage that Susie caused.

SERVANTS AND INDEPENDENT CONTRACTORS

Most workers are either servants or independent contractors. The distinction among the terms *agent, servant,* and *independent contractor* is confusing, partly because authors and judges apply differing definitions to these terms and partly because common usage differs from legal usage. This text uses the definitions of the *Restatement (Second) of Agency.* Using legal definitions, servants and employees are synonymous. We generally use the term "servant" to describe someone who is subject to the control of his or her "master."

Servants

A master is a special type of principal who has the right to tell his or her agent both what to do and how to do it. The agent then falls into a special class of agents called *servants* or *employees.* The more modern term is "employee." A master (employer) has a right to control how the task is done by the servant (employee). The actual exercise of this control is not necessary; it is sufficient that the master has the *right* to control. Thus, interns in hospitals, airline pilots, sales clerks, and officers of corporations are servants.

The distinction between servants and independent contractors is important, because a principal is rarely liable for the unauthorized *physical* acts of an agent who is not a servant. Consequently, a principal generally will not be liable for the torts of an independent contractor. Principals sometimes label a worker as an independent contractor in an attempt to escape liability, but the courts will look behind the label and make a judgment about the true nature of the relationship. The distinction between servants and independent contractors is also important in determining rights and benefits under unemployment insurance laws, workers' compensation laws, and similar statutes.

The distinction between an independent contractor and a servant is represented in Figure 33.2. Remember that this distinction is material only when the question is who may be responsible for the physical acts of the worker.

FIGURE 33.2   Distinction Between Servants and Independent Contractors

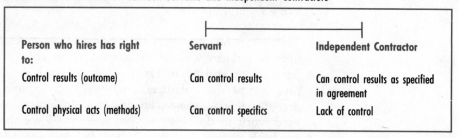

Person who hires has right to:	Servant	Independent Contractor
Control results (outcome)	Can control results	Can control results as specified in agreement
Control physical acts (methods)	Can control specifics	Lack of control

When the worker has entered into a contract for her employer, whether she is a servant or an independent contractor is irrelevant.

Independent Contractors

An *independent contractor* is hired to complete a task for someone else. The physical acts of the independent contractor are not controlled or subject to the control of the hiring party. The independent contractor *relies on his or her own expertise to determine the best way to complete the job.* Anyone who contracts to do work for another is either a servant or an independent contractor. Courts look at many factors in distinguishing between the two, as illustrated by the next case.

F.A.S. International, Inc. v. *Reilly*
427 A.2d 392 (Conn. 1980)

FACTS   F.A.S. operated three correspondence schools—Famous Artists School, Famous Writers School, and Famous Photographers School. F.A.S. used practicing professionals to analyze and critique their students' correspondence lessons. The professionals had no regular office hours. They took the work to their homes, offices, or studios and returned it to F.A.S. when completed. F.A.S. did not supply office space or equipment, but they did supply stationery. The professionals were given only one or two assignments at a time. They were not expected to complete a certain number of assignments per day. F.A.S. did not guarantee that they would receive a minimum amount of work to do. The professionals were paid only for the lessons that they completed. They had no paid vacations, holidays, sick leave, overtime pay, or fringe benefits. F.A.S. did not withhold social security or federal income tax from their pay. Most of the professionals also had independent businesses or worked for others.

ISSUE   Were the professionals working for F.A.S. as servants?

HOLDING   No. The court held that they were independent contractors.

REASONING   This case arose because of a complaint from the administrator of the state unemployment compensation fund. Under Connecticut law, the court stated, the term *employees* should be defined more liberally in reference to unemployment compensation than in reference to other situations. However, it should not be construed unrealistically. Nonetheless, the court held that the common law relationship of master and servant did not exist in this case. The fundamental distinction between a servant and an independent contractor depends on the existence of the right to control the means and the methods of work. Some states require very little supervision in order to find control. Connecticut applies the common law rule. The state supreme court has adopted this definition: "[A]n independent contractor is one who, exercising an independent employment, contracts to do a piece of work according to his own methods and without being subject to the control of his employer, except as to the result of his work." The basic principles of this definition have not been modified. Even with a liberal interpretation of the terms, these professionals were not servants.

FIGURE 33.3   Independent Contractors May Also Be Agents

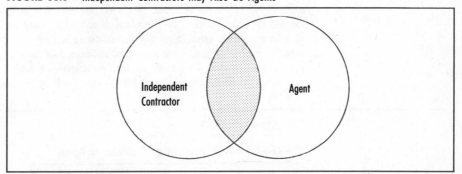

The shaded area indicates independent contractors who are also agents.

Independent contractors may be agents, but that is not a necessary condition of being an independent contractor. This is shown in Figure 33.3. If the independent contractorntractor does not represent the hiring party or act for her in relation to third parties, he is not her agent. Consequently, he does not owe her any **fiduciary duties**. For example, a nonagent independent contractor who is building a house on an owner's lot cannot bind the owner to a contract.

Fiduciary duty   The duty to exercise the highest degree of loyalty.

Independent contractors who are agents (1) have fiduciary duties and (2) can bind their principals to contracts. For example, attorneys owe their clients fiduciary duties when they work out a settlement and then agree to it on the client's behalf. On the other hand, attorneys are not employees. Legal clients cannot control when their attorneys come to work in the morning or how long a lunch break they take. These relationships are represented in Figure 33.4.

The following case addressed the issue of whether an independent contractor was an agent.

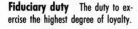

Canton Lutheran Church v. *Sovik, Mathre, Sathrum & Quanbeck*
507 F. Supp. 873 (D. S.D. 1981)

FACTS   A church wanted to build an addition to its principal structure. It entered into a contract with Sovik, Mathre, Sathrum & Quanbeck for professional services as an architect. Later, it entered into a contract with a builder to construct the building that the architect had designed. The architect agreed to be responsible for supervision of the work. The architect signed a certificate that the addition was substantially completed in accordance with the specifications. The building addition cracked because the concrete contained calcium chloride. The building specifications did not call for the use of calcium chloride, and its use was not authorized.

ISSUE   Did the architect have a fiduciary duty to the church?

HOLDING   Yes. The architect was an agent and as such owed a fiduciary duty to the principal.

REASONING   An architect preparing a plan for a landowner generally acts as an independent contractor. With respect to the architect's duty to supervise the builder, the architect generally acts as an agent, thus serving as a representative of the party for whom the job is being completed. In such a case, there is a fiduciary duty. This is especially true when the architect has agreed to guard against deficiencies in the work of the builder by supervising the builder's work. The relationship, then, is one of trust and confidence. South Dakota law defines a fiduciary, in part, as an agent. In this case, there was sufficient evidence that the architect breached its fiduciary duty. It appeared that the architect had fraudulently concealed the builder's breach of contract. This issue was returned to the trial court.

FIGURE 33.4   Is the Independent Contractor an Agent?

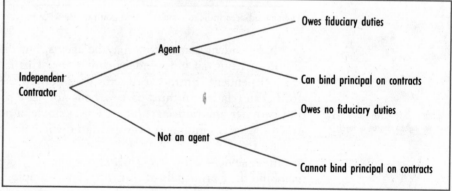

When the legal questions are ones of fiduciary duties or contracts, we will simply call the worker an agent instead of the cumbersome term independent contractor agent.

Responsibility for Independent Contractors

Contract Liability   Principals who engage independent contractors as agents will be liable on the contract *if* the contract was authorized. Authorization is discussed in detail in Chapter 34. This liability complies with the general rule for agents.

Tort Liability   A person who hires an independent contractor usually is not responsible for the independent contractor's physical wrongdoings. Courts make exceptions when the independent contractor was hired to engage in ultrahazardous activities or to commit a crime. The hiring party will be responsible if the hiring party actually directs the independent contractor to do something careless or wrong or if the hiring party sees the independent contractor do something wrong and does not stop it. Recently, courts have also held hiring parties liable for their failure to adequately supervise independent contractors and for carelessly selecting their independent contractors.

In many states, the trend has been to increase the number of situations in which a person who hires an independent contractor may be held liable. One method that is used by courts is to reduce the standard from ultrahazardous activities to hazardous activities. In other words, a person will be liable when he hires an independent contractor to engage in hazardous activities. The court seemed to be applying the hazardous activities standard in the following case.

Henderson Brothers Stores, Inc. v. Smiley
174 Cal. Rptr. 875 (Cal. App. 1981)

FACTS Smiley, a licensed roofing contractor, was hired to reroof MacDonald's building with asphalt. The asphalt must be heated to the melting point in a large tar kettle. Smiley was using such a kettle. He had placed it in a passageway between MacDonald's building and Henderson's warehouse. The kettle suddenly erupted and shot flames ten to twenty feet in the air, setting fire to the Henderson's building. This type of eruption is very common in the use of a tar kettle. The normal operation of tar kettles in roofing work presents a significant, recognizable danger of fire. Setting the thermostat too high, allowing the tar level in the kettle to be too low, and allowing carbon to build up increases this risk. There is evidence that all three occurred in this case.

ISSUE Did the hot roofing operation involve a special danger of fire so that MacDonald should be liable for the acts of its independent contractor, Smiley?

HOLDING Yes. MacDonald should be liable for the acts of its independent contractor.

REASONING The general rule is that there is no vicarious liability for the person who hires an independent contractor. American courts recognize a number of exceptions to this rule. One such exception to the general rule of nonliability is where the contractor is engaged in the performance of "inherently dangerous" work. This is also called the "peculiar risk" doctrine. Under the *Restatement (Second) of Torts,* the hiring party is directly liable for failing to provide in the agreement with the independent contractor for the independent contractor to take appropriate precautions in cases of "peculiar risk." It is not necessary for the application of this rule that the work be of the type that cannot be done without a risk of harm to others. The rule is based on the negligent failure of the employer or the contractor to take appropriate special precautions.

The independent contractor will also be liable for his wrongdoings. In fact, in the previous case Henderson was also suing Smiley, the roofing contractor.

DUTIES OF THE AGENT TO THE PRINCIPAL

The agent must protect the interests of the principal, as the duties discussed in the following sections show. Some of the duties overlap. In fact, when an agent breaches one duty, most likely others have been breached as well.

Duty of Good Faith

The duty of good faith is also called the fiduciary duty, and the rule is that every agent owes the principal the obligation of faithful service. The most common violations of this duty include concealing essential facts that are relevant to the agency, obtaining secret profits, and self-dealing. Suppose the principal was looking for a parcel of agricultural land, and the agent located a suitable parcel. The agent arranged for its sale to the principal without first informing the principal that the agent owned a one-third interest in the parcel. This would be a violation of the agent's fiduciary duty to the principal.

Duty of Loyalty

An agent has a duty to be loyal to the principal and to look out for the principal's best interests. Thus, an agent must not compete with the principal, work for someone who is competing with the principal, or act to further the agent's own interests. For example, suppose Lucy, the principal, has asked her agent to purchase a parcel of land that would be a good location for a shopping center. The agent discovers a good parcel at an excellent price. The agent has a duty not to buy it for himself unless he specifically asks Lucy for permission to disregard these rules and she grants that permission.

In the following case, we see another type of breach of the duty of loyalty. Here the agent did not provide loyal service because he concealed essential facts and did not perform the purpose of the agency.

Black v. *Dahl*
625 P.2d 876 (Alaska 1981)

FACTS   Dahl rented and operated Illiamna Lake Lodge on a long-term lease. Dahl was behind in his lease payments and was in danger of losing his entire investment. He contacted Black, a real estate salesman, about finding a purchaser for Dahl's interest. They entered into an agreement under which Black would receive a 10-percent commission if he located a buyer. Black located two partners who were interested in the premises. These partners wanted to see the financial records and to make a physical inspection. Dahl was not informed of these requests. Black also told the partners that if they delayed ten to fifteen days, they could acquire the lease for $10,000 less. When Dahl asked Black about the progress on the negotiations, Black indicated that he guessed the partners were not interested. Dahl lost his financial interest because he defaulted on the lease. After the default, the partners purchased the lease from others. Dahl did not share in these proceeds.

ISSUE   Did Black violate his duty of loyalty as an agent?

HOLDING   Yes. Black did not protect Dahl's interest.

REASONING Black owed Dahl a duty to try to find a buyer for Dahl's interest in the premises. Once a buyer was located, Black had a duty to use due diligence to close the transaction. Black violated his duty. In fact, he discouraged the buyers from completing the purchase until after Dahl had lost his interest by default.

---

(3) The agent also has a duty not to divulge secret information that gives the principal an advantage over the competition. These are commonly called trade secrets. The duties of loyalty and good faith are very similar. If an agent has violated one, there is a good chance the agent has violated them both.

Duty to Obey All Lawful Instructions

(4) Agents must follow all *lawful* instructions as long as doing so does not subject them to an unreasonable risk of injury, even if agents think the instructions are capricious or unwise. Agents need not follow instructions that are outside the course and scope of the agency relationship. They must repay their principals for damages suffered because they failed to follow instructions.

Duty to Act with Reasonable Care

(5) An agent has a duty to act as a reasonably careful agent would under the same circumstances. Again, if the agent fails to live up to this obligation and it causes the principal a loss, the agent will be obliged to reimburse the principal.

Duty to Segregate Funds

Trust Arrangement whereby one person holds legal title for another person with equitable title.

(6) The agent has a duty to keep personal funds separate from the principal's funds. If the agent wrongfully uses the principal's funds to purchase something, the court may impose a **trust** and treat the matter as though the purchase were originally made for the benefit of the principal. Such a trust—that is, a trust imposed by a court for the purpose of preventing unjust enrichment—is called a *constructive trust*. (Constructive trusts are discussed in Chapter 53.)

Duty to Account for Funds

(7) An agent has a duty to account for money received. This is really a combined function of delivery of the funds and record keeping. The funds usually must be delivered to the principal (or an authorized third party). If the money was received while the agent was not in the course and scope of the employment, the agent has a duty to turn the proceeds over to the third party. An example would be an agent who was not working when she received the funds.

Duty to Give Notice

(8) The duty to give notice requires that an agent will inform the principal about crucial facts that are discovered in the scope of the agent's employment. For example, if a tenant gives an apartment manager notice that the tenant will move out at the end of the month, it is assumed that the manager will inform the owner. In fact, the principal may be bound by this notice even though the agent failed to inform the principal. It is said that the notice is "imputed" to the principal.

The California Raisin Bowl is an annual, postseason, college football game sponsored, at least in part, to raise funds for charities. In 1990, $50,000 of Cal Bowl money was deposited with Money Management Administrators (MMA). The interest rate was substantially above the bank rate; however, the account was not insured. Dennis Frye, an accountant and the bowl treasurer, made this investment decision. According to Frye, "he 'checked out' the firm by talking to people he knew in the financial industry, and he didn't uncover anything to indicate the investment was risky." About nine months later in the spring of 1991, Cal Bowl was able to withdraw the entire investment and approximately 10.25 percent interest.

Frye says that beginning in August, 1990, he believes that his instructions from the full executive committee were to limit investments with MMA to $50,000. Consequently, in April, 1991, Frye again invested $50,000 with MMA. Frye said, "We had the success of the year before. So we went with them again . . ." The Cal Bowl has not been so fortunate with their 1991 investment. MMA has filed bankruptcy and is being investigated for possible criminal misconduct. On May 7, 1991, the California Department of Corporations ordered MMA to stop selling promissory notes and investment contracts because its offerings were not registered as securities. Frye claims that he was not aware of this action. The $50,000 donation promised to the local children's hospital may never be received by them.

The Cal Bowl itself is having money problems. They currently owe $49,000 to California State University, Fresno for costs incurred for the most recent game; they owe $10,000 to the children's hospital for office space; the California Raisin Advisory Board has dropped its sponsorship of the game; and their receipts were less than expected. The paid executive director has resigned.

John Sirman, bowl director, said that he warned the executive committee at their meeting in August, 1990, that money earmarked for charities should be kept in insured investment accounts. (The committee did not take formal action.) In August, 1991, when Frye made his report to the executive committee, Sirman was quite upset. Sirman said, "I thought we were no longer supposed to be investing with them. I really was excited about it, because there were rumblings about Money Management having problems and because I thought we had agreed in 1990 to pull out of there." Sirman again issued his warning.

Frye did not worry about the second investment until September, 1991, when he read a newspaper article about a suit that MMA filed. When Frye contacted MMA, they indicated that the investment would be returned. From September, 1991, until January, 1992, Cal Bowl representatives, including the office manager and Frye, made numerous phone calls, and sent letters and faxes to MMA seeking the return of the funds. In January, MMA filed bankruptcy. The loss was not disclosed to the full executive committee until March, 1992.

Neale Stoner, the paid executive director at the time, denies that he was responsible for investment decisions. He claims that the executive board had that responsibility. Stoner does not remember signing the checks to MMA, as contended by Frey.

John Higginbotham, a stockbroker, has been on the board since it was formed. He said, "This is my business, investments. If this had been brought up in a board meeting, I certainly would have said, 'Let me check into this' or 'Let us do some research on this.'"

If you were the judge deciding this case, what would you decide and why? Who, if anyone, is responsible for the loss?

Source: "Cal Bowl's investments criticized," Jeanie Borba, *The Fresno Bee,* Thursday, May 21, 1992, page A1.

DUTIES OF THE PRINCIPAL TO THE AGENT

A principal has an obligation to compensate the agent under the terms of their agreement. Recall that some agents are not entitled to compensation. Other types of agents are entitled to compensation under special arrangements that developed under common law. These unique situations are usually also mentioned in the written contract. For example, in some states real estate agents are entitled to their commissions if they find a buyer who is ready, willing, and able to buy the parcel. This is true even if the transfer does not occur because of destruction of the building, the buyer's inability to obtain a loan, or some other circumstance. Some states follow a different rule, whereby a sale must close before a commission is earned.

A principal also has an obligation to provide the agent with a reasonably safe place to work and safe equipment to use. This is especially true for agents who are servants.

TERMINATION OF THE AGENCY RELATIONSHIP

Agreement of the Parties

An agency relationship is governed in the first instance by the agreement between the principal and the agent. It is usually based on a contract that is established for a set period. For example, if a real estate agent has a listing to sell a house according to certain terms, one of the terms may be the period for which the contract is going to run, say ninety days; that agreement will terminate at the end of ninety days.

The parties can agree to amend the agency agreement to terminate the agency relationship early or to extend it. For example, if the house that we just referred to was not sold in ninety days, the owner and agent could specifically extend the agency agreement for another sixty days.

If the parties consent to the continuation of the agency relationship beyond the period originally stated and they have not specifically altered the terms and conditions of the original agreement, this consent may be implied as a renewal of the original contract for the same period and under the same conditions.

Agency at Will

If the agency agreement does not specify a set date, a set period, or a set occurrence that will terminate it, the relationship is an *agency at will. Either party can terminate the relationship by giving notice to the other*. This is consistent with the theory that agency is a voluntary relationship between the parties.

The concept of an agency at will is changing, and some states are holding an employer liable if an employee is fired for the wrong reason.[5] Most court cases involve servants instead of independent contractors.[6] The court dealt with an agency at will in the following case.

Savodnik v. Korvettes, Inc.
488 F. Supp. 822 (E.D. N.Y. 1980)

FACTS   Morton Savodnik was employed by Korvettes from 7 October 1963 to 26 January 1977, when he received his termination notice. During that period, he received frequent promotions and annual increases in pay. He was never fined, demoted, or warned about his job performance. Savodnik claimed that he suffered a heart attack because of his termination. He had participated in Korvettes' retirement plan and would have been entitled to the money Korvettes contributed to the plan in his name after fifteen years of employment. Savodnik alleged that Korvettes fired him to prevent him from receiving their contribution. Korvettes did not deny this.

ISSUE   Did Korvettes lawfully fire Savodnik?

[5]On 8 August 1991, the National Conference of Commissioners on Uniform State Laws approved the Model Employment Termination Act 2 (Proposed Official Draft 1991), which addresses these issues.

[6]The courts generally use the terms *employer* and *employee* when discussing both agency at will and wrongful discharge.

HOLDING   No. Korvettes needs a valid reason to fire Savodnik.

REASONING   Under the traditional doctrine of employment at will, the employer or the employee could terminate the contract at will and without reason. However, this doctrine is undergoing dynamic development. In many states, the courts are rewriting the traditional doctrine based on careful assessments of what would benefit the economic system and the public good. Courts are allowing an employee to recover when the firing is based on retaliation, bad faith, or an attempt to avoid paying an employee's commissions. Since this is an issue governed by state law, the court in this case was bound by New York law. New York courts have not yet recognized a cause of action for wrongful firing or abusive discharge. New York **precedents** indicate a willingness to recognize this tort cause of action. The court found that Mr. Savodnik was a model employee for over thirteen years and that Korvettes had no justification for firing him; in addition, Korvettes had a pattern of firing employees to avoid giving them rights in the company retirement plan.

Precedents Prior court cases that control the decision in court.

(These parties were also involved in a trial on related issues, which was reported at 489 F. Supp. 1010 [E.D. N.Y. 1980].)

---

unlawful discharge

There are other prohibitions on firing agents at will. If the agent was fired on the basis of sex, race, religion, or national origin or some other violation of civil rights, the courts may decide that the principal may not terminate the relationship. Notice that wrongful discharge has been used to prevent employers from firing employees, but employees in an employment at will are still free to quit at any time and for any reason.

Fulfillment of the Agency Purpose

Logically, an agency relationship will terminate when the purpose for which it was created has been fulfilled. There would be no sense in continuing the relationship beyond that point.

Revocation

Principals can revoke or terminate the authority of their agents to act for the principal. They should directly notify their agents of the termination. The notice that the agency relationship is being terminated should be clear and unequivocal. Indirect notice will sometimes be sufficient—for example, hiring a second agent to complete all the duties of the first agent. Due to the agent's obligation to obey, the principal can terminate the agency at any time. This is true even though there was an agreement that the agency relationship should continue longer. Even a statement in the agreement that the agency cannot be terminated would not affect the principal's ability to terminate it. Although the principal may have the *ability* to terminate the agency, he or she may not have the legal *right* to do so; in such a case, the agency would be terminated, but the principal would be liable for damages if this termination was a breach of contract.

Renunciation

Renunciation occurs when the agent notifies the principal that he or she will no longer serve as an agent. In other words, the agent resigns. Since an agency relationship is voluntary, an agent may renounce. However, the agent may be liable to the principal if the renunciation is a breach of their contract.

Operation of Law

Operation of law denotes an automatic occurrence that does not require the action of any person. Operation of law generally will terminate an agency relationship under any one of the following circumstances:

1. when the agent dies
2. when either party becomes insane
3. when the principal becomes bankrupt
4. when the agent becomes bankrupt, if the bankruptcy affects the agency
5. when the agency cannot possibly be performed (for example, when the subject matter of the agency is destroyed)
6. when an unusual and unanticipated change in circumstances occurs that destroys the purpose of the agency relationship
7. when a change in law makes completion of the agency relationship illegal

The traditional rule was that the death of the principal would also terminate the agency relationship immediately. Because this rule can cause hardship, many states modified their law to take a more liberal approach. Under this more liberal rule, the death of the principal will not immediately terminate the agency relationship *if* immediate termination would cause a hardship.

When the relationship is terminated by the operation of law, it is usually not necessary to give notice to the other party or to the public at large. This rule is discretionary, and a court may decide to require notice if its absence would cause a great hardship.

Importance of Notice

When an agent or a principal terminates the agency relationship early, the agent or principal has a duty to notify the other party so that the other party does not waste effort on a relationship that no longer exists.

It may be crucial to notify third parties even if it is not legally required, as in termination by operation of law. The agent may find it advantageous to do so, but the principal will find it even more important. If the principal fails to notify a third party, the third party may transfer money, like a rent payment, to the agent with the expectation that the agent will forward the funds to the principal. If the agent is unhappy with the termination, the agent may unlawfully abscond with the money.

The notice may take various forms. The preferred method is to personally notify the third person by mail, telephone, or telegram. Personal notice is generally required for all third parties who have had dealings with the agent. The advantage of using the telephone is that it is fast, but there is no written proof of the notification; the third party may deny receiving the notice. Notice should be given promptly, since one of its purposes is to prevent losses caused by a disgruntled agent who feels that the termination was unjust.

The law also accepts notice by publication (also called constructive notice). Usually such notice is published in the legal notices in the newspaper. This is the only type of notice that is practical for members of the public, who are aware of the agency but who have not had previous dealings with the agent.

The principal will be protected if the third party actually knows that the agency relationship has been terminated even if the third party did not receive notice from the principal (that is, the third party may have heard about the termination from the agent or from someone else).

Breach of Agency Agreement

If the principal revokes the agent's authority wrongfully, the agent can sue for breach of contract. If there is an anticipatory breach and the principal notifies the agent in advance of the breach, the agent can sue the principal immediately for the anticipated damages. The agent, at his or her election, may decide to wait until after the contract period and then sue for actual damages. In either case, the agent has an obligation to mitigate damages or to keep them as low as possible by searching for another similar position with another principal in the same locality.

SPECIAL SITUATIONS

Most agency relationships are formed for the benefit of the principal, but some are formed for the protection and benefit of the agent. The latter most commonly occur when the agent has loaned money to the principal, and the principal is securing the loan with collateral.

The mere statement in a contract that an agency is irrevocable will not make it true. Courts will analyze the facts to make sure that the agent has an *interest* in the collateral itself. Many court cases of this type arise because the principal wishes to terminate the agency relationship and the agent wishes to prevent the termination. Two special situations do restrict the principal's *ability* to terminate the agency relationship: (1) agency coupled with an obligation and (2) power coupled with an interest.

Agency Coupled with an Obligation

Suppose Paula needed cash for an investment. Since the banks would not lend Paula the money, she decided to borrow the $50,000 from Angela for two years. Angela insisted on having collateral, so Paula gave Angela the right to sell her building if Paula did not repay the loan in two years. Angela was entitled to take her $50,000 and her expenses out of the sale, but she had to give the rest of the money to Paula. In this situation, Paula, the principal, had an *obligation* to her agent, Angela, to repay the $50,000. Angela could, if necessary, sell the property to obtain payment. Although a principal cannot terminate such an arrangement at will, the death of a party or a bankruptcy that affects the agency could terminate it.

Power Coupled with an Interest

Power coupled with an interest is similar to an agency coupled with an obligation, but it is more formal and the "agent's" rights are better protected. The parties have a power coupled with an interest if the "agent's" interest is taken through some formal document—for example, if Angela's interest had been taken through a mortgage on Paula's property. It also differs from an agency coupled with an obligation in that the death or bankruptcy of a party would not terminate it. As the name implies, it is not actually an agency relationship.

SUMMARY

Agency relationships center on the agreement between a principal and an agent that the agent shall act for the benefit of the principal. The principal must have capacity to consent to the relationship. The agent need not have contractual capacity. An agent who does not receive compensation is a gratuitous agent.

In analyzing the legal rights of the parties, it is important to determine whether the worker is a servant or an independent contractor. An independent contractor is hired to complete a job. The hiring party does not direct how the independent contractor does the task. In contrast, a principal can exert a great deal of control over a servant and how the servant performs assigned duties. Because the principal can control the servant, the principal is more likely to be held financially responsible for the servant's physical acts.

An agent has a duty to act in good faith, to act loyally, to obey all lawful instructions, to act with reasonable care, to segregate funds, to account for all funds, and to give notice.

An agency relationship may terminate at a specified time agreed on by the parties, at the will of the parties, or after the purpose of the agency has been fulfilled. It may be revoked or renunciated by one of the parties or terminated by operation of law. The method of termination will depend, at least in part, on the terms of the agreement.

A principal generally has the power to terminate an agency relationship even if the termination is wrongful. The principal does not have the power to terminate either an agency coupled with an obligation or a power coupled with an interest without the agent's consent.

DISCUSSION QUESTIONS

1. Tom purchased a new home through Gary, his realtor. The house needed a lot of work, so Tom arranged for George to paint the interior, for Harry to repair the furnace, for his own sons to plant grass in the back yard, and for Martha to clean the interior. Based on normal hiring relationships, who are agents, servants, or independent contractors, and why? Are the agents special agents or general agents, and why?

2. Tommy hired Jack to deliver one cord of pine wood for the fireplace in the house he rented. Jack usually just dumped the wood in the driveway—a practice known as a driveway delivery. However, this time he decided to help Tommy stack the wood in the garage. Tommy was standing in the garage as Jack backed the truck into position. Jack backed the truck too far, damaging both the truck and the garage wall. Was Jack a servant or an independent contractor? Who is liable to the injured third person (the landlord), and why? Who would have been liable if the truck had injured Tommy? Why?

3. Kurt was going to Lake Tahoe for a week's vacation. His friend Karen gave him $5 to bet on a particular football game while he was there. Kurt forgot all about placing the bet. If he had placed the bet, Karen would have won $15,000. What rights does Karen have? If Karen's team had lost, what rights would Karen have then?

4. Ronnie worked for Acme Grocery Store. One day while Ronnie was unloading produce from a truck, Jimmy stopped to talk to him. Jimmy got in the truck, and as he was handing the boxes to Ronnie, Jimmy carelessly dropped a box on a person walking down the alley. Who is responsible for the injury, and why? Is it relevant that Jimmy was not being paid? If so, why?

5. Peter hired Andy to purchase some goods for him on the open market. While Andy was obtaining prices from vendors, Ted offered Andy a $100 rebate if Andy purchased the goods from Ted. Andy did and kept the $100 for himself. What are the rights of the parties? Why?

6. Elaine worked as a travel agent for Travel Enterprises, Inc. As an incentive, a cruise ship line offered travel agents one free passage on a cruise for every twenty-five paying passengers they book on the line. The cruise ship line felt that this practice is good public relations. Elaine has earned two free passages. Who is entitled to these passages, and why?

7. After nine years of marriage, Jill and John have decided to get a divorce. Their neighbor Charlie, who is an attorney, is going to do the legal work for both parties and handle the property settlement. Are there any problems with this arrangement? Why?

8. Brad called Marty, his stockbroker, to tell him that Ellen, Brad's friend, was going to purchase some stock from Marty. Brad directed Marty to charge the purchases against the brokerage account of Brad and his wife, Sue. What is the broker's responsibility to Brad and his wife? What advice would you give Marty?

9. Steve managed a 200-unit apartment complex. The owners wanted to convert the apartments to condominiums. The city council was going to have a hearing on the issue. Instead of sending the notice to the owners, the council sent the notice to Steve. What are the rights and obligations of the parties? Why?

10. Sarah signed a written contract stating that her agency relationship would last for four years and that she would have the irrevocable right to take orders from homemakers for aluminum pots and pans for her principal. In an attempt to economize, her principal fired her. What rights does Sarah have?

CASE PROBLEMS

1. Resnik worked for Day Realty as a licensed real estate salesperson. Resnik claimed that Day did not pay him the commission to which he was entitled and filed a complaint with the state labor commissioner. Since the state labor commissioner had jurisdiction only over cases involving employees, it was important to determine whether Resnik was an employee or an independent contractor. Under the applicable state law, a real estate salesperson cannot contract in his or her own name; can be employed only by a licensed real estate broker; can work under only one broker; and must allow his or her license to remain with the broker. If the broker fails to supervise the salesperson adequately, the broker's own license may be revoked or suspended. The Resnik-Day contract specifically said that Resnik was an independent contractor. Is Resnik an employee or an independent contractor? Why? (*Resnik* v. *Anderson and Miles,* 167 Cal. Rptr. 340 [Cal App. 1980].)

2. Hill purchased some furniture from Grant's. The furniture was defective, so Hill contacted the seller, who assured her that they would send someone to repair the furniture. The repairman, Newman, identified himself as being from Grant's. Shortly after Newman left, an explosion and fire started in Hill's apartment and burned

her severely. It was allegedly caused by the negligence of the repairman. Was Newman a servant or an independent contractor? Is Grant Furniture Company liable for Newman's actions? (*Hill* v. *Newman,* 316 A.2d 8 [N.J. Super. 1973].)

3. The attendant at a service station fatally shot Mrs. Giles's son. Under the lease agreement and the dealer contract, the oil company did not have the right to control the day-to-day operations of the service station and its employees. It was not in the custom of exercising such control. Was the attendant an employee of the oil company? Should the oil company be held liable? (*Giles* v. *Shell Oil Corporation,* 487 A.2d 610 [D.C. App. 1985].)

4. The cable splicers established their own work schedules and hired their own employees. They were highly skilled specialists who provided their own tools and trucks. They did not need routine supervision. The splicers bid for the jobs on a flat sum and were paid each week for the work that had been satisfactorily completed. Twenty percent of the contract price was held back until the job was completed. The splicers did not work on the contractor's premises, and they could work for several contractors simultaneously. Were the cable splicers employees of the contractor and therefore covered by the state unemployment compensation law? (*D.O. Creasman Electronics, Inc.* v. *State Department of Labor,* 458 So.2d 894 [Fla. App. 1984].)

5. Personnel employed by an independent security agency committed intentional torts. The security agency had been hired by the owners of the property for the purpose of protecting their premises and their invitees. Under these circumstances should the owner be liable for the acts of the security personnel? (*Peachtree-Cain Co.* v. *McBee,* 327 S.E.2d 188 [Ga. 1985].)

6. Anthony hired Jo'Dee to excavate a swimming pool site. Jo'Dee did not have the necessary state license to do excavation work. Anthony exercised the right to control Jo'Dee's work. A truck owned by one of the partners of Jo'Dee and driven by Zaugg struck a motorcycle ridden by Foss. Zaugg, an employee of Jo'Dee, was returning to the construction site after dumping a load of debris from the excavation. Zaugg turned left across Foss's lane without signaling or seeing Foss. Foss was killed in the accident. The truck driver had been instructed not to drive the truck. Were Zaugg and Jo'Dee independent contractors of Anthony at the time of the accident? (*Foss* v. *Anthony Industries,* 189 Cal. Rptr. 31 [Cal. App. 1983].)

7. The Silvas wanted to sell a parcel of real estate, and they listed it for sale with Bisbee, who worked for Midkiff Realty. A joint venture was formed for the purpose of purchasing this property. Bisbee was to manage this joint venture and in exchange was to receive 10 percent of the profits. The buyers and sellers agreed on a purchase price of $100,000 and terms. The Silvas were never informed that the purchaser was part of a joint venture or that Bisbee had an interest in the joint venture. There was substantial evidence that Bisbee believed that the property was worth more than $100,000 at the time of the sale. Did Bisbee breach her fiduciary duty to the Silvas? (*Silva* v. *Bisbee,* 628 P.2d 214 [Haw. App. 1981].)

8. The Wilsons borrowed money from Household Finance Corporation (HFC). At the time of the loan HFC sold the Wilsons a group creditor's disability policy. HFC was a major beneficiary under the insurance. West Coast Life Insurance Company provided the insurance. Claims were supposed to be made through HFC. Mr. Wilson became permanently disabled and so notified HFC. West Coast Life Insurance failed to make the payments under the policy, so HFC brought legal action against the Wilsons in Small Claims Court for the unpaid payments. Did HFC owe a duty of good faith and fair dealing to the Wilsons? Did HFC breach its fiduciary duty to the Wilsons? (*Wilson* v. *Household Finance Corporation,* 182 Cal. Rptr. 590 [Cal. App. 1982].)

9. Kinmon contracted with J. P. King Auction Company (King) to sell some real estate. The auction contract did not state that a minimum price would be realized. It indicated that the property would be sold for the highest price obtainable. Kinmon told King that he expected to receive $103,500 for the property. The auctioneer indicated that the property would sell for its highest price on the date of sale. During the bidding, Kinmon went up to the auctioneer and stated that if the property brought less than $70,000, "I will take you to [the] Supreme Court." King went on with the auction and sold the property to the highest bidder for $35,000. Did Kinmon effectively revoke the agency relationship? (*Kinmon* v. *J. P. King Auction Company, Inc.,* 276 So.2d 569 [Ala. 1973].)

10. From 1953 until July, 1967, Geary worked as a sales representative for United States Steel Corporation (USS). Geary, an agent at will, sold tubular products to the oil and gas industry. USS designed a new product for use under high pressure. Geary believed that this new product had not been adequately tested and cre-

ated a serious danger to users. He voiced his concerns to his superiors and was told to sell the product. He then contacted the vice-president in charge of the product to get action. The product was withdrawn from the market. Geary was fired. Under the circumstances, was Geary entitled to protection from being fired? Should he be protected from being fired? (*Geary* v. *United States Steel Corporation,* 319 A.2d 174 [Pa. 1974].)

CHAPTER 34

Agency: Liability for Contracts

OUTLINE

A FRAMEWORK FOR CONTRACTUAL LIABILITY

An agent may have many and varied duties, which may include forming contracts for the principal. This chapter deals with the liability of the agent, the principal, and the third party for the proper performance of these contracts. In applying rules of law, the court often is influenced by the reasonable expectations of the third party; that is, how the third party perceives the situation. The distinction between servants and nonservants is not significant when the agent has entered into a contract; the courts will treat them the same. The distinction *is* significant if the agent commits a tort. Both classes of workers may enter into contracts for their principals. Since the distinction is irrelevant in contract cases, it is logical to use the term *agent* in this chapter. The prime issue for consideration is whether the principal authorized the agent to enter into the contract. Another important factor is whether the principal's identity is to be revealed to the third party. The principal then will be classified as a disclosed, an undisclosed, or a partially disclosed principal. The status of the principal in this regard is determined when the agent and the third party enter the contract; the legal relationships are fixed at that time.

IMPOSING LIABILITY ON THE PRINCIPAL

Regardless of the principal's classification, the principal will not be liable for every act committed by his or her agent or for every contract signed by the agent. To determine whether the principal should be held liable, the court will examine whether the agent was authorized to enter into this type of contract. Authority can be established in a number of different ways, normally referred to as types of authority, and often they overlap in a given situation. The types of authority are summarized in Figure 34.1 and discussed in detail on the following pages.

For the third party to recover a judgment against the principal, all that needs to be shown is that *one* type of authority exists. Generally, authority to act as an agent includes authority to act only for the benefit, not the detriment, of the principal.

Express Authority
Express authority occurs when *the principal informs the agent that the agent has authority to engage in a specific act or to do a particular task*. Generally, express authority need not be in writing, and in most cases it is not. For example, a principal may say to her secretary, "Please order more stationery." Courts often strictly construe the words the principal uses when giving the authority. If the principal says to the agent, "Locate premises for another card shop," usually the court will interpret this to mean that the agent is authorized only to *find* the premises and not actually to purchase the store. Therefore,

FIGURE 34.1   Rights of a Third Party to Sue a Principal

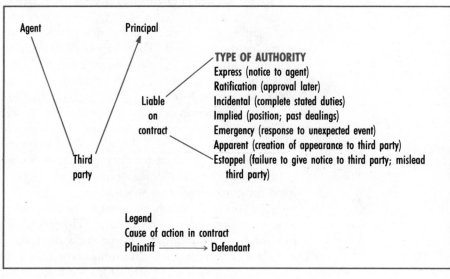

an agent should interpret the instructions narrowly or ask for clarification of the scope of authority involved.

Ratification Authority

Ratification authority occurs when *the agent does something that was unauthorized at the time, and the principal approves it later*. It is approval by the principal after the contract was formed by the agent and after the principal has knowledge of the material facts.

When a principal ratifies a contract, the principal must ratify the whole agreement. The principal cannot elect to ratify parts of the contract and disregard the less advantageous parts.

The principal does not need to communicate the ratification verbally to anyone.[1] Generally, ratification may occur by an express statement or may be implied by the principal's clear indication through his or her conduct of an intent to affirm. An example of the latter would be if the principal retained and used goods delivered under an agreement after learning of the contract and its terms. Another example would be if the principal initiated a lawsuit to enforce the agreement. The ratification needs to follow the same form that the original authorization would have required. In a limited number of situations, the ratification will have to be in writing. If the agent–third-party contract must be in writing under the Statute of Frauds, then the ratification must be written too.

Courts have imposed additional limitations on the doctrine of ratification.

[1]*Restatement (Second) of Agency* (Philadelphia: American Law Institute, 1958), Section 97.

Both the principal and the agent must have been capable of forming a contract when the original contract occurred *and* when it was ratified. This relation-back doctrine is applied to ratified contracts. It states that if the contract is properly ratified, it is as if the contract were valid the whole time. Modern courts will not apply this doctrine if it would harm an innocent party who obtained rights in the contract between the time of the original contract formation and the ratification.

Ratification cannot occur if important contract terms are concealed from the principal. Ratification will be effective only if the principal knows all the relevant facts. Also, the agent must have **purported** to act for the principal when the agent entered into the contract. If the agent did not reveal his or her agency capacity or if the agent was working for an undisclosed principal, there can be no ratification.

Purported   Gave the impression that; reputed.

Incidental Authority

Incidental authority reasonably and necessarily arises in order to enable the agent to complete his or her assigned duties. Suppose an agent is provided with merchandise that is to be sold door to door. The agent will reasonably and necessarily have incidental authority to deliver the merchandise and to collect the purchase price. Another example would be a builder who is hired as an on-site supervisor for a construction job. To complete the job, the supervisor would have incidental authority to hire, fire, and direct other employees on the site. No one realistically expects the supervisor to construct the building alone. The supervisor also would have incidental authority to purchase supplies.

Although in its reasoning the court in the following case referred to authority, which may be "implied" from the facts, the case really centered on the issue of incidental authority.

St. Ann's Home for the Aged v. Daniels
420 N.E.2d 478 (Ill. App. 1981)

FACTS   Daniels arranged to have his mother hospitalized in 1977. When she was ready to be released, Dr. Smith, the physician in charge of the case, told Daniels that his mother should not return to her own apartment. Dr. Smith suggested that she be placed in St. Ann's and said that he could arrange this. Daniels agreed. Dr. Smith was a neighbor of the Danielses as well as their family physician. When Daniels returned from a business trip, he found that his mother had been admitted to St. Ann's, and he indicated that this arrangement was satisfactory.

ISSUE   Did Dr. Smith have authority to bind Daniels to pay for his mother's care?

HOLDING   Yes. He did have this authority.

REASONING   Dr. Smith was acting as Daniels's agent. An agency relationship does not depend only on an express statement, it may also be implied from the facts. It may be shown by reference to the situation of the parties, their acts, and other relevant circumstances. Daniels admitted that he had told Dr. Smith to go ahead and make the arrangements to have his mother placed in St. Ann's. Daniels did not have to expressly say that he would be responsible for the costs. A principal is bound by the acts he or she expressly authorizes the agent to do. A principal is also bound by the agent's normal acts that are necessary to complete performance.

Implied Authority

Implied authority is based on the agent's position or on past dealings between the agent and the third party. One type of implied authority arises when an agent is given a title and a position. It will be implied that the agent can enter into the same types of contracts that people with this title normally can. A vice-president of sales and marketing will have implied authority to purchase advertising in newspapers and on radio and to contract with an advertising agency for a new ad campaign. The agent will have this authority because *most* vice-presidents of sales and marketing have such authority. It is customary. When the principal gave the agent the title, the agent received the implied power that goes with it.

Implied authority may exist because of a series of similar dealings in the past between the agent and the third party. If the principal did not object to the past transactions, it is assumed that the principal authorized the earlier contracts and that this type of transaction is within the agent's power. For example, if a secretary customarily orders office supplies for a business on a monthly basis, the secretary has implied authority to continue to order office supplies in this manner.

Implied authority may exceed actual expressed authority. If the third party reasonably believed that the agent had this particular authority and was unaware that it was lacking, the third party can recover on the basis of this implied authority.

Emergency Authority

Emergency authority is inherent in all agency relationships. It need not be expressed. *It provides the agent with authority to respond to emergencies even though the principal and agent never discussed the type of emergency or how to respond to it.* Suppose the owner of a jewelry shop leaves his manager in charge and goes out for supper. While the owner is absent, a fire starts in the stock room. In an effort to contain the fire, the manager rushes to the hardware store next door and charges four fire extinguishers. The principal—the owner—will have to pay for the fire extinguishers. The manager had emergency authority to purchase them.

Emergency authority will be found when all the following circumstances exist:

1. when an emergency or unexpected situation occurs that requires prompt action

2. when the principal cannot be reached in sufficient time for a response or advice

3. when the action taken by the agent was reasonable in that situation and it was *expected* to benefit the principal

Apparent Authority   *Apparent authority* occurs when *the principal creates the appearance that an agency exists or that the agent has broader powers than he or she actually has.* Here, the representation of authority is made to the third party rather than to the agent.[2] Apparent authority is based on the conduct of the principal; the conduct must cause a reasonable third party to believe that a particular person has authority to act as the principal's agent. An agent with apparent authority may or may not have actual authority.

Apparent authority may be created by intentional or careless acts of the principal and reasonable reliance by the third party. Obviously, if the third party knew the agent did not have this authority, the reliance would not be reasonable.

In some cases, apparent authority exists even though there is no real agent. The person acting in the agent's role may be considered a "purported agent" (that is, one who claims to be an agent). Sometimes this purported agent is an agent who has been terminated, and sometimes the person never was an agent. For example, suppose a company fires a sales representative but neglects to collect its samples, displays, and order forms from the representative. The ex-representative then takes a number of customer orders and disappears with the cash deposits. The company will have to return the deposits or credit the deposits to the customers' orders, because the ex-representative still had apparent authority to take orders. To prevent this situation, the company should have required the ex-representative to return all its sales materials.

When an agency relationship is terminated, a principal should take certain steps to terminate apparent authority. The principal should inform the agent that the relationship is terminated, call or send notices to people who have dealt with that agent, and sometimes advertise in newspapers and journals that the relationship is terminated. The principal should collect all identification tags, samples, displays, order forms, and any other materials that could be used as evidence of the agency's relationship.

Sometimes the purported agent never was employed by the principal, and yet the principal's conduct may cause the principal to be liable for the "agent's" actions. For example, a large and often understaffed department store does not require its clerks to wear identifying jackets or vests or even name tags. A customer selects some merchandise and walks toward a cash register. Another customer steps behind the cash register, rings up the sale, puts the merchandise in the bag, and pockets the payment. The store cannot charge the customer again for the merchandise. It is bound by the acts of the purported agent.

Before they apply apparent authority, some courts require that the principal's actions give rise to a reasonable belief in the agent's authority and that there be detrimental reliance on the part of the third party.[3] A number of

[2]Warren A. Seavey, *Handbook of the Law of Agency* (St. Paul, Minn.: West, 1964), Section 8D, p. 19.
[3]*General Overseas Films, Ltd.* v. *Robin International, Inc.*, 542 F. Supp. 684 (S.D. N.Y. 1982), p. 688, fn. 2.

factors need to be considered, but the existence of apparent authority is a factual issue to be determined in each case.

A third party must act reasonably or the court will not apply the concept of apparent authority. The third party must take into consideration the facts and circumstances surrounding the transaction and the type of authority involved. Sometimes, based on the information available, the third party must investigate further before reasonably relying on apparent authority. In the following case, the court examined the reasonableness of the third party's behavior. The transactions in this case are diagramed in Figure 34.2.

General Overseas Films, Ltd. v. *Robin International, Inc.*
542 F. Supp. 684 (S.D. N.Y. 1982)

FACTS   General Overseas Films, Ltd. (GOF), acting through Robert Haggiag, agreed to lend $500,000 to Robin International, Inc. (Robin). Robin was owned and controlled by Nicholas Reisini. Reisini asked whether Haggiag would extent the payment dates if Reisini could provide a guarantee from Anaconda. Reisini introduced Haggiag to Charles Kraft, vice-president and treasurer of Anaconda. Kraft told Haggiag that Anaconda would guarantee Robin's debt to GOF up to the amount of $1 million. After some partial payments and numerous extensions, Robin was unable to pay off and GOF filed suit on the guarantee.

ISSUE   Did Kraft have the authority to bind Anaconda on the loan guarantee?

HOLDING   No. Kraft did not have such authority.

REASONING   Kraft did not have express authority to guarantee a loan. Article 9 of Anaconda's by-laws authorized the treasurer to borrow money for Anaconda; it did not authorize the treasurer to guarantee loans to another corporation. Moreover, Kraft did not have apparent authority to guarantee a loan. Guaranteeing a loan made to another corporation is an extraordinary power and is not normally inferred from an agency relationship. Usually it must be specifically stated, especially in a case such as this one, where there was no logical business connection between Anaconda, Robin, and the loan. Apparent authority is based on the principal's action or inaction that allows the

FIGURE 34.2   Legal Relationships in *General Overseas Films, Ltd.* v. *Robin International, Inc.*

Note: The numbers in circles indicate the order of events.

agent to mislead others. Article 9 of Anaconda's by-laws did not manifest the authority to guarantee the debt of another corporation, and Anaconda did not clothe Kraft with this type of authority. Haggiag did not exercise due care in relying on the guarantee. He should have realized that Anaconda's guarantee was unusual, and he should have required additional information about Anaconda and Robin's business relationship and about Kraft's authority to make the guarantee. Haggiag knew that his bank would not accept Kraft's guarantee without additional proof of Kraft's authority. A third party who deals with an agent must make a reasonable effort to discover the actual scope of authority. Haggiag did not.

Apparent authority may be used to hold a principal liable on contracts entered into by the agent. It *ordinarily* will not be used to make a principal liable for physical harm caused by the agent through negligence, assault, trespass, and similar torts.

Authority by Estoppel

Authority by estoppel prevents a principal who has misled a third party from denying the agent's authority. It is also called ostensible authority. It occurs when the principal *allows* the purported agent to pass himself or herself off as an agent and does not take steps to prevent the purported agent's representation.

Estoppel authority may occur by itself or in conjunction with other types of authority. When there is only estoppel authority and no other authority, it will be used solely for the protection of the third party. It will not constitute the basis of a successful lawsuit by the principal against the third party. It creates rights for the third party and liabilities for the principal. It protects the third party and allows the third party reimbursement for injuries. As with other doctrines of agency law, the courts are weighing the respective rights of two relatively innocent people—the third party and the principal. The purported agent could be sued for fraud, but generally that person cannot be located or has insufficient funds to cover the losses caused.

Authority by estoppel, symbolized in Figure 34.3, is illustrated in the following example.

FIGURE 34.3 Authority by Estoppel

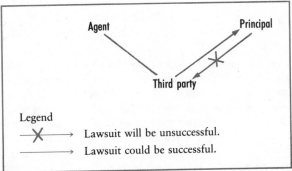

Roy was walking to class one Wednesday when he passed Grace and David, who were standing next to Roy's car. He overheard Grace pointing out all the car's features to David. It was evident that Grace was trying to sell the car to David on Roy's behalf. Roy thought this amusing and did not stop to clarify the situation. He went to class instead. He later learned that David made a $200 down payment on the car and that Grace disappeared with the money.

In a lawsuit between David and Roy, David would prevail. The court would apply agency by estoppel and decide that Roy is estopped (prevented) from denying that Grace was his agent. Roy knew that Grace was representing herself as Roy's agent, and Roy easily could have denied this. Roy's failure to speak helped to cause David's loss. The court would protect David from a loss by allowing him to recover.

Imputing the Agent's Knowledge to the Principal

In addition to being liable for contracts entered into by an agent, a principal may be legally responsible for information known to the agent but not actually known by the principal. This concept is called *imputing knowledge*. Because an agent has a duty to inform the principal about important facts that relate to the agency, it will be assumed that the agent has performed this duty. If the agent fails to perform this duty and the failure causes a loss, the principal—not the third party—should suffer the loss. Courts justify this result because the principal selected the agent, placed the agent in a position of authority, and had (legal) control over the agent.

The agent's knowledge is not always imputed to the principal. Before a principal will be bound by knowledge received by the agent, generally the agent must have actual or apparent authority to receive this type of knowledge. In addition, the information received by the agent must relate to the subject matter of the agency. For example, if the principal owns a real estate firm, a movie theater, and a hardware store, and the agent works in the hardware store, knowledge that the agent obtains about the real estate firm will not be imputed to the principal. The knowledge must be within the scope of the agency. The court examined this issue in the following case.

Ford Motor Credit Company v. Weaver
680 F.2d 451 (6th Cir. 1982)

FACTS   Weaver Farms purchased two Ford tractors and other farm equipment from Cleveland Ford Tractor (CFT), Inc. on an installment sale. One provision of the installment sale contract was that the contract would be assigned to Ford Motor Credit Company (FMCC), and it was. CFT and FMCC have the same parent corporation. FMCC frequently purchases commercial paper from CFT. FMCC has the right of first refusal on commercial paper that CFT creates, and customers leave contracts and payments at CFT for FMCC. Weaver Farms filed a petition for a Chapter 11 bankruptcy. FMCC was listed as a creditor, but its bankruptcy notice was delivered to CFT.

ISSUE   Should notice delivered to CFT be imputed to FMCC?

HOLDING   No, it should not.

REASONING   Notice or knowledge of an agent may be imputed to the principal in certain situations. It is imputed when the agent acquired the notice or knowledge while acting within the scope of his or her authority and when the knowledge pertains to matters within the scope of that authority. Just because an agent can collect payments for another, it does not follow that the agent can accept legal notice. This general rule is applicable in bankruptcy cases. CFT did not have actual or implied authority to collect the outstanding balance, receive legal notices for FMCC, or represent FMCC in any bankruptcy proceeding. CFT could act as a repository and accept individual payments, but that is a different type of authority. There was no apparent authority to accept legal notice in this case.

DISCLOSED PRINCIPAL

When an agent clearly discloses that he or she is representing a principal and identifies the principal, the principal is *disclosed*. In these situations, the principal may be bound to the contract by any of the types of authority that have been discussed.

Liability of the Agent

Normally when an agent indicates that he or she is entering into a contract on behalf of the disclosed principal, the agent will not be liable on the contract. It is clearly understood that the third party should look to the principal alone for performance. As with most legal rules, there are exceptions. Here are the most common exceptions. If the agent fails to represent his capacity as such, the agent will be personally bound. In addition the agent will be bound if he intended to be bound. For example, the agent may say, "You can rely on me," or "You have my word on it." Why would an agent want to be liable on the principal's contract? Why would an agent want to undertake additional liability? An agent might do this if it is necessary to make a sale. The prospective buyer may be unsure about the principal and her reputation or financial backing. Perhaps the prospect has a long working relationship with the agent, so the prospect is persuaded by the agent's guarantee of performance. The agent doesn't really have valid grounds to complain if he is accepted at his word. The third party generally would prefer to sue the principal on the contract instead of the agent since the principal often has more assets.

The third party, then, has legal rights against both the agent and the disclosed principal. This does not mean that the third party can collect twice. The third party must make an *election* to sue either the agent *or* the principal. Obviously, an important factor in this decision is who has the funds to pay a judgment. If the third party sues the principal and loses, she will be barred from then suing the agent. The reverse is also true. The act of filing a suit against one is considered an election.

Warranty of Authority   Whenever an agent of a disclosed principal enters into a contract, the agent makes all of the following implied warranties. These warranties are not stated by the agent; they are implied by the situation.

1. The disclosed principal exists and is competent.
2. The agent is an agent for the principal.
3. The agent is authorized to enter into this type of contract for the principal.

The third party can sue the agent to recover for losses that were caused by the breach of warranty of authority. Perhaps the third party had losses because she did not receive the goods that were covered by the contract. Further, suppose the principal is not responsible for the losses because the agent was not authorized to enter into this type of contract. The third party can sue the agent.

If the agent fears that he does not have the authority to enter into this type of contract, he may be concerned about the warranties of authority. He would be wise, then, to negate the warranties. This can be accomplished by stating that there is no warranty or by specifically stating to the third party the limitations on the agent's actual authority. The latter condition is illustrated in the following example.

Rhoda hires Beth as an agent and tells her to locate a parcel of agricultural real estate. Beth locates a parcel that meets Rhoda's specifications. The owner of the parcel wants Beth to sign the purchase contract, but Beth is not sure whether she has authority to sign. If she fully and truthfully discloses the situation surrounding her authority, Beth would negate the *implied* warranty of authority. If the owner still wished to sign the contract with Beth, the owner would assume the responsibility and the loss if the contract were not authorized. Here the owner would be relying on his own judgment.

The agent may be liable for fraud if he intentionally misrepresents his authority. The agent's liability is shown in Figure 34.4.

Liability of the Third Party   *Lawsuit by the Principal*   When a principal has been disclosed from the beginning, the third party realizes, or should realize, that the principal has an interest in the contract. The principal can successfully sue the third party on the contract if the agent was authorized to enter into this type of contract for the principal. In other words, the third party will be liable if there is express, implied, incidental, emergency, apparent, or ratification authority. The third party will not be liable if the only type of authority is estoppel authority.

FIGURE 34.4   Rights of a Third Party to Sue an Agent of a Disclosed Principal

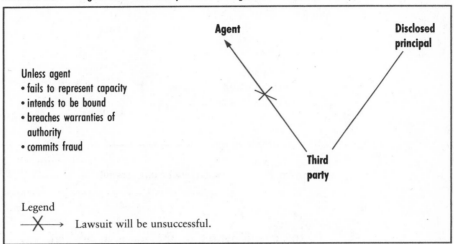

Unless agent
• fails to represent capacity
• intends to be bound
• breaches warranties of
  authority
• commits fraud

Agent

Disclosed principal

Third party

Legend

——X——➤   Lawsuit will be unsuccessful.

Lawsuit by the Agent   Normally the agent has no right to sue the third party on a contract. An agent *may* successfully sue the third party if the agent can show that she has an interest in the contract. The most common type of interest would be one in which the agent was entitled to a commission on a sale. For example, a real estate broker (the agent) entered into a contract on behalf of a homeowner (the principal). The agent was entitled to a 6 percent commission payable from the proceeds of the sale. The buyer (the third party) breached the contract. The agent could sue to recover the lost commission. (In this type of case, the principal may decide that it is not worth suing, but the agent may feel that it is.)

An agent may successfully sue the third party when the agent intended to be bound. This rule is based on equitable principles. If the agent is liable to the third party, the third party should be liable to the agent, too. In some cases, a principal may assign to the agent the right to file the lawsuit. In these cases, also, the agent could sue on the contract. These relationships are illustrated in Figure 34.5.

UNDISCLOSED PRINCIPAL

An *undisclosed* principal is one whose existence and identity are unknown to the third party. There are many reasons why a principal would want to be undisclosed—to negotiate a better deal or simply to negotiate a deal, or to conceal an investment in a project or a donation to a charity. For example, Thomas, a politician, wants to invest in a racetrack. He is aware that race-

FIGURE 34.5   Rights of an Agent of a Disclosed Principal to Sue a Third Party

Agent

Disclosed
principal

Unless agent
• has an interest
• intends to be bound

Third
party

Legend
————X——→   Lawsuit will be unsuccessful.

tracks and betting on the horses have an unsavory reputation, so he hires an agent to negotiate the investment for him. Thomas buys the investment through his agent and thus remains anonymous.

Liability of the Agent

When the principal is completely undisclosed, the third party believes that she is contracting with the agent and that the agent is dealing for himself. Based on her knowledge, that assumption is reasonable. If there is a default on the contract, the third party can sue the agent. As far as the third party is concerned, there were only two parties to the contract: The third party and the agent. The court dealt with such an issue in the case that follows.

Murphy v. Dell Corporation
440 A.2d 223 (Conn. 1981)

FACTS   DeLisa, an agent for Dell Corporation, entered into a contract with Murphy. There was conflicting testimony over whether DeLisa indicated his role as Dell Corporation's agent. The lawsuit originally was filed against Dell Corporation and DeLisa. Murphy withdrew the complaint against Dell Corporation.

ISSUE   Is DeLisa personally liable for the balance due on the contract?

HOLDING   Yes. He is personally liable.

REASONING   The trial court concluded that Murphy did not "notice" that the contract was with Dell Corporation and that DeLisa failed to disclose his representative capacity. "The law is settled that where an agent contracts in his own name, without disclosing his representative capacity, the agent is personally liable on the contract." The trial court decided the questions of fact in favor of Murphy. Their decision must be upheld unless it is clearly erroneous.

Liability of the Principal

If the third party later discovers the identity of the principal, the third party can sue the principal. The principal will be held liable if the agent was authorized to enter into this type of contract for the principal. The third party must make an *election* to sue either the agent *or* the principal. There is one exception, and that is if the third party sues the agent and loses *before* discovering the principal. In that case, the third party is not considered to have made an election and will be permitted to sue the principal later.

Liability of the Third Party

The third party may not be the one who suffers damages because of a breach of contract but may, in fact, be the one who committed the breach. Since the third party thought he was liable to the agent, it is reasonable to allow the agent to sue him. The law allows this action.

Under some circumstances, the undisclosed principal may, in her own name, also be able to sue the third party. There are some limitations, however. The principal can file a lawsuit by herself only if the contract is assignable. (See Chapter 15 for a discussion of assignable contracts.) If it is assignable, the position of the third party would not be jeopardized by either the assignment or the suit by the principal. The agent could assign the contract to someone else, so the agent should be able to "transfer" the contract rights to the principal. This relationship is shown in Figure 34.6. The third party will have to pay for the damages only once.

Assignable Capable of being transferred legally.

The principal may not be able to sue in her own name because the contract is not assignable, or the principal may still wish to keep her identity secret. Then the principal can arrange for her agent to file the lawsuit in the agent's name.

FIGURE 34.6 Rights of an Undisclosed Principal

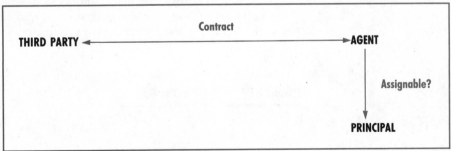

PARTIALLY DISCLOSED PRINCIPAL

A *partially disclosed principal* is one whose existence is known to the third party but whose identity is not. In other words, the agency is disclosed, but the principal is undisclosed. An example would be Robert Smith's signing a contract as "Robert Smith, agent." The rules that are applied to partially disclosed principals are similar to those applied to undisclosed principals. The principal may be sued if the contract is breached, and the suit will be successful if the principal authorized the actions of the agent. Once again, the third party must make an election whether to sue the principal or the agent. If the principal suffers damages, he can sue the third party. The contract need not be assignable because the third party knew that another party in interest was involved.

The general rule is that when an agent is working for a partially disclosed principal, the agent will be personally liable on the contract. The third party is probably relying on the agent's reputation and credit. It is unlikely that the third person is relying on the reputation and credit of the unrevealed principal. The exception would be if the contracting parties agreed that the agent would not be held liable. This may occur if the agent indicated that he or she would not be bound and the third person did not object to this limitation.

CONTRACT BETWEEN THE PRINCIPAL AND THE AGENT

The Need for a Writing

The agency relationship is consensual in nature. It actually will be a contract if the principal and agent both give up consideration, which is generally the case. As with other contracts, the Statute of Frauds may apply and require written evidence of the contract. The provisions of the Statute of Frauds that are most likely to be applicable are those relating to contracts that cannot possibly be performed within one year and contracts involving the sale of real estate. Even if the Statute of Frauds does not apply, it is wise to write the contractual provisions.

The equal dignities rule also requires that some agency agreements be in writing. This rule states that the agent-principal contract deserves (requires) the same dignity as the agent–third-party contract, as shown in Figure 34.7:

FIGURE 34.7   Equal Dignities Rule

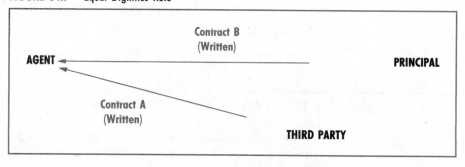

If contract A must be written, then contract B must be written. For example, if the agent is hired to locate and purchase goods costing over $500, the UCC Statute of Frauds requires that the agent–third-party contract also be in writing so the principal-agent contract should also be in writing.

Covenants Not to Compete

Some employment contracts contain *covenants* (promises) that the agent will not work for a competing firm. It may provide that (1) the agent will not "moonlight" with the competition or (2) the agent will not compete with the principal after this employment relationship is terminated. Some contracts do both. The second provision is usually applicable if the agent either quits or is fired. It commonly specifies a time period for which the competition is to be restricted and the area in which the competition is not allowed. For example, "If this employment is terminated by the employee or the employer, then the employee shall not establish or obtain employment with another cable television company in Chicago, Illinois." This restriction may seem harsh if the agent's skills are valuable only to a cable television company.

There are competing legal considerations in disputes about these covenants. On the one hand, the agent did agree not to compete. Perhaps he was desperate for the position and felt that he would not get it without signing the covenant. The agent may not have had equal bargaining power with the principal. Generally, parties *are* bound by their contract provisions. On the other hand, it would be a hardship on the agent to unduly restrict his ability to locate another job. In addition, it would be detrimental to society if people were not allowed to seek the positions for which they are most highly qualified. For these reasons, courts scrutinize covenants not to compete to determine whether the covenant is legal. Courts do not favor covenants not to compete. The covenant will be illegal if the court concludes that it is against public policy.

To determine whether the covenant is against public policy, the court will examine its reasonableness. It will look at the situation surrounding the employment to see whether the principal has a legitimate interest in preventing the competition.

Covenants not to compete are also prevalent in contracts in which the owner of a business sells the business to a buyer and the buyer obtains a promise that the previous owner will not compete with her. In such cases, the buyer has an interest in not having competition from the seller. Generally, the buyer pays a larger purchase price so that the seller will sell the **goodwill** of the business *and* sign a covenant not to compete with the buyer. Courts are more inclined to enforce covenants not to compete in these contexts.

There are additional requirements for a valid covenant not to compete. The time and area specifications of the covenant must be reasonable. What is reasonable depends on the type of employment. Covenants containing time periods of two to five years are generally acceptable to the courts. The limitation is really the time period during which the agent would be able to draw

Goodwill The good name and reputation of a business and thereby the ability to attract clients.

contacts away from the principal or the time period in which these contacts would still have value. For example, suppose a dentist who just graduated went to work for a dental partnership. He agreed to sign a covenant not to compete when he accepted the position. After he left the partnership, how long would he have to leave the community before most of his former patients would find a new dentist? Would two weeks be too short? Would three years be too long? (The answer would be affected to some extent by the type of dental practice the partnership had.)

The covenant also must be reasonable in the area specified. The standard is: If the agent moved, how far could she still attract the contacts? The answer will depend on the field of the agent's expertise. For example, a patient might travel halfway across the country to see a world-famous heart transplant specialist, but many patients will not even go across town to see a general practitioner.

If the principal has a legitimate business interest and the covenant is reasonable, the principal could sue the breaching agent or former agent for an injunction or contract damages. However, a principal may structure a covenant not to compete that is too broad. The courts apply one of two approaches in such cases. One is to declare the covenant void and to ignore it. The agent then can do whatever he wishes with impunity. A less common approach is for the court to reform (modify) the contract to make its restrictions reasonable.

Courts may examine the following criteria in determining whether to enforce a covenant not to compete in an employment contract:

1. Is the restraint reasonable in the amount of protection it affords, or is it excessive?

2. Is the restraint unreasonable because it is unduly harsh on the agent?

3. If the agent worked for a competitor, would that threaten irreparable injury to the principal?

4. Is the agency relationship of a unique and unusual type?

Some state statutes hold that a principal cannot prevent an ordinary employee from engaging in competition once the employment is over.[4] (Covenants not to compete are also discussed in Chapter 12.)

A covenant not to compete is not required in order to prevent an agent from divulging trade secrets or customer lists after the employment is terminated. Under common law, this behavior is a violation of the agent's duties of loyalty.

The following case dealt with the issue of a covenant not to compete.

---

[4]See, for example, California Business and Professions Code, Section 16600.

Holiday Food Co., Inc. v. *Munroe*
426 A.2d 814 (Conn. Super. 1981)

FACTS Munroe worked as a salesperson for Holiday Food, a company that sold and delivered frozen foods. Munroe never examined or used the customer list that the company made available to its sales staff. His supervisor provided him with the names and addresses of contacts, which he kept in a personal notebook. During his employment with Holiday Food, Munroe expressly refused to sign a covenant not to compete. When he left to start a competing frozen-food business, Munroe took his notebook with him and started to call on his old contacts.

ISSUE Did Munroe violate his duties when he solicited orders from his old customers?

HOLDING No. Munroe did not violate his duties to Holiday Food.

REASONING Unless the name of a customer is a trade secret, former employees can contact customers who used to order from them. A trade secret may include any formula, device, pattern, or compilation of information that people use to get an edge over their competitors. Unless there is a covenant not to compete, agents may compete with principals after the agency is terminated. They may not use trade secrets revealed to them or surreptitiously discovered by them. Customer lists may or may not be trade secrets, depending on the facts of a particular case. Courts may examine the extent to which the employee-employer relationship was a confidential one, how the employee acquired the information, the former employee's personal relationship with the customers, and the unfair advantage obtained by the former employee. An appellate court should not overturn a trial court's decision unless it is clearly erroneous. The trial court's decision that the customer list was not a trade secret was upheld in this case.

SUMMARY

A disclosed principal is one whose identity and existence are known to the third party. A partially disclosed principal is one whose existence is known but whose identity is not. When the principal is undisclosed, the third party thinks he is dealing only with the agent. In the last case, the agent will be bound on the contract because the agent is a "party" to it. The type of principal affects the rights and obligations of the agent, the principal, and the third party.

When the principal has been disclosed, the principal can sue and be sued on the contract if there is express, implied, incidental, emergency, apparent, or ratification authority. These types of authority often overlap. If only authority by estoppel exists, it will be applied to protect a third party but not to protect the principal. Information received by the agent in the course and scope of the job generally will be imputed to the principal. Usually the agent of a disclosed principal will not be bound on the contract itself, but the agent may be responsible for breach of warranty of authority. The third party will be liable to the principal on the contract and to the agent if the agent had an interest or intended to be bound. In situations of undisclosed or partially disclosed principals, the agent will be held liable.

The agency agreement must be in writing if this is required by either the Statute of Frauds or the equal dignities rule. Covenants not to compete may be valid if the principal has a legitimate interest in preventing the competition, provided that the limitation is reasonable in the length of time and the area specified.

DISCUSSION QUESTIONS

1. What is a partially disclosed principal? How might partial disclosure occur?

2. Ted farmed 200 acres of grapes. His neighbor had an additional 100 acres of grapes, which were for sale. Since Ted and his neighbor had been feuding for twelve years, the neighbor would not sell the land to Ted. Ted hired Rose to act as his agent without revealing Ted's identity. Rose bought the land and started to transfer it to Ted. The neighbor tried to stop the transfer. What would be the legal rights of the parties in this situation?

3. How do the rights and liabilities of an agent to a partially disclosed principal differ from those of an agent to an undisclosed principal?

4. Sally, a secretary, ordered four reams of erasable typing paper and had it delivered to her home. Sally had the bill sent to her employer. Based on the information provided, did Sally have authority to do this? Why or why not? What additional information would be helpful? Why?

5. What is the difference between implied authority and implied ratification?

6. Besides collecting samples, displays, and order forms, what else should a principal do to terminate the apparent authority of an agent?

7. Bonnie was buying a house through Angie, who was a real estate agent. Angie recommended that they have an appliance inspector examine the house before the sale was completed. Angie made the arrangements. Joe, the inspector, said that all the major appliances were in proper working order. The sales transaction was completed, and Bonnie is now living in the house. Joe has not been paid yet. By whom is he entitled to be paid? Why?

8. Why are warranties of authority applicable only when there is a disclosed principal?

9. Would it be reasonable if a fast-food chain required all new employees to sign an agreement that they would not work for another fast-food restaurant for six months after leaving the chain? Would it be legal? Could an ex-employee legally reveal the recipe for the chain's special blend of eleven herbs and spices? Why or why not?

10. Lisa had some charges on her telephone bill that she did not understand. The bill stated that billing inquiries should be made by calling (412) 312-2941. She called the number and spoke with Janet. Janet said that she would remove the charges. The charges have not been removed. Is Lisa entitled to have them removed? Do you think Janet had authority for her statement? Why or why not?

CASE PROBLEMS

1. Taylor, a district manager for Pargas, Inc., diverted checks into his personal account at Rapides Bank. The payee on these checks was his employer. He endorsed the checks with a rubber stamp that had Pargas's name and address on it. Rapides Bank never obtained a corporation resolution authorizing Taylor to endorse the checks. There was no authorization for Taylor to deposit these checks to his personal account. Should Rapides Bank or Pargas suffer the loss? (*Pargas, Inc.* v. *Estate of Taylor,* 416 So.2d 1358 [La. App. 1982].)

2. Horowytz opened a checking account with Bank of America. The account documents indicated that Ho-

rowytz was doing business under the trade name of E.D.S. The signature card indicated that J. Pearl, Horowytz's father, had power of attorney. The card stated that Pearl had authority to sign and endorse checks, notes, and drafts and transact all business with the bank. It did not specifically state that Pearl had authority to borrow money on Horowytz's credit. Did Pearl have authority to borrow money that Horowytz would have to repay? (*Bank of America, National Trust and Savings Association* v. *Horowytz,* 248 A.2d 446 [N.J. County Ct. 1968].)

3. Hill purchased some furniture from Grant's. The furniture was defective, so Hill contacted the seller, who assured her that they would send someone to repair the furniture. The repairman, Newman, identified himself as being from Grant's. Shortly after Newman left, an explosion and fire started in Hill's apartment and burned her severely. It was allegedly caused by the negligence of the repairman. Did Newman have apparent authority? Was he an apparent agent for Grant's? Is Grant Furniture Company liable for Newman's actions? (*Hill* v. *Newman,* 316 A.2d 8 [N.J. Super. 1973].)

4. The defendant owned two farms and hired Berry to operate them. Berry and his family lived in the house on the main farm. In 1953, Berry asked the plaintiff to bale the hay "on the hill." Plaintiff did so and then made out a bill for the defendant. This bill was paid about a month later. In 1954, Berry asked the plaintiff if he would "bale the hay on the hill the same as last year." The plaintiff baled the hay and presented the bill as he had done before. When the defendant returned from a trip, he refused to pay. The defendant claimed that he was leasing the farms to Berry in 1954 and selling some of the crops and livestock to him. Thus, Berry was the owner of the hay in 1954. The defendant did not give the plaintiff any notice that there was a new business arrangement with Berry; there was no apparent change in the operation of the farm. Should the defendant be liable to the plaintiff for the bill? (*Record* v. *Wagner,* 128 A.2d 921 [N.H. 1957].)

5. Walker left his trailer at the Pacific Mobile Homes, Inc. lot to be sold on consignment. Walker dealt with Robert Stewart, who was seen on the lot on numerous occasions. There was a sign on the lot that indicated that the whole business was an enterprise of Pacific Mobile Homes, Inc. Stewart used the principal's forms and stationery to write up a consignment agreement. Stewart seemed to be the only person present on the lot and seemed to be in control of the office. Later, Henderson

telephoned Walker in Oregon and asked him if he had left his trailer on consignment. Henderson explained that Stewart was no longer at Pacific Mobile Homes and that Henderson was now the manager. He informed Walker that the trailer had been sold. Walker received a few payments, and Henderson absconded with the rest of the funds. Shelly, president of Pacific Mobile Homes, testified that neither salesman had authority to complete a sale; Shelly had to sign all sales documents. Shelly said that his company forbade its salesmen to take trailers on consignment and that he did not know anything about Walker's trailer. Would a reasonable person assume that Stewart and Henderson had authority from the mobile home company to buy, sell, and deliver trailers for cash, on credit, consignment, or in exchange? (*Walker* v. *Pacific Mobile Homes, Inc.,* 413 P.2d 3 [Wash. 1966].)

6. Morrow was planning a business trip to Honduras in a private plane and wanted flight insurance. He discussed the matter with Bennett, who was the attendant at the insurance counter in the airport and who sold insurance from a number of different companies. Bennett selected an insurance policy for Morrow and completed the application. In the space provided for flight information, Bennett wrote "private air." The printed policy stated that it covered only travel on an aircraft operated by a scheduled air carrier. It also stated that the insurance agent could not vary the terms of the policy. Morrow died when the private plane crashed. Did Bennett have implied or apparent authority to issue insurance coverage to Morrow? Why or why not? (*Travelers Insurance Company* v. *Morrow,* 645 F.2d 41 [10th Cir. 1981].)

7. Cecka instructed the account representatives to sell short seven contracts for April cattle. He told them to sell out the contracts before any loss occurred in excess of $2100. He then told them to buy seven contracts of April cattle and "to maintain my same relative position" by selling short contracts for October cattle. A cattle contract is the trading unit used on the Chicago Mercantile Exchange; cattle are traded on a "contract basis," not by total poundage; a "contract" represents a standard poundage that is set by the Chicago Mercantile Exchange. Between April and October, there was an increase in poundage and margin requirements for the type of cattle contracts in which Cecka had invested. Poundage was increased from 25,000 to 40,000. The account representatives failed to inform Cecka about this change. Cecka did not tell the account representa-

tives to maintain the same dollar or poundage position. Cecka did not tell the representatives how many contracts to buy. Did the account representatives violate their duty to Cecka? Were they obligated to tell him about this change? (*Cecka* v. *Beckman & Co., Inc.*, 104 Cal. Rptr. 374 [Cal. App. 1972].)

8. At the suggestion of Petrich, a real estate broker, Chapple decided to build a movie theater on an unimproved lot that she owned and to rent the theater to Rodriques. When the construction bids were in, Chapple felt the lowest bid was still too high, and she asked Petrich to negotiate with Big Bear (the lowest bidder) to obtain a lower price. Big Bear prepared a list of modifications and presented them at a meeting attended by Petrich, Rodriques, and the architect. Those present at the meeting agreed to reduce the capacity of the air conditioner from a twenty-ton capacity to an eight-ton capacity. Chapple was not informed of this agreement. She signed a written contract to have Big Bear construct a movie theater that would have a twenty-ton-capacity air-conditioning unit. Rodriques signed an addendum to the contract calling for a reduction to an eight-ton air conditioner. No one asked Chapple to sign the addendum. An eight-ton unit was used. Could Chapple successfully sue for breach of contract, or did someone, acting as her agent, authorize the change of plans? What type of authority did the agent have? Should knowledge about this change be imputed to Chapple? (*Chapple* v. *Big Bear Super Market No. 3*, 167 Cal. Rptr. 103 [Cal. App. 1980].)

9. Snelling and Snelling, Inc. licensed PPS to operate an employment agency in Pittsburgh. The contract between them stated, in part, that it was a license agreement; that the licensee was not authorized to act for or on behalf of Snelling in any matter whatsoever; that the licensee could not change location without Snelling's written approval; that the licensee could not use any name or service mark other than that of Snelling and Snelling; that the licensee had to use Snelling's training manuals and procedures; that the licensee had to advertise in the Yellow Pages following a form required by Snelling; that the licensee had to obtain insurance naming Snelling as an additional insured; and that the licensee had to promptly notify Snelling of any claims under the insurance. When a dispute arose over PPS's placement practices, the plaintiff filed suit against PPS and Snelling and Snelling. Process for both defendants was served at the PPS office. Was this adequate service of process on Snelling and Snelling, or should the lawsuit against Snelling and Snelling be dismissed? Did PPS have the authority to act as Snelling's agent in accepting service of process? (*Sauers* v. *Pancoast Personnel, Inc.*, 439 A.2d 1214 [Pa. Super. 1982].)

10. Continental sued Grovijohn and his new employer, Amoco Chemicals, to enforce a covenant not to compete. Grovijohn was a plant manager in the plastic beverage bottle division of Continental. He was never employed there as an engineer or a technician. Grovijohn had agreed not to disclose, "directly or indirectly," or "use outside of the Continental organization during or after [his] employment, any confidential information" without Continental's consent. Amoco hired Grovijohn as a plant manager. There was no evidence that Grovijohn intended to reveal confidential information or that Amoco intended to use confidential information. Should Amoco be prevented from employing Grovijohn in this capacity? (*Continental Group, Inc.* v. *Amoco Chemicals Corp.*, 614 F.2d 351 [3rd Cir. 1980].)

CHAPTER 35

Agency: Liability for Torts

O U T L I N E

AGENT'S LIABILITY

Agents often engage in physical activities or labor on behalf of the principal. These activities bring the agent into close contact with the general public. When the agent is careless or overly aggressive, there is a good chance that some members of the public will be injured. This chapter deals with the agent's and the principal's responsibility to the public for these injuries when they occur.

Vicarious liability Legal responsibility for the wrong committed by another person.

Vicarious liability for torts involves different policy considerations from those surrounding an agent's ability to bind the principal in business dealings with third persons. In contract matters, there is a conscious desire to interact with the public and a conscious decision to enter into business arrangements with the public by means of the agent. In most tort situations, neither the principal nor the agent desires that the tort occur. But once the tort has occurred, someone has to suffer the financial burden, even if that someone is the innocent victim. Who should pay? The principal? The agent? Or the third person?

The general rule of tort law is that everyone is liable for his or her own torts. This general rule is followed in agency law. Since the agent committed the tort, the agent is liable for the harm that occurs. The fact that the agent is working for the principal at the time of the tort does not alter the general rule.

PRINCIPAL'S LIABILITY: *RESPONDEAT SUPERIOR*

When the agent commits a tort that harms a third person, the agent should be responsible for the harm. However, in agency law, there are some circumstances in which the principal is also held liable for the torts committed by the agent. Notice that in these situations the *principal* is being held liable for the conduct of the *agent*. Since the agent is also liable for the tortious conduct, the liability is said to be *joint and several*. This means that either party may be held liable (several liability), or that both parties may be held liable (joint liability).

The theory under which *principals are held liable for the torts of their agents* even though the principals are not personally at fault is known as *respondeat superior*. Literally, it means "let the master answer." It is also referred to as a "deep-pockets" theory, based on the belief that the principal's pockets are deeper (that is, they hold more money) than those of the agent. The law generally involves an attempt to balance competing interests, which can clearly be seen in the application of the *respondeat superior* doctrine. For example, if a victim has suffered $175,000 in injuries from an automobile accident caused by the negligence of an agent, and the agent has a total net worth of only $50,000, the victim cannot be fully compensated by the agent.

[handwritten margin notes: NOT unlimited / DEGREE OF CONTROL]

However, if the principal is a multimillion-dollar corporation, the principal could fully compensate the victim. In these circumstances, the court must evaluate all the facts and determine whether *respondeat superior* should be applied in this particular case. This chapter will generally use the traditional terms *master* and *servant* because these are the terms used in the court decisions and the *Restatement (Second) of Agency*.

Respondeat superior has been justified on numerous grounds in court opinions and in legal treatises. These justifications include

[handwritten margin notes: "SCOPE" of "Employment"]

1. The master will be more careful in choosing servants.
2. The master will be more careful in supervising servants.
3. The liability for servants is a cost of conducting business.
4. The master is the person benefiting from the servant's actions.
5. The master can purchase liability insurance.
6. The person with the power to control should be the person to bear financial responsibility.
7. The master can better afford the costs, especially when compared to an innocent third person who has been injured by the servant's conduct, and so should pay.

Strict liability Liability for an action simply because it occurred, not because it is the fault of the person who must pay.

Respondeat superior is not based on the idea that the principal did anything wrong. Rather, it involves a special application of the doctrine of **strict liability**. Simply put, the master hired the servant; the servant did something wrong; the master should pay. "But for" the existence of the agency, no harm would have resulted. Someone should pay; the master is best able to pay and afford the loss; therefore, the master will have to pay. However, *respondeat superior* does require a *wrongful act* by a servant for which the master can be held liable. The following case dealt with such an issue.

[handwritten note: motivation — was it for the benefit of employer]

Morrison v. Concord Kiwanis Club
279 S.E.2d 96 (N.C. App. 1981)

FACTS Barbara Ann Morrison and her sister were attending the Kiwanis Camp for handicapped children. Barbara had had physical disabilities resulting from cerebral palsy since birth. She was generally confined to a wheelchair. Her mother described Barbara's balance control problem to Westbrook, a camp counselor, when she brought the children to the camp. It was not camp policy to require a completed camp registration form or a doctor's medical statement. Barbara's mother was told that the children would be active and play ball, go canoeing, and swim. Later that day Barbara wanted to swing on a little stagecoachlike glider. The counselors tried to dissuade her, but she was insistent. Wilson, the camp director, asked if she had been on a swing glider before. Barbara said she had, and this was confirmed by her sister. Wilson carried Barbara over and put her on the swing. She held onto the seat. She seemed secure, so Wilson pulled the swing back a few inches and let it go. Wilson and Westbrook were standing at opposite sides of the swing. Barbara fell off the seat and onto the floor of the swing. No one was able to catch her in time. She suffered injuries and was taken to the hospital.

ISSUE   Is the Kiwanis Club responsible based on *respondeat superior?*

HOLDING   No. The Kiwanis Club is not responsible.

REASONING   *Respondeat superior* is based on the concept that the employer is liable for the torts of its employees. Here there was no evidence that the employees accidentally or intentionally committed a tort. The jury specifically found that the employees—the camp director and the camp counselor—were not negligent. The Kiwanis Club might have been responsible because of its *own* negligence in hiring employees, in training employees, or in not establishing admissions procedures, if they were the proximate cause of the injury. The plaintiff did not prove that theory of recovery.

Respondeat superior does not make the principal an insurer for all acts of the agent. The principal is liable only for those actions that are in the *course* and *scope* of the employment. Therefore, the issue in most cases in which the agent committed the tort, but the suit is against the principal, involves a decision as to whether the agent was in the course and scope of employment when the tort was committed. To resolve this question, it is important to know the agent's duties, working hours, state of mind, deviation from route, assigned location, and the principal's right to control the agent. It is immaterial if the principal fails to exert actual control over how the agent completes the tasks as long as the principal has the right to use this control. The principal's *right to control* is really what distinguishes "servant" and "nonservant" agents. A principal who has the right to control may be called a *master,* and the agent may be called a *servant. Respondeat superior* applies only to servant agents. It does not apply to nonservant agents because the principal lacks control and thus is not a master.

In the following case, the court examined the course and scope of a servant's employment.

Bowers v. Potts
617 S.W.2d 149 (Tenn. App. 1981)

FACTS   Potts was employed as foreman for J. W. Petty Construction Company, which was laying an underground conduit for South Central Bell. The job required the extraction of dirt, which was stored at two locations so that it could later be replaced in the trenches. Petty had promised any excess dirt to South Central Bell and to Smyrna Hardware and Lumber Company. Terrell knew that Potts was supplying dirt and contacted Potts about hauling some to Terrell's property. Potts agreed to do this in his spare time for $10 or $15 per load. Potts was hauling the dirt to Terrell's on a Saturday, his day off, using his own truck to do so, when he had an accident with another vehicle. Weatherly, the driver of the other vehicle, died at the scene. Bowers, Weatherly's **personal representative,** filed this suit for wrongful death.

Personal representative   A person who handles the financial affairs of someone who has died.

ISSUE	Was Potts in the course and scope of his employment for Petty?
HOLDING	No. Potts was acting for himself, not for Petty.
REASONING	Potts was being paid by Terrell and not by Petty. Potts worked for Petty on weekdays and not on Saturday. Potts was not at the location where he conducted work for Petty. There is no evidence that this activity helped Petty or was strongly motivated by an intent to help Petty. Potts did it to help himself and Terrell. There is no competent testimony to support the idea that Potts's activities were authorized, permitted, known, or ratified by Petty, nor did Potts's actions benefit Petty. When the conduit was finished, Petty had to correct the dirt stockpile deficiency. The deficiency was caused, at least in part, by Potts's decision. Potts was held liable for his negligence, but Petty was not.

Factors Listed in the Restatement of Agency

The *Restatement (Second) of Agency* indicates the factors that should affect the determination of whether an agent is in the scope of her employment. The factors include the following:

General Statement

(1) Conduct of a servant is within the scope of employment if, but only if:
- (a) it is of the kind he is employed to perform;
- (b) it occurs substantially within the authorized time and space limits;
- (c) it is actuated, at least in part, by a purpose to serve the master; and
- (d) if force is intentionally used by the servant against another, the use of force is not unexpectable by the master. . . .[1]

Kind of Conduct Within Scope of Employment . . .

(2) In determining whether or not the conduct, although not authorized, is nevertheless so similar to or incidental to the conduct authorized as to be within the scope of employment, the following matters of fact are to be considered:
- (a) whether or not the act is one commonly done by such servants;
- (b) the time, place and purpose of the act;
- (c) the previous relations between the master and the servant;
- (d) the extent to which the business of the master is apportioned between different servants;
- (e) whether or not the act is outside the enterprise of the master or, if within the enterprise, has not been entrusted to any servant;
- (f) whether or not the master has reason to expect that such an act will be done;
- (g) the similarity in quality of the act done to the act authorized;
- (h) whether or not the instrumentality by which the harm is done has been furnished by the master to the servant;

[1]*Restatement (Second) of Agency* (Philadelphia: American Law Institute, 1958), Section 228(1). Copyright 1958 by The American Law Institute. Reprinted with the permission of The American Law Institute.

(i) the extent of departure from the normal method of accomplishing an authorized result; and

(j) whether or not the act is seriously criminal.[2]

In many cases, certain factors may indicate that the servant is within the scope of employment while other factors may indicate the contrary. For example, the master did furnish the truck, but she had no reason to suspect that the servant would engage in this conduct. No one or two of these factors are controlling. The judge or jury should weigh all the factors involved and reach a decision. Since the triers of fact exercise a lot of discretion in these cases, fact situations that seem very similar may result in different decisions by the court.

Time and Place of Occurrence

Two of the factors analyzed by the courts in determining course and scope of employment are whether the tort occurred on the work premises and whether it occurred during work hours, or in the words of the *Restatement,* the time and place of the act.[3] These factors were influential in the following case.

Chastain v. Litton Systems, Inc.
694 F.2d 957 (4th Cir. 1982)

FACTS   Beck was an employee of Litton Systems, Inc. On the day in question, Litton Systems was having its annual pre-Christmas party. Employees were to clock in and out that day in order to be paid for a full day of work, but they did not have to perform any actual work. Litton provided music, food, and beverages. Beck became intoxicated at the party. About one hour and twenty minutes after he left, while driving his van, Beck ran through a red light and hit another car. He killed the occupants of that car, and their husbands filed this suit.

ISSUE   Is Litton responsible for the accident based on *respondeat superior?*

HOLDING   Perhaps. The case should be returned to the trial court for a decision on the facts.

REASONING   Litton would be responsible for the negligent or willful acts of its employees in the scope of their employment. North Carolina courts have not decided whether an employer who provides alcoholic beverages is liable to innocent victims who are injured. State law imposes liability on businesses that serve and charge for alcoholic beverages, but not on social hosts. This situation is similar to that of a business that serves drinks. Whether Litton was advancing a business purpose is a question of fact to be decided by a jury. Beck's activities may have been within the course and scope of his employment. The time that should be examined is the time during which he became intoxicated. The United States Supreme Court denied Litton's petition for writ of certiorari. (462 U.S. 1106 [1983].)

---

[2]Ibid., Section 229(2).
[3]Ibid., Section 229(2)(b).

In *Chastain*, the court obviously focused on the place where the drinking occurred.

**Failure to Follow
Instructions**

A master can be held liable for a servant's acts even though the master instructed the servant not to commit torts generally or not to perform a specific act. The disobedience of the servant does not necessarily exempt the master from liability, as illustrated in the following example.

Larry worked as a dock worker. According to the contract, he was paid on an hourly basis. During idle hours, when there were no ships to load or unload, the dock workers commonly sat at their cranes, swinging the loading hooks around above the dock. On one such occasion, a stranger, unfamiliar with operations there, walked down the dock and was hit by the hook attached to Larry's crane. The stranger was hospitalized with serious injuries. Is the master liable for the injuries?

Yes. Larry was at work during normal working hours. He was using a crane supplied by his master. The master was aware of the dock workers' habit of swinging the loading hooks and had told them to stop it. However, he had not enforced that rule.

Failure to Act

A master can also be held liable under *respondeat superior* when the servant fails to act as directed. For example, a railroad switch operator was supposed to throw a switch on the track at the same time every day. One day he carelessly failed to do so, a train derailed as a result, and passengers on the train were injured. The master (the railroad) is liable for the servant's negligence in failing to act as instructed.

Respondeat superior does not decrease the servant's liability for wrongdoing, but it makes an additional party, the master, also liable. In many legal situations, such as the one just described, multiple parties are liable in a single occurrence.

Two Masters

Another problem that sometimes arises is deciding *who* the master is. Who controls the manner in which the servant will do the work? The master, or employer, is the one who not only can order the work done, but also can order how it will be done.

One would not expect a problem in determining who the master is, but resolution of the problem is not simple in cases of borrowed servants. In such a case, who is the master? Is it the lending master, the borrowing master, or both? Again, the important factors are the course of the employment and the ability to control the servant. Consider the following example.

Jerry worked for Typewriter, Inc., which was having its office remodeled by Interiors Redone. Since the contractors doing the work were a little short-handed, Jerry's supervisor told him to help them. In this situation, Typewriter, Inc. would be referred to as the general master and Interiors Redone as Jerry's special master. (The meanings of general and special are similar to those used in Chapter 33.) Jerry is labeled a borrowed servant. After painting the walls in the main lobby, Jerry negligently failed to put up Wet Paint signs. A customer leaned against the wall and ruined his clothes. Who was Jerry's master at the time of his negligent act?

Some courts would decide that both Typewriter, Inc. and Interiors Redone are liable. Jerry was subject to the control of both, and his actions benefited both. Other courts would conclude that Interiors Redone is liable because Jerry was working *primarily* in their business at the time of the negligence. Still other courts would hold Typewriter, Inc. liable because ultimately Jerry was subject to their control and they supplied his paycheck.

The following case involved the issue of which master employed a worker who negligently caused an injury.

Krzywicki v. Tidewater Equipment Co., Inc.
600 F. Supp. 629 (D. Maryland 1985)

FACTS   A longshoreman, Krzywicki, suffered extensive injuries when a crane operator dropped a 2½-ton load of cargo directly on him. Krzywicki was a member of a gang of longshoremen supplied to Prudential Lines by Atlantic and Gulf Stevedores, Inc. The barge was owned by Prudential Lines, Inc. The crane was owned by Tidewater and was furnished to Prudential under a written lease. The crane operator, George Eberling, was loading the barge at the time. Jocelyn Taylor, the signalman, was employed as a longshoreman by Atlantic and Gulf. Eberling and Taylor were working under a system in which Eberling would move a load of cargo over the barge and lower it unless he observed a signal to stop. In this case he did not observe a signal to stop, since Taylor temporarily left his station to go to the restroom. Taylor was determined not to have been negligent in causing the accident. Krzywicki was determined not to have been negligent in moving across the barge when he knew that a signalman was on duty who would alert the crane operator if men were under the load. Krzywicki had a right to reasonably assume that a warning would be given if he were in a danger zone and that the load would not be lowered. Krzywicki is now permanently disabled and unable to return to work.

ISSUE   Who was the master of Eberling, the crane operator?

HOLDING   He was the servant of the crane owner, Tidewater.

REASONING   Eberling knew that there were longshoremen working in the barge whom he could not see. It was negligent to load the barge unless there was a negative signal that it was unsafe to lower the load. The court concluded that this was true whether or not this was the practice in this port. Affirmative signals should have been used. Standard crane signal procedures called for affirmative signals if it was okay to lower the load.
If Eberling had been paying attention, he would have noticed that the signalman was not in position. He had a

duty to find out who was acting as signalman. Taylor was not in position. Eberling wrongly assumed that some other longshoremen standing on the pier were acting as signalmen even though neither one of them had given him a signal.

Under the borrowed servant doctrine, the parties may allocate between themselves the risk of any loss caused by the employee's negligent acts. One of the factors to be considered was whether there was a meeting of the minds between the parties as to the status of the employee in question. One factor that is important is whose work is being performed. This is usually decided by who had the power to direct and control the servant. Another factor to be considered is whether one or both parties carried liability insurance that would cover the risk of loss. Eberling was the servant of his general employer, Tidewater. He was paid by Tidewater; Tidewater had the right to discharge him; Tidewater selected him for this job; Tidewater had employed him for a considerable period of time; Tidewater owned the crane; and the benefit to Prudential was for only a short period of time. The work was for the benefit of Prudential, but Prudential did not have control over the crane operations. Eberling, a skilled crane operator, was free to operate the crane in accordance with his own judgment. Both Prudential and Tidewater had liability insurance; they agreed that Eberling should remain the servant of Tidewater. Eberling was not a borrowed servant of the barge owner at the time of the accident.

A shipowner has no duty to be present during the complete loading operation or to inspect the equipment. It is reasonable for him to rely on the harbor workers to avoid unreasonable risks.

When analyzing a complicated fact pattern such as the one in *Krzywicki*, drawing a diagram of the relationships is helpful. An example is shown in Figure 35.1. As you can see from the figure, this case contains at least three instances of potential borrowed servants.

To avoid the uncertainties caused by borrowed servants, prudent employers enter into agreements about which master will be liable and/or which master will obtain liability insurance for the servant's acts.

A closely related problem occurs when one servant appoints another ser-

FIGURE 35.1 Legal Relationships in *Krzywicki* v. *Tidewater Equipment Co., Inc.*

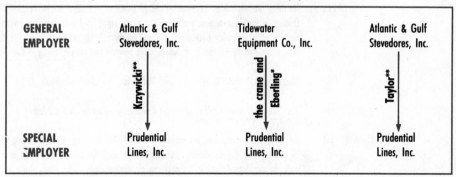

*According to the court, the crane and Eberling were loaned to Prudential Lines, Inc. under a written contract. The parties had agreed that Eberling would remain the servant of Tidewater Equipment.

**The court focused on the status of Eberling, because he was the one who was determined to be negligent. However, Krzywicki and Taylor also were potential borrowed servants.

vant (a subservant) to complete his tasks. Under *respondeat superior,* who is responsible for the torts of the subservant? If the servant had authority to appoint the subservant, the master will be held liable for the subservant. However, if the servant lacked authority, generally the servant herself will be liable as the "master" under *respondeat superior.* The primary reason for this is because the servant is the one with the right to control the subservant.

Crimes and Intentional Torts

Assault A threat to touch someone in an undesired manner.

Battery Unauthorized touching of another person without legal justification or that person's consent.

Courts are more reluctant to hold a master liable under *respondeat superior* for intentional wrongs such as **assault** and **battery** than they are for negligence on the part of the servant. In fact, some courts still follow the traditional rule that a master is not responsible for the intentional acts of his servant. However, the modern view is that a master is liable if the servant advanced the master's interests or the servant believed that her conduct was advancing the master's interests. Consequently, masters can be held liable under *respondeat superior* for intentional acts such as slander, libel, invasion of privacy, and assault and battery. Many criminal acts are also torts, and the master may be held civilly liable under *respondeat superior* for the financial losses suffered by the victim of the servant's criminal act. *Respondeat superior* is not used to impose criminal liability on the master.

The issue in the following case was whether the master could be held civilly liable for an intentional act by a servant (a professional baseball player). Notice that the servant is also being sued, as can be inferred from the name of the case.

Cause be civil responsibility for criminal act of employee

Manning v. Grimsley
643 F.2d 20 (1st Cir. 1981)

FACTS Manning attended a professional baseball game at Fenway Park in Boston. As Grimsley, a pitcher for the Baltimore Orioles in that game, was warming up in the right-field bull pen, the spectators in the nearby stands continuously heckled him. Grimsley periodically turned to stare at them. His catcher left and walked over to the bench. Grimsley wound up and threw the ball, which went toward the stands, through the fence, and hit Manning.

ISSUE Could the Baltimore Orioles be held liable for Grimsley's conduct?

HOLDING Yes. The Baltimore Orioles could be financially liable for his conduct.

REASONING Under Massachusetts law, an employer can be liable for damages resulting from an assault by an employee. It must be proved that the employee's assault was in response to the plaintiff's conduct, which at the time was interfering with the employee's ability to perform his duties successfully. Here there was sufficient evidence that Grimsley was responding to the heckling, which might have annoyed him and interfered with his ability to perform his duties successfully. The court held that Manning was entitled to a jury trial on the factual issue and returned the case to the trial court for a decision on the facts.

Courts will hold a master liable for some of a servant's serious wrong-doings, but not for others. The question is often one of degree. How serious was the tort or crime? Should the master have expected it? Is there much variance between the assigned tasks and the wrongdoing?

DIRECT LIABILITY OF THE PRINCIPAL

The agent must be a servant before *respondeat superior* will be applied. However, principals may be held *directly* responsible, as well as strictly liable, for some of the wrongs committed by their agents, even if the agents are not servants. For example, the principal is liable if the principal *instructed* the agent to commit the wrong, did not properly supervise the agent, ratified or approved the agent's tort, or was negligent in the selection of the agent. The following example illustrates a principal's negligence in the selection of an agent.

The Great Escape, a neighborhood bar, hired Barry to work as a bouncer in the evenings. Barry was 6'4" and weighed 280 pounds. One evening the bartender noticed that Carl, a customer, was drunk and was becoming loud and obnoxious. The bartender, who was Barry's supervisor, asked Barry to evict him. When Barry asked Carl to leave, Carl swung at Barry but was so drunk that he missed. Barry swung back and continued to hit Carl until Carl collapsed. Carl later died from the injuries received. Is the Great Escape civilly liable for Carl's death?

Yes. The court held that even though Barry had never beaten a customer, the owner of the bar knew that Barry had a hot temper and was often involved in fights. Barry did not have the proper disposition for this job, and the owner should have realized that.

Conspiracy A situation in which two or more people plan to engage in an illegal activity.

Solicitation A situation in which one person convinces another to engage in criminal activity.

The rules of agency are not the only rules of law that may be involved when an agent commits a crime. Often a principal will be criminally liable based on his or her own fault. If a principal directs or encourages an agent to engage in criminal activity, the principal will probably be held personally liable for such acts as **conspiracy, solicitation,** or accessory to the crime. In addition, some criminal statutes create liability for the principal even though the principal does not intend to violate the statute or does not know of the illegal act or condition. For example, state liquor laws often state that tavern or restaurant owners are liable if minors are served alcohol in their bars. In most states, this is true whether or not the owner approved of such action or even knew that it had occurred. Other examples include statutes that prohibit the sale of impure food or beverages no matter who is at fault. The purpose of these statutes is to stimulate principals' interest so that they *care* whether these activities occur in their establishments.

INDEMNIFICATION

When a master pays a third person under *respondeat superior* for injuries caused by the servant's unauthorized acts, the master is entitled to *indemnification (the right to be repaid)* from the servant. Unlike most other theories, *respondeat superior* is not based on the fault of the master; here the master only provided payment for the servant's fault. The master should be entitled to recover from the person who caused the loss—the servant—so the law allows the master to recover. As a practical matter, the master generally will have insurance to cover the payment. Furthermore, the servant normally will not have sufficient funds to make the payment. If the servant is still employed by the master, the master may be able to withhold part of the reimbursement from each paycheck until the master is completely repaid. However, continuing to employ the servant may increase the likelihood that the master will be liable for the next wrongdoing by the servant.

Sometimes a servant may be entitled to indemnification from the master if the servant paid the third person who was injured by the servant's tort. It would depend on the particular facts of the case. Such cases are based either on contract law or on the law of restitution.[4] Courts are influenced by what they believe to be just, considering the business and the nature of the particular relationship.[5] Under the *Restatement (Second) of Agency,* an agent is entitled to indemnification if the agent, at the direction of the principal, commits an act that constitutes a tort, but the agent believes that it is not tortious.[6] Obviously if an agent completes a task that he or she knows to be illegal or tortious, the agent is not entitled to indemnification. An illustration follows:

John, a junior in high school, worked for Cutter's Appliance store. Willy had not been making the monthly payments on a color television that he had bought at the store. Mr. Cutter told John to go to Willy's home to repossess the television. He also told John that the store still owned the television and that any amount of force was allowed in retaking possession. When Willy resisted, John shoved the door open, pushed Willy out of the way, and took the television. Under state law, these acts constituted trespass, assault and battery, and use of unlawful force to repossess goods. If John pays Willy

[4]Warren A. Seavey, *Handbook of the Law of Agency* (St. Paul, Minn.: West, 1964), Section 168, p. 265.
[5]*Restatement (Second) of Agency,* Section 438(2)(b).
[6]Ibid., Section 439(c) and Comment on Clause (c).

for his injury, John has a right to indemnification, *if* the trier of fact believes that John was, in *good faith,* following Mr. Cutter's instructions.

As another example, suppose Peggy, a principal, told Simon, her agent, that she had obtained permission to drive trucks across land owned by someone else, in order to commence her mining operation. In fact, she had not obtained permission. Simon would unintentionally commit trespass if he drove his truck across the other person's property. If Simon were required to pay that person for the trespass, he would be entitled to indemnification from Peggy, as he was following her instructions in good faith.

Figure 35.2 illustrates the relationships between the primary parties when the agent commits a tort. The agent's right to indemnification is questionable because the courts require that the agent follow the principal's instructions in good faith before receiving indemnification. The principal's right to indemnification is questionable because, realistically, many agents cannot afford to reimburse the principal.

FIGURE 35.2   Liability for Tortious Injury to a Third Person

YOU BE THE JUDGE

On January 15, 1992, Johnny Carson said on the "Tonight Show" that Mr. Blackwell labeled Mother Teresa a "nerdy nun." Mr. Blackwell, as he is known, is a fashion critic and has become famous by bashing celebrities in his annual 10 worst-dressed women list. Johnny said "Did

> you see what he said about Mother Teresa? 'Miss nerdy nun is a fashion no-no.' Come on now, that's just too much. That's right, that's Mr. Blackwell, that's the guy I'm talking about."
>
> Mr. Blackwell filed a $11 million lawsuit against Johnny Carson and NBC. According to the suit, "Mr. Blackwell did not make any statement about Mother Teresa." Mr. Blackwell "holds Mother Teresa in high regard and has never maligned her or her saintly work."
>
> How would you decide this case, and why?

Source: "Mr. Blackwell isn't amused; Johnny sued" appearing in *The Fresno Bee*, Thursday, March 19, 1992, page A2.

INJURY ON THE JOB

An employer has a duty to provide employees with a reasonably safe place to work and reasonably safe equipment to use at work, considering the nature of the employment. If this is not possible, the employer should warn employees about unsafe conditions that they may not discover even if they are reasonably careful.[7]

Although courts *sometimes* apply similar rules to employees and independent contractors, there are distinct differences in their legal relationships. Nevertheless, courts have on occasion allowed independent contractors to recover for injuries sustained on the job.[8]

If an employee is hurt at work, the employer could utilize a number of defenses to avoid reimbursing the employee for the injury and for any medical bills. Negligence by the employee or the employee's assumption of the known risk would be two such defenses. For example, the employee might have been driving a truck too fast for icy road conditions or might not have been wearing safety goggles provided by the employer. Assumption of the risk, contributory negligence, and its modern counterpart—comparative negligence—are discussed in detail in Chapter 3.

At common law, the *fellow employee doctrine* also acted to bar recovery by the employee. Traditionally, this concept was called the fellow servant doctrine. More recent court cases and treatises call it the fellow employee doctrine. Under this theory an employee could not recover for work-related injuries if they were caused by another servant of the same master. Like as-

[7]Ibid., Section 492.
[8]*Rodney* v. *U.S.*, 77-4028 (9th Cir. 1980); *Cioll* v. *Bechtel Corp.*, No. 733794 (San Francisco City Super. Ct., 23 April 1981).

sumption of the risk, this doctrine acts as a complete bar to recovery. This rule is applicable to many work-site accidents. Most of the time when an employee is injured on the job, the injury is caused not by the employer, but by another employee at the job site. One justification suggested for this doctrine is that the employer is often remote from the work site. The employee, on the other hand, is likely to know of hazards at work and to know of careless fellow employees. Another justification used to support the doctrine is that an employee "assumed the risk" of being injured by co-workers. The existence of the fellow employee doctrine encouraged the spread of state workers' compensation statutes.

Workers' compensation
Payments to injured workers based on the state statute.

In some cases the injured employee would be covered by workers' compensation. In some states, particular types of workers are not covered under the workers' compensation statutes. For example, in New Mexico agricultural workers are not covered under the state statute.

These statues may seem to be the opposite extreme from the fellow employee doctrine. They are not based on the fault of the employer, and the employer's negligence need not be shown in court. The worker needs only to show that his or her injury was caused in the course and scope of the job. In many states these statutes were intended to be economic insurance for workers. These statutes exist in most states and provide for a fixed schedule of compensation for listed injuries. Workers can easily determine how much they are entitled to receive; this procedure allows the quick settlement of claims and discourages many lawsuits. When workers' compensation statutes are applicable, legal action against the employer based on common law theories generally is prohibited.

The state statutes vary in format. Some have organized a fund to which the employers contribute, and injured employees collect from the fund. Some states allow employers to purchase insurance or to establish their own funds. In most states, the employee is allowed to recover even if he or she was negligent in causing the injury, assumed the risk, or was injured by a fellow servant. The injured employee generally receives compensation according to a schedule of payments depending on the type of disability and how long the employee was out of work.

Workers' compensation statutes vary in the following respects:

1. Some cover only major industrial occupations.
2. Some exclude small shops with few employees.
3. Some exclude injuries caused intentionally by the employer or other workers.

Because of the variety, it is important to examine the particular statute at issue.

If the workers' compensation statute does not apply, generally the employee will be permitted to sue based on common law theories. (Workers' compensation is also discussed in Chapter 48.)

SUMMARY

An agent is liable for his or her own tortious and criminal acts. The fact that the agent was working at the time is immaterial. The fact that the principal may also be liable to the third party is immaterial as well.

A principal may be liable for the acts of her agents. Much of this liability is based on the doctrine of *respondeat superior*. A master is liable for the torts committed by a servant if the servant was acting in the course and scope of the employment. Many factors are used in analyzing what activity is "in the course and scope of employment." A principal may also be held liable if she commits a tort or a crime; this liability is not based on *respondeat superior*. It includes situations in which a principal is negligent in selecting an agent or directs an agent to commit a crime or a tort.

Even though a court holds a master liable to the third party under *respondeat superior,* this does not mean that the master necessarily will bear the ultimate loss. The master generally will be entitled to indemnification from the servant, although such indemnification may not be practical.

The principal has a duty to provide a reasonably safe place to work.

DISCUSSION QUESTIONS

1. David hired Annabelle as a housekeeper. Her main duties were to remain in the house and clean, prepare meals, and do the laundry. One afternoon, Annabelle received a call from One-Day Drycleaners. David's suit was ready to be picked up. Annabelle decided to go and get the suit in her car. On the way home, she ran a red light and hit Julie's car. The police officer who came to the scene said that Annabelle's intoxication was the main cause of the accident. Annabelle had had a few drinks with her lunch. David knew that Annabelle had a drinking problem when he hired her and that she was trying to reform. Who is responsible for the damage to Julie's car, and why?

2. Cindy had just started working as an accountant for Big Eight Accounting Firm. On her first audit, Cindy's supervisor sent her to get the coffee and doughnuts every morning. One morning on the way to get the doughnuts, Cindy did not notice that the traffic had stopped in front of her, and she collided with Claudia's car. Who is responsible for the damage to Claudia's car, and why?

3. Cindy prepared a joint tax return for Sammy and Lenora Johnson during her first year at Big Eight. She did not prepare the return correctly, and the IRS assessed $4000 more in taxes and penalties. What rights do the Johnsons have? Why?

4. The employees at an Atlantic City casino "assisted" a compulsive gambler in losing millions of dollars that the gambler had embezzled from his employer. This was in violation of the state gambling regulations pertaining to credit regulations and cash procedures. Should the casino be held liable for the acts of its employees? Why

or why not? Should the employees be held liable? Why or why not?

5. After class in the afternoon, Jim had a job delivering floral arrangements for Flowers by Flo. Flo often told Jim not to take friends in the truck when he made deliveries. One day Jim saw Nanci, a classmate, waiting for the bus. He was going toward her home, so he gave her a ride. Jim carelessly drove off the side of the road, and Nanci was injured. Who is liable to Nanci for her injuries, and why?

6. Janet works as Bill's secretary at Waincoat, Inc. Bill forgot to buy his wife a birthday present, so he sent Janet out to buy one at lunch. While Janet was looking in the jewelry store for a present, she carelessly burned another customer's suit with her cigarette. Who is liable for the damage to the suit, and why?

7. Randy worked as a stock boy in the produce department of May Fair Market. The store prided itself on having the best produce in town. Caroline, a customer, came into the grocery store and started to complain about the quality of the produce generally and of the lettuce specifically. When Randy could not stand her tirade any more, he pushed Caroline, and she fell and broke her ankle. Who is liable to Caroline, and why?

8. Saul worked for Central Cable Co. installing cable television in residential areas. The company needed water to repave the street after the cable was installed. Without permission, Saul used water from Rosemary's tap. When Rosemary got home from work and saw this, she was furious. Her water bill was based on usage, and Saul had been using her water all day. Who is liable to Rosemary, and why?

9. Jeff made deliveries for Superior Meat Packing Company. On Wednesday, he complained to the company mechanic that his truck was not braking correctly. The mechanic said he would check it out immediately. On Thursday afternoon, the brakes failed, and Jeff was unable to stop the truck. He collided with a telephone pole and suffered neck and back injuries. Who is liable? Why?

10. Neal was stationed on the aircraft carrier USS Archer. One night in August, they were having night maneuvers so the pilots and crew could practice night takeoffs and landings. One of the planes crashed on the deck, injuring a number of people and killing Neal. The investigation revealed that some of the crew were suffering from fatigue and some were under the influence of narcotics. Can Neal's wife and children recover? From whom and why?

CASE PROBLEMS

1. Roland had an interview with the personnel department of the sawmill. They discussed working hours, benefits, and the required physical examination. The physical would be completed at the company's expense. On his way to Western Clinic for the physical, Roland negligently allowed the car he was driving to roll backward, and it crushed McLean against a building. Who should be liable to McLean, and why? (*McLean* v. *St. Regis Paper Company*, 496 P.2d 571 [Wash. App. 1972].)

2. Anthony hired Jo'Dee to excavate a swimming pool site. Jo'Dee did not have the necessary state license to do excavation work. A truck owned by one of the partners of Jo'Dee and driven by Zaugg struck a motorcycle ridden by Foss. Zaugg was returning to the construction site after dumping a load of debris from the excavation. This task was necessary to the completion of the job. Zaugg turned left across Foss's lane without signaling or seeing Foss. Foss was killed in the accident. Zaugg had been instructed not to drive the truck. Should Anthony be held responsible under *respondeat superior*? Should Jo'Dee be held responsible under *respondeat superior*? Was Zaugg acting outside his scope of employment? (*Foss* v. *Anthony Industries*, 189 Cal. Rptr. 31 [Cal. App. 1983].)

3. A car driven by Appling, a lawyer employed by Richman and Garrett, collided with the car in which the Wanks were riding. Appling had gone to lunch with a representative of one of the firm's clients and a number of other business contacts. At the lunch Appling had consumed several alcoholic drinks. Between 3:30 and 4:00 that afternoon, Appling called the office and spoke to one of the partners to advise him that he would not be coming back to the office. The partner asked Appling to stay where he was and someone would come to get him. Appling rejected that suggestion and drove himself

in his own automobile. The accident occurred between 6:30 and 6:45 P.M. Appling does not remember where he was going at the time of the accident. There was evidence at the time of trial that Appling had had another accident earlier that afternoon in the parking lot of another restaurant. Is the law firm liable for the alleged negligent driving of Appling? (*Wank* v. *Richman and Garrett*, 211 Cal. Rptr. 919 [Cal. App. 1985].)

4. Sams was a pastor of a church and Calhoun was a member of his congregation. Calhoun often mowed the lawns of Sams's rental properties without charge as a favor to Sams. Calhoun's lawn mower was defective because it was missing a protective guard. One day when Calhoun operated the lawn mower on Sams's rental property, it threw up a projectile into Michael Burns's eye. Michael, a six-year-old, had been playing on the sidewalk. Is Sams liable for the injury caused to Michael Burns? (*Burns* v. *Sams*, 458 So.2d 359 [Fla. App. 1984].)

5. Brown had severe mental retardation, which was evidenced by mumbled speech and a nervous, fidgety manner. He was arrested for stealing a money order. Officers Pool and Polidori interrogated Brown and his accomplice. The officers pointed their guns at the two suspects and played with their guns and ammunition during the interrogation. Pool pointed his police revolver at Brown and shot him. Brown died of the wound. Should the civil law doctrine of *respondeat superior* be applied to Pool's behavior? (*Wagstaff* v. *City of Maplewood*, 615 S.W.2d 608 [Mo. App. 1981].)

6. Williams, an employee of Harrison Electrical Constructors, contended that he was injured by an explosion. The explosion allegedly occurred when an Arkansas Mechanical Contractors, Inc. (AMC) welder stuffed paper in the end of a pipe that was being welded. The paper caused the buildup of acetylene gas and the resulting explosion. Williams contended that this was done as a practical joke or to harass Williams because he was not a union member. AMC employees were not authorized to use acetylene gas for any purpose other than cutting steel for welding. All employees were strictly prohibited from using acetylene gas to produce an explosion or for practical jokes. Could AMC be held liable for the act of its employee? (*Williams* v. *Natkin & Co.*, 508 F. Supp. 1017 [E.D. Ark. 1981].)

7. Thompson, a laborer for Seaman Plumbing Company, received injuries when he was buried alive while trying to connect Seafood Haven's sewage line to the municipality's sewer system. It is necessary to slope deep ditches to prevent cave-ins. The ditch in which Thompson was working was not sloped. Thompson was not on the municipality's property and the municipality had not contracted for the work. Who, if anyone, is liable to Thompson for his injuries? (*Thompson* v. *City of Bayou La Batre*, 399 So.2d 292 [Ala. 1981].)

8. Wallace drowned in a swimming pond located on the premises of Sunnyside Beach and Campground. The campground was operated by Wilgus. Wallace was employed by Consolidated Cigar Corporation as a summer worker at a youth farm work camp called Camp Clark. Camp Clark was leased by Consolidated from Clark Brothers and was operated by the Shade Tobacco Growers Agricultural Association in association with Consolidated and others. His employer had a verbal agreement with Wilgus to allow its workers to use the swimming pond. Wallace was not being paid at the time of the drowning. Wallace and two other boys were at the swimming pond under the supervision of two Camp Clark employees at the time. The employer provided supervisors, transportation, and equipment for its employees to use the swimming pond. The purpose was to improve the morale of its workers and to increase productivity. Did the drowning occur during the course of Wallace's employment within the meaning of the Massachusetts Workmen's Compensation Act? (*Wallace* v. *Shade Tobacco Growers, Etc.*, 642 F.2d 17 [1st Cir. 1981].)

9. Karl Cox, Jr. had operated a cotton stripper for at least twenty years of his life, and he had been working for Karl Cox, Sr. for a number of years. He had been operating a cotton stripper in short cotton for a few days before he was hurt. Cotton strippers have a tendency to become clogged, especially in short cotton. Cox, Jr. was operating the stripper when it became clogged. He got off the machine, left it running, and tried to kick the clog loose with his foot. His foot got caught in the machine and was severed. Is the employer liable for the injury to the employee? Are any defenses available to the employer? (*Cox* v. *Cox*, 555 P.2d 378 [N.M. App. 1976].)

10. Nealey was instructed to haul a load of furniture from North Carolina to Texas. Nealey stopped in Mobile, Alabama, and picked up Bryant, a hitchhiker. Bryant and Nealey struck up a friendship and Nealey bought meals for Bryant and let Bryant sleep in the cab of the truck in exchange for Bryant's help in unloading the furniture. Nealey stated that he might be able to

find work for Bryant in North Carolina, so Bryant returned with Nealey instead of getting off at his original destination. One tire blew out on the truck and Nealey elected to drive on to a larger town with only one tire on that axle. Bryant realized that this was dangerous. Bryant was injured when the second tire blew out and the truck rolled over. Under Mississippi law the assumption of risk defense cannot be used in employment relationships. Did an employment relationship exist between Nealey and Bryant? (*Bryant* v. *Nealey*, 599 F. Supp. 248 [N.D. Miss. 1984].)

PART 7
Business Organizations

*T*he owner—or owners—of every business must select some form of business organization. The selection may be made after long and careful deliberation, or it may be made by circumstances and conduct. Too often, the selection is made in a haphazard and reckless manner, without regard for the legal and economic ramifications of the organizational form that has been selected.

Should the entrepreneur "go it alone" in a proprietorship? If so, the entrepreneur will have absolute authority—and no one to help with the really difficult decisions. Should a partnership be formed? For many businesses, the simplicity of a partnership makes it an ideal form, but the entrepreneur should be aware that a partnership entails the sharing of management powers and duties. Should a corporation be formed? The corporation offers many advantages, including the possibility of franchising, but the entrepreneur should be aware of the heavy federal regulation such an organizational form faces.

This part of the text cannot, and will not, tell any businessperson which type of organization should be chosen. No one form is ideal for every business. However, after studying Part 7, a person who is considering the formation of a business should be able to evaluate the advantages and disadvantages of the alternative forms available. Such an evaluation should lead to a carefully considered and intelligent selection, one that is right for *that* person and for *that* particular business.

C H A P T E R 36

Formation of a Partnership

O U T L I N E

HISTORIC OVERVIEW

The partnership as a business form is very old. It can be traced back to ancient Babylon, and perhaps even further. It was known to, and widely used by, the Romans during the height of the Roman Empire. In fact, Roman merchants introduced the partnership throughout Europe as they conducted trade with the peoples conquered by the Roman legions.

Among the nations that "discovered" the Roman partnership was England. Later, the English common law modified this form of organization somewhat and used it in the development of the British Empire. Among the places the English utilized the partnership was the United States, at that time known as "the Colonies."

The United States followed the English common law of partnerships for quite some time. However, partnership law in the United States has now been *codified*. The controlling law today is found in the *Uniform Partnership Act* (UPA) for general partnerships and in either the *Uniform Limited Partnership Act* (ULPA) or the *Revised Uniform Limited Partnership Act* (RULPA) for limited partnerships. The UPA has now been adopted in every state except Georgia and Louisiana and is also followed in Guam, the Virgin Islands, and the District of Columbia. Either the ULPA or the RULPA is followed in every state except Louisiana. The RULPA is currently followed in twenty-two states, with the ULPA followed in the remaining twenty-seven states that have adopted one or the other of the two uniform acts.

Partnerships are formed for a variety of reasons. For example, many **professionals** enter partnerships because they are not allowed to incorporate under some state laws. (The so-called Big 6 CPA firms are all partnerships, so they can conduct business in every state.) Some people enter partnerships to avoid the technical steps and expense required to form a **corporation.** And some people form partnerships because it seems like the thing to do.

A partnership has many of the best features of the other major types of business organizations, but it also has some of the worst features of the other types. The various features of proprietorships, partnerships, limited partnerships, and corporations are compared in Table 36.1. A partnership is relatively easy to form, and the formation is normally informal—as is the case with a **proprietorship.** Like a corporation, a partnership has a wider potential financial base than a proprietorship. And like a corporation, the partnership has more expertise to draw from.

However, a partnership is not *perpetual,* as a corporation may be. A partnership eventually will dissolve. Also, the partners face unlimited liability for business-related conduct, as does a proprietor. In contrast, the shareholders in a corporation have limited liability.

No one business form is perfect. Each has some advantages that the others lack; each has some drawbacks the others avoid. The decision as to the type

Professionals In the sense used here, a member of a "learned profession," such as a doctor, a lawyer, or an accountant.

Corporation An artificial person or legal entity created by or under the authority of a state or nation, composed by a group of persons known as stockholders or shareholders.

Proprietorship A business with legal rights or exclusive title vested in one individual; a solely owned business.

TABLE 36.1 A Comparison of Different Types of Business Organizations

	PROPRIETORSHIP	PARTNERSHIP	LIMITED PARTNERSHIP	CORPORATION
Creation:	Proprietor opens the business, subject to state and local licensing laws, etc.	Partners enter into an agreement, either orally or in writing; no formalities are required.	Partners enter into a partnership agreement and file a written form designating the limited partners and the general partners.	Parties prepare and file *formal* legal documents known as articles of incorporation with the state of incorporation; they must comply with any relevant state or federal security statutes or regulations.
Termination:	Proprietor closes the business; death, insanity, or bankruptcy of the owner also terminates the business.	Partners agree to dissolve the partnership; death, bankruptcy, or withdrawal of any partner also dissolves the partnership. The terms of the agreement or a court order may dissolve the partnership. Liquidation of the assets after a dissolution winds up the business.	Partners follow same procedure as for a partnership, but with a difference in the order of distributing assets in case of a winding up.	Parties close the business, liquidate all business assets, surrender the corporate charter, and distribute the assets as per state law; termination may also be due to state action revoking the charter.
Taxation:	All business profits are taxed as regular income of the owner; there are no federal income taxes on the business, per se.	The business must file a federal tax return, but it is for information only. The income of the business is taxed as regular income to the partners.	The same procedure is followed as for a regular, general partnership.	Normal corporations are taxed as a separate taxable entity; any dividends are taxed to the stockholders. A sub-Chapter S corporation, created by IRS, is taxed as if it were a general partnership despite its corporate status. A sub-Chapter S corporation is treated differently only for federal tax purposes.

TABLE 36.1   **continued**

	PROPRIETORSHIP	PARTNERSHIP	LIMITED PARTNERSHIP	CORPORATION
Liability:	Proprietor is liable for all business assets and then all personal assets of the owner (unlimited personal liability).	Partners are liable for all business assets and then all personal assets of the partners, jointly and severally (unlimited personal liability).	Partners are liable for all business assets and then all personal assets of the *general* partners, jointly and severally; limited partners have limited liability (they are liable only to the extent of their contribution).	Parties are liable for all business assets; stockholders are *not* personally liable for debts of the corporation (limited liability).
Advantages:	Simplicity of creation; complete ownership and control of the firm.	Informality of creation; greater potential for expertise and capital in management (because there is more than one manager).	Somewhat greater flexibility than a general partnership; much greater potential access to capital.	Longevity—potential for perpetual existence; potentially unlimited access to capital and to expertise; freely transferable ownership; limited personal liability of the owners.
Disadvantages:	Limited capital; limited expertise; limited existence (when the owner dies, the business terminates).	Limited existence; lack of flexibility; potential liability.	Some rigidity in ownership and decision making; personal liability of general partners; limited existence.	"Double taxation" (except for subChapter S); much more federal regulation; considerably more state regulation; formality and rigidity of the organization.

of business organization one should choose should never be made lightly or automatically. The "pros" and "cons" of each available alternative should be weighed carefully before a decision is made.

PARTNERSHIPS DEFINED

Section 6(1) of the Uniform Partnership Act defines a partnership. According to this section, a partnership has five characteristics. It is

Uniform Partnership Act

1. an association
2. of two or more persons
3. to carry on a business
4. as co-owners
5. for profit.

The sixteen words set out in this list are deceptively simple. In fact, a tremendous amount of interpretation often is involved in fitting an organization into the definition of a partnership. To illustrate the potential problem, we will discuss the terms in the order listed.

An Association   The courts have consistently held that a partnership must be entered *voluntarily;* that is, no one can be forced to be a partner against his or her will. Thus, "an association" has been interpreted as being "a voluntarily entered association." Being realistic, the courts also realize that people occasionally disagree. The measure of voluntariness is the willingness to associate *at the creation* of the relationship. Later disagreements will not automatically destroy the partnership. Thus, "an association" means a mutual unanimous assent to be partners jointly and severally at the time of agreement.

Of Two of More Persons   *Persons* here is interpreted broadly. It means persons in the biological sense, *or* persons in the legal sense, *or* persons in any other sense—in other words, two or more identifiable entities that elect to associate. Thus, each partner may be a human being, a corporation, a partnership, or even a joint venture.

To Carry on a Business   The third element of the definition has two separate segments. First, it must be determined whether there is a business. A business is defined as any trade, occupation, or profession; so most associations meet this test. Next, it must be determined whether the business is being "carried on." Carrying on implies some continuity. A business must be fairly permanent and long range in order to be carried on. If a business appears to be short term, it is quite possible that the court will rule that no partnership exists. However, if the other elements of a partnership are present, the short-term business may qualify as a joint venture.

As Co-Owners   The fourth element is probably the most important and the most confusing one. Co-ownership is like pornography: It is hard to define, but you know it when you see it.

Co-ownership does not refer to a sharing of title on the assets used in the business. Instead, it refers to a sharing of ownership of the business itself. The business is an intangible asset. A business often *uses* assets of a tangible nature, but it need not *own* any tangible assets. For example, several lawyers may enter a partnership. The partnership owns a business that provides services, and services are intangible. The lawyers may lease an office; they may rent furniture. They may not own a single tangible asset, yet they co-own a business.

How, then, is one to know if people involved in a business are co-owners? The simplest way is to look at the agreement the people made when the business was started. If the agreement states that they are partners, or co-owners, of the business, they are co-owners of the business. But all too often the agreement is ambiguous, unclear, or oral. In such a situation, the agreement is of no help in resolving the co-ownership question. Then the courts must look beyond the agreement.

Profits The gain made in the sale of produce or manufactures, after deducting the value of the labor, materials, rents, and all expenses, together with the interest of the capital expended.

Rebuttable presumption An inference of law that holds good until it is invalidated by proof or a stronger presumption.

The courts normally will look at how the parties treat **profits**. If the parties share profits, or net returns, there is prima facie evidence that a partnership exists—that is, the partnership is presumed to exist unless disproved by evidence to the contrary. The sharing of profits creates a **rebuttable presumption** that a partnership was formed. The burden then shifts to the parties to *disprove,* or to rebut, the presumption.

The UPA recognizes five rebuttals.[1] If one of the parties can prove that profits were shared for one of the reasons listed below, no partnership exists. If such proof is not made, the sharing of profits establishes that a partnership *did* exist. The rebuttal is valid if profits are shared for one of the following purposes:

1. as payment of a debt, by installments or otherwise (a promissory note or a judgment note should be produced as evidence)
2. as payment of wages to an employee or of rent to a landlord
3. as payment of an annuity to the representatives of a deceased partner
4. as payment of interest on a loan (again, some *document* probably will be necessary)
5. as payment of consideration in the sale of goodwill or other property, whether by installment payments or otherwise

In the following case, the sharing of profits established the existence of a partnership. Note how the court determined that "profits" were being shared.

[1]Uniform Partnership Act, Section 7(4).

Stuart v. Overland Medical Center
510 S.W.2d 494 (Mo. 1978)

FACTS   Dr. Stuart, a physician, withdrew from the Overland Medical Center. Upon his withdrawal, he claimed that the medical center was a professional partnership in which he had been a partner prior to his withdrawal and that he wanted to receive his share of the partnership. The Overland Medical Center argued that the arrangement was an expense-sharing operation rather than a partnership, so that Dr. Stuart was not a partner and was not entitled to any share of the business enterprise. Each physician at the center was paid based on that doctor's billings for services rendered less a percentage of those billings applied to the expenses of the center.

ISSUE   Was there a partnership agreement involved in the operation of the Overland Medical Center?

HOLDING   Yes. The Overland Medical Center was a partnership, and Dr. Stuart was a partner in that partnership.

REASONING   A partnership agreement need not be written in order to be valid and enforceable. The sharing of profits operates as prima facie evidence of the existence of a partnership, and in this case the doctors were sharing "profits," albeit in a strange manner. The share of income each doctor allocated to expenses was in no way related to the expenses that doctor had actually incurred. Thus, any one doctor's contribution toward expenses could actually help to defray the expenses of another of the doctors. In this manner, there was a sharing of profits. Since the medical center presented no evidence to rebut this presumption, the center is deemed to be a partnership, and Dr. Stuart is entitled to a share of the assets of the business.

For Profit   The fifth and final element of the definition of a partnership is probably the easiest to show. A partnership is operated "for profit." All that is needed is a profit *motive*. If the business was created to generate profits and to return these profits to the owners of the business, this test of the existence of a partnership is satisfied. Thus, nonprofit associations cannot, by definition, be partnerships. However, an unprofitable business can be a partnership, provided that profits are the goal of the business. The court is looking at the motive of the organization, not the "bottom line."

Uniform Limited Partnership Act

A limited partnership is set up in accordance with the controlling state laws governing limited partnerships—either the Uniform Limited Partnership Act (followed in twenty-seven states) or the Revised Limited Partnership Act (followed in twenty-two states). In Louisiana, which still follows its own statutes, neither of the uniform acts applies. Any parties who plan to establish a limited partnership need to check the applicable statute for the jurisdiction in which the limited partnership will be created in order to determine which statute will control.

Limited partner   A limited-partnership member who furnishes certain funds to the common stock and whose liability extends no further than the funds furnished.

Under Section 1 of the ULPA, a limited partnership can be created by two or more persons, as long as at least one person is designated a **limited partner.**

With this one exception—the classification of partners—a limited partnership has the same characteristics as a general partnership set up under the UPA. However, a limited partnership is more formal than a general partnership. In order to set up a limited partnership, the partners must sign and swear to a written certificate that details all the important elements of the partnership agreement. This certificate must be filed with the correct public official, as specified in the statutes of the state where the limited partnership is created.

A limited partner is so called because that partner has *limited liability*. A limited partner is not personally liable for any obligations of the partnership. However, there is a price to pay for this protection. A limited partner is precluded from management of the business. A limited partner who takes part in management loses the limited status[2] and may be treated as a *general* partner, subject to unlimited personal liability—but only in dealings with third persons who knew of the involvement of the limited partner in the management of the business. Limited partners who act as agents or employees of a general partner or of the firm or who advise the general partners about business are not considered to be "involved in management."

Revised Uniform Limited Partnership Act

In 1976, the National Conference of Commissioners on Uniform State Laws approved a Revised Uniform Limited Partnership Act (RULPA). This Revised Act was made available to the states in 1977 and by the end of 1985 had been adopted by twenty-two states. Although most of the topical coverage is essentially the same, there are some technical differences between the ULPA and the RULPA. For example, under RULPA, the certificate of agreement forming the limited partnership must be filed with the secretary of state for the state in which the limited partnership is formed. The Revised Act calls for profits and losses to be shared on the basis of capital contributions unless the agreement specifies some other distribution. The distribution of assets upon termination of the entity and the liquidation of its assets is treated differently under the Revised Act from the way it is treated under the ULPA. One of the interesting aspects of RULPA is found in Section 1105, which specifies that any cases not provided for in the Revised Act are to be governed by the provisions of the ULPA.

Throughout the three chapters on partnerships (36, 37, and 38), any major differences between the ULPA and the RULPA are discussed. If the coverage is essentially the same, no distinction between the two acts is mentioned.

PARTNERSHIP PROPERTY

Although a partnership is not required to own property, most partnerships do in fact own some property. Even if the partnership chooses not to own

[2]Ibid., Section 303.

property, it must have access to possession and use of some physical assets. And this access and use *may* lead to ownership, at least under the UPA and in the eyes of the court.

Partnership property is defined in Section 8 of the UPA. Under this section, the following kinds of property are deemed to be *partnership* property (owned by the partnership):

1. all property originally contributed to the partnership as a partner's capital contributions
2. all property acquired *on account of* the partnership
3. all property acquired with partnership funds, unless a contrary intention is shown
4. any interest in real property that is acquired in the partnership name
5. any conveyance to a partnership in the partnership name, unless a contrary intention is shown

If an individual partner wants to retain personal ownership but *allows* the partnership to *use* property, that partner should be extremely cautious. Unless the intention is made obvious, the property he thought he still owned may legally belong to the partnership. (The reason this is so important will be discussed at length in Chapter 38, on dissolution.)

THE PARTNERSHIP AGREEMENT

A partnership is created by *agreement* of the partners. The agreement is a contract. Unless it falls within the Statute of Frauds, it may be oral. In other words, no formality is required in setting up a general partnership. (Note, however, the formal requirements for creating a limited partnership, which we have already discussed.)

A reasonably prudent, cautious person would be expected to take great care in negotiating the basic partnership agreement and then reducing the agreement to written form. Yet all too often a partnership is begun with little or no detailed negotiation. And even if the parties are very careful, situations may arise that never were considered and therefore are not covered by the agreement. To minimize the harm such situations could create, the UPA imposes certain rules to be followed *unless* the agreement provides otherwise and specifies certain areas that the agreement must cover.

Imposed Rules

Unless the agreement between the parties says otherwise, the following rules are imposed by operation of law:

1. Each partner is entitled to an equal voice in the management of the business.
2. Each partner is entitled to an equal share of profits, without regard to capital contributions.
3. Each partner is expected to share any losses suffered by the business in the same proportion as profits are to be shared.
4. The books of the partnership are to be kept at the central office of the business.

In addition, some rules are imposed and *must be followed* by the partners, no matter what the agreement says. Any attempt to modify these rules in the agreement is contrary to public policy, so that the modification would be deemed *void*. Among these rules are the following:

1. Each partner is deemed to be an *agent* for the partnership and for each partner, as long as the partner is acting in a business-related matter.
2. Each partner is personally, *unlimitedly liable* for torts or contracts for which the partnership has too few assets to cover the debt or liability.
3. Each partner is expected to devote service to the partnership only and not to any competing business ventures.

Express Terms

In addition to those terms imposed by law, the partnership agreement should cover some other areas. For instance, the agreement should designate the *name* of the business. This name cannot be deceptively similar to the name of any other company or business, and it cannot mislead the public as to the nature of the business. (If a limited partnership is involved, the name should reflect that fact.)

The agreement should cover the *duration* of the business. How long will the partnership last? Such an understanding in the beginning can avoid serious disagreements later. It also should cover the *purpose* of the business. Knowing what you are trying to do not only makes it easier to operate a business but also helps to avoid any controversies later.

Finally, the agreement should discuss in detail how, or if, a partner *can withdraw* from the business. In this area, the rights of a withdrawing partner should be very carefully spelled out so that no one, including a court, will misconstrue the agreement's terms.

Of course, any other items the partners feel should be included can be discussed, agreed on, and included. In fact, the more detailed the original agreement, the better. A carefully drawn, well-thought-out agreement cannot be anything but helpful to all partners.

In the following case, violations of the partnership agreement led to a lawsuit and a judicially ordered dissolution of the partnership.

Altman v. Altman
653 F.2d 755 (1981)

FACTS   From 1952 to 1973, Sydney and Ashley Altman operated a number of partnerships engaged in real estate construction and management in southeast Pennsylvania. The brothers shared equally in the management and control of the business. They received equal salaries and equal reimbursement for certain personal expenses. In January, 1973, Sydney moved to Florida to establish residence in order to obtain a divorce. The brothers agreed that Sydney should commute to Pennsylvania to continue working until he established his residency. For the first six months, Sydney returned to Pennsylvania every week to work for two or three days. In July the brothers agreed that Sydney needed to return only once a month, and subsequently Sydney was advised by counsel to remain in Florida until the divorce was final. In November, 1973, Sydney told Ashley that he was considering retiring from the business and remaining in Florida permanently. Ashley agreed to consult with the firm's accountant to develop a mutually acceptable retirement agreement. At that point their stories diverged. Ashley claimed that Sydney accepted the accountant's recommendations and retired, effective 31 December 1973. Sydney claimed that the brothers never agreed, and that in the fall of 1974, Ashley presented Sydney with a one-sided retirement proposal prepared at Ashley's direction by the firm's attorney. At that point, Sydney sued for a court-ordered dissolution, alleging that Ashley had violated the partnership agreements, misappropriated partnership assets, and excluded Sydney from the business. Ashley denied all of the allegations, insisting that Sydney had retired as of 31 December 1973, thus dissolving the partnerships and ending the agreements.

ISSUE   Had the partnership been dissolved as of 31 December 1973, or was the partnership, and its agreements, still in effect?

HOLDING   The partnerships had not been dissolved, so that the agreements were still in effect, and therefore Ashley had violated the agreements.

REASONING   Ashley argued that Sydney had retired, as shown by his absence from the firm's office from October, 1973, to September, 1975, the time of the filing of this suit. His absence meant that Ashley had been left to manage the business alone for nearly two years and served as evidence that Sydney had retired. However, the trial court felt that Sydney's denial of his retirement was more credible than was Ashley's testimony to the contrary. In addition, a document prepared by the firm's attorney in September, 1974, which proposed a "plan to clarify the [retirement] situation," casts doubt on Sydney's retirement. Further, Ashley made no attempt to buy Sydney out or to settle business matters with Sydney. Thus, proof of a retirement and dissolution prior to the institution of these proceedings was inadequate. Turning to the alleged violations of the agreements, the court found that Ashley had paid himself a salary well in excess of that agreed to by the partners. His argument that he was doing more work and therefore deserved more money is not justified under Pennsylvania law. Similarly, Ashley violated the agreement in the matter of reimbursing himself for his personal expenses to a greater degree than Sydney was reimbursed. As a result, Sydney's request for a judicial dissolution is granted. In addition, Ashley must account for and return the excess compensation and the excess reimbursements for distribution in the final settlement of the partnership estate.

TAXATION

For taxation purposes, the partnership form of business is neither an advantage nor a disadvantage. Basically, the partnership is not taxed, but the individual partners are taxed on the receipts of the firm. The federal income tax rules and regulations do not recognize the partnership as a taxable entity. The firm must file a federal tax return, but the return is for information purposes only. Each partner is taxed on his or her share of the firm's profits for the year, whether these profits are distributed to the partners or not. Each partner is also taxed on the capital gains—or allowed to take the deductions for capital losses—the firm experiences during the tax year.

Many states treat the partnership as a mere conduit for the transfer of income to the partners. In these states, the partnership is not taxed, but the partners are taxed on the firm's income whether it is distributed or retained by the firm for reinvestment or expansion.

OTHER TYPES OF BUSINESS ORGANIZATIONS

Three other types of business organizations exist that are very similar to partnerships. In a partnership by estoppel, a partnership is imposed by law even though the parties have not entered into a partnership agreement. Joint ventures are sufficiently different from partnerships to merit separate legal treatment. Mining partnerships are treated in a special manner because of the special problems they have presented historically.

Partnerships by Estoppel

Estoppel A person's own act or acceptance that stops or closes that person's mouth to allege or plead the truth; a bar or impediment that precludes allegation or denial of a certain fact or state of facts.

Technically, no partnership can exist without an agreement. However, a third person who is dealing with someone who *claims* to be a partner may be able to proceed against the partnership and/or the alleged partners. Such a situation may lead to a partnership by **estoppel**.

Suppose person D calls on person X. D tells X that he (D) is a partner in firm ABC. In fact, D is *not* a partner. Suppose further that X signs a contract, expecting ABC to perform the contract as signed. Is X entitled to performance from ABC? On the basis of these facts, the answer would be a resounding NO! Since the firm, ABC, did nothing to cause X to believe that D was a partner, ABC is not estopped from denying that D is a partner or from refusing the contract.

But what if X telephoned the firm, and the firm claimed that D was a partner? Now X could hold ABC to the contract. ABC would be estopped from denying that D was a partner. To use estoppel, three facts must be shown:

1. that someone who is not a partner was *held out* to be a partner
2. that the third person justifiably relied on the holding out
3. that the person will be harmed if no liability is imposed

In the following case, estoppel was used to hold the partnership liable.

Volkman v. DP Associates
268 S.E.2d 265 (N.C. App. 1980)

FACTS

The Volkmans entered into a contract with David McNamee for construction advice in the building of a residence. Prior to signing the contract, McNamee told the Volkmans that he was going into business with Philip Carroll. Subsequently, and still before the contract was signed, the Volkmans received correspondence from McNamee on DP Associates letterhead. (The Volkmans testified that they believed the "DP" was derived from the first names of the individual defendants, David and Philip.) Prior to signing the contract at the DP Associates office, McNamee introduced the Volkmans to Carroll, who said, "I hope we'll be working together." Carroll also allegedly stated that, while McNamee was the person the Volkmans would be working with, he would also be available. The Volkmans reviewed the written contract at the DP offices. McNamee suggested that DP should serve as virtual general contractor and said he needed to check the forms with Phil. Once the contract was signed and work began, the Volkmans had other opportunities to see Carroll at the DP office and to discuss the construction project with him. When the contract was breached, the Volkmans sued both McNamee and Carroll, seeking to hold them jointly and severally liable as partners. Carroll moved for a summary judgment releasing him and presented evidence that he had never been a partner with McNamee and should not be held liable in the case. The trial court agreed with Carroll and entered an order dismissing him from the suit.

ISSUE

Was Carroll a partner or a partner by estoppel, so that he was properly a party defendant in this case?

HOLDING

Sufficient evidence was presented to justify denial of the motion for summary judgment on the issue of partnership by estoppel.

REASONING

The appellate court felt that Carroll had the burden of disproving his status as a partner. Partnership by estoppel can be found based on the words or the conduct of one party that leads the other party to reasonably believe the representations to be true, to the detriment of that other person. In this case there were sufficient allegations that Carroll had been present in the offices of DP Associates and had conducted himself in a manner that led the Volkmans to reasonably believe that he was, in fact, a partner with McNamee. In addition, there is the issue of apparent or ostensible authority. Based on his conduct, Carroll may be liable to the Volkmans without reference to estoppel. At the least, the Volkmans presented a sufficient prima facie case to justify going to the jury. The lower court's granting of the motion for summary judgment is reversed.

Notice the difference in the conduct of the purported partner in the following case, and how the court found that a partnership by estoppel was not present due to that difference in conduct.

Cox Enterprises, Inc. v. *Filip*
538 S.W.2d 836 (1976)

FACTS   Trans Texas Properties, a business owned and operated by Filip, wanted to place some advertisements in the *Austin American-Statesman*, a newspaper owned by Cox Enterprises. One of the employees of Trans Texas told the newspaper that Elliot, who was not a general partner, was a co-owner of Trans Texas. The employee had no authority to make such a representation concerning Elliot, and Elliot was not aware that such claims were being made. The newspaper relied on Elliot's "status" as an owner of the business, and on Elliot's financial condition in agreeing to run the advertisements for Trans Texas on credit. The newspaper made no effort to verify the relationship between Elliot and Trans Texas. The advertisements were run in the newspaper, but Trans Texas never paid for the ads. Cox sued Filip and Elliot for the debt, alleging that they were doing business as Trans Texas. Elliot denied liability since he was not an owner of the business or in any way involved with the business.

ISSUE   Did the facts justify treating Elliot as a partner by estoppel?

HOLDING   No. Elliot did not consent to being held out as a partner of the firm.

REASONING   Cox Enterprises argued that it had relied on Elliot's status as a co-owner in extending the credit to Trans Texas and that it was harmed as a result of its reliance. Cox also asserted that Elliot was negligent in not discovering that he was being represented as a partner in the firm and that Elliot had an affirmative duty to seek out the third parties to whom he had been represented as a partner. Cox felt that by acting in this "negligent" manner, Elliot was estopped to deny his status as a partner. The court disagreed with the positions put forward by Cox. Elliot never consented to being held out as a partner, was not aware of this particular situation, and had no duty to seek out any and every third person who might think he was a partner. Cox had acted improperly by merely accepting the fact that Elliot was a partner without any efforts to verify this information.

Joint Ventures

Joint Venture   A commercial or maritime enterprise undertaken by several persons jointly; an association of two or more persons to carry out a single business enterprise for profit.

A **joint venture** has all the characteristics of a partnership except one. It is *not* set up to "carry on a business." A joint venture, by definition, is *set up to carry out a limited number of transactions, very commonly a single deal.* As soon as that deal (or those transactions) is completed, the joint venture terminates. The reason this form is important is that the agency power of the joint venture is limited; thus, a member of the venture is not as likely to be held responsible for the conduct of the other members of the venture. Also, the death of a joint venturer does not automatically dissolve the joint venture. In all other respects, partnership law is applied.

Mining Partnerships

Mining partnership   An association of several owners of a mine for cooperation in working the mine.

A **mining partnership** is a uniquely American creation. A mining partnership *is* a partnership, but it has special characteristics not found in a nonmining partnership. In a regular partnership, no partner can sell his interest or leave his interest to his heirs in a will. In a mining partnership, the sale of an interest or the bequeathing of an interest by will is permitted.

One theory about how this special treatment evolved is that during the California gold rush, after partners discovered gold, one partner would suddenly and "mysteriously" have a fatal accident, which left the mine to the surviving partner. In an effort to extend the life span of successful miners, the mining partnership laws were developed. The death of a partner merely brought *another* partner, the deceased partner's heir, into the business. Thus, no advantage was gained by the death of a partner.

SUMMARY

Every business enterprise must have an organizational form. Partnerships fall between the two extremes of organizational form—that is, proprietorships and corporations. A partnership has the advantages of being easily formed and of having multiple contributors, whose different opinions and expertise are always available. A partnership has the disadvantages of somewhat limited existence and unlimited personal liability for each partner.

A partnership is defined in the Uniform Partnership Act as an association of two or more persons carrying on a business as co-owners for profit. This definition requires that the partners voluntarily agree to enter the business and that the business be somewhat permanent in nature. Co-ownership is the key element of the definition. This element is so important that a sharing of profits by the people involved creates a presumption of co-ownership, which in turn creates a presumption that a partnership exists.

A limited partnership is similar to a regular, or general, partnership with two major exceptions: There must be at least one limited partner who may not participate in the management of the business, and somewhat formal documents must be prepared and correctly filed in order to establish the limited partnership.

Partnership property is a confusing area. Any property owned by the business belongs to the partners together, not to any one partner individually. Five different tests are applied by the courts to decide whether any particular asset belongs to the partnership.

Partners are expected to comply with the basic partnership agreement at all times. However, the law imposes some duties on the partners in the event the agreement does not cover certain areas of responsibility. Some of these rules are followed unless the partners agree otherwise. Some of the rules *must* be followed as a matter of law.

In some enterprises, no regular partnership agreement is involved, but it appears that a partnership exists. The first of these is a partnership by estoppel: There is no partnership agreement, but the parties act as if there were an agreement, to the detriment of some third party. The other two types of organizations are joint ventures and mining partnerships. Both have special rules that separate them from ordinary general partnerships.

DISCUSSION QUESTIONS

1. Why are so many professional businesses (law offices, doctors' offices, and so on) partnerships rather than corporations?

2. List some of the advantages and disadvantages of the partnership form of business organization.

3. Under Section 6 of the UPA, what are the five characteristics of a partnership?

4. How do the courts decide whether the people involved in a business are co-owners of that business?

5. How is a mining partnership different from a general partnership?

6. Bob, Carol, and Ted set up a partnership. Later, Bob and Ted wanted to bring in Alice as a fourth partner. Carol objected to allowing Alice to enter. A vote was taken, and Alice got two votes of approval and one of disapproval. Will Alice be admitted as a fourth partner? Explain your answer.

7. Ed, Tim, and Dennis had a business concept they were sure would be successful if they could establish it properly. Unfortunately, they were short of capital and could not afford to begin the business without financial support. Marge was willing to put up the necessary capital, but she was unwilling to face the liability of a general partner. Marge has agreed to be a limited partner in the business. What must the parties do to establish a limited partnership under the ULPA? Must they do anything differently under the RULPA?

8. Larry and Darrin formed a partnership. Darrin contributed $10,000. Larry let the partnership use an office building he owned, rent free. Three years later, the business dissolved. Darrin claims the building is partnership property. Larry claims he still owns the building personally. Who is correct, and why?

9. Sam and Ruth enter a partnership. Sam does not want Ruth to be his agent or to participate in managing the business. What should he do to see that his wishes are carried out?

10. Tim and Margie are partners. In order to get a loan, they tell the bank Denise is also a partner. Relying on Denise's credit, the bank makes the loan. Tim and Margie default, and the bank sues Denise. What must the bank prove in order to hold Denise liable for the loan?

CASE PROBLEMS

1. Herbst owned a farm that was operated by Parzych. Parzych operated the farm to pay off a debt of $6000 he owed Herbst. The debt was to be repaid by an equal share of profits from the farming operation. Parzych purchased some supplies from Rosenberger on credit. When Parzych did not pay the bill, Rosenberger sued Herbst for the debt. Rosenberger contended that since Parzych and Herbst shared profits, they must be partners. Is this contention correct? (*Rosenberger v. Herbst*, 232 A.2d 634 [Pa. 1967].)

2. Anderson Hay & Grain Co. extended credit to Ruidoso Downs Feed Concession, a business apparently being operated by Dunn and Welch. The credit was extended on the basis of Dunn's financial responsibility, and Dunn was the person contacted for payments on the account. On at least one prior occasion, Dunn and Welch had entered a contract in which each had been designated as the "party of the second part." When the Anderson bill was not paid, Anderson brought suit against Dunn for the balance due. Dunn denied that he and Welch were partners and refused to pay the bill. Given that Dunn and Welch were *not* partners in this

case, on what basis may Anderson Hay & Grain attempt to collect from Dunn? How is the court likely to rule in this case? (*Anderson Hay & Grain Co.* v. *Dunn*, 467 P.2d 5 [N.M. 1970].)

3. Gail Neild and Charles Wolfe planned to marry. They moved into an apartment in New York City, signing a lease in the name of Charles Wolfe. Since Wolfe's salary was twice as large as Neild's, they agreed that Wolfe would pay two-thirds of the rent and Neild would pay one-third. Several years later the relationship deteriorated. Neild went to England for four months to visit her family, and on her return Wolfe refused to let her into the apartment. Soon after, the apartment building was converted to a cooperative, and the tenants were given the opportunity to purchase their apartments at a price well below fair market value. Wolfe purchased his apartment. Neild sued Wolfe, claiming that they were partners in the apartment and that she was entitled to one-third of the difference between the purchase price of the apartment and its fair market value. Were Wolfe and Neild partners in this apartment? What factors will the court examine in deciding this case? [*Neild* v. *Wolfe*, 445 N.Y.S.2d 934 [N.Y. Sup. Ct. 1981].)

4. Young Lumber Co. and Altman entered into an agreement whereby Altman was to supervise a job Young Lumber was obligated to perform. Altman was to receive one-half of the profits from the job. All bills were to be paid by Young Lumber. Does this agreement create a partnership? Explain. (*United States* v. *Young Lumber Co.*, 376 F. Supp. 1290 [S.C. 1974].)

5. Harber, Pittman, and Calvert orally agreed to build and sell houses as partners. Harber then withdrew $6000 from the partnership account to purchase three lots on which to construct houses. The deeds to the lots were listed in Harber's name alone, as were the titles to the three houses when they were built. Harber then sold the properties at a profit. Is Harber entitled to keep all the profits for himself? (*Davis* v. *Pioneer Bank & Trust Co.*, 272 So.2d 430 [La. 1973].)

6. Acruem was a partnership formed in 1967. The partnership certificate filed with the county clerk's office listed three partners: Ackman, Rubin, and Emil. Emil immediately assigned each of his two children one-half of his 25-percent interest in the partnership. Emil would remain as nominal partner, making all business decisions with respect to the business. (Ackman and Rubin had been informed of this arrangement prior to the formal execution of the partnership agreement, and

neither had objected to the arrangement.) Emil's children made all contributions and payments to the business through their father and received their shares of partnership income directly from the business. One of Emil's children, Judy Tenney, had a personal liability insurance policy from Insurance Company of North America (INA) that covered any losses for which the policy holder became personally liable due to personal injury. A fire at Acruem in 1969 resulted in numerous lawsuits against the partners for liability. Tenney paid $141,000 as her share of the personal liability claims of the firm and submitted a claim to INA for indemnification. INA refused to pay the claim, alleging that Tenney was not a partner and therefore not legally liable for the claims. Is INA correct, or is Tenney a partner and therefore personally liable? Explain your answer. (*Tenney* v. *Insurance Company of North America*, 409 F. Supp. 746 [N.Y. 1975].)

7. Adams and Wolff were partners in an automobile body and repair shop. The partnership failed to pay social security taxes or unemployment insurance contributions that had been withheld from the pay of the shop's employees. According to the terms of the partnership, Wolff was responsible for collecting and paying these federal taxes. The government obtained a tax lien on the assets of the business and levied the lien against a bank account owned by Adams. Adams claimed that the tax liability was one owed by Wolff alone, without regard to the partnership, due to the language of the partnership agreement. Is Adams correct in his assertion? (*Adams* v. *United States*, 328 F. Supp. 228 [D.C. Neb. 1971].)

8. Accountants Kelley and Galloway formed a partnership to conduct their business. Eventually they hired Smith as an employee of the firm. Although Smith was only an employee, Kelley and Galloway held Smith out to the public as a partner, and Smith consented to this holding out. Smith resigned from the firm and filed suit against the partnership, claiming that he was a partner by estoppel and entitled to a share of the assets of the business. Is Smith entitled to a share of the firm? Explain fully. (*Smith* v. *Kelley*, 465 S.W.2d 39 [Ky. 1971].)

9. OWLP was a limited partnership in Hawaii that owned the Outrigger Hotel. In 1974, OWLP entered into an agreement with Hotel Operating Company (HOC) that called for HOC and OWLP to jointly manage the Outrigger and to share revenues in a set proportion. For the next three years the business was

operated according to the agreement. In 1977, Hawaii's director of taxes brought suit against OWLP for unpaid general excise taxes for the years 1974 through 1977. He claimed that HOC merely provided services to OWLP, and that OWLP was responsible for the taxes on all of the gross revenues. OWLP paid general excise taxes on its share of the revenues of the hotel during that period and denied its liability for the nearly $200,000 in unpaid excise taxes. If HOC and OWLP were partners or joint venturers, OWLP was not liable. If OWLP was the owner, and HOC merely provided services, OWLP was liable. How should the court resolve this case? What factors will be decisive in the court's determination? (*In re O.W. Limited Partnership,* 668 P.2d 56 [Ha. App. 1983].)

10. P & M Cattle Company, a partnership consisting of Bill Poage and L. W. Maxfield, was in the business of raising and selling cattle. It entered into the following contract:

Contract—Rusty Holler (60 Bar Ranch)
        L. W. Maxfield and Bill Poage

Rusty to furnish grass for est 1000 yr st and 21 heifers—Maxfield and Poage to furnish money for cattle plus trucking and salt—and max of $300 per month for labor

Rusty to take cattle around May 1st and cattle to be sold at a time this fall to be agreed upon by all parties involved

Cost of cattle plus freight—salt and labor to be first cost

Net money from sale of cattle less first cost to be split 50-50 between Rusty (1/2) and Maxfield and Poage (1/2) (death loss to be first cost)

The contract was signed by all parties. When the business venture lost $89,500, P & M sued Holler for his share of the loss, claiming that the contract represented a partnership agreement and that losses were to be shared, just as profits were to be shared. Was this a partnership agreement, so that Holler was liable for the loss? Why or why not? (*P & M Cattle Co.* v. *Holler,* 559 P.2d 1019 [Wyo. 1977].)

CHAPTER 37

Operation of a Partnership

OUTLINE

RIGHTS OF THE PARTNERS

A person who enters a partnership acquires certain rights. Some of these rights are gained through the agreement, and some are gained through the terms of the UPA. This book cannot cover all the rights that the partners might decide to cover in the agreement, but it can examine those rights imposed by operation of law.

Management

By virtue of status as a partner, each partner is entitled to an equal voice in management. In conducting ordinary business of the partnership, a majority vote controls. In order to conduct any extraordinary business, a unanimous vote is required.[1] A matter is considered extraordinary if it changes the basic *nature* or the basic *risk* of the business.

While the UPA requires that each partner be given an equal voice in managing the business, the partners are allowed to agree on the definition of equal. Such an agreement can be beneficial to a dynamic business. If the partnership is forced to conduct its business by majority vote, opportunities could be lost because a vote might not be taken quickly enough.

To avoid this problem, many partnership agreements *define* the management voice of each partner. It should be remembered that such a definition must be included in the agreement to be valid. For instance, a partnership composed of A, B, C, and D might provide the following management divisions:

1. A is in charge of purchasing.
2. B is in charge of marketing.
3. C is in charge of accounting and personnel.
4. D is in charge of paper clips and office neatness.
5. Any other areas are governed by a vote.

Under such an agreement, B could make marketing decisions *immediately,* without the necessity of a meeting among the partners to vote on some marketing question. Likewise, A could decide matters concerning purchasing; C could make personnel decisions; and D could dust the furniture without consulting with the other partners.

Reimbursement

Capital contribution Money expended in acquiring, equipping, and promoting an enterprise.

Each partner is entitled to repayment by the partnership for any money spent to further the interests of the partnership. In addition, each partner is entitled to interest on the advances or payments made, unless the agreement says otherwise. Each partner is also entitled to a return of his or her **capital con-**

[1]Uniform Partnership Act, Section 18(h).

tribution at the close of the partnership, provided enough money is present to repay each partner after all liabilities have been satisfied.[2]

Profits and Losses

Unless the agreement says otherwise, each partner is entitled to an *equal* share of the profits of the business. The profits are *not* automatically divided in the same percentage as capital contributed. Nor are they automatically divided in any other unequal manner. This is the *only* remuneration to which any partner is always entitled.[3] No partner is automatically permitted to draw a salary from the business even if that partner devotes extra time to running the business. However, the agreement can be worded in such a manner that a partner receives a salary from the business, with the remaining profits then divided in some predetermined manner. But such a salary provision must be expressly set out in the agreement. Losses are divided among the partners in the same ratio as profits would have been shared.

Books and Records

Each partner is entitled to free access to the books and records of the business. This includes the right to inspect the records and to copy them as the partner sees fit. Along a related line, each partner is expected to give, and entitled to receive, detailed information on any matter that affects the partnership.[4]

Partnership Property

Tenancy in partnership A special form of ownership of property, found only in partnerships, in which each partner has an equal right to possess and to use partnership assets for partnership purposes, and which carries a right of survivorship.

Each partner is a co-owner of partnership property with the other partners. The ownership is defined as **tenancy in partnership**.[5] This tenancy *entitles the partner to possess the property for partnership purposes*, but *not* to possess it for nonpartnership purposes. However, if all the partners *agree* to a nonpartnership usage, such a usage is allowed.

This tenancy also carries with it a right of survivorship. This means that if a partner dies, the *other partners* own the property. It is *not* inherited by the heirs of the deceased partner if any other partners are still surviving. Thus, the last surviving partner will own the partnership individually. The heirs of the last partner may not possess the property except for partnership purposes.

Right to an Account

Any partner is entitled to a formal *account*—that is, a statement or record of business transactions or dealings—if he or she feels mistreated in the partnership.[6] Specifically, any partner who is excluded from the business or from use of business properties is entitled to an account. And the UPA provides for an account in any other circumstances that render it just and reasonable. In effect, any time there is an internal argument or disagreement about the business operation, the courts will say an account is just and reasonable.

[2]Ibid., Section 18(a), (b), (c).
[3]Ibid., Section 18(f).
[4]Ibid., Sections 19, 20.
[5]Ibid., Section 25.
[6]Ibid., Section 22.

Each partner is a fiduciary for every other partner and is expected to account to the other partners and to the partnership for any benefits received or any profits derived without the knowledge and consent of the other partners.[7] In the following case, a partner was accused of violating his fiduciary duty and of deriving a secret profit from partnership affairs.

Marsh v. Gentry
642 S.W.2d 574 (Ky. 1982)

FACTS	Marsh and Gentry formed a partnership with the purpose of buying and selling race horses. During the course of their partnership, they purchased a mare, Champagne Woman, and her foal, Excitable Lady. Two years later, the partners put Excitable Lady up for sale in an auction. Gentry then bought Excitable Lady at the auction, without telling Marsh that he intended to bid on the filly. The following year, Marsh learned that Gentry had purchased the filly, but Gentry claimed to have sold her in the interim. Marsh learned that Gentry still owned the horse only when Excitable Lady won the Debutante Stakes at Churchill Downs the following summer. Marsh then filed suit against Gentry.
ISSUES	Did Gentry violate his fiduciary duty to Marsh? Is Marsh entitled to an accounting?
HOLDINGS	Yes, to both issues. Gentry violated his duty to his partner, and his partner is entitled to an accounting to discover the extent of the damages.
REASONING	A partner must act as a fiduciary toward his other partners and must account for any benefits derived or profits earned without the consent of the other partners. Here, Gentry purchased a horse being sold by the partnership without telling his partner that he intended to bid on the horse, which was a violation of his fiduciary duty. He then retained ownership of the horse after claiming that he had sold her and raced her in stakes races without revealing his ownership or sharing any of the profits from the racing successes of the horse. Marsh is entitled to an accounting and to a division of profits from the transactions.

Because They were in Horse Business (handwritten margin note)

DUTIES OF THE PARTNERS

Agency Duties

Each partner is an *agent* of the partnership and of every other partner. Thus, any conduct by a partner that is *apparently* authorized is binding on the partnership. And since each partner is *personally* liable for partnership debts, such an act makes each partner at least *potentially* personally liable.

This is obviously a possible financial hazard to the partners. To reduce somewhat the danger that could be presented by a reckless partner, the UPA restricts *some* agency power. Under Section 9(3), there is no apparent au-

[7]Ibid., Section 21.

thority to do any of five specific acts unless *unanimously* approved. These five acts are as follows:

Assignment for the benefit of creditors   An assignment in trust made by debtors for the payment of their debts.

Goodwill   The fixed and favorable consideration of customers arising from established and well-conducted business.

1. making an **assignment for the benefit of creditors** by transferring partnership property to a trust for the creditors of the business
2. selling or otherwise disposing of the **goodwill** of the business
3. performing any act that would make it impossible to carry on the business
4. confessing a judgment against the partnership
5. submitting a partnership claim to arbitration

Notice the scope of these acts. The first three frustrate business, and the last two remove the partners' right to their "day in court." With these five exceptions, any other act of a partner that is within the scope of apparent authority is binding.

For example, a partner may sell and convey real property owned in the partnership name.[8] The conveyance may be made in the business name *or in the name of the partner.* In either case, the conveyance is valid, even if unauthorized, if the grantee has passed title on to an innocent third party in a subsequent sale. If the grantee is still in possession of the property, the other partners can recover the property, provided the sale was not authorized.

Admission   A statement that will be accepted in court as evidence.

Also, if a partner makes an **admission** about partnership affairs, and the admission is within the partner's authority, the partnership is bound.[9] The firm will have to honor the admission and uphold it if it was within the admitting partner's authority, even if it harms the business.

Since each partner is an agent, *notice* given to any partner on a partnership matter is as good as notice given to each of the partners.[10] This is simply the application of basic agency law to a partnership/agency situation. Similarly, knowledge gained, or *remembered,* while one is a partner is imputed to each partner.

If a partner acts, or fails to act, in the course and scope of the business, and the act or omission causes harm to a third person, each partner is as liable to the third person as the partner who committed the tort.[11] The partners face joint and several liability. They can be sued together or separately for the harm. Thus, the injured party might be harmed by partner A but sue only partners B and C and win the suit. In such a case, B and C would have to pay for the harm caused by A even though A was not named as a defendant. Again, this is merely an application of agency law principles to the partnership setting.

[8]Ibid., Section 10.
[9]Ibid., Section 11.
[10]Ibid., Section 12.
[11]Ibid., Section 13.

Likewise, if a partner *misapplies* money or property of a third person that is in the possession of the partnership, the partnership is liable. All the partners, or each of them, may have to answer for the breach of trust of one of them.[12] Again the liability is joint and several.

It should be obvious by now that being a partner *may* be hazardous to your financial health. Even if you are a careful, painstaking, and cautious person, you face potential financial liability, maybe even disaster, from the conduct of your partners. What rights do you have that protect you? What rights are available for the protection of *any* partner from the excesses of another member of the partnership?

One right protects the other partners and the partnership from a creditor of a partner. Suppose that Al, Bill, and Cindi are partners. The business is very profitable, and Bill and Cindi are solvent. However, Al is in deep financial trouble. Several of Al's creditors sue Al to collect their claims. They win the suit, only to discover that Al cannot pay the judgment from his personal assets. Can these creditors foreclose on Al's share of the partnership assets? No. All the creditors can do is to get a **charging order** from a court.[13] Under a charging order, the debtor/partner's *profits* are paid to the creditors until the claims are fully paid. Thus, the partnership can continue, and Bill and Cindi are protected. Only Al, the debtor, suffers.

On the other hand, suppose that the partnership is in financial difficulty, but that some of the partners are solvent. Can the partnership's creditors proceed directly against the individual partners, bypassing or ignoring the assets of the firm? No. The creditors of the firm must first proceed against the assets of the firm. The following case illustrates this point.

Charging order   An order granted to a judgment creditor that the property of the judgment debtor shall stand charged with the payment of the amount for which judgment shall have been recovered, with interest.

Horn's Crane Service v. Prior
152 N.W.2d 421 (Neb. 1967)

FACTS   Prior and Cook were two of three partners in a partnership. The business entered a written contract with Horn's Crane Service and received supplies and services from Horn. When the firm failed to pay Horn's, Horn's immediately sued Prior and Cook individually and personally on the debt. Prior and Cook defended on the basis that Horn's must first proceed against the business assets before it can proceed against the personal assets of the individual partners.

ISSUE   May a partnership creditor proceed directly against the partners as individuals if the firm defaults on its obligations?

HOLDING   No. The creditor must first proceed against the partnership assets or allege that the partnership has too few assets to permit a recovery.

---

[12]Ibid., Section 14.
[13]Ibid., Section 28.

REASONING   The creditor extended credit to the partnership, so that the partners are entitled to expect the business assets will be used to cover the obligation as far as possible. To permit the creditor to bypass the firm and proceed directly against the individual partners is unfair. Such conduct benefits the unsued partners disproportionately and harms the sued partners disproportionately. The case was dismissed for failure to state a proper cause of action.

Fiduciary Duties

Another protection given to the partners is the legal status assigned to each partner. Each member of a partnership is a *fiduciary* of the other partners and of the business itself.[14] The fiduciary position carries with it certain responsibilities and certain duties. As was shown in *Marsh* v. *Gentry*, each partner is required to account for, and to surrender to the firm, any profits derived from the business or from the use of business assets. No partner is allowed to have a conflict of interest with the partnership. And each partner is entitled to indemnification from a partner who causes a loss or liability from misconduct in the course and scope of employment.

RIGHTS OF THIRD PERSONS

While the partners are dealing internally, they are each aware of the rights and duties of one another. Each partner should know the terms of the basic agreement and the limits of his or her authority. However, a third person who deals with the partnership has no such advantage. Any nonpartner who deals with the firm must rely on *appearances*. As a result, a third person who deals with the partnership may be given certain rights by the court that are specifically denied by the basic partnership agreement.

Contracts

As noted earlier, each partner is an agent of the partnership. Thus, if a partner negotiates a contract on behalf of the partnership, that partner is negotiating as an agent. From agency law, we know that if the agent has the *apparent authority* to perform an act, the principal is bound by the act. The same rule applies here. If the partner has the apparent authority to enter the contract, the partnership is bound to honor the contract.

In many instances, the partner has the *actual* authority to enter the contract. If so, the partnership is obviously bound, and the partner who negotiated the contract is no more liable than the other partners.

In some cases, the partner has the apparent authority to enter the contract but lacks the actual authority. (Recall, for example, the division of duties discussion earlier in the chapter.) Under these circumstances, the partnership will still have to honor the contract with the third person. But the partner

[14]Ibid., Section 21.

who negotiated the contract will be liable to the partnership for any losses that arise because the partner exceeded his or her authority.

In still other cases, the partner does not have even apparent authority; if a contract is negotiated, the negotiating partner is personally obligated to perform, but the firm is *not* liable on the agreement.

When the court examines these agreements, the apparent authority of the partner is of overriding importance. To help in deciding the scope of authority, courts often look at the type of business the firm is conducting. If the partnership buys and sells as its primary business purpose, the court views the partnership (unofficially) as a *trading* partnership. If the primary business purpose is to provide services, the court views it (unofficially) as a *nontrading* partnership. In a trading partnership, the partners are presumed to have broad powers. In a nontrading partnership, partners are deemed to have much narrower powers. A partner in a trading partnership is presumably authorized to perform *any* management-related duties. In contrast, a partner in a nontrading business is apparently authorized to do only those things reasonably necessary to further the main business purpose of the partnership.

A third person who is dealing with a partnership for the first time needs to exercise care. The partner with whom the third person is dealing may exceed his or her authority, and the third person will find that the contract entered is not binding on the partnership. The next case dealt with such a situation.

Jolly v. Kent Realty, Inc.
729 P.2d 310 (Ariz. App. 1986)

FACTS   Seven parties entered into a partnership or a joint venture in January, 1979. (The parties signed a "Joint Venture Agreement" specifying that the agreement was between "co-investors and *not* between partners." Despite this agreement, the court assumed that the parties had formed a partnership because the agreement did not restrict the involvement of the investors to a single transaction, but implied that it was to be ongoing.) The first act of the group was to acquire an apartment complex in Phoenix. The group agreed to allow Kent Realty (one of the partners) to manage the property for a fee before profits were divided. The group further agreed that all decisions affecting the investment must be referred to the entire group, with majority of ownership interests voted controlling the decisions so made. In January and February, 1984, Jolly and Kent, nominally acting for Kent Realty, engaged in negotiations for the sale of the property to Jolly on behalf of Sunny Hills Association. Jolly made a written offer to purchase the property for $900,000. The offer was submitted on a standard real estate form. Kent did not accept the offer, but instead submitted a written counteroffer on a preprinted "Supplement" form. Jolly did not execute this form, but instead submitted yet another counteroffer on a "Supplement" form. Again, the form was not executed; instead, Kent submitted another "Supplement" form serving as a counteroffer and establishing a deadline for acceptance two days later. Kent's signature appeared on this form, as it had on the earlier form he had submitted. Jolly signed this fourth form in the space indicated for the buyer to sign. Below the line for the buyer's signature was a "Final Acceptance by Seller" section that was left blank on the form Jolly signed. The next week Jolly opened an escrow account at Western Title Agency and made a partial inspection of the property. Several days later Kent informed Jolly that the property was "in a partnership and that he needed to obtain the partners' approval for the sale." That approval was not forthcoming, and Kent subsequently refused to perform the contract. Jolly sued for specific performance.

ISSUES   Did the writings between Jolly and Kent satisfy the Statute of Frauds? Did Kent have the actual or the apparent authority to sell the property on behalf of his fellow investors?

HOLDINGS   Yes, the writings were sufficient to satisfy the Statute of Frauds. No, Kent did not have the actual or the apparent authority to bind the group to the contract with Jolly.

REASONING   Jolly had not signed each of Kent's submissions, but Jolly was not the party being sued. Kent raised the Statute of Frauds as a defense when, in fact, it was Kent's signature that was needed, and Kent had signed. As for the authority of Kent to bind the group, such authority would be apparent only if the group normally dealt in selling real estate and if Kent's conduct was the usual way the group did business. In fact, the history of the group revealed that no property had ever been sold, so that the sale was unusual. Given that this was an unusual business transaction of the group, the sale could not be authorized without the approval of the co-owners. Since such approval was not given, Kent lacked the requisite apparent authority, and the contract was not binding on the co-owners.

Borrowing in the Partnership Name

Perhaps the most important area in which the court applies the trading-versus-nontrading distinction is in the borrowing of money. In a trading partnership, the firm deals from inventory. Inventory must be purchased. Purchases require money. Thus, a partner has the apparent authority to borrow money in the firm name.

In a nontrading partnership, money is not as obviously needed. As a result, the courts are less apt to impose liability on the firm for a loan that was made to a single partner even though that partner borrowed the money in the partnership name.

Torts and Crimes

Tort feasor   A wrongdoer; one who commits or is guilty of a tort.

Again, it must be pointed out that each partner is an agent for every other partner. Under agency law, a *tort* committed by an agent leaves the agent liable as the **tort feasor**. And it may leave the principal liable, jointly and severally with the agent, under the theory of *respondeat superior*. If the injured person can establish that the partner was performing in "the course and scope of employment," the firm and each of the partners are liable for the tort. If the tort is willful and malicious, the firm is normally not liable. The following hypothetical cases help to illustrate these points.

Mary, Ned, and Oscar are partners. Ned is driving to a business meeting to represent the firm in some negotiations. On the way to the meeting, Ned runs a stop sign and hits Sam. Since Ned was on a job-related errand, all three partners are liable to Sam, as is the partnership itself.

Mary, Ned, and Oscar are still partners. Oscar is driving to a business meeting to represent the firm. On the way, Oscar sees Tom crossing the street. Oscar is still angry at Tom for an insult from long ago. Oscar accelerates the car and *intentionally* runs over Tom. Since the tort was willful and malicious, neither Mary nor Ned nor the firm is liable to Tom.

If the willful and malicious tort is one that furthers any business interests of the firm, the other partners *may* be liable. If the intentional tort is not related to the business purpose, the other partners could still be held liable, provided that they assent to or ratify the conduct. Otherwise, the other partners face no liability for intentional torts. The following case illustrates this concept.

Vrabel v. *Acri*
103 N.E.2d 564 (Ohio 1952)

FACTS   Florence and Michael Acri owned and operated a restaurant and bar as partners. They worked together in the cafe for some time before marital problems led to a separation. After the separation, Michael operated the cafe alone, with no help from Florence. Vrabel and a friend stopped at the bar for a drink. While they were seated at the bar, Michael Acri shot and killed Vrabel's companion and then assaulted and injured Vrabel. Michael was sent to prison, and Vrabel sued Florence for damages, alleging that since she was still Michael's partner, she was liable for Michael's tort.

ISSUE   Is Florence liable for a malicious tort committed by her partner that was not within the scope of normal partnership business?

HOLDING   No. Since Florence neither assented to nor ratified the conduct, she is not liable.

REASONING   Michael's attack against Vrabel and his friend was not within the scope of operating a cafe. Such conduct was a clear departure from his employment and from his business purpose. It would be improper in this case to hold that the principal or partner ratified the conduct. Florence never assented to, participated in, or ratified the assaults. Thus, she was not liable.

Mens rea   A guilty mind; a guilty or wrongful purpose; a criminal intent.

Aid and abet   To help, assist, or facilitate the commission of a crime; to promote the accomplishment of a crime.

If a partner commits a crime, what liability do the noncriminal partners face? For most crimes, the other partners are *not* liable. Most crimes require **mens rea** (*criminal intent*). To be convicted of such a crime, a person must commit it or **aid and abet** in its commission. Unless evidence of involvement is shown, only the partner who committed the criminal act will be liable.

However, some crimes can be committed *without* criminal intent. Such crimes are normally *regulatory* in nature; these crimes involve violations of administrative areas rather than violations in traditional criminal areas. If one of these crimes is committed, *all* the partners are criminally liable.

SUMMARY

Each partner has certain rights in the business by virtue of his or her status as a partner. These rights may be limited or defined by the agreement. If there is no agreement to limit the rights, each partner has an equal voice in management, a right to an equal share of profits or losses, equal access to books and records of the firm, and an equal right to use partnership property for partnership purposes. They also have a right to be reimbursed for expenditures and a right to an account.

Each partner is an agent for every other partner and is a principal of every other partner. As a result, all the regular rules of agency apply. Each partner is a fiduciary of the other partners.

When a partner deals with some third party, the firm is bound by the conduct if it was apparently or actually authorized. Again, agency principles apply to the torts of a partner. If the tort is in the course and scope of employment, the partners are jointly and severally liable. If it is beyond the scope of employment, only the tort feasor is liable, unless the other partners ratify the conduct.

Any liability for crimes committed by a partner is not imposed on the nonacting partners unless they ratify the conduct.

DISCUSSION QUESTIONS

1. What is a partner's management right in a partnership?

2. If a partner advances money to further the partnership interests, what is the partner entitled to receive?

3. The partnership agreement is silent as to profits and losses. Bob put up 50 percent of the money for the business, and Sam and Sue each put up 25 percent. The firm netted $12,000. How much should each partner receive? Explain.

4. Scott felt Mel and Nancy were cheating him in their partnership. He asked to see the books and records to determine whether he was being cheated. Mel and Nancy refused to allow Scott to examine the books. What rights can Scott assert?

5. Denise and Vicki formed a partnership. Two years later, Vicki bought herself a new car, paying for it with a partnership check. If the partnership dissolves, what are Denise's rights in the car? Explain.

6. Tim and Ed were partners. Tim got tired of the business and sold it to Dan. Ed objected to the sale and sued to have it declared void. Dan claims Tim had the apparent authority to sell. How should the court rule, and why?

7. Margaret and Barbara are partners. Barbara called a customer and said the firm would not be able to deliver certain goods on time. The customer immediately sued for anticipatory breach. Margaret objects to the suit, saying the customer has no grounds to expect a breach. Do you agree? Explain.

8. Terry is a partner with Debbie and Donna. Terry learns of a fact that affects the business but does not tell Debbie or Donna. Terry dies, and Debbie and Donna

are sued on the basis of the information Terry had received. Can Debbie and Donna successfully assert their ignorance of the fact?

9. April, Jim, and Dan were partners in a retail business. Dan went to the bank and borrowed $10,000 to "buy more goods." The loan was made in the partnership name. Dan took the money to Las Vegas and lost it all at the roulette table. If the bank sues April and Jim on the loan, what should be the result? Explain.

10. Paul and Alma are partners. Paul commits a fraud in negotiating a contract for the firm. If the defrauded party sues Alma, who should win, and why? What are the rights and liabilities of all three parties?

CASE PROBLEMS

1. Carlson and Teegardin were partners in CIT, a real estate developing firm. Carlson entered into a contract with Ball to sell Ball a house in a CIT development, with the sale "contingent upon approval of the subdivision by county commissioners." The original closing date for the sale could not be met by CIT due to its inability to get the required approval of the commissioners. Ball agreed to give CIT more time to get the approval needed. Soon thereafter, Teegardin informed Ball that the house would cost an additional $8000. When Ball refused to pay the added amount, the real estate agent informed Ball that CIT had terminated the contract. Ball sued for specific performance, and was informed that since only Carlson had signed the contract, CIT was not bound to the agreement. Did Carlson have the necessary apparent authority to bind CIT to the contract with Ball? Explain your answer. (*Ball* v. *Carlson,* 641 P.2d 303 [Colo. 1981].)

2. Phillips and Harris were partners in a used car dealership. Rather than drive their own personal cars, both partners regularly drove cars the business was trying to sell. While driving a car the business had for sale, Phillips was involved in an accident. The passengers in the other car sued the partnership as well as Phillips. Harris contended that the accident was not within the course of employment and that the business should not be liable. Is this contention correct? What factors will influence the decision in this case? (*Phillips* v. *Cook,* 210 A.2d 743 [Md. 1965].)

3. Hodge entered into a contract with Voeller to purchase land owned by a partnership. Voeller was the managing general partner of the partnership, which owned and operated a drive-in movie theater. Voeller signed the contract in the partnership's name and on behalf of the partnership and his partners. One of the partners objected to the sale, and the deed was not transferred to Hodge. Hodge has sued for specific performance of the contract. How will the court resolve this case? What factors will the court examine in reaching its decision? (*Hodge* v. *Garrett,* 614 P.2d 420 [1980].)

4. Kaneco was a limited partnership involved in the oil and gas industry. Kaneco hired Winterhawk to operate its business, agreeing to pay a management and administration fee based on a percentage of drilling and completion costs. In order to acquire funding for its projects, Kaneco obtained a loan from the bank, secured with letters of credit. The loan proceeds were paid directly to Winterhawk by the bank, as per Kaneco's instruction. Winterhawk misappropriated substantial amounts of the loan proceeds, and Kaneco was placed in a poor financial position. Eventually Kaneco had difficulty making its payments on the loan, and the bank informed the general partners that the loan would be called since the loan balance exceeded the value of the letters of credit. Kaneco sought an injunction to prevent the bank from calling the loan or calling the letters of credit. Kaneco argued that the general partners were not jointly and severally liable for the loan balance. How should the court resolve this case? Why? (*Kaneco Oil & Gas, Ltd., II* v. *University National Bank,* 732 P.2d 247 [Colo. App. 1986].)

5. Lyle, Peters, and Barton were the partners in a firm that built packing crates and wood products. Barton, without the knowledge of the other partners, entered into a contract with Bole that called for the firm to sell lumber to Bole. In exchange, Bole paid Barton in advance for the lumber to be delivered. Bole never received the lumber, and Barton never accounted to the firm for the money Bole had paid. Bole sued the partnership for the lumber, or for the damages suffered due to nondelivery. Lyle and Peters deny any liability. What

result should occur and why? (*Bole* v. *Lyle,* 287 S.W.2d 931 [Tenn. 1956].)

6. Amerco filed a lawsuit against Bohonus, a member of a partnership, for a personal, nonbusiness claim. Amerco won the lawsuit, obtaining a judgment against Bohonus. The judgment was not satisfied, and Amerco then sought to enforce the judgment against the partnership property of Bohonus. The trial court ordered the sale of partnership property to satisfy the debt Bohonus owed Amerco. The remaining partners objected to this judicial sale, claiming that the court lacked the authority to sell the partnership assets for a personal liability of a partner. What should the appellate court do? What are the rights of the partners, the firm, and Amerco? (*Bohonus* v. *Amerco,* 602 P.2d 469 [Ariz. 1979].)

7. Mr. and Mrs. Soden were partners in the operation of an apartment building. Starkman, one of the tenants, refused to pay her rent for July until Mr. Soden made some repairs to her apartment as he had promised. While Mr. Soden was out of town, Mrs. Soden once again asked for the July rent, and was again refused. At that point, Mrs. Soden took a broom and beat Starkman with it. Starkman has sued both Mr. and Mrs. Soden for the tort. Was Mrs. Soden acting within the course and scope of her authority so that the partnership and each partner are bound by her tort? Explain. (*Soden* v. *Starkman,* 212 So.2d 763 [Fla. 1969].)

8. Maclay, his wife, and his children were all patients of the Kelsey Clinic. Maclay felt that Dr. Brewer, one of the partners in the clinic, was attempting to alienate the affections of Mrs. Maclay. Maclay went to see Dr. Kelsey, a senior partner in the clinic, with his suspicions, but Dr. Kelsey did nothing about the matter. Al-leging that the affair between his wife and Dr. Brewer still continued after his discussion with Dr. Kelsey, Maclay sued Dr. Brewer and the clinic for the tort of alienation of affections. Assuming that Dr. Brewer was, in fact, guilty of the tort, should the clinic be held liable due to the status of Dr. Brewer as a partner? Explain fully. (*Kelsey-Seybold Clinic* v. *Maclay,* 466 S.W.2d 716 [Tex. 1971].)

9. Corsicana Ready Mix was a partnership with two partners. Corsicana entered into a contract with Trinity to purchase goods on open account. Trinity alleged that the partnership breached the contract and filed suit for damages. The partners each individually filed answers to the complaint, but did not file an answer in the name of the business. As a result, Trinity moved for a default judgment, arguing that he had sued the firm and not the individuals who owned the firm, and since no answer was filed on behalf of the firm, the defendant had defaulted. The partners argued that they had met the spirit, if not the letter, of the law by filing their answers individually, and a default judgment would not be fair to them. How should the court rule in this case? Explain your answer fully. (*Corsicana Ready Mix* v. *Trinity Metroplex Division, General Portland, Inc.* 559 S.W.2d 423 [Tex. 1977].)

10. William and Charlotte operated the Davis Nursing Home as a partnership. William entered into a contract with Feingold to sell Feingold the nursing home, its assets, and its goodwill. Charlotte was unaware of the contract and refused to consent to the sale when she learned of it. Feingold has sued for specific performance of the contract. Who will prevail? (*Feingold* v. *Davis,* 282 A.2d 291 [Pa. 1971].)

CHAPTER 38

Termination of a Partnership

O U T L I N E

TYPES OF TERMINATIONS

Partnerships, like all good—and many bad—things, eventually must end. However, the ending of a partnership is different from what most people expect. The partnership may end while the business enterprise continues. If so, a dissolution occurs. Or the partnership and the business enterprise may both end. If so, a dissolution and a winding up occur. These variations in the termination of a partnership are the focus of this chapter.

DISSOLUTION

Technically, a *dissolution* "is the change in the relation of the partners caused by any partner ceasing to be associated in the carrying on as distinguished from the winding up of the business."[1] This means that *any time a partner leaves the business, the partnership is dissolved*. The change in the relations of the partners changes the partnership.

The fact that a partner "leaves" the business does not mean that the *business* must cease to exist. The remaining partners may be allowed to continue the business, or they may be required to terminate the business. What they may or may not do depends on the method and manner of dissolution.

Section 31 of the UPA lists several different causes of dissolution. Any of these events will cause a dissolution of the partnership, but they may not require a **winding up** of the business. We shall examine these causes of dissolution next.

Winding up Setting the accounts and liquidating the assets of a partnership or corporation for the purpose of making distribution and dissolving the concern.

Without Violation of the Agreement

A dissolution may be caused by the terms of the partnership agreement. For example, the time period set up in the agreement may expire, or the original purpose of the partnership may be fulfilled. If a partnership was established to operate for two years, and two years have elapsed, the partnership is dissolved. If a partnership was established to sell 100 parcels of land, and all the land has been sold, the partnership is dissolved. Of course, a new agreement could be made to extend the time or to modify the purpose, if the partners so desire.

If the agreement does not specify a particular time period or a particular, limited purpose, a partner may simply decide to quit. Unless the agreement denies this right to withdraw, such a decision operates as a dissolution without violation of the agreement.

All the partners may decide to terminate the partnership. If they do so, the partnership is dissolved without violating the agreement. This is true *even if* a definite time period was set and that time has not yet expired. And it is

[1]Uniform Partnership Act, Section 29.

true even if a particular purpose was declared and the purpose has not yet been achieved.

Finally, a partnership is dissolved without violation of the agreement if any partner is expelled from the partnership by the other partners, *provided that* the expulsion is permitted by the agreement. Thus, if X, Y, and Z vote to remove Q from the firm, *and the agreement permits such a vote,* the partnership is dissolved without violation of the agreement.

Normally, a dissolution that does not violate the agreement will lead to a winding up *unless* the agreement itself provides for a continuation of the business. If the agreement does not specify that a continuation is permitted, the partner who causes the dissolution may demand that a winding up take place. Such a demand must be obeyed, even though it normally will harm the remaining partners, who may wish to continue the business. Thus, every partnership agreement should contain some provisions for continuing the business. (Of course, an *expelled* partner cannot demand a winding up of the business if the expulsion was done in good faith by the other partners.)

In Violation of the Agreement

No one can be forced to be a partner against his or her will. Thus, any partner has the *power* to withdraw from any partnership at any time—but a partner does not have the *right* to withdraw at any time. A withdrawing partner may be violating the terms of the partnership agreement by withdrawing. If so, the remaining partners may continue the business if they desire, even though the partnership has been (technically) dissolved. The partner who withdrew in violation of the agreement has no right to demand or require a winding up.

Similarly, the partner who withdraws in violation of the agreement does not have the right to demand that the business be continued. Once a partner withdraws in violation of the agreement, the remaining innocent partners may decide to do whatever they feel is most appropriate. In the following case, a partner who withdrew in violation of the agreement learned that, on his withdrawal, all the options belonged to the remaining partners.

Ohlendorf v. *Feinstein*
636 S.W.2d 687 (Mo. 1982)

FACTS   The Missouri State Highway Commission was accepting bids on seven tracts of land. Feinstein's bid of just over $568,000 was accepted by the Commission. Upon learning that his bid had been accepted, Feinstein entered into a partnership with Ohlendorf and Whaley to sell the land. Several months later Ohlendorf notified the other partners that he was withdrawing from the partnership due to differences of opinion. Ohlendorf also informed the Commission that the partnership would not close the sale of the seven tracts of land. After this, Ohlendorf sued the other two partners to recover his capital contributions. The other partners refused to return his capital and countersued Ohlendorf for damages and for lost profits from the aborted purchase so that they could wind up the partnership affairs.

ISSUE   Did the remaining partners have a duty to continue the business so as to mitigate the damages faced by Ohlendorf?

HOLDING   No. Ohlendorf's withdrawal in violation of the agreement permitted the remaining partners to either continue the business or wind it up at their option.

REASONING   The UPA specifically allows the remaining partners to elect their remedies when a partner withdraws in violation of the partnership agreement. They may continue the business if they so desire and seek damages from the withdrawing partner. Or they may elect to wind up the business and sue the withdrawing partner for damages caused by the wrongful withdrawal. The mere fact that continuing the business would likely result in profits to the remaining partners is irrelevant. When Ohlendorf withdrew, he placed the other partners in a position to decide how to proceed. They chose to sue for damages, as was their right under the law. Their selection must be sustained under the provisions of the UPA.

By Operation of Law   A partnership may also be dissolved by operation of law, if any one of the following three events occurs:

1. Something happens that makes it unlawful for the business to continue or for the partners to continue the business. Thus, a law that prohibited anyone from selling rabbits would terminate a partnership in the rabbit-selling business. And a partnership that lost its import license would be dissolved even though importing itself was still legal.
2. A partner dies.
3. A partner or the partnership goes bankrupt.

By Court Order   The final method for dissolving a partnership is by court order. As explained in Section 32 of the UPA, a court will order a dissolution only if *asked* to do so. The person who wants to dissolve the partnership must petition the court; the court will not go out looking for partnerships that need to be dissolved.

Most commonly, the petitioning person is one of the partners or a representative of one of the partners. Even if a petition is filed, dissolution is not automatic. The court must have *grounds* to grant the request. The following grounds will justify a dissolution by court decree:

1. insanity of any partner
2. incapacity, other than insanity, of a partner that prevents that partner from performing the contractual duties called for in the agreement
3. misconduct by any partner that will make continued operation of the business difficult
4. intentional or repeated breach of the agreement by a partner, or any behavior that makes the continuation of the business impossible or impractical
5. evidence that the business can be continued only at a loss with no prospect of a profit turnaround in the near future

6. any other circumstances that make a dissolution equitable in the eyes of the court

It should be noted that insanity does *not* automatically dissolve the partnership; a petition must be filed seeking dissolution. If the remaining partners wish to continue the business with an insane partner, they have the right to do so.

It is also possible that some person may "purchase" the interest of a partner and then decide to seek a court-ordered dissolution.[2] Such a court order may be granted only if one of two sets of circumstances can be shown:

At will Having no specific date or circumstances that would bring about a dissolution.

1. The agreement had a specific term, or a particular purpose, and it has been fulfilled or satisfied.
2. The partnership was a partnership **at will** at the time of the purchase.

CONTINUATION OF THE BUSINESS

Once a dissolution occurs, a very important decision must be made. Will the business terminate through a winding up, or will the business continue? In most cases, an ongoing business is more valuable than the assets that make up the business; the sum is greater than its parts. Thus, the remaining partners normally will want to continue operating the business if they can possibly do so. However, this may not be satisfactory to a withdrawing partner. For this reason, the partners should consider the problem of a continuation when they draw up the original agreement, and they should make provisions for the problem at that time.

The remaining partners have the *right* to elect to continue the business under any one of the following circumstances:

1. The withdrawing partner withdraws in violation of the agreement.
2. The withdrawing partner consents to the continuation when he or she could have demanded a termination and winding up.
3. The agreement permits a continuation following a dissolution.

Unless one of these circumstances occurs, a dissolution will be followed by a winding up.

Withdrawing Partners

Any time the business is continued following a withdrawal, the continuing partners have a duty to the withdrawing partner. The withdrawing partner must be both indemnified (that is, secured against anticipated losses) and bought out. The purpose of the indemnification is to protect the withdrawing

[2]Ibid., Sections 27, 28.

⟨1⟩ partner from any claims of creditors of the partnership. The withdrawing partner is still liable for any debts owed that arose during membership in the partnership and association with the business. Without an indemnification agreement, a withdrawing partner might be tempted to force a winding up in order to minimize potential liability. But the indemnification agreement is assurance that the continuing partners will repay for any losses the withdrawing partner may suffer on account of partnership obligations.

⟨2⟩ Withdrawing partners also are entitled to payment for their interest in the business, including any undistributed profits, at the time of withdrawal. However, if a withdrawal is in violation of the partnership agreement, the continuing partners may deduct *damages,* based on breach of contract theories, from the payment to adequately cover the harm caused by the breach. The following case illustrates this point.

Grund v. *Wood*
490 P.2d 955 (Colo. 1971)

FACTS Grund was one of several partners in a medical partnership. The written partnership agreement included a covenant not to compete by practicing medicine within five miles of the partnership clinic for two years following withdrawal. It further provided for liquidated damages of up to $15,600 for violating the restrictive covenant. Grund had signed the agreement. He withdrew from the firm and began practicing medicine within five miles of the clinic within two years of his withdrawal. Grund sued to recover his share of the assets, and the partnership paid him his share less the $15,600 stipulated in the agreement. Grund then sued to recover the $15,600.

ISSUE Was Grund entitled to the $15,600 the partnership had withheld?

HOLDING No. The partnership was merely enforcing its rights under the agreement for a withdrawal in violation of the agreement.

REASONING The convenant not to compete was an entirely proper contract provision, and the liquidated damages clause was based on a reasonable method of establishing damages where the proof of damages would be very difficult to ascertain. Grund signed the agreement, he knew the terms, and he violated the agreement. The court held that he could not recover the $15,600.

The continuing partners may pay former partners in a lump sum and settle the matter. If they do not, or cannot, make a lump-sum payment, the withdrawing partners are allowed to elect how payment will be made. They can either receive interest on the unpaid portion until they receive payment in full or elect to receive a portion of profits that corresponds to their unpaid portion of the value of their share until they are paid in full. However, this election must be made at the time of withdrawal, and once made, it cannot be changed unless the continuing partners agree to the change.

Entering Partners

Occasionally, a new partner is brought into the business. When this happens, a continuation obviously occurs. No one would want to enter a business in order to see it go through a winding up. The continuation is treated slightly differently when a new partner enters the firm. As a partner, the new entrant is liable for the debts of the partnership. But the existing creditors did not rely on the new partner's credit when they decided to extend credit. As a result, it seems unfair to impose unlimited liability on the new partner. UPA Section 41(7) resolves this problem by specifying that the new partner is liable to preexisting creditors only up to the amount of his or her capital contribution. In other words, an entering partner has limited liability to preexisting creditors but still faces unlimited personal liability with respect to future creditors.

WINDING UP

Winding up is *the termination of the business enterprise.* In winding up, one must **marshal** and **liquidate** the assets of the business and then distribute the proceeds of this process to the proper parties.

General Partnerships

Marshal   To arrange assets or claims in such a way as to secure the proper application of the assets to the claims.

Liquidate   To assemble and mobilize assets, settle with creditors and debtors, and apportion the remaining assets, if any, among stockholders or owners.

The priority for distributing the proceeds is set out in UPA Section 40. The first priority is claims owed to creditors who are not partners. If the proceeds are sufficient to pay this class entirely, they will be so paid. Any surplus carries over to the next priority class. Any deficit will cause two things to happen: a pro rata distribution of the proceeds within the class and a collection of the balance from the personal assets of the partners, jointly and severally.

The second priority to receive the proceeds is claims owed to the partners *as creditors* of the business. Again, any surplus will be applied to the next priority class. And again, any deficit will be made up from the personal assets of the partners. It should be noted that a partner who wishes to be treated as a creditor of the firm will need to present clear and convincing evidence of the debt. It is normally presumed that any monies advanced to the firm were advanced as a capital contribution, not as a loan. The court probably will demand some written proof, such as a promissory note, that the funds were meant as a loan. Without such proof, the partner is likely to find that what he or she thought was a loan was, in the eyes of the court, a capital contribution.

The third priority is return of the capital contributions of the partners. Any surplus will be carried over to the fourth and final priority. Any deficit will be allocated among the partners pro rata. The fourth and final priority category is profits. Any monies left over after all the other classes have been satisfied will be distributed as profits, according to the terms of the partnership agreements. There can be no deficit here.

The creditors of the partnership have first claim on any partnership assets, as well as a secondary claim on the partnership assets that reflect the interest of the indebted partner in the business. However, the claims by individual creditors against partnership shares are limited by UPA Section 28. Usually, the individual creditor is given a charging order by the court while the business is in operation in order to minimize the disruption of normal business operations.

The examples that follow illustrate how the various interested parties may be treated in a dissolution of a partnership and a winding up of the business. In each example, there are three partners—X, Y, and Z—whose net worths are shown in the first example. In addition, each partner has made the capital contributions specified, and X has made a loan to the firm. Notice the effect the different asset positions of the partners have on the partners individually.

PARTNERS	PERSONAL ASSETS	PERSONAL LIABILITIES	NET WORTH
X	$100,000	$ 20,000	$80,000
Y	80,000	40,000	40,000
Z	40,000	100,000	(60,000)

Each partner contributed $50,000 to the partnership; profits and losses are to be shared equally. X loaned the firm $30,000 (there is a signed promissory note for this loan).

The partnership has $200,000 in proceeds and $290,000 in liabilities to regular creditors, plus the $30,000 owed to X.

Step 1. Partnership proceeds are distributed to regular creditors (priority 1), leaving a deficit of $90,000.

Step 2. Each partner *owes* an additional $30,000 to priority 1 creditors. However, Z has no money, and so X and Y will have to pay the full $90,000 between them (X will pay $50,000 and Y will pay $40,000) and hold claims against Z (X for $20,000, and Y for $10,000). Both Y and Z are now insolvent.

Step 3. Under priority 3, X, Y, and Z each owe X $10,000. X "pays" himself, and Y and Z each owe X $10,000.

The partnership has $309,000 in proceeds and $300,000 in regular liabilities, plus the $30,000 owed to X.

Step 1. The priority 1 debts are paid in full, and the $9000 surplus is carried over.

Step 2. Priority 2 debts are paid until the money runs out. Thus, X receives the $9000 left from priority 1 and is still owed $21,000. X "pays" himself $7000; Y pays X $7000; Z owes $7000. Z is insolvent, and X probably will not collect.

The partnership has $500,000 in proceeds, $200,000 in regular liabilities, and the $30,000 owed to X.

Step 1.   Priority 1 debts are paid in full, with a surplus left of $300,000.

Step 2.   Priority 2 debts are paid in full (X gets his $30,000), leaving a $270,000 surplus.

Step 3.   Priority 3 is taken care of next. Each partner receives a full return of his capital contribution, leaving a surplus of $120,000.

Step 4.   The final priority is satisfied; the $120,000 is distributed as profits, with $40,000 going to each of the partners.

In addition, the regular individual creditors will also be paid in full in this case, as follows. X received:

$ 30,000 loan payment
50,000 return of capital
40,000 profits
80,000 net worth
$200,000 net worth

Y and Z received:

$ 50,000 return of capital
40,000 profits
$ 90,000 distribution

Y had a net worth of $40,000, which has increased to $130,000. Z had a net worth of ($60,000), which has increased to $30,000.

The following case dealt with the claims of partners as creditors of the partnership.

In re Hess
1 F.2d 342 (D.C. Pa. 1923)

FACTS   Weir, Ligo, Hess, and Hanna were partners. Weir withdrew from the firm, selling his interest to the remaining partners. Later Ligo withdrew, again selling his interest to the remaining partners. Neither Weir nor Ligo was paid in cash; instead, both took promissory notes. Hess and Hanna later went bankrupt, and Weir and Ligo sought payment along with the regular creditors of the business.

ISSUE   Were the claims of Weir and Ligo properly filed against the partnership?

HOLDING   Yes. However, they were not on an equal standing with the creditors who had not been partners.

REASONING   Although both Weir and Ligo have provable, valid claims, they will not be permitted to compete with the regular creditors of the firm. Weir, having withdrawn first, takes precedence over Ligo, but Weir must wait until all the creditors with claims predating his retirement have been paid. Ligo must wait until Weir has been paid and until all creditors whose claims arose after Weir retired, but before Ligo withdrew, have been paid. Subject to these restrictions, Weir and Ligo are entitled to assert their respective claims against the partnership.

Limited Partnerships

The distribution of assets in a limited partnership is substantially different from that in a normal general partnership. Under ULPA Section 23, the assets are distributed in the following order:

1. claims of creditors who are not partners
2. income owed to limited partners
3. capital contributions of the limited partners
4. loans made to the firm by any partners
5. profits owed to general partners
6. capital contributions of the general partners

As in the liquidation of a general partnership, no category receives any proceeds until each higher-priority category has been paid in full.

Under the Revised Uniform Limited Partnership Act, the distribution of proceeds is treated differently. The Revised Act calls for distribution in the following order:

1. claims of nonpartner creditors and claims of partners as creditors
2. any amounts owed to former partners prior to their withdrawal from the firm
3. return of capital contributions of all partners
4. the remainder distributed as profits to all of the partners

The examples that follow illustrate how various interested parties may be treated in a dissolution of a limited partnership and a winding up of the business under both the ULPA and the RULPA. In each example there are two general partners—Alice and Bob—and two limited partners—Chuck and Diane. The financial positions and contributions of each of the four are set out in the first example.

PARTNERS	PERSONAL ASSETS	PERSONAL LIABILITIES	NET WORTH
Alice	$150,000	$ 75,000	$ 75,000
Bob	375,000	135,000	240,000
Chuck	100,000	150,000	(50,000)
Diane	200,000	185,000	15,000

Each partner contributed $75,000 to the firm. The general partners are to receive 30 percent of profits each, and the limited partners are to receive 20 percent of profits each. Chuck has loaned the firm an additional $50,000 and has a signed promissory note.

The partnership has $400,000 in proceeds and $500,000 in liabilities to nonpartner creditors. Under the ULPA, distribution is as follows:

Step 1. Claims of creditors who are not partners are satisfied first. This amount is $500,000, and there are only $400,000 in proceeds, so each creditor receives 80 percent of his or her claim from proceeds, with the balance of $100,000 owed by the general partners from personal assets. Alice and Bob each contribute $50,000, and this priority is satisfied.

Step 2. Income owed to limited partners is paid next (none in this example).

Step 3. The general partners are liable personally for the capital contributions of limited partners ($150,000). Alice only has $25,000 remaining, so Bob is liable for the remaining $125,000.

Step 4. Loans made by partners are the fourth priority. The general partners are liable personally for the $50,000 owed to Chuck. Since only Bob has any funds left, Bob pays.

Step 5. Profits owed to general partners are distributed (none in this example).

Step 6. Return of capital of general partners is satisfied last. The general partners are personally liable for this $150,000 as well.

Under the RULPA, the distribution would be as follows:

Step 1. Claims of creditors, both partner and nonpartner, are first priority. Here the $400,000 in proceeds would be allocated to the $550,000 in credit owed, at approximately 73 percent each. The balance of $150,000 would be owed by the general partners individually. Since Alice and Bob have the funds, they share this liability equally.

Step 2. Amounts owed to former partners are paid next (none in this example).

Step 3. Capital contributions of all partners are returned. Since the firm has no money left, the general partners would be personally liable for this $300,000 claim. (Bob would "pay" himself, and he would pay Chuck and Diane. Since Alice already owes Bob from Step 1, she would not collect from Bob.)

Step 4. Remaining funds are distributed as profits (none in this example).

The partnership has $500,000 in proceeds and $100,000 in liabilities to nonpartner creditors. Each limited partner is guaranteed profits of at least 20 percent of investment per year, and no profits have been distributed for the past year. Under the ULPA, the distribution would be as follows:

Step 1. Claims of creditors who are not partners are satisfied. The full $100,000 is paid, with $400,000 left for the next level.

Step 2. Income owed to limited partners, at 20 percent of capital contribution (minimum) guaranteed, is $15,000 each, or $30,000 total. This is paid, with $370,000 remaining.

Step 3. Capital contributions of the limited partners ($150,000) is also paid in full, with $220,000 left.

Step 4. Loans made to the firm by partners are paid. This $50,000 is paid to Chuck, leaving $170,000.

Step 5. Profits owed to general partners are $20,000, to be divided equally between Alice and Bob.

Step 6. Capital contributions of $150,000 by the general partners are paid, spending the last of the proceeds.

Under the RULPA, the distribution would be as follows:

Step 1. Claims of creditors are satisfied first. The entire $150,000 owed would be paid, leaving $350,000.

Step 2. Any amounts owed to former partners are paid (none in this example).

Step 3. Capital contributions of all partners are returned. The entire $300,000 would be paid, leaving a balance of $50,000.

Step 4. The balance is distributed as profits. Each general partner gets $15,000 (30 percent each), and each limited partner gets $10,000 each (20 percent each).

SUMMARY

When a partnership undergoes a change in the relationship among the partners, a dissolution occurs. Thus, a withdrawal by any partner is a dissolution, whether the agreement allows such conduct or not. Likewise, a dissolution will occur when the purpose of the agreement has been carried out or when its time has expired. A dissolution will occur by operation of law if a partner dies, if any partner goes bankrupt, or if the purpose becomes illegal. Finally, a dissolution can occur by court order.

When a dissolution occurs, the remaining partners may be allowed to continue the business. If the business is continued, the withdrawing partner must be bought out and indemnified.

Often the partnership must be wound up if a dissolution occurs. In a winding up, the assets of the firm must be marshaled and liquidated, and the proceeds must be distributed according to law. The proceeds must be used first to pay debts that the partners owe to nonpartner creditors. Next, the creditors who are also partners must be paid. After that, the partners recover their capital contributions. Anything left is distributed as profits.

DISCUSSION QUESTIONS

1. A, B, and C agreed to be partners for five years. After the five years had elapsed, B and C wanted to continue the business. A wanted to withdraw. May A withdraw and dissolve the partnership within the terms of the agreement? Explain.

2. X, Y, and Z formed a partnership for the purpose

of selling 500 mobile homes. After selling 200 of the homes, all three partners decided that things were not working out. If all three agree to dissolve, is the dissolution in violation of the agreement? Explain.

3. Ruth, Sam, and Tom formed a partnership. Sam refused to abide by the rules and terms of the agreement. After repeated efforts to persuade Sam to change his attitude, Ruth and Tom agreed to expel Sam from the firm. What rights may Sam assert at this time?

4. Abner, Bert, and Lois were partners in a bakery. Abner suffered a nervous breakdown and was placed in a mental institution. Abner's wife demanded Abner's share of the business, alleging that Abner's insanity had dissolved the partnership. Discuss her allegation.

5. Scott was in a partnership. He was also heavily in debt. One of his creditors went to court and got a charging order against Scott's share of the business. Under what circumstances can this creditor seek a court-ordered dissolution of the business?

6. Maria entered an existing partnership as a new partner in 1979. She contributed $20,000 at that time. By 1983, her share had grown to $50,000. How much can creditors who had claims predating Maria's entry into the firm collect from Maria's share of the business? From her personal assets?

7. In the winding up of a partnership, how can the creditors of individual partners gain access to partnership assets? Explain fully.

8. Robin was one of two members of a partnership. The partnership and Robin's partner both became bankrupt. Robin had $100,000 above her total personal liabilities. The partnership still owed $40,000, the other partner still owed $40,000, and both had been totally wiped out of assets. What will happen to Robin's $100,000? What rights will this give to Robin?

9. Given the following figures, work out the final financial position of each of the partners (net worth, cash, amounts owed, amounts receivable) following a winding up of their business:

	Bill	Charles	Larry	BCL Partnership
Assets	$70,000	$50,000	$50,000	$200,000
Liabilities	20,000	45,000	85,000	190,000
Capital contribution	50,000	25,000	25,000	
Profits	50%	25%	25%	

10. Given the following figures, work out the final financial position of each of the partners (net worth, amounts owed, amounts receivable) following a winding up of their business under both the ULPA and the RULPA.

	Beth	Cheryl	Linda	B & C
	(General Partners)		(Limited Partner)	(The Firm)
Assets	$67,500	$123,250	$ 87,900	$350,000
Liabilities	24,000	101,000	86,400	200,000
Capital contribution	50,000	50,000	100,000	
Loans to firm	0	5,000	7,000	
Share of profits	35%	35%	30%	

CASE PROBLEMS

1. Nestle and Ellis formed a partnership, Red Rocks Meat and Deli, which they operated from a building leased from Wester. In 1978, Nestle withdrew from the business, selling his interest to Herline. Ellis and Herline agreed that Nestle should be released from any and all liabilities of the firm. Subsequently Herline also withdrew, and Ellis continued the business as a proprietorship. In 1980, Ellis and Wester renegotiated the lease,

giving the firm additional space and increasing the total rent due under the lease agreement. When Ellis fell behind in his rent payments under the new lease, Wester filed suit against Nestle, arguing that he was liable for the lease jointly and severally with Ellis due to their partnership. Nestle denied that he was liable for the rent since he had withdrawn from the firm two years earlier. How should the court resolve this case? What factors will be decisive in deciding the case? Why? (*Webster & Co.* v. *Nestle,* 669 P.2d 1046 [Colo. App. 1983].)

2. Davis and Shipman entered a partnership in 1954. The following year, the partnership dissolved, with Shipman continuing the business under its original name. Shipman agreed with Davis that Shipman would pay all existing debts. However, Shipman defaulted on some of the loans, and the creditors sued Shipman and Davis. Davis contended that he was not liable for any of the debts after his withdrawal from the firm. Is Davis correct? (*Credit Bureau of Merced County* v. *Shipman,* 334 P.2d 1036 [Cal. 1959].)

3. Gauldin and Corn were partners in raising hogs and cattle on land that was part of a larger holding belonging to Corn. While operating the business, the partners spent over $10,000 in improvements to the land (a machine shed and a cargill) that became a part of the land to which they were attached. When the business was dissolved, the partners agreed to the distribution of all "movable assets," but did not agree about the two buildings placed on the land. Gauldin claimed that the buildings were partnership property and asserted a claim for one-half of their value. Corn contended that the buildings belonged to him as accruals to his holdings to make up for the fact that he did not charge the partnership rent for the use of the land that he owned. What should the court decide in this case? (*Gauldin* v. *Corn,* 595 S.W.2d 329 [Mo. App. 1980].)

4. The State House Inn was built and operated as the sole asset of a partnership that consisted of forty-nine partners. One of the partners was Polikoff. After several years of operation, the people who originally planned the inn and created the partnership formed a corporation and attempted to transfer the partnership assets to the new corporation. Polikoff objected to the incorporation and sought a court-ordered winding up of the business. What should the court do in this case? (*Polikoff* v. *Levy,* 270 N.E.2d 540 [Ill. 1971].)

5. Barclay and Barrie were partners. Their partnership agreement provided that the firm was to operate for five years and that each partner was to give reasonable time and attention to the operation of the business. During the first year of the business, Barrie suffered a stroke that left him paralyzed on one side and therefore unable to devote any time or energy to the business. Barrie's mental abilities were unimpaired, and the doctors forecast a full physical recovery within the term of the agreement. Nonetheless, Barclay sought a court-ordered dissolution of the partnership owing to Barrie's inability to perform as agreed. Should the court grant the dissolution? Explain your answer fully. (*Barclay* v. *Barrie,* 102 N.E. 602 [N.Y. 1913].)

6. C. L. Barnhouse Company was a limited partnership with two general partners and three limited partners. One of the limited partners was a trust created by Kilpatrick and represented by the trustee, Kilpatrick's son. The Kilpatrick trust stated that on the death of Kilpatrick the trust was to terminate and all trust assets were to be distributed to the beneficiaries. The partnership agreement provided that the partnership was to terminate on the death of any of the partners, limited or general. It also specified that, on the termination of the partnership, the capital contributions of each partner were to be returned, and then all other assets were to be distributed as per the agreement. Kilpatrick died in December, and the general partners notified the limited partners that Kilpatrick's death terminated the limited partnership. The trustee argued that the death of Kilpatrick did not terminate the limited partnership. Did the death of Kilpatrick, which terminated her trust, serve to dissolve the limited partnership as well? Why? (*Porter* v. *Barnhouse,* 354 N.W.2d 227 [Iowa 1984].)

7. Groff borrowed money from Citizens Bank, pledging as security certain specified cattle that he owned and, as additional security, "all cattle after acquired." Soon after, Groff entered into a cattle-feeding business as a partner or joint venturer with Pickering. Groff and Pickering often purchased cattle from Agri-Tech, with Morgan Bank providing purchase money financing in exchange for purchase money security interests. Eventually Groff encountered financial difficulties and filed for bankruptcy. Citizens Bank argued that all the cattle Groff owned, both individually and in association with Pickering, were the collateral for the loan and properly subject to repossession by Citizens Bank. Morgan Bank claimed that the cattle owned by Groff and Pickering were business assets, and since Citizens Bank was an individual creditor of Groff, Citizens Bank's claim was subordinate to the claim of Morgan on these cattle. Which bank has the better argument? How will the court

resolve this case? (*In re Groff,* 898 F.2d 1475 [10th Cir. 1990].)

8. Williams and Burrus desired to begin a restaurant and bar as partners. Under state law, Williams was not allowed to own a liquor license, so Burrus obtained the required license in his own name, with no mention of WIlliams or his interest in the business. Once the business began, Burrus refused to give Williams his share of the profits as per their agreement or to buy out Williams and then to operate the business as a proprietorship. As a result, Williams filed suit for a court-ordered dissolution and for an accounting. Discuss the rights of the two parties to this partnership. (*Williams v. Burrus,* 581 P.2d 164 [Wash. 1978].)

9. Clyde and Graydon Bohn formed a partnership to operate a farm. The partnership agreement included a buy-out provision that was to be based on "the capital amount" of the partnership. Clyde died, and Graydon offered the estate $135,000 to "buy out" the interest of Clyde. The estate refused the offer, asserting that the "buy out" price should be one-half the fair market value

of the partnership. The net fair market value of the farm as of the date of Clyde's death was $1,500,000. An accountant testified that the phrase used in the partnership agreement, "the capital amount," has no known definition in the accounting profession. What should the court decide is the proper amount to be paid in order to allow Graydon Bohn to "buy out" the interest of his deceased partner and continue to operate the business? Why? (*Bohn v. Bohn Implement Co.,* 325 N.W.2d 281 [N.D. 1982].)

10. Taylor and Bryan were partners. The partnership had no debts and had a bulldozer as its only remaining asset. Each partner filed suit seeking a dissolution and damages. The judge denied the damage claims asserted by each of the partners, awarded the bulldozer to Taylor, and ordered Taylor to pay Bryan one half the fair market value of the bulldozer. Taylor objected to the judge's ruling, arguing that the bulldozer should be sold and the proceeds divided between the partners. What should the appellate court rule? (*Taylor v. Bryan,* 664 S.W.2d 52 [Mo. 1984].)

CHAPTER 39

Formation of a Corporation

OUTLINE

IMPORTANCE OF CORPORATIONS

In 1990, corporations in the United States produced $3,198.6 billion worth of products and services. This production, coupled with the fact that corporations made $247.8 billion in profits before taxes in 1990, graphically illustrates the fact that corporations currently represent a vitally important form of business organization in the United States.[1] An understanding of the essentials of the formation of a corporation therefore seems warranted.

We define a *corporation* as an *artificial person created under the statutes of a state or a nation, organized for the purpose set out in the application for corporate existence.* United States corporations, while subject to applicable federal statutes, primarily are entities derived from state law and thus enjoy certain powers granted to them by state law. One of a corporation's unique features stems from its separateness from the people who own it. That is, a corporation exists in its own right as a legal person distinct from the shareholders. Even though it exists only in contemplation of law, as a legal person it possesses certain attributes and powers that have led to its increasing popularity as a form of business organization. This chapter will explore how and why this growth has occurred.

(margin handwritten notes)
1) artificial person
2) statutes of state nation
3) purpose in applic.

HISTORY

No exact moment of recorded history pinpoints the existence of the first corporation. But some evidence suggests that people recognized the concept of corporate personality to some extent as early as the time of Hammurabi (about 2083 B.C.). Certainly by Roman times, vestiges of corporateness had appeared through imperial **fiat.** From its very origins, then, the concept of corporateness depended on legislative grant. Canon law, borrowing from the Romans, distinguished between the "corporation sole" (composed of a single person, usually a high-ranking church officeholder) and the "corporation aggregate" (composed of several persons). The *fiction theory*—that a corporation is an artificial legal person separate from its shareholders—probably developed from the papacy's desire to accommodate priests who had taken vows of poverty forbidding them to hold property. Since controlling the activities and finances of these clergymen was very lucrative, the church devised ways (the corporation) to allow church officers to own property. This separation of the artificial person from the natural persons associated with it spawned the modern view that the corporation, not the shareholders, owns the corporate property and that shareholders ordinarily are not liable for debts incurred by the corporation. The development of the law merchant, the fore-

Fiat An order issued by legal authority.

---

[1]U.S. Department of Commerce, Bureau of Economic Analysis, *Survey of Current Business* (Washington, D.C.: U.S. Government Printing Office, October, 1991).

runner of modern commercial law, mirrored these and similar views of corporateness.

By the seventeenth century, English monarchs had tightened control over corporations, which were deemed to exist by virtue of "concessionary grants" of power from the state. Not surprisingly, the *concession theory* was part of the common law heritage that remained with American colonists after they had asserted their independence from Britain. At first, Americans viewed corporations with suspicion because several well-known, unsavory schemes had been perpetrated through use of the corporate form. But such suspicions gradually relaxed as the advantages of corporations, such as the potential to raise **capital,** became apparent. However, as the corporate form developed, each state jealously guarded its power over these artificial creatures. This careful regulation of corporations, augmented now by federal securities statutes, remains an essential characteristic of the law of corporations.

Capital Corporate assets or property of a fixed or permanent nature used in carrying on a business.

ADVANTAGES

The popularity of the corporation as a business form results from its comparative advantages over other types of business organizations. One advantage is the insulation from liability provided by the corporate form. As mentioned earlier, corporate debts are the responsibility of the corporation. Since the shareholders' liability ordinarily is limited to the amount of their investment, creditors of the corporation normally cannot reach the shareholders' personal assets to pay for corporate debts.

Related to the idea of insulation from liability is the second advantage, the centralization of management functions. In other business forms such as partnerships, *all* the general partners have an equal voice in the management of the firm's affairs. Centralizing the management functions in a small group of persons possessing management expertise avoids some of the friction that may plague some partnerships.

Continuity of existence is viewed as a third advantage. The corporation continues to exist in the eyes of the law even after the deaths of the officers, directors, or shareholders or the withdrawal of their shares. This potential for perpetual existence provides stability.

Correlating with this factor is the fourth advantage, free transferability of shares, which in turn opens up new possibilities for access to outside capital. These attributes unquestionably convince many large and small businesses to employ the corporate form. However, in a given situation, a sole proprietorship (a business enterprise owned and run by one person) or a partnership (discussed in Chapters 36–38) may better suit the business's needs. Businesspeople should seek the advice of a lawyer, accountant, or other investment adviser before deciding which form of business enterprise to use.

One reason for this caution derives from the fact that distinct disadvantages may result from choosing the corporate form. The tax treatment of corporations stemming from the law's recognition of corporations as separate entities for federal income tax purposes represents one such negative aspect. The corporation pays taxes on all its income as earned; and this income, when distributed to shareholders in the form of dividends, produces taxable income for the shareholders. This structure in effect brings about so-called double taxation. Moreover, because corporate losses are not passed through to the shareholders, shareholders do not receive the tax advantages that would otherwise accompany such losses. The creation of what the Internal Revenue Code terms an "S" corporation (regular corporations are dubbed "C" corporations) may offset these tax drawbacks and thereby give relief from these burdensome results. Subchapter S of the Internal Revenue Code permits certain corporations to avoid corporate income taxes and, at the same time, to pass operating losses on to their shareholders. In this sense, federal tax laws covering S corporations are analogous to the laws covering partnerships but are uniquely corporate at the same time. Attaining S corporation status involves an elective procedure and the necessity of strict compliance with statutory dictates in order to achieve this status.

The federal tax laws limit eligibility for Subchapter S election to domestic small business corporations having thirty-five or fewer shareholders (individuals, estates, and certain trusts qualify as shareholders, but partnerships, corporations, and nonqualifying trusts do not) and only one class of stock issued and outstanding. Moreover, the presence of even one nonresident alien shareholder or passive investment income in excess of statutory limitations make the corporation ineligible for S status. In order to make a proper election, all shareholders must consent to the election; and the filing must be timely and proper. Once an election occurs, renewals are unnecessary; S status remains in effect as long as none of the events that can trigger loss of the election (an excessive number of shareholders or passive investment income, for example) occurs.

CORPORATE NATURE

As mentioned, the corporation is an invisible, intangible, artificial person. Therefore, it ordinarily enjoys most of the rights that natural (flesh-and-blood) persons possess. For example, it is a citizen and a resident of the state in which it has been incorporated. Thus, under the Fourth Amendment, it cannot be the object of unreasonable searches or seizures. Similarly, under the Fourteenth Amendment, it must be afforded its rights of due process and equal protection. In addition, a corporation takes on the nationality of either the nationality and/or the residence of the persons controlling it (called the "aggregate test") or the nation in which it was incorporated or where it has its principal place of business (dubbed the "entity" test).

A landmark case illustrating some of these concepts follows.

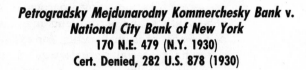

Petrogradsky Mejdunarodny Kommerchesky Bank v. National City Bank of New York
170 N.E. 479 (N.Y. 1930)
Cert. Denied, 282 U.S. 878 (1930)

FACTS　Petrogradsky, a Russian bank, sued a New York bank for a $66,749.45 balance standing to its credit. In 1917, as a result of the Bolshevik Revolution, the Russian bank's assets had been confiscated and its stock canceled. On this basis, the New York bank had said the Russian bank as a corporation had been dissolved and no longer was a juristic (legal) person. Therefore, the New York bank had refused to pay the credit balance.

ISSUE　Had the Russian bank ceased to exist as a legal person?

HOLDING　No. It continued to exist. Hence, the American bank would have to pay the Russian bank the amount in dispute.

REASONING　The Russian bank had not ceased to exist as a legal person. Indeed, the law presumes that a corporation continues perpetually. If assets remain either in the domicile or elsewhere, there is no dissolution, either virtual or legal. Since there is no indication that pre-Bolshevik Russian law regarding juristic personality differs from American law, the presumption of continuance of corporate personality must tilt the balanced scales. Therefore, the corporation survives in such a sense and to such a degree that it can still be dealt with as a person in lands that do not recognize the decrees of the Bolsheviks.

FORMATION

The process of forming a corporation involves complicated issues that demand the attention of well-versed professionals. One of these considerations consists of choosing the most desirable type of corporation for the particular circumstances.

Types of Corporations

The *public-issue private corporation* is the best-known type of private corporation. We are all familiar with American Telephone & Telegraph (AT&T), General Motors (GM), International Business Machines (IBM), General Electric (GE), and other large public-issue corporations. The central advantage of public-issue corporations is their access to capital in the form of new shares. Yet the shareholder has very little say in the management of such giant concerns. For this reason, there is another type of private corporation, the *close corporation*. This form limits the management of the firm to a select few shareholders and restricts the transferability of shares in order to consolidate control. Close corporations allow a firm to enjoy many of the advantages of the corporate form (such as favorable tax treatment) without giving up the day-to-day control more appropriately associated with sole proprietorships or partnerships. An inherent disadvantage of close corporations, on the other hand, stems from a lack of free transferability of shares; these shares are often not as liquid or salable as those of public-issue corporations.

public issue private ③
Close
professional
municipal (public)

Private corporations may also include *professional corporations,* those organized for conducting a particular occupation or profession. Doctors, lawyers, dentists, and accountants may find it advantageous financially (because of tax and pension benefits, for example) to form such corporations. Most states have special statutes regulating professional corporations. Typically, these statutes limit share ownership in such corporations to duly-licensed professional persons. Despite the limited liability offered by the corporate form, under these statutes the professional is ordinarily personally liable for his or her own malpractice or similar torts as well as for any such acts performed by others who are under the professional's supervision.

④ A city is an example of a *public* or *municipal corporation.* We often call public utilities *quasi-public corporations* because they are private corporations that nevertheless furnish public services such as electricity, gas, or water.

Corporations such as the ones we have described are generally for profit. But nonprofit corporations, or those organized for charitable purposes, also exist. Special statutes in some jurisdictions regulate educational institutions, charities, private hospitals, fraternal orders, religious organizations, and other types of nonprofit corporations.

Promoters

Despite the negative connotation of the word, *promoters* may be vital to the formation of the corporation, practically speaking. Although the law does not require the services of promoters as a precondition to incorporating, promoters *begin the process of forming a corporation by procuring subscribers for the stock or by taking other affirmative steps toward incorporating.* Thus, promoters facilitate the creation of the corporation by bringing interested parties together and by "midwifing" the venture until the corporation is formed. We can also label promoters *preincorporators.*

Promoters' activities bring up a host of legal issues. Since the promoter is working on behalf of an entity not yet created, questions arise as to who is liable on contracts made on the corporation's behalf before its inception: The promoter or the corporation? The general rule is that the promoter will be liable for goods and services rendered to him or her before the corporation's formation. However, the corporation may become liable for the promoter's contracts (and possibly torts) after formation by adoption or **ratification** of the promoter's contract, novation, or release. In most cases, this liability is joint and does not (except for novations and express releases of liability) eliminate the promoter's personal liability.

Ratification The acceptance of and the binding to an act that was unauthorized when committed and that was voidable before the ratification.

The possibility of double-dealing inheres in the process of promotion. For this reason, the law treats promoters as owing fiduciary duties to the corporation. Therefore, the promoter must act in good faith, deal fairly, and make full disclosure to the corporation. Despite several older, complicated cases, the liability of promoters as fiduciaries is not as pervasive a problem today as in the past because of the disclosures mandated by the Securities Act of 1933. But, in occasional cases, the promoter has to give back to the corporation secret profits, embezzled funds, and other damages. Therefore, anyone desiring to act as a promoter should seek professional advice beforehand.

Articles of Incorporation

We call the document that signals the official existence of the corporation the *articles of incorporation*. State statutes prescribe the contents of the articles; but, as Figure 39.1 illustrates, typically the articles include the name of the corporation, its purpose, its duration, the location of its principal office or

FIGURE 39.1 Articles of Incorporation

ARTICLES OF INCORPORATION
OF

_____

These Articles of Incorporation have been prepared in order to form a corporation in keeping with the provisions of the Indiana General Corporation Act, as amended (Act).

ARTICLE I
Name

The name of the corporation is _____ (Corporation).

ARTICLE II
Purposes

The Corporation shall engage in the business of _____.

However, it shall also be able to transact any lawful business for which corporations may be incorporated under the Act.

ARTICLE III
Term of Existence

The Corporation shall have perpetual existence.

ARTICLE IV
Resident Agent and Principal Office

The post office address of the principal office of the Corporation is _____.

The name and address of the Corporation's Resident Agent for service of process is _____

_____.

ARTICLE V
Authorized Shares of Stock

The Corporation shall have authority to issue one thousand shares of common stock having no par value. Owners of these shares of common stock shall have the right at every meeting of the shareholders to one vote for each share of stock listed in their name on the books of the Corporation. No shares of stock held in the name of the Corporation or not issued by the Corporation shall be entitled to any voting rights.

The Board of Directors shall be entitled to authorize the issuance of the stock of the Corporation in such a manner as to take advantage of Section 1244 of the Internal Revenue Code.

Subject to the provisions of ARTICLE XI, shares of the capital stock of the Corporation may be issued by the Corporation for such amount of consideration as may be fixed from time to time by the Board of Directors and may be paid in money, in other property, or in services already performed by the Corporation.

FIGURE 39.1   continued

ARTICLE VI
Requirements Prior to Doing Business

The Corporation will not begin business until consideration having value of at least One Thousand Dollars ($1000) has been received for the issuance of shares of stock.

ARTICLE VII
Board of Directors

Section 1. Names and Post Office Addresses of the Initial Board of Directors.   The names and post office addresses of the initial Board of Directors of the Corporation are as follows:

Name	**Street No. or Building**	**City**	**State**	**Zip**

Section 2. Qualifications of Directors.
None.

Section 3. Number and Election of Directors.   The Board of Directors of the Corporation shall consist of not less than one nor more than _____ members. It shall initially consist of _____ member(s). The directors shall have the power to have the bylaws specify the exact number of directors. Directors shall be elected annually by a majority of the shares of stock represented at the annual meeting of shareholders. They shall hold office either until the next annual meeting of the shareholders or until their replacements are properly elected.

Any director or the entire Board of Directors may be removed at any time either at an annual or special meeting of the Corporation's shareholders called for that purpose. The removal shall be by the affirmative vote of the holders of the majority of the outstanding shares and shall be effective immediately even if a successor is not elected simultaneously. Any vacancy on the Board of Directors shall be filled only by the shareholders either at the annual meeting or a special meeting of the shareholders called for that purpose.

Directors need not be shareholders of the Corporation.

ARTICLE VIII
Name and Address of Incorporator

Name	**Street No. or Building**	**City**	**State**	**Zip**

ARTICLE IX
Provisions for Regulation of Business and Conduct of Affairs of Corporation

Meetings of shareholders and directors may be held outside the state of Indiana.

Any contract or other transaction between the Corporation and any of its directors shall be valid for all purposes, even though the director is present at the meeting of the Board of Directors which acts upon the contract or transaction and notwithstanding his participation, if the fact of his interest shall be disclosed or known to the Board of Directors.

FIGURE 39.1   continued

ARTICLE X
Indemnification of Members of Board of Directors

In furtherance and not in limitation of the powers conferred by applicable law, the Board of Directors of the Corporation is expressly authorized to provide indemnification to directors, officers, and employees to the full extent permitted by Indiana law, it being the policy of the Corporation to safeguard its directors, officers, and employees from expense and liability for actions they take in good faith in furtherance of the interests of the Corporation and its shareholders.

ARTICLE XI
Requirement of Greater Than a Majority Vote

The affirmative vote of holders of _____% of the outstanding shares entitled to vote shall be necessary for any of the following corporate actions:

1. an increase or decrease in the number of members of the Board of Directors
2. the classification of members of the Board of Directors into groups
3. the issuance of shares of common stock including treasury stock
4. the amendment of these Articles of Incorporation
5. merger or consolidation of the Corporation
6. reduction or increase of the stated capital of the Corporation
7. sale, lease, or exchange of the major portion of the assets of the Corporation
8. dissolution of the Corporation
9. the employment and compensation of any officers of the Corporation

As the Incorporator of this Corporation, I verify and affirm that subject to the penalties of perjury the facts contained herein are true and, in witness whereof, sign these Articles of Incorporation this _____ day of _____, 19___.

_____

This instrument prepared by _____ of Roemer and Mintz, Attorneys-at-Law, 1400 St. Joseph Bank Building, South Bend, Indiana 46601.

Courtesy of Charles Roemer, Roemer and Mintz, Attorneys-at-Law, South Bend, Indiana.

Registered agent Person designated by a corporation to receive service of process within the state.

Stated capital The amount of consideration received by the corporation for all shares of the corporation.

registered agent (also called *resident agent*), its powers, its capital structure (that is, the number of shares and minimum **stated capital**), its directors and their names (these people are usually the incorporators), and the signatures of the incorporators (in most jurisdictions they do not have to be shareholders). Once the incorporators file the articles with the appropriate state official (ordinarily the secretary of state) and pay all the required filing fees, the state issues a formal certificate of incorporation, or license.

Certificate of Incorporation

In most states, corporate existence begins at the issuance of the certificate of incorporation by the secretary of state in the state of incorporation. After it issues such a certificate, the state normally will not interfere with this grant of power. Unless the corporation by its conduct poses a definite and serious danger to the welfare of the state's citizens (for example, by engaging in wholesale fraud), the state will honor the certificate and allow the corporation to conduct its usual business without impediment. Figure 39.2 represents a typical certificate of incorporation.

Organizational Meeting

In some jurisdictions, official corporate existence begins, not on the issuance of the certificate of incorporation, but after the first organizational meeting of the corporation. This is an important meeting because during it bylaws are adopted, the preincorporation agreements are approved, and officers are elected.

Bylaws

Bylaws are *the rules and regulations adopted by a corporation for the purpose of self-regulation, especially of day-to-day matters not covered by other documents.* These ordinarily are not filed in a public place as are the articles of incorporation. Rather, they constitute the corporation's internal rules for the governance of its own affairs. They must, however, be consistent with the jurisdiction's corporate statute and the corporation's articles. Bylaws typically cover the location of the corporation's offices and records; describe the meetings of the shareholders and the directors; set out the powers and duties of the board of directors, officers, and executive committee; establish the capitalization of the corporation; and fix the methods for conducting the corporation's business, such as execution of contracts and deeds and notices of meetings.

DE JURE VERSUS *DE FACTO* CORPORATE STATUS

As we have seen, it is relatively easy to obtain corporate status if one carefully follows the required statutory procedures. Nevertheless, because ours is not a perfect world, it is still necessary to examine the consequences of failure to comply with such statutory requirements. *Defective incorporation,* as this concept is called, may be a matter of degree. If the defect in formation (or noncompliance with the incorporation statute) is slight, the law characterizes the corporation as *de jure (valid by law).* The general rule is that where substantial compliance with all steps necessary for incorporation has occurred, the resultant entity is a *de jure corporation.* If an address is wrong in a provision mandating an address or a relatively insignificant provision has been overlooked, courts will not invalidate corporate status. Such minor flaws ordinarily will not cause the loss of de jure status.

Sometimes, however, the defect involved is so serious that the law cannot consider the corporation a de jure one. Corporateness and all its attributes may still be retained, however, if certain conditions are met: (1) A law under which the business could have been incorporated exists, (2) there was a good-

Figure 39.2 Certificate of Incorporation

STATE OF INDIANA

OFFICE OF THE SECRETARY OF STATE

CERTIFICATE OF INCORPORATION

OF

...., INC.

....

I, EDWIN J. SIMCOX, *Secretary of State of Indiana, hereby certify that Articles of Incorporation of the above Corporation, in the form prescribed by my office, prepared and signed in duplicate by the incorporator(s), and acknowledged and verified by the same, have been presented to me at my office accompanied by the fees prescribed by law; that I have found such Articles conform to law; that I have endorsed my approval upon the duplicate copies of such Articles; that all fees have been paid as required by law; that one copy of such Articles has been filed in my office; and that the remaining copy of such Articles bearing the endorsement of my approval and filing has been returned by me to the incorporator(s) or his(their) representatives; all as prescribed by the provisions of the* INDIANA GENERAL CORPORATION ACT ....

...., *as amended.*
NOW, THEREFORE, *I hereby issue to such Corporation this Certificate of Incorporation, and further certify that its corporate existence has begun.*

In Witness Whereof, I have hereunto set my hand and affixed

the seal of the State of Indiana, at the City of Indianapolis,

this ....*day of*

...................................., *19*......

Edwin J. Simcox
EDWIN J. SIMCOX, *Secretary of State*

By ....
Deputy

Courtesy of Douglas D. Germann, Sr., Attorney-at-Law, Mishawaka, Indiana.

faith effort to comply with the statute, and (3) there was some use or exercise of corporate powers. Such entities are called *de facto corporations (corporations in fact if not in law)*. Only the state can attack the existence of a de facto corporation. Hence, if the state does not bring an action to dissolve its certificate (or its charter), the firm will enjoy all the powers and privileges that inhere in the corporate form.

This result is probably fair. Even if the defects in compliance are serious, if both the entity and third parties have previously dealt with each other in the belief that corporateness exists, fulfilling the expectations of the parties seems justifiable. Yet the law should scrutinize the parties' nonfulfillment of statutory dictates in order to avoid the frustration of legislative intent. In recent years, statutory provisions have increasingly reflected the view that the issuance of a certificate of incorporation will create a presumption that the corporation has been validly formed (that is, it has attained de jure status) except in actions brought by the state. If the state has taken no action and has issued no certificate, the presumption is that corporate status is as yet unrealized. In this case, third parties can hold individual shareholders personally liable. These developments have greatly eroded the importance of the de facto doctrine; but, as the next case illustrates, some courts have continued to make distinctions between de jure and de facto corporations. It is therefore important to understand both the historical backdrop and the modern trends in this area of the law.

Bankers Trust Company of Western New York v. Zecher
426 N.Y.S.2d 960 (N.Y. Sup. Ct. 1980)

FACTS   A bank sued for repossession of restaurant equipment that was security for an $11,136.31 loan made to Roseberry Inn, Inc. Zecher, one of the owners of the inn, countered with the assertion that the bank could have acquired no interest in the equipment because Roseberry Inn, Inc. was not a legally existing entity at the time the security agreement had been entered into, as it had not yet filed a certificate of incorporation with the secretary of state. The facts showed that the certificate of incorporation had been executed on 24 July 1975, the date of the security agreement, but had not been filed with the state until 30 July 1975.

ISSUE   Was Roseberry Inn, Inc. a corporation at the time of the formation of the contract?

HOLDING   Yes. It was a corporation at that time.

REASONING   To show the existence of a de facto corporation, it was necessary to show the existence of a law under which the corporation might have been organized, an attempt to organize the corporation, and an exercise of corporate powers thereafter. Because there had been a good-faith attempt to comply and numerous examples of use of the corporate name, the corporation was a de facto corporation as of 24 July 1975. The corporation was therefore liable to the bank.

FIGURE 39.3　Achievement of Corporate Status

DE JURE CORPORATE STATUS *A corporation valid in law*	*DE FACTO* CORPORATE STATUS *A corporation valid in fact if not in law*
a. Presence of perfect (or, alternatively, substantial) compliance with all steps necessary for incorporation. b. Articles of incorporation validly filed with appropriate state official. c. Certificate of incorporation issued by appropriate state official and/or organizational meeting held. d. Corporate existence genuine; cannot be attacked by anyone.	a. Attempt to achieve at least substantial compliance with all steps necessary for incorporation. b. Attainment of *de jure* status impossible owing to seriousness of defects. c. Corporateness nonetheless recognized under following conditions: 　1. existence of a law under which the business could have been incorporated; 　2. a good-faith effort to comply with the statute; 　3. some use (or exercise) of corporate powers [i.e., belief that corporate status achieved held by both the entity and third parties dealing with it]. d. Corporate existence genuine; cannot be attacked by anyone but the state [In some states presumption of attainment of *de jure* status on issuance of certificate of incorporation unless state is plaintiff].
Shareholders *Not* Personally Liable For Corporate Debts	**Shareholders *Not* Personally Liable For Corporate Debts**

DISREGARDING THE CORPORATE ENTITY

We have just seen that the law sometimes will recognize corporateness when incorporation has been defective. Now we will examine situations that call for disregarding the corporate entity even when compliance with the incorporation statute has been correct.

The usual rule is that the shareholders in a corporation enjoy limited liability. Because the corporation is a separate entity from the shareholders, the law normally will not be interested in who owns or runs the corporation. Sometimes, though, it will be necessary to "pierce the corporate veil" (the shield that keeps the corporation and its shareholders' respective liabilities separate) in order to serve justice. For example, when the corporate form is being used to defraud others or for similar illegitimate purposes, courts may pierce the corporate veil to place liability on the shareholder who is using the corporate form impermissibly. If Roberts is the sole shareholder in an association that is so thinly capitalized initially that it cannot reasonably meet its obligations, or if Roberts is "draining off" the corporation's assets for his personal use, the law *may* fix personal liability for the obligations incurred on Roberts, despite the corporate form. If Roberts instead can reasonably meet his obligations and does not drain off corporate assets, his having as a goal the limitation of his liability is valid. In this case, there will be no personal liability. Courts therefore must examine the facts closely to see if a particular situation justifies disregard of corporateness or not. Put another way, if the corporation is a mere "shell" or "instrumentality" or in reality is the "alter ego" of the shareholder, courts can use their powers of equity to impose liability on the controlling shareholders.

This is not to say that close ("one-person") corporations are always candidates for disregard of the corporate entity—quite the contrary. The usual rule is that the law will not disregard corporateness if there has been no domination by the shareholder for an improper purpose (such as fraud or evasion of obligations) and resultant injury to the corporation (such as mismanagement), third parties, or the public at large. Courts will uphold corporateness as long as the controlling shareholder keeps corporate affairs and transactions separate from personal ones, adequately capitalizes the business initially and forgoes the draining off of corporate assets, incorporates for legitimate reasons (tax savings, limitation of liability, and so on), and directs the policies of the corporation toward its own interests, not personal ones. These same principles in general apply to situations involving parent-subsidiary (that is, affiliated) companies, another potentially troublesome area for deciding whether corporateness should be retained or disregarded.

Note how the court applied these concepts in the following case.

Evans v. Multicon Construction Company
574 N.E.2d 395 (Mass. App. Ct. 1991)

FACTS   More than a decade after initiating action, Robert Evans, a subcontractor, on 9 August 1978 won a judgment of $124,176.45 against Multicon Construction Corporation (MCC). By that time, MCC, an Ohio corporation, had ceased doing business in Massachusetts and, if it existed at all, was an empty shell. Evans therefore sought alternative sources of recovery by invoking Rule 69 under Massachusetts's rules of civil procedure, which rule, in aid of a judgment, makes available postjudgment discovery and equips the court with "all the traditional flexibility of a court of equity," including enforcement of orders of the court against persons who may not originally have been parties.

Under Rule 69, Evans argued that MCC had been a sham corporation functioning as a front for John W. Kessler and Peter H. Edwards, the original partners who had organized MCC. Evans claimed that the factors typically utilized in piercing the corporate veil—common ownership; pervasive control; intermingling of personal and business assets, activity, or management; thin capitalization; nonobservance of corporate formalities; absence of corporate records; nonpayment of dividends; insolvency at the time of the litigated transaction; siphoning away of corporate assets by dominant shareholders; nonfunctioning officers and directors; use of the corporation for the transactions of the dominant shareholders; and use of the corporation in promoting fraud—justified a court's holding Edwards and Kessler personally liable for the judgment that Evans had won against MCC.

ISSUE

Should a court pierce the corporate veil to hold the officers of MCC personally liable?

HOLDING

No. The evidence showed that the bases in law for so holding were insufficient to permit a court to disregard corporateness.

REASONING

The court noted that rare, particular situations may warrant disregard of separate corporate entities; i.e., allow a court to pierce the corporate veil. Occasion for doing so arises when (1) related business entities are actively and pervasively controlled by the same controlling persons, with fraudulent or injurious consequences by reason of the relationship among those business entities; or (2) confused intermingling of activity exists between two or more corporations engaged in a common enterprise, resulting in substantial disregard of the separate nature of the corporate entities or serious ambiguity about the manner and capacity in which the various corporations and their respective representatives are acting. Other precedents further break these criteria down into twelve factors that courts should consider in deciding whether to penetrate the corporate form: (1) common ownership; (2) pervasive control; (3) confused intermingling of business activity, assets, or management; (4) thin capitalization; (5) nonobservance of corporate formalities; (6) absence of corporate records; (7) nonpayment of dividends; (8) insolvency at the time of the litigated transaction; (9) siphoning away of corporate assets by the dominant shareholders; (10) nonfunctioning of officers and directors; (11) use of the corporation for transactions of the dominant shareholders; and (12) use of the corporation in promoting fraud. In the present case, a court must consider the factors of MCC's operations in view of these criteria. For example, common ownership existed among MCC and its related companies—Georgetown, Multicon, and MPI (MCC's parent company)—in the sense that Edwards and Kessler were a significant presence in all of them. But Edwards and Kessler had partners in Multicon and Georgetown to whom they owed a fiduciary duty. Edwards and Kessler could not, and did not, run MCC as their own enterprise; MCC had to deliver value to the various limited partnerships for which it had served as a construction company. Moreover, the several entities in the Multicon complex were operated on an arm's length basis from one another. Edwards and Kessler maintained pervasive control from 1966 through 1970. There was no confused intermingling of business activity, assets, or management. MCC did not engage in identifying and acquiring project locations, the formation of local partnerships, advertising, or property management. While initial capital was unquestionably thin, i.e., $500, the pertinent question is whether it was too thin. A review of activities shows that, during its corporate life, MCC did not ever want for assets. The observance of corporate formalities occurred. Furthermore, separate tax returns for each company were meticulously filed. Throughout its years of activity in Massachusetts, MCC also filed the appropriate corporate certificates with the secretary of the commonwealth. At the time of the litigated transaction, MCC was not insolvent. MCC's cash position at the end of 1966 was $121,762.67 and at the end of 1967, $275,731.43. There was no suggestion that MCC during that period, or at any time while it was active, had experienced difficulty in paying debts as they became due, a test of insolvency. For the years in question, assets and liabilities were in close balance, but those assets remained sufficient to pay existing debts as they became absolute and matured. At the end of its active period, in December 1973, MCC showed assets in excess of liabilities and retained earnings of $1,109. In the cases in which courts have penetrated the corporate veil, finagling, an element of dubious manipulation and contrivance that confuses corporate identities and causes third parties uncertainty, exists. Here, no one suggests that Evans thought he was doing excavation work for Multicon, Georgetown, or Edwards and Kessler. He entered into a conventional subcontracting arrangement with a general contracting corporation, MCC, and was not misled into doing so on the basis of who was interested in Georgetown (the owner) or Multicon (Georgetown's general partner). Hence, the contract between Evans and MCC and the manner in which MCC had functioned in the Multicon enterprise would not justify looking beyond MCC to its parent MPI or to Edwards and Kessler, who had been the sole stockholders of MCC at the time of contracting. The risk that a defendant, without fraud and in the normal course of business operations, may become unable to answer to a judgment is inherent in any civil litigation. But that in itself can never form the basis for piercing the corporate veil in the absence of evidence supporting such a result.

FIGURE 39.4   Piercing the Corporate Veil

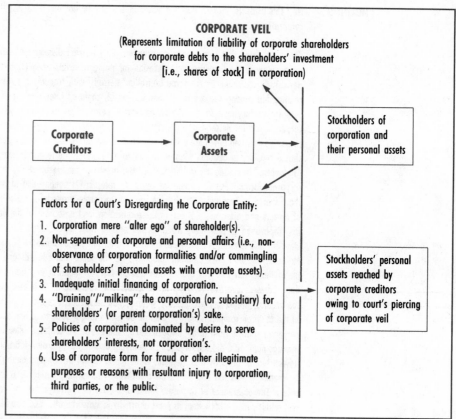

CORPORATE POWERS

As we learned earlier, the articles of incorporation may set forth the powers of the corporation. Such provisions actually may be redundant because state statutes normally set out what corporations can do permissibly. These *express powers* include the ability to conduct business, to exist perpetually (unless the articles define a shorter period or the state dissolves the corporation), to sue and be sued, to use the corporate name or seal, and to make bylaws.

In addition, corporations possess *implied powers* to do everything reasonably necessary for the conduct of the business. Typical implied powers consist of holding or transferring property, acquiring stock from other corporations, borrowing money, executing commercial paper, issuing bonds, effecting loans, reacquiring the corporation's own shares, and contributing to charity. Statutes may enumerate these and other implied powers.

ULTRA VIRES

As noted earlier, the powers of corporations were more heavily circumscribed years ago than they are today. Since the strict application of the concession theory had held that corporate status was a privilege (in contrast to a right), acts outside the boundaries established by law for the corporation were *ultra vires (beyond the scope or legal power of a corporation as established by the corporation's charter or by state statute)* and therefore void. When sued, corporations could use ultra vires as a defense to enforcement of a contract. With the advent of implied powers, and a consequent relaxation of the concession theory and a widening of permissible corporate purposes, a corporation's use of this doctrine for avoidance of contractual duties has become largely outmoded. Thus, the modern trend is to curtail application of the ultra vires doctrine as a defense and in general to uphold the validity of actions taken by the corporation unless the action is a public wrong or forbidden by statute. Sometimes, however, the result depends on whether the transaction is executory or executed.

Injunctive actions Lawsuits asking a court of equity to order a person to do or to refrain from doing some specified act.

Shareholder **injunctive actions** against the corporation, shareholder suits on behalf of the corporation to recover damages occasioned by an impermissible act, and proceedings by the state to dissolve the corporation because of repeated violations of applicable law constitute practically the only areas that remain possibilities for application of the doctrine. Not surprisingly, then, state statutes abolishing the defense of ultra vires usually exempt these three situations from the statute's coverage.

The court in the following case considered the ultra vires defense in reaching its conclusions of law.

Goebel v. Blocks and Marbles Brand Toys, Inc.
568 N.E.2d 552 (Ind. App. 1991)

FACTS Mark Launer incorporated Blocks and Marbles Brand Toys, Inc. (Blocks and Marbles) in 1985, operated it, and served as its sole director and president until March or April, 1986. On 20 May 1986, he executed an agreement with Lawrence E. Goebel to employ Goebel as president and chief operating officer. The term of the agreement commenced 1 April 1986 and was to terminate on 31 December 1991. Goebel began his duties in April, 1986. On 3 February 1987, the corporation amended its bylaws and expanded the board of directors from one person to not less than three nor more than five persons. Launer resigned as director and sold his stock in Blocks and Marbles. The new board elected Goebel president for a one-year term. The directors remaining after Launer's resignation apparently did not become aware of Goebel's employment agreement of 20 May 1986 until sometime in 1988. Although the 20 May 1986 employment agreement provided for Goebel to receive a salary of $5000 per month plus 25 percent of the annual pre-tax profits in excess of $150,000, Goebel received substantially less than the agreed salary in 1986 and 1987. Nevertheless, he told an accountant and outside auditors preparing financial statements for each year not to show any accrued salary as a liability of the corporation. In February, 1989, four members of the five-member board of directors resigned and a new board was elected. On 14 March 1989, this new board voted to terminate Goebel's employment effective 31 March 1989. Contending he was owed additional salary for 1986 and 1987, Goebel, on 12 July 1989, filed a notice of intention to hold a corporate employee's lien on Blocks and Marbles's corporate property. In addition, relying on an arbitration provision in the 20 May 1986 contract, Goebel filed a request for arbitration of his dispute with Blocks and Marbles. The company argued that Goebel's employment contract was ultra vires because it had violated both the corporation's own bylaws and an Indiana statute mandating that the president be chosen from the corporation's directors.

ISSUE   Was Blocks and Marbles's contract with Goebel ultra vires and hence unenforceable?

HOLDING   No. Although Blocks and Marbles could have sued Launer for causing or authorizing an ultra vires act, because Goebel probably had not known of the contract's invalidity, the corporation could not use the ultra vires defense against Goebel for his role in entering into the employment contract.

REASONING Blocks and Marbles argued that the corporation could not legally enter into the agreement to employ a president because the contract had directly violated both the statute under which the corporation had been created and the corporation's own bylaws. Blocks and Marbles made the following arguments: (1) The directors' minutes had not shown a resolution authorizing the contract to make Goebel president or the creation of the additional office of chief operating officer; (2) the directors' minutes had not shown approval of the employment contract; (3) the secretary had not attested to the execution of the employment agreement, as required by the bylaws; (4) any blanket ratification of action by shareholders could not be considered ratification of the employment agreement because the shareholders had been unaware of the material fact of the existence of the agreement; (5) Launer had lacked authority to enter into the employment agreement as a shareholder or on behalf of shareholders because Launer had failed to pay his subscription for his shares of capital stock and had not been lawfully issued shares of stock; and (6) Goebel had been a shareholder and, therefore, an insider improperly contracting with the corporation without the consent and approval of all the shareholders. Blocks and Marbles contended that Indiana law permits the company to challenge the employment agreement as an ultra vires act of the corporation and an insider transaction by Goebel. The pertinent Indiana statutory provision states that a corporation in a proceeding against a former director, officer, employee, or agent may challenge its own power to act. The Official Comment to this statute notes that the suit against the director or other agent is for "authorizing or causing the corporation to engage in an ultra vires act. . . ." Otherwise, "the validity of corporate action may not be challenged on the ground that the corporation lacks or lacked power to act." Thus, although Blocks and Marbles could have sued Launer for causing or authorizing ultra vires acts, Blocks and Marbles could not defend against Goebel or sue him for authorizing or causing the corporation to enter into an employment agreement with himself. Although the record indicates that not all the stockholders knew of the contract, Launer had had apparent authority to enter into the contract. And Goebel could not have been presumed to know of the agreement's invalidity. Thus, Blocks and Marbles could not rely on the ultra vires defense here.

TORTS AND CRIMES

Older precedents had held that a corporation was not answerable for torts and crimes because these were ultra vires acts (so called because a corporation lacked the power to commit torts and crimes). Today, the rule is much different: Corporations are vicariously liable for the torts of their employees by virtue of the doctrine of *respondeat superior*. They are also liable for the criminal acts of their directors, officers, and other agents. It is easy to understand why this would be so in nonintentional torts (such as negligence) or criminal statutes involving nonintent, *mala prohibita* situations (such as violations of environmental statutes or antitrust laws). But it is harder to accept the imposition of a corporation's liability for its agents' intentional torts or crimes that require showings of intent, such as **larceny**. In these cases, in contrast to situations in which the conduct is not willful, courts generally will avoid holding the corporation liable unless a high-ranking official (a "superior servant") has committed the acts and the corporation has intended to retain the benefits of or has participated in the tort or crime.

A factually novel case that illustrates some of these points follows.

Larceny A felonious taking of the personal property of another person with the intent to deprive the owner of possession and to convert it to one's own use.

United States v. LBS Bank–New York, Inc.
757 F. Supp. 496 (E.D. Pa. 1990)

FACTS A jury convicted LBS Bank–New York, Inc. (LBS) of conspiring to defraud the United States by filing false and fraudulent currency transaction reports (CTRs) and/or failing to file reports of apparent crimes. On appeal, LBS argued that the jury should have acquitted it because insufficient evidence had existed to establish that a single agent of LBS had had the specific intent to defraud the government, as required for conviction under 18 U.S.C. Section 371. It argued that Vinko Mir, the bank's chairman, was the only agent of LBS about whom the government had presented any evidence of specific criminal intent that could have been imputed to the bank and that the government could not rely on this evidence to sustain LBS's conviction because the jury, in acquitting Vinko Mir, had found that Mir had not possessed this requisite intent.

ISSUE Could the government successfully prosecute a bank for conspiracy to defraud the United States in circumstances in which the jury had acquitted the bank's chairman of the same charge?

HOLDING Yes. An appellate court could use evidence of the officer's conduct to sustain a verdict against the corporate defendant, despite the fact that the jury had acquitted the officer.

REASONING In determining whether sufficient evidence supports the jury verdict, the court must decide whether the verdict can be sustained on evidence of Vinko Mir's specific intent or whether the evidence necessarily must be disregarded owing to Mir's acquittal. LBS asserted that evidence of Mir's intent cannot be used to sustain the verdict against the bank; that is, the guilt of a corporate defendant cannot be predicated on the acts of an agent acquitted by the jury of the same charge. The bank's position, however, runs contrary to the rulings of the vast majority of the courts of appeals. More importantly, it is contrary to the rulings of the Supreme Court in several recent cases in which the

Court held that acquittal does not necessarily indicate that the jury had found insufficient evidence on that count; rather, the acquittal simply could be a product of juror lenity. The Supreme Court has instructed, therefore, that an acquittal should not mandate a reversal of a finding of guilt on another count that is dependent on the same factual finding. Under this rationale, a court, in attempting to determine whether sufficient evidence supports the conviction of a corporate defendant, remains free to consider all the evidence presented at trial, including evidence that concerns the acts of corporate agents whom the jury had acquitted. For this reason, the court concludes that evidence of Vinko Mir's conduct can be used to sustain a verdict against LBS, despite the fact that Mir himself was acquitted. A review of the evidence presented at trial relating to Mir's activities reveals that there is sufficient evidence relating to Mir on which the jury reasonably could have convicted LBS. There was also sufficient evidence presented from which a jury could reasonably conclude that Mir had known that the bank had filed false CTRs. The government additionally presented sufficient evidence from which a jury could conclude that Mir had known that two different individuals had attempted to defraud the United States through the filing of false CTR forms and that Mir had intended to help effectuate at least one of their objectives.

FOREIGN CORPORATIONS

A corporation usually will be incorporated in the state in which it will carry out most of its business. However, the fact that some jurisdictions are more hospitable to corporations than others tempers this generalization.

For instance, some jurisdictions may allow favorable tax treatment of corporations or may lower the minimum stated capital requirements. Delaware is one such jurisdiction. When the corporation is *operating within the state of its incorporation,* it is called a *domestic corporation.* We already have seen how the state can, through its incorporation laws, regulate the activities of its domestic corporations.

A state also can require *foreign corporations (ones not incorporated in that state)*[2] to "qualify" before "doing business" in that state. *Qualification* usually involves filing required forms, paying fees and taxes, and appointing a resident agent (for service of process). A state cannot require qualification of wholly interstate corporations because such actions would conflict with the commerce clause of the Constitution. The amount of activity that will constitute *doing business* has spawned a great deal of litigation, despite the fact that state statutes generally try to define this term. The term most commonly means that *a foreign corporation is transacting in the state a substantial portion of its ordinary corporate business.* Maintaining bank accounts, conducting sales through independent contractors, holding meetings of directors or shareholders, or maintaining or defending court actions will not amount to "doing business" for qualification (but may for jurisdiction or taxation) purposes.

Noncompliance with qualification statutes may bar a corporation from

[2]Corporations incorporated under the laws of other nations are generally known as *alien* corporations.

maintaining (but not defending) court actions in the state or may result in criminal penalties (fines). Moreover, lack of qualification may impose on the directors, officers, and shareholders personal liability for corporate debts.

The following case illustrates some of the foregoing principles.

Sierra Glass & Mirror v. Viking Industries, Inc.
808 P.2d 512 (Nev. 1991)

FACTS   Viking Industries, Inc. (Viking) is an Oregon corporation that manufactures and sells windows to buyers in thirty different states. Viking brought a breach of contract action against Sierra Glass & Mirror (Sierra), a Nevada company, when Sierra refused to pay for windows delivered. A bench trial resulted in a $53,529 verdict in which the court awarded Viking the contract price of $31,958.08, minus the salvage value that Viking had received, plus shipping costs, interest, and attorneys' fees. Throughout the course of the trial, Sierra had asserted that Viking was not entitled to bring this action in a Nevada court because it is a foreign corporation doing business in Nevada and had failed to comply with Nevada law. A state statute precludes foreign corporations doing business in Nevada from commencing an action in Nevada courts if that corporation has not filed qualifying documents with the secretary of state. The evidence produced at trial revealed the following about Viking's associations with Nevada: Its total sales volume amounts to approximately $20 million in the thirty states in which it conducts business. Of that amount, about $3 million stems from sales in Nevada. At the time the cause of action arose, Viking had one sales representative, Linda Aronsohn, who worked in Nevada. She resided in Las Vegas and spent two weeks per month calling on customers and visiting sales prospects in Reno and Las Vegas. Viking maintained a listed telephone in Las Vegas at Aronsohn's home address. Nevada customers placed orders through Aronsohn, who then phoned the orders and sent the checks to Portland. Viking characterized its contacts with Nevada as purely interstate and thus beyond the state's ability to require it to qualify as a foreign corporation.

ISSUE   Did Viking's connections with Nevada require it to qualify as a foreign corporation before it could bring an action against Sierra to recover the contract price of goods delivered?

HOLDING   No. Although Viking's activities in Nevada appeared to be continuous and systematic, Viking had not so localized itself into the community that its activities in Nevada had taken on an intrastate quality. Hence, Viking's connections with Nevada would not prohibit its bringing suit in Nevada courts, despite its failure to qualify.

REASONING   Viking asserted that its associations with Nevada are purely interstate and therefore subject only to federal regulation under the Commerce Clause. To minimize restrictions on the flow of interstate commerce, states may not impose their filing statutes on companies who send salespeople into the forum state to promote interstate trade. However, when the quantity of business in the forum state becomes substantial, the nature of the business becomes intrastate, subjecting the company to the forum state's regulation of foreign corporations. Therefore, the test to determine if a company is doing business in a state is two-pronged. Courts look first to the nature of the company's business functions in the forum state and then to the quantity of business conducted in the forum state. In *Eli Lilly*, the leading precedent in this area, the U.S. Supreme Court found that the out-of-state company was doing business in the state because (1) it had maintained an office and telephone in the state; (2) the lessor of the office had been a company's employee; (3) the office had employed a secretary and eighteen other salaried workers, many of whom had resided in the forum state; (4) these employees had done promotional and informational work and had received orders for plaintiff's products; and (5) even though the company had sold only to wholesalers, its employees had promoted the products by contacting retailers who bought products intrastate. Viking's activities in Nevada at the time this suit arose were not as pervasive as the factors listed in *Eli Lilly*. Instead, its conduct lay somewhere between the purely interstate transactions of a company that takes orders from the forum state and fills them through its operations in the foreign state and the intrastate nature of a company that has an actual employee soliciting a large quantity of business within the forum state. Hence, because Viking's activities are interstate, but substantial, Viking sits right on the fence between doing business and not doing business in Nevada. As noted, U.S. Supreme Court precedents have determined that states may impose their regulations on interstate commerce as long as the state legislation does not express hostility toward interstate commerce in violation of the Commerce Clause. However, state statutes do violate the Commerce Clause when applied to defeat a transaction that is part of interstate commerce. In *Allenberg Cotton Co.* v. *Pittman,* 419 U.S. 20 (1974), a Tennessee cotton merchant brought suit against a Mississippi cotton grower who had breached a contract. The Supreme Court found that even though the merchant had conducted regular business in Mississippi and had stored a continuous supply of inventory there, the nature of the merchant's business was interstate because he had not sold the cotton within Mississippi. According to the Court, a regulatory statute cannot defeat a "transaction which, though having intrastate aspects, was in fact 'a part of interstate commerce.' " Many state courts have followed the *Allenberg* lead and have determined that something more than continuous business in the forum state is necessary before the state may subject foreign corporations to its statutes. The general consensus of state courts is that whether a company is doing business must be decided on a case-by-case basis. Courts must consider factors such as the quantity of business, the firm's permanence and number of employees, and the presence of a company office. The main question, however, centers on whether the company has *localized* its business in the forum state. In this case, Viking had conducted a large volume of interstate transactions with Nevada; but it had not maintained an office here, and it had had only one agent soliciting contracts in Reno and in Las Vegas. Therefore, although Viking had conducted continuous business here, it had not localized itself into the Nevada community. In rebuttal, Sierra asserted that Nevada law has stricter filing requirements than many other states, since NRS 80.015, enacted in 1989, defines "not doing business" quite narrowly by actually listing activities for which foreign companies need not file. This statute states that activities that do not constitute doing business in Nevada include sales through independent contractors, advertising in and shipping goods to Nevada, and isolated transactions completed within thirty days. Sierra asks this court to consider the factors listed in NRS 80.015 as instructive on the definition of doing business in Nevada, even though the statute was enacted after the commencement of this suit. However, before the legislature enacted NRS 80.015, Nevada had no analogous statute. Therefore, a court cannot impute knowledge of those factors to Viking. More to the point, although Viking's activities are predominately interstate, its high volume of sales in Nevada approaches a quantity that may subject a company to regulation. Unlike the firm in *Eli Lilly,* Viking had only one Nevada employee instead of eighteen and only contacted companies who would buy products directly from Viking. Yet this transaction with Sierra amounted to only about 1/100 of Viking's total sales volume in Nevada for 1983. In addition, Ms. Aronsohn was not an independent contractor but an employee of Viking who had lived and worked in Nevada. Although Viking's activities would appear to be continuous and systematic, it had not so localized itself into the community that its activities had taken on an intrastate quality. Therefore, Sierra was liable for breach of contract because Viking's connections with Nevada had not prohibited it from bringing suit in Nevada courts.

STATE AND FEDERAL SECURITIES LAWS

To protect the public from fraudulent schemes, states also regulate the issuance of corporate securities. Although the content of these statutes varies from state to state, these laws emphasize antifraud and registration provisions. Such statutes are called *blue sky* laws because the securities are often worth no more than pieces of the "blue sky."

Federal laws apply in the area that the states cannot regulate—that is, in interstate commerce. The Securities Act of 1933 and the Securities Exchange Act of 1934, covering original issues of securities and secondary distributions, respectively, represent the most significant federal statutes in the securities area. We will discuss these state and federal securities laws in detail in Chapters 41 and 44; they are mentioned here because corporations may find themselves subject to these provisions.

SUMMARY

A corporation is an artificial entity created by the state and endowed with certain powers by the state. The historical development of corporations illustrates an acceptance of the "fiction" (or "entity" theory) of corporations— that is, that the corporation is an entity separate and distinct from its shareholders. As a business form, corporations have the advantages of limited liability, centralization of management functions, continuity of existence, free transferability of shares, and sometimes favorable tax treatment. There are various types of "for-profit" corporations: public-issue private corporations, close corporations, professional corporations, public corporations, and quasi-public corporations. Nonprofit corporations exist in all jurisdictions as well.

Promoters facilitate the formation of corporations. Although the corporation is generally not liable for the promoter's activities, in some cases it will be.

The filing of the articles of incorporation signals the corporation's official beginning, but some jurisdictions require the issuance of a certificate of incorporation or an organizational meeting before the corporation can attain corporate status. In general, corporate status will not be lost if substantial compliance with incorporation statutes occurs; the courts will view the entity as a de jure (legal) corporation. Courts will even grant de facto (in fact but not in law) corporations corporate status on the fulfillment of certain requirements. But the issuance of a certificate of incorporation will eliminate the need for resort to the de facto doctrine in some jurisdictions. This development actually represents the modern trend: To presume de jure status in such circumstances except in actions brought by the state. At times, however, courts will disregard corporate status even when complete compliance with the statute has taken place. "Piercing the corporate veil" in order to impose personal liability on a shareholder will occur when the corporate form becomes the means for furthering illegitimate ends.

Corporations enjoy certain express and implied powers. Years ago courts held that corporations were not responsible for ultra vires acts (those beyond the power of the corporation), but the law now limits the application of this doctrine to a few specialized situations. Corporations may be liable for the torts and crimes of their agents and employees; but, when instituting corporate liability, courts often distinguish between torts and crimes that require specific intent and those that do not.

States can require foreign corporations to "qualify" in their jurisdictions if these corporations transact a substantial amount of business in those states. State and federal securities laws represent additional methods of regulating corporations.

DISCUSSION QUESTIONS

1. What is a corporation? How did the concept of a corporation evolve?
2. Name five advantages of corporations as business associations.
3. Name and define the various types of corporations.
4. Discuss the rights and duties of promoters.
5. Enumerate in general the contents of articles of incorporation.
6. How does a de jure corporation differ from a de facto corporation? What requirements are necessary for a corporation to acquire de facto status?

7. Under what circumstances will a court or the state "pierce the corporate veil"?
8. Discuss the express and implied powers of corporations.
9. What is the ultra vires doctrine, and what are the circumstances in which it may be applied?
10. Discuss the concepts of "foreign" corporations and "qualification" in other jurisdictions.

CASE PROBLEMS

1. James E. McFadden, Inc. (McFadden) sued United States Fidelity and Guaranty Company (USF&G), a bonding firm, for monies owed to it for construction work McFadden had done for Baltimore Contractors, Inc. (Baltimore). Although USF&G had provided no bonding services for Baltimore on the project in question, McFadden sued USF&G on the theory that USF&G had so completely taken control of Baltimore in 1980 that Baltimore had been a mere instrumentality or alter ego of USF&G. Among other things, USF&G's 1980 agreement with Baltimore had contained provisions for transferring all funds paid to Baltimore to USF&G in order to cover construction contracts bonded by USF&G; turning over all profits from joint ventures to USF&G to be applied to reducing Baltimore's line of credit; allowing USF&G to complete projects in Baltimore's name and at Baltimore's expense if Baltimore failed to complete them; installing an accounting system satisfactory to USF&G, including the sending of monthly financial statements to USF&G; and authorizing USF&G to have prompt access to all project sites bonded by it and to all Baltimore's books, records, and other job accounts. Baltimore alleged that these provisions, plus the lack of a scheduled repayment plan, demonstrated

that Baltimore had relinquished control to USF&G. USF&G, in contrast, argued that the provisions had merely served as a vehicle by which it could minimize its losses if Baltimore failed to repay the $20 million loan from USF&G that had been the subject of the 1980 agreement. Were the business affairs of Baltimore and USF&G so entwined that a court should pierce the corporate veil and impose liability on USF&G in these circumstances? (*James E. McFadden, Inc.* v. *Baltimore Contractors, Inc.,* 609 F. Supp. 1102 [E.D. Pa. 1985].)

2. Samuel Cross was a member in good standing of the Midtown Club, Inc. (Midtown), a Connecticut corporation in Stamford. The certificate of incorporation had stated that the sole purpose of the corporation was "to provide facilities for the serving of luncheon or other meals to members." Neither the certificate of incorporation nor the bylaws of the corporation had contained any qualifications for membership, nor had either contained any restrictions on the luncheon guests members could bring to the club. Cross sought to bring a female to lunch with him, and both he and his guest were refused seating at the luncheon facility. Cross then wrote twice to the president of the corporation to protest the action, but he received no reply to either letter. On three

different occasions, Cross submitted applications for membership on behalf of a different female, and only on the third of those occasions did the board process the application, which it then rejected. Shortly after these occurrences, the board of directors conducted two separate pollings of its members, one by mail, the other by a special meeting held to vote on four alternative proposals to amend the bylaws of the corporation concerning the admission of women members and guests. None of these proposed amendments to the bylaws received the required number of votes for adoption. Following that balloting, the plaintiff again wrote to the president of the corporation and asked that the directors stop interfering with his rights as a member to bring women guests to the luncheon facility and to propose women for membership. The president replied that "the existing bylaws, house rules, and customs continue in effect, and therefore [the board] consider[s] the matter closed." Cross sued the corporation on the rationale that Midtown had committed an ultra vires act in excluding women members. Should Cross win on this theory? (*Cross* v. *Midtown Club, Inc.*, 365 A.2d 1227 [Conn. Super. 1976].)

3. Michael Kvassay, d/b/a Kvassay Exotic Food (Kvassay), had contracted in 1984 to sell 24,000 cases of baklava to Great American Foods, Inc. (Great American) at $19 per case. Under the contract, the sales were to occur over a one-year period; and Great American was to be Kvassay's only customer. The contract included the following clause: "If Buyer refuses to accept or repudiates delivery of the goods sold to him, under this Agreement, Seller shall be entitled to damages, at the rate of $5.00 per case, for each case remaining to be delivered under this Contract." Problems arose early in this contractual relationship, with checks issued by Great American being dishonored for insufficient funds. Frequently, one of Great American's owners, the Murrays, issued a personal check for the amount due. After producing approximately 3000 cases, Kvassay stopped producing the baklava because Great American refused to purchase any more of the product. The Murrays had formed Sunshine Ceramics, Inc. in 1974. The company had been inactive during the late 1970s and early 1980s and therefore had failed to make a number of required corporate filings. In August, 1984, the name of the corporation had been changed to Great American Foods, Inc. The Murrays also had operated fast food restaurants in Wichita under the name of Great American Subs, Inc. and had controlled an entity named Murray

Investments. The Murrays had conducted business for all of their entities and personal business from one street location in Wichita. In August, 1984, the Murrays had opened a bank account in the name of Great American Distributors, Inc., although they never had filed any incorporation papers. The Murrays had frequently paid the bills of their various entities with personal checks and often had written checks to themselves on corporate accounts. In addition, at various times, one entity had paid the Murrays' personal expenses or the expenses of other Murray entities. In April, 1985, Kvassay filed suit for damages arising from the collapse of his baklava baking business; a jury awarded him $35,673.99 in damages. The trial judge also allowed Kvassay to pierce Great American's corporate veil in order to hold the Murrays personally liable for the corporate debts. Great American argued on appeal that Kvassay had experienced no fraud or injustice and that, in addition, no "causal nexus" had existed between Kvassay's decision to enter into the contract and the corporate failings that had come to light during the trial. Kvassay claimed that the corporate entity involved had served as a "facade for the operations of the Murrays" and had worked to Kvassay's injustice "by inducing him to enter into the contract" at issue. How should the appellate court rule in this case? (*Kvassay* v. *Murray*, 808 P.2d 896 [Kan. App. 1991].)

4. A federal district court issued two grand jury subpoenas, one addressed to a corporation calling for testimony and production of the corporation's business records and the other addressed to the "Custodian of Records," also calling for testimony and production of the corporation's business records. The custodian, who was the majority shareholder and sole operating officer and director of the corporation, which had only three shareholders, moved to quash (i.e., cancel) the subpoena for the corporation's records. He argued that the corporation was essentially a one-man operation much akin to a sole proprietorship, and thus to compel the corporation to produce its records would be to force the custodian to act to incriminate himself in violation of a recent Supreme Court precedent. According to this precedent, the custodian insisted, a sole proprietor could assert the Fifth Amendment privilege against self-incrimination because, although the contents of the subpoenaed records were not privileged, the testimonial character of the act of producing the records was. Was the shareholder's contention that this privilege applied when corporate records are subpoenaed persuasive? (*In*

re Two Grand Jury Subpoenae Duces Tecum, 769 F.2d 52 [2nd Cir. 1985].)

5. Albion Cranson wanted to incorporate a business called Real Estate Service Bureau. With the help of an attorney, he prepared articles of incorporation, which he thought the attorney had sent to the appropriate state office on 1 May 1961. Cranson conducted all transactions on behalf of the corporation, including the purchase of eight typewriters from International Business Machines Corporation (IBM), between May and November 1961. At no time did Cranson assume any personal obligations regarding the typewriters. Unknown to Cranson, his attorney had not filed the articles of incorporation until 24 November 1961. In the meantime, Cranson's business began to fail; and IBM sued Cranson for the $4333.40 due on the typewriters. Would only Real Estate Service Bureau be liable for this debt, or could IBM also sue Cranson personally? (*Cranson v. International Business Machines Corporation,* 200 A.2d 33 [Md. 1964].)

6. Jesse Morgan signed a promissory note in his capacity as president of Beefmastor, Inc. on 19 November 1970. The note represented partial payment for Smith's business, which was located in Georgia. Beefmastor, Inc. subsequently was incorporated on 31 December 1970. After making some payments, Beefmastor, Inc. defaulted on the note. Smith then sued Morgan. Could Morgan, the promoter, be held personally liable in these circumstances? (*Smith v. Morgan,* 272 S.E.2d 602 [N.C. App. 1980].)

7. First National Bank of Boston (First National) wished to spend money to publicize its views on a proposed constitutional amendment that would have permitted the Massachusetts legislature to impose a graduated tax on the income of individuals. A Massachusetts law prohibited banks and certain other associations from making contributions or expenditures "for the purpose of . . . influencing or affecting the vote on any question submitted to the voters, other than one materially affecting any of the property, business, or assets of the corporation." Another section of the statute stated that a question concerning tax matters was not a question that fell within the statutory exemption. Any corporation violating the statute could receive a maximum fine of $50,000, and directors and officers violating it faced fines of $10,000, imprisonment for up to one year, or both. After First National had made its wishes known to Bellotti, the attorney general of Massachusetts, he informed the bank that he would enforce the statute

against it if it attempted to disseminate its views in violation of the statute. First National sued, arguing that the statute had unconstitutionally deprived it of its First Amendment right to express its views on issues of public importance. First National contended that as a legal person it possesses First Amendment rights just as natural persons do. Bellotti argued that Massachusetts had the right to limit commercial speech in this context because wealthy and powerful corporations had the resources to drown out other points of view, thereby undermining democratic processes. Who had the more persuasive viewpoint, First National or Bellotti? (*First National Bank of Boston v. Bellotti,* 435 U.S. 765 [1978].)

8. McElfish was the president and a primary stockholder of Gags Enterprises, Inc. (Gags). Gags owned the Sandspur Bar in Melbourne, Florida. The bar had a studio apartment attached to the back, which was occupied at various times by McElfish, who acted as the bar's manager. As he had done on other occasions, McElfish invited Schroeder to go with him to a party at another lounge in Melbourne to assist him in entertaining business clients. After the party, they returned to the apartment at the Sandspur. An argument arose between them that resulted in McElfish's inflicting numerous personal injuries on Schroeder. McElfish explained that he had been trying to remove Schroeder from the premises because she was rowdy and intoxicated and that he had wanted to lock up the bar for the evening. Should Gags be liable for the $31,500 in compensatory damages and $30,000 in punitive damages awarded by the jury to Schroeder? (*Kent Insurance Company v. Schroeder,* 469 So.2d 209 [Fla. Dist. Ct. App. 1985].)

9. William Ruszkowski and his wife own A-1 Contracting, Inc. (A-1). Mr. Ruszkowski claims that he was injured while using a circular saw in connection with his employment at A-1. In his complaint, he sets forth causes of action in negligence and breach of warranty against the defendant, Sears, Roebuck and Company (Sears), for the manufacture, sale, and distribution of a defectively designed product. Sears's answer contains general denials and several affirmative defenses, one of which calls for reducing any recovery received by Ruszkowski owing to Ruszkowski's culpable fault. New York law allows a manufacturer/seller of a product that has allegedly injured an employee at his or her place of employment to implead (i.e., to bring a new party into the lawsuit on the ground that this new party ultimately

may be liable to the impleading party) the employer in order to receive indemnification from the employer in the event the manufacturer/seller is found liable to the employee. Ruszkowski contends that if the court allows this third party action to stand, the result may be inequitable because whatever allocation of fault the court or the jury makes in the main action will then carry over to the third party action. According to Ruszkowski, if, for example, the decision maker finds that the plaintiffs are 30 percent negligent and are awarded $10,000, this award will be reduced to $7000, to be paid by Sears. Sears, in turn, may then recover $3000 from A-1; so the net final effect is that the plaintiffs will recover $4000, owing to the doubling of the allocation of fault, once as plaintiff/employee and once as impleaded employer. In essence, then, in requesting a dismissal of the third party action, Ruszkowski is asking the court to disregard the corporate status of A-1 for Ruszkowski's own benefit. Will a court accept Ruszkowski's argument in this case? (*Ruszkowski* v. *Sears, Roebuck and Co.,* 571 N.Y.S.2d 187 [Sup. 1991].)

10. Posadas de Mexico, S.A., de C.V. (Posadas) owned and operated hotels located exclusively in Mexico. As a corporation organized under the laws of Mexico and having its principal place of business in Mexico City, Posadas contended that it never had maintained an office, employees, or a telephone listing in New York. Posadas further claimed that it is not licensed to do business in New York, does not conduct any intrastate business in the state, and is engaged entirely in international commerce with the United States. Notwithstanding these assertions, Posadas admitted having maintained bank accounts in New York for the limited purpose of accepting deposits from United States clients for its hotels in Mexico. For the convenience of Americans wishing to make reservations to stay in the Mexican hotels, Posadas entered into business relationships with several New York corporations as independent contractors to take reservations and accept deposits in the United States on its behalf. Posadas gave these independent contractors the right, during their period of engagement with Posadas, to use the Posadas trademark and trade name. One of the independent contractors engaged by Posadas to handle reservations and hotel deposits on its behalf, Terence W. Rufer Associates, Inc. (Rufer, Inc.), provided accounting, credit, collection, marketing, and reservation services to Mexican hotels managed by Posadas. In particular, Rufer, Inc. collected checks for third parties managed by Posadas. Their agreement also obligated Rufer, Inc. to remit checks collected by it to Posadas by depositing these checks in certain bank accounts for which only officers of Posadas had signature authority. After the contractual relationship between Posadas and Rufer, Inc. had terminated by its terms on 31 October 1986, Posadas alleged, Rufer Inc.'s officers, Rufer and Dukes, had commingled these checks with their own personal assets. As a consequence of Rufer and Dukes's activities, Posadas sought compensatory and actual damages in the amount of $221,122.31, plus interest from the date of the alleged conversions, and $150,000 in punitive damages. Dukes and Rufer argued that Posadas's failure to qualify as a foreign corporation under New York law would preclude it from bringing suit in New York courts. Would a court find this argument persuasive? (*Posadas de Mexico, S.A., de C.V.* v. *Dukes,* 757 F. Supp. 297 [S.D. N.Y. 1991].)

CHAPTER 40

Operation of a Corporation

OUTLINE

SHAREHOLDERS AS OWNERS OF THE CORPORATION

If you or someone in your family owns stock in a private or publicly held corporation, you already know that the shareholders are the "owners" of the corporation. Your holding share (stock) certificates, such as the one pictured in Figures 40.1 and 40.2, signify that you own a portion of the corporate entity. Moreover, ownership of shares confers on the shareholder certain rights, which we shall discuss in this chapter. Interestingly, however, ownership of shares does not allow the shareholder to claim a specific asset of the corporation (say, a building) as his or hers. You may recall from Chapter 39 that corporate property remains the corporation's; for this reason, shareholders cannot transfer title of such property to others. Thus, even though you can sell your car (assuming it belongs to you) to a friend, as a stockholder in PAK Corporation, you cannot transfer the car to that same friend as if it were a corporate asset. On the other hand, the portion of the ownership of the cor-

FIGURE 40.1 Stock Certificate (Front)

Courtesy of Charles Roemer, Roemer and Mintz, Attorneys-at-Law, South Bend, Indiana.

FIGURE 40.2   Stock Certificate (Back)

Courtesy of Charles Roemer, Roemer and Mintz, Attorneys-at-Law, South Bend, Indiana.

1) VOTE
2) DIVIDENDS
3) % of Liquidate assets.

poration indicated by a share generally entitles the shareholder to vote on certain corporate issues, to receive dividends, and to obtain, upon the corporation's liquidation, the percentage of corporate assets represented by the shares.

At the outset, then, you should be aware that the shareholders, although the ultimate "owners" of the corporation, exert only indirect control over the day-to-day operations and overall policies of the firm. As you will see in Chapter 41, the officers and the board of directors, not the shareholders, bear the responsibilities for these functions. Shareholders, with the exception of controlling shareholders in a close corporation (a "one-person" or "family" corporation), ordinarily have no voice in the management of the corporation. Yet the shareholders form the bedrock of corporate structure because they select the directors, who in turn choose the officers. Additionally, the board of directors and the officers are ultimately answerable to the shareholders.

Although proprietorships in 1988 outnumbered corporations about four to one (see Figure 40.3), corporations are rising in popularity as a form of

FIGURE 40.3 Proprietorships, Partnerships, and Corporations by Numbers and Percentages, 1988

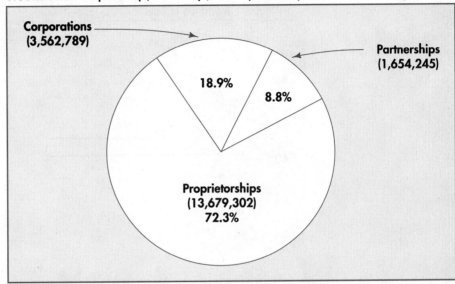

Source: U.S. Internal Revenue Service, *Statistics of Income, Business Income Tax Returns* and *Statistics of Income, Corporation Income Tax Returns* (Washington, D.C.: U.S. Government Printing Office, various years).

business organization. Therefore, it is a good idea to understand the basis of the operation of corporations from the shareholders' point of view. In terms of numbers, the rate of growth for corporations slowed between 1970 and 1988 compared to proprietorships. During that period, corporations increased by about 114 percent, and proprietorships grew by about 137 percent.[1] (Between 1960 and 1984, the number of corporations had almost tripled; but the number of proprietorships had increased only by about one-fourth.[2]) In terms of sales, however, the figures illustrated in Figure 40.4 reflect continual corporate growth and dominance. Total sales receipts for corporations indicate a 452 percent increase between 1970 and 1988, compared to an increase of 238 percent for proprietorships.[3]

We most often think of corporate America in terms of huge corporations like American Telephone & Telegraph (AT&T), General Motors (GM), or International Business Machines (IBM), but government statistics show that about 23 percent of all corporations have sales of under $25,000 per year, and 40 percent sell less than $100,000. Indeed, only about 17 percent have

[1]U.S. Internal Revenue Service, *Statistics of Income, Business Income Tax Returns* and *Statistics of Income, Corporation Income Tax Returns* (Washington, D.C.: U.S. Government Printing Office, various years).
[2]Ibid.
[3]Ibid.

FIGURE 40.4   A Comparison of Proprietorships, Partnerships, and Corporations: Percentage Breakdown of Sales Receipts, 1970–1988

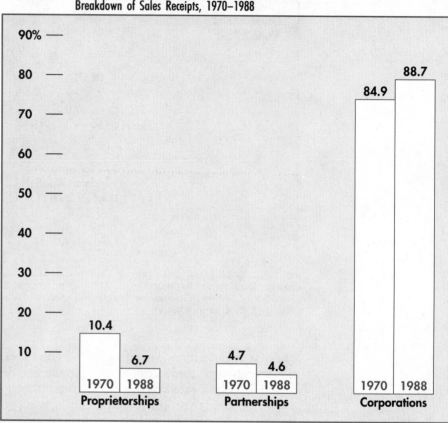

Source: U.S. Internal Revenue Service, *Statistics of Income, Business Income Tax Returns* and *Statistics of Income, Corporation Income Tax Returns* (Washington, D.C.: U.S. Government Printing Office, various years).

sales of $1 million or more.[4] From such statistics, we can deduce that relatively small corporations form the backbone of corporate America and that many of these are probably closely held rather than public-issue corporations, given their size.

In this chapter, we will discuss the general operation of the corporation and the shareholders' rights and duties without differentiating between public-issue and close corporations, unless the concept under discussion seems especially well-suited to close corporations and the preservation of the special management functions associated with them.

[4]Ibid.

	RIGHTS AND DUTIES OF SHAREHOLDERS

Types of Stock Owned

Shareholders exert indirect control over the corporation by virtue of their ownership of shares; the more they own, the more power they wield. A shareholder may own *common stock,* which allows the shareholder to receive dividends, to vote on corporate issues, and to receive property on the corporation's liquidation. Or the shareholder may own *preferred stock,* which, as its name suggests, confers priority with regard to dividends, voting, or liquidation rights. Furthermore, within the preferred stock, there may be several classes, or series, that set out different gradations of priority for each class. Under most state statutes, the corporate articles of incorporation must spell out the preferences; such preferences generally will not be implied.

The most common preference right involves priority with regard to *dividends* (cash, property, or other shares that the board of directors declares as payment to shareholders). For example, preferred stockholders may receive dividends paid at a specified rate (for example, 7 percent) before any other classes of stock receive dividends. Should any dividends remain after payment to the various classes of preferred and common stockholders, preferred shareholders often have *participation* rights; that is, they can take part in this further distribution of dividends rather than having their dividend rights restricted to the preferred stock dividend. In addition to dividend and participation rights, preferred shareholders receive corporate assets before any other stockholders do on the liquidation of the corporation. After the debts of the corporation are paid, preferred shareholders are the first to receive the **par value** of their stocks (plus any outstanding dividends); common stockholders receive assets only if sufficient assets to pay their stocks' par values remain. Should there be additional assets after payment to the common stockholders, the preferred and common shareholders normally share this balance in proportion to the shares that each holds individually. Preferred shareholders also may enjoy *conversion* rights (the option to change preferred stock into common stock or corporate bonds) and/or *redemption* rights (the enforced repurchase of shares by the corporation in certain authorized circumstances).

The following case involved an allegedly invalid issuance of preferred stock.

Par value The face value assigned to a stock and printed on the stock certificate.

STAAR Surgical Company v. Waggoner
588 A.2d 1130 (1991)

FACTS   STAAR Surgical Company (STAAR) faced severe financial difficulties in 1987. A write-down of its accounts receivable left the company's line of credit with the Bank of New York (BONY) undercollateralized by almost $2 million. As a consequence, BONY allegedly demanded Thomas R. Waggoner's personal guarantee to secure all of STAAR's debts to the bank. Waggoner, STAAR's president and CEO, in December, 1987, advised the STAAR board that he would guarantee the debts only if he were given voting control of the company while the guarantees were outstanding. Although Waggoner and the board generally concluded at the end of the meeting that STAAR would issue some type of convertible securities to Waggoner in exchange for his guarantee, the two sides never formally adopted this understanding. Nonetheless, at a hastily called and poorly organized meeting four days later, the board passed a "resolution" giving Waggoner and his wife newly created shares of preferred stock that would be convertible into 2 million shares of common stock if the guarantees Waggoner had made were not removed within thirty days. The STAAR board never formally adopted this resolution, and only Waggoner signed the minutes. Some STAAR board members, dissatisfied with the terms of this preferred stock transaction, called a board meeting for 11 January 1988. At that meeting, the board attempted to delay the conversion feature of the preferred stock. On 19 January 1988, however, Waggoner exercised his conversion option and received 2 million shares of STAAR common stock. Allegedly, Waggoner's action was authorized pursuant to the resolution and the certificate of designation because STAAR had failed to replace Waggoner's guarantee within the prescribed time limits. In August, 1989, the Waggoners attempted to exercise the voting provisions of the remainder of their preferred shares by removing STAAR's board. The directors, aided by two shareholders, contested this election under Delaware statutory law. The Court of Chancery subsequently invalidated the super voting provisions of the preferred shares. The Waggoners then filed an action to compel STAAR to convene a shareholders' meeting. STAAR answered the Waggoners' claim by denying that the Waggoners even owned the 2 million STAAR shares. The Waggoners next moved for an order determining their right to vote the disputed shares. The Court of Chancery ruled that despite the invalidity of the Waggoners' preferred shares, equity entitled the Waggoners to own and vote the disputed 2 million common shares that had been derived from the invalid preferred stock.

ISSUE   Were the Waggoners, as a matter of equity, entitled to own and vote disputed common shares that had been derived from invalid preferred stock?

HOLDING   No. The board's failure to adopt a resolution and certificate of designation authorizing the issue of stock as required under state law made the stock so issued void and a nullity.

REASONING   A corporation can, under Delaware corporate law, issue more than one class of stock, including preferred shares with a conversion feature. Although the STAAR certificate of incorporation authorized the board to issue, by resolution, "blank check" preferred stock, Delaware law requires a board resolution specifically authorizing the issue of such preferred stock. A board resolution must underlie any issue of convertible securities as well. Moreover, Delaware law requires the corporation to issue a certificate of designation in conjunction with such board resolutions. Waggoner conceded that the STAAR board had never formally adopted either the board resolution on 17 December 1987 or the certificate of designation. STAAR contended that the board's failure to adopt the resolution and the certificate of designation had rendered the preferred shares void, thus invalidating the common stock. The Waggoners, in contrast, focused on the common stock and not the preferred shares. They asserted that even if the board had failed to effect technical compliance with the law, the STAAR directors had all agreed at the 17 December 1987 board meeting to issue Waggoner 2 million shares of common stock as compensation for his guarantee of the BONY loans. Therefore, Waggoner claimed, it had been clear to all the parties that he would eventually receive the 2 million shares if STAAR could not find alternate financing for the loan. However, the preferred convertible shares originally issued to the Waggoners were invalid and void under Delaware law. No compliance with the terms of the relevant Delaware statutes ever occurred, as the directors had never formally adopted either the 17 December 1987 resolution or the certificate of designation. The issuance of corporate stock is an act of fundamental legal significance having a direct bearing on questions of corporate governance, control, and the capital structure of the enterprise. Hence, the law properly requires certainty in such matters. Finally, it is a basic concept of Delaware corporation law that in the absence of a clear agreement to the contrary, preferred stock rights are in derogation of the common law and must be strictly construed. Moreover, this principle of strict construction applies with equal force to the creation of preferred stock and its attendant rights, powers, designations, and preferences. Accordingly, a board's failure to adopt a resolution and certificate of designation designed to amend the fundamental document that imbues a corporation with its life and powers and defines the contract with its shareholders would not constitute a mere "technical" error. Stock issued in violation of Delaware law is void. A court—even in the would-be exercise of its equitable powers—cannot imbue void stock with the attributes of valid shares.

**Shareholders'
Meetings**

Notice   In general, shareholders' meetings may not occur unless the corporation has sent written notice of the meeting to all shareholders of record. Statutory and bylaw provisions often spell out the procedures for giving notice. Such notice ordinarily contains the time, date, and place of the meeting, as well as a statement of the purpose of the meeting. Most statutes require at least ten days' notice before a meeting can legitimately be conducted, but shareholders can expressly waive this requirement in writing before or after the meeting, or they can impliedly waive it by not protesting the lack of notice.

Quorum   Shareholder meetings cannot take place in the absence of a quorum. State statutes and corporate bylaws or articles usually state the percentage of outstanding shares, or shares entitled to vote, that will constitute a quorum. A majority of such votes usually will be necessary for a quorum; yet the Model Business Corporation Act sanctions articles that set the quorum requirement at a mere one-third of all outstanding shares.[5] *Dissident shareholders* (that is, those who disagree with the actions of management) may prevent a quorum by not attending meetings; but the law remains unsettled as to whether a subsequent walkout of dissident shareholders, once a quorum is present, will invalidate the meeting.

Election and Removal of Directors   One of the foremost powers held by shareholders is their capacity to elect and remove directors. Although the articles of incorporation usually designate the people who are to serve as the initial directors, these directors may serve only until the first annual meeting. At that time, the shareholders may elect some (or all) of them to the board of directors. If vacancies occur on the board because of deaths or resignations, the shareholders normally fill these vacancies. However, the articles of incorporation or bylaws may permit the directors to fill these posts. Directors usually serve staggered terms. This means that only a certain proportion of directors (for example, one-third) will be up for reelection at any given meeting. Such staggered terms ensure continuity of leadership on the board. In recent years, there has been a trend toward adding "**outsiders**" on the board of directors.

"Outsiders"   Directors who are not shareholders or officers.

---

[5]The Model Business Corporation Act (1969) began as a drafting effort in 1943 by the American Bar Association's Section on Corporation, Banking, and Business Law; its intent was to modernize corporate law and to achieve greater uniformity among jurisdictions by creating a statute that balances the interests of the state, the corporation, the shareholders, and management. Most of the states follow either the older Model Business Corporation Act (MBCA) or the 1984 version, the Revised Model Business Corporation Act (RMBCA).

Shareholders have *inherent* power (that is, power regardless of the articles or bylaws) to remove a director for cause. Previous cases have upheld the exercise of such rights when directors have engaged in embezzlement or other misconduct, have failed to live up to their duties to the corporation, or have undertaken unauthorized acts. The director, of course, may appeal his or her removal to a court of law. Statutes, articles of incorporation, and bylaws may also allow removal without cause.

Amendment of the Bylaws   Bylaws are provisions intended to regulate the corporation and its management. To be valid, bylaws must comply with state incorporation statutes and the articles of incorporation. Shareholders retain inherent power to amend (or repeal) bylaws, but they must do so in accordance with the proportion of outstanding shares mandated by state law.

In the following case, a shareholder alleged that the proposed amendments to the articles and the bylaws that dealt with various issues concerning the corporation's directors were unreasonable and hence invalid.

Stroud v. Milliken Enterprises, Inc.
585 A.2d 1306 (Del. Ch. 1988)

FACTS   W. B. Dixon Stroud, Jr. and other stockholders of Milliken Enterprises, Inc. (Milliken) sued Milliken, arguing that the proposed amendments to Milliken's certificate of incorporation and bylaws were invalid as a matter of law. Specifically, Stroud claimed that certain requirements of the proposed amendments were unlawful: (1) restriction on the number of members of the board of directors; (2) division of directors into three classes, with each director serving a three-year term; (3) enumeration of unreasonable qualifications for directors; and (4) provisions calling for automatic termination on a director's failure to remain qualified.

ISSUE   Were the restrictions set out in the proposed amendments unreasonable and hence void as a matter of law?

HOLDING   No. The board of directors of a corporation has the power to fix the number of directors within the restrictions imposed by the corporation's certificate of incorporation, and the certificate can lawfully provide for reasonable qualifications for the directors who are to serve on the board.

REASONING   Stroud first argued that the proposed amended Article of Incorporation No. 11 provides invalid and unreasonable qualifications for directors by requiring that the board of directors consist of nine to thirteen members, to be fixed by a majority vote of directors. Unquestionably, Delaware law allows the board to fix the number of directors within the restrictions imposed by the certificate of incorporation. Proposed Article 11(b) provides that the corporation will divide the directors into three classes, with each director serving a three-year term. This is lawful under Delaware law as well. Stroud focused most of his objections on proposed Article of Incorporation No. 11(c), which creates three categories for directors. Category 1 requires that directors in that category consist of individuals who have held line positions in other businesses or institutions and who are not officers, employees, or stockholders of Milliken. A majority of the directors must be from Category 1. At least three directors must come from Category 2, individuals who are beneficial stockholders of Milliken. No more than two directors can come from Category 3, which will be chosen from the chairman of the board, the chairman of the executive committee, and the president of Milliken. If an individual is qualified to be a director under both Categories 2 and 3, he or she will be deemed to be qualified only under Category 2. Proposed Article of Incorporation No. 11(c) further provides that if a director fails to remain qualified pursuant to the requirements of the category from which he or she was elected, he or she will automatically cease to be a director. Stroud claimed that proposed Article of Incorporation No. 11(c) (1) illegally requires qualifications for directors, (2) is impermissibly vague, (3) permits the incumbent board to decide whether an individual is qualified under one of the three categories, (4) excludes shareholders from being directors unless they fit within one of the categories, (5) is contradictory in allowing a chairman of the board to be nominated to the board, and (6) automatically causes director removal. Most of Stroud's objections to proposed Article of Incorporation No. 11(c) concerned the allegedly arbitrary qualifications set for directors. Delaware's general corporation law, however, expressly authorizes qualifications for directors: "Directors need not be stockholders unless so required by the Certificate of Incorporation or the bylaws. The Certificate of Incorporation or bylaws may prescribe other qualifications for directors." Contrary to Stroud's assertions, therefore, the certificate of incorporation can provide for reasonable director qualifications. Moreover, the requirement that Category 1 directors be from "line," as opposed to "staff," positions is sufficiently clear. The most elementary of businesses recognizes the distinction between those in "line" positions and those in "staff" positions. Stockholders, under Delaware law, do not have a fundamental right to be directors. Hence, Stroud's assertion that the proposed Article deprived stockholders of becoming directors is further rebuked by the requirements of Category 2, that at least three directors must be stockholders. Stroud also claimed that the restrictions placed on director qualifications are unreasonable and arbitrary. Here, under the procedures proposed, the majority of stockholders must still approve each nominee; and the nominees, as well as the stockholders, are likely to be aware of the qualifications. Stroud also challenged the proposed article by claiming that an automatic termination of directors because of a loss of qualification violates the provisions of Delaware law and is inconsistent with the right of the stockholders to remove directors. The relevant statute provides in part: "Any director or the entire board of directors may be removed, with or without cause, by the holders of a majority of the shares then entitled to vote at an election of directors, except as follows: (1) Unless the Certificate of Incorporation otherwise provides, in the case of a corporation whose board is classified as provided in subsection (d) of this section, shareholders may effect such removal only for cause." Proposed Article of Incorporation No. 11(c) provides an additional method of removal of a director. It expressly states: "Any director who, at any time during his term of office, fails to remain qualified under the Category under which he qualified at the time of his last election shall automatically cease to be a director of the corporation." The certificate of incorporation will provide for automatic termination upon a predetermined occurrence. In short, only the failure to remain qualified will cause a director to be removed. This is akin to a resignation rather than a removal. Moreover, realistically speaking, this is a privately held corporation in which Roger, Gerrish, and Minot Milliken control over 50 percent of the outstanding common and preferred stock; hence, their nominees are going to be elected. In addition, the nominees will likely be aware of their qualifications. The qualifications also will have the result of assuring the presence of outside independent directors—a goal to be commended, not prevented. Accordingly, under the circumstances, the qualifications in issue are not unreasonable. Stroud finally argued that proposed Article of Incorporation 11(c) is internally inconsistent with proposed Article 11(f), which allows the stockholders to remove directors for cause on a 75-percent vote. However, proposed Article 11(f) merely provides an alternative method of termination that is permitted by statute. The stockholders' right to remove directors for cause therefore does not preclude the automatic termination of a director upon his or her failure to remain qualified under one of the three categories set forth in proposed Article of Incorporation No. 11.

Proxy A person appointed and designated to act for another, especially at a public meeting, such as a meeting of the shareholders of a corporation; the document or instrument used to appoint someone to act in a representative capacity as a proxy.

Voting The voting rights exercised by shareholders at meetings allow them indirect control of the corporation and the board of directors. All shareholders of record as of the date of the shareholders' meeting ordinarily appear on the voting list and can vote. Shareholders can either be present at the meeting and vote in person, or they can assign their voting rights to others, who then vote their shares for them by **proxy.** If distant shareholders in public-issue corporations do not want to participate personally in the meeting, they may sign a document called a proxy, giving the proxy holder authority to act as their agent. Figures 40.5 and 40.6 show such a document. Whoever controls large blocs of proxies in a public-issue corporation may in effect thereby dictate the outcome of the election. For this reason, management (and sometimes dissident stockholders) in such corporations may solicit proxy votes in order to consolidate voting power. Not surprisingly, then, bloody proxy wars have occurred at various times in United States corporate history. Because of these high stakes and the accompanying possibilities for abuse, federal law now ensures that proxy solicitations will be carried out fairly. Chapter 44 discusses these provisions. Within the corporation, impartial parties called inspectors, judges, or tellers oversee the election to ensure fairness.

In most corporate matters, a shareholder can cast one vote for each share held. This is called *straight voting*. Unless the voting involves an extraordinary corporate matter (such as dissolution, merger, amendment of articles of incorporation, or sale of substantially all the assets), the decision made by a majority generally controls. Thus, votes of over 50 percent for any ordinary corporate matter usually become binding on the corporation; in extraordinary matters, statutes may require a higher proportion (for example, two-thirds) of votes for the action taken to be legally binding. In straight voting, therefore, unless otherwise indicated, a plurality of votes (or shares) cast determines the outcome of an issue.

To offset shareholders who own large blocs of votes and who may therefore be able to control appreciably the outcomes of elections, most state stat-

FIGURE 40.5   Proxy (Front)

ST. JOSEPH BANCORPORATION, INC.
COMMON STOCK PROXY SOLICITED ON BEHALF OF THE BOARD OF DIRECTORS

The undersigned Shareholder of ST. JOSEPH BANCORPORATION, INC., South Bend, Indiana, does hereby nominate, constitute and appoint Richard A. Rosenthal, Arthur H. McElwee, Jr., or either of them (with full power to act alone), my true and lawful attorney(s) and proxy(ies), with full power of substitution, for me and in my name, place and stead to vote all of the shares of common stock of said Bancorporation, standing in my name on its books, at the annual meeting of its shareholders to be held in the Center for Continuing Education at the University of Notre Dame, on April 19, 1983 at 7:30 o'clock p.m., and at any adjournments thereof, upon all subjects that may properly come before the meeting including the matter described in the proxy statement furnished herewith, subject to any directions indicated below, with all powers the undersigned would possess if personally present.

ELECTION OF DIRECTORS — Frederick K. Baer, Roy L. Beck, Edwin S. Ehlers, Jack E. Ellis, James W. Frick, Gerald Hammes, V. Robert Hepler, Gerald A. Hickey, William P. Johnson, Jr., Gerald A. Kamm, Edward A. Mangone, Daniel A. Manion, Arthur H. McElwee, Jr., Godfrey V. Miholich, Joseph C. Miller, Joseph H. Nash, Robert W. O'Connor, Samuel Raitzin, Richard A. Rosenthal, Frank E. Sullivan and Phillip A. Traub.

☐ VOTE FOR all nominees listed above, except vote withheld from (to withhold authority to vote for any individual nominee, write in the name on the line below):

_____

☐ VOTE WITHHELD from all nominees.

(continued on reverse side)

Courtesy of Trustcorp Bank, South Bend, Indiana (formerly St. Joseph Bank and Trust Company, South Bend, Indiana).

FIGURE 40.6   Proxy (Back)

IF NO DIRECTIONS ARE GIVEN, THE PROXIES WILL VOTE FOR THE ELECTION OF ALL LISTED NOMINEES. THE BOARD OF DIRECTORS RECOMMENDS A VOTE "FOR" ALL NOMINEES LISTED ON THE REVERSE SIDE. THE UNDERSIGNED HEREBY REVOKES ANY PROXY HERETOFORE GIVEN IN RESPECT OF THE SAME SHARES OF STOCK.

Dated: _____ , 1983   _____ (L.S.)

_____ (L.S.)
Please sign your name in the same manner as it appears on your stock certificate. When signing for a corporation or partnership or as agent, attorney or fiduciary, please state your full title as such. If your stock stands in the names of two or more persons, it is necessary that each sign this Proxy.

PLEASE DATE, SIGN AND MAIL THIS PROXY PROMPTLY IN THE ENCLOSED ENVELOPE.

Courtesy of Trustcorp Bank, South Bend, Indiana (formerly St. Joseph Bank and Trust Company, South Bend, Indiana).

utes today either permit or require *cumulative voting*. Cumulative voting applies only to the election of directors and becomes a method for ensuring some minority representation on the board. The following example illustrates the difference between straight and cumulative voting. Assume that at the annual shareholders' meeting, three directors will be elected from a field of six candidates—U, V, W, X, Y, and Z. Under straight voting, shareholder A, who owns 100 shares, can cast 100 votes for each of three directors, say U, V, and W. If, instead, cumulative voting is used, A can cast 300 votes for U or can divide 300 votes among any three candidates in any proportion he or she wishes (for example, 150 for U, 100 for V, and 50 for Y). In this fashion, A's votes "accumulate"—hence, the term *cumulative voting*. The ability of a minority shareholder to have an impact on the election of directors thus becomes more potent under cumulative voting than under straight voting. To dilute the "prominority" effects of cumulative voting, management may stagger the terms of directors, reduce or enlarge the size of the board, or remove directors elected by the minority. To counter such steps, lawmakers in many jurisdictions have passed statutory provisions that protect cumulative voting rights by making such steps illegal or by using statutorily enacted formulas that safeguard the beneficial effects of cumulative voting.

Voting trusts, like proxies and cumulative voting, represent devices used to consolidate votes for control. A shareholder can create a voting trust by transferring to **trustees** the shares he or she owns. Once the shareholder has entered into such an agreement, or trust, the shareholder has no right to vote the shares until the trust terminates. However, the trustees issue a "voting

Trustees   Persons in whom a power is vested under an express or implied agreement in order to exercise the power for the benefit of another.

trust certificate" to the shareholder to indicate that the shareholder retains all rights incidental to share ownership except voting. In contrast to proxies, which are generally revocable, voting trusts are normally irrevocable. State statutes, however, usually limit the duration of voting trusts to a specified time period, such as ten years (with possible extensions).

Pooling agreements are similar to voting trusts. In such agreements, shareholders agree to vote the shares each owns in a specified way. As we will see in Chapter 41, both voting trusts and pooling agreements remain valid and enforceable as long as they do not in effect preempt the directors' managerial functions. This may happen if the shareholders who enter into these arrangements are also directors. For example, it is legal for the shareholders to agree through voting trusts or pooling agreements to vote for director A at the annual meeting's election of directors (even if director A is also one of the shareholders who enters into the arrangement). But if the shareholders' agreements involve their pledging to bring about the dismissal of the current chief executive officer of the corporation, voting trusts or pooling arrangements to this effect normally will be unenforceable because selection of officers is ordinarily a function of the directors.

Shareholders of close corporations probably utilize voting trusts and pooling arrangements more than their counterparts in publicly held corporations. Because modern statutes recognize the unique status of close corporations—that is, that they are more similar to partnerships than are most corporate entities—some states will enforce agreements that bind the shareholders as if they were directors in those situations in which all the shareholders are parties to the agreement. Such statutory developments illustrate the law's ability to change whenever reality dictates such modifications.

The judge in the following case applied some of the principles just discussed in resolving the issue that was in dispute.

Adler v. Svingos
436 N.Y.S.2d 719 (N.Y. App. Div. 1981)

FACTS Adler, Shaw, and Svingos owned an equal number of shares in 891 First Ave. Corp., a restaurant. They had entered into an agreement stating that all corporate operations, including changes in corporate structure, would require the unanimous consent of the parties. When Adler and Shaw tried to sell the business, Svingos objected, relying on the shareholders' agreement. Adler and Shaw brought a court action to declare the agreement void because it violated a statutory provision stating that only articles of incorporation can legally allow greater than normal voting requirements for shareholder action. The plaintiff shareholders thus alleged that the unanimous voting provision of the shareholders' agreement was void.

ISSUE Was a unanimous voting provision that had not been included within the corporate articles but had instead been set out in a shareholders' agreement void and unenforceable?

HOLDING No. The agreement was enforceable because the parties had intended to accomplish the purely ministerial act of amending the certificate of incorporation.

REASONING Because the New York corporate statute allowed greater than normal voting requirements in the certificate of incorporation, the plaintiffs could be ordered to file the appropriate amendments necessary to reform the certificate of incorporation. In addition, since they had given their consent to the agreement, the plaintiffs could not now use the omission of the agreement's provisions from the certificate to justify the sale of the business without Svingos's consent. The fact that the parties had put the record of their undoubted agreement in the wrong place would permit the ordering of the purely ministerial act of amending the articles of incorporation. Accordingly, the shareholders' agreement remained valid and binding on the parties.

Dividends

We discussed earlier the various types of stock (preferred or common) that the corporation can issue. We also learned that preferred stock may be divided further into various classes or series. The right to receive *dividends—a portion of a corporation's profits paid out to its shareholders on a pro rata basis, as voted by the board of directors*—ultimately may hinge on the type of stock owned by the shareholders.

Most shareholders buy shares in "for-profit" public-issue corporations primarily to receive dividends. Such shareholders normally care less about the control functions their shares represent than about the financial aspects of their shares—namely, dividends. Thus far, we have spoken of a *right* to receive dividends, but that constitutes a very loose use of the term. Actually, no "right" to receive dividends without fail exists. The power to declare dividends resides with the board of directors. In the absence of demonstrated bad faith on the directors' part, shareholders cannot compel the directors to declare dividends. The directors alone decide, first, *if* dividends will be distributed. If so, they also determine the timing, type, and amount of the dividend. Of course, shareholders hope to receive from their investment in the corporation the financial profits represented by dividends. *Cash dividends* are the most common type. However, the dividend may also take the form of *property* or *stocks*. For example, assume shareholder Barney of XYZ Corporation has received shares in Erstwhile Corporation, a subsidiary of XYZ, or, alternatively, shares in XYZ; this is called a *stock dividend*.

If cash dividends are involved, the directors must make certain that the dividends have been paid from a *lawful source*. In general, statutes limit the sources of dividends to *current net profits* (those earned in the preceding accounting period) or *earned surplus* (the sum of the net profits retained by the corporation during all previous years of existence). Any declaration of dividends that will impair the corporation's *original capital structure* (the number of shares originally issued times their stated value) is illegal and may subject the directors and shareholders to personal liability. Similarly, payment of dividends during the corporation's insolvency or any payment that will bring about insolvency is illegal.

As noted earlier, preferred stockholders enjoy priority with regard to distribution of dividends. They also receive protection from the rules that limit the source of dividends because directors normally cannot declare dividends if the declaration will thereby jeopardize the liquidation preferences of the preferred shareholders. Once a dividend is lawfully declared, preferred stockholders receive their dividends first. Common stockholders receive dividends only if adequate funds remain after the preferred stockholders have been paid. Sometimes preferred stockholders have *participating* preferred stock. This means they not only receive their original dividend but also share (or "participate") with the common stockholders in any dividends that are paid after the common stockholders have received their original dividends. In other words, participating preferred stockholders may be able to dip twice into the dividend fund. Usually preferred stock is nonparticipating, however.

We should note one last wrinkle in declaring preferred dividends. Preferred dividends may be *cumulative,* which means that the sum (or accumulation) of all preferred dividends that were not paid in a given year must be paid before common shareholders receive any dividends. In contrast, *noncumulative* preferred dividends permit the preferred stockholder to receive only the dividend preferences for the *current accounting period;* and the common stockholders then receive their dividends should any funds remain. Under this type of preference, the preferred shareholders lose all dividends for any years in which the directors have chosen not to declare a dividend.

Figure 40.7 sets out a flowchart that summarizes the various forms dividends may take.

Preemptive Stock Rights

Sometimes it is necessary for a corporation to increase its capital by issuing new shares. Since this is an extraordinary matter involving amendment of the articles of incorporation (the original number of shares and their par value would change with this new capitalization), shareholders must vote on the issuance of these new shares. A shareholder's interest in this matter extends beyond voting rights. A simple example will illustrate this point. Assume Bonnie owns 10 shares of Samp Corporation. Samp's original capitalization involved 100 shares sold at $100 each ($10,000 stated capital). At that time, Bonnie owned 10 percent of Samp Corporation (10 shares/100 total shares). If Samp issues another 100 shares as a result of the amending of the articles, Bonnie then will own 5 percent of the corporation (10 shares/200 total shares). As a result of this new capitalization, her voting power has decreased proportionately; and so has her right to receive a higher amount of dividends and a higher proportion of corporate assets in the event of liquidation. Early on, common law courts, realizing the inherent unfairness of this sequence of events, began to protect the Bonnies of the corporate world by a doctrine called *preemptive rights*. These courts promoted the notion that the right of first refusal inheres in stock ownership; hence, before the corporation can sell to anyone else, it must offer to sell to Bonnie the number of shares that will restore her total share of ownership to the proportion she held before this

FIGURE 40.7 Dividends: A Flowchart

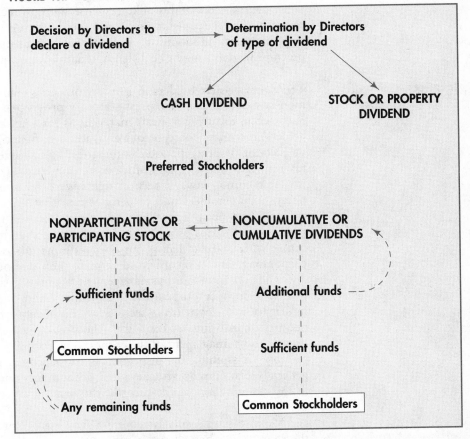

new issuance. Bonnie in effect can "preempt" the rights of other would-be purchasers of the stock because she can purchase before they get a chance to do so. Nevertheless, once the corporation has notified Bonnie of her preemptive rights, she has a limited time to exercise them. If she does not take advantage of the offer, she waives her rights of preemption.

Preemptive rights normally apply only to shares issued for cash and will not apply to shares issued in exchange for property (such as a commercial building) or services (such as shares issued to lure a chief executive officer to Samp), or to shares issued as share dividends, or to *treasury stock* (stock originally issued but subsequently reacquired by the corporation). In this last situation, there is no new issue and hence no reduction in Bonnie's proportionate interest in Samp Corporation. In the other situations in which Samp issues shares for consideration other than money, preemptive rights may cripple the corporation's financing efforts and obstruct the corporation's legitimate, profit-maximizing activities, such as acquiring property and recruiting top-flight executives. Because of the possible frustration of these worthwhile aims, courts and statutes alike dispense with protecting Bonnie's preemptive rights in these circumstances despite the dilution of her proportional ownership interests. In addition, judicial and statutory treatment of Bonnie's preemptive rights might be different if Samp were a publicly held corporation.

Inspection of Corporate Records

The rights of shareholders to inspect corporate records arise from both common law doctrines and express statutory provisions. In general, shareholders have access to such corporate materials as stockholder lists; minutes of shareholders' meetings; board or officers' meetings; financial records, such as books of account or other periodic summaries; and business documents, including tax returns, contracts, and office correspondence or memoranda.

At common law, inspection rights were qualified (rather than absolute) because shareholders had to demonstrate that the reason for inspection involved a "proper purpose"; that is, the motivation for the inspection related to his or her status as a shareholder. Seeking shareholder lists for communicating with shareholders about corporate matters or attempting to examine corporate financial records to determine the value of shares, the propriety of dividends, or possible mismanagement ordinarily signals requests that will qualify as proper purposes. On the other hand, a shareholder's asking for information to learn trade secrets for the benefit of the corporation's competitors or to bring "strike suits" (those without any real merit) in order to impede the management of the corporation normally will constitute improper purposes. Assuming the inspection is for a proper purpose, the shareholder generally can employ attorneys and accountants and other personnel to aid in the examination of the records, the making of copies or summaries, and the like.

Most statutes similarly require a showing of "proper purpose," but once the shareholder has alleged a proper purpose, they may shift the burden of proof to the corporation to show an "improper" purpose on the shareholder's part. Sometimes statutes make the burden of proof, or the party who has the burden, dependent on the type of record being requested. Statutes may also restrict inspection rights only to certain shareholders (for example, those who have held their shares for at least six months or who own at least 5 percent of the outstanding shares). However, these statutory restrictions do not eliminate the shareholder's common law inspection rights. But, as mentioned, the shareholder, not the corporation, will have the burden of proving proper purpose under these common law doctrines. Federal securities law and state statutes that mandate annual disclosure of profits and losses, officer compensation, and the like have made inspection rights somewhat less important: The information made available to the shareholder under these statutes encompasses the type of information that shareholders in the past could learn about only by exercising their rights of inspection.

The case that follows illustrates some of these concepts involving the right of inspection. As you read it, consider as well whether you think the agreement between the Sadlers and AT&T was unethical.

Sadler v. *NCR Corporation*
928 F.2d 48 (2d Cir. 1991)

FACTS NCR Corporation (NCR), a large computer company, maintains at least eight offices in New York and conducts substantial business there. NCR has 75,000 shareholders. AT&T, the well-known telecommunications company, is a New York corporation whose principal executive officers reside in New York City. AT&T became a beneficial owner of 100 shares of NCR stock on 21 November 1990. The Sadlers are New York residents who own more than 6000 shares of NCR stock and were record holders of NCR stock for more than six months prior to this lawsuit. On 6 December 1990, AT&T began a tender offer for the shares of NCR, offering to purchase all the common stock of NCR for $90 per share. In compliance with Rule 14d-5 of the Securities and Exchange Commission, NCR mailed the offer to purchase to all NCR stockholders. The NCR board rejected the tender offer and declined to redeem a **"poison pill"** shareholders' rights plan, which presented and continues to present an obstacle to a hostile tender offer. AT&T responded to this opposition by soliciting NCR shareholders to convene a special meeting of stockholders to replace a majority of the NCR directors as a means of removing this barrier to the tender offer. Soon after soliciting calls for a special meeting, AT&T submitted to NCR requests for a special meeting from holders of more than half of NCR's stock. NCR subsequently scheduled a special meeting for 28 March 1991, the date selected for its annual meeting. Beginning in early January, 1991, AT&T and the Sadlers, acting at AT&T's request, sought from NCR a stockholder list and related materials to facilitate communication with owners of NCR shares because it would need 80 percent of all outstanding shares in order to replace the board at the special meeting. In addition to the list of record owners, AT&T sought a magnetic computer tape of the list and daily transfer sheets showing changes in shareholders from the date of demand to the date of the annual meeting. AT&T also sought two other lists, a "CEDE list" and a "NOBO list." A CEDE list identifies the brokerage firms and other record owners who have bought shares in a street name for their customers and who have placed those shares in the custody of depository firms such as Depository Trust Co.; these shares are reflected in the corporation's records only under the names of the nominees used by such depository firms. A NOBO list (nonobjecting beneficial owners) contains the names of those owning beneficial interests in the shares of a corporation who have given consent to the disclosure of their identities. The Securities and Exchange Commission requires brokers and other record holders of stock in a street name to compile a NOBO list at a corporation's request. Upon NCR's refusal to produce the requested materials, the Sadlers and AT&T sued, relying on Section 1315 of the New York Business Corporation Law. NCR argued that the Sadlers were not qualified under Section 1315 to obtain NCR's shareholder list and that the NOBO list was not producible under Section 1315 because it was not then in existence and would require compilation.

Poison pill Any strategy adopted by the directors of a target firm in order to decrease their firm's attractiveness to an acquiring firm during an attempted hostile takeover.

ISSUES Were the Sadlers qualified to inspect NCR's shareholder list? Could a court require NCR to compile a NOBO list?

HOLDINGS Yes to both questions. Because the Sadlers could turn over the shareholder list (once received) to others involved in the proxy contest, their agreement with AT&T, though it had given considerable control to AT&T in exchange for limiting the Sadlers' potential financial exposure, was proper, particularly since nothing in the agreement created the risk of using the statute for an improper purpose or in bad faith.

REASONING Whether New York law entitles the Sadlers to require NCR to assemble a NOBO list presented a more substantial question. The parties agreed that section 1315 applies to NOBO lists in a corporation's possession; but at the time of the demand, NCR did not have a NOBO list in its possession. However, a corporation can obtain a NOBO list, normally within ten days, by requesting compilation of the list by firms that offer data processing services for this task. NCR interpreted Section 1315 as being limited to production of lists in existence, as distinguished from those readily capable of being compiled. NCR contended that no court has ever required a corporation to compile a NOBO list and relied on a New York decision for the proposition that stockholders are not entitled to have such lists compiled. AT&T construed these decisions more narrowly, found them distinguishable, and argued that New York would require compilation of a NOBO list in this case, owing to the NCR requirement that directors may be replaced at a special meeting only on the affirmative vote of 80 percent of the stockholders. The text of Section 1315 does not resolve the dispute, although a narrow reading of its terms might favor NCR. The statute could be read to be limited to production or examination of lists already in existence and could also be limited to lists reflecting the names and addresses of owners of record. But New York courts have made clear that they favor the liberal construction of this statute in order to facilitate communication among shareholders on issues respecting corporate affairs. A narrow reading of Section 1315 would therefore not accord with New York law. As to both sets of information (the CEDE list and the NOBO list), the underlying data exist in discrete records readily available to be compiled into an aggregate list. Nor are the functions of the lists significantly dissimilar. Both facilitate direct communication with stockholders, at least, in the case of a NOBO list, with those beneficial owners who have indicated no objection to disclosure of their names and addresses. Hence, New York law would apply Section 1315 to permit a qualifying shareholder to require the compilation and production of such a list. Even if the statute might not require compilation of NOBO lists routinely, compilation was properly ordered in this case. The effect of NCR's 80-percent rule is to count as a "no" vote on the replacement of directors any share uncast at the special meeting. Thus, the shares of nonvoting beneficial owners who might oppose management if solicited by management opponents armed with a NOBO list are counted in favor of management. Denying such opponents an opportunity to contact the NOBOs is inconsistent with the statute's objective of seeking, to the extent possible, to place shareholders on an equal footing with management in obtaining access to shareholders. In effect, NCR already has the votes of those NOBOs who, for lack of solicitation, decline to vote. As to them, NCR has all the access it needs. Hence, the Sadlers qualify under Section 1315 of the New York corporate statute as persons entitled to obtain a "record" of NCR's shareholders. The Sadlers are residents of New York and have owned NCR stock for six months prior to their demand. The corporation whose stockholder list they seek does business in New York. Moreover, the fact that the Sadlers had entered into an agreement with AT&T (which was unqualified under Section 1315, since it had not held its shares for six months) whereby the Sadlers would demand that NCR provide the shareholder list to AT&T in exchange for the Sadlers' reimbursement and indemnification from AT&T would not disqualify the Sadlers from invoking Section 1315. Though that arrangement gave AT&T considerable control over the demand, particularly the right reasonably to refuse settlement of the demand or any litigation arising from it, the Sadlers had agreed to that control in exchange for AT&T's assurance that they would incur no financial exposure. Since New York wishes to accord its residents the rights specified in Section 1315, it is not likely to impose any restrictions on their exercise of that right, other than those specified in the statute, unless necessary to prevent the statute from being used in bad faith. Nothing in the arrangement between the Sadlers and AT&T creates a risk of using the statute for an improper purpose or in bad faith. The demanding stockholder is entitled to turn the list over to others involved in a proxy contest, and he or she may make reasonable arrangements to avoid his or her own financial exposure.

The next case shows an interesting twist to the issue of shareholder inspection rights. (The attorney-client privilege is discussed in Chapter 6.)

In re LTV Securities Litigation
89 F.R.D. 595 (N.D. Tex. 1981)

FACTS

Class action   A lawsuit filed by some members of a group on behalf of all the members of the same group.

A group of buyers and sellers of various securities of LTV and some of LTV's shareholders brought a **class action** alleging a conspiracy by LTV to defraud shareholders by overvaluing the inventories of Jones & Laughlin Steel Co., one of LTV's subsidiaries, through a series of accounting manipulations. LTV refused to disclose certain information, asserting the attorney-client privilege.

ISSUE   Would the attorney-client privilege bar a shareholder's right to discover the minutes of board of directors and audit committee meetings, as well as other formal LTV records?

HOLDING   Yes. A valid attorney-client privilege would take precedence over a shareholder's statutory inspection rights.

REASONING   The right of a shareholder to inspect a corporation's "stock ledger" or "list of stockholders" is nearly absolute. But when a shareholder asks to inspect other books and records, even assuming a proper purpose for such requests, the right to inspect must be balanced against the interests of the corporation in nondisclosure. If directors can confer in confidence with counsel and be protected under the attorney-client privilege, such a privilege should also cover the recording of those confidences, such as minutes of board meetings. In the absence of a showing of a special need for the minutes or a lack of other means to obtain the underlying information sought, inspection rights under these circumstances should be denied.

Transfer of Shares

As discussed earlier, ownership of share (stock) certificates signifies ownership of a portion of the corporate entity. Thus, these shares are the shareholder's property. Like other owners of property who have the right to transfer the property (by gift or sale) to others, shareholders generally can transfer their shares to someone else. Figure 40.8 illustrates that a transfer of shares generally occurs through endorsement and delivery of the stock certificate in conjunction with a surrender of the certificate for subsequent reissue to the new owner by the corporation's secretary or, in a large corporation, by its transfer agent. Stock exchange rules regulate the conduct of transfer agents, who are professionals who help the corporate secretary with the myriad of details attendant on large-scale transfers (that is, the buying and selling) of stocks. Because of the administrative headaches associated with transfers of stock in these situations, including the cumbersomeness of actual physical transfers of stock certificates, present-day techniques (such as a brokerage firm's holding title to stock through bookkeeping entries rather than actual transfers of certificates) will probably lead ultimately to the abolition of stock certificates and their replacement by computer printouts.

Despite these new developments, the right to transfer stock in general remains otherwise unfettered. Restrictions placed on the stock, however, may limit this right of transferability.

It is not hard to understand why restrictions on the transferability of stock may be advisable. Such restrictions commonly occur in close corporations. We have already discussed the fact that close corporations are like partnerships in that the controlling shareholders actively take part in the day-to-day management of the corporation. Consequently, shareholders in close corporations often attempt to preserve their control over the affairs of the corporation through voting trusts and pooling arrangements. Such attempts at consolidation of power will be meaningless without restrictions on the stock's transferability. To illustrate, in the absence of such restrictions, stockholder A in Family Corporation can transfer his or her shares to another person and

FIGURE 40.8   Stock Certificate Record of Transfer

PASTE CANCELLED CERTIFICATE IN THIS SPACE

Certificate No._____ For _____ Shares

Dated _____ 19__

Issued to _____

Transferred from	IF NOT AN ORIGINAL ISSUE SHOW DETAILS OF TRANSFER BELOW			
	Original Certificate No.	Date	No. of Origl. Shares	No. of Shrs Transf'd.

New Certificate Issued to	IF THIS CERTIFICATE IS SURRENDERED FOR TRANSFER SHOW DETAILS	
	No. of New Certificate	No. of Shares Transferred

Received this Certificate _____ 19__

Surrendered this Certificate _____ 19__

Courtesy of Charles Roemer, Roemer and Mintz, Attorneys-at-Law, South Bend, Indiana.

thereby force the original three stockholders of Family Corporation to include this previously unknown (and presumably unwanted) shareholder in corporate decisions about corporate affairs. Restrictions on stock transfers within close corporations help to avoid such unhappy results. Such restrictions result from shareholder agreements and are legal if the restrictions are reasonable.

Courts try to balance the legitimate interests of the shareholders in limiting the corporation to a few congenial shareholders and the right of a shareholder to transfer his or her property (called the "right of alienation"), a right considered in our legal system as inherent in the ownership of property. A right of "first refusal"—that is, the shareholder who wishes to sell must first offer his or her shares to the corporation or to the other shareholders—is enforceable as a valid restriction on transfer because it is a reasonable restraint on **alienation**. In contrast, a restriction that states that "these shares are nontransferable" will probably be unreasonable and therefore unenforceable.

Alienation The transfer of ownership to another.

It follows that even a reasonable restriction (such as "future sale or disposition of these shares shall take place in accordance with the shareholder agreement that controls them; and sale of them cannot take place until the holder of them offers them to the corporation or to each other shareholder, on the same terms") must appear conspicuously on the stock certificate if the restriction is to be valid. Such conspicuous notice is meant to protect any subsequent purchaser of the shares by informing him or her of the restricted nature of the stock. If this notice of restriction on transfer is missing, the purchaser will not have to abide by the restriction unless he or she otherwise has notice of the restriction. However, if the restriction is reasonable and appears on the face of the stock certificate, the corporation can refuse to transfer the shares to the purchaser. The purchaser's remedy will involve forcing shareholder A to give back the money paid to A for the shares.

If the transfer satisfies all legal requirements, including the applicable provisions of Article 8 of the UCC and state securities laws, the purchaser (transferee) pays the price asked; and shareholder A (transferor) endorses and delivers the stock to the purchaser. Then the corporation, when notified, must register the transfer and change corporate records to denote the new ownership in order to guarantee to the new owner the rights incidental to stock ownership in Family Corporation.

Liquidation

The process of *liquidation* consists of the *winding up of the affairs of a business in order to go out of business; that is, the marshaling of assets and the subsequent reduction of those assets to cash in order to pay the claims of creditors*. During this "winding up," the corporation pays all debts and creditors from the corporate assets and then distributes any remaining assets to the shareholders. The process of dissolution, which denotes the end of the corporation's legal existence, may immediately precede or follow liquidation. Though the terms *dissolution* and *liquidation* are often used together, they are not synonymous. We will discuss dissolution here and in Chapter 42.

Throughout the liquidation period, the corporation has all the rights and powers reasonably necessary to effect liquidation. Moreover, during this period, the corporation can sue and be sued. Under most statutes, the board of directors continues the management of the corporation unless a court has ordered the dissolution and liquidation. In the latter case, the court may appoint a special person (called a **receiver**) to oversee the liquidation. If the directors unlawfully continue the business of the corporation after dissolution and beyond the time reasonably necessary to wind up the corporation's affairs, they may become personally liable for the corporation's debts. Caution among the directors (and controlling shareholders) is therefore in order during the liquidation process.

Receiver An unbiased person appointed by a court to receive, preserve, and manage the funds and property of a party.

State statutes normally protect creditors during liquidation by requiring the corporation to notify creditors of dissolution and liquidation so that these creditors can file their claims against the corporation during this time period. A creditor who receives notice but does not file a claim may lose the right to sue later on this claim. Retention of this right, on the other hand, allows the creditor to recoup from shareholders any distributions of corporate assets that have occurred before payment of creditors' claims. To protect creditors, the law characterizes the illegal distributions as held "in trust" for the benefit of the creditors because the creditors have rights superior to those of the stockholders in these instances. The directors also may incur liability for distributions illegally declared up to the amount of claims that remain unpaid.

After the corporation has satisfied its debts to its creditors, the shareholders ordinarily receive the proportion of the remaining net assets represented by their respective share ownership. However, as discussed earlier, the articles of incorporation may set out one or more classes of shares as meriting liquidation preferences over another class or classes of shares. For instance, preferred stockholders usually receive their shares of the net assets before holders of common stock do. (Note, however, that preferred shareholders *never* receive payment before creditors do.) But if the preferred shareholders do not enjoy liquidation preferences, they will participate with the common shareholders on a share-for-share basis. Sometimes the articles give to the preferred shareholders both liquidation preferences and participation rights with the common shareholders. Because cash is the usual method for satisfying liquidation preferences, it may be necessary for the corporation to sell its assets to raise the amount required to take care of these preferences. Under most statutes, the corporation can distribute property instead of cash in satisfying liquidation preferences; but it will be illegal to favor some shareholders through grants of property (as when a corporation gives controlling shareholders valuable patents or trademarks) while doling out cash to minority shareholders.

In the following case, the controlling shareholders paid a steep price—personal liability—for failing to dissolve the corporation and for continuing the corporation's existence after the termination of the corporation's right to do business. Note that the shareholders had engaged in more activities than were appropriate for liquidation and/or dissolution.

Nabakowski v. 5440 Corporation
503 N.E.2d 218 (Ohio App. 1986)

FACTS   In 1981, G. John Harris and Marlene Harris (the Harrises) incorporated the 5400 Corporation (the Corporation) for the purpose of managing a building located at 4900 Euclid Avenue. Eventually, this closely held corporation became a lottery sales agent for the Ohio lottery. As a result, a ticket issuing machine (TIM) was placed on the corporate premises so that the corporation could operate a daily game terminal there. G. John Harris hired his son, Mark, to run the daily lottery operations, including the TIM. On 4 November 1983, the state canceled the corporation's charter owing to the nonpayment of its franchise taxes. However, the corporation continued its daily operations. Indeed, on 3 September 1984, Mark Harris initiated a scheme whereby the TIM would spew tickets continuously and Mark would electronically place these bets in the group of tickets eligible to win the lottery. A computer repairman discovered this deception on 4 September 1984, while responding to a service call that had arisen from a blown fuse. He notified the Lottery Commission (the Commission), which quickly deactivated the TIM and filed charges against Mark for his theft of $200,000 in tickets. Nabakowski, the director of the Lottery Commission, also sued the Corporation and the Harrises for defrauding the Commission; and a jury found G. John Harris and Marlene Harris personally liable for $187,000.

ISSUE

Could the controlling shareholders and officers of a corporation that had continued to conduct business after the cancellation of the corporate charter be found personally liable for corporate obligations?

HOLDING

Yes. After the termination of the corporation's charter, the authority of the corporation to do business had ceased, and the principals were personally liable for the corporate obligations incurred.

REASONING

According to Ohio law, after the cancellation of a corporation's articles of incorporation, the corporation should cease to do business and should do only such acts as are required to wind up its business. Moreover, after such a cancellation of the corporate charter, the officers who carry on new business do so as individuals, lose the protection of the Ohio Corporation Act, and thereby accept personal liability for the obligations they incur. In this instance, the Harrises, in their capacity as shareholders and officers of a corporation whose charter had been canceled, had hired Mark Harris to be in charge of the lottery terminal. They also had renewed their contract with the Lottery Commission knowing that their corporation was not in good standing with the state. Consequently, they had become liable for any obligations arising pursuant to their contract with the Lottery Commission. The Harrises could not claim the potential benefits that might flow to the corporation from Mark Harris's scheme to defraud the Lottery Commission while simultaneously disowning the consequences of the corporation's illegal operations. The Harrises as principals, with either passive or active knowledge of the scheme to defraud, therefore had become liable personally for their employee Mark's actions when they had elected to continue doing business with the Commission after their charter had been canceled.

LIABILITIES

As we learned in Chapter 39, one of the most significant advantages of the corporation as a type of business association is the limited liability afforded to shareholders. In other words, the shareholders risk only their investment. Except for situations in which courts can disregard the corporate entity, shareholders normally do not become personally liable for corporate debts. In this section, we will look at some other circumstances that may cause a shareholder to be personally liable for obligations of the corporation.

Watered Stock

At the time of the formation of the corporation, the articles of incorporation spell out the *capital structure* of the corporation. In brief, the money to operate the corporation initially results from the issuance of securities to investors. The authorization for such securities ordinarily occurs early in the process of the corporation's formation, probably by board action at the organizational meeting. Most authorities classify securities into two main types: *debt securities* and *equity securities*. Bonds are examples of debt securities. Those investors who hold bond securities have lent money to the corporation and thus are creditors of the sort who will have claims on the corporate assets superior to the claims of shareholders in the event of liquidation. Bond holders normally do not enjoy ownership rights in the corporation but instead stand in a creditor-debtor relationship with the corporation. In contrast, equity securities create a shareholder relationship. The investor pays for the securities in exchange for shares (or stock) issued in the investor's name. As discussed previously, ownership of these shares confers on the equity holder (shareholder) certain ownership rights in the corporation. The consideration the corporation receives for these shares constitutes the stated capital of the corporation. The board of directors establishes a fixed value of each share of such capital stock (for example, $10 per share). This is called *par value* stock. The corporation may also issue *no–par value* stock, which has no fixed value but may be sold at whatever price the directors deem reasonable (called "stated value"). No–par value shares permit a corporation to issue stock in return for corporate assets that currently are worth little but have the possibility of high, though speculative, returns (such as corporate assets in the form of high-technology developments).

If no statutory provisions to the contrary exist, the corporation may issue shares in exchange for any lawful consideration, including cash received, property received, or services actually rendered. Just as the board of directors generally sets the price of the shares, it also normally fixes the value of the property received or services rendered. As long as the board makes these decisions in good faith and in the absence of fraud, courts will not use these decisions to impose legal liability on the directors.

However, the shareholder who receives *shares of a corporation that are issued as fully paid when in fact the full par or stated value has not been paid by the purchaser* owns *watered stock*. The shareholder is personally liable for the deficiency, that is, "the water." For example, if a shareholder pays $8 per share and the par value or stated value is $10 per share, the shareholder is liable to the corporation for $2 per share. Watered stock problems normally arise in situations in which services have been rendered in exchange for stock. If the corporation issues $4000 worth of its shares in exchange for A's making a high-technology machine later found to be worth $2000, A will be liable for $2000 worth of watered stock. Usually A's liability is to the corporation, but some states will allow corporate creditors to impose liability on A when the corporation is insolvent and unable to meet its obligations as they come due. In some jurisdictions, such creditors can hold shareholders liable for the amounts by which their shares are watered. However, B, a later purchaser from A, normally will not be liable for watered stock because the rule regarding watered stock applies only to initial corporate issuances and purchases of stock, rather than to later transfers of the stock.

The use of no–par value stock and the impact of federal and state securities regulation have greatly reduced the incidence of suits alleging liability for watered stock. Still, shareholders should be aware of this legal doctrine.

Stock Subscriptions

Stock subscriptions are "agreements" by investors ("subscribers") to purchase shares in a corporation. The law views a subscription as an offer, and most state statutes make subscriptions irrevocable for a certain period unless the subscription itself provides otherwise. A subscriber may enter into such "agreements" either before or after the corporation's formation. If the stock subscription occurs before the corporation's formation (usually as a result of promoters' activities), some states treat the subscription as an offer that is automatically accepted by the corporation on its formation. Other states require formal acceptance of the subscription/offer before a valid contract between the subscriber and the corporation arises.

Because an accepted stock subscription constitutes a contract, various types of liabilities arise upon the breach of the subscription contract. Thus, the corporation can sue the subscriber for the subscription price if the subscriber refuses to pay the agreed price. In some cases, creditors of a corporation that has become insolvent may force the subscriber to pay the amount owed on the subscription. (By the same token, the subscriber can sue the corporation if the corporation refuses to issue the shares that are the object of the subscription.)

As in the case of watered stock, securities laws have reduced the incidence of shareholder liability for stock subscriptions.

Illegal Dividends

We noted earlier that cash dividends must be paid from a lawful source. Any declaration of dividends that will impair the original capital structure of the corporation is illegal and may subject both the directors and the shareholders to personal liability. Shareholders who receive an illegal dividend are absolutely liable for its return if the corporation is insolvent when the dividend is paid. In such cases, the corporation's creditors can sue the shareholders directly for the amount of the illegal dividend. If the corporation is instead solvent when the illegal distribution takes place and remains solvent even after it, only shareholders who *knew* the dividend was illegal (for example, because it is from an improper source) must repay the dividends to the corporation. Innocent shareholders can retain the dividends. Directors who have been held liable for distributing illegal dividends can force shareholders who knew of the illegal dividends to pay the amounts received back to the directors. The shareholders and directors thus share liability in such circumstances.

Dissolution

Dissolution signals the legal termination of the corporation's existence. It may occur voluntarily (by actions of the incorporators or shareholders) or involuntarily (by court actions initiated by the state or a shareholder). It is important to note that majority (or controlling) shareholders may incur liability if the purpose of the dissolution is to "freeze out" minority stockholders and to strip them of rights or profits they would otherwise enjoy. The basis of this liability is that controlling shareholders owe fiduciary duties to minority shareholders. Generally speaking, controlling shareholders must exert control for the benefit of *all* shareholders, not just for themselves. Dissolutions that prejudice minority shareholders' interests while greatly enhancing majority shareholders' interests may subject the latter to personal liability if minority shareholders sue.

In the following case, the court imposed liability for claims that had arisen after the dissolution of the two corporations involved, despite the possible prejudice to the former shareholders' interests.

Peñasquitos v. Superior Court (Barbee)
812 P.2d 154 (Cal. 1991)

FACTS   Several owners of single-family homes in San Diego County brought suit on a variety of legal theories against Peñasquitos, Inc. (Peñasquitos) and Crow Pacific Development Corporation (Crow Pacific) to recover damages for construction defects. Crow Pacific had built the homes on lots graded and prepared by Peñasquitos; the homes were all located within a subdivision commonly known as "Peñasquitos Bluffs, Unit No. 4." Unfortunately, both corporations had dissolved before the homeowners' discovery of the construction defects. When these homeowners brought suit for construction defects against these corporations, the corporations argued that they could not be sued because both had dissolved.

ISSUE   Could the parties sue the dissolved corporations on claims that had arisen after the dissolutions?

HOLDING   Yes. California's statutory scheme reveals a legislative intent to permit parties to bring suit against dissolved corporations for damages that occur or are discovered after dissolution.

REASONING   The common law treated the dissolution of a corporation like the death of a natural person: Once it had dissolved, a corporation ceased to exist and could not sue or be sued; and any actions pending against it abated. However, California abandoned the common law rule governing the effect of a corporation's dissolution by the enactment of former Civil Code Section 399 in 1929. This statutory scheme for the postdissolution survival of corporations has endured with relatively few changes. Section 1905, subdivision (b) now provides that when the certificate of dissolution is filed, "the corporate existence shall cease, *except for the purpose of further winding up if needed*" (italics added). Section 2010, subdivision (a) further explains the purposes for which the corporate existence continues after dissolution: "A corporation which is dissolved nevertheless continues to exist for the purpose of winding up its affairs, prosecuting and *defending actions* by or *against it* and enabling it to collect and *discharge obligations,* dispose of and convey its property and collect and divide its assets, but not for the purpose of continuing business except so far as necessary for the winding up thereof" (italics added). Section 2010 permits parties to sue dissolved corporations. Therefore, a court must determine whether these postdissolution actions are limited to those brought on predissolution claims, that is, claims that arose before the corporation filed its notice of dissolution. On its face, Section 2010 draws no distinction between pre- and postdissolution claims. This is particularly significant in view of the language of Section 2011, subdivision (9a), which limits postdissolution actions against the dissolved corporation's shareholders to those on causes of action "arising prior to [the corporation's] dissolution." The legislature's use of this restrictive language in the provision governing suits against shareholders, while omitting it from the provision governing suits against the dissolved corporations themselves, strongly implies that the legislature did not intend to restrict suits against dissolved corporations to those on predissolution claims. As California precedents hold, "Where a statute, with reference to one subject contains a given provision, the omission of such provision from a similar statute concerning a related subject . . . is significant to show that a different intention existed." Courts in other jurisdictions have construed statutes with language similar to Section 2010 to permit actions on postdissolution claims. Moreover, the drafters of the 1984 Revised Model Business Corporation Act (the Act) have abandoned the distinction drawn in earlier versions between pre- and postdissolution causes of action. Under Section 14.07, subdivision (c) of the Act, a dissolved corporation may be sued on any cause of action—whether arising before or after dissolution—so long as the plaintiff files the action within five years after the date of publication of the notice of dissolution. The comment to this provision explains that although a five year cut-off is itself arbitrary, presumably the great bulk of postdissolution claims will arise during this period. This provision provides a reasonable compromise between the competing considerations of assuring the availability of a remedy to injured plaintiffs and a period of repose after which dissolved corporations may distribute remaining assets free of all claims and shareholders may receive them secure in the knowledge that they may not be reclaimed. Hence, Section 2010 permits the assertion of postdissolution claims against dissolved corporations. California state statutes permit the corporate existence to continue indefinitely for the purpose of such actions. Hence, a review of the California statutory scheme leads to the conclusion that, by the terms of the Corporation Code, the legislature has decided not to permit a dissolved corporation to make its final exit as long as obligations resulting from its predissolution activities remain undischarged. Although the law generally precludes an injured party whose claim arises after dissolution from pursuing a dissolved corporation's assets in the hands of its former shareholders, there is no legal barrier to a suit against a dissolved corporation itself for injury or damage that is caused by the corporation's predissolution activities but occurs or is discovered after the dissolution.

SUMMARY

The shareholders of a corporation, although the ultimate owners of the corporation, exert only indirect control over the day-to-day operation and overall policies of the firm. Yet ownership of shares carries with it certain rights. The types of rights shareholders enjoy may vary depending on the type of stock involved. Ownership of common stock permits the shareholder to receive dividends without priority over other shares and to vote on corporate issues. In contrast, ownership of preferred stock confers priority as to dividends, voting, or liquidation rights. In addition, preferred stock may have participation rights, conversion rights, and/or redemption rights.

Shareholders' meetings provide the vehicle by which both common and preferred stockholders exercise their most significant control over the corporation. Corporate bylaws usually require an annual meeting (primarily for election of directors) and may authorize special meetings in appropriate circumstances. Such meetings ordinarily cannot occur in the absence of prior notice or a quorum. One of the shareholders' foremost powers involves the election and removal of directors. Shareholders have inherent power to remove a director for cause and may have power to remove a director without cause. Shareholders may also amend or repeal bylaws.

All shareholders of record as of the date of the shareholders' meeting customarily appear on the voting list and can vote. Shareholders can cast their votes either in person or by proxy. Federal securities laws now cover proxy solicitations. For most corporate matters, straight voting is used. However, for the election of directors, many state statutes either permit or require cumulative voting. Cumulative voting protects the interests of minority shareholders but may be countered by such strategies as staggered terms for directors. Other devices used to consolidate control of corporate affairs through voting include voting trusts and pooling arrangements. These devices are especially useful in close corporations.

Dividends represent financial returns on shareholders' investments. Yet shareholders cannot compel directors to declare dividends; the directors alone have this power. The board also must make certain that dividends, if declared, have been paid from a lawful source. Dividends may be cumulative or noncumulative.

When a corporation increases its capital by issuing new shares, shareholder approval is necessary. To protect a shareholder's proportionate interest in the corporation when recapitalization occurs, the doctrine of preemptive rights is ordinarily applicable.

Shareholders' rights to inspect corporate records arise from both common law doctrines and express statutory provisions. Ordinarily, if a shareholder can demonstrate a "proper purpose" for requesting access to the records, the shareholder will be able to examine certain corporate documents.

Shares, because they are property, generally can be transferred by the shareholder. But in certain circumstances, restrictions on the transferability of shares seem warranted.

The process of liquidation (or "winding up") occurs when the corporation pays all debts and creditors from the corporate assets and then distributes any remaining assets to the shareholders. Directors may incur personal liability if they continue the business of the corporation beyond the time reasonably necessary to wind up the corporation's affairs. Creditors who have preserved their claims against the corporation can recoup from shareholders any distributions of assets that occurred prior to payment of creditors. Directors may also incur liability for the remaining unpaid claims. After creditors' claims have been satisfied, the shareholders normally receive the proportion of the remaining net assets represented by their respective share ownership, subject to any liquidation preferences that the corporation has authorized.

Shareholders may be liable to the corporation or creditors for "watered stock," and a subscriber may be liable to the corporation or to creditors if the subscriber breaches a stock subscription. Declaration and distribution of illegal dividends may subject both directors and shareholders to personal liability. Controlling shareholders may incur liability if the purpose of the corporation's dissolution is to "freeze out" minority stockholders and to strip these stockholders of rights or profits they would otherwise enjoy.

DISCUSSION QUESTIONS

1. Explain the boundaries of the rights conferred by ownership of shares. Then name and define the various types of stocks.

2. What is a *quorum,* and how does this term relate to shareholder meetings?

3. Describe the power of shareholders to remove and elect directors.

4. Explain what the following have to do with shareholders' meetings: (a) proxies, (b) straight voting, (c) cumulative voting, (d) voting trusts, and (e) pooling agreements.

5. Describe the process by which dividends reach stockholders.

6. What are "preemptive rights"?

7. Explain how a shareholder secures the right to inspect corporate documents.

8. In what situations may transfers of shares be restricted?

9. Explain what *liquidation* of the corporation means.

10. How can liability arise for "watered stock," stock subscriptions, illegal dividends, and dissolution?

CASE PROBLEMS

1. Harold L. Jones incorporated and operated Confection Products Corporation (CPC) as a candy manufacturing business. Jones also incorporated and operated Tom Sawyer Enterprises, Ltd. (TSE) as a sales arm of CPC. Jones owned 100 percent of TSE. During 1974, Mercantile Trust Company National Association (Mercantile) made several loans totaling $128,000 to CPC and secured these loans by liens on the inventory and accounts receivable of CPC and TSE. Jones signed a personal guarantee on these loans in his corporate capacity as owner of 78 percent of the stock of CPC and not individually. Also during 1974, CPC and TSE's candy operations encountered serious financial difficulties, and Jones attempted to get a long-term loan guaranteed by the Small Business Administration (SBA). Jones sent to Mercantile a completed SBA loan application together with a chattel mortgage on all of the candy manufacturing equipment of TSE. When Mercantile could not obtain an SBA loan for the corporations, Janice Rennie, its loan officer, recorded the chattel mortgage as additional collateral for the previous Mercantile loans to CPC. Since Mercantile had failed to obtain a long-term SBA loan for CPC and TSE, Jones went to other banks and lending institutions in an attempt to obtain long-term financing. Jones claimed that he had been unable to obtain long-term financing owing to the wrongfully recorded chattel mortgage on TSE's candy manufacturing equipment. At trial, a jury found that the chattel mortgage on equipment of TSE tendered to Mercantile was to be used in connection with obtaining long-term financing and not as additional security for the original loans to CPC. CPC, TSE, and Jones in his individual capacity sued Rennie and Mercantile for misrepresentation, slander of title, interference with business relationships, and negligent handling of the lien papers. Could Jones, as a shareholder, successfully sue Mercantile in his individual capacity for damages done to CPC and TSE? (*Jones* v. *Rennie,* 690 S.W.2d 164 [Mo. App. 1985].)

2. The directors of Datapoint Corporation (Datapoint) had adopted a bylaw that in effect limited the taking of corporate action by written shareholder consent in lieu of a shareholder meeting for sixty days. The bylaw furthermore deferred the effectiveness of any consent actions until the termination of any lawsuits brought to challenge such consent actions. A Delaware law conferred on shareholders the right to take corporate action through such consents in lieu of a meeting. Datapoint had adopted this bylaw in order to repel hostile takeover attempts and to give the corporation time to defeat any such shareholder action initiated by a hostile offeror through solicitations of Datapoint's own proxies or revocations of outstanding shareholder consents. Did the board have the power to pass this bylaw? (*Datapoint Corporation* v. *Plaza Securities Company,* 496 A.2d 1031 [Del. 1985].)

3. In 1989, Rodney Logal made three written requests to the chairman and chief executive officer of Inland Steel Industries, Inc. (ISI) to inspect certain corporate records of ISI and Inland Steel Company (ISC). Logal

was and had been for the past thirty years an employee of ISC and an ISC stockholder from 1958 until 1986. At the 1986 annual meeting, ISC's shareholders had approved a corporate restructuring plan. This reorganization created ISI, which now serves as a holding company for the stock of ISC as well as for two other corporations. Upon this reorganization, Logal's stock holdings in ISC became stock holdings in ISI. At the time of filing his lawsuit, Logal owned 2112 shares of ISI's common stock and no longer owned any stock in ISC. Logal stated that in 1986, the two defendant firms had closed the No. 3 Open Hearth Facility (the Facility) located in East Chicago, Indiana. According to Logal, the Facility represented one of three basic types of steel-making furnaces that the defendant firms had employed to produce semifinished steel from melted steel scrap metal. In Logal's view, the Facility, which had produced 20 percent of the defendants' steel in 1985, produced the highest quality steel more economically and efficiently than that produced by the defendants' other plants. Logal claimed that the decision to close the Facility had resulted from fraud or gross mismanagement that had caused great losses of revenue for ISC and derivative losses to ISI and its shareholders. Specifically, Logal pointed to the restraints on the firms' steel-making capacity after the closing of the Facility, the defendants' purchase of steel from outside sources for exportation, the defendants' inability (as a consequence of this shutdown) to take advantage of the market, and the firms' increasing involvement with the Japanese. Accordingly, Logal sought to inspect the defendants' books and records relating to the closing of the Facility in order to determine whether such fraud or gross mismanagement had occurred and, if so, to use this information in instituting shareholder derivative proceedings. The trial court had determined that Logal had not acted in bad faith in filing suit, but that he had brought the lawsuit to satisfy his own personal curiosity about the recent events he had witnessed or heard about. Would Logal's motives as construed by the trial court suffice as a "proper purpose" so as to enable Logal to examine the defendants' books and records? (*Logal* v. *Inland Steel Industries, Inc.*, 568 N.E.2d 152 [Ill. App. 1991].)

4. At the time of his death in 1956, Walter J. Klassen had owned and held in his name shares of stock in Chemical Fund, Inc., now the Alliance Fund, Inc. (the Fund). Upon the probate of his estate, the shares were transferred and delivered to the trustees of a testamentary trust he had established. The litigants described the

Fund as an "open-end, diversified investment company or mutual fund registered with the federal Securities & Exchange Commission (SEC) under the Investment Company Act of 1940. . . ." Its capital gains distributions were automatically reinvested to purchase more shares in the Fund unless the shareholder had elected in writing to have the disbursement in cash. Conversely, the Fund paid income dividends that were disbursed in cash unless the shareholder had elected in writing to have the dividends reinvested in shares of stock. The trust at no time filed a writing that would have changed the method of disbursements. The trust had in its possession 683 shares of stock in the Fund held since 29 December 1959. The last receipt by the trust of a reinvested capital gains distribution was of 21 shares on 29 December 1959. On 12 January 1960, the trust received $2.06, which was a fractional cash payment on the capital gains distribution after the automatic reinvestment by purchase of whole shares. The inexplicable then occurred: A blackout of communication or correspondence between the Fund and the trust for a period of twenty-three years. The trust apparently made no inquiries of the Fund, and the Fund neither credited nor paid the trust any of the capital gains distributions or income dividends declared through the years. In a financial statement on 22 February 1983, trustee Ray C. Wagner indicated that he had written to the Fund's research department in an effort to discover what had occurred with the stock. He had not received a reply at that time, and the record remained silent on whether he ever received one or further pursued the matter. The current trustee, Carolee Sauder Leek, wrote the Fund on 15 January 1985 regarding liquidating the stock held in the Fund. On 22 June 1988, the Fund indicated it would not pay accrued distributions and dividends on the 683 shares of stock. The trust filed this litigation on 7 June 1989. At trial, the Fund asserted that, because it had paid dividends through 1959, and trust records had projected a sale of the stock in 1964, and the trustee had made no inquiry from 1960 until 1983, the Fund was entitled to a presumption that the stock had been sold or otherwise transferred. Leek argued that a stockholder such as Klassen was under no obligation to draw or demand his dividends within any prescribed period. According to Leek, the debt that a declared dividend creates is equivalent to the obligation of a bank to its depositors. Hence, in her view, it is not subject to limitation until the shareholder has made a demand on the corporation and there has been a refusal to pay. The trial court had allowed Leek's claim for accrual of all capital gains distributions, which, including two stock splits and reinvestment, amounted to the current value of 10,857 shares totaling $61,667.76. The court also had awarded all income dividends, which totaled $13,863.66. Should the appellate court uphold this result? (*Leek* v. *Alliance Fund, Inc.*, 806 P.2d. 491 [Kan. App. 1991].)

5. Saxon Industries, Inc. (Saxon) was a publicly held Delaware corporation in the paper distribution and converting business. Since April, 1982, it had operated as debtor-in-possession in a voluntary Chapter 11 bankruptcy reorganization. Saxon's last shareholders' meeting had occurred on 21 June 1981. After filing for Chapter 11 reorganization in April, 1982, new management, experienced in restoring financially troubled companies, was retained. Although no stockholders' meetings were held, the Saxon Board eventually elected five new directors. Under new management Saxon sold several unprofitable operations, and for the first six months of the 1984 fiscal year showed operating profits in excess of $4 million with annual sales of approximately $400 million. Despite such progress, Saxon's shareholders' deficit remained at approximately $200 million. When Alco Standard Corporation agreed to buy Saxon, NKFW Partners (NKFW) sued to compel an election of directors. By then, over thirty-one months had elapsed since Saxon's last annual meeting. Saxon argued that the shareholders should air their grievances in bankruptcy court rather than in a shareholders' meeting because NKFW's only purpose for requesting the meeting was to achieve for the stockholders a more substantial payment in the reorganization. Saxon further contended that allowing the shareholders' grievances to be aired in the bankruptcy forum, as opposed to a stockholders' meeting, would be more suitable because the bankruptcy court would consider and weigh the competing demands and relative equities of all the interested parties. Delaware law called for annual stockholders' meetings and permitted courts to order such meetings if the directors had failed to call the meetings. Would the insolvency of the corporation divest the corporation's stockholders of their right to elect directors at an annual meeting? (*Saxon Industries* v. *NKFW Partners*, 488 A.2d 1298 [Del. 1984].)

6. At the opening of the 2 November 1989 annual meeting of the Center for Communications and Development/KMOJ Radio (CCD/KMOJ), a nonprofit corporation, the president of the board of directors announced the suspension of the right to vote of two directors. Several directors protested the suspension as a violation of the bylaws. When the president refused to reconsider this matter, seven of the thirteen directors left the meeting. The seventh departing director requested that the record of the meeting reflect that she had not been part of the decision and that she had "challenged the quorum of those remaining." The president continued the meeting, and the board added four new directors and reelected the president for another term. The seven directors who had left the meeting brought a lawsuit to enjoin the president and new directors from acting on behalf of the corporation until a procedurally correct annual meeting could be held. They also sought a temporary injunction to prohibit the president from decreasing community programming on the radio station or significantly altering the station's operations or policies. Minnesota corporate statutes provided for enactment of bylaws "for the purpose of administering and regulating the affairs of the corporation," if the bylaws were "not inconsistent with law or the articles of incorporation." Section 5.5 of CCD/KMOJ's bylaws stated: "Once established, a quorum remains established until the adjournment of the meeting or *until a member calls for a quorum count and one is found lacking*" (emphasis added). The trial court had granted a summary judgment against the departing directors. Would you agree that the facts were so clear that the court's granting summary judgment against the seven directors who had left the meeting was appropriate? (*Johnson* v. *Edwards*, 467 N.W.2d 333 [Minn. App. 1991].)

7. A shareholder brought suit to set aside an authorization for a mortgage given by the directors and officers of a corporation. New York corporate law allowed a board of directors to authorize mortgages on corporate property without either the votes or the consent of the shareholders unless the certificate of incorporation provided otherwise. Although the corporation's certificate failed to restrict the board's authority to mortgage corporate property, a clause in the bylaws restricted any corporate action without a majority vote of the shareholders. In these circumstances, should a court uphold the mortgage authorization? *Chiulli* v. *Reiter*, 570 N.Y.S.2d 821 [A.D. 2 Dept. 1991].)

8. Southwest Breeders, Inc. (Southwest Breeders), an Oklahoma corporation, had offered to sell shares of its stock to Jack Agosta. At the time, Southwest Breeders's articles of incorporation allowed the corporation,

through its officers and directors, to issue no more than 50,000 shares of its stock at $1 per share. On 31 March 1986, Agosta purchased 15,000 shares of the stock. Agosta later discovered that the officers and directors had, on 27 December 1985, issued to themselves 1,370,000 shares at below par value, clearly in excess of the amount allowed by the articles of incorporation. Southwest Breeders subsequently filed an amendment of its articles of incorporation with the secretary of state that authorized it to increase the number of shares of its stock from 50,000 to 50,000,000. Agosta filed suit to rescind his contract, seeking $6000 in damages for his purchase of the overissued stock. Agosta then filed a motion for summary judgment, which the trial court sustained on the ground that the sale of the overissued stock to Agosta constituted a sale of nonexistent stock for which the officers and directors remained personally liable. On appeal, Southwest Breeders alleged that the trial court had erred in characterizing the sale of stock to Agosta as unauthorized and therefore void. How should the appellate court rule? (*Agosta* v. *Southwest Breeders, Inc.,* 810 P.2d 377 [Okla. App. 1991].)

9. Dynamics Corporation of America (DCA) sued CTS Corporation (CTS) to compel CTS to afford it inspection rights as a shareholder of CTS. DCA had begun to acquire CTS stock in 1980, and litigation was still pending between the parties regarding this proposed acquisition. The information requested by DCA included (a) all records and minutes of the 1981 CTS annual meeting of shareholders; (b) books of account reflecting all expenditures for research and development since January, 1978, and all legal fees paid or incurred in connection with claims and suits asserted by CTS against DCA; (c) all fees paid or owed to Goldman, Sachs & Company since 11 August 1980; and (d) the minutes of all regular and special meetings of the board of directors of CTS since 11 August 1980. CTS through its CTS Knights subsidiary and DCA through its Reeves Hoffman Division were direct and substantial competitors in markets for the sale of quartz crystals and electronic quartz crystal products, and DCA was also a potential competitor of CTS in other lines of business. Indeed, DCA had previously hired away from CTS Knights one of its key engineering employees for the Reeves Hoffman Division. In addition, it had been established that CTS's books of account did not contain separate notations for research and development expenditures. That information was contained in work papers prepared by CTS accountants, including the names of

CTS employees who were engaged in research and development, the salaries of each, and the activities on which CTS was expending its research and development efforts. CTS considered this information confidential and protected it as such. Copies of the minutes of the 1981 meeting had been offered to all shareholders at the 1982 annual meeting, and DCA's president and general counsel had been in attendance at that meeting. CTS asserted that Goldman, Sachs & Company had been retained for litigation advice, including the DCA suit in federal court, and that the minutes of directors' meetings reflected legal advice received by CTS regarding the federal litigation with DCA as well as tentative CTS business plans. Given these facts, how should the court rule on DCA's suit? (*Dynamics Corporation of America* v. *CTS Corporation,* 479 N.E.2d 1352 [Ind. App. 1985].)

10. On 8 April 1966, Phillip B. Ingle, James H. Glamore (the sole stockholder of Glamore Motor Sales, Inc.), and the corporation entered into an agreement whereby Ingle, the corporation's general manager, was to purchase twenty-two of the one hundred outstanding shares of the corporation's common stock. The agreement also made Ingle a director and secretary of the corporation and gave him the option to purchase eighteen additional shares of the corporation's stock. The agreement provided that "in the event that INGLE shall cease to be an employee of the corporation for any reason [James H. Glamore] shall have the option, for a period of 30 days after such termination of employment, to purchase all of the shares of stock then owned by INGLE." Pursuant to the terms of the 1966 agreement, the plaintiff purchased an additional eighteen shares of stock. An agreement was drawn up in 1973 reflecting this change in circumstances by acknowledging that the plaintiff then owned forty of the one hundred outstanding shares of stock. The repurchase provision in the 1973 agreement was identical to that of the 1966 agreement. On 1 January 1982, the corporation issued sixty more shares of stock. James H. Glamore purchased twenty-two shares and his two sons (defendants William B. Glamore and Robert L. Glamore) purchased nineteen shares each. An agreement dated 1 January 1982, between Ingle, James H. Glamore, William B. Glamore, Robert L. Glamore, and the corporation, reflected that change. Again, the agreement contained the identical repurchase provision language. On 9 May 1983, at a special meeting of the board of directors of the corporation, Ingle's employment with the corporation was terminated. On 1 June 1983, James H. Gla-

more notified Ingle that he was exercising his option to purchase all of Ingle's stock. Ingle then sued, arguing that the alleged breach of the 1982 agreement and his termination had resulted from Glamore's desire to exercise the option to purchase Ingle's stock. Was Ingle's interpretation of the agreement—that Glamore could only repurchase the shares if the corporation had good cause for discharging Ingle—correct? (*Ingle* v. *Glamore Motor Sales, Inc.,* 490 N.Y.S.2d 240 [N.Y. App. Div. 1985].)

C H A P T E R 41

Management of a Corporation

O U T L I N E

BOARD OF DIRECTORS

The right to manage the affairs of the corporation falls squarely on the board of directors. Although shareholders, the ultimate "owners" of the corporation, retain the power to elect and remove directors, this prerogative does not give shareholders a direct voice in management. Nor can shareholders compel the board to take any action: The directors are not agents of the shareholders; they owe loyalty primarily to the corporation. (As noted before, however, different rules may apply if the corporation is a close corporation.)

Rights and Duties

Number and Qualifications   The articles of incorporation usually name the initial directors. Older statutes required at least three directors, but the modern trend—due, no doubt, in part to the increased numbers of close corporations—is to permit as few as one or two directors. To avoid deadlocks, the articles or bylaws usually authorize an uneven number of directors.

Unless otherwise provided in the relevant statutes, articles, or bylaws, directors need not be either shareholders in the corporation or residents of the state where the corporation has its principal place of business. Where qualifications are necessary, the election of unqualified persons is voidable, not void. Until the corporation employs proper proceedings to displace the unqualified directors, the law considers them de facto directors (that is, directors in fact if not in law). Consequently, most of their acts as directors are effective; and de facto directors must live up to the same corporate duties and standards that qualified directors do. Directors generally have the right to appoint interim replacements on the board when vacancies arise owing to the death, resignation, or incapacity of a director.

Term of Office   Directors serve for the time specified in state statutes, unless the articles or bylaws limit the term to a shorter period. Directors usually serve for one year unless the corporation has set up a "classified board" (a board divided into classes of directors with staggered election dates; for example, three directors elected every year for three-year terms). Directors continue to hold office until the shareholders elect their successors and the latter take office. Thus, sitting directors do not automatically drop off the board at the end of their terms.

Sometimes shareholders remove directors before their terms on the board end. As discussed in Chapter 40, shareholders may remove directors for cause (which was the only basis for removal at common law). Modern statutes relax this standard by permitting a majority of shareholders to remove directors at any time during their terms without cause. However, in those jurisdictions that require cumulative voting, directors cannot be removed if the number of votes cast against the removal would have elected those directors to the board. Directors who have been removed ordinarily can seek court review of such dismissals.

Meetings   Traditionally, the board could validly exercise its powers only when acting collectively, not individually. The law emphasized the value of decision making arrived at through collective debate, deliberation, and judgment. For this reason, statutes set out rules permitting the board to act only when it was formally convened. Moreover, directors traditionally had to be present to vote (they could not vote by proxy or send substitutes to deliberate for them) and could do so only at a duly announced and formalized meeting.

Today, most modern statutes dispense with the formalities previously required of directors' meetings. Thus, even though the bylaws usually fix the times for regular or special board meetings, statutes today allow meetings to occur even without prior notice. To be a valid meeting, however, either before or after the meeting each absent director—*in writing*—must waive the right to prior notice, consent to the meeting, or approve the minutes of the meeting. Similarly, some states even allow the board to act without a meeting, assuming the articles or bylaws permit informal action, as long as all directors consent and file their consents in the corporate minute book. In fact, telephone conference calls suffice in several states. Given this decided trend toward informality, the board can hold its meetings anywhere unless the articles or bylaws declare otherwise. Meetings outside the corporation's state of incorporation or principal place of business are, in general, perfectly legal.

Unless the articles or bylaws set a higher or lower percentage, a simple majority of the directors ordinarily constitutes a quorum. Actions taken by a quorum of directors are binding on the corporation. Yet two questions may still arise in any discussion about quorums. First, may directors who intentionally miss a meeting to prevent a quorum later question the validity of the action taken at the meeting? Since different cases have produced different results, it may be prudent to check the law on this matter for your particular jurisdiction. Second, may directors count toward the quorum (or vote) if the board will be voting on matters in which they are personally interested? Modern statutes generally allow directors to participate as long as compliance with statutory provisions meant to ensure fairness to the corporation (such as disclosure of the interest) has occurred. If there is no such statute, the case results vary from jurisdiction to jurisdiction. Some cases have allowed the interested directors to be counted; other cases have not.

Normally each director casts his or her own vote in person. Directors ordinarily cannot vote by proxy. Whether interested directors can vote depends on the relevant statutes and case law of the appropriate jurisdiction, as noted above. Directors usually cannot agree in advance about how they will vote on corporate matters. Such a formal agreement is not binding because it is void on public policy grounds; directors owe fiduciary duties to the corporation and must be free to exercise their judgment in a totally unrestricted fashion. Such agreements may be valid, however, among directors in a close corporation if all the shareholders/directors agree to the plan.

Delegation of Duties Most statutes authorize the board of directors to delegate managerial authority to officers and executive (or other) committees. Such delegation of duties ensures the smooth running of the day-to-day affairs of the corporation and promotes efficiency by utilizing the expertise of the various committee members (as in a salary committee). You are probably familiar with such committee structures in noncorporate arenas. If no statutory provisions specifically allow delegation of duties, courts will interpret any attempts at delegation very strictly. Moreover, if the delegation becomes too broad and pervasive, such actions will probably be void, owing to this relinquishment of the board's management functions. Similarly, attempts to place control of the corporation in fewer persons than the entire board of directors will be illegal (even in close corporations), since the corporation deserves the best efforts of all its directors, who in turn owe fiduciary duties to the corporation. Delegation of authority to persons outside the directorial ranks (except for officers), such as **arbitrators** or management consultants, therefore becomes extremely difficult to justify legally.

Arbitrators Independent persons chosen by the parties or appointed by statute and to whom the issues are submitted for nonjudicial settlements of cases or controversies.

Compensation In times past, the corporation had no duty to compensate directors for their services. Older cases had held that directors would not be paid for their services unless the articles or bylaws authorized the compensation before the directors had rendered the services. Even under these circumstances, however, directors could receive payment for extraordinary services taken at the board's request (such as recruitment of executive officers), despite the lack of a prearranged, specific agreement, on quasi-contractual grounds (see Chapter 8 for a discussion of quasi contract). Today, although many corporations still pay their directors little or no compensation for their services, an increasing number of corporations do pay rather hefty sums. Since directors today often are not substantial shareholders and since they are subject to ever-expanding duties and concomitant possibilities of liability, compensation seems defensible.

The directors normally determine the salaries of the officers of the corporation. Questions of possible conflicts of interest may arise when directors also serve as officers, because in effect the directors will be participating in the fixing of their own salaries. As noted earlier in the discussion of quorum requirements, statutes may empower interested directors to vote on these issues as long as disclosure of the interest has been made (the possible conflicts of interest here should be obvious) and the transaction is otherwise fair to the corporation. The board can hire officers to serve for periods longer than the board's tenure as long as the period involved is reasonable in length. Likewise, the amount of compensation paid to officers also must be reasonable. Otherwise, the compensation package (fixed salary, bonuses, share options, profit sharing, annuities, deferred compensation plans, and so on) may be attacked as a "waste" of corporate assets by the directors. Corporate salaries in the millions of dollars are not uncommon today. Moreover, it has become a relatively common strategy for the board to give "golden parachutes"—hefty, guaranteed salary packages—to their chief executive officers when the board's corporation is the target of a hostile takeover attempt. Since the acquirer will be obligated to pay these inflated salaries after the acquisition, golden parachutes become a strategy for fending off the would-be takeover. Golden parachutes, as you would expect, raise controversial questions about possible conflicts of interest and possible waste of corporate assets because the officers will be receiving money for doing no work after their severance from the corporation. The emergence of such stratagems illustrates once again the ever-changing, dynamic nature of the legal institution and its attempts to answer new questions of law.

YOU BE THE JUDGE

Charles Zwick served as Southeast Banking Corp.'s chairman and chief executive officer. He was ousted from his $500,000 a year job in January, 1991 and signed a severance agreement of $1.25 million, consisting of monthly payments of $41,667 spread over two and a half years. Once the leading corporate lender in Florida, Southeast's banks were now failing. Due to pressure from regulatory entities such as the comptroller of the currency and from shareholders, Southeast stopped paying Zwick the agreed upon sum after only a few months. Zwick then sued Southeast for breach of contract. The comptroller of the currency argued that regulators had not exceeded their lawful powers by cracking down on golden parachutes extended to departing executives at failing institutions. Zwick's attorney, however, maintained that regulators had been, in these circumstances, unlawfully interfering with valid and legal contracts when they had brought pressure to bear on companies to cease payments under these severance arrangements.

If you were sitting in judgment on this dispute, how would you decide it?

Source: "Firms Rethink Lucrative Severance Pacts for Top Executives as Criticism Swells," Joann S. Lublin, in *The Wall Street Journal*, November 11, 1991, page B-1.

Liabilities

State corporation statutes, common law doctrines, and federal securities and antitrust laws may impose liability on a director for noncompliance with the duties or requirements set out in those doctrines and statutes. Directors, by the very nature of their positions, make numerous decisions, collectively and individually. Increasingly, the performance of these duties subjects directors to possible personal liability, either individually or with the other members of the board who have approved or engaged in the forbidden conduct. Directors must use great caution in order to avoid liability in the form of civil damages or criminal fines.

Although not always the case, today it is legal—indeed, common—for corporations to indemnify (pay back or reimburse) their directors for liabilities accruing from their corporate positions. Through indemnification, directors receive from the corporation the losses and expenses incurred from litigation brought against them personally for actions undertaken in behalf of the corporation in the directors' corporate capacities. Statutes may limit the right of indemnification in certain circumstances. For instance, indemnification for criminal fines may be unavailable when directors have engaged in unlawful activities that they knew at the time were illegal. Statutes often empower corporations to purchase "D and O liability insurance" for their directors, officers, and other employees to cover nonindemnifiable liabilities.

In the next case, the judge awarded both compensatory and punitive damages against several directors for breaching their fiduciary duties (a topic discussed later in this chapter).

W & W Equipment Co., Inc. v. Mink
568 N.E.2d. 564 (Ind. App. 1 Dist. 1991)

FACTS   In 1960, Winter and Wraight entered into a partnership as manufacturers' representatives for waste water treatment equipment. The partnership was incorporated as W & W Equipment in the late 1960s. The firm sought out and hired Mink in 1977 when Wraight began to consider retirement. In January, 1980, the new W & W Equipment Co., Inc. (W & W) was formed. Winter and Wraight each owned 40 percent of the stock of this new corporation, and Mink owned 20 percent. Each shareholder was both an officer and a director of W & W. Secrest, legal counsel for W & W, became the fourth director and officer of W & W. Capitalized in part by a loan from the old corporation, W & W continued to receive the income generated from accounts set up before it had come into existence. When Wraight retired in 1984, the corporation redeemed his shares of stock at book value, as provided for in the stock purchase agreement. Mink and Winter purchased these shares in such a manner that each became a 50-percent shareholder of the corporation. Wraight went off the payroll and moved to California, although he remained a member of the board of directors in order to protect his personal interest in the loan from the old corporation to W & W. Winter indicated that he would be retiring in 1987; and, based on this plan, Mink entered into negotiations with Henry P. Thompson Co. (HPT) to establish a joint venture. Formed in 1985 on the premise that Winter would retire in 1987, the joint venture's board of directors consisted of Winter, Mink, and two individuals from HPT. Winter opposed but did not veto the joint venture, which was financially successful. In early 1986, a dispute arose between Mink and Winter concerning Winter's retirement, in particular concerning the valuation of Winter's stock. Mink initially proposed valuing Winter's stock at book value, which was approximately $15,000 at that time; but he eventually offered to pay Winter $50,000 for the stock. However, Winter wanted to be paid $250,000 for his shares, because he believed he should receive half the value of the corporation on his retirement. During the ensuing negotiations, Winter indicated that if Mink did not pay him the price he wanted, he would simply remove Mink from the business, open up a post office box to collect the accounts receivable, and obtain the amount of money he wanted in that manner. On 9 March 1987, Secrest prepared for Wraight a Waiver of Notice and Consent to Action by the Board of Directors. This notice requested Wraight's consent to the removal of Mink as a director of the joint venture and as an officer and signatory for W & W. Wraight signed the consent; and neither Winter nor Secrest, who had communicated with Mink frequently during the time, mentioned the waiver to Mink. In fact, the firm sent the notice of the board meeting for these purposes to Mink's home while he was vacationing out of state. Prior to the board meeting, checks for final payment of the loan from the old corporation were drafted; but Winter voided the checks. Wraight thus remained a director of the corporation. When Winter informed the HPT members of the joint venture that he was going to take control of W & W, the HPT members terminated the joint venture. Nine days after the joint venture's termination, the W & W board meeting was held. In a summary fashion with no discussion, Secrest and Winter voted to remove Mink as an officer and signatory for W & W and as director of the joint venture. Wraight's vote for Mink's removal, obtained by consent, was also counted. Mink cast the sole vote against his removal and immediately filed the lawsuit that is the subject of this appeal. After the filing of this lawsuit, Winter terminated Mink as an employee of W & W. Mink continued to come to work for a period of time, but Winter obtained a temporary restraining order (TRO) to prevent Mink from coming to work. Winter had obtained this order from a judge different from the one already assigned to the pending lawsuit, and neither Winter nor Secrest had informed the TRO judge that there was a pending lawsuit involving these parties or that Mink was a 50-percent shareholder of W & W. Winter subsequently increased his own salary and began winding up the corporation without ever paying a dividend to its shareholders. As of 31 May 1988, Winter had received $113,015.97 from W & W and Mink had received $18,000 since the filing of this action. W & W had $386,421.63 in remaining assets. Mink's lawsuit sought compensatory damages from Winter, Wraight, and Secrest for breach of fiduciary duty as well as the dissolution of W & W. Mink also asked for punitive damages against Winter and Secrest. Winter, Wraight, and Secrest filed a counterclaim against Mink alleging breach of fiduciary duty and conversion of corporate funds. The court found that Mink had suffered a loss of $420,000. Hence, the judge awarded Mink W & W's remaining assets of $386,421.63 and a judgment of $33,578.37 against Winter, Wraight, and Secrest. The court also imposed punitive damages of $20,000 against Winter and Secrest and ordered the dissolution of W & W. Finally, the court found in favor of Mink on the counterclaim against him.

ISSUES

Had Mink improperly brought a direct (i.e., an individual) action rather than a derivative (i.e., one brought by a shareholder on behalf of the corporation) action? Had Winter, Secrest, and Wraight breached their fiduciary duty to Mink?

HOLDINGS

No. The facts showed that Mink had properly sued directly (rather than derivatively) here. Moreover, Winter, Secrest, and Wraight's breach of their fiduciary duty to Mink had justified Mink's receiving both compensatory and punitive damages.

REASONING

Fiduciary duties Obligations arising from parties' occupying positions of trust and confidence vis-à-vis each other.

Derivative suit A suit filed by a shareholder on behalf of the corporation to enforce a corporate cause of action.

Winter, Secrest, and Wraight argued that the trial court's finding that they had breached their **fiduciary duties** to Mink is contrary to law and unsupported by the evidence. Before a court can determine whether a breach of a fiduciary duty has occurred, it must determine whether a fiduciary duty exists. W & W was a close corporation, as it had only two shareholders, and the shares were not publicly traded. Shareholders in a close corporation stand in a fiduciary relationship to one another and, as such, must deal fairly, honestly, and openly with the corporation and with their fellow shareholder. Winter, as a fellow shareholder, owed a fiduciary duty to Mink. Wraight, however, was only a director of W & W at the time of the events in question, not a shareholder. He argued that under Indiana law, a director owes a fiduciary duty to the corporation and its shareholders and that the corporation or the shareholders may bring a **derivative suit** for a director's breach of his or her fiduciary duty. He contended, nonetheless, that a director owes no duty to individual shareholders. In other words, Wraight claimed that Mink should have brought a derivative action instead of an individual action (i.e., a direct suit). In general, shareholders cannot maintain actions in their own name to redress injuries to the corporation. A single derivative action generally is required in order to further sound policy considerations, one of which is the avoidance of multiple shareholder lawsuits. Authorization of shareholder actions in their own names would constitute authorization of multitudinous litigation and disregard for the corporate entity. Other reasons underlying the general rule that shareholders are limited to bringing a derivative action include: The protection of corporate creditors by putting the proceeds of the recovery back into the corporation; the protection of the interests of all the shareholders rather than allowing one shareholder to prejudice the interests of other shareholders; and the adequate compensation of the injured shareholder by increasing the value of the shares when recovery is put back into the corporation. However, the reasons for requiring a derivative action are not present in this case. There are only two shareholders, and Mink is the sole injured shareholder. Since none of the underlying reasons for requiring a derivative action is present here, the law would not require Mink to bring a derivative action. While the better practice would be to bring a derivative action, given the facts of this case, a court should not exalt form over substance. Winter, Secrest, and Wraight next argued that the court had improperly based its decision that they had breached their duty to Mink on Mink's termination from his job and on the existence of a tort action for freeze-out. Yet their contention is untenable because the nature of the fiduciary duty remains the same regardless of whether it arises in the capacity of a director, officer, or shareholder in a close corporation. As Indiana precedents hold, "The fiduciary must deal fairly, honestly and openly with his corporation and fellow stockholders. He must not be distracted from the performance of his official duties by personal interests." The testimony at trial indicated that Winter, Wraight, and Secrest had not dealt honestly with Mink. The trial court found that Winter, Wraight, and Secrest had schemed to remove Mink from W & W without discussing their plans with him. They had timed the notice to be sent to his home while he was on vacation in order to give him as little notice as possible of the upcoming corporate actions. The trial court's findings moreover demonstrated that Winter had not been honest with Mink about the value of his stock; Winter had simply demanded $250,000 for his stock and had not informed Mink that this price represented the upper limit mentioned to Winter by the accountant. In addition, Winter had threatened to use the courts against Mink to bleed the company of its assets. The trial court found that Winter had terminated Mink simply to get him out of the way, and then Winter had begun paying himself more money. These actions did not constitute dealing fairly, honestly, and openly with the corporation and fellow stockholders, as mandated by Indiana precedents. Such precedents further hold, "Once it is established that one with a fiduciary duty has attempted to benefit from a questioned transaction, the law presumes fraud." The burden of proof then shifts to the fiduciary to overcome the presumption of fraud by showing the actions taken resulted from honesty and good faith. However, none of the evidence sufficed to permit the overcoming of this presumption. Rather, Mink's termination apparently represented part of an overall scheme to allow Winter to receive a desired amount of money on his retirement. Winter, Wraight, and Secrest next argued that the court had improperly resolved this case by awarding dissolution of the corporation and damages to Mink. When the basis of liability is a failure to conform to a fiduciary duty, the measure of damages is the entire loss sustained. A damage award does not require any specific degree of certainty, provided the evidence (as opposed to conjecture or speculation) supports the amount awarded. In the present case, the trial court found Mink had suffered $420,000 in compensatory damages. The court could have based its finding on the evidence that the corporation was worth $500,000 prior to the breaches, that Mink should receive one-half of this amount, or $250,000, and that he should receive $170,000 in damages owing to the lost value of the joint venture. Moreover, the court might have rested its decision on its findings that, since the filing of this action, Winter had received $113,015.97 from the corporation and Mink $18,000. Either way, the court's award remained defensible. Winter and Secrest finally argued that the trial court had erred in assessing punitive damages against them. But as settled law holds, punitive damages are recoverable on clear and convincing evidence that the defendant acted with malice, fraud, gross negligence, or oppression that was not the result of mistake of law or fact, honest error of judgment, overzealousness, mere negligence, or other human failing. Thus, the trial court had properly concluded that Winter and Secrest's conduct in scheming and removing Mink from the corporation solely so that Winter could receive the amount of money he wanted on his retirement had not constituted honest errors of judgment, mistake, or such other human failing but instead had represented the oppressive and malicious acts generally associated with punitive damages awards.

Other Rights

Because directors alone have the right to declare dividends, they (as well as the shareholders) may be personally liable for improper dividends.

Directors, like shareholders, may enter into agreements about how they will vote as directors. But if such agreements unduly fetter the board's managerial functions, the agreements will be void on public policy grounds. These agreements ordinarily will be valid, however, in close corporations in which all the shareholders/directors have assented to the terms.

The rights of directors to inspect corporate records are even more compelling than shareholders' rights because access to corporate records is essential if directors are to discharge their fiduciary duties and decision-making functions. Unlike shareholders' rights, many states characterize the directors' right of inspection as absolute. Yet this right would be unavailable in some states if directors abuse the right by attempting to use it for an improper purpose that damages the corporation, such as misappropriation of trade secrets or confidential trade information.

OFFICERS

Who Really "Manages" the Corporation?

The selection or removal of officers represents an important managerial function of the board of directors. While directors are responsible for the overall policies of the corporation, officers conduct the day-to-day operations of the firm and execute the policies established by the board. These lines of authority are well established in American law. Nevertheless, you may have heard of a "rubber stamp" board—that is, a board that merely approves as corporate policy the directions suggested by the officers. Although such situations no doubt actually exist, it is important to understand that such management constitutes a perversion of the usual corporate roles: The directors should manage, and the officers should carry out the management goals delegated to them by the directors.

Rights and Duties

Qualifications   Officers are agents of the corporation and therefore must live up to the fiduciary duties placed on agents. Statutes often name the officers that a corporation must have, and either these statutes or the corporate bylaws usually spell out the respective officers' authority. Typical officers include president, vice-president, secretary, and treasurer (or comptroller). The top executive may also be called the chairman of the board, the chief executive officer, or the general manager. The same person ordinarily can serve as more than one officer, but some statutes prohibit the same person from serving as both president and secretary.

Term of Office   The board ordinarily appoints the officers, who serve at the will of the directors. (Some modern statutes, on the other hand, allow the shareholders to elect the officers.) Either the board or the president can appoint junior or senior officers. Officers usually serve at the pleasure of the board because the board in most jurisdictions can remove officers with or without cause, even when the officer has a valid employment contract. But after such removal without cause, the corporation may be liable in damages to the former officer for breach of the employment contract. As we shall see later, the directors normally escape personal liability if they have removed the officer in accordance with the "business judgment rule"; that is, they have exercised due care while making corporate decisions. In rare instances, the state, the courts, or the shareholders can remove officers. These instances nearly always involve a removal "with cause."

Compensation   In earlier times, officers, like directors, traditionally served without pay because they usually were shareholders who could expect their investment in the corporation to multiply by virtue of their work on the corporation's behalf. Thus, there was no need to supplement these corporate profits with a salary. Today, since neither directors nor officers must also be shareholders, the corporation usually pays a prearranged, fixed salary (recall in this context the possible existence of so-called golden parachutes as well). In addition, the corporation commonly adds to this salary profit-sharing plans, bonuses, share options, deferred compensation plans, pensions, annuities, and other fringe benefits like health care and expense accounts. Such compensation packages often turn out to be substantial indeed. Compensation, to be lawful, should be reasonable and not represent waste of corporate assets. If waste is present, both directors and officers may be liable to the corporation for this waste. Courts have even ordered the officers to return to the corporation the amounts deemed excessive compensation.

Agency Law   Because officers are agents of the corporation, they have authority to bind the corporation. It would probably benefit you at this point to review the material on agency in Chapters 33–35. Briefly, an officer's authority may be actual (either express or implied) or apparent. *Express authority* derives from state statutes, the articles, or the bylaws. Any of these three sources may spell out the duties, responsibilities, and authority of the respective officers, although the bylaws are the most common source. In these situations, the corporation has determined the boundaries within which the officer shall act on behalf of the corporation. *Implied authority* is also known as *inherent authority.* By virtue of their office or title, presidents have inherent authority to direct corporate meetings and to act on behalf of the corporation with regard to transactions occurring in the ordinary and regular course of business. For instance, it normally will be part of a president's authority to hire real estate brokers for the purpose of selling corporate property. Yet the president cannot validly sell or mortgage corporate assets without the approval of the board (and sometimes that of the shareholders). The president can have authority, however, to bind the corporation to sale or services contracts arising in the usual course of business (for instance, the president of a grain elevator can authorize purchases of wheat from local farmers). Courts sometimes uphold expansions of authority for presidents who are chief executive officers or general managers.

Vice-presidents normally possess no authority by virtue of their office but of course will enjoy the authority the president has if they succeed to the presidency owing to the president's absence, resignation, or death. Similarly, neither the treasurer nor the secretary can normally bind the corporation. The law ordinarily limits them to fairly ministerial intracorporate functions; but some jurisdictions give the treasurer authority to write, accept, endorse, and negotiate corporate checks and promissory notes.

Corporate officers may have *apparent authority* to bind the corporation. Apparent authority arises when the corporation by its actions indicates to a third party that an officer or agent is empowered to engage in certain transactions on behalf of the corporation. For example, if the corporation has customarily allowed the president to buy property on the corporation's behalf without prior board approval, the president in this instance will have apparent authority to bind the corporation to such a real estate transaction. The corporation cannot later allege lack of actual authority as a defense to consummation of the sale. Likewise, the seller of the property may use the theory of estoppel (the corporation is prevented from denying a defense otherwise available to it) to counter a defense of lack of actual authority. Estoppel may be used when the third party has been damaged because of the third party's good faith in and reasonable reliance on the corporation's creation of circumstances that appear to clothe the officer with apparent authority. In fact, estoppel may bind the corporation to transactions that result from unauthorized acts of the officer. Subsequent ratification (approval) of previously unauthorized acts will also bind the corporation. Even if the president had no authority to buy real estate, a later board resolution that approves the sale constitutes a ratification and binds the corporation to the completion of the transaction.

The court grappled with the concept of authority in deciding the case that follows.

First Interstate Bank of Texas, N.A. v. First National Bank of Jefferson
928 F.2d 153 (5th Cir. 1991)

FACTS   In 1982, the Louisiana Public Facilities Authority (LPFA) agreed to issue $3 million worth of industrial bonds and lend the proceeds to New Orleans Property Development (NOPD). NOPD needed the funds to develop a hotel in New Orleans and sought a lender, i.e., someone to purchase the bonds. In February, 1982, NOPD submitted a loan application to First National Bank of Jefferson (FNJ) for the full $3 million. On 12 March, FNJ, through Stratton Orr, sent to NOPD a commitment letter agreeing to purchase the entire $3 million bond issue. NOPD accepted FNJ's offer. Before FNJ sent the commitment letter to NOPD, First Interstate Bank of Texas, N.A. (First Interstate), notified FNJ that it was willing to purchase only $1 million of the bond issue. First Interstate later agreed to purchase $2 million of the bond issue. First Interstate asserted that it had conditioned its agreement to purchase the additional $1 million in bonds on FNJ's commitment to buy First Interstate's NOPD bonds in the future if First Interstate desired to sell them. One of the parties had instructed Butler & Binion, the law firm representing FNJ and First Interstate, to reduce to writing the oral agreement that FNJ would buy, on First Interstate's demand, the entire $2 million of NOPD bonds held by First Interstate. The attorneys sent a draft of the agreement, styled a Bond Purchase Agreement (BPA), to FNJ senior vice-president John Boyd. Boyd, who was Orr's supervisor, had assumed the NOPD account when Orr had left FNJ. According to Boyd, he had discussed the agreement with FNJ president Arceneaux, who had given Boyd the impression that execution of the BPA was an "acceptable approach." On 4 May, First Interstate and FNJ signed an agreement with NOPD and LPFA in which First Interstate agreed to purchase $2 million worth of bonds and FNJ $1 million. The parties closed the NOPD transaction on 29 July. On that day, FNJ, through Boyd, and First Interstate, through vice-president Robert LaRue, signed the separate BPA, which is at issue in this suit. In this document, FNJ agreed to purchase all of First Interstate's NOPD bonds on First Interstate's demand. In August, 1988, First Interstate demanded that FNJ buy its bonds pursuant to the 29 July 1982 BPA. When FNJ refused and asserted that it was not bound by the BPA because Boyd did not have the authority to sign the agreement for FNJ, First Interstate filed this suit to enforce the BPA. When the trial court granted FNJ's motion for a directed verdict, First Interstate appealed.

ISSUE

Had FNJ given Boyd, a senior vice-president of the bank, authority to execute the BPA at issue?

HOLDING

Yes. The bank's sending Boyd to the closing with a certification that Boyd, as a senior vice-president, was acting in behalf of the FNJ board of directors had clothed Boyd with authority to sign the BPA, without which agreement First Interstate would not have consented to buy the NOPD bonds.

REASONING

Louisiana law, which governs the analysis here, recognizes two types of authority—actual and apparent—under agency law. Actual authority can be express or implied. The district court had held that Boyd lacked express actual authority to execute the BPA because no corporate resolution or bylaw specifically authorized the transaction. A principal, however, can confer actual authority orally. For instance, Boyd testified that FNJ had authorized him to sign the BPA. Boyd said that he had discussed the NOPD transaction, including the BPA, with Arceneaux and other FNJ officers, despite Arceneaux's denying such discussions. The district court had weighed Boyd's testimony, but had "considered it very weak." However, given the corroborating evidence, it was sufficiently strong for a reasonable jury to credit it, since Boyd's position in the FNJ hierarchy would lend credence to his assertion that the bank had authorized him to sign the BPA. LaRue had understood from this conversation that First Interstate would buy $2 million of the bonds if FNJ would agree to the buy-back provision. A jury could infer that if Arceneaux had participated in negotiating the buy-back agreement, FNJ must have authorized Boyd to consummate the transaction. The record also demonstrated that the BPA had not obligated FNJ any further than its 12 March commitment letter to NOPD, in which FNJ had agreed to buy the entire $3 million bond issue. Arceneaux had conceded that the letter had bound FNJ to take the entire issue. Thus, the 29 July BPA had not extended FNJ's obligation on the bonds beyond its 12 March commitment. Both agreements had made FNJ the principal lender on a $3 million loan. In sum, the evidence had presented a jury question as to whether FNJ had given Boyd express actual authority to execute the BPA. Furthermore, the issue of implied actual authority merited scrutiny as well. Implied authority is actual authority inferred from the circumstances and the nature of the agency. An agent is vested with the implied authority to do all those things necessary or incidental to the agency assignment. Implied authority connotes permission from the principal for the agent to act, though that permission is not expressly set forth orally or in writing. First Interstate had argued that a juror might infer from the nature of the bank's business and Boyd's position in that business that Boyd had had implied actual authority to sign the BPA. However, the Louisiana Civil Code, which provides in part that "the power [of agency] must be *express* for the following purposes: . . . To contract a loan or acknowledge a debt" (emphasis added) would prevent First Interstate from recovering under an implied actual authority theory. Hence, the district court had correctly declined to submit this theory to the jury. First Interstate's final argument centered on apparent authority. A corporation will be liable to a third party even for the unauthorized acts of its agent under the doctrine of apparent authority if (1) the corporation manifests the agent's authority to the third party and (2) the third party reasonably relies on the agent's purported authority as a result of the manifestation. Indeed, First Interstate had also introduced sufficient evidence to create a jury question regarding Boyd's apparent authority to bind FNJ. When FNJ had hired Boyd as a senior vice-president, it had manifested to the public that Boyd had the authority to bind the bank in agreements necessary to conduct the bank's business. On the day of the NOPD closing, FNJ specifically had manifested to First Interstate that Boyd had authority to execute the necessary closing papers on behalf of FNJ, since FNJ had sent Boyd and one of its trust officers to the closing with a certification that Boyd was its senior vice-president acting on behalf of FNJ's board of directors. The jury was entitled to conclude that when FNJ had sent Boyd to the closing with a certificate of his authority, the bank also was manifesting Boyd's authority to sign the BPA, without which First Interstate would not have agreed to buy the NOPD bonds. A jury could also find that First Interstate had bought $2 million of the bond issue in reliance on FNJ's commitment to purchase these bonds at any time and that First Interstate's reliance on these manifestations had been reasonable. FNJ had argued that the doctrine of apparent authority would not apply in this case because First Interstate had not inquired into the extent of Boyd's authority. FNJ maintained that Louisiana imposes an absolute duty on a third party to inquire about an agent's authority. However, a third party can rely on the apparent authority of an agent until something occurs that would cause a reasonable person to inquire further into the circumstances. Here, a jury could conclude that First Interstate need not have made further inquiry. Because a reasonable jury could conclude that Boyd had had apparent authority to bind FNJ on the BPA, the trial court had inappropriately directed a verdict in favor of FNJ.

Liabilities   Officers who attempt to contract on behalf of the corporation without authority to do so may be personally liable to the other contracting party. Similarly, nondisclosure of the fact that the officer is acting on behalf of the corporation, even when the officer's actions are authorized, will lead to the personal liability of the officer. Officers who commit torts may be personally liable to the injured party, although, as you may recall from Chapter 35, the corporation may also be liable for torts committed by the officer during the scope of his or her employment under the doctrine of *respondeat superior*. Thus, a bank president who converts funds to his or her own use may be liable to the depositor, as may the bank under *respondeat superior*. Yet, as the following case illustrates, if the officer actively participates in the tort, a court may impose liability solely on the officer.

National Acceptance Company of America v. Pintura Corporation
418 N.E.2d 1114 (Ill. App. 1981)

FACTS

Converted Tortiously exercised unlawful dominion over the property of another to the harm of that person.

Nieto, the president of and sole shareholder in Pintura Corporation, allegedly **converted** checks belonging to National Acceptance Company of America (National Acceptance) by endorsing them and placing them in Pintura's account instead of sending them to the rightful **assignee,** National Acceptance Company. The latter sued Pintura and also sued Nieto for personal liability.

ISSUE

Was Nieto personally liable for the monies allegedly converted when he realized no personal benefits from the alleged conversion?

HOLDING

Assignee The recipient of a legal transfer of one's legal rights under a contract.

Yes. Because the evidence showed that Nieto as a corporate officer had converted five checks on behalf of the corporation, his active participation in this tort rendered him personally liable for those funds, even though there was no proof that he had personally benefited from the funds.

REASONING

Corporate officers will not be liable for the corporation's torts simply by virtue of the office, but officers will be individually liable for the corporation's torts in which they actively participate. Moreover, liability for conversion generally does not require that the converter personally benefit from the conversion, since the essence of conversion is not the acquisition of property by the wrongdoer but the deprivation of the owner's property. Because the assignee corporation, National Acceptance, had not authorized Nieto's endorsement and deposit of checks into Pintura's account, Nieto was the proximate cause of National Acceptance's loss and could be held individually liable for the conversion carried out on behalf of Pintura Corporation.

In the next case, high-ranking managerial agents, as well as the corporations, faced possible criminal liability for murder and involuntary manslaughter, respectively.

People v. *O'Neil*
550 N.E.2d 1090 (Ill. App. 1990)

FACTS   Film Recovery Systems, Inc. (Film Recovery) was engaged in the business of extracting, for resale, silver from used x-ray and photographic film. Metallic Marketing Systems, Inc. (Metallic Marketing) operated out of the same premises and owned 50 percent of the stock of Film Recovery. The recovery process involved "chipping" the film product and soaking the granulated pieces in large open bubbling vats containing a solution of water and sodium cyanide. The cyanide solution caused the release of silver contained in the film. A continuous flow system pumped the silver-laden solution into polyurethane tanks that contained electrically charged stainless steel plates to which the separated silver adhered. Workers removed the plates from the tanks to another room where the accumulated silver was scraped off. On the morning of 10 February 1983, shortly after he had disconnected a pump on one of the tanks and had begun to stir the contents of the tank with a rake, Stefan Golab became dizzy and felt faint. He left the production area to rest in the lunchroom area of the plant. Golab eventually lost consciousness, and paramedics summoned to the plant could not revive him. He was pronounced dead on arrival at the hospital. The Cook County medical examiner, after receiving the toxicological report, determined at the autopsy that Golab had died from acute cyanide poisoning through the inhalation of cyanide fumes in the plant air. A Cook County grand jury subsequently charged defendants Steven O'Neil, Charles Kirschbaum, Daniel Rodriguez, Gerald Pett, and Michael T. Mackay with murder, stating that, as individuals and as officers and high managerial agents of Film Recovery, they had knowingly created a strong probability of Golab's death by failing to disclose to Golab that he was working with cyanide and by failing to advise him about, train him to anticipate, or provide adequate equipment to protect him from the attendant dangers involved. The grand jury also charged Film Recovery and Metallic Marketing with involuntary manslaughter, stating that, through the reckless acts of their officers, directors, agents, and others, all acting within the scope of their employment, the corporate entities had, on 10 February 1983, unintentionally killed Golab. Finally, the grand jury charged both individual and corporate defendants with reckless conduct as to twenty other Film Recovery employees based on the same conduct alleged in the murder indictment, but expanding the time of that conduct to "on or about March 1982 through March 1983." O'Neil, Kirschbaum, and Rodriguez each received sentences of 25 years' imprisonment for murder and 14 concurrent 364-day imprisonment terms for reckless conduct. In addition, O'Neil and Kirschbaum were each fined $10,000 with respect to the murder convictions and $14,000 with respect to the convictions for reckless conduct. Film Recovery and Metallic Marketing were each fined $10,000 for the convictions for involuntary manslaughter and $14,000 for the reckless conduct convictions. On appeal, the defendants claimed that their convictions must be reversed and the cause remanded for retrial because of the allegedly inconsistent judgments rendered. The defendants also contended that the evidence presented at trial had been insufficient to support the convictions. Specifically, the defendants argued that the judgments for murder and reckless conduct against O'Neil, Kirschbaum, and Rodriguez were inconsistent because, under Illinois statutes, the offense of murder requires a knowing and intentional act, but reckless conduct does not. The defendants then asserted that since both convictions had arisen from the same acts of the individual defendants, O'Neil, Kirschbaum, and Rodriguez could not be responsible for intentional and unintentional conduct at the same time and, therefore, the judgments for murder and reckless conduct against them were inconsistent. Defendants relied on the same logic to support the contention that the murder convictions against O'Neil, Kirschbaum, and Rodriguez were inconsistent with the convictions for involuntary manslaughter against the corporate defendants. To arrive at that conclusion, however, defendants first stressed that the corporate defendants could be culpable only through the acts and omissions of the individual defendants, since, under Illinois precedents, the mind and mental state of a corporation is the collective mind and mental state of its board of directors or high managerial agents. Further noting that involuntary manslaughter is premised on unintended and reckless conduct, the defendants reasoned that the convictions against the corporate entities for that offense were inconsistent with the individual defendants' convictions for murder because both offenses had been based on the same conduct: the acts of the individual defendants.

ISSUE   Were the convictions of the corporate entities, Film Recovery and Metallic Marketing, for involuntary manslaughter inconsistent with the convictions of the individual corporate officers for murder?

HOLDING   Yes. Since the record failed to disclose that a high managerial agent of the corporation, other than the individual defendants, might have engaged in conduct that would provide a foundation for a charge of involuntary manslaughter against the corporation arising from the death of one of its employees, a conviction on that charge would be inconsistent with the convictions of the individual defendant corporate officers for murder.

REASONING   The pertinent statutes provide: "A person who kills an individual without lawful justification commits murder if, in performing the acts which cause the death: He *knows* that such acts create a strong probability of death or great bodily harm to that individual" (emphasis added). Moreover, "[a] person who *unintentionally* kills an individual without lawful justification commits involuntary manslaughter if his acts whether lawful or unlawful which cause the death are such as are likely to cause death or great bodily harm to some individual, and he performs them *recklessly*" (emphasis added). Furthermore, "[a] person who causes bodily harm to or endangers the bodily safety of an individual by any means commits reckless conduct if he performs *recklessly* the acts which cause the harm or endanger safety, whether they otherwise are lawful or unlawful" (emphasis added). The murder indictment states that on 10 February 1983, defendants O'Neil, Kirschbaum, Rodriguez, Pett, and Mackay, acting as individuals and as officers and high managerial agents of Film Recovery, committed murder in that they had knowingly created a strong probability of Stefan Golab's death. The involuntary manslaughter indictment against Film Recovery and Metallic Marketing asserted that, on 10 February 1983, they "unintentionally killed Stefan Golab by authorizing, requesting, commanding and performing certain acts of commission and acts of omission by [their] officers, board of directors and high managerial agents, . . . who acting within the scope of their employment . . . performed the said acts recklessly in such manner as was likely to cause death and great bodily harm to some individual and . . . caused the death of Stefan Golab." The indictment did not otherwise specify the nature of the acts. With regard to the consistency of the judgments for murder and reckless conduct against O'Neil, Kirschbaum, and Rodriguez, acting solely in their individual capacities, the corresponding indictments differ only in one respect. The murder indictment is limited to the individual defendants' conduct on 10 February 1983, while the reckless conduct indictments concern conduct over a period of time from March, 1982, through March, 1983, which would include the date of Golab's death. In all other respects, the indictment uses as its foundation the same conduct for both offenses against the individual defendants. Although the indictments for both offenses are therefore based on identical acts of the individual defendants, it is conceivable that, owing to the mutual exclusiveness of the mental states required to sustain each, the evidence in the record might reconcile the apparent inconsistency in the convictions for those offenses. A careful review of the record, however, does not reveal that, as to the individual defendants, evidence existed to establish, separately, the defendants' mental states to support the separate offenses of murder and reckless conduct. In short, the individual defendants had not possessed mental states on 10 February 1983 that were different from mental states during the period of March, 1982, to March, 1983, such as might support separate offenses of murder and reckless conduct. Those who testified as to the working conditions in the plant had established the following: The firms had not told the employees that they were working with cyanide or that the compound put into the vats could be harmful when inhaled; although ceiling fans existed above the vats, ventilation in the plants was poor; the defendant firms had not given the employees any safety instruction, goggles to protect their eyes, or protective clothing and, as a result, workers' clothing would become wet with the solution used in the vats; small puddles of that solution as well as film chips had lain on the plant floor around the vats; the solution had burned exposed skin; a strong and foul odor had permeated the plant; the condition of the air in the plant had made breathing difficult and painful; and, finally, workers had experienced dizziness, nausea, headaches, and bouts of vomiting. Because the offenses of murder and reckless conduct require mutually exclusive mental states and because the same evidence of the individual defendants' conduct had been used to support both offenses and had not established, separately, each of the requisite mental states, the convictions were legally inconsistent. To the extent the involuntary manslaughter indictment contemplates the conduct of others, as well as the individual defendants convicted of murder, as providing a basis for corporate criminal responsibility, it is possible the judgments against the corporate defendants for involuntary manslaughter could be consistent with the judgments for murder against the individual defendants. A corporation is criminally responsible whenever any of its high managerial agents possesses the requisite mental state and is responsible for a criminal offense while acting within the scope of his or her employment. To the extent the record discloses that the conduct of a high managerial agent of Film Recovery or Metallic Marketing, other than individual defendants O'Neil, Kirschbaum, and Rodriguez, might provide a foundation for the charge of involuntary manslaughter, that judgment would not be inconsistent with the judgment for murder against the individual defendants. Here, however, the record was devoid of any evidence on which to conclude that the conduct of a high managerial agent, apart from that of the individual defendants found guilty of murder, had provided the basis for establishing criminal responsibility against the corporate defendants for Golab's death. And, because the trial court had used the same conduct to support offenses that have mutually exclusive mental states, the judgments rendered for both offenses were legally inconsistent.

FIDUCIARY DUTIES OWED TO THE CORPORATION

As you may recall from *W & W Equipment*, directors, officers, and controlling shareholders owe assorted duties to the corporation and sometimes to shareholders and creditors. These are called *fiduciary* duties because the directors, officers, and controlling shareholders occupy a position of trust and faith with regard to the corporation and other constituencies. Generally speaking, these obligations fall into three broad categories: the duty of obedience, the duty of diligence (or due care), and the duty of loyalty. These duties may arise from statute, but more often they issue from decisional law.

Obedience

Directors, officers, controlling shareholders, and other corporate managers must restrict their actions and those of the corporation to lawful pursuits. Any action taken beyond the scope of the corporation's power is an illegal, ultra vires act. Violation of a positive rule of law or statute by definition constitutes an illegal act. Any such actions by managers violate their duty of obedience and may subject them to personal liability.

Diligence

Because corporate managers act on behalf of the corporation, they are obligated to perform their duties with the amount of diligence or due care that a reasonably prudent person would exercise in the conduct of his or her own personal affairs or in the same or similar circumstances. You have probably noticed the familiar ring of this language. We talked about this kind of standard when we discussed negligence. Basically, the duty of due care obliges a corporate manager to perform his or her duties in a nonnegligent fashion. Note that the law does not expect a director, officer, or controlling shareholder to be perfect or all-knowing. Honest errors of judgment will not lead to liability for breach of the duty of diligence. If liability were imposed in such situations, who would ever consent to be a director or officer?

Instead, the law excuses the conduct if the manager has made the error in good faith and without being clearly and grossly negligent. This is called the "business judgment rule." Needless to say, whether the manager's decision satisfies the business judgment rule or, in contrast, is grossly negligent and hence unacceptable becomes a question of fact. Nonattendance at corporate meetings or inattention to corporate affairs leading to ill-preparedness may cause the manager to incur liability for breach of the duty of diligence or due care. Similarly, failure to fire an obviously unworthy employee, failure to obtain casualty insurance, failure to heed warning signs suggesting illegal conduct (such as embezzlement), or reliance on unreasonable statements by attorneys or accountants may lead to liability. The manager will nonetheless incur liability only for such losses as his or her own negligent conduct causes. Consequently, if a director formally dissents about a matter that is later held to be negligent, that director will avoid liability. It is usually no defense that the director was a "figurehead" or served without pay; but a manager's reliance on *reasonable* expert reports, such as those by accountants or attorneys, usually exonerates the manager from liability unless violations of securities acts are involved.

The following dispute centered on the possible application of the business judgment rule to a decision made by the directors.

NCR Corporation v. American Telephone and Telegraph Company
761 F. Supp. 475 (S. D. Ohio 1991)

FACTS   American Telephone and Telegraph Company (AT&T) is a New York corporation with its principal place of business in New York City. NCR Corporation (NCR), a leader in the computer field, develops, manufactures, markets, installs, and services business information processing systems for worldwide markets from its principal place of business in Dayton, Ohio. NCR first began considering the implementation of an employee stock ownership plan (ESOP) in 1986, when management mentioned the idea as one of several possible defenses that the firm could raise in case of a hostile takeover attempt. The study of a potential ESOP carried over into 1989. During that time period, both Charles E. Exley, Jr., NCR's CEO and chairman of the board, and a steering committee agreed that an ESOP would be of at least some benefit if another firm should attempt a takeover. However, a number of "technical" difficulties persuaded the board of directors that an ESOP was not appropriate at that time. During the entire period from 1986 to mid-1989, the firm discussed the ESOP concept primarily in the context of potential takeover defenses, even though top employee benefits personnel saw no compelling reason to change benefits. In mid-1989 the board discontinued its studies on the advisability of an ESOP and ignored the topic until AT&T's tender offer. Beginning in mid-November, 1990, AT&T made unsolicited proposals to NCR to purchase all of NCR's outstanding common stock in exchange for AT&T stock. On 5 December 1990, the NCR board of directors announced that it had rejected AT&T's $90 per share stock-for-stock offer as inadequate; and the NCR board recommended that shareholders similarly reject that offer. NCR's charter required a "supermajority" vote of 80 percent of all outstanding voting shares to replace a majority of directors at a special meeting. Since it was necessary to obtain 80 percent of the outstanding shares, as opposed to 80 percent of the shares actually voted, shares not voted at a special meeting would become the functional equivalent of votes cast for the incumbent board. At each of the past four NCR shareholder meetings, the total voter turnout had been less than 80 percent. On 21 January 1991, AT&T delivered to NCR written requests for a special meeting, which requests represented over 25 percent of NCR's outstanding voting stock. Because NCR believed AT&T could have the required number of votes by the 28 March 1991 annual meeting, NCR began reconsidering in December, 1990, the concept of establishing an ESOP as a takeover defense, not as an employee benefits option. During this period, James McElwain, NCR's vice-president for personnel and education, expressed misgivings about the ESOP. At the 20 February 1991 board meeting, in conjunction with a presentation on the proposed ESOP, the directors received "board books," which did not contain a great deal of substantive information regarding the specifics of the proposed ESOP. Nonetheless, following this presentation, the board voted unanimously to adopt the proposal. No benefits personnel made a presentation at either the January or February board meetings, and board members received no information concerning McElwain's reservations about the ESOP. Although McElwain was present at the February meeting, no one directed any questions to him. At both the January and February meetings, the board discussed the usefulness of the ESOP as a reaction to AT&T's takeover attempt. In the period between mid-1989, when the board had tabled the ESOP idea, and the adoption of the ESOP in 1991, changes in tax laws and accounting rules had caused ESOPs to become less attractive financing options. As a result, investment bankers had experienced a dramatic downturn in the number of ESOPs being established by major corporations. Yet the board was apparently unaware or only vaguely aware of these developments. On 20 February 1991, nine days before the record date of 1 March, NCR authorized the issue of 5,509,641.873 shares of preferred stock for an aggregate price of $500 million. Since the ESOP in question was a leveraged ESOP, all shares were issued at once. The 5.5 million share block (over twenty times larger than the ESOP originally considered in 1986 and 1989) put about 8 percent of the outstanding NCR voting stock into employee hands while diluting outstanding common stock shares by approximately 6 percent. Unleveraged ESOPs enjoyed substantial tax advantages not available to leveraged ESOPs. Specifically, if NCR's stock rose in the manner predicted by NCR's financial advisors, NCR would forego potentially hundreds of millions of dollars in tax savings by leveraging its ESOP. In short, the size of the ESOP was apparently not related to benefits objectives but, rather, was an attempt to place as large a number of shares into friendly hands as possible. NCR could also have lessened the dilutive effect of the ESOP by initiating a stock repurchase but had declined to do so. Some shareholders subsequently sued, arguing that the ESOP was invalid.

ISSUE   Would the business judgment rule uphold the decision of the directors of NCR, who had proposed an ESOP as a defensive measure to thwart AT&T's proposed takeover of NCR?

HOLDING   No. Despite the absence of bad faith on the directors' part in adopting the ESOP, the business judgment rule would not protect the transaction owing to the fact that the directors had failed to act in an informed fashion.

REASONING   Under Maryland precedents, it is a well-settled rule that "in all cases, the business judgment rule creates the presumption that directors act in good faith." This presumption is heightened where, as here, the majority of the board members are independent outside directors. In order to rebut a business judgment claim, the party challenging the validity of a board's actions must produce evidence sufficient to rebut the presumption that the directors have acted in accordance with their fiduciary duties. The heart of the fiduciary duty imposed on directors of publicly held corporations is the obligation to act in a manner they reasonably believe to be in the best interests of the corporation. This duty is plainly composed of two separate elements, one subjective and the other objective. A director may take no action on behalf of a corporation unless he or she is of the belief that such action is in the corporation's best interests. However, the second condition implicit in the director's fiduciary duty is that his or her belief be reasonable. Applying the first prong of this test to the facts of the case at bar, it was clear that NCR's outside directors, accomplished and respected in their various fields and independent of NCR's management, would have had little to gain by acting improperly. The business judgment rule serves to uphold the decisions of a board that acts "on an informed basis, in good faith and in the honest belief that the action taken was in the best interests of the company." Any decision undertaken on the basis of insufficient knowledge is inherently unreasonable; hence, the business judgment rule provides no protection for directors who have made an unintelligent or unadvised judgment. In the present case, the record is rife with references to information that was readily available but was either not presented to the outside directors by management or, if it was presented, was not duly considered by the board. Despite the fact that NCR management was aware that the proposed ESOP was dilutive of common stock, management sought no fairness opinion. This is more remarkable given the apparent advantages that the preferred shares enjoy over common stock under the ESOP. The board members are sophisticated businesspersons who have some familiarity with the concept of fairness opinions. Yet there was no discussion at any of the board meetings regarding the lack of such an opinion. Management did not offer an explanation for the absence of one, and no outside director asked. By 1990, the number of companies seeking to implement ESOPs had dropped dramatically owing in large part to changes in tax laws and accounting rules that made ESOPs a much less attractive financing alternative. In structuring its ESOP, NCR employed the aid of two of the most prominent investment banking firms in the country. Yet the board members were, at best, only vaguely familiar with these significant developments. Furthermore, there were numerous problems with the issue of the preferred stock under Maryland law. NCR management was aware, based on consultations with its financial advisors, that an unleveraged ESOP was an available and advantageous option. First, a smaller number of shares could be issued initially. Moreover, the number of shares issued annually could be adjusted to meet the company's actual benefits needs, a particularly attractive option given the fact that NCR had no idea how many employees might actually enroll in the plan. In addition to eliminating the risk of overfunding, an unleveraged ESOP would have allowed NCR to avail itself of tax deductions for depreciation, a savings of potentially hundreds of millions of dollars over the life of the ESOP. However, no one ever presented the board with a meaningful comparison of the two types of ESOPs. The NCR ESOP had a number of unusual features that distinguished it from other ESOPs—indeed, that made it unprecedented (such as the heavy voting provisions, the redemption premium, and the preferred stock's higher dividend yield and price "floor"). As directors, the NCR board had a fiduciary duty to the shareholders. While that duty would not necessarily mandate that the board follow every directive of the majority of shareholders, it surely included some obligation at least to ensure that principles of corporate democracy were not unduly submerged in an attempt by management to entrench itself. Yet the board uncritically accepted the bald assertion that the ESOP would not affect the vote without pausing to question the source of that conclusion. In light of the fact that 70 percent of NCR's shareholders had tendered shares even before AT&T had been able to solicit proxies from individual and retail holders, there should have been at least some informed debate by the directors regarding their duty to the shareholders. The business judgment rule would not protect the transaction because the board had failed to act in an informed capacity. This seems to be the fault both of NCR's management, which did not make the board aware of key information, and of the board itself, which did not ask questions, consider certain consequences, or examine the plan with a critical eye. Under Maryland precedents, in order to determine if the plan was valid, a court must determine if the ESOP had the effect of consolidating or perpetuating management control. The evidence overwhelmingly demonstrated that the primary purpose of the ESOP was to entrench NCR management, in contravention of the principles of corporate democracy. In summary, the evidence had shown the following: The board sought no fairness opinion; a legal opinion regarding the validity of the offer was quickly negotiated; the benefits people were not consulted to any significant degree; there was a general unfamiliarity with the changes in tax laws and accounting rules and no conception of how the plan would be received by employees; and the features of the preferred stock—e.g., the heavy voting provision, the reset provision that negates the risk of market fluctuations, the higher dividend—all were dilutive of the common stock. Finally, these features also created a potential conflict of interest between the two classes of stock. The ESOP was similarly unfair to NCR itself, for the corporation, not the beneficiaries of the stock issue, would foot the bill. Given the plan's internal leveraging, no new capital would flow into the company. Simply put, NCR had locked itself into a large ESOP that NCR could not adjust to meet actual needs. The firm, in deciding to leverage the plan, also had lost significant tax advantages. Hence, AT&T had met its burden of proof of demonstrating that the primary purpose of the NCR ESOP was not benefits related but, rather, an attempt by NCR management to impede corporate democracy and to perpetuate its control of the company. Therefore, AT&T merited a permanent injunction invalidating NCR's ESOP and enjoining the preferred shares issued thereunder from voting at the 28 March 1991 special meeting.

Loyalty

Because directors, officers, and controlling shareholders enjoy positions of trust with the corporation, they must act in good faith and with loyalty toward the corporation and its shareholders. The undivided loyalty expected of fiduciaries means that managers must place the interests of the corporation above their own personal interests. Sometimes these corporate interests and personal interests collide, and it becomes necessary to resort to applicable statutes and decisional law. Usually such collisions involve (1) corporate opportunities or (2) conflicts of interest.

The *corporate opportunity* doctrine forbids directors, officers, and controlling shareholders from diverting to themselves business deals or expectancies that in fairness or in justice belong to the corporation. Personal gains at the expense of the corporation represent a breach of the manager's fiduciary duties.

A corporate opportunity commonly will be found if the manager discovers the opportunity in his or her capacity as director and it is reasonably foreseeable that the corporation would be interested in the opportunity because it relates closely to the corporation's line of business. For example, if Wanda is a director in a real estate development corporation (Real Property Corp.) and Ray offers to sell property to Wanda because he knows she is a director of Real Property, Wanda should not buy the property for herself, since to do so will violate her duty of loyalty. If the corporation would reasonably be interested in the land for its corporate development program, Wanda must disclose this opportunity to the corporation. Once she has given the corporation this "right of first refusal," Wanda ordinarily can purchase the property *if* the corporation refuses the opportunity or is financially unable to effect the purchase.

Constructive trust A trust imposed by law to prevent the unjust enrichment of the purported owner of the "trust" property.

Upon Wanda's breach of the duty of loyalty, corporate remedies include damages (the profits Wanda makes as a result of the sale) or the imposition of a **constructive trust** (a court will treat Wanda as a trustee who is holding the property for the benefit of the corporation). A court then can force Wanda to convey the property to Real Property Corp. and to pay Real Property any profits realized on the transaction.

In the case that follows, the court applied some of these principles.

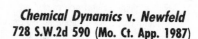

Chemical Dynamics v. *Newfeld*
728 S.W.2d 590 (Mo. Ct. App. 1987)

FACTS   Chemical Dynamics, Inc., which did business as the The Shultz Co., was a close corporation with forty shares, twenty-three of which were held by the Schultz family. A. Y. (Abe) Schultz, Sol Schultz, and Lawrence Newfeld were the managing officers and directors of the corporation. On 6 December 1967, the corporation leased a building for use as its offices and its manufacturing facilities. The lease contained an option provision whereby the corporation could purchase the property for $300,000. In 1970, when the corporation had experienced financial difficulties and had been unable to pay the rent as due, Sol Schultz assigned the lease and purchase option to Newfeld in exchange for Newfeld's advancing the corporation the $21,492.38 needed to avoid the firm's eviction from the building. The owners notified Newfeld in February, 1973, of their willingness to sell the building, even though the option to purchase had already expired. In October, 1973, Newfeld, with the help of Harry and Sol Schultz, purchased the property. In 1975, after all the creditors had been paid, Abe Schultz demanded the return of the property to the corporation. When Newfeld refused to do so, Abe, on behalf of the corporation, sued Newfeld for usurpation of the corporate opportunity represented by the purchase of the property.

ISSUE   Had Newfeld breached his fiduciary duty to the corporation by allegedly seizing for his own benefit the business opportunity of purchasing the building leased by the corporation?

HOLDING   No. Newfeld's purchase had not constituted a corporate opportunity.

REASONING   The corporate opportunity doctrine forbids a corporate director from acquiring for his or her own benefit an opportunity that would have been valuable and germane to the corporation's business, unless that opportunity is first offered to the corporation. If, however, a business opportunity is presented to an officer in his or her individual capacity, rather than in his or her official capacity as an officer or director, the opportunity is that of the officer and not that of the corporation. The test of whether a particular opportunity is an individual or corporate one is largely a question of fact. The pivotal question in this case centers on whether the option to purchase the building constituted a corporate opportunity. On 20 November 1970, the corporation had been in severe financial straits; eviction from its business quarters had been imminent. The corporation had not had the money, the means, or the credit to come up with the money for the back rent. Newfeld had been willing to invest his own funds to save a corporation that was operating at a loss and unable to pay its creditors. Because Newfeld had risked his own money when other experienced businessmen had refused to do so, the assignment of the lease constituted consideration for the business risk Newfeld had been willing to take. Moreover, by A. Y. Schultz's own admission, the corporation had not been in the financial position to buy the building until 1975, two years after the purchase by Newfeld. Hence, Newfeld had not appropriated a business opportunity from the corporation. Rather, he had merely exercised his rights under the lease that the corporation had freely assigned to him. The fact that Sol Schultz and Harry Schultz had helped Newfeld in financing the purchase was also immaterial. Had Newfeld not funded the corporation in 1970, a real danger existed that the corporation could not have continued and that, by 1973, the investment of every shareholder would have been lost. Given these facts, Newfeld was under no duty to exercise the option for the benefit of the corporation. Because the option to purchase the building was an opportunity that had belonged to him in his individual capacity, rather than in his official capacity, Newfeld had not usurped a corporate opportunity so as to justify the imposition of a constructive trust.

Read the following case, which deals with an alleged violation of the fiduciary duty of loyalty, and then ask yourself how you would decide the case if you were the judge.

Steelvest, Inc. v. Scansteel Service Center, Inc.
807 S.W.2d 476 (Ky. 1991)

FACTS   Scanlan had been employed by Steel Suppliers, Inc. (Steel Suppliers), a company engaged in the warehousing and distributing of structural steel, for thirty years and had acted as president and a director. On 21 November 1984, Steelvest, Inc. (Steelvest), a corporation owned by Lucas, purchased the assets of Steel Suppliers for approximately $5 million. After this purchase, Steelvest continued Steel Suppliers, Inc. as a separate, unincorporated division under the same name. At Lucas's request, Scanlan agreed to stay on as president and general manager of Steel Suppliers. He also subsequently became a director of Steelvest and a member of its executive committee. Scanlan's employment with Steel Suppliers continued for eleven months after the purchase by Steelvest. During these eleven months of employment, Scanlan began to formulate a plan to start and incorporate his own steel business, which would compete directly with Steelvest. Toward this end, Scanlan sought the advice of counsel, contacted potential investors, and sought financing. He disclosed none of these activities to any representative of Steelvest. Furthermore, he recruited two chief executive officers of major clients of Steelvest to invest in his new company. Scanlan resigned from his employment with Steel Suppliers and Steelvest on 15 October 1985. One day prior to this, on 14 October, Scanlan had completed most of the necessary arrangements for setting up his new business, including the signing of documents for the purchase of property to be used as the site for the business. Immediately after Scanlan's resignation from Steelvest, he, along with the other investors, incorporated Scansteel Service Center, Inc. (Scansteel), which began actual operations soon after. Nine office and supervisory employees of Steelvest resigned to take employment with Scansteel. Soon after Scanlan's resignation and the formation of Scansteel, Steelvest began experiencing financial difficulties, which eventually forced it to file for bankruptcy. On 2 June 1986, Steelvest instituted this action against Scansteel and Scanlan, alleging a breach of fiduciary duties by Scanlan and a conspiracy on the part of the investors and the bank that had provided the financing for the formation of Scansteel. The circuit court granted the defendants' motions for summary judgment, which decision the court of appeals upheld.

ISSUE   Had Scanlan breached his fiduciary duties to Steelvest by planning and organizing a directly competitive business?

HOLDING   Maybe yes, maybe no. Because genuine issues of fact existed as to this question, the trial court had improperly granted summary judgment in favor of Scansteel and Scanlan.

REASONING   Whether Scanlan, in fact, breached any fiduciary duty to Steelvest by preparing to incorporate his own steel business while still employed with Steelvest constitutes the central issue in this case. If Scanlan was not guilty of any such breach, the other entities, likewise, would not be held responsible for the ensuing civil violations. Generally, in the absence of a contractual provision to the contrary, corporate fiduciaries, such as directors or officers, remain free to resign and form an enterprise that competes with the corporation after they sever their connection with it. Kentucky law has, however, recognized that directors and officers of a corporation may not set up, or attempt to set up, an enterprise that competes with the business in which the corporation is engaged while they are still serving as directors and officers. Thus, they should terminate their position/status as directors or officers when they first make arrangements or begin preparations to compete directly with the employer corporation. In this case, Scanlan was not a mere employee; to the contrary, he served the corporation as both a director and an officer. This relationship provides for an established basis of fiducial confidence. Scanlan, therefore, owed a duty of loyalty and faithfulness to the corporation and a duty not to act against the employer's interest. This concern for the integrity of the employment relationship has led courts to establish a rule that demands of a corporate officer or employee an undivided and unselfish loyalty to the corporation. A direct corollary of this general principle of loyalty is that a corporation officer or other higher-echelon employee is barred from actively competing with his or her employer during the tenure of the employment, even in the absence of an express covenant so providing. Thus, prior to termination of employment, an employee must not solicit for himself or herself business which the position requires the employee to obtain for the employer. The employee must refrain from actively and directly competing with the employer for customers and employees, and must continue to exert his or her best efforts on behalf of the employer. The facts disclose that Scanlan, while still employed with Steelvest, made certain plans, arrangements, and preparations for setting up his own business to compete with Steelvest. He sought legal and accounting advice, made active efforts to acquire bank financing, and recruited investors, two of whom, coincidentally, had served as the chief executive officers of Steelvest's major customers. Scanlan failed to disclose such activities to any representative of Steelvest. There is also some evidence indicating that, prior to his resignation from Steelvest, Scanlan indicated to prospective investors and to bank personnel that he would bring with him some of the present employees of Steelvest. Shortly after Scanlan had resigned from Steelvest, nine office and supervisory employees coincidentally left the company to work for Scansteel. Therefore, genuine issues of material fact respecting Scanlan's alleged breach of fiduciary duty existed; thus, the summary judgment granted in his favor was erroneous.

The most common example of a possible *conflict of interest* occurs when a director, officer, or controlling shareholder personally contracts with the corporation. As an illustration, let us assume that George is a director of Real Property Corporation and that he is willing to sell a piece of his own property to the corporation. Because of his personal interests, George will undoubtedly hope to make as much money as possible on the transaction. Yet his position as a director of Real Property Corporation obligates him to accept as low a price as possible in order to benefit the company. George obviously faces a difficult dilemma. Most states will allow the transaction if George makes a full disclosure of his interest to the board of directors of Real Property Corporation before the board begins its deliberations on the proposed contract and if the resultant contract is fair and reasonable to the corporation. However, whenever George does not fully disclose his interest or if the terms of the contract are unfair or unreasonable, the contract will be voidable by the corporation.

An additional concern in these situations stems from whether George (who is called an "interested" director) should be allowed to vote on the contract. At common law, George could not vote—or even be counted toward the quorum—at the meeting where the matter was to be discussed. Although modern statutes (and articles or bylaws) vary, in general, George can vote and be counted toward the quorum if, as noted earlier, he discloses his interest and the resultant contract is fair to the corporation.

As mentioned in Chapter 40, the duty of loyalty also prohibits directors, officers, or controlling shareholders from prejudicing minority shareholders' rights by "freezing out" minority shareholders through such actions as forcing dissolution of the corporation or changing liquidation preferences.

In the context of corporate takeovers, allegations of breach of fiduciary duties commonly arise. As the sophistication of both the "raider" and the target corporation has increased, directors of the latter have responded creatively (and metaphorically) to mount a host of defensive moves meant to blunt the would-be acquiring firm's appetite for the target corporation. The development of exotic (but apt) terms such as **greenmail** and poison pill to describe these thrusts and countermeasures masks the more important issue

Greenmail A term describing the process by which a firm threatens a corporate takeover by buying a significant portion of a corporation's stock and then selling it back to the corporation at a premium when the corporation's directors and executives, fearing for their positions, agree to buy the firm out.

of whether the law will approve of these deterrent efforts. The next case is illustrative of a typical poison pill.

Unocal Corporation v. Mesa Petroleum Company
493 A.2d 946 (Del. 1985)

FACTS   On 8 April 1985, Mesa Petroleum Company (Mesa), the owner of approximately 13 percent of Unocal Corporation's (Unocal's) stock, commenced a two-tier "front-loaded" cash tender offer for 64 million shares, or approximately 37 percent of Unocal's outstanding stock, at a price of $54 per share. The "back-end," or second tier of the offer, consisted of "junk bonds" that would change Unocal's capitalization significantly from its present structure. Unocal's board of directors met on 13 April 1985 to consider the Mesa tender offer. The next day the board passed a resolution providing that if Mesa acquired 64 million shares of Unocal stock through its own offer, Unocal would buy the remaining 49 percent outstanding for an exchange of debt securities having an aggregate par value of $72 per share. The board resolution also stated that the offer would be subject to other conditions, including the exclusion of Mesa from the proposal. When Unocal initiated its exchange offer on 17 April 1985, Mesa immediately filed suit. On 22 April, the Unocal board met again and, on the advice of its investment bankers, waived the Mesa exclusion as to 50 million shares. This fact notwithstanding, Mesa in its lawsuit contended that (1) Unocal's discriminatory exchange offer violated the fiduciary duties Unocal owed it, and (2) the directors' conduct fell outside the application of the business judgment rule because the directors, by tendering their own shares, would derive a financial benefit that was not available to all shareholders.

ISSUES   Did the Unocal board have the power and duty to adopt a defensive self-tender offer to oppose a takeover threat it perceived to be harmful to the corporation? If so, was its action entitled to the protection of the business judgment rule?

HOLDING   Yes. Delaware law gives the board inherent power to deal selectively with its stockholders, provided that the directors have not acted solely to entrench themselves in office. Indeed, the board's power to act arises from its fundamental duty and obligation to protect the corporation's stockholders from perceived harm, irrespective of its source. Since the board's actions had been reasonable in relation to the threat posed and had been motivated by a good faith concern for the welfare of the corporation and its stockholders, the business judgment rule was available to the directors as a defense.

REASONING   The business judgment rule is a presumption that, in making a business decision, the directors of a corporation have acted on an informed basis, in good faith, and in the honest belief that the action taken was in the best interests of the company. In such circumstances, the judiciary should not substitute its judgment for that of the board if the latter's decision can be attributed to any rational business purpose. Here, the Unocal directors had concluded that the value of Unocal was substantially above the $54 per share, cash, "front-end" offer. Furthermore, they had determined that the subordinated securities to be exchanged in Mesa's announced squeeze-out of the remaining shareholders in the "back-end" tier of the merger were "junk bonds" worth far less than $54. Such a two-tier offer ordinarily represents a classic coercive measure designed to stampede shareholders into tendering at the first tier, even if the price is inadequate, out of fear of what they will receive at the back end of the transaction. Wholly beyond the coercive aspect of an inadequate two-tier tender offer, this threat had been posed by a corporate raider with a national reputation as a "greenmailer." Hence, in adopting the selective exchange offer, the board's stated objective had been either to defeat the inadequate Mesa offer or, should the offer still succeed, to provide the 49 percent of its stockholders, who would otherwise be forced to accept "junk bonds," with $72 worth of senior debt. Both purposes were valid, and such efforts would have been thwarted by Mesa's participation in the exchange offer in several respects. First, if Mesa could have tendered its shares, Unocal would have been effectively subsidizing the former's continuing effort to buy Unocal stock at $54 per share. Second, Mesa could not have, by definition, fit within the class of shareholders being protected from its own coercive and inadequate tender offer. Thus, the board's decision to offer what it had determined to be the fair value of the corporation to the 49 percent of its shareholders who would otherwise have been forced to accept highly subordinated "junk bonds" was reasonable and consistent with the directors' duty to ensure that the minority stockholders received equal value for their shares. Thus, the Unocal directors possessed the power to oppose the Mesa tender offer and to undertake a self-tender offer made in good faith and upon a reasonable investigation pursuant to a clear duty to protect the corporate enterprise. Further, the selective stock repurchase plan chosen by Unocal was reasonable in relation to the threat that the board rationally and reasonably had believed was posed by Mesa's inadequate and coercive two-tier tender offer. Under those circumstances, the board's action was entitled to be measured by the standards of the business judgment rule. Thus, unless it were shown by a preponderance of the evidence that the directors' decisions had been primarily based on perpetuating themselves in office, or some other breach of fiduciary duty such as fraud, overreaching, lack of good faith, or being uninformed, a court should not have substituted its judgment for that of the board. Given the lower courts' findings that the exchange offer had been predicated on the board's good faith belief that the Mesa offer was inadequate, that the board's action had been informed and taken with due care, that Mesa's prior activities had justified a reasonable inference that its principal objective was greenmail, and implicitly, that the substance of the offer itself had been reasonable and fair to the corporation and its stockholders if Mesa were included, it would have been inappropriate to hold that the Unocal directors had acted in such a manner as to have passed an unintelligent and unadvised judgment. Hence, the directors could rely on the business judgment rule to justify their actions.

LIABILITY UNDER FEDERAL SECURITIES LAWS

Corporate managers who violate the Securities Act of 1933 (the '33 Act) and the Securities Exchange Act of 1934 (the '34 Act) may incur liability as well. Because both acts will be discussed in Chapter 44, it is sufficient to note here the broad outlines of possible liability.

Registration statements
Formal statements about securities that are filed by corporations with the Securities and Exchange Commission before offering an issue of securities for sale to the public.

The '33 Act is basically a disclosure statute and thus requires that **registration statements** be filed with the Securities and Exchange Commission (SEC), the federal agency that oversees the enforcement of federal securities laws, whenever certain securities are initially offered to the public through the mails or through interstate commerce. The '33 Act also requires that any information that goes into the prospectus (the description of the securities that is given to every prospective purchaser of the securities) be true. False or misleading assertions in either the registration statement or the prospectus or any material omissions in these documents may subject a wide array of corporate personnel to liability. Directors, officers, attorneys, and auditors/accountants—anyone who has signed the registration statement or provided expert information incorporated either in this statement or in the prospectus (such as investment bankers)—may incur liability.

The '34 Act augments the '33 Act by regulating securities after their initial issue. Congress designed this act to prohibit fraud in the national markets that trade stocks and to ensure the fairness of securities transactions generally.

FIGURE 41.1 Management of the Corporation

DIRECTORS **OFFICERS**

Duties/Responsibilities
1. Management of corporation and setting of overall policies.
2. Delegation of managerial authority to officers and executives.
3. Selection and/or possible removal of officers.
4. Determination of officers' salaries.
5. Obligation to exercise independent, disinterested judgment.

Duties/Responsibilities
1. Oversight of day-to-day operations of the firm.
2. Execution of policies established by board of directors.
3. Fulfillment of agents' applicable duties.

Liability
1. Failure to abide by applicable fiduciary duties.
2. Failure to comply with securities laws.
3. Indemnification and/or insurance possibly available to offset personal liability.

Rights
1. Authority to bind corporation in certain situations owing to agency.
2. Compensation.
3. Court review of removal in certain situations.

Rights
1. Actions by a quorum of directors generally binding on corporation.
2. Appointment of interim replacements on board when vacancies arise.
3. Declaration of dividends.
4. Inspection of corporate records.
5. Court review of removal in certain situations.

FIDUCIARY DUTIES

Diligence
Obliges managers to perform their duties with due care; i.e., in a non-negligent fashion.

Loyalty
Obliges managers to show undivided loyalty to corporation; i.e., to place corporate interests above their own personal interests.

Obedience
Obliges managers to avoid illegal and/or ultra vires acts.

Business Judgment Rule (BJR)
Covers errors made by managers in exercise of good faith and in the absence of clear and gross negligence; if applicable, exonerates managers from personal liability.

Situations Giving Rise to Potential Breach

Corporate Opportunities
Managers' diversion to themselves of deals or expectancies that in fairness and justice belong to the corporation.

Conflicts of Interest
Personal interests of managers at odds with corporation's interests; necessitates full disclosure to corporation of conflicts.

Freeze-outs of Minority Shareholders
Actions by managers that prejudice minority shareholders' rights; e.g., changing liquidation preferences to benefit controlling shareholders at expense of minority shareholders.

Section 10b of the '34 Act, and especially Rule 10b-5 of this section, prohibits deceitful and fraudulent purchases or sales of securities made on the basis of "material inside information." This prevents "insiders"—usually directors, officers, dominant shareholders, or other corporate personnel—from buying or selling stock on the basis of information that is not yet available to the investing public. "Insiders" must either disclose the "material inside information" or abstain from securities activity until the information reaches the investing public. Insiders (and "tippees," those who have learned material information from "insiders") face liability for violation of Section 10b and Rule 10b-5.

Directors, officers, and stockholders who own 10 percent or more of a corporation's stock may incur liability for violations of Section 16b of the '34 Act. Section 16b forbids "short-swing profits," those profits realized by these three classes of insiders on any purchase and sale (or vice versa) of the corporation's stock within a six-month period. Insiders violating this section must return their profits to the corporation. This represents yet another method for protecting the investing public from market manipulations by those who *may*, by virtue of their positions, have access to material inside information.

As mentioned in Chapter 40, proxy solicitations also fall within the purview of the '34 Act. Section 14a requires that proxy solicitations sent to shareholders be accurate and truthful so that shareholders can make an informed decision about how they wish their proxies to be voted. False and misleading proxy statements ordinarily make corporate managers subject to personal liability.

These federal laws, supplementing as they do state securities law and state corporate and decisional law, round out our discussion of the various ways directors, officers, controlling shareholders, and other corporate personnel may incur liability. Corporate managers should tread warily in these areas.

SUMMARY

The right to manage the corporation falls squarely on the board of directors. Shareholders cannot compel directors to take any action, because the directors are not the agents of the shareholders but, rather, owe loyalty primarily to the corporation. The modern trend is to lower the number of directors and to lessen the traditionally stringent rules concerning directors' qualifications. Directors generally are qualified to appoint replacements on the board when vacancies arise due to death, resignation, or incapacity. Directors usually serve for one year unless the corporation has established a "classified" board. In many jurisdictions, shareholders can remove a director with or without cause.

Today, most modern statutes dispense with the formalities required of directors' meetings in the past. Directors' meetings may even occur without prior notice if the directors subsequently manifest their consent to the meeting.

Unless the articles or bylaws set a higher or lower percentage, a simple majority of the directors ordinarily constitutes a quorum. Actions taken by a quorum of directors are binding on the corporation. Normally, each director casts his or her vote in person. Except in close corporations, directors' prior agreements about how they will vote on corporate matters are void on public policy grounds.

Most statutes authorize the board of directors to delegate managerial authority to officers and executive committees. Broad delegations of authority to persons outside the directorial ranks are usually invalid.

Directors may or may not receive compensation from the corporation. The directors normally determine officers' compensation. Such compensation packages are usually legal if reasonable in amount. Otherwise, a shareholder can attack the compensation as a "waste" of corporate assets.

Performance of directorial duties may lead to personal liability for directors. Sometimes, though, the corporation will indemnify the directors for liabilities accruing from their corporate positions. Directors have the right to declare dividends, enter into agreements, and inspect corporate records.

Officers are agents of the corporation and thus must live up to the fiduciary duties placed on agents. The board ordinarily appoints the officers, who serve at the will of the directors. Officers may bind the corporation by express, implied, or apparent authority. But the unauthorized acts of officers may make them personally liable to the other contracting party.

Directors, officers, and controlling shareholders owe fiduciary duties to the corporation. Broadly speaking, these duties fall into three categories: The duty of obedience, the duty of diligence (or due care), and the duty of loyalty. The duty of obedience forbids ultra vires acts. The "business judgment rule" constitutes a defense to liability for violation of the duty of diligence. Under this rule, the manager will not be liable if he or she makes an erroneous decision in good faith and without clear and gross negligence. The duty of loyalty, among other things, precludes directors, officers, and controlling shareholders from usurping corporate opportunities or prejudicing the corporation because of undisclosed conflicts of interest.

Corporate managers may also be liable for violations of the federal securities laws' registration, antifraud, and proxy solicitation rules.

DISCUSSION QUESTIONS

1. Describe the various powers vested in directors.
2. In what ways have statutes dispensed with the formalities previously required of directors' meetings?
3. What are the boundaries of directors' delegations of authority to officers and corporate committees?

4. Explain briefly directors' responsibilities regarding officers' compensation and their own salaries.
5. Briefly enumerate the rights and liabilities of directors. How do officers' rights and liabilities differ from those of directors?

6. Name and define the three sources of an officer's authority to bind the corporation.

7. Explain the three broad categories of fiduciary duties owed to the corporation by directors, officers, and controlling shareholders.

8. What is the "business judgment rule"?

9. Explain how a corporate manager may "usurp a corporate opportunity."

10. In what ways can corporate managers prevent charges of conflicts of interest from being levied against them?

CASE PROBLEMS

1. Wilhite was the president of Growers Supply, Inc. (Growers Supply), a wholesale garden and lawn supply business. Panzico was a shareholder who had another business for which he made purchases from Growers Supply. In 1977 and 1978, Panzico approached Wilhite about withdrawing from the corporation. On 31 May 1978, Panzico allegedly surrendered his $8750 worth of stock to Wilhite as partial payment on his account with Growers Supply and paid the remaining balance of $5920.14 on 5 June 1978. Panzico continued to make purchases for his business after this date but otherwise had no connection with Growers Supply. After two years passed, the other corporate shareholder, McCarty, purchased the accounts receivable of the firm, which had gone bankrupt. McCarty then sued Panzico for $8750 on the rationale that he had been unaware of Wilhite's acceptance of the stock surrender and that Wilhite's authority as president had not extended to the acceptance of surrendered stock as partial payment of a debt. How should the court rule in this case? (*McCarty* v. *Panzico,* 467 So.2d 1229 [La. Ct. App. 1985].)

2. The Greenblatt family had controlled Amfesco Industries, Inc., a corporation engaged in the manufacture of athletic and casual footware for ninety years. Going public in 1971, the firm sold one-third of its stock to public investors; and the families of defendants David and Allan Greenblatt retained the remaining two-thirds in equal shares. In June, 1982, David Greenblatt acquired his brother's shares through a leveraged buyout using the corporation's assets. After the corporation purchased Allan Greenblatt's stock for $12,720,000, David Greenblatt sought to refinance the corporation's debt by selling new shares to public investors. The plaintiff, the secured creditors' committee in subsequent bankruptcy proceedings, contended that after Allan Greenblatt had resigned, leaving David in complete control of the company, David had operated the company solely for his own pecuniary advantage. According

to the committee, he purportedly had extracted kickbacks from commissioned salespersons and had concealed a decline in the company's earnings caused by the lifting of embargo restrictions on foreign competitors. In order to delay revealing the corporation's declining prospects until his own stock holdings could be liquidated, David Greenblatt and the other directors also had purportedly portrayed the corporation as a growing and profitable enterprise while at the same time incurring additional liabilities for capital improvements that the company could never repay. The committee further alleged that, for three years following the leveraged buyout, the directors had made public offerings of newly issued corporate stock to provide the corporation with the equity capital needed to refinance the leveraged buyout debt and also to provide it with new capital to conceal operating losses. They also had made secondary offerings of stock owned by David Greenblatt's family to enable them to sell those holdings before the corporation's losses became known. Despite these operating losses, the defendants had invested more than $20 million of the corporation's funds in useless new production facilities. The committee asserted that the defendants also had caused the corporation to incur over $37 million in bank debts that it could not repay and had induced public investors to pay more than $21 million for virtually worthless corporate stock. At the same time, the defendants allegedly had granted themselves increased bonuses, salaries, and other forms of compensation until 1985, when the corporation filed for bankruptcy. In these circumstances, could the directors invoke the business judgment rule to insulate themselves from personal liability? *Amfesco Industries, Inc.* v. *Greenblatt,* 568 N.Y.S.2d 593 [A.D. 1 Dept. 1991].)

3. Leader and other former minority shareholders of Hycor, Inc. (Hycor) sued the majority shareholders for their actions in amending the articles of incorporation and the resultant recapitalization of the corporation from

the original authorized capital stock of 2 million shares with a par value of $.01 to five hundred shares with a par value of $40. Under the amended articles, each "old share" would be worth 1/4000 of a "new share." In addition, no capital shares would be recognized after the recapitalization (or "reverse stock split"); each holder of a fractional share would instead receive $5 on the surrender of each "old" share certificate. The majority shareholders justified their action of "going private" as a result of the poor market performance of the stock and the low dividends produced in the past. What legal theory should the minority shareholders have used in contesting these actions? (*Leader* v. *Hycor, Inc.,* 479 N.E.2d 173 [Mass. 1985].)

4. Shields was the president and a board member of Production Finishing Corporation (Production Finishing) from January, 1974, through August, 1981. Production Finishing at that time was responsible for most, if not all, of the polishing work in the Detroit area with the exception of the polishing work for Ford Motor Company (Ford), which had its own polishing plant in Monroe, Michigan. A long-standing objective of Production Finishing was to obtain the Ford business if Ford ever decided to cease its operations in that area. Shields, as a representative of Production Finishing, approached Ford on a regular basis with proposals to let Production Finishing do its polishing work. When Shields learned that Ford was considering ceasing its polishing operations, he brought this information to the attention of Production Finishing's board of directors at a meeting on 29 April 1981. Pursuant to the board's request, Shields then contacted the manager of the Ford Motor Monroe Plant and arranged a meeting at which Production Finishing's proposal to obtain Ford's polishing business was discussed. The manager did not favor the proposal because, with the Ford business, Production Finishing would have a monopoly in the area. On the basis of this statement, at some point in the discussion, Shields asked the manager if Ford would let him do the work in his individual capacity. Shields incorporated Flat Rock Metal on 8 July 1981, with the intent that Flat Rock would perform the polishing services for Ford. Shields, as the president and controlling stockholder of Flat Rock, throughout his dealings with Ford, did not inform the Production Finishing board of directors that Ford had refused to give its business to Production Finishing or that Shields was pursuing the Ford opportunity on his own account. However, Shields did disclose his intentions to Omer O'Neil and informed O'Neil of

Ford's refusal in this regard when he asked O'Neil to leave Production Finishing and go with him to his new company. O'Neil was never a member of the board of directors and, in fact, reported to Shields at Production Finishing. Should a court hold Shields liable for breach of fiduciary duties for his failure to disclose Ford's refusal to Production Finishing, or did he satisfy this duty of disclosure by informing O'Neil of this refusal? (*Production Finishing Corporation* v. *Shields,* 405 N.W.2d 171 [Mich. App. 1987].)

5. Eli W. Kaufman, a former vice-president and general sales manager in the radio division of CBS, Inc. (CBS), sought indemnification from CBS for his share of costs incurred in defending and settling a suit brought against him by a female employee. At a well-attended business dinner, in an apparent attempt to be humorous, he had grabbed a piece of the female subordinate's clothing and had made a lewd remark about her in public. The New York statute allowed indemnification whenever the corporate officer had acted in good faith for a purpose reasonably believed to be in the best interests of the corporation. Were Kaufman's actions within the scope of this statutory provision so as to warrant indemnification? (*Kaufman* v. *CBS, Inc.,* 514 N.Y.S.2d 620 [N.Y. Civ. Ct. 1987].)

6. Doemling incorporated Specialty Plastics, Inc. (Specialty) in 1975 to manufacture and sell plastic containers to another business he owned, Imaging Systems Corp. Doemling was the sole shareholder of Specialty and served on its board of directors. When Specialty declared bankruptcy in December, 1982, Doemling was serving as its president. In early 1981, Doemling personally purchased a B75 and a B100 blow molder and related equipment and leased both machines to Specialty. During the lease term, Specialty was responsible for the equipment's installation, maintenance, and repair. In June, 1982, Doemling personally purchased a Uniloy 300 blow molder and related equipment and leased it to Specialty. Doemling purchased all of this equipment in his personal capacity; Specialty's board of directors had approved none of the leases. In December, 1982, Doemling unilaterally terminated Specialty's leases on the B100 blow molder and the Uniloy 300 blow molder. He sold the B100 molder to a third party for $65,000 and the Uniloy 300 for $72,500. These sales resulted in substantial personal profits ($38,000) for Doemling. On 1 May 1984, Doemling unilaterally terminated Specialty's remaining lease on the B75 blow molder. He sold the B75 to a third party for $85,000

and thus realized an additional profit of $50,500. During the course of the three leases, Specialty had paid Doemling a total of $24,300 in rental payments. Specialty also had expended an additional $23,331 for the installation, maintenance, and repair of the three blow molders and related equipment. When Specialty filed for bankruptcy under Chapter 11, the bankruptcy court concluded that Doemling had usurped a corporate opportunity that had properly belonged to Specialty. It therefore ordered Doemling to disgorge any profits he had made through this opportunity and to pay Specialty all the money he had received in rent; all the profits he had realized as a result of the sale of the three blow molders; and all the money Specialty had spent for the installation, repair, and maintenance of the machines. The bankruptcy court further found that Doemling's actions with regard to the purchase and leasing of these machines had constituted defalcation (misconduct, moral dereliction) and therefore held that Doemling's obligation to repay these monies was nondischargeable in bankruptcy. Should the appellate court uphold the bankruptcy court's decision? (*Committee of Unsecured Creditors of Specialty Plastics, Inc.* v. *Doemling,* 127 Bankr. 945 [W.D. Pa. 1991].)

7. n 1984, the directors of Household International, Inc. (Household) approved a preferred stock rights dividend plan (the "Rights Plan") in an attempt to prevent hostile takeovers. Although very complicated, the "Rights Plan" basically set out a process by which shareholders could both exchange a new series of preferred stock upon the payment of an exercise price of $100 per share and purchase the common stock of the acquiring corporation at a price reflecting a market value of twice the exercise price of the right. In other words, a Household shareholder could buy $200 worth of the acquiring corporation's common stock for $100. The exercise of these rights could occur only if a corporation gained control of 20 percent of Household's common shares or made a tender offer for 30 percent of Household's outstanding stock. Should neither of these "triggering events" occur, the rights could not be exercised. Moran, one of the two directors who had voted against the "Rights Plan," had argued that it would cost the shareholders their ability to sell their shares to an acquiring company at a premium over market value and thus would deprive shareholders of significant property rights without their approval. Would the business judgment rule protect the directors' actions in these circumstances? (*Moran* v. *Household International, Inc.,* 490

A.2d 1059 [Del. Ch. 1985], aff'd 500 A.2d 1346 [Del. 1985].)

8. When Pantry Pride Inc. (Pantry Pride) had made a hostile tender offer for Revlon, Inc. (Revlon), Revlon had adopted a "poison pill" Note Purchase Rights Plan in order to thwart the takeover and the allegedly grossly inadequate offer ($45 per share). The Note Purchase Rights Plan consisted of a self-tender for 10 million shares on 29 August 1985, each share paid for with one subordinated note worth $47.50 plus 1/10 of a $9 cumulative convertible preferred share valued at $100 per share. Revlon shareholders thereupon tendered 87 percent of the approximately 33 million outstanding shares. The notes contained covenants limiting Revlon from incurring additional debt, selling assets, or paying dividends without the independent board members' approval. For the next two months, while Revlon continued to search for a "white knight," Pantry Pride increased its offer, culminating in a price of $56.25 on 7 October. Forstmann Little & Co. (Forstmann) offered to pay $57.25 per share on 12 October in exchange for Revlon's waiving the loan covenants, Revlon's giving it a "lock-up" option on two divisions (which would allow Forstmann to buy these for $100–175 million below their appraised value), and Revlon's accepting a "no-shop" provision (i.e., Revlon would promise to refrain from seeking a more attractive offer). Forstmann, in turn, promised to support the notes' par value because the announcement of the covenant waiver had resulted in a sagging market price owing to threatened litigation by the holders of the notes. The directors argued that they had fulfilled their duties of care and loyalty by entering into negotiations with a "white knight" in order to protect the noteholders. However, Pantry Pride, in seeking injunctive relief from the Note Purchase Rights Plan, argued that the "lock-up"/"no shop" provisions authorized by the Revlon board would not satisfy either the board's duty of care or the business judgment rule because, once the board had authorized the sale of the company to a third party, its responsibilities under *Unocal* had changed. Pantry Pride reasoned that the original threat posed by Pantry Pride—the break-up of the company—had become a reality that even the directors had accepted. Selective dealing to fend off a hostile but determined bidder was no longer a proper objective. Instead, obtaining the highest price for the benefit of the stockholders should have been the central theme guiding director action. According to Pantry Pride, the noteholders required no further pro-

tection, and when the Revlon board entered into an auction-ending lock-up agreement with Forstmann on the basis of impermissible considerations at the expense of the shareholders, the directors had breached their primary duty of loyalty. Favoritism for a white knight to the total exclusion of a hostile bidder might be justifiable when the latter's offer would adversely affect shareholder interests; but when bidders had made relatively similar offers, or dissolution of the company had become inevitable, the directors could not fulfill their enhanced *Unocal* duties by playing favorites with the contending factions. Rather, the directors must allow market forces to operate freely to bring the target's shareholders the best price available for their equity. Should a court uphold Pantry Pride's contentions? (*Revlon, Inc.* v. *MacAndrew & Forbes Holdings, Inc.*, 506 A.2d 173 [Del. 1986].)

9. Highland Community Bank is a successful minority bank in the southern part of Chicago. Its president and CEO, George Brokemond, decided in 1983 to experiment with creating a separate marketing staff in the bank. He hired Linda Hurley to head up the new staff; and on 1 March 1984, Hurley hired Marjorie Price, the plaintiff, for the marketing staff. Price at the time was working in a different capacity for Continental Bank; but Continental had just announced a reduction in force that would abolish Price's job, and her prospects for finding another job within Continental were shaky. She initially accepted a substantial reduction in salary to come to Highland—from $37,500 to $25,000. According to Price's testimony, which Hurley corroborated, Price had accepted a lower salary than she was getting at Continental in part because Price had been promised an incentive-compensation plan, which she had not had at Continental. Price remained at Highland Community Bank for two years and eight months, leaving voluntarily to accept a marketing position at another minority bank in Chicago. She received no incentive compensation at Highland—indeed, no incentive-compensation plan was ever put into effect—and this, she testified, constituted the determining factor in her decision to leave. Price ultimately brought suit against the bank and Brokemond on the grounds of fraud and breach of contract. She claimed that Brokemond, in two letters to her, had promised her an incentive-compensation plan. In contrast, Brokemond viewed the terms sketched in one of his letters as preliminary thoughts, tentative and nonbinding, speculative and ruminative. He testified that he had never progressed to the point of settling on the terms of the program and putting it into effect. This alleged inaction had stemmed in part from his dissatisfaction with the marketing staff, which he regarded as an experiment and ultimately as a failed experiment. Brokemond avowedly considered himself the principal marketer of the bank's products and doubted whether the bank could ever justify the cost of the marketing department; indeed, the bank ultimately abolished this department. Would both Brokemond and the bank face liability for fraud in these circumstances? (*Price* v. *Highland Community Bank*, 722 F. Supp. 454 [N.D. Ill. 1989].)

10. James Covington, the owner of Mexico Feed and Seed Company (Mexico), in the mid-1960s entered into an oral lease agreement with Jack Pierce, the president of Pierce Oil Waste Service, Inc. (PWOS), for the placement by PWOS of waste oil tanks on a parcel of land owned by Covington and used as the site for Mexico. During 1967–1976, PWOS employees hauled various types of oils, including transformer oils. Many transformers contained PCBs (polychlorinated byphenyls) during that time. One of PWOS's customers was Mid-Mo Electric Company (Mid-Mo), a rebuilder of transformers. A PWOS driver pumped waste oil directly out of transformers at Mid-Mo and hauled the oil to the Mexico site. In 1985, PCBs were found at the Mid-Mo location, later designated as a PCB Superfund site. During that time, PWOS drivers also hauled oil from Findett, a company that reclaimed fluids from Monsanto Company. Until about 1979, Monsanto was the major manufacturer of PCBs in the United States. PWOS drivers also regularly collected oil from other companies using products showing the presence of PCBs and in fact never rejected any customers' oil because of its contents. Mexico never used the PWOS tanks for its own purposes, never agreed to accept ownership of the tanks in lieu of rental payments, and never listed the tanks as an asset of Mexico Feed and Seed Company or of James and Mary Covington. In June and July, 1984, a representative of the U. S. Environmental Protection Agency inspected the Mexico site for the presence of PCBs, which federal regulations list as "hazardous substances." At the time of the inspection, waste oil sludge, which can contain PCBs, was present in all four tanks; and water dripped from the valve of one of the tanks. The inspection revealed that two of the tanks contained high concentrations of PCBs (80 percent and 74 percent) and that the other two tanks contained traces of PCBs. A chemist with the EPA who had conducted tests on the

samples taken from the site testified that an area becomes a cleanup site when the soil contains 50 parts per million of PCBs. Samples of soil from the tank area revealed 330 parts per million of PCBs. The chemist concluded that the Mexico site was contaminated and that the contamination area radiated out from the tanks for about 100 feet. Moreover, the incorporation of the PCBs into the environment over a period of time (weathering) had occurred, indicating that the initial point of contamination had begun as much as twenty years before. The United States "cleaned up" the site and incurred response costs of over $1,024,321.79 under the Comprehensive Environmental Response, Compensation and Liability Act (CERCLA). Congress had enacted CERCLA in 1980 as a response to hazardous waste problems. According to 42 U.S.C. Section 9607(a), the United States is authorized to sue to recover for damage to natural resources and for "all costs of removal or remedial action." A liable person is "any person who at the time of the disposal of any hazardous substance owned or operated any facility at which such hazardous substances were disposed of." Was Jack Pierce, the president of PWOS, liable under CERCLA? (*United States* v. *Mexico Feed and Seed Company,* 764 F. Supp. 565 [E.D. Mo. 1991].)

CHAPTER 42

Dissolution, Merger, Consolidation, and Other Acquisitions

OUTLINE

FUNDAMENTAL CHANGES IN CORPORATE STRUCTURE

In Chapter 40, we briefly touched on the subject of dissolution when we discussed shareholders' rights in the event of the liquidation of the corporation. So far, though, we have paid scant attention to fundamental changes in the corporate structure that may endanger the rights of shareholders and creditors. Actions bringing about some of these fundamental changes—dissolution, merger and consolidation, sale of substantially all the corporate assets, and stock acquisition—form the central focus of this chapter.

DISSOLUTION

As noted earlier, dissolution involves termination of the corporation as a legal entity, or juristic person. The term *dissolution* is not synonymous with *liquidation,* which refers to the winding up or termination of the corporation's business or affairs. To coin a metaphor, if the filing of the articles of incorporation represents the "alpha" of corporate existence, dissolution represents the "omega." Corporate existence remains impervious to most events, including such unusual occurrences as bankruptcy or the cessation of business activities. Dissolution, then, because it represents an extraordinary circumstance, or an organic change in corporate structure, must occur formally in order to have legal effect. Dissolutions are of two types: voluntary and involuntary.

Voluntary Dissolution   As we learned in Chapter 39, corporations theoretically can exist perpetually. On the other hand, a corporation's articles may limit the period of corporate life to, say, ten years. Alternatively, the incorporators may decide at some point to end the corporation's existence, even though the articles specify the perpetual duration of the corporation. In both cases, such voluntary dissolutions must be carried out through formal procedures. Statutes ordinarily set out the requirements for these nonjudicial, voluntary dissolutions. Typically, these statutes mandate board action recommending dissolution, shareholder voting to approve the dissolution (usually by the holders of two-thirds of the outstanding shares), and/or filing of a notice to creditors prior to dissolution. On compliance with these and any other necessary procedures, a certificate of dissolution should be filed with the secretary of state or other designated state officer. At this time, the dissolution is legally effective. Remember, though, that liquidation may follow or precede dissolution; so it is possible that some limited corporate activity may occur after dissolution. On voluntary liquidation, the shareholders share proportionately—subject, of course, to any liquidation preferences—in the net assets of the corporation that remain after satisfaction of creditors' claims. As discussed in earlier chapters, courts will prohibit dissolutions that "freeze out" minority shareholders, especially if a controlling shareholder has initiated the dissolution. Also, be aware that the rules regarding dissolutions may vary when a close corporation, instead of a publicly held corporation, is involved.

Involuntary Dissolution

Occasionally, the state, the shareholders, or the corporation's creditors may request the dissolution of the corporation. Such judicial proceedings are involuntary because this time the corporation itself is not asking for dissolution; rather, other constituents are requesting a court to terminate the corporation's existence because of corporate wrongdoings or prejudice to shareholders or creditors. Involuntary dissolutions by their very nature occur less frequently than voluntary ones.

Dissolution at the Request of the State   Because the corporation is a creation of the state, the state retains the power to rescind the corporation's certificate when the corporation's actions present a clear danger to the public. For instance, the state may ask for involuntary dissolution of a corporation that has engaged in systematic securities fraud. More often, however, grounds for involuntary dissolution involve noncompliance with state requirements, such as failure to pay taxes or to file annual reports. In lieu of petitions for involuntary dissolution, the state may seek suspension of the corporation. Suspension works as a deprivation of the corporation's right to conduct its business and certain other powers, but it is not as drastic or as permanent a remedy as dissolution. On compliance with corporate statutes, the state can order a reinstatement of the corporation.

A rather novel case dealing with these issues follows.

Benton v. County of Napa
277 Cal. Rptr. 541 (Cal. App. 1 Dist. 1991)

FACTS

On 1 September 1987, the County of Napa (Napa County) granted a use permit to Whitbread of California, Inc. (Whitbread) allowing it to construct and operate a winery and related facilities on property near Soda Canyon Road. The permit was valid for one year. On 1 February 1988 the state suspended Whitbread's corporate powers as a result of its failure to pay corporate taxes. On 5 July Napa County amended its ordinance pertaining to the expiration of use permits, permitting administrative approval of extensions. The previous ordinance had required a duly noticed public hearing as a precondition of an extension. The amended ordinance was to take effect on 4 August. In July, Whitbread filed requests for an administrative extension of the permit and for **tolling** of the use permit to allow the permit to remain valid until after the resolution of a lawsuit between Whitbread and nearby property owners Benton and Schreuder. By a letter dated 1 August, Napa County granted administrative approval of the permit extension. On 30 August, the Napa County board of supervisors approved the request for tolling the use permit after holding a public hearing on the matter. On 14 December, Schreuder sent a letter asking Napa County to declare that Whitbread's use permit had expired on 1 September because of the suspension of its corporate powers. Apparently, Whitbread first learned of this suspension on its receipt of a copy of Schreuder's letter. On 22 December Whitbread revived its corporate status by paying the back taxes owed. By 23 February 1989, when Schreuder had received no response to his 14 December letter, he sent a second letter to Napa County counsel, repeating his earlier request. On 12 May 1989, Schreuder filed an administrative appeal of the extension and tolling approvals with the

Tolling Removing a bar to an action in order to allow something to remain in effect.

county. On 20 June 1989, Whitbread requested another administrative amendment of the use permit, effectively tolling the expiration of the use permit until all administrative and judicial actions concerning the permit had been finally resolved in Whitbread's favor. On 7 July 1989, the county approved the requested administrative amendment. On 13 September 1989, Benton and Schreuder petitioned for a revocation of Napa County's issuance of the extension, effectively revoking the underlying use permit and any related construction permits. Benton and Schreuder argued that Whitbread had lacked the legal authority to request an extension or tolling of the use permit in 1988 when its corporate powers had been suspended. After a hearing, the trial court found that Whitbread's December, 1988, revivor of corporate powers had retroactively validated its earlier requests for extension and tolling. The court also ruled that the board had had authority to act regardless of whether Whitbread's corporate powers had been suspended. Benton and Schreuder appealed this decision.

ISSUE   Did the December reinstatement of Whitbread's corporate status after the expiration of the use permit in September retroactively validate the August extension?

HOLDING   Yes. The issuance of the certificate of revivor on 22 December 1988 reinstated all of Whitbread's powers, including the August extension.

REASONING   Under California law, the corporate powers, rights, and privileges of a domestic corporation may be suspended for the nonpayment of corporate taxes. The Franchise Tax Board transmits the names of such corporations to the secretary of state, whose certificate constitutes prima facie evidence of suspension. A taxpayer that has had its corporate powers suspended may be relieved from suspension if it pays the taxes, penalties, and interest owed. Once payment has been made, the Franchise Tax Board issues a certificate of revivor, which serves as prima facie evidence of reinstatement. The legal rights of a suspended corporation are then revived. In the case at bar, Whitbread's powers became reinstated on 22 December 1988 when it obtained a certificate of revivor. On the issuance of this certificate, Whitbread, like any other taxpayer, became reinstated, without prejudice to any action, defense, or right accruing by reason of the original suspension. If it pays its taxes and obtains a certificate of revivor during the pendency of an action, a corporation may be allowed to carry on litigation, even to the extent of validating otherwise invalid prior proceedings. The purpose of the suspension of corporate power is to induce the payment of taxes. That purpose ordinarily is satisfied by a rule viewing a corporation's tax delinquencies, after correction, as mere irregularities. Indeed, it accomplishes little to impose additional penalties after the payment of the taxes. Moreover, the cases dealing with this topic have created a distinction between procedural and substantive acts. The revival of corporate power validates any procedural step taken on behalf of the corporation while it was under suspension; hence, procedural acts in the prosecution or defense of a lawsuit are validated retroactively by corporate revival. Indeed, most litigation activity has been characterized as procedural for the purposes of corporate revival. For example, a judgment obtained during suspension is validated by a subsequent revivor. However, substantive defenses accruing during corporate suspension may not be applied to the benefit of the now-revived corporation. For example, the statute of limitations is regarded as a substantive defense, not a procedural right. Thus, revival cannot be given a retroactive effect to permit the filing of an action at a time of incapacitation to toll the running of the statute of limitations. In other words, if an action is commenced during the period of suspension and the corporate powers are revived after the limitations period expires, the revival does not toll the running of the limitations period. Benton likened Whitbread's extension and tolling to a statute of limitations and characterized Whitbread's acts as substantive, rather than procedural. However, the limitations cases are distinguishable from the case at bar. Whitbread argued that the time for exercising its use permit had been tolled not as a result of its suspension of corporate power, but as a result of the county's approval of its request for an extension and tolling. It did not seek to take advantage of its failure to pay its taxes in a timely fashion. Rather, Whitbread merely sought to validate actions taken during its suspension in order to give those actions the effect that they would otherwise have. The trial court agreed with this assessment of the matter, since the extension does not establish any new substantive rights; it merely extends rights already granted for a longer period of time. Hence, Whitbread's application for the extension and the tolling constituted procedural acts. On the revival of its corporate status, these interim acts were as valid as if Whitbread's status had never been suspended.

Dissolution at the Request of Shareholders Shareholders can petition the courts for dissolution of the corporation. We already have briefly touched on some of the situations that can precipitate such shareholder actions; examples include "freeze-outs" (or oppression) of minority shareholders' interests as well as allegations of corporate waste of assets. Statutes usually authorize judicial dissolution for these and other examples of corporate mismanagement, but courts will sometimes order dissolutions in similar circumstances even in the absence of express statutory provisions. Deadlock among directors or shareholders constitutes an additional ground for involuntary dissolution. Courts will intervene when a shareholder can show that the deadlock among directors or controlling shareholders has so paralyzed the corporation that it can no longer conduct its business advantageously. When corporate strife has reached these levels, courts may order involuntary dissolution. Alternatively, some state statutes permit the appointment of a provisional, or temporary, director who breaks the deadlock and thus allows the corporation to continue functioning.

Other statutory methods for limiting a court's ordering of involuntary dissolution in these circumstances consist of provisions allowing holders of a majority of the corporation's outstanding shares to purchase the shares owned by the shareholders who are requesting dissolution and/or provisions setting out a minimum number of shareholders (for example, one-third of the corporate shareholders) who must join in the petition for involuntary dissolution before it can be presented to a court. In contrast to these potential impediments to maintaining an action for involuntary dissolution, shareholders in close corporations frequently agree in advance that upon the occurrence of a certain event, such as deadlock, each shareholder will be able to request dissolution. Courts ordinarily enforce such agreements.

Dissolution at the Request of Creditors The theory of corporate personality normally prevents creditors from compelling the involuntary dissolution of the corporation. But statutes requiring prior notice to creditors protect creditors' rights during dissolution and liquidation, as do statutes allowing the appointment of a receiver who takes over the corporation's business and conducts it for the benefit of the creditors. Possibly, creditors also can petition for the involuntary bankruptcy of the corporation to preserve their rights. Neither the appointment of a receiver nor the institution of involuntary bankruptcy proceedings results in the dissolution of the corporation, however. As we have seen, formal statutory procedures spell out the necessary steps for effecting this fundamental change in corporate structure.

As the following case shows, courts are reluctant to force dissolution and do so only if they have no other alternative.

Application of Ng
572 N.Y.S.2d 295 (A.D. Dept. 1991)

FACTS

The 168½ Delancey Street Corporation, formed in 1975, consisted of fifty shares of common stock distributed in five blocks of ten shares each to Vincent Sang, Wai-Ling Sang (his wife), Manolo Ng (Vincent's father-in-law), Shum Yuk Fu (Vincent's wife's uncle), and Shum Chu Wig (Vincent's wife's cousin). Vincent Sang had contributed all the money for the renovation of the building, and the shares were to be held in trust for him as the **beneficial owner**. In 1985, Manolo Ng died, and Yoet Ngor Ng, his wife, became the record owner of Manolo Ng's ten shares. In February, 1988, Shum Yuk Fu and Shum Chu Wig transferred their combined total of twenty shares to Vincent's wife, Wai-Ling Sang. According to Yoet Ngor Ng, this transfer was accomplished by fraud. The present dispute arose after this twenty-share transfer and after Yoet had loaned $20,000 to pay corporate debts in 1988. The Sangs alleged that Yoet had prevailed on her daughter by threats and telephone harassment to convey to Yoet fifteen shares of the twenty that the Shums had earlier conveyed to the Sangs. Wai-Ling Sang transferred the shares, which gave Yoet control of twenty-five of the fifty authorized shares in the corporation. The Sangs contested the validity of the transfer of these fifteen shares. Indeed, William Sang, the secretary of the corporation, had refused to sign the certificates for the transfer of the fifteen shares to his grandmother. In January, 1990, one year after the alleged transfer, Wai-Ling Sang stated in a letter to the corporation's attorney that the transfer was void, owing to lack of consideration, and that her signature had been procured by improper means. The evidence indicated that neither Yoet nor her husband had ever contributed any funds to the corporation other than the $20,000 loan in 1988. Furthermore, Yoet did not deny that the transfer of the fifteen shares lacked consideration. In May, 1990, Yoet Ngor Ng petitioned for the dissolution of 168½ Delancey Street Corporation on the grounds that directors' and shareholders' meetings had not been held in two years, that the shareholders were hopelessly deadlocked, that the payment of dividends had ceased in 1989, and that the corporation either was not collecting the rent from the commercial tenant or was diverting this rent. The Sangs claimed that because the tenant, the Apollo Restaurant, had been experiencing financial difficulties, they had decided eviction would not be prudent in light of the weak market for commercial space. The lower court had granted the petition for dissolution, finding, without elaboration, that owing to an irreconcilable deadlock and internal dissensions among the shareholders with respect to the management of the corporate affairs, dissolution would serve the best interests of the shareholders. The Sangs appealed, arguing the lower court should have conducted a hearing before ordering dissolution.

Beneficial owner One who does not have title to the property but who has rights in the property; the equitable, as opposed to the legal, owner of the property.

ISSUE

In the circumstances of this case, should a court grant dissolution without first conducting a hearing to determine the disputed factual issues present in the record?

HOLDING

No. Because a court should grant the ultimate remedy of dissolution only as a last resort, the court had erred in failing to hold a hearing beforehand.

REASONING

With respect to 168½ Delancey Street Corporation, the order directs the sale of corporate property, including the Apollo Restaurant, despite Vincent Sang's prima facie showing of the elements of a constructive trust: i.e., the existence of a confidential relationship, an express promise, a transfer in reliance on that promise, and unjust enrichment. Settled precedents hold that a court should impose the ultimate remedy of dissolution and forced sale of corporate assets only as a last resort. On this record it appears that the financial management of the corporation had been conducted somewhat loosely from the inception. In addition to the failure to observe corporate formalities, failure to collect rents or pay dividends forms the gist of the petition. Yet family members had from time to time occupied many of the apartments without paying rent. Indeed, even Yoet had enjoyed this perquisite until she had moved out when relations soured; and her son had continued to reside there. Factual issues of waiver and estoppel were thus present and precluded the granting of dissolution, particularly since the Sangs had submitted a business justification for their alleged failure to collect rent from the single commercial tenant.

MERGER AND CONSOLIDATION

Like dissolutions, mergers and consolidations bring about fundamental, or organic, changes in the corporation's structure. Dissolution is also related to these two concepts because dissolution of a corporation (or corporations) occurs automatically on either a merger or a consolidation, and the procedures for carrying out a merger or consolidation are similar to dissolution procedures.

Technically, a *merger* differs from a consolidation. In a merger, *one corporation* (called the "acquirer" or "acquiring" firm) *purchases another firm* (called the "acquired" or "disappearing" firm) *and absorbs it into itself.* This new entity is called the *survivor corporation;* the "acquired" firm no longer exists.

A *consolidation* is similar, except that in a consolidation *two or more existing corporations combine to form a wholly new corporate entity.* Since most statutes treat the procedures for mergers and consolidations as if the two were identical transactions, this part of our discussion will focus only on mergers. But, as noted, they are analytically different ways of bringing about major changes in corporate structure, as Figures 42.1 and 42.2 illustrate.

FIGURE 42.1 Structural Changes as a Result of Merger

Lucky Corporation
(Acquirer or Acquiring Firm)

and

Shamrock, Inc.
(Acquired or Disappearing Firm)

Lucky Corporation
(Survivor)

Rationales for Merger

The last two decades have witnessed a phenomenal upsurge in the number of mergers—for reasons with which you, as business students, are no doubt familiar.

FIGURE 42.2   Structural Changes as a Result of Consolidation

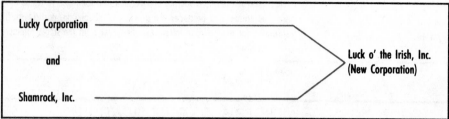

Economies of Scale   *Economies of scale* refer to reductions in per-unit costs resulting from larger plant size. A merger may permit a firm to achieve economies of scale and thus to compete much more efficiently: The larger the firm, the easier it is for the firm to receive discounts on sales and advertising and thereby to achieve lower costs. Accumulation of resources resulting from merged firms also facilitates access to financing. Two beer producers who have just merged generally present a more attractive credit risk for lending institutions than you would if you were attempting to get capital for your wine business currently run from your basement. Bigness may also spawn more research and development. A merged firm ordinarily has more funds to spend on these activities and can utilize its capital in this manner. The capital in your struggling wine business, in contrast, typically goes for electricity, rent, and other overhead costs. You may want to invest in research on capping methods or grape hybrids, but economies of scale make such research and development much more feasible in large firms. Mergers between manufacturers and customers (called "vertical" mergers) may lessen transaction costs and bring about economies of scale in this fashion also. As you will learn in Chapter 46, a firm can use economies of scale to drive out smaller, less efficient firms because of the dominance it may achieve owing to its size and wealth ("deep pockets"). The antitrust laws serve to protect the process of competition from the retaliatory, abusive conduct in which large firms may engage. In the absence of antitrust concerns, mergers to effect economies of scale are legally sound, indeed customary.

Knowledge   A common merger scenario involves a larger company that attempts to merge with a smaller company because the latter possesses valuable technological information or "know-how." An established computer firm, for instance, may find a merger with a software firm valuable if the software firm has made technological breakthroughs deemed valuable by the computer firm. Thinking back to economies of scale for a moment, in a given case it may well be cheaper for the computer firm to purchase this software firm and its patents, trademarks, and trade secrets than to expend the funds for the research and development it would take to approximate the software. Furthermore, the merged firm may be able to retain the staff of the smaller firm and thereby realize further future gains from these persons' collective expertise and inventive capacities.

Diversification   The decade of the 1970s marked a large increase in the number of mergers undertaken for the purpose of diversification. Many firms jumped into areas previously unrelated to their principal lines of business through **conglomerate mergers.** Sears, Roebuck, long a retail merchandising mainstay, now sells insurance, stocks, and real estate because of its recent mergers. Many other firms have undergone similar expansions of their business interests. Diversification minimizes the risks that are inherent in a firm's restricting itself to one industry and the risks caused by economic cycles. Sears's diversification allows it to offset any losses in retail sales caused by seasonal buying with insurance and brokerage sales, which are not tied to the same cycles. Critics of diversification have argued, however, that diversification dilutes capital markets by making it easier for a diversified company to hide its actual profits and losses. These authorities maintain that lending institutions' abilities to assess the credit-riskiness of diversified companies are impaired by mergers aimed at diversification. This estimation, coupled with some experts' fears about the implications of the excessive concentrations of economic power represented by diversified companies, has led some to argue for heightened antitrust enforcement against conglomerate mergers. But the present enforcement posture appears to reject such fears.

Competition   Inherent in a great deal of what we have discussed so far is an underlying desire to control, if not curtail, competition. One firm clearly does not want to be at the mercy of another firm in times of scarcity. Therefore, a merger between a supplier of aluminum and a fabricator of aluminum, for instance, seems a viable strategy for cutting down on some of the supply side uncertainties. Naturally, though, antitrust concerns may also lurk in mergers designed to control the competitive process; so caution is warranted.

Other Rationales   Other rationales for mergers include tax savings, utilization of cash-rich assets to pump up concerns that need such assets for expansion and growth, and preservation of management prerogatives. Critics of the last rationale have argued that many mergers occur because of the egos of important management officials who want to become the executive officers of even bigger companies. Such "power trips," these critics assert, lead to such socially undesirable consequences as the possible sacrifice of shareholders' interests, personnel displacement, and the uprooting of smaller corporations from the local community of which they were an integral part. The previously mentioned controversies over hostile takeovers, "golden parachutes," "poison pills," and defensive mergers (that is, mergers in which corporation A merges with corporation C to avoid A's being taken over by corporation B) often surface in such criticisms as well. You can probably recall the newspaper accounts of recent takeover attempts that have raised similar issues.

Conglomerate mergers
Mergers between noncompeting firms in different industries.

Procedure

Board of Directors   Whatever the rationale for the merger, once the firms have decided to merge, state statutes set out the steps that must be followed in bringing about the merger. Such statutes generally require that each corporation's board of directors adopt a merger plan that names each corporation and signifies the name of the surviving corporation, the appropriate terms and conditions of the merger, the method for converting the acquired firm's securities into the securities of the acquiring firm (stock for cash, stock for stock, and the like), and any amendments to the articles of the acquiring corporation that have resulted from the merger.

As the following case illustrates, thorny problems can arise from these seemingly straightforward actions.

Jewel Companies v. Pay Less Drug Stores Northwest, Inc.
741 F.2d 1555 (9th Cir. 1984)

FACTS   In September, 1979, Pay Less Drug Stores (Pay Less) retained the investment banking firm of Goldman, Sachs & Co. to locate a merger partner. Jewel Companies (Jewel), a Chicago-based company engaged primarily in the retail grocery business, was included among the companies contacted. On 9 November 1979, Jewel and Pay Less agreed to a tax-free merger. The merger agreement was executed in writing, formally approved by both boards of directors, signed on behalf of each corporation by its respective president, and made public in a press release on 9 November 1979. Articles 9.9 and 10.5 of the Jewel–Pay Less merger agreement obligated the board of directors of each firm to "use its best efforts to fulfill those conditions . . . over which it has control or influence and to consummate the Merger." Pay Less further obligated itself under Article 9 to forbear from the sale or transfer of any of its properties or assets and from entering into or terminating any contract other than in the ordinary course of business. The merger agreement moreover provided that Pay Less could not "agree to, or make any commitment to" effect any sale, transfer, or extraordinary action prohibited in Article 9. However, when the Jewel–Pay Less merger agreement was publicly announced, Pay Less Drug Stores Northwest, Inc.'s (Northwest's) management made public its intention to make a competing bid in a press release issued 31 December 1979. This release further noted that Northwest had conditioned its merger offer on Pay Less's board's abandonment of the proposed merger with Jewel. When Pay Less ultimately merged with Northwest, Jewel then sued Northwest for damages arising from Northwest's allegedly tortious interference with contract and prospective commercial advantage. The district court granted Northwest's motion for a summary judgment.

ISSUE   Was an exclusive merger agreement, that is, one in which the board of directors had agreed to forbear from entering into competing and inconsistent agreements until the shareholders' vote had occurred, lawful under California law?

HOLDING   Yes. California corporate statutes permitted a board's entering into an exclusive merger contract.

REASONING   An exclusive, board-negotiated merger agreement may confer considerable benefits on the shareholders of a firm. For example, a potential merger partner might be reluctant to agree to a merger unless it were confident that its offer would not be used by the board simply to trigger an auction for the firm's assets. Therefore, an exclusive merger agreement might be necessary to secure the best offer for the shareholders of a firm. In that sense, permitting a board of directors to decide that a proposed merger transaction was in the best interests of its shareholders at a given time and to agree to refrain from entering into competing contracts until the shareholders had considered the proposal would not conflict in any way with the board's fiduciary obligations. Furthermore, in many ways, shareholders might have more safeguards from market losses in board-negotiated transactions than in others.

According to the court, even after the merger agreement had been signed, a board could not, consistent with its fiduciary obligations to its shareholders, withhold information regarding a potentially more attractive competing offer. While the board could bind itself to exert its best efforts to consummate the merger under California law, it could only bind the corporation temporarily, and in limited areas, pending shareholder approval. Hence, the shareholders retained the ultimate control over the corporation's assets. They remained free to accept or reject the merger proposal presented by the board, to respond to a merger proposal or tender offer made by another firm subsequent to the board's execution of an exclusive merger agreement, or to hold out for a better offer. Given the benefits that might have accrued to shareholders from an exclusive merger agreement, such an agreement would not compromise their legal rights. Therefore, the district court's fears that exclusive merger agreements are anticompetitive and contrary to public policy because they subvert the welfare of shareholders were unfounded. Yet the conclusion that, under California law, the Pay Less board could lawfully commit itself to submit the Jewel proposal to its shareholders on an exclusive basis would not answer the question of whether such an exclusive arrangement was intended by the parties to the transaction at issue. Because the record had not demonstrated conclusively whether the parties had intended that the Jewel–Pay Less agreement would obligate the Pay Less board to abstain from negotiating or executing a competing merger agreement with the board of another firm, summary judgment was inappropriate. Finally, the district court's ruling—that even if the Jewel–Pay Less agreement were binding and valid, Northwest's interference with that agreement would have been justified—lacked legal authority because such a holding would be akin to the "law of the jungle." Indeed, the district court's ruling—that society's interests in promoting "healthy competition" among those seeking to take over existing companies would justify interference with an otherwise valid merger agreement between the boards of directors of two corporations—squarely conflicted with California law. On this alternative basis, the district court's granting of a summary judgment for Northwest was erroneous as well.

The case that follows, one of the most well-publicized decisions in recent years, illustrates the financial and legal risks attendant on a company's canceling its merger with one firm in order to unite with another. This case also underscores the federal courts' reluctance to usurp state courts' jurisdiction over issues important to the respective states unless a clear need to do so exists.

Pennzoil Company v. Texaco, Inc.
107 S.Ct. 1519 (1987)

FACTS   Getty Oil Co. (Getty) and Pennzoil Company (Pennzoil) negotiated an agreement under which Pennzoil was to purchase about three-sevenths of Getty's outstanding shares for $110 a share. However, Texaco, Inc. (Texaco) eventually purchased the shares for $128 a share. Pennzoil subsequently filed a complaint against Texaco alleging that Texaco had tortiously induced Getty to breach the contract to sell its shares to Pennzoil. In that suit, Pennzoil sought actual damages of $7.53 billion and punitive damages in the same amount. In 1985, a jury returned a verdict in favor of Pennzoil, finding actual damages of $7.53 billion and punitive damages of $3 billion. The parties anticipated that the judgment, including prejudgment interest, would exceed $11 billion. Moreover, this expected judgment would give Pennzoil, as a judgment creditor, the right to secure a lien on all of Texaco's real property located in any county in Texas and to obtain a writ of execution allowing it to take possession of Texaco's assets. To avoid the execution of such a judgment, under Texas law, Texaco could have filed a bond in the amount of the judgment. In this case, because the amount of the bond required by law would have been more than $13 billion, it was clear that Texaco would not have been able to post it. As a result of the business community's assessment that Pennzoil would be able, under the lien and bond provisions of Texas law, to commence enforcement of the judgment before Texaco's appeals had been resolved, Texaco began experiencing the negative effects of the jury's verdict almost immediately. Among other things, its stock prices dropped; it had difficulty obtaining credit; and its bond rating was lowered. Texaco therefore asked the federal courts to enjoin Pennzoil from taking any action to enforce the judgment. Pennzoil argued that, under the so-called abstention doctrine, the federal courts should abstain from enjoining the execution of its judgment pending state court proceedings.

ISSUE   Could the federal courts lawfully enjoin Pennzoil, which had prevailed in a trial in state court, from executing the judgment in its favor pending an appeal of that judgment to a state appellate court?

HOLDING   No. The lower federal courts should have abstained from hearing the case under the abstention doctrine.

REASONING   The courts below should have abstained under the principles of federalism enunciated in *Younger* v. *Harris*, 401 U.S. 37 (1971). Both the district court and the court of appeals had failed to recognize the significant interests harmed by their unprecedented intrusion into the Texas judicial system. Similarly, neither of those courts had applied the appropriate standard in determining whether adequate relief was available in the Texas courts. Abstention under *Younger* therefore was warranted whenever the state's interests in the proceeding were so important that exercise of the federal judicial power would have disregarded the **comity** between the states and the federal government. Another important reason for abstention was to avoid unwarranted determinations of federal constitutional questions. When federal courts interpret state statutes in a way that raises federal constitutional questions, "a constitutional determination is predicated on a reading of the statute that is not binding on state courts and may be discredited at any time—thus essentially rendering the federal court decision advisory and the litigation underlying it meaningless." *Moore* v. *Sims*, 442 U.S. 415, 428 (1979). Moreover, this concern had special significance in this case because Texaco had chosen not to present to the Texas courts the constitutional claims asserted in this suit. Thus, it was impossible to be certain that the governing Texas statutes and procedural rules actually raised these claims. Moreover, the Texas Constitution contains an "open courts" provision that appears to address Texaco's claims more specifically than the due process clause of the Fourteenth Amendment does. Hence, upon this case's being filed in federal court, it was entirely possible that the Texas courts could have resolved it on state statutory or constitutional grounds, without reaching the federal constitutional questions Texaco had raised. Furthermore, the state retained an important interest in enforcing the order and judgments of its courts; federal injunctions that interfered with the execution of state judgments would have challenged the very process by which those judgments had been obtained. As long as those challenges related to pending state proceedings, proper respect for the ability of state courts to resolve federal questions presented in state court litigation mandated that the federal courts stay their hand. Nonabstention, therefore, would have disregarded the comity between the states and the federal government. Lastly, abstention under *Younger* was appropriate because Texaco had presented no evidence to buttress its contention that Texas courts would have been unable to hear its constitutional claims within the limited time available to it. When a litigant has made no effort to present its claims in state court, federal courts should assume that state procedures will afford an adequate remedy, in the absence of unambiguous authority to the contrary, and thus should abstain under *Younger*.

Comity   The principle that obliges the federal government to give effect to the laws and decisions of a state out of respect for the state.

Shareholders   After each of the boards of directors has adopted a merger plan, the shareholders of both corporations ordinarily must approve the merger. As with dissolutions, normally the holders of two-thirds of the outstanding shares must approve this fundamental change, although in some states approval by a bare majority of the holders of the outstanding stock will suffice. In some states, however, statutory provisions dispense with the necessity for shareholder approval in "short-form" mergers (those involving a merger between a subsidiary and a parent company that owns 90 to 100 percent of the subsidiary's stock). Since the parent's ownership interest is so high, a vote of approval would be a mere formality; requiring such a vote thus makes little practical sense. Once all the required steps have been followed, the directors file the plan with the appropriate state office. After the state approves this plan, the surviving corporation receives a "certificate of merger" and can begin conducting business.

Effect of Merger

Once the state issues the certificate of merger, the acquired corporation ceases to exist; only one corporation survives. The survivor takes on all the assets, rights, and liabilities of the disappearing (acquired) corporation by operation of law. This means, among other things, that creditors of the acquired corporation are now the creditors of the survivor corporation. Similarly, pending damages suits (such as a products liability case) against the acquired corporation, if successful, will be paid by the survivor corporation.

Appraisal Rights

Appraisal rights The rights in certain extraordinary corporate activities to have a security evaluated and the appraisal value paid to the owner.

Market value The current price the stock would sell for on a stock exchange.

Thus far, we have discussed the positive side of a merger; that is, we have examined the merger only from the point of view of those who want it. However, in any given merger, there will be persons who object to, or dissent from, the merger. Because many people believe it is unfair to require someone to become a shareholder in a new corporation that may be totally different from the one in which he or she has originally invested, statutes in most states give dissenting shareholders **appraisal rights**. Appraisal rights *allow dissenters to sell their shares back to the corporation for cash for the fair market value of the shares*. In this way, a dissenting shareholder can avoid becoming a shareholder in the survivor corporation and can, at the same time, protect his or her original investment.

To be eligible for appraisal rights, a shareholder ordinarily must follow a set statutory procedure. Although the respective state statutes vary regarding the steps with which a dissenting shareholder must comply, in general such statutes require the dissenter to send a written notice of his or her objection to the merger before the meeting at which the merger will be considered. Next, the shareholder must make a written demand on the corporation for the fair value of the shares after the merger has been approved. The corporation must then make a written offer to purchase at a price it believes represents the fair value (or the fair market value) of the shares. If the corporation and the dissenting shareholder disagree about the fair value of the shares, either party may petition a court to determine the fair value of the shares in an appraisal proceeding. Valuation of shares is quite complicated, but this task becomes somewhat easier if the stock is traded on the New York or American Stock Exchanges; in such cases, a court will place great importance on the market price of the stock when assigning a fair value to the stock. Otherwise, a court usually will arrive at its valuation determination by weighing a number of factors, including market price, investment value, net asset value, and dividends.

Some jurisdictions deny appraisal rights for certain types of mergers (for example, shareholders of the parent company in a "short-form" merger may have no appraisal rights) and certain types of corporations (those with stock listed on a national securities exchange or those with more than 2000 shareholders). Since appraisal rights generally represent the exclusive remedy for a dissenting shareholder who opposes a merger, it is important for the shareholder to use vigilance in complying with the strict statutory provisions and short time periods involved.

Note that the courts in the next two cases had to grapple with these issues of appraisal rights in arriving at their decisions.

McCall v. McCall Enterprises, Inc.
578 So.2d 260 (La. App. 3 Cir. 1991)

FACTS When Cameron Crew Boats, Inc. (Cameron) was incorporated on 3 March 1966, the company issued 100 shares of stock—twenty five shares to Norman McCall, ten shares to Gladys McCall, and the remaining shares to other shareholders. Norman McCall served as the president and a director of Cameron. In December, 1970, Claude V. McCall, Sr., the father of the plaintiffs, acquired ownership of the ten shares held by Gladys McCall. Subsequently, Claude McCall sold 2.46 shares to Norman McCall, leaving him (Claude) with 7.54 shares. These shares were inherited by plaintiffs Mary Diane McCall Armand, Charles McCall, and Claude McCall, Jr. on the deaths of their parents, Claude V. and Diana McCall. In December, 1984, McCall Enterprises, Inc. (McCall Enterprises) began acquiring shares of stock in Cameron and by June, 1988, owned more than 90 percent of the firm's shares. On 8 June 1988, McCall Enterprises merged with Cameron, with McCall Enterprises becoming the successor corporation. On 9 June 1988, McCall Enterprises filed the necessary documentation with the secretary of state and at the same time mailed a copy of the documentation to each shareholder. The articles of merger set the fair cash value of the shares of Cameron at $7406.75 per share. The plaintiffs decided to dissent from the merger and to file suit for a court appraisal of the fair cash value of their Cameron shares. The plaintiffs filed a demand for the fair cash value of their shares with the corporation on 28 June 1988 and filed the bank acknowledgment, required by law, on 30 June 1988. On 1 July 1988, McCall Enterprises disagreed with the value demanded. The plaintiffs filed this suit for the fair cash value of their shares on 29 August 1988. McCall Enterprises argued that the plaintiffs had failed to satisfy the statutory requirements for a court appraisal, since the plaintiffs had not filed suit within twenty days of the delivery of the certificate of merger to the secretary of state. The plaintiffs countered that the twenty-day period had begun to run from the time the secretary of state had issued the certificate and that their filing therefore had been timely.

ISSUE Did the relevant time period for filing suit begin running at the time of the secretary of state's issuance of the merger certificate?

HOLDING No. The relevant time period began when the corporation had delivered the merger certificate to the secretary of state. Hence, the plaintiffs had not made a timely demand on the corporation as required by Louisiana law.

REASONING The pertinent Louisiana statute provides: "If a corporation has become a party to a merger . . . , the shareholders of any subsidiaries party to the merger shall have the right to dissent. . . ." and sets out the procedural requirements necessary for a dissenting shareholder to file a suit for a court appraisal of the fair cash value of the dissenting shareholder's shares of stock. In the case of a merger, the dissenting shareholder need not file an objection with the corporation nor vote against the merger, but need only file with the corporation, within twenty days after a copy of the merger certificate has been mailed to him or her, a demand in writing for the cash value of his or her shares as of the day before the certificate was filed with the secretary of state, and fulfill some other technical requirements. In this case, the trial judge held that the plaintiffs had lost their right to pursue the action within the twenty days allowed. Plaintiffs argued on appeal that the defendant had not mailed them a copy of the merger certificate, as required. They claimed that, for this reason, the time had not begun to run on 9 June 1988 and that their demand had fallen within the twenty days and therefore had been timely. They based this argument on the contention that the merger certificate referred to in the relevant statute is the certificate issued by the secretary of state. However, this reference actually means the certificate delivered to the secretary of state by the defendant and not the certificate issued by the secretary of state. In addition, no useful purpose would be served by sending to the minority shareholders the certificate issued by the secretary of state. The certificate submitted to the secretary of state and sent to the minority shareholders contains the information necessary for them to determine if a suit for a court appraisal is the route they want to take; in contrast, the certificate issued by the secretary of state does not contain any vital information necessary to make this decision. These facts notwithstanding, the plaintiffs further argued that they had substantially complied with the statute's prerequisites. On 28 June 1988, the last day of the twenty-day period, plaintiffs filed with the corporation a demand for the fair cash value of their shares. With the demand, the statute also required them to deliver to the corporation the acknowledgment of the escrow bank or trust company. In the instant case, the plaintiffs did not deliver this acknowledgment until 30 June 1988, after the twenty-day period set forth in the statute. In short, the language of the statute sets forth a mandatory time period, which the plaintiffs did not meet. Plaintiffs' failure to fulfill a necessary prerequisite for filing suit for an appraisal of the fair market value of their shares of stock resulted in a conclusive presumption that they had acquiesced in the corporate action proposed or taken, including the case value set by the board for their shares. Thus, plaintiffs lost their right to bring an action for a court appraisal of the fair cash value of their shares by failing to satisfy the statutory prerequisites for filing suit.

Egret Energy Corporation v. *Peierls*
796 P.2d 25 (Colo. App. 1990)

FACTS Following a completed merger with Target Oil & Gas, Inc., Egret Energy Corporation (Egret), the surviving corporation, brought an action to determine the value of the shares held by the dissenting shareholders. Peierls, one such dissenting shareholder, complied with the statutory requirements (by notifying the corporation of his demand for payment and depositing his shares within thirty days of the shareholders' meeting) and mailed a demand letter. On 3 June 1985, Egret mailed to Peierls (and the other dissenters) the accrued interest. Peierls believed Egret owed him more interest and on 7 June requested additional information so he could determine whether the interest had been properly computed. The relevant statute provides: "Within sixty days after receiving a demand for payment pursuant to subsection (7) of this section, if any such demand for payment remains unsettled, the corporation shall file in an appropriate court a petition requesting that the fair value of the shares and interest thereon be determined by the court." The statutory sixty-day period for filing an action to determine fair value expired on 5 July 1985, but Egret did not file this action until 24 July 1985. According to the statute, "If the corporation fails to file a petition as provided in paragraph (a) of this subsection (8), each dissenter who has made a demand and who has not already settled his claim against the corporation shall be paid by the corporation the amount demanded by him [or her] with interest and may sue therefore in an appropriate court." Peierls filed an answer and counterclaim in which he requested that, pursuant to the provisions of this subsection, a court award him the amount demanded with interest. Egret argued that Peierls's 7 June letter constituted a subsection (7) demand letter that had extended the period for filing this action.

ISSUE   Would Peierls's second letter, in which he had requested more information so that he could determine whether interest had been properly computed on the corporation's remittance of the value of his shares, constitute a "demand letter" that would extend the sixty-day period for filing an action to determine the fair value of the dissenting shareholders' shares?

HOLDING   No. This communication did not constitute a demand letter; hence, Colorado law entitled Peierls to have his shares valued at the amount demanded, since the corporation had not mailed the letter within the sixty-day period as provided for by statute.

REASONING   According to Colorado precedents, "[w]here the word 'shall' is used in a statute, it is presumed to be mandatory." Furthermore, separate clauses within a statute should be interpreted to give effect to the entire statute. The statute clearly states that if the action is not filed within the sixty-day period provided for, the dissenter shall be paid the amount demanded by him or her with interest. Here, then, the presumption that "shall" is a mandate remains unrebuttable. Peierls's 7 June letter was not mailed within the thirty-day period provided for in subsection (7), and it therefore did not qualify as a demand letter. It was merely evidence that Peierls's demand remained unsettled. The court, without a hearing, had approved the appraiser's report that the stock had a value of $.813 per share and had ordered Egret to pay the dissenters on the basis of this evaluation. The statute also provides that costs and expenses, including the fees of the appraiser and the experts, shall be assessed against the corporation "except that any part of the costs and expenses may be apportioned and assessed as the court may deem equitable against all or some of the dissenters who are parties and whose action in demanding supplemental payment the court finds to be arbitrary, vexatious, or not in good faith." The trial court had found Peierls's action to be arbitrary, vexatious, and not in good faith and had accordingly assessed him 75 percent of the expert's fees. On appeal, Peierls argued this decision had constituted reversible error, since Peierls was merely exercising the rights given to him and other dissenters by statute. As Colorado precedents hold, "[t]he mere fact that the stockholders took advantage of the statutory remedy and pursued that remedy with great vigor is not in and of itself evidence of bad faith." Given Peierls's entitlement to summary judgment, the trial court should have assessed the costs and expenses against Egret. Therefore, the judgment is reversed and the cause remanded to the trial court for further proceedings to determine the amount due Peierls per share and the interest due Peierls.

In the following case, the court actually ordered an appraisal-like remedy.

Weinberger v. UOP, Inc.
457 A.2d 701 (Del. 1983)

FACTS   Weinberger was a former shareholder of William B. UOP, Inc. (UOP) which, through a merger, had become a wholly owned subsidiary of Signal. UOP's minority shareholders at the time of the merger had been paid $21 per share for their former interests in UOP. Weinberger sued to set aside the merger on the grounds that the $21-per-share price paid to the UOP minority shareholders was grossly inadequate and rendered the merger unfair. Alternatively, Weinberger asked for damages.

ISSUE   Was the merger fair to the UOP minority shareholders?

HOLDING   No. The merger was unfair to the UOP minority shareholders because the price paid for the shares was inadequate.

REASONING   The evidence indicated that the inside directors had withheld information showing that payment of $24 per share would have been a good investment for Signal. Accordingly, the merger did not meet the fairness test due to this breach of the fiduciary duties owed by UOP's board (which had been substantially controlled by Signal) to UOP's minority shareholders. Therefore, on remand, the lower court should have conducted appraisal-like hearings in order to decide the damages necessary to compensate Weinberger and the other minority shareholders of UOP for the directors' unfair dealings and the unfair price paid by them.

In determining the value of shares in a statutory appraisal proceeding, a court retains broad discretionary powers, as the following case illustrates.

Alabama By-Products Corporation v. Neal
588 A.2d 255 (Del. 1991)

FACTS   Minority shareholders, including Neal, challenged an appraisal, pursuant to Delaware statutes, of approximately 120,000 shares of the stock of Alabama By-Products Corporation (ABC). Following a short-form merger between ABC and Drummond Holding Corporation (Drummond) effective 13 August 1985, Drummond absorbed ABC. The ABC minority shareholders were cashed out, pursuant to the merger, and received $75.60 per share. That consideration reflected the $75.00 per share paid to ABC shareholders pursuant to a tender offer less than six months earlier, plus a $.60 quarterly dividend omitted in 1985. After a six-day trial, the Court of Chancery had concluded that the fair value of ABC stock on 13 August 1985 was $180.67 per share and that Neal and the other minority shareholders were entitled to that amount plus interest. But according to ABC, the Court of Chancery had injected an inapposite consideration into the determination of fair value, thereby skewing the statutory appraisal process. Specifically, ABC contended that the Court of Chancery's reliance on evidence of wrongdoing in the merger, when determining value in a statutory appraisal proceeding, had constituted an error of law that would mandate reversal.

ISSUE   Had the Court of Chancery inappropriately considered the majority shareholders' wrongdoing when determining the value of the dissenting shareholders' stock in a statutory appraisal hearing?

HOLDING   No. Although minority shareholders ordinarily cannot litigate such claims of unfair dealing in the context of a statutory appraisal of the value of the shares upon a merger, a court can admit evidence of unfair dealing by majority shareholders in a statutory appraisal action for the purpose of impeaching the majority shareholders' credibility.

REASONING   According to Delaware precedents, including the *Weinberger* case, an appraisal action is "entirely a creature of statute." It is a limited legislative remedy intended to provide shareholders who dissent from a merger and who assert the inadequacy of the offering price with an independent judicial determination of the fair value of their shares. The governing statute provides that "the Court shall appraise the shares, determining their fair value exclusive of any element of value arising from the accomplishment or expectation of the merger or consolidation. . . ." Accordingly, the value of the appraisal of the dissenting shareholders' shares on the date of the merger is the only litigable issue in a statutory appraisal under Section 262. *Weinberger* and other cases note that appraisal may be an inadequate remedy in certain cases, "particularly where fraud, misrepresentation, self-dealing, deliberate waste of corporate assets, or gross and palpable overreaching are involved." Nevertheless, this Court has consistently held that a *"statutory appraisal is limited* to 'the payment of the fair value of the shares . . . by the surviving or resulting corporation. . . .' " Thus, claims for unfair dealing cannot be litigated in the context of a *statutory* appraisal. The Court of Chancery properly dismissed Neal's claim for unfair dealing by noting that "to authorize the joinder of appraisal and unfair dealing actions as proposed here would result in a hybrid appraisal action, effectively broadening the legislative remedy. . . ." However, the Court of Chancery then stated that "if corporate fiduciaries engage in self-dealing and fix the merger price by procedures not calculated to yield a fair price, these facts should, and will, be considered in assessing the credibility of the corporations' valuation contentions." ABC submitted that this statement is contrary to the limited inquiry permitted by Delaware's appraisal statute and provided the improper premise on which the Court of Chancery had mistakenly pursued an inquiry into the claims of wrongdoing in the merger when making this determination of fair value. ABC maintained that, even assuming a factual basis for a finding of unfair dealing, any acts of unfair dealing in the merger process can never be considered in an appraisal proceeding. ABC argued that such a conclusion follows **ipso facto,** since "claims" for unfair dealing cannot be litigated in a statutory appraisal proceeding. The minority shareholders argued that evidence concerning acts of unfair dealing with respect to the merger had been introduced here for two distinct purposes: first, in support of the unfair dealing claim and, second, to impeach the credibility of ABC's valuation contentions. These same shareholders rightly submitted that after the dismissal of their unfair dealing claim from the appraisal proceeding, the Court of Chancery nevertheless was entitled to consider the evidence of unfair dealing for the alternate purpose for which it had been introduced; i.e., to impeach ABC's credibility. Although the justiciable issue in an appraisal action is a limited one, the statute specifically provides that the Court of Chancery must consider "all relevant factors" when it determines the fair value of shares that are subject to appraisal. Nothing in the appraisal statute or in prior holdings suggests that the Court of Chancery may not consider ABC's conduct at the time of the merger in assessing the credibility of ABC's testimony in support of its valuation contentions in an appraisal proceeding. Indeed, the weight ascribed to expert valuations necessarily depends on the validity of the assumptions underlying them. Where those assumptions are values supplied by others, the conduct of such other persons becomes probative of their credibility and of the information being supplied to the expert. The credibility of ABC remained squarely at issue in this appraisal proceeding because the experts retained by ABC had relied on information supplied to them by the corporation. The Court of Chancery considered each factual premise on which the parties had disagreed, resolving some of the evidentiary disputes based on Neal's evidence and some based upon ABC's evidence. The Court of Chancery's fifty-three-page opinion reflects its careful factual findings regarding the fair value of ABC's stock from the record documentary evidence, the weighing of expert testimony, and the credibility of other witnesses, including ABC's representatives. Where factual determinations turn on a question of credibility and the acceptance or rejection of testimony by the trier of fact, a court will accept them, since it is well settled under Delaware precedents that the trier of fact is the sole judge of the credibility of witnesses and the weight to be accorded their testimony and is responsible for resolving conflicts in the evidence. The Court of Chancery's decision in this appraisal proceeding was not arbitrary, as the record supports its factual findings; and its valuation of ABC's shares is the product of an orderly and logical deductive process. Therefore, the decision of the Court of Chancery merits affirmance.

Ipso facto By the mere effect of an act or a fact.

SALE OF SUBSTANTIALLY ALL THE ASSETS

Rather than acquiring another firm through a merger, a corporation can instead buy all, or substantially all, of another firm's assets. For example, a shipping company may buy the ships of a rival company as an alternative to merging with it. This method of acquisition enjoys favor because it is procedurally simpler than a merger. Approval by the shareholders of the acquired firm ordinarily is necessary, but approval by the acquiring firm's shareholders is not. Even then, a sale of substantially all the assets made in the regular course of the corporation's business (as when a corporation is formed to build a tanker, and the tanker is then sold to an oil company) would not normally require shareholder approval. Shareholder approval thus becomes necessary only in the event of a fundamental change in the corporate structure—the disposal of operating assets in order to terminate the business activities of the corporation. Most states provide appraisal rights for dissenting shareholders in these circumstances as well. In addition, various methods of protecting creditors find expression in the statutes governing sales of substantially all the assets. In a merger, the acquiring firm takes on all the liabilities of the acquired firm by operation of law; but since this is not ordinarily the case when all or substantially all the assets are sold, corporate statutory provisions, UCC Article 6's provisions on bulk transfers, and decisional law have been developed to give creditors remedies if such sales prejudice their rights.

The purchaser's potential liability for the alleged contracts of the selling corporation represents the focus of the next case.

Conrad v. Rofin-Sinar, Inc.
762 F. Supp. 167 (E.D. Mich. 1991)

FACTS   In early 1985, Conrad applied for a job as a laser systems salesperson with the Industrial Laser Division (ILD) of Spectra Physics, Inc. (Spectra). As a division, ILD had no separate corporate existence. During the application process, Conrad asked about job security. Herbert Dwight, the president of Spectra, told Conrad that he would remain employed as long as he did a good job selling laser systems. Shortly after beginning his employment, Conrad received a personnel manual describing Spectra's policies and practices. It listed specific grounds for discipline and provided for formal yearly performance reviews. A separate manual for ILD listed the same reasons for discipline as the Spectra manual itself and provided for progressive discipline before termination. In March, 1988, Spectra sold all its ILD assets to Siemens Capital Corporation (Siemens), which in turn incorporated Rofin-Sinar, Inc. (Rofin-Sinar) specifically to continue the business of ILD. Rofin-Sinar informed Spectra's customers that ILD "has been sold and is now Rofin-Sinar." All the supervisory personnel who worked at ILD continued to work for Rofin-Sinar in the same or similar capacities. Before the asset sale, Spectra had given notices to its employees stating that their employment with Spectra was terminated and that they would be offered employment by Rofin-Sinar. However, no evidence suggested that Rofin-Sinar had issued policy statements that it would adopt any "just cause" employment contracts allegedly in effect prior to the asset sale. The asset purchase agreement stated that Rofin-Sinar reserved the right to terminate Spectra employees and that Rofin-Sinar retained Spectra employees under the "terms and conditions of employment as it may determine in its discretion." After the asset sale, Conrad continued to work without interruption at the same salary; under the same commission plan; and with the same reporting requirements, vacation plan, hire date, employee number, personnel file, supervisor, office, car, and insurance deductions. Rofin-Sinar never asked or required him to file an employment application or a W-4 income tax form for the firm. On 11 May 1988 (before the sale), Spectra had placed Conrad on probation as a result of a performance review for the period ending 31 March 1988. After the effective date of the purchase of the ILD assets, Rofin-Sinar continued Conrad's probationary period. Rofin-Sinar retained and relied on Spectra's personnel manual; and it also used the personnel codes, personnel forms, and expense reports contained in it. In terminating Conrad on 27 January 1989, Rofin-Sinar followed the termination and exit interview procedures contained in the personnel manual. A Spectra employee profile form was generated containing Conrad's original hire date, department number, and employee number. The form indicated the termination reason as "42," the code in the personnel manual for "poor performer." Simply put, Rofin-Sinar had not developed any additional or different personnel practices before Conrad's termination. Moreover, it had not notified employees of any changes in personnel policies. The precipitating factor in Conrad's discharge was that he allegedly had withheld information concerning Ford Motor Company's (Ford's) plans to purchase a competitive laser system, although Conrad testified that he had not failed to communicate this information to

Rofin-Sinar. Conrad had satisfactorily completed his probationary period, and Rofin-Sinar had not given him any written notice of performance problems between 11 May 1988 and his termination. Furthermore, Conrad's sales performance had met the goals established by his supervisors. In fact, at the time of his termination, Conrad had been negotiating the sale of two large laser systems; after his termination, Rofin-Sinar had received the purchase orders for these two systems, and Conrad received no commissions on these sales. Conrad sued for wrongful discharge. Rofin-Sinar, in moving for a summary judgment, claimed that the alleged "just cause" contract had not bound it because a representative of Conrad's previous employer, the Industrial Laser Division (ILD) of Spectra Physics Inc., not Rofin-Sinar, had entered into the alleged contract with Conrad.

ISSUE   Had Rofin-Sinar, the purchaser of ILD's assets, impliedly agreed to assume liability under an alleged "just cause" employment contract between the selling corporation and its employee?

HOLDING   Maybe yes, maybe no. Therefore, the granting of a summary judgment in favor of Rofin-Sinar would be inappropriate in these circumstances, since evidence from which the finder of fact could reasonably conclude that the purchaser (Rofin-Sinar) had acceded to most, if not all, of the seller's personnel practices, including honoring any "just cause" employment contracts, had been present here.

REASONING   The Michigan Supreme Court has held that an employee can enforce an employer's promise not to terminate employment except for just cause. *Toussaint* v. *Blue Cross & Blue Shield of Michigan*, 408 Mich. 579, 191 N.W.2d 880 (1980). According to *Toussaint*, such an enforceable agreement can result from either: 1) an employer's "express agreement, oral or written" or 2) "an employee's legitimate expectations grounded in an employer's policy statements." Applying this standard, a reasonable trier of fact might conclude that an implied "just cause" employment contract had existed between Spectra and Conrad. The record contained undisputed evidence that Dwight, the president of Spectra, had promised Conrad he would remain employed as long as he did a good job. This fact alone would support a verdict that Conrad had had a "just cause" employment contract with Spectra. Furthermore, Spectra had adopted other policies that might have given Conrad a "legitimate expectation" that he had a "just cause" employment contract. In particular, its personnel manual had listed grounds for discipline, which would enhance an employee's legitimate expectation that he or she would be terminated only for just cause. The personnel manual also had provided for annual performance reviews. In addition, as Conrad's probation and the personnel manual suggested, Spectra had provided for progressive discipline prior to termination. Michigan precedents hold that a policy of terminating employees only after a graduated series of disciplinary measures contributes to the legitimate expectation that the employee will be terminated only for cause. Ordinarily, a purchaser of assets does not assume the liabilities of the selling corporation. However, under Michigan law, a purchaser of assets assumes the selling corporation's liabilities where: 1) there is an express or implied assumption of liability; 2) the transaction amounts to a consolidation or merger; 3) the transaction is fraudulent; 4) some of the elements of a purchase in good faith are lacking, or where the transfer is without consideration and the creditors of the transferor are not provided for; or 5) the transferee corporation is a mere continuation or reincarnation of the old corporation. The issue of whether the purchasing corporation agrees to assume the predecessor corporation's liabilities is a question of fact for the jury; the presence of such an intention moreover depends on the facts and circumstances of each case. Here, a material fact as to whether Rofin-Sinar had impliedly agreed to assume liability under the alleged "just cause" employment contract between Conrad and Spectra existed. Kay Cooper, Rofin-Sinar's vice-president of human resources, had submitted an affidavit in which she made the conclusory statement that Rofin-Sinar had not adopted the policies of Spectra. Nevertheless, a reasonable trier of fact could conclude from the undisputed facts that Rofin-Sinar had impliedly agreed to assume liability under the contract. For instance, the period of transition after the sale of the ILD assets represented one of continuity in which Rofin-Sinar had availed itself of many of Spectra's practices, policies, and workforce. Rofin-Sinar had failed to promulgate new personnel policies, and it never had disclaimed liability under any "just cause" employment contracts that may have existed. Furthermore, it had used Spectra's personnel manual, which fact ordinarily indicates the existence of a "just cause" contract. Plus, upon Rofin-Sinar's purchase of the ILD assets, Conrad remained on probation. Significantly, too, the same persons remained employed in upper management with Rofin-Sinar after the asset purchase sale. Continued employment of upper management is evidence of a successor company's intent to assume liability under certain agreements. All these undisputed facts, when considered in toto, would allow a finder of fact to conclude reasonably that Rofin-Sinar had acceded to most, if not all, of Spectra's personnel practices, including honoring any alleged "just cause" employment contracts. Hence, the granting of a summary judgment in Rofin-Sinar's favor in these circumstances would be inappropriate.

STOCK ACQUISITION

An alternative method for acquiring the business of another corporation involves stock acquisitions. Instead of buying substantially all the assets of a corporation, the acquiring corporation's directors may decide to buy the stock of the acquired corporation. Since the acquisition implicates only the latter corporation's individual shareholders, who can decide for themselves whether to sell at the price offered for the stock, the directors of the acquired corporation have no right to approve or disapprove the stock acquisition. Similarly, there are usually no requirements of shareholder approval or appraisal rights. However, the federal securities laws may apply to such corporate takeovers, as we will see in Chapter 44.

Because sales of substantially all the assets and stock acquisitions may have the ultimate effect of mergers, some companies have characterized their acquisitions in one of these fashions in order to avoid the strict statutory procedures required of mergers. Transactions that take the *form* of sales of assets or stocks but nevertheless have the *effect* of mergers are called *de facto mergers*. Because shareholders and creditors can be injured through de facto mergers, courts in jurisdictions that recognize the doctrine can set the transactions aside and require compliance with the relevant merger statutes (shareholder approval, appraisal rights, and so on).

A famous case involving a de facto merger follows.

Farris v. *Glen Alden Corp.*
143 A.2d 25 (Pa. 1958)

FACTS The officers of Glen Alden Corp. (Glen Alden) entered into a "reorganization agreement" with the officers of List Industries Corporation (List). Glen Alden was a coal company, and List was a more diversified company owning interests in textiles, theaters, real estate, and gas and oil. Glen Alden's shareholders approved the transaction. As a result of the reorganization agreement, Glen Alden acquired most of the assets and all the liabilities of List, and List was dissolved. Farris, a shareholder in Glen Alden, sought an injunction against the reorganization, stating that it was actually a merger and that it had not given appraisal rights to dissenting shareholders. Glen Alden argued that the transaction was a purchase of corporate assets with respect to which shareholders had no rights of dissent or appraisal.

ISSUE Was the transaction a purchase of assets or instead a de facto merger?

FIGURE 42.3 Fundamental Changes in Corporate Structure

MERGER OR CONSOLIDATION

Rationales:
- Economies of scale
- Knowledge (i.e., acquisition of "know-how")
- Diversification
- Securing of competitive advantages
- Tax savings
- Utilization of assets
- Preservation of management prerogatives

Formalities:
- Both boards' adoption of merger plan
- Both corporations' shareholder approval (usually ⅔ of outstanding shares or more needed) unless short-form merger involved
- Filing of plan with state
- Issuance of certificate of merger
- Provision of appraisal rights to dissenting shareholders and compliance with statutory procedures covering such rights, including:
  a) Dissenting shareholders' written notice of objection to merger
  b) Dissenting shareholders' written demand on corporation for fair value/fair market value of shares
  c) On failure to agree, either corporation or dissenting shareholders' petition court for an appraisal proceeding

Effect:
- Assets, rights, and liabilities of acquired firm assumed by surviving firm by operation of law
- Dissolution of acquired firm

SALE OF SUBSTANTIALLY ALL THE ASSETS

Formalities:
- Simpler than merger procedures
- Approval only by seller's shareholders (i.e., approval of buyer's shareholders unnecessary)
- Provision of appraisal rights to seller's dissenting shareholders and compliance with applicable statutory procedures
- Compliance with statutory provisions protecting creditors' rights
- Formalities not applicable to sale of substantially all the assets made in the regular course of business

Effect:
- Liabilities of seller ordinarily not assumed by purchaser by operation of law

STOCK ACQUISITION

Formalities:
- Simpler than procedures for merger or sale of substantially all the assets
- Compliance with state statutes and federal securities laws (if applicable) necessary
- Neither board action nor shareholder approval by either corporation needed; necessary only for shareholders of target firm to decide to sell to would-be acquirer or refrain from selling
- Transactions sometimes deemed stock acquisitions to avoid compliance with statutory formalities applicable to mergers; such *de facto* mergers generally set aside by courts and compliance with relevant statutes mandated

DISSOLUTION

Voluntary (initiated by shareholders)	Involuntary (initiated by shareholders or other entities)

Formalities:
- Board recommendation
- Shareholder approval (usually ⅔ of outstanding shares or more needed)
- Filing of notice to creditors
- Filing of certificate of dissolution
- Liquidation of corporation (before or after dissolution)
	Types:
	- At request of state, owing to:
	  a) Securities fraud; or
	  b) Noncompliance with state statutory procedures (e.g., failure to pay taxes or to file annual reports)
	- At request of shareholders, owing to
	  a) Mismanagement; or
	  b) Deadlock among directors or controlling shareholders so serious as to warrant dissolution
	- At request of creditors, owing to the need to preserve creditors' rights

HOLDING   The transaction was a de facto merger that should have followed the statutory procedures required of mergers in order to be legal.

REASONING   Farris would be a shareholder in a much different type of corporation once the transaction was consummated. The new company would be twice as large but would have seven times the long-term debt held by Glen Alden before the reorganization. Control of Glen Alden would also pass to the List directors, who would have a majority of the directorships on the new board of directors. Farris's proportionate interest in Glen Alden would be reduced to only two-fifths of what it had been before the reorganization, and the value of his shares would be substantially reduced. Hence, the transaction was in a reality a merger, and Glen Alden should have accorded Farris his statutorily required appraisal rights.

SUMMARY

Dissolution involves the termination of the corporation as a legal person. Dissolution is not synonymous with the term *liquidation,* which refers to the winding up of the corporation's business. Dissolutions may be either voluntary or involuntary. Statutes set out the formal requirements for a voluntary dissolution. Typically, voluntary dissolution involves board action, shareholder approval, and notice to creditors. Upon voluntary dissolution, the shareholders share proportionately in the net assets of the corporation that remain after satisfaction of creditors' claims. Involuntary dissolutions—those effected by judicial proceedings—occur less frequently than voluntary dissolutions.

The state can rescind or suspend the corporation's certificate when the corporation's actions present a clear danger to the public. Upon compliance with corporate statutes, the state often orders the corporation's reinstatement. Shareholders also can petition the courts for dissolution of the corporation because of corporate oppression, mismanagement, or deadlock among directors or shareholders. Statutes sometimes limit the conditions under which shareholders can petition for involuntary dissolution. Creditors normally cannot compel involuntary dissolution of the corporation. Neither the appointment of a receiver nor the institution of involuntary bankruptcy proceedings results in the dissolution of the corporation.

Mergers and consolidations can bring about fundamental changes in the corporation's structure. Technically, mergers and consolidations differ, since in a merger one firm absorbs another, while in a consolidation both firms combine to produce a wholly new entity. The upsurge in mergers stems from a desire to effect economies of scale, to gain technical knowledge, to diversify, to control competition, and to avoid taxes. The negative aspects of mergers include the possible sacrifice of shareholders' interests, personnel displacement, and the uprooting of firms from the local community.

State statutes set out the procedures necessary for bringing about a merger. The directors ordinarily adopt a merger plan, which the shareholders of both firms must approve. Shareholder approval is not necessary in "short-form" mergers. After the state approves the filed merger plan, the surviving corporation receives a "certificate of merger" and can begin conducting business. At this time, the acquired corporation ceases to exist. The surviving corporation takes on all the assets, rights, and liabilities of the transferor (i.e., acquired) corporation by operation of law.

Most state statutes permit appraisal rights for stockholders who object to the merger. Appraisal rights allow dissenters to sell their shares back to the corporation for cash equal to the shares' fair market value. To be eligible for appraisal rights, shareholders usually must follow a set statutory procedure. If the corporation and dissenting shareholders cannot agree about the fair market value of the shares, either party may petition a court to determine their value in an appraisal proceeding. Appraisal rights normally are not available for certain types of mergers and certain types of corporations.

Rather than merging, a corporation instead can buy all or substantially all the assets of another firm. This method of acquisition entails far fewer procedures than a merger. Nevertheless, most statutes in this area try to protect creditors' rights when such sales take place. Stock acquisitions are also simpler than mergers but may be subject to federal securities laws.

Care must be taken to avoid de facto mergers, transactions taking the form of a sale of substantially all the assets or a stock acquisition but nevertheless having the effect of a merger. Because noncompliance with merger statutes can prejudice the rights of shareholders and creditors, courts may set such de facto mergers aside and order compliance with the procedures mandated by the merger statute.

DISCUSSION QUESTIONS

1. What is dissolution?
2. Who can bring about an involuntary dissolution, and how is this done?
3. Explain why creditors ordinarily cannot cause dissolution.
4. How does a merger differ from a consolidation?
5. List and explain four rationales for mergers.
6. What procedures must a corporation generally follow to merge with another company?

7. Explain the meaning and importance of appraisal rights.
8. Why in a given case would a sale of substantially all the corporate assets be preferable to a merger?
9. List one major drawback of a stock acquisition as a substitute for a merger.
10. Explain the legal significance of a de facto merger.

CASE PROBLEMS

1. Roberta Hesek, the surviving spouse of David Hesek, a shareholder in 245 South Main Street, Inc., petitioned the court for judicial dissolution of the corporation. The remaining shareholders, in turn, sought a court order compelling Roberta to resell her husband's shares pursuant to a stock redemption agreement executed by her deceased husband in 1973. The corporation's shareholders had entered into agreements in 1970 and 1973 providing for the redemption of corporate stock on the death of a shareholder. Accord-

ingly, on the death of Roberta's husband, the corporation had given timely notice of its intent to redeem the husband's shares of stock and had tendered the agreed-on price. In these circumstances, did Roberta, as the surviving spouse of a shareholder, have standing to petition for judicial dissolution of the corporation? (*Hesek v. 245 South Main Street, Inc.*, 566 N.Y.S.2d 127 [A.D. 4 Dept. 1991].)

2. Monahan Building Maintenance, Inc. (Monahan Building) provided commercial cleaning services. In 1977, Monahan Building purchased substantially all the assets of Monahan Commercial Cleaners, Inc. (Monahan Cleaners), including a cleaning contract with Sage Realty. Monahan Building hired over 90 percent of Monahan Cleaners' employees and assumed the collective bargaining agreement that covered these employees, including lobby attendants. Under this contract, Sage had dictated the job standards for the lobby attendant position, including the uniforms worn by the lobby attendants. Hasselman was a lobby attendant who, as part of the employment contract, had been made to wear a revealing outfit. She had been the object of sexual harassment as a result of this uniform, but neither Sage nor Monahan Cleaners had done anything about her complaints. After she had been discharged for not wearing the uniform, she had sued Sage and Monahan Cleaners for sexual discrimination. Could Monahan Building, the successor corporation, now be liable for Monahan Cleaners' discriminatory acts? (*Equal Employment Opportunity Commission v. Sage Realty Corporation*, 507 F. Supp. 599 [S.D. N.Y. 1981].)

3. Dayton sued Peck, Stow and Wilcox Co. (PSW-1) under products liability law for personal injuries he suffered in 1976 while operating a metal-shearing machine manufactured by the firm. PSW-1 had manufactured the machine in question in 1957. In 1963, PSW-1 had sold its assets for cash to Veeder-Root, which had never manufactured metal-shear machinery. The purchase agreement had expressly provided that Veeder-Root would not be liable for any claims based on negligence or products liability. As part of the transaction, Veeder-Root had set up a new corporation, Peck, Stow and Wilcox Co. (PSW-2), to carry on the business of PSW-1. The shareholders, officers, and directors of PSW-1 had not become shareholders, officers, or directors of PSW-2; the purchase also had left the shareholders' relationship to their respective companies unchanged. In addition, PSW-1 had undergone no liquidation or dissolution at that time. In 1966, Veeder-Root had merged with PSW-2; and the metal-shear business had been carried on by Veeder-Root's Peck, Stow and Wilcox Division. In the same year, Veeder-Root had changed its name to Veeder Industries, Inc. (Veeder). In 1975, Veeder had sold all the assets of its Peck, Stow and Wilcox Division to P.S.&W. Co. (PSW-3), a corporation formed to make the purchase. As part of the sales agreement, Veeder had agreed to retain responsibility for liabilities arising from products manufactured or sold by its Peck, Stow & Wilcox Division before 1 December 1975. With this transaction, Veeder's involvement with the manufacture and sale of metal-shear machinery had ceased. Dayton argued that Veeder should be liable for his injuries because the "purchase" of PSW-1 by Veeder actually had been a merger. Do you agree? (*Dayton v. Peck, Stow, and Wilcox Company*, 739 F.2d 690 [1st Cir. 1984].)

4. Davis and Levy were the sole shareholders of Shayne-Levy Associates, Inc. (Shayne-Levy), which functioned as a sales representative in the knit goods industry. Davis, who held 18.36 percent of the stock, handled the foreign business, consisting primarily of an account with Kowa Trading Corp. (Kowa). Levy, who owned the balance of the stock, handled the domestic business, primarily the Star Knitwear, Inc. (Star) account, which provided 50 percent of Shayne-Levy's gross income. Each individual earned his own commissions and did not have to account to the other. Levy also held one-third of the stock in Star. When Levy suggested in 1983 that Shayne-Levy should drop the foreign business as unprofitable, Davis left the corporation's employ and joined Kowa. Levy, with the aid of a new corporate accountant, began to alter the corporate structure to increase the perquisites to him and his family and to shelter the income he derived therefrom. These actions in actuality amounted to a siphoning away and "wasting" of a substantial portion of the firm's assets. The perquisites shared by Davis and Levy in an earlier day in no way resembled the wholesale dissipation that took place at Levy's behest, for the benefit of himself and his family, after Davis's departure. Although the corporation had the right, under a 1970 shareholders' agreement, to buy out Davis's interest within sixty days of termination of his employment at the book value of the firm as of the last day of the month preceding such termination, it failed to exercise this right in a timely manner, thereby forgoing its rights under the agreement. The parties nevertheless entered into negotiations for a buy-out. However, when the corporate accountant offered him only $4000, Davis sought judicial relief. After lengthy hearings, the referee reached an adjusted valuation

twenty times greater than the amount Shayne-Levy had offered. The lower court confirmed this finding and entered judgment against the corporation in that amount. In light of the referee's confirmed findings, namely that Levy had looted the corporate defendant by completely controlling the corporation and that his actions might have rendered it unable to pay this judgment, the appeals court joined Levy to the suit. The court did this in order to afford complete relief to Davis by making Levy jointly and severally liable with the corporation. In these circumstances, was the court's reasoning persuasive? (*Matter of Davis,* 571 N.Y.S.2d 234 [A.D. 1 Dept. 1991].)

5. In 1985, First Florida Banks, Inc., a registered bank holding company, together with the board of directors of its subsidiary banks, decided to merge the subsidiary banks into the company's lead bank, First Florida Bank, N.A. (known at the time as First National Bank of Florida). Lewis State Bank was one of the twelve subsidiaries to be merged into First Florida Bank, N.A. (First Florida). Since First Florida owned virtually all the stock, substantially more than the required two-thirds of Lewis State Bank's outstanding common stock voted in favor of the merger in July, 1985. Under the terms of the merger, Lewis State Bank's minority shareholders were to receive cash for their shares; and the majority shareholders would receive stock in the merged bank. George Lewis and others, however, voted their Lewis State Bank shares against the merger. Subsequently, these plaintiffs perfected their rights as dissenting shareholders under the applicable statutes. The cash that First Florida had offered to minority shareholders in the merger agreement represented $21 per share, based on the $20.78 book value of each outstanding share of Lewis State Bank's common stock as of 31 March 1985. By dissenting, the plaintiffs rejected First Florida's $21 per-share offer. First Florida asked the state comptroller of the currency to appraise the dissenters' shares. The comptroller subsequently allowed each party to submit materials for use in conducting the appraisal. Ultimately, the comptroller appraised the stock at $17.23 per share. In June, 1987, the plaintiffs instituted this action, seeking judicial review of the comptroller's approval of the merger and appraisal of their Lewis State Bank stock. On 4 April 1989, the district court entered a final order affirming the comptroller's actions. On appeal, Lewis and the other dissenting shareholders argued that majority stockholders may not freeze out minority shareholders during a merger by requiring them

to take cash over their objection, thus permitting the majority to become 100-percent owners of the merged corporation. Further, if minority stockholders object to taking stock in the merged corporation, they can be required to take cash, but when they want stock in the merged corporation, they are entitled to even treatment with all other holders of like stock. Should the court agree with Lewis and the other dissenting shareholders' reasoning? (*Lewis* v. *Clark,* 911 F.2d 1558 [11th Cir. 1990].)

6. Davis Aircraft Products Co., Inc. (Davis) was engaged in the business of designing, manufacturing, and selling restraints used in aircraft. Prior to November, 1984, Davis had conducted its manufacturing operations out of a building located in Northport, New York. When the Northport facility required extensive repairs, Davis commenced a search for a new building. Subsequently, it purchased a building in Bohemia, New York, that Davis's president viewed as a more efficient facility. After the purchase, Davis continued in the same business as before the move and did not discontinue any of its former operations. Dukas, a shareholder, alleged that the transaction was voidable because the corporation had not obtained the required authorization from its shareholders. Was Davis's purchase a sale of substantially all its assets such as to require shareholder approval of the transaction? (*Dukas* v. *Davis Aircraft Products Co., Inc.,* 516 N.Y.S.2d 781 [N.Y. App. Div. 1987].)

7. Keenan, the corporate president of Superior Grain Company, Inc. (Superior), had executed a broker contract with American River Transportation Company (American) on 5 November 1987, which contract provided for the shipment of soybeans on two barges. The barge freight totaled $21,447.24. At the time of the contract's execution, Superior had merged into Keenan Cotton Gin & Grain Elevator, Inc. No one was aware of the merger other than Keenan and his CPA. The broker contract listed American as the "seller" and Superior /Robert Keenan as the "buyer." Keenan stated in his deposition that he had read the broker's contract, had known what it contained, and had signed it. He further stated by deposition that he had continued to do business under the name of Superior until July, 1988, and had never notified Marine Freight Exchange, Inc. (the broker) or American that Superior had merged into another corporation. The barge freight was never paid, and Keenan admitted there was no reason to doubt the accuracy of the charges. American contended the above

facts were sufficient for the trial court to rule as a matter of law that Keenan was personally liable for the debt incurred on behalf of Superior. According to American, upon Superior's merger with Keenan Cotton Gin & Grain Elevator, Inc., Superior had ceased to exist and any contracts entered into by or on behalf of Superior would involve contracts with a nonexistent entity. The former Arkansas statute under which the merger had occurred provided as follows: "The separate existence of all corporations parties to the plan of merger or consolidation, except the surviving or new corporation, shall cease." In these circumstances, should the court hold Keenan personally liable to American for the nonpayment of the barge freight charges? (*Keenan* v. *American River Transportation Company*, 799 S.W.2d 801 [Ark. 1990].)

8. The plaintiffs—Warner Communications, Inc. (Warner); Time Warner, Inc. (Time); and TW Sub Inc. (TW Sub)—all of which are Delaware corporations, sought a declaratory judgment that Chris-Craft Industries, Inc. (Chris-Craft) and its controlled subsidiary, BHC, Inc. (BHC), the related holders of Warner Communications, Inc.'s Series B Variable Rate Cumulative Convertible Preferred stock (Series B Preferred), are not entitled to a class vote on a proposed merger among Warner, its controlling shareholder Time Incorporated (now renamed Time Warner, Inc.) and TW Sub Inc., a wholly owned subsidiary of Time Warner. The Series B Preferred was issued pursuant to a 1983 exchange agreement among Warner, Chris-Craft, and BHC. Under that exchange agreement, Warner obtained BHC preferred stock convertible into 42.5 percent of BHC's outstanding common stock; and BHC obtained the entire issue—15,200,000 shares—of Warner's Series B Preferred stock. The certificate of designation creating the Series B Preferred entitles each share of that stock to a quarterly dividend equal to the greater of (a) $0.125 or (b) 200 percent of the regular quarterly dividend, if any, payable on a share of Warner common stock. Each share is convertible into common stock pursuant to a complex formula; and each carries the same voting rights as the common stock, unless a dividend is in default. In that event, the Series B Preferred stock "voting as a class" elects three directors. Section 3.3 of the certificate of designation creates a right in the holders of the Series B Preferred to participate with other holders of Warner preferred stock in a class vote under certain circumstances; moreover, Section 3.4(i) of the certificate creates a right in the holders of Series B Preferred stock alone

to a series vote in certain circumstances. Time and Warner subsequently executed an amended merger agreement that contemplated a two-step transaction by which Time would acquire all the outstanding stock of Warner. The first step was completed on 24 July 1989, when Time purchased 100 million shares of Warner common stock, representing approximately 50 percent of such Warner's stock, at $70 per share in cash. Under the amended merger agreement, a merger in which TW Sub will be merged into Warner (which will survive as a wholly owned subsidiary of Time) would follow the tender offer. The Warner common stock, other than that held by Time, will be converted into securities, cash, or other property. The Warner Series B Preferred is to be converted into Time Series BB Preferred stock. The parties have stipulated that the holders of the Warner Series B Preferred will be adversely affected by the back-end merger. The amended merger agreement provides further that shares of Warner common stock and Warner Series B Preferred Stock, the holders of which comply with all provisions of the general corporation law concerning appraisal rights, will not be converted in the back-end merger. BHC and the other defendants contended that BHC is entitled to a class vote on the proposed merger under two distinct provisions of Warner's certificate of incorporation. First, the defendants argued that Section 3.3(i) of the certificate of designation gives BHC the right to a class vote, since this section protects against *any corporate action* that alters or changes "any rights or preferences" of the preferred stock so as to adversely affect the preferred shareholders. The proposed merger, it submitted, will alter the rights of the Series B Preferred (presumptively in an adverse way) by substituting a new security—Time BB Preferred—for the Series B Preferred. Thus, it concluded, Section 3.3(i) requires that BHC be afforded the opportunity to vote on that merger separately. Second, defendants maintained that Section 3.4(i) of the certificate of designation entitles BHC to a vote on the back-end merger because the merger will admittedly amend the Warner certificate of incorporation. Plaintiffs asserted that Section 3.4(iii) is the pertinent provision; and, as such, it grants no right to vote on the back-end merger to the Series B Preferred shareholders. As to BHC's claim that Sections 3.3(i) and 3.4(i) do grant it the right to a class vote in these circumstances, Warner answered first that Section 3.3(i) protects only the rights and preferences of the entire class of preferred stock, not the rights and preferences granted to one or more particular series of preferred stock. The only right or preference necessarily shared by every series of preferred stock, plaintiffs submitted, is the right to share ratably in dividends and asset distribution in certain circumstances. The merger will not affect that right, they claimed, because an identical provision in the Time charter will protect the Time Series BB Preferred. Second, the plaintiffs argued that Section 3.4(i), which requires supermajority approval by the Series B Preferred shares in order to amend Warner's certificate of incorporation or bylaws "so as to affect adversely" the Series B Preferred, does not grant defendants a vote in the back-end merger because it is the merger, rather than the amendments to the certificate of incorporation, that presumably will adversely affect the defendants. How should the court rule on this declaratory judgment? (*Warner Communications, Inc. v. Chris-Craft Industries, Inc.*, 583 A.2d 962 [Del. Ch. 1989].)

9. Rosenblatt, a minority shareholder in Skelly Oil Company (Skelly), brought a class action against Getty Oil Company (Getty) challenging the fairness of the merger of Getty and Skelly. Getty, before the merger, had been a major Skelly shareholder. The evidence showed that, prior to the initiation of merger negotiations, Getty had known that it would be sued. Thus, it had sought to structure the transaction to meet the standards imposed by Delaware law. At the initial meeting held on 15 July 1976, Getty and Skelly management had been given a legal research memorandum on valuation methods approved by Delaware courts. Moreover, Getty had been cognizant of the potential conflicts among the interlocking managements of both companies. Accordingly, at the 15 July 1976 meeting, when Getty had designated Kenneth Hill of Blyth Eastman as its chief negotiator, Hill had immediately resigned from Skelly's board, on which he had served for ten years. Similarly, a partner in the law firm Hays, Landsman & Head had resigned from the Skelly board because the law firm had been representing Getty. As to the structure of the actual negotiations, Getty and Skelly had agreed on 15 July 1976 to have Dolyer & McNaughton, a well-known petroleum engineering firm, estimate their respective reserves and analyze their future prospects. Getty and Skelly also had agreed to evaluate separately their respective surface assets and then negotiate those values. As a result of hard bargaining, the parties had accepted a stock exchange ratio of .5875 Getty shares for one share of Skelly, after Getty had advocated a .5 and Skelly a .7 ratio. On these facts, did Rosenblatt have a good cause of action? (*Rosenblatt v. Getty Oil Company*, 493 A.2d 929 [Del. 1985].)

10. Bowman and Bridges were shareholders, directors, and employees of State Bank of Keysville (the Bank). In 1979, the Bank proposed to merge with NB Corporation. After learning of Bowman and Bridges's opposition to the merger, the president of the Bank told them that their voting against the merger would have a definite adverse effect on their jobs. Both women executed their proxy cards in favor of the merger against their will, under duress, and out of fear of losing their jobs. At the special meeting on 26 June 1979, 2008 shares of the Bank's common stock, including their eleven shares, were voted in favor of the merger proposal. This was eight votes more than the number necessary to constitute the required two-thirds majority for approval of the plan. Two days after the special meeting, however, Bowman and Bridges wrote a joint letter to the Bank president stating that their proxies were invalid, illegally obtained, improper, and null and void. Accordingly, they wrote, only 1997 votes had been cast in favor of the merger, three less than the votes necessary for approval. On 6 July 1979, the Bank board voted to abandon the merger. The merger was aborted, according to Bowman and Bridges's allegations, because the Bank had feared that the illegal activities involved in obtaining the proxies of stockholders, including the plaintiffs, would be discovered. Six days later, the Bank's directors, by a five to four vote, decided to discharge the plaintiffs from their employment with the Bank. The women sued, arguing that the Bank, in discharging employees who were also shareholders, had acted in violation of securities and corporation laws because the Bank had acted against employees who had been merely exercising their protected rights as shareholders in questioning the manner in which proxies had been obtained for a proposed merger. The Bank argued that the women were employees-at-will who could be fired at any time. Should Bowman and Bridges receive damages? (*Bowman v. State Bank of Keysville*, 331 S.E.2d 797 [Va. 1985].)

CHAPTER 43

Franchising

OUTLINE

THE SIGNIFICANCE OF FRANCHISING AS A BUSINESS METHOD

Although franchising began in America over a century ago when breweries licensed beer gardens as a means of distributing their products, franchising did not become recognized as a distinct method of doing business until after World War II.[1] Since then, and especially in the last fifteen years, franchising has contributed significantly to the United States' achieving its position as the world's largest market. Presently more than 2000 U.S. companies encompassing over forty different economic sectors use the franchise method for distributing their goods or services both domestically and internationally.[2] Among the types of businesses that use franchise systems are the following: automobile dealerships; gasoline stations; restaurants; convenience stores; soft drink bottlers; nonfood merchandising businesses (such as drug, electronics, cosmetics, and home furnishings companies); travel agencies; hotels, motels, and campgrounds; automobile and truck rental services; printing and copying services; tax preparation firms; real estate businesses; accounting firms; cleaning services; lawn and garden services; laundry services; equipment rentals; early childhood education and daycare centers; and beauty salons.

According to estimates of the International Franchise Association Educational Foundation, Inc., franchises overall would sell $716.7 billion worth of such goods and services in 1990, 114 percent higher than the level of sales at the beginning of the 1980s. The number of persons employed in franchising systems was 7.7 million in 1988.[3] Figure 43.1 shows that by 1990, franchises would account for approximately 34 percent of all retail sales in the United States ($615.1 billion of the $1,813 billion total in retail sales).

As these statistics demonstrate, franchising has developed into an important and popular method of marketing and distribution. In this chapter, we examine why this has occurred.

DEFINITION

No universally accepted definition of the word *franchise* exists. The following definition, taken from the Washington Franchise Investment Protection Act, Section 19.100.010(4), is typical:

> "Franchise" means an oral or written contract or agreement, either expressed or implied, in which a person grants to another person a license to use a

[1]Harold Brown, *Franchising—Realities and Remedies,* 2nd ed. (New York: Law Journal Press, 1978), p. 1.
[2]International Franchise Association Educational Foundation, Inc., and Horwath International, *Franchising in the Economy 1988–1990* (Washington, D.C., 1990), p. 13.
[3]Ibid., p. 1.

FIGURE 43.1 Franchising as a Percentage of Retail Sales, 1990

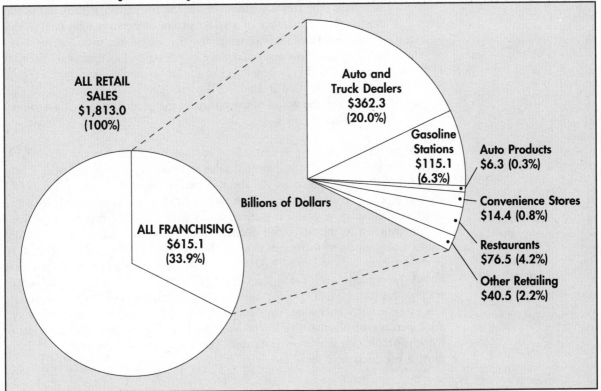

ALL RETAIL SALES $1,813.0 (100%)

ALL FRANCHISING $615.1 (33.9%)

Billions of Dollars

Auto and Truck Dealers $362.3 (20.0%)

Gasoline Stations $115.1 (6.3%)

Auto Products $6.3 (0.3%)

Convenience Stores $14.4 (0.8%)

Restaurants $76.5 (4.2%)

Other Retailing $40.5 (2.2%)

Source: International Franchise Association Educational Foundation, Inc., and Horwath International, *Franchising in the Economy 1988–1990* (Washington, D.C., 1990), p. 11.

trade name, service mark, trade mark, logotype or related characteristic in which there is a community interest in the business of offering, selling, distributing goods or services at wholesale or retail, leasing or otherwise and in which the franchisee is required to pay, directly or indirectly, a franchise fee.

Service marks Distinctive symbols designating the services offered by a particular business or individual.

Trademarks Distinctive marks or symbols used to identify a particular company as the source of its products.

Logotypes Identifying symbols.

Service marks, trademarks, and **logotypes** are symbols that identify the origin of goods and services. The person or firm that grants a franchise to another is called the *franchisor*. The person receiving the franchise is known as the *franchisee*. Franchises, or retail businesses involving sales of products or services to consumers, fall into two general categories:

1. *Distributorships* (also called *product* or *trade name franchises*), in which a manufacturer/franchisor licenses a franchisee to sell its product either exclusively or with other products. The franchisee often has the exclusive right to sell the product in a designated area or territory.

2. *Chain-style businesses* (also called *business format franchises*), in which a franchisee operates a business under the franchisor's trade name and is identified as a member of a select group of persons who deal in this particular business. In exchange for the franchise, the franchisee ordinarily must follow a standardized or prescribed format as to methods of operation and may be subject to the franchisor's control with regard to the materials used in making the product, site selection, the design of the facility, the hours of the business, the qualifications of personnel, and the like.[4]

Distributorships were estimated to account for 70.2 percent of all franchise sales in 1990, with total annual sales by these types of franchisors reaching $503 billion—an increase of about 4 percent over the figures for 1989.[5] However, the overall number of such establishments has decreased since 1972 due to the closings of gasoline stations and automobile and truck dealerships.[6]

In contrast to the predicted decrease in distributorships, chain-style franchises were expected to increase in number to almost 393,000 in 1990, a 16 percent increase over 1988.[7] In 1990, annual sales were expected to increase about 11 percent over the figures for 1989, totaling $213.2 billion.[8] Large franchisors (those with 1000 or more units each) should continue to dominate this category of franchising; they accounted for 51.7 percent of total sales and 53.2 percent of all chain-style establishments in 1988.[9] Most of these large franchisors engage either in restaurant businesses or in the retailing of automotive products and services.

BENEFITS OF FRANCHISING

Whatever form the particular franchise takes, the advantages of a franchise system as a method of doing business make it attractive to both potential franchisees and franchisors.

The benefits to franchisees include the following:

1. the opportunity to start a business despite limited capital and experience

---

[4]Gladys Glickman, *Franchising*, vol. 15 of *Business Organizations* (New York: Matthew Bender, 1983), Section 2.02.
[5]International Franchise Association Educational Foundation, Inc., and Howarth International, *Franchising*, p. 90.
[6]Ibid., p. 94.
[7]Ibid., p. 12.
[8]Ibid.
[9]Ibid., p. 13.

2. the goodwill that results from marketing a nationally known, high-quality trademark or service mark, which not only benefits the individual franchisees but also raises customer acceptance throughout the system

3. the availability of the franchisor's business expertise in such areas as inventory control, warehousing, advertising, market research, and product innovation

4. an assured supply of materials, the use of bulk buying techniques, and access to training and supervision

The benefits to franchisors include:

1. the franchisee's investment of capital

2. the goodwill and other advantages flowing from the franchisee's entrepreneurial abilities, including the enhanced value of the trademark or service mark

3. the availability of an assured distribution network, which brings about economies of scale in labor costs, produces a more certain demand curve, and reduces wide fluctuations in sales

4. a larger asset base, which makes the franchisor better able to secure credit, enhance profits, avoid financial risks, attract the best talent, lobby for favorable legislation, and defray litigation costs[10]

The franchisor and franchisee are able to accomplish more together than they can through individual effort. In an era of increasing vertical integration, some observers have seen franchising as the last bastion for the independent businessperson. Franchising provides independent businesspersons with the means of opening and operating their own businesses, and it allows small businesses to compete with mammoth corporations. In addition, franchising fosters the expansion of an established product or service. It may also bring about the rescue of an otherwise failing business.

By lowering barriers to entry, franchising as a type of business system furthers many of the antitrust policies you will learn about in Chapter 46. It thus provides societal and economic benefits to the public at large as well as to individual consumers. On the other hand, the franchisor's often extensive control over the franchisee's conduct of the business together with other aspects of the franchisor-franchisee relationship have spawned complicated legal questions. We will consider some of these issues in the remainder of this chapter.

[10]Brown, *Franchising,* pp. 6–12.

FRANCHISING COMPARED WITH OTHER BUSINESS RELATIONSHIPS

A franchise generally involves a form of marketing or distribution in which one party grants to another the right or privilege to do business in a specified manner in a particular place over a certain period of time. It has sometimes been difficult to distinguish such a relationship from other types of business relationships. The distinction may nonetheless be legally important, since in recent years about one-third of the states have passed laws dealing specifically with franchising, and the Federal Trade Commission has established regulations covering franchising. Until trouble develops, the two parties may consider the holder of the right to do business in a prescribed manner as an independent contractor. But when the grantor terminates its business relationships with the holder, the holder may try to characterize the relationship as a franchise in order to fall under the protection of such statutes. Even before the relationship between the two parties sours, government agencies tend to view the relationship as one of employment, not of independent contracting. If the holder of the privilege is an employee or agent rather than an independent contractor, the law requires the grantor to pay withholding and social security taxes, federal minimum wages, and workers' compensation. In addition, in such circumstances the grantor may be subject to the provisions of other labor laws and private antitrust suits.

It is especially difficult to classify the relationship if the holder of the privilege is a distributor. As we have already noted, a distributor may be a franchisee. Yet it is also possible that a distributor is instead an employee, a **consignee,** or an independent contractor, depending on the details surrounding the distributor's relationship with its supplier. As you would expect, courts delve deeply into the particular facts at issue (most notably evidence of the grantor's degree of control over the distributor) in making such determinations.

Still, the law is fairly well settled with regard to certain issues: **Cooperatives, concessionaires,** joint ventures, general partnerships (although a partnership can act either as a franchisor or a franchisee), and sales agencies ordinarily are not deemed franchises. And, as you will learn in Chapter 44, a franchise agreement does not usually amount to a security under federal or state law because the distributors/franchisees invest their own efforts in the franchise and do not expect to obtain benefits solely from the efforts of others. In other words, the "passive investment" component generally associated with certain types of securities remains unsatisfied in the typical franchising arrangement.

In the following case, the court had to decide whether the business relationship in dispute involved a franchise arrangement.

Consignee   A person to whom goods are shipped for sale and who generally can return all unsold goods to the consignor.

Cooperatives   Groups of individuals, commonly laborers or farmers, who unite in a common enterprise and share the profits proportionately.

Concessionaires   Operators of refreshment centers.

Blankenship v. Dialist International Corporation
568 N.E.2d 503 (Ill. App. 5 Dist. 1991)

FACTS   Blankenship and Cronin, vice-president and national sales manager of Dialist International Corporation (Dialist International) entered into a distributor's agreement naming Blankenship as the sales representative of Dialist International for a specified territory. In return, Blankenship paid Dialist International $15,000. Thereafter, Blankenship met with Cronin and received a detailed explanation of the Dialist system and instruction on how to market the product, a list-finder device designed for attachment to telephones. Cronin also provided Blankenship with a binder that contained promotional materials; letters from proposed customers; and samples of Dialist advertising, cost sheets, and purchase orders. On attempting to market the Dialist, Blankenship encountered difficulties regarding the credibility of the company. Herman L. Smith, president of Dialist International, provided Blankenship with a letter vouching for the credibility of Dialist International. In March, 1987, Blankenship sued Dialist International, Smith, and Cronin for rescission of the distributorship agreement and for damages under section 21 of the Franchise Disclosure Act (the Act). Blankenship asserted that the agreement had constituted a sale of the franchise and because the sale had violated Section 4 of the Act, he was entitled to the return, with interest, of the full amount paid by him for the franchise, plus attorneys' fees and costs. On 13 April 1989, the trial court granted summary judgment for Blankenship for the $15,000 plus interest.

ISSUE   Had Blankenship and Dialist entered into a franchise agreement?

HOLDING   Yes. The agreement between the parties had satisfied the statutory requirements for the creation of a franchise under Illinois law.

REASONING   The defendants argued that the affidavit and supporting documents submitted by Blankenship had failed to establish that a franchise agreement had existed between the parties under Illinois law. The definition of franchise set forth in Section 3 of the Act reads:

> (1) "Franchise" means a contract or agreement, either expressed or implied, whether oral or written, between two or more persons by which: (a) a franchisee is granted the right to engage in the business of offering, selling or distributing goods or services, under a marketing plan or system prescribed or suggested in substantial part by a franchisor; and (b) the operation of the franchisee's business pursuant to such plan or system is substantially associated with the franchisor's trademark, service mark, trade name, logo-type, advertising, or other commercial symbol designating the franchisor or its affiliate; and (c) the person granted the right to engage in such business is required to pay a fee of $100 or more.

Thus, by statutory definition, a franchise exists where an agreement meets these three objective criteria. Section 3 of the Act defines a marketing plan as "[a] plan relating to some aspect of the conduct of a party to a contract in conducting business, including but not limited to (a) specification of price, or special pricing systems or discount plans, (b) use of particular sales or display equipment or merchandising devices, (c) use of specific sales techniques, (d) use of advertising or promotional materials or cooperation in advertising efforts." Hence, the agreement at issue in the present case satisfies the statutory requirement of a marketing plan or system. When Blankenship encountered difficulty regarding the credibility of Dialist International, its president, Smith, had assisted Blankenship by furnishing a letter asserting the company's integrity and financial responsibility. These representations amply satisfy the statutory requirement of the existence of a marketing plan or system. The second statutory criterion concerns the use of a trade name or other commercial symbol designating the franchise or its affiliate. The "Dialist Agreement" had granted to Blankenship "the distributorship and authority to sell Cooperative Dialists." Moreover, all the promotional materials provided to Blankenship refer to the product as Dialist. Furthermore, Blankenship had been instructed to rely on the purported good name of Dialist and the company of the same name in marketing the product. Given the strong association between the Dialist name and the nature of the product to be distributed and the promised benefits to be derived from being identified with Dialist International, Blankenship's business had been substantially associated with the trade name Dialist such as to satisfy the second statutory requirement. The final statutory requirement is that Blankenship must have paid a fee of $100 or more to be granted the right to engage in the business. Blankenship asserted, and the defendants did not dispute, that he had paid $15,000 for the right to engage in his business. Thus, inasmuch as Blankenship had asserted facts sufficient to satisfy each criterion in the statutory definition, no genuine issue of material fact had existed as to the applicability of the Act. Therefore, the trial court had not erred in entering summary judgment for Blankenship.

SETTING UP THE FRANCHISING RELATIONSHIP

Franchisors usually recruit franchisees by advertising their particular business. The franchisor then sends "franchise kits" to those who answer the advertisement. Typically, this franchise kit points out in glowing terms the potential for success in this particular industry. To the uninitiated layperson or the businessperson with little previous experience and limited capital—those who may be most inclined to enter a franchising arrangement—the franchisor's promotional documents, market studies, and statistics seem highly persuasive. Even at the outset, then, the franchisee relies heavily on the franchisor for guidance. But the pervasiveness of the franchisor's control often leads to later legal difficulties, as we will see.

Although many variables are involved, the details of a franchising arrangement usually follow a pattern. Once the parties have established initial contact and have decided to enter into a franchising relationship, the parties usually first sign a detailed agreement. In this agreement, the franchisor grants to the franchisee the right to use the mark or standardized product or service in exchange for a franchise fee. The franchisor then uses its real estate expertise to designate a specific franchise location, designs and arranges for the standardized construction of the facility, and installs fixtures and equipment therein. The franchisor intensively advertises the product in exchange for an advertising fee (usually a percentage of gross sales) paid by the franchisee. In addition, the franchisor creates training programs, prepares training manuals, and sets out stringent guidelines—even for the hiring of personnel, personnel's dress and grooming standards, and the like—for the day-to-day operation of the business.

Once the franchise becomes operative, the franchisee must follow the procedures set out in the franchisor's confidential operating manual or risk termination of the franchise. This manual usually mandates strict accounting procedures and authorizes the franchisor to inspect the books and records at any time. The franchisee typically pays a set **royalty fee** (usually based on a

Royalty fee Payment made in exchange for the grant of a right or a license.

certain percentage of the gross sales) on a monthly or semimonthly basis to the franchisor. The franchise agreement normally obligates the franchisee to secure liability insurance to protect the franchisee and franchisor against casualty losses and tort suits. The franchisee usually has the responsibility of meeting state requirements regarding workers' compensation.

The last two areas ordinarily covered in the franchise agreement—quality control and termination—pose most of the potential legal problems. It is easy to understand the franchisor's desire for quality control: Only by maintaining uniform standards of quality and appearance can the franchisor preserve its reputation and foster the public's acceptance of its product. For this reason, franchisors typically obligate the franchisee to buy products and supplies from them at set prices or from suppliers who can meet the franchisor's exacting specifications and standards. Forcing franchisees to buy only from their own franchisors would probably constitute antitrust violations, a topic we shall discuss later in this chapter. (As the law currently stands, the same would be true if the franchisor set resale prices for the franchisee; nevertheless, the franchisor can within the law *suggest* resale prices.) Critics of franchising have argued that, practically speaking, the franchisee would have a difficult, if not impossible, time finding a supplier who would meet the franchisor's specifications, with the result that, under the guise of quality control, franchisees often must pay inflated prices for supplies.

The termination provisions of a franchising agreement also constitute legal pitfalls for the unwary. The franchise agreement ordinarily sets out the duration of the franchise (say, ten years) and usually contains provisions for renewals after this time period has passed. As part of the covenants, or promises, made about the term of the agreement, the franchisee usually agrees to a covenant not to compete for a set time period after the termination of the franchise. The conditions of default, such as a franchisee's insolvency or failure to pay monthly or semimonthly fees when due, that lead to termination are reproduced in the franchise agreement. In these and other "for cause" situations, the agreement normally calls for the franchisor to give the franchisee time (for example, ten days) to cure these instances of default. Most agreements provide for notice of termination, and the existing state laws on franchising generally set out a required notice period (say, ninety days) before the franchisor can effect a termination.

When prospective franchisees lack business acumen, they are likely to accept without question the thirty-to-fifty-page agreement that the franchisor typically offers. This disparity in bargaining power has led to the passage of state and federal laws and the promulgation of administrative regulations designed to protect franchisees when they enter their agreements (through mandated disclosures) and upon termination (through notice provisions). Courts, too, have increasingly tried to protect franchisees by closely scrutinizing franchise agreements. In the following case, the court dealt with the issue of whether the franchisor had breached its alleged promise to select a suitable site for its franchisee's ice cream store.

Brennan v. Carvel Corporation
929 F.2d 801 (1st Cir. 1991)

FACTS   In 1977, Robert and Joanne Brennan responded to a newspaper advertisement describing Carvel Corporation (Carvel) franchise opportunities. On 24 April 1977, the Brennans met with Richard Monaco, an assistant to Carvel's vice-president and sales manager, who gave the Brennans a Carvel informational brochure and a Carvel disclosure statement. The brochure stated that "Carvel employs its own Real Estate location experts [who are] . . . dedicated to helping its owner-operators succeed in their stores." The disclosure statement stated in paragraph 11: "Carvel will assume responsibility for selecting, obtaining and negotiating a suitable location for the Carvel Store. When a location has been approved, Carvel will negotiate a rental arrangement, prepare and approve lease documents, and handle the closing and signing of the lease. A one-time real estate fee of $2,500.00 is paid by the Licensee." Paragraph 23 of the disclosure statement provided: "Earnings and/or profits, if any, of a Carvel Store are the responsibility of the Licensee and no representations or statements of projected earnings or profits are made to Licensees with respect to Carvel retail manufacturing stores." The Brennans, on 21 May 1977, again met with Monaco and gave him a $1000 deposit on a Carvel franchise. The Brennans and Carvel entered into a deposit agreement, which was attached to the Carvel disclosure statement. The agreement stated that "the Applicant understands that, in reliance upon this application, a substantial amount of time and effort shall be exerted in seeking, surveying and showing a location suitable for a Carvel Store." At this meeting, the Brennans told Monaco that they knew of available retail space at 195 State Street in Boston, Mass. Monaco stated that he would not approve a location for the Carvel franchise until the proposed site was "studied, evaluated, and approved" by Carvel; hence, the Brennans continued to look at other possible locations for their Carvel store. On 16 July 1977, the Brennans met at the 195 State Street location with Monaco, Urezzio (Carvel's vice-president), and the Brennan's attorney. At the meeting, Urezzio approved the 195 State Street location and, according to the testimony of the Brennans, stated that "everything [checked] out" and that "he had never approved a site which had failed." But the evidence indicated that, at the time that Urezzio approved the site, he had not believed that the store could succeed on foot traffic alone; rather, he had thought that the Brennans would have to generate additional business in the form of office and institutional (O and I) sales. Carvel had located most of its stores in suburban locations where 70 percent of the sales of a typical Carvel franchise consisted of take-home sales. The 195 State Street site, located in downtown Boston, was not conducive to such take-home sales. On 28 October 1977, the Brennans, accompanied by their lawyer, attended the closing for their store. At the closing, the Brennans and Carvel entered into a franchise agreement. The franchise agreement contained a merger clause in paragraph 27 stating, "This Agreement contains all oral and written agreements, representations and arrangements between the parties hereto, and any rights which the respective parties hereto may have had under any other previous contracts are hereby canceled and terminated, and no representations or warranties are made or implied, except as specifically set forth herein. This Agreement cannot be changed or terminated orally." The franchise agreement, in paragraph 34, also contained a statement repeating Carvel's disclaimer of any guarantee of success. At the closing, the Brennans in addition signed several sales contracts, one of which assessed a $2500 real estate services fee. Yet neither the franchise agreement nor the sales contracts contained any description of the real estate services so provided. The Brennans testified that they worked very hard at making the business a success. They pursued O and I sales and, by the time of the store's closing, had obtained over thirty O and I accounts. While these efforts had helped their business, the promotions and other efforts had not generated enough income to make the Carvel store successful. In 1980, the Brennans closed their store; and in 1981 they brought suit against Carvel and Raymond Urezzio, Carvel's vice-president and sales manager, for, among other things, breach of contract and promissory estoppel. At the close of the nonjury trial, the district court entered judgment in favor of the Brennans on the breach of contract claim and granted the Brennans $780,406.70. Carvel appealed this result.

ISSUE   Had Carvel breached its contract to select, evaluate, and approve a suitable site for the Brennans' franchise?

HOLDING   Yes. The insufficient foot traffic—which Carvel's representatives had recognized—made the site chosen unsuitable for the Brennans' ice cream store. Thus, Carvel had breached its contract with the Brennans.

REASONING   Carvel asserted that the franchise agreement entered into between the Brennans and Carvel was an integrated contract into which all prior agreements between the parties had merged and, therefore, as a matter of law, had discharged any prior contractual duty that Carvel had had to find the Brennans a suitable site. Under the parol evidence rule, "a binding integrated agreement discharges prior agreements to the extent that it is inconsistent with them" (*Restatement (Second) of Contracts* Section 213[1]). Nevertheless, the parol evidence rule does not apply to a collateral agreement; i.e., a separate contract between the parties. An examination of the deposit agreement demonstrated that the deposit agreement entered into by the Brennans and Carvel and Carvel's promise to select, evaluate, and approve a suitable site for the Brennans' ice cream store had constituted a separate contract, or an agreement collateral to the franchise agreement. Furthermore, other materials indicated that the Brennans and Carvel had intended to form a separate contract requiring Carvel to select, evaluate, and approve a suitable site or location for the Brennans' store. Moreover, the disclosure statement specifically stated that Carvel would "assume responsibility for selecting, obtaining and negotiating a suitable location for the Carvel Store." In addition, the sales contract required the Brennans to pay a $2500 fee for real estate services, but did not describe the services provided. Carvel nonetheless argued that, owing to the merger clause, the franchise agreement had discharged any prior contract entered into between the Brennans and Carvel. Here, despite the existence of this merger clause, the Brennans and Carvel had not intended that the franchise agreement should constitute the entire agreement between them. Therefore, the finding of the district court—that the Brennans and Carvel had entered into a separate contract collateral to the franchise agreement in which Carvel promised to select, evaluate, and approve a suitable location for the Brennans' ice cream store—was not clearly erroneous. Carvel contended that, even if the Brennans and Carvel had entered into a separate and enforceable contract for the selection, evaluation, and approval of a suitable site, Carvel had not breached that contract, since the district court had erroneously concluded that the site was unsuitable. Carvel asserted that a suitable location or site is one that "is properly zoned, has the necessary electrical and mechanical facilities to operate a Carvel ice cream store, and . . . has enough space to house both the factory facility and retail sales." The evidence presented at trial indicated that, under the circumstances, a "suitable site" means one that is in a location with adequate traffic or population, or other appropriate characteristics, in which a Carvel franchise may succeed. Although the evidence had shown that the Brennans knew that a Carvel franchise could fail, Carvel nevertheless had contracted to approve a "suitable site." In its informational brochure, Carvel had stated that it employed "Real Estate location experts," and, in the deposit agreement, Carvel had stated that "a substantial amount of time and effort" would be used in selecting a suitable site. Furthermore, based on its interpretation of a "suitable site," the district court had not erred in concluding that Carvel had breached the contract to select, evaluate, and approve a suitable location for the Brennans' ice cream store, since the 195 State Street site was not a suitable location for a Carvel store; there was insufficient foot traffic at the 195 State Street site and, to succeed, the Brennans would have had to make the majority of their business O and I sales, even though Carvel's operations were not primarily directed toward O and I sales. Finally, the court had credited the testimony that the Brennans worked hard at their ice cream store and that the store's failure was not attributable to any lack of effort or mismanagement. Carvel, however, contended that the principles of waiver and estoppel would bar the Brennans' claims against Carvel because the Brennans, who had initially mentioned the 195 State Street site, had recognized many of the shortcomings of the site in advance. Under Massachusetts law, the burden of proving waiver is on the party who makes the assertion. In order to establish waiver, the party must show clear, decisive, and unequivocal conduct indicating that the opposing party would not insist that the contractual provision at issue be performed. It is evident that, under the standards established by Massachusetts law, Carvel had not shown that the Brennans had waived their rights concerning the contract provision requiring Carvel to select, evaluate, and approve a suitable site for their ice cream store. Indeed, the evidence indicated that the Brennans had sought Carvel's approval for the site and had viewed Urezzio's approval as very important. In essence, estoppel requires that a party who makes a representation of fact cannot later deny that fact, if the opposing party has justifiably relied upon the representation. Hence, the Brennans had not waived their right to assert, nor were they estopped from asserting, that Carvel had failed to approve a "suitable site" for the Brennans' ice cream store.

Most litigation involving franchises has centered on the termination provisions in the franchising agreement. Because termination can leave the franchisee with little to show after years of effort and expense, courts, whenever possible, try to find a basis of relief so the franchisee is not without a remedy. The following case involved such an issue.

ABA Distributors, Inc. v. *Adolph Coors Company, Inc.*
542 F. Supp. 1272 (W.D. Mo. 1982)

FACTS   ABA Distributors, Inc. (ABA) was a Missouri beer distributor authorized to distribute Adolph Coors Company, Inc. (Coors) beer. From 1 June 1973 to 21 March 1980, Coors had not sold beer in any states east of the Mississippi River, nor had it had any distributors in that territory. ABA had become a Coors distributor on 1 June 1978 for the territory in and around Kansas City, Missouri. ABA had invested over $1.4 million in order to obtain the Coors distributorship. In January, 1979, and January, 1980, Coors officials told the president of ABA that Coors believed ABA had been distributing Coors products outside its assigned geographic territory. ABA denied these allegations. In March, 1980, a Coors official orally announced to a group of distributors at a conference in Phoenix that any distributor selling outside its assigned geographic area would be terminated immediately and without notice once Coors discovered such a fact. From February, 1979, to March, 1980, a private investigator hired by Coors maintained surveillance on ABA's warehouse. On 8 March 1980, the investigator called Coors's counsel to report that three small trucks had left the ABA warehouse and had delivered beer to a large trailer truck parked several blocks away. The investigator had made no inquiries at ABA about this delivery and had not attempted to find out the destination of the trailer truck. Nevertheless, without any further investigation by Coors, Coors officials called the president of ABA to Golden, Colorado, on 19 March 1980 and terminated ABA's distributorship. At this meeting, Coors officials did not charge that ABA had sold Coors beer out of state but charged instead that ABA had been dishonest with regard to out-of-state-sales. Coors temporarily divided ABA's distributorship between two other distributors. Coors sent ABA a letter of termination on 21 March 1980, effective immediately without notice. ABA's franchise agreement with Coors provided for termination on thirty days' notice unless the franchisee had engaged in violations of law, dishonesty, or moral turpitude or had been convicted of a felony. In these "for cause" circumstances, termination could be immediate. ABA argued that since its conduct had not fallen into any of these categories, Coors's termination of its distributorship had breached the franchise agreement.

ISSUE   Had Coors wrongfully terminated ABA's distributorship by breaching the franchise agreement?

HOLDING   Yes. Coors's conduct had violated both Missouri common law and statutory law.

REASONING   Coors had breached the fiduciary duty of good faith and fair dealing that it owed ABA under Missouri law when it attempted, without actual knowledge of any facts to support the grounds stated in its letter of 21 March 1980, to terminate ABA without notice under the agreement. Both common law contract law and Missouri's UCC Section 1-203 imposed an obligation of good faith on Coors. Because Missouri's franchise law applied to beer distributorships, the ninety days' notice required under this statute would invalidate the thirty days' notice provision in Coors's agreement even if Coors had complied with the provisions of its agreement. Therefore, under applicable Missouri law, Coors's attempt to terminate ABA without notice had breached its fiduciary duty to ABA—the duty of fair dealing and good faith it owed to ABA—and the franchise statute's requirement of at least ninety days' notice before an attempted termination. For these reasons, the 21 March 1980 notice of termination was set aside, and Coors was ordered to give ABA the opportunity to sell its distributorship according to the provisions on transferability within the distributorship agreement. Furthermore, Coors must avoid any unreasonable withholding of approval of any prospective buyers ABA might find. Should a good-faith disagreement in this regard arise, however, either party could invoke the arbitration provision of the agreement. This disposition of the dispute represented a more effective remedy than money damages, which would have been inadequate because, unlike a sale of the distributorship, such damages would not have allowed ABA to recoup its substantial investment in Coors products.

Although courts will, whenever possible, try to find a basis of relief for the franchisee, they will not force franchisors to stick with obviously inept franchisees. The following case illustrates this point.

Foreign Motors, Inc. v. Audi of America, Inc.
755 F. Supp. 30 (D. Mass. 1991)

FACTS   Foreign Motors, Inc. (FMI), the plaintiff, commenced this action in response to an attempt by the defendants, Audi of America, Inc. and Volkswagen of America, Inc. (hereinafter collectively referred to as "Audi"), to terminate FMI's franchise to sell, lease, and service Audi automobiles as of 15 January 1991. Plaintiff's complaint alleged that Audi had terminated FMI's franchise arbitrarily and without good cause in violation of the Massachusetts regulatory statute. In addition, Audi had breached the contract and breached the duty of good faith and fair dealing. FMI sought an injunction to **stay** this termination, pending final resolution of its dispute with Audi. FMI had operated in Boston, Mass., for many years as an authorized dealer of certain imported luxury cars. Under individual dealer agreements, FMI sold, leased, and serviced automobiles for BMW, Mercedes-Benz, Porsche, and Audi. In October, 1986, the owners of FMI agreed to sell 12.5 percent of FMI's stock to MBPA Corporation (MBPA), a company wholly owned by Herbert G. Chambers, and to grant MBPA an option to purchase the remaining FMI stock. In March, 1987, MBPA exercised its option to purchase the remaining stock; and on 6 November 1987, Chambers, through MBPA, became the sole owner of FMI. FMI's sale to Chambers was subject to certain existing agreements concerning the business operations of FMI. Specifically, FMI's prior owners had entered into three agreements—an asset purchase agreement, an extension agreement, and a lease—with Bahig F. Bishay, another automobile dealer who had sought to purchase FMI but whose proposed purchase had been rejected. Chambers had been fully apprised of these agreements and had agreed to purchase FMI, subject to the constraints the agreements imposed. In December, 1986, Bishay commenced two court actions (the "Bishay litigation"), alleging that FMI had breached its obligations to Bishay and seeking transfer of the FMI franchise from Chambers to Bishay. In 1988, the trial court ordered that the three agreements between FMI and Bishay continue in force, beyond their expiration, pending final resolution of the Bishay litigation. In 1990, the special master assigned to the Bishay litigation recommended the dismissal of Bishay's claims. Should the final resolution of this litigation turn out favorably for FMI, Chambers would be discharged of any obligations under the existing agreements with Bishay. At the time Chambers purchased FMI and entered into a new Audi dealer agreement with Audi, both parties were aware that the franchise consistently had experienced financial and operational difficulties, including massive operating losses, high employee turnover, and poor customer satisfaction ratings. Since acquiring ownership of FMI, Chambers apparently had invested $6.4 million to recapitalize FMI and to fund the accrued losses. He also had replaced sales and service employees to improve the quality of customer service.

Stay   Suspend.

Nevertheless, the franchise continued to fall below Audi's established capital requirements, sales objectives, and performance standards. Thus, FMI continuously failed to achieve compliance with the terms of the Audi dealer agreement. In this case, FMI argued that its shortcomings are substantially attributable to the constraints imposed on its operations by the Bishay litigation. FMI contended that Audi should not penalize FMI for failing to attain certain rigid objectives that FMI could not reasonably attain under the conditions imposed by the Bishay litigation, particularly when Audi had full knowledge of FMI's peculiar situation. In light of the fact that the resolution of the Bishay litigation remained close at hand and that Chambers then would have the opportunity to implement more dramatic changes in the business, FMI submitted that Audi should not terminate FMI's franchise at this time. Moreover, FMI alleged that Audi's decision to terminate stems from improper motives, i.e., that Audi terminated FMI's franchise on learning that Chambers might seek to sell FMI. According to FMI, Chambers had carried FMI through its serious difficulties, and now that FMI might be marketable, Audi desired the opportunity to reap any benefits. Audi responded that, despite the steadfast assistance of Audi and its executives, FMI had never satisfied the requirements of its dealer agreement with Audi. Audi had appreciated the constraints imposed on FMI as a result of the Bishay litigation and had adjusted its performance expectations accordingly. However, according to Audi, FMI's deficiencies had persisted. In view of the poor performance and unprofitability of the FMI franchise, Audi claimed that it had made a business determination to terminate FMI.

ISSUE   Should the court issue an injunction to stay Audi's termination of FMI's franchise due to the absence of good cause to support such a termination?

HOLDING   No. FMI would not suffer irreparable injury, as it would still have a franchise from three other manufacturers; and money damages would suffice to compensate for any loss of revenue owing to the termination of the franchise. Moreover, Audi had demonstrated good cause in noting that Chambers's equity in the dealership had represented only 26.3 percent of Audi's working capital, FMI's working capital had stood at only 15.4 percent of Audi's requirements, and FMI had attained only 23.2 percent of its projected sales.

REASONING   Although FMI argued that it deserved an injunction to stay Audi's attempted termination of its franchise given FMI's poor customer service ratings vis-à-vis its Audi customers, the extent of harm to the dealership's reputation or goodwill as a result of the termination of its Audi franchise would remain speculative. Hence, FMI could not demonstrate that it would suffer irreparable harm in the absence of a stay of termination necessary to support the granting of an injunction. Massachusetts statute Chapter 93B prevents a manufacturer from terminating a franchise agreement with an automobile dealer "without good cause," but the statute does not define specifically what the term "good cause" means. The legislature has provided some guidance, directing the court to consider "all pertinent circumstances," including, but not limited to, the amount of business transacted by the dealer, the level of investments made, the adequacy of the services provided, and the existence of any breach of the terms of the franchise agreement. In addition, Massachusetts courts, grappling with the somewhat analogous concepts of "due cause" and "just care," have taken into account both the business judgment of the decision maker and the economic realities confronting the business. Audi insisted that it had had legitimate and compelling business reasons for terminating the FMI franchise. In particular, Audi stressed, the sales record of FMI consistently had fallen below Audi's established sales objectives. The most recent statistics showed that FMI had attained only 23.2 percent of its projected sales, while dealers in the Boston metropolitan area and the Atlantic Zone had reached 85.3 percent and 77.8 percent of their objectives, respectively. FMI's customer satisfaction ratings and its service record also remained deficient. Moreover, Chambers's equity in FMI was $638,544, only 26.3 percent of Audi's capital requirements, while FMI's working capital stood at only 15.4 percent of Audi's requirement. In sum, FMI had experienced, and continued to experience, serious operational difficulties; and the franchise had continually failed to comply with the performance standards set out in the Audi dealer agreement. Repeated correspondence with and assistance from Audi executives had been unsuccessful in bringing about any change. In light of the overwhelming evidence of FMI's deficiencies, Audi had had sound business reasons and sufficient "good cause" to terminate FMI. Although Chapter 93B unquestionably seeks to protect automobile dealers from the "inequitable consequences of overweening economic power wielded by manufacturers," it does not purport to shield them entirely from adverse decisions formulated on legitimate business and economic grounds. Hence, a court should not force Audi to continue the franchise where FMI's chronically and irremediably poor performance justifiably caused Audi substantial concern. Moreover, whatever harm FMI may suffer by having its franchise terminated does not constitute irreparable injury. First, the loss of the Audi franchise may result in reduced revenue, but FMI will not go out of business altogether; FMI will still be able to deal in BMW, Mercedes-Benz, and Porsche automobiles, and money damages will suffice to compensate for any loss of additional revenue attributable to Audi sales. Given that FMI had failed to demonstrate both irreparable injury and a likelihood of success on the claim, a court should not order the relief sought by the plaintiff. Should plaintiff's claims be successful, the plaintiff will receive adequate money damages to compensate for any lost revenue from Audi sales or any lost income from a sale of the franchise.

DECISIONAL LAW AND STATUTES AFFECTING FRANCHISING

As the *ABA Distributors* and *Foreign Motors* cases illustrate, courts have been sensitive to the issue of damages in the franchising context. This is particularly true in circumstances involving terminations, because upon termination the franchisee may be left with nothing. Termination provisions, especially when coupled with transferability terms that allow the franchisor to reject potential buyers, may clothe the franchisor with an inordinate amount of power vis-à-vis the franchisee. As we have seen, courts can turn to common law, their own powers of equity, and/or applicable statutes in shaping relief. Some of the statutes mentioned earlier were designed by their drafters to correct perceived abuses and overreaching by franchisors; indeed, few regulations pertain to the conduct of franchisees. Clearly, such statutes have improved the bargaining position of franchisees, but some critics have argued that they also make franchise systems more rigid and encourage litigation. Some state legislatures have passed special laws to protect automobile dealers from excessive competition by requiring that notice be given to established automobile dealers and to the state motor vehicle regulatory agency before a franchisor can establish a new dealership or relocate an existing one. This notice provision allows established dealers to object to the granting of any additional dealership licenses and thereby to protect their economic stakes in a particular territory. In *New Motor Vehicle Board of California* v. *Orrin W. Fox Co.*,[11] the Supreme Court upheld a California statute of this type even though Fox argued that the statute was violative of the antitrust laws and unconstitutional on grounds of due process.

On the federal level, the Automobile Dealers' Franchise Act, also known as the Automobile Dealers' Day in Court Act (15 U.S.C. Section 1221), in a similar vein allows a terminated dealer to bring an action in federal court asking for retention of the franchise if the dealer can prove that the franchisor has conducted the termination in bad faith and coercively. The federal Petroleum Marketing Practices Act (15 U.S.C. Section 2801) protects motor fuel distributors and dealers from arbitrary terminations as well. However, even

[11]439 U.S. 96 (1978).

with these statutes, courts have allowed franchisors to terminate franchisees for such reasons as misconduct or failure to meet sales quotas, to observe quality standards, to maintain appropriate investment levels, and the like. Nevertheless, the presence of these laws helps to ensure that the bargaining power between franchisors and franchisees will be more commensurate and balanced. The following case illustrates these points.

Union Oil Company of California v. *O'Riley*
276 Cal. Rptr. 483 (Cal. App. 2 Dist. 1991)

FACTS   On 22 June 1981, O'Riley entered into a franchise lease with Union Oil Company of California (Union Oil) wherein he agreed to operate a Union Oil station in the city of Wilmington. O'Riley began his franchise as a full-service station. Van der Valk, the Union Oil area manager in charge of the service stations in O'Riley's area, met with him often and suggested that the station become a self-service station. O'Riley, however, had no intention of becoming self-service and told Van der Valk so. When O'Riley next placed an order for delivery of gasoline, it was not delivered. He was informed that a credit hold had been placed on his order and that he would have to speak to Van der Valk. Unable to contact Van der Valk, O'Riley finally spoke to Bill Thomas, the Union Oil retail representative. Thomas, after assuring O'Riley there was no "hold" on his fuel load, attempted to reach Van der Valk. Thomas later informed O'Riley that Van der Valk was on vacation and that the terminal would not release O'Riley's order without Van der Valk's authorization. Meanwhile, O'Riley ran out of fuel and was forced to close the station. When Van der Valk returned, he lifted the hold and apologized, explaining that it had been a mistake. Some time later, forty-eight hours before the 4th of July, O'Riley placed an order for gas. He prepared the payment for the previous load, but the load was not delivered during the three-day holiday weekend. Later, he was told the load had mistakenly been delivered to another station, which had not ordered gas. O'Riley found this explanation unbelievable because he knew a load would not be delivered without a payment in the lock-box for a previous load. Just prior to the 4th of July, O'Riley had had another discussion with Van der Valk in which Van der Valk once more had recommended that O'Riley's station become self-service. When O'Riley had again declined, Van der Valk had been unhappy. In September, 1981, O'Riley agreed to convert the station to self-service. Van der Valk told him that when he stopped servicing cars and selling tires and other accessories, Union Oil would reduce his rent by $500 per month, and within thirty days would install automated pumps, increase the fuel capacity, and install freeway signs and other self-service signs around the station. He also stated that Union Oil would give O'Riley credit for, or purchase, his inventory. The two men shook hands on the deal. When O'Riley ceased selling tires and other accessories and closed his mechanical bays, Union Oil lowered his rent but did nothing else. Though O'Riley inquired on a daily basis about the work Union Oil had agreed to do, Union Oil never fulfilled its promises. By November, 1981, O'Riley had concluded that Union Oil was not going to live up to its end of the bargain. He had a heated discussion with Van der Valk, informed him that he would place his franchise up for sale, and repeated that he would seek legal advice. In December, 1981, O'Riley was hospitalized for back surgery. While in the hospital, he received several calls from Union Oil demanding payment for a load that Union Oil said had been delivered between 1 and 6 December. O'Riley asked who had ordered the gas and why it had been delivered without payment for the previous load. Union Oil responded that the delivery was related to a tank test it had performed, although no one from Union Oil had given O'Riley notice about performing any such test. Union Oil claimed O'Riley owed between $24,000 and $34,000. In the meantime, the station was running low on gas; therefore, O'Riley attempted to place an order. Union Oil refused to deliver until he had paid for the gas that had been delivered. O'Riley left the hospital on 15 December and stayed in bed until 20 December. His mail that day included a notice of default under the station lease, which requested a $1648.09 payment due on 1 December; a second notice of default requesting a $10,609.10 payment due on 6 December; and a third notice of default stating that his lease would be terminated by 21 December

1981 and requesting a $24,095.02 payment. The third notice carried a date of 16 December 1981. None of these notices was personally delivered to him by Union or sent via certified mail. Rather, Union Oil had sent all the notices to the service station. The station was seized on 21 December 1981, and on 13 September 1982, Union Oil filed a complaint against O'Riley alleging that he owed $23,466.41 with interest. O'Riley cross-complained against Union Oil, alleging that Union Oil had violated the provisions of the federal Petroleum Marketing Practices Act (PMPA) when it had terminated his franchise, that Union Oil had breached certain of its contractual obligations, and that Union Oil had made promises it had not intended to keep. After a trial, the jury returned a special verdict in favor of Union Oil on its complaint in the amount of $15,869.68; against O'Riley on his causes of action for breach of contract and fraud; and in favor of O'Riley on his PMPA claims. The court awarded O'Riley attorneys' fees of $40,000, punitive damages of $40,500, and expert witness fees of $2625. Union Oil moved for judgment notwithstanding the verdict or, in the alternative, for a new trial. On the denial of these motions, Union Oil filed a timely notice of appeal.

ISSUE

Had Union Oil violated the PMPA when it attempted to terminate O'Riley's franchise?

HOLDING

Yes. In failing to give O'Riley ninety days' notice before termination, Union Oil had violated the act.

REASONING

By a special verdict the jury had found that O'Riley owed Union Oil $15,869.68 for the gas that had been delivered to effectuate the tank tests and further found that Union Oil had deliberately created this indebtedness and had used it as the basis for its decision to terminate the franchise. Union Oil, however, asserted that O'Riley had had two choices once the gas was delivered. He could have refused to accept the unordered gasoline or have sold the gas to the public. Having sold the gasoline, O'Riley had thereby accepted it within the meaning of the California Commercial Code. O'Riley thus had chosen to become indebted to it, according to Union Oil. No one questioned that O'Riley had owed Union Oil for the gasoline, and the jury so found. The heart of Union Oil's argument centered on its denial that it had deliberately created the indebtedness so it could have a basis for terminating O'Riley's franchise agreement. To reach this conclusion, the jury apparently had believed the testimony of O'Riley regarding the various disagreeable incidents that had occurred between O'Riley and Union Oil. The fact that Union Oil had arranged for the testing of the tanks and the related delivery of the unordered gasoline when O'Riley was hospitalized constituted further evidence that Union Oil had not been treating O'Riley in a fair manner. Hence, the jury had not erred in coming to the conclusion that Union Oil had "deliberately created" this indebtedness; indeed, substantial evidence existed to support this finding. In its special verdict, the jury had found that Union Oil had not given O'Riley ninety days' notice, had not personally delivered notice to O'Riley, and had not been excused from personal delivery of the notice to him. The jury had found that Union Oil had violated the PMPA when it gave O'Riley, at the most, five days' notice of its intention to terminate the franchise and, without excuse, had failed to serve O'Riley personally with the notice. Union Oil asserted that the shortened notice of the instant case had been reasonable under the circumstances (a "drafting error") and cited cases holding that a "reasonable" standard applies. Yet Union Oil offered no explanation of how the drafting error had occurred. In any event, because the jury had found no reason to excuse Union Oil from personally delivering the notice of termination to O'Riley, a permitted inference is that if it had been asked whether five days' notice was reasonable, the jury would have responded negatively. Finally, Union Oil objected to the $40,500 punitive damages award, asserting that substantial evidence had not supported the jury's finding that Union Oil had deliberately created the indebtedness on which it had based its termination of O'Riley's franchise or that it had willfully disregarded the requirements of the PMPA. Yet the evidence indicated that Union Oil had ignored the ninety days' notice requirement. Indeed, its notice included preprinted language stating that Union Oil views as "unreasonable" the giving of ninety days' notice whenever a franchise is indebted to it. This language constituted evidence that Union Oil had willfully ignored the PMPA's requirements whenever a franchisee owed it money. In addition, Union Oil representatives had repeatedly threatened O'Riley with termination of his franchise because of unhappiness with his complaints. Thus, Union Oil had apparently terminated O'Riley's franchise in retaliation for his complaints. Most important, this type of retaliatory termination is exactly the sort of conduct that Congress had enacted the PMPA to prevent.

The Federal Trade Commission has promulgated a trade regulation rule on franchise disclosure meant to satisfy the same aims. This 1979 rule, and state laws that mandate similar disclosure provisions, have helped to do away with the abuses associated with the sale of franchises. Continuing investigations of the franchise industry under the power to prohibit deceptive and unfair trade practices granted to the Federal Trade Commission by the Federal Trade Commission Act should effectively reinforce these other regulatory measures.

In addition, antitrust laws, such as the Sherman Antitrust Act and the Clayton Act, may apply to various aspects of the franchising relationship. We learned earlier that, as a condition of using their trademark or service mark, franchisors often attempt to impose on franchisees territorial restrictions and restrictions on supplies or prices that may run afoul of the antitrust laws. Consumer protection statutes may also affect the franchising relationship: Franchises that extend credit on installments or through charge accounts may be subject to various truth-in-lending statutes. In addition to its requirement of good faith, the UCC's warranty provisions and its section on unconscionability may be applicable to franchising. Since the law on franchising at this time appears to be unsettled yet proliferating, a thoughtful examination of such laws by franchisors and franchisees alike seems warranted.

The next case involved an alleged violation of state antitrust laws.

Yamaha Store of Bend, Oregon, Inc. v. *Yamaha Motor Corporation, U.S.A.*
798 P.2d 656 (Or. 1990)

FACTS   Yamaha Motor Corporation (Yamaha), the United States distributor for Yamaha motorcycles, published a list of the prices that it charged its dealers for motorcycles. Yamaha Store of Bend, Oregon, Inc. (Yamaha/Bend), a retail Yamaha motorcycle dealer from 1978 to 1983, purchased motorcycles, parts, and accessories from Yamaha for resale in Bend, Oregon, and the surrounding area. In June, 1982, the largest Portland-area Yamaha dealer went out of business. That dealer had about 550 new 1980, 1981, and 1982 motorcycles in its inventory, which Yamaha repossessed. In July, 1982, Yamaha sold those repossessed motorcycles to Beaverton Honda (Beaverton) at prices substantially below Yamaha's regular dealer list prices. Yamaha did not offer to sell any of the repossessed motorcycles at the lower prices to Yamaha/Bend or to any of its other dealers. Yamaha also provided Beaverton with advantageous credit terms and advertising support. Beaverton then changed its name to Beaverton Honda-Yamaha and became metropolitan Portland's largest Yamaha dealer. Beaverton subsequently sold the repossessed motorcycles at retail prices close to other dealers' wholesale costs for the same models. Beaverton advertised its low prices extensively in Portland newspapers and on Portland television stations. Since Yamaha/Bend's customers were aware of Beaverton's lower prices, Yamaha/Bend reduced its own prices and, in some cases, sold motorcycles at or below actual costs. Beaverton sold at least two motorcycles to customers with Bend addresses and several others to customers residing in Yamaha/Bend's central Oregon market area. When Yamaha/Bend sued Yamaha for price discrimination allegedly violative of the Oregon Anti-Price Discrimination Law, the jury awarded Yamaha/Bend a verdict on both the price discrimination and breach of contract claims. At trial, Yamaha had moved for a directed verdict on Yamaha/Bend's price discrimination claim, arguing that as a matter of law Yamaha/Bend and Beaverton were not "competitors," a necessary element of an Oregon statutory price discrimination claim. The trial court had denied that motion, and the court of appeals had affirmed that denial. Yamaha then argued that the court of appeals had erred in holding that actual competition between Yamaha/Bend and Beaverton had existed.

ISSUE Had the plaintiff presented sufficient evidence of actual competition between it and the other Yamaha dealer to whom Yamaha had granted more favorable prices to support a price discrimination claim?

HOLDING Yes. The two dealers were in actual competition for the purposes of the Oregon Anti-Price Discrimination Law; hence, the trial court had properly directed a verdict in the plaintiff's favor on this issue.

REASONING Yamaha argued that the question of whether Beaverton's competitive market had included the Bend area hinged on how many actual sales Beaverton had made to Bend area residents. Pointing to evidence showing that out of more than 800 sales, Beaverton had sold only two motorcycles to Bend residents, Yamaha claimed that this evidence had established as a matter of law that Yamaha/Bend and Beaverton were not competitors. Yamaha also alleged that it was not sufficient for the plaintiff to show the effects of Beaverton's advertising campaign on the plaintiff's competitive position (e.g., that Bend area residents would shop in the Portland area or that they knew about Beaverton's lower prices and expected the plaintiff to meet them), since the relevant federal precedents had held that a few "crossover" sales do not prove actual competition. These federal cases are inapposite, however, because they are concerned with exclusive geographic market areas having defined boundaries. No such clearly defined market areas are involved here. The rationale behind the requirement for actual competition in the same market area is that if the favored and disfavored buyers, here Beaverton and the plaintiff, do not in fact compete for the same customers, there cannot be a reasonable probability of harm to competition. Yamaha clearly had sold 1980, 1981, and 1982 motorcycles to Beaverton at prices significantly lower than the prices Yamaha had charged Yamaha/Bend for the same models. Furthermore, Yamaha also had given Beaverton advantageous credit terms not given to the plaintiff. Beaverton then had advertised the sale of its lower-priced motorcycles extensively in Portland newspapers and on Portland television stations, media that Yamaha acknowledged had "statewide" coverage. The Honda motorcycle dealer in Bend had testified that 75 percent of his competition came from Portland-area motorcycle dealers and that Portland pricing directly affected his own prices because, in order to make a sale, he often had to match Portland dealers' prices. A former Oregon Yamaha district manager, who was the Oregon Kawasaki district manager at the time of Yamaha's sale to Beaverton, had testified that the predictable effect of Yamaha's sale to Beaverton was to put all other dealers in Beaverton's market at a competitive disadvantage. One of Yamaha/Bend's owners had testified that Beaverton's advertising of its lower prices actually forced the plaintiff to lower its own prices. Of twelve Yamaha dealers in northwestern Oregon before the challenged sale to Beaverton, some started closing up within a few months after the sale; and all twelve were out of business by the time this case had come to trial. Yamaha/Bend's expert witness, an economist, had testified that the relevant competitive market was wherever the impacts of a price differential are felt; that Beaverton's extensive advertising of its low prices would have an impact on the plaintiff; that competition in the Bend area definitely would be lessened; and that the effect was a foreseeable, natural, and necessary consequence of Beaverton's extensive advertising of its low prices. He also had testified that the foreseeable consequences to the plaintiff would include diversion of sales, negative customer relations, and the depressed value of the plaintiff's new and used motorcycle inventory because the Bend area is reasonably in the Portland market area. Beaverton's advertisements in *The Oregonian* proclaimed, "We're your #1 in the U.S.A. Yamaha connection." Hence, the trial court and the court of appeals had correctly found that evidence in the record had existed from which a jury could find that the Bend area was part of Beaverton's market; that Beaverton competed with plaintiff for customers from the Bend area; that Yamaha discriminated in the prices it had charged Beaverton and plaintiff for 1982 motorcycles; and that such discrimination had the proscribed effect on competition delineated in the Oregon Anti-Price Discrimination Law. The trial court therefore had not erred in denying Yamaha's motion for a directed verdict.

CHALLENGES TO FRANCHISING REGULATORY STATUTES

Some franchisors have bridled at the passage of such franchising statutes because they perceive them as serious limitations on their freedom to contract and to manage their businesses. Consequently, franchisors have raised constitutional arguments against these laws. The parts of the Constitution relied on in these challenges include the following:

1. *Impairment of the obligation of contracts.* The Constitution prohibits a state from passing a law that makes substantive changes in contractual rights.

2. *Due process.* The Fourteenth Amendment bans vague, standardless laws.

3. *Federal supremacy.* Article VI of the Constitution makes federal law the supreme law of the land. Thus, a state franchising law that conflicts with a federal law (say, the Lanham Act's regulation of trademarks) will be unconstitutional.

4. *Interstate commerce.* Article I, Section 8, of the Constitution prohibits the states from placing undue burdens on interstate commerce.

As the following case shows, such arguments can be successful.

Southland Corporation v. Keating
465 U.S. 1 (1984)

FACTS   The Southland Corporation (Southland) is the owner and franchisor of 7-Eleven convenience stores. Southland's standard franchise agreement provides each franchisee with a license to use certain registered trademarks, a lease or sublease of a convenience store owned or leased by Southland, inventory financing, and assistance in advertising and merchandising. The franchisees operate the stores, supply bookkeeping data, and pay Southland a fixed percentage of gross profits. The franchise agreement also contains the following provision requiring arbitration: "Any controversy or claim arising out of or relating to this Agreement or the breach thereof shall be settled by arbitration in accordance with the rules of the American Arbitration Association . . . and judgment upon any award rendered by the arbitrator may be entered in any court having jurisdiction thereof." Keating was a 7-Eleven franchisee. In May, 1977, he filed a class action against Southland on behalf of a class of 800 California franchisees, alleging, among other things, fraud, oral misrepresentation, breach of contract, breach of fiduciary duty, and violation of the disclosure requirements of the California Franchise Investment Law. Southland asserted as an affirmative defense to this suit the franchisee's failure to arbitrate and moved to compel arbitration. The trial court granted Southland's motion to compel arbitration of all claims except those based on the California Franchise Investment Law. This statute provides: "Any condition, stipulation or provision purporting to bind any person acquiring any franchise to waive compliance with any provision of this law or any rule or order hereunder is void." After a trial and appeals, the California Supreme Court interpreted this statute to require judicial consideration of claims brought under the state statute and accordingly refused to enforce the parties' contract to arbitrate such claims. In so doing, California's highest court rejected the state appellate court's holding that the California Franchise Investment Law did not invalidate arbitration agreements and that if it had rendered such agreements involving commerce unenforceable, such a result would conflict with Section 2 of the United States Arbitration Act.

ISSUE   Was the California Franchise Investment Law in conflict with federal law and thus unconstitutional?

HOLDING   Yes. This state law directly conflicted with the Federal Arbitration Act and thereby violated the Supremacy Clause.

REASONING   Congress's enactment of Section 2 of the Federal Arbitration Act represented a declaration of a national policy favoring arbitration and a withdrawal of the power of the states to require a judicial forum for the resolution of claims that the contracting parties had agreed to resolve by arbitration. A portion of Section 2's language—"an agreement in writing to submit to arbitration an existing controversy arising out of such a contract, transaction, or refusal, shall be valid, irrevocable, and enforceable, save upon such grounds as exist at law or in equity for the revocation of any contract"—stood as clear evidence that Congress had mandated the enforcement of arbitration agreements and that such clauses should be revoked only upon "grounds as exist at law or in equity for the revocation of any contract." Nothing in the Act indicated that the broad principle of enforceability had been subject to any additional limitations under state law. Indeed, the legislative history revealed that Congress had meant to remedy two problems in enacting the Federal Arbitration Act: The old common law hostility toward arbitration and the failure of state arbitration statutes to mandate enforcement of arbitration agreements. To confine the scope of the Act to arbitrations sought to be enforced in federal courts would frustrate what Congress had intended as a broad enactment appropriate in scope to meet the large problems Congress was addressing. Accordingly, Justice O'Connor's interpretation of the Federal Arbitration Act as a procedural statute applicable only in federal courts was erroneous. Under her interpretation, claims brought under the California Franchise Investment Law would not be arbitrable when they had been raised in state court. But it was clear beyond question that if this suit had been brought as a diversity action in a federal district court, the arbitration clause would have been enforceable. Because the interpretation given to the Federal Arbitration Act by the California Supreme Court would therefore encourage and reward **forum shopping,** to attribute to Congress the intent, in drawing on the comprehensive powers of the Commerce Clause, to create a right to enforce an arbitration contract and yet make the right dependent for its enforcement on the particular forum in which it is asserted would be inappropriate. And since the overwhelming proportion of all civil litigation in this country is in state courts, Congress apparently had not intended to limit the Arbitration Act to disputes subject only to *federal* court jurisdiction, since such an interpretation would frustrate congressional intent to place "[a]n arbitration agreement . . . upon the same footing as other contracts, where it belongs." Rather, Congress, in creating a substantive rule applicable in state as well as federal courts, had intended to foreclose state legislative attempts to undercut the enforceability of arbitration agreements. Therefore, for these reasons, the California Franchise Investment Law violated the Supremacy Clause of the Constitution.

Forum shopping Choosing the court or place of jurisdiction that will be most favorable to the litigant.

THE FRANCHISING ENVIRONMENT

Ownership Trends

Since 1975, there has been a demonstrated increase in conversions of company-owned franchise units to franchisee-owned ones. According to industry sources, this increase has probably occurred because most of the units that companies have repurchased have represented temporary buy-backs for legitimate business reasons rather than the companies' desire to withdraw from the franchise system or to operate these units permanently themselves. The rate for renewal

FIGURE 43.2   International Franchising, 1988

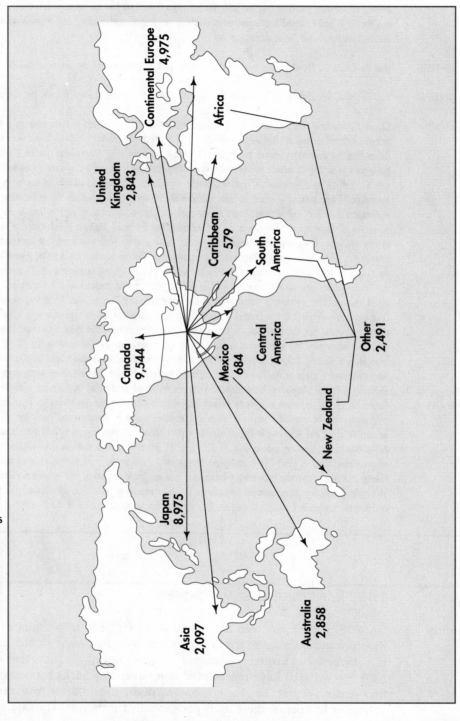

Source: International Franchise Association Educational Foundation, Inc., and Horwath International, *Franchising in the Economy 1988–1990* (Washington, D.C., 1990), pp. 99–100. Number of franchising companies = 374; number of franchising outlets = 35,046.

in 1988 was 90 percent.[12] Approximately 16 percent of the nonrenewals resulted from franchisors' objections; the remainder stemmed from the franchisees' decisions not to renew or from mutual agreement between the franchisor and franchisee.[13] Franchisees initiated approximately 57 percent of the terminations in 1988, compared with approximately 43 percent initiated by the franchisors.[14] Taken together, these statistics indicate overall stability in the field of franchising.

International Markets

Government studies suggest that U.S. franchisors will continue to pierce international markets, despite the numerous problems inherent in complying with the local laws of other nations. Canada continues to be the most important market for U.S. franchisors. As Figure 43.2 shows, Canada in 1988 represented about one-third of all U.S. international outlets, Japan constituted the second-largest foreign outlet, and Australia ranked third. Interestingly, Canada, Mexico, Japan, the United Kingdom, and the continental European countries are, in a similar fashion, setting up an increasing number of franchises in the United States. The international ramifications of franchising thus should become even more significant as the growth of communication and transportation systems continues to narrow the gap among consumer preferences around the world and as the advantages of franchising become more apparent to our international neighbors. This is a development that promises to be well worth watching.

SUMMARY

Franchising has become a significant method of doing business both in the United States and abroad. A franchise is an agreement in which one person pays a fee in exchange for a license to use a trademark, service mark, or logotype while engaged in distributing goods or services. The person or firm granting the franchise is called the franchisor; the person receiving the franchise is known as the franchisee. Franchises fall into two general categories: distributorships or chain-style businesses. The advantages of franchising make it an attractive method of doing business for both franchisees and franchisors.

Courts have had some problems in distinguishing franchise relationships from other types of business relationships, such as independent contracting. Yet such a distinction may be important under state and federal franchising laws, tax laws, labor laws, and antitrust laws. Some areas of the law are settled: Cooperatives, concessionaires, joint ventures, general partnerships, and

---

[12]International Franchise Association Educational Foundation, Inc., and Horwath International, *Franchising*, p. 108.
[13]Ibid.
[14]Ibid., p. 109.

sales agencies generally are not deemed the legal equivalent of a franchise; and a franchise is not considered a security.

The franchisor strictly controls the franchise relationship in order to assure product uniformity and protect the goodwill associated with its trademark or service mark. Two areas ordinarily covered in the franchise agreement—quality control and termination—pose the most legal problems. State and federal laws may cover these two aspects of the agreement, and a wise franchisor should take care not to run afoul of these laws by pressing for unreasonable provisions or terms. Special industry laws at both the federal and state levels may also protect franchisees. The Federal Trade Commission's franchise disclosure regulations, antitrust laws, consumer protection statutes, and the UCC constitute further bases for controlling abusive behavior by franchisors. Franchisors have challenged such statutes on constitutional grounds, sometimes successfully.

For the last few years, the franchising industry has witnessed an increase in conversions of company-owned units to franchisee-owned ones. Although some franchisors fail, other industry statistics indicate overall stability in the franchising field; for example, nonrenewals are usually franchisee-initiated. The international aspects of franchising should continue to gain in significance in the coming decades as more sophisticated communication and transportation systems allow for global dissemination of goods and services.

DISCUSSION QUESTIONS

1. Name eight different types of businesses that use franchising as their distributional method. Then list and describe the two main classifications of franchises.
2. Define the word *franchise*.
3. Describe four benefits of franchising for the franchisee and franchisor, respectively.
4. For what purposes does the law make distinctions between franchising and other types of business relationships, such as independent contracting?
5. Briefly explain the steps involved in setting up a franchising arrangement and describe what areas the franchising agreement normally covers.

6. Discuss why quality control and termination clauses are important to franchisors and how these same provisions nevertheless pose legal pitfalls for franchisors.
7. Enumerate the types of statutes that franchisees can use to curb the power of franchisors.
8. What four constitutional bases have franchisors used to challenge franchising statutes?
9. List some of the current trends in franchising regarding renewal and termination decisions.
10. Name the three most important international markets for United States franchisors.

CASE PROBLEMS

1. The FTC in December, 1983, charged Royco Automobile Parts, Inc., of Jacksonville, Fla. (Royco), and Robert W. Sowerby, a director and president of Royco, with violating the FTC franchise rule by failing to fur- nish prospective franchise purchasers with specific documents. The FTC also claimed that the defendants had violated the FTC Act by representing, contrary to fact, that a prospective franchisee could reasonably expect to

gross over $164 and net over $45 per account per week; that Royco franchises earned the highest rate of return in the auto parts industry, 300 percent per year; that an investment in a Royco franchise was riskless because Royco agreed to reimburse the franchisee if the investment is unsuccessful; that Royco provided its franchisees with experienced "locators" who in turn provided financially secure accounts, training and advice, advertising and other support, and special manufacturers' discounts; and that Royco shipped initial parts inventories within three to ten days. Was the FTC correct? If so, should a court make the defendants pay $567,200 to franchisees victimized by these alleged misrepresentations and a $400,000 penalty for violating the franchise rule? (*U.S.* v. *Royco Automobile Parts, Inc.,* 49 *Antitrust & Trade Regulation Report* [BNA], 213, 25 July 1985 [M.D. Fla. 1985].)

2. A class action was instituted against Montgomery Ward Catalog Sales (Montgomery Ward) on the ground that its catalog sales agency program had stated that the business entities created under the program were franchises within the meaning of the Illinois Franchise Act. All the named class representatives operated franchises outside of Illinois; hence, Montgomery Ward argued that the provisions regarding termination and nonrenewal of the relationships were not applicable to causes of action asserted on behalf of agencies located outside of Illinois. However, the class representatives noted that the contracts with Montgomery Ward provided that the agreements would be governed by the laws of Illinois. Should a court give extraterritorial effect to the Illinois Act? (*In re Montgomery Ward Catalog Sales Litigation,* 680 F. Supp. 182 [E.D. Pa. 1987].)

3. On 19 November 1984, Yamaha Motor Corporation, U.S.A. (Yamaha) and Northshore Cycles, Inc. (Northshore) entered into a dealer agreement. The dealer agreement contains no provision specifying its term or duration but, to the contrary, provides that it "shall continue until terminated as provided herein." The dealer agreement provides for "Termination for Cause (Immediate Effect)" on the basis of any one of several enumerated occurrences; for "Termination—General Non Performance" on the failure of either party to fulfill the responsibilities and obligations of the dealer agreement (at least sixty days' prior written notice is required); and for "Termination—Death, Incapacity," which allows Yamaha to terminate the agreement on at least fifteen days' prior written notice in the event of the death, physical or mental incapacity, or dissociation of certain individuals affiliated with Northshore. The dealer agreement also permits Yamaha to terminate by giving the dealer at least sixty days' prior written notice if Yamaha should offer a new or modified form of agreement to all its dealers. Notably, the dealer agreement fails to provide for unilateral termination without cause. Because the agreement is "open ended," having no term specified, it contains no express provisions for extension or renewal, whether automatic or otherwise. The dealer agreement contains a provision for repurchase of products by Yamaha on termination of the arrangement with a franchise such as Northshore; but the provision clearly gives Yamaha the "option, but not the obligation, to repurchase" products from the dealer. While this dealer agreement was in full force and effect, the Louisiana legislature adopted a statute obligating manufacturers of motorcycles to repurchase inventories on the termination of a dealership. The statute became effective on 1 September 1988. On 5 April 1989, a letter to Yamaha from Northshore advised Yamaha of Northshore's decision to terminate its operations as a new motorcycle dealer thirty days following the date of the letter. On 30 May 1989, a follow-up letter to Yamaha from Northshore purported to comply with the notification provision of the statute, including mail delivery of Northshore's final parts inventory. Yamaha accepted Northshore's request to terminate the dealer agreement but declined to repurchase Northshore's inventory. In November, 1989, Northshore filed suit against Yamaha, seeking to compel Yamaha to repurchase the parts listed on the final inventory submitted by Northshore and, in addition, to pay certain penalties prescribed in the statute plus additional damages. Article I, Section 10, Clause 1, of the U.S. Constitution prohibits the several states from passing any "Law Impairing the Obligation of Contracts." The substantive provision of the Louisiana statute, requiring the manufacturer to repurchase inventory from the dealer, appears to violate this constitutional prohibition if such repurchase obligation were enforced against a manufacturer whose contract with the dealer had pre-dated the effective date of the statute. When the district court dismissed the case on this constitutional basis, the dealer appealed. How should the circuit court of appeals rule in this case? (*Northshore Cycles, Inc.* v. *Yamaha Motor Corporation, U.S.A.,* 919 F.2d 1041 [5th Cir. 1990].)

4. In 1974, Ernst and Barbara Ann Larese entered into a ten-year franchise agreement with Creamland Dairies (Creamland). The franchise agreement provided that the

franchisee "shall not assign, transfer or sublet this franchise, or any of [the] rights under this agreement, without the prior written consent of [Creamland] and Baskin Robbins, any such unauthorized assignment, transfer or subletting being null and without effect." In February and August, 1979, the Lareses attempted to sell their franchise rights, but Creamland refused to consent to the sale. They subsequently charged Creamland with interfering with their contractual relations with the prospective buyers by unreasonably withholding consent to the sale. Should a court impose a "reasonableness" standard on this "consent to transfer" clause, or did the clause give Creamland an absolute, unqualified right to refuse to consent to proposed sales of the franchise rights? (*Larese* v. *Creamland Dairies, Inc.,* 767 F.2d 716 [10th Cir. 1985].)

5. Cullen sued BMW of North America, the franchisor, for damages resulting from the fraudulent conduct of its franchisee, Bavarian Auto Sales. Cullen had paid $18,000 for a new BMW but had received neither the car nor his money back. Cullen argued that BMW should be liable for the $18,000 because it had negligently created a situation that allowed its franchisee to defraud customers. Cullen alleged that BMW had allowed customers to rely on the good reputation of BMW in dealing with Bavarian Auto Sales, even though BMW knew of five prior incidents in which the franchisee had failed to deliver cars that had been paid for and despite the franchisee's failure to make payments to BMW for over six months. Because BMW could have foreseen his ultimate injury at its franchisee's hands, Cullen argued that BMW had been negligent and should be liable to him. Should this theory be successful? (*Cullen* v. *BMW of North America, Inc.,* 691 F.2d 1097 [2d Cir. 1982], cert. denied 460 U.S. 1070 [1983].)

6. Carolina Truck & Body Company, Inc. (Carolina) and General Motors Corporation (GMC) entered into a renewal contract in 1975 entitling Carolina to sell heavy-duty trucks manufactured by GMC. From 1950 until that time, Carolina had been a franchisee, selling light- and medium-duty GMC trucks. On 1 November 1985, the two firms entered into a renewal heavy-duty franchise agreement (the heavy-duty addendum), which had a term of five years to and including 31 October 1990. This heavy-duty addendum gave Carolina the nonexclusive right to purchase and sell new heavy-duty truck motor vehicles marketed by GMC Truck & Coach Operation of General Motors Corporation. The addendum also stated that it would remain in effect unless

cancelled. In August, 1985, owing to an economic decline in its share of the heavy-duty truck market during the 1980s, GMC and Volvo Truck Corporation (Volvo) met to consider forming a joint venture in the area of heavy-duty truck manufacturing. GMC notified Carolina and its other heavy-duty franchise dealers as early as 7 November 1986 that the heavy-duty addendum would be cancelled no later than 31 December 1987 because of GMC's plans to cease manufacturing heavy-duty trucks. GMC conclusively notified Carolina of such cancellation on 23 December 1986. When Carolina subsequently sought a joint venture franchise from Volvo GM (the new joint venture) for heavy-duty trucks, Carolina learned that it would not receive such a franchise. GMC had no role in the daily operation of Volvo GM and had no control over any of Volvo GM's decisions relating to its dealers. On 31 December 1987, GMC stopped marketing all its heavy-duty truck models, no longer shipped these models to any of its dealers nationwide, and cancelled all heavy-duty addenda as of that date. Carolina sued GMC for wrongful termination of Carolina's franchise. Carolina asserted that GMC's actions in discontinuing its heavy-duty truck models and cancelling Carolina's heavy-duty truck addendum had failed to comply with the relevant North Carolina statutes because neither good cause nor good faith had underlaid GMC's actions. In these circumstances, would a franchisor's cancellation of a franchise for the sale of heavy-duty trucks, owing to the discontinuance of a product line, satisfy the "good cause" and "good faith" standard mandated by North Carolina statutes? (*Carolina Truck & Body Company, Inc.* v. *General Motors Corporation,* 402 S.E.2d 135 [N.C. App. 1991].)

7. In December, 1979, Gyp-Crete Corp. (Gyp-Crete) and McKeown Distributors, Inc. (McKeown) of Windsor, Connecticut, entered into a distributorship agreement giving McKeown the nontransferable right to sell Gyp-Crete brand gypsum cement in New England and New York for ten years. John P. McKeown, Sr. was the company's sole owner and operator. Paragraph 14 of the agreement gave Gyp-Crete the right to terminate the agreement on the transfer of a majority of the voting stock in McKeown or in the event "its ownership or control is in any way substantially changed." Paragraph 15 of the agreement barred assignment and delegation of the distributor's duties unless there was an assignment to John McKeown, Sr.'s two sons and Gyp-Crete gave prior written consent. There were no provisions in

the agreement relating to sales quotas, management training, and financial support from Gyp-Crete or to the hiring of employees. Paragraph 2(B) of McKeown's contracts with its three customers contained a clause providing that if McKeown sold the product to anyone else within the customer's assigned territory, McKeown would pay that customer 90 percent of the sales price less cost. Gyp-Crete ultimately became concerned about the quality of the product and the competence and experience of its distributors and applicators. John McKeown, Sr., who handled all technical and quality control aspects of applying Gyp-Crete flooring, died on 3 July 1981. On 5 August, Gyp-Crete notified McKeown that it was terminating the agreement pursuant to paragraphs 14 and 15 and that the termination would take effect in thirty days. Gyp-Crete subsequently notified McKeown's customers that McKeown was no longer Gyp-Crete's distributor, offered to supply them and became the distributor of its products in McKeown's former territory, and charged McKeown's former customers about 20 percent less than they had been charged by McKeown. McKeown sued Gyp-Crete under the Connecticut Franchise Act, which defines a franchise in part as the operation of a business pursuant to "a marketing plan or system prescribed in substantial part by a franchisor" where such operation is "substantially associated" with the franchisor's trademark. Was McKeown a franchisee of Gyp-Crete? (*McKeown Distributors, Inc.* v. *Gyp-Crete Corporation*, 618 F. Supp. 632 [D. Conn. 1985].)

8. Lippo operated a Mobil Oil Corp. (Mobil) service station in Schaumburg, Ill., from 1974 until 1982. The franchise was governed by a series of documents executed on 1 March 1979. Paragraph 6 of the retail dealer contract imposed a duty not to sell non-Mobil products through Mobil equipment or under Mobil signs and gave Mobil a right of immediate termination if the provisions of the paragraph were violated. Article 4A of a supplemental agreement provided that if either party defaulted in the performance of any obligation under the franchise relationship and if the default continued uncorrected for ten days after written notification of the default, the aggrieved party could on written notice terminate the franchise relationship. On 29 September 1980, Lippo purchased 7500 gallons of non-Mobil gasoline. This gasoline was delivered to the station at 2:00 p.m. and sold to the public through Mobil equipment and under Mobil's signs until 4:00 p.m. on the following day. Under Mobil's direction, Lippo then covered

Mobil's pumps and signs with plastic and masking tape. He continued to sell the remaining non-Mobil gasoline and sold Mobil gasoline that was delivered on 1 October. On 12 November 1980, Mobil sent Lippo a notice of termination based on his sale of non-Mobil gasoline. The notice charged Lippo with violating the service station lease and the retail dealer contract. Lippo then sued Mobil, arguing that the attempted termination violated the Petroleum Marketing Practices Act (PMPA). Mobil argued that misbranding was such a serious violation of the agreement that it could not be cured and that, even if the default were cured, Mobil had not violated the PMPA. Who had the better argument? (*Lippo* v. *Mobil Oil Corporation*, 776 F.2d 706 [7th Cir. 1985].)

9. McDonald's Systems, Inc.'s (McDonald's) standard franchise agreement requires franchisees to purchase only "approved menu items," and the only approved sugar-sweetened cola is Coca-Cola. Although McDonald's neither sells Coca-Cola to its franchisees nor receives any rate or commission on Coca-Cola's sales to franchisees, Martino, a franchisee, argued the restriction was nonetheless illegal because McDonald's has an economic interest in Coca-Cola syrup sales to franchisees in the form of payments of advertising allowances by Coca-Cola to be used in the promotion of McDonald's products. Until the end of 1972, the advertising allowances had been paid directly to OPNAD, a national advertising fund separate from McDonald's. But beginning in 1973, Coca-Cola had paid the allowance directly to the franchisees, which they used to defray OPNAD contributions or for cooperative regional advertising or individual advertising programs. Martino contended that because McDonald's controls OPNAD, the Coca-Cola requirement leads to advertising allowances that are funneled into advertising controlled by McDonald's, thus primarily benefiting McDonald's. In addition, Martino characterized the Coca-Cola requirement as a vertical restraint restricting the ability of a franchisee or a syrup seller other than Coca-Cola, or both, to compete. McDonald's showed that its purchases had no substantial effect on the rest of the cola syrup market. Was Martino correct in claiming that this contractual provision violates the antitrust laws? (*Martino* v. *McDonald's System, Inc.*, 625 F. Supp. 356 [N.D. Ill. 1985].)

10. Tynan was the sole owner of Towne Chevrolet (Towne), a former General Motors (GM) franchisee that had sold all its assets in July, 1985. In December, 1985, Tynan had entered into a conditional agreement with

another GM franchisee, J & B Chevrolet and Olds, Inc. (J & B), to purchase that dealership. Tynan had formed L. T. Chevrolet and Olds, Inc. to acquire the assets of J & B. The sale was contingent on GM's issuance and execution of a franchise agreement with Tynan. Citing its past relationship with him, GM ultimately refused the franchise proposal offered by Tynan. J & B, which the parties agreed had standing to sue GM under the New Jersey Franchise Practices Act (the Act), had not challenged GM's decision. Rather, J & B had exercised its right to terminate the agreement with Tynan and had sold its business to a third party whom GM had accepted as a franchisee. Tynan sued, and the trial court found that since "Tynan was not a GM franchisee" on 21 January 1986, having sold the Towne franchise, he would have no standing under the Act to challenge GM's decision. Nonetheless, Tynan argued that his status as a contract purchaser of a franchise would entitle him to the protections of a franchisee. He claimed that the legislature had intended to protect the persons who would suffer from the arbitrary conduct of franchisors with respect to the transfer of a franchise, particularly since only the transferor and transferee can be hurt by the wrongful denial of consent. GM maintained, however, that only a franchisor can offer a franchise and therefore Tynan was not a franchisee with respect to the J & B transaction. GM pointed to a New Jersey statute that distinguishes between a franchisee and a "proposed transferee" or "prospective transferee." According to GM, a purchaser does not become a franchisee within the meaning of the Act until offered a franchise by the franchisor. The trial court found that, given the ordinary and well-understood implication of the word "offer," only the one who holds the ownership rights to a franchise can offer it to a third party. Hence, it concluded that Tynan was not a franchisee within the definition of the relevant New Jersey statute. The judge also cited the language in another statute to support the proposition that a franchisee is in a different class from a prospective transferee. The judge further reasoned that a court's entertaining suits by prospective purchasers would be contrary to the purpose of the legislation; i.e., the protection of the public welfare by defining the relationship and responsibilities between franchisors and franchisees, not hopeful third parties. The judge also suggested that a franchisee should not be required to litigate with the franchisor over the lack of consent to transfer and noted that the Act allows a franchisee to elect between litigation and the less burdensome transfer to a third party acceptable to the franchisor. Given these arguments, for whom should the appellate judge rule in this case? (*Tynan* v. *General Motors Corporation,* 591 A.2d 1024 [N.J. Super. A.D. 1991].)

C H A P T E R 44

Securities Regulation

O U T L I N E

FEDERAL LAWS

In Chapters 40 and 41, we briefly examined some provisions of the 1933 and 1934 Securities Acts. It is not possible in one chapter to discuss fully the complex interplay of federal and state securities laws, but we will attempt in this chapter to understand the broad outlines of this complicated area of the regulation of business.

Securities regulation has come to be known as "federal corporate law." This label stems in large measure from the extensive federal laws and the rules set forth by the *Securities and Exchange Commission* (SEC), the federal agency charged with primary responsibility for the enforcement and administration of federal laws covering securities, public utility holding companies, trust indentures, investment companies, and investment advisers. The SEC consists of five members appointed by the president for five-year terms. To ensure impartiality, securities law requires that no more than three of the commissioners be members of the same political party. The SEC and its staff have generally enjoyed a high-quality reputation among those in the securities field.

The Securities Act of 1933

The Securities Act of 1933 (the '33 Act) defines a *security* as "any note, stock, treasury stock, bond, debenture, evidence of indebtedness, . . . or participation in any profit-sharing agreement, . . . investment contract, . . . fractional undivided interest in oil, gas, or other mineral rights, or, in general, any interest or instrument commonly known as a 'security.' " Subsequent case decisions have made it clear that the essence of a security involves an investment in a common enterprise whereby the investor has no managerial functions but instead expects to profit solely from the efforts of others.[1] For this reason, court interpretations of what constitutes a security based on this so-called economic reality test have been broad and far-reaching. Courts have construed investments in condominiums, citrus groves, and cattle, when others have been employed to manage such assets, as securities subject to federal securities laws.

The '33 Act is basically a disclosure statute meant to protect the unsophisticated investing public. It ensures such protection by requiring the registration of most securities when they are initially offered and by enforcing various antifraud provisions.

In the following case, the court had to decide in its threshold analysis whether certain promissory notes would constitute "securities" under federal law. If so, the '34 Act's antifraud provisions were applicable. Notice the detailed analysis the Court followed in reaching its conclusion.

---

[1]The Supreme Court in *Gould* v. *Ruefenacht,* 471 U.S. 701 (1985), held that where an instrument bears the label "stock" and possesses all the characteristics typically associated with stock, the instrument is a "security"; a court need not look beyond the character of the instrument to the economic substance of the transaction in such cases.

Reves v. Ernst & Young
494 U.S. 56 (1990)

FACTS

Uncollateralized Having no underlying security to guarantee performance.

The Farmers Co-operative of Arkansas and Oklahoma (The Co-Op) is an agricultural co-operative that, at the time relevant here, had approximately 23,000 members. In order to raise money to support its general business operations, the Co-Op sold promissory notes payable on demand by the holder. Although the notes were **uncollateralized** and uninsured, they paid a variable rate of interest that the Co-Op adjusted monthly to keep it higher than the rate paid by local financial institutions. The Co-Op offered the notes to both members and nonmembers, marketing the scheme as an "Investment Program." Advertisements for the notes read in part: "YOUR CO-OP has more than $11,000,000 in assets to stand behind your investments. The Investment is not Federal [sic] insured but it is . . . Safe . . . Secure . . . and available when you need it." Despite these assurances, the Co-Op filed for bankruptcy in 1984. At the time of the filing, over 1600 people held notes worth a total of $10 million. After the Co-Op's filing for bankruptcy, Reves and others, a class of holders of the notes, filed suit against Arthur Young & Co. (Arthur Young), the firm that had audited the Co-Op's financial statements (and the predecessor to Ernst & Young). Reves alleged that Arthur Young had intentionally failed to follow generally accepted accounting principles in its audit in an effort to inflate the assets and net worth of the Co-Op. Reves maintained that, if Arthur Young had properly treated the assets in the audits, he (Reves) would not have purchased the demand notes because the Co-Op's insolvency would have been apparent. On the basis of these allegations, Reves claimed that Arthur Young had violated the antifraud provisions of the '34 Act as well as Arkansas's securities laws. Reves and the others prevailed at trial on both their federal and their state claims, receiving a $6.1 million judgment. Arthur Young appealed, claiming that the demand notes did not constitute "securities" under either federal law or Arkansas law and that the statutes' antifraud provisions therefore did not apply. A panel of the Eighth Circuit Court of Appeals, agreeing with Arthur Young on both the state and federal issues, reversed.

ISSUE

Were the notes issued by the Co-Op "securities" within the meaning of the '34 Act?

HOLDING

Yes. The demand notes issued by the Co-Op fell under the "note" category of instruments that are "securities."

REASONING

This case requires a decision as to whether the note issued by the Co-Op is a "security" within the meaning of the '34 Act. Section 3(a)(10) of the Act, the starting point for analysis, states, as does the '33 Act, that

> the term "security" means any note, stock, treasury stock, bond, debenture, certificate of interest or participation in any profit-sharing agreement or in any oil, gas, or other mineral royalty or lease, any collateral-trust certificate, preorganization certificate or subscription, transferable share, investment contract, voting-trust certificate, certificate of deposit . . . or in general, any instrument commonly known as a "security"; or any certificate of interest or participation in, temporary or interim certificate for, receipt for, or warrant or right to subscribe to or purchase, any of the foregoing; but shall not include currency or any note, draft, bill of exchange, or banker's acceptance which has a maturity at the time of issuance of not exceeding nine months. . . .

Congress's purpose in enacting the securities laws was to regulate investments, in whatever form they are made and by whatever name they are called. A commitment to an examination of the economic realities of a transaction does not necessarily entail a case-by-case analysis of every instrument, however. Some instruments obviously fall within the class Congress intended to regulate because they are by their nature investments. For example, in *Landreth Timber Co.* v. *Landreth*, 471 U.S. 681 (1985), the Supreme Court held that an instrument bearing the name "stock" that, among other things, is negotiable, offers the possibility of capital appreciation, and carries the right to dividends contingent on the profits of a business enterprise, is plainly within the class of instruments Congress intended the securities laws to cover. *Landreth Timber* does not signify a lack of concern with economic reality; rather, it signals a recognition that stock is, as a practical matter, always an investment if it has the economic characteristics traditionally associated with stock. Unlike "stock," the term " 'note' may now be viewed as a relatively broad term that encompasses instruments with widely varying characteristics, depending on whether issued in a consumer context, as commercial paper, or in some other investment context." Thus, notes are used in a variety of settings, not all of which involve investments. Consequently, they are not securities per se but must be defined using the "family resemblance" test. Under that test, a note is presumed to be a security unless it bears a strong resemblance, determined by examining four specified factors, to one of a judicially crafted list of categories of instruments that are not securities. If the instrument is not sufficiently similar to a listed item, a court must decide whether another category should be added by examining the same factors. Applying the family resemblance approach, one can conclude that the notes at issue here constitute "securities." Given the facts of this case, an examination of the four relevant factors provides few reasons to treat the notes as nonsecurities: (1) The Co-Op sold them to raise capital, and purchasers bought them to earn a profit in the form of interest, so that they are most naturally conceived as investments in a business enterprise; (2) there was "common trading" of the notes, which were offered and sold to a broad segment of the public; (3) the public reasonably perceived from advertisements for the notes that they were investments, and there were no countervailing factors that would have led a reasonable person to question this characterization; and (4) there was no risk-reducing factor that would make the application of the Securities Acts unnecessary, since the notes were uncollateralized and uninsured and would escape federal regulation entirely if a court held the Acts inapplicable. Ernst & Young's contention that the notes fall within the statutory exception for "any note . . . which has a maturity at the time of issuance of not exceeding nine months" is incorrect, since this argument rests entirely on the premise that Arkansas's statute of limitations for suits to collect demand notes—which are due immediately—is determinative of the notes' "maturity," as that term is used in the federal Securities Acts. The "maturity" of notes is a question of federal law, and Congress could not have intended that the Acts be applied differently to the same transactions depending on the accident of which state's law happened to apply. Since, as a matter of federal law, the words of the statutory exception are far from plain with regard to demand notes, courts must interpret the exclusion in accordance with the exception's purpose. Even assuming that Congress had intended to create a bright-line rule exempting from coverage all notes of less than nine months' duration on the ground that short-term notes remain sufficiently safe that the Securities Acts need not apply, that exemption would be inapplicable to the notes at issue here. These do not necessarily have short terms, since the note holders might just as easily make their demands years from now or even decades in the future.

Securities exchanges Organized secondary markets in which investors buy and sell securities at central locations.

Procedures   Section 5 is the heart of the '33 Act. It provides that any security that is not exempt must be registered with the SEC before it can be sold through the mails or through any facility of interstate commerce, such as **securities exchanges.** The corporation issuing the security must file a *registration statement* with the SEC and provide investors and would-be investors with a *prospectus*—a document presented by a corporation or its agents announcing the issue of corporate securities, stating the nature of the securities and the financial status of the issuing firm, and asking the general public to purchase the securities covered. The registration statement contains detailed information about the plan for offering and distributing the security; the names and salaries of managers and others who control the corporation; a description of the security; and information about the issuer and its business, including detailed financial reports. The prospectus must contain similar information in summary form. The underlying purpose of both the registration statement and the prospectus is the protection of the unsophisticated investor. These documents purport to inform a prospective investor of everything he or she should know before purchasing a security. Some critics argue, however, that the SEC requires so much information that an unsophisticated investor can make little sense of the myriad details that appear in the statement and the prospectus. These commentators believe the SEC's "overregulation" has actually undercut the worthy purposes of the '33 Act.

Some activities can take place before the filing of the registration statement. For example, if the *issuer* (the corporation selling the stock) has decided to distribute the securities itself during this prefiling period, it can enter into negotiations with **underwriters,** who may agree to handle the stock offering for the issuer. The SEC has twenty days in which to examine the registration statement. If the registration statement is complete and accurate, it becomes effective at the end of this twenty-day waiting period. During this period, the issuer or underwriter can accept oral purchase orders, but the SEC limits written advertisements to "tombstone ads," so called because they are boxed in the shape of a tombstone, and preliminary "red herring" prospectuses, so dubbed because of red lettering on them, to the effect that a registration statement has been filed but is not yet effective. After the registration statement becomes effective, the issuer or underwriter must provide every would-be investor with a prospectus before any sale can occur; otherwise, the sale of the securities will not be legal. These rules reinforce the '33 Act's "truth-in-securities" policies.

Exemptions The '33 Act exempts certain *classes* of securities from the registration and prospectus requirements discussed above. It is important to note, however, that there are *no* exemptions from the antifraud provisions, which we will examine in the next section. The exemptions include securities issued by federal and state governments and banks; short-term commercial paper; issues by nonprofit organizations; issues by savings and loan associations subject to state or federal regulation; issues by common carriers subject to the jurisdiction of the Interstate Commerce Commission; insurance policies and certain annuities subject to regulation by state and federal authorities; and intrastate issues of securities.

In addition, the '33 Act exempts certain *transactions:* private offerings (those that do not involve public offerings of securities, as is the usual case); transactions by persons other than issuers, underwriters, or dealers; certain brokers' and dealers' transactions; and small public issues. The SEC has established prerequisites and complex rules that must be followed in order to secure exemption from the registration process for these and certain other transactions. For instance, in one famous case, Ralston Purina Co. had sold nearly $2 million of stock to its "key employees" without registration. The "key employees" who had purchased the stock had included shop and dock foremen, stenographers, copywriters, clerical assistants, and veterinarians. Ralston Purina had maintained these were "private offering" transactions because the offer had not been made to all its employees and hence had not

Underwriters Persons or institutions that insure the sale of corporate securities by agreeing to sell securities to the public and to buy those not sold.

been a public offering subject to registration under the '33 Act. Asserting that the aim of the '33 Act is to protect investors by promoting full disclosure of information thought necessary for informed investment decisions, the Supreme Court concluded that Ralston Purina had not shown that the employees involved here had enjoyed access to the kind of information that registration would disclose. Thus, the Court held that this attempted private offering (or "private placement") was not a bona fide exempt transaction and that registration should have occurred.[2]

Antifraud Provisions   In addition to registration requirements, the '33 Act contains several antifraud provisions. Section 12 prohibits oral or written misstatements of material facts or omissions of material facts necessary to keep the statements from being misleading in the circumstances in which they were made. Section 17 is a general antifraud provision that makes it unlawful for any person to use the mails or interstate commerce to employ any device or scheme that will defraud another person or to engage in any transaction, practice, or course of business that defrauds or deceives the purchaser. Basically, then, Section 17 makes illegal any form of fraud, untrue statement of a material fact, or omission of a material fact involving the sale of any securities in interstate commerce or through the mail. Because of the complexities inherent in the issuance of securities, anyone who contemplates issuing securities should seek the counsel of professionals who specialize in the securities field.

Liabilities and Remedies   The potential liabilities spawned by the '33 Act also pose a significant reason for seeking competent advice. Section 11 imposes civil liability for any registration statement that contains untrue statements of a material fact or omissions of material facts that would make the registration statement misleading in the circumstances in which a purchaser buys the securities. Such a purchaser can receive as damages an amount not exceeding the price paid for the securities. Section 11 places liability on every person who signed the registration statement; on every person who was a director or was named in the registration statement as about to become a director; on every accountant, engineer, appraiser, or any other professional expert whose statement or report appears in the registration statement; and on every underwriter. All such persons, except the issuer, may escape liability by showing that they acted with "due diligence." This statutory defense of "due diligence" varies as to the type of defendant involved and whether the misrepresentations or omissions are found in the "expertised" or "nonexpertised" portions of the registration statement. The defense generally is available to anyone who, after reasonable investigation, had reasonable grounds to believe, and did believe, that the registration statement was accurate and did not omit material facts that were either required or necessary to make the statement not mis-

[2]*Securities and Exchange Commission v. Ralston Purina Co.*, 346 U.S. 119 (1953).

leading. Additionally, Section 12 exacts civil liability from any person who sells securities through the mails or in interstate commerce by means of a prospectus or oral communication that includes misrepresentations or omissions of necessary material facts. Such persons can avoid liability if they can show that they did not know, and in the exercise of reasonable care could not have known, about the untruths or omissions. The injured party can sue only the person who actually sold the security but can recover the price paid for the security. Section 17's antifraud provisions may be used as a basis for criminal liability. Moreover, Section 24 sets up criminal sanctions for willful violations of the '33 Act.

The case that follows illustrates many of the principles that we have just discussed.

Escott v. *BarChris Construction Corporation*
283 F. Supp. 643 (S.D. N.Y. 1968)

FACTS
The purchasers of certain securities of BarChris Construction Corporation sued under Section 11 of the '33 Act, alleging that the registration statement filed with the SEC about these stocks had contained materially false statements and material omissions. The defendants included the persons who had signed the registration statement (primarily directors and officers), the underwriters (investment bankers), and Peat, Marwick, Mitchell & Co. (BarChris's auditors).

ISSUES
Had the registration statement included materially false statements and material omissions? If so, had the defendants successfully shown the statutory defense—that is, that they had acted with due diligence?

HOLDINGS
Yes. The registration statement had included materially false statements and material omissions. No. Only the outside directors had been able to sustain even a part of their "due diligence" defense (and they could show due diligence only with respect to the "expertised" portion of the registration statement).

REASONING
The registration statement had contained materially false statements and material omissions. A material fact is a fact that, had it been correctly stated or disclosed, would have deterred the average prudent investor from purchasing the securities in question. Therefore, BarChris's overstatement of its sales and gross profits and its understatement of its liabilities in 1961 had satisfied this definition. But the prospectus statements about BarChris's status in December 1960 had been rather minor errors and hence nonmaterial. However, the prospectus's 1961 balance sheet had contained material errors. Nonetheless, although the "due diligence" statutory defense had been available to all the defendants except the issuer, BarChris, none of the inside directors and officers had sustained the due diligence defense with respect to either the "expertised" (that is, the financial reports prepared by accountants) or the "unexpertised" portions of the registration statement. The outside directors similarly had not sustained their due diligence defense with regard to the unexpertised part of the registration statement, primarily because they had neither familiarized themselves with its contents nor questioned its major points. On the other hand, the outside directors had shown due diligence regarding the "expertised" portion of the statement because of their confidence in the auditors, Peat, Marwick, Mitchell & Co. Like the inside directors and officers, the underwriters and the auditors had failed to establish the due diligence defense with respect to either portion of the registration statement.

**The Securities
Exchange Act
of 1934**

While the 1933 Act deals with the initial issuance of securities, the Securities Exchange Act of 1934 (the '34 Act) regulates the secondary distribution of securities. As such, the '34 Act's jurisdiction extends to the registration and distribution of securities through national stock exchanges, national securities associations, brokers, and dealers. The '34 Act also supervises proxy solicitations of registered securities, regulates tender offers, limits insider trading, forbids short-swing profits, and in general tries to eliminate fraud and manipulative conduct with respect to the sale or purchase of securities. Thus, in many ways the '33 and '34 Acts are similar and supplement each other. But the reach of the '34 Act, with its supervision of national exchanges and over-the-counter sales of securities, is even broader than that of the '33 Act.

Registration and Reporting   The '34 Act requires any issuer who trades securities on a national stock exchange to register with the SEC. In addition, any firm engaged in interstate commerce with total assets of over $5 million and at least 500 shareholders must comply with Section 12's registration provisions. For violations of Section 12, the SEC can revoke or suspend the registration of the security involved.

Like the '33 Act, the '34 Act tries to ensure that the investing public will have sufficient information about publicly traded securities when these investors make their decisions about whether to buy stocks. Hence, the '34 Act mandates certain disclosures by firms covered by the Act when the securities are listed with national exchanges or traded over the counter. Basically, these obligatory disclosures include detailed registration statements similar to the information required under the '33 Act as well as annual and quarterly reports. SEC Forms 8-A, 8-K, 10-K, and 10-Q, which companies use for compiling this information, are complex and contain substantial amounts of facts and figures relating to the companies' businesses. (Some companies may utilize EDGAR, the SEC's electronic data-gathering system, which it has employed experimentally for certain filings.) Other SEC provisions impose liability on the company for damages resulting from an investor's reliance on misleading statements contained in any such documents.

Proxy Solicitations   As discussed in Chapter 40, a proxy is an assignment by the shareholder of the right to vote the shares held by the shareholder. Since proxies become a device for consolidating corporate power and control, one cannot underestimate their importance both to management and to those who wish to oust the present management ("dissident" shareholders). Because of the high stakes involved for both competing factions, it is vitally important that the information provided to shareholders be accurate. If shareholders receive misleading information, they will make their decision regarding who should be given their proxies—management or dissidents—in ignorance of the true facts. To prevent such abuses, Section 14 of the '34 Act makes it illegal for a company registered under Section 12 to solicit proxies in a manner that would violate the SEC rules and regulations that protect the investing public. Section 14 also sets out rules mandating disclosure of pertinent information to shareholders at corporate meetings even when there will be no solicitation of proxies.

The disclosure required of proxy solicitations includes a proxy statement, which contains detailed information, and a proxy form, on which the shareholder can note his or her approval or disapproval of each proposal that will be voted on at the corporation's meeting. Before the corporation (or dissidents) sends proxies to shareholders, the SEC must approve the statement and the form. These preliminary proxies must be filed with the SEC at least ten days before they are sent to shareholders. If the meeting involves the election of directors, any proxy statement must also include an annual report detailing, among other things, the financial aspects of the company. Similarly, as mentioned earlier, any proxy contest requires full disclosure of all pertinent facts regarding the matters under consideration, such as the identity of all participants in the proxy contest and the reasons for the proxy solicitation.

Section 14 also authorizes the inclusion of shareholder proposals of no more than 500 words in any management-backed proxy solicitation. This SEC rule allows a shareholder to express an opinion regarding the recommendations management has made without incurring the significant costs involved in an independent proxy solicitation. This aspect of Section 14 thus attempts to preserve the balance of power between management and insurgents in order to safeguard the democratic aspects of the corporation. As you would expect, management usually opposes the inclusion of such proposals. SEC rules authorize exclusion of proposals that are not "proper subjects" for action by shareholders, proposals that center on personal claims or grievances, proposals that are not significantly related to the corporation's business or are beyond the corporation's power to bring about (that is, proposals that primarily promote economic, political, racial, religious, or social causes), and proposals that are substantially similar to a proposal submitted but not approved within the past five years. In disputes over whether the corporation can exclude the proposal, the SEC normally decides who is correct. Management bears the burden of proof regarding why the proposal was properly excluded. Shareholder proposals have dealt with management compensation, company policies allegedly leading to discrimination or pollution, and even opposition to the Vietnam War. Shareholder proposals usually are unsuccessful.

The corporation ordinarily pays for the expenses incurred in proxy contests if either management or the insurgents win. The law is unsettled as to whether the corporation should pay the costs of a contest if management loses, but the trend is to make the corporation (not the managers themselves) pay even in those circumstances.

Liability for misleading proxy statements or those that omit a material fact necessary to make the statement true and not misleading is absolute. Any person who sells or buys securities in reliance on such statements can recover from the corporation.

The following case involves many of these concepts. The case itself is long and complex, but the court's treatment of the concepts makes it well worth reading.

Virginia Bankshares, Inc. v. *Sandberg*
111 S.Ct. 2749 (1991)

FACTS
As part of a proposed "freeze-out" merger, in which First American Bank of Virginia (the Bank) would be merged into Virginia Bankshares, Inc. (VBI), a wholly owned subsidiary of First American Bankshares, Inc. (FABI), the Bank's executive committee and board approved a price of $42 per share for the minority stockholders, who would lose their interests in the Bank after the merger. Although Virginia law required only that the merger proposal be submitted to a vote at a shareholders' meeting, preceded by a circulation of an informational statement to the shareholders, the Bank directors nevertheless solicited proxies for voting on the proposal. Their solicitation urged the proposal's adoption and stated that the plan had been approved because of its opportunity for the minority shareholders to receive a "high" value for their stock. Sandberg, a shareholder, did not give her proxy and filed suit in district court after the approval of the merger, seeking damages from the Bank's action of soliciting proxies by means of allegedly materially false or misleading statements in violation of Section 14(a) of the Securities Exchange Act of 1934 and the Securities and Exchange Commission's Rule 14(a)-9. Among other things, she alleged that the directors believed they would have no alternative but to recommend the merger if they wished to remain on the board. At trial, she obtained a jury instruction, based on language in *Mills* v. *Electric Auto-Lite Co.*, that she could prevail without showing her own reliance on the alleged misstatements, as long as they were material and the proxy solicitation was an "essential link" in the merger process. She was awarded an amount equal to the difference between the offered price and her stock's true value. The court of appeals affirmed, holding that certain statements in the proxy solicitation, including the one regarding the stock's value, were materially misleading; and that Sandberg (and the other shareholders) could maintain the action even though their votes had not been needed to effectuate the merger.

ISSUES
Would a statement couched in conclusory or qualitative terms purporting to explain the directors' reasons for recommending a certain corporate action be materially misleading and within the meaning of Rule 14a-9? Could causation of damages compensable under Section 14(a) be shown by a member of a class of minority shareholders whose votes had not been required by law or any corporate bylaw to authorize the corporate action subject to the proxy solicitation?

HOLDINGS
Yes to the first question, no to the second. Although knowingly false statements of reasons may be actionable even though conclusory in form, Sandberg had failed to demonstrate the equitable basis required to extend the Section 14(a) private action to such shareholders when any indication of congressional intent to do so is lacking.

REASONING
Section 14(a) of the Securities Exchange Act of 1934 authorizes the SEC to adopt rules for the solicitation of proxies and prohibits their violation. In *J.I. Case Co.* v. *Borak*, 377 U.S. 426 (1964), the Supreme Court first recognized an implied private right of action for the breach of Section 14(a) as implemented by SEC Rule 14a-9, which prohibits the solicitation of proxies by means of materially false or misleading statements. The court of appeals had affirmed VBI and FABI's liability for two statements found to have been materially misleading in violation of Section 14(a) of the Act, one of which was that the "Plan of Merger has been approved by the Board of Directors because it provides an opportunity for the Bank's public shareholders to achieve a high value for their shares." VBI and FABI argued that statements of opinion or belief incorporating indefinite and unverifiable expressions cannot be actionable as misstatements of material fact within the meaning of Rule 14a-9 and that such a declaration of opinion or belief should never be actionable when placed in a proxy solicitation incorporating statements of fact sufficient to enable

readers to draw their own, independent conclusions. The meaning of the materiality requirement for liability under Section 14(a) was discussed at some length in *TSC Industries, Inc.* v. *Northway, Inc.* where the Supreme Court held a fact to be material "if there is a substantial likelihood that a reasonable shareholder would consider it important in deciding how to vote." There is no room to deny that a statement of belief by corporate directors about a recommended course of action, or an explanation of their reasons for recommending it, can take on just that importance. Shareholders know that directors usually have knowledge and expertise far exceeding the normal investor's resources, and the directors' perceived superiority is magnified even further by the common knowledge that state law customarily obliges them to exercise the judgment in their shareholders' interest. Naturally, then, the share owner faced with a proxy request will think it important to know the directors' beliefs about the course they recommend and their specific reasons for urging the stockholders to embrace it. But, assuming materiality, the question remains whether statements of reasons, opinions, or beliefs are statements "with respect to . . . material facts" so as to fall within the strictures of the rule. VBI and FABI argued that wasteful litigation of amorphous issues outside the readily provable realm of fact would attend the court's recognition of liability here on proof that the directors had not recommended the merger for the stated reason, and they cite the authority of *Blue Chip Stamps* v. *Manor Drug Stores* as setting out sound policy grounds for placing such statements outside the scope of the rule. Granted, *Blue Chip Stamps* is instructive, as illustrating a line between what is and is not manageable in the litigation of facts; but it does not support VBI and FABI's position. Reasons for directors' recommendations or statements of belief are characteristically matters of corporate record subject to documentation, to be supported or attacked by evidence of historical fact outside a plaintiff's control. Such evidence would include not only corporate minutes and other statements of the directors themselves, but circumstantial evidence bearing on the facts that would reasonably underlie the reasons claimed and the honesty of any statement that those reasons are the basis for a recommendation or other action, a point that becomes especially clear when the reasons or beliefs go to valuations in dollars and cents. It is inappropriate to argue, as VBI and FABI do, that the quoted statement on which liability was predicated did not express a reason in dollars and cents, but focused instead on the "indefinite and unverifiable" term, "high value," much like the similar claims that the merger's terms were "fair" to shareholders. The objection ignores the fact that such conclusory terms in a commercial context are reasonably understood to rest on a factual basis that justifies them as accurate, the absence of which renders them misleading. Provable facts either furnish good reasons to make a conclusory commercial judgment, or they count against it; and expressions of such judgments can be uttered with knowledge of truth or falsity just like more definite statements and defended or attacked through the orthodox evidentiary process that either substantiates their underlying justifications or tends to disprove their existence. In this case, whether $42 was "high" and the proposal "fair" to the minority shareholders depended on whether provable facts about the Bank's assets, and about actual and potential levels of operation, substantiated a value that was above, below, or more or less at the $42 figure, when assessed in accordance with recognized methods of valuation. Sandberg and the other shareholders had adduced evidence for just such facts in proving that the statement was misleading about its subject matter and a false expression of the directors' reasons. Whereas the proxy statement described the $42 price as offering a premium above both book value and market price, the evidence indicated that a calculation of the book figure based on the appreciated value of the Bank's real estate holdings had eliminated any such premium. The evidence on the significance of market price showed that one expert had conceded that the market was closed, thin, and dominated by FABI—facts omitted from the statement. There was, indeed, evidence of a "going concern" value for the Bank in excess of $60 per share of common stock—another fact never disclosed. The question arises, then, whether disbelief, or undisclosed belief or motivation, standing alone, should be a sufficient basis to sustain an action under Section 14(a), in the absence of proof by the sort of objective evidence described above that the statement also expressly or impliedly asserted something false or misleading about its subject matter. Proof of mere disbelief or belief undisclosed should not suffice for liability under Section 14(a). If nothing more had been required or proven in this case, reversal for that reason would be justified. To recognize liability on mere disbelief or undisclosed motive without any demonstration that the proxy statement was false or misleading about its subject would authorize Section 14(a) litigation confined solely to what one skeptical court spoke of as the "impurities" of a director's "unclean heart." This would cross the line that *Blue Chip Stamps* sought to draw. Therefore, disbelief or undisclosed motivation, standing alone, is insufficient to satisfy the element of fact that must be established under Section 14(a). Although a misleading statement will not always lose its deceptive edge simply by joinder with others that are true, the true statements may discredit the other one so obviously that the risk of real deception drops to nil. Since liability under Section 14(a) must rest not only on deceptiveness but on materiality as well (i.e., according to *TSC Industries* it has to be significant enough to be important to a reasonable investor deciding how to vote), VBI and FABI are on perfectly firm ground in their argument that publishing accurate facts in a proxy statement can render a misleading proposition too unimportant to lead to liability. But not every mixture with the true will neutralize the deceptive. If it would take a financial analyst to spot the tension between the one and the other, whatever is misleading will remain materially so; and liability should follow. The point of a proxy statement, after all, should be to inform, not to challenge the reader's critical wits. Only when the inconsistency would exhaust the misleading conclusion's capacity to influence the reasonably astute shareholder would a Section 14(a) action fall on the element of materiality. The evidence invoked by VBI and FABI in the instant case fell short of compelling the jury to find the facial materiality of the misleading statement neutralized. The directors claimed to have made an explanatory disclosure of further reasons for their recommendation when they said they would keep their seats following the merger, but they failed to mention that they would have no expectation of doing so without supporting the proposal. The proxy statement did not speak factually about the merger price in describing it as higher than share prices in recent sales, and it also failed to mention the closed market domination of FABI. The claim that the merger price exceeded book price was controverted. Finally, the solicitation omitted any mention of the bank's value as a going concern at more than $60 a share, compared to the merger price of $42. *J.I. Case Co.* v. *Borak* did not address the requisites of causation or define the class of plaintiffs eligible to sue under Section 14(a). *Mills* v. *Electric Auto-Lite Co.* provided greater clarity, with the court addressing the sufficiency of proof that misstatements in a proxy solicitation were responsible for damages claimed from the merger subject to complaint. The court held that causation of damages by a material proxy misstatement could be established by showing that minority proxies necessary and sufficient to authorize the corporate acts had been given in accordance with the tenor of the solicitations. The court described such a causal relationship by calling the proxy solicitation an "essential link" in the accomplishment of the transaction. Sandberg and the other shareholders addressed the open question from *Mills* by proffering two theories that the proxy solicitation had been an "essential link" under the *Mills* causation test. First they asserted that VBI and FABI would have been unwilling to proceed with the merger without the approval manifested by the minority shareholders' proxies, which could not have been obtained without the solicitation's misstatements and misleading omissions. In the alternative, they argued that the proxy statement had constituted an essential link between the directors' proposal and the merger because it had represented the means to satisfy a state statutory requirement of minority shareholder approval as a condition of saving a merger. Although Sandberg and the other shareholders proffered each of these theories as establishing a chain of causal connection, neither theory presented the proxy solicitation as essential in the sense of *Mills's* causal sequence, in which the solicitation links a directors' proposal with the votes legally required to authorize the action proposed. The theory of causal necessity derived from the requirements of Virginia law dealing with postmerger ratification seeks to identify the essential character of the proxy solicitation from its function in obtaining the minority approval that would preclude a minority suit attacking the merger. This theory of causation rests upon the proposition that Section 14(a) should provide a federal remedy whenever a false or misleading proxy statement results in a loss under state law or a shareholder plaintiff's state remedy for the enforcement of a state right. Assuming the soundness of Sandberg's characterization of the proxy statement as materially misleading, the very terms of the Virginia statute indicate that a favorable minority vote induced by the solicitation would not suffice to render the merger vulnerable to later attack on the ground of the conflict. The statute bars a shareholder from seeking to avoid a transaction tainted by a director's conflict if, for example, the minority shareholders ratified the transaction following the disclosure of the material facts of the transaction and the conflict. Assuming that the material facts about the merger had not been accurately disclosed, the minority votes were inadequate to ratify the merger under state law; and there was no loss of a state remedy to connect the proxy solicitation with harm to minority shareholders irredressable under state law. Nor is there a claim here that the statement misled Sandberg and the other shareholders into entertaining a false belief that they had no chance to upset the merger, until the time for bringing suit had run out. Therefore, the judgment of the court of appeals is reversed.

Tender Offers In addition to regulating proxies, since 1968, the Williams Act, codified in Sections 13 and 14, has also regulated *tender offers* or *takeover bids,* whether hostile or friendly, wherein *one publicly held corporation (the* "*tender offeror") attempts to acquire control of another publicly held company* (the "target"). Section 14, in conjunction with Section 13, sets forth filing and registration requirements for any person who becomes the owner of more than 5 percent of any class of securities registered under Section 12. In general, these provisions force the offeror to provide the target company's shareholders with the names of the offerors and their interests, the purpose of the takeover, the method of disposing of the target firm's stocks and assets, and so forth. Additionally, any statements the management of the target firm makes in opposition to the merger must also be filed with the SEC. Provisions for liability under this aspect of the '34 Act are similar to those instituted for violations of the proxy rules.

The Supreme Court recently answered the numerous questions that had arisen about the constitutionality of state regulation of tender offers or takeovers in a case involving Indiana's statute.

CTS Corporation v. Dynamics Corporation of America
107 S.Ct. 1637 (1987)

FACTS The federal Williams Act and implementing regulations govern hostile corporate stock tender offers by requiring, among other things, that offers remain open for at least twenty business days. The Indiana Act concerning Control Share Acquisitions applies to certain business corporations chartered in Indiana that have specified levels of shares or shareholders within the state and that opt into the Act's protection. The Indiana Act provides that the acquisition of "control shares" in such a corporation—shares that, but for the Act, would bring the acquiring entity's voting power to or above certain threshold levels—does not include voting rights unless a majority of all preexisting disinterested shareholders so agree at their next regularly scheduled meeting. However, the stock acquiror can require a special meeting within fifty days by following specified procedures. Dynamics Corporation of America (Dynamics) announced a tender offer that would have raised its ownership interest in CTS Corporation above the Indiana Act's threshold. At the same time, Dynamics also filed suit in federal court alleging federal securities violations by CTS. After CTS opted into the Indiana Act, Dynamics amended its complaint to challenge the Act's validity under the federal Williams Act and the Commerce Clause.

Preemption Doctrine providing that, as to certain matters, federal law takes precedence over state laws.

ISSUE Was the Indiana takeover statute invalid owing to its **preemption** by the Williams Act or its unconstitutionality under the Commerce Clause?

HOLDING No. The Indiana Act is consistent with the provisions and purposes of the Williams Act and is not preempted thereby. Furthermore, the Act does not violate the Commerce Clause.

REASONING The Indiana Act is consistent with the provisions and purposes of the Williams Act and is not preempted by this federal law. Because the Indiana Act protects independent shareholders from the coercive aspects of tender offers by allowing them to vote as a group, it furthers the Williams Act's basic purpose of placing investors on an equal footing with takeover bidders. Moreover, the Indiana Act avoids the problems that had led to a finding of preemption for other state takeover statutes, since it neither gives management or the offeror an advantage in communicating with shareholders nor imposes an indefinite delay on offers. Moreover, the possibility that the Indiana Act will delay some tender offers does not mandate preemption. The state Act neither imposes an absolute fifty-day delay on the consummation of tender offers nor precludes offerors from purchasing shares as soon as federal law permits. Hence, it does not conflict with the shorter, twenty-day period established by federal law. If a tender offeror fears an adverse shareholder vote, it can condition the tender offer on the shares receiving voting rights within a specified period and thus avoid the fifty-day period. Furthermore, even assuming that the Indiana Act does impose some additional delay, only "unreasonable" delays conflict with the Williams Act. Here, it cannot be said that a fifty-day delay was unreasonable, since that period fell within the sixty-day maximum period Congress had established for tender offers. If the Williams Act were construed to preempt any state statute that causes delays, it would preempt a variety of state corporate laws of hitherto unquestioned validity. The longstanding prevalence of state regulation in this area suggests that, if Congress had intended to preempt all such state laws, it would have said so. The Indiana Act likewise does not violate the Commerce Clause. The Act's limited effect on interstate commerce is justified by the state's interest in defining attributes of its corporations' shares and in protecting shareholders. Moreover, the Act does not discriminate against interstate commerce, as it has the same effect on tender offers whether or not the offeror is an Indiana resident. That the Act may apply most often to out-of-state entities who launch most hostile tender offers is irrelevant, since a claim of discrimination is not established by the mere fact that the burden of a state regulation falls on some interstate companies. Furthermore, the Act does not create an impermissible risk of inconsistent regulation of tender offers by different states. It simply and evenhandedly exercises the state's firmly established authority to define the voting rights of shareholders in Indiana corporations and thus subjects such corporations to the law of only one state. The court of appeal's holding that the Act unconstitutionally hinders tender offers ignores the fact that a state, in its role as overseer of corporate governance, enacts laws that necessarily affect certain aspects of interstate commerce, particularly with respect to corporations with shareholders in other states. A state has interests in promoting stable relationships among the parties involved in its corporations and in ensuring that investors have an effective voice in corporate affairs. The Indiana Act validly furthers these interests by allowing shareholders collectively to determine whether the takeover is advantageous to them. The argument that Indiana has no legitimate interest in protecting nonresident shareholders is unavailing, since the Act applies only to corporations incorporated in Indiana that have a substantial number of shareholders in the state. Even if the Act should decrease the number of successful tender offers for Indiana corporations, this would not offend the Commerce Clause. The Act does not prohibit any resident or nonresident from offering to purchase, or from purchasing, shares in Indiana corporations, or from attempting thereby to gain control. Rather, it merely provides regulatory procedures designed for the better protection of the corporations' shareholders. Thus, the Indiana Control Share Acquisitions provisions of the Act evenhandedly determine the voting rights of shares of Indiana corporations. As such, the Act does not conflict with the provisions or purposes of the Williams Act. To the limited extent that the Act affects interstate commerce, this is justified by the state's interests in defining the attributes of shares in its corporations and in protecting shareholders. Congress has never questioned the need for state regulation of these matters; nor does such regulation offend the Constitution.

Insider Trading   As mentioned in Chapter 41, directors, officers, and controlling shareholders may violate the federal securities laws if they engage in "insider trading." We noted then that the '34 Act makes such activities illegal and sets out possibilities of far-ranging liability. Section 10b of the '34 Act makes unlawful any manipulative or deceptive device used through the mails or in interstate commerce in connection with the purchase or sale of any security. SEC Rule 10b-5 augments Section 10b by providing for liability for any fraudulent or deceitful activity that involves misleading material facts or omissions of material facts that would make a statement misleading in the circumstances in which it was made.

When material inside information is involved, the insider must *either* publicly disclose the information to ensure that the investing public that does not have access to the information will remain free from prejudice *or* abstain from trading in the securities. But it is nevertheless difficult to judge when information is important enough to be considered "material." The *Basic Incorporated* case, which follows, provides some guidelines in this important area.

Basic Incorporated v. *Levinson*
108 S.Ct. 978 (1988)

FACTS   Basic Incorporated (Basic) was a public-issue corporation that provided materials for the manufacture of steel. In 1976, Basic held meetings with representatives of Combustion Engineering Co. (Combustion) regarding the possibility of a merger. During 1977 and 1978, Basic made three public statements denying that it was engaged in merger negotiations. Yet, on 18 December 1978, Basic asked the New York Stock Exchange to suspend trading in its shares and issued a release stating that it had been "approached" by another company concerning a merger. On 19 December, Basic's board endorsed Combustion's offer of $46 per share for its common stock and on the following day publicly announced the company's approval of Combustion's tender offer for all the outstanding shares of Basic. Levinson and other Basic shareholders who had sold their stock after Basic's final public statement on 21 October 1977, and before the suspension of trading in December, 1978, sued Basic and its board of directors for violations of Section 10b of the 1934 Act and Rule 10b-5 allegedly stemming from Basic's denials of the merger negotiations prior to the official announcement.

ISSUE   Did Basic's denials about the preliminary merger negotiations constitute material misrepresentations under Section 10b and Rule 10b-5?

HOLDING   Yes. Information concerning the existence and the status of preliminary merger discussions would be significant to a reasonable investor's trading decision. Consequently, Basic's inaccurate and incomplete statements were material and thus violative of Section 10b and Rule 10b-5.

REASONING   As the *SEC* v. *Texas Gulf Sulphur* case had shown, the materiality requirement of Rule 10b-5 with respect to contingent or speculative information or events depends on the facts. Whether merger discussions in a particular case are material therefore is similarly fact specific. Generally, in order to assess the probability that the event will occur, a fact finder will need to look to indicia of interest in the transaction at the highest corporate levels. Board resolutions, instructions to investment bankers, and actual negotiations between principals or their intermediaries may serve as indicia of such interest. To assess the magnitude of the transaction to the issuer of the securities allegedly manipulated, a fact finder will need to consider such facts as the size of the two corporate entities and the stocks' potential premium over market value. No particular event or factor short of closing the transaction need be either necessary or sufficient by itself to render merger discussions material. Rather, materiality depends on the significance the reasonable investor would place on the withheld or misrepresented information. If, as noted in the *TSC Industries, Inc.* v. *Northway, Inc.* case, there is a substantial likelihood that the disclosure of the omitted fact would have been viewed as significant by a reasonable investor, the information is material. Hence, there is no valid justification for artificially excluding from the definition of materiality information concerning merger discussions, which would otherwise be considered significant to the trading decision of a reasonable investor, merely because the parties (or their representatives) had failed to reach an agreement-in-principle as to the price and structure.

The courts in this case had accepted a presumption, created by the fraud-on-the-market theory and subject to rebuttal by Basic, that persons who had traded Basic shares had done so in reliance on the integrity of the price set by the market, but that because of Basic's material misrepresentations that price had been fraudulently depressed. Requiring plaintiffs to show a speculative state of facts—that is, how they would have acted if omitted material information had been disclosed or if the misrepresentations had not been made—would place an unnecessarily unrealistic evidentiary burden on the Rule 10b-5 plaintiff who had traded on an impersonal market. Because most publicly available information is reflected in market price, an investor's reliance on any public material misrepresentations, therefore, may be presumed for purposes of a Rule 10b-5 action. Nevertheless, any showing that severs the link between the alleged misrepresentation and either the price received (or paid) by plaintiffs, or their decision to trade at a fair market price, will be sufficient to rebut the presumption of reliance. In summary, the standard of materiality set forth in *TSC Industries, Inc.* v. *Northway* will govern future Section 10b and Rule 10b-5 cases. Thus, materiality in the merger context depends on the probability that the transaction will be consummated and its significance to the issuer of the securities. Materiality therefore depends on the facts and must be determined on a case-by-case basis. Courts may apply a presumption of reliance supported by the fraud-on-the-market theory; that presumption, however, is rebuttable.

Although Section 10b does not expressly provide for civil liability, it, as a broad antifraud provision, applies to any manipulative or deceptive device used in connection with any purchase or sale of any security by any person; there are no exemptions from coverage. Similarly, Rule 10b-5 has been applied to the activities of corporate *insiders*—directors, officers, controlling shareholders, employees, lawyers, accountants, bankers, consultants, and anyone else who has access to material inside information that may affect the price of the stock. Before the *Chiarella* case, which follows, persons considered insiders included even those who purchased or sold stock based on tips provided directly or indirectly by directors, officers, and the like. Hence, the SEC would have considered a barber—who buys stock on the basis of market information learned from overhearing a director's discussion of an upcoming business trip—an insider as well. The *Chiarella* case has cast some doubt on whether such remote "tippees" will be liable in the future. The SEC nevertheless is continuing to prosecute such people as the barber for securities violations unless they either "disclose" or "abstain."

Chiarella v. *United States*
445 U.S. 222 (1980)

FACTS   Chiarella was a printer who worked for a firm that printed takeover bids. Although the identities of the firms had been left blank, Chiarella was able to deduce the names of the target companies from other information contained in the documents he was preparing for printing. Without disclosing his knowledge, Chiarella purchased stock in the target companies and sold the stock when the takeover attempts became public knowledge. Chiarella thereby gained $30,000 in fourteen months. The SEC indicted him on seventeen counts of violating Section 10b and Rule 10b-5 of the '34 Act.

ISSUE   Were Section 10b and Rule 10b-5 applicable to Chiarella, who had been neither an insider nor a "tippee" recipient of confidential information from the target company?

HOLDING   No. Section 10b and Rule 10b-5 were not applicable to Chiarella because he was not a corporate insider; rather, he was a complete stranger who had dealt with the sellers only through impersonal market transactions.

REASONING   The fraudulent conduct prohibited by Section 10b and Rule 10b-5 had not occurred here. Although past administrative and judicial interpretations had established that silence in connection with the purchase or sale of securities might operate as a fraud actionable under Section 10b, the element required to make silence fraudulent—a duty to disclose—was absent in this case. Chiarella had been a complete stranger to the sellers of the target company's securities and thus was not in a fiduciary relationship with them. Hence, affirming Chiarella's conviction would recognize a general duty between all participants in market transactions to forgo actions based on material, nonpublic information. The imposition of such a broad duty, departing as it would from the established doctrine that duty arises from a specific relationship between two parties, would be ill-advised.

The Supreme Court's decision in *Dirks* v. *Securities and Exchange Commission* appears to reinforce *Chiarella* by emphasizing the basic principle that only *some* persons, under *some* circumstances, will be barred from trading while in possession of material nonpublic information.

Dirks v. Securities and Exchange Commission
463 U.S. 646 (1983)

FACTS   In 1973, Raymond Dirks was an officer of a New York broker-dealer firm that specialized in providing investment analysis of insurance company securities to institutional investors. On 6 March Ronald Secrist, a former officer of Equity Funding of America (Equity Funding), told Dirks that the assets of Equity Funding, a diversified corporation primarily engaged in selling life insurance and mutual funds, had been vastly overstated as the result of fraudulent corporate practices. Stressing that various regulatory agencies had failed to act on similar charges made by Equity Funding employees, Secrist urged Dirks to verify the fraud and to disclose it publicly. Dirks then visited Equity Funding's headquarters in Los Angeles and interviewed officers and employees of Equity Funding. Although neither Dirks nor his firm owned or traded any Equity Funding stock, some of Equity Funding's clients and investors had sold their holdings in Equity Funding as a result of information that Dirks had shared with them during his investigation. Dirks also urged the *Wall Street Journal* to write a story about the fraud allegations. Eventually, the California insurance authorities uncovered evidence of the fraud, after which the SEC had filed a complaint against Equity Funding. The SEC also investigated Dirks's involvement, finding that he had repeated confidential corporate information in violation of securities rules. However, since he had played an important role in bringing Equity Funding's massive fraud to light, the SEC merely **censured** him.

Censured Formally reprimanded for specific conduct.

ISSUE   Did the disclosure of material nonpublic information received from insiders of a corporation with whom Dirks had no connection to investors who had relied on the information in trading in the shares of the corporation violate the '33 and '34 Acts?

HOLDING No. Dirks, as a tippee of inside material nonpublic information, in these circumstances had had no duty to abstain from use of the inside information where the tippers had been motivated by a desire to expose fraud rather than from a desire either to receive personal benefits or to bestow valuable information on him so that he could derive monetary benefits from what they had told him. Thus, Dirks's conduct had not violated the antifraud provisions of the '33 and '34 Acts.

REASONING *Chiarella* had held that a duty to disclose under Section 10b would not arise from the mere possession of nonpublic market information but rather from a relationship between the parties. Therefore, in determining whether a tippee had been under an obligation to disclose or abstain, it was necessary to ascertain whether the insider's "tip" had constituted a breach of the insider's fiduciary duty. In the absence of a personal gain to the insider, there would be no breach of duty to the stockholders. Similarly, in the absence of such a breach by the insider, there could be no derivative breach by someone like Dirks. Thus, tippees in Dirks's position had inherited no duty to disclose or abstain until a breach of the insider's fiduciary duty had occurred. The appellate court's affirmance of Dirks's censure by the SEC was therefore in error.

The *Chiarella* and *Dirks* cases thus appear to limit significantly the concept of who an "insider" is for Section 10b purposes. According to *Chiarella*, "outsiders"—those who are not in positions of trust or confidence within the companies involved in the litigation—are devoid of any duties to abstain from trading on nonpublic material information, unless they are actual "tippees" of insiders. Reinforcing *Chiarella*, *Dirks* holds that tippees of insiders who have divulged material inside information out of motives other than personal gain may avoid liability as well. Because the tippees' potential liability derives from the insiders' fiduciary duties to the corporation, the absence of any breach of those duties by the insiders leads to a finding of no breach on the tippees' part either.

The SEC, however, is continuing to prosecute outsiders and their tippees on the theory that outsiders' misappropriation of nonpublic material information works a fraud on the securities market or constitutes fraud as to the employers of the persons being sued. As such, the SEC reasons, this fraudulent conduct violates the securities laws' insider trading prohibitions. The SEC's aggressive posture in this context is particularly noteworthy, given the absence of authoritative Supreme Court rulings or legislation regarding the legal validity of the so-called misappropriation (or fraud-on-the-market) theory (although Congress has considered legislation to amend the securities laws to reflect the SEC's position). The doctrinal development of these insider trading precedents and the resultant interplay among the Supreme Court, Congress, and the SEC regarding this area of the law underscore both the important public policy aspects of the law's treatment of insider trading and the significant interrelationships of the various components of our legal system that are empowered to address this issue.

Note how the court in the next case uses these principles in disposing of the issues (the SEC's rulemaking authority and the possible application of the misappropriation theory) before it.

United States v. Chestman
60 U.S.L.W. 2245 (October 22, 1991)

FACTS Keith Loeb's wife, Susan, was the niece of the president and controlling shareholder of the target corporation. The government presented evidence that Susan's mother, Shirley Witkin (the sister of the target's president), had told her of the impending favorable sale of the target, but had added that Susan should tell no one except her husband. The next day, Susan told Loeb of the sale and admonished him not to tell anyone because "it could possibly ruin the sale." Loeb testified that he telephoned broker Robert Chestman the next day and told Chestman that he "had some definite, some accurate information" that the target was being sold at a "substantially higher" price than the market value of its stock. That day, Chestman purchased shares of the target for himself and for Loeb. A jury later convicted Chestman of ten counts of fraudulent trading in connection with the tender offer in violation of Rule 14e-3(a), ten counts of securities fraud in violation of '34 Act Rule 10b-5, and other offenses. The government based its Rule 10b-5 case against Chestman on the misappropriation theory, which holds that one who misappropriates nonpublic information in breach of a fiduciary duty and trades on that information to his or her own advantage violates Section 10(b) and Rule 10b-5. Chestman challenged his convictions for fraudulent trading in connection with a tender offer by claiming that the SEC had exceeded its rulemaking authority under section 14(e) when it had adopted Rule 14e-3 in its present form. Specifically, Chestman asserted that the rule improperly imposes liability in three ways: (1) in the absence of either a duty to disclose or a fiduciary duty; (2) for trading while in the possession of material nonpublic information, whether or not such information is used in effecting the transaction; and (3) on the basis of a "quasi-negligence standard."

ISSUE Was 1934 Securities Exchange Act Rule 14e-3(a), which bars trading on the basis of material nonpublic information concerning a tender offer that the trader knows or has reason to know has been acquired from an insider of the offeror or issuer or their agent, within the Securities and Exchange Commission's rulemaking authority under Sections 14(e) and 23(a)(1) of '34 Act, even though it dispenses with the common law fraud element of breach of fiduciary duty?

HOLDING Yes. Nothing in the legislative history of Section 14(e) indicates that the SEC frustrated congressional intent by enacting Rule 14e-3(a). On the contrary, the legislative history that exists suggests that Congress intended to grant the SEC broad rulemaking authority.

REASONING Section 14(e) of the '34 Act prohibits the making of material misstatements or omissions of fact in connection with tender offers. It further provides: "The Commission shall . . . by rules and regulations define, and prescribe means reasonably designed to prevent, such acts and practices as are fraudulent, deceptive, or manipulative." Section 23(a)(1) of the '34 Act authorizes the SEC "to make such rules and regulations as may be necessary or appropriate to implement the provisions of this chapter for which [it is] responsible or for the execution of the functions invested in [it] by this chapter." One violates Rule 14e-3(a) if he or she trades on the basis of material nonpublic information concerning a pending tender offer that he or she knows or has reason to know has been acquired "directly or indirectly" from an insider of the offeror or issuer or someone working on the insider's behalf. Rule 14e-3(a) is a disclosure provision. It therefore creates a duty in traders within its ambit to abstain or disclose, without regard to whether the trader owes a preexisting fiduciary duty to respect the confidentiality of the information. Chestman claimed that the SEC had exceeded its authority in drafting Rule 14e-3(a) by dispensing with one of the common law elements of fraud, breach of fiduciary duty. However, the plain language of Section 14(e) represents a broad delegation of rulemaking authority. It is difficult to see how the power to "define" fraud could mean anything less than the power to set forth the meaning of "fraud" in the tender offer context. This delegation of rulemaking responsibility becomes a hollow gesture if Congress had meant to confine the SEC's rulemaking authority by common law definitions of fraud. Moreover, the SEC's power to "prescribe means reasonably designed to prevent" fraud extends the agency's rulemaking authority further. The verb "prevent" has a plain meaning: to keep from happening or existing especially by precautionary measures. A delegation of authority to enact rules "reasonably designed to prevent" fraud, then, necessarily encompasses the power to proscribe conduct outside the purview of fraud, be it common law or SEC-defined fraud. Because the operative words of the statute, "define" and "prevent," have clear connotations, the language of the statute is sufficiently clear to be dispositive. In short, nothing in the legislative history of Section 14(e) indicates that the SEC frustrated congressional intent by enacting Rule 14e-3(a). To the contrary, what legislative history there is suggests that Congress intended to grant the SEC broad rulemaking authority. Turning now to Chestman's Rule 10b-5 convictions, it is clear that the government had based its case against Chestman on the misappropriation theory, which provides that one who misappropriates nonpublic information in breach of a fiduciary duty and trades on that information to his or her own advantage violates Section 10(b) and Rule 10b-5. Although Chestman is the defendant here, the alleged misappropriator was Loeb. The application of the misappropriation theory—and its predicate requirement of fiduciary breach—in the context of family relationships represents a case of first impression in this circuit. Under the misappropriation theory of liability, a person violates Rule 10b-5 when he or she misappropriates material nonpublic information in breach of a fiduciary duty or similar relationship of trust and confidence and uses that information in a securities transaction. Cases in this circuit previously have held that the predicate act of fraud may be perpetrated on the source of the nonpublic information, even though the source may be unaffiliated with the buyer or seller of securities. To date the application of this theory has occurred only in the context of employment relationships. Regarding the central inquiry here—what constitutes a fiduciary or similar relationship of trust and confidence in the context of Rule 10b-5 criminal liability—one can state with confidence that the two factors at play here do not in themselves create the necessary relationship. First, fiduciary duty cannot be imposed unilaterally by entrusting a person with confidential information. Second, marriage does not necessarily create a fiduciary relationship. It is therefore clear that the relationships involved here—those between Loeb and his wife and between Loeb and his wife's family—were not traditional fiduciary relationships. However, the misappropriation theory requires a court to consider not only whether a fiduciary relationship exists but also whether a "similar relationship of trust and confidence" exists. A fiduciary relationship involves discretionary authority and dependency: One person depends on another (the fiduciary) to serve his or her interests. What has been said of an agent's duty of confidentiality applies with equal force to other fiduciary relations: "An agent is subject to a duty to the principal not to use or to communicate information confidentially given him [or her] by the principal or acquired by him [or her] during the course of or on account of his [or her] agency" (*Restatement (Second) of Agency,* Section 395). A "similar relationship of trust and confidence" must share these qualities. Here, the evidence remains insufficient to establish a fiduciary relationship or its functional equivalent between Loeb and his wife's family. The government presented only two pieces of evidence on this point. The first was that Loeb was an extended member of the family, specifically the family patriarch's "nephew-in-law." The second concerned the patriarch's discussions of the business with family members. Kinship alone does not create the necessary relationship. The government, however, proffered nothing more to establish a fiduciary-like association. It did not show that Loeb had been brought into the family's inner circle, whose members, it appears, discussed confidential business information either because they were kin or because they worked together with the patriarch. Loeb was not an employee of the family, and there was no showing that he had participated in confidential communications regarding the business. Rather, the critical information was gratuitously communicated to him. And this disclosure did not serve the interests of the patriarch, his children, or the company. Nor was there any evidence that the alleged relationship was characterized by any influence or reliance. Moreover, Loeb's status as his wife's husband could not in itself establish a fiduciary status. Neither, absent a pre-existing fiduciary relation or an express agreement of confidentiality, could the coda "Don't tell." That leaves the unremarkable testimony that Loeb and his wife had shared and maintained generic confidences before. The jury was not told the nature of these past disclosures and therefore could not reasonably find a relationship that had inspired fiduciary, rather than normal marital, obligations. Because Loeb owed neither his wife nor her family a fiduciary duty or its functional equivalent, he had not defrauded them by disclosing news of the pending tender offer to Chestman. In the absence of a predicate act of fraud by Loeb, the alleged misappropriator, Chestman, could not be derivatively liable as Loeb's tippee or as an aider and abettor.

The following case, which owes a large debt analytically to both *Chiarella* and *Dirks*, employs the common law doctrine of *in pari delicto*, a concept we discussed in Chapter 12, in the context of insider trading. It also shows that, *Chiarella* and *Dirks* notwithstanding, tippees of corporate insiders who have provided tips containing false and incomplete information may sue these insiders for their losses.

Bateman Eichler, Hill Richards, Inc. v. Berner
472 U.S. 299 (1985)

FACTS Berner and other investors sued Bateman Eichler, Hill Richards, Inc. (Bateman Eichler) for trading losses resulting from an alleged conspiracy between Lazzaro, a broker employed by Bateman Eichler, and Neadeau, the president of T.O.N.M. Oil & Gas Exploration Corporation (T.O.N.M.). Berner contended that Lazzaro and Neadeau had divulged false and incomplete information on the pretext that it was accurate inside information about a gold strike that T.O.N.M. would soon announce. Berner and the others, relying on this information, had bought T.O.N.M. stock, which had decreased substantially below the purchase price when the mining venture had fallen through. The district court dismissed Berner's suit and absolutely barred him and the others from any recovery because they had been **in pari delicto** with Lazzaro and Neadeau. However, the court of appeals refused to allow the *in pari delicto* doctrine to be used as a defense to shield the violators from the reach of the securities laws' sanctions.

In pari delicto Equally at fault or equally wrong.

ISSUE Did the common law *in pari delicto* defense bar a private damages action under the federal securities laws against corporate insiders and broker-dealers who had fraudulently induced investors to purchase securities by misrepresenting that they had been conveying material nonpublic information about the issuer?

HOLDING No. A private action for damages on the grounds of Berner's own culpability would be barred only where, as a direct result of his own actions, Berner bore at least substantially equal responsibility for the violations he had sought to redress and where preclusion of the suit would not significantly interfere with the effective enforcement of the securities laws and the protection of the investing public.

REASONING The common law defense at issue in this case derives from the Latin, *in pari delicto potior est conditio defendentis:* "In a case of equal or mutual fault . . . the position of the [defending] party . . . is the better one." This defense is grounded on two premises: first, that courts should not lend their good offices to mediating disputes among wrongdoers; and, second, that denying judicial relief to an admitted wrongdoer is an effective means of deterring illegality. Traditionally, the *in pari delicto* defense was narrowly limited to situations in which the plaintiff truly bore at least substantially equal responsibility for his injury, because in such cases it did not always follow that the wrongdoers stood *in pari delicto,* for there might be, and often were, very different degrees of guilt. Notwithstanding these traditional limitations, many judges had given the *in pari delicto* defense a broad application to bar actions where plaintiffs simply had been involved generally in the same sort of wrongdoing as defendants. Using this latter rationale, Bateman Eichler had argued both that Berner was an ordinary tippee who had acted voluntarily in choosing to trade on inside information and that Section 10b and Rule 10b-5 would apply to any violations without recognizing gradations of culpability in support of its contention that Berner's fault had been equal to that of Lazzaro and Neadeau. However, such precedents as *Chiarella* and *Dirks* mandate the rejection of this contention in the context of insider trading cases because a person whose liability is solely derivative cannot be said to be as culpable as one whose breach of duty gave rise to that liability in the first place. Moreover, insiders and broker-dealers who selectively disclose material nonpublic information commit a potentially broader range of violations than do tippees who trade on the basis of that information. Although a tippee trading on insider information will be, in many circumstances, guilty of fraud against individual shareholders, the insider in disclosing such information is not only guilty of fraud, but also frequently violates fiduciary duties toward the issuer itself. And in cases in which the tipper intentionally conveys false or materially incomplete information to the tippee, the tipper commits an additional violation: fraud against the tippee. Such conduct is particularly egregious when committed by a securities professional, who owes a duty of loyalty and fair dealing to his or her client. In the absence of other culpable actions by a tippee that can fairly be said to outweigh these violations by such insiders and broker-dealers, the tippee properly cannot be characterized as being of substantially equal culpability as his or her tippers. Nothing in the facts of this case shows anything to the contrary either. Finally, denying the *in pari delicto* defense in such circumstances will best promote the primary objective of the federal securities laws—protection of the investing public and the national economy through the promotion of a high standard of business ethics in every facet of the securities industry; the *in pari delicto* defense, by denying any incentive to a defrauded tippee to bring suit against his or her defrauding tipper, will significantly undermine this important goal. The deterrence of insider trading most frequently will be maximized by bringing enforcement pressures to bear on the sources of such information: corporate insiders and broker-dealers. Allowing tippees to sue broker-dealers without making the *in pari delicto* defense available to the latter will "nip in the bud" the first step in the chain of dissemination of material inside information. For these reasons, the public interest will most frequently be advanced if defrauded tippees are permitted to bring suit and to expose illegal practices by corporate insiders and broker-dealers to full public view for appropriate sanctions.

Short-Swing Profits   Section 16b is also aimed at gains by corporate insiders. This provision of the '34 Act requires everyone who is directly or indirectly the owner of more than 10 percent of any security registered under Section 12 or who is a director or officer in a so-called Section 12 corporation to make periodic filings with the SEC. In these SEC filings, they must disclose the number of shares owned and any changes in the amount of shares held. This section, designed to prevent unfair use of information obtained by virtue of an inside position in the corporation, forces insiders to disgorge or return to the corporation any profits they realize from the purchase or sale of any security that takes place in any time period of less than six months—that is, *short-swing profits*. Section 16b does not apply to any transaction in which the beneficial owner was not an owner at both the time of purchasing and the time of selling; on the other hand, directors and officers face liability if they held their positions at the time either of sale or of purchase. Interestingly, though, Section 16b covers transactions that fit the enumerated criteria even when the transactions were not actually based on inside information. It is, then, in essence a preventive section. Thus, if director Wallis sells stock in Continuing Corp. for $5000 and five months later buys an equal number of shares for $3000, Wallis will have to pay to the corporation the $2000 in profits so realized.

A recent case invoking the law under Section 16b follows.

Colan v. Mesa Petroleum Company
941 F.2d 933 (9th Cir. 1991)

FACTS   In October, 1984, Mesa Partners II was formed and began accumulating stock in Unocal Corporation (Unocal). On 14 February 1985, Mesa Partners II filed a Schedule 13D statement with the SEC in which it reported that it had acquired 7.3 percent of Unocal's common stock for investment purposes. By 22 February 1985, Mesa Partners II owned 17 million shares of Unocal's common stock, representing 9.7 percent of the outstanding shares. Unocal then initiated defensive measures in order to discourage a perceived takeover threat by Mesa Partners II. On 25 February 1985, Unocal amended its bylaw concerning the procedures for nominating directors and making shareholder proposals. On 22 March 1985, Mesa Partners II acquired a total of 6.7 million shares of Unocal common stock at $48.10 per share. This transaction increased Mesa Partners II's shares to 23.7 million and its ownership interest to 13.6 percent of Unocal's common stock. On 28 March 1985, Mesa Partners II amended its Schedule 13D statement, stating that it "may seek to obtain control of the company [Unocal] or to participate in the formulation, determination or direction of the basic business decisions of the Company." Mesa Partners II also indicated that it intended to solicit proxies to gain postponement of the annual Unocal shareholders' meeting then scheduled for 29 April 1985. On 8 April 1985, Mesa Partners II made a tender offer to purchase 64 million shares of Unocal common stock at $54 per share. Unocal's board of directors recommended that Unocal's shareholders reject Mesa Partners II's tender offer as inadequate and not in their best interests. On 16 April 1985, Unocal offered to exchange a package of its debt securities for up to 87.2 million shares (approximately one-half) of Unocal's outstanding common stock. This offer originally was conditioned on Mesa Partners II's "acceptance for payment of 64,000,000 Shares pursuant to the Mesa Offer." Unocal modified its offer on 23 April 1985 to provide for the purchase of "up to 50 million shares of its common stock in exchange for $72 per share in senior secured notes, whether or not Mesa purchased the 64 million shares it was seeking through its tender offer." Unocal stated in its offer that one of its express purposes was "to make it more difficult for Mesa Bidders to complete the Mesa Offer." Unocal therefore expressly excluded Mesa Partners II from participating in its exchange offer. On 22 April 1985, Mesa Partners II challenged its exclusion from Unocal's tender offer in a Delaware state court. On 29 April 1985, the Court of Chancery temporarily restrained Unocal from proceeding with the offer unless it included Mesa Partners II. On 17 May 1985, the Delaware Supreme Court reversed the Court of Chancery and held that Unocal was not prohibited by law from excluding Mesa Partners II from its tender offer. Following the Delaware Supreme Court's decision, representatives of Mesa Partners II contacted Unocal and sought to reopen negotiations. After several rounds of negotiations, the parties reached an agreement on 20 May 1985. Pursuant to the agreement, the "Mesa Entities" were allowed to participate in Unocal's self-tender offer; Mesa Partners II agreed to terminate its tender offer; and, in addition, Mesa Partners II agreed that it would not participate in any proxy solicitation and would not acquire any additional Unocal shares for a period of twenty-five years. Mesa Partners II also agreed that for a period of ten years, it would vote its Unocal stock on all matters in the same way and "in the same proportion as the votes cast by holders of Shares other than the Mesa Entities." In addition, Mesa Partners II agreed to strict controls on its ability to sell its Unocal common stock. On the same day, Mesa Partners II exchanged approximately 7.8 million shares of Unocal common stock for negotiable debt securities. Mesa Asset Company sold these debt securities on 3 July 1985 for approximately $589 million. On 3 June 1986, David Colan, a Unocal shareholder, filed a derivative action on behalf of Unocal, alleging violations of Section 16(b) by the Mesa defendants. The action sought recovery of short-swing profits realized by Mesa. On 25 September 1989, the Mesa defendants filed a motion for summary judgment, in which they argued that the exchange of their common stock for Unocal's debt securities was not a sale within Section 16(b) because the exchange fell within the "unorthodox transaction" defense to Section 16(b) liability. Unocal appealed the district court's granting of a summary judgment to the Mesa defendants.

ISSUE   Was the exchange of the Mesa defendants' common stock for negotiable debt securities a "sale" within Section 16(b) of the Securities Exchange Act of 1934?

HOLDING   Yes. This exchange constituted a sale within Section 16(b) and did not fall into the "unorthodox transaction" exception to the rule. Hence, it represented a violation of the '34 Act.

REASONING   Unocal argued that the district court had erred in concluding that the "unorthodox transaction" defense to an action for disgorgement of short-swing profits by a beneficial owner is applicable if the facts in the record in this matter are viewed in the light most favorable to the Mesa defendants. Unocal asked for a summary judgment in its favor on the ground that the exchange of the Mesa defendants' common stock for negotiable debt securities was a "sale" within Section 16(b). Unocal asserted that the "unorthodox transaction" defense to an action brought pursuant to Section 16(b) is not applicable to a self-tender offer in which a beneficial owner exchanges its common stock for negotiable debt securities issued as a result of a recapitalization of the issuer. Section 16(b) of the '34 Act provides that an issuer may recover any profits realized by a beneficial owner from the sale of the issuer's equity securities within a six-month period. A beneficial owner is a shareholder who owns, directly or indirectly, more than 10 percent of any class of equity security. Moreover, "[t]he objective standard of Section 16(b) imposes strict liability upon substantially all transactions occurring within the statutory time period, regardless of the intent of the insider or the existence of actual speculation." Section 16(b) has been referred to as a "crude rule of thumb." Furthermore, the application of Section 16(b)'s bright-line rule is "mechanical." Where a transaction involving an equity security falls within the objective standards established by Congress for Section 16(b), liability attaches. The '34 Act broadly defines "sale" as "any contract to sell or otherwise dispose of" any security. A "sale" has been deemed to occur "when an insider becomes irrevocably entitled to receive a sum certain for his [or her] security." The Mesa defendants conceded, at oral argument, that their exchange of Unocal equity stock for debt securities pursuant to Unocal's self-tender offer was a "sale" if Section 16(b) is given a literal interpretation. But the Mesa defendants contended that their 20 May 1985 exchange of stock for nonconvertible debt securities falls within the "unorthodox transaction" defense to Section 16(b) liability. The exchange of stock for debt securities was not an involuntary or automatic transaction. Unocal did not merge into a new corporation so as to compel its shareholders to exchange their stock. Moreover, the Mesa defendants filed a suit in Delaware seeking an injunction to force Unocal to permit the Mesa defendants to participate in Unocal's tender offer; in short, the Mesa defendants had the choice of participating in the tender offer or holding onto their stock. The record shows that it was anticipated that Unocal's stock would sell at $30 per share as a result of the exchange set forth in the tender offer. One of the choices available to the Mesa defendants was to buy up Unocal's stock at the reduced price of $30 per share and acquire control of the corporation. Once in control of Unocal, the Mesa defendants would have the option of selling off Unocal's assets and thereby recouping any of their losses in the value of the stock purchased prior to the self-tender offer. The evidence is undisputed that the Mesa defendants initiated negotiations with Unocal, seeking participation in the self-tender offer. The parties dealt at arm's length in the negotiations that followed. Unocal was concerned that if the Mesa defendants were excluded, they might buy up the devalued shares at a bargain price and seize control of the corporation. The record conclusively shows that the Mesa defendants voluntarily exchanged their common stock for negotiable debt securities. The exchange in the matter was not the inexorable consequence of corporate machinations that had forced the stockholders to exchange their shares as the result of the dissolution of the corporation. Here, the beneficial owners controlled their own destiny and skillfully negotiated a beneficial result. Moreover, the facts in this matter do not come within the Supreme Court's holding that an involuntary transaction that results from a merger is "unorthodox." The cases that have applied the "unorthodox transaction" defense to a short-swing sale by a beneficial owner have characterized it as a narrow exception to Section 16(b). Those courts that have directly addressed the issue of Section 16(b) liability in a tender offer or hostile takeover contest have concluded that the disposition of shares pursuant to a tender offer, or in the face of defeat in a takeover contest, is not an "unorthodox transaction." The evidence is undisputed that the Mesa defendants made a voluntary business decision to persuade Unocal to permit them to participate in the corporation's self-tender offer. As a result, the Mesa defendants exchanged common stock, whose value was subject to the risks of a free market, for negotiable debt securities of a higher current value with fixed payments and interest rates. The record also shows that the Mesa defendants shrewdly calculated their options, which included a complete buy-out of all of Unocal's stock or acceptance of the self-tender offer because of undisclosed tax advantages. Therefore, the exchange of the Mesa defendants' stock for Unocal's negotiable debt securities was a sale within Section 16(b) and did not constitute an "unorthodox transaction." Consequently, the order granting summary judgment in favor of the Mesa defendants is reversed; the order denying Unocal's cross motion for a summary judgment is reversed with directions to enter an order granting Unocal's motion for a summary judgment.

Liabilities and Remedies The '34 Act creates a private right of action for those who have dealt in securities on the basis of misleading registration statements (liability pursuant to Sections 12 and 18), tender offers (Section 13), and proxy solicitations (Section 14). Under Section 16b, the corporation or a shareholder suing in a derivative action for the benefit of the corporation may recover short-swing profits realized by officers, directors, and shareholders controlling at least 10 percent of the securities involved. Private actions under Section 10b and Rule 10b-5, the catchall antifraud provision, may be brought by any purchasers or sellers of any securities against any person who has engaged in fraudulent conduct, including a corporation that has bought or sold its own shares. The early Section 10b cases, such as the *Texas Gulf Sulphur* case cited in the *Basic* decision, had expansively imposed liability under Section 10b and Rule 10b-5. However, the Supreme Court, in *Ernst & Ernst* v. *Hochfelder,* has limited the reach of Section 10b by requiring a private person to prove that the securities law violator intended to deceive, manipulate, or defraud the injured party.[3] After *Hochfelder,* proof of negligent conduct alone will not constitute a violation of Section 10b. Similarly, the holding in the case that follows, *Santa Fe Industries, Inc.* v. *Green,* which refused to extend Section 10b's prohibition against manipulative and deceptive conduct to management's alleged violations of fiduciary duties, signals somewhat of a retreat from the Court's prior, ever-expanding view of possible liability under Section 10b.

Yet the Court's recent opinion that apparently allows securities cases to be brought under the Racketeer Influenced and Corrupt Organizations Act (RICO)[4] and the SEC's ability (under the Insider Trading and Securities Fraud Enforcement Act of 1988) to penalize inside traders up to three times the amount of the profit gained or the loss avoided as a result of the unlawful purchase or sale suggests the availability of potent remedies to discourage securities laws violations. To illustrate, some commentators argue that Drexel, Burnham, Lambert Inc.'s recent decision to plead guilty to six criminal counts and to pay a record-breaking $650 million in fines and restitutions for securities violations stemmed from its desire to avoid further indictments under RICO.

[3]425 U.S. 185 (1976); reh'g. denied, 425 U.S. 986 (1976).
[4]*Sedima S.P.R.L.* v. *Imrex Co., Inc.,* 105 S.Ct. 3275 (1985).

Santa Fe Industries, Inc. v. *Green*
430 U.S. 462 (1977)

FACTS   Green and other minority stockholders of Kirby Lumber Corp. (Kirby) argued that Sante Fe Industries, Inc.'s (Sante Fe's) "short-form merger" with Kirby had involved a fraudulent appraisal of the fair market value of Kirby's stock. Green asserted that the purpose of this fraudulent appraisal had been to freeze out the minority stockholders in violation of Section 10b and Rule 10b-5 of the Securities Exchange Act of 1934, whose provisions, respectively, make it "unlawful for any person . . . [t]o use or employ . . . any manipulative or deceptive device or contrivance in contravention of [SEC rules]" or to use any "artifice to defraud" or to act in a way "which operates or would operate as a fraud or deceit."

ISSUE   Would the term *fraud* in Section 10b and Rule 10b-5 of the '34 Act encompass a breach of fiduciary duty in connection with a securities transaction?

HOLDING   No. Section 10b or Rule 10b-5 reaches only conduct involving manipulation or deception; so a breach of fiduciary duty by majority stockholders, without any deception, misrepresentation, or nondisclosure, would not violate the statute or the rule.

REASONING   The recent *Ernst & Ernst* v. *Hochfelder* case had made clear that the term *fraud* in Rule 10b-5 refers to manipulative or deceptive conduct. Thus, Green's attempt to bring within the reach of the rule all breaches of fiduciary duty in connection with a securities transaction would result in an impermissible interpretation of the securities laws. Such a breach of fiduciary duty would fall under the '34 Act's coverage only if the conduct were manipulative or deceptive. In contrast, any such breach of fiduciary duty by majority shareholders in the absence of deception, misrepresentation, or nondisclosure would not violate the '34 Act. Moreover, private causes of action under the '34 Act should not be implied when what is at issue—here, the fairness of the transaction—is at best a subsidiary concern of the federal legislation. This was especially true, when, as in this case, the cause of action is one traditionally relegated to state law. A decision in favor of Green would federalize corporate conduct customarily left to state regulation and would extend Section 10b and Rule 10b-5 to cover transactions involving internal corporate mismanagement.

Securities and Exchange Commission Actions

Consent decree   An agreement sanctioned by a court that in effect is an admission by the parties that the decree represents a just determination of their rights based on the real facts of the case, if such facts had actually been proved.

The '34 Act empowers the SEC to conduct investigations of possible violations of the securities laws. Many times such investigations lead to censure or, alternatively, culminate in a **consent decree** signed by the alleged wrongdoer in exchange for less stringent sanctions. But the SEC also can order an administrative hearing conducted by an administrative law judge to determine if penalties are in order with respect to any security, person, or firm registered with the SEC. As mentioned earlier, revocation of registration or suspension of distribution of the security (or the activities of the person or firm) are two of the enforcement powers that the SEC possesses. The SEC itself may review the hearing officer's decision and, if necessary, modify the sanctions originally levied. A party adversely affected by a final SEC order can seek review of such orders in a circuit court of appeals. Besides administrative proceedings, the SEC can bring court actions to enjoin violations of the securities laws on a "proper showing" of a reasonable likelihood of further violations. The SEC also can refer cases to the Justice Department, which then mounts criminal actions against willful violators of securities laws and rules. A crackdown on Wall Street insider-trading abuses led to successful cases against well-known traders Ivan Boesky, Dennis Levine, and Michael Milken, to name a few.

STATE REGULATION

Because the assorted federal statutes preserve the states' power to regulate securities activities, any transactions involving securities may be subject to state law as well as federal law. Such state laws, often called "blue sky" laws, though varied, normally include three types of provisions: (1) antifraud stipulations, (2) registration requirements for brokers and dealers, and (3) registration prerequisites for the sale and purchase of securities. With respect to the last, three methods of securities registration ordinarily exist: notification (a streamlined method for securities with a stable earnings record), qualification (a formalized program similar to the procedures mandated by the '33 Act), and coordination (a regimen that directs the issuer to file with the state a copy of the prospectus filed with the SEC under the '33 Act). State laws frequently exempt from registration the same classes of securities exempted from the '33 Act and additionally often exempt stocks listed on major stock exchanges. Exempted transactions customarily include private placements, or limited offerings, and isolated nonissuer transactions. State laws generally provide for sanctions and liabilities similar to those imposed under federal law, but the small securities staffs in most states make the possibility of civil liability a more potent deterrent for violations. In 1956, the National Conference of Commissioners on Uniform State Laws drafted a Uniform Securities Act meant for adoption by the states. This attempt at uniformity for resolving securities questions among the various states has not been wholly successful, however.

THE FOREIGN CORRUPT PRACTICES ACT

One additional topic merits our attention before we leave the subject of securities laws. On 19 December 1977, President Jimmy Carter signed into law the Foreign Corrupt Practices Act (FCPA). The FCPA resulted from post-Watergate congressional hearings about questionable payments made to foreign officials by hundreds of United States firms, including Exxon, Northrop Corporation, Lockheed Aircraft Company, Gulf Oil, and GTE Corp. Testimony revealed that such companies had given foreign officials large payments, or bribes, in order to land sizable contracts for themselves. In their own defense, these United States firms had argued that foreign officials often demanded such payments as a condition of doing business and that without such "grease" payments, or sums paid to facilitate transactions by minor governmental functionaries, bureaucratic red tape would have brought all their business dealings to a complete halt.

Congressional investigators found that such questionable payments had often taken the form of secret slush funds, dubious transfers of funds or assets between subsidiaries and parent companies, improper invoicing procedures (for example, false payments for goods or services that were never received), and bookkeeping practices designed to camouflage improper payments or procedures. Indeed, these corrupt practices by United States corporations had even extended to payments made to engineer the overthrow of foreign governments hostile to the business interests of the firms involved and to attempts to keep competitors out of certain foreign countries through bribery of the appropriate foreign officials. To compound the improprieties, these same firms had often deducted such so-called business expenses from their tax returns. Since accounting irregularities, including secret funds and falsified or inadequate books, formed the vehicle by which firms most often had effected these questionable payments and bribes, Congress attempted to put an end to these practices by enacting the FCPA, which contains both antibribery provisions and accounting standards.

The FCPA itself amends Sections 13a and 13b-2 of the Securities Exchange Act of 1934. The FCPA's antibribery sections provide criminal penalties for actions taken by issuers (that is, firms subject to the '34 Act) or any domestic concern (even those not subject to the '34 Act) when an officer, director, employee, agent, or stockholder acting on behalf of such businesses corruptly uses the mail or any instrumentality of interstate commerce either to offer or actually to pay money (or anything of value) to any foreign official for the purpose of influencing the foreign official to assist the firm "in obtaining or retaining business for or with, or directing business to, any person."[5] In addition, it is unlawful under the FCPA to offer or to give payments or gifts for similar purposes to any foreign political party (or officials or candidates thereof) or to any person who the United States concern knows will transmit the payment or thing of value to any of the classes of persons specifically prohibited from receiving such bribes.[6] Gifts or payments that are lawful under the written laws and regulations of the foreign country involved or that constitute bona fide reasonable expenditures (such as travel or lodging) incurred by such persons during the performance of a contract with the foreign government do not fall within the FCPA's proscriptions. Moreover, these antibribery provisions do not extend to payments made to these classes of persons when the payments' purpose is to expedite or facilitate the performance of routine governmental action. Hence, "grease" payments to obtain permits or licenses to do business in the foreign country, visas, work orders, phone service, police protection, or inspections are legal as long as the em-

[5]15 United States Code Section 78(dd-1), (dd-2).
[6]Ibid.

ployee receiving them is not a person who is known as someone who is acting as a conduit for governmental officials to whom the FCPA forbids corrupt payments or gifts. However, decisions by foreign officials to award or continue business with a particular party are not included in the definition of "routine governmental action."[7] Purely commercial bribery of corporate officials who have no governmental connections and who do not act as conduits for governmental officials thus appears to be legal, but business records should reflect such payments in order to comply with the FCPA's accounting standards described below. Recent amendments to the FCPA empower the attorney general, after consultation with the SEC and others, to issue guidelines describing specific types of conduct that would satisfy the strictures of the Act and, when requested by firms, to issue opinions as to whether certain specified prospective conduct by these firms would conform with the Act. Once promulgated, these regulations and advisory opinions should greatly facilitate U.S. firms' attempts to comply with the FCPA.

Although all individuals and domestic concerns (whether these latter be corporations, partnerships, sole proprietorships, or any other sort of association) are subject to the FCPA antibribery provisions, only issuers subject to SEC jurisdiction must comply with the FCPA's accounting standards. These record-keeping standards require issuers to do the following:

(A) make and keep books, records, and accounts, which, in reasonable detail, accurately and fairly reflect the transactions and dispositions of the assets of the issuer; and

(B) devise and maintain a system of internal accounting controls sufficient to provide reasonable assurances that—

   (i) transactions are executed in accordance with management's general or specific authorization;

   (ii) transactions are recorded as necessary (I) to permit preparation of financial statements in conformity with generally accepted accounting principles or any other criteria applicable to such statements, and (II) to maintain accountability for assets;

   (iii) access to assets is permitted only in accordance with management's general or specific authorization; and

   (iv) the recorded accountability for assets is compared with the existing assets at reasonable intervals and appropriate action is taken with respect to any differences.[8]

Because they largely eliminate the possibility of secret slush funds for bribing foreign officials, these provisions serve a beneficial purpose. Yet the statute gives no specific guidelines for setting up a particular internal control system. Rather, it leaves the choice of the particular system to the individual

[7]Ibid.
[8]Ibid., Section 78(m).

firm. The statute's vagueness therefore has created confusion on the part of some businesspeople as to what type of record-keeping system will suffice. Given the FCPA's criminal penalties for knowingly failing to comply, this is not an idle worry.

Further compounding such worries is the SEC's promulgation of far-ranging regulations designed to promote the reliability of the information requested in the FCPA's record-keeping provisions. These regulations prohibit both the falsification of accounting records and misleading statements made by an issuer's directors or officers to auditors or accountants during the preparation of required documents and reports.

The FCPA's imposition of criminal penalties—setting corporate fines of a maximum of $2 million for violations and a maximum of five years' imprisonment and/or $100,000 in fines for willful violations by corporate individuals—and individual civil penalties not to exceed $10,000 should adequately deter U.S. corporations and corporate personnel engaged in international business from such illegal activities. Adding further strength to the criminal penalties is the FCPA's prohibition of a corporation's indemnification of its employees against liability under this Act.[9] Other remedies available under the '34 Act, such as injunctions, also may be used in the enforcement of the FCPA by the Justice Department and the SEC, which share enforcement responsibilities under it.

Critics of the FCPA argue that its provisions and resultant regulations have greatly increased both American businesses' costs of doing business and the enforcement agencies' costs, all of which negatively affect the American public. On the other hand, such laws and supplementary regulations carry the attendant advantages of heightened investor information and fewer scandals involving American bribery of foreign officials.

Since the FCPA is of relatively recent vintage, case law interpreting it is sparse. And because of the legal, social, and ethical issues it represents, it promises to remain a controversial law for some time to come. An early case construing the FCPA follows.

Clayco Petroleum Corporation v. Occidental Petroleum Corporation
712 F.2d 404 (9th Cir. 1983)

FACTS   Clayco Petroleum Corporation (Clayco) and Bruce Clayman, the founder and principal shareholder of Clayco, filed an antitrust suit against Occidental Petroleum Corporation, Occidental of Umm Al Qaywayn, Inc., and Armand Hammer (Occidental), charging Occidental with making secret payments to an official of Umm Al Qaywayn in order to obtain unlawfully an offshore oil concession. The plaintiffs claimed that Occidental had conspired to make and

[9]Ibid., Section 78(ff).

had made secret payments in England and Switzerland totalling $417,000 to Sheikh Sultan bin Ahmed Muallah (Sultan), Umm Al Qaywayn's petroleum minister and son of its ruler, Sheikh Ahmed al Muallah (Ahmed). The complaint further alleged that only through these unlawful and anticompetitive actions had the defendants secured the valuable offshore oil concession. The 11 December 1978 edition of the *Oakland Tribune* had contained a story stating that Occidental had distributed about $30 million under "questionable legal circumstances" and that Dr. Armand Hammer, Occidental's chief executive officer, had personally disbursed $217,000 to the Sultan in a London hotel room in 1969. The article also reported that the Sultan had received a second payment of $200,000 in Switzerland. The article stated, "Hammer paid the initial $217,000 as part of a $1.7 million deal with the sheikdom . . . for an oil gas concession." In 1977, the SEC commenced an action against Occidental, alleging violations of the Securities Exchange Act of 1934 and the rules promulgated thereunder, based on illegal or questionable payments made by Occidental. Occidental consented to the entry of a permanent injunction and agreed to conduct an internal investigation of the alleged illegal payments and to prepare for the SEC and Occidental's stockholders a special report describing such payments. This so-called Payments Report, when completed, revealed various illegal payments. A Source Memorandum annexed to the Payments Report further recited that Occidental's $200,000 payment in Switzerland had been of "uncertain legality" and had been inaccurately described and documented on Occidental's books. The plaintiffs alleged that the $417,000 in payments, plus "entertainment" expenses, constituted bribes to induce the Sultan and his father to award the concession to Occidental. The plaintiffs contended that Occidental, its subsidiary, and Dr. Hammer had conspired to prevent competition and to deprive the plaintiffs of the concession in violation of the Sherman Act, the Robinson Patman Act, California state law, and common law. The defendants countered with the contention that the act-of-state doctrine would bar the plaintiffs' action. The district court, in granting the defendants' motion to dismiss, had stated that the case implicated an exercise of sovereignty—the award of the offshore oil concession—and that adjudication would interfere with U.S. foreign policy. The court had noted further that plaintiffs' obligation to prove that they had been damaged by defendants' conduct would necessitate review of the ethical validity of the sovereign's conduct and thus involve the application of the act-of-state doctrine. The court also had refused to apply a commercial exception to the act-of-state doctrine.

ISSUES　　Did the defendants' actions in this case fall outside the **act-of-state doctrine?** Alternatively, would the Federal Corrupt Practices Act (FCPA) eliminate the application of the act-of-state doctrine in private suits based on foreign payments?

HOLDINGS　　No to both questions. Because the defendants' actions had implicated sovereign activity that effectuated "public" rather than "private" interests, the act-of-state doctrine would cover their actions and immunize them from private lawsuits. Moreover, nothing in the legislative history of the FCPA would indicate that Congress had intended to abrogate the application of the act-of-state doctrine in private lawsuits based on foreign payments.

REASONING　　The act-of-state doctrine was first enunciated in *Underhill* v. *Hernandez*, 168 U.S. 250 (1897): "Every sovereign state is bound to respect the independence of every other sovereign state, and the courts of one country will not sit in judgment on the acts of the government of another, done within its own territory. The doctrine is a function of our system of separation of powers and as such has 'constitutional' underpinnings." *Banco Nacional de Cuba* v.

Act-of-state doctrine　In international law, this doctrine states that courts of another nation have no jurisdiction over the acts of a sovereign government/state that are performed within that sovereign state's borders.

Sabbatino, 376 U.S. 398 (1964). It recognizes that judicial examination of the acts of foreign governments may hinder the executive and legislative branches' conduct of foreign policy. *Sabbatino* prescribed a flexible approach to the doctrine, the critical element being the potential for interference with our foreign relations. Without sovereign activity effectuating "public" rather than "private" interests, the act-of-state doctrine does not apply. That test is met here; hence, the plaintiffs wrongly characterized the actions in dispute as devoid of any sovereign policy decisions. This case differed from those relied on by the plaintiffs in which sovereign activity had merely formed the background to the dispute or in which the only governmental actions were the neutral application of the laws. In those cases, the governmental activity had not constituted "a considered policy decision by a government to give effect to its political and public interests . . ." and so had fallen outside the "type of sovereign activity that would be of substantial concern to the executive branch in its conduct of international affairs." It is clear that judicial scrutiny of sovereign decisions allocating the benefits of oil development would embarrass the political branches of our government in the conduct of foreign policy. The plaintiffs argued that the examination of foreign governmental action that this case requires is not intrusive enough to warrant an act-of-state defense because the concern here is the motivation behind the sovereign's act rather than its legal validity. Although precedents hold that motivation and validity are "[un]equally protected by the act of state doctrine," these opinions do not foreclose the application of the act-of-state doctrine to cases in which a court must scrutinize motivation but not validity. These decisions instead note that where the motivation for the sovereign act would be subject to a limited examination in order to measure the plaintiff's damages, and the adjudication would result in no embarrassment to executive department action, the act-of-state doctrine would not foreclose such inquiry. In this case, however, the very existence of plaintiffs' claim depended on establishing that the motivation for the sovereign act had involved bribery; thus, embarrassment would presumably result from adjudication. Plaintiffs thus could not argue that inquiry into motivation in this case is valid. Finally, in an effort to invoke exceptions to the act-of-state doctrine, the plaintiffs contended that an exception for purely commercial acts should apply in this case. The plaintiffs submitted that the passage of the FCPA has created an exception to the act-of-state doctrine that should apply in this case. The FCPA prohibits bribery of a foreign official for the purpose of obtaining or retaining business. The act moreover provides for severe criminal penalties including fines and imprisonment. In addition, the attorney general may bring a civil action to enjoin impending violations. Congress intended the FCPA to stop bribery of foreign officials and political parties by domestic corporations. Bribery abroad—considered a "severe" U.S. foreign policy problem—embarrasses friendly governments, causes a decline of foreign esteem for the United States, and casts suspicion on the activities of our enterprises, giving credence to our foreign opponents. The FCPA thus represents a legislative judgment that our foreign relations will be bettered by a strict antibribery statute. There is no question, however, that any prosecution under the act entails risks to our relations with the foreign governments involved. The Justice Department and the SEC, which share enforcement responsibilities under the FCPA, coordinate enforcement of the act with the State Department, thus recognizing the potential foreign policy problems of these actions. Therefore, any governmental enforcement represents a judgment regarding the wisdom of bringing a proceeding, in light of the exigencies of foreign affairs. Act-of-state concerns thus remain inapplicable since the purpose of the doctrine is to prevent the judiciary from interfering with the political branch's conduct of foreign policy. Here, however, the proceedings involved a private lawsuit rather than a public enforcement action. It is the screening of governmental proceedings, with State Department consultation, that distinguishes FCPA enforcement from private suits. Hence, in private suits, the act-of-state doctrine remains necessary to protect the proper conduct of national foreign policy. Hence, the plaintiff's contentions that, in enacting the FCPA, Congress had intended to abrogate the act-of-state doctrine in private suits based on foreign payments would find no support in the legislative history. Thus, because the act-of-state doctrine applies, the trial court's decision to dismiss the action merits affirmance.

Compare and contrast the result in the *Clayco* case with the court's decision in the following more recent FCPA opinion.

Lamb v. *Phillip Morris, Inc.*
915 F.2d 1024 (6th Cir. 1990)

FACTS   Plaintiffs Lamb and Willis, along with various other Kentucky growers, produce burley tobacco for use in cigarettes and other tobacco products. Defendants Phillip Morris, Inc. (Phillip Morris) and B.A.T. Industries (B.A.T.) routinely purchase such tobacco not only from the Kentucky markets serviced by the plaintiffs but also from producers in several foreign countries. Thus, tobacco grown in Kentucky competes directly with tobacco grown abroad, and any purchases from foreign suppliers necessarily reduce the defendants' purchases of domestic tobacco. On 14 May 1982, a Phillip Morris subsidiary known as C.A. Tabacalera National and a B.A.T. subsidiary known as C.A. Cigarrera Bigott, SUCS. entered into a contract with La Fundacion Del Niño (the Children's Foundation) of Caracas, Venezuela. The agreement was signed on behalf of the Children's Foundation by the organization's president, the wife of the then president of Venezuela. Under the terms of the agreement, the two subsidiaries would make periodic donations to the Children's Foundation, totalling approximately $12.5 million. In exchange, the subsidiaries would obtain price controls on Venezuelan tobacco, would eliminate controls on retail cigarette prices in Venezuela, would receive tax deductions for the donations, and would receive assurances that existing tax rates applicable to tobacco companies would not be increased. According to the plaintiffs' complaint, the defendants had arranged similar contracts in Argentina, Brazil, Costa Rica, Mexico, and Nicaragua. In the plaintiffs' view, the donations promised by the defendant's subsidiaries amounted to unlawful inducements designed and intended to restrain trade. The plaintiffs asserted that such arrangements would result in the artificial depression of tobacco prices to the detriment of domestic tobacco growers, while ensuring lucrative retail prices for tobacco products sold abroad. The plaintiffs therefore sought redress in the form of treble damages and injunctive relief principally for the former result—the reduction in domestic tobacco prices—which, according to the plaintiffs, constituted violations of federal antitrust laws. The plaintiffs later amended their complaint to include a claim under the FCPA. On 28 June 1989, the district court dismissed the plaintiffs' antitrust claims as barred by the act-of-state doctrine and dismissed the FCPA claim as an impermissible private action. The plaintiffs appealed this decision.

ISSUES   Did the act-of-state doctrine preclude domestic tobacco producers from bringing an antitrust action against tobacco importers based on the claim that the importers' subsidiaries had made contributions to foreign charities in exchange for the foreign government's imposition of price controls on foreign tobacco and the elimination of controls on retail cigarette prices? Did the FCPA in such circumstances create an implied private right of action in favor of these domestic tobacco producers?

HOLDINGS   No to both issues. The act-of-state doctrine remained inapplicable to the circumstances of this case because the domestic tobacco producers' claims had merely called into question the contracting parties' motivations and the resulting anticompetitive effects of their agreement, not the validity of any foreign sovereign act. But the FCPA would not apply here, either, to create a private right of action, since Congress had primarily designed the FCPA to protect the integrity of American foreign policy in domestic markets rather than to prevent the use of foreign resources to reduce production costs.

REASONING   According to precedent, "The act-of-state doctrine in its traditional formulation precludes the courts of this country from inquiring into the validity of the public acts a recognized foreign sovereign power committed within its own territory." *Banco Nacional de Cuba* v. *Sabbatino*, 376 U.S. 398 (1964). However, "the act-of-state doctrine is not a jurisdictional limit on courts, but rather is a prudential doctrine designed to avoid judicial action in sensitive areas." Although the act-of-state doctrine typically involves an assessment of "the likely impact on international relations that would result from judicial consideration of the foreign sovereign's act," the defendants in this case must establish the factual predicate for the application of the act-of-state doctrine. Although act-of-state analysis is not generally guided by "an inflexible and all-encompassing rule," the Supreme Court recently indicated that, as a threshold matter, "act of state issues only arise when a court must decide—that is, when the outcome of the case turns upon—the effect of official action by a foreign sovereign." Here, the defendants had failed to make such a showing. Because the antitrust claims at issue in this suit merely call into question the contracting parties' motivations and the resulting anticompetitive effects of their agreement, not the validity of any foreign sovereign act, the district court erred in applying the act-of-state doctrine to dismiss the plaintiffs' claims. The defendants rightly contended that the FCPA had been designed with the assistance of the SEC to aid federal law enforcement agencies in curbing bribes of foreign officials. According to the Senate report regarding the FCPA, the direct prohibition against the payment of overseas bribes by any U.S. business concern and the resulting enactment of the FCPA represent a legislative endeavor to promote confidence in international trading relationships and domestic markets. Moreover, the authorization of stringent criminal penalties amplifies the foreign policy and law enforcement considerations underlying the FCPA. The House Conference report refers to the "jurisdictional, enforcement, and diplomatic difficulties" of broadening the FCPA's reach, thereby addressing concerns typically of special interest to law enforcement officials. In light of these comments and the general tenor of the FCPA itself, which requires the attorney general to participate actively in encouraging and supervising compliance with the act, it becomes clear that Congress designed the FCPA primarily to protect the integrity of American foreign policy and domestic markets rather than to prevent the use of foreign resources to reduce production costs. The plaintiffs, therefore, as competitors of foreign tobacco growers and suppliers of the defendants, could not claim the status of intended beneficiaries of the congressional enactment under scrutiny. Despite the paucity of authority in the legislative history for their position, the plaintiffs by identifying one isolated comment in an earlier House report, asserted that Congress had fully intended to permit private rights of action under the FCPA. The plaintiffs' assertion that this single remark would mandate recognition of a private right of action was erroneous. Because the potential for recovery under federal antitrust laws in this case belies the plaintiffs' contention that an implied private right of action under the FCPA is imperative, the absence of state laws proscribing bribery of foreign officials is not of significance. More importantly, since none of the factors traditionally relied on supports the creation of a private right of action theory here, the district court's dismissal of the FCPA claim merits affirmance.

SUMMARY

The Securities Act of 1933 and the Securities Exchange Act of 1934 extensively regulate securities. In essence, a "security" involves an investment in an enterprise whereby the investor has no managerial functions but instead expects to profit solely from the efforts of others. The '33 Act is basically a disclosure statute meant to protect the unsophisticated investing public. The '33 Act, in furtherance of this purpose, requires the filing of a detailed registration statement with the SEC and the furnishing of a prospectus to all potential investors. Until the registration statement becomes effective, selling and promotional activities remain limited.

The '33 Act exempts certain classes of securities from the registration and prospectus requirements: small public offerings, distributions of close corporation securities, short-term commercial paper, intrastate issues, issues by nonprofit organizations, and securities issued by the federal and state governments. The '33 Act in addition exempts certain transactions, such as private offerings. The '33 Act also contains several antifraud provisions. Civil liability may attend violations of the '33 Act. One section places liability on everyone who signed the registration statement, was named as a director, contributed an expert opinion to the statement, or underwrote the issue. All such persons, except the issuer, may escape liability by showing they acted with "due diligence." Other sections establish civil and criminal liability.

The '34 Act regulates the secondary distribution of securities. Its reach is therefore even broader than the '33 Act. The '34 Act covers proxy solicitations and tender offers, limits insider trading, forbids short-swing profits, and in general tries to eliminate fraud and manipulative conduct with respect to the sale or purchase of securities. Any issuer who trades securities on a national stock exchange must register with the SEC, according to the '34 Act. Like the '33 Act, the '34 Act mandates certain disclosures by the firms that it covers when the securities are listed with the national stock exchanges or traded over the counter.

Regulation of proxy solicitations is an important facet of the '34 Act. The '34 Act authorizes the inclusion of shareholder proposals that involve "proper subjects" in management proxy solicitations in order to further the democratic aspects of corporations. Liability for misleading proxy statements is absolute, as is liability for misleading statements made during tender offers or takeover bids. The '34 Act also prohibits insider trading because of the injury to the investing public that may otherwise ensue. When material inside information is involved, the insider must either publicly disclose the information or refrain from trading in the securities. Directors, officers, and beneficial shareholders in certain corporations must refrain from buying or selling securities within a six-month period under the '34 Act's section on short-swing profits. Possible liability under the '34 Act is far-reaching, despite the existence of some Supreme Court decisions suggesting less expansive impositions of liability in the future.

The Securities and Exchange Commission (SEC) can conduct administrative hearings with respect to securities violations and can seek injunctions to stop continued violations.

State securities laws, called "blue sky" laws, usually set up antifraud provisions and registration requirements for brokers and dealers and for the sale of securities. These laws vary greatly in form and reach. The Uniform Securities Act, meant to eliminate the lack of uniformity among state securities laws, has not been wholly successful.

Since 1977, the Foreign Corrupt Practices Act (FCPA) has forbidden American businesses to make corrupt payments to foreign officials for the purpose of obtaining foreign business. Noncompliance with the FCPA's antibribery provisions and record-keeping standards may subject individuals or corporations to civil or criminal penalties.

DISCUSSION QUESTIONS

1. What, essentially, is a security?
2. Explain the primary purposes of the Securities Act of 1933 and the Securities Exchange Act of 1934.
3. List the types of information contained in the registration statement under the '33 Act.
4. What are "tombstone ads" and "red herring" prospectuses?

5. List the '33 Act's exempt classes of securities and transactions.
6. Explain what a proxy is and describe the SEC rules surrounding proxy solicitations.
7. What are the '34 Act's provisions regarding insider trading?

8. Discuss the laws regarding short-swing profits and why the '34 Act prohibits these profits.

9. Enumerate the liabilities and remedies possible under both the '33 and '34 Acts.

10. Explain the enforcement powers held by the Securities and Exchange Commission and how state regulation of securities differs from federal regulation.

CASE PROBLEMS

1. R. Foster Winans was a reporter for the *Wall Street Journal (WSJ)* and one of the writers of the "Heard on the Street" securities column. The government sued him and others for participating in a scheme to trade in securities based on information misappropriated from the *WSJ* in violation of its conflicts-of-interest policy. The information allegedly stolen from the paper had concerned the timing, content, and tenor of market-sensitive stories scheduled to appear in the column. Winans and others tipped by Winans had traded in the stocks featured in the column just before the column had appeared and had realized thousands of dollars in profits as a result. The government argued that Winans's misappropriation of this market-sensitive confidential information had operated as a fraud on the *WSJ* in connection with the purchase and sale of securities in the featured stocks. Winans contended that as a noninsider who had owed no duty to the corporations he had written about, and as a nontippee of any corporate inside information, the *Chiarella* and *Dirks* cases' holdings would exonerate him from liability. Should a court use this "misappropriation" theory to impose securities laws and mail fraud liability on Winans? (*Carpenter* v. *United States,* 108 S.Ct. 316 [1987].)

2. The Securities and Exchange Commission (SEC), as part of its statutory authority to conduct nonpublic investigations of possible violations of the securities laws, often issues subpoenas to obtain relevant information under those investigative powers. When Jerry T. O'Brien learned that he was the target of an investigation involving the issuance of a subpoena to a third party, he argued that he must be given notice of this fact in order for the subpoena to comply with the Fifth Amendment due process clause, the Sixth Amendment confrontation clause, the Fifth Amendment self-incrimination clause, SEC statutes, and prior decisional law. Should the Court impose such a notice requirement on the SEC's subpoena power? (*Securities and Exchange Commission* v. *O'Brien,* 467 U.S. 735 [1984].)

3. Borak was a shareholder in J. I. Case Co. (Case). He sued for damages resulting from the merger of Case and American Tractor Company on the grounds of breach of fiduciary duties by directors and misrepresentations contained in management's proxies. Borak also sued to invalidate the merger. Case contended that Section 14 of the '34 Act did not authorize a private cause of action such as Borak's. Do federal courts have the power to order remedial relief of the type Borak sought? (*J. I. Case Co.* v. *Borak,* 377 U.S. 426 [1964].)

4. Sinay, Rosenberg, and Halye purchased Lamson and Session Company (Lamson) common stock. The named plaintiffs purchased their shares on 1 November 1988 (Rosenberg); 6 March 1989 (Sinay); and 16 June 1989 (Halye). In their complaints, the plaintiffs alleged securities fraud pursuant to Section 10(b) of the '34 Act and Rule 10b-5. The plaintiffs did not assert that fraud had been committed individually upon them because they had relied on statements by defendants when they had purchased their shares. Instead, they contended that Lamson and the other defendants had engaged in a course of conduct that had artificially inflated the common stock's market price (i.e., the plaintiffs asserted a "fraud on the market" theory). Following several November, 1986, acquisitions, Lamson's earnings had dramatically increased. On 24 October 1988, Lamson had publicly disclosed that its performance during the first three quarters had been "gratifying," although it was experiencing a "normal seasonal decline" in its commercial and residential markets that would last "into the first quarter of 1989." On 23 December 1988, Lamson had reported that it was having a "tremendous year." On 21 February 1989, Lamson had stated that it was pleased with the 1988 results and that it planned to continue to develop its position in the domestic and worldwide transportation markets. In an April, 1989, interview with the Dow Jones News Service, Schulze, a Lamson officer, had noted that Lamson "does not quarrel with analysts' earnings estimates for 1989 in the area of $1.50 to $1.60. . . ." Schulze had further asserted that Lamson was "counting on new products to offset a weaker construction market for 1989." Notwithstanding these positive forecasts, Lamson's financial condition began to erode in 1989. Owing to prolonged higher interest rates, the construction market failed to rebound after the winter slowdown. Moreover, Lamson experienced severe labor problems at its Midland plant. The plaintiffs claimed that the defendants knew or should have known that the construction market's decline would be long term and that a major and devastating strike would occur. Therefore, according to the plaintiffs, the defendants deceived the market by failing to issue sufficient cautionary statements concerning Lamson's future. Should the court hold the defendants liable for securities violations based on a corporate officer's statements of honestly held views derived from information currently before the corporation? (*Sinay* v. *Lamson & Sessions Company,* 948 F.2d 1037 [6th Cir. 1991].)

5. In December, 1982, Burlington Northern, Inc. (Burlington) made a hostile tender offer for El Paso Gas Co. (El Paso) to which a majority of El Paso's shareholders ultimately subscribed. However, Burlington did not accept the tendered shares, and instead, in January, 1983 after negotiations with El Paso, announced a new and friendly takeover agreement. Pursuant to this agreement, Burlington, in January, rescinded the December tender offer and substituted a new one, which soon was oversubscribed. The rescission of the first tender offer caused a diminished payment to those shareholders who had tendered during the first offer, because those shareholders who retendered had been forced to sell fewer shares. Schreiber filed suit on behalf of herself and other similarly situated shareholders alleging that Burlington, El Paso, and members of El Paso's board had violated Section 14(e)'s prohibition against "fraudulent, deceptive or manipulative acts or practices . . . in connection with any tender offer." Schreiber claimed that Burlington's withdrawal of the December tender offer, coupled with the substitution of the January tender offer, had constituted a "manipulative" distortion of the market for El Paso stock. Burlington argued that the term "manipulative" required acts involving misrepresentation or nondisclosure, neither of which had been present in the offer in dispute. In addition, Burlington contended that courts should not read the term "manipulative" as an invitation to oversee the substantive fairness or the quality of tender offers, a matter better left to the mar-

ketplace, according to the company. Who had the more persuasive argument, Schreiber or Burlington? (*Schreiber* v. *Burlington Northern, Inc.,* 472 U.S. 1 [1975].)

6. In 1976, Pepsico, Inc. (Pepsico) agreed to sell Lee Way Motor Freight, Inc. (Lee Way) to Commercial Lovelace Motor Freight, Inc. (CL). Shortly after taking over Lee Way's operations, CL began soliciting Lee Way employees to participate in a wage reduction program (the Program) that had been in place at CL since 1983. The Program, which was optional for Lee Way's union employees, provided each participating union employee with an interest both in CL's existing company-administered employee stock ownership plan (CL ESOP) and a profit-sharing plan in return for the individual employee's agreement to a 17.35-percent reduction in the wages due him or her under the union's collective bargaining agreement. CL represented to Lee Way employees that the company would probably fail if they did not enroll in the Program. All the plaintiffs in this action individually elected to participate in the Program. Less than a year later, CL merged with Lee Way and filed for bankruptcy. Lee Way's former assets allegedly were reacquired by Pepsico. In this action, Uselton and 485 former union employees of Lee Way alleged that Pepsico's sale of Lee Way to CL and its subsequent reacquisition of Lee Way's assets on CL's rapid demise had amounted to a sham transaction designed to disguise Pepsico's intended and ultimately successful liquidation of Lee Way. In their federal securities claim, the plaintiffs alleged that their interests in the CL ESOP had constituted "investment contracts" subject to federal securities regulation pursuant to Section 2(1) of the '33 Act. The plaintiffs further submitted that CL's solicitation of Lee Way employees to accept an interest in the CL ESOP as part of the Program had amounted to a sale of an unregistered security and securities fraud in violation of Sections 5 and 17(A) of the '33 Act. Was the CL ESOP—a voluntary, contributory employee benefit plan—a security? (*Uselton* v. *Commercial Lovelace Motor Freight, Inc.,* 940 F.2d 564 [10th Cir. 1991].)

7. In February, 1988, Chrysler adopted a shareholder rights plan (the Plan), commonly known as a "poison pill." Under the Plan, Chrysler stockholders received one preferred share purchase right on each outstanding share of Chrysler common stock. Each purchase right could be exercised following certain triggering events; that is, ten days after the first public disclosure that a person or group had acquired, or had obtained the right

to acquire, beneficial ownership of 30 percent or more of Chrysler's outstanding common stock, or ten days after the first public disclosure or actual commencement of a tender or exchange offer intended to result in the offeror's becoming the beneficial owner of 30 percent or more of Chrysler's outstanding common stock. Additionally, the Plan provided that, following certain events, the poison pill preferred purchase rights would entitle holders to exercise "flip-in" rights to buy Chrysler common stock at one-half the market value or, alternatively, "flip-over" rights to buy common shares in an entity whose announced or actual acquisition of Chrysler common stock had triggered the exercise of the purchase rights. In 1989, Chrysler amended the Plan to reduce the threshold of an acquiring entity's beneficial ownership in Chrysler needed to trigger the exercise of shareholder rights under the Plan from 30 percent to 20 percent. The 1989 amendments also added an additional "flip-in" event. On 14 December 1990, Chrysler issued a press release announcing further amendments to the Plan. This release, which is the focus of the shareholders' federal securities fraud claim, announced an unsolicited stock purchase by Kirk Kerkorian that gave Kerkorian over 9 percent of Chrysler's outstanding common stock. As a result of the purchase, the press release stated, Chrysler's board of directors had adopted amendments to the company's share purchase rights plan. The amendments reduced from 20 percent to 10 percent the threshold of beneficial ownership at which the rights "flip in." The release concluded with a company statement: "The amendments adopted today *are intended to enhance the ability of Chrysler's Board to act in the best interest of all the Company's shareholders if someone should seek to obtain a position of control or substantial influence over Chrysler.*" Lewis and other shareholders alleged that the italicized language in the press release constituted fraud in violation of Section 10(b) and Rule 10b-5. Specifically, Lewis claimed that the corporation's alleged failure to say how management might use the Plan (or poison pill) to its own advantage represented an actionable omission of a material fact and therefore securities fraud, particularly since the press release had affirmatively portrayed the amendments to the plan as being in the shareholders' best interest. Moreover, Lewis alleged that Chrysler's failure to disclose the costs of the Plan to the shareholders had violated the securities laws as well. How should the appellate court rule on Lewis's claims? (*Lewis v. Chrysler Corporation*, 949 F.2d 644 [3rd Cir. 1991].)

8. Texas Gulf Sulphur Company (TGS) had discovered valuable mineral resources through an exploratory drill hole in Ontario, Canada. The defendants, TGS officers and geologists, had attempted to keep this ore strike confidential. They and certain of the persons to whom they had given tips purchased shares of TGS during the drilling efforts. In response to a newspaper article that had speculated about a rich TGS strike, the defendants on 12 April 1964 issued a press release regarding the Canadian drilling operations. Some investors took the release to be optimistic; others thought it painted a gloomy picture of the drilling prospects. A few days later, an official TGS press statement trumpeted a 25-million-ton ore strike. The SEC maintained that the 12 April press release had been materially false and misleading, that the defendants had realized that it had been so, and that the issuance of the press release had violated Section 10b and Rule 10b-5 of the Securities Exchange Act of 1934. What was the standard for deciding whether the press release had violated Section 10b and Rule 10b-5 of the '34 Act? (*Securities and Exchange Commission* v. *Texas Gulf Sulphur Company*, 401 F.2d 833 [2d Cir. 1968], cert. denied, 404 U.S. 1005 [1971], reh'g. denied 404 U.S. 1064 [1972].)

9. The International Brotherhood of Teamsters, Chauffeurs, Warehousemen, and Helpers of America (Teamsters) set up a noncontributory, compulsory pension plan for employees represented by the Chicago local. Under this plan, employees had no choice as to participation in it and did not have the option of demanding that the employer's contribution be paid directly to them as a substitute for pension eligibility. The employees paid nothing to the plan themselves. Daniel had been denied a pension on his retirement because of a break in the twenty years of continuous service required for pension eligibility. He subsequently sued the Teamsters, arguing that the pension plan was a security and that certain misstatements and omissions by Teamsters' officials violated Section 10b of the '34 Act and Section 17 of the '33 Act. Was the pension plan in question a security? (*International Brotherhood of Teamsters, Chauffeurs, Warehousemen & Helpers of America* v. *Daniel*, 439 U.S. 551 [1979].)

10. Huddleston sued Herman & MacLean, the accounting firm, which had issued an opinion regarding the financial information contained in the registration statement of Texas International Speedway, Inc. (TIS) when TIS had offered its securities for sale. Huddleston and other purchasers brought a class action under Sec-

tion 10b of the '34 Act on the rationale that representations made in the registration statement and prospectus had defrauded them. Herman & MacLean argued that Huddleston had been limited to the express remedy for misstatements in registration statements that Section 11 of the '33 Act enumerates. In other words, Herman & MacLean submitted that an action for fraud accruing from a registration should be exempt from liability under Section 10b because such conduct was actionable under Section 11. Were the remedies provided by Section 10b and Section 11 exclusive or cumulative? If they were cumulative, should a plaintiff have a higher burden of proof under a 10b action, since fraud actions at common law would impose a higher standard of proof? (*Herman & MacLean* v. *Huddleston,* 459 U.S. 375 [1983].)

PART 8

Government Regulations

As technology developed and businesses grew large and powerful, the operation of a business became less personal, and the scope of business operations expanded. Many people felt that the individual was being sacrificed on the altar of profits: The "almighty dollar" was becoming more important than the nation's people. As a result, government imposed its power and prestige on the business environment to balance the interests of society more evenly with the interests of business.

This part of the text explores some of the government regulations that have developed in response to social demands. The initial area of government regulation dealt with antitrust law, which endeavored to protect competition in the business setting. Once competition was attained and protected, social demands changed: People wanted to protect the consumer as well as the environment. Again government intervened, regulating these areas as business affected them. Society also called for labor regulations that protect the worker from management and management from the worker. Once again, government intervened with regulations designed to resolve these problems.

CHAPTER 45

An Introduction to Government Regulation

OUTLINE

HISTORIC PERSPECTIVE

In the United States today, business is heavily regulated by government. Local regulations tell a business where it may do business; state regulations deal with the selling of securities, loan rates, and highway weight limits; federal regulations deal with pollution, the safety of employees, consumer protection, and labor negotiations. These are only a few of the regulated areas and topics. The influence of government regulations is pervasive: It covers nearly every aspect of the business situation. However, this has not always been the case.

As is often mentioned in American history texts, America was built on a **laissez-faire** economy. Business was run by businessmen, government was run by politicians, and the two groups left one another alone. Buyers were often ignored, with **caveat emptor** being the rule of the land. Workers were virtually unprotected. If they did not like their jobs, they could quit. If they did not work, they were fired. If they joined a union, they were fired—*and* they quite often faced criminal conspiracy charges. The nineteenth century was a great time to be an American entrepreneur, especially a wealthy one.

Unfortunately for business, these easy times came to an end. Too many "captains of industry" were viewed as "robber barons." Too many workers were abused or mistreated. Too little land was left for westward migration. By the end of the nineteenth century, the voice of the regulators was beginning to be heard.

Laissez-faire A term meaning "hands-off"; a government attitude that business operates best when uninhibited by the government.

Caveat emptor A term meaning "let the buyer beware"; a reference to the fact that the buyer had very few, if any, remedies if the product was defective.

SHOULD GOVERNMENT REGULATE BUSINESS?

For decades people have been asking the question, "Should government regulate business?" The answer to this question is obviously "yes." It is also obviously "no." The answer depends on who is being asked the question, what type of regulation is being discussed, and which level of government is involved. It also depends to some degree on whether the business is involved in international trade, national trade, or regional/local trade. Many factors must be considered before an answer to the basic question can be given, and that answer may vary over time as the circumstances of the business change.

History shows that some regulation or intervention probably is necessary. Unless some protections are provided against business excesses, society is likely to suffer. But history also shows that too much intervention probably is as bad as too little. Government cannot run business as effectively as businesspeople can. Overregulated businesses are likely to suffer financial problems; underregulated businesses tend to create social problems. Somewhere between these extremes a happy medium must exist, and it needs to be reached for the well-being of business, government, and society to be attained and maximized.

SOURCES OF GOVERNMENT POWER

The primary source of power for government regulation of business is found in the commerce clause of the United States Constitution. Article I, Section 8, Clause 3, of the Constitution states: "The Congress shall have power . . . to regulate commerce with foreign nations, and among the several states." In addition, Article I, Section 8, gives Congress the power to levy taxes. These two powers, taken together, form the foundation of federal government regulation of business.

The history of the commerce clause has been checkered. The Supreme Court has interpreted it, expanded the interpretation, contracted the interpretation, and then expanded it again. In 1824, the Supreme Court had its first occasion to interpret the commerce clause. Chief Justice Marshall's opinion in *Gibbons* v. *Ogden* defined commerce as "the commercial intercourse between nations, in all its branches, . . . regulated by prescribing rules for carrying on that intercourse."[1] Marshall went on to note that the federal government could regulate commerce that *affected* other states, even if that commerce was local in nature.

As a result of this interpretation, federal power to regulate business was viewed as a broad power for nearly three-quarters of a century. The Interstate Commerce Act of 1887 permitted the Interstate Commerce Commission (ICC) to regulate local railroad rates and local railroad safety because interstate rates and safety were directly affected.[2] The federal government also was allowed to regulate local grain and livestock exchanges since they were involved in transactions that affected the rest of the nation.

However, not all court opinions of the period were in favor of regulation. In 1873, the Supreme Court decided *In re State Freight Tax*.[3] The Court opinion stated that *among* (from the commerce clause) meant *between*. As a result, the opinion held that the federal government could regulate only **interstate** commerce. As an added contraction of the federal power to regulate business, the Supreme Court limited the definition of commerce. In its 1888 opinion in *Kidd* v. *Pearson*, the Court ruled that commerce meant **transportation**.[4] As a result of these two opinions, federal regulation of business was suddenly restricted to actual interstate transportation and did not reach business deals that *affected* interstate business but that were conducted entirely in one state. Such transactions were defined as **intrastate** and therefore beyond the scope of federal regulation.

It was under this new, restricted definition that the Sherman Act was passed in 1890 (see Chapter 46 for a detailed treatment of this act). The

Interstate Between two or more states; between a point in one state and a point in another state.

Transportation Carrying or conveying from one place to another; the removal of goods or persons from one place to another.

Intrastate Begun, carried on, and completed wholly within the boundaries of a single state.

[1] Wheat (22 U.S.) 1 (1824).
[2] 24 Stat. 379 (1887).
[3] 15 Wall. (82 U.S.) 232 (1873).
[4] 128 U.S. 1 (1888).

Sherman Act and many later federal statutes were interpreted narrowly or were held unconstitutional under this new definition of the federal authority to regulate business.

This narrow view of federal power did not change again until 1937. In the opinion from *NLRB* v. *Jones & Laughlin Steel Corp.*, which overturned fifty years of narrow interpretation, Chief Justice Hughes said:

> When industries organize themselves on a national scale, making their relation to interstate commerce the dominant factor in their activities, how can it be maintained that their industrial relations constitute a forbidden field into which Congress may not enter when it is necessary to protect interstate commerce from the paralyzing consequences of industrial war?[5]

So the Court came full circle. Possibly the most picturesque definition of interstate commerce today, and of the federal power to regulate such commerce, was provided by Justice Jackson. In *United States* v. *Women's Sportswear Manufacturers Ass'n.*, a local price-fixing arrangement was challenged under the Sherman Act; in upholding the right of the government to regulate the case, Justice Jackson stated: "If it is interstate commerce that feels the pinch, it does not matter how local the operation which applies the squeeze."[6]

The following case illustrates the current Supreme Court view of interstate commerce.

Equal Employment Opportunity Commission v. Ratliff
906 F.2d 1314 (9th Cir. 1990)

FACTS   Several former employees of the Grecian Spa fitness club in Tempe, Arizona, filed a claim with the Equal Employment Opportunity Commission (EEOC) alleging sexual harassment and retaliatory discharges in violation of Title VII of the Civil Rights Act of 1964. The EEOC filed a claim on behalf of the employees. Grecian Spa denied the presence of the jurisdictional requirements, thus denying the right of the EEOC to file the claims. Specifically, Grecian Spa denied that it employed at least fifteen people or that it affected commerce, both required under the act. The trial court issued a summary judgment to Grecian Spa for lack of subject matter jurisdiction, agreeing that the spa was not engaged in a business affecting commerce. The EEOC appealed.

ISSUE   Did Grecian Spa engage in an industry that affected commerce and, therefore, fall within the jurisdiction of the EEOC?

HOLDING   The current state of law would seem to indicate that it did, so that the summary judgment awarded on this issue was improper.

REASONING   Congress passed the Civil Rights Act of 1964 based on its authority under the commerce clause. In Title VII, Congress prohibited discrimination in any "industry affecting commerce." The Supreme Court has interpreted "industry affecting

[5]301 U.S. 1 (1937).
[6]336 U.S. 460, 464 (1949).

commerce" to indicate Congress's intent to exercise its regulatory power to "the fullest jurisdictional breadth constitutionally permissible under the Commerce Clause." Based on prior cases, the "affects commerce" jurisdictional obstacle is very low. In the context of Title VII cases, jurisdictional requirements are to be construed liberally to effect the remedial purpose of the statute. In this case, Grecian Spa had Nautilus equipment. Nautilus equipment is not manufactured in Arizona, and therefore the equipment had moved in interstate commerce to get to the Grecian Spa. In addition, fitness clubs as an industry are involved in an activity that "affects commerce," so it would seem that each individual fitness club would also affect commerce. The summary judgment is reversed.

One of the early cases decided under the Civil Rights Act of 1964, and one of the cases relied on by the court in deciding the *Ratliff* case, was *Heart of Atlanta Motel,* which follows. Note again how the court "finds" an interstate commerce connection.

Heart of Atlanta Motel v. United States
379 U.S. 241, 85 S.Ct. 348 (1964)

FACTS   The Heart of Atlanta Motel had a policy of refusing service to blacks. The federal government challenged this policy, asserting a violation of the Civil Rights Act of 1964. The government argued that the motel was involved in interstate commerce and that federal intervention was therefore permitted by the commerce clause. The motel argued that it was purely intrastate and therefore exempt from federal regulation.

ISSUE   Was the motel involved in interstate commerce and therefore subject to federal regulation?

HOLDING   Yes. Because the motel served interstate travelers, it was involved in interstate commerce.

REASONING   The motel was readily accessible from two interstate highways. It advertised in national magazines and placed billboards on federal highways. Approximately 75 percent of its guests were from outside the state of Georgia. To allow such discrimination would discourage travel by the black community. The motel was set up to serve interstate travelers, it drew much of its business from interstate travelers, and it was involved in interstate commerce. The discriminatory practice in room rentals was prohibited.

SCOPE OF GOVERNMENT POWER

The preceding cases, *Ratliff* and *Heart of Atlanta,* point out just how broadly the commerce clause can be interpreted. Using such a broad interpretation as a basis for regulation, the federal government can affect many activities. Under such an approach, virtually *any* aspect of commercial dealing can be brought under federal supervision and control. How much of this potential regulatory power has government decided to exercise? The next three chapters, although not exhausting the scope of federal regulatory coverage, should illustrate how widespread this power has become. The following topics are covered.

Business Dealings

Antitrust law is designed to regulate *business dealings*. The most important of the laws include the following:

Trusts   Associations having the power or tendency to create a monopoly, to control production, or to interfere with free trade.

Monopolize   To get, have, or exploit a monopoly; to get full possession or control of; to dominate completely.

1. the Sherman Act, dealing with **trusts** and attempts to **monopolize**
2. the Clayton Act, dealing with price discrimination, exclusive dealings, tying contracts, and interlocking directorates
3. the Federal Trade Commission Act, covering unfair trade practice

(These topics are discussed in Chapter 46.)

YOU BE THE JUDGE

A professional licensing group has been formed called the American Society of Composers, Authors, and Publishers. This group signs contracts with composers, authors, and publishers of music, and agrees to represent them in their copyright negotiations and to collect the royalties owed to them. Due to the number of members who have signed contracts, the Society is able to exert tremendous power in dealings with radio stations, jukebox distributors, and businesses where copyrighted music is played. The businesses that want to play copyrighted music can either pay a flat weekly rate to the Society, or they can attempt to negotiate every royalty agreement with the individual copyright holder.

Suppose a major telecommunication network has filed suit, alleging that the Society is engaged in illegal price fixing and is monopolizing the music industry, in violation of the federal antitrust laws. How would you rule in this case, and why?

Source: "Royalties' High Value," *U.S. News & World Report*, February 3, 1992, page 46.

Consumer and Environmental Protections

In the area of *consumer protection*, the federal government regulates such activities as the following:

1. labeling and packaging of products
2. consumer credit, through such provisions as the Truth-in-Lending Act
3. the reporting of the credit standing of consumers, through the Fair Credit Reporting Act
4. debt collection practices, through the Fair Debt Collection Practices Act

In the area of *environmental protection,* government regulations cover the following:

1. clean air, with such laws as the Clean Air Act and its amendments
2. water pollution, through the Clean Water Act and related statutes
3. noise pollution, with several noise control acts
4. pesticides, through laws such as the Federal Insecticide, Fungicide, and Rodenticide Act

(Consumer and environmental protections are covered in Chapter 47.)

Labor and Employment

Chapter 48 discusses labor and employment in the context of such statutes as the Wagner Act and the Taft-Hartley Act. The chapter also looks at topics such as Social Security and OSHA from the federal realm and workers' compensation and unemployment provisions at the state level.

The area of government regulation of business is clearly broad and varied. These chapters are not designed to be exhaustive; they are intended as a mere introduction, an "appetizer" of sorts. Many books that treat these topics in much greater detail are available for the interested reader.

ADMINISTRATIVE AGENCIES

Much of the work of regulating business is conducted by administrative agencies. Most of us are familiar with the three official branches of American national government—legislative, executive, and judicial—but we may tend to overlook the *unofficial* fourth branch, the administrative. The administrative branch of government has been especially active since the 1930s. The Great Depression and the presidency of Franklin Delano Roosevelt saw a tremendous growth in the use of administrative agencies as a major means of regulation. A great deal of government intervention in the business sphere is conducted through administrative agencies. As a result, some understanding of administrative law is essential to an understanding of government regulation of business.

Delegated Assigned responsibility and/or authority by the person or group normally empowered to exercise the responsibility or authority.

Quasi-legislative Partly legislative; empowered to enact rules and regulations but not laws.

Quasi-judicial Partly judicial; empowered to hold hearings but not trials.

Administrative agencies are set up by Congress; and since Congress "creates" them, Congress can terminate them. Hence, they are not an independent branch of government. They have only as much authority as is **delegated** to them by the legislature, and as a result they must answer to Congress for their conduct. Congress establishes a basic policy or standard and then authorizes an agency to carry it out.

Once established, the agency will have certain **quasi-legislative** and **quasi-judicial** powers. The agency is allowed to pass rules and regulations within its area of authority and to hold hearings when it feels the rules and regulations have been violated. The power of the Congress to abolish the agency and the power of the courts to review the agency's conduct are considered a sufficient control device. It is believed that the agency will not exceed its authority or abuse its discretion as long as these two *official* branches of government are keeping a watchful eye on the agency's conduct.

Some constitutional provisions also limit the power of administrative agencies. Both the Fifth and the Fourteenth Amendments to the United States Constitution require that due process of law and equal protection under the law be given to each person. The courts hold that agency action must satisfy these criteria. Of special importance is due process, which has two elements: procedural and substantive.

Procedural Due Process

An agency must provide for *fairness* in its proceedings to ensure procedural due process. If a person is facing a proceeding that affects his or her rights, that person is entitled to a full due process hearing. Due process includes the right to present witnesses, the right to cross-examine witnesses, the right to an attorney, and possibly other rights, as well. If the agency is involved in a less personal proceeding, such as rule making or fact finding, fewer personal protections are needed. Notice of the time, place, and purpose of the meeting might be adequate for procedural due process if the agency's proceeding is not directed at personal conduct. However, as noted, as the conduct of the agency becomes more closely related to personal conduct, the amount of procedural due process required increases to the point where it may require a full adversarial proceeding with witnesses, evidence, and attorneys.

In the following case, a procedural due process challenge was raised against the validity of Section 3 of the Robinson-Patman Act.

United States v. National Dairy Products Corporation
372 U.S. 29, 83 S.Ct. 594 (1963)

FACTS   National Dairy Products Corporation (National Dairy) was charged with selling its products at a price below cost in an alleged effort to destroy competition. The conduct was challenged under Section 3 of the Robinson-Patman Act, which prohibits selling goods at "unreasonably low prices for the purpose of destroying competition or eliminating a competitor." National Dairy moved for a dismissal of the indictment on the grounds that the statute is unconstitutionally vague and indefinite. The district court granted the motion for dismissal, and the case was appealed directly to the Supreme Court.

ISSUE   Is the language of the statute unreasonably vague and indefinite, and thus violative of procedural due process?

HOLDING   No. The language of the statute gave the defendant sufficient warning as to the types of conduct prohibited and did not deprive the defendant of due process of law.

REASONING   National Dairy urged that the statute be tested solely "on its face" and argued that "unreasonably low prices" is unconstitutionally vague and indefinite on its face. Admittedly, if the language is read literally and without reference to any other standards, it appears to be unduly vague. However, if read in context, the language of the statute provides a defendant with sufficient warning as to the prohibited conduct. Selling below cost, unless mitigated by some acceptable business exigency, has been viewed historically as a predatory business practice. The language used in the act is sufficiently specific for the case in point. "This opinion is not to be construed, however, as holding that every sale made below cost constitutes a violation of [section] 3. . . . But sales made below cost without legitimate commercial objective and with specific intent to destroy competition would clearly fall within the prohibitions of [section] 3." The District Court's dismissal of the indictment is reversed.

Substantive Due Process

Substantive due process normally refers to the *content* of the rules and regulations. The agency may enact only rules and regulations that bear a rational relationship to the agency's purpose or function. Furthermore, these rules and regulations must focus on the particular problem being treated. If the regulations are too broad, they violate the substantive due process provisions. Likewise, they are prohibited if they unfairly discriminate against one person or group. The rules and regulations must not be arbitrary or capricious.

The following case illustrates how the courts treat the topic of substantive due process. The case deals with a state statute rather than an administrative regulation, but a similar analysis would be used if administrative conduct were involved.

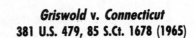

Griswold v. Connecticut
381 U.S. 479, 85 S.Ct. 1678 (1965)

FACTS The state of Connecticut passed a law prohibiting the use of contraceptives and also prohibiting the counseling of people on their use. Griswold was the executive director of Planned Parenthood, and Buxton was a doctor, a professor at Yale Medical School, and the medical director of Planned Parenthood. Both were arrested and convicted of violating the anticontraception statute. Both challenged the statute as unconstitutional because it violated the due process clause of the Fourteenth Amendment.

ISSUE May a state prohibit any and all use of contraceptives within the scope of the Fourteenth Amendment?

HOLDING No. The statute as written denied substantive due process of law.

REASONING A married couple is entitled to certain realms of privacy, and this statute infringes on that realm. The statute had the maximum destructive effect on the couple's privacy and was unreasonably broad. The Court held that the statute was unconstitutional and reversed the convictions.

Judicial Review

If someone is dissatisfied with treatment received at the hands of an administrative agency, that person may ask the court to review the proceedings. However, the court will review the proceedings only from the point of view of their legality. *Issues of fact* are normally not subject to judicial review. The court is required to follow the *substantial evidence rule,* which states that the agency's findings of fact must be followed if they are based on substantial evidence. This means that judicial review normally will focus on four possible areas of agency error:

1. The agency violated procedural due process.
2. The agency violated substantive due process.
3. The agency violated the Constitution.
4. The agency exceeded its authority.

Although judicial review of agency action is limited, the court will review the actions of an agency in some situations. The next case illustrates such a situation. Notice how the court justified its decision to review the case.

Mullin v. *Skinner*
756 F. Supp. 904 (E.D. N.C. 1990)

FACTS   The federal government and the government of North Carolina decided to construct a high-rise, fixed-span bridge at the island of Sunset Beach, N.C. In developing the plans for the bridge, the government decided that an environmental impact statement would not be necessary since the preliminary environmental assessment had indicated that there would be no significant effect on the quality of the human environment or on the ecological environment of the island. Numerous parties joined to seek declaratory and injunctive relief and to halt the development of the bridge until a full environmental impact statement was prepared and approved. Sunset Beach is a small barrier island off the coast of North Carolina. The island comprises environmentally sensitive wetlands on the northern side and sandy beaches on the southern side. A variety of threatened and endangered species live on Sunset Beach. The island is presently attached to the mainland by a pontoon swing-span bridge that will accommodate traffic only in one direction at a time and must be closed to traffic while allowing boats to pass through its movable span.

ISSUE   Was the decision of the defendants not to order an environmental impact statement at variance with the law?

HOLDING   Yes. The administrative process followed in this case was arbitrary and capricious.

REASONING   The court's sole function in reviewing agency action in this situation was to determine if the decision reached was "arbitrary, capricious, an abuse of discretion, or otherwise not in accordance with law." The court can disturb an agency's decision only if the decision was not based on relevant factors or was a clear error of judgment. In reviewing an agency decision under the National Environmental Policy Act, the court must ensure that the agency has taken a hard look at the environmental consequences of the proposed action. Common sense dictates that the proposed bridge will increase access, thus spurring development of Sunset Beach. This development, in turn, will increase the demand for water, sewer, and other services at the island. Given the popularity of North Carolina's beaches, the likelihood of demand for growth and development, and the inevitable strains that would be placed on the region, the decision to forego an environmental impact statement is arbitrary and capricious. The injunctive relief is granted and the defendants are ordered to prepare the necessary studies and statements before approval for the bridge will be considered.

As a result of the restricted nature of judicial review and the pervasive nature of administrative agencies in the business world, this area of regulation has become very important today. A person who plans to advance very far in business would be well advised to study administrative law in some detail. This introductory coverage should serve to whet the appetite, but it hardly satisfies the need.

SUMMARY

Government regulation of business is a fact of life in the modern business environment. Whether regulation takes the form of local zoning ordinances, state income taxation, or federal antitrust regulation, businesses today must deal with it. And the only way to deal with government regulation is to recognize and understand it.

Federal regulation of business is based on both the commerce clause of the United States Constitution, which authorizes Congress to "regulate commerce among the several states," and Congress's taxing power, also included in the Constitution. Most regulation is based on the commerce clause.

The commerce clause has been interpreted in such a way that federal regulation is permitted only if *interstate* commerce is involved. To qualify as interstate, the transaction must directly affect citizens of at least two different states or countries.

If an interstate connection is present, federal regulation may be applied. The federal government regulates many aspects of business, including business dealings in violation of the antitrust laws and aspects relating to consumer and environmental protection and labor and employment practices.

Much of the actual regulation of business is carried out by administrative agencies. Administrative agencies are created by Congress, and Congress then delegates to the agencies the authority to carry out certain duties. Agencies are involved in a large number of regulatory areas. These agencies are required to assure due process of law in carrying out their responsibilities, and they are subject to judicial review to ensure that they conduct themselves properly.

DISCUSSION QUESTIONS

1. How would you define the word "commerce"? How is "commerce" defined by the U.S. Supreme Court? Is the Court's definition too broad, too narrow, or an appropriate definition of the term?

2. What sorts of conduct are considered interstate commerce, and therefore subject to federal regulation, by the U.S. Supreme Court? Is the Court's treatment appropriate in this area?

3. What powers are possessed by administrative agencies? From what source or sources do administrative agencies derive their powers?

4. Explain procedural due process. Why is procedural

due process important to a person or to a business in a regulatory environment?

5. Explain substantive due process. Why is substantive due process important to a person or to a business in a regulatory environment?

6. Suppose that the federal government decides that too many narcotics are being smuggled into the country on small planes. In an effort to stop this drug traffic, the appropriate administrative agency prohibits "all small planes" from flying over the national borders. How could this rule be challenged? Explain.

7. How may judicial review be used to prevent the abuse of power by administrative agencies?

8. Assume that the Federal Trade Commission, the agency charged with regulating trade practices, felt that XYZ Corporation was involved in unfair trade practices. Could the commission publish a notice that it was holding hearings concerning XYZ and then prosecute XYZ for its alleged wrongful conduct? Explain your answer.

9. Assume that the Constitution did not contain a "commerce clause." How might national business practices be different in the absence of this federal authority to regulate business?

10. What is to prevent any of the states from enacting tariffs and other barriers to trade to favor the business of that one state over the businesses of other states? What rights does a state have to regulate the trade within that state?

CASE PROBLEMS

1. An Oklahoma statute prohibited any person who was not a licensed optometrist or ophthalmologist from fitting eyeglass frames or replacing lenses in frames. Several opticians challenged this statute under the due process clause of the Constitution. What result should be reached by the court? (*Williamson* v. *Lee Optical Co.*, 348 U.S 483 [1955].)

2. Darby operated a lumber mill in Georgia. He employed workers at less than the federally prescribed minimum wage and had them work more than the federally prescribed maximum number of hours per week. Both federal criteria were to be found in the Fair Labor Standards Act. Because of these violations by Darby, Congress prohibited Darby from shipping his lumber to any other state unless he complied with the standards of the federal statute. Darby challenged this prohibition. How should the court resolve this case? (*United States* v. *Darby*, 312 U.S. 100 [1941].)

3. The Lake Nixon Club, near Little Rock, Arkansas, was an amusement and recreation area. The club operated as a private club, with a membership fee of $25 charged to prospective members when they joined the club. The club membership was restricted to Caucasian applicants. When the club was challenged for violation of the Civil Rights Act of 1964 under the *Heart of Atlanta Motel* precedent, the club defended its position by alleging that it was not a public accommodation nor did it cater to interstate travelers. What should the court

consider in deciding this case? How should the court rule? (*Daniel* v. *Paul*, 395 U.S. 298 [1969].)

4. Metropolitan Edison was a privately owned and operated utility company that held a certificate of public convenience from the Pennsylvania Utility Commission. Among the communities receiving electricity from Metropolitan Edison was York, Penn. Jackson, a resident of York, had her account with Metropolitan terminated due to delinquent payments. She opened a new account under the name of Dodson, another occupant of the residence. One year later Dodson moved from the address, and service continued although no payments were made. When Metropolitan asked Jackson where Dodson was living, she replied that she did not know. A few days later, and without notice to Jackson, Metropolitan discontinued service to her address. She has sued, seeking damages and an injunction to require Metropolitan to continue to provide service, due to a denial of due process. Jackson contends that she was entitled to notice and a hearing before service could properly be discontinued. She also alleges that Metropolitan is so connected to the state of Pennsylvania that its conduct is the equivalent of state action. Metropolitan denies her allegations. Was the conduct of Metropolitan the equivalent of state action, so that the denial of due process argument can be asserted? Explain fully. (*Jackson* v. *Metropolitan Edison Company*, 419 U.S. 345 [1974].)

5. Grubb borrowed $55.94 from Dollar Loan Company. The loan carried a specified interest rate of 65.46%. On the loan fee, Dollar Loan used the words "loan fee" rather than "prepaid finance charges" as required by the Truth-in-Lending Act. Does such wording by Dollar Loan violate the Truth-in-Lending Act? Is this the sort of transaction the federal government should be able to regulate as part of its concern with consumer protection? (*Grubb* v. *Oliver Enterprises, Inc.,* 358 F. Supp. 970 [D.C. N.D. Ga. 1972].).

6. Sail'er Inn, the holder of an on-sale liquor license, hired several women to work as bartenders in its establishment. The state statute prohibited women from being hired as bartenders unless the women so hired were the licensees, the wives of licensees, or the sole shareholders of a licensee corporation. The state Department of Alcoholic Beverage Control attempted to revoke the license of Sail'er Inn due to the hiring of the women. Sail'er Inn filed suit to prevent the revocation of its license, and asserted that the Civil Rights Act of 1964 prohibited it from discriminating against women. In this conflict between federal and state regulation of a business, which regulation should be followed, and why? (*Sail'er Inn, Inc.* v. *Kirby,* 485 P.2d 529 [Cal. 1971].)

7. Victoria D. was born to Carole D., who was married to and living with Gerald D. in California. Despite Gerald's claims that Victoria was his daughter, blood tests established a 98-percent-plus probability that Michael H., with whom Carole had an adulterous affair, was the true father. During Victoria's first three years, she and Carole lived at various times with Gerald and with Michael, each of whom claimed to be Victoria's father. Michael has filed a filiation action to establish his paternity and to acquire visitation rights. Victoria, through her court-appointed guardian ad litem, filed a cross complaint seeking filiation rights with both Gerald and Michael. Gerald asserted that under California law a child born to a married woman who is living with her husband who is neither impotent nor sterile is presumed to be the child of that marriage. The court agreed with Gerald, issuing a summary judgment in his favor and denying visitation rights to Michael. Michael and Victoria both appealed, arguing that the summary judgment was a denial of due process and equal protection. How will the court resolve this case? Is there a constitutional right to visitation between a child and his or her natural parent? Does the California statute deny due process rights to the natural parent in situations such as this one? (*Michael H.* v. *Gerald D.,* 491 U.S. 110 [1989].)

8. Mr. Azizi illegally entered the United States in early 1986. Soon after, the Immigration and Naturalization Service (INS) instituted a deportation proceeding against him, issuing an order to show cause and giving him notice of a hearing. Mr. Azizi admitted that he had illegally entered the country and applied for political asylum. While his application for political asylum was pending, Mr. Azizi married Saboet Elmazi, a naturalized U.S. citizen. In January, 1987, Mr. Azizi's application for political asylum was denied. The new Mrs. Azizi then filed a petition for an immigrant visa for her husband as an "immediate relative." However, under the Immigration Marriage Fraud Amendments, an alien who marries a citizen during the pendency of deportation proceedings must reside outside the United States for two years before INS will consider a petition for an "immediate relative" visa. The Azizis have challenged the deportation order of the INS and the denial of the "immediate relative" visa, asserting that they have been denied due process and equal protection. They point out that an alien who marries a U.S. citizen while no deportation hearing is pending is given a two-year conditional period to remain in the country, and if the marriage is still intact at the end of the two years, the conditional status is removed. They argue that the deportation order discriminates against people facing deportation hearings in an unfair manner and without any rational basis. Is this rule a denial of due process and equal protection, or is it a legitimate exercise of power by the government? (*Azizi* v. *Thornburgh,* 908 F.2d 1130 [2d Cir. 1990].)

9. A Connecticut statute requires out-of-state shippers of beer to affirm that their posted prices for products sold to Connecticut wholesalers are no higher than the prices at which the products are sold in the bordering states of Massachusetts, New York, and Rhode Island. The Beer Institute (a trade association) filed suit against the state, challenging the statute under the commerce clause. Is the statute a proper exercise of state authority, or is it a violation of the commerce clause that unduly interferes with interstate commerce? (*Healy* v. *The Beer Institute, Inc.,* 491 U.S. 324 [1989].)

10. Willner passed the New York Bar examination, but was denied admission to the Bar due to the adverse report of the Committee on Character and Fitness. Willner asked for, and was given, a hearing by the commit-

tee to appeal its report. At that hearing, Willner was informed that a particular attorney had written a negative letter about Willner. Willner was not allowed to confront the author of the letter or to ascertain and contest of the bases for the negative recommendation the committee. Willner has challenged the committee's recommendation as a denial of due process. What result should occur? (*Willner* v. *Committee on Character and Fitness,* 373 U.S. 96 [1963].)

CHAPTER 46

Antitrust Legislation

OUTLINE

THE BASIS OF REGULATORY REFORM

For the first 114 years of United States history, business had a fairly free field in which to work. There was little federal regulation and little effective state regulation. The courts and the federal government took a "hands off" attitude toward business. In such an environment, Cornelius Vanderbilt, buccaneering railroad tycoon of the 1800s, was able to crow, "What do I care about the law? Hain't I got the power?"

The tide began to turn in the late 1800s as the public tired of the irresponsible behavior of some of the so-called robber barons. The press began to call for reforms and for public protection from "big business." Finally, in 1890, a beachhead was established. The assault on business had begun. Government regulation of business was to become a major factor in the management of commercial affairs. All the regulations that affect business today, all the government inputs and interventions that confront the modern businessperson, can be traced back to *the* cornerstone of business regulation. The law that changed American business so dramatically was the Sherman Antitrust Act.

THE SHERMAN ACT

Pure-competition economy
An economy in which no single business has enough power to affect supply or demand and in which prices are set by the market in perfect equilibrium.

Section 1

Congress passed the Sherman Antitrust Act in 1890. The purpose of the act was to preserve the economic ideal of a **pure-competition economy**. To reach this ideal, the Sherman Act prohibits combinations that *restrain trade,* and it prohibits attempts to *monopolize* any area of commerce. Violations of the act can result in fines, imprisonment, injunctive relief, and civil damages.

The Sherman Act is a fairly short statute, but its few words cover a great number of actions. Section 1 states:

> Every contract, combination in the form of trust or otherwise, or conspiracy, in restraint of trade or commerce among the several States, or with foreign nations, is hereby declared to be illegal.

Because nearly every contract can be viewed as a restraint of trade, if this section were to be interpreted literally, virtually all business dealings that affect interstate commerce would be prohibited. For example, a customer who contracts to buy some item from seller 1 normally will *not* buy the same type of item from any of the competitors of seller 1. As a result, the courts initially interpreted the Sherman Act very narrowly; this worked in such a way that the act was virtually negated.

The courts eventually found a comfortable middle ground. To give the act the scope that Congress had intended, the courts developed the "rule of reason" as a means of applying the provisions of Section 1. Under this test, not *every* "contract, combination, or conspiracy" is prohibited. Rather, only those "contracts, combinations, or conspiracies" that *unreasonably* restrain interstate commerce are prohibited. If a firm can show that its conduct was reasonable, it can avoid a prosecution under Section 1.

This defense provided business with an opportunity that it lost no time in using to its best advantage. Given a sufficient amount of time to prepare a defense, almost any business can show that its conduct was "reasonable" under the circumstances. Because of the results that the rule of reason produced, the courts had to reevaluate their approach. The amended approach retained the rule of reason but added a new category: The courts declared some conduct to be so lacking in social value as to be an automatic violation of Section 1. These actions, called *per se violations,* tend to directly contradict the economic model of pure competition.

The next case dealt with one type of per se violation, price fixing.

Goldfarb et ux. v. *Virginia State Bar et al.*
95 S.Ct. 2004 (1975)

FACTS　The Goldfarbs wanted to purchase a home in Fairfax County, Virginia. The financing agency required them to obtain title insurance, which required a title examination. By state law, only a member of the Virginia Bar Association could legally perform the title examination. When the Goldfarbs contacted a local attorney, he quoted them a fee as established by the county bar association, 1 percent of the value of the property, for a title examination. The Goldfarbs decided to shop around for a lower fee, but every attorney who quoted a fee to them quoted the same fee, that fee published by the Fairfax County Bar Association. The Goldfarbs retained the first attorney to whom they had spoken, obtained their title examination, and then sued the state and county bar associations, alleging an illegal price-fixing arrangement in violation of Section 1 of the Sherman Act.

ISSUE　Was the imposition of a minimum fee schedule by the Fairfax County Bar Association and the adherence to that fee schedule by members of the association an illegal price-fixing agreement?

HOLDING　Yes. The habitual setting of prices at a fixed percentage without regard to the efforts required or any other variable constituted a price-fixing agreement in violation of the law.

REASONING　The Court found that the "suggested minimum fee schedule" resulted in a rigid price floor maintained by the state's attorneys, with each attorney adhering to the schedule both to comply with the announced professional norms and to avoid "fee wars" with the other members of the bar association. Further, since only a member of the Virginia Bar Association may provide the service of title examinations and since a title examination is required to purchase real property in the state of Virginia, a price-fixing scheme existed that no prospective purchaser of real property could escape or avoid. The provision of a title examination is a "service," and that service is performed for a fee, which places it within the definition of "commerce." This price fixing is an unreasonable restraint on commerce and constitutes a violation of the Sherman Act, Section 1.

As noted in the preceding case, the court restricted the availability of the "rule of reason" defense for alleged Sherman Act violations by the imposition of *per se* violations. The acts that are deemed to be *per se* violations are acts that are inherently contradictory to the economic theory of pure competition. If a firm is found guilty of a *per se* violation it is not permitted to defend its conduct; it will be found guilty of violation of the Sherman Act.

The *per se* violations under the Sherman Act, Section 1, are as follows:

1. *horizontal price fixing* (agreements on price among competitors)
2. *vertical price fixing* (agreements on price among suppliers and customers)
3. *horizontal market divisions* (agreements among competitors on who can sell in which region)
4. *group boycotts* (agreements among competitors not to sell to a particular buyer or not to buy from a particular seller)

Clearly, few businesses would be careless (or stupid) enough to actually overtly agree to such conduct. As a result, the courts have had to infer such agreements from the conduct of the parties. If the courts find such conduct to be **conscious parallelism,** a violation may occur. Conscious parallelism, by itself, is not conclusive proof of a violation of Section 1. However, it is to be weighed—and weighed heavily—by the courts in determining whether a Section 1 violation is present. Generally, conscious parallelism coupled with some other *fact,* however slight, is sufficient to support a jury verdict of price fixing in violation of Section 1. But if the conduct is **price leadership,** no violation is present. How can anyone distinguish conscious parallelism from price leadership? There is no answer to this problem; it poses a Gordian knot for the court every time it is raised.

The two hypothetical cases that follow show the problem of deciding whether conduct is permitted or prohibited.

Conscious parallelism Intentional establishment of the price set by another; a form of *tacit* price fixing.

Price leadership Recognition of the power of a competitor and establishment of a price similar to that set by the competitor to avoid a price war.

Alpha, Beta, and Gamma are concrete producers in Minnesota, Iowa, and Wisconsin, respectively. All three must compete with Omega, a concrete producer with plants in all three states. Alpha, Beta, and Gamma agree that each company will sell *only* in its home state, so that each can reduce expenses and thus compete more effectively with Omega. Before the agreement, each of the small companies had 10 percent of the market, and Omega had 70 percent. After the agreement, each of the small companies had 17 percent, and Omega had 49 percent.

Despite this apparent increase in competition, the conduct of Alpha, Beta, and Gamma is a *per se* violation of Section 1 of the Sherman Act because it is a horizontal market division.

Al, Bob, and Charlie are cement salesmen in Michigan, Ohio, and Indiana, respectively. They all work for Oscar Concrete, a cement producer with plants in all three states. Oscar tells them that Al is to sell cement only in Michigan, Bob is to sell only in Ohio, and Charlie is to sell only in Indiana. This is a horizontal market division, but since only one firm is involved, it is *not* a violation of Section 1.

Section 2

Section 2 of the Sherman Act is nearly as brief as Section 1 and is equally as broad. Section 2 makes the following provision:

> Every person who shall monopolize, or attempt to monopolize, or combine or conspire with any other person or persons, to monopolize any part of the trade or commerce among the several States, or with foreign nations, shall be deemed guilty of a misdemeanor.

It should be noted that Section 2 can be violated either by one person acting alone or by multiple parties acting in concert. In contrast, Section 1 can be violated only by multiple parties acting together. (To avoid confusion, remember that it takes 2 people to violate Section 1; it takes only 1 person to violate Section 2.)

Many people have the mistaken idea that monopolies are prohibited by Section 2. In fact, there is no law against having monopoly power. The prohibition in Section 2 is against *monopolizing*. That is, seeking a monopoly and attempting to keep a monopoly once one is attained are illegal. Having a monopoly, however, is not illegal.

In the following case, the court dealt with the monopolizing issue.

United States v. Aluminum Company of America
148 F.2d 416 (2d Cir. 1945)

FACTS Aluminum Company of America (Alcoa) was founded in 1888 as the Pittsburgh Production Company. It was engaged in the production and sale of "ingot" aluminum from the beginning. It changed its name in 1907. The two patents that made the production of aluminum economically feasible both belonged to Alcoa, and the (legal) exploitation of these patents allowed Alcoa to develop a legal monopoly over the manufacturing of aluminum in the United States until 1909, when the second of the two patents expired. From 1909 to 1912, Alcoa retained its monopoly position by admittedly illegal methods, but these methods were discontinued and forbidden after a consent decree entered by Alcoa in 1912. In 1940, the Justice Department filed an action against Alcoa alleging that Alcoa had continued to monopolize the aluminum market in violation of Section 2 of the Sherman Act. The government argued that the relevant product market was "virgin" ingot, and the relevant geographic market was the United States. Given this market definition, Alcoa controlled over 90 percent of the **relevant market**. Further, Alcoa's market share had fallen below 80 percent only three times in the years from 1912 through 1938. Throughout the period, Alcoa had regularly increased its productive capacity whenever the demand for aluminum grew and had managed

Relevant market The area in which a product is sold, including geographic area and all competitive and substitute products.

to anticipate every increase in demand with new and expanded capacity. The government claimed that Alcoa's constant domination of the market was evidence of monopolizing and sought a court-ordered dissolution of the company. Alcoa insisted that its size alone, without more, was insufficient to prove monopolization on its part.

ISSUE

Was Alcoa guilty of monopolizing the relevant market, or had its monopoly power and position been "thrust upon" it?

HOLDING

Alcoa was guilty of monopolizing in violation of Section 2 of the Sherman Act.

REASONING

The court began with the premise that, had a firm combined several independent firms into one large company that controlled 90 percent of the market, that firm would be guilty of monopolizing. However, size does not establish guilt; there must also be some evidence of exclusion of competition. In addition, the growth must be something other than "natural" or "normal," and wrongful intent or unduly coercive means must be shown. The court noted that "the successful competitor, having been urged to compete, must not be turned upon when he wins." But it also noted, "Mere size . . . is not an offense against the Sherman Act unless magnified to the point at which it amounts to a monopoly. . . . But size carries with it an opportunity for abuse that is not to be ignored when the opportunity is proved to have been utilized in the past." In 1912 Alcoa had two plants and produced 42 million pounds of ingot. In 1940, it had five plants and produced 327 million pounds, an eight-fold increase. In the meantime, not a single pound of ingot had been produced by anyone else in the United States. Such an increase and such undisturbed control of the market did not fall undesigned into Alcoa's lap; rather, it resulted from a persistent desire to maintain the control with which the firm was vested in 1912. As the court stated:

> We need charge it with no moral derelictions after 1912; we may assume that all it claims for itself is true. The only question is whether it falls within the exception established in favor of those who do not seek, but cannot avoid, the control of a market. It seems to us that question scarcely survives its statement. It was not inevitable that it should always anticipate increases in the demand for ingot and be prepared to supply them. Nothing compelled it to keep doubling and redoubling its capacity before others entered the field. It insists that it never excluded competitors; but we can think of no more effective exclusion than progressively to embrace each new opportunity as it opened, and to face every newcomer with new capacity already geared into a great organization, having the advantage of experience, trade connections and the elite of personnel. Only in case we interpret "exclusion" as limited to maneuvers not honestly industrial, but actuated solely by a desire to prevent competition, can such a course, indefatigably pursued, be deemed not "exclusionary." So to limit it would in our judgment emasculate the Act; would permit just such consolidations as it was designed to prevent.

The court found Alcoa guilty of monopolizing, but the dissolution issue was denied due to changes in the aluminum market during World War II.

If a firm is found to dominate an industry, it is also found to possess monopoly power. As a rule of thumb, 70 percent of the **relevant market** is deemed to be monopoly power. When such power is present, there is a presumption that Section 2 was, or is, violated. However, a number of defenses exist to rebut this presumption. The dominant firm may argue that it is not attempting to retain its power, or that it acquired its position legally, or that its position was "thrust upon" it. Any of these defenses is sufficient to prevent a Section 2 prosecution.

The next hypothetical case shows how the defense can be applied.

Ralph developed a new product, Kleenzall, which does what any other soap or cleanser does, except that it does it better and is cheaper. Kleenzall is good for washing dishes, clothes, floors, walls, and even hair. Kleenzall is so good a product that Ralph soon had 95 percent of every cleanser and soap market. The major soap producers sued Ralph for monopolizing the industry in violation of the Sherman Act, Section 2.

Ralph is not guilty. He did nothing wrong in acquiring his market share. This monopoly was "thrust upon" him by sheer efficiency. (However, if Ralph subsequently takes steps to prevent other firms from entering the cleanser market, or acts in any manner that seems to be precluding or preventing competition, he may be found guilty of monopolizing. Possessing his monopoly power is legal, but attempting to retain it is illegal!)

Sanctions

When a Sherman Act violation is shown, both criminal and civil remedies are available. An individual can be fined up to $100,000 and can receive up to three years in prison; a corporation that is convicted can be fined up to $1 million. Moreover, an injunction can be issued against the prohibited conduct. As a final disincentive, any harmed parties can recover treble damages plus attorney's fees. This means an injured firm can take its damages, multiply them by three, and then add attorney's fees. In at least one case, damages assessed exceeded $200 million. Needless to say, such damages strongly discourage prohibited conduct.

YOU BE THE JUDGE

Atari was one of the early competitors in the home video game market. Nintendo entered this United States market some time after Atari, but rapidly gained a lion's share of the market. By the late 1980's, Nintendo controlled approximately 90 percent of the U.S. market, and was able to maintain prices on its products for over four years. At the same time the prices of virtually every other consumer electronic product were falling.

Atari alleged that Nintendo had illegally tied up the market by signing exclusive licensing agreements for home video games with the premier video game manufacturers. It was claimed that this conduct injured Atari by forcing it from the industry. As a result, Atari is seeking $160 million in damages. Nintendo asserted that Atari was indecisive, tried to compete as cheaply as possible, and was not willing to fight to increase market share.

Assuming that Atari filed an antitrust case, how would you rule, and why?

Source: "Atari Corp. Fails To Prove Losses in Antitrust Suit," Richard B. Schmidt, *The Wall Street Journal*, May 4, 1992, page A3.

THE CLAYTON ACT

By 1914, Congress realized that the Sherman Act alone was not sufficient to solve the major business problems of the country. The Sherman Act was *remedial* in nature: If a problem existed, the Sherman Act could be used to help correct the problem. Unfortunately, it is possible (if not probable) that by the time the "remedy" is sought the injured party has suffered irreparable harm or has ceased to exist as a business entity. Nothing, however, was available to *prevent* a problem from developing. In an effort to correct this regulatory deficiency, Congress decided to enact some preventive legislation. The result was the Clayton Act, which was designed to nip problems "in their incipiency." The Clayton Act has four major provisions, each dealing with a different potential problem.

Section 2

Price discrimination The practice of discriminating among competing customers by offering them the same product at different prices.

The first regulating section of the Clayton Act, Section 2, prohibits **price discrimination**. The original Section 2 made it illegal for a seller to discriminate in price between different purchasers unless the price difference could be justified by a difference in costs. This provision soon placed a number of sellers in a terrible bind. Major purchasers often demanded special prices from sellers. If the sellers refused, they lost the business; if they agreed, they violated the law. As a result, Section 2 was amended in 1936 when the Robinson-Patman Act became law. Under the Robinson-Patman Act, buyers were prohibited from knowingly accepting a discriminatory price. In addition, the act prohibited such indirect benefits as dummy brokerage fees and promotional kickbacks.

A person accused of price discrimination can defend against the charge by showing that he or she is meeting, but *not* beating, the price being offered by a competitor. The accused can also defend by showing that the lower price is being offered because of obsolescence, seasonal variations, or damage to the goods being sold.

The following case involved a major price-discrimination scheme.

Utah Pie Co. v. Continental Baking Co.
386 U.S. 685 (1967)

FACTS   Utah Pie Co. was a local bakery operating in the Salt Lake City area. It began producing frozen pies in 1957, with immediate success. In 1958, Utah Pie built a new plant and gained a competitive edge over its three major competitors, Pet, Continental, and Carnation. The three major competitors each independently lowered their prices in the Utah market in an effort to cut into Utah Pie's market share. Utah Pie filed suit against all three, alleging violations of the Robinson-Patman Act.

ISSUE   Did the special prices offered by the three major producers in the Utah market amount to unlawful price discrimination?

HOLDING	Yes. Each of the three discriminated in price in violation of the Robinson-Patman Act.
REASONING	There was evidence that Pet's prices in Utah were lower than the prices it charged for the same products in California or in other western markets. Pet also had admitted to sending spies into Utah Pie so that it could gain information to use against Utah Pie. Moreover, Pet suffered losses on its sales in Salt Lake City during the entire challenged period. Continental's share of the market was small from 1957 through 1960. In 1961, Continental lowered its price in Salt Lake City to $2.85 per dozen on frozen pies. This price was below its cost and was offered only in Salt Lake City. Utah Pie was forced to lower its prices to their lowest point ever ($2.75 per dozen) to compete. Carnation also offered lower prices in Utah than in any other regional market. Its pies were sold below cost—as much as $0.50 per dozen less than in other western markets.

The court held that sellers may not sell like goods to different buyers at different prices if the result harms competition. The fact that Utah Pie was expanding its sales volume was not enough to deny recovery. The Utah Pie market had a dramatically declining price during this period, and the decline was due to predatory price discrimination.

The Robinson-Patman Act also changed the standards needed to show a violation. Under the original Section 2, it had been necessary to show that *general competition* had been harmed, but under the Robinson-Patman Act, it is sufficient to prosecute on a showing that a *competitor* was injured.

The following example illustrates this point.

Bill's Bathtub Boutique is the largest customer of Paula's Porcelain Palace. Bill's biggest competitor is Dan's Discount Tub Store. Bill tells Paula that unless she gives him a 10 percent price reduction, he will take his business elsewhere. If Paula gives Bill this price reduction and does not give the same reduction to Dan, both Bill and Paula will be in violation of the Robinson-Patman Act.

Section 3

The second major prohibition under the Clayton Act is found in Section 3. This section bans exclusive-dealing contracts and tying arrangements when their "effect may be to substantially lessen competition or tend to create a monopoly." Notice again the preventive intent of the act: Actual harm need not be shown, merely the likelihood that harm will eventually occur.

In an **exclusive-dealing contract,** one party requires the other party to deal with him, and him alone. For example, the seller tells the buyer that unless the buyer buys *only* from the seller, and not from the seller's competitors, the seller will not deal with the buyer. For such a demand to be effective, the seller must be in a very powerful market position.

In a **tying arrangement,** one party—usually the seller—refuses to sell one product unless the buyer also takes a second product or service from the seller. For example, a manufacturer of cosmetics might refuse to sell a facial moisturizer unless the buyer agrees to purchase the manufacturer's soap. Usually, for this sort of arrangement to work, the seller needs a highly valued, unique

Exclusive-dealing contract An agreement between two parties in which one party agrees not to do business with the other party's competitors but to deal exclusively with that party.

Tying arrangement An agreement between two parties in which one party's purchase of a product or service from the other party is contingent on purchasing a second product or service from that other party.

product to which he or she can tie a commonly available product. As a defense to a charge that such an arrangement lessens competition or creates a monopoly, the seller may attempt to show that the tied product is tied for quality-control reasons. To do so, the seller must prove that no competitors produce a competing product that works adequately with the controlled product.

Technological advances seem to provide special opportunities for tying contracts and exclusive-dealing arrangements. In the following case, the court was faced with an alleged Sherman Act violation and an allegedly illegal tying contract.

Digidyne Corporation v. Data General Corporation
734 F.2d 1336 (9th Cir. 1983)

FACTS   Data General manufactured a computer system known as NOVA. The system consisted of a NOVA CPU, designed to perform a particular "instruction set" or group of tasks, and a copyrighted NOVA operating system called RDOS that contained the basic commands for operation of the system. Data General refused to license its RDOS system to anyone who did not also purchase the Data General NOVA CPU. Digidyne produced an emulator NOVA CPU designed to perform the NOVA instruction set, but it could not compete in the market without access to the RDOS system. Digidyne argued that, since Data General refused to license the use of its RDOS to anyone who did not purchase the NOVA CPU, Data General was guilty of an illegal tying contract under Section 3 of the Clayton Act and of violations of Section 1 of the Sherman Act.

ISSUE   Was Data General guilty of creating an illegal tying contract in this situation?

HOLDING   Yes.

REASONING   A tying contract is illegal if it is shown to restrain competition unreasonably or is illegal *per se,* without such a showing if certain prerequisites are met. . . . The prerequisites are: (1) the separate products, the purchase of one (tying product) being conditioned on purchase of the other (tied product); (2) sufficient economic power with respect to the tying product to restrain competition appreciably in the tied product; and (3) an effect upon a substantial amount of commerce in the tied product. . . . These prerequisites were satisfied in this case. We therefore do not consider whether competition was in fact unreasonably restrained.

The copyright protection of the RDOS system created a presumption of economic power sufficient to render the tying arrangement illegal per se. At that point, the burden shifted to Data General to disprove illegality. Its assertion that it needed to tie the products to recover its research and development costs was not sufficient to rebut the presumption. Data General failed to carry its burden and was found guilty of an illegal tying contract in violation of Section 3 of the Clayton Act.

Section 7   The third major section of the Clayton Act, Section 7, deals with mergers. As originally written, the only prohibited type of merger was one in which the stock of another firm was acquired if its effect might be "substantially to lessen competition, or [to] tend to create a monopoly." This prohibition was so narrow that it was rather easily evaded by merging firms.

To broaden the scope of the law, Congress amended Section 7 in 1950 by passing the Cellar-Kefauver Act. The amended Section 7 prohibits the acquisition of stock *or assets* of another firm that may tend to have a negative effect on *any line of commerce*. As a result, firms are now subject to Section 7 in almost any type of merger—horizontal, vertical, or conglomerate. A *horizontal merger* is one between competing firms; a *vertical merger* is one between a firm and one of its major suppliers or customers; a *conglomerate merger* is one between firms in two noncompetitive industries.

As a challenge to a merger, the government might argue that a "concentration trend" would be established, or that one of the firms was a "potential entrant" into one of the industries affected by the merger. As a defense to a challenged merger, the merging firms might raise the "failing-company" doctrine, showing that without the merger one of the firms would have gone out of business.

The following case illustrates the potential-entrant doctrine.

United States v. Falstaff Brewing Corporation
410 U.S. 526 (1973)

FACTS   Falstaff was the fourth-largest brewer in the United States, but it did not sell any beer in New England. Falstaff decided to enter the New England beer market by merging with a strong regional brewer. After some investigation, Falstaff decided that a merger with Narragansett would be the best way to enter the market. Narragansett was the largest beer supplier in New England at the time of the merger with Falstaff. The United States challenged the merger as a violation of Section 7 of the Clayton Act.

ISSUE   Was Falstaff a "potential entrant" into the New England market, so that its merger was improper?

HOLDING   Yes. Falstaff was the nearest major brewer to New England that did not yet compete there. As such, it had to be considered a potential entrant.

REASONING   The number of brewers in New England had decreased from thirty-two in 1935 to only six in 1964. Even though Falstaff alleged that it would never have entered the New England market unless it did so by acquisition, it was still a potential entrant and a potential competitor of the six breweries operating there at the time. The other brewers in New England could not know what Falstaff had decided. Falstaff was known to be interested in the New England market; its location on the very border of New England was certain to make the firms located there behave as if Falstaff might enter the market. Because of its size, its locations, and its interest, Falstaff was a potential entrant into the market.

The following examples show the failing-company doctrine and the concentration trend.

Fred's Stereo is in severe financial difficulty. Irv's Interstate Sound Store, the largest stereo dealer in the region, buys Fred's. Under the failing-company doctrine, if Fred's would have gone bankrupt, the merger with Irv's is probably permissible.

The belt business is made up of many small producers of belts. The leather industry is made up of many small producers of leather. Bertha's Belts, the tenth largest belt producer, wants to merge with Lanny's Leather, the fourth largest leather producer. Such a merger would not greatly alter the position of the other firms in either industry.

The government could probably successully challenge this merger as a first step toward a concentration trend that would eventually harm competition in both industries by reducing the number of firms in each.

Section 8

The final substantive section of the Clayton Act is Section 8. This section prohibits *interlocking directorates*. That is, no one may sit on the boards of directors of two or more competing corporations if either of the firms has capital and surplus in excess of $1 million, if a merger between them would violate any antitrust law.

THE FEDERAL TRADE COMMISSION ACT

The year 1914 was a very busy one for antitrust regulation. Congress passed not only the Clayton Act but also the Federal Trade Commission Act. The Federal Trade Commission Act did two important things:

1. It created the Federal Trade Commission (FTC) to enforce antitrust laws, especially the Clayton Act.
2. In Section 5, it provided a broad area of prohibitions to close loopholes left by other statutes.

Section 5 of the FTC Act prohibits "unfair methods of competition" and "unfair and deceptive trade practices." This broad language permits the FTC to regulate conduct that technically might be beyond the reach of the other, more specific antitrust statutes.

The area of unfair and deceptive trade practices was intentionally made broad and somewhat vague to grant the FTC the leeway to proceed against any commercial practices that seem to be unfair or deceptive *under the circumstances*. If the statute had been specific, businesspeople could have found methods to circumvent it, methods that might be unfair or deceptive but within the technical limits of the law. The strength of the law has been its breadth, as well as the willingness of the FTC to attack practices that had been followed for many years.

To further strengthen the FTC position, a violation can be found without proof of any actual deception. A mere showing that there is a "fair possibility" that the public will be deceived is sufficient to establish that the conduct is unfair and deceptive. And if a representation made by a company is ambiguous, with one honest meaning and one deceptive meaning, the FTC will treat it as deceptive and as a material aspect of the transaction, so that remedies are available.

If the FTC opposes a business practice as unfair or deceptive, it issues a *cease-and-desist order*. The business must stop the challenged conduct or face a fine for disobeying the order. The fine is $5000 per violation. This sounds small until it is realized that each *day* the order is ignored constitutes a separate violation. Thus, ignoring the order for one week would cost $35,000 in fines; for a month, $150,000 in fines; and so on.

In recent years, the FTC has become particularly concerned about two business practices: deceptive advertising and "bait-and-switch" advertising. In an effort to force truth in advertising, the FTC has been carefully studying the commercials run by corporations and ordering *corrective advertising* in many cases in which the advertising was deemed especially misleading. The case that follows is one of the best known in this area. In it, the FTC attacked Warner-Lambert for the ads it had run for one of its products, Listerine.

Warner-Lambert Co. v. FTC
562 F.2d 749 (D.C. Cir. 1977)

FACTS   Warner-Lambert is the producer of Listerine mouthwash. Listerine has been produced, without a change in the formula, since 1879. And, from 1879 to 1972, it was represented as a beneficial treatment for colds, cold symptoms, and sore throats. In 1972, the FTC issued a cease-and-desist order prohibiting such advertising claims in the future. In addition, the FTC ordered Warner-Lambert to run *corrective advertising* to remove any impression by the public that Listerine was a cold and sore throat medicine. Warner-Lambert agreed to stop the advertisements but objected to running the corrective advertisements.

ISSUE   May the FTC require corrective advertising to remedy the harm done by prior misleading or deceptive advertising?

HOLDING   Yes. The FTC may order corrective advertising in appropriate cases.

REASONING   The ingredients in Listerine are not of sufficient quantity to have any therapeutic effect. Even if the quantities were sufficient, gargling would not allow the ingredients to reach the affected areas. Moreover, the germs Listerine reputedly kills have no effect on either colds or sore throats. The FTC has the power to shape remedies to fit the problem presented. Corrective advertising is an appropriate remedy to inform past *and* future consumers of prior deceptive advertisings and beliefs created by the advertiser. Corrective advertising is not a violation of the First Amendment. Rather, it is a necessary step to remove from the public mind a false belief placed there by the wrongdoer. The court ruled that Warner-Lambert would have to run corrective advertising. All Listerine ads would have to state: "Listerine will not help prevent colds or sore throats or lessen their severity." This correction had to appear in every advertisement until Warner-Lambert had run $10 million worth of advertisements.

Bait-and-switch advertising involves advertising a product at an especially enticing price to get the customer into the store (the "bait") and then talking the customer into buying a more expensive model (the "switch") because the advertised model is sold out or has some alleged defect. An advertiser who refuses to show the advertised item to the customer or who has insufficient quantities on hand to satisfy reasonable customer demand is engaging in an unfair trade practice in violation of Section 5 of the FTC Act.

Some common law unfair trade practices should also be mentioned, such as palming off goods and violating trade secrets. *Palming off* involves advertising, designing, or selling goods as if they were the goods of another. Basically, the person who is palming off goods is fraudulently taking advantage of the goodwill and brand loyalty of the imitated producer. This practice also frequently involves patent, copyright, or trademark infringements.

Trade secrets are special processes, formulas, and the like that are guarded and treated confidentially by the holder of the trade secret. Employers of a firm that has trade secrets must not betray their loyalty to the firm by revealing the trade secrets to others. To do so is a tort, and the employee can be held liable for any damages suffered by the employer. In addition, the firm or person who receives the information is guilty of appropriating the trade secret, and use of the secret can be stopped by injunctions; the recipient of the information will also be liable for damages suffered by the trade-secret holder.

As we just mentioned, palming off frequently involves the infringement of a patent, a copyright, or a trademark. These three areas, along with a few others such as service marks and trade names, are protected by federal statutes and are registered with the United States Patent Office.

A *patent* is a federally created and protected monopoly power given to inventors. If a person invents something that is new, useful, and not obvious to a person of ordinary skill in the industry, the inventor is entitled to a patent. In exchange for making the method of production public, the patent grants the inventor an exclusive right to use, make, or sell the product for seventeen years. If anyone violates this exclusive right, the patent holder can file an infringement suit. If the court upholds the patent, the infringer will be enjoined from further production and will be liable for damages to the holder of the patent.

A *copyright,* protected by the Copyright Office in the Library of Congress, is the protection given to writers, artists, and composers. The creator of a book, song, work of art, or similar item has the exclusive right to the profits from the creation for the life of the creator plus fifty years. Any infringement can result in an infringement action in federal court, with injunctive relief and damages being awarded to the holder of the copyright.

A *trademark* is a mark or symbol used to identify a particular brand name or product. Copying the trademark of a competitor or using a symbol deceptively similar to that of a competitor is a violation of the Lanham Act of 1946, and the violator is subject to an injunction and the imposition of damages.

EXEMPTIONS

Some conduct appears to violate various antitrust rules, and yet the actor is never challenged for the conduct. Many people are confused by this lack of action, asking why that party is allowed to do something when others are not allowed to do the same thing. The reason is probably that the particular party belongs to a group specifically exempted from antitrust coverage.

Labor unions are exempt from the provisions of the Sherman Act by the Norris-LaGuardia Act, passed in 1932. They are also exempt from the Clayton Act by Section 6 of the Clayton Act. The exemption applies only to "labor disputes" and normal union activities. Farm cooperatives are also exempt from antitrust coverage so long as they are engaged in the sale of farm produce. (There are a number of other exemptions, but they have little impact on business law.)

SUMMARY

Since 1890, the federal government has been attempting to regulate business to ensure competition. This legislative effort is referred to as antitrust law. The cornerstone of antitrust law is the Sherman Act, which prohibits joint conduct that unreasonably restricts competition or attempts to monopolize any area of commerce. Some conduct is considered so lacking in social value that it constitutes a per se violation. Other questionable conduct is measured under the rule of reason. If a violation is found, injured parties are entitled to treble damages.

As the Sherman Act was found to be insufficient to prevent many violations, Congress enacted several other statutes to help protect the competitive ideal. One of these statutes is the Clayton Act, which prohibits price discrimination (by means of the Robinson-Patman Act), exclusive-dealing contracts and tying arrangements, a number of mergers (by means of the Cellar-Kefauver Act), and interlocking directorates.

As a means of protecting competition, Congress passed the Federal Trade Commission Act. This act has two major aspects: It created the Federal Trade Commission to act as a watchdog in the antitrust area, and it prohibits unfair and deceptive trade practices.

DISCUSSION QUESTIONS

1. Section 1 of the Sherman Act is intended to protect competition by prohibiting restraints of trade. In order to apply this section, the court uses the so-called rule of reason. What is the rule of reason, and how does it affect Section 1 of the Sherman Act?

2. What is "conscious parallelism," and how does it relate to the Sherman Act? What is "price leadership," and how does it relate to the Sherman Act?

3. How can a firm totally dominate an industry and not be guilty of monopolizing in violation of Section 2 of the Sherman Act?

4. What were the major *new* prohibitions that the Robinson-Patman Act added to Section 2 of the Clayton Act?

5. What did the FTC Act prohibit in an effort to close the antitrust loopholes?

6. What is a "bait-and-switch" maneuver, and why is such conduct treated as an unfair trade practice under the provisions of the Federal Trade Commission Act?

7. Anna and Bruce are competitors in the frozen quiche market. They agree to charge the same price for their products and to compete only in quality and advertising. What antitrust laws, if any, have they violated?

8. Samantha is a major shirt manufacturer. She sells shirts at one price but gives a quantity discount on orders of 5000 shirts or more. Only 2 of Samantha's customers, out of 600 customers, can take advantage of this quantity discount. Is Samantha in violation of any antitrust laws?

9. Mort is one of many producers of sugar cane. He developed a new machine for processing sugar cane that was much faster and much cheaper than any other machine. Mort leased his machine to processors only if the processors bought all their sugar cane from Mort. What antitrust questions are raised by Mort's conduct?

10. Arctic Airlines advertises that it "gets you there ON TIME more often than any other airline." In fact, Arctic has a very bad record of arriving on time. What might the FTC do to Arctic in regard to this advertising campaign?

CASE PROBLEMS

1. Burke owned and operated a vending and catering service in the Los Angeles area. The Musicks operated a competing business. The Musicks claim that from 1985 through 1988 they were threatened and harassed by employees and agents of Burke while they were attempting to serve their customers. They also alleged that Burke engaged in price discrimination and other illegal practices and tactics. The Musicks sued Burke for allegedly violating the Sherman Act, the Clayton Act, and the Robinson-Patman Act. Burke defended on the basis of a lack of jurisdiction, alleging that he was engaged in a purely local business. He also argued that his competitive activities were permissible under the rule of reason. Should the court grant Burke's motion for summary judgment in this case? (*Musick* v. *Burke*, 913 F.2d 1390 [9th Cir. 1990].)

2. Weinberg was on the boards of directors of Sears, Roebuck and of B. F. Goodrich. The government sued both companies, seeking a ruling that Weinberg could not sit on both boards under the Clayton Act. Both Sears and Goodrich sold major home appliances and automobile parts. Was this enough to classify them as competitors, so that they violated Section 8 of the Clayton Act? (*United States* v. *Sears, Roebuck & Co.*, 111 F. Supp. 614 [S.D. N.Y. 1953].)

3. Faulkner is an advertising agency in Baltimore. Faulkner was engaged exclusively in the business of creating and placing advertising for local Nissan dealers until October, 1988. Prior to 1988, Nissan advertising had been conducted on two distinct levels: national advertising that was developed, placed, and paid for by Nissan and local advertising that was obtained and paid for by individual Nissan dealerships. In May, 1988, Nissan announced a new "local market advertising" plan that was to take effect 1 October, 1988. Under the plan, Nissan was going to increase the wholesale price of its products in order to pay for increased advertising developed by Nissan and its ad agency. This new advertising was for both national and local use. At the same time, Nissan discontinued its prior habit of providing contributions to local dealers to develop and pay for their advertising campaigns. As a result, the Baltimore

Nissan dealers stopped using Faulkner for their advertising. Faulkner has sued Nissan, alleging that this arrangement is an illegal tying contract. How will the court resolve this case? What factors will the court examine in reaching its decision? (*Faulkner Advertising Associates, Inc.* v. *Nissan Motor Corporation,* 905 F.2d 769 [4th Cir. 1990].)

4. The Fedders Corporation advertised that its air-conditioning equipment was unique in possessing "reserve cooling power." In fact, Fedders had no evidence that established its equipment as unique. The FTC issued a cease-and-desist order against the advertisements. Fedders challenged the issuance of the cease-and-desist order even though it admitted that its advertising was "misleading." Was the FTC conduct appropriate in this case? (*Fedders Corp.* v. *FTC,* 529 F.2d 1398 [2d Cir. 1976].)

5. Kodak controlled 82 percent of the film market, 61 percent of the camera market, and 67 percent of the color print market. Kodak then introduced a new camera, the "110 Instamatic," and the film that it required, controlling 100% of these submarkets. Berkey filed suit against Kodak, alleging violations of the Sherman Act, Sections 1 and 2. Is Kodak guilty of a Section 2 violation, monopolization? Discuss fully. (*Berkey Photo, Inc.* v. *Eastman Kodak Co.,* 603 F.2d 263 [2d Cir. 1979].)

6. The regional beer distributors in central California decided among themselves to stop allowing the use of short-term trade credit without interest to the beer retailers of the region. The beer retailers objected to this decision, arguing that it constituted an illegal price-fixing agreement among the distributors in violation of Section 1 of the Sherman Act. Analyze the case and decide which side should prevail. (*Catalano, Inc.* v. *Target Sales,* 446 U.S. 635 [1980].)

7. The Jefferson Parish Hospital has a contract with a firm of anesthesiologists requiring that all anesthesiological services for the hospital's patients are to be performed by the firm. Hyde, an anesthesiologist who was not a member of the firm, applied for admission to the hospital staff. The application was denied because of the contract. As a result, Hyde filed suit against the hospital and the firm, alleging that the contract was a violation of Section 1 of the Sherman Act. It was also alleged that this was an illegal tying contract in violation of Section 3 of the Clayton Act. Did this contract constitute a violation of either or both of these antitrust statutes? Why? (*Jefferson Parish Hospital District No. 2* v. *Hyde,* 466 U.S. 2 [1984].)

8. Tampella is a Finnish corporation that manufactures and sells hardrock hydraulic underground drilling rigs (HHUDR) throughout the world. Hughes, a Texas-based corporation, owned a French subsidiary, Secoma, that was also involved in the HHUDR industry. In 1989, when Tampella proposed the acquisition of Secoma, the United States Justice Department challenged the proposed acquisition under Section 7 of the Clayton Act. According to the Justice Department, the acquisition would substantially lessen competition in the HHUDR market in the United States. Between 1986 and 1989, only four firms sold HHUDRs in the United States, and annual sales varied from twenty-two units to forty-three units. Each HHUDR unit costs several hundred thousand dollars, and the purchasers are all highly sophisticated and knowledgeable in the industry. Given these factors, does this acquisition violate Section 7 of the Clayton Act? (*United States* v. *Baker Hughes, Inc.,* 908 F.2d 981 [D.C. Cir. 1990].)

9. Brown Shoe Company wanted to merge with Kinney. At the time of the proposed merger, Brown was the number three shoe retailer in the country and the number four shoe manufacturer. Kinney was the number eight shoe retailer in the country and the number twelve manufacturer. Both companies were in good financial condition, and there were no indications that either was about to fail in the foreseeable future. The government challenged the merger as a violation of Section 7 of the Clayton Act. Brown responded that the merger would have little effect on the total shoe market in the United States and that the companies were not truly competitors since Kinney sold low-price shoes while Brown sold medium-price shoes. Do you find Brown's arguments persuasive? Should the merger be blocked? (*Brown Shoe Co.* v. *United States,* 370 U.S. 294 [1962].)

10. The commercial printing industry in the United States has two major methods for printing, gravure and web offset. Gravure (or rotogravure) printing has nine commercial printing companies in this country. Two of the nine firms, R. R. Donnelley and Sons Company and Meredith Corporation, reached an agreement in which Donnelley would take over all the commercial printing operations of Meredith. The FTC objected to the agreement, alleging that the effect would be to substantially lessen competition in a line of commerce, commercial printing. Donnelley and Meredith objected, arguing that limiting the line of commerce to gravure printing is unrealistic and distorts the overall effect on the industry of the proposed takeover. Gravure printing only rep-

resents 16 percent of all commercial printing in the country. If the takeover is allowed to stand, Donnelley would be the number one gravure commercial printer in the country, but would still possess only 8 percent of the total commercial printing industry market. Is the FTC definition of the relevant line of commerce appropriate in this case, or has the FTC defined the line of commerce too narrowly? Discuss fully. (*Federal Trade Commission v. R. R. Donnelley & Sons Co.,* 1990–2 Trade Cases [CCH] 69,240 [Nov. 20, 1990].)

CHAPTER 47

Consumer and Environmental Protection

OUTLINE

NEW AREAS FOR GOVERNMENT REGULATION

The second half of the twentieth century is witnessing a new revolution in business law. This revolution is not nearly as dramatic, or as obvious, as the antitrust revolution of the early part of the century, but its ultimate effect may be greater. The revolution involves two major areas of social reform legislation. The first, consumer protection, affects the relationship between a business and its customers. The second, environmental protection, affects the production process. Both are concerned with the ethereal concept known as "quality of life." Both have been hailed as a panacea by some and condemned as a Pandora's box by others. In reality, they are probably neither a cure-all for society's ills nor a curse-all intent on destroying business.

The U.S. Administrative Procedure Act, 5 U.S.C. 553, provides, inter alia:

§553. Rule Making

(b)   General notice of proposed rule making shall be published in the Federal Register, unless persons subject thereto are named and either personally served or otherwise have actual notice thereof in accordance with law . . .

(d)   The required publication or service of a substantive rule shall be made not less than thirty days before its effective date, except—

(3)   as otherwise provided by the agency for good cause found and published with the rule.[1]

The following case discusses what constitutes "good cause" for making an agency ruling effective in less than thirty days.

United States Steel Corp. v. Environmental Protection Agency
605 F.2d 283 (7th Cir. 1979)

FACTS   The EPA made an air quality regulation effective immediately instead of the usual thirty days after publication in the Federal Register. U.S. Steel attacked the agency for lacking the "good cause" required by law for bypassing the usual thirty-day waiting period.

ISSUE   Did the EPA have "good cause" for bypassing the thirty-day waiting period?

HOLDING   Yes. Numerous circumstances provide good cause for bypassing the waiting period.

REASONING   The Administrative Procedure Act; 5 U.S.C. 553, provides federal administrative agencies with broad power to determine what constitutes "good cause." The legislative history of the statute reflects that

[1]Sept. 6, 1966, P.L. 89-554, §1, 80 Stat. 383.

> Many rules . . . may be operative in less than thirty days because of inescapable or unavoidable limitations of time, because of demonstrable urgency of the conditions they are designed to correct, and because the parties subject to them may during the usually protracted hearing and decision procedures anticipate the regulation.

CONSUMER PROTECTION

As indicated in our discussion of warranty and product liability in Chapter 21, concern for the consumer has a relatively long legal history. But that concern has been for an *injured* consumer only. Over the past several years, the legislature, deciding that other consumer protections were also needed, has enacted a new wave of consumer protection statutes.

Consumer Credit

Consumer credit in the United States is a very big business. Many consumers rely on the use of credit to purchase various goods and appliances, from air conditioners to automobiles to televisions and stereos, and much more. For many years, such purchases were regulated only at the state level. This led to a great variety of regulation and to differing treatment in different states of consumers who had entered virtually identical transactions. While some variety still exists, several federal regulations now in effect have helped to level the treatment of consumers in different states in certain respects. We will discuss some of the most important of these federal statutes.

Federal Consumer Credit Protection Act   In 1968, Congress enacted the Federal Consumer Credit Protection Act (FCCPA), 15 U.S.C. 1601 et seq. The FCCPA deals with the rights of consumers to know and understand the credit terms to which they are agreeing before they agree. Under this act, the creditor must inform the consumer of the finance charges involved in the transaction, and the information must be put in terms of an annual percentage rate (APR). In addition, the consumer must be made aware of *when* finance charges are imposed, *how* they are calculated, and any other relevant details of the credit arrangement.

The following case shows how this statute can be applied.

Chapman v. *Miller*
575 S.W.2d 581 (Tex. App. 1978)

FACTS   Miller entered into a retail installment contract to purchase a used car from Chapman Motor Sales. The contract called for a $200 down payment, followed by six weekly payments of $25 and then eighteen monthly payments of $70.47. Miller managed to make the payments until the sixth month. At that time, Miller defaulted, and Chapman repossessed the car, demanding the entire balance due from Miller. When Miller was unable to make the demanded payment, Chapman sold the car for the balance due from Miller, plus $19.69. Miller challenged the entire transaction, alleging that Chapman had violated the Federal Consumer Credit Protection Act.

ISSUE   Is an inadequate disclosure of the seller's security interest a violation of the Federal Consumer Credit Protection Act?

HOLDING   Yes. The contract used by Chapman inadequately provided full disclosure of all terms to the customer.

REASONING   The customer signed on the front of the contract form provided by Chapman and the signature did not follow "the full content of the document." Any violation of the disclosure requirements, even a minor one, defeats the purpose of the law. The penalty was twice the finance charges on the loan, plus court costs and attorney fees. (_Note:_ The law did not negate the repossession and sale of the car by Chapman. It merely penalized him for inadequate disclosure.)

Fair Credit Billing Act   As a complement to the FCCPA, Congress enacted the Fair Credit Billing Act, 15 U.S.C. 1601 et seq., in 1975. This act specifies the rights of both the creditor and the consumer/debtor if there is any dispute about a credit account or a credit bill. The consumer is told _exactly_ how to complain about any alleged errors in the credit bill (these normally will be errors on a charge account), and the creditor is required to respond to the complaint in a timely manner. The creditor must either explain the error or correct it. The creditor may _not_

1. try to collect the amount involved in the dispute until the dispute is settled
2. restrict the consumer's use of his or her credit account during the controversy, except for an unrelated but justifiable cause
3. report that the consumer is in arrears or that his or her bill is delinquent because of nonpayment of the disputed amount

Once the controversy is resolved, the parties continue their dealings as they had before the controversy arose.

Uniform Consumer Credit Code   The Uniform Consumer Credit Code (UCCC) was proposed in 1968. This code was intended to do for consumer credit law what the Uniform Commercial Code has done for commercial law. It was, and is, a codification of the major consumer credit areas and the various court rulings and statutes that have governed these areas. The intent was to establish a nationally recognized set of laws so that consumer credit law could become uniform. To date, the UCCC has not been widely adopted, although it is often referred to by legal writers and legal practitioners.

Equal Credit Opportunity Act   In an effort to ensure civil rights in the consumer credit world, Congress passed the Equal Credit Opportunity Act, 15

U.S.C. 1691 et seq. This act prohibits the denial of credit by any business that regularly extends credit to any applicant on the basis of sex, marital status, race, religion, national origin, or age. When a customer applies for credit, the business has thirty days in which to reply to the application. If the company denies the application, it must specify the reasons for the denial.

In the following case, a California federal court considered the question of whether the statute applies to leases as well as sales.

Brothers v. *First Leasing*
724 F.2d 789 (9th Cir. 1984), cert. denied 469 U.S. 832

FACTS	Federal district court dismissed the plaintiff's claim that her lease application had been denied on the basis of sex or marital status in violation of the Equal Credit Opportunity Act.
ISSUE	Does the ECOA apply to consumer leases?
HOLDING	Yes.
REASONING	Congress did not explicitly include references to leases in the statute. However, failure to do so does not mean that Congress intended to exclude leases. Congress used the broad term "credit transaction" as within the jurisdiction of the statute, and lease applications fall within this broad definition.

Fair Credit Reporting Act When a person applies for credit, an investigation usually is conducted into the applicant's financial history and affairs. The accuracy of the information is obviously very important in the decision-making process. In an effort to protect the consumer from inaccurate records and from improper denials of credit, Congress passed the Fair Credit Reporting Act in 1970, 15 U.S.C. 1681 et seq. This act has very broad provisions designed to ensure that the person being investigated is being given the benefit of honest and accurate information, which can be used in a meaningful manner. The purpose of the statute is to protect the reputations of consumers. It gives consumers the right to fair treatment by businesses by respecting the confidentiality, accuracy, relevancy, and proper utilization of credit information.

The act prohibits the use of obsolete material in any credit report. It also requires that the consumer be given written notice *beforehand* that an investigation will, or might, be conducted. The consumer has the right to discover the types of information in the credit record as well as the sources of the information and to find out who has received the information during the previous six months (or the previous two years, if the information was received by a potential employer).

If the consumer disagrees with the information contained in the records, the consumer can notify the reporting company of the disagreement, and the reporting company must reinvestigate the challenged material. If the reinvestigation shows that the original information was not accurate, it must be changed to reflect the truth. If the reinvestigation supports the original information's accuracy, the consumer must be so notified; the consumer then may submit a written explanation of the information. This written statement *must* be included in the files and provided to any potential creditors.

Fair Debt Collection Practices Act   As a final protection of consumers in the credit area, Congress passed the Fair Debt Collection Practices Act in 1977. This act is intended to eliminate the threatening, harassing, and abusive debt collection practices of the past. No longer may a collector make excessive numbers of phone calls or harassing phone calls to the debtor. No longer may a collector visit the debtor's neighbors, telling them that the debtor is a "deadbeat" who fails to repay debts and obligations.

Debt collectors Businesses that collect accounts due and payable but do *not* extend the credit being collected.

The act applies only to **debt collectors** (collection agencies), not to the actual creditor. Under the law, the debt collector may not bother the debtor at inconvenient times, such as during working hours or very late at night. If the debtor informs the collector that he or she has an attorney, the collector may communicate *only* with that attorney, not with the debtor; and the debt collector may not use any collection techniques deemed to be unfair, deceptive, or harassing. Should the collector violate these rules, the debtor can sue for damages and normally will collect a fairly substantial verdict.

The following case discusses the interesting question of whether a state university's withholding of a college transcript is within the statute's jurisdiction.

Juras v. Aman Collection Service, Inc.
829 F.2d 739 (9th Cir. 1987)

FACTS   Juras, the debtor-plaintiff, brought an action against a state university for, inter alia, withholding a transcript containing a description of courses taken and grades received. The transcript was held as "security" against an outstanding debt.

ISSUE   Is a college transcript a "security" and thus subject to the FDCPA?

HOLDING   No.

REASONING   Security refers to "property belonging to a debtor that provides some assurance of repayment." A transcript, on the other hand, is a reflection of a service performed by the university. If a transcript could be considered property, it would be owned by the university and not by Juras.

Product Safety

The area of product safety has become increasingly important. Consumers who are injured by defectively manufactured, designed, or packaged products have a number of different possible remedies to choose from—some at common law, some under the Uniform Commercial Code, and some under recently enacted federal statutes.

Magnuson-Moss Warranty Act–Consumer Product Waranty Act   The Magnuson-Moss Warranty Act–Consumer Product Warranty Act, discussed in Chapter 21, requires that the retailer disclose to the consumer the types of warranties provided in the sale of consumer goods. The disclosure must be made at the time of the sale. This statute has done a great deal to minimize, if not to eliminate, the use of hidden disclaimers of warranties.

Consumer Product Safety Act   In 1972, the Consumer Product Safety Act, 15 U.S.C. 2051 et seq., became law. This act was designed to protect consumers from injuries resulting from the use of dangerous consumer goods. The act also created the Consumer Product Safety Commission, which encourages the following endeavors:

1. research into the causes and the possible prevention of consumer product-related injuries
2. the development of uniform safety standards in consumer products
3. the development of comparison standards for consumers so that the relative safety of different products can be compared

Enforcement and Remedies

Each of these consumer protection statutes provides for different remedies or enforcement provisions. For example, the Federal Consumer Credit Protection Act has no provision for the consumer to collect damages if the creditor fails to comply with the provisions of the law. However, the creditor is subject to a penalty of twice the finance charge, with a minimum of $100 and a maximum of $1000, plus attorneys' fees.

The Fair Debt Collection Practices Act is enforced by the Federal Trade Commission. If a debt collector violates the provisions of this act, the injured, harassed, or otherwise harmed consumer may recover damages plus attorney's fees. In addition, if the *collector* sues the consumer to collect on a debt, and the consumer can prove that the suit itself is harassing or otherwise improper, the consumer can recover attorney's fees, and the suit will be dismissed. The commission has the power to ban consumer products that it determines to be hazardous. Using that power, the Commission has banned unstable refuse bins, extremely flammable contact adhesives, lead-containing paint, products containing asbestos, and certain all-terrain vehicles.

ENVIRONMENTAL PROTECTION

In many areas of the United States, the environment has taken a great deal of abuse. For many years, the sheer size of the country and the ease of migration contributed to the decline of the nation's environment. If an area became too dirty, crowded, or polluted for a comfortable life, the residents could simply pack up their belongings and move to a new, cleaner, less crowded area. As the population grew and the land began to fill up, such migration became less of an option. When all of the free homestead lands were finally occupied, the ability to move west and then start afresh virtually ended. For the first time, people were forced to remain in an environment after it had become fouled.

Some of the horror stories about the environment are almost legendary. Los Angeles has been noted for its smog. Akron, Ohio, smells like burning rubber; when the wind is right, Akron can be smelled before it is seen from the highway. From about twenty miles away, Gary, Indiana, looks like a large gray mushroom on the horizon. Pittsburgh was once infamous for its soot and black skies. And Cleveland's *river* once caught on fire! However, the situation is far from hopeless. Any recent visitor to either Cleveland or Pittsburgh can attest to what is possible if the local citizens decide to re-create a pleasant environment.

Congress has "helped" to persuade businesses that they should cooperate with the citizenry in re-creating a livable environment. For the past several decades, federal environmental regulation has been increasing. We will discuss some of the more important of these laws in this section.

National Environmental Policy Act

The National Environmental Policy Act (NEPA) became law in 1970. This act has two major components. First, it established the Council on Environmental Quality (CEQ), an advisory council that operates under the president. The purpose of the CEQ is to help ensure that the various environmental laws are obeyed. The CEQ has no actual powers of enforcement; rather, it advises the president on environmental policy. The actual task of enforcing federal environmental regulations falls to the Environmental Protection Agency (EPA), which was established by executive order in 1970. The EPA also sets national pollution standards.

The second major component of NEPA is the requirement that before any federal laws, recommendations, or activities that may affect the environment can be undertaken, an *environmental impact statement* must be prepared. At the very least, the environmental impact statement must do the following:

1. describe the anticipated impact the proposed conduct will have on the environment

2. describe any *unavoidable* consequences of the conduct

3. examine possible alternative methods of achieving the desired goals

4. distinguish between long-term and short-term environmental effects
5. describe resource commitments that could not be reversed by the conduct

Once the statement is prepared, the EPA must analyze and evaluate the proposed conduct from an environmental perspective. In addition, other interested parties (local governments, citizens' groups, and the like) can comment on the proposal and their feelings about it. Only after all this has been done and the plan has been approved can the federal proposal proceed.

In the following case, the lack of a proper environmental impact statement prevented federal action.

Natural Resources Defense Council, Inc. v. *Morton*
458 F.2d 827 (D.C. Cir. 1972)

FACTS   The Department of the Interior planned to sell some offshore oil lands for development. In connection with the sale, an environmental impact statement was prepared by Morton, the secretary of the interior. The Natural Resources Defense Council, a citizens' group, objected to the environmental impact statement, arguing that the statement failed to adequately explore available alternatives.

ISSUE   How fully must an environmental impact statement examine alternatives under NEPA?

HOLDING   Since the environmental impact statement is intended to be the environmental source material for decision making, it must fully examine obvious alternatives.

REASONING   The statement prepared by the Department of the Interior discussed problems presented by possible oil pollution, but that was the only thing discussed in detail. It failed to discuss the effect of the sale in meeting energy needs and its effect on market prices. It also failed to fully detail the alternatives raised within the report. The statement need not be exhaustive, but it must contain sufficient information to allow a reasonable weighing of the factors involved and a reasonable decision based on those factors. The court granted an injunction until the department could prepare an adequate environmental impact statement.

Air

Pollution   Impurities, dirt, or contamination.

Clean Air Act and Amendments   Congress passed the Clean Air Act in 1963. This act was designed to provide federal assistance to the various states in combating multistate air **pollution**. The primary aim of the law was to control air pollution at its source, which was generally viewed as a *local* problem, although one with wide-ranging effects. Since the problem was local in nature, the solutions were to be developed by state and local governments. However, it quickly became apparent that the legislature had not gone far enough in the original law. As a result, various changes in the act were introduced over the years.

The act was first amended in 1963, in the Clean Air Act of 1963, and next in 1965 in the Motor Vehicle Air Pollution Control Act, followed by the Clean Air Act of 1966. Still dissatisfied, Congress quickly followed with the Air Quality Act of 1967, the Clean Air Amendments of 1970, the Energy Supply and Environmental Coordination Act of 1974 (ESECA), and the 1977 amendments to the Clean Air Act. The 1990 amendments to the statute deal with four main areas: acid rain, alternative fuel sources, smog, and toxic industrial emissions. As a result of this legislation, the United States will have greatly cleaned its air by the time it enters the twenty-first century.

The total coverage of the Clean Air Act and its various amendments is substantially beyond the scope of this book. A review of some of its major goals, however, is appropriate and relevant. For example, the 1970 amendments demanded that automobile emissions of carbon monoxide and hydrocarbons had to be reduced 90 percent by 1975. This was a direct effort to combat the increasingly prevalent smog problem in urban areas. The 1977 amendments were designed to *maintain* air quality that exceeded federal standards and to *improve* air quality that fell below federal standards in urban areas.

The following case shows one way in which these laws have been used.

Ethyl Corp. v. Environmental Protection Agency
541 F.2d 1 (D.C. Cir. 1976)

FACTS   Under the Clean Air Act, the EPA is empowered to regulate gasoline additives that are considered a danger to public health. As one step in this direction, the EPA ordered annual reductions in the lead content in gasoline. Ethyl Corporation was a major producer of gasoline additives that increased octane rating. It objected to the reductions in lead ordered by the EPA.

ISSUE   Was the EPA's conduct in ordering a reduction in lead additives to gasoline an abuse of its discretion?

HOLDING   No. The EPA acted in a proper manner and obeyed all the procedural rules it needed to follow.

REASONING   Environmental protection is a developing field. The agencies that must protect the environment are forced to decide on the basis of predictions based on less than complete evidence. Looking at both sides of the issue, the EPA had carefully examined the issue of public health with regard to lead additives to gasoline. On the basis of this examination, the EPA determined that lead additives endanger public health. The court had to *presume* that the agency acted properly unless contrary evidence was produced. After reviewing the evidence, the court could not say that the EPA had acted improperly, and so the ruling was upheld.

Other regulations deal with aircraft emissions, "stationary emission sources" (smokestacks and the like), and the use of lead and other additives in fuel. In addition, various national standards exist for a number of major pollutants, as well as guidelines for the acceptable levels of each of them. In addition, the nation has been divided into a number of "atmospheric regions," each of which is expected to develop its own plan to attain the desired levels of compliance with these rules and regulations.

Noise Control Act In 1972, Congress found that noise presents an increasing danger to the nation's health and welfare. Although the primary responsibility for noise control rests with the states, federal action was essential because of the need to deal with the problem uniformly. The administrator of the Environmental Protection Agency has the power to set noise emission standards for products distributed in interstate commerce, standards for railroad noise and motor carrier noise, and standards for the labeling of products that emit noise.

The following case demonstrates the reach of our nation's noise control law.

Recreation Vehicle Industry Association v. Environmental Protection Agency
653 F.2d 562 (D.C. Cir. 1981)

FACTS The EPA failed to include motor homes on its published list of major noise sources. When the EPA attempted to control the noise emissions of motor homes by classifying them as "medium and heavy trucks" the motor home association sued the EPA for attempting to regulate motor homes when they were not mentioned as a major source of noise.

ISSUE Could the EPA regulate motor home noise?

HOLDING Yes.

REASONING The EPA did list medium and heavy trucks as a major source of noise. Although motor homes were not specifically mentioned, neither were fire engines, trash-removal vehicles, cement-mixers, or many other kinds of specialized vehicles that could be considered under the broad category of "medium and heavy trucks." The vast majority of motor homes are built on medium or heavy truck frames; therefore, motor homes are included.

Water *Clean Water Act* Most people who are aware of federal regulations concerning water pollution seem to believe the Clean Water Act of 1972, 33 U.S.C. 1251 et seq., was the first federal water pollution law. In fact, Congress began to regulate water quality in 1886 with the River and Harbor Act. The River and Harbor Act required that anyone dumping refuse into any navigable waters had to have a permit, and the permit limited the refuse that could be dumped. The act was amended in 1899, and in 1965 Congress passed the Federal Water Pollution Control Act to further strengthen these previous laws by expanding the power of the federal government in limiting any dumpings in navigable waterways.

The 1972 Clean Water Act was designed to clean up America's waters. The act set timetables for compliance with its various goals. These timetables were pushed back by amendments to the act passed in 1977. The act includes the following goals:

1. to make the waters safe for swimming and recreational use
2. to protect types of wildlife that rely on the waters
3. to eliminate dumping in the waterways
4. to mandate use of the "best available technology" by governmental and industrial groups that discharge pollutants into the waterways during the interim until all such dumpings and discharges are banned

To date, the goals have not been satisfactorily met, but some progress has been made. The statute was further amended in 1981 to include municipal waste water treatment construction grants.

Safe Drinking Water Act   The Safe Drinking Water Act, passed in 1986, charges the Environmental Protection Agency with the duty to establish national standards for drinking water. This is another example of federalism at work: The EPA sets the standards and the states enforce those standards.

Land

Public domain   Lands that are open to public use.

The protection and preservation of land has been the most obvious area of federal environmental regulation. As early as the presidency of Theodore Roosevelt, there was concern for some protection of the environment and for some preservation of America's natural resources. The **public domain,** land owned and/or controlled by the federal government, comprises nearly 725 million acres; to put this into some perspective, federally controlled land, national parks, and wildlife refuges occupy about as much land as is contained in the subcontinent of India.

In addition to the obvious federal regulation and control of these federal lands, a number of federal statutes regulate how private land can be used and what can be used on private land. We will discuss some of the more important of these regulations here.

Toxic Substances Control Act   Congress passed the Toxic Substances Control Act in 1976, 15 U.S.C. 2601 et seq. The act had two major goals. The first was to regulate the use of chemicals known to be toxic in nature. The second, and more important, goal was to create a method for testing new chemical compounds. Under this second aspect, the manufacturers of any new compounds were to determine what effect the compound might have on people or on the environment before the compound could be made available for public use. This portion of the act has done a great deal of good by preventing the introduction of potentially toxic substances into the streams of commerce and showing the harmlessness of some other new substances currently being used.

The following case demonstrates the importance of the testing provisions contained in the statute.

Ausimont U.S.A., Inc. v. Environmental Protection Agency
838 F.2d 93 (3d Cir. 1988)

FACTS   Chemical manufacturers petitioned for review of the EPA's action requiring the manufacturers to conduct extensive testing of chemical substances known as fluoroalkenes in order to ascertain their potential for harm. The manufacturers contended that neither the existence of toxicity in any known threatening amounts nor harm from exposure to the substances was known, and therefore such an expensive procedure was not justified.

ISSUE   Does the statute provide the EPA with sufficient discretion to mandate the testing?

HOLDING   Yes.

REASONING   The court found: "We can agree with petitioners that Congress did not intend EPA to direct expensive experimentation based on mere speculation . . . but . . . Congress chose . . . to deal with the pervasive nature of scientific uncertainty and the inherent limitations of scientific knowledge by vesting in the Administrator the discretion to deal with uncertainty in each case." The action of the EPA is not unreasonable.

Federal Insecticide, Fungicide, and Rodenticide Act   In 1947, Congress passed a law, 7 U.S.C. 136, to regulate the use of insecticides, fungicides, and rodenticides—substances used to kill insects, fungi, and rodents, respectively. This act was amended and strengthened in 1972 when the Federal Environmental Pesticide Control Act was passed. These two laws are designed to regulate the production and use of insecticides and related products to protect the environment.

Solid Waste Disposal Act   Congress decided in 1965 to encourage recycling of solid wastes and at the same time to discourage their improper disposal. To this end, the Solid Waste Disposal Act, 42 U.S.C. 6901 et seq., became law. The three main aspects of this act are (1) federal encouragement of recycling and other uses of solid waste, (2) federal aid and control in setting up new technology for efficient disposal of unusable waste, and (3) prohibition of future open dumping on the land and elimination of present open dumps. Included in this area are the selection and treatment of landfills, the discovery of uses for waste products, and federal aid to local governments in handling waste products. The statute was amended in 1970, 1976, and 1978.

YOU BE THE JUDGE

A state is planning to build a toxic waste incinerator in a previously selected location. The selected site is approximately halfway between two major cities in the state. The closest community to the selected site has a population composed primarily of minority group members. Several national leaders of various minority groups are leading a demonstration against the construction of the incinerator, alleging that its construction is a form of "toxic racism."

The local residents are seeking an injunction against construction of the incinerator, alleging racism and violation of their civil rights in selecting this particular site. Should an injunction be issued in this case?

Source: "A whiff of discrimination?", Michael Satchell, *U.S. News & World Report,* May 4, 1992, page 34.

Resource Conservation and Recovery Act   Congress was so pleased with the gains realized under the Solid Waste Disposal Act that in 1976 it enacted the Resource Conservation and Recovery Act, 42 U.S.C. 6901 et seq. Once again, the target was solid waste. Under this act, the EPA issues permits for solid waste disposal at federal facilities and also reviews state action in treating nonfederal solid waste disposal.

Superfund   Reacting to the tremendous pressure brought by environmental groups to solve the problem of hazardous waste disposal sites and the potentially serious adverse effects they will have on the future health of the American population, the Congress enacted the Superfund in 1980. The fund's proper name is the Comprehensive Environmental Response, Compensation, and Liability Act (CERCLA), 43 U.S.C. 9601. Under the act, the president is authorized to clean up areas that were once hazardous waste disposal sites. The manner in which this is accomplished is by utilizing the Hazardous Substance Response Trust Fund. The trust is funded by the penalties the government receives when it successfully sues the firms that caused the damage. The statute was amended in 1986, thereby extending and expanding the jurisdiction of the EPA.

Enforcement and Remedies

The enforcement provisions of the federal environmental protection laws are somewhat varied. Under NEPA, interested groups can force compliance with the EPA. They can force the filing of an environmental impact statement and then a full public hearing before the objectionable conduct can be carried out. Injunctive relief until compliance is the basic remedy here.

Under the Clean Air Act and its amendments, the primary means of forcing compliance is through a suit filed by citizens or by a government agency. As a general rule, damages are recoverable only under a common law nuisance action, not under federal law.

Under the different water pollution statutes, citizens can enforce the law by suing to seek compliance, and a guilty firm can be fined; again, damages normally would have to be recovered under common law property right principles. However, the fines for noncompliance can be quite heavy. A first offense carries a minimum fine of $25,000. Subsequent convictions carry fines of up to $50,000 per day and up to two years in prison.

SUMMARY

Over the past several years, a growing body of law has been concerned with consumer protection. Laws protecting the environment have also grown tremendously. These two areas reflect a new trend in federal legislation—a move to improve the quality of life.

In the area of consumer protection, legislation has taken two major directions: consumer credit protection and product safety. The consumer credit protection area requires, among other things, that a full disclosure of credit and finance terms and charges be given to the consumer; that the consumer be told how to object to billing errors *without penalty;* that all consumers be treated fairly in credit applications, without regard to age, sex, race, or marital status; that the consumer be allowed to examine and explain a credit report; and that the consumer be protected from unfair debt collection practices. The area of product safety is addressed by the Magnuson-Moss Warranty Act and the Consumer Product Safety Act. Both are designed to protect consumers from defective products and to inform the consumer about where and how defective products can be reported.

Environmental protection is aimed at preserving and protecting the nation's air, water, and land from pollution, waste, and abuse. The Clean Air Act is designed to ensure that we can continue to breathe in the future. The Clean Water Act is aimed at making our waterways suitable for recreational use and safe for fish and fowl. Land protection aims at regulating solid waste disposal and reducing toxic substances. To implement these protections, the Environmental Protection Agency was created to oversee the National Environmental Policy Act.

DISCUSSION QUESTIONS

1. A credit card customer disagrees with the monthly bill received from the company and then takes the proper steps in objecting to it. What may the company do? What may the company not do?

2. Fred was denied credit with a local store. The denial was based on a poor credit report the store received from the local credit bureau. Fred believes that the information in the credit bureau files is inaccurate. What are Fred's available rights in this matter?

3. David is several months behind in his payments to Sam's Store. Sam's turns the account over to Debtor Collection Service (DCS) for collection. DCS calls David's employer asking for help in collecting the bill, calls David late at night asking for payment, and interviews

David's neighbors about any money he may owe them. What may David do?

4. Julia received a loan the terms of which are in violation of the Federal Consumer Credit Protection Act. If Julia sues the creditor for these violations, what can she recover?

5. The Clean Air Act was amended in 1970. One of the amendments dealt with automobile exhaust emissions. What was the stated goal of this amendment?

6. Federal regulation of water pollution began with the River and Harbor Act of 1886. What did this act do in its efforts to minimize water pollution in federal waters?

7. What are the major goals of the Clean Water Act of 1972?

8. How has the Toxic Substances Control Act of 1976 been used to protect the environment from potentially toxic substances?

9. Under the provisions of the National Environmental Policy Act, an environmental impact statement must be filed with the Environmental Protection Agency before certain federal conduct is permitted. What must this environmental impact statement include?

10. If a firm is found guilty of violating the Clean Water Act, what possible penalties does it face for a first offense? For any subsequent offenses?

CASE PROBLEMS

1. Representatives of Associates Discount made a number of telephone calls to Callarama, to Callarama's wife, and to several of Callarama's relatives in trying to collect an unpaid account owed to Associates Discount. The phone calls were threatening, harassing, and obscene. They were also malicious and damaging. Callarama sued Associates for damages, and Associates moved to dismiss, alleging that Callarama had no legal remedies available. What should be the result? (*Callarama v. Associates Discount Corp. of Delaware, Inc.*, 329 N.Y.S.2d 711 [1972].)

2. The Tennessee Valley Authority was building a dam on the Little Tennessee River. If the dam were completed, an endangered species of fish would be irreparably injured. Several environmental agencies attempted to prevent the completion of the dam. Could the dam be halted by the courts once it was nearing completion? (*Tennessee Valley Authority v. Hill*, 437 U.S. 153 [1978].)

3. New York City enacted an ordinance regulating permissible levels of exhaust emissions for taxicabs. The taxi owners challenged the ordinance, arguing that the federal Clean Air Act had overridden the local ordinance. Is this contention correct? (*Allway Taxi, Inc. v. City of New York*, 340 F. Supp. 1120 [S.D. N.Y. 1973].)

4. The Consumer Product Safety Act calls for product safety to be specified in terms of performance requirements rather than design requirements. The Consumer Product Safety Commission (CPSC) ordered that all power lawn mowers produced after 1981 must have a "blade-control system" that prevents the blade from turning after the controls are released. Southland Mower Co. challenged this rule, alleging that it was a design requirement rather than a performance requirement and therefore beyond the authority of the CPSC. What should be the result? (*Southland Mower Co. v. Consumer Product Safety Commission*, 619 F.2d 499 [5th Cir. 1980].)

5. The Attorney General of Colorado sued a health club for allegedly violating the Colorado Consumer Protection Act. According to the Attorney General, the health club has periodically advertised, through various means, in an effort to increase memberships. On occasion these advertisements have offered special reduced rates and/or free memberships to people making further inquiries. However, according to the complaint, there were "strings" attached to accepting the reduced rates or the free memberships. The most common "string" was that the offer was tied to a regular membership, with full fees. As a result, the Attorney General alleged that the club used bait-and-switch advertising and was, therefore, engaged in deceptive trade practices in violation of the statute. The health club defended by complaining that the statute as written was unconstitutionally vague, failing to indicate precisely which practices were forbidden and which were permissible. The trial court agreed with the health club, and dismissed the complaint. The state then appealed to the Colorado Supreme Court.

What action should the Colorado Supreme Court take in this matter? (*People* v. *Gym of America, Inc.*, 493 P.2d 660 [Colo. 1972]).

6. Perez was accused of loan sharking (making usurious loans, usually very short-term with high daily interest) and was convicted of violating the Federal Consumer Credit Protection Act by engaging in his loan sharking activities. Perez challenged the constitutionality of the federal statute and the ability of the federal government to prosecute him for an activity that was purely local in nature and thus exempt from federal regulation. Can Perez be convicted of a violation of the Federal Consumer Credit Protection Act for a purely local activity? (*Perez* v. *United States*, 91 S.Ct. 1357 [1971].)

7. Charles entered into a contract with Drauss and signed the agreement at the appropriate place. The contract was printed on both the front and the back of the form that Charles signed, but the signature line was on the front. However, the text of the front incorporated the back side of the document by reference. Charles later objected to the terms of the contract and sought relief under the Federal Consumer Credit Protection Act. Drauss defended by arguing that the terms on the back were incorporated by reference and further that Charles had read none of the contract, so Charles could not object to that portion on the back. How should this case be resolved? (*Charles* v. *Drauss Co., Ltd.*, 572 F.2d 544 [5th Cir. 1978].)

8. Arco suffered an accidental oil spill at an off-shore drilling site. Arco complied fully with the federal reporting and cleaning requirements for such a spill, but after this was done, the region was still polluted by the accidentally spilled oil. The federal government assessed monetary damages against Arco, with the money to be used to pay for additional cleanup of the area. Arco objected to this assessment for damages when there was absolutely no showing of fault or negligence by Arco in relation to the spill. The government based its right to

make the assessment on the Federal Water Pollution Control Act Amendments of 1972. Should the government be able to assess Arco for the cleanup in this set of circumstances? (*United States* v. *Atlantic Richfield Co.*, 429 F. Supp. 830 [E.D. Pa. 1977].)

9. Louisiana Power & Light (LPL) acquired property for the right-of-way in order to install transmission lines along the Mississippi River. Once the right-of-way property was acquired, LPL filed an application for permits with the U.S. Army Corps of Engineers to ensure that there was no violation of either the Rivers and Harbors Act or the Clean Water Act. The Corps of Engineers reviewed the applications and determined that there was no significant environmental threat, and thus, there was no need for LPL to prepare an environmental impact statement for the project. Notice of the pending issuance of permits was announced publicly, and comments were invited. No objections were made until the permits were issued, at which point a nonprofit environmental protection group filed suit to block construction of the transmission lines. According to this group, the Corps of Engineers' decision to permit the group to discharge "fill" material (as called for in one of the permits) violated the provisions of the Clean Water Act, and the issuance of the permit was arbitrary and capricious. The trial court dismissed the complaint on the grounds that the Corps of Engineers had been neither arbitrary nor capricious, and the environmental group appealed to the Fifth Circuit Court of Appeals. What decision should this court reach? (*Save Our Wetlands, Inc.* v. *Sands*, 718 F.2d 1096 [5th Cir. 1983].)

10. A trade association of lawn mower manufacturers sought a court order voiding the designation of lawn mowers as a "major source of noise" and, therefore, subject to the Noise Control Act. What should result? Why? (*Outdoor Power Equipment Institute, Inc.* v. *Environmental Protection Agency*, 438 F. Supp. 1092 [D.C. 1977].)

C H A P T E R   48

Labor and
Fair Employment
Practices

O U T L I N E

LABOR

Federal Statutes

Unions are a commonplace fact of life in the United States today. But it was not always so. Violence and bloody battles between employers and pro-union workers marked the rise of unionism in this country. The courts were as hostile as most employers to unions. In fact, in the 1800s and early 1900s, both state and federal courts viewed workers' concerted activities (strikes, **picketing,** and the like) as common law criminal conspiracies, tortious interference with contract, or antitrust violations. Although Congress had passed the Clayton Act in 1914 in part to shield unions from liability under the antitrust laws, subsequent Supreme Court decisions had narrowed this newly won statutory protection. Congress responded to these developments by passing the Norris-LaGuardia Act in 1932. This act immunized certain activities—peaceful refusals to work, **boycotts,** and picketing, for example—from federal court action. The act barred the issuance of injunctions in the context of labor disputes and thus allowed employees to organize and to engage in collective bargaining free from employer or court intervention as long as the concerted activity did not involve **wildcat strikes,** violence, sabotage, trespass, and the like. The Norris-LaGuardia Act signaled a policy aimed at keeping the courts out of the labor field. Free from regulation, then, employees and employers fought for their respective goals by using the economic weapons appropriate to each side: from the unions, strikes, picketing, and boycotts; and from the employer, discharges of employees.

Picketing Union activity in which persons stand near a place of work affected by an organizational drive or a strike in order to influence workers on union causes.

Boycotts Concerted refusals to deal with firms in order to disrupt the business of those firms.

Wildcat strikes Unauthorized withholdings of services of labor during the term of a contract.

The Wagner Act (1935) Congress passed the Wagner Act, also called the National Labor Relations Act, in 1935. This legislation heralded the beginning of an affirmative—as opposed to a neutral—approach to labor organizations. In Section 7 of the Wagner Act, Congress approved the right of employees to organize themselves and "to form, join, or assist labor organizations, to bargain collectively through representatives of their own choosing, and to engage in concerted activities for the purpose of collective bargaining or other mutual aid or protection."

The right to refrain from engaging in concerted activities is protected as well. Buttressing Section 7 is Section 8, which enumerates employer **unfair labor practices,** such as coercion of or retaliation against employees who exercise their Section 7 rights, domination of unions by employers, discrimination in employment (hiring and firing, for instance) designed to discourage union activities, and refusals by employers to bargain collectively and in good faith with employee representatives (that is, with unions). Section 9 sets out the process by which the employees in the appropriate bargaining unit can conduct secret elections for choosing their representative in the collective bargaining process. The Wagner Act also established a new administrative agency, the National Labor Relations Board (NLRB), to oversee such elections and also to investigate and remedy unfair labor practices. Section 10 permits ju-

Unfair labor practices Employer *or* union activities that are prohibited by law as injurious to labor policies.

dicial review of any NLRB order in the appropriate federal circuit court of appeals. A 1937 case, *NLRB* v. *Jones & Laughlin Steel Corp.*, upheld the constitutionality of the Wagner Act.[1]

The Taft-Hartley Act (1947)   Unions grew appreciably in size and power after the passage of the Wagner Act. As a result, the power balance between employees and employers became so "pro-union" that in 1947 Congress passed legislation meant to counter the perceived excesses of the NLRB and pervasive court deference to its orders. The Taft-Hartley Act, also called the Labor-Management Relations Act (LMRA), attempted to curb union excesses by amending Section 8 of the Wagner Act to prohibit certain unfair labor practices by unions, including engaging in **secondary boycotts,** forcing an employer to discriminate against employees on the basis of their union affiliation or lack of union affiliation, refusing to bargain in good faith, requiring an employer to pay for services not actually performed by an employee ("featherbedding"), and **recognitional picketing.** Congress also amended Section 7 to allow employees to refrain from joining a union and participating in its collective activities.

In addition, the Taft-Hartley Act cut back the authority of the NLRB by separating its functions: The Office of General Counsel took on prosecution of the board's unfair labor practices cases, leaving to the five-person board the decision-making (or adjudicatory) function. This significantly changed the nature of the NLRB, which, under the Wagner Act, had served simultaneously as both prosecutor and decision maker. The Taft-Hartley Act also empowered courts of appeals to set aside NLRB findings in unfair labor practices cases, authorized district courts to issue labor injunctions requested by the NLRB for the purpose of stopping unfair labor practices, set out the possibility of fines and imprisonment for anyone resisting NLRB orders, and provided for civil remedies for private parties damaged by secondary boycotts or various union activities.

Other sections protect the employer's right of free speech (by refusing to characterize as unfair labor practices an employer's expressions of its opinions about unionism when they contain no threats of reprisal), preserve the employees' rights to engage in peaceful **informational picketing,** and prohibit "closed shop" agreements (contracts that obligate the employer to hire and retain only union members). "Union shop" clauses (provisions that require an employee, after being hired, to join a union in order to retain his or her job) are legal. The Taft-Hartley Act also created a Federal Mediation and Conciliation Service for settling disputes between labor and management. To foster conciliation efforts further, the act established a "cooling-off" period before strikes could occur in certain circumstances. It also preserved the power of states, under their "right-to-work" laws, to invalidate other union devices designed to consolidate the unions' hold on workers.

Secondary boycotts   Union activities meant to pressure parties not involved in the labor dispute and to influence the affected employer.

Recognitional picketing   Prohibited picketing in which a union attempts to force recognition of a union different from the currently certified bargaining representative.

Informational picketing   Picketing for the purpose of truthfully advising the public that an employer does not employ members of, or have a contract with, a labor organization.

[1]301 U.S. 1 (1937).

The Landrum-Griffin Act (1959) By the 1950s, Congress had unearthed substantial corruption among union leadership. Union members had been prejudiced by officers' plundering of union treasuries and by these officers' often tyrannical treatment of the rank-and-file members. In 1959, to end these abuses, Congress responded with the Landrum-Griffin Act, also called the Labor-Management Reporting and Disclosure Act (LMRDA). As this latter title suggests, the act requires extensive reporting of financial affairs, allows civil and criminal sanctions for financial wrongdoings by union officers, and mandates democratic procedures in the conduct of union affairs by providing a "bill of rights" for union members regarding elections and meetings. In addition, the Landrum-Griffin Act amended portions of the Taft-Hartley Act to outlaw "hot cargo" clauses (that is, provisions in contracts requiring the employer to cease doing business with nonunion companies).

The following recent case illustrates the scope of the LMRDA.

Sheet Metal Workers International Association v. Lynn
109 S.Ct. 639 (1989)

FACTS In June, 1981, Edward Lynn was elected to a three-year term as a business representative of Local 75 of the Sheet Metal Workers' International Association (the Local), an affiliate of the Sheet Metal Workers' International Association (the International). Lynn became instrumental in organizing fellow members of the Local who were concerned about a financial crisis plaguing the Local. These members, who called themselves the Sheet Metal Club Local 75 (the Club), published leaflets that demonstrated, on the basis of Department of Labor statistics, that the Local's officials had spent far more than had the officials of two other sheet metal locals in the area. The Club urged the Local's officials to reduce expenditures rather than increase dues to alleviate the Local's financial problems. Most of the Local's members apparently agreed, for they defeated three successive proposals to increase dues. Following the third vote, the Local's officials, including Lynn, requested action from the International's general president "to put this local on a sound financial basis." The general president placed the Local under a trusteeship and delegated to the trustee, Richard Hawkins, the authority "to supervise and direct" the affairs of the Local, "including, but not limited to, the authority to suspend local union . . . officers, business managers, or business representatives." Within a month of his appointment, Hawkins decided that a dues increase was needed to rectify the Local's financial situation. Recognizing that he lacked authority to impose a dues increase unilaterally, Hawkins submitted a proposal to that effect to the Local's executive board, which approved the proposal. A special meeting was convened to put the dues proposal to a membership vote. Prior to the meeting, Hawkins advised Lynn that he expected Lynn's support. Lynn responded that he first wanted a commitment to reduce expenditures, which Hawkins declined to provide. Lynn spoke in opposition to the dues proposal at the special meeting. In a secret ballot vote, the members defeated the proposal. Five days later, Hawkins notified Lynn that he was being removed "indefinitely" from his position as business representative specifically because of his outspoken opposition to the dues increase. After exhausting his intra-union remedies, Lynn brought suit in district court under Section 102 of the LMRDA, claiming that his removal from office violated the act's Title I free speech provision. The district court granted summary judgment for the International, reasoning that "[a] union member's statutory right to oppose union policies affords him no protection against dismissal from employment as an agent of the union because of such opposition." The court of appeals reversed, holding that the dismissed union employee was an elected, rather than an appointed, official and removal of the former "can only impede the democratic governance of the union." The court also rejected the contention that Lynn's removal had been valid because it had been carried out under the trusteeship, stating that a trustee may not remove an elected local officer "in retaliation for the exercise of a right protected by the LMRDA, such as free speech."

ISSUE   Did the removal of a business representative of the union, occasioned by his opposition to a dues increase, violate the business representative's free speech rights under the LMRDA?

HOLDING   Yes. The removal of an elected business agent, in retaliation for statements he had made at a union meeting in opposition to a dues increase sought by the union trustee, would violate the LMRDA.

REASONING   The legislation that evolved into Title I of the LMRDA, the "Bill of Rights of Members of Labor Organizations," was adopted as an amendment on the Senate floor by "legislators [who] feared that the bill did not go far enough because it failed to provide general protection to union members who spoke out against the union leadership." Designed to guarantee every member equal voting rights, rights of free speech and assembly, and a right to sue, the amendment was "aimed at enlarged protection for members of unions paralleling certain rights guaranteed by the Federal Constitution." In providing such protection, Congress sought to further the basic objective of the LMRDA: "ensuring that unions [are] democratically governed and responsive to the will of their memberships." The International and the Local argued that Lynn's Title I rights were not "infringed" because Lynn, like other members of the Local, had been free to undertake the following actions: Attending the special meeting, expressing his views on Hawkins's dues proposal, or casting his vote. Furthermore, Lynn had remained a member of the Local. Under this view, Lynn's status as an elected, rather than an appointed, official was essentially immaterial and the loss of union employment could not amount to a Title I violation. However, this argument is unpersuasive. Lynn attended the special meeting, expressed his views in opposition to Hawkins's dues proposal, and cast his vote. In taking these actions, Lynn "was exercising . . . membership right[s] protected by Section 101(a)." Given that Lynn was removed from his post as a direct result of his decision to express disagreement with Hawkins's dues proposal at the special meeting and that his removal presumably discouraged him from speaking out in the future, Lynn had paid a price for the exercise of his membership rights. The consequences of the removal of such an elected official are much different from LMRDA precedents that permitted newly elected officers to discharge the appointed staffs of the ousted incumbents. To begin with, the removal of an elected official like Lynn denies the union members the representative of their choice. Indeed, Lynn's removal deprived the membership of his leadership, knowledge, and advice at a critical time for the Local. His removal, therefore, hardly was "an integral part of ensuring a union administration's responsiveness to the mandate of the union election." Furthermore, the potential chilling effect on Title I free speech rights becomes more pronounced on the discharge of elected officials. Not only is the fired official likely to be chilled in the exercise of his or her own free speech rights, but so are the members who voted for him or her. Seeing Lynn removed from his post just five days after he had led the fight to defeat yet another dues increase proposal, other members of the Local may have concluded that one challenged the union's hierarchy, if at all, at one's peril. This is precisely what Congress had sought to prevent when it had passed the LMRDA, for it had "recognized that democracy would be assured only if union members are free to discuss union policies and criticize the leadership without fear of reprisal." Lynn's retaliatory removal therefore stated a cause of action under Section 102. The unions next contended that, even if the removal of an elected official for the exercise of his or her Title I rights ordinarily states a cause of action under Section 102, a different result obtained here because Lynn's removal had occurred during the trusteeship lawfully imposed under Title III of the LMRDA. However, nothing in the language of the LMRDA or its legislative history suggests that Congress intended Title I rights to fall by the wayside on the imposition of a trusteeship. Section 101(a)(3) of Title I guarantees to the members of a local union the right to vote on any dues increase, and, as the unions conceded at oral argument, this critical Title I right does not vanish with the imposition of a trusteeship. A trustee seeking to restore the financial stability of a local union through a dues increase thus is required to seek the approval of the union's members. In order to ensure that the union members' democratic right to decide on a dues proposal is meaningful, the right to exchange views on the advantages and disadvantages of such a measure must be protected. A trustee should not be able to control the debate over an issue that by statute is beyond his or her control. In the instant case, Lynn's statements concerning the proposed dues increase were entitled to protection. Nothing in the International's constitution suggests that the nature of Lynn's office changed once the trusteeship was imposed so as to obligate Lynn to support Hawkins's positions. Thus, at the special meeting, Lynn remained free to express the view apparently shared by a majority of the Local's members that the best solution to the Local's financial problems lay not in a dues increase but in a reduction of expenditures. Under these circumstances, Hawkins had violated Lynn's Title I rights under the LMRDA when he had removed Lynn from his post.

Scope   Taken together, these acts cover almost all employers and employees, excluding federal, state, and local government employers and employees; employers covered under the Railway Labor Act; agricultural workers; domestic workers; independent contractors; and most supervisors. Even though government workers are not covered, they can organize themselves under the authority of Executive Order 11491, entitled Labor-Management Relations in the Federal Service, promulgated in 1969. In addition, about two-thirds of the states have enacted laws permitting collective bargaining in the public sector for state and municipal employees. Such executive orders and statutes ordinarily forbid strikes by public employees (such as police officers and firefighters), but such strikes nevertheless have occurred in recent years. The arrival of collective bargaining in the public sector is fairly new, but it promises to have significant implications for the future as our economy becomes more service-oriented and the number of government employees proliferates.

Although it is impossible to describe fully the pervasive regulation of labor embodied in the Wagner Act, the Taft-Hartley Act, and the Landrum-Griffin Act, we will highlight a few of the more important issues.

Questions invariably arise when the employees select their bargaining representative. The Wagner Act sets forth the procedures that must be followed during this process. Briefly, these procedures include, on a required showing of employee interest, the union's petitioning for an election that will lead to its recognition as the exclusive bargaining representative of the employees. The NLRB decides whether the election has been conducted validly and, if so, certifies the union as the exclusive bargaining agent. The employer, who ordinarily resists the election-representation process, may attempt to "decertify" the union by arguing that the employees do not constitute an appropriate bargaining unit (that is, the employees have different duties, skills, or responsibilities) or that the union has engaged in unfair labor practices. The NLRB initially adjudicates such complaints, but the circuit courts of appeals can review final NLRB orders. In many cases, the employer prevails. Not to be outdone, unions usually have alleged unfair labor practices by employers during the certification process. In other words, these affairs often become real donnybrooks of contradictory allegations because each side is fighting for the economic power signified by union representation or the lack of such representation.

The certification process may raise property issues as well, since organizers ordinarily wish to distribute union literature to employees in firms where they hope ultimately to hold a certification election. The right to engage in protected activity mandated by the Wagner Act thus clashes with the employer's property rights and the efficient conduct of its business. Board decisions generally invalidate the soliciting of employees and the distributing of literature during working hours and in working areas as long as such restrictions do not unduly interfere with the free exercise of employee rights guaranteed by the Wagner Act. As mentioned earlier, during this process, it is likewise permissible for the employer to state its views about unionism unless these statements convey a threat against pro-union employees or promise a benefit to anti-union employees.

The next case involves the court's resolution of these very issues.

Lechmere, Inc. v. *National Labor Relations Board*
60 U.S.L.W. 4145 (January 27, 1992)

FACTS   Lechmere, Inc. (Lechmere) owns and operates a retail store located in a shopping plaza in a large metropolitan area. Lechmere is also part owner of the plaza's parking lot, which is separated from a public highway by a 46-foot wide grassy strip, almost all of which is public property. In a campaign to organize Lechmere employees, nonemployee union organizers placed handbills on the windshields of cars parked in the employees' part of the parking lot. After Lechmere had denied the organizers access to the lot, they distributed handbills and picketed from the grassy strip. In addition, they were able to contact directly 20 percent of the employees. The union filed an unfair labor practice charge with the National Labor Relations Board (the Board), alleging that Lechmere had violated the NLRA by barring the organizers from its property. An administrative law judge ruled in the union's favor, recommending that the Board order Lechmere to cease and desist from barring the organizers from the parking lot. The Board affirmed, and the court of appeals enforced the Board's order. The Supreme Court granted Lechmere's petition for certiorari.

ISSUE   Had Lechmere committed an unfair labor practice by barring nonemployee union organizers from its property?

HOLDING   No. By its plain terms, the NLRA confers rights only on employees, not on unions or their nonemployee organizers. Thus, as a rule, an employer cannot be compelled to allow nonemployee organizers onto his or her property. Only when reasonable access to employees is infeasible does it become appropriate to balance Section 7 and private property rights, and the facts in this case do not justify application of this inaccessibility exception.

REASONING   Section 7 of the NLRA provides in relevant part that "employees shall have the right to self-organization, to form, join, or assist labor organizations." Section 8(a)(1) of the act, in turn, makes it an unfair labor practice for an employer "to interfere with, restrain, or coerce employees in the exercise of rights guaranteed in [Section 7]." By its plain terms, then, the NLRA confers rights only on employees, not on unions or their nonemployee organizers. In cases involving employee activities, the Board can balance the conflicting interests of employees to receive information on self-organization on the company's property from fellow employees during nonworking time with the employer's right to control the use of his or her property. Cases involving nonemployee activities, however, do not authorize the Board to engage in that same balancing. By reversing the Board's interpretation of the statute for failing to distinguish between the organizing activities of employees and nonemployees, the Court interpreted Section 7 as speaking to the issue of nonemployee access to an employer's property. Section 7 simply does not protect nonemployee union organizers except in the rare case where "the inaccessibility of employees makes ineffective the reasonable attempts by nonemployees to communicate with them through the usual channels." This reference to "reasonable" attempts represents a commonsense recognition that unions need not engage in extraordinary feats to communicate with inaccessible employees rather than endorsement of the view that the act protects "reasonable" trespasses. Where reasonable alternative means of access exist, Section 7 guarantees do not authorize trespasses by nonemployee organizers, even "under . . . reasonable regulations" established by the Board. To say that Supreme Court precedents require accommodation between employees and employers' rights is a true but incomplete statement, for the cases also go far in establishing the locus of that accommodation where nonemployee organizing is at issue. As long as nonemployee union organizers have reasonable access to employees outside an employer's property, the requisite accommodation has taken place. It is only where such access is infeasible (for example, in logging camps or mountain resort hotels) that it becomes necessary and proper to take the accommodation inquiry to a second level, balancing the employees and employers' rights. The Board's conclusion in this case that the union had no reasonable means short of trespass to make Lechmere's employees aware of its organizational efforts misapprehends the limited scope of this inaccessibility exception. Because the employees in this case do not reside outside Lechmere's property, they are presumptively not "beyond the reach" of the union's message. Indeed, the union's success in contacting a substantial percentage of them directly, via mailings, phone calls, and home visits suggests their accessibility. Such direct contact, of course, is not a necessary element of "reasonably effective" communication; signs or advertising also may suffice. Access to employees, not success in winning them over, is the critical issue—although success, or lack thereof, may be relevant in determining whether reasonable access exists. Because the union in this case had failed to establish the existence of any "unique obstacles" that had frustrated access to Lechmere's employees, the Board erred in concluding that Lechmere had committed an unfair labor practice by barring the nonemployee organizers from its property.

Once the bargaining representative has been empowered, the Wagner Act requires *good-faith bargaining* by both the employer and the union. This is, of course, a nebulous term; but, in essence, it mandates both sides' meeting and discussing certain issues with as much objectivity as possible. The duty to bargain in good faith does not absolutely presume agreement between the parties. Under this duty, an employer cannot bypass the union to deal directly with the employees.

The Wagner Act requires good-faith bargaining over "wages, hours, and other terms and conditions of employment." Basically, then, the duty to bargain covers only those topics that have a direct impact on the employees' job security. Decisions that are not essentially related to conditions of employment but rather are managerial decisions "which lie at the core of entrepreneurial control"[2] fail to suffice as mandatory bargaining subjects. Pay differentials for different shifts, piecework and incentive plans, transfers, fringe benefits, and severance pay would be mandatory subjects. It has been more difficult for courts to classify bonuses and meals provided by the employer. Managerial decisions to terminate the company's business or to shut down a plant are ordinarily *permissive,* or nonmandatory, subjects. However, an employer might be forced to bargain about the effects of such decisions, such as **severance pay,** which impinge on the "conditions of employment."

Although the labor laws view collective bargaining as the parties' meeting,

Severance pay Wages paid on termination of one's job.

[2]*Fibreboard Paper Products Corp.* v. *NLRB,* 379 U.S. 203, 223 (1964).

Lockouts Plant closings or other refusals by employers to furnish work to employees during labor disputes.

asserting their positions, stating their objections to the other party's position, and disclosing the information necessary for each side to arrive at an informed decision, both sides can permissibly use economic weapons outside the bargaining room. Hence, employee strikes or work stoppages and employer **lockouts** do not in themselves violate the duty to bargain in good faith. An employer's unilateral granting of a wage increase without notice to the union during the process of negotiations does constitute bad-faith bargaining, however. On the other hand, such unilateral changes made after bargaining has reached an impasse are legal.

The NLRB can require either side who has refused, directly or indirectly, to bargain in good faith to begin bargaining and to cease and desist from any unfair labor practice that has accompanied the "bad-faith" bargaining. The board also can use such powers for ending violations of any of the employer or union unfair labor practices enumerated earlier that have occurred outside the bargaining context. But NLRB orders are not self-enforcing and become law only when imposed by a federal circuit court of appeals. Because litigation is time consuming, these limitations on the NLRB's enforcement powers sometimes make policing the actions of maverick employers or unions difficult. Board hearings and resultant orders, if resisted, bring on court scrutiny. If the court affirms the NLRB order, the court issues an injunction. In the meantime, however, the allegedly unfair labor practices may have continued and may have successfully stifled the employer or employee interests at issue.

The following case illustrates the NLRB's power in enforcing the Wagner Act.

Pattern Makers' League of North America, AFL-CIO
v. National Labor Relations Board
473 U.S. 95 (1985)

FACTS The Pattern Makers' League of North America, AFL-CIO (the League), a labor union, provided in its constitution that resignations were not permitted during a strike or when a strike was imminent. The League had fined ten of its members who, in violation of this provision, had resigned during a strike and had returned to work. The National Labor Relations Board (the Board) held that these fines had been imposed in violation of Section 8 of the National Labor Relations Act, which states that a union commits an unfair labor practice if it restrains or coerces employees in the exercise of their Section 7 rights, including the right to "refrain from any or all [concerted] activities."

ISSUE Could the Board construe Section 8 as prohibiting the fining of employees who had tendered resignations under a union constitutional provision that made such resignations invalid?

HOLDING Yes. The Board's construction of Section 8 was reasonable in these circumstances and the Board thus had the power to prohibit the union's imposition of fines on the individuals who had resigned in violation of the union's constitution.

REASONING When employee members of a union refuse to support a strike (whether or not a rule prohibits returning to work during a strike), they are refraining from "concerted activity." Therefore, the League's imposing fines on these employees for returning to work restrained the exercise of their Section 7 rights. Indeed, if the terms *refrain* and *restrain or coerce* are interpreted literally, fining employees to enforce compliance with any union rule or policy would violate the act. Furthermore, the inconsistency between union restrictions of the right to resign and the well-established policy of voluntary unionism would support the Board's conclusion that the union's constitutional provision was invalid. The three arguments the union had advanced to support its actions—(1) union rules restricting the right to resign were protected by the proviso to Section 8(b)(1)(A), (2) the legislative history of the act showed that Congress had not intended to protect the right of union members to resign, and (3) labor unions should be allowed to restrict the right to resign because other voluntary associations are permitted to do so—warranted rejection. The statutory proviso clearly states that nothing in Section 8(b)(1)(A) shall "impair the right of a labor organization to prescribe its own rules with respect to the acquisition or retention of membership therein." However, the union's contention that because the constitutional provision in dispute had placed restrictions on the right to withdraw from the union, it had amounted to a "rul[e] with respect to the . . . retention of membership" within the meaning of the proviso was erroneous: Neither the Board nor the court had ever interpreted the proviso as allowing unions to make rules restricting the right to resign. Rather, the operative assumption had always been that "rules with respect to the . . . retention of membership" were those that provide for the expulsion of employees from the union. In addition, the legislative history of the Taft-Hartley Act was consistent with this interpretation, and this same rationale supported the striking down of the union's second argument. Decisional law formed the basis for the rejection of the union's third contention, since the Board's interpretation of the act takes precedence over common law statements about association members' rights. Hence, the prior judicial decisions relating to the fining of union members and the Board's consistent interpretation of Section 8(b)(1)(A) as prohibiting the imposition of fines on employees who had tendered resignations invalid under a union constitution supported deference to the Board's decision in this case.

State Law

The supremacy clause of the Constitution empowers Congress to pass laws, such as the federal labor laws, that will preempt the states' regulation of labor. Supreme Court decisions construing the labor laws (which are silent on the issue of preemption) have held that federal preemption powers are broad. Federal laws ordinarily will oust the states' jurisdiction in activities that are arguably protected or arguably prohibited by the federal labor statutes because of the NLRB's expertise and a desire for uniformity of case results. Matters that only peripherally affect the federal statutory scheme or matters that are of deep local concern may constitute legitimate state interests that state law (and courts) may therefore regulate. The law in this area is unsettled and the cases controversial; generally, however, state courts may adjudicate lawsuits involving damages from violence or other criminal or tortious activity, retaliatory discharges, and those causes of action covering all employers and employees exempted under federal statutes.

Preemption issues occupied the Supreme Court's attention in the following case.

United Steel Workers of America v. *Rawson*
110 S.Ct. 1904 (1990)

FACTS   Survivors of miners killed in an underground fire filed a state law wrongful death action in Idaho state court against the United Steel Workers of America (the Union), the miners' exclusive bargaining agent, alleging that the Union's fraudulent and negligent acts in connection with mine safety inspections conducted by its representatives pursuant to the collective-bargaining agreement with the mine's operator had proximately caused the miners' deaths. On remand from an Idaho Supreme Court decision that federal labor law had not preempted the claims, the trial court granted summary judgment for the Union. It found the record devoid of evidence supporting the fraud claim and urged the Idaho Supreme Court to reconsider its decision on the negligence claim. The Idaho Supreme Court upheld the trial court's summary judgment on the fraud claim but again concluded that the survivors' negligence claim was not preempted, holding that the Union may be liable under state law for the negligent inspection of the mine where the survivors' **decedents** had worked. According to the Supreme Court of Idaho, although federal law unquestionably imposed on the Union a duty of fair representation of the miners, the survivors' claims were "not necessarily based on the violation of the duty of fair representation" nor was such "the only duty owed by a union to its members."

Decedents Deceased persons.

ISSUE

Would Section 301 of the Labor Management Relations Act (LMRA) preempt (and thus bar) a negligence-based court action that the survivors had filed in state court?

HOLDING

Yes. Nothing in the Union's collective-bargaining agreement suggested that the agreement had created rights directly enforceable by an individual against the Union; neither would the Union's duty of fair representation encompass the survivors' claims of negligence by the Union.

REASONING

This dispute arose out of an underground fire that had occurred on 2 May 1972 at the Sunshine Mine in Kellogg, Idaho, causing the deaths of ninety-one miners. The survivors of four of the deceased miners filed this state law wrongful death action in Idaho state court. Their complaint alleged that the fraudulent and negligent acts of the Union had proximately caused the miners' deaths. As to the negligence claim, the complaint specifically alleged that the Union had, through a collective-bargaining agreement negotiated with the operator of the Sunshine Mine, caused to be established a joint management/labor safety committee intended to exert influence on management concerning mine safety measures; that members of the safety committee designated by the Union had been inadequately trained on mine safety issues; and that the Union, through its representatives on the safety committee, had negligently performed inspections of the mine, failing to uncover obvious and discoverable deficiencies. Section 301 of the LMRA states: "Suits for violation of contracts between an employer and a labor organization representing employees in an industry affecting commerce as defined in this Act, or between any such labor organizations, may be brought in any district court of the United States having jurisdiction of the parties, without respect to the amount in controversy or without regard to the citizenship of the parties." Over thirty years ago, this Court held that Section 301 not only provides the federal courts with jurisdiction over controversies involving collective-bargaining agreements but also authorizes the courts to fashion "a body of federal law for the enforcement of these collective bargaining agreements." Since then, the Court has made clear that Section 301 remains a potent source of federal labor law, for though state courts have concurrent jurisdiction over controversies involving collective-bargaining agreements, state courts must apply federal law in deciding those claims; and indeed federal law under Section 301 would entirely displace any state law cause of action for violation of collective-bargaining agreements. Only the federal law fashioned by the courts under Section 301 governs the interpretation and application of collective-bargaining agreements. The Supreme Court has the preemptive force of Section 301 that extends beyond state law contract actions. For example, *Allis-Chalmers Corp.* v. *Lueck,* 471 U.S. 202 (1985) held that a state law tort action against an employer may be preempted by Section 301 if the duty to the employee of which the tort is a violation is created by a collective-bargaining agreement and without existence independent of the agreement. Any other result would "allow parties to evade the requirements of Section 301 by relabeling their contract claims as claims for tortious breach of contract." The court acknowledged that in the present case, the Union's representatives had been participating in the inspection process pursuant to the provisions of the collective-bargaining agreement and that the agreement had determined the nature and scope of the Union's duty. If the Union had failed to perform a duty in connection with inspection, that duty had arisen out of the collective-bargaining agreement signed by the Union as the bargaining agent for the miners. Clearly, federal law would govern the enforcement of that agreement and the remedies for its breach. Preemption by federal law cannot be avoided by characterizing the Union's negligent performance of what it does on behalf of the members of the bargaining unit pursuant to the terms of the collective-bargaining contract as a state law tort. Accordingly, this suit, if it is to go forward at all, must proceed as a case controlled by federal rather than state law. However, the Union insisted that the case against it may not go forward even under federal law. It argued first that only the duty of fair representation governs the exercise of its representational functions under the collective-bargaining contract and that a member may not sue it under Section 301 for breach of contract. Second, the Union submitted that even if it may be sued under Section 301, the labor agreement contains no enforceable promise made by it to the members of the unit in connection with inspecting the mine. Third, the Union asserted that as the case now stands, it is charged with only negligence, which is insufficient to prove a breach of its duty of fair representation. The duty of fair representation is of major importance, but a breach occurs "only when a union's conduct toward a member of the collective bargaining unit is arbitrary, discriminatory, or in bad faith." The courts have in general assumed that mere negligence, even in the enforcement of a collective-bargaining agreement, would not state a claim for breach of the duty of fair representation, a view the Court endorses here as well. In performing its functions under the collective-bargaining agreement, the Union did, as it conceded, owe the miners a duty of fair representation; but the survivors' allegation of mere negligence would not state a claim for violation of that duty. Indeed, the survivors never specifically relied on the federal duty of fair representation, nor did they allege that the Union had improperly discriminated among its members or had acted in an arbitrary and capricious fashion in failing to exercise its duties under the collective-bargaining agreement. The survivors did, of course, allege that the Union had committed fraud on the membership in violation of state law, a claim that might implicate the duty of fair representation. The Supreme Court of Idaho held, however, that the lower court had properly entered summary judgment on this claim because the survivors had failed to demonstrate specific facts showing the existence of a genuine issue for trial. In the absence, then, of any challenge to this aspect of the judgment by the survivors, the judgment of the Supreme Court of Idaho warrants reversal.

EMPLOYMENT

Fair Employment Practices Laws

In addition to the extensive federal and state regulation of labor, several federal and state statutes designed to ensure equal employment opportunity for persons historically foreclosed from the workplace have come into existence since 1964. Foremost among these laws is the Civil Rights Act of 1964. Title VII of that statute prohibits discrimination in employment on the basis of race, color, religion, sex, or national origin. Under Title VII, it is an unlawful employment practice for any employer to make decisions to hire; discharge; compensate; or establish the terms, conditions, or privileges of employment for any employee based on the categories just enumerated. In addition, an employer cannot segregate, limit, or classify employees or applicants for employment in discriminatory ways. A union cannot discriminate against or refuse to refer for employment or apprenticeship programs any individual because of race, color, religion, sex, or national origin. And employment agencies cannot discriminate with respect to referrals for jobs or use advertisements indicating a discriminatory preference or limitation. None of the three groups— employers, unions, or employment agencies—can discriminate against any individual because the individual has opposed unlawful employment practices either. An employer who relegates blacks to manual labor jobs or an employment agency or labor organization that refers only white males for executive jobs or only women for nursing or secretarial jobs will be in violation of Title

VII. Title VII's coverage extends in general to employers in interstate commerce who have at least fifteen employees for at least twenty weeks per year, to any national or international labor organizations that consist of at least fifteen members or that operate a hiring hall, and to employment agencies that regularly procure employees for employers or work opportunities for potential employees. Because of amendments added in 1972, Title VII currently covers most federal, state, and local governmental and educational employees as well.

Title VII authorized the creation of the Equal Employment Opportunity Commission (EEOC), a bipartisan, five-member group appointed by the president. Since 1979, the EEOC has served as the enforcement agency for Title VII, the Equal Pay Act, the Age Discrimination in Employment Act, the Rehabilitation Act of 1973, the Americans with Disabilities Act of 1990, the Civil Rights Act of 1991, and other statutes. Complaints by individual grievants or charges filed by the EEOC or state fair employment or human rights commissions may trigger the EEOC's jurisdiction.

The jurisdictional requirements for successful suits under Title VII are complex. In brief, a charge must be filed within 180 days or 300 days after the alleged discrimination has occurred, the latter time period being applicable in so-called deferral states (those that have their own fair employment practices commissions). In deferral states, the local commission has exclusive jurisdiction for sixty days, at which point the EEOC has concurrent jurisdiction over the charge. If the EEOC has retained jurisdiction for at least 180 days and has decided there is no reasonable cause to file an action on behalf of the grievant, the EEOC may issue a "right-to-sue" letter to the grievant. Within ninety days of receiving the right-to-sue letter, the grievant must file suit in the appropriate district court or lose, generally speaking, the right to sue. Practically, however, the process almost never works this quickly (the EEOC's case backlog is almost legendary). Indeed, five to six years may elapse before resolution of the allegations occurs. Moreover, because the process is oriented to grievants and because judges do not expect laypersons to write complaints that resemble legal briefs, courts give grievants considerable leeway in describing and recognizing when discrimination has arguably happened. In addition, the conciliation orientation of the process makes it possible for the grievance to be cleared up before litigation becomes necessary. Still, it is important to remember the procedural pitfalls that dot this entire area of the law.

Jurisdictional issues provide the primary focus of the following case.

Yellow Freight System, Inc. v. Donnelly
110 S.Ct. 1566 (1990)

FACTS   Colleen Donnelly, a qualified dock worker, in 1982 applied for work at Yellow Freight System, Inc.'s (Yellow Freight's) facility four blocks from her home. The company had no vacancies but assured her that she would be the first person hired when the situation changed. Yellow Freight maintained this position in response to Donnelly's inquiries over the next eighteen months while at the same time hiring a number of men. The firm hired Donnelly only after she had filed a complaint with the EEOC in 1984. On 15 March 1985, the EEOC issued a notice of right to sue. The notice did not identify the forum in which Donnelly might sue, but it did advise her that she "must do so within ninety days" or she would lose that right. Within the ninety-day period, on 22 May 1985, Donnelly filed a complaint in the circuit court of Cook County, Illinois, alleging that Yellow Freight had discriminated against her on the basis of her sex in violation of the Illinois Human Rights Act. Yellow Freight filed a motion to dismiss on the ground that Donnelly had not exhausted her state administrative remedies. Donnelly countered with a motion to amend her complaint to allege that the facts already pleaded also constituted a violation of Title VII of the Civil Rights Act of 1964. However, Donnelly did not file this motion within the ninety-day period. Yellow Freight removed the case to federal court and moved to dismiss the amended complaint on the ground that the original filing in the state court could not toll the ninety-day limitation period because the state court lacked jurisdiction over a Title VII claim. The district court rejected this jurisdictional argument and, after a trial on the merits, entered judgment for Donnelly. The court of appeals for the seventh circuit affirmed.

ISSUE   Do federal courts have exclusive jurisdiction over Title VII cases?

HOLDING   No. The legislative history of Title VII is devoid of language that expressly confines jurisdiction to federal courts or that ousts state courts of their presumptive jurisdiction.

REASONING Under our system of dual sovereignty, the U.S. Supreme Court has consistently held that state courts have inherent authority, and are thus presumptively competent, to adjudicate claims arising under the laws of the United States. To give federal courts exclusive jurisdiction over a federal cause of action, Congress must, in an exercise of its powers under the supremacy clause, affirmatively divest state courts of their presumptively concurrent jurisdiction. The enforcement provisions of Title VII provide that "each United States district court and each United States court of a place subject to the jurisdiction of the United States shall have jurisdiction of actions brought under this subchapter." Unlike a number of statutes in which Congress has unequivocally stated that the jurisdiction of the federal courts is exclusive, Title VII contains no language that expressly confines jurisdiction to federal courts or ousts state courts of their presumptive jurisdiction. The omission of any such provision is strong, and arguably sufficient, evidence that Congress had no such intent. Like its plain text, the legislative history of the act affirmatively describes the jurisdiction of the federal courts but is completely silent on any role of the state courts over Title VII claims. Moreover, no incompatibility between the procedures provided in Title VII and state court jurisdiction over these claims exists. Yellow Freight correctly noted that Section 706(c) of the Act requires the EEOC to delay any action on a discrimination charge for at least sixty days to give state or local agencies an opportunity to remedy the allegedly unlawful practice prior to any federal action. The action by the EEOC, in contrast, is a predicate for litigation based on the federal statute. When the right to sue under Title VII arises, the fact that both a state agency and the EEOC have failed to resolve the matter does not affect the question of what judicial forum should or may entertain the action. Congress employed a similar scheme in the Age Discrimination in Employment Act, in which complaints must be screened through both state and federal agencies, although concurrently, before an action may be brought "in any court of competent jurisdiction." Nor does the act's provision for appeals and references to injunctive relief and appointment of masters preclude concurrent state court jurisdiction. Although it may be assumed that federal judges will have more experience in Title VII litigation than state judges, that constitutes merely one factor that the plaintiff may weigh when deciding where to file suit or that may motivate a defendant to remove a case to federal court. The presumption that state courts are just as able as federal courts to adjudicate Title VII claims remains uncontradicted. In sum, although Yellow Freight has made a persuasive showing that most legislators, judges, and administrators who have been involved in the enactment, amendment, enforcement, and interpretation of Title VII expected that such litigation would be processed exclusively in federal courts, such anticipation does not overcome the presumption of concurrent jurisdiction that lies at the core of our federal system. The judgment of the court of appeals therefore warrants affirmance.

Many employment practices that seem neutral may in fact lead to discrimination. For instance, in the early 1970s, several cases involving testing procedures and required high school diplomas arose. These cases show that selection criteria that seem outwardly neutral may foreclose blacks and other protected persons from jobs merely because statistically fewer blacks than whites are graduated from high school. Such selection criteria as requiring a certain score on an aptitude test or a high school diploma may "operate as 'built-in' headwinds for minority groups and [may be] unrelated to measuring job capability. . . . [Title VII] proscribes not only overt discrimination but also practices that are fair in form, but discriminatory in operation. The touchstone is business necessity. If an employment practice which operates to exclude [minorities] cannot be shown to be related to job performance, the practice is prohibited."[3]

Any job requirement that prevents a disproportionate number of blacks or other minorities from securing employment or promotions has a *disparate impact* (that is, an unequal effect) on minorities and may be illegal. The employer then has the burden of proving that the requirement is job related. The EEOC has issued guidelines for selecting employees, but these guidelines do not have the force of law. Nonetheless, courts may give these EEOC guidelines considerable deference if they so wish.

Besides liability imposed for disparate impact, employers may, in addition, be liable for *disparate treatment* of their employees. Such cases ordinarily arise when an employer allows whites or males to break rules without punishment but institutes penalties if blacks or women break the same rules. A 1976 case, *McDonald* v. *Santa Fe Trail Transportation Co.,* also held that whites can sue for racial discrimination when they receive disparate treatment.[4] In this case, the employer had accused two whites and one black of misappropriating a shipment of antifreeze. Both white employees had been fired, but the black worker had been retained. The Supreme Court concluded that Title VII prohibits all forms of racial discrimination, including "**reverse discrimination**" of this type.

The allegations of "reverse discrimination" that spring from another source—affirmative action plans—pose some of the most controversial issues in the area of fair employment practices involving race. Title VII places on the employer the duty to maintain a racially balanced workforce. Yet if the employer takes affirmative steps to bring about such racial balance, say by slotting certain apprentice openings for blacks, such actions may adversely affect white incumbents who wish to take part in these training programs. Two diametrically opposed policies clash here: the interests of the minority candidate who has in the past been disadvantaged because of race and the white incumbent worker who has taken no part in this discrimination but who now must lose employment opportunities in order to bring about equality

Reverse discrimination
Claims by whites that they have been subjected to adverse employment decisions because of their race and the application of employment discrimination statutes designed to protect minorities.

---

[3]*Griggs* v. *Duke Power Co.,* 401 U.S. 424, 431–432 (1971).
[4]427 U.S. 273 (1976).

of opportunity for black workers. In these situations, whites occasionally have brought suits alleging "reverse discrimination." A famous 1978 case, *Regents of the University of California* v. *Bakke,* involved a white student who alleged that the University of California at Davis had discriminated against him on the basis of his race in violation of the Fourteenth Amendment by rejecting his application for medical school and admitting sixteen minority students with credentials inferior to his.[5] The Supreme Court, in a very complex opinion, held that university quota systems that absolutely prefer minority candidates (the university had reserved sixteen spots out of one hundred for minorities) are illegal but that a university may take race into account in the admissions process.

The issue of "reverse discrimination" becomes even thornier in the private sector, where employers may face charges by the EEOC if they do not aggressively engage in affirmative action and may face suits by white workers alleging "reverse discrimination" if they do. In the case that follows, the Supreme Court dealt with this particular issue.

United Steelworkers of America v. Weber
443 U.S. 193 (1979), reh'g denied 444 U.S. 889 (1979)

FACTS　The United Steelworkers of America and Kaiser Aluminum & Chemical Corporation (Kaiser) had entered into a master collective bargaining agreement covering fifteen Kaiser plants. The agreement had included an affirmative action plan aimed at eliminating racial imbalances in Kaiser's workforce. This plan had reserved for black employees 50 percent of the openings in Kaiser training programs until Kaiser's percentage of skilled black craftworkers equaled the percentage of blacks in the local labor force. Brian Weber, a white worker who had had more seniority than some of the black workers selected for the training program, was rejected as a trainee. Weber sued, alleging that Kaiser's affirmative action plan constituted "reverse discrimination" against white workers and violated Title VII's ban on discrimination because of race in the selection of apprentices for training programs.

ISSUE　Did Kaiser's voluntary, race-conscious affirmative action plan violate Title VII?

HOLDING　No. Title VII's prohibition against racial discrimination does not condemn all private, voluntary, race-conscious affirmative action plans.

REASONING　Title VII's prohibition against racial discrimination must be read against the historical context of the Civil Rights Act of 1964. An examination of that source makes it clear that an interpretation of Title VII that forbids all race-conscious affirmative action plans must be rejected. Since one of the purposes of Title VII involves opening up job opportunities traditionally closed to blacks, Kaiser's self-evaluation efforts to eliminate its racially imbalanced workforce were appropriate. Because the Kaiser plan opened up opportunities for blacks without unnecessarily trammeling the interests of white workers, its affirmative action plan was legal.

[5]438 U.S. 265 (1978).

Bona fide occupational qualification A defense to charges of discrimination based on religion, sex, or national origin but not to charges of racial discrimination; a situation in which one of these categories is essential to the performance of the job.

Besides racial discrimination, Title VII also prohibits religious discrimination. Sincere religious beliefs (or the lack thereof) are protected under Title VII. Typically, cases involving this protected category occur when a job shift necessitates work on the day the employee considers his or her Sabbath. If a person's religion forbids work on Fridays after sundown, for instance, Title VII mandates that the employer make a "reasonable accommodation" to the employee's beliefs unless to do so would pose an "undue hardship" on the conduct of the business. A 1977 case, *Trans World Airlines, Inc.* v. *Hardison*, has severely undercut the guarantees represented by Title VII, however, by holding that an employer does not have to undertake an accommodation that requires more than a minimal expense or that violates a collective-bargaining agreement.[6] Furthermore, educational institutions may make religion a **bona fide occupational qualification** (BFOQ) under other provisions of Title VII. The University of Notre Dame, for example, can hire only Catholic professors if it so wishes.

Bona fide occupational qualifications may also constitute a *limited* defense to charges of sex discrimination. It is not a violation of Title VII for a movie director to cast only women in women's roles, for instance. Issues implicating the ban on sex discrimination include stereotypes about ability to perform (such as an employer who thinks only men can be telephone "linemen" and only women can be telephone operators), height/weight requirements that are not job related (women are usually smaller than men), and so-called sex-plus cases. In the last, the employer adds a selection criterion for women that is not added for men (as when women with preschool-aged children are not hired, but men who have such children are).

One unanswered question under Title VII involves whether the theory of comparable worth, which allows employees to compare their wages to those of other workers who perform dissimilar jobs of equal value (or intrinsic worth) to the employer in order to prove sex-based wage discrimination, will ultimately enjoy widespread judicial and legislative approval. The ensuing legal developments in this area bear watching. There is little uncertainty, however, with regard to pregnancy: The Pregnancy Discrimination Act of 1978 dictates that an employer treat pregnancy in the same fashion as any other disability. To do otherwise will constitute actionable sex discrimination. Recent Title VII cases also have protected women from sexual harassment in the workplace by imposing on employers liability for sexual advances or requests for sexual favors made by their agents and supervisory employees and for sexual misconduct that creates an intimidating, hostile, or offensive working environment for women.

Title VII's ban on national origin discrimination similarly prevents harassment in the form of ethnic slurs based on the country in which one was born or the country from which one's ancestors came. Repeated Polish jokes and other derogatory statements directed at one's ethnic origins in a given

NATIONAL ORIGIN — ETHNIC SLURS !

[6]432 U.S. 63 (1977).

case may constitute national origin discrimination. National origin discrimination often takes the form of "covert discrimination." To illustrate, height/ weight requirements may foreclose Spanish-surnamed Americans from employment opportunities, as may language difficulties or accents. If an employer bases an adverse employment decision on such criteria, the employer must prove that the criteria are job related. Narrow BFOQs may exist in national origin cases. It is legal to hire a French person to be a French chef, for example. It is also legal to refuse to hire non-American citizens because the prohibition against national origin discrimination does not include citizenship.[7] (Such a refusal to hire may violate the Immigration Reform and Control Act of 1986, however.) Likewise, it is not a violation of Title VII for an employer to refuse to hire persons who are unable to obtain security clearances because they have relatives in countries that are not on friendly terms with the United States.

In addition to Title VII, several other federal statutes protect various classes of persons. The Equal Pay Act of 1963 prohibits discrimination in wages on the basis of sex. Therefore, men and women performing work in the same establishment under similar working conditions must receive the same rate of pay if the work requires equal skill, equal effort, and equal responsibility. Different wages may be paid if based on seniority, merit, piecework, or any factor other than sex (for example, participation in training programs). The Age Discrimination in Employment Act of 1967 in general protects workers from age forty to age seventy from adverse employment decisions based on age. BFOQs based on safety or human and economic risks—age fifty-five retirement for police officers, for instance—may be upheld, as may differentiation in age based on a bona fide seniority system and discharges or disciplinary actions undertaken with good cause.

The Rehabilitation Act of 1973 directs federal contractors to take affirmative action with respect to "otherwise qualified" handicapped individuals. A handicapped individual includes any person who "has a physical or mental impairment which substantially limits one or more of such person's major life functions, has a record of such impairment, or is regarded as having such an impairment." The Vietnam Era Veterans' Readjustment Assistance Act, various executive orders, and the Civil Rights Acts of 1866 and 1871 form alternative bases for guaranteeing equal access to the workplace. State law often augments this extensive federal scheme, as well.

The Americans with Disabilities Act of 1990 (the ADA), which became law on 26 July 1990, seeks to redress discrimination against individuals with disabilities and to guarantee such individuals equal access to public services (including public accommodations and transportation), public services operated by private entities, and telecommunications relay services, to name a few. Title I, which prohibits employment discrimination, adopts the Rehabilitation Act of 1973's definition of handicap but uses the more up-to-date term "disability." The ADA also imports the "reasonable accommodation" concept

[7]*Espinoza* v. *Farah Manufacturing Company, Inc.*, 414 U.S. 86 (1973).

from the Rehabilitation Act in requiring an employer to provide "reasonable accommodation to the known physical or mental limitations" of a person with a disability unless such accommodation "would impose an undue hardship on the operation of the business" of the covered entity. Reasonable accommodation under the ADA includes such actions as making existing facilities accessible to and usable by persons with disabilities, restructuring jobs, and providing part-time or modified work schedules. However, the act does not require the employer to implement any job accommodation if the employer can demonstrate that the accommodation would impose an "undue hardship" on the operation of the business. The ADA defines "undue hardship" as an action requiring "significant difficulty or expense" with reference to the following factors: 1) the nature and cost of the accommodation; 2) the size, type, and financial resources of the specific facility where the accommodation would have to be made; 3) the size, type, and financial resources of the covered employer; and 4) the covered employer's type of operation, including the composition, structure, and functions of its workforce and the geographic separateness and administrative or fiscal relationship between the specific facility and the covered employer. The legislative history indicates that the "significant difficulty or expense" standard encompasses any "action that is unduly costly, extensive, substantial, disruptive, or that will fundamentally alter the nature of the program." Significant, too, is the fact that in defining "undue hardship," Congress rejected all attempts to put a cap on the level of difficulty or expense that would constitute an "undue hardship," including an amendment that would have created a presumption that the cost of any accommodation exceeding 10 percent of the annual salary of the position in question would constitute an "undue hardship." The employment discrimination provisions under Title I became effective on 26 July 1992 for employers with twenty-five or more employees for each working day in each of twenty or more calendar weeks in the current or preceding calendar year. After 26 July 1994, the coverage will extend to employers with fifteen or more employees working the requisite amount of hours. The ADA subsequently will cover an estimated 3.9 million business establishments and 666,000 employers. Like the Civil Rights Act of 1964, the ADA covers, in addition to employers, employment agencies, labor organizations, and joint labor-management committees but exempts religious entities. Thus, the ADA's coverage goes beyond that of the Rehabilitation Act of 1973, which applies only to employers doing business with the federal government.

At the congressional hearings for the ADA, experts testified that it potentially covers about 43 million Americans and that its enactment therefore may cause a flood of litigation. Indeed, the EEOC itself has predicted that complainants will file between 12,000 and 15,000 charges during the first year the statute takes effect. As with any new legislation, the overall impact of the ADA remains unclear. In addition to the costs associated with the hiring process and those resulting from the predicted increases in litigation under the act, the expenses of converting existing facilities in order to make them accessible to individuals with disabilities obviously concern many employers, particularly small firms. Yet data from a 1982 survey of federal contractors showed that the compliance costs/workplace changes for half of the companies amounted to zero dollars and for 30 percent of the companies less than $500. In only 8 percent of the cases the changes cost more than $2000.

The ADA in many ways represents "an emancipation proclamation" for individuals with disabilities. The act was inspired by and shares many of the goals and concepts of prior civil rights legislation, but its innovative approaches more highly define and refine the parameters marked out by its antidiscrimination statutory precursors. It represents a second-generation civil rights statute that may well serve as a bellwether for future legislation of this type. It stands as a powerful constraint on the stereotypic assumptions that often infect employers' and others' considerations of individuals with disabilities. It thereby helps to guarantee what most of us already take for granted—that qualified individuals (with disabilities) will be given the opportunity to participate in the workplace as productive, contributing individuals.

Congress enacted the Civil Rights Act of 1991 on 7 November 1991 after a two-year struggle. Interestingly, Congress passed this act in part to overturn a series of 1989 and 1991 Supreme Court cases that had significantly eroded the rights of complainants alleging employment discrimination. The act reflected Congress's displeasure with the present Court's judicial attitude toward civil rights cases. The act, in its amendments of Title VII, reaffirms the holdings of such cases as *Griggs* v. *Duke Power Co.* The new act's amendments to Section 1981 of the Civil Rights Act of 1866 also specify that this statute covers all forms of racial discrimination in employment (including racial harassment). However, the act mandates the impartial use of tests and thus prohibits "race norming" of employment tests. In other words, employers must record and report actual scores and will be unable to adjust scores, use different cutoff scores, or otherwise adjust the results of employment-related tests on the basis of race, color, religion, sex, or national origin in order to assure minority inclusion in the applicant pool. In a similar vein, the act effects no changes in the law regarding what constitutes lawful affirmative action and/or illegal reverse discrimination. It also restricts challenges to court-ordered consent decrees by individuals who had a reasonable opportunity to object to such decrees or whose interests were adequately represented by another party. The act broadens the scope of federal antidiscrimination law. It makes clear that Americans employed abroad by American-owned or -contolled firms can avail themselves of the protection of Title VII, the ADA, and the Age Discrimination in Employment Act (ADEA), unless compliance with these laws would constitute a violation of the host country's laws. The act extends coverage of the antidiscrimination laws to congressional employees and executive-branch political appointees and sets up discrete internal mechanisms for addressing such claims. The act broadens the categories of victims who can seek compensatory and punitive damages based on intentional discrimination, although it provides for caps of $50,000–$300,000 (depending on the size of the employer's workforce) for discrimination based on the complainant's disability, sex, or religion. Any complainant eligible for compensatory or punitive damages may request a jury trial as well. The act also allows successful complainants to recover expert witness fees in addition to attorneys' fees. Other amendments deal with the availability of interest payments for delayed awards, extensions of filing deadlines for lawsuits brought against the government, notification by the EEOC to the complainant when the EEOC dismisses charges under the ADEA, and a longer statute of limitations period for a claimant to bring an action under the ADEA. The act obligates the EEOC to establish a Technical Assistance Training Institute for entities covered by the laws the EEOC enforces. The act in addition mandates an EEOC outreach/education program for individuals who have historically been the object of employment discrimination. Title II of the act, the Glass Ceiling Act of 1991, sets up a commission to study why impediments to the advancement of women and minorities exist and to make recommendations for eliminating such barriers. Businesses that show substantial efforts to advance such groups to management and decision-making positions in business are eligible to receive national awards recognizing their efforts.[8] Given the newness of this landmark legislation, subsequent court decisions will serve to answer the various questions spawned by the act. Watch for these developments.

The following case is significant in the areas of fair employment practices and gender-based employment policies.

International Union, UAW v. Johnson Controls, Inc.
111 S.Ct. 1196 (1991)

FACTS   A primary ingredient in Johnson Controls, Inc.'s (Johnson Controls's) battery manufacturing process is lead, occupational exposure to which entails health risks, including the risk of harm to a fetus carried by a female employee. After eight of its employees had become pregnant while maintaining blood lead levels exceeding that noted by the Occupational Safety and Health Administration (OSHA) as critical for a worker planning to have a family, Johnson Controls announced a policy barring all women, except those whose infertility could be medically documented, from jobs involving actual or potential lead exposure exceeding the OSHA standard. The International Union UAW (UAW), a group including employees affected by the company's fetal-protection policy, filed a class action in the district court, claiming that the policy constituted sex discrimination violative of Title VII of the Civil Rights Act of 1964. The court granted summary judgment for Johnson Controls, and the court of appeals affirmed. The latter court held that the proper standard for evaluating the policy was the business necessity inquiry applied by other circuits; that Johnson Controls was entitled to summary judgment because the UAW had failed to satisfy its burden of persuasion as to each of the elements of the business necessity defense under the relevant Supreme Court precedents; and that even if the proper evaluation standard consisted of bona fide occupational qualification (BFOQ) analysis, Johnson Controls still would deserve summary judgment because its fetal-protection policy is reasonably necessary to further the industrial safety concern that represents the essence of the firm's business.

[8]*BNA Employee Relations Weekly* (Special Supplement: Civil Rights Act of 1991), vol. 9 (11 November 1991), pp. S-1–S-6.

ISSUE   Did Johnson Controls's sex-specific fetal protection policies, in which the company excluded fertile female employees from certain jobs due to its concern for the health of the fetuses the women might conceive, violate Title VII's ban on sex discrimination?

HOLDING   Yes. By excluding women with childbearing capacity from lead-exposed jobs, Johnson Controls's policy creates a facial classification based on gender and explicitly discriminates against women on the basis of their sex under Title VII. Moreover, in using the words "capable of bearing children" as the criterion for exclusion, the policy explicitly classifies on the basis of potential for pregnancy, which classification must be regarded, under the Pregnancy Discrimination Act, in the same light as explicit sex discrimination.

REASONING   The bias in Johnson Controls's policy is obvious. The company gives fertile men, but not fertile women, a choice as to whether they wish to risk their reproductive health for a particular job. Section 703(a) of the Civil Rights Act of 1964 prohibits sex-based classifications in terms and conditions of employment, in hiring and discharging decisions, and in other employment decisions that adversely affect an employee's status. Johnson Controls's fetal-protection policy therefore explicitly discriminates against women on the basis of their sex. The policy excludes women with childbearing capacity from lead-exposed jobs and so creates a facial classification based on gender. Nevertheless, the court of appeals assumed, as did the two appellate courts that already had confronted the issue, that sex-specific fetal-protection policies do not involve facial discrimination. These courts analyzed the policies as though they were facially neutral and had only a discriminatory effect on the employment opportunities of women. Consequently, the courts looked to see if each employer in question had established the business necessity justification for its policy. The business necessity standard is more lenient for the employer than the statutory BFOQ defense. The courts assumed that because the asserted reason for the sex-based exclusion (protecting women's unconceived offspring) was ostensibly benign, the policy was not sex-based discrimination. That assumption, however, was incorrect. First, Johnson Controls's policy classifies on the basis of gender and childbearing capacity rather than fertility alone. The company does not seek to protect the unconceived children of all its employees. Despite evidence in the record about the debilitating effect of lead exposure on the male reproductive system, Johnson Controls is concerned only with the harms that may befall the unborn offspring of its female employees. Johnson Controls's policy is therefore facially discriminatory because it requires only a female employee to produce proof that she is not capable of reproducing. The Pregnancy Discrimination Act of 1978 (PDA), in which Congress explicitly provided that, for purposes of Title VII, discrimination "on the basis of sex" includes discrimination "because of or on the basis of pregnancy, childbirth, or related medical conditions" also bolsters this conclusion. According to other Supreme Court precedents, the PDA has now made clear that, for all Title VII purposes, discrimination based on a woman's pregnancy is, on its face, discrimination because of her sex. Its use of the words "capable of bearing children" illustrates that Johnson Controls explicitly classified on the basis of potential for pregnancy. Under the PDA, such a classification must be regarded, for Title VII purposes, in the same light as explicit sex discrimination. Because the firm chose to treat all its female employees as potentially pregnant, that choice evinces discrimination on the basis of sex. Furthermore, the absence of a malevolent motive does not convert a facially discriminatory policy into a neutral policy with a discriminatory effect. Whether an employment practice involves disparate treatment through explicit facial discrimination does not depend on why the employer discriminates but rather on the explicit terms of the discrimination. In short, the beneficence of an employer's purpose does not undermine the conclusion that an explicit gender-based policy is sex discrimination under Section 703(a) and thus may be defended only as a BFOQ. Simply put, Johnson Controls's policy "does not pass the simple test of whether the evidence shows 'treatment of a person in a manner which but for that person's sex would be different.' " Therefore, Johnson Controls's fetal-protection policy constitutes sex discrimination forbidden under Title VII unless the firm can establish that sex is a BFOQ. Under Section 703(e)(1) of Title VII, an employer may discriminate on the basis of "religion, sex, or national origin in those certain instances where religion, sex, or national origin is a bona fide occupational qualification [BFOQ] reasonably necessary to the normal operation of that particular business or enterprise." Does Johnson Controls's fetal-protection policy represent one of those "certain instances" that come within the BFOQ exception? The BFOQ defense is written narrowly, and this Court has read it narrowly. This emphasis on the restrictive scope of the BFOQ defense is grounded in both the language and the legislative history of Section 703. The wording of the BFOQ defense contains several terms of restriction that indicate that the exception reaches only special situations. The statute thus limits the situations in which discrimination is permissible to "certain instances" in which sex discrimination is "reasonably necessary" to the "normal operation" of the "particular" business. Each one of these terms—"certain," "normal," "particular"—prevents the use of general subjective standards and favors an objective, verifiable requirement. But the most telling term is "occupational"; this indicates that these objective, verifiable requirements must concern job-related skills and aptitudes. Johnson Controls argues that its fetal-protection policy falls within the so-called safety exception to the BFOQ. Furthermore, Supreme Court cases have stressed that discrimination on the basis of sex because of safety concerns is allowed only in narrow circumstances. Third-party safety considerations properly enter into the BFOQ analysis in such cases because they go to the core of the employee's job performance. Moreover, that performance involves the central purpose of the enterprise. In the present case, the unconceived fetuses of Johnson Controls's female employees, however, are neither customers nor third parties whose safety is essential to the business of battery manufacturing. No one can disregard the possibility of injury to future children. The BFOQ, however, is not so broad that it transforms this deep social concern into an essential aspect of batterymaking. Supreme Court holdings make clear that the safety expectation is limited to instances in which sex or pregnancy actually interferes with the employee's ability to perform the job. This approach is consistent with the language of the BFOQ provision itself, for it suggests that permissible distinctions based on sex must relate to the ability to perform the duties of the job. Johnson Controls suggests, however, that the Court expand the exception to allow fetal-protection policies that mandate particular standards for pregnant or fertile women. However, such an expansion contradicts not only the language of the BFOQ and the narrowness of its exception but the plain language and history of the PDA. Moreover, the PDA's amendment to Title VII contains a BFOQ standard of its own: Women who are either pregnant or potentially pregnant must be treated like others "similar in their ability . . . to work." In other words, women who are as capable of doing their jobs as their male counterparts may not be forced to choose between having a child and having a job. The legislative history of the PDA therefore counsels against expanding the BFOQ to allow fetal-protection policies. The legislative history states that employers may not require a pregnant woman to stop working at any time during her pregnancy unless she is unable to do her work. Employment late in pregnancy often imposes risks on the unborn child, but Congress has indicated that the employer may take into account only the woman's ability to get her job done. With the PDA, Congress makes clear that the decision to become pregnant or to work while being either pregnant or capable of becoming pregnant is reserved for each individual woman to make for herself. Thus, the employer must direct its concerns about a woman's ability to perform her job safely and efficiently to these aspects of the woman's job-related activities that fall within the "essence" of the particular business. Consequently, here, Johnson Controls has failed to establish a BFOQ. Fertile women, as far as appears in the record, participate in the manufacture of batteries as efficiently as anyone else. Johnson Controls's professed moral and ethical concerns about the welfare of the next generation do not suffice to establish a BFOQ of female sterility. Decisions about the welfare of future children must be left to the parents who conceive, bear, support, and raise them rather than to the employers who hire those parents. Congress has mandated this choice through Title VII, as amended by the PDA. Although Johnson Controls has attempted to exclude women because of their reproductive capacity, Title VII and the PDA simply do not allow a woman's dismissal because of her failure to submit to sterilization. Nor can concerns about the welfare of the next generation be considered a part of the "essence" of Johnson Controls's business. In conclusion, a word about tort liability and the increased cost of fertile women in the workplace is perhaps necessary. One of the lower court judges in this case expressed concern about the employer's tort liability and concluded that liability for a potential injury to a fetus is a social cost that Title VII does not require a company to ignore. It is correct to say that Title VII does not prevent the employer from having a conscience. The statute, however, does prevent sex-specific fetal-protection policies. And these two aspects of Title VII do not conflict. Moreover, in the absence of negligence, it would be difficult for a court to find liability on the part of the employer. If, under general tort principles, Title VII bans sex-specific fetal-protection policies, the employer fully informs the woman of the risk, and the employer has not acted negligently, the basis for holding an employer liable seems remote at best. Although the issue is not before us, the concurrence in this case observes that "it is far from clear that compliance with Title VII will preempt state tort liability." The cases relied upon by the concurrence to support its prediction, however, are inapposite. If state tort law furthers discrimination in the workplace and prevents employers from hiring women who are capable of manufacturing the product as efficiently as men, then it will impede the accomplishment of Congress's goals in enacting Title VII. Because Johnson Controls has failed to assert that it faces any costs from tort liability, the pre-emption question is not before the Court; therefore, the concurrence's speculation appears unfounded as well as premature. Of course, this case does not involve costs so prohibitive as to threaten the survival of the employer's business. Yet the Court's prior holdings that the incremental cost of hiring women cannot justify discriminating against them merits reiteration. Hence, the conclusion that Title VII forbids sex-specific fetal-protection policies is neither remarkable nor unprecedented. Concern for a woman's existing or potential offspring historically has been the excuse for denying women equal employment opportunities. Congress in the PDA prohibited discrimination on the basis of a woman's ability to become pregnant. In this case, the Court does no more than hold that the PDA means what it says. It is no more appropriate for the courts than it is for individual employers to decide whether a woman's reproductive role is more important to herself and her family than her economic role. Congress has left this choice to the woman as hers to make. Therefore, the judgment of the court of appeals is reversed and the case remanded for further proceedings consistent with this opinion.

YOU BE THE JUDGE	The New York Human Rights Commission recently filed 62 civil complaints against Delta Air Lines. Each complaint carried a potential liability of $100,000. According to these complaints, Delta interviewers had asked job applicants questions concerning birth control, abortions, and sexual preferences. One interviewer allegedly questioned a female applicant about her son's relationship with his biological father.

If the Commission could prove that Delta's interviewers had actually asked such questions, would these pre-hiring inquiries demonstrate job discrimination on the company's part?

Assuming these complaints were filed in court, how would you decide and why? Did Delta behave *ethically* if its interviewers asked these questions? |

Source: "Job Interviews Pose Rising Risk to Employers," Junda Woo, *The Wall Street Journal*, March 11, 1992, pages B1 and B5.

The Occupational Safety and Health Act

Congress passed the Occupational Safety and Health Act, better known as OSHA, in 1970. This act attempts to assure safe and healthful workplace conditions for working men and women by authorizing enforcement of the standards developed under the act (through the Occupational Safety and Health Administration); by assisting and encouraging the states in their efforts to assure safe and healthful working conditions; and by providing for research, information, education, and training in the field of occupational safety and health (through NIOSH, the National Institute for Occupational Safety and Health). The act covers most employers and employees, including agricultural employees, nonprofit organizations, and professionals (such as doctors, lawyers, accountants, and brokers). In fact, the act reaches almost any employer who employs at least one employee and whose business in any way affects interstate commerce. Atomic energy workers are exempted, however.

Because personal illnesses and injuries arising from the workplace produce significant burdens in terms of lost production, lost wages, medical expenses, and disability payments, Congress designed an act meant to highlight the existence of such factors and to provide standards for preventing future illnesses, injuries, and losses. To this end, OSHA sets out methods by which employers can reduce workplace hazards and foster attention to safety. The act further authorizes the secretary of labor to set mandatory occupational safety and health standards for businesses covered under the act and to create an Occupational Safety and Health Review Commission for hearing appeals from OSHA citations and penalties.

In trying to ensure that no employee suffers diminished health, functional capacity, or life expectancy as a result of work experiences, OSHA requires each employer to furnish a safe and healthful workplace for its employees, one that is free from "recognized hazards" that may cause or are likely to cause death or serious physical harm to employees. Excessive toxic substances in the air would be an example of a "recognized hazard."

OSHA allows inspectors to enter the workplace to inspect for compliance with regulations. As the following case indicates, on an employer's refusal to admit the inspector, OSHA regulations now require a warrant. But the standards for demonstrating the need for the warrant are relatively easy to meet and do not ordinarily impede OSHA's functions very much. Employers normally do not know in advance of an inspector's arrival. By writing to the secretary of labor, employees may request an inspection if they believe a violation that threatens physical harm exists.

Marshall v. Barlow's, Inc.
436 U.S. 307 (1978)

FACTS   Barlow, the owner of an electrical and plumbing business in Pocatello, Idaho, refused to allow an OSHA inspector to view the working areas of his business without a search warrant. An OSHA regulation permitted such inspections without a warrant. Barlow sued the Department of Labor, asserting that such inspections violated his Fourth Amendment guarantees against unreasonable searches and seizures.

ISSUE   Did the OSHA regulation authorizing warrantless inspections violate the Fourth Amendment?

HOLDING   Yes. Such warrantless searches violate the Fourth Amendment, so OSHA will have to amend its regulations to require warrants when entry to business premises is refused.

REASONING   Warrantless searches of commercial premises are just as illegal as warrantless searches of private homes would be. The secretary of labor's argument that the element of surprise, so essential to the proper enforcement of OSHA, will be lost if warrants are required is therefore unsupportable. Moreover, most businesspersons will allow the search even in the absence of a warrant. Should a businessperson's refusal necessitate a warrant, OSHA can obtain one without demonstrating probable cause in the criminal sense; indeed, OSHA need not always show specific evidence of an existing violation but can show instead that the business has been chosen for inspection in accordance with an OSHA general administrative plan. Finally, OSHA is empowered to secure *ex parte warrants* (that is, warrants issued to OSHA without the businessperson's having prior notice or opportunity to object to the warrant's issuance) once entry has been refused.

Inspections typically involve a tour through the business and an examination of each work area for compliance with OSHA standards. After the inspector has informed the employer of the reason for the inspection, the inspector will give the employer a copy of the complaint (if one is involved) or the reason for the inspection if it results from an agency general administrative plan. When an employee has initiated the complaint, OSHA will withhold the employee's name by request. An employer representative and an employee-selected representative generally accompany the inspector on this walk-around tour. The inspector may order some violations, such as blocked aisles, locked fire exits, or unsanitary conditions, to be corrected immediately. The inspector additionally reviews the records OSHA requires the employer to maintain, including records of deaths, injuries, illnesses, and employee exposure to toxic substances. After the inspection, the inspector and employer engage in a closing conference, during which they discuss probable violations and methods for eliminating these violations. The inspector then files his or her report with the commission. Citations and proposed penalties may be issued to the employer, and a copy of these will be sent to the complaining party if there is one. Normally, no citation is issued if a violation of a standard or rule lacks an immediate or direct relationship to safety or health, although a notice of a minimal violation (without a proposed penalty) may be sent to the employer even in these situations. OSHA requires the prominent posting of citations in the workplace.

Penalties, when imposed, are severe: fines of up to $70,000 for each violation may be levied for willful or repeated violations. An employer will also be fined up to $7000 for each serious violation—one in which there is a "substantial probability" that the consequences of an accident resulting from the violation will be death or serious harm. Employers can defend by showing they did not, and could not with the exercise of "reasonable diligence," know about the condition or hazard. For even nonserious violations (such as a failure to paint steps and banisters or to post citations), fines of up to $7000 are possible. Prison terms are possible in the event of willful violations that cause an employee's death. The OSHA Commission assesses these penalties in light of the size of the employer's business, the seriousness of the violation, the presence or absence of employer good faith, and the past history of violations. An employer may contest any penalties by resorting to the procedures established by the commission. In general, these require an investigation and a decision by an administrative law judge. The commission, in turn, can review this decision. If the employer still disagrees with the decision, he or she can appeal to the appropriate federal circuit court of appeals for review.

Employers may request temporary exemptions from OSHA standards on proof of inability to comply because of the unavailability of materials, equipment, or personnel to effect the changes within the required time. Permanent exemptions may be granted when the employer's method of protecting employees is as effective as that required by the standard. Needless to say, such exemptions are not granted retroactively. Other provisions of OSHA protect employees from discrimination or discharge based on filing a complaint, testifying about violations, or exercising any rights guaranteed by the act. The act prohibits employees from stopping work or walking off the job because of "potential unsafe conditions at the workplace" unless the employee, through performance of the assigned work, would subject "himself [or herself] to serious injury or death from a hazardous condition at the workplace." The *Whirlpool Corp.* v. *Marshall* case, which follows, involved an interpretation of this aspect of the act and its attendant regulations.

Whirlpool Corp. v. *Marshall*
445 U.S. 1 (1980)

FACTS   Two maintenance workers at the Whirlpool plant in Marion, Ohio, were told to remove objects from an overhead mesh screen designed to catch appliance components that move along an overhead conveyor belt. Several employees had been injured in falls from the screen because it was necessary to step onto the mesh screen in order to retrieve the objects. Indeed, one employee had recently died from falling through the mesh screen. Because they feared serious injuries, the two maintenance men refused to step onto the screen. They were given reprimands and were ordered to punch out six hours early. The secretary of labor sued Whirlpool for discrimination against the employees who, the secretary believed, had merely utilized the rights guaranteed them under the Occupational Safety and Health Act. The secretary also issued a regulation that protected the right of employees to choose not to perform work because of a reasonable apprehension of injury or death when less drastic alternatives were unavailable. This regulation, the secretary maintained, protected the employees from adverse employment consequences. Whirlpool had argued that the secretary had no right to promulgate this regulation.

ISSUE   Did the secretary of labor have the authority to promulgate a regulation that would permit workers' refusals to perform in hazardous situations?

HOLDING   Yes. The regulation providing for refusals to perform in dangerous situations was a right afforded by the Occupational Safety and Health Act.

REASONING   The promulgation of the regulation was a valid exercise of the authority granted the secretary of labor under the Occupational Safety and Health Act. Moreover, the regulation itself represented a permissible interpretation of the act in light of its fundamental purpose of preventing occupational deaths and serious injuries.

Social Security

The Social Security Act, first enacted in 1935 as part of Roosevelt's "New Deal" policies, has spawned numerous controversies. Current debate about social security centers on fears that the system will become bankrupt and on proposed plans to allay this possibility. By "social security," most people mean the federal old-age, survivors', and disability insurance benefits plan. Broad in scope, social security benefits today are payable to workers, their dependents, and their survivors. Through the Supplemental Security Income Program (SSI) administered by the Department of Health and Human Services, the federal social security system also makes payments to the blind, the disabled, and the aged who are in need of these benefits. The states can also supplement this pervasive federal scheme if they so choose.

In general, federal social security benefits are computed on the worker's earning records. A "fully insured" worker is one who has worked at least forty quarters (ten years). To use 1992 as an example, a worker will earn one quarter of coverage for each $570 in earnings, whether wages, farm wages, or income from self-employment, up to a maximum of four quarters. "Fully insured" workers who receive retirement benefits include retired workers, sixty-two years or older; their spouses, or divorced spouses, sixty-two or older; spouses of any age if caring for a child entitled to benefits; and children or grandchildren under eighteen (or nineteen if a student) or of any age if disabled before age twenty-two. Additionally, survivors' benefits go to certain classes of fully insured workers, as do disability benefits for qualified workers. One should be aware, however, that computing social security benefits involves complicated arithmetical formulas noting the worker's age; date of retirement, disability, or death; and yearly earnings history. Cost-of-living escalators tied to the **consumer price index** in certain circumstances may raise benefits as well.

Consumer price index Measurement of how the price of a group of consumer goods changes between two time periods.

Disability benefits—those granted to a worker who has been disabled at least five months—are computed in a similar manner, subject to some limitations for younger disabled workers. Additionally, for eligibility, the worker must prove that he or she can no longer engage in substantial gainful employment. The disability must be expected to last at least twelve months or to result in death. Finally, the worker must have sufficient quarters of coverage to be considered "fully insured" if near retirement age and must have worked at least twenty quarters of the last forty quarters before the disability began. Blind persons and some younger workers who become disabled face less stringent eligibility requirements. Receipt of benefits paid under workers' compensation or other federal, state, or local disability plans may lessen the amount of benefits received from social security.

Monthly payments made to a retired or disabled worker's family or to the survivors of an insured worker are equal to a certain percentage (usually 50 or 75 percent) of the worker's benefits. For example, if a worker were entitled to $379 per month in benefits, the worker's wife or divorced wife who was married to the worker for at least ten years and is not now married would receive $189.50 or $284.25 in monthly benefits. The act limits the amount one family can receive in total benefits. Similarly, benefits for a non-disabled child who is no longer attending high school normally end at age eighteen. Lump-sum death benefits to eligible persons cannot exceed $255. Earnings realized by retired persons between sixty-five and sixty-nine could not exceed $9,360 in 1990 without loss of benefits. The Social Security Administration (SSA) will reduce from the benefits of any worker who makes more than this amount one dollar for every three dollars over the limit. Social security coverage extends to most types of employment and self-employment; among those excluded are employees of the federal government and railroad workers.

Those who have been denied benefits may utilize certain administrative steps to appeal an SSA decision. Usually, such persons file a request for reconsideration within sixty days of the date of the initial determination. The agency then conducts a thorough and independent review of the evidence. After this reconsideration, a person who remains adversely affected can file for a hearing or review by an administrative law judge. After the hearing, the administrative law judge issues a written decision that sets out his or her findings of fact in understandable language. All parties receive copies of this decision. The decision is binding unless appealed to the Appeals Council of the SSA or to a federal district court.

The taxes paid by employees and employers on wages earned by workers not only fund social security retirement benefits but also help provide qualified persons with hospital insurance. Called Medicare, this protection normally is available to persons sixty-five years or older and to some disabled persons under sixty-five. Medicare covers doctors' services, hospital care, some nursing home care, certain home health services, and hospice care. In 1989, the tax rate paid was 7.51 percent on a maximum of $48,000 in employee wages.

In addition to receiving Medicare, qualified persons can pay for a government-subsidized plan called supplementary medical insurance to cover medical services beyond hospitalization, such as doctors' services and related medical expenses involving outpatient and rehabilitation costs. Another program, Medicaid, provides broad medical assistance to "categorically needy" individuals.

Unemployment Insurance

In addition to retirement, disability, and Medicare benefits, the Social Security Program covers unemployment insurance through the Federal Unemployment Tax Act. Unemployment insurance represents a coordinated federal and state effort to provide economic security for temporarily unemployed workers. The funds used in the unemployment insurance system come from taxes, or "contributions," paid predominantly by employers. In a few states, employees also pay these taxes. Those contributing pay federal taxes, which the government uses to administer the federal/state program, as well as state taxes, which the state uses to finance the payment of weekly benefits to unemployed workers.

Various credits allowed under federal law significantly reduce the amount of taxes paid in federal contributions. Essentially, computation of the taxes is based on a specified percentage of wages paid by the employer/employees. "Wages" include anything paid as compensation for employment and thus may include salaries, fees, bonuses, and commissions. Since 1983, the amount of wages subject to federal taxes for unemployment compensation is at most $7000 for each employee per calendar year. Many states' taxable wage bases are higher than this federal figure. State contribution rates may vary, but most have set a standard rate (such as 5.4 percent).

State rates, almost without exception, utilize "experience rating" or "merit rating" systems whereby the rate employers pay reflects each individual employer's experience with unemployment. Under such systems, employers whose workers suffer the most involuntary unemployment pay higher rates than employers whose workers suffer less unemployment. Since the aim of unemployment compensation involves the achievement of regular employment and the prevention of unemployment, such systems provide incentives to employers to keep their workforces intact and thereby to perpetuate the goals of these laws.

State provisions regarding the criteria for eligibility and the amount of benefits vary greatly. For instance, in different jurisdictions, unemployment compensation may not be available to employees discharged for cause, to those who quit their jobs without cause, or to those who refuse to seek or accept a job for which they are qualified. The plaintiff in the following case challenged the state's denial of unemployment compensation benefits on constitutional grounds.

Frazee v. *Illinois Department of Employment Security*
109 S.Ct. 1514 (1989)

FACTS   In April, 1984, William Frazee refused a temporary retail position offered him by Kelly Services because the job would have required him to work on Sunday. Frazee told Kelly Services that, as a Christian, he could not work on "the Lord's day." Frazee then applied to the Illinois Department of Employment Security for unemployment benefits, claiming that there was good cause for his refusal to work on Sunday. His application was denied. Frazee appealed this denial of benefits to the Department of Employment Security's Board of Review, which also denied his claim. The Board of Review concluded that Frazee had refused an offer of suitable work without good cause. The state circuit court affirmed, thereby rejecting Frazee's claim based on the free exercise clause of the First Amendment. The Illinois appellate court characterized Frazee's refusal to work as resting on his "personal professed religious belief," although it stated that it did "not question the sincerity of the plaintiff."

ISSUE   Did this denial of unemployment compensation benefits violate the First Amendment?

HOLDING Yes. The denial of unemployment compensation benefits to Frazee on the ground that his refusal to work was not based on the tenets or dogma of an established religious sect violated the free exercise clause of the First Amendment as applied to the states through the Fourteenth Amendment.

REASONING The Illinois Unemployment Insurance Act provides: "An individual shall be ineligible for benefits if he has failed, without good cause, either to apply for available, suitable work when so directed . . . or to accept suitable work when offered him. . . ." To the Illinois court, Frazee's position that he was "a Christian" and as such felt it wrong to work on Sunday was insufficient cause to refuse the position offered. For a free exercise clause claim to succeed, said the Illinois appellate court, "the injunction against Sunday labor must be found in a tenet or dogma of an established religious sect. [Frazee] does not profess to be a member of any such sect." The Illinois Supreme Court denied Frazee leave to appeal. Apropos of the issue here, several recent Supreme Court cases have held that a state's denial of unemployment compensation benefits violates the free exercise clause of the First Amendment as applied to the states through the Fourteenth Amendment. In each of those cases, the appellant had been "forced to choose between fidelity to religious belief and employment," and the Court concluded that "the forfeiture of unemployment benefits for choosing the former over the latter [had brought] unlawful coercion to bear on the employee's choice." It is true, as the Illinois court noted, that each of the claimants in those cases was a member of a particular religious sect; but none of those decisions turned on that consideration or on any tenet of the sect involved that forbade the work the claimant had refused to perform. Rather, those cases rested on the fact that each of the claimants had held a sincere belief that religion required him or her to refrain from the work in question. Nowhere did any of those cases suggest that unless a claimant belongs to a sect that forbids what his job requires, his belief, however sincere, must be deemed a purely personal preference rather than a religious belief. Of course, "only beliefs rooted in religion are protected by the free exercise clause"; secular views do not suffice. And one cannot underestimate the difficulty of distinguishing between religious and secular convictions and in determining whether a professed belief is sincerely held. States are clearly entitled to assure themselves that there is an ample predicate for invoking the free exercise clause. But such problems about sincerity or about the religious nature of Frazee's convictions are not at issue here, since the lower courts did not question his sincerity and the state conceded it. Frazee asserted that he was a Christian but did not claim to be a member of a particular Christian sect. Undoubtedly, membership in an organized religious denomination, especially one with a specific tenet forbidding members to work on Sunday, would simplify the problem of identifying sincerely held religious beliefs. But the notion that to claim the protection of the free exercise clause one must be responding to the commands of a particular religious organization must be rejected. Here, Frazee's refusal was based on a sincerely held religious belief. Supreme Court precedents entitled Frazee to invoke First Amendment protection. The state did not appear to defend this aspect of the decision. In its brief and at oral argument, the state conceded that the free exercise clause does not demand adherence to a tenet or dogma of an established religious sect. Instead, the state proposed its own test for identifying a "religious" belief, asserted that Frazee had not met such a test, and asked for affirmance on this basis. The state recognized Frazee's conviction as religious but nonetheless found it to be inadequate because it did not represent a tenet of a religious organization of which he was a member. That ground for decision was clearly erroneous. State interests sufficiently compelling to override a legitimate claim to the free exercise of religion may exist, but no such interest has been presented here. The judgment of the Illinois appellate court is therefore reversed and the case remanded for further proceedings not inconsistent with this opinion.

**Workers'
Compensation**

Workers' compensation statutes are not the same as unemployment statutes, although both concern the welfare of workers. Workers' compensation laws in the various states attempt to reimburse workers for injuries or death arising in the employment context. "Compensation" in this area does not therefore refer to wages or salaries but rather to the money paid by the employer to indemnify the worker for employment-related injury or death. The employer usually self-insures, buys insurance, or pays money into a state insurance fund at a "merit" or "experience" rate, as discussed earlier, reflective of the employer's actual incidence of employee injuries. Injured workers then receive compensation for their injuries in the form of medical care and disability benefits, the latter often based on a specific statutory scale (such as 60 percent of average weekly wages up to $100 in average weekly wages for twenty-six weeks), through administrative proceedings in front of a workers' compensation board.

Workers' compensation acts thus impose strict liability on the employer for injuries to employees during the scope of their employment. These laws first arose out of lawmakers' concern for employees injured as a result of increased industrial mechanization, but these acts serve other functions as well. For instance, through such statutes, employees can receive compensation without engaging in costly litigation, and the employer can recoup the costs of workers' compensation by passing these costs on to consumers. Both sides benefit, since the employee receives reimbursement for the injuries suffered and the employer's liability to the employee usually ends there; that is, the statutes ordinarily prohibit the employee from suing the employer in a court of law. Such acts, then, are grounded in public policy concerns.

The classes of employees covered by such acts depend on the particular statute involved. Agricultural, domestic, or casual laborers often are not covered because the right to compensation ordinarily depends on the nature of the work performed, the regularity of such work, and/or whether the worker was working as an independent contractor for someone else when injured. To be covered, an employee ordinarily must be a "worker"—that is, a person who performs manual labor or similar duties. For this reason, workers' compensation statutes would seemingly not cover directors, officers, or stockholders. Yet under the "dual capacity" doctrine, such persons can receive compensation if they are performing the ordinary duties of the business when injured. For example, a general manager of a tree-pruning service who is injured while pruning trees will be able to recover. If the general manager were instead working as an independent contractor (not for the corporation), he or she normally would be ineligible to receive workers' compensation.

In general, however, just about any employment-related injury or disease makes the covered employee eligible for workers' compensation. For this reason, even a negligent employee usually can recover for injuries suffered while in the employment relationship. Contrast this statutory result with what would have occurred at common law: The employer could have used the employee's contributory negligence as a complete bar to recovery. Recent decisions have allowed recoveries for occupational diseases such as asbestosis, for work-related stress, and even for injuries suffered before or after working hours. Although workers' compensation takes the place of an employee's suing the employer for the injuries suffered, employees still can maintain product liability suits against manufacturers or suppliers and also can sue any fellow employees who cause their injuries.

SUMMARY

The Wagner Act, the Taft-Hartley Act, and the Landrum-Griffin Act set out a pervasive federal scheme for the regulation of labor. This blueprint of federal labor law broadly regulates employees' rights to organize and to engage in concerted activities in furtherance of their objectives. Both employees and employers are protected from unfair labor practices. The National Labor Relations Board retains jurisdiction over labor disputes, oversees elections, arbitrates disputes about the duty to bargain, and almost wholly preempts the states' jurisdiction over labor matters, except for criminal violations or torts, retaliatory discharges, and the like.

A host of federal statutes extensively regulates fair employment practices. Title VII of the Civil Rights Act of 1964 prohibits employment discrimination based on race, color, religion, sex, or national origin by employers, labor organizations, or employment agencies. The Equal Employment Opportunity Commission enforces many of these federal laws and sets out the complex procedures with which a grievant must comply. Employment criteria that have a disparate impact on minorities are illegal unless the employer can show that the criteria are job related. Employers also may be liable for the disparate treatment of their employees. The issue of "reverse discrimination" remains controversial in the Title VII context. Limited defenses based on bona fide occupational qualifications (BFOQs) are available for the protected categories of religion, sex, and national origin; a BFOQ can never be based on race, however. The Equal Pay Act, the Age Discrimination in Employment Act, the Rehabilitation Act of 1973, the Americans with Disabilities Act of 1990, the Civil Rights Act of 1991, and other federal statutes protect qualified individuals against employment discrimination. State law often supplements this comprehensive federal scheme.

The Occupational Safety and Health Act attempts to ensure safe and healthful working conditions for American workers. Inspections of the workplace provide a mechanism for realizing this statutory goal. Warrantless inspections conducted after the owner refuses entry to the inspector are illegal. Workers, in contrast, can legally walk off the job if performance of the work assignment can lead to serious injury or death.

Federal and state social security benefits aid workers, the disabled, the blind, and the aged. Computations of benefits are complex. Those who have been denied benefits may utilize certain administrative steps to appeal such agency decisions. Because both employers and employees must pay social security and hospital care taxes on wages earned by the workers, the record-keeping burdens posed by such provisions have nettled employers.

Unemployment insurance is designed to provide economic security for temporarily unemployed workers. The contributions paid into the insurance fund stem from a specified percentage of wages paid by the employer or employee. State taxable wage bases may differ from the federal figure, and state provisions regarding the criteria for eligibility and the amount of benefits vary greatly.

State workers' compensation statutes attempt to reimburse workers for injuries or death resulting from the employment relationship. In return, such statutes generally prohibit the employee from suing the employer in a court of law. The classes of employees covered in such acts depend on the particular statute involved; but eligible employees may recover for occupational diseases, injuries resulting from the employee's own negligence, and injuries sustained before or after working hours. Workers' compensation statutes ordinarily do not preclude an employee's maintaining either a product liability suit against a manufacturer or a suit against a fellow employee who caused the injuries at issue.

DISCUSSION QUESTIONS

1. List some of the rights guaranteed and the practices prohibited by the Wagner, Taft-Hartley, and Landrum-Griffin acts.
2. Describe some of the issues and enforcement problems involved in the collective-bargaining process.
3. Explain the boundaries of state regulation of labor.
4. What are the protected classes of employees under Title VII?
5. Define and describe the two methods by which an employee can show liability for discrimination on the basis of the protected categories set out in Title VII.

6. Why is the issue of "reverse discrimination" such a difficult problem?
7. Define the term *bona fide occupational qualification*.
8. Name some other statutes that guarantee fair employment, and explain how these more recent ones build on previous fair employment statutes.
9. Describe a typical OSHA inspection.
10. Name the classes of persons eligible for social security, unemployment insurance, and workers' compensation.

CASE PROBLEMS

1. Approximately two months before a vote on unionization, the employer, Wiljef, read to its employees a corporate bylaw stating: "Section 2—Corporate Dissolution. Wiljef Transportation, Inc. hereby expresses as a matter of corporate policy that operations will cease and the corporation will be dissolved in the event of unionization of its employees. As hereby authorized by the Board of Directors, this bylaw may be announced to the employees of Wiljef Transportation, Inc. at any time deemed appropriate by the Board." The firm had adopted the bylaw in 1979, and the announcement occurred in 1988. In the ensuing union representation election, the employees rejected unionization. The Supreme Court, in addressing the tension between an employer's right to announce the probable consequences

of unionization and the employees' right to organize without threat of retaliation had made the following points. On the one hand, the employer's right to communicate its views to its employees is firmly established in the First Amendment and is recognized in Section 8(c) of the NLRA, which provides that "the expressing of any views, argument, or opinion . . . shall not constitute or be evidence of an unfair labor practice . . . if such expression contains no threat of reprisal or force or promise of benefit." On the other hand, the exceptions to the freedom of expression recognized in Section 8(c) reflect the right of employees to associate free of coercion by the employer. Section 8(a)(1) of the NLRA codifies that right by declaring that it is an unfair labor practice to interfere with, restrain, or coerce employees who are exercising their right to organize in unions. The difficulty in attempting to reconcile these two rights lies in determining when speech becomes essentially coercive rather than factually informative or predictive so as to fall outside the protection of the First Amendment and violate the NLRA. The issue in this case centered on whether the announcement of the bylaw constituted a "permitted prediction" of plant closure or a "proscribed threat." The NLRB had held that the announcement represented a threat in violation of Section 8(a)(1) of the NLRA, and Wiljef had appealed to the Seventh Circuit Court of Appeals. How should that court rule in this case? (*Wiljef Transportation Incorporated* v. *National Labor Relations Board*, 946 F.2d 1308 [7th Cir. 1991].)

2. To celebrate a new supplier agreement, New River Industries, Inc. (New River), an acetate fiber manufacturer, announced that it would serve refreshments to its employees. New River issued tickets redeemable in the lunchroom for free ice cream cones. Some employees ridiculed the ice cream cones and suggested writing a letter to "thank" the company for its generosity. Smith drafted a letter, and Simpson agreed to type it. Smith posted the letter on an open bulletin board. This letter and several subsequent copies were removed from the open bulletin board and from a locked bulletin board. The final copy had a handwritten notation at the bottom: "United NRI Workers Vote Union on 1 January." Simpson and Smith, both valued employees, were dismissed for violation of plant rules (posting an unauthorized notice that disrupted the workforce and derogating and undermining management and fellow employees). Simpson filed an unfair labor practice charge with the NLRB. An administrative law judge (ALJ) found that Smith and Simpson had been discharged for union activity in violation of the NLRA and for other "concerted activities." Section 7 of the NLRA provides that an activity, to be protected, must be "for the purpose of collective bargaining or other mutual aid or protection." According to Supreme Court precedents, the "mutual aid or protection" clause of Section 7 protects employees who "seek to improve terms and conditions of employment or otherwise improve their lot as employees through channels outside the immediate employee-employer relationship." Did Simpson and Smith's preparation of a sarcastic letter that was critical of the employer's gift of free ice cream cones to employees constitute protected concerted activity within the meaning of the NLRA? (*New River Industries, Inc.* v. *National Labor Relations Board*, 945 F.2d 1290 [4th Cir. 1991].)

3. Gene Arline (Arline) had taught elementary school in Nassau County, Florida, from 1966 until 1979, when she was discharged after having suffered a third relapse of tuberculosis within two years. Arline argued that the school board had dismissed her solely on the basis of her illness, which she contended was a handicap under the Rehabilitation Act of 1973. The school board asserted that a contagious disease was not protectable under the act and that, in any event, Arline was not a "handicapped" individual because she was not "qualified" to teach owing to her disease. Was Arline a handicapped person under the Rehabilitation Act of 1973? (*School Board of Nassau County, Florida* v. *Arline*, 107 S.Ct. 1123 [1987], reh'g denied 107 S.Ct. 1913 [1987].)

4. The United States Customs Service (Service), which has as its primary enforcement mission the interdiction and seizure of illegal drugs smuggled into the country, implemented a drug-screening program requiring urinalysis tests of Service employees seeking transfer or promotion to positions having a direct involvement in drug interdiction or requiring the incumbent to carry firearms or to handle "classified" material. Among other things, the program required that an applicant be notified that his or her selection was contingent on successful completion of drug screening; set forth procedures for collection and analysis of the requisite samples and procedures designed both to ensure against adulteration or substitution of specimens and to limit the intrusion on employee privacy; and provided that test results may not be turned over to any other agency, including criminal prosecutors, without the employee's written consent. The National Treasury Employees Union, a federal employees' union, and one of its officials filed suit on behalf of Service employees seeking covered positions, alleging that the drug-testing program violated the Fourth Amendment because the program required no warrant, no probable cause, and no level of individualized suspicion before an individual was tested. The district court agreed and enjoined the program. The court of appeals vacated the injunction, however, holding that, although the program effects a search within the meaning of the Fourth Amendment, such searches are reasonable in light of their limited scope and the Service's strong interest in detecting drug use among employees in the covered positions. Von Raab, the commissioner of the United States Customs Service, also argued in behalf of the program that, given the national crisis in

law enforcement caused by the smuggling of illicit narcotics, the government has a compelling interest in ensuring that front-line interdiction personnel are physically fit and have unimpeachable integrity and judgment. According to Von Raab, the government also has a compelling interest in preventing the risk to the life of the citizenry posed by the potential use of deadly force by persons suffering from impaired perception and judgment. In Von Raab's view, these governmental interests outweigh the privacy interests of those seeking promotion to such positions, who have a diminished expectation of privacy with respect to the intrusions occasioned by a urine test by virtue of the special, and obvious physical and ethical, demands of the position. How should the Supreme Court rule in this case? (*National Treasury Employees Union* v. *Von Raab,* 489 U.S. 656 [1989].)

5. Sidney Taylor, vice-president of Capital City Federal Saving and Loan Association (Capital City), asked Mechelle Vinson to apply for employment with Capital City. Vinson was hired as a teller-trainee, and Taylor became her supervisor at the Northeast Branch. She was promoted successively to teller, head teller, and assistant branch manager. After Vinson had worked at the Northeast Branch for four years, she took an indefinite sick leave and was discharged two months later for excessive use of that leave. Vinson subsequently brought an action under Title VII against Taylor and Capital City, alleging that Taylor had sexually harassed her. Vinson contended that Taylor had asked her to have sexual relations with him, claiming that she "owed him" because he had obtained the job for her, and that after initially declining his invitation she ultimately had yielded, but only because she had been afraid that continued refusals would jeopardize her employment. She further asserted that she had been forced to submit to sexual advances by Taylor at the Northeast Branch both during and after business hours and that often Taylor had assaulted or raped her. In addition, she said that Taylor had caressed her on the job, had followed her into the ladies' room when she had been there alone, and at times had exposed himself to her. Capital City argued that it should not be held liable for its supervisor's sexual harassment owing to its lack of actual knowledge of the conduct. Would you agree? Also, should a successful sexual harassment case be dependent on the alleged victim's suffering a loss of employment or promotions? (*Meritor Savings Bank* v. *Vinson,* 477 U.S. 57 [1986].)

6. As part of the 1980 settlement of a Title VII lawsuit filed by Carl Stotts, a black firefighter, against the Memphis, Tenn., Fire Department, the city agreed to a court-imposed consent decree whereby the city promised to promote thirteen individuals, to provide back-pay for eighty-two others, and to increase minority representation in each job classification of the fire department to approximate the proportion of blacks in the labor force in Shelby County, Tenn. The 1980 decree also established hiring and promotion goals with respect to blacks. In May, 1981, owing to projected budget deficits, the city announced layoffs in city government. Layoffs were to be based on the "last-hired, first-fired" rule under which city-wide seniority, determined by each employee's length of continuous service, would be the factor in deciding who would be laid off. Following this announcement, the district court entered an order prohibiting the layoffs of black employees. The order led to the layoffs or demotions of nonminority employees who had attained more seniority than minority employees who had been retained. Was it legal under Title VII to deny nonminority employees the benefits of their seniority in order to provide a remedy in a case alleging a pattern or practice of discrimination where the black employees protected from layoffs were not identifiable victims of discrimination? (*Firefighters Local Union No. 1784* v. *Stotts,* 467 U.S. 561 [1984].)

7. Transportation Agency of Santa Clara County, Calif. (the Agency) adopted an affirmative action plan that allowed it to consider sex as one factor whenever it made promotions to positions within traditionally segregated job classifications in which women had been significantly underrepresented. In selecting applicants for the position of road dispatcher, the Agency passed over Paul Johnson to promote a female applicant, Diane Joyce. Before Joyce, women had held none of the 238 skilled craftworker positions in the Agency. Although both individuals were qualified for the job, Johnson had scored slightly higher on the interview than Joyce. When the Agency nonetheless promoted Joyce, Johnson sued, arguing that the Agency's affirmative action plan violated Title VII of the Civil Rights Act by taking sex into account for promotions. Was he correct? (*Johnson* v. *Transportation Agency, Santa Clara County, California,* 107 S.Ct. 1442 [1987].)

8. Forth Worth Bank and Trust (the Bank) hired Clara Watson, who is black, as a proof operator in August, 1973. In January, 1976, the Bank promoted Watson to a teller position in the Bank's drive-in facility. In Feb-

ruary, 1980, she sought to become supervisor of tellers in the main lobby; however, the Bank selected a white male for this job. Watson then applied for a position as supervisor of the drive-in bank, but this position went to a white female. In February, 1981, after Watson had served for about a year as a commercial teller in the Bank's main lobby and informally as the assistant to the supervisor of tellers, the Bank promoted the man holding that position. Watson applied for the vacancy, but the Bank instead selected the white female who had served as the supervisor of the drive-in bank. Watson then sought the position vacancy created at the drive-in, but a white male won that job. The Bank, which has about eighty employees, had not developed precise and formal criteria for evaluating candidates for the positions for which Watson had unsuccessfully applied. Rather, it had relied on the subjective judgment of supervisors who were acquainted with the candidates and with the nature of the jobs to be filled. All the supervisors involved in denying Watson the four promotions at issue were white. Watson initially filed a discrimination charge with the EEOC. After exhausting her administrative remedies, she filed a lawsuit in the district court. She alleged that the Bank had unlawfully discriminated against blacks in hiring, compensation, initial placement, promotions, terminations, and other terms and conditions of employment. The district court concluded that Watson had failed to establish a prima facie case of racial discrimination in hiring, since the percentage of blacks in the Bank's workforce approximated the percentage of blacks in the metropolitan area where the Bank is located. The district court addressed Watson's individual claims under the evidentiary standards that apply in a discriminatory treatment case and determined, on the evidence presented at trial, that Watson had established a prima facie case of employment discrimination but that the Bank had met its rebuttal burden by presenting legitimate and nondiscriminatory reasons for each of the challenged promotion decisions. The court also concluded that Watson had failed to show that these reasons had been pretexts for racial discrimination and dismissed Watson's lawsuit. A divided panel of the Court of Appeals for the Fifth Circuit affirmed the district court's conclusion that Watson had failed to prove her claim of racial discrimination. Although Watson argued that the district court had erred in failing to apply disparate impact analysis to her claims of discrimination in promotion, the majority of the court of appeals panel held that "a Title VII challenge to an allegedly discretionary promotion system is properly analyzed under the disparate treatment model rather than the disparate impact model." Other courts of appeals, however, had held that disparate impact analysis could be applied to hiring or promotion systems that involve the use of "discretionary" or "subjective" criteria. Apropos of these precedents, Watson claimed that subjective selection methods are at least as likely to have discriminatory effects as the kind of objective tests at issue in *Griggs* and other disparate impact cases. Furthermore, she argued, if courts confine disparate impact analysis to objective tests, employers will be able to substitute subjective criteria having substantially identical effects; and *Griggs* will become a dead letter. The Bank argued that conventional disparate treatment analysis is adequate to accomplish Congress's purpose in enacting Title VII and that subjective selection practices would be so impossibly difficult to defend under disparate impact analysis that employers would be forced to adopt numerical quotas in order to avoid liability. Whose arguments should the Supreme Court endorse—Watson or the Bank's? (*Watson* v. *Fort Worth Bank & Trust*, 487 U.S. 977 [1988].)

9. The Office of Civil Rights (OCR) of the United States Department of Education had employed Debra Mc-Wright as an equal opportunity specialist in its Chicago office between 14 February 1977 and 17 March 1983. As an infant, she had contracted polio, which left her with various permanent physical handicaps, including an inability to bear children. The OCR had hired McWright as a "handicapped individual" pursuant to Section 501 of the Rehabilitation Act of 1973. McWright informed her immediate supervisor, OCR branch chief Catherine Martin, in July, 1982, that she was seeking an adoption and would request maternal child care extended leave if a child were placed with her and her husband. In September, McWright told Martin and Martin's supervisor, Mary Frances O'Shea, that she had been accepted as an adoptive parent. In November, 1982, McWright filed applications for annual leave of four weeks and extended leave without pay but did not list any particular dates because she did not yet know when the child placement would occur; total leave time would amount to about four months. In December, 1982, Martin gave McWright three options: She could take immediate annual and extended leave, she could specify a future certain date to begin them, or she could take them on short notice in the future on the condition that she complete her then pending assignments before

taking the time off. McWright considered the first two alternatives unacceptable and therefore agreed to the third. The next day, Martin gave McWright three new civil rights violation case assignments, which might have taken McWright a year or more to complete, according to McWright. After learning on 5 January 1983 that a child would soon be available, McWright resubmitted her leave application, seeking four weeks' annual leave from 11 January to 7 February and seeking three months' extended leave without pay from 8 February to 17 May. Martin denied the request for annual leave, and O'Shea denied the request for leave without pay. The OCR gave McWright four days off with pay after an adoptive son was placed with McWright and her spouse on 11 January. McWright's renewed request for leave was informally approved on 7 February 1983, on the condition that she work at home during the annual leave period. She accepted, began her annual leave the following day, and worked at home. Her request for leave without pay from 10 March to 29 June was approved unconditionally on 28 February 1983. However, on 10 March, Martin informed McWright that she must complete her pending civil rights violation assignments before her three months' leave could begin and submitted the necessary paperwork requesting cancellation of McWright's leave without pay. McWright alleged that these actions had caused her to suffer physical and emotional exhaustion preventing her from returning to work at the OCR. She informed her supervisors on 17 March 1983 that she would be forced to resign unless she received leave without pay; but the OCR denied her request for leave. McWright resigned her position that day. She subsequently filed suit against the OCR, alleging that it had failed to accommodate her handicap (her inability to bear children) when it had refused to waive two conditions it normally required for maternal child care leave (but which McWright had been unable to meet): Medical certification and specification in advance of the leave period. She further alleged disparate treatment. She claimed that the OCR had consistently granted the extended leave requests of biological mothers, that the OCR had not required biological mothers to complete their pending work beforehand, and that the OCR had not obligated biological mothers to work at home on an uncompensated basis while on leave. As a result of the OCR's alleged failure to accommodate and its disparate treatment of her, McWright claimed that her working conditions had become unreasonable and that her resignation therefore had constituted a constructive discharge (i.e., her resignation had been forced on her by the circumstances and was tantamount to the OCR itself firing her). Would McWright win on appeal? (*McWright* v. *Alexander,* 771 F. Supp. 256 [N.D. Ill. 1991].)

10. When Congress in 1978 amended the Age Discrimination in Employment Act (ADEA) to prohibit most mandatory retirements of individuals between forty and seventy, a Federal Aviation Administration regulation prohibited anyone from serving after age sixty as a captain or first officer on a commercial carrier. This regulation did not affect flight engineers. In response to the ADEA 1978 amendment, Trans World Airlines (TWA) modified its retirement procedures. Under TWA's modified plan, flight engineers were permitted to continue work after age sixty. Captains and first officers had to bid to obtain flight engineer status prior to reaching age sixty, and vacancies were filled only as they occurred. A captain who had been displaced for any reason other than age would not have to resort to the bidding procedure; these captains automatically displaced less senior flight engineers. Thurston and other captains who had been involuntarily retired on reaching age sixty and who thereby had been denied opportunities to "bump" less senior flight engineers sued the airline, contending that its policies had violated the ADEA. Were they correct? Was TWA's retirement policy justified either as a BFOQ or as part of a bona fide seniority system? (*Trans World Airlines, Inc.* v. *Thurston,* 469 U.S. 111 [1985].)

PART 9
Property Protection

When a society forms, it must go through certain stages. When primitive people first began to form tribes, they had a reason for seeking companionship—survival. A tribe allowed for more hunters, and therefore for more food. The larger numbers of people making up the tribe also provided for better defense, more children, and a better chance of perpetuating the species. However, tribal existence also led to internal conflicts, which led to a need for the formation of law. The earliest laws were undoubtedly designed to keep peace within the tribal unit.

Once peace was attained, and human beings began to feel personally secure, their attention shifted. Being assured of peace, they began to seek ways to acquire wealth, and to protect their wealth once they did acquire it. Thus developed the laws of property protection. And once their property was protected, human beings began to seek means for assuring that their families would be protected should some disaster befall them. From this desire came the laws of trusts, wills, estates, and insurance.

When people have no personal security, property is relatively unimportant. Once personal security is provided for, property protection becomes relatively important. This part of the text deals with the bases of property protection in our society.

49
REAL PROPERTY AND JOINT OWNERSHIP

50
PERSONAL PROPERTY AND BAILMENTS

51
INSURANCE

52
WILLS AND ESTATES

53
TRUSTS AND TRUST ADMINISTRATION

CHAPTER 49

Real Property and Joint Ownership

OUTLINE

PROPERTY RIGHTS

There are two distinctly different meanings for *property*. One meaning is the object that is subject to ownership, the valuable asset. The second meaning is the group of rights and interests that are protected by the law. A multitude of rights are associated with property ownership. Ownership entitles a person to use the property personally, to give someone else the use of the property, to rent the use of the property to someone else, or to use the property to secure a loan. The owner may sell the property, make improvements to the property, or abandon the property. Ownership of real estate often entitles the owner to continued use and enjoyment of the property in its present condition. For example, suppose you owned a house with a beautiful view of the mountains. If someone purchased an adjacent lot and started constructing a three-story house that would block your view, you could sue for an injunction to prohibit that person from interfering with the view. Such a lawsuit would be successful in some states.

REAL PROPERTY DEFINED

This chapter deals with *real property* or, as it is commonly called, real estate. There are significant differences between real and personal property. Real property is *land and things that are permanently attached to land,* including buildings, roadways, and storage structures. Personal property, on the other hand, consists of movable goods. Property that is permanently attached to buildings is also considered real property and is called a *fixture.* In determining whether an item is a fixture or a household good, courts will look at the reasonable expectations and understanding of most people. For instance, most people would be shocked if they bought a house and, when they moved in, discovered that the sellers had removed the handles on the kitchen cabinets and the plates over the light switches. The same buyers would expect the sellers to remove the tables, chairs, and other furniture. Ceiling lights are fixtures; table lamps are household goods. Plants in a flower bed are real property; plants in pots are personal property. Wall-to-wall carpeting is real property; area rugs are personal property. Refrigerators, mirrors, and paintings are generally personal property but may be real property if they are an integral part of the building.

A fixture is property that at one time was movable and independent of real estate but became attached to it. Examples are water heaters, central air-conditioning units, furnaces, built-in ovens, installed dishwashers, bathroom sinks, and copper pipes for plumbing. A builder who is constructing a house will buy a water heater, take it to the construction site, and permanently attach it to the plumbing lines and the gas or electric lines. After the personal property has been attached, it becomes a fixture.

In determining whether property is personal property or a fixture, courts also consider another factor: How much damage would occur if the property in question were removed. For example, would the building be damaged by the removal of a brick fireplace? What would the wall look like after the fireplace was removed?

Another issue concerns plants: Are they real property or personal property? Real estate includes plants that are growing on the land, such as fruit and shade trees, tomatoes, strawberries or artichokes, and trees that are being grown for timber. If a farmer sells land with crops still growing on it, the farmer is clearly selling real estate. Sometimes a farmer or another landowner may sell the plants but keep the land. In this case, did the landowner sell real or personal property? The common law rule is that if the plants were still growing when the **title** passed to the buyer, the sale was of real estate. If the title passed after the plants were severed from the land, the sale was of personal property. This rule is difficult to apply because in many instances the buyer and seller never discuss when title should pass.

Title The legal recognition of property ownership.

For this reason, the Uniform Commercial Code uses a different test, one that is much easier to apply. Under the UCC test, the determining factor is *who* is going to remove the plants or trees. If the *buyer* is going to remove them, the buyer has purchased real property. If the *seller* is going to remove them, the buyer has purchased personal property. After defining the difference between real and personal property, the UCC generally is not concerned with real estate, although some sections of the UCC do discuss fixtures and crops. A few states still follow the common law.

Property laws vary from state to state. The laws of a state where the real property is located govern the transaction, regardless of the residence of the owner. For example, if you live in Utah but own land in Ohio, Ohio law governs your transactions with respect to the Ohio real property.

ACQUISITION OF REAL PROPERTY

Original Occupancy

Original occupancy (original entry) occurs when the government allows *the private ownership of land that was previously owned by the government*. In the United States, title may have been acquired by grant from either the United States government or the other countries that colonized here. Original occupancy may be accomplished under an outright grant to specific people or families, or it may have occurred under **homestead entry laws.**

Homestead entry laws Laws that allowed settlers to claim public lands by entering, filing an application, and paying any fees.

Voluntary Transfer by the Owner

The owner of real property may sell, trade, or give title to another by executing (signing) a deed. The recipient can be another private individual, a business entity, or a government body. In any of these cases, the transfer of title is made by the execution and delivery of a written deed of conveyance. A *deed* is the type of title evidence that is used for real estate, and it indicates who owns the land. A written document is required by the Statute of Frauds. This document must adequately describe the property that is being transferred. Documents that transfer important interests in real estate must also be in writing. An example of this type of document is a mortgage, which is a loan of money secured by real estate.

A deed describes the land being transferred and generally includes the following items:

1. the names of the grantor (transferor) and the grantee (transferee)
2. the amount of consideration, if any, that was paid by the grantee
3. a statement that the grantor intended to make the transfer (commonly called words of conveyance)
4. an adequate description of the property (the street address by itself will not be sufficient; usually this description contains information provided by a private or government survey)
5. a list and description of any ownership rights that are not included in the conveyance (such as mineral rights, oil rights, or **easements**)
6. the quantity of the estate conveyed
7. any covenants or warranties from the grantor or grantee (some may be implied under the state law; others may be expressed in the deed, such as the grantee can never allow alcohol to be sold on the premises; usually the deed specifies that these covenants are binding on the grantee and his or her heirs and assigns)
8. the signature of the grantor or grantors

Easements Rights to the access and use of someone else's real estate.

Types of Deeds A *warranty deed* contains a number of implied covenants (or promises) made by the grantor to the effect that a good and marketable title is being conveyed. All the following covenants are included:

1. covenant of title (the grantor owns the estate or interest that he or she is purporting to convey)
2. covenant of right to convey (the grantor has the power, authority, and right to transfer this interest in the property)
3. covenant against encumbrances (there are no encumbrances on the property except for those listed on the deed; encumbrances would include easements, mortgages, and similar restrictions on ownership)
4. covenant of quiet enjoyment (the grantor promises that the grantee's possession or enjoyment of the property will not be disturbed by another person with a lawful claim of title)
5. covenant to defend (the grantor promises to defend the grantee against any lawful or reasonable claims of a third party against the title of the grantee)

A *grant deed* contains fewer promises than a warranty deed. Basically, it includes only a covenant that the grantor has not conveyed this property interest to anyone else. The grantor also promises that all the encumbrances are listed on the deed.

With a *quitclaim deed,* the grantor makes no promises about his or her interest in the property. The grantor simply releases any interest that he or she has.

Delivery of the Deed   To complete a transfer of real property, the grantor *must* deliver the deed to the grantee or have it delivered to the grantee by a third party. The delivery evidences the grantor's intention to transfer the property.

Instead of handing the deed directly to the grantee, the grantor may use a third person to make the transfer. Sometimes, as in a sales transaction, it is important to use an impartial third party to assist in the transfer and to protect both the buyer and seller. This third party is charged with the obligation of supervising the transfer, including such activities as collecting the deed, collecting the funds, checking that utility bills and liens have been paid, checking that back taxes have been paid, prorating real estate taxes, prorating interest payments if a mortgage is being assumed, and checking that the parties have fulfilled any conditions such as repairs and inspections of the premises. This procedure is called an escrow and is a common method of transferring property in some states. The person who supervises this type of delivery may be an attorney, an *escrow officer* (an employee of a bank or escrow company who oversees the escrow transaction), or another agent.

Escrow Period when buyer and seller prepare for the exchange of real estate.

Recording of the Deed   Recording is accomplished by giving the deed to the proper authority, usually the county clerk or county recorder. The recorder files the deed or a copy of it in a deed book. Deed books usually are arranged in chronological order. The recorder also enters information about the transfer in an index, which is organized by the names of the grantors and grantees or by the location of the property. The index makes locating information about a particular parcel easy. The recording gives the whole world notice of the transfer to this grantee. Recording is not a legal prerequisite to the transfer, but it does establish the grantee's interest in the property, and in many states recorded deeds have priority over unrecorded deeds.

Transfer by Will or Intestate Succession

A person can arrange to leave real property by provisions in a valid will. If a person does not have a valid will, the property will pass by the intestate succession statute of the state where the property is located. This statute will determine who inherits the property if a valid will does not exist. (Wills are discussed in detail in Chapter 52.)

PROTECTION OF REAL PROPERTY

Real property is subject to loss by operation of law; it can also be lost due to actions of the government, actions of another person, or actions of nature. This loss is generally involuntary on the part of the owner. To prevent it, the owner should be alert to these potential causes of loss.

Involuntary Transfers by Operation of Law

If the owner is in default on a mortgage or trust deed, the owner may lose the property. The lender may institute foreclosure proceedings and take possession of the real estate. The lender must follow the appropriate state laws. Usually, the property will be sold at a foreclosure sale.

If the owner has not paid a legal judgment, the judgment creditor may ask the court for a writ of execution. Following state procedures, the sheriff will attach the property and sell it at a judgment sale. (Under state law, some property, both real and personal, may be exempt from attachment under a judgment sale.)

If the owner has not paid people who supplied labor or materials for the premises, these suppliers may also be able to force a sale under state law. These workers may have mechanics' liens for the value of the supplies or services rendered to improve the property. Even if they do not force a sale of the real property, generally they can prevent a voluntary sale of the property unless they are paid from the proceeds.

Involuntary Transfers by Government Action

Government bodies may take all or part of the owner's property by eminent domain. The government can also "take" the owner's land by restricting the manner in which it is used.

Government bodies have *the right to take private lands if they are necessary for public use*. This is called the right of *eminent domain*. Under this doctrine the government must have a legitimate public use for the land and must pay the owner a reasonable amount for it.

Zoning and planning laws restrict how property may be used. They may prevent certain types of structures from being built on the property; for example, some areas may be limited to single-family residences. Or they may not allow certain industries to operate plants in particular areas because of the air pollution that these plants would cause. Sometimes they restrict the number and placement of establishments that sell alcohol. Commonly, bars are not allowed within one-quarter mile of public schools. In order to be valid, zoning and planning laws must be based on a compelling state interest, and the restrictions must be reasonable.

Adverse Possession

✗ *Adverse possession* occurs when *someone tries to take title and possession of real estate from the owner*. A person who has physical possession of real property has better legal rights to that property than anyone else, except for the true owner and people who claim possession through the true owner. If the possession is of an adverse nature and if the possession is for a sufficient length of time, the adverse possessor may actually take ownership from the true owner.

For possession to be adverse, it must be _actual, open,_ and _notorious._ *Actual* possession means that the adverse possessor is actually on the land and is using the real estate in a reasonable manner for that type of land—as a residence, a farm, a ranch, or a business office. It is not sufficient that the adverse possessor states that he or she is using the land; actual use is required.

The possession must be _open;_ that is, it must be obvious that the adverse possessor is on the property. It will not be sufficient if the person stays out of sight during the day and walks around the property only at night. Openness is required to reasonably put the owner and the rest of the world on notice that the adverse possessor is using the property.

The possession must also be _notorious,_ which means that it is adverse or hostile to the true owner. Generally, people who occupy or use the property with the owner's permission, such as co-owners and renters, cannot be adverse possessors.

The required holding period varies from state to state and is specified by state statute. The period may range from five to thirty years. Entry under _color of title_ may affect the holding period. Entering under color of title means that the holder thought that he or she had a legal right to take possession of the real property and had title to it. For example, a person with a defective deed would enter under color of title. Some states specify a shorter holding period if the holder entered under color of title and/or if the holder paid real estate taxes. In some states, the payment of real estate taxes is a necessary requirement for adverse possession; in others, color of title is required.

The possession must be continuous for the specified time period. The adverse possessor may leave the property for short periods to go to work, to classes, or on a brief vacation, for example, but he or she may not leave the property for an extended period of time.

The constitutionality of these laws was addressed in the case that follows.

Lucas v. South Carolina Coastal Council
60 U.S.L.W. 4842 (1992)

FACTS In the late 1970's, Lucas and others were involved in extensive residential development on the Isle of Palms, a barrier island east of Charleston, South Carolina. In 1986 Lucas paid $975,000 for two residential lots for his own investment. His intent was to build single-family homes on the lots and he had architectural drawings prepared. When he purchased the lots, the property was not subject to the State's requirements for building in coastal regions because this area was not defined as a critical area. Owners in critical areas were required to obtain building permits from the South Carolina Coastal Council. At the time of the purchase, the lots were zoned for single-family residential use and there were no other restrictions on them. In 1988 the legislature passed the Beachfront Management Act, based on an official report that the stated beaches were seriously eroding. The Act directed the Council to establish a baseline and the Act permanently prohibited the building of _any_ inhabitable structures between the baseline and the ocean. This was because the area was not stabilized as described by the Act, and the legislature concluded that the setback lines were required to protect people and property from storms, high tides and beach erosion. There were *no* exceptions allowed under the Act. When the Council established the baseline, the lots owned by Lucas were in this region where development was prohibited. In 1990, after this lawsuit was commenced, the State legislature amended the Beachfront Management Act to authorize the Council to issue special permits for the construction or reconstruction of single-family residences.

ISSUE

Did the State take Lucas's property in violation of the Takings Clause of the Fifth Amendment? Must the State pay Lucas for the lots because the Act deprived him of all economically viable use of the property?

HOLDING

Yes. There appears to be a taking in violation of the Takings Clause. The latter questions are to be decided on **remand.**

REASONING

Remand   Returning a case to the lower court for additional hearings.

A citizen understands that the State has power over the bundle of rights that he acquires when he obtains title to property. He necessarily expects that his uses of the property will be restricted from time to time by the State exercising its police power. A person purchases property subject to these powers, for example, the power to control harmful and noxious uses of the land. In developing this theory, the concept of noxious uses was used to describe when the exercise of police power would require compensation. Compensation was not required when the legislature is trying to curtail noxious uses. The State does not have to compensate the property owner every time the State exercises its police power in the interest of protecting the health, safety, morals, or general welfare. '' . . . [T]he Fifth Amendment is violated when land-use regulation 'does not substantially advance legitimate state interests *or denies an owner economically viable use of his land* '.'' The State cannot enact a regulation that removes all economic use of the property *after* an owner has acquired it. The court has not clarified what constitutes a legitimate state interest in exercising its police power. Lucas did not contend that the State, in this instance, lacked the power to pass such a statute, but he claimed that this action removed all the value of his property and he was entitled to just compensation. Property interests *can* be regulated; however, at a certain point the regulation will be considered a taking. The court has not established a description of the exact point where a taking occurs, but has engaged in individual factual determinations. The court has traditionally resorted to the existing rules or understandings to interpret regulations that are not takings of property and, consequently, not entitled to compensation. It has established two general categories where compensation is required. The first is when the regulation subjects the owner to a physical invasion of his property. The second is when the regulation denies the owner all the economically beneficial or productive use of his land. In analyzing a total taking, the court will ordinarily examine ''among other things, the degree of harm to public lands and resources, or adjacent private property, posed by the claimant's proposed activities, . . . the social value of the claimant's activities and their suitability to the locality in question, . . . the relative ease with which the alleged harm can be avoided through measures taken by the claimant and the government (or adjacent private landowners) alike.'' The fact that other similarly situated landowners engage in the same use indicates a lack of a common law prohibition; however, new knowledge may change what uses are permitted. The test of whether a regulation denies all economic uses is rather straightforward. However, it is not always applied consistently. In some cases, it is difficult to determine what is a property interest and what is a loss of value. These problems are not posed in this case. The Act required Lucas to leave his land substantially in its natural, undeveloped form. In addition, the trial court concluded that the construction ban left his property valueless. The case is reversed and remanded. In order to win on remand, South Carolina must present the principles of nuisance and property law that prohibit the building of residences on Lucas's lots under the current conditions and circumstances of the property. In other words, the State must show that Lucas acquired the property subject to these restrictions. Also, the State must show the court that the decisions of its legislators are correct. This is the only way that the State can prove that the prohibition on building residences on the lots is not a taking.

The Lucas case provides some insight into the types of land use regulations that exist.

The policy behind the doctrine of adverse possession is to encourage the use of land, a very valuable resource. The doctrine tends to encourage the use of land by someone else if the owner is not using it. As the old adage says, possession may be nine-tenths of the law. This applies only to privately owned real property; government land may not be taken by adverse possession.

Easements

In some situations a person may be *entitled to use the land of another in a particular manner*. This right is called an *easement*. An easement is not a right to *own* the property. It is the right to *use* the property in a particular manner. An easement may belong to a particular person, or it may run with the land. The latter means that the easement belongs to the owner of a particular parcel of land, called the *dominant parcel*. The parcel that is subject to the easement is the *servient parcel*.

An easement may be an *express* easement; that is, it was stated by the person who created the easement. Or an easement can be created by *prescription*, much like adverse possession: A person starts to use the servient parcel openly and, after the state's statutory period, will be entitled to continue the use. An easement can also be created by *necessity*, the most common example of which occurs when an owner divides a parcel and deeds a landlocked portion to someone else: The only method of access is across the servient estate. A requirement for an easement by necessity is that both parcels were originally one large parcel.

Easements can also be created by *implication*. Again, this occurs when a parcel is divided, and the owner of the dominant parcel needs to use the servient parcel. However, the need is not required to be as great as it is for an easement by necessity. As an example of an easement by implication, suppose an owner of a parcel of land decides to sell the northeast corner of the parcel. The owner had previously run a sewer system from this northeast corner to the main sewer line through the rest of the parcel. The buyer can reasonably expect to use the same sewer line when he or she owns the northeast corner. It would be *possible* to run a new sewer line to the northeast corner, but it was implied that the new owner could use the existing one. Easements also are created by *contract*, when an owner of property sells someone a right to use it. For example, an owner may sell an easement to an oil company to come onto the property to drill exploratory oil wells.

The issue in the following case was whether an easement existed.

Helms v. Tullis
398 So.2d 253 (Ala. 1981)

FACTS   The Helmses owned a forty-acre tract of land. They moved a house trailer onto the land so that they could reside there. They wanted to have electrical service on the land, but it was necessary to run a power line to their property. The most efficient way to do this was to run the line over property owned by the Tullises. The Helmses told the power company that they owned all the land to the main road. The power company began installing the line and cutting down trees on the Tullises' property. The Tullises stopped them.

ISSUE	Do the Helmses have the right to have a power line run across the Tullises' property?
HOLDING	No. They are not entitled to run a power line across the Tullises' property.
REASONING	Easements are the only basis on which the Helmses would have been entitled to have a power line run across the Tullises' property. Easements may be acquired in a variety of ways, but the only two methods that would have been possible in this case are easements by necessity or by implication. Easements by necessity are recognized by the courts only when there is a real necessity. Mere convenience is not enough. Here the land could have been used even without electricity. In addition, such an easement requires that the parcel subject to the easement and the parcel entitled to the easement were originally parts of the same parcel. Easements by implication also require this original unity of ownership. In addition, there must have been open, visible, and continuous use of the one parcel for the benefit of the other. This use must be reasonably necessary to the estate needing the easement. The Helmses did not meet either set of requirements.

The manner and type of use is restricted by the easement. A person who exceeds the amount of use that is allowed under the easement will lose the easement, and his or her rights will be extinguished. For example, suppose Mary has an easement that authorizes the use of a neighbor's road to get to her house. Mary opens a restaurant on her premises, thereby greatly increasing the traffic on her neighbor's road. This excessive use of the road will extinguish Mary's easement.

Transfers by Action of Nature

A person who owns land next to a stream or other body of water may find that soil is being lost into the water or that the water is depositing soil next to the land. If the water slowly washes the soil away, the original owner has lost the land. The person who owns the property where this soil is deposited is now the owner. The gradual building up of soil at the new site is called *accretion.* If the build-up occurs at an imperceptibly slow rate, it is called *alluvion. Avulsion* occurs when a severe flood or storm swiftly causes a change in the course of the body of water. In this case, there is no change in the title. If the original owner can locate the property, he or she can reclaim it. *Reliction* occurs when the water level recedes or drops. The owner of the river bed now owns this exposed land. These rights vary from state to state. States that are subject to severe water shortages may have different rules.

RENTAL OF REAL PROPERTY

Types of Tenancies

The owner of real property may decide to allow another person or persons to use the property. The owner is willing to exchange temporary possession of the property for money or other consideration. There are several basic types of tenancies, which are based on the length of the rental period. These include tenancies for a fixed term, periodic tenancies, tenancies at will, and tenancies at sufferance.

A *tenancy for a fixed term* is a tenancy for a set period of time; the beginning and ending dates are established. Generally, the Statute of Frauds requires a written lease if the tenancy is for one year or longer. Such tenancies automatically end at the set time. (Some states have set a maximum allowable term for a tenancy for a fixed term.) If the tenant has not vacated the premises by the end of the lease period, the landlord can explicitly execute a new lease with the tenant or can elect to treat the tenant's actions as an implicit renewal of the lease for another term of the same length. This second, or implicit, type of renewal cannot exceed one year, however, due to the provisions of the Statute of Frauds.

A *periodic tenancy* starts at a specific time and continues for successive periods until terminated. It may be established to run from year to year, month to month, week to week, or for some similar period. It may be terminated by either party after proper notice. The lease normally specifies how much notice is necessary and to whom the notice should be addressed. The beginning date is specified, but the ending date is not.

A *tenancy at will* can be terminated any time at the desire of either the landlord or the tenant.

A *tenancy at sufferance* is one in which the tenant entered into possession properly and with the landlord's permission, but wrongfully remained in possession after the period of the tenancy.

Rights and Duties of Tenants

The tenant rents the right to exclusive possession and control of the premises, which means that the tenant is the only one entitled to be in possession. At common law, the landlord is not entitled to enter the premises. However, the landlord often obtains permission from the tenant to enter the premises either on an ad hoc basis or because such a right is reserved in the lease. Even at common law, the landlord does have the right to enter the premises in case of an emergency.

If the tenant is a business, it may need to install trade fixtures, such as neon signs, commercial refrigeration units, and industrial ovens. If a tenant attaches trade fixtures to the property, the tenant is allowed to remove them before the end of the lease. But if the removal causes any damage, the tenant must repair the damage.

Under a normal lease, the landlord must put the property into good condition for the purposes specified in the lease and must maintain it in good condition. Tenants do not have an obligation to make major improvements or repairs. However, a tenant may contractually agree to make certain modifications or improvements. For example, in exchange for an exceptionally low rent, a tenant might agree to remodel a property at his or her own expense. In such a case, it is wise to specify who will pay for these improvements and who will get the benefit of them at the end of the lease.

Warranty of Habitability Some states have held that an implied warranty of habitability exists in residential housing leases. That is, the landlord impliedly promises that the premises will be fit for living—for example, that the heating system will work, that there will be running water, and that there will be indoor plumbing. When the courts recognize this warranty, the tenant can use a breach as a basis for terminating a lease, as a means of reducing the rent, or as a defense for nonpayment of the rent.

Constructive Eviction   Most states recognize an implied covenant that the owner will protect the tenant's right to quiet enjoyment (use) of the premises. Constructive eviction occurs when the owner does not protect this interest of the tenant and allows a material interference with the tenant's enjoyment of the premises. Suppose, for example, that you rent an apartment and that living next door to you is a person whose habit of playing drums in the middle of the night is interfering with your sleep. Although your neighbor's behavior is in violation of the lease, the landlord will not enforce the lease provisions. The landlord's behavior constitutes constructive eviction, and you may move out without any further liability to pay rent. However, if you do not take some action promptly, the court may decide that you waived your right to complain about the noise.

Assignments and Subleases   The transfer of the tenant's entire interest in the lease is an *assignment*. If the tenant transfers only part and retains some interest, the transfer is a *sublease*. (Note that this terminology is slightly different from that in Chapter 15.) Ordinarily assignments and subleases are allowed unless the lease specifically provides that they are not. Most leases do prohibit assignments and subleases without the prior written approval of the landlord.

Rights and Duties of Landlords

Landlords have the right to retake possession of their property at the end of the lease's term. In most rental situations, the landlord expressly reserves the right to terminate the lease if the tenant breaches any promises contained in it, including the promise to adequately care for the property.

Rent   Rent is the compensation that the landlord receives from granting the right to use his or her property. Most leases require the tenant to pay the rent in advance. Many landlords require that tenants pay the first and last month's rent in advance, which provides added protection for the landlord. If the tenant is behind in paying the rent, it usually takes a number of weeks to force the tenant to leave the premises. If the tenant has not paid the rent, the landlord has a number of available options. The landlord can sue for the rent that has not been paid or can start procedures to have the tenant evicted (removed) from the premises. In some states, the landlord has a lien on the tenant's personal belongings that are on the premises. This allows a form of self-help called a lockout. The landlord locks the tenant out of the premises while all the tenant's personal property is inside. In the following case, the court examined the legality of a lockout.

Spinks v. *Taylor*
278 S.E.2d 501 (N.C. 1981)

FACTS Because Spinks had not paid her rent, the landlord had her apartment padlocked when she was not there. Spinks claimed that she asked the manager to allow her to enter the apartment to get some clothes, but the manager would not allow this. The trial judge issued a decision for the landlord and did not allow the jury to decide this issue.

ISSUE Was there evidence to support the idea that the padlocking was illegal?

HOLDING Yes. The judge should have let the jury decide based on the evidence.

REASONING States use the following rules to determine the amount of self-help allowed to a landlord who is entitled to possession of the premises:

1. A landlord may use necessary and reasonable self-help.

2. A landlord must rely only on the remedies provided by the courts.

3. Or a landlord may gain possession by *peaceable* means.

North Carolina applies the last approach. Under North Carolina law, a landlord cannot retake possession against the will of the tenant. Since there was evidence that the padlocking was against Spinks's will, the court ruled that this case should be referred to a jury to determine if the landlord used peaceable means.

Damage by the Tenant The landlord has the right to collect from the tenant for any damage caused by the tenant. For example, if Rudy, a tenant, negligently fills his waterbed, and it leaks and causes substantial damage to the premises, Rudy is liable for the damage. Tenants are also responsible for any damage caused to the premises by their guests. This right to collect exists at common law and is usually stated in the lease. The tenant is responsible for damage caused negligently or intentionally but not for ordinary wear and tear—the deterioration that occurs through ordinary usage.

Security Deposits For protection, the landlord usually will collect a security deposit. This money is to be used to make repairs after the tenant has vacated the premises. It is for damage negligently or intentionally caused by the tenant. It is not to be used to clean the premises or to repair normal wear and tear. It generally cannot be used to repaint walls that have become dirty through normal use. It can be used to replace doors in which holes have been punched. The money that remains should be returned to the tenant within a reasonable period after the tenancy terminates. Some states have statutes that establish how long the landlord may legally keep the security deposit.

Duty to Protect Tenants and Their Guests Landlords generally have the same responsibility to their tenants' guests as they do to the tenants themselves.

The landlord does not warrant that the premises are safe, but the landlord does have the duty to warn the tenant of *latent defects*—defects that are not immediately obvious and of which the tenant may not be aware. This duty of the landlord extends only to latent defects that the landlord knew or should have known existed.

Rights After Abandonment by a Tenant   If the tenant wrongfully abandons the premises during the term of the lease, the landlord has two options. The landlord can make a good-faith effort to find a suitable tenant, but if one cannot be found, the landlord can leave the premises vacant and collect the rent from the tenant who abandoned the premises. The tenant is legally obligated to pay the rent, and the landlord can obtain a court judgment for the payment. If the tenant can be located and is solvent, the landlord will be able to collect. If the landlord is able to rerent the premises, he or she is technically renting the premises in the tenant's behalf. If a lower rent is obtained, the tenant is liable for the difference.

Under the second option, the landlord can repossess the premises and rerent them on his or her own behalf. The original tenant who abandoned the premises is relieved of any liability for additional rent. If the landlord is able to rerent the premises for more money, that is to the landlord's benefit. As the next case indicates, there may be a factual issue whether the rerenting is for the landlord or the tenant.

Dahl v. Comber
444 A.2d 392 (Me. 1982)

FACTS   Dahl constructed a building for Comber's business. This building was leased to Comber for a five-year term. The business had difficult times and defaulted on the lease. Dahl tried to rent the building but was able to find only temporary tenants.

ISSUE   Did Dahl rerent the premises for his own benefit?

HOLDING   No. It was rerented for Comber.

REASONING   The lower court found that Dahl was rerenting for the benefit of his tenant. The evidence was sufficient to support this conclusion. The lease stated that any surrender had to be in writing and had to be signed by the landlord. When a tenant tries to surrender the premises to the landlord, the landlord can decide whether or not to accept the surrender. The landlord can accept the surrender and then rerent the premises in the landlord's behalf. Or the landlord can refuse the surrender and hold the tenant liable for any shortages in rent. In this case, the landlord was mitigating damages by rerenting the property in the tenant's behalf. Such an action does not disturb the tenant's underlying responsibility to pay the rent.

Legislative Trends

Landlord and tenant laws are undergoing change. Two federal statutes address discrimination in housing—the Civil Rights Act of 1866 and the Civil Rights Act of 1968. The 1968 Fair Housing Act, which is contained in the latter Civil Rights Act, is the basis for most of the recent litigation and is the more comprehensive of the two acts. As originally passed, it prohibits discrimination based on race, color, religion, and national origin. Discrimination based on sex was added in 1974, and, in 1988, discrimination based on familial status was included. Familial status includes having children under 18 years of age. The 1988 amendment also improved the act by providing three methods for enforcement: 1) The Department of Housing and Urban Development may initiate a lawsuit in federal court or before an administrative law judge, *if* all the parties agree; 2) The person subjected to the discrimination may file a suit in either state or federal court, and the court may award actual damages, punitive damages, or equitable relief; 3) The United States Attorney General may file a suit if there is a pattern or practice of discrimination. As with most statutes, there are exceptions. For example, single family units owned by a private investor with less than four houses *may* be exempt from the act as a whole and housing only for the elderly (over 62 years of age) is exempt from the age discrimination provision.

Some states are very protective of the tenant's rights. Recent examples of protenant legislation include laws that require the payment of interest on security deposits and rent control statutes that prohibit landlords from raising the rent. Although rent control was intended to protect tenants, many economists argue that it does not have this protective effect. They argue that instead it creates a shortage of rental housing, because investors would prefer to make other investments that would provide a higher rate of return. Other states are more protective of the landlord.

YOU BE THE JUDGE

In November, 1990, Timus was looking for a new home for herself and her 7-year-old son and her 3-year-old daughter. Timus had a steady job as a secretary for the United States Labor Department. She attempted to rent a one-bedroom apartment in Mount Rainier, Maryland for $395 a month. The building was managed by William J. Davis, Inc., a large property management company. Timus claims the resident manager told her, "This is an all-adult building. No children allowed." When Timus was interviewed she said that she felt degraded when she was told that she could live in the apartment, but that her children could not. She said, "When you're welcome, your children should be. They're part of you. We are one. We're a family. We belong together."

Timus filed suit under the 1988 amendment to the federal Fair Housing Act of 1968. The amendment prohibits discrimination on the basis of "familial status," which it defines as having children under 18 years of age. The act contains an exception for housing designed only for people 62 years of age or older. The proponents of the legislation indicated that it is common to discriminate against families. The property owners and managers who were opposed to the legislation claimed that children are noisy, undisciplined, and often damaged the property.

Part of Timus' case included records of the property owners and the Davis company executives which indicated their preferences in tenants. The Davis company contended that the resident manager was not authorized to exclude families with children. However, Timus presented company documents requesting that children not be allowed in some of the buildings. These statements were attributed to the resident manager's supervisor.

As part of the Davis company's defense, the company indicated that it was aware of the 1988 amendment; that there were some children in apartments at the Mount Rainier building; and that there were children in other buildings managed by the company.

Suppose you were a legislator when the 1988 amendment was proposed. Would you vote in favor of the amendment? Why or why not? How would you decide if you were a juror in the Timus case, and why?

Source: "Renter, family win $2.4 million housing bias suit," Robert Pear, New York Times, *The Fresno Bee,* Thursday, July 16, 1992, page A1.

JOINT OWNERSHIP OF PROPERTY

Joint ownership exists when two or more people have concurrent title to property; that is, they own the property at the same time. There are four forms of joint ownership: tenancy in common, joint tenancy with rights of survivorship, tenancy by the entireties, and community property. Generally, these forms of joint ownership can exist with personal property as well as with real property. Most of these forms can be created voluntarily by the tenants, or they can be created by someone else for the tenants.

A legal characteristic of most forms of joint ownership is that each of the co-owners (the tenants) has an undivided right to use the whole property. Thus, the parcel described on the deed is not divided equally among the tenants; instead, each of them has the right to use all the property. If there is a dispute about the use of the property that the tenants are unable to resolve among themselves, they can file their complaint with the court. The primary remedies available to resolve such a dispute are (1) to sell the property and divide the proceeds or (2) to divide the property equitably and give each tenant a separate parcel. Either of these would be considered an action for partition. Note that because the usable value of adjoining portions may differ, the separate segments may differ in size and shape.

TABLE 49.1 Comparison of Forms of Joint Ownership

Remember that since property rights are governed by state law, sometimes there is a wide variation from state to state.

	TENANCY IN COMMON	JOINT TENANCY WITH RIGHTS OF SURVIVORSHIP	TENANCY BY THE ENTIRETIES	COMMUNITY PROPERTY
REQUIREMENTS FOR CREATION				
Requires equal ownership interests		**	X	X
Restricted to married couples			X	X
Limited to two people			X	X
Restricted to human beings		*	X	X
Applicable to both real and personal property	X	*	*	X
RIGHTS OF ONE TENANT ACTING ALONE TO TRANSFER OR ENCUMBER HIS/HER SHARE WITHOUT THE CONSENT OF THE OTHERS				
May use the whole property (undivided right to the whole)	X	X	X	X
May be transferred by will	X			X
May not be transferred by will		X	X	
Will pass to surviving tenants at death, if there is no valid will[1]		X	X	*[2]
Will pass to intestate heirs at death, if there is no valid will	X			*[2]
May be sold during life	X[3]	*		*/**
May be mortgaged or assigned during life	X[3]	*		*
May be transferred by gift during life	X[3]	*		
May be attached by a creditor of a tenant	X	X		

Legend

X The trait applies to the specific form of joint ownership.

* This is true in most states.

**This is true in many situations.

[1]In some types of tenancies, courts would say the interest "remains" with the surviving cotenants instead of "passing" to the surviving cotenants.

[2]Most community property states have different intestate succession provisions for the passage of separate property and community property. The community property commonly passes to the surviving spouse.

[3]Generally, a tenant in common will have this power. However, in many states if the tenancy in common is between spouses and consists of real estate, the signature of the second spouse will be required.

Tenancy in Common

A tenancy in common occurs when *two or more people own the same property*. Each tenant has an undivided right to use the whole property. Usually, a tenancy in common is indicated by words like "Bennett and McCormick, as tenants in common" on the deed or other evidence of title. If the deed simply says "Bennett and McCormick," most courts will presume that they are tenants in common.

There is no legal limit on the number of tenants in a tenancy in common. Practically speaking, however, if there are too many tenants, conflicts will probably arise among them regarding the use of the property. Each tenant may sell, assign, or give away his or her interest. A tenant may also will away the interest in a valid will. If the tenant has no valid will, the interest in the tenancy will pass to his or her heirs under the state intestate succession statute. A creditor of an individual tenant can attach his or her interest in the tenancy in common.

Tenants in common do not have to have equal interests in the property. For example, if there are four tenants in common, one may have a one-half interest, one may have a one-quarter interest, and the other two may have a one-eighth interest each.

Joint Tenancy with Rights of Survivorship

A joint tenancy with rights of survivorship occurs when *two or more people own property together*. Again, there is no legal maximum number of tenants, but, of course, the practical question of how many co-tenants can get along with each other remains. As in a tenancy in common, each tenant has an undivided right to use the whole property. Generally, each tenant has an equal interest in the property. Joint tenancies differ from tenancies in common in that when one tenant dies, his or her interest passes to the remaining co-tenants. The survivors continue to hold an undivided interest in the whole property. Generally, a will does not have any effect on a joint tenancy with right of survivorship. (There is a movement in the American legal community that advocates changing state laws regarding the ability to will joint tenancies and insurance policies. Some courts are devising theories to the same effect.) The interest in the property will pass from one tenant to another immediately on death by operation of law. Eventually the tenant who outlives the others will own the complete interest. In most states, corporations are not allowed to be joint tenants because corporations do not die.

Because of the survivorship feature, joint tenancies often are used as substitutes for wills. Given the potential for disputes during life, however, this practice may be unwise. In most states, if a joint tenant wrongfully causes the death of another joint tenant, he or she will not be allowed to benefit and will be prevented from taking the **decedent**'s interest.

Decedent   A person who has died.

Joint tenancies may be divided during a court action for partition. In most states, a joint tenant can sell, make a gift of, or assign his or her interest during his or her life. A creditor of the joint tenant can attach the interest. A transferee of the joint tenant will take the interest as a tenant in common. A transferee would include a purchaser, a donee, an assignee, or a creditor who obtained rights through the attachment procedure. The transferee would not receive the survivorship rights of a joint tenant because the other joint tenants never agreed to share the risk of survivorship with the transferee.

Tenancy by the Entireties

In a *tenancy by the entireties, two tenants, who must be husband and wife, share the property*. Each tenant is a joint owner in the whole property. This type of ownership has a survivorship feature. If one spouse dies, the survivor receives the whole property. Unlike joint tenants with rights of survivorship, many states allow a tenant who wrongfully caused the death of his or her spouse, and co-tenant, to benefit and to take title to the whole. Generally, only creditors of the family unit can attach entireties property. One spouse normally cannot unilaterally dispose of his or her interest unless the parties obtain a legal separation or a divorce. The tenants can, however, agree to sever the tenancy. A valid will does not affect distribution of entireties property. Tenancies by the entireties are not recognized in all states, for example **community property states** do not have entireties property ownership.

Community property states
States that recognize community property for married couples.

Community Property

Community property is recognized in eight states—Arizona, California, Idaho, Louisiana, New Mexico, Texas, and Washington and the Commonwealth of Puerto Rico. This discussion will emphasize the general features of community property law. Community property laws vary from state to state. Louisiana community property law is most dissimilar, because it is based on Louisiana's French heritage. The community property laws in the other states are based predominantly on Spanish civil law.[1]

Community property is a form of co-ownership that can occur only between husband and wife. It is based on the concept that financially the marriage is a partnership. One-half of most of the property that is acquired or accumulated during marriage belongs to each spouse. Technically, this assumes that one-half of each asset belongs to the husband and one-half belongs to the wife. Thus, most states require that both the husband and the wife sign any deeds to transfer real property. In most states, this requirement does not extend to personal property. In fact, the names of both spouses do not have to appear on the community property or on any title evidence to the property. For example, although a paycheck may bear the name of only one spouse, it is nonetheless community property and as such belongs to both spouses. The primary source of community property for most couples is wages and earnings.

This is not meant to imply that a married couple will have only community property. Each may own property separately as in **separate property states.** Separate property would normally include the following:

Separate property states
States that do not recognize community property rights.

---

[1]For an excellent discussion of the historical basis for community property law in each state, see chapters 1–3, *Community Property Law in the United States,* by W.S. McClanahan, The Lawyers Cooperative Publishing Co. and Bancoft-Whitney Co., (1982).

1. property owned by either spouse before their marriage
2. property given to one spouse alone by gift, by will, or by intestate succession
3. property that is acquired with separate property funds

In addition, in some states—California, for example—income, rents, or profits earned from separate property is also separate property; in other states—Idaho, Texas, Louisiana—this income would be community property if received during the marriage. In Louisiana, a husband or wife can file a declaration that this income should be separate property instead of community property. All property other than that mentioned here is usually community property.

For most purposes, a husband and wife can contractually agree to split their community property into two shares of separate property. However, if they are careless and mix their respective separate properties and/or community property, it may all become community property. If the property becomes so mixed that it cannot be separated into community and separate property, the courts say that it is hopelessly commingled and treat all of it like community property. Distinguishing separate and community property was an issue in the next case.

Potthoff v. Potthoff
627 P.2d 708 (C.A. Ariz. 1981)

FACTS   Gertrude and Herbert Potthoff were unable to agree on a property settlement in their divorce. They maintained one basic bank account, but Herbert was the only one who could withdraw from the account. Into the account they deposited funds from Herbert's medical practice, loan proceeds, proceeds from the sale of stock, stock dividends, interest income, and proceeds from the sale of Gertrude's separate property. From this account, they paid the expenses of the medical practice, living expenses, costs of investments, and costs of real estate. Before the Potthoffs's marriage, Herbert had purchased property on which he built the Palm Grove Shopping Center with his separate funds. He also spent considerable time and effort making it a successful investment.

ISSUES   Was the bank account community property? Was the Palm Grove Shopping Center separate property?

HOLDINGS   Yes, to both. The bank account was hopelessly commingled; the real property was purchased and improved with separate property funds.

REASONING   Due to the various transactions involving separate and community funds and loss of banking records, the bank account was commingled. The entire amount becomes community property if the funds become so commingled that the identity of the separate funds would be lost, which occurred in this case. The Palm Grove property, however, was purchased before the marriage and was built with separate funds. Thus, it was separate property. Under Arizona law, to the extent that separate property is improved by community funds, the community has a lien on the property for the amount of those funds. To the extent that Herbert's efforts improved the property, this increase in value was community property.

A couple begins to form community property once they are married. In most situations, they stop forming community property once they establish separate residences. In a divorce proceeding, the community property usually is divided.

89%

Community property does not have a survivorship feature. A spouse can will his or her share of the community property to someone else. If the decedent does not have a valid will, most intestate succession statutes provide that the property will pass to the surviving spouse.

The National Conference of Commissioners on Uniform State Law (NCCUSL) adopted a proposal entitled the Uniform Marital Property Act (UMPA).[2] When it is enacted by a state legislature, it will modify the property rights of married couples and make the state more like a community property state. Wisconsin adopted the UMPA in 1983.[3] To date, it is the only state that has enacted the complete act.

Distinguishing Among the Forms of Joint Ownership

The words used on the deed or other title evidence are controlling as to whether the tenants are tenants in common, joint tenants with rights of survivorship, or tenants by the entireties. If the language on the deed is not clear, under state law there will be a presumption as to the form of joint ownership. If the tenants are husband and wife, most states will presume that the property is community property or entireties property. If the state recognizes neither form of ownership, it would presume a joint tenancy with the right of survivorship. If the tenants are not related to each other by marriage, most states would presume that they are tenants in common.

SUMMARY

Property ownership includes title to the property and the right to control possession of the property. Real property consists of land and objects that are built on the land, are growing on the land, and/or are permanently attached to the land. A fixture is property that was personal in nature before it was permanently attached to a building.

Real property can be acquired by a grant from the government or by transfer from the owner. An owner may trade, sell, give, or will the property or leave it to another person by intestate succession. Lifetime transfers will be described in a deed; the deed will be delivered to the grantee; and, in most cases, the deed will be recorded. Although not legally required, recording is for the protection of the grantee and the public.

---

[2]For a copy of the Act as adopted by the NCCUSL and a listing of the states that have adopted the complete act, see 9A Uniform Laws Annotated (U.L.A.) p. 97 (1987) and pocket parts.
[3]Wisconsin 1983, Act 186, Effective 1-1-86, W.S.A. 766.001 to 766.97.

An owner who is not careful may lose title to or use of the property. This loss can be caused by unpaid debts, by government restrictions on the use of the land, or by eminent domain. An owner may also lose his or her interest by the adverse possession of another person or by natural erosion.

An owner can enter into a rental agreement called a lease. Under a lease, a tenant is entitled to the exclusive possession of the owner's real estate. The lease is the contract that will govern many terms of the landlord-tenant relationship. Under modern law, the landlord must repair the premises. A tenant who negligently or intentionally damages the property will be liable for the cost of repairs. The landlord may require a security deposit in order to have funds for making such repairs. The tenant is justified in leaving the premises when there is constructive eviction. A landlord can evict a tenant if the tenant fails to pay the rent.

Two or more people can own an interest in the same piece of property at the same time. These people are called co-tenants. They may be tenants in common, in which case each tenant owns an undivided right in the whole parcel and there are no survivorship rights. Or they may be joint tenants with rights of survivorship. Such tenants can dispose of their interests during life; at death, their interest will pass to the remaining co-tenants by operation of law. Tenants in a tenancy by the entireties must be husband and wife. In community property states, a husband and wife can create community property. Most of the assets that they acquire during marriage will be community property.

DISCUSSION QUESTIONS

1. After Al's mother and father died, Al, who was responsible for their estate, decided to sell their home. After locating buyers for the property and entering into a sales contract with them, Al went to the premises and started to remove the petunias, his father's prize-winning roses, and a load of topsoil that was on the flower beds. The buyers were unhappy about this. Who has the right to these things? Why?

2. Are crops real or personal property? Why is this distinction important?

3. Describe the typical provisions that would be included in a deed.

4. Kim moved onto a piece of real estate in California. He began to use the property in an open, actual, and notorious manner and continued to do so for five years. He also paid the real estate taxes on this parcel. The applicable holding period is five years. Who owns this parcel? Why? Is it material that Nancy, the original owner, also paid real estate taxes? What are the legal rights of the parties? Why?

5. Jack and Rosie are neighbors. In 1970, Rosie built a fence around her property. She did not have the boundary surveyed. The fence was built four feet into Jack's property. Who owns this four-foot strip of land now? Why?

6. Why is it difficult for a lessee (tenant) to be successful as an adverse possessor?

7. How does avulsion differ from accretion?

8. Why might a person want to establish a joint tenancy with another person who is not related to him or her?

9. How is community property made or acquired in a community property state?

10. Why would a person prefer to establish a tenancy in common instead of a joint tenancy with rights of survivorship?

CASE PROBLEMS

1. Private citizens wanted to enter the common areas of a multibusiness office complex to make antiabortion statements. The protesters carried signs and placards and shouted at prospective patients of Cherry Hill Women's Center, one of the ten tenants on the property. These protesters did not have the permission of the owner of the property. Does the landowner have the right to keep the protesters off the property? (*Brown* v. *Davis*, 495 A.2d 900 [N.J. Super. 1984].)

2. Jon and Marion Kubichan owned and occupied a parcel of residential property. During their ownership, they designed and built a fountain pond in their backyard. The Kubichans did not enclose the pond with a fence, but at the time of the accident it had been enclosed. The builders had not obtained the permit that was required by a city rule. Later, the Kubichans sold the property to Goldman, who then entered into a lease-option with the Reids. While the Reids occupied the property they made changes in the exterior of the pond but not in its interior. A toddler, twenty-two months old, was visiting the property with his parents and his siblings. He fell into the pond and suffered severe brain damage and quadriplegia. The pond allegedly was deceptive in nature because it appeared much shallower than it was and it lacked safety features. Is the seller liable for creating an unreasonably dangerous condition on the real estate? (*Preston* v. *Goldman*, 210 Cal. Rptr. 913 [Cal. App. 1985].)

3. Dorothy Karell purchased 18.917 acres in 1958 and received a warranty deed. Rena West and her partner purchased the adjoining 3.783-acre tract. The 18.917 acres owned by Karell was enclosed by a fence that also enclosed a portion of West's 3.783 acres. Karell rented the property to various tenants from 1958 until 1972. The tenants lived in the house on the 18.917 acres. One or two of the tenants kept livestock or grew crops. In 1970 Karell contracted to sell Howl the sand and topsoil from the land enclosed in the fence. Who owns that portion of the 3.783 acres that is enclosed in the fence? Is Karell liable for the sand and topsoil that was removed by Howl? (*Karell* v. *West*, 616 S.W.2d 692 [Tex. App. 1981].)

4. Bernard Guynan owned a parcel of real estate. In September, 1955, he gave his son Edward permission to build a concrete block house on a portion of the property. Edward constructed the house at his own expense and lived in it from 1957 to 1960. Then he began leasing the house and collecting the rent. When Bernard died in 1970, his wife Anne obtained title to the property. She allowed Edward to continue to rent the property to others. During this time, either Anne or Bernard had paid the real estate taxes. When a disagreement arose between Anne and Edward, Anne filed a lawsuit to have Edward and his tenants removed from the premises. Is Edward entitled to the building and real estate based on adverse possession? Why or why not? (*Guynan* v. *Guynan*, 305 N.W.2d 882 [Neb. 1981].)

5. The landlord ordered a notice to quit to be served on the tenant on 24 October 1983. A summary process action was begun on 5 December 1983. The tenant initiated this lawsuit to require the landlord to make certain repairs. Does the tenant have the potential right to have the premises repaired? (*Rivera* v. *Santiago*, 495 A.2d 1122 [Conn. App. 1985].)

6. Mary Stoiber, a tenant of a residential parcel of real estate, sued for damages from her former landlord and the rental agents who managed the property. Stoiber was sued under an unlawful detainer action by Earley, the owner of the premises. The unlawful detainer action was filed after the Kern County Health Department ordered that the premises be vacated and destroyed within thirty days because of numerous housing code violations. Stoiber alleged that she had complained about the condition of the property to Earley's agents. She further alleged that the faulty plumbing had caused discomfort and annoyance and the flooding had damaged her furnishings. Did Stoiber have a cause of action for breach of the warranty of habitability? What should be her measure of damages? (*Stoiber* v. *Honeychuck*, 162 Cal. Rptr. 194 [Cal. App. 1980].)

7. The landlord owned a thirty-six-unit apartment complex. Becker, one of his tenants, slipped and fell against his glass shower door and broke his arm. The shower doors were made of untempered glass. The glass doors were installed before the landlord purchased the premises, and he didn't know that they were made of untempered glass. One of the witnesses testified that tempered glass and untempered glass look the same except for the small identification mark in one corner. It was agreed that, had the shower door been made of tempered glass, the extent of the injury would have been reduced. Should the landlord be liable for latent defects

in rental units if the defects existed when the tenant leased the premises? (*Becker* v. *IRM Corp.,* 698 P.2d 116 [Cal. 1985].)

8. Jackson and Chapman purchased a property on or about 5 June 1984. The property was purchased subject to the lease of the Postal Service and other tenants. The Postal Service was notified of the change of ownership of the premises. It then failed to pay rent to anyone for about six months while it waited for an official notice of the change of ownership on its own forms. The landlords filed a forcible entry and detainer action against the Postal Service. Should they win the suit? (*Jackson* v. *United States Postal Service,* 611 F.Supp. 456 [D.C. Tex. 1985].)

9. A Connecticut state statute provided that the lessee was to be given a five-day notice to quit for nonpayment of rent. The lease provided that whenever the lease terminated by the lapse of time or by breach of any of the promises in the lease, the tenant waived all rights to notice. Did the lease provisions effectively waive the protections granted by state law? (*Sandrew* v. *Pequot Drug, Inc.,* 495 A.2d 1127 [Conn. App. 1985].)

10. Mrs. York and Mr. York were parties to an action for divorce and the division of property. Mrs. York's father testified that he had meant to give the Yorks' residence to his daughter as her sole and separate property. The property was deeded to both the husband and the wife by the wife's parents. Is the residence community property or separate property? Originally, Mr. York and his brother purchased York Tire Company and operated it as a partnership. The partnership was owned half by the brother and half by Mr. and Mrs. York, as community property. Mrs. York traded her interest in York Tire Company for Mr. York's interest in Air Speed Oil Company. Mr. York later bought his brother's interest with a $15,000 note. He paid off the note with cash and earnings from the tire company. Later, Mr. York incorporated the business by taking the assets of the old York Tire Company and adding two service stations that were owned as community property. Is the business community property or separate property? (*Marriage of York,* 613 S.W.2d 764 [Tex. App. 1981].)

CHAPTER 50

Personal Property
and Bailments

OUTLINE

OWNERSHIP OF PROPERTY

Classifications of Property

The concepts of property rights and joint ownership discussed in the context of real property in Chapter 49 apply to personal property as well. As we noted in that chapter, real estate is land and everything built on the land or permanently attached to the land or to the buildings. *All property that is not classified as real property is personal property.*

Personal property is divided into two categories: tangible and intangible. *Tangible* personal property is property that *is movable and can be felt, tasted, or seen.* It has texture, color, temperature, and similar characteristics. Examples of tangible personal property include textbooks, pens, briefcases, calculators, lamps, and chairs.

Intangible personal property cannot be reduced to physical possession. It cannot be held in a person's hand. It may, however, be reduced to legal possession and is often very valuable. Intangible personal possessions include such things as patent rights, copyrights, accounts receivable, and corporate goodwill. The distinction between tangible and intangible personal property is usually not significant and does not govern the parties' legal relationships.

The traditional label for personal property is "chattels." Chattels are divided into chattels real, chattels personal, and chattels personal in action. A *chattel real involves an interest in land, but the chattel itself is personal*—for example, a leasehold or other legal right to use land. The owner of the chattel real does not own the land but does have valuable legal rights. *Chattels personal are tangible, movable personal property,* such as desks, chairs, chalk, and erasers. A *chattel personal in action,* also called a *chose in action, is the right to file a lawsuit* or to bring legal action.

Components of Ownership

The three components of ownership that are important with respect to real property are also important with respect to personal property. These components are ownership, possession, and title. *Ownership includes all the rights* related to the ownership of property. *Possession includes the right to control the property by having it in one's custody* or by directing who shall have custody of it. The concept of *title includes both the current legal ownership of the property and the method of its acquisition.* Title evidence or title also refers to the written evidence of ownership that appears on a certificate of title for property, such as a "pink slip" for an automobile.

ACQUISITION OF PERSONAL PROPERTY BY INDIVIDUALS

Original Possession

Original possession occurs when the owner is the first person to possess the property. In other words, the owner created the ownership rather than receiving it by transfer from another person. One way to obtain ownership by original possession is to create the property through physical or mental labor;

an artist, for example, acquires ownership through original possession by creating a painting or a sculpture.

Ownership by original possession can also be acquired by taking something that has never been owned before and reducing it to possession, as when someone pans for gold in a wilderness area and takes possession of any nuggets found.

When a person creates property, there is usually no dispute about who actually owns it. Disputes do arise, however, when people are hunting or trapping wild animals. For example, suppose that a group of hunters are about to trap a fox when a farmer spots the fox near some chicken coops and shoots it. A dispute then ensues about who owns the fox. The court would decide that the farmer owned the fox and its pelt because the hunters had not reduced the fox to their possession. The farmer had taken control over it first.

Voluntary Transfers of Possession

Individuals can acquire real and personal property by having it transferred to them voluntarily by the previous owner. The transfer can occur by *purchase, gift, gift causa mortis, inheritance,* or *intestate succession.*

Purchases The most common way to acquire property owned by another is to purchase it. When property is sold by the previous owner, there is an exchange of consideration: The buyer gives up one form of property, often money, and the seller gives up another form of property. (Sometimes the parties exchange services for the property. Bartering is becoming increasingly popular for goods.)

Gifts A person can also obtain ownership of property through a gift. The person who transfers the property is called the *donor* and the person who receives the property is called the *donee.*

Three requirements must be satisfied for a valid transfer by gift. First, the donor (the previous owner) must *intend* to make a gift—that is, to transfer the property without full and fair consideration. In most gift situations, the donor is freely giving up the property without receiving any consideration at all. Sometimes it is difficult to determine whether the intent of the donor was to make a gift or to sell or to lend the property. This is particularly true if the donor has died or if the donor and the donee had a disagreement. However, if the transfer is to be treated as a valid gift, it must be shown that the donor's intent was to make a gift.

The second requirement for a valid transfer by gift is that the donor *deliver* the gift property to the donee. When the donor hands the gift to the recipient, *actual delivery* occurs. Sometimes actual delivery is not possible because of the situation of the parties or the type of property being transferred. In such situations, *constructive delivery* may be sufficient. For example, if a hospitalized man had some stocks and bonds in his safe deposit box and wanted to give them to his son, he could give his son the keys and a note that would allow him access to the box, thereby effecting constructive delivery of the gift property.

Transfer tax   Tax on the ability to transfer assets.

The third requirement for a valid gift is *acceptance* by the donee. The donee must be willing to take the property from the donor. In most cases, this is not a problem. However, a donee may refuse to accept a gift if the donee feels that it would "obligate" him or her to the donor, as when a sales agent making a bid for a contract offers the purchasing agent a two-week vacation in Hawaii. Sometimes a donee may refuse a gift because the gift property has no use or value to the donee or would create legal liabilities for the donee. For instance, a donee might refuse a gift of tenements that were substandard housing and had many building code violations.

A transfer by gift may be subject to a **transfer tax,** that is, a gift tax. If so, usually the donor must pay the tax. Most state and federal gift taxes also apply when the donor receives nominal consideration but the transfer is for less than full and adequate consideration. For example, if a donor transfers a diamond ring worth $700,000 to a donee for $5, the value of the gift will be treated as the fair market value of the ring ($700,000) less the $5 that was paid for it. Any gift tax would be figured on this amount ($699,995) and the donor would pay the tax. The gift is not subject to income tax when it is received by the donee.

If the donor intends to make a gift and delivers the property, and the donee accepts the property, the transfer is a valid gift. Once a gift has been completed, it generally cannot be revoked. The donor cannot legally take the property back from the donee, no matter how much the donor wants or needs to have it returned. For example, if Silvia gave her sister $100 as a birthday present and later Silvia lost her job and desperately needed the money, she would not be entitled to it. If her sister decided to give the money back, she would be making a separate gift, this one to Silvia. In most cases a completed gift, also called an *executed gift,* is final. However, the gift can be set aside or revoked if the donee engaged in fraud, duress, or undue influence that resulted in the making of the gift.

A promise to make a gift at some time in the future is not binding on the promisor. The promisor can change his or her mind with impunity. An executory promise to make a gift is enforceable in the case of promissory estoppel, however. (This concept was discussed in Chapter 10.)

Certain types of property require special formalities before the owner can make gifts of them. To transfer a chose in action (a right to bring legal action), the transferor must make an assignment of the right. An *assignment* is a formal transfer of a contract right. (Assignments are discussed in detail in Chapter 15.) To transfer **negotiable instruments,** the transferor must make either an assignment or a negotiation. A *negotiation* is an endorsement or notation on the document that it should be paid to a specific person or that it should be paid to the bearer or holder. (The bearer or holder is the person who is in possession of the document.)

Gifts fall into three categories: inter vivos gifts, testamentary gifts, or gifts causa mortis. *Inter vivos* gifts are made while the transferor is still alive; they are lifetime gifts. *Testamentary* gifts are completed when the owner dies; they

Negotiable instruments   Transferable documents used as credit instruments and as substitutes for money, including checks, drafts, promissory notes, and certificates of deposit.

are the types of gifts that a person puts in a will and are commonly called testamentary transfers. These transfers do not actually take place until death. Gifts *causa mortis* must meet special requirements about the donor's intention.

Gifts Causa Mortis Gifts causa mortis occur while the property owner is still alive. The donor is making the gift because he or she expects to die soon. Generally the donor is contemplating death from a specific cause. The requirements for a gift causa mortis are that the donor must intend to make the gift; the gift must be made in contemplation of death; the gift property must be actually or constructively delivered; and the donor must die from the contemplated cause. If the donor does not die from the contemplated cause, the gift may be revoked. In this case, the donor or the donor's estate can reclaim the gift property. Since the donor was motivated, at least in part, by the expectation of death, it is logical that if the donor does not die, he or she should be able to get the property back.

The following hypothetical case shows the conditional nature of a gift causa mortis.

Betty, aged eighty-eight, was in the hospital and doing very poorly. The doctor told her she would probably not survive another stroke. She felt that she would very likely have another stroke before the end of the week. When her son Charles came to visit her, she told him that she wanted him to have her new color television since she would no longer need it. Charles was reluctant to take the television, but Betty insisted that she was not going to recover, and she gave him the key to go get the television.

However, Betty did recover, and when she returned home, she decided she wanted her television back. Since it was a gift causa mortis, Betty would be entitled to have it returned. She did not die as she anticipated.

Suppose Charles had gone to the hospital to take Betty home when she was discharged. While walking across the street to the car, Betty was hit and killed by a reckless driver. The gift to Charles could be revoked because Betty did not die from the contemplated cause. If her other relatives sued to have Charles return the television, legally Charles would lose, and the television would be included with the rest of Betty's estate.

A gift causa mortis is a *legal* concept and is distinct from various tax concepts that require lifetime gifts to be included in the estate for tax purposes.

Inheritances A person can receive property from the estate of someone who dies. If the person who died had a valid will covering the property, the recipient specified in the will receives the property by inheritance. Like gifts, inheritances may be subject to state and/or federal transfer taxes.

Property Received by Intestate Succession   The property of a person who dies without a valid will is transferred to recipients by intestate succession. The people who receive this property are specified in the state intestate succession statute. As with other death-time transfers, this transfer may be subject to estate or inheritance taxes. Transfers by wills and intestate succession statutes are discussed in greater detail in Chapter 52.

Involuntary Transfers of Possession

Sometimes the transfer of property or the custody of property to a recipient is not completely voluntary on the part of the true owner. Such a situation occurs when there is accession or confusion or when property is abandoned, lost, or mislaid.

Accession   *Accession* occurs when a person takes property that he or she does not own and adds to it. For example, a person takes some lumber and makes it into a dining room table. The legal question that arises is: Who owns the dining room table? Should it be the person who owned the lumber or the person who worked on the lumber and changed its nature? The courts examine a number of factors in making their decision on this question; the most important is whether the worker knew that he or she had no right to the lumber. As with many legal problems, the courts weigh the conflicting equities.

The next hypothetical case shows one way in which accession can occur.

Ed ordered some plywood from Pay Less Hardware that was to be delivered while he was at work. When he got home from work, some plywood was piled in his driveway, and he began using it to build his children a toy chest. However, the plywood was Ed's neighbor's—it has been delivered to the wrong address.

Ed was not guilty of willful misconduct. He did not mean to misappropriate someone else's plywood. He reasonably believed that the plywood was his. Title *may* pass from the owner of the plywood to Ed because of Ed's work effort.

Title normally will remain with the rightful owner of the lumber and will not be transferred to the laborer. Depending on the circumstances, the courts may determine that the laborer is an innocent trespasser. An innocent trespasser does not acquire title simply by adding labor and additional materials. The innocent trespasser *will* acquire title under any of the following conditions:

1. Because of the work effort, the original property has lost its identity. (The innocent trespasser took iron ore and made it into steel.)

2. There is a great difference in the relative values between the original property and the new property. (The innocent trespasser took a rough diamond and cut and polished it into a beautiful pear shape.)

3. A completely new type of property has been created and the innocent trespasser added the major portion of it. (The innocent trespasser placed her notebook on a table in the library. After selecting a couple of references, the trespasser sat down and started to write her research paper. Much later the trespasser discovered that she had sat at the wrong table and used someone else's notebook.)

If the innocent trespasser does acquire title by accession, the trespasser will be obligated to pay the rightful owner for the value of the property taken. This value will be computed on the worth of the property at the time the trespasser took it. These cases are really exceptions to the general rule; the trespasser usually does not acquire title.

If title to the property stays with the original owner, the innocent trespasser can recover for the value of the services rendered in improving the property. If the owner were allowed to keep these improvements without payment, the owner would have an unjust enrichment and the innocent trespasser would suffer an unjust loss. The owner is obligated to pay for the reasonable value of the improvements. This is similar to the theory underlying quasi contracts.

A *willful* trespasser—one who knows he or she has no right to the property—cannot acquire title to the new property. The transfer of title under such conditions would permit willful trespassers to benefit from their wrongdoings and might even encourage them to try such an action again.

A willful trespasser is liable for any damages that he or she caused and will not be entitled to any compensation for improvements made to the property. Suppose, for example, Marti took some bricks that she found in a neighbor's yard. She knew she was not entitled to the bricks, but since she did not think her neighbor wanted them, she decided to go ahead and use them to build a barbecue. Although heavy, the barbecue is movable, and the neighbor is entitled to have it. Marti is not entitled to any money for her labor in building the barbecue. If the neighbor incurs any financial damages because he was planning to use the bricks in another manner, he can recover the damages from Marti.

In rare instances, title may pass to the willful trespasser because the owner decides not to contest the trespasser's title. In other words, the owner does not want the improved property. However, the original owner may collect the value of the improved property from the willful trespasser. In our example, if the neighbor decides that he does not want the barbecue, he may let the title pass to Marti by default and can collect from Marti the value of the brick barbecue instead of the value of the bricks alone. Such action will occur at the option of the original owner.

Some legal disputes involve cases in which a third party has purchased the property created by the trespasser. Generally, the dispute is between the original owner and the third-party purchaser. To be protected, the third party must be a *bona fide purchaser for value.* (A bona fide purchaser for value is a person who buys property in good faith, for a reasonable value, and without actual or constructive knowledge that there is anything wrong with the transfer.) The bona fide purchaser will have the same rights and liabilities as the trespasser. If the original owner could have received the property back from the trespasser, he or she can get it back from the bona fide purchaser. Good-faith purchasers do have the right to remove any additions or improvements that they have made themselves if this can be done without harming the original property.

Confusion   *Confusion* occurs when the personal, fungible property of two or more people is mixed together and cannot be separated. *Fungible property* includes such things as sand, gravel, wheat, corn, rye, oil, and gasoline. It generally consists of very small particles or grains. When wheat of the same type and quality belonging to two different farmers is mixed together, confusion occurs: The particles of wheat cannot be separated and returned to their respective owners.

Confusion may be caused by the wrongdoing of one of the owners or may occur without any misconduct. For example, farmers often store their fungible crops, such as corn, in the same storage bin or silo. If confusion occurs *without misconduct,* the farmers will receive an undivided interest in the new confused mass. If the corn in the bin is sold, the farmers will divide the proceeds in proportion to the amount that they put into the bin. If there are any losses, the farmers will divide the losses proportionately.

If the confusion is caused by *intentional wrongdoing,* different rules apply. If the new mixture is not divisible, title to the whole mass will pass to the innocent party. Therefore, it is to the wrongdoer's benefit to show that the new mass is divisible. If the wrongdoer can prove that the new mass is divisible and that the mixture has at least the same *unit value* (value per ton, pound, gallon, and the like) as the property belonging to the innocent party, the wrongdoer will be entitled to a share of the new mass. If the wrongdoer can clearly prove how much was added, the court can award the wrongdoer that share. If the wrongdoer can identify only the relative proportion of his or her share, the wrongdoer will be allowed to recover a proportional share. In either case, the proof must be clear and convincing. The following case involved an analysis of the proof.

Exxon Corporation v. *West*
543 S.W.2d 667 (C.A. Tex. 1976),
cert. denied, 434 U.S. 875 (1977)

FACTS   Exxon had an agreement to take gas from the Wests' property and to pay them a royalty on it. During the contract term, the Texas Railroad Commission authorized the use of this same reservoir under the Wests' property for gas storage purposes. Exxon began injecting gas into the reservoir for storage, which created a mixture of native gas and injected gas.

ISSUE   Are the Wests entitled to royalties on all the gas drawn from the reservoir?

HOLDING   No. The gas in the reservoir had been confused, but the resulting mass could be divided.

REASONING   The court held that Exxon intentionally caused confusion of the injected gas and the native gas. The Wests were entitled to royalties on the native gas. Exxon had the burden of proving how much gas was subject to the royalties. Exxon provided expert testimony by their geologist and their petroleum engineer, who studied and testified about the maximum amount of native gas and the probable amount of native gas in the reserve. Since the Wests did not offer any contradictory testimony, the court held that Exxon's witnesses had to be believed. The amount of native gas did not need to be proved with exact certainty. In such a case, reasonable certainty is sufficient.

Abandoned Property   Sometimes an owner is no longer interested in owning a piece of personal property. She may *abandon* it by throwing it away without intending to reclaim it or by relinquishing it to someone else without intending to retake possession. If the property is relinquished to someone else, that person will become the new owner of the property. Generally, this type of transfer will be considered a gift. If the property is thrown away, the person who finds the property and reduces it to possession will acquire title. The property will once again be subject to original possession.

The following case involved an alleged abandonment of a property right.

Dodd, Mead & Company, Inc. v. Lilienthal
515 F. Supp. 105 (S.D. N.Y. 1981)

FACTS   Lilienthal, the author of *The Zionist Connection*, contracted with Dodd, Mead & Company (Dodd, Mead) for the publication of his book. Under the contract, Dodd, Mead had the exclusive right to print, publish, and sell the book in the United States and Canada. Dodd, Mead obtained the copyright on the book. They printed and distributed 14,500 copies of it and spent more than $66,000 in manufacturing and promoting it. When the book was no longer available in bookstores or from Dodd, Mead, Lilienthal began printing it himself.

ISSUE   Had Dodd, Mead abandoned their copyrighted interest in the book?

HOLDING   No. There was no evidence of a relinquishing of rights by the publisher.

REASONING   For the holder of a copyright to abandon this property right, he or she must perform some overt act. This act must manifest an intent to surrender rights in the copyrighted material. Mere inaction is not sufficient. The court held that Dodd, Mead never abandoned the copyright and that there was no evidence to suggest that Dodd, Mead intended to give up its exclusive right to publish the book. Dodd, Mead was entitled to an injunction and money damages.

Lost or Mislaid Property   *Lost* property is property that has been unintentionally lost by the true owner. The owner does not know where the property was lost or where it may be retrieved. A person who finds lost property has good title to the property. The true owner is the only one with better title than the finder. The finder of lost property generally is entitled to keep possession of it unless a statute prevents such possession.

Mislaid property is property that was intentionally set somewhere by the owner. The manner of placement and the location of the property indicates whether the owner merely forgot to pick up the property or lost it. The owner of mislaid property usually will be able to remember where the property was left and will reclaim it. The finder of mislaid property has good title against everyone except the true owner.

There is a critical distinction between *title* to the property and *possession* of the property. Although the finder of the mislaid property has good title, he or she is not entitled to possession. The owner of the premises where the property is found or the person in charge of the premises is entitled to hold the mislaid property. The reason is that when the true owner remembers where the mislaid property was left, he or she will return to that location to retrieve it. It is logical to leave the personal property on the premises to make it easier for the true owner to reclaim it. Note that the owner of the premises is entitled to hold mislaid property, but not lost property. If the finder of the lost or mislaid property was a trespasser on the property, the owner of the premises has title to the personal property that was found.

To increase the likelihood that the true owner will be able to reclaim the property, some state statutes and local ordinances require the finder of lost and/or mislaid property to complete certain steps before becoming the final owner. These statutes generally have two requirements:

1. that a specified type of notice be placed in the newspaper
2. that the property be given to the police to be claimed by the true owner

If the property is not claimed within a stated period, the police will allow the finder to claim it.

PROTECTION OF PERSONAL PROPERTY

If an owner of personal property fails to protect the property adequately, it may be taken by someone else. Sometimes this taking is legal, but often it is not. In either case, the owner will suffer a temporary or permanent loss. To protect against such a loss, the owner should be aware of the means—legal or illegal—by which property may be taken. These include *conversion, escheat, judicial sale,* and *mortgage foreclosure* or *repossession of property.*

Conversion

Conversion occurs when one person takes the personal property of the owner. It is unauthorized and unjustified interference, permanent or temporary, with the owner's use and control of property. According to court opinions, a transitory interference would constitute trespass to personal property rather than conversion. A more lengthy interference—but not necessarily a permanent one—would be conversion. Under the theory of conversion, the owner can sue the taker for the return of the property or for money to replace the property. Conversion is the tort equivalent of a number of crimes, including theft, armed robbery, embezzlement, and obtaining property by false pretenses. In a criminal proceeding, the state would protect its interest in having citizens abide by the law. In a civil proceeding, the individual would protect his or her property rights.

Conversion *can* occur when the owner of personal property voluntarily releases the property to another person, who then uses the property in a manner different from that originally authorized. For example, if the owner of an automobile left the automobile with a car dealer for repairs and the dealer used it as a demonstrator, the dealer would be liable if the automobile was damaged while a prospective customer was taking it for a test drive.

In the following case, a lessee was found to have converted the leased property.

Swish Manufacturing Southeast
v. Manhattan Fire & Marine Insurance Company
675 F.2d 1218 (11th Cir. 1982)

FACTS Swish Manufacturing owned a corporate aircraft. Swish entered into a contract with Wings whereby Wings could lease the aircraft whenever Wings wanted it. Under the lease, Wings could not use the aircraft to transport cargo or for unlawful purposes. Swish received an insurance endorsement on the aircraft that excluded loss due to conversion. Wings took the aircraft to the Bahamas in order to smuggle marijuana. The plane was seized by Bahamian police and was damaged while in their custody.

ISSUE Was the aircraft converted by Wings?

HOLDING Yes. The unauthorized use was a conversion.

REASONING Conversion is the unauthorized assumption and exercise of the right of ownership of someone else's personal property. This exercise is contrary to the owner's right. Misuse or excessive use may be conversion. Unauthorized use that causes damage to a chattel constitutes a conversion. The degree of deviation between actual use and permitted use will be important. Here the court found that the deviation was great; conversion had occurred.

In a suit for conversion, the owner generally would prefer to have the personal property returned and repaired, if necessary. Another option available to the owner under the laws of most states is to force the wrongdoer to keep the personal property and to pay for it. The price will be the value at the time the property was taken. This remedy is performed only at the election of the owner. It is not available at the request of the wrongdoer.

Escheat

When the rightful owner of property cannot be located, the property will *escheat,* or revert, to the state government. The effect of escheat is that the property is given to the government. Usually it is in someone else's custody, but possession will be transferred to the state. The policy behind this doctrine is that the state is more deserving of the property than anyone else if the correct owner cannot be found. Escheat tends to occur when a person dies and the heirs or relatives cannot be located. It also may occur when a person does not keep careful financial records and so forgets about small bank accounts, stocks and bonds, or other assets. The following example shows another way in which escheat might occur.

Best Deal Bank offered charge cards to its customers. The bank had a number of credits for these charge accounts but was unable to locate the customers. The total amount of the credits was in excess of $100,000. The state wanted this money to escheat to it. As might be expected, the bank contested the escheat in court, claiming that it was still trying to locate the true owners. The bank was not successful in the lawsuit.

Escheat is governed by the appropriate state statute. Often, escheated property becomes part of the state's general fund. For a specified period after the escheat, the rightful owner can claim the property from the state. The rightful owner will need adequate proof of identity and of a right to the property.

Judicial Sale

When a person loses a civil lawsuit, the court may order that person to make payment to the other party. This is called a judgment. If the person does not make the required payment, additional action may be necessary. This action commonly consists of an execution of judgment. The person who is entitled to payment procures a writ of execution from the clerk of court's office. With this writ, the sheriff can seize the debtor's property and sell it. The money is then given to the judgment creditor to satisfy the judgment. This is called a *judicial sale* or a *sheriff's sale.* If the sale price exceeds the total owed to the judgment creditor, the costs of the sheriff's office, and the costs of the execution, the excess will generally be transferred to the owner. The treatment of this excess is governed by state law and by the type of judgment. Notices of judicial sales are often included with other legal notices in the newspaper. A purchaser at a judicial sale buys the rights that the seller (the sheriff) had to sell. The sheriff's office generally does not warrant (promise) that it is entitled to sell the property. In addition, the true owner may have a limited period within which he or she may redeem the property, even if it is in the hands of a third-party purchaser. The amount of repayment to the third party is governed by state law.

**Mortgage
Foreclosure
or Repossession
of Property**

A lender who wants to protect an interest in a loan may create a security interest in some collateral. If the lender follows the requirements for creating and perfecting a security interest, the lender will have a security interest in the property. If the borrower does not repay the loan under the terms of the contract, the lender can repossess (retake) the property. Usually the lender prefers to have cash and thus will sell the collateral. If the collateral is real estate, the loan will be called a *mortgage,* and taking possession of the property will be called a *mortgage foreclosure.* A person who buys repossessed property or foreclosed property buys only the seller's legal interest. The purchaser may lose the property if the foreclosure or repossession was wrongful.

**YOU BE
THE
JUDGE**

The *Medina Journal-Register* carried the following advertisement:

YOUR NAME MAY BE WORTH MONEY

THE PERSONS whose names and last known addresses are set forth below appear from the records of Metropolitan Life Insurance Company to be entitled to abandoned property in amounts of fifty dollars or more.

Name and Address	Name and Address
Barry, Cathie 11778 Platten Rd., Lydonville	Garling, Carrie RFD 5 Harrison Rd., Medina
Boksene, Frank RFD 1, Medina	
Brady, John 138 Wood Rd., Albion	Schenk, Kevin, A. 16710 Skillington Rd., Holley
	Schreibel, Kathryn RF 6, Median
Clark, Ronald Lot 7 W. Academy St., Albion	
	Zollweg, Louis A. 409 Park Ave., Medina

A report of abandoned property has been made to the Comptroller of the State of New York pursuant to Sec. 701 and 1316 of the Abandoned Property Law of the State of New York. A list of the names of persons appearing from the records of the said life insurance company to be entitled thereto is on file and open to public inspection at the Home Office of the Company located at One Madison Ave., in the City of New York, New York, where such abandoned property is payable.

Such abandoned property will be paid on or before August 31st next to persons establishing to the satisfaction of the Company their right to receive the same.

On or before the succeeding September 10th, such remaining abandoned property will be paid to the Comptroller of the State of New York, and Metropolitan Life Insurance Company shall thereupon cease to be liable therefor.

Write Metropolitan Life Insurance Company, PLI Claims Advisory-Unclaimed Funds Unit, 501 Route 22 West, Bridgewater, NJ 08807, or telephone (908) 253-2208 or 2209.

GET MET. IT PAYS.®
✳ MetLife®

Suppose a court suit were filed concerning the rights of a named person and his family, Metropolitan Life Insurance Company, and the State of New York? What would you decide and why? Would your answer differ if Metropolitan Life Insurance Company had noted elsewhere in its files that the named person had died and had cited the correct name and address of his personal representative?

Source: "Your Name May Be Worth Money," *Medina Journal-Register*, Monday, May 4, 1992, page 6.

BAILMENTS OF PERSONAL PROPERTY

A *bailment* arises when a person lends personal property to someone else. The *bailor* is the owner of the property, and the *bailee* is the one who has possession of (but not title to) the property. Whenever an owner allows another person to have custody of the owner's personal property, a bailment exists. It is understood that the bailee is to use the property in a specific way. For example, if the attendants of a parking garage drive a customer's car for any purpose other than parking or safeguarding it, they breach their duty as bailees. It is further understood that the bailee is to return the property at the end of the bailment.

If the borrower is giving up consideration, a contract exists. If Elizabeth rents a car from Zeta Car Rental Company, a bailment relationship exists. Elizabeth is the bailee and Zeta Car Rental Company is the bailor. Their relationship will be governed by both the rules of bailments and the rules of contracts. However, a contract is not a requirement for a bailment. A bailment can occur gratuitously.

All the following elements are necessary for a bailment:

1. The bailor must retain title.
2. The possession of the property must be delivered to the bailee.
3. The bailee must accept possession.
4. The bailee must have possession of the property for a specific purpose and must have temporary control of the property.
5. The parties must intend that the property will be returned to the bailor unless the bailor directs that the property be given to another person.

A bailment is not a sale of personal property. A sale is a permanent change of possession, includes a transfer of title, and requires an exchange of consideration.

A controversial question is whether parking in a garage constitutes a bailment or the rental of a space to park a car. The following is one court's opinion.

Parking Management, Inc. v. Gilder
343 A.2d 51 (D.C. App. 1975)

FACTS   Gilder parked his car in a garage managed by Parking Management, Inc. (PMI). The garage was enclosed in the Washington Hilton Hotel. When Gilder arrived at the garage, one of the attendants directed him to a space, where Gilder parked the car. Gilder took the key with him. At that time, a manager, a cashier, and three attendants were on duty. The trunk of Gilder's car was pried open while it was parked in the garage.

ISSUE   Did Gilder have a bailment relationship with PMI?

HOLDING   Yes. PMI had created a bailment relationship under these circumstances.

REASONING   The theory that parking in a garage is a lease or a license situation is outmoded. When the owner parks the car and takes the key, the relationship is not always a lease. Unlike the usual tenant of real estate, the owner does not have an adequate opportunity to protect the car. By definition, the owner will always be away from the car once it has been parked. In addition, there is usually no fixed term for the parking of the car. The car owner cannot remove the car until the parking fee is paid. Here Gilder was under the impression that PMI was providing security. In fact, the job descriptions indicated that part of the employees' jobs included providing security.

Bailee's Duty of Care

Disputes often arise when the property is damaged while in the hands of the bailee. In a lawsuit, the issue would be whether or not the bailee took proper care of the property. The answer would depend on provisions in the local statutes, the language of any bailment contract, and the type of bailment.

Classifications of Bailments

Bailments are divided into types based on who benefits from the bailment relationship. The classification affects the bailee's obligation and his or her liability if any damage occurs to the property. This responsibility is illustrated in Table 50.1.

Bailor Benefit Bailments   When the bailment is established solely to benefit the bailor, the bailee will be responsible only for gross negligence in caring for the property. For example, Daniel asks Sue to take his portable computer to the parking lot and put it in his car. Daniel is the only one benefiting from this bailment. Sue will be responsible for damage to the computer only if she is grossly negligent in completing the task. Suppose she carefully places the computer next to the trunk and opens the trunk with the key. While she is doing this, a third person steals the computer. Sue will not be liable because she was not grossly negligent. If she had placed Daniel's computer in the middle of the road before she opened the trunk, and another car had run over it, a court would probably find Sue guilty of gross negligence and therefore hold her liable. Remember that this decision ultimately will be for the trier of fact in a court case to make. What is considered to be negligence will depend on the circumstances and the evidence presented.

Mutual Benefit Bailments   When a bailment is established for the benefit of both the bailor and the bailee, it is called a mutual benefit bailment. Both parties expect to gain from the bailment relationship. In such bailments, the bailee is responsible for ordinary negligence. A mutual benefit bailment occurs, for example, when the owner of a suit takes it to a dry cleaning establishment. The owner will benefit by having the suit cleaned and pressed. The dry cleaners will benefit because they are going to be paid. The dry cleaners will be responsible if they carelessly clean the suit in cleaning fluid that is too hot and causes the suit to shrink.

Bailee Benefit Bailments   When a bailment is established solely for the benefit of the bailee, it is called a bailee benefit bailment. The bailee will be responsible for slight negligence in caring for the property. Suppose Jeanette needed a car to drive downtown for a job interview, but her car was in the garage waiting to be repaired. Paula, her roommate, agreed to lend Jeanette her car. This bailment was created for Jeanette's benefit only. It is thus a bailee benefit

TABLE 50.1   The Responsibility of the Bailee

TYPE OF BAILMENT	WHO WILL BENEFIT	THE BAILEE WILL BE LIABLE FOR . . .
Bailor benefit	Bailor (owner)	Gross negligence
Mutual benefit	Bailor and bailee	Ordinary negligence
Bailee benefit	Bailee (possessor)	Slight negligence

bailment. If Jeanette causes an accident because she is listening to the radio on high volume, she will have to pay for the damage to Paula's car.

Limitations on a Bailee's Liability

Some states and localities have statutes that provide maximum limits on the liability of the bailee in certain types of bailments.

If the bailment is based on a contract, the terms of the contract may increase or decrease the liability of the bailee. A bailee who is a quasi-public bailee generally will not be allowed to limit his or her liability contractually unless specifically permitted to do so by statute. A quasi-public bailee is one offering services to the public; for example, a common carrier, a garage, a hotel, or a public parking lot. Even when a statute permits a bailee to restrict liability, any limitation on liability must be reasonable.

A private bailee can restrict his or her liability under the terms of the agreement if this restriction does not conflict with the real purpose of the contract between the bailee and the bailor. The bailee must inform the bailor of any limitation on the bailee's liability. Most courts hold that a printed ticket stub or a posted notice on the premises does not adequately inform the bailor of the limitations *unless* the bailor's attention is directed to the sign or the ticket stub.

Termination of a Bailment

A bailment will terminate at the end of the period that the parties specify or when a specified condition occurs. If the bailment was for an indefinite time, it may be terminated at the will of either the bailor or the bailee. A bailment will terminate when the purpose or performance of the bailment has been completed. If either party causes a material breach of the bailment relationship, the victim may terminate the bailment and the wrongdoer will be liable for any damages he or she caused. The bailment will terminate if the bailed property is destroyed or becomes unfit or unsuitable for the purpose of the bailment. Generally, a bailment will also terminate by operation of law if death, insanity, or bankruptcy of either party makes performance by the bailee impossible.

Bailee's Duty to Return the Property

A bailee has a general duty to return the bailor's property to the bailor. There are exceptions to this rule. The bailee is not liable to the bailor if the property is lost, destroyed, or stolen through no fault of the bailee. The bailee is not liable if the property is taken away by legal process, such as an attachment for a sheriff's sale. The bailee is not liable if the property is claimed by someone who has a better legal right to possession than the bailor has.

Sometimes a bailee has a duty to return the property to someone other than the bailor. There may be a duty to "return" the property to a transferee who has bought the property from the bailor. A common business example is when a warehouse or common carrier has an obligation to hold personal property and then transfer it to a purchaser who presents a receipt or bill of lading. These situations are discussed in detail in Chapter 19.

The following case dealt with the liability of a bailee for failure to return the property.

Vilner v. Crocker National Bank
152 Cal. Rptr. 850 (Cal. App. 1979)

FACTS   Vilner, the operator of a restaurant, used the Crocker National Bank's night depository on a regular basis. On the occasion in question, he unlocked the night depository at Crocker's Novato branch and placed in it a locked bag containing $7976.36. After closing the depository, he heard what sounded like a bag dropping into the box. He reopened the depository and did not see his bag. The bag was not recovered.

Before that night, the bank had received at least four complaints by customers at other branches that deposits into the night depository were lost. On two occasions, customers had informed Crocker that bags had lodged in the depository at the Novato branch. Crocker did not take any action to correct these problems.

ISSUE   Is Crocker liable for not returning the bailed property?

HOLDING   Yes. The bailee did not adequately explain its failure to return the property.

REASONING   If a bailor can establish that the property was delivered to the bailee and that the bailor subsequently demanded its return, the bailee must explain its failure to return the property. The bailee must explain why the bailed property disappeared and offer evidence to show that failure to return the property was due to some specific casualty like theft or fire. When the bailee cannot deliver the property on demand, the bailee must show that it is without fault. The bailee must explain why delivery of the property is impossible in order to show that the bailee is not responsible for the loss of the bailed property.

The bailee does not have to return the property if the bailee has a lien on the property. Many states have statutes that allow the bailee to keep the property in his or her possession until the bailor pays for the bailment. This is called a *possessory lien*. If the bailor fails to make payment, most statutes will permit the bailee to sell the property. A common type of bailee's lien is a mechanic's lien, which arises when services have been performed on the property. For example, if a garage repairs an automobile and the owner does not have the money to pay for the repairs, the garage can keep the automobile until the owner does pay. In most cases, the bailee will lose the lien if the bailee willingly releases the goods to the bailor—that is, if the bailor comes to reclaim the property and the bailee releases it without receiving payment. Generally, there is no bailee's lien if the bailor and bailee originally agreed that the bailor was going to pay on credit.

SUMMARY

Personal property is classified into tangible and intangible property based on its physical characteristics. Discussions of legal interests in property revolve around ownership rights, title, and possession. Often, one person has title to property, but someone else has possession. Title to personal property can be acquired by original possession, by voluntary transfer directly from the owner to the transferee, or by involuntary transfer from the owner. A transferee of personal property generally will not have any better title than the transferor had. This will be true even though the transferee thought that the transferor had good title. This limitation on title is especially important in judicial sales, sales of repossessed property, conversion, confusion, and accession.

A bailment is a special legal relationship that occurs when the owner-bailor transfers the possession of personal property to someone else, the bailee. The owner keeps title. After the purpose of the bailment has been completed, possession generally will be returned to the owner. The duty of the bailee to protect the property will be affected by whether it is a bailor benefit bailment, a mutual benefit bailment, or a bailee benefit bailment.

DISCUSSION QUESTIONS

1. What are the differences between title and possession?

2. What happens if the donor of a gift causa mortis dies but not from the expected cause? Who is likely to complain in such a situation?

3. What are the policies underlying the rules about accession?

4. James took a piece of rough turquoise stone, polished it, and set it in a silver setting in a necklace. James reasonably believed that he had found the stone on public land. In reality, he had found it on private land, where the owner, who had mined it, had placed it in a pile for polishing. Who owns the jewelry and why? What are the legal rights of the parties?

5. What rights do the owners have when confusion occurs and no one is guilty of misconduct?

6. Is an umbrella on a desk likely to be lost or mislaid property? Why? If the umbrella is on the floor, is it likely to be lost or mislaid property? Why?

7. Ric went to José's Mexican Restaurant for lunch. He hung his coat on the coat rack provided for that purpose. When he got ready to leave, Ric walked out and left his coat. Dennis found the coat. Who is entitled to title of the coat? Why? Who is entitled to possession of the coat? Why?

8. Define escheat. When would it occur?

9. What are the requirements for a bailment relationship?

10. What legal rights does a bailor have when a bailee has damaged the property or allowed someone else to damage it?

CASE PROBLEMS

1. In 1971, Treasure Salvors located an anchor from the *Nuestra Señora de Atocha*. Since that time, Treasure Salvors has continued to conduct salvage operations in the wreck area and has retrieved numerous artifacts. Frick and a number of other defendants began salvage operations 1500 yards from the location where the second anchor was discovered. Are the Treasure Salvors entitled to conduct their salvage operation free from interference from Frick? Do they have ownership rights in the wreck? (*Treasure Salvors, Inc.* v. *Unidentified Wrecked and Abandoned Sailing Vessel,* 640 F.2d 560 [5th Cir. 1981].)

2. Honea was the administrator of the estate of her father, W. E. Smith. Honea filed suit against Scarbrough to recover an amount she claimed was owed by Scarbrough. Smith had purchased a used car, whose title was issued in the name of Scarbrough's daughter. Scarbrough and his daughter had executed a note that provided for thirty-six monthly installments of $125 each, a total of $4500, to be paid to Smith for the car.

Smith had given the original copy of the note to Scarbrough's daughter and kept the carbon copy for himself. Scarbrough's daughter had made one payment on the note when Smith died. This payment was made by a check, which was cashed by Smith. Did Smith intend to make a gift when he delivered the note? (*Scarbrough* v. *Honea,* 331 S.E.2d 80 [Ga. App. 1985].)

3. Kaiser wrote a check to the land title company for $14,692.16, as payment for the home his nephew was buying. He also wrote a check for $2308 to his nephew for furnishings. The alleged oral loan agreement provided for 300 monthly payments. The nephew issued 44 monthly checks to his uncle after the transaction. A number of these checks carried the notation "for house." After Kaiser's death, the nephew quit making the monthly payments. The nephew claimed that the money advanced by Kaiser was a gift, not a loan. Is the nephew correct in his assertion? (*Estate of Kaiser* v. *Gifford,* 692 S.W.2d 525 [Tex. App. 1 Dist. 1985].)

4. The personal representative of Shepard brought a suit for amounts loaned by Shepard to Jacobson. Shepard made the loans by writing checks to Jacobson or his creditors. Some of the checks had the notation "loan" on them. The loans were not evidenced by a note. Shepard had made statements during her life that the debt was forgiven. This evidence was not contradicted. Did Shepard make a valid gift to the debtor of the amount that he owed her? (*Guardian State Bank & Trust* v. *Jacobson,* 369 N.W.2d 80 [Neb. 1985].)

5. Kenneth Simkin initiated a lawsuit against his former wife, Barbara Norcross. Simkin wanted the return of his sailing vessel, a Morgan sloop. He had left the vessel in good condition tied to a jetty. He had the owner's permission to dock his vessel in this manner. When Simkin returned to his vessel, it was gone. It was later found in the custody of his wife. Did Simkin abandon his vessel? Did Simkin intend to give the vessel to his former wife? (*Simkin* v. *Norcross,* 610 F. Supp. 691 [D.C. Fla. 1985].)

6. Chemical Sales Company, a Missouri corporation, was engaged in the business of distributing cleaning products in the St. Louis area. Diamond Chemical Company is a New Jersey corporation engaged in the business of producing cleaning products. Diamond was the primary supplier for Chemical Sales. Chemical Sales began having financial difficulties. To ensure that it would have a continuous supply of products, Chemical Sales entered into an agreement allowing Diamond to manage Chemical Sales' business and receive a security

interest in Chemical Sales' inventory and accounts receivable. The relationship did not work out, and the key officers of Chemical Sales quit their jobs. Diamond Chemical then terminated Chemical Sales' business and sold its assets. A demand was made on Diamond Chemical for an accounting, which was not given. Did Diamond Chemical wrongfully convert Chemical Sales' property? Did Chemical Sales abandon its property? (*Chemical Sales Co., Inc.* v. *Diamond Chemical Co.,* 766 F.2d 364 [8th Cir. 1985].)

7. The Controller of the state of California, Kenneth Cory, started a lawsuit to recover funds held by Golden State Bank. The funds consisted of $157,765.47 set aside because of money orders sold by the bank that were still uncashed after seven years. The bank wanted to deduct $143,133.22 in service charges before remitting (transferring) the funds to the state. Should the funds escheat to the state of California? If so, how much should be given to the state? (*Cory* v. *Golden State Bank,* 157 Cal. Rptr. 538 [Cal. App. 1979].)

8. Goldbaum rented two safe deposit boxes in the bank. He stored rare medals and coins in these boxes. The leases for the boxes stated that "Lessors shall have no liability for loss from fire, water, radiation, the forces of nature. . . ." The bank's sprinkler system failed and water flooded these boxes. Should the bank be liable for the damage? Was the bank a bailee? (*Goldbaum* v. *Bank Leumi Trust Company of New York,* 543 F. Supp. 434 [S.D. N.Y. 1982].)

9. Monroe rented a Roto-tiller from East Bay Rental Service. East Bay employees did not give him any instructions on the proper use of the tiller and did not warn him about the dangers involved in its use. Monroe was injured while using the tiller. Did a bailment relationship exist? If so, what type of bailment relationship existed? Should East Bay Rental Service be held liable? (*Monroe* v. *East Bay Rental Service,* 245 P.2d 9 [1st Dist., Div. 2 1952].)

10. On receiving a shipping order, Delta obtained a cargo container from Imparca, a commercial shipper. The cargo container was loaded and sealed by Delta and then delivered into the possession of Imparca by Delta's agent. The container was placed on a vessel chartered by Imparca, and Imparca issued a clean bill of lading. The bill of lading indicated that the carrier, Imparca, discharged its duties when it delivered the container into the custody of government authorities at the named port, as it was required to do by the laws of the foreign port. The 20-foot cargo container was placed

on the dock in Puerto Cabello in the custody of the Instituto Nacional De Puertos (INP). INP was responsible for the operation of this seaport, including stevedoring, warehousing, and receiving and delivering cargo. The goods subsequently disappeared, and the consignee sought recourse from Imparca. Should the carrier be responsible for the disappearance of the goods in this case? (*Allstate Insurance Co.* v. *Imparca Lines,* 646 F.2d 166 [5th Cir. 1981].)

C H A P T E R   51

Insurance

O U T L I N E

THE CONCEPT OF INSURANCE

The existence of *risk* creates the need, or at least the desire, for insurance. Automobile accidents occur with alarming regularity, normally causing substantial property damage to at least one automobile and frequently to more. Fires burn down homes or businesses, presenting the owner with the potential for economic ruin. People die, leaving behind unpaid bills and very often a family with one less wage earner. Or the death leaves a gaping hole in the management of the business that employed and relied on the deceased.

Risks cannot be totally avoided. When a loss occurs as a result of risk, the victim must somehow finance the loss. There are two basic ways to do so: through self-financing or through risk sharing. Self-financing is expensive and potentially disastrous. The feared event may occur before the self-financing person has been able to **amortize** fully for the potential loss. Risk sharing therefore is a more satisfying alternative to many people. The most common form of risk sharing is through insurance.

Insurance is a type of *contract*. Basically, people who share a common risk contribute to a fund set up to cover the losses that will be felt if the common risk occurs. Any member of the group who suffers a loss due to the occurrence of the common risk can withdraw money from the fund to cover the loss. The amount each person contributes is based on the likelihood of the event's occurrence and also on the value of the property or other interest being protected.

Although people can form their own insurance groups, most would rather deal with a company established for the express purpose of providing insurance protection. Since insurance companies normally can provide coverage over a wider geographic area than a group of individuals could reach, the risk-sharing proportions are usually smaller for each individual insured party. And since the insurance company is an expert in the field, it can establish standards that help minimize the risk faced by members of the covered group. In addition, the insurance company's expertise allows for a more scientific rate-setting mechanism allowing the risk funds contributed by the insured parties to be as low as possible while still providing adequate coverage.

Amortize To provide for the gradual extinguishing of a debt by contributing funds to a sinking fund or similar account.

FORMATION OF THE INSURANCE CONTRACT

Because of public policy considerations, the insurance contract is heavily regulated by state law. An insurance company must comply with the applicable state law in creating the contract with the **insured**. However, because of the potential for fraud and for the huge losses being assumed by the insurance company, state statutes also give the **insurer** some special protections in the formation of the contract.

Insured The person protected by the insurance policy.

Insurer The person or corporation who provides the protection called for by an insurance contract.

Offer and Acceptance

Premiums The monies that the insured pays to retain an insurance contract with the insurer.

The concepts of offer and acceptance are applied in a special way to insurance contracts. The insurance company has an obvious desire to control the nature and extent of its potential liability. This control is important because the company is liable for the risk insured against as soon as the contract is formed, even though most of the **premiums** the company expects to receive have not yet been paid. If the covered risk occurred at this time, the liability of the company would greatly exceed the premiums paid by the insured.

The problem is compounded when the company itself cannot analyze the insured person before the insurance goes into effect. Insurance is generally sold by an agent who represents the insurance company in its dealings with the insured. The agent is the person who speaks to the customer, but the company is the one facing the potential for liability if a claim arises. To what extent can the agent bind the company? The answer depends on the type of insurance sought by the customer.

The agent generally has the power to bind the company to an insurance contract immediately if the insurance is for *property* or *liability* coverage. When the customer completes an application, the customer has made an *offer*. When the agent accepts a premium, or even when the agent agrees to accept a premium later, the insurance company is deemed to have accepted the offer. At that point, a contract exists and the customer is immediately covered for the named risk. The reason for this immediate coverage is that under state law the insurer can cancel a property protection or liability contract fairly easily if the risk is unacceptable to the insurer.

On the other hand, the law places many restrictions on the power of the insurer to cancel a *life insurance* policy. As a result, life insurance companies prefer to investigate a life insurance application before being bound to insurance coverage. When the customer completes and tenders an application for life insurance, the law treats the application as an *inquiry*. The insurance company, not the agent, studies the application. If the company feels that the applicant presents a reasonable risk, the company makes an offer in the form of a policy. The customer then can accept the offer and create a contract by accepting delivery of the contract. Another approach is to treat the customer as an offeror and the application as an offer, but to restrict the authority of the agent. In this case, only the company is empowered to accept the offer; acceptance is shown by the issuance of a policy. In either case, the customer is *not* protected immediately, in contrast to the provisions of property insurance policies. To alleviate this problem, many life insurance companies allow the agent to issue a **binder**, a short-term life insurance policy that provides some coverage for the applicant during the insurance company's investigation of the application.

Binder A short-term commitment to provide insurance coverage in some limited form pending the final entry into a permanent insurance contract.

Avoiding Liability

Since insurance policies are contracts, many of the rules of contract law apply to insurance. Situations that would create voidable contracts often create voidable insurance coverage as well. Fraud on the part of the applicant allows the insurer to avoid the contract. However, the company that provides life insur-

Incontestability clause A clause in an insurance policy that limits the time during which the insurer may challenge coverage.

ance must discover the fraud within a reasonable time (normally three years) in order to avoid the policy. After that, the **incontestability clause** makes the policy "incontestable." Fraud in the filing of a claim is also grounds for avoidance of the coverage. And intentional destruction of the insured property by the insured is not covered by most policies.

Sometimes the court must decide what to do when one of the insured parties has committed a wrongful act but another insured on the same policy has not. The following case shows how one court resolved such a problem.

Ryan v. MFA Mutual Insurance Company
610 S.W.2d 428 (Tenn. App. 1980)

FACTS   Ryan had an argument with his wife and left his home. After he left, his wife started a fire that damaged the house and some of its contents. Mr. Ryan filed a claim on the insurance policy that covered the house. The policy was in the names of Mr. and Mrs. Ryan.

ISSUE   Can Mr. Ryan, an innocent coinsured, collect on a policy when the jointly insured party started the fire?

HOLDING   Yes. Mr. Ryan was not guilty of any wrongdoing.

REASONING   This was a case of first impression in Tennessee. A split of authority among the states had resolved the question. The former majority rule was that the innocent coinsured was barred from recovery because of the wrongdoing of the other coinsured. A new rule that allowed recovery by the innocent party had emerged over the preceding two years. Allowing the innocent party to recover would not benefit the wrongdoer in this case. When an insurance policy is ambiguous or unclear, it must be construed against the insurer. The intentional destruction of property by one of the coinsured should not be interpreted to deny recovery by the other coinsured unless the policy specifically so states. The policy here did not so state. The court held that Mr. Ryan was entitled to recovery for the damages to his property interest as covered by the policy.

One party to a normal contract is excused from performance if the other party has failed to perform. The same rule is applied in insurance. If the insured fails to pay premiums when they are due, the insurance company is justified in thereafter refusing to pay claims filed under the policy.

An insured normally is required to provide prompt notification of any claims to be filed under the policy. The purpose is to allow the insurer an opportunity to investigate the claim and to collect any evidence it may need. Failure of the insured to provide the required notice in a timely manner may discharge the liability of the insurance company even though the occurrence is one the policy was designed to protect against.

Insurable Interest   In most states, gambling contracts are illegal and void on public policy grounds. What separates an insurance contract from a gambling contract is the requirement that a person must have an insurable interest in the object being insured for the policy to be valid and enforceable. If this requirement did not exist, it would be potentially profitable for someone to sit at the nearest airport and purchase flight insurance on the life of every passenger on a particular flight in the hope that the plane would crash. To improve the possibility of such a crash, the person might be encouraged to "arrange" a crisis on the plane. Obviously, such conduct is against public policy.

An insurable interest exists if the person purchasing the insurance has a financial or an equitable interest in the person or property being insured. That is, the purchaser must have an actual, lawful, and substantial economic interest in the safety and the preservation of the person or property being insured. An insurable interest pinpoints the exact nature of the purchaser's interest in the insured object and the exact nature of the possible loss that is being protected against by the policy.

Under property and liability insurance policies, the purchaser must have an insurable interest at two distinct times: When the policy is purchased and when the loss occurs. The absence of an insurable interest at either time will void the policy, and no claims will be honored. Obviously, the owner of property has an insurable interest in that property. Less obviously, the renter of property has an insurable interest in the property rented; a lien holder has an insurable interest in the property covered by the lien; a secured creditor has an insurable interest in the collateral; and a bailee has an insurable interest in the bailed item. Furthermore, since property and liability insurance policies are designed to *indemnify* the insured party for losses actually suffered, the insurable interest is limited to the amount of loss actually suffered or to some percentage of that amount.

The requirements for an insurable interest in life insurance are slightly different from those for property and liability insurance. As will be discussed later, several types of life insurance policies are treated as investments, in contrast to the indemnity purpose of property insurance. As a result, the purchaser of a life insurance policy need have an insurable interest in the life of the insured only at the time the policy is issued. If such an interest exists at the time of issue but is later extinguished, the policy will still remain in effect and will be fully enforceable, provided that the premiums have been paid as due. Thus, the purchaser can still collect the amount of the policy on the death of the insured even though no insurable interest exists at the time of the death—unless the purchaser intentionally caused the death of the insured.

Again, a person obviously has an insurable interest in his or her own life. And it is fairly obvious that a spouse has an insurable interest in the life of his or her spouse. Likewise, parents have an insurable interest in the lives of their children. And, generally, children have an insurable interest in the lives of their parents. A corporation has an insurable interest in the lives of its key executives, usually high-ranking officers on whom the corporation relies for its continued success. And a partnership, or the partners of the partnership, has an insurable interest in the life of each of the partners. Finally, a creditor has an insurable interest in the life of a debtor, but only to the extent of the debt.

Unlike property insurance, which is designed to indemnify the insured for a readily measured loss, life insurance is difficult if not impossible to value. Because there is no way to measure the value of a human life, life insurance policies are "valued" by the purchaser when the policy is purchased. Basically, the value placed on the insured life is decided by the amount the purchaser is willing to pay in premiums. The amount of the premiums is determined by the age, health, occupation, and other factors affecting the life of the insured. Life insurance policies normally are valued in increments of $1000, and a minimum amount usually is required by the company. For example, the policy may be for as little as $5000 or for as much as the national debt—provided that the purchaser is willing and able to pay the requisite premiums.

LIFE INSURANCE

Life insurance is the one type of insurance that the insurer *knows* it will have to pay off, provided that the policy remains in effect. When an insured person dies, the insurer must pay the face amount of the policy (or more) to the named beneficiary. Of course, insurance companies use such things as **mortality tables** to determine the likelihood of death for any particular insured and to establish the insurance rate, or premium.

Mortality tables Bases for determining the expected life span of a person of ordinary health.

However, there is more to life insurance than the calculation of premiums. The primary purpose of most insurance policies covering the life of the purchaser is *investment*. In other words, the insured plans to pay premiums for some time period and then to receive an income or other return for the investment. There are four basic types of life insurance, three of which have investment overtones. The investment rights are spelled out in the standard provisions of the policies.

Ordinary Life Insurance

Beneficiary The person named or designated by the insured as the intended recipient of any insurance proceeds or benefits if the insured risk occurs.

Perhaps the most common type of life insurance purchased by an individual is ordinary life insurance, also called whole life or straight life insurance. The basic concept is that the insured will pay premiums for his or her entire life, and on the insured's death the face amount of the policy will be paid to the **beneficiary.** Most insurance companies consider the age of either ninety-nine or one hundred an "entire life." Thus, if the insured pays premiums until the age of ninety-nine (or one hundred), the insurer then will pay the face amount of the policy to the insured and cancel the coverage. An ordinary life policy is also an investment policy.

Limited-Payment Life Insurance

A limited-payment life insurance policy is similar to a whole life policy in all respects except one. The insured pays all the premiums called for in an ordinary life policy, but pays them in a limited time. Whereas a whole life policy calls for payments until age ninety-nine, a limited-payment life policy might call for all premiums to be paid in twenty years or by age fifty-five. At that point, the insured has a fully paid policy that will be honored on the death of the insured. Or the insured can take advantage of the investment aspects of the policy.

Endowment Life Insurance

In an endowment policy, the insured pays premiums for a fixed time period; at the end of that period, the insured will receive the face amount of the policy from the insurer, and all coverage will terminate. If the insured dies during the period, the insurance company will pay the beneficiary the face amount of the policy. During the endowment period, this type of policy has an investment aspect.

Term Life Insurance

The least expensive form of life insurance is term life insurance. Most group insurance policies are term insurance. This type of insurance has no investment value; hence, the insurance company does not have to set aside funds to provide for the investment aspect required by the other types of life insurance. The term life insurance policy covers the life of the insured for a preset time period, normally for one or five years. If the insured dies during the term of the policy, the insurer must pay the face amount of the policy to the beneficiary. If the insured does not die, the policy expires at the end of the time period. No accumulated values or any coverage will remain. This type of insurance is especially appealing to young adults living on tight budgets. The coverage is inexpensive, but if something does happen to the insured, the beneficiaries will receive the full amount of the insurance.

Standard Provisions

Grace period A preset time period beyond the premium due date during which the insurance remains in effect, permitting the insured to pay the premium with some delay without losing coverage.

Life insurance policies normally provide a **grace period** (usually thirty days) after the premium due date, during which the insured can pay the premium and keep the policy in effect. The policy may exclude certain risks, such as death resulting from military service and suicide by the insured. However, suicide may be excluded only for the period of time before the incontestability clause goes into effect—commonly either two or three years—because suicide is a part of the data in the mortality table. This means that if the insured commits suicide within those two or three years of the policy issue date, the company does not have to pay, but if the suicide occurs after that, the company must honor the policy as written.

Another aspect of the incontestability clause is that the insurance company must challenge any misstatements of fact or concealments by the insured within the stated period or it cannot argue them. The only things the incontestability clause does not cover are lack of an insurable interest and misstatements of age. If the insured misstates his or her age, the only thing that can be done is to modify the policy to reflect the true age of the insured.

The standard life insurance policy (except for term insurance) also contains a **nonforfeiture clause**. This clause guarantees the insured that the investment rights cannot be lost, or forfeited, after the policy has been in effect

Nonforfeiture clause A contract clause assuring that the insured will not forfeit any built-up values if the policy expires or lapses.

Cash value   The built-up value
of the policy based on its investment
portion of the premiums paid.

for three years. These investment rights are reflected in the **cash value** of the policy. If the insured stops paying premiums after the policy has been in effect for three full years, the insured can take the cash value built up in the policy in one of three ways:

1. *cash surrender*—giving up the coverage for the built-up cash value of the policy
2. *extended term insurance*—buying the coverage called for in the policy in term insurance for as long as the cash value will purchase it
3. *paid-up insurance*—purchasing a policy that is in effect until the death of the insured for whatever amount the cash value will cover

In addition, the insured may have options on how to treat dividends paid on the policy by the company. The dividends may be used to reduce future premiums; they may be left with the company to accrue interest; or they may be paid to the insured in cash.

PROPERTY INSURANCE

Property insurance is designed as an indemnification protection against certain predetermined risks faced by the insured. The risk of loss faced by the insured is spread over a group of persons who face the same or a similar risk. The coverage does not normally apply if the insured intentionally destroys the insured property, but it does protect in the event the insured is negligent. The concept of insurable interest is important at two times in property insurance coverage: When the policy is issued and when the loss occurs.

Although an almost infinite number of property insurance areas exist, only three will be examined here. Property and/or liability policies have been issued against damage to the legs of dancers, against injury to the hands of pianists, and even against impairment of the fertility of thoroughbred horses "retired" to stud. Virtually anything the human mind can envision can be insured against—provided that the insured is willing to pay the premium the insurer will charge for assuming the liability if the event occurs. However, most of us are more likely to insure our house, our car, and other equally common items.

Fire Insurance

Most homes in this country are covered by fire insurance policies. The coverage provides protection in the form of indemnification for losses caused by a *hostile* fire, but not for damages caused by a *friendly* fire. In addition, extended coverage endorsements normally provide protection for damage due to smoke, heat, water, and chemicals resulting from a hostile fire. Contrary to popular belief, fires may not be hostile in every circumstance. A fire is friendly, not hostile, if it is burning where it is intended to burn. Thus, damage to a flue caused by fire in a fireplace is not covered by one's fire insurance policy. But if the fire escapes the hearth and spreads to the carpet, it has become hostile. Once it escapes the area where it is meant to be contained, it is deemed hostile, and the damage therefore is covered by a standard fire insurance policy.

Most fire insurance policies are either blanket policies or specific policies. In addition, they are either valued policies or open policies. Thus, you may have a blanket, valued policy; a blanket, open policy; a specific, valued policy; or a specific, open policy.

A *blanket* policy is applied to a class of property, normally at a specified location, rather than to specific articles of property. Coverage of furnishings or clothing normally would be blanket coverage. Coverage of a rare stamp collection would more likely be a *specific* policy, covering specified articles or things.

A *valued* policy is one with a predetermined total value for the insured property. This value is the amount to be used in case of a total loss.

An *open* policy does not predetermine the value of the insured property. Rather, it commonly establishes a maximum value the insurer will pay on total loss of the property, but the insured must establish the fair market value of the destroyed property at the date of loss. If the fair market value exceeds the maximum, the maximum will control. If the fair market value is below the maximum, the fair market value will control.

In either a valued or an open policy, if the loss is less than total, the insured can recover only the amount of the loss actually sustained up to the policy maximum.

Coinsurance clause A clause dividing the potential risk between the insured and the insurer in the event of partial loss or destruction of the insured property.

Many fire insurance policies have a **coinsurance clause.** This clause requires the insured to maintain a minimum amount of coverage as set out in the clause, such as 80 percent of the total value of the property. If the insured maintains the minimum coverage, the company will honor the policy up to its limits. But if the insured has less than the required insurance, the insured must bear a portion of the loss personally. The following standard formula is used to determine how much of the loss must be borne by the insured:

$$\text{Actual loss suffered} \times \frac{\text{amount of insurance carried}}{\text{coinsurance \% } \times \text{ value of property}} = \text{recovery.}$$

For example, George had an 80 percent coinsurance clause, property worth $50,000, insurance of $35,000, and a loss of $20,000:

$$\$20,000 \times \frac{\$35,000}{80\% \times \$50,000} = \$20,000 \times \frac{\$35,000}{\$40,000} = \$17,500.$$

George would recover $17,500 from the insurance company and would have to pay the remaining $2,500 personally. If he had maintained the 80 percent coverage required by the policy, he would have recovered the full $20,000 loss from the insurer.

Fire insurance is normally nonassignable without the prior permission of the insurance company. The coverage is deemed personal between the insured and the insurer. One of the reasons the insurance company assumed the risk is the character of the insured. To allow free substitution of the covered person with another would unduly expose the insurer to risks it might not have been willing to assume. Of course, once a loss has occurred, the proceeds are freely assignable by the insured. At that point, the duty of the insurer is fixed, and the assignment does no harm to its duty.

The insurer can cancel a fire insurance policy on delivery of notice to the insured, and a refund of any unearned premium will be paid to the insured. There is usually a short time period, such as ten days, before the coverage is canceled to allow the insured time to shop for another insurer.

Marine Insurance

Marine insurance protects ships at sea and the cargo or freight on such ships from standard "perils of the sea." The coverage includes such risks as shipwreck, fire, and piracy. It excludes damage due to normal action of wind and waves and to ordinary wear and tear, as well as losses due to delays caused by ordinary weather problems. When most international business was conducted by transportation via the sea lanes, marine insurance was extremely important. Its current importance is primarily in the area of oil shipments, although many other types of cargo still move by sea.

Most marine insurance policies are valued policies; the insurer and the insured agree in advance to the value of the property insured. In addition, the policy will be either a time policy or a voyage policy. In a *time* policy, the insurance coverage is for a preset time period, at the expiration of which the insurance will lapse, even if the ship covered is in the middle of the ocean. In contrast, a *voyage* policy covers a ship until a specified voyage ends, regardless of the time it takes to complete the trip.

To obtain a marine insurance policy, the insured must warrant that the ship is seaworthy. This warranty includes at a minimum that the ship is competent to resist ordinary wind and waves, that it is properly equipped and has an adequate crew, and that the captain is both competent and of "good moral character." Breach of the warranty voids the policy coverage.

Finally, the typical marine insurance policy does not cover all contingencies; it does, however, provide for the allocation of loss when that loss is not covered by the insurance policy. If the ship or cargo is damaged, the loss will be borne proportionately in some instances and individually in others. If the loss or damage is intentionally incurred by the captain to ensure the general safety of the ship and cargo, such as when the captain must jettison some cargo in order to save the ship during a storm, the parties will share the loss. This situation is covered in a "general average" clause, which provides that the owners of the ship and the owners of the cargo will share the losses incurred in proportion to the value of property saved by the act of the captain.

On the other hand, if the loss is not intentionally caused and the policy does not cover it, a "particular average" clause states that the loss is borne exclusively by the owner of the lost or damaged property.

Automobile Insurance

Automobile insurance may be the most widely owned type of insurance in the United States. Nearly every driver has insurance coverage for times when the driver is operating an automobile, either in his or her own name or on the policy of another person, such as a parent or an employer. State statutes require that a driver either have liability insurance or provide self-insurance adequate to cover potential liability that the driver may incur.

The minimum coverage any driver should have is for liability and property damage. This basic coverage protects the driver in the event that he or she causes harm to the person or property of another. That is, if the driver is at fault in an accident, the insurance coverage, at least up to the policy limits, will indemnify the driver if he or she is sued by the injured party. Most states require a minimum amount of liability and property damage coverage. For example, Virginia requires a minimum coverage of $25,000 per person and $50,000 per accident in personal liability and $20,000 per accident in property damage coverage; a person who is involved in an accident and does not have this minimum coverage must post a bond or deposit in order to continue operating an automobile on Virginia highways.

Liability and property coverage provides for protection from the "other guy" in the accident, but it does nothing for the driver or the damaged auto. For this reason, many people add at least a collison clause and often elect a comprehensive clause, as well. Collision coverage provides for insurance coverage on the driver's car in the event of an accident, even if the driver is "at fault." These clauses normally have a **deductible amount,** such as $500. Such a deductible would require the insured to pay the first $500 in collision damages before the insurance policy protection could be exercised. The deductible is designed to discourage petty claims and to help reduce the cost of the insurance.

Deductible amount Amount of damages to be paid by the insured before any liability of the insurer can be enforced.

A comprehensive coverage clause protects the automobile owner from any loss or damage except collision or accident. Thus, fire damages, theft, explosion, and vandalism are covered by this clause, and there is normally no deductible amount. Great care should be exercised in selecting this particular type of coverage. Many items are excluded by the policy, and often the insured purchases comprehensive coverage to protect only those excluded items. For example, many companies do not cover theft of tape decks, CB radios, or other electronic add-ons. Similarly, some policies do not cover "mag wheels" or other custom touches the owner has added to personalize the auto. The buyer needs to shop carefully before deciding to purchase comprehensive insurance coverage. The following case illustrates one situation in which a comprehensive policy may be worthwhile.

Edwards v. State Farm Mutual Automobile Insurance Company
296 N.W.2d 804 (Iowa 1980)

FACTS   Edwards negotiated the sale of his car to Davis. Davis gave Edwards a check for $3400, the purchase price, and Edwards signed the title and gave Davis possession of the car. Davis's check was returned for lack of funds in the account. The trial court concluded, based on the testimony, that Davis had committed fraud. Neither Davis nor the car could be located. Edwards filed a claim under the comprehensive coverage of his policy.

ISSUE   Is Edwards entitled to collect under the theft provisions of the policy?

HOLDING   Yes. The insured automobile was "stolen" under the terms of the policy.

REASONING   Because the term *theft* was not defined in the policy, the court defined it broadly and in a manner most favorable to the insured. The court reasoned that the insurer could have avoided this problem by defining theft in the policy. Although lawyers would not interpret theft as including fraud or obtaining property by false pretenses, most nonlawyers would. The court believed that it should define theft according to its popular meaning. It also noted that the courts and the legislature have recently been broadening the definition of theft. The court concluded that the insurer was incorrect in arguing that this situation fell under the conditional-sale exclusion of the policy: Edwards did not intend to create a security interest in the car; he intended to sell it outright.

Several states have moved into a contemporary area of automobile insurance known as "no-fault." The concept here is that each insured party will collect from his or her own insurance company in the event of an accident without regard to which party was the cause of the accident (that is, was "at fault"). In the event of an accident, each party submits a claim to his or her insurer, and the matter is ideally settled quickly, equitably, and inexpensively.

Finally, drivers should at least consider coverage against **uninsured motorists.** This coverage protects an insured party who is unlucky enough to be involved in an accident in which the other person is both at fault and without insurance. In such an event, the insured submits a claim to the insurer, and the insurer then covers the damages incurred by the insured in the accident. The insurer then assumes the rights of the insured against the uninsured motorist who was at fault in the accident.

Uninsured motorists Persons operating automobiles without any insurance coverage for any accidents they may cause or become party to.

WARRANTIES, WAIVERS, AND ESTOPPEL

Warranties are extremely important in insurance contracts. The warranties in a policy set up the conditions that must exist, or that may not exist, before a claim made on the insurer will be valid. These warranties must be expressed in, or attached to, the policy itself. No implied warranties will be found by the courts. If the insured breaches a warranty, the insurance company has the option of avoiding the policy at its election without any challenge by the insured unless the insurer is liable because of a waiver of the warranty or an estoppel. Warranties are classified as either affirmative or continuing. An *affirmative* warranty is one that must exist at the time the policy is entered into by the parties. A *continuing* warranty is one that must be satisfied during the entire period of the insurance coverage.

Waiver comes into play when the insurer could have avoided liability but the conduct of the insurer waived this ability. Estoppel applies when the insurer is not allowed to avoid the liability (that is, is estopped from avoiding the liability). Technically, *waiver* involves voluntary conduct by the insurer in not asserting a defense. *Estoppel* means that the conduct of the insurer prevents the assertion of any power of avoidance on the policy.

Normally, a waiver will be found when the insurance company agent neglects to enforce a warranty included in the policy. For example, the agent delivers a policy to the insured even though the agent knows that the insured does not have the fire alarm system required before delivery of the policy. The lack of a fire alarm is a breach of warranty by the insured, but the conduct of the agent has waived this requirement, and the breach cannot be asserted by the insurer in the event of a claim filed by the insured.

An estoppel normally will be found in situations in which the insurer acts in a manner that the insured relies on, and subsequently the insurer attempts to deny liability because the insured failed to perform some act. Suppose, for example, that the insured is involved in an automobile accident. The insurer tells the insured that the company will gather all the evidence necessary to defend the case and that the insured needs to do nothing. Later the insurer attempts to deny liability, asserting that the insured failed to cooperate fully in the investigation. The conduct of the company would estop it from denying liability under these facts.

YOU BE THE JUDGE

An insurance company issued a policy to a company involved in the wholesaling of diamonds. The policy protected the diamond company against loss or theft, and included, as a condition of coverage, that the diamond merchant would have at least two employees on duty at all times while the establishment was open for business.

On the date in question, the company had two employees on duty. One of these employees, the president of the company, went to the restroom, leaving the other employee alone in the store. During the absence of the president, an armed gunman entered the store and robbed it. A claim was filed with the insurer in a timely and proper manner. The insurer denied liability, citing the failure of the company to have two employees "on duty" at the time of the robbery. According to the insurer, the failure to have two employees "on duty" voided the policy, relieving the insurer of liability.

Suppose the diamond wholesaler has sued seeking recovery under the policy. How will you resolve the case?

Source: "Whew; judge rules potty breaks OK," Associated Press, *Roanoke Times & World News,* May 6, 1992, page B5.

THE NEW EMPHASIS ON GOOD FAITH

Several cases over the past few years have imposed a new type of liability on insurance companies. These cases have held that an insurance company has a duty to act in good faith in its dealings with the insured and that a failure to do so amounts to a "civil tort" for which the insurer can be held liable for amounts beyond the maximum limits of the policy. Included have been a fire insurance coverage case in which the company refused to pay the policy amount because a replacement asset could be obtained for less than the amount of the policy; a fire insurance policy case in which the insurer refused to pay because the insured had been arrested (wrongfully) for arson, but later was acquitted; and an automobile insurance policy case in which the insurer refused to pay the claim of the insured, asserting that the uninsured motorist involved in the accident might have been insured, even though no one was aware of who that insurer was, and placing the onus on the insured to determine if that was in fact the case.

The following case was one of the first in which the issue of the good faith of the insurer was an issue. Notice how the court treated the bad faith of the insurer.

Gruenberg v. Aetna Insurance Company
510 P.2d 1032 (Cal. 1973)

FACTS   Gruenberg was the owner-operator of a restaurant and cocktail lounge in Los Angeles. Gruenberg purchased fire insurance on his business from several insurers, including Aetna. Seven months later the business burned. Gruenberg was informed of the fire and went to the scene. While there he argued with a member of the arson squad of the fire department and was arrested. Investigators for Aetna informed the fire department that Gruenberg had excessive fire insurance, and on the basis of this information Gruenberg was arrested and charged with arson and with defrauding an insurance company, both felonies under California law. The insurer demanded that Gruenberg appear to answer questions in its office before the arraignment for the felony charges. Under the advice of his attorney, Gruenberg refused to do so. The criminal charges were dismissed for lack of probable cause, but the insurance company denied liability due to Gruenberg's failure to submit to their examination as demanded.

ISSUE   Is the insurance company liable for damages for its bad-faith refusal to honor the terms of the insurance contract?

HOLDING   Yes. A failure to act in good faith by an insurance company is a breach of contract and a tort against the insured.

REASONING   An insurance policy contract carries an implied covenant of good faith and fair dealing. An unreasonable withholding of the payments due under the policy is a breach of the implied covenants and as such gives rise to a cause of action *in tort* for the breach. Further, the duty is nonconsensual in origin, being present whether the party agrees to it or not. Gruenberg had done nothing improper, and the insurer had acted in bad faith. Gruenberg was entitled to damages.

A number of states also allow an insured person to recover a penalty amount from the insurance company if the company refuses to pay benefits without proper cause. The penalty normally will be assessed if the company's refusal to pay benefits is "not in good faith," is "arbitrary and capricious," or is "vexatious." The penalty amount usually is stated as a percentage of the portion of the claim by the insured that is not disputed or disputable. This percentage ranges from 10 percent to 25 percent, depending on the jurisdiction. Although such a penalty normally is not as beneficial to the insured as a claim for the tort of bad faith, it does provide another alternative to the insured who has filed a claim and had payment improperly refused.

Not all states have embraced the concept of the tort of "bad faith" in insurance. Some states have specifically rejected the *Gruenberg* precedent, as the following case shows.

D'Ambrosio v. Pennsylvania National Mutual Casualty Insurance Company
431 A.2d 966 (Pa. 1981)

FACTS   D'Ambrosio purchased an insurance policy from Pennsylvania National Mutual Casualty Insurance Company to cover his motor boat and outboard motor. The boat and motor were damaged in a severe storm, and D'Ambrosio filed a claim for the damages. The company denied liability, and D'Ambrosio then filed suit seeking $932.23, the cost of the repairs plus interest, attorneys' fees, and costs. He also filed an action for trespass, alleging that his claim was summarily denied, even though the insurer could not or would not produce any evidence that it had legitimate reasons to deny his claim, and seeking compensatory and punitive damages for the bad faith of the insurance company in denying his claim.

ISSUE   Should the insurance company be held liable for the "new tort" of bad faith in this case?

HOLDING   No. The Pennsylvania legislature had provided adequate recourse for insured persons, and the courts refused to recognize the "new tort" of bad faith.

REASONING   Pennsylvania's Unfair Insurance Practices Act prohibited unfair or deceptive practices or acts, including unfair claim settlement practices. When an allegation of a violation of this statute is made to the state insurance commissioner, he or she is empowered to investigate to impose sanctions including cease and desist orders, and to suspend or revoke licenses. The commissioner may also seek judicial imposition of civil penalties of up to $5000 for each knowing violation. The court did not feel that the judiciary should supplement this legislative enactment with a "new tort" to afford extra protection to insured individuals and specifically rejected the precedent established in *Gruenberg* v. *Aetna Insurance Co.* (D'Ambrosio's initial complaint, amended complaint, and appeal contained numerous contradictions. He stated that he was told why the claim was denied, gathered additional evidence on his own, and submitted this additional evidence in support of his claim; he was again denied. There was a strong dissent in which two of the justices felt that following the California precedent as a supplement to the state's Unfair Insurance Practices Act would be appropriate for cases in which the insurer acted in bad faith.)

SUMMARY

Insurance is a legal and contractual arrangement for risk sharing, the spreading of risk among people who share a common potential for financial loss. The insurance contract is heavily regulated by state laws because of public policy considerations. Of special concern are the requirements of offer and acceptance and the requirement of an insurable interest in the insured before an insurance policy can be purchased.

This chapter covered two broad types of insurance: life insurance and property insurance. (Numerous other types of insurance, such as health, disability, unemployment, workers' compensation, and social security, were not covered since they are beyond the scope of this text.) Life insurance is primarily thought of as an investment by the insured. The only exception is term insurance, which has no cash or investment value.

Property insurance is used primarily to indemnify the insured if the insured event occurs. The most important types of property insurance are designed to cover fires, marine shipments, and automobiles.

Insurance companies require certain warranties as a condition to providing coverage. Breach of these warranties operates as an avoidance of liability unless the insurer is liable because of a waiver of the warranty or an estoppel.

DISCUSSION QUESTIONS

1. Why do insurance companies use coinsurance clauses?

2. What are the differences between a coinsurance and a deductible clause?

3. How will a court interpret an ambiguous clause in an insurance contract? Why?

4. Should a wife be allowed to recover from her insurance company for theft of her personal property if her husband was the thief and the policy was issued to the two of them as jointly insured parties?

5. Laura's automobile insurance policy includes a comprehensive coverage rider. Laura recently parked her car in a restaurant parking lot. When she returned to the lot after dinner, she discovered that her car had been vandalized. She filed a claim with her insurance company under the comprehensive coverage provisions. Her

insurance company is denying liability and has refused to pay Laura for the damages she has suffered. What rights might Laura be able to assert against the company? What might she be able to recover from the company? Explain fully.

6. Eileen has invested heavily in the stock market, partly because she believes that the president's economic policies will lead to a booming economy. She now desires a life insurance policy on the president's life to protect her investment. Does Eileen have an insurable interest in the life of the President of the United States?

7. Richard, who lives in Boston, wants to buy property insurance from Larry's of Lisbon. The policy would pay Richard $100,000 if any radioactive debris falls on Moscow, Idaho, at any time during the 1990s. Richard owns no property in Idaho, nor does he have any relatives there. What public policy arguments against the policy could be asserted?

8. Donna left her automobile in a parking lot at the local shopping center. When she returned, the automobile was gone. What types of insurance coverage should Donna have on her automobile policy in order to recover for the theft of her car?

9. Carl would like to assure his newborn son of a college education by being able to pay the tuition when his son is old enough to enter college. Carl knows that he could save enough money over the next twenty years, but he is afraid that if he dies the money will not be available. What type of life insurance policy should Carl consider to ensure that the amount will be available in twenty years or sooner if Carl should die prematurely?

10. Rhonda, a recent college graduate, has a new job. As part of her financial planning she would like to purchase as much life insurance as she can obtain for the lowest possible price. What type of policy should she purchase?

CASE PROBLEMS

1. While driving a car owned and insured by his father, Elmer was involved in an accident in which he was at fault. Elmer was covered by his father's policy. When the father reported the accident to his insurer, the insurer informed him that the policy was being canceled due to a material misrepresentation made on the application. There was, in fact, a material misrepresentation on the application. Can the company cancel the policy after the accident has been reported? (*Hawkeye-Security Ins. Co. v. Government Emp. Ins. Co.*, 207 Va. 944, 154 S.E.2d 173 [1967].)

2. Leuchtenmacher was killed in an automobile accident with an underinsured motorist. The estate settled with the driver of the other car for the $55,000 liability limit on his policy. The estate then sued Farm Bureau, the deceased's insurer, for benefits allegedly due under its policy coverage. Farm Bureau objected to any action against it until the estate had sued the other driver and determined the total amount of damages owed. Is the argument of Farm Bureau persuasive? How should the court resolve this case? (*Leuchtenmacher* v. *Farm Bureau Mutual Insurance Company*, 46 N.W.2d 291 [Iowa 1990].)

3. Mann's automobile was insured under a policy issued by State Farm Insurance. Mann advertised the car

for sale. A prospective buyer looked at the car and then negotiated with Mann concerning the sale price and method of payment. Eventually Mann was persuaded to accept a personal check from the buyer for the sale price. Mann delivered the keys, a bill of sale, and a receipt to the buyer. The check subsequently was dishonored by the drawee bank, and Mann was unable to recover the automobile. At that point, Mann filed a claim with State Farm Insurance under this policy, alleging that the car had been stolen. State Farm denied liability, claiming that this situation did not amount to a "theft" as provided for in the policy and arguing that the loss was expressly not covered since the car was in the possession of another person under a conditional sales contract. On the refusal of State Farm to settle the claim, Mann amended his petition, seeking additional damages from State Farm for allegedly acting in bad faith in refusing to pay the claim under the contract. Was this a theft, and therefore covered under the policy, or a conditional sales contract, and therefore not covered under the policy? Did State Farm act in bad faith in refusing to honor the claim as submitted? Explain your answers. (*Mann* v. *State Farm Mutual Insurance Company*, 698 P.2d 925 [Okla. 1985].)

4. Youse had a very valuable ring insured against any

damages, including damage from fire. He accidentally dropped the ring into a trash incinerator, and it was destroyed. When Youse filed a claim, the insurer denied liability since the fire was not hostile and was therefore outside the coverage of the insurance policy. Who should prevail? (*Youse* v. *Employers Fire Insurance Co.,* 172 Kan. 111, 238 P.2d 472 [1951].)

5. Betty Kulubis sued John Kulubis for a divorce. On being served with the divorce citation, John set fire to their mobile home, destroying it and all of the personal property in it. Betty had no knowledge of, and did not participate in, the destruction of the mobile home or the property contained therein. The mobile home was insured by Texas Farm Insurance under a policy that named both parties as the insureds. Betty filed a claim for losses suffered, as required under the terms of the policy, and Texas Farm Insurance refused to pay since the damages were intentionally caused by an insured party. Is Betty entitled to recovery of her losses under the insurance policy in this case? Explain. (*Kulubis* v. *Texas Farm Bureau Underwriters Insurance Company,* 706 S.W.2d 953 [Tex. 1986].)

6. Dixon borrowed money from Citizens Discount Company, using a truck and feed mill as collateral. Dixon obtained a fire insurance policy on the truck and mill, naming Citizens Discount as the loss payee. A short time later, the truck and mill were destroyed in a fire and Dixon notified the insurance company, requesting the $11,000 the valued policy called for in the event of a total loss. The insurance company refused to pay the $11,000, offering instead to pay $2,000 (the value asserted by the insurance company) or to replace the lost property. Dixon refused this counteroffer and sued the insurer. How should the court resolve this case? (*Citizens Discount and Investment Corp.* v. *Dixon,* 499 S.W.2d 231 [Mo. 1973].)

7. Peterson entered into a contract with the U.S. Forest Service to build a highway beside a pipe and trestle owned by the Nevada Power Company. As part of the contract, Peterson agreed to a liquidated damages clause covering any damages done to the pipe and trestle during the construction. Peterson then obtained a liability policy from USF&G to cover the liquidated damages. During the construction some damage occurred, and Peterson notified USF&G. However, USF&G refused to pay the claim, and as a result Peterson lost the contract and then went bankrupt. Peterson has sued USF&G for consequential damages based on the bad faith of the insurer in refusing to honor the insurance policy. What should be the result? (*United States Fidelity & Guarantee Company* v. *Peterson,* 540 P.2d 1070 [Nev. 1975].)

8. Houghton applied for a health insurance policy with AGLIC in response to an advertisement run by AGLIC. The policy was advertised as a "new Federal Medicare supplemental Major Medical insurance program that pays up to $250,000 in benefits." Houghton paid the premiums, and a policy was issued to her. By the terms of the policy, AGLIC reserved the right to decline to renew the policy by giving Houghton thirty days' written notice, but only if it canceled all of the issued policies bearing the same form number in effect in the insured's state. (Houghton's policy was the only policy issued by AGLIC in Pennsylvania.) In March, 1979, Houghton suffered a stroke, with resulting brain damage, while in the hospital for treatment of a hip injury. On 30 November 1979, AGLIC sent Houghton written notice of its intent not to renew her policy and canceled her coverage as of 31 December 1979. AGLIC made all required payments under the policy through the date of coverage, but refused to make any payments for expenses incurred after the coverage date. Houghton sued for post-cancellation expenses incurred on her behalf, arguing that the expenses were based on an illness or injury that occurred during the policy's coverage and therefore should be covered even after the policy was canceled. How will the court resolve this case? Why? (*Houghton* v. *American Guaranty Life Insurance Company,* 692 F.2d 289 [3d. Cir. 1982].)

9. Donald Spreen and his wife were at a party with, among others, William and Edna King. During the course of the evening, William King allegedly made a crude remark concerning Spreen's wife, and Spreen struck King. King sued Spreen for assault and battery, and Spreen filed a cross-complaint against the Hartford Fire Insurance Company, which had issued a liability insurance policy to Spreen covering his liability for bodily injury or property damages caused "accidentally" by Spreen. The insurer had denied liability since the injury was caused intentionally. Should the insurer have to cover this situation? Explain your answer. (*Hartford Fire Insurance Company* v. *Spreen,* 343 So.2d 649 [Fla. App. 1977].)

10. Butler purchased an Austin-Healey automobile for $3500. Unknown to Butler, the car had been stolen. Butler purchased an automobile insurance policy from

Farmers Insurance to cover the car. Two years after Butler purchased the car, the true owner repossessed it from Butler. Butler filed a claim with his insurer for the loss, and the insurance company refused to pay, alleging that Butler did not have an insurable interest in the automobile and that the policy was therefore invalid and unenforceable. Did Butler have an insurable interest in the car? (*Butler* v. *Farmers Insurance Company of Arizona,* 616 P.2d 46 [Ariz. 1980].)

CHAPTER 52

Wills and Estates

OUTLINE

THE TRANSFER OF AN ESTATE

Almost everyone has an estate, no matter how modest it might be. It may consist only of some favorite compact disks, a television, and a ten-speed bike. At the opposite extreme, it may consist of some office buildings, rental houses, and sizable money market accounts. This chapter deals with what happens to an estate when someone dies and with techniques for transferring an estate to family members and friends. The discussion will be general because the rules vary significantly from state to state.

Under the U.S. Constitution, property transfers, including wills, are governed by state law. The **probate codes** in the states vary greatly. The *Uniform Probate Code is a statute drafted by the National Conference of Commissioners on Uniform State Laws (NCCUSL) for adoption by the states as their probate code.* Its purposes are to unify the state laws and to respond to complaints that probate procedures are too complicated, costly, and time consuming. It was first introduced in 1966. The following states have adopted all or almost all of the Uniform Probate Code: Alaska, Arizona, Colorado, Idaho, Maine, Michigan, Minnesota, Montana, Nebraska, New Jersey, New Mexico, North Dakota, Pennsylvania, South Carolina, and Utah. The District of Columbia and all the other states, except Louisiana, have adopted some sections of the code.[1] This chapter will include many aspects of the Uniform Probate Code owing to the number of states which have adopted it.

Probate codes State statutes that deal with the estates of testators and incompetents.

WILLS

In a will, a person indicates who should inherit his or her property at death. The law that controls the validity of a person's will is the law of his or her **domicile.** A will provides an opportunity to name a guardian for any minor children the person may have. In fact, a will is the only way parents can specify who will raise their minor children if they both die. If parents do not use this technique for naming a guardian, the court will appoint one, and the court may not select the best alternative. For example, grandparents may no longer be physically or emotionally capable of raising young children. Since the court is not likely to be aware of these problems, the court may appoint the grandparents as guardians. The parents (and the courts) have the option of dividing the guardian's duties and appointing someone to care for the children's physical needs while appointing someone else to care for their financial needs and manage their inheritance. This option is valuable if one person is not competent in both areas but would be very competent in one area.

A will is also the place to name a **personal representative** for the estate.

Domicile One's permanent legal residence.

Personal representative A person who manages the financial affairs of the estate.

[1]Data provided by NCCUSL office, Chicago, IL (July 17, 1992).

The personal representative nominated in the will is generally the one appointed by the court, if he or she is able to serve. The judge will appoint someone else if the nominee is dead, disabled, or incompetent. The will also should contain a **residuary clause** for all the property that is not specifically mentioned elsewhere in the will. (It is not advisable to include burial instructions in a will because often the will is not located and read until after the funeral. Such instructions are better contained in a separate document, with copies distributed to the personal representative, close family members, and the attorney.)

Residuary clause A clause that disposes of the remainder of an estate.

Some changes in family relationships affect the validity of a will. Children who are born after a will is executed (signed) receive a share of the estate as after-born children. After-born children generally are entitled to their **intestate share.** If a marriage occurs after a will has been executed, the new spouse also will take a share of the estate. A divorce will change an existing will, too. In most states, a divorce with a property settlement will revoke gifts willed to the ex-spouse; however, a few states, including California, still require a revocation by the **testator** or **testatrix.** (In this chapter, we will use the term *testator* to refer to a man or a woman.) In the following case, a will was revoked by a divorce.

Intestate share Portion of the estate that a person is entitled to inherit if there is no valid will.

Testator A man who makes a will.

Testatrix A woman who makes a will.

Estate of Liles
435 A.2d 379 (D.C. App. 1981)

FACTS   Roscoe and Mary Liles were married in 1945. They had no children. In 1972 Roscoe executed a will leaving his estate to his wife if she survived him. In 1975 Mary left Roscoe because he threatened her, and in 1977 she received a divorce. The divorce court divided their property. Roscoe died in 1978.

ISSUE   Should Roscoe's 1972 will be accepted as valid?

HOLDING   No. Roscoe and Mary's divorce revoked this will.

REASONING   Under common law, certain changes in the marital or family status of a decedent revoke a will. In most states, a divorce and a property division revoke a prior will leaving assets to an ex-spouse. The property agreement settles their financial obligations to each other. If they still wish assets to go to an ex-spouse, they can execute a new will. Since the will is invalid, Roscoe died intestate.

To make changes in a will, it is not necessary to write a completely new document. The testator can simply make the desired changes in a **codicil.** The codicil also acts as a confirmation of the will provisions that are not changed. To be valid, a codicil must satisfy the same requirements as a will. The following case shows how a court will interpret a will and a codicil together.

Codicil A separate written document that changes an existing will.

Matter of Estate of Eickholt
365 N.W.2d 44 (Iowa App. 1985)

FACTS

Executor A personal representative named in a will.

Ademption Gift in a will that is not possible because the asset is no longer part of the estate.

Mary Eickholt signed a will in 1980. It provided that one-half of her farm should go to her brother and one-half to her sister and that the residue of her estate should be divided between them. In 1981, she signed a codicil providing that the residue of her estate should go to four of her nephews. The same codicil directed the **executor** to sell her farm and to divide the proceeds with the rest of the residue. The attorney who drafted both documents testified at trial that Mary understood that her brother and sister would still receive the farm. The attorney could not remember if he explained to her the effect that a sale of the farm would have on this bequest.

ISSUE

Was Mary's brother entitled to one-half of the proceeds from the farm, or was there an **ademption** of that gift?

HOLDING

The sale proceeds were part of the residuary estate. Ademption had occurred.

REASONING

The testator's intention is controlling in the interpretation of a will. Outside evidence, such as the attorney's testimony, may not be presented to prove the testator's intent or to contradict the will. Courts will not use oral testimony to create a will that the testator might have desired but did not make. Courts lack the power to remake a will even if they think a different disposition of property should have been made. When construing a will and codicil, the court interprets them as one instrument, executed on the date of the codicil. Each part should be interpreted in relation to the other. Provisions in a codicil substitute for provisions in a will only to the extent that they are incompatible with the will. The will and the codicil do not create two residues. The residuary clause in the codicil is clearly inconsistent with the residuary clause in the will. There can be only one residuary clause, so the one in the codicil controls since it is more recent. (Mary's sister did not object to the interpretation of the will since most of the nephews named in the will were her sons.)

The testator may destroy the effect of a will by making a new will and stating in that new will that the old will is revoked. This is commonly called a revocation clause. If the new will does not specifically revoke the old will, the courts in some states will try to interpret the two wills together. In such a case, the new will revokes the older one only to the extent that they contain contradictory or inconsistent provisions. A testator can also cancel an old will by physically destroying the signed original, with the intention of revoking it.

Wills can be categorized by the manner in which they were formed. Generally, wills will be *formal, holographic,* or *nuncupative.* Wills also can be categorized by the type of dispositions they contain.

Formal Wills

The most common type of will is called a *formal,* or attested, will. It is generally drafted by an attorney and printed by the attorney's staff. A will prepared by a competent attorney who understands the technical requirements of the applicable state statutes and the terminology of wills is more likely to achieve the desired results than one prepared by a layperson. Familiarity with the terminology of wills is important because the words used in the will often have a special significance that differs from their ordinary meaning.

A will *can* be a very lengthy document, and it must be executed in strict compliance with the procedures specified in the state statute. Generally, the testator must sign the will at the end of the document in the presence of at least two witnesses. The testator *must* ask these two individuals to act as witnesses to the will. The witnesses must be disinterested persons; that is, they must have no interest in any of the property passing under the will or by intestate succession. The primary purposes of witnesses are to swear that the signatures are valid and to swear that the testator was lucid and seemed competent. In most states, the will also must be dated.

California, Maine, and Wisconsin have a special type of formal will called a *statutory will*. This will is named a statutory will because it was approved by the state legislature, and the language in the will is included in the state probate statute. Printing companies in the state can print form wills using the approved language. A will form is sold to an individual testator who fills in the appropriate names and executes the will. Since this is a formal will, it must be witnessed by two disinterested witnesses.

Holographic Wills

Holographic wills (called olographic wills, in some states) are required to be written, signed, and usually dated in the testator's own handwriting. Although not universally accepted, they are allowed in a number of states, including Alaska, Arizona, Arkansas, California, Idaho, Kentucky, Louisiana, Mississippi, Montana, Nevada, New Jersey, North Carolina, North Dakota, Oklahoma, Pennsylvania, South Dakota, Tennessee, Texas, Utah, Virginia, West Virginia, and Wyoming. Holographic wills also are allowed under the Uniform Probate Code, Section 2-503.

A testator who writes a holographic will runs the risk of not expressing his or her intentions properly and not complying with the technical requirements. The testator may not be able to take advantage of techniques to reduce costs and taxes because of lack of familiarity with them. An attorney or an accountant with tax expertise may be able to make recommendations that will greatly reduce the taxes.

Most of the states that allow holographic wills require that they be dated. They do not, however, have to be witnessed. Traditionally, holographic wills have to be written completely in the testator's hand with no printed or typed matter included at all. Recently, some courts and legislatures have become more lenient about accepting printed matter on a holographic will. For example, the California legislature enacted a statutory change requiring only that the signature and the material provisions be in the testator's handwriting.[2] Also, a court may accept the will if the printed matter is surplusage (that is, not an integral part of the will). Many of the states that allow holographic wills require that the will be kept with the important papers of the **decedent**. The purpose of this requirement is to help establish the testator's intent to make a will and to ascertain that the document was important to him or her.

Decedent A person who has died.

[2]California Probate Code, Section 6111(a).

Nuncupative Wills

Nuncupative, or oral, wills are permitted in a number of states under limited circumstances. Usually, nuncupative wills can be used only to dispose of personal property; this is true in Kansas, Nebraska, Virginia, and Washington. However, Georgia allows real property to pass in this manner. Some states place a limit on the value of the property transferred by a nuncupative will. The Uniform Probate Code makes no provision for nuncupative wills, and many states do not permit them.

Nuncupative wills also are restricted to certain situations. Generally, an oral will is valid (1) if it is made by a civilian who anticipates death from an injury received the same day or (2) if it is made by a soldier in the field or a sailor on a ship who is in peril or in fear of death. Because of the dangers inherent in military service and duty at sea, some states recognize a separate category of wills called "soldiers' and sailors' wills." These states may exempt soldiers and sailors from the usual requirements for oral or written wills.[3]

A nuncupative will must be heard by two or three disinterested witnesses, one of whom must have been asked by the decedent to act as a witness. This requirement is helpful in distinguishing between nuncupative wills and oral instructions to change a written will or a plan to change a will. Many statutes require that the nuncupative will be written down within thirty days and/or *probated* (that is, established in probate court as genuine and valid) within six months from the time it was spoken.

Matching Wills

Wills also can be categorized by the type of dispositions they contain. For example, married couples or business partners may have matching provisions in their wills. Matching wills are appropriate when the people who make the wills have identical testamentary objectives. For this reason, they are also called *reciprocal* wills. These wills may be mutual, joint, or contractual.

Mutual wills are separate wills in which the testators, usually a husband and wife, have matching provisions in their respective wills. For example, the separate will of each spouse might provide for "the transfer of my assets to my spouse. If my spouse does not survive me, then my assets shall be divided equally among my children."

In *joint* wills, two people sign the same document as their last will and testament. Usually, the dispositive provisions are the same. Joint wills are not recommended. Many state courts have difficulty analyzing the legal relationship between the two signers. The difficulty normally arises after the first person dies and the second person wants to change the will. The issue is whether the second person can change the will or is contractually obligated to leave it as it is. This conflict may cause court trials and appeals. As is the case with any lengthy trial and appeal, a large amount of the estate may be expended in trying to resolve the legal rights of the parties.

In *contractual* wills, people enter into a valid contract in which one or more of them promise to make certain dispositions in their wills. This agree-

[3]79 American Jurisprudence 2d, Wills, Sections 733, 740.

ment must meet the usual requirements for a valid contract, including consideration and the absence of fraud and undue influence. This arrangement lacks flexibility, but it may be desirable in some situations. If it is desirable, it is preferable to make a separate agreement to avoid the interpretive problems of joint wills.

REQUIREMENTS FOR A VALID WILL

The requirements for a valid will vary from state to state and apply to formal, holographic, and nuncupative wills. A person must be an adult at the time the will is executed for it to be valid. The modern rule is that anyone eighteen or older can execute a valid will. This age is used in the Uniform Probate Code and the Model Execution of Wills Act. The Model Act, written by the NCCUSL, is intended as an example for states to follow in drafting their own laws. All states have now adopted the age of 18, with the following exceptions: Alabama (age 19), Louisiana (age 16), and Wyoming (age 19).[4]

Testamentary capacity Sufficient mental capability or sanity to execute a valid will.

A testator must also have **testamentary capacity.** The statement often recited in wills that the testator is of sound mind and body is not necessary. A person need not be physically healthy to write or sign a valid will. A statement declaring testamentary capacity is not required. However, *actual* testamentary capacity is. When such capacity is called into question, it is narrowly defined by the courts. The common requirements are that the person understood the nature and extent of his or her assets, knew who his or her close relatives were, and understood the purpose of a will.[5] In many states, even a prior adjudication of incompetency will not automatically invalidate a will on the grounds of insanity. If a decedent is suspected of having been incompetent when he or she executed the will, some relatives probably will contest the will. One of the purposes of the disinterested witnesses is to be able to testify about the testator's competency. In the following case, the capacity of the testator was at issue.

Koonce v. Mims
402 So.2d 942 (Ala. 1981)

FACTS   James Koonce was admitted to the hospital for emphysema and heart trouble. While he was in the hospital, he had an attorney write a will, leaving his estate to his two sisters, Edith K. White and Nannie Sue Mims. He signed the will on October 22, 1974. His physician, who had treated him for twenty years, saw him the day after the signing of the will. In April 1976, he married Hazel Thomas Koonce. He died September, 1978; his sisters filed the will for probate and Hazel filed a will contest. The physician was permitted to testify at trial.

[4]*The Book of The States,* 1990–91 Edition, Volume 28, The Council of State Governments, Lexington, Kentucky, 1990 at 417.
[5]79 American Jurisprudence 2d, Wills, Section 733, 740.

ISSUE   Was the trial court correct in concluding that Koonce was competent to execute a valid will?

HOLDING   Yes. Competency is presumed unless there is evidence to the contrary.

REASONING   Witnesses are allowed to testify as to competency as long as the jury makes the ultimate decision on testamentary capacity. A person contesting a will on the grounds of incompetency must present some evidence to that effect. Otherwise, it will be presumed that a person of legal age is competent. Sufficient evidence must be presented before the issue of testamentary capacity is referred to the jury for decision. (The Alabama Supreme Court does not address whether Hazel would be entitled to a spousal election against the will. It is assumed that she initiated this law suit because her share would be larger if James had died intestate.)

As noted earlier, formal and holographic wills must be signed by the testator. Many states require that the signature appear at the end of the document. In the following case, the court stressed the importance of a proper signature and strict compliance with the technical requirements of the state statute.

In re Pavlinko's Estate
148 A.2d 528 (Pa. 1959)

FACTS   Vasil and Hellen Pavlinko spoke very little English. They went to an attorney to have wills drawn. He discussed their wishes with them in their native language and drafted two wills. The provisions were similar. They wanted to leave their assets to each other. When both were dead, they wished to make token gifts to Vasil's brother and sister; the rest was to go to Hellen's brother. At the signing of the wills, each accidentally signed the other's will. Hellen died first; her will was not reviewed by the probate court.

ISSUE   Can the court accept the will Vasil signed?

HOLDING   No. The will was not signed by the testator of that will.

REASONING   To be valid, a will must be signed at the end. Vasil did not sign *his* will at the end. The will that he signed was void of legal effect, and it did not make sense because of the references to "my husband." Despite Vasil's clear intentions, the statute of wills had to be given effect. Its purpose is to prevent fraud.

TESTAMENTARY DISPOSITIONS AND RESTRICTIONS

A person has quite a bit of freedom in the dispositions that he or she may make in a will. These provisions are very important to the testator, and the court generally will give effect to them. But a person's ability to make testamentary dispositions is not limitless; there are some restrictions. The restrictions vary from state to state, but some are common. One concerns willing

Trust An arrangement in which one person or business holds property and invests it for another.

Honorary trust An arrangement that does not meet trust requirements and thus is not enforceable, although it may be carried out voluntarily.

Community property A special form of joint ownership between husband and wife.

Common law states States that do not recognize community property law.

Heirs Persons who inherit property from the decedent.

too large a portion of the estate to charity to the detriment of the family. (The prohibitions on such dispositions are called *mortmain,* or fear of death, statutes, and they operate to restrict the types and amounts of charitable gifts.) Another widely prohibited disposition is a **trust** that was established for too long a period of time. The allowable length of time is specified in the rule against perpetuities. (This rule is quite complex, and a discussion of it is outside the scope of this book.) In addition, most states do not allow the testator to will money to pets. Animals are not legal beneficiaries under wills or trusts. However, some states do allow the testator to establish an **honorary trust** for the benefit of the animal. These trusts, where permitted, are limited to an amount of assets that is not excessive with respect to the animal's reasonable needs. Will provisions can be set aside if they are against public policy. Examples would be provisions that encourage beneficiaries to get divorced or that separate children from their parents. Obviously, a person cannot will away someone else's property (for example, the spouse's half of the **community property**) or property that passes by operation of law, as in a joint tenancy with rights of survivorship.[6]

If a testator suspects that the will will be contested, a no-contest clause may be inserted in the will. Basically, such a clause indicates that if a person contests the validity of the will in court, that person will not inherit any assets from the estate. The no-contest clause is used as a threat by the testator, and in that sense it may be effective; however, many states do not enforce no-contest clauses, or they make exceptions to them. Regardless of a state's approach to no-contest clauses, if the person is successful in having the will declared invalid, that person can inherit. Depending on the circumstances, he or she may inherit under a prior will or under the state intestate succession statute.

Contrary to popular belief, a person does not have to leave assets to family members and other relatives. In **common law states,** there is an exception to this rule for a spouse: A widow or widower who is not willed at least a statutory minimum amount often can *elect against the will* (that is, choose to take a preset minimum percentage of the estate rather than the amount provided by the will). Other family members may be excluded, but a testator should mention them and the fact that they are being excluded. This is often accomplished by leaving them a nominal amount, such as $5 or $10. If the testator fails to do this, the omitted family members can claim that they were *pretermitted* (forgotten) **heirs.** Courts generally will award intestate shares to pretermitted heirs on the grounds that the omission was a mistake. In addition, the omission of a close family member can indicate that the testator was incompetent.

Actual heirs may receive their shares under different theories or philosophies. In writing a will, a testator may select between per capita (per head)

[6]A movement in the American legal community advocates changing state laws regarding the ability to will joint tenancies and insurance policies.

or per stirpes (per line) distribution of assets. In per capita distribution, each beneficiary in the group described receives an equal share no matter how many generations he or she is below the decedent. For example, in a gift to the decedent's children and grandchildren, each one would receive an equal share. This is true whether or not the beneficiary's parent is alive. In contrast, in a per stirpes distribution to the decedent's children and grandchildren, each child of the decedent receives an equal share. If any child has already died, his or her children would equally divide that child's share. If a child is still alive, his or her offspring would not directly receive any assets. This is also called taking by **right of representation.** This distinction between a per stirpes and a per capita gift made to children and grandchildren is shown in Figure 52.1.

Right of representation
Right of children to inherit what their parent would have inherited if the parent had not died.

Wills can be set aside (ignored) by the court if they were signed because of fraud in the inducement, fraud in the execution, duress, or undue influence. (These concepts are discussed in detail in Chapter 13. They are used in wills cases in much the same manner as they are used in contract situations.) The following case involved the setting aside of a will on the grounds of undue influence.

Erb v. *Lee*
430 N.E.2d 869 (Mass. App. 1982)

FACTS   The decedent, approximately eighty-five years of age, hired Bates as her housekeeper in 1969 or 1970. Erb, the decedent's attorney, was appointed her conservator in 1973. Bates began to harass the decedent for money and property, so Erb fired Bates at the decedent's request. Bates called the decedent and harassed her and demanded back wages. About five months later, Bates returned, fired her successor, and again began keeping house for the decedent. In 1974 the decedent met with her attorney because she wanted to draft a new will making Bates the primary beneficiary instead of the decedent's grandson. Bates was not present at the meeting or at the execution of the will.

ISSUE   Was the trial judge correct in deciding that Bates had exerted undue influence?

HOLDING   Yes. The testatrix would not have acted in this manner of her own free will.

REASONING   The person contesting a will has the burden of proof. Undue influence will not be presumed just because of a decedent's advanced age or because someone had the opportunity to exercise undue influence. The overriding factors in this case were the decedent's weakened mental condition and Bates's threats and harassment, her meddling in the decedent's affairs, her frightening phone calls, and her domineering personality. Bates's failure to testify about her relationship with the decedent may have been construed against her. Furthermore, a person does not have to be physically present when the will is executed to exert undue influence.

FIGURE 52.1 Testamentary Distributions to Surviving Children and Grandchildren

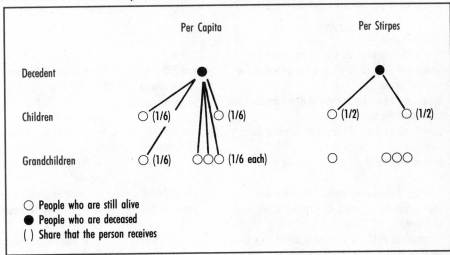

INTESTATE SUCCESSION

For various reasons, many people fail to sign or to execute a valid will. States provide for the transfer of the assets of these people by the intestate succession statute. People who die without a valid will are said to have died intestate. Sometimes, especially with holographic wills, people fail to provide for the disposition of *all* their assets. In a properly drafted will, such disposition is assured by the use of a residuary clause that states: "I leave all the rest and residue of my estate to. . . ." Any assets *not* covered by the will provisions will pass by intestate succession.

The intestacy statutes vary from state to state. Passage of personal property is governed by the intestate law of the decedent's domicile. Real property is governed by the intestate law where the property is located. Some states have different provisions for the passage of personal property and the passage of real property within their control.

Community property states provide for different chains of distribution for community property and separate property. As previously mentioned, community property is a form of joint ownership between husband and wife. In states that allow this form of joint ownership, most property that is acquired during marriage is owned one-half by the husband and one-half by the wife. (Community property is discussed in greater detail in Chapter 49.)

Generally, legislators enact a statute to dispose of property in the manner they think most people would desire. For example, under the Uniform Probate

FIGURE 52.2   Intestate Succession Under the Uniform Probate Code

SURVIVORS	SPOUSE'S SHARE	REMAINDER OF ESTATE TO OTHERS
Spouse (if there is no issue or parent of decedent)	100%	not applicable
Spouse and issue, all of whom are also issue of the surviving spouse	first $50,000, plus ½ the balance	to the issue, if they are of the same degree of kinship, equally*
Spouse and issue, one or more of whom are not issue of the surviving spouse	½ to the spouse	to the issue, if they are of the same degree of kinship, equally*
Spouse and parent(s) (if there is no surviving issue)	first $50,000, plus ½ the balance	to parent or parents equally
Issue of decedent (if there is no surviving spouse)	not applicable	to the issue, if they are of the same degree of kinship, equally*
Parent(s) (if there is no surviving spouse or issue)	not applicable	to parent or parents equally
Issue of parents (if there is no surviving spouse, issue, or parents)	not applicable	to the issue of the parents or either parent by representation*
Grandparents and issue of grandparents (if there is no surviving spouse, issue, parents, or issue of a parent)	not applicable	½ to paternal grandparent(s) or to their issue* if they are both deceased; ½ to maternal grandparent(s) or to their issue* if they are both deceased; if there is no grandparent or issue on one side, that share goes to the other side

*These transfers are made per capita at each generation.

This is a representation of the Uniform Probate Code, Section 2-101 through 2-103. It does not reflect the alternative provisions for community property states.

Copyright © 1987 Kent Publishing Company.

Issue Lineal descendants, such as children, grandchildren, and great-grandchildren.

Code, if the decedent leaves a surviving spouse but no surviving **issue** or parent(s), the surviving spouse takes all the intestate property.[7] If there are surviving issue who are issue of both the decedent and the surviving spouse, the spouse takes the first $50,000 plus one-half the balance of the estate. The issue would share the rest by a system called *per capita at each generation*.[8] These provisions are applicable to separate property states and to separate property in community property states under the Uniform Probate Code. Figure 52.2 details the Uniform Probate Code provisions.

Probate hearings are a series of hearings in probate court in which the judge makes sure that the estate is being properly administered. The judge will conduct a hearing if any interested party contests the validity of the will. The judge confirms whether the will is valid and was properly executed under state law. Even after the judge has accepted the validity of the will, this judicial

[7]Uniform Probate Code, Section 2-102(1).
[8]Ibid., Section 2-102(3), 2-103, 2-106 as amended in 1990.

order can be revoked if it is shown that the will was fraudulently offered for probate. The judge also ascertains that the representative has advertised in the appropriate newspapers in order to locate the creditors of the deceased, ascertains that only lawful creditors are paid, and ascertains that the proper beneficiaries are paid. (It should be noted that if a creditor does not file a claim in a timely manner, the claim thereafter will be barred.)

ESTATE ADMINISTRATION AND PROBATE

The concept of administering an estate is relatively simple. The representative of the estate must collect the assets of the decedent, collect money owed to the decedent, pay the debts owed by the decedent, pay the necessary expenses of administration, and pay any state or federal taxes. It is often necessary to sell assets to make these disbursements. The remaining assets are then distributed to the proper beneficiaries. A court generally will oversee this procedure through probate hearings.

A decedent's estate usually is administered by a personal representative. The representative has fiduciary duties to the lawful beneficiaries of the estate. If the decedent had a valid will that named a representative, that person will be called an *executor*. A court-appointed representative will be called an *administrator*. The administrator will be appointed following any guidelines provided in the state probate code. (Some localities still use the more traditional terminology of calling male representatives executors or administrators, and female representatives executrixes or administratrixes.) Some states require that an executor or an administrator reside in the same state as the decedent. There usually is a minimum age of eighteen.

Surcharged Required to pay for failure to follow fiduciary duties.

Malfeasance The incorrect performance of a duty.

These personal representatives are responsible for the proper administration and probate of the estate. They must make sure that the duties previously mentioned in this section are properly completed. Personal representatives have a large responsibility for which they receive a fee. They can be **surcharged** from personal funds if they do not perform their duties properly. Some common areas of **malfeasance** include failure to pay taxes; failure to probate the will; failure to sell assets that are declining in value; failure to minimize taxes; failure to sell assets at a fair price; self-dealing, such as selling estate or trust assets to oneself or to a friend; and fraud. (The duties of an executor or administrator are discussed in greater detail in Chapter 53.)

In many jurisdictions, the judge can reduce the commissions paid to the personal representative and the fees paid to the attorney and accountant if they are excessive. Executors, administrators, and, in many states, the attorneys usually are paid according to a percentage of the value of the assets in the estate. In some states, the maximum fees are established in the probate code.

AVOIDING PROBATE

Estate tax   A tax assessed on the total net value of the estate.

Inheritance tax   A tax assessed on individual transfers of estate assets to particular people.

Many people believe that it is wise to avoid probate. Property that is held as entireties property or as a joint tenancy with rights of survivorship and life insurance paid to a named beneficiary is not subject to probate. If a person places assets into a trust while alive, these assets will not be probated. Another option of the property owner is to enter into a valid contract that provides, in part, for the passage of property at the owner's death. All these arrangements may act as substitutes for a valid will and, depending on state law, may escape the technical requirements of the state statute of wills. However, even assets that are not subject to probate may still be subject to an **estate tax** and/or an **inheritance tax.**

Avoiding probate of an estate may reduce the amount of time necessary for the administration of that estate. In the case of joint tenancies with rights of survivorship, one owner will have immediate access to these assets at the other owner's death, although some states restrict this immediate access for bank accounts and safe deposit boxes. One can maintain more privacy by avoiding probate, which is an important consideration for some people. Probate, like most court proceedings, is part of the public record; anyone who is so inclined can read the will and the inventory of assets. Costs usually are involved in the probate of an estate; some, such as fees for filing court documents, are nominal. The amount of some fees may be based on the amount of probate assets; avoiding probate or reducing the amount of probate assets would eliminate or reduce these costs. Probate costs increase markedly when lawsuits arise concerning the validity of the will or its interpretation. These *will contests* reduce the amount of assets to be distributed to the beneficiaries. Sometimes these contests are caused by poorly drafted wills or holographic wills. Probate costs and taxes may increase significantly if a person dies intestate or without prudent estate planning.

Avoiding probate does have some disadvantages. The extent to which these items are disadvantageous will depend on the people involved and the method used to avoid probate. Some of the techniques—for example, establishing and operating out of a trust—require additional paperwork and attention to detail. Avoiding probate may also create a higher inheritance or estate tax liability on the decedent's estate or on the estates of other family members. In probate, the creditors of the decedent are located and paid, and the estate is discharged of all further liability to them. Without probate, there is no discharge from potential creditors' claims. In addition, the purpose of probate is to protect lawful beneficiaries and creditors. This may be particularly important when beneficiaries are not knowledgeable or are confused. The court can intervene to protect them from unscrupulous people. Unfortunately, this purpose is not always served effectively under some state probate codes and procedures.

Thus, it is not always advantageous to avoid probate. As with any estate planning decision, consideration must be given to the individuals and the assets involved. One factor that is often overlooked is that an asset's status as a probate or nonprobate asset does *not* avoid the estate or inheritance taxation on it.

SUMMARY

A will states how a person would like to have property pass at his or her death. For a will to be valid, a person must intend it to be his or her will. The person must have testamentary capacity. The will must conform to the state's statutory requirements. Some legal documents, such as trusts and deeds for property, can act as substitutes for wills. In the absence of a valid will, the property will pass by intestate succession, which is controlled by state law.

A formal will, which is drafted by an attorney, the state legislature, or the testator, signed by the testator, and witnessed by two disinterested witnesses, is the most common type of will. Some states also permit nuncupative (oral) wills and holographic (handwritten) wills.

Most estates are subject to probate proceedings. During the hearings, the probate court oversees the proper administration of the estate by the personal representative. The representative must pay debts, collect assets, pay taxes, and distribute assets to the beneficiaries.

DISCUSSION QUESTIONS

1. What is necessary for a formal will to be valid?
2. What types of wills were involved in *In re Pavlinko's Estate*, 148 A.2d 528 (Pa. 1959)?
3. What advantages do formal wills have over other types of wills?
4. List all the types of provisions that should be included in a will. Explain each one.
5. Where should a testator or testatrix keep a holographic will? Why?
6. Why does the omission of a close family member in a will create the appearance of incompetency?
7. Rachael bequeaths the remainder of her estate "to Bank of America in trust to pay all the income to Bill for life, and on Bill's death to transfer the remainder to Bill's issue who are still alive." Bill dies without having any issue. The will has no provision controlling this situation. What will happen? Why?
8. What would be the intestate distribution under the Uniform Probate Code if a husband dies survived by his wife and their children?
9. Brian had inherited a million dollars from his parents' estate. Brian, who has an extremely low IQ, wants to have his attorney write a will leaving his estate to his gardener and excluding his nieces and nephews. Could such a will be valid? If so, under what circumstances?
10. What are the advantages and disadvantages of probating a will?

CASE PROBLEMS

1. In the common law state of Mississippi, a husband and wife separated and established different homes. Neither one filed for a divorce or remarried. Fifteen years after the separation, the wife died testate. Her will provided gifts to three friends. Is her husband entitled to share in her estate because he received insufficient gifts in her will? Should he be so entitled? (*Tillman* v. *Williams*, 403 So.2d 880 [Miss. 1981].)

2. Clara Hicks resided in a nursing home at the time she executed a will in 1977. She was eighty-seven at that time. The will was read to her at the time of execution, and she indicated her approval of the will provisions leaving a larger share to one particular nephew. That nephew visited her at least once a week and responded to her needs and requests. Dr. Hicks, who visited her monthly in the nursing home, testified at trial that he thought that she was competent and that she understood her affairs. Did Clara Hicks have testamentary capacity? Was Clara Hicks subjected to undue influence? (*Estate of Hicks*, 327 S.E.2d 345 [S.C. 1985].)

3. George Tourville had executed a will in which one of his nephews received 25 percent of the estate; Mary, Tourville's sister and that nephew's mother, received 55 percent; and Eileen, Tourville's other living sister, received 20 percent. The nephew had managed the testator's affairs prior to death. He also helped write the paragraph of the will that left assets to himself and was present when the will was prepared. Was the nephew guilty of exerting undue influence? (*In re Estate of Tourville*, 366 N.W.2d 380 [Minn. App. 1985].)

4. Francis and Anna McGrath agreed to sell their restaurant and store. The buyers were to pay $15,000 at the time of the sale and $45 a week until the rest of the sale price was paid off. The sales contract stated that these payments would cease when both Francis and Anna had died. Must this provision comply with the statute of wills? (*McGrath* v. *McGrath*, 220 A.2d 760 [N.H. 1966].)

5. The decedent's will provided that one of his children should receive $2000 on condition that she remarry one of "true Greek blood and descent and of Orthodox religion" after her first marriage was terminated by death or divorce. On the date of the decedent's death, she was married to a man who was not Greek. Should the probate court enforce such a provision? Why or why not? (*In re Estate of Keffalas*, 233 A.2d 248 [Pa. 1967].)

6. McAboy's will was not probated when she died in 1972. This situation was discovered in 1974 by Upchurch, an attorney who was researching the ownership of a parcel of real estate. Upchurch obtained the original of McAboy's 1961 will from McAboy's attorney and a *copy* of her 1964 will from the executrix. The copy of the 1964 will was probated under the state procedures for a lost will. Three and one-half years after the probate court's order, the *original* of the 1964 will was located. On the original, the testatrix had signed a statement that this will was void and withdrawn and that her old will was republished (that is, acknowledged as valid again). Should the court order accepting the 1964 will be set aside on the grounds of fraud? (*Larkin* v. *Ruffin*, 398 So.2d 676 [Ala. 1981].)

7. Mr. and Mrs. Diller had signed *mutual* wills designating that the bulk of their estate go to their children. Mr. Diller died with an estate of approximately $6 million. He was survived by his wife, his son, and his daughter. After his death, Mrs. Diller married Mr. Friedman, who was an insurance salesman and a purported estate planner. Mr. Friedman arranged for the new Mrs. Friedman to meet with attorneys whom he had selected. These attorneys drafted wills and trusts that provided substantial benefits for Mr. Friedman to the disadvantage of Mrs. Friedman's children and other heirs. The new will included a no-contest clause. Mr. Friedman threatened to leave Mrs. Friedman if she did not sign the new will, and so she signed it. Should the daughter contest the will? Should the court enforce the no-contest clause? (*Estate of Friedman*, 161 Cal. Rptr. 311 [Cal. App. 1979].)

8. At the age of ninety, the testator signed a will leaving his estate to his step-great-grandchildren. Ten days later the testator executed a will naming his next-door neighbor as his sole beneficiary. In this will he specifically revoked his prior wills. The neighbor did not order the will prepared, but she did drive the testator to the attorney's office. The neighbor lived next door to the testator for ten years. During the last year or so, the neighbor was hired to provide meals and general care for the testator. The testator said that his step-great-grandchildren did not care anything about him and that he did not want them to have his money. He also said that he wanted his money to go to someone who helped him. Was the testator competent to execute a will? Did

the neighbor exert undue influence? (*Edwards* v. *Vaught,* 681 S.W.2d 322 [Ark. 1984].)

9. Mr. Nassano signed two copies of his will. The original was kept by the attorney. The copy was kept by Nassano. Nassano wrote on the duplicate copy of his will, "This *Will,* and *all* other *Wills* Made by me are *Null* and *Void* Signed by me this Seventh Day of June 1979 Bernard Nassano June-7-1979 BN BN." Nassano signed this statement. Did Nassano effectively cancel his will? (*Will of Nassano,* 489 A.2d 1189 [N.J. Super. A.D. 1985].)

10. Mr. Wetzel's parents signed a single testamentary instrument in 1955. It was properly executed under the laws of Texas, where they lived at the time. This joint and mutual will provided for gifts in Wetzel's favor after both parents had died. When Wetzel's mother died, the 1955 will was not probated, but Wetzel's father did accept the benefits provided for him under this will. Was the joint and mutual will binding on Wetzel's father, or could he replace it with his 1972 will? (*Wetzel* v. *Watson,* 328 S.E.2d 526 [W.Va. 1985].)

CHAPTER 53

Trusts and Trust Administration

OUTLINE

TRUST CHARACTERISTICS

A trust is a fiduciary relationship where specific property is transferred to the care of a trustee, or manager. Trusts may be voluntary arrangements created by the property owner, or they may be legal arrangements imposed by the courts or implied by the law in order to reach a fair result. In a trust, legal title and equitable ownership rights are split between two or more people. One person has the legal right to the asset; another person has the beneficial right to the use and enjoyment of the asset.

EXPRESS TRUSTS

Trusts that are *created voluntarily by the owner of the property* are called *express trusts*. The owner transfers real or personal property to a trustee for the benefit of a named person. During the period of the trust, the trustee manages the property and pays the income to the people specified in the **trust deed**. *If the trust is to take effect during the owner's life,* it is called an *inter vivos* trust. *If it is to take effect at death,* it is called a *testamentary* trust. Testamentary trusts are usually included as part of the will and do not have a separate trust deed.

Trust deed   A legal document that specifies the recipients of a trust, their interests, and how the trust should be managed; also called a deed of trust.

Generally, at least three people are needed for an express trust: a creator, a trustee, and one or more beneficiaries. A creator may also be called a settler or a trustor. A *creator* is one who establishes the trust and is usually the person who puts assets into the trust. The *trustee,* who may be a person or a business entity, is in charge of managing the assets. *Corpus, res,* or *principal* are the names used for the assets. The *beneficiaries* are the recipients. Depending on the trust instrument, the beneficiaries may receive the income from the assets, the assets themselves, or both. Consideration is not required to establish a trust.

To be valid, a trust must meet a few requirements. The intention or purpose of the creator must be expressed—for example, by stating that "this trust is established for my children's college educations." In many cases, though, the courts have concluded that the intention of the creator may be inferred from his or her actions if it was not stated. Creators commonly establish trusts for one of three purposes: To provide for more than one beneficiary; to protect beneficiaries from themselves and from overreaching by others; and to legally avoid taxes.

Most trust deeds must be in writing because they cannot possibly be performed within one year. Even if a writing were not required by the Statute of Frauds, it would be foolish not to write down the trust provisions. Many potential legal problems do not arise until after the creator has died. Trusts generally contain lengthy and complex provisions about what the trustee can and cannot do; these certainly should be reduced to writing.

A trust may terminate when its purpose is completed or when its term is over. Under some circumstances, the trust may terminate by mutual agreement of all the beneficiaries, or when it becomes uneconomical. Depending on the trust deed, the trustee, the creator, or someone else may have the power to terminate the trust. When the trust is terminated, the trust assets are transferred to the specified **remainder beneficiaries.**

Remainder beneficiaries
Persons with an interest in what remains in the trust corpus after use by the income beneficiaries.

There are various categories of express trusts, based on the clauses contained in the trust deed. A specific trust may contain provisions in more than one of these categories. This sampling of trust provisions indicates the variety that is possible with trusts.

Private Trusts

A *private trust* is one that is *not for the general public good.* The beneficiaries of this type of trust are individual citizens and not society as a whole. A private trust is limited by the time period specified by the *rule against perpetuities.* The *rule against perpetuities is really a common law rule that prohibits the remote vesting of trust or property interests.* It requires that an interest vest within the time limit set by the rule. The rule does not apply to interests that are already vested, i.e., nonforfeitable, even if the beneficiary will not receive the vested interest until far into the future. Section 1 of the Uniform Statutory Rule Against Perpetuities states the general rule as "A nonvested property interest is invalid unless: (1) when the interest is created, it is certain to vest or terminate no later than 21 years after the death of an individual then alive; or (2) the interest either vests or terminates within ninety years after its creation." The Uniform Statutory Rule Against Perpetuities with 1990 Amendments, drafted by the NCCUSL, has been adopted in California, Colorado, Connecticut, Florida, Georgia, Indiana, Massachusetts, Michigan, Minnesota, Montana, Nebraska, Nevada, New Jersey, North Dakota, Oregon, and South Carolina.[1]

Accumulation Trusts

Income beneficiaries Persons with an income interest in the trust.

A trust that will accumulate income is called an *accumulation trust.* The trustee will not disburse the income to or for the use of the **income beneficiaries** or remainder beneficiaries. The earnings will be reinvested in the trust for the period of time specified. Most states restrict the length of time that a private trust can accumulate income to the identical time period prescribed by the *rule against perpetuities.*

Sprinkling Trusts

A *sprinkling trust* is one that *gives the trustee the power to determine which income beneficiaries should receive income each year and how much they should receive.* A prudent creator should provide the trustee with some standards to use in making this decision. Income that is not distributed in any particular year will be added to the corpus, as in an accumulation trust.

---

[1]8A U.L.A. (Uniform Laws Annotated)—Estate, Probate and Related Laws—1 S.P., page 342.

Spendthrift Trusts

As the name implies, a *spendthrift trust* is established when *one or more of the beneficiaries are spendthrifts* and need to be protected from their own imprudent spending habits. They are permitted in most but not all states. This type of trust also may be used if the beneficiary is unduly subject to over-reaching by family members and friends. Generally, the beneficiary cannot anticipate the receipt of income or corpus from a spendthrift trust, cannot assign it to creditors or borrow against it, and will not necessarily receive all the income earned in any one year. Income will be paid to the beneficiary only when actually necessary. The trustee often will pay it directly to the creditor for services ordered by the trustee. Under some circumstances, creditors may be able to attach the trust assets.

Discretionary Trusts

A *discretionary trust allows the trustee to pay or not to pay the income or principal at his or her discretion.* It is commonly used in states that either don't allow, or greatly restrict, spendthrift trusts. In these situations the creator generally names an affectionate family member as an alternate beneficiary and, when the primary beneficiary has problems with creditors, the trustee makes the distributions to the "alternate." It is hoped that the alternate will feel a moral obligation to care for the primary beneficiary.

Revocable Trusts

A *revocable trust* is one that *can be revoked or canceled by the creator.* In rare instances, the creator may give this power to another individual. This trust usually becomes permanent and irrevocable at the death of the creator.

Irrevocable Trusts

An *irrevocable trust* is one that *may not be terminated during the specified term of the trust.* Once the assets are placed in trust, they must stay there for the term of the trust under the conditions specified in the trust deed.

Whether a trust is revocable or irrevocable depends on the trust document. It is always wise to specify this aspect of the trust; otherwise, the trust will be governed by state law. In most states, the trust will be irrevocable unless the creator has stated a contrary intention in the trust deed. In a minority of states, including California, it will be presumed to be revocable unless a contrary intention is expressed.

Charitable Trusts

A *charitable trust* is one in which *money is given to a charity for a public purpose.* A charity is a corporation organized for religious, charitable, scientific, literary, or educational purposes, including the encouragement of art and the prevention of cruelty to children or animals. Charities also include the United States or any state or political subdivision or any veterans' organization or its departments or posts.[2] Transfers to charities, either outright or in trust, may pass tax free. However, the strict requirements of the Internal Revenue Service must be met. In addition, the charitable organization must

---

[2]Internal Revenue Code, Section 2055.

qualify under state and federal rules. An organization that qualifies for federal tax purposes may not qualify for state tax purposes. The opposite is also true. California, for example, requires that the organization be a California charity or a national charity that is going to use the assets in California. To qualify for favorable tax treatment under federal law, a trust with charitable and noncharitable beneficiaries must meet the stringent requirements imposed by the 1969 Tax Reform Act. In most states, charitable trusts are excluded from the *rule against perpetuities* (which is discussed in the following sections).

Cy pres doctrine   Doctrine holding that the court will modify the trust in order to follow the creator's intention as closely as possible.

If the original charitable purpose cannot be fulfilled, a court of equity may apply the *cy pres* doctrine. The application of the doctrine means that the court will try to follow the transferor's intention as closely as possible. This is usually accomplished by substituting another charitable beneficiary with a similar purpose for the charity initially specified. Before a substitution can occur, it must be shown that the original charity no longer exists or that the original terms no longer apply. In the following case, the *cy pres* doctrine was used to implement the creator's charitable intent.

Wesley United Methodist Church v. *Harvard College*
316 N.E.2d 620 (Mass. 1974)

FACTS   Colson died in 1968. In his will, which had been written in 1957, he provided for a scholarship fund to be established and administered by the Wesley United Methodist Church Board of Trustees. The fund was to provide one $500 scholarship per year from trust income to a male member of the congregation who was attending Harvard College. The trust corpus was generating $3200 of income per year, the tuition at Harvard had risen to $2600 per year, Harvard was admitting women as well as men, and no member of the congregation had applied for the scholarship by 1973, the date the trial began. The trustees requested a modification of the trust under the *cy pres* doctrine. The family of the creator petitioned for a cancellation of the old trust and the "establishment" of an implied trust in their favor.

ISSUE   Should the *cy pres* doctrine be applied to alter the terms of the original charitable trust?

HOLDING   Yes. The original trust terms are now impractical, but the original charitable purpose is still valid.

REASONING   The court found that the original trust terms that restricted the recipients of the scholarship to male members of the congregation and the amount of the scholarship to $500 per year were no longer realistic. The original charitable intent of the creator was obvious and the original purpose was still valid, but the original terms were too narrow. Therefore, under the *cy pres* doctrine, the court ruled that the trustees could now apply the earnings from the trust fund at their discretion, and in unlimited amount, to any deserving applicant for the scholarship. In addition, applicants could be either male or female and need not be a member of the congregation of the particular church.

ADVANTAGES OF TRUSTS

One of the advantages of trusts over other methods of transferring assets is the flexibility that trusts permit. With an outright gift, the gift property belongs to the beneficiary. If that transfer turns out to be inappropriate, the transferor cannot change it. With gifts in trust, the trustee maintains control over the assets under the instructions in the trust deed, and the trustee does not relinquish control for a certain period of time. For example, a trust can be established for one's children so that each will receive a third of their share of the corpus when they are twenty-five, thirty, and thirty-five.

Another aspect of the flexibility of trusts is that payment to a trust does not have to occur all at one time. A trust deed can be written to permit the creator to add assets to the trust later. In fact, the trust deed can be written so that other people can add assets to the creator's trust. Moreover, trust income can be paid out to the income beneficiaries equally, based on percentages, or based on need. They can receive the income in a lump sum at the end of the trust, annually, quarterly, monthly, or as needed.

DISADVANTAGES OF TRUSTS

The flexibility of trusts has been stressed as an advantage to this method of transferring assets. By the same token, lack of flexibility may be a disadvantage. If a trust is irrevocable and an emergency arises or circumstances change, the trustee generally will be bound to act as specified in the trust deed. If the creator did not anticipate this occurrence in the trust deed, the trustee may not be able to modify his or her actions to fit the situation.

Another disadvantage of trusts is that of fees. Rarely is a trustee willing to undertake the responsibility of being a trustee without receiving a fee. The next case involved a suit for fees by the trustee.

Estate of Gump
180 Cal. Rptr. 219 (Cal. App. 1982)

FACTS   Wells Fargo Bank was the trustee of a testamentary trust under Gump's will. The trustee filed its eighth annual accounting, which included a request for $32,689 compensation for the trustee. The trustee was awarded $10,000 in fees by the probate court. In accordance with the trust deed, the trustee was managing some real estate occupied by a retail store. The retail store underpaid its rent under the formula provided by the lease. The bank negligently accepted the underpayment as full payment of the rent.

ISSUE   Did the probate court unduly penalize the negligent trustee?

HOLDING   Yes. The probate court did not adequately compensate the trustee, and the penalty imposed was disproportionate under the circumstances.

REASONING   Unless the will provides otherwise, a testamentary trustee is entitled to reasonable compensation for services. The probate court has broad discretion in this matter. Its decision should not be disturbed unless it abuses its discretion. It may properly consider customary charges in the private sector based on the value of trust assets and the success or failure of the trustee's administration. The probate court can charge the trustee for shortages. This may be accomplished by denying part or all of the compensation rendered in conjunction with the mismanaged trust asset. In this case, the trustee was also **surcharged** $7300, but the record did not disclose why. Generally, a trustee's liability is limited to the loss actually suffered by the beneficiaries, unless the trustee acted fraudulently or personally benefited. The appellate court held that that was not the situation in this case, and so the additional loss to the trustee of $7300 could not be justified.

Surcharge Required payment for failure to follow fiduciary duties.

Another disadvantage of trusts is that they may increase the amount of taxes that must be paid. This depends on the nature and the terms of the trust. Under the tax codes, trusts are taxed in complex ways. Before establishing a trust, one should determine 1) who will pay income tax on its income, 2) who will have the advantage of any tax deductions, 3) whether it will be subject to gift taxes, 4) whether it will be subject to estate or inheritance taxes when the creator or a beneficiary dies, and 5) whether it will be subject to any *generation skipping transfer taxes*. This is a *tax imposed on some trust (and nontrust) transfers to a recipient who is two or more generations younger than the donor.* For instance, the donor makes a gift to his granddaughter. All of the tax considerations listed above are complex with varying tax rates, deductions, exclusions, exemptions, and credits.

SELECTION OF TRUSTEES AND EXECUTORS

Since trustees and executors have broad powers and broad discretion, it is important to select them wisely. Successor trustees and executors may also be named in a trust or a will in case the first person named is unable or unwilling to serve as the personal representative. If a decedent does not have a valid will naming a suitable executor, the probate court will appoint an administrator for the estate. In such a case, the owner of the assets will have no say in the selection. Administrators, executors, and trustees may be referred to as *fiduciaries,* since each one has a fiduciary duty to protect the rights of the creator and the beneficiaries.

The legal requirements for such fiduciaries are very simple. In most states, the fiduciary must be over eighteen years of age. Some states also require that the fiduciary be a resident of the state. It generally simplifies transactions if the fiduciary does reside in the state.

A common consideration in selecting a fiduciary is whether to select a corporate fiduciary, such as the trust department of a bank, or an individual fiduciary, such as a family member or a friend. A corporate fiduciary usually does not die or dissolve, often has the expertise needed to do a good job, and does not need to be bonded for the faithful performance of its duties. Although corporate trustees may last forever, individual trust officers do not. Often a creator or testator will select a bank because of past dealings with a particular trust officer. It is wise to remember that the trust officer may leave or die. Moreover, some corporate trust departments do not earn a very good rate of return on the assets that they invest. The same may be true, though, for any individual trustee. Corporate trustees will require a fee, but they may be willing to negotiate and handle the trust for a smaller fee. Many states have statutes that prescribe the maximum fees.

Individual trustees may be willing to serve without fees. They also may have more knowledge about the business and family members than corporate trustees have. In addition, they may be personally concerned for the well-being of the beneficiaries. They may, however, be biased toward certain beneficiaries. In fact, they may be so closely involved with the family that they will be subject to overreaching by family members.

A decision to choose a corporate trustee may be affected by the selection of individuals available in that capacity. A trustee should be honest, mature, competent, impartial, and knowledgeable and should have the ability and time to make sound business decisions. Obviously, the final selection of any personal representative should depend on the facts and circumstances of each case.

DUTIES OF TRUSTEES

The trustee has two primary duties in relation to the property in his or her care. First, the trustee is supposed to preserve and protect the trust corpus. This includes identifying the assets, protecting them, and safeguarding them. The other primary function of the trustee is to make the assets productive. In other words, the trustee is supposed to invest and manage the assets to produce income for the beneficiaries. This task must be accomplished without violating the trustee's other duties.

The trustee has some other, more specific duties. They include an obligation to follow the terms of the trust and a duty of care that must be exercised in administering someone else's property. The rule, as stated in a majority of the courts, is that a trustee must exercise the degree of *care, skill, and prudence* that a reasonably prudent businessperson would exercise in dealing with his or her own property. This standard is applied whether or not the person actually possesses the necessary skill and knowledge.

The trustee also has a duty of loyalty. There are, in reality, two aspects of this duty. One is an obligation not to take advantage of situations involving conflicts of interest. In many instances, the trustee has an obligation to avoid even potential conflicts of interest. Obviously, then, a trustee should not personally enter into a transaction with the trust. Such a transaction usually is a breach of fiduciary duty and is voidable. The other aspect of the duty of loyalty is to be as impartial as possible among the beneficiaries. Impartiality is not always possible because there is a natural conflict between the income beneficiaries and the remainder beneficiaries. (Remainder beneficiaries are also called principal beneficiaries or corpus beneficiaries.)

In the following case, the trustee breached its duty of loyalty.

Northwestern Mutual Life Insurance Company v. Wiemer
421 N.E.2d 1002 (Ill. App. 1981)

FACTS   Mr. and Mrs. Wiemer entered into a trust agreement with Havana Bank, as trustee, to enable them to purchase and work a farm. Later, as part of the financial arrangement, Northwestern Mutual executed a $70,000 first mortgage of the farm; Havana had the second mortgage. After Mr. Weimer died, Havana took $8000 from the trust account and paid itself part of its own second mortgage. Consequently, the trust was unable to make the next payment to Northwestern, and Northwestern foreclosed on the first mortgage.

ISSUE   Did the trustee breach its trust duties?

HOLDING   Yes. The trustee was guilty of self-dealing in violation of its duty of loyalty.

REASONING   Havana had drafted the trust document and was trustee under it. Havana knew a payment would be due soon. Havana had three possible options: to apply all the funds to the first mortgage; to pay the regular payment on the first mortgage and pay the rest to itself; or to pay the entire amount to Mrs. Wiemer. Instead, it applied the funds for its own personal gain. This was a classic case of self-dealing and breach of trust. It was also a violation of the trust document, which stated that the first mortgage should be paid first. The court ruled that Mrs. Wiemer was entitled to damages.

Notice that the Wiemers entered into an express trust as part of a loan arrangement (and not part of an estate plan).

It is commonly stated that a trustee has a duty not to delegate, but this is really just a cautionary note. Not every act of trust administration must be completed by the trustee personally. A trustee may delegate to others the performance of any act or the exercise of any power when it is consistent with the trustee's general duty of care owed to the beneficiaries. In other words, the trustee may employ agents when a reasonably prudent owner of the same type of property acting with similar objectives would employ agents. In addition, the trustee must exercise due care in selecting and supervising agents.

The trustee must be careful in selecting trust investments. This generally includes a duty to diversify the type of investments. *The statutes in many states list or define what investments a trustee may make.* These are often called *legal investments.* A creator may grant a trustee the specific power to invest in nonlegal investments. Such a provision gives the trustee broader investment power, *but* it does not remove the general obligation to invest wisely. Obviously, the duty to invest wisely does not imply that the trustee guarantees that all investments will increase in value or that no money will be lost. Generally, trustees limit themselves to conservative investments. The standard test of whether a trustee has fulfilled this obligation is whether other prudent investors, *at that time,* would have chosen other, better investments; the judgment should not be made by hindsight.

As pointed out in *Estate of Gump,* the trustee may be surcharged for unwise investment decisions. In these cases, the trustee must pay personally for any losses caused by negligent decisions. The trustee may not offset profits on other investments against these losses.

The trustee has a duty to maintain clear and accurate records regarding the administration of the trust. This obligation, called the *duty to account,* includes recording the location and type of assets and the receipt and expenditure of income. In some jurisdictions, the trustee must file periodic accountings with the court. In others, it is sufficient for the trustee to account to the trust beneficiaries.

The trustee must not mix his or her personal funds with trust funds, a situation known as *commingling of assets.* The trustee may not borrow money or mortgage trust property unless that power was expressly provided in the trust document. The trustee *will* have the incidental authority to carry out ordinary duties.

The trustee in the following case failed to act prudently and to protect the interests of the beneficiary. Figure 53.1 illustrates the relationships between the parties.

Hatcher v. United States National Bank of Oregon
643 P.2d 359 (Or. App. 1982)

FACTS Hatcher was a remainder beneficiary of the irrevocable inter vivos trust that her stepfather had created. The sole asset in the trust was stock in a closely held corporation. The trust owned approximately 78 percent of the outstanding shares in the corporation. The corporation offered to buy the trust's stock for $800,000, no money down, with 8.5 percent interest to be amortized by twenty equal annual payments. The corporate trustee, United States National Bank of Oregon, asked one of its financial analysts to determine whether the offer was satisfactory. The analyst was not asked for an independent evaluation of net worth, and he did not do one. He used the book value with the tax assessor's values for the real estate and reported that the offer was fair and reasonable. The trustee then made a counteroffer based on the same terms except for an 8.75 percent interest rate, which the corporation accepted. The only security for the payment was a pledge of stock. The agreement contained no controls on corporate salaries, dividends, or borrowing. Later, when the corporation had difficulty repaying loans, the trustee agreed to **subordinate** trust claims to claims of the trustee's commercial department. The commercial department would have to approve any payments to the trustee in excess of $10,000 per year. The trustee did not receive any payment in exchange for this subordination.

Subordinate Give priority to the claims of another; agree to collect only after another collects.

FIGURE 53.1   Legal Relationships in *Hatcher* v. *United States National Bank of Oregon*

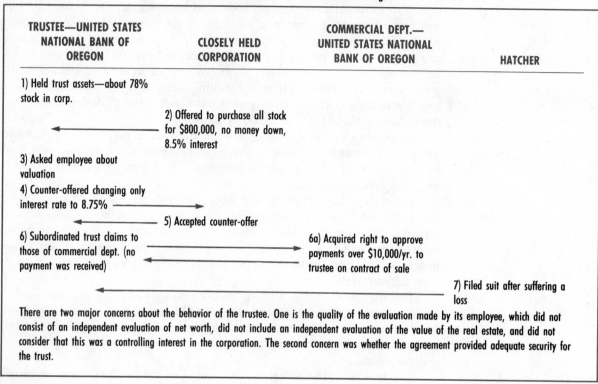

TRUSTEE—UNITED STATES NATIONAL BANK OF OREGON	CLOSELY HELD CORPORATION	COMMERCIAL DEPT.— UNITED STATES NATIONAL BANK OF OREGON	HATCHER
1) Held trust assets—about 78% stock in corp.			
	2) Offered to purchase all stock for $800,000, no money down, 8.5% interest		
3) Asked employee about valuation			
4) Counter-offered changing only interest rate to 8.75%			
	5) Accepted counter-offer		
6) Subordinated trust claims to those of commercial dept. (no payment was received)		6a) Acquired right to approve payments over $10,000/yr. to trustee on contract of sale	
			7) Filed suit after suffering a loss

There are two major concerns about the behavior of the trustee. One is the quality of the evaluation made by its employee, which did not consist of an independent evaluation of net worth, did not include an independent evaluation of the value of the real estate, and did not consider that this was a controlling interest in the corporation. The second concern was whether the agreement provided adequate security for the trust.

ISSUE   Did the trustee breach its fiduciary duty to the plaintiff (the remainder beneficiary)?

HOLDING   Yes. The trustee failed to act in a prudent manner.

REASONING   Oregon statute ORS 128.057 requires trustees to act as reasonable and prudent persons would, "not in regard to speculation but in regard to the permanent disposition of their funds, considering the probable income as well as the probable safety of the capital." The *Restatement (Second) of Trusts,* Section 227, Comment d, suggests an additional requirement for corporate trustees: "If the trustee is a bank or trust company, it must use in selecting investments the facilities which it has or should have, and it may properly be required to show that it has made a more thorough and complete investigation than would ordinarily be expected from an individual trustee." Accordingly, the court held that Hatcher should recover for her losses due to the corporate trustee's negligence in not determining whether the price offered represented the stock's fair market value, not testing the market for other potential buyers, not following appropriate procedures to determine fair market value, not utilizing a real estate appraisal by an independent appraiser or the trustee's real estate staff, not considering the fact that this was a controlling interest, not considering the corporation's reputation (goodwill), not bargaining for better terms, not bargaining for a higher interest rate considering the terms, not anticipating the necessity to subordinate, and accepting the terms of the subordination without consideration.

POWERS OF TRUSTEES

Trustees' powers are based on two primary sources: The trust instrument and the applicable state law. An additional source consists of those powers implied by law because they are necessary or appropriate to carry out the purposes of the trust. (Compare these powers with the incidental and implied powers discussed in Chapter 34.) A trustee who is uncertain about his or her powers may request clarification from the court.

Courts have developed general concepts about the powers that may be implied under state law. These powers may vary from state to state. The most common implied powers are the power to sell assets, the power to lease assets, and the power to incur reasonable expenses. Generally, there is no power to borrow money or to mortgage property. A trustee will not have implied powers if they would conflict with the trust deed or the purpose of the trust.

Invade the corpus Remove assets from the principal of the trust.

Unless there is an express trust provision to the contrary, the trustee will not have the power to **invade the corpus.** However, trust deeds commonly specify that the trustee *can* invade the corpus for the benefit of one or more of the income beneficiaries. *This power generally means that assets will be converted into cash and that the cash will be taken out of the trust.* The money may be given directly to the beneficiary or spent on the beneficiary's behalf. It is advisable for the trust deed to provide a standard so that the trustee and the courts can determine whether the invasion is appropriate. The common standards are called **ascertainable standards.** A body of case law enables both the trustee and the courts to interpret these standards. "The trustee can invade the corpus for the health, education, support, or maintenance of my children" is an example of an ascertainable standard.

Ascertainable standards Words that restrict the trustee's decisions about distributions.

The trust document often includes a list of additional powers given to the trustee. The trustee may utilize these additional powers unless they are against public policy.

RIGHTS AND DUTIES OF BENEFICIARIES

Unless the beneficiary is also serving in some other capacity, he or she has no obligation to the trust. The beneficiary's rights to income and corpus are determined by the trust document and applicable state law.

IMPLIED TRUSTS

Express trusts are voluntarily and intentionally created by the owner of the assets. They are based on the owner's actual intention. Implied trusts are created by operation of law. They are either implied by the law or imposed by the courts. Implied trusts *may* arise in the context of an express trust, but that is not a requirement.

Resulting Trusts

A *resulting trust* is based on the owner's presumed intention and *occurs when the owner of property disposes of the property, but the disposition is not complete.* The owner fails to make a complete, effective disposition of all of his or her equitable interests. However, a disposition *will be* considered complete if the state rules of trust construction determine who receives the equitable interest under the trust. A portion of the owner's interest *reverts* to the owner or the owner's heirs. This situation most commonly occurs under any one of the following conditions:

1. The owner did not state who should acquire a beneficial interest, such as a remainder interest; for example, the owner transfers a vacation home to a cousin for ten years.
2. The owner did not state what should happen under certain unanticipated situations; for example, if a child dies before his or her parents.
3. The express trust is not enforceable because it is not in the proper form; for example, the owner failed to name the beneficiaries.
4. The express trust fails completely or in part because it is illegal, impractical, or impossible or because a beneficiary refuses an interest in the trust; for example, a charitable purpose becomes impractical and the court finds *cy pres* inapplicable. This is the remedy sought by the family members in *Wesley United Methodist Church* v. *Harvard College.*

Resulting trusts also may occur when a person purchases real property with his or her own money and puts the title in the name of another person. The law presumes that the purchaser intended that the recipient should hold the property as "trustee" for the purchaser. This is often called a *purchase money resulting trust.* Such a presumption may be rebutted by evidence that the purchaser had a different intention. In many states, the courts will presume that the purchaser intended a gift if the purchaser and transferee are closely related.

Resulting trusts occur only if the proper owner has been acting in good faith.

Constructive Trusts

A *constructive trust* is often more remote than a resulting trust from express trusts and other forms of property disposition. It *arises by operation of law and serves to redress a wrong or to prevent an unjust enrichment.* It is actually an equitable remedy. It is imposed by a court of equity when a person gains legal title to property but has an equitable duty to transfer the property to someone else. This can occur in any of the following situations:

1. A person takes title as a trustee, but the trust is not enforceable; for example, a trustee receives assets under an oral trust which is unenforceable under the Statute of Frauds. To allow the trustee to keep the property would create unjust enrichment.

2. A person obtains property by breaching a fiduciary duty; for example, an employee embezzles company funds.

3. A person either is guilty of a wrong or would receive unjust enrichment. Depending on state law, the person may be guilty of fraud, conversion, theft, duress, or murder of the transferor. Some situations may involve mistake. For example, the transferor may have owned two lots and sold one lot to the transferee, but the deed mistakenly mentioned two lots. The court would impose a constructive trust on the second lot for the benefit of the transferor.

Constructive trusts are not limited to these situations, which are intended to be illustrative. The following case shows one way in which the court might determine that a constructive trust is needed in order to prevent an unjust enrichment.

In re Estate of Mahoney
220 A.2d 475 (Vt. 1966)

FACTS The decedent died intestate of a gunshot wound. His wife was convicted of manslaughter and sentenced to jail. The decedent was survived by his wife, his mother, and his father. His estate was worth about $3885.

ISSUE Can the decedent's wife inherit from his estate despite the manslaughter conviction?

HOLDING Yes. The widow will inherit. The trial court may impose a constructive trust.

REASONING Under the Vermont intestacy statute, the widow would inherit the estate. Vermont does not have a "slayer's statute," which would prevent the inheritance. A slayer should not be allowed to benefit from the wrong. Legally, the title would pass to the widow. The decedent's parents could petition the court of equity to have a constructive trust imposed on the estate for their benefit. The court of equity would determine whether the widow intended to kill the decedent. If so, a trust could be imposed.

As with other equitable remedies, constructive trusts are created to correct unfair results.

SUMMARY

An express trust is an arrangement whereby the owner of assets voluntarily places the legal ownership in a trustee and the equitable ownership in one or more beneficiaries. Creators are motivated to establish trusts for many purposes including: To protect beneficiaries from themselves and creditors; to free beneficiaries from the responsibilities of asset management; to split an asset or estate among multiple beneficiaries; to test a pattern of transfers before finalizing it; to save taxes; and to increase flexibility. The trustee is obligated to manage the trust assets prudently. Trusts can be flexible and made to accommodate numerous situation. However, they may be expensive because of trustee's fees and added tax burdens. Care must be utilized in selecting an appropriate trustee, since a trustee has a lot of discretion in how to manage the trust. The trustee must exercise due care in selecting investments for the trust. He or she may be surcharged for making the wrong selection.

The two types of implied trusts are not created voluntarily, but arise by operation of law. A resulting trust occurs when a person makes an incomplete transfer of assets. Constructive trusts are imposed by courts of equity to correct a wrong or to prevent unjust enrichment.

DISCUSSION QUESTIONS

1. What parties are involved in the formation of an express trust? What role does each party serve?
2. What is an inter vivos trust? What are some of its advantages and disadvantages?
3. How does the *cy pres* doctrine work in charitable trusts?
4. Why is a duty of loyalty imposed on a trustee? What effect does this duty have?
5. Compare and contrast spendthrift trusts and discretionary sprinkling trusts.
6. Executors and trustees may be asked to serve without fees. Why would they be reluctant to do so? Under what circumstances might they be willing to do so?

7. Are you qualified to act as executor or trustee of your parents' estate? Why or why not?
8. Is it just to impose a high duty of care on a trustee who does not possess the necessary background? Why or why not?
9. A trustee has a duty to exercise care, skill, and prudence. What are these duties? How do they differ?
10. A constructive trust may arise when the court cannot enforce an express trust because the trust lacks a writing required by the Statute of Frauds. Explain why this would be a good application of the constructive trust doctrine.

CASE PROBLEMS

1. Kemske established an irrevocable inter vivos trust for the benefit of his daughter and grandchildren. The corporate trustee was State Bank. State Bank was owned by State Bond. State Bond had three mutual funds, including Common Stock Fund. Kemske knew about the interrelationships between the two companies. The trust deed stated that the trustee was authorized to invest in State Bond and the mutual funds of State Bond. Should

this authorization be valid? Why or why not? Under what circumstances, if any, could it be valid? (*Matter of Irrevocable Inter Vivos Trust, Etc.*, 305 N.W.2d 755 [Minn. 1981].)

2. The decedent died intestate, and his wife was appointed administrator of his estate. She continued to operate his motorcycle business for twenty months after his death. During this time, she paid herself a salary in excess of $30,000 plus fringe benefits and had the use of a company car. When the business continued to lose money, she abandoned it. She did not liquidate the remaining assets or pay corporate debts. Did the administrator breach her fiduciary duties? Why or why not? Should a personal representative continue the operation of a business under any circumstances? If so, when and why? (*In re Estate of Kurkowski*, 409 A.2d 357 [Pa. 1979].)

3. Decedent's trustees, Lamb and Millikan (decedent's attorney), loaned two-thirds of the decedent's trust funds to a borrower and took as security a second mortgage on a parcel of real estate. The trustees based the loan on casual conversations with the borrower and did not require a credit check of the borrower or an appraisal of the property. The borrower, who was another client of Millikan, was having financial difficulty because another lender had reneged on a loan commitment. There were six notices of default and three lawsuits pending against the borrower at the time of the loan. Did the trustees violate their duty to act as prudent investors? (*Matter of Estate of Collins*, 139 Cal. Rptr. 644 [Cal. App. 1977].)

4. Parker was trustee of Hamon's testamentary trust. As such, she loaned trust funds secured by real estate. The trustee did not speak to the borrower until after the loan had been made. The trustee did receive a written application from the borrower, which was approved by the trustee's attorney. She did not inspect the land herself. Her main source of information was Muncy, whom she had known for thirty years. She also received a written report about the land from three men she did not know. Based on this information, she loaned a substantial amount of money on practically valueless land. Did Parker violate her duty to the trust beneficiary? (*Estate of Hamon*, 60 Cal. App. 154 [1922].)

5. Fidelity National Bank was named as the original trustee of Dunham's testamentary trusts. When Fidelity refused to serve, the court appointed Louisiana National Bank as trustee, but the trust funds were never transferred to this trustee. At the time of this lawsuit,

there were a number of other unresolved cases involving this trust, including whether the trusts should be partitioned and whether two individual co-trustees should be removed. Provisional trustees were named for the purpose of the lawsuits. Was Louisiana National Bank in breach of its duty because it did not demand that funds be transferred to it? Why or why not? (*Matter of Succession of Dunham*, 399 So.2d 221 [La. App. 1981].)

6. Devon National Bank was the trustee of the Zarkins' land trust. The trust property was the Zarkins' residence. Home Federal Savings and Loan held the first mortgage, and Devon held the second mortgage. Devon purchased the trust property after there had been a decree of foreclosure initiated by the first mortgagee. Did the trustee breach its duties to the Zarkins? If so, what remedies should the Zarkins have, and why? (*Home Federal Savings and Loan Association of Chicago* v. *Zarkin*, 432 N.E.2d 841 [Ill. 1982].)

7. Security Pacific National Bank was named as the trustee of the decedent's testamentary trust. It decided to sell the lemon groves owned by the trust. Another branch of the bank loaned $115,000 of the bank's funds to the ultimate purchaser of these groves and took back a deed of trust covering the trust property. This loan enabled the purchaser to acquire the trust property. The bank earned between $2004.50 and $2274.00 interest on this loan. The trust did not earn income or interest while the property was in escrow because the trustee surrendered the right to collect income. Did Security Pacific violate its duty to the trust by dealing with the trust property for its own benefit? Did it breach its duty of loyalty? Should the fact that the bank did not know its action was wrong be relevant to a lawsuit based on a trustee's duty to avoid self-dealing in connection with trust property? (*Estate of Pitzer*, 202 Cal. Rptr. 855 [Cal. App. 1984].)

8. The trust of Roberta Switzer provided for her children and contained a spendthrift provision. It stated that the interests of the beneficiaries could not be subject to claims of the beneficiaries' creditors or to legal process or be voluntarily or involuntarily assigned, alienated, or encumbered. It also stated that the trustees should use their discretion in paying as much as necessary for the maintenance, support, and education of each living child. Her son, George, filed a petition in bankruptcy. He was twenty-seven at the time, and under the trust he was not entitled to receive a share of the trust assets yet. Should the court attach George's interest to pay for the necessities provided to him? Should

public policy favor the trust provisions or the bankruptcy trustee? (*Erickson* v. *Bank of California, N.A.,* 643 P.2d 670 [Wash. 1982].)

9. Guynan owned a parcel of real estate. In September, 1955, he gave his son Edward permission to construct a concrete block house on a portion of the property. Edward constructed the house at his own expense and lived in it from 1957 to 1960, after which time he rented the house and collected the rentals. When Guynan died in 1970, his wife, Anne, obtained title to the property. Anne allowed Edward to continue to rent the property to others. Because of a disagreement between Anne and her son, Anne filed a lawsuit to have Edward and his tenants removed from the premises. Should the court impose a resulting trust or a constructive trust in Edward's favor? Why or why not? (*Guynan* v. *Guynan,* 305 N.W.2d 882 [Neb. 1981].)

10. Tenna Manufacturing Company was considering selling small motors to a buyer on credit. An agent for Tenna contacted Columbia Union National Bank by phone about the buyer's credit worthiness. Tenna was going to be an unsecured creditor. A bank employee assured Tenna that the buyer had good credit, was current on loans, had good customers, and had a good balance on its account. At least some of this information was misleading in a material way. About two months after Tenna sold the small motors to the buyer, the bank called its secured loan to the buyer and seized all the buyer's assets, including the motors. When the motors were sold, the bank received the proceeds. Does Tenna have any legal recourse against the bank? What trust theory, if any, should apply? (*Tenna Manufacturing Co.* v. *Columbia Union National Bank,* 484 F. Supp. 1214 [W.D. Mo. 1980].)

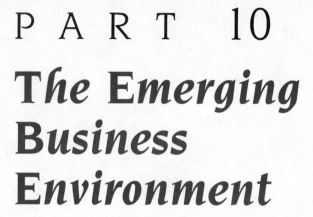

PART 10

The Emerging Business Environment

*T*he computer age has spawned an entirely new era, with new legal problems. Many of these "new" problems merely require a redefined application of "old" principles. In Chapter 54, the era of computers and the law is introduced.

In addition, the world has become smaller in the twentieth century. Advances in communications and in travel have made the entire planet readily accessible to many people and to many businesses. In addition, the reconstruction following World War II has led to a great deal of international trade. Investors today are willing and able to invest in business opportunities in foreign nations as well as in domestic businesses.

Businesses today commonly own plants in several nations. Because of the increasingly multinational character of business, no text on business law can be truly complete or comprehensive without touching on international business. This final part of the text introduces the topic and some of the problems that the area presents to the legal system. While the coverage is brief, at least the seed is planted. Serious students can easily expand their knowledge through independent study.

54
COMPUTERS AND THE LAW

55
INTERNATIONAL BUSINESS

C H A P T E R 54

O U T L I N E

INTRODUCTION

The pervasity of the influence of computers on our lives probably defies description. The strange words that pepper our everyday speech—*software, hardware, bytes, input, output, electronic bulletin boards, mainframes, PCs, minis*—graphically illustrate the primacy of computers in our world. We use computers in the classroom, in our public libraries, for our own personal uses, and for numerous other daily activities, including medical diagnoses. Without computers, the telecommunications, financial, insurance, airline, and newspaper industries and a myriad of other businesses and multinational corporations would undoubtedly grind to a near halt. The government itself holds so much information about us on computer tapes that Congress and state legislatures have passed statutes designed to protect our privacy. And no one believes the amount of computer-generated data will decrease in the foreseeable future.

Nonetheless, the industry itself shows signs of turmoil. Rapid technological and commercial changes have resulted in lowered profitability (if not actual losses) for virtually all U.S. and European computer companies. Slackening demand, the spread of open systems (networks based on standard industry components), and the proliferation of low-cost, high-powered systems have fueled this decline and resultant industry stagnation. Computer companies generally have responded to these lower profit margins in three ways: restructuring (that is, reductions in the workforce), price cutting of unprecedented dimensions, and consolidations (for example, AT&T's acquisition of NCR). Although authorities had estimated that the information industry would grow by 15 percent annually (from the 3.9 percent of the U.S. gross national product attributable to this industry in 1984) to reach $300 billion in worldwide total revenues in 1985 and a whopping $1 trillion in the early 1990s, the industry has failed to reach these optimistic levels.[1] In fact, worldwide, sales reached $649 billion in 1992.[2] The PC boom, resulting from the efforts of entrepreneurial startup companies such as Apple and Commodore, has overtaken the traditional mainframe and minicomputer manufacturers, including IBM, Unisys, Digital Equipment, Wang, Groupe Bull, and Olivetti.[3] Advances in the power of such microprocessors (or PCs) and the emergence of open-based systems has led to a shift away from mainframes and a near saturation of the market (that is, a virtual one-to-one ratio of computers to users).[4] The worldwide recession, dissatisfied customers whose expectations of increased productivity never materialized, and downward-spiraling prices represent formidable hurdles for today's computer manufacturers. Still, the companies that can adjust to this transitional period—perhaps through the

---

[1]*Standard & Poor's Industry Surveys,* June 6, 1985, p. C73.
[2]*Standard & Poor's Industry Surveys,* October 17, 1991, p. C75.
[3]Ibid., p. C76.
[4]Ibid.

development of networked computers—will emerge as stronger entities. Consumers, of course, will be the clear winners in this wrenching period of change.[5] Nonetheless, although optimism among manufacturers remains guarded, experts continue to believe that the information-processing industry will dominate all other industries in the world by the end of the century; and if it does not already affect the daily life of every person now, the information industry certainly will affect all our lives by the end of the century.

Besides market forces, the computer industry also raises noneconomic issues involving regulation/deregulation, privacy, equity, and sovereignty. In fact, these issues have led in many instances to the erection of nontariff trade barriers to transborder data flows. It is easy to forget that we as Americans view privacy much differently from others in our "global village." For example, even though we would probably reject governmental restrictions meant to impede the free flow of information across our country and across national borders, many other countries do not share our misgivings about this type of regulation of information. These countries also would generally favor the creation of governmental commissions to administer privacy laws and to protect citizens' interests, while we would very likely balk at the institution of such governmental controls.

Similarly, the lesser-developed, so-called third-world countries fear the United States's telecommunications dominance, especially our power in the "information era." Their "have not" status alarms them because they believe their lack of access to computer technologies carries with it significant cultural and economic repercussions. Similarly, other countries view U.S.-generated data processing as a threat to their sovereignty because of the challenges these **data banks** pose to these countries' comparatively fledgling information industries. Canadian banking legislation, for instance, requires that all data processing leading to the preparation of banking statements be carried out in Canada. Not only does such legislation protect Canadian jobs, it also avoids the effects of what Canada has dubbed "cultural imperialism," or "Americanized" interpretations of data.

As American technology increasingly permits the beaming of the latest merchandise lines and items across international borders through "electronic catalogues," or teletext and videotext technologies, we can expect such criticisms to proliferate. Since many countries do not welcome this type of information, the erection of further barriers to impede such transborder data flows may follow as a consequence. Indeed, for some American firms these barriers are already a reality. For example, Japan in the late 1970s made it difficult for American firms to connect to its international record carrier unless each leased circuit terminated at a single facility in the U.S. Similarly, France has proposed to levy taxes on information flows across its borders. A host of international organizations and numerous committees within the executive and legislative branches of our government therefore are directing their con-

Data banks Central depositories for information.

[5]Ibid., p. C77.

certed efforts to a consideration of the problems spawned by the computer age. You presumably will be able to witness the resolution of these profound issues as they unfold on the world stage.

Interesting though it is to ponder the multifaceted questions arising from the computer age, we will confine our examination of this important topic to the legal issues inherent in this subject. We can divide these issues into five main areas: the intellectual property aspects of computers (copyrights, patents, trade secrets, and unfair competition); contract law, particularly the Uniform Commercial Code; tort law; statutory protection (invasion of privacy, antitrust, and criminal law); and constitutional law. The national movement toward total computer literacy for all Americans presupposes an understanding of the legal ramifications spawned by the information era. Hence, this chapter's focus on some of the more significant elements of computers and the law should facilitate your comprehension of this noteworthy topic.

INTELLECTUAL PROPERTY ASPECTS OF COMPUTERS

Copyrights

As we learned in Chapter 46, federal law protects the holders of copyrights and patents. Congress as early as 1790 exercised the power granted to it by the Constitution in conferring statutory protection on artistic works created by writers, artists, and composers. The copyright laws protect "any original works of authorship fixed in any tangible medium of expression [including literary works]. . . ."[6] Hence, copyright laws traditionally have protected only *expressions* of ideas, not the ideas themselves. Plans, methods, systems, or devices are not copyrightable either.

The most important of the early copyright laws, the Copyright Act of 1909, remained virtually unchanged until 1 January 1978, when the present copyright statute, the Copyright Act of 1976, became effective. (Vestiges of the 1909 Act in reality remain with us, since it still covers works created prior to 1 January 1978.) Although it was unclear whether computer programs were copyrightable under the 1909 Act, the Copyright Office began accepting computer programs for registration as books as early as 1964, despite the misgivings of register officials.[7] At the time of the passage of the 1976 Act, the "jury" (in the form of the National Commission on New Technological Uses [CONTU]) was still out on the copyrightability of computer software. However, the Computer Software Copyright Act of 1980 amended the 1976 Act by adding the phrase "computer program" and certain other provisions exempting the copying of computer programs from the Act's infringement provisions. As a result of these amendments, few doubts remain today as to the

---

[6]17 U.S.C. §102 (West 1985).
[7]Scott, *Computer Law*, at 3-6. Copyright © 1984 John Wiley & Sons, Inc.

copyrightability of computer programs, despite the omission of this phrase from the listed categories of proper subject matters for copyright protection.

Under the 1980 amendments, "[a] 'computer program' is a set of statements or instructions to be used directly or indirectly in a computer in order to bring about a certain result."[8] According to the 1980 amendments, computer data bases are also copyrightable under Section 103(b) as "compilations" or "derivative works." Infringements of copyrights (for example, unauthorized copying, distribution, or derivation) do not occur if the owner (i.e., a copyright holder) of a copy of a computer program only makes or authorizes the making of a new copy (or adaption) when the copy is an essential step in the utilization of the program in conjunction with a machine (i.e., for use with the owner's computer) or for archival purposes (i.e., for making backup copies in case the original copy is accidentally destroyed).[9] The "fair use" doctrine (whereby, for instance, your professor uses computer software for an in-class performance or display) and the right of libraries to reproduce and distribute copyrighted works, including computer software in some circumstances, apparently do not constitute infringements either.[10] The Act presently does not differentiate between human-readable or machine-readable copies for infringement purposes; copies in either form may constitute infringements unless the copying falls into one of these exemptions.

Yet controversies still abound due to the fact that the 1976 Act continues the long-standing expression/idea dichotomy of copyright law. This duality (that the program as written is protectable but the unique ideas contained in the program are not) of course looms as a significant impediment to software developers who wish to copyright their manuals, since it is easy to produce competing products once the ideas underlying the original package become known. Thus, even though the manuals will be copyrightable on the developers' meeting the required statutory criteria, the formats may not be. Similarly, the audiovisual display aspects of a video game may be copyrightable whereas the idea (a crazy character that "munches" everything, for instance) behind the game (or the game per se) ordinarily will be ineligible for copyright protection.[11] The same may be true in general of flowcharts, components of machines, and printed circuit boards that do not have computer programs embedded in them: These normally are uncopyrightable.[12] The unsettled state of the law in this area merely complicates developers' problems.

The case that follows represents one of the most significant recent decisions regarding the application of the copyright laws to computer software, particularly computer operating systems. Note that the opinion addresses the important issue of whether an *object code*, which is not readable by people,

---

[8]17 U.S.C. Section 101 (West 1985).
[9]Ibid. at Section 117.
[10]Ibid. at Sections 107 and 108.
[11]Scott, *Computer Law,* at 3-89—90. Copyright © 1984 John Wiley & Sons, Inc.
[12]Ibid. at 3-32.

is a "writing" within the Copyright Act's coverage and hence copyrightable or instead, given its normal use, a "method of operation" or a "system," which would be uncopyrightable.

Apple Computer, Inc. v. Franklin Computer Corp.
714 F.2d 1240 (3d Cir. 1983), cert. dismissed, 464 U.S. 1033 (1984)

FACTS

Operating system computer programs Collections of systems software programs designed to help someone else program or use a computer and which allow the computer to execute programs and manage programming tasks.

Apple Computer, Inc. (Apple) filed suit against Franklin Computer Corp. (Franklin) for copyright infringement owing to Franklin's copying of fourteen of Apple's **operating system computer programs** for use with Franklin's ACE 100 personal computer. Franklin admitted it had copied Apple's programs and **ROM chips** but argued it had done so because it had not been feasible for Franklin to write its own operating system programs. Franklin also asserted that the Apple programs did not constitute copyrightable subject matter because the **object code** on which the programs had relied was not a "writing" and that the programs were "processes," "systems," or "methods of operation" unprotected by law.

ISSUE

Were the Apple programs protected under the copyright laws?

HOLDING

Yes. Computer programs, whether in **source code** or in object code embedded in ROM chips, are "literary works" protected under the Copyright Act of 1976 from unauthorized copying from either their object code or source code version.

REASONING

ROM chips (*Read Only Memory* chips) Computer chips on which the data and information used to run computer operating systems are affixed; chips that can be "read" by a computer program but generally cannot be changed or altered.

Object code Translation of source code into lower-level language, consisting of numbers and symbols that the computer interprets into electronic impulses (machine language).

Source code Human-readable version of the program that gives instructions to the computer.

The lower court had been wrong in stating, in effect, that programs expressed in object code, as distinguished from source code, were uncopyrightable. Rather, the legislative history of the Copyright Act and recent amendments supported the conclusion that a computer program, whether in object code or source code, is a "literary work" protected from unauthorized copying from either its object or source code version. Thus, earlier holdings that a computer program in object code embedded in a ROM chip is an appropriate subject of copyright protection were reaffirmed. Franklin's contention that computer operating systems, as opposed to application programs, are nonproper subjects of the copyright laws regardless of the language or medium in which they are fixed because they are either "processes," "systems," or "methods of operation" that are per se excluded from protection under Section 102(b) of the Copyright Act was incorrect. Moreover, Franklin's concession that application programs (which generally perform a certain task for the computer user, such as word processing or checkbook balancing) are appropriate subjects for copyright protection was inconsistent with its position that operating system programs are not. Since both types of programs instruct the computer to do something, it therefore makes no difference whether the instructions involve directions to do a certain task or the translation of high-level language from source code to object code. The fact that the instructions are etched in a ROM chip and are used to activate the computer did not make the operating system program either a "process," "system," or "method of operation" or part of a "machine," all of which are statutorily uncopyrightable. Franklin's argument that the ROM chip is a utilitarian device whose practical usage precludes copyrightability was equally unconvincing. But Franklin's contention that a systems operating program amounts to an idea rather than the means of the expression of an idea was more persuasive. If other programs can be written or created that perform the same functions as the copyright holder's operating system program, the program is an expression of an idea and hence copyrightable. Because the lower court had made no findings as to whether some or all of Apple's operating programs represented the only means of expression of the ideas underlying them, this issue was not fit for appellate review but could be decided on remand. Since Franklin had been unable to prove its contentions that operating system programs are per se uncopyrightable, the lower court's denial of Apple's request for a preliminary injunction to stop Franklin's copying of Apple's programs warranted reversal.

The more recent case that follows utilizes many of the same concepts.

Lotus Development Corporation v. Paperback Software International
740 F. Supp. 37 (D. Mass. 1990)

FACTS   Lotus Development Corporation (Lotus) had created Lotus 1-2-3, a spreadsheet program that also carried out other tasks, including limited data base management and graphics creation. Paperback Software International (Paperback) had developed VP-Planner, another integrated application program that admittedly had copied many of the salient features of Lotus 1-2-3. At a bench trial, Lotus argued that Paperback's copying of Lotus 1-2-3's command and menu sequence had constituted copyright infringements. Paperback countered that its actions had been within the law because Lotus's electronic spreadsheet represented a useful (or functional) article that would not merit copyright protection.

ISSUE   Was the electronic spreadsheet Lotus 1-2-3 copyrightable?

HOLDING   Yes. Lotus 1-2-3's menu command structure, including the choice of command terms, the structure and order of those terms, their presentation on the screen, and the long prompts, was copyrightable; the menu command structure was capable of being expressed in many (though not unlimited) ways; it was an original and nonobvious way of expressing the command structure; and it represented a substantial part of the spreadsheet program.

REASONING   The parties agreed, as a general proposition, that literal manifestations of a computer program, including both source code and object code, if original, are copyrightable. In addition, the law entitles flowcharts, if sufficiently detailed and original, to copyright protection. Paperback, the defendant, vigorously disputed, however, the copyrightability of any nonliteral elements of computer programs. That is, the defendant asserted that only literal manifestations of computer programs are copyrightable. Lotus, the plaintiff, maintained that copyright protection extends to all elements of computer programs that embody original expression, whether literal or nonliteral, including any original expression embodied in a program's "user interface." One difficulty with the plaintiff's argument involves the amorphous nature of "nonliteral" elements of computer programs. Unlike the written code of a program or a flowchart that can be printed on paper, nonliteral elements—including such elements as the overall organization of a program, the structure of a program's command system, and the presentation of information on the screen—may be less tangibly represented. Whether these elements are copyrightable and, if so, how one may identify the nonliteral elements that are copyrightable remain central to deciding this case. Under the copyright law, codified in Title 17 of the United States Code, Congress has broad—though not unlimited—authority to grant copyright monopolies as needed to promote progress. If Congress were to determine that copyright protection is unnecessary to promote the progress of computer programming, Congress could, without offending the Constitution, provide no copyright protection for computer programs. At the other extreme, if Congress were to find that strong copyright protection is necessary to promote the progress of computer programming, Congress could provide for expansive copyright protection for all aspects of computer programs, again without having strayed beyond the bounds of the constitutionally permissible. Because this constitutional grant of power authorizes Congress to take either path (or to chart some middle course), this case does not raise constitutional questions. Rather, the issues at stake here involve statutory interpretation. In construing the relevant statutory mandates, courts must be faithful to the statutory language and mindful of both the ultimate goal of copyright law—the advancement of public welfare—and Congress's chosen method of achieving this goal—private reward to the individual author. Rather than itself drawing the boundary line between the copyrightable and noncopyrightable elements of computer programs, Congress has mandated that courts use an evaluative standard in determining this boundary line. When statutes establish evaluative standards for deciding cases, courts by necessity must locate boundaries in uncharted terrain, using the markers that Congress has placed. Moreover, courts may not disregard or relocate any marker Congress has placed. The fewer markers Congress has placed, the more critical it becomes that courts assure that no marker escapes notice. This inquiry has received heightened attention in this case because the defendant contended that extending copyright protection to nonliteral elements of computer programs is contrary to the objectives and policies of copyright law as expressed in the copyright statute and in precedents. The plaintiff, in disputing the defendant's conclusion, did not contest the underlying premise of this contention. Defendants suggested that the user interface of Lotus 1-2-3 is a useful, functional object like the functional layout of gears in an "H" pattern on a standard transmission, the functional assignment of letters to keys on a standard QWERTY keyboard, and the functional configuration of controls on a musical instrument (such as the keys of a piano). Simply put, the defendant submitted that anything that is useful is a "useful article"; nothing about a "useful article" is ever copyrightable; because 1-2-3 is useful, and is an article, it is not copyrightable. However, a more sensible interpretation of the statutory mandate posits that the mere fact that an intellectual work is useful or functional—whether it is a dictionary, directory, map, book of meaningless code words, or computer program—does not eliminate the possible copyrightability of all the elements of the work. Furthermore, the statute does not bar copyrightability merely because the originality of the expression becomes associated with the usefulness of the work to a degree and in dimensions previously unachieved by other products in the market. To hold otherwise would be to deny copyright protection to the most original and least obvious products of the creative mind merely because the marketplace accepts them as distinctively "functional." Such a rule would grant copyright protection for only those products that fall far short of being the best available. Rather than promoting and encouraging both the development and disclosure of the best, such a rule would offer incentives to market only the second, or third, or tenth best, and to hold back the best for fear that it is too good for copyrightability. The computer programs at issue in this case are expressions of the idea of a computer program for an electronic spreadsheet. The defendant was quite correct in asserting that the idea of developing an electronic spreadsheet is not copyrightable owing to the fact that the core idea of such a spreadsheet is both functional and obvious, even to computer users who claim no technical competence. Thus, even though programs like VisiCalc, 1-2-3, Multiplan, SuperCalc4, and Excel remain distinct in their structure, appearance, and method of operation, each is, at the most basic level, just a different way of expressing the same idea: the electronic spreadsheet. It does not follow, however, that every possible method of designing a metaphorical spreadsheet is obvious, or that no form of expressing the idea of the spreadsheet metaphor can possibly have such originality in pressing beyond the obvious as is required for copyrightability, or that no special form of metaphorical spreadsheet can possibly be a distinctive expression of a particular method of preparing financial information. The issue here is whether Lotus 1-2-3 goes beyond those details essential to any expression of the idea to include, in addition, substantial elements of expression, distinctive and original, that thus become copyrightable. The menu structure of 1-2-3, taken as a whole—including the choice of command terms, the structure and order of those terms, their presentation on the screen, and the long prompts—constitutes an aspect of 1-2-3 that is not present in every expression of an electronic spreadsheet. It thus meets the requirements of the first and second elements of the legal test for copyrightability (originality and nonobviousness, respectively). Finally, the court must consider the third element of the legal test: whether the structure, sequence, and organization of the menu command system is a substantial part of the alleged copyrighted work. That the answer to this question is yes is incontrovertible. The user interface of 1-2-3 constitutes its most unique element and the aspect that has made 1-2-3 so popular. That the defendant went to such trouble to copy that element is a testament to its substantiality. Accordingly, evaluation of the third element of the legal test weighs heavily in favor of Lotus. Taking account of all three elements of the legal test, the fact finder correctly concluded that the plaintiffs had established the copyrightability of the user interface of 1-2-3. Given, then, the defendant's admission that it had copied Lotus 1-2-3's arrangement (and names) of commands and menus so as to effect such compatibility as would allow users to switch from 1-2-3 to VP-Planner without requiring retraining in the operation of VP-Planner, the evidence established that the defendant had engaged in illegal copyright infringement. Thus, the defendant's proof that VP-Planner has many features that differ from Lotus 1-2-3 is off point. The more relevant question is: Does it have significant features that are substantially similar? On the record before the court, there is no genuine dispute of material fact on this question; hence, the answer to this question must be yes. The defendant argued that 1-2-3, and specifically, 1-2-3's menu structure and macro command facility, has set a de facto industry standard for all electronic spreadsheets. Thus, the defendant had had no choice, it argued, but to copy these expressive elements from 1-2-3. Had it not copied these elements (including the macro facility), users, who had been trained in 1-2-3 and had written elaborate macros to run on 1-2-3 spreadsheets, would be unwilling to switch to VP-Planner; VP-Planner, then, would become a commercial failure. Yet neither the factual nor the legal predicate of this argument is supportable. First, the defendant's argument ignores the commercial success of Excel, an innovative spreadsheet program that is incompatible with 1-2-3, in both its menu structure and its macro command facility. Second, the defendant had legally available alternatives to direct copying. Moreover, to the extent that VP-Planner represents an incremental improvement upon 1-2-3 because of its multidimensional database capabilities, the defendant could have 1) sought a license to use 1-2-3's menu structure and command facility; 2) offered to sell its new expression of ideas to Lotus for inclusion in future versions of 1-2-3; or 3) marketed VP-Planner as an "add-in" to 1-2-3. By arguing that 1-2-3 was so innovative that it had occupied the field and had set a de facto industry standard, and that, therefore, the defendant had been free to copy plaintiff's expression, the defendant had flipped copyright law on its head. Copyright protection would be perverse if it only protected mundane increments while leaving unprotected as part of the public domain those advancements that are more strikingly innovative. The particular way the defendant proposed that the court resolve this dispute would reduce copyright protection far below the mandate of the Copyright Act and must, as a consequence, be rejected.

As the *Lotus* case illustrates, copyright claims represent a fertile area for litigation. Apple Computer, Inc., Microsoft Corporation, and Hewlett-Packard Company have recently litigated the copyrightability of the visual display aspects of computer user interfaces. Given the huge economic stakes and the ever-changing technology involved in such cases, companies presumably will continue this zealous protection of their rights through resort to the courts. These developments should be interesting.

Beyond the 1976 Copyright Act and its amendments, international protection of copyrighted works, including computer software, derives from the Berne Convention and the Universal Copyright Convention. Proposed amendments to GATT (the General Agreement on Trade and Tariffs) to cover intellectual property (including computer programs) and the European Economic Community's (EEC's) "Directive on the Legal Protection of Computer Software," slated to cover EEC members as of 1 January 1993, represent other promising initiatives in the international arena as well.[13]

Patents

The same provision of the Constitution that provides the basis for copyright protection furnishes the grounds for patents. Congress has the power to promote the progress of science and the useful arts by securing to inventors (rather than authors) the exclusive right to their respective discoveries (rather than writings). Today, most experts lump the terms *useful arts, inventors,* and *discoveries* with patent rights and leave the promotion of science through writings to copyright law.

---

[13]*Scott on Computer Law*, 2d. ed., at 3-243, 249–51. Copyright © 1991 Prentice Hall Law and Business.

Since the first patent statute in 1790, the statutory categories of patentable subject matter have consisted of (1) any process (the earlier term was *art,* but the term *process* now includes a process, art, or method), (2) machine, (3) manufacture, (4) composition of matter, and (5) any new and useful improvement thereon.[14] Neither the old law nor the significant amendments to the patent laws contemplated the inclusion of computer or program-related inventions within these classifications. As a result, by the 1960s, the Patent Office (PO) and the Court of Customs and Patent Appeals (CCPA) had drawn strict battle lines regarding the patentability of computer programs and other software. The CCPA was for it; the PO against it.[15] Although it was clear that computer programs could fill the first requirement of patentability, that is, that they could potentially arise under one of the four categories of patentable subject matter ("process" or "machine," presumably), doubts existed as to whether software could fulfill the remaining four conditions of patentability: (1) utility, (2) novelty, (3) nonobviousness, and (4) adequate disclosure. Those arguing for patentability viewed computer systems consisting of both hardware and software as either a process (a method for operating a machine) or as a physical component of the hardware itself and thus protected by the "machine" requirement, with the program being one element in the overall apparatus. Other authorities, however, relegated computer software to areas lying outside patent protection by characterizing software as ideas standing alone, laws of nature, scientific truths or principles, algorithms (mathematical formulas), mental steps, printed matter, functions of a machine, and/or methods of doing business.[16] Indeed, for many years that was the fate that befell program-related invention cases, since questions arose as to whether an invention containing as one of its elements a computer program implementing such an algorithm was patentable.

Preempt Seize upon to the exclusion of others.

Many precedents relied on the so-called preemption test in which the PO was obliged to examine whether the patent claim on the software would wholly **preempt** the other uses of the algorithm (i.e., calculations, formulas, or equations). If so, the invention fell into one of the categories of nonstatutory subject matter and was unpatentable because the claim merely recited a mathematical algorithm. If, instead, the algorithm was but one of several steps or procedures leading to the transformation of the data into a wholly different state or thing, the invention complied with the statutory subject matter and was patentable. After several cases in the 1970s holding computer-related inventions unpatentable, the Supreme Court in the following case accepted the preemption test in holding the claim patentable.

[14]Scott, *Computer Law,* at 4-5. Copyright © 1984 John Wiley & Sons, Inc.
[15]Ibid. at 4-3.
[16]Ibid. at 4-10.

Diamond v. *Diehr*
450 U.S. 175 (1981)

FACTS   Diehr filed a patent application for a process for molding raw, uncured synthetic rubber into cured precision products. Diehr claimed its invention ensured the production of molded articles that were properly cured by a process that fed temperatures inside mold presses into a computer. Repeated calculations of the cure time through use of a mathematical equation enabled the computer to signal a device to open the press at the proper time. Diehr contended that this process of measuring temperatures inside the mold cavity, feeding the information to a digital computer for constant recalculation of the cure time, and the signaling by the computer to open the press were all new in the art. The patent examiner characterized Diehr's claim as being based on a computer program for operating a rubber-molding process and thus rejected it as one predicated on nonstatutory subject matter. However, the Court of Customs and Patent Appeals reversed, owing to its view that Diehr's claim did not constitute a mathematical algorithm or an improved method of calculation but rather an improved process for molding rubber articles by solving a practical problem that had arisen in the molding of rubber products.

ISSUE   Was a process for curing synthetic rubber that included in several of its steps the use of a mathematical formula and a programmed digital computer patentable subject matter?

HOLDING   Yes. Because Diehr was not attempting to patent a mathematical formula but instead an industrial process that implemented or applied that mathematical formula as a means of transforming or reducing an article to a different state or thing, Diehr's claim constituted patentable subject matter under the Patent Act.

REASONING   Answering this issue involved construing Section 101 of the patent laws, which provides: "Whoever invents or discovers any new and useful process, machine, manufacture, or composition of matter, or any new and useful improvement thereof, may obtain a patent therefor, subject to the conditions and requirements of this title." Earlier cases had defined a "process" as an act or series or acts performed on the subject matter to be transformed and reduced to a different state or thing. If new and useful, these cases had declared, a process was just as patentable as a piece of machinery; and it mattered not whether the machinery suitable for performing the process was new or patentable. Therefore, industrial processes such as Diehr's were among the types that had historically been eligible to receive the protection of the patent laws. The fact that several steps of the process had used a mathematical equation and a programmed digital computer would not alter this conclusion. Even though mathematical formulas, like laws of nature, natural phenomena, and abstract ideas, are nonpatentable subject matter, Diehr had not sought to patent a mathematical formula; rather, Diehr had requested patent protection for a process of curing synthetic rubber. And, although Diehr's process had employed a well-known mathematical equation, Diehr had not endeavored to preempt (or foreclose from others) the use of that equation except in conjunction with all the other steps in the claimed process. In addition, a claim encompassing subject matter otherwise statutory would not become nonstatutory simply because it had used a mathematical formula, computer program, or digital computer. The engrafting of Section 102's requirement of novelty and Section 103's requirement of nonobviousness onto Section 101's last phrase was unnecessary; hence, a rejection of patent protection on either of these grounds would not affect the determination of whether the invention fell into a category of protectable subject matter under Section 101. Whenever a claim containing a mathematical formula implements or applies that formula in a structure or process that, when considered as a whole, is performing a function the patent laws were designed to protect (i.e., transforming or reducing an article to a different state or thing), the claim satisfies Section 101. Because Diehr's claim was not an attempt to patent a mathematical formula but rather a claim involving an industrial process for the molding of rubber products, the judgment of the Court of Customs and Patent Appeals was affirmed.

Compiler program One that converts a high-level programming language into binary or machine code.

Note that *Diamond* v. *Diehr* involved the question of the patentability of a computer program used as an integral part of a machine. A subsequent CCPA decision, *In re Pardo*,[17] answered the question of whether a **compiler program**, one designed to translate source code to object code, could alone constitute patentable subject matter by holding that it could.

Trade Secrets

We have already seen some of the limitations on protection of software under copyright law (only the written expression of the software and not the ideas embodied in it are protectable) and patent law (strict compliance with statutory requirements is necessary for patentability). However, various state and common law doctrines, such as trade secrets, unfair competition, and misappropriation, may apply to certain aspects of software, including know-how, information, and ideas, and thus encompass concepts too nebulous for copyright or patent protection. These doctrines may cover computer hardware as well.

According to the *Restatement (First) of Torts,* Section 757, Comment (b), a trade secret may include:

> any formula, pattern, device or compilation of information which is used in one's business, and which gives [one] an opportunity to obtain an advantage over competitors who do not know or use it. The subject matter of a trade secret must be secret. . . . so that, except by the use of improper means, there would be difficulty in acquiring the information. In determining whether given information is a trade secret courts generally consider:
>
> 1. The extent to which the information is known outside the owner's business
> 2. The extent to which it is known by employees and others involved in the business
> 3. The extent of measures taken by the owner to guard the secrecy of the information
> 4. The value of the information to the owner and to its competitors
> 5. The amount of effort or money expended by the owner in developing the information
> 6. The ease or difficulty with which the information could be properly acquired or duplicated by others.

The owner of software who decides to resort to trade secret protection may find it advantageous, since it avoids the public registration required to devise and enforce rights under the patent and copyright laws.[18] However, because maintaining the secrecy of the proprietary information in question may be

[17]684 F.2d 912 (CCPA 1982).
[18]*Kewanee Oil Co.* v. *Bicron Corp.,* 416 U.S. 470 (1974), held that federal patent laws do not preempt state trade secret laws.

difficult and because lack of secrecy constitutes one of the primary defenses to a charge of trade secret misappropriation, the owner of the trade secret should implement various mechanisms to ensure secrecy. Actions that employers can take to protect trade secrets about software (or hardware) include the creation of nondisclosure, noncompete, and confidentiality agreements with employees. Employers should also limit physical access to areas where the development of **proprietary** software is taking place as well as to storage areas. All software and documents containing trade secrets should bear proprietary labels, and the software should use **encrypted code** so that only those who have the key for unscrambling it can make the program intelligible. Constant reminders to employees about secrecy obligations and exit interviews with departing employees regarding the information the company considers proprietary constitute recommended policies for employers intent on ensuring secrecy as well.

Proprietary Characterized by private, exclusive ownership.

Encrypted code Code typed in one set of symbols and interpreted by the machine as another; used for security.

The licensing of software mandates special steps by the owner of the software in order to preserve secrecy. Besides restricting disclosures by the licensee, the licensor/owner should limit the rights the licensee retains in the software by virtue of the license, prohibit copying except for use or archival purposes, formulate special coding techniques to identify misappropriated software, distribute the software in object code as opposed to source code, and stipulate that the breach of any confidentiality provision will result in the immediate termination of the licensing agreement.

Courts in fact base trade secret protection on several theories—property, contract, and tort—although courts prefer to utilize the latter two in deciding disputes about computer software. (Indeed, courts often apply the two theories interchangeably.) It is easier for a court to discern a relationship between the owner of the trade secret and the person or entity using or disclosing the trade secret than it is for a court to ascribe property concepts to the trade secret because of the difficulty of determining where general information (which is unprotectable) leaves off and proprietary information in the form of the trade secret (which is protectable) begins. Courts often derive these relationships impliedly from the parties' status as employer/employee, vendor/buyer, and the like. However, the parties cannot enjoy a confidential relationship unless a protectable trade secret first exists. Once it does, though, the trade secret may last perpetually until the owner loses the differential advantage it affords. This loss may occur through another party's independent discovery of the secret or any other legitimate means, such as reverse engineering or the public dissemination of the knowledge underlying the trade secret through either a failure to keep the information secret or flaws in the methods the owner has employed to ensure secrecy. Mass distribution of software copies to those with whom the software owner has a confidential relationship generally does not eliminate trade secret protection as long as the owner has otherwise taken precautions to preserve secrecy.

Note how the court used many of these principles in deciding the next case.

ISC–Bunker Ramo Corporation v. Altech, Inc.
765 F. Supp. 1310 (N.D. Ill. 1990)

FACTS ISC-Bunker Ramo Corporation (ISC) produces complex computer systems specifically intended for financial institutions such as banks and savings and loans. ISC designs, manufactures, installs, updates, maintains, and services these systems. ISC invests a substantial amount of money not only on the original design of its systems, but also on the continual update, refinement, and improvement of those systems. In this manner, ISC seeks to make its systems the most efficient, the most reliable, and, thus, the most desirable to the financial community. ISC designed what is referred to in the industry as a "proprietary architecture" computer system, which means that ISC did not make the design of its computer system available to outsiders so that they could create software to run on the system. While most of the component parts used as the "building blocks" of the ISC computers are generally available on the open market, the design of the use and interrelationships of the components is original to ISC and is kept confidential. ISC also creates original computer programs to operate its computer systems. Since 1970, ISC has developed five basic computer systems. The development of new hardware systems requires the development of new software, and developments in software design in turn allow new hardware to be designed to take advantage of the additional software capability. Consequently, as ISC developed each new computer system, it had to develop new software to operate those systems and various kinds of software for each system. As ISC's computer hardware evolved, the diagnostic software had also undergone modification and redesign. In addition to hardware and software, ISC's "product support" group had had to develop the tools and expertise necessary to support the installation, repair, maintenance, and improvement of ISC's hardware systems and software. Among other things, they developed all the service manuals and technical bulletins on how to install, repair, maintain, and upgrade ISC computer systems. They also developed and implemented extensive formal training programs and procedures in order to teach the conventionally skilled computer service engineer all the special knowledge, skills, and procedures he or she would need in order to work with ISC's systems. Since the service manuals for ISC's computer hardware were far too voluminous for ready access and use, ISC's support engineers created a separate compilation containing the technical information from all the service manuals that a field service engineer would most commonly need in performing installation, repair, and maintenance services. This compilation, called the Field Service Pocket Reference Guide (sometimes referred to as The Guide), had gone through several revisions to accommodate the changes and updates to ISC's computer systems. ISC's training school issued and used ISC's field service manuals and The Guide as reference materials. Each course outline detailed the ISC reference manuals to be used in that training curriculum. ISC invested still more time, effort, and resources in the development of its service manuals, The Guide, and its continuing programs to isolate and solve service and maintenance problems, which are reflected in the updated versions of the service manuals and The Guide. Altech, Inc. (Altech) had copied The Guide, had hired ex-ISC employees in violation of their employment agreements, and had unlawfully obtained and used ISC's diagnostic software. ISC claimed that Altech's actions amount to misappropriation of trade secrets and therefore sought a preliminary injunction against Altech.

ISSUE In these circumstances, should a court issue a preliminary injunction prohibiting Altech from misappropriating ISC's trade secrets?

HOLDING Yes. ISC had established the likelihood of prevailing on the merits of its claims that Altech had been misappropriating trade secrets; that Altech would continue to misappropriate, use, and disclose trade secrets unless enjoined by a court; and that, without an injunction, ISC stood to lose the value of its trade secrets, which ISC had developed at enormous cost over many years.

REASONING ISC's Guide, service manuals, and technical bulletins comprised compilations of valuable technical information and procedures. ISC compiled them at great effort and expense, and they represented extremely useful tools for its business. Thus, these compilations fall squarely with the Illinois statutory definition of a trade secret. The compilations would constitute trade secrets of ISC even if ISC had not developed virtually all the technical information and procedures set forth in them. The effort of compiling useful information is, in and of itself, entitled to protection even if the information is otherwise generally known. But here, ISC also developed virtually all the technical information and procedures set forth in its compilations. That information and those procedures, independently, constituted ISC trade secrets. The voluminousness and vastness of this information did not detract from its status as a trade secret; rather, these facts merely confirmed the huge and continual effort by ISC to create the information and procedure in the first instance. ISC moreover undertook reasonable efforts to keep its compilations, technical information, and procedures from becoming generally known outside of ISC and those third parties who by contract (i.e., license), custom, and usage or by fiduciary duty remained obligated not to use or disclose such information in the absence of ISC's consent. ISC does not distribute its service manuals or technical bulletins to its customers, except for those customers who are on ISC's self-maintenance program and have confidentiality agreements with ISC. The Guide is never given to a customer. The customers receive only "user guides" that tell them how to use the equipment. They do not receive the extensive manuals and information on how to install, maintain, repair, and upgrade the systems. ISC has similarly taken reasonable efforts to maintain the secrecy of the design and logic of its computer programs. ISC's computer programs are distributed only in object code, which is not intelligible to human beings. ISC tightly controls the source code for ISC's IDOS programs and its workstation and branch concentrator operating systems. Access to IDOS source code is limited to a select number of employees in ISC's headquarters. The IDOS source code is not sent to ISC employees in the field, nor is it provided to third parties. Source code for ISC's other operating systems is also maintained in ISC's headquarters, and access is similarly restricted. ISC's efforts to maintain the secrecy of its service manual, The Guide, the technical information and procedures contained therein, and its computer programs have been not only reasonable but successful as well. ISC has more than 2500 customers, many of whom have multiple locations. ISC has more than 1000 employees and hundreds of field service engineers and support personnel. Nonetheless, as the evidence shows, ISC's secrecy measures have been sufficient to cause the industry to acknowledge that ISC's computer systems and its software are "proprietary." Other than ISC's proprietary publications and software, there are no readily available sources for the information, technology, and procedures contained within ISC's service manuals, The Guide, or ISC's software. Altech's own conduct confirmed that ISC's procedures have been successful. Altech admitted that it does not have any service manuals for ISC's computer systems except for The Guide. Altech acknowledged that it had "found" only one copy of The Guide and then had made copies of it for each of Altech's field service engineers. The copy that Altech conceded it had had contained "proprietary" notices, which Altech had unsuccessfully attempted to obliterate in the process of copying and then redistributing it to Altech's employees. Similarly, the information in ISC's computer programs, including the programs' logic and design, was not generally known. Altech conceded that it does not know that information and does not create its own programs. Rather, Altech unlawfully obtained, copied, and distributed ISC's programs to Altech employees. Altech also hired ex-ISC employees, who had been extensively trained by ISC. In this manner, Altech had available to it, and to all of its field service engineers, the most current ISC technology relating to the most current ISC computer systems. Although Altech had attempted at the hearing to find and focus on "leaks" in ISC's security procedures, in order to demonstrate that such procedures were not "reasonable," the evidence showed the contrary. ISC's technology remains generally perceived in the industry as "proprietary," and Altech had to obtain and disseminate that information in an unauthorized fashion. Moreover, the evidence showed that Altech had copied The Guide, had provided it to at least ten ex-ISC employees, had unlawfully obtained and used ISC's diagnostic software, and had hired ex-ISC employees—in direct violation of these employees' employment agreements—rather than engage in its own research, development, and training programs. The evidence therefore demonstrated that ISC has suffered and will continue to suffer irreparable injury for which it has no adequate remedy at law unless Altech is preliminarily enjoined from infringing ISC's copyrighted works. ISC's efforts to maintain the confidentiality of its trade secrets, which were not generally known, have been reasonable and have successfully preserved their trade secret status. ISC's partial disclosures to third parties who are under obligations of confidentiality do not alter the trade secret status of ISC's computer programs, compilations, technical information, and procedures. Altech's contention that ISC's trade secrets had not been sufficiently confidential, or that Altech had not known that ISC had considered and treated its computer programs, compilations, technical information, and procedures as confidential remained untenable, particularly since Altech had intentionally obliterated ISC's "proprietary" legends from The Guide before copying and disseminating it to ex-ISC employees, among others. Hence, the balance of hardships would favor ISC. Without an injunction, it stood to lose the value of its trade secrets that it had developed at enormous cost over many years. Altech had no equitable standing to complain of being deprived of the use of information, manuals, software, and procedures that it had had no right to use and appropriate in the first instance. Altech made no investment in generating those materials and information and knew that the ISC employees it had hired had been obligated to keep all such matters confidential. The public interest therefore favored the issuance of an injunction. The purpose behind the Uniform Trade Secrets Act is to foster the development of new technology. That purpose is achieved by protecting the investment of companies like ISC that undertake to do so. ISC therefore has met all the prerequisites to merit preliminary injunctive relief on its trade secret claims.

Unfair Competition

Although our system of law allows rather free-wheeling activities in the name of "competition," some conduct goes so far beyond reasonable that courts will give remedies to those injured by such activities as soliciting a former employer's customers or employees, an employee's competing with his or her employer while still in the employ of the latter, wrongful terminations by the employer, and "palming off" one's goods as those of another.[19] The common law and statutory restrictions on "unfair competition" often form the legal bases on which aggrieved persons sue in these circumstances. Misappropriation, another basis for relief, derives from the common law principles of unfair competition and often becomes a "catch-all" theory used in situations in which patent, copyright, and trade secret law do not cover the aspect of the business in dispute. In the context of computer software, then, courts may find actionable misappropriation if the plaintiff has invested substantial amounts of time and money in developing the software (that is, a property interest is present) and the defendant has appropriated the software with a minimum of effort and expense to the injury of the plaintiff. Courts are sensitive to the time and effort necessary to develop software systems and, thus, during litigation (under the so-called head start doctrine) sometimes issue injunctions against a competitor's use of the software for at least the time it would have taken the competitor to develop the software independently.

However, this area of the law remains unsettled because of the ambiguities arising from fairly recent Supreme Court holdings and the 1976 Copyright Act. Under the so-called *Sears-Compco* doctrine,[20] even though the states retain an interest in preventing their citizens from being misled as to the source of the goods, state unfair competition laws cannot impose liability for, or prohibit the copying of, unpatented or uncopyrighted items. Thus, in certain cases federal law preempts state law claims based on unfair competition doctrines. But these decisions leave us with scant guidance as to when this

[19]Scott, *Computer Law*, at 5-26–27. Copyright © 1984 John Wiley & Sons, Inc.
[20]*Sears, Roebuck & Co.* v. *Stiffel Co.*, 376 U.S. 225 (1964); *Compco Corporation* v. *Day-Brite Lighting, Inc.*, 376 U.S. 234 (1964).

preemption occurs. Similarly, the 1976 Copyright Act provides for the preemption of state law whenever state law creates legal or equitable rights that are equivalent to any of the exclusive rights enumerated under certain provisions of the Act.[21] Yet courts are split on the issue of when to apply the preemption doctrine in cases of alleged unfair competition and misappropriation. Caution is therefore warranted in these areas.

The Semiconductor Chip Protection Act of 1984

Congress's enactment of the Semiconductor Chip Protection Act of 1984, which took effect on 8 January 1985,[22] as an amendment to the copyright laws, affords developers of integrated circuits a ten-year monopoly over their resultant semiconductor chips. Although it contains ideas common to copyright, patent, and trade secret law, this act creates a new class of intellectual property law. Congress directed the legislation at chip pirates (both domestic and international), who in the past had merely taken chips apart, reconstructed the circuit design on the chip (known as the mask), and then made copies of the original chip. Obviously, as long as copyright law did not protect semiconductor chips (they were deemed utilitarian/useful articles and hence uncopyrightable even though the circuit diagrams might be), the incentive for pirates to reap profits by copying while at the same time avoiding the mammoth costs associated with developing the chips clearly existed. The act eliminates this result by prohibiting reverse engineering that has as its end purpose the copying of the chip but preserves current law by allowing reverse engineering leading to the creation of a new chip.[23]

The act itself protects only mask works, or the layouts of the integrated circuits that appear on the chips; it does not protect the semiconductor chips themselves, any other product that performs the function of chips (such as circuit boards), or works embodied in mask works (such as computer programs).[24] Indeed, not all mask works are protected either. For instance, if the mask work is not "fixed" in a semiconductor chip (as would be the case in information merely stored on diskettes) or if, analogous to the patent law's requirements of novelty and nonobviousness, the mask work embodies designs that are commonplace and unoriginal, the act would be inapplicable.[25]

The duration of the protection is ten years from the time of registration or the first commercial exploitation of the mask work, whichever occurs first.[26] The process of registration contains special procedures for protecting proprietary information. The same remedies generally available under the copyright laws relating to infringement (injunctions, damages, attorneys' fees, and import exclusion and seizure) apply in this context, except that criminal sanc-

[21]17 U.S.C. Section 301 (West 1985).
[22]Ibid. at Section 913(a).
[23]Ibid. at Section 906.
[24]Scott, *Computer Law,* at 12-9. Copyright © 1984 John Wiley & Sons, Inc.
[25]Ibid. at 12-10.
[26]17 U.S.C. Section 904(a), (b) (West 1985).

tions are unavailable.[27] Some provisions of the act protect the mask works of nonpirating foreign companies under certain circumstances as well. Although interpretive questions undoubtedly will arise as the first cases begin to appear under this act, you should particularly note this statute because it represents the first federal intellectual property law in over one hundred years. One recent case that interpreted this act follows.

Brooktree Corporation v. *Advanced Micro Devices, Inc.*
757 F. Supp. 1088 (S.D. Cal. 1990)

FACTS   Brooktree Corporation (Brooktree) is a California corporation in the business of designing, manufacturing, and selling semiconductor chip products used in computer graphic displays. Advanced Micro Devices, Inc. (AMD) is a competitor and one of the five largest manufacturers of chip products in the United States, with sales almost thirty times that of Brooktree. Brooktree originally brought this action for infringement of mask works by AMD. Brooktree alleged that between 1981 and 1986, it had invested approximately $3.8 million in developing integrated circuit chips that convert digital graphics image information to analog information at high frequencies for display on very high resolution computer video screens. It further claimed that its chip had captured this niche market previously dominated by AMD. Brooktree asserted that AMD had introduced pirated chips at lower prices in an attempt to recapture its lost market. These pirated chips allegedly consisted of copies of two of Brooktree's chips, which represented 40 percent of Brooktree's sales. Brooktree submitted that AMD's unlawful conduct had caused irreparable injury, including damages of over $2,753,000 in the previous six months; lost sales; and lost ability to expand or go public owing to lost profits. It further claimed that its total $30 million investment since 1981 was in jeopardy, as the firm had only recently reached profitability and thus did not have the strength to weather the loss of sales stemming from AMD's conduct. Finally, Brooktree alleged that AMD's pirating had damaged Brooktree's other products, as Brooktree had been forced to cut the cost of all its chips in order to keep its cost structure in line. The jury found AMD liable on all but one of the patent claims and on all the mask work claims; the jury also concluded that AMD's infringement of Brooktree's patents had been willful. The jury then awarded damages of over $25 million to Brooktree. AMD subsequently brought a motion for judgment notwithstanding the verdict (JNOV) or, in the alternative, for a new trial, based on several grounds, including the allegations that no reasonable jury could have found that AMD had failed to prove its reverse engineering defense and that no reasonable jury could have found that Brooktree had proved mask work infringement.

ISSUE   Did the circumstances warrant a judgment notwithstanding the verdict (JNOV) in this case?

HOLDING   No. AMD had failed to prove its reverse engineering defense under the Semiconductor Chip Act. Moreover, a reasonable jury could have found that AMD had willfully infringed Brooktree's patents. Hence, a JNOV would be inappropriate.

REASONING   When a party moves for JNOV, the trial court must consider all the evidence in the light most favorable to the nonmover, must draw reasonable inferences favorable to the nonmover, must not determine the credibility of witnesses, and must not substitute its own choice for that of the jury between conflicting elements in evidence. Thus, JNOV is proper only if the evidence permits only one reasonable conclusion as to the verdict. Conversely, the trial court must deny the motion if reasonable minds could differ over the verdict; in short, the court should grant the motion only if it is firmly convinced that reasonable people could not have reached the verdict brought in by the jury. Defendant

---

[27]Ibid. at Sections 910 and 911. The act also contains a statutory damages provision (the amount awarded cannot exceed more than $250,000) as an alternative to a lawsuit for actual damages.

AMD argued that no substantial evidence would support the jury's mask work verdict and that its "condemnation" of AMD's reverse engineering would run counter to the purpose of the Semiconductor Chip Act (the Chip Act). The crux of AMD's argument included the following: (1) Where reverse engineering has been shown, the test for determining infringement is whether the mask work is substantially identical to the registered mask work. (2) Given the evidence of AMD's photographic analysis of one of the chips in question, BT451, its introduction of a "second source product" that had directly competed with Brooktree's device, and its substantial investment in developing this second source product (along with an accompanying paper trail), no reasonable jury could find that AMD had failed to prove its reverse engineering defense. (3) AMD's mask work, given the over fifty differences between the two mask works, had not been substantially identical to Brooktree's mask work. Brooktree, in answer to AMD's reverse engineering argument, argued first that the Chip Act prohibits more than the production of perfect copies of patented mask works and allows the production of reverse engineered mask works only if the resulting product is an "original." Brooktree also noted that AMD had already presented its reverse engineering defense to the jury, that Brooktree had strongly contested at least two of the elements of that defense (whether the AMD analysis of Brooktree's mask work had constituted the type contemplated by the Chip Act and whether the mask works were "original"), and that the jury had received AMD's instruction regarding the reverse engineering defense. In Brooktree's view, the jury simply had decided that Brooktree's arguments and evidence had been stronger and that AMD had failed in its attempt to prove its reverse engineering defense. Given these facts, AMD had not made out a case for the granting of the JNOV on these grounds. AMD also had asked for a JNOV on the issue of willfulness, arguing that Brooktree had not proved by clear and convincing evidence that AMD's infringement had been willful. In so arguing, AMD maintained that because it had learned of the patent only at the onset of this litigation and because its defenses had lacked frivolousness, as a matter of law its infringement of the Brooktree patents had not been willful. It is clear, as a matter of law and logic, that AMD could not be held to have willfully infringed the Brooktree patents before it became aware of them. However, once it had become aware of these patents, whether or not AMD's continued production constituted willful infringement depended on the "totality of the circumstances." The circumstances to be considered do include the continued production of the allegedly infringing products during the course of the litigation. Thus, although it is not a universal rule that continued manufacture of the product leads to a conclusion of willfulness, such manufacture constitutes evidence to be considered in making that determination. The same is true of the failure to seek a legal opinion as to the validity and infringement of the Brooktree patents once AMD had been put on notice. During the course of the trial, both parties had presented evidence on the willfulness issue, including evidence regarding the time at which AMD had become aware of Brooktree's patents and whether AMD had held a good-faith belief in the validity and infringement of those patents. Given "the totality of the circumstances" standard, the evidence presented during trial, and the jury's instructions reflecting the case law, a reasonable jury could have found that AMD had willfully infringed Brooktree's patents. Accordingly, AMD's motion for a JNOV on the issue of willfulness must be denied.

CONTRACT LAW

**General
Considerations**

Since the law of contracts concerning computers theoretically should vary little from contracting for any other kind of equipment or goods, you should be fairly familiar with this dimension of computer law from our discussions in Parts 2 and 3 of this text. In practice, however, computer-related contract law encompasses some pitfalls not common to the rest of contract law due to the technology, the structure of the computer industry, and the relationship

Boilerplate Standard contract language found in all instruments of a like nature.

between the vendor and the purchaser. For instance, vendors of computers especially benefit from the **boilerplate** phrases you have encountered in our earlier examination of contract principles because the wide array of mainframes, minis, and micros (PCs)—not to mention the numerous peripherals—may overwhelm even the bravest soul.

Choosing a computer, as you know, can be a very intimidating experience. Hence, when the sales representative presents you with a preprinted standard form contract containing confusing and ambiguous jargon, you may lack the knowledge and familiarity with computers to enable you to question or interpret its provisions. Moreover, since the relationship between the vendor and buyer presupposes continuity (in that the vendor typically assumes the responsibility for the ongoing maintenance of the hardware and software), adding to the buyer's worries is the fact that the vendor may go out of business in the future and thus fail to provide the maintenance responsibilities contemplated in their initial agreement. To use the jargon of the industry, the "shakeouts" that have caused major companies (including Xerox, General Electric, and RCA), as well as numerous other producers of mainframes, micros, minis, and PCs to leave the industry, reinforce a buyer's apprehensions. And, in some cases, the buyer's virtual dependence on the computer for the firm's survival as a business places even more of a burden on the purchaser, since a series of computer malfunctions (or "system crashes") may lead eventually to the firm's bankruptcy and dissolution. Thus, we cannot emphasize enough the importance of understanding in advance your firm's (or your personal) current and future data processing needs.

If the purchase of a system is afoot, senior executive and technical people (or a hired consultant), in addition to an attorney who has experience in computer contracts, should spearhead this effort by ascertaining such information as the computer's slowest acceptable response time, the highest number of customers for the next ten years, or the largest number of pages of information needed within any twenty-four hour period of time. Once the buyer has defined the minimum and maximum requirements of the system, ordinarily the buyer sends requests for proposals to potential vendors. Negotiations—sometimes long and drawn out—usually follow. If the parties can reach agreement on these and other issues, the vendor and buyer then enter into a contract reflecting those terms and the schedule for implementing the contract. In addition to price and the items and services the vendor must provide, including hardware, software, and maintenance, the contract should list the payment schedule (with the final payment's being contingent on the system's being properly installed, thoroughly tested, and fully operational); the functional specifications of the system's elements; a timetable for each aspect of the system mentioned in the contract (including remedies for failure to live up to the timetable); acceptable testing procedures for each element of the system; and general remedies covering each party's failure to perform completely all the steps enumerated in the contract.

Once the contract embodies the phases contemplated by the parties, the contract itself becomes the document to which the parties (especially the buyer) can resort for guidance during the implementation phase. Finally, the contract should set out the terms of the parties' relationship during the post-acceptance portion of the contract. This is reached when the system is up and functioning in accordance with the contractual provisions but during which the buyer's use may necessitate maintenance or other support services by the vendor. One who plans to lease rather than purchase the system should take into account the foregoing general considerations and in addition bear in mind the contract's assignment provisions; the existence of "hell or high water" clauses (those stating that the vendor or lessor's default will not release the buyer or lessee from its unconditional obligation to pay according to the terms of the contract); terms relating to maintenance and return condition; taxes, loss, and insurance responsibilities; purchase options; and so forth.[28]

The Uniform Commercial Code

As we saw in Part 3 of this text, the Uniform Commercial Code (UCC) in Article Two applies to transactions in goods. Generally, this means sales of goods, or "all things (including specially manufactured goods) which are movable at the time of identification to the contract for sale."[29] Computer hardware is clearly a type of goods. This remains true even though the transactions relating to hardware may also involve the provision of services, such as installation, training, and maintenance. As long as the "goods" component of the transaction predominates over the "services" aspect, most courts allow the Code to cover the transaction. The law is not as clear, however, with regard to software, since software ordinarily involves both tangible property (the medium on which the software is stored) and the previously mentioned services. In this case, courts make distinctions based on the types of software: bundled (whether prewritten or custom) and unbundled. Bundled software refers to the practice of selling computer hardware, software, and support services for one price. (Bundling, because it may violate the antitrust laws in that buyers or lessees who do not want certain components of the bundling must nonetheless pay the full price, is not as common as it once was.)

Courts also split on whether Article Two of the Code covers leases of equipment and software licenses, but in general courts will more readily apply Article Two in the former context than in the latter. The warranty provisions of the Code involving express warranties and the implied warranty of merchantability ordinarily apply to computer hardware and software. The implied warranty of fitness for a particular purpose, which usually involves the buyer's reliance on the seller to furnish or select suitable goods and the seller's knowledge of the buyer's particular purpose, may in a given case be especially relevant to transactions involving hardware and software. Although the UCC

---

[28]Scott, *Computer Law*, at 6-17. Copyright © 1984 John Wiley & Sons, Inc.
[29]Uniform Commercial Code, Section 2-105.

permits the exclusion of warranties in certain circumstances, courts are sometimes hostile to these attempted exclusions. Thus, both vendor and buyer should check carefully any purported warranty disclaimers. "Shrink-wrap" or "box-top" licenses, through which vendors attempt to limit the further distribution of their software sold in retail stores by placing a copy of the licensing agreement inside the package, pose similar problems of enforceability for vendors, since courts may deem these agreements adhesion contracts because of the lack of any meaningful bargaining power on the purchaser's part.

Buyers also may utilize the remedies sections of the UCC, namely rejection and revocation of acceptance, for example; and on breach of the contract (by the vendor's negligent performance or complete nonperformance of the contract) may sue the vendor for damages, including incidental and consequential damages if warranted by the circumstances. Vendors may in general limit these remedies by contract unless a court subsequently construes the limitation as unconscionable or the remedy fails of its essential purpose. Nonetheless, reasonable liquidated damages clauses, whereby the parties agree in advance that upon breach a certain sum of money will be paid to the injured party, seem particularly appropriate in computer contracts because losses accruing from late delivery, nondelivery, or malfunctions involve damages that are by definition difficult to determine with certainty beforehand. Courts also may order specific performance, injunctive relief, restitution, rescission, and replevin in a given case.

TORT LAW

Although there are comparatively few cases involving tort law in the computer field, as we learned in Chapter 3, tort law can form the basis for civil (as opposed to criminal) liability. Vendors of computers, then, may become the objects of lawsuits alleging negligence, intentional torts (such as conversion, defamation, fraud, and invasion of privacy), and strict liability. Defective hardware or improperly designed software; negligent use of a computer in circumstances in which a third party relies on computer-generated data and as a result suffers losses; and negligent nonuse of a computer in such areas as air or railroad traffic control, stock trading, and hospital care may lead to liability as well if losses ensue. Thus, failure to acquire sufficient insurance coverage based on an appraisal that used computer-generated, incorrect data may lead to the imposition of liability for damages incurred as a result of the failure to act. But whether computer programmers are professionals and thus potentially liable under malpractice theories remains an open question.

However, the law is clearer in other contexts. For example, computer salespersons must be careful not to become overly zealous in their representations about the system's capabilities because such statements, coupled with the seller's knowledge that the statements are false and the buyer's justifiable reliance on the representations to his or her detriment, may leave the vendor open to liability under fraud. The damages courts have awarded in fraud cases have even included punitive damages. The intentional tort of conversion occurs whenever former employees appropriate computer programs owned by their former employers. Similarly, court actions involving defamation can possibly derive from computer messages displayed on terminals and perhaps even from mathematical configurations as long as their defamatory content is discernible and no privilege covers the generation of the information. Credit reporting agencies should take special care in this context.

In addition to such intentional torts, defectively manufactured computer equipment may give rise to strict liability as well. The health care profession's increasing reliance on sophisticated computerized equipment exposes both the profession and the manufacturer to liability if, for instance, a CAT scanner or intensive-care monitoring equipment should malfunction. The imposition of strict liability in situations involving only economic harm as opposed to personal injury may be more questionable, however.

STATUTORY PROTECTION

The common law theories that we have just examined are fully applicable to computers and have enriched the legal environment of this important industry. But legislative enactments relating to privacy, antitrust, and criminal law represent increasingly significant sources of law for this area as well.

Invasion of Privacy

Invasion of privacy, although it may give rise to liability under intentional tort common law theories, is more appropriately discussed in the statutory context. But even though numerous statutes concern themselves with this subject nowadays, the concept of privacy, jealously guarded by each of us individually, has evolved slowly in the law. Indeed, the Constitution does not even mention the term. The Supreme Court did not recognize the concept until the mid-1960s, but since that time Congress has enacted several significant privacy laws that affect not only us as citizens but also the computer industry:

—Freedom of Information Act—with some exceptions, opens up federal governmental records to public inspection

—Fair Credit Reporting Act of 1970—regulates the information practices of consumer reporting agencies like credit bureaus and the practices of those who use these reports

—Family Educational Rights and Privacy Act of 1974—affords parents of dependent students and students over eighteen the right to inspect, correct, and control somewhat the disclosure of information in educational records

—Privacy Act of 1974—assures informational privacy in computerized record-keeping systems by agencies of the executive branch, independent regulatory agencies, and the Federal Reserve Bank and provides remedies for violations including injunctive relief, damages, and attorneys' fees as well as criminal sanctions

—Right to Financial Privacy Act of 1978—specifies the circumstances in which the government, including the Internal Revenue Service, can gain access to individuals and partnerships' financial records and sets out the civil remedies available against violators

—Electronic Fund Transfer Act of 1978—regulates the rights, liabilities, and responsibilities of participants in electronic fund transfer systems in order to promote individual consumers' rights and makes available civil and criminal remedies for violations.[30]

These laws attempt to balance individuals' rights to privacy with the government's and other institutions' legitimate needs to collect and maintain information about people by guaranteeing to these individuals the right to know how other entities are using information about them and by protecting the individual from unwarranted or excessive collection or dissemination of personal information. And although it has always been difficult to safeguard privacy, the pervasity of high-speed, low-cost computers in businesses and homes has elevated computer-related privacy violations to a national concern.

Intrusion, whether by unauthorized access to a data base contained on one's computer, unwanted collection of data on one's personal habits or lifestyle, or unauthorized removal of data from a computer, either electronically or manually (through the removal of the software containing the data from the system itself), is one type of violation. The emergence of "hackers" or "electronic vandals" who engage in such activities for amusement has occupied the public press's attention for the last few years. Besides intrusion, interception of information consisting of unauthorized access by an employee or other person at the computer site, unauthorized access from a different location through a remote terminal, or monitoring and interception of information flowing between computers raise additional privacy issues.

Finally, the existence of large aggregations of information in the form of tax, credit, military, medical, employment, and governmental records (such as census tracts and vital statistics) leaves open the possible misuse of infor-

---

[30]Scott, *Computer Law,* at 7-39–43; 48–50. Copyright © 1984 John Wiley & Sons, Inc.

mation. In this context, you may have already experienced the annoyances that result when a group to which you belong sells your name and address to another entity. As we have already seen in the coverage of specific statutes, corollaries of this potential problem of misuse are the individual's right to be informed of the content of the information being maintained about him or her (including who has access to it) and the right to correct erroneous information contained in the data files. This aspect of privacy also covers the right of the individual to demand that certain information (say, credit ratings) be included in these records to facilitate the individual's daily affairs. Because the technology itself makes such storage and retrieval of information speedy and relatively cheap and because existing technology allows the storage of a twenty-page dossier on every American on a magnetic tape less than a mile long, the safeguards mentioned earlier of limiting access to these data and assuring mechanisms to correct erroneous information and to eliminate "stale" information become all the more significant.

Antitrust Law

Besides privacy statutes, the federal and state antitrust statutes we examined in Chapter 46 also may cover the activities of firms in the computer field. For instance, the Sherman Act prohibits price fixing, group boycotts, monopolization, tying arrangements, and certain wrongful terminations of distributors. The Clayton Act augments this extensive federal regulatory scheme by also prohibiting tie-ins and certain exclusive dealing arrangements as well as mergers that would substantially lessen competition or tend to create a monopoly. Bundling, or the practice of selling a number of products or services for a single price, may raise antitrust concerns if courts construe the practice as an illegal tying arrangement. To constitute such an arrangement there must be two separate and distinct products, and the seller must condition the sale of the desired product (the tying product) on the purchase of the less desirable product (the tied product). Generally, before courts will find violations of the antitrust laws, the seller must wield sufficient economic power in the market for the tying product to restrain competition appreciably in the market for the tied product, and the seller's activities must affect a not-insubstantial amount of commerce in that market. The Robinson-Patman Act prohibits price discrimination unless the price differential is cost justified or made in good faith to meet (but not beat) the price offered by a competitor. Similarly, the Federal Trade Commission Act makes illegal unfair methods of competition and unfair or deceptive trade practices in or affecting interstate commerce. The Supreme Court's recent sanctioning of the application of the Racketeer Influenced and Corrupt Organizations (RICO) Act in the civil law context holds wide-ranging implications for the possible imposition of liability in computer-related fields if, for example, a sales representative uses the mail or a telephone to engage in fraudulent representations about computer products.

The following case illustrates some of these points.

Digidyne Corporation v. Data General Corporation
734 F.2d 1336 (9th Cir. 1984), reh'g denied 473 U.S. 926 (1985)

FACTS

Central processing units The main units of the computer hardware that control the interpretation and execution of program instructions, including memory.

Data General Corporation (Data General) manufactured a computer system known as NOVA, consisting of NOVA **central processing units** (CPUs) designed to perform a particular "instruction set" or group of tasks and a copyrighted NOVA operating system called RDOS containing the basic commands for operating the system. Digidyne Corporation (Digidyne) produced NOVA CPUs designed to perform the NOVA instruction set and thus to make use of Data General's RDOS. Data General licensed its RDOS system only to purchasers of its own NOVA CPUs.

ISSUE

Did Data General's refusal to license its NOVA operating system software except to purchasers of its NOVA CPUs constitute an unlawful tying arrangement under Section One of the Sherman Act and Section Three of the Clayton Act?

HOLDING

Yes. Data General's copyright, its reliance on trade secrecy, and its policies gave it sufficient economic power over NOVA purchasers to constitute an illegal tie-in.

REASONING

The settled rule is that a tying arrangement is illegal if it unreasonably restrains competition or is illegal per se without the showing of an unreasonable restraint on competition if (1) the arrangement involves separate products and the purchase of the other (the tied product), (2) sufficient economic power with respect to the tying product to restrain competition appreciably in the tied product exists, and (3) the arrangement affects a substantial amount of commerce in the tied product. The evidence was persuasive, therefore, that Digidyne had proved a per se violation in this case. Moreover, proof of the seller's power to fix prices was not required to show per se illegality. Rather, what was required was the seller's special ability—usually called *market power* or *leverage*—to force a purchaser to do something it would not do in a competitive market. This need not consist of a restraint on competition that is substantial in terms of the entire market for the tied product but instead only that a substantial amount of volume (a dollar-volume that is more than *de minimus*) is foreclosed. Here, there was abundant evidence showing that Data General's RDOS was distinctive, particularly desirable to a number of buyers, and not readily reproducible by other sellers. The fact that the RDOS could not be produced without infringing Data General's copyright and utilizing Data General's trade secrets had satisfied the rule that the requisite economic power would be presumed when the tying product is patented or copyrighted. The fact that many of Data General's customers were also "locked into" the

Original equipment manufacturers (OEMs) A misnomer referring to vendors who assemble computer systems from components originally manufactured by other suppliers.

use of RDOS, since, as **original equipment manufacturers** (OEMs) they had combined RDOS and NOVA CPUs with their application software and thus could abandon their application software that was compatible with Data General's RDOS only at a substantial cost, had magnified Data General's leverage power. Data General's potential power to coerce had also been evident from its requiring all licensees either to purchase its CPUs and a set quantity of other peripheral hardware as a condition of receiving RDOS or to pay a program license charge, which was in the nature of a penalty. Hence, despite the availability of comparable or functionally equivalent operating systems, Data General's RDOS, which was available only from the defendant, had been sufficiently attractive to some customers to enable the defendant to require those who had wished to buy it also to buy from Data General NOVA instruction set CPUs they might otherwise have bought from others. Accordingly, this power had constituted evidence of an illegal tying arrangement under the Sherman and Clayton Acts.

Criminal Law

The criminal law also addresses computer-related crimes. For the imposition of criminal liability, the state or federal government must prove criminal intent and an act that violates a statute. In the late 1970s, as the first cases involving computer-related crimes arose, the coverage of many state laws failed to encompass such things as theft of computer time or services because the statutes in question applied only to the theft of tangible, not intangible, property. Another limitation on the imposition of liability flowed from many statutes' requirement that the theft involve something worth a particular dollar value. Consequently, it was difficult to say whether a given computer theft involved only the value of the paper (which would in most states merely amount to a misdemeanor) or instead the value of the intellectual property represented in the paper (which would sometimes amount to a felony whenever certain computer programs worth millions of dollars were involved). Nowadays, federal statutes and statutes in about three-fifths of the states address these issues in making theft of computer time and services actionable under the criminal law.

Fictitious payee A recipient of payments who has no right to the payments.

Unauthorized access by use of false pretenses or wiretapping for the purpose of committing criminal acts such as embezzlement constitute illegal acts in most jurisdictions. Similarly, instances of so-called data diddling, or the introduction of fraudulent data into a computer system for criminal purposes such as payments to a **fictitious payee** or through vandalism, as demonstrated by recent cases in which teenage "hackers" have invaded corporate and military files, violate criminal statutes. Crimes involving programming have spawned a variety of colorful names to describe the scams: "the Trojan Horse" (alteration of instructions in the program prior to the program's execution so that instructions self-destruct upon the program's execution); "the logic bomb" (an addition to a computer system timed to be executed at a scheduled moment to effect transfer of funds or to sabotage systems by erasing tapes or crashing the system); "the trapdoor" (compromises of a system effected by unauthorized access to passwords or the like); and "the salami technique" (hard-to-detect theft accomplished by "small slices," for example, by rounding down interest in accounts by minuscule amounts and depositing these amounts in the account of the perpetrator).[31] Many of these so-called computer "viruses" that can erase, alter, or destroy data and software have "infected" national research and business computer networks in recent years. Computer experts are currently working hard to develop failsafe "antidotes" for these "outbreaks." Estimates of the cost of computer crime range from $100 million to $3 billion per year.[32]

The physical destruction of data by disgruntled employees, political protestors, or terrorists, though usually covered by existing vandalism statutes, has resulted in the enactment of special statutes in many jurisdictions. The Counterfeit Access Device and Computer Fraud and Abuse Act of 12 October 1984 establishes criminal liability for unauthorized access to or use of a computer to obtain national security information or financial information protected by the Right to Financial Privacy Act or the Fair Credit Reporting Act. This law also criminalizes conduct used to modify or destroy information

[31]Ibid. at 8-10–11.
[32]Bureau of Justice, U.S. Department of Justice, *Computer Crime: Electronic Fund Transfer Systems and Crime* (Washington, D.C.: U.S. Government Printing Office, 1982), p. 83.

in or otherwise affect government computers or their operations. Although this enactment represents the first federal crime law dealing solely with computers per se, you should recall that numerous federal statutes, in addition to specific state laws covering computer-related crimes, apply directly or indirectly to these sorts of activities.

CONSTITUTIONAL LAW

You may remember that we discussed some of the constitutional aspects of the regulation of business in Chapter 45. The constitutional law dimensions of computers so far have received only slight attention. Nonetheless, you should be aware that the electronic publishing aspects of computer-related technologies (teletext and videotext systems, for example) raise not only privacy concerns of the type we examined earlier but also First Amendment issues. Should we regulate these systems as we would any other communications medium like television, or should we instead analogize these systems to newspapers, which we have traditionally exempted from governmental regulation?

Besides the First Amendment, the Fourth Amendment may apply to the computer industry as well. Although some precedents already exist, courts in the future undoubtedly will continue to grapple with such issues as whether the Fourth Amendment protects computer records from unreasonable searches and seizures and whether it is possible to base warrants on the strength of computer-generated (as opposed to personal) information. In addition, they also will need to decide the specificity of detail required for the lawful search of a computer or facilities containing computerized records and the evidentiary issues that underlie these types of records (for example, does the Fourth Amendment permit law enforcement officers to use civilian computer experts to facilitate such searches?).

The due process clause may protect those who have been deprived of property, for example, as a result of computer-generated shut-off notices and the subsequent shut-offs of utilities. The same may be true of persons deprived of governmental benefits by computer-generated erroneous information without the persons' having an opportunity to correct the records that formed the basis for the adverse decisions.

YOU BE THE JUDGE

Electronic mail—or "e-mail"—provides a quick medium of communication for office workers across the country. The Bush Administration is no exception; thousands of staffers and other governmental workers use e-mail everyday for routine matters. Yet, according to some people, many of these "routine matters" may well take on national significance.

For example, investigators uncovered e-mail messages from then U.S. National Security Adviser John Poindexter, Oliver North, and dozens of other officials that ultimately led to the unraveling of the Iran-Contra scandal. Without such backup computer tapes, governmental lawyers would have lost potentially valuable evidence. The Iran-Contra e-mail saga takes on new relevance in the wake of the Bush Administration's articulated position that the Federal Records Act—which obligates U.S. governmental offices to preserve important documents for posterity's sake—does not apply to e-mail. Characterizing e-mail as a mode of communication for purely trivial matters (akin to secretarial phone messages), the Bush Administration contends that few historical gems would ever be unearthed in e-mail records. Besides, the Administration notes, those in the executive branch who utilize e-mail are presently under express orders to print out and preserve any messages of possible historical value. In contrast, historians and librarians vehemently argue for the Federal Record Act's application to e-mail. They contend that the most significant historical information oftentimes surfaces in seemingly inconsequential documents. Far from being trivial, these groups submit that e-mail may well contain historical bombshells of momentous importance.

Several national associations representing historians and librarians have filed a lawsuit to block the Bush Administration's proposed erasure of all e-mail backup tapes.

How would you resolve this case?

Source: "Historians Crusade to Preserve 'E-Mail,' " Michael W. Miller, *The Wall Street Journal*, March 31, 1992, page B-1.

SUMMARY

The pervasity of the influence of computers in our lives conjures up a whole host of economic and noneconomic issues as well as legal questions. Despite early doubts about the copyrightability of computer programs, these programs merit copyright protection today. No infringement of the copyright laws occurs when the copy is made for use with a machine or for archival purposes. Moreover, computer-related programs can be patentable as long as the claim does more than merely recite a mathematical algorithm; it must instead use an algorithm (or a mathematical formula) as one of the steps leading to the transformation of the data into a wholly different state or thing.

Various state and common law doctrines, such as trade secrets, unfair competition, and misappropriation, may apply to certain aspects of software and form the basis for protecting the owner's interest in the software in circumstances in which copyright or patent protection would be unavailable. The Semiconductor Chip Protection Act of 1984 protects most mask works, or the layouts of the integrated circuits embedded on the chips, for a period of ten years. The only new intellectual property law in over one hundred years, this act should reduce the incidence of domestic and international chip piracy.

Computer-related contract law encompasses some pitfalls not common to contract law in general because of the technology, the structure of the industry, and the special relationship between the vendor and the purchaser. The Uniform Commercial Code applies to the sale of computer hardware and may cover the sale of software as well. Vendors' attempts to exclude warranties and to force "shrink-wrap" licenses on buyers may be legally unenforceable.

Tort law may also apply to computer-related transactions. Various statutes exist to protect the individual from invasions of privacy that may occur from the collection and maintenance of computer data. Furthermore, federal and state antitrust laws may cover the activities of firms in the computer field as well. Illegal tying arrangements represent one common type of antitrust violation in this area. Various state and federal laws address the problem of computer-related crimes. The constitutional law dimensions of computers will merit increased attention in the future as computer technology becomes even more pervasive in our daily lives.

DISCUSSION QUESTIONS

1. Discuss some of the economic and noneconomic issues computers pose.

2. In what two circumstances will the copying of computer programs be statutorily exempt from claims of copyright infringement?

3. What were the bases for the early doubts about the patentability of computer programs?

4. List five steps the owners of trade secrets can take to ensure secrecy.

5. Discuss some of the special concerns that underlie the contracting process for computers.

6. What are software "shrink-wrap" or "box-top" licenses? Are they enforceable against the buyers of such software?

7. Name at least three methods by which computers can be used to invade one's privacy.

8. Explain how an illegal tying arrangement may crop up in the sale of computers and related software.

9. What were the early limitations on the law's ability to impose liability for computer-related crimes?

10. Briefly discuss the constitutional dimensions of computer law.

CASE PROBLEMS

1. Michael McGraw worked for the City of Indianapolis as a computer operator. Because the City leased computer services on a fixed charge or flat rate basis, the expense to it was not dependent on use. The City provided McGraw with a terminal at his desk and assigned a portion of the computer's information storage capacity, called a "private library," for his utilization in performing his duties. McGraw, when hired, had received a handbook that spelled out the general prohibition against the unauthorized use of City property. McGraw began a business venture and used the City's computer to store his personal business records. After

his supervisor became aware of his unauthorized activities and reprimanded him several times, McGraw was discharged for unsatisfactory job performance. However, McGraw's use of the computer had not been cited as a basis for this discharge. Following his discharge, McGraw asked a former co-worker to secure for him a print-out of his business data and to erase them from McGraw's library. The co-worker instead turned the print-out over to McGraw's former supervisor. As a result, McGraw subsequently was charged with theft under the criminal law. In Indiana, the statutory elements of theft include the unauthorized control over another's property with the intent to deprive the other of any part of its value or use. Had McGraw, by his unauthorized use of the City's computer, intended to deprive the City of any part of its value or use? (*State v. McGraw,* 480 N.E.2d 552 [Ind. 1985].)

2. Kevin Martin was a passenger in a car that had been driven through a red light. When the driver was arrested, Martin was asked for identification and gave his driver's license to the arresting officer. A computer check on the license revealed an outstanding Alabama warrant for Martin's arrest. Based on this warrant, the officer arrested Martin and searched him. This search subsequently revealed a brown pouch containing heroin. There was actually no outstanding warrant on Martin, as he had served time in Alabama and had been released some months earlier. However, the computer records had not been corrected until the day after Martin's arrest. Was Martin's arrest invalid because it was based on erroneous computer information? (*Martin v. State,* 424 So.2d 994 [Fla. App. 1983].)

3. Abele had made improvements to existing computerized axial tomography, or CAT scans, by reducing the exposure to x-rays while enhancing the reliability of the images produced. Abele admitted that his application had used algorithms, or mathematical calculations, but only after an x-ray beam produced by a CAT scan had passed through an object and had been detected upon its exit. After these data-gathering steps had occurred, the mathematical algorithm portion of the invention (a computer) was used to obtain data that were then displayed on a television screen for diagnostic purposes. Did Abele's application constitute patentable subject matter? (*In re Abele,* 684 F.2d 902 [C.C.P.A. 1982].)

4. During 1973–1974, Bernard Tureen had a health insurance policy with the All-American Insurance Company (All-American). In those years, Tureen had two heart attacks and made disability claims against All-

American for benefits. All-American hired Equifax, Inc. (Equifax), a consumer reports firm that investigates and provides information to employers, insurers, and merchants for their use in decision making, to investigate Tureen's claims. Equifax searched its own files and reported to All-American that Tureen had applied for insurance twenty-three times since 1949. All-American retained this report in its claims department and did not disseminate its contents to anyone else. Tureen sued Equifax for invasion of privacy on the basis of the investigative report and the statements about his past insurance history. Had Equifax, by collecting and retaining Tureen's past insurance history, committed this tort? (*Tureen v. Equifax, Inc.,* 571 F.2d 411 [8th Cir. 1978].)

5. When Ashton-Tate Corp. (Ashton-Tate) sued Fox Software, Inc. (Fox) for copyright infringement, Fox used as its affirmative defense Ashton-Tate's alleged misconduct in its dealings with the U.S. Copyright Office. Specifically, Fox claimed that when Ashton-Tate had filed its original applications for copyright, it had repeatedly failed to disclose material information, including the fact that it had derived its dBase line of computer software programs from JPLDIS, a public-domain computer software program developed by the Jet Propulsion Laboratory, and the fact that the dBase III program had been derived from dBase II. According to Fox, Ashton-Tate's repeated failure to disclose such material information was done knowingly and with an intent to deceive. Fox therefore urged the court to invalidate Ashton-Tate's copyrights on its dBase line of computer software programs owing to this allegedly inequitable conduct. Should the court grant Fox's motion for summary judgment based on Fox's contentions? (*Ashton-Tate Corp. v. Fox Software, Inc.,* 760 F. Supp. 831 [C.D. Cal. 1990].)

6. AccuSystems, Inc. (AccuSystems) and its sole shareholder William Selden sued Honeywell Information Systems, Inc. (Honeywell) for fraud arising from the sale of computer hardware and software to AccuSystems. Beard, a Honeywell salesperson, had made a visit to Selden's former employer's payroll processing operations and had told Selden that Honeywell's TL-6 system would be better suited to the firm's business, as it could handle thirty-two terminals on line. Beard also had stated that the TL-6 system had been extensively tested and furnished to other locations where it was working well. When Selden shortly thereafter formed AccuSystems, he bought a TL-6 system. Following installation, AccuSystems experienced serious difficulties

with the TL-6 system: It failed when more than three terminals were in operation, and it could process only simple programs. The evidence revealed that Accu-Systems had been the first installation site for the TL-6 system, and no testing of the system had been undertaken until a year after AccuSystems's purchases. Could AccuSystems prove fraud in these circumstances? (*AccuSystems, Inc.* v. *Honeywell Information Systems, Inc.,* 580 F. Supp. 474 [S.D. N.Y. 1984].)

7. Convoy Company (Convoy) entered into a contract with a firm named WOFAC whereby WOFAC agreed to design a computerized load makeup and rerouting system for use in Convoy's motor vehicle transport business. Convoy then entered into a second contract with Univac (Sperry Rand Corporation) for the computer hardware to be used with WOFAC's software. Because the system never functioned properly, Convoy sued WOFAC for $516,129.09 in actual damages and more than $1,000,000 in lost profits and punitive damages. After Convoy settled with WOFAC for $354,500, Convoy then sued Univac for $216,398.61 in actual damages. The trial judge reentered judgment for Convoy against Univac for that amount, which included the electronic data processing staff and salaried supervisory staff costs associated with the unsatisfactory computer system. Were these costs recoverable as damages? (*Convoy Company* v. *Sperry Rand Corporation,* 601 F.2d 385 [9th Cir. 1979], modified in part 672 F.2d 781 [9th Cir. 1982].)

8. Apple Computer, Inc. (Apple) manufactures small computers that it markets through a network of independent local outlets. Apple banned mail-order sales of computers to ensure the proper support for the buyer after the sale. Apple contended that only through face-to-face transactions would its retail dealers be able to assess the needs of prospective purchasers, assemble the particular packages to meet those needs, supply hands-on instruction and training, and follow up on any servicing needs. Apple also meant its policy as protection of its dealers against the profit erosion caused by "free-riding" mail order dealers. O.S.C. Corporation (O.S.C.), one of the authorized dealers Apple had terminated due to O.S.C.'s violation of the ban, sued Apple for alleged antitrust violations. Should a court find in O.S.C.'s favor? (*O.S.C. Corporation* v. *Apple Computer, Inc.,* 792 F.2d 1464 [9th Cir. 1986].)

9. Time and Space Processing, Inc. (TSP) and Secure Services Technology, Inc. (SST) both manufactured a facsimile (fax) machine, the TEMPEST, consisting of specialized equipment for the secure transmission and receipt of sensitive or classified documents. American and NATO agencies and qualified private government contractors purchase TEMPEST machines. TSP had entered the TEMPEST facsimile machine market in May, 1987. At that time, only three manufacturers—SST, Valutec, and Ricoh Corporation—inhabited the market. Since the U.S. government had previously purchased TEMPEST machines from each of the manufacturers in the market, TSP's successful market entry depended on achieving interoperability with the SST, Valutec, and Ricoh machines. A so-called handshake protocol (T.30) permits interoperability between TEMPEST machines. Adherence to the phase order and the signal parameters of the T.30 protocol is crucial for interoperability. If a facsimile machine does not "recognize" an incoming signal, it will not respond appropriately; and interoperability will not be achieved. The timing and order parameters, therefore, are crucial to interoperability. For flexibility, however, the T.30 protocol does permit slight variations in specific signals. SST took advantage of these limited opportunities to vary the content and timing of various signals within the constraints of the T.30 protocol. SST claimed that these variations in timing and content, collectively referred to as "protocol variations," deserved trade secret protection. And because the content variations can be transcribed into alphanumeric form, SST also claimed copyright protection. TSP apparently was successful in achieving interoperability with the Ricoh and Valutec machines and believed it also had achieved interoperability with the SST-T1, the SST TEMPEST facsimile machine. In March, 1988, the Air Force expressed an interest in purchasing TSP's TEMPEST machines and requested that TSP demonstrate the interoperability of the SST and TSP machines. This demonstration occurred through the transmission of test documents from an SST fax machine at a government facility to a TSP machine at TSP's plant. TSP achieved substantial, but not complete, interoperability with the SST-T1. Nonetheless, TSP began marketing its TEMPEST facsimile machine as being interoperable with SST's TEMPEST machines. Among those who purchased the TSP facsimile machine was the Air Force Logistics Command (AFLC). In early 1989, the AFLC discovered that an interoperability problem still existed between the TSP and SST facsimile machines and asked TSP to remedy this. TSP was loaned a government-owned SST-T1 to allow TSP to make whatever adjustments might be required to achieve complete interoper-

ability with the SST machine. At that point, SST's representatives discovered for the first time that TSP had somehow gained possession of an SST TEMPEST facsimile machine. SST sells its TEMPEST machines only to government agencies. However, no contract provisions prohibiting the government from supplying the SST facsimile machines to third parties existed; neither the facsimile machines nor the operator's manual had contained any restrictive or proprietary legends or any copyright notices, and SST had not notified the government prior to the sale that SST claimed or might claim proprietary rights in the SST-T1 TEMPEST facsimile machine. SST asserted that it had chosen not to take these precautions because the government and the other TEMPEST machine manufacturers generally had understood that the information contained in the handshake protocol was proprietary information. SST also submitted that it had taken sufficient measures to ensure that its handshake protocol remained secret in its dealing with other TEMPEST machine manufacturers. Furthermore, a complex security system guards all of SST's facilities. Since the inception of its dispute with TSP, SST had begun placing proprietary legends and copyright marks on all its facsimile machines. SST filed this suit alleging claims of trade secret misappropriation and conversion. How should a court rule on these claims? (*Secure Services Technology, Inc.* v. *Time and Space Processing, Inc.*, 722 F. Supp. 1354 [E.D. Va. 1989].)

10. A. I. Root Company (Root) sued Computer/Dynamics, Inc. (CDI) for antitrust violations allegedly resulting from CDI's proposed sale of software to Root. Root had been using a set of computer programs known as the Basic Operating Software System (BOSS) to operate machines that it had purchased from MAI dealers (including CDI). These programs constituted the operating software necessary to operate the computer generally and to support applications software (or programs that performed specific data-processing tasks). Root had approached CDI for the reconfigured BOSS software necessary to operate properly its newly purchased Basic Four Model 730B. Root alleged that CDI had offered to sell the reconfigured BOSS software only if Root would sign licensing agreements concerning the applications software that would require Root to (1) use only computer hardware manufactured by MAI with Root's applications software and (2) purchase for a "transfer fee" CDI's programming services each time Root acquired an updated or different Basic Four computer. Root contended that these terms constituted an unlawful tying arrangement by conditioning the sale of the reconfigured BOSS software (the tying product) on Root's signing the application software license (the tied product). Should a court agree with Root's claim? (*A. I. Root Company* v. *Computer/Dynamics, Inc.*, 806 F.2d 673 [6th Cir. 1986].)

CHAPTER 55

International Business

OUTLINE

BUSINESS IN A GLOBAL VILLAGE

If ten years ago a business forecaster had predicted the end of the Cold War, the political collapse of the Soviet Union, the dismantling of *apartheid* in South Africa, and a strong, unified European market, she might have been told to sell her story to the supermarket tabloid newspapers. Yet these changes represent only some of the massive political and economic shifts that have occurred around the world in recent years. You could add to that list the destruction of the Berlin Wall and of East Germany, the separatist referendum in Quebec, the split of Czechoslovakia into two countries, and the cruel civil wars in such countries as the former Yugoslavia and Somalia. In 1997, Hong Kong, the Asian economic powerhouse, will revert to the control of the Chinese government. The last fifteen years of our century is a time of unprecedented political and economic change.

All these events create both opportunities and risks for United States businesses. For example, the changes in the former Soviet Union created new opportunities for companies such as Pepsico and McDonald's to develop substantial business activities. On the other hand, such events as the war in the former Yugoslavia have destroyed factories and offices of foreign businesses, killed employees, and prevented goods from entering and leaving the area. Viewed from a long-term perspective, however, opportunities for U.S. businesses to compete in global markets have never been better.

If U.S. businesses have learned one lesson in the past few years, it is that, as Marshall McLuhan once said, we all live in a "global village." Companies such as Coca-Cola and General Electric feature global advertising strategies. Other companies, including all major U.S. auto companies, have joint manufacturing and marketing agreements with their Japanese competitors. In many cases, such typically American companies as McDonald's, General Motors, and Digital Equipment find most of their revenues or profits coming from overseas operations.

In 1989, the United States alone exported $603 billion in goods, services, and income and imported $698 billion. Investment in the United States doubled in the 1985–1990 period. The United States currently imports thirteen of the thirty-six minerals considered to be essential for our military weaponry. Marshall McLuhan was right: We are so economically interdependent on one another that we do live in a global village.

To succeed in the business world of the next century, every businessperson must be familiar with the basic rules for international business. This chapter will introduce you to those rules.

GOING GLOBAL

As communications and transportation have improved, buyers and sellers in different markets more easily find each other to do business. As a result, the global marketplace has opened to businesses of all sizes, selling goods, services, and technology.

A business has many options when it decides to "go global." As it develops its international customer base, the business will often change the way it organizes itself, generally moving from simpler selling relationships toward direct investments in major foreign markets.

Direct Sales

Most businesses start their international operations simply by selling to foreign customers. They may exhibit their products at international trade fairs, or a buyer may visit a potential seller on a buying trip, or be referred by another satisfied customer. Like any direct selling relationship, the parties govern their rights and obligations using a contract. Many of the concerns a seller or buyer would have in a local transaction are the same in an international transaction. Others, however, are special to the international transaction.

Governing law   Suppose that Acme Novelties, Inc., a company based in Arizona, is selling a variety of items to Coyote Enterprises, a Mexican business. What happens if the goods are defective, and Coyote rejects them? Whose law will govern the rights and obligations of the parties? Mexican law could be very different from Arizona law.

Historically, smart traders would specify in their contracts which law would govern the transaction. As you will see in later cases in this chapter, their contracts often would also call for any disputes to be arbitrated, rather than using unfamiliar court systems.

In 1988, the United Nations Convention on the International Sale of Goods (CISG) went into effect. This provides a law of sales contracts much like Article 2 of the Uniform Commercial Code, specifically for contracts between businesses in countries that have approved the CISG. In the United States, the CISG replaces the Uniform Commercial Code in any transaction with a business from another CISG country. Fortunately, the CISG follows many Uniform Commercial Code provisions, so it is familiar to many domestic managers.

As of late 1991, twenty-six countries had ratified the CISG, including the United States and other such important trading countries as China, France, and several republics of the former Soviet Union. Over the next several years, the CISG will likely become the law in most Western European countries, the former socialist countries in Europe, and in several more Asian countries.

Agents and Distributors

As a business grows, it may decide that it needs a more systematic effort to find customers in foreign markets. Often, it will turn to people or businesses in other major markets, to act as a go-between in bringing foreign buyers to the company's products.

An agent is a person or company who finds buyers on behalf of the seller, and usually is paid a commission for the resulting sales. The sales contract still remains between the buyer and seller, although in a few cases, the agent has the authority to accept orders on the seller's behalf. The buyer gets the goods directly from the seller, and looks to the seller to solve any problems with the sale.

A distributor, by contrast, buys goods from the seller, and resells them directly to customers. The distributor bears the risk that the goods won't sell, or that customers don't pay for goods. Generally, customers look to the distributor for service after the sale.

Licensing and Franchising

Businesses with intellectual property rights—such as patents, copyrights, and trademarks—sometimes find it best to sell to a foreign business the right to make, copy, or market the products covered by those rights. For example, the publisher of this book might sell the rights to a Russian publisher to reproduce and market it in Russia. Generally, the buyer of the rights will pay a fee plus a royalty—that is, a percentage of the price or profit on any copy sold.

One very popular form of licensing in international business is the franchise. United States fast-food businesses have used franchising as the major method of entering foreign markets. In a franchise, the license covers primarily the trademarks, e.g., brand names such as Big Mac, Whopper, or even Century 21. In return for a fee and royalty paid to the franchisor, the franchisee earns the benefit of the reputation of the trademarks, national and international advertising, and a wide customer base. Many U.S.-based franchisors have identified their largest growth opportunities as coming from international franchising.

Joint Ventures

In Chapter 36, you learned that a joint venture is "an association of two or more persons to carry out a single business enterprise for profit." In international business, joint ventures are viewed somewhat more broadly than that definition implies. The concept covers businesses such as General Motors and Toyota, who together built a plant in California to manufacture Corollas and Novas on the same production lines. It also covers groups of companies that cooperate in research and development activities and even those that jointly market products. The joint venture has proven itself a successful way for companies to enter new markets, as they get the benefit of local expertise from their joint venture partners.

Subsidiaries

In many instances, a growing international business will decide to incorporate an operation separately in another country. If the business controls the new corporation, then it is the *parent,* and the new corporation is the *subsidiary.* A subsidiary may be wholly owned by the parent company, or the parent company may have partial ownership. In some countries, foreign businesses must involve local owners in the ownership and management of subsidiaries.

UNITED STATES ANTITRUST LAWS

Does the law of the United States, or of any other sovereign nation, end at its borders? You have seen movie scenes of automobile chases in which the sheriff of one county has to stop his hot pursuit at the border of his county and depend on the cooperation of the sheriff of the adjoining county to take up the chase to apprehend the person he was chasing. Do nations work that way too, or is there some other way that "domestic" law can be applied internationally? The following case attempted to answer that question.

Timberlane v. Bank of America
549 F.2d 597 (9th Cir. 1976)

FACTS A lumber company filed an action alleging violations of the Sherman Antitrust Act arising out of activities in another country. The district court dismissed the action for lack of subject matter jurisdiction. The plaintiff appealed.

ISSUE Does the Sherman Antitrust Act have extraterritorial jurisdiction?

HOLDING Yes, although if foreign interests outweigh American interests, the court should not exercise its power.

REASONING The court reasoned, "There is no doubt that American antitrust laws extend over some conduct in other nations. . . . That American law covers some conduct beyond the nation's borders does not mean that it embraces all, however . . . it is evident that at some point the interests of the United States are too weak and the foreign harmony incentive for restraint too strong to justify an extraterritorial assertion of jurisdiction. . . . What that point is or how it is determined is not defined by international law." The test is, "Does the alleged restraint affect, or was it intended to affect, the foreign commerce of the United States?"

Accordingly, the United States does have laws with extraterritorial application. These laws fall into two broad categories: crimes and torts. Since the United States antitrust laws fall into both categories, they do have extraterritorial implications.

The Sherman Act states in its first section that "every contract, combination . . . or conspiracy in restraint of trade or commerce among the several States, or with foreign nations, is declared to be illegal." United States courts have not been in full agreement, however, on the meaning of that statute with respect to international commerce. Among American courts, there is no consensus on how far the jurisdiction should extend. Some courts use the "direct and substantial effect" test. That test examines the effect on United States foreign commerce as a prerequisite for proper jurisdiction. Other courts have used a different test that looks at whether a conspiracy exists that adversely affects American commerce. In general, however, most courts prefer to evaluate and balance the relevant considerations in each case. The courts determine whether the contacts and interests of the United States are sufficient to support the exercise of extraterritorial jurisdiction. However, in the following case, the Supreme Court allowed an alleged violation of the Sherman Act to be decided by a Japanese arbitration.

Mitsubishi Motors Corp. v. *Soler Chrysler-Plymouth, Inc.*
473 U.S. 614 (1985)

FACTS A Puerto Rican corporation entered into a contract with a Swiss corporation and a Japanese corporation. The Japanese corporation was a joint venture between the Swiss corporation and another Japanese corporation. The contract provided that in the event of a dispute it would be referred to the Japanese Arbitration Association for resolution. A dispute arose and the Japanese corporation sought a U.S. district court order compelling arbitration in Japan. The Puerto Rican corporation stated that antitrust claims could not be settled by arbitration. The district court ordered arbitration. The court of appeals reversed the district court. The case was then heard by the Supreme Court.

ISSUE Are antitrust claims subject to arbitration clauses?

HOLDING Yes. Claims arising under the Sherman Act are arbitrable.

REASONING The court was asked "whether an American court should enforce an agreement to resolve antitrust claims by arbitration when that agreement arises from an international transaction." There is a federal policy that favors arbitration, and "(t)here is no reason to depart from these guidelines when a party bound by an arbitration agreement raises claims founded on statutory rights."

THE "RULES OF THE GAME"

At one time, it was necessary to know the laws of all the countries involved in an international transaction. Because of the complexity of that matter as well as the increased number of countries in the world since the end of World War II, countries in common geographical areas have banded together to form economic unions to facilitate and expedite trade. At this time, the two most significant regional groupings are the European Community (EC), currently made up of twelve Western European nations, and the North American Free Trade area, which includes the United States, Canada, and Mexico. Other groups in Asia, Africa, and Latin America are now looking to these two major regional groups to create a legal foundation for their own free trade areas.

European Community The EC was created by the Treaty of Rome in 1957. Currently, the member states are Belgium, Denmark, France, Greece, Germany, Ireland, Italy, Luxembourg, The Netherlands, The United Kingdom, Spain, and Portugal. At the time this book went to press, several other nations—including Sweden, Norway, Finland, and Austria—had applied to join the EC, and Switzerland was preparing for a referendum on joining the EC. Several former socialist nations of Eastern Europe and republics of the former Soviet Union also had indicated their interest in joining the EC.

The EC has its own legislative, executive, and judicial branches. The purpose of the community is to establish a common customs tariff for outside nations and to eliminate tariffs among EC members. The treaty also covers the free movement of workers, goods, and capital. It is aimed at accomplishing international cooperation. The EC is governed by the Council of Ministers, the Commission, the Assembly, and the Court of Justice.

The Council of Ministers   The Council of Ministers is the legislative branch of the EC. Each country sends a cabinet-level official to the Council, to represent its interests in the EC. Each country includes a permanent representative, but the actual Council members will change depending on the issue. For example, if the Council is considering agricultural matters, the Minister of Agriculture from each country would attend. If the matter involved the environment, then the Ministers for the Environment would attend from each country.

The Council issues directives and regulations. Directives are instructions to each member country, generally asking it to bring its laws into harmony with overall EC policy. The EC has issued directives on insider trading, product liability, and television broadcasting, to name just a few examples. Countries may continue their own way of handling these issues, as long as their laws conform to the overall policy of the EC. By contrast, Council regulations are superior to each nation's law, and each nation must specifically comply with the terms of the regulation. For example, the EC has a merger control regulation requiring EC approval of mergers that might tend to restrict competition; this extends to all countries in the EC.

The Commission   The Commission is composed of seventeen persons, at least one from each member nation, but they do not represent that nation as do the members of the Council of Ministers. Rather, they represent the EC as a whole. The Commission has two functions in the EC. First, it proposes legislation to the Council. The Council members cannot create directives or regulations by themselves, but must act only on matters coming to them from the Commission. Second, the Commission enforces EC law. It has the power to impose substantial fines on businesses violating EC law. In the areas of agriculture and competition law (the EC name for antitrust law), the Council has delegated to the Commission the powers to create the detailed regulation. It also has the power to issue exemptions from the competition law to businesses.

The European Parliament   The European Parliament has 518 members elected by voters in the member nations. The Parliament has not yet found its role as a legislative body. It has the right to consult with the Council on legislation and to propose amendments to legislation. It also approved parts of the EC budget, and can vote no confidence in the Council, which would then be compelled to resign as a group.

The Court of Justice   The Court of Justice functions in much the same way as the United States Supreme Court does; it is the final arbiter of all disputes. *Once the Court of Justice makes a ruling, it becomes the domestic law of all the member nations.* In order to accomplish this tremendous feat, all the member nations had to give up some of their sovereignty. The law is now applied in all twelve countries and to their approximately 320 million citizens; as such, its market is larger than that of the United States.

Figure 55.1 depicts the European Community.

The Treaty of Rome established four main EC objectives for freedom of movement of goods, people, services, and capital. Since the Treaty, the EC has developed a large body of law designed to achieve these four objectives. In 1986, the EC adopted the Single European Act, mandating the creation of

FIGURE 55.1   The European Community

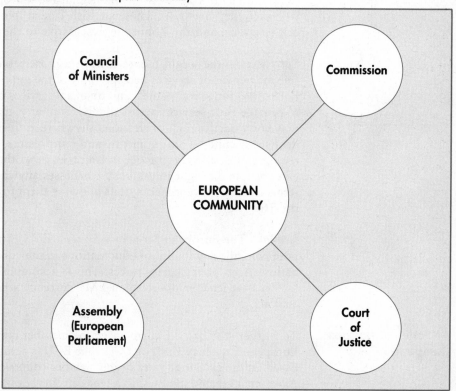

a unified market by the end of 1992. In 1991, the heads of state of the EC member countries signed the Maastricht Treaty on European Political and Monetary Union, which strengthened the EC institutions, and provided for a common currency, called the European Currency Unit (ECU), by the close of the decade. At this time, the Maastricht agreement has run into some trouble in the ratification process, but many of its objectives will most likely go forward.

Goods   The EC has a customs union that is designed to eliminate customs duties among all member nations. In addition, the union has a common tariff with respect to trade between member nations and nonmember nations. As a result, no burdens are placed on trade between member nations, but a burden is placed on trade with countries outside the EC.

Persons   One of the benefits of citizenship in an EC member country is the right to free movement anywhere within the Community. EC nationals and their families may reside anywhere in the EC. Students may enroll in vocational programs anywhere in the EC. Workers may work anywhere in the EC without work permits, on the same terms as nationals of that country. One of the more controversial provisions of the Maastricht agreement allows any EC national to vote in both municipal and European Parliament elections wherever they may live. Thus, an Irish citizen living in Rome could vote in city elections, and for Rome's representative to the European Parliament.

Services   As the world moves toward a more service-oriented economy, the free movement of services becomes part of the importance of EC membership. Banks, insurance companies, and financial services businesses are now entitled to provide their services across the EC. Similarly, many kinds of professionals may now practice their professions anywhere in the EC. For example, doctors, dentists, architects, travel agents, and hairdressers, once they meet minimum requirements, all may practice in countries other than their own. The EC also gives people the right to establish businesses anywhere in the EC on the same terms as local entrepreneurs, thus allowing them to operate freely throughout the EC.

Capital   The European Monetary System (EMS) was created in 1979. Its purpose is to allow only limited fluctuations in the currencies of various member nations from preset parity prices. This is accomplished through a joint credit facility that lends support to an EMS currency when it needs an infusion of capital.

EC Rules of Business Competition

To further stabilize the currency of the member countries, the EC created the European Currency Unit, or ECU. The ECU is actually a basket of currencies, based on the exchange rates of the member countries. In 1992, the Maastricht Agreement created the ECU as a real currency, designed to replace the pounds, marks, pesos, and francs used in the Community. The estimated savings to business is very high. For example, if a business started today with an Irish pound, then exchanged that currency in each of the member countries, by the time it became an Irish pound again, more than half the value would be lost just to money-changing charges. Already, some businesses are accounting and issuing bonds in ECUs.

To create a truly common market, the EC needs extensive rules on competition. The Treaty of Rome set up the basic structure of EC competition law, the Council has issued a large body of directives and regulations, and the Commission, as the law's main enforcer, has issued regulations and decisions implementing the law.

In a manner similar to U.S. antitrust law, Article 85 of the Treaty of Rome prohibits agreements, contracts, cartels, and joint activities that intend to restrict or distort competition within the EC. For example, price fixing, limiting or allocating markets, tying arrangements, and price discrimination are all prohibited under Article 85. However, Article 85 recognizes that some contracts benefit consumers by improving production or distribution of goods, or by promoting product improvements. The Commission, therefore, can exempt activities from Article 85, either by issuing an individual exemption for a particular situation, or a block exemption for similarly situated businesses. An example of a block exemption would be the Commission guidelines for franchises; these tell potential franchise businesses which contract provisions are acceptable and which will bring Commission action. The following case illustrates the application of the exemption process.

Re the Agreement Between Moosehead Breweries, Ltd. and Whitbread and Company
[1990] O.J. L100/32, (1991) 4 C.M.L.R. 391
Commission of the European Communities

FACTS   Moosehead licensed its trademark rights and secret brewing process to Whitbread, giving Whitbread the exclusive right to make and sell Moosehead beer in the United Kingdom. Whitbread agreed not to brew or sell any other Canadian beer in the United Kingdom, and agreed to purchase brewers' yeast only from Moosehead. The two companies applied to the EC Commission for an individual exemption from Article 85.

ISSUE   Should the companies receive an exemption from Article 85?

HOLDING   Yes, the agreement meets the requirements for exemption from the competition law.

REASONING   "The clauses to the agreement which are restrictive of competition are indispensable in order to give Whitbread sufficient confidence to invest substantial sums in the launch of a new beer onto an already competitive market. . . ." The agreement makes Canadian beer available both fresher and cheaper for the United Kingdom market. "Through the agreement, the product will automatically benefit from Whitbread's comprehensive distribution network. . . . [T]he Commission considers that the agreement is likely to contribute to the improvement in the distribution of the product in the area."

Article 86 The second major EC competition law is Article 86 of the Treaty of Rome. It bars one or more companies from using a dominant market position to restrict or distort trade. Prohibited abuses of dominant positions would include tying arrangements, price fixing, price discrimination, and other conduct similar to that prohibited under United States antitrust law.

Both buyers and sellers can have dominant positions. The Commission and the European Court of Justice have defined dominance by a practical test: A firm or firms having the power to "act without taking into account their competitors, purchasers or suppliers" (*Europemballage Corp. and Continental Can Co., Inc. v. Commission,* (1973) E.C.R. 215). Thus, no specific market share is required; instead, the Commission will look at the firm's power to control suppliers and customers, and its ability to prevent competition.

Negative Clearance A business concerned about its actions violating either Article 85 or Article 86 can apply to the Commission for a negative clearance. A negative clearance means that the Commission has reviewed the proposed conduct, and, if the business does what it has indicated, the Commission will not begin prosecution.

Extraterritoriality The EC position on the reach of its power to regulate competition has expanded considerably over the last twenty years. It now appears that conduct anywhere can be subject to EC competition rules if it is intended to affect and does affect the EC market. The following case should serve as a warning to companies who engage in activities lawful in their home country but that also affect the European market.

Re Wood Pulp Cartel et al. v. *E.C. Commission*
[1988] 4 C.M.L.R. 901
European Court of Justice

FACTS The Commission charged forty-one wood pulp producers, all operating outside the EC, with violating Article 85 by taking concerted action to set prices for wood pulp sold to EC customers. The producers claimed that the EC had no jurisdiction, since all the price-fixing activity took place outside the EC. The Commission fined thirty-six of the producers, who then appealed to the Court.

ISSUE Does Article 85 reach conduct occurring outside the Community?

HOLDING   Yes, when that conduct is intended to affect the Community.

REASONING   Where the wood pulp producers "sell directly to purchasers established in the Community and engage in price competition in order to win orders from those customers, that constitutes competition within the Common Market. It follows that where those producers concert on the prices to be charged to their customers in the Community and put that concertation into effect by selling at prices which are actually coordinated, they are taking part in a concertation which has the object and effect of restricting competition within the Common Market. . . ."

NORTH AMERICAN FREE TRADE

One powerful alternative to the EC is the free trade partnership now being formed in North America. The first piece of the new partnership went into effect in 1989, with the ratification of the Canada–U.S. Free Trade Agreement. Like the EC, one major purpose of the Free Trade Agreement was the elimination of tariffs on sales of goods between the United States and Canada. The agreement calls for the elimination of all tariffs between the two countries by 1998. As a practical matter, most tariffs are now gone. Goods qualify for tariff-free treatment if they are 50% North American in content.

Also like the EC, the Canada–U.S. Free Trade Agreement makes it easier for Canadian and United States citizens to work in each other's countries, and also makes it easier for investments to flow across the border.

Unlike the EC, however, the Free Trade Agreement does not set up a host of new institutions, or require the two countries to give up much sovereignty. The only new institutions are binational panels of experts convened as needed to resolve trade disputes between the two countries. The expert panels replace the court systems for both countries in eligible cases.

As this book went to press, Mexican negotiators had joined their Canadian and American counterparts in the North American Free Trade Agreement. If ratified by all three countries, this would create a free trade area similar to the one created by the Canada–U.S. agreement, large enough to compete successfully with Asian and European markets. The fate of a North American agreement is not at all certain, however. U.S. environmental and labor groups object to Mexico's reputation for having a lax legal environment, while Canadians worry about more jobs moving South.

THE GENERAL AGREEMENT ON TARIFFS AND TRADE

The General Agreement on Tariffs and Trade (GATT) provides a worldwide framework for international trade. The GATT promotes free trade by seeking to reduce tariffs and quotas. It promotes fair trade by defining such trade practices as unfair government subsidies of exports and dumping (selling goods below fair value on a foreign market). It also provides panels to resolve trade disputes.

The GATT works through "rounds" of discussions, where countries agree to reduce tariffs for all GATT members. The most recent round, known as the Uruguay Round, also raised non–goods-related issues such as trade-related intellectual property rights, investment protection, services, and agricultural subsidies. At press time, the Uruguay Round was not completed, and was at some risk of failing to achieve an agreement. If the GATT collapses, regional trading groups will most likely take its place, but will not be as effective at promoting world-wide free trade.

IMPORTS

All goods imported into a country must "pass" customs. Passing customs usually means paying a certain sum of money known as a tariff or duty at the port of entry based on the type and value of the goods. For example, when Subaru imported the BRAT motor vehicle into this country, it had to be decided whether the BRAT was a truck or a sports car since the duty that had to be paid would differ depending on the category to which it rightfully belonged. Once the type of import is determined, the analysis turns to its valuation. Is the proper valuation its wholesale value at point of origin or destination, its retail value at point of origin or destination, or a combination of those factors? In general, the transaction value of the goods is used. The *transaction value* is the price the importer paid for the goods plus certain other necessary and related expenses. The U.S. Customs Court has exclusive jurisdiction over civil actions challenging administrative decisions of the U.S. Customs Service.[1]

EXPORTS

All exports leaving the United States must be licensed. For most goods and technology, the licensing process simply involves stamping a general license statement on the export documents. Some goods and technology, however, require validated licenses issued by the Commerce Department, which maintains a Commodity Control List giving the licensing status of thousands of export items. Businesses that export in violation of the export licensing policy face criminal prosecution and loss of export privileges.

United States exports are regulated for three purposes. The first is to protect the nation in time of short supply. For example, Alaskan crude oil may be exported only if it does not affect our domestic supply. The second

[1] 28 U.S.C. 1582 (a).

purpose protects national security. For example, exporting nuclear material to Iraq would not be permitted. The third purpose furthers United States foreign policy interests. For example, exports of all products to Libya were banned in 1986 as a response to Libya's support of terrorism.

Export controls have not always worked very well. Investigations after the Persian Gulf War in 1991 showed that several companies exported material to help Iraq build nuclear, chemical, and other weapons systems. Even more problematic is the fact that banned products are sometimes available from businesses in other countries. The Western powers have a Coordinating Committee (COCOM) that is supposed to regulate products that are most sensitive for security purposes. Since the collapse in 1989 of the U.S.S.R. and the Eastern European communist countries, export licenses have become significantly easier to obtain for products going to such countries as Poland, Hungary, and Russia.

LETTERS OF CREDIT

International traders also face special problems when paying for goods, services, and technology. In a domestic transaction, a seller easily has the ability to check the buyer's creditworthiness. If the buyer wrongfully rejects the goods, the seller is probably familiar enough with the market to know how to resell the goods, or can have them returned fairly easily. In an international transaction, however, the seller will find it harder to check the buyer's financial status, harder to collect unpaid amounts from a foreign buyer, and more expensive or difficult to resell or reship rejected goods.

To solve these problems posed by the international marketplace, buyers and sellers often use *letters of credit* to pay for goods, services, or technology. The contract between buyer and seller will require the buyer to get a letter from its bank. The letter is the bank's promise that it will pay the contract price upon the seller's presentation of documents specified in the contract. To protect itself, the buyer will carefully specify which documents the seller must present to the bank to get payment. If the seller doesn't want to collect from a foreign bank, the contract can require the buyer to have a bank convenient to the seller that will confirm the letter of credit.

Suppose that Salesco, Inc., in California, contracts with Buyco, in Australia, for the sale of 5000 electric motors at a total price of U.S. $25,000. The sales contract that Buyco will pay uses a letter of credit issued by First Australia Bank, and is confirmed by First San Diego Bank. The sales contract also specifies that payment will be made upon presentation of an invoice, packing list, export declaration, and negotiable on-board bill of lading (indicating the goods had been loaded on the ship).

Buyco would go to its bank, First Australia, which would for a fee issue a letter stating the terms as specified in the contract. The bank would send

FIGURE 55.2   Transfers Involved in a Typical Letter of Credit

Legend
———— flow of goods
------- flow of documents
——— flow of money

that letter to First San Diego Bank, which would then write a letter to Salesco confirming the terms of the original letter of credit. Once Salesco obtained all the documents specified in the letter, it would go to its bank, First San Diego, which would compare the documents with the list in the letter of credit. If the documents were in order, First San Diego would pay Salesco, then forward the documents to First Australia, which would get payment from Buyco, then give Buyco the documents so it could take delivery of the motors. Figure 55-2 indicates how the transaction would work.

As you can see, sellers are pleased to use letters of credit. They are paid for goods even before the buyer receives them, and they are paid even if the goods are defective. Buyers protect themselves by specifying carefully which documents are required, and, in some instances, by requiring a third party to inspect the goods as they are loaded for shipment. Buyers are also protected by the legal obligation that the documents the seller presents must strictly comply with the documents required in the letter of credit before the bank can pay the seller. The following case illustrates this strict compliance rule.

Beyene v. *Irving Trust Co.*
762 F.2d 4 (2d Cir. 1985)

FACTS   Beyene, the seller, contracted to sell two prefabricated houses to Mohammed Sofan, a resident of Yemen. Sofan obtained a letter of credit from the Yemen Bank for Reconstruction and Development, which was confirmed by Irving Trust Co. in New York. When Beyene presented the documents to Irving Trust for payment, the bank noticed that the bill of lading listed the party to be notified on arrival of the goods was misspelled as Mohammed Soran. It refused to pay.

ISSUE Does the misspelled name give Irving the right to refuse to pay the letter of credit?

HOLDING Yes. The seller's documents must strictly comply with the letter of credit.

REASONING "The issuing bank, or a bank that acts as a confirming bank for the issuer, takes on an absolute duty to pay the amount to the credit of the beneficiary (seller), so long as the beneficiary complies with the terms of the letter." Even though the mistake may have been merely a typographical error, "literal compliance is generally 'essential so as not to impose an obligation upon the bank that it did not undertake and so as not to jeopardize the bank's right to indemnity from its customer.'"

LABOR

More recent actions by the courts and Congress suggest a willingness to extend the protection of U.S. labor laws to Americans working for United States companies abroad. In 1991, Congress amended Title VII of the Civil Rights Act of 1964 to extend protection against employment discrimination to Americans working for United States companies abroad. The following case illustrates the extraterritorial application of another labor law.

Vermilya-Brown Co. v. Connell
335 U.S. 377 (1948)

FACTS The plaintiffs were hired in New York City and employed by the defendant in Bermuda. Suit was brought with respect to overtime pay based on the Fair Labor Standards Act.

ISSUE Do United States labor laws have extraterritorial jurisdiction?

HOLDING Yes, if the workers are working in United States–controlled areas.

REASONING A controversy as to the geographical application of the statute had to be considered together with an executive agreement that authorized the United States to enact legislation with respect to United States–leased areas in Bermuda. Since the United States can regulate the actions of United States citizens outside the United States, the leased areas within Bermuda were subject to the legislation.

INFORMATION AND TECHNOLOGY

Historically, patent, copyright, and trademark protection extended only within the boundaries of each country. An inventor who wanted to protect an invention in many other countries would have to obtain a patent in each country. To complicate matters, some countries did not recognize exclusive patent rights in some kinds of products, such as pharmaceuticals. These countries felt it more important to deliver life-saving drugs to their people than to protect the profits of the pharmaceutical companies. The following case illustrates the traditional limits of legal protection for patents.

Deepsouth Packing Co. v. Laitram Corp.
406 U.S. 518 (1972)

FACTS Both the plaintiff and the defendant held patents on machines that devein shrimp more efficiently than other machines or hand labor. Laitram's patent claim was superior to Deepsouth's in this country but not outside the United States.

ISSUE Is Deepsouth Packing's absence from the United States market because of Laitram's superior patent rights also preventing it from exporting its machines overseas?

HOLDING No. United States patent laws apply only within the United States.

REASONING The patent statute (35 U.S.C. 154) entitles a patentee to a grant throughout the United States only. United States patents do not apply to United States competition in international commerce. Since there is no common law right, only a statutory one, it is clear that the power of the statute pertains to United States territory only.

Today, although no worldwide intellectual property rights exist, a real trend has grown toward international protection of copyrights, patents, and trademarks. In 1988, for example, the United States became the eightieth member of the Berne Convention for the Protection of Literary and Artistic Works. A copyright holder who publishes a book in the United States will now have the right to go to another member country and receive the same protection there as local authors.

The area of patent law is also moving toward international protection. The European Patent Convention allows only one filing and one patent examination to obtain protection in fourteen countries. Similarly, the Patent Cooperation Treaty also allows only one patent application and examination to serve as a basis for patent filings in up to forty-seven countries, as of 1991. The issue of drug patent recognition is being negotiated at the Uruguay Round of GATT talks, and may reach some resolution soon.

Trademark law has also moved toward some international recognition, though not as quickly as the other areas of intellectual property protection. The Madrid Agreement—to which twenty-nine countries (but not the United States) belonged as of 1991—allows one application to provide protection in all member countries. The EC has moved toward an EC-wide recognition of trademarks, but does not yet have uniformity.

United States businesses have faced serious problems in recent years with counterfeit goods. Levi Strauss, Apple Computer, and other companies have reported large revenues lost due to imports that counterfeit company trademarks or patents. The United States has toughened its enforcement of the laws designed to oppose these counterfeiters. Section 337 of the Tariff Act of 1930 was amended in 1988 to allow any owner of a registered U.S. intellectual property right, who believes that an import infringes that right, to apply to the International Trade Commission for an order banning the goods. This order can also fine the importer up to $100,000 per day or twice the domestic value of the goods. In addition, Congress amended the Trade Act of 1974 with a section called "Special 301" requiring the U.S. Trade Representative to identify countries that do not protect United States intellectual property rights. Once identified, the United States will negotiate improvements with those countries. If no improvements result, the United States must retaliate against those countries. Special 301 has been effective in getting many countries to improve their intellectual property laws.

NATIONALIZATION

Nationalization of privately owned business entities is a risk that exists primarily in developing countries. *Nationalization* is the act of converting privately owned businesses into governmentally owned businesses. In general, international trade can be carried on without fear of nationalization; the exporter merely ensures that payment is guaranteed before shipment of goods. However, international investment is not so simple a matter. To build and operate an aluminum plant or an oil refinery requires a large investment of capital. If, during the time the investment is paying for itself, it is nationalized, the result is usually a loss to the investor. It is for that reason, as well as for others, that international investment decisions usually require a shorter payback period than national investment decisions.

Is nationalization legal? It depends on your perspective. For the most part, from the viewpoint of the country that nationalizes a private property, some act of the legislature or head of state makes it "legal" within that country. From the viewpoint of international law, however, it may not be legal. If it does not comply with international law, it is termed a **confiscation**, not a nationalization. If it does comply with international law, it is called an **expropriation**. The key element is whether the state had a proper public purpose and, in addition, whether "just compensation" was paid for the property. No matter what it is called, there is little that can be done about it if it occurs.

One means of insuring an investment against the risk of loss is by utilizing the facilities of the Overseas Private Investment Corporation (OPIC). OPIC furnishes low-cost insurance against nationalization; confiscation; lack of convertibility of foreign earnings; and general loss due to insurrection, revolution, or war. OPIC currently insures over 400 projects in fifty countries.

Confiscation A taking of private property by the government in violation of international law.

Expropriation A taking of private property by the government not in violation of international law.

ACT OF STATE DOCTRINE

One reason for the importance of seeking insurance protection for overseas investments is the Act of State doctrine. The doctrine states that every sovereign state is bound to respect the independence of every other sovereign state, and the courts of one country will not sit in judgment on the acts of the government of another performed within its own borders. The concept of the Act of State doctrine is imbedded in the notion of sovereign immunity. Certainly each sovereign state recognizes all other states' **sovereignty.** But the Act of State doctrine is not a specific rule of international law. International law does not require that nations follow this rule, and in the United States, the Constitution does not require it. Judicial decisions of the United States, however, have recognized the doctrine. The doctrine is based on the theory that each nation is not qualified to question the actions of other nations taken on their own soil. In fact, denouncing the public decisions of other nations can have a decidedly adverse effect on the conduct of a nation's foreign policy. The following case illustrates a modern application of the doctrine.

Sovereignty The power each country has to control its own people and activities.

Banco Nacional de Cuba v. *Sabbatino*
376 U.S. 398 (1964)

FACTS Cuba expropriated the property of a Cuban corporation, the capital stock of which was principally owned by United States residents. The American residents filed suit to recover proceeds in a United States district court against the corporation, which was an instrumentality of the Cuban government.

ISSUE Will the judiciary of one country examine the validity of a taking of property within the territory of another country?

HOLDING No. Even if the court technically has jurisdiction, it should leave such matters to the executive branch.

REASONING The judiciary will not examine the validity of a taking of property by a foreign government if that taking was within its own territory. This is applicable if the United States diplomatically recognizes the foreign government at the time of the taking. The only grounds on which the United States could examine the taking is if a treaty or other unambiguous agreement gave it the power to do so. Furthermore, this is true if the taking is alleged to be in violation of international law.

But what about a situation in which an American bank held promissory notes issued by a group of Costa Rican banks payable in the United States in United States dollars? Would there be a lack of jurisdiction if the Costa Rican government, after the notes were signed, refused to make the payments in United States dollars? Does the Act of State doctrine apply? The Second Circuit said an emphatic "no" when it held that the situs (location) of the debt was in the

United States and not Costa Rica and, therefore, the doctrine did not apply. See *Allied Bank* v. *Banco Credito,* 757 F.2d 516 (2d Cir. 1985).

SOVEREIGN IMMUNITY

In the traditions of international law, all nations are equal and sovereign. Thus, a nation is immune from suit for its actions, either by individuals or by other countries. To be sued, a nation must agree to give up its sovereign immunity. For example, the United States passed the Federal Tort Claims Act to allow individuals to sue our government for wrongful acts. On an international level, the doctrine of sovereign immunity causes businesses some trouble, especially because many governments operate businesses such as airlines, banks, auto companies, and even computer firms.

The United States has taken actions to limit the effect of sovereign immunity in our courts. In 1976, Congress enacted the Foreign Sovereign Immunities Act, which declared that United States courts would not recognize sovereign immunity when the sovereign engaged in commercial, rather than political, activities. So, for example, a state-owned bank could be subject to suit over its failure to pay a letter of credit. The United States has also negotiated many bilateral investment treaties, containing provisions for other governments to waive their right to claim sovereign immunity.

DISPUTES

The best method of resolving an international dispute is by providing for that contingency at the time of creating the international transaction. Three principal options for settling a dispute are available: the International Court of Justice, national courts, and arbitration.

The International Court of Justice

The International Court of Justice (ICJ) has limited value in solving international business disputes. A private person has no standing before the ICJ. Only nations may appear before the court. A private person who has a grievance against a state not his own must first secure the agreement of his own state to present his claim. If his state asserts his claim, the issue then becomes whether the other state wants to allow the matter to appear before the ICJ for resolution. If it does not, that is the end of the matter. This procedure is established in the United Nations Charter, since the ICJ is an agency of the United Nations. Each state must agree to be bound by the court's decision; if they do not so agree, there is no jurisdiction to hear the claim. Figure 55.3 lists the authorities the ICJ uses in reaching its decisions.

FIGURE 55.3   The International Court of Justice

I	International Conventions (treaties)	The Court will use these authorities irrespective of whether the parties agree or not
II	International Custom (general practice accepted as law)	
III	General Legal Principles (recognized by civilized nations)	
IV	Judicial Decisions and Teachings of Experts (after it examines I, II, and III)	
V	*Ex Aequo et Bono* (that which is just and fair)	The Court will use this authority only if the parties agree

National Courts

A private person usually can resort to settlement of a dispute with a foreign nation by seeking redress through the courts of that state. Private persons can sometimes obtain adequate relief in their native state's judicial system. For example, a favorable judgment from a United States court may be filed in another country and, under certain conditions, can execute on assets in the foreign country on the basis of the other country's judicial decision. United States courts are likely to enforce a judgment obtained in another country following a full and fair trial, before an impartial court, with an opportunity for the defendant to be heard. A biased or corrupt court, or a case that didn't give a defendant an adequate chance to defend against the claims of the plaintiff, would probably lead a United States court to require a plaintiff to retry the entire claim, rather than enforce the prior judgment.

The recognition of foreign judgments is not a matter of international law,

Comity The informal and voluntary recognition of the sovereignty of another nation.

but rather a matter of **comity.** As the Supreme Court stated, in the landmark case of *Hilton* v. *Guyot,* 159 U.S. 113 (1895), comity is "the recognition which one nation allows within its territory to the . . . acts of another nation, having due regard both to international duty and convenience, and to the rights of its own citizens, or other persons. . . ." Comity is a matter of respect, good will, and courtesy which one nation gives to another, at least partly with the hope that the other nation will return the favor.

Arbitration

For variety of reasons, a particular international dispute may not be appropriate for resolution in the ICJ or national courts. In that case, international arbitration might be the correct course of action. Many international commercial contracts include provisions for using arbitration. Over sixty countries, including the United States, have signed the 1958 United Nations Convention on the Recognition and Enforcement of Foreign Arbitration Awards (T.I.A.S. 6997). The countries who have signed this Convention have agreed to use their court systems to recognize and enforce arbitration decisions.

The specification in an international contract of referral of disputes to arbitration or to a particular court may be strictly interpreted, as the following case illustrates.

M/S Bremen v. *Zapata Off-Shore Co.*
407 U.S. 1 (1972)

FACTS   A German corporation agreed to tow the off-shore drilling rig of the Zapata Co. to the Adriatic Sea. The contract provided that any dispute arising from it must be decided by the London Court of Justice. The rig was seriously damaged while being towed, and a dispute arose. Zapata sued the German corporation in a United States district court in Florida, alleging negligence and breach of contract. The German corporation moved to dismiss the suit on the basis of the contract clause.

ISSUE   Should the contract clause be specifically enforced?

HOLDING   Yes. Both parties agreed to it at the time of the contract.

REASONING   The clause should be specifically enforced unless Zapata can show that its enforcement would be unreasonable, unjust, fraudulent, or overreaching.

SUMMARY

We live in an interdependent world. Consequently, businesspersons should be aware of the international implications of their business dealings. In addition to being familiar with the laws and customs of the countries where they do business, managers must be aware that competition and labor laws, among others, may reach beyond national borders.

Global and regional trade organizations, such as the GATT, the EC, and the North American Free Trade Area, are becoming much more important in the world economy. They provide businesses with frameworks for trade and, increasingly, with efficient access to large markets. These organizations will serve as models for others all over the world in years to come.

One risk to international business investment is that of nationalization. Nationalization is the taking of private property. If the nationalization complies with international law, it is called an expropriation. If it does not, it is called a confiscation. The Act of State doctrine is used to justify the position that one country will not stand in judgment of the actions of other countries carried on within their own territories. Sovereign immunity is a rule of international law that states that a country cannot be sued unless it allows itself to be sued.

International law provides three mechanisms for the resolution of international disputes. The International Court of Justice (ICJ) is the appropriate forum when one nation sues another, provided that each nation agrees to the suit. Domestic courts are used for the resolution of disputes between citizens of different nations. Lastly, arbitration is used in international as well as domestic disputes.

DISCUSSION QUESTIONS

1. How would you apply the term *global village* to international business?

2. What arguments can you make for restricting a nation's laws to its territorial limits?

3. What is the modern significance of the Treaty of Rome?

4. What are the main differences between Article 85 and Article 86? How can a business be sure that its activities won't violate either section?

5. Two corporations, one organized in Belgium and the other in Great Britain, seek to merge. They are both in the computer software business. The Belgium corporation has 15 percent of the EC market, and the British corporation has 30 percent. What problems do these facts raise with respect to the Treaty of Rome?

6. Is it appropriate to penalize a seller of goods for a simple typographical error in a letter of credit?

7. An American corporation wishes to export a new computer microchip outside the United States. Do you envision any problems in complying with United States law?

8. You are an executive with an international publishing house. What steps would you take to ensure that your publishing and royalty rights were protected in the world markets?

9. You are a financial adviser to a multinational manufacturing corporation. What considerations would enter into your thinking with respect to a decision to invest $500 million in the nation of Chad?

10. The president has the power under current federal law to enter into foreign trade agreements with foreign governments. In so doing, the president can modify existing duties and import restrictions. Should the president use that power if country X is flooding the United States market with goods that are cheaper than similar United States–made goods? Discuss. (19 U.S.C. § 1351.)

CASE PROBLEMS

1. Is a nationalization a sovereign act, or is it commercial in nature? (*Carey* v. *National Oil Corp.*, 453 F. Supp. 1097 [S.D. N.Y. 1978].)

2. During the Spanish-American War, United States naval vessels captured two Spanish fishing vessels and their cargoes as prizes of war. If a rule of international law is that fishing vessels are exempt from capture as prizes of war, how should a United States court decide the fate of the fishing vessels? (*The Paquette Habana* v. *The Lola*, 175 U.S. 677 [1900].)

3. During Prohibition, the United States Coast Guard seized two vessels nineteen miles off the coast of the United States. The vessels were seized because they were carrying cargoes of whiskey bound for the United States. If the cargo had arrived in the United States, it would have violated federal law, which prohibited alcohol as a subject of commerce. At the time of the seizure, boundaries of the United States extended to twelve miles off the coast. Was the seizure valid? (*The Over the Top Schroeder* v. *Bissell* (5 F.2d 838 [D. Conn. 1925].)

4. Should nations use their status as nation-states in the international community to protect the private business interests of their citizens in international legal tribunals, or should they leave private interests alone? (*Barcelona Traction, Light, & Power Co., Ltd., Belgium* v. *Spain* [1970 I.C.J. Rep. 3].)

5. The American Civil Liberties Union sued on behalf of itself and other bank depositors to restrain the enforcement of the foreign transaction reporting requirements of the Currency and Foreign Transactions Reporting Act as a violation of the Fourth Amendment. Is the reporting requirement a general search warrant? Why or why not? (*California Bankers Association* v. *Shultz*, 416 U.S. 21 [1974].)

APPENDIX A

The Uniform Commercial Code

ARTICLE 1

GENERAL PROVISIONS

PART 1

Short Title, Construction, Application and Subject Matter of the Act

Section 1–101. Short Title

This Act shall be known and may be cited as Uniform Commercial Code.

Section 1–102. Purposes; Rules of Construction; Variation by Agreement

(1) This Act shall be liberally construed and applied to promote its underlying purposes and policies.

(2) Underlying purposes and policies of this Act are

(a) to simplify, clarify and modernize the law governing commercial transactions;

(b) to permit the continued expansion of commercial practices through custom, usage and agreement of the parties;

(c) to make uniform the law among the various jurisdictions.

(3) The effect of provisions of this Act may be varied by agreement, except as otherwise provided in this Act and except that the obligations of good faith, diligence, reasonableness and care prescribed by this Act may not be disclaimed by agreement but the parties may by agreement determine the standards by which tne performance of such obligations is to be measured if such standards are not manifestly unreasonable.

(4) The presence in certain provisions of this Act of the words "unless otherwise agreed" or words of similar import does not imply that the effect of other provisions may not be varied by agreement under subsection (3).

(5) In this Act unless the context otherwise requires

(a) words in the singular number include the plural, and in the plural include the singular;

(b) words of the masculine gender include the feminine and the neuter, and when the sense so indicates words of the neuter gender may refer to any gender.

Section 1–103. Supplementary General Principles of Law Applicable

Unless displaced by the particular provisions of this Act, the principles of law and equity, including the law merchant and the law relative to capacity to contract, principal and agent, estoppel, fraud, misrepresentation, duress, coercion, mistake, bankruptcy, or other validating or invalidating cause shall supplement its provisions.

Section 1–104. Construction Against Implicit Repeal

This Act being a general act intended as a unified coverage of its subject matter, no part of it shall be deemed to be impliedly repealed by subsequent legislation if such construction can reasonably be avoided.

Section 1–105. Territorial Application of the Act; Parties' Power to Choose Applicable Law

(1) Except as provided hereafter in this section, when a transaction bears a reasonable relation to this state and also to another state or nation the parties may agree that the law either of this state or of such other state or nation shall govern their rights and duties. Failing such agreement this Act applies to transactions bearing an appropriate relation to this state.

(2) Where one of the following provisions of this Act specifies the applicable law, that provision governs and a contrary agreement is effective only to the extent permitted by the law (including the conflict of laws rules) so specified:

> Rights of creditors against sold goods. Section 2–402.
>
> Applicability of the Article on Bank Deposits and Collections. Section 4–102.
>
> Bulk transfers subject to the Article on Bulk Transfers. Section 6–102.
>
> Applicability of the Article on Investment Securities. Section 8–106.
>
> Policy and scope of the Article on Secured Transactions. Section 9–103.

Section 1–106. Remedies to Be Liberally Administered

(1) The remedies provided by this Act shall be liberally administered to the end that the aggrieved party may be put in as good a position as if the other party had fully performed but neither consequential or special nor penal damages may be had except as specifically provided in this Act or by other rule of law.

(2) Any right or obligation declared by this Act is enforceable by action unless the provision declaring it specifies a different and limited effect.

Section 1–107. Waiver or Renunciation of Claim or Right After Breach

Any claim or right arising out of an alleged breach can be discharged in whole or in part without consideration by a written waiver or renunciation signed and delivered by the aggrieved party.

Section 1–108. Severability

If any provision or clause of this Act or application thereof to any person or circumstances is held invalid, such invalidity shall not affect other provisions or applications of the Act which can be given effect without the invalid provision or application, and to this end the provisions of this Act are declared to be severable.

Section 1–109. Section Captions

Section captions are parts of this Act.

PART 2

General Definitions and Principles of Interpretation

Section 1–201. General Definitions

Subject to additional definitions contained in the subsequent Articles of this Act which are applicable to specific Articles or Parts thereof, and unless the context otherwise requires, in this Act:

(1) "Action" in the sense of a judicial proceeding includes recoupment, counterclaim, setoff, suit in equity and any other proceedings in which rights are determined.

(2) "Aggrieved party" means a party entitled to resort to a remedy.

(3) "Agreement" means the bargain of the parties in fact as found in their language or by implication from other circumstances including course of dealing or usage of trade or course of performance as provided in this Act (Sections 1–205 and 2–208). Whether an agreement has legal consequences is determined by the provisions of this Act, if applicable; otherwise by the law of contracts (Section 1–103). (Compare "Contract".)

(4) "Bank" means any person engaged in the business of banking.

(5) "Bearer" means the person in possession of an instrument, document of title, or security payable to bearer or indorsed in blank.

(6) "Bill of lading" means a document evidencing the receipt of goods for shipment issued by a person engaged in the business of transporting or forwarding goods, and includes an airbill. "Airbill" means a document serving for air transportation as a bill of lading does for marine or rail transportation, and includes an air consignment note or air waybill.

(7) "Branch" includes a separately incorporated foreign branch of a bank.

(8) "Burden of establishing" a fact means the burden of persuading the triers of fact that the existence of the fact is more probable than its non-existence.

(9) "Buyer in ordinary course of business" means a person who in good faith and without knowledge that the sale to him is in violation of the ownership rights or security interest of a third party in the goods buys in ordinary course from a person in the business of selling goods of that kind but does not include a pawnbroker. All persons who sell minerals or the like (including oil and gas) at wellhead or minehead shall be deemed to be persons in the business of selling goods of that kind. "Buying" may be for cash or by exchange of other property or on secured or unsecured credit and includes receiving goods or documents of title under a pre-existing contract for sale but does not include a transfer in bulk or as security for or in total or partial satisfaction of a money debt.

(10) "Conspicuous": A term or clause is conspicuous when it is so written that a reasonable person against whom it is to operate ought to have noticed it. A printed heading in capitals (as: NON-NEGOTIABLE BILL OF LADING) is conspicuous. Language in the body of a form is "conspicuous" if it is in larger or other contrasting type or color. But in a telegram any stated term is "conspicuous." Whether a term or clause is "conspicuous" or not is for decision by the court.

(11) "Contract" means the total legal obligation which results from the parties' agreement as affected by this Act and any other applicable rules of law. (Compare "Agreement.")

(12) "Creditor" includes a general creditor, a secured creditor, a lien creditor and any representative of creditors, including an assignee for the benefit of creditors, a trustee in bankruptcy, a receiver in equity and an executor or administrator of an insolvent debtor's or assignor's estate.

(13) "Defendant" includes a person in the position of defendant in a cross-action or counterclaim.

(14) "Delivery" with respect to instruments, documents of title, chattel paper or securities means voluntary transfer of possession.

(15) "Document of title" includes bill of lading, dock warrant, dock receipt, warehouse receipt or order for the delivery of goods, and also any other document which in the regular course of business or financing is treated as adequately evidencing that the person in possession of it is entitled to receive, hold and dispose of the document and the goods it covers. To be a document of title a document must purport to be issued by or addressed to a bailee and purport to cover goods in the bailee's possession which are either identified or are fungible portions of an identified mass.

(16) "Fault" means wrongful act, omission or breach.

(17) "Fungible" with respect to goods or securities means goods or securities of which any unit is, by nature or usage of trade, the equivalent of any other like unit. Goods which are not fungible shall be deemed fungible for the purposes of this Act to the extent that under a particular agreement or document unlike units are treated as equivalents.

(18) "Genuine" means free of forgery or counterfeiting.

(19) "Good faith" means honesty in fact in the conduct or transaction concerned.

(20) "Holder" means a person who is in possession of a document of title or an instrument or an investment security drawn, issued or indorsed to him or to his order or to bearer or in blank.

(21) To "honor" is to pay or to accept and pay, or where a credit so engages to purchase or discount a draft complying with the terms of the credit.

(22) "Insolvency proceedings" includes any assignment for the benefit of creditors or other proceedings intended to liquidate or rehabilitate the estate of the person involved.

(23) A person is "insolvent" who either has ceased to pay his debts in the ordinary course of business or cannot pay his debts as they become due or is insolvent within the meaning of the federal bankruptcy law.

(24) "Money" means a medium of exchange authorized or adopted by a domestic or foreign government as a part of its currency.

(25) A person has "notice" of a fact when

    (a)   he has actual knowledge of it; or

    (b)   he has received a notice or notification of it; or

    (c)   from all the facts and circumstances known to him at the time in question he has reason to know that it exists.

A person "knows" or has "knowledge" of a fact when he has actual knowledge of it. "Discover" or "learn" or a word or phrase of similar import refers to knowledge rather than to reason to know. The time and circumstances under which a notice or notification may cease to be effective are not determined by this Act.

(26) A person "notifies" or "gives" a notice or notification to another by taking such steps as may be reasonably required to inform the other in ordinary course whether or not such other actually comes to know of it. A person "receives" a notice or notification

when

    (a)   it comes to his attention; or

    (b)   it is duly delivered at the place of business through which the contract was made or at any other place held out by him as the place for receipt of such communications.

(27) Notice, knowledge or a notice or notification received by an organization is effective for a particular transaction from the time when it is brought to the attention of the individual conducting that transaction, and in any event from the time when it would have been brought to his attention if the organization had exercised due diligence. An organization exercises due diligence if it maintains reasonable routines for communicating significant information to the person conducting the transaction and there is reasonable compliance with the routines. Due diligence does not require an individual acting for the organization to communicate information unless such communication is part of his regular duties or unless he has reason to know of the transaction and that the transaction would be materially affected by the information.

(28) "Organization" includes a corporation, government or governmental subdivision or agency, business trust, estate, trust, partnership or association, two or more persons having a joint or common interest, or any other legal or commercial entity.

(29) "Party", as distinct from "third party", means a person who has engaged in a transaction or made an agreement within this Act.

(30) "Person" includes an individual or an organization (See Section 1–102).

(31) "Presumption" or "presumed" means that the trier of fact must find the existence of the fact presumed unless and until evidence is introduced which would support a finding of its nonexistence.

(32) "Purchase" includes taking by sale, discount, negotiations, mortgage, pledge, lien, issue or re-issue, gift or any other voluntary transaction creating an interest in property.

(33) "Purchaser" means a person who takes by purchase.

(34) "Remedy" means any remedial right to which an aggrieved party is entitled with or without resort to a tribunal.

(35) "Representative" includes an agent, an officer of a corporation or association, and a trustee, executor or administrator of an estate, or any other person empowered to act for another.

(36) "Rights" includes remedies.

(37) "Security interest" means an interest in personal property or fixtures which secures payment or performance of an obligation. The retention or reservation of title by a seller of goods notwithstanding shipment or delivery to the buyer (Section 2–401) is limited in effect to a reservation of a "security interest". The term also includes any interest of a buyer of accounts or chattel paper which is subject to Article 9. The special property interest of a buyer of goods on identification of such goods to a contract for sale under Section 2–401 is not a "security interest", but a buyer may also acquire a "security interest" by complying with Article 9. Unless a lease or consignment is intended as security, reservation of title thereunder is not a "security interest" but a consignment is in any event subject to the provisions on consignment sales (Section 2–326). Whether a lease is intended as security is to be determined by the facts of each case; however, (a) the inclusion of an option to purchase does not of itself make the lease one intended for security, and (b) an agreement that upon compliance with the terms of the lease the lessee shall become or has the option to become the owner of the property for no additional consideration or for a nominal consideration does make the lease one intended for security.

(38) "Send" in connection with any writing or notice means to deposit in the mail or deliver for transmission by any other usual means of communication with postage or cost of transmission provided for and properly addressed and in the case of an instrument to an address specified thereon or otherwise agreed, or if there be none to any address reasonable under the circumstances. The receipt of any writing or notice within the time at which it would have arrived if properly sent has the effect of a proper sending.

(39) "Signed" includes any symbol executed or adopted by a party with present intention to authenticate a writing.

(40) "Surety" includes guarantor.

(41) "Telegram" includes a message transmitted by radio, teletype, cable, any mechanical method of transmission, or the like.

(42) "Term" means that portion of an agreement which relates to a particular matter.

(43) "Unauthorized" signature or indorsement means one made without actual, implied or apparent authority and includes a forgery.

(44) "Value". Except as otherwise provided with respect to negotiable instruments and bank collections (Sections

3-303, 4-208 and 4-209) a person gives "value" for rights if he acquires them

(a)   in return for a binding commitment to extend credit or for the extension of immediately available credit whether or not drawn upon and whether or not a charge-back is provided for in the event of difficulties in collection; or

(b)   as security for or in total or partial satisfaction of a pre-existing claim; or

(c)   by accepting delivery pursuant to a pre-existing contract for purchase; or

(d)   generally, in return for any consideration sufficient to support a simple contract.

(45) "Warehouse receipt" means a receipt issued by a person engaged in the business of storing goods for hire.

(46) "Written" or "writing" includes printing, typewriting or any other intentional reduction to tangible form.

Section 1-202.   Prima Facie Evidence by Third Party Documents

A document in due form purporting to be a bill of lading, policy or certificate of insurance, official weigher's or inspector's certificate, consular invoice, or any other document authorized or required by the contract to be issued by a third party shall be prima facie evidence of its own authenticity and genuineness and of the facts stated in the document by the third party.

Section 1-203.   Obligation of Good Faith

Every contract or duty within this Act imposes an obligation of good faith in its performance or enforcement.

Section 1-204.   Time; Reasonable Time; "Seasonably"

(1)   Whenever this Act requires any action to be taken within a reasonable time, any time which is not manifestly unreasonable may be fixed by agreement.

(2)   What is a reasonable time for taking any action depends on the nature, purpose and circumstances of such action.

(3)   An action is taken "seasonably" when it is taken at or within the time agreed or if no time is agreed at or within a reasonable time.

Section 1-205.   Course of Dealing and Usage of Trade

(1)   A course of dealing is a sequence of previous conduct between the parties to a particular transaction which is fairly to be regarded as establishing a common basis of understanding for interpreting their expressions and other conduct.

(2)   A usage of trade is any practice or method of dealing having such regularity of observance in a place, vocation or trade as to justify an expectation that it will be observed with respect to the transaction in question. The existence and scope of such a usage are to be proved as facts. If it is established that such a usage is embodied in a written trade code or similar writing the interpretation of the writing is for the court.

(3)   A course of dealing between parties and any usage of trade in the vocation or trade in which they are engaged or of which they are or should be aware give particular meaning to and supplement or qualify terms of an agreement.

(4)   The express terms of an agreement and an applicable course of dealing or usage of trade shall be construed wherever reasonable as consistent with each other; but when such construction is unreasonable express terms control both course of dealing and usage of trade and course of dealing controls usage of trade.

(5)   An applicable usage of trade in the place where any part of performance is to occur shall be used in interpreting the agreement as to that part of the performance.

(6)   Evidence of a relevant usage of trade offered by one party is not admissible unless and until he has given the other party such notice as the court finds sufficient to prevent unfair surprise to the latter.

Section 1-206.   Statute of Frauds for Kinds of Personal Property Not Otherwise Covered

(1)   Except in the cases described in subsection (2) of this section a contract for the sale of personal property is not enforceable by way of action or defense beyond five thousand dollars in amount or value of remedy unless there is some writing which indicates that a contract for sale has been made between the parties at a defined or stated price, reasonably identifies the subject matter, and is signed by the party against whom enforcement is sought or by his authorized agent.

(2)   Subsection (1) of this section does not apply to contracts for the sale of goods (Section 2-201) nor

of securities (Section 8–319) nor to security agreements (Section 9–203).

Section 1–207. Performance or Acceptance Under Reservation of Rights

A party who with explicit reservation of rights performs or promises performance or assents to performance in a manner demanded or offered by the other party does not thereby prejudice the rights reserved. Such words as "without prejudice", "under protest" or the like are sufficient.

Section 1–208. Option to Accelerate at Will

A term providing that one party or his successor in interest may accelerate payment or performance or require collateral or additional collateral "at will" or "when he deems himself insecure" or in words of similar import shall be construed to mean that he shall have power to do so only if he in good faith believes that the prospect of payment or performance is impaired. The burden of establishing lack of good faith is on the party against whom the power has been exercised.

Section 1–209. Subordinated Obligations

An obligation may be issued as subordinated to payment of another obligation of the person obligated, or a creditor may subordinate his right to payment of an obligation by agreement with either the person obligated or another creditor of the person obligated. Such a subordination does not create a security interest as against either the common debtor or a subordinated creditor. This section shall be construed as declaring the law as it existed prior to the enactment of this section and not as modifying it. Added 1966.

Note: *This new section is proposed as an optional provision to make it clear that a subordination agreement does not create a security interest unless so intended.*

ARTICLE 2
SALES

PART 1
Short Title, Construction and Subject Matter

Section 2–101. Short Title

This Article shall be known and may be cited as Uniform Commercial Code — Sales.

Section 2–102. Scope; Certain Security and Other Transactions Excluded from This Article

Unless the context otherwise requires, this Article applies to transactions in goods; it does not apply to any transaction which although in the form of an unconditional contract to sell or present sale is intended to operate only as a security transaction nor does this Article impair or repeal any statute regulating sales to consumers, farmers or other specified classes of buyers.

Section 2–103. Definitions and Index of Definitions

(1) In this Article unless the context otherwise requires

  (a) "Buyer" means a person who buys or contracts to buy goods.

  (b) "Good faith" in the case of a merchant means honesty in fact and the observance of reasonable commercial standards of fair dealing in the trade.

  (c) "Receipt" of goods means taking physical possession of them.

  (d) "Seller" means a person who sells or contracts to sell goods.

(2) Other definitions applying to this Article or to specified Parts thereof, and the sections in which they appear are:

  "Acceptance." Section 2–606.
  "Banker's credit." Section 2–325.
  "Between merchants." Section 2–104.
  "Cancellation." Section 2–106(4).
  "Commercial unit." Section 2–105.
  "Confirmed credit." Section 2–325.
  "Conforming to contract." Section 2–106.
  "Contract for sale." Section 2–106.
  "Cover." Section 2–712.
  "Entrusting." Section 2–403.
  "Financing agency." Section 2–104.
  "Future goods." Section 2–105.
  "Goods." Section 2–105.
  "Identification." Section 2–501.
  "Installment contract." Section 2–612.
  "Letter of credit." Section 2–325.
  "Lot." Section 2–105.
  "Merchant." Section 2–104.
  "Overseas." Section 2–323.
  "Person in position of seller." Section 2–707.
  "Present sale." Section 2–106.
  "Sale." Section 2–106.
  "Sale on approval." Section 2–326.

"Sale or return." Section 2–326.
"Termination." Section 2–106.

(3) The following definitions in other articles apply to this Article:

"Check." Section 3–104.
"Consignee." Section 7–102.
"Consignor." Section 7–102.
"Consumer goods." Section 9–109.
"Dishonor." Section 3–507.
"Draft." Section 3–104.

(4) In addition Article 1 contains general definitions and principles of construction and interpretation applicable throughout this Article.

Section 2–104.   Definitions: "Merchant"; "Between Merchants"; "Financing Agency"

(1) "Merchant" means a person who deals in goods of the kind or otherwise by his occupation holds himself out as having knowledge or skill peculiar to the practices or goods involved in the transaction or to whom such knowledge or skill may be attributed by his employment of an agent or broker or other intermediary who by his occupation holds himself out as having such knowledge or skill.

(2) "Financing agency" means a bank, finance company or other person who in the ordinary course of business makes advances against goods or documents of title or who by arrangement with either the seller or the buyer intervenes in ordinary course to make or collect payment due or claimed under the contract for sale, as by purchasing or paying the seller's draft or making advances against it or by merely taking it for collection whether or not documents of title accompany the draft. "Financing agency" includes also a bank or other person who similarly intervenes between persons who are in the position of seller and buyer in respect to the goods (Section 2–707).

(3) "Between merchants" means in any transaction with respect to which both parties are chargeable with the knowledge or skill of merchants.

Section 2–105.   Definitions: Transferability; "Goods"; "Future" Goods; "Lot"; "Commercial Unit"

(1) "Goods" means all things (including specially manufactured goods) which are movable at the time of identification to the contract for sale other than the money in which the price is to be paid, investment securities (Article 8) and things in action. "Goods" also includes the unborn young of animals and growing crops and other identified things attached to realty as described in the section on goods to be severed from realty (Section 2–107).

(2) Goods must be both existing and identified before any interest in them can pass. Goods which are not both existing and identified are "future" goods. A purported present sale of future goods or of any interest therein operates as a contract to sell.

(3) There may be a sale of a part interest in existing identified goods.

(4) An undivided share in an identified bulk of fungible goods is sufficiently identified to be sold although the quantity of the bulk is not determined. Any agreed proportion of such a bulk or any quantity thereof agreed upon by number, weight or other measure may to the extent of the seller's interest in the bulk be sold to the buyer who then becomes an owner in common.

(5) "Lot" means a parcel or a single article which is the subject matter of a separate sale or delivery, whether or not it is sufficient to perform the contract.

(6) "Commercial unit" means such a unit of goods as by commercial usage is a single whole for purposes of sale and division of which materially impairs its character or value on the market or in use. A commercial unit may be a single article (as a machine) or a set of articles (as a suite of furniture or an assortment of sizes) or a quantity (as a bale, gross, or carload) or any other unit treated in use or in the relevant market as a single whole.

Section 2–106.   Definitions: "Contract"; "Agreement"; "Contract for Sale"; "Sale"; "Present Sale"; "Conforming" to Contract; "Termination"; "Cancellation"

(1) In this Article unless the context otherwise requires "contract" and "agreement" are limited to those relating to the present or future sale of goods. "Contract for sale" includes both a present sale of goods and a contract to sell goods at a future time. A "sale" consists in the passing of title from the seller to the buyer for a price (Section 2–401). A "present sale" means a sale which is accomplished by the making of the contract.

(2) Goods or conduct including any part of a performance are "conforming" or conform to the contract when they are in accordance with the obligations under the contract.

(3) "Termination" occurs when either party pursuant to a power created by agreement or law puts an end

to the contract otherwise than for its breach. On "termination" all obligations which are still executory on both sides are discharged but any right based on prior breach or performance survives.

(4) "Cancellation" occurs when either party puts an end to the contract for breach by the other and its effect is the same as that of "termination" except that the cancelling party also retains any remedy for breach of the whole contract or any unperformed balance.

Section 2–107. Goods to Be Severed from Realty; Recording

(1) A contract for the sale of minerals or the like (including oil and gas) or a structure or its materials to be removed from realty is a contract for the sale of goods within this Article if they are to be severed by the seller but until severance a purported present sale thereof which is not effective as a transfer of an interest in land is effective only as a contract to sell.

(2) A contract for the sale apart from the land of growing crops or other things attached to realty and capable of severance without material harm thereto but not described in subsection (1) or of timber to be cut is a contract for the sale of goods within this Article whether the subject matter is to be severed by the buyer or by the seller even though it forms part of the realty at the time of contracting, and the parties can by identification effect a present sale before severance.

(3) The provisions of this section are subject to any third party rights provided by the law relating to realty records, and the contract for sale may be executed and recorded as a document transferring an interest in land and shall then constitute notice to third parties of the buyer's rights under the contract for sale.

PART 2

Form, Formation and Readjustment of Contract

Section 2–201. Formal Requirements; Statute of Frauds

(1) Except as otherwise provided in this section a contract for the sale of goods for the price of $500 or more is not enforceable by way of action or defense unless there is some writing sufficient to indicate that a contract for sale has been made between the parties and signed by the party against whom enforcement is sought or by his authorized agent or broker. A writing is not insufficient because it omits or incorrectly states a term agreed upon but the contract is not enforceable under this paragraph beyond the quantity of goods shown in such writing.

(2) Between merchants if within a reasonable time a writing in confirmation of the contract and sufficient against the sender is received and the party receiving it has reason to know its contents, it satisfies the requirements of subsection (1) against such party unless written notice of objection to its contents is given within ten days after it is received.

(3) A contract which does not satisfy the requirements of subsection (1) but which is valid in other respects is enforceable

(a) if the goods are to be specially manufactured for the buyer and are not suitable for sale to others in the ordinary course of the seller's business and the seller, before notice of repudiation is received and under circumstances which reasonably indicate that the goods are for the buyer, has made either a substantial beginning of their manufacture or commitments for their procurement; or

(b) if the party against whom enforcement is sought admits in his pleading, testimony or otherwise in court that a contract for sale was made, but the contract is not enforceable under this provision beyond the quantity of goods admitted; or

(c) with respect to goods for which payment has been made and accepted or which have been received and accepted (Section 2–606).

Section 2–202. Final Written Expression: Parol or Extrinsic Evidence

Terms with respect to which the confirmatory memoranda of the parties agree or which are otherwise set forth in a writing intended by the parties as a final expression of their agreement with respect to such terms as are included therein may not be contradicted by evidence of any prior agreement or of a contemporaneous oral agreement but may be explained or supplemented

(a) by course of dealing or usage of trade (Section 1–205) or by course of performance (Section 2–208); and

(b) by evidence of consistent additional terms unless the court finds the writing to have been intended also as a complete and exclusive statement of the terms of the agreement.

Section 2–203. Seals Inoperative

The affixing of a seal to a writing evidencing a contract for sale or an offer to buy or sell goods does not constitute the writing of a sealed instrument and the law with respect to sealed instruments does not apply to such a contract or offer.

Section 2-204. Formation in General

(1) A contract for sale of goods may be made in any manner sufficient to show agreement, including conduct by both parties which recognizes the existence of such a contract.

(2) An agreement sufficient to constitute a contract for sale may be found even though the moment of its making is undetermined.

(3) Even though one or more terms are left open a contract for sale does not fail for indefiniteness if the parties have intended to make a contract and there is a reasonably certain basis for giving an appropriate remedy.

Section 2-205. Firm Offers

An offer by a merchant to buy or sell goods in a signed writing which by its terms gives assurance that it will be held open is not revocable, for lack of consideration, during the time stated or if no time is stated for a reasonable time, but in no event may such period of irrevocability exceed three months; but any such term of assurance on a form supplied by the offeree must be separately signed by the offeror.

Section 2-206. Offer and Acceptance in Formation of Contract

(1) Unless otherwise unambiguously indicated by the language or circumstances

(a) an offer to make a contract shall be construed as inviting acceptance in any manner and by any medium reasonable in the circumstances;

(b) an order or other offer to buy goods for prompt or current shipment shall be construed as inviting acceptance either by a prompt promise to ship or by the prompt or current shipment of conforming or non-conforming goods, but such a shipment of non-conforming goods does not constitute an acceptance if the seller seasonably notifies the buyer that the shipment is offered only as an accommodation to the buyer.

(2) Where the beginning of a requested performance is a reasonable mode of acceptance an offeror who is not notified of acceptance within a reasonable time may treat the offer as having lapsed before acceptance.

Section 2-207. Additional Terms in Acceptance or Confirmation

(1) A definite and seasonable expression of acceptance or a written confirmation which is sent within a reasonable time operates as an acceptance even though it states terms additional to or different from those offered or agreed upon, unless acceptance is expressly made conditional on assent to the additional or different terms.

(2) The additional terms are to be construed as proposals for addition to the contract. Between merchants such terms become part of the contract unless:

(a) the offer expressly limits acceptance to the terms of the offer;

(b) they materially alter it; or

(c) notification of objection to them has already been given or is given within a reasonable time after notice of them is received.

(3) Conduct by both parties which recognizes the existence of a contract is sufficient to establish a contract for sale although the writings of the parties do not otherwise establish a contract. In such case the terms of the particular contract consist of those terms on which the writings of the parties agree, together with any supplementary terms incorporated under any other provisions of this Act.

Section 2-208. Course of Performance or Practical Construction

(1) Where the contract for sale involves repeated occasions for performance by either party with knowledge of the nature of the performance and opportunity for objection to it by the other, any course of performance accepted or acquiesced in without objection shall be relevant to determine the meaning of the agreement.

(2) The express terms of the agreement and any such course of performance, as well as any course of dealing and usage of trade, shall be construed whenever reasonable as consistent with each other; but when such construction is unreasonable, express terms shall control course of performance and course of performance shall control both course of dealing and usage of trade (Section 1-205).

(3) Subject to the provisions of the next section on modification and waiver, such course of performance shall be relevant to show a waiver or modification of any term inconsistent with such course of performance.

Section 2-209. Modification, Rescission and Waiver

(1) An agreement modifying a contract within this Article needs no consideration to be binding.

(2) A signed agreement which excludes modification or rescission except by a signed writing cannot be otherwise modified or rescinded, but except as between

merchants such a requirement on a form supplied by the merchant must be separately signed by the other party.

(3) The requirements of the statute of frauds section of this Article (Section 2–201) must be satisfied if the contract as modified is within its provisions.

(4) Although an attempt at modification or rescission does not satisfy the requirements of subsection (2) or (3) it can operate as a waiver.

(5) A party who has made a waiver affecting an executory portion of the contract may retract the waiver by reasonable notification received by the other party that strict performance will be required of any term waived, unless the retraction would be unjust in view of a material change of position in reliance on the waiver.

Section 2–210. Delegation of Performance; Assignment of Rights

(1) A party may perform his duty through a delegate unless otherwise agreed or unless the other party has a substantial interest in having his original promisor perform or control the acts required by the contract. No delegation of performance relieves the party delegating of any duty to perform or any liability for breach.

(2) Unless otherwise agreed all rights of either seller or buyer can be assigned except where the assignment would materially change the duty of the other party, or increase materially the burden or risk imposed on him by his contract, or impair materially his chance of obtaining return performance. A right to damages for breach of the whole contract or a right arising out of the assignor's due performance of his entire obligation can be assigned despite agreement otherwise.

(3) Unless the circumstances indicate the contrary a prohibition of assignment of "the contract" is to be construed as barring only the delegation to the assignee of the assignor's performance.

(4) An assignment of "the contract" or of "all my rights under the contract" or an assignment in similar general terms is an assignment of rights and unless the language or the circumstances (as in an assignment for security) indicate the contrary, it is a delegation of performance of the duties of the assignor and its acceptance by the assignee constitutes a promise by him to perform those duties. This promise is enforceable by either the assignor or the other party to the original contract.

(5) The other party may treat any assignment which delegates performance as creating reasonable grounds for insecurity and may without prejudice to his rights against the assignor demand assurances from the assignee (Section 2–609).

PART 3

General Obligation and Construction of Contract

Section 2–301. General Obligations of Parties

The obligation of the seller is to transfer and deliver and that of the buyer is to accept and pay in accordance with the contract.

Section 2–302. Unconscionable Contract or Clause

(1) If the court as a matter of law finds the contract or any clause of the contract to have been unconscionable at the time it was made the court may refuse to enforce the contract, or it may enforce the remainder of the contract without the unconscionable clause, or it may so limit the application of any unconscionable clause as to avoid any unconscionable result.

(2) When it is claimed or appears to the court that the contract or any clause thereof may be unconscionable the parties shall be afforded a reasonable opportunity to present evidence as to its commercial setting, purpose and effect to aid the court in making the determination.

Section 2–303. Allocation or Division of Risks

Where this Article allocates a risk or a burden as between the parties "unless otherwise agreed", the agreement may not only shift the allocation but may also divide the risk or burden.

Section 2–304. Price Payable in Money, Goods, Realty, or Otherwise

(1) The price can be made payable in money or otherwise. If it is payable in whole or in part in goods each party is a seller of the goods which he is to transfer.

(2) Even though all or part of the price is payable in an interest in realty the transfer of the goods and the seller's obligations with reference to them are subject to this Article but not the transfer of the interest in realty or the transferor's obligations in connection therewith.

Section 2–305.   Open Price Term

(1) The parties if they so intend can conclude a contract for sale even though the price is not settled. In such a case the price is a reasonable price at the time for delivery if

(a)   nothing is said as to price; or

(b)   the price is left to be agreed by the parties and they fail to agree; or

(c)   the price is to be fixed in terms of some agreed market or other standard as set or recorded by a third person or agency and it is not so set or recorded.

(2) A price to be fixed by the seller or by the buyer means a price for him to fix in good faith.

(3) When a price left to be fixed otherwise than by agreement of the parties fails to be fixed through fault of one party the other may at his option treat the contract as cancelled or himself fix a reasonable price.

(4) Where, however, the parties intend not to be bound unless the price be fixed or agreed and it is not fixed or agreed there is no contract. In such a case the buyer must return any goods already received or if unable so to do must pay their reasonable value at the time of delivery and the seller must return any portion of the price paid on account.

Section 2–306.   Output, Requirements and Exclusive Dealings

(1) A term which measures the quantity by the output of the seller or the requirements of the buyer means such actual output or requirements as may occur in good faith, except that no quantity unreasonably disproportionate to any stated estimate or in the absence of a stated estimate to any normal or otherwise comparable prior output or requirements may be tendered or demanded.

(2) A lawful agreement by either the seller or the buyer for exclusive dealing in the kind of goods concerned imposes unless otherwise agreed an obligation by the seller to use best efforts to supply the goods and by the buyer to use best efforts to promote their sale.

Section 2–307.   Delivery in Single Lot or Several Lots

Unless otherwise agreed all goods called for by a contract for sale must be tendered in a single delivery and payment is due only on such tender but where the circumstances give either party the right to make or demand delivery in lots the price if it can be apportioned may be demanded for each lot.

Section 2–308.   Absence of Specified Place for Delivery

Unless otherwise agreed

(a)   the place for delivery of goods is the seller's place of business or if he has none his residence; but

(b)   in a contract for sale of identified goods which to the knowledge of the parties at the time of contracting are in some other place, that place is the place for their delivery; and

(c)   documents of title may be delivered through customary banking channels.

Section 2–309.   Absence of Specific Time Provisions; Notice of Termination

(1) The time for shipment or delivery or any other action under a contract if not provided in this Article or agreed upon shall be a reasonable time.

(2) Where the contract provides for successive performances but is indefinite in duration it is valid for a reasonable time but unless otherwise agreed may be terminated at any time by either party.

(3) Termination of a contract by one party except on the happening of an agreed event requires that reasonable notification be received by the other party and an agreement dispensing with notification is invalid if its operation would be unconscionable.

Section 2–310.   Open Time for Payment or Running of Credit; Authority to Ship Under Reservation

Unless otherwise agreed

(a)   payment is due at the time and place at which the buyer is to receive the goods even though the place of shipment is the place of delivery; and

(b)   if the seller is authorized to send the goods he may ship them under reservation, and may tender the documents of title, but the buyer may inspect the goods after their arrival before payment is due unless such inspection is inconsistent with the terms of the contract (Section 2–513); and

(c)   if delivery is authorized and made by way of documents of title otherwise than by subsection (b) then payment is due at the time and place at which the buyer is to receive the documents regardless of where the goods are to be received; and

(d)   where the seller is required or authorized to ship the goods on credit the credit period runs from the time of shipment but post-dating the invoice or delaying its dispatch will correspondingly delay this starting of the credit period.

Section 2–311.   Options and Cooperation Respecting Performance

(1)   An agreement for sale which is otherwise sufficiently definite (subsection (3) of Section 2–204) to be a contract is not made invalid by the fact that it leaves particulars of performance to be specified by one of the parties. Any such specification must be made in good faith and within limits set by commercial reasonableness.

(2)   Unless otherwise agreed specifications relating to assortment of the goods are at the buyer's option and except as otherwise provided in subsections (1)(c) and (3) of Section 2–319 specifications or arrangements relating to shipment are at the seller's option.

(3)   Where such specification would materially affect the other party's performance but is not seasonably made or where one party's cooperation is necessary to the agreed performance of the other but is not seasonably forthcoming, the other party in addition to all other remedies

(a)   is excused for any resulting delay in his own performance; and

(b)   may also either proceed to perform in any reasonable manner or after the time for a material part of his own performance treat the failure to specify or to cooperate as a breach by failure to deliver or accept the goods.

Section 2–312.   Warranty of Title and Against Infringement; Buyer's Obligation Against Infringement

(1)   Subject to subsection (2) there is in a contract for sale a warranty by the seller that

(a)   the title conveyed shall be good, and its transfer rightful; and

(b)   the goods shall be delivered free from any security interest or other lien or encumbrance of which the buyer at the time of contracting has no knowledge.

(2)   A warranty under subsection (1) will be excluded or modified only by specific language or by circumstances which give the buyer reason to know that the person selling does not claim title in himself or that he is purporting to sell only such right or title as he or a third person may have.

(3)   Unless otherwise agreed a seller who is a merchant regularly dealing in goods of the kind warrants that the goods shall be delivered free of the rightful claim of any third person by way of infringement or the like but a buyer who furnishes specifications to the seller must hold the seller harmless against any such claim which arises out of compliance with the specifications.

Section 2–313.   Express Warranties by Affirmation, Promise, Description, Sample

(1)   Express warranties by the seller are created as follows:

(a)   Any affirmation of fact or promise made by the seller to the buyer which relates to the goods and becomes part of the basis of the bargain creates an express warranty that the goods shall conform to the affirmation or promise.

(b)   Any description of the goods which is made part of the basis of the bargain creates an express warranty that the goods shall conform to the description.

(c)   Any sample or model which is made part of the basis of the bargain creates an express warranty that the whole of the goods shall conform to the sample or model.

(2)   It is not necessary to the creation of an express warranty that the seller use formal words such as "warrant" or "guarantee" or that he have a specific intention to make a warranty, but an affirmation merely of the value of the goods or a statement purporting to be merely the seller's opinion or commendation of the goods does not create a warranty.

Section 2–314.   Implied Warranty: Merchantability; Usage of Trade

(1)   Unless excluded or modified (Section 2–316), a warranty that the goods shall be merchantable is implied in a contract for their sale if the seller is a merchant with respect to goods of that kind. Under this section the serving for value of food or drink to be consumed either on the premises or elsewhere is a sale.

(2) Goods to be merchantable must be at least such as

(a) pass without objection in the trade under the contract description; and

(b) in the case of fungible goods, are of fair average quality within the description; and

(c) are fit for the ordinary purposes for which such goods are used; and

(d) run, within the variations permitted by the agreement, of even kind, quality and quantity within each unit and among all units involved; and

(e) are adequately contained, packaged, and labeled as the agreement may require; and

(f) conform to the promises or affirmations of fact made on the container or label if any.

(3) Unless excluded or modified (Section 2–316) other implied warranties may arise from course of dealing or usage of trade.

Section 2–315. Implied Warranty: Fitness for Particular Purpose

Where the seller at the time of contracting has reason to know any particular purpose for which the goods are required and that the buyer is relying on the seller's skill or judgment to select or furnish suitable goods, there is unless excluded or modified under the next section an implied warranty that the goods shall be fit for such purpose.

Section 2–316. Exclusion or Modification of Warranties

(1) Words or conduct relevant to the creation of an express warranty and words or conduct tending to negate or limit warranty shall be construed wherever reasonable as consistent with each other; but subject to the provisions of this Article on parol or extrinsic evidence (Section 2–202) negation or limitation is inoperative to the extent that such construction is unreasonable.

(2) Subject to subsection (3), to exclude or modify the implied warranty of merchantability or any part of it the language must mention merchantability and in case of a writing must be conspicuous, and to exclude or modify any implied warranty of fitness the exclusion must be by a writing and conspicuous. Language to exclude all implied warranties of fitness is sufficient if it states, for example, that "There are no warranties

which extend beyond the description on the face hereof."

(3) Notwithstanding subsection (2)

(a) unless the circumstances indicate otherwise, all implied warranties are excluded by expressions like "as is", "with all faults" or other language which in common understanding calls the buyer's attention to the exclusion of warranties and makes plain that there is no implied warranty; and

(b) when the buyer before entering into the contract has examined the goods or the sample or model as fully as he desired or has refused to examine the goods there is no implied warranty with regard to defects which an examination ought in the circumstances to have revealed to him; and

(c) an implied warranty can also be excluded or modified by course of dealing or course of performance or usage of trade.

(4) Remedies for breach of warranty can be limited in accordance with the provisions of this Article on liquidation or limitation of damages and on contractual modification of remedy (Sections 2–718 and 2–719).

Section 2–317. Cumulation and Conflict of Warranties Express or Implied

Warranties whether express or implied shall be construed as consistent with each other and as cumulative, but if such construction is unreasonable the intention of the parties shall determine which warranty is dominant. In ascertaining that intention the following rules apply:

(a) Exact or technical specifications displace an inconsistent sample or model or general language of description.

(b) A sample from an existing bulk displaces inconsistent general language of description.

(c) Express warranties displace inconsistent implied warranties other than an implied warranty of fitness for a particular purpose.

Section 2–318. Third Party Beneficiaries of Warranties Express or Implied

Note: *If this Act is introduced in the Congress of the United States, this section should be omitted. (States to select one alternative.)*

Alternative A

A seller's warranty whether express or implied extends to any natural person who is in the family or household of his buyer or who is a guest in his home if it is reasonable to expect that such person may use, consume or be affected by the goods and who is injured in person by breach of the warranty. A seller may not exclude or limit the operation of this section.

Alternative B

A seller's warranty whether express or implied extends to any natural person who may reasonably be expected to use, consume or be affected by the goods and who is injured in person by breach of the warranty. A seller may not exclude or limit the operation of this section.

Alternative C

A seller's warranty whether express or implied extends to any person who may reasonably be expected to use, consume or be affected by the goods and who is injured by breach of the warranty. A seller may not exclude or limit the operation of this section with respect to injury to the person of an individual to whom the warranty extends. As amended 1966.

Section 2–319.   F.O.B. and F.A.S. Terms

(1) Unless otherwise agreed the term F.O.B. (which means "free on board") at a named place, even though used only in connection with the stated price, is a delivery term under which

> (a)   when the term is F.O.B. the place of shipment, the seller must at that place ship the goods in the manner provided in this Article (Section 2–504) and bear the expense and risk of putting them into the possession of the carrier; or

> (b)   when the term is F.O.B. the place of destination, the seller must at his own expense and risk transport the goods to that place and there tender delivery of them in the manner provided in this Article (Section 2–503);

> (c)   when under either (a) or (b) the term is also F.O.B. vessel, car or other vehicle, the seller must in addition at his own expense and risk load the goods on board. If the term is F.O.B. vessel the buyer must name the vessel and in an appropriate case the seller must comply with the provisions of this Article on the form of bill of lading (Section 2–323).

(2) Unless otherwise agreed the term F.A.S. vessel (which means "free alongside") at a named port, even though used only in connection with the stated price, is a delivery term under which the seller must

> (a)   at his own expense and risk deliver the goods alongside the vessel in the manner usual in that port or on a dock designated and provided by the buyer; and

> (b)   obtain and tender a receipt for the goods in exchange for which the carrier is under a duty to issue a bill of lading.

(3) Unless otherwise agreed in any case falling within subsection (1)(a) or (c) or subsection (2) the buyer must seasonably give any needed instructions for making delivery, including when the term is F.A.S. or F.O.B. the loading berth of the vessel and in an appropriate case its name and sailing date. The seller may treat the failure of needed instructions as a failure of cooperation under this Article (Section 2–311). He may also at his option move the goods in any reasonable manner preparatory to delivery or shipment.

(4) Under the term F.O.B. vessel or F.A.S. unless otherwise agreed the buyer must make payment against tender of the required documents and the seller may not tender nor the buyer demand delivery of the goods in substitution for the documents.

Section 2–320.   C.I.F. and C. & F. Terms

(1) The term C.I.F. means that the price includes in a lump sum the cost of the goods and the insurance and freight to the named destination. The term C. & F. or C.F. means that the price so includes cost and freight to the named destination.

(2) Unless otherwise agreed and even though used only in connection with the stated price and destination, the term C.I.F. destination or its equivalent requires the seller at his own expense and risk to

> (a)   put the goods into the possession of a carrier at the port for shipment and obtain a negotiable bill or bills of lading covering the entire transportation to the named destination; and

> (b)   load the goods and obtain a receipt from the carrier (which may be contained in the bill of lading) showing that the freight has been paid or provided for; and

> (c)   obtain a policy or certificate of insurance, including any war risk insurance, of a kind and on terms then current at the port of shipment in the usual amount, in the currency of the contract,

shown to cover the same goods covered by the bill of lading and providing for payment of loss to the order of the buyer or for the account of whom it may concern; but the seller may add to the price the amount of the premium for any such war risk insurance; and

(d)   prepare an invoice of the goods and procure any other documents required to effect shipment or to comply with the contract; and

(e)   forward and tender with commercial promptness all the documents in due form and with any indorsement necessary to perfect the buyer's rights.

(3) Unless otherwise agreed the term C. & F. or its equivalent has the same effect and imposes upon the seller the same obligations and risks as a C.I.F. term except the obligation as to insurance.

(4) Under the term C.I.F. or C. & F. unless otherwise agreed the buyer must make payment against tender of the required documents and the seller may not tender nor the buyer demand delivery of the goods in substitution for the documents.

Section 2–321.   C.I.F. or C. & F.: "Net Landed Weights"; "Payment on Arrival"; Warranty of Condition on Arrival

Under a contract containing a term C.I.F. or C. & F.

(1) Where the price is based on or is to be adjusted according to "net landed weights", "delivered weights", "out turn" quantity or quality or the like, unless otherwise agreed the seller must reasonably estimate the price. The payment due on tender of the documents called for by the contract is the amount so estimated, but after final adjustment of the price a settlement must be made with commercial promptness.

(2) An agreement described in subsection (1) or any warranty of quality or condition of the goods on arrival places upon the seller the risk of ordinary deterioration, shrinkage and the like in transportation but has no effect on the place or time or identification to the contract for sale or delivery or on the passing of the risk of loss.

(3) Unless otherwise agreed where the contract provides for payment on or after arrival of the goods the seller must before payment allow such preliminary inspection as is feasible; but if the goods are lost delivery of the documents and payment are due when the goods should have arrived.

Section 2–322.   Delivery "Ex-Ship"

(1) Unless otherwise agreed a term for delivery of goods "ex-ship" (which means from the carrying vessel) or in equivalent language is not restricted to a particular ship and requires delivery from a ship which has reached a place at the named port of destination where goods of the kind are usually discharged.

(2) Under such a term unless otherwise agreed

(a)   the seller must discharge all liens arising out of the carriage and furnish the buyer with a direction which puts the carrier under a duty to deliver the goods; and

(b)   the risk of loss does not pass to the buyer until the goods leave the ship's tackle or are otherwise properly unloaded.

Section 2–323.   Form of Bill of Lading Required in Overseas Shipment; "Overseas"

(1) Where the contract contemplates overseas shipment and contains a term C.I.F. or C. & F. or F.O.B. vessel, the seller unless otherwise agreed must obtain a negotiable bill of lading stating that the goods have been loaded on board or, in the case of a term C.I.F. or C. & F., received for shipment.

(2) Where in a case within subsection (1) a bill of lading has been issued in a set of parts, unless otherwise agreed if the documents are not to be sent from abroad the buyer may demand tender of the full set; otherwise only one part of the bill of lading need be tendered. Even if the agreement expressly requires a full set

(a)   due tender of a single part is acceptable within the provisions of the Article on cure of improper delivery (subsection (1) of Section 2–508); and

(b)   even though the full set is demanded, if the documents are sent from abroad the person tendering an incomplete set may nevertheless require payment upon furnishing an indemnity which the buyer in good faith deems adequate.

(3) A shipment by water or by air or a contract contemplating such shipment is "overseas" insofar as by usage of trade or agreement it is subject to the commercial, financing or shipping practices characteristic of international deep water commerce.

Section 2–324.   "No Arrival, No Sale" Term

Under a term "no arrival, no sale" or terms of like meaning, unless otherwise agreed,

(a) the seller must properly ship conforming goods and if they arrive by any means he must tender them on arrival but he assumes an obligation that the goods will arrive unless he had caused the non-arrival; and

(b) where without fault of the seller the goods are in part lost or have so deteriorated as no longer to conform to the contract or arrive after the contract time, the buyer may proceed as if there had been casualty to identified goods (Section 2–613).

Section 2–325. "Letter of Credit" Term; "Confirmed Credit"

(1) Failure of the buyer seasonably to furnish an agreed letter of credit is a breach of the contract for sale.

(2) The delivery to seller of a proper letter of credit suspends the buyer's obligation to pay. If the letter of credit is dishonored, the seller may on seasonable notification to the buyer require payment directly from him.

(3) Unless otherwise agreed the term "letter of credit" or "banker's credit" in a contract for sale means an irrevocable credit issued by a financing agency of good repute and, where the shipment is overseas, of good international repute. The term "confirmed credit" means that the credit must also carry the direct obligation of such an agency which does business in the seller's financial market.

Section 2–326. Sale on Approval and Sale or Return; Consignment Sales and Rights of Creditors

(1) Unless otherwise agreed, if delivered goods may be returned by the buyer even though they conform to the contract, the transaction is

(a) a "sale on approval" if the goods are delivered primarily for use, and

(b) a "sale or return" if the goods are delivered primarily for resale.

(2) Except as provided in subsection (3), goods held on approval are not subject to the claims of the buyer's creditors until acceptance; goods held on sale or return are subject to such claims while in the buyer's possession.

(3) Where goods are delivered to a person for sale and such person maintains a place of business at which he deals in goods of the kind involved, under a name other than the name of the person making delivery, then with respect to claims of creditors of the person conducting the business the goods are deemed to be on sale or return. The provisions of this subsection are applicable even though an agreement purports to reserve title to the person making delivery until payment or resale or uses such words as "on consignment" or "on memorandum". However, this subsection is not applicable if the person making delivery

(a) complies with an applicable law providing for a consignor's interest or the like to be evidenced by a sign, or

(b) establishes that the person conducting the business is generally known by his creditors to be substantially engaged in selling the goods of others, or

(c) complies with the filing provisions of the Article on Secured Transactions (Article 9).

(4) Any "or return" term of a contract for sale is to be treated as a separate contract for sale within the statute of frauds section of this Article (Section 2–201) and as contradicting the sale aspect of the contract within the provisions of this Article on parol or extrinsic evidence (Section 2–202).

Section 2–327. Special Incidents of Sale on Approval and Sale or Return

(1) Under a sale on approval unless otherwise agreed

(a) although the goods are identified to the contract the risk of loss and the title do not pass to the buyer until acceptance; and

(b) use of the goods consistent with the purpose of trial is not acceptance but failure seasonably to notify the seller of election to return the goods is acceptance, and if the goods conform to the contract acceptance of any part is acceptance of the whole; and

(c) after due notification of election to return, the return is at the seller's risk and expense but a merchant buyer must follow any reasonable instructions.

(2) Under a sale or return unless otherwise agreed

(a) the option to return extends to the whole or any commercial unit of the goods while in substantially their original condition, but must be exercised seasonably; and

(b) the return is at the buyer's risk and expense.

Section 2–328.   Sale by Auction

(1) In a sale by auction if goods are put up in lots each lot is the subject of a separate sale.

(2) A sale by auction is complete when the auctioneer so announces by the fall of the hammer or in other customary manner. Where a bid is made while the hammer is falling in acceptance of a prior bid the auctioneer may in his discretion reopen the bidding or declare the goods sold under the bid on which the hammer was falling.

(3) Such a sale is with reserve unless the goods are in explicit terms put up without reserve. In an auction with reserve the auctioneer may withdraw the goods at any time until he announces completion of the sale. In an auction without reserve, after the auctioneer calls for bids on an article or lot, that article or lot cannot be withdrawn unless no bid is made within a reasonable time. In either case a bidder may retract his bid until the auctioneer's announcement of completion of the sale, but a bidder's retraction does not revive any previous bid.

(4) If the auctioneer knowingly receives a bid on the seller's behalf or the seller makes or procures such a bid, and notice has not been given that liberty for such bidding is reserved, the buyer may at his option avoid the sale or take the goods at the price of the last good faith bid prior to the completion of the sale. This subsection shall not apply to any bid at a forced sale.

PART **4**

Title, Creditors and Good Faith Purchasers

Section 2–401.   Passing of Title; Reservation for Security; Limited Application of This Section

Each provision of this Article with regard to the rights, obligations and remedies of the seller, the buyer, purchasers or other third parties applies irrespective of title to the goods except where the provision refers to such title. Insofar as situations are not covered by the other provisions of this Article and matters concerning title became material the following rules apply:

(1) Title to goods cannot pass under a contract for sale prior to their identification to the contract (Section 2–501), and unless otherwise explicitly agreed the buyer acquires by their identification a special property as limited by this Act. Any retention or reservation by the seller of the title (property) in goods shipped or delivered to the buyer is limited in effect to a reservation of a security interest. Subject to these provisions and to the provisions of the Article on Secured Transactions (Article 9), title to goods passes from the seller to the buyer in any manner and on any conditions explicitly agreed on by the parties.

(2) Unless otherwise explicitly agreed title passes to the buyer at the time and place at which the seller completes his performance with reference to the physical delivery of the goods, despite any reservation of a security interest and even though a document of title is to be delivered at a different time or place, and in particular and despite any reservation of a security interest by the bill of lading

(a)   if the contract requires or authorizes the seller to send the goods to the buyer but does not require him to deliver them at destination, title passes to the buyer at the time and place of shipment; but

(b)   if the contract requires delivery at destination, title passes on tender there.

(3) Unless otherwise explicitly agreed where delivery is to be made without moving the goods,

(a)   if the seller is to deliver a document of title, title passes at the time when and the place where he delivers such document; or

(b)   if the goods are at the time of contracting already identified and no documents are to be delivered, title passes at the time and place of contracting.

(4) A rejection or other refusal by the buyer to receive or retain the goods, whether or not justified, or a justified revocation of acceptance revests title to the goods in the seller. Such revesting occurs by operation of law and is not a "sale".

Section 2–402.   Rights of Seller's Creditors Against Sold Goods

(1) Except as provided in subsections (2) and (3), rights of unsecured creditors of the seller with respect to goods which have been identified to a contract for sale are subject to the buyer's rights to recover the goods under this Article (Sections 2–502 and 2–716).

(2) A creditor of the seller may treat a sale or an identification of goods to a contract for sale as void if as against him a retention of possession by the seller is fraudulent under any rule of law of the state where the goods are situated, except that retention of possession in good faith and current course of trade by

a merchant-seller for a commercially reasonable time after a sale or identification is not fraudulent.

(3) Nothing in this Article shall be deemed to impair the rights of creditors of the seller

   (a)   under the provisions of the Article on Secured Transactions (Article 9); or

   (b)   where identification to the contract or delivery is made not in current course of trade but in satisfaction of or as security for a pre-existing claim for money, security or the like and is made under circumstances which under any rule of law of the state where the goods are situated would apart from this Article constitute the transaction a fraudulent transfer or voidable preference.

Section 2–403.   Power to Transfer; Good Faith Purchase of Goods; "Entrusting"

(1) A purchaser of goods acquires all title which his transferor had or had power to transfer except that a purchaser of a limited interest acquires rights only to the extent of the interest purchased. A person with voidable title has power to transfer a good title to a good faith purchaser for value. When goods have been delivered under a transaction of purchase the purchaser has such power even though

   (a)   the transferor was deceived as to the identity of the purchaser, or

   (b)   the delivery was in exchange for a check which is later dishonored, or

   (c)   it was agreed that the transaction was to be a "cash sale", or

   (d)   the delivery was procured through fraud punishable as larcenous under the criminal law.

(2) Any entrusting of possession of goods to a merchant who deals in goods of that kind gives him power to transfer all rights of the entruster to a buyer in ordinary course of business.

(3) "Entrusting" includes any delivery and any acquiescence in retention of possession regardless of any condition expressed between the parties to the delivery or acquiescence and regardless of whether the procurement of the entrusting or the possessor's disposition of the goods have been such as to be larcenous under the criminal law.

(4) The rights of other purchasers of goods and of lien creditors are governed by the Articles on Secured Transactions (Article 9), Bulk Transfers (Article 6) and Documents of Title (Article 7).

PART 5
Performance

Section 2–501.   Insurable Interest in Goods; Manner of Identification of Goods

(1) The buyer obtains a special property and an insurable interest in goods by identification of existing goods as goods to which the contract refers even though the goods so identified are non-conforming and he has an option to return or reject them. Such identification can be made at any time and in any manner explicitly agreed to by the parties. In the absence of explicit agreement identification occurs

   (a)   when the contract is made if it is for the sale of goods already existing and identified;

   (b)   if the contract is for the sale of future goods other than those described in paragraph (c), when goods are shipped, marked or otherwise designated by the seller as goods to which the contract refers;

   (c)   when the crops are planted or otherwise become growing crops or the young are conceived if the contract is for the sale of unborn young to be born within twelve months after contracting or for the sale of crops to be harvested within twelve months or the next normal harvest season after contracting whichever is longer.

(2) The seller retains an insurable interest in goods so long as title to or any security interest in the goods remains in him and where the identification is by the seller alone he may until default or insolvency or notification to the buyer that the identification is final substitute other goods for those identified.

(3) Nothing in this section impairs any insurable interest recognized under any other statute or rule of law.

Section 2–502.   Buyer's Right to Goods on Seller's Insolvency

(1) Subject to subsection (2) and even though the goods have not been shipped a buyer who has paid a part or all of the price of goods in which he has a special property under the provisions of the immediately preceding section may on making and keeping good a tender of any unpaid portion of their prices recover

them from the seller if the seller becomes insolvent within ten days after receipt of the first installment on their price.

(2) If the identification creating his special property has been made by the buyer he acquires the right to recover the goods only if they conform to the contract for sale.

Section 2–503.   Manner of Seller's Tender of Delivery

(1) Tender of delivery requires that the seller put and hold conforming goods at the buyer's disposition and give the buyer any notification reasonably necessary to enable him to take delivery. The manner, time and place for tender are determined by the agreement and this Article, and in particular

   (a)   tender must be at a reasonable hour, and if it is of goods they must be kept available for the period reasonably necessary to enable the buyer to take possession; but

   (b)   unless otherwise agreed the buyer must furnish facilities reasonably suited to the receipt of the goods.

(2) Where the case is within the next section respecting shipment tender requires that the seller comply with its provisions.

(3) Where the seller is required to deliver at a particular destination tender requires that he comply with subsection (1) and also in any appropriate case tender documents as described in subsections (4) and (5) of this section.

(4) Where goods are in the possession of a bailee and are to be delivered without being moved

   (a)   tender requires that the seller either tender a negotiable document of title covering such goods or procure acknowledgment by the bailee of the buyer's right to possession of the goods; but

   (b)   tender to the buyer of a non-negotiable document of title or of a written direction to the bailee to deliver is sufficient tender unless the buyer seasonably objects, and receipt by the bailee of notification of the buyer's rights fixes those rights as against the bailee and all third persons; but risk of loss of the goods and of any failure by the bailee to honor the non-negotiable document of title or to obey the direction remains on the seller until the buyer has had a reasonable time to present the document or direction, and a

refusal by the bailee to honor the document or to obey the direction defeats the tender.

(5) Where the contract requires the seller to deliver documents

   (a)   he must tender all such documents in correct form, except as provided in this Article with respect to bills of lading in a set (subsection (2) of Section 2–323); and

   (b)   tender through customary banking channels is sufficient and dishonor of a draft accompanying the documents constitutes non-acceptance or rejection.

Section 2–504.   Shipment by Seller

Where the seller is required or authorized to send the goods to the buyer and the contract does not require him to deliver them at a particular destination, then unless otherwise agreed he must

   (a)   put the goods in the possession of such a carrier and make such a contract for their transportation as may be reasonable having regard to the nature of the goods and other circumstances of the case; and

   (b)   obtain and promptly deliver or tender in due form any document necessary to enable the buyer to obtain possession of the goods or otherwise required by the agreement or by usage of trade; and

   (c)   promptly notify the buyer of the shipment.

Failure to notify the buyer under paragraph (c) or to make a proper contract under paragraph (a) is a ground for rejection only if material delay or loss ensues.

Section 2–505.   Seller's Shipment Under Reservation

(1) Where the seller has identified goods to the contract by or before shipment:

   (a)   his procurement of a negotiable bill of lading to his own order or otherwise reserves in him a security interest in the goods. His procurement of the bill to the order of a financing agency or of the buyer indicates in addition only the seller's expectation of transferring that interest to the person named.

   (b)   a non-negotiable bill of lading to himself or his nominee reserves possession of the goods as security but except in a case of conditional delivery (subsection (2) of Section 2–507) a non-negotiable bill of lading naming the buyer as consignee reserves no security interest even though the seller retains possession of the bill of lading.

(2) When shipment by the seller with reservation of a security interest is in violation of the contract for sale it constitutes an improper contract for transportation within the preceding section but impairs neither the rights given to the buyer by shipment and identification of the goods to the contract nor the seller's powers as a holder of a negotiable document.

Section 2–506. Rights of Financing Agency

(1) A financing agency by paying or purchasing for value a draft which relates to a shipment of goods acquires to the extent of the payment or purchase and in addition to its own rights under the draft and any document of title securing it any rights of the shipper in the goods including the right to stop delivery and the shipper's right to have the draft honored by the buyer.

(2) The right to reimbursement of a financing agency which has in good faith honored or purchased the draft under commitment to or authority from the buyer is not impaired by subsequent discovery of defects with reference to any relevant document which was apparently regular on its face.

Section 2–507. Effect of Seller's Tender; Delivery on Condition

(1) Tender of delivery is a condition to the buyer's duty to accept the goods and, unless otherwise agreed, to his duty to pay for them. Tender entitles the seller to acceptance of the goods and to payment according to the contract.

(2) Where payment is due and demanded on the delivery to the buyer of goods or documents of title, his right as against the seller to retain or dispose of them is conditional upon his making the payment due.

Section 2–508. Cure by Seller of Improper Tender or Delivery; Replacement

(1) Where any tender or delivery by the seller is rejected because non-conforming and the time for performance has not yet expired, the seller may seasonably notify the buyer of his intention to cure and may then within the contract time make a conforming delivery.

(2) Where the buyer rejects a non-conforming tender which the seller had reasonable grounds to believe

would be acceptable with or without money allowance the seller may if he seasonably notifies the buyer have a further reasonable time to substitute a conforming tender.

Section 2–509. Risk of Loss in the Absence of Breach

(1) Where the contract requires or authorizes the seller to ship the goods by carrier

(a) if it does not require him to deliver them at a particular destination, the risk of loss passes to the buyer when the goods are duly delivered to the carrier even though the shipment is under reservation (Section 2–505); but

(b) if it does require him to deliver them at a particular destination and the goods are there duly tendered while in the possession of the carrier, the risk of loss passes to the buyer when the goods are there duly so tendered as to enable the buyer to take delivery.

(2) Where the goods are held by a bailee to be delivered without being moved, the risk of loss passes to the buyer

(a) on his receipt of a negotiable document of title covering the goods; or

(b) on acknowledgment by the bailee of the buyer's right to possession of the goods; or

(c) after his receipt of a non-negotiable document of title or other written direction to deliver, as provided in subsection (4)(b) of Section 2–503.

(3) In any case not within subsection (1) or (2), the risk of loss passes to the buyer on his receipt of the goods if the seller is a merchant; otherwise the risk passes to the buyer on tender of delivery.

(4) The provisions of this section are subject to contrary agreement of the parties and to the provisions of this Article on sale on approval (Section 2–327) and on effect of breach on risk of loss (Section 2–510).

Section 2–510. Effect of Breach on Risk of Loss

(1) Where a tender or delivery of goods so fails to conform to the contract as to give a right of rejection the risk of their loss remains on the seller until cure or acceptance.

(2) Where the buyer rightfully revokes acceptance he may to the extent of any deficiency in his effective

insurance coverage treat the risk of loss as having rested on the seller from the beginning.

(3) Where the buyer as to conforming goods already identified to the contract for sale repudiates or is otherwise in breach before risk of their loss has passed to him, the seller may to the extent of any deficiency in his effective insurance coverage treat the risk of loss as resting on the buyer for a commercially reasonable time.

Section 2–511. Tender of Payment by Buyer; Payment by Check

(1) Unless otherwise agreed tender of payment is a condition to the seller's duty to tender and complete any delivery.

(2) Tender of payment is sufficient when made by any means or in any manner current in the ordinary course of business unless the seller demands payment in legal tender and gives any extension of time reasonably necessary to procure it.

(3) Subject to the provisions of this Act on the effect of an instrument on an obligation (Section 3–802), payment by check is conditional and is defeated as between the parties by dishonor of the check on due presentment.

Section 2–512. Payment by Buyer Before Inspection

(1) Where the contract requires payment before inspection non-conformity of the goods does not excuse the buyer from so making payment unless

(a) the non-conformity appears without inspection; or

(b) despite tender of the required documents the circumstances would justify injunction against honor under the provisions of this Act (Section 5–114).

(2) Payment pursuant to subsection (1) does not constitute an acceptance of goods or impair the buyer's right to inspect or any of his remedies.

Section 2–513. Buyer's Right to Inspection of Goods

(1) Unless otherwise agreed and subject to subsection (3), where goods are tendered or delivered or identified to the contract for sale, the buyer has a right before payment or acceptance to inspect them at any reasonable place and time and in any reasonable manner.

goods to the buyer, the inspection may be after their arrival.

(2) Expenses of inspection must be borne by the buyer but may be recovered from the seller if the goods do not conform and are rejected.

(3) Unless otherwise agreed and subject to the provisions of this Article on C.I.F. contracts (subsection (3) of Section 2–321), the buyer is not entitled to inspect the goods before payment of the price when the contract provides

(a) for delivery "C.O.D." or on other like terms; or

(b) for payment against documents of title, except where such payment is due only after the goods are to become available for inspection.

(4) A place or method of inspection fixed by the parties is presumed to be exclusive but unless otherwise expressly agreed it does not postpone identification or shift the place for delivery or for passing the risk of loss. If compliance becomes impossible, inspection shall be as provided in this section unless the place or method fixed was clearly intended as an indispensable condition failure of which avoids the contract.

Section 2–514. When Documents Deliverable on Acceptance; When on Payment

Unless otherwise agreed documents against which a draft is drawn are to be delivered to the drawee on acceptance of the draft if it is payable more than three days after presentment; otherwise, only on payment.

Section 2–515. Preserving Evidence of Goods in Dispute

In furtherance of the adjustment of any claim or dispute

(a) either party on reasonable notification to the other and for the purpose of ascertaining the facts and preserving evidence has the right to inspect, test and sample the goods including such of them as may be in the possession or control of the other; and

(b) the parties may agree to a third party inspection or survey to determine the conformity or condition of the goods and may agree that the findings shall be binding upon them in any subsequent litigation or adjustment.

PART **6**

Breach, Repudiation and Excuse

Section 2–601. Buyer's Rights on Improper Delivery

Subject to the provisions of this Article on breach in installment contracts (Section 2–612) and unless otherwise agreed under the sections on contractual limitations of remedy (Sections 2–718 and 2–719), if the goods or the tender of delivery fail in any respect to conform to the contract, the buyer may

(a)   reject the whole; or

(b)   accept the whole; or

(c)   accept any commercial unit or units and reject the rest.

Section 2–602. Manner and Effect of Rightful Rejection

(1) Rejection of goods must be within a reasonable time after their delivery or tender. It is ineffective unless the buyer seasonably notifies the seller.

(2) Subject to the provisions of the two following sections on rejected goods (Sections 2–603 and 2–604),

(a)   after rejection any exercise of ownership by the buyer with respect to any commercial unit is wrongful as against the seller; and

(b)   if the buyer has before rejection taken physical possession of goods in which he does not have a security interest under the provisions of this Article (subsection (3) of Section 2–711), he is under a duty after rejection to hold them with reasonable care at the seller's disposition for a time sufficient to permit the seller to remove them; but

(c)   the buyer has no further obligations with regard to goods rightfully rejected.

(3) The seller's rights with respect to goods wrongfully rejected are governed by the provisions of this Article on seller's remedies in general (Section 2–703).

Section 2–603. Merchant Buyer's Duties as to Rightfully Rejected Goods

(1) Subject to any security interest in the buyer (subsection (3) of Section 2–711), when the seller has no agent or place of business at the market of rejection a merchant buyer is under a duty after rejection of goods in his possession or control to follow any reasonable instructions received from the seller with respect to the goods and in the absence of such instructions to make reasonable efforts to sell them for the seller's account if they are perishable or threaten to decline in value speedily. Instructions are not reasonable if on demand indemnity for expenses is not forthcoming.

(2) When the buyer sells goods under subsection (1), he is entitled to reimbursement from the seller or out of the proceeds for reasonable expenses of caring for and selling them, and if the expenses include no selling commission then to such commission as is usual in the trade or if there is none to a reasonable sum not exceeding ten per cent on the gross proceeds.

(3) In complying with this section the buyer is held only to good faith and good faith conduct hereunder is neither acceptance nor conversion nor the basis of an action for damages.

Section 2–604. Buyer's Options as to Salvage of Rightfully Rejected Goods

Subject to the provisions of the immediately preceding section on perishables if the seller gives no instructions within a reasonable time after notification of rejection the buyer may store the rejected goods for the seller's account or reship them to him or resell them for the seller's account with reimbursement as provided in the preceding section. Such action is not acceptance or conversion.

Section 2–605. Waiver of Buyer's Objections by Failure to Particularize

(1) The buyer's failure to state in connection with rejection a particular defect which is ascertainable by reasonable inspection precludes him from relying on the unstated defect to justify rejection or to establish breach

(a)   where the seller could have cured it if stated seasonably; or

(b)   between merchants when the seller has after rejection made a request in writing for a full and final written statement of all defects on which the buyer proposes to rely.

(2) Payment against documents made without reservation of rights precludes recovery of the payment for defects apparent on the face of the documents.

Section 2–606. What Constitutes Acceptance of Goods

(1) Acceptance of goods occurs when the buyer

(a)   after a reasonable opportunity to inspect the goods signifies to the seller that the goods are conforming or that he will take or retain them in spite of their nonconformity; or

(b)   fails to make an effective rejection (subsection (1) of Section 2–602), but such acceptance does not occur until the buyer has had a reasonable opportunity to inspect them; or

(c)   does any act inconsistent with the seller's ownership; but if such act is wrongful as against the seller it is an acceptance only if ratified by him.

(2)   Acceptance of a part of any commercial unit is acceptance of that entire unit.

Section 2–607.   Effect of Acceptance; Notice of Breach; Burden of Establishing Breach After Acceptance; Notice of Claim or Litigation to Person Answerable Over

(1)   The buyer must pay at the contract rate for any goods accepted.

(2)   Acceptance of goods by the buyer precludes rejection of the goods accepted and if made with knowledge of a non-conformity cannot be revoked because of it unless the acceptance was on the reasonable assumption that the non-conformity would be seasonably cured but acceptance does not of itself impair any other remedy provided by this Article for non-conformity.

(3)   Where a tender has been accepted

(a)   the buyer must within a reasonable time after he discovers or should have discovered any breach notify the seller of breach or be barred from any remedy; and

(b)   if the claim is one for infringement or the like (subsection (3) of Section 2–312) and the buyer is sued as a result of such a breach he must so notify the seller within a reasonable time after he receives notice of the litigation or be barred from any remedy over for liability established by the litigation.

(4)   The burden is on the buyer to establish any breach with respect to the goods accepted.

(5)   Where the buyer is sued for breach of a warranty or other obligation for which his seller is answerable over

(a)   he may give his seller written notice of the litigation. If the notice states that the seller may come in and defend and that if the seller does not do so he will be bound in any action against him by his buyer by any determination of fact common to the two litigations, then unless the seller after seasonable receipt of the notice does come in and defend he is so bound.

(b)   if the claim is one for infringement or the like (subsection (3) of Section 2–312) the original seller may demand in writing that his buyer turn over to him control of the litigation including settlement or else be barred from any remedy over and if he also agrees to bear all expense and to satisfy any adverse judgment, then unless the buyer after seasonable receipt of the demand does turn over control the buyer is so barred.

(6)   The provisions of subsections (3), (4) and (5) apply to any obligation of a buyer to hold the seller harmless against infringement or the like (subsection (3) of Section 2–312).

Section 2–608.   Revocation of Acceptance in Whole or in Part

(1)   The buyer may revoke his acceptance of a lot or commercial unit whose non-conformity substantially impairs its value to him if he has accepted it

(a)   on the reasonable assumption that its non-conformity would be cured and it has not been seasonably cured; or

(b)   without discovery of such non-conformity if his acceptance was reasonably induced either by the difficulty of discovery before acceptance or by the seller's assurances.

(2)   Revocation of acceptance must occur within a reasonable time after the buyer discovers or should have discovered the ground for it and before any substantial change in condition of the goods which is not caused by their own defects. It is not effective until the buyer notifies the seller of it.

(3)   A buyer who so revokes has the same rights and duties with regard to the goods involved as if he had rejected them.

Section 2–609.   Right to Adequate Assurance of Performance

(1)   A contract for sale imposes an obligation on each party that the other's expectation of receiving due performance will not be impaired. When reasonable grounds for insecurity arise with respect to the performance of either party the other may in writing demand adequate assurance of due performance and until he receives such assurance may if commercially

reasonable suspend any performance for which he has not already received the agreed return.

(2) Between merchants the reasonableness of grounds for insecurity and the adequacy of any assurance offered shall be determined according to commercial standards.

(3) Acceptance of any improper delivery or payment does not prejudice the aggrieved party's right to demand adequate assurance of future performance.

(4) After receipt of a justified demand failure to provide within a reasonable time not exceeding thirty days such assurance of due performance as is adequate under the circumstances of the particular case is a repudiation of the contract.

Section 2–610.   Anticipatory Repudiation

When either party repudiates the contract with respect to a performance not yet due the loss of which will substantially impair the value of the contract to the other, the aggrieved party may

> (a) for a commercially reasonable time await performance by the repudiating party; or

> (b) resort to any remedy for breach (Section 2–703 or Section 2–711), even though he has notified the repudiating party that he would await the latter's performance and has urged retraction; and

> (c) in either case suspend his own performance or proceed in accordance with the provisions of this Article on the seller's right to identify goods to the contract notwithstanding breach or to salvage unfinished goods (Section 2–704).

Section 2–611.   Retraction of Anticipatory Repudiation

(1) Until the repudiating party's next performance is due he can retract his repudiation unless the aggrieved party has since the repudiation cancelled or materially changed his position or otherwise indicated that he considers the repudiation final.

(2) Retraction may be by any method which clearly indicates to the aggrieved party that the repudiating party intends to perform, but must include any assurance justifiably demanded under the provisions of this Article (Section 2–609).

(3) Retraction reinstates the repudiating party's rights under the contract with due excuse and allowance to the aggrieved party for any delay occasioned by the repudiation.

Section 2–612.   "Installment Contract"; Breach

(1) An "installment contract" is one which requires or authorizes the delivery of goods in separate lots to be separately accepted, even though the contract contains a clause "each delivery is a separate contract" or its equivalent.

(2) The buyer may reject any installment which is non-conforming if the non-conformity substantially impairs the value of that installment and cannot be cured or if the non-conformity is a defect in the required documents; but if the non-conformity does not fall within subsection (3) and the seller gives adequate assurance of its cure the buyer must accept that installment.

(3) Whenever non-conformity or default with respect to one or more installments substantially impairs the value of the whole contract there is a breach of the whole. But the aggrieved party reinstates the contract if he accepts a non-conforming installment without seasonably notifying of cancellation or if he brings an action with respect only to past installments or demands performance as to future installments.

Section 2–613.   Casualty to Identified Goods

Where the contract requires for its performance goods identified when the contract is made, and the goods suffer casualty without fault of either party before the risk of loss passes to the buyer, or in a proper case under a "no arrival, no sale" term (Section 2–324) then

> (a) if the loss is total the contract is avoided; and

> (b) if the loss is partial or the goods have so deteriorated as no longer to conform to the contract the buyer may nevertheless demand inspection and at his option either treat the contract as avoided or accept the goods with due allowance from the contract price for the deterioration or the deficiency in quantity but without further right against the seller.

Section 2–614.   Substituted Performance

(1) Where without fault of either party the agreed berthing, loading, or unloading facilities fail or an agreed type of carrier becomes unavailable or the agreed manner of delivery otherwise becomes commercially impracticable but a commercially reasonable substitute is available, such substitute performance must be tendered and accepted.

(2) If the agreed means or manner of payment fails because of domestic or foreign governmental regulation, the seller may withhold or stop delivery unless the buyer provides a means or manner of payment which is commercially a substantial equivalent. If delivery has already been taken, payment by the means or in the manner provided by the regulation discharges the buyer's obligation unless the regulation is discriminatory, oppressive or predatory.

Section 2–615.   Excuse by Failure of Presupposed Conditions

Except so far as a seller may have assumed a greater obligation and subject to the preceding section on substituted performance:

(a)   Delay in delivery or non-delivery in whole or in part by a seller who complies with paragraphs (b) and (c) is not a breach of his duty under a contract for sale if performance as agreed has been made impracticable by the occurrence of a contingency the non-occurrence of which was a basic assumption on which the contract was made or by compliance in good faith with any applicable foreign or domestic governmental regulation or order whether or not it later proves to be invalid.

(b)   Where the causes mentioned in paragraph (a) affect only a part of the seller's capacity to perform, he must allocate production and deliveries among his customers but may at his option include regular customers not then under contract as well as his own requirements for further manufacture. He may so allocate in any manner which is fair and reasonable.

(c)   The seller must notify the buyer seasonably that there will be delay or non-delivery and, when allocation is required under paragraph (b), of the estimated quota thus made available for the buyer.

Section 2–616.   Procedure on Notice Claiming Excuse

(1)   Where the buyer receives notification of a material or indefinite delay or an allocation justified under the preceding section he may by written notification to the seller as to any delivery concerned, and where the prospective deficiency substantially impairs the value of the whole contract under the provisions of this Article relating to breach of installment contracts (Section 2–612), then also as to the whole,

(a)   terminate and thereby discharge any unexecuted portion of the contract; or

(b)   modify the contract by agreeing to take his available quota in substitution.

(2)   If after receipt of such notification from the seller the buyer fails so to modify the contract within a reasonable time not exceeding thirty days the contract lapses with respect to any deliveries affected.

(3)   The provisions of this section may not be negated by agreement except in so far as the seller has assumed a greater obligation under the preceding section.

PART 7

Remedies

Section 2–701.   Remedies for Breach of Collateral Contracts Not Impaired

Remedies for breach of any obligation or promise collateral or ancillary to a contract for sale are not impaired by the provisions of this Article.

Section 2–702.   Seller's Remedies on Discovery of Buyer's Insolvency

(1)   Where the seller discovers the buyer to be insolvent he may refuse delivery except for cash including payment for all goods theretofore delivered under the contract, and stop delivery under this Article (Section 2–705).

(2)   Where the seller discovers that the buyer has received goods on credit while insolvent he may reclaim the goods upon demand made within ten days after the receipt, but if misrepresentation of solvency has been made to the particular seller in writing within three months before delivery the ten day limitation does not apply. Except as provided in this subsection the seller may not base a right to reclaim goods on the buyer's fraudulent or innocent misrepresentation of solvency or of intent to pay.

(3)   The seller's right to reclaim under subsection (2) is subject to the rights of a buyer in ordinary course or other good faith purchaser under this Article (Section 2–403). Successful reclamation of goods excludes all other remedies with respect to them.

Section 2–703.   Seller's Remedies in General

Where the buyer wrongfully rejects or revokes acceptance of goods or fails to make a payment due on or before delivery or repudiates with respect to a part or the whole, then with respect to any goods directly affected and, if the breach is of the whole contract

(Section 2–612), then also with respect to the whole undelivered balance, the aggrieved seller may

(a) withhold delivery of such goods;

(b) stop delivery by any bailee as hereafter provided (Section 2–705);

(c) proceed under the next section respecting goods still unidentified to the contract;

(d) resell and recover damages as hereafter provided (Section 2–706);

(e) recover damages for non-acceptance (Section 2–708) or in a proper case the price (Section 2–709);

(f) cancel.

Section 2–704. Seller's Right to Identify Goods to the Contract Notwithstanding Breach or to Salvage Unfinished Goods

(1) An aggrieved seller under the preceding section may

(a) identify to the contract conforming goods not already identified if at the time he learned of the breach they are in his possession or control;

(b) treat as the subject of resale goods which have demonstrably been intended for the particular contract even though those goods are unfinished.

(2) Where the goods are unfinished an aggrieved seller may in the exercise of reasonable commercial judgment for the purposes of avoiding loss and of effective realization either complete the manufacture and wholly identify the goods to the contract or cease manufacture and resell for scrap or salvage value or proceed in any other reasonable manner.

Section 2–705. Seller's Stoppage of Delivery in Transit or Otherwise

(1) The seller may stop delivery of goods in the possession of a carrier or other bailee when he discovers the buyer to be insolvent (Section 2–702) and may stop delivery of carload, truckload, planeload or larger shipments of express or freight when the buyer repudiates or fails to make a payment due before delivery or if for any other reason the seller has a right to withhold or reclaim the goods.

(2) As against such buyer the seller may stop delivery until

(a) receipt of the goods by the buyer; or

(b) acknowledgment to the buyer by any bailee of the goods except a carrier that the bailee holds the goods for the buyer; or

(c) such acknowledgment to the buyer by a carrier by reshipment or as warehouseman; or

(d) negotiation to the buyer of any negotiable document of title covering the goods.

(3) (a) To stop delivery the seller must so notify as to enable the bailee by reasonable diligence to prevent delivery of the goods.

(b) After such notification the bailee must hold and deliver the goods according to the directions of the seller but the seller is liable to the bailee for any ensuing charges or damages.

(c) If a negotiable document of title has been issued for goods the bailee is not obliged to obey a notification to stop until surrender of the document.

(d) A carrier who has issued a non-negotiable bill of lading is not obliged to obey a notification to stop received from a person other than the consignor.

Section 2–706. Seller's Resale Including Contract for Resale

(1) Under the conditions stated in Section 2–703 on seller's remedies, the seller may resell the goods concerned or the undelivered balance thereof. Where the resale is made in good faith and in a commercially reasonable manner the seller may recover the difference between the resale price and the contract price together with any incidental damages allowed under the provisions of this Article (Section 2–710), but less expenses saved in consequence of the buyer's breach.

(2) Except as otherwise provided in subsection (3) or unless otherwise agreed resale may be at public or private sale including sale by way of one or more contracts to sell or of identification to an existing contract of the seller. Sale may be as a unit or in parcels and at any time and place and on any terms but every aspect of the sale including the method, manner, time, place and terms must be commercially reasonable. The resale must be reasonably identified as referring to the broken contract, but it is not necessary that the goods be in existence or that any or all of them have been identified to the contract before the breach.

(3) Where the resale is at private sale the seller must give the buyer reasonable notification of his intention to resell.

(4) Where the resale is at public sale

(a)   only identified goods can be sold except where there is a recognized market for a public sale of futures in goods of the kind; and

(b)   it must be made at a usual place or market for public sale if one is reasonably available and except in the case of goods which are perishable or threaten to decline in value speedily the seller must give the buyer reasonable notice of the time and place of the resale; and

(c)   if the goods are not to be within the view of those attending the sale the notification of sale must state the place where the goods are located and provide for their reasonable inspection by prospective bidders; and

(d)   the seller may buy.

(5) A purchaser who buys in good faith at a resale takes the goods free of any rights of the original buyer even though the seller fails to comply with one or more of the requirements of this section.

(6) The seller is not accountable to the buyer for any profit made on any resale. A person in the position of a seller (Section 2–707) or a buyer who has rightfully rejected or justifiably revoked acceptance must account for any excess over the amount of his security interest, as hereinafter defined (subsection (3) of Section 2–711).

Section 2–707.   "Person in the Position of a Seller"

(1) A "person in the position of a seller" includes as against a principal an agent who has paid or become responsible for the price of goods on behalf of his principal or anyone who otherwise holds a security interest or other right in goods similar to that of a seller.

(2) A person in the position of a seller may as provided in this Article withhold or stop delivery (Section 2–705) and resell (Section 2–706) and recover incidental damages (Section 2–710).

Section 2–708.   Seller's Damages for Non-Acceptance or Repudiation

(1) Subject to subsection (2) and to the provisions of this Article with respect to proof of market price (Section 2–723), the measure of damages for non-acceptance or repudiation by the buyer is the difference between the market price at the time and place for tender and the unpaid contract price together with any incidental damages provided in this Article (Section 2–710), but less expenses saved in consequence of the buyer's breach.

(2) If the measure of damages provided in subsection (1) is inadequate to put the seller in as good a position as performance would have done then the measure of damages is the profit (including reasonable overhead) which the seller would have made from full performance by the buyer, together with any incidental damages provided in this Article (Section 2–710), due allowance for costs reasonably incurred and due credit for payments or proceeds of resale.

Section 2–709.   Action for the Price

(1) When the buyer fails to pay the price as it becomes due the seller may recover, together with any incidental damages under the next section, the price

(a)   of goods accepted or of conforming goods lost or damaged within a commercially reasonable time after risk of their loss has passed to the buyer; and

(b)   of goods identified to the contract if the seller is unable after reasonable effort to resell them at a reasonable price or the circumstances reasonably indicate that such effort will be unavailing.

(2) Where the seller sues for the price he must hold for the buyer any goods which have been identified to the contract and are still in his control except that if resale becomes possible he may resell them at any time prior to the collection of the judgment. The net proceeds of any such resale must be credited to the buyer and payment of the judgment entitles him to any goods not resold.

(3) After the buyer has wrongfully rejected or revoked acceptance of the goods or has failed to make a payment due or has repudiated (Section 2–610), a seller who is held not entitled to the price under this section shall nevertheless be awarded damages for non-acceptance under the preceding section.

Section 2–710.   Seller's Incidental Damages

Incidental damages to an aggrieved seller include any commercially reasonable charges, expenses or commissions incurred in stopping delivery, in the transportation, care and custody of goods after the buyer's breach, in connection with return or resale of the goods or otherwise resulting from the breach.

Section 2–711. Buyer's Remedies in General; Buyer's Security Interest in Rejected Goods

(1) Where the seller fails to make delivery or repudiates or the buyer rightfully rejects or justifiably revokes acceptance then with respect to any goods involved, and with respect to the whole if the breach goes to the whole contract (Section 2–612), the buyer may cancel and whether or not he has done so may in addition to recovering so much of the price as has been paid

    (a) "cover" and have damages under the next section as to all the goods affected whether or not they have been identified to the contract; or

    (b) recover damages for non-delivery as provided in this Article (Section 2–713).

(2) Where the seller fails to deliver or repudiates the buyer may also

    (a) if the goods have been identified recover them as provided in this Article (Section 2–502); or

    (b) in a proper case obtain specific performance or replevy the goods as provided in this Article (Section 2–716).

(3) On rightful rejection or justifiable revocation of acceptance a buyer has a security interest in goods in his possession or control for any payments made on their price and any expenses reasonably incurred in their inspection, receipt, transportation, care and custody and may hold such goods and resell them in like manner as an aggrieved seller (Section 2–706).

Section 2–712. "Cover"; Buyer's Procurement of Substitute Goods

(1) After a breach within the preceding section the buyer may "cover" by making in good faith and without unreasonable delay any reasonable purchase of or contract to purchase goods in substitution for those due from the seller.

(2) The buyer may recover from the seller as damages the difference between the cost of cover and the contract price together with any incidental or consequential damages as hereinafter defined (Section 2–715), but less expenses saved in consequence of the seller's breach.

(3) Failure of the buyer to effect cover within this section does not bar him from any other remedy.

Section 2–713. Buyer's Damages for Non-Delivery or Repudiation

(1) Subject to the provisions of this Article with respect to proof of market price (Section 2–723), the measure of damages for non-delivery or repudiation by the seller is the difference between the market price at the time when the buyer learned of the breach and the contract price together with any incidental and consequential damages provided in this Article (Section 2–715), but less expense saved in consequence of the seller's breach.

(2) Market price is to be determined as of the place for tender or, in cases of rejection after arrival or revocation of acceptance, as of the place of arrival.

Section 2–714. Buyer's Damages for Breach in Regard to Accepted Goods

(1) Where the buyer has accepted goods and given notification (subsection (3) of Section 2–607) he may recover as damages for any non-conformity of tender the loss resulting in the ordinary course of events from the seller's breach as determined in any manner which is reasonable.

(2) The measure of damages for breach of warranty is the difference at the time and place of acceptance between the value of the goods accepted and the value they would have had if they had been as warranted, unless special circumstances show proximate damages of a different amount.

(3) In a proper case any incidental and consequential damages under the next section may also be recovered.

Section 2–715. Buyer's Incidental and Consequential Damages

(1) Incidental damages resulting from the seller's breach include expenses reasonably incurred in inspection, receipt, transportation and care and custody of goods rightfully rejected, any commercially reasonable charges, expenses or commissions in connection with effecting cover and any other reasonable expense incident to the delay or other breach.

(2) Consequential damages resulting from the seller's breach include

    (a) any loss resulting from general or particular requirements and needs of which the seller at the time of contracting had reason to know and which could not reasonably be prevented by cover or otherwise; and

(b)   injury to person or property proximately resulting from any breach of warranty.

Section 2-716.   Buyer's Right to Specific Performance or Replevin

(1) Specific performance may be decreed where the goods are unique or in other proper circumstances.

(2) The decree for specific performance may include such terms and conditions as to payment of the price, damages, or other relief as the court may deem just.

(3) The buyer has a right of replevin for goods identified to the contract if after reasonable effort he is unable to effect cover for such goods or the circumstances reasonably indicate that such effort will be unavailing or if the goods have been shipped under reservation and satisfaction of the security interest in them has been made or tendered.

Section 2-717.   Deduction of Damages from the Price

The buyer on notifying the seller of his intention to do so may deduct all or any part of the damages resulting from any breach of the contract from any part of the price still due under the same contract.

Section 2-718.   Liquidation or Limitation of Damages; Deposits

(1) Damages for breach by either party may be liquidated in the agreement but only at an amount which is reasonable in the light of the anticipated or actual harm caused by the breach, the difficulties of proof of loss, and the inconvenience or nonfeasibility of otherwise obtaining an adequate remedy. A term fixing unreasonably large liquidated damages is void as a penalty.

(2) Where the seller justifiably withholds delivery of goods because of the buyer's breach, the buyer is entitled to restitution of any amount by which the sum of his payments exceeds

(a)   the amount to which the seller is entitled by virtue of terms liquidating the seller's damages in accordance with subsection (1), or

(b)   in the absence of such terms, twenty per cent of the value of the total performance for which the buyer is obligated under the contract or $500, whichever is smaller.

(3) The buyer's right to restitution under subsection (2) is subject to offset to the extent that the seller establishes

(a)   a right to recover damages under the provisions of this Article other than subsection (1), and

(b)   the amount or value of any benefits received by the buyer directly or indirectly by reason of the contract.

(4) Where a seller has received payment in goods their reasonable value or the proceeds of their resale shall be treated as payments for the purposes of subsection (2); but if the seller has notice of the buyer's breach before reselling goods received in part performance, his resale is subject to the conditions laid down in this Article on resale by an aggrieved seller (Section 2-706).

Section 2-719.   Contractual Modification or Limitation of Remedy

(1) Subject to the provisions of subsections (2) and (3) of this section and of the preceding section on liquidation and limitation of damages,

(a)   the agreement may provide for remedies in addition to or in substitution for those provided in this Article and may limit or alter the measure of damages recoverable under this Article, as by limiting the buyer's remedies to return of the goods and repayment of the price or to repair and replacement of non-conforming goods or parts; and

(b)   resort to a remedy as provided is optional unless the remedy is expressly agreed to be exclusive, in which case it is the sole remedy.

(2) Where circumstances cause an exclusive or limited remedy to fail of its essential purpose, remedy may be had as provided in this Act.

(3) Consequential damages may be limited or excluded unless the limitations or exclusion is unconscionable. Limitation of consequential damages for injury to the person in the case of consumer goods is prima facie unconscionable but limitation of damages where the loss is commercial is not.

Section 2–720.   Effect of "Cancellation" or "Rescission" on Claims for Antecedent Breach

Unless the contrary intention clearly appears, expressions of "cancellation" or "rescission" of the contract or the like shall not be construed as a renunciation or discharge of any claim in damages for an antecedent breach.

Section 2–721.   Remedies for Fraud

Remedies for material misrepresentation or fraud include all remedies available under this Article for nonfraudulent breach. Neither rescission or a claim for rescission of the contract for sale nor rejection or return of the goods shall bar or be deemed inconsistent with a claim for damages or other remedy.

Section 2–722.   Who Can Sue Third Parties for Injury to Goods

Where a third party so deals with goods which have been identified to a contract for sale as to cause actionable injury to a party to that contract

(a)   a right of action against the third party is in either party to the contract for sale who has title to or a security interest or a special property or an insurable interest in the goods; and if the goods have been destroyed or converted a right of action is also in the party who either bore the risk of loss under the contract for sale or has since the injury assumed the risk as against the other;

(b)   if at the time of the injury the party plaintiff did not bear the risk of loss as against the other party to the contract for sale and there is no arrangement between them for disposition of the recovery, his suit or settlement is, subject to his own interest, as a fiduciary for the other party to the contract;

(c)   either party may with the consent of the other sue for the benefit of whom it may concern.

Section 2–723.   Proof of Market Price: Time and Place

(1)   If an action based on anticipatory repudiation comes to trial before the time for performance with respect to some or all of the goods, any damages based on market price (Section 2–708 or Section 2–713) shall be determined according to the price of such goods prevailing at the time when the aggrieved party learned of the repudiation.

(2)   If evidence of a price prevailing at the times or places described in this Article is not readily available the price prevailing within any reasonable time before or after the time described or at any other place which in commercial judgment or under usage of trade would serve as a reasonable substitute for the one described may be used, making any proper allowance for the cost of transporting the goods to or from such other place.

(3)   Evidence of a relevant price prevailing at a time or place other than the one described in this Article offered by one party is not admissible unless and until he has given the other party such notice as the court finds sufficient to prevent unfair surprise.

Section 2–724.   Admissibility of Market Quotations

Whenever the prevailing price or value of any goods regularly bought and sold in any established commodity market is in issue, reports in official publications or trade journals or in newspapers or periodicals of general circulation published as the reports of such market shall be admissible in evidence. The circumstances of the preparation of such a report may be shown to affect its weight but not its admissibility.

Section 2–725.   Statute of Limitations in Contracts for Sale

(1)   An action for breach of any contract for sale must be commenced within four years after the cause of action has accrued. By the original agreement the parties may reduce the period of limitation to not less than one year but may not extend it.

(2)   A cause of action accrues when the breach occurs, regardless of the aggrieved party's lack of knowledge of the breach. A breach of warranty occurs when tender of delivery is made, except that where a warranty explicitly extends to future performance of the goods and discovery of the breach must await the time of such performance the cause of action accrues when the breach is or should have been discovered.

(3)   Where an action commenced within the time limited by subsection (1) is so terminated as to leave available a remedy by another action for the same breach such other action may be commenced after the expiration of the time limited and within six months after the termination of the first action unless the termination resulted from voluntary discontinuance or from dismissal for failure or neglect to prosecute.

(4)   This section does not alter the law on tolling of the statute of limitations nor does it apply to causes of action which have accrued before this Act becomes effective.

ARTICLE 2A

LEASES

PART 1

General Provisions

Section 2A–101. Short Title

This Article shall be known and may be cited as the Uniform Commercial Code—Leases.

Section 2A–102. Scope

This Article applies to any transaction, regardless of form, that creates a lease.

Section 2A–103. Definitions and Index of Definitions

(1) In this Article unless the context otherwise requires:

(a) "Buyer in ordinary course of business" means a person who in good faith and without knowledge that the sale to him [or her] is in violation of the ownership rights or security interest or leasehold interest of a third party in the goods buys in ordinary course from a person in the business of selling goods of that kind but does not include a pawnbroker. "Buying" may be for cash or by exchange of other property or on secured or unsecured credit and includes receiving goods or documents of title under a pre-existing contract for sale but does not include a transfer in bulk or as security for or in total or partial satisfaction of a money debt.

(b) "Cancellation" occurs when either party puts an end to the lease contract for default by the other party.

(c) "Commercial unit" means such a unit of goods as by commercial usage is a single whole for purposes of lease and division of which materially impairs its character or value on the market or in use. A commercial unit may be a single article, as a machine, or a set of articles, as a suite of furniture or a line of machinery, or a quantity, as a gross or carload, or any other unit treated in use or in the relevant market as a single whole.

(d) "Conforming" goods or performance under a lease contract means goods or performance that are in accordance with the obligations under the lease contract.

(e) "Consumer lease" means a lease that a lessor regularly engaged in the business of leasing or selling makes to a lessee, except an organization, who takes under the lease primarily for a personal, family, or household purpose, if the total payments to be made under the lease contract, excluding payments for options to renew or buy, do not exceed $25,000.

(f) "Fault" means wrongful act, omission, breach, or default.

(g) "Finance lease" means a lease in which (i) the lessor does not select, manufacture or supply the goods, (ii) the lessor acquires the goods or the right to possession and use of the goods in connection with the lease, and (iii) either the lessee receives a copy of the contract evidencing the lessor's purchase of the goods on or before signing the lease contract, or the lessee's approval of the contract evidencing the lessor's purchase of the goods is a condition to effectiveness of the lease contract.

(h) "Goods" means all things that are movable at the time of identification to the lease contract, or are fixtures (Section 2A–309), but the term does not include money, documents, instruments, accounts, chattel paper, general intangibles, or minerals or the like, including oil and gas, before extraction. The term also includes the unborn young of animals.

(i) "Installment lease contract" means a lease contract that authorizes or requires the delivery of goods in separate lots to be separately accepted, even though the lease contract contains a clause "each delivery is a separate lease" or its equivalent.

(j) "Lease" means a transfer of the right to possession and use of goods for a term in return for consideration, but a sale, including a sale on approval or a sale or return, or retention or creation of a security interest is not a lease. Unless the context clearly indicates otherwise, the term includes a sublease.

(k) "Lease agreement" means the bargain, with respect to the lease, of the lessor and the lessee in fact as found in their language or by implication from other circumstances including course of dealing or usage of trade or course of performance as provided in this Article. Unless the context clearly indicates otherwise, the term includes a sublease agreement.

(l) "Lease contract" means the total legal obligation that results from the lease agreement as affected by this Article and any other applicable rules of law. Unless the context clearly indicates otherwise, the term includes a sublease contract.

(m) "Leasehold interest" means the interest of the lessor or the lessee under a lease contract.

(n) "Lessee" means a person who acquires the right to possession and use of goods under a lease. Unless the context clearly indicates otherwise, the term includes a sublessee.

(o) "Lessee in ordinary course of business" means a person who in good faith and without knowledge that the lease to him [or her] is in violation of the ownership rights or security interest or leasehold interest of a third party in the goods leases in ordinary course from a person in the business of selling or leasing goods of that kind but does not include a pawnbroker. "Leasing" may be for cash or by exchange of other property or on secured or unsecured credit and includes receiving goods or documents of title under a pre-existing lease contract but does not include a transfer in bulk or as security for or in total or partial satisfaction of a money debt.

(p) "Lessor" means a person who transfers the right to possession and use of goods under a lease. Unless the context clearly indicates otherwise, the term includes a sublessor.

(q) "Lessor's residual interest" means the lessor's interest in the goods after expiration, termination, or cancellation of the lease contract.

(r) "Lien" means a charge against or interest in goods to secure payment of a debt or performance of an obligation, but the term does not include a security interest.

(s) "Lot" means a parcel or a single article that is the subject matter of a separate lease or delivery, whether or not it is sufficient to perform the lease contract.

(t) "Merchant lessee" means a lessee that is a merchant with respect to goods of the kind subject to the lease.

(u) "Present value" means the amount as of a date certain of one or more sums payable in the future, discounted to the date certain. The discount is determined by the interest rate specified by the parties if the rate was not manifestly unreasonable at the time the transaction was entered into; otherwise, the discount is determined by a commercially reasonable rate that takes into account the facts and circumstances of each case at the time the transaction was entered into.

(v) "Purchase" includes taking by sale, lease, mortgage, security interest, pledge, gift, or any other voluntary transaction creating an interest in goods.

(w) "Sublease" means a lease of goods the right to possession and use of which was acquired by the lessor as a lessee under an existing lease.

(x) "Supplier" means a person from whom a lessor buys or leases goods to be leased under a finance lease.

(y) "Supply contract" means a contract under which a lessor buys or leases goods to be leased.

(z) "Termination" occurs when either party pursuant to a power created by agreement or law puts an end to the lease contract otherwise than for default.

(2) Other definitions applying to this Article and sections in which they appear are:

"Accessions". Section 2A–310(1).
"Construction mortgage". Section 2A–309(1)(d).
"Encumbrance". Section 2A–309(1)(e).
"Fixtures". Section 2A–309(1)(a).
"Fixture filling". Section 2A–309(1)(b).
"Purchase money lease". Section 2A–309(1)(c).

(3) The following definitions in other Articles apply to this Article:

"Accounts". Section 9-106.
"Between merchants". Section 2–104(3).
"Buyer". Section 2–103(1)(a).
"Chattel paper". Section 9–105(1)(b).
"Consumer goods". Section 9–109(1).
"Documents". Section 9–105(1)(f).
"Entrusting". Section 3–403(3).
"General intangibles". Section 9–106.
"Good faith". Section 2–103(1)(b).
"Instruments". Section 9–105(1)(i).
"Merchant". Section 2–104(1).
"Mortgage". Section 9–105(1)(j).
"Pursuant to commitment". Section 9–105(1)(k).
"Receipt". Section 2–103(1)(c).
"Sale". Section 2–106(1).
"Sale on Approval". Section 2–326.
"Sale or Return". Section 2–326.
"Seller". Section 2–103(1)(d).

(4) In addition Article 1 contains general definitions and principles of construction and interpretation applicable throughout this Article.

Section 2A–104.   Leases Subject to Other Statutes

(1) A lease, although subject to this Article, is also subject to any applicable:

(a) Statute of the United States;

(b) Certificate of title statute of this State: (list any certificate of title statutes covering automobiles, trailers, mobile homes, boats, farm tractors, and the like);

(c) Certificate of title statute of another jurisdiction (Section 2A–105); or

(d) Consumer protection statute of this State.

(2) In case of conflict between the provisions of this Article, other than Sections 2A–105, 2A–304(3) and 2A–305(3), and any statute referred to in subsection (1), the provisions of that statute control.

(3) Failure to comply with any applicable statute has only the effect specified therein.

Section 2A–105. Territorial Application of Article to Goods Covered by Certificate of Title

Subject to the provisions of Sections 2A–304(3) and 2A–305(3), with respect to goods covered by a certificate of title issued under a statute of this State or of another jurisdiction, compliance and the effect of compliance or noncompliance with a certificate of title statute are governed by the law (including the conflict of laws rules) of the jurisdiction issuing the certificate until the earlier of (a) surrender of the certificate, or (b) four months after the goods are removed from that jurisdiction and thereafter until a new certificate of title is issued by another jurisdiction.

Section 2A–106. Limitation on Power of Parties to Consumer Lease to Choose Applicable Law and Judicial Forum

(1) If the law chosen by the parties to a consumer lease is that of a jurisdiction other than a jurisdiction in which the lessee resides at the time the lease agreement becomes enforceable or within 30 days thereafter or in which the goods are to be used, the choice is not enforceable.

(2) If the judicial forum chosen by the parties to a consumer lease is a forum that would not otherwise have jurisdiction over the lessee, the choice is not enforceable.

Section 2A–107. Waiver or Renunciation of Claim or Right After Default

Any claim or right arising out of an alleged default or breach of warranty may be discharged in whole or in part without consideration by a written waiver or renunciation signed and delivered by the aggrieved party.

Section 2A–108. Unconscionability

(1) If the court as a matter of law finds a lease contract or any clause of a lease contract to have been unconscionable at the time it was made the court may refuse to enforce the lease contract, or it may enforce the remainder of the lease contract without the unconscionable clause, or it may so limit the application of any unconscionable clause as to avoid any unconscionable result.

(2) With respect to a consumer lease, if the court as a matter of law finds that a lease contract or any clause of a lease contract has been induced by unconscionable conduct or that unconscionable conduct has occurred in the collection of a claim arising from a lease contract, the court may grant appropriate relief.

(3) Before making a finding of unconscionability under subsection (1) or (2), the court, on its own motion or that of a party, shall afford the parties a reasonable opportunity to present evidence as to the setting, purpose, and effect of the lease contract or clause thereof, or of the conduct.

(4) In an action in which the lessee claims unconscionability with respect to a consumer lease:

(a) If the court finds unconscionability under subsection (1) or (2), the court shall award reasonable attorney's fees to the lessee.

(b) If the court does not find unconscionability and the lessee claiming unconscionability has brought or maintained an action he [or she] knew to be groundless, the court shall award reasonable attorney's fees to the party against whom the claim is made.

(c) In determining attorney's fees, the amount of the recovery on behalf of the claimant under subsections (1) and (2) is not controlling.

Section 2A–109. Option to Accelerate at Will

(1) A term providing that one party or his [or her] successor in interest may accelerate payment or performance or require collateral or additional collateral "at will" or "when he [or she] deems himself [or herself] insecure" or in words of similar import must be construed to mean that he [or she] has power to do so only if he [or she] in good faith believes that the prospect of payment or performance is impaired.

(2) With respect to a consumer lease, the burden of

establishing good faith under subsection (1) is on the party who exercised the power; otherwise the burden of establishing lack of good faith is on the party against whom the power has been exercised.

PART **2**

Formation and Constuction of Lease
Contract

Section 2A–201.   Statute of Frauds

(1) A lease contract is not enforceable by way of action or defense unless:

(a)   The total payments to be made under the lease contract, excluding payments for options to renew or buy, are less than $1,000; or

(b)   There is a writing, signed by the party against whom enforcement is sought or by that party's authorized agent, sufficient to indicate that a lease contract has been made between the parties and to describe the goods leased and the lease term.

(2) Any description of leased goods or of the lease term is sufficient and satisfies subsection (1)(b), whether or not it is specific, if it reasonably identifies what is described.

(3) A writing is not insufficient because it omits or incorrectly states a term agreed upon, but the lease contract is not enforceable under subsection (1)(b) beyond the lease term and the quantity of goods shown in the writing.

(4) A lease contract that does not satisfy the requirements of subsection (1), but which is valid in other respects, is enforceable:

(a)   If the goods are to be specially manufactured or obtained for the lessee and are not suitable for lease or sale to others in the ordinary course of the lessor's business, and the lessor, before notice of repudiation is received and under circumstances that reasonably indicate that the goods are for the lessee, has made either a substantial beginning of their manufacture or commitments for their procurement;

(b)   If the party against whom enforcement is sought admits in that party's pleading, testimony or otherwise in court that a lease contract was made, but the lease contract is not enforceable under this provision beyond the quantity of goods admitted; or

(c)   With respect to goods that have been received and accepted by the lessee.

(5) The lease term under a lease contract referred to in subsection (4) is:

(a)   If there is a writing signed by the party against whom enforcement is sought or by that party's authorized agent specifying the lease term, the term so specified;

(b)   If the party against whom enforcement is sought admits in that party's pleading, testimony, or otherwise in court a lease term, the term so admitted; or

(c)   A reasonable lease term.

Section 2A–202.   Final Written Expression: Parol or Extrinsic Evidence

Terms with respect to which the confirmatory memoranda of the parties agree or which are otherwise set forth in a writing intended by the parties as a final expression of their agreement with respect to such terms as are included therein may not be contradicted by evidence of any prior agreement or of a contemporaneous oral agreement but may be explained or supplemented:

(a)   By course of dealing or usage of trade or by course of performance; and

(b)   By evidence of consistent additional terms unless the court finds the writing to have been intended also as a complete and exclusive statement of the terms of the agreement.

Section 2A–203.   Seals Inoperative

The affixing of a seal to a writing evidencing a lease contract or an offer to enter into a lease contract does not render the writing a sealed instrument and the law with respect to sealed instruments does not apply to the lease contract or offer.

Section 2A–204.   Formation in General

(1) A lease contract may be made in any manner sufficient to show agreement, including conduct by both parties which recognizes the existence of a lease contract.

(2) An agreement sufficient to constitute a lease contract may be found although the moment of its making is undetermined.

(3) Although one or more terms are left open, a lease contract does not fail for indefiniteness if the parties have intended to make a lease contract and there is a reasonably certain basis for giving an appropriate remedy.

Section 2A–205. Firm Offers

An offer by a merchant to lease goods to or from another person in a signed writing that by its terms gives assurance it will be held open is not revocable, for lack of consideration, during the time stated or, if no time is stated, for a reasonable time, but in no event may the period of irrevocability exceed 3 months. Any such term of assurance on a form supplied by the offeree must be separately signed by the offeror.

Section 2A–206. Offer and Acceptance in Formation of Lease Contract

(1) Unless otherwise unambiguously indicated by the language or circumstances, an offer to make a lease contract must be construed as inviting acceptance in any manner and by any medium reasonable in the circumstances.

(2) If the beginning of a requested performance is a reasonable mode of acceptance, an offeror who is not notified of acceptance within a reasonable time may treat the offer as having lapsed before acceptance.

Section 2A–207. Course of Performance or Practical Construction

(1) If a lease contract involves repeated occasions for performance by either party with knowledge of the nature of the performance and opportunity for objection to it by the other, any course of performance accepted or acquiesced in without objection is relevant to determine the meaning of the lease agreement.

(2) The express terms of a lease agreement and any course of performance, as well as any course of dealing and usage of trade, must be construed whenever reasonable as consistent with each other; but if that construction is unreasonable, express terms control course of performance, course of performance controls both course of dealing and usage of trade, and course of dealing controls usage of trade.

(3) Subject to the provisions of Section 2A–208 on modification and waiver, course of performance is relevant to show a waiver or modification of any term inconsistent with the course of performance.

Section 2A–208. Modification, Rescission and Waiver

(1) An agreement modifying a lease contract needs no consideration to be binding.

(2) A signed lease agreement that excludes modification or rescission except by a signed writing may not be otherwise modified or rescinded, but, except as between merchants, such a requirement on a form supplied by a merchant must be separately signed by the other party.

(3) Although an attempt at modification or rescission does not satisfy the requirements of subsection (2), it may operate as a waiver.

(4) A party who has made a waiver affecting an executory portion of a lease contract may retract the waiver by reasonable notification received by the other party that strict performance will be required of any term waived, unless the retraction would be unjust in view of a material change of position in reliance on the waiver.

Section 2A–209. Lessee Under Finance Lease as Beneficiary of Supply Contract

(1) The benefit of the supplier's promises to the lessor under the supply contract and of all warranties, whether express or implied, under the supply contract, extends to the lessee to the extent of the lessee's leasehold interest under a finance lease related to the supply contract, but subject to the terms of the supply contract and all of the supplier's defenses or claims arising therefrom.

(2) The extension of the benefit of the supplier's promises and warranties to the lessee (Section 2A–209(1)) does not: (a) modify the rights and obligations of the parties to the supply contract, whether arising therefrom or otherwise, or (b) impose any duty or liability under the supply contract on the lessee.

(3) Any modification or rescission of the supply contract by the supplier and the lessor is effective against the lessee unless, prior to the modification or rescission, the supplier has received notice that the lessee has entered into a finance lease related to the supply contract. If the supply contract is modified or rescinded after the lessee enters the finance lease, the lessee has a cause of action against the lessor, and against the supplier if the supplier has notice of the lessee's entering the finance lease when the supply contract is modified or rescinded. The lessee's recovery from such action shall put the lessee in as good a position as if the modification or rescission had not occurred.

Section 2A–210. Express Warranties

(1) Express warranties by the lessor are created as follows:

   (a) Any affirmation of fact or promise made by the lessor to the lessee which relates to the goods and becomes part of the basis of the bargain creates an express warranty that the goods will conform to the affirmation or promise.

(b)   Any description of the goods which is made part of the basis of the bargain creates an express warranty that the goods will conform to the description.

(c)   Any sample or model that is made part of the basis of the bargain creates an express warranty that the whole of the goods will conform to the sample or model.

(2)   It is not necessary to the creation of an express warranty that the lessor use formal words, such as "warrant" or "guarantee," or that the lessor have a specific intention to make a warranty, but an affirmation merely of the value of the goods or a statement purporting to be merely the lessor's opinion or commendation of the goods does not create a warranty.

Section 2A–211.   Warranties Against Interference and Against Infringement; Lessee's Obligation Against Infringement

(1)   There is in a lease contract a warranty that for the lease term no person holds a claim to or interest in the goods that arose from an act or omission of the lessor, other than a claim by way of infringement or the like, which will interfere with the lessee's enjoyment of its leasehold interest.

(2)   Except in a finance lease there is in a lease contract by a lessor who is a merchant regularly dealing in goods of the kind a warranty that the goods are delivered free of the rightful claim of any person by way of infringement or the like.

(3)   A lessee who furnishes specifications to a lessor or a supplier shall hold the lessor and the supplier harmless against any claim by way of infringement or the like that arises out of compliance with the specifications.

Section 2A–212.   Implied Warranty of Merchantability

(1)   Except in a finance lease, a warranty that the goods will be merchantable is implied in a lease contract if the lessor is a merchant with respect to goods of that kind.

(2)   Goods to be merchantable must be at least such as

(a)   Pass without objection in the trade under the description in the lease agreement;

(b)   In the case of fungible goods, are of fair average quality within the description;

(c)   Are fit for the ordinary purposes for which goods of that type are used;

(d)   Run, within the variation permitted by the lease agreement, of even kind, quality, and quantity within each unit and among all units involved;

(e)   Are adequately contained, packaged, and labeled as the lease agreement may require; and

(f)   Conform to any promises or affirmations of fact made on the container or label.

(3)   Other implied warranties may arise from course of dealing or usage of trade.

Section 2A–213.   Implied Warranty of Fitness for Particular Purpose

Except in a finance lease, if the lessor at the time the lease contract is made has reason to know of any particular purpose for which the goods are required and that the lessee is relying on the lessor's skill or judgment to select or furnish suitable goods, there is in the lease contract an implied warranty that the goods will be fit for that purpose.

Section 2A–214.   Exclusion or Modification of Warranties

(1)   Words or conduct relevant to the creation of an express warranty and words or conduct tending to negate or limit a warranty must be construed wherever reasonable as consistent with each other; but, subject to the provisions of Section 2A–202 on parol or extrinsic evidence, negation or limitation is inoperative to the extent that the construction is unreasonable.

(2)   Subject to subsection (3), to exclude or modify the implied warranty of merchantability or any part of it the language must mention "merchantability," be by a writing, and be conspicuous. Subject to subsection (3), to exclude or modify any implied warranty of fitness the exclusion must be by a writing and be conspicuous. Language to exclude all implied warranties of fitness is sufficient if it is in writing, is conspicuous and states, for example, "There is no warranty that the goods will be fit for a particular purpose."

(3)   Notwithstanding subsection (2), but subject to subsection (4),

(a)   Unless the circumstances indicate otherwise, all implied warranties are excluded by expressions like "as is," or "with all faults," or by other language that in common understanding calls the lessee's attention to the exclusion of warranties and makes plain that there is no implied warranty, if in writing and conspicuous;

(b) If the lessee before entering into the lease contract has examined the goods or the sample or model as fully as desired or has refused to examine the goods, there is no implied warranty with regard to defects that an examination ought in the circumstances to have revealed; and

(c) An implied warranty may also be excluded or modified by course of dealing, course of performance, or usage of trade.

(4) To exclude or modify a warranty against interference or against infringement (Section 2A–211) or any part of it, the language must be specific, be by a writing, and be conspicuous, unless the circumstances, including course of performance, course of dealing, or usage of trade, give the lessee reason to know that the goods are being leased subject to a claim or interest of any person.

Section 2A–215. Cumulation and Conflict of Warranties Express or Implied

Warranties, whether express or implied, must be construed as consistent with each other and as cumulative, but if that construction is unreasonable, the intention of the parties determines which warranty is dominant. In ascertaining that intention the following rules apply:

(a) Exact or technical specifications displace an inconsistent sample or model or general language of description.

(b) A sample from an existing bulk displaces inconsistent general language of description.

(c) Express warranties displace inconsistent implied warranties other than an implied warranty of fitness for a particular purpose.

Section 2A–216. Third-Party Beneficiaries of Express and Implied Warranties

Alternative A

A warranty to or for the benefit of a lessee under this Article, whether express or implied, extends to any natural person who is in the family or household of the lessee or who is a guest in the lessee's home if it is reasonable to expect that such person may use, consume, or be affected by the goods and who is injured in person by breach of the warranty. This section does not displace principles of law and equity that extend a warranty to or for the benefit of a lessee to other persons. The operation of this section may not be excluded, modified, or limited, but an exclusion, modification, or limitation of the warranty, including any with respect to rights and remedies, effective against the lessee is also effective against any beneficiary designated under this section.

Alternative B

A warranty to or for the benefit of a lessee under this Article, whether express or implied, extends to any natural person who may reasonably be expected to use, consume, or be affected by the goods and who is injured in person by breach of the warranty. This section does not displace principles of law and equity that extend a warranty to or for the benefit of a lessee to other persons. The operation of this section may not be excluded, modified, or limited, but an exclusion, modification, or limitation of the warranty, including any with respect to rights and remedies, effective against the lessee is also effective against the beneficiary designated under this section.

Alternative C

A warranty to or for the benefit of a lessee under this Article, whether express or implied, extends to any person who may reasonably be expected to use, consume, or be affected by the goods and who is injured by breach of the warranty. The operation of this section may not be excluded, modified, or limited with respect to injury to the person of an individual to whom the warranty extends, but an exclusion, modification, or limitation of the warranty, including any with respect to rights and remedies, effective against the lessee is also effective against the beneficiary designated under this section.

Section 2A–217. Identification

Identification of goods as goods to which a lease contract refers may be made at any time and in any manner explicitly agreed to by the parties. In the absence of explicit agreement, identification occurs:

(a) When the lease contract is made if the lease contract is for a lease of goods that are existing and identified;

(b) When the goods are shipped, marked, or otherwise designated by the lessor as goods to which the lease contract refers, if the lease contract is for a lease of goods that are not existing and identified; or

(c)   When the young are conceived, if the lease contract is for a lease of unborn young of animals.

Section 2A–218.   Insurance and Proceeds

(1)   A lessee obtains an insurable interest when existing goods are identified to the lease contract even though the goods identified are nonconforming and the lessee has an option to reject them.

(2)   If a lessee has an insurable interest only by reason of the lessor's identification of the goods, the lessor, until default or insolvency or notification to the lessee that identification is final, may substitute other goods for those identified.

(3)   Notwithstanding a lessee's insurable interest under subsections (1) and (2), the lessor retains an insurable interest until an option to buy has been exercised by the lessee and risk of loss has passed to the lessee.

(4)   Nothing in this section impairs any insurable interest recognized under any other statute or rule of law.

(5)   The parties by agreement may determine that one or more parties have an obligation to obtain and pay for insurance covering the goods and by agreement may determine the beneficiary of the proceeds of the insurance.

Section 2A–219.   Risk of Loss

(1)   Except in the case of a finance lease, risk of loss is retained by the lessor and does not pass to the lessee. In the case of a finance lease, risk of loss passes to the lessee.

(2)   Subject to the provisions of this Article on the effect of default on risk of loss (Section 2A–220), if risk of loss is to pass to the lessee and the time of passage is not stated, the following rules apply:

(a)   If the lease contract requires or authorizes the goods to be shipped by carrier

(i)   And it does not require delivery at a particular destination, the risk of loss passes to the lessee when the goods are duly delivered to the carrier; but

(ii)   If it does require delivery at a particular destination and the goods are there duly tendered while in the possession of the carrier, the risk of loss passes to the lessee when the goods are there duly so tendered as to enable the lessee to take delivery.

(b)   If the goods are held by a bailee to be

delivered without being moved, the risk of loss passes to the lessee on acknowledgment by the bailee of the lessee's right to possession of the goods.

(c)   In any case not within subsection (a) or (b), the risk of loss passes to the lessee on the lessee's receipt of the goods if the lessor, or, in the case of a finance lease, the supplier, is a merchant; otherwise the risk passes to the lessee on tender of delivery.

Section 2A–220.   Effect of Default on Risk of Loss

(1)   Where risk of loss is to pass to the lessee and the time of passage is not stated:

(a)   If a tender or delivery of goods so fails to conform to the lease contract as to give a right of rejection, the risk of their loss remains with the lessor, or, in the case of a finance lease, the supplier, until cure or acceptance.

(b)   If the lessee rightfully revokes acceptance, he [or she], to the extent of any deficiency in his [or her] effective insurance coverage, may treat the risk of loss as having remained with the lessor from the beginning.

(2)   Whether or not risk of loss is to pass to the lessee, if the lessee as to conforming goods already identified to a lease contract repudiates or is otherwise in default under the lease contract, the lessor, or, in the case of a finance lease, the supplier, to the extent of any deficiency in his [or her] effective insurance coverage may treat the risk of loss as resting on the lessee for a commercially reasonable time.

Section 2A–221.   Casualty to Identified Goods

If a lease contract requires goods identified when the lease contract is made, and the goods suffer casualty without fault of the lessee, the lessor or the supplier before delivery, or the goods suffer casualty before risk of loss passes to the lessee pursuant to the lease agreement or Section 2A–219, then:

(a)   If the loss is total, the lease contract is avoided; and

(b)   If the loss is partial or the goods have so deteriorated as to no longer conform to the lease contract, the lessee may nevertheless demand inspection and at his [or her] option either treat the lease contract as avoided or, except in a finance lease that is not a consumer lease, accept the goods with due allowance from the rent payable for the balance of the lease term for the deterioration or the deficiency in quantity but without further right against the lessor.

PART 3

Effect of Lease Contract

Section 2A–301.   Enforceability of Lease Contract

Except as otherwise provided in this Article, a lease contract is effective and enforceable according to its terms between the parties, against purchasers of the goods and against creditors of the parties.

Section 2A–302.   Title to and Possession of Goods

Except as otherwise provided in this Article, each provision of this Article applies whether the lessor or a third party has title to the goods, and whether the lessor, the lessee, or a third party has possession of the goods, notwithstanding any statute or rule of law that possession or the absence of possession is fraudulent.

Section 2A–303.   Alienability of Party's Interest Under Lease Contract or of Lessor's Residual Interest in Goods; Delegation of Performance; Assignment of Rights

(1) Any interest of a party under a lease contract and the lessor's residual interest in the goods may be transferred unless

(a) The transfer is voluntary and the lease contract prohibits the transfer; or

(b) The transfer materially changes the duty of or materially increases the burden or risk imposed on the other party to the lease contract, and within a reasonable time after notice of the transfer the other party demands that the transferee comply with subsection (2) and the transferee fails to comply.

(2) Within a reasonable time after demand pursuant to subsection (1)(b), the transferee shall:

(a) Cure or provide adequate assurance that he [or she] will promptly cure any default other than one arising from the transfer;

(b) Compensate or provide adequate assurance that he [or she] will promptly compensate the other party to the lease contract and any other person holding an interest in the lease contract, except the party whose interest is being transferred, for any loss to that party resulting from the transfer;

(c) Provide adequate assurance of future due performance under the lease contract; and

(d) Assume the lease contract.

(3) Demand pursuant to subsection (1)(b) is without prejudice to the other party's rights against the transferee and the party whose interest is transferred.

(4) An assignment of "the lease" or of "all my rights under the lease" or an assignment in similar general terms is a transfer of rights, and unless the language or the circumstances, as in an assignment for security, indicate the contrary, the assignment is a delegation of duties by the assignor to the assignee and acceptance by the assignee constitutes a promise by him [or her] to perform those duties. This promise is enforceable by either the assignor or the other party to the lease contract.

(5) Unless otherwise agreed by the lessor and the lessee, no delegation of performance relieves the assignor as against the other party of any duty to perform or any liability for default.

(6) A right to damages for default with respect to the whole lease contract or a right arising out of the assignor's due performance of his [or her] entire obligation can be assigned despite agreement otherwise.

(7) To prohibit the transfer of an interest of a party under a lease contract, the language of prohibition must be specific, by a writing, and conspicuous.

Section 2A–304.   Subsequent Lease of Goods by Lessor

(1) Subject to the provisions of Section 2A–303, a subsequent lessee from a lessor of goods under an existing lease contract obtains, to the extent of the leasehold interest transferred, the leasehold interest in the goods that the lessor had or had power to transfer, and except as provided in subsection (2) and Section 2A–527(4), takes subject to the existing lease contract. A lessor with voidable title has power to transfer a good leasehold interest to a good faith subsequent lessee for value, but only to the extent set forth in the preceding sentence. When goods have been delivered under a transaction of purchase the lessor has that power even though:

(a) The lessor's transferor was deceived as to the identity of the lessor;

(b) The delivery was in exchange for a check which is later dishonored;

(c)   It was agreed that the transaction was to be a "cash sale"; or

(d)   The delivery was procured through fraud punishable as larcenous under the criminal law.

(2)   A subsequent lessee in the ordinary course of business from a lessor who is a merchant dealing in goods of that kind to whom the goods were entrusted by the existing lessee before the interest of the subsequent lessee became enforceable against the lessor obtains, to the extent of the leasehold interest transferred, all of the lessor's and the existing lessee's rights to the goods, and takes free of the existing lease contract.

(3)   A subsequent lessee from the lessor of goods that are subject to an existing lease contract and are covered by a certificate of title issued under a statute of this State or of another jurisdiction takes no greater rights than those provided both by this section and by the certificate of title statute.

Section 2A–305.   Sale or Sublease of Goods by Lessee

(1)   Subject to the provisions of Section 2A–303, a buyer or sublessee from the lessee of goods under an existing lease contract obtains, to the extent of the interest transferred, the leasehold interest in the goods that the lessee had or had power to transfer, and except as provided in subsection (2) and Section 2A–511(4), takes subject to the existing lease contract. A lessee with a voidable leasehold interest has power to transfer a good leasehold interest to a good faith buyer for value or a good faith sublessee for value, but only to the extent set forth in the preceding sentence. When goods have been delivered under a transaction of lease the lessee has that power even though:

(a)   The lessor was deceived as to the identity of the lessee;

(b)   The delivery was in exchange for a check which is later dishonored; or

(c)   The delivery was procured through fraud punishable as larcenous under the criminal law.

(2)   A buyer in the ordinary course of business or a sublessee in the ordinary course of business from a lessee who is a merchant dealing in goods of that kind to whom the goods were entrusted by the lessor obtains, to the extent of the interest transferred, all of the lessor's and lessee's rights to the goods, and takes free of the existing lease contract.

(3)   A buyer or sublessee from the lessee of goods that are subject to an existing lease contract and are covered by a certificate of title issued under a statute of this State or of another jurisdiction takes no greater rights than those provided by this section and by the certificate of title statute.

Section 2A–306.   Priority of Certain Liens Arising by Operation of Law

If a person in the ordinary course of his [or her] business furnishes services or materials with respect to goods subject to a lease contract, a lien upon those goods in the possession of that person given by statute or rule of law for those materials or services takes priority over any interest of the lessor or lessee under the lease contract or this Article unless the lien is created by statute and the statute provides otherwise or unless the lien is created by rule of law and the rule of law provides otherwise.

Section 2A–307.   Priority of Liens Arising by Attachment or Levy on, Security Interests in, and Other Claims to Goods

(1)   Except as otherwise provided in Section 2A–306, a creditor of a lessee takes subject to the lease contract.

(2)   Except as otherwise provided in subsections (3) and (4) of this section and in Sections 2A–306 and 2A–308, a creditor of a lessor takes subject to the lease contract:

(a)   Unless the creditor holds a lien that attached to the goods before the lease contract became enforceable, or

(b)   Unless the creditor holds a security interest in the goods that under the Article on Secured Transactions (Article 9) would have priority over any other security interest in the goods perfected by a filing covering the goods and made at the time the lease contract became enforceable, whether or not any other security interest existed.

(3)   A lessee in the ordinary course of business takes the leasehold interest free of a security interest in the goods created by the lessor even though the security interest is perfected and the lessee knows of its existence.

(4)   A lessee other than a lessee in the ordinary course of business takes the leasehold interest free of a security interest to the extent that it secures future advances made after the secured party acquires knowledge of the lease or more than 45 days after the lease contract becomes enforceable, whichever first occurs, unless the future advances are made pursuant to a

commitment entered into without knowledge of the lease and before the expiration of the 45-day period.

Section 2A–308.   Special Rights of Creditors

(1) A creditor of a lessor in possession of goods subject to a lease contract may treat the lease contract as void if as against the creditor retention of possession by the lessor is fraudulent under any statute or rule of law, but retention of possession in good faith and current course of trade by the lessor for a commercially reasonable time after the lease contract becomes enforceable is not fraudulent.

(2) Nothing in this Article impairs the rights of creditors of a lessor if the lease contract (a) becomes enforceable, not in current course of trade but in satisfaction of or as security for a pre-existing claim for money, security, or the like, and (b) is made under circumstances which under any statute or rule of law apart from this Article would constitute the transaction a fraudulent transfer or voidable preference.

(3) A creditor of a seller may treat a sale or an identification of goods to a contract for sale as void if as against the creditor retention of possession by the seller is fraudulent under any statute or rule of law, but retention of possession of the goods pursuant to a lease contract entered into by the seller as lessee and the buyer as lessor in connection with the sale or identification of the goods is not fraudulent if the buyer bought for value and in good faith.

Section 2A–309.   Lessor's and Lessee's Rights When Goods Become Fixtures

(1) In this section:

(a) Goods are "fixtures" when they become so related to particular real estate that an interest in them arises under real estate law;

(b) A "fixture filing" is the filing, in the office where a mortgage on the real estate would be recorded or registered, of a financing statement concerning goods that are or are to become fixtures and conforming to the requirements of subsection (5) of Section 9–402;

(c) A lease is a "purchase money lease" unless the lessee has possession or use of the goods or the right to possession or use of the goods before the lease agreement is enforceable;

(d) A mortgage is a "construction mortgage" to the extent it secures an obligation incurred for the construction of an improvement on land including the acquisition cost of the land, if the recorded writing so indicates; and

(e) "Encumbrance" includes real estate mortgages and other liens on real estate and all other rights in real estate that are not ownership interests.

(2) Under this Article a lease may be of goods that are fixtures or may continue in goods that become fixtures, but no lease exists under this Article of ordinary building materials incorporated into an improvement on land.

(3) This Article does not prevent creation of a lease of fixtures pursuant to real estate law.

(4) The perfected interest of a lessor of fixtures has priority over a conflicting interest of an encumbrancer or owner of the real estate if:

(a) The lease is a purchase money lease, the conflicting interest of the encumbrancer or owner arises before the goods become fixtures, the interest of the lessor is perfected by a fixture filing before the goods become fixtures or within ten days thereafter, and the lessee has an interest of record in the real estate or is in possession of the real estate; or

(b) The interest of the lessor is perfected by a fixture filing before the interest of the encumbrancer or owner is of record, the lessor's interest has priority over any conflicting interest of a predecessor in title of the encumbrancer or owner, and the lessee has an interest of record in the real estate or is in possession of the real estate.

(5) The interest of a lessor of fixtures, whether or not perfected, has priority over the conflicting interest of an encumbrancer or owner of the real estate if:

(a) The fixtures are readily removable factory or office machines, readily removable equipment that is not primarily used or leased for use in the operation of the real estate, or readily removable replacements of domestic appliances that are goods subject to a consumer lease, and before the goods become fixtures the lease contract is enforceable; or

(b) The conflicting interest is a lien on the real estate obtained by legal or equitable proceedings after the lease contract is enforceable; or

(c) The encumbrancer or owner has consented in writing to the lease or has disclaimed an interest in the goods as fixtures; or

(d) The lessee has a right to remove the goods as against the encumbrancer or owner. If the lessee's right to remove terminates, the priority of the interest of the lessor continues for a reasonable time.

(6) Notwithstanding paragraph (a) of subsection (4) but otherwise subject to subsections (4) and (5), the interest of a lessor of fixtures is subordinate to the conflicting interest of an encumbrancer of the real estate under a construction mortgage recorded before the goods become fixtures if the goods become fixtures before the completion of the construction. To the extent given to refinance a construction mortgage, the conflicting interest of an encumbrancer of the real estate under a mortgage has this priority to the same extent as the encumbrancer of the real estate under the construction mortgage.

(7) In cases not within the preceding subsections, priority between the interest of a lessor of fixtures and the conflicting interest of an encumbrancer or owner of the real estate who is not the lessee is determined by the priority rules governing conflicting interests in real estate.

(8) If the interest of a lessor has priority over all conflicting interests of all owners and encumbrancers of the real estate, the lessor or the lessee may (a) on default, expiration, termination, or cancellation of the lease agreement by the other party but subject to the provisions of the lease agreement and this Article, or (b) if necessary to enforce his [or her] other rights and remedies under this Article, remove the goods from the real estate, free and clear of all conflicting interests of all owners and encumbrancers of the real estate, but he [or she] must reimburse any encumbrancer or owner of the real estate who is not the lessee and who has not otherwise agreed for the cost of repair of any physical injury, but not for any diminution in value of the real estate caused by the absence of the goods removed or by any necessity of replacing them. A person entitled to reimbursement may refuse permission to remove until the party seeking removal gives adequate security for the performance of this obligation.

(9) Even though the lease agreement does not create a security interest, the interest of a lessor of fixtures is perfected by filing a financing statement as a fixture filing for leased goods that are or are to become fixtures in accordance with the relevant provisions of the Article on Secured Transactions (Article 9).

Section 2A–310. Lessor's and Lessee's Rights When Goods Become Accessions

(1) Goods are "accessions" when they are installed in or affixed to other goods.

(2) The interest of a lessor or a lessee under a lease contract entered into before the goods became accessions is superior to all interests in the whole except as stated in subsection (4).

(3) The interest of a lessor or a lessee under a lease contract entered into at the time or after the goods became accessions is superior to all subsequently acquired interests in the whole except as stated in subsection (4) but is subordinate to interests in the whole existing at the time the lease contract was made unless the holders of such interests in the whole have in writing consented to the lease or disclaimed an interest in the goods as part of the whole.

(4) The interest of a lessor or a lessee under a lease contract described in subsection (2) or (3) is subordinate to the interest of

(a) A buyer in the ordinary course of business or a lessee in the ordinary course of business of any interest in the whole acquired after the goods became accessions; or

(b) A creditor with a security interest in the whole perfected before the lease contract was made to the extent that the creditor makes subsequent advances without knowledge of the lease contract.

(5) When under subsections (2) or (3) and (4) a lessor or a lessee of accessions holds an interest that is superior to all interests in the whole, the lessor or the lessee may (a) on default, expiration, termination, or cancellation of the lease contract by the other party but subject to the provisions of the lease contract and this Article, or (b) if necessary to enforce his [or her] other rights and remedies under this Article, remove the goods from the whole, free and clear of all interests in the whole, but he [or she] must reimburse any holder of an interest in the whole who is not the lessee and who has not otherwise agreed for the cost of repair of any physical injury but not for any diminution in value of the whole caused by the absence of the goods removed or by any necessity for replacing them. A person entitled to reimbursement may refuse permission to remove until the party seeking removal gives adequate security for the performance of this obligation.

PART 4

Performance of Lease Contract:
Repudiated, Substituted and Excused

Section 2A–401. Insecurity: Adequate Assurance of Performance

(1) A lease contract imposes an obligation on each party that the other's expectation of receiving due performance will not be impaired.

(2) If reasonable grounds for insecurity arise with respect to the performance of either party, the insecure

party may demand in writing adequate assurance of due performance. Until the insecure party receives that assurance, if commercially reasonable the insecure party may suspend any performance for which he [or she] has not already received the agreed return.

(3) A repudiation of the lease contract occurs if assurance of due performance adequate under the circumstances of the particular case is not provided to the insecure party within a reasonable time, not to exceed 30 days after receipt of a demand by the other party.

(4) Between merchants, the reasonableness of grounds for insecurity and the adequacy of any assurance offered must be determined according to commercial standards.

(5) Acceptance of any nonconforming delivery or payment does not prejudice the aggrieved party's right to demand adequate assurance of future performance.

Section 2A–402. Anticipatory Repudiation

If either party repudiates a lease contract with respect to a performance not yet due under the lease contract, the loss of which performance will substantially impair the value of the lease contract to the other, the aggrieved party may:

(a) For a commercially reasonable time, await retraction of repudiation and performance by the repudiating party;

(b) Make demand pursuant to Section 2A–401 and await assurance of future performance adequate under the circumstances of the particular case; or

(c) Resort to any right or remedy upon default under the lease contract or this Article, even though the aggrieved party has notified the repudiating party that the aggrieved party would await the repudiating party's performance and assurance and has urged retraction. In addition, whether or not the aggrieved party is pursuing one of the foregoing remedies, the aggrieved party may suspend performance or, if the aggrieved party is the lessor, proceed in accordance with the provisions of this Article on the lessor's right to identify goods to the lease contract notwithstanding default or to salvage unfinished goods (Section 2A–524).

Section 2A–403. Retraction of Anticipatory Repudiation

(1) Until the repudiating party's next performance is due, the repudiating party can retract the repudiation unless, since the repudiation, the aggrieved party has cancelled the lease contract or materially changed the aggrieved party's position or otherwise indicated that the aggrieved party considers the repudiation final.

(2) Retraction may be by any method that clearly indicates to the aggrieved party that the repudiating party intends to perform under the lease contract and includes any assurance demanded under Section 2A–401.

(3) Retraction reinstates a repudiating party's rights under a lease contract with due excuse and allowance to the aggrieved party for any delay occasioned by the repudiation.

Section 2A–404. Substituted Performance

(1) If without fault of the lessee, the lessor and the supplier, the agreed berthing, loading, or unloading facilities fail or the agreed type of carrier becomes unavailable or the agreed manner of delivery otherwise becomes commercially impracticable, but a commercially reasonable substitute is available, the substitute performance must be tendered and accepted.

(2) If the agreed means or manner of payment fails because of domestic or foreign governmental regulation:

(a) The lessor may withhold or stop delivery or cause the supplier to withhold or stop delivery unless the lessee provides a means or manner of payment that is commercially a substantial equivalent; and

(b) If delivery has already been taken, payment by the means or in the manner provided by the regulation discharges the lessee's obligation unless the regulation is discriminatory, oppressive, or predatory.

Section 2A–405. Excused Performance

Subject to Section 2A–404 on substituted performance, the following rules apply:

(a) Delay in delivery or nondelivery in whole or in part by a lessor or a supplier who complies with paragraphs (b) and (c) is not a default under the lease contract if performance as agreed has been made impracticable by the occurrence of a contingency the nonoccurrence of which was a basic assumption on which the lease contract was made or by compliance in good faith with any applicable foreign or domestic governmental regulation or order, whether or not the regulation or order later proves to be invalid.

(b)   If the causes mentioned in paragraph (a) affect only part of the lessor's or the supplier's capacity to perform, he [or she] shall allocate production and deliveries among his [or her] customers but at his [or her] option may include regular customers not then under contract for sale or lease as well as his [or her] own requirements for further manufacture. He [or she] may so allocate in any manner that is fair and reasonable.

(c)   The lessor seasonally shall notify the lessee and in the case of a finance lease the supplier seasonally shall notify the lessor and the lessee, if known, that there will be delay or nondelivery and, if allocation is required under paragraph (b), of the estimated quota thus made available for the lessee.

Section 2A–406.   Procedure on Excused Performance

(1)   If the lessee receives notification of a material or indefinite delay or an allocation justified under Section 2A–405, the lessee may by written notification to the lessor as to any goods involved, and with respect to all of the goods if under an installment lease contract the value of the whole lease contract is substantially impaired (Section 2A–510):

(a)   Terminate the lease contract (Section 2A–505(2)); or

(b)   Except in a finance lease that is not a consumer lease, modify the lease contract by accepting the available quota in substitution, with due allowance from the rent payable for the balance of the lease term for the deficiency but without further right against the lessor.

(2)   If, after receipt of a notification from the lessor under Section 2A–405, the lessee fails so to modify the lease agreement within a reasonable time not exceeding 30 days, the lease contract lapses with respect to any deliveries affected.

Section 2A–407.   Irrevocable Promises: Finance Leases

(1)   In the case of a finance lease that is not a consumer lease the lessee's promises under the lease contract become irrevocable and independent upon the lessee's acceptance of the goods.

(2)   A promise that has become irrevocable and independent under subsection (1):

(a)   Is effective and enforceable between the parties, and by or against third parties including assignees of the parties, and

(b)   Is not subject to cancellation, termination, modification, repudiation, excuse, or substitution without the consent of the party to whom the promise runs.

PART 5

Default

A. In General

Section 2A–501.   Default: Procedure

(1)   Whether the lessor or the lessee is in default under a lease contract is determined by the lease agreement and this Article.

(2)   If the lessor or the lessee is in default under the lease contract, the party seeking enforcement has rights and remedies as provided in this Article and, except as limited by this Article, as provided in the lease agreement.

(3)   If the lessor or the lessee is in default under the lease contract, the party seeking enforcement may reduce the party's claim to judgment, or otherwise enforce the lease contract by self-help or any available judicial procedure or nonjudicial procedure, including administrative proceeding, arbitration, or the like, in accordance with this Article.

(4)   Except as otherwise provided in this Article or the lease agreement, the rights and remedies referred to in subsections (2) and (3) are cumulative.

(5)   If the lease agreement covers both real property and goods, the party seeking enforcement may proceed under this Part as to the goods, or under other applicable law as to both the real property and the goods in accordance with his [or her] rights and remedies in respect of the real property, in which case this Part does not apply.

Section 2A–502.   Notice After Default

Except as otherwise provided in the Article or the lease agreement, the lessor or lessee in default under the lease contract is not entitled to notice of default or of notice of enforcement from the other party to the lease agreement.

Section 2A–503.   Modification or Impairment of Rights and Remedies

(1)   Except as otherwise provided in this Article, the lease agreement may include rights and remedies for default in addition to or in substitution for those provided in this Article and may limit or alter the measure of damages recoverable under this Article.

(2) Resort to a remedy provided under this Article or in the lease agreement is optional unless the remedy is expressly agreed to be exclusive. If circumstances cause an exclusive or limited remedy to fail of its essential purpose, or provision for an exclusive remedy is unconscionable, remedy may be had as provided in this Article.

(3) Consequential damages may be liquidated under Section 2A–504, or may otherwise be limited, altered, or excluded unless the limitation, alteration, or exclusion is unconscionable. Limitation of consequential damages for injury to the person in the case of consumer goods is prima facie unconscionable but limitation of damages where the loss is commercial is not.

(4) Rights and remedies on default by the lessor or the lessee with respect to any obligation or promise collateral or ancillary to the lease contract are not impaired by this Article.

Section 2A–504. Liquidation of Damages

(1) Damages payable by either party for default, or any other act or omission, including indemnity for loss or diminution of anticipated tax benefits or loss or damage to lessor's residual interest, may be liquidated in the lease agreement but only at an amount or by a formula that is reasonable in light of the then anticipated harm caused by the default or other act or omission.

(2) If the lease agreement provides for liquidation of damages, and such provision does not comply with subsection (1), or such provision is an exclusive or limited remedy that circumstances cause to fail of its essential purpose, remedy may be had as provided in this Article.

(3) If the lessor justifiably withholds or stops delivery of goods because of the lessee's default or insolvency (Section 2A–525 or 2A–526), the lessee is entitled to restitution of any amount by which the sum of his [or her] payments exceeds:

(a) The amount to which the lessor is entitled by virtue of terms liquidating the lessor's damages in accordance with subsection (1); or

(b) In the absence of those terms, 20 percent of the then present value of the total rent the lessee was obligated to pay for the balance of the lease term, or, in the case of a consumer lease, the lesser of such amount or $500.

(4) A lessee's right to restitution under subsection (3) is subject to offset to the extent the lessor establishes:

(a) A right to recover damages under the provisions of this Article other than subsection (1); and

(b) The amount or value of any benefits received by the lessee directly or indirectly by reason of the lease contract.

Section 2A–505. Cancellation and Termination and Effect of Cancellation, Termination, Rescission, or Fraud on Rights and Remedies

(1) On cancellation of the lease contract, all obligations that are still executory on both sides are discharged, but any right based on prior default or performance survives, and the cancelling party also retains any remedy for default of the whole lease contract or any unperformed balance.

(2) On termination of the lease contract, all obligations that are still executory on both sides are discharged but any right based on prior default or performance survives.

(3) Unless the contrary intention clearly appears, expressions of "cancellation," "rescission," or the like of the lease contract may not be construed as a renunciation or discharge of any claim in damages for an antecedent default.

(4) Rights and remedies for material misrepresentation or fraud include all rights and remedies available under this Article for default.

(5) Neither rescission nor a claim for rescission of the lease contract nor rejection or return of the goods may bar or be deemed inconsistent with a claim for damages or other right or remedy.

Section 2A–506. Statute of Limitations

(1) An action for default under a lease contract, including breach of warranty or indemnity, must be commenced within 4 years after the cause of action accrued. By the original lease contract the parties may reduce the period of limitation to not less than one year.

(2) A cause of action for default accrues when the act or omission on which the default or breach of warranty is based is or should have been discovered by the aggrieved party, or when the default occurs, whichever is later. A cause of action for indemnity accrues when the act or omission on which the claim for indemnity is based or should have been discovered by the indemnified party, whichever is later.

(3) If an action commenced within the time limited

by subsection (1) is so terminated as to leave available a remedy by another action for the same default or breach of warranty or indemnity, the other action may be commenced after the expiration of the time limited and within 6 months after the termination of the first action unless the termination resulted from voluntary discontinuance or from dismissal for failure or neglect to prosecute.

(4) This section does not alter the law on tolling of the statute of limitations nor does it apply to causes of action that have accrued before this Article becomes effective.

Section 2A–507. Proof of Market Rent: Time and Place

(1) Damages based on market rent (Section 2A–519 or 2A–528) are determined according to the rent for the use of the goods concerned for a lease term identical to the remaining lease term of the original lease agreement and prevailing at the time of the default.

(2) If evidence of rent for the use of the goods concerned for a lease term identical to the remaining lease term of the original lease agreement and prevailing at the times or places described in this Article is not readily available, the rent prevailing within any reasonable time before or after the time described or at any other place or for a different lease term which in commercial judgment or under usage of trade would serve as a reasonable substitute for the one described may be used, making any proper allowance for the difference, including the cost of transporting the goods to or from the other place.

(3) Evidence of a relevant rent prevailing at a time or place or for a lease term other than the one described in this Article offered by one party is not admissible unless and until he [or she] has given the other party notice the court finds sufficient to prevent unfair surprise.

(4) If the prevailing rent or value of any goods regularly leased in any established market is in issue, reports in official publications or trade journals or in newspapers or periodicals of general circulation published as the reports of that market are admissible in evidence. The circumstances of the preparation of the report may be shown to affect its weight but not its admissibility.

PART B. Default by Lessor

Section 2A–508. Lessee's Remedies

(1) If a lessor fails to deliver the goods in conformity

to the lease contract (Section 2A–509) or repudiates the lease contract (Section 2A–402), or a lessee rightfully rejects the goods (Section 2A–509) or justifiably revokes acceptance of the goods (Section 2A–517), then with respect to any goods involved, and with respect to all of the goods if under an installment lease contract the value of the whole lease contract is substantially impaired (Section 2A–510), the lessor is in default under the lease contract and the lessee may:

    (a) Cancel the lease contract (Section 2A–505(1));

    (b) Recover so much of the rent and security as has been paid, but in the case of an installment lease contract the recovery is that which is just under the circumstances;

    (c) Cover and recover damages as to all goods affected whether or not they have been identified to the lease contract (Sections 2A–518 and 2A–520), or recover damages for nondelivery (Sections 2A–519 and 2A–520).

(2) If a lessor fails to deliver the goods in conformity to the lease contract or repudiates the lease contract, the lessee may also:

    (a) If the goods have been identified, recover them (Section 2A–522); or

    (b) In a proper case, obtain specific performance or replevy the goods (Section 2A–521).

(3) If a lessor is otherwise in default under a lease contract, the lessee may exercise the rights and remedies provided in the lease contract and this Article.

(4) If a lessor has breached a warranty, whether express or implied, the lessee may recover damages (Section 2A–519(4)).

(5) On rightful rejection or justifiable revocation of acceptance, a lessee has a security interest in goods in the lessee's possession or control for any rent and security that has been paid and any expenses reasonably incurred in their inspection, receipt, transportation, and care and custody and may hold those goods and dispose of them in good faith and in a commercially reasonable manner, subject to the provisions of Section 2A–527(5).

(6) Subject to the provisions of Section 2A–407, a lessee, on notifying the lessor of the lessee's intention to do so, may deduct all or any part of the damages resulting from any default under the lease contract from any part of the rent still due under the same lease contract.

Section 2A–509. Lessee's Rights on Improper Delivery; Rightful Rejection

(1) Subject to the provisions of Section 2A–510 on default in installment lease contracts, if the goods or the tender or delivery fail in any respect to conform to the lease contract, the lessee may reject or accept the goods or accept any commercial unit or units and reject the rest of the goods.

(2) Rejection of goods is ineffective unless it is within a reasonable time after tender or delivery of the goods and the lessee seasonably notifies the lessor.

Section 2A–510. Installment Lease Contracts: Rejection and Default

(1) Under an installment lease contract a lessee may reject any delivery that is nonconforming if the nonconformity substantially impairs the value of that delivery and cannot be cured or the nonconformity is a defect in the required documents; but if the nonconformity does not fall within subsection (2) and the lessor or the supplier gives adequate assurance of its cure, the lessee must accept that delivery.

(2) Whenever nonconformity or default with respect to one or more deliveries substantially impairs the value of the installment lease contract as a whole there is a default with respect to the whole. But, the aggrieved party reinstates the installment lease contract as a whole if the aggrieved party accepts a nonconforming delivery without seasonably notifying of cancellation or brings an action with respect only to past deliveries or demands performance as to future deliveries.

Section 2A–511. Merchant Lessee's Duties as to Rightfully Rejected Goods

(1) Subject to any security interest of a lessee (Section 2A–508(5)), if a lessor or a supplier has no agent or place of business at the market of rejection, a merchant lessee, after rejection of goods in his [or her] possession or control, shall follow any reasonable instructions received from the lessor or the supplier with respect to the goods. In the absence of those instructions, a merchant lessee shall make reasonable efforts to sell, lease, or otherwise dispose of the goods for the lessor's account if they threaten to decline in value speedily. Instructions are not reasonable if on demand indemnity for expenses is not forthcoming.

(2) If a merchant lessee (subsection (1)) or any other lessee (Section 2A–512) disposes of goods, he [or she] is entitled to reimbursement either from the lessor or the supplier or out of the proceeds for reasonable expenses of caring for and disposing of the goods and, if the expenses include no disposition commission, to such commission as is usual in the trade, or if there is none, to a reasonable sum not exceeding 10 percent of the gross proceeds.

(3) In complying with this section or Section 2A–512, the lessee is held only to good faith. Good faith conduct hereunder is neither acceptance or conversion nor the basis of an action for damages.

(4) A purchaser who purchases in good faith from a lessee pursuant to this section or Section 2A–512 takes the goods free of any rights of the lessor and the supplier even though the lessee fails to comply with one or more of the requirements of this Article.

Section 2A–512. Lessee's Duties as to Rightfully Rejected Goods

(1) Except as otherwise provided with respect to goods that threaten to decline in value speedily (Section 2A–511) and subject to any security interest of a lessee (Section 2A–508(5)):

(a) The lessee, after rejection of goods in the lessee's possession, shall hold them with reasonable care at the lessor's or the supplier's disposition for a reasonable time after the lessee's seasonable notification of rejection;

(b) If the lessor or the supplier gives no instructions within a reasonable time after notification of rejection, the lessee may store the rejected goods for the lessor's or the supplier's account or ship them to the lessor or the supplier or dispose of them for the lessor's or the supplier's account with reimbursement in the manner provided in Section 2A–511; but

(c) The lessee has no further obligations with regard to goods rightfully rejected.

(2) Action by the lessee pursuant to subsection (1) is not acceptance or conversion.

Section 2A–513. Cure by Lessor of Improper Tender or Delivery; Replacement

(1) If any tender or delivery by the lessor or the supplier is rejected because nonconforming and the time for performance has not yet expired, the lessor or the supplier may seasonably notify the lessee of the lessor's or the supplier's intention to cure and may then make a conforming delivery within the time provided in the lease contract.

(2) If the lessee rejects a nonconforming tender that

the lessor or the supplier had reasonable grounds to believe would be acceptable with or without money allowance, the lessor or the supplier may have a further reasonable time to substitute a conforming tender if he [or she] seasonably notifies the lessee.

Section 2A–514. Waiver of Lessee's Objections

(1) In rejecting goods, a lessee's failure to state a particular defect that is ascertainable by reasonable inspection precludes the lessee from relying on the defect to justify rejection or to establish default:

    (a) If, stated seasonably, the lessor or the supplier could have cured it (Section 2A–513); or

    (b) Between merchants if the lessor or the supplier after rejection has made a request in writing for a full and final written statement of all defects on which the lessee proposes to rely.

(2) A lessee's failure to reserve rights when paying rent or other consideration against documents precludes recovery of the payment for defects apparent on the face of the documents.

Section 2A–515. Acceptance of Goods

(1) Acceptance of goods occurs after the lessee has had a reasonable opportunity to inspect the goods and

    (a) The lessee signifies or acts with respect to the goods in a manner that signifies to the lessor or the supplier that the goods are conforming or that the lessee will take or retain them in spite of their nonconformity; or

    (b) The lessee fails to make an effective rejection of the goods (Section 2A–509(2)).

(2) Acceptance of a part of any commercial unit is acceptance of that entire unit.

Section 2A–516. Effect of Acceptance of Goods; Notice of Default; Burden of Establishing Default After Acceptance; Notice of Claim or Litigation to Person Answerable Over

(1) A lessee must pay rent for any goods accepted in accordance with the lease contract, with due allowance for goods rightfully rejected or not delivered.

(2) A lessee's acceptance of goods precludes rejection of the goods accepted. In the case of a finance lease, if made with knowledge of a nonconformity, acceptance cannot be revoked because of it. In any other case, if made with knowledge of a nonconformity, acceptance cannot be revoked because of it unless the acceptance was on the reasonable assumption that the nonconformity would be seasonably cured. Acceptance does not of itself impair any other remedy provided by this Article or the lease agreement for nonconformity.

(3) If a tender has been accepted:

    (a) Within a reasonable time after the lessee discovers or should have discovered any default, the lessee shall notify the lessor and the supplier, or be barred from any remedy;

    (b) Except in the case of a consumer lease, within a reasonable time after the lessee receives notice of litigation for infringement or the like (Section 2A–211) the lessee shall notify the lessor or be barred from any remedy over for liability established by the litigation; and

    (c) The burden is on the lessee to establish any default.

(4) If a lessee is sued for breach of a warranty or other obligation for which a lessor or a supplier is answerable over:

    (a) The lessee may give the lessor or the supplier written notice of the litigation. If the notice states that the lessor or the supplier may come in and defend and that if the lessor or the supplier does not do so he [or she] will be bound in any action against him [or her] by the lessee by any determination of fact common to the two litigations, then unless the lessor or the supplier after seasonable receipt of the notice does come in and defend he [or she] is so bound.

    (b) The lessor or the supplier may demand in writing that the lessee turn over control of the litigation including settlement if the claim is one for infringement or the like (Section 2A–211) or else be barred from any remedy over. If the demand states that the lessor or the supplier agrees to bear all expense and to satisfy any adverse judgment, then unless the lessee after seasonable receipt of the demand does turn over control the lessee is so barred.

(5) The provisions of subsections (3) and (4) apply to any obligation of a lessee to hold the lessor or the supplier harmless against infringement or the like (Section 2A–211).

Section 2A–517.   Revocation of Acceptance of Goods

(1) A lessee may revoke acceptance of a lot or commercial unit whose nonconformity substantially impairs its value to the lessee if he [or she] has accepted it:

(a)   Except in the case of a finance lease, on the reasonable assumption that its nonconformity would be cured and it has not been seasonably cured; or

(b)   Without discovery of the nonconformity if the lessee's acceptance was reasonably induced either by the lessor's assurances or, except in the case of a finance lease, by the difficulty of discovery before acceptance.

(2) Revocation of acceptance must occur within a reasonable time after the lessee discovers or should have discovered the ground for it and before any substantial change in condition of the goods which is not caused by the nonconformity. Revocation is not effective until the lessee notifies the lessor.

(3) A lessee who so revokes has the same rights and duties with regard to the goods involved as if the lessee had rejected them.

Section 2A–518.   Cover; Substitute Goods

(1) After default by a lessor under the lease contract (Section 2A–508(1)), the lessee may cover by making any purchase or lease of or contract to purchase or lease goods in substitution for those due from the lessor.

(2) Except as otherwise provided with respect to damages liquidated in the lease agreement (Section 2A–504) or determined by agreement of the parties (Section 1–102(3)), if a lessee's cover is by lease agreement substantially similar to the original lease agreement and the lease agreement is made in good faith and in a commercially reasonable manner, the lessee may recover from the lessor as damages (a) the present value, as of the date of default, of the difference between the total rent for the lease term of the new lease agreement and the total rent for the remaining lease term of the original lease agreement and (b) any incidental or consequential damages less expenses saved in consequence of the lessor's default.

(3) If a lessee's cover is by lease agreement that for any reason does not qualify for treatment under subsection (2), or is by purchase or otherwise, the lessee may recover from the lessor as if the lessee had elected not to cover and Section 2A–519 governs.

Section 2A–519.   Lessee's Damages for Nondelivery, Repudiation, Default and Breach of Warranty in Regard to Accepted Goods

(1) Except as otherwise provided with respect to damages liquidated in the lease agreement (Section 2A–504) or determined by agreement of the parties (Section 1–102(3)), if a lessee elects not to cover or a lessee elects to cover and the cover is by lease agreement that for any reason does not qualify for treatment under Section 2A–518(2), or is by purchase or otherwise, the measure of damages for non-delivery or repudiation by the lessor or for rejection or revocation of acceptance by the lessee is the present value as of the date of the default of the difference between the then market rent and the original rent, computed for the remaining lease term of the original lease agreement together with incidental and consequential damages, less expenses saved in consequence of the lessor's default.

(2) Market rent is to be determined as of the place for tender or, in cases of rejection after arrival or revocation of acceptance, as of the place of arrival.

(3) If the lessee has accepted goods and given notification (Section 2A–516(3)), the measure of damages for nonconforming tender or delivery by a lessor is the loss resulting in the ordinary course of events from the lessor's default as determined in any manner that is reasonable together with incidental and consequential damages, less expenses saved in consequence of the lessor's default.

(4) The measure of damages for breach of warranty is the present value at the time and place of acceptance of the difference between the value of the use of the goods accepted and the value if they had been as warranted for the lease term, unless special circumstances show proximate damages of a different amount, together with incidental and consequential damages, less expenses saved in consequence of the lessor's default or breach of warranty.

Section 2A–520.   Lessee's Incidental and Consequential Damages

(1) Incidental damages resulting from a lessor's default include expenses reasonably incurred in inspection, receipt, transportation, and care and custody of goods rightfully rejected or goods the acceptance of which is justifiably revoked, any commercially reasonable charges, expenses or commissions in connection with effecting cover, and any other reasonable expense incident to the default.

(2) Consequential damages resulting from a lessor's default include:

(a)   Any loss resulting from general or particular requirements and needs of which the lessor at the time of contracting had reason to know and which could not reasonably be prevented by cover or otherwise; and

(b)   Injury to person or property proximately resulting from any breach of warranty.

Section 2A–521.   Lessee's Right to Specific Performance or Replevin

(1)   Specific performance may be decreed if the goods are unique or in other proper circumstances.

(2)   A decree for specific performance may include any terms and conditions as to payment of the rent, damages, or other relief that the court deems just.

(3)   A lessee has a right of replevin, detinue, sequestration, claim and delivery, or the like for goods identified to the lease contract if after reasonable effort the lessee is unable to effect cover for those goods or the circumstances reasonably indicate that the effort will be unavailing.

Section 2A–522.   Lessee's Right to Goods on Lessor's Insolvency

(1)   Subject to subsection (2) and even though the goods have not been shipped, a lessee who has paid a part or all of the rent and security for goods identified to a lease contract (Section 2A–217) on making and keeping good a tender of any unpaid portion of the rent and security due under the lease contract may recover the goods identified from the lessor if the lessor becomes insolvent within 10 days after receipt of the first installment of rent and security.

(2)   A lessee acquires the right to recover goods identified to a lease contract only if they conform to the lease contract.

C.   Default by Lessee

Section 2A–523.   Lessor's Remedies

(1)   If a lessee wrongfully rejects or revokes acceptance of goods or fails to make a payment when due or repudiates with respect to a part or the whole, then, with respect to any goods involved, and with respect to all of the goods if under an installment lease contract the value of the whole lease contract is substantially impaired (Section 2A–510), the lessee is in default under the lease contract and the lessor may:

(a)   Cancel the lease contract (Section 2A–505(1));

(b)   Proceed respecting goods not identified to the lease contract (Section 2A–524);

(c)   Withhold delivery of the goods and take possession of goods previously delivered (Section 2A–525);

(d)   Stop delivery of the goods by any bailee (Section 2A–526);

(e)   Dispose of the goods and recover damages (Section 2A–527), or retain the goods and recover damages (Section 2A–528), or in a proper case recover rent (Section 2A–529).

(2)   If a lessee is otherwise in default under a lease contract, the lessor may exercise the rights and remedies provided in the lease contract and this Article.

Section 2A–524.   Lessor's Right to Identify Goods to Lease Contract

(1)   A lessor aggrieved under Section 2A–523(1) may:

(a)   Identify to the lease contract conforming goods not already identified if at the time the lessor learned of the default they were in the lessor's or the supplier's possession or control; and

(b)   Dispose of goods (Section 2A–527(1)) that demonstrably have been intended for the particular lease contract even though those goods are unfinished.

(2)   If the goods are unfinished, in the exercise of reasonable commercial judgment for the purposes of avoiding loss and of effective realization, an aggrieved lessor or the supplier may either complete manufacture and wholly identify the goods to the lease contract or cease manufacture and lease, sell, or otherwise dispose of the goods for scrap or salvage value or proceed in any other reasonable manner.

Section 2A–525.   Lessor's Right to Possession of Goods

(1)   If a lessor discovers the lessee to be insolvent, the lessor may refuse to deliver the goods.

(2)   The lessor has on default by the lessee under the lease contract the right to take possession of the goods. If the lease contract so provides, the lessor may require the lessee to assemble the goods and make them available to the lessor at a place to be

designated by the lessor which is reasonably convenient to both parties. Without removal, the lessor may render unusable any goods employed in trade or business, and may dispose of goods on the lessee's premises (Section 2A–527).

(3) The lessor may proceed under subsection (2) without judicial process if that can be done without breach of the peace or the lessor may proceed by action.

Section 2A–526.   Lessor's Stoppage of Delivery in Transit or Otherwise

(1) A lessor may stop delivery of goods in the possession of a carrier or other bailee if the lessor discovers the lessee to be insolvent and may stop delivery of carload, truckload, planeload, or larger shipments of express or freight if the lessee repudiates or fails to make a payment due before delivery, whether for rent, security or otherwise under the lease contract, or for any other reason the lessor has a right to withhold or take possession of the goods.

(2) In pursuing its remedies under subsection (1), the lessor may stop delivery until

(a)   Receipt of the goods by the lessee;

(b)   Acknowledgment to the lessee by any bailee of the goods, except a carrier, that the bailee holds the goods for the lessee; or

(c)   Such an acknowledgment to the lessee by a carrier via reshipment or as warehouseman.

(3) (a) To stop delivery, a lessor shall so notify as to enable the bailee by reasonable diligence to prevent delivery of the goods.

(b)   After notification, the bailee shall hold and deliver the goods according to the directions of the lessor, but the lessor is liable to the bailee for any ensuing charges or damages.

(c)   A carrier who has issued a nonnegotiable bill of lading is not obliged to obey a notification to stop received from a person other than the consignor.

Section 2A–527.   Lessor's Rights to Dispose of Goods

(1)   After a default by a lessee under the lease contract (Section 2A–523(1)) or after the lessor refuses to deliver or takes possession of goods (Section 2A–525 or 2A–526), the lessor may dispose of the goods concerned or the undelivered balance thereof by lease, sale or otherwise.

(2)   Except as otherwise provided with respect to damages liquidated in the lease agreement (Section 2A–504) or determined by agreement of the parties (Section 1–102(3)), if the disposition is by lease agreement substantially similar to the original lease agreement and the lease agreement is made in good faith and in a commercially reasonable manner, the lessor may recover from the lessee as damages (a) accrued and unpaid rent as of the date of default, (b) the present value as of the date of default of the difference between the total rent for the remaining lease term of the original lease agreement and the total rent for the lease term of the new lease agreement, and (c) any incidental damages allowed under Section 2A–530, less expenses saved in consequence of the lessee's default.

(3)   If the lessor's disposition is by lease agreement that for any reason does not qualify for treatment under subsection (2), or is by sale or otherwise, the lessor may recover from the lessee as if the lessor had elected not to dispose of the goods and Section 2A–528 governs.

(4)   A subsequent buyer or lessee who buys or leases from the lessor in good faith for value as a result of a disposition under this section takes the goods free of the original lease contract and any rights of the original lessee even though the lessor fails to comply with one or more of the requirements of this Article.

(5)   The lessor is not accountable to the lessee for any profit made on any disposition. A lessee who has rightfully rejected or justifiably revoked acceptance shall account to the lessor for any excess over the amount of the lessee's security interest (Section 2A–508(5)).

Section 2A–528.   Lessor's Damages for Nonacceptance or Repudiation

(1)   Except as otherwise provided with respect to damages liquidated in the lease agreement (Section 2A–504) or determined by agreement of the parties (Section 1–102(3)), if a lessor elects to retain the goods or a lessor elects to dispose of the goods and disposition is by lease agreement that for any reason does not qualify for treatment under Section 2A–527(2), or is by sale or otherwise, the lessor may recover from the lessee as damages for non-acceptance or repudiation by the lessee (a) accrued and unpaid rent as of the date of default, (b) the present value as of the date of default of the difference between the total rent for the remaining lease term of the original lease agreement and the market rent at the time and place for tender computed for the same lease term,

and (c) any incidental damages allowed under Section 2A–530, less expenses saved in consequence of the lessee's default.

(2) If the measure of damages provided in subsection (1) is inadequate to put a lessor in as good a position as performance would have, the measure of damages is the profit, including reasonable overhead, the lessor would have made from full performance by the lessee, together with any incidental damages allowed under Section 2A–530, due allowance for costs reasonably incurred and due credit for payments or proceeds of disposition.

Section 2A–529. Lessor's Action for the Rent

(1) After default by the lessee under the lease contract (Section 2A–523(1)), if the lessor complies with subsection (2), the lessor may recover from the lessee as damages:

    (a) For goods accepted by the lessee and for conforming goods lost or damaged within a commercially reasonable time after risk of loss passes to the lessee (Section 2A–219), (i) accrued and unpaid rent as of the date of default, (ii) the present value as of the date of default of the rent for the remaining lease term of the lease agreement, and (iii) any incidental damages allowed under Section 2A–530, less expenses saved in consequence of the lessee's default; and

    (b) For goods identified to the lease contract if the lessor is unable after reasonable effort to dispose of them at a reasonable price or the circumstances reasonably indicate that effort will be unavailing, (i) accrued and unpaid rent as of the date of default, (ii) the present value as of the date of default of the rent for the remaining lease term of the lease agreement, and (iii) any incidental damages allowed under Section 2A–530, less expenses saved in consequence of the lessee's default.

(2) Except as provided in subsection (3), the lessor shall hold for the lessee for the remaining lease term of the lease agreement any goods that have been identified to the lease contract and are in the lessor's control.

(3) The lessor may dispose of the goods at any time before collection of the judgment for damages obtained pursuant to subsection (1). If the disposition is before the end of the remaining lease term of the lease agreement, the lessor's recovery against the lessee for damages will be governed by Section 2A–527 or Section 2A–528.

(4) Payment of the judgment for damages obtained

pursuant to subsection (1) entitles the lessee to use and possession of the goods not then disposed of for the remaining lease term of the lease agreement.

(5) After a lessee has wrongfully rejected or revoked acceptance of goods, has failed to pay rent then due, or has repudiated (Section 2A–402), a lessor who is held not entitled to rent under this section must nevertheless be awarded damages for non-acceptance under Sections 2A–527 and 2A–528.

Section 2A–530. Lessor's Incidental Damages

Incidental damages to an aggrieved lessor include any commercially reasonable charges, expenses, or commissions incurred in stopping delivery, in the transportation, care and custody of goods after the lessee's default, in connection with return or disposition of the goods, or otherwise resulting from the default.

Section 2A–531. Standing to Sue Third Parties for Injury to Goods

(1) If a third party so deals with goods that have been identified to a lease contract as to cause actionable injury to a party to the lease contract (a) the lessor has a right of action against the third party, and (b) the lessee also has a right of action against the third party if the lessee:

    (i) Has a security interest in the goods;

    (ii) Has an insurable interest in the goods; or

    (iii) Bears the risk of loss under the lease contract or has since the injury assumed that risk as against the lessor and the goods have been converted or destroyed.

(2) If at the time of the injury the party plaintiff did not bear the risk of loss as against the other party to the lease contract and there is no arrangement between them for disposition of the recovery, his [or her] suit or settlement, subject to his [or her] own interest, is as a fiduciary for the other party to the lease contract.

(3) Either party with the consent of the other may sue for the benefit of whom it may concern.

AMENDMENT XXVII

No law varying the compensation for the services of Senators and Representatives shall take effect, until an election of Representatives shall have intervened.

ARTICLE **3**

COMMERCIAL PAPER

PART **1**

Short Title, Form and Interpretation

Section 3–101.   Short Title

This Article shall be known and may be cited as Uniform Commercial Code — Commercial Paper.

Section 3–102.   Definitions and Index of Definitions

(1) In this Article unless the context otherwise requires

(a)   "Issue" means the first delivery of an instrument to a holder or a remitter.

(b)   An "order" is a direction to pay and must be more than an authorization or request. It must identify the person to pay with reasonable certainty. It may be addressed to one or more such persons jointly or in the alternative but not in succession.

(c)   A "promise" is an undertaking to pay and must be more than an acknowledgment of an obligation.

(d)   "Secondary party" means a drawer or endorser.

(e)   "Instrument" means a negotiable instrument.

(2) Other definitions applying to this Article and the sections in which they appear are:

"Acceptance." Section 3–410.
"Accommodation party." Section 3–415.
"Alteration." Section 3–407.
"Certificate of deposit." Section 3–104.
"Certification." Section 3–411.
"Check." Section 3–104.
"Definite time." Section 3–109.
"Dishonor." Section 3–507.
"Draft." Section 3–104.
"Holder in due course." Section 3–302.
"Negotiation." Section 3–202.
"Note." Section 3–104.
"Notice of dishonor." Section 3–508.
"On demand." Section 3–108.
"Presentment." Section 3–504.

"Protest." Section 3–509.
"Restrictive indorsement." Section 3–205.
"Signature." Section 3–401.

(3) The following definitions in other Articles apply to this Article:

"Account." Section 4–104.
"Banking day." Section 4–104.
"Clearing house." Section 4–104.
"Collecting bank." Section 4–105.
"Customer." Section 4–104.
"Depositary bank." Section 4–105.
"Documentary draft." Section 4–104.
"Intermediary bank." Section 4–105.
"Item." Section 4–104.
"Midnight deadline." Section 4–104.
"Payor bank." Section 4–105.

(4) In addition, Article 1 contains general definitions and principles of construction and interpretation applicable throughout this Article.

Section 3–103.   Limitations on Scope of Article

(1) This Article does not apply to money, documents of title or investment securities.

(2) The provisions of this Article are subject to the provisions of the Article on Bank Deposits and Collections (Article 4) and Secured Transactions (Article 9).

Section 3–104.   Form of Negotiable Instruments; "Draft"; "Check"; "Certificate of Deposit"; "Note"

(1) Any writing to be a negotiable instrument within this Article must

(a)   be signed by the maker or drawer; and

(b)   contain an unconditional promise or order to pay a sum certain in money and no other promise, order, obligation or power given by the maker or drawer except as authorized by this Article; and

(c)   be payable on demand or at a definite time; and

(d)   be payable to order or to bearer.

(2) A writing which complies with the requirements of this section is

    (a) a "draft" ("bill of exchange") if it is an order;

    (b) a "check" if it is a draft drawn on a bank and payable on demand;

    (c) a "certificate of deposit" if it is an acknowledgment by a bank of receipt of money with an engagement to repay it;

    (d) a "note" if it is a promise other than a certificate of deposit.

(3) As used in other Articles of this Act, and as the context may require, the terms "draft", "check", "certificate of deposit" and "note" may refer to instruments which are not negotiable within this Article as well as to instruments which are so negotiable.

Section 3–105. When Promise or Order Unconditional

(1) A promise or order otherwise unconditional is not made conditional by the fact that the instrument

    (a) is subject to implied or constructive conditions; or

    (b) states its consideration, whether performed or promised, or the transaction which gave rise to the instrument, or that the promise or order is made or the instrument matures in accordance with or "as per" such transaction; or

    (c) Refers to or states that it arises out of a separate agreement or refers to a separate agreement for rights as to prepayment or acceleration; or

    (d) states that it is drawn under a letter of credit; or

    (e) states that it is secured, whether by mortgage, reservation of title or otherwise; or

    (f) indicates a particular account to be debited or any other fund or source from which reimbursement is expected; or

    (g) is limited to payment out of a particular fund or the proceeds of a particular source, if the instrument is issued by a government or governmental agency or unit; or

    (h) is limited to payment out of the entire assets of a partnership, unincorporated association, trust or estate by or on behalf of which the instrument is issued.

(2) A promise or order is not unconditional if the instrument

    (a) states that it is subject to or governed by any other agreement; or

    (b) states that it is to be paid only out of a particular fund or source except as provided in this section.

Section 3–106. Sum Certain

(1) The sum payable is a sum certain even though it is to be paid

    (a) with stated interest or by stated installments; or

    (b) with stated different rates of interest before and after default or a specified date; or

    (c) with a stated discount or addition if paid before or after the date fixed for payment; or

    (d) with exchange or less exchange, whether at a fixed rate or at the current rate; or

    (e) with costs of collection or an attorney's fee or both upon default.

(2) Nothing in this section shall validate any term which is otherwise illegal.

Section 3–107. Money

(1) An instrument is payable in money if the medium of exchange in which it is payable is money at the time the instrument is made. An instrument payable in "currency" or "current funds" is payable in money.

(2) A promise or order to pay a sum stated in a foreign currency is for a sum certain in money and, unless a different medium of payment is specified in the instrument, may be satisfied by payment of that number of dollars which the stated foreign currency will purchase at the buying sight rate for that currency on the day on which the instrument is payable or, if payable on demand, on the day of demand. If such an instrument specifies a foreign currency as the medium of payment the instrument is payable in that currency.

Section 3–108. Payable on Demand

Instruments payable on demand include those payable at sight or on presentation and those in which no time for payment is stated.

Section 3–109. Definite Time

(1) An instrument is payable at a definite time if by its terms it is payable

    (a) on or before a stated date or at a fixed period after a stated date; or

    (b) at a fixed period after sight; or

    (c) at a definite time subject to any acceleration; or

    (d) at a definite time subject to extension at the option of the holder, or to extension to a further definite time at the option of the maker or acceptor or automatically upon or after a specified act or event.

(2) An instrument which by its terms is otherwise payable only upon an act or event uncertain as to time of occurrence is not payable at a definite time even though the act or event has occurred.

Section 3–110. Payable to Order

(1) An instrument is payable to order when by its terms it is payable to the order or assigns of any person therein specified within reasonable certainty, or to him or his order, or when it is conspicuously designated on its face as "exchange" or the like and names a payee. It may be payable to the order of

    (a) the maker or drawer; or

    (b) the drawee; or

    (c) a payee who is not maker, drawer or drawee; or

    (d) two or more payees together or in the alternative; or

    (e) an estate, trust or fund, in which case it is payable to the order of the representative of such estate, trust or fund or his successors; or

    (f) an office, or an officer by his title as such in which case it is payable to the principal but the incumbent of the office or his successors may act as if he or they were the holder; or

    (g) a partnership or unincorporated association, in which case it is payable to the partnership or association and may be indorsed or transferred by any person thereto authorized.

(2) An instrument not payable to order is not made so payable by such words as "payable upon return of this instrument properly indorsed."

(3) An instrument made payable both to order and to bearer is payable to order unless the bearer words are handwritten or typewritten.

Section 3–111. Payable to Bearer

An instrument is payable to bearer when by its terms it is payable to

    (a) bearer or the order of bearer; or

    (b) a specified person or bearer; or

    (c) "cash" or the order of "cash", or any other indication which does not purport to designate a specific payee.

Section 3–112. Terms and Omissions Not Affecting Negotiability

(1) The negotiability of an instrument is not affected by

    (a) the omission of a statement of any consideration or of the place where the instrument is drawn or payable; or

    (b) a statement that collateral has been given to secure obligations either on the instrument or otherwise of an obligor on the instrument or that in case of default on those obligations the holder may realize on or dispose of the collateral; or

    (c) a promise or power to maintain or protect collateral or to give additional collateral; or

    (d) a term authorizing a confession of judgment on the instrument if it is not paid when due; or

    (e) a term purporting to waive the benefit or any law intended for the advantage or protection of any obligor; or

    (f) a term in a draft providing that the payee by indorsing or cashing it acknowledges full satisfaction of an obligation of the drawer; or

    (g) a statement in a draft drawn in a set of parts (Section 3–801) to the effect that the order is effective only if no other part has been honored.

(2) Nothing in this section shall validate any term which is otherwise illegal.

Section 3–113. Seal

An instrument otherwise negotiable is within this Article even though it is under a seal.

Section 3–114. Date, Antedating, Postdating

(1) The negotiability of an instrument is not affected by the fact that it is undated, antedated or postdated.

(2) Where an instrument is antedated or postdated the time when it is payable is determined by the stated date if the instrument is payable on demand or at a fixed period after date.

(3) Where the instrument or any signature thereon is dated, the date is presumed to be correct.

Section 3–115. Incomplete Instruments

(1) When a paper whose contents at the time of signing show that it is intended to become an instrument is signed while still incomplete in any necessary respect it cannot be enforced until completed, but when it is completed in accordance with authority given it is effective as completed.

(2) If the completion is unauthorized the rules as to material alteration apply (Section 3–407), even though the paper was not delivered by the maker or drawer; but the burden of establishing that any completion is unauthorized is on the party so asserting.

Section 3–116. Instruments Payable to Two or More Persons

An instrument payable to the order of two or more persons

(a) if in the alternative is payable to any one of them and may be negotiated, discharged or enforced by any of them who has possession of it;

(b) if not in the alternative is payable to all of them and may be negotiated, discharged or enforced only by all of them.

Section 3–117. Instruments Payable with Words of Description

An instrument made payable to a named person with the addition of words describing him

(a) as agent or officer of a specified person is payable to his principal but the agent or officer may act as if he were the holder;

(b) as any other fiduciary for a specified person or purpose is payable to the payee and may be negotiated, discharged or enforced by him;

(c) in any other manner is payable to the payee unconditionally and the additional words are without effect on subsequent parties.

Section 3–118. Ambiguous Terms and Rules of Construction

The following rules apply to every instrument:

(a) Where there is doubt whether the instrument is a draft or a note the holder may treat it as either. A draft drawn on the drawer is effective as a note.

(b) Handwritten terms control typewritten and printed terms, and typewritten control printed.

(c) Words control figures except that if the words are ambiguous figures control.

(d) Unless otherwise specified a provision for interest means interest at the judgment rate at the place of payment from the date of the instrument, or if it is undated from the date of issue.

(e) Unless the instrument otherwise specifies two or more persons who sign as maker, acceptor or drawer or indorser and as a part of the same transaction are jointly and severally liable even though the instrument contains such words as "I promise to pay."

(f) Unless otherwise specified consent to extension authorizes a single extension for not longer than the original period. A consent to extension, expressed in the instrument, is binding on secondary parties and accommodation makers. A holder may not exercise his option to extend an instrument over the objection of a maker or acceptor or other party who in accordance with Section 3–604 tenders full payment when the instrument is due.

Section 3–119. Other Writings Affecting Instrument

(1) As between the obligor and his immediate obligee or any transferee the terms of an instrument may be modified or affected by any other written agreement executed as a part of the same transaction, except that a holder in due course is not affected by any limitation of his rights arising out of the separate written agreement if he had no notice of the limitation when he took the instrument.

(2) A separate agreement does not affect the negotiability of an instrument.

Section 3–120.   Instruments "Payable Through" Bank

An instrument which states that it is "payable through" a bank or the like designates that bank as a collecting bank to make presentment but does not of itself authorize the bank to pay the instrument.

Section 3–121.   Instruments Payable at Bank

Note: *If this Act is introduced in the Congress of the United States, this section should be omitted. (States to select either alternative.)*

Alternative A

A note or acceptance which states that it is payable at a bank is the equivalent of a draft drawn on the bank payable when it falls due out of any funds of the maker or acceptor in current account or otherwise available for such payment.

Alternative B

A note or acceptance which states that it is payable at a bank is not of itself an order or authorization to the bank to pay it.

Section 3–122.   Accrual of Cause of Action

(1)   A cause of action against a maker or an acceptor accrues

(a)   in the case of a time instrument on the day after maturity;

(b)   in the case of a demand instrument upon its date or, if no date is stated, on the date of issue.

(2)   A cause of action against the obligor of a demand or time certificate of deposit accrues upon demand, but demand on a time certificate may not be made until on or after the date of maturity.

(3)   A cause of action against a drawer of a draft or an indorser of any instrument accrues upon demand following dishonor of the instrument. Notice of dishonor is a demand.

(4)   Unless an instrument provides otherwise, interest runs at a rate provided by law for a judgment

(a)   in the case of a maker, acceptor or other primary obligor of a demand instrument, from the date of demand;

(b)   in all other cases from the date of accrual or the cause of action.

PART **2**

Transfer and Negotiation

Section 3–201.   Transfer: Right to Indorsement

(1)   Transfer of an instrument vests in the transferee such rights as the transferor has therein, except that a transferee who has himself been a party to any fraud or illegality affecting the instrument or who as a prior holder had notice of a defense or claim against it cannot improve his position by taking from a later holder in due course.

(2)   A transfer of a security interest in an instrument vests the foregoing rights in the transferee to the extent of the interest transferred.

(3)   Unless otherwise agreed any transfer for value of an instrument not then payable to bearer gives the transferee the specifically enforceable right to have the unqualified indorsement of the transferor. Negotiation takes effect only when the indorsement is made and until that time there is no presumption that the transferee is the owner.

Section 3–202.   Negotiation

(1)   Negotiation is the transfer of an instrument in such form that the transferee becomes a holder. If the instrument is payable to order it is negotiated by delivery with any necessary indorsement; if payable to bearer it is negotiated by delivery.

(2)   An indorsement must be written by or on behalf of the holder and on the instrument or on a paper so firmly affixed thereto as to become a part thereof.

(3)   An indorsement is effective for negotiation only when it conveys the entire instrument or any unpaid residue. If it purports to be of less it operates only as a partial assignment.

(4)   Words of assignment, condition, waiver, guaranty, limitation or disclaimer of liability and the like accompanying an indorsement do not affect its character as an indorsement.

Section 3–203.   Wrong or Misspelled Name

Where an instrument is made payable to a person under a misspelled name or one other than his own he may indorse in that name or his own or both; but signature in both names may be required by a person paying or giving value for the instrument.

Section 3–204.   Special Indorsement; Blank Indorsement

(1)   A special indorsement specifies the person to whom or to whose order it makes the instrument payable. Any instrument specially indorsed becomes payable to the order of the special indorsee and may be further negotiated only by his indorsement.

(2)   An indorsement in blank specifies no particular indorsee and may consist of a mere signature. An instrument payable to order and indorsed in blank becomes payable to bearer and may be negotiated by delivery alone until specially indorsed.

(3)   The holder may convert a blank indorsement into a special indorsement by writing over the signature of the indorser in blank any contract consistent with the character of the indorsement.

Section 3–205.   Restrictive Indorsements

An indorsement is restrictive which either

(a)   is conditional; or

(b)   purports to prohibit further transfer of the instrument; or

(c)   includes the words "for collection", "for deposit", "pay any bank", or like terms signifying a purpose of deposit or collection; or

(d)   otherwise states that it is for the benefit or use of the indorser or of another person.

Section 3–206.   Effect of Restrictive Indorsement

(1)   No restrictive indorsement prevents further transfer or negotiation of the instrument.

(2)   An intermediary bank, or a payor bank which is not the depository bank, is neither given notice nor otherwise affected by a restrictive indorsement of any person except the bank's immediate transferor or the person presenting for payment.

(3)   Except for an intermediary bank, any transferee under an indorsement which is conditional or includes the words "for collection", "for deposit", "Pay any bank", or like terms (subparagraphs (a) and (c) of Section 3–205) must pay or apply any value given by him for or on the security of the instrument consistently with the indorsement and to the extent that he does so he becomes a holder for value. In addition such transferee is a holder in due course if he otherwise complies with the requirements of Section 3–302 on what constitutes a holder in due course.

(4)   The first taker under an indorsement for the benefit of the indorser or another person (subparagraph (d) of Section 3–205) must pay or apply any value given by him for or on the security of the instrument consistently with the indorsement and to the extent that he does so he becomes a holder for value. In addition such taker is a holder in due course if he otherwise complies with the requirements of Section 3–302 on what constitutes a holder in due course. A later holder for value is neither given notice nor otherwise affected by such restrictive indorsement unless he has knowledge that a fiduciary or other person has negotiated the instrument in any transaction for his own benefit or otherwise in breach of duty (subsection (2) of Section 3–304).

Section 3–207.   Negotiation Effective Although It May Be Rescinded

(1)   Negotiation is effective to transfer the instrument although the negotiation is

(a)   made by an infant, a corporation exceeding its powers, or any other person without capacity; or

(b)   obtained by fraud, duress or mistake of any kind; or

(c)   part of an illegal transaction; or

(d)   made in breach of duty.

(2)   Except as against a subsequent holder in due course such negotiation is in an appropriate case subject to rescission, the declaration of a constructive trust or any other remedy permitted by law.

Section 3–208.   Reacquisition

Where an instrument is returned to or reacquired by a prior party he may cancel any indorsement which is not necessary to his title and reissue or further negotiate the instrument, but any intervening party is discharged as against the reacquiring party and subsequent holders not in due course and if his indorsement has been cancelled is discharged as against subsequent holders in due course as well.

PART 3

Rights of a Holder

Section 3–301.   Rights of a Holder

The holder of an instrument whether or not he is the owner may transfer or negotiate it and, except as otherwise provided in Section 3–603 on payment or satisfaction, discharge it or enforce payment in his own name.

Section 3–302. Holder in Due Course

(1) A holder in due course is a holder who takes the instrument

   (a)   for value; and

   (b)   in good faith; and

   (c)   without notice that it is overdue or has been dishonored or of any defense against or claim to it on the part of any person.

(2) A payee may be a holder in due course.

(3) A holder does not become a holder in due course of an instrument:

   (a)   by purchase of it at judicial sale or by taking it under legal process; or

   (b)   by acquiring it in taking over an estate; or

   (c)   by purchasing it as part of a bulk transaction not in regular course of business of the transferor.

(4) A purchaser of a limited interest can be a holder in due course only to the extent of the interest purchased.

Section 3–303. Taking for Value

A holder takes the instrument for value

   (a)   to the extent that the agreed consideration has been performed or that he acquires a security interest in or a lien on the instrument otherwise than by legal process; or

   (b)   when he takes the instrument in payment of or as security for an antecedent claim against any person whether or not the claim is due; or

   (c)   when he gives a negotiable instrument for it or makes an irrevocable commitment to a third person.

Section 3–304. Notice to Purchaser

(1) The purchaser has notice of a claim or defense if

   (a)   the instrument is so incomplete, bears such visible evidence of forgery or alteration, or is otherwise so irregular as to call into question its validity, terms or ownership or to create an ambiguity as to the party to pay; or

   (b)   the purchaser has notice that the obligation of any party is voidable in whole or in part, or that all parties have been discharged.

(2) The purchaser has notice of a claim against the instrument when he has knowledge that a fiduciary has negotiated the instrument in payment of or as security for his own debt or in any transaction for his own benefit or otherwise in breach of duty.

(3) The purchaser has notice that an instrument is overdue if he has reason to know

   (a)   that any part of the principal amount is overdue or that there is an uncured default in payment of another instrument of the same series; or

   (b)   that acceleration of the instrument has been made; or

   (c)   that he is taking a demand instrument after demand has been made or more than a reasonable length of time after its issue. A reasonable time for a check drawn and payable within the states and territories of the United States and the District of Columbia is presumed to be thirty days.

(4) Knowledge of the following facts does not of itself give the purchaser notice of a defense or claim

   (a)   that the instrument is antedated or postdated;

   (b)   that it was issued or negotiated in return for an executory promise or accompanied by a separate agreement, unless the purchaser has notice that a defense or claim has arisen from the terms thereof;

   (c)   that any party has signed for accommodation;

   (d)   that an incomplete instrument has been completed, unless the purchaser has notice of any improper completion;

   (e)   that any person negotiating the instrument is or was a fiduciary;

   (f)   that there has been default in payment of interest on the instrument or in payment of any other instrument, except one of the same series.

(5) The filing or recording of a document does not of itself constitute notice within the provisions of this Article to a person who would otherwise be a holder in due course.

(6) To be effective notice must be received at such time and in such manner as to give a reasonable opportunity to act on it.

Section 3–305. Rights of a Holder in Due Course

To the extent that a holder is a holder in due course he takes the instrument free from

(1) all claims to it on the part of any person; and

(2) all defenses of any party to the instrument with whom the holder has not dealt except

(a) infancy, to the extent that it is a defense to a simple contract; and

(b) such other incapacity, or duress, or illegality of the transaction, as renders the obligation of the party a nullity; and

(c) such misrepresentation as has induced the party to sign the instrument with neither knowledge nor reasonable opportunity to obtain knowledge of its character or its essential terms; and

(d) discharge in insolvency proceedings; and

(e) any other discharge of which the holder has notice when he takes the instrument.

Section 3–306. Rights of One Not Holder in Due Course

Unless he has the rights of a holder in due course any person takes the instrument subject to

(a) all valid claims to it on the part of any person; and

(b) all defenses of any party which would be available in an action on a simple contract; and

(c) the defenses of want or failure of consideration, non-performance of any condition precedent, non-delivery, or delivery for a special purpose (Section 3–408); and

(d) the defense that he or a person through whom he holds the instrument acquired it by theft, or that payment or satisfaction to such holder would be inconsistent with the terms of a restrictive indorsement. The claim of any third person to the instrument is not otherwise available as a defense to any party liable thereon unless the third person himself defends the action for such party.

Section 3–307. Burden of Establishing Signatures, Defenses and Due Course

(1) Unless specifically denied in the pleadings each signature on an instrument is admitted. When the effectiveness of a signature is put in issue

(a) the burden of establishing it is on the party claiming under the signature; but

(b) the signature is presumed to be genuine or authorized except where the action is to enforce the obligation of a purported signer who has died or become incompetent before proof is required.

(2) When signatures are admitted or established, production of the instrument entitles a holder to recover on it unless the defendant establishes a defense.

(3) After it is shown that a defense exists a person claiming the rights of a holder in due course has the burden of establishing that he or some person under whom he claims is in all respects a holder in due course.

PART 4
Liability of Parties

Section 3–401. Signature

(1) No person is liable on an instrument unless his signature appears thereon.

(2) A signature is made by use of any name, including any trade or assumed name, upon an instrument, or by any word or mark used in lieu of a written signature.

Section 3–402. Signature in Ambiguous Capacity

Unless the instrument clearly indicates that a signature is made in some other capacity it is an indorsement.

Section 3–403. Signature by Authorized Representative

(1) A signature may be made by any agent or other representative, and his authority to make it may be established as in other cases of representation. No particular form of appointment is necessary to establish such authority.

(2) An authorized representative who signs his own name to an instrument

(a) is personally obligated if the instrument neither names the person represented nor shows that the representative signed in a representative capacity;

(b) except as otherwise established between the immediate parties, is personally obligated if the instrument names the person represented but does not show that the representative signed in a representative capacity, or if the instrument does not name the person represented but does show that the representative signed in a representative capacity.

(3) Except as otherwise established the name of an organization preceded or followed by the name and office of an authorized individual is a signature made in a representative capacity.

Section 3–404.   Unauthorized Signatures

(1) Any unauthorized signature is wholly inoperative as that of the person whose name is signed unless he ratifies it or is precluded from denying it; but it operates as the signature of the unauthorized signer in favor of any person who in good faith pays the instrument or takes it for value.

(2) Any unauthorized signature may be ratified for all purposes of this Article. Such ratification does not of itself affect any rights of the person ratifying against the actual signer.

Section 3–405.   Impostors; Signature in Name of Payee

(1) An indorsement by any person in the name of a named payee is effective if

(a)   an impostor by use of the mails or otherwise has induced the maker or drawer to issue the instrument to him or his confederate in the name of the payee; or

(b)   a person signing as or on behalf of a maker or drawer intends the payee to have no interest in the instrument; or

(c)   an agent or employee of the maker or drawer has supplied him with the name of the payee intending the latter to have no such interest.

(2) Nothing in this section shall affect the criminal or civil liability of the person so indorsing.

Section 3–406.   Negligence Contributing to Alteration or Unauthorized Signature

Any person who by his negligence substantially contributes to a material alteration of the instrument or to the making of an unauthorized signature is precluded from asserting the alteration or lack of authority against a holder in due course or against a drawee or other payor who pays the instrument in good faith and in accordance with the reasonable commercial standards of the drawee's or payor's business.

Section 3–407.   Alteration

(1) Any alteration of an instrument is material which changes the contract of any party thereto in any respect, including any such change in

(a)   the number or relations of the parties; or

(b)   an incomplete instrument, by completing it otherwise than as authorized; or

(c)   the writing as signed, by adding to it or by removing any part of it.

(2) As against any person other than a subsequent holder in due course

(a)   alteration by the holder which is both fraudulent and material discharges any party whose contract is thereby changed unless that party assents or is precluded from asserting the defense;

(b)   no other alteration discharges any party and the instrument may be enforced according to its original tenor, or as to incomplete instruments according to the authority given.

(3) A subsequent holder in due course may in all cases enforce the instrument according to its original tenor, and when an incomplete instrument has been completed, he may enforce it as completed.

Section 3–408.   Consideration

Want or failure of consideration is a defense as against any person not having the rights of a holder in due course (Section 3–305), except that no consideration is necessary for an instrument or obligation thereon given in payment of or as security for an antecedent obligation of any kind. Nothing in this section shall be taken to displace any statute outside this Act under which a promise is enforceable notwithstanding lack or failure of consideration. Partial failure of consideration is a defense pro tanto whether or not the failure is in an ascertained or liquidated amount.

Section 3–409.   Draft Not an Assignment

(1) A check or other draft does not of itself operate as an assignment of any funds in the hands of the drawee available for its payment, and the drawee is not liable on the instrument until he accepts it.

(2) Nothing in this section shall affect any liability in contract, tort or otherwise arising from any letter of

credit or other obligation or representation which is not an acceptance.

Section 3–410.   Definition and Operation of Acceptance

(1) Acceptance is the drawee's signed engagement to honor the draft as presented. It must be written on the draft, and may consist of his signature alone. It becomes operative when completed by delivery or notification.

(2) A draft may be accepted although it has not been signed by the drawer or is otherwise incomplete or is overdue or has been dishonored.

(3) Where the draft is payable at a fixed period after sight and the acceptor fails to date his acceptance the holder may complete it by supplying a date in good faith.

Section 3–411.   Certification of a Check

(1) Certification of a check is acceptance. Where a holder procures certification the drawer and all prior indorsers are discharged.

(2) Unless otherwise agreed a bank has no obligation to certify a check.

(3) A bank may certify a check before returning it for lack of proper indorsement. If it does so the drawer is discharged.

Section 3–412.   Acceptance Varying Draft

(1) Where the drawee's preferred acceptance in any manner varies the draft as presented the holder may refuse the acceptance and treat the draft as dishonored in which case the drawee is entitled to have his acceptance cancelled.

(2) The terms of the draft are not varied by an acceptance to pay at any particular bank or place in the United States, unless the acceptance states that the draft is to be paid only at such bank or place.

(3) Where the holder assents to an acceptance varying the terms of the draft each drawer and indorser who does not affirmatively assent is discharged.

Section 3–413.   Contract of Maker, Drawer and Acceptor

(1) The maker or acceptor engages that he will pay the instrument according to its tenor at the time of his engagement or as completed pursuant to Section 3–115 on incomplete instruments.

(2) The drawer engages that upon dishonor of the draft and any necessary notice of dishonor or protest he will pay the amount of the draft to the holder or to any indorser who takes it up. The drawer may disclaim this liability by drawing without recourse.

(3) By making, drawing or accepting the party admits as against all subsequent parties including the drawee the existence of the payee and his then capacity to indorse.

Section 3–414.   Contract of Indorser; Order of Liability

(1) Unless the indorsement otherwise specifies (as by such words as "without recourse") every indorser engages that upon dishonor and any necessary notice of dishonor and protest he will pay the instrument according to its tenor at the time of his indorsement to the holder or to any subsequent indorser who takes it up, even though the indorser who takes it up was not obligated to do so.

(2) Unless they otherwise agree indorsers are liable to one another in the order in which they indorse, which is presumed to be the order in which their signatures appear on the instrument.

Section 3–415.   Contract of Accommodation Party

(1) An accommodation party is one who signs the instrument in any capacity for the purpose of lending his name to another party to it.

(2) When the instrument has been taken for value before it is due the accommodation party is liable in the capacity in which he has signed even though the taker knows of the accommodation.

(3) As against a holder in due course and without notice of the accommodation oral proof of the accommodation is not admissible to give the accommodation party the benefit of discharges dependent on his character as such. In other cases the accommodation character may be shown by oral proof.

(4) An indorsement which shows that it is not in the chain of title is notice of its accommodation character.

(5) An accommodation party is not liable to the party accommodated, and if he pays the instrument has a right of recourse on the instrument against such party.

Section 3–416.   Contract of Guarantor

(1) "Payment guaranteed" or equivalent words added to a signature mean that the signer engages that if the

instrument is not paid when due he will pay it according to its tenor without resort by the holder to any other party.

(2) "Collection guaranteed" or equivalent words added to a signature mean that the signer engages that if the instrument is not paid when due he will pay it according to its tenor, but only after the holder has reduced his claim against the maker or acceptor to judgment and execution has been returned unsatisfied, or after the maker or acceptor has become insolvent or it is otherwise apparent that it is useless to proceed against him.

(3) Words of guaranty which do not otherwise specify guarantee payment.

(4) No words of guaranty added to the signature of a sole maker or acceptor affect his liability on the instrument. Such words added to the signature of one of two or more makers or acceptors create a presumption that the signature is for the accommodation of the others.

(5) When words of guaranty are used presentment, notice of dishonor and protest are not necessary to charge the user.

(6) Any guaranty written on the instrument is enforcible notwithstanding any statute of frauds.

Section 3–417. Warranties on Presentment and Transfer

(1) Any person who obtains payment or acceptance and any prior transferor warrants to a person who in good faith pays or accepts that

(a) he has a good title to the instrument or is authorized to obtain payment or acceptance on behalf of one who has a good title; and

(b) he has no knowledge that the signature of the maker or drawer is unauthorized, except that this warranty is not given by a holder in due course acting in good faith

(i) to a maker with respect to the maker's own signature; or

(ii) to a drawer with respect to the drawer's own signature, whether or not the drawer is also the drawee; or

(iii) to an acceptor of a draft if the holder in due course took the draft after the acceptance or obtained the acceptance without knowledge that the drawer's signature was unauthorized; and

(c) the instrument has not been materially altered, except that this warranty is not given by a holder in due course acting in good faith

(i) to the maker of a note; or

(ii) to the drawer of a draft whether or not the drawer is also the drawee; or

(iii) to the acceptor of a draft with respect to an alteration made prior to the acceptance if the holder in due course took the draft after the acceptance, even though the acceptance provided "payable as originally drawn" or equivalent terms; or

(iv) to the acceptor of a draft with respect to an alteration made after the acceptance.

(2) Any person who transfers an instrument and receives consideration warrants to his transferee and if the transfer is by indorsement to any subsequent holder who takes the instrument in good faith that

(a) he has a good title to the instrument or is authorized to obtain payment or acceptance on behalf of one who has good title and the transfer is otherwise rightful; and

(b) all signatures are genuine or authorized; and

(c) the instrument has not been materially altered; and

(d) no defense of any party is good against him; and

(e) he has no knowledge of any insolvency proceeding instituted with respect to the maker or acceptor or the drawer of an unaccepted instrument.

(3) By transferring "without recourse" the transferor limits the obligation stated in subsection (2)(d) to a warranty that he has no knowledge of such a defense.

(4) A selling agent or broker who does not disclose the fact that he is acting only as such gives the warranties provided in this section, but if he makes such disclosure warrants only his good faith and authority.

Section 3–418. Finality of Payment or Acceptance

Except for recovery of bank payments as provided in the Article on Bank Deposits and Collections (Article 4) and except for liability for breach of warranty on presentment under the preceding section, payment or acceptance of any instrument is final in favor of a holder in due course, or a person who has in good faith changed his position in reliance on the payment.

Section 3–419. Conversion of Instrument; Innocent Representative

(1) An instrument is converted when

(a) a drawee to whom it is delivered for acceptance refuses to return it on demand; or

(b) any person to whom it is delivered for payment refuses on demand either to pay or to return it; or

(c) it is paid on a forged indorsement.

(2) In an action against a drawee under subsection (1) the measure of the drawee's liability is the face amount of the instrument. In any other action under subsection (1) the measure of liability is presumed to be the face amount of the instrument.

(3) Subject to provisions of this Act concerning restrictive indorsements a representative, including a depositary or collecting bank, who has in good faith and in accordance with the reasonable commercial standards applicable to the business of such representative dealt with an instrument or its proceeds on behalf of one who was not the true owner is not liable in conversion or otherwise to the true owner beyond the amount of any proceeds remaining in his hands.

(4) An intermediary bank or payor bank which is not a depositary bank is not liable in conversion solely by reason of the fact that proceeds of an item indorsed restrictively (Sections 3–205 and 3–206) are not paid or applied consistently with the restrictive indorsement of an indorser other than its immediate transferor.

PART 5

Presentment, Notice of Dishonor and Protest

Section 3–501. When Presentment, Notice of Dishonor, and Protest Necessary or Permissible

(1) Unless excused (Section 3–511) presentment is necessary to charge secondary parties as follows:

(a) presentment for acceptance is necessary to charge the drawer and indorsers of a draft where the draft so provides, or is payable elsewhere than at the residence or place of business of the drawee, or its date of payment depends upon such presentment. The holder may at his option present for acceptance any other draft payable at a stated date;

(b) presentment for payment is necessary to charge any indorser;

(c) in the case of any drawer, the acceptor of a draft payable at a bank or the maker of a note payable at a bank, presentment for payment is necessary, but failure to make presentment discharges such drawer, acceptor or maker only as stated in Section 3–502 (1)(b).

(2) Unless excused (Section 3–511)

(a) notice of any dishonor is necessary to charge any indorser;

(b) in the case of any drawer, the acceptor of a draft payable at a bank or the maker of a note payable at a bank, notice of any dishonor is necessary, but failure to give such notice discharges such drawer, acceptor or maker only as stated in Section 3–502 (1)(b).

(3) Unless excused (Section 3–511) protest of any dishonor is necessary to charge the drawer and indorsers of any draft which on its face appears to be drawn or payable outside of the states, territories, dependencies, and possessions of the United States, the District of Columbia and the Commonwealth of Puerto Rico. The holder may at his option make protest of any dishonor of any other instrument and in the case of a foreign draft may on insolvency of the acceptor before maturity make protest for better security.

(4) Notwithstanding any provision of this section, neither presentment nor notice of dishonor nor protest is necessary to charge an indorser who has indorsed an instrument after maturity.

Section 3–502. Unexcused Delay; Discharge

(1) Where without excuse any necessary presentment or notice of dishonor is delayed beyond the time when it is due

(a) any indorser is discharged; and

(b) any drawer or the acceptor of a draft payable at a bank or the maker of a note payable at a bank who because the drawee or payor bank becomes insolvent during the delay is deprived of funds maintained with the drawee or payor bank to cover the instrument may discharge his liability by written assignment to the holder of his rights against the drawee or payor bank in respect of such funds, but such drawer, acceptor or maker is not otherwise discharged.

(2) Where without excuse a necessary protest is delayed beyond the time when it is due any drawer or indorser is discharged.

Section 3–503.   Time of Presentment

(1) Unless a different time is expressed in the instrument the time for any presentment is determined as follows:

(a)   where an instrument is payable at or a fixed period after a stated date any presentment for acceptance must be made on or before the date it is payable;

(b)   where an instrument is payable after sight it must either be presented for acceptance or negotiated within a reasonable time after date or issue whichever is later;

(c)   where an instrument shows the date on which it is payable presentment for payment is due on that date;

(d)   where an instrument is accelerated presentment for payment is due within a reasonable time after the acceleration;

(e)   with respect to the liability of any secondary party presentment for acceptance or payment of any other instrument is due within a reasonable time after such party becomes liable thereon.

(2) A reasonable time for presentment is determined by the nature of the instrument, any usage of banking or trade and the facts of the particular case. In the case of an uncertified check which is drawn and payable within the United States and which is not a draft drawn by a bank the following are presumed to be reasonable periods within which to present for payment or to initiate bank collection:

(a)   with respect to the liability of the drawer, thirty days after date or issue whichever is later; and

(b)   with respect to the liability of an indorser, seven days after his indorsement.

(3) Where any presentment is due on a day which is not a full business day for either the person making presentment or the party to pay or accept, presentment is due on the next following day which is a full business day for both parties.

(4) Presentment to be sufficient must be made at a reasonable hour, and if at a bank during its banking day.

Section 3–504.   How Presentment Made

(1) Presentment is a demand for acceptance or payment made upon the maker, acceptor, drawee or other payor by or on behalf of the holder.

(2) Presentment may be made

(a)   by mail, in which event the time of presentment is determined by the time of receipt of the mail; or

(b)   through a clearing house; or

(c)   at the place of acceptance of payment specified in the instrument or if there be none at the place of business or residence of the party to accept or pay. If neither the party to accept r pay nor anyone authorized to act for him is present or accessible at such place presentment is excused.

(3) It may be made

(a)   to any one of two or more makers, acceptors, drawees or other payors; or

(b)   to any person who has authority to make or refuse the acceptance of payment.

(4) A draft accepted or a note made payable at a bank in the United States must be presented at such bank.

(5) In the cases described in Section 4–210 presentment may be made in the manner and with the result stated in that section.

Section 3–505.   Rights of Party to Whom Presentment Is Made

(1) The party to whom presentment is made may without dishonor require

(a)   exhibition of the instrument; and

(b)   reasonable identification of the person making presentment and evidence of his authority to make it if made for another; and

(c)   that the instrument be produced for acceptance or payment at a place specified in it, or if there be none at any place reasonable in the circumstances; and

(d)   a signed receipt on the instrument for any partial or full payment and its surrender upon full payment.

(2) Failure to comply with any such requirement invalidates the presentment but the person presenting

has a reasonable time in which to comply and the time for acceptance or payment runs from the time of compliance.

Section 3–506. Time Allowed for Acceptance or Payment

(1) Acceptance may be deferred without dishonor until the close of the next business day following presentment. The holder may also in a good faith effort to obtain acceptance and without either dishonor of the instrument or discharge of secondary parties allow postponement of acceptance for an additional business day.

(2) Except as a longer time is allowed in the case of documentary drafts drawn under a letter of credit, and unless an earlier time is agreed to by the party to pay, payment of an instrument may be deferred without dishonor pending reasonable examination to determine whether it is properly payable, but payment must be made in any event before the close of business on the day of presentment.

Section 3–507. Dishonor; Holder's Right of Recourse; Term Allowing Re-Presentment

(1) An instrument is dishonored when

(a) a necessary or optional presentment is duly made and due acceptance or payment is refused or cannot be obtained within the prescribed time or in case of bank collections the instrument is seasonably returned by the midnight deadline (Section 4–301); or

(b) presentment is excused and the instrument is not duly accepted or paid.

(2) Subject to any necessary notice of dishonor and protest, the holder has upon dishonor an immediate right of recourse against the drawers and indorsers.

(3) Return of an instrument for lack of proper indorsement is not dishonor.

(4) A term in a draft or an indorsement thereof allowing a stated time for re-presentment in the event of any dishonor of the draft by nonacceptance if a time draft or by nonpayment if a sight draft gives the holder as against any secondary party bound by the term an option to waive the dishonor without affecting the liability of the secondary party and he may present again up to the end of the stated time.

Section 3–508. Notice of Dishonor

(1) Notice of dishonor may be given to any person who may be liable on the instrument by or on behalf of the holder or any party who has himself received notice, or any other party who can be compelled to pay the instrument. In addition an agent or bank in whose hands the instrument is dishonored may give notice to his principal or customer or to another agent or bank from which the instrument was received.

(2) Any necessary notice must be given by a bank before its midnight deadline and by any other person before midnight of the third business day after dishonor or receipt of notice of dishonor.

(3) Notice may be given in any reasonable manner. It may be oral or written and in any terms which identify the instrument and state that it has been dishonored. A misdescription which does not mislead the party notified does not vitiate the notice. Sending the instrument bearing a stamp, ticket or writing stating that acceptance or payment has been refused or sending a notice of debit with respect to the instrument is sufficient.

(4) Written notice is given when sent although it is not received.

(5) Notice to one partner is notice to each although the firm has been dissolved.

(6) When any party is in insolvency proceedings instituted after the issue of the instrument notice may be given either to the party or to the representative of his estate.

(7) When any party is dead or incompetent notice may be sent to his last known address or given to his personal representative.

(8) Notice operates for the benefit of all parties who have rights on the instrument against the party notified.

Section 3–509. Protest; Noting for Protest

(1) A protest is a certificate of dishonor made under the hand and seal of a United States consul or vice consul or a notary public or other person authorized to certify dishonor by the law of the place where dishonor occurs. It may be made upon information satisfactory to such person.

(2) The protest must identify the instrument and certify either that due presentment has been made or the reason why it is excused and that the instrument has been dishonored by nonacceptance or nonpayment.

(3) The protest may also certify that notice of dishonor has been given to all parties or to specified parties.

(4) Subject to subsection (5) any necessary protest is due by the time that notice of dishonor is due.

(5) If, before protest is due, an instrument has been noted for protest by the officer to make protest, the protest may be made at any time thereafter as of the date of the noting.

Section 3–510.   Evidence of Dishonor and Notice of Dishonor

The following are admissible as evidence and create a presumption of dishonor and of any notice of dishonor therein shown:

(a) a document regular in form as provided in the preceding section which purports to be a protest;

(b) the purported stamp or writing of the drawee, payor bank or presenting bank on the instrument or accompanying it stating that acceptance or payment has been refused for reasons consistent with dishonor;

(c) any book or record of the drawee, payor bank, or any collecting bank kept in the usual course of business which shows dishonor, even though there is no evidence of who made the entry.

Section 3–511.   Waived or Excused Presentment, Protest or Notice of Dishonor or Delay Therein

(1) Delay in presentment, protest or notice of dishonor is excused when the party is without notice that it is due or when the delay is caused by circumstances beyond his control and he exercises reasonable diligence after the cause of the delay ceases to operate.

(2) Presentment or notice or protest as the case may be is entirely excused when

(a) the party to be charged has waived it expressly or by implication either before or after it is due; or

(b) such party has himself dishonored the instrument or has countermanded payment or otherwise has no reason to expect or right to require that the instrument be accepted or paid; or

(c) by reasonable diligence the presentment or protest cannot be made or the notice given.

(3) Presentment is also entirely excused when

(a) the maker, acceptor or drawee of any instrument except a documentary draft is dead or in insolvency proceedings instituted after the issue of the instrument; or

(b) acceptance or payment is refused but not for want of proper presentment.

(4) Where a draft has been dishonored by nonacceptance a later presentment for payment and any notice of dishonor and protest for nonpayment are excused unless in the meantime the instrument has been accepted.

(5) A waiver of protest is also a waiver of presentment and of notice of dishonor even though protest is not required.

(6) Where a waiver of presentment or notice or protest is embodied in the instrument itself it is binding upon all parties; but where it is written above the signature of an indorser it binds him only.

PART 6

Discharge

Section 3–601.   Discharge of Parties

(1) The extent of the discharge of any party from liability on an instrument is governed by the sections on

(a) payment or satisfaction (Section 3–603); or

(b) tender of payment (Section 3–604); or

(c) cancellation or renunciation (Section 3–605); or

(d) impairment of right of recourse or of collateral (Section 3–606); or

(e) reacquisition of the instrument by a prior party (Section 3–208); or

(f) fraudulent and material alteration (Section 3–407); or

(g) certification of a check (Section 3–411); or

(h) acceptance varying a draft (Section 3–412); or

(i) unexcused delay in presentment or notice of dishonor or protest (Section 3–502).

(2) Any party is also discharged from his liability on an instrument to another party by any other act or agreement with such party which would discharge his simple contract for the payment of money.

(3) The liability of all parties is discharged when any party who has himself no right of action or recourse on the instrument

    (a) reacquires the instrument in his own right; or

    (b) is discharged under any provision of this Article, except as otherwise provided with respect to discharge for impairment of recourse or of collateral (Section 3−606).

Section 3−602. Effect of Discharge Against Holder in Due Course

No discharge of any party provided by this Article is effective against a subsequent holder in due course unless he has notice thereof when he takes the instrument.

Section 3−603. Payment or Satisfaction

(1) The liability of any party is discharged to the extent of his payment or satisfaction to the holder even though it is made with knowledge of a claim of another person to the instrument unless prior to such payment or satisfaction the person making the claim either supplies indemnity deemed adequate by the party seeking the discharge or enjoins payment or satisfaction by order of a court of competent jurisdiction in an action in which the adverse claimant and the holder are parties. This subsection does not, however, result in the discharge of the liability

    (a) of a party who in bad faith pays or satisfies a holder who acquired the instrument by theft or who (unless having the rights of a holder in due course) holds through one who so acquired it; or

    (b) of a party (other than an intermediary bank or a payor bank which is not a depositary bank) who pays or satisfies the holder of an instrument which has been restrictively indorsed in a manner not consistent with the terms of such restrictive indorsement.

(2) Payment or satisfaction may be made with the consent of the holder by any person including a stranger to the instrument. Surrender of the instrument to such a person gives him the rights of a transferee (Section 3−201).

Section 3−604. Tender of Payment

(1) Any party making tender of full payment to a holder when or after it is due is discharged to the extent of all subsequent liability for interest, costs and attorney's fees.

(2) The holder's refusal of such tender wholly discharges any party who has a right of recourse against the party making the tender.

(3) Where the maker or acceptor of an instrument payable otherwise than on demand is able and ready to pay at every place of payment specified in the instrument when it is due, it is equivalent to tender.

Section 3−605. Cancellation and Renunciation

(1) The holder of an instrument may even without consideration discharge any party

    (a) in any manner apparent on the face of the instrument or the indorsement, as by intentionally cancelling the instrument or the party's signature by destruction or mutilation, or by striking out the party's signature; or

    (b) by renouncing his rights by a writing signed and delivered or by surrender of the instrument to the party to be discharged.

(2) Neither cancellation nor renunciation without surrender of the instrument affects the title thereto.

Section 3−606. Impairment of Recourse or of Collateral

(1) The holder discharges any party to the instrument to the extent that without such party's consent the holder

    (a) without express reservation of rights releases or agrees not to sue any person against whom the party has to the knowledge of the holder a right of recourse or agrees to suspend the right to enforce against such person the instrument or collateral or otherwise discharges such person, except that failure or delay in effecting any required presentment, protest or notice of dishonor with respect to any such person does not discharge any party as to whom presentment, protest or notice of dishonor is effective or unnecessary; or

    (b) unjustifiably impairs any collateral for the instrument given by or on behalf of the party or any person against whom he has a right of recourse.

(2) By express reservation of rights against a party with a right of recourse the holder preserves

(a) all his rights against such party as of the time when the instrument was originally due; and

(b) the right of the party to pay the instrument as of that time; and

(c) all rights of such party to recourse against others.

PART 7

Advice of International Sight Draft

Section 3–701. Letter of Advice of International Sight Draft

(1) A "letter of advice" is a drawer's communication to the drawee that a described draft has been drawn.

(2) Unless otherwise agreed when a bank receives from another bank a letter of advice of an international sight draft the drawee bank may immediately debit the drawer's account and stop the running of interest pro tanto. Such a debit and any resulting credit to any account covering outstanding drafts leaves in the drawer full power to stop payment or otherwise dispose of the amount and creates no trust or interest in favor of the holder.

(3) Unless otherwise agreed and except where a draft is drawn under a credit issued by the drawee, the drawee of an international sight draft owes the drawer no duty to pay an unadvised draft but if it does so and the draft is genuine, may appropriately debit the drawer's account.

PART 8

Miscellaneous

Section 3–801. Drafts in a Set

(1) Where a draft is drawn in a set of parts, each of which is numbered and expressed to be an order only if no other part has been honored, the whole of the parts constitutes one draft but a taker of any part may become a holder in due course of the draft.

(2) Any person who negotiates, indorses or accepts a single part of a draft drawn in a set thereby becomes liable to any holder in due course of that part as if it were the whole set, but as between different holders in due course to whom different parts have been ne-

gotiated the holder whose title first accrues has all rights to the draft and its proceeds.

(3) As against the drawee the first presented part of a draft drawn in a set is the part entitled to payment, or if a time draft to acceptance and payment. Acceptance of any subsequently presented part renders the drawee liable thereon under subsection (2). With respect both to a holder and to the drawer payment of a subsequently presented part of a draft payable at sight has the same effect as payment of a check notwithstanding an effective stop order (Section 4–407).

(4) Except as otherwise provided in this section, where any part of a draft in a set is discharged by payment or otherwise the whole draft is discharged.

Section 3–802. Effect of Instrument on Obligation for Which It Is Given

(1) Unless otherwise agreed where an instrument is taken for an underlying obligation

(a) the obligation is pro tanto discharged if a bank is a drawer, maker or acceptor of the instrument and there is no recourse on the instrument against the underlying obligor; and

(b) in any other case the obligation is suspended pro tanto until the instrument is due or if it is payable on demand until its presentment. If the instrument is dishonored action may be maintained on either the instrument or the obligation; discharge of the underlying obligor on the instrument also discharges him on the obligation.

(2) The taking in good faith of a check which is not postdated does not of itself so extend the time on the original obligation as to discharge a surety.

Section 3–803. Notice to Third Party

Where a defendant is sued for breach of an obligation for which a third person is answerable over under this Article he may give the third person written notice of the litigation, and the person notified may then give similar notice to any other person who is answerable over to him under this Article. If the notice states that the person notified may come in and defend and that if the person notified does not do so he will in any action against him by the person giving the notice be bound by any determination of fact common to the two litigations, then unless after seasonable receipt of the notice the person notified does come in and defend he is so bound.

Section 3–804. Lost, Destroyed or Stolen Instruments

The owner of an instrument which is lost, whether by destruction, theft or otherwise, may maintain an action in his own name and recover from any party liable thereon upon due proof of his ownership, the facts which prevent his production of the instrument and its terms. The court may require security indemnifying the defendant against loss by reason of further claims on the instrument.

Section 3–805. Instruments Not Payable to Order or to Bearer

This Article applies to any instrument whose terms do not preclude transfer and which is otherwise negotiable within this Article but which is not payable to order or to bearer, except that there can be no holder in due course of such an instrument.

ARTICLE 4

BANK DEPOSITS AND COLLECTIONS

PART 1

General Provisions and Definitions

Section 4–101. Short Title

This Article shall be known and may be cited as Uniform Commercial Code — Bank Deposits and Collections.

Section 4–102. Applicability

(1) To the extent that items within this Article are also within the scope of Articles 3 and 8, they are subject to the provisions of those Articles. In the event of conflict the provisions of this Article govern those of Article 3 but the provisions of Article 8 govern those of this Article.

(2) The liability of a bank for action or nonaction with respect to any item handled by it for purposes of presentment, payment or collection is governed by the law of the place where the bank is located. In the case of action or non-action by or at a branch or separate office of a bank, its liability is governed by the law of the place where the branch or separate office is located.

Section 4–103. Variation by Agreement; Measure of Damages; Certain Action Constituting Ordinary Care

(1) The effect of the provisions of this Article may be varied by agreement except that no agreement can disclaim a bank's responsibility for its own lack of good faith or failure to exercise ordinary care or can limit the measure of damages for such lack or failure; but the parties may by agreement determine the standards by which such responsibility is to be measured if such standards are not manifestly unreasonable.

(2) Federal Reserve regulations and operating letters, clearing house rules, and the like, have the effect of agreements under subsection (1), whether or not specifically assented to by all parties interested in items handled.

(3) Action or non-action approved by this Article or pursuant to Federal Reserve regulations or operating letters constitutes the exercise of ordinary care and, in the absence of special instructions, action or non-action consistent with clearing house rules and the like or with a general banking usage not disapproved by this Article, prima facie constitutes the exercise of ordinary care.

(4) The specification or approval of certain procedures by this Article does not constitute disapproval of other procedures which may be reasonable under the circumstances.

(5) The measure of damages for failure to exercise ordinary care in handling an item is the amount of the item reduced by an amount which could not have been realized by the use of ordinary care, and where there is bad faith it includes other damages, if any, suffered by the party as a proximate consequence.

Section 4–104. Definitions and Index of Definitions

(1) In this Article unless the context otherwise requires

    (a) "Account" means any account with a bank and includes a checking, time, interest or savings account;

    (b) "Afternoon" means the period of a day between noon and midnight;

    (c) "Banking day" means that part of any day on which a bank is open to the public for carrying on substantially all of its banking functions;

    (d) "Clearing house" means any association of banks or other payors regularly clearing items;

(e) "Customer" means any person having an account with a bank or for whom a bank has agreed to collect items and includes a bank carrying an account with another bank;

(f) "Documentary draft" means any negotiable or nonnegotiable draft with accompanying documents, securities or other papers to be delivered against honor of the draft;

(g) "Item" means any instrument for the payment of money even though it is not negotiable but does not include money;

(h) "Midnight deadline" with respect to a bank is midnight on its next banking day following the banking day on which it receives the relevant item or notice or from which the time for taking action commences to run, whichever is later;

(i) "Properly payable" includes the availability of funds for payment at the time of decision to pay or dishonor;

(j) "Settle" means to pay in cash, by clearing house settlement, in a charge or credit or by remittance, or otherwise as instructed. A settlement may be either provisional or final;

(k) "Suspends payments" with respect to a bank means that it has been closed by order of the supervisory authorities, that a public officer has been appointed to take it over or that it ceases or refuses to make payments in the ordinary course of business.

(2) Other definitions applying to this Article and the sections in which they appear are:

"Collecting bank." Section 4–105.
"Depositary bank." Section 4–105.
"Intermediary bank." Section 4–105.
"Payor bank." Section 4–105.
"Presenting bank." Section 4–105.
"Remitting bank." Section 4–105.

(3) The following definitions in other Articles apply to this Article:

"Acceptance." Section 3–410.
"Certificate of deposit." Section 3–104.
"Certification." Section 3–411.
"Check." Section 3–104.
"Draft." Section 3–104.
"Holder in due course." Section 3–302.
"Notice of dishonor." Section 3–508.
"Presentment." Section 3–504.
"Protest." Section 3–509.
"Secondary party." Section 3–102.

(4) In addition Article 1 contains general definitions and principles of construction and interpretation applicable throughout this Article.

Section 4–105.   "Depositary Bank"; "Intermediary Bank"; "Collecting Bank"; "Payor Bank"; "Presenting Bank"; "Remitting Bank"

In this Article unless the context otherwise requires:

(a) "Depositary bank" means the first bank to which an item is transferred for collection even though it is also the payor bank;

(b) "Payor bank" means a bank by which an item is payable as drawn or accepted;

(c) "Intermediary bank" means any bank to which an item is transferred in course of collection except the depositary or payor bank;

(d) "Collecting bank" means any bank handling the item for collection except the payor bank;

(e) "Presenting bank" means any bank presenting an item except a payor bank;

(f) "Remitting bank" means any payor or intermediary bank remitting for an item.

Section 4–106.   Separate Office of a Bank

A branch or separate office of a bank [maintaining its own deposit ledgers] is a separate bank for the purpose of computing the time within which and determining the place at or to which action may be taken or notices or orders shall be given under this Article and under Article 3.

Note: *The brackets are to make it optional with the several states whether to require a branch to maintain its own deposit ledgers in order to be considered to be a separate bank for certain purposes under Article 4. In some states, "maintaining its own deposit ledgers" is a satisfactory test. In others, branch banking practices are such that this test would not be suitable.*

Section 4–107.   Time of Receipt of Items

(1) For the purpose of allowing time to process items, prove balances and make the necessary entries on its books to determine its position for the day, a bank may fix an afternoon hour of two P.M. or later as a cut-off hour for the handling of money and items and the making of entries on its books.

(2) Any item or deposit of money received on any

day after a cut-off hour so fixed or after the close of the banking day may be treated as being received at the opening of the next banking day.

Section 4–108. Delays

(1) Unless otherwise instructed, a collecting bank in a good faith effort to secure payment may, in the case of specific items and with or without the approval of any person involved, waive, modify or extend time limits imposed or permitted by this Act for a period not in excess of an additional banking day without discharge of secondary parties and without liability to its transferor or any prior party.

(2) Delay by a collecting bank or payor bank beyond time limits prescribed or permitted by this Act or by instructions is excused if caused by interruption of communication facilities, suspension of payments by another bank, war, emergency conditions or other circumstances beyond the control of the bank provided it exercises such diligence as the circumstances require.

Section 4–109. Process of Posting

The "process of posting" means the usual procedure followed by a payor bank in determining to pay an item and in recording the payment including one or more of the following or other steps as determined by the bank:

(a) verification of any signature;

(b) ascertaining that sufficient funds are available;

(c) affixing a "paid" or other stamp;

(d) entering a charge or entry to a customer's account;

(e) correcting or reversing an entry or erroneous action with respect to the item.

PART 2

Collection of Items: Depositary and Collecting Banks

Section 4–201. Presumption and Duration of Agency Status of Collecting Banks and Provisional Status of Credits; Applicability of Article; Item Indorsed "Pay Any Bank"

(1) Unless a contrary intent clearly appears and prior to the time that a settlement given by a collecting bank for an item is or becomes final (subsection (3)

of Section 4–211 and Sections 4–212 and 4–213) the bank is an agent or sub-agent of the owner of the item and any settlement given for the item is provisional. This provision applies regardless of the form of indorsement or lack of indorsement and even though credit given for the item is subject to immediate withdrawal as of right or is in fact withdrawn; but the continuance of ownership of an item by its owner and any rights of the owner to proceeds of the item are subject to rights of a collecting bank such as those resulting from outstanding advances on the item and valid rights of setoff. When an item is handled by banks for purposes of presentment, payment and collection, the relevant provisions of this Article apply even though action of parties clearly establishes that a particular bank has purchased the item and is the owner of it.

(2) After an item has been indorsed with the words "pay any bank" or the like, only a bank may acquire the rights of a holder

(a) until the item has been returned to the customer initiating collection; or

(b) until the item has been specially indorsed by a bank to a person who is not a bank.

Section 4–202. Responsibility for Collection; When Action Seasonable

(1) A collecting bank must use ordinary care in

(a) presenting an item or sending it for presentment; and

(b) sending notice of dishonor or non-payment or returning an item other than a documentary draft to the bank's transferors (or directly to the depositary bank under subsection (2) of Section 4–212; *see note to Section 4–212*) after learning that the item has not been paid or accepted as the case may be; and

(c) settling for an item when the bank receives final settlement; and

(d) making or providing for any necessary protest; and

(e) notifying its transferor of any loss or delay in transit within a reasonable time after discovery thereof.

(2) A collecting bank taking proper action before its midnight deadline following receipt of an item or payment acts seasonably; taking proper action within a reasonably longer time may be seasonable but the bank has the burden of so establishing.

(3) Subject to subsection (1)(a), a bank is not liable for the insolvency, neglect, misconduct, mistake or default of another bank or person or for loss or destruction of an item in transit or in the possession of others.

Section 4–203.   Effect of Instructions

Subject to the provisions of Article 3 concerning conversion of instruments (Section 3–419) and the provisions of both Article 3 and this Article concerning restrictive indorsements only a collecting bank's transferor can give instructions which affect the bank or constitute notice to it and a collecting bank is not liable to prior parties for any action taken pursuant to such instructions or in accordance with any agreement with its transferor.

Section 4–204.   Methods of Sending and Presenting; Sending Direct to Payor Bank

(1) A collecting bank must send items by reasonably prompt method taking into consideration any relevant instructions, the nature of the item, the number of such items on hand, and the cost of collection involved and the method generally used by it or others to present such items.

(2) A collecting bank may send

(a)   any item direct to the payor bank;

(b)   any item to any non-bank payor if authorized by its transferor; and

(c)   any item other than documentary drafts to any non-bank payor, if authorized by Federal Reserve regulation or operating letter, clearing house rule or the like.

(3) Presentment may be made by a presenting bank at a place where the payor bank has requested that presentment be made.

Section 4–205.   Supplying Missing Indorsement; No Notice from Prior Indorsement

(1) A depositary bank which has taken an item for collection may supply any indorsement of the customer which is necessary to title unless the item contains the words "payee's indorsement required" or the like. In the absence of such a requirement a statement placed on the item by the depositary bank to the effect that the item was deposited by a customer or credited to his account is effective as the customer's indorsement.

(2) An intermediary bank, or payor bank which is not a depositary bank, is neither given notice nor otherwise affected by a restrictive indorsement of any person except the bank's immediate transferor.

Section 4–206.   Transfer Between Banks

Any agreed method which identifies the transferor bank is sufficient for the item's further transfer to another bank.

Section 4–207.   Warranties of Customer and Collecting Bank on Transfer or Presentment of Items; Time for Claims

(1) Each customer or collecting bank who obtains payment or acceptance of an item and each prior customer and collecting bank warrants to the payor bank or other payor who in good faith pays or accepts the item that

(a)   he has a good title to the item or is authorized to obtain payment or acceptance on behalf of one who has a good title; and

(b)   he has no knowledge that the signature of the maker or drawer is unauthorized, except that this warranty is not given by any customer or collecting bank that is a holder in due course and acts in good faith

(i)   to a maker with respect to the maker's own signature; or

(ii)   to a drawer with respect to the drawer's own signature, whether or not the drawer is also the drawee; or

(iii)   to an acceptor of an item if the holder in due course took the item after the acceptance or obtained the acceptance without knowledge that the drawer's signature was unauthorized; and

(c)   the item has not been materially altered, except that this warranty is not given by any customer or collecting bank that is a holder in due course and acts in good faith

(i)   to the maker of a note; or

(ii)   to the drawer of a draft whether or not the drawer is also the drawee; or

(iii)   to the acceptor of an item with respect to an alteration made prior to the acceptance if the holder in due course took the item after the acceptance, even though the acceptance provided "payable as originally drawn" or equivalent terms; or

    (iv)   to the acceptor of an item with respect to an alteration made after the acceptance.

(2) Each customer and collecting bank who transfers an item and receives a settlement or other consideration for it warrants to his transferee and to any subsequent collecting bank who takes the item in good faith that

    (a)   he has a good title to the item or is authorized to obtain payment or acceptance on behalf of one who has a good title and the transfer is otherwise rightful; and

    (b)   all signatures are genuine or authorized; and

    (c)   the item has not been materially altered; and

    (d)   no defense of any party is good against him; and

    (e)   he has no knowledge of an insolvency proceeding instituted with respect to the maker or acceptor or the drawer of an unaccepted item.

In addition each customer and collecting bank so transferring an item and receiving a settlement or other consideration engages that upon dishonor and any necessary notice of dishonor and protest he will take up the item.

(3) The warranties and the engagement to honor set forth in the two preceding subsections arise notwithstanding the absence of indorsement or words of guaranty or warranty in the transfer or presentment and a collecting bank remains liable for their breach despite remittance to its transferor. Damages for breach of such warranties or engagement to honor shall not exceed the consideration received by the customer or collecting bank responsible plus finance charges and expenses related to the item, if any.

(4) Unless a claim for breach of warranty under this section is made within a reasonable time after the person claiming learns of the breach, the person liable is discharged to the extent of any loss caused by the delay in making claim.

Section 4–208. Security Interest of Collecting Bank in Items, Accompanying Documents and Proceeds

(1) A bank has a security interest in an item and any accompanying documents or the proceeds of either

    (a)   in case of an item deposited in an account to the extent to which credit given for the item has been withdrawn or applied;

    (b)   in case of an item for which it has given credit available for withdrawal as of right, to the extent of the credit given whether or not the credit is drawn upon and whether or not there is a right of charge-back; or

    (c)   if it makes an advance on or against the item.

(2) When credit which has been given for several items received at one time or pursuant to a single agreement is withdrawn or applied in part the security interest remains upon all the items, any accompanying documents or the proceeds of either. For the purpose of this section, credits first given are first withdrawn.

(3) Receipt by a collecting bank of a final settlement for an item is a realization on its security interest in the item, accompanying documents and proceeds. To the extent and so long as the bank does not receive final settlement for the item or give up possession of the item or accompanying documents for purposes other than collection, the security interest continues and is subject to the provisions of Article 9 except that

    (a)   no security agreement is necessary to make the security interest enforceable (subsection (1)(b) of Section 9–203); and

    (b)   no filing is required to perfect the security interest; and

    (c)   the security interest has priority over conflicting perfected security interests in the item, accompanying documents or proceeds.

Section 4–209. When Bank Gives Value for Purposes of Holder in Due Course

For purposes of determining its status as a holder in due course, the bank has given value to the extent that it has a security interest in an item provided that the bank otherwise complies with the requirements of Section 3–302 on what constitutes a holder in due course.

Section 4–210. Presentment by Notice of Item Not Payable by, Through or at a Bank; Liability of Secondary Parties

(1) Unless otherwise instructed, a collecting bank may present an item not payable by, through or at a bank by sending to the party to accept or pay a written notice that the bank holds the item for acceptance or payment. The notice must be sent in time to be received on or before the day when presentment is due and the bank must meet any requirement of the party to

accept or pay under Section 3–505 by the close of the bank's next banking day after it knows of the requirement.

(2)   Where presentment is made by notice and neither honor nor request for compliance with a requirement under Section 3–505 is received by the close of business on the day after maturity or in the case of demand items by the close of business on the third banking day after notice was sent, the presenting bank may treat the time as dishonored and charge any secondary party by sending him notice of the facts.

Section 4–211.   Media of Remittance; Provisional and Final Settlement in Remittance Cases

(1)   A collecting bank may take in settlement of an item

(a)   a check of the remitting bank or of another bank on any bank except the remitting bank; or

(b)   a cashier's check or similar primary obligation of a remitting bank which is a member of or clears through a member of the same clearing house or group as the collecting bank; or

(c)   appropriate authority to charge an account of the remitting bank or of another bank with the collecting bank; or

(d)   if the item is drawn upon or payable by a person other than a bank, a cashier's check, certified check or other bank check or obligation.

(2)   If before its midnight deadline the collecting bank properly dishonors a remittance check or authorization to charge on itself or presents or forwards for collection a remittance instrument of or on another bank which is of a kind approved by subsection (1) or has not been authorized by it, the collecting bank is not liable to prior parties in the event of the dishonor of such check, instrument or authorization.

(3)   A settlement for an item by means of a remittance instrument or authorization to charge is or becomes a final settlement as to both the person making and the person receiving the settlement

(a)   if the remittance instrument or authorization to charge is of a kind approved by subsection (1) or has not been authorized by the person receiving the settlement and in either case the person receiving the settlement acts seasonably before its midnight deadline in presenting, forwarding for collection or paying the instrument or authorization, — at the time the remittance instrument

or authorization is finally paid by the payor by which it is payable;

(b)   if the person receiving the settlement has authorized remittance by a nonbank check or obligation or by a cashier's check or similar primary obligation of or a check upon the payor or other remitting bank which is not of a kind approved by subsection (1)(b), — at the time of the receipt of such remittance check or obligation; or

(c)   if in a case not covered by sub-paragraphs (a) or (b) the person receiving the settlement fails to seasonably present, forward for collection, pay or return a remittance instrument or authorization to it to charge before its midnight deadline — at such midnight deadline.

Section 4–212.   Right of Charge-Back or Refund

(1)   If a collecting bank has made provisional settlement with its customer for an item and itself fails by reason of dishonor, suspension of payments by a bank or otherwise to receive a settlement for the item which is or becomes final, the bank may revoke the settlement given by it, charge back the amount of any credit given for the item to its customer's account or obtain refund from its customer whether or not it is able to return the items if by its midnight deadline or within a longer reasonable time after it learns the facts it returns the item or sends notification of the facts. These rights to revoke, charge-back and obtain refund terminate if and when a settlement for the item received by the bank is or becomes final (subsection (3) of Section 4–211 and subsections (2) and (3) of Section 4–213).

[(2) Within the time and manner prescribed by this section and Section 4–301, an intermediary or payor bank, as the case may be, may return an unpaid item directly to the depositary bank and may send for collection a draft on the depositary bank and obtain reimbursement. In such case, if the depositary bank has received provisional settlement for the item, it must reimburse the bank drawing the draft and any provisional credits for the item between banks shall become and remain final.]

Note: *Direct returns is recognized as an innovation that is not yet established bank practice, and therefore Paragraph 2 has been bracketed. Some lawyers have doubts whether it should be included in legislation or left to development by agreement.*

(3)   A depositary bank which is also the payor may charge-back the amount of an item to its customer's account or obtain refund in accordance with the section

governing return of an item received by a payor bank for credit on its books (Section 4–301).

(4) The right to charge-back is not affected by

   (a)   prior use of the credit given for the item; or

   (b)   failure by any bank to exercise ordinary care with respect to the item but any bank so failing remains liable.

(5) A failure to charge-back or claim refund does not affect other rights of the bank against the customer or any other party.

(6) If credit is given in dollars as the equivalent of the value of an item payable in a foreign currency the dollar amount of any charge-back or refund shall be calculated on the basis of the buying sight rate for the foreign currency prevailing on the day when the person entitled to the charge-back or refund learns that it will not receive payment in ordinary course.

Section 4–213.   Final Payment of Item by Payor Bank; When Provisional Debits and Credits Become Final; When Certain Credits Become Available for Withdrawal

(1) An item is finally paid by a payor bank when the bank has done any of the following, whichever happens first:

   (a)   paid the item in cash; or

   (b)   settled for the item without reserving a right to revoke the settlement and without having such right under statute, clearing house rule or agreement; or

   (c)   completed the process of posting the item to the indicated account of the drawer, maker or other person to be charged therewith; or

   (d)   made a provisional settlement for the item and failed to revoke the settlement in the time and manner permitted by statute, clearing house rule or agreement.

Upon a final payment under subparagraphs (b), (c) or (d) the payor bank shall be accountable for the amount of the item.

(2) If provisional settlement for an item between the presenting and payor banks is made through a clearing house or by debits or credits in an account between them, then to the extent that provisional debits or credits for the item are entered in accounts between the presenting and payor banks or between the pre-

senting and successive prior collecting banks seriatim, they become final upon final payment of the item by the payor bank.

(3) If a collecting bank receives a settlement for an item which is or becomes final (subsection (3) of Section 4–211, subsection (2) of Section 4–213) the bank is accountable to its customer for the amount of the item and any provisional credit given for the item in an account with its customer becomes final.

(4) Subject to any right of the bank to apply the credit to an obligation of the customer, credit given by a bank for an item in an account with its customer becomes available for withdrawal as of right

   (a)   in any case where the bank has received a provisional settlement for the item, — when such settlement becomes final and the bank has had a reasonable time to learn that the settlement is final;

   (b)   in any case where the bank is both a depositary bank and a payor bank and the item is finally paid, — at the opening of the bank's second banking day following receipt of the item.

(5) A deposit of money in a bank is final when made but, subject to any right of the bank to apply the deposit to an obligation of the customer, the deposit becomes available for withdrawal as of right at the opening of the bank's next banking day following receipt of the deposit.

Section 4–214.   Insolvency and Preference

(1) Any item in or coming into the possession of a payor or collecting bank which suspends payment and which item is not finally paid shall be returned by the receiver, trustee or agent in charge of the closed bank to the presenting bank or the closed bank's customer.

(2) If a payor bank finally pays an item and suspends payments without making a settlement for the item with its customer or the presenting bank which settlement is or becomes final, the owner of the item has a preferred claim against the payor bank.

(3) If a payor bank gives or a collecting bank gives or receives a provisional settlement for an item and thereafter suspends payments, the suspension does not prevent or interfere with the settlement becoming final if such finality occurs automatically upon the lapse of certain time or the happening of certain events (subsection (3) of Section 4–211, subsections (1)(d), (2) and (3) of Section 4–213).

(4) If a collecting bank receives from subsequent parties

settlement for an item which settlement is or becomes final and suspends payments without making a settlement for the item with its customer which is or becomes final, the owner of the item has a preferred claim against such collecting bank.

PART **3**

Collection of Items: Payor Banks

Section 4–301.   Deferred Posting; Recovery of Payment by Return of Items; Time of Dishonor

(1) Where an authorized settlement for a demand item (other than a documentary draft) received by a payor bank otherwise than for immediate payment over the counter has been made before midnight of the banking day of receipt the payor bank may revoke the settlement and recover any payment if before it has made final payment (subsection (1) of Section 4–213) and before its midnight deadline it

(a)   returns the item; or

(b)   sends written notice of dishonor or non-payment if the item is held for protest or is otherwise unavailable for return.

(2) If a demand item is received by a payor bank for credit on its books it may return such item or send notice of dishonor and may revoke any credit given or recover the amount thereof withdrawn by its customer, if it acts within the time limit and in the manner specified in the preceding subsection.

(3) Unless previous notice of dishonor has been sent an item is dishonored at the time when for purposes of dishonor it is returned or notice sent in accordance with this section.

(4) An item is returned:

(a)   as to an item received through a clearing house, when it is delivered to the presenting or last collecting bank or to the clearing house or is sent or delivered in accordance with its rules; or

(b)   in all other cases, when it is sent or delivered to the bank's customer or transferor or pursuant to his instructions.

Section 4–302.   Payor Bank's Responsibility for Late Return of Item

In the absence of a valid defense such as breach of a presentment warranty (subsection (1) of Section 4–207), settlement effected or the like, if an item is presented on and received by a payor bank the bank is accountable for the amount of

(a)   a demand item other than a documentary draft whether properly payable or not if the bank, in any case where it is not also the depositary bank, retains the item beyond midnight of the banking day of receipt without settling for it or, regardless of whether it is also the depositary bank, does not pay or return the item or send notice of dishonor until after its midnight deadline; or

(b)   any other properly payable item unless within the time allowed for acceptance or payment of that item the bank either accepts or pays the item or returns it and accompanying documents.

Section 4–303.   When Items Subject to Notice, Stop-Order, Legal Process or Setoff; Order in Which Items May Be Charged or Certified

(1) Any knowledge, notice of stop-order received by, legal process served upon or setoff exercised by a payor bank, whether or not effective under other rules of law to terminate, suspend or modify the bank's right or duty to pay an item or to charge its customer's account for the item, comes too late to so terminate, suspend or modify such right or duty if the knowledge, notice, stop-order or legal process is received or served and a reasonable time for the bank to act thereon expires or the setoff is exercised after the bank has done any of the following:

(a)   accepted or certified the item;

(b)   paid the item in cash;

(c)   settled for the item without reserving a right to revoke the settlement and without having such right under statute, clearing house rule or agreement;

(d)   completed the process of posting the item to the indicated account of the drawer, maker or other person to be charged therewith or otherwise has evidenced by examination of such indicated account and by action its decision to pay the item; or

(e)   become accountable for the amount of the item under subsection (1)(d) of Section 4–213 and Section 4–302 dealing with the payor bank's responsibility for late return of items.

(2) Subject to the provisions of subsection (1) items may be accepted, paid, certified or charged to the

indicated account of its customer in any order convenient to the bank.

PART **4**

Relationship Between Payor Bank and Its Customer

Section 4–401.   When Bank May Charge Customer's Account

(1) As against its customer, a bank may charge against his account any item which is otherwise properly payable from that account even though the charge creates an overdraft.

(2) A bank which in good faith makes payment to a holder may charge the indicated account of its customer according to

   (a)   the original tenor of his altered item; or

   (b)   the tenor of his completed item, even though the bank knows the item has been completed unless the bank has notice that the completion was improper.

Section 4–402.   Bank's Liability to Customer for Wrongful Dishonor

A payor bank is liable to its customer for damages proximately caused by the wrongful dishonor of an item. When the dishonor occurs through mistake liability is limited to actual damages proved. If so proximately caused and proved damages may include damages for an arrest or prosecution of the customer or other consequential damages. Whether any consequential damages are proximately caused by the wrongful dishonor is a question of fact to be determined in each case.

Section 4–403.   Customer's Right to Stop Payment; Burden of Proof of Loss

(1) A customer may by order to his bank stop payment of any item payable for his account but the order must be received at such time and in such manner as to afford the bank a reasonable opportunity to act on it prior to any action by the bank with respect to the item described in Section 4–303.

(2) An oral order is binding upon the bank only for fourteen calendar days unless confirmed in writing within that period. A written order is effective for only six months unless renewed in writing.

(3) The burden of establishing the fact and amount of loss resulting from the payment of an item contrary to a binding stop payment order is on the customer.

Section 4–404.   Bank Not Obligated to Pay Check More than Six Months Old

A bank is under no obligation to a customer having a checking account to pay a check, other than a certified check, which is presented more than six months after its date, but it may charge its customer's account for a payment made thereafter in good faith.

Section 4–405.   Death or Incompetence of Customer

(1) A payor or collecting bank's authority to accept, pay or collect an item or to account for proceeds of its collection if otherwise effective is not rendered ineffective by incompetence of a customer of either bank existing at the time the item is issued or its collection is undertaken if the bank does not know of an adjudication of incompetence. Neither death nor incompetence of a customer revokes such authority to accept, pay, collect or account until the bank knows of the fact of death or of an adjudication of incompetence and has reasonable opportunity to act on it.

(2) Even with knowledge a bank may for ten days after the date of death pay or certify checks drawn on or prior to that date unless ordered to stop payment by a person claiming an interest in the account.

Section 4–406.   Customer's Duty to Discover and Report Unauthorized Signature or Alteration

(1) When a bank sends to its customer a statement of account accompanied by items paid in good faith in support of the debit entries or holds the statement and items pursuant to a request or instructions of its customer or otherwise in a reasonable manner makes the statement and items available to the customer, the customer must exercise reasonable care and promptness to examine the statement and items to discover his unauthorized signature or any alteration on an item and must notify the bank promptly after discovery thereof.

(2) If the bank establishes that the customer failed with respect to an item to comply with the duties imposed on the customer by subsection (1) the customer is precluded from asserting against the bank

   (a)   his unauthorized signature or any alteration

on the item if the bank also establishes that it suffered a loss by reason of such failure; and

(b)   an unauthorized signature or alteration by the same wrongdoer on any other item paid in good faith by the bank after the first item and statement was available to the customer for a reasonable period not exceeding fourteen calendar days and before the bank receives notification from the customer of any such unauthorized signature or alteration.

(3)   The preclusion under subsection (2) does not apply if the customer establishes lack of ordinary care on the part of the bank in paying the item(s).

(4)   Without regard to care or lack of care of either the customer or the bank a customer who does not within one year from the time the statement and items are made available to the customer (subsection (1)) discover and report his unauthorized signature or any alteration on the face or back of the item or does not within three years from that time discover and report any unauthorized indorsement is precluded from asserting against the bank such unauthorized signature or indorsement or such alteration.

(5)   If under this section a payor bank has a valid defense against a claim of a customer upon or resulting from payment of an item and waives or fails upon request to assert the defense the bank may not assert against any collecting bank or other prior party presenting or transferring the item a claim based upon the unauthorized signature of alteration giving rise to the customer's claim.

Section 4-407.   Payor Bank's Right to Subrogation on Improper Payment

If a payor bank has paid an item over the stop payment order of the drawer or maker or otherwise under circumstances giving a basis for objection by the drawer or maker, to prevent unjust enrichment and only to the extent necessary to prevent loss to the bank by reason of its payment of the item, the payor bank shall be subrogated to the rights

(a)   of any holder in due course on the item against the drawer or maker; and

(b)   of the payee or any other holder of the item against the drawer or maker either on the item or under the transaction out of which the item arose; and

(c)   of the drawer or maker against the payee or

any other holder of the item with respect to the transaction out of which the item arose.

PART 5

Collection of Documentary Drafts

Section 4-501.   Handling of Documentary Drafts; Duty to Send for Presentment and to Notify Customer of Dishonor

A bank which takes a documentary draft for collection must present or send the draft and accompanying documents for presentment and upon learning that the draft has not been paid or accepted in due course must seasonably notify its customer of such fact even though it may have discounted or bought the draft or extended credit available for withdrawal as of right.

Section 4-502.   Presentment of "On Arrival" Drafts

When a draft or the relevant instructions require presentment "on arrival", "when goods arrive" or the like, the collecting bank need not present until in its judgment a reasonable time for arrival of the goods has expired. Refusal to pay or accept because the goods have not arrived is not dishonor; the bank must notify its transferor of such refusal but need not present the draft again until it is instructed to do so or learns of the arrival of the goods.

Section 4-503.   Responsibility of Presenting Bank for Documents and Goods; Report of Reasons for Dishonor; Referee in Case of Need

Unless otherwise instructed and except as provided in Article 5 a bank presenting a documentary draft

(a)   must deliver the documents to the drawee on acceptance of the draft if it is payable more than three days after presentment; otherwise, only on payment; and

(b)   upon dishonor, either in the case of presentment for acceptance or presentment for payment, may seek and follow instructions from any referee in case of need designated in the draft or if the presenting bank does not choose to utilize his services it must use diligence and good faith to ascertain the reason for dishonor, must notify its transferor of the dishonor and of the results of its effort to ascertain the reasons therefor and must request instructions.

But the presenting bank is under no obligation with respect to goods represented by the documents except to follow any reasonable instructions seasonably received; it has a right to reimbursement for any expense incurred in following instructions and to prepayment of or indemnity for such expenses.

Section 4–504. Privilege of Presenting Bank to Deal with Goods; Security Interest for Expenses

(1) A presenting bank which, following the dishonor of a documentary draft, has seasonably requested instructions but does not receive them within a reasonable time may store, sell, or otherwise deal with the goods in any reasonable manner.

(2) For its reasonable expenses incurred by action under subsection (1) the presenting bank has a lien upon the goods or their proceeds, which may be foreclosed in the same manner as an unpaid seller's lien.

ARTICLE 5

LETTERS OF CREDIT

Section 5–101. Short Title

This Article shall be known and may be cited as Uniform Commercial Code — Letters of Credit.

Section 5–102. Scope

(1) This Article applies

    (a) to a credit issued by a bank if the credit requires a documentary draft or a documentary demand for payment; and

    (b) to a credit issued by a person other than a bank if the credit requires that the draft or demand for payment be accompanied by a document of title; and

    (c) to a credit issued by a bank or other person if the credit is not within subparagraphs (a) or (b) but conspicuously states that it is a letter of credit or is conspicuously so entitled.

(2) Unless the engagement meets the requirements of subsection (1), this Article does not apply to engagements to make advances or to honor drafts or demands for payment, to authorities to pay or purchase, to guarantees or to general agreements.

(3) This Article deals with some but not all of the rules and concepts of letters of credit as such rules or concepts have developed prior to this act or may hereafter develop. The fact that this Article states a rule does not by itself require, imply or negate application of the same or a converse rule to a situation not provided for or to a person not specified by this Article.

Section 5–103. Definitions

(1) In this Article unless the context otherwise requires

    (a) "Credit" or "letter of credit" means an engagement by a bank or other person made at the request of a customer and of a kind within the scope of this Article (Section 5–102) that the issuer will honor drafts or other demands for payment upon compliance with the conditions specified in the credit. A credit may be either revocable or irrevocable. The engagement may be either an agreement to honor or a statement that the bank or other person is authorized to honor.

    (b) A "documentary draft" or a "documentary demand for payment" is one honor of which is conditioned upon the presentation of a document or documents. "Document" means any paper including document of title, security, invoice, certificate, notice of default and the like.

    (c) An "issuer" is a bank or other person issuing a credit.

    (d) A "beneficiary" of a credit is a person who is entitled under its terms to draw or demand payment.

    (e) An "advising bank" is a bank which gives notification of the issuance of a credit by another bank.

    (f) A "confirming bank" is a bank which engages either that it will itself honor a credit already issued by another bank or that such a credit will be honored by the issuer or a third bank.

    (g) A "customer" is a buyer or other person who causes an issuer to issue a credit. The term also includes a bank which procures issuance or confirmation on behalf of that bank's customer.

(2) Other definitions applying to this Article and the sections in which they appear are:

    "Notation of credit." Section 5–108.
    "Presenter." Section 5–112(3).

(3) Definitions in other Articles applying to this Article and the sections in which they appear are:

    "Accept" or "acceptance." Section 3–410.
    "Contract for sale." Section 2–106.
    "Draft." Section 3–104.

"Holder in due course." Section 3–302.
"Midnight deadline." Section 4–104.
"Security." Section 8–102.

(4) In addition, Article 1 contains general definitions and principles of construction and interpretation applicable throughout this Article.

Section 5–104. Formal Requirements; Signing

(1) Except as otherwise required in subsection (1)(c) of Section 5–102 on scope, no particular form of phrasing is required for a credit. A credit must be in writing and signed by the issuer and a confirmation must be in writing and signed by the confirming bank. A modification of the terms of a credit or confirmation must be signed by the issuer or confirming bank.

(2) A telegram may be a sufficient signed writing if it identifies its sender by an authorized authentication. The authentication may be in code and the authorized naming of the issuer in an advice of credit is a sufficient signing.

Section 5–105. Consideration

No consideration is necessary to establish a credit or to enlarge or otherwise modify its terms.

Section 5–106. Time and Effect of Establishment of Credit

(1) Unless otherwise agreed a credit is established

    (a) as regards the customer as soon as a letter of credit is sent to him or the letter of credit or an authorized written advice of its issuance is sent to the beneficiary; and

    (b) as regards the beneficiary when he receives a letter of credit or an authorized written advice of its issuance.

(2) Unless otherwise agreed once an irrevocable credit is established as regards the customer it can be modified or revoked only with the consent of the customer and once it is established as regards the beneficiary it can be modified or revoked only with his consent.

(3) Unless otherwise agreed after a revocable credit is established it may be modified or revoked by the issuer without notice to or consent from the customer or beneficiary.

(4) Notwithstanding any modification or revocation of a revocable credit any person authorized to honor or negotiate under the terms of the original credit is entitled to reimbursement for or honor of any draft or demand for payment duly honored or negotiated before receipt of notice of the modification or revocation and the issuer in turn is entitled to reimbursement from its customer.

Section 5–107. Advice of Credit; Confirmation; Error in Statement of Terms

(1) Unless otherwise specified an advising bank by advising a credit issued by another bank does not assume any obligation to honor drafts drawn or demands for payment made under the credit but it does assume obligation for the accuracy of its own statement.

(2) A confirming bank by confirming a credit becomes directly obligated on the credit to the extent of its confirmation as though it were its issuer and acquires the rights of an issuer.

(3) Even though an advising bank incorrectly advises the terms of a credit it has been authorized to advise the credit is established as against the issuer to the extent of its original terms.

(4) Unless otherwise specified the customer bears as against the issuer all risks of transmission and reasonable translation or interpretation of any message relating to a credit.

Section 5–108. "Notation Credit"; Exhaustion of Credit

(1) A credit which specifies that any person purchasing or paying drafts drawn or demands for payment made under it must note the amount of the draft or demand on the letter or advice of credit is a "notation credit".

(2) Under a notation credit

    (a) a person paying the beneficiary or purchasing a draft or demand for payment from him acquires a right to honor only if the appropriate notation is made and by transferring or forwarding for honor the documents under the credit such a person warrants to the issuer that the notation has been made; and

    (b) unless the credit or a signed statement that an appropriate notation has been made accompanies the draft or demand for payment the issuer may delay honor until evidence of notation has been procured which is satisfactory to it but its obligation and that of its customer continue for a reasonable time not exceeding thirty days to obtain such evidence.

(3) If the credit is not a notation credit

(a)   the issuer may honor complying drafts or demands for payment presented to it in the order in which they are presented and is discharged pro tanto by honor of any such draft or demand;

(b)   as between competing good faith purchasers of complying drafts or demands the person first purchasing has priority over a subsequent purchaser even though the later purchased draft or demand has been first honored.

Section 5–109.   Issuer's Obligation to Its Customer

(1)   An issuer's obligation to its customer includes good faith and observance of any general banking usage but unless otherwise agreed does not include liability or responsibility

(a)   for performance of the underlying contract for sale or other transaction between the customer and the beneficiary; or

(b)   for any act or omission of any person other than itself or its own branch or for loss or destruction of a draft, demand or document in transit or in the possession of others; or

(c)   based on knowledge or lack of knowledge of any usage or any particular trade.

(2)   An issuer must examine documents with care so as to ascertain that on their face they appear to comply with the terms of the credit but unless otherwise agreed assumes no liability or responsibility for the genuineness, falsification or effect of any document which appears on such examination to be regular on its face.

(3)   A non-bank issuer is not bound by any banking usage of which it has no knowledge.

Section 5–110.   Availability of Credit in Portions; Presenter's Reservation of Lien or Claim

(1)   Unless otherwise specified a credit may be used in portions in the discretion of the beneficiary.

(2)   Unless otherwise specified a person by presenting a documentary draft or demand for payment under a credit relinquishes upon its honor all claims to the documents and a person by transferring such draft or demand or causing such presentment authorizes such relinquishment. An explicit reservation of claim makes the draft or demand non-complying.

Section 5–111.   Warranties on Transfer and Presentment

(1)   Unless otherwise agreed the beneficiary by transferring or presenting a documentary draft or demand for payment warrants to all interested parties that the necessary conditions of the credit have been complied with. This is in addition to any warranties arising under Articles 3, 4, 7 and 8.

(2)   Unless otherwise agreed a negotiating, advising, confirming, collecting or issuing bank presenting or transferring a draft or demand for payment under a credit warrants only the matters warranted by a collecting bank under Article 4 and any such bank transferring a document warrants only the matters warranted by an intermediary under Articles 7 and 8.

Section 5–112.   Time Allowed for Honor or Rejection; Withholding Honor or Rejection by Consent; "Presenter"

(1)   A bank to which a documentary draft or demand for payment is presented under a credit may without dishonor of the draft, demand or credit

(a)   defer honor until the close of the third banking day following receipt of the documents; and

(b)   further defer honor if the presenter has expressly or impliedly consented thereto.

Failure to honor within the time here specified constitutes dishonor of the draft or demand and of the credit [except as otherwise provided in subsection (4) of Section 5–114 on conditional payment].

Note: *The bracketed language in the last sentence of subsection (1) should be included only if the optional provisions of Section 5–114 (4) and (5) are included.*

(2)   Upon dishonor the bank may unless otherwise instructed fulfill its duty to return the draft or demand and the documents by holding them at the disposal of the presenter and sending him an advice to that effect.

(3)   "Presenter" means any person presenting a draft or demand for payment for honor under a credit even though that person is a confirming bank or other correspondent which is acting under an issuer's authorization.

Section 5–113.   Indemnities

(1)   A bank seeking to obtain (whether for itself or another) honor, negotiation or reimbursement under

a credit may give an indemnity to induce such honor, negotiation or reimbursement.

(2) An indemnity agreement inducing honor, negotiation or reimbursement

(a)   unless otherwise explicitly agreed applies to defects in the documents but not in the goods; and

(b)   unless a longer time is explicitly agreed expires at the end of ten business days following receipt of the documents by the ultimate customer unless notice of objection is sent before such expiration date. The ultimate customer may send notice of objection to the person from whom he received the documents and any bank receiving such notice is under a duty to send notice to its transferor before its midnight deadline.

Section 5–114.   Issuer's Duty and Privilege to Honor; Right to Reimbursement

(1)   An issuer must honor a draft or demand for payment which complies with the terms of the relevant credit regardless of whether the goods or documents conform to the underlying contract for sale or other contract between the customer and the beneficiary. The issuer is not excused from honor of such a draft or demand by reason of an additional general term that all documents must be satisfactory to the issuer, but an issuer may require that specified documents must be satisfactory to it.

(2)   Unless otherwise agreed when documents appear on their face to comply with the terms of a credit but a required document does not in fact conform to the warranties made on negotiation or transfer of a document of title (Section 7–507) or of a security (Section 8–306) or is forged or fraudulent or there is fraud in the transaction

(a)   the issuer must honor the draft or demand for payment if honor is demanded by a negotiating bank or other holder of the draft or demand which has taken the draft or demand under the credit and under circumstances which would make it a holder in due course (Section 3–302) and in an appropriate case would make it a person to whom a document of title has been duly negotiated (Section 7–502) or a bona fide purchaser of a security (Section 8–302); and

(b)   in all other cases as against its customer, an issuer acting in good faith may honor the draft or demand for payment despite notification from the customer of fraud, forgery or other defect not apparent on the face of the documents but a court of appropriate jurisdiction may enjoin such honor.

(3)   Unless otherwise agreed an issuer which has duly honored a draft or demand for payment is entitled to immediate reimbursement of any payment made under the credit and to be put in effectively available funds not later than the day before maturity of any acceptance made under the credit.

[(4) When a credit provides for payment by the issuer on receipt of notice that the required documents are in the possession of a correspondent or other agent of the issuer

(a)   any payment made on receipt of such notice is conditional; and

(b)   the issuer may reject documents which do not comply with the credit if it does so within three banking days following its receipt of the documents; and

(c)   in the event of such rejection, the issuer is entitled by charge back or otherwise to return of the payment made.]

[(5) In the case covered by subsection (4) failure to reject documents within the time specified in subparagraph (b) constitutes acceptance of the documents and makes the payment final in favor of the beneficiary.]

Note: *Subsections (4) and (5) are bracketed as optional. If they are included, the bracketed language in the last sentence of Section 5–112(1) should also be included.*

Section 5–115.   Remedy for Improper Dishonor or Anticipatory Repudiation

(1)   When an issuer wrongfully dishonors a draft or demand for payment presented under a credit the person entitled to honor has with respect to any documents the rights of a person in the position of a seller (Section 2–707) and may recover from the issuer the face amount of the draft or demand together with incidental damages under Section 2–710 on seller's incidental damages and interest but less any amount realized by resale or other use or disposition of the subject matter of the transaction. In the event no resale or other utilization is made the documents, goods or other subject matter involved in the transaction must be turned over to the issuer on payment of judgment.

(2)   When an issuer wrongfully cancels or otherwise

repudiates a credit before presentment of a draft or demand for payment drawn under it the beneficiary has the rights of a seller after anticipatory repudiation by the buyer under Section 2–610 if he learns of the repudiation in time reasonably to avoid procurement of the required documents. Otherwise the beneficiary has an immediate right of action for wrongful dishonor.

Section 5–116.   Transfer and Assignment

(1) The right to draw under a credit can be transferred or assigned only when the credit is expressly designated as transferable or assignable.

(2) Even though the credit specifically states that it is nontransferable or nonassignable the beneficiary may before performance of the conditions of the credit assign his right to proceeds. Such an assignment is an assignment of an account right under Article 9 on Secured Transactions and is governed by that Article except that

   (a)   the assignment is ineffective until the letter of credit or advice of credit is delivered to the assignee which delivery constitutes perfection of the security interest under Article 9; and

   (b)   the issuer may honor drafts or demands for payment drawn under the credit until it receives a notification of the assignment signed by the beneficiary which reasonably identifies the credit involved in the assignment and contains a request to pay the assignee; and

   (c)   after what reasonably appears to be such a notification has been received the issuer may without dishonor refuse to accept or pay even to a person otherwise entitled to honor until the letter of credit or advice of credit is exhibited to the issuer.

(3) Except where the beneficiary has effectively assigned his right to draw or his right to proceeds, nothing in this section limits his right to transfer or negotiate drafts of demands drawn under the credit.

Section 5–117.   Insolvency of Bank Holding Funds for Documentary Credit

(1) Where an issuer or an advising or confirming bank or a bank which has for a customer procured issuance of a credit by another bank becomes insolvent before final payment under the credit and the credit is one to which this Article is made applicable by paragraphs (a) or (b) of Section 5–102(1) on scope, the receipt or allocation of funds or collateral to secure or meet obligations under the credit shall have the following results:

   (a)   to the extent of any funds or collateral turned over after or before the insolvency as indemnity against or specifically for the purpose of payment of drafts or demands for payment drawn under the designated credit, the drafts or demands are entitled to payment in preference over depositors or other general creditors of the issuer or bank; and

   (b)   on expiration of the credit or surrender of the beneficiary's rights under it unused any person who has given such funds or collateral is similarly entitled to return thereof; and

   (c)   a charge to a general or current account with a bank if specifically consented to for the purpose of indemnity against or payment of drafts or demands for payment drawn under the designated credit falls under the same rules as if the funds had been drawn out in cash and then turned over with specific instructions.

(2) After honor or reimbursement under this section the customer or other person for whose account the insolvent bank has acted is entitled to receive the documents involved.

ARTICLE 6
BULK TRANSFERS

Section 6–101.   Short Title

This Article shall be known and may be cited as Uniform Commercial Code — Bulk Transfers.

Section 6–102.   "Bulk Transfer"; Transfers of Equipment; Enterprises Subject to This Article; Bulk Transfers Subject to This Article

(1) A "bulk transfer" is any transfer in bulk and not in the ordinary course of the transferor's business of a major part of the materials, supplies, merchandise or other inventory (Section 9–109) of an enterprise subject to this Article.

(2) A transfer of a substantial part of the equipment (Section 9–109) of such an enterprise is a bulk transfer if it is made in connection with a bulk transfer of inventory, but not otherwise.

(3)   The enterprises subject to this Article are all those whose principal business is the sale of merchandise from stock, including those who manufacture what they sell.

(4)   Except as limited by the following section all bulk transfers of goods located within this state are subject to this Article.

Section 6–103.   Transfers Excepted from This Article

The following transfers are not subject to this Article:

(1)   Those made to give security for the performance of an obligation;

(2)   General assignments for the benefit of all the creditors of the transferor, and subsequent transfers by the assignee thereunder;

(3)   Transfers in settlement or realization of a lien or other security interest;

(4)   Sales by executors, administrators, receivers, trustees in bankruptcy, or any public officer under judicial process;

(5)   Sales made in the course of judicial or administrative proceedings for the dissolution or reorganization of a corporation and of which notice is sent to the creditors of the corporation pursuant to order of the court or administrative agency;

(6)   Transfers to a person maintaining a known place of business in this State who becomes bound to pay the debts of the transferor in full and gives public notice of that fact, and who is solvent after becoming so bound;

(7)   A transfer to a new business enterprise organized to take over and continue the business, if public notice of the transaction is given and the new enterprise assumes the debts of the transferor and he receives nothing from the transaction except an interest in the new enterprise junior to the claims of creditors;

(8)   Transfers of property which is exempt from execution.

Public notice under subsection (6) or subsection (7) may be given by publishing once a week for two consecutive weeks in a newspaper of general circulation where the transferor had its principal place of business in this state an advertisement including the names and addresses of the transferor and transferee and the effective date of the transfer.

Section 6–104.   Schedule of Property, List of Creditors

(1)   Except as provided with respect to auction sales (Section 6–108), a bulk transfer subject to this Article is ineffective against any creditor of the transferor unless:

(a)   The transferee requires the transferor to furnish a list of his existing creditors prepared as stated in this section; and

(b)   The parties prepare a schedule of the property transferred sufficient to identify it; and

(c)   The transferee preserves the list and schedule for six months next following the transfer and permits inspection of either or both and copying therefrom at all reasonable hours by any creditor of the transferor, or files the list and schedule in (*a public office to be here identified*).

(2)   The list of creditors must be signed and sworn to or affirmed by the transferor or his agent. It must contain the names and business addresses of all creditors of the transferor, with the amounts when known, and also the names of all persons who are known to the transferor to assert claims against him even though such claims are disputed. If the transferor is the obligor of an outstanding issue of bonds, debentures or the like as to which there is an indenture trustee, the list of creditors need include only the name and address of the indenture trustee and the aggregate outstanding principal amount of the issue.

(3)   Responsibility for the completeness and accuracy of the list of creditors rests on the transferor, and the transfer is not rendered ineffective by errors or omissions therein unless the transferee is shown to have had knowledge.

Section 6–105.   Notice to Creditors

In addition to the requirements of the preceding section, any bulk transfer subject to this Article except one made by auction sale (Section 6–108) is ineffective against any creditor of the transferor unless at least ten days before he takes possession of the goods or pays for them, whichever happens first, the transferee gives notice of the transfer in the manner and to the persons hereafter provided (Section 6–107).

[Section 6–106.   Application of the Proceeds

In addition to the requirements of the two preceding sections:

(1)   Upon every bulk transfer subject to this Article

for which new consideration becomes payable except those made by sale at auction it is the duty of the transferee to assure that such consideration is applied so far as necessary to pay those debts of the transferor which are either shown on the list furnished by the transferor (Section 6–104) or filed in writing in the place stated in the notice (Section 6–107) within thirty days after the mailing of such notice. This duty of the transferee runs to all the holders of such debts, and may be enforced by any of them for the benefit of all.

(2) If any of said debts are in dispute the necessary sum may be withheld from distribution until the dispute is settled or adjudicated.

(3) If the consideration payable is not enough to pay all of the said debts in full distribution shall be made pro rata.]

Note: *This section is bracketed to indicate division of opinion as to whether or not it is a wise provision, and to suggest that this is a point on which State enactments may differ without serious damage to the principle of uniformity.*

In any State where this section is omitted, the following parts of sections, also bracketed in the text, should also be omitted, namely: Sections 6–107(2)(e), 6–108(3)(c), and 6–109(2). In any State where this section is enacted, these other provisions should be also.

Optional Subsection (4)

[(4) The transferee may within ten days after he takes possession of the goods pay the consideration into the (specify court) in the county where the transferor had its principal place of business in this state and thereafter may discharge his duty under this section by giving notice by registered or certified mail to all the persons to whom the duty runs that the consideration has been paid into that court and that they should file their claims there. On motion of any interested party, the court may order the distribution of the consideration to the persons entitled to it.]

Note: *Optional subsection (4) is recommended for those states which do not have a general statute providing for payment of money into court.*

Section 6–107.   The Notice

(1) The notice to creditors (Section 6–105) shall state:

(a) that a bulk transfer is about to be made; and

(b) the names and business addresses of the transferor and transferee, and all other business names and addresses used by the transferor within three years last past so far as known to the transferee; and

(c) whether or not all the debts of the transferor are to be paid in full as they fall due as a result of the transaction, and if so, the address to which creditors should send their bills.

(2) If the debts of the transferor are not to be paid in full as they fall due or if the transferee is in doubt on that point then the notice shall state further:

(a) the location and general description of the property to be transferred and the estimated total of the transferor's debts;

(b) the address where the schedule of property and list of creditors (Section 6–104) may be inspected;

(c) whether the transfer is to pay existing debts and if so the amount of such debts and to whom owing;

(d) whether the transfer is for new consideration and if so the amount of such consideration and the time and place of payment; [and]

[(e) if for new consideration the time and place where creditors of the transferor are to file their claims.]

(3) The notice in any case shall be delivered personally or sent by registered or certified mail to all the persons shown on the list of creditors furnished by the transferor (Section 6–104) and to all other persons who are known to the transferee to hold or assert claims against the transferor.

Section 6–108.   Auction Sales; "Auctioneer"

(1) A bulk transfer is subject to this Article even though it is by sale at auction, but only in the manner and with the results stated in this section.

(2) The transferor shall furnish a list of his creditors and assist in the preparation of a schedule of the property to be sold, both prepared as before stated (Section 6–104).

(3) The person or persons other than the transferor who direct, control or are responsible for the auction are collectively called the "auctioneer". The auctioneer shall:

(a) receive and retain the list of creditors and prepare and retain the schedule of property for the period stated in this Article (Section 6–104);

(b) give notice of the auction personally or by registered or certified mail at least ten days before it occurs to all persons shown on the list of creditors and to all other persons who are known to him to hold or assert claims against the transferor; [and]

[(c)   assure that the net proceeds of the auction are applied as provided in this Article (Section 6–106).]

(4)   Failure of the auctioneer to perform any of these duties does not affect the validity of the sale or the title of the purchasers, but if the auctioneer knows that the auction constitutes a bulk transfer such failure renders the auctioneer liable to the creditors of the transferor as a class for the sums owing to them from the transferor up to but not exceeding the net proceeds of the auction. If the auctioneer consists of several persons their liability is joint and several.

Section 6–109.   What Creditors Protected [Credit for Payment to Particular Creditors]

(1)   The creditors of the transferor mentioned in this Article are those holding claims based on transactions or events occurring before the bulk transfer, but creditors who become such after notice to creditors is given (Sections 6–105 and 6–107) are not entitled to notice.

[(2) Against the aggregate obligation imposed by the provisions of this Article concerning the application of the proceeds (Section 6–106 and subsection (3)(c) of 6–108) the transferee or auctioneer is entitled to credit for sums paid to particular creditors of the transferor, not exceeding the sums believed in good faith at the time of the payment to be properly payable to such creditors.]

Section 6–110.   Subsequent Transfers

When the title of a transferee to property is subject to a defect by reason of his non-compliance with the requirements of this Article, then:

(1)   a purchaser of any of such property from such transferee who pays no value or who takes with notice of such non-compliance takes subject to such defect, but

(2)   a purchaser for value in good faith and without such notice takes free of such defect.

Section 6–111.   Limitation of Actions and Levies

No action under this Article shall be brought nor levy made more than six months after the date on which the transferee took possession of the goods unless the transfer has been concealed. If the transfer has been concealed, actions may be brought on levies made within six months after its discovery.

Note to Article 6: *Section 6–106 is bracketed to indicate division of opinion as to whether or not it is a wise provision, and to suggest that this is a point on which State enactments may differ without serious damage to the principle of uniformity.*

In any State where Section 6–106 is not enacted, the following parts of sections, also bracketed in the text, should also be omitted, namely: Sections 6–107(2)(e), 6–108(3)(c), and 6–109(2). In any State where Section 6–106 is enacted, these other provisions should be also.

ARTICLE **7**

WAREHOUSE RECEIPTS, BILLS OF LADING AND OTHER DOCUMENTS OF TITLE

PART **1**

General

Section 7–101.   Short Title

This Article shall be known and may be cited as Uniform Commercial Code — Documents of Title.

Section 7–102.   Definitions and Index of Definitions

(1)   In this Article, unless the context otherwise requires:

(a)   "Bailee" means the person who by a warehouse receipt, bill of lading or other document of title acknowledges possession of goods and contracts to deliver them.

(b)   "Consignee" means the person named in a bill to whom or to whose order the bill promises delivery.

(c)   "Consignor" means the person named in a bill as the person from whom the goods have been received for shipment.

(d)   "Delivery order" means a written order to deliver goods directed to a warehouseman, carrier or other person who in the ordinary course of business issues warehouse receipts or bills of lading.

(e)   "Document" means document of title as defined in the general definitions in Article 1 (Section 1–201).

(f)   "Goods" means all things which are treated

as movable for the purposes of a contract of storage or transportation.

(g) "Issuer" means a bailee who issues a document except that in relation to an unaccepted delivery order it means the person who orders the possessor of goods to deliver. Issuer includes any person for whom an agent or employee purports to act in issuing a document if the agent or employee has real or apparent authority to issue documents, notwithstanding that the issuer received no goods or that the goods were misdescribed or that in any other respect the agent or employee violated his instructions.

(h) "Warehouseman" is a person engaged in the business of storing goods for hire.

(2) Other definitions applying to this Article or to specified Parts thereof, and the sections in which they appear are:

"Duly negotiate." Section 7–501.
"Person entitled under the document." Section 7–403(4).

(3) Definitions in other Articles applying to this Article and the sections in which they appear are:

"Contract for sale." Section 2–106.
"Overseas." Section 2–323.
"Receipt" of goods. Section 2–103.

(4) In addition Article 1 contains general definitions and principles of construction and interpretation applicable throughout this Article.

Section 7–103. Relation of Article to Treaty, Statute, Tariff, Classification or Regulation

To the extent that any treaty or statute of the United States, regulatory statute of this State or tariff, classification or regulation filed or issued pursuant thereto is applicable, the provisions of this Article are subject thereto.

Section 7–104. Negotiable and Non-Negotiable Warehouse Receipt, Bill of Lading or Other Document of Title

(1) A warehouse receipt, bill of lading or other document of title is negotiable

(a) if by its terms the goods are to be delivered to bearer or to the order of a named person; or

(b) where recognized in overseas trade, if it runs to a named person or assigns.

(2) Any other document is non-negotiable. A bill of lading in which it is stated that the goods are consigned to a named person is not made negotiable by a provision that the goods are to be delivered only against a written order signed by the same or another named person.

Section 7–105. Construction Against Negative Implication

The omission from either Part 2 or Part 3 of this Article of a provision corresponding to a provision made in the other Part does not imply that a corresponding rule of law is not applicable.

PART 2

Warehouse Receipts: Special Provisions

Section 7–201. Who May Issue a Warehouse Receipt; Storage Under Government Bond

(1) A warehouse receipt may be issued by any warehouseman.

(2) Where goods including distilled spirits and agricultural commodities are stored under a statute requiring a bond against withdrawal or a license for the issuance of receipts in the nature of warehouse receipts, a receipt issued for the goods has like effect as a warehouse receipt even though issued by a person who is the owner of the goods and is not a warehouseman.

Section 7–202. Form of Warehouse Receipt; Essential Terms; Optional Terms

(1) A warehouse receipt need not be in any particular form.

(2) Unless a warehouse receipt embodies within its written or printed terms each of the following, the warehouseman is liable for damages caused by the omission to a person injured thereby:

(a) the location of the warehouse where the goods are stored;

(b) the date of issue of the receipt;

(c) the consecutive number of the receipt;

(d) a statement whether the goods received will be delivered to the bearer, to a specified person, or to a specified person or his order;

(e) the rate of storage and handling charges, except that where goods are stored under a field warehousing arrangement a statement of that fact is sufficient on a non-negotiable receipt;

(f) a description of the goods or of the packages containing them;

(g) the signature of the warehouseman, which may be made by his authorized agent;

(h) if the receipt is issued for goods of which the warehouseman is owner, either solely or jointly or in common with others, the fact of such ownership; and

(i) a statement of the amount of advances made and of liabilities incurred for which the warehouseman claims a lien or security interest (Section 7–209). If the precise amount of such advances made or of such liabilities incurred is, at the time of the issue of the receipt, unknown to the warehouseman or to his agent who issues it, a statement of the fact that advances have been made or liabilities incurred and the purpose thereof is sufficient.

(3) A warehouseman may insert in his receipt any other terms which are not contrary to the provisions of this Act and do not impair his obligation of delivery (Section 7–403) or his duty of care (Section 7–204). Any contrary provisions shall be ineffective.

Section 7–203. Liability for Non-Receipt or Misdescription

A party to or purchaser for value in good faith of a document of title other than a bill of lading relying in either case upon the description therein of the goods may recover from the issuer damages caused by the non-receipt or misdescription of the goods, except to the extent that the document conspicuously indicates that the issuer does not know whether any part or all of the goods in fact were received or conform to the description, as where the description is in terms of marks or labels or kind, quantity or condition, or the receipt or description is qualified by "contents, condition and quality unknown", "said to contain" or the like, if such indication be true, or the party or purchaser otherwise has notice.

Section 7–204. Duty of Care; Contractual Limitation of Warehouseman's Liability

(1) A warehouseman is liable for damages for loss of or injury to the goods caused by his failure to exercise such care in regard to them as a reasonably careful man would exercise under like circumstances but unless otherwise agreed he is not liable for damages which could not have been avoided by the exercise of such care.

(2) Damages may be limited by a term in the warehouse receipt or storage agreement limiting the amount of liability in case of loss or damage, and setting forth a specific liability per article or item, or value per unit of weight, beyond which the warehouseman shall not be liable; provided, however, that such liability may on written request of the bailor at the time of signing such storage agreement or within a reasonable time after receipt of the warehouse receipt be increased on part or all of the goods thereunder, in which event increased rates may be charged based on such increased valuation, but that no such increase shall be permitted contrary to a lawful limitation of liability contained in the warehouseman's tariff, if any. No such limitation is effective with respect to the warehouseman's liability for conversion to his own use.

(3) Reasonable provisions as to the time and manner of presenting claims and instituting actions based on the bailment may be included in the warehouse receipt or tariff.

(4) This section does not impair or repeal . . .

Note: *Insert in subsection (4) a reference to any statute which imposes a higher responsibility upon the warehouseman or invalidates contractual limitations which would be permissible under this Article.*

Section 7–205. Title Under Warehouse Receipt Defeated in Certain Cases

A buyer in the ordinary course of business of fungible goods sold and delivered by a warehouseman who is also in the business of buying and selling such goods takes free of any claim under a warehouse receipt even though it has been duly negotiated.

Section 7–206. Termination of Storage at Warehouseman's Option

(1) A warehouseman may on notifying the person on whose account the goods are held and any other person known to claim an interest in the goods require payment of any charges and removal of the goods from the warehouse at the termination of the period of storage fixed by the document, or, if no period is fixed, within a stated period not less than thirty days after the notification. If the goods are not removed before the date specified in the notification, the warehouseman may sell them in accordance with the provisions of the section on enforcement of a warehouseman's lien (Section 7–210).

(2) If a warehouseman in good faith believes that the goods are about to deteriorate or decline in value to less than the amount of his lien within the time prescribed in subsection (1) for notification, advertisement and sale, the warehouseman may specify in the notification any reasonable shorter time for removal of the goods and in case the goods are not removed, may sell them at public sale held not less than one week after a single advertisement or posting.

(3) If as a result of a quality or condition of the goods of which the warehouseman had no notice at the time of deposit the goods are a hazard to other property or to the warehouse or to persons, the warehouseman may sell the goods at public or private sale without advertisement on reasonable notification to all persons known to claim an interest in the goods. If the warehouseman after a reasonable effort is unable to sell the goods he may dispose of them in any lawful manner and shall incur no liability by reason of such disposition.

(4) The warehouseman must deliver the goods to any person entitled to them under this Article upon due demand made at any time prior to sale or other disposition under this section.

(5) The warehouseman may satisfy his lien from the proceeds of any sale or disposition under this section but must hold the balance for delivery on the demand of any person to whom he would have been bound to deliver the goods.

Section 7–207. Goods Must Be Kept Separate; Fungible Goods

(1) Unless the warehouse receipt otherwise provides, a warehouseman must keep separate the goods covered by each receipt so as to permit at all times identification and delivery of those goods except that different lots of fungible goods may be commingled.

(2) Fungible goods so commingled are owned in common by the persons entitled thereto and the warehouseman is severally liable to each owner for that owner's share. Where because of overissue a mass of fungible goods is insufficient to meet all the receipts which the warehouseman has issued against it, the persons entitled include all holders to whom overissued receipts have been duly negotiated.

Section 7–208. Altered Warehouse Receipts

Where a blank in a negotiable warehouse receipt has been filled in without authority, a purchaser for value and without notice of the want of authority may treat the insertion as authorized. Any other unauthorized alteration leaves any receipt enforceable against the issuer according to its original tenor.

Section 7–209. Lien of Warehouseman

(1) A warehouseman has a lien against the bailor on the goods covered by a warehouse receipt or on proceeds thereof in his possession for charges for storage or transportation (including demurrage and terminal charges), insurance, labor, or charges present or future in relation to the goods, and for expenses necessary for preservation of the goods or reasonably incurred in their sale pursuant to law. If the person on whose account the goods are held is liable for like charges or expenses in relation to other goods whenever deposited and it is stated in the receipt that a lien is claimed for charges and expenses in relation to other goods, the warehouseman also has a lien against him for such charges and expenses whether or not the other goods have been delivered by the warehouseman. But against a person to whom a negotiable warehouse receipt is duly negotiated a warehouseman's lien is limited to charges in an amount or at a rate specified on the receipt or if no charges are so specified then to a reasonable charge for storage of the goods covered by the receipt subsequent to the date of the receipt.

(2) The warehouseman may also reserve a security interest against the bailor for a maximum amount specified on the receipt for charges other than those specified in subsection (1), such as for money advanced and interest. Such a security interest is governed by the Article on Secured Transactions (Article (9).

(3) (a) A warehouseman's lien for charges and expenses under subsection (1) or a security interest under subsection (2) is also effective against any person who so entrusted the bailor with possession of the goods that a pledge of them by him to a good faith purchaser for value would have been valid but is not effective against a person as to whom the document confers no right in the goods covered by it under Section 7–503.

(b) A warehouseman's lien on household goods for charges and expenses in relation to the goods under subsection (1) is also effective against all persons if the depositor was the legal possessor of the goods at the time of deposit. "Household goods" means furniture, furnishings and personal effects used by the depositor in a dwelling.

(4) A warehouseman loses his lien on any goods which he voluntarily delivers or which he unjustifiably refuses to deliver.

Section 7–210. Enforcement of Warehouseman's Lien

(1) Except as provided in subsection (2), a warehouseman's lien may be enforced by public or private

sale of the goods in block or in parcels, at any time or place and on any terms which are commercially reasonable, after notifying all persons know to claim an interest in the goods. Such notification must include a statement of the amount due, the nature of the proposed sale and the time and place of any public sale. The fact that a better price could have been obtained by a sale at a different time or in a different method from that selected by the warehouseman is not of itself sufficient to establish that the sale was not made in a commercially reasonable manner. If the warehouseman either sells the goods in the usual manner in any recognized market therefor, or if he sells at the price current in such market at the time of his sale, or if he has otherwise sold in conformity with commercially reasonable practices among dealers in the type of goods sold, he has sold in a commercially reasonable manner. A sale of more goods than apparently necessary to be offered to insure satisfaction of the obligation is not commercially reasonable except in cases covered by the preceding sentence.

(2) A warehouseman's lien on goods other than goods stored by a merchant in the course of his business may be enforced only as follows:

(a) All persons known to claim an interest in the goods must be notified.

(b) The notification must be delivered in person or sent by registered or certified letter to the last known address of any person to be notified.

(c) The notification must include an itemized statement of the claim, a description of the goods subject to the lien, a demand for payment within a specified time not less than ten days after receipt of the notification, and a conspicuous statement that unless the claim is paid within the time the goods will be advertised for sale and sold by auction at a specified time and place.

(d) The sale must conform to the terms of the notification.

(e) The sale must be held at the nearest suitable place to that where the goods are held or stored.

(f) After the expiration of the time given in the notification, an advertisement of the sale must be published once a week for two weeks consecutively in a newspaper of general circulation where the sale is to be held. The advertisement must include a description of the goods, the name of the person on whose account they are being held, and the time and place of the sale. The sale must take place at least fifteen days after the first publication. If there is no newspaper of general circulation

where the sale is to be held, the advertisement must be posted at least ten days before the sale in not less than six conspicuous places in the neighborhood of the proposed sale.

(3) Before any sale pursuant to this section any person claiming a right in the goods may pay the amount necessary to satisfy the lien and the reasonable expenses incurred under this section. In that event the goods must not be sold, but must be retained by the warehouseman subject to the terms of the receipt and this Article.

(4) The warehouseman may buy at any public sale pursuant to this section.

(5) A purchaser in good faith of goods sold to enforce a warehouseman's lien takes the goods free of any rights of persons against whom the lien was valid, despite noncompliance by the warehouseman with the requirements of this section.

(6) The warehouseman may satisfy his lien from the proceeds of any sale pursuant to this section but must hold the balance, if any, for delivery on demand to any person to whom he would have been bound to deliver the goods.

(7) The rights provided by this section shall be in addition to all other rights allowed by law to a creditor against his debtor.

(8) Where a lien is on goods stored by a merchant in the course of his business the lien may be enforced in accordance with either subsection (1) or (2).

(9) The warehouseman is liable for damages caused by failure to comply with the requirements for sale under this section and in case of willful violation is liable for conversion.

PART 3

Bills of Lading: Special Provisions

Section 7–301.   Liability for Non-Receipt or Misdescription; "Said to Contain"; "Shipper's Load and Count"; Improper Handling

(1) A consignee of a non-negotiable bill who has given value in good faith or a holder to whom a negotiable bill has been duly negotiated relying in either case upon the description therein of the goods, or upon the date therein shown, may recover from the issuer damages caused by the misdating of the bill or the nonreceipt or misdescription of the goods, except to the extent that the document indicates that the

issuer does not know whether any part or all of the goods in fact were received or conform to the description, as where the description is in terms of marks or labels or kind, quantity, or condition or the receipt or description is qualified by "contents or condition of contents of packages unknown", "said to contain", "shipper's weight, load and count" or the like, if such indication be true.

(2) When goods are loaded by an issuer who is a common carrier, the issuer must count the packages of goods if package freight and ascertain the kind and quantity if bulk freight. In such cases "shipper's weight, load and count" or other words indicating that the description was made by the shipper are ineffective except as to freight concealed by packages.

(3) When bulk freight is loaded by a shipper who makes available to the issuer adequate facilities for weighing such freight, an issuer who is a common carrier must ascertain the kind and quantity within a reasonable time after receiving the written request of the shipper to do so. In such cases "shipper's weight" or other words of like purport are ineffective.

(4) The issuer may by inserting in the bill the words "shipper's weight, load and count" or other words of like purport indicate that the goods were loaded by the shipper; and if such statement be true the issuer shall not be liable for damages caused by the improper loading. But their omission does not imply liability for such damages.

(5) The shipper shall be deemed to have guaranteed to the issuer the accuracy at the time of shipment of the description, marks, labels, number, kind, quantity, condition and weight as furnished by him; and the shipper shall indemnify the issuer against damage caused by inaccuracies in such particulars. The right of the issuer to such indemnity shall in no way limit his responsibility and liability under the contract of carriage to any person other than the shipper.

Section 7–302.   **Through Bills of Lading and Similar Documents**

(1) The issuer of a through bill of lading or other document embodying an undertaking to be performed in part by persons acting as its agents or by connecting carriers is liable to anyone entitled to recover on the document for any breach by such other persons or by a connecting carrier of its obligation under the document but to the extent that the bill covers an undertaking to be performed overseas or in territory not contiguous to the continental United States or an undertaking including matters other than transportation this liability may be varied by agreement of the parties.

(2) Where goods covered by a through bill of lading or other document embodying an undertaking to be performed in part by persons other than the issuer are received by any such person, he is subject with respect to his own performance while the goods are in his possession to the obligation of their issuer. His obligation is discharged by delivery of the goods to another such person pursuant to the document, and does not include liability for breach by any other such persons or by the issuer.

(3) The issuer of such through bill of lading or other document shall be entitled to recover from the connecting carrier or such other person in possession of the goods when the breach of the obligation under the document occurred, the amount it may be required to pay to anyone entitled to recover on the document therefor, as may be evidenced by any receipt, judgment, or transcript thereof, and the amount of any expense reasonably incurred by it in defending any action brought by anyone entitled to recover on the document therefor.

Section 7–303.   **Diversion; Reconsignment; Change of Instructions**

(1) Unless the bill of lading otherwise provides, the carrier may deliver the goods to a person or destination other than that stated in the bill or may otherwise dispose of the goods on instructions from

(a)   the holder of a negotiable bill; or

(b)   the consignor on a non-negotiable bill notwithstanding contrary instructions from the consignee; or

(c)   the consignee on a non-negotiable bill in the absence of contrary instructions from the consignor, if the goods have arrived at the billed destination or if the consignee is in possession of the bill; or

(d)   the consignee on a non-negotiable bill if he is entitled as against the consignor to dispose of them.

(2) Unless such instructions are noted on a negotiable bill of lading, a person to whom the bill is duly negotiated can hold the bailee according to the original terms.

Section 7–304.   **Bills of Lading in a Set**

(1) Except where customary in overseas transportation, a bill of lading must not be issued in a set of parts. The issuer is liable for damages caused by violation of this subsection.

(2) Where a bill of lading is lawfully drawn in a set

of parts, each of which is numbered and expressed to be valid only if the goods have not been delivered against any other part, the whole of the parts constitute one bill.

(3) Where a bill of lading is lawfully issued in a set of parts and different parts are negotiated to different persons, the title of the holder to whom the first due negotiation is made prevails as to both the document and the goods even though any later holder may have received the goods from the carrier in good faith and discharged the carrier's obligation by surrender of his part.

(4) Any person who negotiates or transfers a single part of a bill of lading drawn in a set is liable to holders of that part as if it were the whole set.

(5) The bailee is obliged to deliver in accordance with Part 4 of this Article against the first presented part of a bill of lading lawfully drawn in a set. Such delivery discharges the bailee's obligation on the whole bill.

Section 7–305.   Destination Bills

(1) Instead of issuing a bill of lading to the consignor at the place of shipment a carrier may at the request of the consignor procure the bill to be issued at destination or at any other place designated in the request.

(2) Upon request of anyone entitled as against the carrier to control the goods while in transit and on surrender of any outstanding bill of lading or other receipt covering such goods, the issuer may procure a substitute bill to be issued at any place designated in the request.

Section 7–306.   Altered Bills of Lading

An unauthorized alteration or filling in of a blank in a bill of lading leaves the bill enforceable according to its original tenor.

Section 7–307.   Lien of Carrier

(1) A carrier has a lien on the goods covered by a bill of lading for charges subsequent to the date of its receipt of the goods for storage or transportation (including demurrage and terminal charges) and for expenses necessary for preservation of the goods incident to their transportation or reasonably incurred in their sale pursuant to law. But against a purchaser for value of a negotiable bill of lading a carrier's lien is limited to charges stated in the bill or the applicable tariffs, or if no charges are stated then to a reasonable charge.

(2) A lien for charges and expenses under subsection (1) on goods which the carrier was required by law

to receive for transportation is effective against the consignor or any person entitled to the goods unless the carrier had notice that the consignor lacked authority to subject the goods to such charges and expenses. Any other lien under subsection (1) is effective against the consignor and any person who permitted the bailor to have control or possession of the goods unless the carrier had notice that the bailor lacked such authority.

(3) A carrier loses his lien on any goods which he voluntarily delivers or which he unjustifiably refuses to deliver.

Section 7–308.   Enforcement of Carrier's Lien

(1) A carrier's lien may be enforced by public or private sale of the goods, in bloc or in parcels, at any time or place and on any terms which are commercially reasonable, after notifying all persons known to claim an interest in the goods. Such notification must include a statement of the amount due, the nature of the proposed sale and the time and place of any public sale. The fact that a better price could have been obtained by a sale at a different time or in a different method from that selected by the carrier is not of itself sufficient to establish that the sale was not made in a commercially reasonable manner. If the carrier either sells the goods in the usual manner in any recognized market therefor or if he sells at the price current in such market at the time of his sale or if he has otherwise sold in conformity with commercially reasonable practices among dealers in the type of goods sold he has sold in a commercially reasonable manner. A sale of more goods than apparently necessary to be offered to ensure satisfaction of the obligation is not commercially reasonable except in cases covered by the preceding sentence.

(2) Before any sale pursuant to this section any person claiming a right in the goods may pay the amount necessary to satisfy the lien and the reasonable expenses incurred under this section. In that event the goods must not be sold, but must be retained by the carrier subject to the terms of the bill and this Article.

(3) The carrier may buy at any public sale pursuant to this section.

(4) A purchaser in good faith of goods sold to enforce a carrier's lien takes the goods free of any rights of persons against whom the lien was valid, despite noncompliance by the carrier with the requirements of this section.

(5) The carrier may satisfy his lien from the proceeds of any sale pursuant to this section but must hold the balance, if any, for delivery on demand to any person

to whom he would have been bound to deliver the goods.

(6) The rights provided by this section shall be in addition to all other rights allowed by law to a creditor against his debtor.

(7) A carrier's lien may be enforced in accordance with either subsection (1) or the procedure set forth in subsection (2) of Section 7– 210.

(8) The carrier is liable for damages caused by failure to comply with the requirements for sale under this section and in case of willful violation is liable for conversion.

Section 7–309.   Duty of Care; Contractual Limitation of Carrier's Liability

(1) A carrier who issues a bill of lading whether negotiable or non-negotiable must exercise the degree of care in relation to the goods which a reasonably careful man would exercise under like circumstances. This subsection does not repeal or change any law or rule of law which imposes liability upon a common carrier for damages not caused by its negligence.

(2) Damages may be limited by a provision that the carrier's liability shall not exceed a value stated in the document if the carrier's rates are dependent upon value and the consignor by the carrier's tariff is afforded an opportunity to declare a higher value or a value as lawfully provided in the tariff, or where no tariff is filed he is otherwise advised of such opportunity; but no such limitation is effective with respect to the carrier's liability for conversion to its own use.

(3) Reasonable provisions as to the time and manner of presenting claims and instituting actions based on the shipment may be included in a bill of lading or tariff.

PART 4
Warehouse Receipts and Bills of Lading: General Obligations

Section 7–401.   Irregularities in Issue of Receipt or Bill or Conduct of Issuer

The obligations imposed by this Article on an issuer apply to a document of title regardless of the fact that

(a)   the document may not comply with the requirements of this Article or of any other law or regulation regarding its issue, form or content; or

(b)   the issuer may have violated laws regulating the conduct of his business; or

(c)   the goods covered by the document were owned by the bailee at the time the document was issued; or

(d)   the person issuing the document does not come within the definition of warehouseman if it purports to be a warehouse receipt.

Section 7–402.   Duplicate Receipt or Bill; Overissue

Neither a duplicate nor any other document of title purporting to cover goods already represented by an outstanding document of the same issuer confers any right in the goods, except as provided in the case of bills in a set, overissue of documents for fungible goods and substitutes for lost, stolen or destroyed documents. But the issuer is liable for damages caused by his overissue or failure to identify a duplicate document as such by conspicuous notation on its face.

Section 7–403.   Obligation of Warehouseman or Carrier to Deliver; Excuse

(1) The bailee must deliver the goods to a person entitled under the document who complies with subsections (2) and (3), unless and to the extent that the bailee establishes any of the following:

(a)   delivery of the goods to a person whose receipt was rightful as against the claimant;

(b)   damage to or delay, loss or destruction of the goods for which the bailee is not liable [, but the burden of establishing negligence in such cases is on the person entitled under the document];

Note: *The brackets in (1)(b) indicate that State enactments may differ on this point without serious damage to the principle of uniformity.*

(c)   previous sale or other disposition of the goods in lawful enforcement of a lien or on warehouseman's lawful termination of storage;

(d)   the exercise by a seller of his right to stop delivery pursuant to the provisions of the Article on Sales (Section 2–705);

(e)   a diversion, reconsignment or other disposition pursuant to the provisions of this Article (Section 7–303) or tariff regulating such right;

(f)   release, satisfaction or any other fact affording a personal defense against the claimant;

(g)   any other lawful excuse.

(2)   A person claiming goods covered by a document of title must satisfy the bailee's lien where the bailee so requests or where the bailee is prohibited by law from delivering the goods until the charges are paid.

(3)   Unless the person claiming is one against whom the document confers no right under Section 7–503(1), he must surrender for cancellation or notation of partial deliveries any outstanding negotiable document covering the goods, and the bailee must cancel the document or conspicuously note the partial delivery thereon or be liable to any person to whom the document is duly negotiated.

(4)   "Person entitled under the document" means holder in the case of a negotiable document or the person to whom delivery is to be made by the terms of or pursuant to written instructions under a non-negotiable document.

Section 7–404.   No Liability for Good Faith Delivery Pursuant to Receipt or Bill

A bailee who in good faith including observance of reasonable commercial standards has received goods and delivered or otherwise disposed of them according to the terms of the document of title or pursuant to this Article is not liable therefor. This rule applies even though the person from whom he received the goods had no authority to procure the document or to dispose of the goods and even though the person to whom he delivered the goods had no authority to receive them.

PART **5**

Warehouse Receipts and Bills of Lading: Negotiation and Transfer

Section 7–501.   Form of Negotiation and Requirements of "Due Negotiation"

(1)   A negotiable document of title running to the order of a named person is negotiated by his indorsement and delivery. After his indorsement in blank or to bearer any person can negotiate it by delivery alone.

(2)   (a)   A negotiable document of title is also negotiated by delivery alone when by its original terms it runs to bearer.

(b)   When a document running to the order of a named person is delivered to him the effect is the same as if the document had been negotiated.

(3)   Negotiation of a negotiable document of title after it has been indorsed to a specified person requires indorsement by the special indorsee as well as delivery.

(4)   A negotiable document of title is "duly negotiated" when it is negotiated in the manner stated in this section to a holder who purchases it in good faith without notice of any defense against or claim to it on the part of any person and for value, unless it is established that the negotiation is not in the regular course of business or financing or involves receiving the document in settlement or payment of a money obligation.

(5)   Indorsement of a non-negotiable document neither makes it negotiable nor adds to the transferee's rights.

(6)   The naming in a negotiable bill of a person to be notified of the arrival of the goods does not limit the negotiability of the bill nor constitute notice to a purchaser thereof of any interest of such person in the goods.

Section 7–502.   Rights Acquired by Due Negotiation

(1)   Subject to the following section and to the provisions of Section 7–205 on fungible goods, a holder to whom a negotiable document of title has been duly negotiated acquires thereby:

(a)   title to the document;

(b)   title to the goods;

(c)   all rights accruing under the law of agency or estoppel, including rights to goods delivered to the bailee after the document was issued; and

(d)   the direct obligation of the issuer to hold or deliver the goods according to the terms of the document free of any defense or claim by him except those arising under the terms of the document or under this Article. In the case of a delivery order the bailee's obligation accrues only upon acceptance and the obligation acquired by the holder is that the issuer and any indorser will procure the acceptance of the bailee.

(2)   Subject to the following section, title and rights so acquired are not defeated by any stoppage of the goods represented by the document or by surrender of such goods by the bailee, and are not impaired even though the negotiation or any prior negotiation constituted a breach of duty or even though any person has been deprived of possession of the document by misrepresentation, fraud, accident, mistake, duress, loss, theft or conversion, or even though a previous sale

or other transfer of the goods or document has been made to a third person.

Section 7–503.   Document of Title to Goods Defeated in Certain Cases

(1) A document of title confers no right in goods against a person who before issuance of the document had a legal interest or a perfected security interest in them and who neither

(a)   delivered or entrusted them or any document of title covering them to the bailor or his nominee with actual or apparent authority to ship, store or sell or with power to obtain delivery under this Article (Section 7–403) or with power of disposition under this Act (Sections 2–403 and 9–307) or other statute or rule of law; nor

(b)   acquiesced in the procurement by the bailor or his nominee of any document of title.

(2)   Title to goods based upon an unaccepted delivery order is subject to the rights of anyone to whom a negotiable warehouse receipt or bill of lading covering the goods has been duly negotiated. Such a title may be defeated under the next section to the same extent as the rights of the issuer or a transferee from the issuer.

(3)   Title to goods based upon a bill of lading issued to a freight forwarder is subject to the rights of anyone to whom a bill issued by the freight forwarder is duly negotiated; but delivery by the carrier in accordance with Part 4 of this Article pursuant to its own bill of lading discharges the carrier's obligation to deliver.

Section 7–504.   Rights Acquired in the Absence of Due Negotiation; Effect of Diversion; Seller's Stoppage of Delivery

(1) A transferee of a document, whether negotiable or non-negotiable, to whom the document has been delivered but not duly negotiated, acquires the title and rights which his transferor had or had actual authority to convey.

(2)   In the case of a non-negotiable document, until but not after the bailee receives notification of the transfer, the rights of the transferee may be defeated

(a)   by those creditors of the transferor who could treat the sale as void under Section 2–402; or

(b)   by a buyer from the transferor in ordinary course of business if the bailee has delivered the goods to the buyer or received notification of his rights; or

(c)   as against the bailee by good faith dealings of the bailee with the transferor.

(3)   A diversion or other change of shipping instructions by the consignor in a non-negotiable bill of lading which causes the bailee not to deliver to the consignee defeats the consignee's title to the goods if they have been delivered to a buyer in ordinary course of business and in any event defeats the consignee's rights against the bailee.

(4)   Delivery pursuant to a non-negotiable document may be stopped by a seller under Section 2–705, and subject to the requirement of due notification there provided. A bailee honoring the seller's instructions is entitled to be indemnified by the seller against any resulting loss or expense.

Section 7–505.   Indorser Not a Guarantor for Other Parties

The indorsement of a document of title issued by a bailee does not make the indorser liable for any default by the bailee or by previous indorsers.

Section 7–506.   Delivery Without Indorsement: Right to Compel Indorsement

The transferee of a negotiable document of title has a specifically enforceable right to have his transferor supply any necessary indorsement but the transfer becomes a negotiation only as of the time the indorsement is supplied.

Section 7–507.   Warranties on Negotiation or Transfer of Receipt or Bill

Where a person negotiates or transfers a document of title for value otherwise than as a mere intermediary under the next following section, then unless otherwise agreed he warrants to his immediate purchaser only in addition to any warranty made in selling the goods

(a)   that the document is genuine; and

(b)   that he had no knowledge of any fact which would impair its validity or worth; and

(c)   that his negotiation or transfer is rightful and fully effective with respect to the title to the document and the goods it represents.

Section 7–508.   Warranties of Collecting Bank as to Documents

A collecting bank or other intermediary known to be entrusted with documents on behalf of another or with collection of a draft or other claim against delivery of documents warrants by such delivery of the documents only its own good faith and authority. This rule applies even though the intermediary has purchased or made advances against the claim or draft to be collected.

Section 7–509. Receipt or Bill: When Adequate Compliance with Commercial Contract

The question whether a document is adequate to fulfill the obligations of a contract for sale or the conditions of a credit is governed by the Articles on Sales (Article 2) and on Letters of Credit (Article 5).

PART 6
Warehouse Receipts and Bills of Lading: Miscellaneous Provisions

Section 7–601. Lost and Missing Documents

(1) If a document has been lost, stolen or destroyed, a court may order delivery of the goods or issuance of a substitute document and the bailee may without liability to any person comply with such order. If the document was negotiable the claimant must post security approved by the court to indemnify any person who may suffer loss as a result of non-surrender of the document. If the document was not negotiable, such security may be required at the discretion of the court. The court may also in its discretion order payment of the bailee's reasonable costs and counsel fees.

(2) A bailee who without court order delivers goods to a person claiming under a missing negotiable document is liable to any person injured thereby, and if the delivery is not in good faith becomes liable for conversion. Delivery in good faith is not conversion if made in accordance with a filed classification or tariff or, where no classification or tariff is filed, if the claimant posts security with the bailee in an amount at least double the value of the goods at the time of posting to indemnify any person injured by the delivery who files a notice of claim within one year after the delivery.

Section 7–602. Attachment of Goods Covered by a Negotiable Document

Except where the document was originally issued upon delivery of the goods by a person who had no power to dispose of them, no lien attaches by virtue of any judicial process to goods in the possession of a bailee for which a negotiable document of title is outstanding unless the document be first surrendered to the bailee or its negotiation enjoined, and the bailee shall not be compelled to deliver the goods pursuant to process until the document is surrendered to him or impounded by the court. One who purchases the document for value without notice of the process or injunction takes free of the lien imposed by judicial process.

Section 7–603. Conflicting Claims; Interpleader

If more than one person claims title or possession of the goods, the bailee is excused from delivery until he has had a reasonable time to ascertain the validity of the adverse claims or to bring an action to compel all claimants to interplead and may compel such interpleader, either in defending an action for nondelivery of the goods, or by original action, whichever is appropriate.

ARTICLE 8
INVESTMENT SECURITIES

PART 1
Short Title and General Matters

Section 8–101. Short Title

This Article shall be known and may be cited as Uniform Commercial Code — Investment Securities.

Section 8–102. Definitions and Index of Definitions

(1) In this Article unless the context otherwise requires

  (a) A "security" is an instrument which

    (i) is issued in bearer or registered form; and

    (ii) is of a type commonly dealt in upon securities exchanges or markets or commonly recognized in any area in which it is issued or dealt in as a medium for investment; and

    (iii) is either one of a class or series or by its terms is divisible into a class or series of instruments; and

    (iv) evidences a share, participation or other interest in property or in an enterprise or evidences an obligation of the issuer.

  (b) A writing which is a security is governed by this Article and not by Uniform Commercial Code — Commercial Paper even though it also meets the requirements of that Article. This Article does not apply to money.

(c)   A security is in "registered form" when it specifies a person entitled to the security or to the rights it evidences and when its transfer may be registered upon books maintained for that purpose by or on behalf of an issuer or the security so states.

(d)   A security is in "bearer form" when it runs to bearer according to its terms and not by reason of any indorsement.

(2)   A "subsequent purchaser" is a person who takes other than by original issue.

(3)   A "clearing corporation" is a corporation all of the capital stock of which is held by or for a national securities exchange or association registered under a statute of the United States such as the Securities Exchange Act of 1934.

(4)   A "custodian bank" is any bank or trust company which is supervised and examined by state or federal authority having supervision over banks and which is acting as custodian for a clearing corporation.

(5)   Other definitions applying to this Article or to specified Parts thereof and the sections in which they appear are:

"Adverse claim." Section 8–301.
"Bona fide purchaser." Section 8–302.
"Broker." Section 8–303.
"Guarantee of the signature." Section 8–402.
"Intermediary bank." Section 4–105.
"Issuer." Section 8–201.
"Overissue." Section 8–104.

(6)   In addition Article 1 contains general definitions and principles of construction and interpretation applicable throughout this Article.

Section 8–103.   Issuer's Lien

A lien upon a security in favor of an issuer thereof is valid against a purchaser only if the right of the issuer to such lien is noted conspicuously on the security.

Section 8–104.   Effect of Overissue; "Overissue"

(1)   The provisions of this Article which validate a security or compel its issue or reissue do not apply to the extent that validation, issue or reissue would result in overissue; but

(a)   if an identical security which does not constitute an overissue is reasonably available for

purchase, the person entitled to issue or validation may compel the issuer to purchase and deliver such a security to him against surrender of the security, if any, which he holds; or

(b)   if a security is not so available for purchase, the person entitled to issue or validation may recover from the issuer the price he or the last purchaser for value paid for it with interest from the date of his demand.

(2)   "Overissue" means the issue of securities in excess of the amount which the issuer has corporate power to issue.

Section 8–105.   Securities Negotiable; Presumptions

(1)   Securities governed by this Article are negotiable instruments.

(2)   In any action on a security

(a)   unless specifically denied in the pleadings, each signature on the security or in a necessary indorsement is admitted;

(b)   when the effectiveness of a signature is put in issue the burden of establishing it is on the party claiming under the signature but the signature is presumed to be genuine or authorized;

(c)   when signatures are admitted or established production of the instrument entitles a holder to recover on it unless the defendant establishes a defense or a defect going to the validity of the security; and

(d)   after it is shown that a defense or defect exists the plaintiff has the burden of establishing that he or some person under whom he claims is a person against whom the defense or defect is ineffective (Section 8–202).

Section 8–106.   Applicability

The validity of a security and the rights and duties of the issuer with respect to registration of transfer are governed by the law (including the conflict of laws rules) of the jurisdiction of organization of the issuer.

Section 8–107.   Securities Deliverable; Action for Price

(1)   Unless otherwise agreed and subject to any applicable law or regulation respecting short sales, a person obligated to deliver securities may deliver any security of the specified issue in bearer form or registered in the name of the transferee or indorsed to him or in blank.

(2) When the buyer fails to pay the price as it comes due under a contract of sale the seller may recover the price

(a) of securities accepted by the buyer; and

(b) of other securities if efforts at their resale would be unduly burdensome or if there is no readily available market for their resale.

PART 2
Issue — Issuer

Section 8–201. "Issuer"

(1) With respect to obligations on or defenses to a security "issuer" includes a person who

(a) places or authorizes the placing of his name on a security (otherwise than an authenticating trustee, registrar, transfer agent or the like) to evidence that it represents a share, participation or other interest in his property or in an enterprise or to evidence his duty to perform an obligation evidenced by the security; or

(b) directly or indirectly creates fractional interests in his rights or property which fractional interests are evidenced by securities; or

(c) becomes responsible for or in place of any other person described as an issuer in this section.

(2) With respect to obligations on or defenses to a security a guarantor is an issuer to the extent of his guaranty whether or not his obligation is noted on the security.

(3) With respect to registration of transfer (Part 4 of this Article) "issuer" means a person on whose behalf transfer books are maintained.

Section 8–202.   Issuer's Responsibility and Defenses; Notice of Defect or Defense

(1) Even against a purchaser for value and without notice, the terms of a security include those stated on the security and those made part of the security by reference to another instrument, indenture or document or to a constitution, statute, ordinance, rule, regulation, order or the like to the extent that the terms so referred to do not conflict with the stated terms. Such a reference does not of itself charge a purchaser for value with notice of a defect going to the validity of the security even though the security expressly states that a person accepting it admits such notice.

(2) (a) A security other than one issued by a government or governmental agency or unit even though issued with a defect going to its validity is valid in the hands of a purchaser for value and without notice of the particular defect unless the defect involves a violation of constitutional provisions in which case the security is valid in the hands of a subsequent purchaser for value and without notice of the defect.

(b) The rule of subparagraph (a) applies to an issuer which is a government or governmental agency or unit only if either there has been substantial compliance with the legal requirements governing the issue or the issuer has received a substantial consideration for the issue as a whole or for the particular security and a stated purpose of the issue is one for which the issuer has power to borrow money or issue the security.

(3) Except as otherwise provided in the case of certain unauthorized signatures on issue (Section 8–205), lack of genuineness of a security is a complete defense even against a purchaser for value and without notice.

(4) All other defenses of the issuer including non-delivery and conditional delivery of the security are ineffective against a purchaser for value who has taken without notice of the particular defense.

(5) Nothing in this section shall be construed to affect the right of a party to a "when, as and if issued" or a "when distributed" contract to cancel the contract in the event of a material change in the character of the security which is the subject of the contract or in the plan or arrangement pursuant to which such security is to be issued or distributed.

Section 8–203.   Staleness as Notice of Defects or Defenses

(1) After an act or event which creates a right to immediate performance of the principal obligation evidenced by the security or which sets a date on or after which the security is to be presented or surrendered for redemption or exchange, a purchaser is charged with notice of any defect in its issue or defense of the issuer

(a) if the act or event is one requiring the payment of money or the delivery of securities or both on presentation or surrender of the security and such funds or securities are available on the date set for payment or exchange and he takes the security more than one year after that date; and

(b) if the act or event is not covered by paragraph (a) and he takes the security more than two years after the date set for surrender or presentation or the date on which such performance became due.

(2) A call which has been revoked is not within subsection (1).

Section 8–204. Effect of Issuer's Restrictions on Transfer

Unless noted conspicuously on the security a restriction on transfer imposed by the issuer even though otherwise lawful is ineffective except against a person with actual knowledge of it.

Section 8–205. Effect of Unauthorized Signature on Issue

An unauthorized signature placed on a security prior to or in the course of issue is ineffective except that the signature is effective in favor of a purchaser for value and without notice of the lack of authority if the signing has been done by

(a) an authenticating trustee, registrar, transfer agent or other person entrusted by the issuer with the signing of the security or of similar securities or their immediate preparation for signing; or

(b) an employee of the issuer or of any of the foregoing entrusted with responsible handling of the security.

Section 8–206. Completion or Alteration of Instrument

(1) Where a security contains the signatures necessary to its issue or transfer but is incomplete in any other respect

(a) any person may complete it by filling in the blanks as authorized; and

(b) even though the blanks are incorrectly filled in, the security as completed is enforceable by a purchaser who took it for value and without notice of such incorrectness.

(2) A complete security which has been improperly altered even though fraudulently remains enforceable but only according to its original terms.

Section 8–207. Rights of Issuer with Respect to Registered Owners

(1) Prior to due presentment for registration of transfer of a security in registered form the issuer or indenture trustee may treat the registered owner as the person exclusively entitled to vote, to receive notifications and otherwise to exercise all rights and powers of an owner.

(2) Nothing in this Article shall be construed to affect the liability of the registered owner of a security for calls, assessments or the like.

Section 8–208. Effect of Signature of Authenticating Trustee, Registrar or Transfer Agent

(1) A person placing his signature upon a security as authenticating trustee, registrar, transfer agent or the like warrants to a purchaser for value without notice of the particular defect that

(a) the security is genuine; and

(b) his own participation in the issue of the security is within his capacity and within the scope of the authorization received by him from the issuer; and

(c) he has reasonable grounds to believe that the security is in the form and within the amount the issuer is authorized to issue.

(2) Unless otherwise agreed, a person by so placing his signature does not assume responsibility for the validity of the security in other respects.

PART 3
Purchase

Section 8–301. Rights Acquired by Purchaser; "Adverse Claim"; Title Acquired by Bona Fide Purchaser

(1) Upon delivery of a security the purchaser acquires the rights in the security which his transferor had or had actual authority to convey except that a purchaser who has himself been a party to any fraud or illegality affecting the security or who as a prior holder had notice of an adverse claim cannot improve his position by taking from a later bona fide purchaser. "Adverse claim" includes a claim that a transfer was or would be wrongful or that a particular adverse person is the owner of or has an interest in the security.

(2) A bona fide purchaser in addition to acquiring the rights of a purchaser also acquires the security free of any adverse claim.

(3) A purchaser of a limited interest acquires rights only to the extent of the interest purchased.

Section 8–302. "Bona Fide Purchaser"

A "bona fide purchaser" is a purchaser for value in good faith and without notice of any adverse claim who takes delivery of a security in bearer form or of one in registered form issued to him or indorsed to him or in blank.

Section 8–303. "Broker"

"Broker" means a person engaged for all or part of his time in the business of buying and selling securities, who in the transaction concerned acts for, or buys a security from or sells a security to a customer. Nothing in this Article determines the capacity in which a person acts for purposes of any other statute or rule to which such person is subject.

Section 8–304. Notice to Purchaser of Adverse Claims

(1) A purchaser (including a broker for the seller or buyer but excluding an intermediary bank) of a security is charged with notice of adverse claims if

(a) the security whether in bearer or registered form has been indorsed "for collection" or "for surrender" or for some other purpose not involving transfer; or

(b) the security is in bearer form and has on it an unambiguous statement that it is the property of a person other than the transferor. The mere writing of a name on a security is not such a statement.

(2) The fact that the purchaser (including a broker for the seller or buyer) has notice that the security is held for a third person or is registered in the name of or indorsed by a fiduciary does not create a duty of inquiry into the rightfulness of the transfer or constitute notice of adverse claims. If, however, the purchaser (excluding an intermediary bank) has knowledge that the proceeds are being used or that the transaction is for the individual benefit of the fiduciary or otherwise in breach of duty, the purchaser is charged with notice of adverse claims.

Section 8–305. Staleness as Notice of Adverse Claims

An act or event which creates a right to immediate performance of the principal obligation evidenced by the security or which sets a date on or after which the security is to be presented or surrendered for redemption or exchange does not of itself constitute any notice of adverse claims except in the case of a purchase

(a) after one year from any date set for such presentment or surrender for redemption or exchange; or

(b) after six months from any date set for payment of money against presentation or surrender of the security if funds are available for payment on that date.

Section 8–306. Warranties on Presentment and Transfer

(1) A person who presents a security for registration of transfer or for payment or exchange warrants to the issuer that he is entitled to the registration, payment or exchange. But a purchaser for value without notice of adverse claims who receives a new, reissued or re-registered security on registration of transfer warrants only that he has no knowledge of any unauthorized signature (Section 8–311) in a necessary indorsement.

(2) A person by transferring a security to a purchaser for value warrants only that

(a) his transfer is effective and rightful; and

(b) the security is genuine and has not been materially altered; and

(c) he knows no fact which might impair the validity of the security.

(3) Where a security is delivered by an intermediary known to be entrusted with delivery of the security on behalf of another or with collection of a draft or other claim against such delivery, the intermediary by such delivery warrants only his own good faith and authority even though he has purchased or made advances against the claim to be collected against the delivery.

(4) A pledgee or other holder for security who re-delivers the security received, or after payment and on order of the debtor delivers that security to a third person makes only the warranties of an intermediary under subsection (3).

(5) A broker gives to his customer and to the issuer and a purchaser the warranties provided in this section and has the rights and privileges of a purchaser under this section. The warranties of and in favor of the broker acting as an agent are in addition to applicable warranties given by and in favor of his customer.

Section 8–307. Effect of Delivery Without Indorsement; Right to Compel Indorsement

Where a security in registered form has been delivered to a purchaser without a necessary indorsement he may become a bona fide purchaser only as of the time the indorsement is supplied, but against the transferor the transfer is complete upon delivery and the purchaser has a specifically enforceable right to have any necessary indorsement supplied.

Section 8–308. Indorsement, How Made; Special Indorsement; Indorser Not a Guarantor; Partial Assignment

(1) An indorsement of a security in registered form is made when an appropriate person signs on it or on a separate document an assignment or transfer of the security or a power to assign or transfer it or when the signature of such person is written without more upon the back of the security.

(2) An indorsement may be in blank or special. An indorsement in blank includes an indorsement to bearer. A special indorsement specifies the person to whom the security is to be transferred, or who has power to transfer it. A holder may convert a blank indorsement into a special indorsement.

(3) "An appropriate person" in subsection (1) means

(a) the person specified by the security or by special indorsement to be entitled to the security; or

(b) where the person so specified is described as a fiduciary but is no longer serving in the described capacity — either that person or his successor; or

(c) where the security or indorsement so specifies more than one person as fiduciaries and one or more are no longer serving in the described capacity, — the remaining fiduciary or fiduciaries, whether or not a successor has been appointed or qualified; or

(d) when the person so specified is an individual and is without capacity to act by virtue of death, incompetence, infancy or otherwise, — his executor, administrator, guardian or like fiduciary; or

(e) where the security or indorsement so specifies more than one person as tenants by the entirety or with right of survivorship and by reason of death all cannot sign, — the survivor or survivors; or

(f) a person having power to sign under applicable law or controlling instrument; or

(g) to the extent that any of the foregoing persons may act through an agent, — his authorized agent.

(4) Unless otherwise agreed the indorser by his indorsement assumes no obligation that the security will be honored by the issuer.

(5) An indorsement purporting to be only of part of a security representing units intended by the issuer to be separately transferable is effective to the extent of the indorsement.

(6) Whether the person signing is appropriate is determined as of the date of signing and an indorsement by such a person does not become unauthorized for the purposes of this Article by virtue of any subsequent change of circumstances.

(7) Failure of a fiduciary to comply with a controlling instrument or with the law of the state having jurisdiction of the fiduciary relationship, including any law requiring the fiduciary to obtain court approval of the transfer, does not render his indorsement unauthorized for the purposes of this Article.

Section 8–309. Effect of Indorsement Without Delivery

An indorsement of a security whether special or in blank does not constitute a transfer until delivery of the security on which it appears or if the indorsement is on a separate document until delivery of both the document and the security.

Section 8–310. Indorsement of Security in Bearer Form

An indorsement of a security in bearer form may give notice of adverse claims (Section 8–304) but does not otherwise affect any right to registration the holder may possess.

Section 8–311. Effect of Unauthorized Indorsement

Unless the owner has ratified an unauthorized indorsement or is otherwise precluded from asserting its ineffectiveness

(a) he may assert its ineffectiveness against the issuer or any purchaser other than a purchaser for value and without notice of adverse claims who has in good faith received a new, reissued or re-registered security on registration of transfer; and

(b) an issuer who registers the transfer of a security upon the unauthorized indorsement is subject to liability for improper registration (Section 8–404).

Section 8–312.   Effect of Guaranteeing Signature or Indorsement

(1) Any person guaranteeing a signature of an indorser of a security warrants that at the time of signing

(a)   the signature was genuine; and

(b)   the signer was an appropriate person to indorse (Section 8–308); and

(c)   the signer had legal capacity to sign.

But the guarantor does not otherwise warrant the rightfulness of the particular transfer.

(2) Any person may guarantee an indorsement of a security and by so doing warrants not only the signature (subsection 1) but also the rightfulness of the particular transfer in all respects. But no issuer may require a guarantee of indorsement as a condition to registration of transfer.

(3) The foregoing warranties are made to any person taking or dealing with the security in reliance on the guarantee and the guarantor is liable to such person for any loss resulting from breach of the warranties.

Section 8–313.   When Delivery to the Purchaser Occurs; Purchaser's Broker as Holder

(1) Delivery to a purchaser occurs when

(a)   he or a person designated by him acquires possession of a security; or

(b)   his broker acquires possession of a security specially indorsed to or issued in the name of the purchaser; or

(c)   his broker sends him confirmation of the purchase and also by book entry or otherwise identifies a specific security in the broker's possession as belonging to the purchaser; or

(d)   with respect to an identified security to be delivered while still in the possession of a third person when that person acknowledges that he holds for the purchaser.

(e)   appropriate entries on the books of a clearing corporation are made under Section 8–320.

(2) The purchaser is the owner of a security held for him by his broker, but is not the holder except as specified in subparagraphs (b), (c) and (e) of subsection (1). Where a security is part of a fungible bulk the purchaser is the owner of a proportionate property interest in the fungible bulk.

(3) Notice of an adverse claim received by the broker or by the purchaser after the broker takes delivery as a holder for value is not effective either as to the broker or as to the purchaser. However, as between the broker and the purchaser the purchaser may demand delivery of an equivalent security as to which no notice of an adverse claim has been received.

Section 8–314.   Duty to Deliver, When Completed

(1) Unless otherwise agreed where a sale of a security is made on an exchange or otherwise through brokers

(a)   the selling customer fulfills his duty to deliver when he places such a security in the possession of the selling broker or of a person designated by the broker or if requested causes an acknowledgment to be made to the selling broker that it is held for him; and

(b)   the selling broker including a correspondent broker acting for a selling customer fulfills his duty to deliver by placing the security or a like security in the possession of the buying broker or a person designated by him or by effecting clearance of the sale in accordance with the rules of the exchange on which the transaction took place.

(2) Except as otherwise provided in this section and unless otherwise agreed, a transferor's duty to deliver a security under a contract of purchase is not fulfilled until he places the security in form to be negotiated by the purchaser in the possession of the purchaser or of a person designated by him or at the purchaser's request causes an acknowledgment to be made to the purchaser that it is held for him. Unless made on an exchange a sale to a broker purchasing for his own account is within this subsection and not within subsection (1).

Section 8–315.   Action Against Purchaser Based upon Wrongful Transfer

(1) Any person against whom the transfer of a security is wrongful for any reason, including his incapacity, may against any one except a bona fide purchaser reclaim possession of the security or obtain possession of any new security evidencing all or part of the same rights or have damages.

(2) If the transfer is wrongful because of an unauthorized indorsement, the owner may also reclaim or obtain possession of the security or new security even from a bona fide purchaser if the ineffectiveness of

the purported indorsement can be asserted against him under the provisions of this Article on unauthorized indorsements (Section 8–311).

(3) The right to obtain or reclaim possession of a security may be specifically enforced and its transfer enjoined and the security impounded pending the litigation.

Section 8–316.   Purchaser's Right to Requisites for Registration of Transfer on Books

Unless otherwise agreed the transferor must on due demand supply his purchaser with any proof of his authority to transfer or with any other requisite which may be necessary to obtain registration of the transfer of the security but if the transfer is not for value a transferor need not do so unless the purchaser furnishes the necessary expenses. Failure to comply with a demand made within a reasonable time gives the purchaser the right to reject or rescind the transfer.

Section 8–317.   Attachment or Levy upon Security

(1) No attachment or levy upon a security or any share or other interest evidenced thereby which is outstanding shall be valid until the security is actually seized by the officer making the attachment or levy but a security which has been surrendered to the issuer may be attached or levied upon at the source.

(2) A creditor whose debtor is the owner of a security shall be entitled to such aid from courts of appropriate jurisdiction, by injunction or otherwise, in reaching such security or in satisfying the claim by means thereof as is allowed at law or in equity in regard to property which cannot readily be attached or levied upon by ordinary legal process.

Section 8–318.   No Conversion by Good Faith Delivery

An agent or bailee who in good faith (including observance of reasonable commercial standards if he is in the business of buying, selling or otherwise dealing with securities) has received securities and sold, pledged or delivered them according to the instructions of his principal is not liable for conversion or for participation in breach of fiduciary duty although the principal had no right to dispose of them.

Section 8–319.   Statute of Frauds

A contract for the sale of securities is not enforceable by way of action or defense unless

(a) there is some writing signed by the party against whom enforcement is sought or by his authorized agent or broker sufficient to indicate that a contract has been made for sale of a stated quantity of described securities at a defined or stated price; or

(b) delivery of the security has been accepted or payment has been made but the contract is enforceable under this provision only to the extent of such delivery or payment; or

(c) within a reasonable time a writing in confirmation of the sale or purchase and sufficient against the sender under paragraph (a) has been received by the party against whom enforcement is sought and he has failed to send written objection to its contents within ten days after its receipt; or

(d) the party against whom enforcement is sought admits in his pleading, testimony or otherwise in court that a contract was made for sale of a stated quantity of described securities at a defined or stated price.

Section 8–320.   Transfer or Pledge Within a Central Depository System

(1) If a security

(a) is in the custody of a clearing corporation or of a custodian bank or a nominee of either subject to the instructions of the clearing corporation; and

(b) is in bearer form or indorsed in blank by an appropriate person or registered in the name of the clearing corporation or custodian bank or a nominee of either; and

(c) is shown on the account of a transferor or pledgor on the books of the clearing corporation;

then, in addition to other methods, a transfer or pledge of the security or any interest therein may be effected by the making of appropriate entries on the books of the clearing corporation reducing the account of the transferor or pledgor and increasing the account of the transferee or pledgee by the amount of the obligation or the number of shares or rights transferred or pledged.

(2) Under this section entries may be with respect to like securities or interests therein as a part of a fungible bulk and may refer merely to a quantity of a particular security without reference to the name of the registered owner, certificate or bond number or the like and, in appropriate cases, may be on a net basis taking into account other transfers or pledges of the same security.

(3) A transfer of pledge under this section has the effect of a delivery of a security in bearer form or duly indorsed in blank (Section 8–301) representing the amount of the obligation or the number of shares or rights transferred or pledged. If a pledge or the creation of a security interest is intended, the making of entries has the effect of a taking of delivery by the pledgee or a secured party (Sections 9–304 and 9–305). A transferee or pledgee under this section is a holder.

(4) A transfer or pledge under this section does not constitute a registration of transfer under Part 4 of this Article.

(5) That entries made on the books of the clearing corporation as provided in subsection (1) are not appropriate does not affect the validity or effect of the entries nor the liabilities or obligations of the clearing corporation to any person adversely affected thereby.

PART **4**

Registration

Section 8–401. Duty of Issuer to Register Transfer

(1) Where a security in registered form is presented to the issuer with a request to register transfer, the issuer is under a duty to register the transfer as requested if

(a)   the security is indorsed by the appropriate person or persons (Section 8–308); and

(b)   reasonable assurance is given that those indorsements are genuine and effective (Section 8–402); and

(c)   the issuer has no duty to inquire into adverse claims or has discharged any such duty (Section 8–403); and

(d)   any applicable law relating to the collection of taxes has been complied with; and

(e)   the transfer is in fact rightful or is to a bona fide purchaser.

(2) Where an issuer is under a duty to register a transfer of a security the issuer is also liable to the person presenting it for registration or his principal for loss resulting from any unreasonable delay in registration or from failure or refusal to register the transfer.

Section 8–402. Assurance that Indorsements Are Effective

(1) The issuer may require the following assurance that each necessary indorsement (Section 8–308) is genuine and effective:

(a)   in all cases, a guarantee of the signature (subsection (1) of Section 8–312) of the person indorsing; and

(b)   where the indorsement is by an agent, appropriate assurance of authority to sign;

(c)   where the indorsement is by a fiduciary, appropriate evidence of appointment or incumbency;

(d)   where there is more than one fiduciary, reasonable assurance that all who are required to sign have done so;

(e)   where the indorsement is by a person not covered by any of the foregoing, assurance appropriate to the case corresponding as nearly as may be to the foregoing.

(2) A "guarantee of the signature" in subsection (1) means a guarantee signed by or on behalf of a person reasonably believed by the issuer to be responsible. The issuer may adopt standards with respect to responsibility provided such standards are not manifestly unreasonable.

(3) "Appropriate evidence of appointment or incumbency" in subsection (1) means

(a)   in the case of a fiduciary appointed or qualified by a court, a certificate issued by or under the direction or supervision of that court or an officer thereof and dated within sixty days before the date of presentation for transfer; or

(b)   in any other case, a copy of a document showing the appointment or a certificate issued by or on behalf of a person reasonably believed by the issuer to be responsible or, in the absence of such a document or certificate, other evidence reasonably deemed by the issuer to be appropriate. The issuer may adopt standards with respect to such evidence provided such standards are not manifestly unreasonable. The issuer is not charged with notice of the contents of any document obtained pursuant to this paragraph (b) except to the extent that the contents relate directly to the appointment or incumbency.

(4)   The issuer may elect to require reasonable assurance beyond that specified in this section but if it does so and for a purpose other than that specified in subsection 3(b) both requires and obtains a copy of a will, trust, indenture, articles of co-partnership, by-laws or other controlling instrument it is charged with notice of all matters contained therein affecting the transfer.

Section 8–403.   Limited Duty of Inquiry

(1) An issuer to whom a security is presented for registration is under a duty to inquire into adverse claims if

> (a) a written notification of an adverse claim is received at a time and in a manner which affords the issuer a reasonable opportunity to act on it prior to the issuance of a new, reissued or re-registered security and the notification identifies the claimant, the registered owner and the issue of which the security is a part and provides an address for communications directed to the claimant; or

> (b) the issuer is charged with notice of an adverse claim from a controlling instrument which it has elected to require under subsection (4) of Section 8–402.

(2) The issuer may discharge any duty of inquiry by any reasonable means, including notifying an adverse claimant by registered or certified mail at the address furnished by him or if there be no such address at his residence or regular place of business that the security has been presented for registration of transfer by a named person, and that the transfer will be registered unless within thirty days from the date of mailing the notification, either

> (a) an appropriate restraining order, injunction or other process issues from a court of competent jurisdiction; or

> (b) an indemnity bond sufficient in the issuer's judgment to protect the issuer and any transfer agent, registrar or other agent of the issuer involved, from any loss which it or they may suffer by complying with the adverse claim is filed with the issuer.

(3) Unless an issuer is charged with notice of an adverse claim from a controlling instrument which it has elected to require under subsection (4) of Section 8–402 or receives notification of an adverse claim under subsection (1) of this section, where a security presented for registration is indorsed by the appropriate person or persons the issuer is under no duty to inquire into adverse claims. In particular

> (a) an issuer registering a security in the name of a person who is a fiduciary or who is described as a fiduciary is not bound to inquire into the existence, extent, or correct description of the fiduciary relationship and thereafter the issuer may assume without inquiry that the newly registered

owner continues to be the fiduciary until the issuer receives written notice that the fiduciary is no longer acting as such with respect to the particular security;

> (b) an issuer registering transfer on an indorsement by a fiduciary is not bound to inquire whether the transfer is made in compliance with a controlling instrument or with the law of the state having jurisdiction of the fiduciary relationship, including any law requiring the fiduciary to obtain court approval of the transfer; and

> (c) the issuer is not charged with notice of the contents of any court record or file or other recorded or unrecorded document even though the document is in its possession and even though the transfer is made on the indorsement of a fiduciary to the fiduciary himself or to his nominee.

Section 8–404.   Liability and Non-Liability for Registration

(1) Except as otherwise provided in any law relating to the collection of taxes, the issuer is not liable to the owner or any other person suffering loss as a result of the registration of a transfer of a security if

> (a) there were on or with the security the necessary indorsements (Section 8–308); and

> (b) the issuer had no duty to inquire into adverse claims or has discharged any such duty (Section 8–403).

(2) Where an issuer has registered a transfer of a security to a person not entitled to it the issuer on demand must deliver a like security to the true owner unless

> (a) the registration was pursuant to subsection (1); or

> (b) the owner is precluded from asserting any claim for registering the transfer under subsection (1) of the following section; or

> (c) such delivery would result in overissue, in which case the issuer's liability is governed by Section 8–104.

Section 8–405.   Lost, Destroyed and Stolen Securities

(1) Where a security has been lost, apparently destroyed or wrongfully taken and the owner fails to

notify the issuer of that fact within a reasonable time after he has notice of it and the issuer registers a transfer of the security before receiving such a notification, the owner is precluded from asserting against the issuer any claim for registering the transfer under the preceding section or any claim to a new security under this section.

(2) Where the owner of a security claims that the security has been lost, destroyed or wrongfully taken, the issuer must issue a new security in place of the original security if the owner

(a) so requests before the issuer has notice that the security has been acquired by a bona fide purchaser; and

(b) files with the issuer a sufficient indemnity bond; and

(c) satisfies any other reasonable requirements imposed by the issuer.

(3) If, after the issue of the new security, a bona fide purchaser of the original security presents it for registration of transfer, the insurer must register the transfer unless registration would result in overissue, in which event the issuer's liability is governed by Section 8–104. In addition to any rights on the indemnity bond, the issuer may recover the new security from the person to whom it was issued or any person taking under him except a bona fide purchaser.

Section 8–406. Duty of Authenticating Trustee, Transfer Agent or Registrar

(1) Where a person acts as authenticating trustee, transfer agent, registrar, or other agent for an issuer in the registration of transfers of its securities or in the issue of new securities or in the cancellation of surrendered securities

(a) he is under a duty to the issuer to exercise good faith and due diligence in performing his functions; and

(b) he has with regard to the particular functions he performs the same obligation to the holder or owner of the security and has the same rights and privileges as the issuer has in regard to those functions.

(2) Notice to an authenticating trustee, transfer agent, registrar or other such agent is notice to the issuer with respect to the functions performed by the agent.

ARTICLE 9
SECURED TRANSACTIONS; SALES OF ACCOUNTS AND CHATTEL PAPER

PART 1
Short Title, Applicability and Definitions

Section 9–101. Short Title

This Article shall be known and may be cited as Uniform Commercial Code — Secured Transactions.

Section 9–102. Policy and Subject Matter of Article

(1) Except as otherwise provided in Section 9–104 on excluded transactions this Article applies

(a) to any transaction (regardless of its form) which is intended to create a security interest in personal property or fixtures including goods, documents, instruments, general intangibles, chattel paper or accounts; and also

(b) to any sale of accounts or chattel paper.

(2) This Article applies to security interests created by contract including pledge, assignment, chattel mortgage, chattel trust, trust deed, factor's lien, equipment trust, conditional sale, trust receipt, other lien or title retention contract and lease or consignment intended as security. This Article does not apply to statutory liens except as provided in Section 9–310.

(3) The application of this Article to a security interest in a secured obligation is not affected by the fact that the obligation is itself secured by a transaction or interest to which this Article does not apply.

Section 9–103. Perfection of Security Interest in Multiple State Transactions

(1) Documents, instruments and ordinary goods.

(a) This subsection applies to documents and instruments and to goods other than those covered by a certificate of title described in subsection (2), mobile goods described in subsection (3), and minerals described in subsection (5).

(b) Except as otherwise provided in this subsection, perfection and the effect of perfection or non-perfection of a security interest in collateral are governed by the law of the jurisdiction where the collateral is when the last event occurs on which is based the assertion that the security interest is perfected or unperfected.

(c) If the parties to a transaction creating a purchase money security interest in goods in one jurisdiction understand at the time that the security interest attaches that the goods will be kept in another jurisdiction, then the law of the other jurisdiction governs the perfection and the effect of perfection or non-perfection of the security interest from the time it attaches until thirty days after the debtor receives possession of the goods and thereafter if the goods are taken to the other jurisdiction before the end of the thirty-day period.

(d) When collateral is brought into and kept in this state while subject to a security interest perfected under the law of the jurisdiction from which the collateral was removed, the security interest remains perfected, but if action is required by Part 2 of this Article to perfect the security interest,

  (i) if the action is not taken before the expiration of the period of perfection in the other jurisdiction or the end of four months after the collateral is brought into this state, whichever period first expires, the security interest becomes unperfected at the end of that period and is thereafter deemed to have been unperfected as against a person who became a purchaser after removal;

  (ii) if the action is taken before the expiration of the period specified in subparagraph (i), the security interest continues perfected thereafter;

  (iii) for the purpose of priority over a buyer of consumer goods (subsection (2) of Section 9–307), the period of the effectiveness of a filing in the jurisdiction from which the collateral is removed is governed by the rules with respect to perfection in subparagraphs (i) and (ii).

(2) Certificate of title.

(a) This subsection applies to goods covered by a certificate of title issued under a statute of this state or of another jurisdiction under the law of which indication of a security interest on the certificate is required as a condition of perfection.

(b) Except as otherwise provided in this subsection, perfection and the effect of perfection or non-perfection of the security interest are governed by the law (including the conflict of laws rules) of the jurisdiction issuing the certificate until four months after the goods are removed from that jurisdiction and thereafter until the goods are registered in another jurisdiction, but in any event not beyond surrender of the certificate. After the expiration of that period, the goods are not covered by the certificate of title within the meaning of this section.

(c) Except with respect to the rights of a buyer described in the next paragraph, a security interest, perfected in another jurisdiction otherwise than by notation on a certificate of title, in goods brought into this state and thereafter covered by a certificate of title issued by this state is subject to the rules stated in paragraph (d) of subsection (1).

(d) If goods are brought into this state while a security interest therein is perfected in any manner under the law of the jurisdiction from which the goods are removed and a certificate of title is issued by this state and the certificate does not show that the goods are subject to the security interest or that they may be subject to security interests not shown on the certificate, the security interest is subordinate to the rights of a buyer of the goods who is not in the business of selling goods of that kind to the extent that he gives value and receives delivery of the goods after issuance of the certificate and without knowledge of the security interest.

(3) Accounts, general intangibles and mobile goods.

(a) This subsection applies to accounts (other than an account described in subsection (5) on minerals) and general intangibles (other than uncertificated securities) and to goods which are mobile and which are of a type normally used in more than one jurisdiction, such as motor vehicles, trailers, rolling stock, airplanes, shipping containers, road building and construction machinery and commercial harvesting machinery and the like, if the goods are equipment or are inventory leased or held for lease by the debtor to others, and are not covered by a certificate of title described in subsection (2).

(b) The law (including the conflict of laws rules) of the jurisdiction in which the debtor is located governs the perfection and the effect of perfection or non-perfection of the security interest.

(c) If, however, the debtor is located in a jurisdiction which is not a part of the United States, and which does not provide for perfection of the security interest by filing or recording in that jurisdiction, the law of the jurisdiction in the United

States in which the debtor has its major executive office in the United States governs the perfection and the effect of perfection or non-perfection of the security interest through filing. In the alternative, if the debtor is located in a jurisdiction which is not a part of the United States or Canada and the collateral is accounts or general intangibles for money due or to become due, the security interest may be perfected by notification to the account debtor. As used in this paragraph, "United States" includes its territories and possessions and the Commonwealth of Puerto Rico.

(d) A debtor shall be deemed located at his place of business if he has one, at his chief executive office if he has more than one place of business, otherwise at his residence. If, however, the debtor is a foreign air carrier under the Federal Aviation Act of 1958, as amended, it shall be deemed located at the designated office of the agent upon whom service of process may be made on behalf of the foreign air carrier.

(e) A security interest perfected under the law of the jurisdiction of the location of the debtor is perfected until the expiration of four months after a change of the debtor's location to another jurisdiction, or until perfection would have ceased by the law of the first jurisdiction, whichever period first expires. Unless perfected in the new jurisdiction before the end of that period, it becomes unperfected thereafter and is deemed to have been unperfected as against a person who became a purchaser after the change.

(4) Chattel paper.

The rules stated for goods in subsection (1) apply to a possessory security interest in chattel paper. The rules stated for accounts in subsection (3) apply to a non-possessory security interest in chattel paper, but the security interest may not be perfected by notification to the account debtor.

(5) Minerals.

Perfection and the effect of perfection or non-perfection of a security interest which is created by a debtor who has an interest in minerals or the like (including oil and gas) before extraction and which attaches thereto as extracted, or which attaches to an account resulting from the sale thereof at the wellhead or minehead are governed by the law (including the conflict of laws rules) of the jurisdiction wherein the wellhead or minehead is located.

(6) Uncertificated securities.

The law (including the conflict of laws rules) of the jurisdiction of organization of the issuer governs the perfection and the effect of perfection or nonperfection of a security interest in uncertificated securities. Amended in 1972 and 1977.

Section 9–104. Transactions Excluded from Article

This Article does not apply

(a) to a security interest subject to any statute of the United States to the extent that such statute governs the rights of parties to and third parties affected by transactions in particular types of property; or

(b) to a landlord's lien; or

(c) to a lien given by statute or other rule of law for services or materials except as provided in Section 9–310 on priority of such liens; or

(d) to a transfer of a claim for wages, salary or other compensation of an employee; or

(e) to a transfer by a government or governmental subdivision or agency; or

(f) to a sale of accounts or chattel paper as part of a sale of the business out of which they arose, or an assignment of accounts or chattel paper which is for the purpose of collection only, or a transfer of a right to payment under a contract to an assignee who is also to do the performance under the contract or a transfer of a single account to an assignee in whole or partial satisfaction of a pre-existing indebtedness; or

(g) to a transfer of an interest in or claim in or under any policy of insurance, except as provided with respect to proceeds (Section 9–306) and priorities in proceeds (Section 9–312); or

(h) to a right represented by a judgment (other than a judgment taken on a right to payment which was collateral); or

(i) to any right of set-off; or

(j) except to the extent that provision is made for fixtures in Section 9–313, to the creation or transfer of an interest in or lien on real estate, including a lease or rents thereunder; or

(k) to a transfer in whole or in part of any claim arising out of tort; or

(l) to a transfer of an interest in any deposit account (subsection (1) of Section 9–105), except as provided with respect to proceeds (Section 9–306) and priorities in proceeds (Section 9–312).

Section 9–105.   Definitions and Index of Definitions

(1) In this Article unless the context otherwise requires:

(a) "Account debtor" means the person who is obligated on an account, chattel paper or general intangible;

(b) "Chattel paper" means a writing or writings which evidence both a monetary obligation and a security interest in or a lease of specific goods, but a charter or other contract involving the use or hire of a vessel is not chattel paper. When a transaction is evidenced both by such a security agreement or a lease and by an instrument or a series of instruments, the group of writings taken together constitutes chattel paper;

(c) "Collateral" means the property subject to a security interest, and includes accounts and chattel paper which have been sold;

(d) "Debtor" means the person who owes payment or other performance of the obligation secured, whether or not he owns or has rights in the collateral, and includes the seller of accounts or chattel paper. Where the debtor and the owner of the collateral are not the same person, the term "debtor" means the owner of the collateral in any provision of the Article dealing with the collateral, the obligor in any provision dealing with the obligation, and may include both where the context so requires;

(e) "Deposit account" means a demand, time, savings, passbook or like account maintained with a bank, savings and loan association, credit union or like organization, other than an account evidenced by a certificate of deposit;

(f) "Document" means document of title as defined in the general definitions of Article 1 (Section 1–201), and a receipt of the kind described in subsection (2) of Section 7–201;

(g) "Encumbrance" includes real estate mortgages and other liens on real estate and all other rights in real estate that are not ownership interests;

(h) "Goods" includes all things which are movable at the time the security interest attaches or which are fixtures (Section 9–313), but does not include money, documents, instruments, accounts, chattel paper, general intangibles, or minerals or the like (including oil and gas) before extraction.

"Goods" also includes standing timber which is to be cut and removed under a conveyance or contract for sale, the unborn young of animals, and growing crops;

(i) "Instrument" means a negotiable instrument (defined in Section 3–104), or a certificated security (defined in Section 8–102) or any other writing which evidences a right to the payment of money and is not itself a security agreement or lease and is of a type which is in ordinary course of business transferred by delivery with any necessary indorsement or assignment;

(j) "Mortgage" means a consensual interest created by a real estate mortgage, a trust deed on real estate, or the like;

(k) An advance is made "pursuant to commitment" if the secured party has bound himself to make it, whether or not a subsequent event of default or other event not within his control has relieved or may relieve him from his obligation;

(l) "Security agreement" means an agreement which creates or provides for a security interest;

(m) "Secured party" means a lender, seller or other person in whose favor there is a security interest, including a person to whom accounts or chattel paper have been sold. When the holders of obligations issued under an indenture of trust, equipment trust agreement or the like are represented by a trustee or other person, the representative is the secured party;

(n) "Transmitting utility" means any person primarily engaged in the railroad, street railway or trolley bus business, the electric or electronics communications transmission business, the transmission of goods by pipeline, or the transmission or the production and transmission of electricity, steam, gas or water, or the provision of sewer service.

(2) Other definitions applying to this Article and the sections in which they appear are:

"Account." Section 9–106.
"Attach." Section 9–203.
"Construction mortgage." Section 9–313(1).
"Consumer goods." Section 9–109(1).
"Equipment." Section 9–109(2).
"Farm products." Section 9–109(3).
"Fixture." Section 9–313(1).
"Fixture filing." Section 9–313(1).
"General intangibles." Section 9–106.
"Inventory." Section 9–109(4).
"Lien creditor." Section 9–301(3).

"Proceeds." Section 9–306(1).
"Purchase money security interest." Section 9–
    107.
"United States." Section 9–103.

(3) The following definitions in other Articles apply to this Article:

"Check." Section 3–104.
"Contract for sale." Section 2–106.
"Holder in due course." Section 3–302.
"Note." Section 3–104.
"Sale." Section 2–106.

(4) In addition Article 1 contains general definitions and principles of construction and interpretation applicable throughout this Article. Amended in 1972 and 1977.

Section 9–106.   Definitions: "Account"; "General Intangibles"

"Account" means any right to payment for goods sold or leased or for services rendered which is not evidenced by an instrument or chattel paper, whether or not it has been earned by performance. "General intangibles" means any personal property (including things in action) other than goods, accounts, chattel paper, documents, instruments, and money. All rights to payment earned or unearned under a charter or other contract involving the use or hire of a vessel and all rights incident to the charter or contract are accounts.

Section 9–107.   Definitions: "Purchase Money Security Interest"

A security interest is a "purchase money security interest" to the extent that it is

(a)   taken or retained by the seller of the collateral to secure all or part of its price; or

(b)   taken by a person who by making advances or incurring an obligation gives value to enable the debtor to acquire rights in or the use of collateral if such value is in fact so used.

Section 9–108.   When After-Acquired Collateral Not Security for Antecedent Debt

Where a secured party makes an advance, incurs an obligation, releases a perfected security interest, or otherwise gives new value which is to be secured in whole or in part by after-acquired property his security interest in the after-acquired collateral shall be deemed to be taken for new value and not as security for an antecedent debt if the debtor acquires his rights in such collateral either in the ordinary course of his business or under a contract of purchase made pursuant to the security agreement within a reasonable time after new value is given.

Section 9–109.   Classification of Goods; "Consumer Goods"; "Equipment"; "Farm Products"; "Inventory"

Goods are

(1) "consumer goods" if they are used or bought for use primarily for personal, family or household purposes;

(2) "equipment" if they are used or bought for use primarily in business (including farming or a profession) or by a debtor who is a non-profit organization or a governmental subdivision or agency or if the goods are not included in the definitions of inventory, farm products or consumer goods;

(3) "farm products" if they are crops or livestock or supplies used or produced in farming operations or if they are products of crops or livestock in their unmanufactured states (such as ginned cotton, woolclip, maple syrup, milk and eggs), and if they are in the possession of a debtor engaged in raising, fattening, grazing or other farming operations. If goods are farm products they are neither equipment nor inventory;

(4) "inventory" if they are held by a person who holds them for sale or lease or to be furnished under contracts of service or if he has so furnished them, or if they are raw materials, work in process or materials used or consumed in a business. Inventory of a person is not to be classified as his equipment.

Section 9–110.   Sufficiency of Description

For the purposes of this Article any description of personal property or real estate is sufficient whether or not it is specific if it reasonably identifies what is described.

Section 9–111.   Applicability of Bulk Transfer Laws

The creation of a security interest is not a bulk transfer under Article 6 (see Section 6–103).

Section 9–112.   Where Collateral Is Not Owned by Debtor

Unless otherwise agreed, when a secured party knows that collateral is owned by a person who is not the debtor, the owner of the collateral is entitled to receive from the secured party any surplus under Section 9–502(2) or under Section 9–504(1), and is not liable for the debt or for any deficiency after resale, and he has the same right as the debtor

(a) to receive statements under Section 9–208;

(b) to receive notice of and to object to a secured party's proposal to retain the collateral in satisfaction of the indebtedness under Section 9–505;

(c) to redeem the collateral under Section 9–506;

(d) to obtain injunctive or other relief under Section 9–507(1); and

(e) to recover losses caused to him under Section 9–208(2).

Section 9–113. Security Interest Arising Under Article on Sales

A security interest arising solely under the Article on Sales (Article 2) is subject to the provisions of this Article except that to the extent that and so long as the debtor does not have or does not lawfully obtain possession of the goods

(a) no security agreement is necessary to make the security interest enforceable; and

(b) no filing is required to perfect the security interest; and

(c) the rights of the secured party on default by the debtor are governed by the Article on Sales (Article 2).

Section 9–114. Consignment

(1) A person who delivers goods under a consignment which is not a security interest and who would be required to file under this Article by paragraph (3)(c) of Section 2–326 has priority over a secured party who is or becomes a creditor of the consignee and who would have a perfected security interest in the goods if they were the property of the consignee, and also has priority with respect to identifiable cash proceeds received on or before delivery of the goods to a buyer, if

(a) the consignor complies with the filing provision of the Article on Sales with respect to consignments (paragraph (3)(c) of Section 2–326) before the consignee receives possession of the goods; and

(b) the consignor gives notification in writing to the holder of the security interest if the holder has filed a financing statement covering the same

types of goods before the date of the filing made by the consignor; and

(c) the holder of the security interest receives the notification within five years before the consignee receives possession of the goods; and

(d) the notification states that the consignor expects to deliver goods on consignment to the consignee, describing the goods by item or type.

(2) In the case of a consignment which is not a security interest and in which the requirements of the preceding subsection have not been met, a person who delivers goods to another is subordinate to a person who would have a perfected security interest in the goods if they were the property of the debtor.

PART 2
Validity of Security Agreement and Rights of Parties Thereto

Section 9–201. General Validity of Security Agreement

Except as otherwise provided by this Act a security agreement is effective according to its terms between the parties, against purchasers of the collateral and against creditors. Nothing in this Article validates any charge or practice illegal under any statute or regulation thereunder governing usury, small loans, retail installment sales, or the like, or extends the application of any such statute or regulation to any transaction not otherwise subject thereto.

Section 9–202. Title to Collateral Immaterial

Each provision of this Article with regard to rights, obligations and remedies applies whether title to collateral is in the secured party or in the debtor.

Section 9–203. Attachment and Enforceability of Security Interest; Proceeds; Formal Requisites

(1) Subject to the provisions of Section 4–208 on the security interest of a collecting bank, Section 8–321 on security interests in securities and Section 9–113 on a security interest arising under the Article on Sales, a security interest is not enforceable against the debtor or third parties with respect to the collateral and does not attach unless:

(a) the collateral is in the possession of the secured party pursuant to agreement, or the debtor has signed a security agreement which contains a description of the collateral and in addition, when the security interest covers crops growing or to be grown or timber to be cut, a description of the land concerned;

(b) value has been given; and

(c) the debtor has rights in the collateral.

(2) A security interest attaches when it becomes enforceable against the debtor with respect to the collateral. Attachment occurs as soon as all of the events specified in subsection (1) have taken place unless explicit agreement postpones the time of attaching.

(3) Unless otherwise agreed a security agreement gives the secured party the rights to proceeds provided by Section 9–306.

(4) A transaction, although subject to this Article, is also subject to . . . .,* and in the case of conflict between the provisions of this Article and any such statute, the provisions of such statute control. Failure to comply with any applicable statute has only the effect which is specified therein.

Note: *At * in subsection (4), insert reference to any local statute regulating small loans, retail installment sales and the like.*

Section 9–204. After-Acquired Property; Future Advances

(1) Except as provided in subsection (2), a security agreement may provide that any or all obligations covered by the security agreement are to be secured by after-acquired collateral.

(2) No security interest attaches under an after-acquired property clause to consumer goods other than accessions (Section 9–314) when given as additional security unless the debtor acquires rights in them within ten days after the secured party gives value.

(3) Obligations covered by a security agreement may include future advances or other value whether or not the advances or value are given pursuant to commitment (subsection (1) of Section 9–105).

Section 9–205. Use or Disposition of Collateral Without Accounting Permissible

A security interest is not invalid or fraudulent against creditors by reason of liberty in the debtor to use, commingle or dispose of all or part of the collateral (including returned or repossessed goods) or to collect or compromise accounts or chattel paper, or to accept the return of goods or make repossessions, or to use,

commingle or dispose of proceeds, or by reason of the failure of the secured party to require the debtor to account for proceeds or replace collateral. This section does not relax the requirements of possession where perfection of a security interest depends upon possession of the collateral by the secured party or by a bailee.

Section 9–206. Agreement Not to Assert Defenses Against Assignee; Modification of Sales Warranties Where Security Agreement Exists

(1) Subject to any statute or decision which establishes a different rule for buyers or lessees of consumer goods, an agreement by a buyer or lessee that he will not assert against an assignee any claim or defense which he may have against the seller or lessor is enforceable by an assignee who takes his assignment for value, in good faith and without notice of a claim or defense, except as to defenses of a type which may be asserted against a holder in due course of a negotiable instrument under the Article on Commercial Paper (Article 3). A buyer who as part of one transaction signs both a negotiable instrument and a security agreement makes such an agreement.

(2) When a seller retains a purchase money security interest in goods the Article on Sales (Article 2) governs the sale and any disclaimer, limitation or modification of the seller's warranties.

Section 9–207. Rights and Duties When Collateral Is in Secured Party's Possession

(1) A secured party must use reasonable care in the custody and preservation of collateral in his possession. In the case of an instrument or chattel paper reasonable care includes taking necessary steps to preserve rights against prior parties unless otherwise agreed.

(2) Unless otherwise agreed, when collateral is in the secured party's possession

(a) reasonable expenses (including the cost of any insurance and payment of taxes or other charges) incurred in the custody, preservation, use or operation of the collateral are chargeable to the debtor and are secured by the collateral;

(b) the risk of accidental loss or damage is on the debtor to the extent of any deficiency in any effective insurance coverage;

(c) the secured party may hold as additional security any increase or profits (except money) received from the collateral, but money so received, unless remitted to the debtor, shall be applied in reduction of the secured obligation;

(d)   the secured party must keep the collateral identifiable but fungible collateral may be commingled;

(e)   the secured party may repledge the collateral upon terms which do not impair the debtor's right to redeem it.

(3)   A secured party is liable for any loss caused by his failure to meet any obligation imposed by the preceding subsections but does not lose his security interest.

(4)   A secured party may use or operate the collateral for the purpose of preserving the collateral or its value or pursuant to the order of a court of appropriate jurisdiction or, except in the case of consumer goods, in the manner and to the extent provided in the security agreement.

Section 9–208.   Request for Statement of Account or List of Collateral

(1)   A debtor may sign a statement indicating what he believes to be the aggregate amount of unpaid indebtedness as of a specified date and may send it to the secured party with a request that the statement be approved or corrected and returned to the debtor. When the security agreement or any other record kept by the secured party identifies the collateral a debtor may similarly request the secured party to approve or correct a list of the collateral.

(2)   The secured party must comply with such a request within two weeks after receipt by sending a written correction or approval. If the secured party claims a security interest in all of a particular type of collateral owned by the debtor he may indicate that fact in his reply and need not approve or correct an itemized list of such collateral. If the secured party without reasonable excuse fails to comply he is liable for any loss caused by the debtor thereby; and if the debtor has properly included in his request a good faith statement of the obligation or a list of the collateral or both the secured party may claim a security interest only as shown in the statement against persons misled by his failure to comply. If he no longer has an interest in the obligation or collateral at the time the request is received he must disclose the name and address of any successor in interest known to him and he is liable for any loss caused to the debtor as a result of failure to disclose. A successor in interest is not subject to this section until a request is received by him.

(3)   A debtor is entitled to such a statement once every six months without charge. The secured party may require payment of a charge not exceeding $10 for each additional statement furnished.

PART 3

Rights of Third Parties: Perfected and Unperfected Security Interests; Rules of Priority

Section 9–301.   Persons Who Take Priority over Unperfected Security Interests; Rights of "Lien Creditor"

(1)   Except as otherwise provided in subsection (2), an unperfected security interest is subordinate to the rights of

(a)   persons entitled to priority under Section 9–312;

(b)   a person who becomes a lien creditor before the security interest is perfected;

(c)   in the case of goods, instruments, documents, and chattel paper, a person who is not a secured party and who is a transferee in bulk or other buyer not in ordinary course of business or is a buyer of farm products in ordinary course of business, to the extent that he gives value and receives delivery of the collateral without knowledge of the security interest and before it is perfected;

(d)   in the case of accounts and general intangibles, a person who is not a secured party and who is a transferee to the extent that he gives value without knowledge of the security interest and before it is perfected.

(2)   If the secured party files with respect to a purchase money security interest before or within ten days after the debtor receives possession of the collateral, he takes priority over the rights of a transferee in bulk or of a lien creditor which arise between the time the security interest attaches and the time of filing.

(3)   A "lien creditor" means a creditor who has acquired a lien on the property involved by attachment, levy or the like and includes an assignee for benefit of creditors from the time of assignment, and a trustee in bankruptcy from the date of the filing of the petition or a receiver in equity from the time of appointment.

(4)   A person who becomes a lien creditor while a security interest is perfected takes subject to the security

interest only to the extent that it secures advances made before he becomes a lien creditor or within 45 days thereafter or made without knowledge of the lien or pursuant to a commitment entered into without knowledge of the lien.

Section 9–302. When Filing Is Required to Perfect Security Interest; Security Interests to Which Filing Provisions of This Article Do Not Apply

(1) A financing statement must be filed to perfect all security interests except the following:

(a) a security interest in collateral in possession of the secured party under Section 9–305;

(b) a security interest temporarily perfected in instruments or documents without delivery under Section 9–304 or in proceeds for a 10 day period under Section 9–306;

(c) a security interest created by an assignment of a beneficial interest in a trust or a decedent's estate;

(d) a purchase money security interest in consumer goods; but filing is required for a motor vehicle required to be registered; and fixture filing is required for priority over conflicting interests in fixtures to the extent provided in Section 9–313;

(e) an assignment of accounts which does not alone or in conjunction with other assignments to the same assignee transfer a significant part of the outstanding accounts of the assignor;

(f) a security interest of a collecting bank (Section 4–208) or in securities (Section 8–321) or arising under the Article on Sales (see Section 9–113) or covered in subsection (3) of this section;

(g) an assignment for the benefit of all the creditors of the transferor, and subsequent transfers by the assignee thereunder.

(2) If a secured party assigns a perfected security interest, no filing under this Article is required to order to continue the perfected status of the security interest against creditors of and transferees from the original debtor.

(3) The filing of a financing statement otherwise required by this Article is not necessary or effective to perfect a security interest in property subject to

(a) a statute or treaty of the United States which provides for a national or international registration or a national or international certificate or title or which specifies a place of filing different from that specified in this Article for filing of the security interest; or

(b) the following statutes of this state; [list any certificate of title statute covering automobiles, trailers, mobile homes, boats, farm tractors, or the like, and any central filing statute*.]; but during any period in which collateral is inventory held for sale by a person who is in the business of selling goods of that kind, the filing provisions of this Article (Part 4) apply to a security interest in that collateral created by him as debtor; or

Note: *It is recommended that the provisions of certificate of title acts for perfection of security interests by notation on the certificates should be amended to exclude coverage of inventory held for sale.*

(c) a certificate of title statute of another jurisdiction under the law of which indication of a security interest on the certificate is required as a condition of perfection (subsection (2) of Section 9–103).

(4) Compliance with a statute or treaty described in subsection (3) is equivalent to the filing of a financing statement under this Article, and a security interest in property subject to the statute or treaty can be perfected only by compliance therewith except as provided in Section 9–103 on multiple state transactions. Duration and renewal or perfection of a security interest perfected by compliance with the statute or treaty are governed by the provisions of the statute or treaty; in other respects the security interest is subject to this Article.

Section 9–303. When Security Interest Is Perfected; Continuity of Perfection

(1) A security interest is perfected when it has attached and when all of the applicable steps required for perfection have been taken. Such steps are specified in Sections 9–302, 9–304, 9–305 and 9–306. If such steps are taken before the security interest attaches, it is perfected at the time when it attaches.

(2) If a security interest is originally perfected in any way permitted under this Article and is subsequently perfected in some other way under this Article, without an intermediate period when it is unperfected, the security interest shall be deemed to be perfected continuously for the purposes of this Article.

Section 9–304. Perfection of Security Interest in Instruments, Documents, and Goods Covered by Documents; Perfection by Permissive Filing; Temporary Perfection Without Filing or Transfer of Possession

(1) A security interest in chattel paper or negotiable documents may be perfected by filing. A security interest in money or instruments (other than certificated securities or instruments which constitute part of chattel papers can be perfected only by the secured party's taking possession, except as provided in subsections (4) and (5) of this section and subsections (2) and (3) of Section 9–306 on proceeds.

(2) During the period that goods are in the possession of the issuer of a negotiable document therefor, a security interest in the goods is perfected by perfecting a security interest in the document, and any security interest in the goods otherwise perfected during such period is subject thereto.

(3) A security interest in goods in the possession of a bailee other than one who has issued a negotiable document therefor is perfected by issuance of a document in the name of the secured party or by the bailee's receipt of notification of the secured party's interest or by filing as to the goods.

(4) A security interest in instruments (other than certificated securities) or negotiable documents is perfected without filing or the taking of possession for a period of 21 days from the time it attaches to the extent that it arises for new value given under a written security agreement.

(5) A security interest remains perfected for a period of 21 days without filing where a secured party having a perfected security interest in an instrument (other than a certificated security), a negotiable document or goods in possession of a bailee other than one who has issued a negotiable document therefor

    (a) makes available to the debtor the goods or documents representing the goods for the purpose of ultimate sale or exchange or for the purpose of loading, unloading, storing, shipping, transshipping, manufacturing, processing or otherwise dealing with them in a manner preliminary to their sale or exchange, but priority between conflicting security interests in the goods is subject to subsection (3) of Section 9–312; or

    (b) delivers the instrument to the debtor for the purpose of ultimate sale or exchange or of presentation, renewal, or registration of transfer.

(6) After the 21 day period in subsections (4) and (5) perfection depends upon compliance with applicable provisions of this Article. Amended in 1972 and 1977.

Section 9–305. When Possession by Secured Party Perfects Security Interest Without Filing

A security interest in letters of credit and advices of credit (subsection (2)(a) of Section 5–116), goods, instruments (other than certificated securities), money, negotiable documents or chattel paper may be perfected by the secured party's taking possession of the collateral. If such collateral other than goods covered by a negotiable document is held by a bailee, the secured party is deemed to have possession from the time the bailee receives notification of the secured party's interest. A security interest is perfected by possession from the time possession is taken without relation back and continues only so long as possession is retained, unless otherwise specified in this Article. The security interest may be otherwise perfected as provided in this Article before or after the period of possession by the secured party. Amended in 1972 and 1977.

Section 9–306. "Proceeds"; Secured Party's Rights on Disposition of Collateral

(1) "Proceeds" includes whatever is received upon the sale, exchange, collection or other disposition of collateral or proceeds. Insurance payable by reason of loss or damage to the collateral is proceeds, except to the extent that it is payable to a person other than a party to the security agreement. Money, checks, deposit accounts, and the like are "cash proceeds". All other proceeds are "non-cash proceeds".

(2) Except where this Article otherwise provides, a security interest continues in collateral notwithstanding sale, exchange or other disposition thereof unless the disposition was authorized by the secured party in the security agreement or otherwise, and also continues in any identifiable proceeds including collections received by the debtor.

(3) The security interest in proceeds is a continuously perfected security interest if the interest in the original collateral was perfected but it ceases to be a perfected security interest and becomes unperfected ten days after receipt of the proceeds by the debtor unless

(a)   a filed financing statement covers the original collateral and the proceeds are collateral in which a security interest may be perfected by filing in the office or offices where the financing statement has been filed and, if the proceeds are acquired with cash proceeds, the description of collateral in the financing statement indicates the types of property constituting the proceeds; or

(b)   a filed financing statement covers the original collateral and the proceeds are identifiable cash proceeds; or

(c)   the security interest in the proceeds is perfected before the expiration of the ten day period.

Except as provided in this section, a security interest in proceeds can be perfected only by the methods or under the circumstances permitted in this Article for original collateral of the same type.

(4)   In the event of insolvency proceedings instituted by or against a debtor, a secured party with a perfected security interest in proceeds has a perfected security interest only in the following proceeds:

(a)   in identifiable non-cash proceeds and in separate deposit accounts containing only proceeds;

(b)   in identifiable cash proceeds in the form of money which is neither commingled with other money nor deposited in a deposit account prior to the insolvency proceedings;

(c)   in identifiable cash proceeds in the form of checks and the like which are not deposited in a deposit account prior to the insolvency proceedings; and

(d)   in all cash and deposit accounts of the debtor in which proceeds have been commingled with other funds, but the perfected security interest under this paragraph (d) is

(i)   subject to any right to set-off; and

(ii)   limited to an amount not greater than the amount of any cash proceeds received by the debtor within ten days before the institution of the insolvency proceedings less the sum of (I) the payments to the secured party on account of cash proceeds received by the debtor during such period and (II) the cash proceeds received by the debtor during such period to which the secured party is entitled under paragraphs (a) through (c) of this subsection (4).

(5)   If a sale of goods results in an account or chattel paper which is transferred by the seller to a secured party, and if the goods are returned to or are repossessed by the seller or the secured party, the following rules determine priorities:

(a)   If the goods were collateral at the time of sale, for an indebtedness of the seller which is still unpaid, the original security interest attaches again to the goods and continues as a perfected security interest if it was perfected at the time when the goods were sold. If the security interest was originally perfected by a filing which is still effective, nothing further is required to continue the perfected status; in any other case, the secured party must take possession of the returned or repossessed goods or must file.

(b)   An unpaid transferee of the chattel paper has a security interest in the goods against the transferor. Such security interest is prior to a security interest inserted under paragraph (a) to the extent that the transferee of the chattel paper was entitled to priority under Section 9–308.

(c)   An unpaid transferee of the account has a security interest in the goods against the transferor. Such security interest is subordinate to a security interest asserted under paragraph (a).

(d)   A security interest of an unpaid transferee asserted under paragraph (b) or (c) must be perfected for protection against creditors of the transferor and purchasers of the returned or repossessed goods.

Section 9–307.   Protection of Buyers of Goods

(1)   A buyer in ordinary course of business (subsection (9) of Section 1–201) other than a person buying farm products from a person engaged in farming operations takes free of a security interest created by his seller even though the security interest is perfected and even though the buyer knows of its existence.

(2)   In the case of consumer goods, a buyer takes free of a security interest even though perfected if he buys without knowledge of the security interest, for value and for his own personal, family or household purposes unless prior to the purchase the secured party has filed a financing statement covering goods.

(3)   A buyer other than a buyer in ordinary course of business (subsection (1) of this section) takes free of a security interest to the extent that it secures future advances made after the secured party acquires knowl-

edge of the purchase, or more than 45 days after the purchase, whichever first occurs, unless made pursuant to a commitment entered into without knowledge of the purchase and before the expiration of the 45 day period.

Section 9–308.   Purchase of Chattel Paper and Instruments

A purchaser of chattel paper or an instrument who gives new value and takes possession of it in the ordinary course of his business has priority over a security interest in the chattel paper or instrument

(a)   which is perfected under Section 9–304 (permissive filing and temporary perfection) or under Section 9–306 (perfection as to proceeds) if he acts without knowledge that the specific paper or instrument is subject to a security interest; or

(b)   which is claimed merely as proceeds of inventory subject to a security interest (Section 9–306) even though he knows that the specific paper or instrument is subject to the security interest.

Section 9–309.   Protection of Purchasers of Instruments, Documents and Securities

Nothing in this Article limits the rights of a holder in due course of a negotiable instrument (Section 3–302) or a holder to whom a negotiable document of title has been duly negotiated (Section 7–501) or a bona fide purchaser of a security (Section 8–302) and such holders or purchasers take priority over an earlier security interest even though perfected. Filing under this Article does not constitute notice of the security interest to such holders or purchasers. Amended in 1977.

Section 9–310.   Priority of Certain Liens Arising by Operation of Law

When a person in the ordinary course of his business furnishes services or materials with respect to goods subject to a security interest, a lien upon goods in the possession of such person given by statute or rule of law for such materials or services takes priority over a perfected security interest unless the lien is statutory and the statute expressly provides otherwise.

Section 9–311.   Alienability of Debtor's Rights: Judicial Process

The debtor's rights in collateral may be voluntarily or involuntarily transferred (by way of sale, creation of a security interest, attachment, levy, garnishment or other judicial process) notwithstanding a provision in the security agreement prohibiting any transfer or making the transfer constitute a default.

Section 9–312.   Priorities Among Conflicting Security Interests in the Same Collateral

(1) The rules of priority stated in other sections of this Part and in the following sections shall govern when applicable: Section 4–208 with respect to the security interests of collecting banks in items being collected, accompanying documents and proceeds; Section 9–103 on security interests related to other jurisdictions; Section 9–114 on consignments.

(2) A perfected security interest in crops for new value given to enable the debtor to produce the crops during the production season and given not more than three months before the crops become growing crops by planting or otherwise takes priority over an earlier perfected security interest to the extent that such earlier interest secures obligations due more than six months before the crops become growing crops by planting or otherwise, even though the person giving new value had knowledge of the earlier security interest.

(3) A perfected purchase money security interest in inventory has priority over a conflicting security interest in the same inventory and also has priority in identifiable cash proceeds received on or before the delivery of the inventory to a buyer if

(a)   the purchase money security interest is perfected at the time the debtor receives possession of the inventory; and

(b)   the purchase money secured party gives notification in writing to the holder of the conflicting security interest if the holder had filed a financing statement covering the same types of inventory (i) before the date of the filing made by the purchase money secured party, or (ii) before the beginning of the 21 day period where the purchase money security interest is temporarily perfected without filing or possession (subsection (5) of Section 9–304); and

(c)   the holder of the conflicting security interest receives the notification within five years before the debtor receives possession of the inventory; and

(d)   the notification states that the person giving the notice has or expects to acquire a purchase money security interest in inventory of the debtor, describing such inventory by item or type.

(4) A purchase money security interest in collateral other than inventory has priority over a conflicting security interest in the same collateral or its proceeds if the purchase money security interest is perfected at the time the debtor receives possession of the collateral or within ten days thereafter.

(5) In all cases not governed by other rules stated in this section (including cases of purchase money security interests which do not qualify for the special priorities set forth in subsections (3) and (4) of this section), priority between conflicting security interests in the same collateral shall be determined according to the following rules:

(a) Conflicting security interests rank according to priority in time of filing or perfection. Priority dates from the time a filing is first made covering the collateral or the time the security interest is first perfected, whichever is earlier, provided that there is no period thereafter when there is neither filing nor perfection.

(b) So long as conflicting security interests are unperfected, the first to attach has priority.

(6) For purposes of subsection (5) a date of filing or perfection as to collateral is also a date of filing or perfection as to proceeds.

(7) If future advances are made while a security interest is perfected by filing, the taking of possession, or under Section 8–321 on securities, the security interest has the same priority for the purposes of subsection (5) with respect to the future advances as it does with respect to the first advance. If a commitment is made before or while the secured interest is so perfected, the security interest has the same priority with respect to advances made pursuant thereto. In other cases a perfected security interest has priority from the date the advance is made. Amended in 1972 and 1977.

Section 9–313. Priority of Security Interests in Fixtures

(1) In this section and in the provisions of Part 4 of this Article referring to fixture filing, unless the context otherwise requires

(a) goods are "fixtures" when they become so related to particular real estate that an interest in them arises under real estate law;

(b) a "fixture filing" is the filing in the office where a mortgage on the real estate would be filed or recorded of a financing statement covering goods which are or are to become fixtures and conforming to the requirements of subsection (5) of Section 9–102;

(c) a mortgage is a "construction mortgage" to the extent that it secures an obligation incurred for the construction of an improvement on land including the acquisition cost of the land, if the recorded writing so indicates.

(2) A security interest under this Article may be created in goods which are fixtures or may continue in goods which become fixtures, but no security interest exists under this Article in ordinary building materials incorporated into an improvement on land.

(3) This Article does not prevent creation of an encumbrance upon fixtures pursuant to real estate law.

(4) A perfected security interest in fixtures has priority over the conflicting interest of an encumbrancer or owner of the real estate where

(a) the security interest is a purchase money security interest, the interest of the encumbrancer or owner arises before the goods become fixtures, the security interest is perfected by a fixture filing before the goods become fixtures or within ten days thereafter, and the debtor has an interest of record in the real estate or is in possession of the real estate; or

(b) the security interest is perfected by a fixture filing before the interest of the encumbrancer or owner is of record, the security interest has priority over any conflicting interest of a predecessor in title of the encumbrancer or owner, and the debtor has an interest of record in the real estate or is in possession of the real estate; or

(c) the fixtures are readily removable factory or office machines or readily removable replacements of domestic appliances which are consumer goods, and before the goods become fixtures the security interest is perfected by any method permitted by this Article; or

(d) the conflicting interest is a lien on the real estate obtained by legal or equitable proceedings after the security interest was perfected by any method permitted by this Article.

(5) A security interest in fixtures, whether or not perfected, has priority over the conflicting interest of an encumbrancer or owner of the real estate where

(a) the encumbrancer or owner has consented in writing to the security interest or has disclaimed an interest in the goods as fixtures; or

(b) the debtor has a right to remove the goods as against the encumbrancer or owner. If the debtor's right terminates, the priority of the security interest continues for a reasonable time.

(6) Notwithstanding paragraph (a) of subsection (4) but otherwise subject to subsections (4) and (5), a security interest in fixtures is subordinate to a construction mortgage recorded before the goods become fixtures if the goods become fixtures before the completion of the construction. To the extent that it is given to refinance a construction mortgage, a mortgage has this priority to the same extent as the construction mortgage.

(7) In cases not within the preceding subsections, a security interest in fixtures is subordinate to the conflicting interest of an encumbrancer or owner of the related real estate who is not the debtor.

(8) When the secured party has priority over all owners and encumbrancers of the real estate, he may, on default, subject to the provisions of Part 5, remove his collateral from the real estate but he must reimburse any encumbrancer or owner of the real estate who is not the debtor and who has not otherwise agreed for the cost of repair of any physical injury, but not for any diminution in value of the real estate caused by the absence of the goods removed or by any necessity of replacing them. A person entitled to reimbursement may refuse permission to remove until the secured party gives adequate security for the performance of this obligation.

Section 9–314.   Accessions

(1) A security interest in goods which attaches before they are installed in or affixed to other goods takes priority as to the goods installed or affixed (called in this section "accessions") over the claims of all persons to the whole except as stated in subsection (3) and subject to Section 9–315(1).

(2) A security interest which attaches to goods after they become part of a whole is valid against all persons subsequently acquiring interests in the whole except as stated in subsection (3) but is invalid against any person with an interest in the whole at the time the security interest attaches to the goods who has not in writing consented to the security interest or disclaimed an interest in the goods as part of the whole.

(3) The security interests described in subsections (1) and (2) do not take priority over

(a) a subsequent purchaser for value of any interest in the whole; or

(b) a creditor with a lien on the whole subsequently obtained by judicial proceedings; or

(c) a creditor with a prior perfected security interest in the whole to the extent that he makes subsequent advances

if the subsequent purchase is made, the lien by judicial proceedings obtained or the subsequent advance under the prior perfected security interest is made or contracted for without knowledge of the security interest and before it is perfected. A purchaser of the whole at a foreclosure sale other than the holder of a perfected security interest purchasing at his own foreclosure sale is a subsequent purchaser within this section.

(4) When under subsections (1) or (2) and (3) a secured party has an interest in accessions which has priority over the claims of all persons who have interests in the whole, he may on default subject to the provisions of Part 5 remove his collateral from the whole but he must reimburse any encumbrancer or owner of the whole who is not the debtor and who has not otherwise agreed for the cost of repair of any physical injury but not for any diminution in value of the whole caused by the absence of the goods removed or by any necessity for replacing them. A person entitled to reimbursement may refuse permission to remove until the secured party gives adequate security for the performance of this obligation.

Section 9–315.   Priority When Goods Are Commingled or Processed

(1) If a security interest in goods was perfected and subsequently the goods or a part thereof have become part of a product or mass, the security interest continues in the product or mass if

(a) the goods are so manufactured, processed, assembled or commingled that their identity is lost in the product or mass; or

(b) a financing statement covering the original goods also covers the product into which the goods have been manufactured, processed or assembled.

In a case to which paragraph (b) applies, no separate security interest in that part of the original goods which has been manufactured, processed or assembled into the product may be claimed under Section 9–314.

(2) When under subsection (1) more than one security interest attaches to the product or mass, they rank equally according to the ratio that the cost of the goods to which each interest originally attached bears to the cost of the total product or mass.

Section 9–316.   Priority Subject to Subordination

Nothing in this Article prevents subordination by agreement by any person entitled to priority.

Section 9–317.   Secured Party Not Obligated on Contract of Debtor

The mere existence of a security interest or authority given to the debtor to dispose of or use collateral does not impose contract or tort liability upon the secured party for the debtor's acts or omissions.

Section 9–318.   Defenses Against Assignee; Modification of Contract After Notification of Assignment; Term Prohibiting Assignment Ineffective; Identification and Proof of Assignment

(1) Unless an account debtor has made an enforceable agreement not to assert defenses or claims arising out of a sale as provided in Section 9–206 the rights of an assignee are subject to

(a) all the terms of the contract between the account debtor and assignor and any defense or claim arising therefrom; and

(b) any other defense or claim of the account debtor against the assignor which accrues before the account debtor receives notification of the assignment.

(2) So far as the right to payment or a part thereof under an assigned contract has not been fully earned by performance, and notwithstanding notification of the assignment, any modification of or substitution for the contract made in good faith and in accordance with reasonable commercial standards is effective against an assignee unless the account debtor has otherwise agreed but the assignee acquires corresponding rights under the modified or substituted contract. The assignment may provide that such modification or substitution is a breach by the assignor.

(3) The account debtor is authorized to pay the assignor until the account debtor receives notification that the amount due or to become due has been assigned and that payment is to be made to the assignee. A notification which does not reasonably identify the rights assigned is ineffective. If requested by the account debtor, the assignee must seasonably furnish reasonable proof that the assignment has been made and unless he does so the account debtor may pay the assignor.

(4) A term in any contract between an account debtor and an assignor is ineffective if it prohibits assignment of an account or prohibits creation of a security interest in a general intangible for money due or to become due or requires the account debtor's consent to such assignment or security interest.

PART 4

Filing

Section 9–401.   Place of Filing; Erroneous Filing; Removal of Collateral

First Alternative Subsection (1)

(1) The proper place to file in order to perfect a security interest is as follows:

(a) when the collateral is timber to be cut or is minerals of the like (including oil and gas) or accounts subject to subsection (5) of Section 9–103, or when the financing statement is filed as a fixture filing (Section 9–313) and the collateral is goods which are or are to become fixtures, then in the office where a mortgage on the real estate would be filed or recorded;

(b) in all other cases, in the office of the [Secretary of State].

Second Alternative Subsection (1)

(1) The proper place to file in order to perfect a security interest is as follows:

(a) when the collateral is equipment used in farming operations, or farm products, or accounts or general intangibles arising from or relating to the sale of farm products by a farmer, or consumer goods, then in the office of the . . . . in the county of the debtor's residence or if the debtor is not a resident of this state then in the office of the . . . . in the county where the goods are kept, and in addition when the collateral is crops growing or to be grown in the office of the . . . . in the county where the land is located;

(b) when the collateral is timber to be cut or is minerals or the like (including oil and gas) or accounts subject to subsection (5) of Section 9–103, or when the financing statement is filed as a fixture filing (Section 9–313) and the collateral is goods which are or are to become fixtures, then in the office where a mortgage on the real estate would be filed or recorded;

(c)   in all other cases, in the office of the [Secretary of State].

Third Alternative Subsection (1)

(1) The proper place to file in order to perfect a security interest is as follows:

(a)   when the collateral is equipment used in farming operations, or farm products, or accounts or general intangibles arising from or relating to the sale of farm products by a farmer, or consumer goods, then in the office of the . . . . in the county of the debtor's residence or if the debtor is not a resident of this state then in the office of the . . . . in the county where the goods are kept, and in addition when the collateral is crops growing or to be grown in the office of the . . . . in the county where the land is located;

(b)   when the collateral is timber to be cut or is minerals or the like (including oil and gas) or accounts subject to subsection (5) of Section 9–103, or when the financing statement is filed as a fixture filing (Section 9–313) and the collateral is goods which are or are to become fixtures, then in the office where a mortgage on the real estate would be filed or recorded;

(c)   in all other cases, in the office of the [Secretary of State] and in addition, if the debtor has a place of business in only one county of this state, also in the office of . . . . of such county, or, if the debtor has no place of business in this state, but resides in the state, also in the office of . . . . of the county in which he resides.

Note: *One of the three alternatives should be selected as subsection (1).*

(2) A filing which is made in good faith in an improper place or not in all of the places required by this section is nevertheless effective with regard to any collateral as to which the filing complied with the requirements of this Article and is also effective with regard to collateral covered by the financing statement against any person who has knowledge of the contents of such financing statement.

(3) A filing which is made in the proper place in this state continues effective even though the debtor's residence or place of business or the location of the collateral or its use, whichever controlled the original filing, is thereafter changed.

Alternative Subsection (3)

[(3) A filing which is made in the proper county continues effective for four months after a change to another

county of the debtor's residence or place of business or the location of the collateral, whichever controlled the original filing. It becomes ineffective thereafter unless a copy of the financing statement signed by the secured party is filed in the new county within said period. The security interest may also be perfected in the new county after the expiration of the four-month period; in such case perfection dates from the time of perfection in the new county. A change in the use of the collateral does not impair the effectiveness of the original filing.]

(4) The rules in Section 9–103 determine whether filing is necessary in this state.

(5) Notwithstanding the preceding subsections, and subject to subsection (3) of Section 9–302, the proper place to file in order to perfect a security interest in collateral, including fixtures, of a transmitting utility is the office of the [Secretary of State]. This filing constitutes a fixture filing (Section 9–313) as to the collateral described therein which is or is to become fixtures.

(6) For the purposes of this section, the residence of an organization is its place of business if it has one or its chief executive office if it has more than one place of business.

Note: *Subsection (6) should be used only if the state chooses the Second or Third Alternative Subsection (1).*

Section 9–402.   Formal Requisites of Financing Statement; Amendments; Mortgage as Financing Statement

(1) A financing statement is sufficient if it gives the name of the debtor and the secured party, is signed by the debtor, gives an address of the secured party from which information concerning the security interest may be obtained, gives a mailing address of the debtor and contains a statement indicating the types, or describing the items, of collateral. A financing statement may be filed before a security agreement is made or a security interest otherwise attaches. When the financing statement covers crops growing or to be grown, the statement must also contain a description of the real estate concerned. When the financing statement covers timber to be cut or covers minerals or the like (including oil and gas) or accounts subject to subsection (5) of Section 9–103, or when the financing statement is filed as a fixture filing (Section 9–313) and the collateral is goods which are or are to become fixtures, the statement must also comply with subsection (5). A copy of the security agreement is sufficient as a financing statement if it contains the above information and is signed by the debtor. A carbon, photographic

or other reproduction of a security agreement or a financing statement is sufficient as a financing statement if the security agreement so provides or if the original has been filed in this state.

(2) A financing statement which otherwise complies with subsection (1) is sufficient when it is signed by the secured party instead of the debtor if it is filed to perfect a security interest in

(a) collateral already subject to a security interest in another jurisdiction when it is brought into this state, or when the debtor's location is changed to this state. Such a financing statement must state that the collateral was brought into this state or that the debtor's location was changed to this state under such circumstances; or

(b) proceeds under Section 9–306 if the security interest in the original collateral was perfected. Such a financing statement must describe the original collateral; or

(c) collateral as to which the filing has lapsed; or

(d) collateral acquired after a change of name, identity or corporate structure of the debtor (subsection (7)).

(3) A form substantially as follows is sufficient to comply with subsection (1):

Name of debtor (or assignor) . . . .
Address . . . .
Name of secured party (or assignee) . . . .
Address . . . .

1. This financing statement covers the following types (or items) of property:

(Describe) . . . .

2. (If collateral is crops) The above crops are growing or are to be grown on:

(Describe Real Estate) . . . .

3. (If applicable) The above goods are to become fixtures on (Where appropriate substitute either "The above timber is standing on . . ." or "The above minerals or the like (including oil and gas) or accounts will be financed at the wellhead or minehead of the well or mine located on . . .")

(Describe Real Estate) . . . .

and this financing statement is to be filed [for record] in the real estate records. (If the debtor does not have an interest of record) The name of a record owner is . . . .

4. (If products of collateral are claimed) Products of the collateral are also covered.

(use whichever is applicable)

. . . .
Signature of Debtor (or Assignor)

. . . .
Signature of Secured Party (or Assignee)

(4) A financing statement may be amended by filing a writing signed by both the debtor and the secured party. An amendment does not extend the period of effectiveness of a financing statement. If any amendment adds collateral, it is effective as to the added collateral only from the filing date of the amendment. In this Article, unless the context otherwise requires, the term "financing statement" means the original financing statement and any amendments.

(5) A financing statement covering timber to be cut or covering minerals or the like (including oil and gas) or accounts subject to subsection (5) of Section 9–103, or a financing statement filed as a fixture filing (Section 9–313) where the debtor is not a transmitting utility, must show that it covers this type of collateral, must recite that it is to be filed [for record] in the real estate records, and the financing statement must contain a description of the real estate [sufficient if it were contained in a mortgage of the real estate to give constructive notice of the mortgage under the law of this state]. If the debtor does not have an interest of record in the real estate, the financing statement must show the name of a record owner.

(6) A mortgage is effective as a financing statement filed as a fixture filing from the date of its recording if

(a) the goods are described in the mortgage by item or type; and

(b) the goods are or are to become fixtures related to the real estate described in the mortgage; and

(c) the mortgage complies with the requirements for a financing statement in this section other than a recital that it is to be filed in the real estate records; and

(d) the mortgage is duly recorded.

No fee with reference to the financing statement is required other than the regular recording and satisfaction fees with respect to the mortgage.

(7) A financing statement sufficiently shows the name of the debtor if it gives the individual, partnership or corporate name of the debtor, whether or not it adds other trade names or names of partners. Where the debtor so changes his name or in the case of an or-

ganization its name, identity or corporate structure that a filed financing statement becomes seriously misleading, the filing is not effective to perfect a security interest in collateral acquired by the debtor more than four months after the change, unless a new appropriate financing statement is filed before the expiration of that time. A filed financing statement remains effective with respect to collateral transferred by the debtor even though the secured party knows of or consents to the transfer.

(8) A financing statement substantially complying with the requirements of this section is effective even though it contains minor errors which are not seriously misleading.

Section 9–403. What Constitutes Filing; Duration of Filing; Effect of Lapsed Filing; Duties of Filing Officer

(1) Presentation for filing of a financing statement and tender of the filing fee or acceptance of the statement by the filing officer constitutes filing under this Article.

(2) Except as provided in subsection (6) a filed financing statement is effective for a period of five years from the date of filing. The effectiveness of a filed financing statement lapses on the expiration of the five year period unless a continuation statement is filed prior to the lapse. If a security interest perfected by filing exists at the time insolvency proceedings are commenced by or against the debtor, the security interest remains perfected until termination of the insolvency proceedings and thereafter for a period of sixty days or until expiration of the five year period, whichever occurs later. Upon lapse the security interest becomes unperfected, unless it is perfected without filing. If the security interest becomes unperfected upon lapse, it is deemed to have been unperfected as against a person who became a purchaser or lien creditor before lapse.

(3) A continuation statement may be filed by the secured party within six months prior to the expiration of the five year period specified in subsection (2). Any such continuation statement must be signed by the secured party, identify the original statement by file number and state that the original statement is still effective. A continuation statement signed by a person other than the secured party of record must be accompanied by a separate written statement of assignment signed by the secured party of record and complying with subsection (2) of Section 9–405, including payment of the required fee. Upon timely filing of the continuation statement, the effectiveness of the original

statement is continued for five years after the last date to which the filing was effective whereupon it lapses in the same manner as provided in subsection (2) unless another continuation statement is filed prior to such lapse. Succeeding continuation statements may be filed in the same manner to continue the effectiveness of the original statement. Unless a statute on disposition of public records provides otherwise, the filing officer may remove a lapsed statement from the files and destroy it immediately if he has retained a microfilm or other photographic record, or in other cases after one year after the lapse. The filing officer shall so arrange matters by physical annexation of financing statements to continuation statements or other related filings, or by other means, that if he physically destroys the financing statements of a period more than five years past, those which have been continued by a continuation statement or which are still effective under subsection (6) shall be retained.

(4) Except as provided in subsection (7) a filing officer shall mark each statement with a file number and with the date and hour of filing and shall hold the statement or a microfilm or other photographic copy thereof for public inspection. In addition the filing officer shall index the statement according to the name of the debtor and shall note in the index the file number and the address of the debtor given in the statement.

(5) The uniform fee for filing and indexing and for stamping a copy furnished by the secured party to show the date and place of filing for an original financing statement or for a continuation statement shall be $ . . . . if the statement is in the standard form prescribed by the [Secretary of State] and otherwise shall be $ . . . ., plus in each case, if the financing statement is subject to subsection (5) of Section 9–402, $ . . . . The uniform fee for each name more than one required to be indexed shall be $ . . . . The secured party may at his option show a trade name for any person and an extra uniform indexing fee of $ . . . . shall be paid with respect thereto.

(6) If the debtor is a transmitting utility (subsection (5) of Section 9–401) and a filed financing statement so states, it is effective until a termination statement is filed. A real estate mortgage which is effective as a fixture filing under subsection (6) of Section 9–402 remains effective as a fixture filing until the mortgage is released or satisfied of record or its effectiveness otherwise terminates as to the real estate.

(7) When a financing statement covers timber to be cut or covers minerals or the like (including oil and gas) or accounts subject to subsection (5) of Section

9–103, or is filed as a fixture filing, [it shall be filed for record and] the filing officer shall index it under the names of the debtor and any owner of record shown on the financing statement in the same fashion as if they were the mortgagors in a mortgage of the real estate described, and, to the extent that the law of this state provides for indexing of mortgages under the name of the mortgagee, under the name of the secured party as if he were the mortgagee thereunder, or where indexing is by description in the same fashion as if the financing statement were a mortgage of the real estate described.

Note: *In states in which writings will not appear in the real estate records and indices unless actually recorded, the bracketed language in subsection (7) should be used.*

Section 9–404.   Termination Statement

(1) If a financing statement covering consumer goods is filed on or after . . . . , then within one month or within ten days following written demand by the debtor after there is no outstanding secured obligation and no commitment to make advances, incur obligations or otherwise give value, the secured party must file with each filing officer with whom the financing statement was filed, a termination statement to the effect that he no longer claims a security interest under the financing statement, which shall be identified by file number. In other cases whenever there is no outstanding secured obligation and no commitment to make advances, incur obligations or otherwise give value, the secured party must on written demand by the debtor send the debtor, for each filing officer with whom the financing statement was filed, a termination statement to the effect that he no longer claims a security interest under the financing statement, which shall be identified by file number. A termination statement signed by a person other than the secured party of record must be accompanied by a separate written statement of assignment signed by the secured party of record and complying with subsection (2) of Section 9–405, including payment of the required fee. If the affected secured party fails to file such a termination statement as required by this subsection, or to send such a termination statement within ten days after proper demand therefor, he shall be liable to the debtor for one hundred dollars, and in addition for any loss caused to the debtor by such failure.

(2) On presentation to the filing officer of such a termination statement he must note it in the index. If he has received the termination statement in duplicate, he shall return one copy of the termination statement to the secured party stamped to show the time of receipt thereof. If the filing officer has a microfilm or other photographic record of the financing statement, and of any related continuation statement, statement of assignment and statement of release, he may remove the originals from the files at any time after receipt of the termination statement, or if he has no such record, he may remove them from the files at any time after one year after receipt of the termination statement.

(3) If the termination statement is in the standard form prescribed by the [Secretary of State], the uniform fee for filing and indexing the termination statement shall be $ . . . . and otherwise shall be $ . . . . , plus in each case an additional fee of $ . . . . for each name more than one against which the termination statement is required to be indexed.

Note: *The date to be inserted should be the effective date of the revised Article 9.*

Section 9–405.   Assignment of Security Interest; Duties of Filing Officer; Fees

(1) A financing statement may disclose an assignment of a security interest in the collateral described in the financing statement by indication in the financing statement of the name and address of the assignee or by an assignment itself of a copy thereof on the face or back of the statement. On presentation to the filing officer of such a financing statement the filing officer shall mark the same as provided in Section 9–403(4). The uniform fee for filing, indexing and furnishing filing data for a financing statement so indicating an assignment shall be $ . . . . if the statement is in the standard form prescribed by the [Secretary of State] and otherwise shall be $ . . . . , plus in each case an additional fee of $ . . . . for each name more than one against which the financing statement is required to be indexed.

(2) A secured party may assign of record all or part of his rights under a financing statement by the filing in the place where the original financing statement was filed of a separate written statement of assignment signed by the secured party of record and setting forth the name of the secured party of record and the debtor, the file number and the date of filing of the financing statement and the name and address of the assignee and containing a description of the collateral assigned. A copy of the assignment is sufficient as a separate statement if it complies with the preceding sentence. On presentation to the filing officer of such a separate statement, the filing officer shall mark such separate statement with the date and hour of the filing. He

shall note the assignment on the index of the financing statement, or in the case of a fixture filing, or a filing covering timber to be cut, or covering minerals or the like (including oil and gas) or accounts subject to subsection (5) of Section 9–103, he shall index the assignment under the name of the assignor as grantor and, to the extent that the law of this state provides for indexing the assignment of a mortgage under the name of the assignee, he shall index the assignment of the financing statement under the name of the assignee. The uniform fee for filing, indexing and furnishing filing data about such a separate statement of assignment shall be $ . . . . if the statement is in the standard form prescribed by the [Secretary of State] and otherwise shall be $ . . . . , plus in each case an additional fee of $ . . . . for each name more than one against which the statement of assignment is required to be indexed. Notwithstanding the provisions of this subsection, an assignment of record of a security interest in a fixture contained in a mortgage effective as a fixture filing (subsection (6) of Section 9–402) may be made only by an assignment of the mortgage in the manner provided by the law of the state other than this Act.

(3) After the disclosure or filing of an assignment under this section, the assignee is the secured party of record.

Section 9–406. Release of Collateral; Duties of Filing Officer; Fees

A secured party of record may by his signed statement release all or a part of any collateral described in a filed financing statement. The statement of release is sufficient if it contains a description of the collateral being released, the name and address of the debtor, the name and address of the secured party, and the file number of the financing statement. A statement of release signed by a person other than the secured party of record must be accompanied by a separate written statement of assignment signed by the secured party of record and complying with subsection (2) of Section 9–405, including payment of the required fee. Upon presentation of such a statement of release to the filing officer he shall mark the statement with the hour and date of filing and shall note the same upon the margin of the index of the filing of the financing statement. The uniform fee for filing and noting such a statement of release shall be $ . . . . if the statement is in the standard form prescribed by the [Secretary of State] and otherwise shall be $ . . . . , plus in each case an additional fee of $ . . . . for each name more than one against which the statement of release is required to be indexed.

[Section 9–407. Information from Filing Officer]

[(1) If the person filing any financing statement, termination statement, statement of assignment, or statement of release, furnishes the filing officer a copy thereof, the filing officer shall upon request note upon the copy the file number and date and hour of the filing of the original and deliver or send the copy to such person.]

[(2) Upon request of any person, the filing officer shall issue his certificate showing whether there is on file on the date and hour stated therein, any presently effective financing statement naming a particular debtor and any statement of assignment thereof and if there is, giving the date and hour of filing of each such statement and the names and addresses of each secured party therein. The uniform fee for such a certificate shall be $ . . . . if the request for the certificate is in the standard form prescribed by the [Secretary of State] and otherwise shall be $ . . . . Upon request the filing officer shall furnish a copy of any filed financing statement or statement of assignment for a uniform fee of $ . . . . per page.]

Note: *This section is proposed as an optional provision to require filing officers to furnish certificates. Local law and practices should be consulted with regard to the advisability of adoption.*

Section 9–408. Financing Statements Covering Consigned or Leased Goods

A consignor or lessor of goods may file a financing statement using the terms "consignor," "consignee," "lessor," "lessee" or the like instead of the terms specified in Section 9–402. The provisions of this Part shall apply as appropriate to such a financing statement but its filing shall not of itself be a factor in determining whether or not the consignment or lease is intended as security (Section 1–201(37)). However, if it is determined for other reasons that the consignment or lease is so intended, a security interest of the consignor or lessor which attaches to the consigned or leased goods is perfected by such filing. Added in 1972.

PART 5

Default

Section 9–501. Default; Procedure When Security Agreement Covers Both Real and Personal Property

(1) When a debtor is in default under a security agreement, a secured party has the rights and remedies

provided in this Part and except as limited by subsection (3) those provided in the security agreement. He may reduce his claim to judgment, foreclose or otherwise enforce the security interest by any available judicial procedure. If the collateral is documents the secured party may proceed either as to the documents or as to the goods covered thereby. A secured party in possession has the rights, remedies and duties provided in Section 9–207. The rights and remedies referred to in this subsection are cumulative.

(2) After default, the debtor has the rights and remedies provided in this Part, those provided in the security agreement and those provided in Section 9–207.

(3) To the extent that they give rights to the debtor and impose duties on the secured party, the rules stated in the subsections referred to below may not be waived or varied except as provided with respect to compulsory disposition of collateral (subsection (3) of Section 9–504 and Section 9–505) and with respect to redemption of collateral (Section 9–506) but the parties may by agreement determine the standards by which the fulfillment of these rights and duties is to be measured if such standards are not manifestly unreasonable:

> (a)   subsection (2) of Section 9–502 and subsection (2) of Section 9–504 insofar as they require accounting for surplus proceeds of collateral;

> (b)   subsection (3) of Section 9–504 and subsection (1) of Section 9–505 which deal with disposition of collateral;

> (c)   subsection (2) of Section 9–505 which deals with acceptance of collateral as discharge of obligation;

> (d)   Section 9–506 which deals with redemption of collateral; and

> (e)   subsection (1) of Section 9–507 which deals with the secured party's liability for failure to comply with this Part.

(4) If the security agreement covers both real and personal property, the secured party may proceed under this Part as to the personal property or he may proceed as to both the real and the personal property in accordance with his rights and remedies in respect of the real property in which case the provisions of this Part do not apply.

(5) When a secured party has reduced his claim to judgment the lien of any levy which may be made upon his collateral by virtue of any execution based upon the judgment shall relate back to the date of the perfection of the security interest in such collateral. A judicial sale, pursuant to such execution, is a foreclosure

of the security interest by judicial procedure within the meaning of this section, and the secured party may purchase at the sale and thereafter hold the collateral free of any other requirements of this Article.

Section 9–502.   Collection Rights of Secured Party

(1) When so agreed and in any event on default the secured party is entitled to notify an account debtor or the obligor on an instrument to make payment to him whether or not the assignor was therefore making collections on the collateral, and also to take control of any proceeds to which he is entitled under Section 9–306.

(2) A secured party who by agreement is entitled to charge back uncollected collateral or otherwise to full or limited recourse against the debtor and who undertakes to collect from the account debtors or obligors must proceed in a commercially reasonable manner and may deduct his reasonable expenses of realization from the collections. If the security agreement secures an indebtedness, the secured party must account to the debtor for any surplus, and unless otherwise agreed, the debtor is liable for any deficiency. But, if the underlying transaction was a sale of accounts or chattel paper, the debtor is entitled to any surplus or is liable for any deficiency only if the security agreement so provides.

Section 9–503.   Secured Party's Right to Take Possession After Default

Unless otherwise agreed a secured party has on default the right to take possession of the collateral. In taking possession a secured party may proceed without judicial process if this can be done without breach of the peace or may proceed by action. If the security agreement so provides the secured party may require the debtor to assemble the collateral and make it available to the secured party at a place to be designated by the secured party which is reasonably convenient to both parties. Without removal a secured party may render equipment unusable, and may dispose of collateral on the debtor's premises under Section 9–504.

Section 9–504.   Secured Party's Right to Dispose of Collateral After Default; Effect of Disposition

(1) A secured party after default may sell, lease or otherwise dispose of any or all of the collateral in its then condition or following any commercially reasonable preparation or processing. Any sale of goods is subject to the Article on Sales (Article 2). The proceeds of disposition shall be applied in the order following to

(a) the reasonable expenses of retaking, holding, preparing for sale or lease, selling, leasing and the like and, to the extent provided for in the agreement and not prohibited by law, the reasonable attorneys' fees and legal expenses incurred by the secured party;

(b) the satisfaction indebtedness secured by the security interest under which the disposition is made;

(c) the satisfaction of indebtedness secured by any subordinate security interest in the collateral if written notification of demand therefor is received before distribution of the proceeds is completed. If requested by the secured party, the holder of a subordinate security interest must seasonably furnish reasonable proof of his interest, and unless he does so, the secured party need not comply with his demand.

(2) If the security interest secures an indebtedness, the secured party must account to the debtor for any surplus, and, unless otherwise agreed, the debtor is liable for any deficiency. But if the underlying transaction was a sale of accounts or chattel paper, the debtor is entitled to any surplus or is liable for any deficiency only if the security agreement so provides.

(3) Disposition of the collateral may be by public or private proceedings and may be made by way of one or more contracts. Sale or other disposition may be as a unit or in parcels and at any time and place and on any terms but every aspect of the disposition including the method, manner, time, place and terms must be commercially reasonable. Unless collateral is perishable or threatens to decline speedily in value or is of a type customarily sold on a recognized market, reasonable notification of the time and place of any public sale or reasonable notification of the time after which any private sale or other intended disposition is to be made shall be sent by the secured party to the debtor, if he has not signed after default a statement renouncing or modifying his right to notification of sale. In the case of consumer goods no other notification need be sent. In other cases notification shall be sent to any other secured party from whom the secured party has received (before sending his notification to the debtor or before the debtor's renunciation of his rights) written notice of a claim of an interest in the collateral. The secured party may buy at any public sale and if the collateral is of a type customarily sold in a recognized market or is of a type which is the subject of widely distributed standard price quotations he may buy at private sale.

(4) When collateral is disposed of by a secured party after default, the disposition transfers to a purchaser for value all of the debtor's rights therein, discharges the security interest under which it is made and any security interest or lien subordinate thereto. The purchaser takes free of all such rights and interests even though the secured party fails to comply with the requirements of this Part or of any judicial proceedings

(a) in the case of a public sale, if the purchaser has no knowledge of any defects in the sale and if he does not buy in collusion with the secured party, other bidders or the person conducting the sale; or

(b) in any other case, if the purchaser acts in good faith.

(5) A person who is liable to a secured party under a guaranty, indorsement, repurchase agreement or the like and who receives a transfer of collateral from the secured party or is subrogated to his rights has thereafter the rights and duties of the secured party. Such a transfer of collateral is not a sale or disposition of the collateral under this Article.

Section 9–505. Compulsory Disposition of Collateral; Acceptance of the Collateral as Discharge of Obligation

(1) If the debtor has paid sixty per cent of the cash price in the case of a purchase money security interest in consumer goods or sixty per cent of the loan in the case of another security interest in consumer goods, and has not signed after default a statement renouncing or modifying his rights under this Part a secured party who has taken possession of collateral must dispose of it under Section 9–504 and if he fails to do so within ninety days after he takes possession the debtor at his option may recover in conversion or under Section 9–507(1) on secured party's liability.

(2) In any other case involving consumer goods or any other collateral a secured party in possession may, after default, propose to retain the collateral in satisfaction of the obligation. Written notice of such proposal shall be sent to the debtor if he has not signed after default a statement renouncing or modifying his rights under this subsection. In the case of consumer goods no other notice need be given. In other cases notice shall be sent to any other secured party from whom the secured party has received (before sending his notice to the debtor or before the debtor's renunciation of his rights) written notice of a claim of an interest in the collateral. If the secured party receives

objection in writing from a person entitled to receive notification within twenty-one days after the notice was sent, the secured party must dispose of the collateral under Section 9–504. In the absence of such written objection the secured party may retain the collateral in satisfaction of the debtor's obligation.

Section 9–506.   Debtor's Right to Redeem Collateral

At any time before the secured party has disposed of collateral or entered into a contract for its disposition under Section 9–504 or before the obligation has been discharged under Section 9–505(2) the debtor or any other secured party may unless otherwise agreed in writing after default redeem the collateral by tendering fulfillment of all obligations secured by the collateral as well as the expenses reasonably incurred by the secured party in retaking, holding and preparing the collateral for disposition, in arranging for the sale, and to the extent provided in the agreement and not prohibited by law, his reasonable attorneys' fees and legal expenses.

Section 9–507.   Secured Party's Liability for Failure to Comply with This Part

(1) If it is established that the secured party is not proceeding in accordance with the provisions of this Part disposition may be ordered or restrained on appropriate terms and conditions. If the disposition has occurred the debtor or any person entitled to notification or whose security interest has been made known to the secured party prior to the disposition has a right to recover from the secured party any loss caused by a failure to comply with the provisions of this Part. If the collateral is consumer goods, the debtor has a right to recover in any event an amount not less than the credit service charge plus ten per cent of the principal amount of the debt or the time price differential plus ten per cent of the cash price.

(2) The fact that a better price could have been obtained by a sale at a different time or in a different method from that selected by the secured party is not of itself sufficient to establish that the sale was not made in a commercially reasonable manner. If the secured party either sells the collateral in the usual manner in any recognized market therefor or if he sells at the price current in such market at the time of his sale or if he has otherwise sold in conformity with reasonable commercial practices among dealers the type of property sold he has sold in a commercially reasonable manner. The principles stated in the two preceding sentences with respect to sales also apply as may be appropriate to other types of disposition. A disposition which has been approved in any judicial proceeding or by any bona fide creditors' committee or representative of creditors shall conclusively be deemed to be commercially reasonable, but this sentence does not indicate that any such approval must be obtained in any case nor does it indicate that any disposition not so approved is not commercially reasonable.

[Articles 10 and 11 are not included.]

APPENDIX B

The Constitution of the United States of America

We the people of the United States, in Order to form a more perfect Union, establish Justice, insure domestic Tranquility, provide for the common defense, promote the general Welfare, and secure the Blessings of Liberty to ourselves and our posterity, do ordain and establish this Constitution for the United States of America.

ARTICLE I

Section 1. All legislative Powers herein granted shall be vested in a Congress of the United States, which shall consist of a Senate and House of Representatives.

Section 2. The House of Representatives shall be composed of Members chosen every second Year by the People of the several States, and the Electors in each State shall have the Qualifications requisite for Electors of the most numerous Branch of the State Legislature.

No person shall be a Representative who shall not have attained to the Age of twenty five Years, and been seven Years a Citizen of the United States, and who shall not, when elected, be an Inhabitant of that State in which he shall be chosen.

Representatives and direct Taxes shall be apportioned among the several States which may be included within this Union, according to their respective Numbers, *which shall be determined by adding to the whole Number of free Persons, including those bound to Service for a Term of Years, and excluding Indians not taxed, three fifths of all other Persons.*[1] The actual Enumeration shall be made within three Years after the first Meeting of the Congress of the United States, and within every subsequent Term of ten Years, in such Manner as they shall by Law direct. The Number of Representatives shall not exceed one for every thirty Thousand, but each State shall have at Least one Representative; and until such enumeration shall be made, the State of New Hampshire shall be entitled to chuse three, Massachusetts eight, Rhode-Island and Providence Plantations one, Connecticut five, New-York six, New Jersey four, Pennsylvania eight, Delaware one, Maryland six, Virginia ten, North Carolina five, South Carolina five, and Georgia three.

When vacancies happen in the Representation from any State, the Executive Authority thereof shall issue Writs of Election to fill such Vacancies.

The House of Representatives shall chuse their Speaker and other Officers; and shall have the sole Power of Impeachment.

Section 3. The Senate of the United States shall be composed of two Senators from each State *chosen by the Legislature thereof,*[2] for six Years; and each Senator shall have one Vote.

Immediately after they shall be assembled in Consequence of the first Election, they shall be divided as

[1] See Amendment XIV. Throughout, italics indicate passages altered by amendments.
[2] See Amendment XVII.

A-131

equally as may be into three Classes. The Seats of the Senators of the first Class shall be vacated at the Expiration of the second Year, of the second Class at the Expiration of the fourth Year, and of the third Class at the Expiration of the sixth Year, so that one third may be chosen every second Year *and if Vacancies happen by Resignation, or otherwise, during the Recess of the Legislature of any State, the Executive thereof may make temporary Appointments until the next Meeting of the Legislature, which shall then fill such Vacancies.*[3]

No Person shall be a Senator who shall not have attained to the Age of thirty Years, and been nine Years a Citizen of the United States, and who shall not, when elected, be an Inhabitant of that State for which he shall be chosen.

The Vice President of the United States shall be President of the Senate, but shall have no Vote, unless they be equally divided.

The Senate shall chuse their other Officers, and also a President pro tempore, in the Absence of the Vice President, or when he shall exercise the Office of President of the United States.

The Senate shall have the sole Power to try all Impeachments. When sitting for that Purpose, they shall be on Oath or Affirmation. When the President of the United States is tried, the Chief Justice shall preside: And no Person shall be convicted without the Concurrence of two thirds of the Members present.

Judgment in Cases of Impeachment shall not extend further than to removal from Office, and disqualification to hold and enjoy any Office of honor, Trust or Profit under the United States; but the Party convicted shall nevertheless be liable and subject to Indictment, Trial, Judgment and Punishment, according to Law.

Section 4.   The Times, Places and Manner of holding Elections for Senators and Represenatives, shall be prescribed in each State by the Legislature thereof; but the Congress may at any time by Law make or alter such Regulations, except as to the Places of chusing Senators.

The Congress shall assemble at least once in every Year, and such Meeting shall be on the first Monday in December, unless they shall by Law appoint a different Day.[4]

Section 5.   Each House shall be the Judge of the Elections, Returns and Qualifications of its own Members, and a Majority of each shall constitute a Quorum to do Business; but a smaller Number may adjourn from day to day, and may be authorized to compel the Attendance of absent Members, in such Manner, and under such Penalties as each House may provide.

[3] Ibid.
[4] See Amendment XX.

Each House may determine the Rules of its Proceedings, punish its Members for disorderly Behaviour, and, with the Concurrence of two thirds, expel a Member.

Each House shall keep a Journal of its Proceedings, and from time to time publish the same, excepting such Parts as may in their Judgment require Secrecy; and the Yeas and Nays of the Membership of either House on any question shall, at the desire of one fifth of those present, be entered on the Journal.

Neither House, during the Session of Congress, shall, without the Consent of the other, *adjourn* for more than three days, nor to any other Place than that in which the two Houses shall be sitting.

Section 6.   The Senators and Representatives shall receive a Compensation for their Services, to be ascertained by Law, and paid out of the Treasury of the United States. They shall in all Cases, except Treason, Felony and Breach of the Peace, be privileged from Arrest during their Attendance at the Session of their respective Houses, and in going to and returning from the same; and for any Speech or Debate in either House, they shall not be questioned in any other Place.

No Senator or Representative shall, during the Time for which he was elected, be appointed to any civil Office under the Authority of the United States, which shall have been created, on the Emoluments whereof shall have been encreased during such time; and no Person holding any Office under the United States, shall be a Member of either House during his Continuance in Office.

Section 7.   All Bills for raising Revenue shall originate in the House of Representatives; but the Senate may propose or concur with Amendments as on other Bills.

Every Bill which shall have passed the House of Representatives and the Senate, shall, before it become a Law, be presented to the President of the United States; if he approve he shall sign it, but if not he shall return it, with his Objections to that House in which it shall have originated, who shall enter the Objections at large on their Journal, and proceed to reconsider it. If after such Reconsideration two thirds of that House shall agree to pass the Bill, it shall be sent, together with the Objections, to the other House, by which it shall likewise be reconsidered, and if approved by two thirds of that House, it shall become a Law. But in all such Cases the Votes of both Houses shall be determined by Yeas and Nays, and the Names of the Persons voting for and against the Bill shall be entered on the Journal of each House respectively. If any Bill shall not be returned by the President within ten Days (Sundays excepted) after it shall have been presented to him, the Same shall be a Law, in like Manner as if he had signed it, unless the Congress by their Adjournment prevent its Return, in which Case it shall not be a Law.

Every Order, Resolution, or Vote to which the Concurrence of the Senate and House of Representatives may be necessary (except on a question of Adjournment) shall be presented to the President of the United States; and before the Same shall take Effect, shall be approved by him, or being disapproved by him, shall be repassed by two thirds of the Senate and House of Representatives, according to the Rules and Limitations prescribed in the Case of a Bill.

Section 8.   The Congress shall have Power To lay and collect Taxes, Duties, Imposts and Excises, to pay the Debts and provide for the common Defence and general Welfare of the United States; but all Duties, Imposts and Excises shall be uniform throughout the United States;

To borrow Money on the credit of the United States;

To regulate Commerce with foreign Nations, and among the several States, and with the Indian Tribes;

To establish a uniform Rule of Naturalization, and uniform Laws on the subject of Bankruptcies throughout the United States;

To coin Money, regulate the Value thereof, and of foreign Coin, and fix the Standard of Weights and Measures;

To provide for the Punishment of counterfeiting the Securities and current Coin of the United States;

To establish Post Offices and post Roads;

To promote the Progress of Science and useful Arts, by securing for limited Times to Authors and Inventors the exclusive Right to their respective Writings and Discoveries;

To constitute Tribunals inferior to the supreme Court;

To define and punish Piracies and Felonies committed on the high Seas, and Offences against the Law of Nations;

To declare War, grant Letters of Marque and Reprisal, and make Rules concerning Captures on Land and Water;

To raise and support Armies, but no Appropriation of Money to that Use shall be for a longer Term than two Years;

To provide and maintain a Navy;

To make Rules for the Government and Regulation of the land and naval Forces;

To provide for calling forth the Militia to execute the Laws of the Union, suppress Insurrections and repel Invasions;

To provide for organizing, arming, and disciplining, the Militia, and for governing such Part of them as may be employed in the Service of the United States, reserving to the States respectively, the Appointment of the Officers, and the Authority of training the Militia according to the discipline prescribed by Congress;

To exercise exclusive Legislation in all Cases whatsoever, over such District (not exceeding ten Miles square) as may, by Cession of particular States, and the Acceptance of Congress, become the Seat of the Government of the United States, and to exercise like Authority over all Places purchased by the Consent of the Legislature of the State in which the Same shall be, for the Erection of Forts, Magazines, Arsenals, dock-Yards, and other needful buildings; — And

To make all Laws which shall be necessary and proper for carrying into Execution the foregoing Powers, and all other Powers vested by this Constitution in the Government of the United States, or in any Department or Officer thereof.

Section 9.   The Migration or Importation of such Persons as any of the States now existing shall think proper to admit, shall not be prohibited by the Congress prior to the Year one thousand eight hundred and eight, but a Tax or duty may be imposed on such Importation, not exceeding ten dollars for each Person.

The Privilege of the Writ of Habeas Corpus shall not be suspended, unless when in Cases of Rebellion or Invasion the public Safety may require it.

No Bill of Attainder or ex post facto Law shall be passed.

No Capitation, or other direct, Tax shall be laid, unless in Proportion to the Census or Enumeration herein before directed to be taken.[5]

No Tax or Duty shall be laid on Articles exported from any State.

No Preference shall be given by any Regulation of Commerce or Revenue to the Ports of one State over those of another; nor shall Vessels bound to, or from, one State, be obliged to enter, clear, or pay Duties in another.

No Money shall be drawn from the Treasury, but in Consequence of Appropriations made by Law; and a regular Statement and Account of the Receipts and Expenditures of all public Money shall be published from time to time.

No Title of Nobility shall be granted by the United States; And no Person holding any Office of Profit or Trust under them, shall, without the Consent of the Congress, accept of any present, Emolument, Office, or Title, of any kind whatever, from any King, Prince, or foreign State.

[5]See Amendment XVI.

Section 10. No State shall enter into any Treaty, Alliance, or Confederation; grant Letters of Marque and Reprisal; coin Money; emit Bills of Credit; make any Thing but gold and silver Coin a Tender in Payment of Debts; pass any Bill of Attainder, ex post facto Law, or Law impairing the Obligation of Contracts, or grant any Title of Nobility.

No State shall, without the Consent of the Congress, lay any Imposts or Duties on Imports or Exports, except what may be absolutely necessary for executing its inspection Laws; and the net Produce of all Duties and Imposts, laid by any State on Imports or Exports, shall be for the Use of the Treasury of the United States; and all such Laws shall be subject to the Revision and Controul of the Congress.

No State shall, without the Consent of Congress, lay any Duty of Tonnage, keep Troops, or Ships of War in time of Peace, enter into any Agreement or Compact with another State, or with a foreign Power, or engage in War, unless actually invaded, or in such imminent Danger as will not admit of delay.

ARTICLE II

Section 1. The executive Power shall be vested in a President of the United States of America. He shall hold his Office during the Term of four Years, and, together with the Vice President, chosen for the Same Term, be elected, as follows.

Each State shall appoint, in such Manner as the Legislature thereof may direct, a Number of Electors, equal to the whole Number of Senators and Representatives to which the State may be entitled in the Congress; but no Senator or Representative, or Person holding an Office of Trust or Profit under the United States, shall be appointed an Elector.

The Electors shall meet in their respective States, and vote by Ballot for two Persons of whom one at least shall not be an Inhabitant of the same State with themselves. And they shall make a List of all the Persons voted for, and of the Number of Votes for each; which List they shall sign and certify, and transmit sealed to the Seat of the Government of the United States, directed to the President of the Senate. The President of the Senate shall, in the Presence of the Senate and House of Representatives, open all the Certificates, and the Votes shall then be counted. The Person having the greatest Number of Votes shall be the President, if such Number be a Majority of the whole Number of Electors appointed; and if there be more than one who have such Majority, and have an equal Number of Votes, then the House of Representatives shall immediately chuse by Ballot one of them for President; and if no Person have a Majority, then from the five highest on the List the said House shall in like Manner chuse the President. But in chusing the President, the Votes shall be taken by States, the Representation from each State having one Vote; a quorum for this Purpose shall consist of a Member or Members from two thirds of the States, and a Majority of all the States shall be necessary to a Choice. In every Case, after the Choice of the President, the Person having the greatest Number of Votes of the Electors shall be the Vice President. But if there should remain two or more who have equal Votes, the Senate shall chuse from them by Ballot the Vice President. [6]

The Congress may determine the Time of chusing the Electors, and the Day on which they shall give their Votes; which Day shall be the same throughout the United States.

No Person except a natural born Citizen, or a Citizen of the United States, at the time of the Adoption of this Constitution, shall be eligible to the Office of President; neither shall any Person be eligible to that Office who shall not have attained the Age of thirty five Years, and been fourteen Years a Resident within the United States.

In Case of the Removal of the President from Office, or of his Death, Resignation, or Inability to discharge the Powers and Duties of the said Office, the same shall devolve on the Vice President, and the Congress may by Law provide for the Case of Removal, Death, Resignation or Inability, both of the President and Vice President, declaring what Officer shall then act as President, and such Officer shall act accordingly, until the Disability be removed, or a President shall be elected. [7]

The President shall, at stated Times, receive for his Services, a Compensation, which shall neither be encreased nor diminished during the Period for which he shall have been elected, and he shall not receive within that Period any other Emolument from the United States, or any of them.

Before he enter on the Execution of his Office, he shall take the following Oath or Affirmation: — ''I do solemnly swear (or affirm) that I will faithfully execute the Office of President of the United States, and will to the best of my Ability, preserve, protect and defend the Constitution of the United States.''

Section 2. The President shall be Commander in Chief of the Army and Navy of the United States, and of the Militia of the several States, when called into the actual Service of the United States; he may require the Opinion, in writing, of the principal Officer in each of the executive Departments, upon any Subject relating to the Duties of their respective Offices, and

---

[6] See Amendment XII.
[7] See Amendment XXV.

he shall have Power to grant Reprieves and Pardons for Offences against the United States, except in Cases of Impeachment.

He shall have Power, by and with the Advice and Consent of the Senate, to make Treaties, provided two thirds of the Senators present concur; and he shall nominate, and by and with the Advice and Consent of the Senate, shall appoint Ambassadors, other public Ministers and Consuls, Judges of the supreme Court, and all other Officers of the United States, whose Appointments are not herein otherwise provided for, and which shall be established by Law; but the Congress may by Law vest the Appointment of such inferior Officers, as they think proper, in the President alone, in the Courts of Law, or in the Heads of Departments.

The President shall have Power to fill up all Vacancies that may happen during the Recess of the Senate, by granting Commissions which shall expire at the End of their next Session.

Section 3. He shall from time to time give to the Congress Information of the State of the Union, and recommend to their Consideration such Measures as he shall judge necessary and expedient; he may, on extraordinary Occasions, convene both Houses, or either of them, and in Case of Disagreement between them, with Respect to the Time of Adjournment, he may adjourn them to such Time as he shall think proper; he shall receive Ambassadors and other public Ministers; he shall take Care that the Laws be faithfully executed, and shall Commission all the Officers of the United States.

Section 4. The President, Vice President and all civil Officers of the United States, shall be removed from Office on Impeachment for, and Conviction of, Treason, Bribery, or other high Crimes and Misdemeanors.

ARTICLE III

Section 1. The judicial Power of the United States, shall be vested in one supreme Court, and in such inferior Courts as the Congress may from time to time ordain and establish. The Judges, both of the supreme and inferior Courts, shall hold their Offices during good Behaviour, and shall, at stated Times, receive for their Services, a Compensation, which shall not be diminished during their Continuance in Office.

Section 2. The judicial Power shall extend to all Cases, in Law and Equity, arising under this Constitution, the Laws of the United States, and Treaties

made, or which shall be made, under their Authority; — to all Cases affecting Ambassadors, other public Ministers and Consuls; — to all Cases of admiralty and maritime Jurisdiction; — to Controversies to which the United States shall be a Party; — to Controversies between two or more States, — *between a State and Citizens of another State,* [8] — between Citizens of different States, — between Citizens of the same State claiming Lands under Grants of different States, *and between a state, or the Citizens thereof, and foreign States, Citizens or Subjects.* [9]

In all Cases affecting Ambassadors, other public Ministers and Consuls, and those in which a State shall be Party, the supreme Court shall have original Jurisdiction. In all other Cases before mentioned, the supreme Court shall have appellate Jurisdiction, both as to Law and Fact, with such Exceptions, and under such Regulations as the Congress shall make.

The Trial of all Crimes, except in Cases of Impeachment, shall be by Jury; and such Trial shall be held in the State where the said Crimes shall have been committed; but when not committed within any State, the Trial shall be at such Place or Places as the Congress may by Law have directed.

Section 3. Treason against the United States, shall consist only in levying War against them, or in adhering to their Enemies, giving them Aid and Comfort. No Person shall be convicted of Treason unless on the Testimony of two Witnesses to the same overt Act, or on Confession in open Court.

The Congress shall have Power to declare the Punishment of Treason, but no Attainder of Treason shall work Corruption of Blood, or Forfeiture except during the Life of the Person attainted.

ARTICLE IV

Section 1. Full Faith and Credit shall be given in each State to the public Acts, Records, and judicial Proceedings of every other State. And the Congress may by general Laws prescribe the Manner in which such Acts, Records and Proceedings shall be proved, and the Effect thereof.

Section 2. The Citizens of each State shall be entitled to all Privileges and Immunities of Citizens in the several States.

A Person charged in any State with Treason, Felony, or other Crime, who shall flee from Justice, and be found in another State, shall on Demand of the ex-

[8] See Amendment XI.
[9] Ibid.

ecutive Authority of the State from which he fled, be delivered up, to be removed to the State having Jurisdiction of the Crime.

No Person held to Service or Labour in one State under the Laws thereof, escaping into another, shall, in Consequence of any Law or Regulation therein, be discharged from such Service or Labour, but shall be delivered up on Claim of the Party to whom such Service or Labour may be due.[10]

Section 3. New States may be admitted by the Congress into this Union; but no new State shall be formed or erected within the Jurisdiction of any other State; nor any State be formed by the Junction of two or more States, or Parts of States, without the Consent of the Legislatures of the States concerned as well as of the Congress.

The Congress shall have Power to dispose of and make all needful Rules and Regulations respecting the Territory or other Property belonging to the United States; and nothing in this Constitution shall be so construed as to Prejudice any Claims of the United States, or of any particular State.

Section 4. The United States shall guarantee to every State in this Union a Republican Form of Government, and shall protect each of them against Invasion, and on Application of the Legislature, or of the Executive (when the Legislature cannot be convened) against domestic Violence.

ARTICLE V

The Congress, whenever two thirds of both Houses shall deem it necessary, shall propose Amendments to this Constitution, or on the Application of the Legislatures of two thirds of the several States, shall call a Convention for proposing Amendments, which, in either Case, shall be valid to all Intents and Purposes, as Part of this Constitution, when ratified by the Legislatures of three fourths of the several States, or by Conventions in three fourths thereof, as the one or the other Mode of Ratification may be proposed by the Congress; Provided that no Amendment which may be made prior to the Year One thousand eight hundred and eight shall in any Manner affect the first and fourth Clauses in the Ninth Section of the first Article; and that no State, without its Consent, shall be deprived of its equal Suffrage in the Senate.

ARTICLE VI

All Debts contracted and Engagements entered into, before the Adoption of this Constitution, shall be as

[10]See Amendment XIII.

valid against the United States under this Constitution, as under the Confederation.

This Constitution, and the laws of the United States which shall be made in Pursuance thereof; and all Treaties made, or which shall be made, under the Authority of the United States, shall be the supreme Law of the Land; and the Judges in every State shall be bound thereby, any Thing in the Constitution or Laws of any State on the Contrary notwithstanding.

The Senators and Representatives before mentioned, and the Members of the several State Legislatures, and all executive and judicial Officers, both of the United States and of the several States, shall be bound by Oath or Affirmation, to support this Constitution; but no religious Test shall ever be required as a Qualification to any Office or public Trust under the United States.

ARTICLE VII

The Ratification of the Conventions of nine States, shall be sufficient for the Establishment of this Constitution between the States so ratifying the Same.

Done in Convention by the Unanimous Consent of the States present the Seventeenth Day of September in the Year of our Lord one thousand seven hundred and Eighty seven and of the Independence of the United States of America the Twelfth. IN WITNESS whereof we have hereunto subscribed our Names. [Signatures omitted.]

Articles in Addition to, and Amendment of, the Constitution of the United States of America, Proposed by Congress and Ratified by the Legislatures of the Several States, Pursuant to the Fifth Article of the Original Constitution

AMENDMENT I

Congress shall make no law respecting an establishment of religion, or prohibiting the free exercise thereof; or abridging the freedom of speech, or of the press; or the right of the people peaceably to assemble, and to petition the Government for a redress of grievances. [The first ten amendments were ratified on 15 December 1791.]

AMENDMENT II

A well regulated militia, being necessary to the security of a free State, the right of the people to keep and bear arms, shall not be infringed.

AMENDMENT III

No Soldier shall, in time of peace be quartered in any house, without the consent of the owner, nor in time of war, but in a manner to be prescribed by law.

AMENDMENT IV

The right of the people to be secure in their persons, houses, papers, and effects, against unreasonable searches and seizures, shall not be violated, and no warrants shall issue, but upon probable cause, supported by oath or affirmation, and particularly describing the place to be searched, and the persons or things to be seized.

AMENDMENT V

No person shall be held to answer for a capital, or otherwise infamous crime, unless on a presentment or indictment of a Grand Jury, except in cases arising in the land or naval forces, or in the militia, when in actual service in time of war or public danger; nor shall any person be subject for the same offense to be twice put in jeopardy of life or limb; nor shall be compelled in any criminal case to be a witness against himself, nor be deprived of life, liberty, or property, without due process of law; nor shall private property be taken for public use, without just compensation.

AMENDMENT VI   1963

In all criminal prosecutions, the accused shall enjoy the right to a speedy and public trial, by an impartial jury of the State and district wherein the crime shall have been committed, which district shall have been previously ascertained by law, and to be informed of the nature and cause of the accusation; to be confronted with the witnesses against him; to have compulsory process for obtaining witnesses in his favor, and to have the assistance of counsel for his defence.

AMENDMENT VII

In Suits at common law, where the value in controversy shall exceed twenty dollars, the right of trial by jury shall be preserved, and no fact tried by a jury, shall be otherwise reexamined in any Court of the United States, than according to the rules of the common law.

AMENDMENT VIII

Excessive bail should not be required, nor excessive fines imposed, nor cruel and unusual punishment inflicted.

AMENDMENT IX

The enumeration in the Constitution, of certain rights, shall not be construed to deny or disparage others retained by the people.

AMENDMENT X

The powers not delegated to the United States by the Constitution, nor prohibited by it to the States, are reserved to the States respectively, or to the people.

AMENDMENT XI (1798)

The Judicial power of the United States shall not be construed to extend to any suit in law or equity, commenced or prosecuted against one of the United States by Citizens of another State, or by Citizens or Subjects of any Foreign State.

AMENDMENT XII (1804)

The Electors shall meet in their respective states, and vote by ballot for President and Vice-President, one of whom, at least, shall not be an inhabitant of the same state with themselves; they shall name in their ballots the person voted for as President, and in distinct ballots the person voted for as Vice-President, and they shall make distinct lists of all persons voted for as President, and of all persons voted for as Vice-President, and of the number of votes for each, which lists they shall sign and certify, and transmit sealed to the seat of the government of the United States, directed to the President of the Senate; — The President of the

Senate shall, in the presence of the Senate and House of Representatives, open all the certificates and the votes shall then be counted; — The person having the greatest number of votes for President, shall be the President, if such number be a majority of the whole number of Electors appointed; and if no person have such majority, then from the persons having the highest numbers not exceeding three on the list of those voted for as President, the House of Representatives shall choose immediately, by ballot, the President. But in choosing the President, the votes shall be taken by states, the representation from each state having one vote; a quorum for this purpose shall consist of a member or members from two-thirds of the states, and a majority of all the states shall be necessary to a choice. *And if the House of Representatives shall not choose a President whenever the right of choice shall devolve upon them, before the fourth day of March next following, then the Vice-President shall act as President, as in the case of the death or other constitutional disability of the President.*[11] — The person having the greatest number of votes as Vice-President, shall be the Vice-President, if such number be a majority of the whole number of Electors appointed, and if no person have a majority, then from the two highest numbers on the list, the Senate shall choose the Vice-President; a quorum for the purpose shall consist of two-thirds of the whole number of Senators, and a majority of the whole number shall be necessary to a choice. But no person constitutionally ineligible to the office of President shall be eligible to that of Vice-President of the United States.

AMENDMENT XIII (1865)

Section 1.   Neither slavery nor involuntary servitude, except as a punishment for crime whereof the party shall have been duly convicted, shall exist within the United States, or any place subject to their jurisdiction.

Section 2.   Congress shall have power to enforce this article by appropriate legislation.

AMENDMENT XIV (1868)

Section 1.   All persons born or naturalized in the United States, and subject to the jurisdiction thereof, are citizens of the United States and of the State wherein they reside. No State shall make or enforce any law which shall abridge the privileges or immunities of citizens of the United States; nor shall any State deprive

[11]See Amendment XX.

any person of life, liberty, or property, without due process of law; nor deny to any person within its jurisdiction the equal protection of the laws.

Section 2.   Representatives shall be apportioned among the several States according to their respective numbers, counting the whole number of persons in each State, excluding Indians not taxed. But when the right to vote at any election for the choice of electors for President and Vice President of the United States, Representatives in Congress, the Executive and Judicial officers of a State, or the members of the Legislature thereof, is denied to any of the male inhabitants of such state, being twenty-one years of age, and citizens of the United States, or in any way abridged, except for participation in rebellion, or other crime, the basis of representation therein shall be reduced in the proportion which the number of such male citizens shall bear to the whole number of male citizens twenty-one years of age in such State.

Section 3.   No person shall be a Senator or Representative in Congress, or elector of President and Vice President, or hold any office, civil or military, under the United States, or under any State, who, having previously taken an oath, as a member of Congress, or as an officer of the United States, or as a member of any State legislature, or as an executive or judicial officer of any State, to support the Constitution of the United States, shall be engaged in insurrection or rebellion against the same, or given aid or comfort to the enemies thereof. But Congress may by a vote of two-thirds of each House, remove such disability.

Section 4.   The validity of the public debt of the United States, authorized by law, including debts incurred for payment of pensions and bounties for services in suppressing insurrection or rebellion, shall not be questioned. But neither the United States nor any State shall assume or pay any debt or obligation incurred in aid of insurrection or rebellion against the United States, or any claim for the loss or emancipation of any slave, but all such debts, obligations and claims shall be held illegal and void.

Section 5.   The Congress shall have power to enforce, by appropriate legislation, the provisions of this article.

AMENDMENT XV (1870)

Section 1.   The right of citizens of the United States to vote shall not be denied or abridged by the United States or by any State on account of race, color, or previous condition of servitude.

Section 2.   The Congress shall have the power to enforce this article by appropriate legislation.

AMENDMENT XVI (1913)

The Congress shall have power to lay and collect taxes on incomes, from whatever source derived, without apportionment among the several States, and without regard to any census or enumeration.

AMENDMENT XVII (1913)

The Senate of the United States shall be composed of two Senators from each State, elected by the people thereof, for six years; and each Senator shall have one vote. The electors in each State shall have the qualifications requisite for electors of the most numerous branch of the State legislatures.

When vacancies happen in the representation of any State in the Senate, the executive authority of such State shall issue writs of election to fill such vacancies: *Provided,* That the legislature of any State may empower the executive thereof to make temporary appointments until the people fill the vacancies by election as the legislature may direct.

This amendment shall not be so construed as to affect the election or term of any Senator chosen before it becomes valid as a part of the Constitution.

AMENDMENT XVIII (1919)

Section 1.   *After one year from the ratification of this article the manufacture, sale, or transportation of intoxicating liquors within, the importation thereof into, or the exportation thereof from the United States and all territory subject to the jurisdiction thereof for beverage purposes is hereby prohibited.*

Section 2.   *The Congress and the several States shall have concurrent power to enforce this article by appropriate legislation.*

Section 3.   *This article shall be inoperative unless it shall have been ratified as an amendment to the Constitution by the legislatures of the several States, as provided in the Constitution, within seven years from the date of the submission hereof to the States by the Congress.*[12]

[12]See Amendment XXI.

AMENDMENT XIX (1920)

The right of citizens of the United States to vote shall not be denied or abridged by the United States or by any State on account of sex.

Congress shall have the power to enforce this article by appropriate legislation.

AMENDMENT XX (1933)

Section 1.   The terms of the President and Vice President shall end at noon on the 20th day of January, and the terms of Senators and Representatives at noon on the 3rd day of January, of the years in which such terms would have ended if this article had not been ratified, and the terms of their successors shall then begin.

Section 2.   The Congress shall assemble at least once in every year, and such meeting shall begin at noon on the 3rd day of January, unless they shall by law appoint a different day.

Section 3.   If, at the time fixed for the beginning of the term of the President, the President elect shall have died, the Vice President elect shall become President. If a President shall not have been chosen before the time fixed for the beginning of his term, or if the President elect shall have failed to qualify, then the Vice President elect shall act as President until a President shall have qualified; and the Congress may by law provide for the case wherein neither a President elect nor a Vice President elect shall have qualified, declaring who shall then act as President, or the manner in which one who is to act shall be selected, and such person shall act accordingly until a President or Vice President shall have qualified.

Section 4.   The Congress may by law provide for the case of the death of any of the persons from whom the House of Representatives may choose a President whenever the rights of choice shall have devolved upon them, and for the case of the death of any of the persons from whom the Senate may choose a Vice President whenever the right of choice shall have devolved upon them.

Section 5.   Sections 1 and 2 shall take effect on the 15th day of October following the ratification of this article.

Section 6.   This article shall be inoperative unless it shall have been ratified as an amendment to the Constitution by the legislatures of three-fourths of the several States within seven years from the date of its submission.

AMENDMENT XXI (1933)

Section 1. The eighteenth article of amendment to the Constitution of the United States is hereby repealed.

Section 2. The transportation or importation into any State, Territory, or possession of the United States for delivery or use therein of intoxicating liquors, in violation of the laws thereof, is hereby prohibited.

Section 3. This article shall be inoperative unless it shall be ratified as an amendment to the Constitution by conventions in the several States, as provided in the Constitution, within seven years from the date of the submission hereof to the States by the Congress.

AMENDMENT XXII (1951)

Section 1. No person shall be elected to the office of the President more than twice, and no person who has held the office of President, or acted as President, for more than two years of a term to which some other person was elected President shall be elected to the office of the President more than once. But this Article shall not apply to any person holding the office of President when this Article was proposed by the Congress, and shall not prevent any person who may be holding the office of President, or acting as President, during the term within which this Article becomes operative from holding the office of President or acting as President during the remainder of such term.

Section 2. This article shall be inoperative unless it shall have been ratified as an amendment to the Constitution by the legislatures of three-fourths of the several States within seven years from the date of its submission to the States by the Congress.

AMENDMENT XXIII (1961)

Section 1. The District constituting the seat of Government of the United States shall appoint in such manner as the Congress may direct:

A number of electors of President and Vice President equal to the whole number of Senators and Representatives in Congress to which the District would be entitled if it were a State, but in no event more than the least populous State; they shall be in addition to those appointed by the States, but they shall be considered, for the purposes of the election of President and Vice President, to be electors appointed by a State; and they shall meet in the District and perform such duties as provided by the twelfth article of amendment.

Section 2. The Congress shall have power to enforce this article by appropriate legislation.

AMENDMENT XXIV (1964)

Section 1. The right of citizens of the United States to vote in any primary or other election for President or Vice President, for electors for President or Vice President, or for Senator or Representative in Congress, shall not be denied or abridged by the United States or by any State by reason of failure to pay any poll tax or other tax.

Section 2. The Congress shall have power to enforce this article by appropriate legislation.

AMENDMENT XXV (1967)

Section 1. In case of the removal of the President from office or of his death or resignation, the Vice President shall become President.

Section 2. Whenever there is a vacancy in the office of the Vice President, the President shall nominate a Vice President who shall take office upon confirmation by a majority vote of both Houses of Congress.

Section 3. Whenever the President transmits to the President pro tempore of the Senate and the Speaker of the House of Representatives his written declaration that he is unable to discharge the powers and duties of his office, and until he transmits to them a written declaration to the contrary, such powers and duties shall be discharged by the Vice President as Acting President.

Section 4. Whenever the Vice President and a majority of either the principal officers of the executive departments or of such other body as Congress may by law provide, transmit to the President pro tempore of the Senate and the Speaker of the House of Representatives their written declaration that the President is unable to discharge the powers and duties of his office, the Vice President shall immediately assume the powers and duties of the office as Acting President.

Thereafter, when the President transmits to the President pro tempore of the Senate and the Speaker of the House of Representatives his written declaration that no inability exists, he shall resume the powers and duties of his office unless the Vice President and a majority of either the principal officers of the executive department or of such other body as Congress may by law provide, transmit within four days to the President pro tempore of the Senate and the Speaker of the House of Representatives their written declaration that the President is unable to discharge the powers and duties of his office. Thereupon Congress shall decide the issue, assembling within forty-eight hours for that purpose if not in session. If the Congress, within twenty-one days after receipt of the latter written declaration, or, if Congress is not in session, within twenty-one days after Congress is required to assemble, determines by two-thirds vote of both Houses that the President is unable to discharge the powers and duties of his office, the Vice President shall continue to discharge the same as Acting President; otherwise, the President shall resume the powers and duties of his office.

AMENDMENT XXVI (1971)

Section 1.   The right of citizens of the United States, who are eighteen years of age or older, to vote shall not be denied or abridged by the United States or by any State on account of age.

Section 2.   The Congress shall have the power to enforce this article by appropriate legislation.

Proposed Amendment (1972)

Resolved by the Senate and House of Representatives of the United States of America in Congress assembled (two-thirds of each House concurring therein), That the following article is proposed as an amendment to the Constitution of the United States, which shall be valid to all intents and purposes as part of the Constitution when ratified by the legislatures of three-fourths of the several States within seven years from the date of its submission by the Congress.[13]

Section 1.   Equality of rights under the law shall not be denied or abridged by the United States or by any State on account of sex.

Section 2.   The Congress shall have the power to enforce, by appropriate legislation, the provisions of this article.

Section 3.   This amendment shall take effect two years after the date of ratification.

Proposed Amendment (1978)

Section 1.   For purposes of representation in the Congress, election of the President and Vice President, and article V of this Constitution, the District constituting the seat of government of the United States shall be treated as though it were a State.

Section 2.   The exercise of the rights and powers conferred under this article shall be by the people of the District constituting the seat of government, and as shall be provided by the Congress.

Section 3.   The twenty-third article of amendment to the Constitution of the United States is hereby repealed.

Section 4.   This article shall be inoperative, unless it shall have been ratified as an amendment to the Constitution by the legislatures of three-fourths of the several States within seven years from the date of its submission.

[13]In 1978 Congress extended the deadline for ratification of the Equal Rights Amendment to 30 June 1982; although defeated at that time, it is still active as a proposed amendment.

AMENDMENT XXVII

No law varying the compensation for the services of Senators and Representatives shall take effect, until an election of Representatives shall have intervened.

APPENDIX C

The Uniform Partnership Act[1]

PART 1

Preliminary Provisions

Section 1. Name of Act

This act may be cited as Uniform Partnership Act.

Section 2. Definition of Terms

In this act, "Court" includes every court and judge having jurisdiction in the case.

"Business" includes every trade, occupation, or profession.

"Person" includes individuals, partnerships, corporations, and other associations.

"Bankrupt" includes bankrupt under the Federal Bankruptcy Act or insolvent under any state insolvent act.

"Conveyance" includes every assignment, lease, mortgage, or encumbrance.

"Real property" includes land and any interest or estate in land.

Section 3. Interpretation of Knowledge and Notice

(1) A person has "knowledge" of a fact within the meaning of this act not only when he has actual knowledge thereof, but also when he has knowledge of such other facts as in the circumstances shows bad faith.

(2) A person has "notice" of a fact within the meaning of this act when the person who claims the benefit of the notice:

(a) states the fact to such person; or

(b) delivers through the mail, or by other means of communication, a written statement of the fact to such person or to a proper person at his place of business or residence.

Section 4. Rules of Construction

(1) The rule that statutes in derogation of the common law are to be strictly construed shall have no application to this act.

(2) The law of estoppel shall apply under this act.

(3) The law of agency shall apply under this act.

(4) This act shall be so interpreted and construed as to effect its general purpose to make uniform the law of those states which enact it.

(5) This act shall not be construed so as to impair the obligations of any contract existing when the act goes into effect, nor to affect any action or proceedings begun or right accrued before this act takes effect.

Section 5. Rules for Cases Not Provided for in This Act

In any case not provided for in this act the rules of law and equity, including the law merchant, shall govern.

---

[1] Source: National Conference of Commissioners of Uniform State Laws.

PART 2

Nature of Partnership

Section 6.   Partnership Defined

(1)   A partnership is an association of two or more persons to carry on as co-owners a business for profit.

(2)   But any association formed under any other statute of this state, or any statute adopted by authority, other than the authority of this state, is not a partnership under this act, unless such association would have been a partnership in this state prior to the adoption of this act; but this act shall apply to limited partnerships except in so far as the statutes relating to such partnerships are inconsistent herewith.

Section 7.   Rules for Determining the Existence of a Partnership

In determining whether a partnership exists, these rules shall apply:

(1)   Except as provided by section 16, persons who are not partners as to each other are not partners as to third persons.

(2)   Joint tenancy, tenancy in common, tenancy by the entireties, joint property, common property, or part ownership does not of itself establish a partnership, whether such co-owners do or do not share any profits made by the use of the property.

(3)   The sharing of gross returns does not of itself establish a partnership, whether or not the persons sharing them have a joint or common right or interest in any property from which the returns are derived.

(4)   The receipt by a person of a share of the profits of a business is prima facie evidence that he is a partner in the business, but no such inference shall be drawn if such profits were received in payment:

   (a)   as a debt by installments or otherwise,

   (b)   as wages of an employee or rent to a landlord,

   (c)   as an annuity to a widow or representative of a deceased partner,

   (d)   as interest on a loan, though the amount of payment vary with the profits of the business,

   (e)   as the consideration for the sale of a goodwill of a business or other property by installments or otherwise.

Section 8.   Partnership Property

(1)   All property originally brought into the partnership stock or subsequently acquired by purchase or otherwise, on account of the partnership, is partnership property.

(2)   Unless the contrary intention appears, property acquired with partnership funds is partnership property.

(3)   Any estate in real property may be acquired in the partnership name. Title so acquired can be conveyed only in the partnership name.

(4)   A conveyance to a partnership in the partnership name, though without words of inheritance, passes the entire estate of the grantor unless a contrary intent appears.

PART 3

Relations of Partners to Persons Dealing with the Partnership

Section 9.   Partner Agent of Partnership as to Partnership Business

(1)   Every partner is an agent of the partnership for the purpose of its business, and the act of every partner, including the execution in the partnership name of any instrument, for apparently carrying on in the usual way the business of the partnership of which he is a member binds the partnership, unless the partner so acting has in fact no authority to act for the partnership in the particular matter, and the person with whom he is dealing has knowledge of the fact that he has no such authority.

(2)   An act of a partner which is not apparently for the carrying on of the business of the partnership in the usual way does not bind the partnership unless authorized by the other partners.

(3)   Unless authorized by the other partners or unless they have abandoned the business, one or more but less than all the partners have no authority to:

   (a)   assign the partnership property in trust for creditors or on the assignee's promise to pay the debts of the partnership,

   (b)   dispose of the good-will of the business,

   (c)   do any other act which would make it impossible to carry on the ordinary business of a partnership,

   (d)   confess a judgment,

   (e)   submit a partnership claim or liability to arbitration or reference.

(4)   No act of a partner in contravention of a restriction

on authority shall bind the partnership to persons having knowledge of the restriction.

Section 10.   Conveyance of Real Property of the Partnership

(1) Where title to real property is in the partnership name, any partner may convey title to such property by a conveyance executed in the partnership name; but the partnership may recover such property unless the partner's act binds the partnership under the provisions of paragraph (1) of section 9, or unless such property has been conveyed by the grantee or a person claiming through such grantee to a holder for value without knowledge that the partner, in making the conveyance, has exceeded his authority.

(2) Where title to real property is in the name of the partnership, a conveyance executed by a partner, in his own name, passes the equitable interest of the partnership, provided the act is one within the authority of the partner under the provisions of paragraph (1) of section 9.

(3) Where title to real property is in the name of one or more but not all the partners, and the record does not disclose the right of partnership, the partners in whose name the title stands may convey title to such property, but the partnership may recover such property if the partners' act does not bind the partnership under the provisions of paragraph (1) of section 9, unless the purchaser or his assignee, is a holder for value, without knowledge.

(4) Where the title to real property is in the name of one or more or all the partners, or in a third person in trust for the partnership, a conveyance executed by a partner in the partnership name, or in his own name, passes the equitable interest of the partnership, provided the act is one within the authority of the partner under the provisions of paragraph (1) of section 9.

(5) Where the title to real property is in the names of all the partners a conveyance executed by all the partners passes all their rights in such property.

Section 11.   Partnership Bound by Admission of Partner

An admission or representation made by any partner concerning partnership affairs within the scope of his authority as conferred by this act is evidence against the partnership.

Section 12.   Partnership Charged with Knowledge of or Notice to Partner

Notice to any partner of any matter relating to partnership affairs, and the knowledge of the partner acting in the particular matter, acquired while a partner or then present to his mind, and the knowledge of any other partner who reasonably could and should have communicated it to the acting partner, operate as notice to or knowledge of the partnership, except in the case of a fraud on the partnership committed by or with the consent of that partner.

Section 13.   Partnership Bound by Partner's Wrongful Act

Where, by any wrongful act or omission of any partner acting in the ordinary course of the business of the partnership or with the authority of his co-partners, loss or injury is caused to any person, not being a partner in the partnership, or any penalty is incurred, the partnership is liable therefor to the same extent as the partner so acting or omitting to act.

Section 14.   Partnership Bound by Partner's Breach of Trust

The partnership is bound to make good the loss:

(a) where one partner acting within the scope of his apparent authority receives money or property of a third person and misapplies it; and

(b) where the partnership in the course of its business receives money or property of a third person and the money or property so received is misapplied by any partner while it is in the custody of the partnership.

Section 15.   Nature of Partner's Liability

All partners are liable

(a) jointly and severally for everything chargeable to the partnership under sections 13 and 14.

(b) jointly for all other debts and obligations of the partnership; but any partner may enter into a separate obligation to perform a partnership contract.

Section 16.   Partner by Estoppel

(1) When a person, by words spoken or written or by conduct, represents himself, or consents to another representing him to any one, as a partner in an existing partnership or with one or more persons not actual partners, he is liable to any such person to whom such representation has been made, who has, on the faith of such representation, given credit to the actual or apparent partnership, and if he has made such representation or consented to its being made in a public manner he is liable to such person, whether the representation has or has not been made or communicated to such

person so giving credit by or with the knowledge of the apparent partner making the representation or consenting to its being made.

(a) When a partnership liability results, he is liable as though he were an actual member of the partnership.

(b) When no partnership liability results, he is liable jointly with the other persons, if any, so consenting to the contract or representation as to incur liability, otherwise separately.

(2) When a person has been thus represented to be a partner in an existing partnership, or with one or more persons not actual partners, he is an agent of the persons consenting to such representation to bind them to the same extent and in the same manner as though he were a partner in fact, with respect to persons who rely upon the representation. Where all the members of the existing partnership consent to the representation, a partnership act or obligation results; but in all other cases it is the joint act or obligation of the person acting and the persons consenting to the representation.

Section 17.   Liability of Incoming Partner

A person admitted as a partner into an existing partnership is liable for all the obligations of the partnership arising before his admission as though he had been a partner when such obligations were incurred, except that this liability shall be satisfied only out of partnership property.

PART 4

Relations of Partners to One Another

Section 18.   Rules Determining Rights and Duties of Partners

The rights and duties of the partners in relation to the partnership shall be determined, subject to any agreement between them, by the following rules:

(a) Each partner shall be repaid his contributions, whether by way of capital or advances to the partnership property and share equally in the profits and surplus remaining after all liabilities, including those to partners, are satisfied; and must contribute towards the losses, whether of capital or otherwise, sustained by the partnership according to this share in the profits.

(b) The partnership must indemnify every partner in respect of payments made and personal liabilities reasonably incurred by him in the ordinary and proper conduct of its business, or for the preservation of its business or property.

(c) A partner, who in aid of the partnership makes any payment or advance beyond the amount of capital which he agreed to contribute, shall be paid interest from the date of the payment or advance.

(d) A partner shall receive interest on the capital contributed by him only from the date when repayment should be made.

(e) All partners have equal rights in the management and conduct of the partnership business.

(f) No partner is entitled to remuneration for acting in the partnership business, except that a surviving partner is entitled to reasonable compensation for his services in winding up the partnership affairs.

(g) No person can become a member of a partnership without the consent of all the partners.

(h) Any difference arising as to ordinary matters connected with the partnership business may be decided by a majority of the partners; but no act in contravention of any agreement between the partners may be done rightfully without the consent of all the partners.

Section 19.   Partnership Books

The partnership books shall be kept, subject to any agreement between the partners, at the principal place of business of the partnership, and every partner shall at all times have access to and may inspect and copy any of them.

Section 20.   Duty of Partners to Render Information

Partners shall render on demand true and full information of all things affecting the partnership to any partner or the legal representative of any deceased partner or partner under legal disability.

Section 21.   Partner Accountable as a Fiduciary

(1) Every partner must account to the partnership for any benefit, and hold as trustee for it any profits derived by him without the consent of the other partners from any transaction connected with the formation, conduct, or liquidation of the partnership or from any use by him of its property.

(2) This section applies also to the representatives of a deceased partner engaged in the liquidation of the af-

fairs of the partnership as the personal representatives of the last surviving partner.

Section 22.   Right to an Account

Any partner shall have the right to a formal account as to partnership affairs:

(a)   if he is wrongfully excluded from the partnership business or possession of its property by his co-partners,

(b)   if the right exists under the terms of any agreement,

(c)   as provided by section 21,

(d)   whenever other circumstances render it just and reasonable.

Section 23.   Continuation of Partnership Beyond Fixed Term

(1)   When a partnership for a fixed term or particular undertaking is continued after the termination of such term or particular undertaking without any express agreement, the rights and duties of the partners remain the same as they were at such termination, so far as is consistent with a partnership at will.

(2)   A continuation of the business by the partners or such of them as habitually acted therein during the term, without any settlement or liquidation of the partnership affairs, is prima facie evidence of a continuation of the partnership.

PART 5

Property Rights of a Partner

Section 24.   Extent of Property Rights of a Partner

The property rights of a partner are (1) his rights in specific partnership property, (2) his interest in the partnership, and (3) his right to participate in the management.

Section 25.   Nature of a Partner's Right in Specific Partnership Property

(1)   A partner is co-owner with his partners of specific partnership property holding as a tenant in partnership.

(2)   The incidents of this tenancy are such that:

(a)   A partner, subject to the provisions of this act and to any agreement between the partners, has an equal right with his partners to possess specific partnership property for partnership purposes; but he has no right to possess such property for any other purpose without the consent of his partners.

(b)   A partner's right in specific partnership property is not assignable except in connection with the assignment of rights of all the partners in the same property.

(c)   A partner's right in specific partnership property is not subject to attachment or execution, except on a claim against the partnership. When partnership property is attached for a partnership debt the partners, or any of them, or the representatives of a deceased partner, cannot claim any right under the homestead or exemption laws.

(d)   On the death of a partner his right in specific partnership property vests in the surviving partner or partners, except where the deceased was the last surviving partner, when his right in such property vests in his legal representative. Such surviving partner or partners, or the legal representative of the last surviving partner, has no right to possess the partnership property for any but a partnership purpose.

(e)   A partner's right in specific partnership property is not subject to dower, curtesy, or allowances to widows, heirs, or next of kin.

Section 26.   Nature of Partner's Interest in the Partnership

A partner's interest in the partnership is his share of the profits and surplus, and the same is personal property.

Section 27.   Assignment of Partner's Interest

(1)   A conveyance by a partner of his interest in the partnership does not of itself dissolve the partnership, nor, as against the other partners in the absence of agreement, entitle the assignee, during the continuance of the partnership, to interfere in the management or administration of the partnership business or affairs, or to require any information or account of partnership transactions, or to inspect the partnership books; but it merely entitles the assignee to receive in accordance with his contract the profits to which the assigning partner would otherwise be entitled.

(2)   In case of a dissolution of the partnership, the assignee is entitled to receive his assignor's interest and may require an account from the date only of the last account agreed to by all the partners.

Section 28. Partner's Interest Subject to Charging Order

(1) On due application to a competent court by any judgment creditor of a partner, the court which entered the judgment, order, or decree, or any other court, may charge the interest of the debtor partner with payment of the unsatisfied amount of such judgment debt with interest thereon; and may then or later appoint a receiver of his share of the profits, and of any other money due or to fall due to him in respect of the partnership, and make all other orders, directions, accounts and inquiries which the debtor partner might have made, or which the circumstances of the case may require.

(2) The interest charged may be redeemed at any time before foreclosure, or in case of a sale being directed by the court may be purchased without thereby causing a dissolution:

(a) with separate property, by any one or more of the partners, or

(b) with partnership property, by any one or more of the partners with the consent of all the partners whose interests are not so charged or sold.

(3) Nothing in this act shall be held to deprive a partner of his right, if any, under the exemption laws, as regards his interest in the partnership.

PART 6

Dissolution and Winding Up

Section 29. Dissolution Defined

The dissolution of a partnership is the change in the relation of the partners caused by any partner ceasing to be associated in the carrying on as distinguished from the winding up of the business.

Section 30. Partnership Not Terminated by Dissolution

On dissolution the partnership is not terminated, but continues until the winding up of partnership affairs is completed.

Section 31. Causes of Dissolution

Dissolution is caused:

(1) without violation of the agreement between the partners,

(a) by the termination of the definite term or particular undertaking specified in the agreement,

(b) by the express will of any partner when no definite term or particular undertaking is specified,

(c) by the express will of all the partners who have not assigned their interests or suffered them to be charged for their separate debts, either before or after the termination of any specified term or particular undertaking,

(d) by the expulsion of any partner from the business bona fide in accordance with such a power conferred by the agreement between the partners.

(2) in contravention of the agreement between the partners, where the circumstances do not permit a dissolution under any other provision of this section, by the express will of any partner at any time;

(3) by any event which makes it unlawful for the business of the partnership to be carried on or for the members to carry it on in partnership;

(4) by the death of any partner;

(5) by the bankruptcy of any partner or the partnership;

(6) by decree of court under section 32.

Section 32. Dissolution by Decree of Court

(1) On application by or for a partner the court shall decree a dissolution whenever;

(a) a partner has been declared a lunatic in any judicial proceeding or is shown to be of unsound mind,

(b) a partner becomes in any other way incapable of performing his part of the partnership contract,

(c) a partner has been guilty of such conduct as tends to affect prejudicially the carrying on of the business,

(d) a partner wilfully or persistently commits a breach of the partnership agreement, or otherwise so conducts himself in matters relating to the partnership business that it is not reasonably practicable to carry on the business in partnership with him,

(e) the business of the partnership can only be carried on at a loss,

(f) other circumstances render a dissolution equitable.

(2) On the application of the purchaser of a partner's interest under sections 27 and 28:

(a) after the termination of the specified term or particular undertaking,

(b) at any time if the partnership was a partnership at will when the interest was assigned or when the charging order was issued.

Section 33.   General Effect of Dissolution on Authority of Partner

Except so far as may be necessary to wind up partnership affairs or to complete transactions begun but not then finished, dissolution terminates all authority of any partner to act for the partnership,

(1) with respect to the partners,

(a) when the dissolution is not by the act, bankruptcy or death of a partner; or

(b) when the dissolution is by such act, bankruptcy or death of a partner, in cases where section 34 so requires.

(2) with respect to persons not partners, as declared in section 35.

Section 34.   Right of Partner to Contribution from Co-Partners after Dissolution

Where the dissolution is caused by the act, death or bankruptcy of a partner, each partner is liable to his co-partners for his share of any liability created by any partner acting for the partnership as if the partnership had not been dissolved unless

(a) the dissolution being by act of any partner, the partner acting for the partnership had knowledge of the dissolution, or

(b) the dissolution being by the death or bankruptcy of a partner, the partner acting for the partnership had knowledge or notice of the death or bankruptcy.

Section 35.   Power of Partner to Bind Partnership to Third Persons after Dissolution

(1) After dissolution a partner can bind the partnership except as provided in Paragraph (3)

(a) by any act appropriate for winding up partnership affairs or completing transactions unfinished at dissolution;

(b) by any transaction which would bind the partnership if dissolution had not taken place, provided the other party to the transaction

(i) had extended credit to the partnership prior to dissolution and had no knowledge or notice of the dissolution; or

(ii) though he had not so extended credit, had nevertheless known of the partnership prior to dissolution, and, having no knowledge or notice of dissolution, the fact of dissolution had not been advertised in a newspaper of general circulation in the place (or in each place if more than one) at which the partnership business was regularly carried on.

(2) The liability of a partner under Paragraph (1b) shall be satisfied out of partnership assets alone when such partner had been prior to dissolution

(a) unknown as a partner to the person with whom the contract is made; and

(b) so far unknown and inactive in partnership affairs that the business reputation of the partnership could not be said to have been in any degree due to his connection with it.

(3) The partnership is in no case bound by any act of a partner after dissolution

(a) where the partnership is dissolved because it is unlawful to carry on the business, unless the act is appropriate for winding up partnership affairs; or

(b) where the partner has become bankrupt; or

(c) where the partner has no authority to wind up partnership affairs; except by a transaction with one who

(i) had extended credit to the partnership prior to dissolution and had no knowledge or notice of his want of authority; or

(ii) had not extended credit to the partnership prior to dissolution, and, having no knowledge or notice of his want of authority, the fact of his want of authority has not been advertised in the manner provided for advertising the fact of dissolution in Paragraph (1b ii).

(4) Nothing in this section shall affect the liability under Section 16 of any person who after dissolution represents himself or consents to another representing him as a partner in a partnership engaged in carrying on business.

Section 36.   Effect of Dissolution on Partner's Existing Liability

(1) The dissolution of the partnership does not of itself discharge the existing liability of any partner.

(2) A partner is discharged from any existing liability upon dissolution of the partnership by an agreement to that effect between himself, the partnership creditor and the person or partnership continuing the business; and such agreement may be inferred from the course of dealing between the creditor having knowledge of the dissolution and the person or partnership continuing the business.

(3) Where a person agrees to assume the existing obligations of a dissolved partnership, the partners whose obligations have been assumed shall be discharged from any liability to any creditor of the partnership who, knowing of the agreement, consents to a material alteration in the nature or time of payment of such obligations.

(4) The individual property of a deceased partner shall be liable for all obligations of the partnership incurred while he was a partner but subject to the prior payment of his separate debts.

Section 37.   Right to Wind Up

Unless otherwise agreed the partners who have not wrongfully dissolved the partnership or the legal representative of the last surviving partner, not bankrupt, has the right to wind up the partnership affairs; provided, however, that any partner, his legal representative or his assignee, upon cause shown, may obtain winding up by the court.

Section 38.   Rights of Partners to Application of Partnership Property

(1) When dissolution is caused in any way, except in contravention of the partnership agreement, each partner, as against his co-partners and all persons claiming through them in respect of their interests in the partnership, unless otherwise agreed, may have the partnership property applied to discharge its liabilities, and the surplus applied to pay in cash the net amount owing to the respective partners. But if dissolution is caused by expulsion of a partner, bona fide under the partnership agreement and if the expelled partner is discharged from all partnership liabilities, either by payment or agreement under section 36(2), he shall receive in cash only the net amount due him from the partnership.

(2) When dissolution is caused in contravention of the partnership agreement the rights of the partners shall be as follows:

(a) Each partner who has not caused dissolution wrongfully shall have,

   (i) all the rights specified in paragraph (1) of this section, and

   (ii) the right, as against each partner who has caused the dissolution wrongfully, to damages for breach of the areement.

(b) The partners who have not caused the dissolution wrongfully, if they all desire to continue the business in the same name, either by themselves or jointly with others, may do so, during the agreed term for the partnership and for that purpose may possess the partnership property, provided they secure the payment by bond approved by the court, or pay to any partner who has caused the dissolution wrongfully, the value of his interest in the partnership at the dissolution, less any damages recoverable under clause (2a ii) of this section, and in like manner indemnify him against all present or future partnership liabilities.

(c) A partner who has caused the dissolution wrongfully shall have:

   (i) if the business is not continued under the provisions of paragraph (2b) all the rights of a partner under paragraph (1), subject to clause (2a ii), of this section,

   (ii) if the business is continued under paragraph (2b) of this section the right as against his co-partners and all claiming through them in respect of their interests in the partnership, to have the value of his interest in the partnership, less any damages caused to his co-partners by the dissolution, ascertained and paid to him in cash, or the payment secured by bond approved by the court, and to be released from all existing liabilities of the partnership; but in ascertaining the value of the partner's interest the value of the good-will of the business shall not be considered.

Section 39.   Rights Where Partnership Is Dissolved for Fraud or Misrepresentation

Where a partnership contract is rescinded on the ground of the fraud or misrepresentation of one of the parties thereto, the party entitled to rescind is, without prejudice to any other right, entitled,

(a) to a lien on, or a right of retention of, the surplus of the partnership property after satisfying the partnership liabilities to third persons for any sum of money paid by him for the purchase of an interest in the partnership and for any capital or advances contributed by him; and

(b) to stand, after all liabilities to third persons have been satisfied, in the place of the creditors of the partnership for any payments made by him in respect of the partnership liabilities; and

(c) to be indemnified by the person guilty of the fraud or making the representation against all debts and liabilities of the partnership.

Section 40.   Rules for Distribution

In settling accounts between the partners after dissolution, the following rules shall be observed, subject to any agreement to the contrary:

(a) The assets of the partnership are:

(i)   the partnership property,

(ii) the contributions of the partners necessary for the repayment of all the liabilities specified in clause (b) of this paragraph.

(b) The liabilities of the partnership shall rank in order of payment, as follows:

(i)   those owing to creditors other than partners,

(ii) those owing to partners other than for capital and profits,

(iii) those owing to partners in respect of capital,

(iv) those owing to partners in respect of profits.

(c) The assets shall be applied in the order of their declaration in clause (a) of this paragraph to the satisfaction of the liabilities.

(d) The partners shall contribute, as provided by section 18(a) the amount necessary to satisfy the liabilities; but if any, but not all, of the partners are insolvent, or, not being subject to process, refuse to contribute, the other partners shall contribute their share of the liabilities, and, in the relative proportions in which they share the profits, the additional amount necessary to pay the liabilities.

(e) An assignee for the benefit of creditors or any person appointed by the court shall have the right to enforce the contributions specified in clause (d) of this paragraph.

(f) Any partner or his legal representtive shall have the right to enforce the contributions specified in clause (d) of this paragraph, to the extent of the amount which he has paid in excess of his share of the liability.

(g) The individual property of a deceased partner shall be liable for the contributions specified in clause (d) of this paragraph.

(h) When partnership property and the individual properties of the partners are in possession of a court for distribution, partnership creditors shall have priority on partnership property and separate creditors on individual property, saving the rights of lien or secured creditors as heretofore.

(i) Where a partner has become bankrupt or his estate is insolvent the claims against his separate property shall rank in the following order:

(i)   those owing to separate creditors,

(ii) those owing to partnership creditors,

(iii) those owing to partners by way of contribution.

Section 41.   Liability of Persons Continuing the Business in Certain Cases

(1) When any new partner is admitted into an existing partnership, or when any partner retires and assigns (or the representative of the deceased partner assigns) his rights in partnership property to two or more of the partners, or to one or more of the partners and one or more third persons, if the business is continued without liquidation of the partnership affairs, creditors of the first or dissolved partnership are also creditors of the partnership so continuing the business.

(2) When all but one partner retire and assign (or the representative of a deceased partner assigns) their rights in partnership property to the remaining partner, who continues the business without liquidation of partnership affairs, either alone or with others,

creditors of the dissolved partnership are also creditors of the person or partnership so continuing the business.

(3) When any partner retires or dies and the business of the dissolved partnership is continued as set forth in paragraphs (1) and (2) of this section, with the consent of the retired partners or the representative of the deceased partner, but without any assignment of his right in partnership property, rights of creditors of the dissolved partnersip and of the creditors of the person or partnership continuing the business shall be as if such assignment has been made.

(4) When all the partners or their representatives assign their rights in partnership property to one or more third persons who promise to pay the debts and who continue the business of the dissolved partnership, creditors of the dissolved partnership are also creditors of the person or partnership continuing the business.

(5) When any partner wrongfully causes a dissolution and the remaining partners continue the business under the provisions of section 38(2b), either alone or with others, and without liquidation of the partnership affairs, creditors of the dissolved partnership are also creditors of the person or partnership continuing the business.

(6) When a partner is expelled and the remaining partners continue the business either alone or with others, without liquidation of the partnership affairs, creditors of the dissolved partnership are also creditors of the person or partnership continuing the business.

(7) The liability of a third person becoming a partner in the partnership continuing the business, under this section, to the creditors of the dissolved partnership, shall be satisfied out of partnership property only.

(8) When the business of a partnership after dissolution is continued under any conditions set forth in this section the creditors of the dissolved partnership, as against the separate creditors of the retiring or deceased partner or the representative of the deceased partner, have a prior right to any claim of the retired partner or the representative of the deceased partner against the person or partnership continuing the business, on account of the retired or deceased partner's interest in the dissolved partnership or on account of any consideration promised for such interest or for his right in partnership property.

(9) Nothing in this section shall be held to modify any right of creditors to set aside any assignment on the ground of fraud.

(10) The use by the person or partnership continuing the business of the partnership name, or the name of a deceased partner as part thereof, shall not of itself make the individual property of the deceased partner liable for any debts contracted by such person or partnership.

Section 42. Rights of Retiring or Estate of Deceased Partner When the Business Is Continued

When any partner retires or dies, and the business is continued under any of the conditions set forth in section 41(1, 2, 3, 5, 6), or section 38(2b) without any settlement of accounts as between him or his estate and the person or partnership continuing the business, unless otherwise agreed, he or his legal representative as against such persons or partnership may have the value of his interest at the date of dissolution ascertained, and shall receive as an ordinary creditor an amount equal to the value of his interest in the dissolved partnership with interest, or, at his option or at the option of his legal representative, in lieu of interest, the profits attributable to the use of his right in the property of the dissolved partnership; provided that the creditors of the dissolved partnership as against the separate creditors, or the representative of the retired or deceased partner, shall have priority on any claim arising under this section, as provided by section 41(8) of this act.

Section 43. Accrual of Actions

The right to an account of his interest shall accrue to any partner, or his legal representative, as against the winding up partners or the surviving partners or the person or partnership continuing the business, at the date of dissolution, in the absence of any agreement to the contrary.

PART 7
Miscellaneous Provisions

Section 44. When Act Takes Effect

This act shall take effect on the . . . . day of . . . . one thousand nine hundred and . . . .

Section 45. Legislation Repealed

All acts or parts of acts inconsistent with this act are hereby repealed.

The Revised Uniform Limited Partnership Act with the 1985 Amendments[1]

ARTICLE 1

GENERAL PROVISIONS

Section 101. Definitions

As used in this [Act], unless the context otherwise requires:

(1) "Certificate of limited partnership" means the certificate referred to in Section 201, and the certificate as amended or restated.

(2) "Contribution" means any cash, property, services rendered, or a promissory note or other binding obligation to contribute cash or property or to perform services, which a partner contributes to a limited partnership in his capacity as a partner.

(3) "Event of withdrawal of a general partner" means an event that causes a person to cease to be a general partner as provided in Section 402.

(4) "Foreign limited partnership" means a partnership formed under the laws of any state other than this State and having as partners one or more general partners and one or more limited partners.

(5) "General partner" means a person who has been admitted to a limited partnership as a general partner in accordance with the partnership agreement and named in the certificate of limited partnership as a general partner.

[1] Source: National Conference of Commissioners on Uniform State Laws.

(6) "Limited partner" means a person who has been admitted to a limited partnership as a limited partner in accordance with the partnership agreement.

(7) "Limited partnership" and "domestic limited partnership" mean a partnership formed by two or more persons under the laws of this State and having one or more general partners and one or more limited partners.

(8) "Partner" means a limited or general partner.

(9) "Partnership agreement" means any valid agreement, written or oral, of the partners as to the affairs of a limited partnership and the conduct of its business.

(10) "Partnership interest" means a partner's share of the profits and losses of a limited partnership and the right to receive distribution of partnership assets.

(11) "Person" means a natural person, partnership, limited partnership (domestic or foreign), trust, estate, association, or corporation.

(12) "State" means a state, territory, or possession of the United States, the District of Columbia, or the Commonwealth of Puerto Rico.

Section 102. Name

The name of each limited partnership as set forth in its certificate of limited partnership:

(1) shall contain without abbreviation the words "limited partnership";

(2) may not contain the name of a limited partner

unless (i) it is also the name of a general partner or the corporate name of a corporate general partner, or (ii) the business of the limited partnership had been carried on under that name before the admission of that limited partner;

(3) may not be the same as, or deceptively similar to, the name of any corporation or limited partnership organized under the laws of this State or licensed or registered as a foreign corporation or limited partnership in this State; and

(4) may not contain the followng words [here insert prohibited words].

Section 103.   Reservation of Name

(a) The exclusive right to the use of a name may be reserved by:

(1) any person intending to organize a limited partnership under this [Act] and to adopt that name;

(2) any domestic limited partnership or any foreign limited partnership registered in this State which, in either case, intends to adopt that name;

(3) any foreign limited partnership intending to register in this State and adopt that name; and

(4) any person intending to organize a foreign limited partnership and intending to have it register in this State and adopt that name.

(b) The reservation shall be made by filing with the Secretary of State an application, executed by the applicant, to reserve a specified name. If the Secretary of State finds that the name is available for use by a domestic or foreign limited partnership, he [or she] shall reserve the name for the exclusive use of the applicant for a period of 120 days. Once having so reserved a name, the same applicant may not again reserve the same name until more than 60 days after the expiration of the last 120-day period for which that applicant reserved that name. The right to the exclusive use of a reserved name may be transferred to any other person by filing in the office of the Secretary of State a notice of the transfer, executed by the applicant for whom the name was reserved and specifying the name and address of the transferee.

Section 104.   Specified Office and Agent

Each limited partnership shall continuously maintain in this State:

(1) an office, which may but need not be a place of its business in this State, at which shall be kept the records required by Section 105 to be maintained; and

(2) an agent for service of process on the limited partnership, which agent must be an individual resident of this State, a domestic corporation, or a foreign corporation authorized to do business in this State.

Section 105.   Records to Be Kept

(a) Each limited partnership shall keep at the office referred to in Section 104(1) the following:

(1) a current list of the full name and last known business address of each partner, separately identifying the general partners (in alphabetical order) and the limited partners (in alphabetical order);

(2) a copy of the certificate of limited partnership and all certificates of amendment thereto, together with executed copies of any powers of attorney pursuant to which any certificate has been executed;

(3) copies of the limited partnership's federal, state and local income tax returns and reports, if any, for the three most recent years;

(4) copies of any then effective written partnership agreements and of any financial statements of the limited partnership for the three most recent years; and

(5) unless contained in a written partnership agreement, a writing setting out:

(i) the amount of cash and a description and statement of the agreed value of the other property or services contributed by each partner and which each partner has agreed to contribute;

(ii) the times at which or events on the happening of which any additional contributions agreed to be made by each partner are to be made;

(iii) any right of a partner to receive, or of a general partner to make, distributions to a partner which include a return of all or any part of the partner's contribution; and

(iv) any events upon the happening of which the limited partnership is to be dissolved and its affairs wound up.

(b) Records kept under this section are subject to inspection and copying at the reasonable request and at the expense of any partner during ordinary business hours.

Section 106.   Nature of Business

A limited partnership may carry on any business that a partnership without limited partners may carry on except [here designate prohibited activities].

Section 107.   Business Transactions of Partner with Partnership

Except as provided in the partnership agreement, a partner may lend money to and transact other business with the limited partnership and, subject to other applicable law, has the same rights and obligations with respect thereto as a person who is not a partner.

ARTICLE 2

FORMATION; CERTIFICATE OF LIMITED PARTNERSHIP

Section 201.   Certificate of Limited Partnership

(a) In order to form a limited partnership, a certificate of limited partnership must be executed and filed in the office of the Secretary of State. The certificate shall set forth:

(1)   the name of the limited partnership;

(2)   the address of the office and the name and address of the agent for service of process required to be maintained by Section 104;

(3)   the name and the business address of each general partner;

(4)   the latest date upon which the limited partnership is to dissolve; and

(5)   any other matters the general partners determine to include therein.

(b) A limited partnership is formed at the time of the filing of the certificate of limited partnership in the office of the Secretary of State or at any later time specified in the certificate of limited partnership if, in either case, there has been substantial compliance with the requirements of this section.

Section 202.   Amendment to Certificate

(a)   A certificate of limited partnership is amended by filing a certificate of amendment thereto in the office

of the Secretary of State. The certificate shall set forth:

(1)   the name of the limited partnership;

(2)   the date of filing the certificate; and

(3)   the amendment to the certificate.

(b) Within 30 days after the happening of any of the following events, an amendment to a certificate of limited partnership reflecting the occurrence of the event or events shall be filed:

(1)   the admission of a new general partner;

(2)   the withdrawal of a general partner; or

(3)   the continuation of the business under Section 801 after an event of withdrawal of a general partner.

(c)   A general partner who becomes aware that any statement in a certificate of limited partnership was false when made or that any arrangements or other facts described have changed, making the certificate inaccurate in any respect, shall promptly amend the certificate.

(d) A certificate of limited partnership may be amended at any time for any other proper purpose the general partners determine.

(e) No person has any liability because an amendment to a certificate of limited partnership has not been filed to reflect the occurrence of any event referred to in subsection (b) of this section if the amendment is filed within the 30-day period specified in subsection (b).

(f) A restated certificate of limited partnership may be executed and filed in the same manner as a certificate of amendment.

Section 203.   Cancellation of Certificate

A certificate of limited partnership shall be cancelled upon the dissolution and the commencement of winding up of the partnership or at any other time there are no limited partners. A certificate of cancellation shall be filed in the office of the Secretary of State and set forth:

(1)   the name of the limited partnership;

(2)   the date of filing of its certificate of limited partnership;

(3)   the reason for filing the certificate of cancellation;

(4)   the effective date (which shall be a date certain) of

cancellation if it is not to be effective upon the filing of the certificate; and

(5) any other information the general partners filing the certificate determine.

Section 204.   Execution of Certificates

(a) Each certificate required by this Article to be filed in the office of the Secretary of State shall be executed in the following manner:

(1) an original certificate of limited partnership must be signed by all general partners;

(2) a certificate of amendment must be signed by at least one general partner and by each other general partner designated in the certificate as a new general partner; and

(3) a certificate of cancellation must be signed by all general partners.

(b) Any person may sign a certificate by an attorney-in-fact, but a power of attorney to sign a certificate relating to the admission of a general partner must specifically describe the admission.

(c) The execution of a certificate by a general partner constitutes an affirmation under the penalties of perjury that the facts stated therein are true.

Section 205.   Execution by Judicial Act

If a person required by Section 204 to execute any certificate fails or refuses to do so, any other person who is adversely affected by the failure or refusal may petition the [designate the appropriate court] to direct the execution of the certificate. If the court finds that it is proper for the certificate to be executed and that any person so designated has failed or refused to execute the certificate, it shall order the Secretary of State to record an appropriate certificate.

Section 206.   Filing in Office of Secretary of State

(a) Two signed copies of the certificate of limited partnership and of any certificates of amendment or cancellation (or of any judicial decree of amendment or cancellation) shall be delivered to the Secretary of State. A person who executes a certificate as an agent of fiduciary need not exhibit evidence of his [or her] authority as a prerequisite to filing. Unless the Secretary of State finds that any certificate does not conform to law, upon receipt of all filing fees required by law he [or she] shall:

(1) endorse on each duplicate original the word

"Filed" and the day, month and year of the filing thereof;

(2) file one duplicate original in his [or her] office; and

(3) return the other duplicate original to the person who filed it or his [or her] representative.

(b) Upon the filing of a certificate of amendment (or judicial decree of amendment) in the office of the Secretary of State, the certificate of limited partnership shall be amended as set forth therein, and upon the effective date of a certificate of cancellation (or a judicial decree thereof), the certificate of limited partnership is cancelled.

Section 207.   Liability for False Statement in Certificate

If any certificate of limited partnership or certificate of amendment or cancellation contains a false statement, one who suffers loss by reliance on the statement may recover damages for the loss from:

(1) any person who executes the certificate, or causes another to execute it on his behalf, and knew, and any general partner who knew or should have known, the statement to be false at the time the certificate was executed; and

(2) any general partner who thereafter knows or should have known that any arrangement or other fact described in the certificate has changed, making the statement inaccurate in any respect within a sufficient time before the statement was relied upon reasonably to have enabled that general partner to cancel or amend the certificate, or to file a petition for its cancellation or amendment under Section 205.

Section 208.   Scope of Notice

The fact that a certificate of limited partnership is on file in the office of the Secretary of State is notice that the partnership is a limited partnership and the persons designated therein as general partners are general partners, but it is not notice of any other fact.

Section 209.   Delivery of Certificates to Limited Partners

Upon the return by the Secretary of State pursuant to Section 206 of a certificate marked "Filed," the general partners shall promptly deliver or mail a copy of the certificate of limited partnership and each certificate of amendment or cancellation to each limited partner unless the partnership agreement provides otherwise.

ARTICLE 3

LIMITED PARTNERS

Section 301. Admission of Limited Partners

(a) A person becomes a limited partner:

(1) at the time the limited partnership is formed; or

(2) at any later time specified in the records of the limited partnership for becoming a limited partner.

(b) After the filing of a limited partnership's original certificate of limited partnership, a person may be admitted as an additional limited partner:

(1) in the case of a person acquiring a partnership interest directly from the limited partnership, upon compliance with the partnership agreement or, if the partnership agreement does not so provide, upon the written consent of all partners; and

(2) in the case of an assignee of a partnership interest of a partner who has the power, as provided in Section 704, to grant the assignee the right to become a limited partner, upon the exercise of that power and compliance with any conditions limiting the grant or exercise of the power.

Section 302. Voting

Subject to Section 303, the partnership agreement may grant to all or a specified group of the limited partners the right to vote (on a per capita or other basis) upon any matter.

Section 303. Liability to Third Parties

(a) Except as provided in subsection (d), a limited partner is not liable for the obligations of a limited partnership unless he [or she] is also a general partner or, in addition to the exercise of his [or her] rights and powers as a limited partner, he [or she] participates in the control of the business. However, if the limited partner participates in the control of the business, he [or she] is liable only to persons who transact business with the limited partnership reasonably believing, based upon the limited partner's conduct, that the limited partner is a general partner.

(b) A limited partner does not participate in the control of the business within the meaning of subsection (a) solely by doing one or more of the following:

(1) being a contractor for or an agent or employee of the limited partnership or of a general partner or being an officer, director, or shareholder of a general partner that is a corporation;

(2) consulting with and advising a general partner with respect to the business of the limited partnership;

(3) acting as surety for the limited partnership or guaranteeing or assuming one or more specific obligations of the limited partnership;

(4) taking any action required or permitted by law to bring or pursue a derivative action in the right of the limited partnership;

(5) requesting or attending a meeting of partners;

(6) proposing, approving, or disapproving, by voting or otherwise, one or more of the following matters:

(i) the dissolution and winding up of the limited partnership;

(ii) the sale, exchange, lease, mortgage, pledge, or other transfer of all or substantially all of the assets of the limited partnership;

(iii) the incurrence of indebtedness by the limited partnership other than in the ordinary course of its business;

(iv) a change in the nature of the business;

(v) the admission or removal of a general partner;

(vi) the admission or removal of a limited partner;

(vii) a transaction involving an actual or potential conflict of interest between a general partner and the limited partnership or the limited partners;

(viii) an amendment to the partnership agreement or certificate of limited partnership; or

(ix) matters related to the business of the limited partnership not otherwise enumerated in this subsection (b), which the partnership agreement states in writing may be subject to the approval or disapproval of limited partners;

(7) winding up the limited partnership pursuant to Section 804; or

(8) exercising any right or power permitted to limited partners under this [Act] and not specifically enumerated in this subsection (b).

(c) The enumeration in subsection (b) does not mean that the possession or exercise of any other powers by a limited partner constitutes participation by him [or her] in the business of the limited partnership.

(d) A limited partner who knowingly permits his [or her] name to be used in the name of the limited partnership, except under circumstances permitted by Section 102(2), is liable to creditors who extend credit to the limited partnership without actual knowledge that the limited partner is not a general partner.

Section 304. Person Erroneously Believing Himself [or Herself] Limited Partner

(a) Except as provided in subsection (b), a person who makes a contribution to a business enterprise and erroneously but in good faith believes that he [or she] has become a limited partner in the enterprise is not a general partner in the enterprise and is not bound by its obligations by reason of making the contribution, receiving distributions from the enterprise, or exercising any rights of a limited partner, if, on ascertaining the mistake, he [or she]:

(1) causes an appropriate certificate of limited partnership or a certificate of amendment to be executed and filed; or

(2) withdraws from future equity participation in the enterprise by executing and filing in the office of the Secretary of State a certificate declaring withdrawal under this section.

(b) A person who makes a contribution of the kind described in subsection (a) is liable as a general partner to any third party who transacts business with the enterprise (i) before the person withdraws and an appropriate certificate is filed to show withdrawal, or (ii) before an appropriate certificate is filed to show that he [or she] is not a general partner, but in either case only if the third party actually believed in good faith that the person was a general partner at the time of the transaction.

Section 305. Information

Each limited partner has the right to:

(1) inspect and copy any of the partnership records required to be maintained by Section 105; and

(2) obtain from the general partners from time to time

upon reasonable demand (i) true and full information regarding the state of the business and financial condition of the limited partnership, (ii) promptly after becoming available, a copy of the limited partnership's federal, state and local income tax returns for each year, and (iii) other information regarding the affairs of the limited partnership as is just and reasonable.

ARTICLE 4

GENERAL PARTNERS

Section 401. Admission of Additional General Partners

After the filing of a limited partnership's original certificate of limited partnership, additional general partners may be admitted as provided in writing in the partnership agreement or, if the partnership agreement does not provide in writing for the admission of additional general partners, with the written consent of all partners.

Section 402. Events of Withdrawal

Except as approved by the specific written consent of all partners at the time, a person ceases to be a general partner of a limited partnership upon the happening of any of the following events:

(1) the general partner withdraws from the limited partnership as provided in Section 602;

(2) the general partner ceases to be a member of the limited partnership as provided in Section 702;

(3) the general partner is removed as a general partner in accordance with the partnership agreement;

(4) unless otherwise provided in writing in the partnership agreement, the general partner: (i) makes an assignment for the benefit of creditors; (ii) files a voluntary petition in bankruptcy; (iii) is adjudicated a bankrupt or insolvent; (iv) files a petition or answer seeking for himself [or herself] any reorganization, arrangement, composition, readjustment, liquidation, dissolution or similar relief under any statute, law, or regulation; (v) files an answer or other pleading admitting or failing to contest the material allegations of a petition filed against him [or her] in any proceeding of this nature; or (vi) seeks, consents to, or acquiesces in the appointment of a trustee, receiver, or liquidator of the general partner or of all or any substantial part of his [or her] properties;

(5) unless otherwise provided in writing in the partnership agreement, [120] days after the commencement of any proceeding against the general partner seeking reorganization, arrangement, composition, readjustment, liquidation, dissolution or similar relief under any statute, law, or regulation, the proceeding has not been dismissed, or if within [90] days after the appointment without his [or her] consent or acquiescence of a trustee, receiver, or liquidator of the general partner or of all or any substantial part of his [or her] properties, the appointment is not vacated or stayed or within [90] days after the expiration of any such stay, the appointment is not vacated;

(6) in the case of a general partner who is a natural person,

(i) his [or her] death; or

(ii) the entry of an order by a court of competent jurisdiction adjudicating him [or her] incompetent to manage his [or her] person or his [or her] estate;

(7) in the case of a general partner who is acting as a general partner by virtue of being a trustee of a trust, the termination of the trust (but not merely the substitution of a new trustee);

(8) in the case of a general partner that is a separate partnership, the dissolution and commencement of winding up of the separate partnership;

(9) in the case of a general partner that is a corporation, the filing of a certificate of dissolution, or its equivalent, for the corporation or the revocation of its charter; or

(10) in the case of an estate, the distribution by the fiduciary of the estate's entire interest in the partnership.

Section 403. General Powers and Liabilities

(a) Except as provided in this [Act] or in the partnership agreement, a general partner of a limited partnership has the rights and powers and is subject to the restrictions of a partner in a partnership without limited partners.

(b) Except as provided in this [Act], a general partner of a limited partnership has the liabilities of a partner in a partnership without limited partners to persons other than the partnership and the other partners. Except as provided in this [Act] or in the partnership agreement, a general partner of a limited partnership has the liabilities of a partner in a partnership without limited partners to the partnership and to the other partners.

Section 404. Contributions by General Partner

A general partner of a limited partnership may make contributions to the partnership and share in the profits and losses of, and in distributions from, the limited partnership as a general partner. A general partner also may make contributions to and share in profits, losses, and distributions as a limited partner. A person who is both a general partner and a limited partner has the rights and powers, and is subject to the restrictions and liabilities, of a general partner and, except as provided in the partnership agreement, also has the powers, and is subject to the restrictions, of a limited partner to the extent of his [or her] participation in the partnership as a limited partner.

Section 405. Voting

The partnership agreement may grant to all or certain identified general partners the right to vote (on a per capita or any other basis), separately or with all or any class of the limited partners, on any matter.

ARTICLE 5

FINANCE

Section 501. Form of Contribution

The contribution of a partner may be in cash, property, or services rendered, or a promissory note or other obligation to contribute cash or property or to perform services.

Section 502. Liability for Contribution

(a) A promise by a limited partner to contribute to the limited partnership is not enforceable unless set out in a writing signed by the limited partner.

(b) Except as provided in the partnership agreement, a partner is obligated to the limited partnership to perform any enforceable promise to contribute cash or property or to perform services, even if he [or she] is unable to perform because of death, disability, or any other reason. If a partner does not make the required contribution of property or services, he [or she] is obligated at the option of the limited partnership to contribute cash equal to that portion of the value, as stated in the partnership records required to be kept pursuant to Section 105, of the stated contribution which has not been made.

(c) Unless otherwise provided in the partnership agreement, the obligation of a partner to make a contribution or return money or other property paid or distributed in violation of this [Act] may be compromised only by consent of all partners. Notwithstanding the compromise, a creditor of a limited partnership who extends credit or otherwise acts in reliance on that obligation after the partner signs a writing which reflects the obligation and before the amendment or cancellation thereof to reflect the compromise may enforce the original obligation.

Section 503. Sharing of Profits and Losses

The profits and losses of a limited partnership shall be allocated among the partners, and among classes of partners, in the manner provided in writing in the partnership agreement. If the partnership agreement does not so provide in writing, profits and losses shall be allocated on the basis of the value, as stated in the partnership records required to be kept pursuant to Section 105, of the contributions made by each partner to the extent they have been received by the partnership and have not been returned.

Section 504. Sharing of Distributions

Distributions of cash or other assets of a limited partnership shall be allocated among the partners and among classes of partners in the manner provided in writing in the partnership agreement. If the partnership agreement does not so provide in writing, distributions shall be made on the basis of the value, as stated in the partnership records required to be kept pursuant to Section 105, of the contributions made by each partner to the extent they have been received by the partnership and have not been returned.

ARTICLE 6

DISTRIBUTIONS AND WITHDRAWAL

Section 601. Interim Distributions

Except as provided in this Article, a partner is entitled to receive distributions from a limited partnership before his [or her] withdrawal from the limited partnership and before the dissolution and winding up thereof to the extent and at the times or upon the happening of the events specified in the partnership agreement.

Section 602. Withdrawal of General Partner

A general partner may withdraw from a limited partnership at any time by giving written notice to the other partners, but if the withdrawal violates the part-

nership agreement, the limited partnership may recover from the withdrawing general partner damages for breach of the partnership agreement and offset the damages against the amount otherwise distributable to him [or her].

Section 603. Withdrawal of Limited Partner

A limited partner may withdraw from a limited partnership at the time or upon the happening of events specified in writing in the partnership agreement. If the agreement does not specify in writing the time or the events upon the happening of which a limited partner may withdraw or a definite time for the dissolution and winding up of the limited partnership, a limited partner may withdraw upon not less than six months' prior written notice to each general partner at his [or her] address on the books of the limited partnership at its office in this State.

Section 604. Distribution upon Withdrawal

Except as provided in this Article, upon withdrawal any withdrawing partner is entitled to receive any distribution to which he [or she] is entitled under the partnership agreement and, if not otherwise provided in the agreement, he [or she] is entitled to receive, within a reasonable time after withdrawal, the fair value of his [or her] interest in the limited partnership as of the date of withdrawal based upon his [or her] right to share in distributions from the limited partnership.

Section 605. Distribution in Kind

Except as provided in writing in the partnership agreement, a partner, regardless of the nature of his [or her] contribution, has no right to demand and receive any distribution from a limited partnership in any form other than cash. Except as provided in writing in the partnership agreement, a partner may not be compelled to accept a distribution of any asset in kind from a limited partnership to the extent that the percentage of the asset distributed to him [or her] exceeds a percentage of that asset which is equal to the percentage in which he [or she] shares in distributions from the limited partnership.

Section 606. Right to Distribution

At the time a partner becomes entitled to receive a distribution, he [or she] has the status of, and is entitled to all remedies available to, a creditor of the limited partnership with respect to the distribution.

Section 607.   Limitations on Distribution

A partner may not receive a distribution from a limited partnership to the extent that, after giving effect to the distribution, all liabilities of the limited partnershp, other than liabilities to partners on account of their partnership interests, exceed the fair value of the partnership assets.

Section 608.   Liability upon Return of Contribution

(a) If a partner has received the return of any part of his [or her] contribution without violation of the partnership agreement or this [Act], he [or she] is liable to the limited partnership for a period of one year thereafter for the amount of the returned contribution, but only to the extent necessary to discharge the limited partnership's liabilities to creditors who extended credit to the limited partnership during the period the contribution was held by the partnership.

(b) If a partner has received the return of any part of his [or her] contribution in violation of the partnership agreement or this [Act], he [or she] is liable to the limited partnership for a period of six years thereafter for the amount of the contribution wrongfully returned.

(c) A partner receives a return of his [or her] contribution to the extent that a distribution to him [or her] reduces his [or her] share of the fair value of the net assets of the limited partnership below the value, as set forth in the partnership records required to be kept pursuant to Section 105, of his contribution which has not been distributed to him [or her].

ARTICLE 7

ASSIGNMENT OF PARTNERSHIP INTERESTS

Section 701.   Nature of Partnership Interest

A partnership interest is personal property.

Section 702.   Assignment of Partnership Interest

Except as provided in the partnership agreement, a partnership interest is assignable in whole or in part. An assignment of a partnership interest does not dissolve a limited partnership or entitle the assignee to become or to exercise any rights of a partner. An assignment entitles the assignee to receive, to the extent assigned, only the distribution to which the assignor would be entitled. Except as provided in the partnership agreement, a partner ceases to be a partner upon assignment of all his [or her] partnership interest.

Section 703.   Rights of Creditor

On application to a court of competent jurisdiction by any judgment creditor of a partner, the court may charge the partnership interest of the partner with payment of the unsatisfied amount of the judgment with interest. To the extent so charged, the judgment creditor has only the rights of an assignee of the partnership interest. This [Act] does not deprive any partner of the benefit of any exemption laws applicable to his [or her] partnership interest.

Section 704.   Right of Assignee to Become Limited Partner

(a) An assignee of a partnership interest, including an assignee of a general partner, may become a limited partner if and to the extent that (i) the assignor gives the assignee that right in accordance with authority described in the partnership agreement, or (ii) all other partners consent.

(b) An assignee who has become a limited partner has, to the extent assigned, the rights and powers, and is subject to the restrictions and liabilities, of a limited partner under the partnership agreement and this [Act]. An assignee who becomes a limited partner also is liable for the obligations of his [or her] assignor to make and return contributions as provided in Articles 5 and 6. However, the assignee is not obligated for liabilities unknown to the assignee at the time he [or she] became a limited partner.

(c) If an assignee of a partnership interest becomes a limited partner, the assignor is not released from his [or her] liability to the limited partnership under Sections 207 and 502.

Section 705.   Power of Estate of Deceased or Incompetent Partner

If a partner who is an individual dies or a court of competent jurisdiction adjudges him [or her] to be incompetent to manage his [or her] person or his [or her] property, the partner's executor, administrator, guardian, conservator, or other legal representative may exercise all the partner's rights for the purpose of settling his [or her] estate or administering his [or her] property, including any power the partner had to give an assignee the right to become a limited partner. If a partner is a corporation, trust, or other entity and is dissolved or terminated, the powers of that partner may be exercised by its legal representative or successor.

ARTICLE 8

DISSOLUTION

Section 801.   Nonjudicial Dissolution

A limited partnership is dissolved and its affairs shall be wound up upon the happening of the first to occur of the following:

(1)   at the time specified in the certificate of limited partnership;

(2)   upon the happening of events specified in writing in the partnership agreement;

(3)   written consent of all partners;

(4)   an event of withdrawal of a general partner unless at the time there is at least one other general partner and the written provisions of the partnership agreement permit the business of the limited partnership to be carried on by the remaining general partner and that partner does so, but the limited partnership is not dissolved and is not required to be wound up by reason of any event of withdrawal if, within 90 days after the withdrawal, all partners agree in writing to continue the business of the limited partnership and to the appointment of one or more additional general partners if necessary or desired; or

(5)   entry of a decree of judicial dissolution under Section 802.

Section 802.   Judicial Dissolution

On application by or for a partner the [designate the appropriate court] court may decree dissolution of a limited partnership whenever it is not reasonably practicable to carry on the business in conformity with the partnership agreement.

Section 803.   Winding Up

Except as provided in the partnership agreement, the general partners who have not wrongfully dissolved a limited partnership or, if none, the limited partners, may wind up the limited partnership's affairs; but the [designate the appropriate court] court may wind up the limited partnership's affairs upon application of any partner, his [or her] legal representative, or assignee.

Section 804.   Distribution of Assets

Upon the winding up of a limited partnership, the assets shall be distributed as follows:

(1)   to creditors, including partners who are creditors, to the extent permitted by law, in satisfaction of liabilities of the limited partnership other than liabilities for distributions to partners under Section 601 or 604;

(2)   except as provided in the partnership agreement, to partners and former partners in satisfaction of liabilities for distributions under Section 601 or 604; and

(3)   except as provided in the partnership agreement, to partners first for the return of their contributions and secondly respecting their partnership interests, in the proportions in which the partners share in distributions.

ARTICLE 9

FOREIGN LIMITED PARTNERSHIPS

Section 901.   Law Governing

Subject to the Constitution of this State, (i) the laws of the state under which a foreign limited partnership is organized govern its organization and internal affairs and the liability of its limited partners, and (ii) a foreign limited partnership may not be denied registration by reason of any difference between those laws and the laws of this State.

Section 902.   Registration

Before transacting business in this State, a foreign limited partnership shall register with the Secretary of State. In order to register, a foreign limited partnership shall submit to the Secretary of State, in duplicate, an application for registration as a foreign limited partnership, signed and sworn to be a general partner and setting forth:

(1)   the name of the foreign limited partnership and, if different, the name under which it proposes to register and transact business in this State;

(2)   the State and date of its formation;

(3)   the name and address of any agent for service of process on the foreign limited partnership whom the foreign limited partnership elects to appoint; the agent must be an individual resident of this State, a domestic corporation, or a foreign corporation having a place of business in, and authorized to do business in, this State;

(4) a statement that the Secretary of State is appointed the agent of the foreign limited partnership for service of process if no agent has been appointed under paragraph (3) or, if appointed, the agent's authority has been revoked or if the agent cannot be found or served with the exercise of reasonable diligence;

(5) the address of the office required to be maintained in the state of its organization by the laws of that state or, if not so required, of the principal office of the foreign limited partnership;

(6) the name and business address of each general partner; and

(7) the address of the office at which is kept a list of the names and addresses of the limited partners and their capital contributions, together with an undertaking by the foreign limited partnership to keep those records until the foreign limited partnership's registration in this State is cancelled or withdrawn.

Section 903. Issuance of Registration

(a) If the Secretary of State finds that an application for registration conforms to law and all requisite fees have been paid, he [or she] shall:

    (1) endorse on the application the word "Filed," and the month, day and year of the filing thereof;

    (2) file in his [or her] office a duplicate original of the application; and

    (3) issue a certificate of registration to transact business in this State.

(b) The certificate of registration, together with a duplicate original of the application, shall be returned to the person who filed the application or his [or her] representative.

Section 904. Name

A foreign limited partnership may register with the Secretary of State under any name, whether or not it is the name under which it is registered in its state of organization, that includes without abbreviation the words "limited partnership" and that could be registered by a domestic limited partnership.

Section 905. Changes and Amendments

If any statement in the application for registration of a foreign limited partnership was false when made or any arrangements or other facts described have changed, making the application inaccurate in any respect, the foreign limited partnership shall promptly file in the office of the Secretary of State a certificate, signed and sworn to by a general partner, correcting such statement.

Section 906. Cancellation of Registration

A foreign limited partnership may cancel its registration by filing with the Secretary of State a certificate of cancellation signed and sworn by a general partner. A cancellation does not terminate the authority of the Secretary of State to accept service of process on the foreign limited partnership with respect to [claims for relief] [causes of action] arising out of the transactions of business in this State.

Section 907. Transaction of Business Without Registration

(a) A foreign limited partnership transacting business in this State may not maintain any action, suit, or proceeding in any court of this State until it has registered in this State.

(b) The failure of a foreign limited partnership to register in this State does not impair the validity of any contract or act of the foreign limited partnership or prevent the foreign limited partnership from defending any action, suit, or proceeding in any court of this State.

(c) A limited partner of a foreign limited partnership is not liable as a general partner of the foreign limited partnership solely by reason of having transacted business in this State without registration.

(d) A foreign limited partnership, by transacting business in this State without registration, appoints the Secretary of State as its agent for service of process with respect to [claims for relief] [causes of action] arising out of the transaction of business in this State.

Section 908. Action by [Appropriate Official]

The [designate the appropriate official] may bring an action to restrain a foreign limited partnership from transacting business in this State in violation of this Article.

ARTICLE 10

DERIVATIVE ACTIONS

Section 1001. Right of Action

A limited partner may bring an action in the right of a limited partnership to recover a judgment in its favor if general partners with authority to do so have refused to bring the action or if an effort to cause those general partners to bring the action is not likely to succeed.

Section 1002. Proper Plaintiff

In a derivative action, the plaintiff must be a partner at the time of bringing the action and (i) must have been a partner at the time of the transaction of which he [or she] complains or (ii) his [or her] status as a partner must have devolved upon him [or her] by operation of law or pursuant to the terms of the partnership agreement from a person who was a partner at the time of the transaction.

Section 1003. Pleading

In a derivative action, the complaint shall set forth with particularity the effort of the plaintiff to secure initiation of the action by a general partner or the reasons for not making the effort.

Section 1004. Expenses

If a derivative action is successful, in whole or in part, or if anything is received by the plaintiff as a result of a judgment, compromise or settlement of an action or claim, the court may award the plaintiff reasonable expenses, including reasonable attorney's fees, and shall direct him [or her] to remit to the limited partnership the remainder of those proceeds received by him [or her].

ARTICLE 11

MISCELLANEOUS

Section 1101. Construction and Application

This [Act] shall be so applied and construed to effectuate its general purpose to make uniform the law with respect to the subject of this [Act] among states enacting it.

Section 1102. Short Title

This [Act] may be cited as the Uniform Limited Partnership Act.

Section 1103. Severability

If any provision of this [Act] or its application to any person or circumstance is held invalid, the invalidity does not affect other provisions or applications of the [Act] which can be given effect without the invalid provision or application, and to this end the provisions of this Act are severable.

Section 1104. Effective Date, Extended Effective Date, and Repeal

Except as set forth below, the effective date of this [Act] is _____ and the following acts [list existing limited partnership acts] are hereby repealed:

(1) The existing provisions for execution and filing of certificates of limited partnerships and amendments thereunder and cancellations thereof continue in effect until [specify time required to create central filing system], the extended effective date, and Sections 102, 103, 104, 105, 201, 202, 203, 204 and 206 are not effective until the extended effective date.

(2) Section 402, specifying the conditions under which a general partner ceases to be a member of a limited partnership, is not effective until the extended effective date, and the applicable provisions of existing law continue to govern until the extended effective date.

(3) Sections 501, 502 and 608 apply only to contributions and distributions made after the effective date of this [Act].

(4) Section 704 applies only to assignments made after the effective date of this [Act].

(5) Article 9, dealing with registration of foreign limited partnerships, is not effective until the extended effective date.

(6) Unless otherwise agreed by the partners, the applicable provisions of existing law governing allocation of profits and losses (rather than the provisions of Section 503), distributions to a withdrawing partner (rather than the provisions of Section 604), and distribution of assets upon the winding up of a limited partnership (rather than the provisions of Section 804) govern limited partnerships formed before the effective date of this [Act].

Section 1105. Rules for Cases Not Provided for in This [Act]

In any case not provided for in this [Act] the provisions of the Uniform Partnership Act govern.

Section 1106. Savings Clause

The repeal of any statutory provision by this Act does not impair, or otherwise affect, the organization or the continued existence of a limited partnership existing at the effective date of this Act, nor does the repeal of any existing statutory provision by this Act impair any contract or affect any right accrued before the effective date of this Act.

Glossary

Abandoned property   Property that the owner has discarded with no intention of ever again reclaiming any rights or interests in it.

Abet   To assist or support in the performance of an act or the attainment of a purpose.

Acceleration clause   A clause in a contract that advances the date for payment on the occurrence of a condition or the breach of a duty.

Acceleration of payment   The speeding up of the due date for payment for a contract or for a commercial instrument.

Accept   To agree to, as in an offer.

Acceptance   Compliance with the terms of an offer; the action of a buyer in taking the goods tendered by a seller; the act whereby a drawee agrees to honor a negotiable instrument upon due presentment.

Acceptor   A person who accepts a negotiable instrument or otherwise agrees to be primarily liable for the instrument.

Accession   The acquisition of additional property due to the growth or increase of property already possessed.

The definitions given here are accurate as far as they go, but space limitations prevent complete technical definitions. A student who wants a more detailed definition is advised to consult a legal dictionary such as *Black's Law Dictionary* or *Ballantine's Law Dictionary*.

Accommodation party   A party who signs a commercial paper for the purpose of lending his or her name to another party to the instrument.

Accord   An agreement between two or more parties on the degree of performance that will operate as a full discharge of an obligation.

Accord and satisfaction   The making of a new agreement between two or more parties and the performance of that agreement by the parties (normally used in the area of disputed claims).

Account   To furnish a justifying explanation or analysis for monies spent or actions taken.

Accretion   An addition by growing, especially in the area of real property, where land increases by natural actions and causes.

Actionable   Affording grounds for an action, such as a suit at law.

Actual cause   The act that brings about some end result.

Actual fraud   See **Fraud.**

Adhesion   A firm attachment; a sticking together. When used in reference to a contract, it means a contract whose terms are not open to negotiation — the offeree must "take it or leave it."

Adjudicate   To determine through a judicial proceeding.

Adjunct   Added or joined to another.

Administrative law   The branch of public law that deals with administrative agencies and their actions.

A-165

Administrator (administratrix)   A man (woman) who has been empowered by an appropriate court to handle the estate of a deceased person; a manager of the affairs of another person, in the name of the person so managed.

Admission   Agreement or concession concerning evidence or pleadings without the need to introduce proof.

Adverse possession   A method for gaining title to property by possession/occupancy for a predetermined statutory period. Adverse possession requires that the possessor occupy the property openly, notoriously, hostilely, and continuously for a period specified by state statute.

Advisory opinion   A formal opinion issued by a court at the request of a legislative body or of a government officer concerning a hypothetical fact situation.

Affidavit   A written, sworn statement declaring the facts contained in the statement to be true.

Affirmative defense   A defense to a cause of action that must be raised by the defendant.

After-acquired property   Property gained or possessed following a certain date or event; that which is attained later.

Agency   A legal relationship in which one person is empowered and authorized to represent another, normally in the formation of contracts.

Agent   A person authorized to act for or on behalf of another in the formation of contracts.

Aid   To assist; to provide a person with things necessary to the attainment of a desired end.

Alien   Foreign; owing allegiance to another government.

Alleged   Asserted to be true or factual without any showing of proof.

Allonge   A piece of paper permanently attached to a negotiable instrument to accommodate additional endorsements when the original instrument has no more room for endorsements.

Alluvion   An increase in land by the gradual deposit of substances from the flow of water against the shore. The land so added becomes the property of the owner of the land where the new substances are deposited.

Ambiguity   Doubtful meaning or uncertainty due to obscurity or lack of distinctness.

Amortize   To provide for the gradual extinction of a debt or obligation by periodic contributions to a sinking fund or similar device.

Annuitant   The beneficiary of an annuity.

Annuity   A sum of money payable periodically, commonly annually, to a named person; the contract that creates the obligation to pay the annuitant the periodic payments.

Answer   Any sort of pleading filed by the defendant in a cause of action, but especially the written statement that sets forth the defenses asserted.

Antedated   Predated; given an earlier date than the date on which the event occurred (normally used with reference to a negotiable instrument).

Anticipatory breach   A refusal or rejection by one party to a contract before the time for performance that permits the other party to treat the repudiation as an immediate breach of the contract. Also known as *anticipatory repudiation.*

Antitrust laws   Legislation opposed to the formation or use of trusts or combinations; statutes designed to protect commerce from unfair trade practices or monopolies.

Apparent authority   Authority that the agent appears to possess because of the conduct of the principal and on which the third person relies as being authorized; authority that the agent does not in fact possess but that the third person has been caused to believe does exist.

Appellant   A party who takes an appeal from one court to another.

Appellate court   A court that has the authority to review the action of inferior courts upon proper appeal or writ; a reviewing court.

Appellee   The party in a case against whom an appeal has been taken.

Appraisal right   The right in certain extraordinary corporate activities to have a security evaluated and the appraised value paid to the owner.

Appurtenant   Belonging to; annexed to; adjoining and necessary to the enjoyment of.

Arbitration   A nonjudicial settlement of a case or controversy whereby the parties submit the issues to an independent person chosen by the parties or appointed by statutory authority.

Arraignment   The calling of a defendant before the court to answer to a charge of having committed a crime.

Arson   At common law, the intentional burning of the house or outbuilding of another person. Today, a number of state statutes also include as arson the malicious burning of one's own house or outbuildings.

Articles of incorporation The legal document that must be filed with a designated state official in order to do business as a corporation. The articles must comply with state statutes and must be approved by the state before the corporation legally exists.

Assault An intentional threat to harm another by use of force, together with the apparent means to accomplish the threat, which causes fear that the harm will occur.

Assignee The grantee, or recipient, of an assignment.

Assignment The legal transfer to another of one's rights under a contract.

Assignment for the benefit of creditors An assignment by a debtor of the debtor's assets to a trustee to be used in the satisfaction of the claims of creditors.

Assignor A person who makes an assignment.

Association A voluntary joining together of two or more persons to achieve a common goal.

Assumption of the risk A legal defense to a tort action in which the plaintiff is said to have voluntarily chosen to face the risk or danger that occurred and therefore has no right to complain of its occurrence.

Assurance A guaranty; a promise; a statement that inspires confidence that the assured thing will occur.

Attach To seize property in order to bring it within the jurisdiction of the court.

Attachment The act of attaching; a writ or judicial order directing the taking of persons or property in order to assure jurisdiction by the court.

At will Without a set time period; for as long as is mutually agreeable.

Auction A public sale in which the property being sold goes to the highest bidder.

Avoid To cancel an obligation or duty.

Avulsion The removal of land from the property of one person and the addition of that land to the property of another person by the action of water.

Award The decision entered by an arbitrator or other nonjudicial person in the matter submitted for resolution.

B

Bail Security given for the appearance of a defendant/prisoner in order to secure a release from imprisonment pending the trial.

Bailee The person to whom property is delivered in a bailment, with the understanding that that person will return the property at a later time or will dispose of it according to the directions of the bailor.

Bailment A delivery of goods from one party to another in trust, with no transfer of title occurring.

Bailor The person who delivers the property involved in a bailment to the bailee. A bailor does not need to be the owner of the bailed goods in order to create a valid bailment.

Bankruptcy An area of law designed to give an "honest debtor" a fresh start; the proceedings undertaken against a person or a firm under the bankruptcy laws.

Bar The complete and permanent destruction of an action at law; also, the entire body of attorneys permitted to practice law in a particular jurisdiction.

Bargain (Noun) an agreement between parties that specifies what each is to receive and what each is to perform or deliver. (Verb) to come to terms.

Battery The unauthorized touching of the person of another without legal excuse or the consent of the person so touched.

Beneficiary A person for whom a trust is created; a person designated to receive the proceeds of an insurance policy; a person who receives advantages or profits from another.

Benefit An advantage, profit, or gain; a legal right received from another.

Beyond a reasonable doubt A standard of proof required in criminal proceedings, meaning proof to a moral certainty, proof that is entirely convincing, proof not subject to any other *reasonable* interpretation.

Bilateral Two-sided; reciprocal.

Bilateral contract A contract formed by the exchange of promises by the two parties to the contract; a promise in exchange for a promise.

Binder A temporary contract to provide insurance coverage pending the processing of an application and the issuance of a formal policy.

Blank endorsement A type of endorsement in which the endorser merely writes his or her name without designating the next holder and leaving the instrument payable to bearer.

Board of directors The managers of a corporation; the official governing body of a private corporation elected by the stockholders at the annual meeting of the stockholders.

Bona fide In good faith; honestly; without deceit; innocently.

Bona fide occupational qualification (BFOQ)
A legally justifiable limitation concerning the ability to perform a particular job.

Bona fide purchaser   A person who purchases in good faith, for value, and without notice of any defects or defenses affecting the sale or transaction.

Bond   A written evidence of indebtedness, usually bearing interest, issued by a public or private corporation, and payable at a fixed future date.

Book value   The value of a business, arrived at by deducting liabilities from assets.

Boycott   A concerted refusal to have any dealings with a person or a firm; a conspiracy to disrupt the business of a person or firm.

Breach   The breaking of a duty or right, whether by act or omission; the failure to honor a promise, or any part of a promise, that forms the basis of a contract.

Bribe   Anything of value given or accepted with the corrupt intention of influencing a person in the performance of a public duty or the carrying out of any official actions.

Bulk sale   The sale of all or a substantial part of a merchant's stock in trade not made in the ordinary course of business. Also known as *bulk transfer*.

Burden of proof   The legal duty to prove the truth of facts in dispute in a cause of action in order to prevail in the cause; the amount of proof necessary to carry one's case, such as "beyond a reasonable doubt," or "clear and convincing evidence."

Burglary   The crime of breaking into a building with an intent to steal; at common law, the act of breaking into a dwelling at night with an intent to commit a felony.

Buyer in the ordinary course of business   A purchaser who buys goods or services from a merchant seller in a standard (as opposed to an extraordinary) transaction.

Bylaws   The rules and regulations adopted by a corporation or other association for the purpose of self-regulation, especially of day-to-day matters not covered by other documents.

C

Cancel   To delete or annul; to strike out or obliterate; to revoke.

Cancellation   Any action shown on the face of a contract that indicates an intent to destroy the obligation of the contract.

Capacity   Legal ability to perform an act or to assume an obligation; legal measurement of power, competence, or ability.

Capital contribution   The money invested in a business venture by the owners in return for their shares of ownership; the value of any assets invested in a business venture in lieu of money.

Carrier   See **Common carrier**.

Cases and controversies   Judicial proceedings between parties involving an actual fact situation on justiciable issues, and excluding advisory opinions or hypothetical situations.

Cash   Money; legal tender; official currency.

Cashier's check   A check that is issued by a bank and drawn against the bank's own funds and that is accepted upon issue.

Cash value   The actual market value a thing is worth in a private sale for cash, with no portion of the payment deferred.

Causa mortis   In contemplation of death (normally used in reference to a gift made by the donor because of the donor's expectation of death).

Caveat emptor   Literally, let the buyer beware, meaning that the buyer needs to exercise caution since he or she assumes any and all risks in the transaction.

Caveat venditor   Literally, let the seller beware, meaning that the seller is responsible for any and all defects or deficiencies in the goods being sold.

Certification   The act of certifying something, such as a check, in order to guarantee the signature and the amount appearing on its face.

Certiorari   Literally, to be made informed of; the name of a writ issued by a court in order to review the action of an inferior court in a proceeding.

Charging order   A court order that allows a judgment creditor to receive the profits otherwise owed to the debtor from the operation of a business in which the debtor has an interest, especially the profits of a partnership in which the debtor is a partner.

Charitable subscription   A written and signed commitment to contribute money to a charity.

Charter   A grant by the government that authorizes the creation and operation of a corporation.

Chattel   Articles of personal (as opposed to real) property; any interest in property that is less than a freehold or a fee interest in land.

Chattel mortgage   A mortgage used to create a lien on some right or personal property as security for the payment of a debt or the performance of an obligation.

Chose in action   See **Things in action.**

Circumscribe   To restrict the range or activity of something clearly and definitely.

Civil rights   The personal rights and freedoms guaranteed to the citizens of the United States by the Constitution.

Class action   A lawsuit filed by some members of a group on behalf of all the members of the same group.

Clear and convincing proof   A measure of the burden of proof that must be satisfied in a civil case, which is more than a mere preponderance of the evidence but less than the degree of proof required in a criminal case; proof that is very convincing but not necessarily conclusive.

Clearinghouse   An association of banks and financial institutions that "clears" items, adjusting and paying items among the banks in the city or region.

Closed shop   A business in which the employees must be members of a labor union in order to hold their employment.

Codicil   An addition to a preexisting will used to explain, modify, or supplement the will.

Coinsurance clause   A clause on fire insurance policies that requires that the insured maintain a predetermined percentage of the risk, based on the value of the property, or suffer a reduced coverage from the insurer in the event of a loss.

Collateral   Supplementary; additional; added to; secondary. A collateral *promise* is made secondarily and is added to the primary, or original, promise made by another. Collateral also refers to *security*, things that are given as further assurance that a promise or performance will be forthcoming.

Collective bargaining   Contract negotiations between the management of a company and representatives of labor, or the employees, which determines such things as working conditions, wages, hours, and so on.

Comity   The informal and voluntary recognition of the sovereignty of another nation.

Commercial frustration   Excuse of performance in a contract when the contract depends on the existence of a person or thing and the person or thing ceases to exist; excuse of performance when a contract becomes impossible to perform because of an act of God or a change in the law.

Commercial paper   Negotiable instruments; checks, drafts, notes, and certificates of deposit; instruments that are used as credit instruments and/or as substitutes for money and that are governed by Article 3 of the UCC.

Commercial unit   The size or quantity of packaged goods called for in a contract, such as a *dozen* eggs, a *ton* of coal, and so on.

Commission   A fee paid to an agent or employee for the performance of some task or service; especially, a fee paid as a percentage of the total monies to be received.

Common carrier   A person or firm offering to the general public, for compensation, the service of transporting people or goods.

Common law   Unwritten law; the law as developed by the use of precedent and stare decisis, whereby the court uses the opinions in earlier, similar cases to reach a verdict in a current case.

Common stock   The basic and only necessary ownership class of stock.

Communication   The exchange of knowledge or information between parties; a statement made by one party to another.

Community property   Property held jointly by a husband and wife; normally, property acquired during the marriage and excluding gifts or inheritances received by one spouse only.

Comparative negligence   A means of measuring negligence whereby the negligence of the plaintiff is compared with that of the defendant, and the award to the plaintiff is reduced by the amount of negligence attributed to the plaintiff.

Compensation   Indemnification; payment for services rendered; payment for damages suffered.

Compensatory damages   Those damages necessary to compensate the injured party or to make the injured party whole; actual damages.

Competitors   Persons who offer to perform the same, or a very similar, service and who normally attempt to distinguish their own services on the basis of price, quality, or other differences.

Complaint   The first formal filing of a plaintiff in a civil case, setting out the alleged cause of action and a prayer for relief.

Composition   An agreement between a debtor and his or her creditors whereby each creditor agrees to accept less than is owed in exchange for an earlier payment, and a discharge is granted to the debtor upon the performance of the agreed consideration.

Conclusive presumption   A presumption whose establishment precludes any further evidence or argument to the contrary.

Concurrent jurisdiction   Jurisdiction among several different courts, with the appropriate court being decided by the party who files suit.

Condemnation   The process by which privately held land is taken for a public use despite the owner's objection and lack of consent. See also **Eminent domain.**

Condition   An event whose occurrence will create the obligation to perform a contractual promise or will excuse the performance of a contractual promise.

Conditional sales contract   A sales contract in which the transfer of title to the buyer is subject to a condition, most commonly the payment of the full purchase price by the buyer.

Condition precedent   A condition that must occur before the obligation to perform will exist.

Conditions concurrent   Conditions that are mutually dependent and that must occur at or very near the same time.

Condition subsequent   A condition whose occurrence will excuse the performance of a contractual obligation.

Confession of judgment   A judgment in which the defendant has given the plaintiff written permission to enter a judgment in favor of the plaintiff against the defendant in the event of a lawsuit.

Confirmation   The supporting of a statement with proof; the ratification of a contract that was avoidable; a firming up or finalizing of an agreement that was in doubt.

Confiscation   A taking of private property by the government in violation of international law.

Conforming   In agreement; matching the description; acceptable.

Confusion   A blending, intermixing, or commingling that causes the individual parts to become obscured.

Consent   Voluntary approval of or agreement with the conduct done by, or proposed to be done by, another.

Consent decree   A decree entered by agreement of the parties and in the form of a solemn contract.

Consequential damages   Indirect damages; damages that arise as a consequence of an act or omission and not as a direct result.

Consideration   The legal benefit conferred or the legal detriment assumed as the result of the creation of a contract; the legal measure of value given in a contract.

Consignee   A person to whom goods are shipped.

Consignment   A bailment for the sale of goods. The consignor ships goods to the consignee so that the consignee can sell those goods to purchasers.

Consignor   A person who ships goods to another person.

Consolidate   To combine; to join together; to merge.

Conspicuous   Reasonably calculated to be seen and noticed; expected to convey the information to be imparted; obvious to the eye.

Conspiracy   A combining of two or more persons for the purpose of performing an unlawful act or of violating public policy.

Constitution   A written document that is the supreme law of the jurisdiction it purports to govern.

Constructive condition   A condition imposed by law.

Construction eviction   An inability of the purchasee or lessee to obtain possession or occupancy because of an outstanding claim.

Constructive fraud   An act or omission that operates as would a virtual fraud to the detriment of another or to the detriment of public policy even though the actor did not intend it to be a fraud.

Constructive notice   Information of which a person should have been aware from a review of all the facts and circumstances; information that a person is treated as knowing, whether actually known or not.

Constructive trust   A trust imposed by law to prevent the unjust enrichment of the purported owner of the "trust" property.

Consumer   A user; a person who utilizes economic goods, especially for personal or household use.

Consumer goods   Goods purchased for personal or household use, in contrast to goods purchased for inventory or equipment use.

Consumer price index   Measurement of how the price of a group of consumer goods changes between two time periods.

Contingent   Possible but not assured or definite; subject to the occurrence of a condition.

Contract   A legally enforceable agreement between two or more persons, supported by adequate consideration and having the requisite legal form.

Contract of adhesion   See **Adhesion.**

Contributory negligence   Negligent conduct by the

plaintiff that, taken together with the negligence of the defendant, makes up the proximate cause of the accident; a defense to a lawsuit for negligence in which the defendant shows that the plaintiff was at fault in the occurrence.

Conversion   The unauthorized and wrongful exercise of dominion and control over the personal property of another to the harm of that other person.

Convert   To change the nature of, as from real property to personal property.

Conveyance   A transfer of legal or equitable title.

Copyright   A legally protected, exclusive right to sell, to publish, or to reproduce artistic, musical or literary works for the life of the author plus fifty years.

Corporate charter   The right to conduct business granted to the corporation by the state in which the firm was incorporated, as evidenced by the formal legal papers and documents shown as the charter.

Corporation   An artificial person created under the statutes of a state or federal government, organized for the purpose set out in the application for corporate existence.

Corpus   Literally, body; the principal sum contributed, as to a trust, as distinguished from the income generated by that principal sum.

Counteroffer   A reply to an offer in which the offeree rejects the original offer and substitutes a *new* offer, whereby the former offeree becomes the offeror.

Court of equity   A separate court system developed at common law to administer justice and fairness in cases that were not actionable "at law."

Covenant   A promise, often in writing and under seal, pledging that something has been done or will be done.

Covenant not to compete   A clause in a contract whereby one party agrees not to compete with the other party after the termination of the contract.

Cover   In the law of sales, to purchase similar goods from another source upon the breach of a sales contract by the seller; in insurance, to agree to insure a named asset or thing of value.

Creator   A person who establishes a trust by transferring assets (the corpus) to a trustee for the welfare of the beneficiary.

Credit   The ability to purchase goods or services on time; the opposite of a debt, or a debt looked at from the perspective of the creditor.

Creditor   A person to whom a debt is owed.

Creditor beneficiary   A third party who is designated to receive the benefits of a promise or a performance in satisfaction of a legal obligation owed by one of the parties to the contract.

Crime   An act or conduct against society or the state that is subject to penal sanctions.

Criminal law   The body of law that is designed to protect society at large rather than the individual members of society. Criminal law provides for penal treatment of convicted offenders of the law.

Cruel and unusual punishment   Any punishment or penalty that is disproportionate to the offense, that amounts to barbaric treatment, or that shocks the community standards.

Cumulative voting   A voting method that allows voters to take the total number of votes they are authorized to cast and allocate them in any manner they see fit. They may cast all their votes for one candidate or allocate them in any proportion among the various candidates.

Cure   In the law of sales, the right of the seller to correct any nonconformity of the goods tendered to the buyer in order to avoid a breach of contract.

Current rate   The interest rate that financial institutions are currently charging on loans.

Cy pres doctrine   Literally, as near as possible; a doctrine utilized in equity to carry out the wishes of a testator or of a trustee when the original wish is impossible or when it violates public policy (used especially in the area of charitable trusts when the original beneficiary has been improperly described or has ceased to exist).

D

Damages   Compensation and/or indemnification recovered in a court proceeding for injuries suffered by one person at the hands or by the conduct of another.

D/b/a   Abbreviation for "doing business as"; the name under which a business is conducted.

Deadlock   A tie; a standstill.

Debt   An amount of money owed to another; an obligation.

Debtor   A person who owes an obligation to a creditor.

Debtor in possession   A term used in bankruptcy proceedings to signify that the debtor in a reorganization proceeding is still in control of the business and its assets during the course of the bankruptcy process.

Deceased   A person who has died.

Decedent   Deceased.

Deductible   That which is to be subtracted; a clause in an insurance contract that relieves the insurer of any liability for a specified initial amount of loss.

Deed   The legal instrument by which an owner of land transfers the land to a grantee.

De facto   In fact; in deed; in reality. Contrasted with *de jure,* which means in law, *de facto* normally implies that something is being treated as a fact when it is not technically complete.

Defalcation   A misappropriation or misapplication of monies held by a fiduciary in a fiduciary capacity.

Defamation   A communication, oral or written, that holds a person up to ridicule, humilation, or scorn; a false and malicious attack upon the reputation of another.

Default   A failure to do what should be done, especially in the performance of a contractual obligation, without legal excuse or justification for the nonperformance.

Default judgment   A judgment rendered against a party because of that party's nonappearance in court.

Defendant   The person being sued in a civil action or being charged with a crime in a criminal action; the person from whom remedies or damages are being sought.

Defense   The reason, justification, or excuse for the conduct of the defendant, acceptance of which would shelter the defendant from the damages or remedies being sought in the action.

Defraud   To cheat; to trick; to take property or things of value from another by intentional deception.

De jure   Rightfully; legally; lawfully. Contrasted with *de facto, de jure* means in full compliance with all the requisite technicalities.

Delegate   To assign responsibility or authority to another; to have another act on one's behalf; to transfer the duty to perform to a third party.

Delivery   The intentional transfer of possession to another; the transfer of some thing or some right to another person.

Demand   The assertion of a legal right.

Demand instrument   An instrument that is due and payable at any time; an instrument that can be enforced immediately.

Deposition   Testimony of a witness taken outside of a trial and reduced to a writing and authenticated. A deposition may be used to preserve the testimony of a witness who is not available at trial or to impeach the testimony offered by a witness during the trial.

Depositor   A person who makes a deposit; a bank customer who places funds into an account with the bank for later personal use.

Derivative action   A suit filed by a shareholder on behalf of the corporation to enforce a corporate cause of action.

Destination contract   A contract for the transportation of goods by a common or independent carrier in which the seller remains liable for any losses or damages to the goods until the goods have reached a named destination.

Deterrent   Something that discourages or prevents the occurrence of an act.

Detriment   Loss or harm suffered to a person or a person's property; the forbearance of a legal right.

Diligence   Prudence; care; attention to details and surroundings.

Directors   Persons elected by the shareholders of a corporation to act as a board in managing the affairs of that corporation; managers; supervisors.

Disaffirm   To revoke a prior commitment or promise; to decline to perform what one had previously agreed to perform (most often used in the area of contract law when the disaffirming party asserts a lack of capacity to have entered the contract that is being repudiated).

Discharge   To release from obligation or liability; to excuse from any further duty to perform.

Disclaim   To deny; to renounce; to disavow.

Disclaimer   A statement by a seller, often in writing, that attempts to deny the existence of certain warranty protections that are normally afforded to the buyer.

Disclosed principal   A principal whose existence and identity are made known to the third person with whom the agent is dealing.

Disclosure   A revealing of what would otherwise be unknown.

Discovery   A pretrial procedure for allowing the parties to the litigation to narrow the issues by making one another aware of certain requested information, documents, and so on, and that includes the use of depositions, interrogatories, requests for admissions, and a number of other devices.

Discretion   Wise conduct; caution; exercise of care and concern.

Dishonor   A refusal to accept and/or to pay a negotiable instrument upon due and proper presentment to the drawee or maker.

Dissent   The minority opinion in a court case; the reasoning of the judges who disagreed with the majority position.

Dissolution   The termination of existence of a corporation or partnership, at least in the form previously known and followed. Dissolution does not necessarily mean that the business will cease to operate, only that the prior form no longer exists.

Diversification   The addition of variety, as by the inclusion of a new product line or entry into a new business area; an expansion into new fields and areas of interest.

Diversity of citizenship   A jurisdictional aspect of trials in federal courts wherein the parties on the different sides of a lawsuit are residents of different states.

Divest   To take away from; to deprive; the opposite of invest.

Dividends   A portion of a corporation's profits paid out to its shareholders on a pro rata basis, as voted by the board of directors; in insurance, the refund of excess premiums paid into the company by the policyholders, who are also the owners of the insurance company.

Document   An instrument that may be used as evidence.

Document of title   Written evidence of the legal ownership of a particular asset.

Domestic   Relating to a home, a domicile, or the place of birth or origin.

Domicile   The legal home or residence of a person; the state of incorporation of a corporation.

Donee   The recipient of a gift or a bequest.

Donee beneficiary   A third party who receives the benefits of a contract between two other parties for no reason except the donative intent of the donor.

Donor   A person who gives a gift or makes a bequest.

Double jeopardy   A second prosecution for the same offense or conduct, which is prohibited by the Constitution.

Drawee   The person against whom an order instrument is drawn and who is expected to accept the instrument and to pay it upon maturity and proper presentment.

Drawer   The person who issues an order instrument and who gives the order to pay the instrument to the drawee.

Due diligence   The degree of prudence and care that can reasonably be expected from an ordinary, prudent person under the same circumstances.

Due process   A measure of the appropriateness of a legal proceeding from the perspective of both the court and the individual; the proper exercise of power and authority by the court and the legislature within the rules and principles established by the courts.

Duress   An unlawful imposition whereby a person loses the free exercise of his or her will because of an improper threat made upon the person or upon any other person or thing that is of sufficient importance to the person to constrain the exercise of free will.

Duty   That which a person is expected and required to perform; a legal obligation to perform in a certain manner or to refrain from performing in a certain manner.

E

Easement   The right to use the land of another person, as for ingress and egress; a limited right to use and enjoy the land of another.

Emancipate   To free from the control or power of another; to release from parental care and to make legally independent.

Embezzlement   The fraudulent appropriation of money by a person entrusted with the money.

Eminent domain   The power of a government body to take private property for a public use or benefit, subject to compliance with due process requirements and payment of a fair value.

Employee   A person who occupies some permanent position; a person who accepts a job for wages and operates under the control of the employer.

Employer   One who uses the services of another, usually by hiring the other person to perform for wages.

Employment   The act of hiring employees; the work environment.

Encumbrance   A claim or a right against property owned by another, such as a mortgage or a lien.

Endorsee   A person to whom a document or instrument is endorsed.

Endorsement   The signing of one's name on the

back of a negotiable instrument in order to properly negotiate it to the next holder; a provision added to an insurance contract that alters the nature or the risk of the basic policy.

Endorser   A person who endorses, as by signing his or her name on the back of a negotiable instrument in order to further negotiate it.

Endowment   A life insurance policy that calls for the payment of the face amount of the policy to the insured at a certain age or date or for the payment of the face amount to the beneficiary if the insured dies before that time; the establishment of a fund for the use and benefit of a charitable institution.

Enjoin   To order by means of an injunction.

Entity   A separate being; a thing with a separate and independent legal existence.

Entrustment   The transfer of possession to another person of something that one owns or to which one is entitled, without any transfer of title, as in a consignment.

Equal protection   The requirement that the courts and laws of a state shall apply to all persons within the jurisdiction of the state in like manner, without regard to any extraneous factors such as race, age, or sex; the equality of treatment of all persons who come before the court.

Equipment   The fixed assets of a business, excluding lands and buildings; those assets that a business needs to carry out its commercial function.

Equitable   Fair; just; being a matter for a court of equity and not for a court of law.

Equity   A branch of the legal system designed to provide remedies where no remedy existed at common law; a system designed to provide "fairness" when there was no suitable remedy "at law."

Escheat   The reversion of lands to the state which occurs when a decedent has no legal heirs.

Escrow   A conditional delivery of a deed or of property to a trustee or escrow holder, who in turn delivers it to the grantee upon final performance.

Estate   The assets of a bankrupt; the assets owned by a decedent at the time of death; the interests a person holds in land.

Estoppel   A legal bar that prevents a person from alleging or denying a fact because that person's previous conduct or statements preclude the denial of facts contrary to the conduct or statements.

Eviction   The deprivation of one's right to possess land by court action or order.

Evidence   Any type of proof presented at trial to support a position advocated by the presenting party.

Examiner   A person appointed by the court to look into the affairs and the financial condition of a debtor in a bankruptcy proceeding.

Exchange   To trade; to give something to another, receiving something of equivalent value from the other; to trade foreign currency for domestic currency and domestic currency for foreign currency.

Exclusive-dealing contract   A contract that, by its terms, obligates the promisee to deal with only the promisor in a designated area of trade or commerce.

Exclusive jurisdiction   The right of one court to hear a particular case or controversy, to the exclusion of any and all other courts.

Exculpatory clause   A part of an agreement in which a prospective plaintiff agrees in advance not to seek to hold the prospective defendant liable for certain things for which that person would otherwise be liable.

Excuse   The reason given for not having done something that was to have been done; the rationalization of a nonperformance.

Executed contract   A contract that has been fully performed by all parties to it.

Execution   The full and complete carrying out of some act; a legal remedy for the enforcement of a court's verdict or judgment.

Executor (executrix)   The man (woman) named and appointed in a will by a testator to carry out the administration of the estate as established by the will.

Executory contract   A contract that has been less than fully performed, with performance still to occur.

Exemplary damages   See **Punitive damages.**

Exempt   Excused from a duty or obligation generally imposed on other persons in similar circumstances.

Ex parte   For one party only; without notice to the other side.

Expelled   Ejected; put out; removed.

Expert   A person qualified to testify or to speak as an authority on a given subject because of special skill, training, or knowledge in the subject area.

Export   To send out of the country, especially goods or articles of commerce.

Ex post facto   Literally, after the fact. An ex post facto law is enacted after the action has occurred and often is designed to be retroactive.

Express   Actually stated; clear and definite.

Express authority   Authority actually and truly given to the agent by the principal in the creation of an agency.

Express condition   A condition specifically mentioned in a contract.

Express warranty   A statement about the quality or condition of goods that the seller gives to the buyer at the time of the sale and that is intended as a part of the contract.

Expropriation   A taking of private property by government that is not in violation of international law.

Extension   An addition to something that already exists, as in the granting of additional time to complete a performance or to make a payment.

Extraterritoriality   The state of being exempt from the jurisdiction of local laws or local jurisdiction.

F

Face value   The value dictated by the face of an instrument or document without reference to any external documents.

Fact   Something actual; an actual occurrence.

Factor's lien   A claim or encumbrance on property held by a consignee for compensation owed by the principal.

False imprisonment   The unlawful arrest or detention of a person without permission, a warrant, or legal justification for doing so.

Farm goods   Goods produced by or used in the operation of a farm.

Fellow servant doctrine   A common law defense to a claim for damages by an employee injured on the job; a rule that protects the employer from liability to an employee for job-related injuries caused by a fellow employee.

Felony   A crime punishable by death or incarceration in a penitentiary.

Fiduciary   One who holds a special position of trust or confidence and who is thereby expected to act with the utmost good faith and loyalty.

Filing   The act of placing upon file; the act of depositing something in the custody of a public official to be held as a matter of record.

Finance charge   The consideration paid for the privilege of paying over time rather than paying cash at the time of contract performance; interest on a loan.

Financing statement   A legal document signed by the parties to a secured transaction that describes the collateral involved and that is filed with the appropriate state officials.

Firm offer   An offer made by a merchant to a merchant calling for an irrevocable period in which the offer may be accepted and during which the offer may not be revoked even though there is no consideration for holding it open.

Fixture   An item that was personal property but that has become so permanently attached to real property as to be a part of the real property.

Forbearance   A refraining from acting; the condition of not doing what one would otherwise legally be entitled to do.

Foreclosure   A legal proceeding designed to bar or to extinguish the rights of a mortgagor to the property mortgaged.

Foreign bill   A negotiable bill of exchange drawn in one state or country upon a drawee in another state or country.

Foreign corporation   A corporation incorporated in one state or country and doing business in another state or country.

Foreseeable   Capable of being anticipated as the reasonable result of a particular course of action or of a lack of action.

Forfeiture   The loss of a right or privilege as a penalty for certain conduct.

Forgery   The fraudulent making or altering of a written document or instrument with the intent of affecting the rights and duties of another; the signing of another person's name without permission or authority.

Formal   Of a particular form, as required by law, in order to be valid and enforceable.

Formal will   A testamentary document prepared in strict conformity with the state statute for the preparation of such a document and published and witnessed in its execution.

Franchise   A special privilege granted by a corporation to conduct business under the corporate name.

Fraud   The intentional misstatement of a material fact made for the purpose of inducing the other party to enter an agreement in reliance on the misstated fact; the intentional concealment of a defect whose existence should have been made known to the other party.

Fraudulent conveyance   A transfer of property

made with the intent of defrauding a creditor, of hindering a creditor's efforts to obtain the property transferred, or of placing such property beyond the reach of the creditor.

Fungible   Virtually identical; interchangeable; descriptive of things that belong to a class and that are not identifiable individually.

Future advances clause   A clause commonly used in secured transactions that provides for currently pledged collateral to cover any future credit extended by the covered creditor without need to resort to a subsequent security agreement.

G

Garnishment   A legal proceeding in which assets of a debtor that are in the hands of a third person are ordered held by the third person or turned over to the creditor in full or partial satisfaction of the debt.

General partnership   See **Partnership.**

Gift   An intentional, gratuitous transfer of property from a donor to a donee.

Good faith   Honesty in fact in the transaction; a lack of evil intent or motive.

Goods   Tangible, personal property; things that have a physical being and are movable.

Goodwill   The reputation of a business; the name value of a business; an intangible asset based on community perceptions.

Grace period   An insurance term designating the time period permitted after a premium payment is due during which the insured may tender the premium and retain the insurance coverage.

Grand jury   A jury convened for the purpose of hearing evidence to decide if there is probable cause to believe that a crime has been committed and to issue indictments if it finds the requisite probable cause.

Grant   To bestow on, confer on, or deliver to someone other than the party making the grant.

Grant deed   A deed that transfers an estate in land but with no warranties made by the grantor in the transfer.

Grantee   The recipient of a grant.

Grantor   The person who makes the transfer in a grant.

Gratuitous   Without consideration; not governed by contract law.

Guarantor   One who offers a guaranty by agreeing to pay the debts of another if that person does not pay; a collateral obligor.

Guaranty   A promise to pay the debts or defaults of another on condition that the creditor first attempt to collect the debt from the debtor and be unable to do so.

Guardian   A person legally responsible for taking care of the affairs of another who lacks the legal capacity to do.

H

Habeus corpus   Literally, you should have the body; the technical name for a number of common law writs used to bring a person before a court and subject to its jurisdiction; the right to obtain such a writ as a protection against unlawful imprisonment.

Habitability   Suitability of premises for human occupancy.

Handwritten   Manually subscribed; written by hand, as opposed to being typed, preprinted, or otherwise inscribed by machine.

Harm   Physical or mental damage or injury.

Heir   A person who is designated by statute to receive the assets that are not disposed of by a decedent's will.

Holder   A person who has legally acquired possession of a negotiable instrument by endorsement and/or delivery.

Holder in due course   A holder of a negotiable instrument who acquired possession for value, in good faith, and without notice of any defects or defenses that affect liability on the instrument.

Holographic   Entirely handwritten.

Holographic will   A type of will that is entirely handwritten by the testator, personally and manually, and is dated and signed.

Horizontal merger   A merger between two or more firms at the same level of the distributive chain; a merger between competing firms.

I

Illusory   Falacious; nominal as opposed to substantial; of false appearance.

Impair   To lessen or diminish; to make worse; to interfere with a legal right or remedy.

Impeach   As an aspect of evidence, to challenge the veracity of a witness by using evidence that refutes the witness or his or her testimony.

Implied   Assumed or gathered by a consideration of all the circumstances; not expressed; deduced.

Implied authority   That authority actually given by a principal to an agent but not expressed; the authority reasonably expected to be used and to be necessary in carrying out the purpose of the agency.

Implied consent   Agreement presumed to exist because of the actions or inactions of a party to the agreement.

Implied contract   A contract imposed by law because of the conduct of the parties.

Implied warranty   A warranty protection that unless properly disclaimed by the warrantor is imposed by operation of law because of the nature of the transaction.

Import   Goods or property brought into one country from another country.

Impossibility   Something that cannot possibly be performed because of natural or legal restrictions.

Imposter   A person who assumes a name or an identity not his or her own for the purpose of deceiving another.

Impracticable   Not capable of being performed by the means currently available; commercially unreasonable.

Incidental authority   Actual authority possessed by an agent in minor areas for which no specific directions were given.

Incidental beneficiary   A person who happens to benefit from a contract between two other parties but who was not intended to benefit and who has no legal recourse if the contract is not performed.

Incontestability clause   A clause in an insurance policy that removes the right of the insurer to challenge the application information after some predetermined time period.

Incorporation   The act of forming a corporation by compliance with the applicable state statutes.

Incorporators   Persons who originate a corporation.

Indemnification   Reimbursement to a person for losses sustained; protection from losses or harm.

Independent contractor   A person hired to perform a task for another and who totally controls the means to be used in attaining the desired results, being subject to control of the employer only in regard to the ends to be attained.

Indictment   A formal accusation of criminal conduct issued by a grand jury and then tried before a petit jury.

Informal   Not according to any specific legal form.

Infringement   A violation of a property right of another, especially in the areas of copyrights and patents; an unauthorized use of property belonging to another.

In gross   Personal; not annexed to another person or thing.

Inheritance   Property that a person receives from the estate of a decedent.

Injunction   A writ issued by a court of equity ordering a person to do or to refrain from doing some specified act.

Injury   Wrong or damages done to a person or a person's property or reputation.

In pari delicto   Equally at fault; equally guilty.

In personam   Against a particular person.

Inquiry   A request for information; a question concerning terms or conditions.

In rem   Against a thing; done without regard to any particular person and thus done "against the entire world."

Insane   Of unsound mind; deranged; mad. The term *insane* has many meanings in law, depending upon the circumstances in which it is used. In contract law, it may mean committed to an institution or unable to look out for one's best interests.

Insanity   The state of being insane.

Insider   A person in a position of power; one who has access to information not generally available to the public.

Insolvent   A person unable to pay debts as they come due; one who has liabilities in excess of assets.

Installment note   A negotiable instrument that calls for periodic payments of a debt at predetermined times.

Insurable interest   A legal or equitable interest in the insured property or life; a sufficient connection to the insured property or life to ensure that the contract is to provide for reimbursement of loss and is not a wagering proposition.

Insurance   A method of providing for risk sharing among persons facing the same sort of risk by paying premiums into a fund to be used to reimburse those members of the group harmed by the occurrence of the risk.

Insured   A person protected by an insurance policy.

Insurer   A person who issues an insurance policy.

Intangible property   An asset that does not have physical form or existence.

Intangible right   A right that may be represented

by something such as a writing but that is of value in and of itself without regard to the writing.

Integration   The act of making whole or entire; the entire writing or writings entered into by the parties as their final and complete contract agreement.

Intended beneficiary   A third party who was clearly meant to benefit from the contract by one of the original parties to the contract.

Intent   The purpose for which a person acts; meaning.

Intentional tort   A private or civil wrong done willfully or with reckless disregard for the results that ensue.

Interest   The cost imposed by a creditor for the use of money over time.

Interpretation   The defining, discovering, and explaining of unclear language.

Interrogatory   A series of written questions issued to a party and answered under oath as a portion of the pretrial discovery stage of a lawsuit.

Interstate   Between two or more states or between one state and a foreign country.

Inter vivos   Between living persons; during life.

Intestate   Without a will; a person who dies without leaving a will.

Intestate share   The amount a person inherits from the estate of a decedent who left no valid will; the inheritance provided for in the state statute of descent and distribution.

Intestate succession statute   The state law governing the distribution of the estate of a decedent who left no valid will.

Intoxication   Drunkenness; lack of sobriety; the condition of being under the influence of alcoholic beverages. A number of states also consider being under the influence of a narcotic or illegal controlled substance (drug) as intoxication.

In transit   On the way; being delivered.

Intrastate   Wholly within the borders of one state.

Invasion of privacy   Infringement of the right to be left alone, free from disturbance by others.

Inventory   Stock in trade; goods held for the purpose of resale to customers in the ordinary course of business.

Investigation   A detailed search; a legal inquiry or examination.

Investment security   Bonds, notes, certificates, and other instruments or contracts from which one expects to receive a return primarily from the efforts of others.

Involuntary   Without will; against one's will; not done freely.

Issue   (Noun) one's offspring, progeny. (Verb) to send forth; to originate; to put into circulation. In commercial paper, the issue is the original transfer of a negotiable instrument to the payee or to a remitter.

Issuer   One who officially distributes an item.

J

Jargon   The technical terminology of a particular profession.

Joint and several liability   The liability faced when a creditor may elect to sue each of the debtors individually or to sue all of them together.

Joint liability   The liability faced when a creditor must sue a collection of debtors together and not individually.

Joint tenants   Tenants who acquired title to property at the same time, from the same person, in the same interest, and with the same rights to possession and usage.

Joint venture   A commercial undertaking by two or more persons with a limited time or purpose, which is similar to a partnership but without the continuous nature of a partnership.

Judge   (Noun) the officer who presides over a court of law or equity. (Verb) to decide judicially (properly, to adjudge).

Judgment   The final finding, or opinion, of a court at the conclusion of an action.

Judgment creditor   A creditor who has obtained a court verdict that allows the enforcement of an execution.

Judgment NOV   A judgment *non obstante verdicto*, meaning notwithstanding the verdict; a judgment entered by the court in direct contravention of the jury verdict, normally so entered because the jury verdict is unreasonable under all the facts and circumstances of the case.

Judgment rate   The interest rate imposed and to be paid on a judgment ordered by a court.

Judicial restraint   A doctrine under which the court refuses to enter certain areas in official opinions; the exercise of discretion by a court in determining which cases to hear or which cases to decide.

Judicial review   The examination and hearing of a case, especially by an appellate court.

Junior secured party   Any secured party whose

security interest is subordinate to that of the priority secured party.

Jurisdiction   The power of the court to hear a certain cause of action; the power the court may exercise over a person or thing.

Jurisprudence   The general philosophy of law and the legal system.

Jury   In general, a panel of persons sworn to inquire into certain matters of fact and to render a verdict thereon. Included among the various types of juries are petit juries and grand juries.

Justice   A judge appointed or elected to sit on an appellate court; the conformity of a person's actions to the requirements of law.

Justification   Legal excuse for a course of conduct.

K

Knocking down   The acceptance of a bid made at an auction, signified by a blow of the auctioneer's hammer.

Knowledge   Those things of which a person is aware through perception, experience, education, or exposure.

L

Laissez-faire   A government philosophy of minimizing regulation as much as possible; a government attitude of keeping "hands off" business.

Landlord   A person who owns and leases or rents land to another.

Lapse   The expiration or the loss of an opportunity because of the passage of a time limit within which the opportunity had to be exercised.

Larceny   A felonious taking of the personal property of another person with the intent to deprive the owner of possession and to convert it to one's own use.

Law merchant   A system of laws developed by merchants to regulate commercial transactions at early common law, before such transactions were covered by the courts of either law or equity; the predecessor of modern commercial law.

Lease   Any agreement that establishes a landlord-tenant relationship; contracts that grant the right to use and occupy realty.

Legality   Lawfulness.

Lessee   The person to whom a lease is granted; the tenant.

Lessor   The person who grants a lease; the landlord.

Levy execution   To seize and sell property to satisfy a judgment.

Liability insurance   An insurance policy that protects the insured from a designated potential liability.

Liable   Responsible; subject to an adverse contingency or action.

Libel   A defamation based on the written publication of something that injures the reputation of the plaintiff.

License   Permission; the written document that evidences permission to perform certain acts; the right to use land belonging to another in some manner despite a lack of any estate or title to so use the land.

Lien   A legal charge or encumbrance against property.

Life insurance   An insurance policy that provides for the payment of an amount of money in the event the insured dies during the term of the policy. A number of investment aspects of many life insurance policies distinguish this type of insurance from property and liability insurance.

Limited partner   A partner in a limited partnership who has contributed capital and filed the necessary forms to be classified as limited but who has no voice in management and who faces no personal liability for the debts or other liabilities of the firm.

Limited partnership   A partnership consisting of at least one limited partner, whose risk is restricted to the amount of capital contributed to the firm and who may not take part in the management of the business, and at least one general partner, who is responsible for the management of the firm.

Liquidated   Agreed upon; settled; not in dispute.

Liquidated damages   Damages agreed upon in advance by the parties to a contract and included in the contract as the appropriate measure of damages in the event of a breach; damages preset by the parties because of the anticipated difficulty of establishing damages in the event of a breach.

Liquidated debts   Debts whose amounts are agreed upon by the parties.

Liquidation   The winding up of the affairs of a business in order to go out of business; the marshaling of assets and the subsequent reduction of those assets to cash in order to pay the claims of creditors.

Logotype   An identifying symbol.

Loss The harm or injury that results from a separation; a decrease in size or amount; the amount of a financial liability or setback.

Lost property Property that is accidentally or unintentionally lost by the owner and whose location is unknown and whose recovery is difficult.

Loyalty Faithfulness; adherence to the concept of supporting another over any competing interests; single-minded support and purpose.

M

Maker In negotiable instruments, the person who promises to pay the note or certificate of deposit; the person who developes, creates, or causes to exist.

Mala in se Morally wrong; wrong in and of itself.

Mala prohibita Made wrong by law; pertaining to statutory offenses.

Malfeasance The performance of an illegal act or a morally wrongful act; wrongful conduct.

Mandamus The name of a writ issued by a court of competent jurisdiction ordering the performance of some act, in which the order is directed to an inferior court or to a person or a corporation.

Marshaling of assets The arrangement of a debtor's assets in such a manner as to maximize the protection of the creditors; the gathering and grouping of the assets of the debtor.

Master A principal who has the right to control an agent.

Material Important, essential, or necessary.

Material fact A fact that is a part of the basis of the bargain; a fact without which the contract as entered would not have been made.

Mechanics' lien A statutory protection given to certain builders, artisans, and providers of materials providing for a lien on the building and the land that they have improved.

Mens rea "Guilty mind"; criminal intent; the mental intent that must be shown in order to convict a person of a crime.

Mental distress Suffering in the mind, as opposed to the body; such threats as remove free will.

Merchant A person involved in the trade or commerce of a particular type of goods; one who claims to be an expert in certain types of goods; one who employs an expert in certain types of goods.

Merchantability An implied warranty of quality that warrants to the buyer that the goods are of fair average quality, are fit for their normal use and purpose, and are adequately contained, packaged, and labeled.

Merge To blend; to come together; to combine into one thing.

Merger The absorbing of one thing into another so that only one remains after the merging; in contract law, the extinction of one contract by absorption into another; in corporate and antitrust law, the combining of two or more firms into one resulting firm.

Midnight deadline With respect to a bank, midnight of the next banking day after the day on which it receives the item in question or the notice on which it is acting.

Mining partnership A special form of co-venture that is neither a joint venture nor a partnership in the literal sense and that involves a joint effort to develop a mine or to develop oil or gas leases, with a sharing of profits and a sharing of expenses.

Minor One not yet of legal age; an infant in the law; one lacking the statutory age to be considered an adult.

Minority The period before a person reaches the legal age of majority; the period of legal infancy; the justices who disagree with the majority opinion; the dissent.

Misdemeanor A criminal offense of less severity than a felony and normally punishable by fine or imprisonment in other than a penitentiary.

Misdescription A false description of the subject matter of a contract that causes harm to one of the parties.

Misfeasance Improper performance of some act that could be lawfully performed.

Mislaid property Property placed somewhere and then forgotten by the owner; property intentionally placed but not recovered.

Misrepresentation The misstatement of a material fact in the formation of a contract, made without an intent to deceive.

Mistake An error regarding the truth of facts or of law that causes a person to act or to refrain from acting in a manner other than he or she would have acted had the truth been known.

Mitigation A reduction or a minimizing of loss, liability, or penalty imposed by law.

Money   Legal currency issued by a recognized government entity; legal media of exchange.

Monopolize   To assume complete control over; to attempt to gain or to retain a monopoly.

Monopoly   The power of a firm exclusively to carry on a business or a trade to the exclusion of all competitors.

Moot   Subject to argument; not settled or decided.

Mortgage   A conditional transfer of property as security for a debt; an estate in land created by the granting of the estate but intended as security and becoming void if the debt is repaid.

Mortgagee   The person who receives a mortgage; the creditor.

Mortgage insurance   An insurance policy taken out by a mortgagor to pay off the debt in the event that the insured risk occurs during the mortgage period.

Mortgage note   A promissory note issued in conjunction with a mortgage specifying the terms for repayment of the loan by the debtor in order to cancel the mortgage.

Mortgagor   The person who gives a mortgage as security; the debtor.

N

Nationalization   The act of a government in proclaiming that a business or other property has become the property of the government and that individual owners have been removed from or deprived of the property.

Navigable waters   The commercial waterways of a nation; those streams, rivers, and lakes capable of use in commerce.

Necessary   Needed; inevitable; unavoidable.

Necessity   A controlling force or compulsion that allows for no other course of conduct.

Negligence   A failure to exercise due care under circumstances that require due care and that results in harm to another person.

Negligence per se   Negligence in and of itself without reference to any external factors.

Negligently   Without proper caution and care.

Negotiability   The quality of being transferable by endorsement or delivery.

Negotiable   Transferable by endorsement and delivery so as to give the recipient the rights of the transferor.

Negotiable instruments   Legal instruments governed by Article 3 of the UCC and consisting of notes, drafts, checks, and certificates of deposit.

Negotiation   The act of transferring a negotiable instrument by endorsement or delivery in such a manner that the transferee becomes a holder.

Nolo contendere   A plea of "no contest" entered in a criminal case whereby the defendant agrees to suffer the punishment for the crime charged but does not plead guilty and whereby the case cannot be used as evidence in any later proceedings on the same issue.

Nominal damages   Damages in name; the award given to a plaintiff when no substantial injuries are suffered, consisting of a token sum that the defendant is required to pay in acknowledgment of the wrongful conduct.

Nonassignable   Not subject to being assigned. In contract law, certain rights are nonassignable because of the personal nature of the duty.

Nonconforming   Not in compliance with the terms of the agreement or description.

Nonexempt assets   Those assets of the debtor that may not be protected and retained in a bankruptcy proceeding; those assets that will be liquidated in bankruptcy in order to satisfy the claims of creditors.

Nonforfeiture clause   A clause used in life insurance policies that specifies that certain rights and options of the insured will not be taken away should the policy lapse.

Nonjusticiable   Not properly subject to court action.

No-par value stock   Corporate stock not designated as having a par value; unvalued stock that is sold at some stated value, which is decided by the board of directors at the time of issue.

Notice   The information of which a person should be aware on the basis of knowledge or general observation.

Notorious   Of general notice or knowledge; widely known.

Novation   The substitution of a new contract in place of a preexisting one, whether between the same parties or with new parties replacing one or more of the original ones.

Nuisance   An annoyance or disturbance of a person's use, occupancy, and enjoyment of property that makes the ordinary use or enjoyment uncomfortable or bothersome.

Nuncupative   Oral; verbal; spoken.

Nuncupative will   A will made orally by the testator during his or her last illness or while facing impending death.

O

Obligation   Something a person is bound to do or to refrain from doing; a duty imposed by law or by contract.

Obligee   The person who is to receive the benefit from an obligation or from the performance of an obligation.

Obligor   The person bound by an obligation; the person who is to carry out the duty or to render the benefit.

Occupancy   The taking of possession of property in order to assert a right of ownership; in real property, the exercise of control over land.

Offer   The presentation for acceptance or rejection of a power to create a contract made to the offeree.

Offeree   The person to whom an offer is made.

Offeror   The person who makes an offer to enter into a contract.

Oligopoly   An economic condition in which a small number of firms dominate the market but no one firm controls it.

Omission   A failure to perform; especially, a failure to perform an act required by law.

Operation of law   Certain automatic results that must occur following certain actions or facts because of established legal principles and not as the result of any voluntary choice by the parties involved.

Option   A privilege given to the offeree, for consideration, to accept an offer at any time during a preset period, with the understanding that the offer cannot be revoked during the stated period; a contract to keep an offer open for some agreed-upon time period.

Order   A command or direction; an administrative agency's rules and regulations; a category of negotiable paper in which the drawer commands the drawee to pay a named person.

Order for relief   A bankruptcy judge's decree that the debtor is properly before the court and that control over the procedures to be followed thereafter lies with the bankruptcy court.

Ordinance   A law enacted by a municipal authority.

Output contract   A contract that calls for the buyer to purchase all of the production of the seller during the term of the contract.

Overdraft   A check or draft, honored by the drawee, in excess of the funds to which the drawer is entitled.

Overdue   Not paid when payment was due; delayed beyond maturity; unperformed at the date performance was to have been completed.

P

Paid-in capital   The property contributed to a business venture by the owners of the business as their contributions to the formation of the firm.

Parol evidence   Oral evidence; verbal testimony of witnesses.

Parol evidence rule   A rule that prohibits the introduction of oral evidence that contradicts a complete written contract or agreement unless there is evidence that the writing was the result of fraud, mistake, or accident.

Partially disclosed principal   A principal whose existence is known to the third person at the time of negotiation with the agent but whose identity is not.

Partial performance   Performance of a contractual obligation that is less than full or complete.

Participate   To take part in; to share; to divide in equal shares or proportions.

Partnership   An association of two or more persons as co-owners to carry on a business for profit; a voluntary joining of two or more persons to own and to operate a business venture as equal members.

Party   A person who is directly involved in the performance of any contract or agreement or in the trial, prosecution, or defense of any legal action.

Par value   The face value of a share of stock, not necessarily the same as the price for which the share can be sold.

Past consideration   Purported consideration but in fact no consideration; an attempt to use past conduct as consideration for a present contract.

Patent   (Noun) a government grant of monopoly power to make, to use, or otherwise to enjoy the fruits of one's inventions, provided the invention is new, useful, and not obvious to one of ordinary skill in the field. (Adjective) obvious; manifest; apparent.

Payee   The person designated by the maker or drawer of a negotiable instrument as the person to receive payment or to continue negotiation of the instrument; the person to whose order a negotiable instrument is originally drawn or issued.

Perfection   The act of completing and of moving beyond challenge or defect; in secured transactions, the act of a creditor that serves as notice to the rest of the world that the security interest exists in his or her favor, as by filing.

Performance   The carrying out of what one has agreed to do; the satisfaction of an obligation or contract.

Peril   The risk or hazard against which an insurance policy is issued to the insured.

Perjury   The making of false statements while under oath.

Per se   By itself; taken alone; unconnected to other matters.

Personal defense   In negotiable instruments, a defense that exists between the drawer or maker and the payee or some other party but that does not directly affect the instrument itself; a defense that attacks the underlying obligation but not the validity of the instrument.

Personal property   Anything capable of being owned except land or anything permanently attached to land.

Personal representative   The executor or administrator of a decedent's estate.

Petit jury   "Twelve men good and true"; the ordinary jury called for in a civil or criminal trial; the finders of fact.

Plaintiff   The person who commences a civil cause of action by filing suit against the defendant.

Plea bargaining   A device used in a criminal proceeding whereby the state accepts a guilty plea on a lesser offense in exchange for not bringing the defendant to trial on the greater offense with which he or she was originally charged.

Pledge   A form of perfection in secured transactions whereby the debtor creates a bailment with the creditor, allowing the creditor to retain possession of the collateral until the debt is repaid.

Police power   The authority conferred upon the government to enact the laws necessary to ensure domestic tranquility; the power inherent in the state to protect the lives, health, and property of its citizens by enacting and enforcing laws.

Political question   A nonjusticiable issue; a matter that is purely political in nature and as such is not germane to any legal issues or actions within the jurisdiction of a court.

Pollution   Contamination of the environment; impurity.

Pooling agreement   An agreement between two or more parties to place funds into a common "pool" for allocation for certain uses, as for coverage of losses contemplated and faced by the members of the pooling group.

Possession   The exercise of exclusive physical control over an asset regardless of ownership; physical dominion.

Possessory lien   A statutory claim on property evidenced by the physical control and possession of the creditor and perfected for as long as the creditor retains possession.

Postdated   Dated for a time later than the time of issuance or creation.

Power   The ability or the right to do something. Power does not necessarily mean right; a person may have the power to do a certain thing but doing so will involve the violation of a private civil duty.

Preemption   A seizing for oneself to the exclusion of all others; the right to purchase before others; in corporate law, the right of present stockholders to purchase a new issue of stock before the stock is offered to the general public.

Preference   In bankruptcy, a transfer by the debtor to an unsecured creditor that allows that creditor to receive a greater percentage of his or her claim than is received by other creditors of the same class.

Preferred stock   A class of corporate stock that has rights superior to those of common stock in the areas of dividends and the distribution of corporate assets.

Premium   The cost of insurance coverage paid by the insured to the insurer.

Prepayment clause   A contract clause that allows the debtor to pay the debt before it is due without penalty.

Preponderance of proof   A degree of proof that seems to outweigh that offered by the other side.

Prescription   In real property, the acquisition of an easement by the open, notorious, continuous, and hostile use of the property of another as a matter of right.

Presenter   A person who presents; one who makes a presentment.

Presentment   A demand upon the primary party by the holder of a negotiable instrument for payment and/or acceptance of the instrument.

Price discrimination   The charging of different prices to different purchasers when the price differential is not justified by cost differentials.

Price fixing   An agreement between two or more competing merchants to charge a certain price for goods or services without regard to market pressures or concepts of competition; a per se violation of the Sherman Act when done in interstate commerce.

Price leadership   A position enjoyed by certain firms, by virtue of size, innovations, or ability, to set prices in certain channels of commerce with the understanding or expectation that competing firms will price their products accordingly; the ability to direct the pricing policies of an industry.

Prima facie   At first sight; on its face; something presumed to be true because of its appearance unless disproved by evidence to the contrary.

Primary liability   The liability of the person to be looked to first for payment, who, in commercial paper, is the maker of promise paper or the drawee on order paper.

Principal   In agency law, the person who appoints an agent and bestows authority upon the agent for the purposes set out in the agency agreement.

Priority   Precedence; higher rights; the right to come before another.

Privacy   See **Invasion of privacy.**

Private trust   A trust created for a private purpose and having certain named or readily identifiable beneficiaries.

Privilege   A benefit or advantage enjoyed by some members of a group beyond that enjoyed by the general public; the right enjoyed by certain persons to have particular types of communications treated as confidential, not subject to disclosure.

Privity of contract   The relationship of two or more persons by virtue of the existence of the contract between them.

Probate   (Noun) the legal procedure for establishing that a given written document was the last will and testament of a decedent and that the document is valid. (Adjective) relating to wills and the proof thereof.

Probate court   A court having jurisiction over the estates of decedents.

Procedural law   The body of law that governs *how* legal proceedings are to be conducted.

Proceeds   The property, especially money, received from the sale or disposal of assets.

Profits   The excess in income over expenditures; the gain made in the sale of assets or services; the benefits a person receives from the use of land.

Promise   A showing of an intent to act or to refrain from acting in a certain way made in such a way that the promisee is aware of the commitment.

Promisee   One to whom a promise is made.

Promisor   One who makes a promise.

Promissory estoppel   A doctrine that prohibits a promisor from denying the making of a promise or from escaping the liability for that promise because of the justifiable reliance of the promisee that the promise would be kept.

Promissory note   A written promise to pay a certain sum of money at a future time unconditionally.

Promoter   A person who begins the process of forming a corporation by procuring subscribers for the stock or by taking other affirmative steps toward incorporating.

Property   Anything capable of being owned; anything that has value.

Property insurance   Insurance that covers personal property or buildings and fixtures against certain predetermined risks and hazards.

Proprietorship   The designation for an unincorporated business that has a single owner/manager.

Pro rata   Proportionately; according to percentages.

Prospectus   A document presented by a corporation or its agents announcing the issue of corporate securities, stating the nature of the securities and the financial status of the issuing firm, and asking the general public to purchase the securities covered.

Protest   A formal notice of dishonor of a negotiable instrument made before and attested to by a notary public or a consul of an embassy; a formal declaration of dissent or disagreement regarding some act that has occurred or that is about to occur.

Provable   Capable of being proved; susceptible to being proved.

Proximate cause   An act that naturally and foreseeably leads to harm or injury to another or to an event that injures another.

Proxy   A person appointed and designated to act for another, especially at a public meeting, such as a meeting of the shareholders of a corporation; the document or instrument used to appoint someone to act in a representative capacity as a proxy.

Proxy solicitation   A request contained in the notice of a shareholders' meeting that the shareholder allow some person to act as a proxy for that shareholder at the meeting.

Public corporation   A corporation formed by a federal or state government to carry out a government purpose.

Public domain   All the land owned by the federal government and all land occupied by federal building, arsenals, and docks or for other federal purposes.

Public policy   The general attitude of the public toward certain conduct; the public sense of morality, good conduct, and acceptable behavior to which citizens must conform.

Published   Made public; made generally known.

Punitive damages   Damages awarded to a plaintiff over and above those to which he or she would normally be entitled because of the excessive wrongfulness of the defendant's conduct; damages designed to punish and to make an example of the defendant as a means of discouraging similar conduct by others. Also known as *exemplary damages*.

Purchase money security interest   A security interest in which the credit extended is used to purchase the collateral that is being used as security.

Purchaser   One who acquires property by buying it from a seller for money; one who acquires real property by any method except inheritance.

Q

Qualification   A skill or trait necessary to perform a certain task or to hold a certain office; a modification or limitation of terms used to restrict the scope or meaning of language.

Qualified endorsement   A type of endorsement used on negotiable instruments to remove the contractual liability of the endorsement should the instrument be dishonored.

Quantifiable   Capable of exact statement; measurable; verifiable.

Quasi contract   An equitable remedy to prevent unjust enrichment when no contract was formed but one of the parties has received value knowingly and has not prevented performance by the other party.

Quasi-judicial   "As if" done by a judicial body; pertaining to the hearings, investigations, and ascertaining of facts by administrative bodies in controversies involving administrative agencies in the performance of the duties delegated to them by Congress.

Quasi-legislative   "As if" done by a legislative body; pertaining to the exercise of administrative agencies in enacting regulations within the delegation of authority the agency received from Congress.

Question of fact   A question to be determined by a jury.

Question of law   A question to be decided by the court, in contrast to a question of fact, which is to be determined by the jury.

Quid pro quo   Literally, something for something; the consideration given by each party to a contract in exchange for the consideration given by the other; the bargain element of the contract.

Quiet enjoyment   The right and expectation of a tenant or a purchaser of land to use and enjoy the premises without disturbances or interferences from others; a covenant that is included in leases and deeds.

Quitclaim deed   A deed conveying from the grantor to the grantee such rights as the grantor possesses, if any; a deed of conveyance that carries no warranties or assurances of its validity or genuineness.

Quorum   The number of members or the number of shares that must be present and/or represented at a meeting in order for the meeting to be properly convened and for any business to be properly and legally conducted.

R

Ratification   The acceptance of and the binding to an act that was unauthorized when committed and that was voidable before the ratification. Ratification must be of the *entire* act, not just those parts of benefit to the person who is accepting.

Ratify   To approve and formally sanction.

Real defense   In commercial paper, a defense that attacks the validity of the instrument itself, allowing the maker or drawer to escape liability on the instrument regardless of the status of the holder.

Real property   Land or anything permanently attached to land.

Reasonable and prudent person   A person who before acting gives thought to the consequences of acting; a careful and thoughtful person.

Rebuttable presumption   An assumption of the truth of a matter, based on evidence, that will be accepted as true unless shown to be untrue by other convincing evidence.

Receiver   An unbiased person appointed by a court to receive, preserve, and manage the funds and property of a party involved in litigation.

Receivership   An equitable remedy whereby the court appoints a receiver to manage the property involved pending the outcome of the case.

Reckless   Lacking proper caution; negligent; careless.

Reclaim   To obtain the return of something; to get back.

Reconcile   To make consistent; to settle or resolve; to put into balance or harmony.

Recoupment   A withholding of something that is due; a reduction in the amount allegedly owed because of a counterclaim or a setoff.

Redeem   To buy back; to remove a security interest or a mortgage by paying the total debt due.

Redemption   The act of redeeming or repurchasing; the revocation of a conditional sale by performance of the condition that provided for the revocation.

Reformation   An equitable remedy whereby the court "reforms" a contract in order to remove a mistake and to make the agreement conform to the terms to which the parties originally agreed.

Registered agent   A person designated by a foreign corporation as the proper person upon whom to serve process.

Registration statement   A formal statement complying with statutory information standards that is filed by a corporation in order to offer an issue of securities for sale.

Regulation   An authoritative rule that deals with procedures; an executive rule or order that has the effect of law.

Reimbursement   Repayment for expenditures incurred; indemnification.

Rejection   A refusal to accept what is offered.

Relative   (Noun) kin; family member; a relation by blood or marriage. (Adjective) not capable of exact statement; comparative.

Release   The surrender of a right or claim by the person possessing it to the person who would be obligated to perform; the surrender of a legal claim.

Relevant market   The total market in which a firm operates, including its geographic scope and all competing or substitute products.

Reliance   Dependence; expectation of truth or occurrence.

Reliction   Land that is uncovered by the gradual receding of water.

Remainder beneficiary   The person who is to receive the benefit after the expiration of a prior interest granted in the property, with both interests created at the same time and in the same instrument.

Remand   To send a case back to an inferior court for further action; to return a prisoner to custody pending trial.

Remedy   A method for enforcing a right or preventing a violation of a right; the result of a successful action.

Remitter   The person to whom a bank draft or cashier's check is issued before it is delivered to the payee; the purchaser of such a bank draft or cashier's check.

Remuneration   Salary; wages; compensation.

Renunciation   The abandonment of a right by the possessor of the right.

Reorganization   The restructuring of an insolvent corporation so that the interests of its creditors can be protected and the corporation can continue to exist.

Repentance   A feeling of regret or contrition for past wrongdoing.

Replevin   An action taken to acquire possession of goods that are not necessarily unique but that are currently unavailable in the open market; in the law of sales, a remedy of the buyer when cover is not available and specific performance is not appropriate.

Replevy   To take goods under a writ for replevin.

Repossession   The act of regaining possession; the act of taking possession of collateral upon the default of the debtor in a secured transaction.

Representation   A statement made by an applicant for insurance coverage that allows the insurer to assess the risk and that, if false and material, may allow the insurer to cancel the policy; a statement made to influence the other party to act or to refrain from acting.

Repudiate   To reject, refuse, deny, or disclaim; to refuse to acknowledge or pay.

Repudiation   A rejection; a refusal; a denial of a right or a refusal to perform a duty.

Requirement contract   A contract in which the seller agrees to provide as much of a product or service as the buyer needs during the contract term.

Rescission   An annulment or cancellation; a termination of a contract through restoration of the parties to the status quo.

Reservation of title   A contract clause that leaves title to the sold object with the seller until the buyer has paid the entire purchase price. In secured transaction law, such an effort is treated as a mere security interest, with title transferred to the buyer.

Residuary   Pertaining to the surplus of a decedent's estate after all the debts have been paid and all the legacies distributed and discharged.

Residuary clause   A clause in a will that provides for the disposal of any property left after all bequests and divisions of the estate have been made.

Res judicata   A thing already decided by a judicial action or opinion and that having been decided is final.

Respondeat superior   Literally, let the master answer; a legal doctrine that holds the master liable for the wrongs of the servant, and the principal liable for the wrongs of the agent, provided the wrong was committed in the course and scope of employment.

Restatement   Part of the title of compilations dealing with various areas of law, such as torts and contracts, which detail how the different states have treated topics covered in the volumes and which are used to provide guidance to the courts in resolving cases and controversies in these different areas of law.

Restitution   The return of something; in contract law, the return of any consideration given upon a breach, upon rescission, or upon avoidance of the contract.

Restraint of trade   Any conduct that serves to limit the development of commerce or to interfere with the free flow of commerce.

Restrictive covenant   A promise in a deed whereby the grantee agrees not to do certain things or to use the land in certain ways.

Restrictive endorsement   A type of endorsement that purports to limit or terminate any further negotiation of the instrument; an endorsement that restricts future negotiations to a particular field of commerce, such as banking.

Resulting trust   A trust created by implication of law based on the *presumed* intention of the parties involved, which is inferred from the surrounding facts and circumstances.

Retract   To take back or withdraw, as an offer before its acceptance.

Revenue   Profit; return on investments; income; yield.

Revert   To return to; to go back.

Revest   To vest again; to acquire a right or interest a second time; to regain.

Revocation   The cancellation, rescission, or annulment of something previously done or offered.

Right   A legal power or privilege to do something; justice; that to which a person is entitled.

Risk of loss   Legal responsibility for any damages, loss, or destruction of the subject matter of a contract.

Robbery   A criminal and felonious taking of personal property from a person by force or the threat of force.

Royalty fee   Payment made in exchange for the grant of a right or a license.

Rule against perpetuities   A requirement that an interest in property must vest within a specified time — a life in existence plus twenty-one years — or the interest becomes invalid on the basis of its being contrary to public policy. The rule refers to present possessory interests and not to future interests.

Rule of reason   A defense to an antitrust action used to show that the conduct complained of was reasonable under the circumstances and was the least objectionable of the alternative courses of conduct available to the actor.

S

Sale   The passing of title from the seller to the buyer for a price.

Sale on approval   A sale in which the buyer is allowed some preset time period to test the product before the sale is final.

Sale or return   A sale in which the buyer is allowed to return any goods not resold by the buyer for credit to the buyer's account.

Sanction   (Noun) the penalty imposed for a violation of law as a means of helping in the enforcement of the law. (Verb) to make valid by a formal procedure.

Scienter   Knowledge; especially, one party's prior knowledge of the cause of a subsequent injury to another person.

Seasonably   As quickly as practical; within the appropriate time.

Secondary liability   A liability that does not arise or attach until the occurrence of a condition; the liability faced by each endorser on a negotiable instrument upon proper presentment and dishonor of the instrument.

Secured creditor   A creditor who has access to collateral as a resource to cover the debt upon the default of the debtor.

Secured transactions   Credit arrangements, covered by Article 9 of the UCC, in which the creditor has a security interest in certain assets of the debtor.

Security   Something of value given or pledged to assure the performance of an obligation or the repayment of a debt.

Security agreement   The document executed by the debtor and the creditor in establishing a secured transaction.

Security interest   An interest in personal property or fixtures that secures payment or performance of an obligation.

Seller   A person who transfers property in a contract for the sale of property.

Servant   A person employed to perform services for a master under the control of the master.

Service charge   A fee charged for the performance of a particular service, often added to a basic fee; the charge imposed by a bank on its customer for particular services, such as certifying a check or stopping payment on a check.

Service mark   A distinctive symbol designating the service offered by a particular business or individual.

Service of process   The delivery of a writ or summons to the party or to the address of the party to which it is directed.

Setoff   A demand that the defendant has against the plaintiff and that is deducted from the amount the defendant is to pay to the plaintiff in settlement of the claim.

Settlement   An agreement that settles a dispute as to what each party owes the other.

Settlor   One who creates a trust.

Several liability   The liability faced by each of the parties when the plaintiff may sue any of them and recover the entire judgment from those sued, without having to sue all of the potential defendants.

Share   A proportional ownership of a corporate venture with proportionate rights to management, to profits of the corporation, and to corporate assets upon dissolution.

Shareholder   The owner of a share of a corporation's stock; an investor in a corporation whose investment is made up of ownership shares.

Shipment contract   A contract whereby the seller agrees to put conforming goods into the hands of a shipper and the buyer assumes risk of loss during transit of the goods.

Short-swing profits   Profits made by officers, 10 percent shareholders, insiders, and tippees by the purchase and sale of corporate securities within six months, by matching the high sale and the low purchase prices, and by disregarding any losses.

Signature   Any mark, symbol, or device used with the present intent to authenticate a writing.

Silence   A forbearance from speaking.

Slander   An oral defamation of character; an oral communication that causes a person's reputation to be held up to scorn or ridicule and that is made to any person except the person so scorned or ridiculed.

Sovereign   One possessing supreme power within a given sphere; the government.

Sovereign immunity   The doctrine that protects the state from liability for the performance of its sovereign role; an absolute defense available to the state in lawsuits, provided the government was involved in a government function.

Special endorsement   A type of endorsement used in negotiable instruments whereby the holder designates the next holder of the instrument and another endorsement is needed to further negotiate the instrument.

Specific performance   An equitable remedy provided by the courts when monetary damages would be insufficient and the object of the contract is unique and in which the court orders performance of the contract exactly as agreed.

Standing   The legal right to commence an action based on a showing that the plaintiff has a substantial legal interest that needs to be protected.

Stare decisis   "Let the decision stand"; the policy followed by the courts in deciding current cases on the basis of precedent, thereby not disturbing established policy.

Statement   A declaration of matters of fact; an allegation.

Statute   A law enacted by the legislative branch of the government.

Statute of Frauds   A statute requiring that certain specified types of contracts be in writing in order to be enforceable in court.

Statute of limitations   A statute that provides for a definite time period during which certain legal actions must be commenced and after which they will be barred.

Statutory   Related to or created by statute.

Statutory standard   The general conduct expected of an individual as established by law; the legal measurement of conduct for a given set of circumstances.

Statutory warranties   The warranty protections imposed by law upon the parties to a contract; the quality standards to which a product must adhere in order to comply with the statutory provisions.

Stipend   A fixed sum of money paid periodically.

Stock   The capital fund of a corporation acquired by the sale and distribution of corporate shares; the different classes of shares that a corporation issues to its owners.

Stop payment order   An order given by a drawer of a check to the drawee that a designated check be dishonored upon presentment to the drawee. An oral stop payment order is valid for fourteen days; a written one for six months.

Strict foreclosure   A means of foreclosure that precludes the right of the debtor to redeem the property and that vests title in the creditor.

Strict liability   Liability without fault; liability for which there is no defense assertable by the defendant.

Subject matter jurisdiction   The power of a court to hear only the classes of cases and controversies that are within its jurisdiction, especially important in courts of limited jurisdiction.

Sublease   The lease of all or part of the premises by the lessee for some portion of the unexpired lease period of the lessee's occupancy.

Subpoena duces tecum   An order issued by a court to some designated party to produce specified documents at a trial.

Subrogate   To substitute one person in place of another with reference to rights or claims.

Subscription   The act of writing one's name on a legal document; a written contract in which the subscriber agrees to pay money in exchange for some designated benefit or purpose.

Subsidiary   A corporation controlled by another corporation that owns a majority of the subsidiary corporation's stock.

Substantial performance   Performance of a contract that is less than perfect but that is in compliance with the essential portions of the contract; a good-faith effort to perform a contract, with performance satisfactory and the deviations minor or technical.

Substantive law   The portion of the law that deals with and regulates rights.

Suit   Any legal action in which a plaintiff seeks the enforcement of rights or the granting of remedies.

Sum certain   An amount of money to be paid on a negotiable instrument, with the total amount calculable from the information contained on the face of the instrument.

Summary judgment   A judgment entered by the court when there is no substantial issue of fact present; a judgment by the court on the basis of depositions, discovery, and other nonevidential matters.

Summons   A writ requiring a sheriff to inform the person named that an action has been filed against that person and ordering the person to appear in court to answer the action.

Supremacy clause   The clause in the Constitution that specifies that the federal government is supreme to the state governments and that federal law controls over state law if the federal law is valid.

Surcharge   Required payment for failure to follow fiduciary duties.

Surety   A person who promises to pay or to perform in the event that the principal fails to do so.

Suretyship contract   A contract in which a surety agrees to answer for the debt of another upon the default of the other and in which the surety is entitled to indemnification upon the performance of the obligation.

Suspend   To delay a performance temporarily, with the expectation that performance will occur later.

T

Tenancy   An interest in or possession of land in any manner.

Tenancy in partnership   A form of ownership of partnership property by the partners, with a right of survivorship.

Tenant   One who possesses land belonging to another; the holder of a leasehold estate.

Tenants by the entireties   An estate held by a husband and wife jointly by conveyance and that carries a right of survivorship.

Tenants in common   Co-ownership of real property by two or more persons, with the owners having undivided interests in the land but with title passing to them from different grantors, at different times, or in differing amounts.

Tender   An offer of performance.

Term insurance   A form of life insurance with no investment properties or characteristics that provides coverage for a fixed time period and that is paid only if the loss occurs during that time period.

Testament   The disposition of a testator's personal property according to his or her wishes upon the death of the testator.

Testamentary   Pertaining to a will.

Testamentary capacity   The mental capability required by law in order to make a valid will; the state of being of sufficient age to execute a will and of being aware of the nature of the act.

Testator (testatrix)   A man (woman) who makes a will.

Things in action   A right to receive or to recover money or personal property as the result of a judicial proceeding.

Third-party beneficiary   A person who is not a party to a contract but who will benefit from the performance of the contract; one who derives some gain or benefit from the contractual performance of the parties to the contract.

Time instrument   A negotiable instrument payable at some future, determinable time and not payable upon demand.

Time-price differential sales contract   A contract with a difference in price based on the date of payment, with one price for an immediate payment and another price if the payment is at a later date.

Tippee   One who is not an insider but who receives from an insider information not yet available to the general public; one who receives a tip.

Title   The legal right of ownership and possession of property.

Tort   The breaching of a civil duty that is the proximate cause of harm to some person or the property of some person; failure to exercise due care.

Tort feasor   A person who commits a tort.

Tortious   Wrongful; pertaining to torts.

Trademark   A distinctive mark or symbol used to identify a particular company or its products.

Transferable   Capable of being assigned, transferred, negotiated, or passed from party to party with all the rights of the original holder or party being retained.

Treason   An attempt to overthrow the government by overt acts; betrayal of the government to a foreign government.

Treasury stock   Stock that has been issued by a corporation and then reacquired by the corporation as a part of its treasury.

Treaty   A written contract or agreement entered into by two or more nations for the general welfare of the nations involved.

Treble damages   A statutory remedy in antitrust actions that allows the successful plaintiff to recover three times the damages suffered as a result of the antitrust violation.

Trespass   An unlawful act committed on the person, property, or rights of another; unlawful entry on another's land.

Trial court   The court of first impression; the court in which a cause of action is initiated and that hears evidence and testimony in reaching its verdict.

Trust   A legal relationship in which one party — the trustee — holds legal title to the property, while another party — the beneficiary — holds equitable title to the same property; a combination formed by several corporations by mutual agreement.

Trust deed   A security agreement similar to a mortgage in which a deed is conveyed to a trustee as security for the payment of a debt, with the trustee having the power of sale upon default in the repayment of the debt.

Trustee   The person responsible for performing the purpose of a trust and who administers the trust property for the beneficiary.

Trustee in bankruptcy   The person appointed by the bankruptcy court to act as trustee of the debtor's property for the benefit and protection of the creditors.

Tying arrangement   A contract that requires the buyer to purchase one product from the seller in order to be allowed to purchase a second, difficult-to-obtain product from the same seller.

U

Ultra vires   Beyond the scope or legal power of a corporation as established by the corporation's charter or by state statute.

Unconditional   Not subject to any conditions; under every set of facts or circumstances; in every instance.

Unconscionable   Blatantly unfair and one-sided; so unfair as to shock the conscience.

Unconstitutional   Contrary to a constitution; in violation of a constitution.

Underwriter   The insurer; one who insures another against some risk.

Undisclosed principal   A principal whose existence and identity are unknown to the third person at the time the third person is dealing with the principal's agent.

Undue influence   The control of the free will of another person by unfair or improper persuasion.

Unenforceable   Not subject to performance by judicial intervention; not capable of being implemented under judicial direction.

Unfair trade practice   Any commercial practice that does not allow for the free exercise of trade by competitors; a false, deceptive, or unfair method of gaining trade at the expense of others.

Unilateral   One-sided.

Unilateral contract   A contract in which only one party makes a promise, with the other party's being expected to perform an act in order to accept and thereby create a contract.

Uninsured motorist   An operator of a motor vehicle who is not covered by a valid automobile or vehicular liability insurance policy.

Union shop   A place of employment where only members of a labor union are employed.

Unjust enrichment   The receiving of something of value to which the recipient is not entitled by law or equity; the possession of something to which one is not entitled.

Unliquidated   Not agreed upon; in dispute; subject to controversy or disagreement.

Unqualified endorsement   A type of endorsement that does not qualify the liability of the endorser to the endorsee in the event that the instrument is dishonored.

Unsecured creditor   A general creditor; a creditor who has not entered into a security agreement with the debtor and who does not have specific collateral to rely on in the event of a default by the debtor.

Usage of trade   A practice common to the trade or industry involved or having a generally recognized meaning within the trade or industry.

Usurious contract   A contract that calls for the payment of interest at a rate higher than that permitted under state law.

Usury   The charging of an interest rate in excess of the statutory maximum; the charging of excessive interest.

V

Valid   Legally enforceable; properly executed and formed; legally sufficient.

Value   The worth of an object in terms of money; the consideration necessary to support a simple contract.

Venue   The geographic area in which an action is held and from which the jurors are selected; the court in which an action may be commenced, based upon the convenience of the parties.

Vertical merger   A merger between firms at different levels of the distributive chain.

Vest   To grant a fixed right concerning present or future use; to place in the possession of some authority or person.

Vicarious   Serving in place of someone or something else; acting as a substitute for.

Void   Of no legal effect; invalid; null.

Voidable   Capable of being avoided; cancelable at the option of the disadvantaged party.

Voidable preference   The act of an insolvent debtor of paying one creditor of a class, allowing that creditor to obtain a larger percentage of the debt than other creditors of the same class, within four months of the bankruptcy petition.

Voir dire   The examination of a prospective witness or juror to determine that person's acceptability.

Voluntary   Of one's own free will; spontaneous; intentional.

Voting trust   A commitment by stockholders of a corporation to place their shares in trust so that the shares can be voted as a bloc; a device used to increase the voting power of a group.

W

Waiver   The voluntary surrender of a legal right; the intentional surrender of a right.

Waiver of defenses clause   A clause in a contract whereby one party agrees in advance not to assert certain defenses should a breach occur.

Warehouseman   A person engaged in the business of receiving and storing the goods of others for a fee.

Warranty   A representation that becomes a part of the contract and that is made by a seller of goods at the time of the sale as to the character, quality, or nature of the goods.

Warranty deed   A deed that contains warranties of title from the grantor to the grantee.

Watered stock   Shares of a corporation that are issued as fully paid when in fact the full par or stated value has not been paid by the purchaser.

Will   A written document prepared by a testator to provide for the disposition of the testator's estate upon his or her death.

Winding up   The termination of a business enterprise by marshaling and liquidating the assets and distributing the proceeds according to state law.

Workers' compensation   A type of insurance required by statute to protect workers in the event of injury or illness arising on the job and used in lieu of workers' lawsuits against the employer for such injury or illness.

Working papers   The papers prepared by an accountant in the course of employment that are used to prepare the final reports and that serve as evidence of the care and skill exercised by the accountant in the performance of the job.

Writ   A legal instrument, prepared in the form of a letter and addressed to a sheriff, to some other officer of the court, or to the person directly affected, that requires the performance of a specified act under order of the court.

Writ of execution   A writ used to enforce the judgment of a court.

Writing   A reduction to tangible form.

Wrong   A violation of the legal rights of some other person.

Z

Zoning   A division of the land governed by a city, with certain designated uses being permitted for each area and other uses being declared improper and impermissible; government regulation of permissible land use for the general welfare of the community.

Case Index

Key *a* = annotated and/or case citation
   b = briefed case
   c = case problem

N

Topical Index